W9-AXL-194

About the Authors

Katherine Barber
Heather Fitzgerald
Tom Howell
Robert Pontisso

The lexicographers of the Canadian Oxford Dictionary team have collectively over 30 years of experience editing dictionaries and thesauruses. They have lived in six cities in four provinces, and thus bring a wealth of knowledge of both regional and general Canadian English to the task. Katherine Barber, Editor-in-Chief of Canadian dictionaries since 1991, received the Canadian Booksellers Association's Editor of the Year award in 1999, and is well-known across Canada for frequent appearances on radio and television. In addition to writing Oxford's Canadian dictionaries, the lexicographers are constantly engaged in a reading program to identify new and distinctly Canadian words. They have now read over 9000 Canadian books, magazines, and newspapers.

Colour Oxford Canadian Dictionary of Current English

Ming Cheng .

Colour Oxford Canadian Dictionary

of

Current English

Edited by
Katherine Barber
Heather Fitzgerald
Tom Howell
Robert Pontisso

Editor-in-chief, Canadian Dictionaries
Katherine Barber

OXFORD
UNIVERSITY PRESS

OXFORD
UNIVERSITY PRESS

8 Sampson Mews, Suite 204, Don Mills, Ontario, M3C 0H5

www.oupcanada.com

Oxford University Press is a department of the University of Oxford. It
furthers the University's objective of excellence in research,
scholarship, and education by publishing worldwide in

Oxford New York

Auckland Cape Town Dar es Salaam Hong Kong Karachi
Kuala Lumpur Madrid Melbourne Mexico City Nairobi
New Delhi Shanghai Taipei Toronto

With offices in

Argentina Austria Brazil Chile Czech Republic France Greece
Guatemala Hungary Italy Japan Poland Portugal Singapore South Korea
Switzerland Thailand Turkey Ukraine Vietnam

Oxford is a registered trademark of Oxford University Press
in the UK and in certain other countries

Published in Canada by Oxford University Press

Library and Archives Canada Cataloguing in Publication

Colour Oxford Canadian dictionary of current English /
edited by Katherine Barber ... [et al.].

ISBN: 978-0-19-542843-8

1. English language—Canada—Dictionaries. 2. English language—
Dictionaries. 3. Canadianisms (English)—Dictionaries.
I. Barber, Katherine, 1959-

PE3235.C69 2007   423   C2007-904535-9

Cover Design: Brett J. Miller

2 3 4 - 12 11 10

Printed in China

Colour
Oxford
Canadian
Dictionary
of Current
English

How to use this dictionary

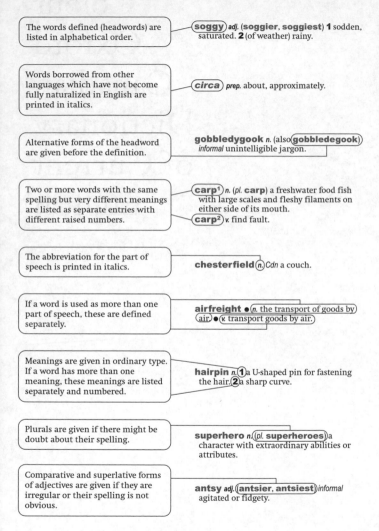

The words defined (headwords) are listed in alphabetical order.

soggy *adj.* (**soggier, soggiest**) **1** sodden, saturated. **2** (of weather) rainy.

Words borrowed from other languages which have not become fully naturalized in English are printed in italics.

circa *prep.* about, approximately.

Alternative forms of the headword are given before the definition.

gobbledygook *n.* (also **gobbledegook**) *informal* unintelligible jargon.

Two or more words with the same spelling but very different meanings are listed as separate entries with different raised numbers.

carp¹ *n.* (*pl.* **carp**) a freshwater food fish with large scales and fleshy filaments on either side of its mouth.
carp² *v.* find fault.

The abbreviation for the part of speech is printed in italics.

chesterfield *n.* *Cdn* a couch.

If a word is used as more than one part of speech, these are defined separately.

airfreight ● *n.* the transport of goods by air. ● *v.* transport goods by air.

Meanings are given in ordinary type. If a word has more than one meaning, these meanings are listed separately and numbered.

hairpin *n.* **1** a U-shaped pin for fastening the hair. **2** a sharp curve.

Plurals are given if there might be doubt about their spelling.

superhero *n.* (*pl.* **superheroes**) a character with extraordinary abilities or attributes.

Comparative and superlative forms of adjectives are given if they are irregular or their spelling is not obvious.

antsy *adj.* (**antsier, antsiest**) *informal* agitated or fidgety.

Derivatives are included without their definition if their meaning can easily be worked out from the meaning of the headword.

avow *v.* admit, confess. (□ **avowal** *n.*)

Derived forms of verbs are given if they are irregular or there might be doubt about their spelling. Where there are three forms, the first is the third person singular, the second is both the past tense and the past participle, and the third is the present participle; where there are more than three forms the past tense and the past participle are clearly labelled.

befall *v.* (**befalls**; *past* **befell**; *past participle* **befallen**; **befalling**) (esp. of something bad) happen to.

Phrases based on the headword are grouped together in alphabetical order after the □ symbol.

hilt *n.* the handle of a sword, dagger, tool, etc. □ **to the hilt** completely.

A label in italics is given if a word is restricted to a particular region, subject area, or style, e.g. *formal* (used in formal and written English), *informal* (used in informal or spoken language), *slang* (very informal or restricted to a particular social group).

baloney *n.* **1** = BOLOGNA. **2** *informal* nonsense.

Entries are sometimes linked by a cross-reference.

garbanzo *n.* (*pl.* **garbanzos**) = CHICKPEA. [*Say* gar BON zo]

Pronunciation is given where it may be tricky.

chlorofluorocarbon = CFC. [*Say* kloro FLORO carbon]

Note on Proprietary Status

Aa

A¹ *n.* (also **a**) (*pl.* **As** or **A's**) **1** the first letter of the alphabet. **2** the sixth note of the C major scale. **3** the first hypothetical person or example. **4** the highest class or category (of marks etc.). **5** a human blood type. □ **from A to B** from one place to another. **from A to Z** over the entire range, completely.

A² *abbr.* **1** ampere(s). **2** answer. **3** atomic (energy etc.).

Å *abbr.* angstrom(s).

A1 *adj. informal* excellent.

a *indefinite article* (also **an** before a vowel) **1** one, some, any. **2** one like or the same. **3** one single. **4** in, to, or for each.

AA *abbr.* **1** Alcoholics Anonymous, an organization that helps alcoholics overcome their addiction through counselling and mutual support. **2** a size of battery. **3** anti-aircraft.

aardvark *n.* an insect-eating mammal, native to Africa. [*Say* ARD vark]

AB¹ *n.* a human blood type.

AB² *abbr.* Alberta.

aback *adv.* □ **take aback** surprise.

abacus *n.* (*pl.* **abacuses**) an oblong frame with rows of beads, used for calculating. [*Say* ABBA cuss]

abalone *n.* a mollusc with a shallow ear-shaped shell. [*Say* abba LONE ee]

abandon ● *v.* **1** give up completely. **2** leave or desert (a person, position, vehicle, ship, etc.). **3** (**abandon oneself**) give in to (a desire etc.) completely. **●** *n.* complete lack of inhibition or restraint. □ **abandonment** *n.*

abandoned *adj.* **1** deserted; left unused. **2** unrestrained, uninhibited.

abase *v.* (**abases, abased, abasing**) **abase oneself** act in a way that shows acceptance of another's power. □ **abasement** *n.*

abashed *adj.* embarrassed and ashamed.

abate *v.* (**abates, abated, abating**) make or become less strong, intense, etc. □ **abatement** *n.*

abattoir *n.* a slaughterhouse. [*Say* ABBA twar]

abbess *n.* (*pl.* **abbesses**) a woman who is the head of an abbey of nuns.

abbey *n.* (*pl.* **abbeys**) **1** the building(s) occupied by a community of monks or nuns. **2** the community itself.

abbot *n.* the head of an abbey of monks.

abbreviate *v.* (**abbreviates, abbreviated, abbreviating**) shorten (a word, phrase, etc.). □ **abbreviation** *n.* [*Say* a BREE vee ate]

ABC *n.* **1** the alphabet. **2** the basics of any subject.

abdicate *v.* (**abdicates, abdicated, abdicating**) **1** give up or renounce (the throne). **2** fail or refuse to perform (a responsibility, etc.). □ **abdication** *n.* [*Say* ABDA kate]

abdomen *n.* **1** the part of the body containing the digestive and reproductive organs. **2** the hinder part of an insect, spider, etc.

abdominal ● *adj.* of or pertaining to the abdomen. **●** *n.* (also **ab**) an abdominal muscle. [*Say* ab DOM in ul]

abduct *v.* kidnap. □ **abductee** *n.* **abduction** *n.* **abductor** *n.* [*Say* ab DUCT]

Abenaki *n.* **1** (*pl.* **Abenaki** or **Abenakis**) a member of an Algonquian-speaking Aboriginal people now living in S Quebec and Maine. **2** their language. □ **Abenaki** *adj.* [*Say* abba NACK ee]

aberration *n.* **1** a departure from what is normal or acceptable. **2** a moral or mental lapse. □ **aberrant** *adj.* [*Say* abba RAY sh'n, a BEAR'nt]

abet *v.* (**abets, abetted, abetting**) (often in **aid and abet**) encourage or assist (esp. an offender or offence). [*Say* a BET]

abhor *v.* (**abhors, abhorred, abhorring**) detest; regard with disgust and hatred. □ **abhorrence** *n.* **abhorrent** *adj.* [*Say* ab HORE]

abide *v.* (**abides, abided, abiding**) **1** tolerate. **2** (foll. by *by*) accept or obey (a rule or decision).

abiding *adj.* lasting; enduring.

ability *n.* (*pl.* **abilities**) **1** capacity or power. **2** cleverness, talent; mental power.

abject *adj.* **1** miserable, wretched. **2** humble. □ **abjection** *n.* **abjectly** *adv.* [*Say* AB ject, ab JECK sh'n]

abjure *v.* (**abjures, abjured, abjuring**)

renounce on oath (an opinion, claim, etc.). [*Say* ab JOOR]

ablaze *adj. & adv.* **1** on fire. **2** glittering, glowing.

able *adj.* (**abler, ablest**) **1** having the capacity or power. **2** having great ability. □ **ably** *adv.*

able-bodied *adj.* **1** not physically handicapped. **2** fit, healthy.

able seaman *n.* (*pl.* **able seamen**) a non-commissioned officer of the second-lowest rank.

ablutions *n.* **1** the ceremonial washing of parts of the body etc. **2** *informal* the act of washing oneself. [*Say* ab LOO sh'n]

ABM *abbr.* ANTI-BALLISTIC MISSILE.

abnegation *n.* renunciation; rejection. [*Say* abna GAY sh'n]

abnormal *adj.* **1** not normal or usual. **2** relating to what is abnormal. □ **abnormality** *n.* (*pl.* **abnormalities**). **abnormally** *adv.*

ABO *adj.* of the system in which blood is classified into four types (A, AB, B, and O).

aboard *adv. & prep.* on or into a ship, aircraft, etc.

abode *n.* a dwelling place; one's home.

abolish *v.* (**abolishes, abolished, abolishing**) put an end to (esp. a custom or institution).

abolition *n.* the act or process of abolishing or being abolished. □ **abolitionist** *n.* [*Say* abba LISH un]

abominable *adj.* **1** causing moral disgust. **2** very bad or unpleasant. □ **abominably** *adv.* [*Say* a BOM in a bull]

abominable snowman *n.* a manlike or bearlike creature said to exist in the Himalaya mountains.

abomination *n.* **1** a thing that causes disgust or hatred. **2** loathing. [*Say* a bomma NATION]

Aboriginal (also **aboriginal**) ● *adj.* **1** (of peoples) inhabiting or existing in a land from the earliest times or from before the arrival of colonists. **2** of or relating to Aboriginal peoples. ● *n.* an Aboriginal inhabitant, esp. of Australia. [*Say* abba RIDGE in ul]

Aboriginal rights *pl. n.* rights enjoyed by a people by virtue of the fact that their ancestors inhabited an area from time immemorial.

Aboriginal title *n.* the communal right of Aboriginal peoples to occupy and use the land inhabited by their ancestors from time immemorial.

Aborigine *n.* (usu. in *pl.*) an Aboriginal inhabitant of Australia. [*Say* abba RIDGE in ee]

abort *v.* **1** end a pregnancy early. **2** cause to end fruitlessly or prematurely. **3** abandon or terminate (a space flight, etc.) before its completion, usu. because of a fault. □ **abortive** *adj.*

abortion *n.* the deliberate ending of a pregnancy. □ **abortionist** *n.*

abound *v.* **1** be plentiful. **2** have something in great numbers or quantities.

about ● *prep.* **1** relating to. **2** at a time near to. **3** in, around, surrounding. **4** here and there in. **5** at a point or points near to. ● *adv.* **1 a** approximately. **b** *informal* used to indicate understatement. **2** all around. **3** on the move. □ **be about to** be on the point of (doing something).

about-face *n.* (also **about-turn**) **1** a turn made so as to face the opposite direction. **2** a change of opinion or policy etc. □ **about-face** *v. & interj.*

above ● *prep.* **1** over; on the top of; higher than. **2** more than. **3** higher in rank, importance, etc., than. **4** too great or good for. ● *adv.* **1** at or to a higher point; overhead. **2** upstairs. **3** (of a text reference) before or earlier in the text. **4** higher than zero on the temperature scale. ● *adj.* mentioned earlier.

above board *adj. & adv.* without concealment; fair or fairly. □ **above-board** *adj.*

abracadabra *interj.* a supposedly magic word used by conjurors.

abrade *v.* (**abrades, abraded, abrading**) scrape or wear away by rubbing. [*Say* a BRAID]

abrasion *n.* **1** the scraping or wearing away (of skin, rock, etc.). **2** a damaged area resulting from this. [*Say* a BRAY zh'n]

abrasive *adj.* **1 a** tending to rub. **b** capable of polishing by rubbing or grinding. **2** harsh or hurtful in manner. □ **abrasive** *n.* [*Say* a BRAY siv]

abreast *adv.* **1** side by side and facing the same way. **2** well-informed, up to date.

abridge *v.* (**abridges, abridged, abridging**) **1** shorten (a book, film, etc.). **2** curtail (liberties, etc.). □ **abridgement** *n.*

abroad *adv.* **1** in or to a foreign country or countries. **2** over a wide area. **3** in circulation.

abrogate *v.* (**abrogates, abrogated, abrogating**) repeal or abolish (a law or custom). □ **abrogation** *n.* [*Say* ABRA gate]

abrupt *adj.* **1** sudden and unexpected; hasty. **2** brief to the point of being rude. **3** steep. □ **abruptly** *adv.* **abruptness** *n.*

ABS *abbr.* anti-lock braking system.

abscess *n.* (*pl.* **abscesses**) a swollen

area full of pus within a body tissue.
□ **abscessed** adj. [Say AB sess]

abscond v. depart hurriedly and secretly, typically to avoid detection or arrest. [Say ab SKOND]

absence n. **1** the state of being away from a place or person. **2** an occasion or period of being away. **3** the non-existence of. [Say AB since]

absent ● adj. **1** not present in a place or at an occasion. **2** (of a part or feature of the body) lacking. **3** inattentive to the matter in hand. ● v. **absent oneself** stay or go away. □ **absently** adv. [Say AB sint for the adjective, ab SENT for the verb]

absentee n. a person not present, esp. one who is absent from work or school. □ **absenteeism** n. [Say ab sin TEE]

absent-minded adj. tending to forget things. □ **absent-mindedly** adv. **absent-mindedness** n.

absinth n. **1** a shrubby plant with a bitter aromatic taste. **2** (usu. **absinthe**) a green aniseed-flavoured potent liqueur based on absinth. [Say AB sinth]

absolute ● adj. **1** complete, perfect. **2** unconditional, unlimited. **3** ruling arbitrarily or with unrestricted power. **4** (of a standard) universally valid; not relative or comparative. ● n. a value, standard, etc., which is objective and universally valid.

absolutely adv. **1** completely, utterly. **2** independently. **3** (no or none) at all.

absolute majority n. a majority over all others combined; more than half.

absolute pitch n. the ability to recognize the pitch of a note or produce any given note.

absolute zero n. the lowest temperature theoretically possible (−273.15°C (or 0 K)).

absolution n. forgiveness, esp. an ecclesiastical declaration of forgiveness of sins.

absolutism n. the principle of absolute government. □ **absolutist** n. & adj.

absolve v. (**absolves, absolved, absolving**) **1 a** set or pronounce free from blame etc. **b** acquit. **2** pardon or give absolution for (a sin etc.).

absorb v. **1** include or incorporate as part of itself or oneself. **2** take in; suck up (liquid, knowledge, etc.). **3** reduce the effect or intensity of; deal easily with. **4** consume (time, resources, etc.). **5** engross the attention of. □ **absorbable** adj. **absorbed** adj. **absorber** n. **absorbing** adj. **absorption** n.

absorbent adj. having a tendency to absorb. □ **absorbency** n. **absorbent** n.

abstain v. **1 a** restrain oneself; refrain

from indulging in. **b** refrain from drinking alcohol. **2** formally decline to vote. □ **abstainer** n. **abstention** n.

abstinence n. the act of abstaining, esp. from food, drugs, or sexual activity. □ **abstinent** adj. [Say AB stin ince]

abstract ● adj. **1 a** to do with or existing in thought or in theory; not tangible or concrete. **b** (of a word) denoting a quality etc. rather than a concrete object. **2** (of art) using shapes and colours to create an effect rather than attempting to represent real life accurately. ● v. take out; remove. ● n. a summary of a book etc. □ **abstractly** adv. [Say ABS tract for the adjective and noun, abs TRACT for the verb]

abstracted adj. inattentive; preoccupied. □ **abstractedly** adv. [Say abs TRACT id]

abstraction n. **1** the quality of dealing with ideas rather than events. **2** (the formation of) an abstract or visionary idea. **3** freedom from representational qualities in art. **4** a state of preoccupation. [Say abs TRACK sh'n]

abstruse adj. hard to understand. [Say abs TRUCE]

absurd adj. **1** (of an idea etc.) wildly unreasonable or inappropriate. **2** (of a person) unreasonable or ridiculous in manner. **3** ludicrous. □ **absurdity** n. **absurdly** adv.

absurdist adj. resembling the characteristics of the theatre of the absurd.

abundance n. **1** a very great quantity. **2** plentifulness of the good things in life; prosperity. □ **abundant** adj. **abundantly** adv.

abuse ● v. (**abuses, abused, abusing**) **1** misuse. **2** treat a person or animal with cruelty or violence. **3** insult verbally. **4** use alcohol or drugs excessively. ● n. **1** incorrect or improper use. **2** unjust or corrupt practice. **3** cruel and violent treatment. **4** insulting language. □ **abuser** n.

abusive adj. **1** (of a situation) involving maltreatment. **2** (of a person) tending to abuse others. **3** using insulting language. **4** (of language) insulting. □ **abusively** adv. **abusiveness** n.

abut v. (**abuts, abutted, abutting**) **1** be located next to. **2** touch or lean upon. [Say a BUT]

abutment n. a structure built to support the lateral pressure of an arch or span.

abuzz adj. in a state of excitement or activity.

abysmal adj. **1** extremely bad. **2** total, utter. □ **abysmally** adv. [Say a BIZ mul]

abyss n. (pl. **abysses**) **1** a deep or

seemingly bottomless gap. **2** an immeasurable depth. **3** a catastrophic situation seen as likely to occur. [*Say* a BISS]

Abyssinian *n.* **1** a native or inhabitant of Abyssinia (a former name for Ethiopia). **2** (also **Abyssinian cat**) a cat with a long slender body, long ears, and short brown hair. [*Say* abba SINNY un]

AC *abbr.* **1** (also **ac**) ALTERNATING CURRENT. **2** air conditioning.

acacia *n.* a usu. thorny tree or shrub with white or yellow flowers. [*Say* a KAY shuh]

academe *n.* the world of learning. [*Say* acka DEEM]

academia *n.* (also **the academy**) the academic world. [*Say* acka DEEMY uh]

academic ● *adj.* **1 a** to do with learning. **b** of or relating to a scholarly institution. **2** not of practical relevance. **3** (of a person) interested in or excelling at scholarly pursuits and activities. ● *n.* a teacher or scholar in a university etc. □ **academically** *adv.*

academics *pl. n.* studies in the humanities or sciences.

academic year *n.* the period during which school is in session (usu. September–June).

academy *n.* (*pl.* **academies**) **1** a place of study or training in a special field. **2** (usu. **Academy**) a society or institution of distinguished scholars, artists, etc. **3** a school (esp. in proper names).

Academy Award *n.* any of the annual awards of the Academy of Motion Picture Arts and Sciences.

Acadian *n.* **1** a native or inhabitant of the former French colony of Acadia in what is now the Maritimes. **2** esp. *Cdn* a francophone descendant of French settlers in Acadia. □ **Acadian** *adj.* [*Say* a KAY dee un]

a cappella *adj. & adv.* (of singing) unaccompanied. [*Say* acka PELLA]

accede *v.* (**accedes, acceded, acceding**) **1** assent or agree. **2** take office, esp. become monarch. [*Say* ack SEED]

accelerate *v.* (**accelerates, accelerated, accelerating**) **1** move or begin to move more quickly. **2** cause to go or happen or reach completion more quickly. □ **accelerated** *adj.* **acceleration** *n.* [*Say* ack SELLA rate]

accelerator *n.* **1** a device for increasing speed, esp. a pedal in a motor vehicle. **2** *Physics* an apparatus for imparting high speeds to charged particles. [*Say* ack SELLA rater]

accent ● *n.* **1** a particular mode of

pronunciation. **2** prominence given to a syllable by stress or pitch. **3** a mark on a letter or word to indicate pronunciation, stress, etc. **4** emphasis. **5** a distinctive or contrasting feature. ● *v.* **1** emphasize. **2** enhance (esp. with a contrasting element).

accentuate *v.* (**accentuates, accentuated, accentuating**) emphasize; make prominent. □ **accentuation** *n.* [*Say* ack SEN choo ate]

accept *v.* **1** consent to receive. **2** give an affirmative answer to. **3 a** regard favourably; treat as welcome. **b** approve for admission. **4 a** believe or receive as valid. **b** be prepared to subscribe to. **5** tolerate; submit to. □ **acceptance** *n.*

acceptable *adj.* **1 a** worthy of being accepted. **b** pleasing. **2** adequate. **3** tolerable. □ **acceptability** *n.* **acceptably** *adv.*

access ● *n.* (*pl.* **accesses**) **1** a way of approaching or reaching or entering. **2** the right or opportunity to reach or use or visit. **3** *Computing* the action or process of obtaining stored documents, data, etc. ● *v.* (**accesses, accessed, accessing**) gain access to (esp. data, a file, etc.).

accessible *adj.* **1** that can readily be reached, entered, or used. **2** posing no obstacles to handicapped people. **3** (of a person) readily available. **4** easy to understand or appreciate. □ **accessibility** *n.*

accession *n.* **1** entering upon an office (esp. the throne) or a condition (as adulthood). **2** a thing added, e.g. a book to a library. [*Say* ack SESSION]

accessory ● *n.* (*pl.* **accessories**) **1** an additional or extra thing. **2 a** small attachment or fitting. **b** a small item of dress, e.g. shoes. **3** a person who helps in or knows about an (esp. illegal) act. ● *adj.* additional; contributing or aiding in a minor way. □ **accessorize** *v.* [*Say* ack SESSA ree, ack SESSA rise]

accident *n.* **1** an event that is without apparent cause, or is unexpected. **2** an unfortunate event brought about unintentionally. **3** an automobile collision or crash.

accidental ● *adj.* happening by accident. ● *n. Music* a sign indicating a momentary departure from the key signature. □ **accidentally** *adv.*

acclaim ● *v.* **1** praise enthusiastically and publicly. **2** hail as. **3** *Cdn Politics* elect without opposition. ● *n.* public praise.

acclamation *n.* **1** *Cdn Politics* the act or an instance of election by virtue of being the sole candidate. **2** loud and eager assent to a proposal. **3** a phrase said or sung by the congregation as part of a liturgy: *the Gospel acclamation.* [*Say* akla MAY sh'n]

acclimatize *v.* (**acclimatizes, acclimatized, acclimatizing**) make or become accustomed to a new climate or to new conditions. □ **acclimatization** *n.* [*Say* a CLIME a tize]

accolade *n.* the awarding of praise; an acknowledgement of merit. [*Say* ACKA laid]

accommodate *v.* (**accommodates, accommodated, accommodating**) **1** provide lodging or room for. **2** adapt, harmonize, reconcile.

accommodating *adj.* fitting in with someone's wishes or demands in a helpful way. □ **accommodatingly** *adv.*

accommodation *n.* **1** temporary lodging. **2** an adjustment or adaptation to suit a special purpose. **3** a convenient arrangement; a compromise.

accompany *v.* (**accompanies, accompanied, accompanying**) **1** go with. **2 a** be done or provided with; supplement. **b** have as a result. **3** support or partner a soloist with an instrumental part. □ **accompaniment** *n.* **accompanist** *n.*

accomplice *n.* a partner in a crime or wrongdoing.

accomplish *v.* (**accomplishes, accomplished, accomplishing**) complete; succeed in doing.

accomplished *adj.* clever, skilled.

accomplishment *n.* **1** the fulfillment (of a task etc.). **2** an acquired esp. social skill. **3** an achievement.

accord ● *v.* **1** agree with or match something. **2** give or grant someone power, status or recognition. ● *n.* **1** agreement, consent. **2** harmony or correspondence. **3** a formal act of agreement; a treaty. □ **of one's own accord** voluntarily. **with one accord** unanimously.

accordance *n.* □ **in accordance with** in a manner corresponding to.

according *adv.* **1** as stated by or in. **2** in a manner corresponding to; in proportion to. □ **accordingly** *adv.*

accordion *n.* a musical instrument played by means of keys, buttons, and pleated bellows. □ **accordionist** *n.*

accost *v.* approach and address (a person), esp. boldly. [*Say* a COST]

account ● *n.* **1** a narration or description. **2** an arrangement with a financial institution or firm by which funds are held on behalf of a customer or goods or services are supplied on credit. **3** a record or statement of money, goods, or services received or expended. ● *v.* consider, regard as. □ **account for 1** serve as or provide an explanation or reason for. **2 a** give a reckoning of (money etc. entrusted). **b** answer for (one's conduct). **3** supply or make up an amount etc. **call to account** require an explanation from (a person). **no accounting for tastes** it's impossible to explain why different people like different things. **of no account** unimportant. **on account of** because of. **on no account** under no circumstances; certainly not. **take account of** (or **take into account**) consider along with other factors.

accountable *adj.* responsible; required to account for one's conduct. □ **accountability** *n.*

accounting *n.* the process of or skill in keeping and verifying accounts. □ **accountant** *n.*

accounts payable *pl. n.* amounts owed by a business to a supplier.

accounts receivable *pl. n.* amounts owed by customers to a business.

accoutrement *n.* additional items of dress or equipment. [*Say* a KOOTRA m'nt, a KOOTER m'nt]

accredit *v.* (**accredits, accredited, accrediting**) **1** officially recognize as meeting certain standards. **2** attribute (a saying etc.) to (a person). □ **accreditation** *n.* **accredited** *adj.*

accretion *n.* **1** the process of growth or increase. **2** a thing formed or added by such growth. [*Say* a CREE sh'n]

accrue *v.* (**accrues, accrued, accruing**) **1** come as a natural increase or advantage, esp. financial. **2** accumulate (esp. interest). □ **accrued** *adj.* [*Say* a CREW]

acculturate *v.* (**acculturates, acculturated, acculturating**) assimilate or cause to assimilate a different culture. □ **acculturation** *n.* [*Say* a CULTURE ate]

accumulate *v.* (**accumulates, accumulated, accumulating**) **1** gradually get more of something. **2** gradually increase. □ **accumulation** *n.* **accumulative** *adj.*

accurate *adj.* **1** correct; lacking errors. **2** conforming exactly with the truth or with a given standard. **3** able to reach a target etc. with precision. □ **accuracy** *n.* **accurately** *adv.*

accursed *adj.* **1** lying under a curse; ill-fated. **2** detestable, annoying. [*Say* a CUR sed *or* a CURST]

accusation n. **1** a charge or claim that someone has done something wrong or illegal. **2** the act of making such a claim. □ **accusatory** adj.

accusative ● n. the case of nouns, pronouns, and adjectives, expressing the object of the verb. ● adj. of or in this case.

accuse v. (**accuses, accused, accusing**) **1** charge (a person etc.) with a fault or crime. **2** lay the blame on. □ **accuser** n. **accusing** adj.

accused n. (pl. same) a person charged with a crime. □ **accused** adj.

accustom v. make (a person, thing, etc.) used to.

accustomed adj. **1** used to. **2** usual.

AC/DC abbr. designating an appliance etc. that can operate on either alternating or direct current.

ace ● n. **1** a playing card, domino, etc., with a single spot. **2 a** a person who excels in some activity, profession, etc. **b** a successful fighter pilot. **3 a** (in racquet sports etc.) a service (or the resultant point scored) that an opponent fails to touch. **4** Golf a hole in one. ● v. (**aces, aced, acing**) **1** informal achieve a high grade in. **2** Tennis etc. score an ace. **3** Golf complete (a hole) in one stroke. ● adj. slang excellent. □ **ace up one's sleeve** (or **in the hole**) something effective kept in reserve.

acerbic adj. critical in a direct and cruel way; biting. □ **acerbically** adv. [Say a SERB ick]

acetaminophen n. a drug used to relieve pain and reduce fever. [Say a seeta MINNA fin]

acetate n. **1** a salt or ester of acetic acid. **2** a fabric or plastic made from this. [Say ASSA tate]

acetic acid n. the clear liquid acid found in vinegar. [Say a SEAT ick]

acetone n. a colourless volatile liquid ketone valuable as a solvent. [Say ASSA tone]

acetylene n. a colourless hydrocarbon gas used in welding. [Say a SETTA leen]

acetylsalicylic acid n. a drug used to relieve pain and reduce fever. Abbreviation: **ASA**. [Say a seetle salla SILL ick]

ache ● n. **1** a continuous or prolonged dull pain. **2** mental distress. ● v. (**aches, ached, aching**) **1** suffer from or be the source of an ache. **2** desire greatly. □ **achingly** adv.

achieve v. (**achieves, achieved, achieving**) **1** reach or attain by effort; earn. **2** accomplish or carry out. □ **achievable** adj. **achievement** n. **achiever** n.

Achilles heel n. a person's weak or vulnerable point. [Say a KILL eez]

Achilles tendon n. the tendon connecting the heel with the calf muscles. [Say a KILL eez]

achoo interj. representing a sneeze.

achy adj. (**achier, achiest**) full of or suffering from aches. [Say AKE ee]

acid ● n. **1** any of a class of substances that are usu. sour and corrosive, and have a pH of less than 7. **2** any sour substance. **3** slang the drug LSD. ● adj. **1** sour. **2** biting, sharp. **3** Chemistry having the essential properties of an acid. □ **acidic** adj.

acid house n. (also **acid rock**) a kind of synthesized music with a simple repetitive beat.

acidify v. (**acidifies, acidified, acidifying**) make or become acid. □ **acidification** n. [Say a SIDDA fie]

acidity n. **1** an acid quality or state. **2** excessive acid in the stomach. [Say a SIDDA tee]

acidly adv. in an unpleasant or critical way.

acid rain n. rain made acidic by industrial pollutants in the atmosphere.

acid test n. a severe or conclusive test.

ackee n. a tropical evergreen tree with bland, leathery fruit edible only when cooked. [Say ACKY]

acknowledge v. (**acknowledges, acknowledged, acknowledging**) **1** recognize; accept; admit the truth of. **2** confirm the receipt of. **3** acknowledge or express gratitude for (a service). **4** recognize as valid.

acknowledgement n. **1** acceptance of the truth or existence of something. **2** the action of acknowledging. **3** a letter confirming receipt of something. **4** an author's statement of gratitude in a book.

acme n. the highest point or period; the peak of perfection. [Say ACK mee]

acne n. a skin condition characterized by red pimples. [Say ACK nee]

acolyte n. **1** a person assisting a priest in a service. **2** an assistant; a beginner. [Say ACKA lite]

acorn n. the fruit of the oak.

acorn squash n. = PEPPER SQUASH.

acoustic ● adj. **1** relating to sound or the sense of hearing. **2** not electrically amplified. **3** used for soundproofing or modifying sound. ● n. **1** the properties or qualities (of a room, hall, etc.) in transmitting sound. **2** the science of sound. □ **acoustical** adj. **acoustically** adv. [Say a COO stick]

acquaint v. make (a person or oneself)

aware of or familiar with. □ **acquainted with** having personal knowledge of.

acquaintance n. **1** a person one knows slightly. **2** the fact or process of being acquainted. **3** knowledge (of a person or thing).

acquiesce v. (**acquiesces, acquiesced, acquiescing**) accept reluctantly but without protest. □ **acquiescence** n. **acquiescent** adj. [Say ack wee ESS]

acquire v. (**acquires, acquired, acquiring**) come to possess.

acquired immune deficiency syndrome n. see AIDS.

acquired taste n. **1** a liking gained by experience. **2** the object of such a liking.

acquisition n. **1** buying or obtaining assets or objects. **2** an asset or object bought or obtained. **3** an act of acquiring. [Say ackwa ZISH un]

acquisitive adj. excessively eager to acquire money or material things. □ **acquisitiveness** n. [Say a QUIZZA tiv]

acquit v. (**acquits, acquitted, acquitting**) **1** declare not guilty. **2** (**acquit oneself**) behave or perform in a specified way.

acquittal n. the process of freeing or being freed from a charge.

acre n. a measure of land, 4,840 sq. yds., 0.405 ha.

acreage n. **1** a number of acres. **2** an extent of land, esp. farmland. **3** a plot of land with an area of approximately one acre. [Say ACRE idge]

acrid adj. having an unpleasantly bitter or pungent taste or smell. [Say ACK rid]

acrimony n. (pl. **acrimonies**) extreme bitterness or ill feeling. □ **acrimonious** adj. **acrimoniously** adv. [Say ACKRA moany]

acrobat n. a performer of feats of agility, esp. in a circus. □ **acrobatic** adj. **acrobatically** adv.

acrobatics pl. n. acrobatic feats or performance.

acronym n. a word formed from the initial letters of other words, e.g. NATO. [Say ACKRA nim]

across prep. & adv. **1** to or on the other side (of). **2** from one side to another side (of).

acrostic n. a poem or word puzzle in which certain letters in each line form a word or words. [Say a CROSS tick]

acrylic ● adj. **1** of synthetic material made from acrylic acid. **2** (of paint) containing acrylic resin. ● n. acrylic plastic, fabric, or paint. [Say a CRILL ick]

acrylic acid n. a pungent liquid organic acid used to make synthetic resins.

acrylic resin n. any of various transparent colourless polymers of acrylic acid.

act ● n. **1** a deed or action. **2** the process of doing something. **3** a performance or performing group. **4** a pretense. **5** a main division of a theatrical production. **6** a law passed formally by a parliament etc. ● v. **1** behave. **2** perform actions or functions; operate effectively. **3** exert energy or influence. **4 a** perform (a part in) a play, film, etc. **b** pretend. □ **act for** be the (esp. legal) representative of. **act out 1** translate (ideas etc.) into action. **2** (esp. of a child or adolescent) misbehave; behave in an anti-social way. **act up** informal misbehave; give trouble. **get one's act together** informal become properly organized. **get in on the act** informal become a participant.

acting ● n. the art or occupation of performing parts in plays, films, etc. ● adj. serving temporarily or on behalf of another.

action n. **1** the fact or process of doing or acting. **2** forcefulness or energy as a characteristic. **3** the exertion of energy or influence. **4** something done; a deed or act. **5** armed conflict. **6** the way in which a machine etc. works. **7** a legal process; a lawsuit. □ **out of action** not working. **take action** act, esp. against something.

actionable adj. giving cause for legal action.

activate v. (**activates, activated, activating**) **1** make active; bring into action. **2** Chemistry cause reaction in. **3** make radioactive. □ **activation** n. **activator** n.

activated carbon n. (also **activated charcoal**) carbon, esp. charcoal, treated to increase its power to adsorb.

active adj. **1 a** energetic. **b** able to move about or accomplish practical tasks. **2** working, operative. **3** not merely passive or inert. **4** of the form of a verb whose grammatical subject is the person or thing that performs the action. □ **actively** adv.

active duty n. = ACTIVE SERVICE.

active service n. full-time service in the armed forces or police.

activism n. the policy or practice of using vigorous action to bring about political or social change. □ **activist** n.

activity n. (pl. **activities**) **1** the condition of being active. **2** vigorous action. **3** a particular occupation or pursuit.

act of God n. a usu. disastrous event caused by uncontrollable natural forces.

actor *n.* a person who acts a part in a play etc., esp. professionally.

ACTRA *abbr.* Alliance of Canadian Cinema, Television and Radio Artists.

actress *n.* (*pl.* **actresses**) a female who acts a part in a play etc., esp. as a profession.

actual *adj.* existing in fact; real.
□ **actualization** *n.* **actualize** *v.* (**actualizes, actualized, actualizing**)

actuality *n.* (*pl.* **actualities**) actual reality as opposed to what was expected or intended.

actually *adv.* as a fact, really; as a matter of fact.

actuary *n.* (*pl.* **actuaries**) a person who analyzes statistics to calculate insurance risks and premiums. □ **actuarial** *adj.* [*Say* ACK choo airy, ack choo AIRY ul]

acuity *n.* sharpness, acuteness.
[*Say* a CUE a tee]

acumen *n.* the ability to make good judgments and take quick decisions.
[*Say* ACK you mun]

acupressure *n.* = SHIATSU.

acupuncture *n.* a system of complementary medicine in which fine needles are inserted in the skin.
□ **acupuncturist** *v.*

acute *adj.* **1** (of a physical sense or faculty) highly developed; keen. **2** shrewd, perceptive. **3** (of a disease) brief but severe. **4** (of a bad situation) present or experienced to a severe degree. **5** (of an angle) less than 90°. □ **acutely** *adv.* **acuteness** *n.*

AD *abbr.* (of a date) of the Christian era.

ad *n. informal* an advertisement.

adage *n.* a traditional saying.
[*Say* AD idge]

adagio *Music & Dance* ● *adv. & adj.* in slow time. ● *n.* (*pl.* **adagios**) an adagio movement or passage. [*Say* a DAZH ee oh *or* a DADGE ee oh]

Adam *n.* □ **not know a person from Adam** be unable to recognize the person in question.

adamant *adj.* stubbornly resolute; resistant to persuasion. □ **adamantly** *adv.*

Adam's apple *n.* a projection of cartilage at the front of the neck.

adapt *v.* **1 a** fit, adjust (one thing to another). **b** make suitable for a new use or purpose. **2** become adjusted to new conditions. □ **adaptive** *adj.*

adaptable *adj.* able to adapt oneself to or be adapted for new conditions.
□ **adaptability** *n.*

adaptation *n.* (also **adaption**) **1** the act or process of adapting or being adapted.

2 a thing made by adapting something else.

adapter *n.* (also **adaptor**) **1** a device for making equipment compatible. **2** a device for connecting several electrical plugs to one socket or for changing voltage or current.

ADD *abbr.* ATTENTION DEFICIT DISORDER.

add *v.* **1** join (one thing to another) as an increase or supplement. **2** put together (two or more numbers) to find their combined value. **3** say in addition. □ **add up 1** find the total of. **2** amount to; constitute. **3** *informal* make sense.
□ **added** *adj.*

addendum *n.* (*pl.* **addenda**) **1** a thing to be added, esp. (in *pl.*) at the end of a book. **2** an appendix; an addition.
[*Say* a DEN dum, a DEN duh]

adder *n.* **1** any of a variety of non-venomous N American snakes. **2** any of various small venomous snakes of Europe and Asia.

addict *n.* **1** a person addicted to a habit, drug, etc. **2** *informal* an enthusiastic devotee of a sport etc. [*Say* ADD ict]

addicted *adj.* **1** physically and mentally dependent on a particular substance. **2** enthusiastically devoted to a particular thing or activity. □ **addiction** *n.* **addictive** *adj.* [*Say* a DICK tid, a DICK shun, a DICK tiv]

addition *n.* **1** the act or process of adding or being added. **2** a person or thing added. □ **in addition** furthermore. □ **additional** *adj.* **additionally** *adv.*

additive *n.* a thing added to improve or alter a substance.

addle-brained *adj.* (also **addle-pated**) silly.

addled *adj.* **1** confused. **2** (of an egg) rotten, producing no chick.

address ● *n.* (*pl.* **addresses**) **1 a** the place where a person lives or an organization is situated. **b** *Computing* the location of an item of stored information. **c** a code representing a person's location on an email network. **2** a speech delivered to an audience. ● *v.* (**addresses, addressed, addressing**) **1** write the name and address of the intended recipient on. **2** direct in speech or writing. **3** speak or write to, esp. formally.
□ **addressable** *adj.*

addressee *n.* the person to whom something (esp. a letter) is addressed.
[*Say* address EE]

adduce *v.* (**adduces, adduced, adducing**) give as an instance or as evidence. [*Say* a DYOOSS]

adenoidal *adj.* **1** suffering from enlarged adenoids. **2** having the nasal tones of a person with enlarged adenoids. [*Say* adda NOID ul]

adenoids *pl. n.* a mass of lymphatic tissue between the back of the nose and the throat. [*Say* ADDA noids]

adept ● *adj.* highly gifted or skilled. ● *n.* a skilled performer, an expert. □ **adeptly** *adv.* **adeptness** *n.*

adequate *adj.* **1** sufficient, satisfactory. **2** barely sufficient. □ **adequacy** *n.* **adequately** *adv.* [*Say* ADDA quit, ADDA kwuh see]

ADHD *abbr.* ATTENTION DEFICIT HYPERACTIVITY DISORDER.

adhere *v.* (**adheres, adhered, adhering**) **1** stick fast to a surface etc. **2** behave according to; follow in detail.

adherence *n.* the fact of behaving according to a particular rule etc., or of following a particular set of beliefs or a fixed way of doing something: *strict adherence to the rules.* [*Say* ad HEAR ince]

adherent *n.* **1** a supporter of a party, person, etc. **2** a devotee of an activity. [*Say* ad HEAR int]

adhesion *n.* **1** the act or process of adhering. **2** the capacity of a substance to adhere. **3** *Medical* a union of surfaces due to inflammation. [*Say* ad HEE zh'n]

adhesive ● *adj.* sticky. ● *n.* a substance used to stick other substances together. □ **adhesiveness** *n.* [*Say* ad HEE siv]

ad hoc *adv. & adj.* for a particular (usu. exclusive) purpose.

adieu ● *interj.* goodbye. ● *n.* (*pl.* **adieus** or **adieux**) a goodbye. [*Say* ad DYOO (*with* OO *as in* FOOT)]

adipose *n.* fatty connective tissue. [*Say* ADDA pose]

Adirondack chair *n.* = MUSKOKA CHAIR [*Say* adda RON dack]

adjacent *adj.* lying near or adjoining. [*Say* a JAY sunt]

adjective *n.* a word or phrase naming an attribute, added to or grammatically related to a noun to modify it or describe it. □ **adjectival** *adj.* **adjectivally** *adv.* [*Say* ADD jick tiv, ad jeck TIE vul]

adjoin *v.* be close to or joined with. □ **adjoining** *adj.*

adjourn *v.* **1** stop a meeting or an official process for a period of time. **2** move to another place, esp. for entertainment etc. □ **adjournment** *n.* [*Say* a JERN]

adjudicate *v.* (**adjudicates, adjudicated, adjudicating**) **1** act as judge in a competition, etc. **2** decide judicially regarding (a claim etc.).

□ **adjudication** *n.* **adjudicator** *n.* [*Say* a JOODA kate]

adjunct *n.* **1** an additional part. **2** an assistant or subordinate. □ **adjunct** *adj.* [*Say* AD junct]

adjust *v.* **1 a** arrange; order. **b** regulate. **2** make suitable or suited. **3** assess (loss or damages). □ **adjustability** *n.* **adjustable** *adj.* **adjuster** *n.* **adjustment** *n.*

adjutant *n.* **1** *Military* an officer who assists superior officers with administrative work. **2** an assistant. [*Say* AD juh t'nt]

ad lib ● *v.* (**ad libs, ad libbed, ad libbing**) speak or perform without formal preparation; improvise. ● *adj.* improvised. ● *n.* something spoken or played without preparation, rehearsal, etc.

admin *n.* *informal* administration.

administer *v.* **1** attend to the running of; manage. **2** be responsible for the implementation of; perform. **3 a** give out, apply (medication etc.). **b** deliver (a rebuke etc.).

administrate *v.* (**administrates, administrated, administrating**) administer; act as an administrator. □ **administrative** *adj.* **administrator** *n.*

administration *n.* **1** management of business, public affairs, etc. **2** those responsible for administering a business, institution, etc. **3** the government in power.

admirable *adj.* **1** deserving admiration. **2** excellent. □ **admirably** *adv.* [*Say* AD meera bull]

admiral *n.* a naval officer of high rank.

admire *v.* (**admires, admired, admiring**) **1** regard with approval or respect. **2** express one's admiration of. □ **admiration** *n.* **admirer** *n.* **admiring** *adj.*

admissible *adj.* **1** worth accepting or considering. **2** *Law* allowable as evidence. **3** having the right to be admitted. □ **admissibility** *n.* [*Say* ad MISSA bull]

admission *n.* **1** an acknowledgement or confession. **2 a** the act of admitting. **b** a fee paid for this. **3** the department responsible for admitting new students, patients, etc.

admit *v.* (**admits, admitted, admitting**) **1** recognize as true. **2** acknowledge responsibility for. **3 a** allow (a person) entrance or access to enter or join. **b** bring (a person) into a hospital for treatment. **4** allow as possible. □ **admittedly** *adv.*

admittance *n.* permission to enter; the process of entering.

admixture *n.* **1** a mixture. **2** a thing added.

admonish *v.* (**admonishes, admonished, admonishing**)

1 reprimand firmly. **2** urge or advise earnestly. □ **admonition** n. **admonitory** adj. [Say ad MON ish, adma NISH un, ad MONNA tory]

ad nauseam adv. to an excessive or tiresome degree. [Say ad NOZZY um]

ado n. fuss. □ **without further ado** immediately. [Say a DOO]

adobe n. **1** a sun-dried brick made from clay and straw. **2** the clay used for making such bricks. [Say a DOE bee]

adolescent ● adj. **1** between childhood and adulthood. **2** of or characteristic of this age. ● n. an adolescent person. □ **adolescence** n. [Say adda LESS int]

Adonis n. (pl. **Adonises**) an extremely handsome young man. [Say a DON niss]

adopt v. **1** legally take another's child and raise it as one's own. **2** choose to follow (a course of action etc.). **3** assume. □ **adoptable** adj. **adoptee** n. **adopter** n. **adoption** n.

adoptive adj. related by adoption.

adorable adj. inspiring great affection. □ **adorably** adv.

adore v. (**adores, adored, adoring**) **1** regard with honour and deep affection. **2** worship as divine. **3** informal like very much. □ **adoration** n. **adoring** adj. **adoringly** adv.

adorn v. make more beautiful or attractive. □ **adornment** n.

adrenal adj. **1** having to do with the two glands above the kidneys that secrete adrenalin. **2** at or near the kidneys. [Say a DREEN ul]

adrenalin n. (also **adrenaline**) a hormone which increases the rate of circulation, respiration, and metabolism. [Say a DRENNEL un]

Adriatic adj. of or relating to Mediterranean Sea between the Balkans and the Italian peninsula. [Say ay dree ATTIC]

adrift adj. **1** drifting, esp. without direction. **2** away from the intended course; lacking purpose.

adroit adj. skilful and clever. □ **adroitly** adv. **adroitness** n. [Say a DROIT]

ADSL abbr. asymmetric digital subscriber line, a technology for transmitting digital information over standard telephone lines, using most of the bandwidth to transmit information to the user and only a small part to receive it from them.

adsorb v. (usu. of a solid) hold (molecules of a gas or liquid or solute) in a thin layer on its surface. □ **adsorption** n.

adulate v. (**adulates, adulated, adulating**) admire and praise very much

or excessively. □ **adulation** n. **adulatory** adj. [Say AD yuh late, ad yuh LAY sh'n, ADYA luh tory]

adult ● adj. **1** mature, grown-up. **2 a** of or for adults. **b** euphemism sexually explicit. ● n. an adult person. □ **adulthood** n.

adulterate v. (**adulterates, adulterated, adulterating**) render something poorer in quality by adding other or inferior ingredients. □ **adulterant** n. **adulteration** n.

adultery n. (pl. **adulteries**) **1** voluntary sexual intercourse between a married person and a person other than his or her spouse. **2** an adulterous act or relationship. □ **adulterer** n. **adulteress** n. **adulterous** adj.

advance ● v. (**advances, advanced, advancing**) **1** move or put forward. **2** make progress. **3 a** pay (money) before it is due. **b** lend (money). **4** give active support to; promote. **5** put forward (a suggestion). ● n. **1** an act of going forward. **2** progress. **3** an amount of money advanced. **4** an attempt to start a sexual relationship. ● adj. done or supplied beforehand. □ **in advance** ahead in place or time. □ **advancement** n.

advanced adj. **1** far on in progress, time, etc. **2** highly developed, complex.

advantage n. **1** a beneficial feature. **2** benefit, profit. **3** superiority. **4** Tennis the next point won after deuce. **5** Hockey numerical superiority, as on a power play. □ **take advantage of 1** make good use of. **2** exploit or outwit, esp. unfairly. □ **advantageous** adj. **advantageously** adv. [Say ad VAN tidge, ad van TAY juss]

advantaged adj. being in a good social or financial situation.

Advent n. **1** Christianity the season before Christmas. **2** Christianity the coming or Second Coming of Christ. **3** (**advent**) the arrival of an important person or thing. [Say AD vent]

Adventist n. a member of a Christian group that believes in the imminent Second Coming of Christ. [Say ad VENT ist]

adventure ● n. **1** an unusual and exciting experience. **2** a daring enterprise; a hazardous activity. **3** enterprise. ● v. (**adventures, adventured, adventuring**) go upon an adventure. □ **adventure** adj. **adventuresome** adj.

adventurer n. a person who seeks adventure, esp. for gain or enjoyment.

adventuress n. (pl. **adventuresses**) **1** derogatory a woman who pursues financial gain or social advancement, esp. by sexual means. **2** a woman who engages in adventures.

adventurous *adj.* **1** willing to take risks; enterprising. **2** full of new, exciting, or dangerous experiences. □ **adventurously** *adv.*

adverb *n.* a word or phrase that modifies or qualifies another word (esp. an adjective, verb, or other adverb) or a word group. □ **adverbial** *adj. & n.*

adversarial *adj.* **1** involving opposition or conflict. **2** (of legal proceedings) in which the parties in a dispute are responsible for finding and presenting evidence.

adversary *n.* (*pl.* **adversaries**) **1** an enemy. **2** an opponent in a sport or game. [*Say* AD vur sairy]

adverse *adj.* preventing success or development; harmful, unfavourable. □ **adversely** *adv.*

adversity *n.* (*pl.* **adversities**) a difficult or unpleasant situation.

advertise *v.* (**advertises**, **advertised**, **advertising**) **1** draw attention to or describe favourably in a public medium to promote sales. **2** make generally or publicly known. **3** seek to fill a vacancy. □ **advertiser** *n.*

advertisement *n.* **1** a public announcement advertising goods or services. **2** a person or thing regarded as a means of recommending something. [*Say* ad VUR tiss m'nt *or* AD vur tize m'nt]

advice *n.* **1** an opinion or recommendation about future action. **2** formal notice of a transaction.

advisable *adj.* recommended, sensible. □ **advisability** *n.*

advise *v.* (**advises**, **advised**, **advising**) **1** give advice to. **2** recommend; offer as advice. **3** inform, notify. □ **adviser** (also **advisor**) *n.* [*Say* ad VIZE]

advised *adj.* behaving as someone, esp. the speaker, would recommend; sensible. □ **advisedly** *adv.*

advisement *n.* □ **take under advisement** reserve judgment while considering.

advisory ● *adj.* having the power to advise. ● *n.* (*pl.* **advisories**) an advisory statement, esp. about bad weather. [*Say* ad VISOR ee]

advocate ● *n.* **1** a person who supports or speaks in favour. **2** a person who pleads for another. **3** a lawyer. ● *v.* (**advocates**, **advocated**, **advocating**) recommend or support by argument. □ **advocacy** *n.* [*Say* ADVA k't *for the noun,* ADVA kate *for the verb,* ADVA kuh see]

adware *n. Computing* software displaying paid advertisements and distributed free of charge (compare SPYWARE).

adze *n.* a tool similar to an axe, used for cutting away the surface of wood. [*Say* ADZ]

Aegean *adj.* of or relating to the Aegean Sea between Greece and Turkey. [*Say* a GEE un]

aegis *n.* (*pl.* **aegises**) the protection, backing, or support of someone. [*Say* EE jiss]

aeon *n.* = EON. [*Say* EE on]

aerate *v.* (**aerates**, **aerated**, **aerating**) **1** introduce a gas into a liquid. **2** introduce air into (soil etc.). □ **aeration** *n.* **aerator** *n.* [*Say* AIR ate]

aerial ● *adj.* **1** by, from, or involving aircraft. **2** existing, moving, taking place, etc. in the air. ● *n.* = ANTENNA 1. [*Say* AIRY ul]

aerie *n.* **1** a nest of a bird of prey, esp. an eagle, built high up. **2** a high place or position. [*Say* AIRY *or* EERIE]

aero- *comb. form* **1** relating to air or the atmosphere. **2** relating to aircraft. [*Say* AIR oh]

aerobatics *pl. n.* feats of expert and usu. spectacular flying and manoeuvring of aircraft. □ **aerobat** *n.* **aerobatic** *adj.* [*Say* air oh BAT ics]

aerobic *adj.* **1** increasing or pertaining to oxygen consumption by the body. **2** of or relating to aerobics. □ **aerobically** *adv.* [*Say* a ROBE ick]

aerobics *pl. n.* exercises, esp. those done to music, designed to increase fitness by sustained aerobic activity. [*Say* a ROBE icks]

aerodynamic *adj.* **1** of aerodynamics. **2** designed to minimize drag. □ **aerodynamically** *adv.* [*Say* air oh die NAM ick]

aerodynamics *pl. n.* **1** the interaction between the air and solid bodies moving through it. **2** the study of this. [*Say* air oh die NAM icks]

aeronautics *pl. n.* the science or practice of motion or travel in the air. □ **aeronautical** *adj.* [*Say* air oh NOT icks]

aerosol *n.* **1** a substance packed under pressure into a container with a device for releasing it as a fine spray. **2** a suspension of particles dispersed in air etc. □ **aerosolize** *v.* [*Say* AIR a sol]

aerospace *n.* **1** the earth's atmosphere and outer space. **2** the technology or industry of flight in the atmosphere and in space. [*Say* AIR oh space]

aesthete *n.* a person who has or professes

to have a special appreciation of beauty. [*Say* ess THEET]

aesthetic ● *adj.* **1** concerned with beauty or the appreciation of beauty. **2** having such appreciation; sensitive to beauty. **3** designed to give pleasure through beauty. ● *n.* **1** (in *pl.*) the philosophy of the beautiful, esp. in art. **2** (in *pl.*) aesthetically pleasing elements. □ **aesthetically** *adv.* **aestheticism** *n.* [*Say* es THETTIC]

aesthetician *n.* **1** a person versed in or devoted to aesthetics. **2** a beautician. [*Say* estha TISH un]

afar *adv.* at or to a distance. □ **from afar** from a distance.

affable *adj.* friendly, good-natured. □ **affability** *n.* **affably** *adv.*

affair *n.* **1** a concern; a matter to be attended to. **2 a** a celebrated or notorious happening. **b** a thing or event of a specified sort. **3** an esp. adulterous love relationship between two people. **4** (in *pl.*) business dealings or matters of public interest.

affect[1] *v.* **1 a** produce an effect on; influence. **b** (of a disease etc.) attack. **2** touch the feelings of. □ **affecting** *adj.* **affectingly** *adv.*

affect[2] *v.* **1** pretend. **2** wear or assume something pretentiously or in order to impress.

affectation *n.* behaviour, speech, etc. that is artificial and designed to impress. [*Say* aff eck TAY shun]

affected *adj.* artificial and designed to impress. □ **affectedly** *adv.*

affectless *adj.* characterized by lack of feeling; emotionless, cold. □ **affectlessness** *n.*

affection *n.* a gentle feeling of fondness or liking.

affectionate *adj.* loving, fond; showing love or tenderness. □ **affectionately** *adv.*

affective *adj. Psychology* relating to moods, feelings, and attitudes.

affidavit *n.* a written statement confirmed by oath, for use as evidence in court. [*Say* affa DAY vit]

affiliate ● *v.* (**affiliates, affiliated, affiliating**) officially link a person, group or oneself to an organization. ● *n.* an affiliated person or organization. □ **affiliated** *adj.* **affiliation** *n.* [*Say* a FILLY ate *for the verb,* a FILLY it *for the noun*]

affinity *n.* (*pl.* **affinities**) **1** a spontaneous or natural liking for or attraction to a person or thing. **2** relationship, esp. by marriage or adoption. **3** resemblance in structure. [*Say* a FINNA tee]

affirm *v.* **1** assert strongly; state as a fact.

2 *Law* confirm, ratify (a judgment). □ **affirmation** *n.*

affirmative ● *adj.* **1** agreeing with or consenting to a statement or request. **2** *Grammar* stating that a fact is so; asserting. ● *n.* **1** an affirmative statement etc. **2** a position of agreement or confirmation. □ **affirmatively** *adv.* [*Say* a FIRMA tiv]

affirmative action *n.* a policy to favour those who often suffer from discrimination, esp. in employment.

affix ● *v.* (**affixes, affixed, affixing**) **1** attach, fasten or join. **2** add or append. ● *n.* (*pl.* **affixes**) a prefix or suffix. □ **affixation** *n.* [*Say* a FIX *for the verb,* AFF ix *for the noun*]

afflict *v.* distress with bodily or mental suffering. □ **affliction** *n.*

affluent *adj.* wealthy, rich. □ **affluence** *n.* [*Say* AFF loo int]

afford *v.* **1 a** have enough money, time, etc., for. **b** be able to do something (esp. without adverse consequences). **2** provide. □ **affordability** *n.* **affordable** *adj.*

affront ● *n.* an action or remark that causes offence. ● *v.* offend or insult. [*Say* a FRONT]

Afghan *n.* **1** (also **Afghani**) a native or national of Afghanistan. **2** the official language of Afghanistan. **3** (**afghan**) a knitted or crocheted blanket. **4** (also **Afghan hound**) a tall hunting dog with long silky hair. □ **Afghan** *adj.* [*Say* AF gan]

aficionado *n.* (*pl.* **aficionados**) a person who is very knowledgeable and enthusiastic about an activity or subject. [*Say* a fisha NADDO *or* a fisha NODDO]

afield *adv.* away from home; to or at a distance.

afire *adv. & adj.* **1** on fire or as if on fire. **2** intensely excited.

aflame *adv. & adj.* **1** in flames. **2** = AFIRE 2.

afloat *adv. & adj.* **1** floating in water or air. **2** on board ship. **3** out of debt or difficulty.

afoot *adv. & adj.* **1** in operation; progressing. **2** stirring; on the move. **3** on foot.

aforementioned *adj.* (also **aforesaid**) previously mentioned.

aforethought *adj.* premeditated.

afoul *adv.* (usu. in **run** or **fall afoul of**) into conflict or difficulty with.

afraid *adj.* **1** alarmed, frightened. **2** unwilling or reluctant for fear of the consequences. □ **be afraid** admit or declare with regret.

A-frame *n.* a house etc. having a frame in the shape of a capital letter A.

afresh *adv.* anew; in a new way.

African *n.* **1** a native or inhabitant of

Africa. **2** a person of African descent.
□ **African** adj.

African-American n. an American
citizen of black African descent.

African-Canadian n. a Canadian citizen
of black African descent.

African violet n. a plant with heart-
shaped velvety leaves, grown as a
houseplant.

Afrikaans n. the language of the
Afrikaner people in South Africa,
developed from Dutch. [Say affra KONCE]

Afrikaner n. an Afrikaans-speaking white
South African. [Say affra CONNER]

Afro n. (pl. **Afros**) a hairstyle of tight curls
formed into a bushy or frizzy mass.

Afro- comb. form African.

Afro-American n. an American black
person. □ **Afro-American** adj.

Afro-Canadian n. & adj. AFRICAN-
CANADIAN.

Afro-Caribbean n. a person of African
descent in or from the Caribbean. □ **Afro-
Caribbean** adj.

aft adv. at or toward the stern of a ship or
tail of an aircraft.

after ● prep. **1** following in time; later than.
2 in view of. **3** in spite of. **4** behind. **5** in
pursuit of. **6** about, concerning. **7** next in
importance to. ● conj., adj. & adv. later in time
(than); following (an event). □ **after all** in
spite of all that has happened or has been
said etc.

afterbirth n. the placenta and fetal
membranes discharged from the uterus
after childbirth.

afterburner n. an auxiliary burner in a jet
engine to increase thrust.

aftercare n. care of a person after a stay
in hospital or on release from prison.

after-effect n. an effect that follows after
an interval.

afterglow n. **1** a light remaining after its
source has disappeared. **2** a feeling of
happiness etc. following a successful event.

after-hours adj. after the usual operating
hours.

afterlife n. life after death.

aftermath n. the consequences or after-
effects of an event, esp. when unpleasant.

afternoon n. the time from noon to
evening.

aftershave n. a scented lotion for use
after shaving.

aftershock n. **1** a lesser shock following
the main shock of an earthquake. **2** an
after-effect.

aftertaste n. a taste lingering in the
mouth after eating or drinking.

afterthought n. something thought of or
added later.

afterwards adv. (also **afterward**) later.

afterword n. concluding remarks in a
book by the author or by someone else.

AG abbr. **1** ATTORNEY GENERAL. **2** Cdn
AUDITOR GENERAL.

again adv. **1** another time; once more. **2** as
in a previous position or condition. **3** in
addition. **4** besides. **5** on the other hand.
□ **again and again** repeatedly.

against prep. **1** in opposition to. **2** in
contact with. **3** to the disadvantage of. **4** in
contrast to. **5** in anticipation of or
preparation for.

agape adv. & adj. gaping, open-mouthed.
[Say a GAPE]

agar n. (also **agar-agar**) a gelatinous
substance obtained from red seaweed, used
as a food thickener, a culture medium, etc.
[Say AY gar]

agate n. any of several varieties of hard
usu. streaked quartz. [Say AG it]

age ● n. **1 a** the length of time that a
person or thing has existed. **b** a particular
point in one's life. **2 a** informal a long time.
b a distinct period of the past. **3** old age.
● v. (**ages, aged**; pres. part. **aging** or
ageing) **1** grow old or appear to grow old.
2 mature. □ **of age** adult (esp. as defined
by law).

aged adj. **1** of the age of. **2** having lived
long; old. [Say AGE ed for sense 2]

ageism n. prejudice or discrimination on
the grounds of age. □ **ageist** adj. & n.
[Say AGE ism, AGE ist]

ageless adj. **1** not aging or appearing to
age. **2** eternal.

agency n. (pl. **agencies**) **1** an
organization or government department
providing a service. **2** a person or business
operating on behalf of another. **3** the duty,
function or office of an agent. **4** action.

agenda n. (pl. **agendas**) **1** a list of things
to be considered or done. **2** an
appointment diary. [Say a JEN duh]

agent n. **1** a person who provides a specific
service etc. **2** a person who acts for or
represents another. **3** a person or thing
that produces an effect. **4** a spy.

age of consent n. the age at which
marriage or consent to sexual intercourse
is valid in law.

age-old adj. having existed for ages.

agglomerate ● v. (**agglomerates,
agglomerated, agglomerating**)
collect or accumulate into a mass. ● n. **1** a
mass or collection of things. **2** a rock
formed of large volcanic fragments.
□ **agglomeration** n.

[*Say* a GLOMMER ate *for the verb*, a GLOMMER it *for the noun*]

agglutinate *v.* (**agglutinates**, **agglutinated**, **agglutinating**) **1** stick together as with glue. **2** (of bacteria etc.) clump together. □ **agglutination** *n.* [*Say* a GLUE tin ate]

aggrandize *v.* (**aggrandizes**, **aggrandized**, **aggrandizing**) **1** increase the power, rank, or wealth of. **2** cause to appear greater than is the case. □ **aggrandizement** *n.* [*Say* a GRAN dize]

aggravate *v.* (**aggravates**, **aggravated**, **aggravating**) **1** make a problem, injury, or offence worse. **2** annoy, exasperate (a person). □ **aggravating** *adj.* **aggravation** *n.*

aggravated assault *n.* *Law* assault in which the victim's injuries or death makes the crime more severe.

aggregate ● *n.* a whole or mass formed by combining several different elements. ● *adj.* formed or calculated by combining many separate items. ● *v.* (**aggregates**, **aggregated**, **aggregating**) combine into one mass. □ **aggregation** *n.* [*Say* AGRA git *for the noun and adjective*, AGRA gate *for the verb*, agra GAY sh'n]

aggression *n.* **1** an unprovoked attack or the practice of making such attacks. **2** hostile behaviour.

aggressive *adj.* **1** forceful; energetic. **2** hostile. □ **aggressively** *adv.* **aggressiveness** *n.*

aggressor *n.* a person or country that attacks without provocation.

aggrieved *adj.* feeling resentment at having been unfairly treated. [*Say* a GREEVD]

aghast *adj.* filled with horror or shock. [*Say* a GAST]

agile *adj.* **1** able to move quickly and gracefully. **2** mentally acute. □ **agilely** *adv.* **agility** *n.* [*Say* ADGE ile *or* ADGE'll, a JILLA tee]

aging *n.* growing or causing to grow old. □ **aging** *adj.*

agitate *v.* (**agitates**, **agitated**, **agitating**) **1** disturb or excite. **2** stir up or attempt to stir up public interest. **3** shake or move briskly. □ **agitated** *adj.* **agitatedly** *adv.* **agitation** *n.*

agitator *n.* **1** a person who agitates for or against a cause. **2** an apparatus for agitating liquid in a washing machine.

agitprop *n.* pro-communist propaganda esp. in Soviet Russia. [*Say* ADGE it prop]

aglow *adj.* glowing.

AGM *abbr.* annual general meeting, a yearly meeting of members or shareholders of a business or organization.

agnostic *n.* a person who believes that nothing is known, or can be known, about God. □ **agnosticism** *n.* [*Say* ag NOSS tik, ag NOSSTA sism]

ago *adv.* earlier, before the present.

agog *adj.* very eager or curious to hear or see something.

agonize *v.* (**agonizes**, **agonized**, **agonizing**) **1** undergo (esp. mental) anguish. **2** cause agony to. □ **agonized** *adj.* **agonizing** *adj.* **agonizingly** *adv.*

agony *n.* (*pl.* **agonies**) **1** extreme mental or physical suffering. **2** the final stages of a painful death.

agoraphobia *n.* an abnormal fear of open spaces or public places. □ **agoraphobic** *adj. & n.* [*Say* a gora FOE bee uh, a gora FOE bick]

agrarian *adj.* of or relating to the land or its cultivation. [*Say* a GRARE ee un]

agree *v.* (**agrees**, **agreed**, **agreeing**) **1** hold a similar opinion. **2** consent. **3 a** become or be in harmony. **b** suit; be good for. **c** *Grammar* have the same number, gender, case, or person as. **4** consent to or approve of. □ **agree to differ** leave a difference of opinion etc. unresolved.

agreeable *adj.* **1** pleasant; enjoyable. **2** willing to agree. **3** acceptable. □ **agreeably** *adv.*

agreement *n.* **1** the act of agreeing. **2** mutual understanding. **3** an arrangement between parties or the contract outlining this. **4** *Grammar* the condition of having the same number, gender, case, or person. **5** a state of being harmonious or consistent.

agribusiness *n.* (*pl.* **agribusinesses**) **1** agriculture conducted on strictly commercial principles. **2** the group of industries dealing with the produce of, and services to, farming.

agriculture *n.* the science or practice of farming. □ **agricultural** *adj.* **agriculturalist** *n.* **agriculturally** *adv.*

agri-food *adj.* esp. *Cdn* concerned with or involved in food production or processing.

agroforestry *n.* agriculture in which there is integrated management of trees or shrubs along with conventional crops or livestock.

agrology *n.* *Cdn* the application of science to agriculture. □ **agrologist** *n.* [*Say* a GRAWLA jee]

agronomy *n.* the science of soil management and crop production. □ **agronomic** *adj.* **agronomist** *n.* [*Say* a GRONNA mee]

aground *adj. & adv.* (of a ship) on or onto the bottom of shallow water.

ah *interj.* expressing surprise, sudden realization, etc.

aha *interj.* expressing triumph, etc.

ahead *adv.* **1** further forward in space or time. **2** in the lead. **3** straight forwards. □ **ahead of 1** further forward or advanced than. **2** before.

ahem *interj.* used to attract attention, express disapproval, etc.

Ahousaht *n.* (also **Ahousat**) a member of the principal group of Nuu-chah-nulth. [*Say* a HOWZ ut]

ahoy *interj.* used to hail a ship or to attract attention.

AI *abbr.* artificial intelligence.

aid ● *n.* **1** help. **2** financial or material help. **3** a person or thing that helps. ● *v.* help, assist. □ **in aid of** in support of.

aide *n.* **1** an assistant. **2** an aide-de-camp.

aide-de-camp *n.* (*pl.* **aides-de-camp**) an officer acting as a confidential assistant to a senior officer. [*Say* aid duh COMP]

AIDS *n.* (also **Aids**) acquired immune deficiency syndrome, a viral disease marked by severe loss of resistance to infection.

ail *v.* trouble or afflict in mind or body.

ailing *adj.* in poor health or condition.

ailment *n.* an illness, esp. a minor one.

aim ● *v.* **1** intend or try. **2** direct or point (a weapon, remark, etc.). **3** seek to attain or achieve. ● *n.* **1** a purpose or intention. **2** the directing of a weapon etc. □ **take aim** direct a weapon etc. at an object.

aimless *adj.* without direction or purpose. □ **aimlessly** *adv.* **aimlessness** *n.*

air ● *n.* **1** an invisible gaseous substance, a mixture mainly of oxygen and nitrogen. **2** the open space above the surface of the earth; the atmosphere. **3 a** a distinctive characteristic. **b** one's manner or bearing. **c** (esp. in *pl.*) an affected manner. **4** a tune or melody. ● *v.* **1** expose to the open air. **2** express publicly. **3** broadcast (a program). □ **in the air** prevalent; gaining currency. **on** (or **off**) **the air** in (or not in) the process of broadcasting. **up in the air 1** aloft. **2** uncertain, undetermined. **walk on air** feel elated. □ **airless** *adj.* **airlessness** *n.*

airbag *n.* a device that inflates on impact to protect a vehicle's occupants in a collision.

airborne *adj.* **1** moving through or carried by the air. **2** (of military activity) involving paratroops.

airbrush ● *n.* (*pl.* **airbrushes**) a device for spraying colour over a surface by means of compressed air, used esp. to retouch photographs. ● *v.* (**airbrushes, airbrushed, airbrushing**) paint with an airbrush.

air command *n.* **1** a major subdivision of an air force. **2** (**Air Command**) the official name for the Canadian air force.

air conditioning *n.* a system or device for lowering temperature and humidity. □ **air-conditioned** *adj.* **air conditioner** *n.*

aircraft *n.* (*pl.* **aircraft**) a machine capable of flight, esp. an airplane or helicopter.

aircraft carrier *n.* a warship that carries and serves as a base for airplanes.

aircrew *n.* the crew of an aircraft.

airdate *n.* the date on which a television or radio program is aired.

airdrop ● *v.* (**airdrops, airdropped, airdropping**) deliver by parachute from an aircraft. ● *n.* a delivery in this way.

Airedale *n.* a large breed of terrier with a rough coat. [*Say* AIR dale]

airfare *n.* the fare for transportation by air.

airfield *n.* an area of land where aircraft take off and land etc.

airflow *n.* a current of air, esp. that encountered by a moving aircraft or vehicle.

airfoil *n.* a structure with curved surfaces, e.g. a wing or tailplane, designed to give lift in flight.

air force *n.* the branch of a nation's armed forces concerned with fighting or defence in the air.

airframe *n.* the body of an aircraft as distinct from its engine(s).

airfreight ● *n.* the transport of goods by air. ● *v.* transport goods by air.

air gun *n.* a gun using compressed air to propel pellets etc.

airhead *n. slang* usu. *derogatory* a foolish person. □ **airheaded** *adj.*

air hockey *n.* a game in which players use paddles to direct a plastic disc supported on a cushion of air over an oblong surface.

air horn *n.* a horn which produces sound by compressed air.

airily *adv.* showing a lack of concern.

airing *n.* **1** exposure to fresh air. **2** public expression of an opinion etc.

air-kiss *v.* pretend to kiss (someone or something) while actually kissing the air, e.g. near their cheek. □ **air kiss** *n.* **air-kisser** *n.*

airlift ● *n.* the transport of troops and supplies by air. ● *v.* transport in this way.

airline *n.* an organization providing regular flights for public use.

airliner *n.* a large passenger aircraft.

airlock *n.* **1** a stoppage of the flow in a pump or pipe, caused by an air bubble. **2** an airtight compartment which permits movement between areas at different pressures.

airmail *n.* a system of transporting mail by air.

airman *n.* (*pl.* **airmen**) a pilot or member of the crew of an aircraft, esp. in an air force.

air mass *n.* a very large body of air with a roughly uniform temperature and humidity.

airplane *n.* a powered flying vehicle with fixed wings.

airplay *n.* broadcasting (of recorded music).

air pocket *n.* an apparent vacuum in the air causing an aircraft to drop suddenly.

airport *n.* a complex of runways and buildings for the takeoff, landing, and maintenance of civil aircraft.

air raid *n.* an attack by military aircraft.

air rifle *n.* a rifle using compressed air to propel pellets etc.

airship *n.* a powered balloon that can be steered.

airsick *adj.* affected with nausea due to travel in an aircraft. □ **airsickness** *n.*

airspace *n.* the air available to aircraft to fly in, esp. the part subject to the jurisdiction of a particular country.

airspeed *n.* the speed of an aircraft relative to the air through which it is moving.

airstream *n.* a current of air.

airstrip *n.* a strip of ground suitable for the takeoff and landing of aircraft.

airtight *adj.* **1** not allowing air to pass through. **2** without weakness.

airtime *n.* **1** time allotted for a broadcast etc. **2** time spent using a cellphone.

air traffic control *n.* an airport department which controls and observes air traffic. □ **air traffic controller** *n.*

airwaves *pl. n.* radio waves used in broadcasting.

airway *n.* **1** a recognized route followed by aircraft. **2** the passage by which air reaches the lungs.

airworthy *adj.* (of an aircraft) fit to fly. □ **airworthiness** *n.*

airy *adj.* (**airier**, **airiest**) **1** spacious and well ventilated. **2** casual, dismissive. **3** delicate; light and thin. □ **airiness** *n.*

airy-fairy *adj. informal* impractical, foolishly idealistic.

aisle *n.* a passage between rows of seats, shelves in a supermarket, etc. [*Say* ILE]

aitch *n.* the letter H.

Aivilik *n.* a branch of the Iglulik Inuit of Canada's Arctic. [*Say* EYE vuh lick]

ajar *adv. & adj.* (of a door) slightly open.

AK-47 *n.* (*pl.* **AK-47s**) a Soviet-designed assault rifle.

a.k.a. *abbr.* also known as.

akimbo *adv.* with hands on the hips and elbows turned outwards. [*Say* a KIM bo]

akin *adj.* of similar character.

alabaster ● *n.* a translucent usu. white form of gypsum. ● *adj.* of or like alabaster. [*Say* ALLA bast er]

à la carte *adv. & adj.* ordered as separately priced item(s) from a menu. [*Say* alla CART]

alacrity *n.* speed or willingness. [*Say* a LACK ruh tee]

à la mode *adj.* **1** in fashion; fashionable. **2** served with ice cream.

alarm ● *n.* **1** a warning of danger etc. **2** a sound or device to warn, alert, or signal. **3** frightened expectation of danger or difficulty. ● *v.* **1** frighten or disturb. **2** warn of danger. □ **alarming** *adj.* **alarmingly** *adv.*

alarmist ● *n.* a person who exaggerates a danger, thus causing needless alarm. ● *adj.* creating needless alarm. □ **alarmism** *n.*

alas *interj.* an expression of regret, sorrow, etc.

alb *n.* a white vestment worn by some Christian clergy.

albacore *n.* a long-finned tuna. [*Say* ALBA core]

Albanian *n.* **1 a** a native or national of Albania. **b** a person of Albanian descent. **2** the language of Albania. □ **Albanian** *adj.* [*Say* al BAINY un]

albatross *n.* (*pl.* **albatrosses**) **1** any of several large seabirds which come ashore only to nest. **2** a source of frustration, guilt, etc. [*Say* ALBA tross]

albedo *n.* (*pl.* **albedos**) the proportion of light or radiation that is reflected by a surface, esp. that of a planet and the moon. [*Say* al BEE doe]

albeit *conj.* though. [*Say* all BE it]

Albertan ● *adj.* of or relating to Alberta. ● *n.* a resident or native of Alberta.

albino *n.* (*pl.* **albinos**) a person or animal born without pigment in the skin, hair, and eyes. [*Say* al BINE oh]

album *n.* **1** a blank book for keeping photographs, stamps, etc. in. **2** a disc or tape comprising several pieces of music.

albumen *n.* **1** egg white. **2** = ENDOSPERM. [*Say* al BYOO m'n]

albumin *n.* any of a class of water-soluble

proteins found in egg white, blood, etc. [Say al BYOO m'n]

alchemy *n.* (*pl.* **alchemies**) the medieval forerunner of chemistry, esp. seeking to turn base metals into gold or silver. □ **alchemical** *adj.* **alchemist** *n.* [Say ALKA mee]

alcohol *n.* **1** (also **ethyl alcohol**) a colourless volatile inflammable liquid forming the intoxicating element in spirits etc. **2** a drink containing this.

alcoholic ● *adj.* relating to alcohol. ● *n.* a person suffering from alcoholism.

alcoholism *n.* an addiction to alcoholic liquor.

alcove *n.* **1** a recess, esp. in the wall of a room. **2** an arbour or shady bower.

aldehyde *n.* any of a class of compounds formed by the oxidation of alcohols. [Say ALDA hide]

al dente *adj.* cooked so as to be still firm when bitten. [Say al DEN tay]

alder *n.* a tree or shrub related to the birch, with catkins and toothed leaves. [Say AWL der]

alderman *n.* (*pl.* **aldermen**) a city councillor. □ **aldermanic** *adj.* [Say AWL der m'n, awl der MANIC]

aldosterone *n.* a steroid hormone isolated from the adrenal gland. [Say awl doe STAIR own]

ale *n.* a beer fermented rapidly at high temperatures.

alert ● *adj.* **1** quick to notice danger or change; vigilant. **2** able to think clearly. ● *n.* an alarm warning of an attack, storm, etc. ● *v.* warn someone of a danger. □ **alertly** *adv.* **alertness** *n.*

Aleut *n.* **1** (*pl.* **Aleut** or **Aleuts**) a member of an Aboriginal people living in the Aleutian Islands and southwestern Alaska. **2** the language of the Aleut. □ **Aleutian** *adj. & n.* [Say AL yoot or a LOOT, a LOO sh'n]

alewife *n.* (*pl.* **alewives**) a fish of the herring family.

alfalfa *n.* a leguminous plant used for fodder, and the sprouts of which are used as a salad vegetable.

alfredo *adj.* designating a sauce of butter, cream, and Parmesan cheese. [Say al FRAY doe]

alfresco *adv. & adj.* in the open air. [Say al FRESS co]

alga *n.* (*pl.* **algae**) a simple, non-flowering, and typically aquatic plant that contains chlorophyll but lacks vascular tissue. □ **algal** *adj.* [Say AL guh *for the singular*, AL jee *for the plural*]

algebra *n.* the branch of mathematics that

uses letters and other general symbols to represent numbers in formulas. □ **algebraic** *adj.* [Say ALJA bruh, alja BRAY ick]

algicide *n.* a substance that destroys algae. [Say ALJA side]

Algonquian *n.* (also **Algonkian**) **1** the largest Aboriginal language group in Canada. **2** (*pl.* **Algonquian** or **Algonquians**) a member of any of the Aboriginal peoples speaking languages of this family. □ **Algonquian** (also **Algonkian**) *adj.* [Say al GON kwee in *or* al GON kee in]

Algonquin *n.* **1** (*pl.* **Algonquin** or **Algonquins**) a member of an Aboriginal people living along the Ottawa River and its tributaries. **2** the dialect of Algonquian spoken by the Algonquin. □ **Algonquin** *adj.* [Say al GON kwin]

algorithm *n.* a process or set of rules used for calculation or problem-solving. □ **algorithmic** *adj.* [Say ALGA rhythm, alga RHYTHMIC]

alias ● *adv.* also known as. ● *n.* (*pl.* **aliases**) **1** an assumed name. **2** *Computing* a command or address which substitutes for another. [Say AILY us]

alibi *n.* (*pl.* **alibis**) **1** a claim or evidence that one was elsewhere when a crime took place. **2** an excuse or justification. [Say ALA bye]

alien ● *adj.* **1** not familiar; unacceptable or repugnant. **2** foreign. **3** of or relating to beings supposedly from other worlds. ● *n.* **1** a resident of a country who is not a naturalized citizen. **2** a being from another world.

alienate *v.* (**alienates**, **alienated**, **alienating**) **1** cause to become hostile. **2** cause to feel isolated or estranged from. □ **alienated** *adj.* **alienation** *n.*

alight¹ *v.* (**alights**, **alighted**, **alighting**) **1** get down (from a vehicle, horse, etc.). **2** come to rest or settle. **3** find by chance; notice.

alight² *adj.* **1** on fire. **2** lighted up; excited.

align *v.* **1** put in a straight line or the correct position in relation to others. **2** (**align oneself with**) give support to a cause etc. □ **alignment** *n.* [Say a LINE]

alike ● *adv.* in a similar way; equally. ● *adj.* similar; indistinguishable.

alimentary canal *n.* the passage along which food passes from the mouth to the anus. [Say ala MENTA ree]

alimony *n.* money paid to a spouse or former spouse after separation or divorce.

alive *adj.* **1** living, not dead. **2 a** (of a thing) existing; continuing. **b** provoking interest.

3 lively, active. **4** aware of. **5** swarming or teeming with. □ **alive and kicking** *informal* very active; lively.

alkali *n.* (*pl.* **alkalis**) **1** a substance that can neutralize acids. **2** a soluble salt existing in arid soil that damages crops. [*Say* ALKA lie]

alkaline *adj.* having the nature of an alkali; having a pH above 7. □ **alkalinity** *n.* [*Say* ALKA line]

alkaloid *n.* any of a series of nitrogenous organic compounds of plant origin, including morphine, quinine, and nicotine. [*Say* ALKA loyd]

alkane *n.* any of a series of saturated hydrocarbons, including methane and ethane. [*Say* AL cane]

alkyd *n.* any of a group of synthetic resins commonly used in paints etc. [*Say* AL kid]

all ● *adj.* **1** the whole amount, quantity, or extent of. **2** any whatever. **3** greatest possible. ● *n.* **1** all or every one of the persons or things concerned; everything. **2** one's whole strength or resources. ● *adv.* **1** entirely. **2** as an intensifier. **2** (in games) on both sides. □ **all along** all the time. **all but** very nearly. **all for** strongly in favour of. **as all get-out** *informal* to a high degree. **all in all** everything considered. **all one** (or **the same**) a matter of indifference. **all over 1** finished. **2** everywhere. **all the same** nevertheless. **all that** *informal* particularly; very. **all there** *informal* mentally alert. **at all** in any way. **in all** altogether. **one and all** everyone.

Allah *n.* the name of the Supreme Being in Islam. [*Say* ALA *or* OLLA]

all-American ● *adj.* **1** (of an athlete) chosen as one of the best in the US. **2** typically or exclusively American. ● *n.* an all-American athlete.

all around *adj.* **1** (of a person) versatile. **2** comprehensive.

allay *v.* (**allays, allayed, allaying**) **1** diminish (fear etc.). **2** alleviate (pain etc.). [*Say* a LAY]

all-Canadian ● *adj.* **1** (esp. of an athlete) chosen as one of the best in Canada. **2** truly, typically, or exclusively Canadian. ● *n.* an all-Canadian athlete.

all-candidates meeting *n.* Cdn a public meeting held during an election campaign at which all candidates for an electoral district are present.

all-clear *n.* a signal that danger or difficulty is over.

all-dressed *adj.* Cdn designating an item of food served with all the optional garnishes.

allegation *n.* an assertion or accusation of wrongdoing, esp. an unproven one. [*Say* ala GAY sh'n]

allege *v.* (**alleges, alleged, alleging**) declare to be the case, esp. without proof. □ **alleged** *adj.* **allegedly** *adv.* [*Say* a LEDGE]

allegiance *n.* **1** loyalty (to a person or cause etc.). **2** duty to a sovereign or government. [*Say* a LEE jince]

allegory *n.* (*pl.* **allegories**) a story, picture, etc., in which each character or event symbolizes an idea or quality. □ **allegorical** *adj.* **allegorically** *adv.* [*Say* ALA gory]

allegretto *adv. & adj.* Music in a fairly brisk tempo. [*Say* ala GRETTO]

allegro Music ● *adv. & adj.* in a brisk tempo. ● *n.* (*pl.* **allegros**) an allegro passage or movement. [*Say* a LEG roe]

allele *n.* one of the (usu. two) alternative forms of a gene that occupy the same relative position on a chromosome. [*Say* AL eel]

alleluia *interj.* God be praised (as an expression of rejoicing etc.). [*Say* ala LOU yuh *or* ollay LOU yuh]

all-embracing *adj.* including everything.

allergen *n.* any substance that causes an allergic reaction. □ **allergenic** *adj.* [*Say* ALLER jin, aller JEN ick]

allergic *adj.* **1** having an allergy to. **2** caused by an allergy.

allergist *n.* a doctor specializing in treating allergies. [*Say* ALLER jist]

allergy *n.* (*pl.* **allergies**) **1** a condition of reacting adversely to certain substances. **2** *informal* a strong dislike.

alleviate *v.* (**alleviates, alleviated, alleviating**) lessen or make less severe. □ **alleviation** *n.* [*Say* a LEEVY ate]

alley *n.* (*pl.* **alleys**) **1** a narrow passageway between or behind buildings. **2** a path in a park or garden. **3** = BOWLING ALLEY. **4** (usu. **Alley**) an area known for a specified characteristic. □ **up one's alley** *informal* suited to one's interests or abilities.

alley cat *n.* a stray cat in an urban area.

alley-oop *n.* Basketball **1** a high lob or pass caught by a leaping teammate. **2** a basket scored by the receiver of such a pass.

alleyway *n.* = ALLEY 1.

alliance *n.* **1 a** formal union or agreement to co-operate for a common purpose. **b** the parties involved. **2** union through marriage.

allied *adj.* **1 a** united or associated in an alliance. **b** (**Allied**) of or relating to the Allies. **2** connected or related. [*Say* AL ide]

Allies *pl. n.* **1** the nations allied against the Central Powers in the First World War.

2 the nations allied against the Axis powers in the Second World War.

alligator *n.* a large reptile similar to a crocodile but with a broader and shorter head.

alliteration *n.* the occurrence of the same sound at the beginning of adjacent words. □ **alliterative** *adj.* [Say a litter AY sh'n, a LITTER a tiv]

all-nighter *n. informal* an event or task that continues throughout the night.

allocate *v.* (**allocates, allocated, allocating**) designate or set aside for a specific purpose. □ **allocation** *n.* **allocator** *n.*

allophone *n. Cdn* (in Quebec) an immigrant whose first language is neither French nor English. □ **allophone** *n.* [Say ALA phone]

allot *v.* (**allots, allotted, allotting**) give or apportion something to someone

allotment *n.* **1** the action of allotting. **2** a portion allotted. **3** a small piece of land.

all-out ● *adj.* total; unrestrained. ● *adv.* (**all out**) with all one's strength; at full speed.

allow *v.* **1** permit. **2** give, provide, or set aside (a sum etc.). **3** admit, concede. **4** take into consideration. □ **allowable** *adj.*

allowance *n.* **1** an amount or sum given regularly to a person. **2** an amount allowed in reckoning. **3** a deduction or discount. **4** tolerance of. □ **make allowances 1** take into consideration. **2** make excuses for (a person etc.).

alloy ● *n.* a metallic substance made by combining two or more elements at least one of which is a metal. ● *v.* mix (metals). [Say AL oy *for the noun,* a LOY *for the verb*]

all-purpose *adj.* suitable for many uses.

all right ● *adv.* **1** satisfactorily. **2** as an intensifier. ● *adj.* satisfactory; safe and sound. ● *interj.* expressing or requesting consent or assent.

All Saints' Day *n.* a Christian festival in honour of the souls in heaven.

allsorts *pl. n.* an assortment, esp. of licorice candies.

All Souls' Day *n.* 2 Nov., a Catholic holy day with prayers for the souls of the dead in purgatory.

allspice *n.* the aromatic spice obtained from the ground berry of the pimento tree.

all-star ● *n.* **1** *Sport* a player on a team of star performers. **2** a superstar. ● *adj.* relating to or consisting of all-stars.

all-terrain vehicle *n.* a vehicle used to travel over rough terrain.

all-time *adj.* (of a record etc.) not surpassed.

all told *adv.* when everything is considered.

allude *v.* (**alludes, alluded, alluding**) **1** suggest indirectly; hint at. **2** mention without discussing at length.

allure *n.* attractiveness, personal charm. □ **allurement** *n.*

alluring *adj.* attractive and exciting; fascinating. □ **alluringly** *adv.*

allusion *n.* an expression designed to call something to mind without mentioning it explicitly. □ **allusive** *adj.*

alluvium *n.* (*pl.* **alluvia** or **alluviums**) a deposit of usu. fine fertile soil left during a time of flood. □ **alluvial** *adj.* [Say a LOOVY um]

ally ● *n.* (*pl.* **allies**) a person, organization or state that co-operates with another. ● *v.* (**allies, allied, allying**) **1** combine or unite a resource with another for mutual benefit. **2** (**ally oneself with**) side with. [Say AL eye *for the noun,* AL eye *or* a LIE *for the verb*]

alma mater *n.* the university, school, or college which one attended. [Say awl ma MOTTER *or* al ma MATTER]

almanac *n.* **1** a calendar listing important dates, astronomical data, etc. **2** an annual book of general information.

almighty *adj.* **1** having complete power. **2** (**the Almighty**) God. **3** *informal* very great.

almond *n.* the oval nut-like seed from the tree *Prunus dulcis.*

almost *adv.* all but; very nearly.

alms *pl. n.* charitable donations of money or food given to the poor. [Say OMZ]

almsgiving *n.* the giving of money to the poor. [Say OMZ giving]

aloe *n.* any plant of the genus *Aloe,* including succulent herbs, shrubs, and trees. [Say AL oh]

aloe vera *n.* a plant yielding a juice used in cosmetics and as a treatment for burns. [Say al oh VERRA]

aloft *adj. & adv.* **1** up in or into the air. **2** upwards.

aloha *interj.* (in Hawaii etc.) a greeting or farewell. [Say a LO haw]

alone ● *adj.* **1** on one's own; without help. **2** lonely and isolated. ● *adv.* only, exclusively. □ **go it alone** act by oneself without assistance. □ **aloneness** *n.*

along ● *prep.* **1** from one end to the other end of. **2** on, beside, or through the length of. **3** during the course of. ● *adv.* **1** onward; into a more advanced state. **2** at or to a particular place; arriving. **3** in company with. □ **along with** in addition to.

alongside ● *adv.* at or to the side. ● *prep.* **1** close to the side of; next to. **2** in close association with.

aloof *adj.* **1** cool and distant. **2** uninterested and not involved. □ **aloofly** *adv.* **aloofness** *n.*

aloud *adv.* audibly.

alpaca *n.* **1** a S American mammal related to the llama. **2** fabric made from its wool. [*Say* al PACKA]

alpha *n.* **1** the first letter of the Greek alphabet (A, α). **2** (as an *adj.*) designating the first. □ **alpha and omega** the beginning and end.

alphabet *n.* the set of letters used in a language.

alphabetical *adj.* (also **alphabetic**) **1** of an alphabet. **2** in the order of the letters of the alphabet. □ **alphabetically** *adv.*

alphabetize *v.* (**alphabetizes, alphabetized, alphabetizing**) arrange in alphabetical order. □ **alphabetization** *n.*

alpha-hydroxy acid *n.* a type of organic acid, some of which are used in exfoliating cosmetics. Abbreviation: **AHA**. [*Say* alfa hy DROXY]

alpha male *n.* **1** the dominant animal within a group of esp. male animals. **2** a man who embodies characteristics thought of as particularly masculine, esp. aggressiveness, dominance, and sexuality.

alphanumeric *adj.* (also **alphanumerical**) containing both alphabetical and numerical symbols. [*Say* alfa new MARE ick]

alpine ● *adj.* **1** of or relating to high mountains. **2** (**Alpine**) of or relating to the Alps. **3** of or relating to competitive downhill or slalom skiing. ● *n.* a plant native to mountain districts.

al Qaeda *n.* a network of Islamic fundamentalist groups advocating and practising terrorism against Western targets and involved in the attacks of September 11th, 2001. [al KYE duh]

already *adv.* **1** before the time in question. **2** as early or as soon as this. **3** used to express impatience etc.

ALS *abbr.* AMYOTROPHIC LATERAL SCLEROSIS.

also *adv.* in addition; likewise; besides.

also-ran *n.* **1** a losing contestant in a race, election, etc. **2** an undistinguished person.

Alt *n.* a key on a computer keyboard which alters the functions of other keys.

Alta. *abbr.* Alberta.

altar *n.* **1** a table or flat-topped block for sacrifice or offering to a deity. **2** *Christianity* a table on which Communion bread and wine are consecrated. □ **lead to the altar** marry.

altar boy *n.* a boy who serves as a priest's assistant in a service.

altarpiece *n.* a piece of art set above or behind an altar.

alter *v.* **1** make or become different; change. **2** modify the style or size of (clothing). □ **alteration** *n.*

altercation *n.* a heated argument or dispute.

alter ego *n.* **1** an intimate and trusted friend. **2** a person's secondary personality.

alternate ● *v.* (**alternates, alternated, alternating**) **1** (of two things) succeed or cause to succeed each other by turns. **2** change repeatedly (between two conditions). ● *adj.* **1** every other. **2** (of two things) following and succeeded by the other. **3** (of a sequence etc.) consisting of alternate things. ● *n.* something that substitutes for another. □ **alternately** *adv.* **alternation** *n.*

alternating current *n.* an electric current that reverses its direction at regular intervals. Abbreviation: **AC**.

alternative ● *adj.* **1** (of one or more things) available instead of another. **2** (of two things) mutually exclusive. **3** of or relating to non-traditional or unconventional practices. ● *n.* **1** any of two or more possibilities. **2** the opportunity to choose between two or more things. □ **alternatively** *adv.*

alternator *n.* a generator that produces an alternating current.

although *conj.* = THOUGH *conj.* 1-3.

altimeter *n.* an instrument for measuring altitude. [*Say* al TIMMA tur]

altitude *n.* **1** the height of an object in relation to a given point, esp. sea level. **2** *Astronomy* the angular distance of a celestial body above the horizon.

alto *n.* (*pl.* **altos**) **1** the lowest adult female or highest adult male singing voice. **2** the member of a family of instruments pitched second- or third-highest.

altogether *adv.* **1** totally, completely. **2** on the whole. **3** in total. □ **in the altogether** *informal* naked.

altruism *n.* selfless concern for the well-being of others. □ **altruist** *n.* **altruistic** *adj.* **altruistically** *adv.* [*Say* AWL true ism *or* AL true ism, awl true ISS tick *or* al true ISS tick]

alum *n.* a double sulphate of aluminum and potassium, with astringent properties. [*Say* AL um]

aluminum *n.* a silvery light and malleable metallic element.

alumna *n.* (*pl.* **alumnae**) a female graduate of a specified university or school. [*Say* a LUMNA *for the singular,* a LUM nee *for the plural*]

alumnus *n.* (*pl.* **alumni**) **1** a graduate of a specified university or other school. **2** a former member of a specified group or organization. [*Say* a LUM nuss *for the singular,* a LUM nigh *for the plural*]

alveolus *n.* (*pl.* **alveoli**) **1** any of the many tiny air sacs of the lungs which allow for rapid gaseous exchange. **2** the bony socket for the root of a tooth. □ **alveolar** *adj.* [*Say* alvy OLE us *for the singular,* alvy OLE ee *for the plural,* alvy OLE er]

always *adv.* **1** at all times; on all occasions. **2** whatever the circumstances.

alyssum *n.* a low-growing plant having very small white or purple flowers. [*Say* a LISS um]

Alzheimer's disease *n.* (also **Alzheimer's**) a serious brain disorder causing progressive mental deterioration in middle or old age. [*Say* ALTS hymers]

AM *abbr.* **1** AMPLITUDE MODULATION. **2** the band of radio stations broadcasting with this system.

am *1st person singular present of* BE.

a.m. *abbr.* before noon.

amalgam *n.* **1** a mixture or blend. **2** an alloy of mercury, used esp. for dental fillings. [*Say* a MAL gum]

amalgamate *v.* (**amalgamates, amalgamated, amalgamating**) combine to form one structure, organization, etc. □ **amalgamation** *n.* [*Say* a MALGA mate]

amaryllis *n.* (*pl.* **amaryllises**) a bulbous plant with showy trumpet-shaped flowers. [*Say* amma RILL iss]

amass *v.* (**amasses, amassed, amassing**) gather together or accumulate over time.

amateur *n.* **1** a person who engages in a pursuit as a pastime rather than for pay. **2** (as an *adj.*) for or done by amateurs. **3** an inept or inexperienced person. □ **amateurish** *adj.* **amateurism** *n.*

amatory *adj.* of or relating to sexual love or desire. [*Say* AMMA tory]

amaze *v.* (**amazes, amazed, amazing**) surprise greatly; overwhelm with wonder. □ **amazement** *n.*

amazing *adj.* **1** causing great surprise. **2** *informal* exceptional. □ **amazingly** *adv.*

Amazon *n.* **1** a member of a mythical race of female warriors. **2** (**amazon**) a very tall, strong woman. □ **Amazonian** *adj.* [*Say* AMMA zon, amma ZONEY un]

ambassador *n.* **1** a diplomat sent as a representative to a foreign country. **2** a representative or promoter of a specified thing. □ **ambassadorial** *adj.* **ambassadorship** *n.*

amber ● *n.* **1** a yellowish translucent fossilized resin. **2** the yellow colour of this. ● *adj.* made of or coloured like amber.

Amber Alert *n.* a public alert issued repeatedly in the event of an abduction

ambergris *n.* a wax-like secretion from the sperm whale used in perfume manufacture. [*Say* AMBER griss *or* AMBER groase]

ambidextrous *adj.* able to use the right and left hands equally well. [*Say* amba DEX truss]

ambience *n.* (also **ambiance**) the surroundings or atmosphere of a place. □ **ambient** *adj.* [*Say* AMBY awnce *or* OMBY awnce *or* AMBY ince, AMBY int]

ambiguity *n.* (*pl.* **ambiguities**) **1** uncertainty or imprecision of meaning. **2** a lack of decisiveness or commitment. [*Say* am big YOO a tee]

ambiguous *adj.* **1** open to more than one interpretation. **2** unclear or inexact. □ **ambiguously** *adv.* **ambiguousness** *n.* [*Say* am BIG you us]

ambition *n.* the determination to achieve success or distinction.

ambitious *adj.* **1** full of ambition. **2** intended to satisfy high aspirations and therefore difficult to achieve. □ **ambitiously** *adv.* **ambitiousness** *n.*

ambivalence *n.* the coexistence in one person of opposing emotions or attitudes. □ **ambivalent** *adj.* **ambivalently** *adv.* [*Say* am BIVVA lince, am BIVVA l'nt]

amble *v.* (**ambles, ambled, ambling**) walk at an easy pace.

ambrosia *n.* **1** (in Greek and Roman mythology) the food of the gods. **2** anything very pleasing to taste or smell. □ **ambrosial** *adj.* [*Say* am BRO zhuh]

ambulance *n.* a vehicle specially equipped for conveying the sick or injured.

ambulatory *adj.* **1** able to walk about. **2** not confining a patient to bed. [*Say* AM byoo luh tory]

ambush ● *n.* (*pl.* **ambushes**) a surprise attack by persons lying in wait. ● *v.* (**ambushes, ambushed, ambushing**) attack by means of an ambush.

ameliorate *v.* (**ameliorates, ameliorated, ameliorating**) *formal* improve. □ **amelioration** *n.* [*Say* a MEELYA rate]

amen *interj.* **1** uttered at the end of a prayer or hymn etc., meaning "so be it". **2** expressing agreement or assent. [*Say* ah MEN *or* ay MEN]

amenable *adj.* **1** willing to co-operate; open to suggestion. **2** capable of being affected by. [*Say* a MENNA bull *or* a MEENA bull]

amend *v.* **1** formally revise or alter (a constitution, legislation, etc.). **2** make minor improvements in. **3** correct errors in. □ **amendable** *adj.*

amendment *n.* **1** a minor improvement in a document. **2** the formal proposal to change a parliamentary bill. **3** an article officially supplementing a constitution. **4** the act or process of improving.

amends *n.* □ **make amends** compensate or make up (for).

amenity *n.* (*pl.* **amenities**) a pleasant or useful feature. [*Say* a MENNA tee]

American ● *adj.* **1** of or relating to the US or its inhabitants. **2** of or relating to the Americas. ● *n.* **1** a native or citizen of the US. **2** a native or inhabitant of the Americas. **3** the English language as used in the US.

Americana *pl. n.* things pertaining to and typical of American culture.

American dream *n.* the traditional American belief in equal opportunity for all.

American eagle *n.* = BALD EAGLE.

American football *n.* a form of football played in the US on a smaller field than Canadian football.

American Indian *n.* (also **North American Indian**) a member of a group of Aboriginal peoples of the western hemisphere, excluding the Inuit and Aleuts.

Americanism *n.* **1** a word or phrase originating in the US. **2** a thing characteristic of or peculiar to the US.

Americanize *v.* (**Americanizes**, **Americanized**, **Americanizing**) make or become American. □ **Americanization** *n.*

Amerindian ● *adj.* of or relating to American Indians. ● *n.* an American Indian. [*Say* amma RINDY un]

amethyst *n.* a precious stone of a violet or purple variety of quartz. [*Say* AMMA thist]

amiable *adj.* friendly and pleasant. □ **amiability** *n.* **amiably** *adv.* [*Say* AIMY a bull]

amicable *adj.* showing or done in a friendly spirit. □ **amicably** *adv.* [*Say* AM ick a bull]

amid *prep.* (also **amidst**) in the middle of.

amide *n.* an organic compound formed from ammonia. [*Say* AM ide *or* AY mide]

amidships *adv.* (also **amidship**) in or into the middle of a ship.

amigo *n.* (*pl.* **amigos**) *informal* a friend or comrade. [*Say* a MEE go]

amino *adj.* of, relating to, or containing the monovalent group -NH₂. [*Say* a MEAN oh]

amino acid *n.* any of a group of organic compounds occurring naturally in plant and animal tissues and forming the basic constituents of proteins.

Amish ● *n.* (**the Amish**) the members of a strict Mennonite group of S Ontario and Pennsylvania. ● *adj.* of or characteristic of this group. [*Say* OMM ish *or* AY mish]

amiss ● *adj.* wrong; out of order. ● *adv.* wrongly; inappropriately. □ **take amiss** be offended by.

amity *n.* a friendly relationship. [*Say* AMMA tee]

ammeter *n.* an instrument for measuring electric current in amperes. [*Say* AMMA tur]

ammo *n.* *informal* ammunition.

ammonia *n.* **1** a colourless alkaline gas with a pungent smell. **2** a solution of ammonia gas in water.

ammonium *n.* the monovalent ion NH_4^+, formed from ammonia. [*Say* a MOANY um]

ammunition *n.* **1** a supply of bullets, shells, etc. **2** points used or usable in an argument.

amnesia *n.* a partial or total loss of memory. □ **amnesiac** *n. & adj.* **amnesic** *adj. & n.* [*Say* am NEE zhuh, am NEEZY ack, am NEE zick]

amnesty *n.* (*pl.* **amnesties**) **1** a general pardon, esp. for political offences. **2** a period during which people may admit an offence without fear of prosecution. [*Say* AMNA stee]

amniocentesis *n.* (*pl.* **amniocenteses**) (also **amnio**) the sampling of amniotic fluid to determine the condition of an embryo. [*Say* amny oh sen TEE sis]

amniotic fluid *n.* the fluid in which a fetus effectively floats within the uterus.

amoeba *n.* (*pl.* **amoebas** or **amoebae**) any usu. aquatic protozoan capable of changing shape. □ **amoebic** *adj.* **amoeboid** *adj.* [*Say* a MEEBA]

amok *adv.* □ **go** (or **run**) **amok 1** be out of control. **2** run about in an uncontrollable rage. [*Say* a MUCK *or* a MOCK]

among *prep.* (also **amongst**) **1** surrounded by. **2** in the number of. **3** in the class or category of. **4** between; shared by.

amoral *adj.* lacking a moral sense; unconcerned with right or wrong. □ **amorality** *n.* [*Say* ay MORAL, ay more AL it ee]

amorous *adj.* feeling or relating to sexual desire. □ **amorously** *adv.* **amorousness** *n.* [*Say* AMMER us]

amorphous *adj.* **1** shapeless. **2** vague, ill-organized. [*Say* a MORF us]

amortize *v.* (**amortizes, amortized, amortizing**) gradually pay off (a debt). □ **amortization** *n.* [*Say* AMMER tize]

amount ● *n.* a quantity, esp. the total number, size or value of things. ● *v.* be equivalent to in number, size, etc. □ **any amount of** a great deal of

amoxicillin *n.* (also **amoxycillin**) a broad spectrum semi-synthetic penicillin. [*Say* a moxa SILL un]

amp *n.* **1** an ampere. **2** an amplifier.

ampere *n.* the SI base unit of electric current. Symbol: **A**. □ **amperage** *n.* [*Say* AM pair]

ampersand *n.* the sign & (= and).

amphetamine *n.* a synthetic drug used esp. as a stimulant. [*Say* am FETTA mean]

amphibian ● *adj.* **1** living or operating both on land and in water. **2** of or relating to amphibians. ● *n.* **1** an animal or creature, including frogs and newts, living both on land and in water. **2** an amphibian vehicle or airplane. [*Say* am FIBBY un]

amphibious *adj.* **1** living in or suited for land and water. **2** (of a military operation) involving forces landed from the sea. [*Say* am FIBBY us]

amphitheatre *n.* (also **amphitheater**) **1** an oval or circular building with tiered seats around a central open space. **2** a piece of level ground surrounded naturally by rising slopes. **3** a lecture hall or part of a theatre with tiered seats. [*Say* AMFA theatre]

amphora *n.* (*pl.* **amphorae** or **amphoras**) a tall ancient Greek jug with two handles. [*Say* AMFA ruh *for the singular*, AMFA ree *for the plural*]

ampicillin *n.* a semi-synthetic penicillin. [*Say* ampa SILL un]

ample *adj.* (**ampler, amplest**) **1** large. **2** enough or more than enough. □ **amply** *adv.*

amplify *v.* (**amplifies, amplified, amplifying**) **1** increase the volume, strength, or intensity of (electrical signals, etc.). **2** enlarge upon or expand. □ **amplification** *n.* **amplifier** *n.*

amplitude *n.* **1** *Physics* the maximum extent of a vibration from the position of equilibrium. **2** *Electricity* the maximum departure of the value of an alternating current or wave from the average.

amplitude modulation *n.* variation of the amplitude of a radio or other wave as a way of carrying information.

amputate *v.* (**amputates, amputated, amputating**) cut off by surgical operation. □ **amputation** *n.*

amputee *n.* a person who has lost a limb etc. by amputation.

amuck *adv.* = AMOK.

amulet *n.* an ornament worn as a charm against evil. [*Say* AM yuh lit]

amuse *v.* (**amuses, amused, amusing**) **1** cause (a person) to find something funny. **2** keep (a person) entertained. □ **amusing** *adj.*

amusement *n.* **1** something that amuses. **2** the state of being amused. **3** a fairground ride or machine.

amusement park *n.* a commercially operated fairground with rides, e.g. Ferris wheel, roller coaster, etc.

amyotrophic lateral sclerosis *n.* a progressive degenerative disease of the central nervous system. [*Say* ammy a TROFF ick]

an *indefinite article* the form of the indefinite article (*see* A) used before words beginning with a vowel sound.

Anabaptism *n.* the doctrine that baptism should only be administered to believing adults. □ **Anabaptist** *n.* [*Say* anna BAP tism]

anabolic steroid *n.* a synthetic steroid hormone used to increase muscle size. [*Say* anna BAWL ick]

anachronism *n.* a person or thing belonging to a period other than that in which it exists. □ **anachronistic** *adj.* [*Say* a NACKRA nism, a nackra NISS tick]

anaconda *n.* a S American boa that kills its prey by constriction. [*Say* anna CONDA]

anaerobic *adj.* growing without air or in oxygen-free conditions. [*Say* anna ROE bick]

anaesthesia *n.* the inability to feel pain, usu. achieved by administering drugs. [*Say* anniss THEEZ ee uh *or* anniss THEEZH yuh]

anaesthetic *n.* a substance that produces insensitivity to pain etc. [*Say* anniss THET ick]

anaesthetist *n.* *Cdn & Brit.* a medical doctor specializing in the administration of anaesthetics. [*Say* a NIECE thuh tist *or* a NESS thuh tist]

anaesthetize *v.* (**anaesthetizes, anaesthetized, anaesthetizing**) administer an anaesthetic to; deprive of feeling. [*Say* a NIECE thuh tize *or* a NESS thuh tize]

anagram *n.* a word or phrase formed by rearranging the letters of another.

anal *adj.* **1** of or relating to the anus. **2** *Psychology* designating or pertaining to a stage of infantile psychological development characterized by a preoccupation with the anus and defecation. **3** *informal* = ANAL-RETENTIVE.

analgesia *n.* the absence or relief of pain. [*Say* annal JEEZ ee uh *or* annal JEECE ee uh]

analgesic ● *adj.* relieving pain. ● *n.* a painkiller. [*Say* annal JEEZ ick *or* annal JEECE ick]

analog *adj.* **1** (also **analogue**) (of a watch, clock, etc.) showing the time using hands rather than displayed digits. **2** operating with signals or information represented by a continuously variable quantity.

analogize *v.* (**analogizes, analogized, analogizing**) compare something with something else to assist understanding. [*Say* a NALA jize]

analogous *adj.* partially similar. □ **analogously** *adv.* [*Say* a NALA gus]

analogue *n.* (*US* **analog**) an analogous or parallel thing. [*Say* ANNA log]

analogy *n.* (*pl.* **analogies**) a comparison between one thing and another to aid explanation. □ **analogical** *adj.* [*Say* a NALA jee]

anal-retentive *adj.* excessively orderly and fussy.

analysis *n.* (*pl.* **analyses**) **1** a detailed examination of the elements or structure of something. **2** *Chemistry* the determination of the constituent parts of something. **3** psychoanalysis.

analyst *n.* **1** a person engaged or skilled in analysis. **2** a psychoanalyst.

analytical *adj.* (also **analytic**) using analysis in order to understand something. □ **analytically** *adv.*

analyze *v.* (**analyzes, analyzed, analyzing**) (also **analyse; analyses, analysed, analysing**) **1** examine in detail the constitution or structure of. **2** examine (a book etc.) critically. **3** psychoanalyze. □ **analyzer** *n.* (also **analyser**)

anaphylactic shock *adj.* an extreme and sometimes fatal allergic reaction to a foreign substance. [*Say* anna fuh LACK tick]

anaphylaxis *n.* (*pl.* **anaphylaxes**) an extreme allergic reaction to a foreign substance to which the body has become hypersensitive. [*Say* anna fuh LAX iss]

anarchism *n.* the doctrine that all government should be abolished. □ **anarchist** *n.* **anarchistic** *adj.* [*Say* ANNER kism, ANNER kist, anner KISS tick]

anarchy *n.* **1** disorder caused by a lack of

authority. **2** absence of government regarded as a political ideal. □ **anarchic** *adj.* [*Say* ANNER kee, an ARE kick]

anathema *n.* (*pl.* **anathemas**) a detested thing or person. [*Say* a NATHA muh]

anatomize *v.* (**anatomizes, anatomized, anatomizing**) examine in detail. [*Say* a NATTA mize]

anatomy *n.* (*pl.* **anatomies**) **1** the scientific study of the bodily structure of humans, animals, and plants, involving dissection. **2** this structure. **3** *informal* a human body. **4** analysis. □ **anatomical** *adj.* **anatomically** *adv.* [*Say* a NATTA me, anna TOM ick ul]

ancestor *n.* **1** any person from whom one is descended. **2** something from which a later species or version has evolved. □ **ancestral** *adj.*

ancestry *n.* (*pl.* **ancestries**) **1** lineage or descent. **2** ancestors collectively.

anchor ● *n.* **1** a heavy metal weight used to moor a ship etc. **2** something that gives stability or security. **3** the main announcer on a news broadcast. ● *v.* **1** secure by or as if by means of an anchor. **2** *Broadcasting* act as an anchor. □ **at anchor** moored by means of an anchor.

anchorage *n.* **1** a place where a ship may be anchored. **2** the act of anchoring.

anchorite *n.* a hermit; a religious recluse. [*Say* ANCHOR ite]

anchorperson *n.* (also **anchorman, anchorwoman**) the main announcer on a news or sports broadcast.

anchovy *n.* (*pl.* **anchovies**) a small Mediterranean fish of the herring family. [*Say* ann CHOVE ee *or* ANCHA vee]

ancient *adj.* **1 a** of long ago. **b** of the world prior to the fall of Rome in 476. **2** having lived or existed long; very old. □ **the ancients** the people of ancient times, esp. the Greeks, Romans, etc.

ancillary *adj.* **1** providing essential support to a central service or industry. **2** associated, secondary. [*Say* ann SILLA ree]

and *conj.* **1 a** connecting words, clauses, or sentences. **b** implying progression, causation, duration, addition, variety, etc. **2** *informal* to. **3** in relation to. □ **and/or** either or both of two stated possibilities.

andante *adv. & adj. Music* in a moderately slow tempo. [*Say* an DAWN tay *or* an DAN tay]

Andean *adj.* of or relating to the Andes. [*Say* an DEE un *or* ANDY un]

androgen *n.* a male sex hormone. □ **androgenic** *adj.* [*Say* ANDRA jen]

androgynous *adj.* having both male and

female characteristics. □ **androgyny** *n.*
[*Say* an DRAW jen iss, an DRAW jen ee]

android *n.* a robot with a human appearance.

anecdote *n.* a short account of an entertaining or interesting incident.
□ **anecdotal** *adj.* [*Say* ANNICK dote, annick DOAT ul]

anemia *n.* a deficiency in the blood resulting in pallor and weariness.
□ **anemic** *adj.* [*Say* a NEEMY uh, a NEEM ick]

anemometer *n.* an instrument for measuring the force of the wind.
[*Say* anna MOMMA ter]

anemone *n.* a plant related to the buttercup, with flowers of various vivid colours. [*Say* a NEMMA nee]

aneroid barometer *n.* an instrument that measures air pressure.
[*Say* ANNA roid]

anesthesia etc. = ANAESTHESIA etc.

anesthesiology *n.* the science of administering anaesthetics.
□ **anesthesiologist** *n.*
[*Say* anniss theezy OLLA jee]

aneurysm *n.* an excessive localized enlargement of a blood vessel.
[*Say* ANYA rism]

anew *adv.* **1** again. **2** in a different way.

angel *n.* **1** a heavenly being serving as a messenger or servant of Gods. **2** a virtuous or obliging person.

angelfish *n.* (*pl.* **angelfish** or **angelfishes**) any of various tropical fish with large fins.

angel food cake *n.* (also **angel cake**) a light cake made of beaten egg whites, sugar, and flour.

angel hair *n.* very fine spaghetti.

angelic *adj.* **1** like or relating to angels. **2** sublimely good, kind, or beautiful.
□ **angelically** *adv.* [*Say* an JELL ick]

angelus *n. Catholicism* a set of prayers commemorating the Incarnation of Jesus.
[*Say* ANJA luss]

anger ● *n.* extreme or passionate displeasure. ● *v.* make angry; enrage.

angina *n.* (also **angina pectoris**) a condition marked by severe pain in the chest. [*Say* an JINE uh (PECKTA riss)]

angiogram *n.* an X-ray of blood and lymph vessels . [*Say* AN jee a gram]

angioplasty *n.* (*pl.* **angioplasties**) surgical repair of a damaged blood vessel.
[*Say* AN jee oh plasty]

angiosperm *n.* any plant producing flowers and reproducing by seeds enclosed within a carpel (*opp.* GYMNOSPERM).
[*Say* AN jee oh sperm]

angiotensin *n.* a powerful substance in the body which results in an increase in blood pressure. [*Say* an jee oh TENSE in]

Angle *n.* (usu. in *pl.*) a member of an ancient Germanic people that settled in eastern Britain in the 5th century.

angle¹ ● *n.* **1 a** the space between two meeting lines or surfaces. **b** the inclination of two lines or surfaces to each other. **2** a corner or sharp projection. **3 a** the direction from which a photograph etc. is taken. **b** the aspect from which a matter is considered. ● *v.* (**angles, angled, angling**) **1** move or place obliquely. **2** present (information) from a particular point of view. □ **angled** *adj.*

angle² *v.* (**angles, angled, angling**) **1** fish with hook and line. **2** seek an objective by devious or calculated means.
□ **angler** *n.*

Anglian *adj.* having to do with the ancient Angles.

Anglican ● *adj.* of or relating to the Church of England or any Church in communion with it. ● *n.* a member of an Anglican Church. □ **Anglicanism** *n.*

anglicism *n.* an English word etc. borrowed into another language.
[*Say* ANGLA sism]

anglicize *v.* (**anglicizes, anglicized, anglicizing**) make English.
[*Say* ANGLA size]

Anglo *n.* (*pl.* **Anglos**) *Cdn informal* an anglophone, esp. in Quebec.

Anglo- *comb. form* **1** English. **2** English or British and.

Anglo-Canadian ● *adj.* **1** of or pertaining to English-speaking Canadians. **2** English (or British) and Canadian. ● *n.* **1** an English-speaking Canadian. **2** a Canadian of English descent.

Anglo-Catholic *n.* a member of a High Church Anglican group which emphasizes its Catholic tradition. □ **Anglo-Catholic** *adj.* **Anglo-Catholicism** *n.*

Anglo-French ● *adj.* **1** English (or British) and French. **2** of Anglo-French. ● *n.* the French language as retained in England after the Norman Conquest.

Anglo-Norman ● *adj.* **1** of the Normans in England after the Norman Conquest. **2** of the dialect of French used by them. ● *n.* the Anglo-Norman dialect.

anglophile *n.* a person who is fond of England or the English. □ **anglophilia** *n.*
[*Say* ANGLO file, anglo FILLY uh]

anglophobia *n.* intense hatred or fear of anglophones, the English, or England.
□ **anglophobic** *adj.* **anglophobe** *n.*
[*Say* angla FOBE ee uh, ANGLA fobe]

anglophone esp. *Cdn* ● *adj.* English-speaking. ● *n.* an English-speaking person. [*Say* ANGLA fone]

Anglo-Saxon ● *adj.* **1** of the Anglo-Saxons. **2** of English descent. ● *n.* **1** a member of the Germanic peoples who settled in Britain before the Norman Conquest. **2** the Old English language.

Angolan ● *n.* a native or inhabitant of Angola. ● *adj.* of Angola or its people. [*Say* ang GO lun]

angora *n.* **1** a fabric made from the hair of the angora goat or rabbit. **2** a long-haired variety of cat, goat, or rabbit. [*Say* ang GORE uh]

angry *adj.* (**angrier, angriest**) **1** feeling, showing or suggesting anger; extremely displeased. **2** inflamed, painful. □ **angrily** *adv.*

angst *n.* **1** a feeling of deep anxiety or dread. **2** *informal* a feeling of persistent worry about something trivial.

angstrom *n.* (also **ångström**) a unit of length equal to 10^{-10} m, used esp. for electromagnetic wavelengths. Symbol: Å. [*Say* ANG strum, ONG strum]

anguish *n.* severe misery or mental suffering. □ **anguished** *adj.*

angular *adj.* **1 a** having angles or sharp corners. **b** (of a person) having sharp features. **2** forming an angle. □ **angularity** *n.*

aniline *n.* a colourless oily liquid, used in making dyes etc. [*Say* ANNA leen *or* ANNA lin]

anima *n.* *Psychology* the part of the psyche which is directed inwards.

animal ● *n.* **1** a living organism which feeds on organic matter, usu. one with specialized sense organs and nervous system. **2** such an organism other than man. **3** a brutish or uncivilized person. **4** *informal* a person or thing of any kind. ● *adj.* **1** characteristic of animals. **2** of animals as distinct from vegetables. **3** physical rather than spiritual or intellectual.

animate ● *adj.* **1** having life. **2** lively and active. ● *v.* (**animates, animated, animating**) **1** give life or vigour to. **2** produce (a film etc.) by animation. □ **animated** *adj.* **animatedly** *adv.* **animator** *n.* [*Say* ANNA mitt *for the adjective,* ANNA mate *for the verb*]

animation *n.* **1** vivacity, ardour. **2** the state of being alive. **3** the technique of filming successive drawings or positions of puppets to create an illusion of movement.

anime *n.* Japanese film and television animation, typically having a science-fiction theme and sometimes including violent or sexual material. [*Say* ANNA may]

animism *n.* the attribution of a living soul to inanimate objects. □ **animist** *n.* **animistic** *adj.* [*Say* ANNA mism, anna MISS tick]

animosity *n.* (*pl.* **animosities**) strong hostility. [*Say* anna MOSSA tee]

animus *n.* **1** animosity or ill feeling. **2** motivation to do something. [*Say* ANNA muss]

anion *n.* a negatively charged ion; an ion that is attracted to the anode in electrolysis (*opp.* CATION). □ **anionic** *adj.* [*Say* AN eye un, an eye ON ick]

anise *n.* an umbel-bearing plant with aromatic seeds. [*Say* ANNIS]

aniseed *n.* the seed of the anise, used to give a licorice-like flavour. [*Say* ANNA seed]

Anishinabe *n.* (*pl.* **Anishinabe**) **1** the preferred name for the Ojibwa living in northern Quebec, Ontario, Manitoba, Saskatchewan, and Alberta. **2** the Algonquian language of this people. □ **Anishinabe** *adj.* [*Say* a nisha NOBBY, a nish NOBBY]

ankh *n.* an ancient Egyptian symbol of life consisting of a looped bar with a shorter crossbar. [*Say* ANK]

ankle *n.* **1** the joint connecting the foot with the leg. **2** the part of the leg between this and the calf.

anklet *n.* an ornament or fetter worn around the ankle.

annals *pl. n.* **1** a narrative of events year by year. **2** historical records.

anneal *v.* heat (metal or glass) and allow it to cool slowly, esp. to toughen it. [*Say* a NEAL]

annelid *n.* an animal with a body made up of ring-shaped segments such as earthworms. [*Say* ANNA lid]

annex ● *n.* (*pl.* **annexes**) **1** a separate or added building. **2** an addition to a document. ● *v.* (**annexes, annexed, annexing**) **1** add or append as a subordinate part. **2** incorporate (a territory of another) into one's own. □ **annexation** *n.*

annexationism *n.* **1** a policy which favours annexation of territory. **2** *Cdn* any of several historical movements favouring Canadian political union with the US. □ **annexationist** *n.*

annihilate *v.* (**annihilates, annihilated, annihilating**) **1** completely destroy; obliterate. **2** defeat utterly; make insignificant. □ **annihilation** *n.* [*Say* a NIGH a late]

anniversary n. (pl. **anniversaries**) **1** the date on which an event took place in a previous year, esp. a wedding. **2** the celebration of this.

Anno Domini adv. in the year of the Christian era. [Say anno DOMMIN ee]

annotate v. (**annotates**, **annotated**, **annotating**) add explanatory notes to (a book etc.). □ **annotation** n. **annotator** n. [Say ANNO tate]

announce v. (**announces**, **announced**, **announcing**) **1** make publicly known. **2** make known the arrival or imminence of. □ **announcement** n.

announcer n. a person who announces, esp. on radio or television.

annoy v. cause slight anger or mental distress to. □ **annoyance** n. **annoying** adj. **annoyingly** adv.

annual ● adj. **1** calculated over or covering a period of a year. **2** occurring every year. **3** living or lasting for one year. ● n. **1** a publication issued once a year. **2** a plant that lives only for a year or less. □ **annually** adv.

annuity n. (pl. **annuities**) **1** a fixed sum of money paid to someone each year. **2** an investment of money entitling the investor to an equal annual sum. [Say a NEW a tee]

annul v. (**annuls**, **annulled**, **annulling**) **1** declare (a marriage etc.) invalid. **2** cancel, abolish. □ **annulment** n. [Say a NULL]

annulus n. (pl. **annuli**) a ring-shaped part. [Say ANYA lus]

Annunciation n. Christianity the occasion on which the angel Gabriel announced to the Virgin Mary that she would give birth to Jesus. [Say a nun see AY sh'n]

anode n. **1** the positive electrode in an electrolytic cell. **2** the negative terminal of a battery (opp. CATHODE). □ **anodic** adj. [Say AN ode, a NOD ick]

anodize v. (**anodizes**, **anodized**, **anodizing**) coat (a metal) with a protective layer by electrolysis. □ **anodizer** n. [Say ANNA dize]

anodyne ● adj. not likely to cause offence or disagreement; dull. ● n. a painkilling drug or medicine. [Say ANNA dine]

anoint v. **1** apply oil or ointment to, esp. as a religious ceremony. **2** choose (a leader etc.) as though by anointing.

anomaly n. (pl. **anomalies**) something that deviates from what is standard or normal. □ **anomalous** adj. **anomalously** adv. [Say a NOMMA lee, a NOMMA lus]

anon. abbr. anonymous.

anonymous adj. **1** not identified by name; of unknown name or origin. **2** having no outstanding or unusual features.

□ **anonymity** n. **anonymously** adv. [Say a NONNA muss, anna NIMMA tee]

anorak n. a waterproof jacket usu. with a hood. [Say ANNA rack]

anorexia n. **1** a lack or loss of appetite for food. **2** (also **anorexia nervosa**) a psychological illness characterized by an obsessive desire to lose weight. [Say anna REXIA (nair VOSA)]

anorexic ● adj. **1** having to do with anorexia. **2** extremely thin. ● n. a person with anorexia. [Say anna REX ic]

another ● adj. **1** an additional; one more. **2** a person like or comparable to. **3** a different. ● pron. **1** an additional one. **2** a different one.

answer ● n. **1** something said or done in reaction to a question or circumstance. **2** the solution to a problem. **3** an equivalent or rival. ● v. **1** make an answer (to). **2** respond to the summons of. **3** be satisfactory for (a purpose). **4** be responsible to or for. □ **answer back** answer impudently.

answerable adj. **1** responsible to. **2** responsible for.

ant n. a small insect living in complex social colonies. □ **have ants in one's pants** fidget.

antacid n. a substance that reduces acidity esp. in the stomach.

antagonism n. active opposition or hostility. [Say an TAG'n ism]

antagonist n. an opponent or adversary. □ **antagonistic** adj. [Say an TAG'n ist]

antagonize v. (**antagonizes**, **antagonized**, **antagonizing**) cause someone to become hostile. [Say an TAG'n ize]

Antarctic ● adj. of the south polar regions. ● n. these regions. [Say ant ARK tic or ant AR tic]

ante ● n. **1** a stake put up by a player in poker etc. before receiving cards. **2** an amount to be paid in advance. ● v. (**antes**, **anted**, **anteing**) put up as an ante. □ **up** (or **raise**) **the ante** increase what is at stake. [Say ANTY]

ante- prefix forming nouns and adjectives meaning "before, preceding".

anteater n. a toothless mammal with a long snout which feeds on ants etc.

antecedent ● n. **1** a thing or event that existed before or logically precedes another. **2** Grammar a word, phrase, etc. to which a following pronoun refers. **3** a person's ancestors. ● adj. preceding in time or order. [Say anty SEED'nt]

antedate v. (**antedates**, **antedated**, **antedating**) **1** exist or occur at a date

earlier than. **2** assign an earlier date to. [*Say* anty DATE]

antelope *n.* (*pl.* **antelope** or **antelopes**) **1** a family of deer-like ruminants abundant in Africa, including gazelles and gnus. **2** = PRONGHORN.

antenna *n.* **1** (*pl.* **antennas**) a metal rod by which radio or television signals are transmitted or received. **2** (*pl.* **antennae**) one of a pair of mobile appendages on the heads of insects, crustaceans, etc. [*For* antennae *say* an TENNY]

anterior *adj.* nearer the front. [*Say* an TEERY er]

anteroom *n.* a small room leading to a main one. [*Say* ANTY room]

anthem *n.* **1** a solemn song expressing loyalty etc., esp. = NATIONAL ANTHEM. **2** a short choral composition set to a passage of scripture.

anther *n.* the tip of a stamen containing pollen.

anthill *n.* a mound-like nest built by ants or termites.

anthologize *v.* (**anthologizes**, **anthologized**, **anthologizing**) compile or include in an anthology. [*Say* ann THOLLA jize]

anthology *n.* (*pl.* **anthologies**) a published collection of poems, stories, etc. □ **anthologist** *n.* [*Say* ann THOLLA jee]

anthracite *n.* a type of coal that burns with little flame and smoke. [*Say* AN thruh site]

anthrax *n.* a lethal disease of sheep and cattle transmissible to humans.

anthropocentric *adj.* regarding human beings as the centre of existence. □ **anthropocentrism** *n.* [*Say* an thruppa SEN trick]

anthropoid ● *adj.* *Biology* **1** esp. *Biology* of or relating to the group of higher primates, which includes monkeys, apes, and humans, esp. designating an ape belonging to the family of great apes. **2** resembling a human being in form. ● *n.* esp. *Biology* a higher primate, esp. an ape. [*Say* ANTHRA poid]

anthropology *n.* **1** the study of human beings, esp. of their societies and customs. **2** the study of the structure and evolution of human beings as animals. □ **anthropological** *adj.* **anthropologist** *n.* [*Say* anthra POLLA jee, anthra POLLA jist]

anthropomorphism *n.* the attribution of human characteristics to a god, animal, or thing. □ **anthropomorphic** *adj.* **anthropomorphize** *v.* [*Say* an thruppa MORF ism]

anti- *prefix* forming nouns and adjectives meaning: **1** opposed to; against. **2** preventing. **3** the opposite of. [*Say* AN tee *or* AN tie]

antibacterial *adj.* active against bacteria, esp. containing an antibiotic that kills bacteria and prevents them from re-establishing themselves.

anti-ballistic missile *n.* a missile designed to intercept and destroy a ballistic missile. Abbreviation: **ABM**. [*Say* anty buh LISS tick]

antibiotic *n.* any of various substances that can inhibit or destroy disease-producing bacteria and fungi. [*Say* by OT ic]

antibody *n.* (*pl.* **antibodies**) any of various blood proteins produced in response to and then counteracting antigens.

antic ● *n.* an absurd or foolish action. ● *adj.* agitated, frenzied.

Antichrist *n.* an opponent of Christ, expected by the early Church to appear before the end of the world.

anticipate *v.* (**anticipates**, **anticipated**, **anticipating**) **1** foresee and deal with ahead of time. **2** expect. **3** look forward to. □ **anticipation** *n.* [*Say* an TISSA pate]

anticipatory *adj.* happening or felt in anticipation of something. [*Say* an TISSA puh tory]

anticlimax *n.* a trivial conclusion to something significant or impressive. □ **anticlimactic** *adj.*

anticoagulant *n.* any drug or substance that retards or inhibits coagulation. [*Say* anty co AG yoo lint]

anticyclone *n.* a weather system with high barometric pressure usu. associated with calm, dry conditions. [*Say* anty SIGH clone]

antidepressant *n.* a drug that alleviates depression.

antidote *n.* **1** a medicine etc. taken or given to counteract poison. **2** anything that counteracts something unpleasant.

antifreeze *n.* a substance added to water to lower its freezing point.

antifungal ● *adj.* preventing fungal growth. ● *n.* a substance, esp. a drug, that is active against fungi.

antigen *n.* a foreign substance, e.g. a toxin, which causes the body to produce antibodies. □ **antigenic** *adj.* [*Say* ANTY jen]

antiglobalization *n.* a political movement opposed to the policies of the International Monetary Fund, the World

Bank, and the World Trade Organization, esp. increased free trade and open markets, and to the increasing international dominance of multinational corporations and financial institutions to the perceived detriment of the environment and to living standards and human rights in poor countries.

anti-hero n. (pl. **anti-heroes**) a central character in a story or drama who lacks conventional heroic attributes.

antihistamine n. a substance that counteracts the effects of histamine, used in treating allergies. [Say anty HISTA min or anty HISTA meen]

anti-inflammatory ● adj. reducing inflammation. ● n. (pl. **anti-inflammatories**) an anti-inflammatory drug. [Say anty in FLAMMA tory]

anti-knock adj. preventing premature combustion in an engine.

anti-lock brake n. an automobile brake which prevents the wheels from locking when braking suddenly.

antimatter n. Physics a hypothetical matter composed solely of antiparticles.

antimony n. a brittle silvery-white metallic element. [Say ANTA moany]

antioxidant n. a substance that inhibits or counteracts oxidation. [Say anty OXA dint]

antiparticle n. Physics an elementary particle having the same mass as a given particle but opposite electric or magnetic properties.

antipasto n. (pl. **antipastos** or **antipasti**) **1** a cold appetizer preceding an Italian meal. **2** a mixture of pickled vegetables served as an appetizer. [Say anty PASS toe for the singular; for ANTIPASTI say anty PASS tee]

antipathy n. (pl. **antipathies**) a strong or deep-seated aversion or dislike. □ **antipathetic** adj. [Say an TIPPA thee (with TH as in THIEF), an tippa THETIC]

anti-personnel adj. designed to kill or injure people rather than to damage buildings or equipment.

antiperspirant n. a substance applied to the skin to prevent or reduce perspiration.

antiphon n. **1** a hymn or psalm, the parts of which are sung alternately by two groups. **2** a Biblical verse sung or recited at a specific moment in a Christian liturgy, e.g. at the beginning of the Mass or before Communion. [Say ANTA fon]

Antipodean ● adj. having to do with Australia or New Zealand. ● n. a person from Australia or New Zealand. [Say an tippa DEE in]

antipodes pl. n. **1** places on opposite sides of the earth. **2** (**Antipodes**) Australia and New Zealand. [Say an TIPPA deez]

antipope n. a person set up as pope in opposition to one canonically chosen.

antipsychotic ● adj. (chiefly of a drug) used to treat psychotic disorders. ● n. an antipsychotic drug.

antiquarian ● adj. of or dealing in antiques or rare books. ● n. (also **antiquary**) a person who studies or collects antiquarian items. [Say anta KWERRY in, ANTA kwerry]

antiquated adj. out of date. [Say ANTA kwated]

antique ● n. an object of considerable age. ● adj. **1** of or existing from an early date. **2** old-fashioned, archaic. ● v. (**antiques**, **antiqued**, **antiquing**) **1** give an antique appearance to artificially. **2** shop for antiques.

antiquity n. (pl. **antiquities**) **1** ancient times, esp. before the Middle Ages. **2** great age. **3** physical remains or customs from ancient times. [Say ann TICKWA tee]

anti-roll bar n. a rubber-mounted bar fitted in the suspension of a vehicle to increase its stability, esp. when cornering.

anti-Semitism n. hatred of Jews; unfair treatment of Jews. □ **anti-Semite** n. **anti-Semitic** adj. [Say anty SEMMA tism, anty SEM ite, anty suh MIT ick]

antiseptic ● adj. **1** preventing the growth of disease-causing micro-organisms. **2** sterile or free from contamination. **3** lacking character or emotion. ● n. an antiseptic substance.

anti-social adj. **1** opposed to normal social practices. **2** not sociable; unfriendly.

antithesis n. (pl. **antitheses**) **1** a person or thing that is the direct opposite of another. **2** contrast or opposition between two things, ideas, etc. □ **antithetical** adj. [Say an TITH uh sis, an TITH uh seez, anta THETIC 'll]

antitrust adj. US opposed to or controlling monopolies (see TRUST n. 6).

antiviral adj. effective against viruses.

antler n. each of the branched horns of a (usu. male) deer. □ **antlered** adj.

antonym n. a word opposite in meaning to another. [Say ANTA nim]

antsy adj. (**antsier**, **antsiest**) informal agitated or fidgety.

anus n. (pl. **anuses**) the opening at the end of the alimentary canal through which solid waste leaves the body.

anvil n. a usu. iron block on which metals are worked in forging.

anxiety n. (pl. **anxieties**) **1** a feeling of

worry or unease. **2** desire to do something. **3** a nervous disorder marked by excessive uneasiness and apprehension. [*Say* angz EYE a tee]

anxious *adj.* **1** worried or troubled. **2** causing or marked by anxiety. **3** *disputed* eager. □ **anxiously** *adv.* [*Say* ANK shus]

any ● *adj.* **1 a** one, no matter which, of several. **b** some **2** a minimal amount of. ● *pron.* any one, number, or amount. ● *adv.* at all, in some degree.

anybody *n. & pron.* **1** a person, no matter who. **2** a person of importance.

anyhow *adv.* **1** anyway. **2** in a disorderly manner or state.

anymore *adv.* (also **any more**) **1** any longer. **2** *informal* nowadays.

anyone *pron.* anybody.

anyplace *adv. informal* anywhere.

anything ● *pron.* whatever thing is chosen. ● *adv.* in any way; at all. □ **anything but** not at all.

any time *adv.* at any time.

anyway *adv.* **1** in any way or manner. **2** at any rate. **3** to resume.

anywhere ● *adv.* **1** in or to any place. **2** to any extent ● *pron.* any place.

A-okay *abbr. informal* excellent; perfect.

aorta *n.* (*pl.* **aortas**) the main artery through which oxygenated air is supplied to the body from the heart. □ **aortic** *adj.* [*Say* ay ORTA]

apace *adv.* swiftly, quickly. [*Say* a PACE]

Apache *n.* **1** (*pl.* **Apache** *or* **Apaches**) a member of an Aboriginal people of the southwestern US. **2** the Athapaskan language of the Apache. □ **Apache** *adj.* [*Say* a PATCH ee]

apart *adv.* **1** separately; not together. **2** into pieces. **3** to or on one side; aside. **4** to or at a distance. **5** from one another. □ **apart from 1** except for. **2** in addition to. □ **apartness** *n.*

apartheid *n.* the former South African policy of segregation and discrimination against non-whites. [*Say* a PAR tite *or* a PAR tide *or* a PAR tate]

apartment *n.* **1** one or more rooms rented and used as a residence. **2** a building other than a house divided into several apartments.

apathy *n.* lack of interest or concern. □ **apathetic** *adj.* [*Say* APPA thee *(with* TH *as in* THIEF*)*, appa THETIC]

apatite *n.* a naturally occurring mineral of calcium phosphate and fluoride. [*Say* APPA tite]

APB *abbr. US* (*pl.* **APBs**) an all-points bulletin, a generally issued alert among police officers.

ape ● *n.* **1** any primate characterized by the absence of a tail. **2** any monkey. **3** a clumsy or stupid person. ● *v.* (**apes**, **aped**, **aping**) imitate, mimic. □ **go ape** *slang* become crazy.

aperitif *n.* an alcoholic drink taken before a meal to stimulate the appetite. [*Say* a perra TEEF]

aperture *n.* **1** an opening; a gap. **2** a variable opening through which light enters a camera. [*Say* APPER chur]

apex *n.* (*pl.* **apexes**) **1** the highest point. **2** a climax; a high point. [*Say* AY pecks]

aphid *n.* a small insect which feeds on the sap of plants. [*Say* AY fid *or* AFF id]

aphorism *n.* a short pithy saying. □ **aphoristic** *adj.* [*Say* AFFER ism]

aphrodisiac ● *adj.* that arouses sexual desire. ● *n.* an aphrodisiac substance. [*Say* afro DEEZY ack *or* afro DIZZY ack]

apiary *n.* (*pl.* **apiaries**) a place where bees are kept. [*Say* APE ee airy]

apiece *adv.* for each one.

aplenty *adv.* in great quantity.

aplomb *n.* assurance or self-confidence. [*Say* a PLOM]

apnea *n.* a temporary cessation of breathing. [*Say* AP nee ah *or* ap NEE ah]

apocalypse *n.* **1** catastrophic destruction, esp. the end of the world. **2** (**the Apocalypse**) another name for the biblical book of Revelation, which describes the destruction of the world. [*Say* a POCKA lips]

apocalyptic *adj.* **1** describing, resembling, or prophesying an apocalypse. **2** momentous or catastrophic. [*Say* a pocka LIP tick]

Apocrypha *pl. n.* **1** those books of the Old Testament which were later rejected from the Jewish canon; most are part of Catholic and Orthodox traditions, but are not included in the Protestant Bible. **2** (**apocrypha**) writings not considered genuine. [*Say* a POCKRA fuh]

apocryphal *adj.* **1** of doubtful authenticity or of the Apocrypha. **2** invented, mythical. [*Say* a POCKRA full]

apogee *n.* **1** the point in a celestial body's orbit where it is furthest from the earth. **2** the highest point or culmination. [*Say* APPA jee]

apolitical *adj.* not interested or involved in politics. [*Say* ay POLITICAL]

apologetic ● *adj.* admitting or showing regret for an offence. ● *n.* reasoned arguments or writings in defence of something. □ **apologetically** *adv.* [*Say* a polla JET ick]

apologist n. a person who defends something by argument. [Say a POLLA jist]

apologize v. (**apologizes, apologized, apologizing**) make an apology; express regret.

apology n. (pl. **apologies**) **1** a regretful acknowledgement of an offence or failure. **2** an assurance that no offence was intended.

apoplectic adj. **1** of or relating to apoplexy. **2** informal enraged. [Say appa PLECK tick]

apoplexy n. a sudden loss of consciousness, sensation, etc. caused by a stroke. [Say APPA plexy]

apostasy n. (pl. **apostasies**) the abandonment of a belief or principle. [Say a POSSTA see]

apostate n. & adj. (a person) who renounces a former belief etc. [Say a POSS tate]

apostle n. **1** (**Apostle**) one of the twelve disciples of Christ, plus Matthias, Paul, and Barnabas. **2** a leader or outstanding figure. [Say a POSSLE]

apostolic adj. **1** of or relating to the Apostles. **2** of the Pope seen as the successor of St. Peter. [Say appa STAW lick]

apostrophe[1] n. a punctuation mark used to indicate the omission of letters or numbers or the possessive case. [Say a POSSTRA fee]

apostrophe[2] n. an exclamatory passage in a speech etc., addressed to an absent person or personified thing. □ **apostrophize** v. (**apostrophizes, apostrophized, apostrophizing**). [Say a POSSTRA fee, a POSSTRA fize]

apothecary n. (pl. **apothecaries**) hist. a person licensed to dispense medicines and drugs. [Say POTH a carry]

apotheosis n. (pl. **apotheoses**) **1** elevation to divine status. **2** a sublime example. [Say a pothy OH sis, a pothy OH seez]

app n. Computing informal application.

Appalachian adj. of or relating to the region of the Appalachian Mountains in eastern N America. [Say appa LAY sh'n]

appall v. greatly dismay or horrify. □ **appalling** adj. **appallingly** adv. [Say a PAUL, a PAUL ing]

Appaloosa n. an American breed of horse with dark spots. [Say appa LOOSSA]

apparatus n. (pl. **apparatuses**) **1** the equipment needed for a particular purpose. **2** complex structure of an organization. [Say appa RAT us or appa RATE us]

apparel n. clothing. [Say a PAIR'll]

apparent adj. **1** readily perceivable. **2** seeming. □ **apparently** adv.

apparition n. **1** a sudden or dramatic appearance. **2** a visible ghost. [Say appa RISH'n]

appeal • v. **1** make a formal request; plead. **2** be of interest; be pleasing. **3** apply (to a higher court) to review or reverse the decision of a lower authority. • n. **1** an urgent or heartfelt request (for financial support etc.). **2** an application to a higher court for a decision to be reversed. **3** attractiveness.

appealing adj. attractive, likeable. □ **appealingly** adv.

appear v. **1** become or be visible. **2** come into view or existence. **3** seem.

appearance n. **1** an act of performing or participating in a public event. **2** the way that someone or something looks or seems. **3** an act of appearing. □ **keep up appearances** maintain an impression of affluence etc. **make** (or **put in**) **an appearance** be present, esp. briefly.

appease v. (**appeases, appeased, appeasing**) **1** pacify or placate, esp. by acceding to demands. **2** satisfy. □ **appeasement** n. **appeaser** n.

appellant n. Law a person who appeals to a higher court. [Say a PELL'nt]

appellate adj. Law concerned with or dealing with appeals. [Say a PELLET]

appellation n. formal a name or title. [Say appa LAY sh'n]

append v. attach or add, esp. to a written document.

appendage n. a smaller or less important part of something larger. [Say a PEN didge]

appendectomy n. (pl. **appendectomies**) the surgical removal of the appendix. [Say appen DECKTA mee]

appendicitis n. inflammation of the appendix. [Say a penda SITE iss]

appendix n. (pl. **appendices** or **appendixes**) **1** a small tube of tissue attached to the lower end of the large intestine. **2** subsidiary matter at the end of a book.

appetite n. **1** a natural desire to satisfy bodily needs, esp. for food or sex. **2** a strong liking or desire.

appetizer n. a small amount of food or drink before a meal.

appetizing adj. pleasing; stimulating an appetite. □ **appetizingly** adv.

applaud v. **1** show approval or praise by clapping. **2** express approval of.

applause *n.* clapping etc. as an expression of approval.

apple *n.* the round fruit of a tree, usu. having thin green or red skin. □ **apples and oranges** completely different things. **apple of one's eye** a cherished person or thing. **upset the apple cart** spoil careful plans.

apple-cheeked *adj.* having round, rosy cheeks.

apple-pie order *n.* perfect order; neatness.

applesauce *n.* **1** mashed stewed apples. **2** *informal* nonsense.

applet *n. Computing* a very small application, esp. a utility program performing one or a few simple functions within a larger program.

appliance *n.* a device used for specific usu. household tasks.

applicable *adj.* relevant or appropriate. □ **applicability** *n.* [Say APP lickable *or* a PLICKABLE, a plick ABILITY]

applicant *n.* a person who applies.

application *n.* **1** the action of applying. **2** a formal request for employment etc. **3** practical use or relevance. **4** effort; hard work. **5** a task that a computer can be programmed to do.

applicator *n.* a device for putting something into or onto something.

applied *adj.* put to practical use rather than theoretical.

appliqué *n.* ornamental work in which fabric shapes are sewn or fixed onto a fabric background. □ **appliquéd** *adj.* [Say APLA kay]

apply *v.* (**applies, applied, applying**) **1** make a formal request for something. **2** have relevance. **3** employ or operate. **4 a** put or spread on. **b** administer. **5** (**apply oneself**) devote oneself.

appoint *v.* **1** assign to (a job). **2** fix, decide on (a time etc.). □ **appointee** *n.* [Say a POINT, a poin TEE]

appointed *adj.* **1** equipped, furnished. **2** decided on beforehand.

appointment *n.* **1** an arrangement to meet. **2** a job or position.

apportion *v.* divide up and share out. □ **apportionment** *n.*

apposite *adj.* apt; well chosen. [Say APPA zit]

apposition *n. Grammar* the placing of a word next to another to qualify or explain the first.

appraisal *n.* **1** an act of assessing. **2** a formal assessment of an employee's performance.

appraise *v.* (**appraises, appraised, appraising**) **1** estimate the quality or value of. **2** consider something so as to make a judgment. □ **appraiser** *n.* **appraisingly** *adv.*

appreciable *adj.* large enough to be noticed; significant. □ **appreciably** *adv.* [Say a PREESHA bull]

appreciate *v.* (**appreciates, appreciated, appreciating**) **1 a** esteem highly; value. **b** be grateful for. **2** understand; recognize. **3** rise in value.

appreciation *n.* **1** favourable or grateful recognition. **2** an esp. favourable estimation or assessment. **3** an increase in value.

appreciative *adj.* feeling or showing gratitude or pleasure. □ **appreciatively** *adv.*

apprehend *v.* **1** understand. **2** seize, arrest. **3** anticipate with uneasiness.

apprehension *n.* **1** uneasiness; dread. **2** understanding. **3** arrest.

apprehensive *adj.* uneasily fearful; dreading. □ **apprehensively** *adv.*

apprentice ● *n.* a person learning a trade from an employer. ● *v.* (**apprentices, apprenticed, apprenticing**) engage or serve as an apprentice. □ **apprenticeship** *n.*

apprise *v.* (**apprises, apprised, apprising**) inform. □ **be apprised of** be aware of.

approach ● *v.* (**approaches, approached, approaching**) **1** come near or nearer. **2** make a tentative proposal or suggestion to. **3** be similar in character etc. to. **4** set about. ● *n.* (*pl.* **approaches**) **1** an act or means of approaching. **2** a way of dealing with something. **3** a sexual advance.

approachable *adj.* **1** friendly; easy to talk to. **2** able to be approached. □ **approachability** *n.*

approbation *n.* approval. [Say appro BAY sh'n]

appropriate ● *adj.* suitable or proper. ● *v.* (**appropriates, appropriated, appropriating**) **1** take possession of, esp. without authority. **2** devote (money etc.) to special purposes. □ **appropriately** *adv.* **appropriateness** *n.* **appropriation** *n.* [Say a PRO pree it *for the adjective*, a PRO pree ate *for the verb*]

approval *n.* **1** the act of approving. **2** a favourable opinion. □ **on approval** (of goods supplied) to be returned if not satisfactory.

approve *v.* (**approves, approved, approving**) **1** confirm; declare acceptable. **2** give or have a favourable opinion.

□ **approve of 1** consider satisfactory; commend. **2** agree to. □ **approvingly** adv.

approximate ● adj. fairly accurate. ● v. (**approximates, approximated, approximating**) bring or come near to. □ **approximately** adv. [Say a PROXA mit for the adjective, a PROXA mate for the verb]

approximation n. an estimate or result that is approximately correct.

appurtenance n. an accessory associated with a particular activity. [Say a PERT'n ince]

Apr. abbr. April.

après-ski n. social activities following a day's skiing. [Say ap ray SKI]

apricot n. a juicy soft fruit, similar to a peach. [Say APRA cot or AYPRA cot]

April n. the fourth month.

April Fool's Day n. April 1, traditionally a day on which people play practical jokes.

a priori adj. & adv. (in a way) based on theoretical reasoning rather than actual observation. [Say ay pry OR eye]

apron n. **1** a garment worn to protect the front of one's clothes. **2** the part of a stage in front of the curtain. **3** the area on an airfield used for manoeuvring or loading aircraft. □ **tied to a person's apron strings** dominated by that person. □ **aproned** adj.

apropos ● adj. appropriate. ● prep. informal with respect to; concerning. ● adv. **1** appropriately. **2** incidentally. [Say apra POE]

apse n. a large recess, arched or with a domed roof, esp. at the eastern end of a church.

apt adj. **1** appropriate. **2 a** inclined. **b** likely. **3** quick to learn. □ **aptly** adv.

aptitude n. a natural ability or talent.

aquaculture n. the cultivation of fish or aquatic plants for human consumption. [Say ACKWA culture]

aquamarine adj. & n. (also **aqua**) a light bluish-green. [Say ackwa MARINE, ACKWA or OCKWA]

aquarium n. (pl. **aquariums** or **aquaria**) **1** a tank of water containing fish or other live aquatic animals and plants. **2** a building in which live aquatic animals are exhibited.

Aquarius n. **1** a constellation (the Water Carrier). **2** a sign of the zodiac, which the sun enters around Jan. 22. □ **Aquarian** n. [Say a KWERRY us, a KWERRY un]

aquatic ● adj. **1** of or relating to water. **2** living in or near water. ● n. an aquatic plant or animal. [Say a KWOT ick]

aqueduct n. an artificial usu. bridge-like

structure for conveying water. [Say ACKWA duct]

aqueous adj. of, containing, or like water. [Say AKE wee us or ACK wee us]

aquifer n. a layer of permeable rock able to store water, through which groundwater moves. [Say ACKWA fur]

Arab ● n. a member of a Semitic people inhabiting the Middle East and North Africa. ● adj. of Arabia or the Arabs.

arabesque n. **1** Dance & Figure Skating a posture with one leg extended straight backwards and usu. raised. **2** a design of intertwined leaves etc. [Say air a BESK]

Arabian ● adj. of or relating to Arabia. ● n. **1** a native of Arabia. **2** (also **Arabian horse**) a breed of horse developed in Arabia noted for its grace and speed.

Arabian camel n. a domesticated camel with one hump, native to the deserts of North Africa and Arabia.

Arabic ● n. the Semitic language of the Arabs. ● adj. of or relating to Arabia.

arabica n. coffee or coffee beans from the most widely grown species of coffee plant. [Say a RABBA kuh]

Arabic numeral n. any of the numerals 0, 1, 2, 3, 4, 5, 6, 7, 8, and 9 (compare ROMAN NUMERAL).

arable adj. **1** (of land) suitable for plowing and cultivation. **2** (of crops) that can be grown on arable land. [Say AIR a bull]

arachnid n. any arthropod of a class including spiders, scorpions, etc. [Say a RACK nid]

-arama comb. form = -RAMA.

Aramaic ● n. an ancient Semitic language, used as a lingua franca in the Near East from the 6th century BC. ● adj. of or in Aramaic. [Say air a MAY ic]

Aran adj. designating a type of thick knitwear with large diamond designs. [Say AIR in]

arbiter n. **1** = ARBITRATOR. **2** a judge; an authority. [Say ARBA ter]

arbitrage n. the buying and selling of stocks in different markets to take advantage of varying prices. □ **arbitrageur** n. [Say ARBA trizh or ARBA tridge, arba truh ZHUR]

arbitrary adj. **1** based on the unrestricted will of a person, not a scheme or plan. **2** established at random. **3** unrestrained and autocratic in the use of authority. □ **arbitrarily** adv. **arbitrariness** n.

arbitration n. the hearing and resolution of a dispute by a referee who has the power to impose a settlement.

arbitrator n. a person appointed to settle a

dispute, usu. with the power to impose a settlement. □ **arbitrate** v.

arbor n. = ARBOUR.

Arbor Day n. a day dedicated annually to public tree planting.

arboreal adj. of, living in, or relating to trees. [Say ar BORRY ul]

arboretum n. (pl. **arboretums** or **arboreta**) a botanical garden devoted to trees. [Say arber EAT'm for the singular; for ARBORETA say arber EETA]

arborio n. a plump, short-grained rice often used in risotto. [Say arb OREO]

Arborite n. Cdn proprietary a plastic laminate used in countertops, tables, etc. [Say ARBER ite]

arborvitae n. any of several evergreen conifers native to North America and N Asia. [Say arber VEE tie or arber VITE ee]

arbour n. **1** a shady garden alcove with a canopy of trees or climbing plants. **2** a metal, wooden, or plastic arch for vines etc. to grow on.

arbutus n. (pl. **arbutuses**) an evergreen tree or shrub having dark green leaves and peeling red bark. [Say ar BYOO tiss]

arc ● n. **1** part of the circumference of a circle or any other curve. **2** any curved shape or course. **3** a luminous discharge between two electrodes. ● v. (**arcs**, **arced**, **arcing**) form an arc.

arcade n. **1** a series of arches supporting or set along a wall. **2** a passageway lined with arches. **3** a public place containing coin-operated video games etc. □ **arcaded** adj.

Arcadian adj. simple and poetically rural. [Say ar KAY dee in]

arcane adj. mysterious; understood by few.

arch[1] ● n. (pl. **arches**) **1** a curved structure spanning an opening, acting as a support for a bridge, roof, floor, etc. **2** something shaped like an arch, esp. the curved bony structure on the underside of the foot or the arrangement of teeth in the mouth. ● v. (**arches**, **arched**, **arching**) **1** form into an arch. **2** span like an arch. **3** form an arch. □ **arched** adj.

arch[2] adj. self-consciously playful or teasing. □ **archly** adv.

arch- comb. form **1** chief, superior. **2** pre-eminent of its kind, extreme.

archaeology n. the study of human history and prehistory through the excavation of sites and the analysis of physical remains. □ **archaeological** adj. **archaeologist** n. [Say arky OLLA jee, arky a LOGICAL, arky OLLA jist]

archaeopteryx n. the oldest known

fossil bird from the Jurassic period. [Say arky OPTA ricks]

archaic adj. **1** antiquated; of an earlier period. **2** (of a word) no longer in ordinary use. [Say ar KAY ick]

archaism n. an archaic word or expression. [Say AR kay ism]

archangel n. an angel of the highest rank. [Say ARK angel]

archbishop n. the chief bishop of an ecclesiastical province.

archdeacon n. a Christian cleric ranking below a bishop.

archdiocese n. the church district for which an archbishop is responsible. [Say arch DIE a siss]

archduke n. hist. a chief duke, esp. as the title of a prince of the Austrian Empire. □ **archduchess** n.

arch-enemy n. (pl. **arch-enemies**) **1** a chief enemy. **2** Satan.

archeology n. = ARCHAEOLOGY. [Say arky OLLA jee]

archery n. shooting with a bow and arrows, esp. as a sport. □ **archer** n.

archetype n. **1** an original which has been imitated. **2** a very typical example of a certain person or thing. □ **archetypal** adj. **archetypical** adj. [Say ARKA type, arka TYPE 'll, arka TYPICAL]

Archimedean adj. of or associated with the Greek mathematician Archimedes (d. 212 BC). [Say arka MEEDIAN]

archipelago n. (pl. **archipelagos**) **1** a group of islands. **2** a sea with many islands. [Say arka PELLA go]

architect n. **1** a person who designs buildings and supervises their construction. **2** a person who brings about a specified thing.

architecture n. **1** the art or science of designing and constructing buildings. **2** the style of a building. **3** buildings collectively. **4** the structure or design of something. □ **architectural** adj.

archive ● n. **1** a collection of historical documents or records. **2** the place where these are stored. **3** Computing a store of data. ● v. (**archives**, **archived**, **archiving**) **1** place or store in an archive. **2** transfer (data) to a storage medium, e.g. from disk to tape. □ **archival** adj. [Say AR kive]

archivist n. a person who maintains and is in charge of archives. [Say ARKA vist]

archrival n. a principal rival.

archway n. a curved structure forming a passage or entrance.

arc lamp n. (also **arc light**) a light source using an electric arc to produce extremely intense white light.

Arctic ● *n.* the area north of the Arctic Circle. ● *adj.* **1** of or native to the Arctic. **2** (**arctic**) (esp. of weather) very cold. [*Say* ARK tick *or* AR tick]

Arctic char *n.* a freshwater fish of the north, with pink flesh similar to salmon.

Arctic Circle *n.* the parallel of latitude 66°33′ north of the equator.

Arctic fox *n.* a small fox whose coat turns white or grey-blue in winter.

Arctic hare *n.* a large hare, whose coat is brown in summer and white in winter.

arc welding *n.* a method of welding using an electric arc to melt metal.

ardent *adj.* zealous, eager; fervent. □ **ardently** *adv.*

ardour *n.* (also **ardor**) passion.

arduous *adj.* difficult and tiring. □ **arduously** *adv.* [*Say* AR joo us *or* ARD you us]

are[1] *2nd singular present & 1st, 2nd, 3rd plural present of* BE.

are[2] *n.* a metric unit of measure equal to 100 square metres. Abbreviation: **a**. [*Say* AIR *or* AR]

area *n.* **1** the extent or measure of a surface. **2** a region or tract. **3** a space allocated for a specific purpose. **4** a part of something. **5** the scope of an activity.

area code *n.* a three-digit code added to local phone numbers to identify a telephone area.

area rug *n.* a rug covering part of a floor only.

areca *n.* a tropical palm native to Asia, the nuts of which are edible. [*Say* AIR icka *or* a REEKA]

arena *n.* **1** a building with an open central area (esp. an ice surface) for sports etc., and seating for spectators. **2** a sphere of action or discussion.

aren't *contr.* **1** are not. **2** am not.

Argentine ● *adj.* of or relating to Argentina. ● *n.* a person from Argentina. [*Say* ARJ'n tine]

Argentinian *adj. & n.* = ARGENTINE. [*Say* arj'n TINNY in]

argh *interj.* expressing usu. feigned pain, disgust, or exasperation.

argillite *n.* a soft rock used in Haida sculpture. [*Say* ARJA lite]

argon *n.* an inert gaseous element used to fill light bulbs, vacuum tubes, etc.

argot *n.* the jargon of a group or class. [*Say* ARGO *or* AR gut]

arguable *adj.* **1** capable of being argued. **2** supportable by argument. □ **arguably** *adv.*

argue *v.* (**argues**, **argued**, **arguing**) **1** exchange views, especially heatedly; quarrel. **2** provide reasons supporting or challenging something. **3** challenge, dispute. **4** treat by reasoning. □ **arguer** *n.*

argument *n.* **1** an exchange of views, esp. a contentious one. **2** a reason advanced; a reasoning process. **3** a summary of the subject matter of a book.

argumentation *n.* **1** methodical reasoning. **2** debate or argument.

argumentative *adj.* **1** fond of arguing. **2** using methodical reasoning. □ **argumentatively** *adv.* **argumentativeness** *n.*

argyle *adj.* (also **argyll**) a knitting pattern with diamonds of various colours on a single background colour. [*Say* AR gile (*with* G *as in* GIVE)]

aria *n.* an accompanied song for solo voice in an opera etc. [*Say* ARRY uh *or* AIRY uh]

arid *adj.* **1** extremely dry, parched. **2** emotionless, not interesting. □ **aridity** *n.* [*Say* AIR id, a RIDDA tee]

Aries *n.* (*pl.* **Aries**) **1** a constellation (the Ram). **2** a sign of the zodiac which the sun enters around 21 March. [*Say* AIR eez]

aright *adv.* rightly.

arise *v.* (**arises**; *past* **arose**; *past participle* **arisen**; **arising**) **1** come into being or come to notice. **2** result. **3** rise.

aristocracy *n.* (*pl.* **aristocracies**) **1** the highest class in certain societies, typically comprising people of noble birth. **2** government by the nobility. [*Say* air iss TOCK ruh see]

aristocrat *n.* a member of the nobility. □ **aristocratic** *adj.* [*Say* uh RISTA crat, air iss tuh CRAT ick]

Aristotelian ● *n.* a disciple or student of the Greek philosopher Aristotle (d. 322 BC). ● *adj.* of Aristotle or his ideas. □ **Aristotelianism** *n.* [*Say* erra sta TEELY in *or* a rista TEELY in]

arithmetic ● *n.* **1** the science of numbers. **2** the use of numbers; computation. ● *adj.* (also **arithmetical**) of or concerning arithmetic. □ **arithmetician** *n.* [*Say* uh RITHMA tick *for the noun*, air ith MET ick *or* air ith MET ick'll *for the adjective*, uh rithma TISH'n]

arithmetic mean *n.* **1** the central number in an arithmetic progression. **2** = AVERAGE *n.* 2.

arithmetic progression *n.* a sequence of numbers in which each differs from the next by a constant quantity.

ark *n.* the ship in which Noah, his family, and the animals were saved from the biblical Flood.

Ark of the Covenant *n.* (also **Ark of**

the Testimony) the wooden chest which in Biblical times contained the Laws given to Moses by God.

arm¹ *n.* **1** each of the two upper limbs of the human body from the shoulder to the hand. **2 a** anything resembling an arm in function or appearance. **b** a sleeve. **c** the side of a chair etc. **3** authority; power. ▢ **an arm and a leg** a large sum of money. **as long as your** (or **my**) **arm** *informal* very long. **at arm's length 1** as far as an arm can reach. **2** far enough to avoid close contact. **give one's right arm** sacrifice a great deal. **in arms** (of a baby) too young to walk. **on one's arm** supported by one's arm. **with open arms** cordially. ▢ **armful** *n.* **armless** *adj.*

arm² ● *n.* **1 a** a weapon. **b** = FIREARM. **2** (in *pl.*) the military profession or a branch of the military. **3** a subdivision of an organization. ● *v.* **1** supply with weapons. **2** supply with tools; equip. **3** make (a bomb etc.) able to explode. ▢ **in arms** armed. **take up arms** begin fighting. **up in arms** actively rebelling or protesting.

armada *n.* a fleet of warships. [*Say* ar MODDA]

armadillo *n.* (*pl.* **armadillos**) an insect-eating mammal covered in bony plates, native to South and Central America.

Armageddon *n.* **1** *New Testament* the last battle between good and evil before the Day of Judgment. **2** a vast and deadly armed conflict. [*Say* arma GED'n]

armament *n.* **1** (often in *pl.*) military weapons and equipment. **2** the process of equipping for war.

armature *n.* **1 a** the rotating coil of an electric motor or generator. **b** any moving part of an electrical machine in which a voltage is induced by a magnetic field. **2** a piece of soft iron placed across the poles of a magnet to preserve its power. **3** *Biology* the protective covering of an animal or plant. [*Say* ARMA chur]

armchair *n.* **1** a usu. upholstered chair with side supports for the arms. **2** (as an *adj.*) theoretical rather than active or practical.

armed *adj.* **1** equipped with or characterized by the use of weapons. **2** equipped, provided or prepared. **3** (of a bomb etc.) activated.

armed forces *pl. n.* (also **armed services**) the combined military services of a country or group of countries.

Armenian ● *n.* **1 a** a native of Armenia. **b** a person of Armenian descent. **2** the language of the Armenian people. ● *adj.* of Armenia, its language, or the Christian Church established there *c.*300. [*Say* ar MEENY in]

armistice *n.* a cessation of armed conflict by common agreement of the opposing sides. [*Say* ARMA stiss]

Armistice Day *n.* the anniversary of the armistice of 11 Nov. 1918 ending the First World War (*compare* REMEMBRANCE DAY).

armload *n.* the quantity that can be carried in the arms; an armful.

armour ● *n.* (also **armor**) **1** protective clothing designed to protect the body in battle **2 a** (also **armour-plate**) a protective metal covering for a tank or other vehicle. **b** armoured vehicles collectively. **3** a protective covering or shell on animals and plants. ● *v.* provide with a protective covering.

armoured *adj.* **1** equipped with a protective covering, esp. of metal: *armoured car.* **2** (of an infantry division etc.) equipped with tanks and other armoured vehicles.

armoury *n.* (also **armory**) (*pl.* **armouries** or **armories**) **1** a place where arms are kept; an arsenal. **2** *Cdn* a place where militia units drill and train.

armpit *n.* **1** the hollow under the arm at the shoulder. **2** *slang* a place considered disgusting or contemptible.

arm's-length *adj.* **1** without friendliness or intimacy. **2** (of commercial relations) with neither party controlled by the other.

arms race *n.* competition between nations in the development and accumulation of weapons.

arm-twisting *n.* persuasion by the use of moral pressure.

arm wrestling *n.* a trial of strength in which two people each try to force the other's forearm down onto a table. ▢ **arm wrestle** *v.* (**arm wrestles, arm wrestled, arm wrestling**)

army *n.* (*pl.* **armies**) **1** an organized force armed for fighting on land. **2** a very large number.

army ant *n.* a blind nomadic tropical ant that forages in large columns.

army surplus *n.* military supplies, such as clothing and camping gear, exceeding the requirements of the forces and sold to the public (also as an *adj.*).

aroma *n.* a distinctive and pleasing smell.

aromatherapy *n.* the use of aromatic plant extracts and essential oils to promote healing or well-being. ▢ **aromatherapist** *n.*

aromatic *adj.* **1** having a pleasant and distinctive smell. **2** (of organic compounds) having an unsaturated ring, esp.

containing a benzene ring.
□ **aromatically** adv. [Say erra MAT ick]

arose past of ARISE.

around ● adv. **1** on every side. **2** in various places. **3** informal available. **4** with circular motion or in a circle. **5** with change to an opposite position. **6** measuring a (specified distance) in girth. ● prep. **1** on or along the circuit of. **2** on every side of; enveloping. **3** near; at a time near to. **4** so as to encircle or enclose. □ **have been around** informal be widely experienced, esp. sexually.

arouse v. (**arouses, aroused, arousing**) **1** evoke or awaken (esp. a feeling etc.). **2** awake from sleep. **3** excite or provoke someone to anger. **4** excite sexually. □ **arousal** n.

arpeggio n. (pl. **arpeggios**) the notes of a chord played or sung in succession. [Say ar PEDGY o]

arraign v. call on to answer a criminal charge before a court. □ **arraignment** n. [Say a RAIN]

arrange v. (**arranges, arranged, arranging**) **1** put into the required order. **2** plan or provide for. **3** come to an agreement. **4** adapt (a composition) for performance with different instruments or voices. □ **arrangement** n. **arranger** n.

arrant adj. downright, notorious. [Say AIR int]

array ● n. **1** an imposing or well-ordered series or display. **2** an ordered arrangement, esp. of troops. **3** attire; an outfit. ● v. **1** dress someone in the clothes specified. **2** set in order.

arrears pl. n. an amount still outstanding, esp. a debt unpaid. □ **in arrears** behind in payments etc.

arrest ● v. **1** seize (a person) and take into custody, esp. by legal authority. **2** stop or check (a process etc.). **3** attract the attention of. ● n. **1** the act of arresting or being arrested. **2** a stoppage of motion.

arresting adj. attracting attention; striking.

arrhythmia n. deviation from the normal rhythm of the heart. [Say a RITH mee uh]

arrival n. **1** the act of arriving; an appearance. **2** a person or thing that has arrived.

arrive v. (**arrives, arrived, arriving**) **1** reach a destination. **2** reach (a conclusion etc.). **3** informal establish one's reputation or position. **4** come.

arrogant adj. behaving in a proud, unpleasant way because convinced of one's superiority. □ **arrogance** n. **arrogantly** adv.

arrow n. **1** a sharp pointed stick shot from a bow. **2** a symbol representing this indicating a direction.

arrowhead n. the pointed end of an arrow.

arrowroot n. **1** a pure edible starch prepared from a Caribbean plant. **2** (also **arrowroot cookie**) a cookie made with arrowroot flour.

arsenal n. **1** a store of weapons and ammunition. **2** a collection of things available for tackling a problem.

arsenic n. a brittle semi-metallic element that produces many highly poisonous compounds. [Say ARSA nick]

arson n. the act of maliciously setting fire to property. □ **arsonist** n.

art n. **1** human creative skill or its application. **2** (**the arts**) the various branches of creative activity, e.g. painting, music, writing, etc. considered collectively. **3** creative activity resulting in visual representation. **4** human workmanship as opposed to the work of nature. **5** a skill, aptitude, or knack. **6** (**arts**) certain branches of (esp. university) study, esp. the fine arts and humanities.

Art Deco n. the predominant decorative art style of the period 1910–30, characterized by bold geometric motifs, colours, etc.

arterial adj. **1 a** of or relating to an artery. **b** (of blood) oxygenated and of a bright red colour. **2** (esp. of a road) main. [Say ar TEERY 'll]

arteriosclerosis n. abnormal thickening and hardening of arterial walls. [Say ar teery o skla ROE sis]

artery n. (pl. **arteries**) **1** any of the muscular-walled tubes forming part of the blood circulation system of the body. **2** a major transport route.

artesian well n. a well bored perpendicularly into water-bearing strata lying at an angle, producing a constant supply of water with little pumping. [Say ar TEE zh'n]

artful adj. **1** skilful, clever. **2** crafty, deceitful. □ **artfully** adv. **artfulness** n.

arthritis n. inflammation of a joint or joints. □ **arthritic** adj. [Say arth RYE tiss, arth RIT ick]

arthropod n. a large phylum of invertebrate animals including insects, spiders, and crustaceans. [Say ARTHRA pod]

artichoke n. a Mediterranean plant cultivated for its large edible flower heads (see also JERUSALEM ARTICHOKE).

article ● n. **1** a particular thing. **2** a piece of writing in a newspaper, magazine, etc.

3 a separate clause or portion of any document. **4** (in *pl.*) the period of apprenticeship of a law student. ● *v.* (**articles**, **articled**, **articling**) **1** bind by a written contract, esp. for a period of training. **2** *Cdn* (of a law student) serve one's period of apprenticeship. □ **article of faith** a firmly held belief.

articulate ● *adj.* **1** able to speak fluently and coherently. **2** (of sound or speech) having clearly distinguishable parts. ● *v.* (**articulates**, **articulated**, **articulating**) **1** pronounce clearly and distinctly. **2** express coherently. □ **articulately** *adv.* **articulation** *n.* [*Say* ar TICK you lit *for the adjective,* ar TICK you late *for the verb,* ar TICK you lit lee, ar tick you LAY sh'n]

articulated *adj.* (of a vehicle) having two or more sections connected by a flexible joint. [*Say* ar TICK you lated]

artifact *n.* a product of human workmanship.

artifice *n.* clever or cunning devices, esp. used to deceive others. [*Say* ARTA fiss]

artificial *adj.* **1** produced by humans and not by nature. **2** formed in imitation of something natural. **3** affected, insincere. □ **artificiality** *n.* **artificially** *adv.*

artificial insemination *n.* a procedure injecting semen into the vagina or uterus other than by intercourse.

artificial intelligence *n.* the capacity of a machine, esp. a computer, to simulate or surpass intelligent human behaviour. Abbreviation: **AI.**

artificial respiration *n.* forcing air into a person's lungs by mechanical or mouth-to-mouth methods.

artillery *n.* **1** large-calibre guns used in warfare on land. **2** a branch of the armed forces that uses these.

artisan *n.* a craftsperson specializing in decorative arts. □ **artisanal** *adj.* [*Say* ARTA zan *or* ARTA san]

artist *n.* **1** a person who practises any of the fine arts. **2** a person in the performing arts. **3** a person who shows great skill in a particular activity. □ **artistry** *n.*

artistic *adj.* **1** having natural skill in art. **2** of art or artists. □ **artistically** *adv.*

artistic director *n.* the director of a performing arts organization in charge of programming and casting decisions etc.

artless *adj.* **1** without guile or deceit. **2** natural and simple. **3** clumsy. □ **artlessly** *adv.*

art nouveau *n.* a European art style of the late 19th century characterized by flowing lines and organic forms. [*Say* art noo VOE]

artsy *adj.* (**artsier**, **artsiest**) (also **arty**) (**artier**, **artiest**) *informal* pretentiously artistic.

artwork *n.* **1** a work of art. **2** the illustrations in a printed work.

arugula *n.* a plant with bitter leaves, used in salads. [*Say* a ROOGA la]

arum *n.* a plant with a white spathe and arrow-shaped leaves. [*Say* AIR um]

Aryan *n.* **1** (in Nazi ideology) a Caucasian not of Jewish descent. **2** a member of a people who invaded northern India in the 2nd millennium BC. □ **Aryan** *adj.* [*Say* AIRY un]

as ● *adv.* used in comparisons to refer to extent. ● *conj.* **1** expressing result or purpose. **2** while. **3 a** in the way that. **b** seeing that. ● *rel. pron.* **1** that, who, which. **2** a fact that. □ **as for** with regard to. **as from** on and after (a date). **as if!** indicating disbelief. **as it were** in a way. **as to** with respect to. **as yet** until now.

ASA *abbr. Cdn* ACETYLSALICYLIC ACID.

asana *n.* any of various postures used in yoga. [*Say* OSSA nuh]

ASAP *abbr.* as soon as possible. [*Say* ay ess ay PEE, AY sap]

asbestos *n.* a non-flammable heat-resistant fibrous silicate mineral used as an insulating material. [*Say* az BEST us]

ascend *v.* **1** rise; move upwards. **2** climb; go up. □ **ascend the throne** become king or queen.

ascendant ● *adj.* **1** rising. **2** predominant. ● *n. Astrology* the point of the ecliptic or sign of the zodiac which is just rising above the eastern horizon. □ **in the ascendant** rising; gaining power or authority. □ **ascendancy** *n.*

ascension *n.* **1** the action of rising to an important position or a higher level. **2** *Christianity* (**Ascension**) **a** the ascent of Christ into heaven after the Resurrection. **b** (also **Ascension Day**) the day on which Christians annually celebrate the Ascension, usu. the fortieth day after Easter.

ascent *n.* **1** a climb or walk to the summit of a mountain or hill. **2** an upward slope. **3** an act of ascending.

ascertain *v.* find out as a definite fact. □ **ascertainable** *adj.* [*Say* asser TAIN]

ascetic ● *n.* a person who practises severe self-discipline, esp. for religious reasons. ● *adj.* abstaining from pleasure. □ **asceticism** *n.* [*Say* a SET ic, a SETTA sism]

ASCII *n. Computing* a standard code for storing and transmitting information. [*Say* ASKY]

ascorbic acid *n.* a vitamin found in citrus fruits and green vegetables. *Also called* VITAMIN C. [*Say* a SCORE bick]

ascot a broad necktie or scarf covering the area of an open neck. [*Say* ASS oot]

ascribe *v.* (**ascribes, ascribed, ascribing**) **1** attribute. **2** regard as belonging. □ **ascribable** *adj.*

aceptic *adj.* free from harmful bacteria, viruses, or other micro-organisms. [*Say* ay SEPTIC]

asexual *adj.* **1** without sex or sexual organs. **2** (of reproduction) not involving the fusion of gametes. **3** without sexuality. □ **asexually** *adv.* [*Say* ay SEXUAL]

ash¹ *n.* (*pl.* **ashes**) **1** the powdery residue left after burning any substance. **2** the remains of the human body after cremation. **3** ash-like material thrown out by a volcano.

ash² *n.* (*pl.* **ashes**) a forest tree with silver-grey bark and hard pale wood.

ashamed *adj.* **1** embarrassed or disconcerted by shame. **2** reluctant.

ashen *adj.* ash-coloured; deathly pale.

Ashkenazi *n.* (*pl.* **Ashkenazim**) a Jew of central, northern, or eastern Europe. □ **Ashkenazic** *adj.* [*Say* ashka NOZZY, ahska NOZZ im]

ashore *adv.* toward or on the shore.

ashram *n.* a place of religious retreat for Hindus. [*Say* ASH rum]

ashtray *n.* a small receptacle for cigarette ash etc.

Ash Wednesday *n. Christianity* the first day of Lent.

ashy *adj.* **1** very pale. **2** covered with ashes.

Asian *n.* **1** a native of Asia. **2** a person of Asian descent. □ **Asian** *adj.*

Asiatic *adj.* Asian. [*Say* ay zhee ATTIC]

aside ● *adv.* **1** to or on one side; away. **2** out of consideration. ● *n.* **1** words spoken in a play to the audience rather than the other characters. **2** an incidental remark. □ **aside from** apart from. **take aside** engage esp. for a private conversation.

asinine *adj.* stupid. [*Say* ASSA nine]

ask *v.* **1** call for an answer. **2** seek to obtain from another person. **3** invite. □ **ask after** inquire about. **ask for it** *slang* invite trouble. **for the asking** (obtainable) for nothing. **I ask you!** an exclamation of disgust, surprise, etc.

askance *adv.* with a look of suspicion or disapproval. [*Say* a SKANCE]

askew *adv. & adj.* not straight or level. [*Say* a SKYOO]

asking price *n.* the price of an object set by the seller.

asleep *adj. & adv.* **1 a** in or into a state of sleep. **b** inactive, inattentive. **2** (of a limb etc.) numb. □ **asleep at the switch** inattentive.

asp *n.* any of several venomous snakes native to Europe, Asia, and North Africa.

asparagus *n.* a plant whose young green or white stems are eaten as a vegetable.

aspartame *n.* a low-calorie sugar substitute. [*Say* ASPER tame]

aspect *n.* **1** a particular part or feature of a matter. **2** an appearance or look. **3** the side of a building facing a particular direction.

aspen *n.* any of several poplars with leaves which tremble in the slightest wind.

asperity *n.* (*pl.* **asperities**) harshness of tone or manner. [*Say* ass PERRA tee]

aspersion *n.* a disparaging remark attacking someone's reputation. [*Say* a SPUR zh'n]

asphalt *n.* a dark bituminous pitch mixed with gravel used for surfacing roads etc. □ **asphalt** *v.* [*Say* ASH fault *or* ASS fault]

asphyxia *n.* a lack of oxygen in the blood caused by suffocation. [*Say* ass FIXIA]

asphyxiate *v.* (**asphyxiates, asphyxiated, asphyxiating**) suffocate. □ **asphyxiation** *n.* [*Say* ass FIXY ate]

aspic *n.* a clear savoury jelly prepared from meat or fish stock or vegetable juice. [*Say* ASS pick]

aspidistra *n.* a bulbous East Asian plant of the lily family with broad tapering leaves. [*Say* aspa DISTRA]

aspirant ● *adj.* having ambitions to achieve something. ● *n.* a person who has ambitions to achieve. [*Say* ASPER int *or* a SPY rint]

aspirate *v.* (**aspirates, aspirated, aspirating**) **1** pronounce with a breath. **2** *Medical* draw (fluid) by suction from a cavity. [*Say* ASPER ate]

aspiration *n.* **1** a strong desire to achieve; an ambition. **2** the act of drawing breath. **3** the act of aspirating. □ **aspirational** *adj.* [*Say* aspa RAY sh'n]

aspire *v.* (**aspires, aspired, aspiring**) have ambition or strong desire. □ **aspiring** *adj.*

Aspirin *n.* (*pl.* **Aspirin** *or* **Aspirins**) *proprietary* **1** acetylsalicylic acid. **2** a tablet of this.

ass *n.* (*pl.* **asses**) **1** a donkey or other small horse with long ears and a braying call. **2** a stupid person. **3** *coarse slang* the buttocks.

assail *v.* **1** make a strong or concerted attack on. **2** (of an unpleasant feeling) overcome someone suddenly. □ **assailant** *n.*

assassin *n.* a killer, esp. of a political or religious leader.

assassinate *v.* (**assassinates, assassinated, assassinating**) kill (a leader) for political or religious motives. □ **assassination** *n.*

assault ● *n.* **1** a violent attack. **2** = SEXUAL ASSAULT. **3** a final effort to reach a (usu. fortified) place esp. in battle. ● *v.* **1** make an assault on. **2** sexually assault. □ **assault and battery** *Law* (in civil law) a threatening act that is followed by physical contact without consent, whether or not harm is caused. □ **assaultive** *adj.*

assault rifle *n.* a lightweight military rifle using high-performance ammunition.

assay ● *n.* a test to determine the composition of a substance, esp. a metal or ore. ● *v.* determine the quality or presence of by testing. [*Say* a SAY *or* ASS ay]

assemblage *n.* **1** a collection or gathering. **2 a** the act of assembling. **b** something made of pieces fitted together.

assemble *v.* (**assembles, assembled, assembling**) **1** gather together; collect. **2** arrange in order. **3** fit together the parts of. □ **assembler** *n.*

assembly *n.* (*pl.* **assemblies**) **1** a group of persons gathered together. **2** (also **Assembly**) a legislative council or deliberative body. **3** the assembling of a machine or its parts.

assembly language *n.* *Computing* a low-level language employing symbols which correspond exactly to groups of machine instructions.

assembly line *n.* a sequence of machines and workers along which products are assembled.

assemblyman *n.* (*pl.* **assemblymen**) a member of an (esp. legislative) assembly.

assent ● *v.* **1** consent. **2** express agreement. ● *n.* **1** acceptance or agreement. **2** consent or sanction, esp. official.

assert *v.* **1** declare; state clearly. **2** (**assert oneself**) (of a person) be confident and forceful; demand recognition. **3** make or enforce a claim to. [*Say* a CERT]

assertion *n.* **1** a confident and forceful statement. **2** the action of asserting. [*Say* a SUR sh'n]

assertive *adj.* having or showing a confident and forceful personality. □ **assertively** *adv.* **assertiveness** *n.* [*Say* a SUR tiv]

assess *v.* (**assesses, assessed, assessing**) **1** estimate the size, quality, or value of. **2** judge or evaluate. **3** fix the amount of (a tax etc.) and impose it.

4 penalize or fine a specific amount. □ **assessment** *n.* **assessor** *n.*

asset *n.* **1 a** a useful or valuable quality. **b** a person or thing possessing such a quality. **2** property and possessions having value.

assiduous *adj.* showing great care and perseverance. □ **assiduously** *adv.* [*Say* a SID yoo us]

assign *v.* **1 a** allot as a share, task, etc. **b** appoint to a position, task, etc. **2** fix (a time etc.). **3** ascribe to (a date etc.). □ **assignable** *adj.*

assignation *n.* an appointment to meet someone in secret. [*Say* assig NATION]

assignment *n.* **1** a task allotted to someone. **2** the action of assigning.

assimilate *v.* (**assimilates, assimilated, assimilating**) **1** absorb and digest (food, information, etc.). **2** absorb (people) into a larger group. **3** make similar to. □ **assimilation** *n.* **assimilationist** *n. & adj.* **assimilative** *adj.* [*Say* a SIMMA late]

Assiniboine *n.* **1** (*pl.* **Assiniboine** or **Assiniboines**) a member of an Aboriginal people living in S Saskatchewan and NE Montana. **2** the Siouan language of the Assiniboine. □ **Assiniboine** *adj.* [*Say* a SINNA boin]

assist ● *v.* **1** help. **2** act as an assistant. ● *n.* **1** *Sport* a play which enables a teammate to score a goal or put out an opponent. **2** an act of helping. □ **assistance** *n.*

assistant *n.* **1** a helper. **2** a person who assists, esp. in a particular role.

assisted suicide *n.* suicide effected with the assistance of another person, esp. a physician.

assize *n.* *Cdn* (usu. in *pl.*) **1** a session of a court. **2** a trial held before a travelling judge. [*Say* a SIZE]

associate ● *v.* (**associates, associated, associating**) **1** connect in the mind. **2** join or combine. **3** (**associate oneself**) declare oneself in agreement. **4** meet frequently or have dealings. ● *n.* **1** a business partner or colleague. **2** a friend or companion. **3** a subordinate member. ● *adj.* **1** joined. **2** allied. **3** of less than full status. □ **associative** *adj.* [*Say* a SO see ate *or* a SO she ate *for the verb,* a SO see it *or* a SO she it *for the noun or adjective;* a SO see a tiv *or* a SO she a tiv]

association *n.* **1** a group of people or organizations united for a joint purpose. **2** a connection or link. **3** the fact of occurring with something else. □ **associational** *adj.*

assorted *adj.* **1** of various sorts. **2** sorted into groups.

assortment *n.* a set of various sorts put together; a mixed collection.

assuage *v.* (**assuages, assuaged, assuaging**) **1** make an unpleasant feeling less intense. **2** satisfy (an appetite or desire). [*Say* a SWAYDGE]

assume *v.* (**assumes, assumed, assuming**) **1** take as true without proof. **2** simulate or pretend. **3** undertake (an office etc.). **4** take on.

assumption *n.* **1** a thing that is accepted as true or certain, without proof. **2** the action of assuming power or responsibility. **3** *Catholicism* (**Assumption**) **a** the reception of the Virgin Mary bodily into heaven. **b** the feast day in honour of this (Aug. 15).

assurance *n.* **1** a positive declaration that a thing is true. **2** confidence or certainty about one's own abilities.

assure *v.* (**assures, assured, assuring**) **1** declare confidently to; convince. **2** make certain of.

assured *adj.* **1** certain, guaranteed. **2** self-confident. □ **rest assured** remain confident. □ **assuredly** *adv.*

Assyrian *n.* **1** an inhabitant of Assyria. **2** the Semitic language of Assyria. □ **Assyrian** *adj.* [*Say* a SEERY in]

astatine *n.* a radioactive element of the halogen family. [*Say* ASTA teen]

aster *n.* a plant with bright daisy-like flowers.

asterisk ● *n.* the symbol (*) used in printing and writing and in computer wild card searches. ● *v.* mark with an asterisk.

astern *adv. Nautical & Aviation* **1** aft; away to the rear. **2** backwards.

asteroid *n.* a small planetary body revolving around the sun, mainly between Mars and Jupiter. □ **asteroidal** *adj.*

asthma *n.* a disorder causing difficulty breathing. □ **asthmatic** *adj.* [*Say* AZMA, azz MAT ic]

astigmatism *n.* a defect in the eye resulting in distorted images. [*Say* a STIGMA tism]

astilbe *n.* a plant with plume-like heads of tiny white, red, orange, or pink flowers. [*Say* a STILL bee]

astonish *v.* (**astonishes, astonished, astonishing**) amaze. □ **astonishing** *adj.* **astonishingly** *adv.* **astonishment** *n.*

astound *v.* overcome with surprise or shock; amaze. □ **astounding** *adj.* **astoundingly** *adv.*

astral *adj.* of, connected with, or consisting of stars. [*Say* ASS trull]

astray *adv. & adj.* **1** into error. **2** away from

the correct path. □ **go astray** be lost or mislaid.

astride *prep.* **1** with a leg on each side of. **2** extending across.

astringent ● *adj.* **1** causing body tissue to contract, esp. to stop bleeding. **2 a** severe, austere. **b** harsh and critical. **3** slightly bitter. ● *n.* an astringent substance. □ **astringency** *n.* [*Say* a STRIN jint, a STRIN jin see]

astrolabe *n.* an instrument formerly used to make astronomical measurements and to aid navigation. [*Say* ASTRA labe]

astrology *n.* the study of the supposed influence of celestial bodies on human affairs. □ **astrologer** *n.* **astrological** *adj.*

astronaut *n.* a person who is trained to travel in a spacecraft.

astronautics *n.* the science of space travel.

astronomical *adj.* (also **astronomic**) **1** of or relating to astronomy. **2** extremely large. □ **astronomically** *adv.*

astronomy *n.* the study of the universe beyond the Earth's atmosphere. □ **astronomer** *n.*

astrophysics *n.* a branch of astronomy concerned with the physical properties of celestial bodies. □ **astrophysical** *adj.* **astrophysicist** *n.*

Astroturf *n. proprietary* a synthetic surface used as a substitute for grass on sports fields etc.

astute *adj.* good at making accurate assessments; shrewd. □ **astutely** *adv.* **astuteness** *n.*

asunder *adv. literary* apart.

asylum *n.* protection, esp. for those pursued by the law. [*Say* a SIGH lum]

asymmetrical *adj.* (also **asymmetric**) **1** lacking symmetry. **2** unequal or unbalanced. □ **asymmetrically** *adv.* [*Say* ay sim METRIC ul]

asymmetry *n.* (*pl.* **asymmetries**) lack of symmetry. [*Say* ay SIMMA tree *or* ass SIMMA tree]

asymptomatic *adj.* producing or showing no symptoms. [*Say* ay simpta MAT ic]

asynchronous *adj.* not happening at the same time. □ **asynchronously** *adv.* [*Say* ay SINKRA nus]

at *prep.* **1** expressing position in space or time. **2** expressing a value, rate, or point in a scale. **3** expressing engagement in a state or activity. **4 a** with or with reference to. **b** by means of. **5** expressing direction towards □ **at it 1** working hard. **2** *informal* repeating a habitual activity. **at that** moreover.

atavism *n.* a reversion to something

ancient or ancestral. □ **atavistic** *adj.*
[*Say* ATTA vism]

ate *past of* EAT.

atelier *n.* a workshop or studio.
[*Say* attle YAY]

Athapaskan *n.* **1** an Aboriginal language group of the subarctic regions of Canada's Northwest. **2** (*pl.* **Athapaskan** or **Athapaskans**) a member of an Athapaskan-speaking people.
□ **Athapaskan** *adj.*

atheism *n.* disbelief in the existence of God or gods. □ **atheist** *n.* **atheistic** *adj.*
[*Say* AY thee ism]

Athenian ● *n.* a native or inhabitant of Athens. ● *adj.* of or relating to ancient or modern Athens. [*Say* a THEENY un]

atherosclerosis *n.* thickening and hardening of the arteries because of the buildup of fatty deposits.
[*Say* atha roe skla ROE sis]

athlete *n.* **1** a person who trains to compete in sports. **2** a person with a natural talent for sports.

athlete's foot *n.* a fungal foot condition causing itching, flaking, etc.

athletic *adj.* **1** of or relating to athletes or athletics. **2** muscular or physically fit. **3** active in, esp. skilled at, sports.
□ **athletically** *adv.* **athleticism** *n.*

athletics *pl. n.* competitive activities requiring physical skill and endurance.

-athon *comb. form* forming nouns denoting an extended event or activity, usu. to raise money for a charity.

athwart *prep.* from side to side of.
[*Say* a THWORT]

Atlantic *adj.* of or adjoining the Atlantic Ocean.

Atlantic provinces *pl. n.* New Brunswick, Nova Scotia, PEI, and Newfoundland (*compare* MARITIMES).

atlas *n.* (*pl.* **atlases**) a book of maps or charts.

ATM *abbr.* (*pl.* **ATMs**) AUTOMATED TELLER MACHINE.

atmosphere *n.* **1 a** the envelope of gases surrounding the earth or another planet. **b** the air in any particular place. **2** the pervading tone or mood. **3** *Physics* a unit of pressure equal to mean atmospheric pressure at sea level, 101.325 kilopascals.

atmospheric *adj.* **1** of, relating to, or occurring in the atmosphere. **2** possessing or evoking a particular tone, mood, etc.
[*Say* atma SFEER ick]

atmospherics *pl. n.* **1** electrical disturbance in the atmosphere. **2** = ATMOSPHERE 2. [*Say* atma SFEER icks *or* atma SFAIR icks]

atoll *n.* a ring-shaped coral reef enclosing a lagoon. [*Say* AT all]

atom *n.* **1** the smallest particle of a chemical element. **2** a very small portion of a thing or quality. **3** *Cdn* **a** a level of children's sports, usu. involving children aged 9–11. **b** a player in this age group.

atomic *adj.* **1** concerned with or using atomic energy. **2** of or relating to an atom or atoms.

atomic bomb *n.* (also **atom bomb**) a bomb involving the release of energy by nuclear fission.

atomic energy *n.* energy obtained by nuclear fission or fusion.

atomic number *n.* the number of protons in the nucleus of an atom.

atomize *v.* (**atomizes, atomized, atomizing**) **1** reduce to very fine particles. **2** break up into small constituent parts.

atomizer *n.* an instrument for emitting liquids as a fine spray.

atonal *adj. Music* not written in any key or mode. □ **atonality** *n.* [*Say* ay TONAL]

atone *v.* (**atones, atoned, atoning**) make amends or reparation. [*Say* a TONE]

atonement *n.* **1** reparation for a wrong. **2** (**the Atonement**) *Christianity* the reconciliation of God and humanity by Jesus Christ.

atop *prep.* on the top of.

ATP *abbr.* adenosine triphosphate, an organic compound important in living cells.

atrial *adj.* having to do with the two upper cavities of the heart. [*Say* AY tree 'll]

atrium *n.* (*pl.* **atriums** *or* **atria**) **1 a** the central court of an ancient Roman house. **b** a central hall or court, often rising through several storeys. **2** a cavity in the body, esp. one of two upper cavities of the heart. [*Say* AY tree um *for the singular; for* ATRIA *say* AY tree uh]

atrocious *adj.* **1** very bad or unpleasant. **2** extremely savage. □ **atrociously** *adv.*
[*Say* a TROE shus]

atrocity *n.* (*pl.* **atrocities**) **1** an extremely wicked or cruel act. **2** a highly unpleasant object. [*Say* a TROSSA tee]

atrophy ● *v.* (**atrophies, atrophied, atrophying**) **1** (of an organ, limb, etc.) waste away. **2** gradually decline in effectiveness or vigour. ● *n.* the process of atrophying. [*Say* ATRA fee]

Atsina *n.* = GROS VENTRE. [*Say* at SEENA]

attaboy *interj.* expressing encouragement or admiration.

attach *v.* (**attaches, attached, attaching**) **1** fasten, join. **2** be very fond of or devoted to. **3** attribute, assign.

4 accompany. **5** (**attach oneself to**) take part in; join. **6** link (an electronic file) to an email message to be sent with it. □ **attachable** adj. **attached** adj.

attaché n. **1** a person appointed to an ambassador's staff. **2** (also **attaché case**) a small flat rectangular case for carrying documents etc. [Say at ash AY]

attachment n. **1** a thing attached or to be attached. **2** affection, devotion. **3** the act of attaching or the state of being attached. **4** something sent as part of an email message.

attack ● v. **1** act violently against. **2** begin a military offensive against. **3** criticize adversely. **4** act harmfully upon. **5** vigorously apply oneself to. ● n. **1** the act or process of attacking. **2** an offensive military operation. **3** gusto, vigour, esp. when starting something. **4** a sudden occurrence of esp. an illness. □ **attacker** n.

attain v. **1** arrive at; reach. **2** gain, accomplish (an aim etc.). □ **attainable** adj. **attainment** n.

attempt ● v. **1** seek to achieve or complete. **2** seek to climb or master. ● n. an act of attempting.

attend v. **1 a** be present at. **b** go regularly to. **2 a** escort, accompany. **b** wait on; serve. **3** turn or apply one's mind to. **4** follow as a result from. □ **attender** n.

attendance n. **1** the act of attending. **2** the number of people present.

attendant ● n. a person employed to wait on others. ● adj. accompanying.

attendee n. a person who attends.

attention n. **1** the act or faculty of applying one's mind. **2** consideration or care. **3** (also **attentions**) **a** ceremonious politeness. **b** wooing, courting. **4** a position standing upright with arms stretched downwards.

attention deficit disorder n. a disorder esp. of children characterized by a short attention span and impulsiveness.

attention deficit hyperactivity disorder n. a behavioural disorder in which the predominant features are inattention, impulsiveness, and hyperactivity.

attentive adj. **1** paying attention. **2** painstakingly polite and considerate. □ **attentively** adv. **attentiveness** n.

attenuate v. (**attenuates**, **attenuated**, **attenuating**) reduce the force, value, or effect of. □ **attenuation** n. [Say a TEN you ate]

attenuated adj. **1** unnaturally thin. **2** weakened in force or effect. □ **attenuation** n.

attest v. **1** confirm the validity or truth of. **2** be evidence of. □ **attestation** n.

attic n. the highest storey of a house.

Attikamek ● n. **1** (pl. **Attikamek** or **Attikameks**) a member of an Aboriginal people living in Quebec. **2** the Algonquian language of this people. ● adj. of the Attikamek or their culture or language. [Say a TICKA meck]

attire ● v. (**attires**, **attired**, **attiring**) dress, esp. in fine clothes. ● n. clothes, esp. fine or formal.

attitude n. **1** a settled opinion or way of thinking. **2** a bodily posture. **3** informal an uncooperative or hostile disposition. □ **attitudinal** adj.

attorney n. (pl. **attorneys**) **1** a person, esp. a lawyer, appointed to act for another in legal matters. **2** US a lawyer. [Say a TURN ee]

Attorney General n. (pl. **Attorneys General**) **1** (in Canada) the minister of the Crown responsible for the administration of justice. **2** a similar chief legal officer in other countries.

attract v. **1** draw or bring to oneself or itself. **2** be attractive to; fascinate. **3** (of a magnet etc.) exert a pull on. □ **attractor** n.

attraction n. **1** the act or power of attracting. **2** a person or thing that attracts.

attractive adj. **1** attracting or capable of attracting; interesting. **2** pleasing to look at. □ **attractively** adv. **attractiveness** n.

attribute ● v. (**attributes**, **attributed**, **attributing**) **1** regard as belonging or appropriate to. **2** caused by. ● n. **1** a characteristic quality. **2** a material object recognized as appropriate to a person, office, etc. □ **attributable** adj.
attribution n. [Say a TRIBUTE for the verb, ATTRA byoot for the noun; ATTRA byoo sh'n]

attributive adj. (of an adjective or noun) preceding the word described. □ **attributively** adv. [Say a TRIBUTE iv]

attrition n. **1** reduction of a workforce without firing personnel, as by not replacing employees who retire etc. **2** wearing down through sustained attack or pressure. See also WAR OF ATTRITION. **3** wearing out, esp. by friction. [Say a TRISH'n]

attune v. (**attunes**, **attuned**, **attuning**) make receptive or aware.

ATV abbr. (pl. **ATVs**) ALL-TERRAIN VEHICLE.

atypical adj. not typical. □ **atypically** adv. [Say ay TYPICAL]

auburn adj. reddish brown.

auction ● n. a sale in which goods are sold

to the highest bidder. ● *v.* sell by auction.
□ **at auction** in an auction sale.
□ **auctioneer** *n.*

audacious *adj.* **1** daring, bold.
2 impudent. □ **audaciously** *adv.*
audacity *n.* [*Say* aw DAY shus,
aw DASSA tee]

audible *adj.* capable of being heard.
□ **audibility** *n.* **audibly** *adv.*

audience *n.* **1** listeners, spectators,
viewers, readers, etc. considered
collectively. **2** a formal interview with a
person in authority.

audio *n.* **1** sound or its reproduction.
2 equipment for electrical reproduction of
sound.

audio- *comb. form* hearing or sound.

audiobook *n.* a recording on audio
cassette or CD of a reading of a book, usu. a
work of fiction.

audiophile *n.* a person who is interested
in high-fidelity sound reproduction.
[*Say* AUDIO file]

audiotape *n.* a magnetic tape on which
sound can be recorded.

audiovisual *adj.* (esp. of teaching
methods) using electrical equipment
directed at the senses of sight and hearing.

audit ● *n.* **1** an official examination and
checking of accounts. **2** a detailed
examination or analysis. ● *v.* (**audits,
audited, auditing**) **1** conduct an audit
(of). **2** attend (a class) without working for
credits.

audition ● *n.* a short performance by a
musician, actor, etc. to demonstrate their
suitability for a role etc. ● *v.* perform or
assess the performance of a candidate at an
audition.

auditor *n.* **1** a person who audits accounts.
2 a person who audits a class.

Auditor General *n.* (*pl.* **Auditors
General**) *Cdn* the official responsible for
auditing the accounts of a (federal or
provincial) government.

auditorium *n.* (*pl.* **auditoriums** or
auditoria) **1** the part of a theatre etc. in
which the audience sits. **2** a building
incorporating a large hall for public
gatherings. **3** a large room, esp. in a school,
used for assemblies etc.

auditory *adj.* of or relating to hearing.

Aug. *abbr.* August.

auger *n.* a tool used for boring holes in
wood, the ground, etc. [*Say* OGGER]

augment *v.* make or become greater;
increase. □ **augmentation** *n.*

augur *v.* be a sign that something will
happen. [*Say* OGGER]

augury *n.* (*pl.* **auguries**) **1** an omen of
what will happen in the future. **2** the
interpretation of omens. [*Say* OG yer ee]

August *n.* the eighth month.

august *adj.* inspiring reverence and
admiration. □ **augustly** *adv.*
[*Say* awe GUST]

Augustan *adj.* connected with the reign of
the Roman emperor Augustus (63 BC–AD
14). [*Say* a GUST'n]

Augustinian ● *adj.* of or relating to St.
Augustine of Hippo (354–430). ● *n.* a
member of a religious order observing
rules derived from St. Augustine's writings.
[*Say* ogga STINNY in]

auk *n.* any of a family of marine diving
birds including the guillemot, puffin, etc.
[*Say* OCK]

aunt *n.* **1** the sister of one's father or
mother. **2** an uncle's wife.

auntie *n.* (also **aunty**) (*pl.* **aunties**) *informal*
= AUNT.

au pair *n.* (*pl.* **au pairs**) a young person
from another country helping with
housework, child care, etc. in exchange for
room and board. [*Say* oh PAIR]

aura *n.* (*pl.* **auras**) **1** the distinctive
atmosphere of a person, place, etc. **2** a
supposed emanation surrounding the body
of a living creature. [*Say* OR uh]

aural *adj.* of or relating to the ear or
hearing. □ **aurally** *adv.* [*Say* ORAL]

aureole *n.* **1** a halo or circle of light, esp.
around a portrayed religious figure. **2** a
corona around the sun or moon.
[*Say* ORY ole]

aurora *n.* (*pl.* **auroras** or **aurorae**) **1** a
luminous phenomenon, usu. of
shimmering coloured streamers, seen in
the upper atmosphere in high latitudes.
2 *literary* the dawn. □ **auroral** *adj.*
[*Say* a RORA *for the singular; for* AURORAE
say a RORY]

aurora borealis *n.* a northern
occurrence of the aurora. *Also called*
NORTHERN LIGHTS.
[*Say* a RORA borry AL iss]

auscultation *n.* the act of listening, esp.
to sounds from the heart, as a part of
medical diagnosis. [*Say* oss cull TAY sh'n]

auspice *n.* □ **under the auspices of**
with the help or protection of.
[*Say* OSS piss]

auspicious *adj.* conducive to success;
favourable. □ **auspiciously** *adv.*
[*Say* oss PISH us]

Aussie *informal* ● *n.* an Australian. ● *adj.*
Australian. [*Say* OZZY *or* OSSY]

austere *adj.* **1** having no comforts or
luxuries; harsh. **2** morally strict. **3** severely

simple; unadorned. □ **austerely** *adv.*
[*Say* oss TEER]

austerity *n.* (*pl.* **austerities**) **1** sternness;
moral severity. **2** frugality. **3** an austere
practice. [*Say* oss TERRA tee]

Australian ● *n.* **1** a native or national of
Australia. **2** a person of Australian descent.
● *adj.* of or relating to Australia.

Australopithecus *n.* an extinct primate
having ape-like and human characteristics.
[*Say* osstra lo PITHA cuss]

Austrian ● *n.* a person from Austria. ● *adj.*
of or relating to Austria.

Austro- *comb. form* **1** Austrian; Austrian and.
2 Australian; Australian and.

autarky *n.* (*pl.* **autarkies**) **1** self-
sufficiency, esp. as an economic system. **2** a
state etc. run according to such a system.
□ **autarkic** *adj.* [*Say* AW tarky, aw TARK ic]

auteur *n.* a director who so greatly
influences the films directed as to rank as
their author. [*Say* oh TURR]

authentic *adj.* **1 a** of undisputed origin;
genuine. **b** reliable or trustworthy. **2** *Music*
performed on instruments dating from the
same period as the piece performed.
□ **authentically** *adv.* **authenticity** *n.*

authenticate *v.* (**authenticates**,
authenticated, **authenticating**)
establish or prove to be authentic.
□ **authentication** *n.*

author ● *n.* **1** a writer, esp. of books. **2** the
originator of an event, a condition, etc. ● *v.*
be the author of. □ **authorial** *adj.*
[*Say* AWE thur, aw THORY ul]

authoritarian ● *adj.* **1** favouring strict
obedience to authority. **2** tyrannical or
domineering. ● *n.* an authoritarian person.
□ **authoritarianism** *n.*
[*Say* a thora TERRY in]

authoritative *adj.* **1** recognized as true or
dependable. **2** commanding or self-
confident. **3** official. □ **authoritatively**
adv. **authoritativeness** *n.*
[*Say* a THORA tay tiv]

authority *n.* (*pl.* **authorities**) **1** the power
or right to enforce obedience. **2** a person or
body having authority. **3 a** an expert in a
particular subject. **b** a book etc. that can
supply reliable information. **4** force or
strength. [*Say* a THORA tee]

authorize *v.* (**authorizes**, **authorized**,
authorizing) give official approval of or
permission to an undertaking or agent.
□ **authorization** *n.*

authorship *n.* the origin of a written
work.

autism *n.* a mental condition
characterized by complete self-absorption
and a reduced ability to communicate with

the outside world. □ **autistic** *adj.*
[*Say* OTT ism, ott ISS tick]

auto ● *n.* (*pl.* **autos**) an automobile. ● *adj.*
automatic.

auto- *comb. form* **1** originating with, induced
by, or pertaining to the self. **2** operating by
itself; automatic. **3** relating to automobiles
or the automobile industry.

autobiography *n.* (*pl.*
autobiographies) **1** a personal account
of one's own life. **2** this as a literary form.
□ **autobiographer** *n.*
autobiographical *adj.*

autobody *n.* the shell of a motor vehicle,
distinguished from its chassis, esp. in
contexts of maintenance or repair.

autocracy *n.* (*pl.* **autocracies**)
1 absolute government by one person. **2** a
state governed in this way.
[*Say* aw TOCKRA see]

autocrat *n.* **1** an absolute ruler. **2** a
dictatorial person. □ **autocratic** *adj.*
[*Say* OTTA crat]

autodial *n.* a facility that enables an
electronic device (as a telephone, fax
machine, modem, etc.) to initiate a
telephone call to a particular number
stored in its memory. □ **autodialler** *n.*
autodialling *n.*

autodidact *n.* a self-taught person.
□ **autodidactic** *adj.* [*Say* otto DIE dact,
otto die DACK tick]

autograph ● *n.* **1** a signature, esp. that of
a celebrity written for an admirer. **2** a
manuscript etc. in an author's own
handwriting. ● *v.* sign.

autoimmune *adj.* (of a disease) caused by
antibodies produced against substances
naturally present in the body.
□ **autoimmunity** *n.* [*Say* otto IMMUNE]

automaker *n.* a company which
manufactures automobiles.

automate *v.* (**automates**, **automated**,
automating) convert to or operate by
automation.

automated teller machine *n.* (also
automated banking machine) a bank
machine.

automatic ● *adj.* **1** operating by itself,
without direct human intervention.
2 a done without conscious thought or
intention. **b** necessary and inevitable. **3** (of
a firearm) self-loading and able to fire
continuously. **4** (of a motor vehicle) using
gears that change automatically. ● *n.* an
automatic gun or a vehicle with automatic
transmission. □ **automatically** *adv.*

automatic pilot *n.* **1** a device for keeping
an aircraft on a set course. **2** the state of

doing something by routine, without concentration.

automation *n.* the use of automatic equipment instead of mental or manual labour.

automatism *n.* **1** *Psychology* the performance of actions without conscious intention. **2** such an action. [*Say* a TOMMA tism]

automaton *n.* (*pl.* **automata** or **automatons**) **1** a moving mechanism which simulates esp. a human being. **2** a person who performs tasks mechanically. [*Say* a TOMMA tawn *for the singular*, a TOMMA tuh *for the plural*]

automobile *n.* a car.

automotive *adj.* concerned with motor vehicles.

autonomic nervous system *n.* the part of the nervous system responsible for control of the involuntary bodily functions. [*Say* otta NOM ic]

autonomous *adj.* **1** having self-government. **2** independent. □ **autonomously** *adv.* [*Say* aw TONNA muss]

autonomy *n.* (*pl.* **autonomies**) **1** the right of self-government. **2** personal freedom or independence.

autopilot *n.* = AUTOMATIC PILOT.

autopsy *n.* (*pl.* **autopsies**) a post-mortem examination conducted to determine the cause of death. [*Say* AW topsy]

autoroute *n.* an expressway in Quebec, France, etc. [*Say* OTTO root]

autumn *n.* **1** the third season of the year, between summer and winter, associated with harvests and falling leaves. **2** a time of maturity or imminent decay. □ **autumnal** *adj.* [*Say* aw TUM n'll]

auxiliary ● *adj.* **1** helpful, giving support. **2** subsidiary, additional. ● *n.* (*pl.* **auxiliaries**) an auxiliary person, group, or thing. [*Say* og ZILLYA ree *or* og ZILLA ree]

auxiliary verb *n.* a verb used in forming tenses, moods, and voices of other verbs, e.g. *will* in *she will go.*

AV *abbr.* = AUDIOVISUAL.

avail ● *v.* **1** help, benefit. **2** (**avail oneself of**) take advantage of. ● *n.* **1** use. **2** (**avails**) esp. *Cdn* proceeds or profits.

available *adj.* **1** capable of being used; obtainable. **2 a** free for consultation. **b** not presently involved in a romantic relationship. □ **availability** *n.*

avalanche *n.* (*pl.* **avalanches**) **1** a mass of snow, ice, etc. tumbling rapidly down a mountainside. **2** an overwhelming quantity.

avant-garde ● *n.* pioneers or innovators esp. in art and literature. ● *adj.* experimental, progressive. □ **avant-gardism** *n.* **avant-gardist** *n.* [*Say* av ont GARD]

avarice *n.* extreme greed for money or material gain. □ **avaricious** *adj.* [*Say* AVVA riss, avva RISH iss]

avatar *n.* **1** *Hinduism* the descent of a deity to earth in bodily form. **2** a movable icon representing a person in cyberspace or virtual reality graphics. [*Say* AVVA tar]

Ave. *abbr.* Avenue.

avenge *v.* (**avenges**, **avenged**, **avenging**) **1** inflict retribution on behalf of. **2** inflict harm in return for an injury or wrong. □ **avenger** *n.*

avens *n.* any of various plants of the genus *Geum.* [*Say* AV 'nz]

avenue *n.* **1** an urban road or street. **2** a road or path with trees along its sides. **3** a way of approaching something.

aver *v.* (**avers**, **averred**, **averring**) *formal* assert or affirm. [*Say* a VUR]

average ● *n.* **1 a** the usual amount, extent, or rate. **b** the ordinary standard. **2** the result of adding several amounts together and dividing the total by the number of amounts. ● *adj.* **1** usual, ordinary. **2** estimated or calculated by average. ● *v.* (**averages**, **averaged**, **averaging**) **1** amount on average to. **2** do on average. **3** estimate the average of. □ **average out** result in an average. **on average** as an average rate or estimate. □ **averagely** *adv.*

averse *adj.* opposed, disinclined. [*Say* a VERSE]

aversion *n.* **1** a dislike or unwillingness. **2** an object of dislike.

avert *v.* **1** turn away (one's eyes etc.). **2** prevent or ward off.

avian *adj.* of or relating to birds. [*Say* AY vee in]

aviary *n.* (*pl.* **aviaries**) a large enclosure for keeping birds. [*Say* AY vee airy]

aviation *n.* **1** the practice of operating aircraft. **2** aircraft manufacture.

aviator *n.* an aircraft pilot.

avid *adj.* **1** eager or enthusiastic. **2** having a desire for. □ **avidity** *n.* **avidly** *adv.*

avocado *n.* (*pl.* **avocados**) (also **avocado pear**) a pear-shaped fruit with rough skin, smooth light green flesh, and a large pit.

avocation *n.* a secondary activity; a hobby. [*Say* avva KAY sh'n]

avoid *v.* **1** keep away or refrain from. **2** escape. □ **avoidable** *adj.* **avoidance** *n.*

avoirdupois *n.* a system of weights based

on a pound of 16 ounces or 7,000 grains. [*Say* avver da POYZ]

avow *v.* admit, confess. □ **avowal** *n.*

avowed *adj.* admitted. □ **avowedly** *adv.* [*Say* a VOWD, a VOW id lee]

avuncular *adj.* (of an older man) benevolent and friendly. [*Say* a VUNK you lur]

aw *interj.* expressing mild protest etc.

AWACS *n.* a long-range radar system for detecting enemy aircraft. [*Say* AY wax]

await *v.* **1** wait (for). **2** be in store for.

awake ● *v.* (**awakes**; *past* **awoke**; *past participle* **awoken**; **awaking**) **1 a** cease to sleep. **b** become active. **2** become aware of. **3** arouse; provoke. ● *adj.* **1** not asleep. **2** aware.

awaken *v.* **1** = AWAKE *v.* **2** make aware.

awakening ● *n.* an arousal from sleep, inaction, ignorance, etc. ● *adj.* coming into existence.

award ● *v.* **1** give as a prize, payment, or penalty. **2** grant (a contract). ● *n.* **1** something awarded. **2** a judicial decision.

aware *adj.* **1** conscious; not ignorant. **2** well-informed. □ **awareness** *n.*

awash *adj.* **1** overrun as if by a flood. **2** covered or flooded with water.

away ● *adv.* **1** to or at a distance from something. **2** towards or into non-existence. **3** constantly, continuously. **4** without delay. **5** *Cdn* (*Nfld & Maritimes*) in a place other than the speaker's home province or Atlantic Canada in general. ● *adj.* *Sport* played in an opponent's venue. □ **away with** let us be rid of.

awe ● *n.* a feeling of respect combined with fear or wonder. ● *v.* (**awes**, **awed**, **awing**) inspire with awe.

awesome *adj.* **1** inspiring awe. **2** *slang* excellent. □ **awesomely** *adv.*

awestruck *adj.* affected or overcome with awe.

awful *adj.* **1** unpleasant or horrible; very bad. **2** *informal* excessive; large. □ **awfulness** *n.*

awfully *adv.* **1** unpleasantly, badly. **2** *informal* very.

awhile *adv.* for an unspecified length of time.

awkward *adj.* **1** difficult to use or deal with. **2** clumsy or bungling. **3** causing or feeling embarrassment. □ **awkwardly** *adv.* **awkwardness** *n.*

awl *n.* a small pointed tool used for piercing holes.

awning *n.* a sheet of canvas, plastic, etc. on a frame used to provide protection from the sun or rain.

awoke *past of* AWAKE.

awoken *past participle of* AWAKE.

AWOL *abbr. informal* absent without leave. [*Say* AY woll]

awry *adv. & adj.* **1** askew; out of the normal position. **2** amiss, wrong. [*Say* a RYE]

aw-shucks *adj. informal* marked by a self-deprecating manner.

axe ● *n.* **1** a chopping tool with a heavy blade. **2** the drastic cutting of expenditure, staff, etc. **3** dismissal, cancellation, etc. ● *v.* (**axes**, **axed**, **axing**) **1** cut drastically. **2** remove or dismiss. □ **an axe to grind** private ends to serve.

Axel *n. Figure Skating* a type of jump.

axial *adj.* **1** forming or belonging to an axis. **2** around an axis. [*Say* AXY 'll]

axil *n.* the upper angle between a leaf and the stem. [*Say* AX 'll]

axiom *n.* an established or widely accepted principle. □ **axiomatic** *adj.* [*Say* AXY um, axy uh MAT ic]

axis *n.* (*pl.* **axes**) **1 a** an imaginary line about which a body rotates. **b** a line which divides a regular figure symmetrically. **2** *Math* a fixed reference line for the measurement of coordinates etc. **3** (**the Axis**) the alliance of Germany and Italy during the Second World War, later extended to include Japan and other countries. [*Say* AX iss *for the singular*, AX eez *for the plural*]

axle *n.* a rod or spindle on which a wheel or group of wheels is fixed.

ayatollah *n.* a Shiite religious leader in Iran. [*Say* eye a TOLA]

aye *interj.* yes (esp. in voting and naval or dialect use). [*Sounds like* EYE]

Ayurveda *n.* a traditional Hindu medicine using naturally based therapies. □ **Ayurvedic** *adj.* [*Say* eye yur VAYDA]

azalea *n.* any of various flowering deciduous shrubs. [*Say* a ZAYLY uh]

azimuth *n.* **1** the angle between the most northerly point of the horizon and the point directly below a given celestial body. **2** the horizontal direction of a compass bearing. □ **azimuthal** *adj.* [*Say* AZZA m'th, azza MOOTH 'll]

Aztec *n.* **1** a member of the Aboriginal people dominant in central and southern Mexico before the Spanish conquest of 1519. **2** the language of the Aztecs. □ **Aztec** *adj.*

azure *n. & adj.* deep sky-blue. [*Say* AZH er *or* AZZ yer]

Bb

B¹ *n.* (also **b**) (*pl.* **Bs** or **B's**) **1** the second letter of the alphabet. **2** the seventh note of the scale of C major. **3** the second hypothetical person or example. **4** the second highest class or category. **5** a human blood type.

B² *abbr.* (also **B.**) **1** Bachelor. **2** bel(s). **3** bishop. **4** bass.

b. *abbr.* **1** born. **2** billion.

B.A. *abbr.* Bachelor of Arts.

baa ● *v.* (**baas, baaed, baaing**) (esp. of a sheep) bleat. ● *n.* (*pl.* **baas**) a sheep's bleat.

baba *n.* **1** (among people of E European descent) grandmother. **2** (among people of Indian descent) father.

baba ghanouj *n.* a dip made from mashed eggplant, tahini, garlic, etc. [*Say* bobba guh NOOSH]

babble ● *v.* (**babbles, babbled, babbling**) **1** talk in an inarticulate manner. **2** chatter excessively. **3** (of a stream etc.) make a murmuring sound. ● *n.* **1 a** incoherent speech. **b** foolish or childish talk. **2** a murmur.

-babble *comb. form* forming nouns denoting the jargon of a group.

babe *n.* **1** a baby. **2** an innocent or helpless person. **3** *slang* an attractive person, esp. a woman.

babel *n.* **1** a confused noise, esp. of voices. **2** a noisy assembly. **3** a scene of confusion. [*Say* BAY bull *or* BABBLE]

babiche *n.* strips of rawhide or sinew used as laces etc. [*Say* ba BEESH]

baboon *n.* **1** a monkey with a long doglike snout and large teeth. **2** an ugly or uncouth person.

babushka *n.* **1** a head scarf tied under the chin. **2** an old Slavic woman. [*Say* ba BOOSH kuh]

baby ● *n.* (*pl.* **babies**) **1** a very young or newly born child or animal. **2** an unduly childish person **3** the youngest member of a family, team, etc. **4** *slang* a person or thing regarded with affection or familiarity. ● *v.* (**babies, babied, babying**) **1** treat like a baby. **2** pamper. □ **throw out the baby with the bathwater** reject the essential with the inessential. □ **babyhood** *n.* **babyish** *adj.*

baby blue *n.* & *adj.* soft, pale blue.

baby blues *pl. n.* **1** *informal* attractive blue eyes. **2** *informal* postpartum depression.

baby bonus *n. Cdn* family allowance or child tax benefit.

baby boom *n.* a temporary marked increase in the birth rate, esp. after 1945. □ **baby boomer** *n.*

baby carriage *n.* (also **baby buggy**) a four-wheeled carriage for a baby.

Babylonian *n.* **1** an inhabitant of the ancient kingdom of Babylon. **2** the language of the Babylonians. □ **Babylonian** *adj.* [*Say* babba LONEY in]

baby's breath *n.* a plant with tiny usu. white flowers.

babysit *v.* (**babysits, babysat, babysitting**) look after a child or children while the parents are out. □ **babysitter** *n.* **babysitting** *n.*

baccalaureate *n.* **1** a bachelor's degree. **2** an examination taken to qualify for higher education. [*Say* backa LORRY it]

baccarat *n.* a card game like blackjack. [*Say* BACKA raw]

bacchanal *n.* an occasion of wild, drunken revelry. [*Say* backa NOL *or* bocka NOL]

bacchanalia *pl. n.* a drunken revelry. □ **bacchanalian** *adj.* & *n.* [*Say* backa NAILY uh]

bachelor *n.* **1** an unmarried man. **2** (also **bachelor's degree**) a degree awarded for the completion of undergraduate studies. **3** (also **bachelor apartment**) *Cdn* an apartment consisting of a single large room serving as bedroom and living room. □ **bachelorhood** *n.*

bachelorette *n.* **1** a young unmarried woman. **2** *Cdn* a very small bachelor apartment.

bacillus *n.* (*pl.* **bacilli**) **1** any rod-shaped bacterium. **2** any pathogenic bacterium. [*Say* ba SILL us, ba SILLY]

bacillus thuringiensis *n.* a bacterium containing a protein toxic to insects, used in pesticides. [*Say* ba SILL us thuh rin jee EN sis]

back ● *n.* **1 a** the rear surface of the human body from the shoulders to the hips. **b** the corresponding part of an animal's body. **c** the spine. **2** any surface regarded as corresponding to the human back. **3** the less active or important part of something, or the part not usually seen. **4** a player positioned behind the front line of play. ● *adv.* **1** to the rear. **2 a** in or into an earlier position. **b** in return. **3** in or into the past. **4** at a distance. **5** in check. ● *v.* **1 a** give support to. **b** bet on the success of. **2** move, or cause to move, backwards. **3 a** put or serve as a back or support to. **b** *Music* accompany. **4** lie at the back of. ● *adj.* **1** situated behind. **2** not current. **3** reversed, backward. □ **back down** withdraw one's claim etc.; concede defeat. **the back of beyond** a very remote or inaccessible place. **back off 1** draw back, retreat. **2** abandon one's intention etc. **back out** withdraw from a commitment. **back up 1** give (esp. moral) support to. **2** *Computing* make a spare copy of. **3** accumulate behind an obstruction. **get** (or **put**) **a person's back up** annoy or anger a person. **get off a person's back** stop troubling a person. **go back on** fail to honour. **pat** (or **slap** or **clap**) **on the back** a gesture of approval or congratulation. **put one's back into** approach with vigour. **with one's back to** (or **up against**) **the wall** in a desperate situation; hard-pressed. □ **backer** *n.* (in sense 1 of *verb*). **backless** *adj.*

back bacon *n.* *Cdn* & *Brit.* round, lean bacon cut from the eye of a pork loin.

backbencher *n.* *Cdn*, *Brit.*, *Austral.*, & *NZ* a member of a legislative assembly who does not hold a government or opposition post. □ **backbench** *n.*

backbiting *n.* speaking maliciously of an absent person.

backboard *n.* **1** *Basketball* the vertical board to which the basket is attached. **2** *Hockey* the boards behind the net. **3** a board forming the back of anything.

backbone *n.* **1** the spine. **2** the main support in a structure etc. **3** firmness of character.

back-breaking *adj.* (esp. of manual work) very hard.

back burner *n.* a position receiving little attention or low priority.

backcatcher *n.* *Cdn* = CATCHER 2.

backcheck *v.* *Hockey* (of a forward) return to the defensive zone and check attacking opponents. ● **backchecker** *n.*

backcountry *n.* an area away from settled districts.

backcourt *n.* **1** *Tennis* the area between the baseline and the service line. **2** *Basketball* the half of the court which a team defends.

backdate *v.* (**backdates**, **backdated**, **backdating**) **1** put an earlier date to. **2** make retroactively valid.

back door ● *n.* an alternative, usu. indirect means of gaining an objective. ● *adj.* (**backdoor**) **1** alternative. **2** underhanded.

backdrop *n.* **1** a large cloth hung across the back of a stage as part of the set. **2** the setting for an event or situation.

backfield *n.* *Football* **1** the area of play behind the line of scrimmage. **2** the players who play in this area.

backfill ● *v.* refill an excavated hole with the material dug out of it. ● *n.* excavated material used to refill an excavation.

backfire ● *v.* (**backfires**, **backfired**, **backfiring**) **1** (of an engine) undergo a improperly-timed explosion. **2** have the opposite effect to what was intended. ● *n.* a improperly-timed explosion in an engine.

backflip *n.* a backwards aerial somersault.

backgammon *n.* a game for two played on a board with pieces moved according to throws of the dice.

background *n.* **1** part of a scene or description that forms a setting for the main characters or events. **2** an inconspicuous or obscure position. **3** a person's education, knowledge, or social circumstances. **4** explanatory information.

backhand ● *n.* **1** (in racquet sports) a stroke performed with the arm initially across and in front of the torso **2** *Hockey* a shot made by striking the puck with the back of the stick's blade. ● *v.* strike with a backhand. □ **backhander** *n.*

backhanded *adj.* indirect; ambiguous.

backhoe *n.* a digging machine.

backing *n.* **1** support. **2** material forming a back or support. **3** musical accompaniment.

backlash *n.* (*pl.* **backlashes**) **1** an excessive or marked adverse reaction. **2** a sudden recoil.

backlight ● *n.* (also **backlighting**) light illuminating something from behind. ● *v.* (**backlights**; *past* and *past participle* **backlit** or **backlighted**; **backlighting**) illuminate from behind. □ **backlit** *adj.*

backlog ● *n.* an accumulation of incomplete work etc. ● *v.* (**backlogs**, **backlogged**, **backlogging**) **1** overload. **2** amass unfinished tasks etc.

back order *n.* a retailer's order yet to be filled by a supplier.

backpack ● *n.* a knapsack. ● *v.* travel or hike with a backpack. □ **backpacker** *n.* **backpacking** *n.*

backpedal *v.* (**backpedals**,

backpedalled, backpedalling) 1 pedal backwards on a bicycle etc. **2** reverse one's previous action or opinion.

backroom *n.* **1** a room at the back of a store etc. **2** a place where secret plans are made.

back seat *n.* □ **take a back seat** occupy a subordinate place.

back-seat driver *n.* **1** a passenger who gives unwanted advice to the driver. **2** a person who criticizes without responsibility.

backside *n. informal* the buttocks.

backslapping *adj.* **1** characterized by (excessive) displays of camaraderie. **2** vigorously hearty.

backslash *n.* (*pl.* **backslashes**) a diagonal line that slopes backwards (\).

backslide *v.* (**backslides, backslid, backsliding**) relapse into bad ways.

backspace ● *v.* (**backspaces, backspaced, backspacing**) move a cursor etc. back one space. ● *n.* the key on a keyboard which performs this function.

backspin *n.* a backward spin imparted to a ball causing it to bounce backwards.

backsplash *n.* (*pl.* **backsplashes**) a covering behind a sink etc. to protect the wall.

backsplit *n. Cdn* a house with floors raised half a storey at the rear.

backstabber *n.* a person who betrays a friend. □ **backstabbing** *n. & adj.*

backstage ● *adv. Theatre* out of view of the audience. ● *adj.* **1** happening or being backstage at a theatre. **2** happening out of the public spotlight.

backstop *n.* **1** a backcatcher. **2** a goaltender. **3** *Sport* a wall, fence, etc. used to keep the ball in the playing area.

backstreet *n.* **1** a street in a quiet part of a city. **2** (as an *adj.*) denoting illicit activity.

backstroke *n. Swimming* a stroke performed on the back.

back-to-back ● *adj.* consecutive. ● *adv.* (**back to back**) **1** with backs adjacent and opposite each other. **2** consecutively.

back to front ● *adv.* with the back at the front. ● *adj.* backwards.

backtrack *v.* **1** retrace one's steps. **2** reverse one's previous action or opinion.

backup *n.* **1** moral or technical support. **2** an alternate kept in reserve. **3** *Computing* the procedure for making security copies of data; these copies. **4** an accumulation (of vehicles etc.) owing to an obstruction. **5** musical accompaniment.

backward ● *adv.* = BACKWARDS. ● *adj.* **1** directed to the rear or starting point. **2** reversed. **3** behind or retarded in progress or development. **4** shy, unassertive. □ **backwardness** *n.*

backwards *adv.* **1** away from one's front. **2 a** with the back foremost. **b** in reverse of the usual way. **3 a** into a worse state. **b** into the past. □ **bend over backwards** *informal* make every effort, esp. to be fair or helpful. **know backwards** be entirely familiar with.

backwash *n.* (*pl.* **backwashes**) **1 a** receding waves created by the motion of a ship etc. **b** a backward current of air created by a moving aircraft. **2** *slang* liquid from the mouth which flows back into the bottle etc. after drinking.

backwater *n.* **1** stagnant water. **2** a place far from the centre of activity.

backwoods *pl. n.* **1** remote land that has not been cleared. **2** any remote or sparsely inhabited region.

backyard *n.* **1** a yard behind a house. **2** a place near at hand.

bacon *n.* cured meat from the back or sides of a pig. □ **bring home the bacon** *informal* make money or achieve success.

bacteria *pl. n.* (*singular* **bacterium**) any of various groups of single-celled micro-organisms, some of which can cause disease. □ **bacterial** *adj.*

bacteriology *n.* the study of bacteria.

Bactrian camel *n.* a camel with two humps, native to central Asia. [*Say* BACK tree un]

bad ● *adj.* (**worse; worst**) **1** inferior, inadequate, defective. **2** unpleasant, unwelcome. **3** harmful. **4** (of food) decayed. **5** *informal* ill, injured. **6** *informal* regretful, ashamed. **7** serious, severe. **8** wicked; naughty. **9** unlikely to be paid. **10** (**badder, baddest**) *slang* admirable, excellent. ● *n.* ill fortune; something bad. □ **in a bad way** ill; in trouble. **not bad** *informal* fairly good. **too bad** *informal* unfortunate, regrettable. □ **badness** *n.*

bad apple *n.* a person whose actions disgrace a group.

bad blood *n.* ill feeling, animosity.

baddie *n. informal* a villain or criminal, esp. in a story, film, etc.

bade *see* BID. [*Say* BADE *or* BAD]

bad faith *n.* intent to deceive.

badge *n.* **1** a distinctive emblem worn as a mark of office etc. **2** any feature which reveals a characteristic quality.

badger ● *n.* an animal related to the weasels, usu. having a grey coat with a white stripe flanked by black stripes on its head. ● *v.* pester, harass.

badlands *pl. n.* extensive, barren, strikingly eroded tracts in arid areas.

badly adv. (**worse**; **worst**) **1** in a bad manner. **2** informal very much. **3** severely.

badminton n. a game in which players use racquets to hit a shuttlecock across a high net.

badmouth v. subject to malicious gossip or criticism.

bad news n. informal an unpleasant person etc.

bad-tempered adj. easily angered or annoyed.

baffle ● v. (**baffles**, **baffled**, **baffling**) confuse or perplex. ● n. (also **baffle plate**) a device used to restrict the flow of fluid, air, etc., through an opening. □**bafflement** n.

bafflegab n. jargon which confuses more than it clarifies.

baffling adj. puzzling, perplexing. □**bafflingly** adv.

bag ● n. **1** a receptacle of flexible material with an opening at the top. **2 a** a piece of luggage. **b** a handbag. **3** slang derogatory a woman who is not pleasant or not attractive. **4** an amount of game or fish taken. **5** baggy folds of skin under the eyes. **6** slang a person's particular interest. ● v. (**bags**, **bagged**, **bagging**) **1** put in a bag. **2** informal **a** attain, secure. **b** apprehend. **c** shoot (game). **3** hang loosely. □**bag and baggage** with all one's belongings. **in the bag** informal as good as secured. **left holding the bag** informal left to face consequences alone.

bagel n. a ring-shaped bread roll that is simmered before baking.

baggage n. **1** luggage packed for travelling. **2** past experiences or ideas perceived as burdensome.

bagged adj. **1** packaged in a bag. **2** informal fatigued, exhausted.

baggy adj. (**baggier**, **baggiest**) **1** (of clothes) loosely fitting. **2** puffed out. □**bagginess** n.

bag lady n. a homeless woman who carries her possessions in shopping bags.

bagman n. (pl. **bagmen**) Cdn a political fundraiser.

bagpipe n. (usu. in pl.) a musical instrument consisting of a windbag connected to drone pipes, and a fingered melody pipe. □**bagpiper** n.

baguette n. a long narrow loaf of French bread. [Say ba GET]

bah interj. expressing contempt or disbelief.

Baha'i n. (pl. **Baha'is**) a member of a monotheistic religion emphasizing the unity of all religions and world peace. □**Baha'ism** n. [Say buh HI]

Bahamian n. a native or national of the Bahamas. □**Bahamian** adj. [Say buh HAY mee un]

bail[1] ● n. **1** the temporary release of an accused person awaiting trial, sometimes after money is paid to guarantee their appearance in court. **2** money paid by or for such a person as security. ● v. **1** release on payment of bail. **2** informal release from a difficulty; come to the rescue of. □**jump** (or **skip**) **bail** fail to appear for trial after being released on bail. **stand** (or **post**) **bail** act as surety (for an accused person).

bail[2] v. scoop water out of a boat etc. □**ball out 1** make an emergency parachute jump from an aircraft. **2** become free of an obligation; end an activity. □**bailer** n.

bailey n. (pl. **baileys**) the outer wall of a castle.

bailiff n. **1** (also **court bailiff**) an officer of the court who serves processes and enforces orders. **2** (also **private bailiff**) Cdn a person who repossesses property for private clients. **3** an official in a court of law who keeps order, looks after prisoners, etc.

bailiwick n. a person's sphere of operations or interest.

bailout n. a financial rescue.

bait ● n. **1** food used to entice prey. **2** something used to lure someone. ● v. **1 a** harass or annoy. **b** torment. **2** put bait on to entice prey.

baitfish n. (pl. **baitfish** or **baitfishes**) any small fish used to lure larger fish.

bake ● v. (**bakes**, **baked**, **baking**) **1 a** cook (food) by dry heat in an oven. **b** undergo the process of being baked. **2** informal be or become very hot in hot weather. **3** harden (clay etc.) by heat. ● n. **1** baked goods. **2** a social gathering at which baked food is eaten.

baked beans pl. n. dried white beans baked in a tomato sauce.

baker n. a person who bakes, esp. professionally.

baker's dozen n. thirteen.

bakery n. (pl. **bakeries**) a place where bread and cakes are made or sold.

bakeshop n. = BAKERY.

baking powder n. a mixture of baking soda and an acid, used to make baked goods rise.

baking soda n. sodium bicarbonate used esp. to make baked goods rise.

baklava n. a rich sweet dessert of flaky pastry, honey, and nuts. [Say BACKLA vuh or backla VAW]

balaclava n. a tight knitted garment covering the whole head with holes for the eyes and mouth. [Say bala CLAVA]

balance ● *n.* **1** an apparatus for weighing. **2** a counteracting weight or force. **3 a** an even distribution; the correct proportion. **b** stability of body or mind. **4** a predominating weight or amount. **5 a** the difference between credits and debits in an account. **b** the amount of money in a bank account. **c** an amount left over, esp. after a payment has been made. ● *v.* (**balances, balanced, balancing**) **1** offset or compare (one thing) with another. **2** counteract or neutralize the weight or importance of. **3** bring into equilibrium. **4** establish equal or appropriate proportions. **5** weigh (arguments etc.) against each other. **6** compare and esp. equalize debits and credits of. □ **in the balance** uncertain; at a critical stage. **off balance 1** in danger of falling. **2** unprepared, confused. **on balance** all things considered. □ **balancer** *n.*

balance beam *n.* a long narrow beam on which gymnasts perform feats of balance.

balance of payments *n.* the difference in value between payments into and out of a country over a period.

balance of power *n.* **1** a situation in which two countries or groups of countries have equal power. **2** the power held by a small group which can give its support to either of two larger groups.

balance of trade *n.* the difference in value between imports and exports.

balance sheet *n.* **1** a written statement of assets and liabilities. **2** an accounting of achievements and failures.

balancing act *n.* the skilful handling of several different tasks simultaneously.

balcony *n.* (*pl.* **balconies**) **1** a platform enclosed by a wall, railing, etc. on the outside of a building. **2** the upper level of seats in a theatre. □ **balconied** *adj.*

bald *adj.* **1** wholly or partly lacking hair. **2** not covered by the usual hair, feathers, features, etc. **3** with the surface worn away. **4** treeless. □ **balding** *adj.* **baldness** *n.*

bald eagle *n.* a N American eagle with a white head and a yellow bill.

balderdash *n.* nonsense.

bald-faced *adj.* shameless.

baldly *adv.* bluntly.

bale ● *n.* a bundle of material tightly wrapped or bound. ● *v.* (**bales, baled, baling**) form into bales. □ **baler** *n.*

baleen *n.* whalebone. [*Say* buh LEEN]

baleen whale *n.* any of various whales having plates of baleen in the mouth for straining plankton from the water.

baleful *adj.* **1** gloomy, menacing. **2** harmful, destructive. □ **balefully** *adv.*

balk ● *v.* **1** refuse to go on. **2** hesitate or be unwilling. **3** *Baseball* commit a balk. ● *n. Baseball* an illegal motion made by a pitcher which allows the baserunners to advance one base. [*Say* BOCK]

Balkan *adj.* of or relating to the people or nations of the Balkan Peninsula. [*Say* BAWL k'n]

balkanize *v.* (**balkanizes, balkanized, balkanizing**) divide (a country etc.) into smaller mutually hostile units. □ **balkanization** *n.* [*Say* BAWLKA nize]

balky *adj.* (**balkier, balkiest**) uncooperative. [*Say* BOCKY]

ball¹ ● *n.* **1** a solid or hollow sphere, esp. for use in a game. **2** a rounded thing or part. **3** a game played with a ball, esp. baseball. **4** *Baseball* a pitch that is not swung at and is not a strike. **5** (in *pl.*) *coarse slang* **a** the testicles. **b** courage. ● *v.* squeeze or form into a ball. □ **the ball is in your court** you must be next to act. **on the ball** *informal* alert. **play ball** *informal* co-operate. **start** (or **keep**) **the ball rolling** begin (or continue) an activity.

ball² *n.* **1** a formal social gathering for dancing. **2** *informal* an enjoyable time.

ballad *n.* **1** a poem or song narrating a popular story. **2** a slow sentimental or romantic song. □ **balladeer** *n.*

ball and chain *n.* **1** a heavy metal ball secured by a chain to the leg of a prisoner etc. **2** *informal* **a** a severe hindrance. **b** *derogatory* a wife.

ball-and-socket joint *n.* a joint in which a rounded end lies in a socket, allowing movement in all directions.

ballast ● *n.* **1** heavy material carried by a ship etc. to secure stability. **2** coarse stone etc. used to form the bed of a railway track etc. ● *v.* make a ship stable using ballast. [*Say* BAL ist]

ball bearing *n.* **1** a bearing in which the parts are separated by a ring of small metal balls which reduce friction. **2** one of these balls.

ballboy *n.* a boy who retrieves balls that go out of play during a game.

ballerina *n.* a female ballet dancer.

ballet *n.* **1 a** a theatrical style of dancing using set steps and gestures. **b** a theatrical work using this form and its music. **2** a company performing ballet. □ **balletic** *adj.* [*Say* BAL ay *or* bal AY, buh LET ick]

ball game *n.* **1** any game played with a ball, esp. baseball. **2** *informal* a particular affair.

ball hockey *n. Cdn* a version of hockey played off the ice (usu. on a paved surface), using a hard plastic or tennis ball in place of a puck.

ballistic *adj.* of or relating to projectiles. □ **go ballistic** *slang* become enraged. [*Say* buh LISS tick]

ballistic missile *n.* a missile which is initially powered and guided but falls under gravity on its target.

ballistics *pl. n.* the science of projectiles and firearms. [*Say* buh LISS ticks]

balloon ● *n.* **1** a small inflatable rubber pouch with a neck, used as a toy or as decoration. **2** a large usu. round bag inflated with hot air or gas to make it rise in the air, often carrying a basket for passengers. **3** an outline enclosing the words or thoughts of characters in a comic strip. ● *v.* **1 a** swell or cause to swell. **b** increase dramatically. **2** travel by balloon. □ **balloonist** *n.* **ballooning** *n. & adj.*

ballot ● *n.* **1** a system of secret voting, usu. by marking a paper. **2 a** a round of voting. **b** the total number of votes recorded. **3** a paper etc. used in voting. ● *v.* (**ballots, balloted, balloting**) vote by ballot.

ballot box *n.* **1** a sealed box which holds completed ballots. **2** an election.

ballpark *n.* **1** a field etc. designed for baseball. **2** *informal* (of a price or cost) approximate.

ballpoint *n.* (also **ballpoint pen**) a pen in which the writing point is a tiny rotating ball.

ballroom *n.* a large room for dancing.

ballroom dancing *n.* formal social dancing for couples.

ballsy *adj.* (**ballsier, ballsiest**) *slang* courageous.

ballyhoo ● *n.* extravagant publicity; hype. ● *v.* (**ballyhoos, ballyhooed, ballyhooing**) publicize extravagantly; hype. □ **ballyhooed** *adj.*

balm *n.* **1** an aromatic ointment for soothing or healing. **2** a fragrant substance which exudes from certain plants. **3** anything that heals or soothes. [*Say* BOM]

balmy *adj.* (**balmier, balmiest**) (of weather) warm. [*Say* BOMMY]

baloney *n.* **1** = BOLOGNA. **2** *informal* nonsense.

balsa *n.* (also **balsa wood**) a tough lightweight wood from a tropical American tree. [*Say* BAWL suh]

balsam *n.* **1** an aromatic resin obtained from various trees and shrubs, used in perfumes and medicines. **2** an ointment. **3** any tree or shrub which yields balsam. [*Say* BAWL sum]

balsam fir *n.* a N American fir that yields balsam.

balsamic vinegar *n.* an aged sweet red wine vinegar. [*Say* bawl SAM ick]

Baltic ● *adj.* of or relating to the Baltic Sea or the Baltic language group. ● *n.* **1** an almost landlocked sea of northern Europe. **2** an Indo-European branch of languages including Lithuanian and Latvian.

baluster *n.* each of a series of often ornamental supports for a railing etc. [*Say* BALA stir]

balustrade *n.* a railing supported by balusters. [*Say* BALA strade]

bam *interj.* **1** expressing the sound of a hard blow. **2** indicating suddenness.

bamboo *n.* a giant woody grass with hollow, jointed stems, used to make furniture etc.

bamboo shoot *n.* a young shoot of bamboo, eaten as a vegetable.

bamboozle *v.* (**bamboozles, bamboozled, bamboozling**) *informal* cheat, swindle.

ban ● *v.* (**bans, banned, banning**) forbid, prohibit. ● *n.* an official or legal prohibition.

banal *adj.* so lacking in originality as to be boring. □ **banality** *n.* (*pl.* **banalities**) [*Say* buh NAL]

banana *n.* **1** a long curved fruit with yellow skin when ripe. **2** (also **banana tree**) any of several treelike plants bearing this fruit.

banana belt *n.* *informal* a region having a relatively warm climate.

banana pepper *n.* a small yellow hot pepper.

banana republic *n.* often *derogatory* a small tropical nation economically dependent on fruit exports etc.

bananas *adj.* *informal* **1** crazy or angry. **2** extremely enthusiastic.

banana split *n.* a dessert consisting of a split banana, ice cream, sauce, etc.

band¹ ● *n.* **1** a flat, thin strip of material used as a fastener, decoration, etc. **2** a stripe of a different colour or material. **3** any long and narrow strip or grouping. **4** a range of frequencies or values in a spectrum or series. **5** a ring without a prominent precious stone. ● *v.* put a band on. □ **banded** *adj.*

band² ● *n.* **1** an organized group of people having a common objective. **2** (in Canada) an Indian community officially recognized by the federal government. **3** a group of musicians playing together. ● *v.* form into a group for a purpose.

bandage ● *n.* a strip of material for

binding or protecting a wound etc. ● *v.*
(**bandages, bandaged, bandaging**)
bind with a bandage.

Band-Aid *n.* **1** *proprietary* an adhesive
bandage for dressing small cuts etc. **2** (also
band-aid) a makeshift or temporary
solution.

bandana *n.* (also **bandanna**) a coloured
handkerchief or head scarf.

B & B *abbr.* **1** (*pl.* **B & B's**) bed and
breakfast. **2** *Cdn* bilingualism and
biculturalism.

band council *n. Cdn* a local form of
Aboriginal government, consisting of a
chief and councillors. □ **band
councillor** *n.*

B and E *abbr.* (*pl.* **B and E's**) *slang*
BREAKING AND ENTERING.

banding *n.* in senses of BAND¹ *v.,* BAND² *v.*

bandit *n.* **1** a robber, esp. a member of a
gang. **2** an outlaw. □ **banditry** *n.*

bandolier *n.* a belt worn diagonally across
the chest with loops or pockets for
ammunition. [*Say* banda LEER]

band saw *n.* an electric saw with a
seamless toothed band.

bandshell *n.* a bandstand in the form of a
large concave shell.

bandstand *n.* a usu. covered outdoor
platform for a band to play on.

bandwagon *n.* a party or cause that is
fashionable or seems likely to succeed.

bandwidth *n.* the range of frequencies
within a given band.

bandy ● *adj.* (**bandier, bandiest**) (also
bandy-legged) (of a person) bowlegged.
● *v.* (**bandies, bandied, bandying**)
1 a pass (a story, rumour, etc.) to and fro.
b throw or pass to and fro. **2** discuss
disparagingly. **3** exchange (blows etc.).

bane *n.* a cause of great distress or
annoyance.

bang ● *n.* **1 a** a loud sudden sound. **b** an
explosion. **2** a sharp blow. **3** *informal* a thrill.
4 (in *pl.*) a fringe of hair cut across the
forehead. ● *v.* **1** strike or shut noisily.
2 make or cause to make a bang. ● *adv.*
1 with a bang or sudden impact. **2** *informal*
exactly. ● *interj.* indicating suddenness or
swiftness. □ **bang on** *informal* exactly right.
bang out *informal* produce quickly and
without attention to detail. **bang up**
damage or injure. **bang for one's buck**
value for one's money.

banger *n.* a thing that makes a banging
noise.

Bangladeshi *n.* (*pl.* **Bangladeshi** or
Bangladeshis) a native or inhabitant of
Bangladesh. □ **Bangladeshi** *adj.*
[*Say* bang gla DESHY]

bangle *n.* a rigid bracelet worn around the
arm or ankle.

bang-up *adj. informal* excellent.

banish *v.* (**banishes, banished,
banishing**) **1** formally expel, esp. from a
country. **2** dismiss from one's presence or
mind. □ **banishment** *n.*

banister *n.* **1** the handrail at the side of a
staircase. **2** an upright supporting a
handrail.

banjo *n.* (*pl.* **banjos** or **banjoes**) a four- or
five-stringed musical instrument with a
circular body and long neck.

bank¹ ● *n.* **1** the sloping ground bordering
a river, lake, etc. **2** a slope or incline. **3** an
underwater ridge of land. **4** a mass of
cloud, fog, etc. ● *v.* **1** heap or rise into
banks. **2** (of a vehicle or aircraft) tilt to one
side while rounding a curve. **3** build (a road
etc.) higher at the outer edge of a bend.
4 heap up (a fire) so that it burns slowly.
5 cause (a puck) to rebound off the boards.

bank² ● *n.* **1** an organization offering
financial services, esp. loans and the
safekeeping of customers' money.
2 something which collects and stores a
product, information, etc. for future use.
3 the banker or dealer in some games. ● *v.*
1 deposit or keep in a bank. **2** engage in
business as a banker. □ **bank on** rely on.
□ **banking** *n.*

bank³ *n.* a row of similar objects.

bankable *adj.* **1** reliable. **2** certain to bring
in a profit. □ **bankability** *n.*

banker *n.* **1** a person who manages or owns
a bank. **2** a keeper of the bank in some
gambling games.

bank machine *n.* esp. *Cdn* = AUTOMATED
TELLER MACHINE.

banknote *n.* a piece of paper money
issued by a central bank.

Bank of Canada *n.* the federally owned
central bank which controls Canada's bank
rate etc.

bank rate *n.* esp. *Cdn* the central bank's
minimum interest rate on short-term loans
to banks etc.

bankroll ● *n.* available funds. ● *v. informal*
support financially.

bankrupt ● *adj.* **1** legally declared unable
to pay debts. **2** exhausted (of a quality etc.);
deficient. ● *n.* a bankrupt person. ● *v.* make
bankrupt. □ **bankruptcy** *n.* (*pl.*
bankruptcies)

banner ● *n.* **1** a large sign or strip of cloth
etc. bearing a slogan or design. **2** a large
newspaper headline, esp. across the top of
the front page. ● *adj.* excellent,
outstanding.

banner ad *n.* an advertisement appearing

as a banner across the top or bottom of a web page.

bannock *n. Cdn* a bread similar to tea biscuits, cooked on a griddle or over a fire.

banns *pl. n.* a notice announcing an intended marriage.

banquet *n.* **1** an elaborate and extensive feast. **2** a ceremonial dinner for many people.

banquet burger *n. Cdn* a hamburger with bacon and cheese.

banquette *n.* an upholstered bench along a wall. [*Say* bang KET]

banshee *n.* (in Gaelic mythology) a female spirit whose wailing warns of death.

bantam *n.* **1** any of several small breeds of domestic fowl. **2** a small but aggressive person. **3** *Cdn* a level of amateur sport, usu. involving children aged 13–15.

bantamweight *n.* **1** a weight class in certain sports between flyweight and featherweight. **2** an athlete of this weight.

banter ● *n.* good-humoured teasing. ● *v.* talk humorously or teasingly.

Bantu *n.* **1** a group of Niger-Congo languages spoken in equatorial and southern Africa. **2** (*pl.* **Bantu** or **Bantus**) a member of the peoples speaking these languages. □ **Bantu** *adj.* [*Say* BAN too]

baptism *n.* **1** a religious rite symbolizing admission to the Christian Church, involving sprinkling with or total immersion in water. **2** any similar rite of initiation, purification, etc. □ **baptismal** *adj.*

Baptist *n.* a member of a Protestant denomination advocating baptism by total immersion.

baptistery *n.* (*pl.* **baptisteries**) (also **baptistry**; *pl.* **baptistries**) the part of a church etc. used for baptism. [*Say* BAP tiss tree]

baptize *v.* (**baptizes, baptized, baptizing**) **1** administer baptism to. **2** give a name or nickname to.

bar¹ ● *n.* **1** a long rigid piece of wood, metal, etc. **2 a** something resembling a bar in being straight and rigid. **b** a band of colour or light. **c** a bank of sand etc. across the mouth of a river or harbour. **3** a barrier or obstruction. **4** a counter, room, or place where alcohol or food and drink is served. **5** a small shop, stall, etc. which sells a particular product. **6** any of the sections of usu. equal time value into which a musical composition is divided. **7 a** a rail in a law court separating the public from the judge, lawyers, etc. **b** an enclosure in which an accused person stands before a court of law. **8** (**the bar**) **a** lawyers collectively.

b the profession of lawyer. ● *v.* (**bars, barred, barring**) **1 a** fasten with a bar or bars. **b** shut or keep in or out. **2** obstruct, prevent. **3** prohibit, exclude. ● *prep.* except. □ **be called** (or **admitted**) **to the bar** be formally admitted into the legal profession. **behind bars** in prison. **raise** (or **lower**) **the bar** increase (or decrease) standards, a level of difficulty or expectations, etc.

bar² *n.* a unit of pressure equal to 100 kilopascals.

barb *n.* **1** a sharp projection near the end of an arrow, fish hook, etc., hindering extraction. **2** a deliberately hurtful remark.

Barbadian *n.* **1** a native or national of Barbados. **2** a person of Barbadian descent. □ **Barbadian** *adj.* [*Say* bar BAY dee in]

barbarian ● *n.* **1** an uncultured or brutish person. **2** (in ancient times) a member of a people not belonging to one of the great civilizations. ● *adj.* **1** rough and uncultured. **2** of or pertaining to uncivilized peoples. [*Say* bar BERRY in]

barbaric *adj.* **1** savagely cruel. **2** rough and uncultured. **3** primitive. [*Say* bar BEAR ick]

barbarism *n.* **1** the absence of civilized standards. **2** a word or expression not considered correct. **3** extreme cruelty or brutality. [*Say* BARBER ism]

barbarity *n.* (*pl.* **barbarities**) savage cruelty. [*Say* bar BERRA tee]

barbarous *adj.* **1** uncivilized. **2** cruel. **3** (esp. of languages) coarse and unrefined. [*Say* BARBER us]

barbecue (also **barbeque**) ● *n.* **1** a meal cooked on an open fire or grill out of doors. **2** a metal appliance with a grill for cooking over charcoal or gas flame. ● *v.* (**barbecues, barbecued, barbecuing**) cook on a barbecue.

barbed *adj.* **1** equipped with barbs. **2** (of a remark etc.) deliberately hurtful.

barbed wire *n.* wire bearing sharp pointed spikes close together.

barbell *n.* a metal bar with a series of weighted discs at each end.

barber ● *n.* a person who cuts men's hair and shaves or trims beards as an occupation. ● *v.* **1** cut the hair or shave the beard of. **2** cut or trim (grass etc.) closely.

barbershop *n.* **1** a shop where a barber works. **2** (also **barbershop quartet**) a style of close harmony singing for four male voices.

barbiturate *n.* a type of drug used in sedatives. [*Say* bar BITCH ur it *or* bar BITCHA rut]

bar code *n.* a code in the form of a

pattern of stripes, used for identification by an optical scanner. □ **bar-coded** *adj.* **bar-coding** *n.*

bard *n.* **1** *hist.* a Celtic minstrel. **2** *literary* a poet. □ **the Bard** Shakespeare. □ **bardic** *adj.*

bare ● *adj.* **1** unclothed or uncovered. **2** without appropriate covering or contents. **3** clear of snow and ice. **4 a** undisguised. **b** unadorned; basic. ● *v.* (**bares, bared, baring**) uncover or reveal. □ **lay bare** expose, reveal. **with one's bare hands** without using tools or weapons. □ **bareness** *n.*

bareback *adj. & adv.* on a horse etc. without a saddle.

bare bones *pl. n.* essential parts or components. □ **bare-bones** *adj.*

barefaced *adj.* shameless and undisguised.

barefoot *adj. & adv.* with nothing on the feet.

bare-handed *adj. & adv.* with bare hands.

bare-knuckle *adj.* (also **bare-knuckled**) **1** *Boxing* without gloves. **2** without niceties.

barely *adv.* **1** only just; scarcely. **2** scantily.

barf *informal* ● *v.* vomit or retch. ● *n.* vomited food etc.

bargain ● *n.* **1** an agreement on the terms of a transaction or sale. **2** something acquired or offered cheaply. ● *v.* discuss the terms of a transaction. □ **bargain for** (or **on**) be prepared for. **bargain on** rely on. **drive a hard bargain** press hard for a deal in one's favour. **into** (or **in**) **the bargain** in addition. □ **bargainer** *n.*

bargain basement *adj.* **1** inexpensive, cheap. **2** of poor quality; inferior.

bargaining chip *n.* something which can be used to advantage in negotiations.

barge ● *n.* **1** a long flat-bottomed boat for carrying freight etc. **2** a long ornamental boat used for ceremony. ● *v.* (**barges, barged, barging**) **1** transport or travel by barge. **2** move clumsily or roughly. **3 a** intrude or interrupt rudely. **b** collide with.

bargoon *n. Cdn slang* a bargain.

bar graph *n.* a graph using bars to represent quantity.

bar-hop *v.* (**bar-hops, bar-hopped, bar-hopping**) *informal* go from one bar to another on a drinking spree.

barista *n.* (*pl.* **baristas**) a person who makes and serves coffee in a specialty coffee shop. [*Say* bar EESTA]

baritone ● *n.* the second-lowest adult male singing voice. ● *adj.* of the second-lowest range. [*Say* BERRA tone]

barium *n.* **1** a white reactive soft metallic element. **2** a mixture of barium sulphate and water which is opaque to X-rays, given to patients requiring radiological examination of the stomach and intestines. [*Say* BERRY um]

bark[1] ● *n.* **1** the sharp cry of a dog, fox, etc. **2** a sound resembling this. ● *v.* **1** give a bark. **2** speak or utter sharply. **3** cough fiercely. □ **one's bark is worse than one's bite** one is not as ferocious as one appears. **bark up the wrong tree** be on the wrong track.

bark[2] ● *n.* the tough outer covering of the trunks and branches of trees etc. ● *v.* **1** graze or scrape (one's shin etc.). **2** strip bark from.

bark[3] *n. literary* a ship or boat.

barker *n.* a person who calls out loudly to attract customers.

barley *n.* any of various hardy cereals with coarse bristles, widely used as food etc.

barmaid *n.* a female bartender.

barman *n.* (*pl.* **barmen**) a male bartender.

bar mitzvah *n.* the religious initiation ceremony of a Jewish boy at the age of 13. [*Say* bar MITSVA]

barn *n.* a large building for housing animals, storing grain, etc.

barnacle *n.* a small marine crustacean which attaches itself permanently to a variety of surfaces. □ **barnacled** *adj.* [*Say* BARNA cull]

barnburner *n. informal* something exciting or successful.

barn owl *n.* an owl with a heart-shaped usu. white face, which frequently nests in farm buildings.

barnstorm *v.* **1** make a rapid tour as a part of political campaigning. **2** tour esp. rural districts giving flying exhibitions, theatrical performances, etc. □ **barnstormer** *n.*

barnyard *n.* **1** the area around a barn. **2** (as an *adj.*) earthy, coarse.

barometer *n.* **1** an instrument measuring atmospheric pressure. **2** anything which indicates change. □ **barometric** *adj.* [*Say* ba ROMMA tur, berra MET rick]

baron *n.* **1** a member of the lowest order of nobility. **2** an important businessman or other influential person.

baroness *n.* (*pl.* **baronesses**) a woman holding the rank of baron or married to a baron.

baronet *n.* a member of the lowest hereditary titled British order, below a baron but above a knight.

baronial *adj.* **1** of or befitting barons. **2** in the turreted style of Scottish country houses. [*Say* ba ROANY ul]

baroque ● *n.* **1** a very ornate style of architecture and art of the late 16th to early 18th century. **2** a style of music from the period 1600–1750. ● *adj.* **1** of or relating to this period or style. **2** highly ornate and complex. [*Say* ba ROKE]

barque *n.* **1** a three-masted sailing ship. **2** *literary* any boat. [*Say* BARK]

barracks *pl. n.* **1** a building or complex used to house soldiers. **2** *Cdn* a building housing a local detachment of the RCMP. [*Say* BARE icks]

barracuda *n.* (*pl.* **barracuda** or **barracudas**) a large, voracious, predatory tropical marine fish. [*Say* berra COODA]

barrage ● *n.* **1** a concentrated artillery bombardment over a wide area. **2** a rapid succession of questions or criticisms. ● *v.* (**barrages, barraged, barraging**) subject to a barrage. [*Say* ba ROZH]

barre *n.* a waist-level horizontal bar used by ballet dancers during exercises. [*Say* BAR]

barred *adj.* **1** marked with bars. **2** closed with a bar.

barrel ● *n.* **1** a cylindrical container usu. bulging out in the middle with flat ends. **2** a measure of capacity, varying from 30 to 40 imperial gallons (136 to 182 litres). **3** a unit of capacity for oil equal to 35 imperial gallons (about 159 litres). **4** the cylindrical tube forming part of an object such as a gun. ● *v.* (**barrels, barrelled, barrelling**) *informal* move quickly. □ **barrel of fun** (or **laughs**) *informal* a great deal of fun. **over a barrel** *informal* in a helpless position.

barrel-chested *adj.* having a large rounded chest.

barrelhead *n.* the flat top of a barrel. □ **on the barrelhead** immediately and up front.

barrel organ *n.* a mechanical musical instrument that plays a tune when a handle is turned.

barrel roll *n.* an aerobatic manoeuvre in which an aircraft rolls on its longitudinal axis.

barren ● *adj.* (**barrener, barrenest**) **1 a** unable to bear young. **b** unable to produce fruit or vegetation. **2** not producing anything useful or successful. **3** devoid, empty. ● *n.* a tract of elevated flat land that supports shrubs but no trees. □ **barrenness** *n.*

Barrens, the *pl. n.* (also **barrens, Barren Grounds, Barren Lands**) *Cdn* the treeless region of N Canada, lying between Hudson Bay and Great Slave and Great Bear lakes.

barrette *n.* a bar-shaped clip for the hair.

barricade ● *n.* a line of objects placed across a street etc. to prevent passage. ● *v.* (**barricades, barricaded, barricading**) **1** block with a barricade. **2** (**barricade oneself in**) shut oneself into a place by blocking all entrances.

barrier *n.* **1** a fence or other obstacle that bars advance or access. **2** an obstacle to communication, transmission, or progress.

barrier reef *n.* a coral reef separated from the shore by a broad deep channel.

barring *prep.* in the absence of.

barrio *n.* (*pl.* **barrios**) (in the US) the Spanish-speaking quarter of a city. [*Say* BAR ee oh]

barrister *n.* (also **barrister-at-law;** *pl.* **barristers-at-law**) a lawyer who pleads cases before the courts. [*Say* BERRA stir]

barrister and solicitor *n. Cdn* a lawyer.

barroom *n.* = BAR[1] 4.

barrow[1] *n.* = WHEELBARROW.

barrow[2] *n.* (in ancient times) a burial mound.

bartender *n.* a person serving drinks at a bar. □ **bartending** *n.*

barter ● *v.* exchange goods or services without using money. ● *n.* trade by exchange of goods.

Bartlett pear *n.* a large, yellow, juicy variety of pear.

basal *adj.* of, at, or forming a base. [*Say* BASE 'll]

basal metabolism *n.* the chemical processes occurring in an organism at complete rest.

basalt *n.* a dark basic volcanic rock. □ **basaltic** *adj.* [*Say* BA salt, ba SALT ick]

base[1] ● *n.* **1** something that supports from beneath or serves as a foundation. **2** a principle or starting point. **3** a centre of operations. **4** a main ingredient of a mixture; an element to which others are added. **5** *Chemistry* a substance capable of combining with an acid to form a salt. **6** *Math* a number in terms of which other numbers are expressed. **7** *Baseball* one of the four stations that must be reached in turn when scoring a run. ● *v.* (**bases, based, basing**) **1** found or establish. **2** station. □ **cover** (or **touch**) **all the bases** *informal* deal with all the related details. **make it to** (or **reach** etc.) **first base** *informal* achieve the first step of an objective etc. **off base** *informal* mistaken; unprepared, unawares. **touch base** *informal* contact or communicate (with someone).

base[2] *adj.* (**baser, basest**) **1** lacking moral worth; ignoble. **2** (of a metal) low in value.

baseball *n.* **1** a game played with teams of nine in which a batter must hit a ball with a bat, and then run around four bases to score a run. **2** the ball used in this game.

baseboard *n.* a strip of wood along the bottom of an interior wall.

base hit *n. Baseball* a hit that enables the batter to reach base without a fielder's error and without forcing out a runner already on base.

baseless *adj.* unfounded.

baseline *n.* **1** a line used as a base or starting point. **2** the area on a baseball diamond within which a runner must remain when running between bases. **3** (in tennis etc.) the line marking each end of the court. **4** something which serves as a basis.

baseman *n.* (*pl.* **basemen**) *Baseball* a player whose position is first, second, or third base.

basement *n.* the lowest floor of a building, at least partly below ground.

baserunner *n. Baseball* a member of the batting team who runs between bases. □ **baserunning** *n.*

bases *pl.* of BASE[1], BASIS.

bash ● *v.* (**bashes, bashed, bashing**) **1 a** strike bluntly or heavily. **b** *informal* attack violently. **2** collide with. **3** (often as **bashing** *n.*) *informal* deride, criticize. ● *n.* (*pl.* **bashes**) **1** a heavy blow. **2** *informal* a party. □ **basher** *n.*

bashful *adj.* shy; easily embarrassed. □ **bashfully** *adv.* **bashfulness** *n.*

basic ● *adj.* **1** forming or serving as a base. **2** fundamental. **3 a** simplest or lowest. **b** vulgar. **4** *Chemistry* having the properties of or containing a base. ● *n.* the fundamental facts or principles. □ **basically** *adv.*

basic training *n.* a period of initial training in the police, armed forces, etc.

basil *n.* an aromatic herb, used as a flavouring in savoury dishes. [*Say* BAZZLE *or* BAYZ'll]

basilica *n.* (*pl.* **basilicas**) **1** an ancient Roman public hall with an apse and colonnades, used as a law court or church. **2** a title of honour awarded to certain Catholic churches by the Pope. [*Say* ba SILLA ca]

basin *n.* **1 a** a wide shallow open container. **b** a bathroom sink. **2** a hollow rounded depression. **3** any sheltered area of water where boats can moor safely. **4** an area drained by a river.

basis *n.* (*pl.* **bases**) **1** the foundation or support of something. **2** the main or determining principle or ingredient. **3** a

starting point . [*Say* BAY sis *for the singular,* BAY seez *for the plural*]

basis point *n.* one-hundredth of one percent.

bask *v.* **1** sit or lie back lazily. **2** derive great pleasure (from).

basket *n.* **1** a container made of interwoven cane etc. **2** a net fixed on a ring used as the goal in basketball. **3** a group, category, or range. **4** a list of items which one has selected for purchase while shopping online. □ **basketful** *n.*

basketball *n.* **1** a game between two teams of five, in which goals are scored by throwing a ball through a basket. **2** the ball used in this game.

basket case *n. informal* a person or thing regarded as useless or unable to cope.

basketry *n.* **1** the art of making baskets. **2** baskets collectively.

basket weave *n.* a weave resembling that of a basket.

basmati *n.* (also **basmati rice**) a kind of rice with very long thin grains. [*Say* bazz MATTY]

Basque *n.* **1** a member of a people inhabiting the western Pyrenees in Spain and France. **2** the language of this people. □ **Basque** *adj.* [*Say* BASK *or* BOSK]

bas-relief *n.* sculpture in which the figures project from the background. [*Say* baw RELIEF]

bass[1] ● *n.* **1** the lowest adult male singing voice. **2** (also **bass line**) the lowest part in harmonized music. **3** an instrument that is the lowest in pitch in its family. **4** a bass guitar or double bass. ● *adj.* **1** lowest in musical pitch. **2** having a deep sound. [*Sounds like* BASE]

bass[2] *n.* (*pl.* **bass** or **basses**) any of various edible freshwater and marine fishes having spiny fins. [*Rhymes with* PASS]

bass[3] *n.* = BASSWOOD. [*Rhymes with* PASS]

bass clef *n. Music* a clef placing F below middle C on the second-highest line of the stave.

basset hound *n.* (also **basset**) a breed of hunting dog with a long body and droopy ears.

bassinet *n.* a portable basket-like bed for a young baby.

bassist *n.* a bass guitar or double bass player.

bassoon *n.* a bass instrument of the oboe family, with a double reed. □ **bassoonist** *n.*

basswood *n.* **1** a N American lime tree with large leaves. **2** its light, soft wood. [*The first part rhymes with* PASS]

bastard ● *n.* **1** a person whose parents are

not married. **2** *coarse slang* **a** an unpleasant or despicable person. **b** a person of a specified kind. ● *adj.* **1** illegitimate. **2** no longer in their pure or original form.

bastardize *v.* (**bastardizes, bastardized, bastardizing**) make impure by adding new elements. □ **bastardization** *n.*

baste¹ *v.* (**bastes, basted, basting**) moisten (meat) with gravy, melted fat, etc. during cooking. □ **baster** *n.*

baste² *v.* (**bastes, basted, basting**) stitch loosely together in preparation for sewing.

bastion *n.* **1** a projecting part of a fortification built at an angle to the line of a wall. **2** something seen as maintaining particular principles, attitudes, etc. [*Say* BASS ch'n]

bat¹ ● *n.* an implement with a rounded usu. wooden handle, used for hitting a ball in various games. ● *v.* (**bats, batted, batting**) **1** hit with or as with a bat. **2** take a turn at batting. □ **bat around** discuss. **go to bat for** *informal* defend the interests of. **right off the bat** immediately.

bat² *n.* a mouselike nocturnal mammal with wings. □ **have bats in the belfry** be eccentric or crazy. **like a bat out of hell** very fast.

bat³ *v.* (**bats, batted, batting**) blink; flutter (one's eyelashes). □ **bat an eye** (or **eyelash** or **eyelid**) *informal* show reaction or emotion.

batch ● *n.* (*pl.* **batches**) **1** a group of things or persons produced or dealt with together. **2** an instalment. **3** a quantity produced by one operation. ● *v.* (**batches, batched, batching**) arrange or deal with in batches.

bated *adj.* □ **with bated breath** very anxiously or eagerly.

bath ● *n.* (*pl.* **baths**) **1** the act of immersing the body for washing etc. **2** = BATHTUB. **3** a vessel containing liquid in which something is immersed; this liquid. **4** = BATHROOM. **5** (usu. in *pl.*) a building with baths or a swimming pool. ● *v.* **1** wash in a bath. **2** take a bath.

bathe *v.* (**bathes, bathed, bathing**) **1** swim. **2** wash oneself. **3** wash with liquid, esp. for cleansing or medicinal purposes. **4** (of sunlight etc.) envelop.

bather *n.* a swimmer. [*Say* BATHE er]

bathetic *adj.* marked by a sudden unintentional change from a serious to a silly mood. [*Say* ba THET ick]

bathhouse *n.* **1** a building with baths for public use. **2** a building for changing clothes at a pool etc.

bathing *n.* **1** the activity of washing oneself in a bath. **2** the activity of swimming in the sea etc. [*Say* BATHE ing]

bathing suit *n.* a garment worn for swimming.

batholith *n.* a dome of igneous rock extending to an unknown depth. [*Say* BATH a lith]

bathos *n.* a lapse in mood from the sublime to the ridiculous. [*Say* BAY thoss]

bathrobe *n.* a loose robe, usu. made of thick terry cloth.

bathroom *n.* **1** a room containing a bath and usu. other washing facilities. **2** a room containing a toilet or toilets. □ **go to the bathroom** *euphemism* urinate or defecate.

bathtub *n.* a tub for bathing in.

bathwater *n.* the water in a bath.

batik *n.* **1** a method of producing coloured designs on textiles by waxing the parts not to be dyed. **2** a piece of cloth treated in this way. [*Say* ba TEEK]

bat mitzvah *n.* **1** a ceremony for a Jewish girl aged twelve years and one day, regarded as the age of religious maturity. **2** the girl undergoing this ceremony. [*Say* bat MITSVA]

baton *n.* **1** a thin stick used by a conductor to direct an orchestra, choir, etc. **2** a short stick passed from runner to runner in a relay race. **3** a stick carried and twirled by a drum major or majorette. **4** a staff of office. **5** a truncheon. [*Say* ba TAWN]

bats *adj. slang* crazy.

batsman *n.* (*pl.* **batsmen**) a person who bats, esp. in cricket.

battalion *n.* **1** a large body of soldiers, esp. forming part of a brigade. **2** a large group of people pursuing a common aim. [*Say* buh TAL y'n]

batten ● *n.* a strip of wood, metal, or plastic for strengthening or securing something. ● *v.* secure with battens. □ **batten down the hatches 1** *Nautical* secure a ship's tarpaulins. **2** prepare for a crisis.

batter¹ *v.* **1** strike repeatedly. **2** (often in *passive*) **a** handle roughly, esp. over a long period. **b** criticize.

batter² *n.* a mixture of flour, egg, milk or water, etc., used for making cakes, to coat food for frying, etc.

batter³ *n.* a player batting, esp. in baseball.

battered¹ *adj.* **1** (of a person, esp. a woman or child) subjected to repeated violence. **2** damaged by age, adversity, or heavy use.

battered² *adj.* coated in batter for frying.

battering ram *n. hist.* a heavy object swung against a door to knock it down.

battery *n.* (*pl.* **batteries**) **1** a device

containing one or more electrical cells, for use as a source of power. **2** an extensive series, esp. of tests. **3 a** a group of heavy guns. **b** an artillery unit of guns, personnel, and vehicles. **4** *Law* an unlawful act of attacking someone, even if no physical harm is done. **5** *Baseball* the pitcher and the catcher. □ **recharge one's batteries** restore one's strength.

batting *n.* **1** the action of hitting with a bat. **2** wadding of cotton etc. prepared in sheets for use in quilts etc.

battle ● *n.* **1** a fight between opposed groups. **2** a prolonged struggle. ● *v.* (**battles, battled, battling**) fight persistently (against). □ **battle it out** fight to a conclusion. **half the battle** the key to the success of an undertaking. □ **battler** *n.*

battleaxe *n.* **1** a large axe used in ancient warfare. **2** *informal* a formidable older woman.

battle cry *n.* a rallying cry or slogan of a group of people.

battledress *n.* combat dress worn by soldiers.

battlefield *n.* (also **battleground**) **1** the piece of ground on which a battle is fought. **2** any area of conflict.

battlement *n.* (usu. in *plural*) a parapet with gaps for firing from, as part of a fortification. □ **battlemented** *adj.*

battle-scarred *adj.* **1** damaged by war. **2** worn out.

battleship *n.* a warship of the most heavily armed class.

batty *adj.* (**battier, battiest**) *informal* crazy.

bauble *n.* a showy trinket. [*Say* BOBBLE]

baud *n.* (*pl.* **baud** or **bauds**) *Computing etc.* a unit of transmission speed for electronic signals, corresponding to one event or bit per second. [*Say* BOD]

bauxite *n.* a claylike mineral from which aluminum is obtained. □ **bauxitic** *adj.* [*Say* BOX ite, box IT ick]

Bavarian ● *adj.* of or relating to Bavaria in southwestern Germany, its people, or their dialect. ● *n.* **1** a native or inhabitant of Bavaria. **2** the dialect of German used there. [*Say* buh VERY un]

bawdy *adj.* (**bawdier, bawdiest**) humorously indecent. [*Say* BODY]

bawdy house *n.* a brothel.

bawl *v.* **1** call or cry out. **2** weep loudly. □ **bawl out** *informal* reprimand angrily.

bay[1] *n.* a broad curved inlet of a sea or lake.

bay[2] *n.* (also **bay laurel** or **bay tree**) a Mediterranean laurel with deep green aromatic leaves used in cooking, and purple berries.

bay[3] *n.* **1** a space created by a window projecting outwards from a wall. **2** a recess. **3** a compartment. **4** an area specially marked off.

bay[4] ● *adj.* (esp. of a horse) dark reddish-brown. ● *n.* a bay horse with a black mane and tail.

bay[5] *v.* **1** howl plaintively. **2** shout, esp. to demand something. □ **at bay 1** cornered. **2** in a desperate situation. **hold** (or **keep**) **at bay** hold off (a pursuer).

bayberry *n.* (*pl.* **bayberries**) **1** a shrub or small tree with aromatic leaves and waxy berries. **2** the fruit of the bay tree. **3** a fragrant Caribbean tree bearing oil.

bayonet ● *n.* a blade attachable to the muzzle of a rifle. ● *v.* (**bayonets, bayonetted, bayonetting**) stab with a bayonet. [*Say* bay uh NET]

bayou *n.* a marshy offshoot of a river etc. in the southern US. [*Say* BY oo]

bayside *adj.* situated at or near a (usu. specified) bay.

Bay Street *n. Cdn* **1** a street in Toronto where the headquarters of many financial institutions and major law firms are located. **2** the interests of major Canadian corporations and banks.

bay window *n.* a window, usu. with glass on three sides, projecting from an outside wall.

bazaar *n.* **1** (esp. in the Middle East) a marketplace. **2** a fundraising sale. **3** a large store.

bazooka *n.* a short-range rocket launcher used against tanks.

BB *n.* (*pl.* **BBs**) a small pellet for shooting out of an air rifle or shotgun.

BBQ *abbr.* (*pl.* **BBQs**) *informal* barbecue.

BBS *abbr.* (*pl.* **BBS's**) bulletin-board service, a computerized system for exchanging software and messages.

BC *abbr.* **1** British Columbia. **2** (of a date) before Christ.

BCE *abbr.* before the Common Era (used for dates before the Christian era, esp. by non-Christians).

be (**am, are, is; was, were; been; being**) ● *v.* **1** exist, live. **2 a** occur; take place. **b** occupy a position in space. **3** remain, continue. **4** linking subject and predicate, expressing: **a** identity. **b** condition. **c** state or quality. **d** opinion. **e** total. **f** cost or significance. ● *aux. v.* **1** with a past participle to form the passive mood. **2** with a present participle to form progressive tenses. **3** with an infinitive to express duty or commitment, intention, possibility, destiny, or hypothesis.

beach ● *n.* a pebbly or sandy shore of a

body of water. ● v. (**beaches, beached, beaching**) run or haul up (a boat etc.) on to a beach.

beach ball n. a large lightweight inflated ball.

beachcomber n. **1** a person who searches beaches for articles of value. **2** a long wave rolling in from the sea. □ **beachcomb** v.

beached adj. (of a sea mammal etc.) stranded on the shore.

beachfront ● n. land that fronts onto a beach. ● adj. located on or overlooking a beach.

beachhead n. **1** a fortified position established on a beach by landing forces. **2** an initial position from which one may advance.

beacon n. **1** a visible warning or guiding device set in a prominent position. **2** a radio transmitter whose signal helps fix the position of a ship, aircraft, etc.

bead ● n. **1 a** a small piece of glass, stone, etc., often threaded with others to make jewellery. **b** (in plural) a string of beads. **c** (in plural) a rosary. **2** a drop of liquid. **3** a small knob on the foresight of a gun. **4** the inner edge of a pneumatic tire. ● v. **1** decorate with beads. **2** string together. □ **draw a bead on** take aim at. □ **beaded** adj.

beading n. **1** decoration in the form of or resembling a row of beads, esp. lace-like looped edging. **2** the bead of a tire.

beadle n. **1** a ceremonial usher in certain universities etc. **2** a Presbyterian church officer attending on the minister. **3** a layperson employed by a church, synagogue, etc., to perform various minor functions. [Say beedle]

beadwork n. ornamental work with beads.

beady adj. (**beadier, beadiest**) (of the eyes) small, round, and bright. □ **beadily** adv.

beady-eyed adj. **1** with beady eyes. **2** observant.

beagle n. a short-legged dog with a short black and white or brown and white coat and floppy ears.

beak n. **1 a** a bird's horny projecting jaws. **b** the similar projecting jaw of other animals, e.g. a turtle. **2** slang a hooked nose. □ **beaked** adj.

beaker n. a lipped cylindrical glass vessel for scientific experiments.

be-all and end-all n. informal a feature of an activity that is more important than anything else.

beam ● n. **1** a long piece of metal or timber used as a support in building. **2** a

ray of light, radiation, or particles. **3** a bright smile. **4** a series of radio or radar signals used to guide a ship or aircraft. **5** the crossbar of a balance, from which the pans or weights are suspended. **6 a** a ship's breadth at its widest point. **b** informal (esp. in **broad in the beam**) the width of a person's hips. **7** (in plural) the horizontal cross timbers of a ship supporting the deck and joining the sides. **8** = BALANCE BEAM. ● v. **1** emit or direct (light, radio waves, etc.). **2 a** shine. **b** look or smile radiantly. □ **beamed** adj.

bean ● n. **1 a** any kind of leguminous plant with edible usu. kidney-shaped seeds in long pods. **b** one of these seeds. **2** a similar seed of coffee and other plants. **3** informal the head. **4** (in plural; with neg.) informal anything at all. ● v. informal hit on the head. □ **be full of beans** informal **1** be lively. **2** talk nonsense. **not a hill of beans** slang an insignificant amount.

beanbag n. **1** a small bag filled with dried beans and used esp. in children's games. **2** a large cushion filled usu. with polystyrene beads and used as a seat.

bean-counter n. informal derogatory a person, esp. an accountant, perceived as placing excessive emphasis on numbers, budgets, etc. □ **bean-counting** n.

bean curd n. = TOFU.

beanie n. a skullcap, esp. of a sort worn formerly by small boys.

bean sprout n. (usu. in plural) a sprout of a bean seed, esp. of the mung bean, eaten raw or cooked.

beanstalk n. the stem of a bean plant.

bear¹ v. (**bears**; past **bore**; past participle **borne**; **bearing**) **1** carry (esp. visibly). **2** show; have as an attribute or characteristic. **3 a** produce, yield (fruit etc.). **b** give birth to. **4 a** support (a weight). **b** endure (an ordeal). **5 a** tolerate. **b** be fit for. **6** retain in memory. **7** veer in a given direction. □ **bear arms** carry weapons; serve as a soldier. **bear away** (or **off**) win. **bear down on** approach rapidly. **bear fruit** have results. **bear in mind** remember and take into account. **bear on** (or **upon**) relate to. **bear out** confirm. **bear up** raise one's spirits. **bear with** tolerate. **bear witness** testify. □ **bearable** adj. **bearer** n.

bear² n. **1** a large mammal with thick fur and a short tail. **2** an uncouth person. **3** a person who sells shares hoping to buy them back later at a lower price. □ **bearish** adj.

bearberry n. (pl. **bearberries**) **1** an evergreen shrub with bright red tart berries. **2** the berries of this plant.

beard ● *n.* hair growing on the chin and lower cheeks. ● *v.* defy. ☐ **bearded** *adj.*

bear hug *n.* a tight embrace.

bearing *n.* **1** a person's bodily attitude. **2** relevance to. **3** a part of a machine that supports a rotating or other moving part. **4** direction or position relative to a fixed point. **5** (in *plural*) one's position relative to one's surroundings. **6** = BALL BEARING.

bear market *n.* a stock market with falling prices.

bearpaw *n.* **1** the paw of a bear. **2** *Cdn* an almost circular, tailless snowshoe.

bear-pit session *n.* *Cdn* an esp. political meeting in which audience members question one or more representatives, leaders, candidates, etc.

bearskin *n.* **1 a** the skin of a bear. **b** a rug etc. made of this. **2** a tall furry hat.

beast *n.* **1** an animal, esp. a large quadruped. **2** an unpleasant person. ☐ **beastly** *adj.*

beat ● *v.* (**beats**; *past* **beat**; *past participle* **beaten**; **beating**) **1** strike repeatedly. **2 a** overcome; defeat. **b** be too hard for. **3** stir (ingredients) vigorously. **4** (often foll. by *out*) shape (metal etc.) by blows. **5** (of the heart etc.) pulsate. **6** move up and down. **7** make (a path etc.) by trampling. ● *n.* **1** the main accent in music or verse. **2 a** a throbbing movement or sound. **b** a brief pause **3 a** an area allocated to a police officer, reporter, etc. **b** a person's habitual round. ● *adj.* **1** *informal* exhausted, tired out. **2** of the beatniks or their philosophy. ☐ **beat around the bush** discuss a matter without coming to the point. **to beat the band** in such a way as to defeat all competition. **beat one's breast** strike one's chest in anguish. **beat it** *informal* go away. **beat a retreat** withdraw. **beat time** indicate or follow a musical tempo with a baton or other means. **beat up** attack and overcome (someone), esp. with punches and kicks. (**it**) **beats me** I do not understand (it). ☐ **beatable** *adj.* **beaten** *adj.* **beating** *n.*

beater *n.* **1** an implement used for beating (e.g. eggs, a drum, etc.). **2** *informal* an old or dilapidated vehicle.

beatific *adj.* **1** *informal* blissful. **2** making blessed. ☐ **beatifically** *adv.* [*Say* bee a TIFF ick]

beatification *n.* **1** *Catholicism* the act of declaring a dead person "blessed", a step towards making them a saint. **2** making or being blessed. ☐ **beatify** *v.* [*Say* bee atta fuh CAY sh'n]

beatitude *n.* **1** blessedness. **2** (**the Beatitudes**) the blessings listed by Jesus in the Sermon on the Mount. [*Say* bee ATTITUDE]

beatnik *n.* a young person, esp. in the 1950s, rejecting conventional society in his or her choice of clothing, habits, and beliefs.

beat-up *adj.* *informal* in a state of disrepair.

Beaufort scale *n.* a scale of wind speed ranging from 0 (calm) to 12 (hurricane). [*Say* BOE fort]

Beaujolais *n.* (*pl.* **Beaujolais**) a red or white burgundy wine from the Beaujolais district of France. [*Say* BOE zhuh lay *or* boe zhuh LAY]

beaut *n.* *informal* an excellent or beautiful person or thing. [*Say* BYOOT]

beauteous *adj.* *literary* beautiful. [*Say* BYOOTY us]

beautician *n.* a person who gives beauty treatment.

beautiful *adj.* **1** delighting the aesthetic senses. **2** enjoyable. **3** excellent. ☐ **beautifully** *adv.*

beautify *v.* (**beautifies**, **beautified**, **beautifying**) make beautiful. ☐ **beautification** *n.*

beauty *n.* (*pl.* **beauties**) **1** a combination of qualities that pleases the senses or intellect. **2 a** an excellent specimen. **b** an attractive feature. **3** a beautiful woman.

beauty queen *n.* the woman judged most beautiful in a contest.

beauty salon *n.* (also **beauty parlour**) an establishment providing beauty treatment.

beauty spot *n.* **1** a place known for its beauty. **2** (also **beauty mark**) a small natural or artificial mark such as a mole on the face.

beauty treatment *n.* the use of cosmetics, hairdressing, etc. to enhance personal appearance.

beaver ● *n.* **1** (*pl.* **beaver** *or* **beavers**) a large broad-tailed semi-aquatic rodent able to gnaw down trees and build dams. **2** its fur. ● *v.* *informal* (usu. foll. by *away*) work hard.

bebop *n.* a type of jazz originating in the 1940s. ☐ **bebopper** *n.* [*Say* BEE bop]

becalmed *adj.* (of sailboats, etc.) deprived of wind and unable to move.

because *conj.* for the reason that. ☐ **because of** by reason of.

beck *n.* ☐ **at a person's beck and call** having constantly to obey a person's orders.

beckon *v.* **1** make a gesture to encourage or tell someone to come nearer. **2** seem appealing.

become *v.* (**becomes**; *past* **became**; *past participle* **become**; **becoming**) **1** begin to be. **2 a** look well on; suit. **b** be suitable for. □ **become of** happen to

becoming adj. **1** flattering the appearance. **2** suitable. □ **becomingly** adj.

becquerel n. *Physics* the SI unit of radioactivity. [*Say* BECKA rell]

B.Ed. abbr. (pl. **B.Ed.'s**) Bachelor of Education.

bed ● n. **1** a piece of furniture etc. used for sleeping or resting on. **2** the bed as a place for sexual intercourse. **3** a place where something is embedded. **4** a foundation, base, or bottom. **5** a plot of land in which plants are grown. ● v. (**beds, bedded, bedding**) **1** provide with or settle in a bed. **2** *informal* have sexual intercourse with. **3** (often foll. by *out*) plant in a garden bed. **4** fix or be fixed firmly.

bed and breakfast n. an establishment providing a night's accommodation and breakfast the next morning.

bedbug n. any of several flat, wingless, bloodsucking insects which infest beds and houses.

bedclothes pl. n. (also **bedcovers**) covers for a bed, such as sheets, blankets, etc.

bedding n. **1** the articles which compose a bed. **2** a layer of straw etc. on which livestock sleep.

bedeck v. adorn. [*Say* be DECK]

bedevil v. (**bedevils, bedevilled, bedevilling**) **1** (of something bad) cause great and continual trouble to. **2** (of a person) torment or harass. [*Say* be DEVIL]

bedfellow n. **1** a person who shares a bed with another. **2** an associate. □ **strange bedfellows** an oddly assorted group of persons, things, etc.

bedlam n. uproar and confusion.

Bedouin n. (pl. **Bedouin**) a member of an Arabic-speaking nomadic people inhabiting the desert regions of the Middle East. □ **Bedouin** adj. [*Say* BED oo in]

bedpan n. a receptacle used by a bedridden patient for urine and feces.

bedraggled adj. untidy. [*Say* be DRAGGLED]

bedridden adj. confined to bed by infirmity.

bedrock n. **1** solid rock underlying soil etc. **2** the underlying principles or facts of a theory, character, etc.

bedroll n. portable bedding rolled into a bundle.

bedroom n. a room for sleeping in.

bedside n. the space beside a bed.

bedside manner n. the manner of a doctor when attending a patient.

bedspread n. a top cover placed over a bed.

bedstead n. a framework supporting the springs and mattress of a bed.

bedtime n. the usual time for going to bed.

bedwetting n. urination in bed while asleep. □ **bedwetter** n.

bee n. **1** a stinging winged insect which collects nectar and pollen and produces wax and honey. **2** a social gathering at which communal work is performed. □ **a bee in one's bonnet** an obsession. **the bee's knees** *slang* something outstandingly good.

beech n. (pl. **beeches**) **1** a large deciduous tree with grey bark and glossy leaves. **2** (also **beechwood**) its wood.

beechnut n. the small rough-skinned fruit of the beech tree.

beef ● n. **1** the flesh of a cow, steer, or bull used as food. **2** (pl. **beeves**) **a** a cow, steer, or bull raised for its meat. **b** its carcass. **3** *informal* muscle; strength. **4** (pl. **beefs**) *slang* a complaint. ● v. *slang* complain. □ **beef up** *informal* strengthen, augment.

beefcake n. *informal* muscular male physique, esp. in photographs.

beefsteak n. a slice of beef, usu. for grilling.

beefsteak tomato n. any of several large and firm varieties of tomato.

beefy adj. (**beefier, beefiest**) **1** like beef. **2** muscular or robust.

beehive n. **1** a structure in which bees are kept. **2** a busy place.

beekeeper n. a person who raises honeybees for their honey and beeswax. □ **beekeeping** n.

beeline n. a straight line between two places. □ **make a beeline for** hurry directly to.

been *past participle of* BE.

beep ● n. **1** a high-pitched noise, esp. one produced electronically. **2** the sound of a car horn. ● v. **1** emit a beep. **2** cause to beep.

beeper n. **1** anything that emits a beep. **2** a pager.

beer n. **1 a** an alcoholic drink made from yeast-fermented malt etc., flavoured with hops. **b** a serving of this. **2** any of several other carbonated drinks flavoured with plant extracts.

beer belly n. a protruding stomach caused by drinking large quantities of beer. □ **beer-bellied** adj.

beer league n. **1** a sports minor league of the lowest rank. **2** a league of recreational hockey, baseball, etc. players.

beernut *n.* a shelled roasted peanut with a crisp sweet coating.

beer parlour *n. Cdn* a room in a hotel or tavern where beer is served.

beer slinger *n. Cdn informal* a bartender. □**beer slinging** *n.*

beery *adj.* (**beerier**, **beeriest**) **1** showing the influence of drink in one's appearance or behaviour. **2** smelling or tasting of beer.

beeswax *n.* the wax secreted by bees to make honeycombs, used to make candles, etc.

beet *n.* a plant with an edible spherical dark red root used as a vegetable. *See also* SUGAR BEET.

beetle ● *n.* an insect with a hard protective case closing over the back wings. ● *v.* (**beetles**, **beetled**, **beetling**) *informal* make one's way hurriedly.

beeves *pl.* of BEEF 2.

befall *v.* (**befalls**; *past* **befell**; *past participle* **befallen**; **befalling**) (esp. of something bad) happen to.

befit *v.* (**befits**, **befitted**, **befitting**) be appropriate for; suit.

before *prep., conj. & adv.* **1** during the time preceding. **2** in front of. **3** rather than.

Before Christ *adv.* (of a date) reckoned backwards from the birth of Christ. Abbreviation: **BC**.

beforehand *adv.* in advance.

befoul *v.* make dirty.

befriend *v.* be or become friendly with.

befuddle *v.* (**befuddles**, **befuddled**, **befuddling**) cause to become unable to think clearly. □**befuddlement** *n.*

beg *v.* (**begs**, **begged**, **begging**) **1** ask for food or money as charity. **2** ask earnestly or humbly. **3** (of a dog) sit up with the front paws raised. **4** take or ask leave (to do something). **5** demand. □**beg off** decline to take part or attend. **beg a person's pardon** apologize. **beg the question 1** *disputed* pose the question. **2** assume the truth of something without arguing it.

beget *v.* (**begets**; *past* **begat** or **begot**; *past participle* **begotten**; **begetting**) **1** be the parent, esp. the father of. **2** cause. □**begetter** *n.*

beggar ● *n.* **1** a person who begs. **2** *informal* a person. ● *v.* reduce to poverty. □**beggars can't be choosers** those without other resources must take what is offered.

beggary *n.* extreme poverty.

begin *v.* (**begins**; *past* **began**; *past participle* **begun**; **beginning**) **1** start; perform the first part of. **2** come into being. **3** start at a certain time. **4 a** start speaking. **b** take the first step. **5** *informal* (usu. with *neg.*) show any attempt or likelihood. □**to begin with** in the first place.

beginner *n.* a person beginning to learn a skill etc.

beginning *n.* **1** the time or place at which anything begins. **2** a source. **3** the first part.

begonia *n.* a plant with bright flowers and waxy leaves. [*Say* buh GOAN ya]

begot *past* of BEGET.

begotten *past participle* of BEGET.

begrudge *v.* (**begrudges**, **begrudged**, **begrudging**) **1** give reluctantly or resentfully. **2** envy (a person) the possession of. □**begrudgingly** *adv.*

beguile *v.* (**beguiles**, **beguiled**, **beguiling**) **1** charm, often in a deceptive way. **2** help time pass pleasantly. **3** trick; cheat. □**beguiling** *adj.* **beguilingly** *adv.* [*Say* be GILE (with G as in GIVE)]

begun *past participle* of BEGIN.

behalf *n.* □**on behalf of 1** in the interests of. **2** as representative of.

behave *v.* (**behaves**, **behaved**, **behaving**) **1 a** act or react (in a specified way). **b** conduct oneself properly. **c** (of a machine etc.) work well. **2** (**behave oneself**) show good manners.

behaviour *n.* (also **behavior**) the way in which someone or something behaves. □**behavioural** *adj.*

behead *v.* cut off the head of (a person), esp. as a form of execution. □**beheading** *n.*

behemoth *n.* a huge creature or thing. [*Say* buh HEE muth]

behest *n.* a request.

behind ● *prep.* **1 a** in, towards, or to the rear of. **b** on the farther side of. **c** hidden by. **2 a** in the past in relation to. **b** late in relation to. **3** inferior to. **4 a** in support of. **b** responsible for. **5** following. ● *adv.* **1 a** in or to or towards the rear. **b** on the further side. **2** remaining after departure. **3 a** in arrears. **b** late in accomplishing a task etc. **4** in an inferior position. **5** following. ● *n. informal* the buttocks. □**behind a person's back** without a person's knowledge.

behold *v.* (**beholds**, **beheld**, **beholding**) see or observe. □**beholder** *n.*

beholden *adj.* having a duty to someone in return for help or service.

behoove *v.* (**behooves**, **behooved**, **behooving**) *formal* **1** be a duty or responsibility. **2** (usu. with *neg.*) be appropriate.

beige *n. & adj.* a very pale yellowish brown.

being *n.* **1** existence. **2** the nature of a person. **3** a human being. **4** anything that exists or is imagined.

bejesus n. (also **bejabbers**) informal used as an intensifier.

bejewelled adj. adorned with jewels.

belabour v. (also **belabor**) **1** argue or elaborate in excessive detail. **2** attack.

Belarusian n. **1** a person from Belarus. **2** the Slavic language of Belarus. □ **Belarusian** adj. [Say bella ROOSE yun]

belated adj. coming late or too late. □ **belatedly** adv. **belatedness** n.

belay v. (**belays, belayed, belaying**) **1** secure (a rope) around a cleat, pin, rock, etc. **2** Nautical halt. [Say be LAY]

bel canto n. a lyrical, smooth style of operatic singing. [Say bell CANTO]

belch ● v. (**belches, belched, belching**) **1** burp. **2 a** (of a chimney, etc.) send (smoke etc.) out or up. **b** gush forth. ● n. a burp.

beleaguered adj. **1** put in a very difficult situation. **2** besieged. [Say be LEE gurd]

belfry n. (pl. **belfries**) a tower or steeple housing bells. [Say BELL free]

Belgian ● n. **1** a person from Belgium. **2** (also **Belgian horse**) a draft horse of a large, heavy, and short-legged breed of Flemish origin. ● adj. of or relating to Belgium.

belie v. (**belies, belied, belying**) **1** fail to give a true notion or impression of. **2** fail to fulfill or justify (a claim or expectation). [Say be LIE]

belief n. **1 a** a firm opinion. **b** an acceptance. **c** a person's religion; religious conviction. **2** (usu. foll. by in) trust or confidence.

believe v. (**believes, believed, believing**) **1** accept as true or as conveying the truth. **2** think, suppose. **3 a** have faith in the existence of. **b** have confidence in. **4** have (esp. religious) faith. □ **make believe** pretend. □ **believability** n. **believable** adj. **believably** adv. **believer** n.

belittle v. (**belittles, belittled, belittling**) dismiss as unimportant or worthless.

bell ● n. **1** a hollow usu. metal object in the shape of a deep upturned cup, made to sound a clear musical note when struck. **2** a sound or stroke of a bell. **3** anything that sounds like or functions as a bell, esp. as a signal. **4 a** any bell-shaped object or part, e.g. of a musical instrument. **b** the corolla of a flower when bell-shaped. ● v. **1** attach a bell to. **2** (foll. by out) form into the shape of the lip of a bell. □ **bells and whistles** informal attractive but non-essential components. **ring a bell** informal

sound familiar. **with bells on** enthusiastically.

Bella Bella n. = HEILTSUK n.

Bella Coola n. = NUXALK n.

belladonna n. **1** a poisonous plant with purple flowers and purple-black berries. **2** a drug prepared from its root and leaves. [Say bella DONNA]

bell-bottom n. **1** a wide flare below the knee of a trouser leg. **2** (in pl.) trousers with bell-bottoms. □ **bell-bottomed** adj.

bellboy n. = BELLHOP.

bellcast adj. designating a style of roof typical of traditional architecture in Quebec, with gables having the shape of a squared-off bell.

belle n. a beautiful woman. [Say BELL]

bellhop n. a hotel employee who helps guests with luggage, etc.

bellicose adj. inclined to war or fighting. □ **bellicosity** n. [Say BELLA cose, bella COSSA tee]

belligerence n. aggressive or warlike behaviour. [Say buh LIDGER ince]

belligerent ● adj. **1** engaged in war or conflict. **2** hostile and aggressive. ● n. a nation or person engaged in war or conflict. □ **belligerently** adv. [Say buh LIDGER int]

bellman n. (pl. **bellmen**) = BELLHOP.

bellow ● v. **1 a** emit a deep loud roar. **b** shout with pain. **2** utter loudly. ● n. a bellowing sound. [Say BELLO]

bellows pl. n. (also treated as sing.) a device with an air bag that emits a stream of air when squeezed.

bell pepper n. see PEPPER n. 2.

bell-ringing n. **1** the ringing of church bells. **2** Cdn the ringing of bells in a legislative assembly to summon members for a vote.

bellwether n. **1** an indicator or predictor of something. **2** the leading sheep of a flock, on whose neck a bell is hung.

belly ● n. (pl. **bellies**) **1** the part of the body just below the chest, containing the stomach and bowels. **2** the stomach. **3 a** cavity or bulging part of anything. ● v. (**bellies, bellied, bellying**) swell or cause to swell. □ **belly up** informal approach closely: bellied up to the bar. **go belly up** informal fail; become bankrupt. □ **bellied** adj.

bellyache informal ● n. a stomach pain. ● v. (**bellyaches, bellyached, bellyaching**) complain noisily. □ **bellyacher** n.

belly button n. informal the navel.

belly dance n. a solo dance of Middle Eastern origin performed by a woman and involving the rippling of the abdominal muscles. □ **belly dancer** n. **belly dancing** n.

bellyflop informal ● n. a dive in which the body lands with the belly flat on the water. ● v. (**bellyflops, bellyflopped, bellyflopping**) perform this dive.

belong v. **1** (foll. by to) **a** be the property of. **b** be assigned to. **c** be a member of. **2** fit or be acceptable in a particular place or situation. **3** (foll. by in, under) be rightly placed or classified. □ **belonging** n.

belongings pl. n. personal possessions.

beloved ● adj. dearly loved. ● n. a dearly loved person. [Say be LUVD or be LOVE id]

below ● prep. at a lower level than. ● adv. **1** to a lower level. **2** further down on a page or later in an article, book, etc. **3** on the lower side. **4** lower than zero on a temperature scale.

belt ● n. **1** a strip of leather, cloth, etc., worn around the waist or from the shoulder to the opposite hip to support clothes, tools, weapons, etc. **2 a** a circular band of material used as a driving medium in machinery etc. **b** a conveyor belt. **3** a seat belt. **4** a strip of reinforcing material. **5** a zone or region of distinct character or occupancy. **6** informal a heavy blow. **7** informal a drink. ● v. **1** put a belt around. **2** fasten with a belt. **3** informal hit hard. **4** informal rush, hurry. **5** drink quickly. □ **below the belt** unfair or unfairly. **belt out** informal sing or utter loudly. **tighten one's belt** curtail expenditure. **under one's belt** **1** (of food or drink) consumed. **2** securely acquired: has a degree under her belt. □ **belter** n.

beluga n. **1** a whale of the Arctic Ocean, found as far south as the St. Lawrence estuary, and white when adult. **2 a** a large kind of sturgeon of the Caspian and Black Seas. **b** caviar obtained from it. [Say buh LOOGA]

belying pres. part. of BELIE. [Say be LYING]

bemoan v. express sorrow over.

bemuse v. (**bemuses, bemused, bemusing**) (usu. as **bemused** adj.) cause puzzlement. □ **bemusedly** adv. **bemusement** n.

bench ● n. **1** (pl. **benches**) a long seat, with or without a back, for several people. **2** a work table used by a carpenter etc., or in a laboratory. **3** (**the bench**) **a** the office or status of a judge. **b** judges and magistrates collectively. **4** Sport **a** a seat used by players when not participating in a game. **b** the substitute players collectively. **5** Parliament a seat. **6** (also **benchland**) a relatively narrow, naturally occurring terrace often backed by a steep slope. ● v.

(**benches, benched, benching**) Sport remove or retire (a player) to the bench esp. for poor performance.

bencher n. **1** (in comb.) Parliament an occupant of a specified bench. **2** Cdn Law a member of the regulating body of the law society in all provinces except New Brunswick.

benchmark n. a standard or point of reference.

bench press ● n. an exercise in which a person lying face upwards on a bench with feet on the floor raises a barbell by extending both arms upward from the chest. ● v. (**bench presses, bench pressed, bench pressing**) raise (a weight) in a bench press.

benchwarmer n. informal an athlete who routinely is not selected to play.

bend ● v. (**bends, bent, bending**) **1** force or be forced into a curve or angle. **2** move or stretch in a curved course. **3** lean or curve the body downwards. **4** direct. ● n. **1** a curved or angled part or course. **2** (**the bends**) informal = DECOMPRESSION SICKNESS. □ **bend someone's ear** talk to someone, esp. in order to ask a favour. **bend the rules** interpret or modify rules etc. to suit oneself. **round the bend** informal crazy, insane. □ **bendable** adj.

bender n. **1** slang a wild drinking spree. **2** an instrument for bending (pipes etc.).

bendy adj. (**bendier, bendiest**) informal soft and flexible.

beneath ● prep. **1** under. **2** unworthy of; too demeaning for. ● adv. underneath.

Benedictine ● n. a monk or nun of an order following the description of monastic life set out by St. Benedict (c. 480–c. 550). ● adj. of St. Benedict or the Benedictines. [Say benna DICK teen]

benediction n. **1** the utterance of a blessing, esp. at the end of a religious service. **2** (**Benediction**) a chiefly Catholic service in which the congregation is blessed with the Host, usu. displayed in a monstrance. **3** the state of being blessed. [Say benna DICK sh'n]

benefaction n. **1** a donation. **2** an act of giving. [Say benna FACTION]

benefactor n. a person who gives support (esp. financial) to a person or cause. □ **benefactress** n. [Say BENNA factor]

benefice n. **1** a position held by a member of the clergy that ensures an income or a specified property. **2** the income from such a position. [Say BENNA fiss]

beneficent adj. **1** generous, actively kind. **2** resulting in good. □ **beneficence** n. **beneficently** adv. [Say buh NEFFA sint]

beneficial adj. advantageous; having benefits. □ **beneficially** adv.

beneficiary n. (pl. **beneficiaries**) **1** a person who receives or is entitled to receive benefits from a will, life insurance policy, etc. **2** a person who benefits from a particular event, action, etc. [Say benna FISHY airy or benna FISHERY]

benefit ● n. **1** advantage or profit. **2** (often in pl.) a payment given by a government or insurer to a person entitled to receive it. **3** (often in pl.) an advantage other than salary associated with a job, e.g. dental coverage, life insurance, etc. **4** an event held in order to raise money for a charity, etc. ● v. (**benefits, benefited, benefiting**) **1** do good to. **2** (often foll. by from, by) receive an advantage. □ **the benefit of the doubt** assumption of a person's innocence, rightness, etc. in the absence of proof to the contrary.

benevolent adj. **1** well meaning. **2** charitable. □ **benevolence** n. **benevolently** adv. [Say buh NEVVA l'nt]

Bengali n. **1** a native of Bengal, a region in the northeast of the Indian subcontinent. **2** the language of this people, descended from Sanskrit. □ **Bengali** adj. [Say ben GALLY or ben GOLLY]

benighted adj. **1** intellectually or morally ignorant. **2** unfortunate.

benign adj. **1** gentle, kindly. **2** (of climate etc.) mild. **3** (of a disease, tumour, etc.) not malignant. **4** harmless. □ **benignly** adv. [Say buh NINE]

bent ● v. past and past participle of BEND v. ● adj. **1** curved or having an angle. **2** determined to do or have. ● n. **1** an inclination or bias. **2** (foll. by for) a talent for something specified. □ **bent out of shape** informal upset or annoyed.

bento box n. a portable lunch of Japanese food, typically rice, vegetables, sashimi, etc. served in a decorated lacquered wood box divided into compartments.

bentonite n. a highly absorbent clay with many uses, esp. as filler, cat litter, etc. [Say BENTA nite]

benzene n. a volatile liquid found in coal tar and petroleum. [Say BEN zeen]

benzodiazepine n. any of a class of compounds used as tranquilizers, including Valium. [Say benzo die AZZA peen]

benzoic acid n. a white crystalline substance used esp. as a food preservative. [Say ben ZO ick]

Beothuk (also **Beothuck**) n. **1** (pl. **Beothuk** or **Beothuks**) a member of an Aboriginal people formerly inhabiting

Newfoundland but extinct since the early 19th century. **2** the Algonquian language of this people. □ **Beothuk** adj. [Say bee OTH uck]

bequeath v. **1** leave to a person by will. **2** hand down to posterity. [Say bee QUEETH]

bequest n. **1** the action of bequeathing. **2** money or property given in a will.

berate v. (**berates, berated, berating**) criticize angrily.

bereaved adj. saddened by the death of a loved one. □ **bereavement** n. [Say be REEVD]

bereft adj. deprived. [Say be REFT]

beret n. a round brimless cap of felt or cloth that is close-fitting and lies flat on the head. [Say buh RAY]

berg n. = ICEBERG.

bergamot n. **1** a citrus tree bearing fruit the oil of which is used esp. in perfumes, Earl Grey tea, etc. **2** any of several plants of the mint family smelling like bergamot. [Say BERGA mot]

beriberi n. a disease causing inflammation of the nerves due to a lack of vitamin B_1 (thiamine). [Say berry BERRY]

berm n. **1 a** a flat strip of land, raised bank, or terrace bordering a river etc. **b** a narrow path or grass strip beside a road. **2** a narrow ledge.

Bermuda shorts pl. n. (also **Bermudas**) knee-length shorts.

berry n. (pl. **berries**) **1** a small round juicy fruit without a stone. **2** Botany a fruit with its seeds enclosed in pulp, e.g. the grape or tomato. □ **berried** comb. form

berserk adj. (esp. in **go berserk**) wild, frenzied.

berth ● n. **1** a fixed bunk on a ship, train, etc., for sleeping in. **2** a ship's place at a wharf. **3** Sport an opportunity for a team or athlete to compete. ● v. moor in a berth. □ **give a wide berth to** avoid.

beryl n. a kind of transparent pale green, blue, or yellow precious stone. [Sounds like BARREL]

beryllium n. a hard white metallic element used in making light corrosion-resistant alloys. [Say buh RILLY um]

beseech v. (**beseeches;** past and past participle **beseeched** or **besought; beseeching**) ask (someone) for something in an anxious way □ **beseeching** adj. **beseechingly** adv.

beset v. (**besets, beset, besetting**) **1** trouble or threaten persistently. **2** surround or hem in.

beside prep. **1** at the side of; near.

2 compared with. **3** irrelevant to. □ **beside oneself** overcome with worry, anger, etc.

besides ● *prep.* **1** in addition to. **2** other than. ● *adv.* in addition.

besiege *v.* (**besieges, besieged, besieging**) **1** surround a place with armed forces in order to capture it or force its surrender. **2** crowd around oppressively. **3** harass with requests.

besmirch *v.* (**besmirches, besmirched, besmirching**) **1** dirty. **2** damage (someone's reputation). [*Say* be SMIRCH]

besotted *adj.* infatuated. [*Say* be SOTTED]

besought *past and past participle of* BESEECH.

bespeak *v.* (**bespeaks;** *past* **bespoke;** *past participle* **bespoken; bespeaking**) suggest; be evidence of.

bespectacled *adj.* wearing eyeglasses.

best ● *adj.* (*superlative of* GOOD) of the most excellent or outstanding or desirable kind. ● *adv.* (*superlative of* WELL¹) **1** in the best manner. **2** to the greatest degree. **3** most usefully. ● *n.* **1** that which is best. **2** the chief merit or advantage. **3** a winning majority of (a certain number of games etc. played). **4** a best performance recorded to date. ● *v. informal* defeat, outwit, outbid, etc. □ **all the best** an expression of goodwill. **at best** on the most optimistic view. **at one's best** in peak condition etc. **be for** (or **all for**) **the best** be desirable in the end. **the best part of** most of. **give a person one's best** express one's best wishes to a person.

best-before date *n.* the date marked on food showing the period after which it will deteriorate.

bestial *adj.* **1** cruel, savage. **2** sexually depraved; lustful. **3** of or like a beast. [*Say* BEESTY ul *or* BESTY ul]

bestiality *n.* (*pl.* **bestialities**) **1** sexual intercourse between a person and an animal. **2** savage or depraved behaviour. [*Say* beesty ALA tee *or* besty ALA tee]

best man *n.* a bridegroom's chief attendant.

bestow *v.* award (a gift, right, etc.). □ **bestowal** *n.* [*Say* buh STOE]

bestride *v.* (**bestrides;** *past* **bestrode;** *past participle* **bestridden; bestriding**) **1** sit or stand astride on or over. **2** dominate.

bestseller *n.* a book or other item that has sold in large numbers. □ **bestselling** *adj.*

bet ● *v.* (**bets;** *past and past participle* **bet** or **betted; betting**) **1** risk a sum of money etc. against another's on the basis of the outcome of an unpredictable event. **2** *informal* feel sure. ● *n.* **1** the act of betting. **2** the money etc. staked. **3** *informal* an opinion, esp. a spontaneous one. **4** *informal* a choice or course of action. □ **you bet** you can be certain. □ **betting** *n.* **bettor** *n.*

beta *n.* **1** the second letter of the Greek alphabet (B, β). **2** the second of a series or set. **3** the second brightest star in a constellation. [*Say* BAY tuh]

beta blocker *n.* a drug used to reduce high blood pressure.

beta carotene *n.* an isomer of carotene found in carrots etc., and converted in the body to vitamin A.

beta test ● *n.* a test of computer hardware or software in the final stages of development, carried out by the users for whom it is intended. ● *v.* submit (a product) to a beta test.

beta version *n.* a version of a computer program or component used in beta testing.

betel *n.* the leaf of an Asian evergreen climbing plant, commonly chewed with parings of the areca nut in Southeast Asia. [*Say* BEETLE]

betel nut *n.* an areca nut.

bête noire *n.* (*pl.* **bêtes noires**) a person etc. one particularly dislikes or fears. [*Say* bet NWAR]

betide *v.* happen to

betoken *v.* indicate or warn.

betray *v.* **1** place in the power of an enemy. **2** be disloyal to. **3** be evidence of. **4** reveal involuntarily or treacherously. □ **betrayal** *n.* **betrayer** *n.*

betrothal *n.* a promise to marry. [*Say* be TROTHE'll (*with* TH *as in* BATHE)]

betrothed *formal* ● *n.* one's fiancé or fiancée. ● *adj.* engaged to be married. [*Rhymes with* CLOTHED]

better ● *adj.* (*comparative of* GOOD) **1** of a more excellent or outstanding or desirable kind. **2** partly or fully recovered from illness. ● *adv.* (*comparative of* WELL¹) **1** in a better manner. **2** to a greater degree. **3** more usefully or advantageously. ● *n.* **1** that which is better. **2** (*usu. in pl.*) one's superior in ability or rank. ● *v.* **1** surpass. **2** improve. **3** (**better oneself**) improve one's position etc. □ **better off** in a better position. **the better part of** most of. **the better to …** so as to … better. **get the better of** win an advantage over. **had better** would find it wiser to.

betterment *n.* improvement.

between ● *prep.* **1 a** at, into, or across a space separating (two things). **b** in the

period separating (two points in time).
2 separating, physically or conceptually.
3 shared by; together with. **4** to and from.
5 taking one and rejecting the other of.
● *adv.* (also **in between**) at a point or in
the area bounded by two or more other
points in space, time, sequence, etc.
□ **between ourselves** (or **you and
me**) in confidence. **between times** (or
whiles) occasionally.

bevel ● *n.* (in carpentry) a sloping surface
or edge. ● *v.* (**bevels, bevelled,
bevelling**) reduce (a square edge) to a
sloping edge. [*Say* BEV'll]

beverage *n.* a drink.

bevy *n.* (*pl.* **bevies**) a group or company of
any kind.

bewail *v.* express great regret or bitterness
over.

beware *v.* be cautious.

bewilder *v.* utterly perplex.
□ **bewildered** *adj.* **bewildering** *adj.*
bewilderingly *adv.* **bewilderment** *n.*

bewitch *v.* (**bewitches, bewitched,
bewitching**) **1** enchant; greatly delight.
2 subject to the influence of magic or
witchcraft. □ **bewitching** *adj.*
bewitchingly *adv.*

beyond ● *prep.* **1** at or to the further side
of. **2** outside the scope, range, or
understanding of. **3** more than. ● *adv.* **1** at
or to the further side. **2** further on. ● *n.*
(**the beyond**) the unknown after death.

bezel *n.* **1** the sloped edge of a chisel. **2** the
oblique faces of a cut gem. **3** a groove
holding a watch glass or gem.
[*Say* BEZZLE]

Bhagavad-Gita *n.* a devotional work, the
most famous religious text of Hinduism.
[*Say* bogga vod GEETA]

bi- *comb. form* forming nouns and adjectives
meaning: **1** two; having two. **2 a** occurring
twice in every one or once in every two.
b lasting for two. **3** in two ways.

biannual *adj.* occurring, appearing, etc.,
twice a year. □ **biannually** *adv.*

bias ● *n.* **1** prejudice in favour of or against
one thing, person, or group compared with
another. **2** an unwanted distortion of a
statistical result. **3** a diagonal line or cut
across the weave of a fabric. ● *v.* (**biases,
biased, biasing**) influence (usu.
unfairly); prejudice. □ **biased** *adj.*

biathlon *n.* an athletic contest in cross-
country skiing and shooting or cycling and
running. □ **biathlete** *n.* [*Say* by ATH lon]

bib *n.* **1** a piece of cloth or plastic fastened
around the neck, esp. of a baby, to keep the
clothes clean during a meal. **2** the top front
part of an apron, overalls, etc. **3** a simple

loose sleeveless jersey worn over sports
attire to identify participants as members
of a team, esp. during practice.

Bible *n.* **1 a** the Christian scriptures
consisting of the Old and New Testaments.
b the Jewish scriptures. **2** (usu. **bible**) any
authoritative book.

Biblical *adj.* (also **biblical**) having to do
with or found in the Bible.
□ **biblically** *adv.*

bibliography *n.* (*pl.* **bibliographies**)
1 a a list of the books referred to in a
scholarly work. **b** a list of the books by a
specific author, or on a specific subject.
2 a the study of books and their
production. **b** any book containing such
information. □ **bibliographic** *adj.*
[*Say* bib lee OGGRA fee]

bibliophile *n.* a person who collects or is
fond of books. [*Say* BIBBLY oh file]

bicameral *adj.* (esp. of a law-making body)
having two chambers.
[*Say* by CAMMER ul]

bicarbonate *n.* **1** *Chemistry* any acid salt of
carbonic acid. **2** (also **bicarbonate of
soda**) = BAKING SODA.
[*Say* by CARBON ate *or* by CARBON it]

bicentenary ● *n.* (*pl.* **bicentenaries**)
1 a two-hundredth anniversary. **2** a
celebration of this. ● *adj.* of a bicentenary.
[*Say* by sen TENNA ree]

bicentennial ● *n.* a two-hundredth
anniversary. ● *adj.* **1** lasting two hundred
years or occurring every two hundred
years. **2** of or concerning a bicentennial.

biceps *n.* (*pl.* **biceps**) the flexor muscle at
the front of the upper arm or at the back of
the thigh.

bicker *v.* quarrel pettily.

bicolour *adj.* (also **bicoloured**) having
two colours.

biconvex *adj.* (esp. of a lens) convex on
both sides.

bicultural *adj.* having or involving two
cultures. □ **biculturalism** *n.*

bicuspid ● *adj.* having two cusps or
points. ● *n.* **1** the premolar tooth in
humans. **2** a tooth with two cusps.
[*Say* by CUSS pid]

bicycle ● *n.* a vehicle with two wheels
held in a frame one behind the other,
propelled by pedals and steered with
handlebars attached to the front wheel.
● *v.* (**bicycles, bicycled, bicycling**) ride
a bicycle. □ **bicyclist** *n.*

bid ● *v.* (**bids, bidding**) **1** (*past and past
participle* **bid**) (often foll. by *for, against*)
offer (a certain price). **2** try to get or do. **3** (*past*
bade, bid; *past participle* **bidden, bid**) utter
(greeting or farewell) to. ● *n.* **1 a** an offer.

b an act of bidding. **2** an attempt. □ **bidder** *n.* **bidding** *n.* [*For* BADE *say* BAYED *or* BAD]

biddable *adj.* obedient.

biddy *n.* (*pl.* **biddies**) *slang derogatory* a woman.

bide *v.* (**bides, bided, biding**) □ **bide one's time** await one's best opportunity.

bidet *n.* a low oval bathroom fixture used for washing the genital and anal regions. [*Say* bid AY]

biennial ● *adj.* **1** recurring every two years. **2** lasting two years. ● *n.* **1** a plant that takes two years to grow. **2** a biennial event. □ **biennially** *adv.* [*Say* by ENNY ul]

bier *n.* a movable frame on which a coffin or a corpse is placed or taken to a grave. [*sounds like* BEER]

biffy *n.* (*pl.* **biffies**) (esp. *West*) *informal* **1** an outhouse. **2** a toilet.

bifidum *n.* a bacterium often added to yogourt as being beneficial to the intestinal flora. [*Say* BIFF id'm]

bifocal ● *adj.* (of a lens) having one part for distant vision and one for near vision. ● *n.* (in *pl.*) bifocal glasses.

bifurcate *v.* (**bifurcates, bifurcated, bifurcating**) divide into two branches. □ **bifurcation** *n.* [*Say* BY fur kate]

big ● *adj.* (**bigger, biggest**) **1** large in size, amount, intensity, etc. **2 a** significant. **b** famous, popular. **3 a** grown up. **b** elder. **4** *informal* **a** boastful. **b** often *ironic* generous. **c** ambitious. ● *adv. informal* in a big manner, esp.: **1** effectively. **2** boastfully. **3** ambitiously. **4** to a considerable extent. ● *n.* (in *pl.*) the major baseball leagues. □ **come up big** *informal* perform successfully when relied upon to do so. **make it big** *informal* achieve great success. **too big for one's britches** (or **boots**) *slang* conceited. □ **bigness** *n.*

bigamy *n.* (*pl.* **bigamies**) the crime of marrying when one is lawfully married to another person. □ **bigamist** *n.* **bigamous** *adj.* [*Say* BIGGA me]

big band *n.* a large jazz or swing orchestra.

big bang *n.* **1** *Astronomy* the violent explosion of all matter from a state of high density and temperature, postulated as the origin of the universe. **2** any sudden or dramatic beginning of drastic change.

Big Brother *n.* **1** a strict dictator or government which keeps the populace under close observation. **2** an adult who befriends a fatherless child, esp. through an agency.

big cheese *n. informal* a very important person.

Bigfoot *n.* = SASQUATCH.

big game *n.* large animals hunted for sport.

big gun *n. informal* **1** an important person, company, etc. **2** *Sport* a high-scoring player.

big head *n. informal* a conceited person. □ **have a big head** be conceited. □ **big-headed** *adj.*

bighorn *n.* a N American wild sheep with large curving horns.

big house *n.* (also **Big House**) **1** *slang* a prison. **2** a communal dwelling, sometimes up to 18 m (60 ft.) in length, used by West Coast Aboriginal peoples.

bight *n.* **1** a curve or recess in a coastline, etc. **2** a loop of rope. [*Sounds like* BITE]

bigmouth *n.* a talkative or boastful person.

bigot *n.* a person intolerant of another's beliefs, race, politics, etc. □ **bigoted** *adj.* **bigotry** *n.* (*pl.* **bigotries**) [*Say* BIG it]

big picture *n.* (**the big picture**) an issue etc. viewed or understood as a whole.

big screen *n.* **1** the screen in a movie theatre. **2** (usu. as **the big screen**) movies collectively, esp. as seen in theatres.

big shot *n. informal* an important person.

Big Sister *n.* an adult who befriends a motherless child, esp. through an agency.

big-ticket *adj.* expensive.

big time *informal* ● *n.* the highest level of success in a profession, esp. entertainment. ● *adv.* as an intensifier. □ **big-time** *adj.* **big-timer** *n.*

big top *n.* the main tent of a circus.

bigwig *n.* (also **big wheel**) *informal* an important person.

bike *informal* ● *n.* a bicycle or motorcycle. ● *v.* (**bikes, biked, biking**) ride a bicycle or motorcycle. □ **biker** *n.*

bikini *n.* **1** a two-piece bathing suit for women. **2** a skimpy bathing suit for men. **3** (as an *adj.*) designating the pubic hairline, esp. of a woman. **4** (as an *adj.*) designating briefs that do not extend above the top of the pelvis.

bilateral *adj.* **1** having or relating to two sides. **2** involving two parties, countries, etc. □ **bilaterally** *adv.* [*Say* by LATERAL]

bile *n.* **1** a bitter alkaline fluid which aids digestion and is secreted by the liver. **2** bad temper.

bi-level ● *adj.* **1** having or functioning on two levels. **2** designating a style of two-storey house in which the lower storey is partially sunk below ground level, and the main entrance is between the two storeys. ● *n.* a bi-level house.

bilge *n.* **1 a** the lowest area inside a ship. **b** the area on the outer surface of a ship's hull where the flat bottom meets the vertical side. **2** (also **bilge water**) filthy

water that collects inside the bilge.
3 *informal* nonsense.

bilharzia *n.* a chronic and debilitating disease of Africa and S America caused by a parasitic flatworm. [*Say* bill HART see uh]

bilingual ● *adj.* **1** able to speak two languages, esp. fluently. **2** spoken or written in or involving two languages. **●** *n.* a bilingual person. □ **bilingualism** *n.* **bilingually** *adv.* [*Say* by LING gwul *or* by LING gyoo ul]

bilingualize *v.* (**bilingualizes**, **bilingualized**, **bilingualizing**) *Cdn* make bilingual. [*Say* by LING gwul ize *or* by LING gyoo ul ize]

bilious *adj.* **1** affected by or associated with nausea and vomiting. **2** bad-tempered. **3** of or like bile; nauseating. **4** (of a colour) lurid or sickly. [*Say* BILL yus *or* BILLY us]

bilk *v. informal* cheat or defraud.

bill¹ ● *n.* **1 a** a printed or written statement of charges for goods or services. **b** the amount owed. **2** = BILL OF EXCHANGE. **3** a draft of a proposed law. **4 a** a printed list, esp. a concert or theatre program. **b** the entertainment itself. **5** a banknote. **6 a** a poster. **b** = HANDBILL. **●** *v.* **1** present publicly. **2** invoice. □ **billable** *adj.*

bill² *n.* **1** the beak of a bird. **2** the muzzle of a platypus. **3** the visor on a baseball cap. □ **bill and coo** behave or talk in a loving, sentimental manner. □ **billed** *adj.*

billboard *n.* a large outdoor board for ads etc.

billet¹ ● *n.* a private home where a student, soldier, etc. is provided with accommodation, usu. without charge. **●** *v.* (**billets, billeted, billeting**) provide or take temporary free lodging.

billet² *n.* **1** a thick piece of wood, esp. one cut for firewood. **2** a metal bar.

billet-doux *n.* (*pl.* **billets-doux**) often *jocular* a love letter. [*Say* billy DOO *for the singular*, billy DOOZ *for the plural*]

billfold *n.* a wallet for keeping paper money.

billiards *n.* **1** any of various games played on an oblong cloth-covered table, with a cue used to strike a number of balls. **2** (**billiard**) (in *comb.*) used in billiards.

billing *n.* **1** *in senses of* BILL¹ *v.* **2** placement in a list of performers.

billion ● *n.* **1** a thousand million (1,000,000,000 or 10^9). **2** (in *pl.*) *informal* a very large number. **●** *adj.* that amount to a billion. □ **billionth** *adj.* & *n.*

billionaire *n.* a person possessing over a billion dollars, pounds, etc.

bill of exchange *n.* a written order to pay a sum on a given date to the signatory or a named payee.

bill of fare *n.* **1** a menu. **2** an offering of entertainment.

bill of health *n.* (**clean bill of health**) a declaration that a person or thing examined has been found to be free of illness or in good condition.

Bill of Rights *n.* (also **bill of rights**) a statement of the rights of a group of people.

billow ● *n.* a large, wavy mass of something, typically cloud, smoke, or steam. **●** *v.* **1** move or flow outward with a wavy motion. **2** (of fabric) fill with air and swell outwards. □ **billowy** *adj.*

billy *n.* (*pl.* **billies**) (also **billycan**) a tin or enamel cooking pot with a lid and wire handle, for outdoor use.

billy goat *n.* (also **billy**; *pl.* **billies**) a male goat.

bimbo *n.* (*pl.* **bimbos**) *slang* usu. *derogatory* (also **bimbette**) a young, sexually attractive, stupid woman.

bimonthly *adj. & adv.* occurring every two months or twice a month.

bin *n.* a large receptacle for storage or for depositing rubbish, recyclables, etc.

binary ● *adj.* **1** related to, composed of, or involving two things. **2** of a system of numbers with 2 as its base, using the digits 0 and 1. **●** *n.* (*pl.* **binaries**) **1** something having two parts. **2** a binary star. **3** a binary number. [*Say* BY na ree *or* BINE a ree]

binary number *n.* (also **binary digit**) one of two digits (usu. 0 or 1) in a binary system of notation.

binational *adj.* involving two nations.

bind ● *v.* (**binds, bound, binding**) **1** (often foll. by *to, on, together*) tie or fasten tightly. **2** restrain; put in bonds. **3 a** cause or cause to cohere. **b** hold by chemical bonding; combine with. **4** hold together as a single mass. **5** compel. **6 a** edge (fabric etc.) with braid etc. **b** fix together and fasten (pages) in a cover. **7** be prevented from moving freely. **●** *n.* **1** a difficult situation. **2** *informal* a nuisance; a restriction.

binder *n.* **1** a detachable cover for sheets of paper, magazines, etc. **2** a substance that acts cohesively.

binder twine *n.* a coarse twine used esp. to tie bales of hay, straw, etc.

binding ● *n.* **1** the strong covering of a book holding the sheets together. **2** the fastening attaching a boot to a ski. **3** a trim for binding raw edges of fabric. **●** *adj.* **1** legally enforceable. **2** causing or tending to stick together.

bindweed *n.* any of various twining plants of the morning glory family, with funnel-shaped flowers.

binge ● *n.* a period of uncontrolled indulgence in some activity, esp. eating or drinking. ● *v.* (**binges, binged, bingeing** or **binging**) eat, etc. in an uncontrolled way. □ **binger** *n.*

bingo ● *n.* a game for any number of players, each having a card of squares with numbers, which are marked off as numbers are randomly drawn by a caller. ● *interj.* indicating a sudden action or event, or satisfaction, etc., as in winning at bingo.

binocular ● *adj.* adapted for or using both eyes. ● *n.* = BINOCULARS.

binoculars *pl. n.* an optical instrument with lenses for each eye, for viewing distant objects.

binomial ● *n.* an algebraic expression of the sum or the difference of two terms. ● *adj.* consisting of two terms. □ **binomially** *adv.* [*Say* by NO me ul]

bio *n.* (*pl.* **bios**) *informal* **1** a biography. **2** biology.

bio- *comb. form* **1** life. **2** of living beings. **3** biology.

biochemistry *n.* the study of the chemical processes of living organisms. □ **biochemical** *adj.* **biochemist** *n.*

biocide *n.* a poisonous substance, esp. a pesticide, herbicide, etc. [*Say* BY a side]

biodegrade *v.* (**biodegrades, biodegraded, biodegrading**) decompose through the action of bacteria etc. □ **biodegradability** *n.* **biodegradable** *adj.* **biodegradation** *n.*

biodiversity *n.* the variety of plant and animal life in the world or in a particular habitat.

bioengineering *n.* **1** = GENETIC ENGINEERING. **2** the use of artificial tissues or organs in the body. **3** the use of organisms or biological processes in industry. □ **bioengineer** *n.* **bioengineered** *adj.*

bioethics *pl. n.* (treated as *sing.*) the ethics of medical and biological research and practice. □ **bioethicist** *n.*

biofeedback *n.* the use of electronic monitoring of a normally automatic bodily function, e.g. temperature, in order to train a person to acquire voluntary control of it.

biogeography *n.* the branch of biology that deals with the geographical distribution of plants and animals.

biography *n.* (*pl.* **biographies**) a written account of a person's life, usu. by another. □ **biographer** *n.* **biographical** *adj.*

biohazard *n.* a risk to human health or the environment arising from biological work.

bioinformatics *n.* the science of collecting and analysing complex biological data such as genetic codes.

biological ● *adj.* **1** (also **biologic**) of or relating to biology or living organisms. **2** (of a parent) related by blood. **3** (of warfare, etc.) using harmful micro-organisms. ● *n.* a biological product, esp. one used therapeutically or in biological control. □ **biologically** *adv.*

biological clock *n.* **1** an innate mechanism controlling the rhythmic physiological activities of an organism, e.g. sleep. **2** an innate mechanism regulating the aging process, esp. in relation to the ability to bear children.

biology *n.* (*pl.* **biologies**) **1** the study of living organisms. **2** the plants and animals of an area. □ **biologist** *n.*

bioluminescence *n.* the emission of light by living organisms such as the firefly and glow-worm. □ **bioluminescent** *adj.* [*Say* bio looma NESS ince]

biomass *n.* **1** the total quantity or weight of organisms in a given area or of a given species. **2** non-fossilized organic matter (esp. regarded as fuel).

biometrics *n.* **1** the application of statistical analysis to biological investigation. **2** technologies for personal identification that use measurements of a part of the human body or characteristics, e.g. fingerprints, irises, keystroke rhythms, voice patterns, etc. □ **biometric** *adj.*

bionic *adj.* having artificial body parts or superhuman powers resulting from these. □ **bionically** *adv.* [*Say* by ON ick]

biophysics *pl. n.* (treated as *sing.*) the science of the application of the laws of physics to biological phenomena. □ **biophysical** *adj.*

biopic *n.* *informal* a biographical film. [*Say* BIO pick]

biopsy ● *n.* (*pl.* **biopsies**) an examination of tissue taken from a living body to discover the presence or extent of a disease. ● *v.* (**biopsies, biopsied, biopsying**) examine for diagnostic purposes. [*Say* BY op see]

biosphere *n.* the regions of the earth's crust and atmosphere occupied by living organisms.

biotech *n.* *informal* biotechnology.

biotechnology *n.* (*pl.* **biotechnologies**) the use of micro-organisms in industry and medicine to produce antibiotics, hormones, etc. □ **biotechnological** *adj.*

biotin *n.* a vitamin of the B complex, found

esp. in egg yolk, liver, and yeast. [*Say* BIO tin]

bipartisan *adj.* of or involving two (esp. political) parties. □ **bipartisanship** *n.*

bipartite *adj.* **1** shared by or involving two parties. **2** consisting of two parts. [*Say* by PAR tite]

biped ● *n.* an animal that walks on two feet. ● *adj.* having two legs. □ **bipedal** *adj.* **bipedalism** *n.* [*Say* BY ped]

biplane *n.* an early type of airplane having two sets of wings, one above the other.

bipolar *adj.* **1** having two poles or extremities. **2** characterized by two extremes. **3** (of psychiatric illness) characterized by both manic and depressive episodes. □ **bipolarity** *n.*

birch *n.* (*pl.* **birches**) **1** a slender tree with thin, peeling bark. **2** (also **birchwood**) its hard wood. **3** a bundle of birch twigs used for flogging.

birchbark *n.* the bark of the birch tree, traditionally used by some Algonquian peoples to make canoes.

bird *n.* **1** a feathered, warm-blooded vertebrate, having a beak and wings, laying eggs, and usu. able to fly. **2** *informal* a person of a specified type. **3** a shuttlecock. **4** *slang* a gesture of contempt made by raising the middle finger.

birdbrain *n.* *informal* a silly or stupid person. □ **birdbrained** *adj.*

bird course *n.* *Cdn derogatory slang* a university or high-school course requiring little work or ability.

bird dog *n.* **1** a hunting dog trained to retrieve birds. **2** *informal* a scout for a sports team etc.

birder *n.* a birdwatcher.

bird flu *n.* avian influenza, esp. disease caused in humans by an avian influenza virus or a closely related virus.

birdhouse *n.* a box designed to attract nesting birds.

birdie ● *n.* **1** *informal* a small bird. **2** *Golf* a score of one stroke under par at any hole. **3** a shuttlecock. ● *v.* (**birdies, birdied, birdieing**) *Golf* play (a hole) in one stroke under par.

birding *n.* birdwatching.

birdlife *n.* the birds of a region collectively.

bird of paradise *n.* (*pl.* **birds of paradise**) any of various birds found chiefly in New Guinea, the males having brilliantly coloured plumage.

bird of prey *n.* (*pl.* **birds of prey**) a bird which hunts animals for food.

birdseed *n.* a blend of seed used in bird feeders.

bird's-eye view *n.* **1** an overhead view (of

a landscape etc.). **2** a general overview (of a subject etc.).

birdsong *n.* the musical call or sound of a bird.

birdwatcher *n.* a person who observes birds in their natural surroundings. □ **birdwatching** *n.*

birl *v.* cause (a floating log) to rotate by using one's feet; spin. □ **birling** *n.* [*Rhymes with* GIRL]

birth ● *n.* **1** the emergence of an infant or other young from the body of its mother. **2** the beginning or coming into existence of something. **3** origin, ancestry. **4** (as an *adj.*) designating the parent who gave birth to or fathered a child. ● *v.* give birth to. □ **birthing** *n.*

birth control *n.* the practice or methods of preventing pregnancy, esp. by contraception.

birthday *n.* the anniversary of a birth.

birthmark *n.* an unusual brown or red mark on one's body at or from birth.

birthplace *n.* **1** the place where a person was born. **2** a place of origin or commencement.

birthright *n.* a right of possession or privilege belonging to one from birth.

birthstone *n.* a gemstone popularly associated with the month of one's birth.

biscotti *pl. n.* hard, dry, Italian cookies. [*Say* biss COTTY]

biscuit *n.* **1** a dry, hard, flat, baked foodstuff. **2** = TEA BISCUIT. □ **have had the biscuit** *Cdn slang* be no longer good for anything; be done for.

bisect *v.* divide into two equal parts.

bisexual ● *adj.* **1** sexually attracted to persons of both sexes. **2** *Biology* having characteristics of both sexes. ● *n.* a bisexual person. □ **bisexuality** *n.*

bishop *n.* **1** a senior member of the Christian clergy, usu. in charge of a diocese. **2** a chess piece which is moved diagonally and has the upper part shaped like a mitre.

bishopric *n.* **1** the office of a bishop. **2** a diocese. [*Say* BISHOP rick]

bismarck *n.* **1** *Alberta, Sask., & US Midwest* a sugar-coated jam-filled doughnut. **2** *Man.* a cream-filled doughnut, often with a chocolate glaze. [*Say* BIZ mark]

bismuth *n.* a brittle reddish-white metallic element. [*Say* BIZ muth]

bison *n.* (*pl.* **bison**) a heavily built bovine with a high shoulder hump, shaggy hair, and a large head with short horns. [*Say* BIZE in *or* BICE in]

bisque[1] *n.* a rich soup usu. made from shellfish. [*Say* BISK]

bisque² *n.* a variety of white porcelain that has not been glazed. [*Say* BISK]

bistro *n.* (*pl.* **bistros**) a small French restaurant with an informal atmosphere. [*Say* BEE stroe *or* BIS troe]

bit¹ *n.* **1** a small piece or quantity. **2 a** a fair amount. **b** *informal* somewhat. **3** a short time or distance. □ **bit by bit** gradually. **do one's bit** *informal* make a useful contribution.

bit² *past of* BITE.

bit³ *n.* **1** a metal mouthpiece on a bridle, used to control a horse. **2** a (usu. metal) tool or piece for boring or drilling. □ **chomp** (or **champ** or **chafe**) **at the bit** be restlessly impatient. **take the bit between** (or **in**) **one's teeth** begin to tackle a task in a determined way.

bit⁴ *n. Computing* a unit of information expressed as a 0 or 1 in binary code.

bitch ● *n.* (*pl.* **bitches**) **1** a female dog or other canine animal. **2** *offensive slang* a malicious, spiteful, or unpleasant woman. ● *v.* (**bitches, bitched, bitching**) *slang* **1** make spiteful comments. **2** complain.

bitchy *adj.* (**bitchier, bitchiest**) *slang* spiteful, bad-tempered. □ **bitchily** *adv.* **bitchiness** *n.*

bite ● *v.* (**bites**; *past* **bit**; *past participle* **bitten; biting**) **1** cut or puncture using the teeth. **2** wound with a sting, fangs, etc. **3** grip. **4** (of fish) accept bait. **5** have an adverse effect. **6** *Curling* (of a rock) come to a stop. **7** *slang* be extremely bad. ● *n.* **1** an act of biting. **2** a wound or sore made by biting. **3 a** a mouthful of food. **b** a snack. **4** the taking of bait by a fish. **5** pungency. **6** incisiveness. **7** a pithy quotation. **8** a portion exacted. **9** = OCCLUSION 1. □ **bite the bullet** *informal* behave bravely or stoically. **bite the dust** *slang* **1** die. **2** fail. **bite one's tongue** refrain from speaking, esp. reluctantly. **once bitten twice shy** an unpleasant experience induces caution. □ **biter** *n.*

biting *adj.* **1** that bites. **2** stinging; intensely cold. **3** sharp. □ **bitingly** *adv.*

bitmap *n.* **1** a representation, e.g. of a computer memory, in which each item is represented by one bit. **2** a graphic display formed by assigning a bit value to each individual pixel. □ **bitmapped** *adj.*

bit part *n.* a minor acting role.

bitten *past participle of* BITE.

bitter ● *adj.* **1** having a sharp pungent taste. **2 a** caused by or showing resentment. **b** difficult to accept. **3 a** virulent. **b** piercingly cold. ● *n.* (in *pl.*) liquor with a bitter flavour used in cocktails. □ **bitterly** *adv.* **bitterness** *n.*

bittern *n.* a marsh bird of the heron family, with a booming call.

bittersweet ● *adj.* **1** sweet with a bitter aftertaste. **2** arousing pleasure tinged with sorrow. ● *n.* a N American climbing vine.

bitty *adj.* (**bittier, bittiest**) *informal* very small.

bitumen *n.* any of various tar-like mixtures derived from petroleum and used for road surfacing and roofing. □ **bituminous** *adj.* [*Say* bit YOU m'n *or* bit OO m'n]

bivalve ● *n.* an aquatic mollusc which has a compressed body enclosed within two hinged shells, e.g. an oyster. ● *adj.* **1** with a hinged double shell. **2** (of a seed capsule) having two valves.

bivouac ● *n.* a temporary open encampment. ● *v.* (**bivouacs, bivouacked, bivouacking**) camp in a bivouac. [*Say* BIVVA wack]

biweekly ● *adv.* **1** every two weeks. **2** twice a week. ● *adj.* produced or occurring biweekly. ● *n.* (*pl.* **biweeklies**) a biweekly periodical.

biz *n. informal* business.

bizarre *adj.* strange; eccentric. □ **bizarrely** *adv.* **bizarreness** *n.*

blab *v.* (**blabs, blabbed, blabbing**) *informal* **1** reveal secrets by indiscreet talk. **2** talk foolishly.

blabber *informal* ● *n.* (also **blabbermouth**) a person who blabs. ● *v.* (often foll. by *on*) talk foolishly.

black ● *adj.* **1** of the darkest colour. **2** very or completely dark. **3** (also **Black**) relating to any of various peoples having dark-coloured skin. **4** angry, threatening. **5** disgraceful, wicked. **6** depressed. **7** portending trouble or difficulty. **8** (of humour) with sinister as well as comic import. **9** without milk. ● *n.* **1** a black colour or pigment. **2** black clothes or material. **3** the credit side of an account. **4** (also **Black**) a black person. ● *v.* make black. □ **black out 1** effect a blackout on. **2** undergo a blackout. **3** obscure with a black mark. □ **blackish** *adj.* **blackly** *adv.* **blackness** *n.*

black and blue *adj.* discoloured by bruises.

black and white ● *n.* writing or printing. ● *adj.* **1** (of film etc.) not in colour. **2** consisting of extremes only, oversimplified.

blackball *v.* **1** reject in a vote. **2** exclude.

black bear *n.* a bear with black or blue-black fur.

black belt *n.* **1** a black belt worn by a martial arts expert. **2** a person qualified to wear this.

blackberry n. (pl. **blackberries**) **1** a thorny shrub related to the raspberry, bearing white or pink flowers. **2** a black fleshy edible fruit of this plant.

blackbird n. any of various birds with mainly black plumage.

black blizzard n. Cdn a dust storm of soil blown by high winds on the prairies.

blackboard n. a board with a dark surface for writing on with chalk.

black box n. a flight recorder in an aircraft.

blackcurrant n. **1** a shrub bearing flowers in racemes. **2** the small dark edible berry of this plant.

Black Death n. a pandemic of bubonic and pneumonic plague that killed perhaps one third of the population of Europe in the mid-14th century and resurfaced throughout the next few centuries.

black diamond n. **1** (in pl.) coal. **2** (as an adj.) designating a particularly difficult ski run.

blacken v. **1** make or become black. **2** defame.

blackened adj. (of food) covered with spices and cooked quickly over high heat.

black eye n. discoloured skin around the eye, esp. resulting from a blow.

black-eyed Susan n. any of several daisy-like plants having yellow flowers with dark centres.

blackfly n. (pl. **blackflies**) any of various gnat-like flies.

Blackfoot n. **1** (pl. **Blackfoot** or **Blackfeet**) a member of a group of N American Aboriginal peoples, now largely found in S Alberta and Montana. **2** = SIKSIKA n. **3** their Algonquian language. □ **Blackfoot** adj.

Black Forest cake n. a layered chocolate cake with a filling of cherries and whipped cream.

Black Forest ham n. a variety of sweetened and smoked ham.

blackguard n. a man who behaves dishonourably. [Say BLAG ard or BLAG erd or BLACK guard]

blackhead n. a black-tipped plug of fatty matter in a skin follicle.

black hole n. **1** a region of space having a gravitational field so intense that no matter and radiation can escape. **2** any inescapable void or place of confinement.

black ice n. thin hard transparent ice, esp. on a road surface or body of water.

blackjack n. **1** a card game in which players try to acquire cards with a face value exceeding the dealer's but no more than 21. **2** a flexible bludgeon of leather-covered lead.

blacklist ● n. a list of persons under suspicion, in disfavour, etc. ● v. put the name of (a person) on a blacklist.

black magic n. magic involving supposed invocation of evil spirits.

blackmail ● n. **1** an extortion of payment in return for not disclosing compromising information etc. **2** the manipulation of someone's feelings to force them to do something. ● v. use blackmail. □ **blackmailer** n.

black mark n. a record of a person's misdemeanour.

black market n. an illegal trade in officially controlled items. □ **black marketeer** n.

blackout n. **1** a loss of vision, consciousness, or memory. **2** a loss of power, radio reception, etc. **3** a compulsory period of darkness as a precaution against air raids. **4** a temporary suppression of the release of information. **5** a period in which discounts, esp. on airfare, do not apply.

blackpoll n. a N American warbler, the male of which has a black crown in spring.

Black Rod n. (also **Usher of the Black Rod** or hist. **Gentleman Usher of the Black Rod**) (in Canada) the principal usher of the Senate, who summons the Commons to the Senate at the opening of Parliament.

black sheep n. informal an unsatisfactory member of a family, group, etc.; an outcast.

blackshirt n. a member of a militant fascist organization.

blacksmith n. **1** a smith who works in iron. **2** = FARRIER 1. □ **blacksmithing** n.

blacktail n. (also **black-tailed deer**) = MULE DEER.

black tea n. tea fully fermented before drying.

blackthorn n. **1** a N American hawthorn. **2** a thorny European shrub, bearing white flowers before small blue-black fruits.

black tie n. **1** a black bow tie worn with a tuxedo etc. **2** (as an adj.) an occasion requiring that men wear a tuxedo (compare WHITE TIE).

blacktop n. asphalt.

Black Watch n. **1** the Royal Highland Regiment of the Canadian Forces. **2** a very dark green and navy blue tartan.

black widow n. a venomous black spider, the female of which usu. devours the male after mating.

bladder n. **1** any of various sacs in some animals, containing urine, bile, or air, esp.

the urinary bladder. **2** an inflated pericarp or vesicle in various plants.

blade ● n. **1 a** the flat cutting edge of a knife, chisel, etc. **b** a razor blade. **2** the flattened functional part of an oar, skate, hockey stick, etc. **3** the flat, narrow leaf of grass and cereals. **4** a cut of beef from behind the neck and above the shoulder. ● v. (**blades, bladed, blading**) = ROLLERBLADE v. □ **bladed** adj. (also in comb.). **blader** n. **blading** n.

blah informal ● n. **1** (also **blah-blah**) pretentious nonsense. **2** (in pl.) a general feeling of depression. ● adj. **1** dull, bland. **2** lacking in enthusiasm. ● interj. (usu. **blah blah blah**) indicating verbose, tedious speech or writing.

blam ● n. a loud sharp sound, as of a gunshot or an explosion. ● v. (**blams, blammed, blamming**) make such a loud sound.

blame ● v. (**blames, blamed, blaming**) **1** assign fault or responsibility to. **2** (foll. by on) assign the responsibility for (an error or wrong) to a person etc. ● n. **1** responsibility for a bad result. **2** the act of blaming. □ **be to blame** be responsible. □ **blameable** adj.

blameless adj. innocent; free from blame. □ **blamelessly** adv. **blamelessness** n.

blameworthy adj. deserving blame. □ **blameworthiness** n.

blanch v. (**blanches, blanched, blanching**) **1** make or become white or pale. **2 a** peel (almonds etc.) by scalding. **b** immerse (vegetables or meat) briefly in boiling water.

bland adj. **1** lacking strong flavour. **2** lacking strong features or qualities. **3** showing no strong emotion. □ **blandly** adv. **blandness** n.

blandishment n. a flattering statement used to persuade or coax.

blank ● adj. **1 a** not written or printed on. **b** containing no recorded sound etc. **2** not filled; empty. **3 a** uninterested; expressionless. **b** void of incident or result. **c** puzzled, nonplussed. **d** having (temporarily) no knowledge or understanding. **4** complete, downright. **5** Curling (of an end) played without either rink scoring a point. ● n. **1** an empty space or period of time. **2** a space left to be filled in a document. **3** a cartridge containing gunpowder but no bullet. **4** euphemism used in place of a noun regarded as coarse. ● v. **1** screen, obscure. **2** Sport defeat without allowing to score. **3** Curling play (an end) without either rink scoring a point. □ **draw a blank** provoke no successful

response; fail. □ **blankly** adv. **blankness** n.

blank cheque n. **1** a cheque with the amount left for the payee to fill in. **2** informal unlimited freedom of action.

blanket ● n. **1** a large piece of woollen or other material used esp. as a bed cover. **2** a type of woollen cloth similar to a woollen blanket. **3** a thick mass or layer. **4** (often as an adj.) traditional Indian life or culture. ● adj. inclusive. ● v. (**blankets, blanketed, blanketing**) cover as if with a blanket.

blank verse n. verse without rhyme.

blare ● v. (**blares, blared, blaring**) make a loud harsh sound. ● n. a loud harsh sound.

blarney ● n. talk which aims to charm or flatter. ● v. (**blarneys, blarneyed, blarneying**) flatter.

blasé adj. indifferent or not impressed as a result of overexposure. [Say blaw ZAY]

blaspheme v. (**blasphemes, blasphemed, blaspheming**) utter blasphemy. □ **blasphemer** n. [Say blass FEEM]

blasphemous adj. sacrilegious against God or sacred things. [Say BLASSFA muss]

blasphemy n. (pl. **blasphemies**) **1** irreverent talk about God or sacred things. **2** something shocking that deeply offends people's idea of what is correct. [Say BLASSFA me]

blast ● n. **1** a strong gust of wind. **2** an explosion, or a destructive wave of air spreading outwards from it. **3** a single loud note emitted by a horn or whistle. **4** informal a good time. ● v. **1** blow up with explosives. **2** create out of or from rocks etc. by blasting. **3** produce loud noise. **4** informal reprimand severely. **5** informal shoot. **6** Sport hit or throw forcefully. **7** destroy, ruin. □ **full blast** informal working at maximum speed. **blast from the past** informal a forcefully nostalgic thing. **blast off** take off from a launching site. □ **blaster** n.

blast furnace n. a smelting furnace into which compressed hot air is driven.

blast-off n. the launching of a rocket etc.

blatant adj. **1** flagrant. **2** completely lacking in subtlety. □ **blatancy** n. **blatantly** adv. [Say BLAY t'nt]

blather ● n. foolish chatter. ● v. chatter foolishly. □ **blathering** n.

blaze[1] ● n. **1** a bright flame or fire. **2** a bright light. **3** an intense outburst (of passion etc.). **4 a** a glow of colour. **b** a bright display. ● v. (**blazes, blazed, blazing**) **1** burn or shine fiercely or brightly. **2** be brilliantly lighted. **3** be

consumed with anger, excitement, etc.
4 show bright colours or light. **5** esp. *Sport* move quickly. □ **blaze away** fire continuously with rifles. **go to blazes** *informal* go to hell.

blaze² ● *n.* **1** a white mark on an animal's face. **2** a mark made on a tree to identify a route. ● *v.* **(blazes, blazed, blazing)** mark (a tree). □ **blaze a trail** (or **path**) **1** mark out a path. **2** be the first to do something.

blazer *n.* **1** a jacket worn as part of a uniform. **2** a plain jacket of a dark solid colour that is not part of a suit.

blazon *v.* display prominently or vividly. [*Say* BLAYZ'n]

bleach ● *v.* **(bleaches, bleached, bleaching)** whiten by a chemical process or by exposure to sunlight. ● *n.* (*pl.* **bleaches**) a bleaching substance used domestically for whitening laundry and as a disinfectant.

bleacher *n.* (usu. in *pl.*) uncovered, tiered bench seating at a sports ground, etc.

bleak *adj.* **1** bare, exposed. **2** unpromising; dreary. **3** cold or harsh. □ **bleakly** *adv.* **bleakness** *n.*

bleary *adj.* **(blearier, bleariest)** (of the eyes) dull or not focused from sleep or tiredness. □ **blearily** *adv.*

bleat ● *v.* **1** (of sheep, goats, etc.) give a tremulous cry. **2** speak or say feebly or plaintively. ● *n.* **1** the sound made by a sheep, goat, etc. **2** a foolish or feeble statement.

bleed ● *v.* **(bleeds, bled, bleeding)** **1** emit blood. **2** draw blood from surgically. **3** extort money from. **4** spend or lose money in large quantities. **5** (of a plant) emit sap. **6 a** (of dye) come out in water. **b** (of colour) run. **7** allow (fluid or gas) to escape from a closed system through a valve etc. ● *n.* an instance of bleeding. □ **one's heart bleeds** usu. *ironic* one is very sorrowful. □ **bleeder** *n.*

bleeding heart *n. informal* a person perceived as overly sentimental, esp. in regard to social problems.

bleep ● *n.* **1** a high-pitched sound made electronically. **2** this sound or the word itself used as a substitute for an expletive. ● *v.* **1** make such a sound. **2** (often foll. by *out*) substitute a bleep for.

blemish ● *n.* (*pl.* **blemishes**) a flaw or defect. ● *v.* **(blemishes, blemished, blemishing)** spoil the perfection of.

blend ● *v.* **1** mix and combine with something else. **2** merge well or imperceptibly. ● *n.* a mixture.

blender *n.* **1** an electric device for chopping or liquefying food. **2** a person or thing that blends.

bless *v.* **(blesses, blessed, blessing)** **1** confer, invoke, or bestow divine favour on. **2** consecrate. **3** call holy; adore. **4** **bless oneself** make the sign of the cross. **5** thank. **6** make happy or successful. □ **(God) bless you! 1** an exclamation of endearment, gratitude, etc. **2** an exclamation made to a person who has just sneezed.

blessed *adj.* **1** sanctified, revered. **2** bringing pleasure or relief. **3** *euphemism* cursed; damned □ **blessedly** *adv.* **blessedness** *n.* [*Say* BLESS id *or* BLEST]

blessing *n.* **1** the act of declaring, seeking, or bestowing (esp. divine) favour. **2** grace said before or after a meal. **3** a thing one is glad of. □ **blessing in disguise** an apparent misfortune with good results.

blew *past of* BLOW¹.

blight ● *n.* **1** any of various plant diseases, esp. caused by fungi. **2** any insect or parasite causing such a disease. **3** a pervasive destructive force. ● *v.* **1** affect a plant with blight. **2** harm or destroy.

blimp *n.* **1** a small non-rigid airship. **2** *informal* an obese person.

blind ● *adj.* **1** lacking the power of sight. **2** ignorant; lacking information. **3** not governed by purpose or reason. **4** concealed, obscured. **5** closed at one end. **6** (of a test) conducted so that the subject or examiner cannot prejudice the results. ● *v.* **1** deprive of sight. **2** rob of judgment. ● *n.* **1 a** a screen for a window. **b** an awning over a store window. **2** something meant to hide the truth. **3** any obstruction to sight or light. ● *adv.* **1** *Aviation* using instruments only. **2** without guidance. **3** to a great extent. □ **turn a blind eye to** pretend not to notice. □ **blindly** *adv.* **blindness** *n.*

blind alley *n.* a course of action leading nowhere.

blind date *n.* a social engagement between two people who have not previously met.

blinder *n. informal* (usu. in *pl.*) = BLINKER *n.* 1.

blindfold ● *v.* deprive (a person) of sight by covering the eyes, esp. with a tied cloth. ● *n.* a bandage or cloth used to blindfold. ● *adj. & adv.* **1** with eyes bandaged. **2** without care or circumspection.

blinding ● *n.* the act of causing blindness. ● *adj.* **1** causing inability to see. **2** dazzlingly bright. **3** extreme; severe. □ **blindingly** *adv.*

blind man's bluff *n.* a game in which a blindfold player tries to catch others while being pushed about by them.

blind side ● *n.* a direction in which one cannot see the approach of danger etc. ● *v.* (usu. **blindside, blindsides, blindsided, blindsiding**) **1** attack or strike on the blind side. **2** surprise.

blind spot *n.* **1** the point of entry of the optic nerve on the retina, insensitive to light. **2** an area where vision is obscured. **3** an area in which a person lacks understanding.

blind trust *n.* a trust independently administering the private business affairs of a person in public office.

bling *n.* (also **bling-bling**) *slang* flashy and expensive clothing or jewellery.

blink ● *v.* **1** shut and open the eyes quickly. **2** look with eyes opening and shutting, esp. in bewilderment. **3** (of a light) flash on and off. **4** back down. ● *n.* **1** an act of blinking. **2** a momentary gleam or glimpse. □ **on the blink** *informal* out of order. **the blink of an eye** a very short time.

blinker ● *n.* **1** (usu. in *pl.*) either of a pair of screens attached to a horse's bridle to prevent it from seeing sideways. **2** a device that blinks, esp. a vehicle's turn signal. ● *v.* obscure with blinkers.

blinkered *adj.* narrow-minded, prejudiced.

blip ● *n.* **1** a short bleep. **2** a small image of an object on a radar screen. **3** a temporary movement in statistics. ● *v.* (**blips, blipped, blipping**) **1** make a blip. **2** (of figures etc.) rise suddenly and temporarily.

bliss *n.* **1** perfect happiness. **2** a state of spiritual blessedness. □ **blissful** *n.* **blissfully** *adv.*

blissed-out *adj.* *slang* in a state of bliss.

blister ● *n.* **1** a small bubble on the skin filled with serum and caused by friction, burning, etc. **2** a similar swelling on any other surface. ● *v.* **1** raise a blister on. **2** form a blister or blisters.

blistering *adj.* very harsh, intense, or fast. □ **blisteringly** *adv.*

blithe *adj.* **1** happy. **2** careless, casual. □ **blithely** *adv.* **blitheness** *n.* [*Rhymes either with* WRITHE *or with the name* SMYTH]

blitz *informal* ● *n.* **1** an intensive or sudden (esp. aerial) attack. **2** *informal* any sudden or concentrated effort. ● *v.* (**blitzes, blitzed, blitzing**) **1** attack, damage, etc. by a blitz. **2** *Football* charge into the offensive backfield.

blitzed *adj.* *slang* drunk.

blitzkrieg *n.* an intense military campaign intended to bring about a swift victory. [*Say* BLITS kreeg]

blizzard *n.* a severe snowstorm with high winds.

bloat *v.* inflate, swell.

blob *n.* **1** a drop of a thick liquid or sticky substance. **2** a roundish mass or shape. □ **blobby** *adj.*

bloc *n.* **1** a group formed to promote a particular purpose. **2** (**Bloc**) (in Canada) = BLOC QUÉBÉCOIS.

block ● *n.* **1** a piece of hard material, esp. with flat sides. **2** a hollow usu. rectangular masonry building unit. **3 a** a large building, esp. when subdivided. **b** = CELLBLOCK. **4 a** an area bounded by (usu. four) streets. **b** the length of one side of this. **5** an obstruction. **6** the metal casting containing the cylinders of an internal combustion engine. **7** a pulley or system of pulleys mounted in a case. **8** a large quantity of things treated as a unit. **9** (also **auction block**) a place or facility for the auction of goods. ● *v.* **1** prevent free movement in. **2** hinder or prevent. ● *adj.* treating (many similar things) as one unit. □ **block out 1 a** shut out. **b** exclude from memory. **2** sketch roughly; plan. □ **blocky** *adj.*

blockade ● *n.* the surrounding or blocking of access to a place to prevent entry and exit of supplies etc. ● *v.* (**blockades, blockaded, blockading**) subject to a blockade.

blockage *n.* an obstruction.

block and tackle *n.* a system of pulleys and ropes, esp. for lifting.

blockbuster *n.* **1** a commercially successful film, book, etc. **2** (also **blockbuster trade**) *Sport* a trade involving several usu. well-known players.

block capitals *pl. n.* capital block letters.

blocker *n.* **1** a person or thing that blocks. **2** *Hockey* a glove with a rectangular pad worn by a goalie to protect the hand holding the stick. **3** *Football* a player whose role is to block the opponent's play.

blockhead *n.* a stupid person. □ **blockheaded** *adj.*

block heater *n.* an electric heater used to warm the engine block of a motor vehicle in winter.

block letters *pl. n.* letters written separately and without serifs.

Block Parent *n.* esp. *Cdn proprietary* one of a number of police-screened volunteers who offer their home, identified by an easily recognizable sign, as an emergency refuge to children or others who are lost or in danger.

Bloc Québécois *n.* a federal political party advocating Quebec separatism, founded in 1990.

blog ● *n.* = WEBLOG. ● *v.* maintain a weblog. □**blogger** *n.*

blond (also **blonde**) ● *adj.* light-coloured; fair. ● *n.* a person with fair hair and skin. □**blondish** *adj.* **blondness** *n.*

Blood *n.* **1** a member of an Aboriginal people of S Alberta. **2** the Algonquian language of the Blood.

blood ● *n.* **1** a usu. red liquid circulating in the arteries and veins of vertebrates that carries oxygen and carbon dioxide. **2** a corresponding fluid in invertebrates. **3** bloodshed, esp. killing. **4** passion, temperament. **5** family descent. **6** a relationship; relations. ● *v.* initiate by experience. □**bad blood** ill feeling. **in one's blood** inherent in one's character. **make one's blood boil** infuriate one. **make one's blood run cold** horrify one. **new** (or **fresh**) **blood** new members admitted to a group. **taste blood** be stimulated by an early success. **young blood** a younger member or members of a group.

blood bank *n.* **1** a place where supplies of blood or plasma for transfusion are stored. **2** any supply of blood for transfusions.

bloodbath *n.* a massacre.

blood brother *n.* a brother by birth or by the ceremonial mingling of blood.

blood-curdling *adj.* horrifying.

blood donor clinic *n.* Cdn a usu. temporary location where people can give blood.

blood group *n.* = BLOOD TYPE.

bloodhound *n.* a large hound of a breed used in tracking, having a very keen sense of smell.

bloodless *adj.* **1** drained of colour. **2** without bloodshed. **3** lacking vitality. □**bloodlessly** *adv.*

bloodletting *n.* **1** the removal of some of a person's blood. **2** bloodshed. **3** *informal* (in a workplace etc.) bitter quarrelling, esp. accompanied by reductions in staff.

bloodline *n.* (usu. in *pl.*) pedigree.

blood money *n.* **1** money paid to the next of kin of a person who has been killed. **2** money paid to a hired murderer.

blood poisoning *n.* a diseased state caused by the presence of micro-organisms or toxins in the blood.

blood pressure *n.* the pressure of the blood in the circulatory system, often measured for diagnosis.

blood relative *n.* (also **blood relation**) a relative by birth.

bloodshed *n.* the killing or wounding of people.

bloodshot *adj.* (of an eyeball) tinged with blood.

blood sport *n.* sport involving the wounding or killing of animals.

bloodstain *n.* a discoloration caused by blood. □**bloodstained** *adj.*

bloodstream *n.* blood in circulation.

bloodsucker *n.* an animal or insect that sucks blood. □**bloodsucking** *adj.*

blood sugar *n.* **1** the amount of glucose in the blood. **2** the glucose itself.

bloodthirsty *adj.* (**bloodthirstier**, **bloodthirstiest**) **1** having a longing for blood. **2** taking pleasure in killing or violence.

blood type *n.* any one of the various types of human blood determining compatibility in transfusion.

blood vessel *n.* a vein, artery, or capillary carrying blood.

bloody ● *adj.* (**bloodier**, **bloodiest**) **1 a** of or like blood. **b** covered with blood. **2 a** involving bloodshed. **b** cruel. **3** *informal* expressing annoyance or antipathy, or as an intensive. ● *adv. informal* as an intensive. ● *v.* (**bloodies**, **bloodied**, **bloodying**) make bloody.

Bloody Caesar *n.* Cdn a drink composed of vodka and tomato clam cocktail, garnished with celery.

Bloody Mary *n.* (*pl.* **Bloody Marys**) a drink composed of vodka and tomato juice.

bloom ● *n.* **1 a** a flower. **b** the state of flowering. **2** a state of loveliness; the prime. **3 a** (of the complexion) a flush; a glow. **b** a delicate powdery surface deposit on fruit etc. **4** a scum formed by the rapid proliferation of microscopic algae on water. ● *v.* **1** bear flowers. **2 a** come into, or remain in, full beauty. **b** flourish; be healthy. □**bloomer** *n.*

bloomers *pl. n.* **1** women's loose-fitting knee-length underpants. **2** *informal* any women's underpants.

blooming *adj.* flourishing; healthy.

bloop Baseball ● *v.* hit (a ball) as a blooper. ● *n.* a blooper (also as an *adj.*).

blooper *n. informal* **1** an embarrassing blunder. **2** Baseball **a** a fly ball hit just beyond the infield. **b** a ball thrown high by the pitcher.

Bloquiste *n.* Cdn a member of the Bloc Québécois. [Say block EEST]

blossom ● *n.* **1** a flower or a mass of flowers, esp. of a fruit tree. **2** the stage or time of flowering. ● *v.* **1** open into flower. **2** reach a promising stage.

blot ● *n.* **1** a spot or stain of ink etc. **2** a moral defect in an otherwise good character. **3** any disfigurement. ● *v.* (**blots**,

blotted, blotting) 1 a stain with ink.
b make blots. **2 a** use blotting paper or
other absorbent material to absorb (liquid).
b (of blotting paper etc.) soak up (liquid).
3 disgrace. □ **blot out 1 a** obliterate.
b obscure. **2** destroy.

blotch ● *n.* (*pl.* **blotches**) **1** a discoloured
or inflamed patch on the skin. **2** an
irregular patch of colour. **●** *v.* (**blotches,
blotched, blotching**) cover with
blotches. □ **blotchy** *adj.* (**blotchier,
blotchiest**)

blotter *n.* **1** a pad of blotting paper. **2** a
record of arrests and charges in a police
station.

blotting paper *n.* absorbent paper used
for soaking up excess ink.

blouse *n.* a woman's upper garment,
resembling a shirt. [*Rhymes either with*
PLOWS *or with* MOUSE]

blow¹ ● *v.* (**blows, blew, blown,
blowing**) **1 a** (of the wind or air) move
along. **b** drive or be driven by an air
current. **2** send out air, esp. through
pursed lips. **3** sound or be sounded by
blowing. **4** clear (the nose) of mucus by
blowing. **5** *slang* depart suddenly from.
6 explode. **7** melt (a fuse) from overloading.
8 shape (glass, etc.) by blowing air in.
9 *informal* squander. **●** *n.* **1** an act of blowing.
2 a gust of wind or air. □ **blow away** *slang*
1 kill or destroy. **2** defeat soundly.
3 impress greatly. **blow off 1** remove or be
removed by the force of an air current.
2 *slang* disregard. **blow over** fade away
without serious consequences. **blow
one's own horn** etc. praise oneself.
blow one's top (or **stack**) *informal*
explode in rage. **blow up 1** explode.
2 inflate; enlarge. **3** *informal* arise.
□ **blower** *n.*

blow² *n.* **1** a hard stroke with a hand or
weapon. **2** a sudden shock or misfortune.
□ **come to blows** end up fighting. **in** (or
at) **one blow** in one operation.

blow-by-blow *adj.* giving all the details in
sequence.

blowdown *n.* the uprooting of trees by the
wind.

blow-dry ● *v.* (**blow-dries, blow-dried,
blow-drying**) arrange (the hair) while
drying it with a hand-held dryer. **●** *n.* an act
of doing this. □ **blow-dried** *adj.* **blow-
dryer** *n.*

blowfish *n.* (*pl.* **blowfish**) = PUFFERFISH.

blowfly *n.* (*pl.* **blowflies**) any of various
flies which deposit their eggs on meat and
carcasses, e.g. the bluebottle.

blowhard *n.* *informal* a boastful person.

blowhole *n.* **1** the nostril of a whale, on
the top of its head. **2** a hole in ice through

which seals or other animals breathe. **3** a
vent for air, smoke, etc., in a tunnel etc.

blown *past participle of* BLOW¹.

blowout *n.* **1** *informal* a burst tire. **2** *informal* a
game, election, etc. with a lopsided result.
3 *informal* an elaborate party or feast. **4** a
rapid uncontrolled upward rush from an
oil or gas well.

blowsy *adj.* (**blowsier, blowsiest**)
1 coarse and red-faced. **2** dishevelled.
[*Rhymes with* LOUSY]

blowtorch *n.* (*pl.* **blowtorches**) a
portable device which creates a very hot
flame, used for welding etc.

blow-up ● *n.* (*pl.* **blow-ups**) **1** an
enlargement. **2** an explosion. **3** *informal* a
quarrel. **●** *adj.* **1** inflatable. **2** enlarged.

BLT *n.* (*pl.* **BLTs**) a bacon, lettuce, and
tomato sandwich.

blubber ● *n.* **1** an insulating layer of fat,
esp. in sea mammals. **2** body fat. **●** *v.* weep
loudly. □ **blubbery** *adj.*

bludgeon ● *n.* a club with a heavy end.
● *v.* **1** beat with a bludgeon. **2** force
someone to do something.
[*Say* BLUDGE *in*]

blue ● *adj.* (**bluer, bluest**) **1** having a
colour between green and violet in the
spectrum, like that of a clear sky.
2 depressed; gloomy. **3** with bluish skin.
4 pornographic. **5** *Cdn & Brit.* politically
conservative. **●** *n.* **1** a blue colour or
pigment. **2** (also **Blue**) *Cdn & Brit.* a
supporter of a Conservative party. **3** (**the
blue**) the clear sky. □ **once in a blue
moon** very rarely. **out of the blue**
unexpectedly. **talk** etc. **a blue streak**
speak etc. in a swift, continuous stream of
words. □ **blueness** *n.*

bluebell *n.* any of several plants with bell-
shaped blue flowers.

blueberry *n.* (*pl.* **blueberries**) **1** a shrub
cultivated for its small, bluish edible fruit.
2 the fruit of this plant.

bluebird *n.* a songbird of the thrush
family, the males having distinctive blue
plumage.

blueblood *n.* a wealthy or aristocratic
person. □ **blue-blooded** *adj.*

bluebottle *n.* any of several large
blowflies with a metallic-blue body.

blue box *n.* *Cdn* a blue plastic box for the
collection of recyclable materials.

blue cheese *n.* a strong cheese produced
with veins of blue mould.

blue chip ● *n.* an investment in a well-
established company thought to be
reliable. **●** *adj.* (usu. **blue-chip**) **1** reliable.
2 of the highest quality.

blue-collar *adj.* of or relating to manual labourers.

bluefin *n.* (*pl.* **bluefin** or **bluefins**) the common tuna.

bluefish *n.* (*pl.* **bluefish**) **1** a voracious blue-coloured marine food fish of the Atlantic and Indian oceans. **2** (also **Boston bluefish**) = POLLOCK.

bluegill *n.* (*pl.* **bluegill** or **bluegills**) a small colourful N American freshwater sunfish.

bluegrass *n.* **1** any of several bluish-green grasses, esp. Kentucky bluegrass. **2** a kind of country music characterized by close harmony and virtuosic playing of banjos, guitars, fiddles, etc.

blue-green algae *pl. n.* = CYANOBACTERIA.

blue jay *n.* a crested jay of central and eastern N America, having a large tail and blue, black, and white plumage.

blue line *n.* *Hockey* **1** a line on the ice surface between the centre and the goal. **2** a team's defencemen collectively.

Bluenose *n.* (also **Bluenoser**) *Cdn informal* a Nova Scotian.

blueprint *n.* **1** a design plan or other technical drawing. **2** something acting as a plan or model.

blue ribbon ● *n.* the highest honour in a competition etc. ● *adj.* (usu. **blue-ribbon**) of the highest quality.

blues *pl. n.* **1** (**the blues**) a bout of depression. **2** (**the blues**; often treated as *sing.*) a melancholic style of popular music. □**bluesy** *adj.*

bluestem *n.* a tall N American grass growing in prairie regions.

blue whale *n.* a baleen whale, the largest of all living animals.

bluey *adj.* = BLUISH.

bluff¹ ● *n.* an attempt to deceive someone into believing that one can or will do something. ● *v.* mislead by bluffing. □**call a person's bluff** challenge a person thought to be bluffing. □**bluffer** *n.*

bluff² ● *n.* **1** a steep cliff or bank. **2** *Cdn* (*Prairies*) a grove or clump of trees. ● *adj.* (of a person) good-naturedly blunt.

bluish *adj.* somewhat blue.

blunder ● *n.* a careless mistake. ● *v.* **1** act ineptly. **2** move about clumsily. □**blunderer** *n.* **blunderingly** *adv.*

blunt ● *adj.* **1** lacking in sharpness. **2** direct, outspoken. **3** short and with a squared-off end. ● *v.* **1** make less sharp. **2** weaken. □**bluntly** *adv.* (in sense 2 of *adjective*). **bluntness** *n.*

blur ● *v.* (**blurs**, **blurred**, **blurring**) **1** make or become less distinct. **2** smear.

● *n.* something that appears or sounds indistinct or unclear. □**blurry** *adj.*

blurb *n.* a promotional description, esp. printed on a book's jacket.

blurt *v.* utter abruptly or thoughtlessly.

blush ● *v.* (**blushes**, **blushed**, **blushing**) **1** develop a pink tinge in the face from embarrassment or shame. **2** be or become red or pink. ● *n.* **1** the act of blushing. **2** a pink tinge. **3** (also **blusher**) a cosmetic used to give a pinkish colour to the cheeks. **4** a fairly sweet, pale pink wine.

bluster ● *v.* **1** talk aggressively to little effect. **2** blow fiercely. ● *n.* loud, aggressive talk with little effect. □**blusterer** *n.* **blustery** *adj.*

B movie *n.* a film regarded as second-rate, esp. one which relies on stereotypes and formulas.

BMX *n.* (*pl.* **BMXs**) **1** organized bicycle racing on a dirt track, esp. for youngsters. **2** the sturdy, manoeuvrable kind of bicycle used for this.

BNA *abbr.* *hist.* British North America.

B.O. *abbr.* *informal* BODY ODOUR.

boa *n.* **1** a large snake that kills prey by coiling itself around it and suffocating it. **2** a long thin scarf made of feathers or fur.

boa constrictor *n.* a large snake native to tropical America and the West Indies, which crushes its prey.

boar *n.* **1** (also **wild boar**) **a** a tusked wild pig. **b** its flesh. **2** a male pig that has not been castrated.

board ● *n.* **1 a** a flat thin piece of sawn timber, usu. long and narrow. **b** a material resembling this, made from compressed or synthetic fibres. **2** a thin slab of wood or similar substance, used for games, displaying notices, etc. **3** the provision of regular meals for payment. **4 a** the directors of a company or other organization. **b** a specially constituted administrative body. **5** (in *pl.*) the fence-like structure enclosing the ice at a skating rink. ● *v.* **1 a** get on or into (a ship, aircraft, etc.). **b** receive passengers. **2 a** receive meals and lodging in return for payment. **b** provide with regular meals. **3** cover with boards. **4** *Hockey* bodycheck (an opponent) into the boards with excessive force. □**across the board** general; generally. **go by the board** be neglected or discarded. **on board 1** on or in a ship, train, etc. **2** present and functioning as a member. **3** *Baseball* on base. **take on board** consider.

boarder *n.* **1** a lodger or a pupil at a boarding school. **2** a person who boards a ship, esp. an enemy. **3** a person who takes part in a sport using a board, such as snowboarding, skateboarding, or surfing.

board foot n. a unit of volume for lumber equal to one square foot of one-inch-thick board.

boarding n. **1** *Hockey* the infraction of bodychecking an opponent into the boards with excessive force. **2** snowboarding.

boarding house n. an establishment providing board and lodging for paying guests.

boarding school n. a school at which pupils are resident during the school term.

board of trade n. = CHAMBER OF COMMERCE.

boardroom n. a meeting room in which the directors of a company etc. convene.

boardwalk n. a walkway of crosswise wooden boards.

boast ● v. **1** talk about oneself with indulgent pride. **2** possess (something praiseworthy). ● n. **1** an act of boasting. **2** something one is proud of. □ **boaster** n.

boastful adj. showing excessive pride in oneself. □ **boastfully** adv. **boastfulness** n.

boat ● n. **1** a small vessel for travelling on water. **2** (in general use) a ship of any size. **3** a boat-shaped container for holding gravy, sauce, etc. ● v. travel or go in a boat, esp. for pleasure. □ **in the same boat** sharing the same (usu. adverse) circumstances. □ **boating** n. **boatload** n.

boater n. **1** a person who boats. **2** a flat-topped hardened straw hat with a brim.

boathouse n. a shed at the edge of a river, lake, etc., for housing boats.

boatman n. (pl. **boatmen**) a man who hires out boats or provides transport by boat.

boat people pl. n. refugees who have fled by sea.

boatswain n. a ship's officer in charge of equipment and crew duties. [Say BOE z'n]

bob¹ ● v. (**bobs, bobbed, bobbing**) move or cause to move quickly up and down. ● n. **1** a bouncing movement, esp. upward. **2** (also **bobber**) a float used in fishing to suspend a line or net at a fixed depth. □ **bob for** try to catch (floating apples etc.) with the mouth, as in a game.

bob² ● n. **1** a short hairstyle hanging evenly all around. **2** a weight on a pendulum, plumb line, or kite tail. **3 a** a short runner on a sled etc. **b** = BOBSLED. ● v. (**bobs, bobbed, bobbing**) cut (hair) short and even all around.

bobbin n. a cylinder or cone holding thread, etc.

bobble¹ ● v. (**bobbles, bobbled,** **bobbling**) **1** move with continual bobbing. **2** mishandle (a ball). ● n. a mistake, esp. a fumble of a ball.

bobble² n. a small woolly or tufted ball as a decoration.

bobby pin n. a flat hairpin of metal bent double.

bobby socks pl. n. socks reaching just above the ankle.

bobcat n. a small lynx with a spotted reddish-brown coat and a short tail.

bobskate n. a child's skate consisting of two parallel blades attached with straps to a shoe etc.

bobsled (also **bobsleigh**) ● n. a mechanically steered and braked sled for two or four people. ● v. (**bobsleds,** **bobsledded, bobsledding**) race in a bobsled. □ **bobsledder** n.

bobwhite n. a N American quail.

bocce n. an Italian form of lawn bowling. [Say BOTCHIE]

bocconcini n. a mild Italian cheese like mozzarella, in the form of a small ball. [Say bock on CHEENY]

bod n. informal a body.

bodacious adj. slang outstanding, excellent. [Say boe DAY shus]

bode v. (**bodes, boded, boding**) suggest a particular outcome.

bodice n. the part of a woman's dress or blouse (excluding sleeves) above the waist. [Say BOD iss]

bodily ● adj. of or concerning the body. ● adv. **1** by taking hold of a person's body, esp. with force. **2** with one's whole body.

body n. (pl. **bodies**) **1 a** the physical structure of a person or an animal. **b** the torso apart from the head and the limbs. **c** a corpse. **2 a** the main or central part of a thing. **b** the bulk or majority. **3 a** an organized group set up for a particular purpose. **b** a collection. **4** a quantity. **5** a piece of matter. **6** informal a person. **7 a** a full, substantial quality of flavour, tone, etc. **b** an appearance of fullness and usu. waviness of the hair. □ **keep body and soul together** keep alive, esp. barely. **over my dead body** informal entirely without my assent. □ **-bodied** comb. form

bodybuilder n. a person who strengthens and enlarges their muscles through exercise. □ **bodybuilding** n.

bodycheck *Hockey* ● n. an attempt to obstruct a player by bumping into them with the shoulder or hip. ● v. hit or obstruct in this way.

bodyguard n. a person or group of persons employed to protect another person.

body language *n.* communication through gestures, posture, and expressions.

body odour *n.* the smell of the human body, esp. when unpleasant.

body piercing *n.* the piercing of holes in parts of the body other than the earlobes in order to insert jewellery.

body politic *n.* organized society.

body shop *n.* a garage where repairs to the bodywork of vehicles are carried out.

bodysuit *n.* a close-fitting one-piece stretch garment worn esp. for sporting activities.

bodysurf *v.* ride the crest of a wave without a surfboard. □**bodysurfer** *n.* **bodysurfing** *n.*

bodywork *n.* **1** the structure of a vehicle body. **2** the manufacture or repair of vehicle bodies.

Boer ● *n.* a South African of Dutch descent. ● *adj.* of or relating to the Boers. [*Say* BORE]

boffo *adj. slang* successful.

bog ● *n.* very soft, wet, spongy ground. ● *v.* (**bogs, bogged, bogging**) **1** make or become unable to proceed. **2** sink into mud or wet ground. □**boggy** *adj.*

bogey[1] *Golf* ● *n.* (*pl.* **bogeys**) a score of one stroke over par. ● *v.* (**bogeys, bogeyed, bogeying**) play (a hole) in one stroke over par.

bogey[2] *n.* (*pl.* **bogeys**) (also **bogeyman**, *pl.* **bogeymen**) **1** an evil or mischievous spirit. **2** an alarming thing.

boggle *v.* (**boggles, boggled, boggling**) *informal* be or cause to be astonished or baffled.

bogus *adj.* not genuine.

Bohemian ● *n.* **1** a native of Bohemia. **2** (also **bohemian**) a socially unconventional person, esp. an artist or writer. ● *adj.* **1** of or characteristic of Bohemia, a region of the Czech Republic, or its people. **2** (also **bohemian**) socially unconventional. □**bohemianism** *n.* (in sense 2). [*Say* boe HEEMY in]

boil[1] ● *v.* **1 a** (of a liquid) reach or cause to reach a temperature at which it bubbles and turns to vapour. **b** (of a vessel) contain boiling liquid. **2** cook in boiling liquid. ● *n.* the act or process of boiling; boiling point. □**boil down 1** reduce volume by boiling. **2** reduce to essentials. **3** (foll. by *to*) amount to.

boil[2] *n.* an inflamed pus-filled swelling caused by infection of a hair follicle etc.

boiler *n.* **1** a strong vessel for generating steam under pressure. **2** a tank for heating water.

boilerplate *n.* **1** a piece of rolled steel for making boilers. **2** a standard form which can easily be replicated. **3** hackneyed or predictable material.

boiling *adj.* (also **boiling hot**) *informal* very hot.

boing *n.* a twanging sound, such as that of a compressed spring suddenly released.

boisterous *adj.* **1** noisy, energetic, and cheerful. **2** (of the sea, etc.) stormy, rough. □**boisterously** *adv.* **boisterousness** *n.* [*Say* BOY stir us]

bok choy *n.* a cabbage-like plant with dark green outer leaves, white stalks, and a yellow centre.

bold ● *adj.* **1** courageous. **2** forthright, impudent. **3** vivid. **4** (also **boldface**) printed in a thick black typeface. ● *n.* (also **boldface**) bold type. ● *v.* (also **boldface**) set in bold type. □**boldly** *adv.* **boldness** *n.*

bole *n.* the stem or trunk of a tree.

bolero *n.* (*pl.* **boleros**) **1** a Spanish dance. **2** a short open jacket. [*Say* buh LAIR oh]

Bolivian *n.* a native or inhabitant of Bolivia. □**Bolivian** *adj.* [*Say* buh LIVVY un]

boll *n.* a rounded capsule containing seeds. [*Sounds like* BOWL]

Bollywood *n.* the Indian popular film industry, based in Bombay, esp. designating very formulaic romantic musicals.

bolo *n.* (*pl.* **bolos**) (also **bolo tie**) a necktie of cord or thick string.

bologna *n.* a smoked luncheon meat made from finely minced pork and beef. [*Say* buh LONEY *or* buh LONA]

Bolshevik ● *n.* **1** *hist.* a member of the radical faction of the Russian socialist party. **2** a Russian communist. **3** (in general use) any revolutionary socialist. ● *adj.* **1** of the Bolsheviks. **2** communist. □**Bolshevism** *n.* **Bolshevist** *n.* [*Say* BOWL shuh vick]

bolster ● *n.* **1** a long, often cylindrical pillow. **2** a pad or support. ● *v.* support, reinforce. [*Say* BOWL stir]

bolt ● *n.* **1** a sliding bar and socket used to fasten a door, gate, etc. **2** a large usu. metal pin with a head, usu. riveted or used with a nut, to hold things together. **3** a discharge of lightning. **4** a roll of fabric, paper, etc. ● *v.* **1** fasten or lock with a bolt. **2 a** dash suddenly away, esp. to escape. **b** (of a horse) suddenly gallop out of control. **3** gulp (food or drink) hurriedly. **4** (of a plant) run to seed. □**a bolt from** (or **out of**) **the blue** a complete surprise. **bolt upright** rigidly, stiffly.

bomb ● *n.* **1 a** a container of material designed to explode on impact or by means of a timer or a remote control. **b** an ordinary object fitted with an explosive device. **2 (the bomb)** nuclear weapons collectively. **3** *informal* a bad failure. **4** *Sport* a long pass, kick, shot or hit. ● *v.* **1** attack with bombs. **2** *informal* fail badly. **3** *informal* move or go very quickly.

bombard *v.* **1** attack with bombs etc. **2** subject to persistent questioning etc. **3** *Physics* direct a stream of high-speed particles at. □ **bombardment** *n.*

bombardier *n.* **1** a member of a bomber crew responsible for sighting and releasing bombs. **2** *Cdn & Brit.* a non-commissioned officer in the artillery, of a rank equivalent to corporal. [*Say* bomba DEER]

bombast *n.* impressive language with little meaning. □ **bombastic** *adj.* **bombastically** *adv.* [*Say* BOM bast, bom BAST ick]

bombed *adj.* **1** *informal* intoxicated. **2** subjected to bombing.

bombed-out *adj.* **1** (of a person) driven out by bombing. **2** (of a building) rendered uninhabitable by bombing.

bomber *n.* **1** an aircraft equipped to carry and drop bombs. **2** a person using bombs, esp. illegally.

bombshell *n.* **1** an overwhelming surprise or shock. **2** an artillery bomb. **3** *informal* a very attractive woman.

bona fide ● *adj.* genuine. ● *adv.* *Law* in good faith. [*Say* BONE uh fide *or* BONNA fide]

bona fides *n.* **1** honest intentions. **2** (as *pl.*) *informal* documentary evidence showing that a person is what they claim to be. [*Say* bone a FIE deez]

bonanza *n.* a source of wealth, profit, or good fortune.

bon appétit *interj.* expressing a wish that someone will enjoy what they are about to eat. [*Say* bon appa TEE]

bonbon *n.* a fancy candy.

bond ● *n.* **1 a** a thing that ties another down or together. **b** (usu. in *pl.*) a thing restraining bodily freedom. **2 a** a uniting force. **b** a restraint; a responsibility. **3** a binding engagement. **4** a certificate issued by a government or a public company promising to repay borrowed money at a fixed rate of interest at a specified time. **5** adhesiveness. **6** a strong force of attraction holding atoms together in a molecule or crystal. ● *v.* **1** bind together with an adhesive. **2** adhere. **3** connect with a bond. **4** place (goods) in bond. **5 a** become emotionally attached. **b** link by an emotional or psychological bond.

bondage *n.* **1** slavery. **2** subjection to constraint, obligation, etc. **3** sexual practice that involves tying up one's partner.

bonded *adj.* **1** (of material) reinforced by or cemented to another. **2** (of a person's or company's behaviour or performance) insured by a deposit of money which is paid to the company in the event of the employee's misconduct, theft, etc. **3** emotionally or psychologically linked. **4** (of a worker or workforce) obliged to work for a particular employer, typically in a condition close to slavery.

bone ● *n.* **1** any of the pieces of hard tissue making up the skeleton in vertebrates. **2 a** the material of which bones consist. **b** a similar substance such as ivory. **3** a strip of stiffening in a corset etc. ● *v.* (**bones**, **boned**, **boning**) remove the bones from. □ **bone of contention** a source or ground of dispute. **bone up** (often foll. by *on*) *informal* study intensively. **close to** (or **near**) **the bone 1** tactless to the point of offensiveness. **2** with little or no money. **have a bone to pick** have a cause for dispute. **make no bones about 1** admit openly. **2** not hesitate. **work one's fingers to the bone** work very hard. □ **boned** *adj.* **boneless** *adj.*

bone-chilling *adj.* **1** extremely cold. **2** frightening.

bone china *n.* fine china made of clay mixed with the ash from bones.

bonehead *informal* ● *n.* a stupid person. ● *adj.* stupid. □ **boneheaded** *adj.*

bone marrow *n.* a soft substance in the cavities of bones, of importance in blood cell formation.

bone meal *n.* crushed bones used as fertilizer.

boner *n.* *informal* a stupid mistake.

boneyard *n.* *informal* a cemetery.

bonfire *n.* a large open-air fire for burning rubbish, as part of a celebration, or as a signal.

bongo *n.* (*pl.* **bongos**) either of a pair of small drums, held between the knees and played with the fingers.

bonhomie *n.* cheerful outgoing friendliness. [*Say* bon om EE]

bonk ● *v.* hit resoundingly. ● *n.* a knock or hit.

bonkers *adj.* *slang* crazy.

bonnet *n.* **1 a** a woman's or child's hat tied under the chin and usu. with a brim framing the face. **b** *informal* any hat. **2** = WAR BONNET.

bonsai *n.* (*pl.* **bonsai**) **1** the art of cultivating ornamental artificially dwarfed varieties of trees and shrubs. **2** a tree or shrub grown by this method. [*Say* BON sigh]

bonspiel n. a curling tournament. [*Say* BON speel]

bonus n. (pl. **bonuses**) **1** an unexpected extra benefit. **2** a sum of money added to a person's wage for good performance.

bonusing n. Cdn an act of subsidizing something to encourage development etc.

bon voyage interj. & n. an expression of good wishes to a departing traveller. [*Say* bon voy OZH]

bony adj. (**bonier**, **boniest**) **1** (of a person) thin with prominent bones. **2** having many bones. **3** of or like bone.

boo ● interj. **1** an expression of disapproval or contempt. **2** a sound intended to surprise. ● n. an utterance of "boo" ● v. (**boos**, **booed**, **booing**) utter a boo or boos. □ **not say boo to a goose** remain silent, esp. from shyness or timidity.

boob n. **1** slang a foolish person. **2** informal a woman's breast.

boo-boo n. informal a mistake.

boob tube n. informal (usu. as **the boob tube**) television; a television set.

booby n. (pl. **boobies**) **1** = BOOB. **2** any of various seabirds related to the gannet.

booby prize n. a prize given to the least successful competitor in a contest.

booby trap ● n. **1** a trap intended to surprise someone as a practical joke. **2** Military a hidden explosive device designed to explode when someone touches it etc. ● v. (usu. **booby-trap**) (**booby-traps**, **booby-trapped**, **booby-trapping**) place a booby trap or traps in or on.

booger n. informal a piece of dried nasal mucus.

boogie ● v. (**boogies**, **boogied**, **boogying**) informal **1** dance enthusiastically to rock music. **2** move or go quickly. ● n. **1** (also **boogie-woogie**) a style of blues or jazz on the piano, marked by a persistent bass rhythm. **2** informal a dance to rock music. [*Say* BOOGY (with OO either as in GOOD or as in FOOD)]

boohoo ● interj. expressing weeping. ● n. (pl. **boohoos**) loud sobbing. ● v. (**boohoos**, **boohooed**, **boohooing**) (esp. of a child) weep loudly.

book ● n. **1 a** a written or printed work consisting of pages glued or sewn together along one side and bound in covers. **b** a literary composition intended for publication. **2** a bound set of blank sheets for writing in. **3** a set of tickets, cheques, etc., bound up together. **4** (in pl.) a set of records or accounts. **5** a main division of a literary work or the Bible. ● v. **1 a** reserve (accommodation, tickets, etc.) **b** engage (a guest etc.) for some occasion. **2** take the

personal details of (an offender). **3** issue a railway etc. ticket to. □ **book off** Cdn stay home from work. **booked up** with all places reserved. **by the book** according to the rules. **in a person's bad** (or **good**) **books** in disfavour (or favour) with a person. **in my book** in my opinion. **on the books 1** publicly recorded. **2** contained in a list of members etc. **throw the book at** informal charge or punish to the utmost. □ **booker** n.

bookbinder n. a person who binds books professionally. □ **bookbinding** n.

bookcase n. a cabinet containing shelves for books.

bookend n. ● a prop placed at the end of a row of books to keep them upright. ● v. serve as or provide with something which frames a larger item on either side.

bookie n. informal = BOOKMAKER.

booking n. an act of reserving accommodations etc. or of buying a ticket in advance.

bookish adj. studious; fond of reading. □ **bookishness** n.

bookkeeper n. a person who keeps accounts for a business, etc. □ **bookkeeping** n.

booklet n. a small book, usu. with paper covers.

bookmaker n. a person who takes bets, calculates odds, and pays out winnings. □ **bookmaking** n.

bookmark ● n. **1** a strip of leather, card, etc., used to mark one's place in a book. **2** an electronic record of a particular website address, etc., enabling quick access by the user. ● v. record a bookmark for (a website).

bookseller n. a person who sells books.

bookshelf n. (pl. **bookshelves**) **1** a single shelf for books, often part of a bookcase. **2** = BOOKCASE.

bookstore n. (also **bookshop**) a store where books are sold.

bookworm n. **1** informal a person who reads a lot. **2** the larva of any moth or beetle which feeds on the paper and glue used in books.

boom[1] ● n. **1** a deep resonant sound. **2** a period of prosperity. ● v. **1** make a deep hollow resonant sound. **2** be suddenly prosperous.

boom[2] ● n. **1** a movable arm used for lifting, manoeuvring a microphone, etc. **2** a floating barrier stretched across a body of water to obstruct navigation, guide floating logs, contain oil spills, etc. **3** a raft of logs fastened together for transportation on water. **4** a pivoted spar to which the foot of a sail is attached. ● v. **1** gather (logs) in a boom. **2** move (logs) by forming them into a boom.

boomer n. = BABY BOOMER.

boomerang ● n. a curved flat hardwood projectile used by Australian Aboriginals to kill prey, and often of a kind able to return in flight to the thrower. ● v. (**boomerangs**, **boomeranged**, **boomeranging**) (of a plan etc.) backfire.

booming ground n. Cdn a section of a lake, river, etc. where logs are collected into booms.

boomy adj. (**boomier**, **boomiest**) **1** having a loud, deep, resonant sound. **2** of or relating to a boom in business etc.

boon n. a beneficial thing.

boondocks pl. n. (also **boonies**) informal rough or isolated country.

boondoggle informal ● n. **1** work of little value done merely to appear busy. **2** a government project with no purpose other than political patronage. ● v. (**boondoggles**, **boondoggled**, **boondoggling**) **1** deceive. **2** do work just to appear busy.

boor n. a rude person. □ **boorish** adj. **boorishly** adv. **boorishness** n.

boost ● v. **1** promote (a person, scheme, etc.) by praise or advertising. **2** increase. **3** push from below. **4** recharge. ● n. **1** a lift or push from below. **2** an improvement in spirits, confidence, etc. **3** an increase. **4** the action of recharging a car battery.

booster n. **1** a device for increasing electrical power or voltage. **2** an auxiliary engine or rocket used to give initial acceleration. **3** a dose of vaccine etc., renewing the effect of an earlier one. **4** a keen promoter.

booster cable n. (usu. in pl.) = JUMPER² 2b.

booster seat n. a small seat placed on another seat to elevate a toddler.

boot¹ ● n. **1** an outer covering for the foot usu. reaching above the ankle. **2** informal a kick. **3** (**the boot**) informal dismissal, esp. from employment. ● v. **1** kick. **2** dismiss (a person) forcefully. □ **put the boots to** kick brutally. **to boot** as well.

boot² ● v. prepare (a computer) for operation by causing an operating system to be loaded into its memory. ● n. the procedure of starting up a computer operating system. □ **bootable** adj.

boot camp n. informal **1** a centre for basic military training. **2** a penal institution subjecting young offenders to rigorous exercise and military-style discipline.

booth n. (pl. **booths**) **1** a small temporary structure for the display or sale of goods.

2 an enclosure for various purposes, e.g. voting. **3** a set of a table and benches in a restaurant etc.

bootie n. **1** a soft woollen or cloth shoe. **2** a woman's short boot.

bootleg ● adj. (esp. of alcohol, recordings, etc.) illicitly produced, transported, or sold. ● n. something produced or sold illegally. ● v. (**bootlegs**, **bootlegged**, **bootlegging**) make, distribute, or smuggle illicit goods (esp. alcohol). □ **bootlegger** n.

bootlicker n. informal a person who behaves obsequiously.

bootstrap n. a loop at the back of a boot used to pull it on. □ **pull oneself up by one's bootstraps** better oneself by one's own efforts.

booty n. **1** plunder gained by force or violence. **2** something gained or won.

booze informal ● n. **1** alcoholic drink. **2** a drinking bout. ● v. (**boozes**, **boozed**, **boozing**) drink alcoholic liquor, esp. excessively. □ **boozer** n. **boozy** adj.

booze can n. Cdn an illegal bar, esp. one operating in a private home.

booze-up n. slang a drinking bout.

bop¹ informal ● n. = BEBOP. ● v. (**bops**, **bopped**, **bopping**) **1** dance, esp. to pop music. **2** move, go.

bop² informal ● v. (**bops**, **bopped**, **bopping**) hit, punch lightly. ● n. a light blow.

borage n. a plant with hairy leaves and bright blue flowers. [Say BORE idge]

borax n. a mineral salt occurring in alkaline deposits, used in making glass, as an antiseptic, and as a household cleanser. [Say BORE ax]

Bordeaux n. (pl. **Bordeaux**) any of various red, white, or rosé wines from the district of Bordeaux in southwestern France. [Say bore DOE for the singular, bore DOZE for the plural]

bordello n. (pl. **bordellos**) a brothel. [Say bore DELLO]

border ● n. **1** an edge or boundary. **2 a** the line separating two areas, esp. countries. **b** the district on each side of this. **3** a decorative edging. **4** a long narrow bed of flowers or shrubs in a garden. ● v. **1** be a border to. **2** provide with a border. **3** (usu. foll. by on, upon) **a** adjoin. **b** come close to being.

border collie n. a long-haired usu. black and white dog.

borderline ● n. **1** a marginal position between two categories. **2** a line marking a boundary. ● adj. on the boundary between two conditions or qualities.

bore¹ ● *v.* (**bores, bored, boring**) **1** make a hole in a thing, esp. with a revolving tool. **2** hollow out. **3** drill a well (for oil etc.). **4** move by burrowing. ● *n.* **1** the hollow of a firearm barrel or of a cylinder in an engine. **2** the diameter of this; the calibre. **3** = BOREHOLE. □ **borer** *n.*

bore² ● *n.* a dull person or thing. ● *v.* (**bores, bored, boring**) cause to lose interest by dullness.

bore³ *n.* a high wave caused by rapidly rising tide entering a long shallow narrow inlet.

bore⁴ *past of* BEAR¹.

boreal *adj.* **1** of the North or northern regions. **2** of the north wind. [*Say* BORRY ul]

boreal forest *n.* the northernmost and coldest forest zone, across N America, Europe, and Asia.

boredom *n.* the state of being bored.

borehole *n.* a deep narrow hole, esp. one made in the earth to find water, oil, etc.

boring *adj.* not interesting; tedious, dull. □ **boringly** *adv.*

born *adj.* **1** existing as a result of birth. **2 a** being such or likely to become such by natural ability or quality. **b** having a specified destiny or prospect. **3** (in *comb.*) of a certain status by birth. **4** created or caused. □ **born and bred** by birth and upbringing. **not born yesterday** *informal* not naive.

born-again *adj.* **1** of or relating to a Christian who has made a new or renewed commitment to esp. evangelical faith. **2** full of new-found zeal for a cause.

borne *n* **1** *past participle of* BEAR¹. **2** (in *comb.*) carried or transported by.

boron *n.* a non-metallic chemical element with semiconducting properties. [*Say* BORE on]

borough *n.* a type of municipal administrative region. [*Say* BURRA]

borrow *v.* **1 a** acquire temporarily with the intention of returning. **b** obtain money in this way. **2** use (an idea, etc.) originated by another; plagiarize. □ **borrowed time** an unexpected extension, esp. before an imminent disaster. □ **borrower** *n.* **borrowing** *n.*

borscht *n.* an originally Eastern European soup with various ingredients including beets and cabbage. [*Say* BORSHT]

bosom *n.* **1 a** a person's breast or chest, esp. a woman's. **b** *informal* each of a woman's breasts. **c** the enclosure formed by a person's breast and arms. **2** an emotional centre, esp. as the source of an enfolding relationship. [*Say* BOOZUM (*with* OO *as in* BOOK)]

bosom friend *n.* (also **bosom buddy**) a very close friend.

bosomy *adj.* (of a woman) having large breasts.

boss¹ ● *n.* (*pl.* **bosses**) a person in charge of employees or an organization. ● *v.* (**bosses, bossed, bossing**) (usu. foll. by *around*) treat in a domineering way.

boss² *n.* (*pl.* **bosses**) a round knob on the centre of a shield, propeller, etc.

bossy *adj.* (**bossier, bossiest**) *informal* domineering; tending to boss. □ **bossily** *adv.* **bossiness** *n.*

Boston bluefish *n.* (*pl.* **Boston bluefish**) *Cdn* = POLLOCK.

Bostonian ● *n.* a native or inhabitant of Boston, Massachusetts. ● *adj.* of or relating to Boston. [*Say* boss TONY in]

bosun (also **bo'sun**) = BOATSWAIN. [*Say* BOE z'n]

botanical ● *adj.* (also **botanic**) **1** of or relating to botany. **2** having to do with plants. ● *n.* a drug etc. derived from parts of a plant.

botany *n.* **1** the study of plants. **2** the plant life of a particular area or time. □ **botanist** *n.*

botch *v.* (**botches, botched, botching**) bungle.

both ● *adj. & pron.* the two, not only one. ● *adv.* with equal truth in two cases.

bother ● *v.* **1 a** give trouble to; disturb. **b** (**bother with**) be concerned with. **2** make an effort. ● *n.* **1** trouble and fuss. **2** a cause of trouble. □ **cannot be bothered** will not make the effort needed.

bothersome *adj.* annoying.

Botox *n. propr.* a drug prepared from the toxin that causes botulism, used medically to treat certain muscular conditions and cosmetically to reduce wrinkles by temporarily paralyzing facial muscles. [*Say* BOE tox]

bottle ● *n.* **1** a container with a narrow neck, for storing liquid, pills, etc. **2** alcoholic drink. ● *v.* (**bottles, bottled, bottling**) **1** put into bottles or jars. **2** (usu. foll. by *up*) conceal (esp. emotions) for a time. □ **bottler** *n.*

bottle-feed *v.* (**bottle-feeds, bottle-fed, bottle-feeding**) feed with milk by means of a bottle equipped with a nipple.

bottleneck *n.* a point at which the flow of traffic, production, etc., is constricted.

bottom ● *n.* **1 a** the lowest point or part. **b** the part on which a thing rests. **c** the underside. **2** *informal* the buttocks. **3** the ground under the water of a lake etc. **4** the basis; the origin. **5** *Baseball* the second half of an inning, in which the home team bats. **6** (in *pl.*) the part of a two-piece garment worn below the waist. **7** the keel or hull of a ship. ● *adj.* **1** lowest. **2** last. □ **be at the bottom of** be the cause of. **bottom falls out** collapse occurs. **bottom out** reach the lowest level. **bottom up** upside down. **get to the bottom of** fully investigate and explain.

bottom-feeder *n.* **1** a fish or other organism feeding near the bottom of a body of water. **2** *derogatory* a person who exploits others. □ **bottom-feeding** *adj.*

bottomland *n.* low-lying, fertile land along a watercourse.

bottomless *adj.* **1** without a bottom. **2** very deep. **3** (of a supply etc.) inexhaustible.

bottom line *n.* **1** the final total of an account or balance sheet. **2** net profit or loss. **3** *informal* the crucial factor.

bottom-up *adj.* proceeding from detail to general theory.

botulism *n.* poisoning caused by a bacterium in poorly preserved food. [*Say* BOTCHA lism]

boudoir *n.* a woman's small private room or bedroom. [*Say* BOO dwar]

bouffant *adj.* puffed out. [*Say* boo FONT]

bougainvillea *n.* a tropical plant with large coloured leaves. [*Say* boo gun VILLY uh]

bough *n.* a branch of a tree. [*Rhymes with* HOW]

bought *past and past participle of* BUY.

bouillon *n.* a clear broth made by cooking meat or fish in water. [*Say* BULL y'n]

boulder *n.* a large stone.

boulevard *n.* **1** a broad urban road. **2** a broad street with trees planted along it. **3** (*esp. Cdn*) **a** a strip of grass between a sidewalk and a roadway. **b** a median separating opposite directions of traffic. [*Say* BULL a vard]

bounce ● *v.* (**bounces, bounced, bouncing**) **1 a** rebound. **b** cause to rebound. **c** move up and down repeatedly. **2** *informal* (of a cheque) be returned by a bank when an account has insufficient funds to meet it. **3** jump or move energetically. **4** (of an email message) be returned to the sender. ● *n.* **1 a** a rebound. **b** the power of rebounding. **c** a springy quality. **2** a boost or rise. **3** *informal* **a** swagger, self-confidence. **b** liveliness. □ **bounce back** regain good health, spirits, etc.

bouncer *n.* a person employed to eject troublemakers from a bar etc.

bouncing *adj.* vigorous and healthy.

bouncy *adj.* (**bouncier, bounciest**) **1** tending to bounce well. **2** cheerful and lively. **3** resilient. □ **bounciness** *n.*

bound[1] ● *v.* **1** leap. **2** walk or run with leaping strides. ● *n.* a leap.

bound[2] ● *n.* (usu. in *pl.*) a limitation; a restriction. ● *v.* **1** limit. **2** be the boundary of. □ **out of bounds 1** outside the part of a playing field, court, etc. in which play is conducted. **2** beyond what is acceptable; forbidden.

bound[3] *adj.* moving in a specified direction or toward a specified goal.

bound[4] ● *v. past and past participle of* BIND. ● *adj.* **1** tied with rope, etc. **2** certain. **3** required; obligated. **4** (in *comb.*) constricted, prevented from advancing. **5** (of the pages in a book etc.) held together by a binding. □ **bound up with** (or **in**) closely associated with.

boundary *n.* (*pl.* **boundaries**) a line marking the limits of an area.

bounden duty *n.* a solemn responsibility.

boundless *adj.* unlimited.

bounteous *adj. literary* **1** abundant. **2** freely given. □ **bounteously** *adv.*

bountiful *adj.* **1** plentiful. **2** giving generously. □ **bountifully** *adv.*

bounty *n.* (*pl.* **bounties**) **1** a reward for the killing of dangerous or undesirable animals. **2** a sum paid for bringing criminals to justice. **3** an act of giving in abundance. **4** an abundance.

bounty hunter *n.* a person who pursues criminals or kills animals for a reward. □ **bounty hunting** *n.*

bouquet *n.* **1** an arrangement of cut flowers. **2** the scent of wine etc. **3** a favourable comment. [*Say* bo KAY *or* boo KAY]

bourbon *n.* whisky distilled from corn mash and rye. [*Say* BUR b'n]

bourgeois *often derogatory* ● *adj.* **1** of or characteristic of the middle class. **2** upholding the interests of the capitalist class. ● *n.* (*pl.* **bourgeois**) a bourgeois person. [*Say* boor ZHWAH]

bourgeoisie *n.* **1** the capitalist class, owning most of society's wealth and means of production. **2** the middle class. [*Say* boor zhwah ZEE]

bout *n.* **1** a short period, esp. of illness or intense activity. **2** a wrestling or boxing match.

boutique *n.* a small shop selling esp. fashionable clothes or accessories. [*Say* boo TEEK]

boutonniere *n.* a flower or flowers worn on a lapel. [*Say* boota NEER]

bouzouki *n.* a long-necked Greek form of mandolin. [*Say* boo ZOOKY]

bovine ● *adj.* **1** of or resembling oxen or cattle. **2** stupid, dull. ● *n.* a bovine animal. [*Say* BOE vine]

bow¹ ● *n.* **1** a knot with a double loop, which can be undone by pulling one end. **2** a device for shooting arrows with a taut string joining the ends of a curved piece of wood etc. **3** a rod with horsehair stretched along its length, used for playing some stringed instruments. **4 a** a shallow curve or bend. **b** a rainbow. ● *v.* **1** use a bow on (a violin etc.). **2** curve outward like a bow. [*Rhymes with* SHOW]

bow² ● *v.* **1 a** incline the head or upper body as a sign of greeting, respect, or shame. **b** bend downward. **2** submit. **3** cause to incline. ● *n.* an act of bowing. □ **bow and scrape** behave obsequiously. **bow out** withdraw. **take a bow** acknowledge applause. [*Rhymes with* HOW]

bow³ *n.* the front end of a boat. □ **shot across the bows** a warning. [*Rhymes with* HOW]

bowdlerize *v.* (**bowdlerizes, bowdlerized, bowdlerizing**) remove improper or offensive material from (a text). [*Say* BOWD lur ize (*the first syllable rhymes with* LOUD)]

bowel *n.* **1 a** the part of the alimentary canal below the stomach. **b** (usu. in *pl.*) the intestines. **2** (in *pl.*) the innermost parts.

bowel movement *n.* an act of defecation.

bower *n.* a secluded place, esp. in a garden, enclosed by foliage. [*Rhymes with* FLOWER]

bowhead *n.* a large baleen whale inhabiting Arctic waters. [*Say* BOE head]

bowl¹ *n.* **1 a** a usu. round deep basin used for food or liquid. **b** the quantity a bowl holds. **2** a round, hollow part of an object. **3 a** a bowl-shaped natural basin. **b** an amphitheatre or stadium.

bowl² ● *v.* **1 a** roll (a ball) along the ground. **b** play a game of bowling. **2** go along rapidly. ● *n.* **1** a hard ball used in lawn bowling. **2** (in *pl.*; usu. treated as *sing.*) = LAWN BOWLING. □ **bowl over 1** knock down. **2** *informal* impress greatly.

bow legs *pl. n.* legs which are curved so as to be wide apart below the knee. □ **bowlegged** *adj.* [*Rhymes with* SHOW]

bowling *n.* a game in which players roll a ball toward usu. five or ten pins with the intent of knocking them down. □ **bowler** *n.*

bowling alley *n.* **1** a long, narrow lane along which the ball is rolled in the game of bowling. **2** a building containing several of these.

bowsprit *n.* a spar running out from a sailing ship's bow to which the stays supporting the forward mast are fastened. [*Say* BOE sprit]

bowstring *n.* the string of an archer's bow.

bow tie *n.* a necktie in the form of a bow (BOW¹ *n.* 1).

box¹ ● *n.* (*pl.* **boxes**) **1** a container with a flat base and sides and usu. a lid. **2** the amount that will fill a box. **3 a** a compartment reserved for an individual or small group in a theatre, sports stadium, or law court, etc. **b** a stall for a horse. **4** an enclosed space. **5** any of various electric or electronic devices housed in a box. **6** an area enclosed by a border on a page or computer screen. ● *v.* (**boxes, boxed, boxing**) **1** put in or provide with a box. **2** (foll. by *in*, *up*, *out*) surround or confine. □ **boxy** *adj.*

box² ● *v.* (**boxes, boxed, boxing**) **1** fight in a boxing match. **2** punch (esp. a person's ear). ● *n.* (*pl.* **boxes**) a punch.

boxcar *n.* an enclosed railway freight car, usu. having sliding doors on the sides.

boxer *n.* **1** a person who participates in boxing. **2** a breed of medium-sized dog with a brown coat and a wrinkled face. **3** (in *pl.*) = BOXER SHORTS.

boxer shorts *n.* men's loose-fitting underwear.

boxing *n.* the sport of fighting with the fists, esp. in padded gloves.

Boxing Day *n.* a holiday celebrated on Dec. 26 or the first weekday after Christmas.

box lacrosse *n. Cdn* (also **boxla**) a form of lacrosse played in an enclosed area by teams of six players.

box office *n.* an office at a theatre etc. where tickets are sold.

boxwood *n.* an evergreen tree or shrub with glossy leaves, popular as hedging.

boy ● *n.* **1** a male child or youth. **2** a male belonging to a specified group. **3** (usu. as a form of address) a male animal. ● *interj.* expressing pleasure etc. □ **boyhood** *n.* **boyish** *adj.* **boyishly** *adv.* **boyishness** *n.*

boycott ● *v.* **1** protest against or punish by a refusal of normal commercial or social relations. **2** refuse to attend (a meeting) or buy (goods) to this end. ● *n.* such a refusal.

boyfriend *n.* **1** a regular male companion or lover. **2** any male friend.

boysenberry *n.* (*pl.* **boysenberries**) **1** a hybrid of several species of bramble. **2** the

large red edible fruit of this plant.
[Say BOYS'n berry]

bozo n. (pl. **bozos**) slang a stupid or
annoying person.

BP abbr. before the present (era).

BQ abbr. (in Canada) BLOC QUÉBÉCOIS.

bra n. (pl. **bras**) an undergarment worn to
support the breasts. □ **braless** adj.

brace ● n. **1 a** a device that clamps or
fastens tightly. **b** a strengthening piece of
iron or timber used in building. **2** (in pl.)
suspenders. **3** (in pl.) an orthodontic
appliance worn on the teeth to straighten
them. **4** a device to support an injured
body part. **5** (pl. **brace**) a pair, often of
birds or mammals killed in hunting. ● v.
(**braces**, **braced**, **bracing**) **1** fasten
tightly. **2** make steady by supporting.
3 (often **brace oneself**) prepare for a
shock etc.

bracelet n. a band worn on the wrist, arm,
or ankle, for decoration or identification.

brachytherapy n. the treatment of
cancer, esp. prostate cancer, by the
insertion of small radioactive implants
directly into the cancerous tissue.

bracing ● adj. invigorating. ● n. a system
or series of braces.

bracken n. a large branching fern with
long coarse fronds.

bracket ● n. **1** a support attached to and
projecting from a vertical surface. **2** a shelf
fixed with such a support to a wall. **3** each
of a pair of marks () [] {} <> used to enclose
words or figures. **4** a group classified as
containing similar elements. ● v.
(**bracketed**, **bracketing**) **1 a** link or
couple with a brace. **b** imply a connection
between. **2** Math enclose in brackets as
having specific relations to what precedes
or follows. **3** enclose on either side.

brackish adj. (of water etc.) slightly salty.
□ **brackishness** n.

bract n. a modified and often brightly
coloured leaf, with a flower or an
inflorescence in its axil.

brag v. (**brags**, **bragged**, **bragging**) say
something boastfully.

braggadocio n. boastful speech and
behaviour. [Say bragga DOE chee oh]

braggart n. a person who boasts about
their achievements or possessions.
[Say BRAG ert]

Brahman n. (also **brahman**) (pl.
Brahmans) a member of the highest
Hindu caste, that of the priesthood.
□ **Brahmanical** adj. [Say BRA m'n,
bra MAN ick]

braid ● n. **1** a length of hair, straw, etc. in
three or more interlaced strands. **2** threads

woven into a decorative band. ● v.
intertwine. □ **braiding** n.

Braille ● n. a written language for the
blind, using raised dots. ● v. print in
Braille. [Say BRAIL]

brain ● n. **1** an organ of soft tissue
contained in the skull, functioning as the
centre of the nervous system. **2 a** a person's
intellectual capacity. **b** (often in pl.)
intelligence. **3** (**the brains**) informal the
main organizer within a group. ● v. **1** dash
out the brains of. **2** strike hard on the head.
□ **on the brain** informal obsessively in one's
thoughts.

brainchild n. (pl. **brainchildren**) informal
an idea or invention thought up by a
particular person.

brain damage n. injury to the brain
permanently impairing its functions.
□ **brain-damaged** adj.

brain-dead adj. **1** having suffered brain
death. **2** informal derogatory stupid.

brain death n. permanent cessation of
the brain functions controlling breathing,
regarded as indicative of death.

brain drain n. informal the loss of skilled
personnel by emigration.

brainless adj. stupid.

brainpower n. mental ability.

brainstorm ● n. **1** a group discussion to
produce ideas. **2** = BRAINWAVE 2. **3** informal
mental confusion. ● v. have a discussion to
produce ideas. □ **brainstorming** n.

brainteaser n. informal a puzzle or
problem.

brain trust n. a group of expert advisers.

brainwash v. (**brainwashes**,
brainwashed, **brainwashing**) subject
to a process by which ideas other than and
at variance with those already held are
implanted in the mind.
□ **brainwashing** n.

brainwave n. **1** (usu. in pl.) an electrical
impulse in the brain. **2** informal a sudden
bright idea.

brainy adj. (**brainier**, **brainiest**) clever.
□ **braininess** n.

braise v. (**braises**, **braised**, **braising**)
fry lightly and then stew slowly in a closed
container.

brake ● n. **1** (often in pl.) a device for
stopping the motion of a mechanism.
2 anything that impedes. ● v. (**brakes**,
braked, **braking**) **1 a** apply a brake.
b slow or stop upon application of a brake.
2 retard or stop with a brake.

brake drum n. a cylinder attached to a
wheel, whose inner surface is gripped by
brake shoes to cause braking.

brakeman n. (pl. **brakemen**) an employee

on a train, responsible for maintenance on a journey.

brake shoe n. a long curved metal block which presses onto a brake drum.

bramble n. **1** any of various thorny shrubs bearing berries, esp. the blackberry. **2** the edible berry of these shrubs. □ **brambly** adj.

bran n. edible husks of grain which are removed when the cereal is milled or ground.

branch ● n. **1** (pl. **branches**) a limb extending from a tree or bough. **2** a river, road, or railway extending out from a main one. **3** a division of a larger group, network, etc. ● v. (**branches, branched, branching**) **1** diverge. **2** divide into branches. □ **branch out** extend one's field of interest. □ **branched** adj.

branch plant n. Cdn a factory etc. owned by a company based in another country.

brand ● n. **1 a** a particular make of goods. **b** an identifying trademark, label, etc. **2** (usu. foll. by of) a characteristic kind. **3** an identifying mark burned on livestock or (formerly) prisoners etc. with a hot iron. **4** (also **branding iron**) an iron used for this. **5** a piece of smouldering wood. ● v. **1** mark with a hot iron. **2** mark with disgrace. **3** assign a trademark or label to. **4** make (a product or line of products) instantly recognizable as being produced by a particular manufacturer etc. □ **brander** n.

brandied adj. preserved or flavoured with brandy.

brandish v. (**brandishes, brandished, brandishing**) flourish threateningly.

brand name n. **1** a proprietary name. **2** a product with such a name.

brand new adj. completely new.

brandy n. (pl. **brandies**) a strong alcoholic liquor distilled from wine or fermented fruit juice.

brant n. an Arctic goose that is smaller and darker than the Canada goose.

brash[1] adj. **1** self-assertive in an overbearing way. **2** vulgar. □ **brashness** n.

brash[2] n. loose broken rock or ice.

brass n. (pl. **brasses**) **1** a yellow alloy of copper and zinc. **2 a** a brass ornament. **b** brass objects collectively. **3** brass wind instruments forming a band or orchestra section. **4** (also **top brass**) informal people in authority. **5** informal effrontery.

brassica n. any of various related plants including broccoli, cabbage, cauliflower, etc. [Say BRASSA kuh]

brassiere n. = BRA.

brass ring n. noteworthy success.

brass tacks pl. n. informal essential details.

brassy adj. (**brassier, brassiest**) **1** impudent. **2** showy. **3** loud and blaring. **4** of or like brass.

brat n. **1** usu. derogatory a child, esp. a badly behaved one. **2** a child brought up in a specified milieu: Forces brat. □ **bratty** adj. **brattiness** n. **brattish** adj.

bratwurst n. a small German pork sausage.

bravado n. boldness intended to impress. [Say bruh VODDO]

brave ● adj. able or ready to endure danger, pain, etc. ● n. hist. a N American Aboriginal warrior. ● v. (**braves, braved, braving**) defy; encounter bravely. □ **brave it out** behave defiantly under suspicion or blame. □ **bravely** adv.

bravery n. **1** brave conduct. **2** a brave nature.

bravo ● interj. expressing approval of a performer etc. ● n. (pl. **bravos**) a cry of bravo.

bravura ● adj. displaying virtuosic skill. ● n. virtuosic skill, esp. in artistic performance. [Say bra VOORA]

brawl ● n. a rowdy fight. ● v. fight or quarrel roughly. □ **brawler** n.

brawn n. muscular strength.

brawny adj. (**brawnier, brawniest**) muscular, strong.

bray ● n. **1** the cry of a donkey. **2** a sound like this cry. ● v. **1** make a braying sound. **2** utter harshly.

brazen ● adj. **1** bold and shameless. **2** made of brass. **3** of or like brass. ● v. (usu. in phr. **brazen it out**) endure a difficult situation by behaving with apparent confidence. □ **brazenly** adv. **brazenness** n. [Say BRAY z'n]

brazier n. **1** a charcoal grill for cooking. **2** a portable heater holding lighted coals. [Say BRAZE yer or BRAY zhur]

Brazilian adj. of or relating to Brazil or its people or culture. □ **Brazilian** n.

Brazil nut n. the large three-sided nut of a S American tree.

breach ● n. (pl. **breaches**) **1** the failure to observe a law, etc. **2** a breaking of relations. **3** a gap, esp. one made by artillery in fortifications. ● v. (**breaches, breached, breaching**) **1** make a gap in. **2** break (an agreement etc.). **3** (of a whale) leap clear out of the water. □ **step into** (or **fill**) **the breach** give help in a crisis, esp. by replacing someone who has dropped out.

bread ● n. **1** baked food made of flour and a liquid and often raised with yeast. **2 a** necessary food. **b** (also **daily bread**) one's livelihood. **3** slang money. ● v. coat with bread crumbs for cooking. □ **break bread** share a meal.

bread and butter ● *n.* an essential element, esp. that which provides one's livelihood. ● *adj.* (usu. **bread-and-butter**) designating something basic and fundamental to one's livelihood.

breadbasket *n.* **1** a basket for bread. **2** a region producing much grain.

breadboard *n.* a board for cutting bread on.

breadbox *n.* (*pl.* **breadboxes**) a container in which bread is kept.

breadfruit *n.* (*pl.* **breadfruit** or **breadfruits**) **1** a tropical evergreen tree bearing edible usu. seedless fruit. **2** this fruit, which when roasted becomes soft like new bread.

breadknife *n.* (*pl.* **breadknives**) a knife with a long saw-like blade, for slicing bread.

breadline *n.* a line of people waiting to receive free food.

breadstick *n.* a long, stick-like piece of crisp bread.

breadth *n.* **1** the distance from side to side of a thing. **2** extent, range.

breadwinner *n.* a person who earns the money to support a family. □ **breadwinning** *n. & adj.*

break ● *v.* (**breaks**; *past* **broke**; *past participle* **broken**; **breaking**) **1 a** separate into pieces under a blow or strain; fracture. **b** make or become inoperative, esp. from damage. **c** break a bone in or dislocate. **d** break the skin of (the head or crown). **2 a** interrupt. **b** have an interval between spells of work. **3** fail to observe (a law etc.). **4 a** make or become subdued or weakened. **b** weaken the effect of (a fall etc.). **c** = BREAK IN 3c. **d** defeat. **5** surpass (a record). **6** (foll. by *with*) cease association with. **7 a** be no longer subject to. **b** (foll. by *of*) cause (a person) to be free of a habit. **8** reveal or be revealed. **9 a** (of the weather) change after a hot spell. **b** (of waves) curl over and dissolve into foam. **c** (of the day) dawn. **d** (of clouds) move apart. **e** (of a storm) begin violently. **10** *Electricity* disconnect (a circuit). **11 a** (of the voice) change with emotion. **b** (of a boy's voice) change in register at puberty. **12 a** (often foll. by *up*) divide into parts. **b** change (a bill) for coins. **13** ruin financially. **14** penetrate by force. **15** decipher (a code). **16** clear (a trail). **17** burst forth. **18 a** (usu. foll. by *free, loose, out,* etc.) escape from constraint suddenly. **b** escape or emerge from. **19** *Billiards etc.* disperse the balls at the beginning of a game. **20** end. **21** (often foll. by *in*) bring (virgin land) under cultivation.

● *n.* **1 a** an act or instance of breaking. **b** a point where something is broken. **2 a** an interval, an interruption. **b** a holiday. **3** a sudden dash. **4** *informal* an opportunity. **5** *Sport* = BREAKAWAY 1. **6** *Billiards etc.* **a** a series of points scored during one turn. **b** the opening shot that disperses the balls. **7** *Electricity* a discontinuity in a circuit. □ **break away** separate. **break the back of 1** overburden (a person). **2** exert (oneself) greatly. **3** do the hardest part of (a task). **break down 1 a** collapse, fail. **b** be overcome by emotion. **2** demolish; force to yield. **3** analyze into components. **4** decompose. **break even** emerge from a transaction etc. with neither profit nor loss. **break the ice 1** begin to overcome shyness, esp. between strangers. **2** make a start. **break in 1** enter premises by force, esp. with criminal intent. **2** interrupt. **3 a** accustom to a habit etc. **b** wear etc. until comfortable. **c** accustom (a horse) to saddle and bridle etc. **break into 1** enter forcibly or violently. **2** suddenly begin. **3** interrupt. **break a leg** (as *interjection*) *Theatre slang* good luck. **break loose 1** escape from constraint or a fixed position suddenly. **2** develop suddenly. **break out 1** escape by force, esp. from prison. **2** begin suddenly; burst forth. **3** become covered in (a rash, pimples, etc.). **4** exclaim. **5** open up (a receptacle) and remove its contents. **break (into) a sweat** begin sweating. **break up 1** break into small pieces. **2** disperse. **3 a** terminate a relationship. **b** cause to do this. **4** (of a frozen body of water) break into blocks of ice at the spring thaw. **5** upset or be upset. **break wind** release gas from the anus. **give me a break** *informal* expressing skepticism, exasperation, etc. □ **breakable** *adj. & n.*

breakage *n.* **1** a broken thing. **2** an action of breaking something or the fact of being broken.

break and enter *n.* = BREAKING AND ENTERING.

breakaway ● *n.* **1** (in hockey etc.) a rush towards the goal having passed all defenders. **2** a radical change from something established. ● *adj.* **1** separated from a larger body. **2** designed to break easily.

breakdance ● *n.* an energetic, acrobatic, solo street dance. ● *v.* (**breakdances**, **breakdanced**, **breakdancing**) dance a breakdance. □ **breakdancer** *n.* **breakdancing** *n.*

breakdown *n.* **1** a mechanical failure. **2** a loss of (esp. mental) health and strength. **3** a collapse. **4** chemical or physical decomposition. **5** a detailed analysis.

breaker *n.* **1** a person or thing that breaks something. **2** a heavy wave that breaks.

break-even ● *adj.* designating the point at which earnings equal expenditures. ● *n.* a break-even point.

breakfast ● *n.* the first meal of the day. ● *v.* have breakfast. □ **eat for breakfast** *slang* destroy or defeat easily.

break-in *n.* an illegal forced entry into premises.

breaking *adj.* (of news etc.) happening at the moment.

breaking and entering *n.* the illegal entering of a building with the intent to commit an indictable offence.

breaking ball *n.* (also **breaking pitch**) *Baseball* a pitch that drops just before reaching the batter.

breaking point *n.* the point of greatest strain, at which a thing breaks or a person gives way.

breakneck *adj.* (of speed) dangerously fast.

breakout *n.* **1** (in hockey etc.) a sudden offensive rush. **2** a forcible escape. **3** an outbreak, esp. of pimples.

breakthrough *n.* a major advance.

breakup *n.* **1** disintegration, collapse. **2** the termination of a relationship. **3** *Cdn* (also **spring breakup**) **a** the breaking of a frozen river etc. into blocks of ice at the spring thaw. **b** the time during which this happens.

breakwater *n.* a structure which breaks the force of waves, esp. at the entrance to a harbour.

bream *n.* (*pl.* **bream**) **1** a carp-like European freshwater fish. **2** (also **sea bream**) a similar marine fish.

breast ● *n.* **1** either of two milk-secreting organs on the upper front of a woman's body. **2** the upper front part of a human or animal's body. **3** the breast as a source of emotion. ● *v.* **1** face, meet in full opposition. **2** reach the top of (a hill). □ **make a clean breast of** confess fully.

breast-beating *n.* an exaggerated display of remorse, etc.

breastbone *n.* a thin flat vertical bone and cartilage in the chest connecting the ribs.

breastfeed *v.* (**breastfeeds, breastfed, breastfeeding**) **1** feed (a baby) with milk from the breast. **2** (of a baby) feed from the breast.

breastplate *n.* a piece of armour covering the chest.

breaststroke *n.* a swimming stroke in which the arms are pushed forwards and then swept back while the legs are tucked in and kicked out.

breath *n.* **1 a** the air taken into or expelled from the lungs. **b** one respiration of air. **2 a** a slight movement of air; a breeze. **b** a whiff of perfume etc. **3** a sign, hint, or suggestion (esp. of a scandalous nature). **4** the power of breathing; life. □ **below** (or **under**) **one's breath** in a whisper. **take one's breath away** astound, delight. **waste one's breath** talk without effect.

breathable *adj.* **1** (of air) fit to be breathed. **2** (of textiles, clothing, etc.) allowing the passage of air and allowing sweat to evaporate. □ **breathability** *n.*

Breathalyzer *n. proprietary* an instrument for measuring the amount of alcohol in a driver's breath.

breathe *v.* (**breathes, breathed, breathing**) **1** take air into and expel it from the lungs. **2** be or seem alive **3 a** utter; say (esp. quietly). **b** express; display. **4** take breath, pause. **5** send out or take in (as if) with exhaled air. **6** be exposed to fresh air. **7 a** (of textiles, clothing, etc.) allow the passage of air and inhibit condensation. **b** (of the skin) absorb oxygen and get rid of moisture. **8** (of wind) blow softly. □ **breathing** *n. & adj.*

breather *n.* **1** *informal* a brief pause for rest. **2** a person or animal that breathes, esp. in a specified way.

breathless *adj.* **1** panting, out of breath. **2** holding the breath because of excitement. □ **breathlessly** *adv.* **breathlessness** *n.*

breathtaking *adj.* awe-inspiring. □ **breathtakingly** *adv.*

breath test *n.* a test of a person's alcohol consumption, using a Breathalyzer.

breathy *adj.* (**breathier, breathiest**) (of a voice etc.) producing a noticeable sound of breathing. □ **breathily** *adv.* **breathiness** *n.*

breech *n.* (*pl.* **breeches**) **1** the back part of a gun barrel. **2** (as an *adj.*) designating a birth in which the baby presents in the birth canal with the buttocks or feet foremost.

breeches *pl. n.* (also **pair of breeches** *singular*) short trousers fastened below the knee.

breed ● *v.* (**breeds, bred, breeding**) **1** give birth to. **2** propagate or cause to propagate. **3 a** yield; result in. **b** spread. **4** arise. **5** bring up. ● *n.* **1** a particular type within a species of animals or plants. **2** a lineage. **3** a sort, a kind. □ **breeder** *n.*

breeding *n.* **1** the process of developing or propagating (animals, plants, etc.). **2** child-bearing. **3 a** upbringing. **b** behaviour, esp. good manners.

breeding ground *n.* an area where an animal, esp. a bird, habitually breeds.

breeze ● *n.* **1** a gentle wind. **2** *informal* an easy task. ● *v.* (**breezes, breezed, breezing**) **1** (foll. by *in, out, along,* etc.) *informal* come or go in a casual manner. **2** (usu. foll. by *through*) emerge successfully and easily from.

breezy *adj.* (**breezier, breeziest**) **1** pleasantly windy. **2** appearing relaxed, informal, and cheerily brisk. □ **breezily** *adv.* **breeziness** *n.*

brekkie *n.* *slang* breakfast.

brethren *pl. n.* *see* BROTHER *n.* 3.

Breton *n.* **1** a native of Brittany in northwestern France. **2** the Celtic language of Brittany. □ **Breton** *adj.* [Say BRET un]

brevity *n.* **1** concise and exact use of words. **2** shortness of time. [Say BREVVA tee]

brew ● *v.* **1 a** make (beer, etc.) by infusion, boiling, and fermentation. **b** make (tea, coffee, etc.) by infusion. **2** undergo either of these processes. **3** gather force. **4** concoct. ● *n.* **1** an amount brewed at one time. **2** what is brewed. **3** beer.

brewer *n.* a person or company that makes beer.

brewery *n.* (*pl.* **breweries**) a place where beer etc. is brewed commercially.

brewpub *n.* a bar with on-site brewing facilities.

brewski *n.* (*pl.* **brewskis**) *slang* a beer.

briar *n.* = BRIER.

bribe ● *n.* a reward for an (often dishonest) action or decision in favour of the giver. ● *v.* (**bribes, bribed, bribing**) persuade by means of a bribe. □ **bribery** *n.*

bric-a-brac *n.* miscellaneous trinkets etc. [Say BRICKA brack]

brick ● *n.* **1** a small rectangular block of fired clay, used in building. **2** a brick-shaped solid object. ● *v.* (foll. by *in, up*) close or block with brickwork. ● *adj.* built of brick. □ **run into a brick wall** encounter an insurmountable obstacle.

brickbat *n.* an uncomplimentary remark.

bricklayer *n.* a worker who builds with bricks. □ **bricklaying** *n.*

bricks and mortar *n.* buildings, esp. housing or traditional retail businesses based in stores, as opposed to electronic retailing.

brickwork *n.* **1** construction using brick. **2** a wall etc. made of brick.

bridal *adj.* of or concerning a bride or a wedding.

bride *n.* a woman on her wedding day and for some time before and after it.

bridegroom *n.* a man on his wedding day and for some time before and after it.

bridesmaid *n.* **1** a girl or woman attending a bride on her wedding day. **2** someone that never quite attains a desired goal.

bridge¹ ● *n.* **1 a** a structure carrying a road, path, or railway across water, a road, etc. **b** anything providing a connection between things. **2** the superstructure on a ship from which the captain and officers direct operations. **3** the upper bony part of the nose. **4** a piece of wood on a violin, guitar, etc. over which the strings are stretched. **5** a dental structure used to cover a gap. ● *v.* (**bridges, bridged, bridging**) **1** be or make a bridge over. **2** span as if with a bridge. □ **cross that bridge when one comes to it** deal with a problem when and if it arises.

bridge² *n.* a card game derived from whist, in which one player's cards are exposed and are then played by his or her partner.

bridge-building *n.* **1** the activity of building bridges. **2** the promotion of friendly relations. □ **bridge-builder** *n.*

bridgehead *n.* a fortified position held on the enemy's side of a river etc., established as a basis for advancing further.

bridle ● *n.* **1** the headgear used to control a horse. **2** a restraining influence. ● *v.* (**bridles, bridled, bridling**) **1** put a bridle on. **2** express offence etc.

brie *n.* a ripened soft cheese with a white mould skin. [Say BREE]

brief ● *adj.* **1** not lasting long. **2** concise in expression. **3** short. ● *n.* **1** (in *pl.*) close-fitting legless underpants. **2** *Law* a written statement of the arguments for a case. **3** instructions. **4** a short news article. ● *v.* instruct in preparation for a task. □ **briefly** *adv.*

briefcase *n.* a flat rectangular case for carrying documents etc.

briefing *n.* **1** a meeting for giving information or instructions. **2** the information given. **3** the action of informing or instructing.

Brier *n.* the bonspiel for the Canadian men's national curling championship. [Rhymes with FIRE]

brier *n.* **1** any prickly bush esp. of a wild rose. **2 a** a white European plant of the heath family. **b** a tobacco pipe made from its root. [Rhymes with FIRE]

brig *n.* **1** a two-masted square-rigged ship. **2** a prison, esp. on a warship.

brigade *n.* **1** a subdivision of an army. **2** an

organized band of workers. **3** *informal* any group of people with a characteristic in common.

brigadier general *n.* (also **Brigadier General**) an officer ranking next above colonel.

brigand *n.* a member of a gang of bandits. □ **brigandage** *n.* [*Say* BRIG und]

brigantine *n.* a two-masted sailing ship. [*Say* BRIG un teen]

bright ● *adj.* **1** giving out or full of light. **2** (of colour) vivid. **3** clever. **4** cheerful. **5** promising. ● *n.* (in *pl.*) **1** bright colours. **2** headlights switched to high beam. □ **bright-eyed and bushy-tailed** *informal* alert and sprightly. **look on the bright side** be optimistic. □ **brightly** *adv.* **brightness** *n.*

brighten *v.* make or become brighter. □ **brightener** *n.*

brilliant *adj.* **1** very bright. **2** outstandingly talented or intelligent. **3** showy. □ **brilliance** *n.* **brilliantly** *adv.*

brim ● *n.* **1** the lip of a cup, bowl, etc. **2** the projecting edge of a hat. ● *v.* (**brims, brimmed, brimming**) fill or be full to the point of overflowing. □ **brimful** *adj.*-**brimless** *adj.* **brimmed** *comb. form*

brimstone *n.* *archaic* sulphur.

brine *n.* **1** water having a high concentration of salt. **2** sea water.

bring *v.* (**brings, brought, bringing**) **1** come carrying or accompanying. **2** cause to be in a particular position or state. **3** cause or result in. **4** be sold for. **5** begin (legal action). **6** provide (evidence). **7** make (something) move in the direction or way specified. □ **bring about** cause to happen. **bring down** *Cdn* present (a budget, law, report, etc.). **bring down the house** get loud applause. **bring forth 1** give birth to. **2** produce. **bring forward 1** move to an earlier time. **2** draw attention to. **bring home to** cause to realize fully. **bring off** achieve successfully. **bring on** cause to happen or appear. **bring out 1** emphasize. **2** publish. **bring over** convert to one's own side. **bring round** (or **around**) **1** restore to consciousness. **2** persuade. **bring to bear** exert influence. **bring to mind** recall; cause one to remember. **bring to pass** cause to happen. **bring up 1** rear (a child). **2** vomit. **3** call attention to. □ **bringer** *n.*

brink *n.* **1** the extreme edge of land before a sudden drop or body of water. **2** the point where a new or unpleasant situation is about to begin.

brinkmanship *n.* the pursuit of a dangerous policy to the brink of catastrophe before stopping.

briny *adj.* (**brinier, briniest**) salty. [*Say* BRINE ee]

brio *n.* vigour or vivacity. [*Say* BREE oh]

briquette *n.* a block of compressed charcoal etc. used as fuel. [*Say* brick ET]

brisk *adj.* **1** active, energetic. **2** cold but pleasantly fresh. **3** slightly abrupt. □ **briskness** *n.* **briskly** *adv.*

brisket *n.* **1** the breast of an animal. **2** a cut of beef used esp. to make corned beef.

bristle ● *n.* **1** a short stiff hair. **2** a stiff animal hair, or a synthetic substitute, used in clumps to make a brush. ● *v.* (**bristles, bristled, bristling**) **1** (of the hair) stand upright, esp. in anger or fear. **2** show irritation. □ **bristling** *adj.* **bristly** *adj.*

bristol board *n.* a kind of fine smooth pasteboard.

Brit *informal* ● *n.* a British person. ● *adj.* British.

britches *pl. n.* *informal* any pants, shorts, or underwear. □ **too big for one's britches** excessively arrogant.

British *adj.* of or relating to Great Britain.

British Columbian *adj.* of or relating to British Columbia. □ **British Columbian** *n.*

British thermal unit *n.* the amount of heat needed to raise 1 lb. of water at maximum density through one degree Fahrenheit. Abbreviation: **BTU**.

Briton *n.* **1** a native or inhabitant of Great Britain. **2** a native of southern Britain before the Roman conquest.

brittle ● *adj.* **1 a** hard but easily broken. **b** insecure; easily damaged. **2** grating or artificial. ● *n.* a brittle candy made from nuts and set melted sugar. □ **brittleness** *n.*

broach *v.* (**broaches, broached, broaching**) **1** raise for discussion. **2** pierce and open (a container) to draw liquid. **3** (of a fish etc.) break the surface of the water.

broad ● *adj.* **1** large in extent from one side to the other. **2** full and clear. **3** unmistakable. **4** general. **5** of or including a great variety. **6** tolerant, liberal. **7** somewhat coarse. **8** (of speech) markedly regional. ● *n.* **1** the broad part of something. **2** *slang offensive* a woman. □ **broadly** *adv.*

broadaxe *n.* a large axe with a broad blade.

broadband *n.* a transmission technique enabling messages to be communicated simultaneously.

broadcast ● *v.* (**broadcasts, broadcast, broadcasting**) **1 a** transmit by radio or television. **b** spread widely. **2** scatter (seeds). ● *n.* a radio or television

program. □ **broadcaster** n.
broadcasting n.

broadcloth n. a fine cloth of wool, cotton and/or silk.

broaden v. make or become broader.

broadleaf ● adj. (also **broad-leaved**, **broad-leafed**) **1** having broad leaves. **2** deciduous and having hard timber. ● n. (pl. **broadleaves**) **1** a broadleaf weed. **2** a broadleaf tree.

broadloom n. carpet woven in broad widths. □ **broadloomed** adj.

broadsheet n. a newspaper printed on large sheets of paper.

broadside ● n. **1** the firing of all guns from one side of a ship. **2** a strongly worded criticism. ● adv. with the side turned towards a given object. ● adj. sideways. ● v. collide with on the side.

broad spectrum adj. (of a drug) effective against a wide range of pathogens.

brocade n. a rich fabric woven with a raised pattern. □ **brocaded** adj. [Say bro CADE]

broccoli n. a vegetable related to the cauliflower, with a loose cluster of green flower buds.

brochette n. chunks of meat threaded on a skewer and grilled. [Say braw SHET or bruh SHET]

brochure n. a pamphlet giving descriptive information.

brogue[1] n. a marked accent, esp. Irish. [Say BROAG]

brogue[2] n. **1** a strong outdoor shoe with ornamental perforated bands. **2** a rough leather shoe. [Say BROAG]

broil v. **1** cook by direct exposure to heat; grill. **2** make or become very hot. □ **broiling** adj.

broiler n. **1** an appliance or the element in an oven used for broiling. **2** a young chicken raised for broiling.

broke ● v. past of BREAK. ● adj. informal having no money. □ **go for broke** slang risk everything in a strenuous effort.

broken ● v. past participle of BREAK. ● adj. **1 a** that has been broken. **b** out of order. **2** reduced to despair. **3** spoken with many mistakes. **4** uneven. **5** divided by separation or divorce. □ **brokenness** n.

broken-down adj. **1** in bad condition. **2** out of order.

broken-hearted adj. overwhelmed with sorrow. □ **broken-heartedness** n.

broker ● n. **1** an agent who buys and sells or acts for others. **2** a member of a stock exchange who deals in stocks and shares. ● v. negotiate, esp. as an intermediary. □ **brokerage** n.

brome n. (also **brome grass**) an oat-like grass of the temperate zone.

bromide n. **1** a compound of bromine. **2** a trite remark. [Say BRO mide]

bromine n. a dark liquid element with a choking smell. [Say BRO mean]

bronc n. informal = BRONCO.

bronchial adj. of or relating to the air passages in the lungs which diverge from the windpipe. [Say BRONKY ul]

bronchitis n. inflammation of the mucous membrane in the bronchial tubes. [Say bron KITE iss]

bronchodilator n. a substance which causes widening of the bronchi. [Say bronco DIE later]

bronchus n. (pl. **bronchi**) any of the major air passages of the lungs, esp. either of the two main divisions of the windpipe. [Say BRON kuss]

bronco n. (pl. **broncos**) a wild or half-tamed horse.

broncobuster n. informal a person who breaks in horses. □ **broncobusting** n.

brontosaurus n. (pl. **brontosauruses**) (also **brontosaur**) a large plant-eating dinosaur of the Jurassic and Cretaceous periods, with a long whip-like tail and trunk-like legs.

bronze ● n. **1** an alloy of copper and tin. **2** its brownish colour. **3** an artwork made of bronze. **4** (also **bronze medal**) a medal usu. awarded to a competitor who comes third (esp. in sport). ● adj. made of or coloured like bronze. ● v. (**bronzes**, **bronzed**, **bronzing**) **1** give a bronze-like surface to. **2** make suntanned.

Bronze Age n. the period preceding the Iron Age, when weapons and tools were usu. made of bronze.

bronzer n. a cosmetic applied to the skin to make it look tanned.

brooch n. (pl. **brooches**) an ornament fastened to clothing with a hinged pin. [Sounds like BROACH]

brood ● n. **1** the young of an animal produced at one hatching or birth. **2** informal the children in a family. **3** (as an adj.) kept for breeding. ● v. **1** (often foll. by on, over, etc.) worry or ponder. **2** (of a bird) sit on eggs to hatch them. **3** (usu. foll. by over) hang or hover closely.

brooding adj. melancholy, sombre. □ **broodingly** adv.

broody adj. (**broodier**, **broodiest**) **1** (of a hen) wanting to brood. **2** depressed.

brook[1] n. a small stream.

brook[2] v. tolerate.

brook trout n. (also **brookie**) a trout

found widely throughout eastern
N America.

broom n. **1** a brush of bristles, straw, etc.
on a long handle, used for sweeping. **2** a
flowering shrub with thin stems and
bright yellow flowers.

broomstick n. the handle of a broom.

broth n. a thin soup of meat or fish stock.

brothel n. a house etc. where prostitution
takes place.

brother ● n. **1** a man or boy in relation to
other children of his parents. **2** a male
colleague or friend. **3** (pl. also **brethren**)
a a member of a male religious order, esp.
a monk. **b** a male fellow Christian. ● interj.
expressing mild annoyance.
□ **brotherly** adj. & adv. **brotherliness** n.

brotherhood n. **1 a** the relationship
between brothers. **b** friendliness;
companionship. **2** a group of people linked
by a common interest etc.

brother-in-law n. (pl. **brothers-in-law**)
1 the brother of one's wife or husband.
2 the husband of one's sister or sister-in-
law.

brought past and past participle of BRING.

brouhaha (pl. **brouhahas**) a noisy and
overexcited reaction. [Say BREW haw haw]

brow n. **1** the forehead. **2** (usu. in pl.) an
eyebrow. **3** the summit of a hill or pass.
4 the edge of a cliff etc.

browbeat v. (**browbeats**; past
browbeat; past participle **browbeaten**;
browbeating) intimidate with words or
looks. □ **browbeater** n.

brown ● adj. **1** having the colour of dark
wood or rich soil. **2** dark-skinned or
suntanned. ● n. a brown colour or
material. ● v. make or become brown by
cooking, sunburn, etc. □ **brownish** adj.
browny adj.

brown bear n. a large bear of northern
N America, Europe, and Asia.

brown cow n. Cdn a cocktail of coffee
liqueur and milk.

brownie n. **1** (usu. **Brownie**; in full
Brownie Guide) a member of the junior
branch of the Guides. **2** a small square of
rich chocolate cake.

brownie point n. informal a notional credit
for something done to please.

brown-nose v. (**brown-noses, brown-
nosed, brown-nosing**) behave
obsequiously in hopes of advancement.
□ **brown-noser** n. **brown-nosing** adj. & n.

brownout n. a temporary reduction in
electrical power.

brown owl n. **1** any of various owls, esp.
the tawny owl. **2** (**Brown Owl**) Cdn an
adult leader of a Brownie pack.

brown rice n. unpolished rice with only
the husk of the grain removed.

brown sugar n. **1** refined sugar to which
molasses has been added. **2** unrefined or
partially refined sugar.

browse ● v. (**browses, browsed,
browsing**) **1** read or survey haphazardly.
2 feed (on vegetation). **3** view (data files) on
a network. ● n. an act of browsing.

browser n. **1** a program used to navigate
the World Wide Web. **2** a person or animal
that browses.

bruise ● n. **1** an area of discoloured skin
on the body, caused by a blow. **2** similar
damage on fruit etc. ● v. (**bruises,
bruised, bruising**) **1** a inflict a bruise
on. **b** hurt mentally. **2** be susceptible to
bruising.

bruiser n. informal a large tough-looking
person.

brunch ● n. a late-morning meal intended
to combine breakfast and lunch. ● v.
(**brunches, brunched, brunching**) eat
brunch.

brunette n. a woman with dark brown
hair.

brunt n. the worst part or initial impact of
an action.

bruschetta n. (pl. **bruschettas**) slices of
toasted bread drizzled with olive oil and
usu. topped with diced tomatoes, garlic,
etc. [Say brew SHETTA or brew SKETTA]

brush ● n. (pl. **brushes**) **1** an implement
with a handle and a block of bristles etc.,
for various purposes. **2** the application of a
brush; brushing. **3** a short esp. unpleasant
encounter. **4** the bushy tail of a fox.
5 undergrowth. ● v. (**brushes, brushed,
brushing**) **1** clean, smooth or apply with a
brush. **2** touch lightly. □ **brush aside**
dismiss curtly. **brush off** rebuff. **brush
up** (usu. foll. by on) revive one's former
knowledge of. □ **brushlike** adj.

brush cut n. a very short haircut.

brushcutter n. a device with blades for
cutting heavy undergrowth.

brushed adj. **1** swept or smoothed with a
brush. **2** (of metallic surfaces) finished with
a non-reflective surface. **3** (of fabric)
brushed so as to raise the nap.

brush-off n. a rebuff; an abrupt dismissal.

brushwork n. the way in which painters
use their brush.

brushy adj. covered with small trees and
shrubs.

brusque adj. abrupt in manner.
□ **brusquely** adv. **brusqueness** n.
[Say BRUSK]

Brussels sprouts pl. n. **1** a vegetable
with small cabbage-like buds close together

along a tall single stem. **2** these buds eaten as a vegetable.

brutal adj. **1** savagely cruel. **2** harsh, merciless. □ **brutality** n. (pl. **brutalities**) **brutally** adv.

brutalize v. (**brutalizes, brutalized, brutalizing**) **1** treat in a cruel manner. **2** make brutal by exposing to violence. □ **brutalization** n.

brute ● n. **1 a** a brutal or violent person or animal. **b** informal an unpleasant person. **2** an animal as opposed to a human being. **3** a large and very strong person etc. ● adj. **1** entirely physical. **2** unreasoning and animal-like. □ **brutish** adj.

B.Sc. abbr. (pl. **B.Sc.'s**) Bachelor of Science.

BT abbr. (also **Bt**) BACILLUS THURINGIENSIS.

BTU abbr. (pl. **BTUs**) BRITISH THERMAL UNIT.

BTW abbr. by the way.

bu. abbr. bushel(s).

bubbe n. (pl. **bubbes**) (also **bubbie**; pl. **bubbies**) a Jewish grandmother. [Say BUBBA, BUBBY]

bubble ● n. **1 a** a thin sphere of liquid enclosing water etc. **b** an air-filled cavity in a liquid or a solidified liquid such as glass. **2** a transparent domed cavity. **3** a state that is unstable and unlikely to last. ● v. (**bubbles, bubbled, bubbling**) **1 a** rise in or send up bubbles. **b** become manifest; arise as if from a depth. **2** make the sound of boiling. **3** be exuberant with laughter etc.

bubble bath n. **1** a preparation for adding to bathwater to make it foam. **2** a bath with this added.

bubble tea n. an originally Taiwanese beverage consisting of cold tea, milk, and cooked tapioca balls, sometimes with fruit flavouring.

bubbly ● adj. (**bubblier, bubbliest**) **1** having or resembling bubbles. **2** full of high spirits. ● n. (pl. **bubblies**) informal sparkling wine, esp. champagne.

bubonic plague n. a form of plague characterized by swellings in the groin or armpits. [Say byoo BON ick or boo BON ick]

buccaneer n. **1** a pirate. **2** a recklessly adventurous person. □ **buccaneering** n. & adj. [Say bucka NEAR]

buck¹ ● n. **1** the male of various animals, esp. the deer. **2** a self-assured young man. ● v. **1** (of a horse) jump upwards with back arched. **2** (usu. foll. by off) throw (a rider etc.) in this way. **3 a** oppose, resist. **b** make one's way with difficulty against. **4** Football charge into (an opponent's line) while carrying the ball. □ **buck up** informal make or become more cheerful.

buck² n. informal a dollar. □ **pass the buck** informal shift responsibility.

bucket n. **1** an open container with a handle, for carrying liquids etc. **2** (in pl.) large quantities of liquid. □ **bucketful** n. (pl. **bucketfuls**)

bucket seat n. a seat with a rounded back to fit one person, esp. in a car.

buckeye n. **1** any of various trees related to the horse chestnut. **2** the shiny brown fruit of this plant.

buckle ● n. a flat frame with a hinged pin, used as a fastener. ● v. (**buckles, buckled, buckling**) **1** (often foll. by up, on, etc.) fasten with a buckle. **2** give way or cause to give way under pressure. □ **buckle down** make a determined effort. **buckle up** fasten one's seat belt.

bucksaw n. a woodcutting saw having the blade set within an H-shaped upright frame.

buckshot n. a coarse lead shot used in shotgun shells.

buckskin n. a soft leather made from the skin of a male deer or sheepskin.

bucktail n. a fishing lure made of hairs from the tail of a deer etc.

buckthorn n. a thorny shrub or small tree bearing black berries used as a laxative.

bucktooth n. (pl. **buckteeth**) an upper front tooth that projects. □ **bucktoothed** adj.

buckwheat n. a cereal plant with seeds used for fodder and for flour.

bucolic adj. relating to an idyllic life in the countryside. [Say byoo COL ick]

bud¹ ● n. an immature shoot from which a stem, leaf, or flower develops. ● v. (**buds, budded, budding**) **1** form a bud or buds. **2** begin to develop. □ **in bud** having newly formed buds.

bud² n. informal (as a form of address) any male.

Buddhism n. a religion or philosophy based on the 5th-century teachings of Gautama Buddha. □ **Buddhist** n. & adj. [Say BOOD ism]

buddy ● n. (pl. **buddies**) **1** informal a close friend. **2** a person's companion for some activity, esp. a dangerous one. ● v. (**buddies, buddied, buddying**) (often foll. by up) become friendly.

budge v. (**budges, budged, budging**) **1 a** make the slightest movement. **b** change one's opinion. **2** cause or compel to budge.

budgerigar n. (also **budgie**) a small Australian parakeet. [Say BUDGE a ree gar]

budget ● n. **1** an estimate of revenue and expenditure for a set period of time. **2** (as an *adj.*) inexpensive. **3** the amount of money needed or available (for a specific item etc.). ● *v.* (**budgets, budgeted, budgeting**) **1** allow for in a budget. **2** plan the allotment of (money, time, etc.). □ **on a budget** with a restricted amount of money. □ **budgetary** *adj.*

budworm *n.* **1** SPRUCE BUDWORM. **2** a larva destructive to the buds of plants.

buff ● *adj.* **1** of a yellowish beige colour. **2** (also **buffed**) *informal* (of a person) having a body with highly sculpted muscles. ● *n.* **1** yellowish beige. **2** *informal* an expert in a specified subject. **3** a thick, soft, yellow leather. ● *v.* **1** polish. **2** make (leather) velvety like buff, by removing the surface. □ **in the buff** *informal* naked.

buffalo *n.* (*pl.* **buffalo** or **buffaloes**) **1** the N American bison. **2** either of two species of ox, the Cape buffalo or the water buffalo.

buffalo grass *n.* a creeping grass of the N American plains.

buffalo jump *n. hist.* a cliff over which Plains Aboriginal peoples drove herds of bison to kill them.

buffer ● *n.* **1** something that protects against or reduces the effect of an impact. **2** a substance that resists changes in pH when an acid or alkali is added. **3** an intermediate memory for the temporary storage of information during data transfers. ● *v.* **1** act as a buffer to. **2** *Chemistry* treat with a buffer.

buffet[1] *n.* **1 a** a meal consisting of several dishes from which guests serve themselves. **b** a table from which such meals are served. **2** a sideboard or cabinet for china etc. [*Say* buff AY]

buffet[2] *v.* (**buffets, buffeted, buffeting**) **1** strike repeatedly. **2** afflict repeatedly. □ **buffeting** *n.* [*Say* BUFF it]

buffoon *n.* a ridiculous person. □ **buffoonery** *n.* **buffoonish** *adj.*

bug ● *n.* **1 a** any small insect. **b** *Zoology* an insect having mouthparts modified for piercing and sucking. **2** *informal* a microorganism or a disease caused by it. **3** a concealed microphone etc. used in surveillance. **4** a malfunction in a computer program etc. **5** *informal* an obsession. ● *v.* (**bugs, bugged, bugging**) **1** *informal* annoy, bother. **2** conceal a microphone in (a room etc.). **3** (often foll. by *out*) (of the eyes) bulge.

bugaboo *n.* (*pl.* **bugaboos**) **1** a bugbear. **2** an object of fear or anxiety.

bugbear *n.* a cause of annoyance or anxiety.

bug-eyed *adj.* having bulging eyes.

bugger ● *n.* **1** *slang* an unpleasant or awkward person or thing. **2** a person who commits buggery. ● *v.* commit buggery with. ● *interj. informal* expressing annoyance. □ **bugger about** (or **around**) (often foll. by *with*) *slang* **1** mess about. **2** mislead; persecute.

buggery *n.* anal intercourse.

buggy[1] *n.* (*pl.* **buggies**) **1** a light horse-drawn vehicle for one or two people. **2** a small, sturdy, esp. open, automobile. **3** = BABY CARRIAGE. **4** a shopping cart.

buggy[2] *adj.* (**buggier, buggiest**) **1** infested with bugs. **2** (of software) having programming errors.

bugle ● *n.* **1** a brass instrument like a small trumpet. **2** the call of a bull elk. ● *v.* (**bugles, bugled, bugling**) **1** sound a bugle. **2** (of a bull elk etc.) make a loud bellowing call. □ **bugler** *n.* [*Say* BYOO gull]

build ● *v.* (**builds, built, building**) **1** construct by putting parts or material together. **2 a** establish, develop, or increase gradually. **b** (often foll. by *on*) base. ● *n.* the size or form of someone or something. □ **build in** (or **into**) incorporate as part of (a structure, plan, etc.). **build on** add (to). □ **builder** *n.* **building** *n.*

buildup *n.* **1** a favourable description in advance. **2** a gradual approach to a climax. **3** an accumulation.

built ● *v.* past and past participle of BUILD. ● *adj.* **1** having a specified build. **2** produced by building.

built-in *adj.* forming an integral part of a something.

built-up *adj.* **1** (of a locality) densely covered by houses etc. **2** increased over a period of time.

bulb *n.* **1** the rounded base of the stem of some plants, from which the roots grow. **2** = LIGHT BULB.

bulbous *adj.* **1** round or bulging at one end. **2** growing from a bulb.

Bulgarian *n.* **1** a person from Bulgaria, or of Bulgarian descent. **2** the language of Bulgaria. □ **Bulgarian** *adj.*

bulge ● *n.* **1** a rounded swelling on a flat surface. **2** *informal* a temporary increase. ● *v.* (**bulges, bulged, bulging**) **1** swell outwards. **2** be full of. □ **bulgy** *adj.*

bulgur *n.* a cereal food of whole wheat partially boiled then dried. [*Say* BUL gur]

bulimia *n.* (also **bulimia nervosa**) a disorder characterized by bouts of extreme overeating, followed by self-induced vomiting or fasting. □ **bulimic** *adj.* & *n.* [*Say* buh LIMMY uh]

bulk ● *n.* **1 a** size (esp. large). **b** a large mass or shape. **c** a large quantity. **2** the greater part. **3** dietary fibre. **4** cargo. ● *v.* **1** seem, as regards size or importance. **2** make (a substance) seem bulkier. **3** combine together. ● *adj.* pertaining to material in bulk. □ **in bulk 1** loose, not packaged. **2** in large quantities. **bulk up** increase in bulk.

bulkhead *n.* a partition separating compartments in a ship, aircraft, etc.

bulky *adj.* (**bulkier, bulkiest**) taking up much space. □ **bulkiness** *n.*

bull[1] ● *n.* **1 a** a male bovine animal that has not been castrated. **b** a large male animal, e.g. a whale or moose. **2** *slang* nonsensical talk or writing. ● *adj.* like that of a bull. □ **bull in a china shop** a reckless or clumsy person. **take the bull by the horns** meet a difficulty boldly.

bull[2] *n.* a papal edict.

bulldog *n.* **1** a sturdy, short dog with a powerful jaw and smooth hair. **2** a tenacious person.

bulldogging *n. slang* = STEER WRESTLING. □ **bulldogger** *n.*

bulldoze *v.* (**bulldozes, bulldozed, bulldozing**) **1** clear with a bulldozer. **2** *informal* use force insensitively.

bulldozer *n.* **1** a tractor with a curved blade at the front for clearing ground. **2** a forceful and domineering person.

bullet *n.* **1** a small projectile fired from a gun. **2** a solid circle printed before an item in a list etc.

bulletin *n.* **1** a short official statement or summary of news. **2** a regular newsletter or report.

bulletin board *n.* **1** a board for displaying notices. **2** a store of information that authorized computer users can access remotely.

bulletproof ● *adj.* **1** impenetrable by bullets. **2** unassailable. ● *v.* make bulletproof.

bullfight *n.* a sport of baiting and killing bulls as a public spectacle. □ **bullfighter** *n.* **bullfighting** *n.*

bullfrog *n.* a large frog with a bellowing call.

bullhead *n.* a N American freshwater catfish.

bullheaded *adj.* obstinate, unthinking. □ **bullheadedly** *adv.* **bullheadedness** *n.*

bullhorn *n.* an electronically amplified megaphone.

bullion *n.* gold or silver in bulk before coining. [Say BULL yun]

bullish *adj.* **1** *Stock Market* associated with a rise in prices. **2** aggressively optimistic. □ **bullishly** *adv.* **bullishness** *n.*

bull market *n.* a market with shares rising in price.

bullock *n.* a castrated male of domestic cattle, raised for beef.

bullpen *n.* **1** *Baseball* **a** an area where pitchers warm up. **b** the relief pitchers on a team. **2** a large cell for holding prisoners temporarily.

bull riding *n.* a rodeo event in which a rider attempts to remain on a bucking bull. □ **bull rider** *n.*

bullring *n.* an arena for bullfights.

bull's eye *n.* **1 a** the centre of a target. **b** a shot etc. hitting this. **2** an accurate guess.

bull snake *n.* a yellowish-brown snake found on the N American prairies.

bull terrier *n.* a stocky, short-haired breed of dog that is a cross between a bulldog and a terrier.

bull trout *n.* a brightly spotted char.

bullwhip ● *n.* a whip with a long heavy lash. ● *v.* (**bullwhips, bullwhipped, bullwhipping**) thrash with such a whip.

bully ● *n.* (*pl.* **bullies**) a person who uses power to coerce others by fear. ● *v.* (**bullies, bullied, bullying**) persecute, oppress, or coerce by force or threats.

bulrush *n.* **1** a slender-stemmed water plant used for weaving. **2** a tall water plant with a brown flower head.

bulwark *n.* **1** a defensive wall. **2** something that acts as a defence. **3** (usu. in *pl.*) a ship's side above deck. [Say BULL work]

bum[1] *n. informal* the buttocks.

bum[2] *informal* ● *n.* **1** a vagrant. **2** a lazy or irresponsible person. **3** an obnoxious person. **4** a person who devotes a lot of time to a specified activity. ● *v.* (**bums, bummed, bumming**) **1** (often foll. by *around*) loaf or wander around. **2** acquire by begging. **3** (foll. by *out*) disappoint. ● *adj.* **1** malfunctioning. **2** worthless. **3** unfair, disappointing. □ **give a person the bum's rush 1** forcibly eject. **2** abruptly dismiss.

bumble *v.* (**bumbles, bumbled, bumbling**) **1** act ineptly. **2** (foll. by *on*) speak incoherently. □ **bumbler** *n.*

bumblebee *n.* a large hairy bee with a loud buzz.

bumbleberry pie *n. Cdn* a pie with a filling of mixed berries, e.g. blackberries, raspberries, blueberries, strawberries, etc.

bumbling *adj.* inept.

bummed *adj. informal* (also **bummed out**) disappointed.

bummer *n. informal* **1** an annoying or disappointing thing. **2** an idler.

bump ● *n.* **1** a dull-sounding blow or collision. **2** a swelling or dent caused by this. **3** an uneven patch on a road, field, etc. ● *v.* **1 a** hit with a bump. **b** collide.

2 hurt or damage by striking. **3** move with much jolting. **4** displace. □ **bump and grind** move to music, esp. as part of an erotic dance. **bump into** *informal* meet by chance. **like a bump on a log** inertly. **bump off** *slang* murder. **bump up** *informal* increase (prices etc.).

bumper *n.* **1** a horizontal bar fixed across the ends of a motor vehicle to reduce damage in a collision. **2** (usu. as an *adj.*) unusually large or fine. □ **bumper to bumper** (of traffic) backed up.

bumper car *n.* each of several small electric cars in an enclosure at an amusement park, driven around and bumped into each other.

bumpkin *n.* an unsophisticated and socially inept rural person.

bumptious *adj.* offensively conceited. □ **bumptiousness** *n.* [*Say* BUMP shuss]

bumpy *adj.* (**bumpier, bumpiest**) **1** having many bumps. **2** affected by bumps. □ **bumpily** *adv.* **bumpiness** *n.*

bum rap *n. informal* **1** imprisonment on a false charge. **2** a false accusation.

bum steer *n. informal* false information.

bun *n.* **1** a small bread roll. **2** (in *pl.*) *informal* the buttocks. **3** hair worn in a tight coil at the back of the head. □ **have a bun in the oven** *slang* be pregnant.

bunch ● *n.* **1** a cluster of things growing or fastened together. **2** a collection; a set or lot. **3** *informal* a group; a gang. **4** *informal* a large amount; lots. ● *v.* (**bunches, bunched, bunching**) **1** make into a bunch or bunches. **2** form into a group. □ **bunchy** *adj.*

bunchberry *n.* (*pl.* **bunchberries**) a low-growing plant of the dogwood family.

bunchgrass *n.* a grass that grows in clumps.

bundle ● *n.* **1** a collection of things tied together. **2** a set of nerve fibres etc. banded together. **3** *informal* a large amount of money. ● *v.* (**bundles, bundled, bundling**) **1** (usu. foll. by *up*) tie in or make into a bundle. **2** throw or push, esp. quickly. **3** send away hurriedly. **4** dress. **5** sell as a unit. □ **bundle up** dress warmly.

bung ● *n.* **1** a stopper for closing a hole in a container. ● *v.* stop with a bung. □ **bunged up** *informal* **1** damaged; malfunctioning. **2** closed, blocked.

bungalow *n.* a low house having only one storey.

bungee cord *n.* strong elasticized cord or cable, used esp. for securing baggage. [*Say* BUN jee]

bungee jump *v.* jump from a high place while attached to it by a bungee cord.

□ **bungee jumper** *n.* **bungee jumping** *n.* [*Say* BUN jee]

bungle ● *v.* (**bungles, bungled, bungling**) **1** mismanage or fail at. **2** make mistakes. ● *n.* bungled work. □ **bungler** *n.*

bunion *n.* a painful swelling on the big toe. [*Say* BUN yun]

bunk¹ ● *n.* a simple bed, esp. one of two or more arranged on top of one another. ● *v.* sleep in a bunk. □ **bunk down** go to bed.

bunk² *n. slang* nonsense.

bunker *n.* **1** a large container for storing fuel. **2** a reinforced underground shelter. **3** a sand-filled hollow on a golf course.

bunkhouse *n.* **1** a house where workers etc. are lodged. **2** *Cdn* = BUNKIE.

bunkie *n. Cdn* a small outbuilding on the property of a summer cottage providing extra sleeping accommodation for guests.

bunny *n.* (*pl.* **bunnies**) **1** *informal* a rabbit. **2** *derogatory* (usu. in *comb.*) a young, attractive woman, esp. one who is sexually available, involved in a particular activity. **3** (as an *adj.*) designating an easy hill for beginner skiers.

Bunsen burner *n.* a small adjustable gas burner used in scientific work.

bunt ● *v.* **1** push with the head or horns. **2** *Baseball* **a** strike (the ball) with the bat without swinging. **b** bunt the ball. ● *n.* **1** an act of bunting. **2** a bunted ball. □ **bunter** *n.*

bunting *n.* **1 a** flags and other decorations. **b** a fabric used for these. **2** (also **bunting bag**) a hooded sleeping bag for infants. **3** a seed-eating bird related to the finch and sparrow.

buoy ● *n.* an anchored float serving as a navigation mark etc. ● *v.* **1** (usu. foll. by *up*) **a** keep afloat. **b** uplift, encourage. **2** mark with a buoy. [*Say* BOY]

buoyant *adj.* **1 a** able to keep afloat or rise to the top of a liquid or gas. **b** (of a liquid or gas) able to keep something afloat. **2** lighthearted. □ **buoyancy** *n.* **buoyantly** *adv.* [*Say* BOY ent]

bur *n.* = BURR *n.* 1-2.

burb *n. informal* (usu. in *pl.*) a suburb.

burble ● *v.* (**burbles, burbled, burbling**) **1** murmur. **2** speak in a rambling way. ● *n.* **1** a murmuring noise. **2** rambling speech.

burbot *n.* a freshwater fish of the cod family. [*Say* BURR bit]

burden ● *n.* **1** a heavy load. **2** an oppressive duty. ● *v.* **1** load with a burden. **2** cause worry or hardship to. □ **burden of proof** the obligation to prove one's case. □ **burdensome** *adj.*

burdock *n.* a plant with large leaves and prickly flowers. [*Say* BURR dock]

bureau n. (pl. **bureaus**) **1 a** a writing desk with an angled top opening downwards to form a writing surface. **b** a chest of drawers. **2 a** an office with a specified function. **b** a government department. [Say BYOOR oh]

bureaucracy n. (pl. **bureaucracies**) **1** a system of government in which most decisions are made by civil servants rather than by elected representatives. **2** the officials of such a government. **3** excessively complicated administrative procedure. [Say byur OCKRA see]

bureaucrat n. an official, esp. one excessively concerned with procedural correctness. □ **bureaucratic** adj. [Say BYUR a crat, byur a CRAT ick]

bureaucratese n. language characteristic of bureaucrats. [Say byur OCK ra TEEZ]

burg n. informal a town.

burgeon v. grow or increase rapidly. □ **burgeoning** adj. [Say BURR jun]

burger n. informal a hamburger.

burgher n. a middle-class town-dweller. [Sounds like BURGER]

burglary n. (pl. **burglaries**) illegal entry into a building to commit theft or do damage. □ **burglar** n.

burgle v. (**burgles, burgled, burgling**) commit burglary.

burgundy n. (pl. **burgundies**) **1** a red wine of Burgundy in east central France. **2** the reddish purple colour of burgundy wine. □ **burgundy** adj.

burial n. **1** the burying of a body. **2** a funeral. [Say BARE ee ul]

burlap n. coarse canvas woven from jute or hemp.

burlesque ● n. **1** comic imitation. **2** a variety show, often including striptease. ● adj. of or like burlesque. ● v. (**burlesques, burlesqued, burlesquing**) make or give a burlesque of. [Say burr LESK]

burly adj. (**burlier, burliest**) big and strong.

Burmese n. (pl. **Burmese**) **1** a person from Burma (now Myanmar) in SE Asia. **2** a member of the largest ethnic group of Burma. **3** the language of this group. □ **Burmese** adj. [Say burr MEEZ]

burn ● v. (**burns**; past and past participle **burned** or **burnt**; **burning**) **1** be or cause to be consumed or damaged by fire. **2** (of fire) glow or blaze with flame. **3** use or be used as a source of energy. **4** scorch. **5** produce (a hole etc.) by fire or heat. **6** colour, tan, or parch with heat or light. **7 a** brand. **b** (foll. by in) imprint. **8** make or

be hot, give or feel a sensation like heat. **9** make or be passionate. **10** slang drive fast. **11** informal anger. **12** (of acid etc.) gradually penetrate (into) causing disintegration. **13** metabolize in the body. **14** copy data onto (a compact disc). **15** Curling touch (a rock in play) with one's foot, broom, etc. ● n. **1 a** a mark or injury caused by burning. **b** a mark or injury caused by friction. **2** an area of forest destroyed by fire. □ **burn one's bridges** (or **boats**) do something which makes turning back impossible. **burn the candle at both ends** exhaust oneself by undertaking too much. **burn a hole in one's pocket** (of money) be quickly spent. **burn the midnight oil** work late into the night. **burn out 1** be reduced to nothing by burning. **2** suffer physical or emotional exhaustion.

burner n. **1** a person or thing that burns. **2 a** the part of a gas stove etc. that emits flame. **b** a heating element on a stovetop. **3** a furnace.

burning adj. **1** ardent. **2** hotly discussed.

burnish ● v. (**burnishes, burnished, burnishing**) polish by rubbing. ● n. the shine on a highly polished surface.

burnout n. **1** physical or emotional exhaustion, esp. caused by stress. **2** depression, disillusionment.

burnt ● v. past and past participle of BURN. ● adj. marked or affected by burning.

burnt-out adj. **1** physically or emotionally exhausted. **2** destroyed by burning so that only a shell remains.

burp ● v. **1** belch. **2** make (a baby) belch. ● n. a belch.

burr ● n. **1** a prickly clinging seed case or flower head. **2** a rough edge left on cut or punched metal, paper, etc. **3** a whirring sound. **4** a swirled pattern in the grain of wood. ● v. make a whirring sound.

burrito n. (pl. **burritos**) a tortilla rolled around a spicy filling of meat, beans, etc. [Say buh REE toe]

burrow ● n. a hole etc. dug by a small animal as a dwelling. ● v. **1** make a burrow. **2** dig. **3** investigate. □ **burrower** n.

bursar n. a financial officer, esp. of a university. [Say BURR sir]

bursary n. (pl. **bursaries**) Cdn a financial award to a university student, esp. one in financial need. [Say BURSA ree]

burst ● v. (**bursts, burst, bursting**) **1** break suddenly and violently apart. **2** move or be opened forcibly or suddenly. **3** (usu. foll. by with) have in abundance. **4** give sudden expression to. ● n. **1** an instance of bursting. **2** a sudden issuing forth. **3** a short period of activity or exertion.

bury v. (**buries**, **buried**, **burying**) **1** place (a dead body) in the earth etc. **2** lose by death. **3** put under ground. **4 a** put out of sight. **b** conceal. **c** forget. **5** involve deeply. □ **bury the hatchet** cease to quarrel. [*Rhymes with* FAIRY *or* FURRY]

bus ● n. (pl. **buses**) **1** a large motor vehicle designed to carry several passengers. **2** a set of conductors carrying data within a computer. ● v. (**buses**, **bused**, **busing**) **1** go or transport by bus. **2** remove dishes etc. in a cafeteria.

busboy n. a waiter's assistant who clears tables etc.

bush ● n. (pl. **bushes**) **1** a shrub or clump of shrubs. **2** Cdn a woodlot. **3** a wild uncultivated district. ● v. (**bushes**, **bushed**, **bushing**) branch or spread like a bush.

bush camp n. Cdn the living quarters, offices, etc., of a mining or lumbering operation in the bush.

bushed adj. **1** informal tired out. **2** forested; wooded. **3** Cdn informal (of a person) **a** living in the bush. **b** insane (due to isolation).

bushel n. **1** (in Canada and other Commonwealth countries) a measure of capacity for grain, fruit, etc., equal to 8 imperial gallons or 36.4 litres. **2** (in the US) a similar unit of measure equal to 64 US pints or 35.24 litres. □ **bushelful** n. (pl. **bushelfuls**)

bush fever n. Cdn a mental disorder caused by protracted isolation in the bush.

bushland n. = BUSH 3.

bush league ● n. = MINOR LEAGUE n. 1. ● adj. inferior, unsophisticated.

bushman n. (pl. **bushmen**) **1** a person who lives or works in the bush, e.g. a logger. **2** (**Bushman**) **a** a member of an aboriginal people in southern Africa. **b** the language of this people.

bush pilot n. a pilot who flies small aircraft into isolated areas.

bush plane n. a small plane used for flying into isolated areas, usu. equipped with floats or skis.

bushwhack v. **1** clear away underbrush etc. **2** ambush.

bushwhacker n. **1** a person who clears land in bush country and settles there. **2** a person who hikes in bush country.

bushy adj. (**bushier**, **bushiest**) **1** like a bush. **2** covered with bush or bushes.

business n. **1** one's regular occupation, profession, or trade. **2** a thing that is one's concern. **3 a** a task or duty. **b** a reason for coming **4** serious activity. **5** derogatory a

matter. **6** volume of trade. **7 a** a company etc. **b** commercial enterprises collectively. **8** patronage. □ **has no business** has no right. **the business end** informal the functional part of a tool or device. **mind one's own business** not meddle.

business class n. a more expensive class of airline seating than economy class, typically with roomier seating, better food, and other advantages.

businesslike adj. efficient, systematic, practical.

businessman n. (pl. **businessmen**) a male businessperson.

businessperson n. (pl. **businesspeople**) a person engaged in commerce, esp. at a senior level.

businesswoman n. (pl. **businesswomen**) a female businessperson.

busk v. perform (esp. music) for voluntary donations, usu. in the street etc. □ **busker** n. **busking** n.

busload n. the number of people travelling in a bus.

buss informal ● n. a kiss. ● v. (**busses**, **bussed**, **bussing**) kiss.

bust[1] n. **1** the human chest, esp. that of a woman. **2** a sculpture of a person's head, shoulders, and chest.

bust[2] informal ● v. (**busts**; past and past participle **busted** or **bust**; **busting**) **1** burst, break. **2 a** raid, search. **b** arrest. **3** tame (esp. broncos). ● n. **1** a failure. **2** a sudden economic downturn. **3** a police raid. **4** a punch; a hit. ● adj. **1** (also **busted**) broken, burst, collapsed. **2** bankrupt. □ **bust a gut 1** become overwrought. **2** exert oneself exceedingly. **3** laugh hysterically. **go bust** become bankrupt.

bustard n. a large, swift-running bird with a stout tapering body.

buster n. **1** a person or thing that busts. **2** informal fellow (used esp. as a disrespectful form of address). **3** (in comb.) something that overpowers an undesirable phenomenon.

bustle ● v. (**bustles**, **bustled**, **bustling**) **1** (often foll. by about) move energetically or noisily. **2** (often foll. by with) (of a place) be full of activity. ● n. excited activity.

bustline n. **1** the shape or outline of a woman's breasts. **2** the part of a garment covering this.

bust-up n. informal **1** a quarrel. **2** a marital separation or other breakup. **3** a collapse.

busty adj. (**bustier**, **bustiest**) (of a woman) having a prominent bust.

busy ● adj. (**busier**, **busiest**) **1** occupied

with an activity or activities. **2** full of activity. **3** (of a street etc.) having heavy traffic. **4** (of patterns etc.) overwhelmed by an excess of detail. **5** employed continuously; not resting. **6** (of a telephone line) already in use. ● *v.* **busy oneself** (**busies, busied, busying**) keep oneself busy. □ **busily** *adv.* **busyness** *n.*

busybody *n.* (*pl.* **busybodies**) a meddling person.

but ● *conj.* **1 a** nevertheless, however. **b** on the other hand. **2** except **3** without. **4** prefixing an interruption ● *prep.* except. ● *adv.* **1** no more than. **2** introducing emphatic repetition. ● *rel. pron.* who not; that not. ● *n.* an objection. □ **but for** without the help or hindrance etc. of. **but one** (or **two** etc.) excluding one (or two etc.) from the number.

butane *n.* a hydrocarbon of the alkane series used in liquefied form as fuel. [*Say* BYOO tane]

butch *slang* ● *adj.* masculine; tough-looking. ● *n.* **1 a** a mannish woman. **b** a mannish lesbian. **2** a tough-looking youth or man.

butcher ● *n.* **1 a** a person whose trade is selling meat. **b** a person who slaughters animals for food. **2** a brutal killer. ● *v.* **1** slaughter or cut up for food. **2** kill (people) wantonly. **3** ruin through incompetence. □ **butchery** *n.*

butler *n.* the principal male servant of a household.

butt[1] ● *v.* **1** hit with the head or horns. **2** project, jut. **3** lie with one end flat against. ● *n.* a rough push with the head or horns. □ **butt in 1** interrupt. **2** push into (a line of people) out of turn. **butt out** cease to interrupt or meddle.

butt[2] *n.* **1** (often foll. by *of*) an object of ridicule etc. **2 a** a mound behind a target to stop stray bullets etc. **b** (in *pl.*) a shooting range. **c** a target.

butt[3] ● *n.* **1** (also **butt end**) the thicker end of a tool or weapon. **2** a cut of pork from the shoulder. **3** the stub of a cigarette etc. **4** *informal* the buttocks. ● *v.* extinguish (a cigarette). □ **butt out** extinguish.

butte *n.* a high isolated hill with steep sides and a flat top. [*Say* BYOOT]

butter ● *n.* a pale yellow edible fatty substance made by churning cream. ● *v.* spread, cook, or serve with butter. □ **butter up** *informal* flatter excessively. **look as if butter wouldn't melt in one's mouth** seem innocent, probably deceptively. □ **buttery** *adj.*

buttercup *n.* a plants bearing yellow cup-shaped flowers.

buttercup squash *n.* a winter squash with dark green skin and orange flesh.

butterfat *n.* the natural fats derived from milk. Abbreviation: **BF.**

butterfingers *n. informal* a clumsy person prone to drop things. □ **butterfingered** *adj.*

butterfly ● *n.* (*pl.* **butterflies**) **1** an insect with a long thin body and four usu. brightly coloured wings. **2** a frivolous person. **3** (in *pl.*) *informal* a nervous sensation felt in the stomach. **4** a swimming stroke in which both arms are lifted out of the water and the legs are kept together while kicking. **5** *Hockey* a kneeling position assumed by a goaltender, with the lower legs spread apart to cover the bottom part of the goal. ● *v.* (**butterflies, butterflied, butterflying**) slice down the centre and spread apart before cooking. □ **butterflied** *adj.*

buttermilk *n.* **1** a slightly acid liquid left after churning butter. **2** a dairy product prepared commercially by adding bacterial culture to milk.

butternut *n.* **1** a deciduous, eastern N American tree of the walnut family. **2** the oily nut of this tree.

butternut squash *n.* a pear-shaped variety of winter squash with light yellowish-brown skin and orange flesh.

butterscotch *n.* **1** a brittle candy made from butter, brown sugar, etc. **2** the flavour of this.

butter tart *n.* Cdn a tart with a filling of butter, eggs, brown sugar, and usu. raisins.

buttock *n.* (usu. in *pl.*) **1** each of two fleshy protuberances on the lower rear part of the human trunk. **2** the corresponding part of an animal.

button ● *n.* **1** a small disc sewn on to a garment to fasten it by being pushed through a buttonhole. **2 a** a knob on a piece of equipment which performs a particular function when pressed. **b** a small box depicted on a computer screen, representing a function which can be selected. **3** a usu. round badge bearing a slogan etc. **4** *Curling* the circular mark in the centre of the house. ● *v.* fasten with buttons. □ **button it** *informal* cease talking. **button one's lip** *informal* remain silent. **button up 1** fasten with buttons. **2** *informal* become silent. **on the button** *informal* exactly on target. □ **buttoned** *adj.*

buttonhole ● *n.* a slit made in a garment to receive a button for fastening. ● *v.* (**buttonholes, buttonholed, buttonholing**) **1** *informal* attract the attention of and detain (a reluctant listener). **2** make buttonholes in.

button mushroom *n.* a young mushroom that has not opened.

buttress ● *n.* **1** a projecting support of stone or brick etc. built against a wall. **2** a source of help or support. **3** a projecting portion of a hill or mountain. ● *v.* **1** support with a buttress. **2** provide with support. [*Say* BUTT riss]

buxom *adj.* (of a woman) large-breasted and healthy-looking.

buy ● *v.* (**buys, bought, buying**) **1** get in return for payment. **2** get (something) by sacrifice or great effort. **3** *informal* accept as true. ● *n. informal* a purchase. □ **buy into** obtain a share in (an enterprise) by payment. **buy it** (also **buy the farm**) (usu. in *past*) *slang* be killed. **buy out** pay (a person, company, etc.) to give up an ownership, interest, etc. **buy time** delay an event etc. temporarily.

buyer *n.* **1** a purchaser. **2** a person who selects and purchases stock for a store etc.

buyer's market *n.* an economic position in which goods are plentiful and cheap and buyers have the advantage over sellers.

buyout *n.* the purchase of a controlling share in a company etc.

buzz ● *n.* **1** a low humming sound. **2** the sound of a buzzer. **3 a** a stir; hurried activity. **b** *informal* a rumour. **c** *informal* publicity, esp. created by word of mouth. **4** *slang* a thrill; a feeling of mild intoxication. **5** (also **buzz cut**) *slang* a very short haircut. ● *v.* (**buzzes, buzzed, buzzing**) **1** make a humming sound. **2 a** signal or call with a buzzer. **b** *informal* telephone. **3 a** (often foll. by *about*) move or hover busily. **b** (of a place) have an air of excitement or activity. **4** (of a person's mind or head) be filled with excited or confused thoughts. □ **buzz off** *slang* go or hurry away.

buzzard *n.* **1** a large bird of prey well adapted for soaring flight. **2** = TURKEY VULTURE.

buzzer *n.* an electromagnetic device that makes a buzzing noise.

buzz saw *n.* a circular saw.

buzzword *n.* a fashionable piece of jargon.

buzzy *adj.* (**buzzier, buzziest**) **1** lively, active. **2** making a buzzing sound.

by ● *prep.* **1** near. **2** through the agency of.

3 as soon as. **4 a** past, beyond. **b** via. **5** in the circumstances of. **6** to the extent of. **7** according to. **8** expressing multiplication. ● *adv.* past. ● *n.* = BYE¹. □ **by and by** before long. **by and large** on the whole. **by the by** (or **bye**) incidentally.

bycatch *n.* fish of species other than that being fished for, caught in fishing nets.

bye¹ *n.* the status of an unpaired competitor in a tournament, who proceeds to the next round as if having won.

bye² *interj.* = GOODBYE.

bye-bye ● *interj. informal* = GOODBYE. ● *n.* (also **bye-byes**) (a child's word for) sleep.

by-election *n.* an election held to fill a vacant seat during a government's term of office.

bygone ● *adj.* past. ● *n.* (in *pl.*) past events, esp. offences. □ **let bygones be bygones** forgive and forget.

bylaw *n.* **1** a rule made by a society etc. for its members. **2** a law made by a body subordinate to a legislature, esp. a municipal government.

byline *n.* **1** a line in a newspaper naming the writer of an article. **2** *Soccer* the goal line or side line.

BYO *abbr. informal* (also **BYOB**) bring your own (bottle of liquor).

bypass ● *n.* **1** a road passing around a town to provide an alternative route for through traffic. **2** any secondary channel etc. to allow a flow when the main one is blocked or cannot be used. ● *v.* (**bypasses, bypassed, bypassing**) **1** go around. **2** provide with a bypass.

by-product *n.* **1** an incidental product made in the manufacture of something else. **2** a secondary result.

bystander *n.* a person who is present but does not take part.

byte *n. Computing* a group of usu. eight binary digits, often used to represent one character.

byway *n.* a minor road.

byword *n.* **1** a notable example. **2** a saying.

Byzantine ● *adj.* **1** relating to the ancient Greek city of Byzantium (now Istanbul). **2** excessively complicated. **3** devious. ● *n.* a citizen of Byzantium. [*Say* BIZZEN teen]

Cc

C¹ *n.* (also **c**) (*pl.* **Cs** or **C's**) **1** the third letter of the alphabet. **2** the first note of the C major scale. **3** the third item in a set. **4** the third highest class (of academic marks etc.). **5** *Math* (usu. **c**) the third known quantity. **6** (as a Roman numeral) 100.

C² *abbr.* **1** Cape. **2** Conservative. **3** Celsius, Centigrade.

c. *abbr.* **1** century; centuries. **2** cent(s). **3** cubic. **4** centi-. **5** cup(s).

c. *abbr. circa.*

CA *abbr.* (*pl.* **CAs**) (in Canada and Scotland) = CHARTERED ACCOUNTANT.

ca. *abbr. circa.*

cab *n.* **1** a taxi. **2** the driver's compartment in a truck, train, etc.

cabal *n.* a secret political group. [*Say* kuh BAL]

cabana *n.* (*pl.* **cabanas**) a small shelter, esp. at a beach or swimming pool. [*Say* kuh BAN uh]

cabaret *n.* **1** a restaurant in which entertainment is provided. **2** the entertainment provided. [*Say* cabba RAY]

cabbage *n.* a plant with thick green or purple leaves eaten as a vegetable.

cabbage roll *n.* (usu. in *pl.*) a boiled cabbage leaf wrapped around a filling and baked.

cabbie *n. informal* a taxi driver.

Cabernet *n.* **1** a variety of black grape (esp. **Cabernet Sauvignon**) used in winemaking. **2** a wine made from these. [*Say* cabber NAY (so veen YON)]

cabin *n.* **1 a** a small shelter or house, esp. of wood. **b** a summer cottage. **2** a compartment in an aircraft or ship for passengers or crew. **3** a driver's cab.

cabinet *n.* **1 a** a cupboard with drawers, shelves, etc., for storing articles. **b** a piece of furniture housing a stereo, television set, etc. **2** (also **Cabinet**) **a** (in Canada, the UK, etc.) a committee of senior government ministers. **b** (in the US) a body of advisers to the President.

cabinetmaker *n.* a person skilled in making furniture and light woodwork. □ **cabinetmaking** *n.*

cabinet order *n. Cdn* = ORDER-IN-COUNCIL.

cabinetry *n.* cabinets or fine woodwork.

cabin fever *n.* lethargy, irritability, anxiety, etc. resulting from long confinement indoors.

cable ● *n.* **1** a thick rope of wire or fibre. **2** an encased group of insulated wires for transmitting electricity. **3** = CABLE TELEVISION. **4** (also **cable stitch**) a knitted stitch resembling twisted rope. ● *v.* (**cables, cabled, cabling**) fasten with a cable.

cable car *n.* a small carriage hung from a cable, drawn up and down a mountainside etc.

cable television *n.* (also **cablevision**) a broadcasting system with signals transmitted and received by cable.

caboodle *n.* □ **the whole (kit and) caboodle** *informal* the whole lot.

caboose *n.* a rail car at the end of the train for housing the crew.

cacao *n.* (*pl.* **cacaos**) **1** a seed pod from which cocoa and chocolate are made. **2** a small evergreen bearing these. [*Say* kuh KA oh]

cache ● *n.* **1** a hiding place. **2** *Cdn* (*North*) something used for storing food, supplies, etc. **3** the contents of a cache. **4** an auxiliary computer memory allowing high-speed retrieval. ● *v.* (**caches, cached, caching**) put in a cache. [*Say* CASH]

cachet *n.* prestige. [*Say* ka SHAY]

cackle ● *n.* a noisy clucking cry or laugh. ● *v.* (**cackles, cackled, cackling**) emit a cackle.

cacophony *n.* (*pl.* **cacophonies**) a harsh discordant mixture of sound. □ **cacophonous** *adj.* [*Say* kuh COFFA nee]

cactus *n.* (*pl.* **cacti** or **cactuses**) a plant with a thick fleshy stem, usu. spines but no leaves, and brilliantly coloured flowers.

cad *n.* a person who behaves dishonourably.

cadaver *n.* a corpse. [*Say* kuh DAV er]

cadaverous *adj.* like a corpse in being very pale and thin. [*Say* kuh DAV er us]

caddis fly *n.* a small nocturnal moth-like insect living near water.

caddy¹ *n.* (*pl.* **caddies**) a small container.

caddy² (also **caddie**) ● *n.* (*pl.* **caddies**) a person who assists a golfer by carrying clubs etc. ● *v.* (**caddies, caddied, caddying**) act as a caddy.

cadence *n.* **1** a modulation or inflection of the voice. **2** the resolution at the end of a musical phrase. **3** rhythm. □ **cadenced** *adj.* [*Say* KAY dinse]

cadenza *n.* (*pl.* **cadenzas**) a virtuosic passage for a solo voice or instrument. [*Say* kuh DEN zuh]

cadet *n.* **1** a young trainee in the police or armed forces. **2** (in Canada) a member of a paramilitary organization for youth aged 12 to 18.

cadge *v.* (**cadges, cadged, cadging**) get or seek by begging or scrounging. □ **cadger** *n.*

cadmium *n.* a soft bluish-white metallic element. [*Say* KAD mee um]

cadre *n.* **1** a small group specially trained for a particular purpose. **2** a group of activists in a political party. [*Say* CAD ruh *or* CAD ray]

Caesar *n.* **1** a title of the Roman emperors. **2** an autocrat. **3** = CAESAR SALAD. **4** *Cdn* = BLOODY CAESAR. [*Say* SEE zur]

Caesarean ● *adj.* **1** of Julius Caesar or the Caesars. **2** (of a birth) effected by Caesarean section. ● *n.* a Caesarean section. [*Say* suh ZERRY un]

Caesarean section *n.* an operation for delivering a child by cutting through the wall of the abdomen.

Caesar salad *n.* a salad of romaine lettuce tossed with Parmesan cheese, garlic croutons, etc.

CAF *abbr.* CANADIAN ARMED FORCES.

caf *n.* *informal Cdn* a cafeteria.

café *n.* **1** a restaurant serving coffee and light meals. **2** a bar or nightclub.

café au lait *n.* strong coffee with an equal portion of hot milk. [*Say* ka fay oh LAY]

cafeteria *n.* **1** a restaurant where customers collect meals at a counter and usu. pay before sitting down. **2** a lunch room in a school, office, etc.

caffeinated *adj.* containing caffeine. [*Say* KAF in ate id]

caffeine *n.* a stimulant found in coffee, tea, etc. [*Say* kaf EEN]

caftan *n.* **1** an ankle-length tunic worn by men in eastern Europe and the Middle East. **2 a** a woman's long loose dress. **b** a loose shirt. [*Say* KAF tan]

cage ● *n.* **1** a structure of bars, wires, etc. used as a place of confinement. **2** a protective structure of strong metal bars. **3** a system of netting or mesh strung around a metal framework. **4** a wire face mask attached to a helmet. ● *v.* (**cages, caged, caging**) place or keep in a cage.

cagey *adj.* (**cagier, cagiest**) *informal* cautious and uncommunicative. □ **cagily** *adv.* **caginess** *n.* (also **cageyness**)

cahoots *pl. n.* □ **in cahoots** *slang* colluding with. [*Say* kuh HOOTS]

caiman *n.* an alligator-like reptile native to South and Central America. [*Say* KAY mun]

cairn *n.* a mound of rough stones as a monument.

caisse populaire *n.* (*pl.* **caisses populaires**) *Cdn* (in Quebec etc.) a co-operative financial institution similar to a credit union. [*Say* kess pop yoo LAIR]

cajole *v.* (**cajoles, cajoled, cajoling**) persuade to do something by coaxing. □ **cajolery** *n.* [*Say* kuh JOLE]

Cajun ● *n.* **1** a descendant of French-speaking settlers expelled from Acadia in the mid-18th century, living esp. in S Louisiana. **2** the French patois of the Cajuns. ● *adj.* **1** of the Cajuns or their language. **2** cooked in a Cajun style, esp. using strong seasonings. [*Say* KAY jun]

cake ● *n.* **1** a baked sweet food usu. containing flour, eggs, sugar, and often fat and leavening. **2** any of several foods in a flat round shape. **3** a flattish compact mass. ● *v.* (**cakes, caked, caking**) **1** form into a compact mass. **2** cover (with a hard or sticky mass). □ **have one's cake and eat it** (**too**) *informal* enjoy two mutually exclusive alternatives. **a piece of cake** *informal* something easily achieved.

cakewalk *n.* *informal* an easy task.

cal (often in *comb.*) calorie(s).

calabash *n.* **1 a** a tropical American tree bearing large gourd-like fruit. **b** this fruit. **2** a vessel made from the shell of this fruit. [*Say* CALA bash]

calabrese *n.* esp. *Cdn* round white crusty Italian bread. [*Say* cala BRAY zay]

calamari *n.* the flesh of the squid when used as food. [*Say* cala MAR ee]

calamine *n.* a pink powder consisting of zinc and iron compounds, used to make a soothing lotion. [*Say* CALA mine]

calamity *n.* (*pl.* **calamities**) a disaster. □ **calamitous** *adj.* [*Say* kuh LAMMA tee]

calcareous *adj.* of or containing calcium carbonate. [*Say* cal KERRY iss]

calcify *v.* (**calcifies, calcified**) **1** harden by deposition of calcium salts. **2** convert to calcium carbonate. **3** make or become inflexible. □ **calcification** *n.* [*Say* CALSA fie]

calcite *n.* natural crystalline calcium carbonate. [*Say* CAL site]

calcium *n.* a greyish-white metallic

element occurring in limestone, animal bones, and teeth.

calcium carbonate *n.* a white solid found as chalk, limestone, and marble.

calculable *adj.* able to be calculated.

calculate *v.* (**calculates, calculated, calculating**) **1** determine by using mathematics or one's judgment. **2** intend for a particular purpose.

calculated *adj.* **1** done knowing the likely consequences. **2** designed. □ **calculatedly** *adv.*

calculating *adj.* scheming.

calculation *n.* **1** a mathematical determination of something. **2** an assessment of the likely results of a course of action.

calculator *n.* a device used for making mathematical calculations.

calculus *n.* (*pl.* **calculi** or **calculuses**) **1** *Math* **a** a particular method of calculation or reasoning. **b** the branch of mathematics concerned with problems involving rates of variation. **2 a** a stone formed esp. in the kidney or gallbladder. **b** a hard deposit of saliva, calcium phosphate, etc. that forms on the teeth. [*Say* CAL cue liss *for the singular,* CAL cue lie *or* CAL cue lisses *for the plural*]

calèche *n.* Cdn a two-wheeled one-horse vehicle used in tourist areas of Quebec. [*Say* ka LESH]

calendar *n.* **1** a system by which the beginning, length, and subdivisions of the year are fixed. **2** a chart or series of pages showing the days, weeks, and months of a year. **3** a timetable of events etc. **4** Cdn a list of courses offered at a university or college. **5** a register of cases for trial, canonized saints, etc.

calender *n.* a machine in which cloth, paper, etc., is pressed by rollers to glaze or smooth it.

calf[1] *n.* (*pl.* **calves**) **1** a young bovine animal. **2** the young of other animals, e.g. seal. **3** (also **calfskin**) the hide of a calf, esp. as leather. **4** a floating piece of ice detached from an iceberg.

calf[2] *n.* (*pl.* **calves**) the fleshy hind part of the human leg below the knee.

Calgarian ● *n.* a person from Calgary. ● *adj.* of or relating to Calgary. [*Say* cal GARE ee un]

calibrate *v.* (**calibrates, calibrated, calibrating**) **1** mark (a gauge) with a standard scale of readings. **2** correlate the readings of (an instrument) with a standard. **3** determine the calibre of (a gun). □ **calibration** *n.* [*Say* CALA brate]

calibre *n.* **1 a** the internal diameter of a

gun or tube. **b** the diameter of a bullet or shell. **2** quality of character.

calico ● *n.* (*pl.* **calicoes** or **calicos**) a cotton fabric with a printed pattern. ● *adj.* **1** made of calico. **2** (of an animal) having irregular patches of colours. [*Say* CALA co]

Californian ● *adj.* of or relating to California. ● *n.* a person from California.

California roll *n.* a type of sushi consisting of rice, avocado, crab, and cucumber rolled in seaweed.

caliper *n.* (usu. in *pl.*) **1** an instrument with hinged legs for measuring diameters. **2** the part of a brake assembly which houses the brake pads.

caliph *n.* hist. the chief Muslim ruler. [*Say* KAY lif *or* CAL if]

calisthenics *pl. n.* gymnastic exercises to achieve bodily fitness and grace of movement. [*Say* cal iss THEN icks]

call ● *v.* **1 a** cry, shout. **b** (of a bird or animal) emit its characteristic cry. **2** phone or radio (someone). **3** bring to one's presence by calling. **4** pay a brief visit. **5** order to take place. **6** name; describe as. **7** guess the outcome. **8** (foll. by *for*) require. **9** read out. **10** (foll. by *on, upon*) appeal to. **11** (of an umpire) **a** assess. **b** officiate (a game). **12** (foll. by *on*) **a** require (of someone) proof or support for a statement. **b** criticize, condemn. ● *n.* **1** a shout or cry. **2** the characteristic cry of a bird or animal. **3** a brief visit. **4** an act of phoning. **5 a** a summons to be present. **b** an appeal to follow a certain profession, principle, etc. **6** a demand. **7** Sport a ruling or decision. **8** a signalling sound. □ **call forth** elicit. **call in 1** withdraw from circulation. **2** seek the advice or services of. **call in** (or **into**) **question** dispute. **call off 1** cancel. **2** order to desist. **call of nature** a need to urinate or defecate. **call the shots** (or **tune**) be in control. **call to mind** cause one to remember. **call up 1** reach by telephone. **2** imagine, recollect. **3** summon, esp. to serve in the army. **4** promote (a player) to the major leagues. **on** (or **at**) **call** (of a doctor etc.) available if required but not formally on duty. □ **caller** *n.*

calla *n.* (*pl.* **callas**) a flower with a white spathe and a yellow spadix, esp. the **calla lily** and the **wild calla**, with a cluster of red berries. [*Say* CALA]

call girl *n.* a female prostitute who accepts appointments by telephone.

calligraphy *n.* **1** fine handwriting. **2** the art of stylized or beautiful handwriting. □ **calligrapher** *n.* **calligraphic** *adj.* [*Say* kuh LIGRA fee, kuh LIGRA fur, cala GRAPH ick]

calling n. **1** a profession or occupation. **2** an inwardly felt call; a vocation.

calling card n. **1** a small card with one's name and often address, presented when visiting. **2 (Calling Card)** proprietary a credit card issued by a telephone company allowing a customer to charge long-distance calls. **3** a distinctive mark or feature.

callous ● adj. unfeeling, insensitive. ● n. = CALLUS 1. □ **callously** adv. **callousness** n.

calloused adj. having an area of hardened skin. [Say CAL ust]

callow adj. inexperienced, immature. [Say CAL oh]

call-up n. **1** the act or process of being summoned to the army or promoted to the major leagues. **2** a person who is called up.

callus n. (pl. **calluses**) a hard thick area of skin or tissue. □ **callused** adj.

calm ● adj. **1** tranquil, windless. **2** (of a person or disposition) not agitated. ● n. **1** stillness. **2** a period without wind or storm. ● v. (often foll. by down) make or become calm. □ **calmly** adv. **calmness** n.

caloric adj. of heat or calories. [Say kuh LORE ick]

calorie n. the amount of energy needed to raise the temperature of 1 kilogram of water through 1°C.

calorific adj. pertaining to or high in calories. [Say cala RIF ick]

calumet n. a N American Aboriginal tobacco pipe, smoked esp. as a sign of peace. [Say CAL yuh mit]

calumny n. (pl. **calumnies**) the making of false and defamatory statements about someone. [Say CAL um nee]

calve v. (**calves, calved, calving**) **1** give birth to a calf. **2** break off or shed (a mass of ice).

calves pl. of CALF¹, ².

Calvinism n. the doctrines of John Calvin (1509–64) or his followers, such as the belief that everything is predestined by God. □ **Calvinist** n. **Calvinistic** adj.

calypso n. (pl. **calypsos**) **1** a kind of West Indian music in syncopated African rhythm. **2** an orchid with pink, slipper-shaped flowers. [Say kuh LIP so]

calyx n. (pl. **calyces** or **calyxes**) sepals collectively, forming the protective layer of a flower in bud. [Say KAY licks for the singular, KAYLA seez for the plural]

cam n. a projection on a rotating part in machinery, shaped to impart motion to the part in contact with it.

camaraderie n. mutual trust and sociability among friends. [Say comma RODDA ree]

camas n. (pl. **camas**) a N American lily with starry blue or purple flowers. [Say CAM iss]

camber ● n. the slightly convex shape of a road surface, ship's deck, etc. ● v. **1** have a camber. **2** give a camber to.

cambium n. (pl. **cambia** or **cambiums**) a cellular plant tissue responsible for the increase in girth of stems and roots. [Say CAMBY um for the singular, CAMBY un or CAMBY umz for the plural]

Cambodian n. **1 a** a person from Cambodia in SE Asia. **b** a person of Cambodian descent. **2** the Khmer language. □ **Cambodian** adj. [Say cam BOADY un]

Cambrian adj. of or relating to the first period of the Paleozoic era, lasting from about 590 to 505 million years BP. [Say CAME bree un]

camcorder n. a portable video camera.

came past of COME.

camel n. **1** a large long-necked mammal with broad cushioned feet, and either one hump (**Arabian camel**) or two humps (**Bactrian camel**). **2** a fawn colour.

camel hair n. **1 a** the hair of a camel. **b** a fabric made of this. **2** a fine soft hair used in artists' brushes.

camellia n. an evergreen shrub with shiny leaves and red, pink, or white rose-like flowers. [Say kuh MEALY uh]

Camembert n. a kind of soft creamy cheese. [Say CAM um bear]

cameo n. (pl. **cameos**) **1** a small piece of hard stone standing out from a background of a different colour. **2** a small character part in a play or film. [Say CAMMY oh]

camera n. a device for taking photographs or for recording moving images. □ **in camera 1** privately. **2** Law in a judge's private room.

cameraman n. (pl. **cameramen**) a camera operator, esp. a male one.

camera operator n. (also **cameraperson** pl. **camerapersons**) a person who operates a film or television camera.

camera-ready adj. Printing suitable for immediate photographic reproduction.

camerawoman n. (pl. **camerawomen**) a female camera operator.

camisole n. a woman's waist-length sleeveless undergarment. [Say CAMMA sole]

camomile n. a daisy-like plant, used in herbal teas and to lighten hair. [Say CAMMA mile]

camouflage ● n. **1** colouring or covering that allows animals, people, or equipment

to blend in with the surroundings.
2 clothing or materials used for this
purpose. ● *v.* (**camouflages**,
camouflaged, **camouflaging**) disguise
by means of camouflage.
[*Say* CAMMA flawzh]

camp[1] ● *n.* **1 a** a temporary lodging, esp.
consisting of tents. **2 a** a complex of
buildings for troops, workers, vacationers,
etc. **b** a summer holiday program for
children, offering recreational or
educational activities. **c** (*N Ont. & Maritimes*) a
summer cottage. **3** the adherents of a
particular party or doctrine regarded
collectively. ● *v.* **1** set up or spend time in a
camp. **2** (often foll. by *out*) lodge in
temporary quarters or in the open.

camp[2] *informal* ● *adj.* **1** (of a man)
ostentatiously and extravagantly
effeminate. **2** done in an exaggerated,
theatrical way. ● *n.* a camp manner. ● *v.*
behave or do in a camp way.

campaign ● *n.* **1** an organized course of
action for a particular purpose. **2** a series of
military operations to achieve an objective.
● *v.* conduct or take part in a campaign.
□ **campaigner** *n.* [*Say* cam PANE]

camper *n.* **1** a person who camps. **2** a
vehicle or trailer equipped for camping.

campfire *n.* an outdoor fire in a camp etc.

camp follower *n.* **1** a civilian, esp. a
prostitute, who provides services to
personnel in a military camp. **2** a person
who associates with a group without being
a full member of it.

campground *n.* an area with facilities for
camping.

camphor *n.* an aromatic, translucent
crystalline substance used in essential oils.
[*Say* CAM fur]

camping *n.* the act of staying outdoors in
a tent.

campion *n.* a plant with pink or white
flowers with notched petals.
[*Say* CAM pee un]

campsite *n.* any place used for camping.

camp stove *n.* a portable cooking stove
used by campers.

campus *n.* (*pl.* **campuses**) **1 a** the
grounds of a university or college. **b** one of
several branches of a large university. **2** a
university or college.

campy *adj.* (**campier**, **campiest**)
1 exaggerated and theatrical, usu. for
humorous effect. **2** ostentatiously
effeminate. □ **campily** *adv.* **campiness** *n.*

camshaft *n.* a shaft with one or more
cams attached.

can[1] *aux. v.* (*3rd singular present* **can**; *past*

could) **1 a** be able to; know how to. **b** be
potentially capable of. **2** be permitted to.

can[2] ● *n.* **1** a cylindrical metal container.
2 (**the can**) *slang* **a** prison. **b** a toilet. ● *v.*
(**canned**, **canning**) **1** put or preserve in a
can or jar. **2** *informal* **a** cease, end. **b** remove.
c fire, dismiss. □ **can it** *informal* be quiet. **in
the can** *informal* completed, ready.
□ **canning** *n.*

Canada Day *n.* the annual holiday
commemorating the creation of the
Dominion of Canada on 1 July 1867
(formerly called DOMINION DAY).

Canada goose *n.* a wild goose with a
brownish-grey back, black head and neck,
and white cheeks and breast.

Canada Pension Plan *n.* a pension
plan funded by contributions from
employees and employers and
administered by the Canadian government.

Canadian ● *n.* a person from Canada.
● *adj.* of or relating to Canada or its people.
□ **Canadianness** *n.*

Canadiana *n.* things pertaining to and
typical of Canadian culture.

Canadian Alliance *n.* a federal political
party (2000-03), which became part of the
Conservative Party of Canada in 2003.

Canadian Armed Forces *n.* an
unofficial name for the Canadian Forces.

Canadian football *n.* a form of football
played on a field 110 by 65 yards with
teams of 12 players having only three
downs in which to progress 10 yards.

Canadian Forces *n.* the official name of
the Canadian military.

Canadianism *n.* **1** a word or expression
originating or used only in Canada.
2 loyalty to Canada. **3 a** the state of being
Canadian. **b** Canadian character or spirit.

Canadianist *n.* a specialist in Canadian
studies.

Canadianize *v.* (**Canadianizes**,
Canadianized, **Canadianizing**) make
or become Canadian in content,
ownership, etc. □ **Canadianization** *n.*

Canadian Shield *n.* a vast area of
extremely old rock surrounding Hudson
Bay, occupying over two-fifths of Canada's
land area and characterized by thin soil,
rock outcrops, countless lakes and rivers,
and, in the southern areas, vast coniferous
forests.

Canadian whisky *n.* = RYE 2.

canal *n.* **1** an artificial inland waterway.
2 a duct or passage in a plant or animal
body.

Can-Am *Cdn* ● *adj.* designating a sporting
event for Canadian and American
participants. ● *n.* a Can-Am event.

canapé *n.* a small cracker or piece of bread with a savoury food on top, served as an hors d'oeuvre. [*Say* CANNA pay]

canard *n.* an unfounded rumour or story. [*Say* kuh NARD]

canary ● *n.* (*pl.* **canaries**) **1** a finch with yellow or yellowish-green plumage and a melodious song. **2** (also **canary yellow**) a bright yellow colour. ● *adj.* bright yellow.

cancan *n.* a lively stage dance with high kicking.

cancel *v.* (**cancels, cancelled, cancelling**) **1 a** announce that (something arranged) will not take place. **b** discontinue. **2** obliterate or delete. **3** mark or pierce so that (a cheque etc.) may not be used again. **4** make void. **5** (often foll. by *out*) neutralize. □ **cancellation** *n.*

cancer *n.* **1** a disease caused by abnormal and uncontrolled division of body cells. **2** an evil influence spreading uncontrollably. **3** (**Cancer**) **a** a constellation (the Crab). **b** the fourth sign of the zodiac, which the sun enters about 21 June. □ **cancerous** *adj.* (in senses 1, 2)

CanCon *n. Cdn informal* Canadian content, esp. with reference to quotas in broadcasting.

candela *n.* the SI unit of luminous intensity. [*Say* can DEELA *or* can DELLA]

candelabra *n.* (*pl.* **candelabras**) (also **candelabrum**, *pl.* **candelabra**) a large branched candlestick or lamp for holding several candles or bulbs. [*Say* canda LABRA]

candid *adj.* **1** straightforward and truthful. **2** (of a photograph) taken informally or secretly. □ **candidness** *n.*

candidate *n.* **1** a person who seeks or is nominated for an office, award, etc. **2** a person or thing likely to gain some distinction or position. **3** a person entered for an examination. □ **candidacy** *n.* [*Say* CANDA date, CAN didda see]

candidly *adv.* in a frank, honest, or open manner.

candied *adj.* **1** (esp. of fruit) preserved with sugar. **2** cooked with a large quantity of sugar.

candle *n.* a stick of wax with a central wick that is lit to produce light as it burns. □ **cannot hold a candle to** is much inferior to.

candlefish *n.* = EULACHON.

candle ice *n.* (also **candled ice**) esp. *Cdn* ice which has deteriorated into candle-like icicles before breaking up.

Candlemas *n. Christianity* a feast with blessing of candles (2 Feb.), commemorating the Purification of the Virgin Mary and the presentation of Christ in the Temple. [*Say* CANDLE muss]

candlestick *n.* a holder for a candle.

can-do *adj. informal* displaying confidence and efficiency.

candour *n.* (also **candor**) the quality of being open and honest. [*Say* CAN dur]

CANDU *n.* (*pl.* **CANDUs**) *proprietary* a nuclear reactor using easily replaceable fuel bundles and a heavy water cooling and moderating system.

C & W *abbr.* country and western.

candy *n.* (*pl.* **candies**) a very sweet confection, often also including chocolate, nuts, etc.

candy cane *n.* a hard, thin, striped candy with a curved end.

candy floss *n.* a fluffy mass of fine threads of sugar wrapped around a stick.

cane ● *n.* **1 a** the hollow jointed stem of giant reeds or grasses, e.g. bamboo. **b** the solid stem of slender palms such as rattan. **2** = SUGAR CANE. **3** material of cane used in wicker furniture etc. **4 a** a cane used as a walking stick etc. **b** any slender walking stick. ● *v.* (**canes, caned, caning**) **1** beat with a cane. **2** weave cane into (a chair etc.).

canine ● *adj.* having to do with dogs. ● *n.* **1** a dog. **2** (also **canine tooth**) a pointed tooth between the incisors and premolars. [*Say* KAY nine]

caning *n.* a beating with a cane as a punishment.

canister *n.* **1** a container, often one of a set, for holding flour, sugar, coffee, tea, etc. **2** a cylinder of shot, tear gas, etc., that explodes on impact.

canker *n.* **1** a destructive fungus disease of trees and plants. **2** an ulcerous ear disease of animals. **3** (also **canker sore**) a small sore on the lips or in the mouth. **4** a corrupting influence. □ **cankerous** *adj.*

CanLit *abbr. Cdn informal* Canadian literature.

cannabis *n.* **1** any hemp plant. **2** a drug obtained from a hemp plant; marijuana. [*Say* CANNA biss]

canned *adj.* **1** supplied in a can. **2** pre-recorded or prepared in advance.

cannellini *n.* (also **cannellini bean**) a kidney-shaped bean of a medium-sized creamy-white variety. [*Say* canna LEE nee]

cannelloni *pl. n.* rolls of pasta stuffed with meat or a vegetable mixture. [*Say* canna LOW nee]

canner *n.* **1** a large cooking vessel in which jars of preserves are immersed in boiling water to be sterilized and vacuum sealed. **2** a person who preserves food by canning: *home canners.*

cannery n. (pl. **canneries**) a factory where food is canned.

cannibal n. **1** a person who eats human flesh. **2** an animal that feeds on flesh of its own species. □ **cannibalism** n. **cannibalistic** adj.

cannibalize v. (**cannibalizes, cannibalized, cannibalizing**) use (a machine etc.) as a source of spare parts for others.

canning n. the process of preserving food in cans etc.

cannon ● n. **1** (pl. **cannon** or **cannons**) a large gun installed on a carriage or mounting. **2** a similar device for discharging a specific substance. **3** an automatic aircraft gun firing shells. ● v. (usu. foll. by *against, into*) collide heavily.

cannonball n. **1** a large usu. metal ball fired by a cannon. **2** a jump (into a pool etc.) with the knees clasped close to the chest.

cannot aux. v. can not.

canny adj. (**cannier, canniest**) shrewd, esp. in business matters. □ **cannily** adv. **canniness** n.

canoe ● n. a small narrow boat with pointed ends that curve upwards, usu. propelled by paddling. ● v. (**canoes, canoed, canoeing**) travel in a canoe. □ **canoeist** n. **canoeing** n.

can of worms n. *informal* a complicated problem.

canola n. a kind of rapeseed yielding an oil used in cooking. [*Say* kuh NO luh]

canon n. **1 a** a general rule or principle by which something is judged. **b** a church decree or law. **2** a member of the clergy who is on the staff of a cathedral. **3 a** a list of sacred books etc. accepted as genuine. **b** a list of literary works etc. considered to be the most important. **4** *Music* a piece with different parts taking up the same theme successively.

canonical adj. (also **canonic**) **1 a** according to canon law. **b** included in the canon of Scripture. **2** authoritative. **3** *Music* in canon form. □ **canonically** adv. [*Say* kuh NONNA cull]

canonize v. **1 a** declare officially to be a saint, usu. with a ceremony. **b** regard as a saint. **2 a** admit to the canon of Scripture. **b** accept as canonical. **3** sanction by Church authority. **4** treat or regard as being above reproach or of great significance. □ **canonization** n.

canon law n. church law.

canopy n. (pl. **canopies**) **1** a covering hung over a throne, bed, etc. **2** *Architecture* a roof-like shelter or projection. **3** the uppermost layers of foliage. **4 a** the expanding part of a parachute. **b** the cover of an aircraft's cockpit. □ **canopied** adj. [*Say* CANNA pee]

cant¹ n. **1** hypocritical and sanctimonious talk. **2** fashionable catchwords. **3** jargon.

cant² ● n. **1** a slanting surface. **2** a partly trimmed log. ● v. be or move in a slanting position.

can't contr. can not.

cantaloupe n. a small round melon with orange flesh. [*Say* CANTA lope]

cantankerous adj. bad-tempered. □ **cantankerously** adv. **cantankerousness** n. [*Say* can TANKA riss]

cantata n. (pl. **cantatas**) a sung narrative composition usu. with chorus and orchestral accompaniment. [*Say* can TATTA]

canteen n. **1** a soldier's or camper's water flask. **2** a restaurant or small shop in a barracks, workplace, etc.

canter ● n. a gentle gallop. ● v. **1** go at a canter. **2** make (a horse) canter.

canticle n. a song with a Biblical text.

cantilever ● n. a long projecting beam or girder fixed at only one end, used in bridge construction. ● v. support by a cantilever.

canto n. (pl. **cantos**) a division of a long poem.

Cantonese ● adj. of Canton (Guangzhou), a city in S China, its inhabitants, their Chinese dialect, or their cuisine. ● n. (pl. same) **1** a native of Canton. **2** the Chinese dialect of SE China and Hong Kong.

cantor n. **1** the leader of the singing in church. **2** a person employed to sing the solo prayers in a synagogue. [*Say* CAN tur]

Canuck *informal* ● n. a Canadian. ● adj. Canadian.

canvas n. **1 a** a strong coarse cloth used for sails, tents, etc. and as a surface for oil painting. **b** a piece of this. **2** an oil painting on canvas.

canvasback n. a wild duck with whitish back feathers.

canvass ● v. (**canvasses, canvassed, canvassing**) **1 a** solicit votes, donations, etc. **b** visit (people or an area) in order to do this. **2** ascertain opinions of. ● n. an attempt to secure votes or ascertain opinions. □ **canvasser** n.

canyon n. a deep gorge. □ **canyonland** n.

cap ● n. **1 a** a soft, brimless hat, usu. with a visor. **b** a mortarboard. **2** a lid or cover. **3** = CROWN n. 7b. **4** the spore-bearing structure surmounting the stipe of a mushroom or toadstool. **5** a tiny explosive device used esp. in toy guns. **6** an upward

limit put on something. ● v. (**caps,
capped, capping**) **1** put a cap on.
2 a form the cap of. **b** surpass, excel.
c complete. □ **cap in hand** humbly. **set
one's cap at** try to attract as a suitor.

capability n. (pl. **capabilities**) the power
or ability to do something.

capable adj. **1** competent, able, gifted.
2 (foll. by of) having the necessary ability.
□ **capably** adv.

capacious adj. roomy.
[Say kuh PAY shuss]

capacitance n. the ability to store an
electric charge. [Say kuh PASSA tunce]

capacitor n. a device used to store an
electric charge. [Say kuh PASSA tur]

capacity ● n. (pl. **capacities**) **1 a** the
ability to do something. **b** the maximum
amount that can be contained or
produced. **c** the volume of a cylinder etc.
2 a position or function. **3** legal
competence. ● adj. filling all available
space.

cape n. **1** a sleeveless cloak. **2** a
promontory. □ **caped** adj.

Cape Bretoner n. a person from Cape
Breton.

Cape Cod n. a style of rectangular house,
usu. one-and-a-half storeys, with a steeply
gabled roof.

Cape Island boat n. (also **Cape
Islander**) Cdn a boat used by inshore
fishermen esp. in Nova Scotia, with a high
prow and a low stern.

capelin n. a smelt-like baitfish of the
North Atlantic. [Say CAPE lun]

caper¹ ● v. skip or dance about in a lively
manner. ● n. **1** a playful jump or leap.
2 a an amusing film or TV drama. **b** informal
an illicit or illegal activity.

caper² n. **1** a bramble-like southern
European shrub. **2** (in pl.) its flower buds
cooked and pickled for use as flavouring.

capillary ● n. (pl. **capillaries**) **1** of one of
the fine branching blood vessels that form
a network between arteries and veins. **2** a
tube having an internal diameter of
hairlike thinness. ● adj. relating to
capillaries. [Say kuh PILLA ree]

capisce interj. slang understand?
[Say kuh PEESH]

capital ● n. **1** the city or town in a
country, province, etc. at which the
principal government institutions are
located. **2** the most noteworthy place for a
specified quality. **3 a** the assets with which
a company starts in business.
b accumulated wealth. **c** money invested or
lent at interest. **4** the holders of wealth as a
class. **5** a capital letter. **6** the section at the

top of a pillar. ● adj. **1** informal excellent,
first-rate. **2** involving or punishable by
death. **3** (of letters of the alphabet) large in
size and of the form used to begin
sentences and names etc. □ **make capital
out of** use to one's advantage.

capital gain n. a profit from the sale of
investments or property.

capital goods pl. n. goods used in
producing commodities.

capitalism n. an economic system in
which a country's trade and industry are
controlled by private owners for profit,
rather than by the state. □ **capitalist** n.
& adj.

capitalize v. (**capitalizes, capitalized,
capitalizing**) **1 a** provide with capital.
b convert into capital. **c** reckon (the value
of an asset) by setting future benefits
against the cost of maintenance. **2 a** write
(a letter of the alphabet) as a capital.
b begin (a word) with a capital letter.
3 profit from. □ **capitalization** n.

Capitol n. a building housing a legislature
in the US.

capitulate v. (**capitulates,
capitulated, capitulating**) cease to
resist something unwelcome.
□ **capitulation** n. [Say kuh PITCHA late]

capon n. a young rooster castrated and
fattened for eating. [Say KAY pawn]

cappuccino n. (pl. **cappuccinos**)
espresso coffee with milk made frothy with
pressurized steam. [Say cappa CHEE no]

capri n. (pl. **capris**) (usu. as an adj.)
women's close-fitting, tapered pants
extending to just above the ankles.
[Say kuh PREE]

caprice n. a whimsical change of mind or
conduct. [Say kuh PREECE]

capricious adj. **1** given to caprice.
2 unpredictable. □ **capriciously** adv.
capriciousness n. [Say kuh PREESH iss
or kuh PRISH iss]

Capricorn n. a constellation and sign of
the Zodiac (the Goat), which the sun enters
around Dec. 22. □ **Capricornian** n. & adj.

caprock n. **1** a hard rock overlying a
deposit of oil, gas, etc. **2** a hard rock at the
top of a hoodoo, butte, etc.

capsize v. (**capsizes, capsized,
capsizing**) overturn.

capstan n. a thick revolving cylinder with
a vertical axis, for winding cable.
[Say CAP stun]

capstone n. **1 a** a stone which caps a
structure. **b** = CAPROCK. **2** a culmination.

capsule n. **1** a small soluble case of gelatin
enclosing a dose of medicine and
swallowed with it. **2** (also **space**

capsule) a detachable compartment of a spacecraft. **3** a dry fruit that releases its seeds when ripe. **4** a concise or highly condensed report.

captain ● n. **1** a chief or leader. **2 a** the person in command of a ship. **b** the pilot of a civil aircraft. **3** (also **Captain**) a middle-ranking officer, esp. in a military organization. **4 a** a foreman. **b** a supervisor of waiters or bellboys. ● v. be captain of. □ **captaincy** n. (pl. **captaincies**)

caption ● n. **1** a brief explanation appended to an illustration etc. **2** wording appearing on a cinema or television screen as part of a film or broadcast. ● v. provide with a caption.

captivate v. (**captivates, captivated, captivating**) **1** overwhelm with charm. **2** fascinate. □ **captivatingly** adv. **captivation** n.

captive ● n. a person or animal that has been taken prisoner. ● adj. **1** imprisoned or confined. **2** in a position of having to comply. **3** of or like a prisoner. □ **captivity** n.

captor n. a person who takes or holds (a person etc.) captive.

capture ● v. (**captures, captured, capturing**) **1 a** take prisoner. **b** seize as a prize. **c** obtain by force. **2** win control of. **3** preserve in permanent form. **4** Physics absorb. **5** cause to be stored in a computer. ● n. **1** the act of capturing. **2** a thing or person captured.

Capuchin n. **1** a friar of a strict branch of the Franciscan order. **2** (**capuchin**) a S American monkey with cowl-like fur on its head. [Say CAP you chin]

car n. **1** a road vehicle with an enclosed passenger compartment, powered by an internal combustion engine. **2** a wheeled vehicle. **3** a railway vehicle. **4** the passenger compartment of an elevator, balloon, etc.

carafe n. **1** a wide-mouthed glass container for beverages. **2** an insulated jug. [Say kuh RAF]

caragana n. (pl. **caraganas**) any Asian leguminous shrub of the genus *Caragana*, esp. the Siberian pea, planted as hedging. [Say care a GANNA]

caramel ● n. **1** sugar or syrup heated until it turns brown. **2** a soft candy made with sugar, butter, milk, etc. ● adj. **1** flavoured with caramel. **2** of the light brown colour of caramel. [Say CARE a mel or CARM ul]

caramelize v. (**caramelizes, caramelized, caramelizing**) **1** convert or be converted into caramel. **2** cook (food) with caramelized sugar or syrup. [Say CARE a muh lize or KARMA lize]

carapace n. the hard upper shell of a turtle or a crustacean. [Say CARE a pace]

Caraquet n. Cdn a small edible oyster found in the waters off New Brunswick. [Say CAR a ket]

carat n. **1** a unit of weight for precious stones, equivalent to 200 milligrams. **2** = KARAT.

caravan n. **1** a company of people with vehicles or pack animals travelling together. **2** a covered motor vehicle with living accommodations. **3** a covered carriage.

caraway n. **1** a plant of the parsley family bearing clusters of tiny white flowers. **2** (also **caraway seed**) this plant's seeds, used for flavouring. [Say CARE a way]

carb n. informal **1** a carburetor. **2** carbohydrate.

carbide n. **1** a compound of carbon with a metal or other element. **2** a very hard material made of cobalt or nickel and carbides of metals, used in cutting tools.

carbine n. a short firearm.

carbohydrate n. any of a large group of energy-producing organic compounds containing carbon, hydrogen, and oxygen. [Say carba HI drate]

carbon n. a non-metallic element occurring naturally as diamond, graphite, and charcoal, and in all organic compounds.

carbon-14 n. a long-lived radioactive carbon isotope of mass 14, used in carbon dating.

carbonara adj. designating a sauce for pasta made of eggs, cream, Parmesan cheese, and pieces of bacon. [Say carba NAR uh]

carbonate ● n. a salt of carbonic acid. ● v. (**carbonates, carbonated, carbonating**) **1** dissolve carbon dioxide in a liquid to make it bubbly. **2** convert into a carbonate. □ **carbonated** adj.

carbon copy n. **1** a copy made with carbon paper. **2** an exact duplicate.

carbon dating n. (also **carbon-14 dating**) a method of estimating the age of organic archaeological specimens by determining the ratio of carbon-14 to another isotope.

carbon dioxide n. a colourless odourless gas occurring naturally and formed by respiration.

carbonic acid n. a very weak acid formed from carbon dioxide dissolved in water. [Say car BON ick]

Carboniferous adj. relating to a period of the Paleozoic era, lasting from about 360 to 286 million years BP when extensive coal-

bearing strata were formed.
[*Say* carba NIFFA riss]

carbonize v. (**carbonizes, carbonized, carbonizing**) **1** convert into carbon by heating. **2** reduce to charcoal or coke.

carbon monoxide n. a toxic gas formed by the incomplete burning of carbon.

carburetor n. an apparatus for controlling the mixture of gasoline and air in an internal combustion engine.
[*Say* CARBA rate ur]

carcass n. (*pl.* **carcasses**) **1** the dead body of an animal. **2** the bones of a cooked bird. **3** the structure or framework of something.

carcinogen n. any substance that produces cancer. □ **carcinogenic** adj. **carcinogenicity** n. [*Say* car SINNA jin, car sinna JEN ick, car sinna juh NISSA tee]

carcinoma n. (*pl.* **carcinomas**) a cancer arising in epithelial tissue or the lining of the internal organs. [*Say* karsa NOMA]

card[1] ● n. **1** thick stiff paper or thin pasteboard. **2** a flat piece of this for writing on or printed with information. **3 a** = PLAYING CARD. **b** (in *pl.*) card playing; a card game. **c** a specified advantageous usu. political card. **4** *informal* an amusing person. **5** a small rectangular piece of plastic issued by a bank etc. with machine-readable data on it. **6** a circuit board. ● v. **1** affix to a card. **2** write on a card. **3** demand identification from. □ **card up one's sleeve** a plan in reserve. **in the cards** possible or likely. **play one's cards right** (or **well**) act carefully and successfully. **put** (or **lay**) **one's cards on the table** reveal one's resources, intentions, etc.

card[2] ● n. **1** a machine that combs and disentangles fibre before spinning. **2** an instrument for raising the nap on cloth. ● v. prepare (fibre) with a card.

cardamom n. (also **cardamon**) a plant of the ginger family, the seeds of which are used as a spice. [*Say* CARDA mum, CARDA mun]

cardboard ● n. pasteboard or stiff paper. ● adj. **1** made of cardboard. **2** lacking depth and realism.

card-carrying adj. **1** registered as a member. **2** devoted.

carded adj. Cdn (of an amateur athlete) receiving government funding to pursue training.

cardholder n. a person who has a specific card.

cardiac ● adj. relating to the heart. ● n. a person with heart disease. [*Say* CAR dee ack]

cardiac arrest n. a sudden cessation of the heartbeat.

cardigan n. a sweater fastening down the front.

cardinal ● n. **1** (as a title **Cardinal**) a leading dignitary of the Catholic Church. **2** a N American songbird, the male of which has scarlet plumage. ● adj. fundamental.

cardinal number n. a number denoting quantity rather than position in a series.

cardinal point n. one of the four main points of the compass: north, south, east, west.

cardinal sin n. **1** = DEADLY SIN. **2** an unforgivable action.

cardio n. *slang* **1** cardiovascular exercise. **2** cardiovascular fitness.

cardiogram n. = ELECTROCARDIOGRAM.

cardiograph n. = ELECTROCARDIOGRAPH. □ **cardiographer** n. **cardiography** n. [*Say* CARDY oh graph, cardy OGRA fur, cardy OGRA fee]

cardiology n. the branch of medicine concerned with heart abnormalities. □ **cardiologist** n. [*Say* cardy OLLA jee, cardy OLLA jist]

cardiopulmonary adj. of the heart and lungs. [*Say* cardy oh PUL muh nerry]

cardiopulmonary resuscitation n. a series of emergency techniques used to revive a patient whose heart has stopped.

cardiovascular adj. relating to the heart and blood vessels. [*Say* cardy oh VASK you lur]

care ● n. **1 a** the process of looking after someone or something. **b** protective guardianship provided by a child welfare agency. **2** serious attention in doing something properly or safely. **3** a troubled state of mind. **4** maintenance. **5** a matter of concern. ● v. (**cares, cared, caring**) **1 a** feel concern. **b** have an objection. **2** feel affection. **3** wish. □ **care for 1** look after. **2** love. **care of** at the address of. **take care 1** be careful. **2** not fail or neglect. **take care of 1** look after. **2** deal with. **3** dispose of.

careen v. rush headlong.

career ● n. **1 a** one's advancement through life. **b** the progress through history of a group or institution. **2** a profession. ● adj. **1 a** pursuing a career. **b** working permanently in a specified profession. **2** *Sport* **a** accumulated over one's career. **b** constituting a high point in one's career. ● v. swerve about wildly.

careerist n. a person concerned with personal advancement. □ **careerism** n.

carefree *adj.* free from anxiety or responsibility.

careful *adj.* **1** painstaking. **2** cautious. **3** done with care and attention. **4** showing concern for. □ **carefully** *adv.* **carefulness** *n.*

caregiver *n.* a person who looks after a child or a sick or elderly person. □ **caregiving** *n.*

careless *adj.* **1** not paying attention. **2** insensitive. **3** inaccurate. **4** lighthearted. **5** (foll. by *of*) not concerned about. □ **carelessly** *adv.* **carelessness** *n.*

care package *n.* a parcel of food, clothing, etc. sent to someone who needs it.

caress ● *v.* (**caresses, caressed, caressing**) touch or stroke gently. ● *n.* a loving touch or kiss.

caretaker *n.* **1** a custodian or janitor. **2** = CAREGIVER. **3** (as an *adj.*) exercising temporary authority. □ **caretaking** *n.*

careworn *adj.* showing the effects of prolonged worry.

cargo *n.* (*pl.* **cargoes** or **cargos**) goods carried on a ship, aircraft, truck, etc.

Caribbean ● *n.* the part of the Atlantic between the southern W Indies and Central America. ● *adj.* relating to this region or its people. [*Say* care a BEE in *or* kuh RIBBY in]

caribou *n.* (*pl.* **caribou**) a subspecies of reindeer inhabiting northern Canada and Alaska.

Caribou Inuit *pl. n.* an inland Inuit people formerly inhabiting the Barrens and relying on caribou for food and clothing.

caricature ● *n.* **1** a grotesque, exaggerated, usu. comic representation of a person. **2** a ridiculously poor imitation. ● *v.* (**caricatures, caricatured, caricaturing**) make or give a caricature of. □ **caricaturist** *n.* [*Say* CARE ick a chur]

caries *n.* (*pl.* **caries**) decay and crumbling of a tooth or bone. [*Say* CARE eez]

carillon *n.* **1** a set of bells sounded either from a keyboard or mechanically. **2** a tune played on bells. [*Say* CARE a lun]

caring *adj.* compassionate. □ **caringly** *adv.*

carjack *v.* hijack a car. □ **carjacker** *n.* **carjacking** *n.*

carload *n.* **1** the quantity of freight that can be shipped in a railway car. **2** the number of people that can travel in an automobile.

Carmelite ● *n.* a monk or nun of a Roman Catholic contemplative order. ● *adj.* relating to the Carmelites. [*Say* KARMA lite]

carnage *n.* the killing of many people or animals.

carnal *adj.* relating to physical, esp. sexual needs and activities. □ **carnality** *n.* **carnally** *adv.* [*Say* CAR null, car NALA tee]

carnation *n.* a cultivated variety of the pink, with showy flowers.

carnival *n.* **1** regular festivities involving processions, music, dancing, etc. **2** a travelling fair with exhibits, rides, and other amusements. **3** *Cdn Figure Skating* a non-competitive performance given by the members of a figure skating club. □ **carnivalesque** *adj.*

carnivore *n.* an animal that eats meat.

carnivorous *adj.* **1** meat-eating. **2** (of a plant) digesting trapped insects or other animal substances. [*Say* car NIV er us]

carob *n.* **1** an evergreen Mediterranean tree bearing edible bean-shaped seed pods. **2** the pod of this tree. **3** the pulp of these pods, used as a substitute for chocolate. [*Say* CARE ub]

carol ● *n.* a song celebrating Christmas. ● *v.* (**carols, carolled, carolling**) **1** sing carols. **2** sing or say joyfully. □ **caroller** *n.*

Carolingian ● *adj.* having to do with the Frankish dynasty, which ruled in western Europe from 750 to 987. ● *n.* a member of the Carolingian dynasty. [*Say* care a LIN gee un]

Carolinian ● *adj.* **1** relating to a deciduous forest region extending from southern Ontario to North and South Carolina. **2** relating to the states of South or North Carolina. ● *n.* a person from South or North Carolina. [*Say* care a LINNY in]

carom ● *n.* *Billiards* a shot in which the cue ball strikes two other balls in succession. ● *v.* (**caroms, caromed, caroming**) **1** *Billiards* make a carom. **2** strike and rebound. [*Say* CARE um]

carotene *n.* an orange-coloured plant pigment found in carrots etc. which is a source of vitamin A. [*Say* CARE a teen]

carotid ● *n.* each of the two main arteries carrying blood to the head and neck. ● *adj.* relating to these arteries. [*Say* kuh ROT id]

carouse ● *v.* (**carouses, caroused, carousing**) **1** participate in a noisy drinking party. **2** drink heavily. ● *n.* a noisy drinking party. [*Say* kuh ROUSE (ROUSE *rhymes with* VOWS)]

carousel *n.* **1 a** a large revolving device in a playground, for children to ride on. **b** a merry-go-round. **2** a rotating conveyor system, esp. for passengers' luggage at an airport. **3** a rotating tray for holding specific objects, esp. on a slide projector or CD player. [*Say* care a SELL *or* CARE a sell]

carp[1] *n.* (*pl.* **carp**) a freshwater food fish with large scales and fleshy filaments on either side of its mouth.

carp[2] *v.* find fault.

carpaccio *n.* a thin strip of marinated raw meat. [*Say* car PATCHY oh]

carpal *adj.* of the bones in the wrist. [*Say* CARP ul]

carpal tunnel syndrome *n.* a painful disorder caused by compression of a major nerve in the wrist, often brought about by overexertion.

carpel *n.* the female reproductive organ of a flower. [*Say* CARP ul]

carpenter ● *n.* a person skilled in woodwork. ● *v.* work as a carpenter. ☐ **carpentry** *n.*

carpet ● *n.* **1 a** thick fabric for covering a floor or stairs. **b** a piece of this. **2** an expanse resembling a carpet in being soft, thick, etc. ● *v.* (**carpets, carpeted, carpeting**) cover with or as with a carpet. ☐ **sweep under the carpet** conceal in the hope that it will be forgotten.

carpetbagger *n.* **1** a political candidate with no local connections. **2** an unscrupulous opportunist.

carpeting *n.* **1** material for carpets. **2** carpets collectively.

carpool *n.* an arrangement between people to travel together in a single vehicle. ☐ **carpool** *v.* **carpooler** *n.* **carpooling** *n.*

carport *n.* a shelter with a roof and open sides, for a car.

carpus *n.* (*pl.* **carpi**) the group of small bones in the wrist. [*Say* CARP iss *for the singular,* CARP eye *for the plural*]

carrageenan *n.* (also **carrageenin**) a mixture of polysaccharides extracted from seaweed and used as a gelling, thickening, and emulsifying agent. [*Say* care a GEEN in]

carrel *n.* a small cubicle or desk with high sides in a library.

carriage *n.* **1** a wheeled passenger vehicle. **2** = BABY CARRIAGE. **3 a** the conveying of goods. **b** the cost of this. **4** (**gun carriage**) a wheeled support for a gun. **5** a person's bearing.

Carrier *n.* (*pl.* **Carrier** or **Carriers**) **1** a member of an Athapaskan people inhabiting the BC interior. **2** the language of this people. ☐ **Carrier** *adj.*

carrier *n.* **1** a person or thing that carries something. **2** a company undertaking to convey goods or passengers for payment. **3** a person or animal that transmits a disease etc. without suffering from it. **4** a mobile electron or hole that carries a charge in a semiconductor. **5** (also **carrier**

wave) a high-frequency electromagnetic wave modulated in amplitude or frequency to convey a signal.

carrier pigeon *n.* a homing pigeon trained to carry messages tied to it.

carrion *n.* **1** dead rotting flesh. **2** something vile.

carrot *n.* **1 a** a cultivated parsley-like plant with a tapering orange-coloured root. **b** this root as a vegetable. **2** a means of enticement.

carrot-and-stick *n.* (used as an *adj.*) designating an approach combining rewards for desirable behaviour and punishment for undesirable behaviour.

carry ● *v.* (**carries, carried, carrying**) **1** support, esp. while moving. **2** convey from one place to another. **3** have on one's person. **4** conduct. **5** (foll. by *to*) continue. **6** involve, imply. **7** (in calculations) transfer (a figure) to a column of higher value. **8 a** (**carry oneself**) conduct oneself. **b** hold (a part of the body) in a specified way. **9** publish or broadcast. **10** (of a retailing outlet) keep a regular stock of. **11** make regular payments towards. **12 a** (of sound) be audible at a distance. **b** (of a missile) travel. **13** (of a gun etc.) propel a specified distance. **14 a** win victory for. **b** win acceptance from. **c** win, capture. **15** be the driving force in. **16** be pregnant with. **17 a** (of a motive, money, etc.) cause or enable (a person) to go to a specified place. **b** (of a journey) bring (a person) to a specified point. **18** sing (a tune) on pitch. ● *n.* (*pl.* **carries**) **1** an act of carrying. **2** *Golf* the distance a ball travels before reaching the ground. **3** a portage between rivers etc. **4** the range of a gun etc. **5** *Football* an act of rushing with the ball. ☐ **carry all before one** overcome all opposition. **carry away 1** remove. **2** inspire. **3** deprive of self-control. **carry the can** *informal* bear the responsibility or blame. **carry the day** be victorious. **carry on 1** continue. **2** engage in. **3** *informal* behave strangely. **4** (often foll. by *with*) *informal* flirt or have a love affair. **5** advance (a process) by a stage. **carry out 1** put into practice. **2** perform or conduct.

carrying charge *n.* **1** the interest on a loan etc. **2** the cost of storing unproductive assets etc.

carrying-on *n.* (also **carryings-on** *pl. n.*) **1** a state of excitement or fuss. **2** a questionable piece of behaviour. **3** a flirtation or love affair.

carry-on ● *adj.* (of a suitcase etc.) suitable for carrying onto an airplane, bus, etc. ● *n.* a carry-on suitcase.

carry-over *n.* something transferred from a previous context.

cart ● *n.* **1** a strong vehicle with two or four wheels for carrying loads, drawn by a horse, ox, etc. **2** a light vehicle for pushing or pulling by hand. **3** a light vehicle with two wheels for driving in, drawn by a single horse. ● *v.* **1** convey in or as in a cart. **2** *informal* carry with difficulty or over a long distance. □ **cart off** remove, esp. by force or unceremoniously. **put the cart before the horse 1** reverse the proper order. **2** take an effect for a cause.

carte blanche *n.* complete freedom to act as one thinks best. [*Say* cart BLONSH]

cartel *n.* a group of manufacturers or suppliers formed to maintain high prices and restrict competition. [*Say* car TELL]

Cartesian ● *adj.* of or relating to the French philosopher René Descartes (1596–1650) or to his mathematical methods. ● *n.* a follower of Descartes. [*Say* car TEE zhin]

Cartesian coordinates *pl. n.* a system for locating a point by reference to its distance from two or three axes intersecting at right angles.

Carthusian ● *n.* a Christian monk or nun of a strictly contemplative order founded in France in 1084. ● *adj.* relating to the Carthusians. [*Say* carth YOOZ ee in]

cartilage *n.* a firm, elastic, semi-opaque connective tissue of the vertebrate body. □ **cartilaginous** *adj.* [*Say* CARTA lidge, carta LADGE uh niss]

cartography *n.* the science or practice of map drawing. □ **cartographer** *n.* **cartographic** *adj.* [*Say* car TOGRA fee, car TOGRA fur, carta GRAPH ick]

carton *n.* a light box or container.

cartoon ● *n.* **1** a humorous drawing in a newspaper, magazine, etc. **2** = COMIC STRIP. **3** an animated film. **4** an artist's full-size preliminary design for a painting, tapestry, etc. ● *v.* draw cartoons. □ **cartoonist** *n.*

cartoonish *adj.* simplified or exaggerated like a comic cartoon. □ **cartoonishly** *adv.*

cartoon-like *adj.* resembling a comic cartoon.

cartoony *adj.* resembling a comic cartoon.

cartridge *n.* **1** a case containing a charge and a bullet or shot, used in firearms. **2** a container holding film, magnetic tape, ink, etc. for insertion into a mechanism.

cartwheel ● *n.* **1** the wheel of a cart. **2** a circular sideways handspring with the arms and legs extended. ● *v.* **1** perform cartwheels. **2** turn end over end.

carve *v.* (**carves**, **carved**, **carving**) **1** cut into or shape (hard material) to produce an object or design. **2** produce by carving. **3** cut (meat etc.) into slices for eating. **4** cut (a way, passage, etc.). □ **carved in stone** unchangeable. **carve out 1** take from a larger whole. **2** establish purposefully. **carve up 1** divide. **2** cut (a person) with a knife. □ **carver** *n.*

carving *n.* a carved object.

CAS *abbr.* (in Canada) Children's Aid Society.

casaba *n.* (*pl.* **casabas**) a melon with a yellow wrinkled skin and whitish flesh. [*Say* kuh SAW buh]

Casanova *n.* (*pl.* **Casanovas**) a man notorious for seducing women. [*Say* cassa NO vuh]

cascade ● *n.* **1** a small waterfall, esp. one in a series. **2** a rapid sequence of things. **3** a thing that falls or hangs in a way suggestive of a waterfall. ● *v.* (**cascades**, **cascaded**, **cascading**) fall in or like a cascade.

cascara *n.* (also **cascara sagrada**) the bark of the western N American buckthorn, used as a laxative. [*Say* cass CAR uh (suh GRODDA)]

case¹ *n.* **1** an example of something occurring. **2** a state of affairs. **3** the circumstances in which one is. **4** a person or their situation as a subject of a doctor's or social worker's attention. **5** a matter under police investigation. **6** a legal action decided in court. **7** a set of facts or arguments, e.g. in a lawsuit. **8** *Grammar* a form of a noun, adjective, or pronoun expressing the relation of a word to others in a sentence. □ **get off** (or **on**) **one's case** *informal* stop (or start) harassing one. **in any case** whatever the truth is. **in case 1** if. **2** lest.

case² ● *n.* a container or covering. ● *v.* (**cases**, **cased**, **casing**) **1** enclose in a case. **2** (foll. by *with*) surround. **3** *slang* reconnoitre.

case history *n.* information about a person for use in medical treatment etc.

casein *n.* the main protein in milk and cheese. [*Say* KAY seen]

case law *n.* the law as established by the outcome of former cases.

caseload *n.* the cases with which a doctor etc. is concerned at one time.

casement *n.* a window hinged to open like a door.

case-sensitive *adj. Computing* differentiating between capital and lower case letters.

case study *n.* **1** a detailed study of the development of a person or thing over time. **2** a particular instance used to illustrate a general principle.

casework *n.* social work concerned with

individuals and their family and background. □ **caseworker** n.

cash ● n. **1** money in coins or banknotes. **2** (also **cash down**) money paid at the time of purchase, as distinct from credit. **3** informal money. **4** Cdn informal = CASH REGISTER. ● v. (**cashes, cashed, cashing**) give or obtain cash for. □ **cash in 1** obtain cash for. **2** informal (usu. foll. by on) profit (from).

cash and carry ● adj. (of a store etc.) operated on a system of cash payments, with no delivery available. ● n. a store where this system operates.

cashback n. **1** a form of incentive offering customers a cash sum after making their purchase or negotiating their loan etc. **2** a facility offered by certain retailers whereby the customer may withdraw cash when making a debit card purchase, the amount of which is added to their bill.

cash cow n. informal a product or operation providing a steady and abundant cash flow.

cashew n. **1** a kidney-shaped nut. **2** the Central and South American evergreen tree that produces it. [Say CASH oo or ka SHOO]

cash flow n. the movement of money in and out of a business.

cashier[1] n. a person handling cash and customer payments in a store, bank, or company.

cashier[2] v. dismiss from the armed forces with disgrace.

cashless adj. functioning without cash.

cash machine n. = AUTOMATED TELLER MACHINE.

cashmere n. a fine soft wool, originally that of a Himalayan goat.

cash register n. a machine used for storing cash, recording the amount of each sale, totalling receipts, etc.

cashspiel n. Cdn a bonspiel in which curlers compete for cash. [Say CASH speel]

cash-strapped adj. extremely short of money.

casing n. a protective or enclosing cover or shell.

casino n. (pl. **casinos**) a venue for gambling at cards, roulette, slot machines, etc.

cask n. a large barrel-like container for liquor.

casket n. **1** a coffin. **2** a small ornamental box for valuables.

Cassandra n. a prophet of disaster. [Say kuh SANDRA]

cassava n. (pl. **cassavas**) **1** a cultivated plant with starchy tuberous roots, or the roots themselves. **2** a starch or flour obtained from these roots. [Say kuh SAW vuh]

casserole n. **1** a covered dish in which food is cooked in an oven. **2** food cooked in such a dish.

cassette n. a sealed case containing a length of audiotape, film, etc., for insertion in a machine.

cassia n. (pl. **cassias**) a tree or shrub yielding a variety of products, esp. senna. [Say CASSY uh]

cassock n. a long church vestment, usu. worn under a surplice. [Say CASS ick]

cast ● v. (**casts, cast, casting**) **1** throw deliberately or forcefully. **2** (often foll. by on, over) **a** direct (one's gaze etc.). **b** cause (light, a shadow, etc.) to appear. **c** express. **3** let down (an anchor etc.). **4 a** throw off, get rid of. **b** leave aside or shed (skin etc.). **5** register (a vote). **6 a** shape (molten material) in a mould. **b** make (a product) in this way. **7** select a performer for a role. ● n. **1** an act of throwing (a fishing line etc.). **2** a throw or a number thrown at dice. **3** Fishing the line thrown, its hook, fly, etc. **4 a** an object made in a mould. **b** solidified plaster etc. protecting a broken limb. **5** the performers taking part in a play, film, etc. **6** form, type, or quality. □ **cast about** search. **cast away 1** reject. **2** shipwreck. **cast in stone** irrevocably set. **cast off 1** abandon. **2** Knitting take the stitches off the needle. **3** set a ship free from a quay etc.

castanets pl. n. a pair of shell-shaped pieces of wood or ivory clicked together with the fingers to accompany Spanish dancing.

castaway ● n. **1** a shipwrecked person. **2** an outcast. **3** a castoff. ● adj. **1** shipwrecked. **2** cast aside.

caste n. **1** each of the Hindu hereditary classes. **2** an exclusive social class. **3** (also **caste system**) a system of such classes. □ **casteism** n. [Say CAST, CAST ism]

caster n. **1** a person who casts. **2** a small swivelled wheel fixed to the underside of furniture. □ **castered** adj. (in sense 2).

castigate v. (**castigates, castigated, castigating**) rebuke severely.

Castilian n. **1** a person from Castile. **2** the language of Castile, standard Spanish. □ **Castilian** adj. [Say ka STILLY in]

casting n. **1** an object made by casting molten metal etc. **2** in senses of CAST v.

cast iron ● n. a hard alloy of iron, carbon, and silicon cast in a mould. ● adj. (also **cast-iron**) **1** made of cast iron. **2** firm, unchangeable.

castle n. **1** a large fortified building or group of buildings. **2** *Chess* = ROOK 1. □ **castles in the air** (or **in Spain**) an unattainable daydream.

cast net n. *Fishing* a net thrown out and immediately drawn in.

cast-off ● adj. abandoned, discarded. ● n. (**castoff**) a cast-off person or thing.

castor[1] n. = CASTER 2.

castor[2] n. (also **castoreum**) a pungent, bitter, reddish-brown substance secreted by beavers, formerly used in medicine and perfumes. [*Say* cass TORY um]

castor oil n. an oil obtained from the seeds of an African shrub, used as a purgative and lubricant.

castrate v. (**castrates**, **castrated**, **castrating**) **1** remove the testicles of. **2** deprive of vigour or power. □ **castration** n.

casual ● adj. **1** due to chance. **2** temporary, occasional. **3 a** unconcerned, uninterested. **b** lacking care or thought. **4** informal, relaxed. ● n. **1** a casual worker. **2** (usu. in pl.) casual clothes or shoes. □ **casually** adv. **casualness** n.

casualty n. (pl. **casualties**) **1** a person killed or injured in a war or accident. **2** a thing lost, badly affected, or destroyed.

casuistry n. the use of clever but unsound reasoning. [*Say* KAZZ you iss tree]

CAT abbr. COMPUTERIZED AXIAL TOMOGRAPHY.

cat n. **1** a small soft-furred four-legged domesticated animal. **2** a wild animal related to or resembling this. □ **cat got your tongue?** *informal* don't you have anything to say? **cat's whiskers** (or **pyjamas** or **meow** or *Cdn* **ass**) *informal* an excellent person or thing. **let the cat out of the bag** reveal a secret, esp. involuntarily. **rain cats and dogs** rain very hard.

cataclysm n. a violent upheaval or disaster. □ **cataclysmic** adj. **cataclysmically** adv. [*Say* CATTA clism, catta KLIZZ mick]

catacomb n. (often in pl.) an underground cemetery consisting of tunnels with recesses for tombs. [*Say* CATTA comb]

Catalan n. **1** a person from Catalonia. **2** the language of Catalonia. □ **Catalan** adj. [*Say* CATTA lan]

catalepsy n. a medical condition in which a person loses consciousness and the body becomes rigid. □ **cataleptic** adj. & n. [*Say* CATTA lep see, catta LEP tick]

catalogue ● n. **1** a complete list of items in alphabetical or other systematic order. **2** a publication describing items for sale.

● v. (**catalogues**, **catalogued**, **cataloguing**) **1** make a catalogue of. **2** enter in a catalogue. □ **cataloguer** n.

catalpa n. (pl. **catalpas**) a tree with trumpet-shaped flowers. [*Say* kuh TAL puh]

catalyst n. **1** a substance that, without itself undergoing any permanent chemical change, increases the rate of a reaction. **2** a person or thing that precipitates a change. [*Say* CATTA list]

catalytic adj. relating to the acceleration of a reaction by a catalyst. [*Say* catta LIT ick]

catalytic converter n. a device fitted in the exhaust system of some motor vehicles which converts pollutant gases into less harmful ones.

catalyze v. (**catalyzes**, **catalyzed**, **catalyzing**) (also **catalyse**; **catalyses**, **catalysed**, **catalysing**) **1** produce (a reaction) by the action of a catalyst. **2** cause an action or process to begin. [*Say* CATTA lize]

catamaran n. a boat with twin hulls in parallel. [*Say* CATTA muh RAN]

catapult ● n. **1** *hist.* a military device for hurling large stones etc. **2** a mechanical device for launching an aircraft. ● v. **1** move suddenly and very fast. **2** throw forcefully.

cataract n. **1** a large waterfall or cascade. **2 a** a disease in which the lens of the eye becomes cloudy, causing partial or total blindness. **b** an area clouded in this way.

catarrh n. inflammation of the mucous membrane of the nose, air passages, etc. □ **catarrhal** adj. [*Say* kuh TAR, kuh TAR ul]

catastrophe n. a great and usu. sudden disaster. □ **catastrophic** adj. **catastrophically** adv. [*Say* kuh TASS truh fee, cat iss TROFF ick]

catatonic ● adj. **1** immobile and not responsive due to illness etc. **2** inert or not emotional. ● n. a person in a catatonic state. [*Say* catta TONIC]

cat burglar n. a burglar who enters by climbing to an upper storey.

catcall ● n. a shrill whistle of disapproval. ● v. make a catcall.

catch ● v. (**catches**, **caught**, **catching**) **1** seize and hold. **2** detect or surprise. **3 a** become infected with. **b** acquire from another's example. **4** be in time to board (a bus etc.) or see (an event). **5** apprehend; capture. **6 a** become fixed or entangled. **b** cause to do this. **c** hit. **7** draw the attention of. **8 a** begin to burn. **b** (of an engine) start. **9** (often foll. by *up*) reach or overtake. **10** (**catch oneself**) stop (oneself) just in time. ● n. (pl. **catches**) **1** an act of catching. **2 a** an amount of fish caught. **b** something worth catching, esp. in marriage. **3** a game in which two players throw a ball back and forth. **4** a hidden difficulty or trick. **5** a device for fastening a door etc. **6** an impediment in the voice, throat, etc. **7** a snag in a sweater etc. **8** a fragment of a song. □ **catch it** *slang* be punished or in trouble. **catch on** *informal* **1** become popular. **2** (of a person) understand what is meant. **catch out 1** detect in a mistake etc. **2** take unawares. **catch up 1 a** reach a person etc. ahead. **b** (often foll. by *with, on*) make up arrears (of work etc.). **2** snatch hurriedly. **3** (often in *passive*) **a** involve; entangle. **b** fasten up.

Catch-22 *n.* (*pl.* **Catch-22s**) a dilemma or circumstance from which there is no escape because of mutually conflicting or dependent conditions.

catch-all *n.* a thing designed to be all-inclusive.

catcher *n.* **1** a person or thing that catches. **2** *Baseball* the fielder positioned behind home plate.

catching *adj.* **1** infectious. **2** likely to be imitated.

catchment *n.* **1** the act or process of collecting water. **2** a place where water is collected. **3** (also **catchment area**) **a** the area from which rainfall flows into a river etc. **b** the area served by a school, hospital, etc.

catchphrase *n.* a phrase or slogan in frequent use.

catch-up *n.* the act of attempting to reach someone or something which is ahead.

catchword *n.* **1** a topical slogan or phrase. **2** a word placed so as to draw attention.

catchy *adj.* (**catchier, catchiest**) (of a tune etc.) easy to remember. □ **catchiness** *n.*

catechism *n.* **1** a summary of the principles of a Christian religion, esp. in the form of questions and answers. **2** esp. *Catholicism* **a** religious instruction. **b** a class in this. [*Say* CATTA kism]

catechize *v.* (**catechizes, catechized, catechizing**) **1** instruct by means of question and answer, esp. from a catechism. **2** put questions to. [*Say* CATTA kize]

categorical *adj.* unconditional, absolute. □ **categorically** *adv.*

categorize *v.* (**categorizes, categorized, categorizing**) place in a category or categories. □ **categorization** *n.*

category *n.* (*pl.* **categories**) a class or division.

cater *v.* **1** provide food, drink, etc. for an

event. **2** meet the needs of. □ **caterer** *n.* **catering** *n.*

caterpillar *n.* **1** the larva of a butterfly or moth. **2 a** an endless steel tread passing around the wheels of a tractor etc. **b** (**Caterpillar**) *proprietary* a vehicle equipped with these treads.

caterwaul ● *v.* make the shrill howl of a cat. ● *n.* a caterwauling noise. [*Say* CATTER wall]

cat fight *n.* **1** a dispute in which the participants are spiteful, malicious, and unrestrained. **2** a malicious fight or dispute between women. **3** a fight between cats.

catfish *n.* (*pl.* same) a fish with whisker-like growths around the mouth.

catgut *n.* a material made from the intestines of sheep etc., and used for sutures, instrument strings, etc.

catharsis *n.* (*pl.* **catharses**) the release of pent-up emotion. [*Say* kuh THARSE iss *for the singular,* ku THARSE eez *for the plural*]

cathartic ● *adj.* **1** providing psychological relief through the open expression of strong emotions. **2** strongly laxative. ● *n.* a laxative drug. □ **cathartically** *adv.* [*Say* ku THART ick]

cathedral *n.* the principal church of a diocese, containing the bishop's throne.

catheter *n.* a tube inserted into the bladder or other body cavity, for removing fluid. [*Say* CATH a tur]

cathode *n.* an electrode with a negative charge. [*Say* CATH ode]

cathode ray tube *n.* a high-vacuum tube in which beams of electrons produce a luminous image on a fluorescent screen, used in televisions etc. Abbreviation: **CRT**.

catholic ● *adj.* **1** (**Catholic**) Roman Catholic. **2** including a wide variety of things. ● *n.* (**Catholic**) a Roman Catholic.

Catholicism *n.* the faith, practice, and church order of the Roman Catholic Church. [*Say* kuh THOLLA sism]

cation *n.* a positively charged ion. □ **cationic** *adj.* [*Say* CAT eye in, cat eye ON ick]

catkin *n.* a spike of silky flowers hanging from a willow or other tree.

catlike *adj.* **1** like a cat. **2** stealthy.

catnap ● *n.* a short sleep. ● *v.* (**catnaps, catnapped, catnapping**) have a catnap.

catnip *n.* a white-flowered herb, having a smell attractive to cats.

CAT scan *n.* a medical examination using an X-ray apparatus which produces a series of detailed cross-sectional pictures of internal organs, esp. the brain. □ **CAT scanner** *n.*

cat's cradle *n.* a child's game in which a loop of string is held between the fingers and patterns are formed.

cattail *n.* = BULRUSH 2.

cattle *pl. n.* bovine animals, e.g. cows, bison, and buffalo.

cattle guard *n.* a ditch covered by metal bars spaced so as to allow vehicles and pedestrians to pass over but not cattle or other animals.

cattleman *n.* (*pl.* **cattlemen**) a person who tends or rears cattle.

catty *adj.* (**cattier, cattiest**) **1** sly, spiteful. **2** catlike. □ **cattily** *adv.* **cattiness** *n.*

catwalk *n.* **1** a raised narrow footway. **2** a narrow platform along which models walk during a fashion show.

Caucasian ● *adj.* **1** relating to light-skinned humans of a race originally inhabiting Europe, N Africa, and the Middle East. **2** relating to the Caucasus region. ● *n.* a Caucasian person. [*Say* caw KAY zhun]

caucus *n.* (*pl.* **caucuses**) **1** the members of a legislature belonging to a particular party. **2** a faction within a larger group, sharing common political goals. **3** a usu. secret meeting of a small group of people. [*Say* CAW cuss]

caught *past and past participle of* CATCH.

caul *n.* **1** a membrane enclosing a fetus. **2** part of this sometimes found on a child's head at birth. [*Sounds like* CALL]

cauldron *n.* a large metal cooking pot.

cauliflower *n.* a variety of cabbage with a large white flower head, eaten as a vegetable.

caulk[1] ● *v.* **1** fill (a seam etc.) with a watertight or airtight material. **2** make watertight or airtight by this method. ● *n.* (also **caulking**) a substance used to caulk. [*Sounds like* COCK]

caulk[2] ● *n.* **1** a spike fitted to a boot to resist slipping. **2** (also **caulk boot**) a boot so equipped, used by loggers. ● *v.* furnish (a boot) with caulks. [*Sounds like* COCK *or* CORK]

causal *adj.* relating to or being a cause. □ **causally** *adv.*

causality *n.* the relation of cause and effect.

causation *n.* **1** the causing of an effect. **2** = CAUSALITY.

causative *adj.* **1** acting as cause. **2** (foll. by *of*) producing.

cause ● *n.* **1** that which produces an effect. **2** a reason considered adequate. **3** a principle or purpose which is advocated.

4 a lawsuit. ● *v.* (**causes, caused, causing**) be the cause of.

cause célèbre *n.* (*pl.* **causes célèbres**) a controversial issue that attracts much attention. [*Say* koz suh LEB *or* koze say LEBRA]

causeway *n.* a raised road over wet ground etc.

caustic ● *adj.* **1** able to burn or corrode organic tissue. **2** bitterly sarcastic. ● *n.* a caustic substance. □ **caustically** *adv.* [*Say* KOSS tick]

caution ● *n.* **1** attention to safety. **2** a warning. ● *v.* warn or admonish. □ **throw caution to the wind** act imprudently on purpose.

cautionary *adj.* serving as a warning.

cautious *adj.* careful. □ **cautiously** *adv.* **cautiousness** *n.*

cavalcade *n.* a procession of riders, vehicles, etc.

cavalier ● *n.* **1** a gallant or fashionable man. **2** *hist.* (**Cavalier**) a supporter of Charles I in the English Civil War (1642–9). ● *adj.* showing a lack of proper concern. □ **cavalierly** *adv.* [*Say* cava LEER]

cavalry *n.* (*pl.* **cavalries**) (usu. treated as *pl.*) **1** soldiers on horseback. **2** soldiers in armoured vehicles. [*Say* CAV ul ree]

cave ● *n.* a large natural underground hollow. ● *v.* (**caves, caved, caving**) explore caves. □ **cave in a** subside, collapse. **b** cause (a wall etc.) to do this. **2** yield to pressure. □ **caving** *n.*

caveat *n.* a warning. [*Say* CAV ee at]

caveat emptor *n.* the buyer alone is responsible if dissatisfied. [*Say* cav ee at EMP tore]

cave-in *n.* **1** a collapse, typically underground. **2** yielding to pressure.

caveman *n.* (*pl.* **cavemen**) a prehistoric human.

cavern *n.* a large cave.

cavernous *adj.* resembling a cavern. □ **cavernously** *adv.*

caviar *n.* the pickled roe of sturgeon or other large fish, eaten as a delicacy. [*Say* CAV ee arr]

cavil ● *v.* (**cavils, cavilled, cavilling**) make petty objections. ● *n.* a trivial objection. [*Say* CAV ul]

cavity *n.* (*pl.* **cavities**) **1** a hollow within a solid body. **2** a decayed part of a tooth.

cavort *v.* **1** behave excitedly. **2** apply oneself to sexual or disreputable pursuits.

caw ● *n.* the harsh cry of a crow etc. ● *v.* utter this cry.

cayenne *n.* (also **cayenne pepper**) a hot-tasting red powder obtained from ground dried chile peppers. [Say kie YEN or KIE yen or kay EN or KAY en]

Cayuga n. (pl. **Cayuga** or **Cayugas**) **1** a member of an Iroquoian people. **2** the language of this people. □ **Cayugan** adj. [Say kay OOGA]

CB abbr. (pl. **CBs**) citizens' band (radio).

CBC abbr. Canadian Broadcasting Corporation.

CC abbr. Companion of the Order of Canada.

cc • abbr. (also **c.c.**) **1** cubic centimetre(s). **2** carbon copy. **•** n. (pl. **cc's**) a cubic centimetre.

CCD abbr. (pl. **CCDs**) charge-coupled device, a light-sensitive grid on a silicon microchip that creates digital signals from images.

CCF abbr. Cdn hist. CO-OPERATIVE COMMONWEALTH FEDERATION. □ **CCFer** n.

CCRA abbr. (in Canada) Canada Customs and Revenue Agency.

CD n. (pl. **CDs**) a compact disc.

Cdn. abbr. Canadian.

CD-ROM n. (pl. **CD-ROMs**) a compact disc with read-only memory.

CE abbr. **1** civil engineer. **2** Common Era.

cease v. (**ceases, ceased, ceasing**) stop.

ceasefire n. **1** an order to stop firing. **2** a period of truce.

ceaseless adj. without end. □ **ceaselessly** adv.

cecum n. (pl. **ceca**) a pouch connected to the join between the small and large intestines. [Say SEEK um for the singular, SEEKA for the plural]

cedar n. **1** any of various coniferous trees with fragrant wood. **2** (also **cedarwood**) its fragrant durable wood.

cedar shake n. a type of cedar shingle.

cedarstrip n. Cdn a technique for making canoes etc. of long strips of cedar.

cede v. (**cedes, ceded, ceding**) give up (power, territory, etc.).

cedilla n. (pl. **cedillas**) a mark written under the letter c to show that it sounds like an "s" (as in soupçon). [Say suh DILLA]

CEGEP abbr. (also **Cegep**) (in Quebec) Collège d'enseignement général et professionnel, a post-secondary educational institution offering university preparation and job training. [Say SEE jep or SAY zhep]

ceilidh n. a party or concert featuring Celtic music and dancing. [Say KAY lee]

ceiling n. **1** the upper interior surface of a room. **2** an upper limit, such as on prices. □ **ceilinged** adj. (in comb.).

ceinture fléchée n. (pl. **ceintures fléchées**) Cdn hist. a long, brightly coloured sash woven with an arrow-shaped pattern and worn around the waist, esp. by voyageurs. [Say san tyoor flay SHAY]

celeb n. informal a celebrity.

celebrant n. **1** a person who performs a rite, esp. a priest who officiates at the Eucharist. **2** a person celebrating something. [Say SELLA brunt]

celebrate v. (**celebrates, celebrated, celebrating**) **1** mark (an occasion) with festivities. **2** perform (a religious ceremony etc.). **3** honour or praise publicly. □ **celebrated** adj. **celebration** n. **celebratory** adj. [Say SELLA brate, SELLA bruh tory]

celebrity n. (pl. **celebrities**) **1** a well-known person. **2** fame. [Say suh LEB ruh tee]

celery n. a vegetable with crisp juicy stalks.

celestial adj. **1** heavenly. **2 a** of the sky. **b** of heavenly bodies. [Say suh LESS chull]

celiac disease n. a disorder of the small intestine, causing failure to digest food properly unless the diet is gluten-free. [Say SEELY ack]

celibate • adj. **1** committed to abstinence from sexual relations and from marriage, esp. for religious reasons. **2** abstaining from sex. **•** n. a celibate person. □ **celibacy** n. [Say SELLA bit, SELLA buh see]

cell n. **1** a small room, esp. in a prison or monastery. **2** a compartment or small section within a larger structure. **3** a small active political group that is part of a larger organization. **4** the basic functional unit of an organism, usu. microscopic, consisting of cytoplasm and a nucleus enclosed in a membrane. **5** a device for generating electricity from chemical energy or light. **6** a cellphone. **7** an atmospheric mass with roughly uniform properties.

cellar • n. **1** a room below ground level in a house. **2** a stock of wine in a cellar. **•** v. store in a cellar.

cellblock n. one of several sections of cells in a large prison.

cello n. (pl. **cellos**) the second-largest instrument of the violin family, held upright on the floor between the knees of the seated player. □ **cellist** n. [Say CHELLO]

Cellophane n. proprietary a thin transparent plastic packaging material. [Say SELLA fane]

cellphone n. a portable telephone which operates by means of a cellular network.

cellular • adj. **1** of or consisting of cells.

2 (of a telephone system) using a number of short-range radio transmitters to cover a large area. ● *n.* a cellphone system. [*Say* SELL yuh lur]

cellulite *n.* fatty tissue regarded as causing a dimpled texture on the skin. [*Say* SELL yuh lite]

celluloid ● *n.* **1** a transparent flammable plastic. **2** motion-picture film. ● *adj.* **1** made of celluloid. **2** relating to motion pictures. [*Say* SELL yuh loid]

cellulose *n.* a carbohydrate forming the main constituent of the cell walls of plants, used making paints, lacquers, and man-made fibres. [*Say* SELL yuh loase]

Celsius *adj.* relating to a scale of temperature on which water freezes at 0° and boils at 100°. [*Say* SELL see us]

Celt *n.* a member of a group of western European peoples esp. in Ireland, Wales, Scotland, Cornwall, Brittany, etc. [*Say* KELT *or* SELT]

Celtic ● *adj.* relating to the Celts. ● *n.* a group of languages spoken by Celtic peoples, including Gaelic, Welsh, and Breton. [*Say* KELL tick *or* SELL tick]

cement ● *n.* **1 a** a powdery substance made by subjecting lime and clay to heat, used to make mortar or concrete. **b** concrete. **2** any substance that hardens and fastens on setting. **3** a uniting factor. ● *v.* **1** fix with cement. **2** establish or strengthen.

cemetery *n.* (*pl.* **cemeteries**) a graveyard.

cenotaph *n.* a tomb-like monument to a person or persons whose bodies are interred elsewhere. [*Say* SENNA taff]

Cenozoic *adj.* relating to the most recent geological era, following the Mesozoic and lasting from about 65 million years ago to the present day. [*Say* senna ZO ick]

censer *n.* a vessel in which incense is burned. [*Say* SEN sir]

censor ● *n.* an official authorized to examine material to be published and to suppress anything considered obscene, a threat to security, etc. ● *v.* **1** act as a censor of. **2** make deletions or changes in. □ **censorial** *adj.* [*Say* SEN sir, sen SORRY ul]

censorious *adj.* severely critical. □ **censoriousness** *n.* [*Say* sen SORRY us]

censorship *n.* the practice of officially examining books, movies, etc. and suppressing unacceptable parts.

censure ● *v.* (**censures**, **censured**, **censuring**) criticize severely. ● *n.* harsh criticism. [*Say* SEN shur]

census *n.* (*pl.* **censuses**) an official count of a population etc. [*Say* SEN suss]

cent *n.* a monetary unit in various countries, equal to one-hundredth of a dollar or other decimal currency unit.

cent. *abbr.* century.

centaur *n. Greek Myth* a creature with the upper body of a man and the lower body of a horse. [*Say* SEN tore]

centenary ● *n.* (*pl.* **centenaries**) a hundredth anniversary. ● *adj.* relating to a centenary. [*Say* sen TENNER ee]

centennial ● *n.* a hundredth anniversary. ● *adj.* relating to a hundredth anniversary.

center etc. = CENTRE etc.

centi- *comb. form* **1** one-hundredth. **2** hundred. Abbreviation: **c**.

centigrade *adj.* = CELSIUS.

centigram *n.* a metric unit equal to one-hundredth of a gram.

centilitre *n.* a metric unit equal to one-hundredth of a litre.

centimetre *n.* a metric unit equal to one-hundredth of a metre.

centipede *n.* a predatory invertebrate with a wormlike body of many segments each with two legs.

central ● *adj.* **1** of, at, or forming the centre. **2** from the centre. **3** most important. **4** denoting a house's heating, air conditioning, or vacuum system in which the rooms are connected via pipes, ducts, or tubes to a single source of heat, cool air, or suction. ● *n. informal* a place with a high concentration of a specified thing. □ **centrally** *adv.*

central bank *n.* a bank operated by the state, which issues currency etc.

Central Canada *n.* see CENTRAL PROVINCES.

centrality *n.* the central position or role of something. [*Say* sen TRALA tee]

centralize *v.* (**centralizes**, **centralized**, **centralizing**) **1** move to a centre. **2 a** concentrate (administration) at a single centre. **b** subject to this system. □ **centralism** *n.* **centralist** *n.* **centralization** *n.* **centralizer** *n.*

central nervous system *n.* the complex of nerve tissues controlling the activities of the body, in vertebrates the brain and spinal cord.

central processing unit *n.* (also **central processor**) the part of a computer in which operations are controlled and carried out.

Central provinces *pl. n.* Ontario and Quebec (*compare* ATLANTIC PROVINCES, WESTERN PROVINCES).

centre (also **center**) ● *n.* **1** the middle point or part. **2** an axis of rotation. **3 a** a main area for an activity. **b** a place with a specified function. **4** a point of concentration or dispersion. **5** a moderate political group. **6** the middle player in a line or group in some games. **7** (as an *adj.*) of or at the centre. ● *v.* (**centres, centred, centring**) **1** (foll. by *in, on, around*) have as its main centre or focus. **2** place in the centre. **3** (foll. by *in* etc.) concentrate. **4** pass (the puck etc.) from the side to the centre of the playing area.

centreboard *n.* a retractable keel on a sailboat.

centred *adj.* **1** having the kind of centre described. **2** having the specified subject as the key element. **3** (of a person) well balanced, serene. □ **centredness** *n.* (in *comb.*)

centrefold *n.* **1** a centre spread of a magazine, often with a portion that folds out. **2** a usu. naked or scantily clad model pictured on such a spread.

centre ice *n.* the central area of a rink.

centreman *n.* (*pl.* **centremen**) = CENTRE *n.* 6.

centre of gravity *n.* a point from which the weight of a body or system may be considered to act.

centrepiece *n.* **1** an ornament for the middle of a table. **2** a principal item.

centre stage ● *n.* **1** the central area on a theatrical stage. **2** the most prominent position. ● *adv.* in or into this position.

centric *adj.* (in *comb.*) **1** having a specified centre or focus. **2** forming an evaluation from a specified viewpoint. □ **centricity** *n.* [*Say* SEN trick, sen TRISSA tee]

centrifugal *adj.* moving away from a centre. [*Say* sen TRIFFA gull *or* sentra FEW gull]

centrifuge ● *n.* a machine with a rapidly rotating device designed to separate liquids from solids or other liquids. ● *v.* (**centrifuges, centrifuged, centrifuging**) **1** subject to the action of a centrifuge. **2** separate by centrifuge. [*Say* SENTRA fuge]

centripetal *adj.* moving towards a centre. [*Say* sen TRIPPA tull]

centrist *n. Politics* a person who holds moderate views. □ **centrism** *n.*

centurion *n.* the commander of a century in the ancient Roman army. [*Say* sen CHURRY in]

century *n.* (*pl.* **centuries**) **1 a** a period of one hundred years. **b** any of the centuries reckoned from the supposed date of the

birth of Christ. **2** a company in the ancient Roman army, originally of 100 men.

CEO *n.* (*pl.* **CEOs**) = CHIEF EXECUTIVE OFFICER

cephalopod *n.* any mollusc of the class that includes octopuses and squids. [*Say* SEFFA luh pod]

ceramic ● *adj.* **1** made of clay hardened by heat. **2** relating to pottery. ● *n.* a ceramic object.

ceramics *pl. n.* **1** ceramic products. **2** (usu. treated as *sing.*) the art of making ceramic articles.

cereal ● *n.* **1** (usu. in *pl.*) a grass producing an edible grain, such as wheat, corn, or rye. **2** a breakfast food made from a cereal. ● *adj.* of edible grain or products of it.

cerebellum *n.* (*pl.* **cerebellums** or **cerebella**) the part of the brain at the back of the skull, which controls muscular activity. [*Say* sare a BELLUM]

cerebral *adj.* **1** of the brain. **2** intellectual. [*Say* suh REE brull *or* SARE a brull]

cerebral cortex *n.* the intricately folded outer layer of the cerebrum.

cerebral palsy *n.* a condition marked by weakness and impaired coordination of the limbs, esp. caused by damage to the brain before or at birth.

cerebrospinal fluid *n.* a clear fluid surrounding the brain and spinal cord. Abbreviation: **CSF.** [*Say* suh ree bro SPINAL]

cerebrum *n.* (*pl.* **cerebra**) the principal part of the brain, located in the front area of the skull. [*Say* su REE brum *or* SARE a brum]

ceremonial ● *adj.* **1** having to do with ceremonies. **2** formal. ● *n.* a ceremony or ceremonies. □ **ceremonially** *adv.*

ceremonious *adj.* done in a way appropriate to formal occasions. □ **ceremoniously** *adv.* **ceremoniousness** *n.* [*Say* sare a MOANY us]

ceremony *n.* (*pl.* **ceremonies**) **1** a formal religious or public rite or occasion celebrating an event. **2** formalities. □ **stand on ceremony** insist on the observance of formalities. **without ceremony** informally.

Cerlox *n. proprietary Cdn* a type of plastic spiral binding with teeth that lock into rectangular holes punched in the paper.

cert *n. slang* (esp. **dead cert**) something certain to happen.

certain *adj.* **1 a** confident, convinced. **b** indisputable. **2 a** that may be relied on. **b** destined. **3** that might be specified, but is not. **4** some but not much.

certainly adv. **1** without doubt. **2** yes.

certainty n. (pl. **certainties**) **1** the state of being certain. **2** a certain prospect. **3** a reliable person or thing.

certifiable adj. **1** able or needing to be certified. **2** informal insane. [Say serta FIE a bull]

certificate n. a formal document attesting a fact, event, or achievement. □ **certification** n.

certified cheque n. a cheque the validity of which is guaranteed by a bank.

certify v. (**certifies, certified, certifying**) **1** attest; attest to. **2** declare by certificate that something or someone meets the specified standards. **3** officially declare insane.

certitude n. a feeling of or belief held with absolute certainty.

cerulean adj. literary deep blue like a clear sky. [Say suh RULEY un]

cervical adj. **1** relating to the neck. **2** relating to the cervix. [Say SURVA cull]

cervix n. (pl. **cervices**) **1** the narrow lower part of the uterus, extending into the vagina. **2** the neck. [Say SIR vicks for the singular, SURVA sees for the plural]

cesium n. a soft silver-white element used in photoelectric cells. [Say SEEZY um]

cessation n. a ceasing. [Say suh SAY sh'n]

cession n. **1** (often foll. by of) the ceding or giving up (of territory etc.). **2** the territory etc. so ceded. [Sounds like SESSION]

cesspit n. **1** a pit for the disposal of refuse. **2** = CESSPOOL.

cesspool n. **1** an underground container for the temporary storage of liquid waste or sewage. **2** a centre of corruption and depravity.

cetacean ● n. a marine mammal of the order that includes whales and dolphins. ● adj. of cetaceans. [Say suh TAY sh'n]

CF abbr. **1** cystic fibrosis. **2** Canadian Forces.

cf. abbr. compare.

CFB abbr. Canadian Forces Base.

CFC n. (pl. **CFCs**) chlorofluorocarbon, a gaseous compound of carbon, hydrogen, chlorine, and fluorine, used in refrigerants etc. and thought to be harmful to the ozone layer.

CFL abbr. Canadian Football League.

CFS abbr. Canadian Forces Station.

Chablis n. (pl. **Chablis**) a dry white wine. [Say sha BLEE for the singular, sha BLEEZ for the plural]

cha-cha (also **cha-cha-cha**) ● n. (pl. **cha-chas**) a ballroom dance with a Latin American rhythm. ● v. (**cha-chas, cha-chaed, cha-chaing**) dance the cha-cha.

chador n. a cloth worn by some Muslim women, wrapped around the body to leave only the face exposed. [Say CHUDDER]

chafe v. (**chafes, chafed, chafing**) **1** make or become sore or damaged by rubbing. **2** rub (esp. the skin) to warm it. **3** make or become annoyed.

chafer n. a large slow-moving beetle.

chaff ● n. **1** the husks of grain separated from the seed by winnowing or threshing. **2** chopped hay and straw used as fodder. **3** lighthearted banter. **4** worthless things. ● v. tease. □ **separate the wheat from the chaff** distinguish valuable things from worthless ones.

chagrin ● n. annoyance or shame. ● v. affect with chagrin. [Say shuh GRIN]

chain ● n. **1 a** a connected flexible series of esp. metal links. **b** something resembling this. **2** (in pl.) **a** fetters used to confine prisoners. **b** any restraining force. **3** a sequence or set. **4** a group of associated stores or other businesses. **5** (in pl.) a set of linked chains fastened around a vehicle's tires to prevent skidding in snow. ● v. **1** secure with a chain. **2** confine or restrict (a person).

chain gang n. a team of convicts chained together and forced to work in the open air.

chain letter n. one of a sequence of letters the recipient of which is requested to send copies to a specific number of other people.

chain-link adj. made of wire in a diamond-shaped mesh.

chain reaction n. **1** a nuclear or chemical reaction in which the products cause a series of further reactions. **2** a series of events, each caused by the previous one.

chainsaw ● n. a motor-driven saw with teeth on an endless chain. ● v. cut with a chainsaw.

chain-smoke v. (**chain-smokes, chain-smoked, chain-smoking**) smoke (cigarettes etc.) continually. □ **chain-smoker** n. **chain-smoking** n.

chair ● n. **1** a separate seat for one person, of various forms, usu. having a back. **2** a professorship. **3** a chairperson. ● v. act as chairperson of. □ **take a chair** sit down.

chairlift n. a series of chairs on an endless cable for carrying passengers up and down a mountain etc.

chairman n. (pl. **chairmen**) **1** a person who presides over a meeting. **2** the permanent president of a committee, board, etc. □ **chairmanship** n.

chairperson n. (pl. **chairpersons** or **chairpeople**) a chairman or chairwoman.

chairwoman n. (pl. **chairwomen**) a female chairperson.

chaise longue n. (pl. **chaise longues** or **chaises longues**) (also **chaise, chaise lounge**) a chair with an extended seat on which to rest the legs. [*Say* shays LONZH *or* shays LONG]

chalcedony n. a type of quartz occurring in several different forms, e.g. agate etc. [*Say* kal SEDDA nee]

chalet n. **1** a wooden house with overhanging eaves, typical of the European Alps. **2** the main building at a ski resort, usu. with rental facilities and a restaurant.

chalice n. *Christianity* a wine cup used in the Eucharist. [*Say* CHAL iss]

chalk ● n. **1** a white soft limestone formed from the skeletal remains of sea creatures. **2** a similar substance made into sticks and used for writing or drawing. ● v. draw or write with chalk. □ **chalk up 1** (foll. by *to*) attribute, charge. **2** register (a score etc.)

chalkboard n. = BLACKBOARD.

chalky adj. (**chalkier, chalkiest**) **1** abounding in chalk. **2** white as chalk. **3** having the consistency of chalk. □ **chalkiness** n.

challah n. (pl. **challahs** or **challoth**) a loaf of usu. braided egg bread, traditionally baked to celebrate the Jewish Sabbath. [*Say* HALLA *for the singular,* HALLAS *or* HALLOT *for the plural*]

challenge ● n. **1 a** a summons to take part in a contest etc. **b** a summons to prove or justify something. **2** a difficult task. ● v. (**challenges, challenged, challenging**) **1 a** invite to take part in a contest etc. **b** invite to prove or justify. **2** dispute. **3** stretch, stimulate. □ **challenger** n.

challenged adj. **1** (of a person) disabled. **2** *jocular* not having a specified quality, e.g. *vertically challenged* for *short*.

challenging adj. stimulating and difficult.

chamber n. **1 a** a hall used by a legislative or judicial body. **b** any of the houses of a parliament. **2** (in pl.) a judge's room used for hearing cases not in court. **3** *Music* (as an adj.) of or for a small group of instruments. **4** the part of a gun that contains the cartridge or shell. **5** a cavity. **6** a space or room constructed for a specific purpose. □ **chambered** adj.

chamberlain n. an officer managing the household of a monarch or noble. [*Say* CHAMBER lin]

chambermaid n. a housemaid at a hotel etc.

chamber of commerce n. an association to promote local commercial interests.

chamber pot n. a receptacle for urine etc., used in a bedroom.

chameleon n. a small lizard that can change colour according to its surroundings. [*Say* kuh MEELY un]

chamois n. (pl. **chamois**) **1** soft leather made from the skin of sheep, goats, etc. **2** an agile goat living in the mountains of Europe and Asia. [*For sense 1 say* SHAMMY *for the singular,* SHAMMIES *for the plural; for sense 2 say* SHAM wah *for the singular,* SHAM wahz *for the plural*]

chamomile n. = CAMOMILE.

champ[1] n. *informal* a champion.

champ[2] v. & n. = CHOMP.

champagne n. a bubbly white wine, often used for celebrations. [*Say* sham PAIN]

champion ● n. **1** someone who has won a competition. **2** a person who fights or argues for a cause or another person. ● v. support the cause of.

championship n. **1** a competition to decide the champion. **2** the position of a champion.

chance ● n. **1 a** a possibility. **b** probability. **2** a risk. **3 a** an unplanned occurrence. **b** the absence of design or cause. **4** an opportunity. **5** the way things happen; fortune; luck. ● adj. fortuitous, accidental. ● v. (**chances, chanced, chancing**) **1** *informal* risk. **2** happen without intention. □ **by any chance** perhaps. **chance on** (or **upon**) happen to find etc. **stand a chance** have a prospect of success etc. **take a chance** (or **chances**) risk failure.

chancel n. a part of some churches near the altar, reserved for the clergy and choir. [*Say* CHAN sul]

chancellor n. **1** the head of government in Germany and Austria. **2** the honorary head of a university. [*Say* CHAN suh lur]

chancery n. (pl. **chanceries**) **1** an office attached to an embassy. **2** the administrative office of a Catholic diocese. [*Say* CHAN sur ee]

chancy adj. (**chancier, chanciest**) risky.

chandelier n. an ornamental hanging lamp with branches for several light bulbs or candles. [*Say* shan duh LEER]

chandler n. **1** a dealer in supplies for ships. **2** a person who makes or sells candles. [*Say* CHAND lur]

change ● n. **1 a** an act or process through which something becomes different. **b** an alteration. **2 a** money given in exchange for money in larger units. **b** money returned as the balance of the sum paid. **3** a new experience; variety. **4 a** an exchange. **b** a replacement set of clothes etc. ● *v.* (**changes, changed, changing**) **1** make or become different. **2** exchange for another; go from one to another. **3 a** give or get change in smaller denominations for **b** exchange (a sum of money) for. **4** put fresh clothes on. □ **change of air** a different climate. **change hands 1** pass to a different owner. **2** substitute one hand for another. **change of heart** a conversion to a different view. **change one's tune** express a very different opinion. □ **changeable** *adj.* **changeless** *adj.* **changer** *n.*

changeling *n.* in folklore, a child that is left by fairies in exchange for another. [*Say* CHANGE ling]

changeover *n.* a change from one system to another.

changeup *n.* in baseball, a slow pitch thrown like a fastball.

channel ● *n.* **1 a** a wide stretch of water joining two larger areas of water. **b** the deeper part of a waterway. **c** the bed of a river stream etc. **2 a** band of frequencies used for broadcasting by a particular station. **3** a way communication may travel. **4** the course in which anything moves. ● *v.* (**channels, channelled, channelling**) **1** guide something in a channel. **2** direct.

channelling *n.* the act of acting as a medium.

channel surfing *n. informal* the act of flipping from one television channel to another. □ **channel surfer** *n.*

chant ● *n.* **1** words sung or shouted repeatedly to the same rhythm. **2** a religious song or prayer. **3** = GREGORIAN CHANT. ● *v.* say, shout, or sing in chant.

Chanukah *n.* = HANUKKAH.

chaos *n.* complete disorder or confusion. [*Say* KAY oss]

chaos theory *n.* the theory that provides mathematical methods to explain the chaotic behaviour of systems.

chaotic *adj.* in a confused or disorderly state. □ **chaotically** *adv.* [*Say* kay OTT ik, kay OTT ik ly]

chap ● *v.* (**chaps, chapped, chapping**) (esp. of the skin) become rough and painful; crack. ● *n. informal* **1** a man or boy. **2** the lower part of the jaw or cheek.

chapati *n.* (*pl.* **chapatis**) a thin flat round whole wheat bread from India. [*Say* chuh POTTY *or* chuh PATTY]

chapel *n.* **1** a small room or building used for worship. **2** a funeral home.

chaperone ● *n.* a person who supervises young people on trips, dates, etc. ● *v.* (**chaperones, chaperoned, chaperoning**) act as a chaperone for someone. [*Say* SHAPPA rone]

chaplain *n.* a member of the clergy whose job is to serve the spiritual needs of people in a chapel, the armed forces, etc. [*Say* CHAP lin]

chapped *adj.* (of the skin) dry and cracking.

chappie *n. informal* = CHAP *n.* 1.

chaps *pl. n.* protective leather coverings for the legs.

chapter *n.* **1** a main division of a book. **2** a local branch of a club or society. **3** the governing body of a cathedral or other religious community. **4** a period of time in history or a person's life. □ **chapter and verse** the exact details of something.

char ● *v.* (**chars, charred, charring**) **1** make or become black by burning. **2** burn to charcoal. ● *n.* (*pl.* **char**) a small trout, esp. the Arctic char.

character ● *n.* **1** all the distinctive qualities etc. of a person or thing. **2** moral strength. **3** reputation. **4** a person in a novel, play, etc. **5** *informal* an unusual person. **6** a printed or written letter or symbol. ● *adj.* (of a supporting role) portraying an eccentric person. □ **characterful** *adj.* **characterless** *adj.*

character assassination *n.* a malicious attempt to harm a person's good reputation.

characteristic ● *adj.* typical, distinctive. ● *n.* a typical or distinctive feature or quality. □ **characteristically** *adv.*

characterize *v.* (**characterizes, characterized, characterizing**) **1** describe the character of. **2** be typical of. □ **characterization** *n.*

charade *n.* an absurd pretense. [*Say* shuh RAID]

charades *n.* a game in which a word or phrase must be guessed from silently acted clues.

charbroil *v.* broil over a charcoal fire etc. □ **charbroiled** *adj.*

charcoal *n.* **1** a porous black substance made by burning wood etc. slowly in an oven with little air. **2** a sketch drawn with charcoal. **3** a dark grey colour.

chard *n.* a kind of beet with edible green leaves and white leaf stalks.

Chardonnay *n.* a dry white wine. [*Say* SHARDA nay]

charge ● *v.* (**charges, charged,**

charging) **1** ask as a price. **2** debit the cost of to. **3** accuse (of an offence). **4** instruct or command. **5** entrust with. **6** make a rushing attack. **7 a** give an electric charge to. **b** (of a battery etc.) receive and store energy. **8** load or fill. • *n.* **1 a** a price asked. **b** a financial liability. **2 a** an accusation. **b** a judge's instructions to a jury. **3 a** a task or duty. **b** care, custody. **c** a person or thing entrusted. **4** an impetuous rush or attack. **5** an amount of explosive needed to fire a gun etc. **6 a** the property of matter that is responsible for electricity. **b** an amount of electricity stored in a battery etc. **7** a thrill. □ **in charge** having command. **take charge** assume control. □ **chargeable** *adj.*

charged *adj.* **1** filled or saturated with. **2** intense, emotional. **3** having an electrical charge.

charger *n.* **1** an apparatus for charging a battery. **2** a horse ridden in battle.

charging *n. Hockey* an illegal play in which a player takes more than two steps or strides before bodychecking an opponent.

chariot *n.* an open two-wheeled vehicle drawn by horses. □ **charioteer** *n.* [*Say* CHERRY it, cherry a TEER]

charisma *n.* great charm or personal power that inspires admiration in others. [*Say* kuh RIZ muh]

charismatic *adj.* **1** having charisma. **2** (of Christian worship) emphasizing the influence of the Holy Spirit on believers. [*Say* care iz MAT ic]

charitable *adj.* **1** relating to a charity. **2** generous. **3** tolerant when judging others. □ **charitably** *adv.*

charity *n.* (*pl.* **charities**) **1** an organization that helps those in need. **2 a** the aim of giving help etc. to people in need. **b** the help or money given in this way. **3** kindness and sympathy towards others. □ **charity begins at home** a person's first duty is to help his or her own family.

charlatan *n.* a person who falsely claims to have a special skill. [*Say* SHARLA tun]

charley horse *n.* a cramp in a muscle, esp. in the leg.

charm • *n.* **1 a** the power of pleasing or attracting people. **b** an attractive quality. **2** a small ornament, esp. one worn for good luck. **3** an object or word believed to have magic power. • *v.* **1** please, attract, or fascinate. **2** control or protect someone with or as if with magic. □ **work like a charm** be immediately successful. □ **charmer** *n.* **charmless** *adj.*

charmed life *n.* a life that has been unusually lucky or happy.

charming *adj.* delightful, attractive, pleasing. □ **charmingly** *adv.*

charnel house *n.* a building where bodies are piled in times of mass death. [*Say* CHAR nul]

chart • *n.* **1** a graph, diagram, or table presenting information. **2** a record of medical information. **3** a map. **4** a weekly etc. list of popular songs or records. • *v.* **1** make a chart or map of. **2** plan a route on a chart.

charter • *n.* **1 a** a written government statement granting certain rights to a town, university, etc. or allowing a new organization to be founded. **b** a written statement of an organization's main functions. **2** (**the Charter**) the Canadian Charter of Rights and Freedoms. **3** the hiring of a bus, airplane, etc. for a special purpose. • *v.* **1** grant a charter to. **2** hire (a bus or aircraft etc.).

charter airline *n.* an airline that sells discounted blocks of seats to tour operators.

chartered accountant *n.* a person who is fully licensed to practise accounting.

chartered bank *n.* (in Canada) a large, privately owned bank established by government charter.

charter member *n.* an original member.

chary *adj.* (**charier, chariest**) cautiously reluctant; wary. [*Sounds like* CHERRY]

chase • *v.* (**chases, chased, chasing**) **1** pursue in order to catch. **2** force to leave; dispel. **3** hurry in pursuit of. **4** *informal* try to get or find. • *n.* an act of pursuing. □ **give chase** pursue; hunt.

chaser *n.* **1** one that chases. **2** *informal* a drink taken after another of a different kind.

chasm *n.* **1** a deep crack or opening in the ground. **2** a wide difference between people or groups. [*Say* KAZ um]

Chassid *n.* (also **Chasid**) = HASID.

chassis *n.* (*pl.* **chassis**) **1** the basic frame of a vehicle. **2** the frame of a stereo, television, etc. [*Say* CHASSY *or* SHASSY *for the singular*, CHASSIES *or* SHASSIES *for the plural*]

chaste *adj.* **1** choosing not to have sex outside marriage or at all. **2** not sexual in nature. **3** simple or unadorned. □ **chastely** *adv.* [*Rhymes with* WASTE]

chasten *v.* **1** cause someone to be regretful or ashamed. **2** punish. [*Say* CHASE un]

chastise *v.* criticize, scold. □ **chastisement** *n.* [*Say* CHASS tize]

chastity *n.* the state of refraining from sex. [*Say* CHASTA tee]

chat • *v.* (**chats, chatted, chatting**)

talk in a friendly, informal way. ● *n.* friendly, informal conversation. □ **chat up** *informal* talk flirtatiously to.

château *n.* (*pl.* **châteaux**) **1** a castle or manor in France. **2** the home of a seigneur or governor in New France. [*Say* sha TOE *or* SHA toe *for the singular,* sha TOZE *or* SHA toze *for the plural*]

chatelaine *n.* the woman in charge of a large house. [*Say* SHATTA lane]

chat room *n.* an area on the Internet etc. where users can communicate.

chattel *n.* a personal possession. [*Say* CHAT ul]

chatter ● *v.* **1** talk quickly or non-stop. **2** (of an animal) emit short quick sounds. **3** (of the teeth) click repeatedly together. ● *n.* **1** chattering talk or sounds. **2** the exchange of electronic communications as intercepted by intelligence agencies. □ **chatterer** *n.*

chatterbox *n.* (*pl.* **chatterboxes**) a talkative person.

chatty *adj.* (**chattier**, **chattiest**) **1** fond of chatting; talkative. **2** informal and lively.

chauffeur ● *n.* a person employed to drive a limousine etc. ● *v.* **1** drive as a chauffeur. **2** transport by car. [*Say* show FUR, SHOW fur]

chauvinism *n.* excessive or prejudiced loyalty to one's own nationality, race, or sex. □ **chauvinist** *n.* **chauvinistic** *adj.* [*Say* SHOW v'n ism]

cheap ● *adj.* **1** inexpensive; charging low prices. **2** of poor quality. **3** *derogatory* stingy with money. **4** worthless or contemptible. ● *adv.* inexpensively. □ **on the cheap** inexpensively. **talk is cheap** actions speak louder than words. □ **cheaply** *adv.* **cheapness** *n.*

cheapen *v.* make less worthy of respect; degrade.

cheapo (also **cheapie**) *informal* ● *adj.* inexpensive or of low quality. ● *n.* (*pl.* **cheapos**) **1** something cheap. **2** a stingy person.

cheap shot *n.* **1** a malicious or cruel comment, action, etc. **2** *Sport* an illegal attack against an unsuspecting player.

cheapskate *n. informal* a stingy person.

cheat ● *v.* **1 a** deceive or trick. **b** deprive of. **2** gain unfair advantage by deception etc. **3** avoid by luck or skill. **4** be sexually unfaithful. **5** lapse from strict adherence to a diet. ● *n.* **1** a person who cheats. **2** a trick, fraud, etc. **3** an act of cheating. □ **cheater** *n.*

Chechen *n.* **1** a member of a Muslim people of the Chechen Republic, an autonomous republic in SE Russia. **2** the Caucasian language of this people. □ **Chechen** *adj.* [*Say* CHETCH enn]

check ● *v.* **1 a** examine the accuracy, quality, or condition of; inspect. **b** make sure; verify. **c** search. **2** stop or slow the progress of. **3** *Chess* move a piece into a position that directly threatens (the opposing king). **4** make a mark next to an item. **5** deposit (a coat etc.) for temporary storage. ● *n.* **1** an act of checking accuracy, quality, condition, etc. **2** a measure to ensure against fraud or abuse. **3** an act of checking progress, motion, etc. **4** *Chess* an act of checking the opposing king. **5** a mark (✓) placed beside an item to indicate that it is correct or has been dealt with. **6** a pattern of small squares. **7** esp. *US* = CHEQUE etc. **8** a bill in a restaurant. ● *interj.* expressing assent. □ **check in 1** register at a hotel, airport, etc. **2** record the arrival of. **check (up) on 1** examine carefully. **2** keep a watch on. **check out 1** leave a hotel etc. after paying the bill. **2 a** investigate. **b** *informal* look at. **3** agree or correspond. **4** borrow (an item) from a library, video store, etc. **in check** under control, restrained.

checked *adj.* having a checkered pattern.

checker *n.* **1** something or someone that checks. **2** a pattern of alternately coloured squares. **3** one of the small round pieces used in the game of checkers.

checkerboard *n.* **1** a board with a pattern of squares of alternating colours. **2** something with a pattern resembling this.

checkered *adj.* **1** marked with a checker pattern. **2** marked by periods of good and bad luck, behaviour, etc.

checkers *n.* a game for two, played on a checkerboard.

check-in *n.* the act of registering one's arrival at a hotel, airport, etc.

checklist *n.* a list of items to be checked.

checkmate ● *n.* *Chess* a situation from which a king cannot escape, indicating that the game is over. ● *v.* (**checkmates**, **checkmated**, **checkmating**) **1** *Chess* put into checkmate. **2** defeat; thwart.

checkout *n.* **1** an act of registering one's departure from a hotel etc. **2** a counter, or the point in an electronic transaction, at which goods are paid for.

checkpoint *n.* a place, e.g. on a border, where travellers are stopped for inspection.

checkup *n.* a thorough medical or dental examination.

cheddar *n.* a firm cheese that ranges in colour from white to orange and becomes stronger tasting with age.

cheder *n.* a Jewish school teaching Hebrew and religious knowledge. [*Say* HEY der]

cheek *n.* **1** the side of the face below the eye. **2** impertinence. **3** *slang* either of the buttocks. □ **cheek by jowl** close together. **turn the other cheek** accept attack etc. meekly.

cheekbone *n.* the bone below the eye.

cheeky *adj.* (**cheekier, cheekiest**) showing a lack of respect, esp. playfully; impertinent. □ **cheekily** *adv.* **cheekiness** *n.*

cheep ● *n.* the weak cry of a young bird. **●** *v.* make such a cry.

cheer ● *n.* **1** a shout of encouragement or approval. **2** cheerfulness. **3** food and drink. **●** *v.* **1 a** applaud with shouts; shout for joy. **b** (also **cheer on**) urge or encourage. **2** (also **cheer up**) make or become less depressed.

cheerful *adj.* **1** noticeably happy. **2** bright, pleasant. **3** not reluctant. □ **cheerfully** *adv.* **cheerfulness** *n.*

cheerleader *n.* **1** a person who leads a crowd in formal cheers at a sporting event. **2** a person who rouses others into action. □ **cheerleading** *n.*

cheerless *adj.* gloomy, dreary.

cheers *interj.* **1** a drinking toast. **2** goodbye (esp. in closing an email).

cheery *adj.* (**cheerier, cheeriest**) **1** lively; in a good mood. **2** that makes people happy. □ **cheerily** *adv.*

cheese ● *n.* **1** a solid or semi-solid food made from milk. **2** (also **big cheese**) *slang* an important person. **●** *v.* (**cheeses, cheesed, cheesing**) *slang* exasperate, annoy. □ **say cheese** smile for a photograph.

cheeseburger *n.* a hamburger topped with melted cheese.

cheesecake *n.* **1** a rich sweet cake made with cream cheese. **2** *informal* the portrayal of women in a sexually provocative manner in photographs.

cheesecloth *n.* thin loosely woven cloth resembling gauze.

cheesed *adj.* (also **cheesed off**) annoyed.

cheesy *adj.* (**cheesier, cheesiest**) **1** like cheese in taste or smell. **2** *slang* of poor quality. **3** *slang* unsophisticated, corny. □ **cheesiness** *n.*

cheetah *n.* a large swift-running cat found in Africa and Asia.

chef *n.* a cook, esp. the chief cook in a restaurant. [*Say* SHEF]

chem *n.* *informal* a chemistry class or course.

chemical ● *n.* **1** any of the elements which constitute all substances. **2** such a

substance considered as an artificial component of food etc. **●** *adj.* of or relating to chemistry or chemicals. □ **chemically** *adv.*

chemical weapon *n.* a weapon that releases a toxic substance, e.g. poison gas.

chemist *n.* a scientist trained in chemistry.

chemistry *n.* (*pl.* **chemistries**) **1** the scientific study of the structure and nature of substances, esp. how they react when combined. **2** the attraction or rapport existing among two or more people.

chemotherapy *n.* (also *informal* **chemo**) the treatment of disease, esp. cancer, by use of highly toxic chemicals. [*Say* KEY moe THAIR uh pee]

cheque *n.* a printed form used to order a bank to pay money from an account to a specified person.

chequebook *n.* a book of forms for writing cheques and recording account activity.

chequing account *n.* a bank account from which money may be withdrawn with cheques.

cherish *v.* (**cherishes, cherished, cherishing**) **1** love and want to protect. **2** keep in one's mind or heart.

Cherokee *n.* **1** (*pl.* **Cherokee** or **Cherokees**) a member of an Iroquoian people living esp. in Oklahoma and North Carolina. **2** the language of this people. □ **Cherokee** *adj.* [*Say* CHAIR uh key]

cherry ● *n.* (*pl.* **cherries**) **1** a small soft round usu. red fruit with a single stone in its centre. **2** the reddish wood of a cherry tree. **●** *adj.* of a light red colour.

cherry-pick *v.* selectively choose the best items, opportunities, etc. from those available.

cherry picker *n.* a crane with a hinged arm and a bucket for raising and lowering workers etc.

cherry tomato *n.* a very small tomato.

chert *n.* a form of quartz like flint.

cherub *n.* (*pl.* **cherubs**) **1** a representation of a winged child. **2** a beautiful or innocent child. □ **cherubic** *adj.* [*Say* CHAIR ub, chair ROO bic]

chess *n.* a game for two, played on a chessboard, in which players attempt to place their opponent's king in checkmate.

chessboard *n.* a board with a pattern of squares of alternating colours, used in the game of chess.

chessman *n.* (*pl.* **chessmen**) any of the 32 pieces used in the game of chess.

chest *n.* **1** the upper part of the body from the neck to the waist. **2** a large strong box. □ **get a thing off one's chest** *informal* talk about a problem. **play** (or **keep**) **close to one's chest** *informal* be cautious or secretive.

chesterfield *n.* Cdn a couch.

chestnut ● *n.* **1** a smooth brown often edible nut inside prickly cases. **2 a** a type of tree producing these nuts. **b** the heavy wood of this tree. **3** a reddish-brown colour. ● *adj.* reddish brown.

chest of drawers *n.* (*pl.* **chests of drawers**) a piece of furniture having a set of drawers in a frame.

chesty *adj.* (**chestier, chestiest**) **1** *informal* having large breasts. **2** *slang* arrogant.

chevron *n.* a V-shaped mark or stripe, esp. on the sleeve of military uniform. [*Say* SHEV run *or* SHEV ron]

chew ● *v.* **1** work (food etc.) between the teeth. **2** shred, mangle, mutilate, etc. **3** think about, discuss. ● *n.* **1** an act of chewing. **2** something intended for chewing. □ **chew the cud** ruminate. **chew the fat** (or **rag**) *slang* chat. **chew out** *informal* reprimand harshly. □ **chewable** *adj.* **chewer** *n.*

chewing gum *n.* flavoured and sweetened gum for chewing.

chewing tobacco *n.* flavoured tobacco designed for chewing.

chewy *adj.* (**chewier, chewiest**) requiring much chewing. □ **chewiness** *n.*

Cheyenne *n.* **1** (*pl.* **Cheyenne** or **Cheyennes**) a member of an Algonquian people of Oklahoma and Montana. **2** their language. □ **Cheyenne** *adj.* [*Say* shy ANN *or* shy ENN]

ch'i *n.* (also **chi**) (in Chinese philosophy) the physical life force that flows through the body. [*Say* CHEE]

Chianti *n.* (*pl.* **Chiantis**) a dry usu. red Italian wine. [*Say* key AN tee]

chic ● *adj.* (**chicer, chicest**) stylish, elegant. ● *n.* stylishness, elegance. [*Say* SHEEK]

chicanery *n.* (*pl.* **chicaneries**) the use of trickery to achieve one's ends. [*Say* shi KAY nuh ree]

Chicano *n.* (*pl.* **Chicanos**) esp. *US* a Mexican-American. [*Say* chick ON oh *or* chick AN oh]

chi-chi *adj.* pretentiously elegant or stylish. [*Say* SHEE shee]

chick *n.* **1** a young or newly hatched bird. **2** *slang* often *offensive* a young woman.

chickadee *n.* any of various small birds with a dark patch on the head and throat.

chicken ● *n.* **1** any of several varieties of domestic fowl raised for their flesh or eggs. **2** *informal* a coward. ● *adj. informal* cowardly.

□ **chicken out** *informal* withdraw from some activity through fear. **count one's chickens (before they're hatched)** be overconfident in anticipating success.

chicken-and-egg *adj.* pertaining to the unresolved question as to which of two things came first.

chicken feed *n.* **1** food for domestic fowl. **2** *informal* a small amount of money.

chicken-hearted *adj.* (also **chicken-livered**) easily frightened; lacking nerve.

chicken pox *n.* an infectious disease with a rash of small blisters.

chicken wire *n.* a light wire netting with a hexagonal mesh.

chickpea *n.* an edible yellowish-brown pea-shaped seed.

chickweed *n.* a common weed with slender stems and tiny white flowers.

chicle *n.* the milky juice of the sapodilla tree (a tropical American evergreen), used in chewing gum. [*Say* CHICK'll *or* CHICK lee]

chicory *n.* a blue-flowered plant grown for its salad leaves and for its root.

chide *v.* (**chides, chided, chiding**) scold, rebuke.

chief ● *n.* **1** a leader, esp. of a tribe, clan, or Aboriginal group. **2** the head of an organization. ● *adj.* **1** first in position, importance, etc. **2** prominent, leading.

chiefdom *n.* the domain of a chief.

chief electoral officer *n.* Cdn an official who oversees the conduct of elections.

chief executive officer *n.* the highest-ranking executive of a corporation etc.

chief justice *n.* the presiding judge of the Supreme Court etc.

chiefly *adv.* above all; mainly.

chief of staff *n.* **1** the senior staff officer of a branch of the armed forces. **2** the head of any government staff.

chieftain *n.* the leader of a tribe or clan; chief.

chiffon *n.* a thin almost transparent fabric made of silk, nylon, etc. [*Say* shif FON]

chigger *n.* the larva of any of various mites.

chihuahua *n.* a very small dog with large eyes and prominent ears. [*Say* chuh WAH wah]

Chilcotin *n.* & *adj.* = TSILHQOT'IN. [*Say* chill KOTE un]

child *n.* (*pl.* **children**) **1** a young human being below the age of puberty. **2** one's son or daughter (at any age). **3** a descendant or product of. □ **childhood** *n.* **childless** *adj.* **childlessness** *n.*

child-bearing ● *n.* the act of giving birth to a child. ● *adj.* of, relating to, or suitable for child-bearing.

childbirth *n.* the act of giving birth to a child.

childish *adj.* immature, silly. □ **childishly** *adv.* **childishness** *n.*

childlike *adj.* like a child, esp. in innocence or frankness.

childproof ● *adj.* **1** unable to be operated or opened by a child. **2** safe for young children. ● *v.* make childproof.

children *pl. of* CHILD.

child's play *n.* an easy task.

child support *n.* money paid by a parent to a divorced spouse for the support of children.

Chilean *n.* **1** a native or national of Chile **2** a person of Chilean descent. □ **Chilean** *adj.* [*Say* CHILLY un *or* chill AY un]

chili *n.* (*pl.* **chilies**) **1** the small pod of a type of pepper plant. **2** a spicy stew made with chilies or chili powder, with or without meat.

chili con carne *n.* a spicy dish of chopped or ground meat, chilies or chili powder, and usu. cooked tomatoes. [*Say* con CAR nee]

Chilkat *n.* a member of the Tlingit people inhabiting the Alaska coast. [*Say* CHILL cat]

chill ● *n.* **1 a** an unpleasant cold sensation. **b** a feverish cold. **2 a** a depressing influence. **b** a feeling of fear or dread. **3** coldness of manner. ● *v.* **1** make or become cold. **2** depress. **3** (also **chill out**) *slang* relax. ● *adj.* chilly. □ **take the chill off** warm slightly. □ **chiller** *n.*

chilling *adj.* frightening or horrifying. □ **chillingly** *adv.*

Chilliwack *n.* **1** a member of a Salishan people, a division of the Halq'emeylem, living in BC. **2** the Halkomelem language of this people. [*Say* CHILL a wack]

chilly *adj.* (**chillier, chilliest**) **1** somewhat cold. **2** unfriendly; not emotional. □ **chilliness** *n.*

chime ● *n.* **1** a set of tuned bells. **2** the sounds given by this. ● *v.* (**chimes, chimed, chiming**) **1** (of bells) ring. **2** sound (a bell etc.) by striking. □ **chime in** interject a remark.

chimera *n.* **1** a mythical female monster with a lion's head, a goat's body, and a serpent's tail. **2** an impossible idea or hope. [*Say* kye MEER uh *or* kim EER uh]

chimes *pl. n.* a musical instrument comprising a set of tuned bells or bars.

chimichanga *n.* a tortilla filled with esp.

meat and deep-fried. [*Say* chimmy CHAN guh]

chimney *n.* **1** a vertical shaft conducting smoke or steam away from a fire, furnace, etc. **2** a glass tube protecting the flame of a lamp.

chimney sweep *n.* a person whose job is removing soot from chimneys.

chimp *n. informal* = CHIMPANZEE

chimpanzee *n.* a black ape with large ears, native to west and central Africa.

chin *n.* the front of the lower jaw. □ **keep one's chin up** *informal* remain cheerful in difficult circumstances. **take it on the chin** *informal* endure misfortune, esp. courageously.

china *n.* **1** a fine white ceramic material. **2** things made from china.

Chinatown *n.* a district of a city in which the population is predominantly Chinese.

chinchilla *n.* **1** a small S American rodent with soft grey fur. **2** the valuable fur of this animal. [*Say* chin CHILL uh]

Chinese *n.* **1** the language of China. **2** (*pl.* **Chinese**) a person of Chinese nationality or descent. □ **Chinese** *adj.*

Chinese checkers *n.* a game in which players attempt to move marbles from one point of a star-shaped board to the opposite one.

Chinese New Year *n.* the start of the New Year in the Chinese calendar, observed officially in late January or early February.

chink ● *n.* **1** a slight ringing sound. **2** a narrow opening or crack. ● *v.* make a slight ringing sound. □ **a chink in one's armour** a weakness.

chinook *n.* **1** a warm wind which blows near the Rocky Mountains. **2** (also **chinook salmon**) a large silver-coloured salmon with black spots. [*Say* shin NOOK]

Chinook Jargon *n.* a language consisting of elements of West Coast Aboriginal languages, English, and French, formerly used by traders.

chinos *pl. n.* khaki-coloured casual pants made from a cotton twill fabric. [*Say* CHEE nose]

chintz *n.* a multicoloured glazed cotton fabric, used for curtains and upholstery. [*Say* CHINTS]

chintzy *adj.* (**chintzier, chintziest**) **1** resembling or decorated with chintz. **2** of poor quality. **3** miserly.

chin-up *n.* an exercise in which one pulls oneself up with one's arms on a horizontal bar.

chinwag *informal* ● *n.* a talk or chat. ● *v.* (**chinwags, chinwagged, chinwagging**) chat or gossip.

chip ● *n.* **1 a** a small piece cut or broken off from a hard material. **b** the place from which a chip has been removed. **2** a crisp deep-fried wafer-thin slice of potato, cornmeal, etc. **3** a small piece of chocolate etc. **4** = FRENCH FRY. **5** a counter used in gambling to represent money. **6** = MICROCHIP. **7** (also **chip shot**) *Sport* a short high shot or kick. ● *v.* (**chips**, **chipped**, **chipping**) **1** cut or break (a piece) from a hard material. **2** cut pieces off (a hard material). **3** be susceptible to being chipped. **4** *Sport* strike or kick (the ball) so that it travels in a short arc. □ **chip in** *informal* contribute (money etc.). **a chip off the old block** a child who resembles a parent. **a chip on one's shoulder** an inclination to feel resentful. **let the chips fall where they may** whatever the consequences. **when the chips are down** when the situation becomes difficult.

chipboard *n.* a rigid sheet made from compressed wood chips.

Chipewyan *n.* (*pl.* **Chipewyans**) **1** a member of an Athapaskan people inhabiting much of northwestern Canada. **2** their language. □ **Chipewyan** *adj.* [*Say* chippa WHY un]

chipmunk *n.* a striped burrowing ground squirrel.

chipotle *n.* a hot red pepper, usu. smoked. [*Say* chip OAT lay]

chipper ● *adj. informal* cheerful and lively. ● *n.* a person or tool that chips timber.

Chippewa *n.* & *adj.* (*pl.* **Chippewa** or **Chippewas**) = OJIBWA. [*Say* CHIPPA wah]

chippy *adj.* (**chippier**, **chippiest**) *Cdn informal* **1** short-tempered or irritable. **2** *Hockey* characterized by rough or dirty play. □ **chippiness** *n.*

chip wagon *n. Cdn* a mobile roadside stand selling french fries etc.

chiropodist *n.* = PODIATRIST. [*Say* shuh ROP uh dist *or* kuh ROP uh dist]

chiropractor *n.* a person who treats disorders of the spine by using the hands to press and move the spine. □ **chiropractic** *n.* [*Say* KYE roe prak ter, kye roe PRAK tik]

chirp ● *v.* **1** (of small birds etc.) emit a short high-pitched note. **2** speak in a cheerful way. ● *n.* a chirping sound.

chirpy *adj.* (**chirpier**, **chirpiest**) *informal* cheerful, lively. □ **chirpily** *adv.*

chirrup ● *v.* (**chirrups**, **chirruped**, **chirruping**) (esp. of small birds) chirp, esp. repeatedly. ● *n.* a chirruping sound. □ **chirrupy** *adj.* [*Say* CHUR up]

chisel ● *n.* a tool with a sharp flat blade for shaping wood etc. ● *v.* (**chisels**, **chiselled**, **chiselling**) cut with a chisel. □ **chiseller** *n.*

chiselled *adj.* (of facial features etc.) strongly defined.

chit *n.* a note showing money owing.

chit-chat *informal* ● *n.* light conversation; gossip. ● *v.* (**chit-chats**, **chit-chatted**, **chit-chatting**) talk informally; gossip.

chitin *n.* a tough semi-transparent substance that is found in the hard shells of crabs, insects, and other arthropods. [*Say* KITE in]

chitter ● *v.* make a chattering or twittering sound. ● *n.* a twittering or chattering sound.

chivalrous *adj.* gallant and courteous. [*Say* SHIV 'll rus]

chivalry *n.* **1** courteous behaviour, esp. that of a man towards women. **2** (in the Middle Ages) the ideal qualities expected of a knight, such as courage, honour, etc. □ **chivalric** *adj.* [*Say* SHIV 'll ree]

chive *n.* (usu. **chives**) a plant of the onion family with long tube-shaped leaves used as flavouring.

chlamydia *n.* **1** (*pl.* **chlamydiae**) any of various parasitic bacteria. **2** a urinary or genital infection caused by these bacteria. [*Say* kluh MIDDY uh *for the singular*, kluh MIDDY ee *for the plural*]

chloride *n.* any compound of chlorine with another element or group. [*Say* KLOR ide]

chlorinate *v.* (**chlorinates**, **chlorinated**, **chlorinating**) combine or treat with chlorine, esp. to disinfect. □ **chlorination** *n.* [*Say* KLOR in ate]

chlorine *n.* a poisonous green gaseous element, used for purifying water, bleaching, etc. [*Say* klor EEN *or* KLOR een]

chlorofluorocarbon = CFC. [*Say* kloro FLORO carbon]

chloroform *n.* a colourless liquid, formerly used as a general anaesthetic. [*Say* KLOR uh form]

chlorophyll *n.* the green pigment found in plants. [*Say* KLOR a fill]

chock *n.* a block or wedge used to prevent a wheel etc. from moving.

chockablock *adj.* completely full.

chock full *adj.* crammed full.

chocoholic *n. informal* a person who likes chocolate a great deal.

chocolate ● *n.* **1 a** a food made from cacao seeds, often combined with sugar etc. **b** a candy or drink made with this. **2** (also **chocolate brown**) dark brown. ● *adj.* **1** made or flavoured with chocolate. **2** (also **chocolate brown**) dark brown. □ **chocolatey** *adj.*

choice ● *n.* **1 a** an act of selecting or deciding between two or more possibilities. **b** something chosen. **2** a range from which to choose. **3** the best or preferred item. **4** the power or right to choose ● *adj.* (**choicer, choicest**) of superior quality; carefully selected. □ **of choice** preferred.

choir *n.* **1** a group of singers. **2** the part of some churches between the altar and the nave. [Say KWIRE]

choke ● *v.* (**chokes, choked, choking**) **1** hinder or impede the breathing of. **2** have trouble breathing. **3** make or become speechless from emotion. **4** retard the growth of or kill (esp. plants) by deprivation. **5** suppress (emotions) with difficulty. **6** *informal* fail to perform effectively under pressure. ● *n.* **1** an action or sound of choking. **2** the valve that controls the intake of air to an engine. □ **choke down** swallow with difficulty. **choke off** impede or stop.

chokecherry *n.* (*pl.* **chokecherries**) a N American cherry tree bearing small bitter cherries.

chokehold *n.* **1** a tight grip around a person's neck, used to restrain them by restricting their breathing. **2** unshakable control.

choker *n.* a close-fitting necklace.

cholera *n.* an infectious and often fatal bacterial disease of the small intestine. [Say CALL er uh]

cholesterol *n.* a substance found throughout the body, believed to be harmful to the arteries in high concentrations. [Say kuh LESS ter all]

chomp ● *v.* munch or chew noisily. ● *n.* a chewing noise or motion. □ **chomp at the bit** be restlessly impatient to start something.

choose *v.* (**chooses**; *past* **chose**; *past participle* **chosen**; **choosing**) **1** select one or more from a number of alternatives. **2** decide. **3** like, prefer. □ **cannot choose but** must. □ **chooser** *n.*

choosy *adj.* (**choosier, choosiest**) *informal* demanding, fussy.

chop ● *v.* (**chops, chopped, chopping**) **1 a** cut or fell by a blow, usu. with an axe. **b** cut into pieces. **2** strike with a short heavy stroke or blow. **3** *informal* remove; reduce by. ● *n.* **1** a cutting blow. **2** a thick slice of meat usu. including a rib. **3** a short downward stroke or blow. **4** the broken motion of waves. **5** (**the chop**) *informal* dismissal or killing.

chopper *n.* **1** a person or tool that chops. **2** *informal* a helicopter.

chopping block *n.* □ **on the chopping block** likely to be eliminated etc.

choppy *adj.* (**choppier, choppiest**) **1** (of water) with a rough surface of small, irregular waves. **2** uneven.

chops *pl. n.* **1** the jaw or mouth. **2** *informal* talent, skill. □ **bust one's chops** *slang* exert oneself. **bust someone's chops** *slang* nag or criticize.

chopstick *n.* each of a pair of thin sticks used as eating utensils, originally in east Asia.

chop suey *n.* a Chinese-style dish usu. of meat, bean sprouts, bamboo shoots, and onions. [Say chop SOO ee]

choral *adj.* of or sung by a choir. [Say CORE ul]

chorale *n.* **1** a grand but simple hymn tune. **2** esp. *US* a choir. [Say core AL]

chord *n.* **1** a group of three or more notes sounded together. **2** *Math* a straight line joining the ends of an arc. □ **strike** (or **touch**) **a chord** evoke some reaction, esp. sympathy. □ **chordal** *adj.*

chore *n.* **1** a routine often daily task. **2** any tedious or unpleasant piece of work.

chorea *n.* a medical disorder characterized by jerky involuntary movements. [Say kuh REE uh]

choreograph *v.* **1** design and arrange movements for dancers or figure skaters. **2** arrange or direct. □ **choreographer** *n.* [Say COREY a graph, corey OGRA fur]

choreography *n.* (*pl.* **choreographies**) **1** the sequence of movements in dance or figure skating. **2** the art of designing such movements. □ **choreographic** *adj.* [Say corey OGRA fee, corey a GRAPHIC]

chorion *n.* the outermost membrane surrounding an embryo. □ **chorionic** *adj.* [Say COREY un, corey ON ick]

chorister *n.* a person who sings in a choir. [Say CORE ist er]

chortle ● *v.* (**chortles, chortled, chortling**) chuckle gleefully. ● *n.* a gleeful chuckle.

chorus ● *n.* (*pl.* **choruses**) **1** a usu. large group of singers; a choir. **2** a piece of music composed for a choir. **3** a part of a song that is sung after each verse. **4** something said by many people together. **5** a group of singers or dancers in a musical, opera, etc. ● *v.* (**choruses, chorused, chorusing**) (of a group) speak or utter simultaneously. □ **in chorus** in unison.

chorus line *n.* a group of esp. female singers and dancers performing in a musical etc.

chose *past of* CHOOSE.

chosen ● *v. past participle of* CHOOSE. ● *adj.* selected or preferred.

chow *n.* **1** *slang* food. **2** (also **chow chow**) a Chinese breed of dog with a tail curled over its back. □ **chow down** eat.

chowder n. a thick soup, usu. containing fish, potatoes, etc.

chow mein n. a Chinese-style dish of fried noodles with chopped meat, seafood, etc. [Say chow MAIN]

chrism n. a consecrated oil used in rites in the Catholic and Orthodox Churches. [Say KRIZ'm]

Christ n. Jesus Christ, the central figure of the Christian religion.

christen v. **1** give a name to, esp. at baptism as a sign of admission to the Christian church. **2** *informal* use for the first time. □ **christening** n. [Say CRISS'n, CRISS'n ing]

Christendom n. the worldwide body of Christians. [Say CRISS'n dum]

Christian ● *adj.* relating to or believing in Christianity or its teachings. ● n. a person who has received Christian baptism or is a believer in Christ. □ **Christianization** n. **Christianize** v. (**Christianizes, Christianized, Christianizing**)

Christianity n. the religion based on the teachings of Christ and his disciples.

Christian Science n. the beliefs and practices of the Church of Christ, Scientist, a Christian sect. □ **Christian Scientist** n.

Christmas n. (*pl.* **Christmases**) (also **Christmas Day**) *Christianity* the annual festival of Christ's birth celebrated on Dec. 25 or Jan. 7. □ **Christmasy** (also **Christmassy**) *adj.*

Christmas cake n. a rich fruitcake eaten at Christmas.

Christmas pudding n. a rich heavy steamed dessert eaten at Christmas.

Christmas tree n. an evergreen or artificial tree set up with decorations at Christmas.

chromatic *adj.* **1** (of a scale) ascending or descending by semitones. **2** pertaining to colour; brightly coloured. [Say crow MAT ik]

chromatography n. a method of analyzing a mixture by passing it through a material through which the components move at different rates. □ **chromatographic** *adj.* [Say crow ma TOG ra fee, CROW muh tuh GRAPH ic]

chrome n. a shiny coating of chromium. □ **chromed** *adj.* [Say KROME]

chromium n. a hard white metallic element used in alloys. [Say CROW me um]

chromosome n. one of the structures within a cell, each consisting of a single strand of DNA. □ **chromosomal** *adj.* [Say CROW muh soam, CROW muh SOAM'l]

chronic *adj.* **1** persisting for a long time. **2** having a chronic complaint. **3** *informal* habitual. □ **chronically** *adv.*

chronic fatigue syndrome n. a disease characterized by extreme fatigue, poor coordination, and general malaise. Abbreviation: **CFS**.

chronicle ● n. **1** a record of events in the order in which they happened. **2** a narrative. ● v. (**chronicles, chronicled, chronicling**) record events in a chronicle. □ **chronicler** n.

chronograph n. **1** a type of very accurate clock. **2** a stopwatch. [Say CRON uh graph or CROW nuh graph]

chronological *adj.* **1** arranged in the order of their occurrence. **2** of or relating to chronology. □ **chronologically** *adv.* [Say kronna LOGICAL]

chronology n. (*pl.* **chronologies**) the arrangement of events etc. in the order of their occurrence. [Say kruh NOLLA jee]

chronometer n. a very accurate clock used esp. in navigation. [Say kruh NOMMA tur]

chrysalis n. (*pl.* **chrysalises**) **1** an insect pupa, esp. of a butterfly or moth. **2** a transitional state. [Say KRISS uh liss *for the singular,* KRISS uh liss ez *for the plural*]

chrysanthemum n. a plant with brightly coloured daisy-like flowers. [Say kris SANTH uh mum]

chub n. **1** a fish with a short, thick body. **2** a short, fat sausage.

chubby *adj.* (**chubbier, chubbiest**) plump and rounded. □ **chubbiness** n.

chuck ● v. **1** *informal* **a** fling or throw carelessly. **b** (also **chuck out**) throw out. **2** touch playfully, esp. under the chin. ● n. **1** a playful touch under the chin. **2** a device for holding e.g. a bit in a drill. **3** a cut of beef from the neck to the sixth rib. **4** *informal* food.

chuckle ● v. (**chuckles, chuckled, chuckling**) laugh quietly. ● n. a quiet laugh.

chuckwagon n. a vehicle carrying provisions etc., as used on a ranch.

chuff v. move with a regular sharp puffing sound.

chug ● v. (**chugs, chugged, chugging**) **1** emit a regular muffled explosive sound, as of an engine running slowly. **2** move with this sound. **3** move slowly but steadily. **4** *slang* drink in large gulps. ● n. a chugging sound.

chugalug v. (**chugalugs, chugalugged, chugalugging**) = CHUG 4.

chum ● n. **1** informal a close friend. **2** chopped fish, used as bait. **3** a salmon of the Pacific coast. ● v. (**chums, chummed, chumming**) **1** associate with. **2** fish using chum as bait.

chummy adj. informal (**chummier, chummiest**) friendly, sociable. □ **chumminess** n.

chump n. informal a gullible or foolish person.

chunk ● n. **1** a thick solid piece. **2** a substantial amount. ● v. break or cut into chunks.

chunky adj. (**chunkier, chunkiest**) **1** containing chunks. **2** thick and solid. **3** stocky.

church n. (pl. **churches**) **1** a building for public (usu. Christian) worship. **2** (also **Church**) the body of all Christians, or a specific Christian group. **3** (also **Church**) institutionalized religion as a political force. □ **churchy** adj.

churchgoer n. a person who goes to church, esp. regularly. □ **churchgoing** n. & adj.

churchman n. (pl. **churchmen**) a male member of the clergy or of a church.

Church of England n. an English branch of Christianity with the monarch as its head.

Church of Jesus Christ of Latter-day Saints n. the official name of the Mormon Church.

churchwarden n. Anglicanism either of two elected lay representatives of a parish.

churchyard n. a yard surrounding a church, esp. a graveyard.

churl n. a rude or boorish person.

churlish adj. ungrateful or ungracious. □ **churlishly** adv. **churlishness** n.

churn ● n. a machine for making butter. ● v. **1** agitate milk or cream to produce butter. **2** upset, agitate. **3** move or be moved about violently. □ **churn out** produce routinely or mechanically.

chute n. **1** a sloping channel for conveying things to a lower level. **2** a slide into a swimming pool. **3** a narrow passage for sheep, horses, or cattle. **4** Cdn a rapid in a river. **5** informal a parachute. [Say SHOOT]

chutney n. (pl. **chutneys**) a spicy sauce made of fruits or vegetables, vinegar, sugar, etc.

chutzpah n. slang shameless boldness. [Say HOOTZ puh (with OO as in HOOK)]

CIA abbr. the Central Intelligence Agency, a US federal agency responsible for government intelligence activities.

ciabatta n. a type of flattish, open-textured Italian bread with a floury crust, made with olive oil. [Say chuh BATTA]

ciao interj. informal **1** goodbye. **2** hello. [Sounds like CHOW]

cicada n. a large insect with a loud shrill sound. [Say sick AID uh]

CIDA abbr. Canadian International Development Agency. [Say SEE dah]

cider n. **1** a thick pure apple juice. **2** (also **hard cider**) an alcoholic drink made from apple juice.

cigar n. a cylinder of rolled tobacco leaves for smoking. □ **close but no cigar** informal almost but not quite successful.

cigarette n. a thin cylinder of finely-cut tobacco rolled in paper for smoking.

cilantro n. fresh coriander. [Say sill AN tro]

cilia pl. n. (singular **cilium**) tiny hairlike vibrating structures on the surface of some cells. □ **ciliary** adj. [Say SILL ee ah for the plural, SILL ee um for the singular, SILLY airy]

ciliate ● adj. (also **ciliated**) having cilia. ● n. a protozoan with cilia. [Say SILLY ate]

cinch ● n. **1** informal **a** a sure thing. **b** an easy task. **2** a girth for a saddle etc. ● v. (**cinches, cinched, cinching**) **1** tighten firmly. **2** slang make certain of.

cinchona n. a S American evergreen tree or shrub, whose bark contains quinine. [Say sing CONE uh]

cinder n. **1** a small piece of partly-burned coal or wood. **2** (in pl.) ashes. □ **cindery** adj.

cinder block n. a standard building block made of cinders mixed with sand and cement.

Cinderella n. a person or thing whose talents or merits go unrecognized, esp. one that succeeds in the end.

cinema n. movies generally; the production of movies.

cinematic adj. of or relating to the cinema. □ **cinematically** adv.

cinematography n. the art or technique of shooting motion pictures. □ **cinematographer** n. **cinematographic** adj. [Say SIN uh muh TOG ruh fee, SIN uh muh TOG ruh fer, SIN uh muh tuh GRAPHIC]

Cineplex n. (pl. **Cineplexes**) proprietary a complex consisting of several movie theatres.

cinnamon n. a spice from the dried and rolled bark of a Southeast Asian tree.

cinquefoil n. a plant with leaves consisting of five leaflets. [Say SINK foil]

cipher *n.* **1 a** a secret code or coded message. **b** the key to a code. **2** a zero. **3** something of no importance. [*Say* SIGH fer]

circa *prep.* about, approximately.

circle ● *n.* **1** a perfectly round shape. **2** a thing or group shaped or arranged in a circle. **3** a group of people having similar interests etc. **4** a period or cycle. ● *v.* (**circles, circled, circling**) move in or form a circle. □ **come full circle** return to the starting point.

circlet *n.* **1** a small circle. **2** a circular band worn around the head.

circuit *n.* **1 a** the distance or a course around something. **b** a racetrack. **2 a** standard series of places visited by athletes, a judge, etc. **3** *Electricity* **a** the path of a current. **b** the apparatus through which a current passes.

circuit board *n.* a thin rigid board containing an electric circuit.

circuit breaker *n.* an automatic device for stopping the flow of current in an electrical circuit.

circuit court *n.* (in Canada) a province's superior court travelling to different communities.

circuitous *adj.* **1** indirect and usu. long. **2** not direct or straightforward. □ **circuitously** *adv.* [*Say* sir CUE it us]

circuitry *n.* (*pl.* **circuitries**) a system of electric circuits.

circular ● *adj.* **1 a** having the form of a circle. **b** moving along a circle. **2** *Logic* (of reasoning) using the point it is trying to prove as evidence for its conclusion. **3** printed for distribution to a large number of people. ● *n.* a circular advertisement or letter. □ **circularity** *n.*

circular saw *n.* a power saw with a toothed disc.

circulate *v.* (**circulates, circulated, circulating**) **1** go around from one place or person etc. to the next. **2** (of blood, sap, etc.) flow through a body, tree, etc. **3** cause to go around. **4** be actively sociable. □ **circulator** *n.*

circulation *n.* **1** the movement of blood from and to the heart, or of sap in a tree, etc. **2 a** the transmission or distribution of news etc.). **b** the number of copies sold, esp. of journals and newspapers. **3** the movement or exchange of currency in a country etc. □ **in** (or **out of**) **circulation** participating (or not participating) in activities etc.

circulatory *adj.* of or relating to the circulation of blood or sap. [*Say* SIR cue la tory]

circumcise *v.* (**circumcises, circumcised, circumcising**) **1** cut off the foreskin of. **2** cut off the clitoris of. □ **circumcision** *n.* [*Say* SIR cum size, sir cum SIZH un]

circumference *n.* the line enclosing a circle; the length of this. [*Say* sir KUM fer ince]

circumflex *n.* (*pl.* **circumflexes**) (also **circumflex accent**) a mark (^) placed over a vowel in some languages, sometimes indicating a change in sound. [*Say* SIR cum flex]

circumlocution *n.* the use of many words where fewer would do; evasive talk. [*Say* SIR kum luh CUE sh'n]

circumnavigate *v.* (**circumnavigates, circumnavigated, circumnavigating**) sail or fly around the world. □ **circumnavigation** *n.* [*Say* sir cum NAVIGATE, sir cum NAVIGATION]

circumpolar *adj.* around or near one of the earth's poles. [*Say* sir cum POLAR]

circumscribe *v.* (**circumscribes, circumscribed, circumscribing**) **1** enclose or outline. **2** confine, restrict. **3** *Math.* draw a figure around another. □ **circumscription** *n.* [*Say* SIR cum scribe, sir cum SCRIP sh'n]

circumspect *adj.* wary, cautious. □ **circumspection** *n.* [*Say* SIR cum spect, sir cum SPEC sh'n]

circumstance *n.* **1** a condition or fact connected with an event or action. **2** one's state of financial or material welfare. □ **under the circumstances** since this is the case. **under** (or **in**) **no circumstances** never. [*Say* SIR cum stance]

circumstantial *adj.* **1** (of evidence etc.) consisting of details that strongly suggest something but do not prove it. **2** detailed. [*Say* sir cum STAN shull]

circumvent *v.* find a way around (a problem or obstacle). [*Say* sir cum VENT]

circus *n.* (*pl.* **circuses**) **1** a travelling show of performing animals, acrobats, clowns, etc. **2** *informal* a situation of chaotic activity.

cirque *n.* a steep-sided hollow at the head of a valley or on a mountainside. [*Say* SURK]

cirrhosis *n.* a chronic disease of the liver caused esp. by alcoholism or hepatitis. [*Say* suh ROE sis]

cirrus *n.* clouds formed at high altitudes as delicate white wisps. [*Say* SEER us]

cisco *n.* (*pl.* **ciscoes**) a N American freshwater whitefish. [*Say* SIS coe]

Cistercian ● *n.* a monk or nun of an

order that is a stricter branch of the Benedictines. ● *adj.* of the Cistercians. [*Say* sis TUR sh'n]

cistern *n.* a tank or reservoir for storing water. [*Say* SIS turn]

citadel *n.* a fortress protecting or overlooking a city. [*Say* SITTA del]

citation *n.* **1** a quotation from or reference to a book or author. **2** a summons to appear in court. **3** a mention in an official report of a praiseworthy act. [*Say* sigh TAY sh'n]

cite *v.* (**cites, cited, citing**) **1** quote a book etc. to support an argument. **2** mention as an example. **3** *Military* praise in an official dispatch. **4** summon to appear in court.

CITES *abbr.* Convention on International Trade in Endangered Species. [*Say* SIGH teez]

citified *adj.* usu. *derogatory* characteristic of an urban environment. [*Say* SITTA fide]

citizen *n.* **1** a person who has full rights as a member of a country. **2** an inhabitant of a city or town. □ **citizenship** *n.*

citizenry *n.* citizens collectively.

citizens' band *n.* a system of local intercommunication by individuals on special radio frequencies. Abbreviation: **CB.**

citric acid *n.* a sharp-tasting acid found in citrus fruit.

citron *n.* a large lemon-like fruit borne on a shrubby tree. [*Say* SIT run]

citronella *n.* a fragrant oil distilled from a south Asian grass and used as an insect repellent etc. [*Say* sitra NELLA]

citrus *n.* (*pl.* **citrus**) **1** a group of trees and shrubs including lemon, lime, orange, grapefruit, and citron. **2** (also **citrus fruit**) fruit from such a tree. □ **citrusy** *adj.*

city *n.* (*pl.* **cities**) **1** a large town. **2 a** the people of a city. **b** the government of a city.

city father *n.* a prominent citizen or elected official of a city.

city hall *n.* the central administrative offices of a municipality.

cityscape *n.* a view of a city.

city slicker *n.* usu. *derogatory* a person with the sophisticated tastes and values often associated with city-dwellers.

city state *n.* an independent state consisting of a city and surrounding territory.

civet *n.* **1** (also **civet cat**) a catlike carnivore, native to Africa and Asia. **2** a musky perfume obtained from this animal. [*Say* SIV et]

civic *adj.* of a city or its citizens. [*Say* SIV ick]

civic centre *n.* a building containing municipal offices or other public facilities.

civic holiday *n. Cdn* a holiday that is commonly observed but not legislated, esp. the first Monday in August.

civics *pl. n.* the study of government and the rights and duties of citizenship.

civil *adj.* **1** of ordinary citizens, as distinct from the military or the Church. **2** occurring between citizens of the same country. **3** polite. **4** *Law* involving civil rather than criminal law. [*Say* SIV ul]

civil code *n.* a body of civil laws (such as the one used in Quebec) based on Roman and Napoleonic law.

civil disobedience *n.* the refusal to comply with certain laws or pay taxes as a political protest.

civil engineer *n.* an engineer who designs roads, bridges, dams, etc. □ **civil engineering** *n.*

civilian ● *n.* a person not in the armed services or the police force. ● *adj.* of or for civilians.

civility *n.* (*pl.* **civilities**) politeness.

civilization *n.* **1 a** an advanced stage of human social development. **b** those peoples regarded as having this. **2** a people (esp. of the past) regarded as an element of social evolution. **3** *informal* populated areas. **4** the act of becoming civilized.

civilize *v.* (**civilizes, civilized, civilizing**) **1** bring to an advanced stage of social or cultural development. **2** improve the behaviour of. □ **civilized** *adj.*

civil law *n.* **1** law concerning private rights and legal remedies. **2** a legal system (e.g. in Quebec) in which laws are set out in a civil code.

civil liberties *n.* fundamental rights, such as freedom of speech, which are protected by the laws of the country. □ **civil libertarian** *pl. n.*

civil liberty *n.* the freedom to exercise civil liberties.

civil rights *pl. n.* the rights of citizens to political and social freedom and equality.

civil servant *n.* a member of the civil service.

civil service *n.* the permanent branches of public service, excluding military and judicial branches and elected politicians.

civil war *n.* a war between citizens of the same country.

clack ● *n.* a sharp sound as of hard objects hitting each other. ● *v.* make a clacking sound. □ **clacker** *n.*

clad *adj.* **1** dressed in a particular manner. **2** covered.

cladding n. a protective covering, esp. for a building.

claim ● v. **1** state as being true, esp. without giving proof. **2** say that one has a right to something. **3** request payment under an insurance policy. **4** (of a disaster) cause the death of. **5** deserve (one's attention). ● n. **1** an assertion that something is true. **2** a demand for something considered one's due. **3** a right to something. **4** a piece of public land granted or taken for mining. □ **lay claim to** declare that one has a right to something. **stake a** (or **one's**) **claim to** see STAKE¹.

claimant n. a person making a claim, esp. in a lawsuit.

clairvoyance n. the power of seeing things beyond the natural range of the senses, such as being able to see into the future. □ **clairvoyant** n. & adj. [Say clair VOY ance]

clam ● n. a usu. edible bivalve mollusc. ● v. (**clams, clammed, clamming**) dig for clams. □ **clam up** informal refuse to talk. **happy as a clam** extremely happy.

clambake n. a seaside picnic at which clams etc. are baked and eaten.

clamber v. climb with difficulty using the hands and feet. [Say CLAM bur or CLAMMER]

clammy adj. (**clammier, clammiest**) unpleasantly damp or slimy. □ **clammily** adv. **clamminess** n.

clamour (also **clamor**) ● n. **1** loud noise, esp. of people shouting. **2** a strong protest or demand. ● v. **1** demand insistently. **2** make a clamour. □ **clamorous** adj.

clamp ● n. a device for holding things together tightly. ● v. **1** fasten together or in place with a clamp. **2** hold something tightly. □ **clamp down** suppress or prevent something.

clampdown n. a severe attempt to restrict something.

clamshell n. a thing with hinged parts that open and close like the shell of a clam.

clan n. **1** the basic social and political organization of many Aboriginal societies. **2** a group of families with a common ancestor.

clandestine adj. secretive. □ **clandestinely** adv. [Say clan DESS tine or clan DESS tin, clan DESS tin lee]

clang ● n. a loud ringing sound. ● v. make a clanging sound.

clangour (also **clangor**) a continuous clanging sound or commotion. □ **clangorous** adj. [Say KLANG ger, KLANG ger us]

clank ● n. a loud sound made by pieces of metal hitting each other. ● v. make or move with a clanking sound. □ **clanky** adj.

clannish adj. usu. derogatory (of a group) tending to exclude others outside the group. □ **clannishness** n.

clap ● v. (**claps, clapped, clapping**) **1** strike the palms of one's hands together esp. to applaud. **2** slap a person lightly, usu. in a friendly way. ● n. **1** the act of clapping. **2** a sudden loud noise, esp. of thunder.

clapboard n. a type of wooden siding used to cover outer walls.

clapper n. the striker of a bell.

claptrap n. nonsense.

claret n. a dry red wine, esp. from Bordeaux. [Say CLAIR it]

clarify v. (**clarifies, clarified, clarifying**) **1** make clearer. **2** remove impurities from. □ **clarification** n.

clarinet n. a woodwind instrument with a single-reed mouthpiece and holes stopped by keys. □ **clarinetist** n.

clarion call n. a strongly expressed request for action. [Say CLAIR ee un]

clarity n. the state or quality of being clear.

clash ● n. **1** a violent confrontation or disagreement. **2** an incompatibility. **3** a loud jarring sound. ● v. (**clashes, clashed, clashing**) **1** come into violent conflict or disagreement. **2** fail to match or look good together. **3** strike together with a loud harsh noise.

clasp ● n. **1** a device for fastening things together. **2** an embrace. **3** a grip or grasp. ● v. **1** hold tightly. **2** place one's hands together. **3** fasten with a clasp. □ **clasp hands** shake hands with affection.

class ● n. (pl. **classes**) **1** a set of things having some property in common. **2 a** a group of people at the same social or economic level. **b** a system that divides people into such groups. **3 a** a group of students taught together. **b** their course of instruction. **4** informal sophistication or stylishness. **5** Biology the second highest group into which animals and plants are divided. ● v. (**classes, classed, classing**) assign to a class or category. ● adj. showing excellence in behaviour or appearance.

class action n. a lawsuit filed by an individual on behalf of a group with a common grievance.

class-conscious adj. aware of belonging to a particular social class. □ **class-consciousness** n.

classic ● adj. **1** judged over time to be of the highest quality. **2** remarkably typical. **3** (of clothes) made in a simple elegant style. ● n. **1** a work of art recognized as being of high quality and lasting value. **2** a thing which is an outstanding example of its kind. **3** a garment in classic style.

classical adj. **1 a** relating to or influenced by ancient Greek or Latin literature, art, or culture. **b** (of language, art, etc.) representing the highest standard within a long-established form. **2 a** (of music) serious and following long-established principles, as opposed to folk, rock, jazz, etc. **b** of the period from c.1750–1800, when forms such as the symphony, concerto, and sonata were standardized. **3** established and widely accepted. □ **classically** adv.

classicism n. the following of ancient Greek or Roman principles and style in art and literature. □ **classicist** n. [Say CLASSA sism, CLASSA sist]

classics n. the works of ancient Greek and Latin writers and philosophers.

classification n. **1** the action classifying. **2** a category into which something is put.

classified ● adj. **1** arranged in classes or categories. **2** (of information etc.) designated as officially secret. ● n. (of newspaper ads) arranged in categories. ● n. a classified ad.

classify v. (**classifies, classified, classifying**) **1** assign to a category. **2** declare information etc. as officially secret. □ **classifiable** adj. **classifier** n.

classism n. prejudice based on social class. □ **classist** adj. & n.

classless adj. making no distinction of classes.

classmate n. a fellow member of a class at school.

classroom n. a room in a school in which classes are taught.

classy adj. (**classier, classiest**) **1** stylish, elegant. **2** admirable.

clastic adj. denoting rocks composed of broken pieces of older rocks.

clatter ● n. **1** a rattling sound like that of hard objects striking each other. **2** noisy talk. ● v. make a clatter.

clause n. **1** a group of words that consists of a subject and predicate and usu. a verb, and which may constitute a sentence or part of a sentence. **2** a paragraph or section in a legal document stating a particular obligation or condition etc.

claustrophobia n. an abnormal fear of confined places. □ **claustrophobic** adj. [Say klostra PHOBIA, klostra FOE bick]

clavicle n. the collarbone. [Say KLAV ick ul]

claw ● n. **1** a curved pointed horny nail on each digit of an animal's foot. **2** the pincers of a shellfish. **3** a device resembling a claw. ● v. **1** scratch, tear, or grab with the claws or fingernails. **2** proceed by or as if by using one's hands or claws. □ **claw back 1** (of a government) recover money paid out in the form of a benefit or allowance, esp. by taxation. **2** regain something lost with great effort.

clawback n. a situation in which the government retrieves money paid out, esp. by taxation.

clawed adj. having claws.

clay n. stiff, sticky earth, which can be moulded when wet and baked to make bricks and pottery. □ **clayey** adj. **claylike** adj.

clay pigeon n. a breakable disc thrown up as a target for shooting.

clean ● adj. **1** free from dirt or contaminating matter. **2** clear. **3** free from obscenity or indecency. **4** attentive to personal hygiene. **5** even; straight. **6** not obstructed. **7** skilful. **8** free from any record of a crime etc. **9** informal free from addiction to drugs. ● adv. **1** so as to be free of dirt, garbage, etc. **2** informal completely. ● v. **1** make or become clean. **2** eat all the food on. ● n. the act of cleaning or being cleaned. □ **clean out 1** clean thoroughly. **2** slang empty or deprive (esp. of money). **clean up 1** restore order or morality to. **2** slang make or acquire as gain or profit. **clean up one's act** begin to behave responsibly. **come clean** informal confess. **make a clean job of** informal do thoroughly. □ **cleanable** adj.

clean-cut adj. (of a person) neat and tidy.

cleaner n. a person or thing that cleans.

cleaners pl. n. an establishment where clothes are dry cleaned. □ **take to the cleaners** slang rob of a great deal of money etc.

cleanliness n. the habit of being or keeping things clean. [Say KLEN lee ness]

cleanly adv. **1** in a clean way. **2** without difficulty. [Say CLEAN lee]

clean room n. a room free from dust and bacteria, used for medical or manufacturing purposes.

cleanse v. (**cleanses, cleansed, cleansing**) **1** make thoroughly clean. **2** rid of something unpleasant or unwanted. **3** free someone of sin or guilt. □ **cleanser** n. [Say KLENZ, KLENZ er]

clean-shaven adj. without a beard or moustache.

clean slate n. an opportunity for a fresh start.

cleanup n. an act of cleaning up.

clear ● adj. **1** free from dirt or

contamination. **2** not dull or cloudy. **3** transparent; smooth. **4** easily perceived or understood; manifest. **5** confident, certain. **6** free from guilt. **7** not obstructed. **8** unencumbered. ● *adv.* **1** clearly. **2** completely. **3** apart, away from. **4** all the way. ● *v.* **1** make or become clear. **2 a** free from prohibition or obstruction. **b** cause people to leave (a room etc.). **3** show or declare to be innocent. **4** approve for special duty, access, etc. **5** pass over or by safely or without touching. **6** make (an amount of money) as a net gain. **7** pass (a cheque). □ **clear the air 1** make the air less humid. **2** disperse an atmosphere of suspicion, tension, etc. **clear the decks** prepare for action, esp. fighting. **clear off 1** get rid of. **2** *informal* go away. **clear out 1** empty. **2** *informal* go away. **clear up 1** tidy up. **2** solve. **3** (of weather) become fine. **clear a thing with** get approval from. **in the clear** free from suspicion or difficulty. □ **clearly** *adv.*

clearance *n.* **1** the action of removing or getting rid of. **2** clear space between objects. **3** special authorization or permission. **4** a sale to get rid of stock.

clear-cut ● *adj.* **1** sharply defined; not vague. **2** of a logging method in which all trees in an area are harvested at the same time. ● *n.* an area of clear-cut forest. ● *v.* (**clear-cuts, clear-cut, clear-cutting**) log an area of forest by cutting all trees. □ **clear-cutting** *n.*

clear-eyed *adj.* **1** having clear eyes. **2** able to make good decisions.

clear-headed *adj.* **1** able to think clearly. **2** well-thought-out.

clearing *n.* a treeless area in a forest.

clearing house *n.* a bankers' institution where cheques and bills from member banks are exchanged.

cleat *n.* **1** a T-shaped projection around which a rope may be secured. **2** a projecting piece on the bottom of a shoe etc. to improve grip; the shoe itself. **3** a projecting piece to improve footing.

cleavage *n.* **1** the hollow between a woman's breasts. **2** a division or splitting. [*Say* KLEEV idge]

cleave[1] *v.* (**cleaves**; *past* **cleaved** or **clove** or **cleft**; *past participle* **cloven** or **cleft** or **cleaved**; **cleaving**) **1** split, esp. along a natural grain or line. **2** make one's way through.

cleave[2] *v.* (**cleaves, cleaved, cleaving**) (foll. by *to*) *literary* adhere.

cleaver *n.* a broad-bladed knife used for chopping meat.

clef *n. Music* a symbol placed at the beginning of a staff, indicating the pitch of the notes written on it.

cleft ● *adj.* split, partly divided. ● *n.* a split or fissure.

cleft palate *n.* a congenital split in the roof of the mouth.

clematis *n.* (*pl.* **clematis**) an esp. climbing plant bearing white, pink, or purple flowers. [*Say* kluh MAT iss *or* KLEM uh tis]

clemency *n.* mercy.

clement *adj.* **1** mild, temperate. **2** merciful. [*Say* KLEM ent]

clementine *n.* a small citrus fruit, related to the tangerine. [*Say* KLEM in tine *or* KLEM in teen]

clench *v.* (**clenches, clenched, clenching**) **1** close the teeth or fingers tightly. **2** grasp firmly.

clergy *pl. n.* the people who have been ordained for religious duties. □ **clergyman** *n.* **clergywoman** *n.*

cleric *n.* a member of the clergy.

clerical *adj.* **1** of or done by an office clerk or secretary. **2** of the clergy. □ **clericalism** *n.* **clericalist** *n.*

clerical collar *n.* a stiff upright white collar, worn by the clergy in some churches.

clerk ● *n.* **1** a person employed in an office, bank, etc., to keep records, accounts, etc. **2** a salesperson in a store. **3** a person who keeps records of a government, court, etc. **4 a** *Cdn* a judge's research assistant. **b** (in full **articled clerk**) a law student who is articling. ● *v.* work as a clerk.

clever *adj.* (**cleverer, cleverest**) **1** quick to understand and learn. **2** skilful. **3** ingenious, cunning. **4** witty. □ **cleverly** *adv.* **cleverness** *n.*

cliché *n.* a phrase or idea that is overused so as to be no longer interesting or effective. □ **clichéd** *adj.* [*Say* klee SHAY *or* KLEE shay]

click ● *n.* **1** a slight sharp sound as of a switch being operated. **2** *Computing* an act of pressing a button on a mouse. ● *v.* **1** make or cause to make a click. **2** *informal* **a** become clear. **b** become friendly. **3** *Computing* **a** press (a mouse button). **b** select (an item on the screen) by so doing. □ **click in** *informal* become active or effective.

clicker *n.* **1** a remote control for a television etc. **2** a person or thing that clicks.

client *n.* a person using the services of a professional person; any customer.

clientele *n.* clients or customers collectively. [*Say* klye 'n TELL *or* klee on TELL]

client-server n. Computing designating a type of system in which a server distributes files and databases to workstations connected to it.

cliff n. a high steep rock face.

cliffhanger n. **1** a story etc. with a strong element of suspense; a suspenseful ending. **2** a situation in which the outcome is uncertain. □ **cliffhanging** adj.

climactic adj. of or forming a climax. [Say clime ACK tic]

climate n. **1** the regular pattern of weather conditions of an area. **2** a region with particular weather conditions. **3** the prevailing trend of opinion. □ **climatic** adj. [Say CLIME it, clime ATTIC]

climate control n. a system for regulating the humidity and temperature of air. □ **climate-controlled** adj.

climatology n. the scientific study of climate. □ **climatologist** n. [Say clime a TOLLA jee, clime a TOLLA jist]

climax ● n. (pl. **climaxes**) **1** the event or point of greatest intensity or interest. **2** an orgasm. **3** Ecology a state of equilibrium reached by a plant community. ● v. (**climaxes**, **climaxed**, **climaxing**) informal bring or come to a climax.

climb ● v. **1** ascend or come up to a higher position. **2** (of a plant) grow up a wall, trellis, etc. **3** make progress from one's own efforts. **4** go or slope upwards. **5** (of numbers) increase. ● n. **1** an ascent by climbing. **2** a place climbed or to be climbed. □ **climb down 1** descend. **2** withdraw from a stance taken up in argument, negotiation, etc. **climb the walls** informal go crazy. □ **climbable** adj. **climber** n.

clime n. literary **1** a region. **2** a climate.

clinch ● v. (**clinches**, **clinched**, **clinching**) **1** confirm or settle an argument etc. conclusively. **2** Sport secure a position on a team etc. ● n. **1** a clinching action. **2** informal an embrace. □ **clincher** n.

cling v. (**clings**, **clung**, **clinging**) **1** hold on tightly. **2** stick closely to. **3** refuse to abandon; remain faithful. **4** be emotionally dependent on.

clingy adj. (**clingier**, **clingiest**) **1** emotionally dependent. **2** (of clothing) sticking to the body.

clinic n. **1** a place where medical treatment etc. or advice is given. **2** a place where a group of doctors or dentists practice together. **3** a conference or short course on a subject.

clinical adj. **1 a** of or for the direct examination and treatment of patients. **b** based on observed symptoms. **2** coldly detached. **3** (of a room etc.) bare. □ **clinically** adv.

clinician n. a doctor having direct contact with and responsibility for patients. [Say klin ISH'n]

clink ● n. **1** a light sharp ringing sound. **2** slang prison. ● v. make or cause to make a clink.

clinker n. **1** a mass of slag or lava. **2** a stony residue from burnt coal. **3** informal a blunder.

clip¹ ● n. **1** a device for holding things together or in place. **2** a piece of jewellery fastened by a clip. ● v. (**clips**, **clipped**, **clipping**) **1** attach with a clip. **2** grip tightly.

clip² ● v. (**clips**, **clipped**, **clipping**) **1** cut with shears or scissors. **2** trim the hair or wool of. **3** informal hit smartly. **4** cut short. ● n. **1** an act of clipping, esp. shearing or haircutting. **2** informal a smart blow. **3** a short sequence from a film etc. □ **clip a person's wings** prevent a person from pursuing ambitions.

clip art n. publicly available artwork that can be copied into documents etc.

clipboard n. **1** a small board with a spring clip for holding papers etc. **2** a feature of some computer programs which temporarily stores extracted text.

clip-clop ● n. a sound like the beat of a horse's hooves. ● v. (**clip-clops**, **clip-clopped**, **clip-clopping**) make such a sound.

clip-on ● adj. attached by a clip. ● n. a thing that attaches by a clip.

clipper n. **1** a person or thing that clips. **2** a fast sailing ship.

clipping n. **1** a short piece clipped from a newspaper etc. **2** (**clippings**) small pieces of grass etc. produced by cutting.

clique n. a small group of people who associate together and do not allow others to join them. □ **cliquey** adj. **cliquish** adj. **cliquishness** n. [Say KLEEK, KLEEK ee, KLEEK ish, KLEEK ish ness]

clitoris n. a small erectile part of the vulva. [Say CLITTER iss]

cloak ● n. **1** an outdoor garment hanging loosely from the shoulders. **2** a covering. **3** something which conceals. ● v. **1** cover with a cloak. **2** cover over. **3** conceal, disguise.

cloak-and-dagger adj. involving plotting and intrigue, esp. espionage.

cloakroom n. a room where outdoor clothes or luggage may be left.

clobber v. informal **1** hit repeatedly; beat up. **2** defeat.

clock ● n. **1** an instrument for measuring

or indicating time. **2** any measuring device resembling a clock, e.g. a speedometer. **3** time. ● v. **1** attain or register a stated total, number, etc. **2** time with a stopwatch. **3** measure the speed of. □ **clean someone's clock** *informal* beat someone soundly. **around the clock** all day and night. **clock in** (or **out**) register one's arrival (or departure) at work. **watch the clock** keep a close watch on the passing of time.

clockwise *adj. & adv.* moving in the same direction as the hands of a clock.

clockwork ● n. a mechanism like that of a mechanical clock. ● adj. **1** driven by clockwork. **2** regular, mechanical. □ **like clockwork** smoothly, regularly.

clod n. **1** a lump of earth etc. **2** *informal* a foolish person.

clodhopper n. **1** *informal* a large heavy shoe. **2** an unsophisticated person.

clog ● n. **1** a shoe with a thick wooden sole. **2** a blockage in a drain etc. ● v. (**clogs, clogged, clogging**) block or become blocked.

cloister ● n. **1** a covered walk around an open courtyard in a convent etc. **2** a convent or monastery. ● v. seclude in or as if in a convent etc. [*Say* CLOY ster]

cloistered *adj.* **1** kept away from the outside world. **2** living in a convent or monastery.

clomp v. walk with heavy steps.

clone ● n. **1** a plant or animal produced from the cells of another to which it is genetically identical. **2** a person or thing regarded as identical with another. ● v. (**clones, cloned, cloning**) produce or copy as a clone. □ **clonal** *adj.*

clonk ● n. an abrupt heavy sound of impact. ● v. make such a sound.

clop ● n. the sound made by a horse's hooves. ● v. (**clops, clopped, clopping**) make this sound.

close¹ ● adj. (**closer, closest**) **1** situated at only a short distance or interval. **2 a** having a strong likeness or connection. **b** in intimate friendship or association. **c** fitting tightly. **d** (of hair etc.) short. **3** in or almost in contact. **4** dense, compact. **5** in which competitors are almost equal. **6** concentrated. **7** (of air etc.) stuffy or humid. ● adv. at only a short distance or interval. □ **closely** *adv.* **closeness** n.

close² ● v. (**closes, closed, closing**) **1 a** shut or be shut. **b** prevent access to. **2 a** bring or come to an end. **b** settle or finalize. **3** cease work or business temporarily or permanently. **4** (of a group of people) come close to or surround. **5** (of stocks etc.) be at a particular price at the

close of a day's trading. **6** withdraw all the money from (a bank account etc.). **7** remove from use or stop using (a room, bed, etc.): *the hospital closed 100 beds.* ● n. a conclusion, an end. □ **close down** discontinue business, esp. permanently. **close one's eyes to** pay no attention to. **close in** come nearer; surround. **close off** prevent access to. **close out** discontinue, terminate. **close ranks** **1** (esp. of soldiers) move closer together. **2** maintain solidarity. □ **closing** n.

close call n. a narrow escape.

closed *adj.* **1** not giving access; shut. **2** self-contained; not communicating with others. **3** *Cdn* (of a mortgage etc.) that may not be paid off before the stated term without a financial penalty.

closed caption n. one of a series of captions along the bottom of a television screen as an aid to the hearing impaired. □ **closed-captioned** *adj.* **closed-captioning** n.

closed-circuit *adj.* (of television) transmitted by wires to a restricted set of receivers.

closed shop n. a place of work etc. where all employees must belong to an agreed labour union.

close-fitting n. (of a garment) fitting close to the body.

close-knit *adj.* (also **closely-knit**) tightly bound or interlocked; closely united.

close-mouthed *adj.* tight-lipped.

close quarters pl. n. a cramped place. □ **at close quarters** very close.

closer n. a person or thing that closes.

close-set *adj.* set close together.

close shave n. *informal* a narrow escape.

closet ● n. **1** a cupboard or wardrobe. **2** a small or private room. **3** (as an *adj.*) secret, covert. ● v. (**closets, closeted, closeting**) shut away, esp. in private conference or study. □ **in the closet** **1** keeping one's homosexuality from public knowledge. **2** hidden from public scrutiny. **out of the closet** **1** into the open. **2** having publicly declared one's homosexuality. □ **closeted** *adj.*

close-up n. **1** a photograph etc. taken at close range. **2** an intimate description.

closure n. **1** the act or process of closing. **2** something that closes or seals. **3** conclusion.

clot ● n. **1** a lump of solidified liquid, esp. blood. **2** a mass of material stuck together. ● v. (**clots, clotted, clotting**) form into clots.

cloth n. (pl. **cloths**) **1** woven or felted

material; a piece of this. **2** a piece of cloth for a particular purpose. **3** the clergy.

clothe v. (**clothes**, **clothed** or formal **clad**, **clothing**) put clothes on; provide with clothes.

clothes pl. n. garments.

clothes horse n. **1** a frame for airing washed clothes. **2** informal a person who has many clothes.

clothesline n. a rope or wire etc. on which laundry is hung to dry.

clothespin n. a device for attaching clothes to a clothesline.

clothier n. a maker or seller of clothes. [Say CLOTHE ee er]

clothing n. clothes collectively. [Say CLOTHE ing]

cloud ● n. **1** a visible mass of condensed watery vapour floating in the atmosphere. **2** any similar mass, esp. of smoke or dust. **3** a great number of insects, birds, etc., moving together. **4** a state of gloom or suspicion. ● v. **1** cover or darken with or as if with clouds. **2** become overcast or gloomy. **3 a** make unclear. **b** distort. □ **on cloud nine** informal extremely happy. **under a cloud** out of favour, under suspicion. **with one's head in the clouds** daydreaming, unrealistic. □ **cloudiness** n. **cloudless** adj. **cloudy** adj. (**cloudier**, **cloudiest**).

cloudberry n. (pl. **cloudberries**) a low-growing plant with a white flower.

cloudburst n. a sudden violent rainstorm.

clout ● n. **1** informal influence. **2** a heavy blow. ● v. hit hard.

clove[1] n. **1** a dried flower bud of a tropical plant, used as a pungent spice. **2** any of the small bulbs making up a compound bulb of garlic, shallot, etc.

clove[2] past of CLEAVE[1].

cloven adj. split, partly divided.

clover n. a small plant with usu. three leaves on each stem, and purple, pink or white flowers. □ **in clover** in ease and luxury.

cloverleaf n. (pl. **cloverleafs**) an intersection of highways with ramps forming the pattern of a four-leaf clover.

clown ● n. **1** a comic entertainer usu. with a painted face and ridiculous clothing. **2** a silly or playful person. ● v. **1** behave like a clown. **2** perform a part etc. like a clown. □ **clownish** adj.

cloying adj. **1** extremely sweet. **2** excessively sentimental. □ **cloyingly** adv.

club ● n. **1** a heavy stick with a thick end, used as a weapon etc. **2** a stick used in a game to strike a ball. **3** a playing card of a suit denoted by a black trefoil. **4** an

association dedicated to a particular activity. **5** an organization where members can meet, eat meals, or stay overnight. **6** an organization offering members certain benefits. **7** a sports team. **8** a nightclub. ● v. (**clubs**, **clubbed**, **clubbing**) **1** beat with or as with a club. **2** combine for joint action. **3** visit nightclubs. □ **join** (or **welcome to) the club** you're not the only one to feel that way. □ **clubber** n.

clubbing n. the practice of frequenting nightclubs.

clubby adj. (**clubbier**, **clubbiest**) **1** friendly with fellow members of a group but not with outsiders. **2** typical of a social club. □ **clubbiness** n.

club foot n. a congenitally deformed foot. □ **club-footed** adj.

clubhouse n. **1** the premises used by a club. **2** the dressing room of a sports team.

club sandwich n. (also **clubhouse sandwich**) a sandwich usu. consisting of bacon, lettuce, tomato, mayonnaise, and poultry served between three slices of bread.

club soda n. soda water.

cluck ● n. a guttural cry like that of a hen. ● v. **1** make a clucking sound. **2** (also **cluck-cluck**) express disapproval etc. by making a similar noise.

clue ● n. a fact or idea that helps to solve a problem, mystery, crime, etc. ● v. (**clues**, **clued**, **clueing**) provide a clue to. □ **clue in** informal inform. **not have a clue** informal be ignorant or incompetent.

clueless adj. informal ignorant, stupid. □ **cluelessly** adv. **cluelessness** n.

clump ● n. **1** a cluster of things or people, esp. of trees, hair, etc. **2** a mass or lump. ● v. **1** form a clump. **2** walk with heavy steps. □ **clumpy** adj.

clumsy adj. (**clumsier**, **clumsiest**) **1** not graceful; awkward. **2** done without skill. **3** tactless. **4** difficult to use or move. □ **clumsily** adv. **clumsiness** n.

clung past and past participle of CLING.

clunk ● n. a dull sound as of thick pieces of metal striking. ● v. **1** make such a sound. **2** move or progress clumsily. □ **clunking** adj.

clunker n. informal a dilapidated automobile or machine.

clunky adj. (**clunkier**, **clunkiest**) informal **1** awkward or clumsy. **2** not sleekly designed.

cluster ● n. a close group of similar things growing or placed together. ● v. **1** form a cluster. **2** gather.

cluster bomb n. an anti-personnel bomb spraying smaller bombs when detonated.

clutch¹ ● v. (**clutches, clutched, clutching**) **1** seize or grasp tightly. **2** snatch suddenly. ● n. (pl. **clutches**) **1** a tight grasp. **2** (in pl.) power or control. **3 a** (in a motor vehicle) a device for connecting and disconnecting the engine to the transmission. **b** the pedal operating this. **4** a decisive situation.

clutch² n. (pl. **clutches**) **1 a** a set of eggs to be hatched at one time. **b** the brood resulting from this. **2** a group of people or items.

clutter ● n. **1** a crowded and untidy collection. **2** an untidy state. ● v. crowd untidily, fill with clutter. □ **cluttered** adj.

cm abbr. centimetre(s).

C-note n. slang a one-hundred-dollar bill.

Co. abbr. **1** company. **2** county. □ **and Co.** informal and the rest of them.

c/o abbr. care of.

co- prefix **1** (forming nouns) joint, mutual; common. **2** (forming adjectives) jointly, mutually. **3** (forming verbs) together with another or others.

coach ● n. (pl. **coaches**) **1** a bus which is comfortably equipped for longer journeys. **2 a** a person who trains or instructs in sports. **b** a private tutor. **3** economy class seating in an aircraft, train, etc. **4** a four-wheeled horse-drawn carriage. ● v. (**coaches, coached, coaching**) **1** train or instruct as a coach. **2** give hints to. □ **coachable** adj. **coaching** n.

coach house n. a building designed to hold horse-drawn carriages.

coachman n. (pl. **coachmen**) the driver of a horse-drawn carriage.

coagulate v. (**coagulates, coagulated, coagulating**) (of a fluid, esp. blood) change to a solid or semi-solid state. □ **coagulation** n. [Say co AG yuh late]

coal n. **1 a** a hard black or blackish rock, mainly carbonized plant matter. **b** a piece of this for burning. **2** (in pl.) burning pieces of coal, wood, etc. in a fire. **3** = CHARCOAL 1. □ **rake** (or **haul**) **over the coals** reprimand severely.

coalesce v. (**coalesces, coalesced, coalescing**) come or combine together to form one whole. □ **coalescence** n. **coalescent** adj. [Say co a LESS, co a LESS unce, co a LESS unt]

coalfield n. an extensive area containing coal.

coalition n. a temporary alliance for combined action. [Say co a LISH'n]

coal tar n. a thick black sticky liquid distilled from coal.

coarse adj. (**coarser, coarsest**) **1** rough or loose in texture; made of large particles. **2** lacking refinement; crude. □ **coarsely** adv. **coarseness** n.

coarsen v. make or become coarse.

coast ● n. the land near the sea; the seashore. ● v. **1** ride or move, usu. downhill, without use of power. **2** make progress without much effort. □ **the coast is clear** there is no danger of being observed or caught. □ **coastal** adj.

coaster n. **1** a small mat for a glass. **2** a sled or toboggan. **3** a ship that travels along the coast from port to port.

coast guard n. (also **Coast Guard**) an organization whose responsibilities include patrolling coastal waters, rescue at sea or on major lakes etc.

coastline n. the line of the seashore.

Coast Salish n. = SNE NAY MUXW.

Coast Tsimshian n. **1** a member of the Tsimshian linguistic group living in northwestern BC. **2** the language of these people.

coat ● n. **1** an outer garment with sleeves. **2** an animal's fur, hair, etc. **3 a** an enclosing layer or covering. **b** a single application of paint etc. ● v. apply a coat of paint etc. to; provide with a layer or covering. □ **coated** adj.

coat check n. a place at a theatre, restaurant, etc. where coats, bags, etc. may be left with an attendant.

coat hanger n. = HANGER 2.

coating n. a thin layer or covering.

coat of arms n. (pl. **coats of arms**) a shield or other arrangement of the heraldic bearings of a person, family, government, etc.

coattail n. each of the flaps from the back of a tailcoat. □ **(riding) on the coattails of** undeservedly benefiting from.

co-author ● n. an author who collaborates with another. ● v. be a co-author of.

coax v. (**coaxes, coaxed, coaxing**) **1** persuade gradually or by flattery. **2** obtain by coaxing. **3** manipulate carefully or slowly. □ **coaxing** n. [Say COKES]

coaxial adj. **1** having a common axis. **2** Electricity (of a cable or line) transmitting by means of two concentric conductors separated by an insulator. [Say co AX ee ul]

cob n. **1** a corncob. **2** a sturdy horse with short legs.

cobalt n. a silvery-white magnetic metallic element, used in alloys and the radioisotope of which is is used in cancer treatment. [Say CO bawlt]

cobalt blue n. a deep-blue pigment containing a cobalt salt.

cobble¹ ● *n.* a small round stone, larger than a pebble. ● *v.* (**cobbles, cobbled, cobbling**) pave with cobblestones.

cobble² *v.* (**cobbles, cobbled, cobbling**) **1** mend or patch up. **2** assemble roughly.

cobbler *n.* **1** a person who mends shoes. **2** a baked dessert of fruit topped with a tea-biscuit crust.

cobblestone *n.* a small rounded stone used for paving.

cobra *n.* a venomous Asian and African snake which can dilate its neck to form a hood. [*Say* CO bra]

cobweb *n.* **1** a fine network of threads spun by a spider. **2** anything compared with a cobweb. □ **cobwebbed** *adj.* **cobwebby** *adj.*

coca *n.* a S American shrub, the dried leaves of which yield cocaine. [*Say* CO kuh]

cocaine *n.* a white crystalline narcotic derived from coca leaves.

cochlea *n.* (*pl.* **cochleae**) the spiral cavity of the internal ear. □ **cochlear** *adj.* [*Say* COCKLY uh *for the singular,* COCKLY ee *for the plural*]

cock ● *n.* **1** a male bird, esp. of a domestic fowl; a rooster. **2** a firing lever in a gun which can be raised to be released by the trigger. **3** *Curling* the position at the end of the rink at which rocks are aimed. **4** a tap or valve controlling flow. ● *v.* **1** raise. **2** turn or move (the eye or ear) attentively. **3** set aslant, or turn up the brim of (a hat). **4** raise the cock of (a gun).

cockade *n.* a rosette etc. worn in a hat as a badge of office etc. □ **cockaded** *adj.*

cock-a-doodle-doo *n.* a rooster's crow.

cockatiel *n.* (also **cockateel**) a small delicately coloured crested Australian parrot. [*Say* cocka TEEL]

cockatoo *n.* an Australian crested parrot.

cockerel *n.* a young rooster. [*Say* COCKER ul]

cocker spaniel *n.* a small breed of spaniel with a silky coat.

cockeyed *adj. informal* **1** crooked, askew. **2** absurd, not practical. **3** drunk. [*Say* COCK eyed]

cockfight *n.* a fight between pitted cocks, often fitted with metal spurs. □ **cockfighting** *n.*

cockle *n.* an edible mollusc with a ribbed bivalve shell. □ **warm the cockles of one's heart** make one contented.

cockney *n.* (*pl.* **cockneys**) **1** a native of the East End of London. **2** the dialect or accent typical of this area. □ **cockney** *adj.* [*Say* COCK nee]

cockpit *n.* **1 a** a compartment for the pilot and crew of an aircraft or spacecraft. **b** the driver's compartment in a race car. **2** a place where cockfights are held.

cockroach *n.* (*pl.* **cockroaches**) any of various flat brown insects resembling a beetle, which infest households etc.

cocksure *adj.* arrogantly confident.

cocktail *n.* **1** a usu. alcoholic drink made by mixing spirits, fruit juices, etc. **2** (in combination) an appetizer. **3** a dish of mixed ingredients. **4** a mixture of substances or factors. **5** a number of different drugs used together to treat a condition.

cocky *adj.* (**cockier, cockiest**) **1** conceited, arrogantly confident. **2** impudent. □ **cockiness** *n.*

coco *n.* (*pl.* **cocos**) (also **coconut palm**) a tropical palm tree bearing coconuts.

cocoa *n.* **1** a powder made from crushed cacao seeds. **2** a hot drink made from this. [*Say* COCO]

cocoa bean *n.* a cacao seed.

cocoa butter *n.* a fatty substance obtained from cocoa beans.

coconut *n.* **1** a large brown seed of the coco, with a hard shell, edible white flesh, and a milky juice. **2** the white flesh of a coconut. □ **coconutty** *adj.*

cocoon ● *n.* **1** a silky case spun by many insect larvae for protection as pupae. **2** anything which encloses or protects like a cocoon. ● *v.* wrap in or form a cocoon.

cocooning *n.* the practice of spending one's leisure time at home instead of going out. □ **cocooner** *n.*

COD *abbr.* **1** collect on delivery. **2** cash on delivery.

cod *n.* (*pl.* **cod**) a large marine food fish.

coda *n.* **1** *Music* the concluding passage of a piece or movement. **2** a concluding event. [*Say* CO duh]

coddle *v.* (**coddles, coddled, coddling**) **1** treat indulgently or over-attentively. **2** cook (an egg) in water below boiling point.

code ● *n.* **1** a pre-arranged system of words, letters, or symbols, used to represent others esp. to ensure secrecy. **2** a set of instructions written in a programming language. **3** a systematic collection of statutes. **4** a set of principles or rules of behaviour. ● *v.* (**codes, coded, coding**) put into code. □ **bring up to code** renovate an older building to make it conform to building code regulations. □ **coder** *n.*

codec *n.* a device that converts an analog signal into an encoded digital form, and

decodes digital signals into analog form.
[*Say* CO deck]

codeine *n.* an alkaloid derived from morphine and used to relieve pain.
[*Say* CO deen]

codependency *n.* excessive emotional or psychological dependence on supporting or caring for a partner.
□ **codependent** *n. & adj.*

code-sharing *n.* the practice of two airlines listing certain flights in a reservation system under each other's names. □ **code-share** *v. & n.*

codfish *n.* (*pl.* **codfish**) = COD.

codger *n.* (usu. in **old codger**) *informal* an esp. old or eccentric person.

codicil *n.* an addition explaining, modifying, or revoking a will or part of one. [*Say* CO duh sill]

codify *v.* (**codifies, codified, codifying**) arrange (laws etc.) systematically into a code. □ **codification** *n.* [*Say* CO duh fie, co duh fuh CAY sh'n]

coed *informal* ● *adj.* **1** coeducational. **2** open to both males and females. ● *n. dated* a female student at a coeducational institution. [*Say* CO ed]

coeducation *n.* the education of male and female students together.
□ **coeducational** *adj.*

coefficient *n.* **1** a quantity multiplying an algebraic expression. **2** *Physics* a multiplier or factor that measures some property.
[*Say* co EFFICIENT]

coerce *v.* (**coerces, coerced, coercing**) persuade or restrain by force.
[*Say* co URSS]

coercion *n.* the act or process of coercing.
□ **coercive** *adj.* **coercively** *adv.* **coerciveness** *n.* [*Say* co UR sh'n, co UR siv]

coeval ● *adj.* having the same age or date of origin. ● *n.* a person of roughly the same age; a contemporary. [*Say* co EVIL]

coexist *v.* **1** exist together. **2** (esp. of nations) exist in mutual tolerance.
□ **coexistence** *n.* **coexistent** *adj.*

co-extensive *adj.* extending over the same space, time, or limits.

coffee ● *n.* **1** a drink made from the roasted and ground seeds of a tropical shrub. **2 a** the shrub yielding these seeds. **b** these seeds. **3** a pale brown colour. ● *adj.* **1** coffee coloured. **2** flavoured with coffee.
□ **wake up and smell the coffee** become aware of realities.

coffee cake *n.* a type of cake or sweet bread with cinnamon sugar.

coffee house *n.* **1** a place serving coffee

and other refreshments. **2** a form of entertainment performed cabaret-style.

coffee shop *n.* a small informal restaurant serving simple meals and beverages.

coffee table *n.* a small low oblong table.

coffee-table book *n.* a large illustrated book for display.

coffer *n.* **1** a box, esp. for valuables. **2** (**coffers**) a treasury or store of funds.

coffin *n.* a long narrow box in which a corpse is buried or cremated.

cog *n.* **1** a wheel or shaft with teeth on its edge which transfers motion by engaging with another series. **2** a person who plays a minor role in an organization.
□ **cogged** *adj.*

cogeneration *n.* the utilization of otherwise wasted energy for heating etc.
[*Say* co GENERATION]

cogent *adj.* clear, logical, and convincing.
□ **cogency** *n.* **cogently** *adv.* [*Say* CO jint, CO jin see]

cogitate *v.* (**cogitates, cogitated, cogitating**) ponder, meditate.
□ **cogitation** *n.* [*Say* CODGE a tate]

cognac *n.* a high-quality brandy, distilled in Cognac in France. [*Say* CON yack *or* CONE yack]

cognate ● *adj.* **1** having the same linguistic family or derivation. **2** related; connected. ● *n.* a cognate word.
[*Say* COG nate]

cognition *n.* the process of acquiring knowledge through thought, experience, and the senses. [*Say* cog NISH'n]

cognitive *adj.* connected with cognition.
□ **cognitively** *adv.* [*Say* COG nuh tiv]

cognizance *n.* **1** knowledge or awareness. **2** *Law* the right of a court to deal with a matter. □ **cognizant** *adj.*
[*Say* COG nizz ince, COG nizz'nt]

cognoscenti *pl. n.* connoisseurs; discerning experts. [*Say* cog nuh SENTY *or* cog nuh SHENTY]

cogwheel *n.* = COG 1.

cohabit *v.* (**cohabits, cohabited, cohabiting**) **1** coexist. **2** live together in a sexual relationship without marriage.
□ **cohabitation** *n.*

cohere *v.* (**coheres, cohered, cohering**) **1** stick together, remain united. **2** be logical or consistent.

coherent *adj.* **1** able to speak intelligibly and articulately. **2** (of speech, an argument, etc.) logical and consistent. **3** forming a whole. □ **coherence** *n.* **coherently** *adv.*
[*Say* co HERE int]

cohesion *n.* **1** the action or fact of forming a united whole. **2** *Physics* the sticking together of particles of the same substance. □ **cohesive** *adj.* **cohesively** *adv.* **cohesiveness** *n.* [Say co HEE zh'n]

coho *n.* (*pl.* **coho** or **cohos**) a salmon of the north Pacific.

cohort *n.* **1** a companion. **2** a group of persons with a shared feature. **3** a band of warriors.

coif[1] *n.* a close-fitting cap, esp. as worn by nuns under a veil. [Say COYF]

coif[2] ● *n.* a hairstyle. ● *v.* (**coifs, coiffed, coiffing**) (usu. as **coiffed** *adj.*) arrange or style (hair). [Say KWOFF]

coiffure ● *n.* a hairstyle. ● *v.* (**coiffures, coiffured, coiffuring**) style (hair). □ **coiffured** *adj.* [Say kwoff YOOR]

coil ● *n.* **1** anything arranged in a joined sequence of loops. **2** a single turn of something coiled. **3 a** (in full **induction coil**) a coil for generating intermittent high voltage from a direct current. **b** any helix of wire through which electric current passes. ● *v.* **1** arrange in a series of concentric loops or rings. **2** twist or be twisted into a spiral shape.

coin ● *n.* **1** a piece of flat usu. round metal used as money. **2** metal money collectively. ● *v.* **1** invent (esp. a new word or phrase). **2** make (metal) into coins. □ **the other side of the coin** the opposite view of the matter. **to coin a phrase** *ironic* introducing a banal remark or cliché.

coinage *n.* **1** the act or process of coining. **2 a** coins collectively. **b** a system of coins in use. **3** a newly invented word or phrase.

coincide *v.* (**coincides, coincided, coinciding**) **1** occur at the same time or in the same place. **2** be in agreement. [Say co in SIDE]

coincidence *n.* a remarkable concurrence of events or circumstances without apparent causal connection. □ **coincidental** *adj.* **coincidentally** *adv.*

coincident *adj.* occurring together in space or time.

coitus *n.* sexual intercourse. □ **coital** *adj.* [Say COY tiss *or* CO it iss, COY tul *or* CO it ul]

coitus interruptus *n.* intercourse in which the penis is withdrawn before ejaculation. [Say inter RUP tiss]

coke[1] ● *n.* a solid substance left after the gases have been extracted from coal, used as fuel. ● *v.* (**cokes, coked, coking**) convert (coal) into coke.

coke[2] *n.* *slang* cocaine.

cokehead *n.* *slang* a person addicted to cocaine.

cola *n.* **1** a small west African tree, bearing seeds containing caffeine. **2** a sweet carbonated drink usu. flavoured with cola seeds.

colander *n.* a container with holes in it, used to drain foods. [Say COLL 'n der]

cold ● *adj.* **1** of or at a low or relatively low temperature. **2** not heated. **3** feeling cold. **4** lacking ardour, friendliness, etc. **5 a** dead. **b** *informal* unconscious. **6** (of a scent in hunting) weak. ● *n.* **1 a** the prevalence of a low temperature. **b** cold weather. **2** an infection, causing runny nose, sneezing, etc. ● *adv.* **1** completely. **2** not rehearsed. □ **cold (hard) cash** cash as opposed to credit. **in cold blood** without feeling; deliberately. **out in the cold** ignored, neglected. **throw** (or **pour**) **cold water on** be discouraging about. □ **coldly** *adv.* **coldness** *n.*

cold-blooded *adj.* **1** having a body temperature varying with that of the environment (e.g. of fish). **2** callous; cruel. □ **cold-bloodedly** *adv.*

cold call *n.* an unsolicited sales call to a prospective customer. □ **cold-call** *v.*

cold-cock *v.* *slang* punch in the head.

cold cuts *pl. n.* slices of cold cooked meats.

cold feet *pl. n.* *informal* loss of nerve or confidence.

cold fish *n.* an unfeeling person.

cold frame *n.* a box-shaped frame with a glass top, placed over plants to protect them.

cold front *n.* the forward edge of an advancing mass of cold air.

cold-hearted *adj.* lacking affection or warmth. □ **cold-heartedly** *adv.* **cold-heartedness** *n.*

cold shoulder ● *n.* a show of intentional unfriendliness. ● *v.* (**cold-shoulder**) be deliberately unfriendly to.

cold sore *n.* inflammation and blisters around the mouth, caused by a virus infection.

cold storage *n.* a state in which something (esp. an idea) is put aside temporarily.

cold sweat *n.* a state of sweating due to fear or illness.

cold turkey *informal* ● *n.* abrupt withdrawal from addictive drugs. ● *adv.* abruptly. □ **go cold turkey** cease completely and abruptly.

cold war *n.* **1** a state of prolonged hostility between nations short of armed conflict. **2** (**Cold War**) relations of this nature between the Soviet Union and the US and their respective allies in the decades following the Second World War. □ **Cold Warrior** *n.*

coleslaw *n.* a salad of shredded raw cabbage with a dressing. [*Say* COLE slaw]

colic *n.* **1** severe spasmodic abdominal pain. **2** a condition in young babies characterized by long, loud crying. □ **colicky** *adj.* [*Say* COLLICK]

coliform *adj.* of or pertaining to a group of bacteria which, when present in water, indicate fecal contamination. [*Say* COLLA form]

coliseum *n.* a large amphitheatre, stadium, etc.

colitis *n.* inflammation of the colon lining. [*Say* kuh LITE iss]

collaborate *v.* (**collaborates**, **collaborated**, **collaborating**) **1** work jointly. **2** co-operate traitorously with an enemy. □ **collaboration** *n.* **collaborationist** *n. & adj.* **collaborative** *adj.* **collaboratively** *adv.* **collaborator** *n.*

collage ● *n.* **1** a form of art in which various materials are arranged and glued to a backing. **2** a collection of unrelated things. ● *v.* (**collages**, **collaged**, **collaging**) arrange in a collage. [*Say* kuh LOZH]

collagen *n.* a protein found in animal connective tissue. [*Say* COLLA jin]

collapse ● *n.* **1** the falling down of a structure etc. **2** a sudden failure or breakdown. **3** a physical or mental breakdown. ● *v.* (**collapses**, **collapsed**, **collapsing**) **1** fall down or cause to fall down. **2** *informal* sit or lie down and relax. **3** (of furniture etc.) be foldable. □ **collapsible** *adj.*

collar ● *n.* **1** the part of a shirt etc. that goes around the neck. **2** a band of material worn around the neck. **3** a band put around the neck of an animal, esp. in order to control or identify it. ● *v.* **1** seize by the collar or neck. **2** capture, arrest. **3** *informal* detain. □ **collared** *adj.* **collarless** *adj.*

collarbone *n.* either of the two curved bones joining the breastbone and the shoulder blade.

collard *n.* (also **collards**, **collard greens**) a variety of cabbage without a distinct heart.

collate *v.* (**collates**, **collated**, **collating**) **1** sort (pages) in the correct order. **2** analyze and compare (texts etc.). **3** assemble from different sources. [*Say* CO late *or* kuh LATE]

collateral ● *n.* security pledged as a guarantee for repayment of a loan. ● *adj.* **1** side by side. **2** additional but subordinate. [*Say* kuh LATTER ul]

collateral damage *n.* injury to civilians as the unintended result of a military attack.

collation *n.* **1** the action of collating something. **2** a light informal meal. [*Say* co LAY sh'n *or* coll AY sh'n]

colleague *n.* a person with whom one works.

collect[1] ● *v.* **1** bring or come together. **2** seek and acquire (e.g. books, stamps) as a hobby. **3 a** demand or obtain (taxes etc.). **b** receive (a prize, payment, etc.). **4** come for and take away. **5 a** (**collect oneself**) regain control of oneself. **b** concentrate. ● *adj. & adv.* (of a telephone call etc.) to be paid for by the recipient.

collect[2] *n.* a short prayer, esp. one assigned to a particular day. [*Say* COLL ect]

collected *adj.* **1** calm; not perturbed. **2** (of literary works) gathered together in one publication.

collectible ● *adj.* worth collecting. ● *n.* an item sought by collectors.

collection *n.* **1** the act of collecting or being collected. **2** any group of things systematically assembled. **3** an accumulation. **4** the collecting of money. **5** the regular removal of mail, garbage, etc.

collective ● *adj.* **1** formed by or constituting a collection. **2** taken as a whole. **3** of or from several individuals; done by or belonging to all members of a group. ● *n.* **1** a co-operative enterprise. **2** (also **collective noun**) a noun that denotes a group of people. □ **collectively** *adv.*

collective agreement *n.* an agreement between a union and an employer.

collective bargaining *n.* the process by which wages etc. are negotiated by a union.

collective memory *n.* the memory of a group of people.

collectivism *n.* collective ownership of land and the means of production. □ **collectivist** *n.*

collectivity *n.* (*pl.* **collectivities**) a group of people bound together by common beliefs or interests. [*Say* coll eck TIVVA tee]

collectivize *v.* (**collectivizes**, **collectivized**, **collectivizing**) organize something on the basis of collective ownership. □ **collectivization** *n.* [*Say* kuh LECK tiv ize]

collector *n.* **1** a person who collects things of a particular type. **2** a person who collects payments etc. **3** a thing that collects. **4** *Cdn* a lane running parallel to the express lanes of a freeway.

college *n.* **1** an establishment for further or higher education or specialized instruction. **2** the buildings or premises of

a college. **3** an organized body of persons with shared functions and privileges.
□ **give a thing the (old) college try** put forth one's best effort.

collegial adj. **1** characterized by collaboration among colleagues. **2** pertaining to a body of colleagues. **3** of a college. □ **collegiality** n. **collegially** adv. [Say kuh LEE jul or kuh LEE jee ul, kuh lee jee ALA tee]

collegiate ● adj. **1** of or pertaining to colleges or universities. **2** constituted of or belonging to colleges. ● n. Cdn (also **collegiate institute**) (in some provinces) a public secondary school. [Say kuh LEE jit]

collide v. (**collides, collided, colliding**) **1** strike together with a violent impact. **2** be in conflict.

collie n. a sheepdog of a breed originating in Scotland, with a pointed nose and long hair.

collier n. a coal miner. [Say COLLY er]

colliery n. (pl. **collieries**) a coal mine. [Say COLL yuh ree]

collision n. **1** an instance of colliding. **2** the clashing of opposed interests.

colloquial adj. used in ordinary or familiar conversation. □ **colloquially** adv. [Say kuh LOKE wee ul, kuh LO kwee ul ee]

colloquialism n. a colloquial word or phrase. [Say kuh LOKE wee ul ism]

colloquium n. (pl. **colloquia**) an academic conference. [Say kuh LOKE wee um]

collude v. (**colludes, colluded, colluding**) conspire together esp. for a fraudulent purpose. [Say kuh LOOD]

collusion n. a secret agreement. [Say kuh LOO zh'n]

cologne n. a dilute solution of alcohol and perfume. [Say kuh LONE]

colon[1] n. a punctuation mark (:) used before a list, a quotation, etc. [Say CO lun]

colon[2] n. the lower part of the large intestine, from the cecum to the rectum. □ **colonic** adj. [Say CO lun, kuh LONNICK]

colonel n. (in Canada and the US) an officer in the armed forces ranking above a lieutenant colonel. [Say KER nul]

colonial ● adj. **1 a** of or relating to a colony or colonies. **b** typical of people living in a colony or former colony. **2** of or relating to the period of a nation's history during which it was under the rule of a mother country. ● n. a person inhabiting a colony.

colonialism n. **1** a policy of acquiring or maintaining colonies. **2** the exploitation of

a people by a larger or wealthier power. □ **colonialist** n. & adj.

colonist n. a settler in or inhabitant of a colony.

colonize v. (**colonizes, colonized, colonizing**) **1** establish a colony in. **2** establish or join a colony. **3** impose a culture on. **4** become established. □ **colonization** n. **colonizer** n.

colonnade n. a row of columns, esp. supporting a roof etc. □ **colonnaded** adj. [Say colla NADE]

colonoscopy n. (pl. **colonoscopies**) a procedure in which an illuminated fibre optic tube is used to examine the colon. [Say col uh NOSCA pee]

colony n. (pl. **colonies**) **1** a group of people who settle in a new territory while retaining ties with a mother country. **2** any country or area subject to colonial rule. **3** a group of people of common nationality, religion, etc. inhabiting a particular area. **4** a group which is segregated from a larger population. **5** a community of plants or animals living close together.

color etc. = COLOUR etc.

coloration n. (also **colouration**) colouring. [Say colour AY sh'n]

coloratura n. **1** elaborate ornamentation of a vocal melody. **2** a singer skilled in this method of singing. [Say colour a TURA]

colossal adj. extremely large. □ **colossally** adv. [Say kuh LOSS ul]

colossus n. (pl. **colossi**) **1** a gigantic person, statue, etc. **2** an extremely powerful person. [Say kuh LOSS iss for the singular, kuh LOSS eye for the plural]

colostomy n. (pl. **colostomies**) an operation on the colon to make an opening in the abdominal wall to provide an artificial anus. [Say kuh LOSS tuh mee]

colour (also **color**) ● n. **1 a** the sensation produced on the eye by rays of light when resolved into different wavelengths. **b** the perception of colour by the eye. **2** one, or any mixture, of the constituents into which light can be separated. **3** a colouring substance. **4** the use of all colours in photography, television, etc. **5** analysis etc. provided by a sports broadcaster as a supplement to the play-by-play. **6** pigmentation of the skin as an indication of race. **7** ruddiness of complexion. **8** distinctive character or timbre. ● v. **1** apply colour to. **2** influence. **3** misrepresent. **4** blush. □ **show one's true colours** reveal one's true character. **under false colours** falsely, deceitfully.

colouration n. = COLORATION.

colour-blind adj. **1** unable to distinguish

certain colours. **2** showing no racial bias.
□ **colour-blindness** n.

coloured (also **colored**) ● adj. **1** having colour(s). **2** (also **Coloured**) offensive wholly or partly of non-white descent. ● n. (also **Coloured**) offensive a coloured person.

colourfast adj. (also **colorfast**) dyed in colours that will not fade or be washed out.

colourful adj. (also **colorful**) **1** having much or varied colour. **2** vivid, lively.
□ **colourfully** adv.

colouring n. (also **coloring**) **1** the act or process of using colour(s). **2** the style in which a thing is coloured. **3 a** facial complexion. **b** natural colour. **4** an artificial colouring agent.

colourize v. (**colourizes, colourized, colourizing**) (also **colorize, colorizes, colorized, colorizing**) colour by means of a computer.

colourless adj. (also **colorless**) **1** without colour. **2** lacking character or interest. **3** dull or pale.
□ **colourlessly** adv.

colt n. **1** a young male horse that has not been castrated. **2** a young, inexperienced person. □ **coltish** adj.

columbine n. a garden plant with pointed blue, pink, or yellow flowers.
[Say CAWL um bine]

column n. **1** an upright pillar supporting a structure or standing alone as a monument. **2** something resembling a column. **3** a vertical division of a page, chart, etc. **4** a part of a newspaper regularly devoted to a particular subject. **5** an arrangement of troops in successive lines.
□ **columnar** adj. **columned** adj.
[Say CAWL um, cawl UM ner]

columnist n. a journalist contributing a regular column to a newspaper etc.
[Say COLL um nist]

coma n. (pl. **comas**) a prolonged deep unconsciousness.

comatose adj. **1** in a coma. **2** drowsy, sleepy. [Say CO muh toce]

comb ● n. **1** a toothed strip of rigid material for tidying and arranging the hair. **2** a device or part of a machine having a similar design or purpose. **3** the red fleshy crest of a fowl, esp. a rooster. ● v. **1** arrange or tidy by drawing a comb through. **2** search thoroughly. □ **comb out 1** tidy and arrange with a comb. **2** remove with a comb.

combat ● n. **1** a fight or contest. **2** an armed encounter with enemy forces (also as an adj.). ● v. (**combats, combatted, combatting**) fight.

combatant ● n. a person engaged in fighting. ● adj. **1** fighting. **2** for fighting.
[Say com BAT'nt]

combative adj. ready or eager to fight.
□ **combativeness** n. [Say k'm BAT iv]

combination n. **1** the act of combining two or more things. **2** a combined state. **3** a combined set of things or people. **4** a sequence of numbers or letters used to open a lock.

combine ● v. (**combines, combined, combining**) **1** join or mix together. **2** possess together. **3** co-operate. **4** harvest by means of a combine. ● n. **1** a combination of esp. commercial interests to control prices etc. **2** a self-propelled machine that reaps and threshes in one operation.

combined adj. **1** united. **2** performed by a group acting together.

combo n. (pl. **combos**) informal **1** a small jazz or dance band. **2** any combination.

comb-over n. a men's hairstyle in which the hair is grown long on the sides then combed over the top of the head to cover a bald spot.

combust v. burn or be burned by fire.
[Say kum BUST]

combustible ● adj. capable of or used for burning. ● n. a combustible substance.
[Say kum BUST a bull]

combustion n. **1** burning. **2** the production of heat from the chemical combination of a substance with oxygen.
[Say kum BUS ch'n]

come v. (**comes**; past **came**; past participle **come**; **coming**) **1** move towards or reach a place. **2** reach or be brought to a specified situation. **3** reach or extend to a specified point. **4** traverse or accomplish. **5** occur, happen. **6** take or occupy a specified position. **7** become perceptible or available. **8** become. **9 a** be descended from; originate from. **b** be the result of. □ **come about** happen. **come across 1** be effective or understood. **2** slang hand over. **3** find by chance. **come again** informal **1** make a further effort. **2** (as imper.) what did you say? **come along 1** arrive, appear. **2** make progress. **3** (as imper.) hurry up. **come back 1** return. **2** become fashionable again. **3** reply, retort. **come by 1** pass. **2** call on. **3** acquire, obtain. **come forward 1** advance. **2** offer one's help, services, etc. **come in 1** enter. **2** take a specified position in a race etc. **3 a** have a useful role or function. **b** prove to be. **4** be received. **come into** receive, esp. as heir. **come off 1** informal succeed. **2** turn out. **come off it** informal an expression of disbelief. **come on 1** continue to come. **2** advance; make progress. **3** begin.

4 expressing encouragement. **5** = COME UPON. **6** make sexual advances to. **come out 1** become known. **2** appear or be published. **3 a** declare oneself; make a decision. **b** openly declare one's homosexuality. **4** make one's debut. **5** be covered with. **6** be solved. **come round 1** pay an informal visit. **2** recover consciousness. **3** be converted to another person's opinion. **come through 1** be successful. **2** survive or overcome. **3** provide support etc. when needed. **come to** recover consciousness. **come to hand** become available. **come to pass** happen, occur. **come to that** informal in fact. **come under 1** be classified as or among. **2** be subject to. **come up 1** come to a place or position regarded as higher. **2** attain wealth or position. **3 a** arise. **b** occur, happen. **4** approach. **5** match (a standard etc.). **6** produce (an idea etc.). **come up against** be faced with. **come upon 1** meet or find by chance. **2** attack by surprise. **have it coming to one** informal be about to get what one deserves. **how come?** informal why? **not know if one is coming or going** be confused from being very busy. **where a person is coming from** a person's meaning, intention, or personality.

comeback n. **1** a return to a previous state. **2** informal a retaliation or retort.

comedian n. **1** a humorous entertainer. **2** an actor in comedy.

comedienne n. a female comedian. [Say kuh meedy EN]

comedown n. **1** a loss of status; decline or degradation. **2** a disappointment. **3** a lessening of the sensations generated by a narcotic drug as its effects wear off.

comedy n. (pl. **comedies**) **1** a play, film, etc., of an amusing or satirical character. **2** an amusing incident in everyday life. **3** humour, esp. in a work of art etc. □ **comedic** adj. [Say COMMA dee, kuh MEE dick]

come-hither adj. informal enticing, flirtatious.

comely adj. (**comelier**, **comeliest**) pleasant to look at. □ **comeliness** n. [Say KUM lee, KUM lee niss]

come-on n. informal **1** something intended to attract or persuade. **2** a remark etc. intended to allure someone sexually.

comer n. **1** a person who comes. **2** informal a person likely to be a success. [Say KUMMER]

comet n. a mass of ice and dust with a long tail, moving about the sun in an eccentric orbit. □ **cometary** adj.

comeuppance n. informal one's deserved fate. [Say come UP ince]

comfort ● n. **1** consolation. **2 a** a state of physical well-being. **b** something that makes life pleasant. **3** a cause of satisfaction. **4** a person who helps one. ● v. console. □ **comforting** adj. **comfortingly** adv. **comfortless** adj.

comfortable adj. **1** giving ease. **2** free from discomfort. **3** informal free from financial concern. **4** with a wide margin. □ **comfortableness** n. **comfortably** adv.

comforter n. **1** someone who comforts. **2** a warm quilt.

comfort zone n. **1** the immediate area around a person. **2** a range of action etc. with which a person feels comfortable.

comfrey n. (pl. **comfreys**) a herb with clusters of usu. white or purple flowers. [Say KUM free]

comfy adj. (**comfier**, **comfiest**) informal comfortable. [Say KUM fee]

comic ● adj. **1** of, or in the style of, comedy. **2** causing or meant to cause laughter. ● n. **1** a professional comedian. **2 a** (**comics**) a section of a newspaper containing comic strips. **b** = COMIC BOOK.

comical adj. causing laughter. □ **comically** adv.

comic book n. a book etc. containing a narrative told through comic strips.

comic relief n. comic episodes in a play etc. intended to offset more serious portions.

comic strip n. a horizontal series of drawings in a comic book, newspaper, etc., usu. telling a story.

coming ● adj. **1** approaching, next. **2** of potential importance. ● n. arrival; approach. □ **coming and going** (or **comings and goings**) activity, esp. intense.

comma n. a punctuation mark (,) indicating a pause between parts of a sentence, or dividing items in a list.

command ● v. **1** give an order. **2** have authority over. **3 a** restrain, master. **b** have at one's disposal (resources etc.). **4** deserve and get (respect etc.). **5** look down over. ● n. **1** an authoritative order. **2** mastery, control. **3** authority, esp. naval or military. **4** Military Cdn one of the three divisions of the Canadian Forces. **5** an instruction causing a computer to perform one of its basic functions.

commandant n. a commanding officer. [Say COMMON dont or common DANT]

command economy n. an economy

which relies on the direction of a central governing body.

commandeer v. **1** seize for military purposes. **2** take possession of without authority.

commander n. a person who commands, esp. a naval officer next in rank below captain. Abbreviation: **Cdr**.

commander-in-chief n. (pl. **commanders-in-chief**) the supreme commander, esp. of a nation's forces.

commanding adj. **1** dignified, exalted. **2** giving a wide view. **3** controlling; superior. □**commandingly** adv.

commanding officer n. the officer in command of a military unit. Abbreviation: **CO**.

commandment n. a command from God.

commando n. (pl. **commandos**) **1** a soldier specially trained for carrying out raids. **2** a unit of such soldiers.

commemorate v. (**commemorates**, **commemorated**, **commemorating**) **1** preserve in memory by some celebration. **2** be a memorial of. □**commemoration** n. [Say kuh MEMMA rate]

commemorative adj. intended to commemorate a person or event. [Say kuh MEMMA ruh tiv]

commence v. (**commences**, **commenced**, **commencing**) formal begin.

commencement n. formal **1** a beginning. **2** a ceremony for the conferral of diplomas.

commend v. **1** entrust. **2** praise. **3** recommend. **4** (**commend itself**) find favour with.

commendable adj. praiseworthy. □**commendably** adv.

commendation n. **1** praise. **2** an award etc. giving public praise. [Say com en DAY sh'n]

commensurate adj. corresponding in size or degree; in proportion. □**commensurately** adv. [Say kuh MEN sur it]

comment ● n. a remark etc. conveying an opinion, criticism, etc. ● v. make (esp. critical) remarks.

commentary n. (pl. **commentaries**) **1** a set of explanatory notes on a text etc. **2** a descriptive spoken account of an event or a performance as it happens. **3** something that serves to illustrate or exemplify something.

commentator n. a person who provides or writes commentaries.

commerce n. buying and selling, esp. on a large scale.

commercial ● adj. **1** of, engaged in, or concerned with, commerce. **2** relating to the production of esp. foodstuffs on an industrial scale. **3** (of radio or television) funded by broadcast advertising. **4** (of an airline etc.) suitable for business or commerce; not private. ● n. a television or radio advertisement. □**commercially** adv. [Say kuh MER sh'll, COMMERCIAL ee]

commercialism n. **1** the principles and practice of commerce. **2** emphasis on financial profit as a measure of worth.

commercialize v. (**commercializes**, **commercialized**, **commercializing**) manage or exploit in a way designed to make a profit. □**commercialization** n. **commercialized** adj. [Say COMMERCIAL ize]

commie slang derogatory communist.

commingle v. (**commingles**, **commingled**, **commingling**) mingle together. [Say kuh MINGLE]

commiserate v. (**commiserates**, **commiserated**, **commiserating**) express or feel pity. □**commiseration** n. [Say kuh MIZZER ate]

commissary n. (pl. **commissaries**) **1** a deputy or delegate. **2** a store for the sale of food etc., esp. to soldiers. [Say COMMA serry]

commission ● n. **1 a** the authority to perform certain duties. **b** an instruction, command, or duty. **2** an order for something to be produced specially. **3** Military a warrant conferring the rank of officer. **4 a** the authority to act as agent for a company. **b** a percentage paid to the agent for selling goods etc. **5** the act of committing. ● v. **1** authorize. **2** give a commission to. **3 a** Military appoint by means of a commission. **b** prepare for active service. **4** bring into operation. □**out of commission** not in service, not working.

commissioner n. **1** a person appointed by, or as a member of, a commission. **2** a representative of the supreme authority in an area etc. **3** (in the OPP and RCMP) the highest ranking officer. **4** a person appointed by an athletic league etc. to perform various administrative and judicial functions.

commit v. (**commits**, **committed**, **committing**) **1** entrust for: **a** safekeeping. **b** treatment. **2** perpetrate (esp. a crime). **3** pledge to a certain course. **4** consign (a person) to a mental hospital, prison, etc. □**commit to memory** memorize.

commitment n. **1** a promise. **2** an engagement or obligation that restricts freedom of action. **3** the willingness to work hard etc.; dedication.

committal *n.* the act of committing a person, esp. to a prison or a mental hospital.

committed *adj.* **1** dedicated to a cause or belief. **2** obliged (to take a certain action).

committee *n.* a body of persons elected or appointed for a specific function from a larger body.

commode *n.* **1** a chest of drawers. **2** a piece of furniture containing a chamber pot. **3** *informal* a toilet. [*Say* kuh MODE]

commodification *n.* the action of turning something into or treating something as a (mere) commodity. □ **commodify** *v.* (**commodifies, commodified, commodifying**) [*Say* kuh modda fuh KAY sh'n, kuh MODDA fie]

commodious *adj.* roomy and comfortable. [*Say* kuh MOADY us]

commodity *n.* (*pl.* **commodities**) **1** a raw material or product that can be bought and sold. **2** a useful thing. [*Say* kuh MODDA tee]

commodore *n.* **1** a naval officer ranking above captain and below rear admiral. **2** the commander of a squadron of vessels. [*Say* COMMA dore]

common ● *adj.* (**commoner, commonest**) **1 a** occurring often. **b** ordinary. **2 a** shared by more than one. **b** affecting the whole community. **3** *derogatory* vulgar. **4** of the most familiar type. ● *n.* **1** (**the Commons**) = HOUSE OF COMMONS. **2** a piece of land set aside for public use. □ **common or garden** *informal* ordinary. **in common 1** in joint use; shared. **2** of joint interest.

commonality *n.* (*pl.* **commonalities**) **1** the sharing of features. **2** a shared feature. [*Say* common ALA tee]

common carrier *n.* a person or company undertaking to transport goods or persons in a specified category.

common denominator *n.* **1** *Math* a common multiple of the denominators of several fractions. **2** a common feature of members of a group.

commoner *n.* one of the common people, as opposed to the aristocracy.

common ground *n.* a view accepted by both sides in a dispute.

common law *n.* **1** law derived from custom and judicial precedent rather than statutes (*compare* CASE LAW, STATUTE LAW). **2** a relationship between cohabiting but unmarried partners, recognized as a marriage in some jurisdictions.

commonly *adv.* usually.

common market *n.* a group of countries imposing few duties on trade with one another.

common noun *n.* (also **common name**) *Grammar* a noun denoting a thing as opposed to a particular individual, e.g. *boy, beauty*.

commonplace ● *adj.* ordinary; trite. ● *n.* **1** an everyday saying. **2** anything usual or trite

common sense ● *n.* sound practical sense, esp. in everyday matters. ● *adj.* = COMMONSENSICAL.

commonsensical *adj.* having or showing common sense. [*Say* common SENSE ick ul]

common share *n.* (also **common stock**) an ordinary capital share in a company, yielding a flexible dividend (*compare* PREFERRED SHARE).

commonwealth *n.* **1** a community of people viewed as a political entity. **2** (**Commonwealth**) (also **the Commonwealth of Nations**) an international association comprising members of the former British Empire.

commotion *n.* noisy disturbance or confusion.

communal *adj.* **1** relating or belonging to a community. **2** of or relating to a commune. □ **communally** *adv.* [*Say* kuh MYOON ul]

commune[1] *n.* a group of people who live together and share responsibilities, possessions, etc. [*Say* COM yoon]

commune[2] *v.* (**communes, communed, communing**) **1** speak confidentially and intimately. **2** feel in close touch. [*Say* kuh MYOON]

communicable *adj.* (of a disease) able to be passed on. [*Say* kuh MYOON ick a bull]

communicate *v.* (**communicates, communicated, communicating**) **1 a** transmit or pass on (information). **b** transmit (heat, motion, disease, etc.). **2** succeed in evoking understanding etc. **3** (of a room etc.) have a common connecting door. □ **communicator** *n.*

communication *n.* **1 a** the action of communicating. **b** a letter or message. **c** the means of sending or receiving information. **2** (in *pl.*) the science, practice, or study of transmitting information.

communicative *adj.* **1** talkative, informative. **2** ready to communicate.

communion *n.* **1** the sharing of intimate thoughts and feelings. **2** the common participation in a mental or spiritual experience. **3** (also **Communion**) (also **Holy Communion**) the service of Christian worship at which bread and wine are consecrated and shared. **4** a relationship of recognition between Christian denominations.

communiqué n. an official communication. [Say kuh MYOON a kay]

communism n. **1** a system of society with the state controlling the means of production and members contributing or receiving according to their abilities and needs. **2** (usu. **Communism**) a system of this kind derived from Marxism. □ **communist** n. **communistic** adj.

community n. (pl. **communities**) **1 a** all the people living in a specific locality. **b** a specific locality. **2** a body of people with a common religion, profession, etc. **3** fellowship of interests etc.; similarity. **4** joint ownership. **5** (**the community**) the public.

community access n. Cdn a type of television programming that is made available to community groups or members of the public.

community centre n. a place providing social and recreational facilities for a neighbourhood.

community college n. a post-secondary institution offering training esp. in specific employment fields.

community hall n. Cdn a hall maintained by a community for community events.

community service n. work, esp. voluntary and unpaid, in the community, esp. as performed as part of a judicial sentence.

commute ● v. (**commutes**, **commuted**, **commuting**) **1** travel to and from one's daily work. **2** Law change (a sentence etc.) to another less severe. **3** change (one thing) for another. ● n. **1** an act of commuting. **2** a distance travelled by a commuter. □ **commuter** n. [Say kuh MUTE, kuh MUTE er]

Comox n. (pl. **Comox** or **Comoxes**) **1** a member of an Aboriginal group living on Vancouver Island. **2** the Salishan language of this people. [Say CO mox]

comp n. informal **1** a competition. **2** a complimentary ticket, pass, etc. **3** a comprehensive examination. **4** compensation.

compact[1] ● adj. **1** closely or neatly packed together. **2** well-fitted and practical though small. **3** (of style etc.) condensed; brief. **4** small but well-proportioned. **5** designating a car larger than a subcompact and smaller than a mid-size. ● v. press firmly together. ● n. **1** a small, flat case for face powder, a mirror, etc. **2** a compact car. □ **compaction** n.

compactly adv. **compactness** n. **compactor** n.

compact[2] n. a formal agreement.

compact disc n. a disc on which information or sound is recorded digitally.

companion n. **1 a** a person who associates or shares with another. **b** a person employed to live with and assist another. **2** a handbook on a particular subject. **3** a thing that matches another. **4** (**Companion**) a member of the highest grade of the Order of Canada. □ **companionable** adj. **companionship** n.

company n. (pl. **companies**) **1 a** a number of people assembled. **b** guests or a guest. **2** companionship. **3** a commercial business. **4** a group of performers. **5** a subdivision of an infantry battalion. □ **be in good company** discover that others have done the same as oneself. **in company** not alone. **keep a person company** accompany a person. **part company 1** separate. **2 a** cease to associate. **b** disagree.

company town n. a town that is dependent upon one company for its employment etc.

comparable adj. **1** fit or able to be compared. **2** similar. □ **comparably** adv. [Say COMP er a bull or COMPARE a bull]

comparative ● adj. **1** perceptible or judged by comparison; relative. **2** of or involving comparison. **3** (of an adjective or adverb) expressing a higher degree of a quality, but not the highest possible (e.g. braver). ● n. the comparative form of an adjective or adverb. □ **comparatively** adv. [Say COMPARE a tiv]

compare v. (**compares**, **compared**, **comparing**) **1** express or estimate the similarities in; liken. **2** bear comparison. **3** be equal or equivalent to. □ **beyond compare** greatly superior. **compare notes** exchange ideas or opinions.

comparison n. **1** an action or instance of comparing. **2** an analogy. **3** the quality of being similar or equivalent. **4** the formation of the comparative and superlative forms of adjectives and adverbs. □ **bear** (or **stand**) **comparison** be able to be compared favourably. **beyond comparison 1** totally different in quality. **2** greatly superior.

compartment n. a separate space within a larger space. □ **compartmental** adj.

compartmentalize v. (**compartmentalizes**, **compartmentalized**, **compartmentalizing**) divide into compartments or categories.

compass n. (pl. **compasses**) **1** (also **magnetic compass**) an instrument showing the direction of magnetic north. **2** an instrument for taking measurements and drawing circles. **3** area, extent; scope.

compassion n. sympathetic pity and concern for the sufferings of others.

compassionate adj. feeling or showing compassion. □ **compassionately** adv.

compatible ● adj. **1 a** able to coexist; well-suited. **b** consistent. **2** capable of being used in combination. ● n. (usu. in comb.) Computing a piece of equipment that can use software etc. designed for another brand of equipment. □ **compatibility** n.

compatriot n. a person of the same country or region. [Say kum PAY tree it]

compel v. (**compels**, **compelled**, **compelling**) **1** force, constrain. **2** bring about by force.

compelling adj. arousing strong interest or admiration. □ **compellingly** adv.

compendium n. (pl. **compendiums** or **compendia**) a collection of detailed items of information. [Say kum PENDY um]

compensate v. (**compensates**, **compensated**, **compensating**) **1** provide something good to balance or reduce the bad effects of damage, loss, etc.; make up for. **2** act so as to neutralize or correct a deficiency, disability, etc.

compensation n. **1 a** the act of compensating. **b** the process of being compensated. **2** something given as a recompense. **3** a salary or wages.

compensatory adj. **1** providing or effecting compensation. **2** (of a payment) intended to compensate someone. **3** reducing or offsetting unpleasant effects. [Say kum PENSA tory]

compete v. (**competes**, **competed**, **competing**) **1** strive for superiority or supremacy. **2** take part (in a contest etc.).

competence n. (also **competency** pl. **competencies**) **1** ability; the state of being competent. **2** Law legal capacity to deal with a matter. [Say COMPA tince]

competent adj. **1 a** adequately qualified or capable. **b** effective. **2** Law legally qualified or qualifying. □ **competently** adv. [Say COMPA tint]

competition n. **1** the activity of competing with others. **2** an event or contest in which people compete. **3** the person, people, or products with which or whom one is competing.

competitive adj. **1** having to do with competition. **2** (of prices etc.) low enough to compete with rival products etc. **3** (of a

person) having a strong urge to win. □ **competitively** adv. **competitiveness** n.

competitor n. **1** a person who competes. **2** a rival, esp. in business.

compilation n. **1** the act of compiling. **2** something compiled, esp. a book etc. [Say compa LAY sh'n]

compile v. (**compiles**, **compiled**, **compiling**) **1** collect material into a list, volume, etc. **2** produce (a machine-coded form of a high-level program). □ **compiler** n.

complacency n. (also **complacence**) a feeling of satisfaction with oneself or with a situation. □ **complacent** adj. **complacently** adv. [Say kum PLAY sun see, kum PLAY sint]

complain v. **1** express dissatisfaction. **2** announce that one is suffering from (an ailment). □ **complainer** n.

complainant n. a plaintiff in certain lawsuits.

complaint n. **1** an act of complaining. **2** a grievance. **3** an ailment or illness.

complement ● n. **1 a** a thing that contributes extra features to something else so as to improve it. **b** one of a pair, or one of two things that go together. **2** (often **full complement**) the number required to make a group complete. **3** a word or phrase added to a verb to complete the predicate of a sentence. ● v. **1** complete. **2** form a complement to.

complementarity n. (pl. **complementarities**) a complementary relationship or situation. [Say compla men TARE a tee]

complementary adj. combining in such a way as to form a complete whole or to improve each other.

complete ● adj. **1** having all its parts. **2** finished. **3** of the maximum extent or degree. ● v. (**completes**, **completed**, **completing**) **1** finish. **2** make whole or perfect. **3** fill in the answers to. □ **complete with** having (as an accessory). □ **completed** adj. **completely** adv. **completeness** n. **completion** n.

complex ● n. (pl. **complexes**) **1** a building, network, etc. made up of related parts. **2** a group of usu. repressed feelings which cause abnormal behaviour or mental states. **3** a preoccupation or obsession. ● adj. **1** consisting of related parts. **2** complicated. □ **complexity** n. **complexly** adv.

complexion n. **1** the condition of the skin, esp. of the face. **2** an aspect; a character. □ **complexioned** adj.

compliance *n.* the action or practice of complying. [*Say* kum PLY unce]

compliant *adj.* **1** ready to agree with others or obey rules, esp. excessively **2** complying with rules or standards. □ **compliantly** *adv.* [*Say* kum PLY unt]

complicate *v.* (**complicates, complicated, complicating**) make or become difficult or confusing.

complicated *adj.* complex; intricate.

complication *n.* **1 a** an involved or confused state. **b** a difficulty. **2** a secondary disease or condition aggravating a previous one.

complicity *n.* partnership in a crime or wrongdoing. □ **complicit** *adj.* [*Say* kum PLISS it ee, kum PLISS it]

compliment ● *n.* **1** an expression of praise. **2** (in *pl.*) **a** formal greetings. **b** praise. ● *v.* congratulate; praise. **compliments of 1** given free of charge. **2** usu. *ironic* thanks to. **pay a compliment to** praise.

complimentary *adj.* **1** praising. **2** free of charge.

comply *v.* (**complies, complied, complying**) act in accordance (with a wish, command, rule, etc.).

component ● *n.* a part of a larger whole. ● *adj.* being part of a larger whole. □ **componentry** *n.*

comport *v. formal* conduct oneself; behave. □ **comportment** *n.* [*Say* kum PORT, kum PORT m'nt]

compose *v.* (**composes, composed, composing**) **1** construct or create (a work of art, esp. poetry or music). **2** constitute; make up. **3** put together to form a whole. **4** (**compose oneself**) calm; settle.

composed *adj.* calm; in control of one's feelings.

composer *n.* a person who composes (esp. music).

composite ● *adj.* **1** made up of various parts. **2** denoting plants of the daisy family. ● *n.* a thing made up of several parts. [*Say* COMPA zit]

composite index *n.* a stock market index based on the performance of a selection of stocks.

composition *n.* **1 a** the act of putting together; formation. **b** something composed; a mixture. **2 a** a literary or musical work. **b** the act of composing. **c** the craft of writing. **d** an artistic arrangement. □ **compositional** *adj.* **compositionally** *adv.*

compost ● *n.* decayed organic matter used to fertilize soil. ● *v.* **1** treat (soil) with compost. **2** make into compost. □ **compostable** *adj. & n.*

composter *n.* (also **compost bin**) a container used to create compost.

composure *n.* calmness; self-control. [*Say* kum POE zhur]

compote *n.* fruit preserved or cooked in syrup. [*Say* COM pote *or* COM pot]

compound ● *n.* **1** a mixture of two or more elements. **2** (also **compound word**) a word made up of two or more existing words. **3** *Chemistry* a substance formed from two or more elements chemically united in fixed proportions. **4** an enclosed area. ● *adj.* **1** made up or consisting of several parts. **2** combined; collective. ● *v.* **1** mix or combine. **2** increase or complicate. **3** make up (a composite whole). **4** increase by compound interest.

compound eye *n.* an eye consisting of numerous visual units, as found in insects.

compound fracture *n.* a fracture in which a broken bone pierces the skin.

compound interest *n.* interest payable on capital and its accumulated interest.

comprehend *v.* **1** grasp mentally; understand (a person or a thing). **2** include; encompass.

comprehensible *adj.* that can be understood. □ **comprehensibly** *adv.*

comprehension *n.* the act or capability of understanding, esp. writing or speech.

comprehensive ● *adj.* **1** complete; including all or nearly all aspects. **2** (of motor vehicle insurance) providing complete protection. ● *n.* (also **comprehensive examination**) a test of one's learning or proficiency in all aspects of a subject. □ **comprehensively** *adv.* **comprehensiveness** *n.*

compress ● *v.* (**compresses, compressed, compressing**) **1** squeeze together. **2** bring into a smaller space or shorter extent. **3** *Computing* condense (data etc.) for easier storage. ● *n.* a cloth or ice pack etc. pressed onto part of the body to relieve inflammation, stop bleeding, etc. □ **compressible** *adj.*

compressed air *n.* air at more than atmospheric pressure.

compression *n.* **1** the act of compressing or being compressed. **2** the reduction in volume (causing an increase in pressure) of the fuel mixture in an internal combustion engine before ignition.

compressor *n.* an instrument or device for compressing.

comprise *v.* (**comprises, comprised, comprising**) **1** consist of, be composed of. **2** make up, compose.

compromise ● *n.* **1** the settlement of a

dispute by each side making concessions. **2** an intermediate state between two things. **3** the acceptance of standards that are lower than desirable. ● v. (**compromises, compromised, compromising**) **1** settle a dispute by mutual concession. **2** bring into disrepute or danger. **3** do something that is against one's principles. **4** weaken (a reputation or principle) by accepting standards that are lower than is desirable. **5** accept standards that are lower than desirable for the sake of expediency. □ **compromiser** n.

comptroller n. (also **controller**) someone in charge of financial affairs. [*Sounds like* CONTROLLER *or like* komp TROLL ur]

compulsion n. **1** the action of compelling. **2** an irresistible urge to do something.

compulsive adj. resulting from or acting on an irresistible urge. □ **compulsively** adv. **compulsiveness** n.

compulsory ● adj. required by law or a rule. ● n. (pl. **compulsories**) (also **compulsory figure**) a specified move that must be performed as a component of a figure skating or synchronized swimming competition.

compunction n. a feeling of guilt that prevents or follows wrongdoing. [*Say* kum PUNK sh'n]

computation n. **1** mathematical calculation. **2** the use of computers. □ **computational** adj.

compute v. (**computes, computed, computing**) **1** reckon or calculate. **2** *informal* make sense. □ **computable** adj.

computer n. an electronic device for storing and processing data.

computer graphics n. visual images produced by means of a computer.

computerize v. (**computerizes, computerized, computerizing**) organize with or convert to a system using computers. □ **computerization** n. **computerized** adj.

computerized axial tomography n. tomography in which the X-ray scanner makes many sweeps of the body to give a cross-sectional image. Abbreviation: **CAT**.

computer language n. any of numerous systems for writing computer programs.

computing n. the use or operation of computers.

comrade n. **1 a** a workmate, friend, or companion. **b** (also **comrade-in-arms**) a fellow soldier etc. **2** a fellow socialist or communist. □ **comradely** adj. **comradeship** n.

con¹ *informal* ● n. **1** a swindle in which the swindler first gains the victim's confidence (also as an adj.). **2** a deception. ● v. (**cons, conned, conning**) **1** swindle. **2** deceive.

con² n. (usu. in pl.) a reason against.

con³ n. *slang* a convict.

concatenate v. (**concatenates, concatenated, concatenating**) link together, interconnect. □ **concatenation** n. [*Say* k'n CATTA nate, k'n catta NATION]

concave adj. having an outline or surface curved inwards (*compare* CONVEX). □ **concavity** n. (pl. **concavities**) [*Say* CON cave, k'n CAVITY]

conceal v. **1** keep secret. **2** not allow to be seen. □ **concealment** n.

concealer n. **1** a cosmetic which covers blemishes. **2** something that conceals.

concede v. (**concedes, conceded, conceding**) **1 a** admit to be true. **b** admit defeat in a match or contest. **2** yield or surrender (a right, a privilege, etc.). **3** *Sport* allow an opponent to score or win.

conceit n. **1** excessive pride in oneself. **2 a** a far-fetched comparison; a confusing metaphor. **b** an artistic device.

conceited adj. full of conceit; vain.

conceivable adj. capable of being imagined. □ **conceivably** adv.

conceive v. (**conceives, conceived, conceiving**) **1** become pregnant. **2** cause an embryo to come into being. **3 a** devise, compose. **b** understand. **4** develop (an emotion, feeling, etc.).

concentrate ● v. (**concentrates, concentrated, concentrating**) **1** focus all one's attention or mental ability. **2 a** bring toward a centre. **b** cause to converge or be focused on. **3** increase the strength of (a liquid etc.). ● n. a concentrated substance or solution. □ **concentrated** adj. **concentrator** n.

concentration n. **1** the act or power of concentrating. **2** a close gathering of people or things. **3** the weight of substance in a given weight or volume of material.

concentration camp n. a camp for the detention or extermination of political prisoners etc., esp. one run by Nazi Germany.

concentric adj. (esp. of circles) having a common centre. □ **concentrically** adv.

concept n. **1** an abstract idea. **2 a** an idea, theme or design, esp. one used to produce something. **b** the product of this.

conception n. **1** the action of conceiving a child or of one being conceived. **2** an idea or plan. **3** an understanding. **4** a concept. □ **no conception of** an inability to imagine.

conceptual *adj.* of mental conceptions or concepts. □ **conceptually** *adv.*

conceptualize *v.* (**conceptualizes, conceptualized, conceptualizing**) form a concept of. □ **conceptualization** *n.*

concern ● *v.* **1 a** be important to. **b** relate to; be about. **2** (**concern oneself**) interest or involve oneself. **3** worry, affect. ● *n.* **1 a** anxiety, worry. **b** solicitude. **2 a** a matter of interest or importance. **b** private business. **3** a business. □ **to whom it may concern** to those who have a proper interest in the matter.

concerned *adj.* **1** involved, interested. **2** troubled, anxious.

concerning *prep.* about, regarding.

concert *n.* **1** a musical performance. **2** a public performance of a variety of entertainments. **3** (as an *adj.*) performing in concerts. □ **in concert** acting jointly.

concerted *adj.* **1** jointly arranged or planned. **2** serious.

concertina *n.* (*pl.* **concertinas**) a musical instrument with bellows, the notes being sounded by buttons. [*Say* con ser TINA]

concertmaster *n.* the principal violin player in an orchestra.

concerto *n.* (*pl.* **concertos** or **concerti**) a composition for one or more solo instruments accompanied by an orchestra. [*Say* k'n CHAIR toe *for the singular; for* CONCERTI *say* k'n CHAIR tee]

concession *n.* **1 a** the action of conceding something. **b** a thing that is granted; a thing conceded. **2 a** a reduction in price for a certain kind of person. **b** the right to use land or other property, granted esp. by a government, for a specific use. **3** a booth or stand where refreshments etc. are sold.

conch *n.* (*pl.* **conches** or **conchs**) a mollusc with a thick heavy spiral shell. [*Say* KONTCH *or* KONK]

concierge *n.* **1** (esp. in France) a caretaker in charge of the entrance of a building. **2** a hotel employee responsible for attending to special needs of guests. **3** an attendant at the entrance to a condominium building. [*Say* kon see AIRZH]

conciliate *v.* (**conciliates, conciliated, conciliating**) **1** mediate an esp. labour dispute. **2** placate. □ **conciliation** *n.* **conciliator** *n.* **conciliatory** *adj.* [*Say* kun SILLY ate, kun silly AY sh'n, kun SILLY ay tur, kun SILLY a tory]

concise *adj.* giving a lot of information clearly and in a few words. □ **concisely** *adv.* **conciseness** *n.*

conclave *n.* **1** a private meeting. **2** the assembly of cardinals for the election of a pope. [*Say* CON clave]

conclude *v.* (**concludes, concluded, concluding**) **1** bring or come to an end. **2** infer (from given premises). **3** settle, arrange (a treaty etc.).

conclusion *n.* **1** a final result; a termination. **2** a judgment reached by reasoning. **3** the summing-up of an argument, book, etc. **4** the settling or arrangement of a treaty. □ **in conclusion** to conclude.

conclusive *adj.* **1** decisive, convincing. **2** (of a victory) achieved easily. □ **conclusively** *adv.*

concoct *v.* **1** make by combining elements not usually mixed together. **2** invent. □ **concoction** *n.*

concomitant ● *adj.* naturally accompanying or associated. ● *n.* a concomitant thing. □ **concomitantly** *adv.* [*Say* k'n COMMA tint]

concord *n.* **1** agreement or harmony. **2** a treaty.

concordance *n.* (a book containing) an alphabetical list of the important words in a text. [*Say* kun CORE dince]

Concord grape *n.* a variety of dark purple grape, used esp. for making juice, jelly, etc.

concourse *n.* **1** an open central area in a large public building etc. **2** an indoor shopping area, often on the lowest level of an office building etc. **3** *formal* a crowd.

concrete ● *adj.* **1** existing in a material form; real. **2** definite. ● *n.* a durable building material made from a mixture of gravel, sand, cement, and water, which forms a stone-like mass when dry. ● *v.* (**concretes, concreted, concreting**) cover with concrete. □ **concretely** *adv.* **concreteness** *n.*

concubine *n.* (among polygamous peoples) a woman who lives with a man but has lower status than his wife or wives. [*Say* CON cue bine]

concur *v.* (**concurs, concurred, concurring**) agree.

concurrence *n.* **1** agreement. **2** an example of two or more things happening at the same time. [*Say* kun CUR ince]

concurrent *adj.* **1** existing or happening at the same time. **2** *Math* (of lines) meeting at or tending toward one point. □ **concurrently** *adv.* [*Say* cun CUR int]

concussion *n.* **1** a period of unconsciousness caused by a blow to the head. **2** a violent shock from a heavy blow.

□ **concussed** adj. [Say k'n KUSH'n, k'n CUSSD]

condemn v. **1** express utter disapproval of. **2** sentence someone to a particular punishment. **3** show or suggest one's guilt. **4** pronounce (a building etc.) unfit to use. **5** doom or assign. □ **condemnation** n. **condemnatory** adj.

condensation n. **1** the act of condensing. **2** any condensed material. **3** a concise summarized version.

condense v. (**condenses, condensed, condensing**) **1** make denser or more concentrated. **2** express in fewer words. **3** reduce or be reduced from a gas or solid to a liquid.

condensed milk n. milk thickened by evaporation and sweetened.

condenser n. **1** an apparatus for condensing vapour. **2** something that condenses.

condescend v. **1** usu. ironic be gracious enough (to do a thing) esp. while showing one's sense of dignity or superiority. **2** derogatory behave as if one is better than other people. □ **condescending** adj. **condescendingly** adv. **condescension** n.

condiment n. a spice or foodstuff used to enhance the flavour of other foods, e.g. salt and pepper etc.

condition ● n. **1** a state of affairs that must exist before something else is possible. **2 a** the state of being or fitness of something. **b** an ailment or abnormality. **3** (in pl.) circumstances affecting something. ● v. **1 a** bring into a good or desired state or condition. **b** make fit. **2** train to adopt certain habits etc. **3** govern, determine. **4** apply conditioner to. □ **in** (or **out of**) **condition** in good (or bad) condition. **on condition that** with the stipulation that. □ **conditioned** adj. **conditioning** n. & adj.

conditional ● adj. **1** subject to one or more conditions. **2** (of a clause, sentence, etc.) expressing a condition on which something depends. ● n. **1** a word, clause, proposition, etc., expressing a condition. **2** Grammar the conditional mood. □ **conditionally** adv.

conditional discharge n. an order made by a criminal court whereby an offender will not be sentenced for an offence unless a further offence is committed within a stated period.

conditional sentence n. **1** Cdn Law a criminal sentence of up to two years that is served in the community rather than in jail under various conditions imposed by the trial judge, such as house arrest,

curfews, community service, etc., the breaching of which may lead to incarceration. **2** Grammar a sentence including a conditional clause.

conditioned reflex n. (also **conditioned response**) a reflex response established by training.

conditioner n. something used to improve the condition of something, esp. hair.

condo n. (pl. **condos**) = CONDOMINIUM 1.

condolence n. an expression of sympathy. [Say k'n DOLE ince]

condom n. a rubber sheath worn during sexual intercourse as a contraceptive or to prevent infection.

condominium n. **1** a building or building complex in which units are individually owned. **2** a unit in such a building or complex.

condone v. (**condones, condoned, condoning**) accept or allow to continue (offensive behaviour etc.).

condor n. a large vulture of S America, having black plumage with a white neck ruff.

conducive adj. contributing or helping. [Say k'n DOO siv or k'n DYOO sive]

conduct ● n. **1** behaviour; way of acting. **2** management or direction (of a business, war, etc.). ● v. **1** direct or manage. **2** carry out or administer. **3** direct the performance of (an ensemble or piece of music). **4** transmit (heat, electricity, etc.) by conduction. **5** (**conduct oneself**) behave in a specified way.

conductance n. the degree to which a material conducts electricity.

conduction n. **1** the transmission of heat or electricity through a substance. **2** the conducting of liquid through a pipe etc.

conductivity n. (pl. **conductivities**) the conducting power of a specified material. □ **conductive** adj.

conductor n. **1** a person who conducts an orchestra or choir etc. **2** a thing that conducts heat or electricity. **3 a** a person who collects fares on a bus etc. **b** a person in charge of a train.

conduit n. **1** a channel or pipe for conveying liquids. **2** something through which anything is conveyed. **3** a tube for protecting insulated electric wires. [Say CON do it or CON dyoo it]

cone n. **1** a solid figure with a circular plane base, tapering to a point. **2** a thing of a similar shape, solid or hollow. **3** the dry fruit of conifers. **4** a conical wafer filled with ice cream. **5** a type of light-sensitive cell in the eye, responsible for sharpness of vision and colour perception.

coneflower n. a daisy-like plant having flowers with cone-like centres.

confab n. *informal* a conversation. [*Say* CON fab]

confection n. **1** a sweet dessert or candy. **2** an elaborate or highly contrived thing.

confectioner n. someone who makes or sells confections.

confectionery n. (pl. **confectioneries**) **1 a** candy and other sweets. **b** a candy store. **2** the art of making candy.

confederacy n. (pl. **confederacies**) **1** an alliance of persons, states, etc. **2** (usu. **Confederacy**) the Confederate states in the US Civil War. [*Say* k'n FEDDER uh see]

confederate ● adj. **1** esp. *Politics* allied; joined by an agreement or treaty. **2** (**Confederate**) being or relating to the eleven southern states which seceded from the US in 1860–61. ● n. **1** (**Confederate**) a supporter of the Confederate states in the US Civil War. **2** an accomplice. □ **confederated** adj. [*Say* k'n FEDDER it, k'n FEDDER ate id]

confederation n. **1** a union or alliance of peoples, countries, unions, etc. **2** (**Confederation**) **a** (in Canada) the federal union of provinces and territories forming Canada. **b** (also **Confederation Day**) (in Canada) the date of the creation of the Dominion of Canada, 1 July 1867. **c** (in Newfoundland) the date of the political union of Newfoundland and Canada, 31 March 1949. **3** the action of joining by an agreement or treaty.

confer v. (**confers**, **conferred**, **conferring**) **1** grant or bestow (a title etc.). **2** converse, consult. □ **conferral** n. [*Say* con FUR, k'n FUR ul]

conference ● n. **1** a meeting for discussion or presentation of information. **2** the linking of several telephones, computer terminals, etc., so that each user may communicate with the others simultaneously (also as an adj.). **3** a division within a sports league. **4** an association of schools, churches, nations, etc. ● v. (**conferences**, **conferenced**, **conferencing**) take part in a conference or conference call.

confess v. (**confesses**, **confessed**, **confessing**) **1** acknowledge or admit (a fault, wrongdoing, etc.). **2** admit reluctantly. **3** declare (one's sins) to a priest.

confession n. **1 a** an act of confessing, esp. a formal statement admitting to a crime. **b** (in pl.) intimate revelations about a person's private life or occupation. **2** a formal admission of one's sins esp. to a priest. **3** (also **confession of faith**) a formal declaration of one's religious beliefs or principles.

confessional ● n. an enclosed stall in a church in which a priest hears confessions. ● adj. **1** of or relating to confession. **2** denominational.

confessor n. a priest who hears confessions.

confetti n. small bits of coloured paper thrown esp. at weddings.

confidant n. a person to whom secrets etc. are confided. [*Say* CONFA dawnt]

confidante n. a female confidant.

confide v. (**confides**, **confided**, **confiding**) **1** tell someone in confidence. **2** *literary* entrust to.

confidence n. **1** firm trust; faith. **2 a** belief in own's own abilities. **b** assurance. **3 a** something told confidentially. **b** the telling of private matters with mutual trust. **4** *Parliament* majority support for a government etc. □ **in confidence** as a secret. **take into one's confidence** confide in.

confidence game n. a swindle in which the victim is persuaded to trust the swindler.

confident adj. **1** feeling or showing confidence; self-assured. **2** assured, trusting. □ **confidently** adv.

confidential adj. **1** spoken, written or kept in confidence. **2** entrusted with secrets. □ **confidentiality** n. **confidentially** adv.

configuration n. **1** an arrangement of parts in a particular form or figure. **2** the design of a computer system or elements of it so that it will accommodate a particular specification.

configure v. (**configures**, **configured**, **configuring**) **1** put together in a certain configuration. **2** interconnect or interrelate (a computer system etc.) so as to fit it for a designated task. □ **configurable** adj.

confine ● v. (**confines**, **confined**, **confining**) **1** (also **confine oneself**) keep or restrict (within certain limits etc.). **2** hold captive. **3** oblige (a person) to remain indoors, in bed, etc. ● n. a limit or boundary.

confinement n. **1** the state of being forced to stay in a confined space. **2** *dated* the time of a woman's giving birth.

confirm v. **1** provide support for the truth or correctness of; make definitely valid. **2** establish more firmly. **3** encourage (a person) in (an opinion etc.). **4** ratify (a treaty etc.). **5** administer the religious rite of confirmation to. □ **confirmatory** adj.

confirmation n. **1** something that confirms something. **2** a religious rite or ceremony admitting a usu. young person as a full member of the Christian Church or other religious community.

confirmed adj. **1** firmly settled in some habit or condition. **2** valid.

confiscate v. (**confiscates, confiscated, confiscating**) **1** take or seize by authority. **2** appropriate to the public treasury. □ **confiscation** n.

conflagration n. a great and destructive fire. [Say confla GRAY sh'n]

conflate v. (**conflates, conflated, conflating**) blend or fuse together. □ **conflation** n.

conflict ● n. **1** a serious disagreement. **2** a violent situation or period of fighting. **3** a situation in which there are opposing ideas, opinions, or wishes. **4** the scheduling of two events at the same time. ● v. **1** be incompatible. **2** struggle or contend. □ **conflicting** adj.

conflicted adj. having or showing confused and mutually inconsistent feelings.

conflict of interest n. (pl. **conflicts of interest**) the situation of a public figure whose private interests might benefit from his or her public actions.

confluence n. **1** the place where two rivers etc. meet. **2** a coming together. [Say CON floo ince]

conform v. **1** comply with socially acceptable conventions or standards. **2** be in accordance with.

conformance n. = CONFORMITY 1, 2.

conformation n. the shape or structure of something, esp. an animal.

conformist ● n. a person who conforms to an established practice. ● adj. conventional. □ **conformism** n.

conformity n. (pl. **conformities**) **1** behaviour that conforms to established conventions. **2** compliance with practices, standards, or laws.

confound v. **1** throw into perplexity or confusion. **2** mix up; confuse. **3** damn (used in mild curses).

confounded adj. informal used to express annoyance.

confront v. **1 a** face in hostility or defiance. **b** face up to and deal with (a problem). **2** (of a difficulty etc.) present itself to. **3** bring (a person) face to face with. **4** meet or stand facing. □ **confrontation** n. **confrontational** adj.

Confucianism n. a system of philosophical and ethical teachings founded by Confucius in China in the 6th century BC. □ **Confucian** adj. **Confucianist** n. & adj. [Say k'n FYOO sh'n ism, k'n FYOO sh'n]

confuse v. (**confuses, confused, confusing**) **1** disconcert, perplex, bewilder. **2** mix up in the mind. **3** make indistinct. **4** throw into disorder.

confused adj. **1** perplexed. **2** unclear. **3** mentally infirm. **4** disorderly. □ **confusedly** adv.

confusing adj. difficult to understand; not clear. □ **confusingly** adv.

confusion n. **1 a** uncertainty. **b** the state of being confused. **2 a** a confused state; disorder. **b** a disorderly jumble. **3** a riot or similar disturbance.

conga n. (pl. **congas**) **1** a Latin American dance usu. performed by people in a single line. **2** (also **conga drum**) a tall drum beaten with the hands.

congeal v. **1** make or become semi-solid by cooling. **2** coagulate. **3** (of ideas etc.) take shape or become fixed. □ **congealed** adj. [Say k'n JEEL]

congenial adj. **1** pleasant because like oneself in temperament or interests. **2** suited or agreeable. □ **congeniality** n. [Say k'n JEENY ul]

congenital adj. **1** (esp. of a disease, defect, etc.) existing from birth. **2** having a specified nature deeply ingrained as if from birth. □ **congenitally** adv.

congested adj. **1** abnormally full of blood. **2** so crowded as to hinder movement. **3** blocked with mucus. □ **congestion** n. **congestive** adj.

conglomerate n. **1** a number of distinct things or parts forming a whole. **2** a corporation formed by the merging of separate firms. **3** a rock made up of small stones held together. □ **conglomeration** n. [Say k'n GLOMMER it]

Congolese ● adj. of or relating to Congo (formerly Zaire), the Republic of the Congo, or the region surrounding the Congo River. ● n. **1** (pl. **Congolese**) a native or resident of these regions. **2** any of the Bantu languages spoken by the Congolese people. [Say konga LEEZ]

congrats interj. informal congratulations.

congratulate v. (**congratulates, congratulated, congratulating**) **1** express pleasure at the happiness or good fortune of. **2** (**congratulate oneself**) feel pride or satisfaction.

congratulation n. **1** the expression of praise and good wishes. **2** (also as interjection; usu. in pl.) words expressing one's praise for an achievement or good wishes on a special occasion.

congratulatory *adj.* expressing congratulations. [*Say* k'n GRATCH'll a tory *or* k'n GRADGE'll a tory]

congregate *v.* (**congregates, congregated, congregating**) collect or gather into a crowd.

congregation *n.* **1** a group of people assembled for religious worship. **2** the process of congregating. **3** a crowd gathered together. □ **congregational** *adj.*

congress *n.* **1** (**Congress**) the national legislative body of the US. **2** the national legislative body in some other countries. **3** a formal meeting between delegates. □ **congressional** *adj.*

congressman *n.* (*pl.* **congressmen**) a member of the US Congress.

congressperson *n.* (*pl.* **congresspersons** *or* **congresspeople**) a member of the US Congress.

congresswoman *n.* (*pl.* **congresswomen**) a female member of the US Congress.

congruent *adj.* **1** in agreement or harmony. **2** *Math* coinciding exactly when superimposed. □ **congruence** *n.* **congruently** *adv.* [*Say* CON groo int *or* con GROO int, CON groo ince *or* con GROO ince]

conic *adj.* of, pertaining to, or resembling a cone.

conical *adj.* cone-shaped.

conifer *n.* any evergreen tree of a group usu. bearing cones, including pines, cedars, etc. □ **coniferous** *adj.* [*Say* CONNA fur, kuh NIFFER us]

conjecture ● *n.* an opinion based on incomplete information; guessing. ● *v.* (**conjectures, conjectured, conjecturing**) form an opinion on incomplete information. □ **conjectural** *adj.* [*Say* k'n JECK chur, k'n JECK chur ul]

conjoin *v.* join, combine.

conjoined twins *pl. n.* twins joined at any part of the body.

conjugal *adj.* of marriage or the relation between husband and wife. [*Say* CONJA gull]

conjugate *v.* (**conjugates, conjugated, conjugating**) **1** inflect (a verb) in its various forms. **2** unite sexually. □ **conjugation** *n.* [*Say* CONJA gate, conja GAY shun]

conjunction *n.* **1** a word used to connect clauses or words (e.g. *and*, *but*, *if*). **2** a combination (of events or circumstances). □ **in conjunction with** together with.

conjunctiva *n.* (*pl.* **conjunctivas** *or* **conjunctivae**) the mucous membrane that covers the front of the eye and lines the inside of the eyelids. □ **conjunctival** *adj.* [*Say* con junc TIVE uh]

conjunctivitis *n.* inflammation of the conjunctiva; pink eye. [*Say* conjunctive ITE iss]

conjuncture *n.* a combination of events; a state of affairs.

conjure *v.* (**conjures, conjured, conjuring**) **1** cause to appear as if by magic. **2** perform tricks which are seemingly magical. **3** call upon (a spirit etc.) to appear. **4** evoke. □ **conjure up 1** cause to appear as if by magic. **2** call to mind; evoke. [*Say* CON jur]

conjuring *n.* the performance of seemingly magical tricks. [*Say* CON juring]

conjuror *n.* (also **conjurer**) a performer of conjuring tricks. [*Say* CON jur er]

conk¹ *v. informal* □ **conk out 1** (of a machine etc.) break down. **2** (of a person) become exhausted. **3** (of a person) fall asleep.

conk² *slang* ● *n.* **1** the head. **2** a blow, esp. on the nose or head. ● *v.* hit, esp. on the head.

con man *n.* (*pl.* **con men**) a man who cheats or tricks someone by first gaining their trust.

connect *v.* **1** join or be joined. **2** associate. **3** (of an airplane etc.) be synchronized at its destination with another airplane etc., so that passengers can transfer. **4** put into communication by telephone. **5** establish contact. **6** establish a rapport. **7** form a logical sequence. **8** *informal* hit or strike effectively. □ **connector** *n.*

connected *adj.* **1** joined in sequence. **2** (of ideas etc.) coherent. **3** related or associated. □ **connectedness** *n.*

connection *n.* **1** the action of linking one thing to another. **2** the point at which two things are connected. **3 a** a link or relationship. **b** a telephone or computer link. **4** arrangement for catching a connecting airplane etc. **5** a relative or associate, esp. one with influence.

connective *adj.* serving or tending to connect. □ **connectivity** *n.*

connive *v.* (**connives, connived, conniving**) **1** conspire. **2** disregard or tacitly consent to (a wrongdoing). □ **connivance** *n.* **conniving** *adj. & n.* [*Say* kuh NIVE, kuh NIVE 'nce]

connoisseur *n.* an expert judge in matters of taste. □ **connoisseurship** *n.* [*Say* conna SIR *or* conna SOOR]

connotation *n.* an idea or feeling which a word evokes in addition to its primary meaning. [*Say* conna TAY sh'n]

connote v. (**connotes, connoted, connoting**) **1** (of a word etc.) imply or suggest in addition to the literal meaning. **2** (of a fact) imply as a consequence. [*Say* kuh NOTE]

conquer v. **1 a** overcome and control by military force. **b** be victorious. **2** overcome by effort. **3** climb (a mountain). **4** gain the admiration of. □ **conquerable** adj. **conqueror** n.

conquest n. **1** the act of conquering. **2** conquered territory. **3** a person that someone has persuaded to love or have sex with them.

conquistador n. (*pl.* **conquistadores** or **conquistadors**) a 16th-century Spanish conqueror of Mexico and Peru. [*Say* con QUISTA dor; *for the plurals say* con quista DOR ez, con QUISTA dors]

consanguinity n. relationship by descent from a common ancestor. [*Say* con san GWINNA tee]

conscience n. **1** a moral sense of right and wrong. **2** an inner feeling as to the goodness of one's behaviour. □ **in all** (or **good** or **all good**) **conscience** in such a way that one's conscience is clear. **on one's conscience** causing one feelings of guilt. [*Say* CON shince]

conscientious adj. **1** careful and thorough in doing one's work or duty. **2** relating to a person's conscience. □ **conscientiously** adv. **conscientiousness** n. [*Say* conshy EN chuss]

conscientious objector n. a person who refuses to serve in the armed forces for reasons of conscience.

conscious adj. **1** awake and aware of one's surroundings. **2** aware. **3** (of actions etc.) intentional. **4** concerned with. □ **consciously** adv.

consciousness n. **1** the state of being conscious. **2** awareness of one's existence. **3** awareness of. **4** the totality of the thoughts and feelings of a person or group.

consciousness-raising n. the activity of increasing esp. social or political awareness.

conscript ● v. enlist by conscription. ● n. a person enlisted by conscription. [*Say* k'n SCRIPT *for the verb,* CON script *for the noun*]

conscription n. compulsory enlistment for military service. [*Say* k'n SCRIP sh'n]

consecrate v. (**consecrates, consecrated, consecrating**) **1** make or declare sacred. **2** (in Christian belief) make (bread and wine) into the body and blood of Christ. **3** devote (one's life etc.) to.

4 ordain (esp. a bishop). □ **consecrated** adj. **consecration** n. [*Say* CONSA crate]

consecutive adj. **1** following continuously, in unbroken sequence. **2** in logical order. □ **consecutively** adv.

consensual adj. of or by consent or consensus. [*Say* k'n SENSUAL]

consensus n. (*pl.* **consensuses**) **1** general agreement. **2** (as an adj.) based on the majority view.

consent ● v. give permission, agree. ● n. agreement or permission.

consequence n. **1** a result or effect. **2 a** importance. **b** social distinction. □ **in consequence** as a result.

consequent adj. **1** following as a consequence. **2** logically consistent. □ **consequential** adj. **consequently** adv. & conj.

conservancy n. (*pl.* **conservancies**) **1** a body concerned with the preservation of natural resources. **2** conservation.

conservation n. preservation, esp. of the natural environment. □ **conservationist** n.

conservative ● adj. **1 a** opposed to rapid change and holding to traditional attitudes. **b** (of taste etc.) sober and conventional. **2** (of an estimate etc.) purposely low; cautious. **3 a** (of a political party) favouring free enterprise and private ownership. **b** (**Conservative**) relating to a Conservative party. **4** tending to conserve. ● n. **1** a conservative person. **2** (**Conservative**) a supporter or member of a Conservative party. □ **conservatism** n. **conservatively** adv.

conservatory n. (*pl.* **conservatories**) **1** a school of esp. classical music. **2** a greenhouse. **3** a glassed-in sunroom in a house.

conserve ● v. (**conserves, conserved, conserving**) **1** store up; protect from harm or overuse. **2** preserve (food, esp. fruit). ● n. a jam-like mixture of several fruits.

consider v. **1** contemplate mentally. **2** examine the merits of. **3** take into account. **4** have the opinion; believe. □ **considered** adj.

considerable adj. great in size, amount, or importance. □ **considerably** adv.

considerate adj. thoughtful toward other people. □ **considerately** adv.

consideration n. **1** careful thought. **2** thoughtfulness for others. **3** a fact or a thing taken into account in deciding something. **4** a payment or reward. □ **in consideration of** in return for; on account of. **under consideration** being considered.

considering *prep.* **1** taking into consideration. **2** *informal* all in all.

consign *v.* **1** commit decisively or permanently. **2** deliver something to a person's custody. [*Say* k'n SIGN]

consignment *n.* **1** a batch of goods consigned. **2** (as an *adj.*) designating a store selling goods on consignment. □ **on consignment** (of goods) delivered to a shop etc. to be sold, with the original seller reimbursed only on sale of the goods.

consist *v.* **1** be composed of. **2** have its essential features as specified.

consistency *n.* (*pl.* **consistencies**) **1** the degree of firmness or viscosity, esp. of thick liquids. **2** the state of being consistent.

consistent *adj.* **1** in harmony; not contradictory. **2** unchanging. □ **consistently** *adv.*

consolation *n.* **1** the comfort received after a loss or disappointment. **2** a consoling thing. □ **consolatory** *adj.* [*Say* k'n SOLLA tory]

consolation prize *n.* a prize given to a competitor who fails to win.

console[1] *v.* (**consoles, consoled, consoling**) comfort, esp. in grief or disappointment. [*Say* k'n SOLE]

console[2] *n.* **1** a panel or unit accommodating a set of controls etc. **2** a cabinet for television or radio equipment etc. **3** a cabinet with the keyboards, pedals, etc., of an organ. [*Say* CON sole]

consolidate *v.* (**consolidates, consolidated, consolidating**) **1** make or become strong or solid. **2** reinforce or strengthen (one's position etc.). **3** combine into one whole. □ **consolidated** *adj.* **consolidation** *n.* **consolidator** *n.*

consommé *n.* a clear soup made with meat stock. [*Say* CONSA may]

consonant ● *n.* **1** a speech sound in which the breath is at least partly obstructed. **2** a letter or letters representing this. ● *adj.* in agreement or harmony.

consort ● *n.* **1** a wife or husband, esp. of royalty. **2** a companion. ● *v.* habitually associate with someone.

consortium *n.* (*pl.* **consortia** or **consortiums**) several large companies in a joint venture. [*Say* k'n SORE tee um *or* k'n SORE sh'm *for the singular,* k'n SORE tee uh *or* k'n SORE shuh *for the plural*]

conspicuous *adj.* **1** clearly visible; attracting notice. **2** remarkable of its kind.

□ **conspicuously** *adv.* [*Say* k'n SPICK you us, k'n SPICK you us lee]

conspiracy *n.* (*pl.* **conspiracies**) **1** a secret plan to commit a crime or do harm. **2** the act of conspiring. [*Say* k'n SPEAR a see]

conspiracy theory *n.* a belief that some covert agency is responsible for an unexplained event.

conspire *v.* (**conspires, conspired, conspiring**) **1** combine secretly to plan and prepare an unlawful or harmful act. **2** (of events or circumstances) seem to be working together, esp. to bring about an unfortunate result. □ **conspirator** *n.* **conspiratorial** *adj.* **conspiratorially** *adv.* [*Say* k'n SPIRE, k'n SPEAR a tor, k'n speera TORY ul]

constable *n.* **1** (in some countries) a police officer of the lowest rank. **2** an officer of the peace with minor judicial duties.

constabulary *n.* (*pl.* **constabularies**) a police force. [*Say* k'n STAB you lerry]

constant ● *adj.* **1** continuous. **2** occurring frequently. **3** unchanging. **4** faithful, dependable. ● *n.* **1** anything that does not vary. **2** *Math* a number or quantity that does not change its value. **3** *Physics* a number expressing a relation, property, etc., and remaining the same in all circumstances. □ **constancy** *n.* **constantly** *adv.*

constellation *n.* **1** a group of stars whose outline forms a particular figure. **2** a group of associated persons, ideas, etc.

consternation *n.* anxiety or dismay.

constipation *n.* a condition in which there is difficulty in emptying the bowels. □ **constipated** *adj.*

constituency *n.* (*pl.* **constituencies**) **1** a body of voters in a specified area who elect a representative to a legislative body. **2** the area represented in this way. **3** a body of supporters etc. [*Say* k'n STITCH oo in see]

constituent ● *adj.* **1** composing a whole. **2** able to make or change a (political) constitution. ● *n.* **1** a member of a constituency. **2** a component part. [*Say* k'n STITCH oo int]

constitute *v.* (**constitutes, constituted, constituting**) **1** be the components of; make up. **2 a** amount to. **b** formally establish.

constitution *n.* **1** the act or method of constituting; composition. **2** the body of fundamental principles etc. according to which a state or organization is governed. **3** a person's physical state. **4** a person's mental makeup.

constitutional ● *adj.* **1** of, consistent with, or authorized by a political constitution. **2** relating to a person's physical or mental state. **●** *n.* a walk taken regularly to maintain good health. □**constitutionality** *n.* **constitutionally** *adv.*

constitutionalism *n.* **1** a constitutional system of government. **2** the adherence to or advocacy of such a system. □**constitutionalist** *n.*

constitutive *adj.* **1** forming esp. an essential part of something. **2** forming an essential element of something. [*Say* k'n STITCH you tiv]

constrain *v.* **1** restrict severely. **2** compel to do something.

constrained *adj.* **1** *in senses of* CONSTRAIN *v.* **2** forced; not natural.

constraint *n.* **1** the act of constraining or being constrained. **2** a limitation. **3** the restraint of natural feelings.

constrict *v.* **1** make or become narrow or tight. **2** restrict, obstruct. □**constriction** *n.* **constrictive** *adj.*

constrictor *n.* any snake that kills by coiling around its prey and compressing it.

construct ● *v.* make by fitting parts together; build, form. **●** *n.* a thing constructed, esp. by the mind. □**constructor** *n.*

construction *n.* **1** the act or a mode of constructing. **2 a** a thing constructed. **b** repair or building work. **3** the building industry. **4** an interpretation or explanation. □**constructional** *adj.*

constructive *adj.* helpful, useful. □**constructively** *adv.*

construe *v.* (**construes**, **construed**, **construing**) **1** interpret. **2** combine (words) grammatically.

consul *n.* an official appointed by a nation to live in a foreign city and protect the interests of the nation's citizens in the region. □**consular** *adj.*

consulate *n.* the building officially used by a consul. [*Say* CONSA lit]

consult *v.* **1** seek information or advice from. **2** have discussions or confer with someone. □**consultation** *n.* **consultative** *adj.*

consultancy *n.* (*pl.* **consultancies**) the professional practice of a consultant.

consultant *n.* a person who gives professional advice or services.

consulting *adj.* giving professional advice to others in the same field.

consume *v.* (**consumes**, **consumed**, **consuming**) **1** eat or drink. **2** use up.

3 completely destroy. **4** engage the full attention of. □**consumable** *adj. & n.*

consumer ● *n.* **1** a person who consumes, esp. one who uses a product. **2** a purchaser of goods or services. **●** *adj.* intended for use by consumers.

consumerism *n.* **1** the protection or promotion of consumers' interests. **2** preoccupation with buying consumer goods. □**consumerist** *adj. & n.*

consummate ● *v.* (**consummates**, **consummated**, **consummating**) **1 a** make (a marriage) legally complete by having sex. **b** give sexual expression to (love etc.). **2** complete. **●** *adj.* **1** complete, perfect. **2** perfectly skilled. □**consummately** *adv.* **consummation** *n.* [*Say* CONSA mate *for the verb*, CONSA mit *for the adjective*]

consumption *n.* **1** the using up of a resource. **2** *hist.* tuberculosis. **3** an amount consumed. **4** the purchase of goods and services by the public. **5** the eating of something.

consumptive *adj. hist.* having tuberculosis.

contact ● *n.* **1** the state of touching, meeting, or communicating. **2** a person who may be communicated with for assistance etc. **3** *Electricity* **a** a connection for the passage of a current. **b** a device for providing this. **4** *informal* a contact lens. **●** *v.* get into communication with.

contact lens *n.* a small lens placed directly on the eyeball to correct vision.

contagion *n.* **1 a** the communication of disease by bodily contact. **b** a contagious disease. **2** the spreading of a harmful idea. [*Say* k'n TAY jin]

contagious *adj.* **1 a** (of a person) likely to transmit disease by contact. **b** (of a disease) transmitted in this way. **2** likely to affect others. □**contagiously** *adv.*

contain *v.* **1** hold; include, comprise. **2** (of measures) consist of or be equal to. **3** prevent (a problem etc.) from spreading or increasing. **4** restrain.

contained *adj.* **1** included, enclosed. **2** restrained.

container *n.* **1** a vessel, box, etc., for holding things. **2** a large box-like receptacle for the transport of goods.

containment *n.* **1** *in senses of* CONTAIN *v.* **2** the action or policy of preventing the expansion of a hostile country or influence.

contaminate *v.* (**contaminates**, **contaminated**, **contaminating**) **1** make impure; pollute. **2** infect. **3** introduce radioactivity into. □**contaminant** *n.* **contamination** *n.*

contemplate v. (**contemplates, contemplating, contemplated**) **1** look at or consider. **2** regard as possible. **3** intend. **4** meditate. □ **contemplation** n.

contemplative ● adj. of or given to contemplation. ● n. a person whose life is devoted to contemplation.
□ **contemplatively** adv.
[Say k'n TEMPLA tiv or CON tum play tiv]

contemporaneous adj. existing or occurring at the same time.
□ **contemporaneously** adv.
[Say k'n tempa RAINY us]

contemporary ● adj. **1** living or occurring at the same time. **2** approximately equal in age. **3** following the latest fashion. **4** living or existing at the present. ● n. (pl. **contemporaries**) **1** a person or thing existing at the same time as another. **2** a person of the same age as another.

contempt n. **1** a feeling that a person or a thing is beneath consideration or worthless. **2** disregard. **3** (also **contempt of court**) disobedience to or disrespect for a court of law. □ **beneath contempt** utterly worthless or despicable.
□ **contemptible** adj. **contemptibly** adv.

contemptuous adj. showing contempt.
□ **contemptuously** adv.

contend v. **1** struggle to surmount a difficulty. **2** engage in a struggle to achieve something. **3** assert. □ **contender** n.

content[1] ● adj. **1** satisfied; happy. **2** willing. ● v. make content; satisfy. ● n. a contented state. □ **to one's heart's content** to the full extent of one's desires.
□ **contentment** n.

content[2] n. **1** what is contained in something. **2** the amount of a particular thing occurring in a substance. **3** the material dealt with in a speech etc. as distinct from its form or style. **4** capacity or volume. **5** (in pl.) (also **table of contents**) a list of the chapters etc. at the front of a book etc.

contented adj. happy, satisfied.
□ **contentedly** adv. **contentedness** n.

contention n. **1** an assertion. **2** a dispute or argument. □ **in contention** competing. **out of contention** having lost any chance of succeeding.

contentious adj. **1** involving heated argument. **2** controversial. **3** likely to argue. □ **contentiously** adv. **contentiousness** n. [Say k'n TEN shus]

contest ● n. **1** a competition etc. **2** a dispute or controversy. ● v. **1** challenge or dispute. **2** debate. **3** contend or compete for. □ **contestable** adj. **contestation** n.

contested adj. [Say CON test for the noun, k'n TEST for the verb, con tess TAY shun]

contestant n. a person who takes part in a contest.

context n. **1** the parts that immediately precede and follow a word or passage and clarify its meaning. **2** the circumstances relevant to something.

contextual adj. connected with a particular context. □ **contextualization** n. **contextualize** v. **contextually** adv.

contiguous adj. **1** touching, adjoining. **2** neighbouring. **3** esp. US describing the continental US. □ **contiguity** n. **contiguously** adv. [Say kun TIG you us, conta GYOO uh tee]

continent[1] n. **1** any of the main continuous expanses of land (Europe, Asia, Africa, N and S America, Australia, Antarctica). **2** (**the Continent**) the mainland of Europe as distinct from the British Isles.

continent[2] adj. **1** able to control movements of the bowels and bladder. **2** exercising self-restraint.
□ **continence** n.

continental ● adj. **1** of or characteristic of a continent. **2** (**Continental**) of or relating to mainland Europe. ● n. an inhabitant of mainland Europe.

continental breakfast n. a light breakfast of coffee, rolls, etc.

continental divide n. the boundary between separate drainage basins on a continent, esp. (**Continental Divide**) that formed by the Rocky Mountains.

continental drift n. the slow movement of the continents over the surface of the earth.

continental shelf n. the area of seabed around a large land mass where the sea is relatively shallow.

contingency n. (pl. **contingencies**) **1** a future event which is possible but cannot be predicted with certainty. **2** a plan for such an event. **3** an incidental expense.
[Say k'n TINGE 'n see]

contingent ● n. **1** a group with a common feature representing a larger body. **2** a force contributed to form part of an army or navy. ● adj. **1** conditional, dependent on. **2** subject to chance.
[Say k'n TINGE 'nt]

continual adj. **1** constantly or frequently recurring. **2** always happening.
□ **continually** adv.

continuance n. **1** a state of continuing in existence or operation. **2** duration. **3** a postponement of legal proceedings.

continuation n. **1** the action of

continuing or the state of being continued.
2 a part that is attached to and an extension of something else.

continue v. (**continues, continued, continuing**) **1** persist in, maintain, not stop. **2** resume or prolong. **3** be a sequel to. **4** remain. **5** *Law* adjourn (proceedings).

continuity n. (pl. **continuities**) **1** the state of being continuous. **2** an unbroken succession. **3** a logical sequence.
[*Say* conta NEW it ee]

continuous adj. **1** unbroken, uninterrupted. **2** continued throughout in time or space. □ **continuously** adv. **continuousness** n.

continuum n. (pl. **continua**) a series of similar items in which each is almost the same as the ones next to it but the last is very different from the first.
[*Say* kun TIN you um, kun TIN you uh]

contort v. twist or be twisted out of normal shape. □ **contorted** adj. **contortion** n.

contortionist n. a person who twists and bends their body into strange and unnatural positions to entertain.

contour n. **1** an outline of the shape of something. **2** the outline of a natural feature. □ **contoured** adj.

contour line n. **1** a line on a map joining points of equal altitude. **2** a line in a painting etc. joining points.

contour map n. a map marked with contour lines.

contra- comb. form against, opposite.

contraband ● n. **1** anything that has been imported or exported illegally. **2** prohibited trade; smuggling. ● adj. **1** forbidden to be imported or exported. **2** concerning traffic in contraband.

contraception n. the use of contraceptives.

contraceptive ● adj. preventing pregnancy. ● n. a device, drug, etc. preventing pregnancy.

contract ● n. **1** a written or spoken agreement intended to be enforceable by law. **2** a document recording this. **3** *informal* an arrangement for someone to be killed in exchange for money. ● v. **1 a** make or become smaller. **b** draw or be drawn together. **2 a** make a contract. **b** enter into a contractual arrangement. **3** catch or develop (a disease). **4** incur (a debt etc.). □ **contractual** adj. **contractually** adv.

contraction n. **1** the process of contracting. **2** the tensing of the muscles in the uterus esp. during labour. **3 a** a shortening of a word. **b** a contracted word or words.

contractor n. a person who undertakes a contract, esp. to provide materials, do building, etc.

contradict v. **1** affirm the contrary of (a statement etc.). **2** deny the truth of a statement made by saying the opposite.

contradiction n. **1** the statement of a position opposite to one already made. **2** a combination of things which are opposed to one another. □ **contradiction in terms** a statement containing two words that contradict each other.

contradictory adj. **1** expressing a denial or opposite statement. **2** mutually opposed or inconsistent. **3** inclined to contradict.

contradistinction n. difference made apparent by contrast.

contrail n. a visible stream of water droplets in the exhaust of an aircraft.
[*Say* CON trail]

contraindicate v. (**contraindicates, contraindicated, contraindicating**) cause (a medication etc.) to be inappropriate. □ **contraindication** n.
[*Say* contra INDICATE]

contralto n. (pl. **contraltos**) the lowest female singing voice. [*Say* kun TRAWL toe *or* kun TRAL toe]

contraption n. often *derogatory* or *jocular* a machine, esp. a strange or particularly intricate one.

contrapuntal adj. using counterpoint.
[*Say* contra PUNT ul]

contrarian ● n. a person who opposes majority opinions, attitudes, etc., esp. in economic matters. ● adj. going against popular opinion or current practice.
[*Say* con TERRY an]

contrary ● adj. **1** opposite in nature, direction or meaning. **2** mutually opposed. **3** (of a wind) unfavourable. **4** *informal* perversely inclined to disagree or to do the opposite of what is expected. ● n. (pl. **contraries**) (usu. as **the contrary**) the opposite. ● adv. in opposition. □ **on the contrary** intensifying a denial of what has just been implied or stated.
[*Say* CON trary *except for sense 4, which is* kun TRERRY, con TRERRY un]

contrast ● n. **1** a juxtaposition showing striking differences. **2** a thing or person noticeably different from another. **3** the degree of difference between tones in a television picture or a photograph. ● v. **1** compare so as to reveal a difference. **2** differ strikingly. □ **contrasting** adj. **contrastingly** adv.

contravene v. (**contravenes, contravened, contravening**) **1** infringe, violate (a law etc.). **2** (of things)

conflict with. □ **contravention** n.
[Say contra VEEN, contra VEN sh'n]

contribute v. (**contributes, contributed, contributing**) **1** give (money etc.) toward a common purpose. **2** help to cause. **3** supply (an article etc.) for publication. □ **contributing** adj. **contribution** n. **contributor** n.
[Say kun TRIB yoot]

contributory adj. **1** contributing to a result; partly responsible for. **2** operated by means of contributions.

contrite adj. very sorry for having done wrong. □ **contritely** adv. **contrition** n.
[Say CON trite or kun TRITE, kun TRISH'n]

contrivance n. **1 a** a device made for a particular purpose. **b** an obviously artificial construction. **2** an elaborate act or plan.
[Say kun TRIVE unce]

contrive v. (**contrives, contrived, contriving**) **1** create or bring about by skill and artifice. **2 a** manage. **b** plot or scheme.

contrived adj. so obviously planned as to seem unnatural.

control ● n. **1** the power of directing; command. **2** the power of restraining, esp. self-restraint. **3** a means of restraint; prevention. **4** (usu. in pl.) a means of regulating prices etc. **5** a device or switch used to control something. **6** (also **control key**) Computing a key which alters the function of other keys. **7** a person or thing used as a standard of comparison for checking the results of a survey or experiment. ● v. (**controls, controlled, controlling**) **1** dominate or have command of. **2** regulate. **3** curb, restrain. □ **out of control** no longer subject to control. **under control** in order. □ **controllability** n. **controllable** adj. **controller** n.

control freak n. informal a person with a near obsessive desire for order and control.

controlled substance n. (also **controlled drug**) a substance the possession of which is restricted by law, e.g. cocaine.

controlling.

controlling interest n. ownership of sufficient stock in a company to exert control over policy etc.

control tower n. a tall structure at an airport etc. from which air traffic is controlled.

controversial adj. causing or subject to dispute. □ **controversialist** n. **controversially** adv.

controversy n. (pl. **controversies**) a prolonged argument, esp. when conducted publicly and over a matter of opinion.
[Say CONTRA versey]

controvert v. **1** deny the truth of. **2** argue about. □ **controverted** adj.

contusion n. a bruise.
[Say kun TYOO zhun]

conundrum n. **1** a riddle. **2** a hard or puzzling question or issue.
[Say kuh NUN drum]

conurbation n. an extended urban area, usu. consisting of several towns merging with the suburbs of a city.
[Say conner BAY sh'n]

convalesce v. (**convalesces, convalesced, convalescing**) recover one's health after illness or medical treatment. [Say conva LESS]

convalescent ● adj. **1** recovering from an illness. **2** pertaining to convalescents. ● n. a convalescing person. □ **convalescence** n.
[Say conva LESS int, conva LESS ince]

convection n. **1** transference of mass or heat within a fluid caused by the tendency of warmer material to rise. **2** the atmospheric process of air transfer, esp. of hot air upward. □ **convective** adj.

convene v. (**convenes, convened, convening**) **1 a** call or arrange (a meeting etc.). **b** call together (people) for a meeting. **2** assemble or meet together. **3** summon before a tribunal.

convener n. = CONVENOR.

convenience n. **1** the quality of being convenient. **2** freedom from difficulty or trouble. **3** an advantage. **4** a device etc. that saves or simplifies effort. □ **at your convenience** when and where it suits you.

convenience store n. a small, conveniently located store with extended hours.

convenient adj. **1 a** serving one's comfort, interests, or needs. **b** easily accessible. **c** suitable. **d** free of trouble or difficulty. **2** available at a suitable time or place. □ **conveniently** adv.

convenor n. a person who arranges meetings.

convent n. **1** a religious community, esp. of nuns, under vows. **2** (also **convent school**) a school attached to and run by a convent.

convention n. **1 a** socially acceptable behaviour. **b** a custom or customary practice. **2** a formal assembly or conference. **3 a** a formal agreement. **b** an agreement between nations.

conventional adj. **1** based on or following convention. **2** (of a person) conforming to social conventions. **3 a** usual. **b** traditional. **4** (of weapons) non-nuclear.

□ **conventionality** *n.*
conventionally *adv.*

conventional wisdom *n.* a common body of accumulated opinion.

conventioneer *n.* a person attending a convention.

converge *v.* (**converges, converged, converging**) **1** come together from different directions so as eventually to meet. **2** (of lines) tend to meet at a point. **3** approach from different directions.
□ **convergence** *n.* **convergent** *adj.*

conversant *adj.* familiar or knowledgeable about a subject etc.
[*Say* k'n VERSE int]

conversation *n.* the informal exchange of ideas by spoken word.
□ **conversational** *adj.*

conversationalist *n.* a person who is fond of or excels at conversing.

converse¹ *v.* (**converses, conversed, conversing**) engage in conversation.
[*Say* kun VERSE]

converse² ● *adj.* opposite. ● *n.* something that is opposite or contrary. □ **conversely** *adv.* [*Say* CON verse, kun VERSE lee]

conversion *n.* **1** the action of converting. **2** an adaptation of a building for new purposes. **3** the changing of funds, units, etc. into others of a different kind.

convert ● *v.* **1** change in form, character, or function. **2** change or cause to change beliefs etc. **3** change (funds, units, etc.) into others of a different kind. **4** adapt a building for a new purpose. **5** be converted or convertible. **6** *Football* complete (a touchdown) by kicking a goal or crossing the goal line. ● *n.* **1** a person who has been converted to a different belief etc. **2** *Cdn Football* the scoring of points after a touchdown by kicking the ball between the uprights (for one point) or by carrying or passing the ball over the defending team's goal line (for two points). □ **converter** *n.*

convertible ● *adj.* **1** that may be converted. **2** (of a car) having a folding or detachable roof. **3** *Cdn* designating a mortgage which may be converted to a longer term without penalty. ● *n.* a car with a folding or detachable roof.
□ **convertibility** *n.*

convex *adj.* having an outline or surface curved like the exterior of a circle (*compare* CONCAVE). □ **convexly** *adv.*

convey *v.* **1** communicate (an idea etc.). **2** transport or carry.

conveyance *n.* **1 a** the act of conveying. **b** the communication (of ideas etc.). **c** transmission. **2** a means of transport. **3** *Law* the transfer of property from one owner to another.

conveyor *n.* **1** a person or thing that conveys. **2** (also **conveyor belt**) a flexible, endless belt used to convey articles or materials.

convict ● *v.* declare guilty, esp. by the verdict of a jury or the decision of a judge. ● *n.* **1** a person found guilty of a criminal offence. **2** a person serving a prison sentence.

conviction *n.* **1** a formal declaration that someone is guilty of a criminal offence. **2** a firm belief or opinion.

convince *v.* (**convinces, convinced, convincing**) persuade (a person) to believe, realize, or agree. □ **convinced** *adj.*

convincing *adj.* **1** persuading by argument or evidence. **2** plausible or seeming worthy of belief.
□ **convincingly** *adv.*

convivial *adj.* **1 a** (of a person) friendly. **b** sociable and lively. **2** festive.
□ **conviviality** *n.* **convivially** *adv.* [*Say* kun VIVVY ul, kun vivvy ALA tee]

convocation *n.* **1** a formal assembly at a university etc. for graduation ceremonies. **2** a large, formal gathering of people.

convoke *v.* (**convokes, convoked, convoking**) *formal* call (people) together to a meeting etc.

convoluted *adj.* **1** (of style, meaning, etc.) complicated, difficult to comprehend. **2** intricately folded or twisted.
[*Say* CONVA loot id]

convolution *n.* **1** a complex or confused condition or issue. **2** a coil or twist.
[*Say* conva LOO sh'n]

convoy ● *n.* a group of ships or vehicles travelling together, typically under armed protection. ● *v.* **1** (of a warship) escort (a vessel). **2** escort, esp. with armed force. □ **in convoy** as a group.

convulse *v.* (**convulses, convulsed, convulsing**) **1** suffer convulsions. **2** laugh or cause to laugh uproariously. **3** throw a country into violent upheaval.
□ **convulsive** *adj.* **convulsively** *adv.*

convulsion *n.* **1** (usu. in *pl.*) violent irregular motion of the body caused by involuntary contraction of muscles. **2** a violent natural disturbance. **3** violent social or political agitation. **4** (in *pl.*) uncontrollable laughter.

coo ● *n.* a soft murmuring sound like that of a dove. ● *v.* (**coos, cooed, cooing**) **1** make a coo. **2** talk in a soft or amorous voice.

cook ● *v.* **1** prepare food for consumption, esp. by heating. **2** (of food) undergo cooking. **3** *informal* falsify or alter (accounts etc.). ● *n.* a person who cooks, esp. professionally. □ **cook a person's**

goose ruin a person's chances. **cook up** *informal* invent or concoct (a story etc.).

cookbook *n.* a book containing recipes and information about cooking.

cooker *n.* a container or device for cooking food.

cookery *n.* the art or practice of cooking.

cookie[1] *n.* **1** a small sweet biscuit. **2** *slang* a person. **3** *Computing* a token or packet of data, passed between computers or programs to allow access or to activate certain features, esp. a packet of data sent by an Internet server to a browser, which is returned by the browser each time it subsequently accesses the same server, thereby identifying the user or monitoring their access to the server. □ **toss** (or **lose**) **one's cookies** *slang* vomit. **the way the cookie crumbles** *informal* how things turn out.

cookie[2] *n.* a cook or cook's assistant.

cookie cutter *n.* **1** a stamp for cutting cookie dough. **2** (as an *adj.*) denoting something mass-produced.

cook-off *n.* a cooking competition.

cookout *n.* a gathering with an open-air cooked meal.

cookware *n.* utensils for cooking, esp. pans etc.

cool ● *adj.* **1** of or at a fairly low temperature. **2** suggesting or achieving coolness. **3** calm, not excited. **4** unfriendly or not enthusiastic. **5** *informal* **a** excellent. **b** following the latest fashions; hip. ● *n.* **1** coolness. **2** a cool place. **3** *slang* calmness, composure. ● *v.* make or become cool. □ **cool as a cucumber** completely unruffled. **cool it** *informal* relax, calm down. □ **coolish** *adj.* **coolness** *n.*

coolant *n.* a fluid used to remove heat from an engine etc.

cooler *n.* **1** a container for keeping things cool. **2** a mixture of wine or spirits and soda water. **3** *slang* prison.

cool-headed *adj.* not easily excited.

coolie *n.* an unskilled labourer in or from India or other Asian countries.

cooling-off period *n.* an interval to allow for a change of mind before commitment to action.

coolly *adv.* **1** in a way that is not friendly or enthusiastic. **2** in a calm manner.

coon *n.* a raccoon.

coop ● *n.* **1** a cage or pen for poultry. **2** a small place of confinement, esp. a prison. ● *v.* **1** put or keep in a coop. **2** confine (a person) in a small space. □ **fly the coop** *informal* leave abruptly.

co-op *n. informal* **1** a co-operative business, store or housing complex. **2** esp. *Cdn* an

educational program in which students alternate terms in the classroom with terms in the workforce in a job related to their studies.

co-operate *v.* (**co-operates, co-operated, co-operating**) **1** work or act together towards the same end. **2** comply with a request. □ **co-operation** *n.* **co-operator** *n.*

co-operative ● *adj.* **1** characterized by co-operation. **2** willing to co-operate. **3** (of a farm, business, etc.) owned and run jointly by its members, with profits shared among them. **4** designating a type of non-profit housing where the housing complex is jointly owned by the occupants. ● *n.* a co-operative institution. □ **co-operatively** *adv.*

Co-operative Commonwealth Federation *n. hist.* (in Canada) a progressive labour party formed in 1932, re-founded as the NDP in 1961.

co-opt *v.* **1 a** absorb into a larger group. **b** adopt. **2** appoint to membership of a body by invitation of the existing members. □ **co-optation** *n.*

coordinate ● *v.* (**coordinates, coordinated, coordinating**) **1** bring (various parts etc.) into an efficient relation. **2** work or act together effectively. ● *adj.* **1** equal in rank or importance. **2** involving coordination. ● *n.* **1** *Math* each of a set of magnitudes used to fix the position of a point, line, or plane. **2** (often in *pl.*) a combination of numbers or letters indicating a place on a map. **3** (in *pl.*) matching items of clothing. □ **coordinated** *adj.* **coordinator** *n.*

coordination *n.* **1** the action of coordinating. **2** the ability to control one's movements properly or effectively.

coot *n.* **1** a dark grey or black marsh bird with a white bill. **2** a scoter. **3** *informal derogatory* a stupid or elderly person.

cootie *n.* **1** *slang* a body louse. **2** any of various indeterminate bugs or germs.

cop *informal* ● *n.* a police officer. ● *v.* (**cops, copped, copping**) **1** catch or arrest (an offender). **2** receive or attain. □ **cop out 1** withdraw. **2** go back on a promise. **cop an attitude** assume an esp. arrogant posture etc. **cop a plea** plea bargain.

copayment *n.* (also **copay**) a payment made by a beneficiary (esp. for health services) in addition to that made by an insurer.

cope[1] *v.* (**copes, coped, coping**) deal effectively with something difficult. □ **coping** *n.*

cope[2] *n.* a long cloak-like vestment worn by a priest in ceremonies etc.

Copernican system n. (also **Copernican theory**) the theory that the planets (including the earth) move around the sun. [Say kuh PURNA kin]

copier n. a machine or person that copies.

co-pilot n. a second pilot in an aircraft.

copious adj. abundant, plentiful. □ **copiously** adv. **copiousness** n. [Say COPE oo us]

cop-out n. an act of copping out.

copper[1] ● n. **1** a red-brown metallic element, used esp. as an electrical conductor and in alloys. **2** a copper or bronze coin, esp. a penny. ● adj. made of or coloured like copper. □ **coppery** adj.

copper[2] n. slang a police officer.

copperhead n. a venomous viper of N America.

Copper Inuit pl. n. an Inuit people living along the Coppermine River in the NWT.

cops and robbers n. a children's game in which the participants act as police officers and criminals.

copse n. a small group of trees. [Say COPS]

Copt n. **1** a native Egyptian in the Hellenistic and Roman periods (from 323 BC to the 4th century AD). **2** a Christian of the Coptic Church.

copter n. informal a helicopter.

Coptic n. the language of the Copts, now used only in the Coptic Church. □ **Coptic** adj.

Coptic Church n. the native Christian Church of Egypt.

copulate v. (**copulates**, **copulated**, **copulating**) have sexual intercourse. □ **copulation** n. [Say COP you late]

copy ● n. (pl. **copies**) **1** a thing made to imitate or be identical to another. **2** a single specimen of a publication. **3 a** matter to be printed in a book, newspaper, etc. **b** the text of an advertisement. ● v. (**copies**, **copied**, **copying**) **1** make a copy of. **2** send a copy of (a letter) to a third party. **3** imitate.

copycat n. informal a person who copies another.

copy-edit v. (**copy-edits**, **copy-edited**, **copy-editing**) edit (copy) for printing. □ **copy editor** n.

copyist n. **1** a person who makes copies. **2** an imitator.

copyright ● n. the exclusive legal right granted to print, publish, perform, film, or record original literary, artistic, or musical material. ● v. secure copyright for (material).

copywriter n. a person who writes esp.

advertising copy for publication. □ **copywriting** n.

coquette n. a woman who flirts. □ **coquettish** adj. **coquettishly** adv. [Say co KET]

coral ● n. **1** a hard substance secreted by various marine creatures as an external skeleton. **2** a reddish-pink colour. **3** the roe of a lobster or scallop. ● adj. **1** of a reddish-pink colour. **2** made of coral.

cord ● n. **1** long thin flexible material made from several twisted strands. **2** a structure in the body resembling a cord. **3 a** ribbed fabric, esp. corduroy. **b** (in pl.) corduroy pants. **4** an insulated electric cable. **5** a measure of cut wood. ● v. fasten or bind with cord. □ **corded** adj.

cordgrass n. a grass growing in wet and marshy ground.

cordial ● adj. **1** heartfelt. **2** friendly. ● n. **1** a fruit-flavoured drink. **2** a comforting medicine. □ **cordiality** n. **cordially** adv. [Say CORE jul or CORDY ul, cordy ALA tee]

cordillera n. a system or group of usu. parallel mountain ranges. □ **cordilleran** adj. [Say cor DILLER uh or cordil YAIR uh]

cordless adj. (of an electrical appliance etc.) working from an internal source of energy etc. (esp. a battery).

cordon ● n. **1** a line or circle of police, soldiers, guards, etc. forming a barrier. **2** an ornamental cord or braid. ● v. enclose or separate with a cordon.

cordon bleu Cooking ● adj. **1** of the highest class. **2** designating a dish consisting of a cutlet of meat stuffed with ham and Swiss cheese, breaded and shallow fried. ● n. a cordon bleu cook. [Say cor don BLOO (with OO as in LOOK)]

corduroy n. **1** a thick cotton fabric with velvety ribs. **2** (in pl.) corduroy pants.

corduroy road n. esp. hist. a road made of tree trunks laid across muddy ground.

cordwood n. wood that is measured in cords.

core ● n. **1** the hard central part of various fruits, containing the seeds. **2** the central or most important part. **3** the central part of the earth. **4** (also **core lanes**) Cdn the express lanes on a highway. **5** the central part of a nuclear reactor. ● v. (**cores**, **cored**, **coring**) remove the core from. □ **corer** n.

coreopsis n. (pl. **coreopsis**) a plant of the daisy family with usu. yellow flowers. [Say cory OP sis]

corgi n. (pl. **corgis**) (also **Welsh corgi**) a short-legged dog with a foxlike head. [Say COR ghee]

coriander n. a parsley-like plant or its seeds used for flavouring in cooking. [Say CORY ander]

Corinthian ● adj. **1** of ancient Corinth. **2** Architecture of an order characterized by ornate decoration. ● n. a native of Corinth. [Say kuh RINTH ee in]

cork ● n. **1** the buoyant light brown bark of the cork oak. **2** a bottle stopper of cork etc. **3** a float of cork used in fishing etc. ● v. close with a cork. □ **put a cork in it** slang be quiet. □ **corky** adj.

corkboard n. board made of compressed cork, used as bulletin boards etc.

corked adj. (of wine) spoiled by a decayed cork.

corker n. informal **1** an excellent person or thing. **2** something that ends a discussion etc.

corking adj. informal strikingly impressive.

corkscrew ● n. a spiral-shaped device for extracting corks from bottles. ● v. twist in a spiral motion.

corm n. an underground swollen stem base of some plants.

cormorant n. a diving water bird with shiny black plumage. [Say CORMER unt]

corn[1] n. **1** a cereal plant yielding edible grains set on a cob. **2** the cob or grains of this.

corn[2] n. a painful area of thickened skin on the foot, caused by pressure.

cornball adj. = CORNY 1.

cornbread n. bread made from cornmeal.

corncob n. the cylindrical centre of an ear of corn, to which grains are attached.

cornea n. (pl. **corneas**) the transparent part of the front of the eyeball. □ **corneal** adj. [Say CORNY uh]

corned beef n. **1** beef brisket cured in brine and boiled. **2** low quality beef preserved in brine and saltpetre, chopped and tinned.

corner ● n. **1** a place where converging sides or edges meet. **2** an angle, esp. where two streets meet. **3** the internal space formed by the meeting of two sides. **4** a difficult position. **5** a secluded or remote place. **6** a monopoly on a stock of a commodity. ● v. **1** force into a difficult or inescapable position. **2 a** establish a monopoly in (a commodity). **b** dominate (the market) in this way. **3** go around a corner. □ **in a person's corner** supporting a person. **turn a** (or **the**) **corner** pass from one situation to a usu. better one.

cornerback n. Football a defensive player covering the sideline behind the line of scrimmage.

cornerstone n. **1 a** a stone that forms the base of a corner of a building. **b** a foundation stone. **2** a vital part.

cornet n. **1** a brass instrument resembling a trumpet but shorter and wider. **2** its player. □ **cornetist** n.

cornflower n. a plant with daisy-like deep-blue flowers.

cornice n. **1** a moulding around the wall of a room just below the ceiling. **2** a horizontal moulded projection crowning a building etc. [Say COR niss]

Cornish ● adj. of or relating to Cornwall. ● n. the ancient Celtic language of Cornwall.

Cornish hen n. a chicken slaughtered at six weeks to provide a single-serving sized bird.

cornmeal n. meal made by grinding corn.

cornrow n. a small tight braid made close to the head.

cornsilk n. the threadlike styles on an ear of corn.

cornstarch n. purified starch from corn, used as a thickener etc.

corn syrup n. glucose syrup often made from corn.

cornucopia n. (pl. **cornucopias**) **1** a symbol of plenty consisting of a goat's horn overflowing with flowers, fruit, and grain. **2** an abundant supply. [Say corn yuh COPEY uh]

corny adj. (**cornier**, **corniest**) **1** informal trite. **2** sentimental. **3** old-fashioned. □ **corniness** n.

corolla n. (pl. **corollas**) the petals of a flower. [Say kuh RAWL uh or kuh ROLE uh]

corollary n. (pl. **corollaries**) a situation, argument, or fact that is the direct result of another. [Say kuh RAWL uh ree]

corona n. (pl. **coronae** or **coronas**) **1 a** a small circle of light round the sun or moon. **b** the rarefied gaseous envelope of the sun. **2** Botany a crown-like outgrowth from the corolla. [Say kuh ROE nuh for the singular; for CORONAE say kuh ROE nee]

coronary ● adj. relating to the arteries which surround and supply the heart. ● n. (pl. **coronaries**) (also **coronary thrombosis**) a blockage of blood flow to the heart caused by a blood clot in a coronary artery. [Say CORA nerry]

coronary bypass n. a surgical procedure to relieve obstruction of the coronary arteries.

coronation n. the ceremony of crowning a sovereign.

coroner n. a public official responsible for

investigating violent, suspicious, or accidental deaths.

coronet *n.* **1** a small crown. **2** a circlet of precious materials. □ **coroneted** *adj.*

corporal[1] *n.* **1** (in Canada) a non-commissioned officer ranking above private. **2** (in some armies and police forces) a member ranking below sergeant.

corporal[2] *adj.* relating to the human body.

corporal punishment *n.* punishment inflicted on the body.

corporate *adj.* **1** of or relating to business corporations. **2** (of a large company etc.) authorized to act as a single entity. **3** of or shared by all the members of a group. □ **corporately** *adv.*

corporate raider *n.* a person who takes control of a company by buying up shares on the stock market.

corporation *n.* a company or group recognized in law as a single entity.

corporatism *n.* a political ideology or system in which business, industry, etc. are organized as corporate entities. □ **corporatist** *adj.*

corps *n.* (*pl.* **corps**) **1** *Military* **a** a body of troops with special duties. **b** a main subdivision of an army in the field. **2** a body of people engaged in a special activity. [*The singular sounds like CORE; for the plural say CORZ*]

corps de ballet *n.* the group of dancers of the lowest rank in a ballet company. [*Say cor duh bal LAY*]

corpse *n.* a dead (usu. human) body.

corpulent *adj.* fat. □ **corpulence** *n.* [*Say CORP you lint, CORP you lince*]

Corpus Christi *n.* *Christianity* a feast commemorating the Eucharist. [*Say corp us KRISS tee*]

corpuscle *n.* a red or white blood cell in vertebrates. □ **corpuscular** *adj.* [*Say CORE pussle, cor PUS kyoo lur*]

corral ● *n.* a pen for horses etc. ● *v.* (**corrals, corralled, corralling**) **1** drive or keep in a corral. **2** *informal* capture; get. [*Say kuh RAL*]

correct ● *adj.* **1** true, right, accurate. **2** proper. **3** in accordance with good standards of taste etc. ● *v.* **1** set right. **2** mark the errors in (a text etc.). **3** substitute the right thing for (the wrong one). **4** admonish or rebuke. **5** counteract. □ **correct for** adjust to compensate for a deviant factor. □ **correctable** *adj.* **correctly** *adv.* **correctness** *n.* **corrector** *n.*

correction *n.* **1** the act or process of correcting. **2** a change that corrects an error. **3** (usu. **corrections**) the treatment of convicted offenders through incarceration etc. □ **correctional** *adj.*

corrective ● *adj.* serving to correct or counteract something unwanted. ● *n.* a corrective measure.

correlate ● *v.* (**correlates, correlated, correlating**) **1** have a mutual relationship, in which one thing affects or depends on another. **2** bring into a mutual relation. ● *n.* each of two related or complementary things. [*Say CORA late for the verb, CORA lit for the noun*]

correlation *n.* **1** a mutual relation between two or more things. **2** the act or process of correlating.

correlative ● *adj.* having a mutual relation; corresponding. ● *n.* a correlative word or thing. [*Say kuh RELATIVE*]

correspond *v.* **1 a** be analogous or similar. **b** match; agree. **c** be in harmony. **2** communicate by exchanging letters etc. □ **corresponding** *adj.* **correspondingly** *adv.*

correspondence *n.* **1** similarity or harmony. **2 a** communication by letters etc. **b** letters.

correspondence course *n.* a course of study conducted by mail or over the Internet.

correspondent *n.* **1** a journalist reporting on a particular subject. **2** a person who communicates with others in writing.

corridor *n.* **1** a passage in a building or train from which doors lead into rooms or compartments. **2** a densely populated belt of land with major transportation routes. **3 a** a strip of territory that runs through that of another state and secures access to the sea or some desired part. **b** a right-of-way reserved for utilities: *hydro corridor*. **4** a route to which aircraft are confined, esp. over a foreign country. **5** an extent of land characterized by a specific activity, e.g. wildlife migration.

corridors of power *pl. n.* the upper echelons of government, business, etc.

corroborate *v.* (**corroborates, corroborated, corroborating**) confirm or give support to (a statement or theory). □ **corroboration** *n.* **corroborative** *adj.* [*Say kuh ROBBA rate*]

corrode *v.* (**corrodes, corroded, corroding**) **1** wear or be worn away, esp. by chemical action. **2** destroy gradually. □ **corroded** *adj.*

corrosion *n.* **1** the process of corroding. **2** damage caused by corroding.

corrosive ● *adj.* **1** tending to corrode or consume. **2** destructive. ● *n.* a corrosive substance.

corrugated *adj.* formed into alternate ridges and grooves. [*Say* CORA gated]

corrupt ● *adj.* **1** influenced by or using bribery or fraudulent activity. **2** morally depraved; wicked. **3** (of a text etc.) made unreliable by errors or alterations. **●** *v.* make or become corrupt. □ **corrupter** *n.* **corruptible** *adj.* **corruptly** *adv.*

corruption *n.* **1** use of corrupt practices. **2** moral deterioration. **3** irregular alteration (of a text, data, etc.) from its original state. **4** decomposition.

corsage *n.* an arrangement of flowers worn pinned to a woman's dress, or on the wrist. [*Say* core SAWZH]

corset *n.* **1** a close-fitting undergarment worn by women to shape and support the torso. **2** a similar garment worn to support the back. □ **corseted** *adj.*

Corsican ● *adj.* of or relating to Corsica. **●** *n.* **1** a native of Corsica. **2** the Italian dialect of Corsica.

cortège *n.* **1** a procession, esp. for a funeral. **2** a person's entourage. [*Say* core TEZH]

cortex *n.* (*pl.* **cortices**) **1** the outer part of an organ, esp. of the brain (**cerebral cortex**). **2** *Botany* **a** an outer layer of tissue immediately below the epidermis. **b** bark. □ **cortical** *adj.* [*Say* CORE tex, CORTA seez, CORE tickle]

corticosteroid *n.* (also **corticoid**) **1** any of a group of steroid hormones produced in the adrenal cortex. **2** an analogous synthetic steroid. [*Say* corta co STEROID]

cortisone *n.* a steroid hormone used medicinally to treat inflammation and allergy. [*Say* CORTA zone]

corundum *n.* extremely hard crystallized aluminum oxide, used esp. as an abrasive. [*Say* kuh RUN dum]

corvette *n.* a small naval escort vessel.

co-sign *v.* sign jointly with another. □ **co-signer** *n.*

cosine *n.* *Math* the ratio of the side adjacent to an acute angle (in a right-angled triangle) to the hypotenuse. [*Say* CO sine]

cosmetic ● *adj.* **1** intended to beautify or improve the body, esp. the face. **2** intended to improve only appearances. **●** *n.* a cosmetic preparation, esp. for the face. □ **cosmetically** *adv.*

cosmic *adj.* **1** of or connected with the cosmos. **2** of or for space travel. **3** immeasurably vast. □ **cosmically** *adv.*

cosmic rays *pl. n.* (also **cosmic radiation** *n.*) radiation from outer space, usu. with high energy and penetrative power.

cosmogony *n.* (*pl.* **cosmogonies**) **1** a theory or account of the origin of the universe. **2** the branch of science that deals with this. [*Say* koz MOGGA nee]

cosmology *n.* (*pl.* **cosmologies**) **1** the study of the origin and development of the universe. **2** a theory of the origin of the universe. □ **cosmological** *adj.* **cosmologist** *n.* [*Say* koz MOLLA jee, cosma LOGICAL, coz MOLLA jist]

cosmonaut *n.* a Russian astronaut.

cosmopolitan ● *adj.* **1 a** familiar with and at ease in many different countries. **b** consisting of people from many parts. **2 a** free from national prejudices. **b** sophisticated; worldly. **●** *n.* **1 a** cosmopolitan person. **2 a** cocktail of vodka, orange liqueur, lime juice, and cranberry juice. □ **cosmopolitanism** *n.* [*Say* cozma POLLA tin]

cosmos¹ *n.* (*pl.* **cosmoses**) **1** the universe, esp. as a well-ordered whole. **2** an ordered system.

cosmos² *n.* (*pl.* **cosmos**) a plant bearing single daisy-like blossoms of various colours.

Cossack ● *n.* a member of a people living on the northern shores of the Black and Caspian seas, originally famous for their military skill. **●** *adj.* of the Cossacks.

cosset *v.* (**cossets, cosseted, cosseting**) care for and protect in an overindulgent way. [*Say* KOSS it]

cost ● *v.* (**costs, cost, costing**) **1** have as a price. **2 a** involve as a loss of. **b** necessitate the expenditure of. **3** (*past* and *past participle* **costed**) fix or estimate the cost of. **4** *informal* be costly. **●** *n.* **1** what a thing costs. **2** a loss or sacrifice; an expenditure of time etc. **3** (in *pl.*) legal or household expenses. □ **at all costs** (or **at any cost**) no matter what the cost or risk may be. **at cost** at the initial cost; at cost price. **at the cost of** at the expense of losing or sacrificing. **cost a person dear** (or **dearly**) involve a person in a high cost or a heavy penalty. **to a person's cost** with loss or disadvantage to a person.

co-star ● *n.* a film, television, or stage star appearing with another. **●** *v.* (**co-stars, co-starred, co-starring**) **1** take part as a co-star. **2** (of a production) include as a co-star.

Costa Rican *n.* a native or inhabitant of Costa Rica. □ **Costa Rican** *adj.* [*Say* costa REEK'n]

cost-benefit *adj.* assessing the relation between the cost of an operation and the value of the resulting benefits.

cost-effective *adj.* effective in relation to

its cost. □ **cost-effectively** *adv.* **cost-effectiveness** *n.*

costing *n.* (often in *pl.*) the cost of producing or undertaking something.

costly *adj.* (**costlier, costliest**) **1** expensive. **2** involving great loss or sacrifice. **3** of great value. □ **costliness** *n.*

cost of living *n.* the level of prices esp. of the basic necessities of life.

cost price *n.* the price paid for a thing by a retailer.

costume ● *n.* **1** a style of dress, esp. that of a particular place, time, etc. **2** an ensemble of unusual clothes worn at Halloween etc. **3** clothing for a particular activity. **4** a performer's clothes worn for a part. ● *v.* (**costumes, costumed, costuming**) provide with a costume. □ **costuming** *n.*

costume jewellery *n.* relatively inexpensive jewellery made to imitate expensive jewellery.

cot *n.* a small folding or portable bed.

cotangent *n.* the ratio of the side adjacent to an acute angle (in a right-angled triangle) to the opposite side. [*Say* CO tangent]

coterie *n.* a group of people who associate closely. [*Say* CO tur ee]

cotoneaster *n.* a shrub bearing usu. bright red berries. [*Say* kuh tony ASTER]

cottage ● *n.* **1** a dwelling used for vacation purposes. **2** a small house, typically one in the country. ● *v.* (**cottages, cottaged, cottaging**) vacation at a cottage. □ **cottager** *n.* **cottaging** *n.*

cottage cheese *n.* soft white cheese made from skimmed milk curds.

cottage industry *n.* a business activity in a home.

cottage roll *n.* *Cdn* a pickled, boneless, prepared ham from the pork butt.

cotter *n.* **1** a bolt for securing parts of machinery etc. **2** (also **cotter pin**) a split pin that opens after passing through a hole.

cotton ● *n.* **1** a soft white fibrous substance covering the seeds of certain plants. **2** (also **cotton plant**) such a plant. **3** thread or cloth made from the fibre. ● *v. informal* take a liking to. □ **cotton on** *informal* begin to understand. □ **cottony** *adj.*

cotton batting *n.* (*Cdn* also **cotton batten**) fluffy cotton wadding.

cotton candy *n.* candy floss.

cottontail *n.* a N American rabbit with a white fluffy underside to the tail.

cottonwood *n.* any of several N American poplars, having seeds covered in white cottony hairs.

cotyledon *n.* an embryonic leaf in seed-bearing plants. [*Say* cotta LEED'n]

couch ● *n.* (*pl.* **couches**) **1** an upholstered piece of furniture for several people; a sofa. **2** a long seat with a headrest at one end, esp. one in a psychiatrist's or doctor's office. ● *v.* (**couches, couched, couching**) express in words of a specified kind.

couch potato *n.* *slang* a person who spends much time watching television.

cougar *n.* a moderately large wild cat with a golden or greyish coat.

cough ● *v.* **1** expel air from the lungs with a sudden sharp sound. **2** (of an engine etc.) make a similar sound. ● *n.* **1** an act of coughing. **2** an illness causing coughing. □ **cough up** (also **cough out**) **1** eject by coughing. **2** *slang* bring out or hand over (money etc.) reluctantly. **3** *slang* yield or eject. □ **cougher** *n.*

could *aux. v.* (*3rd. singular* **could**) past of CAN¹.

couldn't *contr.* could not.

coulee *n.* a deep ravine with steep sides. [*Say* COOLY]

coulis *n.* (*pl.* **coulis**) a purée of fruit etc., thin enough to pour. [*Say* COOLY]

coulomb *n.* the SI unit of electric charge. [*Say* COO lom]

council *n.* **1** an advisory, deliberative, or administrative body of people formally constituted and meeting regularly. **2** the body of people elected to manage the affairs of a municipality.

councillor *n.* a member of a council. □ **councillorship** *n.*

counsel ● *n.* **1** advice. **2** consultation. **3** (*pl.* **counsel**) a lawyer or lawyers. ● *v.* (**counsels, counselled, counselling**) **1** advise. **2 a** give professional advice on social or personal problems. **b** assist in resolving personal difficulties. □ **keep one's own counsel** not confide in others. □ **counselling** *n.*

counsellor *n.* (also **counselor**) **1** a person who counsels or gives counsel. **2** a supervisor of a children's camp.

count¹ ● *v.* **1** determine the total number of. **2** repeat numbers in ascending order. **3** include or be included. **4** consider to be (lucky etc.). **5** have value; matter. **6** rely on. ● *n.* **1 a** the act of counting. **b** a total found by counting. **2** *Law* each charge in an indictment. **3** a count by a referee when a boxer is knocked down. **4** a point under discussion. □ **count against** be reckoned to the disadvantage of. **count one's chickens (before they're hatched)**

be hasty in anticipating good fortune. **count the days** (or **hours** etc.) be impatient. **count down** recite numbers backwards to zero. **count on** (or **upon**) **1** depend on, rely on. **2** make allowance for. **count up** find the sum of. **down** (or **out**) **for the count 1** *Boxing* defeated by being unable to rise within ten seconds. **2** *informal* **a** dead drunk. **b** soundly asleep. **not counting** excluding from the reckoning. **stand up and be counted** state publicly one's support. □ **countable** *adj.*

count[2] *n.* a noble in some countries corresponding in rank to an English earl.

countdown *n.* **1** the act of counting down, esp. at a rocket launch etc. **2** the final moments before any significant event.

countenance ● *n.* **1** the face or its expression. **2** composure. **3** favour; moral support. ● *v.* (**countenances, countenanced, countenancing**) give approval to. [*Say* COUNTA nince]

counter[1] *n.* **1** a long flat-topped surface at a height suitable for working or serving standing up. **2** a small object used for keeping score or marking place in some board games. **3** an apparatus used for counting. **4** a person or thing that counts. □ **over the counter** by ordinary retail purchase. **under the counter** surreptitiously, esp. illegally.

counter[2] ● *v.* speak or act in opposition or response to. ● *adv.* in the opposite direction to or in conflict with. ● *adj.* opposing. ● *n.* a thing which opposes something else.

counter- *comb. form* **1** retaliation, opposition. **2** opposite direction. **3** correspondence, duplication etc.

counteract *v.* act against something in order to reduce its force or neutralize it. □ **counteraction** *n.*

counterattack ● *n.* an attack in reply to an attack. ● *v.* attack in reply.

counterbalance ● *n.* **1** a weight balancing another. **2** an argument, force, etc. that counters another. ● *v.* (**counterbalances, counterbalanced, counterbalancing**) act as a counterbalance to.

counterclaim ● *n.* a claim made against another claim, esp. in law. ● *v.* make a counterclaim (for).

counter-clockwise ● *adv.* in a direction opposite to the movement of the hands of a clock. ● *adj.* moving counter-clockwise.

counterculture *n.* a culture having values that are in opposition to those of the dominant culture. □ **countercultural** *adj.*

counterfeit ● *adj.* (of money etc.) not genuine; forged. ● *n.* a forgery. ● *v.* **1** imitate fraudulently. **2** pretend (feelings etc.). □ **counterfeiter** *n.* **counterfeiting** *n.* [*Say* COUNTER fit]

counter-intelligence *n.* action taken to prevent spying by an enemy.

countermeasure *n.* an action taken to counteract a danger, threat, etc.

counteroffensive *n.* *Military* an attack made against an attacking force.

counterpart *n.* **1** a person or thing that corresponds to another. **2** one of two copies of a legal document.

counterpoint *n.* **1 a** the art or technique of writing or playing a melody in conjunction with another. **b** a melody played in conjunction with another. **2** a contrasting element, theme, etc. **3** contrast.

counterpoise *n.* a counterbalance.

counterproductive *adj.* having the opposite of the desired effect.

Counter-Reformation *n.* *hist.* the reform of the Catholic Church in the 16th and 17th centuries in response to the Protestant Reformation.

counter-revolution *n.* a revolution opposing a former one. □ **counter-revolutionary** *adj. & n.*

countersign *v.* sign (a document previously signed by another).

countersink ● *v.* (**countersinks, countersunk, countersinking**) **1** enlarge and bevel (a hole) so that a screw etc. can be inserted flush with the surface. **2** sink (a screw etc.) in such a hole. ● *n.* a tool used to countersink a hole.

counter-tenor *n.* an adult male alto singing voice.

countertop *n.* the flat working surface of a counter.

countervail *v.* oppose forcefully and usu. successfully.

countervailing duty *n.* a tax put on imports to offset a subsidy in the exporting country.

counterweight *n.* a counterbalancing weight.

countess *n.* **1** the wife or widow of a count or earl. **2** a woman holding the rank of count or earl.

countless *adj.* too many to be counted.

countrified *adj.* often *derogatory* rural or rustic. [*Say* CUN truh fied]

country *n.* (*pl.* **countries**) **1** the territory of a nation with its own government; a nation. **2** rural districts as opposed to cities. **3** the land of a person's birth or citizenship. **4** a territory marked by some particular characteristic. **5** = COUNTRY AND

WESTERN. □**across country** not keeping to roads. **by a country mile** *informal* by a great extent.

country and western *n.* a style of music originating in the rural or southern areas of N America, often accompanied by guitar and dealing with themes of lost love.

country club *n.* a suburban club, with facilities for golf, tennis, etc.

countryman *n.* (*pl.* **countrymen**) **1** a person living in a rural area. **2** (also **fellow-countryman**) a person of one's own or a specific country or region.

country music *n.* = COUNTRY AND WESTERN.

countryside *n.* **1** a rural area or areas. **2** the inhabitants of a rural area.

countrywide *adj.* throughout a nation.

countrywoman *n.* (*pl.* **countrywomen**) **1** a woman living in a rural area. **2** a person of one's own or a specific country.

county *n.* (*pl.* **counties**) any of the territorial divisions of some countries etc., for judicial or local government purposes.

county council *n.* the elected governing body of an administrative county. □**county councillor** *n.*

county seat *n.* (also **county town**) the administrative capital of a county.

coup *n.* **1** a successful move. **2** a coup d'état. [*Say* COO]

coup de grâce *n.* (*pl.* **coups de grâce**) **1** a final stroke, esp. to kill a wounded animal or person. **2** something that puts a definitive end to something. [*Say* coo duh GRASS *or* coo duh GRAWSS]

coup d'état *n.* (*pl.* **coups d'état**) a violent or illegal seizure of power from a government. [*Say* coo day TAW]

coupe *n.* a two-door car with a hard roof. [*Say* COOP]

couple ● *n.* **1 a** two. **b** about two. **2 a** two people who are romantically involved. **b** a pair in dancing etc. ● *v.* (**couples**, **coupled**, **coupling**) **1** fasten or link together; connect. **2** associate in thought. **3** bring or come together as partners. **4** copulate. □**coupler** *n.*

couplet *n.* two successive usu. rhyming lines of verse.

coupling *n.* **1** a device connecting railway cars, machine parts, etc. **2** a thing that couples things together.

coupon *n.* **1** a form or ticket entitling the bearer to something, e.g. a discount on a purchase etc. **2** a detachable portion of a bond etc. given up in return for interest payment. [*Say* COO pon *or* CYOO pon]

courage *n.* the ability to disregard fear; bravery. □**courage of one's convictions** the courage to act on one's beliefs. [*Say* CUR idge]

courageous *adj.* brave. □**courageously** *adv.* [*Say* cur AGE us]

coureur de bois *n. Cdn hist.* (*pl.* **coureurs de bois**) a French or Metis fur trader. [*Say* coo RUR duh BWAH]

courier ● *n.* **1** a messenger who conveys esp. documents from sender to recipient. **2** a person who transports drugs, arms, etc. illegally. ● *v.* ship by courier.

course ● *n.* **1** a continuous onward movement. **2** a direction taken. **3** the ground on which a race, game, etc. takes place. **4** a series of lectures, lessons, etc., in a particular subject. **5** any of the successive parts of a meal. **6** a sequence of medical treatment etc. **7** a channel in which water flows. ● *v.* (**courses**, **coursed**, **coursing**) flow, esp. fast. □**the course of nature** ordinary events. **in the course of** during. **in the course of time** eventually. **of course** as is expected. **run** (or **take**) **its course** (esp. of an illness) complete its natural development.

coursework *n.* the work done during a course of study.

court ● *n.* **1** (also **court of law**) **a** an assembly of a judge or judges and other persons acting as a tribunal in civil and criminal cases. **b** a regular session of a court. **c** a courtroom. **2** a demarcated area for playing games. **3** = ATRIUM 1b. **4 a** the residence, establishment, courtiers, etc. of a sovereign. **b** an assembly held by a sovereign. **5** attention paid to a person. ● *v.* **1 a** try to win the affection or favour of. **b** pay amorous attention to. **2** seek to win. **3** invite (misfortune) by one's actions. □**go to court** take legal action. **hold court** preside over a group of admirers etc. **out of court 1** (of a plaintiff) not entitled to be heard. **2** (of a settlement) arranged before a hearing can take place.

courteous *adj.* polite. □**courteously** *adv.* **courteousness** *n.* [*Say* KER tee us]

courtesan *n. hist.* **1** a prostitute, esp. one with upper-class clients. **2** the mistress of a wealthy man. [*Say* CORTA zan]

courtesy ● *n.* (*pl.* **courtesies**) **1** courteous behaviour. **2** a courteous act. ● *adj.* (esp. of transport) supplied free of charge to people who are already paying for another service. □**as a courtesy** by favour, not by right. **courtesy of** thanks to. [*Say* KER tuh see]

courthouse *n.* a building in which a judicial court is held.

courtier *n.* a person who attends or frequents a sovereign's court. [*Say* CORE tee ur]

courtly *adj.* (**courtlier, courtliest**) polished or refined in manners. □ **courtliness** *n.*

court martial ● *n.* (*pl.* **courts martial**) a judicial court for trying members of the armed services. ● *v.* (**court-martial**) (**court-martials, court-martialled, court-martialling**) try by a court martial.

Court of Appeal *n.* a court of law hearing appeals against judgments in lower courts.

courtroom *n.* the place in which a court of law meets.

courtship *n.* **1 a** courting. **b** the period in which this occurs. **2** an attempt to gain advantage by flattery, attention, etc.

courtyard *n.* an area enclosed by walls or buildings.

couscous *n.* a type of N African pasta in granules made from crushed durum wheat, often steamed and served with meat, vegetables, etc. [*Say* COOSE coose (*rhymes with* GOOSE)]

cousin *n.* **1 a** (also **first cousin**) the child of one's uncle or aunt. **b** any other relative with whom one shares a common ancestor. **2** something related to another by common features etc. or nation. **3** a person of a kindred race or nation.

couth *jocular* ● *adj.* cultured; well-mannered. ● *n.* good manners. [*Rhymes with* YOUTH]

couture *n.* **1** the design and manufacture of fashionable clothes. **2** high fashion. □ **couturier** *n.* [*Say* coo CHOOR, coo TOORY ay]

covalence *n.* **1** the linking of atoms by a covalent bond. **2** the number of pairs of electrons an atom can share with another. [*Say* co VAY lince]

covalent *adj.* **1** relating to chemical bonds. **2** formed by sharing of electrons. □ **covalently** *adv.* [*Say* co VAY lint]

cove *n.* a small, esp. sheltered, bay in a shoreline.

covenant ● *n.* **1** an agreement. **2** *Law* **a** a contract drawn up under a seal. **b** a clause of a covenant. **3** (**Covenant**) *Bible* an agreement between God and a person etc. *See also* ARK OF THE COVENANT. ● *v.* agree, esp. by legal covenant. [*Say* CUVVA nint]

cover ● *v.* **1** protect or conceal by means of a cloth, lid, etc. **2** extend over. **3** protect; clothe. **4** deal with; report on. **5** travel (a specified distance). **6** be enough to pay for. **7** (**cover oneself**) take precautionary measures to protect oneself. **8** deputize or stand in for. **9** protect (an exposed person). ● *n.* **1** something that covers or protects. **2** a hiding place; a shelter. **3** woods or undergrowth. **4 a** a pretense; a screen. **b** a spy's pretended identity. **5** = COVER CHARGE. **6** a recording or performance of a previously recorded song etc. □ **break cover** leave a place of shelter while being chased. **cover one's tracks** conceal evidence of what one has done. **cover up 1** completely cover or conceal. **2** assist in a deception.

coverage *n.* **1** an area or an amount covered. **2** the amount of publicity received. **3** a risk covered by an insurance policy.

coverall *n.* (usu. in *pl.*) a one-piece garment worn to protect other clothing.

cover charge *n.* an extra charge levied per head in a restaurant, nightclub, etc.

covered *adj.* **1** provided with a lid or covering. **2 a** enclosed. **b** (of a ship) decked. **3** enveloped. **4** insured.

cover girl *n.* a female model whose picture appears on magazine covers etc.

covering *n.* anything that covers for protection, concealment, etc.

covering letter *n.* (also **cover letter**) a letter which accompanies a resumé etc.

coverlet *n.* a bedspread.

cover story *n.* **1** a story in a magazine highlighted on the front cover. **2** an invented story intended to mislead.

covert ● *adj.* secret or disguised. ● *n.* a thicket which hides game. □ **covertly** *adv.* [*Say* CO vert, co VERT or CUV ert *for the adjective*, CO vert or CUV ert *for the noun*]

cover-up *n.* **1** an act of concealing circumstances. **2** a loose garment worn to cover a bathing suit, etc.

covet *v.* (**covets, coveted, coveting**) **1** desire something belonging to someone else. **2** long for or desire greatly. □ **coveted** *adj.*

covetous *adj.* **1** wrongfully eager to possess something. **2** greatly desirous (of something). □ **covetously** *adv.* **covetousness** *n.* [*Say* CUVVET us]

covey *n.* (*pl.* **coveys**) **1** a brood of game birds. **2** a small group of people or things. [*Say* CUVVY]

cow[1] *n.* **1** a fully grown female of any bovine animal. **2** the female of other large animals, esp. the moose, elephant, etc. □ **have a cow** *slang* become angry. **till the cows come home** *informal* an indefinitely long time.

cow[2] *v.* (usu. in *passive*) intimidate or frighten into submission.

coward *n.* a person with little courage in the face of danger, pain, etc. □ **cowardly** *adj.*

cowardice *n.* lack of courage.

cowbell *n.* **1** a bell worn round a cow's neck. **2** a similar bell used as a percussion instrument.

cowberry *n.* (*pl.* **cowberries**) an evergreen shrub bearing red berries.

cowbird *n.* any of several N American orioles which lays its eggs in other birds' nests.

cowboy *n.* **1** a person who herds cattle, esp. in western N America. **2** *informal* **a** a person who acts outside of established rules etc. **b** an unscrupulous or reckless person.

cowboy boot *n.* a square-heeled boot with a pointed toe, extending to mid-calf.

cowboy hat *n.* a hat with a high crown and broad brim.

cowcatcher *n.* a metal frame at the front of a locomotive for pushing aside obstacles.

cower *v.* crouch or shrink back in fear. [*Rhymes with* FLOWER]

cowgirl *n.* a woman who herds and tends cattle.

cowhand *n.* a person who tends cattle.

cowhide *n.* **1** leather made from a cow's hide. **2** a leather whip made from this.

Cowichan *n.* (*pl.* **Cowichan**) **1** a member of an Aboriginal people living on SE Vancouver Island. **2** the language of this people, a dialect of Halkomelem. □ **Cowichan** *adj.* [*Say* COW itch un]

Cowichan sweater *n.* Cdn a heavy sweater of wool with animal designs, made by the Coast Salish of the Cowichan valley.

cowl *n.* **1 a** the hood of a monk's habit. **b** a loose hood. **2** a covering of a chimney or ventilating shaft. **3** (also **cowling**) the removable cover of a vehicle or aircraft engine. □ **cowled** *adj.* [*Rhymes with* OWL]

cowlick *n.* a projecting lock of hair.

co-worker *n.* a fellow worker.

cow-pie *n.* (also **cow patty, cow pat**) a flat piece of cow dung.

cowpoke *n.* (also **cowpuncher**) = COWBOY.

cowslip *n.* a primrose with fragrant yellow flowers.

cowtown *n.* a town or city in a cattle area of western N America.

cox ● *n.* (*pl.* **coxes**) a coxswain. ● *v.* (**coxes, coxed, coxing**) act as a cox. □ **coxless** *adj.*

coxcomb *n.* archaic a vain and conceited man.

coxswain *n.* **1** a steersman in a rowboat.

2 the senior petty officer in a small ship. [*Say* COX'n *or* COX swain]

coy *adj.* (**coyer, coyest**) **1** pretending to be shy or modest. **2** irritatingly reticent. □ **coyly** *adv.* **coyness** *n.*

coyote *n.* **1** a wolflike wild dog native to N America. **2** a trickster figure in N American Aboriginal folklore. [*Say* kye OH tee *or* KYE ote]

cozy ● *adj.* (**cozier, coziest**) **1** comfortable, warm, or snug. **2** intimate and friendly. **3** working to the mutual advantage of those involved (used to convey a suspicion of corruption). **4** *derogatory* not difficult or demanding. ● *n.* (*pl.* **cozies**) a cover to keep something hot, esp. a teapot. □ **cozy up to** (**cozies, cozied, cozying**) *informal* ingratiate oneself with. □ **cozily** *adv.* **coziness** *n.*

CPP *abbr.* Canada Pension Plan.

CPR *abbr.* CARDIOPULMONARY RESUSCITATION.

CPU *n.* (*pl.* **CPUs**) CENTRAL PROCESSING UNIT.

crab[1] ● *n.* **1** a ten-footed crustacean having the first pair of legs modified as pincers. **2** (also **crab louse**) (often in *pl.*) a parasitic louse infesting hairy parts of the body. ● *v.* (**crabs, crabbed, crabbing**) fish for crabs. □ **crabber** *n.*

crab[2] *informal* ● *v.* (**crabs, crabbed, crabbing**) find fault, criticize. ● *n.* a bad-tempered person.

crabapple *n.* a small, sour apple.

crabbed *adj.* **1** (of handwriting) cramped and hard to read. **2** = CRABBY.

crabby *adj.* (**crabbier, crabbiest**) surly, irritable. □ **crabbily** *adv.* **crabbiness** *n.*

crabgrass *n.* any of several creeping grasses infesting lawns.

crack ● *n.* **1 a** a sudden sharp noise. **b** (in a voice) a sudden change in pitch. **2** a sharp blow. **3 a** a narrow opening formed by a break. **b** a partial fracture. **4** *informal* a joke or gibe. **5** *informal* **a** an attempt. **b** an opportunity. **6** (also **crack cocaine**) *slang* a potent form of cocaine. ● *v.* **1** break without a complete separation of parts. **2** make or cause to make a sudden sharp sound. **3** break or cause to break with a cracking sound. **4** break down. **5** (of the voice) change tone, become harsh. **6 a** decipher. **b** break into. **7** tell (a joke). **8** *informal* hit hard. ● *adj.* *informal* excellent; first-rate. □ **crack a book** *informal* study or research. **crack down on** *informal* take severe measures against. **crack a smile** *informal* begin to smile. **crack the whip** *informal* exercise authority. **crack up** *informal* **1** suffer a breakdown. **2** laugh or cause to laugh. **get cracking** *informal* begin promptly. **have a crack at** *informal* attempt. **not all it's cracked up to be** *informal* not all a thing seems to be.

crackdown *n.* enforcement of severe or repressive measures (esp. against lawbreakers etc.).

cracked *adj.* **1** having cracks. **2** *informal* eccentric or crazy. **3** varying or broken in tone.

cracked wheat *n.* wheat crushed into small pieces.

cracker *n.* **1 a** a thin, dry biscuit. **b** a cookie. **2** a paper cylinder which, when pulled, makes a sharp noise and releases a small toy etc. **3** a firework exploding with a crack.

crackerjack *slang* • *adj.* exceptionally fine or expert. • *n.* an exceptionally fine thing.

crackers *adj. slang* crazy.

crackhead *n. slang* a habitual user of crack cocaine.

crack house *n.* a place where crack cocaine is sold or used.

crackle • *v.* (**crackles, crackled, crackling**) make short, sharp cracking sounds. • *n.* such a sound. □ **crackly** *adj.*

crackling *n.* the crisp skin of roast pork.

crackpot *slang* • *n.* an eccentric or foolish person. • *adj.* crazy, unworkable.

crack-up *n. informal* **1** a mental breakdown. **2** a car crash.

cradle • *n.* **1 a** a baby's bed on rockers. **b** a place in which a thing begins. **2** a framework resembling a cradle. • *v.* (**cradles, cradled, cradling**) hold gently and protectively. □ **from (the) cradle to (the) grave** from infancy till death. **rob the cradle** become romantically involved with someone much younger.

cradleboard *n.* (among some N American Aboriginal peoples) a board to which an infant is strapped.

craft • *n.* **1 a** a trade or an art. **b** the product of such skill. **2** skill, esp. in practical arts. **3** the activity of producing handiwork. **4** (*pl.* **craft**) a boat, aircraft, or spacecraft. **5** cunning. • *v.* make skilfully.

crafter *n.* = CRAFTSPERSON.

craft shop *n.* **1** a small store selling handicrafts. **2** (also **craft store**) a store selling craft supplies.

craftsman *n.* (*pl.* **craftsmen**) **1** a skilled worker in a particular craft. **2** a person who practises a handicraft.

craftsmanship *n.* **1** the quality of execution in a craft. **2** skilled workmanship.

craftsperson *n.* (*pl.* **craftspeople**) a person who practises a handicraft, esp. an artisan.

crafty *adj.* (**craftier, craftiest**) cunning, wily. □ **craftily** *adv.* **craftiness** *n.*

crag *n.* a steep or rugged rock. □ **craggy** *adj.*

cram *v.* (**crams, crammed, cramming**) **1 a** fill to bursting. **b** force (a thing) into. **2** study hard before a test.

cramp • *n.* **1** a painful involuntary contraction of a muscle or muscles. **2** abdominal pain accompanying menstruation. • *v.* **1** affect with a cramp or cramps. **2** restrict or hamper. □ **cramp a person's style** prevent a person from acting freely.

cramped *adj.* **1** (of handwriting) small and difficult to read. **2** uncomfortably small or crowded.

crampon *n.* a spiked iron plate fixed to a boot for walking on ice etc. [*Say* CRAMP on]

cranberry *n.* (*pl.* **cranberries**) an evergreen shrub producing small tart red berries.

crane • *n.* **1** a machine for moving heavy objects. **2 a** a tall wading bird with long legs and a long neck. **b** = GREAT BLUE HERON. • *v.* (**cranes, craned, craning**) stretch out (one's neck) in order to see.

cranesbill *n.* any of various herbaceous plants having beaked fruits.

cranial *adj.* of or relating to the skull. [*Say* CRAY nee ul]

cranium *n.* (*pl.* **craniums** or **crania**) the part of the skull enclosing the brain. [*Say* CRAY nee um *for the singular; for* CRANIA *say* CRAY nee uh]

crank[1] • *n.* part of an axle or shaft bent at right angles for converting reciprocal into circular motion and vice versa. • *v.* **1** cause to move by means of a crank. **2** start by turning a crank. □ **crank out** *informal* produce quickly in a mechanical fashion. **crank up 1** start or power up. **2** *informal* increase (speed, sound, etc.). **turn one's crank** *slang* please or excite one's interest.

crank[2] • *n.* **1** an eccentric person. **2** a bad-tempered person. • *adj.* of an eccentric etc. person.

crank call *n.* a harassing telephone call usu. made as a prank.

crankcase *n.* a metal covering enclosing an engine's crankshaft, connecting rods, etc.

crankshaft *n.* a shaft driven by a crank.

cranky *adj.* (**crankier, crankiest**) **1** bad-tempered. **2** working badly. □ **crankily** *adv.* **crankiness** *n.*

cranny n. (pl. **crannies**) a small narrow opening or hole.

crap[1] slang ● n. **1 a** feces. **b** an act of defecation. **2** nonsense. **3** something valueless. **4** garbage. ● v. (**craps**, **crapped**, **crapping**) defecate. □ **cut the crap** slang get to the point. □ **crappy** adj.

crap[2] n. (in pl.) a gambling game played with two dice. □ **crap out 1** make a losing throw in craps. **2** informal fail. **shoot craps** play craps.

crape n. **1** CREPE. **2** a fabric, usu. black silk, formerly used for mourning clothes.

crappie n. a N American freshwater sunfish.

crapshoot n. slang a gamble or highly uncertain venture. □ **crapshooter** n.

crash ● v. (**crashes**, **crashed**, **crashing**) **1** make or cause to make a loud smashing noise. **2** (of a vehicle) collide violently with another vehicle, obstacle, etc. **3** (of an aircraft) fall from the sky and hit the land or water. **4** collide violently. **5** undergo financial ruin. **6** informal enter without permission. **7** (of a computer etc.) fail suddenly. **8** slang **a** sleep. **b** stay somewhere temporarily. ● n. (pl. **crashes**) **1** an instance or sound of crashing. **2** (as an adj.) marked by an urgent and concentrated effort. **3** a dramatic decrease in numbers. □ **crash and burn** informal collapse or fail utterly.

crashing adj. informal overwhelming.

crash-land v. (of an aircraft or pilot) make an emergency landing. □ **crash landing** n.

crash test ● v. assess (a product) for safety under severe conditions. ● n. such a test.

crass adj. (**crasser**, **crassest**) **1** not subtle. **2** insensitive, rude. □ **crassly** adv. **crassness** n.

crate ● n. **1** a usu. wooden case or box for transporting goods. **2** slang an old airplane or other vehicle. ● v. (**crates**, **crated**, **crating**) pack in a crate.

crater ● n. **1** the mouth of a volcano. **2** a bowl-shaped cavity created by an explosion or impact. ● v. make a crater or craters in. □ **cratered** adj.

cravat n. a scarf worn inside an open-necked shirt. [Say kruh VAT]

crave v. (**craves**, **craved**, **craving**) **1** feel a powerful desire for. **2** dated ask for. □ **craver** n.

craven ● adj. cowardly. ● n. a cowardly person. □ **cravenly** adv.

craving n. a strong desire or longing.

craw n. the crop of a bird or insect. □ **stick**

in one's craw informal be difficult to accept.

crawfish n. (pl. **crawfish**) a large marine spiny lobster.

crawl ● v. **1** move slowly, esp. on hands and knees. **2** (of an insect etc.) creep. **3** move or progress slowly. **4** informal behave obsequiously. **5** be unpleasantly covered or filled with. **6** feel a creepy sensation. ● n. **1** an act of crawling. **2** a slow rate of movement. **3** a high-speed swimming stroke with alternate overarm movements. □ **crawler** n.

crawl space n. a low, constricted space in a house for access to wiring etc.

crayfish n. (pl. **crayfish**) **1** a small lobster-like freshwater crustacean. **2** a crawfish.

crayon ● n. a stick of coloured wax etc. used for drawing. ● v. (**crayons**, **crayoned**, **crayoning**) draw with crayons.

craze ● v. (**crazes**, **crazed**, **crazing**) make insane. ● n. a usu. temporary enthusiasm.

crazed adj. **1** insane. **2** wildly enthusiastic.

crazy ● adj. (**crazier**, **craziest**) **1** informal **a** insane. **b** foolish, impractical. **2** informal extremely enthusiastic. **3** slang exciting, wild. ● n. (pl. **crazies**) slang a person who is eccentric, unbalanced, etc. □ **crazily** adv. **craziness** n.

crazy eights n. (treated as sing.) a card game in which eight is a wild card.

crazy quilt n. **1** a patchwork quilt made of material of various shapes, sizes, and colours. **2** an apparently random collection.

creak ● n. a harsh scraping or squeaking sound. ● v. make or move with a creak.

creaky adj. (**creakier**, **creakiest**) **1** creaking. **2 a** stiff or frail. **b** (of a practice etc.) outmoded. □ **creakily** adv.

cream ● n. **1 a** the fatty content of milk. **b** this eaten (often whipped) with or as a dessert etc. **2** (usu. as **the cream**) the best or choicest part of something. **3** a creamlike preparation, esp. a cosmetic. **4** a very pale yellow or off-white colour. **5** something with a creamy consistency or containing cream. ● v. **1 a** take the cream from (milk). **b** take the best part from. **2** work (butter) to a creamy consistency. **3** informal defeat decisively. ● adj. pale yellow; off-white.

cream cheese n. a soft, rich, spreadable cheese made from milk or cream.

creamed adj. **1** prepared in a cream sauce. **2** (of honey) whipped or churned. **3** (of cottage cheese) having the curds combined with milk.

creamer n. **1** a jug or container for cream. **2** a non-dairy product used as a substitute for cream.

creamery n. (pl. **creameries**) a factory producing butter or cheese.

cream pie n. a pie with a custard-like filling.

cream puff n. **1** a ball-shaped pastry shell filled with whipped cream etc. **2** informal a weak, ineffectual person.

cream soda n. a vanilla-flavoured soft drink.

creamy adj. (**creamier, creamiest**) like cream in taste, colour, or consistency. □ **creaminess** n.

crease ● n. **1 a** a line in paper, fabric, etc. caused by folding, ironing, etc. **b** a fold or wrinkle. **2** a marked area in front of the goal in hockey or lacrosse. ● v. (**creases, creased, creasing**) **1** make creases in. **2** become creased.

create v. (**creates, created, creating**) **1** cause to exist. **2** have as a result; produce.

creation n. **1 a** the action of creating. **b** a thing which has been created. **2 a** (usu. **the Creation**) the creating of the universe regarded as an act of God. **b** (usu. **Creation**) the universe.

creationism n. a theory that views creation according to a literal interpretation of the Biblical book of Genesis. □ **creationist** n. & adj.

creative adj. **1** of or involving the skilful and imaginative use of something to produce e.g. a work of art. **2** able to create things. **3** inventive. □ **creatively** adv. **creativity** n.

creator n. **1** a person who creates. **2** (**the Creator**) God.

creature n. **1 a** an animal, as distinct from a human being. **b** any living being. **2** a person of a specified kind **3** someone considered to be completely under the control of another. □ **creature of habit** a person set in an unvarying routine.

creature comforts pl. n. material comforts such as good food etc.

crèche n. a usu. three-dimensional depiction of Christ's birth in a stable, with Mary, Joseph, animals, shepherds, etc. [Say CRESH or CRAYSH]

credence n. belief in something as true. □ **give credence to 1** believe. **2** (also **lend credence to**) support the believability of. [Say CREE dince]

credential n. (usu. in pl.) evidence of a person's achievements or trustworthiness. □ **credentialed** adj.

credible adj. **1** believable or worthy of belief. **2** convincing. □ **credibility** n. **credibly** adv.

credit ● n. **1** a source of honour, pride, etc. **2** the acknowledgement of merit. **3** a good reputation. **4 a** a person's financial standing. **b** the power to obtain goods etc. before payment. **5** an acknowledgement of a contributor's services to a film, television program, etc. **6** a reputation for solvency and honesty in business. **7 a** (in bookkeeping) the acknowledgement of being paid. **b** the sum entered. **8** a value ascribed to a course. ● v. (**credits, credited, crediting**) **1** ascribe something to. **2** believe. **3** enter in an account as being paid. □ **do credit to** (or **do a person credit**) enhance the reputation of. **give credit to** believe. **take credit (for)** accept praise or commendation. **to one's credit** in one's praise or defence.

creditable adj. deserving public acknowledgement and praise. □ **creditably** adv.

credit card n. a card authorizing the obtaining of goods on credit.

creditor n. a person to whom a debt is owing.

credit rating n. an estimate of one's suitability to receive credit.

credit union n. a banking co-operative offering financial services to members.

creditworthy adj. considered suitable to receive credit. □ **creditworthiness** n.

credo n. (pl. **credos**) **1** a set of principles held by a specified group. **2** (**Credo**) a prayer summarizing Christian belief. [Say CREE doe or CRAY doe]

credulous adj. too ready to believe things. □ **credulously** adv. **credulity** n. **credulousness** n. [Say CRED you lus, kruh DYOOLA tee]

Cree n. (pl. **Cree** or **Crees**) **1** a member of a part of the Algonquian linguistic family, forming the largest Aboriginal group in Canada. **2** the language of this people. □ **Cree** adj.

creed n. **1** a set of principles or opinions. **2** (often **the Creed**) a prayer summarizing Christian beliefs. **3** a system of religious belief.

creek n. a stream or brook. □ **up the creek** slang in difficulties or trouble. [Rhymes either with SEEK or with SICK]

creep ● v. (**creeps, crept, creeping**) **1** crawl. **2** move slowly or timidly. **3** enter slowly. **4** (of a plant) grow along the ground or up a wall. **5** (of the flesh) feel as if insects etc. were creeping over it. ● n. **1 a** the act of creeping. **b** slow movement. **2** (in pl.; **the creeps**) informal a nervous feeling. **3** *informal* an unpleasant person. **4** a phenomenon characterized by a gradual increase: *cost creep*. □ **creep up on** approach stealthily. □ **creeper** *n.*

creepy *adj.* (**creepier, creepiest**) *informal* causing an unpleasant feeling of fear or unease. □ **creepily** *adv.* **creepiness** *n.*

creepy-crawly *n. informal* (*pl.* **creepy-crawlies**) an insect, worm, etc.

cremate *v.* (**cremates, cremated, cremating**) burn (a corpse etc.) to ashes. □ **cremation** *n.* [*Say* CREAM ate *or* cream ATE]

crematorium *n.* (*pl.* **crematoria** *or* **crematoriums**) a building in which corpses are cremated. [*Say* creama TORY um]

creme *n.* **1** a creamy substance not containing real cream. **2** a cosmetic or ointment having the consistency of cream.

crème brûlée *n.* (*pl.* **crèmes brûlées**) a baked custard topped with caramelized sugar. [*Say* crem broo LAY]

crème caramel *n.* (*pl.* **crème caramels**) a baked custard cooked in a caramel-coated dish. [*Say* crem cara MEL]

crème de la crème *n.* the best part; the elite. [*Say* crem duh luh CREM]

Creole *n.* **1 a** a descendant of European settlers in the W Indies or Central or S America. **b** a white descendant of French settlers in the southern US. **c** a person of mixed European and black descent. **2 a** a language formed from the contact of a European language with an esp. African language. **b** (usu. **creole**) a former pidgin language that has become the native language of a community. □ **Creole** *adj.* [*Say* CREE ole]

creosote *n.* **1** (also **creosote oil**) a dark brown oil distilled from coal tar. **2** a colourless fluid distilled from wood tar. ● *v.* treat with creosote. [*Say* CREE uh sote]

crepe *n.* **1** a light fabric with a wrinkled surface. **2** a thin pancake. **3** (also **crepe rubber**) a very hard-wearing wrinkled sheet rubber used for the soles of shoes etc. **4** (also **crepe paper**) thin crinkled paper. [*Say* CRAPE *or* CREP]

crept *past and past participle of* CREEP.

crescendo ● *n.* (*pl.* **crescendos**) **1** *Music* a passage gradually increasing in loudness. **2 a** progress towards a climax. **b** a climax. ● *v.* (**crescendoes, crescendoed, crescendoing**) increase gradually in loudness or intensity. [*Say* kruh SHENDO]

crescent ● *n.* **1** the curved sickle shape of the waxing or waning moon. **2** anything of this shape. **3** a curving street. ● *adj.* crescent-shaped.

cress *n.* (*pl.* **cresses**) a plant of the cabbage family, usu. with pungent edible leaves.

crest ● *n.* **1 a** a comb or tuft of feathers, fur, etc. on a bird's or animal's head. **b** something resembling this. **2** the top of something. **3** a shield or coat of arms. **4** a line along the top of the neck of some animals. ● *v.* **1** reach the crest of. **2** provide with or serve as a crest. **3** reach its highest level. □ **crested** *adj.*.

crestfallen *adj.* sad and disappointed.

Cretaceous ● *adj.* **1** (**cretaceous**) of the nature of chalk. **2** of or relating to the last period of the Mesozoic era, lasting from about 144 to 65 million years BP. ● *n.* this geological era or system. [*Say* kruh TAY shuss]

Cretan *n.* a native of Crete. □ **Cretan** *adj.* [*Say* CREET'n]

cretin *n.* **1** a person who is deformed and mentally retarded as the result of a thyroid deficiency. **2** *informal derogatory* a stupid person. □ **cretinism** *n.* **cretinous** *adj.* [*Say* CRET'n *or* CREET'n]

crevasse *n.* a deep open crack in a glacier. [*Say* kruh VASS]

crevice *n.* a narrow opening or fissure, esp. in a rock or building etc.

crew[1] ● *n.* **1 a** a group of people operating a ship, aircraft, train, etc. **b** such a group other than the officers. **c** a body of people working together. **2** *informal* a company of people. ● *v.* supply or act as a crew.

crew[2] *past of* CROW[2].

crewcut *n.* a very short haircut.

crewman *n.* (*pl.* **crewmen**) a member of a crew.

crewneck *n.* **1** a close-fitting round neckline. **2** a sweater etc. with a crewneck.

crib ● *n.* **1** a bed with raised sides for a baby. **2** a barred container or rack for animal fodder. **3** *informal* **a** a sheet of notes etc. used by students to cheat on an exam etc. **b** plagiarized work etc. **4** *informal* cribbage. ● *v.* (**cribs, cribbed, cribbing**) *informal* copy something unfairly or without acknowledgement.

cribbage *n.* a card game in which the objective is to reach a certain number of points, counted using pegs in a board.

crib death *n.* = SUDDEN INFANT DEATH SYNDROME.

crick ● *n.* a sudden painful stiffness in the neck or the back etc. ● *v.* produce a crick in.

cricket[1] *n.* any of various grasshopper-like insects which produce a chirping sound.

cricket[2] ● *n.* a game played on a field with two teams of 11 players using a bat, ball, and wickets. ● v. (**crickets, cricketed, cricketing**) play cricket. □ **cricketer** n.

cried past and past participle of CRY.

crier n. **1** a person who cries. **2** an officer who makes public announcements.

crime n. **1 a** an offence punishable by law. **b** illegal acts as a whole. **2** an action considered to be wrong, though not illegal. **3** a shameful act.

criminal ● n. a person who has committed a crime. ● adj. **1** of or relating to crime. **2** having committed a crime. **3** relating to or expert in criminal law. **4** deplorable. □ **criminality** n. **criminally** adv. [Say CRIMMIN 'll, crimmin ALA tee]

Criminal Code n. a federal statute embodying most of Canada's criminal law.

criminalize v. (**criminalizes, criminalized, criminalizing**) **1** turn (an activity) into a criminal offence by making it illegal. **2** turn (a person) into a criminal. □ **criminalization** n.

criminal law n. law concerned with the prosecution of crime (opp. CIVIL LAW 1).

criminal negligence n. Cdn Law an offence involving a wanton or reckless disregard for the lives or safety of others.

criminology n. the scientific study of crime. □ **criminologist** n.

crimp ● v. **1** compress into small folds or ridges. **2** make narrow wrinkles in. **3** make waves in (the hair). ● n. a crimped thing or form. □ **put a crimp in** informal thwart.

crimson ● adj. of a rich deep purplish red. ● n. this colour. ● v. make or become crimson.

cringe v. (**cringes, cringed, cringing**) **1** shrink back or cower in fear or in a servile way. **2** feel excessively embarrassed.

crinkle ● n. **1** a wrinkle or crease. **2** fabric with a wrinkled surface. ● v. (**crinkles, crinkled, crinkling**) form crinkles. □ **crinkly** adj.

crinoline n. a stiffened or hooped petticoat worn to make a skirt stand out. [Say KRINNA lin]

cripes interj. slang expressing surprise, anger, etc.

cripple ● n. a person who is permanently impaired in movement. ● v. (**cripples, crippled, crippling**) **1** cause someone to become unable to walk or move properly. **2** weaken or damage seriously. □ **crippled** adj. **crippling** adj. **cripplingly** adv.

crisis n. (pl. **crises**) **1** a time of danger or great difficulty. **2** the turning point, esp. of a disease. **3** a decisive moment. [Say CRY seez for the plural]

crisis centre n. a place offering counselling, treatment, etc. to people who are victims of (sexual) assault etc.

crisp ● adj. **1** hard but brittle. **2** (of air or weather) dry and cold. **3** brisk and decisive. **4** (of pictures etc.) clear. **5** (of cloth etc.) slightly stiff. **6** (of hair) closely curling. **7** (of produce) firm and fresh. ● n. **1** a baked dessert made of fruit with a crumbly topping. **2** a crisp state or thing. ● v. **1** make or become crisp. **2** curl in short stiff folds or waves. □ **crisply** adv. **crispness** n.

crispbread n. a thin crisp biscuit of crushed rye etc.

crisper n. a compartment in a refrigerator for storing fruit and vegetables.

crispy adj. (**crispier, crispiest**) firm, dry, and brittle. □ **crispiness** n.

criss-cross ● v. (**criss-crosses, criss-crossed, criss-crossing**) **1 a** cross or intersect repeatedly. **b** move crosswise. **2** mark with a criss-cross pattern. ● n. (pl. **criss-crosses**) a pattern of crossing lines. ● adj. crossing; in cross lines. ● adv. crosswise.

criterion n. (pl. **criteria**) a principle or standard that a thing is judged by. [Say cry TEERY in for the singular, cry TEERY uh for the plural]

critic n. **1** a person who expresses an unfavourable opinion. **2** a person who assesses literary or artistic works, restaurants, wines, etc. **3** Cdn an opposition party member monitoring a specific government ministry.

critical adj. **1 a** expressing disapproving comments or judgments. **b** expressing criticism. **c** involving judgment or discernment. **2** skilful at criticism. **3** providing commentary or analysis. **4 a** of or at a crisis. **b** decisive. □ **critically** adv.

critical mass n. **1** the amount of fissile material needed to maintain a nuclear chain reaction. **2** the amount of anything required to achieve a desired effect.

criticism n. **1** fault-finding; disapproval. **2 a** the work of a critic. **b** an article etc. expressing an analytical evaluation of something.

criticize v. (**criticizes, criticized, criticizing**) **1** find fault with. **2** discuss critically.

critique ● n. a detailed analysis and assessment of something. ● v. (**critiques, critiqued, critiquing**) discuss critically. [Say crit EEK]

critter n. informal an animal etc.

croak ● n. a deep hoarse sound as of a frog. ● v. **1** utter a croak. **2** slang die. □ **croaky** adj.

Croat *n. & adj.* = CROATIAN. [*Say* CROW at]

Croatian *n.* **1** a person from Croatia. **2** their language, a form of Serbo-Croat written in the Roman alphabet. ☐ **Croatian** *adj.* [*Say* crow AY sh'n]

crochet ● *n.* a handicraft in which yarn is looped into a fabric using a small hooked rod. ● *v.* (**crochets, crocheted, crocheting**) make in such a way. [*Say* crow SHAY]

crock *n.* **1** an earthenware jar. **2** *informal* something untrue etc.

crocked *adj. slang* drunk.

crockery *n.* earthenware or china dishes.

crocodile *n.* **1** an amphibious reptile with thick scaly skin, long tail, and long jaws. **2** leather from its skin.

crocodile tears *n.* **1** insincere grief. **2** false tears.

crocus *n.* (*pl.* **crocuses**) a spring-flowering plant with white, yellow, or purple flowers.

Crohn's disease *n.* a chronic inflammatory disease of the intestines. [*Rhymes with* BONES]

croissant *n.* a flaky, crescent-shaped bread roll. [*Say* crwah SONN]

crokinole *n. esp. Cdn* a game in which wooden discs are flicked across a round wooden board. [*Say* CROKA nole]

Cro-Magnon ● *adj.* of a tall broad-faced European race who appeared *c.*35,000 years ago. ● *n.* a Cro-Magnon person. [*Say* crow MAG non]

crone *n.* an ugly old woman.

crony *n.* (*pl.* **cronies**) often *derogatory* a close friend or companion. [*Say* CROW nee]

cronyism *n.* the appointment of friends to political posts; patronage. [*Say* CROW nee ism]

crook ● *n.* **1** *informal* **a** a criminal. **b** a swindler. **2** the hooked staff of a shepherd or bishop. **3** a bend, curve, or hook. ● *v.* bend, curve.

crooked *adj.* (**crookeder, crookedest**) **1 a** bent, curved, twisted. **b** deformed. **2** *informal* dishonest. ☐ **crookedly** *adv.* **crookedness** *n.*

croon ● *v.* hum or sing in a low subdued voice. ● *n.* such singing. ☐ **crooner** *n.*

crop ● *n.* **1 a** the produce of cultivated plants. **b** the season's total yield of this. **2** a group or an amount appearing at one time. **3** the stock or handle of a whip. **4** a style of hair cut very short. **5** the pouch in a bird's gullet where food is prepared for digestion. ● *v.* (**crops, cropped, cropping**) **1 a** cut off or cut very short. **b** (of animals) bite off (the tops of plants). **2** trim (a photograph).

3 (of land) bear a crop. ☐ **crop up** appear unexpectedly.

crop-dusting *n.* the sprinkling of powdered insecticide or fertilizer on crops, esp. from the air. ☐ **crop-duster** *n.*

cropper *n.* ☐ **come a cropper** *slang* **1** fail badly. **2** fall heavily.

croquet *n.* a game played on a lawn, in which wooden balls are driven through hoops with mallets. [*Say* crow KAY *or* CROW kay]

cross ● *n.* (*pl.* **crosses**) **1** an upright post with a transverse bar. **2 a** (**the Cross**) in Christianity, the cross on which Christ was crucified. **b** a representation of this. **3** something shaped like a cross. **4** a cross-shaped decoration awarded for personal valour. **5** an animal or plant resulting from cross-breeding. **6** a mixture of two things. ● *v.* (**crosses, crossed, crossing**) **1** go across or to the other side of. **2** place or be across one another. **3** draw a line across. **4** cancel or remove from a list. **5** (**cross oneself**) make the sign of the cross. **6** pass in opposite directions. **7 a** cause to interbreed. **b** cross-fertilize (plants). ● *adj.* **1** angry. **2** reaching from side to side. **3** opposed. ☐ **at cross-purposes** misunderstanding one another. **bear one's cross** accept trials and misfortunes stoically. **cross one's fingers** (or **keep one's fingers crossed**) trust in good luck. **cross the floor** *Cdn & Brit.* join the opposing side in a legislature. **cross one's heart** make a solemn pledge. **cross one's mind** occur to one. **cross paths** (or **cross one's path**) encounter or meet. **cross swords** encounter in opposition. **cross wires** (or **get one's wires crossed**) have a misunderstanding. ☐ **crossly** *adv.*

crossbar *n.* a horizontal bar between two upright bars.

crossbeam *n.* a transverse beam in a structure.

crossbill *n.* a stout finch having a bill with crossed mandibles.

crossbones *n.* a representation of two crossed thigh bones, usu. under the figure of a skull.

crossbow *n.* a bow fixed across a wooden stock, with a mechanism for drawing and releasing the string.

crossbreed ● *n.* an animal, plant, or breed produced by crossing different breeds. ● *v.* (**crossbreeds, crossbred, crossbreeding**) produce by crossing different breeds.

cross-check ● *v.* **1** check by a second or alternative method. **2** (in hockey and lacrosse) obstruct by holding one's stick horizontally in both hands. ● *n.* an instance of cross-checking.

cross-country ● *adj. & adv.* **1** across fields or open country. **2** across a country. ● *adj.* designating skiing done across the countryside using long, narrow skis. ● *n.* (*pl.* **cross-countries**) a cross-country sport or race.

cross-dress *v.* wear clothes usu. worn by a person of the opposite sex. □ **cross-dresser** *n.* **cross-dressing** *n.*

crosse *n.* (in women's field lacrosse) the stick. [*Sounds like* CROSS]

cross-examine *v.* (**cross-examines**, **cross-examined**, **cross-examining**) question (a witness in a law court) esp. to check or discredit their testimony. □ **cross-examination** *n.* **cross-examiner** *n.*

cross-eyed *adj.* having one or both eyes turned inwards towards the nose.

cross-fertilization *n.* **1** fertilization from one of a different species. **2** fruitful interchange of ideas etc. □ **cross-fertilize** *v.* (**cross-fertilizes**, **cross-fertilized**, **cross-fertilizing**)

crossfire *n.* **1** lines of gunfire crossing one another. **2** a situation in which two or more groups are arguing with each other.

crosshairs *n.* **1** a pair of fine wires crossing at right angles at the focus of an optical instrument or gun sight. **2** a representation of this on a computer screen.

cross-hatch *v.* (**cross-hatches**, **cross-hatched**, **cross-hatching**) shade with intersecting sets of parallel lines. □ **cross-hatching** *n.*

crossing *n.* **1** a place where things (esp. roads) cross. **2** a place at which one may cross a street, railway tracks, etc. **3** a journey across water.

cross-legged *adj.* with one leg crossed over the other.

crossover ● *n.* **1** a point or place of crossing. **2** the process of crossing over, esp. from one style or genre to another. ● *adj.* **1** having a part that crosses over. **2** that crosses over.

crosspiece *n.* a transverse beam or other component of a structure etc.

cross-pollinate *v.* (**cross-pollinates**, **cross-pollinated**, **cross-pollinating**) **1** pollinate from another. **2** blend together. □ **cross-pollination** *n.*

cross-reference ● *n.* a reference to another text etc. ● *v.* provide with cross-references.

crossroad *n.* **1** a road that crosses a main road. **2** = CROSSROADS.

crossroads *n.* **1** an intersection of two or more roads. **2** a critical turning point.

cross-section *n.* **1 a** a cutting of a solid at right angles to an axis. **b** a plane surface produced in this way. **2** a representative sample. □ **cross-sectional** *adj.*

cross-stitch ● *n.* a stitch formed of two stitches crossing each other. ● *v.* (**cross-stitches**, **cross-stitched**, **cross-stitching**) sew or embroider with cross-stitches.

crosstown ● *adj.* **1** extending or travelling across a town or city. **2** coming from the other side of a town or city. ● *adv.* across a town or city.

cross-train *v.* **1** train in two or more sports to improve performance. **2** train (an employee etc.) in more than one skill. □ **cross-trainer** *n.* **cross-training** *n.*

crosswalk *n.* a pedestrian crossing.

crossways *adv.* crosswise.

crosswind *n.* a wind blowing across one's direction of travel.

crosswise *adj. & adv.* **1** across; transverse or transversely. **2** in the form of a cross.

crossword *n.* (also **crossword puzzle**) a puzzle of a grid of squares and blanks into which words have to be filled from clues.

crostini *pl. n.* small pieces of toasted bread topped with vegetables etc. [*Say* cross TEENY]

crotch *n.* (*pl.* **crotches**) **1** the place where the legs join the trunk of the human body. **2** the part of a pair of pants, underwear, etc. corresponding to this.

crotchety *adj.* peevish, irritable. □ **crotchetiness** *n.*

crouch ● *v.* (**crouches**, **crouched**, **crouching**) stoop low with the legs bent close to the body, esp. for concealment, or (of an animal) before pouncing; be in this position. ● *n.* (*pl.* **crouches**) an act of crouching; a crouching position.

croup[1] *n.* an inflammation of the larynx and trachea in children. [*Say* CROOP]

croup[2] *n.* the rump esp. of a horse. [*Say* CROOP]

croupier *n.* the person in charge of a gaming table. [*Say* CROOPY ur *or* CROOPY ay]

crouton *n.* a small cube of fried or toasted bread. [*Say* CROO tawn]

Crow *n.* (*pl.* **Crow** *or* **Crows**) **1** a member of an Aboriginal people living in southern Montana. **2** the Siouan language of this people. □ **Crow** *adj.*

crow[1] *n.* a large black bird with a powerful black beak and a raucous caw. □ **as the**

crow flies in a straight line. **eat crow** *informal* be forced to admit a mistake.

crow² ● *v.* **1** (**crows**, *past* **crowed** or **crew**, **crowing**) (of a rooster) utter its characteristic loud cry. **2** express a feeling of happiness or triumph, esp. in a gloating way. ● *n.* **1** a rooster's cry. **2** a happy or triumphant cry.

crowbar *n.* an iron bar with a flattened end, used as a lever.

crowd ● *n.* **1** a large number of people gathered together. **2** an audience. **3** *informal* a particular set of people. **4** (**the crowd**) the multitude of people. **5** a large number. ● *v.* **1 a** come together in a crowd. **b** force one's way. **2 a** force into a confined space. **b** fill with. **3** come aggressively close to. □ **crowd out** exclude by crowding. □ **crowded** *adj.*

crown ● *n.* **1** a monarch's ornamental headdress. **2** (**the Crown**) **a** the monarch. **b** the authority residing in the monarchy. **3 a** a wreath of leaves or flowers etc. worn as an emblem of victory. **b** an award gained by a victory. **4** a crown-shaped thing. **5** the top part of a thing, esp. of the head. **6 a** the highest of an arched thing. **b** a thing that forms the summit. **7 a** the part of a tooth projecting from the gum. **b** an artificial replacement for this. **8** = CROWN ATTORNEY. ● *v.* **1** put a crown on. **2** give a person royal authority. **3** encircle or rest on the top of. **4 a** (often as **crowning** *adj.*) be the finishing touch to. **b** bring to a happy issue.

Crown attorney *n.* (also **Crown counsel**, **Crown prosecutor**) *Cdn* a lawyer who conducts prosecutions on behalf of the Crown.

Crown corporation *n. Cdn* a corporation owned by the federal or provincial governments.

crown jewel *n.* **1** (in *pl.*) the regalia and other jewellery worn by a sovereign on state occasions. **2** the most valuable thing.

Crown land *n.* land owned by a government.

crown prince *n.* a male heir to a throne.

Crown witness *n. Cdn* a witness called to testify by the Crown.

crow's feet *pl. n.* wrinkles at the outer corner of a person's eye.

crow's nest *n.* a platform for a lookout at the masthead of a ship.

crozier *n.* a hooked staff carried by a bishop. [*Say* CROW zhur *or* CROW zee ur]

CRT *abbr.* cathode ray tube.

CRTC *abbr.* Canadian Radio-television and Telecommunications Commission.

crucial *adj.* **1** decisive, critical. **2** very important. □ **crucially** *adv.*

crucible *n.* **1** a container in which metals etc. are heated. **2** a severe trial. [*Say* CROO suh bull]

cruciferous *adj.* of or denoting plants of the cabbage family. [*Say* croo SIFFER us]

crucifix *n.* (*pl.* **crucifixes**) a model of a cross with a figure of Christ on it. [*Say* CROO suh fix]

crucifixion *n.* **1** the execution of a person by crucifying them. **2** (**Crucifixion**) the crucifixion of Christ. [*Say* croo suh FICK shun]

cruciform *adj.* cross-shaped. [*Say* CROO suh form]

crucify *v.* (**crucifies**, **crucified**, **crucifying**) **1** put to death by fastening to a cross. **2 a** cause extreme pain to. **b** persecute. **c** criticize harshly. **3** *slang* defeat thoroughly. [*Say* CROO suh fie]

crud *n. slang* **1** a deposit of dirt etc. **2** something of little value. □ **cruddy** *adj.*

crude ● *adj.* (**cruder**, **crudest**) **1 a** in the natural state; not refined. **b** rough; lacking finish. **2** offensive, indecent. ● *n.* unrefined petroleum. □ **crudely** *adv.* **crudeness** *n.* **crudity** *n.*

crudités *pl. n.* an hors d'oeuvre of mixed raw vegetables. [*Say* croo dee TAY]

cruel *adj.* (**crueller**, **cruellest**) **1** causing pain or suffering. **2** indifferent to or gratified by another's suffering. **3** merciless; harsh. □ **cruelly** *adv.*

cruelty *n.* (*pl.* **cruelties**) cruel behaviour or attitudes.

cruise ● *v.* (**cruises**, **cruised**, **cruising**) **1** make a journey aboard ship calling at a series of ports, esp. for pleasure. **2** travel without a precise destination. **3 a** travel at a moderate speed. **b** *slang* travel about in search of a sexual partner. **4** achieve an objective etc. with ease. ● *n.* **1** a cruising voyage on board a ship. **2** the act or an instance of cruising.

cruise control *n.* a device on some vehicles that maintains a predetermined constant speed.

cruise missile *n.* a low-flying missile which guides itself by reference to the features of the region it crosses.

cruiser *n.* **1** a warship of high speed. **2** a police patrol car.

cruller *n.* a small, twisted doughnut. [*Can be said to rhyme with* DULLER, RULER, *or* FULLER]

crumb ● *n.* **1** a small fragment, esp. of bread. **2** a small particle. ● *v.* cover with or break into crumbs. □ **crumby** *adj.* (**crumbier**, **crumbiest**).

crumble ● *v.* (**crumbles**, **crumbled**, **crumbling**) **1** break or fall into fragments.

2 gradually disintegrate. ● *n.* **1** = CRISP *n.* 1. **2** a crumbly or crumbled substance.

crumbly *adj.* (**crumblier, crumbliest**) easily crumbling.

crummy *adj.* (**crummier, crummiest**) *informal* **1** dirty, squalid. **2** inferior. **3** sick or depressed.

crumpet *n.* a small round bread resembling an English muffin.

crumple ● *v.* (**crumples, crumpled, crumpling**) **1** crush so as to become creased. **2** collapse. ● *n.* a crease or wrinkle. □ **crumply** *adj.*

crumple zone *n.* a part of a motor vehicle designed to crumple easily in a crash.

crunch ● *v.* (**crunches, crunched, crunching**) **1 a** crush noisily with the teeth. **b** grind under foot, wheels, etc. **2** make a crunching sound. **3** *informal* process (numbers or data). ● *n.* (*pl.* **crunches**) **1** a crunching sound. **2** crunchiness. **3** *informal* a shortage. **4** *informal* a decisive event or moment. **5** (often in *pl.*) a half sit-up. □ **cruncher** *n.* **crunchiness** *n.* **crunchy** *adj.* (**crunchier, crunchiest**).

crusade ● *n.* **1** (usu. **Crusade**) any of several medieval military expeditions made by Europeans to take the Holy Land from the Muslims. **2** a vigorous campaign for a cause. ● *v.* (**crusades, crusaded, crusading**) engage in a crusade. □ **crusader** *n.*

crush ● *v.* (**crushes, crushed, crushing**) **1** compress with force or violence. **2** reduce to powder by pressure. **3** crease or crumple. **4** defeat or subdue completely. **5** (usu. in *passive*) humiliate. ● *n.* (*pl.* **crushes**) **1** an act of crushing. **2** a crowded mass of people. **3** *informal* an infatuation. □ **crushable** *adj.* **crusher** *n.*

crust ● *n.* **1 a** the hard outer part of a loaf of bread. **b** a hard dry scrap of bread. **2** pastry, bread, etc. covering, supporting, or encasing a filling. **3** a hard casing of a softer thing. **4** *Geology* the outer portion of the earth. **5** a coating or deposit. ● *v.* **1** form into or cover with a crust. **2** form into a crust.

crustacean *n.* a usu. aquatic, hard-shelled arthropod, e.g. crab, lobster, etc. [*Say* kruh STATION]

crusty *adj.* (**crustier, crustiest**) **1** having a crisp crust. **2** irritable. **3** crust-like. □ **crustiness** *n.*

crutch *n.* (*pl.* **crutches**) **1** a support for a lame person. **2** any support or prop.

crux *n.* (*pl.* **cruxes**) **1** the decisive point at issue. **2** a difficult matter.

cry ● *v.* (**cries, cried, crying**) **1** make a loud or shrill sound. **2** shed tears. **3** say or exclaim loudly. **4** (of a bird etc.) make a loud call. ● *n.* (*pl.* **cries**) **1** a loud utterance of grief, pain, etc. **2** a loud excited utterance. **3** an urgent appeal. **4** a period of weeping. **5 a** public demand. **b** a rallying call. **6** the distinctive call of an animal, esp. of birds. □ **cry one's eyes (or heart) out** weep bitterly. **cry out for** demand as a self-evident requirement. **a far cry 1** a long way. **2** a very different thing. **for crying out loud** *informal* an exclamation of surprise or annoyance.

crybaby *n.* (*pl.* **crybabies**) **1** a person who cries often. **2** a whiny or self-pitying person.

crying *adj.* (of an injustice) demanding redress.

cryogenics *n.* **1** the branch of physics dealing with the production and effects of very low temperatures. **2** = CRYONICS. □ **cryogenic** *adj.* **cryogenically** *adv.* [*Say* cry oh JEN icks]

cryonics *n.* the practice of deep-freezing the bodies of those who have died of an incurable disease, in the hope of a future cure. □ **cryonic** *adj.* [*Say* cry ON icks]

crypt *n.* an underground room or vault beneath a church. [*Say* CRIPT]

cryptic *adj.* **1** obscure in meaning; mysterious. **2** (of a crossword clue etc.) indirect. □ **cryptically** *adv.* [*Say* CRIP tic]

cryptography *n.* the art of writing or solving codes. □ **cryptographer** *n.* **cryptographic** *adj.* [*Say* crip TOGRA fee, crip TOGRA fur, cripta GRAPHIC]

crystal ● *n.* **1** a transparent mineral, esp. quartz. **2 a** highly transparent glass. **b** articles made of this. **3** *Electronics* a crystalline piece of semiconductor. **4** *Chemistry* a piece of a solid substance with a regular internal structure and plane faces arranged symmetrically. ● *adj.* like crystal. □ **crystal clear 1** transparent. **2** readily understood.

crystal ball *n.* a glass globe used for predicting the future.

crystalline *adj.* **1** of or clear as crystal. **2** having the structure and form of a crystal. [*Say* CRISTA line *or* CRISTA leen]

crystallize *v.* (**crystallizes, crystallized, crystallizing**) **1** form or cause to form crystals. **2** make or become clear. **3** coat or impregnate with sugar. □ **crystallization** *n.*

crystallography *n.* the science of crystal structure and properties. □ **crystallographer** *n.* [*Say* crystal OGGRA fee, crystal OGGRA fur]

C-section n. = CAESAREAN SECTION.

CSIS abbr. Canadian Security Intelligence Service. [Say SEE sis]

CT abbr. Medical computerized tomography.

ct. abbr. carat.

CT scan n. = CAT SCAN.

cu. abbr. cubic.

cub ● n. **1** the young of a fox, bear, lion, etc. **2** (**Cub**) a member of the junior level in Scouting. **3** (also **cub reporter**) informal an inexperienced reporter. ● v. (**cubs, cubbed, cubbing**) give birth to (cubs).

Cuban n. a native or national of Cuba. □ **Cuban** adj.

cubbyhole n. **1** a very small room. **2** a small compartment.

cube ● n. **1** a solid contained by six equal squares. **2** the product of a number multiplied by its square. ● v. (**cubes, cubed, cubing**) **1** find the cube of. **2** cut into small cubes.

cube van n. (also **cube truck**) Cdn a truck resembling a van at the front, with a large cube-like storage compartment behind.

cubic adj. **1** cube-shaped. **2** of three dimensions. **3** involving the cube of a number.

cubicle n. a small partitioned space.

cubism n. an early 20th-century style of painting in which objects are shown as made up of geometrical forms. □ **cubist** n. & adj. **cubistic** adj.

cuckold ● n. a man whose wife is unfaithful. ● v. make a cuckold of. [Say CUCK old]

cuckoo ● n. **1** a brown-and-white or greyish bird which leaves its eggs in the nests of small birds and has a distinctive two-note call. **2** informal a crazy person. ● adj. informal crazy.

cucumber n. a long green fleshy fruit eaten as a vegetable or pickled.

cud n. half-digested food returned from the first stomach of ruminants (e.g. cows) to the mouth for further chewing. □ **chew the cud** think or talk reflectively.

cuddle ● v. (**cuddles, cuddled, cuddling**) **1** hold in an affectionate embrace. **2** nestle together. ● n. the action of holding someone close in the arms to show affection. □ **cuddler** n.

cuddly adj. (**cuddlier, cuddliest**) **1** pleasant to cuddle. **2** plump.

cudgel ● n. a short thick stick used as a weapon. ● v. (**cudgels, cudgelled, cudgelling**) beat with a cudgel. [Say CUDGE ul]

cue[1] ● n. **1** a signal for a performer or technician to speak, enter, or execute an action. **2 a** a stimulus. **b** a hint on how to behave. ● v. (**cues, cued, cueing**) **1** give a cue to. **2** put (audio equipment) in readiness to play particular recorded material. □ **on cue** at the correct moment. **take one's cue from** follow the example of.

cue[2] Billiards etc. ● n. a long straight tapering rod for striking the ball. ● v. (**cues, cued, cueing**) **1** strike (a ball) with a cue. **2** use a cue.

cue card n. a small card from which a person reads lines.

cuff[1] ● n. **1** the end part of a sleeve or pant leg. **2** (in pl.) informal handcuffs. **3** an inflatable band used to measure blood pressure. **4** a muscle ringing a joint. ● v. informal put handcuffs on. □ **off-the-cuff** informal without preparation.

cuff[2] ● v. strike with an open hand. ● n. such a blow.

cufflink n. a device of two joined studs etc. to fasten the sides of a cuff together.

cuisine n. a style of cooking, esp. of a particular country or establishment. [Say quiz EEN]

cuke n. informal a cucumber.

cul-de-sac n. (pl. **cul-de-sacs**) a street or passage closed at one end. [Say CULL duh sack]

culinary adj. of or for cooking. [Say CULLA nare ee]

cull ● v. **1** select from a large quantity. **2** select for slaughter or felling. ● n. **1** an act of culling. **2** what is culled. □ **culler** n.

culminate v. (**culminates, culminated, culminating**) (usu. foll. by in) reach its climax. □ **culmination** n. [Say CULMA nate, culma NATION]

culottes pl. n. a woman's garment that hangs like a skirt but has separate legs, like trousers. [Say coo LOTS or COO lots]

culpable adj. deserving blame. □ **culpability** n. **culpably** adv. [Say KULPA bull, kulpa BILLA tee]

culprit n. a person or thing that is responsible for an offence etc.

cult n. **1 a** a system of religious worship directed towards a particular figure or object. **b** a relatively small religious group regarded as strange or sinister. **2 a** fashion or thing popular with a specific section of society. **3** (as an adj.) denoting a person or thing so popularized. □ **cultic** adj. **cultish** adj. **cultishness** n. **cultism** n. **cultist** n.

cultivar n. a plant variety produced in cultivation by selective breeding.

cultivate v. (**cultivates, cultivated, cultivating**) **1** prepare and use (land) for crops or gardening. **2** grow or produce (crops, mussels, bacteria, etc.). **3 a** make more educated and sensitive. **b** nurture. **4** acquire or develop. □ **cultivated** adj. **cultivation** n.

cultivator n. a mechanical implement for breaking up the ground.

cultural adj. **1** relating to artistic activity etc. seen as cultivating the mind. **2** relating to the ideas, customs, etc. in a society or civilization. □ **culturally** adv.

cultural sovereignty n. Cdn the power of a country to maintain independence in its cultural activities from another, culturally dominant, nation.

culture ● n. **1 a** the arts and other manifestations of human intellectual achievement regarded collectively. **b** a refined understanding of this. **2** the behaviour and achievements of a particular time, people, or group. **3** cultivation. **4** a quantity of micro-organisms grown on nutrient material. ● v. (**cultures**, **cultured**, **culturing**) maintain (bacteria etc.) in conditions suitable for growth.

cultured adj. **1** refined and educated. **2** caused to develop by artificial means.

cultured pearl n. a pearl formed by an oyster after the insertion of a foreign body into its shell.

culvert n. an underground channel carrying water across a road etc.

cum prep. (usu. in comb.) with, combined with, also used as.

cumbersome adj. inconvenient or unwieldy. □ **cumbersomely** adv.

cumin n. a plant, or its aromatic seeds used as a curry spice. [Say CUM in or CUE min]

cummerbund n. a wide horizontally pleated sash worn around the waist, esp. with a tuxedo.

cumulative adj. increasing by successive additions. □ **cumulatively** adv. **cumulativeness** n. [Say CUE myoo luh tiv]

cumulus n. a cloud forming rounded masses heaped on a flat base. [Say CUE myuh luss]

cuneiform ● adj. relating to the wedge-shaped writing of ancient Babylonian etc. inscriptions. ● n. cuneiform writing. [Say cue NAY uh form or cue NEE uh form]

cunnilingus n. stimulation of the female genitals using the tongue or lips. [Say cunna LING gus]

cunning ● adj. (**more cunning**, **cunningest**) **1** skilled in achieving one's ends by deceit or evasion. **2** ingenious. ● n. **1** skill in deceit. **2** ingenuity. □ **cunningly** adv.

cup ● n. **1** a small bowl-shaped container, often with a handle, for drinking from. **2 a** its contents. **b** a measure of capacity equal to eight fluid ounces (237 ml). **3** a cup-shaped thing, such as the calyx of a flower or part of a bra. **4** an ornamental trophy. ● v. (**cups**, **cupped**, **cupping**) **1** form (esp. one's hands) into the shape of a cup. **2** take or hold as in a cup. □ **one's cup of tea** informal what interests or suits one.

cupboard n. a recess or piece of furniture with a door, used for storage.

cupcake n. a small cake baked in a cup-shaped mould.

cupidity n. greed for money or possessions. [Say cue PIDDA tee]

cupola n. a rounded dome forming or adorning a roof. [Say CUE puh luh]

cur n. **1** a worthless or snappy dog. **2** a contemptible person.

curable adj. that can be cured.

curare n. a paralyzing poison obtained from S American plants. [Say kyuh RAR ee]

curate[1] n. a member of the clergy assisting a parish priest. [Say CURE it]

curate[2] v. (**curates**, **curated**, **curating**) **1** act as curator of. **2** select and present items for (an exhibition etc.). [Say CURE ate]

curative adj. tending or able to cure.

curator n. **1** an employee of a museum etc. responsible for the collections. **2** a person who curates an exhibition. □ **curatorial** adj. **curatorship** n. [Say CURE ate ur, cure a TORY ul]

curb ● n. **1** the raised, usu. concrete border along the side of a street etc. **2** a check or restraint. **3** a strap etc. fastened to the bit and passing under a horse's lower jaw, used as a check. ● v. restrain.

curbside n. the area adjacent to a curb.

curd n. (often in pl.) a coagulated substance formed by the action of acids on milk, used for making cheese.

curdle v. (**curdles**, **curdled**, **curdling**) make into or become curds. □ **make one's blood curdle** fill one with horror.

cure ● v. (**cures**, **cured**, **curing**) **1** restore to health. **2** eliminate (a disease etc.). **3** preserve by salting, drying, etc. **4 a** vulcanize. **b** harden. ● n. **1** restoration to health. **2** a means of curing a disease.

cure-all n. a universal remedy.

curfew n. **1** a regulation requiring people to remain indoors between specified hours, usu. at night. **2** a requirement that one be home etc. by a certain time.

Curia n. the papal court at the Vatican, by

which the Roman Catholic Church is governed. [*Say* CURE ee uh]

curie *n.* a unit of radioactivity, corresponding to 3.7 × 10^{10} disintegrations per second. [*Say* CURE oo]

curio *n.* (*pl.* **curios**) a rare or unusual object. [*Say* CURE ee oh]

curiosity *n.* (*pl.* **curiosities**) **1** an eager desire to know. **2** a strange thing.

curious *adj.* **1** eager to know. **2** strange.
□ **curiously** *adv.*

curl ● *v.* curve or form into a spiral. **2** move in a spiral form. **3 a** (of the upper lip) be raised slightly as an expression of contempt. **b** cause (the lip) to do this. **4** play curling. ● *n.* **1** a lock of curled hair. **2** anything spiral or curved inwards. **3** a curling movement or act. □ **curl up** lie or sit with the knees drawn up.
□ **curliness** *n.* **curly** *adj.*

curler *n.* **1** a roller etc. for curling the hair. **2** a player in the game of curling.

curlew *n.* (*pl.* **curlew** or **curlews**) a bird with a usu. long beautiful down-curved bill.

curlicue *n.* a decorative curl or twist.

curling *n.* **1** in senses of CURL *v.* **2** a game played on ice, in which large round stones are slid across the surface towards a mark.

curmudgeon *n.* a bad-tempered person.
□ **curmudgeonly** *adj.*
[*Say* cur MUDGE in]

currant *n.* **1** a dried fruit of a small seedless variety of grape. **2** a shrub producing red, white, or black berries.

currency *n.* (*pl.* **currencies**) **1 a** the money in general use in a country. **b** anything seen as a medium through which transactions are completed. **2** the condition of being current.

current ● *adj.* **1** belonging to the present time; happening now. **2** in general circulation or use. ● *n.* **1** a body of water, air, etc., moving in a definite direction. **2** a flow of electrically charged particles. **3** a general tendency or course.

current affairs *pl. n.* esp. *Cdn & Brit.* (also **current events**) events of importance happening at the present time.

currently *adv.* now.

curriculum *n.* (*pl.* **curricula**) **1** the subjects that are studied or prescribed for study. **2** any program of activities.
□ **curricular** *adj.* [*Say* kuh RICK yoo lum *for the singular,* kuh RICK yoo luh *for the plural*]

curriculum vitae *n.* (*pl.* **curricula vitae**) a brief account of one's education, qualifications, and previous occupations. Abbreviation: **CV**
[*Say* kuh rick yoo lum VEE tae]

curry[1] ● *n.* (*pl.* **curries**) a dish of meat, vegetables, etc., cooked in a highly spiced sauce, usu. served with rice. ● *v.* (**curries**, **curried**, **currying**) prepare or flavour with hot-tasting spices.

curry[2] *v.* (**curries**, **curried**, **currying**) groom (a horse) with a curry comb. □ **curry favour** attempt to gain someone's favour by acting obsequiously.

curry comb *n.* a hand-held metal serrated device for grooming horses.

curry powder *n.* a preparation of turmeric, cumin, and other spices for making curry.

curse ● *n.* **1** an appeal to a supernatural power to harm a person or thing. **2** the evil supposedly resulting from a curse. **3** a profane oath. **4** a cause of harm. **5** (**the curse**) *slang* menstruation. ● *v.* (**curses**, **cursed**, **cursing**) **1 a** utter a curse against. **b** (in *imper.*) may God curse. **2** (usu. in *passive*; foll. by *with*) afflict with. **3** say offensive words.

cursed *adj.* damnable. [*Say* CURSE id *or* CURST]

curses *interj.* expressing annoyance.

cursive ● *adj.* (of writing) done with joined characters. ● *n.* cursive writing.

cursor *n.* a movable indicator on a computer screen identifying the position that the program will operate on with the next keystroke.

cursory *adj.* hasty; superficial.
□ **cursorily** *adv.* [*Say* CURSOR ee]

curt *adj.* noticeably or rudely brief.
□ **curtly** *adv.*

curtail *v.* cut short. □ **curtailment** *n.*
[*Say* cur TAIL]

curtain ● *n.* **1** a piece of cloth etc. hung up as a screen, esp. at a window or between the stage and auditorium of a theatre. **2** *Theatre* the rise or fall of the stage curtain between acts or scenes. **3** (in *pl.*) *slang* the end. **4** any concentration of something forming a barrier. ● *v.* (foll. by *off*) shut off with a curtain or curtains.
□ **curtained** *adv.*

curtain call *n.* an appearance by a performer or performers to take a bow at the end of a performance.

curtsy (also **curtsey**) ● *n.* (*pl.* **curtsies** or **curtseys**) a woman's or girl's formal greeting made by bending the knees and lowering the body. ● *v.* (**curtsies**, **curtsied**, **curtsying** or **curtseys**, **curtseyed**, **curtseying**) make a curtsy.

curvaceous *adj. informal* having a shapely, curved figure. [*Say* cur VAY shuss]

curvature *n.* the fact of being curved or

the degree to which something is curved. [*Say* CURVA chur]

curve ● *n.* **1** a line or surface with a gradual deviation from being straight or flat. **2** a curved line on a graph. **3** (also **curveball**) **a** *Baseball* a ball pitched so that it curves away from the side from which it was thrown. **b** something unexpected. ● *v.* (**curves, curved, curving**) form a curve. □ **curved** *adj.*

curvy *adj.* (**curvier, curviest**) **1** having many curves. **2** shapely.

cushion ● *n.* **1** a bag of cloth stuffed with soft material and used as a soft support for sitting etc. **2** a buffer or means of protection against something unpleasant. ● *v.* **1** provide with a cushion or cushions. **2** protect. **3** mitigate the adverse effects of. □ **cushioned** *adj.* **cushioning** *n.* **cushiony** *adj.*

cushy *adj.* (**cushier, cushiest**) *informal* **1** easy and pleasant. **2** soft, comfortable.

cusp *n.* **1** an apex. **2** a pointed part. **3** a cone-shaped prominence on the surface of a tooth. □ **on the cusp** at a point of change. □ **cusped** *adj.*

cuss *informal* ● *n.* (*pl.* **cusses**) **1** an obscene or profane expression. **2** usu. *derogatory* a strange and obstinate person or creature. ● *v.* (**cusses, cussed, cussing**) swear, use foul language.

cussed *adj. informal* awkward and stubborn. □ **cussedly** *adv.* **cussedness** *n.* [*Say* CUSS id]

custard *n.* **1** (also **baked custard**) a baked dish made with milk and eggs. **2** (**custard sauce**) a sweet sauce made with milk and thickened with eggs or cornstarch. □ **custardy** *adj.*

custodial *adj.* **1** relating to legal custody or guardianship. **2** pertaining to the work of a caretaker or janitor. **3** pertaining to imprisonment or forcible institutionalization: *a custodial sentence.*

custodian *n.* **1** a person responsible for or having custody of someone or something. **2** a janitor.

custody *n.* **1 a** legal guardianship. **b** safekeeping, protective care. **2** (often preceded by *in* or *into*) imprisonment. □ **take into custody** arrest.

custom ● *n.* **1 a** a traditional way of doing something, specific to a society, place, or time. **b** a habit. **2** habitual business patronage. **3** (in *pl.*; also treated as *sing.*) **a** a duty on imported or exported goods. **b** the official department that administers this. ● *adj.* CUSTOM-MADE.

customary *adj.* **1** usual. **2** in accordance with custom. □ **customarily** *adv.*

customer *n.* **1** a person who buys goods or

services from a store or business. **2** a person one has to deal with.

customize *v.* (**customizes, customized, customizing**) make or modify according to individual requirements. □ **customizable** *adj.* **customization** *n.* **customized** *adj.*

custom-made *adj.* (also **custom-built** etc.) made to an individual customer's specifications.

cut ● *v.* (**cuts, cut, cutting**) **1** penetrate or wound with a sharp-edged instrument. **2** divide, trim, or be divided with a knife etc. **3** make loose, open, etc. by cutting. **4** (esp. as **cutting** *adj.*) cause sharp pain to. **5** reduce or remove. **6** shape or make by cutting. **7** perform. **8** cross. **9** pass. **10** renounce. **11** deliberately fail to attend. **12** *Film* **a** edit. **b** stop recording. **c** (foll. by *to*) go quickly to (another shot). **13** switch off. **14** dilute. **15** swerve sharply. ● *adj.* **1** divided or separated into pieces. **2** made by cutting. **3** lowered or reduced. ● *n.* **1** an act of cutting. **2** something made by cutting. **3** a stroke with a knife etc. **4 a** a reduction. **b** a cessation. **5 a** an abrupt transition. **b** a single song, piece, etc. on an album etc. **6** the way or style in which something is cut. **7** *informal* a share of profits. **8** *Sport* an exclusion from a team etc. **9** a quantity of timber cut in a season. □ **a cut above** *informal* noticeably superior to. **be cut out** be suited. **cut across** transcend (normal limitations etc.). **cut and dried 1** completely decided. **2** ready-made, lacking freshness. **cut and thrust** a lively interchange of argument etc. **cut both ways 1** serve both sides of an argument etc. **2** have both good and bad effects. **cut a corner** go across and not around a corner. **cut corners** do a task incompletely to save time or money. **cut down 1 a** bring or throw down by cutting. **b** kill, disable; ruin. **2** reduce. **cut a person down to size** *informal* ruthlessly expose someone's limitations. **cut from the same cloth** of the same nature. **cut in 1** interrupt. **2** pull in too closely in front of another vehicle. **3** give a share of profits to. **cut it** *informal* function or perform adequately. **cut it out** (usu. in *imper.*) *informal* stop doing something. **cut loose** act freely. **cut one's losses** (or **a loss**) abandon an unprofitable enterprise before losses become too great. **cut the mustard** *slang* reach the required standard. **cut no ice** *slang* **1** have no influence. **2** achieve little. **cut short** interrupt; terminate prematurely. **cut a** (or **the**) **rug** *slang* dance. **cut (a person) some slack** *slang* allow (somebody) some leeway. **cut one's teeth on** acquire initial experience from (something). **cut to the bone** reduce to a minimum. **cut to the chase** come to the point. **cut up 1** cut into pieces. **2** slash, wound. **3** (usu. in *passive*) distress greatly. **make the cut** *informal* **1** be selected for a team, short list, etc. **2** achieve a specified status.

cut-and-paste *n.* the process of assembling text by adding or combining sections from other texts.

cutaneous *adj.* of the skin. [*Say* cue TAINY us]

cutaway *adj.* **1** with some parts left out to reveal the interior. **2** (of a coat) with the front below the waist cut away.

cutback *n.* a reduction.

cutblock *n.* **1** an area with defined boundaries authorized for logging. **2** *Football* a tackle at or below the knees.

cute *adj.* (**cuter, cutest**) *informal* **1** attractive. **2** endearing, charming. □ **cutely** *adv.* **cuteness** *n.*

cutesy *adj.* (**cutesier, cutesiest**) dainty or quaint to an affected degree.

cuticle *n.* **1** the dead skin at the base of a fingernail or toenail. **2** the epidermis of a body. [*Say* CUE tuh cull]

cutie *n. slang* an attractive person.

cutlass *n.* (*pl.* **cutlasses**) a short sword with a slightly curved blade. [*Say* CUT luss]

cutlery *n.* knives, forks, and spoons for use at table.

cutlet *n.* **1** a thin piece of boneless veal etc. usu. served fried. **2** a flat patty of ground meat or nuts and bread crumbs etc.

cutlette *n. Cdn* a roughly oval-shaped, breaded patty of finely chopped meat.

cutline *n.* **1** a caption to an illustration. **2** a line indicating where a cut should be made. **3** *Cdn* a line cut through the bush, e.g. as a survey line.

cut-off *n.* **1** the point at which something is cut off. **2** a device for stopping a flow. **3** (in *pl.*) shorts made from jeans with the legs cut short. **4** a time after which some action is no longer possible.

cut-out ● *n.* **1 a** a figure cut out of paper etc. **b** a person perceived as characterless. **2** a device for automatic disconnection etc. ● *adj.* of or like a cut-out (in sense 1).

cut-rate *adj.* (also **cut-price**) sold at a reduced price.

cutter *n.* **1** a person or thing that cuts. **2** a light, fast boat. **3** a light horse-drawn sleigh.

cutthroat ● *n.* **1** a murderer. **2** (also **cutthroat trout**) a species of trout with a reddish mark under the jaw. ● *adj.* ruthless and intense.

cutting ● *n.* **1** a piece or section cut from something. **2** a piece cut from a plant for propagation. **3** an excavated channel through high ground for a railway or road. **4** *Forestry* **a** a stand of timber. **b** the site of a logging operation. ● *adj.* causing sharp pain.

cutting edge ● *n.* **1** an edge that cuts. **2** the forefront of a movement. ● *adj.* (**cutting-edge**) pioneering.

cuttlefish *n.* (*pl.* **cuttlefish** or **cuttlefishes**) (also **cuttle**) a swimming marine mollusc resembling a squid, that ejects black fluid when alarmed.

cutworm *n.* any of various caterpillars that eat through young plants level with the ground.

CV *abbr.* (*pl.* **CVs**) CURRICULUM VITAE.

cyanide *n.* a highly poisonous chemical compound. [*Say* SIGH a nide]

cyanobacteria *pl. n.* (*singular* **cyanobacterium**) single-celled organisms capable of photosynthesizing. [*Say* sigh a no BACTERIA *for the plural*, sigh a no BACTERIUM *for the singular*]

cyber- *comb. form* of computers, artificial intelligence or virtual reality.

cybernetics *pl. n.* (usu. treated as *sing.*) the science of communications and automatic control systems in machines and living things. □ **cybernetic** *adj.*

cyberspace *n.* the forum in which the global electronic communications network operates.

cybersquatter *n.* a person who registers brand names etc. as Internet domain names, in the hope of later selling them back to the brand owner at a profit. □ **cybersquatting** *n.*

cyborg *n.* (in science fiction) a person whose physical abilities are extended by machine technology.

cyclamen *n.* a plant, having pink, red, or white flowers with petals folded backwards. [*Say* SICK luh min]

cycle ● *n.* **1 a** a recurrent series or period. **b** the time needed for one such series or period. **2** a series of songs, poems, etc. on a single theme. **3** a bicycle, tricycle, etc. ● *v.* (**cycles, cycled, cycling**) **1** ride a bicycle etc. **2** move in cycles. □ **cycling** *n.*

cyclic *adj.* (also **cyclical**) **1 a** occurring in cycles. **b** having to do with cycles. **2** with constituent atoms forming a ring. [*Say* SIKE lick *or* SICK lick]

cyclist *n.* a rider of a bicycle.

cyclone *n.* **1 a** a system of winds rotating inwards to an area of low barometric pressure. **b** a tornado. **2** a hurricane, esp. in

the Indian Ocean. □ **cyclonic** *adj.*
[*Say* SIGH clone, sigh CLON ick]

Cyclops *n.* (*pl.* **Cyclops**) (in Greek mythology) a member of a race of one-eyed giants. [*Say* SIGH clops]

cyclosporin *n.* a drug used to prevent the rejection of grafts and transplants.
[*Say* sike luh SPORE in]

cygnet *n.* a young swan. [*Say* SIG nit]

cylinder *n.* **1** a three-dimensional body with straight sides and a circular section. **2** a piston chamber in an engine. **3** the rotating part of a revolver which houses the cartridge chambers. □ **cylindrical** *adj.*
[*Say* SILL in dur, sill INDRA cull]

cymbal *n.* a musical instrument consisting of a concave brass or bronze plate, struck with another or with a stick. [*Say* SIM bull]

cynic *n.* **1** a person with little faith in human goodness who doubts sincerity and merit. **2** (**Cynic**) one of a school of ancient Greek philosophers, marked by contempt for ease and pleasure.

cynical *adj.* **1** believing that people are motivated by self-interest. **2** doubtful or sneering. **3** concerned only with one's own interests. □ **cynically** *adv.* **cynicism** *n.*

cypress *n.* (*pl.* **cypresses**) a coniferous tree with hard wood and dark foliage.
[*Say* SIGH priss]

Cypriot *n.* a person from Cyprus.
□ **Cypriot** *adj.* [*Say* SIP ree ut]

Cyrillic *n.* the alphabet used for Russian,
Ukrainian, etc. □ **Cyrillic** *adj.*
[*Say* suh RILL ick]

cyst *n.* an abnormal sac containing fluid, pus, etc. □ **cystic** *adj.* [*Say* SIST]

cystic fibrosis *n.* a hereditary disease characterized by abnormal mucus production which affects esp. the lungs, pancreas, and gastrointestinal tract. Abbreviation: **CF**.

cystitis *n.* a bladder infection.
[*Say* sis TITE iss]

cytology *n.* the microscopic study of cells, esp. to identify disease. □ **cytological** *adj.* **cytologist** *n.* [*Say* sigh TOLLA jee]

cytoplasm *n.* the material within a living cell, apart from its nucleus.
□ **cytoplasmic** *adj.* [*Say* SIGH toe plasm, sigh toe PLASMIC]

czar *n.* **1** *hist.* the title of the emperor of Russia before 1917. **2** a person with great power. □ **czarist** *n.* [*Say* ZAR]

czarina *n.* *hist.* the title of the empress of Russia before 1917. [*Say* zar EENA]

Czech *n.* **1** a person from the Czech Republic or *hist.* Czechoslovakia. **2** the Slavic language spoken in the Czech Republic or *hist.* Czechoslovakia. □ **Czech** *adj.* [*Say* CHECK]

Czechoslovak *n.* (also **Czechoslovakian**) a person from Czechoslovakia. □ **Czechoslovak** *adj.*
[*Say* checko SLOW vack]

Dd

D *n.* (also **d**) (*pl.* **Ds** or **D's**) **1** the fourth letter of the alphabet. **2** the second note of the C major scale. **3** the fourth item in a set. **4** the fourth class (of academic marks etc.). **5** *Math* the fourth known quantity. **6** (as a Roman numeral) 500.

'd *v.* (usu. after pronouns) had, would.

DA *abbr.* (*pl.* **DAs**) *US* district attorney.

dab ● *v.* (**dabs, dabbed, dabbing**) **1** press briefly with a cloth etc. **2** (foll. by *on*) apply by dabbing a surface. **3** (usu. foll. by *at*) pat; tap. ● *n.* **1** a brief application of a cloth etc. to a surface. **2** a small amount. □ **smack dab** *adv. informal* exactly, directly. □ **dabber** *n.*

dabble *v.* (**dabbles, dabbled, dabbling**) **1** (usu. foll. by *in, at*) take a casual interest. **2** splash or move about in a small amount of liquid. □ **dabbler** *n.*

dachshund *n.* a dog with short legs and a long body. [*Say* DACKS hund *or* DOCKS hund]

dad *n. informal* father.

Dada *n.* an early 20th-century artistic movement emphasizing the illogical and the absurd. □ **Dadaism** *n. & adj.*

daddy *n.* (*pl.* **daddies**) *informal* **1** father. **2** the oldest or supreme example.

daddy-long-legs *n.* (*pl.* **daddy-long-legs**) an arachnid with very long thin legs.

daffodil *n.* a bulbous plant with a yellow or white trumpet-shaped flower.

daffy *adj.* (**daffier, daffiest**) *slang* silly, foolish.

dagger *n.* **1** a short stabbing weapon with a pointed and edged blade. **2** a symbol (†) used as a reference mark in printed matter. □ **look daggers at** glare angrily at.

dahlia *n.* a daisy-like plant having many-coloured single or double flowers. [*Say* DAILY uh]

daikon *n.* a long, thin, white oriental radish. [*Say* DIE con]

daily ● *adj.* **1** done etc. every day or every weekday. **2** constant. **3** calculated etc. by the day. ● *adv.* **1** every day. **2** constantly. ● *n.* (*pl.* **dailies**) *informal* a daily newspaper. □ **dailiness** *n.*

dainty ● *adj.* (**daintier, daintiest**) **1** delicately pretty or graceful. **2** (of food) delicious. ● *n.* (*pl.* **dainties**) a choice morsel. □ **daintily** *adv.* **daintiness** *n.*

daiquiri *n.* (*pl.* **daiquiris**) a cocktail of rum and lime juice. [*Say* DACKA ree]

dairy *n.* (*pl.* **dairies**) **1** a building for processing and distributing milk and its products. **2** a store where such products are sold. **3** milk and milk products. **4** (as an *adj.*) containing or concerning milk and its products.

dairying *n.* the activity of producing milk for distribution.

dais *n.* (*pl.* **daises**) a low platform used to support a table, throne, etc. [*Say* DIE iss *or* DAY iss]

daisy *n.* (*pl.* **daisies**) a plant bearing flowers with a yellow disc and white rays. □ **pushing up the daisies** *slang* dead and buried.

daisy chain ● *n.* **1** a string of daisies threaded together. **2** a group of several connected things. ● *v.* (**daisy-chain**) link together in succession. □ **daisy-chained** *adj.*

Dakota *n.* (*pl.* **Dakota** or **Dakotas**) **1** a member of a N American Aboriginal people inhabiting the upper Mississippi and Missouri river valleys. **2** the Siouan language of this people. □ **Dakota** *adj.* [*Say* duh CO tuh]

dal *n.* **1** a kind of lentil or split pea. **2** a dish made with this. [*Sounds like* DOLL]

dale *n.* a broad valley.

dalliance *n.* **1** brief involvement with something. **2** a casual love affair. [*Say* DALLY ince]

Dall sheep *n.* (also **Dall's sheep**) a white sheep of the mountains of northwestern Canada and Alaska. [*Sounds like* DOLL]

dally *v.* (**dallies, dallied, dallying**) **1** waste time frivolously. **2** have a casual sexual relationship with. **3** show a casual interest in something.

Dalmatian *n.* a large dog having white, short hair with dark spots. [*Say* dal MAY sh'n]

dam ● *n.* a barrier constructed to hold back water. ● *v.* (**dams, dammed, damming**) **1** provide or confine with a dam. **2** (often foll. by *up*) obstruct.

damage • n. **1** harm impairing the value or usefulness of something, or the normal function of a person. **2** (in pl.) Law money in compensation for loss or injury. **3** (the damage) informal cost • v. (damages, damaged, damaging) harm. □ damaged adj. damaging adj.

damage deposit n. money given as a deposit against possible future damage to rented property.

damask n. a woven fabric with a pattern visible on both sides. [Say DAM isk]

dame n. slang offensive a woman.

damn • v. **1** curse (a person or thing). **2** doom to hell. **3** condemn. **4** (often as damning adj.) (of evidence etc.) prove to be guilty. • n. slang a negligible amount. • interj. informal expressing emphatic annoyance etc. • adj. & adv. informal = DAMNED. □ damn with faint praise praise with so little enthusiasm as to imply disapproval. I'll be (or I'm) damned if informal I certainly do not, will not, etc.

damnable adj. very bad or unpleasant. [Say DAM nuh bull]

damnation • n. condemnation to hell. • interj. expressing anger. [Say dam NATION]

damned informal • n. (in Christian belief) those condemned by God to suffer eternally in hell. • adj. informal used to emphasize anger. • adv. informal extremely.

damnedest adj. informal most extraordinary. □ do one's damnedest do one's utmost.

damp • adj. slightly wet. • n. moisture in the air, on a surface, or in a solid. • v. **1** moisten. **2** (often foll. by down) take the force or strength out of. □ dampness n.

dampen v. **1** make damp. **2** make less strong or intense.

damper n. **1** a person or thing that reduces enthusiasm. **2** a device that reduces shock or noise. **3** a movable metal plate in a flue to control the draft. **4** a pad for silencing a piano string.

damsel n. archaic or jocular a young unmarried woman.

damselfly n. (pl. damselflies) an insect like a dragonfly.

dance • v. (dances, danced, dancing) **1** move rhythmically to music. **2** move in a lively way. **3** perform (a dance or dancing role). • n. **1** a sequence of steps or bodily motions etc., usu. performed to music. **2** a social gathering for dancing. **3** the art of dancing. **4** music suitable for dancing to. **5** a pattern of small movements etc. performed by an animal or bird. □ dance attendance on try hard to please. □ danceable adj. dancer n. dancey adj.

D & C n. (pl. D & C's) an operation in which the cervix is dilated and the uterine lining scraped off.

dandelion n. a plant with a large bright yellow flower followed by a globular head of seeds with downy tufts.

dander[1] n. □ get one's dander up informal lose one's temper.

dander[2] n. dandruff.

dandle v. (dandles, dandled, dandling) move a young child up and down on one's knees or in one's arms.

dandruff n. dead skin in small scales in the hair.

dandy • n. (pl. dandies) **1** a man unduly devoted to fashionable dress and appearance. **2** informal an excellent thing. • adj. (dandier, dandiest) informal first-rate. □ dandyish adj. dandyism n.

Dane n. a native or national of Denmark.

dang adj. & interj. informal = DAMN.

danger n. **1** liability or exposure to harm. **2** a cause of harm. **3** an unwelcome possibility.

dangerous adj. likely to cause harm. □ dangerously adv. dangerousness n.

dangerous offender n. Cdn Law a person who has been convicted of a serious personal injury offence and constitutes a threat to the life, safety, or well-being of others, and whose history suggests little hope of reform, who is imprisoned indefinitely.

dangle v. (dangles, dangled, dangling) **1** be loosely suspended. **2** suspend loosely. **3** offer enticingly. □ dangly adj.

Danish n. **1** the language of Denmark. **2** (the Danish; treated as pl.) the people of Denmark. **3** (pl. Danishes) (also Danish pastry) a sweet, flaky roll topped with icing, fruit, etc. □ Danish adj.

dank adj. damp and cold. □ dankly adv. dankness n.

dapper adj. neat and trim in appearance.

dapple v. (dapples, dappled, dappling) mark with spots or small patches. □ dappled adj.

dare • v. (dares, dared, daring) **1** have the courage or impudence (to) **2** challenge (a person). • n. **1** an act of daring. **2** a challenge to prove courage. □ I dare say probably.

daredevil • n. a recklessly daring person. • adj. recklessly daring. □ daredevilry n.

daring • n. adventurous courage. • adj. prepared to take risks. □ daringly adv.

dark • adj. **1** with little or no light. **2** of a deep colour. **3** (of skin, hair, or eyes) deep brown or black. **4** gloomy, dismal. **5** evil. **6** angry. **7** remote, little-known. • n.

1 absence of light. **2** nightfall. □ **in the dark 1** without light. **2** lacking information. □ **darkly** adv. **darkness** n.

Dark Ages pl. n. **1** the period in Europe between the fall of the Roman Empire and the high Middle Ages, c.500–1100, seen as lacking culture and learning. **2** (**dark ages**) any period of supposed lack of enlightenment.

darken v. make or become darker. □ **darken a door** appear at a place □ **darkener** n.

dark horse n. a little-known person who is unexpectedly successful.

darkroom n. a room for developing photographic work, with normal light excluded.

darling ● n. **1** a beloved person or thing. **2** a favourite. **3** informal an endearing person or thing. ● adj. **1** beloved, lovable. **2** favourite. **3** informal charming.

darn¹ ● v. mend (knitted material) by interweaving yarn across it. ● n. a darned area in material. □ **darning** n.

darn² v., interj., adj., & adv. informal a milder form of DAMN.

darned adj. & adv. informal a milder form of DAMNED. □ **darndest** adj.

darnel n. a grass planted as pasture or to stabilize soil.

dart ● n. **1** a small pointed object thrown or fired as a weapon. **2 a** a small pointed missile used in the game of darts. **b** (in pl.) an indoor game in which such darts are thrown at a circular target. **3** a sudden rapid movement. ● v. **1** move quickly. **2** direct suddenly.

dartboard n. a circular board marked with numbered segments, used as a target in darts.

darter n. **1** a water bird with a long thin neck. **2** a quick-moving freshwater fish.

Darwinian ● adj. **1** relating to Charles Darwin's theory of evolution. **2** characterized by ruthless competition for survival. ● n. an adherent of Darwin's theory. □ **Darwinism** n. **Darwinist** n. [Say dar WINNY un, DARWIN ism]

dash ● v. (**dashes**, **dashed**, **dashing**) **1** rush. **2** strike or fling with great force. **3** frustrate. **4** splash or splatter. ● n. **1** a rushing movement. **2** a horizontal written or printed stroke to mark a pause or omission. **3** a small amount. **4** impetuous vigour. **5** a sprint. **6** the longer signal of the two used in Morse code. **7** = DASHBOARD. □ **dash off** finish hurriedly.

dashboard n. the surface below the windshield of a motor vehicle or aircraft.

dashing adj. **1** fashionable. **2** attractive in a romantic, adventurous way. □ **dashingly** adv.

dastardly adj. wicked and cruel. [Say DASS turd lee]

data n. **1** quantities or characters operated on by a computer. **2** (treated as sing.) information. **3** (treated as pl.) facts, statistics. **4** pl. of DATUM. [Say DAT uh or DATE uh]

database n. (also **data bank**) an organized store of data on a computer.

datable adj. that can be assigned a date.

date¹ ● n. **1** a day of the month as specified by a number. **2** a day or year when a given event occurred or will occur. **3 a** a social or romantic appointment. **b** a person with whom one has a social engagement. **4** the period to which a work of art etc. belongs. **5** (in pl.) the dates of a person's birth and death, usu. in years. ● v. (**dates**, **dated**, **dating**) **1** mark with a date. **2 a** assign a date to. **b** (foll. by to) assign to a particular time, period, etc. **3** go out on a date or regular dates with a person. **4** have its origins at a particular time. **5** become evidently out of date. **6** expose as being out of date. □ **to date** until now. **up to date** according to the latest requirements, fashion, etc. □ **dating** n.

date² n. a dark oval single-stoned fruit of a palm tree of W Asia and North Africa.

datebook n. an appointment diary.

dated adj. **1** old-fashioned. **2** marked with a date.

dateline ● n. **1** (**Date Line**) the line from north to south partly along the meridian 180° from Greenwich, to the east of which the date is a day earlier than it is to the west. **2** a line at the head of a newspaper article showing the date and place of writing. ● v. (**datelines**, **datelined**, **datelining**) provide with a dateline.

date rape n. the rape of a girl or woman by a person with whom she is on a date.

date square n. Cdn a dessert with an oatmeal base, a date filling, and a crumble topping.

dative ● n. the case of nouns and pronouns indicating an indirect object or recipient. ● adj. of or in the dative. [Say DAY tiv]

datum n. (pl. **data**) **1** a piece of information. **2** a known premise from which inferences may be drawn. [Say DAT um or DATE um]

daub ● v. **1** spread (a thick substance) crudely on a surface. **2** smear (a surface) with paint etc. **3** paint ineptly. ● n. **1** paint etc. daubed on a surface. **2** plaster, clay, etc., for coating a surface. **3** a poor painting.

daughter n. **1** a girl or woman in relation to either or both of her parents. **2** a female descendant. □ **daughterly** adj.

daughter-in-law n. (pl. **daughters-in-law**) the wife of one's son.

daunt v. discourage, intimidate. □ **daunting** adj.

dauntless adj. intrepid, persevering.

davit n. a small crane on a ship. [Say DAV it or DAVE it]

dawdle v. (**dawdles, dawdled, dawdling**) **1** walk or move slowly. **2** waste time. □ **dawdler** n.

dawn ● n. **1** the first light of day. **2** the beginning of something. ● v. **1** (of a day) begin. **2** begin to appear or develop. **3** (often foll. by *on, upon*) become evident to. □ **dawning** n.

day n. **1** the time between sunrise and sunset. **2** a period of 24 hours, esp. from midnight to midnight. **3** the part of a day when work is engaged in. **4** daylight. **5 a** (also in pl.) a period of the past or present. **b** (**the day**) the present time. **6** a point of time. □ **any day** at any time. **at the end of the day** in the final reckoning. **call it a day** end a period of activity. **day and night** all the time. **day by day** gradually. **day in, day out** routinely, constantly. **from day one** from the beginning. **not one's day** a day of successive misfortunes for a person. **win the day** be successful.

daybook n. an appointment diary.

daybreak n. the first appearance of light in the morning.

daycare n. **1** the supervision of children during the workday by people other than their parents. **2** (also **daycare centre**) a place where daycare is provided.

daydream ● n. a pleasant fantasy or reverie. ● v. (**daydreams, daydreamed, daydreaming**) indulge in this. □ **daydreamer** n. **daydreaming** n. & adj.

day job n. a job with regular daytime hours, esp. as opposed to artistic pursuits.

daylight n. **1** the light of day. **2** dawn. **3** a visible gap or interval.

daylights pl. n. informal senses or wits.

daylight saving n. (also **daylight savings**) the achieving of longer evening daylight in summer by setting the time an hour ahead.

daylight time n. (also **daylight saving time**) time as adjusted for daylight saving.

daylong adj. lasting for a day.

Day of Atonement n. = YOM KIPPUR.

Day of Judgment n. = JUDGMENT DAY.

day of reckoning n. the time when something must be atoned for.

day pack n. a small backpack.

day release n. Cdn release of a jailed offender for a short period of time, e.g. to attend school or for employment.

daytime n. the part of the day when there is natural light.

Day-timer n. proprietary an appointment diary.

day-to-day adj. **1** involving daily routine. **2** planning for only one day at a time.

day trader n. a trader who holds stocks very briefly, usu. less than a full day. □ **day trading** n.

daze ● v. (**dazes, dazed, dazing**) stupefy, bewilder. ● n. a state of confusion. □ **dazed** adj. **dazedly** adv.

dazzle ● v. (**dazzles, dazzled, dazzling**) **1** blind temporarily with an excess of light. **2** impress (a person) with any brilliant display. ● n. bright confusing light. □ **dazzled** adj. **dazzlement** n. **dazzler** n. **dazzling** adj. **dazzlingly** adv.

dB abbr. decibel(s).

DC abbr. (also **d.c.**) direct current.

D-Day n. 6 June 1944, on which Allied forces invaded northern France.

DDT abbr. dichlorodiphenyltrichloroethane, an insecticide now banned in many countries.

de- prefix removal or reversal.

deacon n. **1** (in churches with a hierarchy) a minister ranking below priest. **2** (in some Protestant churches) a layperson assisting the minister. [Say DEE kun]

deaconess n. (pl. **deaconesses**) a laywoman with functions similar to a deacon's. [Say dee kun ESS]

deactivate v. (**deactivates, deactivated, deactivating**) make inactive. □ **deactivation** n.

dead ● adj. **1** no longer alive. **2** informal extremely tired or unwell. **3** numb. **4** (foll. by *to*) unconscious of; insensitive to. **5** no longer effective. **6** no longer current. **7** inanimate. **8 a** lacking vigour **b** lacking activity. **9** not functioning. **10** abrupt. ● adv. absolutely, exactly. ● n. (**the dead**) **1** (treated as pl.) those who have died. **2** silence or inactivity. □ **dead in the water 1** (of a ship) motionless. **2** not progressing. **dead to the world** informal fast asleep. **play dead** pretend to be dead by lying still.

deadbeat n. **1** someone who avoids paying debts or child support. **2** a sponging idler.

deadbolt n. a bolt engaged by turning a knob or key, rather than by spring action.

deaden v. **1** deprive of or lose vitality or force. **2** (foll. by *to*) make insensitive.

dead end ● n. **1 a** a closed end of a road, passage, etc. **b** a road with a dead end. **2** a situation offering no prospects of progress. ● v. (**dead-end**) come to an end.

deadfall n. **1** a trap in which a weight falls on large game. **2** a fallen tree or trees, branches, etc.

deadhead ● n. **1** a faded flower head. **2** a useless person. **3** a submerged log hazardous to boats. ● v. remove deadheads from (a plant).

dead heat n. a race in which two or more competitors are exactly level.

dead letter n. a law or practice no longer observed.

deadline n. a time limit for the completion of something.

deadlock ● n. **1** a situation in which no progress can be made. **2** a lock requiring a key to open or close it. ● v. bring or come to a deadlock. □**deadlocked** adj.

deadly ● adj. (**deadlier, deadliest**) **1** causing or able to cause death or serious damage. **2** intense, extreme. **3** extremely accurate. **4** deathlike. **5** informal dreary. ● adv. **1** like death. **2** intensely. □**deadliness** n.

deadly nightshade n. a poisonous plant with purple flowers and purple-black berries.

deadly sin n. a sin regarded as leading to damnation.

dead meat n. informal a person or thing that is doomed.

dead-on adj. **1** exactly right. **2** perfectly on target.

deadpan ● adj. & adv. not showing emotion. ● v. (**deadpans, deadpanned, deadpanning**) say in a deadpan manner.

dead set adj. (foll. by *against*) fiercely opposed.

dead weight n. **1** an inert mass. **2** a burden.

deadwood n. informal one or more useless people or things.

deaf adj. **1** wholly or partly without hearing. **2** refusing to listen. □**deafness** n.

deafen v. **1** (often as **deafening** adj.) overpower with sound. **2** make deaf. □**deafeningly** adv.

deal ● v. (**deals, dealt, dealing**) **1** (foll. by *with*) **a** take measures to put right. **b** do business with. **c** discuss or treat (a subject). **2** (foll. by *in*) be concerned with commercially. **3** distribute. **4** give out (cards) to players for a game. **5** administer. ● n. **1** (usu. **a good** (or **great) deal**)

informal **a** a large amount. **b** to a considerable extent. **2** an agreement. **3** a specified form of treatment given or received. □**it's a deal** informal expressing assent to an agreement.

dealer n. **1** a person dealing in goods. **2** the player dealing at cards. **3** a person who deals in illegal drugs. □**dealership** n. (in sense 1)

dealings pl. n. contacts or transactions.

dealt past and past participle of DEAL.

dean n. **1 a** the head of a university faculty. **b** a college or university official with disciplinary and advisory functions. **2** the head of the chapter of a cathedral. **3** the most senior of a category or body of people.

dear ● adj. **1** much loved. **2** used as a formula of address at the beginning of letters. **3** earnest. **4** expensive. ● n. a dear person. ● adv. at great cost. ● interj. expressing dismay, pity, etc.

dearly adv. **1** fondly. **2 a** earnestly. **b** very much. **3** at great cost.

dearth n. a scarcity. [*Rhymes with* EARTH]

death n. **1** the ending of life. **2** the event that terminates life. **3** the state of being dead. **4** the end of something. □**at death's door** close to death. **be the death of 1** cause the death of. **2** be very harmful to. **do to death** overdo. **put to death** execute. **to death** to the utmost. □**deathless** adj. **deathlike** adj.

deathbed n. a bed where a person is dying or has died.

death knell n. **1** the tolling of a bell to mark a person's death. **2** an event that heralds the end of something.

deathly ● adj. (**deathlier, deathliest**) suggestive of death. ● adv. **1** in a deathly way. **2** extremely.

death row n. a prison block for those sentenced to death.

death sentence n. **1** a judicial sentence of punishment by death. **2** a situation implying imminent death.

death trap n. informal a dangerous building, vehicle, etc.

death wish n. an unconscious wish for one's own death.

debacle n. **1** an utter failure or disaster. **2** a breakup of ice in a river, with resultant flooding. [*Say* duh BOCK ul *or* duh BACK ul]

debark v. **1** = DISEMBARK. **2** remove the bark from (a tree etc.).

debase v. (**debases, debased, debasing**) lower in quality, character, or value. □**debasement** n.

debatable adj. subject to dispute. □**debatably** adv.

debate ● v. (**debates, debated, debating**) **1** discuss or dispute about, esp. formally. **2** ponder (a matter). ● n. **1** a formal discussion on a particular matter, with opposing views presented. **2** argument. □ **debater** n.

debauch ● v. (**debauches, debauched, debauching**) **1** corrupt morally. **2** seduce (a woman). ● n. (pl. **debauches**) a bout of excessive indulgence in sex, alcohol, and drugs. □ **debauched** adj. [Say duh BOTCH]

debauchery n. (pl. **debaucheries**) excessive indulgence in sex, alcohol, and drugs. [Say duh BOTCHA ree]

debenture n. a loan certificate issued by a company. [Say duh BEN chur]

debilitate v. (**debilitates, debilitated, debilitating**) severely weaken. □ **debilitating** adj. **debilitation** n. [Say duh BILLA tate]

debility n. (pl. **debilities**) **1** feebleness, esp. of health. **2** a disability. [Say duh BILLA tee]

debit ● n. **1** an entry in an account recording a sum owed or paid out. **2** the sum recorded. **3** a transaction using a debit card. ● v. (**debits, debited, debiting**) (of a bank) remove money from a customer's account.

debit card n. a card enabling the holder to pay for purchases electronically by transferring funds from a bank account.

debonair adj. confident, stylish, and charming. [Say debba NAIR]

debrief v. discuss a completed mission etc. with. □ **debriefing** n.

debris n. **1** scattered fragments of something destroyed. **2** an accumulation of loose material. [Say duh BREE]

debt n. **1** a sum of money owed. **2** a state of owing money. **3** gratitude for kindness etc. □ **in a person's debt** under an obligation to a person. [Say DET]

debtor n. a person etc. that owes a debt.

debug v. (**debugs, debugged, debugging**) **1** remove defects from (computer software etc.). **2** remove concealed listening devices. □ **debugging** n.

debugger n. a program for debugging.

debunk v. informal expose the false nature of. □ **debunker** n.

debut ● n. **1** a person's first appearance in a role. **2** the first appearance of a young woman of marriageable age in fashionable society. ● adj. first; inaugural. ● v. (**debuts, debuted, debuting**) make a debut. [Say day BYOO or DAY byoo]

debutante n. a (usu. wealthy) young woman making her social debut. [Say DEB you tont]

deca- comb. form (also **dec-** before a vowel) ten.

decade n. **1** ten years. **2** a set of ten Hail Marys as part of the rosary. [Say DECK ade for sense 1, DECK id for sense 2]

decadent ● adj. **1** in a state of moral or cultural deterioration. **2** self-indulgent. **3** (of food) very rich or sweet. ● n. a decadent person. □ **decadence** n. **decadently** adv. [Say DEKKA dint]

decaf informal ● n. decaffeinated coffee. ● adj. decaffeinated.

decaffeinate v. (**decaffeinates, decaffeinated, decaffeinating**) **1** remove the caffeine from. **2** reduce the quantity of caffeine in (usu. coffee). □ **decaffeinated** adj. **decaffeination** n.

decal n. a picture or design transferred from specially prepared paper to the surface of glass, plastic, etc. [Say DEE cal or DECK ul]

decamp v. depart suddenly or secretly.

decant v. pour (liquid) from one container to another. [Say duh CANT]

decanter n. a glass container into which wine or liquor is decanted. [Say duh CANT er]

decapitate v. (**decapitates, decapitated, decapitating**) cut off the head of. □ **decapitation** n. [Say dee CAPPA tate]

decathlon n. an athletic contest in which each competitor takes part in ten events. □ **decathlete** n. [Say duh KATH lon]

decay ● v. **1** rot. **2** decline or cause to decline in quality etc. **3** Physics (of a substance etc.) undergo change by radioactivity. ● n. **1** a rotten or ruinous state. **2** decline in health, quality, etc. **3** Physics change into another substance etc. by radioactivity.

decease n. formal esp. Law death.

deceased ● adj. dead. ● n. (usu. as **the deceased**) a person who has recently died.

deceit n. **1** the act or process of deceiving. **2** a dishonest trick.

deceitful adj. **1** using deceit. **2** intended to deceive. □ **deceitfully** adv. **deceitfulness** n.

deceive v. (**deceives, deceived, deceiving**) **1** make (a person) believe what is false. **2** be unfaithful to, esp. sexually. □ **be deceived** be mistaken. **deceive oneself** persist in a mistaken belief. □ **deceiver** n.

decelerate v. (**decelerates, decelerated, decelerating**) slow

down. □ **deceleration** *n.* **decelerator** *n.*
[*Say* duh SELLA rate]

December *n.* the twelfth month.

decency *n.* (*pl.* **decencies**) **1** decent behaviour. **2** (in *pl.*) the requirements of correct behaviour.

decent *adj.* **1** conforming with current standards of propriety. **2** respectable. **3** of acceptable quality. **4** kind. **5** *informal* sufficiently clothed to see visitors. □ **decently** *adv.*

decentralize *v.* (**decentralizes**, **decentralized**, **decentralizing**) **1** transfer (powers etc.) from a central to a local government etc. **2** move departments of a large organization away from a single administrative centre, usu. granting them some autonomy. □ **decentralization** *n.* **decentralized** *adj.*

deception *n.* **1** the act of deceiving. **2** a thing that deceives.

deceptive *adj.* giving a misleading impression. □ **deceptively** *adv.*

decertify *v.* (**decertifies**, **decertified**, **decertifying**) revoke or renounce certification of (esp. a union). □ **decertification** *n.*

deci- *comb. form* one-tenth.

decibel *n.* **1** a unit (one-tenth of a bel) expressing the power of electrical signals or intensity of sound. **2** *informal* a degree of noise. [*Say* DESSA bull *or* DESSA bell]

decide *v.* (**decides**, **decided**, **deciding**) **1** come to a resolution after consideration. **2** resolve or settle. **3** give a judgment concerning a matter.

decided *adj.* **1** definite, unquestionable. **2** having clear opinions.

decidedly *adv.* undoubtedly.

decider *n.* **1** a contest that settles the winner of a series of contests. **2** a person or thing that decides.

deciduous *adj.* **1** (of a tree) shedding its leaves annually. **2** (of leaves, horns, teeth, etc.) shed periodically. [*Say* duh SIDGE yoo us *or* duh SID yoo us]

decimal ● *adj.* **1** (of a system of numbers etc.) based on the number ten. **2** of tenths or ten. ● *n.* (also **decimal fraction**) a fraction whose denominator is a power of ten, expressed by units to the right of a decimal point. □ **decimally** *adv.*

decimal place *n.* the position of a digit to the right of a decimal point.

decimal point *n.* a period placed before a numerator in a decimal fraction.

decimate *v.* (**decimates**, **decimated**, **decimating**) destroy a large proportion of. □ **decimation** *n.* [*Say* DESSA mate]

decipher *v.* **1** succeed in understanding.

2 convert code into an intelligible script or language. □ **decipherable** *adj.*
[*Say* duh SIGH fur]

decision *n.* **1** the act or process of deciding. **2** a conclusion reached after consideration. **3 a** the settlement of a question. **b** a formal judgment.

decisive *adj.* **1** that decides an issue. **2** able to decide effectively. □ **decisively** *adv.* **decisiveness** *n.*

deck ● *n.* **1** a platform in a ship serving as a floor. **2** anything compared to a ship's deck. **3** a component that carries a CD etc. in sound-reproduction equipment. **4** a pack of cards. **5** a level area without a roof adjoining a house or pool. ● *v.* **1** (often foll. by *out*) decorate, adorn. **2** furnish with or cover as a deck. **3** *slang* knock (a person) to the ground.

deck chair *n.* a folding chair of wood and canvas, of a kind used on deck on passenger ships.

declaim *v.* utter words or a speech in a rhetorical way, as if to an audience.

declamation *n.* **1** the act or art of declaiming. **2** a rhetorical exercise. **3** an impassioned speech. □ **declamatory** *adj.*
[*Say* deckla MAY sh'n, duh CLAMMA tory]

declaration *n.* **1** the act or process of declaring. **2 a** a formal, emphatic, or deliberate statement. **b** a statement asserting a legal right. **3** a written public announcement of intentions etc.

declarative *adj.* **1** making a declaration. **2** *Grammar* (of a sentence) that takes the form of a simple statement.
[*Say* duh CLAIRA tiv]

declare *v.* (**declares**, **declared**, **declaring**) **1** announce or assert. **2** pronounce (a person or thing) to be something. **3** acknowledge possession of (taxable income etc.). **4** (of things) make evident, prove. □ **declare oneself** reveal one's intentions or identity.

declaw *v.* **1** remove the claws from (a cat). **2** remove the force from.

declension *n.* the variation of the form of a noun, pronoun, or adjective, by which its grammatical case, number, and gender are identified. [*Say* duh KLEN sh'n]

declination *n.* **1** the angular distance of a star etc. north or south of the celestial equator. **2** the angular deviation of a compass needle from true north.
[*Say* deckla NAY sh'n]

decline ● *v.* (**declines**, **declined**, **declining**) **1** lose strength, size, numbers, etc. **2** politely refuse. **3** slope downwards or bend down. **4** state the forms of (a noun, pronoun, or adjective) corresponding to cases, number, and gender. ● *n.* **1 a** a decrease in numbers, rates, etc. **b** gradual loss of vigour or excellence. **2** decay, deterioration. □ **decliner** n.

Deco n. (also **deco**) = ART DECO (often as an adj.). [Say DECK oh]

decode v. (**decodes, decoded, decoding**) **1** convert (a coded message) into intelligible language or format. **2** analyze and interpret.

decoder n. **1** a person or thing that decodes (texts etc.). **2** an electronic device for analyzing stereophonic signals and feeding separate amplifier channels. **3** an electronic device that unscrambles encoded transmissions.

decolonize v. (**decolonizes, decolonized, decolonizing**) (of a state) withdraw from (a colony), leaving it independent. □ **decolonization** n.

decommission v. **1** close down (a nuclear reactor etc.). **2** take (a ship or aircraft) out of service.

decompose v. (**decomposes, decomposed, decomposing**) **1** destroy or be destroyed gradually by natural chemical processes. **2** separate (a substance) into its elements. **3** break up. □ **decomposable** adj. **decomposition** n.

decompress v. (**decompresses, decompressed, decompressing**) **1 a** subject to decompression. **b** relieve or reduce the compression on. **2** restore (compacted computer files) to normal size. **3** informal calm down, relax.

decompression n. **1** reduction of (esp. air) pressure. **2** a gradual reduction of air pressure on a person who has been subjected to high pressure (esp. underwater). **3** the restoring of compacted computer files to their normal size.

decompression sickness n. a serious condition that results when too rapid decompression by a diver causes nitrogen bubbles to form in the body tissues.

decongestant n. a medication that relieves nasal congestion. □ **decongestant** adj. [Say dee cun JEST int]

deconstruct v. **1** analyze a text in order to show that there is no fixed meaning within the text but that meaning is created each time in the act of reading. **2** take to pieces. □ **deconstruction** n. **deconstructionism** n. **deconstructionist** adj. & n. **deconstructive** adj.

decontaminate v. (**decontaminates, decontaminated, decontaminating**) remove contamination or dangerous substances from. □ **decontamination** n.

decor n. the decorations and furnishings of a room. [Say day CORE]

decorate v. (**decorates, decorated, decorating**) (often foll. by with) **1** make more attractive by ornamentation etc. **2** apply new paint or wallpaper to. **3** give an award or medal to. □ **decorated** adj.

decoration n. **1** the process or art of decorating. **2** a decorative ornament or pattern. **3** a medal etc. conferred and worn as an honour.

decorative adj. **1** serving to decorate. **2** ornamental rather than practical. □ **decoratively** adv. [Say DECK ruh tiv]

decorative arts pl. n. the arts that produce high-quality objects which are both useful and beautiful, e.g. ceramics, furniture making, etc.

decorator n. **1** an interior designer. **2** a person who decorates.

decorous adj. polite and appropriate. □ **decorously** adv. [Say DECKER us]

decorum n. behaviour required by politeness or decency. [Say duh CORE um]

decoy ● n. **1** a person or thing used to lure an animal or person into a trap. **2** a bird or animal, or an imitation of one, used to attract others. **3** an aircraft, missile, etc. used to distract the enemy, mislead radar, etc. ● v. lure by means of a decoy.

decrease ● v. (**decreases, decreased, decreasing**) make or become smaller, fewer, weaker, less, etc. ● n. the process of reducing or the amount reduced. □ **decreasingly** adv.

decree ● n. **1** an official order issued by a legal authority. **2** a judgment of certain law courts. ● v. (**decrees, decreed, decreeing**) order by decree.

decrepit adj. **1** worn out by age and infirmity. **2** worn out by long use. □ **decrepitude** n. [Say duh CREP it, duh CREPPA tude]

decriminalize v. (**decriminalizes, decriminalized, decriminalizing**) cease to treat (something) as illegal. □ **decriminalization** n.

decry v. (**decries, decried, decrying**) strongly criticize publicly. [Say duh CRY]

decrypt v. decipher or decode. □ **decryption** n.

dedicate v. (**dedicates, dedicated, dedicating**) **1** (foll. by to) devote to a task or purpose. **2** (foll. by to) address (a book, music, etc.) to a patron or friend as a mark of respect etc. **3** (often foll. by to) consecrate with solemn rites (a building etc.) to a god, saint, etc.

dedicated adj. **1** (of a person) devoted to

an aim or vocation. **2** set apart or available only for a particular purpose.

dedication *n.* **1** the quality of being committed to a purpose. **2** the words with which a book etc. is dedicated. **3** a formal public opening of a building etc.

deduce *v.* (**deduces, deduced, deducing**) (often foll. by *from*) draw as a logical conclusion.

deduct *v.* (often foll. by *from*) subtract, take away.

deductible ● *adj.* that may be deducted, e.g. from taxable income. ● *n.* a sum payable by an insured party in the event of a claim.

deduction *n.* **1 a** the act or process of deducting. **b** an amount deducted. **2** the process of drawing a conclusion using information already gained or a general rule. □ **deductive** *adj.* **deductively** *adv.*

deed ● *n.* **1** an action that is performed intentionally. **2** a document under seal often used for a legal transfer of ownership. ● *v.* transfer by legal deed.

deejay *n. informal* a disc jockey.

deem *v.* regard, consider.

de-emphasize *v.* (**de-emphasizes, de-emphasized, de-emphasizing**) reduce the importance given to something. □ **de-emphasis** *n.*

deep ● *adj.* **1** extending or situated far down from the top or in from the surface or edge. **2** extending to or lying at a specified depth. **3** from far down or in. **4** low-pitched. **5 a** intense. **b** vivid, darkly hued. **c** mysterious or obscure. **6** fully absorbed or overwhelmed. **7** profound. **8** *Baseball* relatively far in or into the outfield. **9** *Sport* near to the opposing team's territory. **10** cunning or secretive. ● *n.* **1** (**the deep**) *literary* the sea. **2** the most intense part. ● *adv.* **1** deeply. **2** far down, in, on, or back. □ **go off the deep end** *informal* go crazy. **in deep** inextricably involved or committed. **jump** (**or be thrown**) **in at the deep end** face a difficult situation with little experience.

deepen *v.* make or become deep or deeper.

deep-freeze ● *n.* **1** a refrigerator for freezing and storing food for long periods. **2** a suspension of activity. **3** a period of very cold weather. ● *v.* (**deep-freezes, deep-froze, deep-frozen, deep-freezing**) freeze or store (food) in a deep-freeze.

deep-fry *v.* (**deep-fries, deep-fried, deep-frying**) fry (food) in hot oil or fat deep enough to cover it. □ **deep-fried** *adj.*

deeply *adv.* **1** far down or in. **2** intensely.

deep pocket *n. informal* (usu. in *pl.*)

substantial financial resources. □ **deep-pocketed** *adj.*

deep-rooted *adj.* **1** firmly established. **2** having long roots.

deep-seated *adj.* firmly established.

deep-set *adj.* **1** (of the eyes) set deeply in the sockets. **2** firmly fixed.

deep-six *v.* (**deep-sixes, deep-sixed, deep-sixing**) *slang* **1** defeat thoroughly. **2** discard.

deepwater *n.* water of great depth (often as an *adj.*).

deer *n.* (*pl.* **deer**) a four-hoofed grazing animal, the males of which usu. have deciduous branching antlers.

deer fly *n.* a bloodsucking fly.

deerskin *n.* leather from a deer's skin.

DEET *n.* N,N-diethyl-meta-toluamide, the active ingredient in many insect repellents.

deface *v.* (**defaces, defaced, defacing**) **1** spoil the appearance of something, esp. by drawing or writing on it. **2** make illegible.

de facto ● *adj.* that exists in fact, whether legally acknowledged or not. ● *adv.* in fact, whether by right or not (*compare* DE JURE).

defame *v.* (**defames, defamed, defaming**) attack the good reputation of, esp. unjustly. □ **defamation** *n.* **defamatory** *adj.* [*Say* duh FAME, deffa MAY shun, duh FAMMA tory]

default ● *n.* **1 a** failure to fulfill an obligation. **b** *Sport* failure to compete in or finish a contest, etc. **2** a pre-selected option adopted by a computer program when no alternative is specified by the user. ● *v.* **1** fail to fulfill an obligation, esp. to pay money or to appear in a law court. **2** fail to appear for or complete a contest etc. **3** lose by default. **4** revert automatically to a pre-selected option. □ **by default** because of a lack of opposition or action. □ **defaulted** *adj.* **defaulter** *n.* [*Say* DEE fault, duh FAULT]

defeat ● *v.* **1** overcome in a battle or other contest. **2** frustrate, thwart. **3** reject (a motion etc.) by voting. ● *n.* **1** failure. **2** a victory over something.

defeatism *n.* excessive readiness to accept defeat. □ **defeatist** *n. & adj.*

defecate *v.* (**defecates, defecated, defecating**) discharge feces from the body. □ **defecation** *n.* [*Say* DEFFA kate]

defect ● *n.* a shortcoming, failing, or imperfection. ● *v.* abandon one's country or cause in favour of another. □ **defection** *n.* **defector** *n.*

defective *adj.* imperfect; faulty.

defence *n.* (also **defense**) **1** the act of defending against attack. **2** something that provides protection against attack, disease, etc. **3** the military resources of a country. **4** justification. **5 a** the defendant's case in a lawsuit. **b** the counsel for the defendant. **6** *Sport* the role of or players responsible for defending a goal. **7** (also **defence mechanism**) an unconscious mental process to avoid conflict or anxiety. □ **defenceless** *adj.*

defenceman *n.* (*pl.* **defencemen**) a player in a defensive position in hockey or lacrosse.

defend *v.* **1** (often foll. by *against*, *from*) resist an attack made on; protect (a person or thing) from harm. **2 a** speak or write in favour of. **b** present a (thesis etc.) orally to examiners and answer questions. **3** conduct the case for (a defendant in a lawsuit). **4** *Sport* **a** protect (a goal etc.). **b** compete to retain (a contested title). □ **defendable** *adj.* **defender** *n.*

defendant *n.* a person etc. sued or accused in court.

defense *n.* = DEFENCE.

defensible *adj.* **1** justifiable by argument. **2** that can be easily defended from attack.

defensive *adj.* **1** done or intended to defend. **2** very anxious to challenge or avoid criticism. □ **on the defensive 1** expecting criticism. **2** in an attitude or position of defence. □ **defensively** *adv.* **defensiveness** *n.*

defer *v.* (**defers, deferred, deferring**) **1** put off to a later time. **2** (foll. by *to*) yield. □ **deferral** *n.* [*Say* duh FUR]

deference *n.* courteous regard. □ **in** (or **out of**) **deference to** out of respect for. □ **deferential** *adj.* **deferentially** *adv.* [*Say* DEF rinse, deffer EN sh'll]

defiance *n.* open disobedience.

defiant *adj.* showing defiance. □ **defiantly** *adv.*

defibrillation *n.* the application of an electric shock to the heart to encourage the resumption of coordinated contractions. □ **defibrillator** *n.* [*Say* dee fib ruh LAY sh'n, dee FIB ruh lay tur]

deficiency *n.* (*pl.* **deficiencies**) **1** a lack or shortage. **2** a fault. **3** the amount by which something falls short. [*Say* duh FISHIN see]

deficient *adj.* **1** (usu. foll. by *in*) not having enough of a specified quality or ingredient. **2** inadequate. [*Say* duh FISH int]

deficit *n.* **1** the amount by which a thing is too small. **2** an excess of liabilities or expenditures over assets or income in a given period. **3** a shortage. [*Say* DEFFA sit]

defile ● *v.* (**defiles, defiled, defiling**)

1 make dirty. **2** corrupt morally. **3** make unfit for ritual or ceremonial use. ● *n.* a gorge or narrow passage. □ **defilement** *n.* [*Say* duh FILE]

define *v.* (**defines, defined, defining**) **1** give the exact meaning of. **2** describe or explain the scope etc. of. **3** mark out the limits or outline of. □ **definable** *adj.*

defined *adj.* **1** having a definite outline or form. **2** clearly marked.

definite *adj.* **1** having exact and discernible limits. **2** clearly defined. **3** certain, sure. □ **definiteness** *n.*

definite article *n.* the word (*the* in English) preceding a noun and implying a specific or known instance.

definitely ● *adv.* **1** in a definite manner. **2** without doubt. ● *interj.* yes.

definition *n.* **1 a** the act or process of defining. **b** a statement of the meaning of a word or the nature of a thing. **2** the degree of distinctness in outline of an object or image. □ **by definition** by its very nature.

definitive *adj.* **1** conclusive, final. **2** most complete and authoritative. □ **definitively** *adv.*

deflate *v.* (**deflates, deflated, deflating**) **1 a** let air or gas out of. **b** be emptied of air or gas. **2** lose or cause to lose confidence. **3** *Economics* reduce price levels in an economy. **4** reduce the level of (emotion). □ **deflated** *adj.*

deflation *n.* **1** the action of deflating. **2** a reduction in general level of prices in a country's economy. □ **deflationary** *adj.*

deflect *v.* turn aside from a straight course or intended purpose. □ **deflection** *n.* **deflector** *n.*

deflower *v.* have sex with (a virgin).

defogger *n.* a device in vehicles for clearing condensation from windshields etc.

defoliant *n.* a chemical that strips leaves from trees and plants. [*Say* dee FOLEY int]

defoliate *v.* (**defoliates, defoliated, defoliating**) remove leaves from trees and plants. □ **defoliation** *n.* [*Say* dee FOLEY ate]

deforest *v.* clear land of trees. □ **deforestation** *n.* **deforested** *adj.*

deform *v.* change or spoil the usual shape of. □ **deformation** *n.* **deformed** *adj.* [*Say* duh FORm, def or MAY shun]

deformity *n.* (*pl.* **deformities**) **1** the state of being misshapen. **2** a faulty formation, esp. of body or limb.

defraud *v.* illegally obtain money from (a person) by deception. □ **defrauder** *n.*

defray *v.* provide money to pay (a cost).

defrost ● *v.* **1 a** free (a refrigerator) of

excess frost. **b** remove frost or ice from (a windshield). **2** thaw (frozen food). **3** become unfrozen. ● *n.* a device for defrosting. □ **defroster** *n.* **defrosting** *n.*

deft *adj.* skilful and quick. □ **deftly** *adv.* **deftness** *n.*

defunct *adj.* no longer existing or used. [*Say* duh FUNCT]

defuse *v.* (**defuses, defused, defusing**) **1** remove the fuse from (a bomb) so that it cannot explode. **2** reduce the tension or danger in (a situation.).

defy *v.* (**defies, defied, defying**) **1** resist openly or completely. **2** challenge to do or prove something. **3** challenge the power of (esp. something immutable). [*Say* duh FIE]

degenerate ● *adj.* **1** having very low moral standards. **2** *Biology* having changed to a lower type. ● *n.* an immoral person. ● *v.* (**degenerates, degenerated, degenerating**) (often foll. by *into*) **1** become deficient in the qualities proper to one's kind. **2** deteriorate. **3** revert to a lower type. □ **degeneracy** *n.* **degeneration** *n.* [*Say* duh JENNER it *for the noun and adjective,* duh JENNER ate *for the verb*]

degenerative *adj.* **1** of or tending to decline and deteriorate. **2** characterized by deterioration. [*Say* duh JENNER a tiv]

degradation *n.* **1** a state of complete humiliation. **2** the process of something being damaged or made worse. [*Say* deggra DAY sh'n]

degrade *v.* (**degrades, degraded, degrading**) **1** treat a person as being unworthy of respect. **2** lower in character or quality. **3** break down or deteriorate chemically. □ **degradable** *adj.* **degraded** *adj.*

degrading *adj.* humiliating. □ **degradingly** *adv.*

degree *n.* **1** a stage in a scale, series, or process. **2** a stage in intensity or amount. **3** an academic rank conferred by a college or university after completion of a course. **4** a unit of measurement of angles, one-ninetieth of a right angle. **5** a unit of latitude or longitude. **6** a unit in a scale of temperature, hardness, etc. **7** any of three grades (first, second, third) used to categorize burns. **8** a grade of crime or criminality. **9** any of three stages (positive, comparative, superlative) in the comparison of an adjective or adverb. **10** *Math* the highest power of unknowns or variables in an equation etc. **11** a unit of measurement of alcohol content. □ **by degrees** gradually. **to a degree** somewhat.

dehumanize *v.* (**dehumanizes, dehumanized, dehumanizing**) cause someone to lose their good human qualities. □ **dehumanization** *n.*

dehumidify *v.* (**dehumidifies, dehumidified, dehumidifying**) remove moisture from (esp. air). □ **dehumidifier** *n.*

dehydrate *v.* (**dehydrates, dehydrated, dehydrating**) **1 a** remove water from. **b** make dry, esp. make (the body) deficient in water. **2** lose water □ **dehydrated** *adj.* **dehydration** *n.* **dehydrator** *n.*

de-ice *v.* (**de-ices, de-iced, de-icing**) **1** remove ice from. **2** prevent the formation of ice on.

de-icer *n.* a device or substance for removing ice from a windshield, aircraft, etc.

deify *v.* (**deifies, deified, deifying**) **1** make a god of. **2** regard or worship as a god. □ **deification** *n.* [*Say* DEE a fie, dee if a KAY sh'n]

deign *v.* do something as though one thinks one is too important to do it. [*Say* DANE]

de-index *v.* (**de-indexes, de-indexed, de-indexing**) cancel the indexation to inflation of (pensions or other benefits). □ **de-indexation** *n.*

deism *n.* belief in the existence of a supreme being or creator who does not intervene in the universe. □ **deist** *n.* **deistic** *adj.* [*Say* DEE ism]

deity *n.* (*pl.* **deities**) **1** a god or goddess. **2** (**the Deity**) the Creator, God. [*Say* DEE a tee *or* DAY a tee]

déjà vu *n.* a feeling of having already experienced a present situation. [*Say* day zhah VOO]

dejected *adj.* sad and disappointed. □ **dejectedly** *adv.* **dejection** *n.*

de jure *adj. & adv.* rightfully; by right. [*Say* duh JURY *or* day JURAY]

deke esp. *Hockey slang* ● *n.* a fake shot or movement done to draw a defensive player out of position. ● *v.* (**dekes, deked, deking**) **1** deceive (a defensive player) with a fake shot or movement. **2** avoid (an obstacle or issue). **3** move or go quickly.

delay ● *v.* **1** postpone; defer. **2** make late. **3** loiter; procrastinate ● *n.* **1** the act of delaying. **2** a period of time by which something is late.

delectable ● *adj.* (of food) delicious. ● *n.* (in *pl.*) delicious food, esp. desserts. □ **delectably** *adv.* [*Say* duh LECTA bull]

delegate ● *n.* **1** a person sent to represent others. **2** a member of a committee. ● *v.*

(**delegates, delegated, delegating**)
1 (often foll. by *to*) entrust to another person, typically one less senior. **2** authorize (a person) to do something as a representative.

delegation *n.* **1** a group of delegates. **2** the act of delegating.

delete ● *v.* (**deletes, deleted, deleting**) remove or obliterate (text). ● *n.* (also **delete key**) *Computing* a key which is held down in order to delete text. □ **deletion** *n.*

deleterious *adj.* harmful and damaging. □ **deleteriously** *adv.* [*Say* della TEERY us]

deli *n.* (*pl.* **delis**) a delicatessen.

deliberate ● *adj.* **1** done on purpose. **2** careful or not hurried. ● *v.* (**deliberates, deliberated, deliberating**) think or discuss carefully. □ **deliberately** *adv.* **deliberateness** *n.* [*Say* duh LIBBER it *for the adjective*, duh LIBBER ate *for the noun*]

deliberation *n.* **1** careful consideration. **2** slow and careful action.

deliberative *adj.* having to do with consideration or discussion. [*Say* duh LIBBER a tiv]

delicacy *n.* (*pl.* **delicacies**) **1** fineness or intricacy of structure or texture. **2** a special or expensive food. **3** discretion or sensitivity. [*Say* DELLA kuh see]

delicate *adj.* **1 a** fine in texture or structure. **b** of exquisite quality. **c** subtle; faint. **2 a** not robust. **b** (of a person) susceptible to illness. **3 a** requiring or showing careful handling. **b** (of an instrument) highly sensitive. **4** deft. □ **delicately** *adv.*

delicatessen *n.* **1** a place selling cooked meats, cheeses, and unusual or foreign prepared foods. **2** such foods collectively. [*Say* della kuh TESS in]

delicious *adj.* **1** delightful and enjoyable to the taste or sense of smell. **2** entertaining; very enjoyable. □ **deliciously** *adv.* **deliciousness** *n.*

delight ● *n.* **1** great pleasure. **2** something giving pleasure. ● *v.* **1** (often foll. by *with*) please greatly. **2** take great pleasure; be highly pleased. □ **delighted** *adj.* **delightedly** *adv.*

delightful *adj.* causing great delight. □ **delightfully** *adv.* **delightfulness** *n.*

delimit *v.* (**delimits, delimited, delimiting**) determine the limits of. □ **delimitation** *n.*

delineate *v.* (**delineates, delineated, delineating**) describe, draw, or explain

something in detail. □ **delineation** *n.* [*Say* duh LINNY ate]

delinquent ● *n.* an offender. ● *adj.* **1** guilty of a minor crime. **2** failing in one's duty, esp. to pay money owed. **3** (of a sum of money) not having been paid in time. □ **delinquency** *n.* [*Say* duh LING kwunt]

deliquesce *v.* (**deliquesces, deliquesced, deliquescing**) become liquid. □ **deliquescent** *adj.* [*Say* della KWESS]

delirious *adj.* **1** affected with delirium. **2** wildly excited. **3** (of behaviour) betraying delirium or ecstasy. □ **deliriously** *adv.* [*Say* duh LEERY us]

delirium *n.* **1** a disordered state of mind marked by incoherent speech, hallucinations, and frenzied excitement. **2** great excitement. [*Say* duh LEERY um]

delirium tremens *n.* a condition typical of withdrawal in chronic alcoholics, involving tremors and hallucinations. [*Say* duh leery um TREM enz]

deliver *v.* **1 a** distribute to the addressee or the purchaser. **b** (often foll. by *to*) hand over. **2** present formally. **3** produce. **4 a** give birth to. **b** assist at a birth. **5** launch or aim. **6** save or set free. **7** *informal* (often foll. by *on*) provide (something expected or promised). □ **deliverable** *adj.* **deliverer** *n.*

deliverance *n.* the state of being rescued or set free.

delivery *n.* (*pl.* **deliveries**) **1 a** the delivering of letters, goods, etc. **b** something delivered. **2 a** the process of childbirth. **b** an act of this. **3** the uttering of a speech etc. **4** an act of throwing, esp. of a baseball. **5** provision. **6** the act of giving or surrendering.

dell *n.* a small valley.

delphinium *n.* a plant with tall spikes of usu. blue flowers. [*Say* del FINNY um]

delta *n.* **1** a triangular tract of land formed by a river's diverging outlets. **2** the fourth letter of the Greek alphabet (Δ, δ). □ **deltaic** *adj.* [*Say* del TAY ick]

deltoid *n.* (also **deltoid muscle**) a thick muscle covering the shoulder joint and used for raising the arm away from the body. [*Say* DEL toid]

delude *v.* (**deludes, deluded, deluding**) deceive or mislead.

deluge ● *n.* **1** a great flood. **2** a great outpouring. **3** a heavy fall of rain. ● *v.* (**deluges, deluged, deluging**) **1** overwhelm. **2** flood. [*Say* DEL yoozh *or* DEL yooge]

delusion *n.* **1** a false belief or impression. **2** the act of deluding someone. □ **delusional** *adj.*

deluxe *adj.* **1** of a superior kind. **2** luxurious.

delve *v.* (**delves**, **delved**, **delving**) (often foll. by *in*, *into*) search energetically.

demagogue *n.* a leader or orator who tries to win support by inflaming people's emotions and prejudices. □ **demagogic** *adj.* **demagoguery** *n.* **demagogy** *n.* [*Say* DEMMA gog, demma GODGE ick, demma GOGGA ree, DEMMA godge ee]

demand ● *n.* **1** an insistent and peremptory request. **2** desire for a commodity. **3** an urgent claim or requirement. ● *v.* **1** ask for (something) insistently and urgently. **2** require. □ **in demand** sought after. **on demand** as soon as a demand is made.

demanding *adj.* **1** requiring skill, effort, etc. **2** hard to satisfy. □ **demandingly** *adv.*

demarcate *v.* (**demarcates**, **demarcated**, **demarcating**) mark the limits of something. [*Say* DEE mar kate]

demarcation *n.* a line that separates two things. [*Say* dee mar KAY sh'n]

demean *v.* lower the dignity of. □ **demeaning** *adj.*

demeanour *n.* (also **demeanor**) outward behaviour or bearing. [*Say* duh MEANER]

demented *adj.* **1** *informal* wild and irrational. **2** suffering from dementia. □ **dementedly** *adv.*

dementia *n.* a mental disorder marked by memory disorders, personality changes, and impaired reasoning. [*Say* duh MENSHA]

demerit *n.* **1** a fault or disadvantage. **2** a mark given to an offender, esp. in a school or the armed forces or for traffic offences.

demigod *n.* **1** a partly divine being. **2** *informal* a person of compelling beauty, powers, or personality.

demilitarize *v.* (**demilitarizes**, **demilitarized**, **demilitarizing**) remove a military organization or forces from (an area etc.). □ **demilitarization** *n.*

demineralize *v.* (**demineralizes**, **demineralized**, **demineralizing**) remove minerals from (water etc.). □ **demineralization** *n.* **demineralized** *adj.*

demise *n.* **1** death. **2** termination or failure. [*Say* duh MIZE]

demo *n.* (*pl.* **demos**) *informal* **1** = DEMONSTRATION 1, 2. **2** (often as an *adj.*) demonstrating the capabilities of a group of musicians, computer software, etc. [*Say* DEM oh]

demobilize *v.* (**demobilizes**, **demobilized**, **demobilizing**) release someone from military service. □ **demobilization** *n.*

democracy *n.* (*pl.* **democracies**) **1 a** a form of government in which the power resides in the people and is exercised by them either directly or by means of elected representatives. **b** a state so governed. **2** any organization governed on democratic principles. **3** a classless and tolerant form of society.

democrat *n.* **1** an advocate of democracy. **2** (**Democrat**) (in the US) a member or supporter of the Democratic Party.

democratic *adj.* **1** having to do with democracy. **2** favouring social equality. **3** (**Democratic**) (in the US) of the Democratic Party. □ **democratically** *adv.*

Democratic Party *n.* one of the two main US political parties, considered to support social reform and international commitment.

democratize *v.* (**democratizes**, **democratized**, **democratizing**) make democratic. □ **democratization** *n.* [*Say* dim OCKRA tize]

demodulate *v.* (**demodulates**, **demodulated**, **demodulating**) *Physics* extract (a modulating signal) from its carrier.

demographic ● *adj.* having to do with the structure of populations or population statistics, esp. those showing average age, income, marital status, etc. ● *n.* a demographic category. □ **demographically** *adv.* [*Say* demma GRAPHIC]

demographics *pl. n.* population statistics, esp. those showing average age, income, marital status, etc. [*Say* demma GRAPHICS]

demography *n.* the study of the structure of human populations, using statistics concerning births, deaths, income, disease, etc. □ **demographer** *n.* [*Say* dem OGRA fee]

demolish *v.* (**demolishes**, **demolished**, **demolishing**) **1 a** pull down (a building). **b** completely destroy. **2** refute. **3** overthrow (an institution). **4** *jocular* eat up completely and quickly.

demolition *n.* the action of demolishing or being demolished.

demon *n.* **1** an evil spirit. **2** (often as an *adj.*) a forceful or skilful performer of a specified activity. **3** an evil passion or habit. **4** a cruel or destructive person.

demonic *adj.* having to do with demons. □ **demonically** *adv.*

demonize *v.* (**demonizes**, **demonized**, **demonizing**) portray as wicked and threatening. □ **demonization** *n.*

demonology n. (pl. **demonologies**)
1 the study of demons. **2** belief in demons.
3 the depiction of a group of persons or things as evil. [Say demon OLLA jee]

demonstrable adj. capable of being shown or logically proven.
□ **demonstrably** adv.
[Say duh MON struh bull]

demonstrate v. (**demonstrates,
demonstrated, demonstrating**)
1 show and explain (how something works). **2** logically prove the truth of.
3 show evidence of (feelings etc.). **4** take part in or organize a public demonstration.
□ **demonstrator** n.

demonstration n. **1** a practical exhibition or explanation of something.
2 a public meeting, march, etc., for a political or moral purpose. **3** proof provided by logic, argument, etc. **4** the outward showing of feeling etc. **5** a show of military force.

demonstrative ● adj. **1** showing feelings openly. **2** logically conclusive. **3** serving to point out or exhibit. **4** (of an adjective or pronoun) indicating the person or thing referred to, e.g. this, that, those. ● n. a demonstrative adjective or pronoun.
□ **demonstratively** adv.
demonstrativeness n.
[Say duh MON struh tiv]

demoralize v. (**demoralizes,
demoralized, demoralizing**) destroy (a person's) morale. □ **demoralization** n.
demoralizing adj. **demoralizingly** adv.

demote v. (**demotes, demoted,
demoting**) move someone to a lower position or rank, often as a punishment.
□ **demotion** n.

demur ● v. (**demurs, demurred,
demurring**) raise objections or show reluctance. ● n. (also **demurral**) the act of objecting or hesitating over something.
[Say duh MUR]

demure adj. (**demurer, demurest**)
1 quiet and reserved. **2** affectedly shy and quiet. **3** (of attire) modest. □ **demurely** adv.
demureness n. [Say dem YOOR (YOOR rhymes with POOR)]

demystify v. (**demystifies,
demystified, demystifying**) make something easier to understand.
□ **demystification** n.

den ● n. **1** a wild animal's lair. **2** a room in a home serving as an informal place for reading, pursuing a hobby, etc. **3** a place of crime or vice. ● v. (**dens, denned,
denning**) live in or as if in a den.

denationalize v. (**denationalizes,
denationalized, denationalizing**)
transfer from public to private ownership.

denature v. (**denatures, denatured,
denaturing**) **1** change the natural properties of. **2** make (alcohol) unfit for drinking, esp. by the addition of a toxic or foul-tasting substance. □ **denatured** adj.

Dene n. (pl. **Dene**) a member of a group of Aboriginal peoples of the Athapaskan linguistic family, living esp. in the Canadian north. [Say DEN ay]

dengue n. a tropical viral disease causing fever and acute pains in the joints.
[Say DENG ghee]

deniable adj. that may be denied.
□ **deniability** n.

denial n. **1** the action of declaring something to be untrue. **2** a refusal of a request or wish. **3** a statement that a thing is not true. **4** the usu. subconscious suppression of an unacceptable truth or emotion.

denier¹ n. a person who denies something.
[Say DENY ur]

denier² n. a unit of weight by which the fineness of yarn is measured.
[Say DEN yur]

denigrate v. (**denigrates, denigrated,
denigrating**) criticize unfairly.
□ **denigration** n. **denigrator** n.
[Say DENNA grate]

denim n. **1** a hard-wearing cotton twill fabric. **2** (in pl.) informal jeans made of this.

denizen n. an inhabitant of or frequent visitor to a place. [Say DENNA zin]

denomination n. **1** a branch of the Christian Church. **2** a unit of value, esp. of money. **3** the rank of a playing card within a suit, or of a suit relative to others.

denominational adj. relating to a particular denomination.
□ **denominationalism** n.

denominator n. the number below the line in a fraction.

denote v. (**denotes, denoted,
denoting**) **1** be a sign of. **2** mean, convey.
3 stand as a name or symbol for.
□ **denotation** n.

denouement n. the final unravelling of a plot or complicated situation.
[Say day noo MON]

denounce v. (**denounces, denounced,
denouncing**) **1** accuse publicly;
condemn. **2** inform against.
□ **denouncer** n.

dense adj. (**denser, densest**) **1** closely compacted in substance. **2** crowded together. **3** informal stupid. □ **densely** adv.

density n. (pl. **densities**) **1** the degree of compactness of a substance; mass per unit volume. **2** the quantity of people or things in a given area. **3** informal stupidity.

dent ● *n.* **1** a slight hollow in a surface made by a blow or pressure. **2** a noticeable effect. ● *v.* **1** mark with a dent. **2** have (esp. an adverse) effect on.

dental *adj.* **1** relating to the teeth. **2** relating to dentistry.

dental floss *n.* a strong, soft thread used to clean between the teeth.

denticare *n. Cdn* a plan for providing dental care funded by some provincial governments.

dentine *n.* a hard dense bony tissue forming the bulk of a tooth. [*Say* DEN teen]

dentist *n.* a person who is qualified to treat the diseases and conditions that affect the teeth. □ **dentistry** *n.*

denture *n.* an artificial replacement for one or more teeth attached to a removable plate or frame.

denude *v.* (**denudes, denuded, denuding**) strip something bare. [*Say* duh NUDE]

denunciation *n.* a public condemnation. □ **denunciatory** *adj.* [*Say* duh nun see AY sh'n, duh NUN see a tory]

deny *v.* (**denies, denied, denying**) **1** declare untrue or non-existent. **2** repudiate or disclaim. **3** refuse. □ **deny oneself** go without.

deodorant *n.* a substance that removes or conceals unpleasant smells.

deodorize *v.* (**deodorizes, deodorized, deodorizing**) remove or conceal the smell of. □ **deodorizer** *n.*

deoxygenate *v.* (**deoxygenates, deoxygenated, deoxygenating**) remove oxygen from. □ **deoxygenated** *adj.* [*Say* dee OXYGEN ate]

deoxyribonucleic acid *n. see* DNA. [*Say* dee OXY rye bo new CLAY ick]

depart *v.* **1** leave. **2** (usu. foll. by *from*) diverge; deviate.

departed *adj.* bygone.

department *n.* **1** a branch of an administration. **2** a specialized section of a large store. **3** a subdivision of a company or organization. **4** *informal* an area of special expertise. □ **departmental** *adj.*

department store *n.* a large store stocking many varieties of goods in different departments.

departure *n.* the action of departing.

depend *v.* (usu. foll. by *on, upon*) **1** be controlled or determined by. **2** rely on. □ **it** (or **it all** or **that**) **depends** expressing uncertainty in answering a question.

dependable *adj.* trustworthy and reliable. □ **dependability** *n.* **dependably** *adv.*

dependant *n.* a person who relies on another esp. for financial support.

dependence *n.* the state of being dependent.

dependency *n.* (*pl.* **dependencies**) **1** a country or province controlled by another. **2** the fact or condition of being dependent.

dependent ● *adj.* **1** conditional. **2** unable to do without (esp. a drug). **3** requiring someone or something for support. **4** *Math* (of a variable) having a value determined by another variable. **5** *Grammar* (of a clause, word, etc.) subordinate to a sentence or word. ● *n.* = DEPENDANT. □ **dependently** *adv.*

depersonalize *v.* (**depersonalizes, depersonalized, depersonalizing**) **1** make impersonal. **2** deprive of personality. □ **depersonalization** *n.*

depict *v.* **1** represent in a drawing or painting etc. **2** describe. □ **depiction** *n.*

depilatory ● *adj.* that removes unwanted hair. ● *n.* (*pl.* **depilatories**) a depilatory substance. [*Say* duh PILLA tory]

deplane *v.* (**deplanes, deplaned, deplaning**) disembark or remove from an airplane.

deplete *v.* (**depletes, depleted, depleting**) **1** reduce in number or quantity. **2** exhaust. □ **depleter** *n.* **depletion** *n.*

deplorable *adj.* exceedingly bad. □ **deplorably** *adv.* [*Say* duh PLORE a bull]

deplore *v.* (**deplores, deplored, deploring**) feel or express strong disapproval of something. [*Say* duh PLORE]

deploy *v.* **1** bring or send into position for esp. military action. **2** use effectively. □ **deployment** *n.*

depolarize *v.* (**depolarizes, depolarized, depolarizing**) reduce or remove the polarization of. □ **depolarization** *n.*

depoliticize *v.* (**depoliticizes, depoliticized, depoliticizing**) **1** make non-political. **2** remove from political influence. [*Say* dee puh LITTA size]

depopulate *v.* (**depopulates, depopulated, depopulating**) reduce the population of. □ **depopulation** *n.*

deport *v.* expel from a country. □ **deportation** *n.*

deportee *n.* a person who has been or is being deported.

deportment *n.* **1** a person's behaviour or manners. **2** the way in which a person stands and moves.

depose v. (**deposes, deposed, deposing**) remove from power suddenly and forcefully.

deposit ● n. **1** a sum of money etc. placed in an account in a bank. **2 a** a sum payable as a first instalment on an item bought, or as a pledge for a contract. **b** a returnable sum payable on short-term rentals and certain bottles and containers, refunded when the item is returned. **c** = DAMAGE DEPOSIT. **3** *Cdn & Brit.* a sum of money forfeited by an election candidate if he or she fails to receive a certain proportion of the votes. **4** a natural accumulation of matter. ● v. (**deposits, deposited, depositing**) **1** put or lay down. **2 a** store or entrust for keeping. **b** pay (a sum of money) into a bank account. **3** pay as a deposit. **4** insert (coins) in a vending machine etc. □ **depositor** n.

deposition n. **1** the action of depositing something. **2** *Law* **a** the process of giving sworn evidence. **b** a formal, usu. written, statement to be used as evidence. **3** the action of removing someone from power. [*Say* deppa ZISH un *or* deepa ZISH un]

depot n. **1** a storehouse. **2 a** a bus station. **b** a building where vehicles are housed and serviced. **3** *Military* **a** a storehouse for equipment etc. **b** a military establishment where troops are assembled.

depraved adj. corrupt, esp. morally.

depravity n. moral corruption. [*Say* duh PRAVA tee]

deprecate v. (**deprecates, deprecated, deprecating**) **1** express disapproval of or a wish against. **2** (usu. in comb.) disparage, belittle. □ **deprecatingly** adv. **deprecation** n. **deprecatory** adj. [*Say* DEPRA kate, depra KAY sh'n, DEPRA kuh tory]

depreciable adj. **1** capable of depreciating. **2** able to be depreciated for tax purposes. [*Say* duh PREESHA bull]

depreciate v. (**depreciates, depreciated, depreciating**) **1** diminish in value. **2** make something seem unimportant. **3** reduce the value, as stated in the company's accounts, of a particular asset over a particular period of time. □ **depreciation** n. [*Say* duh PREESHY ate]

depredation n. (usu. in pl.) an act of damaging or harming. [*Say* depra DAY sh'n]

depress v. (**depresses, depressed, depressing**) **1** push or pull down. **2** make dispirited or dejected. **3** *Economics* reduce the activity of (esp. trade).

depressant ● adj. (of a drug) reducing functional or nervous activity. ● n. a depressant drug or substance.

depressed adj. **1** dispirited or miserable. **2** *Psychology* suffering from depression. **3** suffering from economic hardship. **4** pressed down. **5** persistently lower-priced than normal.

depressing adj. causing depression. □ **depressingly** adv.

depression n. **1** *Psychology* a state of extreme sadness, characterized by feelings of hopelessness and inadequacy. **2** a long or severe economic slump. **3** *Meteorology* an area of lower atmospheric pressure. **4** a sunken place or hollow. **5** the action of pressing down on something.

depressive ● adj. **1** tending to depress. **2** *Psychology* having to do with depression. ● n. *Psychology* a person suffering or tending to suffer from depression.

depressor n. **1 a** a muscle that causes the lowering of some part of the body. **b** a nerve that lowers blood pressure. **2** *Medical* an instrument for pressing down an organ etc.

depressurize v. (**depressurizes, depressurized, depressurizing**) cause a drop in the gas or air pressure.

deprivation n. **1** the lack of something considered to be a necessity. **2** the act of depriving. [*Say* depra VAY sh'n]

deprive v. (**deprives, deprived, depriving**) (usu. foll. by of) dispossess; stop from enjoying.

deprived adj. suffering from the lack of things considered necessary.

depth n. **1** the distance from the top or surface to the bottom, or from front to back. **2** extensive and detailed study. **3 a** complexity and profundity of thought. **b** intensity of emotion. **4** an intensity of colour, darkness, etc. **5** (in pl.) a deep, low, or innermost part or place. □ **in depth** thoroughly. **out of one's depth 1** in water over one's head. **2** engaged in something too difficult for one.

depth charge n. an explosive device that detonates under water.

deputation n. a group of people appointed to represent others. [*Say* dep yoo TAY sh'n]

depute v. (**deputes, deputed, deputing**) appoint someone to perform a task for which one is responsible. [*Say* duh PYOOT]

deputize v. (**deputizes, deputized, deputizing**) **1** appoint (a person) to perform a task. **2** temporarily act on behalf of someone else. [*Say* DEP yoo tize]

deputy n. (pl. **deputies**) a person delegated to act for another (also as an adj.).

deputy minister n. Cdn the senior civil servant in a government department.

derail v. **1** leave or cause to leave the rails. **2** obstruct the progress of (a person, plan, etc.). □ **derailment** n.

derailleur n. a device for shifting gears on a bicycle. [Say dee RAILER]

derange v. (**deranges, deranged, deranging**) throw into confusion.

deranged adj. unable to behave and think normally; insane. □ **derangement** n.

Derby n. (pl. **Derbies**) **1** an important annual horse race. **2** (**derby**) a sporting contest open to any participants.

deregulate v. (**deregulates, deregulated, deregulating**) remove regulations or restrictions from. □ **deregulation** n. **deregulator** n.

derelict ● adj. **1** (of property) ruined; dilapidated. **2** negligent. ● n. a social outcast or homeless person. [Say DERRA likt]

dereliction n. **1** the shameful failure to do one's duty. **2** the state of having been abandoned and become dilapidated. [Say derra LICK sh'n]

deride v. (**derides, derided, deriding**) be scornful of.

de rigueur adj. required by custom or etiquette. [Say duh rig UR]

derision n. ridicule; mockery. [Say duh RIZH un]

derisive adj. expressing contempt or ridicule. □ **derisively** adv. [Say duh RICE iv]

derisory adj. **1** scornful. **2** ridiculously small or unimportant. [Say duh RICE a ree]

derivation n. **1** the obtaining of something from a source. **2** the formation of a word from another word or root. [Say derra VAY sh'n]

derivative ● adj. imitative of another's work; unoriginal. ● n. something derived from another source. [Say duh RIVVA tiv]

derive v. (**derives, derived, deriving**) **1 a** get. **b** obtain a substance from something. **2** come or develop from a source. **3** Math obtain from another by a sequence of logical steps. [Say duh RIVE]

dermatitis n. inflammation of the skin as a result of irritation or allergy. [Say durma TITE iss]

dermatology n. the study of the diagnosis and treatment of skin disorders. □ **dermatological** adj. **dermatologist** n. [Say durma TOLLA jee]

dermis n. **1** (in general use) the skin. **2** the thick layer of living tissue below the epidermis that forms the true skin. □ **dermal** adj.

derogatory adj. showing a negative attitude. [Say duh ROGGA tory]

derrick n. **1** a kind of mechanical crane with a movable pivoted arm. **2** the framework over an oil well etc., holding the drilling machinery.

derrière n. informal the buttocks. [Say derry AIR]

derring-do n. heroic courage or action. [Say derring DOO]

dervish n. (pl. **dervishes**) a member of a Muslim fraternity vowed to poverty and austerity.

descant n. an independent melody usu. sung or played above a basic melody. [Say DESS cant]

descend v. **1** go or come down. **2** (usu. foll. by on) make a sudden attack or unwelcome visit. **3** (usu. foll. by from) (often in passive) originate with or derive from (a progenitor or predecessor). **4** (foll. by to) stoop to something unworthy.

descendant n. (often foll. by of) a person, animal, etc. descended from another.

descent n. **1** an action of moving downwards. **2** a downward slope. **3** a decline to a lower condition. **4** a sudden violent attack. **5** family origin.

descramble v. (**descrambles, descrambled, descrambling**) convert or restore (an electronic signal) to intelligible form, esp. through an electronic device. □ **descrambler** n.

describe v. (**describes, described, describing**) **1 a** give a detailed account in words of. **b** (foll. by as) assert to be. **2** mark out or draw (a shape).

description n. **1 a** a spoken or written representation. **b** the action of describing. **2** a sort, kind, or class.

descriptive adj. **1** serving or seeking to describe. **2** describing without expressing judgment. □ **descriptively** adv.

desecrate v. (**desecrates, desecrated, desecrating**) treat (a sacred place or thing) with violent disrespect. □ **desecration** n. [Say DESSA crate]

desegregate v. (**desegregates, desegregated, desegregating**) abolish racial segregation in or of. □ **desegregation** n. [Say dee SEGRA gate]

desensitize v. (**desensitizes, desensitized, desensitizing**) make less sensitive. □ **desensitization** n. [Say dee SENSA tize]

desert[1] v. **1** forsake or abandon. **2** (of a power or faculty) fail (someone). **3** *Military* run away from (one's duty). □ **deserter** n. **desertion** n. [Say duh ZURT]

desert[2] ● n. **1** a dry, barren area of land, often sand-covered. **2** a place that is not interesting. ● *adj.* of or like a desert. [Say DEZ urt]

desert[3] n. (usu. in *pl.*) deserved reward or punishment. [Say duh ZURT]

deserted *adj.* empty, abandoned.

desertification n. the transformation of fertile land into desert. [Say duh zurt iffa KAY sh'n]

desert island n. a remote tropical island presumed to be uninhabited.

deserve v. (**deserves, deserved, deserving**) be entitled to or worthy of. □ **deserved** *adj.* **deservedly** *adj.*

deserving *adj.* worthy of help, praise, etc.

desiccate v. (**desiccates, desiccated, desiccating**) remove the moisture from. □ **desiccated** *adj.* **desiccation** n. [Say DESSA kate]

desideratum n. (*pl.* **desiderata**) something needed and desired. [Say duh zidda RAT um *for the singular*, duh zidda RATTA *for the plural*]

design ● n. **1** a preliminary plan or sketch for the making or production of something. **2 a** the art of planning and creating something in accordance with functional and aesthetic criteria. **b** = INTERIOR DESIGN. **3** the general arrangement or layout of a product. **4** a motif or pattern. **5** a plan, scheme, or intention. ● v. **1** produce a design for. **2** intend for a purpose. □ **by design** on purpose. **have designs on** aim to obtain. □ **designed** *adj.*

designate ● v. (**designates, designated, designating**) **1** appoint to an office or function. **2** mark out clearly. **3** give a name or title to. **4** serve as the name or distinctive mark of. ● *adj.* (placed after noun) appointed to a position but not yet officially occupying it. □ **designated** *adj.* [Say DEZ ig nate *for the verb*, DEZ ig nit *for the adjective*]

designation n. **1** a name, description, or title. **2** the act of designating.

designer n. **1 a** a person who designs things. **b** an interior designer. **2** (as an *adj.*) **a** made by a prestigious designer. **b** trendy. **c** (of chemicals etc.) designed for a specific purpose.

designing *adj.* cunning and deceitful.

desirable *adj.* **1 a** worth having or doing. **b** advisable. **2** arousing sexual desire; very attractive. □ **desirability** n. **desirably** *adv.*

desire ● n. **1** an unsatisfied longing. **2** sexual appetite. **3** something desired. ● v. (**desires, desired, desiring**) **1 a** strongly wish for. **b** feel sexual desire for. **2** request. □ **leave something to be desired** be bad or unacceptable.

desirous *adj.* (usu. foll. by *of*) having desire; wishful. [Say duh ZYE russ]

desist v. cease.

desk n. **1** a piece of furniture with a writing surface and usu. drawers. **2** a service counter in a library, hotel, etc. **3** a section of a news organization.

desktop n. **1** the working surface of a desk. **2** (as an *adj.*) suitable for use on a desk. **3** a desktop computer.

desktop publishing n. the design and production of printed matter using a desktop computer.

desolate ● *adj.* **1** very unhappy. **2** bleak and lonely ● v. (**desolates, desolated, desolating**) devastate, lay waste to. □ **desolated** *adj.* **desolation** n. [Say DESSA lit *for the adjective*, DESSA late *for the verb*]

despair ● n. the complete loss or absence of hope. ● v. (often foll. by *of*) lose or be without hope. □ **despairing** *adj.* **despairingly** *adv.*

desperado n. (*pl.* **desperadoes** or **desperados**) esp. *hist.* a desperate or reckless person, esp. a criminal. [Say despa RODDO *or* despa RADDO]

desperate *adj.* **1** reckless from despair. **2 a** extremely serious. **b** undertaken as a last resort. **3** extreme, excessive. **4** (usu. foll. by *for*) needing very much. □ **desperately** *adv.* **desperation** n.

despicable *adj.* deserving hatred or contempt. □ **despicably** *adv.* [Say duh SPICKA bull]

despise v. (**despises, despised, despising**) hate or feel disgusted by. □ **despised** *adj.*

despite *prep.* in spite of.

despoil v. **1** spoil, destroy. **2** *literary* rob.

despondent *adj.* characterized by loss of courage or enthusiasm. □ **despondency** n. **despondently** *adv.* [Say duh SPON dint]

despot n. an absolute or tyrannical ruler. □ **despotic** *adj.* **despotically** *adv.* **despotism** n. [Say DESS pot, dess POT ick lee]

dessert n. a sweet food eaten at the end of a meal. [Say duh ZURT]

destabilize v. (**destabilizes, destabilized, destabilizing**) **1** upset the stability of. **2** make politically unstable. □ **destabilization** n.

destination n. a place to which a person or thing is going or being sent.

destined adj. **1** having a future decided beforehand. **2** (foll. by *for*) bound (for a certain place). [*Say* DESS tinned]

destiny n. (pl. **destinies**) **1** fate. **2** (often **Destiny**) the power that supposedly predetermines events.

destitute adj. completely impoverished. □ **destitution** n. [*Say* DESTA toot, desta TOO sh'n]

destroy v. **1** demolish; smash to pieces. **2** put an end to. **3** kill. **4** spoil utterly. **5** discredit or ruin.

destroyer n. **1** a person or thing that destroys. **2** a small fast warship.

destruct ● v. destroy deliberately. ● n. an act of destructing.

destruction n. **1** the action of destroying or state of being destroyed. **2** a cause of someone's ruin.

destructive adj. **1** (often foll. by *to, of*) causing destruction. **2** negative and not helpful. □ **destructively** adv. **destructiveness** n.

desultory adj. **1** going from one subject to another in a half-hearted way. **2** lacking purpose or enthusiasm. □ **desultorily** adv. [*Say* DESSLE tory]

detach v. (**detaches, detached, detaching**) **1** unfasten and remove. **2** send (a regiment etc.) on a separate mission. □ **detachable** adj.

detached adj. **1** impartial, not emotional. **2** (esp. of a house) not joined to others.

detachment n. **1** a state of being indifferent or not involved. **2** the act of detaching. **3** a separate unit of an army etc. used for specific purpose. **4** *Cdn* the headquarters of a police district patrolled by the RCMP, OPP, etc.

detail ● n. **1** a small or subordinate particular. **2 a** a minor decoration. **b** a small part of a picture considered in isolation. **3** a small detachment of soldiers. ● v. **1** describe minutely. **2** assign for special duty. **3** decorate with intricate designs.

detailed adj. having many details.

detailing n. the treatment of detail in a work of art etc.

detain v. **1** keep in confinement. **2** delay or keep (someone) waiting.

detainee n. a person detained in custody.

detect v. **1** discover the presence of. **2** discover or investigate (crime etc.). □ **detectable** adj. **detection** n.

detective n. a person employed to investigate crime.

detector n. a device which detects something and usu. then sends out a signal.

détente n. an easing of hostility or strained relations between nations. [*Say* day TONT]

detention n. **1** the state of imprisonment or confinement. **2** the punishment of being kept in school after hours.

detention centre n. an institution for the short-term detention of esp. criminals.

deter v. (**deters, deterred, deterring**) **1** discourage (a person) through fear of the consequences. **2** prevent the occurrence of. [*Say* duh TUR]

detergent n. a chemical substance for removing dirt, grease, etc.

deteriorate v. (**deteriorates, deteriorated, deteriorating**) become worse. □ **deterioration** n.

determinant n. a factor which determines the nature or outcome of something.

determinate adj. having exact and discernible limits. [*Say* duh TURMA nit]

determination n. **1** firmness of purpose. **2 a** the action of establishing or deciding something. **b** the decision etc. reached.

determine v. (**determines, determined, determining**) **1** find out precisely. **2** decide. **3** be a decisive factor in. **4** define the position of.

determined adj. showing determination. □ **determinedly** adv. [*Say* duh TERM ind lee]

determinism n. the doctrine that all events are determined by causes regarded as external to the will. □ **determinist** n. **deterministic** adj.

deterrent ● n. a thing that deters or is intended to deter. ● adj. able or intended to deter. □ **deterrence** n. [*Say* duh TUR int]

detest v. hate, loathe.

detestable adj. deserving intense dislike. □ **detestably** adv.

detonate v. (**detonates, detonated, detonating**) explode or cause to explode. □ **detonation** n. **detonator** n. [*Say* DET'n ate]

detour ● n. a roundabout route, esp. one taken to avoid a blocked road etc. ● v. make or cause to make a detour.

detox *informal* ● n. (pl. **detoxes**) **1** = DETOXIFICATION. **2** a detoxification clinic, program, etc. ● v. (**detoxes, detoxed, detoxing**) detoxify.

detoxification n. **1** the removal of toxic substances or qualities. **2** medical treatment of a drug addict etc. involving abstention from the drug. □ **detoxify** v. [Say dee toxa fuh KAY sh'n, dee TOXA fie]

detract v. diminish or belittle. □ **detraction** n.

detractor n. a person who belittles another.

detriment n. harm or a cause of harm. □ **to the detriment of** to the disadvantage of. □ **detrimental** adj. [Say DETRA mint]

detritus n. **1** matter produced by erosion, such as gravel, silt, etc. **2** debris or decomposed material. [Say duh TRITE us]

deuce[1] n. **1** the two in dice or playing cards. **2** Tennis the score of 40 all, at which two consecutive points are needed to win. [Say DOOCE]

deuce[2] n. informal the Devil. [Say DOOCE or DYOOCE]

deuterium n. a stable isotope of hydrogen with a mass about double that of the usual isotope. [Say due TEERY um]

devalue v. (**devalues, devalued, devaluing**) **1** reduce or underestimate the worth or value of. **2** reduce the value of (a currency) in relation to other currencies or to gold (opp. REVALUE 2). □ **devaluation** n.

devastate v. (**devastates, devastated, devastating**) **1** destroy or ruin. **2** upset deeply. □ **devastating** adj. **devastatingly** adv. **devastation** n.

develop v. (**develops, developed, developing**) **1 a** make or become bigger, fuller, or more advanced. **b** bring or come into existence. **2** begin to suffer from. **3** convert (land) to a new purpose. **4** treat (photographic film) chemically to make the latent image visible. □ **developable** adj. **developer** n.

developing country n. a poorer country seeking to become more advanced and industrialized.

development n. **1** the action or state of developing. **2 a** stage of growth or advancement. **b** a full-grown state. **3** a significant change in a course of action, events, circumstances, etc. **4** the process of developing a photograph. **5** a tract of land with new houses on it. **6** industrialization or economic advancement of a country or area.

developmental adj. **1** pertaining to the process of achieving physical, mental, or social maturity. **2** of or pertaining to development. □ **developmentally** adv.

deviant ● adj. different from what most people consider to be normal and acceptable. ● n. a person or thing which deviates from the normal, esp. from normal social or sexual practices. □ **deviance** n. [Say DEE vee int]

deviate v. (**deviates, deviated, deviating**) turn aside or diverge from. □ **deviation** n. [Say DEE vee ate]

device n. **1** a thing made for a particular purpose. **2** a method of doing something that produces a particular result. **3** an artistic drawing or design. □ **leave a person to his** (or **her**) **own devices** leave a person to do as he or she wishes.

devil n. **1** (usu. **the Devil**) (in Christian and Jewish belief) the supreme spirit of evil; Satan. **2** an evil spirit. **3 a** a wicked or cruel person. **b** a mischievous and clever person. **4** informal a person or animal. **5** informal something difficult or awkward. **6** (**the devil**) informal used as an exclamation of surprise or annoyance □ **between the devil and the deep blue sea** in a dilemma. **a devil of** informal a remarkable or difficult one. **the devil to pay** trouble to be expected. **like the devil** with great energy. **speak of the devil** said when a person appears just after being mentioned.

devilled adj. prepared with spicy seasonings.

devil-may-care adj. cheerful and reckless.

devil's advocate n. a person who expresses an unpopular view in order to provoke argument.

devious adj. not straightforward or sincere; underhand. □ **deviously** adv. **deviousness** n. [Say DEE vee us]

devise v. (**devises, devised, devising**) plan or invent by careful thought. □ **deviser** n. [Say duh VIZE]

devoid adj. totally lacking. [Say duh VOID]

devolution n. the delegation of power by central government to local or regional administration. [Say devva LOO sh'n or deeva LOO sh'n]

devolve v. (**devolves, devolved, devolving**) **1** transfer (duties, power, etc.) to a lower level. **2** pass to (a deputy, successor, etc.).

Devonian n. the fourth period of the Paleozoic era (about 408 to 360 million years ago). □ **Devonian** adj. [Say duh VOE nee un]

devote v. (**devotes, devoted, devoting**) apply or give over to.

devoted adj. very loving or loyal. □ **devotedly** adv.

devotee n. **1** a zealous enthusiast. **2** a strong believer in a religion. [Say dev oh TEE]

devotion n. **1** enthusiastic attachment or

loyalty. **2 a** religious worship. **b** (in *pl.*) prayers. □ **devotional** *adj.*

devour *v.* **1** eat greedily. **2** consume destructively. **3** take in eagerly with the eyes or ears. **4** (usu. in *passive*) absorb the attention of.

devout *adj.* **1** deeply religious. **2** earnestly sincere. □ **devoutly** *adv.*

dew *n.* atmospheric vapour condensing in small drops on cool surfaces at night.

dewdrop *n.* a drop of dew.

dewlap *n.* a loose fold of skin hanging from the throat of cattle, dogs, etc.

deworm *v.* rid (a dog, cat, etc.) of worms. □ **dewormer** *n.* [*Say* dee WURM]

dew point *n.* the temperature at which dew forms.

dewy *adj.* (**dewier, dewiest**) **1 a** wet with dew. **b** moist as if with dew. **2** = DEWY-EYED. **3** of or like dew.

dewy-eyed *adj.* innocently trusting.

dexterity *n.* skill in performing tasks, esp. with the hands. [*Say* deck STAIR a tee]

dexterous *adj.* demonstrating neat skill. □ **dexterously** *adv.* **dexterousness** *n.* [*Say* DECKS truss]

dextrose *n.* a form of glucose. [*Say* DECK strose]

dhal *n.* = DAL. [*Sounds like* DOLL]

dharma *n.* **1** (in Hinduism) the eternal law of the cosmos. **2** (in Buddhism) the true doctrine as preached by the Buddha. [*Say* DARR muh]

dhoti *n.* (*pl.* **dhotis**) the loincloth worn by male Hindus. [*Say* DOE tee]

dhow *n.* a ship with a triangular sail used in the Arabian region. [*Say* DOW, *rhymes with* HOW]

diabetes *n.* (also **diabetes mellitus**) a metabolic disorder in which a lack of the hormone insulin causes sugar and starch not to be properly absorbed. [*Say* die a BEE teez]

diabetic ● *adj.* **1** relating to diabetes. **2** for use by diabetics. ● *n.* a person suffering from diabetes. [*Say* die a BET ick]

diabolical *adj.* (also **diabolic**) **1** of the Devil. **2** wicked. **3** fiendishly cunning. □ **diabolically** *adv.* [*Say* die a BOLLA cull]

diaconal *adj.* of a deacon or deaconess. [*Say* die ACKA null *or* dee ACKA null]

diadem *n.* a crown or headband worn as a sign of sovereignty. [*Say* DIE a dem]

diagnose *v.* (**diagnoses, diagnosed, diagnosing**) make a diagnosis of (a problem). [*Say* die ig NOCE]

diagnosis *n.* (*pl.* **diagnoses**) the identification of an illness or problem by examining the symptoms.

[*Say* die ig NO sis *for the singular*, die ig NO seez *for the plural*]

diagnostic *adj.* of or assisting diagnosis. □ **diagnostically** *adv.* **diagnostician** *n.* [*Say* die ig NOSS tick, die ig noss TISH un]

diagnostics *n.* **1** (treated as *pl.*) *Computing* programs used to detect faults in hardware or software. **2** (treated as *sing.*) the science of diagnosing disease. [*Say* die ig NOSS ticks]

diagonal ● *adj.* **1** crossing a straight-sided figure from corner to corner. **2** oblique. ● *n.* a diagonal line. □ **diagonally** *adv.*

diagram ● *n.* **1** a drawing showing the general appearance or structure of something. **2** a graphic representation of the results of an action or process. ● *v.* (**diagrams, diagrammed, diagramming**) represent by means of a diagram.

diagrammatic *adj.* in the form of a diagram. [*Say* die a gruh MAT ick]

dial ● *n.* **1** a flat plate marked to show time on a clock or measurements of weight, pressure, etc., indicated by a pointer. **2** a disc with numbered holes on a telephone, rotated for each digit to call a telephone number. **3** a rotating knob or button for selecting settings on a washing machine, stove, radio, etc. ● *v.* (**dials, dialed** or **dialled, dialing** or **dialling**) make a telephone call to.

dialect *n.* a form of speech peculiar to a particular region or group. □ **dialectal** *adj.*

dialectic *n.* **1** a method of discovering the truth of ideas by discussion and logical argument. **2** the existence of opposing forces in society etc. □ **dialectical** *adj.*

dialectics *n.* (treated as *sing.* or *pl.*) = DIALECTIC 1.

dialer *n.* (also **dialler**) **1** an electronic device which dials phone numbers automatically. **2** a person who dials a telephone.

dialogue ● *n.* **1** conversation between two or more people, esp. between characters in a novel, play, etc. **2** constructive communication etc. between different people or groups. ● *v.* (**dialogues, dialogued, dialoguing**) take part in a dialogue.

dial tone *n.* an uninterrupted telephone tone indicating that a caller may dial.

dial-up *adj.* relating to a data transmission link using the telephone system.

dialysis *n.* (*pl.* **dialyses**) **1** the separation of particles in a liquid by differences in their ability to pass through a membrane. **2** the purification of blood, e.g. of a person with inadequately functioning kidneys, by this technique. [*Say* die ALA sis *for the singular,* die ALA seez *for the plural*]

diameter *n.* a straight line passing from side to side through the centre of a circle or sphere. [*Say* die AMMA tur]

diametrical *adj.* **1** of or along a diameter. **2** (of opposites) complete.
□ **diametrically** *adv.*
[*Say* die a METRICAL]

diamond ● *n.* **1** a precious stone of great brilliance and hardness, usu. clear and colourless. **2** a rhombus placed with its diagonals horizontal and vertical. **3** *Baseball* the space delimited by the bases. **4** a playing card of a suit denoted by a red rhombus. ● *adj.* **1** made of or set with diamond. **2** rhombus-shaped.

diamond anniversary *n.* the 60th (or 75th) anniversary of something.

diamondback *n.* **1** an edible freshwater turtle native to N America. **2** a N American rattlesnake with diamond-shaped markings.

diaper ● *n.* a folded cloth or disposable absorbent material wrapped around a baby's bottom to retain urine and feces. ● *v.* put a diaper on (a baby).

diaphanous *adj.* light, delicate, and almost transparent. [*Say* die AFFA nuss]

diaphragm *n.* **1** a muscular, dome-shaped partition which separates the thorax from the abdomen. **2** a thin contraceptive cap placed over the cervix. **3** a vibrating disc or cone producing sound waves. **4** a thin sheet of material used as a partition, esp. in a tube or pipe. [*Say* DIE a fram]

diarist *n.* a person who keeps a diary. [*Say* DIE a rist]

diarrhea *n.* **1** a condition of excessively frequent and loose bowel movements. **2** semi-liquid feces characteristic of this condition. □ **diarrheal** *adj.*
[*Say* die a REE uh]

diary *n.* (*pl.* **diaries**) **1** a daily written record of events, feelings, or thoughts. **2** a book for this or for noting future engagements.

Diaspora *n.* **1** (**the Diaspora**) **a** the dispersion of the Jews among the Gentiles. **b** Jews or Jewish communities outside the state of Israel. **2** (also **diaspora**, *pl.* **diasporas**) **a** any group of people similarly dispersed. **b** their dispersion. [*Say* die ASPER uh]

diatom *n.* a microscopic single-celled alga which has a cell wall of silica.
[*Say* DIE a tum]

diatonic *adj.* (of a scale, interval, etc.) involving only notes proper to the prevailing key without chromatic alteration. [*Say* die a TONIC]

diatribe *n.* a forceful and bitter verbal attack.

diazepam *n.* a muscle-relaxant drug used to relieve anxiety. *Also called* VALIUM. [*Say* die AZZA pam]

dibs *pl. n.* slang a first claim or option to use or have something.

dice ● *pl. n.* **1 a** small cubes marked on each side with 1–6 spots, used in games and gambling. **b** one of these cubes. **2 a** game played with such cubes. ● *v.* (**dices, diced, dicing**) **1** cut (food) into small cubes. **2 a** play or gamble with dice. **b** take great risks. □ **no dice** *slang* no success or luck. □ **dicer** *n.*

dicey *adj.* (**dicier, diciest**) *slang* risky; uncertain.

dichotomy *n.* (*pl.* **dichotomies**) a division or contrast between two things.
□ **dichotomous** *adj.* [*Say* die COTTA me]

dick *n. slang* a detective.

dickens *n. informal* (esp. in exclamations) the Devil.

Dickensian *adj.* resembling the novels of Charles Dickens, esp. in terms of poor social conditions or comically repulsive characters. [*Say* duh KENZY un]

dicker *v.* bargain; haggle.

dicotyledon *n.* any flowering plant having two cotyledons (seed leaves).
□ **dicotyledonous** *adj.*
[*Say* die cotta LEE din, die cotta LEE din us]

dicta *pl. of* DICTUM.

Dictaphone *n. proprietary* a machine for recording and playing back dictated words.

dictate ● *v.* (**dictates, dictated, dictating**) **1** say or read aloud (words to be written down or recorded). **2** tell someone what to do, esp. disregarding their wishes. **3** control or determine. ● *n.* (usu. in *pl.*) an order or rule that must be obeyed. □ **dictation** *n.*

dictator *n.* a ruler with unrestricted authority. □ **dictatorial** *adj.*
dictatorially *adv.* [*Say* DICK tater, dicta TORY ul]

dictatorship *n.* **1** a state ruled by a dictator. **2** government by a dictator. [*Say* dick TATER ship]

diction *n.* **1** the manner of pronouncing words. **2** the choice of words in speech or writing.

dictionary *n.* (*pl.* **dictionaries**) a listing of words with their definitions or translations.

dictum *n.* (*pl.* **dicta** or **dictums**) **1** a formal pronouncement from an authoritative source. **2** a saying or maxim.

did *past of* DO¹.

didactic *adj.* **1** intended to teach or give moral instruction. **2** in the manner of a teacher; patronizing. □ **didactically** *adv.* **didacticism** *n.* [*Say* die DACK tick, die DACTA sism]

diddle *v.* (**diddles, diddled, diddling**) *informal* **1** cheat, swindle. **2** (often foll. by *with*) adjust; toy with. **3** waste time. □ **diddler** *n.*

diddly *n. slang* = DIDDLY-SQUAT.

diddly-squat *n. slang* **1** (with *neg.*) anything, the least bit. **2** nothing at all.

didn't *contr.* did not.

die[1] *v.* (**dies, died, dying**) **1** cease to live. **2 a** come to an end. **b** break down. **c** (of a flame) go out. **3** suffer (a specified death). □ **be dying** wish for longingly. **die away** become weaker or more faint. **die off 1** die one after another. **2** fade away gradually. **die out** become extinct. **never say die** keep up courage. **to die for** *informal* extremely desirable.

die[2] *n.* **1** *singular of* DICE *n.* 1a. **2** (*pl.* **dies**) a device for cutting or moulding material, or for stamping a design on coins, medals, etc. □ **the die is cast** an irrevocable step has been taken.

die-cast *adj.* formed by pouring molten metal into a mold.

dieffenbachia *n.* a poisonous tropical American evergreen plant often grown as a houseplant. [*Say* dee fin BACKY uh]

diehard ● *n.* a conservative or stubborn person. ● *adj.* **1** resolutely opposing change. **2** staunchly loyal.

die-off *n.* a sharp decline in a natural population.

diesel *n.* **1** (also **diesel engine**) an internal combustion engine in which the heat of air compression ignites the fuel. **2** a vehicle driven by a diesel engine. **3** (also **diesel fuel**) a petroleum product used as fuel in diesel engines. [*Say* DEEZ ul]

diet[1] ● *n.* **1** the kinds of food that a person or animal habitually eats. **2** a special course of food to which a person is restricted, esp. for medical reasons or to control weight. **3** an activity which forms one's main concern. ● *v.* (**diets, dieted, dieting**) restrict oneself to a diet to control one's weight. ● *adj.* suitable for consumption by someone on a calorie-reduced diet. □ **dieter** *n.*

diet[2] *n.* a legislative assembly in certain countries, e.g. Japan.

dietary *adj.* relating to or provided by diet. [*Say* DIE a terry]

dietary fibre *n.* the part of a foodstuff that cannot be digested or absorbed; roughage.

dietetic *adj.* **1** relating to diet. **2** suitable for a calorie-reduced diet. [*Say* die a TET ick]

dietetics *pl. n.* (usu. treated as *sing.*) the scientific study of diet and nutrition. [*Say* die a TET icks]

dietitian *n.* (also **dietician**) an expert in dietetics. [*Say* die a TISH in]

diff *n. informal* difference

differ *v.* **1** (often foll. by *from*) be unlike. **2** disagree. □ **differing** *adj.*

difference *n.* **1** the state of being unlike. **2** a way in which things differ. **3** the quantity by which amounts differ. **4** a disagreement or dispute. □ **make a** (or **no**) **difference** have a significant (or no) effect (on a person etc.).

different *adj.* **1** (often foll. by *from, than*) unlike; distinguishable (from another). **2** separate; not the same one. **3** *informal* unusual. □ **differently** *adv.*

differential ● *adj.* of, exhibiting, or depending on a difference. ● *n.* **1** difference in an amount, esp. between rates of pay for people doing different work in the same industry. **2** *Math* an infinitesimal difference between successive values of a variable. **3** (also **differential gear**) a gear allowing a vehicle's wheels to rotate at different speeds while cornering. □ **differentially** *adv.* [*Say* diffa REN shull]

differentiate *v.* (**differentiates, differentiated, differentiating**) **1** cause to appear different. **2** find differences. □ **differentiated** *adj.* **differentiation** *n.* [*Say* diffa REN shee ate]

difficult *adj.* **1** needing much effort or skill. **2** troublesome, uncooperative. **3** not easy to satisfy. **4** characterized by hardships.

difficulty *n.* (*pl.* **difficulties**) **1** the state of being difficult. **2** a difficult or dangerous thing. □ **with difficulty** not easily.

diffident *adj.* reserved, lacking self-confidence. □ **diffidence** *n.* **diffidently** *adv.* [*Say* DIFFA dint]

diffract *v.* (of an edge, narrow slit, etc.) break up (light) into a series of dark or light bands or coloured spectra. □ **diffraction** *n.* [*Say* duh FRACT]

diffuse ● *adj.* spread out over a wide area. ● *v.* (**diffuses, diffused, diffusing**) **1** spread or be spread widely. **2** *Physics* become or cause (a fluid, gas, etc.) to become intermingled with a substance by movement. □ **diffused** *adj.* **diffusely** *adv.* **diffuser** *n.* [*Say* dif FYOOSS *for the adjective,* duh FYOOZ *for the verb*]

diffusion *n.* **1** the spreading of something

more widely. **2** *Physics & Chemistry* the intermingling of substances by the natural movement of their particles. [*Say* dif FYOO zhun]

dig ● *v.* (**digs, dug, digging**) **1** break up and move or turn over earth etc. **2** make (a hole etc.) by digging. **3 a** (often foll. by *up, out*) obtain or remove by digging. **b** discover after searching. **4** excavate (an archaeological site). **5** *dated slang* like or understand. **6** thrust or poke. ● *n.* **1 a** thrust or poke. **2** *informal* a pointed remark. **3** an archaeological excavation. **4** (in *pl.*) *informal* lodgings. □ **dig deep 1** draw on one's innermost resources. **2** give generously. **dig in one's heels** be obstinate. **dig in** *informal* begin eating. **dig (oneself) in 1** prepare a defensive trench. **2** establish one's position. **dig one's own grave** cause one's own ruin.

digest ● *v.* **1** assimilate (food) in the stomach and bowels. **2** (of food) undergo digestion. **3** understand and assimilate mentally. ● *n.* a summary of current information etc. □ **digester** *n.* **digestibility** *n.* **digestible** *adj.*

digestion *n.* **1** the process of digesting. **2** the capacity to digest food.

digestive ● *adj.* relating to or aiding digestion. ● *n.* a substance that aids digestion.

digger *n.* a person, machine, or tool that digs.

digit *n.* **1** any numeral from 0 to 9. **2** a finger, thumb, or toe.

digital ● *adj.* **1** relating to a digit or digits. **2** (of a clock etc.) displaying the time with numerical digits. **3** relating to electronic data represented as a series of usu. binary digits etc. **4** having to do with a finger or fingers. ● *n.* a digital device. □ **digitally** *adv.*

digital camera *n.* a camera that records images digitally rather than on photographic film.

digitalis *n.* a drug prepared from foxgloves, used to stimulate the heart muscle. [*Say* didge a TALLIS]

digitalize *v.* (**digitalizes, digitalized, digitalizing**) = DIGITIZE.

digitize *v.* (**digitizes, digitized, digitizing**) convert (data etc.) into digital form. □ **digitization** *n.* **digitizer** *n.*

dignified *adj.* having or showing dignity.

dignify *v.* (**dignifies, dignified, dignifying**) **1** give dignity or distinction to. **2** treat as worthy.

dignitary *n.* (*pl.* **dignitaries**) a person holding high rank or office.

dignity *n.* (*pl.* **dignities**) **1** a composed and serious manner. **2** the state of being worthy of respect. **3** worthiness, excellence. **4** high regard. □ **beneath one's dignity** not considered worthy enough for one to do.

digress *v.* (**digresses, digressed, digressing**) depart from the main subject temporarily. □ **digression** *n.* **digressive** *adj.* [*Say* die GRESS]

digs *pl. n. see* DIG *n.* 4.

Dijon mustard *n.* a mild mustard paste using brown and black varieties of seed blended with white wine. [*Say* dee ZHON]

dike ● *n.* **1** a long wall etc. built to prevent flooding. **2** an artificial watercourse. **3** a defensive barrier. ● *v.* (**dikes, diked, diking**) provide with a dike or dikes.

dilapidated *adj.* in a state of disrepair as a result of neglect. □ **dilapidation** *n.* [*Say* duh LAPPA dated, duh lappa DAY shun]

dilate *v.* (**dilates, dilated, dilating**) **1** widen or enlarge. **2** speak or write at length. □ **dilation** *n.* [*Say* DIE late *or* die LATE, die LAY sh'n]

dilatory *adj.* slow to act or causing delay. [*Say* DILLA tory]

dilemma *n.* **1** a situation in which a choice has to be made between equally undesirable alternatives. **2** a difficult situation.

dilettante *n.* a person who cultivates an area of interest, e.g. the arts, without real commitment or knowledge. □ **dilettantism** *n.* [*Say* DILLA tont]

diligent *adj.* caring and conscientious about one's work. □ **diligence** *n.* **diligently** *adv.* [*Say* DILLA jint]

dill *n.* a herb, the leaves and seeds of which are used for flavouring etc.

dilly *n.* (*pl.* **dillies**) *informal* an excellent person or thing.

dilly-dally *v.* (**dilly-dallies, dilly-dallied, dilly-dallying**) *informal* waste time or be indecisive.

dilute ● *v.* (**dilutes, diluted, diluting**) **1** make (a fluid) weaker by adding water or another solvent. **2** weaken; make less effective. ● *adj.* **1** diluted, weakened. **2** (of a colour) low in saturation. **3** *Chemistry* (of a substance) in solution. □ **diluted** *adj.* **dilution** *n.*

dim ● *adj.* (**dimmer, dimmest**) **1 a** only faintly luminous. **b** obscure; ill-defined. **2** not clearly remembered. **3** *informal* stupid. **4** not seeing clearly. **5** not likely to succeed. ● *v.* (**dims, dimmed, dimming**) make or become less bright. □ **take a dim view of** *informal* **1** disapprove of. **2** feel gloomy about. □ **dimly** *adv.* **dimness** *n.*

dime n. a ten-cent coin. □ **a dime a dozen** cheap and commonplace.

dimension n. **1** a measurable extent, such as length, breadth, depth, etc. **2** (in pl) size, scope, extent. **3** an aspect or feature. □ **dimensional** adj. (also in comb.) **dimensionality** n. **dimensionally** adv. **dimensionless** adj.

dime store n. **1** = FIVE-AND-DIME STORE. **2** (**dime-store**) (as an adj.) cheap, of poor quality.

diminish v. (**diminishes**, **diminished**, **diminishing**) make or become less. □ **diminished** adj. **diminishment** n.

diminuendo n. Music (pl. **diminuendos**) **1** a decrease in loudness. **2** a passage to be performed with such a decrease. [Say dim in yoo EN doe]

diminution n. a reduction. [Say dim in YOO sh'n]

diminutive ● adj. **1** very small. **2** (of a word or suffix) implying smallness. ● n. **1** a word or suffix indicating that something is small. **2** a short informal form of a word. [Say duh MIN you tiv]

dimmer n. (also **dimmer switch**) a device for varying the brightness of an electric light.

dimple ● n. **1** a small dent in the flesh, esp. in the cheeks or chin. **2** a round depression, e.g. in a golf ball. ● v. (**dimples**, **dimpled**, **dimpling**) produce dimples. □ **dimpled** adj. **dimply** adj.

dim sum n. small Chinese dumplings with savoury fillings.

dim-wit n. informal a stupid person. □ **dim-witted** adj.

din ● n. a prolonged loud and distracting noise. ● v. (**dins**, **dinned**, **dinning**) **1** (foll. by into) instill (something) by constant repetition. **2** make a din.

dine v. (**dines**, **dined**, **dining**) **1** eat dinner. **2** give dinner to.

diner n. **1** a person who dines. **2** a small restaurant serving short-order food. **3** a railway carriage equipped as a restaurant.

dinette n. **1** a small room or part of a room used for eating meals. **2** a table and chairs for this. [Say die NET]

ding[1] ● v. make a ringing sound. ● n. a ringing sound, as of a bell.

ding[2] informal ● n. a dent. ● v. **1** make a dent in. **2** hit. **3** make to pay (an excessive amount).

ding-a-ling ● n. **1** the sound of a bell. **2** informal a crazy person. ● adj. crazy.

dingbat n. informal a stupid or eccentric person.

ding-dong ● n. **1** the sound of alternate chimes, as of two bells. **2** slang a crazy person. ● adj. slang crazy.

dinghy n. (pl. **dinghies**) a small boat, esp. an inflatable one. [Say DING ee]

dingo n. (pl. **dingoes**) a wild Australian dog.

dingy adj. (**dingier**, **dingiest**) gloomy and drab. [Say DIN jee]

dining room n. a room in which meals are eaten.

dinky adj. (**dinkier**, **dinkiest**) informal trifling, insignificant.

dinner n. **1** the main meal of the day. **2** a formal meal. □ **done like dinner** Cdn & Austral. informal utterly defeated.

dinnertime n. the time at which dinner is customarily eaten.

dino n. (pl. **dinos**) informal a dinosaur.

dinosaur n. **1** an extinct reptile of the Mesozoic era, often of enormous size. **2** an outdated person or thing.

dint ● n. a dent. ● v. mark with dints. □ **by dint of** by force or means of.

diocesan adj. concerning a diocese. [Say die OSSA sin or die OSSA zin]

diocese n. a district under the care of a bishop. [Say DIE a seez or DIE a sis]

diode n. a semiconductor allowing the flow of current in one direction only and having two terminals. [Say DIE ode]

diorama n. **1** a scenic, partially translucent painting. **2** a representation of a scene with three-dimensional figures and a painted background. **3** a small-scale model or film set. [Say die a RAMA]

dioxide n. an oxide containing two separate atoms of oxygen. [Say die OXIDE]

dioxin n. a highly toxic compound produced as a chemical by-product. [Say die OXIN]

dip ● v. (**dips**, **dipped**, **dipping**) **1** put or let down briefly into liquid etc. **2** lower briefly. **3** sink, drop, or slope downwards. **4** go under water and emerge quickly. **5** (foll. by into) peruse. **6** (foll. by into) **a** reach into (a container) to take something out. **b** spend from one's resources. ● n. **1** an act of dipping or being dipped. **2** a liquid into which something is dipped. **3** a brief swim. **4** a brief downward slope, followed by an upward one. **5** a thick sauce into which food is dipped before eating. **6** an ice cream cone dipped in melted chocolate etc.

diphtheria n. an acute infectious bacterial disease with inflammation of a mucous membrane esp. of the throat. [Say dif THEERY uh or dip THEERY uh]

diphthong n. a sound formed by the combination of two vowels in one syllable (as in coin). [Say DIF thong or DIP thong]

diploid ● *adj.* (of an organism or cell) having two complete sets of chromosomes per cell. ● *n.* a diploid cell or organism. [*Say* DIP loyd]

diploma *n.* a certificate awarded for completing a course of study etc.

diplomacy *n.* **1 a** the management of international relations by negotiation. **b** expertise in this. **2** skill or tact in dealing with people.

diplomat *n.* **1** a government official who conducts negotiations with other countries. **2** a tactful person.

diplomatic *adj.* **1** of or involved in diplomacy. **2** tactful.
□ **diplomatically** *adv.*

dipole *n.* **1** *Physics* two equal and oppositely charged or magnetized poles separated by a distance. **2** (also **dipole antenna**) an antenna composed of two equal straight rods having an electrical connection in the centre. □ **dipolar** *adj.* [*Say* DIE pole]

dipper *n.* **1** a short-tailed songbird which habitually bobs up and down. **2** a ladle. **3** an item of food suitable for dipping.

dippy *adj.* (**dippier, dippiest**) *informal* foolish.

dipstick *n.* **1** a rod for measuring the depth of a liquid. **2** *slang* a fool.

dipsy-doodle esp. *Cdn slang* ● *v.* (**dipsy-doodles, dipsy-doodled, dipsy-doodling**) esp. *Hockey* evade the defending team by using swerving motions and finesse in stickhandling etc. ● *n.* **1** an evasive movement of this type. **2** a tactic designed to outwit opponents or competitors.

dipterous *adj.* having two membranous wings or wing-like appendages. [*Say* DIPTER us]

dire *adj.* (**direr, direst**) **1 a** dreadful. **b** ominous. **2** urgent.

direct ● *adj.* **1 a** going in a straight line or by the shortest route. **b** (of a journey) not involving any changes of airplane, train, etc. **2** straightforward. **3** without intermediaries or interventions. **4** (of descent) lineal, not collateral. **5** exact, complete. **6** (of a quotation etc.) literal; word for word. ● *adv.* in a direct way or by a direct route. ● *v.* **1** guide, esp. with advice. **2** control the movement of. **3 a** administer. **b** supervise (a film, performance, etc.). **4** give an order to. **5** aim towards or address. **6** conduct (a group of musicians). □ **directness** *n.*

direct access *n.* = RANDOM ACCESS.

direct current *n.* an electric current flowing in one direction only. Abbreviation: **DC, d.c.**

direct debit *n. Cdn & Brit.* **1** an arrangement with a bank for the regular debiting of funds from one's account. **2** payment by means of a debit card, allowing for the electronic transfer of funds to a merchant etc.

direct deposit *n.* the electronic transfer of money from one bank account to another.

direction *n.* **1** the act or process of directing. **2** (usu. in *pl.*) an order or instruction. **3 a** a course along which a person or thing moves or looks, or which leads to a destination. **b** the point to or from which a person or thing moves or faces. **4** the tendency taken by events etc. □ **directionless** *adj.*

directional *adj.* **1** of or indicating direction. **2** transmitting or receiving radio or sound waves in or from a particular direction. □ **directionally** *adv.*

directive ● *n.* a general instruction from an authority. ● *adj.* serving to direct.

directly *adv.* **1** without delay. **2** exactly. **3** in a direct manner.

direct mail *n.* unsolicited advertising material mailed to large numbers of prospective customers. □ **direct mailing** *n.*

direct object *n. Grammar* a person or thing directly affected by the action of a verb.

director *n.* **1** a person in charge of an organization, department, etc. **2** a member of a governing board. **3** a person who directs a film etc. **4** a conductor of a choir or of a band etc. in which the director is a performing instrumentalist. □ **directorial** *adj.* **directorship** *n.* [*Say* duh RECK tur, duh reck TORY ul]

directorate *n.* **1** a government body with a specific responsibility. **2** a board of directors. **3** the office of director.

director general *n.* (*pl.* **directors general**) **1** the chief executive of a public organization. **2** *Cdn* a rank in the civil service immediately below assistant deputy minister. **3** (in the SQ) the highest ranking officer.

directory *n.* (*pl.* **directories**) **1 a** a book listing individuals or organizations with details such as telephone numbers. **b** a large board listing names of departments, individuals, etc. and giving their location, esp. in a building. **2** a computer file listing other files or programs etc.

direct payment *n.* DIRECT DEBIT 2

direct tax *n.* a tax paid directly to the government, e.g. income tax.

dirge *n.* **1** a lament for the dead. **2** music

that is too slow and mournful. [*Rhymes with* URGE]

dirigible *n.* an airship.
[*Say* DEER idge uh bull]

dirt *n.* **1** unclean matter that soils. **2 a** soil. **b** earth, gravel, etc., used to surface a road (usu. as an *adj.*). **3** scandalous information. **4** excrement. **5** something considered worthless.

dirt bike *n.* a motorcycle used in cross-country racing.

dirt cheap *adj. & adv. informal* extremely cheap.

dirt poor *adj.* very poor.

dirty ● *adj.* (**dirtier, dirtiest**) **1** unclean. **2** pertaining to or obsessed with sexual activity. **3** nasty, unfair. **4** (of weather) rough, squally. **5** (of a colour) not pure. ● *adv. informal* in a malicious or unfair manner. ● *v.* (**dirties, dirtied, dirtying**) make or become dirty. □ **dirty one's hands** (or **get one's hands dirty**) *informal* acquire practical experience. **do the dirty on** *informal* play a mean trick on. **talk dirty** *informal* use obscene language. □ **dirtiness** *n.*

dirty bomb *n. informal* a conventional weapon containing radioactive material.

dirty laundry *n.* (also **dirty linen**) intimate, scandalous secrets.

dirty look *n. informal* a look of disapproval or disgust etc.

dirty thirties *n. pl.* esp. *Cdn informal* **1** the Great Depression of the 1930s. **2** the years of drought coinciding with this on the Prairies.

dirty word *n.* **1** an indecent word. **2** a thing regarded with dislike or disapproval.

dirty work *n.* unpleasant or illegal activity.

dis *slang v.* (**disses, dissed, dissing**) put (a person etc.) down.

disability *n.* (*pl.* **disabilities**) **1** a physical or mental condition limiting a person's activity or senses. **2** a disadvantage.

disable *v.* (**disables, disabled, disabling**) **1** make unable to function. **2** limit someone in their movements, senses, or activities. □ **disablement** *n.*

disabled *adj.* **1** having a mental or physical disability. **2** made incapable of action or use.

disabuse *v.* (**disabuses, disabused, disabusing**) persuade someone that a belief or idea is mistaken.

disadvantage ● *n.* an unfavourable circumstance or condition. ● *v.* cause disadvantage to. □ **disadvantageous** *adj.*

disadvantaged *adj.* suffering from social or economic deprivation or discrimination.

disaffected *adj.* dissatisfied with one's situation, belief, etc. and therefore not loyal to it. □ **disaffection** *n.*

disagree *v.* (**disagrees, disagreed, disagreeing**) (often foll. by *with*) **1** hold a different opinion. **2** quarrel. **3** not correspond. **4** have an adverse effect upon. □ **disagreement** *n.*

disagreeable *adj.* **1** unpleasant, not to one's liking. **2** quarrelsome. □ **disagreeably** *adv.*

disallow *v.* **1** refuse to allow. **2** annul (a statute) passed by a lower legislative body. □ **disallowance** *n.*

disappear *v.* **1** cease to be visible. **2** cease to exist. **3** go missing. □ **disappearance** *n.*

disappoint *v.* fail to fulfill the hopes of. □ **disappointing** *adj.*

disappointed *adj.* frustrated or saddened by not having one's hopes fulfilled. □ **disappointedly** *adv.*

disappointment *n.* **1** something that disappoints. **2** a feeling of distress etc. resulting from this.

disapprove *v.* (**disapproves, disapproved, disapproving**) have or express an unfavourable opinion. □ **disapproval** *n.* **disapproving** *adj.* **disapprovingly** *adv.*

disarm *v.* **1** deprive of a weapon or weapons. **2 a** (of a nation) reduce one's armed forces or weapons. **b** cause (a nation) to do this. **3** defuse. **4** cause to feel less critical or hostile. **5** deactivate (an alarm system).

disarmament *n.* the reduction of military forces and weapons.

disarming *adj.* reducing suspicion or hostility. □ **disarmingly** *adv.*

disarrange *v.* (**disarranges, disarranged, disarranging**) bring into disorder.

disarray *n.* disorder, confusion.

disassemble *v.* (**disassembles, disassembled, disassembling**) take (a machine etc.) to pieces. □ **disassembly** *n.*

disassociate *v.* (**disassociates, disassociated, disassociating**) = DISSOCIATE. □ **disassociation** *n.*

disaster *n.* **1** a great misfortune. **2** a complete failure.

disastrous *adj.* **1** causing great damage. **2** highly unsuccessful. □ **disastrously** *adv.*

disavow *v.* disclaim knowledge of or support for. □ **disavowal** *n.*
[*Say* dissa VOW]

disband *v.* break up an organization or group.

disbar v. (**disbars, disbarred, disbarring**) deprive (a lawyer) of the right to practise. □ **disbarment** n.

disbelief n. **1** lack of belief. **2** astonishment.

disbelieve v. (**disbelieves, disbelieved, disbelieving**) be unable or unwilling to believe (a person or statement). □ **disbeliever** n. **disbelieving** adj. **disbelievingly** adv.

disburse v. (**disburses, disbursed, disbursing**) pay out (money from a fund). □ **disbursement** n. [Say diss BURSE]

disc n. (also **disk**) **1** a flat thin circular object. **2** a layer of cartilage between vertebrae. **3** a sound or video recording in the form of a disc. **4** = DISK n.

discard ● v. get rid of as unwanted. ● n. a rejected or abandoned thing.

disc brake n. a brake employing the friction of pads against a disc which is attached to the wheel.

discern v. **1** perceive, esp. by sight. **2** recognize or detect. □ **discernible** adj. **discernibly** adv. [Say dis SERN]

discerning adj. showing good judgment. □ **discerningly** adv. **discernment** n. [Say dis SERN ing]

discharge ● v. (**discharges, discharged, discharging**) **1** let go, release from a duty, debt, etc. **2** dismiss from office. **3** fire (a gun, bullet, etc.). **4 a** emit (pus, liquid, etc.). **b** (foll. by into) (of a river) flow into. **5 a** perform (an obligation). **b** pay (a debt). **6** release an electrical charge from. **7** remove cargo from (a ship). ● n. **1** the action of discharging. **2** a flow of liquid or gas out from where it is confined. **3 a** the payment (of a debt). **b** the performance (of a duty). **4** Physics the release of a quantity of electric charge.

disciple n. **1 a** a follower or pupil. **2** a follower of Jesus during his lifetime, esp. one of the Apostles. □ **discipleship** n. [Say dis SIPE ul]

disciplinarian n. a person who upholds firm discipline. [Say dissa plin AIRY in]

disciplinary adj. relating to discipline or punishment. [Say DISSA plin airy]

discipline ● n. **1 a** training of the mind and character to producing self-control, obedience, etc. **b** behaviour resulting from such training. **2** a branch of learning. ● v. (**disciplines, disciplined, disciplining**) **1** punish, reprimand. **2** train to be obedient, self-controlled, etc.

disciplined adj. behaving in a controlled way. [Say DISSA plinned]

disc jockey n. a person who introduces and plays recorded music on radio, at a dance, etc.

disclaim v. deny or disown.

disclaimer n. a statement disclaiming responsibility for something.

disclose v. (**discloses, disclosed, disclosing**) **1** make known. **2** expose to view.

disclosure n. **1** the action revealing information. **2** a revelation.

disco n. informal (pl. **discos**) **1** a place or event at which people dance to recorded popular music. **2** a style of repetitive dance music using electronic instrumentation, popular in the 1970s.

discolour v. (also **discolor**) spoil or cause to spoil the colour of. □ **discoloration** n.

discombobulate v. (**discombobulates, discombobulated, discombobulating**) jocular disturb; disconcert. □ **discombobulation** n.

discomfit v. (**discomfits, discomfited, discomfiting**) make someone feel confused or uneasy. □ **discomfiture** n. [Say dis KUM fit]

discomfort ● n. **1 a** slight pain. **b** mental uneasiness. **2** a lack of physical comfort. ● v. make uneasy.

disconcert v. unsettle, upset. □ **disconcerted** adj. **disconcerting** adj. **disconcertingly** adv. [Say dis kun SERT]

disconnect v. ● **1** break the connection between. **2** become detached. **3** detach from an electrical supply or service network. ● n. **1** an act or instance of disconnecting. **2** a lack of connection; a discrepancy. □ **disconnection** n.

disconnected adj. **1** incoherent and illogical. **2** not connected.

disconsolate adj. unhappy and unable to be comforted. □ **disconsolately** adv. [Say dis CONSA lit]

discontent n. lack of contentment. □ **discontented** adj.

discontinue v. (**discontinues, discontinued, discontinuing**) cease existing, making, or doing something. □ **discontinuation** n.

discontinuity n. (pl. **discontinuities**) a distinct break or change.

discontinuous adj. not continuous.

discord n. **1** disagreement; quarrelling. **2** a harsh-sounding combination of musical notes.

discordant adj. **1** not in agreement; combining strangely or unpleasantly. **2** (of sounds) not in harmony; dissonant. □ **discordance** n. **discordantly** adv. [Say dis CORE dint]

discotheque *n.* = DISCO 1.
[*Say* DISCO teck]

discount ● *n.* a deduction from a bill or amount due. ● *v.* **1** disregard as being unreliable. **2 a** lessen; deduct (esp. an amount from a bill etc.). **b** reduce in price. **3** trade (a bill of exchange before its maturity date) at a price less than its face value. ● *adj.* **1** selling goods below normal retail price. **2** sold below normal retail price. □ **discounter** *n.*

discourage *v.* (**discourages, discouraged, discouraging**) **1** deprive of confidence or enthusiasm. **2** (usu. foll. by *from*) dissuade. **3** oppose or deter. □ **discouragement** *n.* **discouraging** *adj.* **discouragingly** *adv.*

discourse ● *n.* **1** communication in speech or writing. **2** a long and serious discussion. **3** discussion on a specific subject as typified by recurring terms and concepts. ● *v.* (**discourses, discoursed, discoursing**) **1** talk; converse. **2** speak or write learnedly.

discourteous *adj.* impolite; rude. □ **discourteously** *adv.* **discourteousness** *n.*
[*Say* dis COURTEOUS]

discourtesy *n.* (*pl.* **discourtesies**) **1** bad manners; rudeness. **2** an impolite act or remark.

discover *v.* **1 a** become aware of. **b** be the first to find. **2** (in show business) find and promote as a new singer, actor, etc. □ **discoverable** *adj.* **discoverer** *n.*

discovery *n.* (*pl.* **discoveries**) **1** the act of discovering. **2** a person or thing discovered.

discredit ● *n.* **1** harm to reputation. **2** a person or thing causing such harm. ● *v.* (**discredits, discredited, discrediting**) **1** harm the good reputation of. **2** destroy confidence in (an effort, a person, etc.). □ **discredited** *adj.*

discreditable *adj.* tending to bring harm to a reputation.

discreet *adj.* careful not to reveal much, attract attention, or give offence. □ **discreetly** *adv.*

discrepancy *n.* (*pl.* **discrepancies**) a difference between things expected to be the same. [*Say* dis CREP'n see]

discrete *adj.* individually separate and distinct. □ **discretely** *adv.* **discreteness** *n.*

discretion *n.* **1** the quality of being discreet. **2** the power to decide what should be done. □ **at one's discretion** as one pleases. **use one's discretion** act according to one's own judgment.
[*Say* dis CRESH'n]

discretionary *adj.* used whenever necessary. [*Say* dis CRESH'n airy]

discriminate *v.* (**discriminates, discriminated, discriminating**) **1** (often foll. by *between*) make or see a distinction. **2** (usu. foll. by *against*) make an unjust distinction on the basis of race, age, sex, etc. □ **discrimination** *n.*

discriminating *adj.* **1** having good judgment. **2** showing racial etc. discrimination. □ **discriminatingly** *adv.*

discriminatory *adj.* showing unjust discrimination and prejudice.
[*Say* dis CRIMMIN a tory]

discursive *adj.* **1** digressing from subject to subject. **2** fluent and expansive. □ **discursively** *adv.* [*Say* dis CURSE iv]

discus *n.* (*pl.* **discuses**) a heavy thick-centred disc thrown in sporting events. [*Say* DISK iss]

discuss *v.* (**discusses, discussed, discussing**) **1** hold a conversation about. **2** examine by argument.

discussion *n.* **1** a conversation or informal debate. **2** a detailed treatment of a topic in speech or writing.

disdain ● *n.* a feeling of scorn or contempt. ● *v.* consider to be unworthy of one's attention. □ **disdainful** *adj.* **disdainfully** *adv.*

disease *n.* a disorder of a plant, animal, or human, caused by infection, diet, or faulty functioning of a process. □ **diseased** *adj.*

disembark *v.* leave or remove from a ship, aircraft, train, etc. □ **disembarkation** *n.*

disembodied *adj.* **1** coming from a person that cannot be seen. **2** separated from the body or a concrete form. □ **disembodiment** *n.*

disembowel *v.* (**disembowels, disembowelled, disembowelling**) remove the bowels or entrails of. □ **disembowelled** *adj.* **disembowelment** *n.*
[*Say* dissem BOWEL]

disempower *v.* make less powerful or confident. □ **disempowered** *adj.* **disempowerment** *n.*

disenchanted *adj.* no longer feeling enthusiasm for someone or something. □ **disenchantment** *n.*

disenfranchise *v.* (**disenfranchises, disenfranchised, disenfranchising**) deprive of a right, esp. to vote. □ **disenfranchised** *adj.* **disenfranchisement** *n.*
[*Say* dis in FRAN chize]

disengage *v.* (**disengages, disengaged, disengaging**) **1** detach or separate (parts etc.). **2** remove (troops) from

a battle area. □ **disengaged** adj.
disengagement n.

disentangle v. (**disentangles,
disentangled, disentangling**) free
from entanglement.
□ **disentanglement** n.

disequilibrium n. (pl. **disequilibria**) a
lack or loss of equilibrium.
[Say dis equal LIB ree um]

disestablish v. (**disestablishes,
disestablished, disestablishing**) end
the official status of a national Church.
□ **disestablishment** n.

disfavour n. (also **disfavor**) **1** disapproval
or dislike. **2** the state of being disliked.

disfigure v. (**disfigures, disfigured,
disfiguring**) spoil the appearance or
beauty of. □ **disfigured** adj.
disfigurement n.

disfranchise v. (**disfranchises,
disfranchised, disfranchising**) =
DISENFRANCHISE.

disgorge v. (**disgorges, disgorged,
disgorging**) **1** vomit (matter). **2** empty.
3 cause to pour out.

disgrace ● n. **1** the loss of reputation. **2** a
person or thing that brings shame. ● v.
(**disgraces, disgraced, disgracing**)
bring shame on. □ **in disgrace** having
lost respect or reputation.
□ **disgraceful** adj. **disgracefully** adv.

disgruntled adj. irritated, annoyed.
□ **disgruntlement** n.

disguise ● v. (**disguises, disguised,
disguising**) **1** (often foll. by as) alter the
appearance etc. of (someone or something)
to conceal their true identity. **2** misrepresent or
cover up. ● n. **1** something used to disguise.
2 the state of being disguised.
□ **disguised** adj.

disgust ● n. (usu. foll. by at, for) strong
aversion to something that is loathsome.
● v. **1** offend the sensibilities of. **2** cause
nausea and loathing in.
□ **disgustedly** adv.

disgusting adj. arousing disgust.
□ **disgustingly** adv.

dish ● n. (pl. **dishes**) **1** a shallow container
for holding or serving food. **2** food
prepared in a particular way. **3** a dish-
shaped receptacle, object, or cavity. ● v.
(**dishes, dished, dishing**) put (food) into
a dish for serving. □ **dish it out** informal
deal out punishment, criticism, etc. **dish
out** informal distribute. **dish up** serve,
present. **dish the dirt** informal spread
gossip.

disharmony n. (pl. **disharmonies**) a lack
of agreement leading to tension.

dishearten v. cause to lose courage, hope,
etc. □ **disheartening** adj.
dishearteningly adv.

dishevelled adj. unkempt, untidy.
[Say dih SHEV'ld]

dishonest adj. fraudulent or insincere.
□ **dishonestly** adv. **dishonesty** n.

dishonour (also **dishonor**) ● n. a state or
cause of shame or disgrace. ● v. **1** disgrace.
2 treat without respect.

dishonourable adj. (also **dishonorable**)
1 causing disgrace. **2** (of a person)
unprincipled. □ **dishonourably** adv.

dishwasher n. a person or machine that
washes dishes. □ **dishwashing** n.

dishwater n. water in which dishes have
been washed.

disillusion ● n. disappointment upon
realizing that something is not as good as
one believed it to be. ● v. cause someone to
realize that a belief they hold is false.
□ **disillusionment** n.

disincentive ● n. something that
discourages a particular action. ● adj.
tending to discourage.

disinclination n. unwillingness.

disincline v. (**disinclines, disinclined,
disinclining**) make unwilling.
□ **disinclined** adj.

disinfect v. cleanse of infection by
destroying germs. □ **disinfection** n.

disinfectant ● n. a chemical liquid or
spray that destroys germs. ● adj. of
disinfectants or causing disinfection.

disinformation n. deliberately false
information.

disingenuous adj. insincere, esp. by
feigning ignorance. □ **disingenuously**
adv. **disingenuousness** n.
[Say dis in JEN you us]

disinherit v. (**disinherits,
disinherited, disinheriting**) reject as
one's heir. [Say dis in HAIR it]

disintegrate v. (**disintegrates,
disintegrated, disintegrating**) **1** break
up into small parts. **2** Physics (of a nucleus
etc.) emit a smaller particle or divide into
smaller particles. **3** deteriorate rapidly.
□ **disintegration** n.

disinter v. (**disinters, disinterred,
disinterring**) dig up (something buried).
[Say dis in TUR]

disinterest n. **1** impartiality. **2** disputed
lack of interest.

disinterested adj. unbiased; not
influenced by one's own advantage.
□ **disinterestedly** adv.
disinterestedness n.

disjointed adj. incoherent; not properly
connected. □ **disjointedly** adv.
disjointedness n.

disk n. (also **disc**) **1 a** (also **magnetic disk**) a computer storage device consisting of a rotatable disc or discs with a magnetic coating. **b** (also **optical disk**) a smooth non-magnetic disc, esp. a CD-ROM, with data read by laser. **2** = DISC.

disk drive n. *Computing* a device for storing and retrieving data from magnetic or optical disks.

diskette n. = FLOPPY n.

dislike ● v. (**dislikes, disliked, disliking**) have an aversion to. ● n. **1** a feeling of distaste or hostility. **2** an object of dislike. □ **dislikable** adj.

dislocate v. (**dislocates, dislocated, dislocating**) **1** disturb the normal connection of (esp. a joint in the body). **2** disrupt. **3** displace from proper position. □ **dislocation** n.

dislodge v. (**dislodges, dislodged, dislodging**) remove from a fixed position.

disloyal adj. not loyal or faithful. □ **disloyalty** n.

dismal adj. **1** causing or showing gloom. **2** informal feeble. □ **dismally** adv. **dismalness** n.

dismantle v. (**dismantles, dismantled, dismantling**) take apart. □ **dismantler** n.

dismay ● n. consternation or anxiety, usu. caused by something unexpected. ● v. fill with consternation. □ **dismaying** adj. **dismayingly** adv.

dismember v. **1** tear or cut the limbs from. **2** divide up (a country etc.). □ **dismemberment** n.

dismiss v. (**dismisses, dismissed, dismissing**) **1** cause (a person) to leave one's presence. **2** discharge from employment etc., esp. dishonourably. **3** treat as unworthy of consideration. **4** *Law* refuse further hearing to (a case). □ **dismissal** n. **dismissible** adj.

dismissive adj. showing that something is not worth consideration. □ **dismissively** adv. **dismissiveness** n.

dismount ● v. get off a horse, bicycle, etc. ● n. an act of dismounting.

disobedient adj. disobeying; rule-breaking. □ **disobedience** n. **disobediently** adv. [Say dis oh BEEDY int]

disobey v. **1** fail or refuse to obey. **2** be disobedient. [Say dis oh BAY]

disorder ● n. **1** confusion; lack of order. **2** a disturbance or commotion. **3** an illness or disturbance of the normal state of body or mind. ● v. bring disorder to. □ **disordered** adj.

disorderly adj. **1** involving a breakdown of law-abiding behaviour. **2** lacking organization; untidy. □ **disorderliness** n.

disorganized v. lacking organization. □ **disorganization** n.

disorient v. confuse (a person) as to his or her bearings. □ **disorientation** n.

disown v. **1** refuse to having anything to do with (someone). **2** disclaim (an idea etc.).

disparage v. (**disparages, disparaged, disparaging**) regard or represent as being of little worth. □ **disparagement** n. **disparaging** adj. **disparagingly** adv. [Say dis PAIR idge]

disparate adj. **1** very different in kind. **2** made up of very different elements. □ **disparately** adv. [Say DISPA rit]

disparity n. a great difference. [Say dis PAIRA tee]

dispassionate adj. calm, impartial. □ **dispassionately** adv.

dispatch ● v. (**dispatches, dispatched, dispatching**) **1** send off to a destination or for a purpose. **2** kill. **3** perform (a task etc.) promptly. ● n. **1** the act of dispatching. **2 a** an official written message, esp. on military affairs. **b** a report sent from abroad by a journalist. **3** promptness, efficiency.

dispatcher n. a person who coordinates the departure of taxis, buses, trains, etc.

dispel v. (**dispels, dispelled, dispelling**) make a feeling, belief, etc. disappear.

dispensable adj. able to be replaced or done without.

dispensary n. (pl. **dispensaries**) a place where medicines and medical advice are dispensed. [Say dis PENSA ree]

dispensation n. **1** the action of dispensing. **2** an exemption from a usual requirement or rule. **3** (in Christian theology) a divinely ordained order prevailing at a particular time. [Say dis pen SAY sh'n]

dispense v. (**dispenses, dispensed, dispensing**) **1** distribute or deal out. **2** administer (justice, etc.). **3** make up and give out (medicine etc.) according to a doctor's prescription. **4 a** do without. **b** give exemption from (a rule). □ **dispenser** n.

disperse v. (**disperses, dispersed, dispersing**) **1** go or distribute in different directions. **2** (usu. in passive) place at widely separated points. **3** *Chemistry* distribute (small particles) uniformly in a medium. □ **dispersal** n. **disperser** n. **dispersion** n.

dispirited adj. having lost enthusiasm. □ **dispiritedly** adv.

dispiriting adj. discouraging.
□ **dispiritingly** adv.

displace v. (**displaces, displaced, displacing**) **1** move from the usual or accustomed place. **2** take the place of.

displacement n. **1** the action of displacing. **2** the enforced departure of people from their homes. **3** *Physics* the amount by which anything is displaced.

display ● v. show. ● n. **1** an action of showing emotion, skill, etc. **2 a** a performance, show, or event intended for public entertainment. **b** a collection of objects presented for viewing. **3** the data or images on a computer screen etc.

displease v. (**displeases, displeased, displeasing**) make indignant or angry. □ **be displeased** (often foll. by *at, with*) be indignant or dissatisfied.
□ **displeasing** adj.

displeasure n. disapproval; dissatisfaction.

disposable ● adj. **1** intended to be used once and then thrown away. **2** (esp. of financial assets) available for use. ● n. a disposable thing.

disposal n. **1** the action of disposing of something, esp. waste. **2** the sale of shares, property, etc. □ **at one's disposal** available for one's use.

dispose v. (**disposes, disposed, disposing**) **1** make willing; incline. **2** place suitably or in order. □ **dispose of 1 a** deal conclusively with. **b** get rid of. **2** sell. **3** prove to be incorrect. □ **disposed** adj. **disposer** n.

disposition n. **1 a** temperament or character. **b** (often foll. by *to*) a natural tendency. **2** the arrangement or placement of something. **3 a** the transfer of property, esp. in a will. **b** the power to deal with something.

dispossess v. (**dispossesses, dispossessed, dispossessing**) deprive someone of property.
□ **dispossessed** adj. **dispossession** n.

disproportionate adj. too large or small in comparison with something else.
□ **disproportionately** adv.

disprove v. (**disproves, disproved, disproving**) prove false.

disputable adj. open to question.

disputation n. debate or argument.

disputatious adj. **1** (of a person) fond of heated arguments. **2** motivated by or causing strong opinions.
□ **disputatiously** adv.
disputatiousness n.
[*Say* dis pyoo TAY shuss]

dispute ● v. (**disputes, disputed,**

disputing) **1** argue about something. **2** question the truth etc. of. **3** compete for. ● n. **1** a controversy. **2** a disagreement or quarrel. □ **disputed** adj.

disqualify v. (**disqualifies, disqualified, disqualifying**) **1** (often foll. by *from*) bar from a competition because of an infringement of the rules etc. **2** (often foll. by *for, from*) make or pronounce ineligible. **3** (often foll. by *from*) deprive of legal capacity, power, or right.
□ **disqualification** n.

disquiet ● v. worry; make anxious. ● n. anxiety. □ **disquieting** adj.

disquisition n. a long treatise on a subject. [*Say* dis quiz ISH'n]

disregard ● v. pay no attention to. ● n. (often foll. by *of, for*) lack of regard.

disrepair n. the state of being in poor condition.

disreputable adj. **1** of bad reputation. **2** not respectable in appearance.
□ **disreputably** adv.
[*Say* dis REP you tuh bull]

disrepute n. a lack of good reputation. [*Say* dis ree PYOOT]

disrespect ● n. a lack of respect or courtesy. ● v. *informal* have or show no respect for. □ **disrespectful** adj. **disrespectfully** adv.

disrobe v. (**disrobes, disrobed, disrobing**) undress, esp. remove the clothes worn for an official ceremony.

disrupt v. interrupt or disturb (the order of something). □ **disruption** n. **disruptive** adj. **disruptively** adv.

diss v. = DIS v.

dissatisfy v. (**dissatisfies, dissatisfied, dissatisfying**) make discontented. □ **dissatisfaction** n.

dissect v. **1** cut into pieces, esp. to examine the structure of something. **2** examine in detail. □ **dissection** n.
[*Say* die SECT *or* dis SECT]

dissemble v. (**dissembles, dissembled, dissembling**) conceal one's motives. □ **dissembler** n.
[*Say* dis SEM bull]

disseminate v. (**disseminates, disseminated, disseminating**) spread (esp. ideas) widely. □ **dissemination** n. **disseminator** n. [*Say* dis EMMA nate]

dissension n. disagreement within a group.

dissent ● v. **1** think differently, disagree. **2** differ in religious opinion. ● n. disagreement with a widely held or official view. □ **dissenter** n. **dissenting** adj.

dissertation n. a detailed discourse on a subject. [*Say* disser TAY sh'n]

disservice n. a harmful action. [Say dis SERVICE]

dissident ● adj. disagreeing with an established system etc. ● n. a person who opposes official policy. □ **dissidence** n. [Say DIS id int]

dissimilar adj. not similar. □ **dissimilarity** n. (pl. **dissimilarities**)

dissipate v. (**dissipates**, **dissipated**, **dissipating**) 1 be or cause to be dispersed. 2 break up. 3 squander.

dissipated adj. indulging in physical pleasures.

dissipation n. 1 dissipated living. 2 the action of dispersing.

dissociate v. (**dissociates**, **dissociated**, **dissociating**) 1 disconnect or separate. 2 Psychology cause (a person's mind) to develop more than one centre of consciousness. □ **dissociate oneself from** 1 declare oneself unconnected with. 2 decline to support. □ **dissociation** n.

dissolute adj. enjoying immoral activities. [Say DISSA lute]

dissolution n. 1 disintegration; decomposition. 2 the formal end of a partnership, alliance, assembly, etc. 3 coming to an end. 4 immoral living. [Say dissa LOO sh'n]

dissolve v. (**dissolves**, **dissolved**, **dissolving**) 1 disperse or cause to disperse in a liquid. 2 disappear gradually. 3 close down or end (an assembly or agreement). 4 give way (to emotion etc.).

dissonant adj. 1 Music lacking harmony. 2 clashing. □ **dissonance** n. [Say DISSA nint]

dissuade v. persuade against. □ **dissuasion** n. **dissuasive** adj. [Say dis SWADE]

distance ● n. 1 the condition of being far off. 2 a a space or interval between two things. b the length of this. 3 a point far away. 4 avoidance of familiarity. 5 a remoter field of vision. 6 the full length of a race etc. ● v. (**distances**, **distanced**, **distancing**) place far off. □ **at a distance** far off. **keep one's distance** maintain one's reserve.

distant adj. 1 a far away in space or time. b at a specified distance. 2 far apart. 3 not intimate. 4 vague. □ **distantly** adv.

distaste n. (usu. foll. by for) dislike.

distasteful adj. unpleasant or offensive. □ **distastefulness** n.

distemper¹ ● n. a type of paint that is mixed with water and used on walls. ● v. paint (walls etc.) with distemper.

distemper² n. 1 a disease of dogs or cats, causing fever, vomiting, etc. 2 uneasiness.

distend v. swell out by pressure from within. □ **distension** n. [Say dis TEND]

distill v. (**distills**, **distilled**, **distilling**) 1 purify (a liquid) by vaporizing and condensing it. 2 extract the essence of. 3 make (esp. liquor) by distilling raw materials. □ **distillation** n. **distiller** n.

distillate n. a product of distillation. [Say DISTA lit or DISTA late]

distillery n. (pl. **distilleries**) a place where liquor is distilled. [Say dis TILLA ree]

distinct adj. 1 noticeably different or separate. 2 clearly perceptible. □ **distinctly** adv. **distinctness** n.

distinction n. 1 a noticeable difference or contrast. 2 the action of distinguishing. 3 outstanding excellence. 4 an honour.

distinctive adj. having a characteristic that makes something different. □ **distinctively** adv. **distinctiveness** n.

distinguish v. (**distinguishes**, **distinguished**, **distinguishing**) 1 a see or point out the difference of or between. b constitute such a difference. 2 be a characteristic of. 3 make prominent. □ **distinguishable** adj.

distinguished adj. 1 of high standing. 2 commanding great respect.

distort v. 1 put out of shape. 2 misrepresent. 3 alter the form of (sound etc.) during amplification. □ **distorted** adj.

distortion n. 1 the action of distorting. 2 a distorted thing. 3 the characteristic fuzzy sound of electric guitars in heavy metal etc.

distract v. draw away the attention of.

distracted adj. unable to concentrate because one's mind is preoccupied by something else. □ **distractedly** adv.

distraction n. 1 a the act of distracting, esp. the mind. b something that distracts. 2 an amusement. 3 mental agitation. □ **to distraction** almost to madness.

distraught adj. very worried, upset, etc. [Say dis TROT]

distress ● n. (pl. **distresses**) 1 severe trouble, anxiety, or sorrow. 2 Medical the state of an organ that is not functioning normally. ● v. (**distresses**, **distressed**, **distressing**) 1 subject to distress. 2 mark (furniture etc.) to simulate the effects of age and wear. □ **in distress** in danger. □ **distressing** adj. **distressingly** adv.

distressed adj. 1 suffering from distress. 2 impoverished. 3 having simulated marks of age and wear.

distribute v. (**distributes**, **distributed**, **distributing**) 1 share out. 2 spread

throughout a region. **3** divide into parts.
4 supply (goods) to customers.

distribution *n.* **1** the action of
distributing. **2** the way in which something
is distributed. □ **distributional** *adj.*

distributive *adj.* relating to distribution.
[*Say* dis TRIBUTE iv]

distributor *n.* **1** a person or company that
distributes goods. **2** *Electricity* a device in an
internal combustion engine for passing the
current to each spark plug in turn.
[*Say* dis TRIBUTE ur]

district *n.* **1** a territory marked off for
special administrative purposes. **2** an area
which has common characteristics.

district attorney *n.* (in the US) the
prosecuting law officer of a district.
Abbreviation: **DA**.

distrust ● *n.* a lack of trust. ● *v.* have no
trust in. □ **distrustful** *adj.*

disturb *v.* **1** break the rest, calm, order, or
privacy of. **2** worry. **3** move from a settled
position. □ **disturbing** *adj.*
disturbingly *adv.*

disturbance *n.* **1** the interruption of a
settled condition. **2** a breakdown of
peaceful behaviour. **3** the disruption of
healthy function.

disturbed *adj.* **1** *in senses of* DISTURB.
2 emotionally or mentally abnormal.

disulphide *n.* a chemical with two atoms
of sulphur in each molecule.
[*Say* die SULFIDE]

disuse *n.* a disused state. □ **fall into
disuse** cease to be used.

disused *adj.* no longer used.

ditch ● *n.* (*pl.* **ditches**) a long narrow
excavated channel esp. for drainage. ● *v.*
(**ditches, ditched, ditching**) **1** make or
repair ditches. **2** *informal* **a** get rid of.
b abandon. **3** (of an aircraft) make a forced
landing on water. □ **ditcher** *n.*

dither ● *v.* be indecisive. ● *n. informal* a state
of agitation or indecisiveness.
□ **ditherer** *n.* **dithery** *adj.*

dithered *adj.* (of a computer image) shaded
by dithering.

dithering *n.* **1** *in senses of* DITHER *v.*
2 *Computing* a method of creating
continuous colour tones by gradually
spacing single-tone pixels.

Ditidaht *n.* (*pl.* **Ditidaht** or **Ditidahts**) a
member or the language of a Nuu-chah-
nulth people living on southern Vancouver
Island.

ditto *n.* (*pl.* **dittos**) the aforesaid, the same.

ditty *n.* (*pl.* **ditties**) a short simple song.

ditz *n.* (*pl.* **ditzes**) a ditzy person.

ditzy *adj.* (**ditzier, ditziest**) (also **ditsy**,

ditsier, ditsiest) *informal* silly or foolish.
□ **ditziness** *n.*

diuretic ● *adj.* causing increased output
of urine. ● *n.* a diuretic substance.
[*Say* die a RET ick]

diurnal *adj.* **1** of or during the day. **2** daily.
3 active during daylight. □ **diurnally** *adv.*
[*Say* die UR n'll]

diva *n.* (*pl.* **divas**) **1** a great or famous
woman singer. **2** a haughty, spoiled
woman. [*Say* DEEVA]

divalent *adj.* having a valence of two.
[*Say* die VAY lint]

divan *n.* **1** a backless sofa. **2** a bed
consisting of a base and mattress, usu. with
no board at either end. [*Say* dih VAN]

dive ● *v.* (**dives**; *past* **dived** or **dove**; *past
participle* **dived**; **diving**) **1** plunge headfirst
into water. **2** swim or go deeper under
water. **3** plunge steeply downwards
through the air. **4** move quickly downwards
or under cover. **5** fall deliberately so one's
opponent may be penalized. ● *n.* **1** an act
or instance of diving. **2** *informal* a seedy
nightclub etc. □ **dive in** *informal* help
oneself (to food).

dive-bomb *v.* **1** (of an aircraft) bomb (a
target) while diving towards it. **2** (of a bird
etc.) descend rapidly from a height to
attack something. □ **dive-bomber** *n.*

diver *n.* **1** a person who dives. **2** any diving
bird, esp. a loon.

diverge *v.* (**diverges, diverged,
diverging**) **1** proceed in a different
direction or different directions. **2** depart
from a set course. □ **divergence** *n.*
divergent *adj.*

diverse *adj.* unlike in nature or qualities.
□ **diversely** *adv.* [*Say* die VERSE]

diversify *v.* (**diversifies, diversified,
diversifying**) **1** make or become more
varied. **2** spread (resources etc.) over several
enterprises or products.
□ **diversification** *n.*
[*Say* die VERSE if eye]

diversion *n.* **1** the action of turning
something aside from its course.
2 something intended to distract
someone's attention. **3** an activity that is
done for pleasure. **4** an artificial
watercourse that diverts water.
□ **diversionary** *adj.*

diversity *n.* (*pl.* **diversities**) **1** the
condition of being diverse. **2** a variety.
3 ethnic, social, or gender variety in a
group, culture, or institution.
[*Say* die VERSA tee or div VERSA tee]

divert *v.* **1 a** turn aside from a direction or
course. **b** draw the attention of. **2** (often as
diverting *adj.*) entertain; amuse.

□**divertingly** adv. [Say die VERT or div VERT]

divest v. **1** sell off. **2** remove the clothes from. **3** deprive □**divestment** n. [Say die VEST]

divide ● v. (divides, divided, dividing) **1** separate into parts. **2** share out. **3** disagree or cause to disagree. **4** form a boundary between. **5** *Math* **a** find how many times (a number) contains another number. **b** (of a number) be susceptible of division without a remainder. ● n. **1** a **a** dividing line. **b** a separation. **2** a line of high land that separates two river systems.

dividend n. **1** a **a** sum of money to be divided among a number of persons. **b** an individual's share of this. **2** *Math* a number to be divided by a divisor. **3** a benefit from any action. [Say DIVVA dend]

divider n. anything which divides a whole into sections.

divination n. the act of predicting the future, esp. by supernatural means. [Say divva NATION]

divine ● adj. (diviner, divinest) **1** a having to do with God or a god. **b** sacred. **2** excellent. ● v. (divines, divined, divining) **1** discover by guesswork, intuition, etc. **2** foresee. **3** practise divination. **4** discover water by dowsing. ● n. **1** a cleric. **2** (the Divine) providence or God. □**divinely** adv. **diviner** n.

divinity n. (pl. divinities) **1** the state or quality of being a god. **2 a** a god. **b** (as the Divinity) God. **3** the study of religion.

divisible adj. **1** capable of being divided. **2** (foll. by by) *Math* containing (a number) a number of times without a remainder. [Say dih VIZZA bull]

division n. **1** the action of separating or being separated into parts. **2** *Math* the process of dividing one number by another. **3** disagreement or discord. **4** one of two or more parts into which a thing is divided. **5** a major unit of administration or organization. **6** a grouping of teams or athletes within a league. **7** a district defined for administrative purposes. □**divisional** adj.

Divisional Court n. Cdn (in Ontario) a court consisting of tribunals of three judges, which hears appeals from lower provincial courts and provincial administrative tribunals.

division sign n. the sign (÷), placed between two numbers to indicate that the one preceding the sign is to be divided by the one following it.

divisive adj. causing disagreement. □**divisively** adv. **divisiveness** n.

[Say dih VISS iv or dih VICE iv or dih VIZZ iv]

divisor n. a number by which another is to be divided. [Say dih VIZE ur]

divorce ● n. **1** the legal dissolution of a marriage. **2** a severance. ● v. (divorces, divorced, divorcing) **1** separate (from) by divorce. **2** detach.

divorcee n. a divorced person [Say dih vor SAY or dih vor SEE]

divulge v. (divulges, divulged, divulging) reveal (a secret etc.). [Say die VULGE or dih VULGE]

divvy v. informal (divvies, divvied, divvying) divide.

Diwali n. a major Hindu festival with lights, held in October or November. [Say dee WOLLY]

Dixieland n. a kind of jazz with a strong two-beat rhythm.

DIY abbr. do-it-yourself. □**DIYer** n.

dizzy ● adj. (dizzier, dizziest) **1 a** giddy, unsteady. **b** feeling confused. **c** informal scatterbrained. **2** causing giddiness. ● v. (dizzies, dizzied, dizzying) make dizzy. □**dizzily** adv. **dizziness** n. **dizzying** adj. **dizzyingly** adv.

DJ ● n. (pl. DJs) a disc jockey. ● v. (DJs, DJed, DJing) act as a disc jockey.

DNA abbr. (pl. DNAs) deoxyribonucleic acid, a substance carrying genetic information and found in nearly all living cell nuclei.

do¹ ● v. (does; past did; past participle done; doing) **1** perform, carry out. **2** produce, make. **3** bestow, grant; have a specified effect on. **4** act. **5** work at. **6** suffice. **7** deal with. **8 a** traverse (a certain distance). **b** travel at a specified speed. **9** informal act like. **10** informal finish. **11** cook. **12** be in progress **13** informal visit. **14** informal **a** (often as **done** adj.) exhaust. **b** beat up. **c** ruin. **15** slang take (a drug). ● aux. v. **1** used before a verb in questions and negative statements. **2** ellipt. or in place of verb or verb and object. **3** used for emphasis or to give commands. ● n. (pl. dos or do's) **1** informal an elaborate event or operation. **2** informal a hairdo. □**do away with** informal **1** abolish. **2** kill. **do in** slang **a** kill. **b** ruin. **2** informal exhaust, tire out. **do a person out of** informal swindle out of. **do up 1** fasten, secure. **2** informal **a** refurbish, renovate. **b** adorn, dress up.

do² n. (pl. dos) Music **1** (in tonic sol-fa) the first and eighth note of a major scale. **2** the note C in the fixed-do system. [Rhymes with GO]

DOA abbr. dead on arrival.

doable adj. able to be done. [Say DOO a bull]

D.O.B. *abbr.* date of birth.

Doberman *n.* (also **Doberman pinscher**) a breed of large dog with powerful jaws.
[*Say* DOBER m'n (PIN sher)]

doc *n. informal* **1** doctor. **2** buddy, fellow. **3** documentary. **4** *Computing* document.

docile *adj.* quiet and easy to control. □ **docilely** *adv.* **docility** *n.* [*Say* DOSS ile, *or* DOE sile, doss ILLA tee]

dock¹ ● *n.* **1 a** a structure extending out from a shore, either floating or on piles, to which boats are tied. **b** a ship's berth. **2** an artificially enclosed body of water for the loading, unloading, and repair of ships. **3** (in *pl.*) a range of docks with wharves and offices. **4** a platform for loading and unloading trucks etc. **5** = DRY DOCK. ● *v.* **1** bring or come into a dock. **2 a** join (spacecraft) together in space. **b** (of spacecraft) be joined.

dock² *n.* the enclosure for the accused in a criminal court. □ **in the dock** on trial.

dock³ *n.* a plant with a spike of many small, green flowers.

dock⁴ ● *v.* **1** cut short an animal's tail. **2** deduct a part from wages, supplies, etc. ● *n.* the solid bony part of an animal's tail.

docket *n.* **1** a list of causes for trial. **2** *Business* a document that shows what is in a package, which goods have been delivered, etc.

dockside *n.* the area immediately adjacent to a dock.

dockyard *n.* an area with docks and equipment for building and repairing ships.

doctor ● *n.* **1 a** a qualified practitioner of medicine. **b** (esp. as an honorific) a qualified dentist, veterinarian, optometrist, or chiropractor. **2** a person who holds a doctorate. **3** *informal* a person who carries out repairs. ● *v. informal* **1 a** treat medically. **b** (esp. as **doctoring** *n.*) practise as a physician. **2** castrate or spay. **3** mend. **4** tamper with.

doctoral *adj.* of or relating to a doctorate.

doctorate *n.* the highest university degree in any faculty.

Doctor of Philosophy *n.* **1** a doctorate. **2** a person holding such a degree. Abbreviation: **Ph.D.**

doctrinaire *adj.* applying theory without regard to practical considerations.
[*Say* dock trin AIR]

doctrinal *adj.* relating to a doctrine or doctrines. □ **doctrinally** *adv.*
[*Say* dock TRINE ul *or* DOCK trin'll]

doctrine *n.* a principle or principles of religious or political etc. belief.
[*Say* DOCK trin]

docudrama *n.* a dramatized TV film based on real events.
[*Say* DOCK you drama]

document ● *n.* **1** a piece of written or printed matter that provides information or evidence. **2** *Computing* a file. ● *v.* **1** prove with evidence. **2** record in a document. **3** provide with citations or references.

documentarian *n.* (also **documentarist**) someone who makes documentaries.

documentary ● *n.* (*pl.* **documentaries**) a film or broadcast program based on real events, intended primarily to record or inform. ● *adj.* **1** consisting of documents. **2** providing a factual record or report.

documentation *n.* **1** documents produced as evidence of something. **2** the written specification and instructions accompanying a computer program.

dodder *v.* tremble or totter, esp. from age. □ **dodderer** *n.* **doddering** *adj.* **doddery** *adj.*

dodge ● *v.* (**dodges, dodged, dodging**) **1** (often foll. by *about, around*) move quickly to elude a pursuer, blow, etc. **2 a** evade by cunning. **b** elude by a sideways movement. ● *n.* **1** a quick movement to avoid something. **2** a clever trick.

dodger *n.* a person who dishonestly avoids doing something.

dodo *n.* (*pl.* **dodos** or **dodoes**) an extinct large flightless bird native to Mauritius. [*Say* DOE doe]

doe *n.* a female deer, rabbit, etc.

doe-eyed *adj.* having large gentle dark eyes.

doer *n.* **1** a person who does something. **2** a person who acts rather than merely talking. [*Say* DOO ur]

does *3rd singular present of* DO¹.

doesn't *contr.* does not.

doff *v. literary* take off (one's hat).

dog ● *n.* **1** a four-legged flesh-eating animal, often kept as a pet or used for work. **2** the male of any of these animals. **3** *informal* **a** a despicable person. **b** a person of a specified kind. **4** a mechanical device for gripping. **5** *slang* something of poor quality. **6** = HOT DOG *n.* 1. ● *v.* (**dogs, dogged, dogging**) follow closely and persistently. □ **dog in the manger** a person who prevents others from using something, although that person has no use for it. **dog's breakfast** *informal* a mess. **a dog's life** a miserable existence.

dog collar *n.* **1** a collar for a dog. **2** *informal* a stiff upright white collar fastening at the

back, worn by some Christian clergy. **3** a
jewelled band worn around the neck.

dog days *pl. n.* the hottest period of the
year.

dog-eared *adj.* (of a book) with the corners
worn by use.

dog-eat-dog *adj. informal* ruthlessly
competitive.

dogfight *n.* **1** a fight between dogs. **2** a
close combat between fighter aircraft. **3** a
violent and confused fight.

dogfish *n.* (*pl.* **dogfish** or **dogfishes**) a
small shark with a long tail.

dogged *adj.* not giving up easily.
□ **doggedly** *adv.* **doggedness** *n.*
[*Say* DOG id]

doggerel *n.* badly written or ridiculous
poetry. [*Say* DOGGER ul]

doggone *adj. & adv. slang* damned.

doggy ● *adj.* **1** of or like a dog. **2** devoted to
dogs. ● *n.* (also **doggie**) (*pl.* **doggies**) a pet
name for a dog.

doggy bag *n.* a bag for putting leftovers
in to take home.

doghouse *n.* a shelter for a dog. □ **in the
doghouse** *informal* in disgrace.

dogleg ● *n.* a sharp bend like that in a
dog's hind leg. ● *adj.* (also **doglegged**)
bent sharply. ● *v.* (**doglegs**, **doglegged**,
doglegging) bend sharply.

dogma *n.* a belief or set of beliefs held by
an authority, intended to be accepted
without argument.

dogmatic *adj.* **1** firm in one's beliefs
without regard for evidence or other
opinions. **2** relating to dogma.
□ **dogmatically** *adv.* **dogmatism** *n.*
[*Say* dog MAT ick]

do-gooder *n.* a person who zealously tries
to help others. □ **do-good** *adj.* **do-
goodery** *n.* **do-gooding** *n. & adj.*

dog-paddle ● *n.* an elementary
swimming stroke with short quick
movements of the arms and legs beneath
the body. ● *v.* (**dog-paddles**, **dog-
paddled**, **dog-paddling**) swim using
this stroke.

Dogrib *n.* (*pl.* **Dogrib** or **Dogribs**) a
member or the language of a Dene
Aboriginal people living along the north
shore of Great Slave Lake. □ **Dogrib** *adj.*

dog salmon *n.* a salmon of the
N American Pacific coast.

dogsled ● *n.* a sled designed to be pulled
by dogs. ● *v.* (**dogsleds**, **dogsledded**,
dogsledding) travel by dogsled.
□ **dogsledding** *n.*

dog-tired *adj.* utterly exhausted.

dogwood *n.* a shrub or small tree, esp.
bearing a four-petalled white flower.

doh *n.* = DO².

doily *n.* (*pl.* **doilies**) a small ornamental
mat of paper, lace, etc.

doing *n.* **1** an action; the performance of a
deed. **2** activity, effort.

do-it-yourself *adj.* done or to be done by
an amateur at home. □ **do-it-
yourselfer** *n.*

doldrums *pl. n.* (usu. as **the doldrums**)
boredom, sluggishness, or depression.
[*Say* DOLE drums *or* DOLL drums]

dole ● *n.* (usu. as **the dole**) *informal*
benefits that can be claimed by the
unemployed from the government. ● *v.*
(**doles**, **doled**, **doling**) (usu. foll. by *out*)
deal out, distribute.

doleful *adj.* **1** mournful, sad. **2** dreary.
□ **dolefully** *adv.* **dolefulness** *n.*

doll ● *n.* **1** a usu. small model of a human
figure. **2** *informal* an attractive or kind
person. ● *v.* (foll. by *up*) dress up smartly.

dollar *n.* the chief monetary unit of
Canada, the US, Australia, and certain
other countries.

dollhouse *n.* (also **doll's house**) **1** a
miniature toy house for dolls. **2** a very
small house.

dollop ● *n.* **1** a shapeless lump of
something soft, esp. food. **2** something
added as if in dollops. ● *v.* (**dollops**,
dolloped, **dolloping**) serve out in large
shapeless quantities.

dolly *n.* (*pl.* **dollies**) **1** a child's name for a
doll. **2** a small four-wheeled cart for
moving appliances, boxes, etc. **3** a movable
platform for a camera.

Dolly Varden *n.* (*pl.* **Dolly Varden** or
Dolly Vardens) a brightly spotted char of
western N America.

dolomite *n.* a mineral or rock of calcium
magnesium carbonate. □ **dolomitic** *adj.*
[*Say* DOLLA mite *or* DOLA mite,
dolla MIT ick *or* dola MIT ick]

dolphin *n.* a porpoise-like sea mammal
with a slender beak-like snout.

dolt *n.* a stupid person. □ **doltish** *adj.*

-dom *suffix* forming nouns denoting a
condition, place, or class of people.

domain *n.* **1** an area under one rule. **2** a
sphere of control. **3** *Math* the set of possible
values of an independent variable. **4** the
parts of an email address following the @
symbol.

dome ● *n.* **1** a rounded vault as a roof. **2** a
stadium with a domed roof. **3** any natural
raised rounded shape. ● *v.* (**domes**,
domed, **doming**) (usu. as **domed** *adj.*)
cover with or shape as a dome.

domestic ● *adj.* **1** of the home or family
affairs. **2** of or within one's own country.

3 kept by human beings. **4** fond of home life. ● *n.* a household servant. □ **domestically** *adv.*

domesticate *v.* (**domesticates, domesticated, domesticating**) **1** tame. **2** naturalize (a plant etc.). □ **domestication** *n.*

domesticated *adj.* **1** (of an animal or plant) kept by humans for work, food, or companionship. **2** (of a person) skilled at household tasks.

domesticity *n.* home or family life. [*Say* doe mess TISSA tee *or* domma STISSA tee]

domicile *formal* ● *n.* a dwelling place. ● *v.* (**domiciles, domiciled, domiciling**) (usu. as **domiciled** *adj.*) establish or settle in a place. [*Say* DOMMA sile]

dominant *adj.* **1** most important, powerful, influential, or numerous. **2** (of a gene) appearing in offspring even if a contrary gene is also inherited. **3** based on or pertaining to the fifth note of the diatonic scale of any key. □ **dominance** *n.* **dominant** *n.* **dominantly** *adv.*

dominate *v.* (**dominates, dominated, dominating**) **1** have a commanding influence on or position over. **2** be the most influential factor in. □ **dominating** *adj.* **domination** *n.* **dominator** *n.*

domineering *adj.* trying to control other people without considering their wishes.

Dominican[1] *adj.* relating to the Order of Friars Preaching, or a corresponding order of nuns. □ **Dominican** *n.* [*Say* duh MINNA k'n]

Dominican[2] *n.* **1** a person from the island of Dominica in the W Indies. **2** a person from the Dominican Republic in the Caribbean. □ **Dominican** *adj.* [*Say* duh MINNA k'n]

dominion *n.* **1** sovereign authority; control. **2** the territory of a sovereign or government. **3** *hist.* (**the Dominion**) *informal* Canada.

Dominion Day *n. hist.* = CANADA DAY.

domino *n.* (*pl.* **dominoes**) **1** any of 28 small oblong tiles, marked with 0–6 dots on each half. **2** (in *pl.*, usu. treated as *sing.*) a game played with these.

domino effect *n.* the effect of one event triggering a succession of other events.

don[1] *n.* **1** (**Don**) a Spanish title prefixed to a man's first name. **2** an Italian title of respectful address. **3** *Cdn* a senior person in a university residence. **4** a high-ranking member of the Mafia.

don[2] *v.* (**dons, donned, donning**) put on (clothing).

donair *n.* spiced lamb cooked on a spit, served in slices in pita bread. [*Say* doe NAIR]

donate *v.* (**donates, donated, donating**) **1** give (money etc.) voluntarily to a fund. **2** allow (blood or a body organ) to be removed to help somebody who needs it.

donation *n.* **1** the act of donating. **2** something donated.

done ● *v. past participle of* DO[1]. ● *adj.* **1** finished, completed. **2** *informal* socially acceptable. **3 a** (often with *in*) *informal* tired out. **b** (often with *up*) made more attractive. **4** (of food) cooked sufficiently. □ **done for** *informal* **1** in serious trouble. **2** finished, destroyed. **have done with** have finished dealing with.

Don Juan *n.* a man with a reputation for seducing women. [*Say* don WON (WON rhymes with DON)]

donkey *n.* (*pl.* **donkeys**) **1** a domesticated hoofed mammal of the horse family with long ears and a braying call. **2** *informal* a stupid person.

donnybrook *n.* a scene of uproar.

donor *n.* **1** a person who gives or donates something. **2** a person who provides blood for a transfusion, an organ or tissue for transplant, etc.

don't *contr.* do not.

donut *n.* = DOUGHNUT.

doodad *n.* a gadget or ornament not readily nameable.

doodle ● *v.* (**doodles, doodled, doodling**) **1** draw absent-mindedly. **2** waste time. ● *n.* a figure drawn absent-mindedly. □ **doodler** *n.* **doodling** *adj.*

doo-doo *n. slang* **1** excrement. **2** serious trouble.

doofus *n.* (*pl.* **doofuses**) an inept person.

doohickey *n.* (*pl.* **doohickeys**) *informal* an unspecified object or mechanical device.

doom ● *n.* **1** a grim destiny. **2** impending death. ● *v.* (usu. foll. by *to*) condemn to some fate. □ **doomed** *adj.*

doomsayer *n.* a person who predicts disaster. □ **doomsaying** *n.*

doomsday *n.* **1** (in some beliefs) the day at the end of the world, when humankind will be judged. **2** any day of final judgment or dissolution. **3** (also as an *adj.*) a projected time of destruction of the world.

doomy *adj.* **1** suggesting doom. **2** ominous.

door *n.* **1** a barrier for closing and opening an entrance. **2 a** an entrance or exit. **b** a means of access. **c** (**the door**) the entrance to a theatre, club, etc. at which admission must be paid or tickets shown. □ **lay something at a person's door** regard someone as responsible. **open the door**

to create an opportunity for. **out of doors** in or into the open air.

do-or-die adj. undeterred by any danger or difficulty.

doorknob n. a handle which is turned to open or close a door.

doorman n. (pl. **doormen**) an attendant at the entrance to a hotel etc.

doormat n. **1** a mat at an entrance to a building for wiping mud etc. from the shoes. **2** a submissive person.

doornail n. □ **dead as a doornail** completely or unmistakably dead.

doorpost n. (also **door jamb**) each of the uprights of a door frame.

door prize n. something awarded as a prize at a gathering, usu. through a draw.

doorstep n. a step leading up to the outer door of a house. □ **on one's doorstep** very close.

doorstop n. **1** an object placed to keep a door open. **2** a device fixed to prevent a door from opening too widely.

door-to-door ● adj. **1** (of a salesperson) covering each house on a street, in an area, etc. **2** (of journeys, deliveries, etc.) direct. ● adv. (**door to door**) calling at each house in turn.

doorway n. **1** an opening into a building or a room. **2** a means of approach or access.

doozy n. (pl. **doozies**) (also **doozer**) slang something remarkable.

dope ● n. **1 a** slang a narcotic drug, esp. marijuana. **b** a drug taken or given to affect athletic performance etc. **2** slang a stupid person. **3** slang essential facts about a subject. **4** a thick substance used as a lubricant or repellent. ● v. (**dopes, doped, doping**) **1 a** administer drugs to (an athlete, horse, etc.) esp. to improve performance. **b** informal take addictive drugs. **2** informal treat (food or drink) with drugs. **3** informal (foll. by out) figure out. □ **doped up** slang heavily under the influence of drugs. □ **doper** n. **doping** n.

dopey adj. (**dopier, dopiest**) informal **1** stupid. **2 a** half asleep. **b** stupefied by a drug.

Doppler effect n. a change in the frequency of sound, light, etc. as the source and observer move toward or away from each other.

doré n. (pl. **doré** or **dorés**) Cdn the walleye. [Say dor AY]

dork n. slang a socially awkward, often stupid person. □ **dorky** adj. (**dorkier, dorkiest**)

dorm n. informal a dormitory.

dormant adj. **1 a** lying inactive as in sleep. **b** Biology alive but with development

suspended. **2** temporarily inactive. □ **dormancy** n.

dormer n. an upright window in a sloping roof.

dormitory n. (pl. **dormitories**) **1** a university or college residence. **2** a large room containing beds. [Say DORMA tory]

dormouse n. (pl. **dormice**) a small rodent with a long bushy tail.

dorsal adj. Anatomy, Zoology, & Botany of, on, or near the back. □ **dorsally** adv. [Say DOR s'll]

Dorset n. a prehistoric Arctic culture displaced by the Inuit. [Say DOR sit]

dory[1] n. (pl. **dories**) a marine food fish with a flat head.

dory[2] n. (pl. **dories**) a small flat-bottomed fishing boat with high sides.

doryman n. (pl. **dorymen**) Cdn a person who fishes from a dory.

dosage n. the size or frequency of a dose of medicine etc.

dose ● n. **1** an amount of a medicine or drug taken at one time. **2** a quantity of something administered. **3** the amount of radiation received at one time. ● v. (**doses, dosed, dosing**) **1** treat with doses of medicine. **2** divide into, or administer in, doses.

dossier n. a collection of documents about a person or subject. [Say DOSSY ay]

dot ● n. **1 a** a small spot. **b** a period, esp. in an email or web address. **2** the shorter signal of the two used in Morse code. **3** a tiny or apparently tiny object. ● v. (**dots, dotted, dotting**) **1** mark with a dot or dots. **2** occur singly throughout (an area) or over (a surface). □ **on the dot** exactly on time.

dot-com n. a company or website that conducts business on the Internet. □ **dot-commer** n.

dote v. (**dotes, doted, doting**) (foll. by on, upon) be excessively fond of. □ **doting** adj. **dotingly** adv.

dotted line n. a line of dots or dashes on a document. □ **sign on the dotted line** agree formally.

dotty adj. (**dottier, dottiest**) informal **1** confused, esp. due to old age. **2** absurd. **3** (foll. by about, over) infatuated with. □ **dottiness** n.

double ● adj. **1** consisting of two equal or identical parts. **2** twice as much or many. **3** having twice the usual amount. **4** designed or suitable for two people. **5** having some essential part double. ● adv. **1** at or to twice the amount. **2** two at once. ● n. **1** a double quantity or thing. **2** a person or thing looking exactly like another. **3** (in *pl.*) *Sport* a game between two pairs of players. **4** a stand-in for a film actor. **5** *Baseball* a successful hit which allows a player to get to second base safely. ● *v.* (**doubles, doubled, doubling**) **1** make or become double. **2** fold or bend over on itself. **3** (usu. foll. by as) function in an additional capacity. **4** (foll. by *up*) bend or curl up. □ **on** (or **at**) **the double** hurrying. **bent double** folded, stooping. **double back** take a new direction opposite to the previous one. □ **doubleness** *n.*

double agent *n.* a person who pretends to spy for one country while actually working for another one.

double-barrelled *adj.* **1** (of a gun) having two barrels. **2** having two parts.

double bass *n.* the largest and lowest-pitched instrument of the violin family.

double bill *n.* two films, plays, etc. presented to an audience one after the other.

double-blind *adj.* designating a test in which neither the tester nor the subject knows of identities or other factors that might lead to bias.

double-book *v.* accept two reservations, appointments, etc. for the same time.

double-breasted *adj.* (of a coat etc.) having a large overlap of material at the front and two rows of buttons.

double-check *v.* verify twice.

double-click *v. Computing* **1** press and release the button of a mouse twice in quick succession. **2** click on (an icon etc.) in this way.

double-cross ● *v.* (**double-crosses, double-crossed, double-crossing**) deceive or betray. ● *n.* (*pl.* **double-crosses**) an act of doing this.

double date ● *n.* a date on which two couples go together. ● *v.* (**double dates, double dated, double dating**) go on a double date.

double-dealing ● *n.* deceit. ● *adj.* deceitful.

double-decker *n.* **1** a bus having an upper and lower deck. **2** *informal* anything consisting of two layers.

double-dipping *n.* the practice of receiving two incomes, e.g. a pension from a former job and a salary from a current one.

double-double *n.* esp. *Cdn* a cup of coffee with a double serving of both sugar and cream.

double-edged *adj.* **1** having two contradictory aspects. **2** (of a knife etc.) having two cutting edges.

double entendre *n.* a word or phrase open to two interpretations, one usu. indecent. [*Say* double on TONDRA]

double figures *pl. n.* the numbers from 10 to 99.

doubleheader *n.* two games etc. in succession, esp. on the same day.

double helix *n.* a pair of parallel helices with a common axis, esp. in the structure of DNA.

double negative *n.* a negative statement containing two negative elements, e.g. *didn't say nothing.*

doublespeak *n.* = DOUBLE-TALK *n.*

double standard *n.* a rule etc. applied more strictly to some people than to others.

doublet *n. hist.* a man's short close-fitting jacket. [*Say* DUB lit]

double take *n.* a delayed reaction to something, immediately following one's first reaction.

double-talk *n.* deliberately ambiguous or misleading language. □ **double-talking** *adj.*

double-team *v. Basketball etc.* block (an opposing player) with two players. □ **double-teaming** *n.*

doublethink *n.* the capacity to believe two entirely contradictory opinions.

double time *n.* twice the standard rate of pay.

double vision *n.* the simultaneous perception of two images of one object.

double whammy *n. informal* a twofold blow.

doubly *adv.* **1** more than usual. **2** in two ways.

doubt ● *n.* **1** a feeling of uncertainty. **2** an inclination to disbelieve. **3** an uncertain state of affairs. ● *v.* **1** feel uncertain about. **2** hesitate to trust. □ **beyond (a) doubt** certainly. **give (a person) the benefit of the doubt 1** assume innocence. **2** incline to a more favourable judgment. **no doubt** certainly. □ **doubter** *n.* **doubtless** *adv.*

doubtful *adj.* **1** feeling doubt. **2** causing doubt. **3** unreliable. □ **doubtfully** *adv.* **doubtfulness** *n.*

douche ● *n.* **1** a jet of liquid applied to part of the body for cleansing or medicinal purposes. **2** a device for producing such a jet. ● *v.* (**douches, douched, douching**) treat with or use a douche. □ **douching** *n.* [*Say* DOOSH]

dough *n.* **1 a** a thick mixture of flour, water, etc. for baking into bread etc. **b** any soft, pasty mass. **2** *slang* money.

doughnut *n.* **1** a small spongy cake of

sweetened and deep-fried dough. **2** any circular object with a hole in the middle.

doughty *adj.* (**doughtier, doughtiest**) fearless, valiant. [*Say* DOUTY]

doughy *adj.* (**doughier, doughiest**) **1** having the form or consistency of dough. **2** pale and sickly in colour. [*Say* DOE ee]

Douglas fir *n.* (also **Douglas pine** or **Douglas spruce**) a large conifer of western N America, with thick bark.

Doukhobor *n.* a member of an originally Russian Christian sect rejecting church liturgy and secular governments. [*Say* DOOKA bore]

dour *adj.* severe or sullenly obstinate in manner. □ **dourly** *adv.* **dourness** *n.* [*Can be rhymed either with* POWER *or with* POOR]

douse *v.* (**douses, doused, dousing**) **1** soak a person or thing in liquid. **2** extinguish. [*Rhymes with* MOUSE]

dove[1] *n.* **1** a bird with short legs, small head, and a large breast. **2** a gentle person. **3** someone advocating negotiation and conciliation.

dove[2] *past and past participle of* DIVE.

dovetail ● *n.* a wedge-shaped joint formed by interlocking pieces of wood. ● *v.* **1** join together by means of a dovetail. **2** fit together perfectly.

dowager *n.* **1** a widow with a title or property derived from her late husband. **2** *informal* a dignified elderly woman. [*Say* DOW a jer]

dowdy *adj.* (**dowdier, dowdiest**) unfashionable in a way that is not attractive. □ **dowdiness** *n.*

dowel ● *n.* a headless peg of wood, metal, or plastic for holding together components of a structure. ● *v.* (**dowels, dowelled, dowelling**) fasten with a dowel or dowels. □ **dowelled** *adj.* [*Rhymes with* TOWEL]

dowelling *n.* cylindrical rods for cutting into dowels. [*Rhymes with* TOWELLING]

dowitcher *n.* a N American wading bird with a long, straight bill. [*Say* DOW itch ur]

Dow Jones Average *n. proprietary* an index of the average level of share prices on the New York Stock Exchange at any time, based on the daily price of a selection of representative stocks.

down[1] ● *adv.* **1** in, into, or toward a lower place or level. **2** to or in a more southerly place. **3 a** in or into a weaker position. **b** (of a computer system) temporarily unavailable for use. **4** from an earlier to a later time. **5** to a finer consistency or smaller amount or size. **6** in writing. **7** paid; dealt with. **8** *Football* (of the ball) not in play. ● *prep.* **1** downwards along, through, or into. **2** from top to bottom of.

3 along. **4** at or in a lower part of. ● *adj.* **1** directed downwards. **2** depressed. ● *v. informal* **1** bring down. **2** defeat. **3** swallow quickly. ● *n.* **1** *Football* any of a fixed number of attempts (3 in Canadian football, 4 in American football) to advance the ball a total of 10 yards. **2** a reverse of fortune. □ **be down on** *informal* disapprove of. **be down to 1** be attributable to. **2** have used up everything except. **down for the count 1** (of a boxer) knocked unconscious. **2** completely defeated. **down in the dumps** depressed. **down on one's luck** *informal* temporarily unfortunate. **down the road** (or **line**) *informal* in the future. **down tools** *informal* cease work. **down to the wire** *informal* right up to the very last minute. **down with** *interj.* expressing strong disapproval of (a person or thing). **when you get** (or **come**) (**right**) **down to it** in the final analysis.

down[2] *n.* **1** small soft feathers or hairs. **2** a fluffy substance, e.g. thistledown.

down[3] *n.* **1** (usu. in *pl.*) an area of open rolling land. **2** (usu. **the Downs**) undulating chalk and limestone uplands esp. in S England. **3** (in *pl.*) often used in the names of racetracks.

down-and-dirty *adj. informal* highly competitive or unprincipled.

down-and-out ● *adj.* **1** penniless. **2 a** *Boxing* unable to resume the fight. **b** (of a team, business etc.) no longer successful. ● *n.* (also **down-and-outer**) a destitute person.

down-at-the-heels *adj.* **1 a** shabby. **b** dilapidated. **2** (**down-at-heel**) (of shoes) with the heels worn down.

downbeat ● *n. Music* an accented beat, usu. the first of the bar. ● *adj.* pessimistic; gloomy.

downcast *adj.* **1** looking downwards. **2** dejected.

downdraft *n.* a downward current of air.

downer *n. slang* **1** a depressant or tranquilizing drug. **2** something depressing.

downfall *n.* **1** a fall from prosperity or power. **2** a sudden rain.

downfield *adv.* in or towards the opponents' end of a football, soccer, etc. field.

downgrade ● *v.* (**downgrades, downgraded, downgrading**) reduce in rank, importance, or value. ● *n.* **1** an instance of downgrading. **2** a downward gradient.

downhearted *adj.* in low spirits.

downhill ● *adv.* in a descending direction. ● *adj.* **1** sloping down. **2** deteriorating. **3** designating or relating to skiing performed on a steep slope. ● *n. Skiing* a downhill race. □ **go downhill** *informal* decline, deteriorate. □ **downhiller** *n.*

down-home *adj.* unpretentious; unaffected.

down in the mouth *adj. informal* unhappy.

downlink ● *n.* a communications link for signals coming from a satellite to earth. ● *v.* provide with or send by a downlink.

download ● *v.* **1** copy (data) from one storage system or computer to another. **2** *Cdn* shift responsibilities from one level of government to a lower one. ● *n.* a transfer of data. □ **downloadable** *adj.*

down-market *adj. & adv. informal* relating to the less affluent sector of the market.

down payment *n.* a partial payment made at the time of purchase.

downplay *v.* minimize the importance of.

downpour *n.* a heavy fall of rain.

downrigger *n.* a trolling rig consisting of a cable attached underneath a boat to a fishing line.

downright ● *adv.* thoroughly. ● *adj.* **1** complete. **2** straightforward.

downriver *adv. & adj.* at or towards a point nearer the mouth of a river.

downscale ● *adj.* at the lower end of a scale. ● *v.* (**downscales, downscaled, downscaling**) reduce in size or scale.

downshift ● *v.* **1** change to a lower gear in a motor vehicle. **2** slow down; become less busy. ● *n.* a change to a lower gear.

downside *n. informal* the negative aspect of something.

downsize *v.* (**downsizes, downsized, downsizing**) **1** reduce in size. **2** fire (workers). □ **downsizing** *n.*

downspout *n.* a pipe to carry rainwater from an eavestrough to a drain or to ground level.

Down's syndrome *n.* (also **Down syndrome**) a congenital form of mental retardation due to a chromosome defect, causing a flattened facial profile, weak muscles, etc.

downstage *adj. & adv.* at or to the front of the stage.

downstairs ● *adv.* **1** down a flight of stairs. **2** to or on a lower floor. ● *adj.* situated downstairs. ● *n.* the main floor or basement of a house etc.

downstream ● *adv.* in the direction of the flow of a stream etc. ● *adj.* situated or occurring downstream.

downswing *n.* **1** a downward trend in economic conditions. **2** the downward swing of a golf club.

downtime *n.* **1** time during which a machine is unavailable for use. **2** time not spent working.

down-to-earth *adj.* practical; realistic.

downtown ● *adj.* being or located in the central part of a town or city. ● *n.* a downtown area. ● *adv.* in or into a downtown area. □ **downtowner** *n.*

downtrodden *adj.* oppressed; badly treated.

downturn *n.* a decline in economic or other activity.

down under (also **Down Under**) *informal* ● *adv.* in or to Australia or New Zealand. ● *n.* Australia or New Zealand.

downward ● *adv.* (also **downwards**) toward a lower place or level. ● *adj.* directed or moving downward. □ **downwardly** *adv.*

downwind *adv. & adj.* in the direction in which the wind is blowing.

downy *adj.* (**downier, downiest**) **1** of, like, or covered with down. **2** soft and fluffy.

dowry *n.* (*pl.* **dowries**) property or money brought by a bride to her husband at marriage. [*Say* DOW ree]

dowse[1] *v.* (**dowses, dowsed, dowsing**) search for underground water or minerals by holding a Y-shaped stick or rod which dips abruptly when over the right spot. □ **dowser** *n.* [*Rhymes with* PLOWS]

dowse[2] *v.* (**dowses, dowsed, dowsing**) = DOUSE. [*Rhymes with* HOUSE]

doyen *n.* the most senior or prominent male member of a group. [*Say* DOY en *or* doy EN]

doyenne *n.* the most senior or prominent female member of a group. [*Say* doy EN]

doz. *abbr.* dozen.

doze ● *v.* (**dozes, dozed, dozing**) sleep lightly. ● *n.* a short light sleep. □ **doze off** fall lightly asleep.

dozen *n.* (*pl.* **dozen** *or* **dozens**) **1** twelve. **2** *informal* about twelve. **3** (in *pl.*) *informal* very many. □ **by the dozen** in large quantities.

dozy *adj.* (**dozier, doziest**) **1** drowsy; tending to doze. **2** *Brit. & Cdn informal* slow-witted or lazy.

dpi *abbr. Computing* dots per inch.

Dr. *abbr.* **1** Doctor. **2** Drive.

drab ● *adj.* (**drabber, drabbest**) **1** of a dull brownish colour. **2** dreary, dull. ● *n.* fabric of a dull brownish colour. □ **drably** *adv.* **drabness** *n.*

drachma *n.* (*pl.* **drachmas**) **1** the former chief monetary unit of Greece. **2** an ancient Greek coin. [*Say* DRACKMA]

draconian *adj.* very harsh or severe. [*Say* druh CONEY in]

draft ● *n.* **1 a** a preliminary written version of a speech, book, etc. (also as an *adj.*). **b** a drawing of something to be constructed. **2** a current of air in a confined space. **3** a system of selection by which sports teams acquire the rights to new players (also as an *adj.*). **4** esp. *US* compulsory military service. **5** (also **draft beer**) beer drawn from a keg. **6** a single act of drinking. **7** a written order for payment of money by a bank. **8** the depth of water needed to float a ship. ● *v.* **1** prepare a draft of. **2 a** acquire the rights to. **b** *US* conscript for military service. ● *adj.* (of an animal) used for pulling a cart etc. □ **on draft** (of beer etc.) ready to be drawn from a keg. □ **draftee** *n.* **drafter** *n.*

draft dodger *n.* a person who evades compulsory military service, esp. in the US. □ **draft dodging** *n.*

draftsman *n.* (*pl.* **draftsmen**) **1** a person who makes detailed technical plans or drawings. **2** an artist skilled in drawing.

drafty *adj.* (**draftier**, **draftiest**) (of a room etc.) letting in sharp currents of air.

drag ● *v.* (**drags**, **dragged**, **dragging**) **1** pull along with effort or difficulty. **2** trail along the ground. **3** (of time) pass slowly or tediously. **4** use grapnels and nets to search the bottom of a river etc. **5** continue at tedious length. **6** *Computing* move (a window etc.) around the screen using a mouse. **7** draw on (a cigarette etc.). ● *n.* **1** the force resisting the motion of a body through a liquid or gas. **2** *informal* a boring thing. **3** *slang* women's clothes worn by a man. **4** *slang* a draw on a cigarette etc. **5** an obstruction to progress. **6** an apparatus for recovering drowned persons etc. from under water. **7** = DRAGNET 1. □ **drag one's feet** (or **heels**) be deliberately slow to act. **drag out** make something last an unnecessarily long time. **drag up** *informal* deliberately mention.

dragger *n.* a trawler. □ **draggerman** *n.* (*pl.* **draggermen**)

dragnet *n.* **1** a net drawn to trap fish or game. **2** a systematic hunt for criminals etc.

dragon *n.* **1** a mythical fire-breathing reptilian monster. **2** a fierce woman.

dragon boat *n.* a long wooden racing boat with dragon's features carved at its stern and prow.

dragonfly *n.* (*pl.* **dragonflies**) an insect with a long body and two unequal pairs of large wings.

dragoon ● *n.* (often **Dragoon**) a member of any of several cavalry (now armoured) regiments. ● *v.* force into doing something. [*Say* druh GOON]

drag queen *n.* *slang* a male transvestite.

drag race *n.* a race between cars starting from a standstill. □ **drag racer** *n.* **drag racing** *n.*

dragster *n.* a car modified for drag races.

drain ● *v.* **1** draw off liquid from. **2** flow or trickle away. **3** become dry as liquid flows away. **4** exhaust (a person or thing) of strength, resources, etc. **5** gradually disappear. **6** drink the contents of. ● *n.* **1** a channel or pipe for carrying off surplus liquid. **2** a constant outflow. □ **down the drain** *informal* lost, wasted.

drainage *n.* the process of draining.

drainage basin *n.* the area of land drained by a river and its tributaries.

drainer *n.* a device for draining.

drainpipe *n.* a pipe for carrying off water, sewage, etc., from a building.

drake *n.* a male duck.

drama *n.* **1** a play. **2 a** plays as a branch of literature. **b** the art of acting. **3** an exciting or emotional event. **4** dramatic quality. [*Say* DRAMMA *or* DROMMA]

dramatic *adj.* **1 a** of drama. **b** of acting. **2** sudden and exciting. **3** vividly striking. **4** excessively theatrical. □ **dramatically** *adv.* [*Say* druh MAT ick]

dramatics *pl. n.* (often treated as *sing.*) **1** the production and performance of plays. **2** exaggerated or showy behaviour. [*Say* druh MAT icks]

dramatist *n.* a writer of dramas. [*Say* DRAMMA tist]

dramatize *v.* (**dramatizes**, **dramatized**, **dramatizing**) **1** adapt as a dramatic work. **2** express or react to (something) in a dramatic way. □ **dramatization** *n.*

drank *past of* DRINK.

drape ● *v.* (**drapes**, **draped**, **draping**) **1** cover loosely or adorn with cloth etc. **2** place or hang casually. ● *n.* **1** a curtain. **2** the way in which something hangs.

drapery *n.* (*pl.* **draperies**) **1** clothing or hangings arranged in folds. **2** (often in *pl.*) a curtain or hanging.

drastic *adj.* having a strong or far-reaching effect. □ **drastically** *adv.*

drat *informal* ● *v.* (**drats**, **dratted**, **dratting**) curse ● *interj.* expressing anger or annoyance. □ **dratted** *adj.*

draught esp. *Brit.* = DRAFT *n.* 2, 5, 6, 8 & *adj.* [*Sounds like* DRAFT]

draughtsman *n.* (*pl.* **draughtsmen**) esp. *Brit.* = DRAFTSMAN. [*Sounds like* DRAFTSMAN]

draughty *adj.* (**draughtier**, **draughtiest**) esp. *Brit.* = DRAFTY. [*Sounds like* DRAFTY]

draw ● *v.* (**draws**; *past* **drew**; *past participle* **drawn**; **drawing**) **1** pull or drag toward or after one. **2** pull (a thing) up, over, or

across. **3** pull (curtains etc.) open or shut.
4 take (a person) aside. **5** attract. **6** trace.
7 produce (a picture or diagram) by making
lines and marks. **8** proceed, move, come.
9 (foll. by *at, on*) inhale smoke from. **10** take
out (a gun from a holster). **11** obtain.
12 deduce (a conclusion). **13 a** elicit, evoke.
b bring about, entail. **14** haul up (water)
from a well. **15** cause (blood) to flow.
16 (foll. by *on*) make a demand. **17** (of a
ship) require (a specified depth of water) to
float in. **18** *Curling* slide (a rock) so that it
stops in the target area without striking
another rock. ● *n.* **1** an act of drawing. **2** a
person or thing that attracts attention etc.
3 the random selection of lots for a prize.
4 a tied game. **5** a suck on a cigarette etc.
6 the act of removing a gun from its
holster. □ **draw back** withdraw from an
undertaking. **draw the line** set a limit.
draw off 1 drain away (liquid).
2 withdraw (troops). **draw out 1** remove;
pull out. **2** prolong. **3** elicit. **4** induce to
talk. **draw up 1** compose. **2** come to a
halt. **3** make (oneself) stand straight. **4** gain
on or overtake.

drawback *n.* a disadvantage.

drawbridge *n.* a bridge hinged at one end
so as to be raised.

drawdown *n.* **1** a lowering of the water
level in a lake, pond, etc. **2** a withdrawal of
oil from a reservoir. **3** an act of raising
money through loans. **4** a reduction of
troops.

drawer *n.* **1** a storage compartment sliding
in and out of a frame, table, etc. **2** (in *pl.*)
a *hist.* or *jocular* underpants. **b** *slang* pants.

drawing *n.* **1** a picture or diagram made
with a pencil, pen, etc., rather than paint.
2 the art of making such a picture.

drawing board *n.* a large flat board on
which paper is placed for drawing plans
etc. □ **back to the drawing board** back
to begin afresh.

drawing-room *n.* a room in a large
private house in which guests are received
and entertained.

drawl ● *v.* speak with drawn-out vowel
sounds. ● *n.* drawling speech.

drawn ● *v. past participle of* DRAW. ● *adj.*
looking strained from anxiety or pain.

drawn-out *adj.* lasting a very long time.

drawstring *n.* a string that can be pulled
to tighten an opening.

dread ● *v.* fear greatly. ● *n.* **1** great fear.
2 (in *pl.*) = DREADLOCKS. ● *adj.* dreaded.

dreaded *adj.* regarded with fear.

dreadful *adj.* **1** terrible. **2** troublesome.
□ **dreadfully** *adv.* **dreadfulness** *n.*

dreadlocks *pl. n.* a hairstyle in which the

hair is twisted into tight braids or ringlets.
□ **dreadlocked** *adj.*

dream ● *n.* **1** a series of pictures or
feelings occurring in the mind during
sleep. **2** a daydream or fantasy. **3** an
ambition. **4** a beautiful or ideal person or
thing. **5** a state of mind out of touch with
reality. ● *v.* (**dreams**; *past and past participle*
dreamt or **dreamed**; **dreaming**)
1 experience a dream. **2** imagine in or as if
in a dream. **3** be unrealistic. ● *adj.* ideal. □ **a
dream come true** an ideal or desired
situation or thing. **dream in colour** (or
Technicolour) *Cdn* be wildly unrealistic.
dream up imagine. **like a dream**
informal easily, effortlessly. □ **dreamer** *n.*
dreamless *adj.*

dreamboat *n. informal* a very attractive
person.

dream catcher *n.* a webbed hoop
believed by some woodland Aboriginal
groups to protect a person from bad
dreams.

dreamland *n.* **1** an ideal or imaginary
land. **2** sleep.

dreamlike *adj.* as if existing or happening
in a dream rather than in real life.

dreamscape *n.* a dreamed or dreamlike
scene.

dream team *n. slang* a team composed of
the top players in a given sport.

dreamy *adj.* (**dreamier, dreamiest**)
1 preoccupied with and distracted by
pleasant thoughts. **2** imaginative but not
realistic. **3** dreamlike; vague. **4** *informal* very
attractive. **5** *informal* delightful.
□ **dreamily** *adv.*

dreary *adj.* (**drearier, dreariest**) dull,
gloomy. □ **drearily** *adv.* **dreariness** *n.*

dreck *n. slang* garbage; worthless junk.

dredge[1] ● *v.* (**dredges, dredged,
dredging**) **1** mention something (usu.
unpleasant) that has been forgotten.
2 bring up or clear mud etc. from a river,
harbour, etc. ● *n.* an apparatus used to
scoop up mud or objects from a river or sea
floor.

dredge[2] *v.* (**dredges, dredged,
dredging**) coat (food) with flour, sugar,
etc.

dredger *n.* a boat designed for dredging.

dregs *pl. n.* **1** the last drops of a liquid,
together with any sediment. **2** the worst
and most useless parts. □ **drink to the
dregs** consume leaving nothing.

drench *v.* (**drenches, drenched,
drenching**) **1** wet thoroughly. **2** saturate.

dress ● *v.* (**dresses, dressed,
dressing**) **1 a** clothe. **b** put on one's
clothes. **2** decorate. **3** apply ointment, a

bandage, etc. to (a wound) **4 a** add a dressing to (a salad etc.). **b** clean and prepare (poultry etc.) for cooking or eating. ● *n.* (*pl.* **dresses**) **1** a one-piece woman's garment consisting of a bodice and skirt. **2** clothing of a specified kind. □ **dress down** *informal* **1** dress informally. **2** reprimand. **dress up 1** dress (oneself or another) in good clothes or a costume. **2** decorate.

dressage *n.* the training of a horse in obedience and deportment. [*Say* druh SAWZH]

dresser *n.* **1** a chest of drawers. **2** a sideboard with shelves above for plates. **3** a person who dresses in a specified way.

dressing *n.* **1** *in senses of* DRESS *v.* **2 a** a sauce for salads. **b** = STUFFING 2. **3 a** a bandage for a wound. **b** ointment etc. used to clean a wound.

dressing-down *n. informal* a severe reprimand.

dressing gown *n.* a loose usu. belted robe worn over nightwear.

dressing room *n.* a room where athletes or performers change into their uniforms or stage clothes.

dressing table *n.* a table with an upright mirror and usu. drawers underneath.

dressmaker *n.* a person who makes clothes professionally. □ **dressmaking** *n.*

dress rehearsal *n.* the final rehearsal of a play etc., with the performers in costume.

dress shirt *n.* a man's formal long-sleeved shirt.

dress-up *n.* the action of dressing up in costume.

dressy *adj.* (**dressier**, **dressiest**) **1** suitable for a formal occasion. **2** requiring formal dress or one's best clothes. **3** stylish.

drew *past of* DRAW.

dribble ● *v.* (**dribbles**, **dribbled**, **dribbling**) **1** let saliva flow from the mouth. **2** flow or let flow in drops or a trickle. **3** control or advance with a ball by bouncing or slight touches of the feet or stick. ● *n.* **1** the act of dribbling. **2** a small trickling stream. **3** a small amount. □ **dribbler** *n.* **dribbly** *adj.*

dribs and drabs *pl. n. informal* small scattered amounts.

dried *past and past participle of* DRY.

drier[1] *comparative of* DRY.

drier[2] = DRYER.

driest *superlative of* DRY.

drift ● *n.* **1** slow movement. **2** the intention of what is said. **3** a large mass of snow or sand blown by the wind. **4** deviation from an expected course. **5** = CONTINENTAL DRIFT. ● *v.* **1** be carried, esp. by a current of air or water. **2** move passively or aimlessly. **3** pile or be piled by the wind into drifts. **4** (of a current) carry. □ **drift off** fall asleep.

drifter *n.* **1** an aimless or rootless person. **2** a boat used for drift net fishing.

drift net *n.* a large net allowed to drift with the tide to catch herrings etc. □ **drift netter** *n.* **drift netting** *n.*

driftwood *n.* wood floating on, or driven ashore by, water.

drill ● *n.* **1** a tool or machine for boring holes. **2 a** training in military exercises. **b** instruction by means of repeated exercises. **3** *informal* a recognized procedure. **4** a machine used for making furrows, sowing, and covering seed. ● *v.* **1** make (a hole) with a drill. **2** esp. *Military* subject to discipline by drill. **3** impart (knowledge etc.) by repetition etc. **4** hit forcefully. □ **driller** *n.*

drily *adv.* = DRYLY.

drink ● *v.* (**drinks**; *past* **drank**; *past participle* **drunk**; **drinking**) **1** swallow a liquid. **2** take alcohol. **3** (of a plant etc.) absorb (moisture). ● *n.* **1** a liquid for drinking. **2** alcoholic liquor. **3** (**the drink**) *informal* a body of water. □ **drink in** listen to or watch closely or eagerly. **drink to** toast; wish success to. □ **drinkability** *n.* **drinkable** *adj.* **drinker** *n.*

drip ● *v.* (**drips**, **dripped**, **dripping**) **1** fall or let fall in drops. **2** be so wet as to shed drops. ● *n.* **1 a** the action or sound of dripping. **b** a drop of liquid. **2** *informal* an ineffective person. **3** *Medical* = DRIP-FEED *n.* □ **dripping with** full of or covered with.

drip-dry ● *v.* (**drip-dries**, **drip-dried**, **drip-drying**) (of fabric etc.) dry crease-free when hung up to drip. ● *adj.* able to be drip-dried.

drip-feed ● *v.* (**drip-feeds**, **drip-fed**, **drip-feeding**) supply fluid drop by drop into the veins. ● *n.* a device for doing this.

dripping *n.* (often in *pl.*) fat melted from roasted meat and used for cooking.

drippy *adj.* (**drippier**, **drippiest**) **1** tending to drip. **2** *informal* sloppily sentimental. **3** *informal* lacking character.

drive ● *v.* (**drives**; *past* **drove**; *past participle* **driven**; **driving**) **1** urge in some direction. **2** force. **3** operate, or carry in, a motor vehicle. **4** conclude forcibly. **5** set or keep (machinery) going. **6** propel forcefully. **7** float (timber) down a river etc. ● *n.* **1 a** journey in a motor vehicle. **2** motivation and energy. **3 a** a street. **b** = DRIVEWAY. **4** an organized effort to achieve a purpose. **5** the act or an instance of a puck, ball, etc. being driven forwards. **6** the transmission of

power to machinery, wheels, etc.
7 *Computing* a device for handling data on disks or tape. **8** an act of impelling along. **9** *Cdn* = LOG DRIVE. □ **drive at** mean. **drive out** oust; exorcise. □ **driveable** *adj.* (also **drivable**)

drive-by ● *adj.* (of a crime) carried out from a moving vehicle. ● *n.* (pl. **drive-bys**) a drive-by shooting.

drive-in ● *adj.* that can be visited without leaving one's car. ● *n.* a drive-in movie theatre, restaurant, etc.

drivel ● *n.* silly nonsense. ● *v.* (**drivels, drivelled, drivelling**) talk foolishly. □ **drivelling** *adj.* [*Say* DRIV'll]

driven ● *v.* past participle of DRIVE. ● *adj.* **1** (of snow) piled into smooth drifts by the wind. **2** urged on; motivated (by something specified). **3** showing compulsion in behaviour. □ **white** (or **pure**) **as driven snow** immaculately white or pure.

driver *n.* **1** a person who drives a vehicle. **2** *Golf* a club with a flat face and wooden head. **3** *Computing* a program that controls a device. **4** a person who herds an animal. □ **in the driver's seat** in charge. □ **driverless** *adj.*

driver's licence a licence permitting a person to drive a motor vehicle.

driveshaft *n.* a rotating shaft that transmits power esp. to the differential in a motor vehicle.

drive-through ● *adj.* designating a restaurant etc. where customers need not leave their cars. ● *n.* a place offering drive-through service.

drivetrain *n.* the system in a motor vehicle connecting the transmission to the axles.

driveway *n.* **1** a parking area leading to a garage or house. **2** a private lane.

driving *adj.* **1** moving rapidly. **2** energetic. **3** used when driving.

drizzle ● *n.* **1** very fine rain. **2** esp. *Cooking* a fine trickle. ● *v.* (**drizzles, drizzled, drizzling**) fall or sprinkle in fine drops. □ **drizzly** *adj.*

droll *adj.* provoking dry amusement. [*Rhymes with* ROLL]

drone ● *n.* **1** a male honeybee that does no work but mates with fertile females. **2** a continuous low noise. **3** a remote-controlled aircraft or missile. ● *v.* (**drones, droned, droning**) **1** make a deep humming sound. **2** speak in a boring tone.

drool ● *v.* **1** have saliva coming out of the mouth. **2** (often foll. by *over*) show infatuation. ● *n.* saliva.

droop ● *v.* **1** hang or sag, esp. from weariness. **2** lose heart. ● *n.* an act of drooping. □ **drooping** *adj.* **droopy** *adj.*

drop ● *v.* (**drops, dropped, dropping**) **1** fall or cause to fall. **2** make or become lower, weaker, or less. **3** abandon. **4** place or leave (something) without ceremony. **5** lose. **6** mention casually. **7** collapse. ● *n.* **1** a small round or pear-shaped portion of liquid. **2** an instance of falling or dropping. **3** a small drink. **4** an abrupt fall or slope. **5** *informal* a delivery. **6** a lozenge. □ **at the drop of a hat** given the slightest excuse. **drop the ball** make a mess of something. **drop a brick** *informal* make an embarrassing remark. **drop dead** die suddenly. **drop in** (or **by**) *informal* call casually as a visitor. **drop off** *informal* fall asleep. **drop out** *informal* cease to participate. □ **dropped** *adj.*

drop cloth *n.* a sheet of cloth used to protect surfaces.

drop-dead *adj. slang* stunningly good-looking.

drop-in ● *adj.* (of a place) at which one can turn up without prior appointment. ● *n.* *informal* a place or function at which one can turn up informally.

drop kick ● *n.* *Football etc.* a kick made by dropping the ball and kicking it on the bounce. ● *v.* **1** kick (a ball etc.) by means of a drop kick. **2** make a drop kick.

droplet *n.* a tiny drop of liquid.

drop-off *n.* **1 a** an act of delivering something. **b** a place where this can be done. **2** a decline. **3** a cliff.

dropout *n. informal* a person who has dropped out of society or school.

dropper *n.* **1** a device for administering liquid in drops. **2** a person or thing that drops.

droppings *pl. n.* animal or bird dung.

dropsy *n.* (pl. **dropsies**) = EDEMA.

dross *n.* **1** something worthless. **2** waste material. [*Rhymes with* CROSS]

drought *n.* **1** a continuous absence of rain. **2** a prolonged lack of something. [*Rhymes with* SHOUT]

drove[1] *past of* DRIVE.

drove[2] *n.* **1** a large number of people doing the same thing. **2** a flock of animals being driven.

drover *n.* a person who drives herds to market.

drown *v.* **1** die or kill by submersion in liquid. **2** submerge. **3** deaden (grief etc.) with drink. **4** (often foll. by *out*) make (a sound) inaudible by being louder.

drowse *v.* (**drowses, drowsed, drowsing**) be half asleep. [*Rhymes with* PLOWS]

drowsy *adj.* (**drowsier, drowsiest**) sleepy. □ **drowsily** *adv.* **drowsiness** *n.*

drub v. (**drubs**, **drubbed**, **drubbing**)
1 beat someone repeatedly. **2** defeat
thoroughly. **3** criticize harshly.
□**drubbing** n.

drudge n. a person who does hard, dull, or
menial work. □**drudgery** n.

drug ● n. **1** a medicinal substance. **2** a
narcotic, hallucinogen, or stimulant. ● v.
(**drugs**, **drugged**, **drugging**) **1** add a
drug to. **2** administer a drug to.

druggie n. *informal* a drug addict.

druggist n. a pharmacist.

druggy adj. (**druggier**, **druggiest**) *informal*
of or associated with narcotic drugs.

drugstore n. a pharmacy that also sells
cosmetics and other items.

Druid n. a priest in the ancient Celtic
religion. □**Druidic** adj. **Druidical** adj.
Druidism n. [*Say* DROO id, droo ID ick,
droo ID ick'll, DROO id ism]

drum ● n. **1 a** a percussion instrument
sounded by striking a skin stretched across
a hollow frame. **b** a sound made by a drum.
2 a cylinder or barrel. **3** the membrane of
the middle ear. ● v. (**drums**, **drummed**,
drumming) **1** play on a drum. **2** beat, tap,
or thump. **3** make a loud, rhythmic noise.
□**drum into** drive (a lesson) into (a
person) by persistence. **drum up** summon.
□**drummer** n.

drum brake n. a brake in which shoes on
a vehicle press against the drum on a
wheel.

drum dance n. a dance, accompanied by
drumming, combining traditional Inuit
dancing with Scottish and French-
Canadian jigs and reels.

drumlin n. a long low oval mound formed
by glacier action.

drum roll n. a rapid succession of notes on
a drum.

drumstick n. **1** a stick used for beating a
drum. **2** the lower joint of the leg of a
cooked chicken etc.

drunk ● adj. **1** rendered incapable by
alcohol. **2** (often foll. by *with*) overcome with
joy, success, etc. ● n. a habitually drunk
person.

drunkard n. a person who is drunk, esp.
habitually. [*Say* DRUNK erd]

drunken adj. **1** = DRUNK. **2** caused by or
exhibiting excessive or habitual
consumption of alcohol. □**drunkenly** adv.
drunkenness n.

drunk tank n. *slang* a prison cell for
detaining drunkards.

druthers n. *informal* preference. [*Rhymes
with* OTHERS]

dry ● adj. (**drier**; **driest**) **1** lacking
moisture. **2** not sweet. **3** serious and

boring. **4** subtle and ironic. **5 a** prohibiting
the sale of alcoholic drink. **b** sober. **6** solid,
not liquid. **7** (of a cow etc.) not yielding
milk. ● v. (**dries**, **dried**, **drying**) **1** make
or become dry. **2** (usu. as **dried** adj.)
preserve (food etc.) by removing the
moisture. ● n. (*pl.* **dries**) dry ginger ale.
□**dry out** become fully dry or sober. **dry
up 1** make or become dry. **2** (of moisture)
disappear. **3** disappear or cease. □**dryly** adv.
dryness n.

dry clean v. clean (clothes etc.) with
organic solvents without using water.
□**dry cleaner** n. **dry cleaning** n.

dry dock n. an enclosure for repairing of
ships, from which water can be removed.

dryer n. a machine or apparatus for drying
the hair, laundry, etc.

dry fly n. an artificial fishing fly which
floats on the water.

dry ice n. **1** solid carbon dioxide. **2** a fog
produced using this.

dry land n. **1** land as opposed to the sea
etc. **2** (**dryland**) an area where rainfall is
low.

dry rot n. a fungus causing decay of wood
in poorly ventilated conditions.

dry run n. *informal* a rehearsal.

drywall ● n. prefabricated sheets of
plaster sandwiched between heavy paper,
used for interior walls. ● v. install drywall
(on a wall etc.). □**drywaller** n.
drywalling n.

DSL abbr. *Computing* digital subscriber line, a
technology for the high-speed transmission
of digital information over standard
telephone lines.

dual adj. **1** having two parts or aspects.
2 divided in two. □**duality** n. [*Say* DUE ul,
due ALLA tee]

dualism n. **1** the division of something
conceptually into two opposed or
contrasted aspects. **2** *Theology* the theory
that the forces of good and evil are equally
balanced in the universe. □**dualist** n.
dualistic adj. **dualistically** adv.
[*Say* DUE ul ism]

dub[1] v. (**dubs**, **dubbed**, **dubbing**)
1 confer a knighthood upon (a person) with
a sword. **2** give a name to.

dub[2] ● v. (**dubs**, **dubbed**, **dubbing**)
1 provide (a film etc.) with an alternative
soundtrack in a different language. **2** add
(sound effects or music) to a film or a
broadcast. **3** transfer or make a copy of. ● n.
a dubbed tape etc.

dub[3] n. **1** (also **dub music**) a remixed and
altered version of recorded (esp. reggae)
music. **2** (also **dub poetry**) a kind of

performance poetry in Jamaican (or black English) vernacular.

dubbing *n.* an alternative soundtrack to a film etc.

dubious *adj.* **1** hesitating. **2** of questionable value. **3** unreliable. □ **dubiously** *adv.* **dubiousness** *n.* [*Say* DUE bee us]

ducal *adj.* pertaining to a duke. [*Say* DUKE'll]

ducat *n.* a gold or silver coin formerly used in Europe. [*Say* DUCK it]

duchess *n.* (*pl.* **duchesses**) (as a title usu. **Duchess**) **1** a woman holding a rank equivalent to duke. **2** a duke's wife. [*Say* DUTCH iss]

duchy *n.* (*pl.* **duchies**) the territory of a duke or duchess. [*Say* DUTCHIE]

duck[1] *n.* a swimming bird with a broad bill and webbed feet. □ **like a duck to water** adapting very readily. **like water off a duck's back** *informal* (of complaints etc.) producing no effect.

duck[2] ● *v.* **1** dip under water and emerge. **2** stoop suddenly. **3** *informal* (often foll. by *out*) avoid or withdraw. ● *n.* a quick lowering of the head.

duck[3] *n.* a strong linen or cotton fabric.

duckbill *adj.* (also **duck-billed**) having a bill like that of a duck.

duckling *n.* a young duck.

duckweed *n.* a plant growing on the surface of still water.

ducky ● *n.* (*pl.* **duckies**) a toy duck made of plastic, rubber, etc. ● *adj. ironic* fine, splendid.

duct *n.* **1** a channel or tube for conveying air, fluid, cable, etc. **2** a tube or passage in a body or plant. □ **ducting** *n.*

ductile *adj.* **1** pliable, not brittle. **2** (of a metal) able to be drawn out into a thin wire. [*Say* DUCK tile]

duct tape *n.* tape of plastic-backed webbed cloth, used for household repairs. □ **duct-tape** *v.* (**duct-tapes**, **duct-taped**, **duct-taping**)

ductwork *n.* a system of ducts.

dud *n. slang* **1** something that fails to work properly. **2** a dishonoured cheque. **3** (in *pl.*) clothes.

dude *slang* ● *n.* a person, usu. male. ● *v.* (**dudes**, **duded**, **duding**) dress or fix up, esp. in a showy way.

dude ranch *n.* a cattle ranch converted to a vacation resort for tourists.

due ● *adj.* **1** owing as a debt or an obligation. **2** belonging to (a person). **3** proper. **4** attributable to. **5** expected at a certain time. ● *n.* **1** a thing owed to a person. **2** (in *pl.*) **a** what a person owes. **b** a

payment, esp. membership fees. ● *adv.* exactly, directly. □ **due to** because of. **in due course** at the appropriate time. **pay one's dues 1** fulfill one's obligations. **2** undergo hardships to succeed.

due date *n.* the date when something is expected or owing.

duel ● *n.* **1** a private pre-arranged fight between two people, fought with deadly weapons. **2** any contest between two parties. ● *v.* (**duels**, **duelled**, **duelling**) fight a duel or duels. □ **dueller** *n.* **duellist** *n.* [*Say* DUE ul]

due process *n.* (also **due process of the law**) the proper administration of justice through the courts.

duet *n.* a performance by two musicians etc. □ **duettist** *n.* [*Say* due ET]

duff *n.* **1** a boiled pudding. **2** decaying vegetable matter. **3** *informal* buttocks.

duffer *n. slang* an incompetent or stupid person.

duffle *n.* (also **duffel**) **1** a coarse, closely woven woollen cloth. **2** (also **duffle bag**) a large, cylindrical canvas bag.

dug *past and past participle of* DIG.

dugout *n.* **1 a** *Sport* a low shelter for the manager and players at a baseball diamond etc. **b** a roofed trench for sheltering troops. **2** a canoe made from a hollowed out tree trunk. **3** *Cdn* (*Prairies*) a large hole in the ground used to catch and hold rain, spring runoff, etc.

duh *interj.* indicating stupidity or scorn.

du jour *adj.* **1** of the day. **2** trendy. [*Say* doo ZHOOR]

duke ● *n.* **1 a** (as a title usu. **Duke**) a man holding the highest hereditary title of the nobility and ranking next below a prince, esp. in Britain. **b** a sovereign European prince ruling a duchy or small nation. **2** *slang* the fist. ● *v.* (**dukes**, **duked**, **duking**) *slang* fight, esp. with the fists. □ **dukedom** *n.*

dulcimer *n.* **1** a musical instrument with strings struck by small hammers. **2** a zither-like folk instrument, played by plucking or strumming. [*Say* DULLSA mer]

dull ● *adj.* **1** not interesting. **2** cloudy. **3** not sharp or bright. **4** slow to understand. ● *v.* make or become dull. □ **dulled** *adj.* **dullish** *adj.* **dullness** *n.* **dully** *adv.*

dulse *n.* an edible seaweed with red wedge-shaped fronds. [*Rhymes with* PULSE]

duly *adv.* in accordance with what is expected. [*Say* DUE lee]

Duma a legislative body in the ruling assembly of Russia and of some other

republics of the former USSR.
[*Say* DOOMA]

dumb ● *adj.* **1** unable to speak; mute.
2 *informal* stupid. **3** (of a computer terminal etc.) not programmable. ● *v. slang* (usu. foll. by *down*) adapt (a text etc.) to a lower level of understanding. □ **dumbly** *adv.*

dumbbell *n.* **1** a short bar with a weight at each end. **2** *slang* a stupid person.

dumbfound *v.* greatly astonish.

dumbo *n.* (*pl.* **dumbos**) *slang* a stupid person.

dumbstruck *adj.* lost for words.

dummy ● *n.* (*pl.* **dummies**) **1** a model of a human being. **2** an object designed to resemble or take the place of the real one. **3** *informal* a stupid person. **4** *Cdn & Brit.* a baby's soother. **5** *Military* a blank round of ammunition. ● *adj.* sham, fictitious.

dump ● *n.* **1** a site for depositing garbage or waste. **2** a heap of garbage left at a dump. **3** *informal* an unpleasant or dreary place. **4** *Military* a temporary store of weapons or provisions. **5** *Computing* an act of dumping stored data. **6** (also **log dump**) a place where logs are piled. ● *v.* **1** deposit or dispose of. **2** put down firmly. **3** abandon. **4** *Computing* copy to a different location. **5** send (goods) to a foreign market for sale at a low price. □ **dump on** *slang* **1** criticize severely or defeat heavily. **2** thwart. □ **dumping** *n.*

dump-and-chase *adj. Cdn Hockey* designating a strategy of shooting the puck far down the ice and then chasing after it.

dumper *n.* **1** a large metal bin for garbage. **2** a person, company, or thing that dumps garbage etc.

dumping ground *n.* **1** = DUMP 1. **2** a catch-all category or last resort.

dumpling *n.* **1 a** a small piece of dough, sometimes with a filling, boiled in water or in stew. **b** an apple etc. enclosed in dough and baked. **2** *informal* a small fat person.

dumps *pl. n. informal* □ **down in the dumps** depressed.

Dumpster *n. proprietary* a very large garbage container.

dump truck *n.* a usu. open topped truck with a body that tilts for unloading.

dumpy *adj.* (**dumpier, dumpiest**) short, rounded, and stout.

dun *v.* (**duns, dunned, dunning**) make persistent demands on (someone), esp. for repayment.

dunce *n.* a person slow at learning.

dune *n.* a ridge of loose sand etc. formed by the wind.

dune buggy *n.* a low, lightweight motor vehicle with wide tires for recreational driving on sand.

dung *n.* manure.

dungaree *n.* (in *pl.*) pants with a bib, held up by straps over the shoulders.
[*Say* dun ga REE]

dung beetle *n.* a beetle that lays its eggs in dung or rolls up balls of dung for its larvae to feed on.

dungeon *n.* a strong underground cell for prisoners. [*Say* DUN jin]

dunk ● *v.* **1** dip (bread etc.) into soup, coffee, etc. **2** immerse, dip. **3** *Basketball* shoot (the ball) down through the hoop from above. ● *n.* **1** (also **dunk shot** or **slam dunk**) *Basketball* an act of dunking. **2** an act of immersing oneself in a lake etc. □ **dunker** *n.*

dunlin *n.* a long-billed sandpiper.
[*Say* DUN lin]

Dunne-Za *n.* **1** a member of an Aboriginal people of the Peace River area of Alberta and BC. **2** the Athapaskan language of this people. □ **Dunne-Za** *adj.* [*Say* dunna ZAW]

duo *n.* (*pl.* **duos**) a pair, esp. of entertainers.

duodenum *n.* the first part of the small intestine immediately below the stomach.
[*Say* due oh DEE num *or* due ODDA num]

duopoly *n.* (*pl.* **duopolies**) *Economics* a condition in which two suppliers dominate the market. [*Say* due OPPA lee]

Duo-Tang *n. Cdn proprietary* a folder for loose-leaf paper, having three flexible metal fasteners.

dupe ● *n.* a person who is deceived by another. ● *v.* (**dupes, duped, duping**) deceive.

duplex *n.* (*pl.* **duplexes**) **1 a** = SEMI-DETACHED. **b** a residential building divided into two. **2** the capacity of a computer etc. to send and receive data simultaneously. □ **duplexed** *adj.* [*Say* DUE plex]

duplicate ● *adj.* **1** exactly like something else. **2 a** having two corresponding parts. **b** twice the number or quantity. ● *n.* one of two or more things exactly alike. ● *v.* (**duplicates, duplicated, duplicating**) **1** multiply by two. **2** copy. **3** repeat unnecessarily. □ **duplication** *n.*
[*Say* DUE plick it *for the adjective and noun,* DUE plick ate *for the verb*]

duplicator *n.* a machine for making copies.

duplicity *n.* (*pl.* **duplicities**) deceitfulness. □ **duplicitous** *adj.*
[*Say* due PLISS it ee]

durable ● *adj.* able to withstand change, decay, or wear. ● *n.* (in *pl.*; also **durable goods**) goods which remain useful over time. □ **durability** *n.*

duration n. the time during which something continues.

duress n. threats or violence to compel someone. [Say dur ESS or dyur ESS]

during prep. **1** throughout the duration of. **2** at some point in the duration of.

durum n. a kind of hard wheat used to make pasta. [Say DUR um or DYUR um]

dusk n. **1** the darker stage of twilight. **2** = NIGHTFALL.

dusky adj. (**duskier, duskiest**) somewhat dark.

dust ● n. finely powdered earth, dirt, etc. ● v. **1** clear (furniture etc.) of dust. **2** sprinkle with a powdery substance. □ **dust off 1** remove the dust from. **2** use again after a long period of neglect. **in the dust** informal far behind or much inferior. **when the dust settles** when things quieten down. □ **dusting** n.

dustball n. informal a clump of dust, lint, etc.

dust bowl n. an unproductive dry region where vegetation has been lost and soil reduced to dust.

dust bunny n. informal = DUSTBALL.

dust devil n. a small whirlwind common in dry regions.

duster n. **1** a cloth, brush, etc. for dusting surfaces. **2** a person who dusts.

dust jacket n. a removable, usu. decorated paper cover used to protect a book.

dustpan n. a small pan into which dust etc. is brushed from the floor.

dust-up n. informal a fight or quarrel.

dusty adj. (**dustier, dustiest**) **1 a** full of or covered with dust. **b** resembling dust. **2** solemn and not interesting.

Dutch n. **1** the language of the Netherlands. **2** (**the Dutch**; treated as pl.) the people of the Netherlands. □ **go Dutch** share expenses equally. □ **Dutch** adj.

Dutch elm disease n. a fungal disease of elms.

Dutchie n. a square glazed doughnut containing raisins.

Dutch oven n. a large covered container for braising etc.

Dutch Reformed Church n. a Christian denomination based on the teachings of Dutch Calvinists.

dutiable adj. liable to customs taxes or other duties. [Say DUTY a bull]

dutiful adj. **1** observant of one's duty. **2** characteristic of a sense of duty. □ **dutifully** adv. **dutifulness** n.

duty n. (pl. **duties**) **1** a moral or legal responsibility. **2** payment on the import, export, manufacture, or sale of goods. **3** an action required by one's job. **4** (as an adj.) to do with duties or being on duty. □ **on** (or **off**) **duty** engaged (or not engaged) in one's work.

duty-free ● adj. (of goods etc.) exempt from payment of duties. ● n. (also **duty-free shop**) a shop selling merchandise exempt from duty to travellers.

duvet n. a thick soft quilt used instead of an upper sheet and blankets. [Say doo VAY or DOO vay]

DVD n. (pl. **DVDs**) proprietary a digital recording medium similar to a CD but capable of storing a feature film.

dwarf ● n. (pl. **dwarfs** or **dwarves**) **1 a** an abnormally small person. **b** (also as an adj.) an animal or plant much below the ordinary size for the species. **2 a** mythological race of diminutive beings skilled in mining and metalworking. **3** (also **dwarf star**) a small, dense star with low to average luminosity. ● v. (**dwarfs, dwarfed, dwarfing**) **1** restrict the growth of. **2** cause to seem small or insignificant. □ **dwarfed** adj. **dwarfish** adj.

dwarfism n. unusually low stature or small size.

dweeb n. slang a studious or boring person. □ **dweebish** adj. **dweeby** adj. (**dweebier, dweebiest**)

dwell v. (**dwells, dwelt** or **dwelled, dwelling**) literary reside. □ **dwell on** (or **upon**) spend time on; write, brood, or speak at length on. □ **dweller** n.

dwelling n. (also **dwelling place**) a place of residence.

dwindle v. (**dwindles, dwindled, dwindling**) gradually lessen or fade. □ **dwindling** adj.

dye ● n. **1** a substance used to change the colour of hair, fabric, etc. **2** (also **dyestuff**) a substance yielding a dye. ● v. (**dyes, dyed, dyeing**) change the colour of something, esp. by using a special liquid or substance. □ **dyer** n.

dyed-in-the-wool adj. having strong unchangeable beliefs.

dying ● adj. **1** connected with death. **2** about to die. **3** coming to an end. ● n. the cessation of life.

dyke n. = DIKE.

dynamic ● adj. **1** forceful and energetic. **2** (of a process) always changing and progressing. **3** (also **dynamical**) Physics relating to forces producing motion. **4** (also **dynamical**) of or concerning dynamics. **5** Music relating to the volume of sound.

● *n.* a force that stimulates change or progress. □ **dynamically** *adv.*

dynamics *pl. n.* **1** the branch of mechanics concerned with the motion of bodies under the action of forces. **2** the motive forces affecting any sort of behaviour and change. **3** the varying degree of volume of sound in musical performance.

dynamism *n.* energizing action or power. [*Say* DIE nuh mism]

dynamite ● *n.* **1** a high explosive made of nitroglycerine. **2** a potentially dangerous person etc. **3** *informal* a powerful person or thing. ● *v.* (**dynamites**, **dynamited**, **dynamiting**) charge or shatter with dynamite. ● *adj. informal* excellent or powerful. □ **dynamiter** *n.*

dynamo *n.* (*pl.* **dynamos**) **1** a machine converting mechanical into electrical energy. **2** *informal* an energetic person. [*Say* DIE nuh moe]

dynasty *n.* (*pl.* **dynasties**) **1** a line of hereditary rulers. **2** a succession of leaders in any field. □ **dynastic** *adj.* [*Say* DIE nuh stee, die NASS tic]

dysentery *n.* a disease with inflammation of the intestines, causing severe diarrhea. [*Say* DISSIN terry *or* DISSIN tree]

dysfunctional *adj.* not working in a satisfactory way. □ **dysfunction** *n.*

dyslexia *n.* a disorder affecting one's ability to read but not one's general intelligence. □ **dyslexic** *adj. & n.* [*Say* dis LEXIA]

dyspepsia *n.* indigestion. [*Say* dis PEPSI uh]

dyspeptic *adj.* **1** relating to indigestion. **2** ill-tempered. [*Say* dis PEP tick]

dystrophy *n.* a disorder in which an organ or tissue of the body wastes away. [*Say* DISTRA fee]

Ee

E¹ *n.* (also **e**) (*pl.* **Es** or **E's**) **1** the fifth letter of the alphabet. **2** the third note of the scale of C major.

E² *abbr.* (also **E.**) **1** East, Eastern. **2** (also **e**) *slang* the drug ecstasy.

e- *comb. form* electronic.

each ● *adj.* every one of two or more persons or things, regarded separately. ● *pron.* each person or thing. □ **each and every** single.

each other *pron.* one another.

eager *adj.* full of keen desire. □ **eagerly** *adv.* **eagerness** *n.*

eager beaver *n. informal* a very diligent person.

eagle *n.* a large bird of prey with keen vision and powerful flight.

eagle eye *n.* keen sight. □ **eagle-eyed** *adj.*

eaglet *n.* a young eagle. [*Say* EE glit]

ear¹ *n.* **1** the organ of hearing and balance in humans and vertebrates. **2** the faculty for discriminating sounds. **3** an ear-shaped thing, esp. the handle of a jug. □ **all ears** listening attentively. **give ear to** listen to. **have a person's ear** receive a favourable hearing. **have** (or **keep**) **an ear to the ground** be alert to rumours. **out on one's ear** dismissed ignominiously. □ **eared** *adj.*

ear² *n.* the seed-bearing head of a cereal plant.

earache *n.* pain inside the ear.

eardrum *n.* the membrane of the middle ear, which vibrates in response to sound waves.

earflap *n.* a flap on a hat for covering the ear.

earful *n.* (*pl.* **earfuls**) *informal* **1** a lot of talking. **2** a strong reprimand.

earl *n.* a British nobleman ranking between a marquess and a viscount. □ **earldom** *n.*

Earl Grey *n.* a type of tea flavoured with bergamot.

earlobe *n.* the lower soft external part of the ear.

early *adj. & adv.* (**earlier, earliest**) **1** before the expected time. **2** near the beginning of a particular time, period, or sequence. □ **earliness** *n.*

early bird *n. informal* a person who arrives, gets up, etc. earlier than others.

earmark ● *n.* an identifying mark or characteristic. ● *v.* set aside for a purpose.

earmuff *n.* (usu. in *pl.*) either of a pair of connected ear coverings worn for warmth.

earn *v.* **1 a** obtain (income) in return for labour or services. **b** (of capital invested) bring in as interest or profit. **2 a** deserve. **b** incur. □ **earned** *adj.* **earner** *n.*

earnest ● *adj.* very serious and sincere. ● *n.* a token or foretaste. □ **in earnest** with sincere and serious intention. □ **earnestly** *adv.* **earnestness** *n.*

earnings *pl. n.* money earned.

EARP *abbr.* (in Canada) Environmental Assessment and Review Process.

earphone *n.* a receiver (usu. one of a pair) fitted over or inside the ear, used for listening to a radio, stereo, etc.

earpiece *n.* **1** the part of a telephone etc. held to the ear during use. **2** the part of a pair of glasses, a helmet, etc., that fits over the wearer's ear.

ear-piercing ● *adj.* loud and shrill. ● *n.* the piercing of the ears to allow the wearing of earrings.

earplug *n.* soft material placed in the ear to keep out water, noise, etc.

earring *n.* a piece of jewellery worn on the lobe or edge of the ear.

earshot *n.* the distance over which something can be heard.

ear-splitting *adj.* excessively loud.

earth *n.* **1** (also **Earth**) the planet on which we live. **2** the substance of the land surface; soil. **3** the hole of a badger, fox, etc. **4** (**the earth**) *informal* a huge amount. □ **come back** (or **down**) **to earth** return to realities. **gone to earth** in hiding. **on earth** *informal* **1** existing anywhere. **2** as an intensifier.

earthbound *adj.* **1** attached to the earth. **2** moving toward the earth.

earthen *adj.* **1** made of earth. **2** made of baked clay.

earthenware *n.* pottery made of baked clay.

earthling *n.* (in science fiction) a person from this planet.

earthly *adj.* **1** of the earth or human life on earth. **2** *informal* remotely possible.

earthmover *n.* a vehicle or machine for moving earth. □ **earthmoving** *n.*

earthquake *n.* **1** a convulsion of the ground, caused by movements within the earth's crust. **2** a severe upheaval.

earth science *n.* any of the sciences concerned with the earth or its atmosphere. □ **earth scientist** *n.*

earth-shattering *adj.* (also **earth-shaking**) traumatic or shocking. □ **earth-shatteringly** *adv.*

earthward ● *adv.* (also **earthwards**) toward the earth. ● *adj.* directed toward the earth.

earthwork *n.* an artificial bank of earth.

earthworm *n.* a worm living and burrowing in the ground.

earthy *adj.* (**earthier, earthiest**) **1** of or like soil. **2** crude. □ **earthiness** *n.*

earwax *n.* a waxy secretion produced by the ear.

earwig *n.* a small brown insect with two curved pointed parts called pincers at its rear end.

ease ● *n.* **1** absence of difficulty. **2** freedom from problems or toil. ● *v.* (**eases, eased, easing**) **1** relieve from pain or anxiety etc. **2** (often foll. by *off, up*) relax or lessen. **3** *Meteorology* become less severe. **4** move or be moved carefully. □ **at ease 1** free from trouble. **2** *Military* in a relaxed attitude.

easel *n.* a standing frame for supporting an artist's work.

easement *n.* a right-of-way etc. over another's land.

easily *adv.* **1** without difficulty. **2** without doubt.

east ● *n.* **1** the direction in which the sun rises at the equinoxes (cardinal point 90° to the right of north). **2** (usu. **the East**) the regions or countries lying to the east of Europe. **3** the eastern part of a place. ● *adj.* **1** toward or facing east. **2** coming from the east. ● *adv.* toward, at, or near the east.

eastbound *adj. & adv.* directed eastwards.

Easter *n.* a springtime Christian festival commemorating Christ's resurrection.

easterly ● *adj. & adv.* **1** in an eastern position or direction. **2** (of a wind) blowing from the east. ● *n.* (*pl.* **easterlies**) a wind blowing from the east.

eastern *adj.* **1** of, in, or directed toward the east. **2** (**Eastern**) of or in the East. □ **easternmost** *adj.*

Eastern Church *n.* a branch of the Christian Church which developed in Greece and Eastern Europe.

easterner *n.* a person from the east.

Eastern Time *n.* the time in a zone including most of Ontario and Quebec as well as the eastern US. **Eastern Standard Time** is five hours behind GMT; **Eastern Daylight Time** is four hours behind GMT.

East Indian *adj.* relating to the Indian subcontinent or its indigenous peoples or their descendants. □ **East Indian** *n.*

Eastmain Cree *n.* (*pl.* **Eastmain Cree** or **Eastmain Crees**) a member of a Cree people living at the mouth of the Eastmain River on the shore of James Bay. [*Say* EAST main]

east-northeast *n.* the direction midway between east and northeast.

east-southeast *n.* the direction midway between east and southeast.

eastward *adj. & adv.* (also **eastwards**) toward the east. □ **eastwardly** *adj. & adv.*

easy ● *adj.* (**easier, easiest**) **1** not difficult. **2** free from worry or discomfort. **3** easily persuaded or available. ● *interj.* go carefully; move gently. □ **easy on the eye** *informal* pleasant to look at. **go easy** (foll. by *with, on*) be sparing. **I'm easy** *informal* I have no preference. **take it easy 1** proceed carefully. **2** relax. **3** (often as *interjection*) calm down.

easy chair *n.* a large comfortable armchair.

easygoing *adj.* relaxed in manner.

easy listening *n.* tuneful and undemanding music.

easy money *n.* money got without effort.

eat *v.* (**eats**; *past* **ate**; *past participle* **eaten**; **eating**) **1** consume as food. **2** diminish; destroy gradually. **3** *informal* trouble. □ **eat one's heart out** suffer from excessive longing or envy. **eat up 1** consume completely. **2** use or deal with rapidly or wastefully. **3** *informal* receive with vigorous enjoyment. **eat one's words** admit that one was wrong. □ **eatable** *adj.* **eater** *n.* **eating** *adj.*

eatery *n.* (*pl.* **eateries**) *informal* a restaurant.

eats *pl. n.* *informal* food.

eau de cologne *n.* a mild perfume. [*Say* oh duh kuh LONE]

eau de toilette *n.* (*pl.* **eaux de toilette**) a perfume that is slightly stronger than eau de cologne. [*Say* oh duh twah LET]

eaves *pl. n.* the underside of a projecting roof.

eavesdrop *v.* (**eavesdrops, eavesdropped, eavesdropping**) listen

secretly to a conversation.
□ **eavesdropper** n.

eavestrough n. (also **eavestroughing**) (esp. *Cdn*) a shallow trough attached to the eaves of a building to collect runoff from the roof. [*Say* EAVES troff]

ebb ● n. **1** the movement of the tide out to sea (also as an *adj.*). **2** a flowing away; decline. ● v. (often foll. by *away*) **1** (of tidewater) flow out to sea. **2** decline. □ **at a low ebb** in a poor condition. **ebb and flow** decline and upturn in circumstances.

Ebola n. a tropical African virus that causes severe fever and internal bleeding. [*Say* i BOLA]

ebony ● n. (pl. **ebonies**) **1** a heavy hard dark wood. **2** any of various trees producing this. ● adj. **1** made of ebony. **2** black. [*Say* EBBA nee]

ebullient adj. (of a person) enthusiastic and lively. □ **ebullience** n. **ebulliently** adv. [*Say* i BULLY int]

eccentric ● adj. **1** odd or capricious. **2 a** not placed or not having its axis placed centrally. **b** (of an orbit) not circular. ● n. an eccentric person. □ **eccentrically** adv. **eccentricity** n. (pl. **eccentricities**) [*Say* eck SEN trick, eck sen TRISSA tee]

ecclesiastic ● n. a member of the Christian clergy. ● adj. (usu. **ecclesiastical**) of the Christian Church or clergy. □ **ecclesiastically** adv. [*Say* i cleezy ASTICK]

ECE abbr. early childhood education (or educator).

ECG abbr. (pl. **ECGs**) **1** electrocardiogram. **2** electrocardiograph.

echelon n. (often in *pl.*) a level or rank in an organization, in society, etc.; those occupying it. [*Say* ESHA lon]

echinacea n. **1** any of several eastern N American plant, esp. a purple coneflower. **2** a herbal remedy made from its roots. [*Say* ecka NAYSHA]

echo ● n. (pl. **echoes**) **1** the repetition of a sound by the reflection of sound waves. **2** (often in *pl.*) something repeating or reminiscent of something else. ● v. (**echoes**, **echoed**, **echoing**) **1 a** (of a place) resound with an echo. **b** repeated or be repeated. **2** imitate.

echo sounder n. a device for determining the depth of water by measuring the time taken for an echo to be received.

eclair n. an elongated cream puff filled with cream and topped with chocolate icing. [*Say* ay CLAIR or i CLAIR]

eclectic ● adj. deriving ideas or style from a wide variety of sources. ● n. an eclectic person. □ **eclectically** adv. **eclecticism** n. [*Say* i CLECK tick, i CLECK tuh sism]

eclipse ● n. **1** an occasion when the moon, a planet, etc. blocks out light from a similar object. **2** a deprivation of light or the period of this. **3** a sudden loss of importance or prominence. ● v. (**eclipses**, **eclipsed**, **eclipsing**) **1** (of a celestial body) obscure the light from or to (another). **2** outshine, surpass. [*Say* i CLIPS]

ecliptic n. the sun's apparent path among the stars during the year. [*Say* i CLIP tick]

eco n. informal ecology (also as an adj.). [*Say* ECKO or EEKO]

eco- comb. form ecology, ecological.

E. coli n. (in full **Escherichia coli**) a bacterium which can cause severe gastrointestinal disease. [*Say* ee CO lye]

ecology n. (pl. **ecologies**) **1** the branch of biology dealing with the relations of organisms to one another and to their physical surroundings. **2** (also **human ecology**) the study of the interaction of people with their environment. □ **ecological** adj. **ecologist** n. [*Say* i COLLA jee]

e-commerce n. financial transactions conducted over the Internet.

econometrics pl. n. (usu. treated as *sing.*) the branch of economics studying the use of statistics and mathematical methods. □ **econometric** adj. [*Say* i conna METRICS]

economic adj. **1** relating to economics or the economy. **2** profitable. **3** = ECONOMICAL.

economical adj. **1** careful in the use of resources. **2** inexpensive. **3** = ECONOMIC. □ **economically** adv.

economics pl. n. (treated as *sing.*) **1** the social science of the production and distribution of wealth in theory and practice. **2** financial considerations.

economies of scale pl. n. proportionate savings gained by using larger quantities.

economist n. an expert in economics.

economize v. (**economizes**, **economized**, **economizing**) reduce expenses, make savings. □ **economizer** n. **economizing** n.

economy n. (pl. **economies**) **1** the wealth and resources of a community, esp. in terms of the production and consumption of goods and services. **2 a** careful management of resources. **b** (often in *pl.*) a financial saving. **3** the cheapest class of some service or product. **4** (as an *adj.*) offering good value for money.

ecoregion n. a local ecosystem.

ecosphere *n.* the earth's biosphere.
[*Say* EEKO sphere]

ecosystem *n.* a biological community of
interacting organisms and their
environment.

eco-terrorism *n.* **1** violence for
environmentalist ends. **2** politically
motivated damage to the natural
environment. □ **eco-terrorist** *n.*

ecotourism *n.* tourism to unspoiled
natural environments, esp. intended to
support conservation efforts.
□ **ecotourist** *n.*

ecstasy *n.* (*pl.* **ecstasies**)
1 overwhelming joy. **2** rapture supposed to
accompany religious inspiration etc. **3** *slang*
a powerful stimulant and hallucinatory
drug (*see* MDMA). [*Say* ECK sta see]

ecstatic *adj.* very happy or excited.
□ **ecstatically** *adv.* [*Say* ick STATIC]

ECT *abbr.* ELECTROCONVULSIVE THERAPY.

ectopic pregnancy *n.* a pregnancy in
which the fertilized ovum develops outside
the uterus.

ectoplasm *n.* the outer layer of the
cytoplasm in some cells. □ **ectoplasmic**
adj. [*Say* ECTO plasm]

ecumenical *adj.* **1** of or representing the
whole Christian world or several
denominations. **2** promoting Christian
unity. [*Say* eck you MENNA cul *or*
eek you MENNA cul]

ecumenism *n.* the aim of promoting
unity among the world's Christian
Churches. [*Say* eck YOU m'n ism *or*
ECK you m'n ism]

eczema *n.* superficial skin inflammation,
usu. with itching and discharge from
blisters. [*Say* eck ZEE muh]

ed *n. informal* education.

Edam *n.* a firm Dutch cheese, usu. pale
yellow with a red rind. [*Say* EE d'm *or*
EE dam]

eddy ● *n.* (*pl.* **eddies**) **1** a circular
movement of water causing a small
whirlpool. **2** a movement of wind etc.
resembling this. ● *v.* (**eddies, eddied,
eddying**) whirl around.

edelweiss *n.* (*pl.* **edelweiss**) an alpine
plant with woolly white bracts.
[*Say* AID'll vice]

edema *n.* an excess of watery fluid in the
cavities of the body. [*Say* i DEEMA]

Eden *n.* (also **Garden of Eden**) **1** an
unspoiled paradise. **2** the abode of Adam
and Eve in the Biblical account of the
Creation. □ **Edenic** *adj.* [*Say* EE d'n,
ee DEN ick]

edge ● *n.* **1** the outside limit of an object,
area, or surface. **2** a line along which two
surfaces of a solid intersect. **3** the
sharpened side of a blade. **4 a** incisiveness,
excitement. **b** an advantage. ● *v.* (**edges,
edged, edging**) **1** move gradually or
furtively. **2** provide with an edge or border.
3 defeat by a small margin. □ **on edge**
1 tense and irritable. **2** eager. **set a
person's teeth on edge** cause acute
irritation or discomfort. **take the edge
off** dull, weaken. □ **edged** *adj.*

edger *n.* a tool for making, trimming, or
finishing an edge.

edgewise *adv.* (also esp. *Brit.* **edgeways**)
with the edge uppermost or towards the
viewer. □ **get a word in edgewise**
manage to break into a conversation.

edging *n.* **1** something forming an edge.
2 the process of making an edge. **3** *Skiing*
the angling of a ski so that it cuts into the
snow.

edgy *adj.* (**edgier, edgiest**) **1** irritable,
anxious. **2** characterized by sharp
observation or wit. **3** innovative.
□ **edginess** *n.*

edible ● *adj.* fit or suitable to be eaten. ● *n.*
(in *pl.*) things that may be eaten.

edict *n.* an official order or proclamation.
[*Say* EE dict]

edifice *n.* a large, impressive building.
[*Say* EDD i fiss]

edify *v.* (**edifies, edified, edifying**)
instruct and improve morally.
□ **edification** *n.* edifying *adj.*
[*Say* EDDA fie]

edit ● *v.* (**edits, edited, editing**)
1 assemble, prepare, or modify (written
material) esp. for publication. **2** be the
editor of (a newspaper etc.). **3** prepare
(recorded materials etc.) for broadcast.
4 (foll. by *out*) remove (a part) from a text
etc. ● *n.* **1 a** the action of editing. **b** a
change made as a result of editing. **2** an
edited item. □ **editable** *adj.*

edition *n.* **1** a particular form or version of
a publication. **2 a** whole number of copies
of a publication issued at one time. **3** a
particular version or instance of a regular
broadcast.

editor *n.* **1** a person who prepares or selects
texts or recorded material for publication
or broadcasting. **2** a person in charge of a
newspaper or magazine etc. **3** a computer
program enabling the user to edit
something. □ **editorship** *n.*

editorial ● *adj.* **1** of or concerned with
editing or editors. **2** distinguished from
news and advertising matter. ● *n.* a
newspaper article etc. giving the opinion of
an editor. □ **editorialist** *n.*
editorially *adv.*

editorialize v. (**editorializes**, **editorialized**, **editorializing**) express opinions rather than just report the news.

Edmonton n. a person from Edmonton. □ **Edmontonian** adj. [Say ed m'n TONY in]

EDT abbr. Eastern Daylight Time.

educate v. (**educates**, **educated**, **educating**) **1** give intellectual or moral instruction to. **2** instruct for a particular purpose. □ **educated** adj. **educator** n.

education n. **1** the process of teaching or learning. **2** the theory and practice of teaching. □ **educational** adj. **educative** adj.

Edwardian adj. relating to the reign of Edward VII of England (1901–10). [Say ed WAR dee un]

-ee suffix forming nouns denoting: **1** the person affected by the verbal action. **2** a person concerned with or described as.

eel n. a snakelike fish living in fresh water but breeding in warm deep oceans.

eelgrass n. (pl. **eelgrasses**) **1** a marine plant with long ribbon-like leaves. **2** a similar freshwater plant.

eensy adj. (also **eensy-weensy**) informal tiny.

eerie adj. (**eerier**, **eeriest**) inspiring unease. □ **eerily** adv. **eeriness** n.

efface v. (**effaces**, **effaced**, **effacing**) **1** rub or wipe out (a mark). **2** obliterate (a memory etc.). [Say i FACE]

effect ● n. **1** the consequence of an action etc. **2** efficacy. **3** an impression produced on a spectator, hearer, etc. **4** (in pl.) (also **personal effects**) property, luggage, etc. **5** (in pl.) (also **special effects**) the lighting, sound, etc. used in a play, film, etc. **6** a scientific phenomenon. ● v. bring about or accomplish. □ **give effect to** make operative or put into force. **in effect** in practice, if not formally acknowledged. **take effect** become operative. **to that effect** having that result.

effective adj. **1** producing a desired effect. **2** impressively powerful. **3** existing in fact rather than officially. **4** operative. □ **effectively** adv. **effectiveness** n.

effectual adj. effective. □ **effectually** adv.

effeminate adj. (of a man) feminine in appearance or manner. □ **effeminacy** n. **effeminately** adv. [Say if FEMMA nit]

effervesce v. (**effervesces**, **effervesced**, **effervescing**) give off bubbles of gas. □ **effervescence** n. **effervescent** adj. [Say effer VESS]

effete adj. **1** affected. **2** no longer effective. [Say if FEET]

efficacious adj. effective. □ **efficaciously** adv. [Say effa KAY shuss]

efficacy n. the ability of something to produce the desired result. [Say EFFA kuh see]

efficiency n. (pl. **efficiencies**) **1** the quality of being efficient. **2** (also **efficiency unit**) Cdn a hotel room etc. with limited washing and cooking facilities. [Say i FISHIN see]

efficient adj. productive with minimum waste or effort. □ **efficiently** adv. [Say i FISH int]

effigy n. (pl. **effigies**) a sculpture or model of a person. □ **burn in effigy** subject a usu. crude image of a person to a punishment. [Say EFFA jee]

effluent n. sewage or industrial waste discharged into a body of water. [Say EFF loo int]

effluvium n. (pl. **effluvia**) **1** (usu. in pl.) waste material or refuse. **2** an unpleasant or noxious odour or discharge. [Say if LOOVY um, if LOOVY ah]

effort n. **1** strenuous exertion. **2** a vigorous attempt. □ **effortful** adj.

effortless adj. requiring or done with little or no exertion. □ **effortlessly** adv. **effortlessness** n.

effrontery n. (pl. **effronteries**) shamelessly confident and rude behaviour. [Say i FRONTER ee]

effusion n. **1** an instance of giving off a liquid, light, or smell. **2** usu. derogatory an unrestrained flow of speech or writing. [Say e FYOO zh'n]

effusive adj. expressing gratitude, approval, etc. in an unrestrained manner. □ **effusively** adv. **effusiveness** n. [Say e FYOO siv]

e.g. abbr. for example.

egalitarian ● adj. relating to the principle of equal rights and opportunities for all. ● n. a person who advocates egalitarian principles. □ **egalitarianism** n. [Say i gal a TERRY in]

egg[1] n. **1** the more or less spheroidal reproductive body produced by females of animals such as birds, reptiles, fish, etc. and enclosed in a protective layer, shell, or firm membrane. **2** (also **egg cell**) Biology an ovum. □ **with egg on one's face** informal in a condition of looking foolish. □ **eggy** adj.

egg[2] v. (foll. by on) urge.

egghead n. informal an intellectual.

eggnog n. a thick drink of beaten eggs, milk or cream, sugar, flavourings, and usu. rum or brandy.

eggplant *n.* a white or purple fruit eaten as a vegetable.

egg roll *n.* an appetizer consisting of deep-fried egg dough and a savoury filling.

eggs Benedict *n.* a dish of poached eggs, ham, toast, and hollandaise sauce.

eggshell ● *n.* **1** the thin shell of a bird's egg. **2** anything very fragile. ● *adj.* **1** (of china) extremely thin. **2** (of paint etc.) having the slight sheen of a bird's egg. □ **walk on eggshells** proceed cautiously.

ego *n.* (*pl.* **egos**) **1** a person's sense of self-esteem. **2** *Psychology* that part of the mind which mediates between the conscious and the unconscious and is responsible for reality testing and a sense of personal identity. [*Say* EE go]

egocentric ● *adj.* self-centred. ● *n.* an egocentric person. □ **egocentricity** *n.* [*Say* ee go SEN trick, ee go sen TRISSA tee]

egoism *n.* **1** an ethical theory that regards self-interest as the foundation of morality. **2** systematic self-centredness. **3** = EGOTISM. □ **egoist** *n.* **egoistic** *adj.* [*Say* EE go ism]

egomania *n.* obsessive self-centredness. □ **egomaniac** *n.* **egomaniacal** *adj.* [*Say* ee go MANIA]

egotism *n.* **1** the practice of continually talking about oneself. **2** an exaggerated opinion of oneself. **3** extreme selfishness. □ **egotist** *n.* **egotistic** *adj.* **egotistical** *adj.* **egotistically** *adv.* [*Say* EE go tism]

ego trip *informal* ● *n.* an action performed to draw attention to one's abilities, for vanity's sake, etc. ● *v.* (**ego-trip, ego-trips, ego-tripped, ego-tripping**) indulge in an ego trip. □ **ego-tripper** *n.*

egregious *adj.* outstandingly bad. □ **egregiously** *adv.* **egregiousness** *n.* [*Say* i GREEDGE iss]

egret *n.* a heron with long white feathers in the breeding season. [*Say* EE grit]

Egyptian *adj.* relating to Egypt or its language or people. □ **Egyptian** *n.* [*Say* ee JIP shun]

Egyptology *n.* the study of ancient Egypt. □ **Egyptologist** *n.* [*Say* egypt OLLA jee]

eh *interj. informal* **1** inviting assent. **2** *Cdn* ascertaining comprehension etc. **3** expressing inquiry or surprise.

EI *abbr. Cdn* employment insurance.

Eid *n.* = ID.

eider *n.* (also **eider duck**) a large northern sea duck. [*Rhymes with* RIDER]

eight *card. num.* one more than seven, or two less than ten.

eight ball *n.* **1** a billiard game. **2** the black ball, numbered eight, in this. □ **behind the eight ball** in a difficult situation.

eighteen *card. num.* one more than seventeen, or eight more than ten. □ **eighteenth** *ord. num.*

eighteen-wheeler *n. informal* a large transport truck having eighteen wheels.

eighth *ord. num.* constituting number eight in a sequence. □ **eighthly** *adv.*

eighth note *n.* a note having the time value of an eighth of a whole note and represented by a large dot with a hooked stem.

800 number *n.* a toll-free telephone number.

eighty *card. num.* (*pl.* **eighties**) ten less than ninety. □ **eightieth** *adj., n.,* & *adv.*

either ● *adj.* & *pron.* **1** one or the other of two. **2** each of two. ● *adv.* & *conj.* **1** as one possibility. **2 a** any more than the other. **b** moreover. [*Say* EYE ther *or* EE ther]

either-or *n.* a choice that cannot be avoided between alternatives. ● *adj.* involving such a choice.

ejaculate ● *v.* (**ejaculates, ejaculated, ejaculating**) **1** forcefully eject semen on achieving orgasm. **2** suddenly eject (any matter) from a body. **3** utter (words) suddenly. ● *n.* semen that has been ejaculated. □ **ejaculation** *n.* **ejaculator** *n.* [*Say* i JACK you late *for the verb,* i JACK you lit *for the noun,* i jack you LAY sh'n, i JACK you luh tory]

eject ● *v.* **1** send or drive out or away by force. **2** catapult out of an aircraft using a special seat. **3** cause to expel, e.g. a disc from a CD player. ● *n.* a device, command, etc. causing something to be ejected. □ **ejectable** *adj.* **ejection** *n.*

eke *v.* (**ekes, eked, eking**) □ **eke out 1** live with very little money. **2** use sparingly. [*Say* EEK]

EKG *abbr.* (*pl.* **EKGs**) **1** electrocardiogram. **2** electrocardiograph.

elaborate ● *adj.* **1** detailed and complicated. **2** (of an action) lengthy and exaggerated. ● *v.* explain in detail. □ **elaborately** *adv.* **elaborateness** *n.* **elaboration** *n.* [*Say* i LABBA rut *for the adjective,* i LABBA rate *for the verb*]

élan *n.* style, vivacity. [*Say* ay LON]

elapse *v.* (**elapses, elapsed, elapsing**) (of time) pass by. [*Say* i LAPS]

elastic ● *adj.* **1** able to resume its normal bulk or shape after being stretched or squeezed. **2** flexible. **3** springy. ● *n.* **1** elastic cord or fabric. **2** (also **elastic band**) = RUBBER BAND. □ **elasticity** *n.* [*Say* il LASTIC, il lass TISS ity]

elasticized *adj.* **1** (of a fabric) made elastic

by weaving with rubber thread. **2** made stretchy. [*Say* il LASTA sized]

elated *adj.* extremely happy. [*Say* il LATE id]

elation *n.* great happiness and excitement.

elbow ● *n.* **1** the joint between the forearm and the upper arm. **2** an elbow-shaped bend or pipe. **3** a push with an elbow. ● *v.* **1** thrust or jostle. **2** make (one's way) by jostling. □ **out** (**or** (**the**) **elbows 1** worn out; shabby. **2** ragged, poor. **up to the elbows** *informal* busily engaged (in).

elbow grease *n. informal* hard manual work.

elbowing *n. Hockey* the illegal action of fouling an opponent with an elbow.

elbow room *n.* adequate space to move or work in.

elder¹ ● *adj.* (of two indicated persons) of a greater age. ● *n.* (often as **the elder**) **1** the older or more senior of two people. **2** (in *pl.*) **a** persons of greater age or seniority. **b** venerable persons. **3** an administrative official in various churches. **4** a leader or senior figure in an Aboriginal group etc.

elder² *n.* a shrub or tree with white flowers and blue-black or red berries.

elderberry *n.* (*pl.* **elderberries**) the edible berry of the elder.

elderly *adj.* past middle age.

elder statesman *n.* an older experienced person, esp. a politician.

eldest *adj.* first-born or oldest.

El Dorado *n.* (*pl.* **El Dorados**) **1** a fabled city or country abounding in gold. **2** (usu. **Eldorado**) a place of great abundance. [*Say* el duh ROD oh]

elect ● *v.* **1** choose (a person) by vote. **2** choose in preference to an alternative. ● *adj.* **1** *Theology* chosen by God. **2** elected to a position but not yet in office. ● *n.* (**the elect**) a specially chosen group of people. □ **electability** *n.* **electable** *adj.*

election *n.* **1** the procedure whereby someone is elected. **2** the act of electing or the fact of being elected.

electioneer *v.* **1** take part in an election campaign. **2** seek election by currying favour with voters. □ **electioneering** *n.*

elective ● *adj.* **1** filled or appointed by election. **2** having the power to elect. **3** optional. ● *n.* an elective course of study.

elector *n.* a person who has the right to vote.

electoral *adj.* relating to electors or elections. [*Say* il LECTER ul *or* il leck TORE ul]

electorate *n.* the body of persons entitled to vote in a country or constituency. [*Say* il LECTER it]

electric ● *adj.* **1** of, worked by, or charged with electricity. **2** producing electricity. **3** (of a musical instrument) amplified electronically. **4** exciting. ● *n.* **1** an electric car, train, etc. **2** electrical appliances or circuitry.

electrical *adj.* **1** of or concerned with electricity. **2** operating by electricity. □ **electrically** *adv.*

electric chair *n.* a chair used for capital punishment by electrocution.

electric eel *n.* an eel-like freshwater fish native to S America, which can give a severe electric shock.

electric fence *n.* (also **electric fencing**) a fence which gives a mild electric shock to an animal touching it.

electric field *n.* a region in which an electric charge experiences a force.

electric guitar *n.* a guitar in which the vibrations of the strings are converted into electrical signals and amplified.

electrician *n.* a person who installs or maintains electrical equipment.

electricity *n.* **1** a form of energy resulting from the existence of charged particle, either statically as a buildup of charge or dynamically as a current. **2** a supply of electric current for heating, lighting, etc. **3** excitement.

electric shock *n.* **1** a sudden discharge of electricity through a part of the body. **2** = SHOCK TREATMENT 1.

electrify *v.* (**electrifies**, **electrified**, **electrifying**) **1** charge with electricity. **2** convert to the use of electric power. **3** excite. □ **electrification** *n.*

electro- *comb. form* of or relating to electricity.

electrocardiogram *n.* a chart or record produced by an electrocardiograph. Abbreviation: **ECG**, **EKG**. [*Say* electro CARDIO gram]

electrocardiograph *n.* an instrument that records or displays the electric activity of the heart. Abbreviation: **ECG**, **EKG**. □ **electrocardiography** *n.* [*Say* electro CARDIO graph, electro cardy OGGRA fee]

electroconvulsive therapy *n.* a method of treating certain mental illnesses by applying electric shocks to the brain. Abbreviation: **ECT**. [*Say* electro CONVULSIVE]

electrocute *v.* (**electrocutes**, **electrocuted**, **electrocuting**) injure or kill by electric shock. □ **electrocution** *n.*

electrode *n.* a conductor through which electricity enters or leaves something.

electroencephalogram *n.* a record

produced by an electroencephalograph.
Abbreviation: **EEG**.
[*Say* electro en SEFFA luh gram]

electroencephalograph *n.* an
instrument that records or displays the
electrical activity of the brain.
Abbreviation: **EEG**.
□ **electroencephalography** *n.*
[*Say* electro en SEFFA luh graph,
electro en seffle OGGRA fee]

electrologist *n.* a person who removes
excess hair using electrolysis.
[*Say* il leck TRAWLA jist]

electrolysis *n.* **1** the separation of a
liquid into its chemical parts by passing an
electric current through it. **2** the removal
of excess hair by passing an electric current
through the root. [*Say* il leck TRAWLA sis
or ee leck TRAWLA sis]

electrolyte *n.* **1** a liquid which contains
ions and can be decomposed by
electrolysis. **2** (usu. in *pl.*) the ionized
constituents of a living cell etc.
□ **electrolytic** *adj.* [*Say* ELECTRA lite,
electra LIT ick]

electromagnet *n.* a piece of soft iron
that becomes magnetic when an electric
current is passed through the coil
surrounding it.

electromagnetic *adj.* having both an
electrical and a magnetic character or
properties. □ **electromagnetism** *n.*

electromagnetic radiation *n.* a kind
of radiation in which electric and magnetic
fields vary simultaneously.

electromechanical *adj.* of a mechanical
device which is electrically operated.

electromotive force *n.* a difference in
potential that tends to give rise to an
electric current. Abbreviation: **emf, EMF**.
[*Say* electro MOE tiv]

electron *n.* a stable subatomic particle
with a charge of negative electricity.

electronic *adj.* **1** relating to electrons or
electronics. **2** (of a device) using electronic
components. **3** relating to or carried out by
means of a computer. **4** producing sounds
by electronic means. □ **electronically** *adv.*

electronic data interchange *n.* a
computer protocol for the exchange of
electronic information. Abbreviation: **EDI**.

electronic publishing *n.* the
publishing of books etc. in machine-
readable form.

electronics *pl. n.* **1** (treated as *sing.*) a
branch of physics and technology
concerned with the behaviour and
movement of electrons. **2** the circuits used
in this. **3** electronic devices.

electron microscope *n.* a microscope

with high magnification and resolution,
employing electron beams in place of light.

electroplate ● *v.* (**electroplates,
electroplated, electroplating**) coat (a
metal object) with another metal using
electrolysis. ● *n.* electroplated articles.

electroshock ● *n.* = ELECTROCONVULSIVE
THERAPY. ● *adj.* (of medical treatment) by
means of electric shocks.

electrostatic *adj.* relating to stationary
electric charges as opposed to electric
currents. □ **electrostatically** *adv.*
[*Say* electro STATIC]

elegant *adj.* **1** tasteful, stylish. **2** showing
refined grace in movement. **3** of refined
luxury. **4** ingeniously simple and satisfying.
□ **elegance** *n.* **elegantly** *adv.*

elegiac *adj.* having a pleasing quality of
gentle and wistful mournfulness.
□ **elegiacally** *adv.* [*Say* ella JYE ick]

elegy *n.* (*pl.* **elegies**) a poem of serious
reflection, typically a lament for the dead.
[*Say* ELLA jee]

element *n.* **1** a component part or group.
2 any of the hundred or so substances that
cannot be resolved by chemical means into
simpler substances. **3** a resistance wire that
heats up in an electric heater etc. **4** (in *pl.*)
weather. **5** (in *pl.*) the rudiments of
learning. □ **in** (or **out of**) **one's element**
in (or out of) one's preferred surroundings.

elemental *adj.* **1** essential; basic. **2** of the
forces of nature. **3** pertaining to chemical
elements. **4** of the four elements.

elementary *adj.* **1 a** rudimentary,
introductory. **b** simple. **2** of or pertaining
to elementary school. **3** *Chemistry* not
decomposable.

elementary particle *n.* a subatomic
particle.

elementary school *n.* a school offering
primary education.

elephant *n.* (*pl.* **elephants** or **elephant**)
the largest living land animal, with a trunk
and long tusks.

elephant seal *n.* a very large seal, of
which the males have inflatable snouts.

elevate *v.* (**elevates, elevated,
elevating**) raise.

elevated *adj.* **1** high. **2** having a high
moral or intellectual level. **3** higher than
the area around.

elevation *n.* **1** the process, state, or fact of
elevating or being elevated. **2** the height
above a given level. **3** a high position. **4** the
angle of something with the horizontal.

elevator *n.* **1** a platform or compartment
for raising and lowering persons or things
to different floors of a building etc. **2** (also
grain elevator) a tall building for the

storing and discharge of grain. **3** the movable part of a tailplane for changing the pitch of an aircraft.

eleven *card. num.* one more than ten.

eleventh *ord. num.* constituting number eleven in a sequence. □ **the eleventh hour** the last possible moment.

elf *n.* (*pl.* **elves**) **1** a mythological being, esp. one that is small and mischievous. **2** a small person.

elfin *adj.* **1** of or like an elf. **2** small and delicate.

elicit *v.* (**elicits, elicited, eliciting**) draw out or evoke (an answer, response, etc.). [*Say* il LISS it]

elide *v.* (**elides, elided, eliding**) omit (a sound or syllable) when speaking. [*Say* il LIDE]

eligible *adj.* **1** fit or entitled to be chosen for. **2** meeting specified preconditions. **3** desirable or suitable. □ **eligibility** *n.* [*Say* ELLA juh bull, ella juh BILLA tee]

eliminate *v.* (**eliminates, eliminated, eliminating**) **1** remove, get rid of. **2** exclude from consideration. **3** exclude from further participation in a competition etc. by defeat. **4** murder (a rival etc.). **5** discharge from the body. □ **elimination** *n.* **eliminator** *n.*

elision *n.* the omission of a sound or syllable in speech. [*Say* il LIZH un *or* ee LIZH un]

elite ● *n.* 1 (the elite) the best or choice part of a larger body or group. **2** a class or group possessing wealth, power, etc. ● *adj.* of or belonging to an elite. [*Say* il LEET]

elitism *n.* **1** a way of organizing a society etc. so that only a few people have power or influence. **2** a feeling of being better than other people. □ **elitist** *n.* & *adj.* [*Say* il LEET ism]

elixir *n.* **1 a** (also **elixir of life**) a magic liquid supposedly able to prolong life indefinitely. **b** a magical or medicinal potion. **2** a supposed remedy for all ills. [*Say* il LIX ur *or* ee LIX ur]

Elizabethan ● *adj.* of the period of Elizabeth I of England. ● *n.* a person of the time of Elizabeth I. [*Say* il lizza BEETH un]

elk *n.* (*pl.* **elk** *or* **elks**) a very large N American deer the male of which has huge antlers, a shaggy mane, and a loud bugling call.

ellipse *n.* a regular oval resulting when a cone is cut by an oblique plane which does not intersect the base. [*Say* il LIPS]

ellipsis *n.* (*pl.* **ellipses**) **1** the omission of words not needed to complete the construction or sense. **2** a set of dots indicating an omission. [*Say* il LIP sis *for the singular*, il LIP seez *for the plural*]

ellipsoid *n.* a solid of which at least one set of parallel cross-sections are ellipses and the rest circles. □ **ellipsoid** (also **ellipsoidal**) *adj.* [*Say* il LIP soid]

elliptic *adj.* (also **elliptical**) **1** relating to or having the form of an ellipse. **2** (of writing or speech) very concise. □ **elliptically** *adv.* [*Say* il LIP tick]

elm *n.* **1** a shade tree with asymmetrical toothed leaves. **2** (also **elmwood**) its wood.

El Niño *n.* (*pl.* **El Niños**) an irregularly occurring southward current in the Pacific Ocean, associated with weather changes. [*Say* el NEEN yo]

elocution *n.* **1** the art of clear and expressive speech. **2** a particular style of speaking. [*Say* ella CUE sh'n]

elongate *v.* (**elongates, elongated, elongating**) lengthen, prolong. □ **elongated** *adj.* **elongation** *n.* [*Say* ee LONG gate *or* EE long gate, ee long GAY sh'n]

elope *v.* (**elopes, eloped, eloping**) run away secretly, esp. to get married. □ **elopement** *n.*

eloquent *adj.* **1** fluent or persuasive in speaking or writing. **2** clearly expressive or indicative. □ **eloquence** *n.* **eloquently** *adv.* [*Say* ELLA quint, ELLA quince]

else *adv.* **1** besides. **2** instead. □ **or else 1** otherwise. **2** *informal* a warning or threat of the consequences should a previously expressed order not be carried out.

elsewhere *adv.* in or to some other place.

elucidate *v.* (**elucidates, elucidated, elucidating**) explain, clarify. □ **elucidation** *n.* [*Say* il LUCE a date]

elude *v.* (**eludes, eluded, eluding**) **1** escape cleverly from. **2** fail to be grasped by. **3** fail to be attained.

elusive *adj.* difficult to find, catch, or achieve. □ **elusively** *adv.* **elusiveness** *n.* [*Say* il LOO sive *or* ee LOO sive]

elves *pl.* of ELF.

'em *pron. informal* them.

emaciated *adj.* abnormally thin or feeble. □ **emaciation** *n.* [*Say* im MAY see ated, im may see AY sh'n]

email ● *n.* **1** messages distributed by electronic means esp. from one computer system to another. **2** a message sent by email. **3** the email system. ● *v.* send email. □ **emailable** *adj.*

emanate *v.* (**emanates, emanated, emanating**) **1** come (from a source). **2** emit. □ **emanation** *n.* [*Say* EMMA nate, emma NATION]

emancipate *v.* (**emancipates,**

emancipated, emancipating) 1 set free. **2** free from slavery. □ **emancipated** *adj.* **emancipation** *n.*
[*Say* im MAN suh pate, im MAN suh pate id, im man suh PAY sh'n]

emasculate *v.* (**emasculates, emasculated, emasculating**) **1** make weaker or less effective. **2** castrate. **3** deprive (a man) of his male role or identity. □ **emasculation** *n.*
[*Say* im MASS cue late]

embalm *v.* **1** preserve (a corpse) from decay. **2** preserve something in an unchanged state. □ **embalmer** *n.*
[*Say* em BOM]

embankment *n.* an earth or stone bank for keeping back water, or for carrying a road or railway.

embargo ● *n.* (*pl.* **embargoes**) **1** an order prohibiting ships from entering or leaving a country's ports. **2** an official suspension of trade. **3** a prohibition. ● *v.* (**embargoes, embargoed, embargoing**) place under embargo.
[*Say* em BAR go]

embark *v.* **1** go on board a ship or aircraft. **2** begin an activity or undertaking. □ **embarkation** *n.* (in sense 1).

embarrass *v.* (**embarrasses, embarrassed, embarrassing**) cause to feel awkward or ashamed. □ **embarrassingly** *adv.* **embarrassment** *n.*

embarrassed *adj.* **1** feeling awkward or ashamed. **2** having or showing financial difficulties. □ **embarrassedly** *adv.*

embassy *n.* (*pl.* **embassies**) the residence or offices of an ambassador.
[*Say* EMBA see]

embattled *adj.* **1** beset by problems or difficulties. **2** surrounded by enemy forces.

embed *v.* (**embeds, embedded, embedding**) **1** fix firmly in a surrounding mass. **2** fix (an idea, attitude, etc.).

embellish *v.* (**embellishes, embellished, embellishing**) **1** beautify, adorn. **2** add details to (a narrative). □ **embellishment** *n.* [*Say* em BELL ish]

ember *n.* (usu. in *pl.*) a piece of glowing coal or wood in a dying fire.

embezzle *v.* (**embezzles, embezzled, embezzling**) divert (money etc.) fraudulently in violation of trust. □ **embezzlement** *n.* **embezzler** *n.*

embittered *adj.* very hostile or discontented.

emblazon *v.* inscribe a conspicuous design, logo, etc. on a surface.
[*Say* em BLAZE un]

emblem *n.* a symbol or representation identifying an institution etc.
[*Say* EM blum]

emblematic *adj.* **1** that represents or is a symbol of something. **2** that is considered typical. [*Say* embla MAT ick]

embody *v.* (**embodies, embodied, embodying**) **1** give a tangible or visible form to (an idea or quality); be a typical example of. **2** include or contain as a part. □ **embodiment** *n.* [*Say* em BODY, em BODY mint]

embolden *v.* make bold; encourage.
[*Say* em BOWL din]

emboss *v.* (**embosses, embossed, embossing**) carve or mould a raised design on. □ **embosser** *n.* **embossing** *n.*

embrace ● *v.* (**embraces, embraced, embracing**) **1** hold closely in the arms, esp. as a sign of affection. **2** accept eagerly. **3** adopt (a course of action etc.). **4** include, comprise. ● *n.* an act of embracing.

embroider *v.* **1** decorate cloth etc. with needlework. **2** embellish with fictitious additions. [*Say* em BROY dur]

embroidery *n.* (*pl.* **embroideries**) **1** the art of embroidering. **2** embroidered work.
[*Say* em BROY dur ee]

embroil *v.* involve in an argument, conflict, etc.

embryo *n.* (*pl.* **embryos**) **1 a** an offspring that has not been born or hatched. **b** a human offspring in the first eight or twelve weeks from conception. **2** a thing in a rudimentary stage. □ **in embryo** not developed. □ **embryonic** *adj.*
[*Say* EM bree oh, em bree ON ick]

emcee *informal* ● *n.* (*pl.* **emcees**) a master of ceremonies. ● *v.* (**emcees, emceed, emceeing**) act as master of ceremonies.

emerald *n.* **1** a bright green precious stone, a variety of beryl. **2** (also **emerald green**) the colour of this; bright green.

emerg *n.* *Cdn slang* = EMERGENCY 3.

emerge *v.* (**emerges, emerged, emerging**) **1** come into view. **2** (of facts, circumstances, etc.) come to light. **3** become recognized; become apparent. **4** survive an ordeal etc. □ **emergence** *n.*

emergency *n.* (*pl.* **emergencies**) **1** a sudden situation of danger etc., requiring immediate action. **2** (as an *adj.*) characterized by or for use in an emergency. **3** a part of a hospital for handling emergencies.

emergency brake *n.* a brake on a car etc. for use if the main brakes fail.

emergency room *n.* = EMERGENCY 3.

emergent *adj.* **1** becoming apparent. **2** (of

a nation) newly formed or made independent.

emeritus *adj.* retired and retaining one's title as an honour. [*Say* im MERIT us]

emery *n.* a coarse form of corundum used as an abrasive.

emery board *n.* a strip of thin wood or board coated with emery, used as a nail file.

emetic ● *adj.* that causes vomiting. ● *n.* an emetic medicine. [*Say* im MET ick]

emigrant *n.* a person who emigrates.

emigrate *v.* (**emigrates**, **emigrated**, **emigrating**) leave one's own country to settle in another. □ **emigration** *n.*

émigré *n.* an emigrant. [*Say* EMMA gray]

eminence *n.* **1** distinction; recognized superiority. **2** (**Eminence**) a title used in addressing a cardinal. [*Say* EMMA nince]

eminent *adj.* **1** distinguished. **2** used to emphasize the presence of a positive quality. □ **eminently** *adv.* [*Say* EMMA nint]

emir *n.* a title of various Muslim rulers. [*Say* em MEER]

emirate *n.* the rank or domain of an emir. [*Say* EMMA rit *or* EMMA rate]

emissary *n.* (*pl.* **emissaries**) a person sent on a special (usu. diplomatic) mission. [*Say* EM iss airy]

emission *n.* **1** the process or an act of emitting. **2** a thing emitted.

emissive *adj.* having the power to emit. □ **emissivity** *n.* [*Say* im MISS iv, im miss IV a tee]

emit *v.* (**emits**, **emitted**, **emitting**) **1 a** send out. **b** discharge. **2** give forth (a sound). □ **emitter** *n.* [*Say* im MIT, im MIT ur]

Emmenthal *n.* a kind of Swiss cheese. [*Say* EM in tawl]

emollient ● *adj.* that softens or soothes the skin. ● *n.* an emollient cream etc. [*Say* im MOLLY int]

emote *v.* (**emotes**, **emoted**, **emoting**) *informal* show excessive emotion. [*Say* im MOTE *or* ee MOTE]

emoticon *n.* a (usu. sideways) representation of a facial expression constructed out of keyboard characters, added to an esp. email message to indicate tone. [*Say* im MOTE a con *or* ee MOTE a con]

emotion *n.* a strong mental or instinctive feeling such as love or fear. □ **emotionless** *adj.*

emotional *adj.* **1** of or relating to the emotions. **2** liable to or showing excessive emotion. **3** based on emotion. **4** arousing emotion. □ **emotionalism** *n.* **emotionality** *n.* **emotionally** *adv.*

emotive *adj.* **1** of or characterized by emotion. **2** arousing emotion or strong feeling.

empathize *v.* (**empathizes**, **empathized**, **empathizing**) understand and share the feelings of another. [*Say* EMPA thize]

empathy *n.* the ability to empathize. □ **empathetic** *adj.* **empathetically** *adv.* [*Say* EM puth ee, em PATHETIC]

emperor *n.* the male sovereign of an empire.

emphasis *n.* (*pl.* **emphases**) **1** special importance or value attached to something. **2** stress laid on a word or words in speaking. **3** intensity of expression. [*Say* EMFA sis *for the singular*, EMFA seez *for the plural*]

emphasize *v.* (**emphasizes**, **emphasized**, **emphasizing**) bring into special prominence; put emphasis on.

emphatic *adj.* **1** (of language etc.) forcibly expressive. **2** showing or giving emphasis. **3** definite and clear. □ **emphatically** *adv.*

emphysema *n.* enlargement of the air sacs of the lungs causing breathlessness. [*Say* emfa ZEEM uh]

empire *n.* **1** an extensive group of states etc. under a single authority, esp. an emperor. **2** a large commercial organization etc. owned or directed by one person or group. **3** a period of government in which the sovereign is called emperor. **4** (as an *adj.*) denoting a style of dress with a waistline under the bust.

empirical *adj.* (also **empiric**) based on observation or experience rather than theory or logic. □ **empirically** *adv.* [*Say* em PEERA cull]

empiricism *n.* *Philosophy* the theory that all knowledge is derived from sense-experience. □ **empiricist** *n. & adj.* [*Say* em PEERA sism]

emplacement *n.* a platform where a gun is placed for firing.

employ ● *v.* **1** use the services of (a person) in return for payment. **2** use, esp. to good effect. **3** keep occupied. ● *n.* the state of being employed. □ **in the employ of** employed by.

employable *adj.* **1** qualified or available for employment. **2** usable. □ **employability** *n.*

employee *n.* a person employed for wages or salary.

employer *n.* a person or organization that employs people.

employment *n.* **1** the act of employing or the state of being employed. **2** a person's trade or profession.

employment insurance *n. Cdn* a federal government program providing payments to eligible unemployed people.

emporium *n. (pl.* **emporia** or **emporiums**) **1** a specialized retail store etc. **2** a large retail store selling a wide variety of goods. [*Say* em PORE ee um *for the singular,* em PORE ee uh *for the plural*]

empower *v.* **1** authorize. **2** give power to. **3** give strength and confidence to. □ **empowerment** *n.*

empress *n. (pl.* **empresses**) **1** the wife or widow of an emperor. **2** a female sovereign of an empire.

empty ● *adj.* (**emptier, emptiest**) **1** containing nothing. **2** meaningless. **3** *Math* (of a class or set) containing no members or elements. ● *v.* (**empties, emptied, emptying**) **1** make or become empty. **2** transfer (the contents of a container). **3** (of a river) flow into the sea etc. ● *n. (pl.* **empties**) *informal* a container (esp. a bottle) left empty of its contents. □ **run on empty** continue to function though having exhausted all one's resources etc. □ **emptiness** *n.*

empty-handed *adj.* **1** bringing or taking nothing. **2** having achieved or obtained nothing.

empty nest *n.* a household where the children have grown up and left. □ **empty nester** *n.*

emu *n. (pl.* **emus**) a flightless Australian bird related to the ostrich. [*Say* EE myoo *or* EE moo]

emulate *v.* (**emulates, emulated, emulating**) **1** match or surpass. **2** imitate. □ **emulation** *n.* **emulator** *n.* [*Say* EM yoo late]

emulsifier *n.* any substance that stabilizes an emulsion, esp. one used to stabilize processed foods. [*Say* im MULL suh fire]

emulsify *v.* (**emulsifies, emulsified, emulsifying**) make into or become an emulsion. [*Say* im MULL suh fie]

emulsion *n.* **1** a fine dispersion of one liquid in another. **2** a light-sensitive coating for photographic plates or films. [*Say* im MULL shun]

enable *v.* (**enables, enabled, enabling**) **1** give the means or authority to do something. **2** make possible. **3** esp. *Computing* make operational. □ **enabler** *n.*

enact *v.* **1 a** establish (a law etc.). **b** make (a bill etc.) law. **2** play (a part on stage etc.). □ **enactment** *n.*

enamel ● *n.* **1** a glass-like shiny coating on metallic or other surfaces for ornament. **2** a paint that dries to give a smooth hard coat. **3** the hard coating over the crown of a tooth. ● *v.* (**enamels, enamelled, enamelling**) coat with enamel.

enamour *v.* (also **enamor**) **1** inspire with love or liking. **2** charm. [*Say* in AMMER]

encamp *v.* **1** settle in a military camp. **2** lodge in the open in tents.

encampment *n.* a place where troops etc. are encamped.

encapsulate *v.* (**encapsulates, encapsulated, encapsulating**) **1** enclose in or as in a capsule. **2** summarize. □ **encapsulation** *n.*

encase *v.* (**encases, encased, encasing**) **1** put into a case. **2** surround as with a case.

encephalitis *n.* inflammation of the brain. [*Say* en seffa LITE is]

enchant *v.* (usu. in *passive*) **1** delight. **2** bewitch. □ **enchanted** *adj.* **enchantedly** *adv.* **enchantment** *n.*

enchanting *adj.* delightfully charming or attractive. □ **enchantingly** *adv.*

enchilada *n. (pl.* **enchiladas**) a tortilla rolled around a filling, served with chili sauce. □ **the whole enchilada** a thing in its entirety. [*Say* encha LADA]

encircle *v.* (**encircles, encircled, encircling**) **1** surround. **2** form a circle around.

enclave *n.* **1** a portion of territory of one state surrounded by territory of another, as viewed by the surrounding territory. **2** a group of people who are distinct from those surrounding them. [*Say* ON clave *or* EN clave]

enclose *v.* (**encloses, enclosed, enclosing**) **1** surround or close off on all sides. **2** fence in. **3** put in an envelope together with a letter.

enclosure *n.* **1** the act of enclosing. **2** an enclosed area. **3** a thing enclosed with a letter.

encode *v.* (**encodes, encoded, encoding**) **1** put into code or cipher. **2** specify the genetic code for. □ **encoder** *n.*

encomium *n. (pl.* **encomiums** or **encomia**) a formal or high-flown expression of praise. [*Say* en CO me um]

encompass *v.* (**encompasses, encompassed, encompassing**) **1** surround or form a circle about. **2** include comprehensively.

encore ● *n.* **1** a call by an audience for additional performance. **2** such a performance. ● *interj.* again.

encounter ● *v.* **1** meet, come across, esp. unexpectedly. **2** meet as an opponent. ● *n.* **1** a meeting by chance. **2** a confrontation.

3 an act of sexual intercourse. **4** an exposure to something.

encourage v. (**encourages**, **encouraged**, **encouraging**) **1** give courage, confidence, or hope to. **2** urge, advise. **3** stimulate by help etc. **4** promote or assist. □ **encouragement** n. **encourager** n. **encouraging** adj. **encouragingly** adv.

encroach v. (**encroaches**, **encroached**, **encroaching**) **1** intrude, esp. on another's territory or rights. **2** advance gradually beyond due limits. □ **encroachment** n.

encrust v. cover with a crust.

encrypt v. convert (data) into code. □ **encryption** n.

encumber v. burden (someone or something).

encumbrance n. a burden or impediment.

encyclical n. a papal letter addressed to the members of the Catholic Church. [Say en SICK lick ul]

encyclopedia n. (pl. **encyclopedias**) a book or set of books giving information on many subjects. [Say en sike luh PEEDY uh]

encyclopedic adj. **1** of or resembling an encyclopedia. **2** comprehensive. [Say en sike luh PEED ick]

end ● n. **1** the extreme limit or furthest part. **2** death, destruction, downfall. **3** a goal or purpose. **4** a piece left over. **5** (**the end**) informal the limit of what one can endure. **6** a part or share of an activity. **7** one side of a rink, court, or field. **8** Curling one of the frames of a game. **9** Football the lineman positioned furthest from centre. ● v. **1** bring or come to an end. **2** have as a result. **3** eventually do or come to. □ **at an end** exhausted or completed. **at the end of one's rope** (or **tether**) having reached the limits of one's patience etc. **end it** (**all**) informal commit suicide. **end of the road** the point at which a hope etc. has been abandoned. **make ends meet** live within one's income. **no end** informal to a great extent. **no end of** informal much or many of. **on end 1** in an upright position. **2** continuously.

endanger v. **1** place in danger. **2** jeopardize the continuance of (a species etc.). □ **endangerment** n.

endangered species n. a species in danger of extinction.

endear v. make dear to or beloved by.

endearing adj. inspiring love or affection. □ **endearingly** adv.

endearment n. **1** an expression of love. **2** fondness, affection.

endeavour (also **endeavor**) ● v. try earnestly. ● n. an attempt. [Say en DEV ur]

endemic adj. **1** (of a disease, condition, etc.) regularly found in a particular place or among a particular group. **2** (of a plant or animal) native and usu. restricted to a certain area. [Say en DEM ick]

ending n. **1** a termination or conclusion. **2** an end or final part. **3** an inflected final part of a word.

endive n. **1** (also called **Belgian endive**) the crown of the chicory plant used in salads. **2** a curly-leaved plant used in salads. [Say EN dive]

endless adj. **1** infinite, without end. **2** continual, incessant. **3** (of a belt, chain, etc.) having the ends joined for continuous action. □ **endlessly** adv. **endlessness** n.

endnote n. a note printed at the end of a book etc.

endocrine ● adj. (of a gland) secreting directly into the blood. ● n. an endocrine gland. [Say ENDO crine or ENDO crin]

endocrinology n. the study of endocrine glands and hormones. □ **endocrinologist** n. [Say endo crin OLLA jee, endo crin OLLA jist]

endometriosis n. a condition in which endometrial tissue grows in the pelvic cavity. [Say endo mee tree OH sis]

endometrium n. (pl. **endometria**) the mucous membrane lining the uterus. □ **endometrial** adj. [Say endo MEE tree um, endo MEE tree ul]

endoplasm n. the inner fluid of the cytoplasm of some cells. [Say ENDO plazzum]

endorphin n. any of a group of peptide neurotransmitters occurring in the brain and having pain-relieving properties. [Say en DOR fin]

endorse v. (**endorses**, **endorsed**, **endorsing**) **1 a** declare one's approval of. **b** confirm. **2** sign on the back of (a cheque) to make (it) payable to someone.

endorsement n. **1** (Cdn also **endorsation**) an act of endorsing. **2** (also **product endorsement**) a recommendation of a product or service in advertising material. **3** something with which a document etc. is endorsed.

endoscope n. a flexible medical instrument for viewing the internal cavities or hollow organs of the body. □ **endoscopic** adj. **endoscopy** n. (pl. **endoscopies**) [Say ENDO scope, endo SKOP ick, en DOSS kuh pee]

endoskeleton n. an internal skeleton. [Say ENDO skeleton]

endosperm *n.* nutritive material surrounding the germ in plant seeds. [*Say* ENDO sperm]

endothermic *adj.* (of a reaction) absorbing heat. [*Say* endo THERMIC]

endotoxin *n.* a toxin in a bacterial cell. [*Say* ENDO toxin]

endow *v.* **1 a** bequeath or give a permanent income to. **b** establish (an academic chair, prize, etc.) by donating funds. **2** enrich or provide with. □ **endowed** *adj.*

endowment *n.* **1** the action of endowing. **2** property or income with which a person or organization is endowed. **3** a quality or ability.

endpaper *n.* a leaf of paper at the beginning and end of a book, fixed to the inside cover.

end product *n.* the final product.

end run *n.* a tactic or manoeuvre used to achieve one's ends by indirect means.

endurance *n.* the fact or power of enduring something unpleasant, difficult, or painful.

endure *v.* (**endures, endured, enduring**) **1 a** undergo (a difficulty, hardship, etc.). **b** withstand (strain, pressure, etc.). **2** tolerate. **3** remain in existence. **4** submit to. □ **endurable** *adj.* **enduring** *adj.* **enduringly** *adv.*

end-user *n.* the person who is the intended ultimate recipient or user of a product.

end zone *n. Football* the rectangular area between the goal line and the end line.

enema *n.* (*pl.* **enemas**) **1** the injection of liquid into the rectum, esp. to expel the contents. **2** a fluid so injected. [*Say* ENNA muh]

enemy *n.* (*pl.* **enemies**) **1 a** a person or group actively opposed or hostile to someone or something. **b** an adversary or opponent. **2 a** a hostile nation or its armed forces in a time of war. **b** a member of such a force. **3** a thing that harms, injures, or is prejudicial to another. □ **be one's own worst enemy** have the habit of bringing trouble upon oneself by one's own actions or behaviour.

energetic *adj.* showing or involving great energy. □ **energetically** *adv.*

energize *v.* (**energizes, energized, energizing**) **1** infuse energy or vigour into. **2** provide energy for the operation of. □ **energized** *adj.* **energizer** *n.*

energy *n.* (*pl.* **energies**) **1** a person's force, vigour, or capacity for strenuous activity. **2** (in *pl.*) individual powers in use. **3** *Physics* **a** the quantity of work a system is capable

of doing. **b** this ability provided in a readily utilized form, such as an electric current.

enervate *v.* (**enervates, enervated, enervating**) cause someone to feel drained of energy. □ **enervating** *adj.* **enervation** *n.* [*Say* ENNER vate]

enfant terrible *n.* (*pl.* **enfants terribles**) a person whose controversial attitudes, behaviours, etc. shock others. [*Say* on fon tare EEB luh]

enfeeble *v.* (**enfeebles, enfeebled, enfeebling**) weaken. □ **enfeebled** *adj.*

enfold *v.* **1** envelop. **2** clasp someone lovingly in one's arms.

enforce *v.* (**enforces, enforced, enforcing**) **1** compel observance of (a law etc.). **2** force something to happen. □ **enforceability** *n.* **enforceable** *adj.* **enforcement** *n.*

enforcer *n.* **1** a person or thing that enforces. **2** *Hockey* a highly aggressive player who protects other players on his team. **3** a gang member who intimidates others.

enfranchise *v.* (**enfranchises, enfranchised, enfranchising**) **1** grant (a person) the right to vote. **2** *Cdn* give up one's status as an Indian. □ **enfranchisement** *n.*

engage *v.* (**engages, engaged, engaging**) **1** employ or hire. **2** attract or involve (a person's attention, interest, etc.). **3** reserve for one's own use. **4** bring (a component) into operation. **5** enter into combat with. **6** take part in.

engagé *adj.* showing social, moral, or political commitment. [*Say* ong ga ZHAY]

engaged *adj.* **1** under a promise to marry. **2** occupied. **3** actively participating in issues etc. **4** in operation.

engagement *n.* **1** the act or state of engaging or being engaged. **2** an appointment. **3** a betrothal. **4** an encounter between hostile forces. **5** the period during which a performance is being produced.

engaging *adj.* **1** attractive, charming. **2** interesting. □ **engagingly** *adv.*

engender *v.* give rise to; bring about. [*Say* en GENDER]

engine *n.* **1** a machine for producing energy of motion from some other form of energy. **2 a** a railway locomotive. **b** = FIRE ENGINE. **3** a thing that achieves or causes something.

engine block *n.* the metal casting housing the cylinders etc. of an internal combustion engine.

engineer ● *n.* **1** a person qualified in engineering. **2 a** a person who designs or makes engines. **b** a person who maintains or controls an engine or other machine. **3** a soldier in a division of an army that specializes in engineering. ● v. **1** arrange for something to happen or take place. **2** design, make.

engineering n. **1** the application of science for directly useful purposes, as construction, propulsion, etc. **2** the work done by an engineer.

English ● adj. **1** of or relating to England, its language or its people. **2** *Cdn* of or relating to English-speaking Canadians. ● n. **1** the language of England, now used in many varieties around the world. **2 (the English) a** the people of England. **b** English-speaking people. **3** English language or literature as a subject of study. □ **Englishman** n. **Englishwoman** n.

English Canadian n. **1** an English-speaking Canadian. **2** a Canadian of English descent. □ **English Canadian** adj.

English cucumber n. a long seedless variety of cucumber.

English muffin n. a small, round, flat, yeast bread, usu. toasted.

engorge v. (**engorges, engorged, engorging**) cause to swell with fluid. □ **engorged** adj.

engrave v. (**engraves, engraved, engraving**) **1** cut words or designs on a hard surface. **2** cut or produce (a design) for printing. **3** impress deeply or indelibly. □ **engraved** adj. **engraver** n.

engraving n. **1** a print made from an engraved plate. **2** the process or art of cutting a design etc. on metal, stone, etc. **3** an engraved design or inscription.

engross v. (**engrosses, engrossed, engrossing**) absorb the whole attention of. □ **engrossing** adj.

engulf v. **1** surround or cover completely. **2** swallow up or overwhelm. □ **engulfment** n.

enhance v. (**enhances, enhanced, enhancing**) **1** increase the good quality, value or status of. **2** improve (a thing). □ **enhancement** n. **enhancer** n.

enigma n. a puzzling or perplexing person or thing. □ **enigmatic** adj. **enigmatically** adv. [Say en NIGMA, en ig MAT ick]

enjoin v. **1** order or strongly advise someone to do something; say that a particular action or quality is necessary. **2** *Law* prohibit or restrain (a person) by an injunction.

enjoy v. **1** take pleasure in. **2** have the use of (something pleasant). **3** experience. □ **enjoy oneself** experience pleasure. □ **enjoyable** adj. **enjoyableness** n. **enjoyably** adv. **enjoyment** n.

enlarge v. (**enlarges, enlarged, enlarging**) **1 a** make or become bigger. **b** make more comprehensive. **2** describe in greater detail. **3** produce an enlargement of (a photo). □ **enlarged** adj. **enlarger** n.

enlargement n. **1** the process or result of something becoming or being made larger. **2** *Photography* a print that is larger than the original negative.

enlighten v. **1** give someone greater knowledge and understanding. **2** give spiritual knowledge or insight to. □ **enlightening** adj.

enlightened adj. having or showing an understanding that is not based on old-fashioned attitudes.

enlightenment n. **1** knowledge and understanding. **2 (the Enlightenment)** the 18th-century philosophical movement in Europe which emphasized reason and individualism. **3** *Buddhism* a state of pure and unqualified knowledge and insight.

enlist v. **1** enrol in the armed forces. **2** engage (a person etc.) as a means of help or support. □ **enlistment** n.

enliven v. **1** make something more interesting or more fun. **2** make someone more cheerful. □ **enlivening** adj. [Say en LIE v'n]

en masse adv. all together. [Say on MASS]

enmesh v. (**enmeshes, enmeshed, enmeshing**) entangle.

enmity n. (pl. **enmities**) hostility. [Say ENMA tee]

ennoble v. (**ennobles, ennobled, ennobling**) **1** lend greater dignity or nobility to. **2** give the rank of noble to. □ **ennoblement** n. **ennobling** adj. [Say en NOBLE]

ennui n. boredom or mental weariness from lack of occupation etc. [Say on WEE]

enormity n. (pl. **enormities**) **1** monstrous wickedness. **2** an act of extreme wickedness. **3** large size or scale. [Say en NORMA tee]

enormous adj. excessive in size or intensity. □ **enormously** adv. **enormousness** n.

enough ● adj. as much or as many as required. ● n. as much as is needed. ● adv. **1** sufficiently **2** passably. **3** very. □ **enough is enough** stop, no more.

enquire v. = INQUIRE.

enquiry n. = INQUIRY. [Say en QUIRE ee]

enrage v. (**enrages, enraged, enraging**) make very angry. □ **enraged** adj.

enrapture v. (**enraptures, enraptured, enrapturing**) give someone great pleasure.

enrich v. (**enriches**, **enriched**, **enriching**) **1** make wealthy or wealthier. **2 a** enhance or make (a thing) richer. **b** improve the quality or value of. **3** make (a course of study) more challenging. □ **enriched** adj. **enriching** adj. **enrichment** n.

enrol v. (also **enroll**) (**enrols** or **enrolls**, **enrolled**, **enrolling**) **1** enter one's name on a list. **2** join or be recruited as esp. a member, student, etc. □ **enrolment** n.

enrollee n. a person who has officially enrolled in a course etc.

en route adv. on the way. [Say on ROOT]

ensconce v. (**ensconces**, **ensconced**, **ensconcing**) establish or settle comfortably or safely. [Say en SCONCE]

ensemble n. **1** a thing viewed as the sum of its parts. **2** an outfit worn together. **3** a group of actors, dancers, musicians, etc. who perform together. **4 a** a group of singers or musicians. **b** a piece of music sung or played by the whole group of musicians. [Say on SOM bull]

enshrine v. (**enshrines**, **enshrined**, **enshrining**) **1** integrate (a right, principle, etc.) into a law etc. so as to preserve it perpetually. **2** contain in a way that preserves or cherishes. □ **enshrinement** n.

ensign n. **1** a military or naval standard, esp. one showing its nationality. **2** the lowest rank of commissioned officer in the US navy and coast guard. [Say EN sign or EN sin]

enslave v. (**enslaves**, **enslaved**, **enslaving**) **1** cause (a person) to lose freedom of choice or action. **2** reduce (a person) to slavery. □ **enslavement** n.

ensnare v. (**ensnares**, **ensnared**, **ensnaring**) catch in or as in a snare.

ensue v. (**ensues**, **ensued**, **ensuing**) happen afterwards or as a result. □ **ensuing** adj. [Say en SUE]

ensuite Cdn & Brit. ● adv. forming a single unit, with one room leading into another. ● adj. (of a room) adjoining. ● n. an ensuite bathroom. [Say on SWEET]

ensure v. (**ensures**, **ensured**, **ensuring**) **1** make certain that something will occur or be so. **2** secure. **3** make safe from a risk etc.

ENT abbr. Medical ear, nose, and throat.

entail v. **1** necessitate as a consequence or involve in a way that is not avoidable. **2** Law bequeath (property etc.) so that it remains within a family. □ **entailment** n.

entangle v. (**entangles**, **entangled**, **entangling**) **1** cause to get caught in something that is tangled. **2** cause to become tangled. **3** involve in difficulties, a compromising relationship, etc. **4** make tangled, complicated, etc. □ **entanglement** n.

entente n. **1** (also **entente cordiale** (pl. **ententes cordiales**)) a friendly understanding between nations. **2** a group of nations in such a relation. **3** an agreement to co-operate. [Say on TONT (cordy AL)]

enter ● v. **1** go or come in. **2** penetrate. **3 a** write or record information. **b** input (data). **4** register as a competitor. **5** enrol as or become a member of (a society etc.). **6** introduce (a matter etc.) for consideration. **7 a** engage in. **b** subscribe to. **c** form part of (one's plans etc.). **8 a** begin, undertake. **b** assume the functions of. ● n. the key on a computer keyboard which when pressed instructs the computer to execute a command etc.

enterprise n. **1** an undertaking. **2** bold resourcefulness. **3** a business or businesses collectively. □ **enterpriser** n.

enterprising adj. **1** ready to engage in enterprises. **2** imaginative, energetic. □ **enterprisingly** adv.

entertain v. **1** amuse; occupy agreeably. **2 a** receive or treat as a guest. **b** receive guests. **3** give consideration to (an idea).

entertainer n. a person who entertains, esp. professionally.

entertaining adj. amusing. □ **entertainingly** adv.

entertainment n. **1** the action of entertaining. **2** a public performance. **3** amusement.

enthrall v. (**enthralls**, **enthralled**, **enthralling**) captivate. □ **enthralling** adj. [Say en THRAWL]

enthrone v. (**enthrones**, **enthroned**, **enthroning**) install (a king, bishop, etc.) on a throne, esp. ceremonially. □ **enthronement** n.

enthuse v. (**enthuses**, **enthused**, **enthusing**) informal **1** be or make enthusiastic. **2** speak enthusiastically.

enthusiasm n. **1** strong interest or admiration. **2** great eagerness. □ **enthusiast** n. **enthusiastic** adj. **enthusiastically** adv.

entice v. (**entices**, **enticed**, **enticing**) attract by the offer of pleasure or reward. □ **enticement** n. **enticing** adj. **enticingly** adv. [Say en TICE]

entire adj. **1** whole, complete. **2** not broken or decayed. **3** unqualified, absolute.

entirely adv. **1** wholly. **2** solely.

entirety n. (pl. **entireties**) the sum total.

□ **in its entirety** in its complete form. [Say en TIRE tee or en TIE ruh tee]

entitle v. (**entitles**, **entitled**, **entitling**) **1** to give somebody a right to have or do something. **2** give a title to. □ **entitlement** n.

entity n. (pl. **entities**) a thing with distinct existence. [Say ENTA tee]

entomb v. place in or as in a tomb. □ **entombment** n.

entomology n. the study of the forms and behaviour of insects. □ **entomological** adj. **entomologist** n. [Say enta MOLLA jee, enta muh LOGICAL, enta MOLLA jist]

entourage n. people attending an esp. important person. [Say onta RAWZH]

entrails pl. n. the internal bodily organs, esp. the intestines. [Say EN trails]

entrance[1] n. **1** the act of entering. **2 a** a door etc. by which one enters. **b** a point of entering something. **3** the right or privilege of admission.

entrance[2] v. (**entrances**, **entranced**, **entrancing**) fill with wonder and delight. □ **entrancing** adj. **entrancingly** adv. [Say en TRANCE]

entrant n. **1** a person who enters a competition etc. **2** a person who enters, joins, or takes part in something. **3** a product etc. which enters a new market etc. [Say EN trint]

entrap v. (**entraps**, **entrapped**, **entrapping**) **1** catch in or as in a trap. **2** beguile or trick. □ **entrapment** n.

entreat v. ask earnestly.

entreaty n. (pl. **entreaties**) an earnest request.

entree n. **1** the main dish of a meal. **2** the right or privilege of admission. [Say ON tray]

entrench v. (**entrenches**, **entrenched**, **entrenching**) **1** to establish something very firmly so that it is very difficult to change. **2** establish (a military force) in a fortified position. □ **entrench oneself** adopt a well-defended position. □ **entrenched** adj. **entrenchment** n.

entrepreneur n. a person who starts or organizes a commercial business. □ **entrepreneurial** adj. **entrepreneurialism** n. **entrepreneurship** n. [Say ontra pruh NUR, ontra pruh NURRY ul]

entropy n. **1** Physics a thermodynamic quantity representing the lack of availability of a system's thermal energy for conversion into mechanical work. **2** lack of order or predictability.

□ **entropic** adj. [Say ENTRA pee, en TROPIC]

entrust v. make someone responsible for.

entry n. (pl. **entries**) **1** an act of coming or going in. **2** a place of entrance. **3 a** the right, means, or opportunity to enter. **b** the action of undertaking something. **4** an item entered in a list etc. **5** the act of entering (data etc.) into something.

entry-level adj. **1** suitable for inexperienced applicants. **2** relatively low in cost.

entwine v. (**entwines**, **entwined**, **entwining**) **1** to twist or wind together. **2** to be very closely involved with.

enumerate v. (**enumerates**, **enumerated**, **enumerating**) **1** specify (items); mention one by one. **2** Cdn enter (a name) on a list of voters. **3** count. □ **enumeration** n. **enumerator** n. [Say in NEW mur ate, in new mur AY sh'n, in NEW mur ate ur]

enunciate v. (**enunciates**, **enunciated**, **enunciating**) **1** pronounce clearly. **2** set out precisely. □ **enunciation** n. [Say in NUN see ate]

envelop v. (**envelops**, **enveloped**, **enveloping**) wrap up, cover, or surround completely. [Say en VELL up]

envelope n. **1** a folded paper container, usu. with a flap that can be sealed, for a letter etc. **2** Botany any enveloping structure. □ **push** (or **push the edge of**) **the envelope** go to the greatest length that an activity allows. [Say ENVA lope or ONVA lope]

enviable adj. exciting or likely to excite envy. □ **enviably** adv. [Say ENVY a bull]

envious adj. feeling or showing envy. □ **enviously** adv. [Say ENVY us]

environment n. **1** the physical surroundings, conditions, etc., in which a person, animal, or plant lives etc. **2** the area surrounding a place. **3** Computing the overall structure within which a user or program operates. □ **environmental** adj. **environmentally** adv.

environmentalist n. a person who is concerned with the protection of the environment. □ **environmentalism** n.

environmentally friendly adj. (also **environment-friendly**) not harmful to the environment.

environs pl. n. a surrounding district. [Say en VIRE enz]

envisage v. (**envisages**, **envisaged**, **envisaging**) **1** have a mental picture of. **2** contemplate or conceive. [Say en VIZ idge]

envision *v.* envisage, visualize.
[*Say* en VISION]

envoy *n.* a messenger or representative.
[*Say* ON voy *or* EN voy]

envy ● *n.* (*pl.* **envies**) **1** a feeling of
discontented longing aroused by another's
better fortune etc. **2** the object of this
feeling. ● *v.* (**envies**, **envied**, **envying**)
feel envy of.

enzyme *n.* a protein produced by living
cells and functioning as a catalyst in a
specific biochemical reaction.
□ **enzymatic** *adj.* [*Say* EN zime,
enza MAT ick]

Eocene *n.* the second epoch of the Tertiary
period, lasting from about 54.9 to 38
million years BP. □ **Eocene** *adj.*
[*Say* EE oh seen]

eon *n.* **1** a very long or indefinite period.
2 *Astronomy* a billion years. **3** the largest
division of geological time. [*Say* EE on]

epaulette *n.* (also **epaulet**) a decoration
on the shoulder of a coat etc., esp. on a
uniform. [*Say* eppa LET]

épée *n.* *Fencing* a sharp-pointed duelling
sword, often with a blunt end. [*Say* ay PAY]

ephedra *n.* (*pl.* **ephedras**) an evergreen
shrub with trailing stems. [*Say* ef FEDRA]

ephedrine *n.* an alkaloid drug found in
some ephedras, causing constriction of the
blood vessels and widening of the
bronchial passages. [*Say* eff ED rin]

ephemera *pl. n.* things of short-lived
importance or usefulness.
[*Say* ef FEM er uh]

ephemeral *adj.* lasting or of use for only a
short time. [*Say* ef FEM er ul *or*
ef FEEM er ul]

epic ● *n.* **1** a long poem narrating the
deeds of heroic figures or the past history
of a nation. **2** a long film, book, etc.
portraying heroic adventures or covering
an extended period of time. ● *adj.* **1** having
the features of an epic. **2** grand or heroic.
□ **epically** *adv.*

epicentre *n.* **1** the point at which an
earthquake reaches the earth's surface.
2 the centre or heart of something.
[*Say* EPPA centre]

epicure *n.* (also **epicurean**) a person
with refined tastes, esp. in food and drink.
□ **epicurean** *adj.* [*Say* EPPA cure,
eppa CURE ee un]

epidemic ● *n.* **1** a widespread occurrence
of a disease in a community at a particular
time. **2** a wide prevalence of something
undesirable. ● *adj.* widespread.

epidemiology *n.* the study of the spread
and control of diseases and other health-
related factors. □ **epidemiologic** *adj.*

epidemiological *adj.* **epidemiologist**
n. [*Say* eppa deemy OLLA jee,
eppa deemy a LOGIC,
eppa deemy OLLA jist]

epidermis *n.* **1** the outer cellular layer of
the skin. **2** the outer layer of tissue in
plants. □ **epidermal** *adj.*
[*Say* eppa DERMIS, eppa DERMAL]

epidural ● *adj.* **1** on or around the
outermost membrane enveloping the brain
and spinal cord. **2** (of an anaesthetic)
introduced into the space around this
membrane. ● *n.* an epidural anaesthetic,
used esp. in childbirth. [*Say* eppa DUR ul]

epiglottis *n.* (*pl.* **epiglottises**) a flap of
cartilage at the root of the tongue, which is
depressed during swallowing to cover the
windpipe. [*Say* eppa GLOTTIS]

epigram *n.* **1** a short witty poem. **2 a** a
saying or maxim. **b** a pointed and usu.
witty remark. □ **epigrammatic** *adj.*
[*Say* EPPA gram, eppa gruh MAT ick]

epigraph *n.* **1** a quotation at the
beginning of a chapter, book, etc. **2** an
inscription on a statue, building, etc.
[*Say* EPPA graph]

epilepsy *n.* a disorder of the nervous
system causing loss of consciousness or
convulsions. □ **epileptic** *adj.*
[*Say* EPPA lep see, eppa LEP tick]

epilogue *n.* **1** the concluding part of a
literary work. **2** a speech etc. addressed to
the audience at the end of a play.
[*Say* EPPA log]

epinephrine *n.* = ADRENALIN.
[*Say* eppa NEFF rin]

epiphany *n.* (*pl.* **epiphanies**)
1 (**Epiphany**) a Christian festival on Jan. 6
commemorating (in the Orthodox Church)
the baptism of Jesus, or (in the Western
Church) the manifestation of Jesus to the
three wise men. **2** a sudden realization.
[*Say* ep PIFFA nee]

epiphyte *n.* a plant growing but not
parasitic on another. □ **epiphytic** *adj.*
[*Say* EPPA fite, eppa FIT ick]

episcopal *adj.* **1** of a bishop or bishops.
2 (**Episcopal**) of or relating to the
Episcopal Church. [*Say* ep PISKA pull]

Episcopal Church *n.* the Anglican
Church in the US and Scotland.

episcopalian ● *adj.* **1** of or advocating
government of a Church by bishops. **2** of or
belonging to an episcopal Church. ● *n.*
(**Episcopalian**) a member of the
Episcopal Church. [*Say* ep piska PAILY un]

episcopate *n.* **1** the office or tenure of a
bishop. **2** (**the episcopate**) the bishops
collectively. [*Say* ep PISKA pit]

episiotomy n. (pl. **episiotomies**) a surgical cut made at the opening of the vagina during childbirth. [Say ep peezy OTTA me or ep pizzy OTTA me]

episode n. **1** one event or a group of events as part of a sequence. **2** each of the parts of a serial story or broadcast. **3** an incident that is distinct but contributes to a whole.

episodic adj. **1** containing a series of separate parts or events. **2** occurring at irregular intervals. □ **episodically** adv. [Say eppa SOD ick]

epistemology n. the theory of knowledge. □ **epistemological** adj. [Say ep pista MOLLA jee, ep pista muh LOGICAL]

epistle n. **1** formal or jocular a letter. **2** (**Epistle**) any of the letters of the apostles in the New Testament. [Say ep PISSLE]

epitaph n. words written in memory of a person who has died. [Say EPPA taff]

epithelium n. (pl. **epitheliums** or **epithelia**) the thin tissue forming the outer layer of a body's surface and lining many hollow structures. □ **epithelial** adj. [Say eppa THEELY um, eppa THEELY ul]

epithet n. **1** a descriptive word expressing a quality or attribute. **2** such a word as a term of abuse. [Say EP ith et]

epitome n. a perfect example of something. [Say ep PITTA me]

epitomize v. (**epitomizes**, **epitomized**, **epitomizing**) be a perfect example of. [Say ep PITTA mize]

epoch n. **1** a period of time in history. **2** a division of geological time that is a subdivision of a period. □ **epochal** adj. [Say EP ock or EE pock]

eponymous adj. **1** (of a person etc.) giving their name to something. **2** (of a thing) named after a particular person.

epoxy ● n. (pl. **epoxies**) (also **epoxy resin**) a synthetic resin which sets permanently when heated, used as an adhesive. ● v. (**epoxies**, **epoxied**, **epoxying**) secure with epoxy glue etc. [Say ep POXY]

Epsom salts n. (as sing. or pl.) a preparation of magnesium sulphate used medicinally.

equable adj. **1** not easily disturbed or angered. **2** free from fluctuation or variation. □ **equably** adv. [Say EKWA bull]

equal ● adj. **1** identical in amount, size, number, status, etc. **2** evenly balanced. **3** having the same rights or status. **4** applicable to all in the same way. ● n. a person or thing equal to another. ● v. (**equals, equalled, equalling**) **1** be equal to. **2** match or rival. □ **be equal to** have the ability or resources for. □ **equally** adv.

equality n. (pl. **equalities**) the condition of being equal.

equalization payment n. (also **equalization grant**) Cdn a transfer by the federal government of funds to poorer provinces to ensure comparable levels of service and taxation.

equalize v. (**equalizes, equalized, equalizing**) **1** make or become equal. **2** score a goal or point that ties a match. □ **equalization** n.

equalizer n. **1** a thing that equalizes. **2** Electricity a network designed to modify a frequency response. **3** a goal etc. that ties the score in a game.

equal opportunity n. **1** the right to be considered for employment without discrimination on the basis of race, sex, etc. **2** the practice of not discriminating in this way.

equanimity n. mental composure, evenness of temper. [Say ekwa NIMMA tee]

equate v. (**equates, equated, equating**) **1** consider (one thing) as equal to another. **2** be or make equal or equivalent to.

equation n. **1** the process of equating one thing with another. **2** a statement that two mathematical expressions are equal (indicated by the sign =). **3** a formula indicating a chemical reaction.

equator n. an imaginary line around the earth, equidistant from the poles, dividing the earth into northern and southern hemispheres.

equatorial adj. **1** of an equator. **2** situated on or near the earth's equator. [Say ekwa TORY ul or eekwa TORY ul]

equestrian ● adj. **1** of or relating to horses and horseback riding. **2** representing a person on horseback. ● n. a person who is skilled at horseback riding. [Say i KWESTRY in]

equidistant adj. at equal distances. [Say ekwa DISTANT or EEKWA distant]

equilateral adj. having all its sides equal in length. [Say ekwa LATERAL or EEKWA lateral]

equilibrium n. (pl. **equilibria** or **equilibriums**) **1** a state of balance, especially between opposing forces. **2** a state of mental calm. [Say eekwa LIB ree um or ekwa LIB ree um for the singular, eekwa LIB ree uh or ekwa LIB ree uh for the plural]

equine *adj.* of, like, or affecting a horse or horses. [*Say* ECK wine *or* EEK wine]

equinox *n.* (*pl.* **equinoxes**) either of the two occasions in the year, approx. March 21 and Sept.22, when day and night are of equal length. [*Say* EKWA nox *or* EEKWA nox]

equip *v.* (**equips, equipped, equipping**) **1** supply with what is needed. **2** provide with the mental or physical resources needed for a task etc.

equipment *n.* **1** the items needed for a particular purpose. **2** mental or physical resources. **3** the process of equipping or being equipped.

equitable *adj.* characterized by fairness or equity. □ **equitably** *adv.* [*Say* EKWA tuh bull]

equity *n.* (*pl.* **equities**) **1** fairness, impartiality. **2** a system of natural justice allowing a fair judgement in a situation where the existing laws are not satisfactory. **3 a** (also **equity capital**) the value of a company's shares. **b** (**equities**) shares in a company which pay relatively low, profit-related dividends. **4** the value of a property after all debts have been paid. [*Say* EKWA tee]

equivalent *adj.* equal in value, amount, meaning, etc. □ **equivalence** *n.* **equivalency** *n.* **equivalently** *adv.*

equivocal *adj.* **1** (of words etc.) capable of more than one interpretation. **2** (of evidence etc.) of uncertain significance. **3** vague. □ **equivocally** *adv.* [*Say* i KWIV uh cull]

equivocate *v.* (**equivocates, equivocated, equivocating**) use ambiguous language so as to conceal the truth. □ **equivocation** *n.* [*Say* i KWIVVA kate]

ER *n.* (*pl.* **ERs**) an emergency room in a hospital.

-er[1] *suffix* forming nouns denoting: **1 a** a person involved with or in something. **b** an animal or thing that does a specified action or activity. **2 a** a person or thing that has a specified attribute, form, etc. **b** a thing suitable for a specified function. **3 a** person or thing belonging to or connected with. **4** a person belonging to a specified place or group.

-er[2] *suffix* forming the comparative of adjectives and adverbs.

ERA *abbr.* (also **era**) *Baseball* earned run average, the average number of runs scored against a pitcher over nine innings.

era *n.* **1** a usu. lengthy and distinct period of history. **2** a subdivision of an eon in geological time.

eradicate *v.* (**eradicates, eradicated, eradicating**) remove or destroy completely. □ **eradication** *n.* [*Say* i RADDA kate]

erase *v.* (**erases, erased, erasing**) **1** rub out or obliterate. **2** remove all traces of. □ **erasable** *adj.*

eraser *n.* a thing that erases, esp. a piece of rubber used for removing pencil marks.

erasure *n.* **1** an act or instance of erasing. **2** a place or mark left by erasing. [*Say* i RAY shur]

ere *prep. & conj. literary or archaic* before (in time). [*Sounds like* AIR]

erect ● *adj.* **1** upright; not inverted. **2** (of the penis, clitoris, or nipples) enlarged and firm. **3** (of hair) bristling. ● *v.* **1** set in an upright position. **2** build, construct. **3** create, establish.

erectile *adj.* that can be erected or become erect. [*Say* i RECK tile]

erection *n.* **1** the action of erecting a structure or monument. **2** an enlarged and rigid state of the penis.

ergonomics *n.* (treated as *sing.* or *pl.*) the field of study that deals with the relationship between people and their working environment, esp. as it affects efficiency and safety. □ **ergonomic** *adj.* **ergonomically** *adv.* [*Say* urga NOM icks]

ermine *n.* (*pl.* **ermine** or **ermines**) **1** a weasel that has brown fur in the summer turning mainly white in the winter. **2** the white fur of an ermine used in clothing. [*Say* UR min]

erode *v.* (**erodes, eroded, eroding**) **1** wear away; destroy or be destroyed gradually. **2** make or become gradually diminished in value etc. □ **eroded** *adj.*

erogenous *adj.* (esp. of a part of the body) sensitive to sexual stimulation. [*Say* i RODGE uh nus]

eros *n.* romantic or sexual love or desire. [*Say* AIR oss *or* EAR ose (*with* OSE *as in* DOSE)]

erosion *n.* **1** the process of eroding or the result of being eroded. **2** gradual destruction or diminution. □ **erosional** *adj.*

erotic *adj.* relating to sexual desire or excitement. □ **erotically** *adv.* [*Say* i ROT ick, i ROT ick lee]

erotica *n.* erotic literature or art. [*Say* i ROT ick uh]

eroticism *n.* **1** erotic nature or character. **2** the use of erotic images etc. [*Say* i ROTTA sism]

eroticize *v.* make erotic or endow with erotic qualities. □ **eroticized** *adj.* [*Say* i ROTTA size]

err *v.* **1** be mistaken or incorrect. **2** do

wrong. □ **err on the side of** show too much rather than risk showing too little. [*Sounds like* AIR]

errand *n.* a short trip to buy or deliver something etc. □ **errand of mercy** a journey to give help etc.

errant *adj.* **1 a** deviating from an accepted standard. **b** breaking with the dominant pattern etc. **2** *literary* or *archaic* travelling in search of adventure. [*Say* AIR int]

errata *pl. n.* (*singular* **erratum**) errors in a printed text. [*Say* i RATTA *for the plural,* i RAT um *for the singular*]

erratic *adj.* inconsistently variable in conduct, movement, etc.; unpredictable. □ **erratically** *adv.* [*Say* i RAT ick]

erroneous *adj.* incorrect. □ **erroneously** *adv.* [*Say* i RONEY us]

error *n.* **1** a mistake. **2** the condition of being wrong in conduct or judgment. **3** a wrong opinion or judgment. **4** the amount by which something is incorrect. **5** *Baseball* a fielder's misplay allowing a batter to reach base etc.

ersatz *adj.* imitation (esp. of inferior quality). [*Say* AIR zats *or* UR zats]

erstwhile *adj.* former, previous [*Say* URST while]

erudite *adj.* having or showing great knowledge or learning. □ **eruditely** *adv.* **erudition** *n.* [*Say* AIR oo dite *or* AIR you dite, air oo DISH in *or* air you DISH in]

erupt *v.* **1** break out or burst forth suddenly. **2** (of a volcano) become active and eject lava etc. **3** (of a rash etc.) appear on the skin. **4** (of the teeth) break through the gums. □ **eruption** *n.*

erythrocyte *n.* a red blood cell. [*Say* i RITH roe site]

erythromycin *n.* an antibiotic similar in its effects to penicillin. [*Say* i rith roe MICE in]

escalate *v.* (**escalates, escalated, escalating**) to become or make something greater, more serious, etc. □ **escalating** *adj.* **escalation** *n.*

escalator *n.* a moving staircase consisting of an endless chain of steps on a circulating belt.

escapade *n.* a daring or adventurous act. [*Say* ESKA paid]

escape ● *v.* (**escapes, escaped, escaping**) **1** break free or free oneself. **2** leak or seep out. **3** succeed in avoiding (something bad). **4** avoid or elude. **5** elude the memory of. ● *n.* **1** an act of escaping. **2** a means of escaping. **3** a temporary relief from reality. **4** (also **escape key**)

Computing a key which ends the current operation. □ **escaper** *n.*

escapee *n.* a person who has escaped. [*Say* i SCAPE ee *or* ess kay PEE]

escapism *n.* the tendency to seek distraction and relief from reality, esp. through fantasy. □ **escapist** *n. & adj.*

escargot *n.* (*pl.* **escargots** *pronunc.* same) a snail as an item of food. [*Say* es car GO]

escarpment *n.* a long, steep-sided ridge.

Escherichia coli *n.* (also **E. coli**) a species of bacillus which can cause serious disease in humans. [*Say* esha ricky uh CO lie]

eschew *v.* *literary* carefully or deliberately avoid. [*Say* es CHEW]

escort ● *n.* **1** one or more persons, vehicles, etc. accompanying another to provide protection etc. **2** a person accompanying a person of the opposite sex socially. **3 a** a person employed to provide another with entertainment etc. **b** *euphemism* a prostitute. ● *v.* accompany as an escort.

esker *n.* a long, narrow ridge, usu. of sand and gravel.

Eskimo *n.* (*pl.* same or **Eskimos**) **1** (in former use) a member of an Aboriginal people inhabiting northern Canada, Alaska, Greenland, and eastern Siberia. **2** the language of this people. □ **Eskimo** *adj.*

ESL *abbr.* English as a second language.

esophagus *n.* (*pl.* **esophagi** *or* **esophaguses**) the part of the alimentary canal from the mouth to the stomach. [*Say* i SOFFA gus *for the singular,* i SOFFA jie *for the plural*]

esoteric *adj.* intended for or intelligible to only those with special knowledge. [*Say* esso TARE ick *or* ee so TARE ick]

ESP *abbr.* extrasensory perception.

especially *adv.* **1** chiefly, pre-eminently. **2** particularly or much more than in other cases.

Esperanto *n.* an artificial language invented as a means of international communication. [*Say* espa RAN toe]

espionage *n.* the practice of spying or of using spies. [*Say* ESS pee a nozh]

esplanade *n.* a level, open space along a waterfront, where people may walk or drive. [*Say* espla NADE *or* ESPLA nod]

espouse *v.* (**espouses, espoused, espousing**) adopt or support (a cause etc.). □ **espousal** *n.* [*Say* es POWZ, es POW zull]

espresso *n.* (*pl.* **espressos**) strong, concentrated, black coffee made by forcing steam through ground coffee beans. [*Say* es PRESSO]

esprit de corps *n.* loyalty and devotion to a group to which one belongs. [*Say* es pree duh CORE]

Esquimalt *n.* (*pl.* **Esquimalt** or **Esquimalts**) a member of a Salishan Aboriginal group living near Esquimalt, BC. [*Say* esk WYE malt]

-ess *suffix* forming nouns denoting females.

essay ● *n.* **1 a** a written composition on any subject. **b** a short composition in any medium. **2** *formal* an attempt. ● *v. formal* attempt, try. □ **essayist** *n.* [*Say* ESS ay *for the noun*, ess SAY *for the verb*, ESS ay ist]

essence *n.* **1 a** the quality which determines the character of something. **b** the intrinsic nature of something. **2 a** an extract of a plant, drug, etc. usu. obtained by distillation. **b** a perfume or scent. □ **in essence** essentially. **of the essence** very important.

essential ● *adj.* **1** absolutely necessary. **2** fundamental, basic. ● *n.* (esp. in *pl.*) a basic or indispensable element. □ **essentially** *adv.*

essential oil *n.* an oil taken from a plant.

EST *abbr.* **1** Eastern Standard Time. **2** electroshock treatment.

-est *suffix* forming the superlative of adjectives and adverbs.

establish *v.* (**establishes, established, establishing**) **1** found or consolidate on a permanent basis. **2** settle in some capacity. **3** achieve permanent acceptance for. **4 a** validate. **b** ascertain. **5** gain recognition and acceptance. **6** bring about; achieve. **7** enact; decree in law. □ **established** *adj.*

established church *n.* a religious denomination recognized by a national government as its nation's official church.

establishment *n.* **1** the action of establishing something or being established. **2** a business, institution, etc. **3** (also **Establishment**) the group in a society exercising authority, and resisting change.

estate *n.* **1** a property consisting of extensive grounds and usu. a large house. **2** *Law* all of a person's property, esp. at death. **3** a property where grapes, tea, etc. are cultivated.

esteem ● *v.* **1** have a high regard for; respect. **2** *formal* deem. ● *n.* high regard; respect. □ **esteemed** *adj.*

ester *n.* any of a class of organic compounds produced by a reaction between an acid and an alcohol.

esthete etc. = AESTHETE etc. [*Say* ess THEET]

estimable *adj.* worthy of esteem. [*Say* ESS timma bull]

estimate ● *n.* **1** a judgment or calculation of an approximate cost, value, etc. **2** an appraisal. **3** a price specified as that likely to be charged for work ● *v.* (**estimates, estimated, estimating**) **1** form an estimate of. **2** fix (a price etc.) by estimate. □ **estimated** *adj.* **estimation** *n.* **estimator** *n.*

Estonian *n.* **1** a person from Estonia. **2** the language of Estonia, related to Hungarian and Finnish. □ **Estonian** *adj.* [*Say* ess TONY un]

estranged *adj.* **1** no longer close or on friendly terms with. **2** (of a husband or wife) no longer living with his or her spouse. □ **estrangement** *n.*

estrogen *n.* any of various hormones developing and maintaining female characteristics of the body. [*Say* ESTRA jen]

estuary *n.* (*pl.* **estuaries**) the tidal mouth of a large river. □ **estuarine** *adj.* [*Say* ESS choo airy, ESS choo a rine]

ET *abbr.* **1** EASTERN TIME. **2** extraterrestrial.

ETA *abbr.* estimated time of arrival.

et al. *abbr.* and others.

etc. *abbr.* = ET CETERA.

et cetera *adv.* **1** and the rest. **2** and so on. [*Say* et SETTER uh]

etch *v.* (**etches, etched, etching**) **1** engrave (metal, glass, or stone), esp. for printing. **2** impress deeply (esp. on the mind).

etching *n.* **1** a print made from an etched plate. **2** the art of producing these plates.

eternal *adj.* **1** without an end or beginning. **2** essentially unchanging. □ **eternally** *adv.*

eternity *n.* (*pl.* **eternities**) **1** unending time. **2** *Theology* the afterlife. **3** a very long time.

ethane *n.* a colourless odourless gaseous hydrocarbon of the alkane series. [*Say* ETH ane *or* EETH ane]

ethanol *n.* alcohol. [*Say* ETHA nawl]

ether *n.* **1** a colourless volatile organic liquid used as an anaesthetic or solvent. **2** *hist.* the sky or upper regions of the air. [*Say* EETH ur]

ethereal *adj.* extremely delicate and light; heavenly. □ **ethereally** *adv.* [*Say* i THEERY ul, i theery ALA tee]

ethic *n.* a set of moral principles.

ethical *adj.* **1** connected with moral principles. **2** morally correct. □ **ethically** *adv.*

ethicist *n.* a person who studies ethics. [*Say* ETHA sist]

ethics *pl. n.* **1** the science of morals in human conduct. **2** moral principles; rules of conduct. **3** moral correctness.

Ethiopian *n.* a person from Ethiopia. □ **Ethiopian** *adj.* [*Say* eethy OPE ee un]

ethnic ● *adj.* **1** (of a population group) sharing a distinctive cultural and historical tradition. **2** relating to race or culture. **3** (of clothes, music, etc.) influenced by the traditions of a particular people or culture. **4** denoting origin by birth rather than nationality. ● *n.* a member of an (esp. minority) ethnic group. □ **ethnically** *adv.* **ethnicity** *n.* (*pl.* **ethnicities**) [*Say* ETH nik, eth NISSA tee]

ethnic cleansing *n. euphemism* the mass expulsion or extermination of people from opposing ethnic or religious groups within a certain area.

ethnic minority *n.* a group different from the main population of a community by race or cultural background.

ethnocentric *adj.* evaluating other peoples and cultures (esp. negatively) according to the assumptions of one's own culture. □ **ethnocentricity** *n.* **ethnocentrism** *n.* [*Say* ethno SEN trick, ethno sen TRISSA tee]

ethnocultural *adj.* pertaining to or having ethnic groups. [*Say* ethno CULTURAL]

ethnography *n.* the scientific description of peoples and cultures. □ **ethnographer** *n.* **ethnographic** *adj.* [*Say* eth NOGGRA fee, eth NOGGRA fur, ethno GRAPHIC]

ethnology *n.* the branch of knowledge that deals with the characteristics of different peoples and the differences and relationships between them. □ **ethnological** *adj.* **ethnologist** *n.* [*Say* eth NOLLA jee]

ethology *n.* **1** the science of animal behaviour. **2** the science of character formation in human behaviour. □ **ethological** *adj.* **ethologist** *n.* [*Say* eeth OLLA jee, eetho LOGICAL, eeth OLLA jist]

ethos *n.* the characteristic spirit of a community, people, or literary work etc. [*Say* EETH oss]

ethyl *n.* the monovalent radical derived from ethane, present in alcohol. [*Say* ETHEL]

ethylene *n.* a gaseous hydrocarbon occurring in natural gas and crude oil. [*Say* ETHA leen]

ethylene glycol *n.* a colourless viscous liquid used as an antifreeze.

etiology *n.* the scientific study of the causes of disease. □ **etiological** *adj.* [*Say* eaty OLLA jee, eaty oh LOGICAL]

etiquette *n.* **1** the conventional rules of social or official behaviour. **2** the customary behaviour of members of a profession, sports team, etc. towards each other. [*Say* ETTA kit]

Etruscan ● *adj.* of ancient Etruria in W Italy, esp. its pre-Roman civilization. ● *n.* **1** a native of Etruria. **2** the language of Etruria. [*Say* i TRUSS kin]

-ette *suffix* forming nouns meaning: **1** small. **2** imitation or substitute. **3** female.

etymology *n.* (*pl.* **etymologies**) **1** the study of the origin of words and the development of their meanings. **2** the origin of a word and the historical development of its meaning. □ **etymological** *adj.* **etymologically** *adv.* [*Say* etta MOLLA jee, etta muh LOGICAL]

eucalyptus *n.* (*pl.* **eucalyptuses** or **eucalypti**) **1** a tree native to Australasia, cultivated for its timber and for the oil from its leaves. **2** (also **eucalyptus oil**) the essential oil from eucalyptus leaves, used medicinally etc. [*Say* yuke a LIP tuss *for the singular,* yuke a LIP tie *for the plural*]

Eucharist *n.* **1** (in some Christian churches) the sacrament commemorating the Last Supper, in which bread and wine are consecrated and consumed. **2** the consecrated elements. □ **Eucharistic** *adj.* [*Say* YUKE a rist, yuke a RISS tick]

euchre ● *n.* **1** a card game for two to four players played with the highest cards in the deck. **2** an act of euchring or being euchred. ● *v.* (**euchres, euchred, euchring**) **1** (in euchre) prevent from winning three or more tricks. **2** *slang* deceive, outwit. **3** *Cdn slang* ruin. [*Say* YOO cur]

Euclidean *adj.* of the Greek mathematician Euclid (*c.*300 BC). [*Say* yoo KLIDDY un]

eugenics *pl. n.* (treated as *sing.*) the science of improving a population by controlled breeding for desirable inherited characteristics. □ **eugenic** *adj.* **eugenicist** *n.* [*Say* you GENICS, you JENNA sist]

eukaryote *n.* an organism consisting of a cell or cells in which the genetic material is DNA in the form of chromosomes. □ **eukaryotic** *adj.* [*Say* you CARRY oat, yoo carry OTT ick]

eulachon *n.* (*pl.* **eulachon** or **eulachons**) a small oily food fish of the Pacific coast of N America. [*Say* YOOLA con]

eulogize v. (**eulogizes, eulogized, eulogizing**) **1** praise highly. **2** compose or deliver a funeral oration. [*Say* YOOLA jize]

eulogy n. (pl. **eulogies**) a speech or piece of writing in praise of a person esp. one who has just died. [*Say* YOOLA jee]

eunuch n. **1** a castrated man. **2** a person lacking effectiveness. [*Say* YOO nick]

euonymus n. (pl. **euonymus**) a tree, shrub, or ground cover of a genus found throughout the temperate Northern Hemisphere. [*Say* yoo ONNA muss]

euphemism n. a mild or vague expression substituted for one thought to be too harsh or direct. □ **euphemistic** adj. **euphemistically** adv. [*Say* YOOFA mism, yoofa MISS tick]

euphony n. (pl. **euphonies**) pleasantness of sound; harmony. [*Say* YOOFA nee]

euphoria n. an extremely strong feeling of happiness. □ **euphoric** adj. **euphorically** adv. [*Say* yoo FOREY uh]

Eurasian ● adj. **1** of mixed European and Asian parentage. **2** of Europe and Asia. ● n. a Eurasian person. [*Say* yoor ASIAN]

eureka interj. I have found it! (announcing a discovery etc.). [*Say* yoo REEKA]

euro n. (pl. **euros**) the currency unit used by most European Union countries.

Euro- comb. form Europe, European.

Eurocentric adj. **1** having or regarding Europe as its centre. **2** presupposing the supremacy of European culture etc. □ **Eurocentricity** n. **Eurocentrism** n. [*Say* yoor oh SEN trick, yoor oh SEN trism]

European ● adj. of, from, or in Europe. ● n. **1** a person from Europe. **2** a white person. □ **Europeanization** n. **Europeanize** v.

European plan n. a system of charging for a hotel room only without meals. Abbreviation: **EP**.

eurozone n. (also **euroland**) the economic region formed by those member countries of the European Union that have adopted the euro.

eurythmic adj. **1** of or in harmonious proportion. **2** involving harmonious bodily movement, esp. as a system of music education. [*Say* yuh RHYTHMIC]

euthanasia n. an act of painlessly killing a person or animal suffering from an incurable condition. □ **euthanize** v. (**euthanizes, euthanized, euthanizing**) [*Say* yootha NAY zhuh, YOOTHA nize]

eutrophic adj. (of a lake etc.) rich in nutrients and supporting a dense plant population, which kills animal life by depriving it of oxygen. □ **eutrophication** n. [*Say* yoo TROFF ick or yoo TROFE ick, yoo troffa KAY sh'n or you trofe a KAY sh'n]

evacuate v. (**evacuates, evacuated, evacuating**) **1** move from a place of danger to a safer place. **2** empty (the bowels). □ **evacuation** n.

evacuee n. a person evacuated from a place of danger. [*Say* i vac you EE]

evade v. (**evades, evaded, evading**) **1 a** escape from, avoid. **b** avoid doing (one's duty etc.). **c** avoid giving a direct answer to. **2** fail to pay (tax). □ **evader** n.

evaluate v. (**evaluates, evaluated, evaluating**) **1** assess, appraise. **2** find or state the number or amount of. □ **evaluation** n. **evaluative** adj. **evaluator** n.

evanescent adj. quickly fading; having no permanence. [*Say* evva NESS int]

evangelical ● adj. (also **evangelic**) **1** of or according to the teaching of the gospel or Christianity. **2** of a branch of Protestant Christianity emphasizing the authority of Scripture and personal conversion. **3** wanting very much to convert people to one's views etc. ● n. an evangelical person or one who belongs to an evangelical church. □ **evangelicalism** n. **evangelically** adv. [*Say* ee van JELL ik ul or evan JELL ick ul]

evangelist n. **1** a preacher of the Christian gospel. **2** a person engaged in travelling Christian missionary work. **3** a zealous advocate of a cause or doctrine. **4** (**Evangelist**) any of the writers of the four Gospels. □ **evangelism** n. **evangelistic** adj. [*Say* i VAN juh list or ee VAN juh list, i van juh LISS tick or ee van juh LISS tick]

evangelize v. (**evangelizes, evangelized, evangelizing**) **1** preach the Christian gospel to. **2** convert to Christianity. **3** try to win support for a cause. □ **evangelization** n. **evangelizer** n. [*Say* i VAN juh lize or ee VAN juh lize]

evaporate v. (**evaporates, evaporated, evaporating**) **1** turn from liquid into vapour. **2** lose moisture by evaporation. **3** disappear, especially gradually. □ **evaporation** n. **evaporator** n.

evaporated milk n. thick milk which has had some of its liquid removed by evaporation.

evasion n. **1** the act or a means of evading a duty etc. **2** an evasive statement.

evasive adj. **1** not willing to give clear answers to a question. **2** enabling evasion or escape. □ **evasively** *adv.* **evasiveness** *n.* [*Say* i VAY siv]

eve *n.* **1** the evening or day before an event etc. **2** the time just before anything.

even[1] ● *adj.* (**evener, evenest**) **1** level. **2 a** (of an action etc.) uniform. **b** equal in number, amount, value, etc. **c** equally balanced. **3** in the same plane or line. **4** calm. **5 a** (of a number) divisible by two without a remainder. **b** not involving fractions; exact. **6** neither owed nor owing money. **7** (of a bet etc.) as likely to succeed as not. ● *adv.* used for emphasis. ● *v.* make or become even. □ **even so** nevertheless. **even though** despite the fact that. **get** (or **be**) **even with** have one's revenge on. □ **evenness** *n.*

even[2] *n. archaic* or *literary* evening.

even-handed *adj.* impartial, fair. □ **even-handedly** *adv.* **even-handedness** *n.*

evening *n.* **1** the end part of the day. **2** an event happening in the evening.

evening dress *n.* (also **evening clothes, evening wear**) clothes worn for formal occasions in the evening.

evening gown *n.* a woman's long formal dress.

evening primrose *n.* a plant with yellow flowers, from whose seeds an oil is extracted for medicinal use.

evenly *adv.* **1** in a smooth, regular, or equal manner. **2** calmly.

evensong *n.* an esp. Anglican service of evening prayer.

even-steven *adj. informal* **1** having no balance of debt on either side. **2** (of a game etc.) tied.

event *n.* **1** a thing that happens or takes place. **2** a public or social occasion. **3** an item in a sports program. □ **in any event** (or **at all events**) whatever happens. **in the event** as it turns (or turned) out. **in the event of** if (a specified thing) happens. **in the event that** if it happens that.

eventful *adj.* marked by many events or incidents. □ **eventfully** *adv.* **eventfulness** *n.*

eventual *adj.* occurring or existing in due course or at last; ultimate. □ **eventually** *adv.*

eventuality *n.* (*pl.* **eventualities**) a possible event or outcome.

ever *adv.* **1** at all times; always. **2** at any time. **3** as an emphatic word. **4** (in *comb.*) constantly. **5** very; very much. **6** increasingly.

evergreen ● *adj.* **1** (of a plant) retaining green leaves throughout the year. **2** having an enduring freshness or success. ● *n.* an evergreen plant.

everlasting *adj.* lasting forever or a long time. □ **everlastingly** *adv.*

evermore *adv.* forever; always.

every *adj.* **1** each single. **2** each at a specified interval in a series. **3** all possible. □ **every bit as** *informal* quite as. **every now and again** (or **now and then**) from time to time. **every so often** occasionally. **every which way** *informal* **1** in all directions. **2** in a disorderly manner.

everybody *pron.* every person.

everyday *adj.* **1** daily. **2** suitable for ordinary days. **3** commonplace.

Everyman *n.* the ordinary human being.

everyone *pron.* every person. □ **everyone who is anyone** (also **everybody who is anybody**) every person who is important etc.

everything *pron.* **1** all things; all the things of a group. **2** a great deal. **3** the essential consideration.

everywhere *adv.* (also *informal* **everyplace**) in every place.

Everywoman *n.* the typical woman.

evict *v.* legally expel (a tenant) from a property. □ **eviction** *n.*

evidence ● *n.* **1** the available facts etc. indicating whether something is true or valid. **2** *Law* information used to establish facts in a legal investigation or used as testimony in a law court. **3** a sign or indication. ● *v.* be evidence of. □ **call in evidence** *Law* summon as a witness. **in evidence** noticeable. □ **evidentiary** *adj.*

evident *adj.* plain or obvious. □ **evidently** *adv.*

evil ● *adj.* **1** morally bad. **2** harmful or tending to harm. **3** unpleasant. **4** unlucky. ● *n.* **1** wickedness. **2** something morally wrong, harmful, or undesirable. □ **speak evil of** slander. □ **evilly** *adv.*

evildoer *n.* a person who does evil. □ **evildoing** *n.*

evil eye *n.* a gaze superstitiously believed to cause harm.

evil one *n.* the embodiment of evil in certain religious beliefs.

evince *v.* (**evinces, evinced, evincing**) **1** indicate or make evident. **2** show that one has. [*Say* ee VINCE]

eviscerate *v. formal* **1** remove the inner organs of. **2** remove a significant part of something. □ **evisceration** *n.* [*Say* ee VISSER ate]

evocation *n.* an act of evoking. [*Say* ee voe KAY sh'n]

evocative *adj.* tending to evoke.

□ **evocatively** adv. **evocativeness** n. [Say ee VOCKA tiv]

evoke v. (**evokes, evoked, evoking**) inspire or bring to mind.

evolution n. **1** gradual development, esp. from a simple to a more complex form. **2** a process by which different kinds of organism develop from earlier forms. □ **evolutionary** adj. [Say evva LOO sh'n]

evolutionist n. a person who believes in evolution as explaining the origin of species. □ **evolutionism** n.

evolve v. (**evolves, evolved, evolving**) **1** develop gradually. **2** come into being through evolution.

ewe n. a female sheep. [Say YOO]

ewer n. a large pitcher with a wide mouth. [Say YOO ur]

ex[1] n. (pl. **exes**) informal a former spouse, lover, etc.

ex[2] abbr. example.

ex[3] n. (pl. **exes**) Cdn exhibition.

ex- prefix forming nouns meaning "formerly".

exacerbate v. (**exacerbates, exacerbated, exacerbating**) make (something bad) worse. □ **exacerbation** n. [Say ex ASSER bate]

exact ● adj. **1** correct in all details. **2** precise. **3** strict. ● v. **1** demand and get something from someone. **2** inflict (revenge) on someone. □ **exactness** n.

exacting adj. making great demands. □ **exactingly** adv.

exaction n. **1** the action of demanding payment. **2** a sum of money demanded.

exactitude n. the quality of being exact.

exactly adv. **1** accurately, precisely. **2** in exact terms. **3** (said in reply) I agree completely. □ **not exactly** informal by no means.

exactor n. Cdn a bet on the first- and second-place finishers in a race.

exaggerate v. (**exaggerates, exaggerated, exaggerating**) **1** make something seem greater etc. than it really is. **2** enlarge or alter beyond normal proportions. □ **exaggerated** adj. **exaggeratedly** adv. **exaggeration** n. **exaggerator** n.

exalt v. **1** raise in rank or power etc. **2** praise highly. **3** make lofty or noble. [Say ex AWLT]

exaltation n. **1** extreme happiness. **2** the action of exalting. [Say ex awl TAY sh'n]

exam n. = EXAMINATION 2, 3.

examination n. **1** the action of examining. **2** a detailed inspection or investigation. **3** a test of proficiency or knowledge in a certain subject or area. **4** the formal questioning of a witness in court.

examination for discovery n. (pl. **examinations for discovery**) Cdn Law a meeting before a civil trial to disclose evidence that will be presented in court.

examine v. (**examines, examined, examining**) **1** inquire into the nature or condition etc. of. **2** look closely at. **3** test the proficiency of. **4** check the health of by examination. **5** Law formally question in court. □ **examiner** n.

example n. **1** a thing characteristic of its kind or illustrating a general rule. **2** a person, thing, etc., regarded in terms of its fitness to be copied. **3** a circumstance or treatment seen as a warning to others; a person so treated. □ **for example** by way of illustration.

exasperate v. (**exasperates, exasperated, exasperating**) irritate intensely. □ **exasperated** adj. **exasperating** adj. **exasperation** n. [Say ex ASPER ate]

excavate v. (**excavates, excavated, excavating**) **1 a** make (a hole or channel) by digging. **b** dig out material from (the ground). **2** reveal or extract by digging. **3** Archaeology dig systematically into the ground to explore. □ **excavation** n. **excavator** n.

exceed v. **1** be greater or more numerous than. **2** go beyond what is allowed etc. **3** surpass, excel.

exceedingly adv. extremely.

excel v. (**excels, excelled, excelling**) **1** be pre-eminent or the most outstanding. **2** (**excel oneself**) perform exceptionally well.

Excellency n. (pl. **Excellencies**) (usu. preceded by Your, His, Her) a title used in addressing certain high officials, e.g. governors general, ambassadors, and (in some countries) senior Church dignitaries.

excellent adj. extremely good; pre-eminent. □ **excellence** n. **excellently** adv.

except ● v. exclude. ● prep. (also **excepting**) not including. ● conj. with the exception; only.

exception n. a person or thing that is excluded from a general statement or does not follow a rule. □ **take exception** **1** object. **2** be offended (by). **with the exception of** except.

exceptional adj. **1** forming an exception. **2** not typical. **3** unusually good. □ **exceptionally** adv.

excerpt ● n. a short extract. ● v. take an excerpt from a book etc.

excess ● *n.* (*pl.* **excesses**) **1** an amount of something that is more than necessary, permitted, or desirable. **2** the amount by which one quantity exceeds another. **3** outrageous behaviour. ● *adj.* exceeding a set or limited amount. □ **in** (or **to**) **excess** exceeding the proper amount. **in excess of** exceeding.

excess baggage *n.* **1** baggage exceeding a weight allowance and liable to an extra charge. **2** something burdensome.

excessive *adj.* **1** too much. **2** more than what is normal or necessary. □ **excessively** *adv.*

exchange ● *n.* **1** an act of giving one thing and receiving another in its place; a trade. **2** trading an amount in one currency for the same amount in another. **3** a central place where telephone calls are connected. **4** a place where commodities, securities, etc. are bought and sold. **5** a short conversation or correspondence. ● *v.* (**exchanges, exchanged, exchanging**) **1** give or receive (one thing) in place of another. **2** give and receive as equivalents (e.g. things, information, etc.). **3** make an exchange. □ **exchangeable** *adj.* **exchanger** *n.*

exchange rate *n.* the value of one currency in terms of another.

excise[1] *n.* a duty or tax levied on certain goods. [*Say* EK size]

excise[2] *v.* (**excises, excised, excising**) **1** remove (a passage of a book etc.). **2** cut out by surgery. □ **excision** *n.* [*Say* ek SIZE, ek SIZH un]

excitable *adj.* easily excited. □ **excitably** *adv.*

excite *v.* (**excites, excited, exciting**) **1 a** rouse a person's feelings or emotions. **b** arouse sexually. **2** give rise to. **3** promote the activity of. □ **excitation** *n.* **excitedly** *adv.* **excitement** *n.* **exciting** *adj.* **excitingly** *adv.*

exclaim *v.* cry out suddenly.

exclamation *n.* a sudden cry or remark.

exclamatory *adj.* of or serving as an exclamation. [*Say* ex KLAMMA tory]

exclude *v.* (**excludes, excluded, excluding**) **1** remove from consideration. **2** prevent someone or something from entering or taking part in something.

exclusion *n.* **1** the process or state of excluding or being excluded. **2** an item etc. excluded from a contract or insurance policy. □ **to the exclusion of** so as to exclude. □ **exclusionary** *adj.*

exclusive ● *adj.* **1** excluding other things. **2** not including. **3** tending to exclude others. **4** catering for few or select customers. **5** not obtainable or published elsewhere. **6** restricted or limited to. ● *n.* **1** an exclusive story. **2** an item available for sale from only one supplier. □ **exclusively** *adv.* **exclusiveness** *n.* **exclusivity** *n.* [*Say* ex clue SIVVA tee]

excommunicate *v. Christianity* (**excommunicates, excommunicated, excommunicating**) officially exclude from participation in the sacraments and services of the Church. □ **excommunication** *n.*

ex-con *n. informal* a former inmate of a prison.

excoriate *v.* (**excoriates, excoriated, excoriating**) criticize severely. □ **excoriation** *n.* [*Say* ex COREY ate]

excrement *n.* waste matter discharged from the bowels. [*Say* EX kruh mint]

excrescence *n.* **1** a distinct outgrowth on a body or a plant. **2** an ugly or superfluous feature. [*Say* ex CRESS ince]

excrete *v.* (**excretes, excreted, excreting**) expel as waste. □ **excretion** *n.* **excretory** *adj.* [*Say* ex CREET, ex CREE sh'n, EXCRA tory]

excruciating *adj.* (of pain) intense, acute. □ **excruciatingly** *adv.* [*Say* ex KROOSHY ate ing]

exculpate *v.* (**exculpates, exculpated, exculpating**) *formal* show or declare to be not guilty of wrongdoing. □ **exculpation** *n.* **exculpatory** *adj.* [*Say* EX cull pate, ex cull PAY sh'n, ex CULPA tory]

excursion *n.* a short journey taken for pleasure. □ **excursionist** *n.* [*Say* ex CUR zh'n]

excuse ● *v.* (**excuses, excused, excusing**) **1** attempt to lessen the blame attaching to (a person or fault). **2** mitigate. **3** obtain exemption for. **4 a** release from a duty etc. **b** allow to leave. **5** overlook or forgive (a fault). **6** (**excuse oneself**) apologize for leaving. ● *n.* **1** a reason put forward to justify an offence, fault, etc. **2** an apology. **3** *informal* a poor example of. □ **excuse me** a polite apology.

execrable *adj.* **1** of very poor quality. **2** worthy of condemnation. [*Say* EX uh cribble]

execrate *v.* express or feel great loathing for. [*Say* EX uh crate]

execute *v.* (**executes, executed, executing**) **1 a** carry out a sentence of death on (a condemned person). **b** kill as a political act. **2** carry out, perform. **3** make valid by signing, sealing, etc. **4** put into effect (the terms of a will etc.). **5** *Computing* run or process. □ **executable** *adj.*

execution *n.* **1** the act of killing someone, esp. as a legal punishment. **2** the carrying

out or performance of something.
3 technique. **4** the putting into effect of a legal instrument.

executioner *n.* an official who carries out a sentence of death.

executive ● *n.* **1** a senior manager or administrative body in a business etc. **2** the branch of a government concerned with putting laws into effect. ● *adj.*
1 designating the executive branch of government. **2 a** concerned with administration or management. **b** relating to executives.

executive director *n.* a person employed by a non-profit organization to oversee operations and management.

executor *n.* a person appointed in a will to carry out its instructions.
[*Say* eg ZECK yoo tur]

executrix *n.* (*pl.* **executrixes**) a woman appointed as executor.
[*Say* eg ZECK yoo trix]

exemplar *n.* a person or thing serving as a typical example or appropriate model.
[*Say* ex EM plur]

exemplary *adj.* **1** fit to be imitated; outstandingly good. **2** serving as a warning.
[*Say* ex EMPLA ree]

exemplify *v.* (**exemplifies, exemplified, exemplifying**) **1** illustrate by example. **2** be an example of.
□ **exemplification** *n.* [*Say* ex EMPLA fie, ex empla fuh KAY sh'n]

exempt ● *adj.* **1** free from an obligation etc. imposed on others. **2** not liable to. ● *v.* free from an obligation. □ **exemption** *n.*

exercise ● *n.* **1** activity requiring physical effort, done esp. to sustain or improve health. **2** mental or spiritual activity, esp. as practice. **3** a particular task or set of tasks devised as practice. **4** the use of a mental faculty, right, quality, etc. **5** (often in *pl.*) military drills or manoeuvres. **6** a process directed at something specified.
● *v.* (**exercises, exercised, exercising**) **1** use or apply (a faculty, right, etc.). **2** perform (a function). **3** take (esp. physical) exercise. **4** perplex, worry.
□ **exerciser** *n.*

exert *v.* **1** bring to bear (a quality, force, etc.). **2** (**exert oneself**) use one's efforts or endeavours; strive. □ **exertion** *n.*

exfoliant *n.* a cosmetic designed to remove dead cells from the skin.
[*Say* ex FOLEY int]

exfoliate *v.* (**exfoliates, exfoliated, exfoliating**) **1** shed or come off in scales or layers. **2** (of a tree) throw off layers of bark. □ **exfoliation** *n.* [*Say* ex FOLEY ate]

exhale *v.* (**exhales, exhaled, exhaling**) **1** breathe out (esp. air or smoke) from the lungs. **2** give off or be given off in vapour.
□ **exhalation** *n.* [*Say* ex HALE, ex huh LAY sh'n]

exhaust ● *v.* **1** use up completely. **2 a** tire out. **b** drain (soil) of nutritive ingredients. **3** explore a subject thoroughly. **4** draw out (a gas etc.). ● *n.* **1** expelled waste air, esp. from an engine. **2** (also **exhaust pipe**) the pipe, system, etc. by which these are expelled. □ **exhausted** *adj.* **exhaustible** *adj.* **exhausting** *adj.* **exhaustingly** *adv.*

exhaustion *n.* **1** the action of exhausting or state of being exhausted. **2** a state of extreme fatigue.

exhaustive *adj.* thorough; covering all aspects thoroughly. □ **exhaustively** *adv.*

exhibit ● *v.* (**exhibits, exhibited, exhibiting**) **1** display something in a public place. **2** show clearly. ● *n.* **1** a thing or collection forming an exhibition. **2** something produced in a law court as evidence. □ **exhibitor** *n.*

exhibition *n.* **1** a display (esp. public) of works of art etc. **2** *Cdn* a large regional fair, usu. lasting for an extended period. **3** a world's fair. **4** a display or demonstration of a skill etc. **5** (as an *adj.*) denoting games whose outcomes do not affect the teams' standings, esp. those played before the start of a regular season. □ **make an exhibition of oneself** behave so as to appear ridiculous.

exhibitionism *n.* **1** behaviour that is intended to attract attention to oneself. **2** a mental condition characterized by the compulsion to display one's genitals in public. □ **exhibitionist** *n.*

exhilarate *v.* (**exhilarates, exhilarated, exhilarating**) affect with great liveliness or joy. □ **exhilaratingly** *adv.* **exhilaration** *n.* [*Say* ex ILLA rate]

exhort *v.* urge strongly or earnestly.
□ **exhortation** *n.* [*Say* ex ORT, ex or TAY sh'n]

exhume *v.* (**exhumes, exhumed, exhuming**) **1** dig out, unearth. **2** bring to light. □ **exhumation** *n.* [*Say* ex OOM *or* ex YOOM, ex oo MAY sh'n *or* ex yoo MAY sh'n]

exigency *n.* (*pl.* **exigencies**) (usu. in *pl.*) an urgent need or demand.
[*Say* EX idge in see *or* ex IDGE in see]

exile ● *n.* **1** expulsion, or the state of being expelled, from one's native land. **2 a** long absence from home. **b** exclusion. **3** a person who lives in exile. ● *v.* (**exiles, exiled, exiling**) **1** officially expel (a person) from his or her native country etc. **2** exclude from a group etc.

exist *v.* **1** have being. **2** occur; be found. **3** live. □ **existing** *adj.*

existence *n.* **1** the fact or condition of existing. **2** a way of living. **3** all that exists.

existent *adj.* existing, actual.

existential *adj.* **1** of or relating to existence. **2** concerned with existentialism. [*Say* exa STEN shull]

existentialism *n.* a theory emphasizing the existence of the individual person as a free and responsible agent determining their own development in a meaningless world. □ **existentialist** *n. & adj.* [*Say* exa STEN shull ism]

exit ● *n.* **1** a passage or door by which to leave a room etc. **2** the act of going out. **3** the act of departing from. **4** a place where vehicles can leave a highway or major road. ● *v.* (**exits, exited, exiting**) **1** go out of. **2** leave (a highway or major road). **3** terminate (a computer session etc.).

exit poll *n.* an unofficial poll in which voters leaving a polling station are asked how they voted.

exodus *n.* (*pl.* **exoduses**) **1** a mass departure of people. **2** (**Exodus**) *Bible* the departure of the Israelites from slavery in Egypt. [*Say* EXA dus]

exonerate *v.* (**exonerates, exonerated, exonerating**) officially declare free from blame. □ **exoneration** *n.* [*Say* ex ONNA rate]

exorbitant *adj.* (of a price etc.) grossly excessive. □ **exorbitance** *n.* **exorbitantly** *adv.* [*Say* ex ORBA tint, ex ORBA tince]

exorcise *v.* (**exorcises, exorcised, exorcising**) (also **exorcize, exorcizes, exorcized, exorcizing**) **1** endeavour to expel (a supposed evil spirit) from a person or place. **2** remove or free from (an evil influence). □ **exorcism** *n.* **exorcist** *n.*

exoskeleton *n.* a rigid external covering for the body in some invertebrates, esp. arthropods. [*Say* EXO skeleton]

exotic ● *adj.* **1** coming from or characteristic of a foreign or distant place. **2** attractively or remarkably unusual. ● *n.* an exotic person or thing. □ **exotically** *adv.*

exotica *pl. n.* remarkably strange or rare things. [*Say* ex OTT ick uh]

exotic dancer *n.* a stripper.

exoticism *n.* a foreign or unusual character or nature. [*Say* ex OTTA sism]

expand *v.* **1** increase in size, scope, or importance. **2** give a fuller account of. □ **expandable** *adj.* **expander** *n.* **expanding** *n.*

expanse *n.* a wide continuous area or extent.

expansion *n.* **1** the action of becoming larger or more extensive. **2** enlargement of (esp. commercial) operations. **3** increase in the amount of a state's territory etc. **4** a thing formed by expansion. **5** *Sport* the addition of new teams to a league. □ **expansionary** *adj.*

expansionism *n.* a policy of esp. territorial expansion. □ **expansionist** *n.*

expansive *adj.* **1** covering a wide area or large subject area. **2** friendly and willing to talk. □ **expansively** *adv.* **expansiveness** *n.*

expat *n. & adj. informal* = EXPATRIATE. [*Say* EX pat]

expatriate ● *adj.* **1** living abroad. **2** exiled. ● *n.* an expatriate person. [*Say* ex PAY tree it]

expect *v.* **1 a** regard as likely. **b** look for as one's due. **c** look forward to the arrival of. **2** *informal* think, suppose. □ **be expecting** *informal* be pregnant.

expectancy *n.* (*pl.* **expectancies**) **1** a state of expectation. **2** what can reasonably be expected.

expectant *adj.* **1** revealing expectation. **2** expecting the birth of a child. □ **expectantly** *adv.*

expectation *n.* **1** a belief that something will happen or be the case. **2** a hope that something good will happen.

expectorant ● *adj.* causing the coughing out of phlegm etc. ● *n.* an expectorant medicine. [*Say* ex PECTA rint]

expedient ● *adj.* **1** necessary for a particular purpose, but not always fair or right. **2** suitable, appropriate. ● *n.* a means of attaining an end. □ **expediency** (also **expedience**) *n.* [*Say* ex PEEDY int]

expedite *v.* (**expedites, expedited, expediting**) make a process happen more quickly. [*Say* EXPA dite]

expedition *n.* **1** a journey or voyage for a particular purpose. **2** the group undertaking this. **3** promptness. □ **expeditionary** *adj.* [*Say* expa DISH'n, expa DISH'n airy]

expeditious *adj.* quick and efficient. □ **expeditiously** *adv.* [*Say* expa DISH us]

expel *v.* (**expels, expelled, expelling**) **1** compel (a pupil) to leave a school etc. **2** force out or eject. **3** order or force to leave.

expend *v.* spend or use up.

expendable *adj.* of little significance when compared to an overall purpose, and therefore able to be sacrificed.

expenditure *n.* **1** the action of spending funds. **2** a thing (esp. money) expended.

expense *n.* **1** cost incurred. **2** a thing that is a cause of much expense. □ **at the**

expense of so as to cause harm to (something).

expense account *n.* a list of an employee's expenses to be reimbursed by the employer.

expensive *adj.* **1** costing much. **2** charging high prices. □ **expensively** *adv.*

experience ● *n.* **1** actual observation of or contact with facts or events. **2** knowledge or skill resulting from this. **3** an event regarded as affecting one. ● *v.* (**experiences**, **experienced**, **experiencing**) **1** have experience of; undergo. **2** feel (an emotion etc.).

experienced *adj.* **1** having had much experience. **2** skilled from experience.

experiential *adj.* involving or based on experience. □ **experientially** *adv.* [*Say* ex peery EN shull]

experiment ● *n.* **1** a procedure undertaken to make a discovery, test a hypothesis etc., or demonstrate a known fact. **2** a course of action adopted without being sure of its outcome. ● *v.* make an experiment. □ **experimentation** *n.* **experimenter** *n.*

experimental *adj.* **1** based on or making use of experiment. **2 a** used in experiments. **b** based on untested ideas and not yet established. **3** (of art, music, etc.) involving a radically new style. □ **experimentally** *adv.*

experimentalism *n.* the use of experiment or innovation in the arts. □ **experimentalist** *n.*

expert ● *adj.* having or involving special knowledge or skill in a subject. ● *n.* a person having special knowledge or skill. □ **expertly** *adv.* **expertness** *n.*

expertise *n.* expert skill, knowledge, etc. [*Say* ex pur TEEZ]

expiate *v.* (**expiates**, **expiated**, **expiating**) make amends for. □ **expiation** *n.* [*Say* EX pee ate, ex pee AY sh'n]

expiration *n.* **1** expiry. **2** breathing out.

expire *v.* (**expires**, **expired**, **expiring**) **1** (of a period of time etc.) come to an end. **2** (of a document etc.) cease to be valid. **3** (of a person) die. **4** exhale (air) from the lungs.

expiry *n.* (*pl.* **expiries**) **1** the end of the validity or duration of something. **2** death.

explain *v.* **1** make (something) clear with detailed information etc. **2** account for (one's conduct etc.). □ **explain away** give an excuse for (something). **explain oneself** give an account of one's motives or conduct. □ **explainable** *adj.* **explainer** *n.*

explanation *n.* **1** a statement or account that makes something clear. **2** a reason or justification given for an action or belief.

explanatory *adj.* serving to explain. [*Say* ex PLANNA tory]

expletive *n.* a swear word. [*Say* EXPLA tiv *or* ex PLEE tiv]

explicable *adj.* that can be explained. [*Say* ex PLICKA bull *or* EX plicka bull]

explicate *v.* (**explicates**, **explicated**, **explicating**) **1** make clear, explain. **2** analyze in detail. □ **explication** *n.* [*Say* EXPLA kate]

explicit *adj.* **1** expressly stated or conveyed, with no room for confusion. **2** expressing views bluntly. **3** describing or representing sexual activity. □ **explicitly** *adv.* **explicitness** *n.* [*Say* ex PLISS it]

explode *v.* (**explodes**, **exploded**, **exploding**) **1 a** burst or shatter violently with a loud noise owing to a release of internal energy. **b** cause to explode. **2** give vent suddenly to emotion. **3** increase suddenly, esp. in size, numbers, etc. **4** appear suddenly. **5** show to be false or baseless.

exploit ● *n.* a bold or daring feat. ● *v.* **1** make use of (a resource etc.). **2** utilize or take advantage of for one's own ends. □ **exploitable** *adj.* **exploitation** *n.* **exploitative** *adj.* **exploiter** *n.* **exploitive** *adj.*

explore *v.* (**explores**, **explored**, **exploring**) **1** travel (through a country etc.) in order to learn about it. **2 a** inquire (into); investigate thoroughly. **b** experiment. **3** *Surgery* examine (a part of the body) in detail. □ **exploration** *n.* **exploratory** *adj.* **explorer** *n.*

explosion *n.* **1** an act or the action of exploding. **2 a** a sudden outburst of noise. **b** a sudden outbreak of feeling. **3** a sudden, rapid increase.

explosive ● *adj.* **1** able or likely to explode. **2 a** highly controversial. **b** (of a situation etc.) dangerously tense. **3** rapid, sudden; violent. ● *n.* an explosive substance. □ **explosively** *adv.* **explosiveness** *n.*

Expo *n.* (*also* **expo**) (*pl.* **Expos**) **1** a large international exhibition. **2** an exhibition for a specific industry.

exponent *n.* **1** a promoter of an idea, theory, etc. **2** a person who is able to perform a particular activity with skill. **3** a raised symbol beside a numeral indicating how many times it is to be multiplied by itself. [*Say* ex POE nint]

exponential *adj.* **1** of or indicated by a mathematical exponent. **2** (of an increase etc.) more and more rapid.

□ **exponentially** adv. [Say expa NEN chull, expa NEN chuh lee]

export ● v. **1** send out (goods, services, etc.) to another country, esp. for sale. **2** spread (ideas or customs) into another country. **3** *Computing* transmit (data) for use elsewhere. ● n. **1** the process of exporting. **2** an exported article or service. □ **exportable** adj. **exporter** n.

expose v. (**exposes, exposed, exposing**) **1** uncover and make visible. **2** make vulnerable to. **3** subject (a film) to light. **4** reveal the identity or fact of. **5** disclose. **6** leave (a person) in the open to die. □ **expose oneself** display one's genitals publicly. □ **exposed** adj.

exposé n. a media report that reveals something discreditable. [Say expo ZAY]

exposition n. **1** a comprehensive description and explanation of a theory. **2** *Music* the part of a movement in which the principal themes are first presented. **3** a large public exhibition of art or trade goods.

expositor n. a person or thing that explains complicated ideas or theories. □ **expository** adj. [Say ex POZZA tur, ex POZZA tory]

exposure n. **1** the act or condition of exposing or being exposed. **2** the physical condition resulting from being exposed to severe weather conditions. **3** the revelation of an esp. secret identity or fact. **4 a** the action of exposing a film etc. to the light. **b** the extent to which the film is exposed. **5** publicity.

expound v. set out in detail. □ **expounder** n.

express¹ v. (**expresses, expressed, expressing**) **1** convey (thought, feelings, etc.) in words or by gestures etc. **2** (**express oneself**) say what one thinks or means. **3** squeeze out (liquid or air). □ **expressible** adj.

express² ● adj. **1 a** operating at high speed. **b** (of a train, bus, etc.) making relatively few stops before reaching its destination. **c** (of a road etc.) designed for express traffic. **2** definitely stated. **3** done etc. for a special purpose. **4** (of messages etc.) delivered immediately. ● adv. by express courier or train. ● n. (pl. **expresses**) an express train, bus, etc. ● v. (**expresses, expressed, expressing**) send by express courier etc.

expression n. **1** the process or act of expressing. **2** a word or phrase. **3** *Math* a collection of symbols expressing a quantity. **4** the look on someone's face. □ **expressionless** adj.

expressionism n. (also

Expressionism) a style of painting, music, drama, etc., in which an artist or writer seeks to express emotional experience rather than impressions of the external world. □ **expressionist** n. & adj. **expressionistic** adj.

expressive adj. **1** full of expression. **2** serving to express. □ **expressively** adv. **expressiveness** n. **expressivity** n.

expressly adv. **1** clearly, definitely. **2** for a special and deliberate purpose.

expresso n. = ESPRESSO.

expressway n. a highway for fast-moving traffic, esp. in urban areas.

expropriate v. (**expropriates, expropriated, expropriating**) (esp. of a government) take away property from its owner. □ **expropriation** n. [Say ex PRO pree ate]

expulsion n. **1** the action of expelling. **2** (**the Expulsion**) *Cdn Hist.* the eviction of francophones from Acadia in 1755. □ **expulsive** adj. [Say ex PUL shun, ex PULSE iv]

expunge v. (**expunges, expunged, expunging**) **1** erase, remove. **2** wipe out, destroy. [Say ex PUNGE]

expurgate v. (**expurgates, expurgated, expurgating**) remove matter thought to be objectionable from a book etc. [Say EX pur gate]

exquisite adj. **1** extremely beautiful or pleasing. **2** keenly felt. **3** highly sensitive. □ **exquisitely** adv. [Say ex QUIZ it or EX quiz it]

extant adj. (esp. of a document etc.) still existing. [Say EX t'nt or ex TANT]

extempore adj. & adv. without preparation. [Say ex TEMPA ree]

extemporize v. (**extemporizes, extemporized, extemporizing**) improvise. [Say ex TEMPA rize]

extend v. **1** lengthen or make larger in space or time. **2** lay out at full length. **3** reach or be continuous over a certain area. **4 a** have a certain scope. **b** increase the scope of application of. **5 a** offer. **b** accord (financial credit). □ **extendable** adj. **extender** n. **extensible** adj. [Say ex TEND, ex TENSA bull]

extended family n. **1** one's family beyond the nuclear family. **2** such a group living together or near each other.

extension n. **1** the action or process of extending. **2** a part added to something to enlarge or prolong it. **3** a part added on to a building. **4** an application of an existing system to a new area. **5** a subsidiary telephone on the same line. **6** an additional period of time. **7** (also

extension cord) an electrical cable used to plug an appliance etc. into a distant outlet. □ **by extension** taking the same line of argument further.

extensive *adj.* **1** covering a large area. **2** having a wide scope. □ **extensively** *adv.*

extensor *n.* (also **extensor muscle**) a muscle that extends part of the body.

extent *n.* **1** the space over which a thing extends. **2** the width or limits of application.

extenuating *adj.* showing reasons why a wrong or illegal act should be judged less seriously. [*Say* ex TEN yoo ate]

exterior ● *adj.* **1** of or on the outer side. **2** *Film* outdoor. ● *n.* the outward aspect or appearance.

exterminate *v.* (**exterminates, exterminated, exterminating**) **1** destroy utterly. **2** get rid of. □ **extermination** *n.* **exterminator** *n.*

external ● *adj.* **1 a** of or situated on the outside or visible part. **b** coming from the outside or an outside source. **2** relating to a country's foreign affairs. ● *n.* (in *pl.*) **1** the outward features or aspect. **2** external circumstances. □ **externally** *adv.*

external affairs *pl. n.* **1** a country's relations with other countries. **2** (treated as *sing.*) the government department concerned with these.

externalize *v.* (**externalizes, externalized, externalizing**) **1** treat (a fact etc.) as existing outside of oneself. **2** *Psychology* attribute (one's own feelings etc.) to others etc. **3** express (a thought or feeling) in words or actions.

extinct *adj.* **1 a** (of a species, language, etc.) no longer surviving or in existence. **b** (of a family) having no living descendant. **2** (of a volcano) no longer active. **3** terminated, quenched.

extinction *n.* the state or process of being or becoming extinct.

extinguish *v.* (**extinguishes, extinguished, extinguishing**) **1** quench, put out (a flame, light, etc.). **2** destroy, put an end to. **3 a** wipe out (a debt). **b** *Law* nullify or render void. □ **extinguisher** *n.* [*Say* ex TING gwish, ex TING gwish er]

extirpate *v.* (**extirpates, extirpated, extirpating**) **1** search out and destroy completely. **2** do away with. □ **extirpation** *n.* [*Say* EX tur pate]

extol *v.* (**extols, extolled, extolling**) praise enthusiastically. [*Say* ex TOLL]

extort *v.* obtain by force, threats, persistent demands, etc. □ **extortion** *n.*

extortionate *adj.* (of a price etc.) exorbitant. [*Say* ex TORE shun it]

extortionist *n.* a person who extorts esp. money. [*Say* ex TORE shun ist]

extra ● *adj.* additional. ● *adv.* **1** more than the usual or expected amount. **2** additionally. ● *n.* **1** an additional thing, esp. one for which an extra charge is made. **2** a person engaged to fill out a crowd scene in a film or play. **3** a special issue of a newspaper etc.

extra- *comb. form* **1** outside. **2** beyond the scope of.

extract ● *v.* **1** remove or take out with care or effort. **2** obtain with difficulty from a person. **3** obtain (a resource) from the earth. **4** select (a passage of writing, music, etc.) for quotation or performance. **5** obtain (juices etc.) by pressure, distillation, etc. **6** derive (happiness etc.) from a source. ● *n.* **1** an excerpt or short passage taken from a book, piece of music, etc. **2** the concentrated form of the active ingredient of a substance. □ **extractor** *n.*

extraction *n.* **1** the action of extracting. **2** the ethnic origin of someone's family.

extractive *adj.* of, involving, or concerned with the extraction of natural resources or products, esp. non-renewable ones.

extracurricular *adj.* **1** (of an activity) not included in the normal curriculum. **2** outside the normal routine etc. [*Say* extra kuh RICK you lur]

extradite *v.* (**extradites, extradited, extraditing**) hand over (a person accused or convicted of a crime) to the foreign country etc. in which the crime was committed. □ **extradition** *n.* [*Say* EXTRA dite, extra DISH un]

extramarital *adj.* occurring outside marriage. [*Say* extra MARITAL]

extramural *adj.* designating educational activity conducted off the premises of a university, college, or school. [*Say* extra MURAL]

extraneous *adj.* **1** unrelated to the subject being dealt with. **2** of external origin. □ **extraneously** *adv.* [*Say* ex TRAINY us]

extraordinaire *adj.* outstanding in a particular capacity. [*Say* ex TRORE din air]

extraordinary *adj.* **1** unusual, remarkable. **2** exceeding what is usual, esp. to the point of provoking astonishment. □ **extraordinarily** *adv.* [*Say* ex TRORE din airy *or* extra ORDINARY]

extrapolate *v.* (**extrapolates, extrapolated, extrapolating**) use (a fact valid for one situation) to make conclusions about a different or wider

situation. □ **extrapolation** n.
[Say ex TRAPPA late]

extrasensory adj. regarded as derived by
means other than the known senses.
[Say extra SENSA ree]

extrasensory perception n. the
supposed ability to perceive things without
the use of known senses. Abbreviation:
ESP.

extraterrestrial ● adj. **1** existing or
occurring beyond the earth or its
atmosphere. **2** (in science fiction) from
outer space. ● n. a being from outer space.
[Say extra tuh RESS tree ul]

extraterritorial adj. situated or valid
outside a country's territory.
[Say extra TERRITORIAL]

extravagant adj. **1** immoderate,
excessive, or wasteful in use of resources,
esp. money. **2** costing much. **3 a** going
beyond what is reasonable. **b** astonishingly
elaborate or showy. □ **extravagance** n.
extravagantly adv. [Say ex TRAVVA gint,
ex TRAVVA gince]

extravaganza n. an elaborate and
spectacular entertainment.
[Say ex travva GANZA]

extra-virgin adj. (of olive oil) made from
the first pressing, and thus of high quality.

extreme ● adj. **1 a** reaching a high or the
highest degree; very great. **b** (of a case etc.)
highly unusual. **2 a** severe, stringent. **b** (of
a person etc.) not moderate. **3 a** furthest
from the centre or a given point. **b** last,
utmost. **4** Politics radical. **5** designating
sports performed in a hazardous
environment. ● n. **1** (often in pl.) one or
other of two things that are as different
from each other as possible. **2** a thing at
either end of anything. **3** the highest
degree. □ **go to extremes** take an
extreme course of action. **go to the
other extreme** take a diametrically
opposite course of action. **in the
extreme** to an extreme degree.
□ **extremely** adv.

extremist n. **1** a person who holds
extreme political or religious views. **2** a
person who tends to go to extremes.
□ **extremism** n. **extremist** adj.

extremity n. (pl. **extremities**) **1** the
furthest point or limit. **2** (in pl.) the hands
and feet. **3** the degree to which a situation,
a feeling, etc. is extreme.
[Say ex TREMMA tee]

extricate v. free from a difficulty.
□ **extrication** n. [Say EXTRA kate]

extrovert n. an outgoing or sociable
person. □ **extroverted** adj.
[Say EXTRA vert]

extrude v. (**extrudes, extruded,**

extruding) **1** thrust, force out, or expel.
2 shape (metal, plastics, etc.) by forcing
through a die. □ **extruded** adj. **extruder**
n. **extrusion** n. [Say ex TRUDE,
ex TRUE zhun]

exuberant adj. **1** lively, high-spirited,
effusive. **2** growing luxuriously or
profusely. □ **exuberance** n.
exuberantly adv. [Say ex OO bur int or
ex YOO bur int]

exude v. (**exudes, exuded, exuding**)
1 come out or cause to come out slowly;
ooze. **2 a** display (an emotion etc.)
abundantly and openly. **b** (of a place) have a
strong atmosphere of. [Say ex OOD or
ex YOOD]

exult v. show or feel triumphant joy.
□ **exultation** n. **exultant** adj. **exultantly**
adv. [Say ex ULT, ex ul TAY sh'n]

exurb n. a town or community beyond the
suburbs of a large city. □ **exurban** adj.

eye ● n. **1** the organ of sight in humans
and animals. **2 a** sight or the faculty of
sight. **b** perception. **3 a** a mark or spot
resembling an eye. **b** the leaf bud of a
potato. **4** the calm region at the centre of a
storm. **5** the hole in a needle through
which thread is passed. **6** a ring or loop for
a hook etc. to pass through. ● v. (**eyes,
eyed, eyeing**) **1** watch or observe closely.
2 ogle or look at amorously. □ **all eyes**
1 watching intently. **2** general attention.
an eye for an eye retaliation in kind.
have one's eye on aim to procure.
**have eyes bigger than one's
stomach** expect to eat more than one
can. **have an eye to** have as one's
objective. **hit a person (right)
between the eyes** informal be very
obvious or impressive. **keep an eye
open** (or **out**) watch carefully. **keep
one's eyes open** (or **peeled** or
skinned) watch out or be on the alert.
make eyes (or **sheep's eyes**) look
amorously at. **my eye** slang nonsense. **see
eye to eye** be in full agreement. **up to
the** (or **one's**) **eyes in 1** inundated with.
2 to the utmost limit. **with one's eyes
open** with full awareness. **with one's
eyes shut** (or **closed**) easily or with
little effort. □ **eyeless** adj.

eyeball ● n. the firm white sphere of the
eye within the eyelids and socket. ● v. slang
look or stare at. □ **eyeball-to-eyeball**
informal confronting or encountering closely.
to (or **up to**) **the eyeballs** informal to a
great extent.

eyebrow n. the line of hair growing along
the ridge above each eye socket. □ **raise
(one's) eyebrows** cause (or show)
surprise or disapproval.

eye candy *n.* **1** superficially attractive but undemanding visual images. **2** an attractive person or thing.

eye-catcher *n.* a person or thing which catches the eye. □ **eye-catching** *adj.*

eyedropper *n.* = DROPPER 1.

eyeful *n.* (*pl.* **eyefuls**) *informal* **1** a good look at something. **2** a visually striking scene or thing. □ **get an eyeful** take a good, long look.

eyeglass *n.* **1** (in *pl.*) a pair of lenses used to correct defective eyesight. **2** a lens for correcting defective sight.

eyelash *n.* each of the short hairs growing on the edge of the eyelid.

eyelet *n.* **1** a small hole in paper, leather, cloth, etc., for string or rope etc. to pass through. **2** a metal ring reinforcement for this. **3** a form of decoration in embroidery, which produces an open work effect.

eyelid *n.* either of the upper or lower folds of skin that meet when the eye is closed.

eyeliner *n.* a cosmetic applied as a line around the eye.

eye-opener *n.* *informal* a thing that enlightens, surprises, etc. □ **eye-opening** *adj.*

eyepiece *n.* the lens at the end of a telescope etc. to which the eye is applied.

eye-popping *adj.* surprising, astonishing.

eyeshadow *n.* a coloured cosmetic applied to the eyelids.

eyesight *n.* the faculty or power of seeing.

eyesore *n.* a very ugly thing.

eye tooth *n.* a canine tooth. □ **would give one's eye teeth for** would make any sacrifice to obtain.

eyewitness *n.* a person who has personally seen a thing happen and can testify to it.

Ff

F¹ *n.* (also **f**) (*pl.* **Fs** or **F's**) **1** the sixth letter of the alphabet. **2** the fourth note of the C major scale. **3** the lowest academic mark, denoting a failing grade.

F² *abbr.* (also **F.**) **1** Fahrenheit. **2** female.

f *abbr.* (also **f.**) **1** female. **2** *Grammar* feminine. **3** (*pl.* **ff.**) following page etc. **4** *Music* forte. **5** (*pl.* **ff.**) folio. **6** frequency.

fa *n.* **1** (in tonic sol-fa) the fourth note of a major scale. **2** the note F in the fixed-do system.

fab *adj. informal* fabulous.

Fabian *n.* a member or supporter of the Fabian Society, a socialist organization founded to promote gradual political change. □ **Fabian** *adj.* **Fabianism** *n.* [*Say* FAY bee un]

fable *n.* **1** a tale conveying a moral. **2** myths and legendary tales collectively. **3** a lie.

fabled *adj.* **1** famous. **2** celebrated in fable.

fabric *n.* **1** a textile. **2** a structure, esp. the walls, floor, and roof of a building. **3** the essential structure of a thing.

fabricate *v.* (**fabricates**, **fabricated**, **fabricating**) **1** construct or manufacture. **2** invent (a story etc.). □ **fabrication** *n.* **fabricator** *n.*

fabulous *adj.* **1** extraordinary. **2** excellent, marvellous. **3** legendary, mythical. □ **fabulously** *adv.* **fabulousness** *n.*

FAC *abbr. Cdn* Firearms Acquisition Certificate.

facade *n.* **1** the face of a building. **2** an esp. deceptive outward appearance. [*Say* fuh SOD]

face ● *n.* **1** the front of the head from the forehead to the chin. **2** the expression of the facial features. **3** a grimace. **4** the main surface of a thing. **5** the working surface of an implement etc. **6** outward appearance or show. **7** respectable reputation. ● *v.* (**faces**, **faced**, **facing**) **1** look or be positioned towards or in a certain direction. **2** (of an illustration etc.) stand on the opposite page to. **3** confront and deal with. □ **face a charge** (or **charges**) be charged with a crime in court. **face off 1** *Hockey & Lacrosse* start play by a faceoff. **2** contend or compete against. **face up to** confront, accept bravely. **in one's** (or **the**) **face 1** directly at one. **2** irritatingly present. **in face** (or **the face**) **of**
1 despite. **2** when confronted by. **let's face it** *informal* we must be realistic about it. **on the face of it** apparently. **to a person's face** openly in a person's presence. □ **faced** *adj.*

face card *n.* the king, queen, or jack in playing cards.

face cloth *n. Cdn & Brit.* a small cloth for washing one's face etc.

faceless *adj.* remote and impersonal.

facelift *n.* **1** cosmetic surgery to remove wrinkles etc. by tightening the skin of the face. **2** a procedure to improve the appearance of a thing.

face mask *n.* **1** any covering or device to shield or protect the face. **2** (also **facial mask**) a preparation beneficial to the complexion, spread over the face.

faceoff *n.* **1** *Hockey & Lacrosse* the action of starting play by dropping the puck or ball between two opposing players' sticks. **2** a direct confrontation.

facet *n.* **1** a particular aspect. **2 a** one side of something many-sided. **b** any of the faces of a cut gem. □ **faceted** *adj.* (also in *comb.*) [*Say* FASS it]

facetious *adj.* **1** not intended seriously or literally. **2** treating serious issues with inappropriate humour. □ **facetiously** *adv.* [*Say* fuh SEE shuss]

face to face ● *adv.* confronting. ● *adj.* (**face-to-face**) with the people involved facing each other.

face value *n.* the value printed or stamped on money or postage stamps. □ **take** (or **accept**) **at face value** assume something is genuinely what it appears to be.

facial ● *adj.* of or for the face. ● *n.* a beauty treatment for the face. □ **facially** *adv.* [*Say* FAY shull]

facile *adj.* **1** *usu. derogatory* too easily obtained or achieved. **2** (esp. of theory or argument) lacking careful thought. [*Say* FASS ile *or* FASS eel]

facilitate *v.* (**facilitates**, **facilitated**, **facilitating**) **1** make easy or easier. **2** encourage discussion in a group. □ **facilitation** *n.* **facilitator** *n.* [*Say* fuh SILLA tate, fuh silla TAY sh'n, fuh SILLA tay tur]

facility *n.* (*pl.* **facilities**) **1** a natural ability to do something easily. **2** a building, service, equipment, etc. provided for a particular purpose. **3** euphemism (in *pl.*) a toilet or washroom. [*Say* fuh SILLA tee]

facing *n.* **1** an esp. interior layer of material covering part of a garment etc. for contrast or strength. **2** a layer forming the face of a wall etc.

facsimile *n.* an exact copy. [*Say* fack SIMMA lee]

fact *n.* **1** a thing that is known to be true. **2** a thing that is believed or claimed to be true. □ **before** (or **after**) **the fact** before (or after) the occurrence of an event. **facts and figures** precise information etc. **hard fact** (or **facts**) **1** inescapable truth. **2** concrete evidence. **in** (or **in point of**) **fact 1** in reality. **2** in summary.

faction *n.* **1** a small self-interested or dissenting group within a larger one, esp. in politics. **2** dissension within an organization. □ **factional** *adj.* **factionalism** *n.*

fact of life *n.* **1** something unpleasant that must be accepted. **2** (**the facts of life**) information about sexual functions and practices.

factoid *n.* **1** something that is reported so often that it becomes accepted as fact. **2** a trivial fact.

factor ● *n.* **1** a circumstance, fact, etc. contributing to a result. **2** Math a whole number etc. that when multiplied with another produces a given number or expression. **3** a gene etc. determining hereditary character. **4** any of several substances in the blood which contribute to coagulation. **5** Cdn hist. an employee of the Hudson's Bay Company in charge of a trading post. ● *v.* Math resolve into factors or express as a product of factors. □ **factor in** introduce as a factor. **factor out** exclude from an assessment.

factory *n.* (*pl.* **factories**) **1** a building containing equipment for manufacturing or processing. **2** Cdn hist. a main fur-trading post.

factory outlet *n.* a store in which factory-made goods are sold directly by the manufacturer at discount prices.

factory ship *n.* a fishing ship with facilities for immediate processing.

factual *adj.* **1** based on or concerned with fact or facts. **2** actual, true. □ **factuality** *n.* **factually** *adv.* [*Say* FACK choo ul, fack choo ALA tee]

faculty *n.* (*pl.* **faculties**) **1** an aptitude or ability. **2** a basic physical or mental ability. **3 a** a group of university departments concerned with a major division of knowledge. **b** the teaching staff of a university or college.

fad *n.* a craze. □ **faddish** *adj.* **faddishly** *adv.* **faddishness** *n.* **faddism** *n.* **faddist** *n.*

fade ● *v.* (**fades**, **faded**, **fading**) **1** lose or cause to lose colour. **2** lose strength. **3** disappear gradually; grow dim or faint. **4** diminish. **5** Film **a** cause (a picture) to come gradually in or out of view on a screen. **b** make (the sound) more or less audible. ● *n.* an act of causing a film or television picture to fade. □ **fade away** informal languish, grow thin.

fade-out *n.* **1** a filmmaking and broadcasting technique whereby an image or sound is made to fade away. **2** informal a gradual reduction etc.

Fahrenheit *adj.* of or measured on a scale of temperature on which water freezes at 32° and boils at 212° under standard conditions. [*Say* FAIR in hite]

fail ● *v.* **1** be unsuccessful. **2** disappoint; let down. **3** (of supplies, crops, etc.) be or become insufficient. **4** become weaker; break down. ● *n.* a failure in an examination or test. □ **without fail** whatever happens.

failed *adj.* **1** unsuccessful. **2** deficient.

failing ● *n.* a fault or shortcoming; a weakness. ● *prep.* without.

fail-safe *adj.* **1** reverting to a safe condition in the event of a breakdown etc. **2** totally reliable.

failure *n.* **1** lack of success. **2** an unsuccessful person, thing, or attempt. **3** non-performance. **4** breaking down. **5** a cessation in existence or availability.

faint ● *adj.* **1** indistinct; not clearly perceived. **2** (of a person) weak or giddy. **3** slight, remote. **4** feeble. **5** timid. ● *v.* lose consciousness. ● *n.* a sudden loss of consciousness. □ **not have the faintest** informal have no idea. □ **faintly** *adv.* **faintness** *n.*

faint-hearted *adj.* timid.

fair¹ ● *adj.* **1** just; in accordance with the rules. **2** blond; light in complexion. **3** moderately good; average. **4** (of weather) fine and dry. **5** beautiful, attractive. **6** Baseball (of a ball) that lands within the legal area of play. ● *adv.* **1** in a fair manner. **2** exactly. □ **fair and square 1** exactly. **2** honest, above-board. **fair enough** informal that is reasonable. **the fair sex** dated or jocular women. **fair shake** (also **fair crack**) informal a fair opportunity. **no fair** informal (that is) unfair. □ **fairness** *n.*

fair² *n.* **1** a usu. annual exhibition held esp. in rural areas in conjunction with a travelling midway. **2** an exhibition to promote particular products. **3** a periodical gathering for the sale of goods.

fair game n. a thing or person one may legitimately pursue, exploit, etc.

fairground n. a place where a fair is held.

fair-haired adj. **1** having fair hair. **2** favoured.

fairing n. a streamlining structure added to a ship, aircraft, etc.

fairly adv. **1** justly. **2** moderately. **3** to a noticeable degree. **4** used as an intensifier.

fair play n. reasonable treatment or behaviour.

fairway n. **1** the part of a golf course between a tee and its green. **2** a navigable channel for a ship.

fair-weather adj. (of a person) tending to be unreliable in times of difficulty.

fairy ● n. (pl. **fairies**) a small imaginary being with magical powers. **●** adj. **1** of or relating to fairies. **2** delicate, small.

fairy godmother n. a person who provides unexpected help.

fairyland n. **1** the imaginary home of fairies. **2** an enchanted region.

fairy tale ● n. (also **fairy story**) **1** a tale about fairies. **2** an unbelievable story. **●** adj. (**fairy-tale**) **1** of or relating to or resembling a fairy tale. **2** highly unlikely.

fait accompli n. (pl. **faits accomplis**) a thing that has been done and is past arguing or altering. [Say fett a com PLEE]

faith n. **1** complete trust or confidence. **2** strong religious belief. **3** a particular religion.

faithful adj. **1** showing faith. **2** loyal, trustworthy. **3** remaining sexually loyal to one's spouse, lover, etc. **4** true to fact. **5 a** (**the Faithful**) the believers in a religion. **b** (**the faithful**) loyal adherents of a political party. □ **faithfully** adv. **faithfulness** n.

faithless adj. **1** disloyal. **2** without religious faith. □ **faithlessness** n.

fajita n. (pl. **fajitas**) (usu. in pl.) a dish of small strips of grilled meat rolled in a tortilla and garnished with fried vegetables, grated cheese, etc. [Say fuh HEAT uh]

fake ● n. **1** a thing or person that is not genuine. **2** a trick. **●** adj. not genuine. **●** v. (**fakes**, **faked**, **faking**) **1** make (something) appear genuine. **2** pretend to feel or have. **3** Sport deceive by a misleading movement. □ **fake out** slang deceive or trick. □ **faker** n. **fakery** n. (pl. **fakeries**)

fakie n (in skateboarding or snowboarding) a movement in which the board is ridden backwards.

fakir n. a Muslim (or Hindu) holy man who lives by begging. [Say FAY keer or fuh KEER]

falafel n. a spicy fried patty of ground chickpeas, often served in a pita. [Say fuh LAWFUL]

falcon n. a bird of prey with long pointed wings. [Say FAWL kun or FAL kun]

falconry n. the breeding and training of hawks for hunting; the sport of hawking. □ **falconer** n. [Say FAWL kun ree or FAL kun ree, FAWL kun ur or FAL kun ur]

fall ● v. (**falls**; past **fell**; past participle **fallen**; **falling**) **1** descend rapidly. **2** collapse to the ground. **3** become detached and descend. **4** hang down. **5** (of a sound) become lower. **6** occur. **7** decline, diminish. **8** cut down. **9** show dismay or disappointment. **10** be defeated. **11** (foll. by to) begin. **●** n. **1** an act of falling; a sudden rapid descent. **2** autumn. **3** that which falls or has fallen. **4** overthrow, downfall. **5 a** succumbing to temptation. **b** (**the Fall**) in Christian and Jewish theology, the lapse into a sinful state resulting from the first act of disobedience by Adam and Eve. **6** a waterfall. □ **fall away** (of a surface) incline abruptly. **fall back** retreat. **fall back on** have recourse to in difficulty. **fall behind 1** lag. **2** be in arrears. **fall for** informal **1** be captivated or deceived by. **2** admire. **fall afoul** (or **foul**) **of** come into conflict with. **fall in** take one's place in military formation. **fall into place** begin to make sense. **fall in with 1** meet by chance. **2** agree with. **fall off** (of demand etc.) decrease, deteriorate. **fall on 1** attack. **2** be the duty of. **fall out 1** quarrel. **2** Military come into formation. **3** come to pass. **fall over oneself** informal be eager or competitive. **fall short** fail to reach a standard or target. **fall through** fail. **fall to** begin an activity. **take the fall** informal take blame or punishment, esp. for someone else.

fallacious adj. based on a mistaken belief. [Say fuh LAY shuss]

fallacy n. (pl. **fallacies**) **1** a mistaken belief. **2** faulty reasoning; misleading argument. [Say FAL a see]

fallback ● n. a reserve; something that may be used in an emergency. **●** adj. reserve, emergency.

fallen ● v. past participle of FALL. **●** adj. **1** having fallen. **2** killed in war.

faller n. **1** something that falls. **2** a logger who cuts down trees.

fall guy n. slang **1** an easy victim. **2** a scapegoat.

fallible adj. capable of making mistakes. □ **fallibility** n. **fallibly** adv. [Say FAL a bull, fal a BILLA tee]

falling-out *n.* (*pl.* **fallings-out**) a quarrel.

fall-off *n.* a decrease, deterioration, etc.

Fallopian tube *n.* either of two tubes in female mammals along which ova travel from the ovaries to the uterus.
[*Say* fuh LOPEY in]

fallout *n.* **1** radioactive debris caused by a nuclear explosion. **2** the adverse side effects of a situation etc.

fallow ● *adj.* **1 a** (of land) plowed and harrowed but left unsown for a year. **b** uncultivated. **2** inactive. ● *n.* fallow land.
[*Say* FAL oh]

false ● *adj.* **1** not according with fact. **2** sham, artificial. **3** not actually so. **4** improperly so called. **5** deceptive. **6** deceitful or unfaithful. ● *adv.* in a false manner. □ **falsely** *adv.* **falsity** *n.*

falsehood *n.* **1** the state of being false or untrue. **2** a lie. **3** the act of lying.

false memory syndrome *n.* apparent memory of an event that did not occur, created by psychological techniques such as hypnosis etc.

false pretenses *pl. n.* behaviour intended to deceive.

falsetto *n.* (*pl.* **falsettos**) **1** a method of voice production used by male singers to sing notes higher than their normal range. **2** an unnaturally high voice.
[*Say* fawl SET oh]

falsify *v.* (**falsifies, falsified, falsifying**) **1** fraudulently alter or make false. **2** show to be false. □ **falsification** *n.*
[*Say* FALSE a fie, false a fuh KAY sh'n]

falter *v.* **1** stumble, stagger. **2** lose courage. **3** stammer. **4** lose momentum, energy, etc.
[*Say* FAWL tur]

fame *n.* the state of being famous.

famed *adj.* famous.

familial *adj.* having to do with family.
[*Say* fuh MILLY ul]

familiar ● *adj.* **1 a** well known. **b** common; often encountered. **2** knowing a thing well. **3** well acquainted; friendly. **4** excessively informal; impertinent. ● *n.* **1** a close friend. **2** (also **familiar spirit**) a demon supposedly attending and obeying a witch etc. □ **familiarly** *adv.*

familiarity *n.* (*pl.* **familiarities**) **1** the state of being familiar. **2** a close relationship.

familiarize *v.* (**familiarizes, familiarized, familiarizing**) **1** make conversant or well acquainted. **2** make well known or understood.
□ **familiarization** *n.*

family *n.* (*pl.* **families**) **1** a group of people related by blood, marriage, or adoption. **2 a** the members of a household. **b** a person's children. **c** a person's spouse and children. **3** all the descendants of a common ancestor. **4** all the languages derived from a particular early language. **5** a group of objects distinguished by common features. **6** a group of related plants or animals. □ **in the family way** *informal* pregnant.

family allowance *n. Cdn hist.* a monthly payment made by the federal government to mothers of children under 18.

Family Compact *n. Cdn* **1** a name given to the ruling class in Upper Canada in the early 19th century. **2** any influential clique or faction.

family law *n.* the part of the legal system that deals with matters affecting families.

family man *n.* a man having a wife and children.

family planning *n.* the planning of the number of children in a family by using birth control.

family room *n.* a room in a house used by family members for relaxation etc.

family tree *n.* a chart showing relationships and lines of descent.

famine *n.* **1** extreme scarcity of food. **2** a shortage.

famished *adj.* very hungry.

famous *adj.* **1** celebrated; well known. **2** *informal* excellent. **3** notorious. □ **famous last words** (an ironic comment on) an overconfident assumption that may be proved wrong by events. □ **famously** *adv.*

fan¹ ● *n.* **1** an apparatus with rotating blades that creates a current of air. **2** a hand-held folding device for agitating the air to cool oneself. **3** anything spread out like a fan. ● *v.* (**fans, fanned, fanning**) **1 a** blow a current of air on. **b** agitate (the air) with a fan. **2** spread out in the shape of a fan. **3** make more ardent. □ **fan the flames of** increase the intensity of.

fan² *n.* a devotee or admirer of a particular activity, performer, etc.

fanatic ● *n.* **1** a person filled with excessive enthusiasm for something. **2** *informal* a person who is devoted to a hobby, pastime, etc. ● *adj.* excessively enthusiastic. □ **fanatical** *adj.* **fanaticism** *n.* [*Say* fuh NAT ick, fuh NAT ick ul, fuh NATTA sism]

fan belt *n.* a belt that drives a fan to cool the radiator in a motor vehicle.

fancier *n.* **1** a connoisseur or follower. **2** a breeder of a certain type of animal or plant.

fanciful *adj.* **1** existing only in the imagination. **2** over-imaginative and unrealistic. **3** designed or decorated in an odd but creative manner. □ **fancifully** adv.

fancy ● n. (pl. **fancies**) **1** an individual taste. **2** a caprice or whim. **3** a thing favoured. **4** an arbitrary supposition. **5 a** the faculty of using imagination. **b** a mental image. **6** delusion. ● adj. (**fancier**, **fanciest**) **1** elaborate. **2** of high quality or very expensive. ● v. (**fancies**, **fancied**, **fancying**) **1** be inclined to suppose. **2** informal have an unduly high opinion of. **3** (in imperative) an exclamation of surprise. **4** conceive, imagine. □ **catch** (or **take**) **the fancy of** please; appeal to. **take a fancy to** become fond of. □ **fancily** adv.

fancy footwork n. **1** agile use of the feet, esp. in dancing etc. **2** agility in negotiation etc.

fancy-free adj. (often in phr. **footloose and fancy-free**) without (esp. emotional) commitments.

fancy-pants adj. informal hotshot.

fandom n. the world of fans. [Say FAN dum]

fanfare n. **1** a short sounding of trumpets, bugles, etc. **2** an elaborate display.

fang n. **1** a sharply pointed canine tooth. **2** the tooth of a venomous snake, by which poison is injected. □ **bare one's fangs** show oneself ready for confrontation. □ **fanged** adj. **fangless** adj.

fanny n. (pl. **fannies**) slang the buttocks.

fanny pack n. a small pouch worn on a belt around the waist etc.

fantail n. **1** a pigeon with a broad fan-shaped tail. **2** a fan-shaped tail or end. □ **fantailed** adj.

fantasia n. a musical or other composition free in form, often based on several familiar tunes. [Say fan TAY zhuh]

fantasize v. (**fantasizes**, **fantasized**, **fantasizing**) **1 a** daydream. **b** indulge in a sexual fantasy. **2** imagine; create a fantasy about.

fantastic adj. **1** informal excellent, extraordinary. **2** informal very large; lavish. **3** (also **fantastical**) existing only in the imagination; unreal. □ **fantastically** adv.

fantasy n. (pl. **fantasies**) **1** the faculty of inventing images. **2** a sequence of mental images developed in the imagination reflecting a person's desires. **3** a whimsical speculation. **4** a musical composition, free in form. **5** a genre of imaginative fiction involving stories involving magic, mythical creatures, etc.

fantasyland n. an imaginary world where all fantasies are fulfilled.

fanzine n. a magazine for fans. [Say FAN zeen]

FAQ n. frequently asked questions.

far adv. & adj. (**further**, **furthest** or **farther**, **farthest**) at or to or by a great distance or degree. □ **as far as 1** to the distance of. **2** to the extent that. **by far** by a great amount. **far and away** by a very large amount. **far and near** everywhere. **far and wide** over a large area. **far be it from me** I am reluctant to. **far from** tending to the opposite of. **go far 1** achieve much. **2** contribute greatly. **go too far** go beyond reasonable limits etc. **how far** to what extent. **so far 1** to this point. **2** until now. **so** (or **in so**) **far as** (or **that**) to the extent that. **so far so good** progress has been satisfactory so far now.

faraway adj. **1** remote; long-past. **2** (of a look) dreamy. **3** (of a voice) sounding as if from a distance.

farce n. **1** a coarsely comic dramatic work based on ludicrously improbable events. **2** an absurd event.

farcical adj. ridiculous or absurd. [Say FARSA cul]

fare ● n. **1 a** the price a passenger has to pay to be conveyed on public transport. **b** a passenger in a taxi etc. **2** a range of food. **3** something presented to the public, esp. for entertainment. ● v. (**fares**, **fared**, **faring**) **1** progress; get on. **2** happen.

Far East n. China, Japan, and other countries of eastern Asia. □ **Far Eastern** adj.

farewell ● interj. goodbye. ● n. **1** leave-taking. **2** parting good wishes.

far-fetched adj. not convincing, improbable.

far-flung adj. **1** widely distributed. **2** remote.

far gone adj. **1** informal in an advanced state of drunkenness, illness, etc. **2** past.

farm ● n. **1 a** an area of land used for growing crops, rearing animals, etc. **b** a farmhouse. **2** a place for breeding or growing something. ● v. **1** use land for growing crops, rearing animals, etc. **2** breed commercially. **3** (also **farm out**) delegate or subcontract (work) to others. □ **farmer** n. **farming** n.

farmhand n. a worker on a farm.

farmhouse n. a dwelling attached to a farm.

farmland n. land suitable for farming.

farmstead n. a farm and its buildings as a unit. [Say FARM sted]

farm team n. (also **farm club**) a minor-league sports team affiliated with a major-league team.

Far North n. (in Canada) the Arctic and sub-Arctic regions of the country.

far-off adj. remote; distant.

far-out adj. slang **1** unconventional. **2** excellent.

far-reaching adj. **1** extending widely. **2** having important consequences or implications.

farrier n. a smith who shoes horses. [Say FERRY ur]

farrow ● n. a litter of pigs. ● v. (of a sow) give birth to (pigs). □ **farrowing** n.

Farsi n. modern Persian. [Say FAR see]

far-sighted adj. **1** having foresight. **2** able to see distant things more clearly than near ones. □ **far-sightedness** n.

fart coarse slang ● v. **1** emit intestinal gas from the anus. **2** behave foolishly; waste time. ● n. **1** an emission of intestinal gas from the anus. **2** a boring or unpleasant person.

farther = FURTHER adv. 1, adj. 1.

farthest = FURTHEST.

farthing n. hist. (in the UK) a coin worth a quarter of an old penny.

fascia n. (pl. **fascias** or **fasciae**) **1** a flat horizontal band around the edge of a roof. **2** Anatomy a thin sheath of fibrous tissue. [Say FAY shuh or FASHY uh; for sense 2 say FASHY uh]

fascinate v. (**fascinates, fascinated, fascinating**) capture the interest of. □ **fascinated** adj. **fascinating** adj. **fascinatingly** adv. **fascination** n. [Say FASSA nate]

Fascism n. **1** hist. the totalitarian principles etc. of the extreme right-wing nationalist movement in Italy (1922–43). **2** (also **fascism**) **a** any similar movement, e.g. Nazism. **b** derogatory extreme right-wing or authoritarian views. □ **Fascist** n. & adj. (also **fascist**). **Fascistic** adj. (also **fascistic**). [Say FASH ism]

fashion ● n. **1** the current popular custom or style. **2** a manner of doing something. **3** characteristic form. ● v. make into a particular form. □ **after** (or **in**) **a fashion** as well as possible, though not satisfactorily.

fashionable adj. following or influenced by the current fashion. □ **fashionableness** n. **fashionably** adv.

fashionista n. (pl. **fashionistas**) **1** a person employed in the creation or promotion of haute couture. **2** a person much interested in fashion. [Say fashen EESTA]

fashion plate n. a person who consistently dresses in the current fashion.

fast¹ ● adj. **1** moving or capable of moving at high speed. **2** (of a clock etc.) ahead of the correct time. **3 a** (of photographic film) needing only a short exposure. **b** (of a lens) having a large aperture. **4 a** firmly fixed or attached. **b** secure. **5** (of a colour) not fading. **6** involving exciting or shocking activities. ● adv. **1** quickly. **2** firmly. **3** completely. □ **pull a fast one** informal try to gain an unfair advantage.

fast² ● v. abstain from all or some kinds of food or drink. ● n. an act or period of fasting.

fast and furious ● adv. **1** rapidly. **2** eagerly. ● adj. **1** rapid, fast-paced. **2** lively, energetic.

fastball n. **1** a baseball pitch thrown at full speed. **2** Cdn = FAST PITCH.

fast-breeder n. (also **fast-breeder reactor**) a nuclear reactor using neutrons with high kinetic energy.

fasten v. **1** make or become fixed or secure. **2** lock securely. **3** look or think fixedly or intently. **4** single out. □ **fastener** (also **fastening**) n.

fast food n. food prepared for quick sale, esp. in a snack bar or restaurant.

fast-forward ● n. a control on a tape or video player for advancing the tape rapidly. ● adj. designating such a control. ● v. advance rapidly.

fastidious adj. **1** overly scrupulous in matters of cleanliness etc. **2** squeamish. □ **fastidiously** adv. **fastidiousness** n. [Say fas TIDDY us]

fast lane n. **1** a traffic lane on a highway for high-speed driving and passing. **2** a means of rapid progress. **3** a fast lifestyle.

fastness n. **1** a stronghold. **2** the capacity of a dye not to fade or wash out.

fast pitch n. a variety of the game of softball, featuring fast underhand pitching.

fast-talk informal ● v. persuade by rapid or deceitful talk. ● n. (**fast talk**) such talk. □ **fast talker** n. **fast-talking** adj.

fast track ● n. a method etc. which provides rapid results. ● v. (**fast-track**) **1** treat as urgent. **2** advance quickly. □ **fast-tracker** n.

fat ● n. **1 a** a natural oily substance found in the tissue of animals and in some plants. **b** fat from animals or plants, purified and used for cooking. **2** excessive amounts of fat in a person or animal. **3** excess; surplus. ● adj. (**fatter, fattest**) **1** having excessive fat. **2** plump; well fed. **3** containing much fat. **4 a** thick. **b** substantial. **5** informal ironic very little. ● v. (**fats, fatted, fatting**) make or become fat. □ **the fat is in the fire** trouble is imminent. **kill the fatted calf** celebrate, esp. at a prodigal's return.

live off (or **on**) **the fat of the land** have the best of everything.

fatal adj. **1** causing or ending in death. **2** destructive; ruinous. □**fatally** adv.

fatalism n. the belief that all events are predetermined and therefore inevitable. □**fatalist** n. **fatalistic** adj. **fatalistically** adv. [Say FATAL ism]

fatality n. (pl. **fatalities**) **1** a death that is caused by accident, war, etc. **2** deadliness. [Say fay TALLA tee or fuh TALLA tee]

fat cat n. slang derogatory a wealthy and powerful person.

fate n. **1** the things that will happen or have happened to someone. **2** the power that is believed to control everything that happens. □**fated** adj.

fateful adj. important; having far-reaching usu. bad consequences.

fathead n. informal a stupid person.

father ● n. **1 a** a male parent. **b** a man who has care of a child, esp. by adoption or remarriage. **2** a progenitor or forefather. **3** an originator or early leader. **4** (**Fathers**) (also **Fathers of the Church**) early Christian theologians whose writings are regarded as authoritative. **5** (also **Father**) a priest. **6** (**the Father**) (in Christian belief) the first person of the Trinity. **7** a venerable person. ● v. **1** be the father of. **2** behave as a father towards. □**fatherhood** n. **fatherless** adj.

father-in-law n. (pl. **fathers-in-law**) the father of one's husband or wife.

fatherland n. one's native country.

fatherly adj. of or like a father (in affection, care, etc.).

Father of Confederation n. Cdn any of the delegates who represented colonies of British North America at the Charlottetown and Quebec Conferences or the London Conference, which led to Confederation in 1867.

Father Time n. the personification of time as an old man.

fathom ● n. (pl. often **fathom** when preceded by a number) a measure of six feet (1.8 m), used to measure depth. ● v. **1** grasp or comprehend. **2** measure the depth of. [Say FA thum (with TH as in THEM)]

fathomless adj. extremely deep.

fatigue ● n. **1 a** extreme tiredness. **b** a state of indifference. **2** weakness in materials caused by repeated stress. **3 a** a non-military duty in the army, often as a punishment. **b** (in pl.) clothing worn for such a duty usu. in drab colours or camouflage. ● v. (**fatigues, fatigued, fatiguing**) tire, exhaust.

fatso n. (pl. **fatsos**) slang offensive a fat person.

fatten v. **1** make fat. **2** grow or become fat.

fattening adj. high in calories.

fatty ● adj. (**fattier, fattiest**) **1** consisting of or containing fat. **2** marked by abnormal deposition of fat. **3** oily, greasy. ● n. (pl. **fatties**) slang offensive a fat person.

fatty acid n. an organic acid whose molecule contains a hydrocarbon chain.

fatuous adj. very silly; purposeless, idiotic. □**fatuously** adv. [Say FATCH oo us]

fatwa n. (pl. **fatwas**) (in Islamic countries) a ruling on a religious matter. [Say FAT wuh]

faucet n. a tap for running water. [Say FOSSET]

fault ● n. **1** a defect or imperfection. **2** a mistake. **3** responsibility for wrongdoing, error, etc. **4** a break in an electric circuit. **5** Geology an extended break in the continuity of strata. **6** Tennis etc. a service not in accordance with the rules. ● v. **1** find fault with; blame. **2** commit a fault. □**at fault** to blame. **find fault** make an adverse criticism. **to a fault** excessively. □**faultless** adj. **faultlessly** adv.

fault line n. Geology the line of intersection of a fault with the earth's surface.

faulty adj. (**faultier, faultiest**) having faults. □**faultiness** n.

faun n. a minor Roman god with a human face and torso and a goat's horns, legs, and tail.

fauna n. the animal life of a particular region, geological period, or environment. □**faunal** adj.

faux adj. false, imitation. [Say FOE]

faux pas n. (pl. **faux pas**) an embarrassing or tactless act or remark. [Say foe PAW for the singular, foe PAWS for the plural]

fave n. & adj. slang favourite.

favour (also **favor**) ● n. **1** an act of kindness beyond what is usual. **2** approval, goodwill. **3** special treatment. **4** a small gift given to guests at a party. **5** a thing given as a mark of favour or support. **6** (usu. in pl.) sexual relations. ● v. **1** regard or treat with favour. **2** give support or approval to. **3** facilitate, help. **4** oblige. **5** avoid putting too much strain on. □**find favour** be liked; prove acceptable. **in one's favour** to a person's advantage. **out of favour** lacking approval. □**favoured** adj.

favourable adj. (also **favorable**) **1** approving. **2** giving consent. **3** helpful, suitable. □**favourably** adv.

favourite (also **favorite**) ● adj. preferred to all others. ● n. **1** a specially favoured person or thing. **2** a competitor thought most likely to win.

favouritism *n.* (also **favoritism**) the unfair favouring of a person etc. at the expense of another.

fawn¹ *n.* **1** a young deer in its first year. **2** *n. & adj.* a light brown.

fawn² *v.* behave in an obsequious manner. □ **fawning** *adj.* **fawningly** *adv.*

fax ● *n.* (*pl.* **faxes**) **1** an exact copy of a document etc. produced by electronic scanning and transmission. **2** a machine for transmitting and receiving these. ● *v.* (**faxes, faxed, faxing**) send a document in this way. □ **faxable** *adj.*

faze *v.* (**fazes, fazed, fazing**) *informal* disconcert, perturb.

FBI *abbr.* (in the US) Federal Bureau of Investigation.

fealty *n.* (*pl.* **fealties**) **1** *hist.* a feudal tenant's fidelity to a lord. **2** allegiance. [*Say* FEEL tee]

fear ● *n.* **1** an unpleasant emotion caused by the threat of danger, pain, etc. **2** a cause of fear. **3** anxiety for the safety of. **4** likelihood (of something unwelcome). ● *v.* **1** be frightened of. **2** feel anxious about. □ **for fear of** (or **that**) to avoid the risk of (or that). **never fear** there is no danger of that.

fearful *adj.* **1** afraid. **2** terrible. **3** *informal* extremely unwelcome or unpleasant. □ **fearfully** *adv.* **fearfulness** *n.*

fearless *adj.* without fear; brave. □ **fearlessly** *adv.* **fearlessness** *n.*

fearsome *adj.* **1** frightening. **2** inspiring awe. □ **fearsomely** *adv.*

feasible *adj.* **1** easily or conveniently done. **2** likely. □ **feasibility** *n.* **feasibly** *adv.*

feast ● *n.* **1 a** a large or sumptuous meal. **b** a banquet for many guests. **2** a gratification of the senses or mind. **3** an annual religious celebration. ● *v.* **1** partake of a feast. **2** take pleasure in. □ **feast one's eyes** take pleasure in beholding. **feast or famine** either too much or too little.

feat *n.* a noteworthy act or achievement.

feather ● *n.* **1** any of the appendages growing from a bird's skin, consisting of a partly hollow stem fringed with fine strands. **2** one or more of these as decoration etc. **3** something resembling a feather. ● *v.* **1** cover or line with feathers. **2** turn (an oar) to pass through the air edgewise. **3** cause (propeller blades) to rotate with less resistance. **4** (of ink, lipstick, etc.) break into tiny feather-like lines when applied. **5** cut (hair) into wispy feather-like points. □ **a feather in one's**

cap an achievement to be proud of. **feather one's nest** make oneself richer, more comfortable, etc. **ruffle (a person's) feathers** disturb or annoy (a person). □ **feathered** *adj.* **featherless** *adj.* **feathery** *adj.*

featherbed ● *n.* a bed with a mattress stuffed with feathers. ● *v.* (**featherbeds, featherbedded, featherbedding**) provide with advantageous working conditions at the expense of efficiency.

featherweight *n.* **1 a** a weight in certain sports between bantamweight and lightweight. **b** a boxer etc. of this weight. **2** a very light person or thing. **3** (as an *adj.*) trifling or unimportant.

feature ● *n.* **1** a distinctive part of a thing. **2** a distinctive part of the face. **3** something offered for sale as a special. **4** an article in a newspaper or magazine. **5 a** (also **feature film**) a full-length film forming the main item in a movie theatre program. **b** a broadcast devoted to a particular topic. ● *v.* (**features, featured, featuring**) **1 a** give special prominence to. **b** include as a characteristic part. **2** have as or be an important actor, participant, etc. **3** be a feature or special attraction. □ **featured** *adj.* (also in *comb.*). **featureless** *adj.*

feature-length *adj.* of the length of a typical feature film or program.

featurette *n.* **1** a short feature film. **2** a short documentary on some aspect of a film, included on the DVD of the film.

Feb. *abbr.* February.

febrile *adj.* of or relating to fever. [*Say* FEE brile *or* FEB rile]

February *n.* (*pl.* **Februaries**) the second month. [*Say* FEB roo airy *or* FEB yoo airy]

feces *n.* waste matter discharged from the bowels. □ **fecal** *adj.* [*Say* FEE seez, FEEK'll]

feckless *adj.* **1** feeble, ineffective. **2** irresponsible. □ **fecklessly** *adv.* **fecklessness** *n.*

fecund *adj.* **1** fertile. **2** intellectually prolific or creative. □ **fecundity** *n.* [*Say* FEEK'nd *or* FECK'nd, fi CUNDA tee]

fed¹ *past and past participle of* FEED.

fed² *n. slang* **1** *Cdn* (*in pl.*) the federal government. **2** *US* (also **Fed**) a member of the FBI.

federal *adj.* **1** of a system of government in which power is divided between a central government and several regional ones. **2** relating to such a federation. **3** of or relating to the central government in a federation. □ **federally** *adv.*

federalism *n.* **1** a federal system of

government. **2** advocacy of a federal system of government, esp. as opposed to separatism. □ **federalist** *n. & adj.*

federate ● *v.* (**federates, federated, federating**) organize or be organized on a federal basis. ● *adj.* having a federal organization.

federation *n.* **1** a group of states etc. forming a centralized unit, within which each keeps some internal autonomy. **2** an organization within which smaller divisions have some internal autonomy. **3** the action of federating.

fedora *n.* a low soft felt hat with a crown creased lengthwise. [*Say* fuh DORA]

fed up *adj. informal* discontented or bored.

fee *n.* **1** a payment made for professional advice or services. **2** money paid for a privilege, admission, tuition, etc.

feeble *adj.* (**feebler, feeblest**) **1** weak. **2** lacking energy or force. **3** lacking in character or intelligence. □ **feebleness** *n.* **feebly** *adv.*

feeble-minded *adj.* **1** not intelligent. **2** mentally deficient.

feed ● *v.* (**feeds, fed, feeding**) **1** supply with food. **2** eat. **3** nourish; make grow. **4 a** supply. **b** flow or merge into another. **5 a** be nourished by. **b** derive benefit from. ● *n.* **1** food, esp. for farm animals. **2** an act of feeding or of being fed. **3** *informal* a meal. **4** a locally broadcast radio or television program transmitted to a larger audience.

feedback *n.* **1** information about the result of an experiment, performance, etc. **2** the return of a fraction of the output signal of a circuit, amplifier, microphone, etc., to the input of the same device.

feeder *n.* **1** a person who supplies food. **2** a person or thing that feeds in a specified manner. **3** a receptacle from which animals may feed. **4** an animal being fattened for market. **5** a road, bus route, airline, etc. linking outlying districts with a main system **6** a thing which feeds or supplies something.

feeding frenzy *n.* **1** an instance of ravenous eating. **2** *informal* competitive, unscrupulous behaviour.

feedlot *n.* a farming operation where livestock are fed or fattened.

feedstock *n.* raw material to supply a machine etc.

feel ● *v.* (**feels, felt, feeling**) **1** perceive, examine, or search by touch. **2** experience. **3** be emotionally affected by. **4** have a belief or opinion. **5** give an impression of being. **6** have pity or compassion for. ● *n.* **1** an act of feeling. **2** a sensation produced. **3 a** a sensitive appreciation of something. **b** natural ability. □ **feel free** not be

reluctant. **feel like 1** feel as though. **2** desire or have an inclination towards. **feel out** investigate cautiously. **feel up to** feel capable of. **feel one's way** proceed carefully. **make one's influence** (or **presence** etc.) **felt** have a noticeable effect.

feeler *n.* **1** an organ in certain animals for testing things by touch. **2** a tentative proposal, esp. to test opinion.

feel-good *adj. informal* characterized by positive feelings.

feeling ● *n.* **1 a** the capacity to feel. **b** a physical sensation. **2** a particular emotional reaction. **3** a particular sensitivity or aptitude. **4** an opinion or belief. ● *adj.* **1** sensitive, sympathetic. **2** showing emotion. □ **feelingly** *adv.*

feet *pl.* of FOOT.

feign *v.* pretend to be affected by. □ **feigned** *adj.* [*Say* FANE]

feint ● *n.* a sham move etc. to divert attention or fool an opponent. ● *v.* make a feint. [*Sounds like* FAINT]

feisty *adj.* (**feistier, feistiest**) *informal* **1** spirited, energetic. **2** touchy, quarrelsome. □ **feistiness** *n.* [*Say* FICE tee]

feldspar *n.* any of a group of aluminum silicate minerals.

felicitous *adj.* **1** strikingly suitable. **2** pleasing. □ **felicitously** *adv.* [*Say* fuh LISSA tuss]

felicity *n.* (*pl.* **felicities**) **1** intense happiness. **2 a** the quality of being suitable. **b** a well-chosen or successful feature. [*Say* fuh LISSA tee]

feline ● *adj.* **1** of or relating to cats. **2** catlike. ● *n.* any member of the cat family. [*Say* FEE line]

fell¹ *past of* FALL *v.*

fell² *v.* **1** cut down (a tree). **2** knock down.

fell³ *adj.* □ **at** (or **in**) **one fell swoop** all in one go.

fellatio *n.* stimulation of the penis using the mouth. □ **fellate** *v.* (**fellates, fellated, fellating**). [*Say* fuh LAY show]

feller *n.* a person or thing that fells something.

feller-buncher *n.* a large machine used to shear trees and pile them.

fellow ● *n.* **1** *informal* a man or boy. **2** a person in the same position, activity, or otherwise associated with another. **3** a thing of the same kind as another. **4 a** a graduate student receiving a stipend for research. **b** a member of the governing body in some universities. **5** a member of a learned society. ● *adj.* belonging to the same class or activity.

fellowship n. **1** companionship or friendliness. **2** a group of people sharing a common interest or aim. **3 a** an award of money to a graduate student. **b** a post as a fellow in a college etc.

felon n. a criminal. [Say FELL'n]

felony n. (pl. **felonies**) a (usu. violent) crime. [Say FELLA nee]

felquiste n. Cdn hist. a member of the FLQ. [Say fell KEEST]

felt[1] n. a fabric made of wool etc. consolidated by heat and mechanical action so that the fibres become matted. □ **felted** adj.

felt[2] past and past participle of FEEL.

felt pen n. a pen with a writing tip made of felt etc.

female ● adj. **1** of the sex that can bear offspring or produce eggs. **2** (of a plant etc.) bearing fruit or having pistils. **3** of or consisting of women. **4** (of a fitting etc.) manufactured hollow to receive a corresponding, inserted, male part. ● n. a female person, animal, or plant. □ **femaleness** n.

feminine ● adj. **1** of or characteristic of women. **2** having qualities traditionally associated with women. **3** (of a gender of nouns and adjectives in certain languages) treated as female. ● n. **1** Grammar a feminine gender or word. **2** feminine qualities. □ **femininity** n.

feminism n. the advocacy of equality of the sexes. □ **feminist** n. & adj.

feminize v. (**feminizes**, **feminized**, **feminizing**) make more feminine or female. □ **feminization** n. **feminized** adj.

femme fatale n. (pl. **femmes fatales**) a woman to whom a person feels irresistibly attracted. [Say fem fuh TAL]

femur n. (pl. **femurs** or **femora**) the thigh bone. □ **femoral** adj. [Say FEE mur for the singular, FEMMER uh for the plural, FEMMER ul]

fen n. a low and marshy area of land, often subject to frequent flooding.

fence ● n. **1** a barrier enclosing an area of ground. **2** a large, upright obstacle for a horse to jump over. **3** a person who deals in stolen goods. ● v. (**fences**, **fenced**, **fencing**) **1** surround, divide, enclose, etc. with a fence. **2** keep out with or as with a fence. **3** deal in (stolen goods). **4** practise the sport of fencing. □ **(sit) on the fence** (remain) neutral or undecided.

fence-mending n. making peace with an opponent.

fencer n. a person who takes part in the sport of fencing.

fencing n. **1** a set of fences. **2** material for making fences. **3** the sport of engaging in combat with usu. blunted swords.

fend v. **1** support or look after (esp. oneself). **2** ward off, or defend from.

fender n. **1 a** the area around the wheel well of a motor vehicle, bicycle, etc. **b** disputed the bumper of a motor vehicle. **2** a piece of rubber etc. hung over a ship's side to protect it against impact. **3** a low frame bordering a fireplace to keep in falling coals etc.

fender-bender n. slang a usu. minor collision between vehicles.

feng shui n. (in Chinese thought) a system of siting or designing buildings etc. to ensure a favourable flow of energy. [Say feng SHOOEY or fung SHWAY]

Fenian n. a member of the Irish Republican Brotherhood, a militant 19th-c. nationalist organization founded among the Irish in the US. [Say FEENY in]

fennel n. **1** a plant with fragrant seeds and fine leaves with a mild licorice flavour used as flavouring. **2** (also **sweet fennel**) a variety of this with leaf bases eaten as a vegetable.

feral adj. **1** (of animals) wild, but ultimately descended from domesticated animals. **2** resembling a wild animal. [Say FEAR ul or FAIR ul]

ferment ● n. social unrest. ● v. undergo or cause to undergo fermentation. □ **fermented** adj. **fermenter** n.

fermentation n. the chemical breakdown of a substance by micro-organisms such as yeasts and bacteria, esp. of sugar to ethyl alcohol.

fern n. a flowerless plant reproducing by spores and usu. having feathery fronds. □ **ferny** adj.

ferocious adj. **1** savagely fierce, cruel, or violent. **2** characterized by aggression, bitterness, and determination. □ **ferociously** adv.

ferocity n. the state of being ferocious. [Say fur OSSA tee]

ferret ● n. a small half-domesticated animal of the weasel family. ● v. (**ferrets**, **ferreted**, **ferreting**) **1** search out. **2** rummage about. [Say FAIR it]

ferric adj. of or containing iron in a trivalent form (compare FERROUS). [Say FAIR ick]

Ferris wheel n. a fairground ride involving a large, upright wheel revolving on a fixed axle, with seats suspended from its rims.

ferrous adj. **1** (of an alloy etc.) containing iron. **2** of or containing iron in a divalent form (compare FERRIC). [Say FAIR us]

ferrule n. a usu. metal ring or cap strengthening the end of a stick or tube. [Say FAIR ool]

ferry ● n. (pl. **ferries**) **1** (also **ferry boat**) a boat which conveys passengers etc. as a regular service. **2** the service itself. ● v. (**ferries, ferried, ferrying**) **1** convey by ferry. **2** transport from one place to another.

fertile adj. **1** (of soil) producing abundant vegetation or crops. **2 a** (of a person, animal, or plant) able to produce offspring. **b** producing many offspring. **3 a** (of the mind) inventive. **b** conducive to creativity etc. □ **fertility** n. [Say FUR tile or FURTLE, fur TILLA tee]

fertilize v. (**fertilizes, fertilized, fertilizing**) **1 a** make fertile or productive. **b** add fertilizer to. **2** cause to develop a new individual by introducing male reproductive material. □ **fertilization** n.

fertilizer n. a substance added to soil to make it more fertile.

fervent adj. ardent, impassioned. □ **fervently** adv.

fervid adj. intensely enthusiastic or passionate. □ **fervidly** adv.

fervour n. (also **fervor**) passion, zeal. [Say FUR vur]

fescue n. a grass valuable for lawns, pasture, etc. [Say FESS cue]

fess v. (**fesses, fessed, fessing**) (usu. foll. by up) informal confess.

fest n. **1** a festival or special occasion. **2** an activity of a specified type.

fester v. **1** make or become infected and filled with pus. **2** become bitter and angry.

festival ● n. **1** a day or period of celebration. **2** an organized series of concerts, films, etc. ● adj. of or concerning a festival.

festival of lights n. **1** = Hanukkah. **2** = Diwali.

festive adj. **1** of or characteristic of a festival. **2** joyous, cheerful. □ **festively** adv. **festiveness** n.

festivity n. (pl. **festivities**) **1** a celebration. **2** rejoicing, merriment.

festoon ● n. a garland of flowers, leaves, ribbons, etc. hung in a curve. ● v. **1** adorn elaborately with festoons. **2** cover abundantly. [Say fess TOON]

feta n. a very soft, white cheese of Greek origin, made from ewe's or goat's milk. [Say FETTA]

fetal adj. of or pertaining to a fetus. [Say FEET'll]

fetal alcohol syndrome n. a syndrome of birth defects caused by alcohol consumption during pregnancy.

fetal position n. a curled position of the body, resembling that of a fetus in the uterus.

fetch ● v. (**fetches, fetched, fetching**) **1** go for and bring back. **2** sell for (a price). **3** informal give (a blow etc.). ● n. (pl. **fetches**) **1** an act of fetching etc. **2** a game involving fetching, usu. played with a dog. □ **fetch and carry** run backwards and forwards with things or be a mere servant. **fetch up** informal arrive.

fetching adj. attractive. □ **fetchingly** adv.

fete ● n. a festival, fair, or great entertainment. ● v. (**fetes, feted, feting**) honour or entertain lavishly. [Say FATE]

Fête nationale n. (also **Fête nationale du Québec**) (in Quebec) the holiday celebrated on June 24, formerly called St. Jean Baptiste Day. [Say fet nass yuh NAL]

fetid adj. foul smelling. [Say FET id or FEET id]

fetish n. (pl. **fetishes**) **1** Psychology a part of the body, object, etc. acting as a focus for sexual desire. **2** an inanimate object worshipped as having inherent magical powers. **3** an object, principle, etc. evoking obsessive devotion. □ **fetishism** n. **fetishist** n. **fetishistic** adj. [Say FETTISH]

fetishize v. (**fetishizes, fetishized, fetishizing**) **1** make a fetish of. **2** pay undue respect to. □ **fetishization** n. [Say FETTISH ize]

fetlock n. the part of a horse's leg above and behind the hoof where a tuft of hair often grows.

fetter ● n. **1** a shackle or chains put on a prisoner's feet. **2** something that confines, impedes, etc. ● v. **1** bind with fetters etc. **2** restrict or impede.

fettle n. condition.

fettuccine n. (also **fettucini**) pasta made in ribbons. [Say fet oo CHEENY]

fetus n. (pl. **fetuses**) the unborn offspring of a mammal. [Say FEET us]

feud ● n. **1** a prolonged mutual hostility, esp. between two families, tribes, etc. **2** a prolonged or bitter dispute. ● v. take part in a feud.

feudal adj. of, according to, or resembling feudalism.

feudalism n. (also **the feudal system**) the dominant social system in medieval Europe in which the nobility held lands from the Crown in exchange for military service, and lower orders of society held lands from and worked for the nobles.

fever n. **1** an abnormally high body temperature. **2** intense excitement or agitation. □ **feverish** adj. **feverishly** adv.

fevered *adj.* **1** affected with fever. **2** highly excited.

feverfew *n.* a plant with daisy-like flowers, formerly used to reduce fever.

fever pitch *n.* a state of extreme excitement.

few ● *adj.* not many. ● *pron.* (as *pl.*) **1** some, but not many. **2** a small number, not many. **3** (**the few**) **a** the minority. **b** the elect. □ **few and far between** neither numerous nor frequent. **have a few** *informal* take several alcoholic drinks. **quite** (or **not**) **a few** a considerable number.

fey *adj.* **1** otherworldly, whimsical. **2** *usu. ironic* or *derogatory* affected. [*Say* FAY]

fez *n.* (*pl.* **fezzes**) a red brimless felt cap with a flat top and tassel, worn by men in some Muslim countries.

ff. *abbr.* and the following (pages etc.).

fiancé *n.* (*pl.* **fiancés**) a man to whom one is engaged to be married. [*Say* fee ON say *or* fee on SAY]

fiancée *n.* (*pl.* **fiancées**) a woman to whom one is engaged to be married. [*Say* fee ON say *or* fee on SAY]

fiasco *n.* (*pl.* **fiascos**) a complete and ridiculous failure. [*Say* fee ASS co]

fiat *n.* **1** a formal authorization. **2** a declaration by someone in power. [*Say* FEE ut]

fib ● *n.* a trivial lie. ● *v.* (**fibs, fibbed, fibbing**) tell a fib. □ **fibber** *n.*

fibre *n.* **1** a threadlike element or structure in plant or animal tissue. **2 a** a thread or filament forming part of a textile. **b** any material consisting of fibres. **3 a** the texture or structure of a thing. **b** the essence of a person's character. **4** = DIETARY FIBRE. □ **fibred** *adj.* **fibreless** *adj.*

fibreboard *n.* a building material made of compressed usu. wood fibres.

fibreglass *n.* any material consisting of glass filaments woven into a textile or paper, for use as a construction or insulation material.

fibre optics *pl. n.* **1** transmission of information by means of infrared light signals, along a thin glass fibre. **2** the fibres etc. so used. □ **fibre optic** *adj.*

fibril *n.* a small or delicate fibre. [*Say* FIE brill]

fibrillate *v.* (**fibrillates, fibrillated, fibrillating**) (of a muscle, esp. in the heart) undergo a quivering movement or contract irregularly. □ **fibrillation** *n.* [*Say* FIB ruh late]

fibromyalgia *n.* an inflammation of fibrous connective tissue. [*Say* fie bro my AL juh]

fibrosis *n.* (*pl.* **fibroses**) a thickening and scarring of connective tissue. [*Say* fie BROE sis]

fibrous *adj.* consisting of or like fibres. [*Say* FIE brus]

fibula *n.* (*pl.* **fibulae** or **fibulas**) the smaller outer bone of the two bones between the knee and the ankle. □ **fibular** *adj.* [*Say* FIB you luh *for the singular*, FIB you lee *for the plural*]

fickle *adj.* changeable, esp. in loyalty. □ **fickleness** *n.*

fiction *n.* **1** an invented idea, statement or narrative. **2** literature describing imaginary events and people. **3** a false belief or statement. □ **fictional** *adj.* **fictionally** *adv.* **fictionalization** *n.* **fictionalize** *v.* (**fictionalizes, fictionalized, fictionalizing**)

fictitious *adj.* invented rather than true. □ **fictitiously** *adv.* [*Say* fick TISH us]

fictive *adj.* created by imagination; not real.

ficus *n.* (*pl.* **ficus**) a tree or shrub of the mulberry family, including the fig. [*Say* FEE kus *or* FIKE us]

Ficus benjamina *n.* (*pl.* **Ficus benjamina**) a tropical tree with drooping branches. [*Say* FEE kus (*or* FIKE us) benja MEENA]

fiddle ● *n.* **1** a violin. **2** *informal* an act of cheating or fraud. ● *v.* (**fiddles, fiddled, fiddling**) **1 a** play restlessly. **b** move aimlessly. **c** tinker. **2** *slang* cheat. **3** play the fiddle. □ **as fit as a fiddle** in very good health. **play second fiddle** take a subordinate role. □ **fiddler** *n.* **fiddling** *n.*

fiddlehead *n.* the young edible frond of certain ferns.

fiddlesticks *interj.* expressing scorn etc.

fiddly *adj.* (**fiddlier, fiddliest**) *informal* intricate or awkward to do or use.

fidelity *n.* **1** faithfulness, loyalty. **2** sexual faithfulness. **3** exact correspondence to the original. [*Say* fuh DELLA tee]

fidget ● *v.* (**fidgets, fidgeted, fidgeting**) move or act restlessly or nervously. ● *n.* **1** a person who fidgets. **2** bodily uneasiness seeking relief in spasmodic movements. □ **fidgety** *adj.*

fiduciary *adj.* involving trust, esp. concerning the relationship between a trustee and a beneficiary. [*Say* fuh DOOSHY airy *or* fuh DYOOSHY airy]

fief *n.* a piece of land held under the feudal system. □ **fiefdom** *n.* [*Say* FEEF, FEEF dum]

field ● *n.* **1 a** an area of open land, esp. one used for pasture or crops. **b** (as an *adj.*) grown in a field. **2** a piece of land for a specified purpose. **3** the participants in a contest or sport. **4** an area rich in some natural product. **5** an expanse of ice, sky, etc. **6 a** a battlefield. **b** the scene of a campaign. **7** an area of operation or activity. **8** the region in which a force is effective. **9** a range of perception. **10** a part of a record in a database. ● v. **1** *Baseball* **a** act as a fielder. **b** select to play in a game. **b** deploy (an army). **c** propose (a candidate). **3** deal with. □ **in the field 1** on a military campaign. **2** working etc. away from one's laboratory etc. **play the field** *informal* avoid exclusive attachment to one person etc. **take the field 1** begin a campaign. **2** (of a sports team) go on to a playing field. □ **fielder** *n.*

field day *n.* **1** wide scope for action or success. **2** a day devoted to outdoor track and field events.

field goal *n.* **1** *Football* a goal scored by a drop kick or place kick from the field. **2** *Basketball* a two- or three-point basket.

field guide *n.* a book for the identification of birds, flowers, etc.

field hockey *n.* a game played between two teams on a field with curved sticks and a small hard ball.

field of vision *n.* all that is in view through a person's eyes.

fieldstone *n.* unfinished stone.

field test ● *n.* a test of a device etc. in the environment in which it is to be used. ● *v.* test (a device) in this way.

field trial *n.* **1** a competition between gun dogs to determine their hunting ability. **2** = FIELD TEST *n.*

field trip *n.* **1** a school trip to gain knowledge away from the classroom. **2** a research trip.

fieldwork *n.* the practical work of a researcher in the field. □ **fieldworker** *n.*

fiend *n.* **1** an evil spirit. **2** a very wicked or cruel person. **3** *informal* **a** a devotee. **b** an addict. [*Say* FEEND]

fiendish *adj.* **1** extremely cruel or unpleasant. **2** extremely difficult. □ **fiendishly** *adv.* [*Say* FEEND ish]

fierce *adj.* (**fiercer, fiercest**) **1** angry and aggressive. **2** (of a feeling etc.) showing a powerful intensity. **3** unpleasantly strong or intense. □ **fiercely** *adv.* **fierceness** *n.*

fiery *adj.* (**fierier, fieriest**) **1** consisting of or resembling fire. **2 a** flashing, ardent. **b** showing strong emotions, especially anger. [*Say* FIRE ee]

fiesta *n.* (*pl.* **fiestas**) **1** a holiday or festivity. **2** a religious festival in Spanish-speaking countries. [*Say* fee ESTA]

fife *n.* a kind of small shrill flute used in military music.

fifteen *card. num.* one more than fourteen. □ **fifteenth** *ord. num.*

fifth *ord. num.* **1** constituting the number 5 in a sequence. **2** a musical interval spanning five consecutive notes in a scale. □ **take the Fifth** (in the US) exercise the right guaranteed by the Fifth Amendment.

Fifth Amendment *n.* an amendment to the US constitution which states that no person may be compelled to give testimony that might incriminate himself or herself.

fifth column *n.* a group working for an enemy within a country at war etc. □ **fifth columnist** *n.*

fifth wheel *n.* **1** an extra wheel for a four-wheeled vehicle. **2** an extra person or thing. **3** a camper-trailer.

fifty *card. num.* (*pl.* **fifties**) the product of five and ten. □ **fiftieth** *ord. num.*

fifty-fifty ● *adj.* equal, with equal shares or chances. ● *adv.* equally.

fig *n.* **1** a soft pear-shaped fruit with many seeds. **2** (also **fig tree**) a broad-leaved tree bearing these. □ **not care** (or **give**) **a fig** not care at all.

fig. *abbr.* **1** figure. **2** figurative. **3** figuratively.

fight ● *v.* (**fights, fought, fighting**) **1** quarrel or contend with an opponent in a war, battle, etc. **2 a** contend about. **b** maintain (a lawsuit etc.) against an opponent. **3** strive to achieve or overcome something. ● *n.* **1 a** an act of fighting. **b** a boxing match. **c** a battle. **d** an argument. **2** a conflict or struggle. □ **fight back 1** counterattack. **2** (also **fight down**) suppress. **fight off** repel with effort. **fight out** (usu. **fight it out**) settle (a dispute etc.) by fighting.

fighter *n.* **1** a person or animal that fights. **2** a fast military aircraft designed for attacking other aircraft. **3** a person with great determination etc.

fighting chance *n.* an opportunity of succeeding by great effort.

fighting words *pl. n. informal* words likely to provoke a fight.

figment *n.* a thing existing only in the imagination.

Fig Newton *n. proprietary* a small rectangular plain cookie with a filling of figs etc.

figuration *n.* ornamentation by means of figures.

figurative *adj.* **1** (of language) used in a non-literal sense; metaphorical. **2** (of art) showing people or things as they really

look. □ **figuratively** *adv.*
[*Say* FIGURE a tiv]

figure ● *n.* **1 a** the external shape of a thing. **b** bodily shape, esp. of a woman. **2** an unidentified person. **3** an important or well-known personage. **4** an artistic representation of the human form. **5 a** a numerical symbol. **b** an amount of money, a value. **6** *Geometry* a two-dimensional space enclosed by a line or lines. **7** a diagram. **8** (also **figure of speech**) a word or phrase used in a non-literal sense to add interest to speech or writing. ● *v.* (**figures, figured, figuring**) **1** appear or be mentioned. **2** represent in a diagram. **3** imagine. **4** calculate, think, consider. □ **figure on** count on, expect. **figure out 1** work out. **2** understand. **go figure** *informal* it escapes explanation.

figure eight *n.* the shape of the number eight.

figurehead *n.* **1** a leader who has no real power. **2** a carving at a ship's prow.

figure skating *n.* a type of ice skating in which the skater combines a number of movements including steps, jumps, turns, etc. □ **figure skate** *n.* **figure skater** *n.*

figurine *n.* a small esp. ornamental statue.

Fijian *n.* **1** a person from Fiji. **2** the language of Fiji. □ **Fijian** *adj.*
[*Say* fee JEE in]

filament *n.* **1** a slender threadlike body or fibre. **2** a conducting wire in a light bulb etc., which glows white-hot when an electric current passes through it. □ **filamentous** *adj.* [*Say* FILLA mint]

filbert *n.* a hazelnut.

filch *v.* (**filches, filched, filching**) *informal* pilfer, steal.

file¹ ● *n.* **1** a folder etc. for holding loose papers. **2** a set of papers kept in this. **3** a collection of data stored under one name. **4** *Cdn* issues and responsibilities in a specified area, considered collectively. **5** a line of persons or things one behind another. ● *v.* (**files, filed, filing**) **1** place in a file. **2** submit (a petition for divorce etc.). **3** (of a reporter) send (a story etc.) to a newspaper. **4** walk in a line. □ **file away** file or make a mental note of. □ **filer** *n.* **filing** *n.*

file² ● *n.* a tool with a roughened surface for smoothing or shaping wood etc. ● *v.* (**files, filed, filing**) work with a file. □ **file away** remove with a file. □ **filer** *n.*

file server *n.* *Computing* a device which manages access to centralized files in a network.

filet mignon *n.* a small tender piece of beef from the end of the tenderloin. [*Say* fuh LAY mee NYON]

filial *adj.* having to do with the relationship of a child with its parent. [*Say* FILLY ul]

filibuster ● *n.* a long speech made in a parliament in order to delay a vote. ● *v.* deliver a filibuster. [*Say* FILLA buster]

filigree *n.* **1** ornamental work of fine wire. **2** anything delicate resembling this. □ **filigreed** *adj.* [*Say* FILLA gree]

filing *n.* a particle rubbed off by a file.

Filipina *n.* a woman or girl from the Philippines. □ **Filipina** *adj.*
[*Say* filla PEENA]

Filipino *n.* (*pl.* **Filipinos**) a person from the Philippines. □ **Filipino** *adj.*
[*Say* filla PEENO]

fill ● *v.* **1** make or become full. **2** block up (a cavity). **3** appoint a person to (a vacant post). **4** hold (a position). **5** supply (a prescription etc.). **6** occupy (time). **7** satisfy, fulfill. ● *n.* **1** as much as one wants or can bear. **2** material used for filling something. □ **fill the bill** be suitable. **fill in 1** complete (a form, drawing, etc.). **2** fill completely. **3** act as a substitute. **4** *informal* inform more fully. **fill out 1** enlarge to the required size. **2** become enlarged. **3** fill in (a document). **fill up 1** make or become full. **2** fill the fuel tank of (a car etc.).

filler *n.* **1** a substance used to fill holes or cracks or to increase bulk. **2** an item filling space in a newspaper etc.

filles du roi *pl. n.* *Cdn hist.* women of marriageable age sent from France to New France between 1663–73 to be married. [*Say* fee doo RWAH]

fillet ● *n.* **1 a** a fleshy boneless piece of meat from near the loins or the ribs. **b** a boned side of a fish. **2** a headband or ribbon for binding the hair. ● *v.* (**fillets, filleted, filleting**) **1** remove bones from (fish or meat). **2** divide into fillets. [*Say* FILL it; *for the food senses you can also say* fuh LAY]

fill-in *n.* a person or thing put in as a substitute or replacement.

filling *n.* any material that fills, esp. that used to: **1** fill a cavity in a tooth. **2** fill a sandwich or a pie etc.

filling station *n.* a gas station.

fillip *n.* something that adds interest or excitement.

fill-up *n.* **1** a thing that fills something up. **2** the act of filling a fuel tank.

filly *n.* (*pl.* **fillies**) **1** a young female horse. **2** *informal offensive* a girl or young woman.

film ● *n.* **1** a thin coating or covering layer. **2** a strip of plastic or other flexible base coated with light-sensitive emulsion for exposure in a camera. **3 a** a story or event recorded by a camera. **b** (in *pl.*) the cinema industry. **4** a slight haze etc. ● *v.* **1** make a film of. **2** cover or become covered with or as with a film. □ **filmic** *adj.*

filmgoer *n.* a person who frequents the cinema.

filmmaker *n.* a director or producer of films. □ **filmmaking** *n.*

filmography *n.* (*pl.* **filmographies**) a list of films by one director etc.

filmy *adj.* (**filmier, filmiest**) **1** thin and translucent. **2** covered with film.

filo *n.* = PHYLLO. [*Say* FIE lo]

filter ● *n.* **1** a porous device for removing impurities or solid particles from a liquid or gas. **2** = FILTER TIP. **3** a screen or attachment for absorbing light, X-rays, etc. **4** a device for suppressing electrical or sound waves of frequencies not required. **5** a piece of software that processes text, for example to remove unwanted spaces or to format it for use in another application. **6** a functionality in email or Internet searching that automatically sorts email into folders or blocks access to pornographic etc. sites. ● *v.* **1** pass or cause to pass through a filter. **2** make way gradually. **3** leak or cause to leak.

filter tip *n.* a filter attached to a cigarette for removing impurities from smoke. □ **filter-tipped** *adj.*

filth *n.* **1** any very dirty substance. **2** foul or obscene language etc. **3** corruption.

filthy ● *adj.* (**filthier, filthiest**) **1** disgustingly dirty. **2** obscene. ● *adv. informal* extremely. □ **filthily** *adv.* **filthiness** *n.*

filtrate *n.* filtered liquid.

filtration *n.* the process of filtering something.

fin *n.* **1** an organ on various parts of the body of fish etc., used for propelling, steering, and balancing. **2** a small projecting surface on an aircraft etc. for ensuring stability. **3** an underwater swimmer's flipper. **4** a fin-like projection on any device.

finagle *v.* (**finagles, finagled, finagling**) *informal* act or obtain dishonestly. [*Say* fuh NAY gull]

final ● *adj.* **1** situated at the end, coming last. **2** conclusive, decisive. **3** reached as the outcome of a process. ● *n.* **1** (usu. in *pl.*) the last or deciding game etc. in a competition. **2** (usu. in *pl.*) the last examination in an academic course.

finale *n.* **1** the last part of a piece of music, an entertainment, or a public event. **2** a conclusion. [*Say* fuh NALLY]

finalist *n.* a competitor in the final of a competition etc.

finality *n.* (*pl.* **finalities**) the quality of being final.

finalize *v.* (**finalizes, finalized, finalizing**) **1** put into final form. **2** complete.

finally *adv.* **1** after a long time. **2** as the last in a series. **3** used to introduce a final point.

final solution *n.* the policy under the German Nazi regime of exterminating European Jews.

finance ● *n.* **1** the management of money. **2** monetary support for an enterprise. **3** (in *pl.*) the money resources of a country, company, or person. ● *v.* (**finances, financed, financing**) provide capital for. □ **financing** *n.* [*Say* FIE nance *or* fuh NANCE]

finance company *n.* a company that provides money to consumers for purchasing goods on credit.

financial *adj.* of or pertaining to finance. □ **financially** *adv.*

financial institution *n.* a bank or finance company.

financial year *n. Cdn & Brit.* = FISCAL YEAR.

financier *n.* a person who is concerned with or skilled in finance. [*Say* fie nan SEER *or* fin an SEER]

finback *n.* (also **finback whale**) a large baleen whale with a prominent dorsal fin.

finch *n.* (*pl.* **finches**) a small seed-eating songbird with usu. colourful plumage.

find ● *v.* (**finds, found, finding**) **1 a** discover by or as if by search or effort. **b** become aware of. **2 a** perceive or experience. **b** discover to be present. **c** learn through experience, trial, etc. **3** (of a jury, judge, etc.) authoritatively decide and declare to be the case. **4** reach by a natural process. ● *n.* a valuable or interesting discovery. □ **find against** *Law* judge to be guilty. **find for** *Law* judge to be innocent. **find one's feet** grow in ability or confidence. **find it in one's heart** be willing. **find out 1** discover or detect. **2** get information. **find one's way 1** manage to reach a place. **2** be brought or get.

finder *n.* **1** a person or thing which finds. **2** the viewfinder of a camera. □ **finders keepers** *informal* whoever finds a thing is entitled to keep it.

fin de siècle ● *n.* the end of a century. ● *adj.* **1** characteristic of the end of the 19th century. **2** decadent. [*Say* fan duh SYECK luh]

finding *n.* **1** a result or conclusion of an official inquiry. **2** a verdict.

fine¹ ● *adj.* **1** of superior quality. **2** excellent, admirable. **3 a** clear, pure. **b** (of gold or silver) containing a high proportion of pure metal. **4 a** handsome, beautiful. **b** imposing, dignified. **5** in good health or spirits. **6** (of weather) bright and clear. **7 a** extremely thin or slender. **b** having a sharp point. **c** in small particles. **d** (esp. of print) small. **8** capable of delicate perception or discrimination. ● *adv. informal* very well. □ **cut it fine** allow very little time, margin for error, etc. **not to put too fine a point on it** to speak bluntly. □ **finely** *adv.* **fineness** *n.*

fine² ● *n.* a sum of money exacted as a penalty for an offence. ● *v.* (**fines, fined, fining**) impose a fine upon.

fine art *n.* **1** (in *pl.*) those arts appealing to the intellect or the sense of beauty. **2** a high accomplishment.

fine-grained *adj.* **1** having a fine grain. **2** consisting of very small particles.

fine print *n.* the details that are printed in small type and so are easy to overlook in an agreement or contract.

finer points *pl. n.* details appreciated only by those who are very familiar with a thing, field, etc.

finery *n.* showy or elegant dress.

finesse ● *n.* **1** subtle skill in handling people or situations. **2** delicacy, refinement. ● *v.* (**finesses, finessed, finessing**) **1** do in a subtle and delicate manner. **2** evade by finesse.

finest ● *adj. superlative of* FINE¹ *adj.* ● *n.* the police of a specified city.

fine-tooth comb *n.* □ **go over with a fine-tooth comb** check or search thoroughly.

fine-tune *v.* (**fine-tunes, fine-tuned, fine-tuning**) make small adjustments to so as to improve performance. □ **fine tuning** *n.*

finger ● *n.* **1** any of the terminal members of the hand, including or excluding the thumb. **2** an item of food etc. shaped like a finger. **3** the breadth or length of a finger as a unit of measurement. ● *v.* **1** touch or feel with the fingers. **2** *Music* play with the fingers. **3** *informal* indicate (a person or thing) for a specific purpose etc. **4** *slang* identify (a criminal) to the police. □ **have a finger in the pie** be concerned in a matter. **lay a finger on** touch however slightly. **point a** (or **the**) **finger at** identify as responsible. **put one's finger on** identify with precision. **twist** (or **wrap**) **around one's finger** (or **little finger**) **1** persuade (a person) without difficulty. **2** dominate (a person) completely. □ **fingered** *adj.*

fingerboard *n.* a piece of wood on the neck of a stringed instrument against which the strings are pressed to vary the tone.

finger food *n.* food that can be eaten conveniently without cutlery.

fingering *n.* a manner or technique of using the fingers to play a musical instrument etc.

fingerling *n.* any young fish.

fingernail *n.* the nail at the tip of each finger.

fingerpaint ● *n.* a thick, jellylike paint that can be applied with the fingers. ● *v.* apply such paint. □ **fingerpainting** *n.*

fingerprint ● *n.* **1** an impression made on a surface by the fingertips. **2** any distinctive characteristic etc. definitively identifying a particular person etc. ● *v.* record the fingerprints of.

fingertip ● *n.* the tip of a finger. ● *adj.* (of controls etc.) that can be controlled by the fingers. □ **at one's fingertips** readily accessible. **by one's fingertips** barely.

finial *n.* an ornament top or end of a roof or object. [*Say* FINNY ul]

finicky *adj.* **1** fussy. **2** needing much attention to detail.

finish ● *v.* (**finishes, finished, finishing**) **1** come or bring to an end. **2 a** *informal* kill, destroy. **b** consume the whole or the remainder of (food etc.). **3 a** complete the manufacture of by surface treatment. **b** put the final touches to. **4** have no more to do with. ● *n.* **1 a** an end or last stage. **b** the point at which a race or other contest ends. **2** the way in which a manufactured article is finished. **3** a thing which finishes. □ **finished** *adj.* **finisher** *n.*

finishing touch *n.* a detail that completes and enhances a piece of work etc.

finish line *n.* a line which indicates the end of a race.

finite *adj.* **1** having limits or bounds. **2** not infinitely small. □ **finitely** *adv.* [*Say* FIE nite]

fink *slang* ● *n.* **1** an unpleasant person. **2** an informer. ● *v.* **1** inform on. **2** let a person down.

Finn *n.* a person from Finland.

finned *adj.* having a fin or fins.

Finnish ● *adj.* of or relating to Finland, the Finns, or their language. ● *n.* the language of the Finns.

fiord *n.* = FJORD. [*Say* FYORD *or* FEE ord]

fir *n.* (also **fir tree**) an evergreen coniferous tree with needles borne singly on the stems.

fire ● *n.* **1 a** the state of burning, in which substances combine with oxygen, giving out light, heat, and smoke. **b** the flame so produced. **2** a conflagration or destructive burning. **3** fuel in a state of combustion. **4** the firing of guns etc. **5 a** zeal, fervour. **b** liveliness of imagination or inspiration. **c** burning passion or emotion. **6** fever. ● *v.* (**fires, fired, firing**) **1** discharge a gun etc. **2** set fire to. **3** deliver a rapid series (of questions etc.). **4** dismiss from a job. **5** catch fire. **6** (in an engine) undergo ignition of fuel. **7** supply with fuel. **8** inspire or stimulate. **9** bake or dry (pottery etc.). □ **catch fire** begin to burn. **fight fire with fire** use similar strategies as one's opponent does. **fire and brimstone** the torments of hell. **fire away** *informal* begin or go ahead. **fire up 1** *informal* **a** stimulate or excite. **b** start up (an engine etc.). **2** show sudden anger. **fired-up** highly motivated or enthused. **light a fire under** cause to work faster. **set fire to** (or **set on fire**) ignite, cause to burn. **set the world on fire** do something remarkable or sensational. **under fire** being shot at or strongly criticized. □ **firing** *n.*

firearm *n.* (usu. in *pl.*) a portable gun of any sort.

fireball *n.* **1** a large, bright meteor. **2** a ball of flame or fire. **3 a** a very energetic person. **b** a person with a fiery temper.

firebomb ● *n.* a bomb intended to cause a fire. ● *v.* attack with a firebomb.

firebox *n.* (*pl.* **fireboxes**) **1** an enclosed space in which a fire is made. **2** the fuel chamber of a steam engine or boiler.

firebrand *n.* **1** a person who inflames passion, causes trouble, etc. **2** a piece of burning wood.

firebreak *n.* a strip of land cleared to stop fire from spreading.

fire brigade *n.* esp. *Brit.* an organized body of firefighters.

firecracker *n.* a small firework that explodes with a cracking noise.

fire drill *n.* a rehearsal of the procedures to be used in case of fire.

fire engine *n.* a heavy vehicle, usu. red, carrying equipment for fighting fires.

fire escape *n.* an emergency staircase for use to escape from a fire.

fire extinguisher *n.* a portable apparatus for discharging chemicals, water, etc. to put out a fire.

firefight *n.* a skirmish or battle involving the exchange of gunfire.

firefighter *n.* a person whose job is to extinguish fires. □ **firefighting** *n. & adj.*

firefly *n.* (*pl.* **fireflies**) a soft-bodied beetle that produces light.

fire hall *n. Cdn* a fire station.

fire hydrant *n.* a pipe with a valve for drawing water to which a hose can be attached for extinguishing fires.

fireman *n.* (*pl.* **firemen**) **1** a firefighter. **2** a person who tends a furnace or fires.

fireplace *n.* **1** a place for a domestic fire. **2** a structure surrounding this.

firepower *n.* the destructive capacity of guns, missiles, a military force, etc.

fireproof ● *adj.* able to resist fire or great heat. ● *v.* make fireproof. □ **fireproofing** *n.*

fire-resistant *adj.* **1** almost completely non-flammable. **2** = FIRE-RETARDANT. □ **fire-resistance** *n.*

fire-retardant *adj.* capable of slowing the spread of fire.

fire sale *n.* **1** a sale of goods remaining after a fire. **2** a sale of anything at a remarkably low price.

fireside ● *n.* the area around a fireplace (used esp. with reference to a person's home or family life). ● *adj.* **1** situated beside a domestic fire or fireplace. **2** intimate or relaxed.

firestorm *n.* **1** a very intense and destructive fire fanned by strong currents of air. **2** an intense and forceful response.

firewall *n.* **1** a fireproof wall to prevent the spread of fire. **2** *Computing* a system designed to control the passage of information between networks.

firewater *n. informal* strong alcoholic liquor.

fireweed *n.* any of several plants that spring up on burnt land.

firewood *n.* wood used as fuel.

firework *n.* **1** a device containing chemicals that burn or explode spectacularly. **2** (in *pl.*) **a** an outburst of passion, esp. anger. **b** an impressive display of wit or skill.

firing line *n.* **1** the front line in a battle. **2** the forefront of an activity, controversy, etc. □ **on the firing line** subject to challenge, criticism, etc. because of one's position.

firing range *n.* = RANGE *n.* 8.

firing squad *n.* a group of soldiers ordered to shoot a condemned person.

firm¹ ● *adj.* **1 a** hard, resistant to pressure or impact, or of solid structure. **b** securely fixed, stable. **c** steady or controlled. **2** resolute, determined. **3** (of an offer etc.) not liable to cancellation. ● *v.* firmly. ● *v.* make or become firm. □ **a firm hand** strong discipline. **firm up 1** work to improve the condition of muscles etc. **2** put in final, fixed form. **3** strengthen, reinforce. □ **firmly** *adv.* **firmness** *n.*

firm² *n.* a business organization.

firmament *n. literary* the arch or vault of the skies.

firn *n.* crystalline or granular snow.

first ● *adj.* **1 a** coming before all others in time, order, or experience, **b** coming next after a specified time. **2** foremost in rank or importance. **3** *Music* denoting one of two parts for the same instrument or voice. **4** most willing. **5** basic or evident. ● *n.* **1** the first part, the beginning. **2** the first occurrence or place. **3** the first day of a month. **4** first gear. ● *adv.* **1** before all others. **2** before another specified or implied thing etc. **3** for the first time. **4** in preference to something else. □ **at first** at the beginning. **at first hand** coming directly from the original source. **first off** *informal* first of all. **first things first** the most important things first. **from the first** from the beginning. **from first to last** throughout. **in the first place** as the first consideration.

first aid *n.* help given to a sick or injured person until proper medical treatment is available.

first-born ● *adj.* eldest. ● *n.* the eldest child of a person.

first class ● *n.* **1** a set of persons grouped together as the best. **2** the best seating in an airplane, train, etc. **3** the class of mail given priority in handling. ● *adj.* **1** belonging to or travelling by the first class. **2** of the best quality. ● *adv.* by the best form of transport or mail.

first-come, first-served *n.* a system of providing service strictly in the order in which people arrive etc.

first contact *n.* the first interaction between colonizers and an Aboriginal people.

first cousin *n.* the child of one's uncle or aunt.

first-degree *adj.* **1 a** designating the most serious category of crime. **b** (of murder) premeditated. **2** denoting the least serious category of burn, those that affect only the surface of the skin.

first gear *n.* the lowest gear on a car, bicycle, etc.

first generation *adj.* **1** designating the offspring born to immigrants in their adopted country. **2** of or belonging to an initial model, program, etc.

first-hand *adj. & adv.* direct, from the original source or personal experience.

first lady *n.* **1** the leading woman in some

specified activity. **2 (First Lady)** (in the US) the wife of the President.

first line *n.* **1** the preliminary effort, resources, etc. ready for immediate use. **2** the thing, group, etc., which is most advanced.

firstly *adv.* in the first place, first.

first mate *n.* (on a merchant ship) the officer who is second-in-command.

First Meridian *n. Cdn* the north-south line, 97 degrees 27 minutes west, from which land in the prairies is surveyed.

first minister *n. Cdn* **1** the prime minister of Canada. **2** the premier of a province.

First Nation *n. Cdn* **1** (usu. in *pl.*) the Aboriginal peoples of Canada, not including the Inuit or Metis. **2** an Indian band, or an Indian community not having official band status.

first officer *n.* **1** the mate on a merchant ship. **2** the second-in-command to the captain on an aircraft.

first past the post *adj.* (of an electoral system) in which the person or party who gets the most votes is elected.

First Peoples *pl. n.* the Aboriginal peoples of a particular country etc.

first person *n. Grammar* **1** a set of pronouns and verb forms used to refer to a speaker. **2** a way of writing a novel, etc. as if one of the characters is telling the story.

first principles *pl. n.* the fundamental concepts on which a theory or system is based.

first-rate *adj.* of the highest class, excellent.

first-run *adj.* designating the initial period in which a film etc. is first shown publicly.

first-string ● *n.* the primary and usu. starting line of a team. ● *adj.* of or like the first-string.

first thing *informal* ● *n.* (**the first thing**) the most elementary thing. ● *adv.* **1** before anything else. **2** very early in the morning.

First World *n.* the industrialized capitalist countries.

firth *n.* an estuary or narrow inlet of the sea.

fiscal *adj.* **1** of or related to public revenue, usu. taxes. **2** of financial matters. □ **fiscally** *adv.*

fiscal year *n.* a period of twelve months over which accounts are calculated.

fish ● *n.* (*pl.* **fish** or **fishes**) **1** a vertebrate cold-blooded animal with gills and fins living in water. **2** any animal living wholly in water. **3** the flesh of fish as food. ● *v.* (**fishes, fished, fishing**) **1** try to catch fish. **2 a** search or feel for something hidden. **b** try to obtain by indirect means.

□ **a big fish in a small pond** a significant figure in a small group, community, etc. **drink like a fish** drink excessively. **fish out** depopulate through excessive fishing. **fish out of water** a person in an environment or situation that is not familiar. **other** (or **plenty more** etc.) **fish in the sea** other people or things as good as the one lost. **other fish to fry** other matters to attend to. □ **fishing** n. **fishlike** adj.

fishable adj. **1** (of water) able to be fished in. **2** (of fish) able to be caught.

fishbowl n. **1** a bowl for keeping pet fish in. **2** a place, situation, etc. in which one's activities are publicly observed etc.

fish cake n. a small patty of fish and mashed potato.

fisher n. **1 a** a large N American forest-dwelling weasel. **b** its pelt. **2** a fisherman.

fisherman n. (pl. **fishermen**) a person who catches fish as a livelihood or for sport.

fishery n. (pl. **fisheries**) **1 a** a place where fish are reared. **b** an area where fish are caught. **2** the industry of catching or rearing fish.

fish eye n. **1** (also **fish-eye lens**) a wide-angle lens for a camera. **2** an eye of or like that of a fish.

fish farm n. a place where fish are bred for food. □ **fish farmer** n. **fish farming** n.

fish finder n. a device equipped with sonar to locate schools of fish.

fish hook n. a barbed hook for catching fish.

fish hut n. Cdn a small, portable shack used in ice fishing.

fishing camp n. an establishment providing accommodation etc. for sport fishermen.

fishing derby n. a fishing competition.

fishing hole n. **1** a favoured spot for catching fish. **2** an opening cut in ice for ice fishing.

fishing rod n. (also **fishing pole**) a long, tapering rod to which a fishing line is attached.

fishing station n. Cdn a small sheltered cove from which seasonal fishing is undertaken.

fish ladder n. a series of pools built like steps to enable fish to ascend a fall or dam.

fishmonger n. a person who sells fish. [Say FISH mong gur or FISH mung gur]

fishnet n. (often as an adj.) an open, meshed fabric resembling a net.

fish sauce n. a spicy condiment made from fermented anchovies.

fish stick n. a small, oblong piece of fish coated in batter etc. and fried.

fishtail ● v. move or travel with a side-to-side motion. ● n. something shaped like a fish's tail.

fishway n. Cdn a lock built to aid fish in passing a waterfall etc.

fishy adj. (**fishier**, **fishiest**) **1 a** of or like fish. **b** (of an eye) dull. **2** slang of dubious character.

fissile adj. **1** capable of undergoing nuclear fission. **2** (of rock) easily split. [Say FISS ile or FISSLE]

fission n. **1** the splitting of a heavy atomic nucleus, accompanied by a release of energy. **2** the division of a cell into new cells. **3** the action of splitting into pieces. □ **fissionable** adj. [Rhymes either with MISSION or with VISION]

fissure n. an opening made by cracking or splitting. [Say FISHER or FIZHER]

fist n. a tightly closed hand. □ **fisted** adj. **fistful** n.

fistula n. (pl. **fistulas** or **fistulae**) an abnormal or surgically made passage. [Say FIST you luh for the singular; for FISTULAE say FIST you lee]

fit¹ ● adj. (**fitter**, **fittest**) **1** suitable. **2** in good health or athletic condition. **3** proper, becoming. ● v. (**fits**, **fitted**, **fitting**) **1 a** be of the right shape and size for. **b** adjust (an object) to be the right shape or size. **c** (of a component) be correctly positioned. **d** find room for. **2 a** make or be suitable. **b** make ready. **3** supply, furnish. **4** fix in place. **5** try clothing on (a person) in order to adjust it to the right size. **6** be in harmony with. ● n. **1** the way in which something fits. **2** suitability. ● adv. informal in a suitable manner. □ **fit the bill** be suitable. **fit in 1** be compatible or accommodating. **2** find space or time for. **fit out** (or **up**) equip. **see** (or **think**) **fit** decide or choose (a specified course). □ **fitness** n.

fit² n. **1** a sudden seizure. **2** a sudden brief attack of an illness. **3** a sudden short bout or burst. **4** an attack of strong feeling. □ **by** (or **in**) **fits and starts** spasmodically. **have** (or **throw**) **a fit** informal be greatly surprised or outraged.

fitful adj. active or occurring irregularly. □ **fitfully** adv.

fitted adj. made or shaped to fill a space or cover something closely.

fitter n. **1** a person who supervises the fitting of garments. **2** a person who fits together and adjusts machinery.

fitting ● n. **1** the process of having a garment etc. fitted. **2** decorative metal handles etc. on furniture, bathtubs, etc. **3** a

small standard component. ● *adj.* suitable.
□**fittingly** *adv.*

fitting room *n.* a room in a store etc.
where garments are tried on.

five *card. num.* one more than four.
□**fivefold** *adj. & adv.*

five-and-dime store *n.* (also **five-and-
dime, five-and-ten**) a store selling a
wide variety of cheap goods.

Five Nations *pl. n. hist.* the Seneca,
Cayuga, Onondaga, Oneida, and Mohawk,
who formed the League of the Iroquois in
the 16th century.

five-pin bowling *n.* Cdn a variety of
bowling using five pins and a smaller ball
than in 10-pin bowling.

fiver *n.* informal a five-dollar bill.

five-star *adj.* (of a hotel etc.) given five stars
in a grading, indicating the highest quality.

fix ● *v.* (**fixes, fixed, fixing**) **1** repair.
2 put in order, adjust. **3** make firm or
stable. **4** decide or settle on. **5** implant in
the mind. **6 a** direct (a look or the eyes)
steadily. **b** attract and hold (a person's
attention etc.). **7** establish. **8** determine the
exact nature of. **9** informal prepare (food or
drink). **10** informal arrange the result of
fraudulently. **11** make (a pigment etc.) fast
or permanent. **12** castrate or spay (an
animal). ● *n.* (*pl.* **fixes**) **1** informal a position
hard to escape from; a dilemma. **2** informal a
repair. **3** a charted position. **4** slang a dose
of (a narcotic drug etc.) to which one is
addicted. □**be fixed** be disposed or
affected (regarding). **fix up 1** arrange,
prepare. **2** upgrade. □**fixable** *adj.*

fixate *v.* (**fixates, fixated, fixating**) be
or become obsessed with.

fixation *n.* **1** an obsessive interest in
someone or something. **2** the action of
making something firm or stable. **3** the
process by which some plants and micro-
organisms combine chemically with
nitrogen or carbon dioxide to form non-
gaseous compounds.

fixative *n.* a substance used to set or fix
colours etc. [*Say* FIXA tiv]

fixed-do *adj.* applied to a system of reading
music in which C is called "do". [DO *sounds
like* DOE]

fixed income *n.* income from an
investment etc. that is set at a particular
figure.

fixedly *adv.* continually, without looking
away. [*Say* FIX id lee]

fixer *n.* **1** a person or thing that fixes. **2** a
substance used for fixing a photographic
image etc.

fixings *pl. n.* the necessary ingredients for a
dish etc.

fix-it *n.* the action or an act of fixing
something.

fixity *n.* (*pl.* **fixities**) the quality of being
firm and not changing.

fixture *n.* **1** something fixed in position.
2 informal a person or thing established in
one place.

fizz ● *v.* (**fizzes, fizzed, fizzing**) **1** make a
hissing or spluttering sound. **2** (of a drink)
make bubbles. ● *n.* (*pl.* **fizzes**) **1** the sound
of fizzing. **2** bubbles. **3** informal energy.

fizzle ● *v.* (**fizzles, fizzled, fizzling**)
1 make a feeble hissing sound. **2** end feebly.
● *n.* a failure, a fiasco.

fizzy *adj.* (**fizzier, fizziest**) bubbly;
effervescent. □**fizziness** *n.*

fjord *n.* a long, narrow, and deep inlet of
sea between high cliffs. [*Say* FYORD *or*
FEE ord]

flab *n.* informal fat; flabbiness.

flabbergast *v.* overwhelm with
astonishment. [*Say* FLABBER gast]

flabby *adj.* (**flabbier, flabbiest**) **1** (of
flesh etc.) hanging down. **2** (of a person)
having soft fatty flesh; overweight.
3 feeble; lacking vigour. □**flabbiness** *n.*

flaccid *adj.* **1** (of flesh etc.) soft and limp.
2 lacking vigour. [*Say* FLASS id *or*
FLACK sid]

flack¹ *slang* ● *n.* a publicist. ● *v.* **1** act as a
publicist. **2** promote.

flack² *n.* = FLAK.

flag¹ ● *n.* a piece of cloth, attachable to a
pole or rope and used as a country's
emblem or as a standard, signal, etc. ● *v.*
(**flags, flagged, flagging**) **1 a** grow
tired; lose vigour. **b** droop. **2** mark out with
or as if with a flag. □**flag down** signal to
(a driver) to stop. **wave the flag 1** make a
display of one's patriotism. **2** assert one's
allegiance to.

flag² ● *n.* a flat usu. rectangular stone slab
used for paving; a flagstone. ● *v.* (**flags,
flagged, flagging**) pave with flagstones.

flag³ *n.* an iris.

flagellate¹ *v.* (**flagellates, flagellated,
flagellating**) **1** flog (someone), either as a
religious discipline or for sexual pleasure.
2 (**flagellate oneself**) criticize oneself
harshly and publicly. □**flagellation** *n.*
[*Say* FLADGE uh late]

flagellate² ● *adj.* (also **flagellated**)
having flagella. ● *n.* a protozoan having
one or more flagella. [*Say* FLADGE uh lit]

flagellum *n.* (*pl.* **flagella**) a long lash-like
appendage found esp. on microscopic
organisms. [*Say* fluh JELLUM *for the
singular,* fluh JELLA *for the plural*]

flagon *n.* a large bottle or vessel for wine
etc. [*Rhymes with* WAGON]

flagpole n. a pole on which a flag may be hoisted. □ **run something up the flagpole** test (an idea etc.).

flagrant adj. very obvious or unashamed. □ **flagrantly** adv. [Say FLAY grint]

flagship n. 1 a ship, esp. in a fleet, having an admiral on board. 2 something considered a leader or superior example of its kind.

flagstone n. a flat usu. rectangular stone slab used for paving. □ **flagstoned** adj.

flag-waving ● n. an excessive display of patriotism. ● adj. behaving in this manner. □ **flag-waver** n.

flail ● n. a tool used for threshing wheat etc. ● v. 1 beat (grain) with a flail. 2 wave or swing wildly. 3 a move with one's limbs swinging wildly. b struggle to find one's way.

flair n. 1 special talent or ability. 2 stylishness.

flak n. 1 anti-aircraft fire. 2 adverse criticism.

flake ● n. 1 a a small thin light piece of snow. b a similar piece of another material. 2 (in pl.) a flaked breakfast cereal. 3 slang an eccentric person. ● v. (**flakes, flaked, flaking**) come away or separate in flakes. □ **flake out** informal fall asleep.

flaky adj. (**flakier, flakiest**) 1 of or like flakes. 2 slang crazy, eccentric. 3 slang unreliable. □ **flakiness** n.

flambé ● adj. (of food) covered with alcohol and set alight briefly. ● v. (**flambés, flambéed, flambéing**) cover (food) with alcohol and set alight briefly. [Say flom BAY or flam BAY]

flamboyant adj. 1 confident and exciting in a way that attracts attention. 2 bright, colourful, and noticeable. □ **flamboyance** n. **flamboyantly** adv.

flame ● n. 1 ignited gas. 2 a a bright light. b a brilliant orange-red colour. 3 a strong passion. b informal a boyfriend or girlfriend. 4 slang a disparaging message sent by one user of a computer network to another. ● v. (**flames, flamed, flaming**) 1 emit or cause to emit flames. 2 (of an emotion) appear suddenly. 3 shine or glow like flame. 4 send someone an abusive message on the Internet. 5 (of a person's face) suddenly become red. □ **go up in flames** be consumed by fire. □ **flamelike** adj.

flamenco n. (pl. **flamencos**) 1 a style of Spanish guitar music, accompanied by singing and dancing. 2 a strongly rhythmical dance performed to this music. [Say fluh MENG co]

flame-thrower n. a weapon that projects a stream of burning fuel.

flaming adj. 1 covered in flames. 2 informal full of anger. 3 bright red or orange in colour.

flamingo n. (pl. **flamingos** or **flamingoes**) a tall wading bird with pink, scarlet, and black plumage.

flammable adj. easily set on fire. □ **flammability** n.

flan n. an open pastry case containing fruit, jam, or savoury filling.

flange ● n. a projecting flat rim, collar, or rib, used for strengthening or attachment. ● v. (**flanges, flanged, flanging**) provide with a flange. [Say FLANDGE]

flank ● n. 1 a the side of the body between the ribs and the hip. b a cut of meat, esp. beef, from the flank. 2 the side of a mountain, building, etc. 3 the right or left side of an army or group of people. ● v. 1 be situated at both sides of. 2 Military attack down or from the sides.

flanker n. (in football) an offensive player.

flannel n. 1 a kind of soft-woven woollen or synthetic fabric. 2 (also **flannelette**) a napped cotton fabric imitating the texture of flannel. 3 (in pl.) flannel garments.

flap ● v. (**flaps, flapped, flapping**) 1 move up and down when or as if flying. 2 swing or sway about; flutter. ● n. 1 a piece of cloth, wood, paper, etc. hinged or attached by one side only. 2 one up-and-down motion of a wing etc. 3 informal a a panic. b trouble, confrontation. 4 a hinged section of an aircraft wing used to control lift.

flapjack n. a pancake.

flapper n. (in the 1920s) a fashionable and unconventional young woman.

flare ● v. (**flares, flared, flaring**) 1 burn or cause to burn suddenly with a bright flame. 2 burst into anger etc.; burst forth. 3 widen or cause to widen at one end. ● n. 1 a a dazzling irregular flame or light. b a sudden outburst of flame. 2 a device producing a bright flame used as a signal, marker, etc. 3 Astronomy a sudden burst of radiation from a star. 4 a sudden outburst. 5 (in pl.) wide-bottomed pants. □ **flare up** become suddenly angry or active.

flare-up n. an outburst of flame, anger, a disease, etc.

flash ● v. (**flashes, flashed, flashing**) 1 shine with bright but brief light. 2 break suddenly into flame. 3 a burst suddenly into view or perception. b move swiftly. 4 a (of a message, image, etc.) show or be shown briefly. b signal by shining lights. 5 informal show or display briefly or ostentatiously. 6 slang expose one's genitals indecently. ● n. (pl. **flashes**) 1 a sudden bright light or flame. 2 a very brief time.

3 a brief, sudden occurrence. **4** = NEWS FLASH. **5** (also **flashbulb**) *Photography* a device producing a flash of intense light, used for photographing in dim light. **6** *Cdn & Brit.* a coloured patch on a uniform etc. as a distinguishing emblem. **7** a bright patch of colour. **8** (**Flash**) *proprietary* a computer application used to produce animation sequences that can be viewed by a web browser. ● *adj. informal* gaudy; vulgar. □**flash in the pan** a promising start followed by failure.

flashback *n.* **1** a scene in a film, novel, etc. set in a time earlier than the main action. **2** a vivid memory of a past event.

flasher *n.* **1** *slang* a man who indecently exposes his genitals in public. **2 a** an automatic device for switching lights rapidly on and off. **b** a sign or signal, e.g. hazard lights on a vehicle, using this device.

flash flood *n.* a sudden local flood due to heavy rain etc.

flashing *n.* a usu. metallic strip preventing water penetration at the junction of a roof with a wall etc.

flashlight *n.* a portable, battery-powered light.

flash memory *n. Computing* a type of memory that retains data in the absence of a power supply.

flashpoint *n.* **1** the temperature at which vapour from oil etc. will ignite in air. **2** the point at which anger, indignation, etc. becomes uncontrollable. **3** a place or situation which has the potential to explode into sudden violence or controversy.

flashy *adj.* (**flashier, flashiest**) showy; gaudy. □**flashily** *adv.* **flashiness** *n.*

flask *n.* **1** a narrow-necked bulbous bottle. **2** a small bottle of liquor, esp. for carrying in a pocket. **3** = THERMOS.

flat¹ ● *adj.* (**flatter, flattest**)
1 a horizontally level. **b** even. **c** with a level surface and little depth. **2** (of a refusal etc.) unqualified. **3 a** dull, without liveliness. **b** not funny. **4** (of a drink etc.) stale; no longer fizzy. **5** (of a tire) deflated. **6** *Music* below true or normal pitch. **7** not proportional or variable. **8** not glossy; matte. **9** (of prices etc.) inactive. ● *adv.* **1** spread out. **2** *informal* **a** completely, absolutely. **b** exactly. **3** *Music* below the true or normal pitch. ● *n.* **1** the flat part of anything. **2** (usu. in *pl.*) level ground. **3** a note lowered a semitone below natural pitch. **4** a flat tire. **5** a woman's shoe with a low or no heel. **6** a shallow box or container. □**fall flat** not win approval.

flat out **1** at top speed. **2** directly, bluntly. □**flatness** *n.* **flattish** *adj.*

flat² *n.* one or more rooms, rented and used as a residence

flatbed *n.* (also **flatbed trailer** or **flatbed truck**) **1** a trailer or truck with a flat load-carrying area. **2** *Computing* a scanner etc. which keeps paper flat during use.

flatbread *n.* any of various flat, thin breads.

flatcar *n.* a railway car without a roof or raised sides.

flatfish *n.* (*pl.* **flatfish** or **flatfishes**) a marine fish with both eyes on one side of a flattened body.

flat-footed *adj.* **1** having feet with a lower than normal arch. **2** *informal* awkward or unprepared.

flatland *n.* a region of flat land. □**flatlander** *n.*

flatly *adv.* **1** showing little interest or emotion. **2** in a firm and unambiguous manner; absolutely.

flatten *v.* **1** make or become flat. **2** *informal* knock down.

flatter *v.* **1** compliment unduly. **2** (**flatter oneself**) please, congratulate, or delude oneself. **3** make (a person) appear to the best advantage. **4** make (a person) feel honoured. **5** use flattery. □**flatterer** *n.* **flattering** *adj.* **flatteringly** *adv.*

flattery *n.* exaggerated or insincere praise.

flatulent *adj.* **1 a** causing formation of gas in the alimentary canal. **b** suffering discomfort from this. **2** inflated, pretentious. □**flatulence** *n.* [*Say* FLATCH oo lint, FLATCH oo lince]

flatware *n.* domestic cutlery.

flatwater *n.* slowly moving water.

flatworm *n.* a worm with a flattened body, including tapeworms, flukes, etc.

flaunt *v.* display ostentatiously; show off. [*Say* FLONT]

flautist *n.* a flute player. [*Say* FLOT ist *or* FLOUT ist]

flavour (also **flavor**) ● *n.* **1** a distinctive taste. **2** a characteristic or distinctive quality. **3** an indication of the essential character of something. ● *v.* give flavour to. □**flavour of the month** (or **week**) a temporary trend or fashion. □**flavourful** *adj.* **flavourless** *adj.*

flavouring *n.* (also **flavoring**) a substance used to flavour food or drink.

flaw ● *n.* **1** a fault or weakness. **2** a crack or chip in china, weaving defect in cloth, etc. **3** a mistake or shortcoming. ● *v.* mar, weaken, or invalidate. □**flawed** *adj.* **flawless** *adj.* **flawlessly** *adv.*

flax n. (pl. **flaxes**) **1** a blue-flowered plant cultivated for textile fibre and for its seeds. **2** this textile fibre.

flaxen adj. (of hair) pale yellow.

flay v. **1** strip the skin or hide off. **2** criticize severely. **3** peel off.

flea n. a small wingless jumping insect which feeds on human and other blood.

fleabane n. a plant of the daisy family supposed to drive away fleas.

flea-bitten adj. **1** bitten by or infested with fleas. **2** shabby.

flea market n. a usu. outdoor market selling second-hand goods, antiques, etc.

fleck ● n. **1** a small patch of colour or light. **2** a small particle. ● v. cover or mark with flecks.

fledge v. (**fledges, fledged, fledging**) **1** (of a bird) grow feathers. **2** bring up (a bird) until it can fly.

fledged adj. (of a young bird) having wing feathers that are large enough for flight.

fledgling ● n. a young bird. ● adj. new; inexperienced.

flee v. (**flees, fled, fleeing**) go away (from) rapidly.

fleece ● n. **1** the woolly covering of a sheep. **2** a soft warm fabric with a pile. ● v. (**fleeces, fleeced, fleecing**) **1** strip (a person) of money, valuables, etc.; swindle. **2** shear. □ **fleeced** adj. **fleecy** adj. (**fleecier, fleeciest**).

fleet[1] n. **1 a** a number of warships under one commander-in-chief. **b** (**the fleet**) a country's navy. **2** a number of ships, aircraft, buses, etc. operating together or having the same owner.

fleet[2] adj. literary swift; nimble.

fleeting adj. lasting only a short time. □ **fleetingly** adv.

Fleming n. **1** a native of medieval Flanders. **2** a member of a Flemish-speaking people. [Say FLEM ing]

Flemish ● adj. of or relating to Flanders. ● n. **1** the West Germanic language of Flanders. **2** (**the Flemish**) the people of Flanders. [Say FLEM ish]

flesh n. **1 a** the soft, esp. muscular, substance between the skin and bones in a body. **b** plumpness; fat. **2** the body as opposed to the mind or the soul. **3** the pulpy substance of a fruit or a plant. **4 a** the visible surface of the human body. **b** a light brownish pink. □ **flesh out** make or become substantial. **go the way of all flesh** die. **in the flesh** in person. **make a person's flesh creep** frighten or horrify a person. **sins of the flesh** sins related to physical indulgence. □ **fleshed** adj.

flesh and blood ● n. **1** the body or its substance. **2** human nature. ● adj. real; actually living. □ **one's own flesh and blood** near relatives.

fleshly adj. of or relating to the body and its needs.

fleshy adj. (**fleshier, fleshiest**) **1** plump, fat. **2** (of leaves or fruit) pulpy. **3** like flesh.

fleur-de-lys n. (also **fleur-de-lis**) (pl. **fleurs-de-lys** or **fleurs-de-lis**) **1** a figure of a lily composed of three petals bound together near their bases, used as a symbol of Quebec. **2** the flag of the province of Quebec. [Say flur duh LEE or flur duh LEECE for either the singular or the plural]

flew past of FLY[1].

flex v. (**flexes, flexed, flexing**) **1** bend (a joint, limb, etc.). **2** move (a muscle). □ **flex one's muscle(s)** assert one's strength or power.

flexible adj. **1** able to bend without breaking. **2** able to change or be changed to adapt to circumstances; adaptable. **3** (of a person) able to bend and contort the limbs and torso easily. □ **flexibility** n. **flexibly** adv.

flexor n. (also **flexor muscle**) a muscle that bends part of the body.

flextime n. a system of working with the starting and finishing times chosen by the employee.

flick ● n. **1 a** a light, quickly retracted blow with a whip etc. **b** the sudden release of a bent finger or thumb. **2** a sudden movement. **3** a quick turn of the wrist. **4** a slight, sharp sound. **5** informal a movie. ● v. **1** strike or remove with a rapid action of the fingers. **2** give a flick with. **3** activate by flicking a switch. **4** move rapidly. □ **flick through 1** turn over (pages etc.) of. **2** look cursorily through (a book etc.).

flicker ● v. **1** shine or burn unsteadily. **2** quiver; vibrate. **3** (of hope etc.) increase and decrease unsteadily. ● n. **1** a flickering movement or light. **2** a brief period of hope, recognition, etc. **3** a N American woodpecker. □ **flicker out** die away.

flier n. = FLYER.

flight[1] n. **1 a** the action of flying. **b** the passage of a projectile etc. through the air. **2** a journey made through the air or in space. **3** a flock of birds, insects, etc. **4** a series, esp. of stairs between floors. **5** an extravagant soaring. □ **take flight** fly.

flight[2] n. **1** an act of fleeing. **2** a hasty retreat. □ **put to flight** cause to flee. **take flight** flee.

flight attendant n. an airline employee who serves meals etc. during a flight.

flight crew *n.* a team of people who operate an aircraft flight.

flight deck *n.* **1** the deck of an aircraft carrier used as a runway. **2** the cockpit of an aircraft.

flightless *adj.* (of a bird etc.) naturally unable to fly

flight recorder *n.* a device in an aircraft to record technical details during a flight.

flighty *adj.* (**flightier, flightiest**) **1** frivolous, fickle, changeable. **2** crazy. □ **flightiness** *n.*

flim-flam *n.* **1** nonsense. **2** a deception or swindle. □ **flim-flammer** *n.*

flimsy *adj.* (**flimsier, flimsiest**) **1** carelessly assembled; easily damaged. **2** not convincing. **3** (of clothing) thin. □ **flimsily** *adv.*

flinch *v.* (**flinches, flinched, flinching**) **1** draw back; wince. **2** avoid thinking about or doing something unpleasant.

fling ● *v.* (**flings, flung, flinging**) **1** throw or hurl forcefully. **2** (**fling oneself**) rush headlong. **3** utter forcefully. **4** put on or take off (clothes) carelessly or rapidly. **5** put or send suddenly. **6** discard thoughtlessly. ● *n.* **1** a period of indulgence. **2** a short sexual relationship. **3** an energetic, whirling Highland dance.

flint *n.* **1 a** a hard grey stone of nearly pure silica. **b** a piece of this used to form a primitive tool or weapon. **2** a piece of hard alloy used to give an igniting spark in a lighter etc. □ **flinty** *adj.* (**flintier, flintiest**).

flip ● *v.* (**flips, flipped, flipping**) **1 a** turn over with a quick movement. **b** settle a question etc. by flipping a coin. **2** cause to move with a flick of the fingers. **3 a** turn (a page). **b** move through a book etc. **4** change or switch (channels). **5 a** move (a switch etc.). **b** turn on or off by flipping a switch. **6** resell (real estate etc.). **7** *slang* **a** become suddenly excited. **b** = FLIP OUT. ● *n.* **1** an act of flipping over. **2 a** a flick. **b** an act of activating a switch etc. **3** a somersault. **4** *Figure Skating* a type of jump. **5** an act of flipping real estate etc. ● *adj. informal* glib; flippant. □ **flip one's lid** (or **wig**) *slang* = FLIP OUT. **flip out 1** lose self-control. **2** become insane.

flip-flop ● *n.* **1** an abrupt reversal of policy. **2** a usu. rubber sandal with a thong between the big and second toe. **3** a backward somersault. **4** a flapping sound. ● *v.* (**flip-flops, flip-flopped, flip-flopping**) make a flip-flop.

flippant *adj.* treating serious things lightly. □ **flippancy** *n.* **flippantly** *adv.* [*Say* FLIP'nt, FLIP'n see]

flipper *n.* **1** a broadened limb of a seal,

penguin, etc., used in swimming. **2** a flat rubber attachment worn on the foot for underwater swimming. **3** = SPATULA 3.

flip side *n. informal* **1** the music on the second, usu. less commercial side, of a single. **2** the reverse or opposite of something.

flirt ● *v.* **1** show sexual interest in (a person) without serious intent. **2 a** show casual interest in. **b** have a brush with (danger etc.). ● *n.* a person who habitually flirts. □ **flirtation** *n.*

flirtatious *adj.* liking or likely to flirt. □ **flirtatiously** *adv.* **flirtatiousness** *n.* [*Say* flur TAY shus]

flirty *adj.* (**flirtier, flirtiest**). = FLIRTATIOUS.

flit ● *v.* (**flits, flitted, flitting**) **1** move lightly or rapidly. **2** make short flights. ● *n.* an act of flitting. □ **flitter** *n.*

flitter *v.* flit about; flutter.

float ● *v.* **1** rest or move, or cause to rest or move, on the surface of a liquid without sinking. **2** drift. **3** *informal* **a** move in a leisurely or casual way. **b** hover before the eye or mind. **4** be free from attachment, commitment, etc. **5 a** launch. **b** offer (shares etc.) on the stock market. **6 a** (of currency) be allowed to have a fluctuating exchange rate. **b** (of an interest rate) fluctuate according to market conditions. **7** put forward (an idea etc.); circulate. ● *n.* **1** a lightweight object or device designed to float on water. **2** a vehicle carrying a display in a parade etc. **3 a** *Cdn & Brit.* a sum of money used to provide change. **b** petty cash. **4** a soft drink with a scoop of ice cream floating in it. □ **floating** *adj.*

floatation *n.* = FLOTATION.

floater *n.* **1** a person or thing that floats. **2** a voter who is undecided. **3** a person who frequently changes occupation etc.

floating point *n. Computing* a decimal etc. point that does not occupy a fixed position in the numbers processed.

float plane *n.* an airplane equipped with floats so that it can land on water.

flock[1] ● *n.* **1** a number of birds, sheep, or goats moving or kept together. **2** a large crowd of people. **3 a** a Christian congregation under one priest or minister. **b** a number of children, pupils, etc. ● *v.* **1** congregate. **2** move in great numbers.

flock[2] *n.* **1** a lock or tuft of wool, cotton, etc. **2 a** material for quilting and stuffing. **b** powdered wool or cloth, applied to wallpaper, fabrics, etc. □ **flocked** *adj.* **flocking** *n.*

floe *n.* a sheet of floating ice. [*Sounds like* FLOW]

flog v. (**flogs**, **flogged**, **flogging**) **1** beat with a whip, stick, etc. **2** slang **a** sell. **b** publicize; promote. □ **flog to death** informal talk about at tedious length. □ **flogger** n. **flogging** n.

flood ● n. **1 a** an overflowing of water beyond its normal confines. **b** the water that overflows. **2 a** a torrent. **b** something resembling a torrent. **3** the inflow of the tide. **4** (**the Flood**) any universal flood as described by various ancient religious traditions. ● v. **1** cover with or overflow in or as if in a flood. **2** irrigate. **3** deluge with water. **4** arrive in great quantities. **5** become inundated. □ **flooding** n.

floodgate n. **1** a gate opened or closed to admit or exclude water. **2** a restraint or check holding back tears etc.

floodlight ● n. a large powerful light to illuminate a building, stage, etc. ● v. (**floodlights**, **floodlit**, **floodlighting**) illuminate with floodlights.

flood plain n. a relatively flat plain next to a river etc. that is naturally subject to flooding.

floodway n. a channel for diverting flood waters away from a city etc.

floor ● n. **1** the lower surface of a room. **2** the bottom of the sea, a cave, etc. **3** a storey of a building. **4 a** (in a legislative assembly) the part of the house in which members sit. **b** the right to speak next in debate. **5** the minimum of prices, wages, etc. ● v. **1** furnish with a floor. **2** knock (a person) down. **3** informal confound, baffle. **4** push (an accelerator pedal) all the way to floor. □ **from the floor** (of a speech etc.) given by a member of the audience. **take the floor 1** begin to dance. **2** speak in a debate.

floorboard n. **1** a long wooden board used for flooring. **2** the floor of a car etc.

floor hockey n. a form of hockey played on an indoor floor.

flooring n. the materials with which a floor is made or covered.

floor plan n. **1** a diagram of the rooms etc. on one floor of a building. **2** the arrangement of rooms.

floozie n. (also **floozy**) (pl. **floozies**) informal a promiscuous girl or a woman.

flop ● v. (**flops**, **flopped**, **flopping**) **1** sway about heavily or loosely. **2** move in an ungainly way. **3** sit, lie, or fall heavily or suddenly. **4** slang fail; collapse. **5** make a dull sound as of a soft body landing. ● n. **1 a** a flopping movement. **b** the sound made by it. **2** informal a failure.

-flop comb. form Computing floating-point operations per second.

flophouse n. informal a cheap boarding house.

floppy ● adj. (**floppier**, **floppiest**) tending to flop. ● n. (pl. **floppies**) (also **floppy disk**) Computing a flexible removable magnetic disk for storing data.

flora n. (pl. **floras**) **1** the plants of a particular region or period. **2** a catalogue of the plants of a defined area. **3** (also **intestinal flora**) the beneficial bacteria normally present in the intestines.

floral ● adj. having to do with flowers. ● n. something with a floral design.

Florentine ● adj. **1 a** of or relating to Florence. **b** denoting the art etc. developed in Renaissance Florence. **2** (**florentine**) (of a dish) served on a bed of spinach. ● n. **1** a person from Florence. **2** a thin cookie coated on one side with chocolate. [Say FLOR un teen]

floret n. **1** each of the small flowers making up a composite flower head. **2** any of the segments into which a head of broccoli etc. may be divided. **3** a tiny blossom. [Say FLOR it for senses 1 and 3; say flor ET for sense 2]

florid adj. **1** (of a person's complexion) ruddy or flushed. **2** elaborately ornate. [Say FLOR id]

florist n. a person who retails flowers and plants.

floss ● n. (pl. **flosses**) **1 a** the rough silk enveloping a silkworm's cocoon. **b** the silk down in corn. **2** untwisted silk thread used in embroidery. **3** = DENTAL FLOSS. ● v. (**flosses**, **flossed**, **flossing**) clean between (the teeth) with dental floss. □ **flossing** n.

flotation n. **1** the process of launching or financing a commercial enterprise. **2 a** the action of floating. **b** buoyancy.

flotilla n. **1** a fleet of boats or small ships. **2** a small fleet of warships. [Say flo TILLA]

flotsam n. **1** wreckage found floating on the water. **2** (also **flotsam and jetsam**) odds and ends. [Say FLOT sum]

flounce[1] ● v. (**flounces**, **flounced**, **flouncing**) move in an exaggeratedly impatient or angry manner. ● n. an action expressing annoyance or impatience.

flounce[2] n. a frill or wide strip of material gathered and sewn to a skirt, dress, etc. □ **flouncy** adj.

flounder[1] v. **1** struggle or show confusion. **2** manage something badly. **3** stagger clumsily through mud, snow, etc. □ **floundering** n.

flounder[2] n. (pl. **flounder** or **flounders**) a flatfish used for food.

flour ● n. **1** a fine powder obtained by

grinding grain, used for making bread, cakes, etc. **2** a fine powder made from other foodstuffs. ● **v.** sprinkle or cover with flour. □ **floured** adj. **floury** adj. (**flourier, flouriest**).

flourish ● **v.** (**flourishes, flourished, flourishing**) **1 a** grow vigorously. **b** prosper. **c** be in one's prime. **d** be in good health. **2** spend one's life during a specified period. **3** show ostentatiously. **4** wave vigorously. ● **n.** (pl. **flourishes**) **1** an ostentatious gesture with a weapon etc. **2** an ornamental curve of handwriting. **3** a fanfare played by brass instruments. □ **flourishing** adj. [Say FLUR ish]

flout v. openly fail to follow (the law, rules, etc.).

flow ● **v.** **1** glide along as a stream. **2 a** spring or well up. **b** (of blood etc.) be spilled. **3** circulate. **4** move freely and continuously. **5** proceed easily and smoothly. **6** hang easily or gracefully. **7** result from or be caused by. **8** (of the tide) come in. **9** be poured out abundantly. ● **n.** **1 a** a flowing movement in a stream. **b** the quantity that flows. **c** the act of flowing. **2** any continuous movement that denotes a copious supply. **3** the rise of a tide. □ **go with the flow** informal be relaxed and not resist change.

flow chart n. (also **flow diagram**) **1** a diagram showing the different stages through which a process must move. **2** a graphic representation of a computer program in relation to its sequence of functions.

flower ● **n.** **1** the part of a plant from which the fruit or seed develops. **2** a blossom and usu. its stem. **3** a flowering plant. **4 a** the prime in a person's life. **b** the finest thing, embodiment of a quality, etc. **5** (of a plant) the state of being in bloom. ● **v.** **1** (of a plant) produce flowers. **2** develop into. □ **flowered** adj.

flower child n. a hippie, esp. in the late 1960s.

flower girl n. a child bridesmaid.

flowering adj. **1** (of a plant) capable of producing flowers. **2** (of a plant) in bloom.

flowerpot n. **1** a container for growing plants in. **2** Cdn a tall column or island of rock formed by water erosion.

flowery adj. **1** decorated with flowers or floral designs. **2** (of speech, writing, etc.) ornate. **3** full of or like flowers.

flowing adj. **1** (of language etc.) fluent. **2** smoothly continuous. **3** not confined; hanging loosely and gracefully.

flown past participle of FLY[1].

fl. oz. abbr. fluid ounce.

FLQ abbr. (in Canada) FRONT DE LIBÉRATION DU QUÉBEC.

FLQ crisis n. = OCTOBER CRISIS.

flu n. (pl. **flus**) a highly contagious virus infection causing fever and coughing. □ **flu-like** adj.

flub informal ● **v.** (**flubs, flubbed, flubbing**) botch, bungle. ● **n.** a blunder.

fluctuate v. (**fluctuates, fluctuated, fluctuating**) change frequently in size, amount, quality, etc. □ **fluctuation** n. [Say FLUCK choo ate]

flue n. **1** a passage in a chimney for smoke, waste gases, etc. **2** a channel for conveying heat.

fluent adj. **1 a** (of speech, writing, etc.) flowing naturally. **b** able to speak a language easily. **c** articulate. **2** (of movement etc.) easy and graceful. □ **fluency** n. **fluently** adv. [Say FLOO int, FLOO in see]

fluff ● **n.** **1** soft, light, feathery material coming off blankets etc. **2** a piece of downy material. **3** informal a mistake or error. **4** something unimportant or insignificant. ● **v.** **1** make or become fluffy. **2** informal blunder or make a mistake.

fluffy adj. (**fluffier, fluffiest**) **1** of or like fluff. **2** covered in fluff. **3** light and airy. **4** lacking depth. □ **fluffiness** n.

fluid ● **n.** a substance, esp. a gas or liquid, lacking definite shape and capable of flowing. ● adj. **1** able to flow freely. **2** not settled or stable. **3** (of speech etc.) fluent. **4** graceful. □ **fluidity** n. **fluidly** adv.

fluid ounce n. a unit of capacity equal to one-twentieth of an imperial pint (approx. 28.4 ml), or (in the US) equal to one-sixteenth of a pint (approx. 29.6 ml). Abbreviation: **fl. oz.**

fluke[1] n. a piece of luck, an unexpected success.

fluke[2] n. **1** a parasitic flatworm. **2** a flatfish.

fluke[3] n. **1** a broad triangular plate on the arm of an anchor. **2** the barbed head of a lance, harpoon, etc. **3** a lobe of a whale's tail.

flume n. **1** an artificial channel conveying water etc. for industrial use. **2** a deep, narrow channel with a stream running through it. **3** a waterslide at an amusement park or swimming pool.

flummox v. (**flummoxes, flummoxed, flummoxing**) informal bewilder. [Say FLUM ix]

flung past and past participle of FLING.

flunk v. informal fail (in school).

flunky n. (pl. **flunkies**) usu. derogatory a

person who performs relatively menial tasks.

fluorescence *n.* **1** light given out by certain substances as a result of exposure to radiation such as X-rays, ultraviolet light, etc. **2** the property of emitting light in this way. [*Say* flor ESSENCE]

fluorescent ● *adj.* **1** having or showing fluorescence. **2** (of colours) very bright and glowing. ● *n.* (also **fluorescent light, fluorescent bulb**, etc.) a light or bulb radiating largely by fluorescence. [*Say* flor ESS'nt]

fluoridate *v.* (**fluoridates, fluoridated, fluoridating**) add traces of fluoride to. □ **fluoridated** *adj.* **fluoridation** *n.* [*Say* FLORA date]

fluoride *n.* a binary compound of fluorine, used to prevent tooth decay. [*Say* FLOR ide]

fluorine *n.* a poisonous, pale yellow gaseous element. [*Say* FLOR een]

fluoxetine *n.* an organic compound used as an antidepressant (compare PROZAC). [*Say* flu OXA teen]

flurry ● *n.* (*pl.* **flurries**) **1** a short, usu. localized shower of snow. **2** a sudden burst of intense activity. **3** a number of things happening or arriving at once. ● *v.* (**flurries, flurried, flurrying**) **1** agitate or confuse. **2** move quickly and agitatedly.

flush¹ ● *v.* (**flushes, flushed, flushing**) **1 a** (of the face) redden. **b** glow with a warm colour, light, etc. **2 a** cleanse (a toilet etc.) by a rushing flow of water. **b** dispose of in this way. **3** *Computing* cleanse or erase. ● *n.* (*pl.* **flushes**) **1 a** a reddening of the face. **b** a glow of light or colour. **2 a** a sudden rush of water. **b** an act of flushing. **3** a rush of emotion, elation, etc. **4** the freshness and vigour of youth.

flush² *adj.* **1** completely level or continuous with another surface. **2** *informal* having plenty of something. **3** (of text) level with the margin. □ **flushable** *adj.*

flush³ *n.* (*pl.* **flushes**) a hand of cards all of one suit, esp. in poker.

flush⁴ *v.* (**flushes, flushed, flushing**) cause (a game bird) to fly up suddenly. □ **flush out** force (a person) out of hiding etc.

flushed *adj.* glowing or blushing.

fluster ● *v.* make or become agitated or confused etc. ● *n.* a nervous or agitated state. □ **flustered** *adj.*

flute ● *n.* **1 a** a high-pitched woodwind instrument of metal or wood. **b** its player. **2 a** *Architecture* an ornamental vertical groove in a column. **b** any similar groove. **3** a tall narrow wineglass. ● *v.* (**flutes,**

fluted, fluting) make, shape, or carve flutes. □ **fluted** *adj.* **fluting** *n.*

flutist *n.* a flute player.

flutter ● *v.* **1** flap the wings lightly and quickly. **2** fall with a quivering motion. **3** move or cause to move in a quick, irregular way. **4** move about aimlessly and restlessly. **5** (of a pulse or heartbeat) beat irregularly. **6** tremble with excitement. ● *n.* **1** an act of fluttering. **2** tremulous excitement. **3** an abnormally rapid but regular heartbeat. □ **flutter one's eyelashes** blink one's eyes in a coyly flirtatious manner. □ **fluttering** *adj. & n.* **fluttery** *adj.*

flux *n.* (*pl.* **fluxes**) **1 a** a process of flowing. **b** the flowing in of the tide. **2** a stream or flood. **3** continuous change. **4** a substance mixed with a metal etc. to promote fusion. **5** the rate of flow or amount of a fluid, radiation, electric field, etc. across a given area.

fly¹ ● *v.* (**flies**; *past* **flew**; *past participle* **flown**; **flying**) **1** (of a winged creature or aircraft) move through the air. **2** control the flight of or transport in (an aircraft). **3 a** cause to fly or remain aloft. **b** (of a flag etc.) flutter. **4** pass or rise quickly through the air. **5 a** go or move quickly. **b** (of time) pass swiftly. **6 a** flee (from). **b** *informal* depart hastily. **7** attack or criticize fiercely. **8** *Baseball* (*past & past participle* **flied**) hit a fly ball. **9** *informal* meet with approval. ● *n.* (*pl.* **flies**) **1** a zippered or buttoned opening at the crotch of a pair of trousers. **2** a flap of material on a tent, to form a door or repel moisture. **3** (*in pl.*) the space above a theatre stage. **4** *Baseball* a fly ball. □ **fly in the face of** disregard, defy. **fly off the handle** *informal* lose one's temper. **fly the coop** *informal* escape or leave without warning. **on the fly 1** quickly, esp. while on the go. **2** (of something hit or thrown) while still flying through the air.

fly² *n.* (*pl.* **flies**) **1** a flying insect with a single pair of transparent wings and sucking (and often piercing) mouthparts. **2** used in names of flying insects with other characteristics. **3** a fishing bait consisting of a natural or artificial fly. □ **catch flies** *informal* have one's mouth open for a prolonged time. **fly in the ointment** a minor irritation that spoils something. **fly on the wall** an observer who is not noticed. **like flies** in large numbers. **no flies on** *informal* nothing to diminish (a person's) astuteness.

fly-away *adj.* **1** (of hair etc.) loose and difficult to control. **2** (of a person etc.) sudden, impulsive.

fly ball *n.* *Baseball* a ball hit high up into the air.

flyby n. (pl. **flybys**) **1** a flight past a position. **2** a low-level, ceremonial procession of aircraft.

fly-by-night • adj. **1** unreliable or dishonest. **2** short-lived. • n. (also **fly-by-nighter**) an unreliable person.

fly cast v. (**fly casts, fly cast, fly casting**) fish with a rod and artificial flies rather than live bait. □ **fly caster** n. **fly casting** n.

flycatcher n. any of various birds which catch flying insects.

flyer n. informal **1 a** a pilot or aviator. **b** a person or thing that flies. **2** a small advertising leaflet. **3** a fast-moving animal or vehicle. **4** an ambitious person.

fly-fish v. (**fly-fishes, fly-fished, fly-fishing**) fish with an artificial fly as bait. □ **fly-fisher** n. **fly-fisherman** n. **fly-fishing** n.

fly-in • n. (pl. **fly-ins**) **1** the delivery of goods etc. by air to a usu. remote place. **2** a service etc. provided for people who arrive by air. • adj. **1** of or for people arriving by air. **2** accessible only by air.

flying • adj. **1** that flies or flies about. **2** fluttering in the air etc. **3** hasty, brief. **4** travelling swiftly. **5** Figure Skating designating a spin begun with a leap through the air. • n. the action of flying an aircraft, spacecraft, etc. □ **with flying colours** with distinction.

flying buttress n. a usu. arched buttress which slants upwards to a wall.

flying fish n. (pl. **flying fish** or **flying fishes**) any of various tropical fishes capable of gliding above the water by means of wing-like fins.

flying saucer n. any unidentified flying object, popularly supposed to have come from outer space.

flyover n. **1** a flight of aircraft for observation, as part of a military display, etc. **2** (also **flypast**) a ceremonial flight of aircraft past a person or place.

fly rod n. a very light, flexible rod for use in fly casting. □ **fly rodding** n.

flytrap n. a plant that catches flies, esp. the Venus flytrap.

flyway n. the regular line of flight followed by a migrating bird.

flyweight n. **1** a weight in certain sports below bantamweight. **2** an athlete of this weight.

flywheel n. a heavy wheel on a revolving shaft used to regulate machinery or accumulate power.

FM abbr. **1** FREQUENCY MODULATION. **2** radio stations broadcast using this.

FN abbr. Cdn FIRST NATION.

f-number n. Photography the ratio of the focal length to the effective diameter of a lens.

foal • n. the young of a horse or related animal. • v. give birth to a foal. □ **foaling** n. [Rhymes with POLE]

foam • n. **1** a mass of small bubbles formed on or in liquid. **2** a froth of saliva or sweat. **3** solidified rubber (also **foam rubber**) or plastic (also **foam plastic**). **4** any of various chemical substances forming foam. • v. emit foam; froth. □ **foam at the mouth** be very angry. □ **foaming** adj. **foam-like** adj. **foamy** adj. (**foamier, foamiest**)

fob¹ n. **1** (also **fob chain**) a chain attached to a watch for carrying in a waistcoat or waistband pocket. **2** a tab on a key ring.

fob² v. (**fobs, fobbed, fobbing**) □ **fob off 1** deceive into accepting something inferior. **2** palm or pass off.

focaccia n. (pl. **focaccias**) a type of flat Italian bread usu. topped with herbs etc. [Say fuh CATCH uh]

focal adj. relating to a focus.

focal length n. the distance between the centre of a mirror or lens and its focus.

focal point n. = FOCUS n. 1a, 3.

fo'c'sle n. = FORECASTLE. [Say FOKE s'll]

focus • n. (pl. **focuses** or **foci**) **1** Physics **a** the point at which rays or waves from a lens or mirror meet, or from which divergent rays or waves appear to proceed. **b** the distance from a lens etc. to this point (compare FOCAL LENGTH). **2 a** Optics the point at which an object must be situated for a lens or mirror to produce a clear image of it. **b** a state of clear definition. **3** the centre of interest or activity. **4** Math a fixed point with reference to which an ellipse, parabola, or other curve is drawn. **5** Geology the place of origin of an earthquake etc. • v. (**focuses, focused, focusing**) **1** bring into focus etc. **2** adjust the focus of a lens, the eye, etc. **3** concentrate on. **4** converge or make converge to a focus. [For the plural say FOCUS iz or either FOE kye or FOE sigh]

focus group n. a selection of people surveyed for their opinions.

fodder n. **1** dried hay or straw etc. for cattle etc. **2 a** something that feeds (creativity etc.). **b** people viewed as dispensable commodities.

foe n. an enemy or opponent.

foetus n. (pl. **foetuses**) esp. Brit. = FETUS. [Say FEET us]

fog • n. **1 a** a thick cloud of water droplets suspended in the atmosphere at or near the earth's surface, which reduces visibility. **b** an opaque mass of smoke etc. **2** a state of confusion, uncertainty, etc. ● *v.* (**fogs, fogged, fogging**) **1** cover or become covered with condensed vapour. **2** bewilder, confuse. □ **in a fog** puzzled; at a loss. □ **fogging** *n.*

fogey *n.* (*pl.* **fogeys**) (also **fogy**, *pl.* **fogies**) a person with old-fashioned ideas. □ **fogeyish** *adj.* [*Say* FOE ghee]

foggy *adj.* (**foggier, foggiest**) **1** full of fog. **2** vague, confused. □ **not have the foggiest** *informal* have no idea.

foghorn *n.* a deep sounding instrument for warning ships in fog.

fog lamp *n.* a headlight for improving visibility in fog.

fogy *n.* = FOGEY. [*Say* FOE ghee]

foible *n.* a minor weakness or idiosyncrasy. [*Say* FOY bull]

foie gras *n.* a pâté of goose or duck liver. [*Say* fwah GRAH]

foil¹ *v.* prevent the success of.

foil² *n.* **1 a** metal hammered or rolled into a thin sheet. **b** aluminum foil. **2** a person or thing that enhances the qualities of another by contrast.

foil³ *n.* a light blunt-edged fencing sword with a button on its point.

foist *v.* impose (an unwelcome person or thing) on.

folate *n.* a salt or ester of folic acid. [*Say* FOE late]

fold¹ ● *v.* **1** bend or close over. **2** become or be able to be folded. **3** make compact by folding. **4** *informal* **a** collapse, disintegrate. **b** (of an enterprise) go bankrupt. **5** withdraw from play. **6** mix (ingredients) using a gentle turning motion. **7** *literary* embrace. ● *n.* **1** a form or shape produced by draping cloth. **2** a line or crease produced by folding. **3** an area of skin that sags. □ **foldable** *adj.*

fold² *n.* **1** an enclosure for sheep. **2** a body of believers. **3** a community sharing a way of life, values, etc.

-fold *suffix* forming adjectives and adverbs from cardinal numbers, meaning: **1** in an amount multiplied by. **2** consisting of so many parts.

foldaway *adj.* designed to be folded away.

fold-down *adj.* designed to be folded down for use.

folder *n.* **1** a folding cover or holder for loose papers. **2** *Computing* a directory containing related files.

folding *adj.* **1** that can be folded. **2** (of a door) having vertically jointed sections that can be folded together.

fold-out ● *n.* an oversize folded page in a book etc. ● *adj.* designed to be unfolded.

foley *adj.* designating sound effects in a motion picture etc. [*Rhymes with* GOALIE]

foliage *n.* leaves. [*Say* FOLEY idge]

foliate *adj.* decorated with leaves or leaflike patterns. [*Say* FOLEY it]

foliated *adj.* **1** = FOLIATE. **2** *Geology* consisting of thin sheets. [*Say* FOLEY ated]

folic acid *n.* a B vitamin, found in leafy green vegetables and liver. [*Say* FOLLIC *or* FOE lick]

folio *n.* (*pl.* **folios**) **1** a leaf of paper etc. **2** a sheet of paper folded once making two leaves of a book. **3** a book made of such sheets.

folk *n.* (*pl.* **folk** *or* **folks**) **1** people in general. **2** (*usu.* as **folks**) one's parents or relatives. **3** a people. **4** *informal* = FOLK MUSIC. **5** (as an *adj.*) traditional. □ **folkish** *adj.* **folky** *adj.*

folkie *informal* ● *n.* a devotee of folk music. ● *adj.* of or relating to folk music.

folklore *n.* the traditional beliefs, stories, customs, etc. of a people. □ **folkloric** *adj.* **folklorist** *n.*

folk medicine *n.* medicine of a traditional kind.

folk music *n.* **1** traditional music as made by the common people. **2** contemporary music composed in this style.

folk song *n.* **1** a song that has been handed down esp. orally from one generation to the next. **2** a song written in this style. □ **folksinger** *n.*

folksy *adj.* (**folksier, folksiest**) **1** friendly, informal. **2** artificially unsophisticated. □ **folksiness** *n.*

folkways *pl. n.* the traditional behaviour of a people.

follicle *n.* a small cavity, sac, or gland, esp. the gland at the root of a hair. [*Say* FOLLA cull]

follow *v.* **1** go or come after. **2** go along (a route). **3** take as a guide. **4** conform to. **5** practise (a trade or profession). **6** undertake (a course of study etc.). **7** understand. **8** maintain awareness of. **9** be necessarily true as a result of something else. □ **follow one's nose** trust to instinct. **follow on** continue. **follow suit** conform to another person's actions. **follow through** continue (an action etc.) to its conclusion. **follow up** make further investigation of.

follower *n.* **1** an adherent or devotee. **2** a person or thing that follows.

following ● *prep.* coming after; as a sequel to. ● *n.* **1** a body of devotees. **2** that which follows. ● *adj.* that follows or comes after.

follow-on adj. following as the next step in a progression.

follow-the-leader n. a game in which players must do as the leader does.

follow-through n. **1** the continuing of an action or task to its conclusion. **2** a continuation of the movement of a bat etc. after a ball etc. has been struck.

follow-up n. a subsequent or continued action etc.

folly n. (pl. **follies**) **1** foolishness. **2** a foolish act, idea, etc. **3** an ornamental building.

foment v. stir up or worsen trouble etc. [Say foe MENT]

fond adj. **1** having affection or liking for. **2** affectionate. **3** doting. **4** unlikely to be fulfilled. □ **fondly** adv. **fondness** n.

fondant n. **1** a creamy, thick paste made of sugar and water. **2** a candy made of this. [Say FOND'nt]

fondle v. (**fondles, fondled, fondling**) **1** caress. **2** sexually molest by touching etc. **3** touch (a person's genitals) erotically.

fondue n. a dish in which small pieces of food are dipped into melted cheese or other hot sauce. [Say fon DOO]

font¹ n. a receptacle in a church for baptismal water.

font² n. a selection or set of type of one particular face and size.

fontina n. a mild, semi-soft to firm, cow's-milk cheese. [Say fon TEENA]

food n. **1** any substance that can be taken into the body to maintain life and growth. **2** solid nourishment, as opposed to drink. **3** ideas as a resource for thought etc. **4** a nutritive substance absorbed by a plant from the earth or air.

food bank n. a charitable institution which provides food to the needy.

food chain n. a hierarchy of organisms in which each feeds on the next down.

food court n. an area with a variety of fast-food stalls surrounding a shared area.

foodie n. informal a person who is interested in esp. exotic or trendy food.

foodland n. Cdn farmland.

food poisoning n. illness due to bacteria or other toxins in food.

food processor n. a domestic kitchen appliance for chopping, grating, slicing, etc.

foodstuff n. any substance suitable as food.

food web n. a system of interdependent food chains.

fool ● n. a person who acts unwisely. ● v. **1** trick or deceive. **2** act in a joking way. ● adj. informal foolish. □ **act** (or **play**) **the**

fool behave in a silly way. **fool around 1** engage in sexual activity. **2** waste time. **make a fool of** make someone look foolish

foolhardy adj. (**foolhardier, foolhardiest**) rashly or foolishly bold; reckless. □ **foolhardiness** n.

foolish adj. lacking good sense; unwise. □ **foolishly** adv. **foolishness** n.

foolproof adj. so straightforward as to be incapable of misuse.

foolscap n. a type of writing paper measuring 8 1/2 by 14 inches (22 by 35.5 cm). [Say FULL scap or FOOLS cap]

fool's gold n. iron pyrites.

foot ● n. (pl. **feet**) **1** the lower extremity of the leg below the ankle. **2 a** the lower or lowest part of anything. **b** the lower end of a table. **c** the end of a bed. **3** the base of anything vertical. **4** a step, pace, or tread. **5** (pl. **feet** or **foot**) a unit of length equal to 12 inches (30.48 cm). **6** (in poetry) a group of syllables constituting a metrical unit. ● v. **1** (usu. as **foot it**) **a** traverse by foot. **b** dance. **2** pay (a bill). □ **get off on the wrong** (or **right**) **foot** make a bad (or good) start. **get one's feet wet** begin to participate. **have one's** (or **both**) **feet on the ground** be practical. **have a foot in the door** have a prospect of success. **have one foot in the grave** be near death. **my foot!** interj. expressing strong contradiction. **not put a foot wrong** make no mistakes. **on foot** walking. **put one's best foot forward** make every effort. **put one's foot down** informal be firmly insistent. **put one's foot in one's mouth** (also **put one's foot in it**) informal commit a blunder. **set foot in** (or **on**) enter. **think on one's feet** think or react rapidly under stress etc. **under foot** in the way. □ **footed** adj.

footage n. **1** length or distance in feet. **2** an amount of film made for broadcasting etc.

foot-and-mouth disease n. a contagious viral disease of cattle etc.

football n. **1** a game in which each of two teams attempts to move a ball across the other's goal line or into a goal. **2** the inflated ball used in this. □ **footballer** n.

footboard n. **1** a board to support the feet. **2** an upright board at the foot of a bed.

footbridge n. a bridge for use by pedestrians.

foot-dragging n. deliberate reluctance to act or proceed. □ **foot-dragger** n.

footer n. **1** a person or thing of so many feet in length or height. **2** a line of text appearing at the foot of each page of a document etc.

footfall *n.* the sound of a footstep.

foothill *n.* (often in *pl.*) a low hill at the base of a mountain or mountain range.

foothold *n.* **1** a place, esp. in climbing, where a foot can be supported securely. **2** a secure initial position.

footing *n.* **1** a foothold. **2** the basis on which an enterprise is established or operates; a person's status. **3** a foundation resting directly on the earth.

footlights *pl. n.* a row of lights along the front of a stage floor.

footloose *adj.* free to do as one pleases.

footman *n.* (*pl.* **footmen**) a male servant in a house.

footnote ● *n.* **1** a note printed at the foot of a page. **2** a minor or tangential event, comment, etc. ● *v.* (**footnotes**, **footnoted**, **footnoting**) supply with footnotes.

footpad *n. hist.* a highway robber on foot.

footpath *n.* a path for walking along.

footprint *n.* **1** the impression left by a foot or shoe. **2** the surface area taken up by something.

foot race *n.* a running race.

footrest *n.* a support for the feet or a foot.

footsie *n. informal* □ **play footsie with a person** touch or caress a person's feet lightly with one's own feet to express romantic interest.

foot soldier *n.* **1** an infantry soldier. **2** a person who works for a cause at the basic level.

footstep *n.* **1** a step taken in walking. **2** the sound of this. □ **follow** (or **tread**) **in a person's footsteps** do as another person did.

footstool *n.* a stool for resting the feet on.

footwear *n.* anything worn on the feet.

footwork *n.* the use of the feet, esp. skilfully.

fop *n.* a dandy. □ **foppish** *adj.*

for ● *prep.* **1** in the interest or to the benefit of. **2** in defence or favour of. **3** appropriate to. **4** with reference to. **5** in place of. **6** in exchange against. **7 a** as the price of. **b** to the amount of. **8** as a reward for. **9 a** with a view to. **b** on account of. **10** corresponding to. **11** towards. **12** conducive to. **13** through or over (a distance or period). **14** in spite of. ● *conj.* because.

forage ● *n.* **1** food for cattle etc. **2** a wide search to obtain something, esp. food. ● *v.* (**forages**, **foraged**, **foraging**) rummage (esp. for food). □ **forager** *n.* [*Say* FOR idge]

foray *n.* **1** a sudden attack; a raid. **2** a brief, vigorous attempt to be involved in a new activity etc. [*Say* FOR ay]

forbear¹ *v.* (**forbears**; *past* **forbore**; *past participle* **forborne**; **forbearing**) *literary* stop oneself from saying or doing something. [*Say* for BARE]

forbear² *n.* = FOREBEAR. [*Say* FOR bare]

forbearance *n.* patient self-control.

forbid *v.* (**forbids**; *past* **forbade** or **forbad**; *past participle* **forbidden**; **forbidding**) **1** order not to do. **2** refuse to allow. □ **God** (or **heaven**) **forbid** may it not happen! □ **forbidden** *adj.* [*For* forbade *say either* for BADE *or* for BAD]

forbidding *adj.* seeming unfriendly and frightening.

force ● *n.* **1** power; exerted strength. **2** coercion or compulsion. **3 a** military strength. **b** an organized body of soldiers, police, or workers. **4** validity. **5** precise significance. **6** mental strength; influence. **7** *Physics* an influence tending to cause the motion of a body. **8** a person or thing having influence. ● *v.* (**forces**, **forced**, **forcing**) **1** constrain (a person) by force. **2** make a way through or into by force. **3** drive or propel violently. **4** achieve or attain by effort. **5** strain or increase to the utmost. **6** artificially hasten the development of (a plant). **7** (**force oneself on**) rape. **8** *Baseball* cause (a runner) to be put out in a forceout. □ **by force of** by means of. **force a person's hand** make a person act prematurely. **in force 1** valid, effective. **2** in great strength or numbers. **join forces** combine efforts. □ **forced** *adj.*

force-feed *v.* (**force-feeds**, **force-fed**, **force-feeding**) **1** force to take food. **2** compel (a person) to absorb propaganda etc.

force field *n.* (in science fiction) an invisible barrier of force.

forceful *adj.* **1** vigorous, powerful. **2** compelling. □ **forcefully** *adv.* **forcefulness** *n.*

forceout *n. Baseball* (also **force play**) a play in which a runner is put out after being forced (by another runner) to advance.

forceps *n.* (*pl.* **forceps**) a surgical tool for grasping and holding.

forcible *adj.* done by force. □ **forcibly** *adv.*

ford ● *n.* a shallow place where a river or stream may be crossed. ● *v.* cross at a ford.

fore ● *adj.* situated in front. ● *n.* the front part. ● *interj. Golf* a warning to a person in the path of a ball. □ **to the fore** in front; conspicuous.

fore and aft ● *adv.* going from front to rear. ● *adj.* (**fore-and-aft**) **1** (of a sail) set lengthwise. **2** backwards and forwards.

forearm *n.* the part of the arm from the elbow to the wrist.

forebear *n.* (also **forbear**) (usu. in *pl.*) an ancestor. [Say FOR bare]

foreboding ● *n.* an expectation of trouble or evil. ● *adj.* threatening.

forecast ● *v.* (**forecasts**; *past* and *past participle* **forecast** or **forecasted**; **forecasting**) predict; estimate beforehand. ● *n.* a prediction or estimate. □ **forecaster** *n.* **forecasting** *n.*

forecastle *n.* (also **fo'c'sle**) the forward part of a ship below deck. [Say FOKE s'll]

forecheck *v. Hockey* play an aggressive style of defence. □ **forechecker** *n.* **forechecking** *n.*

foreclose *v.* (**forecloses**, **foreclosed**, **foreclosing**) **1** take control of someone's property because they have not paid their mortgage. **2** rule out; exclude. □ **foreclosure** *n.*

foredeck *n.* the deck at the forward part of a ship.

forefather *n.* (usu. in *pl.*) **1** an ancestor. **2** a member of a past generation of a people.

forefinger *n.* the finger next to the thumb.

forefoot *n.* (*pl.* **forefeet**) either of the front feet of an animal.

forefront *n.* **1** the foremost part. **2** the leading position.

foregoing *adj.* previously mentioned.

foregone conclusion *n.* an easily predictable result.

foreground ● *n.* **1** the part of a view or picture that is nearest the observer. **2** the most conspicuous position. ● *v.* place in the foreground.

forehand *n. Tennis etc.* a stroke played with the palm of the hand facing the opponent.

forehead *n.* the part of the face above the eyebrows.

foreign *adj.* **1** having to do with a country or a language other than one's own. **2** of another district, society, etc. **3** not familiar; strange. **4** coming from outside. □ **foreignness** *n.*

foreign affairs *pl. n.* the affairs of a nation that involve its relations with other nations.

foreign aid *n.* money, food, etc. given or lent by one country to another.

foreigner *n.* **1** a person from a foreign country. **2** *informal* a stranger or outsider.

foreign exchange *n.* the currency of other countries.

foreign legion *n.* a body of foreign volunteers in the French army.

foreign minister *n.* (also **foreign**

secretary) esp. *Brit.* a government minister in charge of foreign affairs.

foreign service *n.* the branch of a government concerned with the official representation of a country abroad by diplomats etc.

foreknow *v.* (**foreknows**; *past* **foreknew**; *past participle* **foreknown**; **foreknowing**) know beforehand.

foreknowledge *n.* knowledge of something before it happens

foreleg *n.* each of the front legs of a quadruped.

forelimb *n.* any of the front limbs of an animal.

forelock *n.* a lock of hair growing just above the forehead. □ **touch** (or **tug** etc.) **one's forelock** defer to a person of higher rank.

foreman *n.* (*pl.* **foremen**) **1** a worker with supervisory responsibilities. **2** the head of a jury who speaks on its behalf.

foremost ● *adj.* first in status or position. ● *adv.* in the first place.

forensic ● *adj.* **1** having to do with courts of law. **2** of or employing forensic science. ● *n.* (also **forensics**) **1** forensic science. **2** a forensic science department. [Say fuh REN zick]

forensic accounting *n.* the use of accounting skills to investigate matters of fraud, embezzlement, etc. □ **forensic accountant** *n.*

forensic science *n.* the application of scientific knowledge to the investigation of crime.

foreplay *n.* stimulation preceding sexual intercourse.

forerunner *n.* a person or thing that came before and influenced someone or something; a sign or portent.

foresee *v.* (**foresees**; *past* **foresaw**; *past participle* **foreseen**; **foreseeing**) be aware of beforehand. □ **foreseeable** *adj.*

foreshadow *v.* be a sign or warning of (a future event). □ **foreshadowing** *n.*

foreshore *n.* the part of the shore between high- and low-water marks, or between the water and cultivated or developed land.

foreshorten *v.* show or portray (an object) with the apparent shortening due to visual perspective. □ **foreshortening** *n.*

foresight *n.* the ability to predict and prepare for future events.

foreskin *n.* the fold of skin covering the end of the penis.

forest *n.* a large area covered chiefly with trees and undergrowth. ■ **not see the forest for the trees** be unable to perceive the overall situation because one

is preoccupied with details. □**forested** adj.
forestland n.

forestall v. **1** act in advance of to prevent
someone from doing something. **2** prevent
or obstruct something by taking action
ahead of time. [Say for STALL]

forester n. a person in charge of a forest or
skilled in forestry.

forest fire n. an uncontrolled fire in a
forest.

forest green n. & adj. a dark green colour.

forest ranger n. an official who patrols
and protects a public forest.

forestry n. the science and practice of
planting, caring for, and managing forests.

foretaste n. a sample of something that
lies ahead.

foretell v. (**foretells**; **foretold**;
foretelling) predict or presage.

forethought n. careful thought to make
sure that things are successful in the
future.

forever ● adv. **1** for all future time.
2 continually. **3** informal for an extremely
long time. ● n. informal a very long time.

forevermore adv. an emphatic form of
FOREVER adv. 1.

forewarn v. warn beforehand.
□**forewarned is forearmed** knowing
about problems etc. beforehand makes one
better prepared for them.

foreword n. introductory remarks at the
beginning of a book.

forfeit ● n. **1** a fine or penalty for
wrongdoing. **2** something surrendered as a
penalty. **3** the process of forfeiting. ● adj.
lost or surrendered as a penalty. ● v.
(**forfeits**, **forfeited**, **forfeiting**) lose the
right to or have to pay as a penalty.
□**forfeiture** n. [Say FOR fit, FOR fit chur]

forgave past of FORGIVE.

forge¹ ● v. (**forges**, **forged**, **forging**)
1 produce a copy of (a document or
signature) for deceptive purposes. **2** create.
3 shape (esp. metal) by heating and
hammering. ● n. **1** a blacksmith's
workshop. **2** a furnace for refining metal.
□**forger** n. **forging** n.

forge² v. (**forges**, **forged**, **forging**) move
forward gradually or steadily. □**forge
ahead 1** take the lead. **2** make progress
rapidly.

forgery n. (pl. **forgeries**) **1** the action of
forging, counterfeiting, or falsifying a
document etc. **2** a forged or spurious thing.

forget v. (**forgets**; past **forgot**; past
participle **forgotten** or **forgot**;
forgetting) **1** not remember.
2 inadvertently omit to do or mention.
3 cease to think of. □**forget (about) it!**

informal take no more notice of it. **forget
oneself** act in an unbecoming way.
□**forgettable** adj.

forgetful adj. apt to forget. □**forgetfully**
adj. **forgetfulness** n.

forget-me-not n. a low-growing plant
with small blue flowers.

forgive v. (**forgives**; past **forgave**; past
participle **forgiven**; **forgiving**) **1** cease to
feel angry or resentful towards. **2** pardon
or let off. □**forgivable** adj.
forgiveness n.

forgiving adj. **1** inclined to forgive.
2 tolerant.

forgo v. (**forgoes**; past **forwent**; past
participle **forgone**; **forgoing**) go without
(something desirable).

forgot past of FORGET.

forgotten past participle of FORGET.

fork ● n. **1** an implement with two or more
prongs used for holding food. **2** a similar
much larger instrument used for digging,
lifting, etc. **3** any pronged device or part.
4 a a divergence of anything into two parts,
or a confluence of two parts, esp. rivers,
into one. **b** the place where this occurs.
c either of the two parts. ● v. **1** divide into
two parts. **2** take one or the other road etc.
at a fork. **3** dig or lift etc. with a fork.
□**fork out** (or **up** or **over**) informal hand
over or pay.

forked adj. having a divided or pronged
end.

forked lightning n. a lightning flash in
the form of a zigzag or branching line.

forkful n. (pl. **forkfuls**) the amount that a
fork holds.

forklift n. (also **forklift truck**) a vehicle
with a horizontal fork for lifting and
carrying loads.

forlorn adj. **1** sad and lonely. **2** in a pitiful
state. **3** hopeless. □**forlornly** adv.
[Say for LORN]

form ● n. **1** shape. **2** the mode in which a
thing exists. **3 a** a kind. **b** an artistic or
literary genre. **4** a printed document with
blank spaces for information to be inserted.
5 what is usually done. **6** a formula.
7 behaviour according to custom. **8** (**the
form**) correct procedure. **9** condition of
health and training. **10** general state or
disposition. **11** formality. **12** a mould or
frame on which something is shaped. ● v.
1 make into or take a certain shape. **2** make
up or constitute. **3** train or instruct.
4 develop or establish. **5** embody, organize.
6 take shape or develop.

formal ● adj. **1** following rules or
conventions of behaviour etc. **2** ceremonial.
3 precise or symmetrical. **4** prim in

manner. **5** perfunctory. **6** explicit and definite. **7** (of education) officially given at a school etc. **8** of or concerned with (outward) form or appearance. ● *n.* **1** a dance etc. to which evening dress is worn. **2** an evening gown. □ **formally** *adv.*

formaldehyde *n.* a colourless, pungent, toxic gas used as a disinfectant and preservative. [*Say* for MALDA hide]

formalism *n.* a style in art, music, literature, etc. that pays more attention to rules and outward form than to inner meaning. □ **formalist** *n.*

formality *n.* (*pl.* **formalities**) **1 a** a formal or ceremonial act, regulation, or custom. **b** a thing done simply to follow a rule. **2** the rigid observance of rules or convention. **3** ceremony.

formalize *v.* (**formalizes, formalized, formalizing**) **1** give legal or formal status to. **2** give something a definite shape. □ **formalization** *n.*

format ● *n.* **1** the shape and size of a book etc. **2** the style of an arrangement, design or procedure. **3** *Computing* a defined structure for holding data etc. **4** the medium in which a recording is available. ● *v.* (**formats, formatted, formatting**) **1** arrange or put into a format. **2** *Computing* prepare (a storage medium) to receive data.

formation *n.* **1** the action of forming; the process of being formed. **2** a structure or arrangement. **3** a particular arrangement of troops, aircraft in flight, etc. **4** an assemblage of rocks.

formative *adj.* having a strong influence upon the development of.

former ● *adj.* **1** of or occurring in the past. **2** having been previously. ● *n.* (**the former**) the first or first mentioned of two (*opp.* LATTER *n.*).

formerly *adv.* in the past.

form-fitting *adj.* = CLOSE-FITTING.

Formica *n.* *proprietary* a hard durable plastic laminate used for working surfaces etc. [*Say* for MIKE uh]

formidable *adj.* inspiring fear or respect through being large, powerful, or capable. □ **formidably** *adv.* [*Say* for MIDDA bull *or* FOR midda bull]

formless *adj.* shapeless. □ **formlessness** *n.*

form letter *n.* a standardized letter.

formula *n.* (*pl.* **formulas** or (*esp.* in senses 1, 2) **formulae**) **1** a set of chemical symbols showing the constituents of a substance and their relative proportions. **2** a mathematical rule or law expressed in symbols. **3 a** a fixed form of words. **b** an established or conventional usage. **c** a

method for achieving or calculating something. **4 a** a list of ingredients with which something is made. **b** an infant's liquid food preparation. **5** a classification of race car. [*For* formulae *say* FOR mew lee]

formulaic *adj.* **1** containing a set form of words. **2** produced by closely following a rule or style. [*Say* for mew LAY ick]

formulate *v.* (**formulates, formulated, formulating**) **1** make according to a formula. **2** express clearly and precisely. **3** devise, create. □ **formulation** *n.*

fornicate *v.* (**fornicates, fornicated, fornicating**) have sexual intercourse with someone one is not married to. □ **fornication** *n.* **fornicator** *n.*

for-profit *adj.* designating an institution run to make a profit.

forsake *v.* (**forsakes**; *past* **forsook**; *past participle* **forsaken; forsaking**) **1** give up. **2** abandon.

forsythia *n.* an ornamental shrub bearing yellow flowers. [*Say* for SITH ee uh]

fort *n.* **1** a fortified building or position. **2** *hist.* a trading post.

forte[1] *n.* a thing in which a person excels. [*Say* FOR tay]

forte[2] ● *adj.* performed loudly. ● *adv.* loudly. [*Say* FOR tay]

forth *adv.* **1** forward; into view. **2** onward in time. **3** out from a starting point. □ **and so forth** and so on.

forthcoming *adj.* **1** about to appear or happen. **2** produced when wanted. **3** informative, responsive.

forthright *adj.* direct and outspoken. □ **forthrightly** *adv.* **forthrightness** *n.*

forthwith *adv.* immediately.

fortify *v.* (**fortifies, fortified, fortifying**) **1** provide with defensive works so as to strengthen against attack. **2** strengthen or invigorate; encourage. **3** strengthen the structure of. **4** strengthen (wine) with alcohol. **5** increase the nutritive value of. □ **fortification** *n.*

fortissimo *Music adj. & adv.* very loud or loudly. [*Say* for TISSA moe]

fortitude *n.* moral strength or courage.

fortnight *n.* a period of two weeks. □ **fortnightly** *adj. & adv.*

fortress *n.* (*pl.* **fortresses**) **1** a military stronghold. **2** any place of refuge, security, etc.

fortuitous *adj.* due to or characterized by chance. □ **fortuitously** *adv.* [*Say* for TOO it us *or* for TYOO it us]

fortunate *adj.* **1** lucky. **2** materially well off.

fortunately adv. **1** luckily, successfully. **2** it is fortunate that.

fortune n. **1 a** chance or luck as a force in human affairs. **b** a person's destiny. **2** (**Fortune**) this force personified. **3** luck (esp. favourable) that befalls a person or enterprise. **4** prosperity. **5** great wealth.

fortune cookie n. a small cookie containing a prediction, joke, etc.

fortune teller n. a person who claims to predict future events. □ **fortune-telling** n.

forty card. num. (pl. **forties**) the product of four and ten. □ **fortieth** ord. num.

forty-five n. **1** a small phonograph record played at 45 rpm. **2** a .45 calibre revolver.

fortyish adj. about forty (in age etc.).

forty-ninth parallel n. the parallel of latitude 49° north of the equator, esp. as forming the boundary between Canada and the US.

forum n. (pl. **forums**) **1** a meeting or medium for public discussion. **2** a court or tribunal. **3** hist. a public square or marketplace in an ancient Roman city.

forward ● adj. **1** directed or moving towards a point in advance. **2** situated in front; near or at the front (of a ship etc.). **3** bold in manner. **4** relating to the future. **5** progressing towards maturity or completion. ● n. a player positioned near the front of a team in hockey, soccer, etc. ● adv. **1 a** to the front. **b** into a position for consideration. **2** ahead. **3** onward. **4** towards the future. **5** (also **forwards**) towards the front in the direction one is facing. **6** Nautical & Aviation in, near, or towards the bow or nose. ● v. **1** send (a letter etc.) on to a further destination. **2** promote. **3** advance (a videotape etc.). □ **forwardness** n.

forwarder n. something that dispatches or delivers goods.

forward-looking adj. (also **forward-thinking**) progressive; favouring change.

forwent past of FORGO.

fossil ● n. **1** the remains or impression of a prehistoric plant or animal, usu. petrified. **2** informal an antiquated person or thing. ● adj. of or like a fossil.

fossil fuel n. a natural fuel such as coal or gas formed from the remains of living organisms.

fossilize v. (**fossilizes**, **fossilized**, **fossilizing**) **1** preserve (an animal or plant) so that it becomes a fossil. **2** become a fossil. □ **fossilization** n.

foster ● v. **1 a** promote the growth or development of. **b** encourage. **2** bring up (a child that is not one's own). **3** cherish.

● adj. involving or concerned with fostering a child.

fought past and past participle of FIGHT.

foul ● adj. **1** having a disgusting smell or taste; very unpleasant. **2** angry or disagreeable. **3 a** containing noxious matter. **b** clogged, choked. **4** morally offensive. **5 a** against the rules of a game etc. **b** Baseball relating to a foul ball. **6** (of the weather) bad. ● n. **1** Sport a violation of the rules. **2** a collision or entanglement. ● adv. **1** unfairly. **2** Baseball outside the foul lines. ● v. **1** make or become foul or dirty. **2** Baseball hit a foul ball. **3** Sport commit a foul. **4** become or cause to become entangled, jammed, etc. **5** informal spoil or bungle. □ **cry foul** protest. □ **foulness** n.

foul ball n. Baseball a ball struck so that it falls outside the foul lines.

foul line n. **1** Baseball a line marking the limit of the playing area. **2** Basketball a line on the court from which free throws are made.

foul-mouthed adj. using obscene and offensive language.

foul play n. **1** Sport unfair play. **2** treacherous or violent activity.

foul-up n. a bungled situation.

found¹ past and past participle of FIND.

found² v. **1 a** establish (esp. with an endowment). **b** originate (an institution etc.). **2** be the original builder of (a town etc.). **3** lay the base of. **4 a** be based on (a particular idea). **b** have a basis in.

found³ v. melt and mould metal or glass.

foundation n. **1** the solid base on which a building rests. **2** a base on which other parts are overlaid. **3** a basis or underlying principle. **4 a** the act of establishing (esp. an endowed institution). **b** an institution so founded or one maintained by an endowment. **c** an endowment. **5** a cosmetic applied to the face as a base for other makeup. □ **foundational** adj.

foundation stone n. a stone laid with ceremony to celebrate the founding of a building.

founder¹ n. a person who founds an institution etc.

founder² v. **1** (of a ship) fill with water and sink. **2** (of a plan etc.) fail. **3** fall to the ground, stick fast in mud etc.

founder³ n. the owner or operator of a foundry.

found-in n. Cdn a person arrested for being discovered in a brothel etc.

founding father n. a founder.

foundling n. an abandoned infant of unknown parentage.

foundry *n.* (*pl.* **foundries**) a factory where metal is melted and moulded.

fount *n.* a source of a desirable quality.

fountain *n.* **1 a** a spray or sprays of water made to spout for ornamental purposes. **b** a structure built for this. **2** a structure for the public supply of drinking water. **3** a source

fountainhead *n.* a source or origin.

fountain pen *n.* a pen with a reservoir holding ink.

four *card. num.* one more than three. □ **on all fours** on hands and knees. □ **fourfold** *adj. & adv.*

four-by-four *n.* (also **4 × 4** *pl.* **4 × 4s**) **1** a four-wheeled vehicle with four-wheel drive. **2** wood measuring four inches by four in cross-section.

4-H club *n.* a club for the instruction of young people in citizenry and agriculture.

four-letter word *n.* a short word regarded as coarse or offensive.

four-poster *n.* (also **four-poster bed**) a bed with a post at each corner supporting a canopy.

foursome *n.* **1** a group of four persons. **2** a golf match between two pairs.

four-square ● *adj.* **1** (of a building etc.) square in shape, solid, and strong. **2** (of a person) firm, determined. ● *adv.* resolutely.

four-star *adj.* (of a hotel etc.) given four stars in a grading in which this denotes the highest or second-highest standard.

four-stroke ● *adj.* (of an internal combustion engine) having a cycle of four strokes. ● *n.* a four-stroke engine or vehicle.

fourteen *card. num.* one more than thirteen. □ **fourteenth** *ord. num.*

fourth *ord. num.* **1** corresponding to the number 4 in a sequence. **2** a quarter. **3** an interval or chord spanning four consecutive notes in a scale. □ **fourthly** *adv.*

fourth estate *n.* (also **Fourth Estate**) the press.

four-wheel drive *n.* a system in a motor vehicle which supplies power to all wheels.

four-wheeler *n. slang* **1** a four-wheeled all-terrain vehicle. **2** = FOUR-BY-FOUR 1.

fowl (*pl.* **fowl** or **fowls**) ● *n.* **1** a domestic bird kept for eggs and meat. **2** the flesh of birds as food. **3** a bird or birds collectively. ● *v.* catch or hunt wildfowl.

fowl supper *n.* (also **fall supper**) *Cdn* a fundraising dinner at a church etc., often serving poultry.

fox ● *n.* (*pl.* **foxes**) **1** a dog-like animal with a sharp snout, bushy tail, and usu. red or grey fur. **2** a cunning or sly person. **3** *slang* an attractive young woman. ● *v.* (**foxes**, **foxed**, **foxing**) deceive, baffle, trick.

foxglove *n.* a tall plant with flowers resembling the fingers of a glove.

foxhole *n.* a hole used as a shelter against enemy fire.

foxhound *n.* a kind of hound bred and trained to hunt foxes.

foxlike *adj.* **1** resembling a fox. **2** crafty, cunning.

fox terrier *n.* a short-haired terrier originally used for unearthing foxes.

foxtrot ● *n.* a ballroom dance involving combinations of slow and quick steps. ● *v.* (**foxtrots**, **foxtrotted**, **foxtrotting**) perform this dance.

foxy *adj.* (**foxier**, **foxiest**) **1** of or like a fox. **2** sly or cunning. **3** reddish brown. **4** *slang* sexually attractive. □ **foxiness** *n.*

foyer *n.* an entrance hall in a hotel, theatre, etc. [*Say* FOY ay]

Fr. *abbr.* Father.

fracas *n.* (*pl.* **fracases**) a noisy disturbance or quarrel. [*Say* FRACK us]

fractal *Math* ● *n.* a curve or geometrical figure, each part of which has the same statistical character as the whole. ● *adj.* of a fractal. [*Say* FRACK t'll]

fraction *n.* **1** a number that is not a whole number (e.g. $1/2$, 0.5). **2** a small part or amount. **3** a subdivision of a whole. **4** a portion of a mixture separated by distillation etc.

fractional *adj.* **1** having to do with a fraction. **2** very slight. □ **fractionally** *adv.* (esp. in sense 2).

fractious *adj.* **1** bad-tempered. **2** difficult to control. □ **fractiousness** *n.* [*Say* FRACK shuss]

fracture ● *n.* breakage or breaking, esp. of a bone; a crack or split. ● *v.* (**fractures**, **fractured**, **fracturing**) **1** undergo or cause to undergo a fracture. **2** break or cause to break. **3** (of a group) split into several parts.

fragile *adj.* **1** easily broken. **2** delicate; not strong. **3** vulnerable. □ **fragility** *n.*

fragment ● *n.* **1** a part broken off; a detached piece. **2** an incomplete part. **3** the remains of an otherwise lost or destroyed whole. ● *v.* break or separate into fragments. □ **fragmentary** *adj.* **fragmentation** *n.*

fragrance *n.* **1** a sweet scent. **2** something scented, esp. a perfume etc. [*Say* FRAY grince]

fragrant *adj.* pleasant smelling. □ **fragrantly** *adv.* [*Say* FRAY grint]

frail *adj.* **1** physically weak or delicate. **2** easily damaged or broken. **3** morally weak.

frailty *n.* (*pl.* **frailties**) **1** the condition of being frail. **2** weakness in character or morals.

frame ● *n.* **1** a case or border enclosing a picture, window, etc. **2** the basic rigid supporting structure of anything, e.g. of a building. **3** (in *pl.*) a structure of metal, plastic, etc. holding the lenses of a pair of eyeglasses. **4** a human or animal body. **5** the underlying structure that supports a system or idea. **6** a mental state (esp. in **frame of mind**). **7 a** a single complete image or picture on a cinema film. **b** one of the separate drawings of a comic strip. **8** *Sport informal* an inning, period, etc. **9** any of the ten divisions of a bowling game. ● *v.* (**frames, framed, framing**) **1 a** set in or provide with a frame. **b** serve as a frame for. **2** create or develop (a plan or system). **3** formulate or devise the essentials of. **4** *informal* concoct a false charge or evidence against. **5** articulate (words). ● *adj.* (of a house) made of a wooden frame covered with boards etc. □ **framer** *n.*

frame of reference *n.* a set of standards governing behaviour, judgments, etc.

framework *n.* **1** an essential supporting structure. **2** a basic system.

framing *n.* **1** a framework. **2** the act of framing something.

franc *n.* the chief monetary unit of Switzerland and several other countries (formerly also of France and Belgium).

franchise ● *n.* **1** the right to vote in elections. **2 a** authorization granted to a person or group by a company to sell its goods or services, or by a sports league to operate a team as a member of the league. **b** the business or team granted such authorization. **3** a series of films featuring one or more of the same characters and similar formulaic plots, usually accompanied by various marketing spinoffs. ● *v.* (**franchises, franchised, franchising**) grant a franchise to. □ **franchisee** *n.* **franchisor** *n.* (also **franchiser**)

Franciscan ● *n.* a monk or nun of an order founded by St. Francis of Assisi (c.1181–1226). ● *adj.* of St. Francis or his order. [*Say* fran SIS k'n]

Franco- *comb. form* **1** French; French and; francophone. **2** (**franco-**) regarding France, the French, or French-speakers.

francophile *n.* a person who admires French or francophone culture. □ **francophilia** *n.* [*Say* FRANCO file, franco FILLY uh]

francophone esp. *Cdn* ● *n.* a French-speaking person. ● *adj.* French-speaking.

Francophonie *n. Cdn* **1** (also **la Francophonie, the Francophonie**) a loosely united group of nations in which French is an official or important language. **2** (also **francophonie**) francophones within Canada. [*Say* frank oh foe NEE]

franglais *n.* often *derogatory* **1** a blend of French and English. **2** broken French as spoken by anglophones. [*Say* frong GLAY]

Frank *n.* a member of a Germanic nation that conquered Gaul in the 6th century. □ **Frankish** *adj.*

frank[1] ● *adj.* **1** candid, outspoken. **2** undisguised. ● *v.* stamp (a letter) with an official mark to record the payment of postage. □ **frankness** *n.*

frank[2] *n.* = FRANKFURTER.

Frankenstein *n.* a thing that becomes terrifying to its maker.

frankfurter *n.* a seasoned smoked sausage made of beef and pork.

frankincense *n.* an aromatic substance obtained from trees, used as incense. [*Say* FRANK in sense]

Franklin stove *n.* a cast iron wood stove resembling a fireplace, usu. having doors on the front.

frankly *adv.* **1** in a frank manner. **2** to be frank.

frantic *adj.* **1** wildly excited; frenzied. **2** characterized by great hurry or anxiety. □ **frantically** *adv.*

frat *n. informal* a fraternity.

fraternal *adj.* **1** of or like or suitable to a brother. **2** (of twins) developed from separate ova and therefore not identical. **3** of or concerning a fraternity etc.

fraternity *n.* (*pl.* **fraternities**) **1** a male students' society in a university or college. **2** a religious brotherhood. **3** a group or company with common interests, profession, etc.

fraternize *v.* (**fraternizes, fraternized, fraternizing**) behave in a friendly manner, especially towards someone considered an enemy etc. □ **fraternization** *n.* [*Say* FRATTER nize]

fratricide *n.* **1** the killing of one's brother or sister. **2** a person who does this. **3** the killing of a member of one's own ethnic group, culture, etc. □ **fratricidal** *adj.* [*Say* FRATRA side, fratra SIDE ul]

fraud *n.* **1** criminal deception intended to result in financial or personal gain. **2** a person or thing that is not what it is claimed to be. **3** a dishonest trick. [*Say* FROD]

fraudulent *adj.* intended to deceive someone; involving fraud. □ **fraudulence** *n.* **fraudulently** *adv.* [*Say* FROD you lint, FROD you lince]

fraught adj. **1** filled with (something undesirable). **2** informal causing or affected by great anxiety or distress. [Say FROT]

fray[1] v. **1** (of fabric, rope, etc.) wear through or become worn; unravel. **2** (of nerves etc.) become strained.

fray[2] n. **1** conflict, fighting. **2** a noisy quarrel or brawl.

frazil n. (also **frazil ice**) slushy ice formed in water too turbulent to freeze over. [Say FRAZZLE]

frazzle v. (**frazzles**, **frazzled**, **frazzling**) informal **1** wear out; exhaust. **2** char. □ **to a frazzle** completely; absolutely.

freak ● n. **1** (also **freak of nature**) an abnormally developed individual or thing. **2** an abnormal or bizarre occurrence. **3** informal a an unconventional person. **b** a person with a specified interest. ● v. informal become or make very angry, frightened, etc.

freaking adj. euphemism expressing annoyance.

freakish adj. very strange, unusual. □ **freakishly** adv.

freak-out n. informal an act of freaking out.

freak show n. a sideshow at a fair, featuring people or animals with abnormal features.

freaky adj. (**freakier**, **freakiest**) very odd or eccentric.

freckle ● n. any of a number of light brown spots on the skin. ● v. (**freckles**, **freckled**, **freckling**) spot or be spotted with freckles. □ **freckly** adj.

free ● adj. (**freer**; **freest**) **1** not under the control of another; able to do what one wants. **2** subject neither to foreign domination nor to despotic government. **3 a** unrestricted, unimpeded. **b** at liberty. **c** independent. **4 a** exempt from. **b** not containing or subject to a specified thing. **5** able to take a specified action. **6** unconstrained. **7 a** available without charge. **b** not subject to tax, duty, etc. **8 a** clear of obligations **b** not occupied. **9** lavish, profuse. **10** not observing the strict laws of form; not literal. ● adv. **1** in a free manner. **2** without cost or payment. ● v. (**frees**, **freed**, **freeing**) **1** make free; set at liberty. **2** relieve from. **3** disengage, disentangle. □ **for free** informal free of charge. **free and easy** informal, unceremonious. **free up** informal **1** make available. **2** make less restricted. **it's a free country** informal the action proposed is not illegal or forbidden.

-free comb. form free of or from.

free agent n. **1** a person with freedom of action. **2** a professional athlete who is not under contract to a team. □ **free agency** n.

free association n. any process in which one thought, word, image, etc. suggests the next without following a logical or conscious direction.

freebase slang ● n. cocaine that has been purified by heating with ether. ● v. (**freebases**, **freebased**, **freebasing**) **1** purify (cocaine) for smoking or inhaling. **2** smoke or inhale (freebased cocaine).

freebie informal ● n. a thing provided free of charge. ● adj. free.

freeboard n. the part of a ship's side between the waterline and the deck.

Free Church n. a Church seceding from an established church.

freedom n. **1** the condition of being free. **2 a** personal or civic liberty. **b** absence of slave status. **3** the power of self-determination. **4** the state of being free to act, speak, etc. **5** the condition of being exempt from or not subject to. **6 a** full or honorary participation in. **b** unrestricted use of.

freedom fighter n. a person who takes part in violent resistance to a political system etc.

free enterprise n. a system in which private business operates in competition and largely free of governmental control. □ **free enterpriser** n.

free fall ● n. **1** downward movement under the force of gravity only. **2** any state of falling rapidly. ● v. (**free-fall**, **free-falls**, **free-fell**, **free-falling**) move in a free fall.

free-floating adj. **1** (of an emotion) having no particular cause. **2** (of people) not committed to any particular cause, party, etc.

free-for-all n. (pl. **free-for-alls**) a fight etc. in which many people take part, usu. having no rules.

free-form adj. not in a regular or formal shape or structure.

freehand ● adj. done by hand without special instruments or guides. ● adv. in a freehand manner.

free hand n. freedom to act at one's own discretion.

freehold n. **1** permanent and absolute tenure of land or property with freedom to sell it. **2** land or property held by such tenure. □ **freehold** adj. **freeholder** n.

free kick n. Soccer a set kick allowed to be taken without interference.

freelance ● n. (also **freelancer**) a person offering services on a temporary basis. ● v. (**freelances**, **freelanced**, freelancing) act as a freelance. ● *adv.* as a freelance.

freeloader *n. slang* a person who eats or drinks at others' expense; a sponger. □**freeload** *v.* **freeloading** *n.*

free love *n.* sexual relations unrestricted by marriage.

free lunch *n.* □**there's no (such thing as a) free lunch** nothing is without cost.

freely *adv.* **1** not under the control of another. **2 a** without restriction. **b** in copious amounts. **3** openly and honestly. **4** willingly and readily.

freeman *n.* (*pl.* **freemen**) a person who is not a slave or serf.

free market *n.* a market in which prices are determined by supply and demand. □**free marketeer** *n.*

Freemason *n.* a member of an international fraternity for mutual help and fellowship (the *Free and Accepted Masons*). □**Freemasonry** *n.* [*Say* FREE may sun]

freer *comparative of* FREE.

free radical *n.* an atom without a charge and with one or more unpaired electrons.

free-range *adj.* **1** (of hens etc.) kept in natural conditions with freedom of movement. **2** (of eggs) produced by such birds.

free ride ● *n.* **1** something obtained at no cost or with no effort. **2** (**freeride**) a type of snowboard designed for use on and off piste. ● *v.* snowboard, esp. off the major runs, for fun rather than competition. □**free rider** *n.*

free safety *n. Football* a secondary defensive player who has no assigned position at the snap of the ball.

freesia *n.* a bulbous plant native to Africa, with fragrant coloured flowers. [*Say* FREE zhuh *or* FREEZY uh]

free skate *n.* (also **free skating program**) a part of a figure skating competition in which the elements of a program are chosen freely by the skater.

free speech *n.* the right to express opinions freely.

free spirit *n.* an independent or uninhibited person. □**free-spirited** *adj.*

freest *superlative of* FREE.

free-standing *adj.* **1** not supported by another structure. **2** autonomous.

freestone *n.* a peach or other fruit having a stone to which the flesh does not cling.

freestyle ● *adj.* (of a race or contest) in which all styles are allowed. ● *n.* **1** freestyle swimming or wrestling. **2** the front crawl. □**freestyler** *n.*

free-swimming *adj.* (of an aquatic

organism) capable of swimming around freely; not fixed in one position or attached to any object.

freethinker *n.* a person who rejects dogma or authority. □**freethinking** *n.* & *adj.*

free throw *n. Sport* an unimpeded throw awarded to a player following a foul etc.

free trade *n.* international trade free from protectionist tariffs, quotas, etc. □**free trader** *n.*

free verse *n.* poetry which doesn't rhyme or have a regular rhythm.

free vote *n.* a parliamentary vote in which MPs are not constrained to vote along party lines.

freeware *n.* software available without charge.

freeway *n.* **1** = EXPRESSWAY. **2** a toll-free highway.

free weight *n.* a barbell or other weight not attached to a machine.

freewheeling *adj.* not hampered by rules or responsibilities; allowed to run freely.

free will ● *n.* **1** the power to make one's own decisions without being controlled by fate. **2** the ability to act at one's own discretion. ● *adj.* (usu. **free-will**) voluntary.

freeze ● *v.* (**freezes**; *past* **froze**; *past participle* **frozen**; **freezing**) **1** turn or be turned into ice or another solid by cold. **2** be or feel very cold. **3** cover or become covered with ice. **4** adhere or be fastened by frost. **5** become or make blocked or rigid by ice. **6** preserve (food) by refrigeration below freezing point. **7 a** become motionless through fear, surprise, etc. **b** treat with sudden aloofness or detachment. **8** *informal* make (part of the body) insensitive to pain. **9** prevent (assets etc.) from being converted into money. **10** fix (prices etc.) at a certain level. **11** (of a computer screen) cease to respond. ● *n.* **1** a state of frost or very cold weather. **2** an act of freezing. □**freeze out** *informal* exclude from business, society, etc. **freeze up** obstruct or be obstructed by the formation of ice.

freeze-dry *v.* (**freeze-dries**, **freeze-dried**, **freeze-drying**) preserve by freezing and then drying in a vacuum.

freeze-frame ● *n.* (also as an *adj.*) the facility of stopping a film or videotape to view a motionless image. ● *v.* (**freeze-frames**, **freeze-framed**, **freeze-framing**) use freeze-frame on.

freezer *n.* a refrigerated cabinet or room for preserving food at very low temperatures.

freeze-up *n.* esp. *Cdn* the freezing up of a river, lake, etc.

freezing *adj.* **1** (of temperatures) at or near the freezing point. **2** *informal* (also **freezing cold**) very cold.

freezing point *n.* the temperature at which a liquid, esp. water, freezes.

freezing rain *n.* rain that freezes on impact.

freight ● *n.* **1** goods transported by water, air, or land. **2** the transportation of such goods. **3** a charge for transportation of goods. ● *v.* **1** transport as freight. **2** fill with esp. too much of a particular mood or tone. [*Say* FRATE]

freighter *n.* a ship or aircraft designed to carry freight. [*Say* FRATE er]

French ● *adj.* **1** of or relating to France or its people or language. **2** of or relating to French Canada or French Canadians. ● *n.* **1** the language of France, also used in Canada, Belgium, Switzerland, etc. **2** (**the French**) (treated as *pl.*) **a** the people of France. **b** the people of French Canada. □ **pardon** (or **excuse**) **my French** *informal* excuse my use of coarse language. □ **Frenchness** *n.*

French bread *n.* a long loaf of white bread with a crisp crust.

French Canadian ● *n.* a Canadian whose principal language is French. ● *adj.* (**French-Canadian**) of or relating to French-speaking Canadians.

French door *n.* a long glass door, usu. opening onto a patio or balcony.

French dressing *n.* **1** a creamy, sweet salad dressing, usu. orange in colour. **2** a salad dressing of vinegar and oil, usu. seasoned.

French fact *n. Cdn* (**the French fact**) francophone culture as a distinct component of Canadian society.

French French *Cdn* ● *n.* the French language as spoken in France. ● *adj.* (**French-French**) of or relating to the French people or language of France.

french fry *n.* (*pl.* **french fries**) a strip of potato which has been deep-fried. □ **french-fried** *adj.*

French horn *n.* a valved brass wind instrument with a long, coiled tube and a wide bell.

Frenchify *v.* (**Frenchifies, Frenchified, Frenchifying**) make French in form, character, or manners.

French immersion *n. Cdn* an educational program in which anglophone students are taught entirely in French.

French kiss *n.* a kiss with contact between tongues. □ **French kiss** *v.* (**French kisses, French kissed, French kissing**)

Frenchman *n.* (*pl.* **Frenchmen**) **1** a native or national of France. **2** a francophone.

French regime *n.* the period of French rule in Canadian history, until 1763.

French toast *n.* bread dipped in egg and milk and fried.

French window *n.* = FRENCH DOOR.

Frenchwoman *n.* (*pl.* **Frenchwomen**) **1** a female person from France. **2** a francophone woman.

frenetic *adj.* frantic, frenzied. □ **frenetically** *adv.* [*Say* fruh NET ick]

frenzy *n.* (*pl.* **frenzies**) a state or period of uncontrolled excitement or behaviour. □ **frenzied** *adj.*

Freon *n. proprietary* any of a group of hydrocarbons containing fluorine, chlorine, and sometimes bromine. [*Say* FREE on]

frequency *n.* (*pl.* **frequencies**) **1** the rate at which something happens or is repeated. **2** the state of being frequent. **3 a** *Physics* the rate of recurrence of a vibration, cycle, etc.; the number of repetitions in a given time. **b** the number of cycles per second of a radio wave. **c** a radio channel.

frequency modulation *n.* **1** variation of the frequency of a wave as a way of broadcasting an audio signal by radio. **2** the system using this. Abbreviation: **FM**.

frequent ● *adj.* **1** occurring often or in close succession. **2** habitual, constant. ● *v.* attend or go to habitually. □ **frequently** *adv.* [*Say* FREE quint; *for the verb you can also say* free QUENT]

fresco *n.* (*pl.* **frescoes**) **1** a painting done in watercolour on a wall or ceiling while the plaster is still wet. **2** this method of painting. □ **frescoed** *adj.*

fresh ● *adj.* **1** new. **2 a** other, different. **b** additional. **3** lately arrived from. **4** recently made; not stale or faded. **5 a** (of food) not preserved by drying, freezing, etc. **b** not cooked. **6** not salty. **7** pure, untainted. **8** (of the wind) brisk. **9** *informal* cheeky, presumptuous. ● *adv.* newly, recently. □ **fresh out of 1** recently out of. **2** having just run out of. □ **freshly** *adv.* **freshness** *n.*

freshen *v.* make something fresh or fresher. □ **freshen up** refresh oneself by washing etc. □ **freshener** *n.*

freshet *n.* **1** a rush of fresh water flowing into the sea. **2** the flood of a river from heavy rain or melted snow. [*Say* FRESH it]

fresh-faced *adj.* having a clear and young-looking complexion.

freshman ● *n.* (*pl.* **freshmen**) a first-year

student at university, high school, etc.
● *adj.* **1** of or relating to a freshman.
2 requisite or suitable for first-year students. **3** inexperienced. **4** first.

freshwater *adj.* of or found in fresh water.

fret¹ *v.* (**frets, fretted, fretting**) **1** feel or express anxiety. **2** cause anxiety to.

fret² *n.* each of a sequence of ridges on the fingerboard of some stringed instruments, used to produce the desired notes. □ **fretted** *adj.*

fretboard *n.* a fretted fingerboard on a guitar etc.

fretful *adj.* anxious. □ **fretfully** *adv.* **fretfulness** *n.*

fretwork *n.* patterns cut into wood, metal, etc.

Freudian ● *adj.* **1** relating to Sigmund Freud and his methods of psychoanalysis. **2** possibly revealing one's subconscious thoughts. ● *n.* a follower of Freud or his methods. □ **Freudianism** *n.* [*Say* FROY dee un]

Freudian slip *n.* an unintentional, esp. spoken error that seems to reveal subconscious feelings.

Fri. *abbr.* Friday.

friable *adj.* easily crumbled. [*Say* FRY a bull]

friar *n.* a member of certain religious orders of men.

fricassee ● *n.* a dish of cut white meat served in a thick white sauce. ● *v.* (**fricassees, fricasseed, fricasseeing**) make a fricassee of. [*Say* FRICKA see]

friction *n.* **1** the action of one surface rubbing against another. **2** the resistance an object or surface encounters in moving over another. **3** a conflict or disagreement. □ **frictional** *adj.* **frictionless** *adj.*

Friday ● *n.* the sixth day of the week, following Thursday. ● *adv.* **1** on Friday. **2** (**Fridays**) each Friday.

fridge *n. informal* = REFRIGERATOR 1.

fried ● *adj.* **1** cooked by frying. **2** *informal* exhausted. **3** *slang* intoxicated. ● *v. past and past participle of* FRY¹.

friend *n.* **1** a person with whom one enjoys mutual affection and regard. **2** a sympathizer. **3** an ally, sympathizer, or patron. **4** a romantic or sexual partner. **5** an acquaintance. □ **be friends (with)** be on good or intimate terms (with). □ **friendless** *adj.* **friendship** *n.*

friendly *adj.* (**friendlier, friendliest**) **1** acting kindly. **2 a** on amicable terms. **b** not seriously competitive. **3** (esp. in *comb.*) not harming; helping. □ **friendliness** *n.*

friendship centre *n. Cdn* an institution

providing counselling etc. to Aboriginal people.

frieze *n.* a broad horizontal band of sculpted or painted decoration. [*Sounds like* FREEZE]

frigate *n. Cdn & Brit.* a warship with mixed weapons and equipment. [*Say* FRIG it]

fright *n.* **1** sudden or extreme fear. **2** a shock. **3** a grotesque person. □ **take fright** become frightened.

frighten *v.* be or cause to be afraid. □ **frightening** *adj.* **frighteningly** *adv.*

frightful *adj.* **1** shocking. **2** *informal* extremely bad. □ **frightfully** *adv.* **frightfulness** *n.*

frigid *adj.* **1** extremely cold. **2** (of a woman) unable to be sexually aroused. **3** lacking friendliness. □ **frigidity** *n.* **frigidly** *adv.* [*Say* FRIDGE id, fruh JIDDA tee]

frill *n.* **1** a strip of gathered or pleated material used as a decorative edging. **2** an optional extra that is not essential. □ **frilled** *adj.* **frilly** *adj.*

fringe *n.* **1** an ornamental border of threads, tassels, or twists. **2** a natural border of hair etc. in an animal or plant. **3 a** the outer edge of something. **b** (also as an *adj.*) something non-mainstream. □ **fringed** *adj.*

fringe benefit *n.* an extra benefit given to an employee.

frippery *n.* (*pl.* **fripperies**) an unnecessary or frivolous item.

Frisbee *n. proprietary* a concave plastic disc for skimming through the air as an outdoor game.

frisk ● *v.* **1** search (a person) by feeling quickly over the body. **2** skip or frolic playfully. ● *n.* the act of frisking.

frisky *adj.* (**friskier, friskiest**) **1** lively. **2** *informal* amorous, sexually excited.

frisson *n.* an emotional thrill. [*Say* FREE sawn]

frittata *n.* (*pl.* **frittatas**) an omelette fried with chopped vegetables, meat, etc. [*Say* fruh TATTA]

fritter¹ *v.* (usu. foll. by *away*) waste (money, time, etc.) triflingly.

fritter² *n.* a piece of food coated in batter and deep-fried.

fritz *n.* □ **on the fritz** *slang* broken, defective.

friulano *n. Cdn* a mild, pale yellow, firm cow's-milk cheese. [*Say* free oo LAN oh]

frivolous *adj.* **1 a** silly or wasteful. **b** having no reasonable grounds. **2** foolish, lighthearted. □ **frivolity** *n.* **frivolously** *adv.* [*Say* FRIVVA luss]

frizz • v. (**frizzes, frizzed, frizzing**) form into tight curls. • n. frizzy hair. □ **frizzy** adj.

frizzle • v. (**frizzles, frizzled, frizzling**) **1 a** fry with a sputtering noise. **b** burn. **2** form into tight curls. • n. frizzled hair.

frock n. **1** a monk's or priest's long gown. **2** Brit. a dress.

frock coat n. a usu. double-breasted, long-skirted coat.

frog n. a tailless amphibian with a smooth-skinned body and long legs for jumping. □ **frog in the** (or **one's**) **throat** informal hoarseness. □ **froggy** adj.

frogman n. (pl. **frogmen**) a scuba diver engaged in police or military operations.

frolic • v. (**frolics, frolicked, frolicking**) play about cheerfully. • n. fun, or a fun activity.

from prep. expressing separation or origin.

frond n. the leaf or leaflike part of a palm, fern, or similar plant.

front • n. **1 a** the part of an object that normally presents itself to view or that is normally seen first. **b** the forward-facing part. **c** a position directly ahead. **2 a** face of a building. **3** a main area of fighting in a war. **4** the forward edge of an advancing mass of air. **5** an organized political group. **6** a leading or conspicuous position. **7 a** a false appearance or pretext. **b** something serving as a cover for illegal activities etc. • adj. **1** relating to the front. **2** situated in front. • v. **1** have the front facing a specific direction. **2** (foll. by for) slang act as a front for. **3** furnish with a facing. **4** present or lead. **5** face. □ **in front 1** in the lead. **2** in a position exactly ahead. **in front of 1** ahead of. **2** in the presence of.

frontage n. **1 a** the front of a building. **b** the extent of this. **2** land abutting on a street or on water.

frontal adj. **1** of, at, or on the front. **2** of the front part of the skull. □ **frontally** adv.

frontal lobe n. each of the paired lobes of the brain lying behind the forehead.

front bench n. the seats in Parliament occupied by leading members of the government and opposition. □ **front-bencher** n.

Front de Libération du Québec n. (in Canada) a Quebec separatist terrorist organization esp. active in the 1960s and early 1970s. Abbreviation: **FLQ**. [Say FRON duh lee bay rass YON doo kay BECK]

front end n. **1** the forward part of something. **2** (**front-end**) that part of a computer system that a user deals with directly. **3** (**front-end**) designating charges at the beginning of a transaction.

front-end loader n. a machine with a scoop at the front for digging and loading dirt etc.

frontier • n. **1** the border between two countries. **2** the limits of understanding. **3** the extreme limit of settled land. • adj. relating to the frontier. [Say frun TEER or frawn TEER]

frontiersman n. (pl. **frontiersmen**) a man living on or beyond a frontier.

frontispiece n. an illustration facing the title page of a book etc. [Say FRUN tiss piece]

front line n. **1 a** the line of fighting closest to the enemy. **b** a position closest to a crisis. **2** the most important position.

front-runner n. the candidate, contestant, etc. leading or most likely to succeed. □ **front-running** adj.

front-wheel drive n. a drive system in a car etc. in which power operates through the front wheels.

frosh n. (pl. **frosh**) slang = FRESHMAN n.

frost • n. **1** a deposit of tiny ice crystals formed on surfaces when the temperature falls below the freezing point. **2** a period of cold weather causing frost to form. • v. **1** (usu. foll. by over, up) become covered with frost. **2 a** cover with or as if with frost, powder, etc. **b** freeze. **3** decorate (a cake etc.) with icing.

frostbite n. injury to body tissues caused by intense cold. □ **frostbitten** adj.

frosted adj. **1** covered with frost. **2** (of glass or a window) having a translucent textured surface so that it is difficult to see through. **3** decorated or dusted with icing or sugar.

Frost fence n. Cdn proprietary a chain-link fence.

frost-free adj. **1** experiencing no frost. **2** able to defrost automatically.

frosting n. **1** icing for a cake etc. **2** a rough surface on glass etc. **3** a hair treatment that produces highlights.

frosty adj. (**frostier, frostiest**) **1** very cold. **2** covered with hoarfrost. **3** unfriendly. □ **frostily** adv.

froth • n. **1** a mass of small bubbles on liquid. **2** worthless talk and ideas. • v. form or emit froth.

frothy adj. (**frothier, frothiest**) **1** full of froth. **2** entertaining but insubstantial.

frown • v. **1 a** furrow one's brow to show anger, worry, or deep thought. **b** make a glum expression by turning down the corners of the mouth. **2** express disapproval. • n. a facial expression of worry, thoughtfulness, etc.

froze past of FREEZE.

frozen past participle of FREEZE.

fructose *n.* a simple sugar found in honey and fruits. [*Say* FROOK tose]

frugal *adj.* **1** thrifty. **2** plain and not excessive. □ **frugality** *n.* **frugally** *adv.* [*Say* FROO gull, froo GALA tee]

fruit ● *n.* **1 a** the usu. sweet and fleshy edible product of a plant or tree, containing seed. **b** (in *sing.*) these in quantity. **2** the seed-bearing part of a plant, e.g. an acorn. **3** (usu. in *pl.*) a product of activity. ● *v.* produce fruit. □ **fruiting** *adj.*

fruit bat *n.* a bat with a large snout and large eyes that feeds chiefly on fruit.

fruitcake *n.* **1** a cake containing much dried fruit etc. **2** *slang* an eccentric person.

fruit cocktail *n.* = FRUIT SALAD.

fruit fly *n.* a small fly that feeds on fruit.

fruitful *adj.* **1 a** producing much fruit. **b** fertile. **2** producing good results. □ **fruitfully** *adv.* **fruitfulness** *n.*

fruition *n.* the fulfillment of a plan or project. [*Say* froo ISH un]

fruitless *adj.* **1** useless, unsuccessful. **2** not bearing fruit. □ **fruitlessly** *adv.*

fruit salad *n.* various fruits cut up and served in syrup, juice, etc.

fruity *adj.* (**fruitier, fruitiest**) **1** relating to or resembling fruit. **2** (of a voice etc.) mellow. □ **fruitiness** *n.*

frump *n.* a dowdy, not attractive woman. □ **frumpily** *adv.* **frumpiness** *n.* **frumpy** *adj.* (**frumpier, frumpiest**)

frustrate *v.* (**frustrates, frustrated, frustrating**) **1** upset or discourage. **2** make (efforts) ineffective. **3** prevent (a person) from achieving a purpose. □ **frustrated** *adj.* **frustrating** *adj.* **frustratingly** *adv.* **frustration** *n.*

fry¹ ● *v.* (**fries, fried, frying**) **1** cook or be cooked in hot fat. **2** *informal* overload (electronic components etc.). **3** *slang* electrocute or be electrocuted. **4** *informal* burn or overheat. **5** *slang* destroy. ● *n.* (*pl.* **fries**) **1** (**fries**) french fries. **2** a dish of fried food, esp. meat.

fry² *pl. n.* **1** newly hatched fish. **2** the young of other creatures produced in large numbers, e.g. bees or frogs.

fryer *n.* **1** a pot etc. for frying food in deep fat. **2** a person who fries. **3** a chicken suitable for frying.

frying pan *n.* (also **fry pan**) a flat, shallow pan with a long handle, used for frying food. □ **out of the frying pan into the fire** from a bad situation to a worse one.

f-stop *n.* an f-number setting on a camera.

Ft. *abbr.* **1** Fort. **2** (**ft.**) foot, feet.

FTA *abbr.* Free Trade Agreement.

FTP *Computing* ● *abbr.* file transfer protocol. ● *v.* (**FTP's, FTP'd, FTP'ing**) implement this protocol on (a data item etc.).

fuchsia *n.* **1** a shrub with drooping red or purple or white flowers. **2** a bright purple-pink shade of red. [*Say* FEW shuh]

fuddle *v.* (**fuddles, fuddled, fuddling**) confuse.

fuddy-duddy *slang* ● *n.* (*pl.* **fuddy-duddies**) an old-fashioned person. ● *adj.* quaintly fussy.

fudge ● *n.* **1** a soft candy made with milk, sugar, butter, etc. **2** designating rich chocolate cakes, cookies, sauces, etc. **3** *informal* nonsense. **4** *informal* a piece of dishonesty. ● *v.* (**fudges, fudged, fudging**) **1** put together in a makeshift or dishonest way. **2** deal with vaguely, usu. on purpose. ● *interj.* expressing disbelief or annoyance.

fuel ● *n.* **1** material, esp. oil, gas, etc., burned as a source of heat or power. **2** food as a source of energy. **3** anything that sustains or inflames emotion etc. ● *v.* (**fuels, fuelled, fuelling**) **1** supply with fuel. **2** sustain or inflame. **3** take in or get fuel.

fuel cell *n.* a cell producing an electric current direct from a chemical reaction.

fuel injection *n.* the direct introduction of fuel into the combustion chamber of an internal combustion engine. □ **fuel-injected** *adj.*

fugitive ● *n.* a person who flees from justice etc. ● *adj.* **1** fleeing. **2** quick to disappear.

fugue *n.* a composition in which a short melody or phrase is introduced by one part and successively taken up by others. [*Say* FYOOG]

fulcrum *n.* (*pl.* **fulcrums** or **fulcra**) the point against which a lever turns or is supported. [*Say* FULL crum]

fulfill *v.* (**fulfills, fulfilled, fulfilling**) **1** bring to completion or reality. **2** carry out as required. **3** satisfy. □ **fulfill oneself** develop one's gifts and character to the full. □ **fulfillment** *n.*

fulfilled *adj.* completely happy.

fulfilling *adj.* satisfying.

full¹ ● *adj.* **1** holding all its limits will allow. **2** having eaten all one can. **3** abundant or having an abundance. **4** (foll. by *of*) unable to stop talking or thinking about. **5** complete. **6** strong, intense. **7** plump. **8** (of clothes) not tightly fitting. ● *adv.* **1** very. **2** exactly. □ **full of oneself** selfish, conceited. **full nine yards** *slang* everything. **in full swing** at the height of activity. **to the full** to the utmost extent. □ **fullness** *n.*

full² v. cleanse and thicken (cloth).

fullback n. **1** *Football* a running back who lines up behind the rest of his team at the scrimmage. **2** *Soccer etc.* a defensive player, or a position near the goal.

full blood n. **1** pure descent. **2** a person or animal of unmixed ancestry.

full-blooded adj. **1** of unmixed race. **2** vigorous and without compromise.

full-blown adj. **1** fully developed. **2** (of flowers) very open.

full-bodied adj. rich in quality, tone, flavour, etc.

full bore informal ● adv. at maximum power, speed, etc. ● adj. complete.

full-fledged adj. of full rank or status.

full-grown adj. having reached maturity.

full house n. **1** a maximum or large attendance at a theatre, stadium, etc. **2** *Cards* a poker hand with three of a kind and a pair.

full-length adj. **1** of normal, standard, or maximum length. **2** (of a mirror, portrait, etc.) showing the whole height of the human figure.

full moon n. **1** the moon in its fullest phase, with its whole disc illuminated. **2** the time when this occurs.

full out ● adv. at full power etc. ● adj. (**full-out**) complete.

full-scale adj. **1** not reduced in size. **2** all-out.

full-service adj. designating a gas station, restaurant, etc. where service is provided entirely by staff.

full-time ● adj. using the whole of the available working time. ● adv. on a full-time basis. ● n. (**full time**) the total normal duration of work etc. □ **full-timer** n.

fully adv. **1** completely. **2** no less or fewer than.

fulmar n. a medium-sized seabird with a stout body. [Say FULL mur]

fulminate v. (**fulminates, fulminated, fulminating**) express criticism forcefully. □ **fulmination** n. [Say FULL min ate]

fulsome adj. **1** effusive, overdone. **2** abundant. □ **fulsomely** adv.

fumble ● v. (**fumbles, fumbled, fumbling**) **1** grope about. **2** handle clumsily. **3** *Football etc.* fail to keep hold of a ball after having touched it or transported it. **4** make one's way clumsily. ● n. an act of fumbling. □ **fumblingly** adv.

fume ● n. (usu. in pl.) a gas or vapour, esp. when harmful or unpleasant. ● v. (**fumes, fumed, fuming**) **1** emit fumes. **2** feel great anger.

fumigate v. (**fumigates, fumigated, fumigating**) disinfect with the fumes of certain chemicals. □ **fumigation** n.

fumigator n. [Say FUME a gate]

fun ● n. **1** amusement. **2** playfulness; good humour. **3** (also **fun and games**) lighthearted activities. ● adj. informal amusing, entertaining. ● v. (**funs, funned, funning**) informal have fun □ **make fun of** (or **poke fun at**) mock; ridicule.

function ● n. **1** an activity natural to or a purpose of a person or thing. **2** a formal social event. **3** *Math* a variable quantity regarded in relation to another or others. **4** something dependent on other factors. **5** *Computing* a part of a program that corresponds to a single value. ● v. **1** fulfill a function. **2** operate.

functional adj. **1** relating to the way in which something works. **2** able to work. **3** practical rather than attractive. **4** *Math* of a function. □ **functionality** n. **functionally** adv.

functionalism n. (in the arts) the doctrine that the design of an object should be determined solely by its function, rather than by aesthetic considerations. □ **functionalist** n. & adj.

functionally illiterate adj. unable to read or write well enough to complete everyday tasks.

functionary n. (pl. **functionaries**) a person who performs official functions or duties.

function key n. *Computing* a key which is used to generate instructions.

fund ● n. **1** a permanent stock ready to be drawn upon. **2** a reserve of money or investments. **3** (in pl.) money resources. ● v. provide with money. □ **funded** adj. **funder** n. **funding** n.

fundamental ● adj. of basic importance. ● n. **1** (usu. in pl.) a basic rule etc. **2** the lowest note of a chord. □ **fundamentally** adv.

fundamentalism n. **1** strict maintenance of ancient or fundamental doctrines of a religion. **2** a form of Protestant Christianity which upholds belief in the strict and literal interpretation of the Bible. □ **fundamentalist** n. & adj.

fundraiser n. **1** a person who raises money for a cause. **2** an event held to raise money for something. □ **fundraising** n.

funeral n. a ceremony in which a dead person is usu. buried or cremated.

funeral director n. an undertaker.

funeral home n. (also **funeral parlour**, **funeral chapel**) an establishment where the dead are prepared for burial or cremation.

funerary adj. of or used at a funeral or funerals. [Say FEW nur airy]

funereal adj. having the mournful character appropriate to a funeral. [Say few NEERY ul]

fungicide n. a fungus-destroying substance. □**fungicidal** adj. [Say FUNGA side or FUNJA side]

fungus n. (pl. **fungi** or **funguses**) a spore-producing plant such as a mushroom, that has no leaves or flowers and grows esp. on other plants or on decaying matter. □**fungal**, **fungous** adj. [Say FUN guy or FUN jye for the plural]

funhouse n. (in an amusement park) a building with trick mirrors, shifting floors, etc., designed to scare or amuse patrons as they walk through.

funk n. informal **1** fear, panic. **2** a dejected state of mind. **3** a style of popular music of US black origin. **4** a strong, unpleasant smell.

funky adj. (**funkier**, **funkiest**) **1** (of music) bluesy, with a heavy rhythmical beat. **2** informal **a** fashionable. **b** unconventional. **3** having a strong, unpleasant smell. □**funkily** adv. **funkiness** n.

funnel ● n. **1** a narrow tube or pipe widening at the top, for pouring liquid, powder, etc., into a small opening. **2** a metal chimney on a steam engine or ship. ● v. (**funnels**, **funnelled**, **funnelling**) direct or move through or as if through a funnel or narrow space.

funny ● adj. (**funnier**, **funniest**) **1** amusing. **2** strange. **3** underhand, deceitful. ● n. (pl. **funnies**) (usu. in pl.) informal **1** a comic strip in a newspaper. **2** a joke. □**funnily** adv.

funny bone n. **1** the part of the elbow over which a sensitive nerve passes. **2** a sense of humour.

funny money n. informal inflated or counterfeit currency.

fur n. **1 a** the fine, soft, thick hair of certain animals. **b** the skin of such an animal with the fur on it, used in making garments. **2** a garment made with fur. □**furred** adj.

furball n. **1** an accumulation of fur ingested by a cat etc. during self-grooming and then spit up. **2** a small furry animal.

fur-bearer n. a furred animal. □**fur-bearing** adj.

furbish v. give a fresh look to.

fur brigade n. Cdn hist. a convoy of boats transporting furs to and from isolated trading posts.

furious adj. **1** extremely angry. **2** raging. **3** requiring intense energy. □**furiously** adv. **furiousness** n.

furl v. **1** roll or fold up securely. **2** become furled.

furlong n. an eighth of a mile (201.168 metres).

furlough n. leave of absence. [Say FUR lo]

furnace n. **1** an appliance fired by gas or oil in which air or water is heated to be circulated throughout a building to heat it. **2** an enclosed structure for intense heating by fire.

furnish v. (**furnishes**, **furnished**, **furnishing**) **1** provide (a house, room, etc.) with furniture and fittings. **2** supply; provide. □**furnished** adj.

furnishings pl. n. the furniture and fittings in a house, room, etc.

furniture n. the movable objects that make a room or building suitable for living and working in. □**part of the furniture** informal a person or thing taken for granted.

furor n. an outbreak of great anger or excitement by a number of people.

furrier n. **1** a person who makes, cleans, and repairs fur garments. **2** a person who buys and sells furs.

furrow ● n. **1** a narrow trench made in the ground by a plow. **2** a rut or groove. ● v. **1** plow. **2** make furrows or wrinkles in. □**furrowed** adj.

furry adj. (**furrier**, **furriest**) **1** of or like fur. **2** covered with fur.

fur seal n. a seal with thick fur on the underside used commercially as sealskin.

further ● adv. **1** to or at a greater distance. **2** to a greater extent, more. **3** in addition. ● adj. **1** more distant or advanced. **2** additional. ● v. promote, help on. □**further to** formal following on from.

furthermore adv. in addition, besides.

furthermost adj. at the greatest distance from a central point or implicit standpoint.

furthest ● adj. **1** most distant. **2** longest; most extended in space. ● adv. **1** to or at the greatest distance in space or time. **2** to the highest degree or extent.

furtive adj. **1** attempting to avoid notice or attention. **2** suggestive of guilty nervousness. □**furtively** adv. **furtiveness** n.

fur trade n. the business of trapping, transporting, and selling furs, esp. as carried on between European traders and Aboriginal peoples in N America from the 17th to the 19th century. □**fur trader** n. **fur-trading** n.

fury n. (pl. **furies**) **1** wild and passionate anger. **2** violence of a storm, disease, etc. **3** (**Fury**) (usu. in pl.) (in Greek mythology) one of three goddesses who punished people for wrongdoing. **4** an angry or malignant woman. □**like fury** *informal* with great force or effect.

fuse¹ ● *v.* (**fuses**, **fused**, **fusing**) **1** melt with intense heat. **2** blend or amalgamate into one whole by or as by melting. **3** provide with a fuse. **4** coalesce, join. ● *n.* a device containing a strip of wire that melts and breaks an electric circuit if an excessive current passes through. □**blow a fuse** *informal* **1** cause a fuse to melt by passing excessive current through it. **2** lose one's temper.

fuse² *n.* **1** a device for igniting a bomb or explosive charge, consisting of a length of combustible matter. **2** a component in a bomb that controls the timing of the explosion. □**have a short fuse** anger easily.

fuselage *n.* the main body of an airplane. [*Say* FYOOZ a lazh]

fusible *adj.* easily fused or melted. [*Say* FEW zuh bull]

fusilier *n.* a member of any of several regiments formerly armed with light muskets. [*Say* few zuh LEER]

fusillade ● *n.* **1** a continuous discharge of firearms. **2** a sustained outburst of criticism etc. ● *v.* **1** assault (a place) by a fusillade. **2** shoot down (persons) with a fusillade. [*Say* few zuh LAID *or* few zuh LOD]

fusilli *pl. n.* pasta in the form of short spirals. [*Say* foo ZILLY *or* few ZILLY]

fusion *n.* **1** the process or result of joining two or more things together to form one. **2** a coalition. **3** = NUCLEAR FUSION. **4** a kind of music in which elements of more than one popular style are combined, esp. jazz and rock. **5** (also **fusion cuisine**) a style of cuisine combining ingredients and cooking methods from different countries.

fusion bomb *n.* a bomb deriving its energy from nuclear fusion, esp. a hydrogen bomb.

fuss ● *n.* **1** a display of excitement or worry, esp. of an unnecessary kind. **2** a sustained protest or dispute. ● *v.* (**fusses**, **fussed**, **fussing**) **1 a** make a fuss. **b** busy oneself with trivial things. **c** (of a baby) express unhappiness by whimpering etc. **2** agitate, worry. □**make a fuss** complain vigorously. **make a fuss over** treat with excessive attention.

fuss-budget *n.* *informal* (also **fusspot**) a person given to fussing.

fussy *adj.* (**fussier**, **fussiest**) **1** inclined to fuss. **2** full of unnecessary detail or decoration. **3** difficult to please. □**be not fussy about 1** be indifferent about. **2** not like particularly. □**fussily** *adv.* **fussiness** *n.*

fusty *adj.* (**fustier**, **fustiest**) **1** stale-smelling. **2** antiquated. □**fustiness** *n.*

futile *adj.* useless. □**futilely** *adv.* **futility** *n.* [*Say* FEW tile *or* FEW tul, few TILLA tee]

futon *n.* **1** a mattress that can be rolled up. **2** a bed or couch having such a mattress. [*Say* FOO tawn]

future ● *n.* **1** time still to come. **2** events or conditions existing in the future. **3** a prospect of success etc. **4** the verbal tense expressing things yet to happen. **5** (in *pl.*) goods and stocks sold for future delivery. ● *adj.* **1** expected or existing in the future. **2** *Grammar* describing a future event. □**in future** from now onward.

future-proof ● *adj.* (of a product) unlikely to become obsolete. ● *v.* make (something) future-proof.

future shock *n.* a state of disorientation due to rapid change.

futurism *n.* (also **Futurism**) an early 20th-century artistic movement celebrating and incorporating modern technology.

futurist *n.* **1** (also **Futurist**) a supporter or follower of futurism. **2** a person who studies the future.

futuristic *adj.* **1** suitable for the future. **2** (also **Futuristic**) of futurism. **3** relating to the future. □**futuristically** *adv.*

fuzz ● *n.* **1** a mass of soft light particles; fluff. **2** frizzled hair. **3** *slang* the police. **4** an indistinct sound, image, etc. ● *v.* (**fuzzes**, **fuzzed**, **fuzzing**) make or become fluffy or blurred.

fuzzy *adj.* (**fuzzier**, **fuzziest**) **1 a** like fuzz. **b** frizzy. **2** blurred, indistinct. □**fuzzily** *adv.* **fuzziness** *n.*

FX *abbr.* = SPECIAL EFFECTS.

FYI *abbr.* for your information.

Gg

G¹ *n.* (also **g**) (*pl.* **Gs** or **G's**) **1** the seventh letter of the alphabet. **2** the fifth note in the C major scale.

G² *abbr.* (also **G.**) *informal* a thousand (esp. dollars).

g *symb.* **1** gram(s). **2 a** gravity. **b** acceleration due to gravity.

GAA *abbr.* = GOALS-AGAINST AVERAGE.

gab *n. & v. informal* talk; chatter. □ **gift of the gab** the facility of speaking eloquently or profusely. □ **gabby** *adj.*

gabardine *n.* (also **gaberdine**) **1** a smooth durable twill-woven cloth. **2** a garment made of this, esp. a raincoat. [*Say* GABBER deen]

gabble ● *v.* (**gabbles, gabbled, gabbling**) **1** speak incoherently. **2** (of geese, chickens, etc.) gaggle, cackle, etc. ● *n.* **1** loud unintelligible talk. **2** the inarticulate noises made by some animals.

gable *n.* the triangular upper part of a wall enclosed by the two sloping planes of a ridged roof. □ **gabled** *adj.*

gad *v.* (**gads, gadded, gadding**) (foll. by *about, around*) go about idly or in search of pleasure.

gadfly *n.* (*pl.* **gadflies**) **1** a cattle-biting fly, esp. a horsefly. **2** a person who persistently criticizes others.

gadget *n.* a small mechanical or electronic device.

gadgetry *n.* gadgets collectively.

Gael *n.* a Gaelic Celt. [*Say* GALE]

Gaelic ● *n.* any of the Celtic languages spoken in Ireland and Scotland. ● *adj.* relating to the Celts of Ireland or Scotland, or their languages. [*Say* GAY lick]

gaff ● *n.* **1 a** a stick with an iron hook for landing large fish, seals, etc. **b** a barbed fishing spear. **2** a spar to which the head of a fore-and-aft sail is bent. ● *v.* seize (a fish etc.) with a gaff.

gaffe *n.* an indiscreet act or remark. [*Say* GAFF]

gaffer *n.* **1** the chief electrician in a film or television production unit. **2** an old man.

gag ● *n.* **1** a piece of cloth etc. put in or over the mouth to prevent speaking. **2** a thing or circumstance restricting free speech. **3** a joke or comic scene. ● *v.* (**gags, gagged, gagging**) **1** apply a gag to.

2 silence; deprive of free speech. **3** choke or retch.

gaga *adj. slang* senile or crazy.

gage esp. *US* = GAUGE.

gaggle ● *n.* **1** a flock of geese. **2** *informal* a disorderly, noisy group. ● *v.* (**gaggles, gaggled, gaggling**) (of geese) cackle.

gag order *n. informal* a court order banning the publication of information disclosed at a trial etc.

Gaia 1 *Ecology* the earth perceived as a vast self-regulating organism. **2** (in Greek mythology) the earth personified as a goddess. □ **Gaian** *adj. & n.* [*Say* GUY uh, GUY un]

gaiety *n.* **1** the state of being lighthearted or merry. **2** merrymaking. [*Say* GAY a tee]

gaily *adv.* **1** in a gay or lighthearted manner. **2** with a bright appearance.

gain ● *v.* **1** obtain or secure (something desirable). **2** obtain as an increment or addition. **3** win (a victory). **4** (foll. by *in*) make a specified advance or improvement. **5** (of a clock etc.) have the fault of becoming fast. **6** (often foll. by *on, upon*) come closer to a person or thing pursued. **7** *formal* reach. ● *n.* **1** something gained. **2** an increase, profit, or improvement. **3** the acquisition of wealth. **4** (in *pl.*) sums of money acquired. □ **gainer** *n.*

gainful *adj.* (of employment) paid. □ **gainfully** *adv.*

gainsay *v.* (**gainsays, gainsaid, gainsaying**) contradict. □ **gainsayer** *n.* [*Say* GAIN say]

gait *n.* **1** a manner of walking. **2** a way in which a horse moves, such as a trot.

gaiter *n.* a covering of cloth, leather, etc. for the ankle and lower leg.

gal *n. slang* a girl or woman.

gala *n.* (*pl.* **galas**) **1** a festive or special occasion. **2** a heart-shaped type of crisp, sweet apple with a yellow-orange skin with red streaks. [*Say* GAL uh *or* GALE uh]

galactic *adj.* relating to a galaxy or galaxies.

galaxy *n.* (*pl.* **galaxies**) **1** an independent system of stars, gas, dust, etc., held together by gravitational attraction. **2** (**Galaxy**) = MILKY WAY.

gale n. **1** a very strong wind. **2** Nautical a storm. **3** an outburst, esp. of laughter.

Galician n. hist. **1** a late 19th-century or early 20th-century Slavic immigrant to western Canada, esp. a Ukrainian. **2** the language of Galicians. □ **Galician** adj. [Say guh LISH un]

gall ● n. **1** shamelessly rude behaviour. **2** formal resentment. **3** a swelling on plants and trees caused by insects, disease, etc. **4** the bile of animals. ● v. upset or anger (someone).

gallant ● adj. **1** brave, noble. **2** charmingly attentive, esp. to women. **3** (of a ship, horse, etc.) grand, stately. ● n. a ladies' man; a lover. □ **gallantly** adv. [Say GAL'nt]

gallantry n. (pl. **gallantries**) **1** bravery. **2** polite attention or respect given by men to women. [Say GAL un tree]

gallbladder n. the vessel storing bile to be released into the intestine.

galleon n. hist. a square-rigged ship with three or more decks and masts. [Say GALLEE un]

gallery n. (pl. **galleries**) **1** a room or building for showing works of art. **2** a balcony or upper floor projecting from the inner wall of a hall or church. **3** the highest balcony in a theatre, usu. with the cheapest seats. **4** a covered space for walking in, partly open at the side. **5** (esp. Que., Nfld, & Gulf States) a veranda. **6** Military & Mining a horizontal underground passage. □ **play to the gallery** seek approval by appealing to popular taste.

galley n. (pl. **galleys**) **1** hist. a low flat single-decked vessel using sails and up to three banks of oars. **2** the kitchen in a ship, aircraft, camper, etc.

Gallic adj. **1** French or typically French. **2** of the Gauls. [Say GAL ick]

Gallicism n. a French word or usage. [Say GAL a sism]

galling adj. causing anger or resentment. □ **gallingly** adv. [Rhymes with FALLING]

gallivant v. **1** (often foll. by around) idly search for pleasure. **2** flirt. [Say GAL a vant]

gallon n. **1 a** (also **imperial gallon**) a measure of capacity equal to eight pints and equivalent to 4.55 litres. **b** (also **US gallon**) (in the US) a measure of capacity equivalent to 3.79 litres, used for liquids. **2** (usu. in pl.) informal a large amount.

gallop ● n. **1** the fastest pace of a horse or other quadruped, with all the feet off the ground together in each stride. **2** a ride at this pace. ● v. (**gallops**, **galloped**, **galloping**) **1** a go at the pace of a gallop. **b** make (a horse etc.) gallop. **2 a** run with leaping strides. **b** move rapidly.

gallows pl. n. (usu. treated as sing.) a structure, usu. of two uprights and a crosspiece, for the hanging of criminals. [Say GAL oze]

gallstone n. a small hard mass forming in the gallbladder or bile ducts from bile pigments, cholesterol, and calcium salts.

Gallup poll n. an assessment of public opinion by questioning a representative sample.

galoot n. informal a clumsy person.

galore adv. in abundance.

galosh n. (pl. **galoshes**) (usu. in pl.) a waterproof rubber overshoe.

galumph v. informal move clumsily.

galvanic adj. **1** of or producing an electric current by chemical action. **2** making people react dramatically. □ **galvanically** adv. [Say gal VAN ick]

galvanize v. (**galvanizes**, **galvanized**, **galvanizing**) **1** rouse forcefully. **2** coat with zinc as a protection against rust. □ **galvanizer** n. [Say GALVA nize]

gambit n. **1** a chess opening in which a player sacrifices a piece or pawn to secure an advantage. **2** a move or remark intended to gain an advantage.

gamble ● v. (**gambles**, **gambled**, **gambling**) **1** play games of chance for money. **2 a** bet (money etc.) in gambling. **b** (often foll. by away) lose (assets) by gambling. **3** take great risks in the hope of substantial gain. **4** (foll. by on) act in the expectation of. ● n. **1** a risky undertaking. **2** an act of gambling. □ **gambler** n.

gambol ● v. (**gambols**, **gambolled**, **gambolling**) frolic playfully. ● n. a playful frolic. [Sounds like GAMBLE]

game[1] ● n. **1 a** an amusement, pastime, etc. **b** a form of contest played according to rules. **2** a single portion of play forming a scoring unit in some contests, e.g. tennis. **3** (in pl.) a meeting for athletic etc. contests. **4** a winning score in a game. **5** the apparatus necessary to play a game. **6** one's skill at or style of playing a game. **7 a** a piece of fun. **b** (in pl.) tricks **8** any undertaking regarded as a game. **9** wild animals or birds hunted for sport or food. ● adj. eager and willing. ● v. (**games**, **gamed**, **gaming**) **1** play at games of chance for money. **2** play video or computer games. □ **the game is up** the scheme is revealed or foiled. **give the game away** reveal something one would rather keep hidden. **game over** slang all is lost. **off** (or **on**) **one's game** playing badly (or well). **play the game** behave according to the rules. □ **gameness** n. **gamer** n. **gaming** n.

game² *adj.* (of a leg, arm, etc.) lame, crippled.

game bird *n.* a bird shot for sport or food.

game fish *n.* (*pl.* **game fish** or **game fishes**) a kind of fish caught for sport.

gamekeeper *n.* a person employed to breed and protect game.

gamelan *n.* **1** a kind of Indonesian orchestra including a variety of percussion instruments. **2** a kind of xylophone used in this. [*Say* GAMMA lan]

gamely *adv.* making a brave effort.

game misconduct *n.* *Hockey* a penalty banishing a player for the rest of the current game.

game plan *n.* a plan for success in sport, politics, or business.

game show *n.* a television program in which people compete to win prizes.

gamesmanship *n.* the art of defeating an opponent by psychological ploys etc.

gamete *n.* a cell which unites with another of the opposite sex in sexual reproduction to form a zygote. [*Say* GAM eet]

game warden *n.* an official locally supervising game, hunting and fishing, etc.

gamey *adj.* = GAMY.

gamine ● *n.* a girl with mischievous or boyish charm. ● *adj.* of or like a gamine. [*Say* GAM een]

gamma *n.* **1** the third letter of the Greek alphabet (Γ, γ). **2** the third brightest star in a constellation. **3** designating high-energy electromagnetic radiation of wavelengths shorter than those of X-rays.

gamut *n.* the whole range of anything. □ **run the gamut** experience, include, or perform the complete range. [*Say* GAM ut]

gamy *adj.* (**gamier, gamiest**) having the strong flavour or scent of well aged game. □ **gaminess** *n.*

gander *n.* **1** a male goose. **2** *informal* a look.

gang *n.* **1 a** an organized group of criminals or rowdy youths. **b** *informal* a group of people who regularly associate together. **2** a set of workers, slaves, or prisoners. □ **gang up** *informal* **1** (foll. by *on*) combine against. **2** (often foll. by *with*) act in concert.

gangbuster *informal* ● *n.* a person who takes part in the aggressive breakup of criminal gangs. ● *adj.* (often as **gangbusters**) outstandingly successful. □ **go gangbusters** be vigorously successful. **like gangbusters** energetically.

gangland *n.* the world of organized crime.

gangling *adj.* (of a person) loosely built.

ganglion *n.* (*pl.* **ganglia**) **1** a structure containing a number of nerve cells, often forming a swelling on a nerve fibre. **2** a cyst, esp. on a tendon sheath. [*Say* GANGLY un]

gangly *adj.* (**ganglier, gangliest**) = GANGLING.

gangplank *n.* a plank used for boarding or disembarking from a ship etc.

gangrene *n.* death of body tissue, resulting from obstructed circulation or bacterial infection. [*Say* GANG green]

gangsta *n.* **1** *slang* = GANGSTER. **2** (also **gangsta rap**) a style of rap music, the lyrics of which centre on gang culture, racism, and police brutality.

gangster *n.* a member of a gang of violent criminals. □ **gangsterish** *adj.* **gangsterism** *n.*

gangway ● *n.* **1** an opening by which a ship is entered or left. **2** a bridge laid from ship to shore. **3** a walkway or raised passage. ● *interj.* make way!

ganja *n.* a potent form of marijuana for smoking. [*Say* GAN juh *or* GON juh]

gannet *n.* a large seabird with mainly white plumage. [*Say* GAN it]

gantry *n.* (*pl.* **gantries**) **1** a bridge-like overhead structure supporting railway or road signals etc. **2** a structure supporting a rocket prior to launching. [*Say* GAN tree]

gaol *n.* esp. *Brit.* = JAIL. [*Sounds like* JAIL]

gap *n.* **1** an empty space or interval. **2** a gorge or pass. □ **fill** (or **close** etc.) **the gap** make up a deficiency.

gape ● *v.* (**gapes, gaped, gaping**) **1** be or become open. **2** stare with one's mouth wide open in amazement. ● *n.* a wide-open expanse. □ **gaper** *n.* **gaping** *adj.*

gap-toothed *adj.* having gaps between the teeth.

garage *n.* **1** a building for the storage of a motor vehicle or vehicles. **2** an establishment that sells gasoline, repairs motors, etc. **3** denoting raw, energetic guitar-based rock music. [*Say* guh ROZH *or* guh RODGE *or* guh RADGE *or* guh RAZH]

garage sale *n.* a sale of used household items etc. in the garage or on the lawn of a private house.

garb ● *n.* distinctive clothing. ● *v.* dress in distinctive clothes.

garbage *n.* **1** household waste. **2** anything worthless. **3** nonsense.

garbage disposal *n.* (also **garbage disposer**) a system installed in a kitchen sink, with blades in the drain to mulch refuse.

garbageman *n.* a person employed to remove garbage and transport it to a dump.

garbanzo n. (pl. **garbanzos**) = CHICKPEA. [Say gar BON zo]

garble ● v. (**garbles**, **garbled**, **garbling**) reproduce in a distorted way. ● n. garbled speech or sounds.

garburator n. Cdn a garbage disposal. [Say GARBA rater]

garden ● n. **1** a piece of ground used for growing flowers, vegetables, etc., sometimes including a lawn and often adjoining a house. **2** ornamental grounds laid out for public enjoyment. ● v. cultivate or work in a garden. □ **gardener** n. **gardening** n.

gardenia n. a tree or shrub of warm climates with large fragrant white or yellow flowers. [Say gar DEAN yuh]

garden path n. a path through a garden. □ **lead a person down** (or **up**) **the garden path** mislead a person into error, folly, etc.

garden salad n. a salad made with common garden vegetables.

garden-variety adj. commonplace.

gargantuan adj. enormous. [Say gar GAN choo un]

gargle ● v. (**gargles**, **gargled**, **gargling**) **1** wash one's mouth and throat with a liquid kept in motion by a stream of air which is breathed out. **2** make a sound as when doing this. ● n. **1** a liquid for gargling. **2** the sound of gargling.

gargoyle n. a grotesque face or figure carved on the gutter of a building. □ **gargoylish** adj.

garish adj. overly bright or decorated. □ **garishly** adv. **garishness** n. [Say GARE ish]

garland n. a wreath of flowers, leaves, etc., worn on the head or hung as a decoration. □ **garlanded** adj.

garlic n. a strong-smelling pungent-tasting bulb of a plant of the onion family, used in cooking. □ **garlicky** adj.

garment n. an article of clothing.

garner v. **1** obtain or gather (information etc.). **2** earn, get.

garnet n. **1** a red semi-precious stone. **2** n. & adj. deep red.

garnish ● v. (**garnishes**, **garnished**, **garnishing**) **1** decorate (esp. food). **2** Law serve notice on (a person) for the purpose of legally seizing money. ● n. a decoration for food.

garnishee Law ● n. a third party required to surrender money belonging to a debtor or defendant in compliance with a court order obtained by the creditor or plaintiff. ● v. (**garnishees**, **garnisheed**, **garnisheeing**) recover a debt from (a person, his or her wages) by garnishee order. [Say garnish EE]

garret n. a top-floor or attic room. [Say GARE lt]

garrison ● n. the troops stationed in a fortress, town, etc., to defend it. ● v. provide (a place) with or occupy as a garrison. [Say GARE iss un]

garrotte ● n. a wire or cord used for strangling a person. ● v. (**garrottes**, **garrotted**, **garrotting**) strangle by means of a wire, cord, etc. [Say guh ROT]

garrulous adj. talkative. □ **garrulously** adv. **garrulousness** n. [Say GARE uh lus]

garter n. **1** a band worn to keep a sock, stocking, or shirt sleeve up. **2** a suspender for a sock or stocking.

garter belt n. an undergarment with suspenders for holding up socks or stockings.

garter snake n. a common, harmless N American snake with well-defined lengthwise stripes.

gas ● n. (pl. **gases**) **1** any airlike fluid substance which expands to fill any space available. **2** such a substance used as a fuel, e.g. natural gas. **3 a** gasoline. **b** the gas pedal. **4** gas used as an anaesthetic or as a toxic element in warfare etc. **5** informal pointless idle talk. **6** slang an enjoyable thing. **7** intestinal gas. ● v. (**gases**, **gassed**, **gassing**) **1** harm or kill with poisonous gas. **2** (usu. foll. by up) informal fill (the tank of a motor vehicle) with gasoline. **3** give off gas. **4** informal talk idly. □ **run out of gas** lose one's impetus.

gasbag n. **1** a container of gas. **2** slang an idle talker.

gas bar n. Cdn a gas station consisting of a kiosk and pumps but no garage.

gas chamber n. an airtight chamber that can be filled with poisonous gas to kill people or animals.

gaseous adj. of or like gas. [Say GASSY us or GASH us]

gash ● n. (pl. **gashes**) a long and deep slash or wound. ● v. (**gashes**, **gashed**, **gashing**) make a gash in.

gasket n. a sheet or ring of rubber etc., shaped to seal the junction of metal surfaces. □ **blow a gasket** slang lose one's temper.

gaslight n. **1** a jet of burning gas, usu. heating a mantle, to provide light. **2** light emanating from this. □ **gaslit** adj.

gasoline n. a volatile inflammable liquid obtained from petroleum and used as motor fuel.

gasp ● v. **1** catch one's breath with an open mouth as in exhaustion or astonishment. **2** strain to obtain by gasping. **3** utter with gasps. ● *n.* a convulsive catching of breath.

gas pedal *n.* the accelerator pedal on a motor vehicle.

gaspereau *n.* (*pl.* **gaspereaux**) *Cdn* an alewife. [*Say* GASPER oh]

Gaspesian *adj. Cdn* pertaining to the Gaspé Peninsula. □ **Gaspesian** *n.* [*Say* gas PAY zhun]

gassy *adj.* (**gassier, gassiest**) **1** of, like, or full of gas. **2** *informal* verbose.

gastric *adj.* of the stomach.

gastritis *n.* inflammation of the stomach lining. [*Say* gas TRITE us]

gastro- *comb. form* (also **gastr-** before a vowel) stomach.

gastroenteritis *n.* inflammation of the stomach and intestines, causing vomiting and diarrhea. [*Say* gastro enta RITE us]

gastrointestinal *adj.* relating to the stomach and the intestines. [*Say* gastro INTESTINAL]

gastronomy *n.* **1** the practice, study, or art of eating and drinking well. **2** the cuisine of an area. □ **gastronomic** *adj.* [*Say* guh STRONNA mee, gastra NOM ick]

gastropod *n.* any of a large class of molluscs including snails and slugs. [*Say* GASTRA pod]

gate ● *n.* **1** a hinged barrier used to close an entrance or exit. **2** an opening in a city wall, large building, etc. **3** a place of access to aircraft at an airport or trains at a train station. **4** an electrical circuit with an output which depends on the combination of several inputs. **5 a** the number of people paying to attend a sporting event etc. **b** (also **gate money**) the proceeds taken for admission. **6** a barrier for securing a fair start in a race. **7** *Skiing* a pair of poles on a slalom course through which a skier must pass. ● *v.* (**gates, gated, gating**) *Cdn* retain an inmate in prison by arresting him or her immediately upon release under mandatory supervision.

-gate *comb. form* forming nouns denoting an actual or alleged scandal.

gatecrash *v.* (**gatecrashes, gatecrashed, gatecrashing**) go to a party or social event without being invited. □ **gatecrasher** *n.*

gated *adj.* having a gate or gates to control access or movement.

gatehouse *n.* a house standing by a gateway.

gatekeeper *n.* **1** an attendant at a gate. **2** a thing or person that controls access to or availability of information etc.

gatepost *n.* a post on which a gate is hung or against which it shuts.

gateway *n.* **1** an entrance with or opening for a gate. **2** a structure built over a gate. **3** a means of access. **4** a device or software used to connect two networks.

gather ● *v.* **1** bring or come together. **2** harvest or pick. **3** infer or understand. **4** be subjected to the accumulation or increase of. **5** (often foll. by *up*) summon for a purpose. **6** draw (material) together in folds etc. ● *n.* (in *pl.*) a part of a garment that is gathered or drawn in. □ **gatherer** *n.*

gathering ● *n.* **1** an assembly or meeting. **2** the gathers formed by drawing up a fabric. ● *adj.* increasing in intensity etc.

gator *n. informal* an alligator.

GATT *abbr.* General Agreement on Tariffs and Trade.

gauche *adj.* **1** socially awkward. **2** tactless. [*Say* GOASH]

gaucho *n.* (*pl.* **gauchos**) **1** a cowboy from the S American pampas. **2** (in *pl.*) (also **gaucho pants**) wide, calf-length pants. [*Say* GOW cho]

gaudy *adj.* (**gaudier, gaudiest**) tastelessly or extravagantly bright or showy. □ **gaudily** *adv.* **gaudiness** *n.*

gauge ● *n.* **1** an instrument that measures and gives a visual display of the amount, level, or contents of something. **2** a standard measure, e.g. of thickness. **3** the distance between a pair of rails or the wheels on one axle. **4** a means of estimating or testing. ● *v.* (**gauges, gauged, gauging**) **1** measure exactly. **2** determine the capacity of. **3** estimate or form a judgment of.

Gaul *n.* a person from the ancient European region of Gaul now largely occupied by France.

gaunch *n. Cdn slang* underwear.

gaunt *adj.* **1** lean and haggard. **2** grim or desolate. [*Say* GONT]

gauntlet[1] *n.* **1** a sturdy glove long enough to cover the wrist and part of the forearm. **2** *hist.* an armoured glove. □ **take** (or **pick**) **up the gauntlet** accept a challenge. **throw down the gauntlet** issue a challenge.

gauntlet[2] *n.* **1** a punishment in which the offender must pass between two rows of people and receive blows from them. **2** a series of ordeals. □ **run the gauntlet** be subjected to harsh criticism.

gauze *n.* **1** a thin transparent fabric of silk, cotton, etc. **2** *Medical* thin loosely woven material used for dressings and swabs. **3** a fine mesh of wire etc.

gauzy *adj.* (**gauzier**, **gauziest**) thin and translucent.

gave *past of* GIVE.

gavel *n.* a small hammer used by an auctioneer, judge, etc. to call for attention etc. [*Say* GAV ul]

gawk *v. informal* stare stupidly. □ **gawker** *n.*

gawky *adj.* (**gawkier**, **gawkiest**) awkward or ungainly. □ **gawkiness** *n.*

gay ● *adj.* **1 a** homosexual. **b** pertaining to homosexuals. **2 a** lighthearted and carefree. **b** characterized by cheerfulness. **c** brightly coloured. ● *n.* a homosexual, esp. male. □ **gayness** *n.*

gay bashing *n. informal* unprovoked violence against a homosexual or homosexuals.

gay pride *n.* a sense of strong self-esteem associated with a person's public acknowledgement of their homosexuality.

gaze ● *v.* (**gazes**, **gazed**, **gazing**) look fixedly. ● *n.* a fixed or intent look. □ **gazer** *n.*

gazebo *n.* (*pl.* **gazebos** or **gazeboes**) a small structure offering a wide view of the surrounding area. [*Say* guh ZEE bo]

gazelle *n.* a slender antelope with curved horns and a fawn-coloured coat, common in Africa and Asia. [*Say* guh ZEL]

gazette *n.* a newspaper or journal. [*Say* guh ZET]

gazetteer *n.* a geographical index or dictionary. [*Say* gazza TEER]

gazillion *n. informal* an exaggeratedly large number. □ **gazillionaire** *n.*

gazpacho *n.* (*pl.* **gazpachos**) a Spanish soup made from tomatoes, peppers, cucumbers, garlic, etc., and served cold. [*Say* guh SPATCH oh]

Gbyte *abbr.* gigabyte.

GDP *abbr.* GROSS DOMESTIC PRODUCT.

gear ● *n.* **1** (often in *pl.*) a toothed wheel that works with others to receive and transmit force and motion. **2** a particular setting of engaged gears. **3** a state of speed or activity. **4** a mechanism or set of equipment for a special purpose. **5** belongings. ● *v.* **1** adjust for a purpose or recipient. **2** (often foll. by *up*) equip with gears. □ **gear down** engage a lower gear in a vehicle. **gear up 1** prepare or equip in anticipation of some activity. **2** speed up. **3** engage a higher gear in a vehicle. **give a person the gears** *Cdn* pester, hassle. **in gear 1** with a gear engaged. **2** operating properly. **shift** (or **change** etc.) **gears** change one's pace, direction, strategy, etc.

gearbox *n.* a set of gears with its casing, esp. in a motor vehicle.

gearing *n.* a set or arrangement of gears in a machine.

gearshift *n.* a lever used to engage or change gear.

gearwheel *n.* a toothed wheel in a set of gears.

gecko *n.* (*pl.* **geckos** or **geckoes**) a house lizard with adhesive feet, found in warm climates.

gee *interj. informal* a mild expression of surprise etc.

geek *n. informal* **1** a socially inept person. **2** a person devoted to one usu. technical interest, at the expense of social interaction. □ **geekdom** *n.* **geekiness** *n.* **geekish** *adj.* **geeky** *adj.*

geese *pl. of* GOOSE.

gee whiz *informal* ● *interj.* = GEE. ● *adj.* (usu. as **gee-whiz**) characterized by naive astonishment.

geezer *n. slang* an old man.

Geiger counter *n.* a device for measuring radioactivity. [*Say* GUY gur]

geisha *n.* (*pl.* **geisha** or **geishas**) **1** a Japanese hostess trained in entertaining men with dance and song. **2** a Japanese prostitute. [*Say* GAY shuh]

gel ● *n.* **1** a semi-solid suspension of a solid dispersed in a liquid. **2** a jellylike substance used for setting hair. ● *v.* (**gels**, **gelled**, **gelling**) **1** = JELL. **2** apply gel to.

gelatin *n.* (also **gelatine**) a water-soluble protein obtained by prolonged boiling of animal skin, tendons, ligaments, etc., used in food preparation, photography, glue manufacture, etc. □ **gelatinous** *adj.* [*Say* JELLA tin, jel LATIN us]

gelato *n.* (*pl.* **gelati**) an Italian sherbet-like ice cream. [*Say* jel LATTO]

gelcap *n.* a gelatin capsule containing a medication in liquid or gel form.

geld *v.* **1** castrate. **2** deprive of some essential part.

gelding *n.* a gelded animal, esp. a male horse.

gelignite *n.* a high explosive made from a gel of nitroglycerine. [*Say* JELL ignite]

gem *n.* **1** a precious stone. **2** an outstanding person or thing.

Gemini *n.* (*pl.* **Geminis**) **1 a** a constellation (the Twins). **b** the third sign of the zodiac, which the sun enters about May 21. **2** *Cdn* an award presented by the Academy of Canadian Cinema and Television for excellence in Canadian English-language television. □ **Geminian** *n. & adj.* [*Say* JEM in eye, jemmin EYE un]

gemstone *n.* a gem used in jewellery.

Gen. *abbr.* General.

gendarme n. a police officer in some French-speaking countries. [Say zhon DARM]

gender n. 1 any of various classes (e.g. masculine, feminine, neuter) into which nouns and pronouns are divided. 2 the state of being male or female, esp. in regard to social roles. □ **gendered** adj. **genderless** adj.

gender-bender n. someone or something adopting non-traditional gender roles. □ **gender-bending** n. & adj.

gender-neutral adj. denoting language that cannot be taken to refer to one sex only.

gene n. a unit of heredity forming part of a chromosome and determining a characteristic of an individual.

genealogy n. (pl. **genealogies**) 1 a a line of descent traced continuously from an ancestor. b an account of this. 2 the study and investigation of lines of descent. 3 a plant's or animal's line of development from earlier forms. □ **genealogical** adj. **genealogist** n. [Say jeany OLLA jee or jeany ALA jee, jeany a LOGICAL]

gene mapping n. the determination of a gene's location on a chromosome.

gene pool n. the stock of different genes in an interbreeding population.

genera pl. of GENUS. [Say JENNER uh]

general ● adj. 1 affecting or concerning all or most people or things. 2 involving only the main elements. 3 chief. ● n. 1 (also **General**; abbreviation: **Gen** Cdn or **Gen.**) a military officer of the highest rank. 2 a commander of an army. □ **in general** 1 usually. 2 for the most part.

general anaesthetic n. an anaesthetic that affects the whole body.

General Assembly n. the main deliberative body of the United Nations.

general election n. the election of representatives to a legislature from all constituencies of a country, province, etc.

generalist n. a person competent or knowledgeable in several different fields or activities.

generality n. (pl. **generalities**) 1 a statement that discusses general principles. 2 the quality of being general. 3 most of a group.

generalize v. (**generalizes**, **generalized**, **generalizing**) 1 make a general statement based on specific cases. 2 make more common or widely applicable. 3 (of a disease) spread to other parts of the body. □ **generalization** n.

generally adv. 1 usually; for the most part. 2 without regard to particulars.

general manager n. 1 the member of the administration of a sports team responsible for hiring, firing, trading etc. the players. 2 the person having overall responsibility for the operations of a company etc.

general practice n. 1 the work of a general practitioner. 2 a place where such a doctor works.

general practitioner n. a doctor working in the community and treating cases of all kinds in the first instance.

general public n. the people of a community collectively.

general staff n. the staff assisting a military commander.

general strike n. a strike of workers in most occupations.

generate v. (**generates**, **generated**, **generating**) 1 bring into existence. 2 produce (electricity).

generation n. 1 all the people born at a particular time, regarded collectively. 2 a single step in descent or pedigree. 3 a stage in development. 4 members of a group who became prominent at the same time. 5 the average time in which children grow up and have children of their own (usu. reckoned at about 30 years). 6 the action of producing or generating. □ **generational** adj.

generation gap n. differences in attitudes between people of different generations.

Generation X n. the generation born between the early 1960s and mid-1970s. □ **Generation Xer** n.

generative adj. 1 of or concerning procreation. 2 productive. [Say JENNER a tiv]

generator n. 1 a machine for converting mechanical into electrical energy. 2 a person or thing that generates something.

generic adj. 1 relating to an entire class; not specific. 2 Biology relating to genus. 3 designating a word that can refer to both men and women. 4 (of goods) having no brand name. □ **generically** adv. [Say jen AIR ick]

generous adj. 1 freely giving more than necessary or expected. 2 larger or more plentiful than is usual. 3 kind towards others. 4 a ample, copious. b spacious. □ **generosity** n. **generously** adv.

genesis n. (pl. **geneses**) the origin, or mode of formation, of a thing. [Say JENNA sis for the singular, JENNA seez for the plural]

gene-splicing n. the process of integrating a gene with the genetic material of another organism so that it produces the protein for which the gene codes.

gene therapy *n.* the introduction of normal genes into cells in order to correct genetic disorders.

genetic *adj.* **1** of heredity or genes. **2** of genetics. □ **genetically** *adv.* [Say jen NET ick]

genetically modified *adj.* (also **genetically altered**) **1** (of genetic material) artificially manipulated in order to produce a desired characteristic. **2** (of an organism or cell) containing such genetic material. **3** (of foodstuffs) containing or consisting of genetically altered plant or animal tissue.

genetic code *n.* the means by which genetic information is stored in DNA and RNA.

genetic engineering *n.* the deliberate modification of the characters of an organism by the manipulation of the genetic material. □ **genetically engineered** *adj.*

genetic fingerprinting *n.* (also **genetic profiling**) the analysis of characteristic patterns in DNA as a way of identifying individuals.

genetics *pl. n.* **1** (treated as *sing.*) the study of heredity and the variation of inherited characteristics. **2** (treated as *sing.* or *pl.*) the genetic properties of an organism etc. □ **geneticist** *n.* [Say jen NET icks, jen NETTA sist]

genial *adj.* **1** friendly and cheerful. **2** (of the climate) mild and warm. □ **geniality** *n.* **genially** *adv.* [Say JEANY ul, jeany ALA tee]

genie *n.* **1** (*pl.* **genies** or **genii**) **a** = JINNI. **b** a spirit of Arabian folklore, esp. one capable of granting wishes. **2** (**Genie**) *Cdn* an award presented by the Academy of Canadian Cinema and Television for excellence in filmmaking. [Say JEANY *for the singular,* JEANIES *or* JEANY eye *for the plural*]

genital ● *adj.* of the reproductive organs. ● *n.* (in *pl.*) the external reproductive organs.

genitalia *pl. n.* the genitals. [Say jenna TAIL yuh]

genitive ● *n.* the grammatical case indicating possession or close association. ● *adj.* of or in the genitive. [Say JENNA tiv]

genius *n.* (*pl.* **geniuses**) **1** exceptional natural ability. **2** an exceptionally intelligent or able person.

genocide *n.* the mass extermination of human beings, esp. from a particular

ethnic group or nation. □ **genocidal** *adj.* [Say JENNA side]

genome *n.* **1** the haploid set of chromosomes of an organism. **2** the genetic material of an organism. □ **genomic** *adj.* [Say JEE nome, jee NOM ick]

genotype *n.* the genetic constitution of an individual. [Say JEAN oh type]

genre ● *n.* a style or category of art or literature. ● *adj.* denoting a film etc. following the conventions of a recognizable genre. [Say ZHON ruh]

gent *n. informal* (often *jocular*) a gentleman.

genteel *adj.* ostentatiously refined or polite. □ **genteelly** *adv.*

gentian *n.* a plant with violet or blue trumpet-shaped flowers. [Say JEN sh'n]

Gentile ● *adj.* not Jewish. ● *n.* a person who is not Jewish. [Say JEN tile]

gentility *n.* **1** refined manners and habits. **2** affected or pretentious refinement. **3** people of noble birth. [Say jen TILLA tee]

gentle *adj.* (**gentler, gentlest**) **1** not rough; mild or kind. **2 a** moderate. **b** gradual. **3** of or fit for people of elevated social position. **4** docile. □ **gently** *adv.*

gentleman *n.* (*pl.* **gentlemen**) **1** a man (in polite or formal use). **2** a courteous and honourable man. **3** a man of good social position. □ **gentlemanly** *adj.*

gentleman's agreement *n.* an agreement based upon trust but not legally enforceable.

Gentleman Usher of the Black Rod *n. see* BLACK ROD.

gentrify *v.* (**gentrifies, gentrified, gentrifying**) convert (a poor neighbourhood etc.) into an area of middle-class residence. □ **gentrification** *n.* **gentrifier** *n.* [Say JENTRA fie, jentra fuh KAY sh'n]

gentry *pl. n.* **1** people of high social standing. **2** (in the UK) the class of people next below the nobility.

genuflect *v.* bend the knee to the ground, esp. in worship or as a sign of respect. □ **genuflection** *n.* [Say JEN you fleckt]

genuine *adj.* **1** truly what it is said to be. **2** not sham. **3** sincere. **4** (of a person) free from affectation or hypocrisy. □ **genuinely** *adv.* **genuineness** *n.* [Say JEN you in *or* JEN you ine]

genus *n.* (*pl.* **genera**) a taxonomic category ranking above species and below family, grouping organisms that have common characteristics. [Say JEE nus *or* JEN us *for the singular,* JENNER uh *for the plural*]

geo- *comb. form* **1** earth. **2** global.

geocentric adj. having or considering the earth as the centre.

geochemistry n. the chemistry of the earth and its rocks, minerals, etc. □ **geochemical** adj. **geochemist** n.

geode n. **1** a small cavity lined with crystals or other mineral matter. **2** a rock containing such a cavity. [Say JEE ode]

geodesic ● adj. **1** relating to the branch of mathematics dealing with the shape of the earth or large parts of it. **2** relating to a geodesic line. **3** (of a dome) constructed of struts along geodesic lines. ● n. (also **geodesic line**) the shortest possible line between two points on a curved surface. [Say geo DEE sick or geo DESS ick]

geoduck n. a giant mud-burrowing bivalve mollusc of N America. [Say GOOEY duck]

geography n. **1** the study of the physical features of the earth and of human activity as it relates to these. **2** the arrangement and way in which the physical features of a place are arranged. □ **geographer** n. **geographical** (also **geographic**) adj. **geographically** adv.

geology n. **1** the science of the earth (or another planet etc.), including the composition, structure, and origin of its rocks. **2** the geological features of a district. □ **geological** adj. **geologist** n.

geometric adj. (also **geometrical**) **1** related to geometry. **2** decorated with regular lines and shapes. □ **geometrically** adv.

geometric mean n. the central number in a geometric progression (e.g. 9 in 3, 9, 27).

geometric progression n. a sequence of numbers with a constant ratio between each number and the one before (as 1, 3, 9, 27).

geometry n. (pl. **geometries**) **1** the branch of mathematics concerned with the properties and relations of points, lines, surfaces, and solids. **2** the relative arrangement of objects or parts.

geomorphic adj. relating to the physical features of the earth's surface. [Say geo MORF ick]

geomorphology n. the study of the physical features of the earth's surface and their relation to its geological structures. □ **geomorphological** adj. [Say geo morf OLLA jee]

geophysics n. the science concerned with the physical properties of the earth, including seismology, gravity, magnetism, etc. □ **geophysical** adj. **geophysicist** n.

geopolitics n. **1** the politics of a country as determined by its geographical features.

2 politics on a global scale. □ **geopolitical** adj.

Georgian[1] adj. **1 a** of or characteristic of the time of Kings George I–IV of England (1714–1830). **b** relating to the architecture of this period. **2** of or characteristic of the time of Kings George V and VI of England (1910–52). [Say JORE jin]

Georgian[2] adj. relating to the US state of Georgia. □ **Georgian** n. [Say JORE jin]

Georgian[3] n. **1** a person from Georgia, a country in SE Europe. **2** the language of Georgia. □ **Georgian** adj. [Say JORE jin]

geoscience n. earth sciences, e.g. geology, geophysics. □ **geoscientist** n. [Say geo SCIENCE]

geothermal adj. relating to or produced by the internal heat of the earth.

geranium n. a plant that is widely cultivated for its red, pink, or white flowers. [Say RAINY um]

gerbil n. a mouselike desert rodent. [Say JUR bull]

geriatric ● adj. relating to old age or old people. ● n. an old person, esp. one receiving special care. [Say jerry AT rick]

geriatrics pl. n. (usu. treated as sing.) a branch of medicine or social science dealing with the health and care of old people. [Say jerry AT ricks]

germ n. **1** a micro-organism, esp. one which causes disease. **2 a** a portion of an organism capable of developing into a new one. **b** an embryo of a seed. **3** an original idea etc. from which something may develop.

German n. **1** a person from Germany. **2** the language of Germany, also used in Austria and Switzerland. □ **German** adj.

germane adj. relevant. [Say jur MANE]

Germanic ● adj. **1** of the language group including English, German, Dutch, and the Scandinavian languages. **2** of the Scandinavians, Anglo-Saxons, or Germans. **3** having to do with Germans and Germany. ● n. **1** the Germanic family of languages. **2** the ancient language from which these developed. [Say jur MANIC]

germanium n. a semi-metallic element occurring naturally and used in semiconductors. [Say jur MAINY um]

German measles n. a contagious disease, rubella, resembling a mild form of measles.

German shepherd n. a large dog with a shaggy tail, used as a guard dog and in police work.

germicide n. a substance destroying germs. □ **germicidal** adj. [Say JERMA side, jerma SIDE ul]

germinate v. (**germinates**, **germinated**, **germinating**) **1** sprout, bud, or put forth shoots. **2** come into existence. □**germination** n.

germ warfare n. the systematic spreading of micro-organisms to cause disease in an enemy population.

gerontology n. the scientific study of old age, aging, and old people. □**gerontologist** n. [Say jare un TOLLA jee]

gerrymander ● v. **1** alter the boundaries of (a constituency etc.) so as to favour some party or class. **2** manipulate (a situation etc.) to gain advantage. ● n. this practice. □**gerrymandering** n.

gerund n. a noun formed from a verb, in English ending in -ing. [Say JARE ind]

gesso n. (pl. **gessoes**) plaster of Paris as used in painting as a ground or in sculpture. [Say JESSO]

gestalt n. Psychology an organized whole that is perceived as more than the sum of its parts. [Say guh STAWLT]

Gestapo n. the German secret police under Nazi rule. [Say guh STOPPO]

gestate v. (**gestates**, **gestated**, **gestating**) **1** carry (a fetus) in gestation. **2** develop. [Say JESS tate]

gestation n. **1 a** the process of developing in the womb between conception and birth. **b** this period. **2** the private development of a plan, idea, etc. □**gestational** adj. [Say jess TAY sh'n]

gesticulate v. (**gesticulates**, **gesticulated**, **gesticulating**) use esp. lively gestures instead of or in addition to speech. □**gesticulation** n. [Say jess TICK yoo late]

gesture ● n. **1** a movement of the hand or head to express thought or feeling. **2** an action performed to show one's feelings or intentions. ● v. make a gesture. □**gestural** adj. **gesturally** adv.

gesundheit interj. expressing a wish of good health to a person who has sneezed. [Say guh ZOON tite]

get v. (**gets**; past **got**; past participle **got** or **gotten**; **getting**) **1** come to have. **2** go to reach or catch. **3** prepare. **4** become or cause to become. **5** obtain as a result of calculation. **6** establish or be in communication with; receive (a radio signal etc.). **7** experience or suffer. **8** successfully achieve, bring, place, etc. **9** (preceded by have) **a** possess. **b** be bound or obliged. **10** induce. **11** informal understand. **12** informal inflict punishment or retribution on. **13** informal **a** annoy. **b** affect emotionally. **c** attract. **14** develop an inclination as specified. **15** begin. **16** catch in an argument; puzzle. **17** establish in one's mind. **18** answer. **19** move or come into a particular condition or position. □**be getting on for** be approaching. **get across** communicate or be communicated. **get ahead** be or become successful. **get along** (or **on**) live harmoniously. **get around 1** (also **get about**) **a** travel extensively. **b** manage to walk, move about, etc. **c** be circulated. **2** evade. **get around to** deal with in due course. **get at 1** reach. **2** informal imply. **3** informal criticize. **get away 1** escape. **2** (foll. by with) escape punishment for. **get back 1** move back or away. **2** return. **3** recover (something lost). **4** (usu. foll. by to) contact later. **get back at** informal retaliate against. **get by** informal **1** barely manage. **2** be acceptable. **get down to** begin working on. **get into** become interested in. **get it** slang be punished. **get off 1** informal be acquitted. **2** start. **3** alight; alight from. **get off on** slang be excited or aroused by. **get on 1** make progress. **2** enter. **3** = GET ALONG. **4** (usu. as **getting on**) informal grow old. **get a person out** help a person to leave. **get out of 1** avoid or escape. **2** abandon. **get over 1** recover from. **2** overcome. **3** communicate. **4** overcome one's disbelief about. **get one's own back** informal have one's revenge. **get to 1** reach. **2** annoy. **3** = GET DOWN TO. **have got it bad** (or **badly**) slang be obsessed or affected emotionally. □**getter** n.

get-at-able adj. informal accessible.

getaway n. **1** an escape. **2 a** a place far from work or home, visited for relaxation. **b** a relaxing holiday.

get-go n. informal the very beginning.

get-out n. □**as all get-out** informal to a high degree.

get-together n. informal a social gathering.

getup n. informal a style or arrangement of dress.

get-up-and-go n. informal energy, enthusiasm.

gewgaw n. a gaudy trinket.

geyser n. an intermittently gushing hot spring that throws up a tall column of water. [Say GUY zur]

G-force n. the force of acceleration due to gravity.

GG abbr. **1** Governor General. **2** Cdn = GOVERNOR GENERAL'S AWARD.

Ghanaian adj. relating to Ghana. □**Ghanaian** n. [Say guh NAY un]

ghastly ● adj. (**ghastlier**, **ghastliest**) **1** horrible. **2** deathlike. ● adv. in a ghastly way.

ghee *n.* clarified butter as used in Indian cuisine. [*Say* GEE *(with G as in* GEESE*)*]

gherkin *n.* **1** a small pickled cucumber. **2** a trailing plant with small cucumber-like fruits. [*Say* GUR kin]

ghetto *n.* (*pl.* **ghettos** or **ghettoes**) **1** a part of a city occupied by a minority group. **2** *hist.* an area of a city in which Jews were required to live. **3** a situation in which a group is segregated because of discrimination or its own preference.

ghettoize *v.* (**ghettoizes**, **ghettoized**, **ghettoizing**) restrict to a certain category by prejudice. □ **ghettoization** *n.*

ghost ● *n.* **1** the supposed apparition of a dead person or animal; a disembodied spirit. **2** a faint trace or shadow. ● *v.* ghostwrite. □ **give up the ghost** *informal* die. □ **ghostlike** *adj.*

ghostly *adj.* (**ghostlier**, **ghostliest**) like a ghost.

ghost town *n.* a deserted town.

ghostwrite *v.* write material to be published under another person's name. □ **ghostwriter** *n.*

ghoul *n.* an evil spirit, esp. one preying on corpses. **2** a person morbidly interested in death. □ **ghoulish** *adj.* **ghoulishly** *adv.* **ghoulishness** *n.* [*Say* GOOL]

GI *n.* (*pl.* **GIs**) a private soldier in the US Army.

giant ● *n.* **1** an imaginary being of human form but superhuman size. **2** an abnormally tall or large person, animal, or plant. **3** an exceptionally prominent or able person, company, etc. **4** a large and bright star. ● *adj.* very big or important etc. □ **giantism** *n.* **giant-like** *adj.*

giardia *n.* a microscopic organism found in untreated water. [*Say* jee ARDY uh]

giardiasis *n.* infection of the intestines with giardia, often from drinking untreated lake water, causing diarrhea etc. [*Say* jee arr DIE a sis]

gibber *v.* speak fast and inarticulately. □ **gibbering** *n.* & *adj.* [*Say* JIBBER]

gibberish *n.* unintelligible speech or writing. [*Say* JIBBER ish]

gibbon *n.* a small, slender, tree-dwelling ape native to Southeast Asia. [*Say* GIB un]

gibe *n.* & *v.* = JIBE[1]. [*Say* JIBE]

giblets *pl. n.* the liver, gizzard, heart, neck, etc., of a fowl. [*Say* JIB lits]

GIC *n.* (*pl.* **GICs**) *Cdn* = GUARANTEED INVESTMENT CERTIFICATE.

giddy *adj.* (**giddier**, **giddiest**) **1** having a sensation of whirling and a tendency to fall; dizzy. **2 a** overexcited. **b** (of a person) not serious. □ **giddily** *adv.* **giddiness** *n.*

giddying *adj.* tending to make one giddy.

giddy-up *interj.* (also **giddyap**) commanding a horse to go or go faster.

GIF *n.* **1** *Computing* a format for image files, with built-in data compression. **2** a file in this format. [*Say* GIFF]

gift ● *n.* **1** a thing given freely. **2** a natural ability or talent. **3** an act of giving something as a present. ● *v.* endow with. □ **look a gift horse in the mouth** find fault with what has been given.

gifted *adj.* exceptionally talented. □ **giftedness** *n.*

giftware *n.* goods sold as being suitable as gifts.

gift-wrap ● *v.* (**gift-wraps**, **gift-wrapped**, **gift-wrapping**) wrap attractively as a gift. ● *n.* decorative paper etc. for wrapping gifts.

gig *informal* ● *n.* **1** a live performance by or engagement for a musician or other performer. **2** a job, esp. likely to be temporary. **3** *hist.* a small light carriage with two wheels, pulled by one horse. **4** a gigabyte. ● *v.* (**gigs**, **gigged**, **gigging**) perform in gigs.

giga- *comb. form* **1** denoting a factor of 10^9 (i.e. one billion). **2** *Computing* (in the binary system) denoting a factor of 2^{30} (i.e. 1 073 741 824).

gigabyte *n.* 1 073 741 824 (i.e. 2^{30}) bytes as a measure of data capacity, or loosely 1 000 000 000. [*Say* GIGGA byte *or* JIGGA byte]

gigantic *adj.* very large.

giggle ● *v.* laugh in a half-suppressed, silly manner. ● *n.* **1** such a laugh. **2** *informal* an amusing person or thing. □ **giggler** *n.*

giggly *adj.* (**gigglier**, **giggliest**) laughing a lot in a silly, nervous way.

gigolo *n.* (*pl.* **gigolos**) **1** a young man paid by an older woman to be her escort or lover. **2** a professional male dancing partner or escort. [*Say* JIGGA lo]

gild *v.* (**gilds**, **gilded**, **gilding**) **1** cover thinly with gold. **2** tinge with a golden colour. □ **gild the lily** try to improve what is already excellent. □ **gilding** *n.*

gilded *adj.* **1** covered with a thin layer of gold or gold paint. **2** wealthy and privileged.

gilded cage *n.* a luxurious but restrictive environment.

gill ● *n.* (usu. in *pl.*) **1** the respiratory organ in fishes and other aquatic animals. **2** the vertical radial plates on the underside of mushrooms and other fungi. **3** the flesh below a person's jaws. ● *v.* **1** gut or clean (a fish). **2** catch in a gillnet. □ **to the gills** completely. □ **gilled** *adj.* (also in *comb.*)

Giller Prize *n.* *Cdn* a prize awarded to the

author of the best Canadian novel or short story collection published in English each year.

gillnet *n.* a net suspended vertically to entangle fish by the gills.

gillnetter *n.* **1** a person who fishes using gillnets. **2** a ship or boat designed for fishing with gillnets.

gilt ● *adj.* covered thinly with gold or a gold-like substance. ● *n.* gold or a gold-like substance applied in a thin layer to a surface.

gilt-edged *adj.* **1** (of a page, book, etc.) having a gilded edge. **2** of the highest quality. **3** particularly reliable as an investment.

gimcrack *adj.* showy but flimsy. □ **gimcrackery** *n.* [Say JIM crack]

gimmick *n. informal* a trick or device for attracting attention etc. □ **gimmickry** *n.* **gimmicky** *adj.*

gimp *slang* ● *n.* a lame person or leg. ● *v.* limp, hobble. □ **gimpy** *adj.*

gin¹ *n.* **1** a hard liquor flavoured esp. with juniper berries. **2** = GIN RUMMY.

gin² *n.* **1** a snare or trap. **2** a machine for separating cotton from its seeds.

ginch *n. var. of* GOTCH.

ginger ● *n.* **1** a hot spicy root of a Southeast Asian plant, used in cooking, preserved in syrup, or candied. **2** ginger ale. ● *adj.* of a light reddish-yellow colour. ● *v.* **1** flavour with ginger. **2** *informal* enliven. □ **gingery** *adj.*

ginger ale *n.* a fizzy drink flavoured with ginger extract.

ginger beer *n.* an effervescent, cloudy soft drink strongly flavoured with ginger.

gingerbread *n.* **1** a cake or cookie made with molasses and flavoured with ginger. **2** elaborate carving or other trim on buildings.

gingerly *adv.* carefully.

gingersnap *n.* a brittle, ginger-flavoured cookie.

gingham *n.* a plain-woven cotton cloth, esp. with a checked pattern. [Say GING um]

gingiva *n. Dentistry* the gums. □ **gingival** *adj.* [Say JIN jiv uh or jin JIVE uh, jin JIVE ul]

gingivitis *n.* inflammation of the gums. [Say jin juh VITE is]

ginkgo *n.* (also **gingko**) (*pl.* **ginkgos** or **ginkgoes**) a tree with fan-shaped leaves from which is derived a herbal remedy reputed to improve mental function.

ginormous *adj. slang* very large. [Say jye NOR mus]

gin rummy *n.* a form of rummy in which a player holding cards totalling ten or less may terminate play.

ginseng *n.* a plant whose root is used for medicinal purposes. [Say JIN seng]

gipsy *n.* = GYPSY.

giraffe *n.* a large mammal, the tallest living animal, with a very long neck.

gird *v.* (**girds**, **girded**, **girding**) *literary* **1** encircle with a belt. **2** enclose. **3** (foll. by *for*) prepare. □ **gird** (or **gird up**) **one's loins** prepare for action.

girder *n.* a large iron or steel beam or compound structure for bearing loads.

girdle ● *n.* **1** a woman's corset extending from waist to thigh. **2** a belt worn around the waist. **3** a thing that surrounds like a belt. ● *v.* (**girdles**, **girdled**, **girdling**) **1** surround with or as with a girdle. **2** remove a ring of bark from a branch or tree to kill it.

girl *n.* **1** a female child or youth. **2** *informal* a young (esp. unmarried) woman. **3** *informal* a daughter. **4** *informal* a girlfriend. □ **girlhood** *n.*

girlfriend *n.* **1** a regular female companion or lover. **2** a female friend.

Girl Guide *n.* a member of a girls' organization promoting outdoor activity and community service.

girlie (also **girly**) *informal* ● *adj.* **1** (of a magazine etc.) depicting nude young women in erotic poses. **2** characteristic of or appropriate for a young woman. ● *n.* (*pl.* **girlies**) *offensive* a young woman.

girlish *adj.* of or like a young girl. □ **girlishly** *adv.* **girlishness** *n.*

girth *n.* **1** the distance around a thing. **2** a band around the body of a horse to secure the saddle etc.

GIS *abbr. Cdn* Guaranteed Income Supplement, a federally-supported supplement to monthly pension payments.

gist *n.* the substance or essence of a matter. [Say JIST]

gitch *n. Cdn slang* underwear.

Gitksan *n.* (*pl.* **Gitksan** or **Gitksans**) an Aboriginal group living along the Skeena River in north central BC, or their Tsimshian language. [Say git K'SAWN]

give ● *v.* (**gives**, **gave**, **given**) **1** cause to receive or have. **2** be inclined to. **3** yield as a result. **4** yield to pressure. **5** devote. **6** present; show. **7** be a source of. **8** allow. **9** value. **10** concede. ● *n.* **1** capacity to yield or bend. **2** ability to adapt or comply. □ **give and take** exchange. **give away 1** transfer. **2** betray or expose. **give forth** emit; publish; report. **give the game** (or **show**) **away** reveal a secret. **give in**

yield. **give off** emit (vapour etc.). **give oneself airs** act pretentiously or snobbishly. **give oneself up** surrender. **give or take** *informal* add or subtract (a specified amount) in estimating. **give out** **1** emit; distribute. **2** be exhausted. **give over 1** *informal* abandon (a habit etc.); desist. **2** hand over. **give rise to** cause. **give up 1** resign; surrender. **2** part with. **3** renounce or cease. **what gives?** *informal* what's happening?; what's the problem? □ **giver** *n.*

give-and-take *n.* a discussion, compromise etc.

giveaway *n.* *informal* **1** an inadvertent betrayal or revelation. **2** an act of giving away. **3** something given away free. **4** the inadvertent giving of a puck etc. to an opponent.

given ● *adj.* **1** as previously stated. **2** *Law* (of a document) signed and dated. ● *n.* a known fact or situation.

given name *n.* a name given to a child, distinguished from the surname.

gizmo *n.* (*pl.* **gizmos**) *informal* a gadget.

gizzard *n.* **1** the second part of a bird's stomach, for grinding food usu. with grit. **2** a muscular stomach of some fish, insects, molluscs, etc. **3** *informal* the throat.

glacial *adj.* **1** of or resembling ice. **2** relating to the action of glaciers. **3** extremely slow. □ **glacially** *adv.* [*Say* GLAY shull]

glaciated *adj.* covered or previously covered by glaciers. □ **glaciation** *n.* [*Say* GLAY see ate id]

glacier *n.* a slow-moving river of ice formed by the accumulation and compaction of snow on mountains or near the poles. [*Say* GLAY shur *or* GLAY she ur]

glad¹ *adj.* (**gladder**, **gladdest**) **1 a** pleased. **b** relieved. **c** (usu. foll. by *of*) grateful. **d** willing and eager. **2** giving or expressing joy. □ **give a person the glad eye** *informal* cast an amorous glance at a person. □ **gladly** *adv.* **gladness** *n.*

glad² *n.* *informal* a gladiolus.

gladden *v.* make glad.

glade *n.* an open space in a wood or forest.

glad hand ● *n.* a warm superficial welcome. ● *v.* (**glad-hand**) greet warmly and superficially. □ **glad-hander** *n.*

gladiator *n.* *hist.* a man trained to fight at ancient Roman shows. □ **gladiatorial** *adj.*

gladiolus *n.* (*pl.* **gladioli** *or* **gladioluses**) (also *informal* **gladiola**) a plant of the iris family with brightly coloured flower spikes. [*Say* gladdy OH lus *for the singular,* gladdy OH lie *or* gladdy OH lus is *for the plural*]

glam *informal* ● *adj.* glamorous. ● *n.* glamour.

glamorize *v.* (**glamorizes**, **glamorized**, **glamorizing**) make glamorous.

glamour *n.* (also **glamor**) **1** physical attractiveness, esp. when achieved by makeup, elegant clothing, etc. **2** an attractive or exciting quality, esp. one which is inaccessible to the average person. □ **glamorous** *adj.* **glamorously** *adv.*

glance ● *v.* (**glances**, **glanced**, **glancing**) **1** cast a momentary look. **2** strike or bounce off (an object) obliquely. ● *n.* **1** a brief look. **2** a flash or gleam. □ **at a glance** immediately upon looking. **at first glance** initially. □ **glancing** *adj.* **glancingly** *adv.*

gland *n.* **1** an organ or group of cells secreting substances for use in a body or for ejection. **2** a structure resembling this, such as a lymph gland.

glandular *adj.* relating to a gland or glands. [*Say* GLAND you lur]

glans *n.* (*pl.* **glandes**) the rounded part forming the head of the penis or clitoris. [*Say* GLANZ *for the singular,* GLAN deez *for the plural*]

glare¹ ● *v.* (**glares**, **glared**, **glaring**) **1** look fiercely. **2** shine or reflect light dazzlingly. ● *n.* **1 a** strong fierce light. **b** oppressive public attention. **2** a fierce look.

glare² *adj.* (esp. of ice) smooth and glassy.

glaring *adj.* **1** obvious. **2** shining light oppressively. **3** staring fiercely. □ **glaringly** *adv.*

glasnost *n.* *hist.* (in the former Soviet Union) the policy of more open government and dissemination of information. [*Say* GLAZ nost]

glass *n.* **1** a hard, brittle, usu. transparent substance, made by fusing sand with soda and lime. **2** (often *collect.*) a drinking vessel. **3** (in *pl.*) **a** eyeglasses. **b** binoculars.

glass-blowing *n.* the blowing of semi-molten glass to make glassware. □ **glass-blower** *n.*

glass ceiling *n.* an unacknowledged barrier to progress in a profession, esp. affecting women and members of minorities.

glassed-in *adj.* surrounded by or enclosed in glass.

glasshouse *n.* *Cdn & Brit.* a greenhouse.

glass-making *n.* the manufacture of glass.

glassware *n.* articles made from glass.

glassy *adj.* (**glassier**, **glassiest**) **1** smooth like glass. **2** abstracted; dull.

glaucoma *n.* a condition of the eye with

increased pressure within the eyeball, causing gradual loss of sight. [*Say* glaw COMA]

glaze ● *n.* **1** a glass-like substance used to give a hard shiny surface to pottery. **2** a smooth shiny coating of sugar etc., on food. **3** a thin topcoat of transparent paint used to modify the tone of the underlying colour. **4** a thin coating of ice. ● *v.* (**glazes, glazed, glazing**) **1** fit (a window etc.) with glass. **2** cover with a glaze. **3** (often foll. by *over*) (of the eyes) become fixed or glassy. **4** coat with a thin layer of ice.

glazing *n.* **1** the action of installing windows. **2** windows. **3** material used to produce a glaze.

gleam ● *n.* **1** a faint or brief light. **2** a faint or brief show or expression. ● *v.* **1** emit gleams. **2** shine brightly with reflected light. **3** (of a quality) be indicated.

glean *v.* **1** collect (news, gossip, etc.) in small quantities. **2** gather (ears of grain etc.) after the harvest. □ **gleaner** *n.*

gleanings *pl. n.* things gleaned, esp. facts.

glee *n.* triumphant delight. □ **gleeful** *adj.* **gleefully** *adv.* **gleefulness** *n.*

glen *n.* a narrow valley.

glib *adj.* (**glibber, glibbest**) using words that are clever but not sincere. □ **glibly** *adv.* **glibness** *n.*

glide ● *v.* (**glides, glided, gliding**) **1** move with a smooth continuous motion. **2** fly without engine power. ● *n.* an instance of gliding.

glider *n.* **1 a** an aircraft that flies without an engine. **b** a glider pilot. **2** a person or thing that glides.

glimmer ● *v.* shine faintly or intermittently. ● *n.* **1** a feeble or wavering light. **2** a faint sign (of hope etc.). **3** a glimpse. □ **glimmering** *n. & adj.*

glimpse ● *n.* (often foll. by *of*) **1** a momentary or partial view. **2** a faint and transient appearance. ● *v.* (**glimpses, glimpsed, glimpsing**) **1** see faintly or partly. **2** (often foll. by *at*) cast a passing glance.

glint ● *v.* flash; sparkle; reflect. ● *n.* a brief flash or sparkle of light.

glissando *n.* a continuous rapid slide of adjacent notes upwards or downwards. [*Say* glis SAN doe]

glisten *v.* (of something wet) shine or sparkle.

glitch *n.* a sudden irregularity or malfunction.

glitter ● *v.* **1** shine or sparkle. **2** be showy. ● *n.* **1** a gleam. **2** showiness; splendour. **3** tiny pieces of sparkling material. □ **glittery** *adj.*

glitterati *pl. n. informal jocular* fashionable, wealthy literary or show-business people. [*Say* glitta ROTTY]

glitz *n. informal* extravagant but superficial display. □ **glitzy** *adj.*

gloat *v.* (often foll. by *on, upon, over*) be smug about one's success or another's failure. □ **gloater** *n.* **gloatingly** *adv.*

glob *n.* a lump of semi-liquid substance.

global *adj.* **1** worldwide. **2** relating or applying to the whole of something. □ **globally** *adv.*

globalize *v.* (**globalizes, globalized, globalizing**) make or become global. □ **globalization** *n.*

Global Positioning System *n.* a system using satellites to pinpoint the location of a receiver on the earth's surface.

global warming *n.* the increase in temperature of the earth's atmosphere supposedly caused by the greenhouse effect.

globe *n.* **1** any spherical body; a ball. **2** (**the globe**) the planet earth. **3** a spherical model of usu. the earth, with a map on the surface.

globetrotting ● *n.* frequent and extensive travelling. ● *adj.* engaging in extensive travelling. □ **globetrotter** *n.*

globular *adj.* **1** spherical. **2** composed of globules. [*Say* GLOB yoo lur]

globule *n.* a small globe or round particle. [*Say* GLOB yool]

globulin *n.* any of a group of single proteins found in blood serum. [*Say* GLOB yoo lin]

glockenspiel *n.* a musical instrument containing metal pieces which are struck with small hammers. [*Say* GLOCK un speel]

gloom *n.* **1** darkness; obscurity. **2** sadness.

gloomy *adj.* (**gloomier, gloomiest**) **1** dark; not lighted. **2** depressed. **3** dismal. □ **gloomily** *adv.*

gloop *n. informal* semi-liquid or sticky material. □ **gloopy** *adj.* (**gloopier, gloopiest**)

glop *slang* ● *n.* a liquid or sticky mess. ● *v.* (**glops, glopped, glopping**) **1** scoop or drop (a semi-liquid substance). **2** ooze or splat. □ **gloppy** *adj.*

glorified *adj.* made out to be more splendid than in reality.

glorify *v.* (**glorifies, glorified, glorifying**) **1** exalt to heavenly glory. **2** praise. □ **glorification** *n.*

glorious *adj.* **1** possessing or conferring glory. **2** splendid. □ **gloriously** *adv.*

glory ● *n.* (*pl.* **glories**) **1** high renown or fame. **2** praise and thanksgiving. **3** resplendent majesty. **4** a distinction. **5** the splendour of heaven. **6** *informal* a state of exaltation or happiness. ● *v.* pride oneself.

gloss¹ *n.* **1 a** surface shine or lustre. **b** a smooth finish. **2** deceptively attractive appearance. **3** (also **gloss paint**) paint formulated to give a hard glossy finish. **4** a cosmetic applied to add lustre to skin. □ **gloss over** conceal or evade by mentioning briefly or misleadingly.

gloss² ● *n.* an explanatory word or phrase. ● *v.* (**glosses, glossed, glossing**) add a gloss or glosses to (text etc.).

glossary *n.* (*pl.* **glossaries**) an alphabetical list of terms found in a specific subject or text, with explanations.

glossy ● *adj.* (**glossier, glossiest**) **1** having a shine; smooth. **2** (of paper etc.) smooth and shiny. **3** (of a magazine etc.) printed on such paper. **4** having a deceptively smooth and attractive appearance. ● *n.* (*pl.* **glossies**) *informal* **1** a glossy magazine. **2** a photograph with a glossy surface. □ **glossiness** *n.*

glottis *n.* (*pl.* **glottises**) the part of the larynx made up of the vocal cords and the slit-like opening between them.

glove ● *n.* **1** a covering for the hand, having separate fingers. **2** a padded covering for the hand used in hockey, boxing, etc. ● *v.* (**gloves, gloved, gloving**) **1** (usu. as **gloved** *adj.*) cover or provide with a glove or gloves. **2** catch (a ball, puck, etc.) in a glove. □ **drop the** (or **one's**) **gloves 1** (in hockey) remove one's gloves in order to fight. **2** *Cdn* engage in a debate, confrontation, etc. **fit like a glove** fit exactly. **with the gloves off** mercilessly; unfairly.

glove compartment *n.* (also **glovebox**) a recess for small articles in the dashboard of a motor vehicle.

glow ● *v.* **1 a** throw out light and heat. **b** shine as though heated. **2** (of the cheeks) redden, esp. from cold or exercise. **3** express or experience strong emotion, esp. joy. **4** show a warm colour. ● *n.* **1** a glowing state. **2** a warm, esp. rosy, colour. **3** ardour; passion. **4** a feeling induced by good health, exercise, etc.

glower ● *v.* stare or scowl angrily. ● *n.* a glowering look. □ **gloweringly** *adv.* [*Rhymes with* FLOWER]

glowing *adj.* **1** giving light and heat. **2** expressing pride or praise. □ **glowingly** *adv.*

glow-worm *n.* a soft-bodied beetle with luminescent organs in the abdomen.

glucosamine *n.* a crystalline amino sugar that is derived from glucose and is the principal constituent of chitin. [*Say* glue KOSE a meen]

glucosamine sulphate *n.* a nutritional supplement that is a sulphate of glucosamine and which relieves the symptoms and delays the progress of osteoarthritis.

glucose *n.* **1** a simple sugar containing six carbon atoms. **2** a syrup containing glucose sugars. [*Say* GLUE kose]

glue ● *n.* an adhesive substance used for sticking things together. ● *v.* (**glues, glued, gluing** or **glueing**) **1** fasten or join with glue. **2** keep or put very close. **3** set fixedly.

glue gun *n.* a hand-held tool for melting and applying glue.

gluey *adj.* (**gluier, gluiest**) resembling glue.

glug ● *v.* (**glugs, glugged, glugging**) pour or drink (liquid) with a gurgling sound. ● *n.* such a sound.

glum *adj.* (**glummer, glummest**) looking or feeling dejected. □ **glumly** *adv.* **glumness** *n.*

glut ● *n.* **1** supply exceeding demand. **2** an excessive quantity. ● *v.* (**gluts, glutted, glutting**) **1** overstock with goods. **2** fill to excess. **3** feed or indulge to the full.

glutamate *n.* *see* MONOSODIUM GLUTAMATE. [*Say* GLOOTA mate]

gluten *n.* a mixture of proteins present in cereal grains, responsible for the elasticity of dough. [*Say* GLUE tin]

gluteus *n.* (*pl.* **glutei**) any of the three muscles in each buttock. [*Say* GLUE tee us *for the singular,* GLUE tee eye *for the plural*]

gluteus maximus *n.* (*pl.* **glutei maximi**) **1** the largest and outermost muscle of each buttock. **2** *slang* the buttocks. [*For the plural, say* GLUE tee eye MAXA mye]

glutinous *adj.* sticky; like glue. [*Say* GLUE tin us]

glutton *n.* **1** an excessively greedy eater. **2** (often foll. by *for*) *informal* a person insatiably eager. □ **a glutton for punishment** a person eager to take on hard or unpleasant tasks. □ **gluttonous** *adj.* **gluttonously** *adv.*

gluttony *n.* habitual greed or excess in eating.

glycemic index *n.* the ability of a food to increase blood sugar, calculated as the increase in blood glucose over 2 hours after consuming 50 g of carbohydrate, expressed as a percentage of that after 50 g of glucose. [*Say* glice EEMIC]

glyceride n. any fatty-acid ester of glycerol. [Say GLISSA ride]

glycerine n. (esp. US **glycerin**) = GLYCEROL. [Say GLISSA rin]

glycerol n. a liquid by-product of soap manufacture, used as an emollient and laxative. [Say GLISSA rawl]

glycogen n. a polysaccharide serving as a store of carbohydrates. [Say GLYE kuh jen]

glycol n. an alcohol containing two hydroxyl groups in each molecule. [Say GLYE call]

glyph n. **1** a sculptured character or symbol. **2** a symbol or pictorial representation. □ **glyphic** adj. [Say GLIFF]

GM abbr. (pl. **GMs**) **1** general manager. **2** genetically modified.

gm abbr. gram(s).

GMO abbr. genetically modified organism.

GMT abbr. Greenwich Mean Time.

gnarled adj. knobbly, twisted. [Say NARLD]

gnarly adj. **1** = GNARLED. **2** slang excitingly rough. [Say NARLY]

gnash v. (**gnashes, gnashed, gnashing**) grind (one's teeth) together, esp. in frustration. [Say NASH]

gnat n. a small two-winged biting fly. [Say NAT]

gnaw v. **1 a** wear away by biting. **b** bite, nibble. **2** cause persistent anxiety to. [Say NAW]

gnawing adj. persistent. □ **gnawingly** adv. [Say NAWING]

gneiss n. a metamorphic rock foliated by mineral layers, principally of feldspar, quartz, and mica. [Sounds like NICE]

gnocchi pl. n. an Italian dish of small dumplings usu. made from potato, flour, etc. [Say NYOCKY]

gnome n. a dwarfish legendary creature supposed to guard the earth's treasures underground. [Say NOME]

gnomon n. the pin on a sundial that shows the time by its shadow. [Say NO mon]

gnostic ● adj. **1** relating to knowledge. **2** (**Gnostic**) of or concerning Gnosticism or the Gnostics. ● n. (**Gnostic**) (usu. in pl.) an adherent of Gnosticism. [Say NOSS tick]

Gnosticism n. a heretical movement prominent in the Christian Church in the 2nd century, emphasizing the redeeming power of special knowledge understood by only a few. [Say NOSSTA sism]

GNP abbr. gross national product.

gnu n. a large antelope native to southern Africa. [Sounds like NEW]

GNWT abbr. Cdn Government of the Northwest Territories.

go ● v. (**goes, going, went**; past part. **gone**) **1** move to or from a place. **2** pass into or be in a particular state. **3** lie or extend in a certain direction. **4** come to an end. **5** disappear or be used up. **6** (of time) pass. **7** pass time in a particular way. **8** engage in a specified activity. **9** have a particular outcome. **10** (**be going to be/do**) used to express a future tense. **11** function or operate. **12** match. **13** be acceptable or allowed. **14** fit into or be regularly kept in a particular place. **15** make a specified sound. ● n. (pl. **goes**) informal **1** an attempt. **2** a turn to do or use something. **3** spirit or energy. □ **go about** begin or carry on work at. **go along with** agree to. **go at** energetically attack or tackle. **go back on** fail to keep (a promise). **go down 1** be defeated in a contest. **2** obtain a specified reaction. **go for 1** decide on. **2** attempt to gain. **3** attack. **go halves** or **shares** share something equally. **go in for 1** enter (a contest). **2** like. **going!, gone!** an auctioneer's announcement that bidding is closing or closed. **go into 1** investigate or enquire into. **2** (of a whole number) be capable of dividing another. **go off 1** (of a gun or bomb) explode or fire. **2** esp. Brit. (of food) begin to decompose. **3** informal, esp. Brit. begin to dislike. **go on 1** continue. **2** take place. **go out 1** be extinguished. **2** carry on a regular romantic relationship with someone. **go over** examine or check the details of. **go through 1** undergo (a difficult experience). **2** examine carefully. **3** informal use up or spend. **go under** become bankrupt. **go with 1** give one's consent or agreement to. **2** have a romantic or sexual relationship with. **go without** suffer lack or hardship. **have a go at** esp. Brit. attack or criticize. **have —— going for one** informal be in one's favour. **make a go of** informal be successful in. **no go** informal impossible, hopeless, or forbidden. **on the go** informal very active or busy. **to go** (of food or drink from a restaurant or café) to be eaten or drunk off the premises.

goad ● n. **1** an implement, such as a pointed rod, used for herding cattle etc. **2** anything that torments, incites, or stimulates. ● v. **1** urge on with a goad. **2** (usu. foll. by on, into) irritate; stimulate.

go-ahead ● n. permission to proceed. ● adj. **1** enterprising. **2** Sport designating a goal, run, etc. which puts the scoring team ahead of its opponent.

goal n. **1** the object of an ambition or effort. **2 a** a pair of posts with a crossbar between which the puck or ball has to be sent to score. **b** a successful attempt to score. **3** a point marking the end of a race. **4** the position of goalkeeper.

goalie n. = GOALKEEPER.

goalkeeper n. a player stationed to protect the goal in various sports. □ **goalkeeping** n.

goalless adj. without either team scoring a goal.

goalmouth n. the space directly in front of the goal.

goalpost n. either of the two upright posts of a goal.

goals-against average n. Hockey the average number of goals scored per game against a specified goaltender. Abbreviation: **GAA**.

goaltending n. **1** (esp. in hockey) the action of defending a goal. **2** (in basketball) the illegal blocking of a shot while the ball is descending. □ **goaltender** n.

goat n. a hardy mammal with backward curving horns and (in the male) a beard. □ **get a person's goat** informal irritate a person.

goatee n. a small pointed beard like that of a goat. □ **goateed** adj. [Say go TEE]

goatherd n. a person who tends goats.

gob slang ● n. **1** a lump of esp. slimy or soft matter. **2** slang **a** Cdn spittle. **b** a globule of spittle. **3** (in pl.; foll. by of) lots of. ● v. (**gobs, gobbed, gobbing**) Cdn & Brit. spit.

gobble ● v. (**gobbles, gobbled, gobbling**) **1** eat hurriedly and noisily. **2** (often foll. by up) **a** seize avidly. **b** consume. **3** (of a male turkey) make a swallowing sound in the throat. ● n. a gobbling sound.

gobbledygook n. (also **gobbledegook**) informal unintelligible jargon.

gobbler n. informal a male turkey.

go-between n. an intermediary.

goblet n. a drinking vessel with a foot and a stem.

goblin n. a mischievous dwarf-like creature of folklore.

go-cart n. **1** = GO-KART. **2** a small esp. homemade riding cart.

god n. **1** (in many religions) a superhuman being or spirit worshipped as having power over nature, human fortunes, etc. **2** (God) (in monotheistic religions) the creator and ruler of the universe. **3** an adored, admired, or influential person. **4** (God!) an exclamation of surprise, anger, etc. □ **God knows 1** it is beyond all knowledge. **2** I call God to witness that. **in God's name** an appeal for help. **play God** attempt to control matters traditionally outside the realm of human influence.

godawful adj. slang very unpleasant, inferior, etc.

godchild n. (pl. **godchildren**) a person in relation to a godparent.

goddaughter n. a female godchild.

goddess n. (pl. **goddesses**) **1** a female deity. **2** a woman adored for her beauty.

godfather n. **1** a male godparent. **2** a person directing an illegal organization, esp. the Mafia. **3** the most experienced or influential member of an organization.

God-fearing adj. earnestly religious.

godforsaken adj. **1** (of a place) dismal. **2** remote.

godhead n. **1 a** the state of being God or a god. **b** divine nature. **2** an adored person; an idol. **3** (**the Godhead**) God.

godless adj. **1** wicked. **2** without a god. **3** not recognizing God. □ **godlessness** n.

godlike adj. resembling God or a god.

godly adj. religious. □ **godliness** n.

godmother n. a female godparent.

godparent n. a person who presents a child at baptism and promises to take responsibility for their religious education.

godsend n. an unexpected but welcome thing.

godson n. a male godchild.

Godspeed n. good fortune.

goer n. **1** (often in comb.) a person who attends, esp. regularly. **2** a person or thing that goes.

goes 3rd singular present of GO.

gofer n. informal a person who runs errands.

go-getter n. informal an aggressively enterprising person. □ **go-getting** adj.

goggle ● n. (in pl.) eyeglasses for protecting the eyes from glare, dust, water, etc. ● v. (**goggles, goggled, goggling**) **1** (often foll. by at) stare in surprise or wonder. **2** (of the eyes) protrude.

goggle-eyed adj. having staring or bulging eyes.

go-go adj. **1** (of a dancer) performing at a nightclub in scanty clothing. **2** informal unrestrained; energetic.

going ● n. **1** in senses of GO. **2 a** the condition of the ground for walking, riding, etc. **b** conditions for any activity. ● adj. **1** in or into action. **2** existing, available. **3** current. □ **get going** start. **going for one** informal acting in one's favour. **going on fifteen** etc. approaching one's fifteenth etc. birthday. **going on for** approaching. **going to** intending or intended to; about to; likely to. **to be going on with** to start with.

going concern n. a thriving business.

going-over n. (pl. **goings-over**) informal

1 an inspection or overhaul. **2** a thrashing. **3** a scolding.

goings-on *pl. n.* unusual or undesirable activities.

goitre *n.* a swelling of the neck caused by enlargement of the thyroid. [*Say* GOY tur]

go-kart *n.* a miniature race car with a skeleton body.

gold ● *n.* **1** a yellow precious metal, used as a monetary medium, in jewellery, etc. **2** the colour of gold. **3** coins or articles made of gold. **4** something precious. **5** a gold medal. ● *adj.* **1** made of gold. **2** coloured like gold.

gold card *n.* a credit card issued only to people with a high credit rating and giving benefits not available to holders of the standard card.

gold dust *n.* gold in fine particles as often found naturally.

golden *adj.* **1** made of or resembling gold. **2** precious; excellent. **3** wealthy.

golden age *n.* **1** a supposed past age of happiness and innocence. **2** the period of greatest esp. artistic achievement. **3** old age.

golden boy *n. informal* a popular man or boy.

goldeneye *n.* a duck, the male of which has a large dark head with bright yellow eyes.

golden handshake *n. informal* a payment given as compensation for dismissal or compulsory retirement.

golden jubilee *n.* the fiftieth anniversary of an important event.

golden retriever *n.* a retriever with a thick yellowish coat.

goldenrod *n.* a plant of the daisy family, which bears tall spikes of small bright yellow flowers.

golden rule *n.* a basic principle of action, esp. "do unto others as you would have them do unto you".

golden wedding *n.* the fiftieth anniversary of a wedding.

goldeye *n.* a silvery freshwater fish with a golden iris.

goldfield *n.* a district in which gold is found.

goldfinch *n.* (*pl.* **goldfinches**) a brightly coloured songbird with predominantly yellow plumage.

goldfish *n.* (*pl.* **goldfish**) a small reddish-golden Chinese carp kept for ornament or as a pet.

goldfish bowl *n.* **1** a globular glass container for goldfish. **2** a situation lacking privacy.

gold leaf *n.* gold beaten into a very thin sheet, used for gilding.

gold medal *n.* a medal of gold awarded as a first prize.

gold mine *n.* **1** a place where gold is mined. **2** *informal* a source of wealth or something valuable. □ **gold miner** *n.* **gold mining** *n.*

gold plate ● *n.* **1** vessels made of gold. **2** material plated with gold. ● *v.* (**gold-plate, gold-plates, gold-plated, gold-plating**) plate with gold.

gold-plated *adj.* **1** plated with gold. **2** excessively luxurious.

gold rush *n.* a rush to a newly discovered goldfield.

goldsmith *n.* a person who makes gold articles.

gold standard *n.* a system in which the value of a currency is defined in terms of gold.

golf ● *n.* a game in which a small hard ball is driven with clubs into a series of 18 or 9 holes. ● *v.* play golf. □ **golfer** *n.*

golf club *n.* a long thin club with a metal or wooden head used in golf.

golly *interj.* expressing mild surprise.

gonad *n.* an animal organ producing gametes. [*Say* GO nad]

gonadotropin *n.* (also **gonadotrophin**) any of various hormones stimulating the activity of the gonads. [*Say* go nadda TROE pin, go nadda TROE fin]

gonch *n. var. of* GAUNCH.

gondola *n.* (*pl.* **gondolas**) **1** a light flat-bottomed boat used on Venetian canals, worked by one oar at the stern. **2** an enclosed compartment on a ski lift, or suspended from an airship or balloon. [*Say* GONDA luh]

gondolier *n.* the oarsman on a gondola. [*Say* gonda LEER]

gone ● *v. past participle of* GO. ● *adj.* **1 a** lost; hopeless. **b** dead. **2** used up. **3** *informal* pregnant for a specified time.

goner *n. slang* a doomed person or thing.

gong *n.* a metal disc with a turned rim, giving a resonant note when struck.

gonna *contr. informal* going to.

gonorrhea *n.* (also esp. *Brit.* **gonorrhoea**) a venereal disease with inflammatory discharge from the urethra or vagina. □ **gonorrheal** *adj.* [*Say* gon uh REE uh]

gonzo *adj.* **1** *informal* bizarre; crazy. **2** (of journalism) exaggerated, subjective.

goo *n. informal* a sticky or slimy substance.

goober *n.* (also **goober pea**) **1** a peanut or peanut plant. **2** a stupid or inept person.

good ● adj. (**better, best**) **1** to be desired or approved of. **2** having the required qualities; of a high standard. **3** morally right. **4** well behaved. **5** enjoyable. **6** appropriate. **7** thorough. **8** at least. ● n. **1** that which is morally right or beneficial. **2** merchandise or possessions. □ **as good as** practically. **for good (and all)** permanently. **good** and informal used as an intensifier. **good for 1** beneficial to. **2** reliable or inclined for. **make good 1** make up for. **2** fulfill (a promise).

goodbye ● interj. expressing good wishes on parting etc. ● n. (pl. **goodbyes**) a parting.

good faith n. sincerity of intention.

good form n. what complies with current social conventions. □ **in good form** in a state of good health or training.

good-for-nothing ● adj. worthless. ● n. a worthless person.

Good Friday n. the Friday before Easter Sunday, commemorating the Crucifixion of Christ.

good-hearted adj. kindly.

good-humoured adj. cheerful. □ **good-humouredly** adv.

goodie n. = GOODY n.

goodie bag n. a bag of treats etc., given as a gift or prize.

good-looking adj. handsome; attractive.

good luck ● n. **1** good fortune. **2** an omen of this. ● interj. an exclamation of well-wishing.

goodly adj. (**goodlier, goodliest**) **1** good-looking, handsome. **2** of imposing size etc.

good-natured adj. kind; easygoing. □ **good-naturedly** adv.

goodness ● n. **1** virtue. **2** kindness. **3** what is good or beneficial in a thing. ● interj. (as a substitution for "God").

good riddance interj. expressing welcome relief from an unwanted person or thing.

goods and services tax n. Cdn & NZ a value-added tax levied on a broad range of consumer goods and services. Abbreviation: **GST**.

good-tempered adj. cheerful; not easily annoyed. □ **good-temperedly** adv.

good-time adj. recklessly pursuing pleasure.

goodwill n. **1** kindly feeling. **2** the established reputation of a business etc. as enhancing its value. **3** cheerful consent.

goody ● n. (pl. **goodies**) **1** (usu. in pl.) something good, esp. to eat. **2** = GOODY-GOODY n. **3** informal a hero in a story etc. ● interj. expressing childish delight.

goody-goody informal ● n. (pl. **goody-goodies**) an obtrusively virtuous person. ● adj. smugly virtuous.

goody two-shoes n. = GOODY-GOODY n.

gooey adj. (**gooier, gooiest**) slang **1** viscous, sticky. **2** sentimental. □ **gooeyness** n.

goof informal ● n. **1** a foolish person. **2** a mistake. ● v. **1** (foll. by up) bungle, mess up. **2** (often foll. by off) idle. **3** (foll. by around, about) fool around, mess about.

goofball informal ● n. **1** a blundering person. **2** a pill containing a barbiturate. ● adj. eccentric or silly.

goof-up n. informal a mistake.

goofy adj. (**goofier, goofiest**) silly, ridiculous, odd. □ **goofily** adv. **goofiness** n.

google v. search (a term) on the Internet using the search engine Google.

gook n. slang a slimy substance. [Rhymes with KOOK or COOK]

goon n. slang **1** a person employed to terrorize opponents. **2** informal a hockey player who intimidates with rough play. **3** a stupid person. □ **goony** adj.

goop n. = GLOOP. □ **goopy** adj. (**goopier, goopiest**)

goose ● n. (pl. **geese**) **1 a** a large water bird with short legs and a broad bill. **b** the female of this. **2** informal a silly person. ● v. (**gooses, goosed, goosing**) **1** slang poke (a person) in the buttocks. **2** esp. US informal (often foll. by up) energize or increase.

gooseberry n. (pl. **gooseberries**) the edible yellowish-green juicy berry of a thorny shrub.

goosebumps pl. n. (also **goose pimples, gooseflesh** n.) small bumps appearing on the skin because of cold, fright, etc.

goose egg n. informal **1** a zero score. **2** a lump appearing after a blow to the head.

goosefoot n. (pl. **goosefoots**) a plant of temperate regions with leaves shaped like a goose's foot.

gooseneck n. a long thin flexible metal tube.

goose step ● n. a marching step in which the knees are locked and the legs lifted high. ● v. (**goose-step: goose-steps, goose-stepped, goose-stepping**) march in this way.

gopher n. **1** a buff-coloured ground squirrel of N American prairies. **2** a burrowing rodent of North and Central America, having external cheek pouches. **3** = GOFER.

Gordian knot n. an extremely difficult problem. □ **cut the Gordian knot** solve a problem by force or by evasion.

gore ● n. **1** blood that has been shed. **2** informal carnage. ● v. (**gores**, **gored**, **goring**) pierce with a horn, tusk, etc.

Gore-Tex n. proprietary a breathable laminated waterproof fabric.

gorge ● n. **1** a narrow valley or ravine. **2** a feast. ● v. (**gorges**, **gorged**, **gorging**) (usu. foll. by on) feed greedily. □ **one's gorge rises** one is sickened.

gorgeous adj. **1** strikingly beautiful. **2** very pleasant. □ **gorgeously** adv. **gorgeousness** n.

Gorgonzola n. a type of rich cheese with bluish-green veins. [Say gorgun ZOLA]

gorilla n. (pl. **gorillas**) **1** the largest anthropoid ape, native to Central Africa. **2** informal a heavily built man of aggressive demeanour.

go-round n. each of several recurring turns or chances.

gorp n. = TRAIL MIX.

gorse n. a spiny yellow-flowered shrub found in Europe.

gory adj. (**gorier**, **goriest**) **1** involving or depicting bloodshed. **2** covered in gore. □ **gory details** jocular explicit details.

gosh interj. expressing mild surprise.

goshawk n. a large short-winged hawk, resembling a large sparrow hawk. [Say GOSS hawk]

gosling n. a young goose. [Say GOZZ ling]

gospel n. **1** the teachings of Christ. **2** (**Gospel**) **a** the record of Christ's life and teaching in the first four books of the New Testament. **b** each of these books. **3** (also **gospel truth**) a thing regarded as absolutely true. **4** a principle one advocates. **5** (also **gospel music**) a style of religious music, esp. as originally sung by US Blacks.

gossamer ● n. **1** a filmy substance of small spiders' webs. **2** delicate filmy material. ● adj. light and flimsy. [Say GOSSA mur]

gossip ● n. **1** casual conversation or unproven reports about other people. **2** a person who indulges in gossip. ● v. (**gossips**, **gossiped**, **gossiping**) talk or write gossip. □ **gossiper** n. **gossipy** adj.

got past and past participle of GET.

gotch n. (also **gotchies** pl. n.) Cdn slang underpants.

Goth n. **1** a member of a Germanic tribe that invaded the Roman Empire in the 3rd–5th centuries. **2** (**goth**) **a** a style of rock music derived from punk. **b** a member of a subculture favouring black clothing, metal jewellery, and goth music.

Gothic ● adj. **1** of the Goths or their language. **2** in the style of architecture prevalent in western Europe in the 12th–16th centuries. **3** gloomy and horrifying. ● n. **1** the Gothic language. **2** Gothic architecture. □ **Gothicism** n.

go-to guy n. (also **go-to person** etc.) slang the person most often relied on to accomplish a task.

gotten past participle of GET.

gouache n. **1** a method of painting in opaque pigments ground in water and thickened with a glue-like substance. **2** these pigments. [Say goo AWSH]

Gouda n. a usu. Dutch cheese with a yellow rind. [Say GOO duh]

gouge ● n. **1** a chisel with a concave blade. **2** a groove or mark made by gouging. ● v. (**gouges**, **gouged**, **gouging**) **1** cut with or as with a gouge. **2** force out roughly. **3** informal take an unjustly large sum of money from (someone). □ **gouger** n.

goulash n. (pl. **goulashes**) a Hungarian stew of meat and vegetables. [Say GOO lash]

gourd n. **1** a large hard-skinned fleshy fruit of a climbing or trailing plant. **2** a container made from the hollowed skin of a gourd. [Rhymes with TOURED]

gourmand n. **1** a glutton. **2** a gourmet. [Say goor MOND]

gourmet ● n. a connoisseur of good food. ● adj. **1** (of food) of very high quality. **2** of or suitable for a gourmet. [Say GOOR may]

gout n. **1** a disease causing joints to swell painfully. **2** a drop or spot. □ **gouty** adj.

Gov. abbr. **1** Governor. **2** Government.

govern v. **1** rule or control with authority. **2** control or influence. **3** be a standard or principle for. □ **governability** n. **governable** adj.

governance n. the action or manner of governing.

governess n. (pl. **governesses**) a woman employed to teach children in a private household.

government n. **1 a** the governing body of a state. **b** a particular administration in office. **2** the system by which a state or community is governed. **3** the action or manner of controlling a state. □ **governmental** adj. **governmentally** adv.

Government House n. the official residence of the representative of the Crown, e.g. a Lieutenant-Governor.

Government Leader n. (in Canada) the leader of a Territorial government.

governor n. **1** a person who governs. **2 a** (also **governor-in-chief**) an official governing a province, town, etc. **b** a representative of the Crown in a colony.

3 the executive head of a US state. **4** an officer commanding a fortress or garrison. **5** the head of an institution. **6** *Cdn hist.* **a** the officer in charge of a fort or factory of the Hudson's Bay Company. **b** (also **governor-in-chief**) the Hudson's Bay Company's chief officer in Canada.

Governor General *n.* (*pl.* **Governors General**) the representative of the Crown in a Commonwealth country that regards the Queen as head of state.

Governor General's Award *n. Cdn* an award presented annually by the Governor General in each of several categories of Canadian literature.

Gov. Gen. *abbr.* Governor General.

Govt. *abbr.* (also **govt.**, **gov't.**) government.

gown *n.* **1** a loose flowing esp. formal garment. **2** the official robe of a judge, cleric, member of a university, etc. **3** a protective garment worn in a hospital by surgical staff etc. □ **gowned** *adj.*

goy *n.* (*pl.* **goyim** or **goys**) *slang* a non-Jew. □ **goyish** *adj.* (also **goyishe**) [*For* goyim *say* GOY im; *for* goyishe *say* GOY ish uh]

GP *abbr.* general practitioner.

GPS *abbr.* GLOBAL POSITIONING SYSTEM.

grab ● *v.* (**grabs**, **grabbed**, **grabbing**) **1** seize suddenly or firmly. **2** *slang* attract the attention of. **3** (foll. by *at*) make a sudden snatch at. **4** obtain quickly. ● *n.* **1** a sudden attempt to seize. **2** a mechanical device for clutching. **3** rapacious proceedings in politics or commerce. □ **up for grabs** *slang* easily obtainable. □ **grabber** *n.*

grab bag *n.* **1** a bag of assorted prizes, treats, etc. **2** any assortment.

grabby *adj. informal* **1** tending to grab. **2** attracting attention.

grace ● *n.* **1** elegance and attractiveness. **2** courteous good will. **3** an attractive feature; an accomplishment. **4** (in Christian belief) the favour of God. **5** delay granted as a favour. **6** a short thanksgiving before or after a meal. **7** (**Grace**) (in Greek mythology) each of three beautiful sister goddesses, who bestowed beauty and charm. **8** (**Grace**) (preceded by *His*, *Her*, *Your*) forms of description or address for a duke, duchess, or archbishop. ● *v.* (**graces**, **graced**, **gracing**) (often foll. by *with*) confer honour or dignity on. □ **with good** (or **bad**) **grace** as if willingly (or reluctantly). □ **graceless** *adj.*

graceful *adj.* having or showing grace. □ **gracefully** *adv.* **gracefulness** *n.*

gracious ● *adj.* **1** kindly. **2** (of God) merciful. **3** characterized by elegance. ● *interj.* expressing surprise. □ **graciously** *adv.* **graciousness** *n.*

grackle *n.* a songbird of the N American blackbird family.

grad *n. informal* **1** a university or high school graduate. **2** *Cdn* a graduation ceremony. **3** *Cdn* a dinner followed by a dance to celebrate graduation.

gradation *n.* (usu. in *pl.*) **1** a scale of successive changes, stages, or degrees. **2** a stage in such a scale. [*Say* gray DAY sh'n *or* gruh DAY sh'n]

grade ● *n.* **1** a certain degree in rank, merit, proficiency, quality, etc. **2** a step or stage in a process. **3** a mark indicating the quality of a student's work. **4 a** a class in school, concerned with a particular year's work. **b** (in *comb.*) *Cdn* a school pupil of a specified grade. **5 a** a gradient or slope. **b** the level at which the ground meets the foundation of a building. ● *v.* (**grades**, **graded**, **grading**) **1** arrange in or allocate to grades. **2** pass gradually between grades. **3** give a grade to. **4** level (a road etc.). □ **at grade** on the same level. **make the grade** *informal* reach the desired standard.

grader *n.* **1** a person or thing that grades. **2** (in *comb.*) a school pupil of a specified grade. **3** (in full **road grader**) a vehicle with a heavy blade, used in road construction for levelling the ground.

grade school *n.* elementary school.

gradient *n.* **1 a** a sloping stretch of road, railway, etc. **b** the amount of such a slope. **2** the rate of change in temperature etc. between areas. [*Say* GRAY dee int]

gradual *adj.* **1** taking place slowly or by degrees. **2** not rapid or steep or abrupt. □ **gradually** *adv.*

graduate ● *n.* **1 a** a person who has been awarded an academic degree. **b** relating to education undertaken beyond the bachelor's degree. **2** a person who has completed a course of study. ● *v.* (**graduates**, **graduated**, **graduating**) **1 a** receive an academic degree or a high school diploma. **b** complete a course of study. **2** confer a degree etc. upon. **3** move up to (a higher level). □ **graduation** *n.*

graduated *adj.* **1** arranged in grades or gradations; advancing or proceeding by degrees. **2** marked with lines to indicate degrees, grades, or quantities. **3** (of tax) apportioned according to a scale.

Graeco-Roman *adj.* = GRECO-ROMAN.

graffiti *pl. n.* (often treated as *sing.*) unauthorized writing or drawings on public surfaces. □ **graffitied** *adj.* [*Say* gruh FEETY]

graft¹ ● *n.* **1** a shoot from one plant inserted into another to form new growth. **2** a piece of living tissue, organ, etc., transplanted surgically. ● *v.* **1** insert or transplant something as a graft. **2** insert or fix (a thing) to another.

graft² informal ● n. bribery etc. used to secure illicit gains in politics or business. ● v. seek or make such gains. □ **grafter** n.

graham adj. designating coarse-grained whole wheat flour, or crackers etc. made from this. [Say GRAY um or GRAM]

Grail n. (also **grail**) **1** (in medieval legend) the cup or platter used by Christ at the Last Supper. **2** any object of a quest.

grain n. **1 a** wheat or any other cereal plant used as food. **b** their fruit. **2 a** fruit or seed of a cereal. **3** a small hard particle of salt, sand, etc. **4** the smallest unit of weight in the troy and avoirdupois systems (approx. 0.0648 grams). **5** the smallest possible quantity. **6** the texture of skin, wood, stone, etc. **7** a pattern of lines of fibre in meat, wood, fabric, or paper. □ **against the grain** contrary to one's natural inclination or feeling. □ **grained** adj.

grain elevator n. = ELEVATOR 2.

grainy adj. (**grainier**, **grainiest**) **1** granular. **2** Photography showing visible grains of emulsion. **3** having a rough or gravelly quality. □ **graininess** n.

gram n. a metric unit of mass equal to one-thousandth of a kilogram.

-gram comb. form forming nouns denoting a thing written or recorded.

gramma n. (pl. **grammas**) informal = GRANDMA.

grammar n. **1** the rules in a language for how words are formed and their relation to each other. **2** a person's manner of using grammatical forms. **3** a book on grammar.

grammarian n. an expert in grammar. [Say gruh MARY un]

grammatical adj. **1** relating to grammar. **2** conforming to the rules of grammar. □ **grammaticality** n. **grammatically** adv. [Say gruh MATTA cull, gruh matta CAL a tee]

gramophone n. a device for playing records. [Say GRAMMA phone]

grampa n. (also **gramps**) informal = GRANDPA.

gran n. informal grandmother.

granary n. (pl. **granaries**) a storehouse for grain. [Say GRAIN a ree or GRAN a ree]

grand ● adj. **1 a** splendid, magnificent. **b** large or ambitious in scale. **2** main. **3** of the highest rank. **4** informal excellent. **5** belonging to high society. **6** in names of family relationships, denoting the second degree of ascent or descent. **7** comprehensive, final. **8** Law serious, important. ● n. **1** = GRAND PIANO. **2** (pl.

grand) (usu. in pl.) slang a thousand dollars or pounds. □ **grandly** adv. **grandness** n.

grand chief n. the chief of a grand council or national or regional Aboriginal organization.

grandchild n. (pl. **grandchildren**) a child of one's son or daughter.

grand council n. a group of chiefs representing several different First Nations.

granddad n. (also **grandad**) informal **1** grandfather. **2** an elderly man.

granddaddy n. (pl. **granddaddies**) informal **1** = GRANDDAD. **2** the greatest example of something.

granddaughter n. a female grandchild.

grande dame n. (pl. **grandes dames**) **1** a dignified eminent woman. **2** a venerable institution, hotel, theatre, etc. [Say grond DOM]

grandee n. an eminent person. [Say gran DEE]

grandeur n. **1** splendour and impressiveness. **2** high rank or social importance. [Say GRAND ur or GRAND yur]

grandfather ● n. a male grandparent. ● v. exempt a pre-existing class of people etc. from a new regulation. □ **grandfatherly** adj.

grandfather clock n. a clock in a tall wooden case.

grand finale n. an elaborate, impressive conclusion or finish.

grandiloquent adj. pompous or extravagant in language, style, or manner. □ **grandiloquence** n. **grandiloquently** adv. [Say gran DILLA quint]

grandiose adj. **1** meant to be imposing. **2** ambitious or magnificent. **3** pompous or arrogant. □ **grandiosity** n. [Say grandy OSE or GRANDY ose (with OSE as in GROSS), grandy OSSA tee]

grandkid n. informal = GRANDCHILD.

grandma n. informal grandmother.

grandmaster n. **1** a chess player of the highest class. **2** (**Grand Master**) the head of a military order of knighthood, of Freemasons, etc.

grandmother n. a female grandparent. □ **teach one's grandmother to suck eggs** presume to advise a more experienced person. □ **grandmotherly** adj.

grandpa n. (pl. **grandpas**) informal grandfather.

grandparent n. a parent of one's father or mother.

grand piano n. a large piano with the body and strings arranged horizontally.

Grand Prix *n.* (*pl.* **Grands Prix**) an esp. auto racing event forming part of a world championship. [*Say* gron PREE]

grand slam *n.* **1** *Bridge* the winning of 13 tricks. **2** the winning of all the major championships in a sport in the same year.

grandson *n.* a male grandchild.

grandstand ● *n.* the main stand for spectators at a racetrack etc. ● *v.* seek to impress others. □ **grandstander** *n.*

granite *n.* **1** a granular igneous rock of quartz, mica, feldspar, etc. **2** curling rocks. □ **granitic** *adj.* [*Say* GRAN it, gruh NIT ick]

granny *n.* (also **grannie**) (*pl.* **grannies**) *informal* grandmother.

granny flat *n.* part of a house made into self-contained accommodation, as for an elderly relative.

Granny Smith *n.* a round, bright green apple.

granola ● *n.* a mixture of rolled oats, nuts, raisins, brown sugar, etc. ● *adj. jocular* designating persons with liberal politics, concerns about the environment, etc.

grant ● *v.* **1 a** consent to fulfill. **b** allow to have. **2** give formally. **3** admit as true. ● *n.* **1** a sum of money or tract of land given for any of various purposes. **2** *Law* the documented transfer of the ownership of property from one person to another. □ **take for granted 1** assume to be true. **2** cease to appreciate through familiarity. □ **grantee** *n.* **grantor** *n.*

granular *adj.* **1** of or like granules. **2** having a roughened surface.

granulate *v.* (**granulates**, **granulated**, **granulating**) form into grains. □ **granulation** *n.*

granule *n.* a small grain. [*Say* GRAN yule]

grape *n.* a berry (usu. purple, black, or green) growing on a vine, eaten as fruit or used in making wine.

grapefruit *n.* (*pl.* **grapefruit**) a large yellow citrus fruit with an acid juicy pulp.

grapevine *n.* **1** a vine bearing grapes. **2** *informal* the means of transmission of unofficial information or rumour.

graph ● *n.* a diagram showing the relation between variable quantities, usu. measured along axes at right angles. ● *v.* plot on a graph.

graphic ● *adj.* **1** relating to visual art, esp. writing and drawing. **2** vividly descriptive. ● *n.* a visual image. □ **graphically** *adv.*

graphical *adj.* **1** of or in the form of graphs. **2** graphic.

graphic arts *pl. n.* the visual and technical arts involving design, writing, drawing, printing, etc.

graphics *pl. n.* (usu. treated as *sing.*) **1** the products of the graphic arts, esp. commercial design and illustration. **2** the use of diagrams in calculation and design. **3** (also **computer graphics**) visual images produced or manipulated on computers.

graphite *n.* a crystalline form of carbon used as a solid lubricant, in pencils, and as a moderator in nuclear reactors. [*Say* GRAF ite]

graph paper *n.* paper with intersecting lines forming small squares of equal size, used for graphs.

grapnel *n.* **1** a device with iron claws, attached to a rope and used for dragging or grasping. **2** a small anchor with several flukes.

grappa *n.* a brandy distilled from fermented pressed grapes.

grapple ● *v.* (**grapples**, **grappled**, **grappling**) **1** fight at close quarters or in close combat. **2** (foll. by *with*) deal with a difficult problem etc. ● *n.* **1 a** a hold or grip in or as in wrestling. **b** a contest at close quarters. **2** a grapnel. □ **grappler** *n.*

grappling hook *n.* (also **grappling iron**) = GRAPNEL 1.

grasp ● *v.* **1 a** clutch at. **b** hold firmly. **2** (foll. by *at*) try to seize. **3** understand or realize. ● *n.* **1** a firm hold. **2** (foll. by *of*) **a** mastery. **b** understanding. □ **within one's grasp** capable of being grasped, achieved, or comprehended by one. □ **graspable** *adj.*

grasping *adj.* greedy.

grass ● *n.* (*pl.* **grasses**) **1 a** vegetation consisting of small plants with narrow green blades. **b** any plant of this family, which includes cereals, reeds, and bamboos. **2** pasture land. **3** lawn. **4** *slang* marijuana. ● *v.* (**grasses**, **grassed**, **grassing**) cover with turf. □ **grasslike** *adj.*

grasshopper *n.* **1** a plant-eating insect with legs adapted for jumping. **2** a cocktail usu. consisting of cream, chocolate liqueur, and mint liqueur.

grassland *n.* a large open area covered with grass.

grassroots *pl. n.* **1** a fundamental level. **2** ordinary people; the rank and file.

grassy *adj.* (**grassier**, **grassiest**) covered with or resembling grass.

grate[1] *v.* (**grates**, **grated**, **grating**) **1** reduce to small shreds by rubbing on a serrated surface. **2** rub with a harsh scraping sound. **3** (often foll. by *on*) have an irritating effect. **4** creak.

grate[2] *n.* **1** = GRATING. **2** a frame of metal

bars for holding the fuel in the recess of a fireplace etc.

grateful *adj.* feeling or showing gratitude. □ **gratefully** *adv.*

grater *n.* a device for reducing cheese etc. to small shreds.

gratification *n.* the feeling of pleasure when something goes well. [*Say* grat if a KAY sh'n]

gratify *v.* (**gratifies, gratified, gratifying**) **1** please, satisfy. **2** indulge in (a feeling). □ **gratifying** *adj.* **gratifyingly** *adv.*

gratin *n.* a dish with a crisp brown crust usu. of bread crumbs or melted cheese. [*Say* gra TAN]

grating ● *adj.* **1** sounding harsh. **2** irritating. ● *n.* a framework of parallel or crossed metal bars. □ **gratingly** *adv.*

gratis *adv. & adj.* without charge. [*Say* GRAT iss]

gratitude *n.* thankfulness.

gratuitous *adj.* uncalled for. □ **gratuitously** *adv.* **gratuitousness** *n.* [*Say* gruh TOO it us *or* gruh TYOO it us]

gratuity *n.* (*pl.* **gratuities**) money given in recognition of services. [*Say* gruh TOO it ee *or* gruh TYOO it ee]

grave[1] *n.* **1** a hole dug in the ground for a corpse. **2** (**the grave**) death. □ **turn** (or **roll**) **over in one's grave** (of a dead person) react with imagined disgust at the actions of those still living.

grave[2] *adj.* **1** serious, solemn. **2** extremely serious or threatening. □ **gravely** *adv.*

gravedigger *n.* a person who digs graves.

gravel ● *n.* a mixture of small stones and coarse sand, used for paths and roads. ● *v.* (**gravels, gravelled, gravelling**) lay or strew with gravel.

gravelly *adj.* **1** of or containing gravel. **2** (of a voice) deep and rough-sounding.

graven *adj.* engraved, carved. [*Say* GRAVE un]

graveside *n.* the ground at the edge of a grave.

gravesite *n.* the location of a grave.

gravestone *n.* = TOMBSTONE.

graveyard *n.* **1** a cemetery. **2** *informal* = GRAVEYARD SHIFT. **3** a place for obsolete objects.

graveyard shift *n.* a work shift beginning around midnight and lasting until morning.

gravitas *n.* seriousness. [*Say* GRAVVY tass]

gravitate *v.* (**gravitates, gravitated, gravitating**) **1** (foll. by *to, toward*) be drawn to a place or thing. **2** move or tend by force of gravity toward. [*Say* GRAVVA tate]

gravitation *n.* **1** a force of attraction between any two particles of matter. **2** the effect of this. **3** a natural tendency toward a person etc. □ **gravitational** *adj.* [*Say* gravva TAY sh'n]

gravity *n.* **1** the force that attracts a body toward the centre of the earth or toward any other physical body having mass. **2** importance, seriousness.

Gravol *n. Cdn proprietary* a medication used to counter nausea and vomiting and prevent motion sickness.

gravy *n.* (*pl.* **gravies**) **1** the juices and fat from cooked meat, usu. thickened and used as a sauce. **2** *slang* money easily acquired.

gravy train *n. slang* a source of easy financial benefit.

gray *adj., n., & v.* = GREY.

grayling *n.* a silver-grey freshwater fish with a long high dorsal fin.

graze[1] *v.* (**grazes, grazed, grazing**) **1** feed on growing grass. **2** *informal* snack on small meals or casually sample food. □ **grazer** *n.*

graze[2] ● *v.* (**grazes, grazed, grazing**) **1** scrape and break the skin on (part of the body). **2** touch lightly in passing. ● *n.* a superficial wound.

grease ● *n.* **1** semi-solid oily or fatty matter used as a lubricant etc. **2** the melted fat of a dead animal. ● *v.* (**greases, greased, greasing**) **1** smear or lubricate with grease. **2** smear (a cookie sheet etc.) with fat before using. □ **grease the palm of** *informal* bribe. **like greased lightning** *informal* very fast.

greasepaint *n.* a waxy theatrical makeup.

greasewood *n.* a resinous dwarf shrub of western N America.

greasy *adj.* (**greasier, greasiest**) **1** of, containing, or covered with grease. **2 a** slippery. **b** friendly in a way that seems insincere. □ **greasiness** *n.*

greasy spoon *n. informal* a cheap diner.

great ● *adj.* **1** of an amount, extent, or intensity considerably above average. **2** important, prominent. **3** grand. **4** remarkable or outstanding. **5** skilled. **6** fully deserving the name of. **7** (also **greater**) the larger of the name, species, etc. **8** (**Greater**) (of a city etc.) including adjacent urban areas. **9** *informal* very enjoyable. **10** (in names of family relationships) denoting one degree further removed. ● *n.* an outstanding person or thing. ● *adv. informal* excellently. □ **great**

and small all classes or types. (the)
great and (the) good often *ironic*
distinguished and worthy people. **to a
great extent** largely. □ **greatness** *n.*

great blue heron *n.* a predominantly
greyish blue heron of N America.

great circle *n.* a circle on the surface of a
sphere whose plane passes through the
sphere's centre.

greatcoat *n.* a long heavy overcoat.

Great Dane *n.* a breed of very large,
powerful, short-haired dog.

great deal *n. see* DEAL *n.* 1.

Great Divide *n.* (**the Great Divide**)
1 the boundary between life and death.
2 (usu. **great divide**) the boundary
between two contrasting conditions,
cultures, etc.

great grey owl *n.* a very large grey
hornless owl of northern coniferous
forests.

great horned owl *n.* a large powerful
N American owl with prominent ear tufts.

greatly *adv.* by a considerable amount.

great unwashed *n. informal* (**the great
unwashed**) the lower classes.

Great War *n.* (**the Great War**) the First
World War.

Great White North *n. Cdn jocular* Canada.

great white shark *n.* a large and
dangerous greyish shark, found in
temperate and tropical ocean regions.

grebe *n.* a diving water bird with a long
neck and almost no tail.

Grecian *adj.* following Greek models or
ideals. [*Say* GREE sh'n]

Greco-Roman *adj.* relating to the Greeks
and Romans. [*Say* grecko ROMAN]

greed *n.* an excessive desire, esp. for wealth
or food.

greedy *adj.* (**greedier**, **greediest**)
1 having or showing greed. **2** very keen or
eager. □ **greedily** *adv.* **greediness** *n.*

Greek *n.* **1** a person from Greece. **2** the
ancient or modern language of Greek.
□ **Greek to me** *informal* incomprehensible
to me. □ **Greek** *adj.*

Greek Orthodox Church *n.* (also
Greek Church) the national Church of
Greece.

Greek salad *n.* a salad of lettuce,
tomatoes, cucumbers, olives, feta, and olive
oil vinaigrette.

green ● *adj.* **1** of the colour of grass.
2 covered with leaves or grass. **3** unripe or
unseasoned. **4** not dried, smoked, or
tanned. **5** inexperienced. **6 a** sickly-hued.
b envious. **7** young, flourishing.
8 vegetable. **9 a** (also **Green**) supporting

protection of the environment. **b** (of a
consumer product) not harmful to the
environment. ● *n.* **1** green colour or
material. **2** a grassy area used for a special
purpose. **3** (in *pl.*) green vegetables. **4** a
green light. **5** (also **Green**) a member or
supporter of an environmentalist group or
party. ● *v.* make or become green.
□ **greenish** *adj.* **greenness** *n.*
greeny *adj.*

greenback *n.* **1 a** a US legal tender note.
b the US dollar. **2** a green-backed animal.

green bean *n.* **1** any bean plant grown for
its edible young pods rather than for its
seeds. **2** this pod.

greenbelt *n.* an area of open land around
a city, the development of which is
restricted.

Green Beret *n. informal* an American or
British commando.

green bin *n.* a green plastic bin used for
curbside collection of recyclable or
compostable materials, esp. (in Canada) one
for organic waste.

green card *n. US* a permit allowing a
foreign national to live and work
permanently in the US.

greenery *n.* green foliage etc.

green-eyed *adj.* **1** having green eyes.
2 jealous; envious.

greengrocer *n.* a retailer of fruit and
vegetables.

greenhorn *n.* an inexperienced person.

greenhouse *n.* a transparent glass or
plastic building for growing plants.

greenhouse effect *n.* the heating of the
earth's surface and lower atmosphere
attributed to an increase in carbon dioxide
and other gases, which are more
transparent to incoming solar radiation
than to reflected radiation from the earth.

greenhouse gas *n.* any gas that
contributes to the greenhouse effect.

greenie *n. informal* a person concerned
about environmental issues.

Greenlander *n.* a person from Greenland.

green light ● *n.* **1** a signal to proceed on a
road, railway, etc. **2** *informal* permission to
go ahead. ● *v.* (**green-light**) give approval
for a project to go ahead.

green onion *n.* an immature onion with
slender green hollow leaves.

Green Paper *n. Cdn & Brit.* a preliminary
report of Government proposals, for
discussion.

green pepper *n.* the mild-flavoured
unripe fruit of a sweet pepper.

green room *n.* a room in a theatre,
studio, etc. in which performers may relax
when not on stage etc.

greensward n. grassy turf. [Say GREENS ward]

green tea n. tea made from steam-dried, not fermented, leaves.

green thumb n. informal a talent for gardening. □ **green-thumbed** adj.

Greenwich Mean Time n. the local time on the 0° meridian, used as an international basis of time reckoning. Abbreviation: **GMT**. [Say GREN itch]

greet v. **1** welcome or address politely. **2** receive in a specified way. **3** become apparent to or noticed by. □ **greeter** n.

greeting n. **1** a polite word or sign of welcome. **2** the action of giving such a sign. **3** (often in pl.) an expression of goodwill.

greeting card n. a decorative card sent to convey greetings.

gregarious adj. **1** fond of company; sociable. **2 a** (of animals or birds) living in groups. **b** (of plants) growing in clusters. □ **gregariously** adv. **gregariousness** n. [Say gruh GARRY us]

Gregorian calendar n. the general calendar in use today, with 365 days in standard years and 366 days in leap years. [Say gruh GORY un]

Gregorian chant n. very old church music of western Europe, sung in unison. [Say gruh GORY un]

gremlin n. informal an imaginary mischievous sprite regarded as responsible for mechanical faults.

grenade n. a small bomb thrown by hand (**hand grenade**) or launched mechanically.

grenadier n. hist. **1** a soldier armed with grenades. **2** a soldier selected to be part of an elite unit. [Say grenna DEER]

grenadine n. a sweet red syrup flavoured with pomegranates. [Say GRENNA dean]

grew past of GROW.

grey ● adj. **1** of a colour intermediate between black and white, as of ashes. **2** dull, dismal, depressing. **3 a** (of hair) turning white with age etc. **b** (of a person) having grey hair. **4** nondescript, unable to be identified. ● n. **1** grey colour or material. **2** a grey or white horse. ● v. **1** make or become grey. **2** informal age. □ **greyish** adj.

grey area n. an area of activity that does not easily fit or conform to existing categories or rules.

greybeard n. often derogatory an old man.

Grey Cup n. Cdn **1** the trophy presented each year to the team winning the Canadian Football League championship. **2** the game deciding this championship.

greyhound n. a swift, slender dog used in racing.

grey jay n. a common N American jay, having grey, black, and white plumage, notorious for its boldness at picnic grounds.

grey market n. the unofficial but not illegal buying and selling of goods □ **grey marketer** n.

grey matter n. **1** the darker tissues of the brain and spinal cord. **2** informal intelligence.

grey-scale Computing ● adj. designating the production of black and white images by the assigning of a shade of grey to each pixel. ● n. a grey-scale image.

greystone n. Cdn **1** grey stones used in building walls etc. **2** a house etc. made of greystone.

grey water n. mildly contaminated household waste water.

grey whale n. a large mottled grey baleen whale of north Pacific waters.

grid n. **1 a** a framework of spaced parallel bars. **b** a network of regularly spaced lines crossing at right angles. **2** a network of water mains, gas lines, power lines, etc. **3** an arrangement of town streets in a rectangular pattern. □ **gridded** adj.

griddle n. a flat pan with little or no rim.

gridiron n. **1** a cooking utensil of metal bars for broiling or grilling. **2 a** a football field. **b** informal the game of football. **3** = GRID 3. [Say GRID iron]

gridlock n. **1** a traffic jam affecting a whole network of intersecting streets. **2** = DEADLOCK n. 1. □ **gridlocked** adj.

grid road n. Cdn a road following the surveyed divisions of a township etc.

grief n. **1** deep sorrow or mourning. **2** informal trouble; annoyance. □ **come to grief** meet with disaster. **good grief!** an exclamation of surprise, alarm, etc.

grievance n. **1** a cause for complaint. **2** an official allegation that something is unjust etc.

grieve v. (**grieves**, **grieved**, **grieving**) **1** suffer grief, esp. at another's death. **2** cause grief to. **3** file a grievance (against). □ **griever** n.

grievous adj. very serious and severe. □ **grievously** adv. **grievousness** n.

griffin n. a mythical creature with an eagle's head and wings and a lion's body.

griffon n. **1** a small terrier-like dog with coarse or smooth hair. **2** (also **griffon vulture**) a large brown vulture. [Sounds like GRIFFIN]

grift n. & v. esp. US slang = GRAFT[2]. □ **grifter** n.

grill • n. **1** a cooking apparatus consisting of a series of metal bars over a heat source. **2** a dish of grilled food. **3** a restaurant serving grilled food. • v. **1** cook on a grill. **2** interrogate. □ **grilling** n.

grille n. (also **grill**) **1** a grating or latticed screen. **2** a metal grid protecting the radiator of a vehicle. [Say GRILL]

grilse n. (pl. **grilse**) a young salmon that has returned to fresh water for the first time.

grim adj. (**grimmer**, **grimmest**) **1** stern or forbidding. **2** harsh, unpleasant. **3** joyless. □ **grimly** adv.

grimace • n. a distortion of the face made in disgust, pain, etc. • v. (**grimaces**, **grimaced**, **grimacing**) make a grimace. [Say GRIM iss]

grime n. dirt ingrained in a surface. □ **grimed** adj.

Grim Reaper n. a personification of death.

grimy adj. (**grimier**, **grimiest**) covered with grime.

grin • v. (**grins**, **grinned**, **grinning**) smile broadly, showing the teeth. • n. a broad smile. □ **grin and bear it** take pain etc. stoically.

grinch n. (pl. **grinches**) a person that seeks to deprive others of joy.

grind • v. (**grinds**, **ground**, **grinding**) **1** reduce to small particles by crushing. **2 a** reduce, sharpen, or smooth by friction. **b** rub or rub together gratingly. **3** (often foll. by *down*) oppress. **4 a** (foll. by *out*) produce with effort. **b** (foll. by *on*) (of a sound) continue gratingly. **5** slang rotate the hips in a suggestive manner. • n. **1** a grating sound or motion. **2** informal hard dull work. **3** the fineness of something that has been ground. □ **grind to a halt** stop laboriously. □ **grindingly** adv.

grinder n. **1** a person or thing that grinds. **2** a molar tooth.

grindstone n. a revolving disc used for grinding. □ **keep one's nose to the grindstone** work hard and continuously.

gringo n. (pl. **gringos**) often derogatory a foreigner, esp. a white anglophone, in a Latin American country.

grip • v. (**grips**, **gripped**, **gripping**) **1** take a firm hold of. **2** deeply affect. **3** compel the attention or interest of. • n. **1 a** a firm hold. **b** control. **c** understanding. **2** a part or attachment by which an implement etc. is held. **3** a member of a camera crew responsible for moving and setting up equipment. □ **come to grips with** begin to deal with. **get a grip** gain composure or

control. **in the grip of** dominated or affected by. □ **gripper** n. **gripping** adj.

gripe • v. (**gripes**, **griped**, **griping**) informal complain peevishly. • n. **1** informal **a** a complaint. **b** the act of griping. **2** (usu. in pl.) gastric or intestinal pain. □ **griper** n.

grisly adj. (**grislier**, **grisliest**) causing horror or fear. [Sounds like GRIZZLY]

grist n. **1** grain that is to be or has been ground. **2** malt crushed for brewing. **3** (also **grist for the** (or **one's**) **mill**) a subject to be used, processed, etc.

gristle n. tough cartilaginous tissue in meat. □ **gristly** adj. [Say GRISSLE]

grit • n. **1** small particles of stone or sand. **2** coarse sandstone. **3** (**Grit**) Cdn a supporter or member of the Liberal Party. **4** informal strength of character. • v. (**grits**, **gritted**, **gritting**) clench (the teeth).

grits pl. n. **1** (treated as sing. or pl.) esp. US **a** a coarsely ground grain. **b** = HOMINY. **2** husked oats.

gritty adj. (**grittier**, **grittiest**) **1** containing or covered with grit. **2** courageous. **3** tough and uncompromising, esp. in depicting sordid or ugly details. □ **grittily** adv. **grittiness** n.

grizzled adj. having, or streaked with, grey hair.

grizzly • adj. (**grizzlier**, **grizzliest**) grizzled. • n. (pl. **grizzlies**) (also **grizzly bear**) a large brown bear found in N America and northern Russia.

groan • v. **1** make a deep expressive sound. **2** complain inarticulately. **3** be loaded or oppressed. • n. the sound made in groaning. □ **groaner** n.

groats pl. n. hulled or crushed oats etc.

grocer n. a person who owns or operates a grocery store.

grocery n. (pl. **groceries**) **1** (in pl.) food and other general household supplies. **2** (also **grocery store**) a store selling groceries.

grog n. **1** a drink of liquor and water. **2** informal any alcoholic drink.

groggy adj. (**groggier**, **groggiest**) dazed or unsteady after drunkenness, sleep, etc. □ **groggily** adv.

groin n. **1** the part of the body where the thighs meet the abdomen. **2** the region of the genitals. **3** Architecture an edge formed by intersecting vaults.

grommet n. a protective eyelet in a hole that a rope or cable passes through. [Say GROM it]

groom • n. **1** = BRIDEGROOM. **2** a person employed to take care of horses. • v. **1** brush or clean an animal's coat. **2 a** give a neat or tidy appearance to. **b** maintain (ski or snowmobile trails). **3** train (a person) for a particular purpose. □ **groomer** n.

groomsman n. (pl. **groomsmen**) = BEST MAN.

groove ● n. **1 a** a channel or long narrow hollow. **b** a spiral track cut in a phonograph record. **2** an established routine. **3** Music slang a rhythmic pattern. ● v. (**grooves, grooved, grooving**) **1** make a groove in. **2** slang **a** play or dance to music rhythmically. **b** enjoy oneself.

groovy adj. (**groovier, grooviest**) slang (dated or jocular) fashionable and exciting.

grope ● v. (**gropes, groped, groping**) **1** feel about uncertainly with the hands. **2** search mentally. **3** slang fondle clumsily for sexual pleasure. ● n. an act of groping someone. □ **groper** n.

grosbeak n. a usu. brightly coloured finch-like bird with a heavy bill. [Say GROSS beak]

gross ● adj. **1** repulsively fat. **2** coarse, unrefined. **3** conspicuously wrong. **4** total; not net. **5** slang disgusting. ● v. (**grosses, grossed, grossing**) produce as gross profit or income. ● n. (pl. **gross**) **1** gross income, receipts, etc. **2** twelve dozen. □ **gross out** slang disgust. □ **grossly** adv. **grossness** n.

gross domestic product n. the total value of goods produced and services provided in a country excluding transactions with other countries.

gross national product n. the annual total value of goods produced and services provided in a country.

Gros Ventre n. (pl. **Gros Ventre** or **Gros Ventres**) a member of an Algonquian-speaking Aboriginal people living in Montana and (formerly) in southern Saskatchewan. [Say GROW vont]

grotesque ● adj. **1** comically or repulsively distorted. **2** incongruous. ● n. a grotesque picture or person. □ **grotesquely** adv. [Say grow TESK]

grotesquerie n. (also **grotesquery**) grotesque quality or things. [Say grow TESKER ee]

grotto n. (pl. **grottoes** or **grottos**) a small picturesque cave.

grotty adj. (**grottier, grottiest**) slang unpleasant, dirty, shabby.

grouch informal ● n. (pl. **grouches**) a discontented person. ● v. (**grouches, grouched, grouching**) grumble.

grouchy adj. (**grouchier, grouchiest**) informal discontented, grumpy. □ **grouchily** adv. **grouchiness** n.

ground¹ ● n. **1 a** the solid surface of the earth. **b** an area of land or sea of a specified

kind. **2** soil. **3 a** a position, area, or distance. **b** the extent of a subject etc. dealt with. **4** (often in pl.) a foundation or reason. **5** an area designated for special use. **6** (in pl.) an enclosed area attached to a building. **7** (in pl.) solid particles, esp. of coffee, forming a residue. **8** a connection between an electrical circuit and the earth. ● v. **1 a** ban from flying. **b** informal restrict the esp. social activities of (a child etc.), as a punishment. **2** run aground. **3** instruct thoroughly (in a subject). **4** base (a principle etc.) on. **5** connect (an electrical circuit) to the ground. **6** alight on the ground. □ **break ground** begin excavation. **2** introduce or discover something new. **from the ground up 1** completely. **2** from the basic to the complex. **get off the ground** informal make a successful start. **hold** (or **stand**) **one's ground** not retreat or give way. **lose ground 1** retreat. **2** lose advantage or position. **on the ground** at the point of production or operation. **on one's own ground** on one's own territory or subject. **thin on the ground** not numerous.

ground² past and past participle of GRIND.

groundbreaking ● adj. **1** innovative, pioneering. **2** relating to a groundbreaking. ● n. the act of breaking ground for a new construction project.

ground cover n. **1** a low-growing spreading plant. **2** such plants collectively.

grounded adj. **1** unable, or not allowed, to fly. **2** confined to home outside of school hours as a punishment. **3** sensible, well-balanced. **4** electrically connected with the ground, either directly or through another conductor. □ **groundedness** n. (in sense 3).

grounder n. (also **ground ball**) a ball that is hit along the ground.

ground-fault interrupter n. a circuit breaker integrated into an outlet, esp. for use in bathrooms or outdoors.

groundfish n. (pl. **groundfish** or **groundfishes**) any fish living near the bottom of the sea.

ground glass n. glass with a smooth ground surface that makes it non-transparent.

groundhog n. a woodchuck.

Groundhog Day n. Feb. 2, when the groundhog is said to come out of hibernation.

grounding n. basic training in a subject.

groundless adj. without justification.

groundout n. Baseball a play in which the batter hits a ball along the ground to an infielder and is put out at first base.

groundsheet n. a waterproof sheet placed under a tent etc.

groundskeeper n. a person who maintains a playing field or court etc.

groundspeed n. an aircraft's speed relative to the ground.

ground squirrel n. a squirrel or squirrel-like rodent living in burrows.

groundswell n. **1** a swell of the sea caused by a distant storm etc. **2** a large buildup of public opinion.

groundwater n. water held in soil or rock.

groundwork n. preparatory work.

ground zero n. **1** the point directly under or above an explosion. **2** *informal* the starting point.

group ● n. **1** a number of persons or things located or considered together. **2** a small music band. **3** a set of elements occupying a column in the periodic table and having broadly similar properties. ● v. place in or form into a group.

grouper n. a large fish of the sea bass family.

group home n. a home where unrelated people live together under supervision.

groupie n. *slang* **1** an ardent follower of touring pop groups. **2** a fan or follower.

grouping n. **1** a process of allocation to groups. **2** an arrangement in a group or groups.

groupthink n. poor-quality thinking and decision-making performed by a group of people.

grouse ● n. (*pl.* **grouse**) **1** a game bird with a plump body. **2** a complaint. ● v. (**grouses, groused, grousing**) *informal* complain pettily. [*Rhymes with* MOUSE]

grout ● n. a thin mortar for filling gaps in tiling etc. ● v. provide or fill with grout.

grove n. a small orchard or group of trees.

grovel v. (**grovels, grovelled, grovelling**) behave obsequiously in seeking favour or forgiveness. □ **groveller** n. **grovelling** adj. **grovellingly** adv. [*Say* GROV'll]

grow v. (**grows**; *past* **grew**; *past participle* **grown**; **growing**) **1** increase in size, degree, or in any way measurable. **2** develop or exist naturally. **3** produce or be produced. **4** become gradually. **5** (foll. by *on*) become gradually more favoured by. **6** (in *passive*; foll. by *over, up*) be covered with a growth. **7** cause to grow. □ **grow out of 1** become too large or mature for. **2** be the result of. **grow up 1 a** advance to maturity. **b** (esp. in *imperative*) behave sensibly. **2** arise. □ **grower** n.

growing pains *pl. n.* **1** difficulties in the development of an enterprise etc. **2** pain in the limbs of young children.

growl ● v. make a low guttural, usu. angry, sound. ● n. a growling sound. □ **growler** n.

grown-up ● adj. adult. ● n. an adult person.

grow op n. *Cdn informal* an illegal marijuana-growing operation, usu. in someone's home.

growth n. **1** the process of growing. **2** an increase in size or value. **3** something growing. **4** an abnormal formation, esp. a tumour.

grr *interj.* representing the sound of growling, esp. to express anger or annoyance.

grub ● n. **1** an insect larva. **2** *informal* food. ● v. (**grubs, grubbed, grubbing**) **1** dig superficially. **2** clear away. □ **grubber** n.

grubby adj. (**grubbier, grubbiest**) **1** dirty, grimy. **2** infested with grubs. □ **grubbiness** n.

grubstake *informal* ● n. material supplied to an enterprise in return for a share in the profits. ● v. (**grubstakes, grubstaked, grubstaking**) provide with a grubstake. □ **grubstaker** n.

grudge ● n. a persistent feeling of resentment. ● v. (**grudges, grudged, grudging**) be resentfully reluctant to give, allow, or do (something).

grudging adj. reluctant. □ **grudgingly** adv. **grudgingness** n.

gruel n. a liquid food of oatmeal etc. boiled in milk or water.

gruelling adj. (also **grueling**) extremely demanding. □ **gruellingly** adv.

gruesome adj. horrible, disgusting. □ **gruesomely** adv. **gruesomeness** n.

gruff adj. **1** (of a voice) low and harsh. **2** terse, rough-mannered. □ **gruffly** adv. **gruffness** n.

grumble ● v. (**grumbles, grumbled, grumbling**) **1** complain peevishly. **2** rumble. ● n. a complaint. □ **grumbler** n. **grumbling** adj. & n. **grumblingly** adv.

grump *informal* ● n. **1** a grumpy person. **2** (in *pl.*) a fit of sulks. ● v. **1** be grumpy. **2** utter grumpily.

grumpy adj. (**grumpier, grumpiest**) morosely irritable. □ **grumpily** adv. **grumpiness** n.

grunge n. **1** grime, dirt. **2** (also **grunge rock**) aggressive rock music with a loud and raucous guitar sound. **3** a style of dress associated with this music, characterized by loose-fitting, often second-hand clothes. □ **grunginess** n. **grungy** adj. (**grungier, grungiest**)

grunt ● n. **1** a low guttural sound, esp.

made by a pig. **2** *slang* a low-ranking labourer, soldier, etc. ● *v.* make a low inarticulate sound or grunt.

Gruyère *n.* a firm pale yellow cheese. [*Say* groo YAIR]

gryphon *n.* = GRIFFIN. [*Say* GRIFFIN]

GST *abbr.* Cdn & NZ GOODS AND SERVICES TAX.

G-string *n.* **1** a narrow strip of cloth covering only the genitals and attached to a string around the waist. **2** (usu. **G string**) *Music* a string sounding the note G.

GTA *abbr.* Greater Toronto Area.

guacamole *n.* a dip or spread made from mashed avocado. [*Say* gwocka MOLEY]

guano *n.* (*pl.* **guanos**) the excrement of seabirds, used as fertilizer. [*Say* GWONNO]

guar *n.* a drought-resistant plant grown esp. in the Indian subcontinent for food and as a source of guar gum. [*Say* GWAR (*rhymes with* FAR)]

guarantee ● *n.* **1 a** an assurance that an obligation will be fulfilled or that something is of a specified quality and durability. **b** a document giving such an undertaking. **2** = GUARANTY. **3** a person making a guaranty or giving a security. **4** something that makes an outcome certain. ● *v.* (**guarantees, guaranteed, guaranteeing**) **1** provide a guarantee for something. **2** give a promise or assurance. **3** provide financial security for.

guaranteed investment certificate *n.* Cdn a certificate guaranteeing a fixed interest rate on a sum of money. Abbreviation: **GIC**.

guarantor *n.* a person who gives a guarantee or guaranty. [*Say* GAIR un tor *or* GAIR un ter]

guaranty *n.* (*pl.* **guaranties**) **1** a promise to pay a debt or carry out a duty for another person should they fail to. **2** a thing serving as security for a guaranty. [*Say* GAIR un tee]

guard ● *v.* **1** watch over in order to protect or control. **2** (foll. by *against*) take precautions. ● *n.* **1** a state of vigilance. **2** a person who keeps watch or protects. **3** a body of soldiers etc. serving to protect a place or person. **4** (in *pl.*) (usu. **Guards**) a body of troops nominally employed to guard a ruler. **5** a thing that protects or defends. **6** (often in *comb.*) a device fitted or worn to prevent injury or damage. **7** a defensive player. **8** (in curling) a rock positioned in front of the house to protect those behind it. □ **be on** (or **keep** or **stand**) **guard** keep watch; be vigilant. **lower one's guard** (also **let one's guard down**) reduce vigilance against

attack. **off guard** unprepared for some surprise.

guarded *adj.* **1** cautious, avoiding commitment. **2** defended. □ **guardedly** *adv.* **guardedness** *n.*

guardian *n.* **1** a defender, protector, or keeper. **2** a person legally responsible for someone unable to manage their own affairs. □ **guardianship** *n.*

guardian angel *n.* a spirit conceived as watching over a person or place.

guardrail *n.* a rail fitted as a support or to prevent an accident.

guardsman *n.* (*pl.* **guardsmen**) a soldier belonging to a body of guards.

guar gum *n.* a powder obtained from guar seeds, used in the food, paper, and other industries.

Guatemalan *n.* a person from Guatemala. □ **Guatemalan** *adj.* [*Say* gwotta MOLL un]

guava *n.* (*pl.* **guavas**) the pink-fleshed yellow fruit of a small tropical American tree. [*Say* GWOVVA]

gubernatorial *adj.* esp. US relating to a governor. [*Say* goober nuh TORY ul]

guck *n.* slang a sticky or slimy substance.

guerrilla *n.* **1** a member of a small independent force fighting against the government or regular forces. **2** *informal* an activist using controversial or sensational means. [*Say* gur ILLA]

guess ● *v.* (**guesses, guessed, guessing**) **1** estimate without enough information to be sure. **2** form a hypothesis about. **3** guess correctly. **4** make a conjecture about. **5** *informal* suppose. ● *n.* (*pl.* **guesses**) an estimate or conjecture. □ **guesser** *n.*

guesstimate *informal* ● *n.* an estimate based more on guesswork than calculation. ● *v.* (**guesstimates, guesstimated, guesstimating**) form a guesstimate of. [*Say* GUESS tuh mit *for the noun*, GUESS ti mate *for the verb*]

guesswork *n.* the process or results of guessing.

guest ● *n.* **1** a person (usu. invited) visiting another's house or having a meal etc. at the expense of the inviter. **2** a person lodging at a hotel, boarding house, etc. **3** a person invited to take part in an event, performance, broadcast, etc. ● *v.* be a guest on a radio or television show or in a theatrical performance etc.

guff *n.* slang **1** nonsense. **2** insolent talk. □ **no guff** Cdn **1** a declaration of truthfulness. **2** an expression of mock surprise.

guffaw ● *n.* a boisterous laugh. ● *v.* **1** utter

a guffaw. **2** say with a guffaw. [*Say* guh FAW]

guidance *n.* **1** advice or information aimed at solving a problem. **2** the control of a missile or spacecraft in its course.

guidance counsellor *n.* a person who counsels others regarding career decisions.

guide ● *n.* **1** a person who leads or shows the way. **2** an adviser. **3** a directing principle. **4** a book with essential information on a subject. **5** a structure or marking which directs the position or movement of something. **6 (Guide)** = GIRL GUIDE. ● *v.* (**guides, guided, guiding**) **1 a** act as guide to. **b** arrange the course of (events). **2** be the principle or ground of (an action, judgment, etc.). **3** direct the affairs of.

guidebook *n.* **1** a book of information about a place for visitors. **2** a manual.

guide dog *n.* a dog trained to guide a blind person.

guideline *n.* (often in *pl.*) a principle or criterion directing action.

guild *n.* **1** an association of people for a common purpose. **2** a medieval association of craftsmen or merchants. [*Rhymes with* BUILD]

guile *n.* sly, cunning behaviour. □ **guileful** *adj.* **guileless** *adj.* **guilelessly** *adv.* [*Say* GILE (*with a hard G as in* GIVE)]

guillemot *n.* a diving seabird of the auk family, with a pointed bill, found in the northern latitudes. [*Say* GILLA mot]

guillotine ● *n.* **1** *hist.* a machine with a heavy blade sliding vertically, used for beheading. **2** a device for cutting paper, metal, etc. **3** *Parliament* a fixed time for voting on various parts of a legislative bill. ● *v.* (**guillotines, guillotined, guillotining**) **1** use a guillotine on. **2** *Parliament* end discussion of (a bill) by applying a guillotine. [*Say* GILLA teen *or* GHEE uh teen]

guilt *n.* **1** the fact of having committed an offence. **2 a** culpability. **b** the feeling of this.

guilt trip ● *n.* an intense feeling of guilt. ● *v.* (**guilt-trip**) (**guilt-trips, guilt-tripped, guilt-tripping**) induce a feeling of guilt in.

guilty *adj.* (**guiltier, guiltiest**) **1** responsible for a wrong. **2** affected by guilt. **3** concerning guilt. **4** having committed a (specified) offence. □ **guiltily** *adv.* **guiltiness** *n.* **guiltless** *adj.* **guiltlessly** *adv.*

guinea fowl *n.* (*pl.* **guinea fowl** or **guinea fowls**) a large African game bird with slate-coloured white-spotted plumage. [*Say* GINNY fowl (*with a hard G as in* GIVE)]

guinea hen *n.* a female guinea fowl, esp. as food.

guinea pig *n.* **1** a tailless domesticated S American rodent. **2** a person or thing used in an experiment.

guise *n.* an external form concealing the true nature of something. [*Sounds like* GUYS]

guitar *n.* a usu. six-stringed musical instrument with a fretted fingerboard, played by plucking or strumming. □ **guitarist** *n.*

gulag *n.* **1** (also **Gulag**) *hist.* the system of forced-labour camps in the former Soviet Union. **2** such a camp. [*Say* GOO lag]

gulch *n.* (*pl.* **gulches**) a ravine.

gulf *n.* **1** a stretch of sea consisting of a deep inlet with a narrow mouth. **2 (the Gulf) a** the Gulf of Mexico. **b** the Persian Gulf. **c** the Gulf of St. Lawrence. **3** a deep crack in the ground. **4** a large difference between two people or groups.

gull¹ *n.* any of various kinds of long-winged web-footed birds, usu. having white and black or grey plumage and a bright bill.

gull² *v.* dupe, fool.

gullet *n.* **1** the food passage extending from the mouth to the stomach; the esophagus. **2** the throat.

gullible *adj.* easily persuaded or deceived; credulous. □ **gullibility** *n.* **gullibly** *adv.* [*Say* GULLA bull]

gully *n.* (*pl.* **gullies**) a small ravine. □ **gullied** *adj.*

gulp ● *v.* **1** (often foll. by *down*) swallow greedily, hastily, or with difficulty. **2** stifle. ● *n.* **1** an act of gulping. **2** a large mouthful of a drink. □ **gulper** *n.*

gum¹ ● *n.* **1** a sticky secretion of some trees and shrubs. **2** chewing or bubble gum. **3** (in full **gum arabic**) a gum exuded by some acacias, used as a glue or emulsifier. **4** a eucalyptus. ● *v.* (**gums, gummed, gumming**) smear, fasten, or make waterproof with gum. □ **gum up 1** become clogged. **2** *informal* obstruct.

gum² ● *n.* (usu. in *pl.*) the firm flesh around the roots of the teeth. ● *v.* (**gums, gummed, gumming**) (of someone without teeth) chew using the gums.

gumbo *n.* (*pl.* **gumbos**) **1 a** okra. **b** a spicy chicken or seafood soup thickened with okra, rice, etc. **2** thick clinging mud.

gumboot *n.* a rubber boot.

gumdrop *n.* a soft chewy coloured candy.

gummy¹ *adj.* (**gummier, gummiest**) sticky.

gummy² *adj.* (**gummier, gummiest**) toothless.

gumption *n. informal* spirited initiative and resourcefulness.

gumshoe *n. informal* a detective.

gum tree *n.* a tree exuding gum, esp. a eucalyptus.

gumweed *n.* a plant with dark green gummy leaves and showy yellow flowers with sticky bracts, widespread in W Canada.

gun ● *n.* **1** a weapon with a metal tube from which bullets or other projectiles are propelled by explosive force. **2** any device imitative of this. **3** a device for discharging something under pressure. **4** a gunman. ● *v.* (**guns, gunned, gunning**) **1** shoot with a gun. **2** *informal* accelerate. **3** *informal* (foll. by *for*) go determinedly after, esp. to rebuke. □ **go great guns** *informal* proceed vigorously. **jump the gun** *informal* start prematurely. **stick to one's guns** *informal* maintain one's position under attack. **under the gun** *informal* under pressure.

gunboat *n.* a small vessel armed with guns.

gun dog *n.* a dog bred or trained to assist hunters.

gunfight *n.* a fight with firearms. □ **gunfighter** *n.*

gunfire *n.* the repeated firing of a gun.

gunge *informal* ● *n.* = GUNK *n.* ● *v.* (**gunges, gunged, gunging**) (usu. foll. by *up*) clog with gunge. □ **gungy** *adj.*

gung-ho *adj.* eager.

gunk *slang* ● *n.* sticky or viscous matter. ● *v.* (often foll. by *up*) soil or clog with gunk. □ **gunky** *adj.* (**gunkier, gunkiest**)

gunman *n.* (*pl.* **gunmen**) a person using a gun, esp. to commit a crime.

gunmetal ● *n.* **1** (also **gunmetal grey, gunmetal blue**) a dull bluish-grey colour. **2** an alloy of copper and tin or zinc. ● *adj.* dull bluish grey.

gunnel *n.* = GUNWALE.

gunner *n.* **1** a soldier in the artillery. **2** a person who operates a gun.

gunnery *n.* the design and operation of large guns.

gunny *n.* (*pl.* **gunnies**) **1** coarse sacking, usu. of jute. **2** (also **gunny sack**) a sack made of this.

gunplay *n.* the use of guns.

gunpoint *n.* □ **at gunpoint** threatened with a gun or an ultimatum etc.

gunpowder *n.* an explosive powder made of potassium nitrate, sulphur, and charcoal.

gunrunner *n.* a person engaged in the illegal sale or importing of firearms. □ **gunrunning** *n.*

gunship *n.* a heavily armed helicopter.

gunshot *n.* **1** a shot fired from a gun. **2** the range of a gun.

gun-shy *adj.* **1** frightened by the sound a gun makes. **2** hesitant because of a past unpleasant experience.

gunsight *n.* a sight on a gun (see SIGHT *n.* 6).

gunslinger *n.* esp. *US slang* a gunfighter. □ **gunslinging** *n. & adj.*

gunsmith *n.* a person who makes and sells firearms. □ **gunsmithing** *n.*

gunwale *n.* the upper edge of the side of a boat or ship. [*Say* GUN ul]

guppy *n.* (*pl.* **guppies**) a small freshwater fish of tropical America.

gurdwara *n.* a Sikh temple. [*Say* gurd WAR uh (WAR *rhymes with* FAR)]

gurdy *n.* (*pl.* **gurdies**) *Cdn* a winch on a fishing boat.

gurgle ● *v.* (**gurgles, gurgled, gurgling**) **1** make a bubbling sound, as of water flowing over stones. **2** (of a baby) make a guttural noise indicating happiness. ● *n.* a gurgling sound. □ **gurgly** *adj.*

Gurkha *n.* **1** a member of the principal Hindu race in Nepal. **2** a Nepalese soldier serving in the British army. [*Say* GURKA]

gurney *n.* a wheeled stretcher. [*Say* GURNY]

guru *n.* (*pl.* **gurus**) **1** a Hindu spiritual teacher. **2** an influential teacher or popular expert. **3** each of the ten first leaders of the Sikh religion.

gush ● *v.* (**gushes, gushed, gushing**) **1** emit or flow in a sudden and copious stream. **2** express approval etc. effusively. ● *n.* (*pl.* **gushes**) **1** a sudden or abundant stream. **2** exaggerated effusiveness. □ **gushing** *adj.* **gushy** *adj.*

gusher *n.* an oil well from which oil flows without a pump.

gusset *n.* a piece of material let into a garment etc. to strengthen or enlarge it.

gussy *v.* (**gussies, gussied, gussying**) *informal* dress up, esp. for a special occasion.

gust ● *n.* **1** a sudden strong rush of wind. **2** a burst of rain, sound, emotion, etc. ● *v.* blow in gusts. □ **gusty** *adj.*

gustatory *adj.* concerning taste. [*Say* GUSTA tory]

gusto *n.* enthusiasm or vigour.

gut ● *n.* **1 a** the intestine. **b** *informal* the abdomen or belly. **2** (in *pl.*) the bowel or entrails of something. **3** (in *pl.*) *informal* courage and determination. **4** (as an *adj.*) **a** instinctive. **b** fundamental. ● *v.* (**guts, gutted, gutting**) **1** (often in *passive*) remove or destroy (esp. by fire) the internal fittings of (a house etc.). **2** take out the guts of. **3** remove the essential components of. □ **hate a person's guts** *informal* dislike a person intensely. **have someone's guts for garters** *Cdn & Brit.* be extremely angry at someone. □ **gutted** *adj.*

gut-busting *adj.* **1** hilariously funny. **2** (of food) very dense or rich and filling. □ **gut-buster** *n.*

gutless *adj. informal* lacking courage. □ **gutlessly** *adv.* **gutlessness** *n.*

gut-level *adj.* instinctive.

gutsy *adj.* (**gutsier, gutsiest**) *informal* courageous. □ **gutsiness** *n.*

gutter ● *n.* **1 a** a channel at the side of a street to carry away runoff. **b** *esp. US & Brit.* = EAVESTROUGH. **2** (**the gutter**) a poor or sordid background or environment. **3** any conduit for liquid. **4** the channel at the side of a bowling lane. ● *v.* **1** (of a candle) melt away. **2** (of a candle flame) flicker as the last wax melts away.

gutter press *n.* sensational journalism concerned esp. with the private lives of public figures.

guttersnipe *n.* **1** a street urchin. **2** an ill-mannered vagrant.

guttural *adj.* **1** (of a sound) produced at the back of the throat. **2** (of speech) characterized by guttural sounds. □ **gutturally** *adv.* [Say GUTTER ul]

gut-wrenching *adj.* emotionally devastating.

guy¹ *n.* **1** *informal* a man. **2** (in *pl.*) *informal* a person of either sex.

guy² *n.* a rope or line fixed to the ground to secure a tent etc.

Guyanese *n.* a person from Guyana. □ **Guyanese** *adj.* [Say guy uh NEEZ]

guy wire *n.* a wire or cable used to secure a tent or keep something upright.

guzzle *v.* (**guzzles, guzzled, guzzling**) consume greedily. □ **guzzler** *n.*

Gwich'in *n.* (*pl.* **Gwich'in**) a member or the language of an Aboriginal people living in Alaska, the Yukon, and the NWT. □ **Gwich'in** *adj.* [Say GWITCHEN]

gybe ● *v.* (**gybes, gybed, gybing**) **1** (of a fore-and-aft sail or boom) swing across a following wind. **2** cause (a sail) to do this. **3** change course so that this happens. ● *n.* a change of course causing gybing. [Say JIBE]

gym *n.* *informal* **1** a gymnasium. **2** physical education. **3** gymnastics.

gymnasium *n.* (*pl.* **gymnasiums**) a room or building equipped for gymnastics and other physical exercise.

gymnast *n.* an expert in gymnastics.

gymnastic *adj.* of or involving gymnastics. □ **gymnastically** *adv.*

gymnastics *pl. n.* (also treated as *sing.*) **1** exercises involving physical agility and coordination, usu. in competition. **2** physical or mental agility.

gymnosperm *n.* a plant having seeds unprotected by an ovary. [Say JIM no sperm]

gym shoe *n.* = RUNNING SHOE.

gynecology *n.* (also **gynaecology**) the branch of medicine concerned with conditions and diseases specific to women and girls. □ **gynecological** *adj.* **gynecologist** *n.* [Say guy nuh COLLA jee, guy nuh cuh LOGICAL]

gyp *slang* ● *v.* (**gyps, gypped, gypping**) cheat. ● *n.* an act of cheating. [Say JIP]

Gyproc *n.* = DRYWALL *n.* [Say JIP rock]

gypsum *n.* a soft whitish mineral used in the building industry and to make plaster of Paris. [Say JIP sum]

gypsy *n.* (*pl.* **gypsies**) (also **Gypsy**) a member of a travelling people speaking the Romany language.

gypsy moth *n.* a kind of moth the caterpillars of which are very destructive to foliage.

gyrate *v.* (**gyrates, gyrated, gyrating**) **1** revolve around a fixed point or axis. **2** dance wildly, esp. moving ones hips in a suggestive circular pattern. □ **gyration** *n.*

gyre *esp. literary* ● *v.* (**gyres, gyred, gyring**) whirl, gyrate. ● *n.* a whirling, a vortex. [Say JIRE *(rhymes with FIRE)*]

gyrfalcon *n.* the largest falcon, found in Arctic regions. [Say JUR falcon]

gyro¹ *n.* (*pl.* **gyros**) *informal* **1** = GYROSCOPE. **2** = GYROCOMPASS. [Say JYE roe]

gyro² *n.* (*pl.* **gyros**) a sandwich of pita bread filled with spiced meat etc. [Say YEE roe]

gyrocompass *n.* (*pl.* **gyrocompasses**) a non-magnetic compass giving true north and bearings from it by means of a gyroscope. [Say JYE ro compass]

gyroscope *n.* a wheel or disc mounted so as to spin rapidly about an axis whose orientation is not fixed, used in stabilizers etc. □ **gyroscopic** *adj.* [Say JYE ruh scope]

Hh

H¹ *n.* (also **h**) (*pl.* **Hs** or **H's**) the eighth letter of the English alphabet.

H² *abbr.* (also **H.**) **1** hardness. **2** (of a pencil lead) hard. **3** *slang* heroin.

h *abbr.* (also **h.**) **1** height. **2** hot. **3** hour(s). **4** husband. **5** *Baseball* hit. **6** hundred.

ha¹ *interj.* expressing surprise, triumph, etc.

ha² *abbr.* hectare(s).

habeas corpus *n.* **1** a writ requiring a person to be brought before a judge or into court, esp. to investigate the lawfulness of his or her detention. **2** the right to such a writ. [*Say* HAY be us CORP us]

haberdasher *n.* a dealer in men's clothing. □ **haberdashery** *n.* [*Say* HABBER dasher]

habit *n.* **1** something a person does often. **2** *informal* an addiction to drugs. **3 a** the dress of a particular religious order. **b** (also **riding habit**) an outfit designed to be worn by a rider on horseback. □ **make a habit of** do regularly.

habitable *adj.* suitable for habitation. □ **habitability** *n.*

habitant *n. hist.* (in Canada) a French settler in rural Quebec, esp. a farmer. [*Say* abbey TON (with TON as in French)]

habitat *n.* the natural environment of an animal or plant.

habitation *n.* **1** the state of living somewhere. **2** a home.

habit-forming *adj.* addictive.

habitual *adj.* **1** done as a habit. **2** usual. □ **habitually** *adv.*

habituate *v.* (**habituates**, **habituated**, **habituating**) (often foll. by *to*) make used to something. □ **habituation** *n.* [*Say* huh BICH oo ate]

habitué *n.* a habitual visitor to a place. [*Say* huh BICH oo AY]

hacienda *n.* (in Spanish-speaking countries) a large estate with a house. [*Say* hassy ENDA]

hack¹ ● *v.* **1** chop with heavy blows. **2** shorten (a piece of writing, etc.). **3** use a computer to gain unauthorized access to data. **4** *slang* cope with. **5** cough repeatedly. ● *n.* **1** a rough cut or blow. **2** a short, hard cough. **3** *Curling* an insert in the ice, used to steady the foot. □ **hacker** *n.*

hack² ● *n.* **1 a** a person hired to do dull,

routine work. **b** a mediocre writer. **c** *derogatory* a journalist. **2 a** a taxi. **b** a taxi driver. **3** a horse for ordinary riding. ● *adj.* commonplace; inferior.

hacking *adj.* (of a cough) short, dry, and frequently repeated.

hackle *n.* **1** the neck or saddle feathers of certain birds, e.g. the rooster. **2** (in *pl.*) the hairs along the back of a dog, which rise when it is angry or alarmed. □ **make a person's hackles rise** or **raise some** (or **a person's**) **hackles** anger a person.

hackneyed *adj.* (of a phrase etc.) made trite by overuse. [*Say* HACK need]

hacksaw *n.* a saw with a narrow blade set in a frame, for cutting metal.

hackwork *n.* mediocre esp. literary work done primarily or solely to make money.

had *past and past participle of* HAVE.

haddock *n.* (*pl.* **haddock**) a popular food fish of the North Atlantic, related to the cod. [*Say* HAD ick]

hadn't *contr.* had not.

hafnium *n.* a silvery metallic element used in tungsten alloys for filaments and electrodes. [*Say* HAFNY um]

haft *n.* the handle of a dagger etc.

hag *n.* an ugly old woman.

haggard *adj.* looking exhausted and distraught. [*Say* HAG'rd]

haggis *n.* (*pl.* **haggises**) a Scottish dish consisting of seasoned sheep's or calf's offal mixed with suet and oatmeal.

haggle *v.* (**haggles**, **haggled**, **haggling**) bargain persistently over a price. □ **haggler** *n.* **haggling** *n.*

hagiography *n.* (*pl.* **hagiographies**) **1** the writing of the lives of saints. **2** an idealized biography of any person. □ **hagiographer** *n.* **hagiographic** *adj.* [*Say* haggy OGGRA fee, haggy uh GRAPHIC]

hah *interj.* = HA¹.

Haida *n.* **1** (*pl.* **Haida** or **Haidas**) a member of an Aboriginal people living on the west coast of Canada. **2** the language of this people. □ **Haida** *adj.* [*Say* HI duh]

haiku *n.* (*pl.* **haiku**) **1** a Japanese poem, usu. of 17 syllables. **2** an imitation of this in another language. [*Say* HI koo]

hail¹ ● *n.* **1** pellets of frozen rain falling in showers. **2** a barrage. ● *v.* hail falls.

hail² *v.* **1** describe or greet enthusiastically. **2** attract the attention of. **3** (foll. by *from*) have one's home or origins in. □ **hailer** *n.*

Hail Mary *n.* (*pl.* **Hail Marys**) a prayer to the Virgin Mary used chiefly by Roman Catholics.

hailstone *n.* a pellet of hail.

hair *n.* **1 a** any of the fine threadlike strands growing from the skin of mammals. **b** these collectively. **2** anything resembling a hair. **3** a fine, elongated outgrowth from a plant. **4** a very small quantity or extent. □ **get in a person's hair** annoy someone. **hair of the dog (that bit you)** an alcoholic drink taken to cure a hangover. **let one's hair down** *informal* abandon restraint. **make one's hair stand on end** horrify one. □ **-haired** *comb. form* **hairlike** *adj.*

hairball *n.* a ball of hair collecting in the stomach of a cat etc. as a result of the animal licking its coat.

hairbrush *n.* (*pl.* **hairbrushes**) a brush for smoothing one's hair.

haircut *n.* **1** an act of cutting the hair. **2** the style in which the hair is cut. □ **haircutter** *n.* **haircutting** *n.*

hairdo *n.* (*pl.* **hairdos**) the style of a person's hair.

hairdresser *n.* a person who cuts and styles hair. □ **hairdressing** *n.*

hairline ● *n.* the natural line on the head at which a person's hair stops growing, esp. on the forehead. ● *adj.* very thin.

hairnet *n.* a fine net for holding the hair in place.

hairpiece *n.* a piece of false hair adding to a person's natural hair.

hairpin *n.* **1** a U-shaped pin for fastening the hair. **2** a sharp curve.

hair-raising *adj.* terrifying.

hair shirt *n.* **1** a shirt made of a very rough cloth woven from hair, worn as a form of self-discipline or to punish oneself. **2** (**hair-shirt**) (as an *adj.*) austere, self-sacrificing.

hairsplitting *adj. & n.* quibbling.

hairspray *n.* a fixative solution sprayed to keep hair in place.

hairstyle *n.* a particular way of arranging the hair. □ **hairstyling** *n.* **hairstylist** *n.*

hair-trigger ● *n.* a firearm trigger set for release at the slightest pressure. ● *adj.* easily provoked.

hairy *adj.* (**hairier**, **hairiest**) **1** made of, covered with, or resembling hair. **2** *slang* difficult or frightening. □ **hairiness** *n.*

Haisla *n.* (*pl.* same or **Haislas**) **1** a member of a major language group of northern Wakashan, living in the watershed of the Douglas Channel in NW BC. **2** the language of the Haisla. □ **Haisla** *adj.* [*Say* HICELA]

Haitian *n.* **1** a native of inhabitant of Haiti, a country in the Caribbean. **2** the French-based Creole language spoken in Haiti. □ **Haitian** *adj.* [*Say* HAY sh'n]

hajj *n.* the pilgrimage to Mecca, constituting one of the religious duties of Islam. [*Say* HADGE]

hajji *n.* (*pl.* **hajjis**) a Muslim who has been to Mecca as a pilgrim. [*Say* HADGEY]

hake *n.* any of various food fishes related to the cod.

halal ● *adj.* (of meat) prepared as prescribed by Muslim law. ● *n.* meat prepared in this way. [*Say* hal AL]

halcyon *adj.* **1** peaceful. **2** (of a period) happy. [*Say* HAL see un]

hale *adj.* strong and healthy (esp. in **hale and hearty**).

half ● *n.* (*pl.* **halves**) **1** either of two equal or corresponding parts into which a thing is or might be divided. **2** either of two equal periods of play in sports. ● *adj.* **1** forming a half. **2** partial. ● *adv.* partly. □ **by halves** incompletely. **go halves** (or **half and half**) share equally. **half a chance** *informal* the slightest opportunity. **half past** (of time) thirty minutes past the hour.

half a dozen *n.* six.

half-and-half ● *adv.* in equal parts. ● *adj.* that is half one thing and half another. ● *n.* a mixture of milk and cream having 10% milk fat.

halfback *n.* **1** *Football* a back lined up on one or the other side of the fullback. **2** *Soccer* a player positioned between the forwards and fullbacks.

half-baked *adj.* incompletely developed.

half-breed *n.* *offensive* a person of mixed race.

half-brother *n.* a brother with whom a person has only one biological parent in common.

half-cut *adj.* *Cdn & Brit. slang* fairly drunk.

half-decent *adj.* moderately decent.

half-dozen *n.* six or about six.

half-hearted *adj.* lacking enthusiasm. □ **half-heartedly** *adv.*

half hitch *n.* (*pl.* **half hitches**) a knot formed by passing the end of a rope around its standing part and then through the loop.

half-hour *n.* (also **half an hour**) a period of 30 minutes. □ **half-hourly** *adj. & adv.*

half-life *n.* (*pl.* **half-lives**) **1** the time taken for half of a radioactive substance to decay.

2 the time taken for half of a dose of a drug etc. to disappear in the body.

half-light *n.* dim light, as at dusk.

half-mast *n.* the position of a flag halfway down the mast, as a mark of respect for a person who has died.

half moon *n.* **1** the moon when only half its illuminated surface is visible from earth. **2** a semicircular object.

half note *n. Music* a note having the time value of half a whole note and represented by a hollow ring with a stem.

half-sister *n.* a sister with whom a person has only one biological parent in common.

half-slip *n.* an article of lingerie resembling a skirt, worn underneath dresses and skirts.

half-step *n. Music* a semitone.

half-timbered *adj. Architecture* having walls with a timber frame and a brick or plaster filling. □ **half-timbering** *n.*

halftime *n.* an interval between halves of a sports event.

half-ton *n.* esp. *Cdn* a pickup truck than can carry approximately half a ton.

halftone *n.* **1** an image in which continuous tone is simulated by dots or lines of various sizes. **2** *Music* a semitone.

half-track *n.* a military or other vehicle with wheels at the front and caterpillar tracks at the rear.

half-truth *n.* a statement that conveys only part of the truth, esp. deliberately.

halfway ● *adv.* **1** at or to a point equidistant between two others. **2** to some extent. ● *adj.* equidistant between two points.

halfway house *n.* **1** a residence where ex-prisoners, mental patients, etc. live and receive treatment to help prepare them for their return to society. **2** the halfway point in a progression.

halfwit *n. informal* a stupid person. □ **halfwitted** *adj.*

halibut *n.* (*pl.* **halibut**) a large marine flatfish, used as food. [*Say* HALA b't]

halide *n.* a binary compound of a halogen with another group or element. [*Say* HAL ide *or* HAIL ide]

Haligonian *n.* a person from Halifax, Nova Scotia. □ **Haligonian** *adj.* [*Say* hala GO nee un]

Halkomelem *n.* (*pl.* **Halkomelem**) the Salishan language of the Halq'emeylem. [*Say* hall kuh MAY lum]

hall *n.* **1 a** a corridor. **b** a space just inside the front entrance of a house. **2** a large room or building for meetings, concerts, etc. **3** a building containing lecture rooms etc. at a college or university.

hallelujah *interj. & n.* = ALLELUIA.

hallmark *n.* **1** a mark used for indicating a standard of gold, silver, and platinum. **2** any distinctive feature.

Hall of Fame *n.* (*pl.* **Halls of Fame**) **1** a building with memorials of people who have excelled in a specific activity, esp. a sport. **2** (*usu.* **hall of fame**) a group famous in a particular sphere. □ **Hall of Famer** *n.*

halloo (also **hallo**) ● *interj.* calling attention. ● *v.* (**halloos**, **halloos**, **hallooed**) cry "halloo". [*Say* huh LOO]

hallowed *adj.* **1** respected and important. **2** made holy.

Halloween *n.* the night of 31 October, the eve of All Saints' Day.

hallucination *n.* the perception of an object not actually present. □ **hallucinate** *v.* **hallucinatory** *adj.* [*Say* huh loo sin AY shun, huh LOO sin ate, huh LOO sin a tory]

hallucinogen *n.* a drug causing hallucinations. □ **hallucinogenic** *adj.* [*Say* huh LOO sinna jen, huh loo sinna JEN ick]

hallway *n.* HALL 1.

halo *n.* (*pl.* **halos** or **haloes**) **1** a circle of light surrounding the head of a sacred person. **2** a circle of light around a luminous body, esp. the sun or moon. □ **haloed** *adj.* [*Say* HAY low]

halogen ● *n.* any of the reactive elements fluorine, chlorine, bromine, iodine, and astatine. ● *adj.* using a filament surrounded by a halogen, usu. iodine vapour. [*Say* HALA jen]

Halq'emeylem *n.* (*pl.* same) **1** a member of an Aboriginal people living in southwestern BC. **2** the Salishan language of the Halq'emeylem, particularly the upriver dialect spoken by the Sto:lo. □ **Halq'emeylem** *adj.* [*Say* hall kuh MAIL'em]

halt ● *n.* a temporary stop. ● *v.* **1** stop. **2** cause to stop.

halter ● *n.* **1** a rope or strap with a noose for horses or cattle. **2** (also **halter top**) a style of woman's sleeveless top fastened behind the neck and across the back. ● *v.* put a halter on (a horse etc.).

halting *adj.* slow, hesitant. □ **haltingly** *adv.*

halvah *n.* (also **halva**) a sweet confection of sesame flour and honey. [*Say* HAL vuh]

halve *v.* (**halves**, **halved**, **halving**) **1** divide into two equal parts. **2** reduce by half.

halves *pl.* of HALF.

halyard *n. Nautical* a rope for raising or lowering a sail etc. [*Say* HAL y'rd]

ham n. **1** the upper part of a pig's leg salted and dried or smoked for food. **2** the back of the thigh; the thigh and buttock. **3** *slang* an actor who overacts. **4** *informal* an amateur radio station operator. □ **ham it up** overact. □ **hammy** adj.

hamburger n. (also **hamburg**) **1** a patty of ground beef, seasonings, etc. **2** this fried or grilled and eaten in a soft bread roll. **3** ground beef.

ham-fisted adj. informal = HAM-HANDED. □ **ham-fistedly** adv. **ham-fistedness** n.

ham-handed adj. informal clumsy, bungling. □ **ham-handedness** n.

hamlet n. a small village.

hammer ● n. **1 a** a tool with a heavy metal head at right angles to the handle, used for breaking things and driving in nails. **b** one part of a mechanism that hits another, e.g. one that strikes the strings of a piano. **2** an auctioneer's mallet. **3** a heavy metal ball attached to a wire for throwing in an athletic contest. **4** *Curling* the last rock of an end. ● v. **1** hit repeatedly with or as with a hammer. **2** inculcate (ideas, knowledge, etc.) forcefully. **3** work persistently. □ **hammer and tongs** with vigour. **hammer out 1** make flat or smooth by hammering. **2** work out the details of. **3** play loudly. **under the hammer** to be sold at an auction.

hammer and sickle n. the symbols of the industrial worker and the peasant used as the emblem of the former USSR and of communism.

hammered adj. **1** shaped by hammer. **2** informal drunk.

hammerhead n. a shark with a flattened, laterally elongated head.

hammerlock n. **1** a hold in which an opponent's arm is twisted and bent behind the back. **2** fig. a strong hold.

hammock n. a bed of canvas or rope network, suspended by cords at the ends. [Say HAM ick]

hamper¹ n. **1** a large basket usu. with a hinged lid and containing food. **2** a package of food or other essentials for a needy person. **3** a usu. covered basket or other receptacle for dirty laundry.

hamper² v. impede, hinder.

hamster n. a burrowing rodent with a short tail and large cheek pouches.

hamstring ● n. each of five tendons at the back of the knee. ● v. (**hamstrings**, **hamstrung**, **hamstringing**) **1** cripple by cutting the hamstrings of. **2** prevent the activity of.

Han n. (pl. **Han**) **1** a member of a small Aboriginal group living along the Yukon River. **2** the Athapaskan language of this people. □ **Han** adj. [Say HON]

hand ● n. **1** the end part of the arm beyond the wrist. **2 a** (often in pl.) control. **b** agency or influence. **c** an active role. **3** help. **4** the pointer of a clock or watch. **5 a** skill. **b** a person skilful in some respect. **6** handwriting. **7** a pledge of marriage. **8** a manual labourer. **9** the playing cards dealt to a player. **10** informal applause. **11** the unit of measure of a horse's height, equal to 4 inches (10.16 cm). ● v. deliver; give to. □ **at hand 1** close by. **2** about to happen. **by hand** by a person and not a machine. **hand in glove** in collusion or association. **hand in hand 1** holding hands. **2** in close association. **hand it to** informal acknowledge the merit of (a person). **hand off 1** Football hand (the ball) to another player. **2** give or hand (a thing) to another person. **hand over** deliver; surrender possession of. **hand over fist** informal with rapid progress. **hands down** (esp. of winning) with no difficulty. **hands off 1** a warning not to interfere with something. **2** Computing etc. not requiring manual use of controls. **hands on 1** Computing of or requiring personal operation at a keyboard. **2** involving active participation rather than theory. **hand-to-hand** (of fighting) at close quarters. **have one's hands full** be fully occupied. **have one's hands tied** informal be unable to act. **in hand 1** in reserve. **2** under one's control. **on hand 1** available. **2** present, in attendance. **on one's hands** resting on one as a responsibility. **on the one (or the other) hand** from one (or another) point of view. **out of hand 1** out of control. **2** peremptorily. **to hand** within easy reach. **turn one's hand to** undertake (as a new activity).

handbag n. a woman's purse.

handball n. **1** a game in which a ball is hit with the hand in a walled court. **2** Soccer illegal touching of the ball with the hand or arm.

handbasket n. a small basket. □ **go to hell in a handbasket** degenerate rapidly.

handbill n. a printed notice distributed by hand.

handbook n. a short manual or guidebook.

handbrake n. a brake operated by hand.

handcart n. a small cart pushed or drawn by hand.

handcraft ● n. = HANDICRAFT. ● v. make by handicraft. □ **handcrafted** adj.

handcuff ● n. (in pl.) a pair of lockable

linked metal rings for securing a person's wrists. ● v. **1** put handcuffs on. **2** prevent (a person) from acting freely.

-handed adj. (in comb.) **1** for or involving a specified number of hands. **2** using chiefly the hand specified. □ **-handedly** adv. **-handedness** n. (both in sense 2)

handful n. (pl. **handfuls**) **1** a quantity that fills the hand. **2** a small number or amount. **3** informal a troublesome person or task.

hand grenade n. see GRENADE.

handgrip n. **1** a grasp with the hand. **2** a handle designed for easy holding.

handgun n. a small firearm held in and fired with one hand.

hand-held ● adj. designed to be held in the hand. ● n. a small computer.

handhold n. something for the hands to grip on.

handicap ● n. **1 a** a disadvantage imposed on a superior competitor in order to make the chances more equal. **b** a contest in which this is imposed. **2** the number of strokes by which a golfer normally exceeds par for the course. **3** a thing that makes progress difficult. **4** a physical or mental disability. ● v. (**handicaps**, **handicapped**, **handicapping**) **1** impose a handicap on. **2** place at a disadvantage. □ **handicapped** adj.

handicraft n. **1** a particular skill of making decorative objects by hand. **2** work produced by such a skill.

handiwork n. work done by hand, or by a particular person.

handkerchief n. (pl. **handkerchiefs** or **handkerchieves**) a square of cotton, linen, silk, etc., usu. carried in the pocket for wiping one's nose, etc.

handle ● n. **1** the part by which a thing is held, carried, or controlled. **2** a fact that may be taken advantage of. **3** informal a personal name or title. ● v. (**handles**, **handled**, **handling**) **1** feel or move with the hands. **2** manage. **3** deal in (goods). **4** react or behave. □ **get a handle on** informal understand. □ **handleable** adj. **handled** comb. form **handler** n. **handling** n.

handlebar n. (often in pl.) the steering bar of a bicycle etc., with a grip at each end.

handlogger n. a person who logs by hand. □ **handlogging** n.

handmade adj. made by hand and not by machine.

hand-me-down n. an article of clothing etc. passed on from another person.

handoff n. the act of handing something off to another person.

handout n. **1** something given free to a needy person. **2** a fact sheet etc. distributed to an audience. **3** anything given away free. **4** a payment made by esp. a government to a person, agency, etc. perceived as providing nothing in return.

handover n. the act of handing over (power, possessions, etc.).

hand-pick v. **1** pick (fruit etc.) by hand. **2** choose personally. □ **hand-picked** adj.

handrail n. a narrow rail for holding as a support on stairs etc.

handsaw n. a saw worked by one hand.

hands-down adj. unrivalled, without competition.

handset n. a telephone mouthpiece and earpiece forming one unit.

hands-free adj. designed to be operated without using one's hands.

handshake n. the shaking of a person's hand with one's own as a greeting etc.

hands-off adj. **1** characterized by the lack of intervention. **2** without the use of the hands.

handsome adj. (**handsomer**, **handsomest**) **1** (of a person) good-looking. **2** (of a building etc.) imposing, attractive. **3 a** generous. **b** (of a price, etc.) considerable. □ **handsomely** adv. **handsomeness** n.

hands-on adj. characterized by active participation.

handspring n. a somersault in which one lands first on the hands and then on the feet.

handstand n. an act of balancing upside down on one's hands.

handwashing n. **1** washing of the hands. **2** washing by hand.

handwoven adj. (of cloth) woven by hand, as opposed to by a machine.

hand-wringing n. exaggerated lamentation.

handwriting n. **1** writing with a pen, pencil, etc. **2** a person's particular style of writing. □ **handwriting on the wall** clear signs of approaching disaster. □ **handwritten** adj.

handy adj. (**handier**, **handiest**) **1** convenient to use; useful. **2** placed conveniently. **3** clever with the hands. □ **handily** adv.

handy-dandy adj. informal extremely handy.

handyman n. (pl. **handymen**) a person able or employed to do minor repairs and renovations.

hang ● v. (**hangs**; past and past participle **hung** except in sense 6; **hanging**) **1** suspend or be suspended from above, esp.

with the lower part free. **2** place (a picture) on a wall. **3** set up (a door etc.) on its hinges. **4** attach (wallpaper) in vertical strips to a wall. **5** *informal* attach the blame for (a thing) to (a person). **6** (*past* and *past participle* **hanged**) suspend or be suspended by the neck with a noose until dead. **7** let droop. **8** remain static in the air. **9** be present. **10 a** depend on. **b** listen closely to. **11** prevent (a jury) from reaching a verdict. **12** (also **hang up**) (of a computer) cease to respond to input. **13** (also **hang around**, **hang out**) *slang* associate. ● *n.* **1** the way a thing hangs or falls. **2** a downward droop. □ **get the hang of** *informal* understand or master. **hang a left** (or **right**) *informal* make a left (or right) turn. **hang around 1** loiter. **2** linger near (a person or place). **3** wait. **hang back 1** show reluctance to act or move. **2** remain behind. **hang in** *informal* persevere. **hang loose** *informal* be casual. **hang on** *informal* **1** persevere, esp. with difficulty. **2** continue to grasp. **3** retain. **4** wait for a short time. **hang one's hat** be resident. **hang a person out to dry** abandon a person to a usu. unpleasant fate. **hang together 1** make sense. **2** remain associated. **hang tough** *informal* be or remain inflexible. **hang up 1** hang from a hook, etc. **2** (often foll. by *on*) end a telephone conversation, esp. abruptly. **hang up one's skates** *Cdn* quit or retire. **let it all hang out** *slang* be uninhibited.

hangar *n.* a building with extensive floor area, for housing aircraft etc. [*Say* HANG er]

hangashore *n. Cdn* (*Nfld & Maritimes*) a weak, sickly, or idle person. [*Say* HANG a shore]

hangdog *adj.* having a dejected appearance.

hanger *n.* **1** a person or thing that hangs. **2** a shaped piece of wood or plastic etc. from which clothes may be hung.

hanger-on *n.* (*pl.* **hangers-on**) a follower, esp. an unwelcome one.

hang-glider *n.* **1** a frame with a fabric airfoil stretched over it, from which the operator is suspended and controls flight by body movement. **2** a person who practises hang-gliding. □ **hang-gliding** *n.*

hanging ● *n.* **1** the act or practice of executing a person by hanging. **2** a tapestry hung on a wall etc. ● *adj.* **1** that hangs or is hung; suspended. **2** (of a crime) punishable by hanging. **3** (of a judge, jury, etc.) inclined towards giving a death sentence.

hangman *n.* (*pl.* **hangmen**) **1** an executioner who hangs condemned persons. **2** a word game for two players, in

which the tally of failed guesses is kept by drawing a representation of a body on a gallows.

hangnail *n.* a piece of torn skin at the root of a fingernail, causing soreness.

hangout *n. informal* a place one frequently visits, esp. to relax or socialize etc.

hangover *n.* **1** a severe headache and other after-effects caused by drinking an excess of alcohol. **2** a feeling, custom, habit, etc. that remains from the past, although it is no longer practical or suitable.

hang-up *n. slang* an emotional problem or inhibition.

hanker *v.* long for; crave. □ **hankering** *n.*

hanky *n.* (also **hankie**) (*pl.* **hankies**) *informal* a handkerchief.

hanky-panky *n. slang* naughtiness or dishonesty, esp. sexual misbehaviour.

Hansard *n.* the official record of debates in parliaments in Canada, the UK, and other Commonwealth parliaments. [*Say* HAN serd]

hantavirus *n.* (*pl.* **hantaviruses**) any of various viruses spread esp. by rodents and causing acute respiratory disease, kidney failure, etc. [*Say* HANTA virus]

Hanukkah *n.* the eight-day Jewish festival of lights, usu. in December, commemorating the purification of the Temple in 165 BC. [*Say* HONNA kuh]

haphazard *adj.* with no particular order or plan. □ **haphazardly** *adv.* **haphazardness** *n.*

hapless *adj.* unlucky. □ **haplessly** *adv.* **haplessness** *n.*

haploid ● *adj.* with a single set of chromosomes. ● *n.* a haploid organism or cell.

haplotype *n. Genetics* a set of genetic determinants located on a single chromosome.

happen *v.* **1** occur. **2** become of. **3** (foll. by *to*) be experienced by. **4** (foll. by *on*) encounter by chance. **5** have the (good or bad) fortune to. **6** (foll. by *along*, *by*, etc.) turn up as if by chance. □ **as it happens** in fact.

happening ● *n.* an event or occurrence. ● *adj. slang* exciting, trendy.

happenstance *n.* a thing that happens by chance.

happy *adj.* (**happier**, **happiest**) **1** feeling or showing pleasure. **2 a** fortunate. **b** appropriate, pleasing. **3** *informal* slightly drunk. **4** (in *comb.*) *informal* inclined to use excessively. □ **happily** *adv.* **happiness** *n.*

happy-go-lucky *adj.* cheerfully casual.

happy hour *n.* a period of the day when

drinks are sold at reduced prices in bars, hotels, etc.

happy hunting ground *n.* a place where success or enjoyment is obtained.

hara-kiri *n.* **1** ritual suicide by disembowelment with a sword. **2** a self-destructive action. [*Say* haira KEERY]

harangue ● *n.* **1** a lengthy and earnest speech. **2** a passionate verbal attack. ● *v.* (**harangues, harangued, haranguing**) make a harangue (to). [*Say* huh RANG]

harass *v.* (**harasses, harassed, harassing**) **1** trouble continually. **2** make repeated attacks on. □ **harasser** *n.* **harassing** *n. & adj.* **harassingly** *adv.* **harassment** *n.* [*Say* huh RASS *or* HAIR us]

harbinger *n.* a person or thing that signals the approach of another. [*Say* HAR binge er]

harbour (also **harbor**) ● *n.* a place of shelter for ships. ● *v.* **1** give shelter to. **2** keep in one's mind. **3** come to anchor in a harbour.

harbourfront ● *n.* land adjacent to a harbour. ● *adj.* situated beside a harbour.

harbourmaster *n.* an official in charge of a harbour.

harbour seal *n.* a small seal of coastal marine waters and estuaries.

hard ● *adj.* **1** firm and solid. **2** difficult. **3** difficult to bear; entailing suffering. **4** (of a person) unfeeling. **5** severe, harsh. **6** unpleasant to the senses. **7** a strenuous, enthusiastic, intense. **b** (of a turn) sharp, extreme. **c** *Politics* most radical. **8** a (of liquor) strongly alcoholic. **b** (of a beverage) containing alcohol. **9** potent and addictive. **10** (of pornography) highly explicit. **11** (of water) containing mineral salts that make lathering difficult. **12** indisputable. **13** (of money) **a** in coins as opposed to paper currency. **b** in currency as opposed to cheques etc. ● *adv.* **1** intensely. **2** with difficulty. **3** so as to be hard or firm. **4** in close proximity. **5** with great force. □ **be hard on 1** be difficult for. **2** be severe in one's treatment or criticism of. **3** be unpleasant to (the senses). **be hard put** find it difficult. **hard at it** *informal* busily working. **hard by** near; close by. **a hard case 1** *informal* an intractable person. **2** a case of hardship. **hard done by** unfairly treated **take a hard line** be unyielding in one's position. □ **hardness** *n.*

hard and fast *adj.* definite, unchangeable.

hardback *n.* = HARDCOVER.

hardball ● *n.* **1** = BASEBALL. **2** *slang* uncompromising methods or dealings. ● *adj.* tough.

hardboard *n.* stiff board made of compressed and treated wood pulp.

hard-boiled *adj.* **1** (also **hard-cooked**) (of an egg) boiled until solid. **2** (of a person) tough, cynical.

hard copy *n.* (*pl.* **hard copies**) printed material produced by computer, usu. on paper.

hard core ● *n.* **1** the most committed or uncompromising members of a group. **2** fast punk rock music, more rhythmic than melodic. ● *adj.* (usu. **hard-core**) (of pornography) explicit, obscene.

hardcover *adj. & n.* ● *adj.* (of a book) bound in stiff covers. ● *n.* a hardcover book.

hard disk *n. Computing* a large-capacity rigid usu. magnetic storage disk.

hard-earned *adj.* that has taken great effort to acquire.

hard-edged *adj.* aggressive, uncompromising; not gentle or emotional etc.

harden *v.* **1** make or become hard or harder. **2** (of prices etc.) cease to fluctuate. □ **hardener** *n.*

hard hat *n.* **1** protective headgear worn on construction sites etc. **2** *informal* a construction worker.

hard-headed *adj.* **1** practical. **2** stubborn. □ **hard-headedly** *adv.* **hard-headedness** *n.*

hard-hearted *adj.* unfeeling. □ **hard-heartedly** *adv.* **hard-heartedness** *n.*

hard-hitting *adj.* forceful.

hard knocks *n.* painful or difficult experiences.

hard labour *n.* heavy manual work as a punishment.

hardline *adj.* unyielding. □ **hardliner** *n.*

hard luck *n.* worse fortune than one deserves.

hardly *adv.* **1** scarcely. **2** only with difficulty. **3** almost certainly not. □ **hardly any** almost no; almost none. **hardly ever** very rarely.

hard-nosed *adj. informal* tough-minded.

hard of hearing *adj.* somewhat deaf.

hardpack *n.* snow with a very dense, tightly packed surface.

hard palate *n.* the bony front part of the roof of the mouth.

hard-pressed *adj.* in difficulty or under pressure.

hard rock *n.* rock music with a heavy beat, distorted amplified guitar-playing, and loud vocals.

hardrock mining *n.* mining underground in large formations of esp.

igneous or metamorphic rock.
□ **hardrock miner** n.

hardscrabble adj. yielding a meagre output and requiring much effort.

hard sell n. aggressive salesmanship.

hardship n. severe suffering.

hardtack n. = SHIP'S BISCUIT.

hardtop n. **1 a** a road paved with a hard surface, esp. tar and gravel. **b** the material used for this. **2** a car with a rigid (sometimes detachable) roof.

hard up adj. **1** short of money. **2** (foll. by *for*) at a loss for; lacking.

hardware n. **1** tools, building materials, and household articles. **2** heavy machinery or armaments. **3** the mechanical and electronic components of a computer.

hard-wearing adj. able to stand much wear.

hard-wired adj. **1** involving permanently connected circuits designed to perform a specific function. **2** innate.

hardwood ● n. **1** the wood from a deciduous broadleaf tree. **2** a tree producing such wood. ● adj. **1** made of hardwood. **2** containing hardwoods.

hardy adj. (**hardier, hardiest**) **1** capable of enduring difficult conditions. **2** (of a plant) able to survive outside during winter. □ **hardiness** n.

Hare n. (pl. **Hare** or **Hares**) **1** a member of a Dene Aboriginal group living along the north Mackenzie River. **2** the Athapaskan language of this people.

hare n. a fast-running mammal resembling a large rabbit, with long hind legs.

harebell n. a plant with pale blue bell-shaped flowers.

hare-brained adj. foolish; ill-judged.

Hare Krishna n. **1** a sect devoted to the worship of the Hindu deity Krishna. **2** (pl. **Hare Krishnas**) a member of this sect. [Say har ee KRISHNA]

harelip n. often *offensive* a congenital split in the upper lip. □ **harelipped** adj.

harem n. **1** the separate part of a Muslim household reserved for women. **2** the women living in this area. [Say HAIR um]

hark v. (usu. in *imper.*) listen. □ **hark back** recall an earlier period.

harken v. listen.

harlequin ● n. **1** a mute character in pantomime. **2** a small duck, the male having grey-blue plumage with chestnut and white markings. ● adj. variegated. [Say HARLA quin]

harlot n. a prostitute or promiscuous woman. □ **harlotry** n. [Say HAR lut]

harm ● n. **1** deliberate injury. **2** damage.

3 a bad effect or danger. ● v. cause harm to. □ **do more harm than good** make matters worse (despite good intentions). **out of harm's way** in safety.

harmful adj. causing or likely to cause harm. □ **harmfully** adv.

harmless adj. not able or likely to cause harm. □ **harmlessly** adv.

harmonic ● adj. having to do with musical harmony. ● n. *Music* a higher and quieter note produced when another note is sung or played. □ **harmonically** adv. [Say har MONN ick]

harmonica n. a small rectangular wind instrument with a row of metal reeds that produce different notes. [Say har MONICA]

harmonious adj. **1** sweet-sounding. **2** forming a pleasing whole. **3** free from conflict. □ **harmoniously** adv. [Say har MOANY us]

harmonium n. a keyboard instrument in which the notes are produced by air driven through metal reeds by foot-operated bellows. [Say har MOANY um]

harmonize v. (**harmonizes, harmonized, harmonizing**) **1** add notes to (a melody) to produce harmony. **2** make or be in harmony. **3** make harmonious or consistent. □ **harmonization** n.

harmonized sales tax n. *Cdn* a value-added tax on goods and services combining the GST and the provincial sales tax in Nova Scotia, New Brunswick, and Newfoundland and Labrador. Abbreviation: **HST**.

harmony n. (pl. **harmonies**) **1 a** a combination of simultaneously sounded musical notes to produce chords. **b** the study of this. **c** the parts of a harmonized piece of music other than the melody. **2** the quality of forming a pleasing and consistent whole. **3** agreement. □ **harmonically** adv.

harness ● n. (pl. **harnesses**) **1** the set of straps and fittings by which a horse or other animal is fastened to a cart etc. and controlled. **2** a similar arrangement of straps, such as for fastening a parachute to a person's body. ● v. (**harnesses, harnessed, harnessing**) **1** fit with a harness. **2** make use of (power or resources).

harness race n. a type of horse race in which a horse pulls a two-wheeled vehicle and its driver with a trotting or pacing gait. □ **harness racing** n.

harp ● n. **1** a musical instrument consisting of a frame housing a series of vertical strings, played by plucking with the fingers. **2** (also **mouth harp**) *informal* a harmonica. ● v. (foll. by on, on about) talk repeatedly about. □ **harpist** n.

harpoon ● n. a barbed spear-like weapon with a rope attached, for hunting seals, whales etc. ● v. spear with a harpoon. □ **harpooner** n.

harp seal n. a seal with a harp-shaped dark mark on its back.

harpsichord n. a keyboard instrument with horizontal strings which are plucked mechanically. □ **harpsichordist** n. [Say HARPSA cord]

harpy n. (pl. **harpies**) **1** (in Greek and Roman mythology) a monster with a woman's head and body and bird's wings and claws. **2** an unpleasant woman.

harridan n. a bad-tempered woman. [Say HAIRA d'n]

harrier n. **1** a hound used for hunting hares. **2** a bird of prey with long wings for swooping over the ground.

harrow ● n. a heavy frame with iron teeth dragged over plowed land to break up soil, etc. ● v. pull a harrow over (land). [Say HAIR oh]

harrowing adj. very distressing. □ **harrowingly** adv.

harrumph (also **harumph**) ● v. clear the throat, esp. ostentatiously. ● interj. expressing disapproval. [Say huh RUMF]

harry v. (**harries, harried, harrying**) persistently attack; harass.

harsh adj. **1** unpleasantly rough. **2** severe. □ **harshly** adv. **harshness** n.

hart n. an adult male European red deer.

harum-scarum informal adj. reckless. [Say hair um SCARE um]

harvest ● n. **1 a** the process of gathering in crops etc. **b** the season when this takes place. **2** the season's yield or crop. ● v. **1** gather (crops, timber, etc.) as a harvest. **2** kill or remove (wild animals) for food, sport, or population control. **3** remove (cells, tissues, organs) from a person or animal for transplants, experiments, or other purposes. □ **harvestable** adj. **harvester** n.

harvest moon n. the full moon nearest to the autumnal equinox.

has 3rd singular present of HAVE.

has-been n. informal a person or thing that has lost a former importance.

hash¹ ● n. (pl. **hashes**) **1** a dish of diced cooked meat re-cooked with vegetables. **2 a** a jumble. **b** a mess. ● v. (**hashes, hashed, hashing**) **1** make into a hash. **2** (often foll. by out, over) informal discuss in detail. □ **settle a person's hash** informal deal with and subdue a person.

hash² n. informal hashish.

hash browns pl. n. chopped boiled potatoes, often with onions, fried until brown.

hashish n. a resinous product of hemp, with narcotic effects. [Say ha SHEESH or HASH eesh]

hash mark n. the symbol #.

Hasid n. (pl. **Hasidim**) (also **Hassid**, pl. **Hassidim**) a member of any of several mystical Jewish sects. □ **Hasidic** adj. **Hasidism** n. [Say HASS id for the singular, HASS id im for the plural; huh SID ick, HASS id ism]

hasn't contr. has not.

hasp n. a hinged metal clasp that fits over a staple and can be secured by a padlock.

hassle informal ● n. a prolonged inconvenience. ● v. (**hassles, hassled, hassling**) harass.

haste n. quickness, esp. excessive. □ **in haste** hurriedly. **make haste** hurry. □ **hastily** adv. **hasty** adj.

hasten v. **1** make haste; hurry. **2** cause to happen or be done sooner.

hat n. **1** a covering for the head, often with a brim and worn out of doors. **2** informal a person's function or role, esp. one of several. □ **hat in hand** obsequiously. **hats off** (as interjection; foll. by to) expressing appreciation. **keep it under one's hat** informal keep it secret. **out of a hat** by random selection. **pass the hat** collect money. **take off one's hat to** informal acknowledge admiration for. **throw (or toss) one's hat in the ring** take up a challenge. □ **hatless** adj. **hatted** adj.

hatband n. a band of ribbon etc. around a hat above the brim.

hatch¹ n. (pl. **hatches**) **1 a** an opening in a floor, ceiling, or wall of a building, or the deck of a ship. **b** a trap door or cover for this **2** a door in an aircraft, spacecraft, or submarine. □ **down the hatch** slang drink up!

hatch² v. (**hatches, hatched, hatching**) **1 a** (of a young bird or fish etc.) emerge from the egg. **b** (of an egg) produce a young animal. **2** incubate (an egg). **3** devise (a plot etc.).

hatch³ v. (**hatches, hatched, hatching**) mark with close parallel lines. □ **hatching** n.

hatchback n. **1** a car with a sloping back hinged at the top to form a door. **2** such a hinged door.

hatchery n. (pl. **hatcheries**) a place for hatching eggs, esp. of fish or poultry.

hatchet n. **1** a light short-handled axe. **2** a tomahawk.

hatchet job n. informal a fierce verbal attack on a person, esp. in print.

hatchetman n. (pl. **hatchetmen**) informal **1** a hired killer. **2** a vindictive critic. **3** a person employed to do unpleasant tasks, e.g. reducing staff.

hatchling n. a bird or fish that has just hatched.

hatchway n. an opening in a ship's deck for lowering cargo into the hold.

hate ● v. (**hates, hated, hating**) dislike intensely. ● n. **1** very strong dislike. **2** informal a hated person or thing. □ **hater** n.

hateful adj. **1** arousing hatred. **2** full of hatred. □ **hatefulness** n.

hate mail n. letters sent (usu. anonymously) in which the sender expresses hostility toward the recipient.

hate-monger n. a person who promotes hatred. □ **hate-mongering** n.

hatpin n. a long pin for securing a hat to the head.

hatred n. intense dislike.

hatter n. a maker or seller of hats. □ **mad as a hatter** wildly eccentric.

hat trick n. **1** the scoring of three goals, points etc. by one person during a game. **2** three successes.

haughty adj. (**haughtier, haughtiest**) arrogantly self-admiring and disdainful. □ **haughtily** adv. **haughtiness** n. [Say HOTTY]

haul ● v. **1** pull or drag with effort. **2** transport by truck, cart, etc. **3** informal bring for reprimand or trial. ● n. **1 a** an amount acquired. **b** the quantity of fish caught in one draft of the net. **2** a distance to be traversed. □ **hauler** n.

haulage n. **1** the commercial transport of goods. **2** a charge for this. [Say HAUL idge]

haunch n. (pl. **haunches**) **1** the fleshy part of the buttock with the thigh. **2** the leg and loin of a deer etc. as food.

haunt ● v. **1** (of a ghost) appear regularly at (a place). **2** visit (a place) frequently. **3** return repeatedly and disturbingly to the mind of. **4** cause continued difficulty to. ● n. a place frequented by a person or animal. □ **haunted** adj.

haunting ● adj. poignant, evocative. ● n. a visitation by a ghost. □ **hauntingly** adv.

haute adj. upper-class. [Say OAT or HOAT]

hauteur n. haughtiness of manner. [Say owe TUR]

havarti n. a mild, semi-soft Danish cheese with small holes. [Say huh VARTY]

have ● v. (**has, had, having**) **1** possess. **2** experience. **3** be able to make use of. **4** perform the action indicated by the noun specified. **5** demonstrate. **6** suffer from. **7** cause to be in a particular state. **8** cause to be done for one by someone else. **9** hold in a particular position. **10** be the recipient or host of. **11** eat or drink. **12** tolerate. ● aux. v. used with a past participle to form the perfect, pluperfect, and future perfect tenses, and the conditional mood. ● n. (in pl.) informal people with plenty of money etc. □ **be had** informal be deceived. **had better** would find it prudent to. **have got to** informal = HAVE TO. **have had it** informal **1** have missed one's chance. **2** be no longer useful or appropriate. **3** have been killed, defeated, etc. **4** be fed up with. **have it 1** (foll. by that + clause) express the view that. **2** win a decision in a vote. **3** informal have found the answer etc. **have it coming** can expect unpleasant consequences to follow. **have it in for** informal be hostile toward. **have it out** (often foll. by with) informal attempt to settle a dispute by discussion. **have on 1** be wearing. **2** be committed to. **have out** get (a tooth etc.) extracted. **have something (or nothing) on a person 1** know something (or nothing) discreditable about a person. **2** have an (or no) advantage over a person. **have to** be obliged to.

haven n. **1** a harbour or port. **2** a place of refuge. [Say HAY v'n]

have-not n. (usu. in pl.) informal a person etc. lacking wealth and resources.

have-not province n. Cdn a province whose per capita tax revenue falls below a certain average level and which is therefore entitled to receive equalization payments from the federal government.

haven't contr. have not.

have province n. Cdn a province whose per capita tax revenue exceeds a certain average level and which does not therefore receive equalization payments from the federal government.

havoc n. widespread destruction or disorder. □ **play havoc with** informal cause great difficulty to. **wreak havoc** devastate. [Say HAVE ick]

haw[1] n. the hawthorn or its fruit.

haw[2] interj. expressing hesitation. □ **hum and haw** hesitate, esp. in speaking.

Hawaiian ● n. **1 a** a native of Hawaii, a group of 20 islands in the N Pacific. **b** a person of Hawaiian descent. **2** the language of Hawaii. ● adj. **1** of or relating to Hawaii or its people or language. **2** (of pizza) garnished with ham and pineapple. [Say huh WHY in]

Hawaiian guitar n. a steel-stringed instrument, usu. played by sliding a metal bar along the strings as they are plucked.

Hawaiian shirt *n.* a brightly coloured and gaily patterned shirt.

haw haw *interj.* used to represent the sound of a loud laugh.

hawk[1] ● *n.* **1** a bird of prey with a characteristic curved beak, broad rounded wings, and a long tail. **2** *Politics* a person who advocates an aggressive policy, esp. in foreign affairs. ● *v.* hunt game with a hawk. □ **watch like a hawk** watch intently. □ **hawkish** *adj.* **hawkishness**

hawk[2] *v.* offer (goods) for sale. □ **hawker** *n.*

hawk[3] *v.* **1** clear the throat noisily. **2** bring (phlegm etc.) up from the throat.

hawkweed *n.* a plant of the daisy family, which typically has yellow or orange dandelion-like flowers and often grows as a weed.

hawse *n.* **1** the part of a ship's bows containing holes through which a cable or anchor rope passes. **2** the space between the head of an anchored vessel and the anchors. [*Say* HOZZ]

hawser *n.* a thick rope or cable for mooring or towing a ship. [*Say* HOZZER]

hawthorn *n.* a thorny shrub or tree with white, red, or pink blossoms and small dark red fruit.

hay ● *n.* grass etc. cut and dried for animal fodder. ● *v.* make hay. □ **hit the hay** *informal* go to bed. **make hay (while the sun shines)** seize opportunities for profit or enjoyment. □ **haying** *n.*

hay fever *n.* an allergic reaction to pollen, causing sneezing, watery eyes, etc.

hayfield *n.* a field where hay is made.

haylage *n.* animal feed made from partially dried grass preserved in a silo. [*Say* HAY lidge]

hayloft *n.* = LOFT *n.* 2.

haymaker *n.* **1** a person who tosses and spreads hay to dry after mowing. **2** an apparatus for shaking and drying hay. **3** *slang* a forceful blow. □ **haymaking** *n.*

haymow *n.* hay stored in a stack or barn. [*Say* HAY mow *(with* mow *rhyming either with* WOW *or with* BLOW)]

hayseed *n.* **1** grass seed obtained from hay. **2** *informal* a rustic or yokel.

haystack *n.* a packed pile of hay.

haywire *n.* wire for binding bales of hay, straw, etc. □ **go haywire** go out of control.

hazard ● *n.* **1** a danger. **2** (in *pl.*) (also **hazard lights**) flashing lights on a vehicle, indicating a warning. ● *v.* **1** suggest tentatively. **2** risk. □ **hazardous** *adj.* **hazardously** *adv.*

haze[1] *n.* **1** a thin mist caused by dust, pollutants, etc. **2** mental confusion.

haze[2] *v.* (**hazes, hazed, hazing**) subject (new students etc.) to abuse and ridicule as an initiation.

hazel *n.* **1** a shrub or small tree with broad leaves, bearing round brown edible nuts. **2** a golden-brown or greenish-brown colour.

hazelnut *n.* the fruit of the hazel.

haz-mat *n.* hazardous material.

hazy *adj.* (**hazier, haziest**) **1** misty. **2** vague. **3** uncertain. □ **hazily** *adv.* **haziness** *n.*

HB *abbr.* hard black (pencil lead).

HBC *abbr. Cdn* Hudson's Bay Company.

H-bomb *n.* = HYDROGEN BOMB.

HDTV *abbr.* high-definition television.

he ● *pron.* **1** the man or boy or male animal previously named or in question. **2** a person etc. of unspecified sex, esp. referring to one already named or identified. ● *n.* **1** a male; a man. **2** (in *comb.*) male.

head ● *n.* **1** the part of a human's or an animal's body, containing the brain, mouth, and sense organs. **2** the head regarded as the seat of intellect and memory. **3** *informal* a headache. **4** the front, forward, or upper part of something. **5** a compact mass of leaves or flowers at the top of a stem. **6** the flat end of a drum. **7** the foam on top of a glass of beer etc. **8 a** a person in charge. **b** a position of leadership. **9** an individual regarded as a numerical unit. **10** (as *pl.* **head**) a number of cattle or game as specified. **11** (in *pl.*) the side of a coin bearing an image of a head. **12 a** the source of a river, stream etc. **b** the end of a lake, bay, etc. at which a river enters it. **13** the part of a computer or recorder which transfers information to and from a tape or disk. **14** pressure exerted by a confined body of water or steam. **15** a promontory (esp. in place names). **16** a culmination. **17** the fully developed top of a boil etc. ● *adj.* chief or principal. ● *v.* **1** be at the head of. **2** be in charge of. **3** (often foll. by *for*) direct or move in a specified direction. **4** *Soccer* strike (the ball) with the head. □ **bang one's head against a wall** *informal* be frustrated. **come to a head 1** (of a boil etc.) form pus. **2** reach a climax. **go to one's head 1** make one drunk. **2** make one conceited. **have one's head (screwed) on straight** be sensible. **head and shoulders** *informal* by a considerable amount. **head in the sand** refusal to acknowledge an obvious difficulty. **head off 1** intercept and turn aside. **2** forestall. **head over heels 1** turning over completely in forward motion as in a somersault etc. **2** utterly. **in**

one's head 1 in one's imagination. **2** by mental process without use of physical aids. **keep one's head** remain calm. **keep one's head above water** *informal* **1** keep out of debt. **2** avoid succumbing to difficulties. **keep one's head down** *informal* remain inconspicuous. **lose one's head** lose self-control. **make head(s) or tail(s) of** (usu. with *neg.* or *interrog.*) understand at all. **off the top of one's head** *informal* impromptu. **one's head off** noisily or excessively. **on one's (or one's own) head** as one's sole responsibility. **over one's head 1** beyond one's comprehension. **2** without one's involvement, esp. when one has a right to this. **put heads together** consult together. **turn heads** cause people to notice. □ **headed** *comb. form* **headless** *adj.*

headache *n.* **1** a continuous pain in the head. **2** *informal* something that causes worry or trouble. □ **headachy** *adj.*

headband *n.* a band worn around the head as decoration or to keep the hair off the face.

headbanger *n.* *slang* a fan of heavy metal music.

headbanging *n.* vigorous head-shaking in time to heavy metal music.

headboard *n.* an upright panel forming or placed behind the head of a bed etc.

head-butt ● *v.* attack (another person) by hitting them with one's head. ● *n.* an act of head-butting.

head case *n.* *informal* a mentally unstable person.

headcheese *n.* a jellied preparation of the chopped meat from a boiled pig's head.

headdress *n.* (*pl.* **headdresses**) an ornamental covering for the head.

header *n.* **1** *Soccer* a shot or pass made with the head. **2** *informal* a headlong fall. **3** text appearing at the top of each page of a document etc. (*compare* FOOTER 2).

headfirst *adv. & adj.* **1** with the head foremost. **2** without thinking beforehand.

headgear *n.* something worn on the head.

headhunter *n.* **1** an agency or agent specializing in recruiting skilled staff for an organization etc. **2** a member of a tribe that collects the heads of dead enemies as trophies. □ **headhunt** *v.* **headhunting** *n.*

heading *n.* **1** a title at the head of a page or section of a book, document, menu, etc. **2** a direction or bearing.

headlamp *n.* **1** = HEADLIGHT. **2** a small lamp attached to a hat or strapped to the forehead.

headland *n.* a promontory.

headlight *n.* **1** a strong light at the front of a motor vehicle or railway engine. **2** the beam from this.

headline ● *n.* **1** a heading at the top of a news or magazine article. **2** (in *pl.*) a summary of the most important items of news. ● *v.* (**headlines**, **headlined**, **headlining**) **1** give a headline to. **2** appear as the chief performer (at). □ **hit** (or **make**) **the headlines** *informal* be given prominent attention as news. □ **headliner** *n.*

headlock *n.* a hold with an arm around the opponent's head.

headlong *adv. & adj.* **1** with the head foremost. **2** in a rush.

headman *n.* (*pl.* **headmen**) the chief man of a village, tribe etc.

headmaster *n.* the principal in charge of a school.

headmistress *n.* (*pl.* **headmistresses**) a woman principal in charge of a school.

head of state *n.* (*pl.* **heads of state**) the official leader of a country, who may also be the head of government.

head-on *adj. & adv.* **1** with the front foremost. **2** in direct confrontation.

headphone *n.* (usu. in *pl.*) a pair of earphones joined by a band placed over the head.

headpiece *n.* any covering for the head.

headquarters *n.* (as *sing.* or *pl.*) **1** the administrative centre of an organization. **2** the premises occupied by a military commander and staff. □ **headquarter** *v.*

headrest *n.* a padded support for the head on the back of a seat.

headroom *n.* **1** the space between a person's head and the ceiling or structure above. **2** the clearance between the top of a vehicle and the underside of a structure above.

headset *n.* a set of headphones, often with a microphone attached.

headspace *n.* **1** space left in the top of a jar, bottle, etc. to allow room for expansion of contents. **2** *slang* mindset.

head start *n.* an advantage granted or gained at an early stage.

headstone *n.* a stone slab set up at the head of a grave.

headstrong *adj.* obstinate.

heads-up *informal* ● *n.* a warning. ● *adj.* alert. ● *interj.* (**heads up**) look out!

head-to-head ● *adj.* involving two parties confronting each other. ● *adv.* confronting another party.

headwater *n.* (in *sing.* or *pl.*) streams flowing from the sources of a river.

headway *n.* forward progress.

headwind *n.* a wind blowing from directly in front.

headword *n.* a word forming a heading, e.g. of an entry in a dictionary.

heady *adj.* (**headier**, **headiest**) **1** (of liquor) potent. **2** affecting the senses strongly. **3** exhilarating.

heal *v.* **1** become or cause to become sound or healthy again. **2** put right. □ **healer** *n.* **healing** *n.* & *adj.*

healing circle *n.* **1** a traditional Aboriginal ceremony that promotes emotional healing, in which participants are arranged in a circle and each in turn is invited to speak. **2** any gathering or forum that uses shared prayer, chanting, etc. to promote healing.

health *n.* **1** the state of being well in body or mind. **2** a person's mental or physical condition. **3** soundness, esp. financial or moral. **4** a toast drunk in someone's honour.

health care *n.* the improvement of health, esp. as administered by organized medical services.

health food *n.* natural food eaten for its health-giving qualities.

healthful *adj.* conducive to good health. □ **healthfulness** *n.*

health plan *n.* a medical insurance plan.

healthy *adj.* (**healthier**, **healthiest**) **1** having or promoting good health. **2** beneficial. **3** ample. **4** (of a business etc.) sound. □ **healthily** *adv.* **healthiness** *n.*

heap ● *n.* **1** a **a** collection of things lying haphazardly one on another. **b** an untidy mass of something. **2** *informal* a large number or amount. **3** *slang* an old or dilapidated thing. ● *v.* **1** put in or form a heap. **2** load copiously. **3** offer copiously to.

heaping *adj.* with the contents piled above the brim.

hear *v.* (**hears**, **heard**, **hearing**) **1** perceive (sound) with the ear. **2** listen to. **3** listen judicially to and judge (a case, plaintiff, etc.). **4** be told. **5** (foll. by *from*) be contacted by. □ **have heard of** be aware of. **hear a pin drop** hear the slightest noise. **hear! hear!** *interj.* expressing agreement. **will not hear of** will not allow or agree to. □ **hearable** *adj.* **hearer** *n.*

hearing *n.* **1** the faculty of perceiving sounds. **2** the range within which sounds may be heard. **3** an opportunity to state one's case. **4** an act of listening to evidence.

hearing aid *n.* a small device to amplify sound, worn on the ear by a partially deaf person.

hearken *v.* = HARKEN. [*Say* HARK'n]

hearsay *n.* rumour.

hearse *n.* a vehicle for conveying the coffin at a funeral. [*Rhymes with* PURSE]

heart *n.* **1** a hollow muscular organ that pumps blood around the body. **2** the heart regarded as the centre of feeling and emotion. **3 a** courage or enthusiasm. **b** one's mood. **4 a** the innermost part of something. **b** the essence. **5** a shape representing a heart with two equal curves meeting at a point at the bottom and a cusp at the top. **6** (in *pl.*) one of the four suits in a pack of playing cards. **7** a beloved person. □ **after one's own heart** sharing one's tastes. **at heart** essentially. **break a person's heart** overwhelm a person with sorrow, esp. by ending a romantic relationship. **by heart** in or from memory. **have a heart** be merciful. **have the heart** be insensitive or hard-hearted enough. **have one's heart in one's mouth** be greatly alarmed. **heart to heart** candidly, frankly. **in one's heart of hearts** in one's innermost feelings. **take to heart** be much affected by. **wear one's heart on one's sleeve** make one's feelings apparent.

heartache *n.* anguish or grief.

heart attack *n.* a sudden occurrence of coronary thrombosis usu. resulting in the death of part of a heart muscle.

heartbeat *n.* **1** a pulsation of the heart. **2** the most important part. □ **in a heartbeat** in a very brief moment.

heartbreak *n.* overwhelming sorrow. □ **heartbreaker** *n.* **heartbreaking** *adj.* **heartbroken** *adj.*

heartburn *n.* a burning sensation in the chest resulting from indigestion.

-hearted *comb. form* bearing the characteristics described, esp. in terms of compassion or courage.

hearten *v.* make more cheerful. □ **heartening** *adj.* **hearteningly** *adv.*

heart failure *n.* a severe failure of the heart to function properly.

heartfelt *adj.* deeply felt.

hearth *n.* **1** the floor or surround of a fireplace. **2** this symbolizing the home. [*Say* HARTH]

heartland *n.* the central or most important part of an area.

heartless *adj.* unfeeling, pitiless. □ **heartlessly** *adv.* **heartlessness** *n.*

heart rate *n.* the pulse, calculated by counting the number of beats of the heart per unit of time.

heart-rending *adj.* causing great sorrow. □ **heart-rendingly** *adv.*

heart-searching *n.* the thorough examination of one's own feelings.

heartsick *adj.* very sad.

heart-stopping *adj.* very thrilling.

heartstrings *pl. n.* one's deepest emotions.

heartthrob *n.* **1** *informal* an extremely attractive (usu. male) person. **2** beating of the heart.

heart-to-heart ● *adj.* (of a conversation etc.) intimate. **●** *n.* a candid conversation.

heartwarming *adj.* emotionally uplifting.

heartwood *n.* the dense inner part of a tree trunk yielding the hardest timber.

hearty *adj.* (**heartier, heartiest**) **1** loudly vigorous. **2** (of a meal or appetite) large. **3** warm, sincere. **4** heartfelt, sincere. □ **heartily** *adv.* **heartiness** *n.*

heat *n.* **1** the condition of being hot. **2** *Physics* heat as a form of energy arising from the random motion of molecules. **3** hot weather. **4** strength of feeling. **5** (foll. by *of*) the most intense part of an activity. **6** a preliminary round in a race or contest. **7** the receptive period of the sexual cycle. **8** *slang* criticism; blame. **●** *v.* (often foll. by *up*) **1** make or become hot. **2** inflame; intensify. □ **in the heat of the moment** during intense activity, without pause for thought.

heated *adj.* **1** angry; passionate. **2** made hot. □ **heatedly** *adv.*

heater *n.* a device for warming something.

heath *n.* **1** an area of flattish uncultivated land with low shrubs. **2** any plant growing on a heath, e.g. heather.

heathen ● *n.* **1** *derogatory* a person who does not belong to a widely held religion, as regarded by those that do. **2** an unenlightened person. **●** *adj.* **1** of or relating to heathens; pagan. **2** having no religion. □ **heathenism** *n.* [*Say* HEE then]

heather *n.* an evergreen shrub with purple bell-shaped flowers. [*Rhymes with* WEATHER]

heating *n.* **1** the imparting or generation of heat. **2** equipment used to provide heat.

heat-seeking *adj.* (of a missile etc.) able to detect and home in on heat sent out by a target.

heatstroke *n.* a feverish condition caused by excessive exposure to high temperature.

heave ● *v.* (**heaves**; *past* and *past participle* **heaved** or esp. *Nautical* **hove**; **heaving**) **1** lift or haul with great effort. **2** utter with effort. **3** throw. **4** rise and fall. **5** *Nautical* haul by rope. **6** retch. **7** rise up above the general surface; expand, shift. **●** *n.* an act of heaving. □ **heave in sight** (or **into**

view) come into view. **heave to** esp. *Nautical* come to a standstill. □ **heaver** *n.*

heave-ho *n.* (**the** (**old**) **heave-ho**) *slang* rejection or dismissal.

heaven *n.* **1** (also **Heaven**) the place regarded in various religions as the abode of God or the gods, where good people go after death. **2** a place or state of bliss. **3** (**the heavens**) the sky as the abode of the sun, moon, and stars. □ **in seventh heaven** in a state of ecstasy. **move heaven and earth** make extraordinary efforts. □ **heavenward** *adv.*

heavenly *adj.* **1** of heaven or the heavens. **2** *informal* wonderful.

heavenly body *n.* a natural object in outer space.

heaven-sent *adj.* wonderfully opportune.

heavy ● *adj.* (**heavier, heaviest**) **1 a** of great weight. **b** (of a person) overweight. **2** of great density or mass. **3** abundant. **4** forceful. **5** (of rock music etc.) highly amplified with a strong beat. **6** (of machinery, etc.) very large. **7** needing much physical effort. **8** (foll. by *with*) laden. **9 a** dull; hard to understand. **b** important. **10** (of food) hard to digest. **11** (of ground) difficult to traverse or work. **12 a** oppressive. **b** (of the atmosphere) sultry. **13 a** not graceful. **b** unwieldy. **14** sad. **15** (of sleep) deep. **●** *n.* (*pl.* **heavies**) *informal* a large violent person; a thug. **●** *adv.* heavily (esp. in *comb.*). □ **heavy on** using a lot of. □ **heavily** *adv.* **heaviness** *n.*

heavy-duty *adj.* intended to withstand hard use.

heavy-handed *adj.* clumsy, insensitive, unnecessarily forceful. □ **heavy-handedly** *adv.* **heavy-handedness** *n.*

heavy hitter *n.* *informal* an important or powerful person.

heavy industry *n.* industry producing large, heavy articles and materials in large quantities.

heavy metal *n.* **1** a type of loud, vigorous rock music with a strong fast beat. **2** metal of high density.

heavy-set *adj.* (of a person) stocky.

heavyweight *n.* **1 a** a weight in certain sports, over 81 kg in amateur boxing but differing for professional boxing and wrestling. **b** a sportsman of this weight. **2** someone or something of above average weight. **3** *informal* an influential person.

Hebraic *adj.* having to do with the Hebrew language or people. [*Say* he BRAY ick]

Hebrew ● *n.* **1** a member of a Semitic people having a descent traditionally traced from Abraham, Isaac, and Jacob.

2 the language of this people. ● *adj.* **1** of or in Hebrew. **2** of the Hebrews or the Jews.

heck *informal* ● *interj.* a mild exclamation of surprise. ● *adv.* as an intensifier. □ **what the heck** expressing indifference.

heckle ● *v.* (**heckles, heckled, heckling**) harass (a public speaker). ● *n.* an act of heckling. □ **heckler** *n.*

hectare *n.* a metric unit of land measure, equal to 100 ares (2.471 acres or 10,000 square metres). Abbreviation: **ha**. [*Say* HECK tair]

hectic *adj.* busy and confused. □ **hectically** *adv.*

hecto- *comb. form* a hundred, esp. of a unit in the metric system. Abbreviation: **h**.

hector *v.* bully, intimidate. □ **hectoring** *adj.*

he'd *contr.* **1** he had. **2** he would.

hedge ● *n.* **1** a fence formed by closely growing bushes or shrubs. **2** a protection against possible loss. **3** a statement made to avoid firm commitment. ● *v.* (**hedges, hedged, hedging**) **1** surround with a hedge. **2 a** reduce one's risk of loss on (a bet) by compensating transactions on the other side. **b** avoid a definite commitment. □ **hedge one's bets** protect oneself against loss by supporting more than one side.

hedge fund *n.* an esp. offshore investment fund usu. formed as a private limited partnership that engages in speculation using credit or borrowed capital.

hedgehog *n.* **1** a small mammal with a coat of spines. **2** a porcupine.

hedgerow *n.* a row of bushes etc. forming a hedge.

hedonism *n.* the pursuit of pleasure as the highest good. □ **hedonist** *n.* **hedonistic** *adj.* [*Say* HEED'n ism *or* HED'n ism]

heebie-jeebies *pl. n.* *slang* a state of nervous depression or anxiety.

heed ● *v.* attend to; take notice of. ● *n.* careful attention. □ **heedless** *adj.* **heedlessly** *adv.* **heedlessness** *n.*

hee-haw ● *n.* the bray of a donkey. ● *v.* emit a braying sound.

heel¹ ● *n.* **1** the back part of the foot below the ankle. **2** the part of a shoe or sock covering the heel. **3** a thing like a heel, e.g. the part of the palm next to the wrist. **4** *informal* a person regarded with contempt. ● *v.* **1** renew a heel on (a shoe or boot). **2** (of a dog) follow obediently at a person's heels. □ **at** (*or* **on**) **the heels of** following closely. **cool one's heels** be kept waiting. □ **heelless** *adj.*

heel² ● *v.* (of a ship etc.) lean over to one side. ● *n.* an instance or amount of heeling.

heft ● *v.* lift (something heavy), esp. to judge its weight. ● *n.* *informal* weight, heaviness.

hefty *adj.* (**heftier, heftiest**) **1** large, heavy, powerful. **2** substantial.

hegemony *n.* (*pl.* **hegemonies**) dominance of one group or state over others. [*Say* huh JEMMA nee]

hegira *n.* **1** (**Hegira**) Muhammad's departure from Mecca to Medina in AD 622. **2** a general exodus. [*Say* huh JYE ruh *or* HEDGE i ruh]

heifer *n.* a cow that has not borne a calf, or has borne only one calf. [*Say* HEFFER]

height *n.* **1** the measurement from base to top or from head to foot. **2** the elevation above ground or sea level. **3** (often in *pl.*) **a** a high place. **b** the state of being high above the ground. **4** the top of something. **5 a** the most intense part. **b** an extreme example.

heighten *v.* make or become higher or more intense. □ **heightened** *adj.*

Heiltsuk *n.* (*pl.* **Heiltsuk** *or* **Heiltsuks**) **1** a member of an Aboriginal group living on the coast of BC. **2** the Wakashan language of this people. □ **Heiltsuk** *adj.* [*Say* HAILT sook]

Heimlich manoeuvre *n.* a procedure to dislodge an object from a choking person's windpipe by applying a sudden upward thrust to the victim's abdomen. [*Say* HIME lick]

heinous *adj.* utterly wicked. □ **heinously** *adv.* [*Say* HAY niss]

heir *n.* **1** a person entitled to property or rank as the legal successor of its former owner. **2** a person who continues the work of someone earlier. [*Sounds like* AIR]

heir apparent *n.* (*pl.* **heirs apparent**) **1** an heir whose claim cannot be set aside by the birth of another heir. **2** a person considered likely to succeed to another.

heiress *n.* (*pl.* **heiresses**) a female heir. [*Say* AIR iss]

heirloom *n.* an object that has belonged to a family for several generations. [*Say* AIR loom]

heir presumptive *n.* (*pl.* **heirs presumptive**) an heir whose claim may be set aside by the birth of another heir.

heist *slang* ● *n.* a robbery. ● *v.* rob. [*Say* HICED (*rhymes with* PRICED)]

held *past and past participle of* HOLD¹.

heli- *comb. form* helicopter: *heliport; heli-logging.*

helical *adj.* having the form of a helix; spiral. [*Say* HELL ick ul *or* HEEL ick ul]

helices *pl.* of HELIX. [*Say* HEEL uh seez *or* HELL uh seez]

helicopter ● *n.* a type of aircraft with one or two sets of horizontally revolving blades or rotors. ● *v.* fly by helicopter.

heliocentric *adj.* having, representing, or regarding the sun as centre. [*Say* heely uh SEN trick]

helium *n.* a light colourless gas that does not burn.

helix *n.* (*pl.* **helices**) an object in the shape of a spiral. [*Say* HEE licks *for the singular,* HEEL uh seez *or* HELL uh seez *for the plural*]

hell ● *n.* **1** (in various religions) a place of evil or suffering where wicked people are sent after death. **2 a** a place or state of great suffering. **b** extreme turmoil. **3** criticism, punishment, or difficulty. ● *interj. informal* used as an exclamation of surprise, annoyance, etc. □ **as hell** *informal* as an intensifier. (**come**) **hell or high water** *informal* (through) great difficulties. **for the hell of it** *informal* for fun. **the hell** (usu. preceded by *what, where, who,* etc.) *slang* expressing disbelief, exasperation, etc. **hell** (or **hell-bent**) **for leather** *informal* at full speed. **hell's bells** *slang* expressing anger or annoyance. **not a hope in hell** *informal* no chance at all. **raise hell** *informal* cause trouble, create chaos. **till** (or **until** or **when**) **hell freezes over** *informal* never or to (or at) some date in the impossibly distant future.

he'll *contr.* he will; he shall.

hell-bent *adj. informal* recklessly determined.

hellebore *n.* a poisonous evergreen plant with large white, green, or purplish flowers. [*Say* HELLA bore]

Hellenic *adj.* Greek. [*Say* hell EN ick *or* hell EEN ick]

Hellenism *n.* **1** Greek character or culture (esp. of ancient Greece). **2** the study or imitation of Greek culture. [*Say* HELLEN ism]

Hellenistic *adj.* of or relating to the period of Greek history 323 BC–31 BC. [*Say* hellen ISS tick]

hellfire *n.* the fire regarded as existing in hell.

hellhole *n.* an unbearable place.

hellion *n. informal* a rowdy, troublemaking person. [*Say* HELL yun]

hellish *adj.* **1** of or like hell. **2** *informal* extremely difficult or unpleasant. □ **hellishly** *adv.*

hello *interj.* **1** used as a greeting. **2** used to call attention. **3** used to reproach ignorance or inattention.

hellraiser *n.* a person who causes trouble. □ **hellraising** *adj. & n.*

helm ● *n.* **1** a tiller or wheel for controlling a ship's rudder. **2** a position of leadership. ● *v.* steer; lead.

helmet *n.* a hard or padded protective hat. □ **helmeted** *adj.* **helmetless** *adj.*

helmsman *n.* (*pl.* **helmsmen**) a person who steers a ship.

help ● *v.* **1** make it easier for (someone) to do something. **2** improve (a situation). **3** (usu. with *neg.*) **a** refrain from. **b** not be avoidable. **c** (**help oneself**) extricate oneself from a difficulty. ● *n.* **1** assistance. **2** an employee. □ **can't** (or **cannot**) **help but** be obliged to or unable to do other. **help oneself** (often foll. by *to*) **1** serve oneself (with food). **2** take without seeking help or permission. **not if I can help it** not if I can prevent it. □ **helper** *n.*

helpdesk *n.* a service which helps users who have problems esp. with computers.

helpful *adj.* giving of help; useful. □ **helpfully** *adv.* **helpfulness** *n.*

helping *n.* **1** a portion of food. **2** a portion of something offered.

helpless *adj.* **1** unable to defend oneself or act without help. **2** uncontrollable. □ **helplessly** *adv.* **helplessness** *n.*

helpline *n.* a telephone service providing help and advice.

helpmate *n.* a helpful companion or partner, usu. a husband or wife.

helter-skelter *adj. & adv.* in disorderly haste or confusion.

hem¹ ● *n.* **1** the cut edge of a piece of cloth, turned under and sewn down. **2** HEMLINE. ● *v.* (**hems, hemmed, hemming**) turn under and sew in the edge of. □ **hem in** confine.

hem² ● *interj.* representing a slight cough or clearing of the throat. ● *v.* (**hems, hemmed, hemming**) hesitate in speech. □ **hem and haw** hesitate in speaking, esp. through indecision, disagreement, etc.

he-man *n.* (*pl.* **he-men**) *informal* often *ironic* a particularly strong or virile man.

hematite *n.* ferric oxide occurring as a dark red mineral which is an important ore of iron. [*Say* HEEMA tite]

hematology *n.* the branch of medicine that deals with the blood. [*Say* heema TOLLA jee]

hematoma *n. Medical* a solid swelling of clotted blood within the tissues. [*Say* heema TOE muh]

heme *n.* a non-protein compound containing iron. [*Say* HEEM]

hemi- *comb. form* half.

hemisphere *n.* **1** a half of the earth.

2 (also **cerebral hemisphere**) a half of the cerebrum. **3** half of a sphere. □ **hemispheric** adj. **hemispherical** adj. [Say HEM iss fear]

hemline n. the level of the lower edge of a garment such as a skirt.

hemlock n. **1 a** a highly poisonous plant with fern-like leaves and small white flowers. **b** a poison obtained from this. **2 a** a coniferous tree which has foliage that smells like hemlock when crushed. **b** its wood.

hemo- comb. form blood. [Say HEEMO]

hemoglobin n. a red, oxygen-carrying substance containing iron, present in the red blood cells of vertebrates. [Say HEEMA globe in]

hemophilia n. a usu. hereditary disorder, entailing the failure of the blood to clot normally. □ **hemophiliac** n. [Say heema FEELY uh]

hemorrhage ● n. **1** an escape of blood from a ruptured blood vessel, esp. when profuse. **2** a damaging or uncontrolled outflow of something. ● v. (**hemorrhages, hemorrhaged, hemorrhaging**) **1** undergo a hemorrhage. **2** expend in large amounts. [Say HEM er idge]

hemorrhoid n. (usu. in pl.) swollen veins at or near the anus. [Say HEMMA roid]

hemp n. **1** (also **Indian hemp**) the cannabis plant, esp. when grown for its fibre. **2** its fibre used to make rope and stout fabrics. **3** the drug cannabis.

hen n. **1** a female bird, esp. of a domestic fowl. **2** a female lobster or crab or salmon.

hence adv. **1** from this time. **2** for this reason.

henceforth adv. (also **henceforward**) from this time onward.

henchman n. (pl. **henchmen**) usu. derogatory a trusted supporter or faithful follower.

henge n. a prehistoric monument consisting of a circle of stone or wooden uprights.

henhouse n. a building in which poultry roost.

henna n. **1** a tropical shrub with small pink, red, or white flowers. **2** the reddish dye from this. □ **hennaed** adj.

henpeck v. constantly nag. □ **henpecked** adj.

hep¹ adj. = HIP³.

hep² n. informal hepatitis.

HEPA abbr. high efficiency particulate air. [Say HEPPA]

heparin n. a compound occurring in the liver and other tissues which inhibits blood coagulation. [Say HEPPA rin]

hepatic adj. of or relating to the liver. [Say hep ATTIC]

hepatitis n. inflammation of the liver. [Say heppa TITE iss]

heptagon n. a plane figure with seven sides and angles. □ **heptagonal** adj. [Say HEPTA gon, hep TAGGA nul]

her ● pron. **1** objective case of SHE. **2** informal she. ● poss. adj. **1** of or belonging to her or herself. **2** (**Her**) (in titles) that she is.

herald ● n. **1** an official messenger bringing news. **2** a forerunner. ● v. **1** proclaim the approach of. **2** acclaim. [Say HAIR uld]

heraldic adj. of or concerning heraldry. [Say hair AL dick]

heraldry n. the study of the coats of arms and the history of old families. [Say HAIR uld ree]

herb n. **1** any non-woody seed-bearing plant which dies down to the ground after flowering. **2** any plant with leaves, seeds, or flowers used for flavouring, food, medicine, scent, etc. [Say HERB or ERB]

herbaceous adj. of or like herbs (see HERB 1). [Say her BAY shiss]

herbal ● adj. pertaining to or containing herbs, esp. in therapeutic and culinary use. ● n. a book with descriptions of herbs and their uses. [Say HERB'll or ERB'll]

herbalism n. the study or practice of the medicinal use of plants. □ **herbalist** n. [Say HERB'll ism or ERB'll ism]

herbarium n. (pl. **herbaria**) **1** a systematically arranged collection of dried plants. **2** a book, room, or building for these. [Say her BERRY um]

herbicide n. a substance toxic to plants and used to destroy unwanted vegetation. [Say HER buh side]

herbivore n. an animal that feeds on plants. □ **herbivorous** adj. [Say HERB uh vore, her BIV er us]

Herculean adj. **1** having or requiring great strength or effort. **2** of, like, or pertaining to the mythic hero Hercules. [Say her cue LEE in]

herd ● n. **1** a large number of animals that live or are kept together. **2** derogatory **a** a large number of people. **b** (**the herd**) the majority viewed as mindless followers. ● v. **1** move in a large group. **2** tend (livestock). **3** drive (an animal or person) in a particular direction. □ **herder** n. **herding** n.

herdsman n. (pl. **herdsmen**) the owner or keeper of herds of animals.

here ● adv. **1** in or at or to this place or

position. **2** indicating a person's presence or a thing offered. **3** at this point in the argument, situation, etc. ● *n.* this place. ● *interj.* **1** calling attention **2** indicating one's presence in a roll call. □ **here and there** in various places. **here goes!** *informal* an expression indicating the start of a bold act. **here's to** I drink to the health, success, etc. of. **here we go again** *informal* the same, usu. undesirable, events are recurring. **neither here nor there** of no importance or relevance.

hereabouts *adv.* about or near this place.

hereafter ● *adv.* **1** from now on. **2** after death. ● *n.* life after death.

hereby *adv.* as a result of this. [*Say* HERE by]

hereditary *adj.* **1** able to be passed down from one generation to another. **2** of or relating to inheritance. [*Say* huh REDDA terry]

heredity *n.* **1** the passing on of physical or mental characteristics genetically from one generation to another. **2** these characteristics in an individual. [*Say* huh REDDA tee]

herein *adv. formal* in this document, book, matter, etc. [*Say* here IN]

heresy *n.* (*pl.* **heresies**) **1** a belief or an opinion that is against the principles of a particular religion. **2** opinion at odds with what most believe. [*Say* HERRA see]

heretic *n.* **1** the holder of an unorthodox opinion. **2** *esp. hist.* a person believing in or practising heresy. □ **heretical** *adj.* **heretically** *adv.* [*Say* HERRA tick, huh RET ick ul]

heritable *adj.* transmissible from parent to offspring. □ **heritability** *n.* [*Say* HERRA tuh bull]

heritage *n.* **1 a** things such as works of art and folklore passed on from earlier generations. **b** a nation's buildings etc., esp. when regarded as worthy of preservation. **2** inherited circumstances, benefits, etc.

herky-jerky *adj. slang* (of a movement) spasmodic.

hermaphrodite *n.* **1** a person or animal having both male and female sexual organs. **2** a plant having stamens and pistils in the same flower. □ **hermaphroditic** *adj.* **hermaphroditism** *n.* [*Say* her MAFFRA dite, her maffra DIT ick, her MAFFRA dite ism]

hermetic *adj.* (also **hermetical**) **1** completely airtight. **2** protected from outside influences. □ **hermetically** *adv.* [*Say* her MET ick]

hermit *n.* **1** a person who, from religious motives, has retired into solitude. **2** any person living in solitude.

hermitage *n.* a hermit's dwelling, esp. when small and remote.

hermit crab *n.* a crab that lives in a cast-off mollusc shell for protection.

hernia *n.* (*pl.* **hernias**) the abnormal protrusion of part of an organ through the wall of the cavity containing it. □ **herniated** *adj.* [*Say* HER nee uh, HER nee ate id]

herniated disc *n.* a disc between vertebrae that has become displaced, causing pain because of pressure on the nerves of the spine.

hero *n.* (*pl.* **heroes**) **1** a person distinguished by courage or outstanding achievements. **2** the chief, esp. male, character in a poem, play, story, etc.

heroic ● *adj.* **1** very brave. **2** grand in scale. **3** (of poetry etc.) dealing with heroes. ● *n.* (in *pl.*) heroic behaviour, esp. if reckless. □ **heroically** *adv.*

heroin *n.* a highly addictive drug derived from morphine.

heroine *n.* **1** a woman noted or admired for courage or outstanding achievements. **2** the chief female character in a poem, play, story, etc.

heroism *n.* heroic conduct or qualities.

heron *n.* a large fish-eating wading bird with very long legs, neck, and bill.

hero-worship ● *n.* idealization of an admired person. ● *v.* (**hero-worships**, **hero-worshipped**, **hero-worshipping**) be excessively devoted to (a person). □ **hero-worshipper** *n.*

herpes *n.* (*pl.* **herpes**) any of several infectious diseases caused by a herpesvirus and characterized by outbreaks of blisters on the skin etc. [*Say* HER peez]

herpesvirus *n.* any of a group of related viruses that includes those causing shingles, chicken pox, and herpes simplex. [*Say* HER peez virus]

herring *n.* (*pl.* **herring** or **herrings**) a silvery edible fish that is abundant in coastal waters.

herringbone *n.* **1** any zigzag pattern or arrangement resembling the pattern of a herring's bones. **2** cloth woven in this pattern.

hers *poss. pron.* the one or ones belonging to or associated with her. □ **of hers** of or belonging to her.

herself *pron.* **1 a** *emphatic form of* SHE *or* HER. **b** *reflexive form of* HER. **2** in normal state of body or mind.

hertz *n.* (*pl.* **hertz**) the SI unit of frequency,

equal to one cycle per second. Abbreviation: **Hz**. [*Sounds like* HURTS]

he's *contr.* **1** he is. **2** he has.

hesitant *adj.* tending to be slow in speaking or acting because of uncertainty. □ **hesitancy** *n.* **hesitantly** *adv.* [*Say* HEZZA tint]

hesitate *v.* (**hesitates, hesitated, hesitating**) **1** show or feel indecision or uncertainty. **2** be reluctant. **3** falter or pause momentarily in speech. □ **hesitatingly** *adv.* **hesitation** *n.*

Hesquiaht *n.* (*pl.* **Hesquiaht** or **Hesquiahts**) **1** a member of a Nuu-chah-nulth Aboriginal group living on the west coast of Vancouver Island. **2** their Wakashan language. □ **Hesquiaht** *adj.* [*Say* HESH kwit]

hetero *informal* ● *n.* (*pl.* **heteros**) a heterosexual. ● *adj.* heterosexual. [*Say* HETTER oh]

hetero- *comb. form* other, different.

heterodox *adj.* not conforming with orthodox standards or beliefs. □ **heterodoxy** *n.* [*Say* HETTER uh dox]

heterogeneous *adj.* diverse in character or content. □ **heterogeneity** *n.* **heterogeneously** *adv.* [*Say* hetter uh GENIUS, hetter uh juh NAY uh tee]

heterosexism *n.* prejudice by heterosexuals against homosexuals. □ **heterosexist** *adj.* & *n.* [*Say* hetter oh SEXISM]

heterosexual ● *adj.* **1** sexually attracted to the opposite sex. **2** concerning heterosexual relations or people. ● *n.* a heterosexual person. □ **heterosexuality** *n.* [*Say* hetter oh SEXUAL]

het up *adj. informal* excited, overwrought.

heuristic *adj.* allowing one to discover things for oneself. [*Say* hure ISS tick]

hew *v.* (**hews;** *past* **hewed;** *past participle* **hewn** or **hewed; hewing**) **1 a** (often foll. by *down, away, off*) chop or cut (a thing) with an axe, etc. **b** cut (a block of wood) into shape. **2** (usu. foll. by *to*) conform. □ **hewer** *n.*

hex¹ ● *v.* (**hexes, hexed, hexing**) bewitch. ● *n.* (*pl.* **hexes**) a magic spell.

hex² *adj.* hexagonal.

hexa- *comb. form* (also **hex-** esp. before a vowel) six.

hexagon *n.* a plane figure with six sides and angles. □ **hexagonal** *adj.* [*Say* HEXA gon, hex AGGA nul]

hey *interj.* **1** calling attention or expressing joy, surprise, greeting, etc. **2** expressing greeting. **3** indicating feigned or real

unconcern about something one has just stated.

heyday *n.* the period of one's greatest success, activity, or energy.

HF *abbr.* HIGH FREQUENCY.

hi *interj.* used as a greeting.

hiatus *n.* (*pl.* **hiatuses**) **1** a pause in activity. **2** a gap in a piece of writing where something is missing. [*Say* hi AY tiss]

hibachi *n.* (*pl.* **hibachis**) a small, portable charcoal brazier with a grill. [*Say* huh BOTCH ee]

hibernate *v.* (**hibernates, hibernated, hibernating**) spend the winter in a dormant state. □ **hibernation** *n.*

Hibernian ● *adj.* Irish. ● *n.* a native of Ireland. [*Say* hi BERN ee un]

hibiscus *n.* (*pl.* **hibiscuses**) a plant with large bright-coloured flowers. [*Say* hib ISS cuss *or* high BISS cuss]

hiccup ● *n.* **1** an involuntary spasm of the diaphragm and respiratory organs, with a characteristic gulping sound. **2** a minor difficulty. ● *v.* (**hiccups, hiccuped, hiccuping**) make a hiccup or hiccups.

hick *informal derogatory* ● *n.* a country dweller. ● *adj.* rural or unsophisticated.

hickey *n.* (*pl.* **hickeys**) *informal* a red mark on the skin, caused by biting or sucking during sexual play.

hickory *n.* (*pl.* **hickories**) **1** a N American tree of the walnut family, yielding tough timber and edible nuts (see PECAN). **2** its wood.

hicksville *n. derogatory* a non-urban area.

hidden *past participle of* HIDE¹.

hidden agenda *n.* a secret motive or plan.

hide¹ *v.* (**hides;** *past* **hid;** *past participle* **hidden; hiding**) **1** put or keep out of sight. **2** conceal oneself. **3** keep secret. **4** conceal (a thing) from sight intentionally or not. □ **hide one's light under a bushel** conceal one's merits.

hide² ● *n.* **1** the skin of an animal. **2** *informal* the human skin. ● *v.* (**hides, hided, hiding**) *informal* flog. □ **neither hide nor hair** not the slightest trace.

hideaway ● *n.* a hiding place. ● *adj.* hidden or concealed.

hidebound *adj.* unwilling or unable to change because of convention.

hideous *adj.* **1** repulsive to the senses or the mind. **2** *informal* unpleasant. □ **hideously** *adv.* **hideousness** *n.*

hideout *n. informal* a hiding place.

hidey-hole *n. informal* a hiding place.

hiding¹ *n.* **1** the action of concealing. **2** the state of being hidden.

hiding[2] *n. informal* a thrashing.

hierarchy *n.* (*pl.* **hierarchies**) **1** a system in which people are ranked into different levels of importance from highest to lowest. **2** any classification of things according to their importance. □ **hierarchical** *adj.* [*Say* HIRE arky]

hieroglyph *n.* a picture of an object representing a word, syllable, or sound, esp. as used in ancient Egypt. [*Say* HI ruh glif]

hieroglyphic ● *adj.* of or concerning hieroglyphs. ● *n.* (**hieroglyphics**) **1** hieroglyphs. **2** handwriting that is difficult to read. [*Say* hi ruh GLIF ick]

hi-fi *informal* ● *adj.* of or relating to high fidelity. ● *n.* (*pl.* **hi-fis**) a set of equipment for high-fidelity sound reproduction.

higgledy-piggledy *adv. & adj.* in disorder.

high ● *adj.* **1 a** of great vertical extent. **b** of a specified height. **2** far above ground or sea level etc. **3** extending above the normal level. **4** of exalted, esp. spiritual, quality. **5** great in status. **6** great in amount, proportion, value, size, or intensity. **7** *informal* **a** (often foll. by *on*) intoxicated by alcohol or esp. drugs. **b** exhilarated. **8** (of a sound or note) of high frequency. **9** (of a period or movement) at its peak. **10** (of a gear) having comparatively high output speed relative to input speed. ● *n.* **1** a high, or the highest, level or figure. **2** an area of high barometric pressure. **3** *informal* **a** a euphoric drug-induced state. **b** a state of excitement. ● *adv.* **1** far up. **2** in or to a high degree. **3** at a high price. **4** (of a sound) at or to a high pitch. □ **from on high** from heaven or a high place. **high on the agenda** (or **list**) considered a priority for discussion or action. **on one's high horse** *informal* behaving superciliously.

high and dry *adv.* (usu. in phr. **leave high and dry**) **1** stranded without resources. **2** (of a ship) out of the water, esp. stranded.

high and low *adv.* everywhere.

high and mighty *adj. informal* arrogant.

High Arctic *n.* the part of the Canadian Arctic that lies within the Arctic Circle.

highball *n.* a drink of liquor diluted with a soft drink etc., served with ice.

high beam *n.* (usu. in *pl.*) a bright headlight beam, used for long-range illumination.

highbrow *informal* ● *adj.* intellectual; cultural. ● *n.* an intellectual or cultured person.

highbush *adj.* designating varieties of cranberries or blueberries growing on a relatively tall bush.

high chair *n.* an infant's chair with long legs and a tray, for use at meals.

High Church ● *n.* a tradition within the Anglican Church emphasizing rituals and priestly authority. ● *adj.* of or relating to this tradition.

high-class *adj.* of high quality.

high command *n.* the commander-in-chief and senior staff of a military force.

High Commission 1 an embassy from one Commonwealth country to another. **2** an international commission. □ **High Commissioner** *n.*

High Court *n.* a supreme court of justice for civil cases.

high-definition *adj.* providing a relatively clear image.

high-density *adj.* **1** (of a substance) very dense. **2** accommodating a large number of people in a relatively small area.

high-end *adj.* expensive and of fine quality.

higher *adj.* **1** comparative of HIGH. **2** *Computing* designating software releases that are more recent than one specified.

higher-up *n.* (*pl.* **higher-ups**) *informal* a superior.

highest common factor *n.* the highest number that can be divided exactly into each of two or more numbers.

high explosive *n.* an extremely explosive substance used in shells and bombs.

highfalutin *adj. informal* absurdly pretentious.

high fidelity *n.* the reproduction of sound with little distortion. □ **high-fidelity** *adj.*

high-five *slang* ● *n.* a gesture of celebration or greeting in which two people slap each other's palms with their arms raised. ● *v.* (**high-fives**, **high-fived**, **high-fiving**) **1** greet with a high-five. **2** make a high-five. □ **high-fiving** *n.*

high-flown *adj.* (of language etc.) grand-sounding.

high flyer *n.* a successful and ambitious person. □ **high-flying** *adj.*

high frequency *n.* (*pl.* **high frequencies**) a frequency, esp. in radio, of 3 to 30 megahertz. Abbreviation: **HF**. □ **high-frequency** *adj.*

High German *n.* standard written and spoken German.

high-grade ● *adj.* **1** of good quality. **2** (of ore) rich in metal value. ● *v.* (**high-grades**, **high-graded**, **high-grading**) **1** steal (high-grade ore) from a mine. **2** cut (the best trees) in a forest. □ **high-grading** *n.*

high ground *n.* **1** ground that is naturally elevated. **2** a position of moral superiority.

high-handed *adj.* disregarding others' feelings. □ **high-handedly** *adv.* **high-handedness** *n.*

High Holidays *pl. n.* the Jewish festivals of Rosh Hashanah and Yom Kippur.

high-impact *adj.* **1** (of plastics etc.) able to withstand great impact without breaking. **2** (of exercises) placing great stress on the body. **3** having a great effect.

highjinks *pl. n.* = HIJINKS.

high jump *n.* an athletic event consisting of jumping as high as possible over a bar of adjustable height. □ **high jumper** *n.* **high jumping** *n.*

highland ● *n.* (usu. in *pl.*) **1** an area of high land. **2** (**the Highlands**) **a** the mountainous part of Scotland. **b** any similar area of hilly plateau. ● *adj.* of or in a highland or the Highlands. □ **highlander** *n.*

high-level *adj.* **1** (of negotiations etc.) conducted by high-ranking people. **2** (of a programming language) usu. resembling a standard spoken language.

high life *n.* (also **high living**) a luxurious existence.

highlight ● *n.* **1** an outstanding moment or detail. **2** a light area in a painting. **3** (usu. in *pl.*) a bright tint in the hair. ● *v.* **1** draw attention to. **2** mark with a highlighter.

highlighter *n.* a marker pen which overlays colour on a printed word etc., leaving it emphasized.

highly *adv.* **1** in a high degree. **2** favourably.

High Mass *n.* a Mass in which the prayers are sung rather than spoken.

high-minded *adj.* having strong moral principles. □ **high-mindedly** *adv.* **high-mindedness** *n.*

high muckamuck *n.* = MUCKY-MUCK.

highness *n.* (*pl.* **highnesses**) **1** the state of being high. **2** (**Highness**) a title used in regard to a prince or princess.

high-octane *adj.* **1** (of fuel) of very good quality and very efficient. **2** high-powered.

high-powered *adj.* (also **high-power**) **1** having great power. **2** important or influential.

high pressure ● *n.* **1** a high degree of activity or exertion. **2** a condition of the atmosphere with the pressure above 101.3 kilopascals. ● *adj.* (usu. **high-pressure**) **1** involving a pressure above the ordinary. **2** (of a job, etc.) demanding; stressful. **3** (of a sales technique) forceful, persistent.

high priest *n.* **1** a chief priest in some non-Christian religions. **2** a chief exponent of a political or cultural movement.

high priestess *n.* (*pl.* **high priestesses**) **1** a chief priestess in some non-Christian religions. **2** a woman who is the chief exponent of a political or cultural movement.

high-rise ● *adj.* (of a building) having many storeys. ● *n.* such a building.

high-risk *adj.* involving or exposed to danger.

high road *n.* a direct route.

high roller *n. slang* a person who gambles large sums or spends freely.

high school *n.* a secondary school. □ **high-school** *adj.*

high sea *n.* (also **high seas**) open seas not within any country's jurisdiction.

high season *n.* the period during which the most people travel, book accommodation, etc.

high spirits *pl. n.* vivacity; cheerfulness. □ **high-spirited** *adj.*

high-stick *v.* (**high-sticks, high-sticked, high-sticking**) *Hockey* illegally strike another player with the stick held above shoulder level.

high-strung *adj.* very sensitive or nervous.

hightail *v. informal* □ **hightail it** hurry.

high-tech ● *adj.* having to do with high technology. ● *n.* (**high tech**) = HIGH TECHNOLOGY.

high technology *n.* advanced technological development, esp. in electronics.

high-tensile *adj.* (of metal) very strong under tension.

high tension *n.* = HIGH VOLTAGE.

high tide *n.* **1** the tide at its fullest. **2** the time of this.

high time *n.* a time that is late or overdue.

high-top ● *adj.* designating athletic shoes that come above the ankle bone. ● *n.* (in *pl.*) high-top shoes.

high treason *n. see* TREASON 1.

high voltage ● *n.* electrical potential large enough to cause injury or damage if diverted. ● *adj.* (also **high-voltage**) **1** involving high electrical voltage. **2** displaying a great deal of energy.

high water *n.* = HIGH TIDE.

high-water mark *n.* **1** the level reached by the sea at high tide, or by a lake or river in flood. **2** the highest point of excellence.

highway *n.* **1 a** a main road, esp. one between towns or cities. **b** a public road. **2** a much-travelled route.

highwayman *n.* (*pl.* **highwaymen**) *hist.* a man who held up and robbed travellers.

high wire *n.* a high tightrope.

hi-hat *n.* a pair of cymbals mounted on an

upright rod, clashed together by means of a foot pedal.

hijab *n.* a veil worn by some Muslim women to cover the hair, forehead, etc. [*Say* HIDGE ob]

hijack ● *v.* **1** illegally seize control of (an aircraft in flight etc.). **2** take over (an organization etc.) by force in order to redirect it. ● *n.* an occurrence of hijacking. □ **hijacker** *n.*

hijinks *pl. n. informal* boisterous merrymaking. [*Say* HI jinks]

hike ● *n.* **1** a long walk, esp. in the country, taken for pleasure or exercise. **2** an increase (of prices etc.). ● *v.* (**hikes, hiked, hiking**) **1** go for a long walk. **2** (usu. foll. by *up*) hitch up (clothing etc.). **3** increase (prices etc.). □ **take a hike** *slang* go away. □ **hiker** *n.*

hilarious *adj.* exceedingly funny. □ **hilariously** *adv.* **hilarity** *n.*

hill *n.* **1** a naturally raised area of land, not as high as a mountain. **2** (often in *comb.*) a heap. □ **old as the hills** very ancient. **over the hill** *informal* past the prime of life.

hillbilly esp. *US* ● *n.* (*pl.* **hillbillies**) **1** *informal, often derogatory* a person from a remote area. **2** country music of or like that of the southern US. ● *adj.* relating to hillbillies.

hillock *n.* a small hill. [*Say* HILL uck]

hillside *n.* the sloping side of a hill.

hilltop *n.* the summit of a hill.

hilly *adj.* (**hillier, hilliest**) having many hills.

hilt *n.* the handle of a sword, dagger, tool, etc. □ **to the hilt** completely.

him *pron.* **1** *objective case of* HE. **2** *informal* he.

Himalayan *adj.* relating to the Himalayas, a vast mountain system in southern Asia. [*Say* himma LAY in]

himself *pron.* **1 a** *emphatic form of* HE or HIM. **b** *reflexive form of* HIM. **2** in his normal state of body or mind.

hind[1] *adj.* situated at the back.

hind[2] *n.* a female deer.

hinder[1] *v.* delay, obstruct. [*Say* HIN der]

hinder[2] *adj.* rear, hind. [*Say* HIND er]

Hindi ● *n.* a language of northern India derived from Sanskrit. ● *adj.* of or concerning Hindi. [*Say* HIN dee]

hindmost *adj.* furthest back.

hindquarters *pl. n.* the hind legs and adjoining parts of a quadruped.

hindrance *n.* a thing that hinders. [*Say* HIN drince]

hindsight *n.* wisdom after the event.

Hindu ● *n.* (*pl.* **Hindus**) a follower of Hinduism. ● *adj.* of or concerning Hindus or Hinduism.

Hinduism *n.* the main religious and social system of India, including a belief in reincarnation, the worship of several gods, and an ordained caste system as the basis of society.

Hindustani ● *n. hist.* the Delhi dialect of Hindi, used throughout India as a lingua franca. ● *adj.* of or relating to northwestern India or its people, or Hindustani. [*Say* hindu STANNY]

hinge ● *n.* a movable joint on which something swings open or is closed. ● *v.* (**hinges, hinged, hinging**) **1** (foll. by *on*) depend. **2** attach with or as if with a hinge. □ **hinged** *adj.*

hint ● *n.* **1** a slight or indirect suggestion. **2** a very small trace. **3** a small item of practical information ● *v.* suggest indirectly. □ **hint at** give a slight suggestion of.

hinterland *n.* **1** a remote area. **2** the area around a major town.

hip[1] *n.* **1** a projection of the pelvis and upper thigh bone on each side of the body. **2** the part on each side of the human body between the top of the legs and the waist.

hip[2] *n.* the fruit of a rose.

hip[3] *adj.* (**hipper, hippest**) *slang* **1** fashionable. **2** (often foll. by *to*) aware.

hip hop *n.* a style of popular music of US black origin, featuring rap with an electronic backing. □ **hip-hopper** *n.*

hippie *n. informal* (esp. in the 1960s) a young person who advocated free love, peace, etc., and adopted an unconventional appearance. □ **hippiedom** *n.*

hippo *n.* (*pl.* **hippos**) *informal* a hippopotamus.

hippocampus *n.* (*pl.* **hippocampi**) **1** a sea horse. **2** the part of the brain thought to be the centre of emotion and the autonomic nervous system. [*Say* hippa CAMPUS *for the singular,* hippa CAM pee *for the plural*]

hippopotamus *n.* (*pl.* **hippopotamuses** or **hippopotami**) a large African mammal with a thick skin and massive jaws, living partly in water.

hippy *n.* = HIPPIE.

hipster *n. slang* a person who is hip.

hip waders *pl. n.* waders that come up to the hips.

hire ● *v.* (**hires, hired, hiring**) **1** employ (a person) for wages or a fee. **2** procure temporary use of (a thing) for payment. ● *n.* **1** the action of hiring. **2** a recently hired employee. □ **for** (or **on**) **hire** ready to be hired.

hired gun *n. informal* **1** an expert brought in to resolve complex problems. **2 a** a bodyguard. **b** a hit man or gunfighter.

hired hand *n.* a person employed to do usu. manual work.

hireling *n.* usu. *derogatory* a person who works primarily for monetary gain, esp. doing menial work.

hirsute *adj.* hairy. [*Say* her SUIT]

his *poss. adj.* of or belonging to him. □ **his and hers** (of matching items) for husband and wife.

Hispanic ● *adj.* **1** of or relating to Spain or Spanish-speaking countries. **2** of or relating to Hispanics. ● *n.* a Spanish-speaking person living in the US or Canada. [*Say* hiss PANIC]

hiss ● *v.* (**hisses, hissed, hissing**) **1** make a sharp sound as of the letter *s*, often as a sign disapproval. **2** whisper urgently or angrily. ● *n.* (*pl.* **hisses**) a hissing sound. □ **hissy** *adj.*

histamine *n.* a substance released by cells in response to injury and in allergic and inflammatory reactions. [*Say* HISTA min *or* HISTA mean]

histology *n.* (*pl.* **histologies**) the study of the microscopic structure of tissues. [*Say* hiss TOLLA jee]

historian *n.* an expert in history.

historic *adj.* famous or important in history or potentially so.

historical *adj.* **1** of or concerning history. **2** (of the study of a subject) looking at its development over a period. **3** belonging to or set in the past. □ **historically** *adv.*

history *n.* (*pl.* **histories**) **1 a** a continuous record of past events. **b** the past considered as a whole. **2 a** the study of past events. **b** a critical account of a past event, development, etc. **3** an eventful past. □ **be history** *informal* be no longer existing, or important.

histrionic ● *adj.* excessively dramatic. ● *n.* (in *pl.*) exaggerated behaviour designed to impress. □ **histrionically** *adv.* [*Say* histry ON ick]

hit ● *v.* (**hits, hit, hitting**) **1** strike. **2** affect the feelings, conscience, etc. of a person. **3** *informal* **a** encounter. **b** arrive at. **4** *slang* kill, attack, or rob. **5** occur forcefully to. **6** *informal* give (a person) a playing card, alcoholic drink, etc. **7** *slang* (also foll. by *up*) ask (a person), esp. for money. ● *n.* **1 a** a blow. **b** a collision. **2 a** a shot etc. that hits its target. **3** a popular success, esp. in entertainment. **4** *slang* **a** a contract killing. **b** a dose of something, esp. an illegal drug. **5** *Computing* a instance of identifying an item of data which matches the requirements of a search. **6** an instance of a website being accessed by a user. □ **hit back** retaliate. **hit below the belt 1** esp. *Boxing* hit an opponent below the waist, esp. in the genitals. **2** behave unfairly. **hit the books** study diligently. **hit the deck** *informal* fall to the floor, ground, etc. **hit the ground running** *informal* begin an endeavour with the preparation already completed. **hit home 1** become fully clear. **2** (of remarks etc.) have the intended, often painful, effect. **hit it off** *informal* get on well (with a person). **hit the nail on the head** express the truth precisely. **hit on 1** (also **hit upon**) find, esp. by chance. **2** *slang* make sexual overtures toward. **hit the road** *slang* depart. **hit the sack** (or **hay**) *informal* go to bed. □ **hitter** *n.*

hit-and-miss *adj.* (also **hit-or-miss**) done carelessly or inconsistently.

hit and run *n.* (*pl.* **hit and runs**) a motor vehicle accident in which the driver who caused the accident flees the scene. □ **hit-and-run** *adj.*

hitch ● *v.* (**hitches, hitched, hitching**) **1** fasten with a loop, hook, etc. **2** move with a jerk. **3** *informal* = HITCHHIKE. **4** become caught on something. ● *n.* (*pl.* **hitches**) **1** a temporary obstacle. **2** a knot used to fasten one thing temporarily to another. □ **get hitched** *informal* marry.

hitchhike *v.* (**hitchhikes, hitchhiked, hitchhiking**) travel by seeking free rides in passing vehicles. □ **hitchhiker** *n.* **hitchhiking** *n.*

hi-tech *adj.* = HIGH-TECH.

hither *adv.* to or towards this place.

hither and thither *adv.* to and fro.

hitherto *adv.* until this time.

hit list *n. slang* a list of prospective victims esp. of assassination.

hit man *n.* (*pl.* **hit men**) *slang* a hired assassin.

hit-or-miss *adj.* = HIT-AND-MISS.

Hittite *n.* **1** a member of an ancient, non-Semitic people of Asia Minor and Syria. **2** the Indo-European language of the Hittites. □ **Hittite** *adj.* [*Say* HIT ite]

HIV *abbr.* human immunodeficiency virus, a retrovirus which causes AIDS.

hive *n.* **1 a** a beehive. **b** the bees in a hive. **2** a place full of people working hard. □ **hive off** separate from a larger group.

hives *pl. n.* a rash of itchy red welts caused by allergic reaction, emotional stress, etc.

hiya *interj. informal* a word used in greeting.

HMCS *abbr.* Her (or His) Majesty's Canadian Ship (as a designation for a Canadian naval vessel).

HMS *abbr.* Her (or His) Majesty's Ship.

ho *interj.* expression of admiration or (often repeated as **ho! ho!**), derision or triumph.

hoar *n.* (also **hoarfrost**) frozen water vapour deposited in clear still weather on vegetation etc.

hoard ● *n.* a store of money or valued objects. ● *v.* amass (money, food, etc.) and store away. □ **hoarder** *n.*

hoarding *n.* a temporary board fence erected around a construction site.

hoarse *adj.* (**hoarser, hoarsest**) **1** (of the voice) husky, croaking. **2** having such a voice. □ **hoarsely** *adv.* **hoarseness** *n.*

hoary *adj.* (**hoarier, hoariest**) **1** (of hair) grey or white with age. **2** old and trite. **3** *Botany & Zoology* covered with short white hairs.

hoax ● *n.* (*pl.* **hoaxes**) a humorous or malicious deception. ● *v.* (**hoaxes, hoaxed, hoaxing**) deceive with a hoax. □ **hoaxer** *n.*

hob *n.* a flat metal surface for heating a pan etc.

hobble ● *v.* (**hobbles, hobbled, hobbling**) **1** walk lamely. **2** tie together the legs of a horse etc. to prevent it from straying. **3** hinder or interfere with. ● *n.* **1** an uneven or infirm gait. **2** a rope etc. used for hobbling an animal.

hobby *n.* (*pl.* **hobbies**) a favourite leisure-time activity. □ **hobbyist** *n.*

hobby horse *n.* **1** a child's toy consisting of a long stick with a figure of a horse's head on one end. **2** a favourite topic of conversation. **3** a rocking horse.

hobgoblin *n.* a mischievous imp.

hobnail *n.* a heavy-headed nail formerly used for boot soles. □ **hobnailed** *adj.*

hobnob *v.* (**hobnobs, hobnobbed, hobnobbing**) mix socially or informally.

hobo *n.* (*pl.* **hoboes** or **hobos**) a vagrant.

hock¹ *n.* **1** the joint of a quadruped's hind leg between the knee and the fetlock. **2** a knuckle of pork; the lower joint of a ham.

hock² *v. informal* pawn. □ **in hock 1** in debt. **2** in pawn.

hockey *n.* **1** a game played on ice between two teams of six players each, in which players try to shoot a puck into the opposing team's net with sticks. **2** any of a number of variations of this, such as street hockey. *See also* FIELD HOCKEY.

hocus-pocus *n.* **1** meaningless talk or activity. **2** words uttered by a conjuror when doing a trick. [*Say* hoke us POKE us]

hod *n.* a V-shaped open trough on a pole used for carrying bricks, mortar, etc.

hodgepodge *n.* a mixture of heterogeneous things.

Hodgkin's disease *n.* a disease of the lymphatic system usu. characterized by enlargement of the lymph nodes, liver, and spleen. [*Say* HODGE kins]

hoe ● *n.* a long-handled gardening tool with a thin metal blade. ● *v.* (**hoes, hoed, hoeing**) use a hoe to weed, loosen earth, dig, etc.

hoedown *n.* a lively party with square dancing and music.

hog ● *n.* **1 a** a castrated male pig reared for slaughter. **b** a wild animal of the pig family, e.g. a warthog. **2** *informal* a greedy person. **3** *slang* a large, heavy motorcycle. ● *v.* (**hogs, hogged, hogging**) *informal* hoard selfishly; monopolize. □ **live high on** (or **off**) **the hog** *informal* live luxuriously. **go (the) whole hog** *informal* do something completely or thoroughly.

hog heaven *n. informal* a place or condition of foolish or idle bliss.

hog line *n. Curling* either of two lines drawn across each end of a rink at one sixth of the rink's length from the tee, which a rock must cross to count in the game.

hognose snake *n.* any of several harmless N American snakes which have an upturned snout.

hogshead *n.* **1** a large cask. **2** a measure, varying according to the commodity, but usu. about 220 to 245 litres. [*Say* HOGS head]

hog-tie *v.* (**hog-ties, hog-tied, hog-tying**) **1** secure by fastening the hands and feet or all four feet together. **2** restrain, impede.

hogwash *n. informal* nonsense.

hog-wild *adj. informal* exceedingly excited.

ho-hum ● *adj.* dull, routine, boring. ● *interj.* expressing boredom.

hoi polloi *n.* the common people. [*Say* hoy puh LOY]

hoist ● *v.* **1** raise or haul up. **2** raise by means of ropes and pulleys etc. ● *n.* **1** an apparatus for hoisting. **2** an act of hoisting, a lift. **3 a** the perpendicular height of a flag or sail. **b** the part of a flag nearest the staff. **c** a group of flags raised as a signal.

hoity-toity *adj.* haughty, pretentious.

hokey *adj.* (**hokier, hokiest**) *slang* sentimental, contrived. □ **hokeyness** *n.*

hokum *n. slang* **1** sentimental or unreal material in a film, play, etc. **2** nonsense. [*Say* HOE k'm]

hold¹ ● *v.* (**holds, held, holding**) **1** grasp, carry, or support. **2** keep or detain. **3** have in one's possession. **4** contain or be capable of containing. **5** occupy a job or position. **6** have an opinion. **7** stay or cause to stay at a certain level. **8** adhere or cause to adhere to a commitment. **9** continue to follow a course. **10** arrange and take part in a meeting. **11** regard someone or something with a specified feeling. **12** refrain from adding or using. **13** remain connected by telephone without speaking to someone. ● *n.* **1** an act or manner of grasping someone or something. **2** a handhold. **3** a degree of control. **4** a tentative reservation. □ **get (a) hold of 1** acquire, etc. **2** contact, esp. by telephone. **hold (a thing) against (a person)** resent or regard (a thing) as discreditable to (a person). **hold back 1** impede the progress of. **2** keep (a thing) to oneself. **3** (often foll. by *from*) hesitate; refrain. **hold by** (or **to**) adhere to (a choice, purpose, etc.). **hold court** preside over one's admirers etc., like a sovereign. **hold down 1** *informal* be competent enough to keep (one's job etc.). **2** secure, restrain. **hold everything!** cease action. **hold forth 1** offer (an inducement etc.). **2** usu. *derogatory* speak at length. **hold a person's hand** give a person guidance. **hold one's horses** *informal* stop; slow down. **hold it!** stop. **hold one's nose** compress the nostrils to avoid a bad smell. **hold off 1** delay; not begin. **2** keep one's distance. **hold on 1** keep one's grasp on something. **2** wait. **hold out 1** offer. **2** maintain resistance. **3** persist. **hold out for** continue to demand. **hold out on** *informal* refuse something to (a person). **hold over 1** postpone. **2** retain for an additional period. **hold together 1** cohere. **2** cause to cohere. **3** retain one's composure, esp. in difficult circumstances. **hold one's tongue** *informal* be silent. **hold to ransom 1** keep (a person) prisoner until a ransom is paid. **2** demand concessions from by threats of damaging action. **hold true** (or **good**) be valid. **hold up 1** support. **2** exhibit; display. **3** obstruct. **4** rob using violence or threats. **hold water** (of reasoning) be sound. **hold with** (usu. with *neg.*) *informal* approve of. **left holding the bag** left with unwelcome responsibility. **on hold 1** (when telephoning) waiting to be dealt with. **2** (esp. in phr. **put on hold**) temporarily inactive or receiving little attention. **take hold** become established. **with no holds barred** with no restrictions. □ **holder** *n.*

hold² *n.* a cavity in the lower part of a ship or aircraft.

holding *n.* **1 a** land held by lease. **b** the tenure of land. **2** (usu. in *pl.*) stocks, property, etc. held. **3** *Sport* the illegal restraint of one's opponent. **4** the collection of books etc. in a library.

holdout *n.* **1** an act of resisting something. **2** a person or organization doing this.

holdover *n.* **1** a relic. **2** a person who remains in office etc. beyond the regular term.

holdup *n.* **1** a cause of delay. **2** a robbery, esp. by the use of threats or violence.

hole ● *n.* **1** an empty space in a solid or surface. **2** an animal's burrow. **3** a cavity or receptacle into which the ball must be propelled in various games, e.g. golf. **4** *informal* (also **hole in the wall**) a small, mean, or dingy abode, place of business, etc. **5** a dungeon or prison cell. **6** *informal* an awkward situation. **7** *Golf* the terrain or distance from tee to hole. ● *v.* (**holes, holed, holing**) **1** make a hole or holes in. **2** put into a hole. □ **dig a hole for oneself** put oneself in a predicament. **hole up** *informal* **1** hide oneself. **2** take shelter. **in the hole** *informal* in debt.

hole-in-one *n.* (*pl.* **holes-in-one**) *Golf* a shot from the tee that goes directly into the hole.

holey *adj.* having many holes.

holiday ● *n.* **1 a** a day on which most work and school ceases, esp. in honour of a person or event. **b** a religious festival. **2** (often in *pl.*) a vacation; an extended period of leisure. **3** (in *pl.*) (also **holiday season**) the festive period surrounding Christmas, Hanukkah, and New Year's. **4** (as an *adj.*) festive. ● *v.* spend a holiday.

holier-than-thou *adj. informal* self-righteous.

holiness *n.* **1** sanctity; the state of being holy. **2** (**Holiness**) a title used when referring to or addressing the Pope.

holistic *adj.* taking into account a whole system rather than focusing on one aspect of it. □ **holistically** *adv.* [Say HOLE ism]

hollandaise sauce *n.* a creamy sauce of melted butter, egg yolks, and lemon juice. [Say HOLLAN days]

holler *informal* ● *v.* shout. ● *n.* a loud cry, noise, or shout.

hollow ● *adj.* **1 a** having a hole or cavity inside. **b** having a depression; sunken. **2** (of a sound) echoing, as though made in or on a hollow container. **3** without significance. **4** insincere; false. ● *n.* **1** a hollow place; a hole. **2** a valley; a basin. ● *v.* (often foll. by *out*) make hollow; excavate. □ **hollowness** *n.*

holly *n.* (*pl.* **hollies**) an evergreen shrub, typically having dark green leaves, small white flowers, and red berries, used as a Christmas decoration.

hollyhock *n.* a tall plant of the mallow family, with large showy flowers.

Hollywood *n.* the American motion picture industry or its products.

holocaust *n.* **1** a case of large-scale destruction, esp. by fire or nuclear war. **2 (the Holocaust)** the mass murder esp. of Jews under the Nazi regime 1941–5. **3** a sacrifice consumed by fire. [*Say* HOLLA cost]

Holocene ● *adj.* of or relating to the second epoch of the Quaternary period, lasting from about 10,000 years ago to the present. ● *n.* this geological period. [*Say* HOLLA seen]

hologram *n.* a photographic image formed in such a way that, when suitably lit up, a three dimensional image is seen. □ **holographic** *adj.* **holography** *n.* [*Say* HOLLA gram]

Holstein *n.* (also **Holstein-Friesian**) a large black and white breed of dairy cattle. [*Say* HOLE steen *or* HOLE stine]

holster *n.* a case for a handgun, esp. worn on a belt or under an arm.

holy (holier, holiest) ● *adj.* **1** morally and spiritually excellent or perfect, and to be revered. **2** belonging to or devoted to God. **3** consecrated, sacred. **4** used in exclamations ● *interj.* expressing amazement etc.

Holy Ghost *n.* see HOLY SPIRIT.

holy moly *interj. slang* (also **holy moley**) expressing great surprise, admiration, etc.

holy of holies *n.* **1** the inner chamber of the sanctuary in the Jewish temple. **2** *jocular* a special place that can only be visited by important people. **3** a thing regarded as most sacred.

holy orders *pl. n.* the status of a member of the clergy, esp. the grades of bishop, priest, and deacon.

holy roller *n. slang derogatory* **1** a member of a group characterized by religious excitement. **2** a highly vocal devout person.

Holy Saturday *n.* the day before Easter Sunday.

Holy See *n.* the papacy or the papal court.

Holy Spirit *n.* (in Christian theology) one of the persons of the Trinity, considered as God acting in the world as a spirit.

Holy Thursday *n.* the Thursday before Easter.

Holy Week *n.* the week before Easter.

homage *n.* **1** special honour or respect shown publicly. **2** *hist.* formal public acknowledgement of feudal allegiance. [*Say* HOM idge]

homburg *n.* a man's felt hat with a narrow curled brim and a lengthwise dent in the crown. [*Say* HOM burg]

home ● *n.* **1** the place where one lives. **2** one's family background. **3** an institution for persons needing professional care. **4** the place where a thing originates. **5** = HOME PAGE. **6** *Baseball* = HOME PLATE. ● *adj.* **1 a** of or connected with one's home. **b** carried on, done, or made at home. **2** carried on or produced in one's own country. **3** *Sport* played on one's own ground etc. **4** in the neighbourhood of home. ● *adv.* **1** to or at one's home. **2** to the point aimed at. ● *v.* **(homes, homed, homing) 1** (esp. of a trained pigeon) return home. **2** (often foll. by *on, in on*) (of a vessel, missile, etc.) be guided towards a destination by a landmark, radio beam, etc. □ **come home to** become fully realized by. **home free** assured of success or safety.

home and school *n.* esp. *Cdn* a local association of parents and teachers.

homebody *n.* (*pl.* **homebodies**) a person who likes to stay at home.

homeboy *n.* esp. *US slang* **1** a person from one's own town or neighbourhood. **2** a close friend, esp. a member of one's gang.

homebrew *n.* beer or other alcoholic drink brewed at home. □ **home-brewed** *adv.*

homebuyer *n.* a person who buys a house, condominium, etc.

home care *n.* care, esp. medical care, given or received at home.

home child *n. Cdn* (usu. in *pl.*) one of a number of orphaned or poor children sent from Britain to Canada from about 1850 to the early 1900s.

homecoming *n.* **1** arrival at home. **2** a reunion, esp. of former students.

home economics *pl. n.* (often treated as *sing.*) (also **home ec** *n.*) the study of household management, usu. including cooking, nutrition, sewing, child-raising, budgeting, etc. □ **home economist** *n.*

home fires *pl. n.* □ **keep the home fires burning** maintain a family home, esp. while one of its members is away.

home fry *n.* (*pl.* **home fries**) (usu. in *pl.*) a slice of usu. boiled potato that has been fried in a frying pan rather than deep-fried.

homegirl *n.* esp. *US slang* **1** a girl from one's own town or neighbourhood. **2** a close friend, esp. a member of one's gang.

homegrown *adj.* native to or produced in one's own country, locality, etc.

homeland *n.* **1** one's native land. **2** *hist.* a partially self-governing area in South Africa set aside for indigenous African people under apartheid; they were abolished in 1994. **3** any similar semi-autonomous area.

homeless adj. lacking a home.
□ **homelessness** n.

homely adj. (**homelier, homeliest**) **1** not attractive. **2** simple, plain, unpretentious. **3** comfortable in the manner of a home, cozy.

homemade adj. made at home.

homemaker n. a person who runs a household for their family, esp. as a primary occupation.
□ **homemaking** adj. & n.

homeopath n. a person who practises homeopathy. [Say HOME ee oh path]

homeopathy n. the treatment of disease by minute doses of drugs that in a healthy person would produce symptoms of the disease. □ **homeopathic** adj.
homeopathically adv.
[Say home ee OPP uth ee, homey o PATHIC]

home opener n. a sports team's first home game of a new season.

homeostasis n. the tendency towards a relatively stable equilibrium between interdependent elements. □ **homeostatic** adj. [Say home ee oh STAY sis, home ee oh STATIC]

homeowner n. a person who owns his or her own home. □ **home ownership** n.

home page n. a computer screen that serves as an introduction to a network site.

home plate n. Baseball a base beside which the batter stands and which a runner must reach to score a run.

homer Baseball ● n. a home run. ● v. hit a homer.

Homeric adj. **1** of, or in the style of, the Greek epic poet Homer (c.700 BC) or the epic poems ascribed to him, the Iliad and the Odyssey. **2** epic, large-scale.
[Say hoe MAIR ick]

homeroom n. (at school) the first class of the day, for announcements, opening exercises, etc.

home rule n. a movement for the self-government of a colony, dependent country, etc.

home run n. Baseball a hit that allows the batter to make a complete circuit of the bases.

home-school v. teach one's child in one's own home rather than send him or her to school. □ **home-schooler** n. **home-schooling** n.

home shopping n. shopping carried out from home using catalogues, TV channels, etc.

homesick adj. depressed by longing for one's home. □ **homesickness** n.

homespun ● adj. **1 a** (of cloth) made of

yarn spun at home. **b** (of yarn) spun at home. **2** plain, unsophisticated. ● n. homespun cloth.

homestand n. a series of games played at a team's own venue.

homestead n. **1** an area of public land granted to a settler on certain conditions, e.g. that a certain portion of it be cultivated within a specified time. **2** a house, esp. a farmhouse, and outbuildings.
□ **homestead** v. **homesteader** n.

home stretch n. **1** the straight section of a racetrack leading to the finish line. **2** the final stage or phase of anything.

homestyle adj. (esp. of food) of a kind prepared at home.

home theatre n. a home audio-video system designed to simulate as closely as possible the viewing conditions in a movie theatre, e.g. with a very large flat screen and high quality sound.

hometown n. the town of one's birth or early life or present fixed residence.

homeward ● adv. (also **homewards**) towards home. ● adj. going or leading towards home.

homework n. **1** work to be done at home, esp. by a student. **2** preparatory work or study.

homeworker n. a person who works from home, esp. doing low-paid piecework.

homey adj. (**homier, homiest**) suggesting home; cozy. □ **homeyness** n.

homicide n. the intentional killing of a human being by another. □ **homicidal** adj.
[Say HOMMA side]

homily n. (pl. **homilies**) **1** a sermon. **2** a tedious moralizing discourse. □ **homiletic** adj. [Say HOMMA lee]

homing adj. **1** (of a pigeon) trained to fly home, bred for long-distance racing, carrying messages, etc. **2** (of a weapon) able to find and hit a target electronically.

hominid ● n. a primate of a family which includes humans and their fossil ancestors. ● adj. of this family. [Say HOM in id]

hominy n. esp. US coarsely ground kernels of corn esp. boiled with water or milk.
[Say HOM in ee]

Homo n. any primate of the genus of Homo, including modern humans and various extinct species.

homo n. Cdn homogenized milk typically having a butterfat content of 3.25 percent.

homoerotic adj. concerning or arousing sexual desire in a person of the same sex.
□ **homoeroticism** n. [Say homo EROTIC]

homogeneous adj. consisting of things that are all the same or all of the same type. □ **homogeneity** n.

homogeneously adv.
[Say home uh GENIOUS, home ujuh NAY uh tee]

homogenize v. (**homogenizes, homogenized, homogenizing**) make or become homogeneous.
□ **homogenization** n.
[Say huh MODGE uh nize]

homogenized adj. **1** homogeneous. **2** (of milk) having the fat droplets emulsified, esp. (in Canada) designating homogenized milk with a butterfat content of 3.25 percent. [Say huh MODGE uh nized]

homogenous adj. disputed = HOMOGENEOUS. [Say huh MODGE un us]

homograph n. a word spelled like another but of different meaning or origin, e.g. "palm" (a tree) and "palm" (of the hand). [Say HOMMA graf]

homologous adj. Biology having a related or similar position or structure.
[Say huh MOLLA gus]

homonym n. a word of the same spelling or sound as another but of different meaning, e.g. "palm" (a tree) and "palm" (of the hand), or "deer" and "dear", or "sow" (plant seeds) and "sow" (female pig). [Say HOMMA nim]

homophobia n. prejudice against or fear of homosexuals or homosexuality.
□ **homophobe** n. **homophobic** adj.
[Say home uh PHOBIA]

homophone n. a word having the same sound as another but of different spelling and meaning (e.g. pair, pear).
[Say HOMMA phone]

Homo sapiens n. modern humans regarded as a species. [Say SAY pee enz]

homosexual ● adj. feeling or involving sexual attraction to persons of the same sex. ● n. a homosexual person.
□ **homosexuality** n.

homy adj. (**homier, homiest**) = HOMEY.

Hon. abbr. **1** Honourable. **2** Honorary.

hon n. informal honey (as a term of endearment).

honcho n. slang (pl. **honchos**) a leader.

hone v. (**hones, honed, honing**)
1 sharpen a blade with a stone. **2** make more effective or focused.

honest adj. **1** fair and just in character or behaviour. **2** sincere. **3** fairly earned. **4** (of an act or feeling) showing fairness. **5** (of a thing) simple and straightforward.
□ **honesty** n.

honestly ● adv. **1** in an honest way.
2 really. ● interj. expressing exasperation, dismay, etc.

honest-to-God adj. (also **honest-to-goodness**) informal genuine, real.

honey n. (pl. **honeys**) **1** a sweet sticky yellowish fluid made by bees from nectar. **2** the colour of this. **3** darling.

honeybee n. the common bee, domesticated for its honey.

honeycomb ● n. **1** a structure of hexagonal cells of wax, made by bees to store honey and eggs. **2** a hexagonal pattern. ● v. **1** fill with cavities or tunnels. **2** mark with a honeycomb pattern.
□ **honeycombed** adj.

honeydew n. **1** a sweet sticky substance excreted by aphids onto leaves. **2** a melon with smooth pale skin and sweet green flesh.

honeyed adj. **1** of or containing honey.
2 (of words) intending to please or flatter.

honeymoon ● n. **1** a holiday taken by a newly married couple. **2** an initial period of enthusiasm or goodwill. ● v. spend a honeymoon. □ **honeymooner** n.

honeysuckle n. a shrub with fragrant yellow, orange, white or pink flowers.

honk ● n. **1** the cry of a goose. **2** the sound of a car horn. **3** a sound similar to either of these. ● v. emit or give a honk. □ **honker** n.

honking adj. (also **honkin'**) slang very large.

honky-tonk n. informal **1** ragtime piano music. **2** a cheap or disreputable nightclub.

honorarium n. (pl. **honorariums** or **honoraria**) a voluntary payment for professional services offered without the normal fee. [Say onna RERRY um]

honorary adj. (also **honourary**)
1 conferred as an honour, without the usual requirements, functions, etc. **2** (of an office or its holder) unpaid.

honorific ● adj. (of a title etc.) showing respect for a person. ● n. an honorific.
□ **honorifically** adv. [Say onna RIFFICK]

honour (also **honor**) ● n. **1** high respect; glory. **2** a clear sense of what is morally right. **3** nobleness of mind. **4** an award conferred as a distinction. **5** privilege. **6** (**Honour**) (preceded by your, his, her, etc.) a title of respect given to a lower court judge etc. **7** a person or thing that brings honour. **8** (in pl.) **a** special distinction for proficiency. **b** a course of degree studies more specialized than for a general degree. ● v. **1** respect highly. **2** confer honour on. **3** accept or pay (a bill or cheque) when due. **4** acknowledge. □ **in honour of** as a celebration of.

honourable adj. (also **honorable**)
1 a deserving respect and admiration.
b showing high moral standards.
2 (**Honourable**) a title indicating eminence or distinction, given e.g. to an MP. □ **honourably** adv.

honouree n. (also **honoree**) a person who is honoured.

honour roll n. **1** a list of students who have achieved grades above a certain average. **2** a list of local citizens who served in the armed forces.

hooch n. informal alcoholic liquor, esp. if illicit.

hood[1] n. **1** a covering for the head and neck. **2** a hinged cover over the engine of a motor vehicle. **3** a canopy over a machine etc. **4** the hood-like structure or marking on the head or neck of a cobra, seal, etc. □ **hooded** adj. **hoodless** adj.

hood[2] n. slang a gangster or gunman.

'hood n. esp. US slang a neighbourhood, esp. one in the inner city.

-hood suffix forming nouns: **1** of condition or state. **2** indicating a collection or group.

hooded seal n. a northern seal, the male of which has an inflatable nasal sac.

hoodlum n. **1** a young thug. **2** a gangster. [HOOD rhymes with GOOD or FOOD]

hoodoo n. (pl. **hoodoos**) a column or pinnacle of weathered rock. [Say HOO doo]

hoodwink v. deceive, delude.

hooey n. & interj. slang nonsense, humbug.

hoof ● n. (pl. **hoofs** or **hooves**) the horny part of the foot of a horse, antelope, etc. ● v. (**hoofs**, **hoofed**, **hoofing**) slang kick or shove. □ **hoof it** slang **1** go on foot. **2** dance. □ **hoofed** adj. (also in comb.). [With OO as in HOOD or HOOP]

hoo-ha n. slang (pl. **hoo-has**) a commotion, a row; uproar, trouble.

hook ● n. **1 a** a bent or curved piece of metal or other material, for catching hold or for hanging things on. **b** (also **fish hook**) a bent piece of wire, usu. barbed and baited, for catching fish. **2** a curved cutting instrument. **3** Hockey the illegal act of tugging at the puck carrier with the blade of one's stick. **4** Golf, Baseball, etc. **a** a ball's deviation from a straight line. **b** = HOOK SHOT. **5** Boxing a short swinging blow with the elbow bent and rigid. **6** something that captures attention or entices. ● v. **1** secure, catch, attach, or be attached with a hook. **2** (foll. by *up*) **a** connect or set up (electronic components etc.). **b** attach (a house, vehicle, etc.) to a central source of electricity, water, etc. **c** informal meet or become involved with. **3** Hockey illegally tug at the puck carrier with the blade of one's stick. □ **by hook or by crook** by any means, fair or foul. **get one's hooks on** (or **into**) get hold of. **hook, line, and sinker** entirely. **off the hook** informal **1** no longer in difficulty or trouble. **2** (of a telephone receiver) not on its rest, and so preventing incoming calls. **on the hook** informal responsible for.

hookah n. an oriental tobacco pipe with a long tube passing through water for cooling the smoke. [Say HOOK uh]

hooked adj. **1** hook-shaped. **2** furnished with a hook or hooks. **3** in senses of HOOK v. **4** informal (often foll. by *on*) addicted to or captivated by.

hooker n. slang a prostitute.

hooking n. Hockey the illegal tugging at the puck carrier with the blade of one's stick.

hook shot n. Basketball a one-handed shot in which the player lobs the ball over the head with a sweeping movement of the arm.

hookup n. a connection to an electrical system, communications system, etc.

hookworm n. **1** a parasitic nematode worm that attaches itself with a hooklike mouthpart to the wall of human or animal intestines. **2** a disease caused by one of these, often resulting in severe anemia.

hooky n. □ **play hooky** slang play truant.

hooligan n. a noisy and violent person. □ **hooliganism** n.

hoop ● n. **1** a rigid circular band. **2** a large ring rolled along as a toy or used in exercises. **3** Basketball **a** the round metal frame of the basket. **b** (also **hoops**) the game of basketball. ● v. bind or encircle with hoops.

hoop dance n. a dance among certain N American Aboriginal peoples in which many hoops are suspended from the arms, legs, and body to create patterns. □ **hoop dancer** n.

hoopla n. informal **1** extravagant publicity; hype. **2** commotion; excitement.

hoopster n. slang a basketball player.

hooray interj. = HURRAH.

hoosegow n. slang a prison.

hoot ● n. **1** an owl's cry. **2** the sound made by a train whistle etc. **3** a shout expressing scorn or disapproval. **4** informal **a** a shout of laughter. **b** a cause of laughter or merriment. ● v. utter or produce a hoot.

hootch n. = HOOCH.

hooter n. **1** a person or animal that hoots. **2** (usu. in pl.) slang a woman's breast.

hooves pl. of HOOF.

hop[1] ● v. (**hops**, **hopped**, **hopping**) **1** (of a bird, frog, etc.) spring with two or all feet at once. **2** (of a person) **a** jump on one foot. **b** make small jumps up and down on both feet. **3** move or go quickly. **4** traverse by hopping. **5** informal board (a vehicle, plane, etc.). **6** (usu. as **hopping** n.) (esp. of aircraft) pass quickly from one island etc. to another. ● n. **1** a hopping movement.

2 *informal* an informal gathering for dancing. **3** a bounce of a ball etc.

hop² *n.* a climbing plant whose dried flowers are used to give a bitter flavour to beer. □ **hoppy** *adj.*

hope ● *n.* **1** a feeling of expectation and desire for something to happen. **2** something that gives cause for hope. **3** what is hoped for. ● *v.* (**hopes, hoped, hoping**) **1** (often foll. by *for*) feel hope. **2** expect and desire.

hope chest *n.* a chest containing linen, clothing, china, etc. stored by a woman in preparation for her marriage.

hopeful ● *adj.* **1** feeling hope. **2** inspiring hope. **3** likely to succeed, promising. ● *n.* a person likely to succeed. □ **hopefulness** *n.*

hopefully *adv.* **1** in a hopeful manner. **2** (qualifying a whole sentence) it is to be hoped that.

hopeless *adj.* **1** feeling no hope; despairing. **2** admitting no hope. **3** inadequate. **4** without hope of success; futile. □ **hopelessly** *adv.* **hopelessness** *n.*

Hopi *n.* (*pl.* **Hopi** or **Hopis**) **1** a member of a N American Aboriginal people living chiefly in northeastern Arizona. **2** the language of this people. □ **Hopi** *adj.* [*Say* HOE pee]

hopped up *adj. slang* **1** intoxicated; stimulated with or as with a drug. **2** excited, enthusiastic.

hopper *n.* **1** a person who hops. **2** a container tapering downward, esp. one through which grain passes into a mill.

hopping *adj.* **1** *in senses of* HOP¹. **2** *informal* very active, lively.

hopscotch *n.* a children's game of hopping on one foot into and over squares marked on the ground.

horde *n.* usu. *derogatory* a large group or swarm.

horizon *n.* **1** the line at which the earth and sky appear to meet. **2** range or limit of mental perception, experience, interest, etc. □ **on the horizon** (of an event) just imminent or becoming apparent.

horizontal ● *adj.* parallel to the plane of the horizon, at right angles to the vertical. ● *n.* a horizontal line, plane, etc. □ **horizontally** *adv.*

hork *v. slang* spit.

hormone *n.* **1** a substance transported in tissue fluids such as blood or sap to stimulate cells or tissues into action. **2** (in *pl.*) *informal* the hormones regulating the sex drive. □ **hormonal** *adj.*

hormone replacement therapy *n.*

treatment with estrogens to alleviate menopausal symptoms.

horn *n.* **1 a** a hard usu. pointed permanent outgrowth on the head of cattle and other esp. hoofed mammals. **b** the hard substance of which animal horns are made. **2** each of a deer's antlers. **3** a horny projection on the head of other animals, e.g. a snail's tentacle etc. **4** anything resembling a horn in shape. **5 a** = FRENCH HORN. **b** a wind instrument played by lip vibration, originally made of horn, now usu. of brass. **6** a loudspeaker sounding a warning or other signal. □ **horn in** *slang* **1** (usu. foll. by *on*) intrude. **2** interfere.

horn of plenty a cornucopia. □ **horned** *adj.* **hornless** *adj.*

hornbeam *n.* a tree with a smooth bark and a hard tough wood.

hornbill *n.* a tropical bird with a large bony growth on its large curved bill.

hornblende *n.* a dark brown, black, or green mineral composed of calcium, magnesium, and iron silicates.

hornet *n.* any of various large social wasps with a severe sting.

hornpipe *n.* **1** a lively solo dance traditionally performed by sailors. **2** the music for this.

horn-rimmed *adj.* (esp. of eyeglasses) having rims made of horn or a substance resembling it. □ **horn-rims** *pl. n.*

horny *adj.* (**hornier, horniest**) **1** of or like horn. **2** hard like horn, callous. **3** wearing or having a horn or horns. **4** *slang* **a** sexually excited. **b** lecherous.

horoscope *n.* a forecast of a person's future based on the positions of the stars and planets at the time of birth.

horrendous *adj.* horrifying; awful. □ **horrendously** *adv.*

horrible *adj.* **1** causing or likely to cause horror; hideous, shocking. **2** unpleasant, excessive. □ **horribly** *adv.*

horrid *adj.* **1** horrible, revolting. **2** unpleasant. □ **horridly** *adv.* **horridness** *n.*

horrific *adj.* horrifying. □ **horrifically** *adv.*

horrify *v.* (**horrifies, horrified, horrifying**) arouse horror in; shock, scandalize. □ **horrifying** *adj.* **horrifyingly** *adv.*

horror *n.* **1** an intense feeling of loathing and fear. **2 a** intense dislike. **b** intense dismay. **3** a person or thing causing horror.

hors d'oeuvre *n.* (*pl.* **hors d'oeuvre** or **hors d'oeuvres**) a small item of food served as an appetizer or at a reception etc. [*Say* or DERV]

horse ● *n.* **1** a solid-hoofed plant-eating

quadruped with flowing mane and tail, used for riding and to carry and pull loads. **2** a padded wooden block used for vaulting over by gymnasts. **3** a frame or structure on which something is mounted or supported. ● *v.* (**horses, horsed, horsing**) *informal* (foll. by *around*) fool around. □ **from the horse's mouth** (of information etc.) from the person directly concerned or another authoritative source. □ **horsey** (also **horsy**) *adj.* (**horsier, horsiest**)

horse-and-buggy *adj.* old-fashioned, bygone.

horseback ● *n.* the back of a horse, esp. as sat on in riding. ● *adv.* on horseback.

horse chestnut *n.* **1** a large ornamental tree, with upright conical clusters of esp. white flowers. **2** the edible but bitter dark brown fruit of this.

horsefly *n.* (pl. **horseflies**) a fly, the female of which inflicts a painful bite on horses and other large mammals, including humans, to suck blood.

horseman *n.* (pl. **horsemen**) a rider on horseback.

horsemanship *n.* the art of riding on horseback; skill in doing this.

horseplay *n.* boisterous play.

horsepower *n.* (pl. **horsepower**) an imperial unit for measuring the power of an engine etc., equal to about 750 watts. Abbreviation: **hp**.

horseradish *n.* a plant of the cabbage family, grown for its pungent root which is grated as a condiment.

horse sense *n. informal* plain common sense.

horseshoe *n.* **1** an iron shoe for a horse shaped like the outline of the hard part of the hoof. **2** a representation of this as a good luck charm. **3** an object shaped like C or U (e.g. a magnet). **4** (in pl.) a game in which horseshoes are tossed at an iron stake.

horseshoe crab *n.* a large marine invertebrate with a horseshoe-shaped shell and a long tail spine.

horsewoman *n.* (pl. **horsewomen**) a woman who rides on horseback.

horticulture *n.* the art or science of gardening. □ **horticultural** *adj.* **horticulturist** *n.* (also **horticulturalist**).

hosanna *n. & interj.* (pl. **hosannas**) (esp. in Jewish and Christian worship) a shout of adoration and praise. [Say hoe ZANNA]

hose ● *n.* **1** a flexible tube conveying or spraying water. **2 a** (as pl.) stockings and socks. **b** *hist.* tights. ● *v.* (**hoses, hosed,**

hosing) **1** water or spray or drench with a hose. **2** *slang* deceive, swindle.

hoser *n. Cdn slang* **1** an idiot. **2** an uncultivated person, esp. a stupid, inarticulate, beer-drinking lout.

hosiery *n.* stockings and socks. [Say HOE zuh ree]

hospice *n.* a home for people who are ill (esp. terminally). [Say HOSS piss]

hospitable *adj.* **1** generous and friendly to visitors. **2** (of an environment) pleasant and favourable for living in. □ **hospitably** *adv.* [Say hoss PITTA bull]

hospital *n.* an institution providing medical and surgical treatment and nursing care for ill or injured people.

hospitality *n.* the friendly and generous reception and entertainment of guests or strangers.

hospitalize *v.* (**hospitalizes, hospitalized, hospitalizing**) send or admit (a patient) to hospital. □ **hospitalization** *n.*

Host *n.* the bread that is used in the Christian service of Communion.

host ● *n.* **1 a** a person who receives or entertains a guest. **b** an emcee or interviewer, esp. on television or radio. **c** an animal or plant having a parasite. **2 a** a large number of people or things. **b** (also **heavenly host**) the angels. ● *v.* act as host to (a person) or at (an event).

hosta *n.* a shade-loving perennial garden plant with large leaves and tubular flowers. [Say HOSS tuh]

hostage *n.* a person held in order to try to make others agree to a demand.

hostel *n.* **1** a place providing temporary accommodation for the homeless etc. **2** = YOUTH HOSTEL.

hostess *n.* (pl. **hostesses**) **1** a woman who receives or entertains a guest. **2** a woman who welcomes customers of a restaurant etc.

hostile *adj.* **1** of an enemy. **2 a** (often foll. by *to*) aggressively opposed. **b** showing strong dislike. **3** (of a takeover bid) opposed by the company to be bought. [Say HOSS tile or HOSS tull]

hostility *n.* (pl. **hostilities**) **1** hostile behaviour. **2** (in pl.) acts of warfare.

hot *adj.* (**hotter, hottest**) **1** having a high temperature. **2** feeling or producing an uncomfortable sensation of heat. **3** feeling or showing intense excitement, anger, lust, or other emotion. **4** currently popular, fashionable, or interesting. **5** *informal* (of goods) stolen. □ **blow** (or **run**) **hot and cold** *informal* be alternately enthusiastic and indifferent. **have the hots for** *slang* be sexually attracted to. **hot on the heels of** in close pursuit of. **hot under the collar** feeling anger or embarrassment. **not so hot** *informal* only mediocre.

hot air *n. informal* empty or boastful talk.

hot and sour soup *n.* an Oriental soup having a spicy and slightly acidic broth.

hotbed *n.* (foll. by *of*) an environment promoting the growth of something.

hot-blooded *adj.* ardent, passionate.

hot button *n. informal* an emotionally or politically sensitive topic or issue.

hot cross bun *n.* a sweet bun marked with a cross, traditionally eaten on Good Friday.

hot dog ● *n.* a hot wiener sandwiched in an elongated soft roll. **●** *interj. slang* expressing approval. **●** *v.* (**hot-dog; hot-dogs, hot-dogged, hot-dogging**) *slang* perform stunts. □ **hot-dogger** *n.*

hotel *n.* **1** an establishment providing meals and lodging for payment. **2** *Austral., NZ,* & *Cdn* a tavern.

hotelier *n.* a person who owns or manages a hotel. [*Say* HOTEL ee er]

hot flash *n.* a sudden feeling of heat during menopause.

hotfoot *v.* (**hotfoots, hotfooted, hotfooting**) hurry eagerly.

hothead *n.* an impetuous, fiery, quick-tempered person. □ **hotheaded** *adj.* **hotheadedly** *adv.* **hotheadedness** *n.*

hothouse ● *n.* **1** a heated building, usu. largely of glass, for rearing plants; a greenhouse. **2** an environment that encourages the rapid growth or development of something. **●** *adj.* characteristic of something reared in a hothouse; sheltered, sensitive.

hot key *n. Computing* a key that has been programmed to cause an immediate change such as the execution of a program.

hotline *n.* **1** a direct communication link between heads of government etc., esp. for emergencies. **2** a telephone link specially arranged for a particular purpose.

hotlink *n.* & *v.* = HYPERLINK.

hotly *adv.* **1** eagerly. **2** passionately. **3** angrily.

hot pants *pl. n.* very brief, tight shorts for women.

hot plate *n.* an electrical appliance with a flat surface for cooking.

hot potato *n.* (*pl.* **hot potatoes**) *informal* a controversial or awkward matter or situation.

hot rod *n.* a motor vehicle modified to have extra power and speed. □ **hot rodder** *n.*

hot seat *n. slang* a position of difficult responsibility.

hotshot *informal* **●** *n.* **1** an important or exceptionally able person. **2** a skilful player of football, basketball, etc., esp. one who is showy. **●** *adj.* **1** important, able, expert. **2** displaying skills in a flamboyant manner.

hot spring *n.* a spring of naturally hot water.

hot stuff *n. informal* **1** an important, impressive, or popular person or thing. **2** a sexually attractive person.

hot-tempered *adj.* impulsively angry.

Hottentot *n.* & *adj.* often *offensive* formerly used to refer to a people of southern Africa. [*Say* HOT un tot]

hottie *n. slang* a sexually attractive person.

hot tub *n.* a large tub filled with hot aerated water and used for recreation or physiotherapy.

hot water bottle *n.* a container, usu. made of rubber, filled with hot water, esp. to warm a bed.

hot-wire *v.* (**hot-wires, hot-wired, hot-wiring**) *slang* start the engine of (a car etc.) by bypassing the ignition system.

Houdini *n.* a person skilled at escaping. [*Say* hoo DEENY]

hound ● *n.* **1** a dog used for hunting, esp. one able to track by scent. **2** (usu. in *comb.*) a person keen in pursuit of something. **●** *v.* harass or pursue relentlessly.

hour *n.* **1** a twenty-fourth part of a day and night; 60 minutes. **2** a definite time of day, a specific point in time. **3** a period set aside for some purpose. **4** the present or a particular time. □ **the wee (small) hours** the hours after midnight, usu. 1 to 4 o'clock.

hourglass *n.* (*pl.* **hourglasses**) **1** a reversible device with two connected glass bulbs containing sand that takes an hour to pass from the upper to the lower bulb. **2** (as an *adj.*) narrow in the middle and curving strongly outward above and below.

hourly ● *adj.* **1** done or occurring every hour. **2 a** reckoned hour by hour. **b** (of a worker etc.) hired or paid by the hour. **●** *adv.* every hour.

house ● *n.* **1** a building for human habitation. **2** a building for a special purpose. **3** a building for keeping animals etc. **4** a religious community that occupies a particular building. **5** a family, esp. a royal family. **6** a firm or institution. **7** (**the House**) a legislative or deliberative assembly. **8** an audience in a theatre etc. **9** *Curling* the space within the outermost circle drawn around either tee. **10** = HOUSE MUSIC. **●** *v.* (**houses, housed, housing**)

1 provide (a person, a population, etc.) with accommodation. **2** store (goods etc.). **3** enclose or encase. □ **bring the house down** make the audience laugh or applaud loudly. **clean house 1** do housework. **2** wipe out corruption, inefficiency, etc. **like a house on fire 1** vigorously, fast. **2** successfully, excellently. **on the house** at the management's expense; free. □ **houseful** n.

house arrest n. detention in one's own house etc.

houseboat n. a boat equipped for living in, usu. on inland waters.

housebound adj. unable to leave one's house through illness etc.

housebreaker n. a person who breaks into a house or building intending to steal. □ **housebreaking** n.

housebroken adj. (of a pet) having been trained to urinate and defecate outside or in a litter box.

house call n. a visit made to a patient in his or her own home by a doctor etc.

housecleaning n. **1** the cleaning of the interior of a house or apartment. **2** the revamping of a company, department, etc. by eliminating personnel, reorganizing systems, etc.

housecoat n. a dressing gown.

housedress n. (pl. **housedresses**) a plain dress usu. of light cotton, for wearing around the house.

housefly n. (pl. **houseflies**) a small common fly often found in human habitations.

house guest n. a guest staying for some days in a private house.

household n. a house and/or its occupants. □ **householder** n.

household name n. (also **household word**) **1** a familiar name or saying. **2** a familiar person or thing.

househusband n. a husband who works full-time in the home, managing the household, etc.

housekeeper n. **1** a person employed to manage a household. **2** a person employed to manage the cleaning staff in a hotel, hospital, etc.

housekeeping n. **1** the maintenance of a household, including esp. cleaning chores etc. **2** maintenance, record-keeping, etc. in an organization.

house league n. Cdn **1** a sports league in which the players on all teams are members of the same school, organization, etc. **2** a league in children's sports in which

any child may play without having to pass a tryout.

housemaid n. a female servant in a house, esp. one who cleans rooms etc.

house music n. a form of fast popular dance music.

House of Assembly n. **1** Cdn (in Newfoundland and Nova Scotia) the provincial legislature. **2** the legislature in certain Commonwealth nations.

House of Commons n. (in Canada and the UK) the lower house of Parliament, composed of elected members.

House of Lords n. (in the UK) the chamber of Parliament composed of peers and bishops.

House of Representatives n. the lower house of the US Congress and other legislatures.

houseplant n. a plant suitable for growing indoors.

house-sit v. (**house-sits**, **house-sat**, **house-sitting**) live in and look after a house while its owner is away. □ **house-sitter** n. **house-sitting** n.

Houses of Parliament pl. n. (in Canada and the UK) the central legislative body, composed of a lower elected chamber and an upper appointed chamber.

house-to-house adj. & adv. calling at each house in turn.

house trailer n. **1** a trailer, such as that used in camping. **2** = MOBILE HOME.

house-train v. esp. Brit. train a pet to urinate and defecate outside or in a litter box. □ **house-trained** adj.

housewares pl. n. utilitarian household items, esp. kitchen utensils.

housewarming n. a party celebrating a move to a new home.

housewife n. (pl. **housewives**) a woman (usu. married) managing a household, esp. as her primary occupation. □ **housewifely** adj.

housework n. regular work done in housekeeping, esp. cleaning, laundry, etc.

housing n. **1** houses, apartments, etc. collectively. **2** a rigid casing, esp. for moving or sensitive parts of a machine.

housing development n. the planning and building of a large group of homes in an area.

housing project n. a government-subsidized housing development with relatively low rents.

HOV abbr. (pl. **HOVs**) high-occupancy vehicle.

hove past of HEAVE.

hovel *n.* a small miserable dwelling. [*Say* HUV'll *or* HOV'll]

hover *v.* **1** (of a bird, insect, etc.) maintain a stationary position in the air. **2** wait close at hand, linger. **3** be in an irresolute state; waver.

hovercraft *n.* (*pl.* **hovercraft**) a vehicle that travels over land or water supported on a cushion of air.

how *interrog. adv.* **1** in what way or by what means. **2** in what condition or health. **3** to what extent or degree. **4** the way in which. □ **how about 1** would you like. **2** what is to be done about it. **how do you do** a greeting on first being introduced. **how so?** how can you show that that is so?

however *adv.* **1** nevertheless; yet. **2** in whatever way or to whatever extent.

howitzer *n.* a short, relatively light gun for firing of shells at a high angle. [*Say* HOW itz er]

howl ● *n.* **1** a long loud doleful cry uttered by a dog, wolf, etc. **2** a prolonged wailing noise, e.g. as made by a strong wind. **3** a loud cry of pain, rage, amusement, etc. ● *v.* **1** make a howling sound. **2** (esp. of a child) weep loudly.

howler *n.* **1** *informal* a glaring and usu. amusing mistake. **2** a person or animal that howls.

howling *adj.* **1** that howls. **2** *slang* extreme.

how-to ● *adj.* instructive. ● *n.* (*pl.* **how-tos**) the instructions for doing something.

h.p. *abbr.* (also **HP**) **1** horsepower. **2** high pressure.

HQ *abbr.* headquarters.

hr. *abbr.* (*pl.* **hrs.**) hour.

HR *abbr.* **1** *Baseball* home run. **2** HUMAN RESOURCES.

HRDC *abbr. Cdn* Human Resources Development Canada, the federal government department responsible for employment and income support programs.

HRH *abbr.* Her or His Royal Highness.

HRT *abbr.* = HORMONE REPLACEMENT THERAPY.

HST *abbr. Cdn* HARMONIZED SALES TAX.

HT *abbr. Physics* high tension.

HTML *abbr.* HYPERTEXT MARKUP LANGUAGE.

http *abbr. Computing* hypertext transfer protocol, a protocol that supports the retrieval of data on the Internet.

hub *n.* **1** the central part of a wheel, rotating on or with the axle, and from which the spokes radiate. **2** a central point of interest, importance, activity, esp. an airport with major air traffic etc. **3** *Computing* a common connection point for devices in a network.

hubbub *n.* **1** a confused din, esp. from a crowd of people. **2** a disturbance or uproar.

hubby *n.* (*pl.* **hubbies**) *informal* a husband.

hubcap *n.* a cover for the hub of a vehicle's wheel.

hubris *n.* excessive pride or self-confidence. [*Say* HEW briss]

huck *v. Cdn* (*West*) *informal* throw.

huckleberry *n.* (*pl.* **huckleberries**) any of various low-growing N American shrubs of the heather family with edible dark blue berries.

huckster *n.* an aggressive salesperson or advertiser. □ **hucksterism** *n.*

huddle ● *v.* (**huddles, huddled, huddling**) **1** crowd together; nestle closely. **2** coil one's body into a small space. **3** confer, discuss. ● *n.* **1** (in team sports, esp. football) a gathering of players during a game to receive instructions on the next play. **2** *informal* a close or secret conference. **3** a confused or crowded mass of people or things.

Hudson's Bay blanket *n. Cdn* (also **Hudson's Bay point blanket**) a durable woollen blanket woven in a variety of patterns. □ **Hudson's Bay blanket coat** *n.*

hue *n.* **1** a colour; a particular shade of a colour. **2** a type of belief or opinion. □ **hued** *adj.*

hue and cry *n.* a loud clamour or outcry.

huff ● *v.* **1** give out loud puffs of air, steam, etc. **2** say in an offended or irritated tone. ● *n.* a fit of petty annoyance.

huffy *adj.* (**huffier, huffiest**) **1** apt to take offence. **2** offended. □ **huffily** *adv.*

hug ● *v.* (**hugs, hugged, hugging**) **1** squeeze tightly in one's arms, esp. with affection. **2** keep close to (the shore, curb, etc.). ● *n.* a strong esp. affectionate embrace. □ **huggable** *adj.* **hugger** *n.*

huge *adj.* (**huger, hugest**) **1** extremely large. **2** (of immaterial things) very great. **3** *informal* very popular, fashionable, or important.

hugely *adv.* **1** enormously. **2** very much.

Huguenot *n. hist.* a French Protestant in the 16th or 17th century. [*Say* HEW guh not *or* HEW guh no]

huh *interj.* **1** expressing disgust, surprise, inquiry, etc. **2** inviting assent.

hula *n.* (*pl.* **hulas**) (also **hula-hula** *pl.* **hula-hulas**) a Hawaiian dance with flowing arm and swaying hip movements.

hula hoop *n. proprietary* a large, usu. plastic hoop for spinning around the body by hula-like movements of the waist and hips.

hulk ● *n.* **1** the body of a dismantled ship. **2** *informal* a large unwieldy person or thing. **3** the shell of something abandoned or

destroyed. ● v. **1** move in a clumsy way. **2** be bulky or massive; rise like a hulk.
□ **hulking** adj.

hull ● n. **1** the body or frame of a ship, airship, etc. **2** the outer covering of a fruit or seed. ● v. remove the hulls from (fruit etc.).

hullabaloo n. (pl. **hullabaloos**) informal an uproar or clamour. [Say HULL a buh LOO]

hum ● v. (**hums, hummed, humming**) **1** make a low steady continuous sound like that of a bee. **2** sing (a wordless tune) with closed lips. **3** informal be in an active state. ● n. a humming sound. □ **hum and haw** hesitate, esp. in speaking.
□ **hummable** adj.

human ● adj. **1** of, belonging to, or characteristic of people or humankind. **2** showing (esp. the better) qualities of humankind, e.g. kindness, compassion, etc. ● n. (also **human being**) a person, esp. as distinguished from an animal. □ **humanly** adv. **humanness** n.

human capital n. an individual's or group's training, skills, etc., viewed as a resource contributing to economic growth.

humane adj. **1** benevolent, compassionate. **2** inflicting the minimum of pain.
□ **humanely** adv. **humaneness** n.

humane society n. an organization concerned with the protection and humane treatment of animals.

human immunodeficiency virus n. = HIV.

human interest n. (in a newspaper etc.) reference to personal experience and emotions etc.

humanism n. **1** an outlook or system of thought attaching prime importance to human rather than divine or supernatural matters. **2** a belief or outlook emphasizing common human needs, seeking solely rational ways of solving human problems. **3** (often **Humanism**) a Renaissance cultural movement which revived interest in ancient Greek and Roman thought and literature. □ **humanist** n.

humanitarian ● n. a person who seeks to reduce human suffering and improve life for human beings. ● adj. concerned with human welfare. □ **humanitarianism** n.

humanity n. **1 a** people in general. **b** the state of being a person rather than a god, an animal or a machine. **2** humaneness, kindness. **3** (**humanities**) learning concerned with human culture, such as literature, history, philosophy, etc.

humanize v. (**humanizes, humanized, humanizing**) **1** make human. **2** make more humane or civilized.
□ **humanization** n.

humankind n. human beings collectively.

human nature n. the general characteristics and feelings shared by humankind.

humanoid ● adj. having an appearance or character resembling a human. ● n. a humanoid being.

human race n. the division of living creatures to which people belong; humankind.

human resources pl. n. **1** the personnel or workers in a business, organization, etc. **2** the department in a business, etc. which deals with the hiring, training, etc. of employees.

human rights pl. n. basic rights held to belong to every living person, e.g. the right to freedom etc.

humble ● adj. (**humbler, humblest**) **1** (of a person) not proud; having or showing a low or modest estimate of one's own importance. **2** of low social or political rank. **3** not large or elaborate. ● v. (**humbles, humbled, humbling**) make humble. □ **eat humble pie** make a humble apology; accept humiliation.
□ **humbleness** n. **humbly** adv.

humbug n. **1** deceptive or false talk or behaviour. **2** an imposter. **3** Brit. & Cdn a hard usu. peppermint-flavoured candy. **4** nonsense, rubbish.

humdinger n. slang an excellent or remarkable person or thing.

humdrum adj. boring and always the same.

humerus n. (pl. **humeri**) the bone of the upper arm between the elbow and shoulder. [Sounds like HUMOROUS; for humeri say HUMOUR eye]

humid adj. (of the air or climate) warm and damp.

humidex n. Cdn a scale indicating the personal discomfort level resulting from combined heat and humidity.

humidify v. (**humidifies, humidified, humidifying**) make (air etc.) humid or damp. □ **humidifier** n.

humidity n. (pl. **humidities**) the amount of moisture in the air.

humiliate v. (**humiliates, humiliated, humiliating**) make humble; injure the dignity or self-respect of. □ **humiliating** adj. **humiliatingly** adv. **humiliation** n.

humility n. humbleness; a modest view of one's importance.

hummingbird n. a very small N American bird, which feeds from flowers while hovering and makes a characteristic humming sound.

hummock n. a hillock or knoll; a mound. □ **hummocky** adj. [Say HUM uck]

hummus n. a thick Middle Eastern dip made from ground chickpeas and tahini. [Say HUM us]

humongous adj. slang huge, enormous.

humorist n. a person who is known for his or her humorous writing or talking.

humorous adj. **1** showing humour or a sense of humour. **2** comic, funny. □ **humorously** adv.

humour (also **humor**) ● n. **1** the condition of being amusing or comic. **2** (also **sense of humour**) the ability to perceive or express humour or take a joke. **3** a mood or state of mind. **4** an inclination or whim. **5** (also **cardinal humour**) each of the four chief fluids of the body (blood, phlegm, yellow bile (choler) and black bile (melancholy)) that were formerly believed to determine a person's physical and mental qualities. ● v. agree with someone's wishes in order to keep the person happy. □ **out of humour** displeased. □ **-humoured** adj. **-humouredly** adv. **humourless** adj.

hump ● n. **1** a rounded protuberance on the back of a camel etc., or as an abnormality on a person's back. **2 a** a rounded, raised mound of earth etc. **b** a mountain or mountain range. ● v. **1** informal lift or carry (heavy objects etc.) with difficulty. **2** make or be humped or hump-shaped. □ **over the hump** over the worst. □ **humped** adj.

humpback n. **1** (also **humpback whale**) a large black baleen whale with a dorsal fin forming a hump. **2** = HUNCHBACK. **3** (also **humpback salmon**) = PINK SALMON. □ **humpbacked** adj.

humungous adj. = HUMONGOUS.

humus n. the organic constituent of soil, usu. formed by the decomposition of plants and leaves by soil bacteria. [Say HEW muss]

Hun n. a member of a warlike Asiatic nomadic people who invaded and ravaged Europe in the 4th–5th centuries.

hunch ● v. (**hunches, hunched, hunching**) **1** raise one's shoulders and bend the top of one's body forward. **2** sit with the body hunched. ● n. (pl. **hunches**) **1** an intuitive feeling or conjecture. **2** a hump.

hunchback n. **1** a person having a deformed, humped, or protruding back. **2** such a back. □ **hunchbacked** adj.

hundred card. num. **1** ten more than ninety. **2** used to express whole hours in the 24-hour system. □ **a** (or **one**) **hundred percent 1** entire(ly), complete(ly). **2** (usu. with neg.) fully recovered. □ **hundredfold** adj. & adv. **hundredth** ord. num.

hundredweight n. (pl. **hundredweight** or **hundredweights**) **1** (also **metric hundredweight**) a unit of weight equal to 50 kg. **2** US a unit of weight equal to 100 lb. (about 45.4 kg). Abbreviation: **cwt**.

hung ● v. past and past participle of HANG. ● adj. **1** (of a jury) unable to agree on a verdict. **2** (of an elected body) in which no political party has a clear majority.

Hungarian ● n. **1** a native or national of Hungary. **2** the language of Hungary. ● adj. of or relating to Hungary, its language or people. [Say hung GARY un]

hunger ● n. **1 a** a feeling of pain, weakness, or discomfort, caused by lack of food. **b** lack of food; famine. **2** a strong desire. ● v. **1** (often foll. by for, after) have a craving or strong desire. **2** feel hunger.

hunger strike n. the refusal of food as a form of protest, esp. by prisoners. □ **hunger striker** n.

hungover adj. informal suffering from a hangover.

hungry adj. (**hungrier, hungriest**) **1** feeling or showing hunger; needing food. **2** (also in comb.) eager, greedy, esp. for money, power, etc. □ **hungrily** adv.

hunk n. **1 a** a large piece cut off. **b** a thick or clumsy piece. **2** informal a sexually attractive, well built and ruggedly handsome man.

hunker v. **1** squat or crouch with the haunches nearly touching the heels. **2** hide or take shelter. □ **hunker down** apply oneself.

hunky adj. (**hunkier, hunkiest**) informal (of a man) well built and sexually attractive.

hunky-dory adj. informal excellent.

hunt ● v. **1 a** pursue and kill (wild animals or game) for sport or food. **b** (of an animal) chase (its prey). **2** seek, search. ● n. **1** an act of looking for something; a search. **2** an act of hunting wild animals. □ **hunt down** pursue and capture. □ **hunting** n.

hunted adj. (of a look etc.) expressing alarm or terror as of one being hunted.

hunter n. a person or animal that hunts.

hunter-gatherer n. a member of a people whose mode of subsistence is based on hunting animals and gathering plants etc.

huntsman n. (pl. **huntsmen**) a hunter.

hurdle ● n. **1** each of a series of light frames which athletes in a race must jump over. **2** an obstacle or difficulty. ● v. (**hurdles, hurdled, hurdling**) run in a hurdle race; jump over or clear a hurdle while running. □ **hurdler** n.

hurdy-gurdy *n.* (*pl.* **hurdy-gurdies**) a musical instrument with a droning sound, played by turning a handle with one hand and working keys with the other hand.

hurl ● *v.* **1** throw with great force. **2** utter (abuse etc.) vehemently. **3** *slang* vomit. ● *n.* **1** a forceful throw. **2** the act of hurling. □ **hurler** *n.*

hurly-burly *n.* boisterous activity; commotion.

Huron *n.* **1** (*pl.* **Huron** or **Hurons**) a member of an Aboriginal group formerly living around Lake Simcoe, with present-day populations north of Quebec City and in Oklahoma. **2** the Iroquoian language of this people. □ **Huron** *adj.*

hurrah *interj. & n.* (also **hurray**) an exclamation of joy or approval.

hurricane *n.* a tropical cyclone with winds greater than 65 knots (125 kph) accompanied by heavy rain, esp. one originating in the western North Atlantic.

hurried *adj.* **1** hasty; done rapidly owing to lack of time. **2** pressed for time. □ **hurriedly** *adv.*

hurry ● *n.* (*pl.* **hurries**) haste. ● *v.* (**hurries**, **hurried**, **hurrying**) **1** move or act or cause to move or act with great or undue haste. **2** *Curling* sweep. □ **in a hurry 1** hurrying; in a rushed manner. **2** *informal* easily or readily. **hurry up** make or cause to make haste.

hurt ● *v.* (**hurts**, **hurt**, **hurting**) **1** cause pain or injury to. **2** cause mental pain or distress to (a person, feelings, etc.). **3** suffer physical pain or mental anguish. **4** (foll. by *for*) have a pressing need for. **5** influence or be influenced adversely. ● *n.* **1** bodily or material injury. **2** harm, wrong. ● *adj.* **1** physically injured. **2** emotionally wounded.

hurtful *adj.* causing (esp. mental) hurt.

hurtle *v.* (**hurtles**, **hurtled**, **hurtling**) move or hurl rapidly or with a clattering sound.

husband ● *n.* a married man esp. in relation to his wife. ● *v.* manage carefully with a view to not wasting; use (resources) economically.

husbandry *n.* **1** farming, esp. the raising of livestock. **2** careful use of resources.

hush ● *v.* (**hushes**, **hushed**, **hushing**) make or become silent or quiet. ● *interj.* calling for silence. ● *n.* (*pl.* **hushes**) stillness or silence. □ **hush up 1** be quiet. **2** suppress public mention of (an affair).

hush-hush *adj. informal* highly secret or confidential.

hush money *n.* money paid to someone to prevent them from revealing information.

husk ● *n.* **1** the dry outer covering of some fruits or seeds. **2** the coarse leaves enclosing an ear of corn. ● *v.* remove the husk or outer covering from.

husky[1] *adj.* (**huskier**, **huskiest**) **1** (of a person or voice) sounding rough as if dry in the throat, often because of emotion; hoarse. **2** big and strong. □ **huskily** *adv.*

husky[2] *n.* (*pl.* **huskies**) a breed of dog used in the Arctic for pulling sleds.

hussar *n.* a soldier of a light cavalry regiment. [*Say* hoo ZARR *(with* HOO *as in* HOOK)]

hussy *n.* (*pl.* **hussies**) *derogatory* a wanton or impudent girl or woman.

hustings *n.* the political campaigning leading up to an election, e.g. canvassing and making speeches.

hustle ● *v.* (**hustles**, **hustled**, **hustling**) **1** push or move (someone) in a hurried, esp. rough and aggressive way. **2** move quickly. **3** work hard. ● *n.* (also **hustle and bustle**) busy movement or activity, esp. of many people. □ **hustler** *n.*

hut *n.* a small simple or crude house or shelter.

hutch *n.* (*pl.* **hutches**) **1** a box or cage for keeping small animals, esp. rabbits. **2** a usu. open shelving unit placed on top of a sideboard, desk, etc.

Hutterite *n.* a member of an Anabaptist sect living esp. in rural communal settlements and holding all property in common. □ **Hutterite** *adj.* [*Say* HUTTER ite]

Hutu *n.* (*pl.* **Hutu** or **Hutus**) a member of a Bantu-speaking people forming the majority population in Rwanda and Burundi. [*Say* HOO too]

hyacinth *n.* a bulbous plant with bell-shaped fragrant flowers. [*Say* HI a synth]

hybrid ● *n.* **1** the offspring of two plants or animals of different species or varieties. **2** a thing composed of mixed or incongruous elements. ● *adj.* formed from mixed, esp. incongruous elements. [*Say* HI brid]

hybridize *v.* (**hybridizes**, **hybridized**, **hybridizing**) **1** subject (a species etc.) to crossbreeding. **2 a** produce hybrids. **b** (of an animal or plant) interbreed. □ **hybridization** *n.* [*Say* HI brid ize]

hybrid offence *n.* *Cdn* a crime which may be treated as either a summary conviction offence or an indictable offence.

hydra *n.* (*pl.* **hydras**) a freshwater polyp with a tubular body and tentacles around the mouth. [*Say* HI druh]

hydrangea *n.* (*pl.* **hydrangeas**) a shrub

with clusters of small white, pink, or blue flowers. [*Say* hi DRAIN juh *or* hi DRAIN jee uh]

hydrant *n.* = FIRE HYDRANT.

hydrate ● *n. Chemistry* a compound of water combined with another compound or with an element. ● *v.* (**hydrates, hydrated, hydrating**) **1** combine chemically with water. **2** cause to absorb water. □ **hydrated** *adj.* **hydration** *n.* [*Say* HI drate, hi DRAY sh'n]

hydraulic *adj.* **1** (of water, oil, etc.) conveyed through pipes or channels usu. by pressure. **2** (of a mechanism etc.) operated by liquid moving in this manner. □ **hydraulically** *adv.* [*Say* hi DRAWL ick]

hydraulics *n.* the science of the conveyance of liquids through pipes etc. esp. as motive power. [*Say* hi DRAWL icks]

hydro *n.* **1** *Cdn* electricity. **2** hydroelectricity. □ **hydro** *adj.*

hydrocarbon *n. Chemistry* a compound of hydrogen and carbon.

hydrocephalus *n.* an accumulation of fluid in the brain, esp. in young children, which makes the head enlarge and can cause mental handicap. □ **hydrocephalic** *adj.* [*Say* hydro SEFFA luss, hydro suh FAL ick]

hydrochloric acid *n.* a corrosive acid containing hydrogen and chlorine.

hydrochloride *n.* a compound of an organic base with hydrochloric acid.

hydrocortisone *n.* a steroid hormone used to treat inflammation and rheumatism. [*Say* hydro CORTA zone]

hydrodynamics *n.* the science of forces acting on or exerted by fluids. □ **hydrodynamic** *adj.*

hydroelectric *adj.* **1** generating electricity by utilization of water power. **2** (of electricity) generated in this way. □ **hydroelectricity** *n.*

hydrofoil *n.* a boat equipped with a device consisting of planes for lifting its hull out of the water to increase its speed.

hydrogen *n.* a colourless gaseous element which is the lightest of the chemical elements and occurs in water and all organic compounds. [*Say* HI druh jun]

hydrogenated *adj.* add hydrogen to (an edible oil) to convert it into a saturated fat, usu. solid at room temperature. □ **hydrogenation** *n.* [*Say* hi DRAW jin ate]

hydrogen bomb *n.* an immensely powerful bomb utilizing the explosive fusion of hydrogen nuclei.

hydrogen peroxide *n.* an unstable liquid used in some disinfectants or bleaches.

hydrogen sulphide *n.* a poisonous gas with a disagreeable smell.

hydrography *n.* the science of surveying and charting seas, lakes, rivers, etc. □ **hydrographer** *n.* **hydrographic** *adj.* [*Say* hi DRAW gruh fee, hydro GRAPHIC]

hydro line *n. Cdn* a wire for the transmission of electricity.

hydrology *n.* the science of the properties of the earth's water, esp. of its movement in relation to land. □ **hydrologic** *adj.* **hydrologist** *n.* [*Say* hi DRAWL a jee, hydro LOGIC]

hydrolysis *n.* the chemical reaction of a substance with water, usu. resulting in decomposition. □ **hydrolytic** *adj.* [*Say* hi DRAWL a sis, hydro LIT ick]

hydrolyze *v.* (also **hydrolyse**) subject to or undergo the chemical action of water. [*Say* HYDRO lize]

hydrophobia *n.* **1** a morbid aversion to water, esp. as a symptom of rabies in humans. **2** rabies, esp. in humans. [*Say* hydro FOE be uh]

hydrophobic *adj.* **1** of or suffering from hydrophobia. **2** tending to repel or fail to mix with water. [*Say* hydro FOE bick]

hydroplane ● *n.* a light fast motorboat designed to skim over the surface of water. ● *v.* (**hydroplanes, hydroplaned, hydroplaning**) (of a vehicle) glide uncontrollably on the wet surface of a road.

hydroponics *n.* the process of growing plants in sand, gravel, or liquid, without soil and with added nutrients. □ **hydroponic** *adj.* **hydroponically** *adv.* [*Say* hydro PAWN icks]

hydrostatic *adj.* of the equilibrium of liquids and the pressure exerted by liquid at rest. [*Say* hydro STATIC]

hydrotherapy *n.* the use of water in the treatment of disorders, usu. exercises in swimming pools for arthritic or partially paralyzed patients.

hydroxide *n.* a metallic compound containing oxygen and hydrogen either in the form of the hydroxide ion (OH-) or the hydroxyl group (-OH). [*Say* hi DROX ide]

hydroxyl *n. Chemistry* the monovalent group containing hydrogen and oxygen, as -OH. [*Say* hi DROX'll]

hyena *n.* any of several carnivorous scavenging animals somewhat resembling a dog. [*Say* hi EE nuh]

hygiene *n.* **1** the branch of knowledge that deals with the maintenance of health, esp.

the conditions and practices conducive to it. **2** cleanliness. [*Say* HI jean]

hygienic *adj.* conducive to health; clean and sanitary. □ **hygienically** *adv.* [*Say* hi JEN ick *or* hi JEAN ick]

hygienist *n.* a specialist in the promotion and practice of cleanliness for the preservation of health. [*Say* hi JEN ist *or* hi JEAN ist]

hymen *n.* a membrane which partially closes the opening of the vagina and is usu. broken at the first occurrence of sexual intercourse. [*Say* HI mun]

hymn *n.* **1** a song of praise, esp. to God in Christian worship. **2** a song of praise in honour of a god or other exalted being or thing. [*Say* HIM]

hymnal *n.* a book of hymns. [*Say* HIM nul]

hype *slang* ● *n.* extravagant or intensive publicity promotion. ● *v.* (**hypes**, **hyped**, **hyping**) promote with extravagant publicity.

hyped up *adj. informal* very worried or excited.

hyper *adj. slang* hyperactive, high-strung.

hyperactive *adj.* **1** (of a person, esp. a child) showing constantly active and sometimes disruptive behaviour. **2** abnormally active. □ **hyperactivity** *n.*

hyperbola *n.* (*pl.* **hyperbolas** *or* **hyperbolae**) *Geometry* the curve produced when a cone is cut by a plane nearly parallel to the cone's axis. [*Say* hi PERBA luh *for the singular,* hi PERBA lee *for the plural*]

hyperbole *n.* (*pl.* **hyperboles**) an exaggerated statement not meant to be taken literally, used for emphasis, e.g. "I'm starving to death" said by someone who is merely very hungry. [*Say* hi PERBA lee]

hyperbolic *adj.* **1** of or relating to a hyperbola. **2** of the nature of or using hyperbole; exaggerated. [*Say* hyper BAWL ick]

hyperinflation *n.* monetary inflation at a very high rate.

hyperlink ● *n.* a software link in a hypertext system connecting cross-referenced items. ● *v.* connect by means of a hyperlink.

hyperreal *adj.* (esp. of an artificial environment or an artistic creation) created or represented with such attention to detail as to appear more real than reality. □ **hyperrealistic** *adj.* **hyperreality** *n.* [*Say* hyper REAL]

hypersensitive *adj.* abnormally or excessively sensitive. □ **hypersensitivity** *n.*

hypersonic *adj.* relating to speeds of more than five times the speed of sound (Mach 5).

hypertension *n.* abnormally high blood pressure.

hypertext *n.* a software system allowing extensive cross-referencing between related sections of text and associated graphic material.

Hypertext Markup Language *n.* the system of tagging used in hypertext to indicate how downloaded text should be formatted.

hyperventilate *v.* (**hyperventilates**, **hyperventilated**, **hyperventilating**) breathe at an abnormally rapid rate, resulting in an increased loss of carbon dioxide, and often accompanied by dizziness. □ **hyperventilation** *n.*

hyphen *n.* the sign (-) used to join words semantically or syntactically (as in *pick-me-up*, *rock-forming*), or to divide words into parts between one line and the next.

hyphenate *v.* (**hyphenates**, **hyphenated**, **hyphenating**) **1** write (a compound word) with a hyphen. **2** join (words) with a hyphen. □ **hyphenated** *adj.* **hyphenation** *n.*

hypnosis *n.* a state like sleep in which the subject acts only on external suggestion. [*Say* hip NOCE iss *(*NOCE *rhymes with* GROSS*)*]

hypnotherapy *n.* psychotherapy involving hypnotism. □ **hypnotherapist** *n.* [*Say* hip no THERAPY]

hypnotic ● *adj.* **1** of or producing hypnotism. **2** (of a drug) sleep-inducing. **3** (of a person's gaze, musical rhythms, etc.) producing a trancelike state or fascination. ● *n.* a thing, esp. a drug, that produces sleep. □ **hypnotically** *adv.* [*Say* hip NOT ick]

hypnotism *n.* the study or practice of hypnosis. □ **hypnotist** *n.* [*Say* HIP no tism]

hypnotize *v.* (**hypnotizes**, **hypnotized**, **hypnotizing**) **1** produce hypnosis in. **2** fascinate; capture the mind of (a person). [*Say* HIP no tize]

hypo *n.* (*pl.* **hypos**) *informal* = HYPODERMIC *n.*

hypoallergenic *adj.* having little tendency, or a reduced tendency, to cause an allergic reaction. [*Say* hypo al er JEN ick]

hypochondria *n.* abnormal and unnecessary anxiety about one's health. □ **hypochondriac** *n.* & *adj.* [*Say* hypo CON dree uh]

hypocrisy *n.* (*pl.* **hypocrisies**) behaviour in which someone pretends to have moral standards or opinions that they do not actually have. [*Say* hip OCKRA see]

hypocrite *n.* a person who pretends to have moral standards or opinions that they do not actually have. □ **hypocritical** *adj.* **hypocritically** *adv.* [*Say* HIPPO crit, hippo CRITICAL]

hypodermic ● *adj.* (of a needle, syringe, etc.) used to inject a drug etc. beneath the skin. ● *n.* a hypodermic injection or syringe. [*Say* hypo DERMIC]

hypoglycemia *n.* a deficiency of glucose in the bloodstream. □ **hypoglycemic** *adj.* [*Say* hypo glye SEAMY uh]

hypotenuse *n.* the side opposite the right angle of a right-angled triangle. [*Say* hi POTTA noose *or* -nooz *or* -nyooz]

hypothermia *n.* the condition of having an abnormally low body temperature. □ **hypothermic** *adj.* [*Say* hypo THURR me uh, hypo THURR mick]

hypothesis *n.* (*pl.* **hypotheses**) an idea or explanation that is used as a starting point for further investigation. [*Say* hi PAW thuh sis *for the singular*, hi PAW thuh seez *for the plural*]

hypothesize *v.* (**hypothesizes**, **hypothesized**, **hypothesizing**) assume as a hypothesis. [*Say* hi PAW thuh size]

hypothetical *adj.* **1** based on possible or imagined situations which are not necessarily real or true. **2** of or based on or serving as a hypothesis. □ **hypothetically** *adv.* [*Say* hi puh THET ick'll]

hyssop *n.* a small, bushy, aromatic herb of the mint family, used in cooking and herbal medicine. [*Say* HISSUP]

hysterectomy *n.* (*pl.* **hysterectomies**) the surgical removal of the uterus. [*Say* hista RECTA me]

hysteria *n.* **1** an emotional state, caused by grief or fear etc., accompanied by uncontrollable laughter, weeping, etc. **2** an excited and exaggerated reaction to an event. [*Say* hiss TERRY uh]

hysteric *n.* **1** (in *pl.*) a fit of hysteria. **2** *informal* overwhelming mirth or laughter. [*Say* hiss TARE ick]

hysterical *adj.* **1** of or affected with hysteria. **2** *informal* extremely funny or amusing. □ **hysterically** *adv.* [*Say* hiss TARE ick'll]

Hz *abbr.* hertz.

Ii

I¹ *n.* (also **i**) (*pl.* **Is** or **I's**) **1** the ninth letter of the alphabet. **2** (as a Roman numeral) 1.

I² *pron.* used by a speaker or writer to refer to himself or herself.

I³ *abbr.* **1** Island(s). **2** Isle(s). **3** (in the US) (used in designating highways) interstate.

iambic *adj.* (of poetry etc.) having a metrical pattern of one short (or unstressed) syllable followed by one long (or stressed) syllable. [*Say* eye AM bick]

IBD *abbr.* inflammatory bowel disease.

Iberian ● *adj.* of ancient Iberia, the peninsula now comprising Spain and Portugal; of Spain and Portugal. ● *n.* a native of ancient Iberia.
[*Say* eye BEERY un]

ibex *n.* (*pl.* **ibexes**) a wild goat-antelope with a chin beard and thick curved ridged horns. [*Say* EYE bex]

ibid. *abbr.* in the same book or passage etc.

ibis *n.* (*pl.* **ibises**) a wading bird with a curved bill, long neck, and long legs.
[*Say* EYE biss]

ibuprofen *n.* an analgesic and anti-inflammatory drug used esp. as a painkiller. [*Say* eye byoo PRO fin]

IC *abbr.* integrated circuit.

ICBM *abbr.* (*pl.* **ICBMs**) INTERCONTINENTAL BALLISTIC MISSILE.

ice ● *n.* **1 a** frozen water. **b** a sheet of ice used as a playing surface for hockey, curling, etc. **2** a frozen dessert made of fruit juice or flavoured water and sugar. ● *v.* (**ices**, **iced**, **icing**) **1** mix with or cool in ice. **2** cover or become covered with ice; freeze. **3** spread or cover (a cake etc.) with icing. **4** *Hockey* shoot (the puck) from one's own half of the rink to the far end of the other half. **5** *Cdn* select (a team or individual) to play in a hockey game. □ **on ice 1** (of an entertainment etc.) performed by skaters. **2** *informal* held in reserve; awaiting further attention. **on thin ice** in a risky situation.

ice age *n.* a period when ice sheets were particularly extensive, esp. in the Pleistocene epoch.

iceberg *n.* a large floating mass of ice detached from a glacier or ice sheet. □ **the tip of the iceberg** a small perceptible part of something (esp. a difficulty) the greater part of which is hidden.

iceberg lettuce *n.* any of various crisp lettuces with pale, compact leaves.

icebound *adj.* (of a ship, harbour, coast, etc.) surrounded, obstructed or sealed off by ice.

icebox *n.* (*pl.* **iceboxes**) **1** an insulated chest, cabinet, etc. for storing food, cooled by means of a block of ice. **2** esp. *US* a refrigerator.

icebreaker *n.* **1** a ship specially built or adapted for breaking a channel through ice. **2** something that serves to relieve inhibitions, start a conversation, etc. □ **icebreaking** *n.*

ice cap *n.* a permanent covering of ice e.g. in polar regions.

ice cream *n.* a frozen dessert made of cream or milk, sugar, flavourings or fruit, etc.

ice cube *n.* a small block of ice made in a refrigerator.

ice dancing *n.* (also **ice dance**) a form of esp. competitive figure skating based on ballroom dancing. □ **ice dancer** *n.*

iced tea *n.* (also **ice tea**) a cold drink of sweetened tea, often flavoured with lemon etc.

icefield *n.* **1** an expanse of ice, esp. in polar regions. **2** a large flat area of floating ice.

ice fishing *n.* the act or an instance of fishing through holes cut in the ice on the surface of a lake etc. □ **ice-fish** *v.* **ice fisherman** *n.*

ice fog *n.* fog made up of minute ice crystals suspended in the air.

ice hockey *n.* = HOCKEY 1.

Icelander *n.* **1** a native or national of Iceland. **2** a person of Icelandic descent.

Icelandic ● *adj.* of or relating to Iceland. ● *n.* the Scandinavian language of Iceland. [*Say* ice LAND ick]

ice milk *n.* a sweet frozen food similar to ice cream but containing less butterfat.

ice-out *n.* the time of year at which a body of water becomes free of ice.

ice pack *n.* **1** = PACK ICE. **2** a waterproof package containing ice or another frozen substance, used to cool an injured part of the body or to keep food cold.

ice palace *n.* **1** *Cdn informal* a hockey arena. **2** a large building made or carved from ice.

ice pick *n.* a pointed implement for breaking up pieces of ice.

ice road *n.* *Cdn* a winter road built across frozen lakes, rivers, etc.

ice sheet *n.* a permanent layer of ice covering an extensive tract of land.

ice-skate *v.* skate on ice. □ **ice-skater** *n.*

ice storm *n.* a storm of freezing rain, that leaves a deposit of ice.

ice time *n.* esp. *Hockey* **1** time spent by a hockey etc. player engaged in play. **2** the time during which a team, league, etc. may use an ice rink.

ice water *n.* water from, or cooled by, ice.

Icewine *n.* **1** esp. *Cdn proprietary* a very sweet wine made from ripe grapes left to freeze on the vine before being picked. **2** (**icewine**) a similar wine made in California from artificially frozen grapes.

ichthyology *n.* the study of fish. □ **ichthyologist** *n.* [*Say* ick thee OLLA jee *(with* TH *as in* THIN)]

ichthyosaur *n.* (also **ichthyosaurus**) an extinct marine reptile with a long head, tapering body, four flippers, and usu. a large tail. [*Say* ICK thee a sore *(with* TH *as in* THIN)]

icicle *n.* a hanging tapering piece of ice, formed by the freezing of dripping water.

icily *adv.* in a very cold way.

icing *n.* **1** a spread of sugar with butter or egg whites etc., used as a coating or filling for cakes etc. **2** the formation of ice on a ship or aircraft. **3** the act of icing the puck (see ICE *v.* 4). □ **icing on the cake** an attractive though inessential addition or enhancement.

icing sugar *n.* finely powdered sugar, usu. combined with a little cornstarch, for making icing for cakes etc.

ICJ *abbr.* International Court of Justice.

icky *adj.* (**ickier, ickiest**) *informal* **1** sweet, sticky, sickly. **2** (as a general term of disapproval) nasty, repulsive.

icon *n.* **1** a devotional painting or carving of Christ or another holy figure, esp. in the Eastern Church. **2** an image or statue. **3** a symbol or small graphic representation on a computer screen of a program, option, etc. **4** an object of particular admiration, esp. as a representative symbol of something.

iconic *adj.* **1** constituting a cultural icon. **2** of or pertaining to a computer icon.

iconoclast *n.* **1** a person who attacks cherished beliefs or conventions. **2** a

person who destroys images used in religious worship. □ **iconoclasm** *n.*

iconoclastic *adj.* [*Say* eye CONNA klast, eye conna KLAST ick]

iconography *n.* (*pl.* **iconographies**) **1** the visual images and symbols typical of an art form, an artist, a culture, etc. **2** the illustration of a subject by drawings or figures. □ **iconographic** *adj.* [*Say* ike un OGRA fee, eye conna GRAPHIC]

ICU *abbr.* intensive care unit.

icy *adj.* (**icier, iciest**) **1** very cold. **2** covered with or abounding in ice. **3** (of a tone or manner) unfriendly, hostile.

ID ● *abbr.* identification, identity: *ID card.* ● *v.* (**ID's, ID'd, ID'ing**) identify.

Id *n.* **1** (also **Id ul-Fitr**) a Muslim festival at the end of Ramadan. **2** (also **Id ul-Adha**) a Muslim festival marking the culmination of the annual pilgrimage to Mecca. [*Say* EED, eed ul FITRA, eed ul ODDA]

I'd *contr.* **1** I had. **2** I would.

id *n.* the part of the unconscious mind consisting of a person's basic inherited instincts, needs, and feelings.

id. *abbr.* *idem* (in the same place).

idea *n.* **1** a conception or plan formed by mental effort. **2 a** a mental impression or notion; a concept. **b** a vague belief or fancy. **3** an intention, purpose, or essential feature. □ **that's the idea!** that's the correct way to proceed etc. **what's the big idea?** expressing disapproval of effrontery, stupidity, etc.

ideal ● *adj.* **1** most suitable. **2** impossibly perfect; existing only in the imagination or as an idea. ● *n.* **1** a person or thing regarded as perfect. **2** an actual thing as a standard for imitation. **3** (usu. in *pl.*) an esp. moral standard of perfection.

idealism *n.* **1** the practice of forming or following after ideals, esp. unrealistically (*compare* REALISM). **2** the representation of things in ideal or idealized form. □ **idealist** *n.* **idealistic** *adj.*

idealize *v.* (**idealizes, idealized, idealizing**) consider or represent as perfect or ideal. □ **idealization** *n.*

ideally *adv.* **1** perfectly; in accordance with an ideal. **2** in theory or principle.

identical *adj.* **1** (of different things) exactly alike. **2** (of one thing viewed at different times) one and the same. **3** (of twins) developed from a single fertilized ovum, therefore of the same sex and usu. very similar in appearance. □ **identically** *adv.*

identification *n.* **1** the action of identifying someone or something or the fact of being identified. **2** an official document or other proof of one's identity.

identify v. (**identifies**, **identified**, **identifying**) **1** establish the identity of; recognize. **2** establish or select by consideration, analysis, etc. **3** associate very closely (with a party, policy, etc.). **4** (foll. by *with*) regard oneself as sharing characteristics of (another person). □ **identifiable** adj. **identifier** n.

identity n. (pl. **identities**) **1 a** the quality or condition of being a specified person or thing. **b** individuality, personality. **2** the state of being the same in substance, nature, qualities, etc.; absolute sameness.

identity crisis n. (pl. **identity crises**) profound confusion about one's identity and role in relation to society.

identity theft n. the obtaining of someone's personal information such as social insurance numbers, credit card numbers, bank account numbers, etc. in order to defraud the victim of money or impersonate them. □ **identity thief** n.

ideologue n. a person whose actions are influenced by a strong belief in a set of strict principles. [Say EYE dee a log or IDEA log]

ideology n. (pl. **ideologies**) **1** a system of ideas and principles forming the basis of a political or economic theory. **2** the set of beliefs held by a particular group which are used to justify actions, etc. □ **ideological** adj. [Say eye dee OLLA jee, eye dee a LOGICAL]

ides pl. n. the 15th day of March, May, July or October, or the 13th of other months in the ancient Roman calendar. [Rhymes with HIDES]

idiocy n. (pl. **idiocies**) utter foolishness; idiotic behaviour or actions. [Say IDDY a see]

idiom n. **1** a group of words whose meaning is different from those of the individual words, e.g. *down in the dumps*. **2** a form of expression peculiar to a language, person, or group of people. **3** a characteristic mode of expression in music, art, etc. [Say IDDY um]

idiomatic adj. **1** relating to or conforming to idiom. **2** characteristic of a particular language. [Say iddy a MAT ick]

idiosyncrasy n. (pl. **idiosyncrasies**) **1** a person's particular way of thinking, behaving, etc. that is clearly different from that of others. **2** anything highly individualized or eccentric. □ **idiosyncratic** adj. **idiosyncratically** adv. [Say iddy oh SINK ruh see, iddy oh sin KRAT ick]

idiot n. a stupid person; an utter fool.

idiot box n. (pl. **idiot boxes**) informal television or a television set.

idiotic adj. very stupid. □ **idiotically** adv.

idiot savant n. (pl. **idiot savants**) a person considered mentally retarded but who displays brilliance in a specific area. [Say idiot sa VONT]

idiot string n. (also **idiot strings**) Cdn a string attached to each of two mittens or gloves to prevent the mittens etc. from being lost.

idle ● adj. (**idler**, **idlest**) **1 a** not working, doing nothing. **b** lazy. **2** not in use. **3** (of time etc.) not occupied. **4 a** having no particular purpose. **b** trifling, ineffective, or worthless. ● v. (**idles**, **idled**, **idling**) **1** (of an engine) run slowly without doing any work. **2** be idle. **3** (foll. by *away*) pass (time etc.) in idleness. □ **idleness** n. **idler** n. **idly** adv.

idol n. **1** an image of a deity etc. used as an object of worship. **2** Bible a false god. **3** the object of excessive adulation.

idolatry n. **1** the worship of idols. **2** excessive devotion to or veneration for a person or thing. □ **idolater** n. **idolatrous** adj. [Say eye DOLLA tree]

idolize v. (**idolizes**, **idolized**, **idolizing**) venerate or love extremely or excessively.

idyll n. **1** a short poem etc. that describes a peaceful and happy esp. rustic scene. **2** a happy and peaceful esp. rustic place, event or experience. [Say ID'll]

idyllic adj. peaceful and beautiful; perfect, without problems. □ **idyllically** adv. [Say i DILL ick]

i.e. abbr. that is to say.

if ● conj. **1** on the condition or supposition that. **2** even though. **3** whether. **4** expressing wish or surprise. **5** with implied reservation, and perhaps not. **6** despite being. ● n. **1** a condition or supposition. **2** an uncertainty. □ **if only 1** even if for no other reason than. **2** (often ellipt.) an expression of regret or a wish. **ifs, ands, or buts** (usu. in neg.) reservations, arguments against.

iffy adj. (**iffier**, **iffiest**) informal **1** uncertain, doubtful. **2** of questionable quality.

igloo n. (also **iglu**) **1** a dome-shaped Inuit dwelling built of snow. **2** any other dome-shaped Inuit dwelling.

Iglulik n. (pl. **Iglulik**) (also **Igloolik**, pl. **Igloolik**) **1** a member of an Inuit people inhabiting the eastern Arctic, esp. living on Baffin Island and the Melville Peninsula. **2** their language. [Say ig LOO lick]

igneous adj. (esp. of rocks) produced by volcanic or magmatic action. [Say IG nee us]

ignite v. (**ignites, ignited, igniting**) **1** set fire to; cause to burn. **2** catch fire. **3** provoke or excite. □ **igniter** n.

ignition n. **1 a** the action of igniting the fuel in the cylinder of an internal combustion engine. **b** the mechanism for starting this process. **2** the action of igniting.

ignoble adj. (**ignobler, ignoblest**) dishonourable. □ **ignobly** adv. [Say ig NOBLE]

ignominious adj. shameful, disgraceful, humiliating. □ **ignominiously** adv. [Say igna MINI us]

ignominy n. (pl. **ignominies**) public shame and loss of honour; disgrace. [Say ig NOMMA nee or IGNA mini]

ignoramus n. (pl. **ignoramuses**) an extremely ignorant person. [Say igna RAY muss or igna RAM us]

ignorant adj. **1 a** lacking knowledge or experience. **b** (foll. by of, in) uninformed (about a fact or subject). **2** informal ill-mannered, uncouth. □ **ignorance** n. **ignorantly** adv.

ignore v. (**ignores, ignored, ignoring**) intentionally disregard. □ **ignorable** adj.

iguana n. any of various large lizards having a spiny crest along the back and throat appendages. [Say ig WONNA]

ikon n. = ICON 1, 2.

ileitis n. **1** inflammation of the ileum. **2** = CROHN'S DISEASE. [Say illy ITE iss]

ileum n. (pl. **ilea**) the last portion of the small intestine. [Say ILLY um]

ilium n. (pl. **ilia**) the bone forming the upper part of each half of the pelvis. [Say ILLY um]

ilk n. informal usu. derogatory a family, class, or set.

I'll contr. I will; I shall.

ill ● adj. **1** out of health; sick. **2** (of health) unsound. **3** unfavourable, harmful. ● adv. **1** badly, wrongly, or inefficiently. **2** scarcely. ● n. **1** injury, harm. **2** evil. **3** something unfriendly, unfavourable, or injurious. □ **ill at ease** embarrassed, uneasy. **speak ill of** say something unfavourable about.

ill-advised adj. **1** acting imprudently. **2** (of a plan etc.) not well formed or considered. □ **ill-advisedly** adv.

ill-bred adj. badly brought up, badly behaved.

ill-conceived adj. badly planned or conceived.

ill-considered adj. = ILL-ADVISED 2.

ill-defined adj. not accurately analyzed or described.

ill-disposed adj. unfavourably disposed.

ill effect n. a harmful or unpleasant consequence or result.

illegal ● adj. **1** not legal. **2** contrary to law. **3** Sport against or prohibited by the rules. ● n. an illegal immigrant. □ **illegality** n. (pl. **illegalities**) **illegally** adv.

illegible adj. not legible. □ **illegibility** n. **illegibly** adv.

illegitimate adj. **1** (of a child) born of parents not married to each other. **2** not allowed by a particular set of rules or by law. □ **illegitimacy** n. **illegitimately** adv. [Say illa JITTA mutt, illa JITTA muh see]

ill-equipped adj. not adequately equipped or qualified.

ill-fated adj. unlucky, doomed.

ill feeling n. bad feeling.

ill-founded adj. (of an idea etc.) groundless.

ill-gotten adj. gained dishonestly.

illiberal adj. intolerant, narrow-minded. [Say ill LIBERAL]

illicit adj. **1** unlawful, forbidden. **2** secret. □ **illicitly** adv. [Say ill LISS it]

illiterate ● adj. **1** unable to read or write. **2 a** having or showing little or no education. **b** ignorant in a particular field. ● n. an illiterate person. □ **illiteracy** n. [Say ill LITTER it]

ill-mannered adj. rude.

ill-natured adj. churlish, unkind.

illness n. **1** an ailment. **2** the state of being ill.

illogical adj. devoid of or contrary to logic. □ **illogicality** n. (pl. **illogicalities**). **illogically** adv.

ill temper n. irritability. □ **ill-tempered** adj.

ill-timed adj. done or occurring at an inappropriate time.

ill-treat v. treat badly or cruelly. □ **ill-treatment** n.

illuminate v. (**illuminates, illuminated, illuminating**) **1** light up. **2** help to explain. **3** decorate (a manuscript) with elaborate designs in brilliant colours. □ **illumination** n.

illuminating adj. helping to clarify or explain.

illumine v. (**illumines, illumined, illumining**) literary **1** make bright. **2** enlighten spiritually. [Say ill LOO min]

ill-use ● v. (**ill-uses, ill-used, ill-using**) treat badly. ● n. ill-treatment. □ **ill-used** adj.

illusion n. **1** a false idea or belief. **2** something that seems to exist, but in fact does not. **3** a figment of the imagination. **4** = OPTICAL ILLUSION.

illusionist *n.* a person who produces illusions, esp. a conjuror. □ **Illusionistic** *adj.*

illusive *adj.* deceptive; illusory. [*Say* ill OO siv]

illusory *adj.* based on illusion; not real. [*Say* ill LOOZA ree *or* ill LOOSE a ree]

illustrate *v.* (**illustrates**, **illustrated**, **illustrating**) **1** provide with pictures. **2** serve as an example of. **3** explain or make clear, esp. by examples. □ **illustration** *n.*

illustrative *adj.* (often foll. by *of*) serving as an explanation or example. [*Say* ILL us tray tiv]

illustrator *n.* a person who draws or creates pictures for books, etc.

illustrious *adj.* distinguished, renowned. □ **illustriousness** *n.* [*Say* ill LUSS tree us]

ill will *n.* bad feeling; animosity.

ill wind *n.* an unfavourable circumstance.

I'm *contr.* I am.

image ● *n.* **1** a representation of a person or thing. **2** character or reputation as generally perceived by the public. **3** a picture of someone or something seen on a TV or computer screen, through a lens, or reflected in something. **4** likeness. **5** an idea or mental representation. **6** a typical example. **7** a word or phrase that describes something in an imaginative way. ● *v.* (**images**, **imaged**, **imaging**) **1** make an image of. **2** imagine or form a mental picture of.

imagery *n.* (*pl.* **imageries**) **1** language that produces pictures in the minds of people reading or listening. **2** pictures, photographs. **3** visual images collectively.

imaginary *adj.* existing only in the imagination.

imagination *n.* **1** a mental faculty forming images or concepts of objects not present to the senses. **2** the ability of the mind to be creative or resourceful.

imaginative *adj.* having or showing imagination. □ **imaginatively** *adv.*

imagine *v.* (**imagines**, **imagined**, **imagining**) **1** form a mental image or concept of. **2** think or conceive. **3** guess. **4** suppose, be of the opinion. **5** as an exclamation of surprise. □ **imaginable** *adj.*

imaging *n.* the creation of images of internal organs etc. through tomography etc.

imaginings *pl. n.* things imagined.

imam *n.* **1** a leader of prayers in a mosque. **2** a title of various Muslim leaders, esp. of one succeeding Muhammad as leader of Shiite Islam. [*Say* im MAM]

IMAX *n. proprietary* a technique of widescreen cinematography using 70 mm film.

imbalance *n.* **1** lack of balance. **2** a lack of proportion or relation. □ **imbalanced** *adj.*

imbecile ● *n. informal* a stupid person. ● *adj.* stupid. □ **imbecilic** *adj.* **imbecility** *n.* (*pl.* **imbecilities**) [*Say* IMBA sill *or* IMBA sile, imba SILL ick, imba SILLA tee]

imbed *v.* = EMBED.

imbibe *v.* (**imbibes**, **imbibed**, **imbibing**) **1** drink (esp. alcoholic liquor). **2** absorb or assimilate. □ **imbiber** *n.*

imbroglio *n.* (*pl.* **imbroglios**) a complicated, confused, or embarrassing situation. [*Say* im BRO lee oh]

imbue *v.* (**imbues**, **imbued**, **imbuing**) inspire or permeate. [*Say* im BYOO]

IMF *abbr.* International Monetary Fund.

imitate *v.* (**imitates**, **imitated**, **imitating**) **1** follow the example of; copy the action(s) of. **2** mimic. □ **imitator** *n.*

imitation *n.* **1** an act of imitating a person's speech or mannerisms, esp. for comic effect. **2** a copy. **3** something made to look like something else.

imitative *adj.* imitating; following a model or example.

immaculate *adj.* **1** perfectly clean and tidy. **2** free from flaws or mistakes; perfect. □ **immaculately** *adv.* [*Say* im MACK yoo lit]

Immaculate Conception *n. Catholicism* the doctrine that God preserved the Virgin Mary from the taint of original sin from the moment she was conceived.

immanent *adj.* present within or throughout. [*Say* IMMA nint]

immaterial *adj.* **1** unimportant, irrelevant. **2** without physical form or substance.

immature ● *adj.* **1** not mature, ripe, or fully developed. **2** lacking emotional or intellectual development. □ **immaturity** *n.*

immeasurable *adj.* not measurable; immense. □ **immeasurably** *adv.*

immediate *adj.* **1** occurring or done without delay. **2 a** nearest in time or space. **b** (of family) designating those of closest relation, usu. parents, children, spouses, and siblings. **3** most pressing or urgent. **4** having direct effect. □ **immediacy** *n.* **immediately** *adv.*

immemorial *adj.* very old or long established. [*Say* im MEMORIAL]

immense *adj.* **1** immeasurably large or great. **2** considerable. □ **immensity** *n.*

immensely *adv.* very much.

immerse *v.* (**immerses**, **immersed**, **immersing**) **1** dip or submerge in a liquid. **2** absorb or involve deeply in a particular activity or condition.

immersion *n.* **1** a method of teaching a foreign language by the exclusive use of that language. **2** the action of immersing in a liquid. **3** baptism by immersing the whole person in water. **4** mental absorption in an activity etc.

immigrant *n.* **1** a person who immigrates. **2** an animal or plant that migrates into a given area.

immigrate *v.* (**immigrates, immigrated, immigrating**) **1** come as a permanent resident to a country. **2** (of an animal or plant) migrate to a different geographical region, esp. when this leads to continuous occupation of the area by the species. □ **immigration** *n.*

imminent *adj.* about to happen. □ **imminence** *n.* **imminently** *adv.* [*Say* IM in int]

immobile *adj.* **1** not moving. **2** not able to move or be moved. □ **immobility** *n.* [*Say* im MOE bile *or* im MOE bull, immo BILLA tee]

immobilize *v.* (**immobilizes, immobilized, immobilizing**) make or keep immobile. □ **immobilization** *n.*

immoderate *adj.* excessive; lacking moderation. □ **immoderately** *adv.*

immodest *adj.* **1** lacking modesty. **2** lacking due decency. □ **immodestly** *adv.* **immodesty** *n.* [*Say* im MODEST]

immolate *v.* (**immolates, immolated, immolating**) kill or offer as a sacrifice, esp. by burning. □ **immolation** *n.* [*Say* IMMA late]

immoral *adj.* **1** not conforming to accepted standards of morality. **2** morally wrong, esp. in sexual matters. **3** depraved, dissolute. □ **immorality** *n.* **immorally** *adv.*

immortal ● *adj.* **1 a** living forever. **b** divine. **2** worthy to be famous for all time. ● *n.* an immortal being. □ **immortality** *n.* **immortalize** *v.* (**immortalizes, immortalized, immortalizing**)

immovable *adj.* **1** unable to be moved. **2** unyielding. □ **immovably** *adv.*

immune *adj.* **1** resistant to a particular infection, toxin, etc. **2** free or exempt from or not subject to (some undesirable factor or circumstance). □ **immunity** *n.*

immunize *v.* (**immunizes, immunized, immunizing**) make immune, esp. to infection, usu. by inoculation. □ **immunization** *n.*

immunodeficiency *n.* a reduction in a person's normal immune defences. □ **immunodeficient** *adj.* [*Say* im yoono duh FISHIN see, im yoono duh FISH int]

immunoglobulin *n.* any of a group of structurally related proteins which function as antibodies. [*Say* im yoono GLOB yoo lin]

immunology *n.* the scientific study of resistance to infection in humans and animals. □ **immunological** *adj.* **immunologist** *n.* [*Say* im yoo NOLLA jee]

immunotherapy *n.* (*pl.* **immunotherapies**) the prevention or treatment of disease with substances that stimulate the body's production of antibodies. [*Say* im yoono THERAPY]

immutable *adj.* that cannot be changed; that will never change. □ **immutability** *n.* **immutably** *adv.* [*Say* im MUTE a bull]

imp *n.* **1** a mischievous child. **2** a small mischievous devil or sprite.

impact ● *n.* **1** the action of one body coming forcibly into contact with another. **2** an esp. strong effect or influence. ● *v.* **1** have an impact on. **2** come forcibly into contact with. □ **impactful** *adj.*

impacted *adj.* (of a tooth) wedged between another tooth and the jaw.

impact statement *n.* a formal written account of how a person, place, etc. has been or will be affected by something.

impair *v.* damage or weaken (esp. an ability).

impaired *adj.* **1** *Cdn* (of a driver or driving) adversely affected by alcohol or narcotics, esp. having a blood alcohol level greater than .08. **2** (usu. in *comb.*) disabled, handicapped. **3** that has been impaired. □ **impairment** *n.*

impala *n.* (*pl.* **impala**) a medium-sized reddish-brown grazing antelope of southern and eastern African savannah. [*Say* im PALA]

impale *v.* (**impales, impaled, impaling**) transfix or pierce with a sharp instrument.

impart *v.* **1** communicate (information). **2** give a particular quality to something.

impartial *adj.* treating all sides equally; fair. □ **impartiality** *n.* **impartially** *adv.* [*Say* im PAR shull, im parshy ALA tee]

impassable *adj.* impossible to travel on or through.

impasse *n.* a deadlock. [*Say* IM pass]

impassioned *adj.* ardent.

impassive *adj.* not showing any feeling or emotion. □ **impassively** *adv.*

impasto *n. Art* the process of laying on paint thickly. [*Say* im PASTO]

impatiens *n.* (*pl.* **impatiens**) a colourful, rapidly spreading garden plant. [*Sounds like* IMPATIENCE]

impatient *adj.* **1** lacking patience or

tolerance. **2** restlessly eager.
□ **impatience** n. **impatiently** adv.

impeach v. (**impeaches**, **impeached**, **impeaching**) esp. *US* charge (the holder of a public office) with misconduct. □ **impeachment** n.

impeccable adj. **1** faultless, exemplary. **2** flawlessly clean and tidy. □ **impeccably** adv. [*Say* im PECKA bull]

impecunious adj. having little or no money. [*Say* impa KYOONY us]

impedance n. the total effective resistance of an electric circuit etc. to alternating current. [*Say* im PEE dince]

impede v. (**impedes**, **impeded**, **impeding**) delay or stop the progress of something; hinder.

impediment n. **1** a hindrance or obstruction. **2** a defect in speech, e.g. a lisp or stammer. [*Say* im PEDDA m'nt]

impel v. (**impels**, **impelled**, **impelling**) **1** drive, force, or urge into action. **2** drive forward; propel.

impending adj. (usu. of an unpleasant event) that is going to happen very soon.

impenetrable adj. **1** that cannot be entered, passed through, or seen through. **2** impossible to understand. □ **impenetrability** n. **impenetrably** adv. [*Say* im PENNA truh bull]

imperative ● adj. **1** of vital importance. **2** commanding. **3** *Grammar* expressing a command (e.g. *wait!*). ● n. **1** *Grammar* the imperative mood. **2** a command. **3** an essential or urgent thing. □ **imperatively** adv. [*Say* im PAIR a tiv]

imperceptible adj. **1** that cannot be perceived. **2** very slight, gradual, or subtle. □ **imperceptibly** adv. [*Say* imper SEPTA bull]

imperfect ● adj. **1** not perfect; faulty, incomplete. **2** (of a tense) denoting a (usu. past) action in progress but not completed (e.g. *they were singing*). ● n. the imperfect tense. □ **imperfectly** adv.

imperfection n. **1** incompleteness. **2 a** faultiness. **b** a fault or blemish.

imperial adj. **1** of or characteristic of an empire. **2** of or characteristic of an emperor or empress. **3** (of weights and measures) used or formerly used in the UK and other Commonwealth jurisdictions. [*Say* im PEERY ul]

imperial gallon n. = GALLON 1a.

imperialism n. **1** an imperial rule or system. **2** usu. *derogatory* a policy of extending a country's influence over less developed countries through trade, diplomacy, etc. **3** advocacy or support for imperial interests. □ **imperialist** n. [*Say* im PEERY a lism]

Imperial Order Daughters of the Empire n. a Canadian women's organization founded in 1900, focusing on community affairs.

imperil v. (**imperils**, **imperilled**, **imperilling**) bring or put into danger

imperious adj. overbearing, domineering, expecting obedience. □ **imperiously** adv. **imperiousness** n. [*Say* im PEERY us]

impermanent adj. not permanent. □ **impermanence** n. **impermanently** adv.

impermeable adj. **1** that cannot be penetrated. **2** that does not permit the passage of fluids. [*Say* im PERMY a bull]

impersonal adj. **1** not influenced by, showing or involving human emotions. **2** objective. **3** having no personality; not existing as a person. **4** (of a verb) expressing an action without a definite subject (e.g. *it is snowing*). □ **impersonality** n. **impersonally** adv.

impersonate v. (**impersonates**, **impersonated**, **impersonating**) pretend to be (another person) in order to deceive or entertain others. □ **impersonation** n. **impersonator** n.

impertinent adj. rude or insolent; lacking proper respect □ **impertinence** n. **impertinently** adv.

imperturbable adj. not excitable; calm. □ **imperturbably** adv.

impervious adj. **1** not responsive (to an argument, outside influence, etc.). **2** not allowing water, gas, etc. to pass through. **3** able to withstand wear and tear; resistant. □ **imperviousness** n.

impetigo n. a contagious bacterial skin infection forming pustules and yellow crusty sores. [*Say* impa TIE go]

impetuous adj. acting or done rashly or with sudden energy. □ **impetuously** adv. **impetuousness** n. [*Say* im PETCH oo us]

impetus n. (*pl.* **impetuses**) **1** a driving force or impulse. **2** the force or energy with which a body moves. [*Say* IMPA tuss]

impiety n. (*pl.* **impieties**) a lack of piety or reverence. [*Say* im PIE a tee]

impinge v. (**impinges**, **impinged**, **impinging**) **1** have an esp. negative effect or impact. **2** advance over an area belonging to someone or something else; encroach. **3** strike, come into forcible contact; collide. [*Say* im PINDGE]

impious adj. **1** not pious; lacking reverence for God or a god. **2** wicked, profane.

□ **impiously** adv. **impiousness** n.
[Say IMPY us]

impish adj. mischievous. □ **impishness** n.

implacable adj. that cannot be appeased.
□ **implacably** adv. [Say im PLACKA bull]

implant ● v. **1** instill (a principle, idea, etc.)
in a person's mind. **2 a** insert (tissue, a
substance, or an artificial object) in a living
body. **b** (of a fertilized ovum) become
attached to the wall of the uterus. ● n. a
thing implanted in something else.
□ **implantation** n.

implausible adj. not seeming reasonable
or likely to be true. □ **implausibility** n.
implausibly adv.

implement ● n. **1** a tool or utensil. **2** a
piece of farm machinery. ● v. put (a
decision, plan, etc.) into effect.
□ **implementation** n. **implementer** n.

implicate v. (**implicates**, **implicated**,
implicating) **1** show (a person or thing) to
be concerned or involved (in a charge,
crime, etc.). **2** be affected or involved.
[Say IMPLA kate]

implication n. **1** the conclusion that can
be drawn from something although it is
not directly stated. **2** the state of being
involved in something.
[Say impla KAY sh'n]

implicit adj. **1** implied though not plainly
expressed. **2** essentially connected with;
always to be found in. **3** absolute,
unquestioning. □ **implicitly** adv.
implicitness n. [Say im PLISS it]

implode v. (**implodes**, **imploded**,
imploding) collapse violently inwards.

implore v. (**implores**, **implored**,
imploring) beg earnestly.
□ **imploringly** adv.

implosion n. a bursting or collapsing
inward.

imply v. (**implies**, **implied**, **implying**)
1 suggest rather than state directly.
2 involve as a necessary consequence.
3 insinuate, hint. □ **implied** adj.

impolite adj. rude. □ **impolitely** adv.
impoliteness n.

imponderable adj. difficult or impossible
to assess or estimate.

import ● v. **1** bring in (foreign goods) to a
country. **2** *Computing* bring (files etc.) from
one application into another. ● n. **1** an
imported article. **2** what is implied;
meaning. **3** importance. **4** *Cdn Sport* a player
who is enlisted from elsewhere, esp. a
football player from the US.
□ **imported** adj. **importer** n.
importation n.

important adj. **1** of great effect or
consequence; significant. **2** having high

status or great authority. **3** pretentious,
pompous. **4** of great concern to; highly
prized. □ **importance** n.
importantly adv.

importune v. (**importunes**,
importuned, **importuning**) ask (a
person) pressingly and persistently.
□ **importunate** adj. **importunity** n. (pl.
importunities) [Say im pore CHOON,
im PORCH a nit, im pore CHOONA tee]

impose v. (**imposes**, **imposed**,
imposing) **1** require (a charge or
obligation) to be paid or undertaken.
2 enforce compliance with. **3** demand the
attention or commitment of; take
advantage of.

imposing adj. impressive, esp. in
appearance. □ **imposingly** adv.

imposition n. **1** the action or process of
imposing or of being imposed. **2** an unfair
or resented demand or burden.

impossible adj. **1** not possible; that
cannot occur, exist, or be done. **2** (loosely)
extremely difficult, inconvenient, or
implausible. **3** *informal* outrageous,
intolerable. □ **impossibility** n.
impossibly adv.

imposter n. (also **impostor**) a person
who pretends to be someone else.

impotent adj. **1** unable to take effective
action; helpless or powerless. **2** (of a male)
unable to achieve an erection.
□ **impotence** n. **impotently** adv.
[Say IMPA t'nt]

impound v. **1** confiscate; take legal
possession of. **2** shut up (animals) in a
pound. □ **impoundment** n.

impoverish v. (**impoverishes**,
impoverished, **impoverishing**) **1** make
poor. **2** exhaust the natural fertility of.
3 weaken or reduce the quality of.
□ **impoverished** adj.
impoverishment n.

impracticable adj. impossible in practice.
□ **impracticably** adv.

impractical adj. **1** not sensible or realistic.
2 impossible to do. □ **impracticality** n. (pl.
impracticalities) **impractically** adv.

imprecation n. a spoken curse.
[Say impra KAY sh'n]

imprecise adj. not precise.
□ **imprecisely** adv. **imprecision** n.

impregnable[1] adj. **1** (of a fortress etc.)
that cannot be taken by force. **2** resistant to
attack or criticism. □ **impregnably** adv.
[Say im PREGNA bull]

impregnable[2] adj. that can be
impregnated. [Say im PREGNA bull]

impregnate v. (**impregnates**,
impregnated, **impregnating**) **1** make

(a female) pregnant. **2** fill or saturate. **3** fill (with feelings, qualities, etc.).
□ **impregnation** n.

impresario n. (pl. **impresarios**) an organizer or promoter of theatrical or musical productions.
[Say impra SAR ee oh or impra SARE ee oh]

impress ● v. (**impresses, impressed, impressing**) **1 a** affect or influence deeply. **b** evoke a favourable opinion or reaction from. **2** emphasize (an idea etc.). **3** apply (a mark) to something with pressure. ● n. (pl. **impresses**) a mark made by a seal, stamp, etc.

impression n. **1 a** an effect produced (esp. on the mind or feelings). **b** a striking or positive effect. **2** a notion or belief (esp. a vague or mistaken one). **3** an imitation of a person or sound, esp. done to entertain. **4** a mark impressed.

impressionable adj. easily influenced; susceptible to impressions.
□ **impressionably** adv.

Impressionism n. (also **impressionism**) an artistic style characterized by the depiction of visual impressions in terms of the shifting effect of light and colour.

impressionist ● n. **1** an entertainer who impersonates famous people etc. **2** (**Impressionist**) an artist who uses an Impressionistic style. ● adj. (**Impressionist**) of or relating to Impressionism or Impressionists.

impressionistic adj. **1** (**Impressionistic**) in the style of Impressionism. **2** based on subjective reactions presented in a random way.
□ **impressionistically** adv.

impressive adj. arousing admiration.
□ **impressively** adv. **impressiveness** n.

imprimatur n. **1** Catholicism an official licence to print an ecclesiastical book. **2** official approval. [Say impra MAT er or impra MATE er]

imprint ● v. **1** impress or establish firmly, esp. on the mind. **2** make a stamp or impression on a thing. ● n. **1** a mark produced by pressure on a surface. **2** a lasting impression of some emotion, experience, etc.

imprison v. **1** put into prison. **2** confine; shut up. □ **imprisonment** n.

improbable adj. **1** not likely to be true or to happen. **2** difficult to believe.
□ **improbability** n. **improbably** adv.

impromptu adj. & adv. without preparation; on the spur of the moment.
[Say im PROMP too]

improper adj. **1 a** unseemly; indecent.

b not in accordance with accepted rules of behaviour; dishonest. **2** wrong or incorrect.
□ **improperly** adv.

impropriety n. (pl. **improprieties**) **1** lack of propriety; indecency. **2** an action that is improper, dishonest, or morally wrong.
[Say impra PRY a tee]

improv n. informal improvisation, esp. as a theatrical technique.

improve v. (**improves, improved, improving**) **1** make or become better (than). **2** make (land) more productive or valuable by cultivation, clearing, etc.
□ **improved** adj. **improver** n.

improvement n. **1** the act or process of making something better or becoming better. **2** something that improves. **3** something that has been improved.

improvident adj. not providing for future needs. [Say im PROV a d'nt]

improvise v. (**improvises, improvised, improvising**) **1 a** compose or perform (music, dialogue, etc.) on the spur of the moment, not working from a text or score. **b** say or do (something) without preparation. **2** provide or construct (a thing) from whatever is available, without preparation. □ **improvisation** n. **improvisatory** adj. **improviser** n.

imprudent adj. not showing care for the consequences of an action.
□ **imprudence** n. **imprudently** adv.
[Say im PRUDENT]

impudent adj. not showing due respect for another person. □ **impudence** n. **impudently** adv. [Say IMP yoo d'nt]

impugn v. challenge or call in question (a statement, action, someone's character, etc.). [Say im PYOON]

impulse n. **1** impetus. **2** incitement or stimulus to action arising from a state of mind or feeling. **3** a sudden desire or tendency to act without reflection.
□ **impulsive** adj. **impulsively** adv. **impulsiveness** n.

impunity n. exemption from punishment or from injurious consequences. □ **with impunity** without having to suffer the normal consequences.
[Say im PYOONA tee]

impure adj. **1** mixed with foreign matter. **2 a** dirty or contaminated. **b** ceremonially unclean. **3** not morally pure.
□ **impurely** adv.

impurity n. (pl. **impurities**) **1** the quality or condition of being impure. **2** a thing which spoils the purity of something.

impute v. (**imputes, imputed, imputing**) (foll. by to) regard (esp. something undesirable) as being done or

caused or possessed by. □ **imputation** n.
[Say im PYOOT]

in ● prep. **1** so as to be enclosed,
surrounded, or inside. **2** expressing a
period of time during which an event takes
place. **3** expressing the length of time
before an event is to take place.
4 expressing a state or quality. **5** so as to be
included or involved. **6** indicating the
means of expression used. **7** expressing a
value as a proportion of (a whole). ● adv.
1 expressing the state of being enclosed,
surrounded, or inside. **2** present at one's
home or office. **3** expressing arrival. ● adj.
informal fashionable. □ **be in for** be going to
experience. **in that** for the reason that.
the ins and outs informal all the details.

in. abbr. inch(es).

in- prefix **1** adjectives, meaning "not".
2 nouns, meaning "without, lacking".

inability n. (pl. **inabilities**) the state of
being unable to do something.

inaccessible adj. **1** not accessible. **2** (of a
person) unapproachable. **3** (of language or
a work of art) difficult to understand or
appreciate. □ **inaccessibility** n.
inaccessibly adv.

inaccurate adj. not accurate.
□ **inaccuracy** n. **inaccurately** adv.

inaction n. lack of action where some is
expected or appropriate.

inactivate v. (**inactivates**,
inactivated, **inactivating**) make
inactive or inoperative. □ **inactivation** n.

inactive adj. **1** not active or inclined to act.
2 passive. **3** sedentary. □ **inactivity** n.

inadequate adj. **1** not enough; not good
enough. **2** (of a person) not able to deal
with a situation. □ **inadequacy** n. (pl.
inadequacies). **inadequately** adv.
[Say in ADDA quit]

inadmissible adj. that cannot be
admitted or allowed.
[Say in ad MISSA bull]

inadvertent adj. not resulting from
deliberate planning; unintentional.
□ **inadvertently** adv. [Say in ad VUR t'nt]

inadvisable adj. not advisable.

inalienable adj. that cannot be taken
away. [Say in ALIEN a bull]

inane adj. silly, senseless. □ **inanely** adv.
[Say in ANE]

inanimate adj. **1** not alive, esp. not in the
manner of animals and humans. **2** showing
no sign of life or vitality.
[Say in ANNA mitt]

inanity n. (pl. **inanities**) **1** silliness.
2 something silly or senseless.
[Say in ANNA tee]

inapplicable adj. not applicable.
[Say inna PLICKA bull or in APP licka bull]

inappropriate adj. not appropriate;
unsuitable. □ **inappropriately** adv.
inappropriateness n.

inarticulate adj. **1** unable to speak or
express oneself clearly. **2** not expressed
clearly. □ **inarticulately** adv.
[Say in ar TICK yoo lit]

inasmuch adv. (foll. by as) **1** seeing or
considering that. **2** in so far as.

inattentive adj. not paying due attention;
heedless. □ **inattention** n. **inattentively**
adv. **inattentiveness** n.

inaudible adj. not audible.
□ **inaudibly** adv.

inaugural adj. marking the beginning of
an activity or period of political office.
[Say in OGG yur ul or in OGG ur ul]

inaugurate v. (**inaugurates**,
inaugurated, **inaugurating**) **1** admit (a
person) formally to office. **2** open or
dedicate (a building etc.) by a ceremony.
3 begin, introduce, or initiate (a system,
policy, or period). □ **inauguration** n.
[Say in OGG yur ate or in OGG ur ate]

inauspicious adj. showing signs that the
future will not be good.
[Say in oss PISH us]

inauthentic adj. not authentic.

in-basket n. a tray on a desk etc. for
incoming documents.

in-between ● adj. informal intermediate.
● n. informal a person or thing that occupies
an intermediate position.

inboard ● adj. situated within a boat or
other vehicle. ● adv. within the sides of a
boat etc. ● n. **1** a boat with a motor
mounted within the hull. **2** a motor so
mounted.

inborn adj. innate, existing from birth.

inbound adj. coming in or homeward
bound.

inbox n. the window or file space in which
an individual user's received email
messages etc. are received, displayed, and
stored.

inbred adj. **1** produced by breeding among
closely related individuals. **2** existing from
birth.

inbreeding n. breeding between closely
related animals or persons, often with
undesirable results. □ **inbreed** v.

Inc. abbr. Incorporated.

Inca n. (pl. **Inca** or **Incas**) a member of a
S American Aboriginal people who
established an empire in the central Andes
before the Spanish conquest in the early
16th century. □ **Incan** adj.

incalculable adj. **1** very large or very

great. **2** that cannot be measured or calculated.

incandescent *adj.* **1** (of a light) produced by a glowing white-hot filament. **2** glowing with heat. □ **incandescence** *n.*
[*Say* in can DESS'nt]

incantation *n.* words uttered as a magic spell. □ **incantatory** *adj.*
[*Say* in can TAY sh'n, in CANTA tory]

incapable *adj.* incompetent, not capable. □ **incapably** *adv.*

incapacitate *v.* (**incapacitates, incapacitated, incapacitating**) prevent (a person) from functioning in a normal way. □ **incapacitation** *n.*
[*Say* inca PASSA tate]

incapacity *n.* (*pl.* **incapacities**) inability; lack of the necessary power or resources. [*Say* in CAPACITY]

incarcerate *v.* (**incarcerates, incarcerated, incarcerating**) imprison or confine. □ **incarceration** *n.*
[*Say* in KARSA rate]

incarnate ● *adj.* embodied in human or physical form. ● *v.* (**incarnates, incarnated, incarnating**) **1** embody or represent (a deity or spirit) in human form. **2** put (an idea etc.) into concrete form. **3** be the living embodiment of (a quality etc.).
[*Say* in CAR nit *for the adjective,* in CAR nate *for the verb*]

incarnation *n.* **1** the form assumed by a person or thing at a particular time. **2** the embodiment of a deity etc. in esp. human flesh. **3** a living embodiment (of a quality etc.).

incendiary ● *adj.* **1** designed to cause fires. **2** tending to stir up conflict. ● *n.* (*pl.* **incendiaries**) an incendiary bomb or device. [*Say* in SENDY airy]

incense *v.* (**incenses, incensed, incensing**) **1** a gum or spice producing a sweet smell when burned. **2** the smoke of this used esp. in religious ceremonies.
[*Say* IN sense]

incensed *adj.* enraged. [*Say* in SENSED]

incentive *n.* a thing that motivates or encourages a person to do something.
[*Say* in SEN tiv]

inception *n.* the starting point of an institution or activity. [*Say* in SEP sh'n]

incessant *adj.* unceasing, continual. □ **incessantly** *adv.* [*Say* in SESS'nt]

incest *n.* sexual intercourse between parent and child or grandchild, or siblings or half-siblings.

incestuous *adj.* **1** involving incest. **2** interconnected in an unwholesome way. □ **incestuously** *adv.* **incestuousness** *n.* [*Say* in SESS choo us]

inch ● *n.* (*pl.* **inches**) **1** a unit of linear

measure equal to one-twelfth of a foot (2.54 cm). **2** (as a unit of rainfall) a quantity that would cover a surface to a depth of 1 inch. **3** a small amount. ● *v.* (**inches, inched, inching**) move gradually. □ **by inches 1** only just. **2** gradually. **every inch** entirely. **within an inch of one's life 1** completely, thoroughly **2** almost to death; severely.

inchoate *adj.* **1** just begun or starting to develop. **2** not fully formed or developed; incoherent. [*Say* in CO it *or* in CO ate]

inchworm *n.* a caterpillar which moves by alternately hunching and stretching its body.

incidence *n.* **1** the occurrence, rate, or frequency of something undesirable. **2** *Physics* the way in which esp. a ray of light strikes a surface. [*Say* INSA dince]

incident ● *n.* **1** an esp. minor but noteworthy event or occurrence. **2 a** a military clash. **b** an accident, public disturbance, or other trouble. ● *adj.* **1** resulting from. **2** (of light etc.) falling upon a surface.

incidental ● *adj.* **1** having a minor role in relation to something more important. **2** happening by chance in connection with something else. **3** (of an expense) incurred apart from the main sum disbursed. ● *n.* (usu. in *pl.*) a minor detail, expense, etc.

incidentally *adv.* **1** by the way; as a further thought or unconnected remark. **2** in an incidental way.

incinerate *v.* (**incinerates, incinerated, incinerating**) destroy completely by burning. □ **incineration** *n.* **incinerator** *n.* [*Say* in SINNA rate]

incipient *adj.* just beginning to develop. [*Say* in SIPPY int]

incise *v.* (**incises, incised, incising**) **1** make a cut in. **2** engrave (letters etc.). □ **incised** *adj.* [*Say* in SIZE]

incision *n.* **1** a cut made during surgery. **2** a mark cut into a surface. [*Say* in SIZH un]

incisive *adj.* **1** showing clear thought and good understanding. **2** (of a comment etc.) cutting, penetrating. □ **incisively** *adv.* **incisiveness** *n.*

incisor *n.* a sharp cutting tooth, esp., in humans, any of the eight front teeth. [*Say* in SIZE er]

incite *v.* (**incites, incited, inciting**) urge or stir up. □ **incitement** *n.*

inclement *adj.* (of the weather or climate) severe, esp. cold, rainy, or stormy. [*Say* in CLEM'nt]

inclination *n.* **1** a disposition or tendency. **2** a liking or affection. **3** a leaning, slope, or slant. **4** the action of bending towards something. **5** *Math* the angular difference between two lines or planes. [*Say* in kluh NATION]

incline ● *v.* (**inclines, inclined, inclining**) **1** be disposed; tend. **2** lean in or away from a given direction. **3** bend forward, downward, or toward a thing. ● *n.* a slope, esp. on a road or railway.

inclined *adj.* **1** sloping, slanted. **2** having a natural ability or tendency.

include *v.* (**includes, included, including**) **1** involve or comprise as part of a whole. **2** treat or regard as part of the whole.

including *prep.* taking into account, inclusive of.

inclusion *n.* **1** the action or state of including or being included. **2** a person or thing that is included.

inclusive *adj.* **1** including, comprising. **2** including all the normal services etc. **3 a** not excluding any section of society. **b** (of language) deliberately non-sexist. □ **inclusively** *adv.* **inclusiveness** *n.*

incognito *adj. & adv.* with one's name or identity kept secret. [*Say* in cog NEAT oh]

incoherent *adj.* **1** (of a person) unable to speak intelligibly. **2** (of speech, thought, etc.) disjointed, lacking logic or consistency. □ **incoherence** *n.* **incoherently** *adv.* [*Say* inco HEAR int]

income *n.* the money or other assets received from one's business, work, etc.

income tax *n.* a tax levied on income.

incoming *adj.* **1** coming in. **2** succeeding another person or persons.

incommensurable *adj.* not able to be measured or judged by the same standards. [*Say* inca MEN shurra bull]

incommunicado *adj. & adv.* not wanting or able to communicate with others. [*Say* inca myoona KODDO *or* inca myoona KADDO]

incomparable *adj.* **1** without an equal in quality. **2** totally different in nature or extent. □ **incomparably** *adv.* [*Say* in COM purra bull]

incompatible *adj.* **1** opposed in character. **2** not consistent or in logical agreement. **3** unable to live, work, etc., together in harmony. **4** (of equipment etc.) not capable of being used in combination with some other item. □ **incompatibility** *n.*

incompetent *adj.* not having the necessary skills to do something successfully. □ **incompetence** *n.* **incompetently** *adv.*

incomplete *adj.* **1** not complete. **2** *Football* (of a forward pass) not completed.

□ **incompletely** *adv.* **incompleteness** *n.* **incompletion** *n.*

incomprehensible *adj.* that cannot be understood.

incomprehension *n.* failure to understand.

inconceivable *adj.* impossible to imagine or believe. □ **inconceivably** *adv.*

inconclusive *adj.* not leading to a definite conclusion or result. □ **inconclusively** *adv.* **inconclusiveness** *n.*

incongruous *adj.* not in harmony or in keeping with the surroundings or other aspects of something. □ **incongruity** (*pl.* **incongruities**) *n.* [*Say* in CON grew us, in cun GROOWA tee]

inconnu *n.* (*pl.* **inconnu**) an Arctic freshwater game fish. [*Say* IN canoe]

inconsequential *adj.* trivial, unimportant. [*Say* in consa KWEN shull]

inconsiderate *adj.* **1** lacking consideration for the feelings of others. **2** rash. □ **inconsiderately** *adv.*

inconsistent *adj.* **1** acting in a manner not in keeping with one's usual conduct. **2** not compatible with. **3** (of a single thing) not staying the same throughout. **4** erratic in behaviour or action. □ **inconsistency** *n.* **inconsistently** *adv.*

inconsolable *adj.* that cannot be consoled or comforted. □ **inconsolably** *adv.* [*Say* in cun SOLE a bull]

inconspicuous *adj.* not easily noticed. □ **inconspicuously** *adv.* [*Say* in cun SPICK yoo us]

inconstant *adj.* **1** (of a person) fickle, changeable. **2** variable, irregular. □ **inconstantly** *adv.*

incontestable *adj.* unquestionable, not open to argument. □ **incontestably** *adv.*

incontinent *adj.* **1** unable to control movements of the bowels or bladder or both. **2** lacking self-restraint. □ **incontinence** *n.*

incontrovertible *adj.* indisputable. □ **incontrovertibly** *adv.* [*Say* in contra VERTA bull]

inconvenience ● *n.* **1** trouble or problems. **2** a person or thing that causes problems or difficulties. ● *v.* (**inconveniences, inconvenienced, inconveniencing**) cause trouble or difficulty for someone. □ **inconvenient** *adj.* **inconveniently** *adv.*

incorporate *v.* (**incorporates, incorporated, incorporating**) **1** include something so that it forms a part of something. **2** combine or form into an organization, esp. constitute as a legal

corporation. □ **incorporated** *adj.*
incorporation *n.*

incorrect *adj.* not in accordance with fact
or accepted standards. □ **incorrectly** *adv.*
incorrectness *n.*

incorrigible *adj.* not able to be corrected,
improved, or reformed. □ **incorrigibly** *adv.*
[*Say* in CORA juh bull]

incorruptible *adj.* **1** unable to be
corrupted, esp. unable to be bribed. **2** not
susceptible to decay.
[*Say* in CORRUPT a bull]

increase ● *v.* (**increases**, **increased**,
increasing) **1** make or become greater in
size, amount, etc. **2** intensify (a quality).
● *n.* **1** the act or process of increasing. **2** (of
people, animals, or plants) growth in
numbers. **3** the amount or extent of an
increase. □ **increasingly** *adv.*

incredible *adj.* **1** that cannot be believed.
2 *informal* amazing, extraordinary.
□ **incredibly** *adv.*

incredulous *adj.* **1** unwilling to believe,
skeptical. **2** showing disbelief.
□ **incredulously** *adv.* **incredulity** *n.*
[*Say* in CRED yoo luss, incra DYOOLA tee]

increment *n.* **1** an increase or addition.
2 *Math* a small amount by which a variable
quantity increases. □ **incremental** *adj.*
incrementally *adv.* [*Say* INCRA m'nt,
incra MENTAL]

incriminate *v.* (**incriminates**,
incriminated, **incriminating**) **1** make
someone appear guilty of a crime or
wrongdoing. **2** accuse. □ **incrimination** *n.*
[*Say* in CRIMMIN ate]

incubate *v.* (**incubates**, **incubated**,
incubating) **1** sit on or artificially heat
(eggs) so they will hatch. **2** maintain (cells,
micro-organisms, etc.) in a controlled
environment suitable for growth.
3 undergo incubation. **4** develop or grow
slowly.

incubation *n.* **1** the act of incubating.
2 (also **incubation period**) the period
between exposure to an infection and the
appearance of the first symptoms.

incubator *n.* **1** an apparatus used to
provide a suitable temperature and
environment for a premature or very small
baby. **2** an apparatus used to hatch eggs or
grow micro-organisms.

incubus *n.* (*pl.* **incubi**) **1** a male demon
believed to have sexual intercourse with
sleeping women. **2** a person or thing that
oppresses or troubles like a nightmare.
[*Say* INK yoo bus *for the singular*,
INK yoo bye *for the plural*]

inculcate *v.* (**inculcates**, **inculcated**,
inculcating) urge or impress (a fact,

habit, idea, etc.) persistently.
□ **inculcation** *n.* [*Say* IN cull kate]

incumbent ● *adj.* **1** currently holding
office. **2** resting upon a person as a duty.
● *n.* the holder of an office or post.
□ **incumbency** *n.* [*Say* in CUM b'nt]

incur *v.* (**incurs**, **incurred**, **incurring**)
bring (something unwelcome) upon
oneself. [*Say* in CUR]

incurable *adj.* **1** unable to be cured. **2** not
likely to be reformed. □ **incurably** *adv.*

incursion *n.* **1** an esp. brief invasion or
attack. **2** an interruption or disturbance.

indebted *adj.* **1** owing gratitude or
obligation. **2** owing money.
□ **indebtedness** *n.* [*Say* in DET id]

indecent *adj.* **1** offending against
recognized standards of decency.
2 unbecoming; highly unsuitable.
□ **indecency** (*pl.* **indecencies**) *n.*
indecently *adv.*

indecent exposure *n.* the intentional
act of indecently exposing one's body in
public.

indecipherable *adj.* that cannot be read
or understood.

indecisive *adj.* not decisive. □ **indecision**
n. **indecisiveness** *n.*

indeed *adv.* **1** in truth. **2** expressing
emphasis. **3** admittedly.

indefatigable *adj.* that cannot be tired
out. □ **indefatigably** *adv.*
[*Say* in duh FATTA guh bull]

indefensible *adj.* that cannot be defended
or justified. [*Say* in duh FENCE a bull]

indefinable *adj.* that cannot be defined or
exactly described. [*Say* in duh FINE a bull]

indefinite *adj.* **1** not clearly defined or
stated; vague. **2** of undetermined extent or
number; unlimited. □ **indefinitely** *adv.*
[*Say* in DEFFA nit, in DEFFA nit lee]

indefinite article *n.* *Grammar* a word (*a* or
an in English) preceding a noun and
implying lack of specificity.

indelible *adj.* not able to be forgotten or
removed. □ **indelibly** *adv.*
[*Say* in DELLA bull]

indelicate *adj.* **1** coarse, unrefined.
2 tactless. **3** tending to indecency.

indemnify *v.* (**indemnifies**,
indemnified, **indemnifying**) **1** protect
or secure (a person) against harm, loss, etc.
2 secure (a person) against legal
responsibility for actions. **3** compensate for
a loss etc. [*Say* in DEMNA fie]

indemnity *n.* (*pl.* **indemnities**)
1 a compensation for loss incurred. **b** a
sum paid for this. **2** security against loss.
3 legal exemption from penalties etc. **4** *Cdn*
a salary paid to a Member of Parliament or

of a Legislative Assembly.
[*Say* in DEMNA tee]

indent ● *v.* **1** start (a line of print) further from the margin than other lines. **2** form deep recesses or dents in. ● *n.* an indentation in printing. □ **indentation** *n.*

indenture ● *n.* (usu. in *pl.*) **1** a sealed agreement or contract. **2** a contract binding a person to service. ● *v.* (**indentures, indentured, indenturing**) bind by indentures. □ **indentured** *adj.*

indépendantiste *Cdn* *n. & adj.* (of or relating to) a person who supports Quebec sovereignty. [*Say* an day pon don TEEST]

independence *n.* the state of being or becoming independent.

independent ● *adj.* **1 a** free from outside influence or control. **b** (of a state) self-governing. **2** having or earning enough money to support oneself. **3** unwilling to be under an obligation to others. **4** *Politics* not belonging to or supported by a party. **5** not depending on something else for validity, value, etc. **6** impartial. **7** not part of a chain or large corporate structure. ● *n.* an independent person or organization. □ **independently** *adv.*

in-depth *adj.* thorough.

indescribable *adj.* **1** too unusual or extreme to be described. **2** vague. □ **indescribably** *adv.* [*Say* in DESCRIBE a bull]

indestructible *adj.* that cannot be destroyed. □ **indestructibility** *n.*

indeterminate *adj.* **1** not exactly known or defined. **2** *Math* (of a quantity) not limited to a fixed value. □ **indeterminacy** *n.* [*Say* in DETERMINE it, in DETERMINE a see]

index ● *n.* (*pl.* **indexes** or esp. in technical use **indices**) **1** an alphabetical list of names, subjects, etc. with page references. **2** a usu. alphabetical catalogue of books etc. **3** a scale relating the level of prices, wages, etc. to those at a previous date. **4** *Math* an exponent. **5** a sign or indication of something. ● *v.* (**indexes, indexed, indexing**) **1** record in or provide with an index. **2** relate (wages etc.) to the value of a price index. □ **indexation** *n.* [*For* indices *say* INDA seez]

index card *n.* a small rectangular card made of heavy paper.

index finger *n.* the forefinger.

Indian ● *n.* **1** a person from India. **2 a** a member of the Aboriginal peoples of N and S America other than the Inuit and Metis. **b** any of the languages spoken by these

peoples. ● *adj.* **1** of or relating to India. **2** of the Aboriginal peoples of N and S America.

Indian agent *n.* *Cdn hist.* a person appointed to supervise government programs on a reserve etc.

Indian paintbrush *n.* a chiefly N American plant with brightly coloured bracts.

Indian summer *n.* a period of unusually dry warm weather in late autumn.

India rubber *n.* = RUBBER 1.

indicate *v.* (**indicates, indicated, indicating**) **1** point out; show. **2** be a sign or symptom of. **3** suggest; call for. **4** state briefly. **5** (of a gauge) give as a reading. □ **indication** *n.*

indicative ● *adj.* **1** suggestive. **2** *Grammar* (of a form of a verb) stating a simple fact. ● *n.* *Grammar* the indicative mood. [*Say* in DICKA tiv]

indicator *n.* **1** a person or thing that indicates. **2** a pointer etc. which draws attention or gives warning. **3** a recording instrument attached to an apparatus. **4** a substance which changes colour in the presence of a particular substance, so indicating e.g. acidity.

indices *pl.* of INDEX. [*Say* INDA seez]

indict *v.* formally charge with a crime. □ **indictable** *adj.* [*Say* in DITE, in DITE a bull]

indictment *n.* **1** a formal accusation. **2** something that serves to condemn. [*Say* in DITE m'nt]

indie *informal* ● *n.* an independent record or film company. ● *adj.* **1** not belonging to a major record company or film studio. **2** characteristic of the non-commercial style of indie bands.

indifferent *adj.* **1** having no interest or sympathy; unconcerned. **2** average, mediocre. **3** not very good. □ **indifference** *n.* **indifferently** *adv.*

indigene *n.* a native or aboriginal inhabitant of a region etc. [*Say* INDA jean]

indigenous *adj.* **1** originating or occurring naturally in a place; native. **2** having to do with the aboriginal inhabitants of a region. □ **indigenously** *adv.* [*Say* in DIDGE a nus]

indigent ● *adj.* poor. ● *n.* an indigent person. [*Say* INDA j'nt]

indigestible *adj.* difficult or impossible to digest. [*Say* inda JESTA bull]

indigestion *n.* stomach discomfort associated with difficulty in digesting food. [*Say* inda JES chun]

indignant *adj.* feeling or showing indignation. □ **indignantly** *adv.* [*Say* in DIG nint]

indignation *n.* scornful anger at supposed

unfair conduct or treatment.
[*Say* in dig NATION]

indignity *n.* (*pl.* **indignities**) **1** unworthy treatment. **2** an insult. **3** the humiliating quality of something. [*Say* in DIGNA tee]

indigo *n.* (*pl.* **indigos**) *n. & adj.* (also **indigo blue**) a dark blue colour or dye. [*Say* INDA go]

indirect *adj.* **1 a** not direct. **b** roundabout. **2** (of a route etc.) circuitous. **3** (of lighting) from a concealed source. □ **indirection** *n.* **indirectly** *adv.* **indirectness** *n.*

indirect object *n.* Grammar a person or thing affected by a verbal action but not primarily acted on, e.g. *him* in *give him the book.*

indirect tax *n.* a tax that is paid through an intermediary rather than directly, e.g. sales tax.

indiscreet *adj.* not discreet. □ **indiscreetly** *adv.*

indiscretion *n.* **1** indiscreet conduct. **2** an indiscreet remark etc.

indiscriminate *adj.* done or acting without careful judgement. □ **indiscriminately** *adv.* [*Say* in dis CRIM in ut]

indispensable *adj.* essential. □ **indispensability** *n.* [*Say* in dis PENCE a bull, in dis pence a BILLA tee]

indisposed *adj.* **1** slightly unwell. **2** unwilling.

indisputable *adj.* that cannot be disputed; unquestionable. □ **indisputably** *adv.*

indissoluble *adj.* **1** that cannot be dissolved or destroyed. **2** lasting. □ **indissolubly** *adv.* [*Say* in dis SAWL yoo bull]

indistinct *adj.* **1** not distinct. **2** confused. □ **indistinctly** *adv.*

indistinguishable *adj.* not distinguishable. [*Say* in dis TING wish a bull]

indium *n.* a soft silvery-white metallic element used for electroplating and in semiconductors. [*Say* IN dee um]

individual ● *adj.* **1** single, separate. **2** particular, special. **3** having a distinct character; characteristic. **4** designed for one person. ● *n.* **1** a single human being as distinct from a group. **2** a person. **3** a distinctive or original person. □ **individually** *adv.*

individualism *n.* **1** the quality of being independent and self-reliant. **2** a social theory favouring the free action of individuals. **3** egoism. **4** = INDIVIDUALITY 1. □ **individualist** *n.* **individualistic** *adj.*

individuality *n.* (*pl.* **individualities**)

1 the sum of the attributes which distinguish one person or thing from others. **2** the fact of separate existence.

individualize *v.* (**individualizes, individualized, individualizing**) **1** give an individual character to. **2** personalize or tailor to suit the individual.

individuate *v.* (**individuates, individuated, individuating**) distinguish from others of the same kind. □ **individuation** *n.* [*Say* inda VIDGE oo ate]

indivisible *adj.* **1** not divisible. **2** not able to be distributed among a number. [*Say* inda VIZZA bull]

Indo-Canadian *n.* a Canadian born in the Indian subcontinent. □ **Indo-Canadian** *adj.*

indoctrinate *v.* (**indoctrinates, indoctrinated, indoctrinating**) teach (someone) to accept a doctrine or set of beliefs. □ **indoctrination** *n.* [*Say* in DOCTRINE ate]

Indo-European ● *adj.* of the family of languages spoken over the greater part of Europe and Asia as far as northern India. ● *n.* **1** the Indo-European family of languages. **2** the hypothetical parent language of this family.

indolent *adj.* lazy. □ **indolence** *n.* **indolently** *adv.* [*Say* INDA lint, INDA lince]

indomitable *adj.* impossible to subdue or defeat. [*Say* in DOMMA tuh bull]

Indonesian *n.* a person from Indonesia. □ **Indonesian** *adj.* [*Say* inda NEE zhun]

indoor *adj.* situated, done, or used within a building or under cover.

indoor-outdoor *adj.* designating a sturdy carpet, used both inside and outside.

indoors *adv.* into or within a building.

indubitable *adj.* that cannot be doubted. □ **indubitably** *adv.* [*Say* in DOO bit a bull or in DYOO bit a bull]

induce *v.* (**induces, induced, inducing**) **1** persuade. **2** Medical bring on (labour) artificially. **3** bring about or cause. □ **inducer** *n.*

inducement *n.* **1** an attraction that leads one on. **2** something that persuades someone to do something.

induct *v.* **1** formally give someone a job or position of authority. **2** introduce, initiate, admit. □ **inductee** *n.* [*Say* in DUCKT, in duck TEE]

inductance *n.* **1** the property of an electric circuit that causes an electromotive force to be generated by a change in the current flowing. **2** an inductor.

induction *n.* **1** the process of introducing

someone to a new job, organization, etc.
2 the process of bringing on (esp. labour) by artificial means. **3** the inference of a general law from particular instances. **4** the production of an electric or magnetic state by the proximity (without contact) of an electrified or magnetized body.

inductive adj. **1** (of reasoning etc.) of or based on induction. **2** of electric or magnetic induction. □ **inductively** adv.

inductor n. a component (in a circuit) which possesses inductance.

indulge v. (**indulges**, **indulged**, **indulging**) **1** allow oneself to enjoy the pleasure of. **2** yield freely to. **3** gratify the wishes of. **4** informal take alcoholic liquor.

indulgence n. **1 a** the act of indulging. **b** the state of being indulgent. **2** something indulged in. **3** Catholicism the remission of punishment, still due after absolution.

indulgent adj. **1** ready or too ready to overlook faults etc. **2** indulging or tending to indulge. □ **indulgently** adv.

industrial adj. **1** having to do with industry. **2** designed for industrial use. **3** having highly developed industries. □ **industrially** adv.

industrial arts pl. n. woodworking, metalwork, etc.

industrial design n. the art of designing objects for manufacture. □ **industrial designer** n.

industrialism n. a social system in which manufacturing industries are prevalent.

industrialist n. a person who owns or operates an industrial enterprise.

industrialize v. (**industrializes**, **industrialized**, **industrializing**) **1** introduce industries to (a country etc.). **2** become industrialized. □ **industrialization** n.

Industrial Revolution n. the dramatic transformation of society from an agrarian economy to an industrial one, esp. in Britain from about 1750–1850.

industrial-strength adj. strong, powerful.

industrious adj. hard-working. □ **industriously** adv. **industriousness** n.

industry n. (pl. **industries**) **1 a** a branch of trade or manufacture. **b** trade and manufacture collectively. **c** any commercial undertaking. **2** hard work.

inebriated adj. drunk. □ **inebriation** n. [Say in EE bree ate id, in ee bree AY sh'n]

inedible adj. not suitable for eating. [Say in EDDA bull]

ineffable adj. **1** too great for description in words. **2** that must not be uttered. □ **ineffably** adv. [Say in EFFA bull]

ineffective adj. **1** not producing any or the desired effect. **2** inefficient. □ **ineffectively** adv. **ineffectiveness** n.

ineffectual adj. **1** ineffective. **2** lacking the ability to achieve results. □ **ineffectually** adv.

inefficient adj. failing to make the best use of the available time and resources. □ **inefficiency** n. **inefficiently** adv. [Say in i FISH int, in i FISHIN see]

inelastic adj. **1** not elastic. **2** inflexible. **3** (of demand or supply) not responsive to changes in price.

inelegant adj. not attractive or graceful. □ **inelegantly** adv.

ineligible adj. not eligible (for an office, position, etc.). □ **ineligibility** n. [Say in ELLA juh bull]

ineluctable adj. unable to be resisted or avoided. □ **ineluctably** adv. [Say inna LUCK tuh bull]

inept adj. incompetent. □ **ineptitude** n. **ineptly** adv. **ineptness** n.

inequality n. (pl. **inequalities**) **1** lack of equality. **2 a** difference of rank or circumstance. **b** unfairness.

inequitable adj. unfair, unjust. [Say in ECKWA tuh bull]

inequity n. (pl. **inequities**) unfairness, bias. [Say in ECKWA tee]

ineradicable adj. unable to be eradicated. □ **ineradicably** adv. [Say inna RAD ick a bull]

inert adj. **1** without power to move or act. **2** without active chemical properties. □ **inertly** adv.

inert gas n. = NOBLE GAS.

inertia n. **1** Physics a property in which matter remains in a state of rest or continues moving in a straight line, unless changed by an external force. **2** a tendency to do nothing or remain unchanged. □ **inertial** adj. [Say in URSH uh]

inescapable adj. that cannot be escaped or avoided. □ **inescapability** n. **inescapably** adv.

inessential adj. not necessary.

inestimable adj. too great etc. to be estimated. [Say in ESS timma bull]

inevitable ● adj. impossible to avoid; sure to happen. ● n. (**the inevitable**) that which is inevitable. □ **inevitability** n. **inevitably** adv. [Say in EVVA tuh bull, in evva tuh BILLA tee]

inexact adj. not exact.

inexcusable adj. that cannot be excused or justified. □ **inexcusably** adv.

inexhaustible adj. that cannot be used up. [Say in ex OSS tuh bull]

inexorable adj. that cannot be stopped or changed. □ **inexorably** adv. [Say in EX ur a bull]

inexpensive adj. not expensive, cheap. □ **inexpensively** adv.

inexperience n. lack of experience. □ **inexperienced** adj.

inexpert adj. not skilful; lacking expertise. □ **inexpertly** adv.

inexplicable adj. that cannot be explained. □ **inexplicably** adv. [Say in ex PLICK a bull]

inexpressible adj. ineffable. □ **inexpressibly** adv.

in extremis adj. **1** at the point of death. **2** in great difficulties. [Say in ex TREM iss or in ex TREEM iss]

inextricable adj. too closely linked to be separated. □ **inextricably** adv. [Say in EX trick a bull or in ex TRICK a bull]

infallible adj. **1** incapable of error. **2** sure to succeed. □ **infallibility** n. **infallibly** adv. [Say in FAL a bull, in fal a BILLA tee]

infamous adj. well-known for being bad, wicked, etc. □ **infamously** adv. [Say IN fuh muss]

infamy n. **1** the state of being infamous. **2** evil behaviour. [Say IN fuh mee]

infancy n. (pl. **infancies**) **1** early childhood. **2** an early state in the development of something. [Say IN fan see]

infant n. **1** a very young child or baby. **2** something in an early stage of development.

infanticide n. **1** the practice of killing infants. **2** a person who does this. [Say in FANTA side]

infantile adj. **1** like or characteristic of a child. **2** childish. [Say IN f'n tile]

infantry n. (pl. **infantries**) foot soldiers collectively. □ **infantryman** n. [Say IN fun tree]

infatuated adj. affected by an intense fondness. □ **infatuation** n. [Say in FATCH oo ate id]

infect v. **1** contaminate. **2 a** affect with disease-causing micro-organisms. **b** affect (a computer) with a virus. □ **infective** adj.

infection n. **1** the process of infecting or state of being infected. **2** an infectious disease.

infectious adj. **1** infecting with disease. **2** (of a disease) liable to be transmitted by air, water, etc. **3** quickly affecting others. □ **infectiously** adv.

infer v. (**infers, inferred, inferring**) deduce from facts and reasoning.

inference n. **1** a conclusion reached on the basis of evidence. **2** the process of reaching such a conclusion. [Say IN fur ince]

inferior ● adj. of lower rank, quality, etc. ● n. a person inferior to another, esp. in rank. □ **inferiority** n. [Say in FEARY er, in feary OR a tee]

infernal adj. **1** of hell or the underworld. **2** informal tiresome. □ **infernally** adv. [Say in FUR null]

inferno n. (pl. **infernos**) **1** a raging fire. **2** hell. [Say in FUR no]

infertile adj. not fertile. □ **infertility** n. [Say in FUR tile or in FURTLE, in fur TILLA tee]

infest v. overrun (a place) in large numbers. □ **infestation** n.

infidel n. usu. derogatory a person who does not believe in religion or in a particular religion. [Say IN fuh del]

infidelity n. (pl. **infidelities**) the action of being unfaithful to one's sexual partner. [Say in fuh DELLA tee]

infield n. **1** Baseball the area bounded by the baselines. **2** the fielders stationed in this area. □ **infielder** n.

infighting n. conflict within an organization.

infill ● n. (also **infilling**) **1** material used to fill a hole etc. **2** a house etc. built in the space between existing ones. ● v. fill in.

infiltrate v. (**infiltrates, infiltrated, infiltrating**) **1** enter a place or an organization secretly. **2** pass slowly into something. □ **infiltration** n. **infiltrator** n. [Say IN fill trate]

infinite ● adj. **1** boundless, endless. **2** very great. **3** innumerable. ● n. **1** (**the Infinite**) God. **2** (**the infinite**) infinite space. □ **infinitely** adv. [Say IN fuh nit]

infinitesimal adj. very small. □ **infinitesimally** adv. [Say in finna TESS'm ul, in finna TESS'm ul lee]

infinitive n. the basic form of a verb (e.g. see in we came to see).

infinity n. (pl. **infinities**) **1** the state of being infinite. **2** an infinite number or extent. **3** Math infinite quantity. Symbol: ∞.

infirm adj. physically weak.

infirmary n. (pl. **infirmaries**) **1** a place set aside for those who are ill. **2** a hospital. [Say in FIRM a ree]

infirmity n. (pl. **infirmities**) physical or mental weakness. [Say in FIRM a tee]

inflame v. (**inflames, inflamed, inflaming**) **1** provoke to strong feeling, esp. anger. **2** make worse. **3** cause inflammation in. □ **inflamed** adj.

inflammable *adj.* easily set on fire.

inflammation *n.* a condition in which an area of skin becomes hot, swollen, reddened, etc.

inflammatory *adj.* **1** tending to cause anger etc. **2** causing inflammation.

inflatable ● *adj.* that can be inflated. ● *n.* an inflatable object, esp. a boat.

inflate *v.* (**inflates, inflated, inflating**) **1** distend (a balloon etc.) with air. **2** puff up (an ego). **3 a** bring about inflation (of a currency). **b** raise (prices). **4** exaggerate.

inflated *adj.* **1** swollen, puffed up. **2** (esp. of language etc.) bombastic. **3** (of prices etc.) unreasonably high. **4** exaggerated.

inflation *n.* **1** a general increase in prices. **2** the state of inflating or being inflated. □ **inflationary** *adj.*

inflect *v.* **1** change the pitch of. **2** *Grammar* change the form of (a word) to express tense, gender, etc. **3** bend inwards. **4** influence or modify.

inflection *n.* **1** *Grammar* **a** the practice of inflecting words. **b** an inflected form. **2** a modulation of the voice. □ **inflectional** *adj.*

inflexible *adj.* **1** that cannot be changed or adapted. **2** unwilling to change or adapt. **3** not able to bend. □ **inflexibility** *n.*

inflict *v.* **1** cause (injury, defeat, etc.). **2** impose (something unwelcome) on. □ **infliction** *n.*

inflight *adj.* occurring or provided during an aircraft flight.

inflorescence *n.* **1** the complete flower head of a plant. **2** the process of flowering. [*Say* in flor ESSENCE]

inflow *n.* **1** a flowing in. **2** something that flows in.

influence ● *n.* **1 a** the power or ability to affect someone's beliefs or actions. **b** a thing or person exercising such power. **2** the ability to obtain favours by means of wealth, status, etc. ● *v.* (**influences, influenced, influencing**) **1** have an influence on. **2** persuade (a person) to think or act. □ **under the influence** *informal* inebriated.

influential *adj.* having great influence. [*Say* in floo EN shull]

influenza *n.* the flu. [*Say* in flu ENZA]

influx *n.* (*pl.* **influxes**) **1** a continual entry of people into a place. **2** a flowing in of a substance.

info *n. & comb. form informal* information.

infomercial *n.* a television commercial made to look like a regular program. [*Say* INFO mur shull]

inform *v.* **1** tell. **2** make an accusation.

3 give or supply information. **4** have an influence on.

informal *adj.* **1** without ceremony or formality. **2** (of clothing etc.) casual. **3** (of language etc.) relaxed; not formal. □ **informality** *n.* (*pl.* **informalities**) **informally** *adv.*

informant *n.* **1** a person who gives information. **2** a person who informs against another; an informer.

information *n.* **1** knowledge; news. **2** a booth etc. providing information. **3** computer data. □ **informational** *adj.*

information overload *n.* the provision or receipt of an excessive quantity of information, such that it cannot be processed fully or efficiently by the recipient.

information technology *n.* the study or use of systems (esp. computers, telecommunications, etc.) for storing, retrieving, and sending information.

informative *adj.* giving information.

informed *adj.* **1** with knowledge of the facts. **2** knowledgeable.

informer *n.* a person who informs against another.

infotainment *n.* broadcast material intended to entertain and to inform. [*Say* info TAIN m'nt]

infra- *comb. form* below.

infraction *n.* esp. *Law* a violation or infringement.

infrared ● *adj.* **1** having a wavelength just greater than that of red light but less than that of radio waves. **2** of or using such radiation. ● *n.* the infrared part of the spectrum. [*Say* infra RED]

infrastructure *n.* **1** the basic structures, such as roads, bridges, etc., of a society or enterprise. **2** permanent installations for military etc. operations. □ **infrastructural** *adj.* [*Say* INFRA structure]

infrequent *adj.* not frequent. □ **infrequency** *n.* **infrequently** *adv.*

infringe *v.* (**infringes, infringed, infringing**) **1 a** violate (a law etc.). **b** act in defiance of. **2** encroach on. □ **infringement** *n.*

infuriate *v.* (**infuriates, infuriated, infuriating**) fill with fury. □ **infuriating** *adj.* **infuriatingly** *adv.* [*Say* in FYOORY ate]

infuse *v.* (**infuses, infused, infusing**) **1** fill; spread throughout. **2** steep (herbs, tea, etc.) in liquid to extract the content. **3** instill. [*Say* in FYOOZ]

infusion *n.* **1** a drink prepared by infusing.

2 the process of infusing.
[*Say* in FEW zh'n]

ingenious *adj.* **1** clever; skilful;
resourceful. **2** cleverly contrived.
□ **ingeniously** *adv.* [*Say* in GENIUS]

ingenue *n.* **1** an innocent young woman.
2 a such a part in a play. **b** the actress who
plays this part. [*Say* on zhuh NOO]

ingenuity *n.* (*pl.* **ingenuities**) skill in
devising or contriving.
[*Say* in juh NOO a tee *or*
in juh NYOO a tee]

ingenuous *adj.* **1** innocent; artless. **2** open;
frank. □ **ingenuousness** *n.*
[*Say* in JEN yoo us]

ingest *v.* take in; eat. □ **ingestion** *n.*
[*Say* in JEST]

inglorious *adj.* causing shame.

ingot *n.* a usu. oblong block of gold, silver,
or steel. [*Say* IN gut]

ingrain *v.* implant (a belief etc.)
ineradicably in a person.

ingrained *adj.* **1** deeply rooted. **2** (of dirt
etc.) deeply embedded.

ingrate *n.* an ungrateful person.
[*Say* IN grate]

ingratiate *v.* (**ingratiates, ingratiated,
ingratiating**) □ **ingratiate oneself
with** try to gain favour with someone by
flattering them etc. □ **ingratiating** *adj.*
ingratiatingly *adv.*
[*Say* in GRAY shee ate]

ingratitude *n.* a lack of due gratitude.

ingredient *n.* **1** any of the foods that are
combined to make a dish. **2** a part or
element.

in-group *n.* a small exclusive group of
people.

ingrown *adj.* (of a toenail etc.) grown into
the flesh. □ **ingrowing** *adj.*

inhabit *v.* (**inhabits, inhabited,
inhabiting**) dwell in; occupy.
□ **inhabitable** *adj.* **inhabitant** *n.*
inhabited *adj.*

inhalant *n.* **1** a medicinal preparation for
inhaling. **2** a substance inhaled by drug
abusers. [*Say* in HAY l'nt]

inhale *v.* (**inhales, inhaled, inhaling**)
1 breathe in. **2** *informal* devour (food etc.)
rapidly. □ **inhalation** *n.* [*Say* in HALE,
in huh LAY sh'n]

inhaler *n.* a portable device for
administering a drug to treat asthma etc.

inherent *adj.* existing in something, esp. as
a permanent or characteristic attribute.
□ **inherently** *adv.* [*Say* in HAIR int]

inherit *v.* (**inherits, inherited,
inheriting**) **1** receive (property, rank, etc.)
by legal descent or succession. **2** receive or
have from a predecessor, previous owner,

etc. **3** derive from one's ancestors.
□ **inheritor** *n.*

inheritance *n.* **1** something that is
inherited. **2** the action of inheriting.

inhibit *v.* (**inhibits, inhibited,
inhibiting**) **1** hinder or prevent (an action
or progress). **2** prevent from acting or
expressing oneself freely. □ **inhibited** *adj.*

inhibition *n.* **1** *Psychology* a restraint on the
direct expression of an instinct. **2** a feeling
which prevents one from behaving
naturally. [*Say* in huh BISH'n]

inhibitor *n.* **1** a thing which inhibits. **2** a
substance which slows down a particular
chemical reaction or other process.
□ **inhibitory** *adj.*

inhospitable *adj.* **1** not hospitable. **2** (of a
place) not providing shelter etc.
[*Say* in hoss PITTA bull]

in-house ● *adj.* done or existing within an
organization. ● *adv.* internally.

inhuman *adj.* **1** brutal; unfeeling;
barbarous. **2** not human. **3** not suitable for
humans. □ **inhumanly** *adv.*

inhumane *adj.* not humane.
□ **inhumanely** *adv.*

inhumanity *n.* (*pl.* **inhumanities**)
1 brutality. **2** an inhumane act.

inimical *adj.* harmful. [*Say* in IMM ick ul]

inimitable *adj.* impossible to imitate.
[*Say* in IMM it a bull]

iniquity *n.* (*pl.* **iniquities**) **1** wickedness.
2 a gross injustice. □ **iniquitous** *adj.*
[*Say* ICKWA tee, in ICKWA tus]

initial ● *adj.* existing or occurring at the
beginning. ● *n.* the first letter of a name or
word. ● *v.* (**initials, initialled,
initialling**) mark or sign with one's
initials. □ **initially** *adv.*

initialize *v.* (**initializes, initialized,
initializing**) **1** *Computing* set to or put in
the condition appropriate to start an
operation. **2** format (a disk).
□ **initialization** *n.*

initiate ● *v.* (**initiates, initiated,
initiating**) **1** begin; set going. **2 a** admit (a
person) into a society or group, esp. with a
formal ceremony. **b** introduce to or instruct
in a new activity. ● *n.* a person who has
been initiated; a novice. □ **initiation** *n.*
initiator *n.* [*Say* i NISHY ate *for the verb,*
i NISHY it *for the noun and adjective;*
i nishy AY sh'n]

initiative *n.* **1** the ability to initiate things.
2 a the action of initiating something. **b** a
proposal made by one group, nation, etc. to
another. □ **on one's own initiative**
without being prompted by others. **take
the initiative** be the first to take action.
[*Say* i NISHA tiv]

inject v. **1 a** introduce (a drug or other substance) into the body with a syringe. **b** force a fluid under pressure into something. **2** introduce suddenly. **3** introduce (a new quality etc.). □ **injectable** adj. & n. **injector** n.

injection n. **1 a** the act of injecting. **b** an instance of this. **2** something (to be) injected.

in-joke n. a joke which can be appreciated by only a limited group.

injudicious adj. showing lack of judgment; unwise. [Say in joo DISH us]

injunction n. **1** an authoritative warning or order. **2** Law an official order by a court of law demanding that someone must do or not do something.

injure v. (**injures**, **injured**, **injuring**) **1** do esp. physical harm to; hurt. **2** harm or impair. **3** do wrong to.

injured adj. **1** harmed. **2** offended.

injurious adj. **1** hurtful. **2** (of language) insulting. [Say in JURY us]

injury n. (pl. **injuries**) **1** harm or damage. **2** esp. Law wrongful action or treatment.

injustice n. **1** a lack of justice. **2** an unjust act. □ **do a person an injustice** judge a person unfairly.

ink ● n. **1** a coloured fluid used for writing, drawing, printing, etc. **2** a black liquid ejected by a squid, octopus, etc. to confuse a predator. ● v. **1** mark or go over with ink. **2** apply ink to. **3** informal sign.

ink-jet printer n. a printer that prints characters and graphics by firing ink drops from tiny nozzles.

inkling n. a slight suspicion; a hint.

inky adj. (**inkier**, **inkiest**) of, as black as, or stained with ink.

inlaid ● v. past and past participle of INLAY. ● adj. ornamented by inlaying.

inland ● adj. **1** in the interior of a country. **2** esp. Cdn & Brit. domestic. ● n. the interior. ● adv. in or towards the interior of a country. □ **inlander** n.

Inland Tlingit n. (pl. **Inland Tlingit**) **1** a member of an Aboriginal group living in northern BC and the southern Yukon Territory. **2** the Tlingit language of this people.

in-law ● n. a relative by marriage. ● comb. form related by marriage.

in-law suite n. (also **in-law apartment**) a room or suite forming a small apartment within a house.

inlay ● v. (**inlays**, **inlaid**, **inlaying**) **1** embed (a thing in another) so that the surfaces are even. **2** ornament (a thing) by embedding another material in its surface.

● n. **1** inlaid work. **2** a material used for inlaying.

inlet n. **1** a small arm of the ocean, a lake, or a river. **2** a place or means of entry.

in-line adj. **1** having parts arranged in a line. **2** involving or forming part of a continuous sequence of operations or machines.

in-line skate n. a roller skate having a single line of usu. four rubber wheels. □ **in-line skater** n. **in-line skating** n.

inmate n. a person confined in a prison, hospital, etc.

in memoriam ● prep. in memory of (a dead person). ● n. a written notice etc. in memory of a dead person. [Say in muh MORY um]

inmost adj. innermost.

inn n. **1** a small hotel. **2** a tavern.

innards pl. n. informal **1** entrails. **2** inner workings. [Say IN urdz]

innate adj. inborn; natural. □ **innately** adv. [Say in ATE]

inner ● adj. **1** further in; inside; closest to the centre. **2** (of feelings etc.) deeper, more secret. **3** mental; spiritual. ● n. the inner part.

inner child n. **1** a person's supposed original self. **2** that part of a person which enjoys childish activities.

inner city n. the central area of a city, esp. if impoverished etc.

inner ear n. the semicircular canals and cochlea, which form the organs of balance and hearing.

innermost adj. **1** (of feelings) most private. **2** furthest in.

inner tube n. an inflatable rubber tube in a tire.

inning n. each of the divisions of a baseball game during which both sides have a turn at bat.

innkeeper n. a person who runs an inn.

innocent ● adj. **1** free from moral wrong; sinless. **2** not guilty (of a crime etc.). **3** simple; guileless. **4** not intending to hurt or offend. **5** informal lacking experience etc. ● n. an innocent person, esp. a child. □ **innocence** n. **innocently** adv.

innocuous adj. not harmful or offensive. □ **innocuously** adv. [Say i NOCK yoo us]

innovate v. (**innovates**, **innovated**, **innovating**) **1** bring in new methods, ideas, products, etc. **2** make changes. □ **innovation** n. **innovative** adj. **innovatively** adv. **innovator** n.

Innu ● n. (pl. **Innu**) **1** a member of an Aboriginal people living in Labrador and northern Quebec (see also MONTAGNAIS,

NASKAPI). **2** the Cree language of this people. ● *adj.* of this people. [*Say* IN oo]

innuendo *n.* (*pl.* **innuendoes** or **innuendos**) an indirect remark or hint. [*Say* in yoo END oh]

innumerable *adj.* too many to be counted. [*Say* i NOO mur a bull *or* i NYOO mur a bull]

inoculate *v.* (**inoculates, inoculated, inoculating**) **1** make immune, esp. by injecting a vaccine into. **2** indoctrinate with ideas etc. □ **inoculation** *n.* [*Say* i NOCK yoo late]

inoffensive *adj.* not objectionable or harmful.

inoperable *adj.* **1** *Surgery* that cannot be operated on successfully. **2** that cannot be operated; inoperative. [*Say* in OPERA bull]

inoperative *adj.* not working or taking effect. [*Say* in OPERA tiv]

inopportune *adj.* occurring at an inconvenient time.

inordinate *adj.* beyond normal limits; excessive. □ **inordinately** *adv.* [*Say* in OR din it]

inorganic *adj.* **1** not arising from natural growth. **2** of or denoting chemical compounds not containing carbon. **3** without organized physical structure.

in-patient *n.* a patient who stays in hospital while receiving treatment.

input ● *n.* **1 a** what is put in or taken in by any process or system. **b** the total resources necessary to production. **2** a place or device from which energy, information, etc., enters a system. **3** the information fed into a computer. **4** a contribution. ● *v.* (**inputs**; *past* and *past participle* **input** or **inputted**; **inputting**) **1** put in. **2** supply (data etc. to a computer etc.).

inquest *n.* an inquiry by a coroner's court into the cause of a death.

inquire *v.* (**inquires, inquired, inquiring**) **1** seek information; ask a question. **2** seek information formally. □ **inquirer** *n.* **inquiring** *adj.*

inquiry *n.* (*pl.* **inquiries**) **1** an act or process of inquiring. **2** a question. **3** a formal investigation. [*Say* in QUIRE ee *or* IN kwuh ree]

inquisition *n.* **1** usu. *derogatory* **a** an intensive search or investigation. **b** a relentless or unwelcome questioning. **2** (**the Inquisition**) *Catholicism hist.* an ecclesiastical court established *c.*1232 for the detection of heretics. [*Say* in kwuh ZISH'n]

inquisitive *adj.* **1** seeking knowledge; inquiring. **2** prying. □ **inquisitively** *adv.* [*Say* in KWIZZA tiv]

inquisitor *n.* **1** a person making an inquiry. **2** *hist.* an officer of the Inquisition. [*Say* in KWIZZA tur]

inroad *n.* **1** an encroachment. **2** an advance.

inrush *n.* (*pl.* **inrushes**) an influx. □ **inrushing** *adj.* & *n.*

insane *adj.* **1** mentally deranged. **2** extremely foolish; irrational. □ **insanely** *adv.* **insanity** *n.* (*pl.* **insanities**)

insatiable *adj.* unable to be satisfied. □ **insatiably** *adv.* [*Say* in SAY shuh bull]

inscribe *v.* (**inscribes, inscribed, inscribing**) **1** write or carve (words etc.) on a surface. **2** write a dedication (to a person) in (a book etc.). **3** *Math* draw (a figure) within another so that their boundaries touch but do not intersect.

inscription *n.* **1** words inscribed on a monument, in a book, etc. **2** the act of inscribing.

inscrutable *adj.* impossible to understand or interpret. □ **inscrutably** *adv.* [*Say* in SCREW tuh bull]

inseam *n.* the inner seam on the leg of a pair of pants, extending from crotch to cuff.

insect *n.* **1** an arthropod with six legs and a body divided into three parts (head, thorax, and abdomen). **2** (loosely) any other small invertebrate animal esp. with several pairs of legs.

insecticide *n.* a substance used for killing insects. □ **insecticidal** *adj.* [*Say* in SECTA side, in secta SIDE ul]

insectivore *n.* any animal that feeds on insects. □ **insectivorous** *adj.* [*Say* in SECTA vore, in sec TIVVA russ]

insecure *adj.* **1** uncertain; lacking confidence. **2** not safe, not firm or fixed. □ **insecurely** *adv.* **insecurity** *n.* (*pl.* **insecurities**)

inseminate *v.* (**inseminates, inseminated, inseminating**) introduce semen into (a female). □ **insemination** *n.* [*Say* in SEMMA nate, in semma NATION]

insensible *adj.* **1 a** unconscious. **b** numb; without feeling. **2** unaware; indifferent. □ **insensibility** *n.* (*pl.* **insensibilities**)

insensitive *adj.* **1** having no concern for the feelings of others. **2** not sensitive to physical stimuli. **3** not susceptible or responsive to some physical influence. □ **insensitivity** *n.*

inseparable *adj.* unable or unwilling to be separated. □ **inseparability** *n.* **inseparably** *adv.* [*Say* in SEPPER a bull, in sepper a BILLA tee]

insert ● *v.* **1** place, fit, or thrust (a thing) into another. **2** introduce into a piece of

text etc. ● n. something inserted.
□ **insertion** n.

in-service adj. (of training) intended to take place during the course of employment.

inset ● n. **1** something set in or inserted. **2** a small map, photograph, etc., inserted within the border of a larger one. ● v. (**insets, inset, insetting**) set or put in as an inset; insert.

inshallah interj. if Allah wills it. [Say in SHALA]

inshore ● adj. **1** situated at sea close to the shore. **2** of or pertaining to fishing conducted in coastal waters. ● adv. **1** close to the shore. **2** towards the shore.

inside ● n. **1** the inner side, part, or surface of a thing. **2** the part of a bend nearest to the shorter side of the curve. **3** (usu. in pl.) informal the stomach and bowels. ● adj. **1** situated on or in, or coming from, the inside. **2** available only to those on the inside. ● adv. **1 a** on, in, or to the inside. **b** indoors. **2** slang in prison. ● prep. **1** on the inner side of; within. **2** in less than. □ **inside of** informal in less than.

inside job n. informal a crime committed by or with the help of a person living or working on the premises.

inside out ● adv. with the inner surface turned outwards. ● adj. (**inside-out**) in this condition. □ **know a thing inside out** know a thing thoroughly. **turn inside out 1** turn the inner surface outwards. **2** informal cause confusion.

insider n. **1** a person who is within an organization etc. **2** a person privy to a secret.

insider trading n. Stock Market the illegal use of confidential information for share trading.

inside track n. a position of advantage.

insidious adj. proceeding in a gradual and harmful way. □ **insidiously** adv. [Say in SIDDY us]

insight n. **1** the capacity of perceiving hidden truths, solutions to problems, etc. **2** an understanding of this kind. □ **insightful** adj.

insignia n. a badge or symbol of military rank, office, or membership in an organization. [Say in SIG nee uh]

insignificant adj. **1** unimportant; trifling. **2** (of a person) undistinguished. **3** meaningless. □ **insignificance** n.

insincere adj. not sincere; not candid. □ **insincerely** adv. **insincerity** n.

insinuate v. (**insinuates, insinuated, insinuating**) **1** convey indirectly or obliquely; hint. **2** introduce (oneself etc.)

gradually into (a favourable position). □ **insinuation** n. [Say in SIN yoo ate]

insipid adj. **1** lacking vigour or interest. **2** lacking flavour. [Say in SIP id]

insist v. maintain or demand positively and assertively. □ **insist on** persist in (doing).

insistent adj. **1** insisting; demanding continually. **2** repeated; demanding attention. □ **insistence** n. **insistently** adv.

in situ adv. in its original or proper place. [Say in SIT yoo]

insofar adv. to the extent that.

insole n. **1** a removable sole worn in a boot or shoe. **2** the fixed inner sole of a boot or shoe.

insolent adj. rude, disrespectful. □ **insolence** n. **insolently** adv. [Say IN suh l'nt, IN suh lince]

insoluble adj. **1** unable to be solved. **2** unable to be dissolved in a liquid. [Say in SAUL yoo bull]

insolvent ● adj. unable to pay one's debts. ● n. a debtor. □ **insolvency** n. (pl. **insolvencies**) [Say in SOLVE int, in SOLVE in see]

insomnia n. habitual sleeplessness. □ **insomniac** n. & adj. [Say in SOMNY uh, in SOMNY ack]

insouciant adj. carefree; unconcerned. □ **insouciance** n. **insouciantly** adv. [Say in SOO see int, in SOO see ince]

inspect v. **1** look closely at or into. **2** examine officially. □ **inspection** n.

inspector n. **1** a person who inspects. **2** an official employed to supervise something. **3** a middle-ranking police officer.

inspiration n. **1** a person or thing that inspires. **2** a sudden brilliant or creative idea etc. **3** inhalation. □ **inspirational** adj.

inspire v. (**inspires, inspired, inspiring**) **1** stimulate or arouse (a person) to esp. creative activity or moral fervour. **2 a** animate (a person) with a feeling. **b** create (a feeling) in a person. **3** give rise to. □ **inspirer** n. **inspiring** adj.

inspired adj. **1** showing inspiration. **2** (of a guess) intuitive but accurate.

instability n. (pl. **instabilities**) **1** a lack of stability. **2** weather characterized by precipitation, winds, etc.

install v. (**installs, installed, installing**) **1** place (equipment etc.) in position ready for use. **2** load (software) onto a computer etc. **3** establish (a person etc.) in a new place or role etc. □ **installer** n.

installation n. **1** the action of installing. **2** a piece of equipment etc. installed for use. **3 a** a large work of art specially created for display in a particular site. **b** an exhibition of such works. **4** a military or industrial establishment.

instalment *n.* (also **installment**) **1** one of several usu. equal payments, spread over a period of time. **2** any of several parts of something broadcast or published at intervals.

instance ● *n.* **1** an example or illustration of. **2** a particular case. **3** *Law* a legal suit. ● *v.* (**instances, instanced, instancing**) cite as an instance. □ **for instance** as an example.

instant ● *adj.* **1 a** occurring immediately. **b** designed to produce immediate results. **2** (of food etc.) processed to allow quick preparation. ● *n.* **1** a precise moment of time. **2** a short space of time.

instantaneous *adj.* occurring or done in an instant or instantly. □ **instantaneously** *adv.* [*Say* in st'n TAY nee us]

instantly *adv.* immediately; at once.

instant replay *n.* the recording and immediate broadcasting again of part of a televised sports event, often in slow motion.

instead *adv.* **1** in place of. **2** as an alternative.

instep *n.* the inner arch of the foot between the toes and the ankle.

instigate *v.* (**instigates, instigated, instigating**) **1** bring about; provoke. **2** urge on, incite (a person etc.) to do something. □ **instigation** *n.* **instigator** *n.* [*Say* INSTA gate]

instill *v.* (**instills, instilled, instilling**) **1** gradually introduce (an idea etc.) into a person's mind etc. **2** put in drop by drop.

instinct *n.* **1** an inborn tendency to behave in a certain way. **2** unconscious skill; intuition. □ **instinctual** *adj.*

instinctive *adj.* **1** relating to or prompted by instinct. **2** automatic. □ **instinctively** *adv.*

institute ● *n.* **1** an organization for the promotion of science, education, etc. **2** a unit within a university etc. devoted to advanced teaching and research. ● *v.* (**institutes, instituted, instituting**) **1** establish; found. **2** initiate; begin.

institution *n.* **1** the action of instituting something. **2 a** a society or organization founded esp. for particular purposes. **b** a business etc. providing a service to the public. **3** a residential centre for the care of patients with special needs. **4** an established law or custom.

institutional *adj.* **1** of or like an

institution. **2** typical of institutions. □ **institutionally** *adv.*

institutionalize *v.* (**institutionalizes, institutionalized, institutionalizing**) **1** place or keep in an institution. **2** make institutional. □ **institutionalization** *n.*

institutionalized *adj.* **1** made apathetic and dependent after a long period in an institution. **2** established in practice or custom.

instruct *v.* **1** teach. **2** command. **3** inform of a fact or situation.

instruction *n.* **1** a direction or order. **2** teaching. **3** a direction in a computer program. □ **instructional** *adj.*

instructive *adj.* tending to instruct; enlightening.

instructor *n.* **1** a teacher. **2** a university teacher ranking below assistant professor.

instrument *n.* **1** a tool or implement, esp. for precise work. **2** (also **musical instrument**) a device for producing musical sounds. **3** a thing used in performing an action. **4** a measuring device. **5** a formal, esp. legal, document.

instrumental ● *adj.* **1** serving as a means. **2** (of music) performed on instruments. **3** of an instrument. ● *n.* a piece of music performed by instruments. □ **instrumentalist** *n.*

instrumentation *n.* **1** the arrangement of music for a particular group of musical instruments. **2** the design or use of instruments in industry, science, etc.

insubordinate *adj.* refusing to obey or show respect. □ **insubordination** *n.* [*Say* in suh BOR duh nit, in suh bor duh NAY sh'n]

insubstantial *adj.* **1** lacking solidity; weak, flimsy. **2** not real. **3** not large.

insufferable *adj.* **1** intolerable. **2** unbearably arrogant or conceited etc. □ **insufferably** *adv.*

insufficient *adj.* not sufficient; inadequate. □ **insufficiency** *n.* (*pl.* **insufficiencies**) **insufficiently** *adv.*

insular *adj.* **1** of or like an island. **2** ignorant of or indifferent to things outside one's own experience. □ **insularity** *n.* [*Say* IN sue ler, in sue LERRA tee]

insulate *v.* (**insulates, insulated, insulating**) **1** prevent the passage of heat, sound, etc. from (a room etc.) by interposing non-conductors. **2** detach (something) from its surroundings; isolate. □ **insulator** *n.*

insulation *n.* **1** the action of insulating or the condition of being insulated. **2** materials used for this.

insulin n. **1** a hormone produced in the pancreas, which controls the amount of sugar absorbed by the body. **2** a commercial preparation of this, used in treating diabetes. [Say IN suh lin or IN syuh lin]

insult ● v. **1** speak to or treat with disrespect or abuse. **2** offend. ● n. **1** an insulting remark or action. **2** something so worthless etc. as to be offensive. □ **add insult to injury** behave offensively as well as harmfully. □ **insulting** adj. **insultingly** adv.

insuperable adj. impossible to surmount or overcome. [Say in SUPER uh bull]

insurance n. **1** the act or an instance of insuring property, life, etc. **2 a** a sum paid for this. **b** a sum paid out as compensation for theft, damage, etc. **3** = INSURANCE POLICY. **4** a measure taken to provide for a possible contingency.

insurance policy n. a contract of insurance.

insure v. (**insures, insured, insuring**) **1** arrange for compensation in the event of loss or damage to (property, life, etc.) by regular payments. **2** = ENSURE. □ **insurable** adj. **insured** adj. **insurer** n. [Say in SURE, in SURE uh bull]

insurgent ● adj. rising in active revolt; rebellious. ● n. a rebel; a revolutionary. □ **insurgency** n. (pl. **insurgencies**) [Say in SURGE int, in SURGE in see]

insurmountable adj. unable to be surmounted or overcome.

insurrection n. an uprising against established authority.

intact adj. entire; not damaged.

intake n. **1** the action of taking something in. **2** a number or amount taken in. **3** a place where fluid is taken into a channel or pipe.

intangible ● adj. **1** that exists but that is difficult to describe or measure. **2** (of a business asset) saleable, but having no value in itself. ● n. an intangible thing. □ **intangibly** adv. [Say in TAN juh bull]

integer n. a whole number. [Say INTA jur]

integral ● adj. **1 a** necessary to make a whole complete; fundamental. **b** forming a whole. **c** included as part of the whole. **2** Math of or denoted by an integer. ● n. Math a quantity of which a given function is the derivative, and which may express the area under the curve of a graph of the function. □ **integrally** adv. [For the adjective say INTA grul or in TEG rul; for the noun say INTA grul; in TEGRA lee]

integrate v. (**integrates, integrated, integrating**) **1** combine into a whole. **2** make someone accepted as part of a group. **3** desegregate. □ **integrated** adj. **integrative** adj. **integrator** n. [Say INTA grate, INTA grate iv, INTA grate er]

integrated circuit n. a small chip etc. replacing several separate components in a conventional electrical circuit.

integrated services digital network n. a telecommunications network through which data can be transmitted as digitized signals. Abbreviation: **ISDN**.

integration n. **1** the act or an instance of integrating. **2** the intermixing of persons previously segregated.

integrity n. **1** moral uprightness; honesty. **2** wholeness. **3** the condition of being unified or sound. [Say in TEGRA tee]

intellect n. **1 a** the faculty of reasoning and thinking. **b** a person's mental powers. **2** a clever or knowledgeable person.

intellectual ● adj. **1** of or relating to the intellect. **2** having a highly developed intellect. **3** requiring or engaging the intellect. ● n. **1** a person of superior intelligence. **2** a person interested in intellectual matters. □ **intellectually** adv.

intellectualism n. the exercise of the intellect at the expense of the emotions.

intellectualize v. (**intellectualizes, intellectualized, intellectualizing**) make intellectual.

intellectual property n. Law non-tangible property that is the result of creativity.

intelligence n. **1 a** the intellect; the understanding. **b** wisdom. **2 a** the usu. secret collection of information. **b** information so collected. **c** information in general.

intelligent adj. **1** having intelligence, esp. of a high level. **2 a** (of a device or machine) able to vary its behaviour in response to varying situations and past experience. **b** (esp. of a computer terminal) programmable. **c** equipped with sophisticated technology. □ **intelligently** adv.

intelligentsia n. **1** the class of intellectuals. **2** people doing intellectual work. [Say in tella GENT see uh]

intelligible adj. able to be understood. □ **intelligibility** n. **intelligibly** adv. [Say in TELLA juh bull, in tella juh BILLA bee]

intemperate adj. **1** showing a lack of self-control. **2** characterized by excessive indulgence esp. in alcohol. □ **intemperance** n. [Say in TEMPER it, in TEMPER ince]

intend v. **1** have as one's purpose; propose. **2** design or plan for. **3** mean.

intendant n. (often **Intendant**) hist. a high-ranking administrative official in French, Portuguese, and Spanish settlements.

intended ● adj. **1** intentional. **2** designed, meant. ● n. informal one's fiancé or fiancée

intense adj. **1** existing in a high degree; extremely strong. **2 a** deeply or strongly felt. **b** extremely earnest and serious. **c** expressing strong emotion. **3** requiring a great deal of effort concentrated in a short time. □ **intensely** adv.

intensifier n. **1** a word or prefix used to give force or emphasis. **2** a thing that intensifies.

intensify v. (**intensifies, intensified, intensifying**) **1** make or become more intense. **2** increase the quantity or strength of. □ **intensification** n.

intensity n. (pl. **intensities**) **1** the quality of being intense. **2** concentration of feeling or passion. **3** esp. Physics the measurable amount of some quality.

intensive ● adj. **1** characterized by a great deal of concentrated effort. **2** (of agriculture) aiming to achieve maximum production within a limited area. **3** Economics making much use of. **4** Grammar expressing intensity; giving force. ● n. Grammar an intensifier. □ **intensively** adv.

intensive care n. special medical treatment for a dangerously ill patient.

intent ● n. intention; purpose. ● adj. **1 a** resolved; determined. **b** attentively occupied with. **2** earnest; eager. □ **to** (or **for**) **all intents and purposes** practically; virtually. □ **intently** adv.

intention n. **1** an aim or purpose. **2** the action or fact of intending. **3** informal (usu. in pl.) a man's designs in respect to marriage.

intentional adj. deliberate. □ **intentionality** n. **intentionally** adv.

inter v. (**inters, interred, interring**) deposit (a corpse etc.) in a grave or tomb; bury.

inter- comb. form **1** between. **2** mutually, reciprocally. [Say IN tur]

Interac n. Cdn proprietary a system of payment by means of a debit card.

interact v. **1** act reciprocally; act on each other. **2** work together or communicate. □ **interaction** n.

interactive adj. **1** reciprocally active; influencing each other. **2** (of a computer etc.) allowing a two-way flow of information between it and a user. □ **interactively** adv. **interactivity** n.

interbreed v. (**interbreeds, interbred, interbreeding**) breed with animals of a different race or species to produce a hybrid.

intercalate v. (**intercalates, intercalated, intercalating**) insert (a day etc.) into a calendar. □ **intercalation** n. [Say in TURCA late]

intercede v. (**intercedes, interceded, interceding**) intervene on behalf of another; try to settle a dispute.

intercellular adj. located or occurring between cells.

intercept ● v. **1** seize or stop something going from one place to another. **2** check or stop (motion etc.). **3** overtake and destroy. ● n. Math the point at which a line cuts the axis of a graph. □ **interception** n.

interceptor n. **1** an aircraft used to intercept enemy aircraft. **2** a person or thing that intercepts.

intercession n. **1** the act of interceding. **2** a prayer on behalf of another. □ **intercessor** n.

interchange ● v. (**interchanges, interchanged, interchanging**) **1** exchange (things) with each other. **2** put each of (two things) in the other's place. ● n. **1** a reciprocal exchange between two people etc. **2** an intersection on several levels so that traffic streams do not intersect. □ **interchangeability** n. **interchangeable** adj. **interchangeably** adv.

intercity adj. existing or travelling between cities.

intercom n. a device enabling reciprocal communication by radio or telephone.

interconnect v. connect with each other. □ **interconnected** adj. **interconnectedness** n. **interconnecting** adj. **interconnection** n. **interconnectivity** n.

intercontinental adj. connecting or travelling between continents.

intercontinental ballistic missile n. a ballistic missile able to be sent from one continent to another.

intercourse n. **1** = SEXUAL INTERCOURSE. **2** communication or dealings between people.

intercultural adj. taking place between cultures.

intercut v. (**intercuts, intercut, intercutting**) Film **1** alternate (scenes or shots) with contrasting scenes or shots. **2** switch from one shot or scene to another.

interdependent adj. dependent on each other. □ **interdependence** n. **interdependently** adv.

interdict ● *n.* an authoritative prohibition. ● *v.* **1** prohibit. **2 a** impede (an enemy force). **b** intercept (a prohibited commodity etc.). □ **interdiction** *n.*

interdisciplinary *adj.* of or between more than one branch of learning.

interest ● *n.* **1 a** concern; curiosity. **b** something exciting curiosity or holding the attention. **c** the power of something to hold the attention. **2 a** subject, hobby, etc., in which one is concerned. **3** advantage or profit. **4 a** money paid for the use of money lent. **b** = INTEREST RATE. **5 a a** financial stake. **b** a legal concern, title, or right (in property). ● *v.* **1** excite the curiosity or attention of. **2** cause (a person) to take a personal interest. □ **in the best interests of** to the greatest advantage of. **in the interest** (or **interests**) **of** as something that is advantageous to.

interested *adj.* **1** showing or having interest. **2** having a personal interest in something; not impartial.

interest group *n.* a group of people sharing a common identifying interest or purpose.

interesting *adj.* causing curiosity. □ **interestingly** *adv.*

interest rate *n.* a charge made for borrowing a sum of money for a stated period of time.

inter-ethnic *adj.* occurring or existing between ethnic groups.

interface ● *n.* **1** esp. *Physics* a surface forming a common boundary between two regions. **2** a point where interaction occurs between two things. **3** *Computing* **a** an apparatus for connecting two pieces of equipment so that they can communicate with each other. **b** the way in which a program communicates with the user. ● *v.* (**interfaces, interfaced, interfacing**) **1** connect with (something) by an interface. **2** interact with.

interfacing *n.* **1** a stiffish material between two layers of fabric in collars etc. **2** *in senses of* INTERFACE *v.*

interfaith *adj.* between or involving different religions or members of different religions.

interfere *v.* (**interferes, interfered, interfering**) **1** obstruct a process or activity. **2** become involved, esp. without invitation. **3** *Sport* unlawfully obstruct an opposing player. **4** *Cdn & Brit.* sexually molest. □ **interfering** *adj.*

interference *n.* **1** the action of interfering. **2 a** disturbance of radio signals by the interference of waves from different sources. **b** the distorted reception caused by this. **3** *Physics* the combination of two or more wave motions, producing a new wave pattern. **4 a** *Football* the legal blocking of an opposing player to clear a way for the ball carrier. **b** *Sport* the illegal blocking of an opponent. **5** *Law* sexual abuse of a minor. □ **run interference** intervene on someone's behalf.

interferon *n.* any of various proteins released by cells able to inhibit viral replication. [*Say* inter FEAR on]

intergalactic *adj.* of or situated between galaxies. [*Say* inter GALACTIC]

interim ● *n.* the intervening time. ● *adj.* provisional, temporary. [*Say* INTER im]

interior ● *adj.* **1** inner. **2** remote from the coast or frontier; inland. **3** connected with a country's own affairs. **4** coming from or done inside. ● *n.* **1** the interior part; the inside. **2** the interior part of a country or region. **3** a country's own internal affairs. **4** the inside of a building, room, etc. □ **interiority** *n.* [*Say* in TEERY er, in teery ORRA tee]

interior design *n.* (also **interior decoration**) the decoration or design of the interior of a building etc. □ **interior designer** *n.* (also **interior decorator**).

interject *v.* say suddenly or as an interruption.

interjection *n.* an exclamation (e.g. *hey!*).

interlace *v.* (**interlaces, interlaced, interlacing**) **1** interweave. **2** mingle, intersperse.

inter-lacrosse *n.* a coeducational, non-contact version of lacrosse played indoors or outdoors with a moulded plastic stick and a soft, air-filled ball, and involving continuous running.

interleave *v.* (**interleaves, interleaved, interleaving**) **1** insert leaves between the leaves of (a book etc.). **2** insert something between (the parts of).

interleukin *n.* any of several proteins that regulate the reaction of the body to substances that can cause disease. [*Say* inter LOO kin]

interlink *v.* link or be linked together. □ **interlinked** *adj.*

interlock ● *v.* **1** engage with each other by overlapping or fitting together. **2** be intimately connected. ● *adj.* (of fabric) knitted with closely interlocking stitches. ● *n.* **1** a device for connecting the function of different components. **2** an interlock fabric.

interlocutor *n.* a person who takes part in a conversation. [*Say* inter LOCK you ter]

interloper *n.* a person who interferes in another's affairs.

interlude *n.* **1 a** a period of time or

activity that contrasts with what goes before or after. **b** a temporary amusement. **2** a piece of music played between other pieces or between acts of a play.

intermarry v. (**intermarries**, **intermarried**, **intermarrying**) (of people belonging to different races, religions, etc.) become connected by marriage. □ **intermarriage** n.

intermediary ● n. (pl. **intermediaries**) **1** a person who helps to negotiate between others. **2** something acting between persons or things. ● adj. coming between two or more people or things. [Say inter MEEDY airy]

intermediate ● adj. coming between two things in time, place, character, etc. ● n. an intermediate person or thing.

interment n. burial. [Say in TUR mint]

intermezzo n. (pl. **intermezzi** or **intermezzos**) a short piece of music, either for a solo instrument, or to connect parts of an opera etc. [Say inter METSO]

interminable adj. **1** endless. **2** tediously long. □ **interminably** adv. [Say in TERM in a bull]

intermingle v. (**intermingles**, **intermingled**, **intermingling**) mix together.

intermission n. **1** a pause or break between parts of a play, concert, etc. **2** any pause or break.

intermittent adj. occurring at intervals. □ **intermittently** adv. [Say inter MIT int]

intermix v. (**intermixes**, **intermixed**, **intermixing**) mix together. □ **intermixture** n.

intermodal adj. involving two or more different modes of transport.

intern ● n. **1** a recent medical graduate receiving supervised training in a hospital. **2** a person in any profession gaining practical experience under supervision. ● v. **1** serve as an intern. **2** confine as a prisoner. [Say IN turn *for the noun*, in TURN *for the verb*]

internal adj. **1** of or situated in the inside part. **2** inside of the body. **3** of or relating to affairs within a country; domestic. **4** used or applying within an organization. **5** experienced in one's mind. □ **internally** adv.

internal combustion engine n. an engine in which motive power is generated by the expansion of exhaust gases from the burning of fuel with air inside the engine.

internalize v. (**internalizes**, **internalized**, **internalizing**) make (attitudes, behaviour, etc.) part of one's nature by learning or unconscious assimilation. □ **internalization** n.

internal medicine n. the diagnosis and treatment of diseases of internal organs.

international adj. **1** existing or carried on between nations. **2** agreed on or used by all or many nations. □ **internationally** adv.

International Date Line n. see DATELINE n. 1.

internationalism n. the belief that countries should work together in a friendly way. □ **internationalist** n. & adj.

internationalize v. (**internationalizes**, **internationalized**, **internationalizing**) make something international. □ **internationalization** n.

internecine adj. **1** mutually destructive. **2** (of conflict) happening within a group etc. [Say inter NESS een]

internee n. a prisoner. [Say intern EE]

Internet n. an international computer network linking computers.

Internet café n. a café, bar, etc. where customers can sit at computer terminals to surf the Internet, use email, etc.

Internet Protocol n. a standard that specifies the format and addressing scheme of packets of data sent over the Internet or other network.

Internet service provider n. an organization that provides access to the Internet, usu. on a commercial basis, and usu. also offers services relating to websites etc.

internist n. a specialist in internal medicine.

internment n. confinement; the act of interning someone. [Say in TURN mint]

internship n. **1** the position of an intern. **2** the period of such a position.

interpersonal adj. **1** (of relations) occurring between persons. **2** relating to relationships between people.

interplanetary adj. **1** between planets. **2** relating to travel between planets.

interplay n. the way in which things interact.

Interpol n. the International Criminal Police Organization, which coordinates investigations by police forces of member countries into international crime. [Say INTER pole]

interpolate v. (**interpolates**, **interpolated**, **interpolating**) **1** interject (a remark) in a conversation. **2** insert as something additional or different. **3** estimate (values) from known ones in the same range. **4** insert words in a book etc. □ **interpolation** n. [Say in TERPA late]

interpose v. (**interposes, interposed, interposing**) **1** place or insert (a thing) between others. **2** say (words) as an interruption. **3** exercise (a veto or objection).

interpret v. (**interprets, interpreted, interpreting**) **1** explain the meaning of. **2** perform a piece of music, a dramatic role, etc. **3** translate orally etc. from one language into another. **4** understand (behaviour etc.) in a specified manner. □ **interpretable** adj. **interpretation** n. **interpretative** adj. **interpretive** adj.

interpreter n. **1** a person who translates from one language to another orally or using sign language. **2** a person who explains the meaning of or performs (a role, music, etc.). **3** an employee of a park, museum, etc. who gives tours etc.

interprovincial adj. between provinces.

interracial adj. existing between or affecting different races. [Say inter RACIAL]

interrelate v. (**interrelates, interrelated, interrelating**) relate or connect to another or others. □ **interrelatedness** n. **interrelation** n. **interrelationship** n.

interrogate v. (**interrogates, interrogated, interrogating**) **1** ask questions of (a person) esp. thoroughly or formally. **2** obtain data from (a computer file etc.). □ **interrogation** n. **interrogator** n. [Say in TERRA gate, in terra GAY sh'n, in TERRA gate er]

interrogative ● adj. **1** of or like a question; used in questions. **2** asking a question. ● n. an interrogative word (e.g. what?, why?). [Say inter OGGA tiv]

interrupt v. **1 a** stop the continuous progress of. **b** stop (someone) speaking, by saying or doing something. **2** break the continuity of (a view, line, surface, etc.). □ **interrupter** n. **interruption** n.

intersect v. **1** divide (a thing) by passing or lying across it. **2** (of lines, roads, etc.) cross or cut each other.

intersection n. **1 a** a place where two or more roads intersect. **b** the place where two things intersect or cross. **2** the act of intersecting.

intersession n. Cdn a short university term, usu. in May and June. [Say INTER session]

intersperse v. (**intersperses, interspersed, interspersing**) scatter; place here and there.

interstate ● adj. existing or carried on between states. ● n. US each of a system of highways between states.

interstellar adj. occurring or situated between stars.

interstice n. **1** an intervening space. **2** a chink or crevice. [Say in TUR stiss]

interstitial adj. of, forming, or occupying small gaps. [Say inter STISH'll]

intertextuality n. the relationship between esp. literary texts; the fact of relating or alluding to other texts. □ **intertextual** adj.

intertidal adj. of or relating to the underwater area which is exposed at low tide.

intertwine v. (**intertwines, intertwined, intertwining**) **1** entwine (together). **2** become entwined.

interval n. **1** an intervening time or space. **2** the difference in pitch between two sounds. □ **at intervals** here and there; now and then.

interval house n. Cdn = WOMEN'S SHELTER.

intervene v. (**intervenes, intervened, intervening**) **1** occur in time between events. **2** come between so as to prevent or alter a situation. **3** be situated between things. **4** appear in a lawsuit etc. as a third party. □ **intervenor** n. (also **intervener**)

intervention n. **1** the act or an instance of intervening. **2** interference, esp. by one country in another's affairs. **3** action or an action taken to improve a situation, esp. a medical disorder.

interventionism n. the principle or practice of intervention. □ **interventionist** n. & adj.

interview ● n. **1** a meeting at which a job applicant, student, etc. is questioned to determine their suitability. **2** a conversation between a reporter etc. and a person of public interest. **3** a meeting of persons face to face. **4** a session of formal questioning by the police. ● v. **1** hold an interview with. **2** question. **3** participate in an interview. □ **interviewee** n. **interviewer** n.

interwar adj. existing in the period between two wars, esp. the two world wars.

interweave v. (**interweaves**; past **interwove**; past participle **interwoven**; **interweaving**) **1** weave together. **2** link closely. **3** be or become interwoven.

interwoven adj. **1** woven together; interlaced. **2** closely blended or linked.

intestate ● adj. not having made a will before death. ● n. a person who has died intestate. [Say in TEST ate]

intestine n. (in sing. or pl.) the lower part of

the alimentary canal from the end of the stomach to the anus. □ **intestinal** *adj.* [*Say* in TESS tine *or* in TESS tin, in TESS tin ul]

intifada *n.* a movement of Palestinian uprising in the Israeli-occupied West Bank, beginning in 1987. [*Say* inta FODDA]

intimacy *n.* (*pl.* **intimacies**) **1** close familiarity or friendship. **2** an intimate act or remark. **3** a private cozy atmosphere.

intimate¹ ● *adj.* **1** familiar, close, friendly. **2** private and personal. **3** having sexual relations. **4** (of knowledge) detailed. **5** involving very close connection. **6** cozy; suggesting intimacy. ● *n.* a very close friend. □ **intimately** *adv.*

intimate² *v.* (**intimates**, **intimated**, **intimating**) state indirectly; imply, hint. □ **intimation** *n.* [*Say* INTA mate, inta MAY sh'n]

intimidate *v.* (**intimidates**, **intimidated**, **intimidating**) frighten into doing something. □ **intimidating** *adj.* **intimidatingly** *adv.* **intimidation** *n.* **intimidator** *n.*

into *prep.* **1** expressing motion or direction to a point on or within. **2** expressing direction of attention or state. **3** expressing a change of state. **4** *informal* interested in. **5** after the beginning of.

intolerable *adj.* that cannot be endured. □ **intolerably** *adv.*

intolerance *n.* **1** lack of tolerance for difference of opinion or practice. **2** severe sensitivity or allergy to a substance.

intolerant *adj.* **1** not tolerant. **2** not having the capacity to tolerate or endure a specified thing.

intonation *n.* **1** modulation of the voice; accent. **2** the act of intoning. **3** accuracy of pitch. [*Say* inta NAY sh'n]

intone *v.* (**intones**, **intoned**, **intoning**) **1** recite with prolonged sounds, esp. in a monotone. **2** chant (psalms etc.). **3** utter in a solemn or pompous tone.

intoxicant *n.* an intoxicating substance.

intoxicate *v.* (**intoxicates**, **intoxicated**, **intoxicating**) **1** make drunk. **2** excite or exhilarate. □ **intoxicating** *adj.* **intoxicatingly** *adv.* **intoxication** *n.*

intra- *prefix* forming adjectives meaning "on the inside, within".

intractable *adj.* **1** hard to control or deal with. **2** (of a disease) not easily treated. **3** stubborn. [*Say* in TRACTA bull]

intramural ● *adj.* **1** taking place within a single (esp. educational) institution. **2** forming part of normal university or

college studies. ● *n.* (in *pl.*) intramural sports. [*Say* intra MURAL]

intranet *n. Computing* a communications network within an organization.

intransigent *adj.* uncompromising, stubborn. □ **intransigence** *n.* [*Say* in TRANSA jint, in TRANSA jince]

intransitive *adj.* (of a verb) that does not take or require a direct object.

intrauterine *adj.* within the uterus. [*Say* intra YOO tuh rin *or* intra YOO tuh rine]

intrauterine device *n.* a contraceptive device fitted inside the uterus. Abbreviation: **IUD**.

intravenous ● *adj.* in or into a vein or veins. ● *n.* an intravenous injection or feeding. □ **intravenously** *adv.* [*Say* intra VENUS]

in-tray *n.* = IN-BASKET.

intrepid *adj.* fearless; very brave. □ **intrepidly** *adv.* [*Say* in TREP id]

intricate *adj.* very complicated; detailed in a perplexing way. □ **intricacy** *n.* **intricately** *adv.* [*Say* INTRA kit, IN tricka see]

intrigue ● *v.* (**intrigues**, **intrigued**, **intriguing**) **1** provoke (a person's) interest or curiosity. **2** plot something illegal or harmful. ● *n.* **1** the making of secret plans to cause somebody harm, do something illegal, etc. **2** a secret plan or arrangement. □ **intriguing** *adj.* **intriguingly** *adv.* [*Say* in TREEG *for the verb*, IN treeg *or* in TREEG *for the noun*]

intrinsic *adj.* belonging to or forming part of the real nature of a person or thing. □ **intrinsically** *adv.* [*Say* in TRIN zick]

intro *informal* ● *n.* (*pl.* **intros**) an introduction. ● *adj.* introductory.

intro- *comb. form* into.

introduce *v.* (**introduces**, **introduced**, **introducing**) **1** present (someone) by name to another. **2** announce or present to an audience. **3** bring (a custom, idea, etc.) into use. **4** bring before a legislative assembly. **5** bring (a subject) to the attention of (someone) for the first time. **6** insert; place in. **7** bring in. **8** begin; occur at the start of. □ **introducer** *n.*

introduction *n.* **1** the act or an instance of introducing. **2** a formal presentation of one person to another. **3** an explanatory section at the beginning of a book etc. **4** a preliminary section in a piece of music. **5** an introductory treatise on a subject. **6** a thing introduced.

introductory *adj.* serving as an introduction.

introspection *n.* the examination of

one's own thoughts and feelings.
□ **introspective** adj.

introvert ● n. **1** Psychology a person predominantly concerned with his or her own thoughts and feelings. **2** a shy, quiet person. ● adj. (also **introverted**) typical or characteristic of an introvert.
□ **introversion** n. [Say INTRA vert]

intrude v. **1** come without being invited or wanted. **2** thrust or be thrust into.

intruder n. a person who intrudes, esp. into a building with criminal intent.

intrusion n. **1** the act or an instance of intruding. **2** an unwanted interruption etc.

intrusive adj. **1** unwelcome; having an unwelcome effect. **2** formed by or having to do with an influx of molten rock between strata. □ **intrusively** adv. **intrusiveness** n.

intuit v. understand or work out by instinct. [Say in TOO it or in TYOO it]

intuition n. **1** the power of understanding something immediately, without the need for conscious reasoning or study. **2** an idea gained by this power. [Say into ISH'n]

intuitive adj. **1** of, characterized by, or possessing intuition. **2** capable of being easily understood by intuition.
□ **intuitively** adv. [Say in TOO it iv or in TYOO it iv]

Inuinnaqtun n. an Inuit language spoken in the Coronation Gulf area of the Central Arctic. [Say in noo een ACK toon]

Inuit ● n. (pl. **Inuit**) **1** any of several Aboriginal peoples inhabiting the Arctic coasts of Canada and Greenland. **2** the language of the Inuit; Inuktitut. ● adj. of the Inuit. [Say IN you it or IN oo it]

Inuk n. (pl. **Inuit**) a member of any of the Inuit peoples. [Say in OOK (with OOK as in BOOK)]

inukshuk n. a figure of a human made of stones. [Say in OOK shook (with OOK as in BOOK)]

Inuktitut n. the language of the Inuit. [Say in OOK ti tut (TUT rhymes with PUT)]

inundate v. (**inundates**, **inundated**, **inundating**) **1** flood. **2** overwhelm.
□ **inundation** n. [Say IN un date]

Inupiaq n. an Inuit language spoken in Canada, Alaska, and Greenland.
[Say in OO pee ack]

Inupiat n. (pl. **Inupiat**) **1** a member of an Inuit people inhabiting areas of northern Alaska. **2** the Inuit language spoken by the Inupiat. □ **Inupiat** adj. [Say in OO pee at]

inure v. (**inures**, **inured**, **inuring**) accustom to something unpleasant.
[Say in YUR]

in utero adv. in the womb.
[Say in YOOTER oh]

Inuvialuit n. an Inuit people of the western Canadian Arctic. □ **Inuvialuit** adj. [Say in oovy AL oo it]

Inuvialuktun n. an Inuit language of the western Arctic. [Say in oovy uh LOOK toon]

invade v. (**invades**, **invaded**, **invading**) **1** enter (a country etc.) with intent to control or subdue it. **2** enter in large numbers. **3** (of a disease) attack (a body etc.). **4** encroach upon. □ **invader** n.

invalid[1] n. a person weakened or disabled by illness or injury. [Say INVA lid]

invalid[2] adj. **1** not officially acceptable or usable. **2** not true or logical. [Say in VALID]

invalidate v. (**invalidates**, **invalidated**, **invalidating**) make invalid.
□ **invalidation** n. [Say in VALID ate]

invalidity n. (pl. **invalidities**) **1** lack of validity. **2** the condition of being an invalid. [Say inva LIDDA tee]

invaluable adj. extremely useful; beyond calculable value. □ **invaluably** adv.

invariable adj. **1** unchangeable.
2 constant, fixed. □ **invariably** adv.

invasion n. **1** the act of invading or process of being invaded. **2** an entry of a hostile army into a country or territory. **3** the arrival of a large number of people or things. **4** intrusion.

invasive adj. **1** (of weeds etc.) tending to spread. **2** (of medical procedures etc.) involving the introduction of instruments into the body. **3** tending to invade or intrude. □ **invasiveness** n.

invective n. rude language and unpleasant remarks shouted in anger.

inveigh v. criticize strongly. [Say in VAY]

inveigle v. (**inveigles**, **inveigled**, **inveigling**) persuade by trickery or flattery. [Say in VAY gull]

invent v. **1** create by thought; devise.
2 concoct (a false story etc.). □ **inventor** n.

invention n. **1** the process of inventing. **2** a thing invented; a contrivance. **3** a fictitious statement or story. **4** creativity.

inventive adj. **1** (of a person) having the ability to create or to think originally.
2 showing creativity or original thought.
□ **inventively** adv. **inventiveness** n.

inventory ● n. (pl. **inventories**) **1 a** a complete list of goods in stock etc. **b** the goods listed in this. **2** any list, catalogue, or account. ● v. (**inventories**, **inventoried**, **inventorying**) **1** make an inventory of. **2** enter in an inventory. [Say IN v'n tory]

inverse ● adj. inverted in position, order, or relation. ● n. (often foll. by of) a thing that is the opposite or reverse of another. □ **inversely** *adv.*

inverse proportion *n.* (also **inverse ratio**) a relation between two quantities such that one increases in proportion as the other decreases.

inversion *n.* **1 a** the act of inverting. **b** the state of being inverted. **2** the reversal of a normal order, position, etc. **3** the reversal of the normal order of words, for rhetorical effect. **4** the reversal of the normal variation of air temperature with altitude, i.e. an increase of temperature with height.

invert *v.* **1** turn upside down, inside out, or inward. **2** reverse the position, order, or relation of.

invertebrate ● *adj.* (of an animal) not having a backbone. ● *n.* an invertebrate animal. [*Say* in VERTA brate *or* in VERTA brit]

inverter *n.* an apparatus that converts direct electrical current into alternating current.

invest *v.* **1** put money into shares, property, financial schemes, etc., with the expectation of achieving a profit. **2** *informal* buy (something useful). **3** devote (time or effort) to an enterprise. **4 a** give someone power or authority. **b** provide with (a particular quality). □ **investable** *adj.* **investor** *n.*

investigate *v.* (**investigates, investigated, investigating**) find out information or facts about a person, thing, event, etc. □ **investigation** *n.* **investigator** *n.*

investigative *adj.* (of journalism) investigating and seeking to expose dishonesty, injustice, etc. [*Say* INVEST uh gate iv *or* INVEST uh guh tiv]

investiture *n.* the formal investing of a person with honours or rank. [*Say* INVEST uh chur]

investment *n.* **1 a** the act or process of investing. **b** an instance of this. **2** money etc. invested. **3** property etc. in which money may be invested.

investment bank *n.* a financial institution that specializes in financing commercial loans, mergers and acquisitions, foreign trade, etc. □ **investment banker** *n.* **investment banking** *n.*

inveterate *adj.* **1** (of a person) confirmed in an esp. bad habit etc. **2** (of a feeling or habit) firmly established. [*Say* in VETTER it]

invidious *adj.* unpleasant and unfair; likely to cause resentment or envy. □ **invidiously** *adv.* [*Say* in VIDDY us]

invigorate *v.* (**invigorates, invigorated, invigorating**) give vigour or strength to. □ **invigorating** *adj.* **invigoration** *n.* [*Say* in VIGGER ate]

invincible *adj.* too powerful to be defeated or overcome. [*Say* in VINSA bull]

inviolable *adj.* not to be violated or profaned. □ **inviolability** *n.* [*Say* in VIE uh luh bull]

inviolate *adj.* free or safe from injury or violation [*Say* in VIOLET]

invisible *adj.* **1** unable to be seen, either by nature or because concealed. **2** too small or inconspicuous to be seen or noticed. □ **invisibility** *n.* **invisibly** *adv.*

invitation *n.* **1** the process of inviting or fact of being invited. **2** the spoken or written form in which a person is invited. **3** the action or an act of enticing.

invitational ● *adj.* open only to those invited. ● *n.* an invitational contest etc.

invite ● *v.* (**invites, invited, inviting**) **1** ask (a person) courteously to come, or to do something. **2** make a formal courteous request for. **3** tend to call forth unintentionally (something unwanted). ● *n. informal* an invitation. □ **invitee** *n.* **inviter** *n.*

inviting *adj.* **1** attractive. **2** enticing. □ **invitingly** *adv.*

in vitro *adv.* (of processes) performed or occurring in a test tube or elsewhere outside a living organism. [*Say* in VEE troe]

in vitro fertilization *n.* a method of fertilizing an ovum in a test tube etc. and then implanting it in a uterus.

invocation *n.* **1** the act or an instance of invoking. **2** the act or an instance of calling upon God, a deity, etc. in prayer. [*Say* in voe KAY sh'n]

invoice ● *n.* a list of goods shipped, or services rendered, with prices and charges; a bill. ● *v.* (**invoices, invoiced, invoicing**) **1** make an invoice of. **2** send an invoice to.

invoke *v.* (**invokes, invoked, invoking**) **1** mention or use a law, rule, etc. as a reason for doing something. **2** appeal to as an authority or to support one's opinions or ideas. **3** make someone have a particular feeling; evoke. **4** make a request (for help) to someone, especially a god.

involuntary *adj.* **1** not done willingly or by choice; unintentional. **2** (of a nerve or muscle) not under the control of the will. □ **involuntarily** *adv.*

involve *v.* (**involves, involved, involving**) **1** cause to experience or participate in (a situation, activity, etc.).

2 imply, entail. **3** implicate. **4** include or affect in its operations. □ **involvement** n.

involved adj. **1 a** connected with. **b** implicated. **2** complicated. **3** engaged in a romantic relationship.

invulnerable adj. that cannot be harmed or defeated; safe. □ **invulnerability** n. [Say in VULL ner uh bull, in vull ner uh BILLA tee]

-in-waiting comb. form **1** attending another person. **2** future.

inward ● adj. **1** directed toward the inside; going in. **2** situated within. **3** mental, spiritual. ● adv. (also **inwards**) **1** towards the inside. **2** in the mind or soul.

inwardly adv. **1** towards the inside. **2** in one's mind.

in-your-face adj. slang aggressively blatant or provocative.

I/O abbr. Computing input/output.

IODE abbr. Cdn IMPERIAL ORDER DAUGHTERS OF THE EMPIRE.

iodine n. **1** a non-metallic element of the halogen group, forming black crystals and a violet vapour. **2** a solution of this in alcohol used as an antiseptic. [Say EYE uh dine]

iodized adj. treated with iodine. [Say EYE uh dized]

ion n. an atom, molecule, or group that has lost or gained one or more electrons. □ **ionic** adj. [Say EYE on, eye ON ick]

Ionic adj. of the order of Greek architecture characterized by a column with scroll shapes on the capital. [Say eye ON ick]

ionize v. (**ionizes**, **ionized**, **ionizing**) convert or be converted into an ion or ions. □ **ionization** n. **ionizer** n. [Say EYE uh nize, eye uh nize AY sh'n, EYE uh nize er]

ionosphere n. an ionized region of the atmosphere above the stratosphere. [Say eye ONNA sphere]

iota n. **1** the ninth letter of the Greek alphabet (Ι, ι). **2** the smallest possible amount. [Say eye OAT uh]

IOU n. (pl. **IOUs**) a signed document acknowledging a debt.

IP address n. Computing a unique string of numbers separated by periods that identifies each computer attached to the Internet.

ipso facto adv. **1** by that very fact or act. **2** thereby. [Say ipso FACTO]

IQ abbr. (pl. **IQs**) intelligence quotient, a number denoting the ratio of a person's intelligence to the statistical norm.

Iranian ● adj. **1** of or relating to Iranians or Iran. **2** of the Indo-European group of languages including Persian, Pashto,

Avestan, and Kurdish. ● n. **1** a person from Iran. **2** the Iranian languages. [Say i RAINY in]

Iraqi n. (pl. **Iraqis**) **1** a person from Iraq. **2** the form of Arabic spoken in Iraq. □ **Iraqi** adj. [Say i RACKY or i ROCKY]

irascible adj. easily provoked to anger; irritable. [Say i RASSA bull]

irate adj. extremely angry. [Say eye RATE]

IRC abbr. Internet Relay Chat.

ire n. anger, wrath.

iridescent adj. **1** showing rainbow-like luminous or gleaming colours. **2** changing colour with position. □ **iridescence** n. [Say ir uh DESS'nt, ir uh DESS'nce]

iridium n. a hard white metallic element, used esp. in alloys. [Say ir IDDY um]

iris n. (pl. **irises**) **1** the flat circular coloured membrane behind the cornea of the eye, with the pupil in the centre. **2** a plant with sword-shaped leaves and showy flowers.

Irish ● adj. of or relating to Ireland, its people or language. ● n. **1** (**the Irish**; treated as pl.) people from Ireland. **2** the Celtic language of Ireland. □ **Irishman** n. **Irishness** n. **Irishwoman** n.

Irish coffee n. coffee with Irish whiskey, topped with whipped cream.

Irish moss n. an edible seaweed of the northern hemisphere.

Irish setter n. a breed of dog with a long silky dark red coat.

irk v. annoy. □ **irksome** adj.

iron ● n. **1** a silver-white metallic element, much used for tools and implements. **2** this as a symbol of firmness or strength. **3** a tool or implement made of iron. **4** a household appliance with a heated flat base used to smooth wrinkles from fabric. **5** a golf club with a sloping head which is angled in order to loft the ball. **6** (usu. in pl.) shackles or chains on a prisoner's feet. ● adj. **1** consisting, made of, or resembling iron. **2** firm, inflexible. ● v. smooth (clothes etc.) with an iron. □ **iron in the fire** an undertaking or commitment. **iron out** smooth over (difficulties etc.).

Iron Age n. the period following the Bronze Age when iron replaced bronze in the making of implements and weapons, lasting in Europe from about 1000 BC until the Roman period.

ironclad adj. strict, rigorous, hard and fast.

Iron Curtain n. the notional barrier which existed between the West and the countries of the former Soviet bloc until the decline of Communism.

iron fist n. (also **iron hand**) firmness or ruthlessness.

ironic *adj.* (also **ironical**) **1** using or displaying irony. **2** in the nature of irony. □ **ironically** *adv.*

ironing *n.* **1** the pressing of clothes etc. with a heated iron. **2** clothes etc. which are to be or have just been ironed.

ironist *n.* a person who uses irony. □ **ironize** *v.* (**ironizes, ironized, ironizing**)

Ironman *n.* a triathlon of swimming, cycling, and running.

ironwood *n.* any of various trees with very hard wood.

ironwork *n.* things made of iron.

irony *n.* (*pl.* **ironies**) **1 a** the expression of meaning using language that normally expresses the opposite. **b** an instance of this. **2** a discrepancy between the expected and actual state of affairs.

Iroquoian *n.* **1** a major Aboriginal linguistic group, including Cayuga, Mohawk, Oneida, Onondaga, Seneca, and Tuscarora. **2** a member of the Iroquois. □ **Iroquoian** *adj.* [*Say* irra KWOY in]

Iroquois *n.* (*pl.* **Iroquois**) **1 a** a confederacy of Iroquoian peoples living in Ontario, Quebec, and New York. **b** a member of any of the peoples of this confederacy. **2** any of the languages of these peoples. □ **Iroquois** *adj.* [*Say* IRRA kwah]

irradiate *v.* (**irradiates, irradiated, irradiating**) **1** subject to radiation. **2** make brighter, light up. □ **irradiation** *n.*

irrational *adj.* **1** illogical; unreasonable. **2** not capable of reasoning. **3** *Math* (of a root etc.) not expressible as a ratio of two integers. □ **irrationality** *n.* **irrationally** *adv.*

irreconcilable *adj.* **1** relentlessly hostile. **2** incompatible, unable to be brought into harmony. [*Say* i reck un SILE uh bull]

irrecoverable *adj.* that cannot be recovered. □ **irrecoverably** *adv.*

irredeemable *adj.* too bad to be corrected, improved or saved. □ **irredeemably** *adv.*

irreducible *adj.* that cannot be made smaller or simpler. □ **irreducibly** *adv.* [*Say* i re DUCE uh bull]

irrefutable *adj.* that cannot be refuted or disproved. [*Say* i re FUTE uh bull]

irregular ● *adj.* **1** not regular; not symmetrical, uneven. **2** contrary to a rule or standard. **3** not occurring at regular intervals. **4** (of troops) not belonging to the regular army. **5** (of a word) not conjugated, pluralized, etc. according to the usual rules. **6** (of cloth etc.) flawed or damaged. ● *n.* **1** (in *pl.*) irregular troops. **2** a member

of an irregular military force. □ **irregularity** *n.* (*pl.* **irregularities**) **irregularly** *adv.*

irrelevant *adj.* not relevant. □ **irrelevance** *n.* **irrelevancy** *n.*

irreligious *adj.* **1** indifferent or hostile to religion. **2** lacking a religion.

irreparable *adj.* that cannot be rectified or made good. □ **irreparably** *adv.* [*Say* i REP ruh bull]

irreplaceable *adj.* that cannot be replaced if lost or damaged.

irrepressible *adj.* that cannot be repressed or restrained. □ **irrepressibly** *adv.*

irreproachable *adj.* faultless, blameless.

irresistible *adj.* too strong or tempting to be resisted. □ **irresistibly** *adv.*

irresolute *adj.* hesitant, undecided. □ **irresolution** *n.*

irrespective *adj.* regardless of.

irresponsible *adj.* **1** acting or done without due sense of responsibility. **2** not responsible for one's conduct. □ **irresponsibility** *n.* **irresponsibly** *adv.*

irretrievable *adj.* that cannot be retrieved or restored. □ **irretrievably** *adv.*

irreverent *adj.* lacking reverence; disrespectful. □ **irreverence** *n.* **irreverently** *adv.*

irreversible *adj.* not reversible or able to be altered. □ **irreversibility** *n.* **irreversibly** *adv.*

irrevocable *adj.* not able to be changed, reversed, or recovered. □ **irrevocably** *adv.* [*Say* i REV uh kuh bull *or* i re VOKE uh bull]

irrigate *v.* (**irrigates, irrigated, irrigating**) **1** supply (land or a crop) with water, esp. by means of specially constructed channels or pipes. **2** *Medical* supply (a wound etc.) with a constant flow of liquid. □ **irrigation** *n.* **irrigator** *n.*

irritable *adj.* **1** easily annoyed or angered. **2** very sensitive to contact. □ **irritability** *n.* **irritably** *adv.*

irritable bowel syndrome *n.* a condition involving abdominal pain and diarrhea or constipation.

irritant ● *adj.* causing slight inflammation to the body. ● *n.* **1** an irritant substance. **2** a source of continual annoyance.

irritate *v.* (**irritates, irritated, irritating**) **1** annoy. **2** stimulate discomfort or pain in (a part of the body). □ **irritating** *adj.* **irritatingly** *adv.* **irritation** *n.*

is 3rd singular present of BE.

ISBN *abbr.* (*pl.* **ISBNs**) international standard book number.

ISDN *abbr.* (*pl.* **ISDNs**) INTEGRATED SERVICES DIGITAL NETWORK.

-ish *suffix* forming adjectives: **1** having the qualities or characteristics of. **2** of the nationality of. **3** "somewhat". **4** *informal* denoting an approximate age or time.

Islam *n.* **1** the religion of Muslims, revealed through Muhammad as the Prophet of Allah, the one God. **2** the Muslim world. □ **Islamic** *adj.* [*Say* IZ lam *or* IZ lom, iz LAM ick *or* iz LOM ick]

Islamicist *n.* **1** a person who is an expert in Islamic culture, history, etc. **2** = ISLAMIST.

Islamic state *n.* a state governed under Islamic rather than secular law.

Islamism *n.* a political and cultural movement favouring the establishment of Islamic states. □ **Islamist** *n. & adj.*

island *n.* **1** a piece of land surrounded by water. **2** something resembling an island, esp. in being isolated. **3** a free-standing cupboard unit with a countertop. **4** (in full **traffic island**) a paved or grassed area in a road to divert traffic etc. □ **islander** *n.*

isle *n.* an island. [*Say* I'll]

islet *n.* **1** a small island. **2** *Anatomy* a portion of tissue structurally distinct from surrounding tissues. [*Say* EYE lit]

-ism *suffix* forming nouns, esp. denoting: **1** a system, principle, or movement. **2** a basis of prejudice. **3** a state or quality.

isn't *contr.* is not.

ISO *abbr.* **1** International Organization for Standardization. **2** the numerical exposure index assigned to a photographic film.

iso- *comb. form* **1** equal. **2** *Chemistry* isomeric. [*Say* ICE oh]

isobar *n.* a line on a map connecting positions having the same atmospheric pressure. [*Say* ICE oh bar]

isoflavone *n.* a phytoestrogen found in leguminous plants such as chickpeas and soybeans. □ **isoflavonoid** *n.* [*Say* ice oh FLAY vone ice oh FLAYVA noid]

isolate *v.* (**isolates, isolated, isolating**) **1 a** place apart or alone, cut off. **b** place (someone) in quarantine. **2 a** identify and separate for attention. **b** *Chemistry* separate (a substance) from a mixture. □ **isolator** *n.*

isolated *adj.* **1** lonely; remote. **2** not typical; unique.

isolation *n.* **1** the act or an instance of isolating. **2** the state of being isolated. **3** designating a hospital ward etc. for quarantined patients. □ **in isolation** considered singly, not relatively.

isolationism *n.* the policy of holding

aloof from the affairs of other countries. □ **isolationist** *n. & adj.*

isomer *n.* one of two or more compounds with the same molecular formula but a different arrangement of atoms and different properties. □ **isomeric** *adj.* [*Say* ICE uh mer, ice uh MAIR ick]

isometric *adj.* **1** of or having equal dimensions. **2** (of an exercise) involving contraction of a muscle group against a fixed, immovable resistance. □ **isometrically** *adv.* [*Say* ice uh METRIC]

isopropyl alcohol *n.* a colourless secondary alcohol used in antifreeze and as a solvent. [*Say* ice uh PRO pull]

isosceles *adj.* (of a triangle) having two sides equal. [*Say* eye SOSSA leez]

isotherm *n.* a line (on a map) connecting places having the same temperature. □ **isothermal** *adj.* [*Say* ICE uh therm]

isotonic *adj.* **1** designating a solution having the same osmotic pressure as some particular solution. **2** relating to a solution having the same salt concentration as blood. [*Say* ice oh TONIC]

isotope *n.* each of two or more forms of the same element that contain equal numbers of protons but different numbers of neutrons in their nuclei. □ **isotopic** *adj.* [*Say* ICE uh tope, ice uh TOPIC]

ISP *n.* Internet service provider.

Israeli ● *adj.* relating to the modern state of Israel. ● *n.* (*pl.* **Israelis**) a person from Israel. [*Say* iz RAY lee]

Israelite *n.* a member of the ancient Hebrew nation. □ **Israelite** *adj.* [*Say* IZ ree uh lite]

issue ● *n.* **1 a** a circulation of shares, stamps, etc. **b** a quantity of coins, copies of a newspaper or book etc., circulated at one time. **c** something given out or distributed. **d** each of a regular series of a magazine etc. **2** an outgoing, an outflow; an outlet. **3** an important subject of debate or litigation. **4** a result, outcome, or decision. **5** a problem. **6** *Law* children. ● *v.* (**issues, issued, issuing**) **1** *literary* go or come out. **2 a** send forth; publish. **b** supply, esp. officially. **3** be derived or result. **4** emerge from a condition. □ **at issue 1** under discussion. **2** at variance. **make an issue of** make a fuss about. **take issue** disagree. □ **issuance** *n.* **issuer** *n.*

-ist *suffix* forming personal nouns (and related adjectives) denoting: **1** an adherent of a system etc. in *-ism.* **2** a person who is prejudiced.

isthmus *n.* (*pl.* **isthmuses**) a narrow piece of land connecting two larger bodies of land. [*Say* ISS muss *or* ISTH muss]

IT *abbr.* information technology.

it *pron.* **1** the thing (or occasionally the animal or child) previously named or in question. **2** the person in question. **3** as the subject of an impersonal verb. **4** as a substitute for a deferred subject or object. **5** as a substitute for a vague object. **6** as the antecedent to a relative word. **7** exactly what is needed. **8** (in children's games) a player who has to do something, esp. to catch the others. **9** sex.

ital. *abbr.* italic (type).

Italian *n.* **1** a person from Italy. **2** the Romance language used in Italy.
□ **Italian** *adj.*

Italianate *adj.* of Italian style or appearance. [*Say* ITALIAN ate]

Italian dressing *n.* a salad dressing of oil and vinegar seasoned with garlic, oregano, basil, dill, fennel, and sometimes minced red pepper.

Italian sausage *n.* a pork sausage flavoured with anise or fennel seeds and sometimes hot red pepper flakes.

italic ● *adj.* **1** of the sloping typeface now used esp. for emphasis and in foreign words. **2** (**Italic**) of ancient Italy. ● *n.* a letter in italic type. [*Say* eye TAL ick *or* i TAL ick]

italicize *v.* (**italicizes**, **italicized**, **italicizing**) print in italics.
[*Say* eye TALA size *or* i TALA size]

Italo- *comb. form* Italian; Italian and. [*Say* ITTA low]

itch ● *n.* (*pl.* **itches**) **1** an irritation in the skin. **2** an impatient desire. ● *v.* (**itches**, **itched**, **itching**) **1** feel an itch, causing a desire to scratch it. **2** feel a desire to do something.

itchy *adj.* (**itchier**, **itchiest**) having or causing an itch. □ **have itchy feet** *informal* **1** be restless. **2** have a strong urge to travel.
□ **itchiness** *n.*

it'd *contr.* **1** it had. **2** it would.

-ite *suffix* forming nouns meaning "a person or thing connected with": **1** as natives or residents of a country, city, etc. **2** often *derogatory* as followers of a movement etc.

item *n.* **1** any of a number of enumerated or listed things. **2** an individual article, esp. one for sale. **3** a distinct piece of news etc. **4** a couple in a romantic relationship.

itemize *v.* (**itemizes**, **itemized**, **itemizing**) state or list item by item.

itoration *n.* the repetition of a process or utterance. [*Say* itta RAY shun]

itinerant ● *adj.* **1** travelling from place to place. **2** (of a judge etc.) travelling within a circuit. ● *n.* a person who travels from place to place. [*Say* eye TINNER rit]

itinerary *n.* (*pl.* **itineraries**) **1** a detailed route. **2 a** a record of a journey. **b** a listing of departure and arrival times for a journey. [*Say* eye TINNER airy]

-itis *suffix* forming nouns, esp.: names of inflammatory diseases. [*Say* ITE iss]

it'll *contr.* it will; it shall.

its *poss. adj.* of it; of itself.

it's *contr.* **1** it is. **2** it has.

itself *pron. emphatic and reflexive form of* IT.
□ **by itself** apart from its surroundings, automatically. **in itself** viewed in its essential qualities.

itsy-bitsy *adj.* (also **itty-bitty**) *informal* tiny, insubstantial, slight.

IUD *abbr.* (*pl.* **IUDs**) INTRAUTERINE DEVICE.

IV *adj. & n.* (*pl.* **IVs**) intravenous.

I've *contr.* I have.

IVF *abbr.* in vitro fertilization.

ivory (*pl.* **ivories**) ● *n.* **1** a hard creamy-white substance composing the main part of the tusks of an elephant, walrus, etc. **2** the colour of this. **3 a** an article made of ivory. **b** *slang* a piano key or a tooth. ● *adj.* creamy white. □ **tickle** (or **tinkle**) **the ivories** *informal* play the piano.

ivory tower *n.* a state or place separated from the ordinary world and the harsh realities of life.

ivy *n.* (*pl.* **ivies**) **1** a climbing evergreen plant with dark green, five-pointed leaves. **2** any of various other climbing plants.

Ivy League ● *n.* a group of prestigious universities in the eastern US. ● *adj.* of or relating to these schools or their students.

-ize *suffix* forming verbs, meaning: **1** make or become. **2** treat in such a way. **3 a** follow a special practice. **b** have a specified feeling. **4** affect with or subject to. □ **-izer** *suffix.*

Jj

J¹ *n.* (also **j**) (*pl.* **Js** or **J's**) the tenth letter of the alphabet.

J² *symb.* joule(s).

jab ● *v.* (**jabs**, **jabbed**, **jabbing**) **1** pierce or poke with the end or point of something. **2** punch, esp. with a short, sharp blow. **3** thrust (a thing) hard or abruptly. ● *n.* **1** an abrupt blow with one's fist etc. **2** a satirical or cutting remark.

jabber ● *v.* **1** chatter volubly and incoherently. **2** utter (words) fast and indistinctly. ● *n.* meaningless jabbering.

jacaranda *n.* any tropical American tree with hard scented wood, esp. one with blue trumpet-shaped flowers. [*Say* jacka RANDA]

jack ● *n.* **1** a device for lifting heavy objects, esp. the axle of a vehicle off the ground. **2** a playing card ranking next below queen. **3** a ship's flag flown from the bow and showing nationality. **4** a female connecting device in an electrical circuit. **5** a small starlike piece of metal used in tossing games. ● *v.* **1** raise (a car, etc.) with or as with a jack (in sense 1). **2** *informal* increase (prices etc.).

jackal *n.* a wild dog found in Africa and southern Asia, usu. scavenging for food in packs. [*Say* JACK'll]

Jack and Jill ● *adj.* open to both men and women. ● *n.* (*pl.* **Jack and Jills**) a party held for a couple soon to be married.

jackass *n.* (*pl.* **jackasses**) **1** a male donkey or ass. **2** a stupid person.

jackboot *n.* a large military boot reaching above the knee, esp. as a symbol of fascism. □ **jackbooted** *adj.*

jacket ● *n.* **1 a** a sleeved short outer garment. **b** a thing worn esp. round the torso for protection or support. **2** a casing or covering. **3** the skin of a potato. ● *v.* (**jackets**, **jacketed**, **jacketing**) cover with a jacket. □ **jacketed** *adj.*

Jack Frost *n.* frost personified.

jackhammer ● *n.* a portable pneumatic drill. ● *v.* drill using a jackhammer.

jack-in-the-box *n.* (*pl.* **jack-in-the-boxes**) a toy in the form of a box containing a figure on a spring which pops up when the lid is opened.

jack-in-the-pulpit *n.* any of several small N American woodland plants of the arum family.

jackknife ● *n.* (*pl.* **jackknives**) **1** a large pocket knife. **2** a dive in which the body is first bent at the waist and then straightened. ● *v.* (**jackknifes**, **jackknifed**, **jackknifing**) **1** (of an articulated vehicle) fold against itself in an accident. **2** fold like a jackknife.

jack of all trades *n.* (*pl.* **jacks of all trades**) a person who can do many different kinds of work.

jack-o'-lantern *n.* a lantern made esp. from a hollowed-out pumpkin carved to resemble a face.

Jack pine *n.* a hardy pine with short needles, found in northern N America.

jackpot *n.* a large prize or amount of winnings. □ **hit the jackpot** *informal* **1** win a large prize. **2** have remarkable success.

jackrabbit *n.* any of various large N American prairie hares.

Jacobean *adj.* **1** of the reign of James I of England (1603–25). **2** (of furniture) in the style prevalent then. [*Say* jacka BEE un]

Jacobin *n. hist.* a member of a radical democratic club established in Paris at the start of the French Revolution in 1789. [*Say* JACKA bin]

Jacobite *n.* a supporter of the deposed James II and his descendants in their claim to the British throne. [*Say* JACKA bite]

Jacob's ladder *n.* **1** a plant with rows of slender pointed leaves suggesting a ladder. **2** *Nautical* a rope or chain ladder.

jacquard *n.* a fabric made with an intricate variegated pattern. [*Say* JACK ard]

Jacuzzi *n.* (*pl.* **Jacuzzis**) *proprietary* **1** = WHIRLPOOL 2. **2** = HOT TUB. [*Say* juh COOZY]

jade ● *n.* **1** a hard usu. green stone, used for ornaments etc. **2** the green colour of jade. **3** a worn-out horse. ● *adj.* of the colour jade.

jaded *adj.* tired and bored, usually from having too much of something. □ **jadedness** *n.*

jade plant *n.* a succulent plant with thick dark green leaves.

jaeger *n.* a seabird of the skua family. [*Say* JAY grr]

jag¹ *n.* a sharp projection of rock etc.

jag² *n. informal* a bout of drinking, crying, etc.

jagged *adj.* **1** with an unevenly cut or torn edge. **2** with sharp points. **3** not smooth. □ **jaggedly** *adv.* **jaggedness** *n.*

jaguar *n.* a large feline of Central and South America, mainly yellowish-brown with dark spots. [*Say* JAG war *(*WAR *rhymes with* FAR*)*]

jail ● *n.* a prison for holding people accused or convicted of crime. ● *v.* put in jail. □ **jailer** *n.*

jailbird *n.* a prisoner or habitual criminal.

jailbreak *n.* an escape from jail.

jailhouse *n.* a prison.

Jain ● *n.* an adherent of a religion founded in India, characterized by its stress on non-violence. ● *adj.* of or relating to this religion. □ **Jainism** *n.* **Jainist** *n.* [*Say* JINE]

jalapeno *n.* (*pl.* **jalapenos**) (also **jalapeno pepper**) a very hot green chili pepper. [*Say* hala PEE no *or* hala PAY nyo *or* hala PEE nyo]

jalopy *n.* (*pl.* **jalopies**) *informal* a dilapidated old car etc. [*Say* juh LOPPY]

jam ● *v.* (**jams**, **jammed**, **jamming**) **1 a** squeeze or wedge into a space. **b** become wedged. **2** become or make unable to operate due to a part becoming stuck. **3** push or cram together in a compact mass. **4** push or crowd. **5 a** block (a road etc.) by crowding etc. **b** (of ice, logs, etc.) form an obstruction in a river etc. **6** apply (brakes etc.) forcefully. **7** block (a radio transmission) by causing interference. **8** *informal* improvise with other musicians. ● *n.* **1** a conserve of fruit and sugar. **2** a squeeze or crush. **3** a crowded mass. **4** *informal* an awkward predicament. **5** a stoppage due to jamming. **6** (also **jam session**) *informal* improvised playing by a group of musicians.

Jamaican *n.* **1** a person from Jamaica. **2** the variety of English spoken in Jamaica. □ **Jamaican** *adj.* [*Say* juh MAKE in]

Jamaican patty *n.* a half-moon shaped turnover of yellow pastry with a spicy filling.

jamb *n.* a side post of a doorway, window, etc. [*Say* JAM]

jambalaya *n.* a Cajun dish of rice with shrimps, chicken, etc. [*Say* jam buh LIE uh]

jamboree *n.* **1** a large celebration or party. **2** a large rally of Scouts. [*Say* jam buh REE]

jammies *pl. n. slang* = PYJAMAS 1.

jam-packed *adj. informal* full to capacity.

Jan. *abbr.* January.

Jane Doe *n.* a woman whose name is unknown.

jangle ● *v.* (**jangles**, **jangled**, **jangling**) **1** make, or cause to make, a harsh metallic sound. **2** irritate (the nerves etc.). ● *n.* a harsh metallic sound. □ **jangly** *adj.*

janitor *n.* a caretaker of a building, responsible for its cleaning etc. □ **janitorial** *adj.*

January *n.* (*pl.* **Januaries**) the first month of the year.

japan ● *n.* a hard usu. black varnish, originating in Japan. ● *v.* (**japans**, **japanned**, **japanning**) varnish with japan.

Japanese *n.* (*pl.* **Japanese**) **1** a person from Japan. **2** the language of Japan. □ **Japanese** *adj.*

Japanimation *n.* = ANIME.

jape *n.* a jest or joke. □ **japery** *n.* (*pl.* **japeries**)

japonica *n.* a flowering shrub with bright red flowers. [*Say* juh PONNA cuh]

jar¹ *n.* a container of glass, earthenware, etc., usu. cylindrical.

jar² ● *v.* (**jars**, **jarred**, **jarring**) **1** (of sound, words, etc.) sound discordant or grating. **2** strike or cause to strike with a jolt. **3** send a shock through (a part of the body). **4** (of an opinion, fact, etc.) be at variance. ● *n.* a physical shock or jolt. □ **jarring** *adj.*

jargon *n.* **1** words or expressions used by a particular group that are difficult for others to understand. **2** gibberish. **3** a pidgin. □ **jargony** *adj.*

jasmine *n.* (also **jasmin**) a shrub or climbing plant with fragrant flowers. [*Say* JAZZ min]

jasper *n.* an opaque variety of quartz, usu. red, yellow, or brown.

jaundice ● *n.* **1** yellowing of the skin etc. caused by a bile disorder. **2** envy, resentment. ● *v.* (**jaundices**, **jaundiced**, **jaundicing**) **1** affect with jaundice. **2** affect (a person) with envy or disillusionment. [*Say* JOHN diss]

jaunt ● *n.* a short excursion for enjoyment. ● *v.* take a jaunt.

jaunty *adj.* (**jauntier**, **jauntiest**) **1** cheerful and self-confident. **2** dashing, pert. □ **jauntily** *adv.* **jauntiness** *n.*

Java *n. proprietary* a programming language used esp. for creating applications for the Internet. [*Say* JAV uh]

java *n. slang* coffee. [*Say* JAV uh *or* JOV uh]

Javanese *n.* (also **Javan**) (*pl.* **Javanese**) **1** a person from Java. **2** the language of

central Java. □ **Javanese** *adj.*
[*Say* java NEEZ]

javelin *n.* a light spear thrown in a competitive sport or as a weapon.
[*Say* JAVA lin *or* JAV lin]

Javex *n. Cdn proprietary* chlorine bleach.

jaw ● *n.* **1 a** each of the upper and lower bony structures in vertebrates forming the framework of the mouth and containing the teeth. **b** the parts of certain invertebrates used for the ingestion of food. **2 a** (*in pl.*) the mouth with its bones and teeth. **b** the gripping parts of a tool or machine. **3** *informal* **a** talkativeness. **b** a conversation. ● *v. informal* speak esp. at tedious length.

jawbone *n.* the bone of the lower jaw.

jawbreaker *n. informal* **1** a word that is hard to pronounce. **2** a large, hard candy.

jawed *adj.* having a jaw or the kind of jaw described.

jawline *n.* the outline of the jaw.

jay *n.* any of various medium-sized birds of the crow family, with varied, colourful, plumage.

jaywalk *v.* (of a pedestrian) cross a street at a place other than at an intersection, crosswalk, etc., or against a red light.
□ **jaywalker** *n.* **jaywalking** *n.*

jazz ● *n.* **1** a type of music of African-American origin, characterized by improvisation, syncopated phrasing, etc. **2** (also **jazz ballet, jazz dance**) a style of theatrical dance performed to jazz or popular music. **3** *slang* energy, excitement. ● *v.* (**jazzes, jazzed, jazzing**) play or dance to jazz. □ **all that jazz** all that sort of thing. **jazz up** brighten or enliven.
□ **jazzer** *n.*

jazzman *n.* (*pl.* **jazzmen**) a male jazz musician.

jazzy *adj.* (**jazzier, jazziest**) **1** of or like jazz. **2** *slang* spirited, lively. **3** *slang* flashy, showy.

jealous *adj.* **1** envious or resentful. **2** suspicious or resentful of rivalry in love or affection. **3** fiercely protective (of rights etc.). □ **jealously** *adv.* **jealousy** *n.*

jean *n.* **1** a heavy twilled cotton fabric, now usu. denim. **2** (usu. in *pl.*) pants made of this fabric.

Jeep *n. proprietary* a sturdy, four-wheel drive motor vehicle.

jeepers *interj.* (also **jeepers creepers**) *slang* expressing surprise etc.

jeer ● *v.* **1** speak or call out in derision or mockery. **2** drive or force away by jeering. ● *n.* a scoff or taunt.

jeez *interj. slang* a mild expression of surprise, discovery, etc.

jeezly *adj. Cdn slang* used as an intensifier

Jehovah *n.* a form of the Hebrew name of God used in some translations of the Bible.
[*Say* juh HOVE uh]

Jehovah's Witness *n.* a member of a fundamentalist Christian sect that denies many traditional Christian doctrines and preaches the Second Coming.

Jekyll and Hyde *n.* a person alternately displaying opposing good and evil personalities. [*Say* JECK'll and HIDE]

jell *v. informal* **1 a** set as a jelly. **b** take a definite form. **2** (of people) readily co-operate.

jellied *adj.* **1** set into a jelly. **2** containing jelly.

Jell-O *n. proprietary* a fruit-flavoured gelatin dessert.

jelly *n.* (*pl.* **jellies**) **1 a** a type of jam made of fruit juice and sugar. **b** a dessert made of fruit-flavoured liquid, sugar and gelatin, set to form a semi-solid mass. **2** any substance of a similar consistency.
□ **jellylike** *adj.*

jelly bean *n.* a bean-shaped candy with a hard sugar coating.

jelly doughnut *n.* a round jam-filled doughnut.

jellyfish *n.* (*pl.* **jellyfish** or **jellyfishes**) a marine animal having a jellylike body and stinging tentacles.

jelly roll *n.* a thin layer of sponge cake spread with jam or other filling and rolled up to form a cylindrical cake.

je ne sais quoi *n.* an indefinable something. [*Say* zhuh nuh say KWAH]

jeopardize *v.* (**jeopardizes, jeopardized, jeopardizing**) endanger; put into jeopardy. [*Say* JEP er dize]

jeopardy *n.* **1** danger, esp. of harm or loss. **2** *Law* the risk of being convicted of a criminal offence. [*Say* JEP er dee]

jeremiad *n.* a list of woes.
[*Say* jerra MY ud]

jerk¹ ● *n.* **1** a sharp sudden movement; a muscle twitch. **2** *slang* a fool; a stupid person. ● *v.* move, thrust, or pull with a jerk. □ **jerk around** *slang* deceive or mislead.

jerk² ● *v.* cure (meat) by drying it in slices in the sun. ● *n.* an originally Jamaican method of preparing meat by seasoning it highly with pepper and spices, and barbecuing.

jerkin *n.* a sleeveless jacket.

jerky¹ *adj.* (**jerkier, jerkiest**) having sudden abrupt movements; spasmodic.
□ **jerkily** *adv.*

jerky² *n.* jerked meat.

jerry-built *adj.* badly or hastily built with cheap materials.

jerry can *n.* a kind of gasoline or water can.

jersey *n.* (*pl.* **jerseys**) **1** a soft knitted fabric. **2** a knitted usu. woollen pullover. **3** a distinguishing sweater or shirt worn by members of a team. **4** (**Jersey**) a light brown dairy cow.

Jerusalem artichoke *n.* a species of sunflower with edible tubers.

jest ● *n.* **1 a** a joke. **b** fun. **2 a** banter. **b** an object of derision. ● *v.* joke; make jests.

jester *n. hist.* a professional joker or fool at a medieval court etc.

Jesuit *n.* a member of the Society of Jesus, a Catholic order of priests founded in 1534 to do missionary work. [*Say* JEZH yoo it *or* JEZZ oo it]

jet¹ ● *n.* **1** a stream of liquid or gas shot out, esp. from a small opening. **2** a spout or nozzle for emitting water etc. in this way. **3 a** a jet engine. **b** an aircraft powered by jet engines. ● *v.* (**jets, jetted, jetting**) **1** spurt out or cause to spurt out in jets. **2** travel by jet plane.

jet² ● *n.* **1** a hard black variety of coal that can be highly polished. **2** *n. & adj.* (also **jet black**) a deep glossy black.

jet engine *n.* an engine (esp. of an aircraft) which for forward thrust uses the backward ejection of a high-speed jet of gas.

jet lag *n.* extreme tiredness and disrupted biological rhythms felt after a long flight across several time zones. □ **jet-lagged** *adj.*

jetliner *n.* a commercial airplane equipped with jet engines.

jetsam *n.* discarded material washed ashore, esp. that thrown overboard from a ship. [*Say* JET sum]

jet set *n. informal* wealthy people frequently travelling for pleasure. □ **jet-setter** *n.* **jet-setting** *adj.*

Jet Ski ● *n. proprietary* a jet-propelled watercraft ridden like a motorbike. ● *v.* (**jet ski, jet skis, jet skied, jet skiing**) ride on a jet ski. □ **jet skiing** *n.*

jet stream *n.* **1** a narrow current of very strong winds several miles above the earth. **2** the stream from a jet engine.

jettison ● *v.* **1** throw overboard to lighten an aircraft, ship, etc. **2** release from a spacecraft in flight. **3** get rid of. ● *n.* the act of jettisoning. [*Say* JETTA sun]

jetty *n.* (*pl.* **jetties**) **1** a landing pier. **2** a pier or breakwater constructed to protect a harbour etc.

Jew *n.* a person of Hebrew descent or whose religion is Judaism.

jewel ● *n.* **1 a** a precious stone. **b** this as used as a bearing in watchmaking. **2** pieces of jewellery. **3** something of great beauty or worth. ● *v.* (**jewels, jewelled, jewelling**) adorn or set with jewels. □ **jewel in the crown** the best in a particular group.

jewel box *n.* **1** (also **jewellery box**) a small box for storing jewellery. **2** (also **jewel case**) a plastic case for storing a compact disc.

jeweller *n.* (also esp. *US* **jeweler**) a person who makes or sells jewellery.

jewellery *n.* (also **jewelry**) personal ornaments, often set with jewels, e.g. rings and necklaces. [*Say* JEW luh ree *or* JEW ul ree *or* JULE ree]

Jewish *adj.* **1** of or relating to Jews. **2** of Judaism. □ **Jewishness** *n.*

Jewry *n.* (*pl.* **Jewries**) the Jewish people; Jews collectively.

Jew's harp *n.* a small lyre-shaped musical instrument held between the teeth and struck with the finger.

jib ● *n.* **1** a triangular sail in front of the mast. **2** the projecting arm of a crane. ● *v.* (**jibs, jibbed, jibbing**) (of a sail etc.) gybe.

jibe¹ ● *n.* an instance of mocking or taunting. ● *v.* (**jibes, jibed, jibing**) **1** jeer, mock. **2** sneer at, taunt.

jibe² *v. & n.* (**jibes, jibed, jibing**) = GYBE.

jibe³ *v.* (**jibes, jibed, jibing**) *informal* agree; be in accord.

jiffy *n.* (*pl.* **jiffies**) *informal* a short time; a moment.

jig ● *n.* **1 a** a lively leaping dance. **b** the music for this. **2** a device that holds a piece of work and guides the tools operating on it. ● *v.* (**jigs, jigged, jigging**) **1** dance a jig. **2** move quickly and jerkily up and down. **3** work on with a jig. **4** fish (for) with a jigger. □ **the jig is up** the scheme is revealed or foiled.

jigger¹ ● *n.* **1 a** a small tackle of a double and single block with a rope. **b** a small sail at the stern. **c** a small fishing boat having this. **2 a** a small glass marked for measuring liquor. **b** the quantity of liquor contained in this. **3** *Cdn* **a** a device upon which a gillnet is hung underneath ice. **b** a piece of lead shaped like a fish fastened on the end of a heavy fishing line. **4** someone that jigs. ● *v.* (usu. in phr. **I'll be jiggered**) *slang* confound, damn.

jiggle ● *v.* (**jiggles, jiggled, jiggling**) **1** shake lightly; rock jerkily. **2** fidget. ● *n.* a light shake. □ **jiggly** *adj.*

jigsaw *n.* **1** (also **jigsaw puzzle**) a puzzle consisting of a picture on board or wood etc. cut into irregular interlocking pieces.

2 a machine saw with a fine blade enabling it to cut curved lines in a sheet of wood, metal, etc.

jihad *n.* **1** a holy war undertaken by Muslims against unbelievers. **2** a campaign or crusade in some cause. [*Say* juh HAD]

jihadi *n.* (also **jihadist**) a person taking part in a jihad.

jillion *n. informal* a great many.

jilt *v.* abruptly reject or abandon (a lover etc.).

Jim Crow *n. US* the practice of segregating or discriminating against blacks.

jimmy ● *n.* (*pl.* **jimmies**) a burglar's short crowbar. ● *v.* (**jimmies, jimmied, jimmying**) force open with a jimmy.

jingle ● *n.* 1 a a mixed noise as of metal objects being shaken together. **b** a thing that jingles. **2** a short easily remembered slogan, verse, or tune, esp. as used in advertising. ● *v.* (**jingles, jingled, jingling**) make or cause to make a jingling sound. □ **give a person a jingle** *informal* telephone a person. □ **jingly** *adj.* (**jinglier, jingliest**)

jingo *n.* (*pl.* **jingoes**) a supporter of war; a blustering patriot. □ **jingoism** *n.* **jingoist** *n.* **jingoistic** *adj.*

jink ● *v.* move elusively; dodge. ● *n.* an act of dodging or eluding.

jinni *n.* (also **jinnee, jinn**) (*pl.* **jinn**) (in Muslim mythology) an intelligent being lower than the angels which has power over people. [*Say* jin EE *or* JIN ee]

jinx *informal ● n.* (*pl.* **jinxes**) a person or thing that seems to cause bad luck. ● *v.* (**jinxes, jinxed, jinxing**) bring bad luck to.

jitter *informal ● n.* (**the jitters**) extreme nervousness. ● *v.* be or act nervous. □ **jittery** *adj.*

jitterbug ● *n. hist.* a fast dance popular in the 1940s, performed to swing music. ● *v.* (**jitterbugs, jitterbugged, jitterbugging**) dance the jitterbug.

jiu-jitsu *n.* a Japanese system of unarmed combat. [*Say* joo JIT soo]

jive ● *n.* 1 a jerky lively style of dance esp. popular in the 1950s. **2** music for this dance. **3** a variety of American black English associated with jazz. ● *v.* (**jives, jived, jiving**) **1** dance the jive. **2** play jive music. **3** *slang* **a** mislead, fool. **b** talk nonsense. □ **jiver** *n.*

job ● *n.* 1 a piece of esp. paid work. **2** a paid position of employment. **3** anything one has to do. **b** responsibility. **c** a specified operation or other matter. **4 a** *informal* a difficult task. **b** performance. **5** an item of

work. **6** *slang* a crime. ● *v.* (**jobs, jobbed, jobbing**) **1** do jobs; do piecework. **2** subcontract. □ **get on with the job** continue with one's affairs. **on the job** at work. **out of a job** unemployed. □ **jobbing** *adj.* **jobless** *adj.* **joblessness** *n.*

job action *n.* an organized protest by employees.

jobber *n.* **1** a wholesaler. **2** a worker paid for the amount produced.

job-share ● *v.* (**job-shares, job-shared, job-sharing**) (of two employees) jointly share a full-time position. ● *n.* a job-sharing situation. □ **job-sharer** *n.* **job-sharing** *n.*

jock *n. informal* **1** = JOCKSTRAP. **2** an esp. male athlete or sports fan. **3** an enthusiast or devotee.

jockey ● *n.* (*pl.* **jockeys**) **1** a professional rider in horse races. **2** a person having control or direction of something. ● *v.* (**jockeys, jockeyed, jockeying**) **1** try to gain advantage by skilful manoeuvring. **2** ride as a jockey.

Jockey shorts *pl. n. proprietary* men's or boys' close-fitting underpants with a triangular flap at the front.

jock itch *n.* a fungal infection of the groin area.

jockstrap *n.* an undergarment providing support or protection for the male genitals.

jocular *adj.* **1** said, done, etc. jokingly. **2** fond of joking. □ **jocularity** *n.* **jocularly** *adv.* [*Say* JOCK you ler, jock you LAIR uh tee]

jodhpurs *pl. n.* long breeches for riding etc. that are close-fitting below the knee. [*Say* JOD purrs]

joe *n. slang* **1** a fellow or average man. **2** coffee.

Joe Blow *n. informal* a hypothetical average man.

joe job *n. Cdn informal* a menial or monotonous task.

Joe Public *n. informal* (a member of) the general public.

joey *n.* (*pl.* **joeys**) a young kangaroo.

jog¹ ● *v.* (**jogs, jogged, jogging**) **1** run at a slow, steady pace. **2** proceed, go on one's way. **3** nudge (a person). **4** shake or bump. **5** give a gentle reminder to (one's memory). ● *n.* **1 a** a slow walk or trot. **b** a gentle run taken as exercise. **2** a shake, push, or nudge. □ **jogging** *n.*

jog² ● *n.* 1 a short bend in a road etc., after which it continues in its original direction. **2** a notch or jag in an otherwise level surface or straight line. ● *v.* (**jogs, jogged,**

jogging) bend, turn, or suddenly change direction.

jogger *n.* **1** a person who jogs. **2** *Cdn & Brit.* = RUNNING SHOE.

joggle ● *v.* (**joggles**, **joggled**, **joggling**) shake or move with repeated jerks. ● *n.* a slight shake or jerk.

john *n.* *informal* **1** a toilet. **2** a washroom. **3** a prostitute's customer.

John Doe *n.* **1** a person whose real name is unknown. **2** an anonymous party in a legal action.

johnnycake *n.* a cornmeal bread usu. fried.

Johnny Canuck *n.* *Cdn informal* **1** a person from Canada. **2** a Canadian soldier. **3** Canada personified.

johnny-come-lately *n.* (*pl.* **johnny-come-latelies**) *informal* a newcomer or late-starter.

joie de vivre *n.* healthy and exuberant enjoyment of life. [*Say* zhwah duh VEEVRA]

join ● *v.* **1** put together; fasten, unite. **2** connect by a line etc. **3** become a member or employee of. **4 a** come into the company of. **b** share the company of (a person) for a specified occasion **5** come together, be united. **6** take part with others in an activity etc. **7** unite in marriage etc. ● *n.* a place where things are joined. □ **join forces** combine efforts. **join hands 1 a** clasp each other's hands. **b** clasp one's hands together. **2** combine in an action or enterprise. **join up 1** enlist for military service. **2** unite, connect.

joiner *n.* **1** *informal* a person who readily joins groups etc. **2** a device used for making carpentry joints.

joinery *n.* **1** the construction of wooden furniture etc. **2** carpentry joints collectively.

joint ● *n.* **1** a place at which parts are joined. **2 a** a structure in an animal body which joins two bones. **b** the place of connection of two movable parts in an invertebrate. **3** a large cut of meat. **4** *slang* **a** a place where people go for eating, entertainment, etc. **b** an establishment. **c** prison. **5** *slang* a marijuana cigarette. **6** the part of a stem from which a leaf or branch grows. ● *adj.* **1** held or done by two or more persons etc. **2** sharing with another person in some action, state, etc. **3** of or involving both houses of a bicameral parliament. ● *v.* **1** connect by joints. **2** divide (a body) at a joint or into joints. □ **out of joint 1** (of a bone) dislocated. **2** disordered, out of order. □ **jointed** *adj.* **jointly** *adv.*

joist *n.* each of a series of parallel supporting beams of timber, steel, etc., used in floors, ceilings, etc.

jojoba *n.* an evergreen shrub or tree of the southwestern US, which produces an oil used in cosmetics. [*Say* ho HO buh]

joke ● *n.* **1 a** a thing said or done to excite laughter. **b** a witticism or jest. **2** a ridiculous thing or person. **3 a** something trifling. **b** *informal* something very easy. ● *v.* (**jokes**, **joked**, **joking**) **1 a** make a joke or jokes. **b** utter as a joke. **2** poke fun at; banter. □ **jokey** *adj.* **jokingly** *adv.*

joker *n.* **1** a person who jokes. **2** a playing card usu. with a figure of a jester. **3** an unexpected factor or resource.

jollity *n.* **1** the quality or condition of being jolly. **2** merrymaking. [*Say* JOLLA tee]

jolly[1] ● *adj.* (**jollier**, **jolliest**) **1** cheerful and good-humoured. **2** lively and pleasant. ● *v.* (**jollies**, **jollied**, **jollying**) **1** *informal* keep or make (a person) jolly by friendly behaviour etc. **2** tease. ● *n.* (*pl.* **jollies**) *informal* a thrill.

jolly[2] *n.* (*pl.* **jollies**) (also **jolly boat**) a small light boat carried aboard a ship.

Jolly Jumper *n.* *Cdn proprietary* an infant swing which suspends a baby in a harness, allowing the child to jump etc.

Jolly Roger *n.* a pirates' black flag, usu. with a skull and crossbones.

jolt ● *v.* **1** disturb or shake abruptly and roughly. **2** give a mental shock to. **3** invigorate suddenly. **4** move with a jolt. ● *n.* **1** an abrupt movement or jerk. **2** a surprise or mental shock.

Jordanian *adj.* of or relating to the kingdom of Jordan. □ **Jordanian** *adj.* [*Say* jor DAINY in]

josh *v.* *slang* (**joshes**, **joshed**, **joshing**) **1** tease or joke with. **2** indulge in banter. □ **joshing** *n.*

joss *n.* (*pl.* **josses**) **1** a Chinese figure of a god. **2** (also **joss stick**) a stick of a fragrant substance, burned as incense.

jostle ● *v.* (**jostles**, **jostled**, **jostling**) **1** push, bump, or collide, esp. in a crowd. **2** struggle forcefully for. ● *n.* the act or an instance of jostling. [*Say* JOSSLE]

jot ● *v.* (**jots**, **jotted**, **jotting**) write briefly or hastily. ● *n.* a very small amount. □ **jotting** *n.*

joual *n.* a variety of Canadian French considered to be uneducated, characterized by numerous English borrowings. [*Say* zhoo ALL]

joule *n.* the SI unit of work or energy. [*Say* JOOL]

jounce *v.* (**jounces**, **jounced**, **jouncing**) bump, bounce, jolt. □ **jouncing** *n. & adj.* [*Rhymes with* BOUNCE]

journal n. **1** a daily record of events; a diary. **2 a** a periodical dealing with a specialized subject. **b** an esp. daily newspaper. **3** a book in which business transactions are entered.

journalism n. **1** the work of writing and reporting news items in the press or on television etc. **2** the news media collectively. □ **journalist** n. **journalistic** adj. **journalistically** adv.

journey ● n. (pl. **journeys**) **1** an act of travelling from one place to another. **2** the distance travelled. ● v. (**journeys**, **journeyed**, **journeying**) make a journey. □ **journeyer** n.

journeyman n. (pl. **journeymen**) **1** a person who is qualified to work in a craft or trade under the direction of a more qualified person. **2** a reliable but not outstanding worker.

joust ● n. **1** hist. a combat between two knights on horseback with lances. **2** a verbal, political, etc. encounter or contest. ● v. engage in a joust. □ **jouster** n.

Jove n. □ **by Jove!** an exclamation of surprise or approval.

jovial adj. cheerful and friendly. □ **joviality** n. **jovially** adv. [Say JOE vee ul, joe vee ALA tee]

Jovian adj. of the planet Jupiter. [Say JOE vee in]

jowl n. **1** the cheek, esp. when it is loose and fleshy. **2** the meat of the cheek of a pig. **3** the dewlap of oxen etc. **4** the jaw or jawbone. □ **cheek by jowl** close together. □ **jowly** adj. [Rhymes with HOWL]

joy n. **1** great pleasure; extreme gladness. **2** a cause of joy. **3** informal satisfaction, success. □ **joyless** adj.

joyful adj. feeling or causing joy. □ **joyfully** adv.

joyous adj. characterized by pleasure or joy; joyful. □ **joyously** adv.

joyride informal ● n. **1** a car ride taken for fun and excitement, usu. without the owner's permission. **2** a pleasurable, often exciting experience. ● v. go for a joyride. □ **joyrider** n. **joyriding** n.

joystick n. **1** a lever used to control the movement of an image on a video or computer screen. **2** the control column of an aircraft.

JP abbr. (pl. **JPs**) JUSTICE OF THE PEACE.

JPEG n. **1** a technique and standard for the compression of continuous-tone digital images. **2** an image encoded as a file in this format.

Jr. abbr. Junior.

jubilant adj. rejoicing, joyful. □ **jubilantly** adv. [Say JOOBA lint]

jubilation n. a feeling of great happiness and triumph. [Say joo buh LAY sh'n]

jubilee n. **1** an anniversary, esp. the 25th, 50th, or 60th. **2** a time of rejoicing. [Say jooba LEE or JOOBA lee]

Judaeo- comb. form = JUDEO-.

Judaic adj. of or characteristic of the Jews or Judaism. [Say joo DAY ick]

Judaica pl. n. the literature, customs, etc. which are of particular relevance to Jews or Judaism. [Say joo DAY ick uh]

Judaism n. **1** the religion of the Jews, based on the Old Testament and the Talmud. **2** the cultural practices etc. based on this religion. [Say JOO day ism]

Judas n. (pl. **Judases**) a person who betrays a friend. [Say JOO dis]

judder ● v. (esp. of a mechanism) shake noisily or violently. ● n. an instance of juddering. □ **juddery** adj.

Judeo- comb. form **1** pertaining to the Jews, Judaism, or things Jewish. **2** Jewish and. [Say joo DAY oh]

judge ● n. **1** a public officer who decides cases in a court of justice. **2** a person appointed to decide a competition etc. **3 a** a person who decides anything in question. **b** a person with the knowledge to decide on the merits of something. ● v. (**judges**, **judged**, **judging**) **1 a** try (a cause) in a court of justice. **b** pronounce sentence on (a person). **2** form an opinion about. **3** act as a judge of. **4** conclude or suppose. □ **judgeship** n.

judgment n. (also **judgement**) **1** the critical faculty; discernment. **2** good sense. **3** an opinion or estimate. **4** the decision or sentence of a court of justice. **5** (**Judgment**) = LAST JUDGMENT. □ **pass judgment 1** (of a judge) give a verdict. **2** criticize or condemn someone.

judgmental adj. (also **judgemental**) **1** of, concerning, or by way of judgment. **2** condemning, critical. □ **judgmentally** adv.

Judgment Day n. the time of the Last Judgment.

judicial adj. **1** of or proper to a court of law. **2** invested with the authority to judge causes. **3** having to do with a judge. □ **judicially** adv. [Say joo DISH'll]

judicial review n. Law a procedure by which a superior judicial body may pronounce on (in Canada) the conduct of an inferior court etc.

judiciary n. (pl. **judiciaries**) the judges of a nation collectively. [Say joo DISHA ree or joo DISHY airy]

judicious adj. having or done with good

judgment. □ **judiciously** adv.
[Say joo DISH us]

judo n. a refined form of jiu-jitsu using principles of movement and balance.
[Say JOO doe]

jug n. **1 a** a large, deep vessel, with a narrow neck and usu. a handle. **b** Cdn & Brit. a deep vessel with a handle and a spout shaped for pouring. **2** slang prison. **3** (in pl.) slang a woman's breasts.

juggernaut n. a large and powerful force or movement whose growth cannot be controlled. [Say JUGGER not]

juggle ● v. (**juggles**, **juggled**, **juggling**) **1** perform feats of dexterity, esp. by tossing objects in the air and catching them. **2** continue to deal with (several things) at once. **3** manipulate or misrepresent (facts etc.). ● n. an act of juggling. □ **juggler** n.

jugular ● adj. **1** of the neck or throat. **2** designating a large vein of the neck. ● n. **1** (also **jugular vein**) any of several large veins in the neck. **2** the weakest point in an opponent's argument etc.
[Say JUG yuh ler]

juice ● n. **1** the extractable liquid part of a vegetable or fruit. **2 a** the fluid part of an animal body. **b** the fluid naturally contained in anything. **3 a** a person's vitality or creative faculties. **b** strength or vigour. **4** informal gasoline or electricity. **5** slang influence or money. ● v. (**juices**, **juiced**, **juicing**) extract the juice from. □ **juice up 1** increase the power or performance of. **2** heighten the enthusiasm of.

juiced adj. **1** slang intoxicated. **2** (of fruit etc.) having had its juice extracted.

juicer n. **1** an appliance used to extract juice. **2** an alcoholic.

juicy adj. (**juicier**, **juiciest**) **1** full of juice. **2 a** interesting. **b** racy, scandalous. **3** profitable.

ju-jitsu (also **ju-jutsu**) n. = JIU-JITSU.
[Say joo JIT soo]

juju n. (pl. **jujus**) **1** a magic object of some West African peoples. **2** a supernatural power from this. **3** Music a complex musical style of Yoruba origin. [Say JOO joo]

jujube n. **1** a shrub or tree native to the warmer regions of Eurasia. **2** a small jellylike candy. [Say JOO joob]

jukebox n. a machine that automatically plays a selected musical recording when a coin is inserted.

Jul. abbr. July.

julep n. = MINT JULEP. [Say JOO lip]

Julian calendar n. a calendar introduced by Julius Caesar in 46 BC, in which the year consisted of 365 days.

julienne ● adj. (of a vegetable etc.) cut into thin strips. ● v. (**juliennes**, **julienned**, **julienning**) slice into short, thin strips. □ **julienned** adj. [Say joo lee EN]

July n. (pl. **Julys**) the seventh month.

jumble ● n. a confused state or heap. ● v. (**jumbles**, **jumbled**, **jumbling**) mix up in a confused and disordered way. □ **jumbled** adj.

jumbo informal ● n. (pl. **jumbos**) **1** a large person or thing. **2** (also **jumbo jet**) a very large airliner. ● adj. very large.

jump ● v. **1** move off the ground by sudden muscular effort in the legs. **2** move suddenly or hastily. **3** give a sudden bodily movement from shock etc. **4** undergo a rapid change. **5** change rapidly from one subject to another. **6** rise or increase suddenly. **7** pass over esp. by jumping. **8** skip, ignore. **9** cause to jump. **10** reach a conclusion hastily. **11** attack unexpectedly. **12** start (a car) using jumper cables. **13** (of a nightclub, etc.) pulsate with activity. ● n. **1** the act or an instance of jumping. **2** Sport **a** an act or type of jumping. **b** a distance jumped. **3** an obstacle to be jumped. **4** a sudden bodily movement. **5** an abrupt rise in amount, price, etc. **6** a sudden transition from one thing etc. to another. □ **get** (or **have**) **the jump on** informal get (or have) an advantage over. **jump at** accept eagerly. **jump down a person's throat** informal berate fiercely. **jump for joy** be joyfully excited. **(go) jump in the lake** informal go away. **jump out at 1** grab the attention. **2** suddenly spring out at. **jump out of one's skin** be extremely startled. **jump rope** skip with a skipping rope. **jump to it** informal act promptly.

jump-cut Film ● n. the abrupt transition from one scene to another. ● v. (**jump-cuts**, **jump-cut**, **jump-cutting**) join to others via a jump-cut.

jumped-up adj. informal newly risen in status or importance.

jumper[1] n. a sleeveless dress worn over a shirt.

jumper[2] n. **1** a person or animal that jumps. **2 a** a short wire used to make or break a circuit. **b** (usu. in pl.) (also **jumper cable**) either of a pair of heavy electric cables, used for starting the engine of a vehicle whose battery is dead.

jumping jack n. **1** an exercise performed by jumping with legs spread and arms fully extended. **2** a toy figure with movable limbs esp. attached to strings.

jumping-off point n. (also **jumping-off place** etc.) the place or point from where something is begun or launched.

jump rope n. a skipping rope.

jump-start ● v. **1** start (a motor vehicle) with jumper cables. **2** revitalize or stimulate. **●** n. the action of jump-starting.

jumpsuit n. a one-piece garment for the whole body.

jumpy adj. (**jumpier, jumpiest**) **1** nervous; easily startled. **2** making sudden movements. □ **jumpiness** n.

Jun. abbr. **1** June. **2** (also **jun.**) Junior.

junco n. (pl. **juncos**) any of several small songbirds of Central and North America. [Say JUNK oh]

junction n. **1** a point at which two or more things are joined. **2** a place where things meet, unite, or cross. □ **junctional** adj.

juncture n. **1** a critical point of time. **2** a place where things join. [Say JUNK chur]

June n. the sixth month.

June bug n. (also **June beetle**) a large beetle appearing in early summer.

Jungian ● adj. having to do with the system of analytical psychology of Carl Jung (1875–1961). **●** n. a supporter of Jung or his system. [Say YOONG ee in (with OO as in BOOK)]

jungle n. **1** land overgrown with undergrowth or tangled vegetation. **2** a wild tangled mass. **3** a very competitive or bewildering situation. □ **law of the jungle** a state of ruthless competition. □ **jungly** adj.

jungle gym n. climbing equipment for a children's playground.

junior ● adj. **1 a** inferior in age or position. **b** low or lower in status. **2** having to do with young or younger people. **3** referring to the younger of two people with the same name. **4** smaller than usual. **5** Sport of or for (usu. amateur) athletes under 20 years of age. **6** esp. US of the year before the final year at school. **●** n. **1** a person who holds a low rank in a profession etc. **2** a person who is a specified number of years younger than another. **3** a junior athlete. **4** esp. US a student in the third year of a four-year program. **5** informal a young male child.

Junior A n. Hockey the second- highest level of junior amateur competition.

junior high school n. (also informal **junior high**) a school intermediate between elementary school and high school.

junior minister n. Cdn & Brit. a cabinet minister with responsibility for certain matters within a larger portfolio.

juniper n. an evergreen shrub or tree with dark blue berry-like cones. [Say JOONA purr]

junk¹ ● n. **1** anything regarded as useless or of little value. **2** old or unwanted articles. **3** slang a narcotic drug, esp. heroin. **●** v. discard as junk. □ **junky** adj.

junk² n. a flat-bottomed sailing vessel used in the China seas.

junk bond n. a high-yielding high-risk security.

Junker n. hist. a member of the aristocracy in Prussia. [Say YOON ker (with OO as in BOOK)]

junker n. informal **1** an old, dilapidated car, boat, etc. **2** a junk dealer. [Say JUNK er]

junket ● n. **1 a** an extensive tour taken esp. for promotional purposes. **b** a pleasure outing. **2** a dish of sweetened and flavoured curds. **●** v. (**junkets, junketed, junketing**) go on a pleasure excursion. □ **junketeer** n. [Say JUNK it, junk it EER]

junk food n. food with low nutritional value.

junkie n. informal **1** a drug addict. **2** informal an aficionado of some specified activity.

junk mail n. unsolicited advertising material etc. sent by mail.

junkyard n. a place where junk is collected.

Juno n. Cdn (pl. **Junos**) any of several awards presented by the Canadian Academy of Recording Arts and Sciences for excellence in Canadian music recording. [Say JOO no]

junta n. **1** a political or military faction taking power after esp. a coup. **2** a secretive group. [Say HOONTA (with OO as in BOOK)]

Jurassic adj. the second period of the Mesozoic era, between 213 and 144 million years ago, with evidence of many large dinosaurs, the first birds, and mammals. □ **Jurassic** adj. [Say jur ASS ick]

juridical adj. of judicial proceedings or the law. □ **juridically** adv. [Say jur IDDA cull]

juried adj. judged or selected by a jury.

jurisdiction n. **1** the authority to make legal decisions. **2** an area or country in which a particular system of laws has authority. [Say jur iss DICTION]

jurisprudence n. **1** the theory of law. **2** a legal system. **3** legal decisions collectively. [Say jur iss PRUDENCE]

jurist n. an expert in legal matters.

juror n. a member of a jury. [Say JUR er]

jury ● n. (pl. **juries**) **1** a body of usu. twelve persons sworn to render a verdict in a court of justice. **2** a body of persons selected to judge a competition. **●** v. (**juries, juried, jurying**) select or judge by a jury. □ **the jury is** (or **is still**) **out** a decision has not yet been reached.

jury-rig v. (**jury-rigs, jury-rigged, jury-rigging**) assemble hastily, using materials at hand.

just ● *adj.* **1** right or fair. **2** (of treatment etc.) deserved. **3** (of feelings etc.) well-grounded. ● *adv.* **1** exactly. **2** exactly or nearly at this or that moment; recently. **3** simply, merely. **4** barely. □ **just about** *informal* almost exactly. **just in case** as a precaution. **just now 1** at this moment. **2** a little time ago. **just so 1** exactly arranged. **2** it is exactly as you say. □ **justly** *adv.*

justice *n.* **1** just conduct; fairness. **2** the law and its administration. **3** judgment by legal process. **4 a** a judge. **b** (**Justice**) a title given to an appeal court judge. □ **do justice to** treat fairly or appropriately. **do oneself justice** perform as well as one is able.

Justice of the Peace *n.* a local public official appointed to hear minor cases, take oaths, etc.

justifiable *adj.* that can be justified or defended. □ **justifiably** *adv.*

justified *adj.* **1** right; having a good reason **2** declared or made free from sin in the sight of God. **3** (of text) having been adjusted so that the print fills a space evenly or forms a straight edge at the margin.

justify *v.* (**justifies**, **justified**, **justifying**) **1** show that someone or something is right or reasonable. **2** give an explanation or excuse for. **3** (of God) free from the consequences of sin. **4** adjust (a line of type) to fill a space evenly. □ **justification** *n.*

jut *v.* (**juts**, **jutted**, **jutting**) protrude, project.

Jute *n.* a member of a Germanic tribe that settled in Britain in the 5th–6th centuries. [*Say* JOOT]

jute *n.* **1** a rough fibre made from the bark of a jute plant, made into rope or sacking etc. **2** an Asian plant yielding this fibre. [*Say* JOOT]

juvenile ● *adj.* **1 a** young, youthful. **b** of, for or characteristic of young persons. **2** immature. **3** *Cdn* (of a sports team etc.) involving teenagers. ● *n.* **1** a young person. **2** a young bird, animal, etc.

juvenile delinquency *n.* offences committed by a young person. □ **juvenile delinquent** *n.*

juxtapose *v.* (**juxtaposes**, **juxtaposed**, **juxtaposing**) place close together, esp. to highlight a contrast. □ **juxtaposition** *n.* [*Say* JUXTA pose *or* juxta POSE]

Kk

K¹ *n.* (also **k**) (*pl.* **Ks** or **K's**) the eleventh letter of the alphabet.

K² *abbr.* (also **K.**) **1** kelvin(s). **2** (also **k**) kilobyte. **3** *informal* one thousand dollars. **4** kilometre.

k *symb.* kilo-.

Kabbalah *n.* (also **Kabbala**, **Cabbala**) **1** a Jewish mystical tradition. **2** any obscure doctrine. □ **Kabbalist** *n.* **Kabbalistic** *adj.* [*Say* kuh BOLLA *or* CABBA luh]

kabloona *n.* (*pl.* **kabloona** or **kabloonas** or **kabloonat**) a person who is not Inuit. [*Say* kuh BLUE nuh]

kabob *n.* = KEBAB. [*Say* ka BOB]

kaboom *n.* the sound of an explosion.

kabuki *n.* a form of popular Japanese drama with highly stylized song, acted by males only. [*Say* ka BOO kee]

Kaddish *n.* **1** a Jewish mourner's prayer. **2** a formula of praise used in the synagogue service. [*Say* CAD ish]

Kafkaesque *adj.* nightmarish in a manner characteristic of the fictional world of the Czech novelist Franz Kafka (1883–1924). [*Say* kafka ESK]

kafuffle *n.* *Cdn* = KERFUFFLE.

Kaigani *n.* (*pl.* **Kaigani** or **Kaiganis**) a member of a division of the Haida, who settled on the southern shores of Prince of Wales Island (Alaska). [*Say* ky GANNY]

Kainai *pl. n.* = BLOOD. [*Say* KY nye]

kaiser *n.* **1** *hist.* an emperor, esp. the German Emperor or the Emperor of Austria. **2** (also **kaiser roll**) a large crusty bread roll.

kalamata *n.* a medium-sized variety of purplish-black olive. [*Say* kala MATA]

Kalashnikov *n.* a type of rifle or submachine gun made in Russia. [*Say* kuh LASH ni koff]

kale *n.* a variety of cabbage which forms no compact head.

kaleidoscope *n.* **1** a tube containing mirrors and pieces of coloured glass or paper, whose reflections produce changing patterns when the tube is turned. **2** a constantly changing pattern. □ **kaleidoscopic** *adj.* [*Say* kuh LIE duh scope]

kamikaze ● *n.* *hist.* (during World War II) a Japanese aircraft loaded with explosives

and deliberately crashed on its target. ● *adj.* **1** of or relating to a kamikaze. **2** reckless, dangerous. [*Say* comma COZZY]

Kampuchean *n. & adj.* = CAMBODIAN. [*Say* cam poo CHEE in]

kangaroo *n.* (*pl.* **kangaroos**) **1** a large Australian marsupial with a long tail and strong hind legs that enable it to travel by jumping. **2** *Cdn* designating a hooded garment with a front pouch.

kangaroo court *n.* **1** an illegal court formed by a group to settle disputes among themselves. **2** any trial, court, etc. operating unfairly. **3** a mock trial.

Kanienkehaka *n.* (*pl.* same) **1** the Mohawk people. **2** their Iroquoian language. [*Say* can yen kay HA ka]

kanji *n.* Japanese writing using Chinese characters. [*Say* CAN jee]

kaolin *n.* a fine soft white clay, used esp. for making porcelain and in medicines. [*Say* KAY uh lin]

kappa *n.* the tenth letter of the Greek alphabet (K, κ).

kaput *adj.* *slang* broken; done for. [*Say* kuh PUT]

karaoke *n.* a form of entertainment in which people sing popular songs against a pre-recorded backing. [*Say* carry OAKY]

karat *n.* a measure of purity of gold. Abbreviation: **kt**. [*Sounds like* CARROT]

karate *n.* a Japanese system of unarmed combat using the hands and feet as weapons. [*Say* kuh ROTTY]

karma *n.* **1** *Buddhism & Hinduism* the sum of a person's actions in previous lives, viewed as deciding his or her future fate. **2** destiny. **3** the positive or negative energy felt to be produced by something. □ **karmic** *adj.*

karst *n.* a limestone region with underground drainage and many cavities.

kart *n.* = GO-KART.

kasha *n.* a soft food made of boiled or baked buckwheat. [*Say* COSH uh]

Kashmiri *n.* **1** a person from Kashmir. **2** the language of Kashmir. □ **Kashmiri** *adj.* [*Say* cash MEERY]

Kaska *n.* (*pl.* **Kaska** or **Kaskas**) **1** a member of a Dene Aboriginal group living in northwestern BC. **2** the Athapaskan

language of this people. □ **Kaska** *adj.*
[*Say* CASS kuh]

Kathakali *n.* a form of dramatic dance of southern India. [*Say* catta KAH lee]

kathump *n.* a loud thudding sound, e.g. of a heart beating rapidly.

katydid *n.* any of various green N American grasshoppers. [*Say* KATY did]

kayak ● *n.* **1** an Inuit one-man canoe consisting of a light wooden frame covered with sealskins. **2** a small covered canoe modelled on this, used for sport. ● *v.* (**kayaks, kayaked, kayaking**) **1** travel by kayak. **2** paddle a kayak on. □ **kayaker** *n.* **kayaking** *n.*

kayo *informal* ● *v.* (**kayoes, kayoed, kayoing**) knock out. ● *n.* (*pl.* **kayos**) a knockout.

Kazakh *n.* (also **Kazak**) **1** a member of a Turkic people of central Asia, esp. of Kazakhstan. **2** the language of this people. □ **Kazakh** *adj.* [*Say* kuh ZOCK]

kazoo *n.* a toy or jazz musical instrument consisting of a tube which produces a buzzing noise when hummed into.

KB *abbr.* kilobyte(s).

kebab *n.* a dish of pieces of marinated meat and vegetables cooked on a skewer. [*Say* kuh BOB]

keel *n.* the structure along the base of a ship etc. on which the framework of the whole is built. □ **keel over 1** fall down or over. **2** die. **on an even keel 1** (of a ship) not listing. **2** (of a person) untroubled.

keelhaul *v.* scold or punish severely.

keen¹ *adj.* **1** eager, ardent. **2** fond of or enthusiastic about. **3 a** (of the senses) highly sensitive. **b** (of feelings) intense. **4** intellectually acute. **5** sharp. **6** piercingly cold. □ **keenly** *adv.* **keenness** *n.*

keen² ● *n.* an Irish funeral song accompanied with wailing. ● *v.* **1** make a high-pitched wailing sound. **2** wail in grief for a dead person.

keener *n.* Cdn informal a person, esp. a student, who is extremely eager.

keep ● *v.* (**keeps, kept, keeping**) **1** have charge of; retain possession of. **2** retain or reserve for future use. **3** retain or remain in a specified condition, position, etc. **4** store in a regular place. **5** cause to avoid or abstain from. **6** detain. **7 a** observe (a law etc.). **b** fulfill (a commitment etc.). **8** own and look after. **9 a** provide for the sustenance of. **b** maintain with a supply of. **10** manage (a shop etc.). **11 a** record or regularly make entries in (a diary). **b** maintain (a house). **12** continue to have or follow. **13** maintain (a person) in return for sexual favours. ● *n.* **1** food, clothes, and

other essentials for living. **2** the strongest or central tower of a castle. □ **for keeps** *informal* permanently. **how are you keeping?** how are you? **keep at** persist. **keep back 1** keep at a distance. **2** retard the progress of. **3** conceal. **keep down 1** hold in subjection. **2** keep low in amount. **3** stay hidden. **4** manage not to vomit. **keep one's feet** manage not to fall. **keep on 1** continue to do or use. **2** pester or harass. **keep one's temper** control one's anger. **keep to 1** adhere to. **2** observe (a promise). **3** confine oneself to. **keep to oneself 1** avoid contact with others. **2** refuse to disclose. **keep up 1** maintain (progress etc.). **2** prevent from sinking. **3** keep in repair. **4** carry on (a correspondence etc.). **5** manage not to fall behind. **keep up with the Joneses** strive to compete socially with one's neighbours.

keeper *n.* **1** a person who keeps or looks after something or someone. **2** a device for keeping something in place. **3** *informal* something that one wishes to keep.

keeping *n.* the action of owning or maintaining something. □ **in someone's keeping** being taken care of by someone. **in keeping (with something)** appropriate or expected.

keepsake *n.* a thing kept in remembrance of the giver.

keg *n.* a small barrel.

kelp *n.* any of several large brown seaweeds.

Kelt *n.* = CELT.

kelvin *n.* the SI unit of thermodynamic temperature.

kendo *n.* a Japanese form of fencing with two-handed bamboo swords. [*Say* KEN doe]

kennel ● *n.* **1** a small shelter for a dog. **2** a breeding or boarding establishment for dogs. ● *v.* (**kennels, kennelled, kennelling**) put into or keep in a kennel.

keno *n.* a game of chance resembling bingo. [*Say* KEEN oh]

Kenyan *n.* a person from Kenya. □ **Kenyan** *adj.* [*Say* KEN yin or KEEN yin]

kept *past and past participle of* KEEP.

keratin *n.* a fibrous protein which occurs in hair, feathers, hooves, etc. [*Say* KERRA tin]

kerchief *n.* a cloth used to cover the head. □ **kerchiefed** *adj.* [*Say* KER chiff or KER chief]

kerf ● *n.* a slit made by cutting, esp. with a saw. ● *v.* make a kerf in (a piece of wood etc.).

kerfuffle *n.* *informal* a fuss or commotion. [*Say* ker FUFFLE]

kermode *n.* (also **kermode bear**) a subspecies of the black bear with either black or white fur, found on the west coast of Canada. [*Say* ker MOE dee]

kern *v.* adjust the spacing between (printed characters). □ **kerned** *adj.* **kerning** *n.*

kernel *n.* **1** a central, softer part within a hard shell of a nut, seed, etc. **2** the whole seed of a cereal. **3** the essential part of anything.

kerosene *n.* a petroleum distillate widely used as a fuel and solvent.

kestrel *n.* a small falcon that hunts by hovering. [*Say* KESS trul]

keta *n.* chum salmon. [*Say* KEETA]

ketamine *n.* an anaesthetic and painkilling drug. [*Say* KEETA meen]

ketch *n.* (*pl.* **ketches**) a two-masted fore-and-aft-rigged sailing boat.

ketchup *n.* a thick sauce made from tomatoes, vinegar, sugar, etc.

ketone *n.* any of a class of organic compounds, including acetone. [*Say* KEE tone]

kettle *n.* **1** a vessel with a spout and handle, for boiling water in. **2** a large usu. open pot for cooking foods etc. □ **a different kettle of fish** a different matter altogether. **a pretty** (or **fine**) **kettle of fish** an awkward state of affairs.

kettledrum *n.* a large drum shaped like a bowl with adjustable pitch.

Kevlar *n. proprietary* a synthetic fibre of high tensile strength used in tires etc. [*Say* KEV lar]

kewpie doll *n.* (also **kewpie**) a small chubby doll with a curl or topknot. [*Say* CUE pee]

key¹ ● *n.* (*pl.* **keys**) **1** an instrument, usu. of metal, for moving the bolt of a lock to lock or unlock. **2** a similar implement for operating a switch in the form of a lock. **3** an instrument for grasping screws, pegs, nuts, etc. **4** a lever depressed by the finger in playing the organ, flute, etc. **5** each of several buttons for operating a typewriter or computer. **6** a thing that provides access or understanding. **7 a** a word or system for solving a cipher or code. **b** an explanatory list of symbols used in a map, table, etc. **c** a list of solutions. **8** *Music* a system of notes based on a particular note and making up a scale. **9** (in basketball) the area beneath each basket, extending from the end line to a circle surrounding the free throw line. ● *adj.* essential. ● *v.* (**keys, keyed, keying**) **1** enter (data) by means of a keyboard. **2** link. □ **key** (**in**) **on** focus on. **key up** make nervous or tense. □ **keyless** *adj.*

key² *n.* (*pl.* **keys**) a low-lying island or reef.

keyboard ● *n.* **1** a set of keys on a typewriter, piano, etc. **2** an electronic musical instrument like a piano. ● *v.* enter (data) by means of a keyboard. □ **keyboardist** *n.*

keyhole *n.* **1** a hole by which a key is put into a lock. **2** something shaped like a keyhole.

key lime *n.* a small yellowish tart lime.

Keynesian ● *adj.* of or relating to the theories of the English economist J. M. Keynes (1883–1946). ● *n.* a supporter of these theories. [*Say* KAIN zee in]

keynote *n.* **1** a prevailing tone or idea. **2** (as an *adj.*) intended to set the tone at a meeting or conference. **3** *Music* the note on which a key is based.

keypad *n.* a small keyboard or set of buttons for operating an electronic device, telephone, etc.

key ring *n.* a ring for keeping keys on.

key signature *n.* a combination of sharps or flats after the clef indicating the key of a piece of music.

keystone *n.* **1** the central principle of a policy. **2** a central stone at the top of an arch locking the whole together.

keystroke *n.* a single depression of a key on a keyboard.

keyword *n.* **1** the key to a cipher etc. **2 a** a word of great significance. **b** a word used in searching a computer database.

kg *abbr.* kilogram(s).

KGB *abbr.* the Soviet secret police (1953–91).

khaki ● *adj.* dull brownish yellow. ● *n.* (*pl.* **khakis**) **1** khaki fabric of twilled cotton or wool. **2** a dull brownish-yellow colour. **3** esp. military clothing made from this. [*Say* CACKY *or* COCKY *or* CARKY]

Khalsa *n.* the fraternity of warriors into which Sikh males are initiated at puberty. [*Say* COLLSA]

khan *n.* a title given to rulers and officials in Central Asia etc. [*Say* CON *or* CAN]

khat *n.* **1** the leaves of an Arabian shrub, which are used as a stimulant. **2** the shrub that produces these leaves. [*Say* COT]

Khmer *n.* **1** a native of the ancient Khmer kingdom, or of modern Cambodia. **2** the language of this people. □ **Khmer** *adj.* [*Say* k'MAIR]

kibble *n.* ground meal shaped into pellets.

kibbutz *n.* (*pl.* **kibbutzim**) a collective esp. farming settlement in Israel. [*Say* ki BUTS *for the singular*, ki buts EEM *for the plural* (BUTS *rhymes with* PUTS)]

kibitz *v.* (**kibitzes, kibitzed, kibitzing**) *informal* chat or joke lightheartedly. □ **kibitzer** *n.* [*Say* KIB its]

kibosh v. slang (**kiboshes**, **kiboshed**, **kiboshing**) □ **put the kibosh on** put an end to. [Say KYE bosh]

kick ● v. **1** strike or propel forcibly with the foot. **2 a** strike out with the foot. **b** express dislike of, rebel against. **3** informal give up (a habit). **4** expel or dismiss forcibly. **5** (**kick oneself**) be annoyed with oneself. ● n. **1 a** a blow with the foot. **b** an extension of the leg and foot out from the body. **2** informal **a** a sharp stimulant effect. **b** a pleasurable thrill. **3** the recoil of a gun. □ **kick around** (or **about**) informal **1 a** drift idly from place to place. **b** be unused or unwanted. **2 a** treat roughly. **b** discuss (an idea). **kick at the can** (or **cat**) Cdn informal an opportunity. **kick back 1** recoil. **2** informal relax. **kick the bucket** slang die. **kick in 1** knock down by kicking. **2** slang pay one's share. **3** become activated, start. **kick in the pants** informal **1** a setback seen as an incentive. **2** (also **in the teeth**, **ass**, etc.) a humiliating setback. **kick off 1** (in football or soccer) begin or resume a match. **2** informal begin. **kick up a fuss** informal create a disturbance. **kick up one's heels** have a lively, enjoyable time. □ **kickable** adj. **kicker** n.

kickback n. informal **1** the force of a recoil. **2** money paid illegally to someone in return for work or help; a bribe.

kick-boxing n. a form of martial art that combines boxing with elements of karate. □ **kick-boxer** n.

kickoff n. **1** (in football or soccer) the start or resumption of a match with a kick. **2** an event marking the beginning of a campaign etc.

kickstand n. a rod attached to a bicycle or motorcycle to support the vehicle when stationary.

kick-start ● n. **1** (also **kick-starter**) a device to start the engine of a motorcycle etc. by the downward thrust of a pedal. **2** an impetus given to get a thing started. ● v. **1** start (a motorcycle etc.) in this way. **2** stimulate.

kid[1] n. **1** a young goat. **2** the leather made from its skin. **3** a child or young person. □ **handle with kid gloves** handle in a delicate manner. **kids'** (or **kid's**) **stuff** informal something very simple.

kid[2] v. (**kids**, **kidded**, **kidding**) informal **1** (**kid oneself**) deceive, trick. **2** tease, joke with. □ **no kidding** (also **I kid you not**) informal that is the truth. □ **kidder** n. **kiddingly** adv.

kiddie n. (also **kiddy**) (pl. **kiddies**) informal a child or young person.

kidnap (**kidnaps**, **kidnapped**, **kidnapping**) ● v. carry off (a person etc.) by illegal force, esp. to obtain a ransom. ● n. an instance of kidnapping. □ **kidnapper** n. **kidnapping** n.

kidney n. (pl. **kidneys**) **1** either of a pair of organs which remove wastes from the blood and excrete urine. **2** the kidney of a pig etc. as food. □ **kidney-shaped** adj.

kidney bean n. a dark red kidney-shaped bean.

kidney-shaped adj. shaped like a kidney, with one side curving inward and the other curving outward.

kielbasa n. a type of highly seasoned garlic sausage of Eastern European origin. [Say keel BOSSA]

Kikuyu n. (pl. **Kikuyu** or **Kikuyus**) **1** a member of a Bantu-speaking people constituting the largest ethnic group in Kenya. **2** the language of this people. □ **Kikuyu** adj. [Say kee KOO you]

kill ● v. **1** deprive of life or vitality. **2** put an end to. **3** (**kill oneself**) **a** commit suicide. **b** informal overexert oneself. **c** laugh heartily. **4** informal overwhelm (a person) with an emotion etc. **5** switch off. **6** informal cause pain to. **7** pass (time) usu. while waiting. **8** defeat (a bill in a legislative assembly). **9** neutralize or render ineffective. **10** cancel publication of. **11** Hockey (of a team) endure (a penalty) without being scored on. ● n. **1** an act of killing. **2** an animal or animals killed, esp. by a hunter. □ **dressed to kill** dressed impressively. **kill two birds with one stone** achieve two aims at once. **kill with kindness** spoil with overindulgence.

killdeer n. a large N American plover with a plaintive song.

killer n. **1 a** a person or thing that kills. **b** a murderer. **2** informal **a** an impressive thing. **b** a decisive blow.

killer whale n. a predatory whale with black and white markings and a high narrow dorsal fin.

killifish n. (**killifish** or **killifishes**) **1** a small, often brightly coloured fish found in eastern N America. **2** a brightly-coloured tropical aquarium fish.

killing ● n. **1** in senses of KILL v. **2** a large profit. ● adj. **1** that kills. **2** informal very funny. **3** informal exhausting.

killjoy n. a person who throws gloom over other people's enjoyment.

kiln n. an oven for baking or drying, esp. one for firing pottery etc.

kilo n. (pl. **kilos**) **1** a kilogram. **2** a kilometre.

kilo- comb. form denoting a factor of 1,000. Abbreviation: **k**, or **K** in Computing.

kilobyte *n.* 1,024 bytes as a measure of memory size. Abbreviation: **KB** or **kbyte**.

kilogram *n.* the SI unit of mass, equivalent to 1,000 grams (approx. 2.205 lb.). Abbreviation: **kg**.

kilometre *n.* (also **kilometer**) a metric unit of measurement equal to 1 000 metres. Abbreviation: **km**. [*Say* kuh LOMMA ter *or* KILLA metre, killa METRIC]

kilopascal *n.* a metric unit of pressure equal to 1,000 pascals. [*Say* KILLO pask'll *or* killo pass KAL]

kilowatt *n.* 1,000 watts. Abbreviation: **kW**.

kilowatt hour *n.* a measure of electrical energy equivalent to a power consumption of 1,000 watts for one hour.

kilt *n.* a skirt-like garment, usu. of pleated tartan cloth. □ **kilted** *adj.*

kilter *n.* good working order.

kimberlite *n.* a rare igneous blue-tinged rock sometimes containing diamonds.

kimono *n.* (*pl.* **kimonos**) **1** a long loose Japanese robe worn with a sash. **2** a dressing gown. [*Say* ki MOE no]

kin ● *n.* one's relatives or family. ● *adj.* **1** (of a person) related. **2** similar.

kinase *n.* any of various enzymes that catalyze the transfer of a phosphate group from ATP to another molecule. [*Say* KINE ace *or* KIN ace]

kind¹ *n.* **1 a** a race or species. **b** a natural group of animals, plants, etc. **2** type. **3** character, quality. □ **in kind 1** in the same form, likewise. **2** (of payment) in goods or labour instead of money. **kind of** *informal* to some extent. **of a kind** similar in some important respect.

kind² *adj.* friendly, generous.

kindergarten *n.* a class or school for young children. □ **kindergartner** *n.*

kind-hearted *adj.* of a kind disposition. □ **kind-heartedly** *adv.* **kind-heartedness** *n.*

kindle *v.* (**kindles**, **kindled**, **kindling**) **1** light or set on fire. **2** catch fire. **3** arouse or inspire. **4** become animated. **5** make or become bright. [*Say* KIN d'll]

kindling *n.* small sticks etc. for lighting fires. [*Say* KIND ling (KIND *rhymes with* PINNED)]

kindly¹ *adv.* **1** in a kind manner. **2** used in a polite request. □ **look kindly upon** regard sympathetically. **take a thing kindly** like or be pleased by it. **take kindly to** be pleased by. **thank kindly** thank very much.

kindly² *adj.* (**kindlier**, **kindliest**) kind, kind-hearted.

kindness *n.* (*pl.* **kindnesses**) **1** the state or quality of being kind. **2** a kind act.

kindred ● *n.* **1** one's relatives. **2** a relationship by blood. ● *adj.* **1** related by blood or marriage. **2** allied or similar in character. [*Say* KIN drid]

kindred spirit *n.* a person whose character and outlook are similar to one's own.

kinesiology *n.* the study of the mechanics of human body movements. □ **kinesiologist** *n.* [*Say* kuh nee see OLLA jee *or* kuh nee zee OLLA jee]

kinetic *adj.* of, relating to, or due to motion. □ **kinetically** *adv.* [*Say* kin ET ick]

kinetic energy *n.* energy which a body possesses by virtue of being in motion.

kinetics *pl. n.* **1** = DYNAMICS 1. **2** the branch of chemistry concerned with the rates of chemical reactions. [*Say* kin ET icks]

Kinette *n. Cdn* a member of a women's organization associated with the Kinsmen. [*Say* kin ET]

kinfolk *pl. n.* people to whom one is related by blood.

king ● *n.* **1** (as a title usu. **King**) a male sovereign, esp. the ruler of an independent state. **2** a person or thing pre-eminent in a field or class. **3** a large kind of plant, animal, etc. **4** the most important chess piece, which the opposing side has to checkmate to win. **5** a piece in checkers made by crowning a piece that has reached the far end of the board. **6** a playing card bearing a representation of a king, ranking next below an ace. ● *adj.* denoting a king-size bed etc. (*see* KING-SIZE 2). □ **kingly** *adj.* **kingship** *n.*

kingbird *n.* a large N American tyrant flycatcher, esp. with a grey head and black and yellowish or white underparts.

kingdom *n.* **1** an organized community headed by a king or queen. **2** the territory subject to a king or queen. **3** *Christianity* the spiritual reign of God. **4** a domain belonging to a person, animal, etc. **5** a province of nature. **6** *Biology* the highest category in taxonomic classification.

kingdom come *n.* □ **till kingdom come** forever.

kingfisher *n.* a stocky bird with a long sharp beak, which dives for fish in rivers.

King James Version *n.* (also **King James Bible**) a 1611 English translation of the Bible made under James I.

kingmaker *n.* a person who makes kings, leaders, etc., by using political influence.

kingpin *n.* **1** an essential person or thing.

2 a a main bolt in a central position. **b** a vertical bolt used as a pivot.

king-size *adj.* (also **king-sized**) **1** larger than normal. **2** designating the largest standard size of mattress.

kink ● *n.* **1 a** a short twist or bend in wire or tubing etc. **b** a tight wave in human or animal hair. **2** a flaw or glitch in something. **3** a crick in the neck or back. ● *v.* form or cause to form a kink.

kinky *adj.* (**kinkier, kinkiest**) **1** *informal* **a** given to or involving bizarre or unusual sexual behaviour. **b** (of clothing etc.) bizarre in a sexually provocative way. **2** strange, eccentric. **3** having kinks or twists. □ **kinkiness** *n.*

kinnikinnick *n.* **1** a mixture formerly used by some Aboriginal peoples of N America as a substitute for tobacco or for mixing with it. **2** bearberry. [*Say* kinny kin ICK]

kinsfolk *pl. n.* = KINFOLK.

kinship *n.* **1** blood relationship. **2** the sharing of characteristics.

kinsman *n.* (*pl.* **kinsmen**) **1** a relative. **2** a member of one's own people. **3** (**Kinsman**) *Cdn* a member of a fraternal organization for esp. businessmen and professionals. □ **kinswoman** *n.* (*pl.* **kinswomen**)

kiosk *n.* an open-fronted booth from which refreshments, newspapers, etc. are sold or information is provided. [*Say* KEE osk]

kipper ● *n.* a fish, esp. herring, that has been split, salted and dried or smoked. ● *v.* cure (fish) in this way.

kirk *n.* esp. *Scot.* a church.

kirk session *n.* (in Presbyterian churches) = SESSION 5.

kirpan *n.* the dagger worn by Sikhs as a religious symbol. [*Say* ker PAN *or* ker PON]

kirsch *n.* (*pl.* **kirsches**) a brandy distilled from fermented cherries. [*Say* KEERSH]

kismet *n.* destiny, fate. [*Say* KIZZ met]

kiss ● *v.* (**kisses, kissed, kissing**) **1** touch with the lips, esp. as a sign of love, greeting, or reverence. **2** touch very lightly or briefly. ● *n.* (*pl.* **kisses**) **1** a touch with the lips in kissing. **2** a very light or brief touch. **3** a bite-sized baked meringue or esp. chocolate candy. □ **kiss and tell** recount one's romantic encounters etc. **kiss away** remove (tears etc.) by kissing. **kiss goodbye to** *informal* accept the loss of. **kiss off** *slang* dismiss, get rid of. **kiss up to** *slang* act obsequiously toward. □ **kissable** *adj.* **kissy** *adj.*

kiss-and-cry *n.* (*pl.* **kiss-and-cries**) an area in which figure skaters await the judges' marks at a competition.

kiss-and-tell *adj.* revealing confidential material.

kisser *n.* **1** a person who kisses. **2** *slang* the mouth.

kiss of death *n.* an act or situation which causes ruin.

kiss-off *n.* *slang* an abrupt or rude dismissal.

kiss of life *n.* **1** mouth-to-mouth resuscitation. **2** something which revitalizes.

kit¹ *n.* **1** a set of articles, equipment, etc. needed for a specific purpose. **2** a container for such a set. **3** the clothing, gear, etc. needed for any activity. **4** a set of the parts needed to assemble an item. **5** (in full **drum kit**) a set of drums, cymbals, etc.

kit² *n.* **1** a kitten. **2** a young fox, beaver, etc.

kit bag *n.* a large bag or sack used by soldiers etc.

kitchen *n.* **1** a room where food is prepared and cooked. **2** the staff working in the kitchen of a restaurant etc. □ **everything but the kitchen sink** everything imaginable.

kitchenette *n.* a small kitchen or part of a room fitted as a kitchen.

kitchen garden *n.* a garden where vegetables etc. are grown for personal use.

kitchen-sink *adj.* (in art forms) depicting extreme realism, esp. drab or sordid.

kitchenware *n.* kitchen utensils.

kite ● *n.* **1** a toy consisting of a light frame with thin material stretched over it, flown in the wind at the end of a long string. **2** a bird of prey with long wings and usu. a forked tail. ● *v.* (**kites, kited, kiting**) **1** soar like a kite. **2** originate or pass (fraudulent cheques etc.). □ **go fly a kite** *informal* get lost; go away. **high as a kite** *informal* **1** intoxicated by alcohol or drugs. **2** excited. □ **kiting** *n.*

kith and kin *n.* friends and relations.

kitsch *n.* art or articles that are considered tacky, dated, or overly sentimental. □ **kitschiness** *n.* **kitschy** *adj.* [*Say* KITCH, KITCHY, KITCHY niss]

Kitselas *n.* (*pl.* **Kitselas**) **1** a member of an Aboriginal people living along the Skeena River in northwestern BC. **2** the Tsimshian language of this people. [*Say* KIT sul us]

kitten *n.* **1** a young cat. **2** the young of certain other animals, as the fox etc. □ **have kittens** *informal* be extremely upset or nervous.

kittenish *adj.* **1** playful and lively. **2** flirtatious.

kittiwake *n.* a small gull that nests in colonies on sea cliffs. [*Say* KITTY wake]

kitty[1] *n.* (*pl.* **kitties**) **1** a fund of money for communal use. **2** a pool of money in some card games.

kitty[2] *n.* (*pl.* **kitties**) a pet name for a kitten or cat.

kitty-corner ● *adj.* placed or situated diagonally. ● *adv.* diagonally.

Kitty Litter *n. proprietary* granular material put in a box for a cat to urinate and defecate in indoors.

Kiwanis *n.* a social and charitable organization of business and professional people. [*Say* ki WON iss (WON rhymes with DON)]

kiwi *n.* (*pl.* **kiwis**) **1** a flightless New Zealand bird with hairlike feathers and a long bill. **2 a** a climbing plant bearing fruits with a thin hairy skin, green flesh, and black seeds. **b** (also **kiwi fruit**) this fruit. **3** (**Kiwi**) *informal* a New Zealander.

Klansman *n.* (*pl.* **Klansmen**) a member of the Ku Klux Klan.

Kleenex *n.* (*pl.* **Kleenex** or **Kleenexes**) *proprietary* a disposable paper tissue.

kleptomania *n.* a recurrent urge to steal. □ **kleptomaniac** *n. & adj.*

klezmer *n.* **1** a member of a group of musicians playing traditional eastern European Jewish music. **2** (also **klezmer music**) this type of music. [*Say* KLEZZ mer]

klick *n. slang* a kilometre.

klutz *n.* (*pl.* **klutzes**) *informal* a clumsy, awkward person. □ **klutzy** *adj.* (**klutzier, klutziest**)

km *abbr.* kilometre(s).

knack *n.* **1** a skill at performing a task. **2** a trick or habit of action or speech etc.

knapsack *n.* a bag carried strapped on the back by hikers, students, etc.

knave *n. archaic* a dishonest man. □ **knavery** *n.* **knavish** *adj.*

knead *v.* **1** work (dough, clay, etc.) with the hands. **2** blend or weld together. **3** massage as if kneading.

knee ● *n.* **1** the joint between the thigh and the lower leg. **2** the corresponding joint in other animals. **3** the upper surface of a sitting person's thigh. ● *v.* (**knees, kneed, kneeing**) touch or strike with the knee. □ **bring to its** (or **his** or **her**) **knees** reduce someone to a state of weakness or submission. **learn (something) at one's mother's knee** learn something at an early age. **on bended knee** (also **on one's bended knees**) **1** kneeling. **2** seriously weakened.

kneeboard ● *n.* a short surfboard ridden in a kneeling position. ● *v.* ride a kneeboard. □ **kneeboarding** *n.*

kneecap ● *n.* the convex bone in front of the knee. ● *v.* (**kneecaps, kneecapped, kneecapping**) shoot in the knee or leg as a punishment. □ **kneecapping** *n.*

knee-deep *adj.* **1 a** immersed up to the knees. **b** deeply involved. **2** (of water etc.) so deep as to reach the knees.

knee-high ● *adj.* reaching as high as the knees. ● *n.* a sock reaching just below the knee. □ **knee-high to a grasshopper** very small or very young.

knee-jerk ● *n.* an involuntary kick caused by a blow on the tendon just below the knee. ● *adj.* predictable, automatic.

kneel *v.* (**kneels**; *past and past participle* **knelt** or **kneeled**; **kneeling**) fall or rest on the knees or a knee.

kneeler *n.* **1** a low cushion etc. used for kneeling. **2** a person who kneels.

knell ● *n.* **1** the sound of a bell, esp. when rung solemnly. **2** a sound or sign that is regarded as a solemn warning of the end of something. ● *v.* (of a bell) ring solemnly.

knelt *past and past participle of* KNEEL.

Knesset *n.* the parliament of Israel. [*Say* k'NESS it]

knew *past of* KNOW.

knickerbocker *n.* (in *pl.*) loose-fitting breeches gathered at the knee or calf.

knickers *pl. n.* **1** knickerbockers. **2** a boy's short trousers. □ **get one's knickers in a twist** become agitated or upset.

knick-knack *n.* a small decorative object.

knife ● *n.* (*pl.* **knives**) **1** a cutting instrument consisting of a blade fixed into a handle. **2** a cutting blade forming part of a machine. ● *v.* (**knifes, knifed, knifing**) **1** cut or stab with a knife. **2** *slang* undermine by underhand means. **3** cut or move through like a knife. □ **go under the knife** *informal* have surgery. **like a (hot) knife through butter** easily. **that one could cut with a knife** *informal* (of an accent etc.) very obvious etc. □ **knifelike** *adj.* **knifing** *n.*

knife-edge *n.* **1** the edge of a knife. **2** a position of extreme danger or uncertainty.

knight ● *n.* **1** a man awarded the title *Sir* by a sovereign in recognition of merit or service. **2** *hist.* **a** a man, usu. noble, raised esp. by a sovereign to honourable military rank. **b** a military follower or attendant. **3** *Chess* a piece usu. shaped like a horse's head. ● *v.* confer a knighthood on. □ **knighthood** *n.* **knightly** *adj.*

knight errant *n.* (*pl.* **knights errant**) *hist.* a medieval knight wandering in search of adventures.

knish n. (pl. **knishes**) a dumpling of flaky dough filled with cheese etc. [Say k'NISH]

knit • v. (**knits**; past and past participle **knitted** or **knit**; **knitting**) **1 a** make (a garment etc.) by interlocking loops of yarn with knitting needles or by machine. **b** make (a plain stitch) in knitting. **2 a** contract (the forehead) in vertical wrinkles. **b** frown. **3** make or become close or compact esp. by common interests etc. **4** become joined; heal. • n. knitted material or a knitted garment. □ **knitter** n. **knitting** n.

knitting needle n. a thin pointed rod used esp. in pairs for knitting.

knitwear n. knitted garments.

knives pl. of KNIFE.

knob n. **1 a** a rounded protuberance, esp. at the end or on the surface of a thing. **b** a knob-shaped handle. **c** a knob-shaped attachment for pulling, turning, etc. **2** a small, usu. round, piece of something. **3** a prominent round hill. □ **knobbed** adj. **knobby** adj. (**knobbier, knobbiest**). **knob-like** adj.

knobbly adj. having many small knobs.

knock • v. **1 a** strike (a hard surface) with an audible blow. **b** strike, esp. a door to gain admittance **2** make (a hole, dent, etc.) by knocking. **3** drive (something) by striking. **4** informal criticize. **5** come into collision with something. **6** (of an engine) make a thumping or rattling noise. • n. **1** an act of knocking. **2** an audible sharp blow. **3** the sound of knocking in an engine. **4 a** a setback. **b** adverse criticism. □ **knock around** (or **about**) **1** strike repeatedly. **2** wander aimlessly. **knock back** informal eat or drink, esp. quickly. **knock down 1** strike to the ground with a blow. **2** demolish. **3** (at an auction) sell an item. **4** informal lower the price of. **5** take (machinery etc.) apart for transportation. **knock it off!** stop it! **knock off 1** strike off with a blow. **2** informal finish work. **3** informal rapidly produce (a work of art etc.). **4** deduct from a price. **5** slang **a** steal. **b** copy. **knock (on) wood** knock on something wooden to avert bad luck. **knock out 1** make unconscious. **2** knock down (a boxer) for a count of 10, thereby winning the contest. **3 a** defeat. **b** get rid of; destroy. **4** informal astonish. **5** (**knock oneself out**) informal exhaust. **knock over 1** cause to fall or overturn. **2** slang rob, steal. **knock one's socks off** slang astound, amaze. **knock up** slang make pregnant.

knock-down • adj. **1** (of a blow, argument, etc.) overwhelming. **2** informal (of

a price) very low. • n. an act or instance of knocking down.

knocker n. **1** an instrument hinged to a door for knocking to call attention. **2** a person or thing that knocks. **3** (in pl.) slang a woman's breasts. **4** informal a person who continually finds fault.

knock-kneed adj. having legs that curve inwards at the knees.

knock-off n. informal a copy or imitation.

knockout n. **1** the act of knocking someone out. **2** Boxing etc. a blow that knocks an opponent out. **3** a competition in which the loser in each round is eliminated. **4** informal an outstanding person or thing.

knoll n. a small hill or mound. [Say NOLE]

knot • n. **1 a** a fastening made by looping a piece of string, rope, etc. on itself and tightening it. **b** a set method of tying a knot. **c** a tangle in hair, wool, etc. **2** a unit of a ship's or aircraft's speed equivalent to one nautical mile per hour. **3** a group or cluster. **4** a bond or tie, esp. of wedlock. **5** a hard lump of bodily tissue. **6 a** a knob in a stem, branch, or root. **b** a hard mass where a tree trunk and a branch join. **7** a difficulty; a problem. **8** a sensation of tension felt in the stomach, caused by stress. • v. (**knots, knotted, knotting**) **1 a** tie in a knot. **b** secure with a knot. **2 a** entangle. **b** become entangled. **3** form lumps, knobs, or knots on or in. **4** slang tie (a score etc.). □ **tie in knots** informal baffle or confuse completely. **tie the knot** informal get married.

knothole n. a hole in a piece of timber where a knot has fallen out.

knotty adj. (**knottier, knottiest**) **1** full of knots. **2** hard to explain; puzzling.

know • v. (**knows**; past **knew**; past participle **known**; **knowing**) **1 a** have in the mind; have learned. **b** be aware of. **c** have a good command of. **2** be acquainted or friendly with. **3 a** recognize; identify. **b** be able to distinguish. **4** be subject to. **5** have personal experience of. • n. (in phr. **in the know**) informal having special knowledge. □ **have been known to** have occasionally in the past. **know better than** be wise or well-mannered enough to avoid (specified behaviour etc.). **know by sight** recognize the appearance (only) of. **know of** be aware of. **know one's own mind** be decisive. **know the ropes** (or **one's stuff**) be fully knowledgeable or experienced. **know a thing or two** be experienced or shrewd. **know what's what** have adequate knowledge of the world etc. **not know from** not know anything about. **not want to know**

refuse to take any notice of.
□ **knowable** adj. **knower** n.

know-how n. **1** practical knowledge.
2 natural skill.

knowing ● n. the state of being aware of
any thing. ● adj. **1** cunning. **2** showing
knowledge or awareness. □ **there is no
knowing** no one can tell.
□ **knowingly** adv. **knowingness** n.

know-it-all n. informal a person who seems
or pretends to know everything.

knowledge n. **1 a** awareness or
familiarity gained by experience. **b** a
person's range of information. **2 a** a
theoretical or practical understanding of a
subject, language, etc. **b** the sum of what is
known. □ **come to one's knowledge**
become known to one. **to (the best of)
my knowledge 1** so far as I know. **2** as
I know for certain.

knowledgeable adj. well-informed;
intelligent. □ **knowledgeably** adv.
[Say KNOWLEDGE uh bull]

knowledge-based adj. **1** (of an industry
etc.) producing information rather than
manufactured goods etc. **2** (of a computer
system) incorporating a set of facts etc.
derived from human knowledge.

known ● v. past participle of KNOW. ● adj.
1 publicly acknowledged. **2** Math (of a
quantity etc.) having a value that can be
stated.

know-nothing n. an ignorant person.

knuckle n. **1** the bone at a finger joint.
2 a a projection of the carpal or tarsal joint
of a quadruped. **b** a joint of meat
consisting of this. □ **knuckle down
1** apply oneself seriously. **2** (also **knuckle
under**) give in.

knuckleball n. Baseball a slow pitch made
by gripping the ball with the knuckles or
fingernails and throwing it with little spin.
□ **knuckleballer** n.

knucklehead n. informal a stupid person.

knurl ● n. a small projecting knob, ridge,
etc. ● v. make knurls on the edge of.
□ **knurled** adj.

KO ● n. (pl. **KOs**) a knockout in boxing etc.
● v. (**KO's, KO'd KO'ing**) **1** knock out in
boxing etc. **2** informal destroy, defeat.

koala n. (also **koala bear**) an Australian
bearlike marsupial, which has grey fur and
feeds on eucalyptus leaves.
[Say kuh WOLLA]

Kodiak n. a large variety of grizzly found
in Alaska. [Say KOE dee ack]

kohl n. a black powder used as eye makeup
esp. in Eastern countries. [Say KOLE]

kohlrabi n. (pl. **kohlrabies**) a variety of

cabbage with an edible turnip-like stem.
[Say kole RABBY or kole ROBBY]

koi n. (pl. **koi**) a carp of a large ornamental
variety bred in Japan.

kokanee n. (pl. **kokanee**) a non-migratory
form of sockeye salmon found in lakes.
[Say CO canny or co CANNY]

kolbassa n. a type of highly seasoned
sausage, usu. containing garlic.
[Say co baw SAW or COO buh saw or
ko BASSA]

komatik n. an Inuit sled, usu. pulled by a
dog team or snowmobile.
[Say COMMA tick]

Komodo dragon n. (also **Komodo
monitor**) a large, heavily built, East Indian
monitor lizard. [Say kuh MOE doe]

kook n. slang a strange or eccentric person.

kooky adj. (**kookier, kookiest**) slang
strange, eccentric. □ **kookiness** n.

Kool-Aid n. proprietary a fruit-flavoured
powder mixed with water and sugar to
make a drink.

Kootenay (pl. **Kootenay**) (also
Kootenai, pl. **Kootenai**) = KUTENAI.
[Say COO tuh nay]

Koran n. = QURAN □ **Koranic** adj.
[Say core ANN or kuh RAN, core ANN ick
or kuh RAN ick]

Korean n. **1** a native or national of North
or South Korea. **2** the language of Korea.
□ **Korean** adj. [Say kuh REE in]

kosher ● adj. **1** (of food) prepared in
accordance with Jewish law. **2** informal
correct; genuine; legitimate. ● n. kosher
food. [Say CO sher]

Kosovar ● n. an esp. Albanian-speaking
person from Kosovo. ● adj. of or relating to
Kosovo or its inhabitants. [Say COSSA var]

kowtow ● n. hist. the Chinese custom of
kneeling and touching the ground with
the forehead in worship or submission. ● v.
act obsequiously. [Say COW tow (TOW
rhymes with COW)]

kraft n. (also **kraft paper**) a kind of
strong brown wrapping paper.

kremlin n. **1** a citadel within a Russian
town. **2** (**the Kremlin**) the citadel in
Moscow, housing the Russian government.

krill n. a small shrimp-like crustacean,
important as food for fish, and for some
whales.

krypton n. an inert gaseous element, used
in fluorescent lamps etc. [Say CRIP tonn]

Ktunaxa Kinbasket n. (pl. **Ktunaxa
Kinbasket**) **1** a member of an Aboriginal
people living in southeastern BC and
northeastern Washington. **2** the language
of this people. □ **Ktunaxa Kinbasket** adj.
[Say k'too NOCK aw KIN basket]

kubasa *n. Cdn* a garlic sausage of Ukrainian origin. [*Say* co baw SAW *or* COO buh saw *or* ko BASSA]

kudlik *n.* an Inuit soapstone seal oil lamp. [*Say* COOD lick]

kudos *n. informal* praise and honour. [*Say* COO doze *or* COO dose]

kugel *n.* a baked dish of potatoes or noodles mixed with eggs, cottage cheese, etc. [*Say* COO gull]

Ku Klux Klan *n.* a secret society of white people in the United States, originally formed to harass and intimidate Blacks and other ethnic or religious minorities.

kumquat *n.* an orange-like fruit with a sweet rind and acid pulp. [*Say* KUM kwot]

kung fu *n.* the Chinese form of unarmed combat similar to karate. [*Say* kung FOO]

Kurd *n.* a member of a mainly pastoral Muslim people living chiefly in Kurdistan and other areas of the Middle East. □ **Kurdish** *adj.* [*Rhymes with* BIRD, KURD ish]

Kutchin *n.* (*pl.* **Kutchin**) = GWICH'IN. [*Say* coo CHIN]

Kutenai *n. & adj.* (*pl.* **Kutenai**) = KTUNAXA KINBASKET. [*Say* COO tuh nay]

Kuwaiti *n.* **1** (*pl.* **Kuwaitis**) a native or inhabitant of Kuwait. **2** the dialect of Arabic spoken in Kuwait. □ **Kuwaiti** *adj.* [*Say* coo WAIT ee]

kvetch *slang* ● *v.* (**kvetches, kvetched, kvetching**) complain and whine, esp. continually. ● *n.* (*pl.* **kvetches**) (also **kvetcher**) a person who complains. □ **kvetching** *n.* [*Say* k'VETCH]

kW *abbr.* kilowatt(s).

Kwagiulth *n.* (*pl.* **Kwagiulth**) **1** a member of an Aboriginal people living in parts of coastal BC and northern Vancouver Island. **2** the Kwa-kwa-la language of this people. □ **Kwagiulth** *adj.* [*Say* kwah GHEE oolt]

Kwakiutl *n. & adj.* (*pl.* **Kwakiutl**) = KWAGIULTH. [*Say* kwocky OOTL]

Kwakwaka'wakw *n.* (*pl.* **Kwakwaka'wakw**) a member of an Aboriginal people living in southwestern BC. □ **Kwakwaka'wakw** *adj.* [*Say* kwah KWOCKY wock]

Kwakwala *n.* the Wakashan language of the Kwakwaka'wakw and Kwagiulth. [*Say* kwah KWOLLA]

Kwanza *n.* (also **Kwanzaa**) a festival observed from 26 Dec. to 1 Jan. in celebration of black cultural heritage. [*Say* KWONZA]

kwashiorkor *n.* a form of malnutrition caused by a severe protein deficiency. [*Say* kwoshy OR core]

Kyrie *n.* (also **Kyrie eleison**) a short repeated invocation beginning with the words "Lord, have mercy" used in many Christian liturgies. [*Say* KEERY ay (ay LAY ee sonn)]

Ll

L¹ *n.* (also **l**) (*pl.* **Ls** or **L's**) **1** the twelfth letter of the alphabet. **2** (as a Roman numeral) 50. **3** a thing shaped like an L.

L² *abbr.* (also **L.**) **1** Lake. **2** large. **3** Liberal. **4** litre.

l *abbr.* (also **l.**) **1** left. **2** line. **3** litre(s). **4** length.

la *n. Music* **1** the sixth note of a major scale. **2** the note A in the fixed-do system.

Lab *n.* a Labrador retriever.

lab *n. informal* a laboratory.

lab coat *n.* a usu. white coat, worn to protect clothing esp. in a laboratory etc.

label ● *n.* **1** a small piece of paper, fabric, etc. attached to an object and giving information about it. **2** the name or trademark of a fashion company. **3** a company that produces recorded music. **4** a classifying name applied to a person or thing. ● *v.* (**labels, labelled, labelling**) **1** attach a label to. **2** assign to a category.

labial *adj.* of the lips or a labium. [*Say* LAY bee ul]

labium *n.* (*pl.* **labia**) **1** each of the two pairs of skin folds that enclose the vulva. **2** a lip or lip-like part. [*Say* LAY bee um]

labor etc. = LABOUR etc.

laboratory *n.* (*pl.* **laboratories**) a room or building fitted out for scientific experiments, research, teaching, or the manufacture of drugs and chemicals. [*Say* LABRA tory *or* luh BORA tory]

laborious *adj.* **1** needing hard work or toil. **2** (of speech, writing, etc.) showing obvious signs of effort. □ **laboriously** *adv.* [*Say* luh BORY us]

labour (also **labor**) ● *n.* **1** work; exertion. **2** workers, esp. manual, considered as a class. **3** the process of childbirth. **4** a particular esp. difficult task. **5** (**Labour**) = LABOUR PARTY. ● *v.* **1 a** work hard or exert oneself. **b** do esp. manual work. **2** strive for a purpose. **3** elaborate needlessly. **4** suffer under (a disadvantage or delusion). **5** proceed with trouble or difficulty. □ **labour of love** a task done for pleasure, not reward.

labour board *n.* (also **Labour Relations Board**) a tribunal empowered to mediate and resolve labour disputes.

labour camp *n.* a prison camp enforcing a regime of hard labour.

Labour Day *n.* a holiday in celebration of working people, observed in Canada and the US on the first Monday in September.

laboured *adj.* **1** not natural or spontaneous. **2** slow and difficult.

labourer *n.* (also **laborer**) a person doing unskilled, usu. manual, work.

labour-intensive *adj.* (of a process or industry) having labour as the largest factor or cost.

Labour Party *n.* a British political party formed to represent the interests of ordinary working people.

labour union *n.* an organized association of workers formed to protect and further their rights and interests.

Labrador *n.* (also **Labrador dog**, **Labrador retriever**) a breed of retriever with a black or golden coat often used as a guide dog.

Labradorian *n.* a native or inhabitant of Labrador. □ **Labradorian** *adj.*

Labrador Inuit *n.* **1** the Inuit people living in N Labrador. **2** the language of this people.

Labrador tea *n.* a shrub with fragrant evergreen leaves used to make a herbal tea.

laburnum *n.* a small tree with racemes of golden flowers yielding poisonous seeds. [*Say* luh BURN um]

labyrinth *n.* **1** a complicated irregular network of passages etc.; a maze. **2 a** an intricate or tangled arrangement. **b** a complex or confusing situation. **3** *Anatomy* the complex structure in the inner ear which contains the organs of hearing and balance. **4** any of various devices containing or consisting of winding passages, esp. a series of chambers designed to absorb unwanted vibrations in a loudspeaker. □ **labyrinthine** *adj.* [*Say* LABBER inth, labber INTH ine]

lac *n.* a resinous substance secreted by an Asian insect (the lac insect), used to make varnish and shellac. [*Say* LACK]

lace ● *n.* **1** a fine open fabric, esp. of cotton or silk, made by weaving thread in patterns. **2** a cord or leather strip used to fasten a shoe, skate, garment, etc. ● *adj.*

made of lace. ● v. (**laces, laced, lacing**)
1 fasten or tighten with a lace or laces.
2 a add an ingredient to (a drink, dish, etc.)
to enhance flavour, strength, effect, etc.
b intermingle. **3** *informal* thrash, beat. **4** pass
(a shoelace etc.) through. □ **laced** *adj*.

lacerate v. (**lacerates, lacerated,
lacerating**) **1** tear or cut (esp. flesh or
tissue). **2** distress or cause pain to.
□ **lacerated** *adj*. **laceration** *n*.
[*Say* LASSA rate]

lace-up ● *n*. a shoe, boot, etc. fastened
with a lace. ● *adj*. (of a shoe etc.) fastened by
a lace or laces.

lacewing *n*. a predatory insect with
delicate lace-like wings.

lacing *n*. **1** the action of lacing something.
2 something that laces or fastens.
3 ornamental lace trimming or braiding.

lack ● *n*. an absence, want, or deficiency.
● *v*. be without or deficient in. □ **lack for**
lack.

lackadaisical *adj*. not enthusiastic,
lacking vigour. □ **lackadaisically** *adv*.
[*Say* lacka DAZE ick ul]

lackey *n*. (*pl.* **lackeys**) **1** *derogatory* a person
who is obsequiously willing to obey or
serve others. **2** a servant. [*Say* LACKY]

lacking *adj*. **1** not available, missing.
2 inadequate or deficient.

lacklustre *adj*. (also esp. US **lackluster**)
1 lacking in vitality, force, or conviction.
2 (of the eye, hair, etc.) dull.
[*Say* LACK luster]

laconic *adj*. using very few words to say
something. □ **laconically** *adv*.
[*Say* luh CONNIC]

lacquer ● *n*. **1** a sometimes coloured
varnish made from shellac or synthetic
substances. **2** any of the various resinous
wood varnishes capable of taking a hard
polish. ● *v*. coat with lacquer.
□ **lacquered** *adj*. [*Say* LACKER]

lacrosse *n*. a game in which a ball is
thrown, carried and caught with a stick
having a long handle and a small net at
one end.

lactase *n*. any of a group of enzymes
which catalyze the hydrolysis of lactose.
[*Say* LACK tace]

lactate[1] *v*. (**lactates, lactated,
lactating**) (of mammals) secrete milk.
□ **lactating** *adj*. **lactation** *n*.
[*Say* LACK tate, LACK tate ing,
lack TAY shun]

lactate[2] *n*. any salt or ester of lactic acid.
[*Say* LACK tate]

lactic *adj*. of or obtained from milk.

lactic acid *n*. an organic acid formed in

sour milk, and produced in the muscles
during strenuous exercise.

lactose *n*. a sugar that occurs in milk.
[*Say* LACK tose *or* LACK toze]

lacuna *n*. (*pl.* **lacunae**) **1** a space that is
not filled; a gap. **2 a** a missing portion.
b something missing or left out.
[*Say* luh CUE nuh *for the singular*,
luh CUE nee *for the plural*]

lacy *adj*. (**lacier, laciest**) of, trimmed
with, or resembling lace.

lad *n*. **1 a** a boy or youth. **b** a young son.
2 *informal* a man; a fellow.

ladder *n*. **1 a** a device consisting of a series
of bars, rungs, or steps fixed between two
supports and used for climbing up or
down. **b** anything resembling a ladder. **2** a
series of stages by which one can make
progress in a career etc.

laddie *n*. *informal* a young boy or lad.

lade *v*. (**lades**; *past* **laded**; *past participle*
laden; **lading**) **1** put cargo on board (a
ship). **2** ship (goods) as cargo.

laden *adj*. **1** (in *comb.*) having a high
proportion of the specified thing. **2** heavily
loaded, abundantly filled. **3** burdened.

la-di-da *adj*. *informal* (also **la-de-da, lah-di-
dah**) affectedly genteel or refined.

ladies *pl.* of LADY.

Ladies' Aid *n*. (also **Ladies' Aid
Society**) an organization of women who
support the work of a church by
fundraising etc.

ladies' room *n*. a women's washroom.

ladle ● *n*. a long-handled spoon with a cup-
shaped bowl. ● *v*. (**ladles, ladled,
ladling**) serve or transfer (liquid) with a
ladle. □ **ladleful** *n*. (*pl.* **ladlefuls**) [*Rhymes
with* CRADLE]

lady *n*. (*pl.* **ladies**) **1 a** a woman of superior
social status. **b** a well-mannered and
sophisticated woman. **c** (**Lady**) a title used
by peeresses, female relatives of peers, the
wives of knights, etc. **2** any woman.
3 *informal* **a** a wife or consort. **b** a man's
girlfriend or mistress. **4** the female head of
a household. □ **the Ladies** (or **Ladies'**) a
women's public washroom.

ladybug *n*. a small beetle with domed
wing covers, usu. reddish-brown with black
spots.

ladyfinger *n*. a finger-shaped sponge cake.

lady friend *n*. a regular female
companion or lover.

lady-in-waiting *n*. (*pl.* **ladies-in-
waiting**) a lady attending a queen etc.

ladylike *adj*. with the modesty,
comportment, etc., thought characteristic
of a lady.

ladyship *n*. □ **her** (or **your** or **their**)

ladyship (or **ladyships**) a respectful form of reference or address to a Lady.

lady's slipper *n.* an orchid with a slipper-shaped lip on its flowers, the floral emblem of PEI.

lag ● *v.* (**lags**, **lagged**, **lagging**) fall behind. ● *n.* **1** = LAG TIME. **2** a delay.

lager *n.* (also **lager beer**) a kind of beer, light in colour and body. [*Sounds like* LOGGER]

laggard ● *n.* someone who falls behind others. ● *adj.* slower than desired or expected. [*Say* LAG erd]

lagoon *n.* a bay separated from the sea, a large lake, etc. by a low sandbank or similar barrier.

lag time *n.* a period of time separating two events.

lah = LA.

laid *past and past participle of* LAY[1].

laid-back *adj. informal* relaxed, easygoing.

laid up *adj.* **1** confined to bed, esp. because of illness or injury. **2** (of a vehicle etc.) taken out of service. **3** (of provisions etc.) saved, stored up.

lain *past participle of* LIE[1].

lair *n.* **1** a wild animal's den or resting place. **2** a person's hiding place or secret base.

laissez-faire *n.* **1** the theory or practice of governmental abstention from interference in the workings of the market etc. **2** a policy of leaving things to take their course, without interfering. [*Say* less ay FAIR]

laity *n.* **1** the non-ordained people in the church, as distinct from the clergy. **2** ordinary people, as distinct from professionals or experts. [*Say* LAY uh tee]

lake *n.* a large body of water surrounded by land.

lake effect *n.* the influence of a lake on weather patterns, esp. increasing snowfall and moderating temperature.

lakefront *n.* the shore of a lake.

lakehead *n. Cdn* the area along a lakeshore farthest from the lake's outlet.

lakeland *n.* an area with many lakes.

laker *n. informal* **1** = LAKE TROUT. **2** a ship designed for lakes, esp. the Great Lakes.

lakeshore *n.* the shore of a lake.

lakeside *adj.* beside a lake.

lake trout *n.* a lake-dwelling N American sport fish of the salmon family.

lakeview *adj.* overlooking a lake.

la-la land *n. informal* a fanciful state or dream world.

lam[1] *v.* (**lams**, **lammed**, **lamming**) *slang* hit hard.

lam[2] *n.* □ **on the lam** *slang* in flight, esp. from the police.

lama *n.* (*pl.* **lamas**) a Tibetan or Mongolian Buddhist monk. [*Say* LOMMA *or* LAMMA]

Lamaze *n.* designating a method of childbirth which emphasizes preparation and controlled breathing instead of drugs to control pain. [*Say* luh MOZZ]

lamb *n.* **1** a young sheep. **2** a mild or gentle person, esp. a young child.

lambada *n.* (*pl.* **lambadas**) a fast erotic Brazilian dance. [*Say* lum BODDA]

lambaste *v.* (**lambastes**, **lambasted**, **lambasting**) criticize severely. [*Say* lam BASTE]

lambda *n.* **1** the eleventh letter of the Greek alphabet (Λ, λ). **2** (as λ) the symbol for wavelength. [*Say* LAM duh]

lambent *adj.* **1** (of a soft flame) playing on a surface without burning. **2** softly radiant; lightly brilliant. [*Say* LAM bint]

Lamb of God *n.* **1** a name for Christ. **2** a prayer or hymn beginning with the words "Lamb of God".

lambskin prepared skin from a lamb, with or without the wool.

lamb's lettuce *n.* a plant sometimes used in salad.

lamb's quarters *n.* a plant of the goosefoot family.

lambswool *n.* soft fine wool from a young sheep.

lame *adj.* **1** walking with difficulty because of an injured leg. **2** (of an argument, excuse, etc.) not convincing; weak. **3** contemptibly not fashionable. **4** (of something intended to be entertaining) dull, not inspiring. □ **lamely** *adv.* **lameness** *n.*

lamé *n.* a fabric with gold or silver threads interwoven. [*Say* lam AY *or* LAM ay]

lamebrain *n. informal* a stupid person. □ **lamebrained** *adj.*

lame duck *n.* **1** a disabled or powerless person or thing. **2** a person (esp. the US President) in the final period of office, after the election of a successor.

lament ● *n.* **1** a passionate expression of grief. **2** a song or poem of sorrow. ● *v.* express or feel grief or regret. □ **lamentable** *adj.* **lamentably** *adv.*

lamentation *n.* **1** the action of lamenting. **2** a lament. [*Say* lammen TAY sh'n]

lamented *adj.* recently dead.

lamina *n.* (*pl.* **laminae**) a thin plate or scale. [*Say* LAM uh nuh *for the singular*, LAM uh nee *for the plural*]

laminate ● *v.* (**laminates**, **laminated**, **laminating**) **1** overlay with a thin esp. plastic layer. **2** beat or roll (metal) into thin

plates. **3** split or be split into layers or leaves. ● *n.* a laminated structure or material. □ **lamination** *n.*
[*Say* LAMMA nate *for the verb,* LAMMA nit *for the noun*]

lamp *n.* a device for producing a steady light or heat.

lampblack *n.* a black pigment made from soot.

lamplight *n.* light given by a lamp. □ **lamplit** *adj.*

lampoon ● *n.* a satirical attack. ● *v.* satirize.

lamppost *n.* a tall post supporting a street light.

lamprey *n.* (*pl.* **lampreys**) an eel-like aquatic animal with a sucker mouth.
[*Say* LAM pree]

lampshade *n.* a cover for a lamp, used to soften or direct its light.

LAN *n. Computing* local area network.

lance ● *n.* **1 a** a weapon with a long shaft and a pointed head, used by a horseman in charging. **2** a similar weapon used for spearing a fish etc. ● *v.* (**lances, lanced, lancing**) pierce with or as with a lance or lancet. □ **lance the boil** relieve an unpleasant situation by taking painful measures.

lancer *n. hist.* a soldier of a cavalry regiment armed with lances.

lancet *n.* a small broad double-edged surgical knife with a sharp point.
[*Say* LANCE it]

land ● *n.* **1 a** the solid part of the earth's surface, as opposed to water or air. **b** designating armies rather than navies or air forces. **2 a** an expanse of country; ground. **b** such land as a basis for agriculture etc. **3** a country, nation, or state. **4** landed property. ● *v.* **1** set or go ashore; disembark. **2** (of an aircraft, bird, etc.) alight on the ground or water. **3** bring (a fish) to land. **4** *informal* bring to, reach, or find oneself in a certain situation, place, or state. **5** *informal* deal (a blow etc.). **6** *informal* win or obtain. □ **land of Nod** sleep.

landau *n.* a four-wheeled horse-drawn carriage with folding front and rear hoods.
[*Say* LAN dow *(DOW rhymes with HOW)*]

land bridge *n.* a neck of land joining two large land masses.

land claim *n.* esp. *Cdn* a legal claim by an Aboriginal group concerning the use of an area of land.

landed *adj.* **1** *Cdn* denoting official recognition of immigration to Canada. **2** owning land.

lander *n.* a spacecraft designed to land on the surface of a planet or moon.

landfall *n.* the first approach to land after a journey across water.

landfill ● *n.* **1** refuse disposed of by burying it underground. **2** an area filled in by this process. ● *v.* **1** dispose of in this way. **2** fill with refuse in this way.

Land Forces Command *n. Cdn* the official name for the Canadian army.

landform *n.* a natural feature of the earth's surface.

landholding *n.* **1** a piece of land owned or rented. **2** the owning or renting of land. □ **landholder** *n.*

landing *n.* **1 a** the action of coming to land or the ground. **b** a place in a harbour for disembarking, loading, etc. **2** a level place above or below a flight of stairs. **3** *Cdn* an area where logs are piled before transportation.

landing craft *n.* any of several types of craft for putting troops and equipment ashore.

landing gear *n.* the undercarriage of an aircraft.

landing stage *n.* a platform on which goods and passengers are disembarked.

landlady *n.* (*pl.* **landladies**) a woman who rents land, an apartment, etc., to a tenant.

landless *adj.* not owning land.

landlocked *adj.* **1** almost or entirely enclosed by land. **2** (of fish) living in fresh water cut off from the sea.

landlord *n.* a person who rents land, an apartment, etc., to a tenant.

landlubber *n.* a person not familiar with the sea or sailing.

landmark *n.* **1 a** a conspicuous object in a landscape. **b** an important building, monument, etc. **2** an event marking a stage or turning point in history.

land mass *n.* a continent or other large area of land.

land mine *n.* an explosive mine laid in or on the ground.

landowner *n.* an owner of land. □ **landownership** *n.* **landowning** *adj. & n.*

landscape ● *n.* **1** esp. natural scenery, as seen in a broad view. **2** a picture of this. **3** a page format with the width greater than the height. ● *v.* (**landscapes, landscaped, landscaping**) alter (a piece of land) by landscape gardening. □ **landscaper** *n.* **landscaping** *n.*

landscape architecture *n.* the art of planning and designing parks or large gardens. □ **landscape architect** *n.*

landscape gardening *n.* the art of laying out ornamental grounds or grounds imitating natural scenery. □ **landscape gardener** *n.*

landslide n. **1** the sliding down of a mass of land from a mountain, cliff, etc. **2** an overwhelming majority for one side in an election.

landward ● adj. facing the land, as opposed to the sea. ● adv. (also **landwards**) towards the land.

lane n. **1** a narrow road, street, or path. **2** a division of a road for a stream of traffic. **3** a strip of track or water for each competitor in a race. **4** a regular path or course for ships, aircraft, etc. **5** the long alley down which a bowling ball is thrown.

laneway n. **1** = LANE 1. **2** Cdn a narrow urban street, esp. behind houses or stores.

language n. **1** communication by a system of spoken or written words. **2** the language of a particular community etc. **3** any method of expression. **4** a system of symbols and rules for writing computer programs. □ **speak the same language** have a similar outlook.

language police n. derogatory Cdn (in Quebec) the officials responsible for ensuring that Quebec's language laws are enforced.

languid adj. **1** very slow and relaxed. **2** pleasantly lazy and peaceful. **3** weak or faint from illness or fatigue. □ **languidly** adv. [Say LANG gwid]

languish v. (**languishes, languished, languishing**) **1** be or grow weak. **2** be forced to stay somewhere or suffer something unpleasant for a long time. [Say LANG gwish]

languor n. **1** the state or feeling, often pleasant, of being lazy and lacking energy. **2** an oppressive stillness of the air. □ **languorous** adj. **languorously** adv. [Say LANG grr]

lank adj. **1** (of hair, grass, etc.) long, limp, and straight. **2** thin and tall.

lanky adj. (**lankier, lankiest**) (of limbs, a person, etc.) ungracefully thin and long or tall.

lanolin n. a fat found on sheep's wool and used purified for cosmetics etc. [Say LANNA lin]

lantern n. **1** a portable lamp with a transparent or translucent case protecting a flame. **2** a similar electric etc. lamp.

lanthanide n. any of 15 metallic elements in the periodic table having similar chemical properties. [Say LANTH uh nide]

lanthanum n. a silvery metallic element used in the manufacture of alloys and catalysts. [Say LANTH uh num]

Laotian n. **1** a person from Laos. **2** the language of Laos. □ **Laotian** adj.

[Say LOW sh'n (with LOW rhyming with HOW) or luh OH sh'n]

lap[1] n. **1** the front of the body from the waist to the knees of a sitting person. **2** a condition of extreme comfort, ease, etc. □ **in the lap of the gods** beyond human control.

lap[2] ● n. **1** one circuit of a racetrack etc. **2** a swim from one end of a pool to the other and back again. **3** a swim from one end of a pool to the other. ● v. (**laps, lapped, lapping**) lead or overtake (a competitor in a race) by one or more laps.

lap[3] v. (**lapped, lapping**) **1 a** (usu. of an animal) drink with the tongue. **b** consume (liquid, gossip, praise, etc.) greedily. **2** (of water) move or beat upon a shore with a rippling sound.

laparoscope n. a fibre optic instrument inserted through the abdominal wall to give an interior view of the abdomen. □ **laparoscopic** adj. **laparoscopy** n. (pl. **laparoscopies**) [Say LAPPA ruh scope, lappa ruh SCOPPIC, lappa ROSCA pee]

lapdog n. a small pet dog.

lapel n. the part of the front of a coat which is folded over towards either shoulder. [Say luh PELL]

lapidary adj. **1** concerned with stone or stones. **2** engraved upon stone. **3** (of writing) dignified and concise, suitable for inscriptions. [Say LAPPA derry]

lapis lazuli n. (also **lapis**) **1** a blue mineral used as a gemstone. **2** a bright blue pigment formerly made from this. [Say lappis LAZOO lee]

Lapp n. **1** a member of the indigenous population of the extreme north of Scandinavia. **2** the language of this people. □ **Lapp** adj.

lapse ● n. **1** a slight error; a slip of memory etc. **2** a careless decline into an inferior state. **3** an interval or passage of time. ● v. (**lapses, lapsed, lapsing**) **1** fail to maintain a position or standard. **2** fall back into an inferior or previous state. **3** (of a privilege etc.) become invalid because of disuse, failure to renew, etc.

lapsed adj. having abandoned a formerly adhered-to religion, philosophy, etc.

laptop n. a portable microcomputer.

lapwing n. a plover with black and white plumage, crested head, and a shrill cry.

larceny n. (pl. **larcenies**) the theft of personal property. [Say LARSA nee]

larch n. (pl. **larches**) a coniferous tree with bunches of soft, bright green needles.

lard ● n. the internal fat of the abdomen of pigs, esp. when used for cooking. ● v. **1** insert fat or bacon in (meat etc.) before cooking. **2** embellish with extraneous material, esp. to excess.

larder *n.* **1** a room or cupboard for storing food. **2** a store of food.

large ● *adj.* (**larger, largest**) **1** of considerable or relatively great size or extent. **2** of the larger kind. **3** of wide range; comprehensive. ● *n.* **1** a garment of a size suited for people moderately larger than average. **2** a large serving of a beverage or food. □ **at large 1** at liberty; not confined. **2** as a body or whole. **live large** be very wealthy; have an extravagant lifestyle. □ **largeness** *n.*

large intestine *n.* the cecum, colon, and rectum collectively.

largely *adv.* to a great extent; principally.

largemouth *n.* a N American freshwater bass of the sunfish family.

large-scale *adj.* made or occurring on a large scale or in large amounts.

largesse *n.* (also **largess**) **1** generosity in giving money or gifts. **2** money or gifts given generously. [*Say* lar JESS]

largish *adj.* somewhat large. [*Say* LARGE ish]

largo *Music* ● *adv. & adj.* in a slow tempo and dignified in style. ● *n.* (*pl.* **largos**) a largo passage etc.

lariat *n.* **1** a lasso. **2** a tethering rope, esp. used by cowboys. [*Say* LERRY it]

lark¹ *n.* a small brown songbird which sings while flying.

lark² *informal* ● *n.* a carefree frolic; an amusing incident or practical joke. ● *v.* behave in a playful and mischievous way. □ **larky** *adj.*

larkspur *n.* **1** a plant of the buttercup family, which bears spikes of spurred flowers. **2** a delphinium.

larva *n.* (*pl.* **larvae**) **1** the stage of an insect between egg and pupa, e.g. a caterpillar. **2** an immature form of other animals that undergo some metamorphosis, e.g. a tadpole. □ **larval** *adj.* [*Say* LAR vuh *for the singular,* LAR vee *for the plural*]

laryngitis *n.* inflammation of the larynx, usu. with roughness or loss of the voice. [*Say* lair in JITE us]

larynx *n.* (*pl.* **larynges**) the hollow muscular organ holding the vocal cords. [*Say* LAIR inx *for the singular,* luh RIN jeez *for the plural*]

lasagna *n.* (also **lasagne**) **1** pasta in the form of wide ribbons. **2** a baked dish made from layers of lasagna, usu. filled with tomato sauce, cheese, and ground meat. [*Say* luh ZON yuh]

lascivious *adj.* lustful. □ **lasciviously** *adv.* **lasciviousness** *n.* [*Say* luh SIVVY us]

laser *n.* **1** an intense beam of light with parallel rays of the same wavelength. **2** a device generating this.

laser disc *n.* a disc on which data is recorded digitally and is read optically by a laser beam.

laser printer *n.* a computer printer in which a laser is used to form dots on a photosensitive drum corresponding to the pattern of print required on the page.

lash ● *v.* (**lashes, lashed, lashing**) **1** make a sudden whip-like movement. **2** beat with a whip, rope, etc. **3** (of wind, rain, etc.) pour or rush with great force. **4** fasten with a cord. ● *n.* (*pl.* **lashes**) **1 a** a sharp blow made by a whip, rope, etc. **b** (**the lash**) punishment by whipping. **2** an eyelash. □ **lash out** speak or hit out angrily.

lashing *n.* **1** a beating. **2** a scolding; reprimand.

LASIK *n.* laser in situ keratomileusis, surgery which uses a laser to carve the interior of the cornea. [*Say* LAY zick]

lass *n.* (also **lassie**) *Scot. & Northern England* or *literary* a girl or young woman.

lassitude *n.* weariness in mind or body. [*Say* LASSA tude]

lasso ● *n.* (*pl.* **lassos** or **lassoes**) a rope with a noose at one end, esp. as used for catching cattle. ● *v.* (**lassoes, lassoed, lassoing**) catch with or as with a lasso. [*Say* la SOO *or* LASS oh]

last¹ ● *adj.* **1** after all others; coming at the end. **2** preceding; previous in a sequence. **3** only remaining; final. **4** (**the last**) least likely or suitable. **5** the lowest in rank. ● *adv.* **1** after all others. **2** on the last occasion before the present **3** (esp. in enumerating) lastly. ● *n.* a person or thing that is last, last-mentioned, most recent, the only remaining, etc. □ **at last** (or **long last**) in the end; after much delay.

last² *v.* **1** remain adequate or alive for a specified or considerable time. **2** continue for a specified time.

last³ *n.* a shoemaker's model for shaping or repairing a shoe or boot.

last-ditch *adj.* designating a final effort to avert disaster.

last-gasp *adj.* last-minute.

last hurrah *n.* any final performance, effort, or success.

lasting *adj.* **1** continuing, permanent. **2** durable. □ **lastingly** *adv.*

Last Judgment *n.* (in some beliefs) the judgment of all people at the end of the world.

lastly *adv.* finally.

last minute ● *n.* (also **last moment**)

the time just before an important event. ● *adj.* (**last-minute**) done at the last minute.

last name *n.* surname.

last post *n. Brit. & Cdn* **1** a bugle call marking the hour of retiring at night. **2** this call blown at military funerals etc.

last rites *n.* sacred rites for a person about to die.

Last Supper *n.* the supper eaten by Christ and his disciples on the eve of the Crucifixion.

last word *n.* **1** a final or definitive statement. **2** the latest fashion.

lat *n.* (usu. in *pl.*) *slang* = LATISSIMUS DORSI.

lat. *abbr.* latitude.

latch ● *n.* **1** a bar with a catch and lever used as a fastening for a gate etc. **2** a spring lock requiring a key for opening from the outside. ● *v.* fasten or be fastened with a latch. □ **latch on** *informal* **1** attach oneself (to). **2** obtain, get. **3** associate oneself strongly with. **4** become very interested in.

latchkey *n.* (*pl.* **latchkeys**) a key of an outer door.

latchkey child *n.* (also **latchkey kid**) a child who is alone at home after school until a parent returns from work.

late ● *adj.* (**later**, **latest**) **1** acting, arriving, or happening after the due or usual time. **2** far on in a specified time or period. **3** no longer alive. ● *adv.* (**later**, **latest**) **1** after the due or usual time. **2** far on in time. **3** at or till a late hour. **4** at a late stage of development. **5** formerly but not now. **6** (**later**) subsequently. □ **of late** lately, recently. **the latest** the most recent news, fashion, etc. □ **lateness** *n.*

latecomer *n.* **1** a person who arrives late. **2** a recent arrival.

lately *adv.* not long ago; recently.

late-model *adj.* (of a consumer product) of a recent make.

latent *adj.* existing but not yet developed or manifest; hidden. □ **latency** *n.* **latently** *adv.* [*Say* LAY tint]

lateral ● *adj.* **1** of or to the side or sides. **2** (of movement to a new job) that is neither a promotion nor a demotion. ● *n.* **1** a side part etc., esp. a lateral shoot or branch. **2** *Football* a sideways pass. □ **laterally** *adv.* [*Say* LATTER ul]

lateral thinking *n.* a method of solving problems indirectly or by apparently illogical methods.

latex *n.* (*pl.* **latexes**) **1** a milky fluid found in various plants and trees, used for commercial purposes. **2** a synthetic product resembling this. **3** paint having latex as its binding medium. [*Say* LAY tex]

lath *n.* (*pl.* **laths**) **1** a thin flat strip of wood, esp. part of a supporting framework for plaster. **2** (esp. in phr. **lath and plaster**) laths collectively as a building material.

lathe *n.* a machine for shaping wood etc. by rotating it against a fixed cutting tool. [*Rhymes with* BATHE]

lather ● *n.* **1** a froth produced by agitating soap etc. and water. **2** frothy sweat, esp. of a horse. **3** a state of agitation. ● *v.* **1** (of soap etc.) form a lather. **2** cover with lather. **3** (of a horse etc.) become covered with lather.

Latin ● *n.* **1** the language of ancient Rome and its empire. **2** a native of any of the countries whose language is developed from Latin. ● *adj.* **1** of or in Latin. **2 a** of the peoples using languages developed from Latin. **b** Latin American. **3** of the Roman Catholic Church. **4** of or relating to the Latin alphabet.

Latina *n.* a female Latin American in N America. [*Say* luh TEENA]

Latin America *n.* the parts of the Americas where Spanish or Portuguese is the main language. □ **Latin American** *adj. & n.*

Latino *n.* (*pl.* **Latinos**) a Latin American in N America. [*Say* luh TEENO]

latissimus dorsi *n.* (*pl.* **latissimi dorsi**) either of a pair of large, roughly triangular muscles of the lower back. [*Say* luh TISSA mus DORE sigh *for the singular,* luh TISSA my DORE sigh *for the plural*]

latitude *n.* **1 a** a place's distance north or south of the equator, expressed in degrees. **b** (usu. in *pl.*) regions with reference to their temperature and distance from the equator. **2** freedom to choose what one does or the way that one does it. □ **latitudinal** *adj.*

latke *n.* (in Jewish cooking) a pancake made with grated potato. [*Say* LAT kuh]

latrine *n.* a communal lavatory, esp. in a camp etc. [*Say* luh TREEN]

latte *n.* espresso coffee with hot milk. [*Say* LAT ay *or* LOT ay]

latter ● *n.* (**the latter**) the second of two things mentioned. ● *adj.* **1** nearer to the end. **2** second of two things mentioned.

latter-day *adj.* modern, contemporary.

Latter-day Saint *n.* a member of the Mormon Church (officially called the Church of Jesus Christ of Latter-day Saints).

latterly *adv.* **1** in the latter part of life or of a period. **2** recently.

lattice *n.* **1** a structure of crossed strips with square or diamond-shaped spaces between. **2** something with an open interlaced structure like that of a lattice. □ **latticed** adj. [Say LAT iss]

latticework n. laths arranged in lattice formation. [Say LAT iss work]

Latvian n. **1 a** a native or inhabitant of Latvia. **b** a person of Latvian descent. **2** the language of Latvia. □ **Latvian** adj.

laud v. praise. □ **laudable** adj. **laudably** adv. [Say LOD]

laudanum n. a morphine solution formerly used as a painkiller. [Say LODDA num]

laudatory adj. expressing praise. [Say LODDA tory]

laugh ● v. **1** make the spontaneous sounds and movements usual in expressing lively amusement. **2** (foll. by at) ridicule, make fun of. **3** (in phr. **be laughing**) informal be in a fortunate or successful position. ● n. **1** the sound or act or manner of laughing. **2** informal a comical or entertaining person or thing. □ **laugh all the way to the bank** be in an enviable financial position. **laugh off** get rid of (embarrassment or humiliation) by joking. **laugh out of the other side of one's face** (or **mouth**) change from amusement to displeasure.

laughable adj. ludicrous; highly amusing. □ **laughably** adv.

laugher n. **1** a person who laughs. **2** Sport slang an easily won game; a walkover.

laughing gas n. nitrous oxide as an anaesthetic.

laughingly adv. **1** with amused ridicule or ludicrous inappropriateness. **2** in an amused way; with laughter.

laughingstock n. a person or thing open to general ridicule.

laugh line n. **1** a wrinkle around the eye or mouth formed over the years by smiling. **2** a line in a play, movie, etc. designed to elicit laughter.

laughter n. the act or sound of laughing.

laugh track n. pre-recorded laughter added to a television show to simulate or encourage audience response.

launch ● v. (**launches, launched, launching**) **1** set a vessel afloat. **2** hurl or send forth (a rocket etc.). **3** start or set in motion. **4** formally introduce a new product with publicity etc. **5** begin suddenly (a tirade, speech, song, etc.). ● n. **1 a** the action of launching something. **b** an event at which something is launched. **2** a large motorboat.

launcher n. a structure or device to hold a rocket, missile, etc. during launching.

launching pad n. (also **launch pad**) **1** a platform with a supporting structure, from

which rockets are launched. **2** a starting point for an enterprise etc.

launder v. **1 a** wash and dry (clothes etc.). **b** bear laundering without damage. **2** informal transfer (funds) to conceal their dubious or illegal origin. □ **launderer** n.

launderette n. (also **laundrette**) a laundromat. [Say lon DRET]

laundromat n. an establishment with coin-operated washers and dryers for public use.

laundry n. (pl. **laundries**) **1** clothes etc. to be laundered or just laundered. **2 a** a room or building for washing clothes etc. **b** a business washing clothes etc. commercially.

laundry list n. a long list of assorted items.

laureate n. **1** a person who is honoured for outstanding creative or intellectual achievement. **2** = POET LAUREATE. [Say LORRY it]

laurel n. **1** a bay tree. **2 a** (in sing. or pl.) a crown or wreath of bay leaves used as an emblem of victory or distinction in poetry. **b** (in pl.) honour or distinction. **3** any plant with dark green glossy leaves like a bay tree. □ **rest on one's laurels** be satisfied with what one has done and not seek further success. [Say LORE ul]

Laurentian adj. **1** designating a group of granites found northwest of the St. Lawrence River. **2** of or pertaining to the Laurentian Mountains in Quebec. [Say luh REN sh'n]

lava n. **1** the molten matter which flows from a volcano. **2** the solid substance which it forms on cooling.

lavatory n. (pl. **lavatories**) **1** a toilet. **2** a room or compartment containing one or more toilets. [Say LAV uh tory]

lavender n. **1 a** a small evergreen shrub with narrow leaves and blue, purple, or pink aromatic flowers. **b** its flowers and stalks dried and used to scent clothes etc. **2** the oil obtained from the blossoms of cultivated lavender, used in medicine and perfume. **3** a pale blue colour with a trace of mauve.

lavish ● adj. **1** giving or doing something generously. **2** rich in quality and usu. expensive. ● v. (**lavishes, lavished, lavishing**) bestow or spend (money, effort, praise, etc.) abundantly. □ **lavishly** adv. **lavishness** n.

law n. **1** a rule or system of rules and penalties recognized by a community as regulating the actions of its members. **2** such rules as a subject of study or as the basis of the legal profession. **3** a statement of fact to the effect that a particular natural phenomenon always occurs if certain conditions are present. **4** a rule defining correct procedure in a sport. **5** something having binding force or effect. **6** (**the law**) *informal* the police. □ **lay down the law** be dogmatic or authoritarian. **take the law into one's own hands** redress a grievance by one's own means, esp. by force.

law-abiding *adj.* obedient to the laws.

lawbreaker *n.* a person who breaks the law. □ **law-breaking** *n. & adj.*

lawful *adj.* conforming with, permitted by, or recognized by law. □ **lawfully** *adv.* **lawfulness** *n.*

lawgiver *n.* a person who lays down laws.

lawless *adj.* **1** having no laws or enforcement of them. **2** disregarding laws. □ **lawlessness** *n.*

lawmaker *n.* a legislator. □ **law-making** *adj. & n.*

lawn *n.* **1** an area of grass kept mown. **2** a fine linen or cotton fabric.

lawn bowling *n.* any of several games played on grass or dirt surfaces in which players attempt to roll a ball as close as possible to a smaller ball.

lawn tennis *n.* the usual form of tennis, played on outdoor grass or a hard court.

Law Society *n. Cdn & Brit.* a professional body representing lawyers.

lawsuit *n.* the process of bringing a dispute, claim, etc. before a law court for settlement.

lawyer *n.* a member of the legal profession. □ **lawyerly** *adj.*

lax *adj.* not strict enough in enforcing rules. □ **laxity** *n.*

laxative *n.* a medication promoting bowel movements. □ **laxative** *adj.* [*Say* LAXA tiv]

lay[1] ● *v.* (**lays, laying, laid**) **1** put down, especially gently or carefully. **2** put down and set in position for use. **3** assign or place. **4** present (material) for consideration. **5** (of a female bird, reptile, etc.) produce (an egg) from inside the body. **6** stake (an amount of money) in a bet. **7** *coarse slang* have sexual intercourse with. ● *n.* the general appearance of an area of land. □ **lay off 1** discharge (a worker) because of a shortage of work. **2** *informal* give up. **lay out 1** construct or arrange (buildings or gardens) according to a plan. **2** arrange (material) for printing. **lay up** put out of action through illness or injury.

lay[2] *adj.* **1 a** non-clerical. **b** designating a member of a religious order who is not ordained and is employed in ancillary or manual work. **2** not professionally qualified.

lay[3] *n.* **1** a short lyric or narrative poem meant to be sung. **2** a song.

lay[4] *past of* LIE[1].

layabout *n.* a habitual loafer or idler.

layaway *n.* a method of purchasing by instalments in which the purchaser takes possession after all instalments have been paid.

layer ● *n.* a thickness of matter, esp. one of several, laid over a surface or forming a horizontal division. ● *v.* **1 a** arrange in layers. **b** cut (hair) in layers. **2** form layers. **3** wear several layers of clothing so that layers can be removed or put back on to adjust to temperature variations. □ **layered** *adj.* **layering** *n.*

layette *n.* a set of clothing, toilet articles, and bedclothes for a newborn child. [*Say* lay ET]

layman *n.* (*pl.* **laymen**) **1** any non-ordained member of a church. **2** a person without professional or specialized knowledge in a subject.

layoff *n.* **1** a temporary or permanent dismissal of workers. **2** a period when this is in force.

layout *n.* **1** the arrangement of a site, ground, etc. **2** the way in which printed matter is arranged or set out. **3** something arranged or set out in a particular way.

layover *n.* a period of rest or waiting before a further stage in a journey etc.

layperson *n.* (*pl.* **lay people** or **laypersons**) a layman or laywoman.

layup *n. Basketball* a shot in which the shooter lays the ball against the backboard so it will rebound into the basket.

laywoman *n.* (*pl.* **laywomen**) **1** any non-ordained female member of a church. **2** a woman without professional or specialized knowledge in a subject.

laze *v.* (**lazes, lazed, lazing**) spend time lazily or idly.

lazy *adj.* (**lazier, laziest**) **1** unwilling to work or be active; doing as little as possible. **2** not involving much energy or activity; slow and relaxed. **3** showing a lack of effort or care. □ **lazily** *adv.* **laziness** *n.*

lazybones *n.* (*pl.* **lazybones**) *informal* a lazy person.

Lazy Susan *n.* a revolving stand, cupboard, or shelf in a kitchen.

lb. *abbr.* a pound or pounds (weight).

LCD *abbr.* **1** LIQUID CRYSTAL DISPLAY. **2** lowest common denominator.

lea *n. literary* a piece of meadow. [*Say* LEE]

leach *v.* (**leaches, leached, leaching**) **1** (of chemicals, minerals, etc.) be removed from soil etc. by the action of rainwater. **2** (of a liquid) remove chemicals, minerals,

etc. from soil. □**leachable** *adj.*
leaching *n.*

leachate *n.* liquid that has percolated
through a solid and leached out some of
the constituents. [*Say* LEACH ate]

lead¹ ● *v.* (**leads**, **leading**, **led**) **1** cause (a
person or animal) to go with one. **2** be a
route or means of access. **3** (foll. by *to*)
result in. **4** influence to do or believe
something. **5** be in charge of. **6** have the
advantage in a race or game. **7** have (a
particular way of life). **8** (foll. by *on*) deceive.
9 go or be first. ● *n.* **1** the initiative in an
action. **2** (**the lead**) a position of
advantage in a contest. **3** the chief part in a
play or film. **4** the member of a curling
rink who delivers the first two rocks. **5** a
clue to be followed in solving a problem.
6 the item of news given first. ● *adj.* playing
the chief part in a musical group.

lead² *n.* **1** a heavy bluish-grey soft ductile
metallic element. **2** graphite, esp. as used
in a pencil. **3** bullets collectively. □**get the
lead out** *slang* hurry up. [*Say* LED]

lead crystal *n.* leaded crystal.

leaded *adj.* **1** (of gasoline) containing an
anti-knock lead compound. **2** (of glass or
crystal) containing a high proportion of
lead oxide, making it more refractive. **3** (of
a window) containing panes of glass set in
lead strips.

leaden *adj.* **1** of or like lead. **2** heavy, slow,
burdensome. **3** dull or depressing. **4** lead-
coloured.

leader *n.* **1** a person or thing that leads.
2 the principal player in a music group.
3 the tip or leading section of something
long, e.g. of a roll of film or plant stem. **4** a
length of wire connecting a fishing line to
a hook or fly. □**leaderless** *adj.*
leadership *n.*

leaderboard *n.* a scoreboard, esp. at a
golf course.

leadership convention *n.* *Cdn* a
convention held by a political party to elect
a new leader.

lead-footed *adj.* **1** slow or sluggish.
2 tending to drive too quickly.

lead-in *n.* an introduction, opening, etc.

leading *adj.* **1** chief; most important; most
popular. **2** first in position.

leading lady *n.* the actress who plays the
principal female part in a play or film.

leading man *n.* the actor who plays the
principal male part in a play or film.

leading question *n.* a question that
prompts the (esp. incriminating) answer
wanted.

leading seaman *n.* **1** (also **Leading
Seaman**) a member of the Canadian Navy

of the rank above able seaman and below
master seaman. Abbreviation: **LS**. **2** a
person of similar rank in other navies.

leadoff *adj.* *Baseball* referring to the player
who bats first in an inning.

lead time *n.* the time between the
initiation and completion of a process.
[*Say* LEED]

leaf *n.* (*pl.* **leaves**) **1** a flat green structure
that grows from the stem of a plant. **2** the
state of having leaves out. **3** a single
thickness of paper in a book etc., with each
side forming a page. **4** a very thin sheet of
metal. **5** an extra section inserted to extend
a table. □**leaf through** turn over the
pages of (a book etc.). **take a leaf out of
a person's book** imitate a person. **turn
over a new leaf** improve one's conduct
or performance. □**leafless** *adj.* **leaflike**
adj. **leafy** *adj.* (**leafier**, **leafiest**)

-leafed *comb. form* having the kind or
number of leaves described.

leaflet *n.* **1** a usu. folded sheet of paper
containing printed information. **2** a young
leaf. **3** any division of a compound leaf.

leaf lettuce *n.* lettuce with loose leaves.

leaf mould *n.* soil consisting chiefly of
decayed leaves.

league¹ ● *n.* **1** a collection of people,
countries, etc., combining esp. for mutual
protection or co-operation. **2** a group of
sports teams organized to compete among
themselves. **3** a class or category. ● *v.*
(**leagues**, **leagued**, **leaguing**) join in a
league. □**in league** allied, conspiring.

league² *n.* *archaic* a variable measure of
distance, usu. about three miles (4.8 km).

leaguer *n.* a member of a league.

leak ● *n.* **1** a hole in a pipe, container, etc.,
through which liquid or gas passes
accidentally in or out. **2** the intentional
disclosure of secret information. ● *v.* **1** pass
in or out through a leak. **2** intentionally
disclose (secret information). **3** (often foll.
by *out*) (of a secret) become known. □**take
a leak** *slang* urinate. □**leakage** *n.* **leaker**
n. **leaky** *adj.* (**leakier**, **leakiest**)

leak-proof *adj.* designed so as to prevent
leakage.

lean¹ ● *v.* (**leans**; **leaned** or (esp. *Brit.*)
leant; **leaning**) **1** incline from the
perpendicular. **2** rest or cause to rest for
support against etc. **3** rely on. **4** have a
tendency toward. ● *n.* a deviation from the
perpendicular. □**lean on** *informal* put
pressure on (a person) to act in a certain
way.

lean² ● *adj.* **1** (of a person, animal or meat)
thin; having little fat. **2** meagre; of poor
quality. **3** rendered more efficient through
the reduction of unnecessary costs.

4 marked by austerity and restraint. ● *n.* the lean part of meat. □ **leanness** *n.*

leaning *n.* a tendency or partiality.

lean-to *n.* (*pl.* **lean-tos**) **1** a usu. temporary shelter consisting of an inclined makeshift roof supported at one side by trees, posts, etc. **2** a roof that has a single slope and joins a wall at its upper end. **3** a room or building with such a roof.

leap ● *v.* (**leaps**; *past* and *past participle* **leaped** or **leapt**; **leaping**) **1** jump or spring forcefully. **2** jump across. **3** (of prices etc.) increase dramatically. **4** move quickly or suddenly. **5** spring or arise quickly. ● *n.* **1** a forceful jump. **2** a large, sudden increase. **3** a sudden or dramatic transition. □ **leap to the eye** be immediately apparent. □ **leaper** *n.*

leapfrog ● *n.* a game in which players in turn vault with parted legs over another who is bending down. ● *v.* (**leapfrogs**, **leapfrogged**, **leapfrogging**) **1** perform such a vault. **2** overtake or surpass a competitor.

leap of faith *n.* (*pl.* **leaps of faith**) the action of accepting something that cannot be proven.

leap year *n.* a year, occurring once in four, with 366 days instead of 365.

learn *v.* (**learns**; *past* and *past participle* **learned** or **learnt**; **learning**) **1** gain knowledge or skill by study, experience, or being taught. **2** commit to memory. **3** become aware of by information or from observation. □ **learnability** *n.* **learnable** *adj.* **learner** *n.* **learning** *n.*

learned *adj.* **1** having much knowledge acquired by study. **2** scholarly. **3** acquired by learning or experience; not innate. □ **learnedly** *adv.* **learnedness** *n.* [*Say* LEARN id, *except for sense 3, which is pronounce* LEARND]

learning curve *n.* **1** the rate of progress in learning. **2** a graph of this.

lease ● *n.* **1** an agreement by which the owner of property allows another to use it for a specified time in return for payment. **2** the period of time for which such an agreement is made. ● *v.* (**leases**, **leased**, **leasing**) grant or take on a lease. □ **a new lease on life** a substantially improved prospect of living or of use.

leasehold ● *n.* **1** the holding of property by lease. **2** property held by lease. ● *adj.* held by lease. □ **leaseholder** *n.*

leash ● *n.* (*pl.* **leashes**) a cord for leading or controlling a dog. ● *v.* (**leashes**, **leashed**, **leashing**) **1** put a leash on. **2** restrain.

least ● *adj.* smallest in amount, size, or significance. ● *n.* the least amount. ● *adv.*

in the least degree. □ **at least 1** at all events; anyway. **2** (also **at the least**) not less than. **in the least** (or **the least**) in the smallest degree; at all.

leather *n.* **1** material made from the skin of an animal by tanning. **2** a thing made of leather.

leatherback *n.* a very large turtle that has a thick leathery shell, living esp. in tropical seas.

leather-bound *adj.* (esp. of a book) bound in leather.

leatherette *n.* imitation leather.

leathery *adj.* **1** like leather. **2** (esp. of meat etc.) tough.

leave¹ *v.* (**leaves**, **left**, **leaving**) **1** go away from. **2** cause to or let remain. **3** cease to be at or belong to. **4** abandon, desert. **5** refrain from interfering with. **6** commit or refer to another person. **7 a** abstain from consuming or dealing with. **b** remain over. **8** deposit something to be attended to. **9** cause to be in a specified state. □ **have left** have remaining. **leave alone 1** not interfere with. **2** not have dealings with. **leave be** *informal* refrain from disturbing. **leave it at that** *informal* abstain from comment or further action. **leave out** omit, not include.

leave² *n.* **1** permission. **2 a** permission to be absent from duty, work, etc. **b** the period for which this lasts. □ **on leave** legitimately absent from duty, work, etc. **take one's leave** bid farewell.

leaved *adj.* having leaves of a specified kind or number.

leaven ● *n.* **1** *archaic* leavening. **2** a pervasive transforming influence. ● *v.* **1** cause dough to rise with a leavening substance. **2** modify with a tempering element. [*Say* LEV in]

leavening *n.* **1** a substance, e.g. yeast or baking powder, that causes dough or batter to rise. **2** the action or process of causing fermentation by using leaven. **3** a small amount of a specified quality. [*Say* LEV in ing]

leaves *pl.* of LEAF.

leave-taking *n.* the act of saying goodbye.

leavings *pl. n.* things left over, esp. as worthless.

Lebanese *n.* a native or inhabitant of Lebanon. □ **Lebanese** *adj.* [*Say* lebba NEEZ]

lech *informal* ● *v.* (**leches**, **leched**, **leching**) feel lecherous; behave lustfully. ● *n.* (*pl.* **leches**) a lecher. [*Say* LETCH]

lecher *n.* a lecherous man.

lecherous *adj.* having excessive sexual

desire. □ **lecherously** adv.
lecherousness n.

lechery n. unrestrained indulgence of sexual desire.

lecithin n. a substance widely distributed in animal tissues, egg yolk, and some plants, used as an emulsifier. [Say LESS i thin]

lectern n. a stand with a sloping top from which a speaker can read while standing.

lectionary n. (pl. **lectionaries**) a book containing portions of Scripture for reading at a religious service.

lector n. Catholicism a person designated to read aloud at Mass.

lecture ● n. **1** an educational talk to an audience. **2** a lengthy reprimand. ● v. (**lectures, lectured, lecturing**) deliver a lecture or lectures. □ **lecturer** n. **lectureship** n.

LED abbr. light-emitting diode.

led past and past participle of LEAD¹.

ledge n. **1** a narrow horizontal surface projecting from a wall etc. **2** a shelf-like projection on the side of a rock or mountain. **3** an underwater ridge of rocks. □ **ledged** adj.

ledger n. a book or computer document for recording financial accounts.

lee n. **1** shelter given by a neighbouring object. **2** the side away from the wind.

leech n. (pl. **leeches**) **1** a worm that sucks the blood of animals or people. **2** a person who extorts profit from or sponges off others.

leek n. a vegetable related to the onion, with flat overlapping leaves forming an elongated cylindrical bulb.

leer ● v. look at someone in an unpleasant way with sexual interest or evil intent. ● n. a leering look.

leery adj. (**leerier, leeriest**) wary.

lees pl. n. the sediment of wine etc. [Say LEEZ]

leeward adj. & adv. on or toward the side sheltered from the wind. [Say LEE werd or Nautical LOO erd]

leeway n. **1** allowable deviation or freedom of action. **2** the sideways drift of a ship to leeward of the desired course.

left¹ ● adj. **1** on or toward the west side of a person or thing facing north. **2** (also **Left**) Politics favouring liberal, radical, or socialist policies. ● adv. on or to the left side. ● n. **1** the left side or area. **2** (a turn onto) the road etc. on the left. **3** Boxing a blow with the left hand. **4** (often **Left**) Politics a group or section favouring liberal policies. □ **have two left feet** informal be clumsy.

left² past and past participle of LEAVE¹.

left field n. **1** Baseball the part of the outfield to the left of the batter as he or she faces the pitcher. **2** informal an unconventional position, state, experience, etc. □ **out in left field** slang completely wrong or unconventional. □ **left fielder** n.

left-hand adj. **1** on or toward the left side of a person or thing. **2** to the left. **3** done with the left hand.

left-handed ● adj. **1** using the left hand. **2** designed for use by left-handed people. **3** toward the left. ● adv. with the left hand or to the left side. □ **left-handedly** adv. **left-handedness** n.

left-hander n. **1** a left-handed person. **2** a left-handed blow.

leftie = LEFTY.

leftism n. the principles of the political left, including the promotion of liberalism, socialism, or radical social change. □ **leftish** adj. **leftist** n. & adj.

left-of-centre adj. having somewhat leftist views, policies, etc.

leftover ● n. (usu. in pl.) an item remaining after the rest has been used. ● adj. remaining over, surplus.

leftward ● adv. (also **leftwards**) toward the left. ● adj. going toward or facing the left.

left wing ● n. **1** the radical or socialist section of a political party. **2** Hockey the forward position to the left of centre. **3** the left side of an army. ● adj. (usu. **left-wing**) socialist or radical. □ **left-winger** n.

lefty ● n. (pl. **lefties**) informal **1** a left-handed person. **2** Politics a left-winger. ● adv. esp. Baseball with the left hand or to the left side. □ **lefty** adj.

leg n. **1** each of the limbs on which a person or animal walks and stands. **2** an analogous part of a piece of furniture. **3** a section of a journey or relay race. □ **find one's legs 1** gain momentum. **2** acquire or regain mastery of a skill. **leg it** informal walk or run hard. **not have a leg to stand on** be unable to support one's argument by facts or sound reasons. **on one's last legs** near death or the end of one's usefulness etc.

legacy (pl. **legacies**) ● n. **1** a gift left in a will. **2** something handed down by a predecessor. ● adj. denoting software or hardware that has been superseded but is difficult to replace because of its wide use. [Say LEGGA see]

legal adj. **1** of or based on law; falling within the province of law. **2** permitted by law or the rules. **3** designating a size of paper $8\frac{1}{2}$ by 14 inches (22 by 35.5 cm). □ **legally** adv.

legal aid n. payment from public funds

allowed, in cases of need, to help pay for legal advice.

legalese *n. informal* the technical language of legal documents. [*Say* legal EEZ]

legalism *n.* excessively strict adherence to law or rules. □ **legalist** *n.* **legalistic** *adj.*

legality *n.* (*pl.* **legalities**) **1** lawfulness. **2** an obligation imposed by law. [*Say* li GAL a tee *or* lee GAL a tee]

legalize *v.* (**legalizes**, **legalized**, **legalizing**) make lawful. □ **legalization** *n.*

legal tender *n.* currency that cannot legally be refused in payment of a debt.

legate *n.* a member of the clergy representing the Pope. [*Say* LEG it]

legation *n.* a diplomatic minister and staff. [*say* li GAY sh'n]

legato *adv.* & *adj. Music* in a smooth flowing manner. [*Say* luh GOT toe]

legend *n.* **1 a** a traditional story sometimes popularly regarded as historical; a myth. **b** such stories collectively. **2** a person of the highest renown. **3** a key to the symbols used on a map etc.

legendary *adj.* **1** of or connected with legends. **2** remarkable enough to be a subject of legend. □ **legendarily** *adv.*

legerdemain *n.* **1** sleight of hand. **2** trickery. [*Say* lezh er duh MAIN]

legged *adj.* having legs, esp. of a specified kind or number.

leggings *pl. n.* **1** close-fitting stretch trousers for women or children. **2** an outer garment for keeping the legs warm.

leggy *adj.* (**leggier**, **leggiest**) **1** long-legged, esp. attractively so. **2** long-stemmed.

leghold trap *n.* a type of trap which catches an animal by one of its legs.

Leghorn *n.* a chicken of a small, hardy domestic breed.

legible *adj.* (of handwriting, print, etc.) clear enough to read. □ **legibility** *n.* **legibly** *adv.*

legion ● *n.* **1** a vast multitude or number. **2** (**Legion**) any of various national associations of ex-servicemen and ex-servicewomen. **3** = LEGION HALL. **4** *Roman History* a division of 3,000–6,000 soldiers. **5** a large military force. ● *adj.* great in number.

legionary *n.* (*pl.* **legionaries**) a soldier of a legion. □ **legionary** *adj.*

legion hall *n.* a building housing a local Legion branch, usu. incorporating a bar and banquet hall.

legionnaire *n.* **1** a member of a foreign legion. **2** a member of a Legion. [*Say* lee juh NAIR]

legionnaires' disease *n.* a form of pneumonia spread esp. through air conditioning systems etc.

legislate *v.* (**legislates**, **legislated**, **legislating**) **1** make laws. **2** create or control by means of legislation.

legislation *n.* a law or series of laws.

legislative *adj.* **1** of or empowered to make legislation. **2** of or pertaining to a legislature. □ **legislatively** *adv.*

legislative assembly *n.* the national or provincial etc. body empowered to make laws.

legislative building *n. Cdn* the building in which a provincial legislature meets.

legislator *n.* **1** a member of a legislative body. **2** a person who makes laws.

legislature *n.* **1** the legislative body of a nation, province, etc. **2** *Cdn* = LEGISLATIVE BUILDING. [*Say* LEDGE iss lay chur]

legit *adj. informal* legitimate. [*Say* li JIT]

legitimate ● *adj.* **1** sanctioned or authorized by law, principle, standards, or logic. **2** born of parents married to each other. ● *v.* (**legitimates**, **legitimated**, **legitimating**) make legitimate; justify or make lawful. □ **legitimacy** *n.* **legitimately** *adv.* **legitimating** *adj.* **legitimation** *n.* [*Say* li JITTA mit *for the adjective*, li JITTA mate *for the verb*]

legitimize *v.* (**legitimizes**, **legitimized**, **legitimizing**) **1** make something that is questionable seem acceptable. **2** make something legal. [*Say* li JITTA mize]

legless *adj.* having no legs.

Lego *n. proprietary* a set of interlocking plastic toy building blocks.

legroom *n.* the space available for the legs of a seated person in a car, theatre, etc.

legume *n.* a leguminous plant, esp. its seed, pod, or other edible part. [*Say* LEG yume]

leguminous *adj.* having seeds in pods, e.g. peas and beans. [*Say* luh GYUME in us]

leg-up *n.* **1** an act of helping someone or something to improve their situation. **2** an advantage.

legwork *n.* work that involves tiring movement from place to place.

lei *n.* (*pl.* **leis**) a Polynesian garland of flowers, feathers, shells, etc. [*Say* LAY *or* LAY ee]

leisure *n.* **1** free time. **2** enjoyment of free time. □ **at leisure 1** not occupied. **2** in an easygoing manner. **at one's leisure** when one has time. [*Say* LEEZH er *or* LEZH er]

leisured *adj.* **1** having ample leisure. **2** leisurely. [*Say* LEEZH erd *or* LEZH erd]

leisurely ● *adj.* relaxed and not hurried. ● *adv.* without haste or hurry. [*Say* LEEZH ur lee *or* LEZH ur lee]

leitmotif *n.* (also **leitmotiv**) a recurrent theme in a musical, literary, etc. composition. [*Say* LITE mo teef]

Lekwiltok *n.* (*pl.* **Lekwiltok**) **1** a member of a large group of the Kwakwaka'wakw. **2** their Kwakwala language. [*Say* LECK will tock]

lemming *n.* **1** any of several short-tailed esp. Arctic rodents noted for their periodic mass migrations. **2** a person who unthinkingly joins an esp. destructive mass movement. □ **lemming-like** *adj.*

lemon *n.* **1 a** a pale-yellow thick-skinned oval citrus fruit. **b** the tree that produces this fruit. **2** = LEMON YELLOW. **3** *informal* an unsatisfactory or disappointing product, esp. a defective car. □ **lemon** *adj.* **lemony** *adj.*

lemonade *n.* a usu. sweetened drink made of lemon juice and water.

lemon grass *n.* a tropical grass yielding an oil smelling of lemon.

lemon yellow *n. & adj.* a pale yellow colour.

lemur *n.* a tree-dwelling primate of Madagascar. [*Say* LEE mer]

lend *v.* (**lends**, **lent**, **lending**) **1** grant the use of a thing on the understanding that it shall be returned. **2** allow the use of money at interest. **3** contribute or add a quality to. □ **lend an ear** listen. **lend itself to** allow, be suitable for. □ **lender** *n.* **lending** *n. & adj.*

length *n.* **1 a** the linear extent of a thing. **b** the greater of two or the greatest of three dimensions of a figure. **c** the quality of being long. **2 a** extent from beginning to end, esp. of a period of time, etc.; duration. **b** a period or duration of time, esp. a long period. **3 a** the length of a swimming pool as a measure of the distance swum. **b** the length of a horse etc. as a measure of the lead in a race. **4** a long stretch, piece, or extent of something. **5** a degree of thoroughness in action. □ **at length 1** in detail, without curtailment. **2** after a long time, at last. **length and breadth** the whole area.

lengthen *v.* make or become longer. □ **lengthening** *n. & adj.*

lengthwise ● *adv.* in a direction parallel with a thing's length. ● *adj.* lying or moving lengthwise.

lengthy *adj.* (**lengthier**, **lengthiest**) **1** (of a period of time) long, extended, of unusual length. **2** (of speech, writing, etc.) tedious.

lenient *adj.* (of punishment or an authority) merciful. □ **leniency** *n.* **leniently** *adv.* [*Say* LEENY int]

lens *n.* (*pl.* **lenses**) **1** a piece of a transparent substance with sides curved esp. for focusing light rays in optical instruments, eyeglasses, photography, etc. **2** its lens-shaped structure in the eye. **3** a contact lens.

Lent *n.* *Christianity* the period of fasting and penitence leading up to Easter. □ **Lenten** *adj.*

lent *past and past participle of* LEND.

lentil *n.* **1** a leguminous plant native to the Mediterranean and Africa. **2** its lens-shaped seed, esp. used as food. [*Say* LENT'll]

Leo *n.* (*pl.* **Leos**) a constellation and sign of the zodiac which the sun enters around July 23.

leopard *n.* a large African or Asian cat with either a black-spotted yellowish or all black coat. [*Say* LEP erd]

leopard frog *n.* a N American frog that is green with black pale-ringed blotches.

leopard skin *n.* **1** the skin of a leopard. **2** (also **leopard print**) fabric printed in imitation of a leopard skin.

leotard *n.* **1** a close-fitting one-piece garment worn by dancers, gymnasts, etc. **2** (usu. in *pl.*) heavy tights. [*Say* LEE uh tard]

leper *n.* a person suffering from leprosy. [*Say* LEPPER]

leprechaun *n.* a small, usu. mischievous being of human form in Irish folklore. [*Say* LEPRA con]

leprosy *n.* a contagious bacterial disease that affects the skin, causing disfigurement. [*Say* LEPRA see]

lesbian *n.* a woman who is sexually attracted to other women. □ **lesbian** *adj.* **lesbianism** *n.*

lesion *n.* a region which has suffered damage through injury or disease, such as a wound, ulcer, tumour, etc. [*Say* LEE zh'n]

less ● *adj.* **1** smaller in extent, degree, etc. **2** of smaller quantity, not so much. ● *adv.* to a smaller extent, in a lower degree. ● *pron.* a smaller amount, quantity, or number. ● *prep.* minus. □ **no less** (as an intensifier) what's more.

-less *suffix* forming adjectives and adverbs: **1** from nouns, meaning "not having, without, free from". **2** from verbs, meaning "not affected by or doing the action of the verb".

lessee *n.* a person who holds a property by lease, esp. a tenant. [*Say* less EE]

lessen *v.* make or become less, diminish.

lesser *adj.* **1** not so great or much as the

other or the rest. **2** smaller, inferior, or of lower status or worth.

lesser-known *adj.* known less well than others.

lesson *n.* **1 a** a session of teaching or learning. **b** a thing learned. **2** an event that serves or should serve to warn or encourage. **3** a passage from the Bible read aloud during a church service. □ **learn one's lesson** be wiser as a result of an unpleasant experience. **teach a person a lesson** punish a person, esp. as a deterrent.

lessor *n.* a person who lets a property by lease. [*Say* less OR]

lest *conj.* **1** for fear that. **2** that.

let¹ *v.* (**lets, let, letting**) **1** allow. **2** used to express intention, suggestion, or command. □ **let alone 1** not to mention. **2** = LET BE. **let be** not interfere with, attend to, or do. **let down 1** lower; allow to hang. **2** disappoint. **let go 1** release. **2 a** dismiss from one's thoughts. **b** dismiss (an employee). **let oneself go 1** give way to enthusiasm, impulse, etc. **2** neglect one's appearance. **let loose 1** release or unleash. **2** loosen. **3** (also foll. by *with*) emit abruptly (a scream, tirade, etc.). **let off 1 a** fire (a gun). **b** explode (a bomb or firework). **2** allow or cause (steam, pressure) to escape. **3** not punish. **let on** *informal* **1** reveal a secret. **2** pretend. **let out 1** release from restraint. **2** reveal (a secret etc.). **3** make (a garment) looser esp. by adjustment at a seam. **4** (of a class, meeting, etc.) come to an end. **let (a person) have it** assail with blows or words. **let up** *informal* **1** become less intense or severe. **2** relax one's efforts.

let² *n.* (in tennis, squash, etc.) an obstruction of a ball or a player, e.g. by hitting the net, requiring the ball to be served again.

letdown *n.* a disappointment.

lethal *adj.* causing or sufficient to cause death. □ **lethality** *n.* **lethally** *adv.* [*Say* LEETH'll, lee THALA tee]

lethargy *n.* **1** a lack of energy and enthusiasm; sluggishness. **2** *Medical* a pathological state of sleepiness or deep inactivity. □ **lethargic** *adj.* [*Say* LETH er jee, leth ARJIC]

let's *contr.* let us.

letter ● *n.* **1** a character representing one or more of the sounds used in speech. **2** a written communication, usu. sent by mail or electronically. **3** the precise terms or strict verbal interpretation of a document. **4** (also **letters**) literature. **5** designating a size of paper 8¹⁄₂ by 11 inches (22 by 28 cm). ● *v.* write, paint, inscribe, etc. letters on.

□ **to the letter 1** with adherence to every detail. **2** in accordance with a strict literal interpretation.

letter bomb *n.* a terrorist explosive device disguised as a letter and sent through the mail.

letterbox *n.* (as an *adj.*) designating the fitting of a full motion picture image on a television screen, resulting in strips of unused space along the top and bottom of the screen. □ **letterboxed** *adj.* **letterboxing** *n.*

letter carrier *n.* a person who delivers mail for the postal service.

lettered *adj.* **1** printed, marked, inscribed, etc. with or as with letters. **2** well-read or educated.

letterhead *n.* **1** stationery with a printed heading containing the address etc. of an organization or individual. **2** the heading.

lettering *n.* **1** the process of writing, inscribing, etc. letters. **2** letters written, painted, etc. on something.

lettuce *n.* a plant with crisp edible leaves used in salads.

let-up *n.* *informal* **1** a reduction in intensity or severity. **2** a relaxation of effort.

leukemia *n.* (also esp. *Brit.* **leukaemia**) a malignant disease in which the bone marrow produces increased numbers of leukocytes. [*Say* loo KEEMY uh]

leukocyte *n.* (also **leucocyte**) a white blood cell. [*Say* LOOKA site]

levee¹ *n.* **1** *Cdn* a New Year's Day reception held by the Governor General, a Lieutenant-Governor, a mayor, etc. **2** a formal reception of visitors or guests. [*Say* LEVVY]

levee² *n.* **1** an embankment against flooding. **2** a landing place, a pier, or a quay. [*Say* LEVVY]

level ● *n.* **1 a** a horizontal plane or line. **b** an instrument for producing or testing a horizontal or vertical line. **2** a height or distance from the ground or another base. **3** a position or stage on a scale. **4** a floor within a multi-storey building. ● *adj.* **1** having a flat, horizontal surface. **2** at the same height. **3** not in front of or behind. **4** calm and steady. ● *v.* (**levels, levelled, levelling**) **1** make or become level. **2** aim or direct a weapon, criticism, or accusation. **3** *informal* be frank or honest (with). □ **do one's level best** *informal* do one's utmost. **level off 1** make or become level or smooth. **2** cease or cause to cease ascending or descending. **level out** make or become level; differences, irregularities, etc. from. **on the level** *informal* honest(ly), truthful(ly).

level crossing *n.* *Cdn & Brit.* a place at

which a road and a railway cross each
other at the same level.

level-headed *adj.* mentally balanced,
cool, sensible. □ **level-headedly** *adv.*
level-headedness *n.*

leveller *n.* **1** a person who advocates the
abolition of social distinctions. **2** a person
or thing that levels.

levelly *adv.* in a calm and steady way.

level playing field *n.* a situation in
which everyone has the same
opportunities.

lever ● *n.* **1** a projecting handle moved to
operate a mechanism. **2** a bar resting on a
pivot, used to help lift a heavy object. **3** a
means of exerting pressure on someone to
act in a particular way. ● *v.* **1** use a lever.
2 act on with or as with a lever.
[*Say* LEAVE er *or* LEV er]

leverage ● *n.* **1** the action of a lever. **2** the
power of a lever. **3** advantage for
accomplishing a purpose. ● *v.* use borrowed
capital for (an investment), expecting the
profits to be greater than the interest
payable. [*Say* LEVVER idge *or*
LEAVER idge]

leviathan *n.* **1** an imaginary or real
aquatic animal of enormous size.
2 anything monstrously large.
[*Say* luh VYE uh thun]

levitate *v.* (**levitates, levitated,
levitating**) **1** rise and float in the air.
2 cause to do this. □ **levitation** *n.*
[*Say* LEVVA tate]

levity *n.* the treatment of a serious matter
with humour or irreverence.
[*Say* LEVVA tee]

levy ● *v.* (**levies, levied, levying**) **1** raise
(contributions, taxes) or impose (a fee etc.).
2 *archaic* enlist or enrol (troops etc.). ● *n.* (*pl.*
levies) **1 a** the collecting of a
contribution, tax, etc. **b** a contribution, tax,
etc., levied. **2** *archaic* **a** an act of enlisting
troops. **b** a body of troops enlisted.
[*Say* LEVVY]

lewd *adj.* **1** lustful. **2** indecent, obscene.
□ **lewdly** *adv.* **lewdness** *n.* [*Say* LUDE]

lexical *adj.* of the words of a language.
□ **lexically** *adv.*

lexicography *n.* the compiling, writing,
or editing of dictionaries.
□ **lexicographer** *n.*
[*Say* lexa COGRA fee]

lexicon *n.* **1** a dictionary. **2** the vocabulary
of a person, language, branch of
knowledge, etc. [*Say* LEXA con]

Lhasa *n.* (*pl.* **Lhasas**) (also **Lhasa Apso**
pl. **Lhasa Apsos**) a breed of small long-
coated dog, often gold or grey and white.
[*Say* LASSA (AP so)]

liability *n.* (*pl.* **liabilities**) **1** the state of
being legally responsible for something. **2** a
person or thing that causes one problems.
3 what a person or company is liable for.
[*Say* lie uh BILLA tee]

liable *adj.* **1** legally responsible; subject by
law. **2** exposed or open to (something
undesirable). **3** likely. **4** answerable.
[*Say* LIE uh bull]

liaise *v.* (**liaises, liaised, liaising**)
establish co-operation, act as a link.
[*Say* lee AYZ]

liaison *n.* **1** communication or co-
operation, esp. between groups within an
organization. **2** an illicit sexual
relationship. [*Say* lee AY zon]

liar *n.* a person who tells a lie or lies, esp.
habitually.

lib *n. informal* **1** liberation. **2** a liberal. **3** (**Lib**)
a Liberal.

libation *n.* **1** a drink poured out as an
offering to a god. **2** *jocular* a drink.
[*Say* lie BAY sh'n]

libber *n. informal* an advocate of women's
liberation.

libel ● *n.* **1** *Law* a published false statement
damaging to a person's reputation. **2** (foll.
by *on*) a thing that brings discredit by
misrepresentation etc. ● *v.* (**libels,
libelled, libelling**) **1** harm someone's
reputation by libellous statements.
2 accuse falsely and maliciously. □ **libeller**
n. **libellous** *adj.* **libellously** *adv.*
[*Say* LIE bull]

liberal ● *adj.* **1** given freely or generously.
2 giving freely; generous. **3** open-minded,
not prejudiced. **4** not strict or rigorous; (of
interpretation) not literal. **5** for general
broadening of the mind, not professional
or technical. **6 a** favouring a relaxing of
social traditions and a significant role for
the state in matters of economics and
social justice. **b** (of a political party)
favouring individual liberty and limited
government involvement in economic
affairs. **c** (**Liberal**) relating to a Liberal
party. ● *n.* **1** a person of liberal views.
2 (**Liberal**) a supporter or member of a
Liberal party. □ **liberalism** *n.*
liberally *adv.*

liberal arts *pl. n.* the humanities, esp. as
studied at university, leading to a broad
general education.

liberality *n.* **1** respect for political,
religious or moral views, even if one does
not agree with them. **2** the quality of being
generous.

liberalize *v.* (**liberalizes, liberalized,
liberalizing**) **1** make or become more
liberal or less strict. **2** remove or loosen

restrictions on something, esp. a political or economic system. □ **liberalization** n.

liberate v. (**liberates**, **liberated**, **liberating**) **1** set free. **2** free (a country etc.) from an oppressor. **3** free from rigid social conventions or stigmas. **4** slang jocular steal. □ **liberation** n. **liberationist** n. & adj. **liberator** n.

Liberian n. a native or inhabitant of Liberia. □ **Liberian** adj. [Say lie BEERY in]

libertarian ● n. an advocate of an almost absolute freedom of expression and action. ● adj. believing in free will. □ **libertarianism** n. [Say libber TAIRY in]

libertine ● n. a person who behaves without moral principles esp. in sexual matters. ● adj. characterized by a disregard of morality, esp. in sexual matters. □ **libertinism** n. [Say LIBBER teen or LIBBER tine]

liberty n. (pl. **liberties**) **1** freedom from captivity or slavery. **2** the right to do as one pleases. **3** setting aside of rules or convention, esp. concerning intimacy. □ **at liberty 1** free, not imprisoned. **2** entitled, permitted. **take liberties 1** behave in an unduly familiar manner. **2** deal freely or superficially with rules or facts. **take the liberty** presume, venture.

libidinal adj. of or pertaining to the sex drive. [Say luh BID in ul]

libidinous adj. lustful. [Say luh BID in us]

libido n. (pl. **libidos**) the sexual drive or instinct. [Say luh BEEDO]

Libra n. **1** a constellation traditionally regarded as contained in the figure of scales. **2** the seventh sign of the zodiac, which the sun enters usu. between Sept. 23 and Oct. 22. □ **Libran** n. & adj. [Say LEE bruh]

librarian n. **1** a person trained in the collection and use of information resources. **2** a person in charge of a library. □ **librarianship** n.

library n. (pl. **libraries**) **1 a** a collection of books, periodicals, recordings, electronic reference materials, etc. for use by the public or by members of a group. **b** a person's collection of books. **2** a room containing a collection of books. **3** a series of books issued in similar bindings as a set.

librettist n. a person who writes the words for an opera or a musical.

libretto n. (pl. **librettos** or **libretti**) the text of an opera or other long vocal work. [Say lib RETTO for the singular, lib RETTOS or lib RETTY for the plural]

Libyan adj. **1** of or relating to modern Libya. **2** of ancient northern Africa west of Egypt. □ **Libyan** n. [Say LIBBY in]

lice pl. of LOUSE 1.

licence n. (also esp. US **license**) **1** a permit from an authority to own, use, or do something. **2** freedom to behave as one wants. **3** a writer's or artist's freedom to ignore accepted rules.

licence plate n. an identifying plate fixed to all licensed motor vehicles.

license v. (**licenses**, **licensed**, **licensing**) (also **licence**, **licences**, **licenced**, **licencing**) **1** grant a licence to (a person). **2** authorize the use of premises for sale and consumption of alcohol. **3** authorize the use of a logo or proprietary name on merchandise.

licensed adj. (also **licenced**) **1** having an appropriate licence. **2** having a licence to sell alcohol. **3** bearing a logo, trademark, etc. which the manufacturer was licensed to use.

licensed practical nurse n. a person who has a licence to perform basic nursing tasks.

licensee n. the holder of a licence.

licensor n. a person who licenses something.

licentious adj. sexually promiscuous or immoral. □ **licentiousness** n. [Say lie SEN shus]

lichee n. = LYCHEE. [Say LEE chee]

lichen n. a low, crust-like, leaflike, or branching greenish or yellowish growth on rocks, walls, and trees. □ **lichened** adj. [Say LIKE in]

licit adj. not forbidden. [Say LISS it]

lick ● v. **1** pass the tongue over. **2** touch or move over lightly. **3** informal defeat. **4** informal thrash. **5** informal overcome (a difficulty). ● n. **1** an act of licking with the tongue. **2** = SALT LICK. **3** informal a fast pace. **4** informal a small amount. **5** slang Music a short ornamental solo passage. □ **lick a person's boots** (or **shoes**) show too much respect for someone in authority. **lick one's lips** (or **chops**) **1** look forward to something eagerly. **2** show one's satisfaction. **lick one's wounds** try to recover after defeat. □ **licker** n.

lickety-split informal ● adv. at full speed. ● adj. quick.

licking n. informal **1** a thrashing. **2** a defeat.

licorice n. **1** a plant whose root produces a sweet, chewy, black substance. **2** black rubbery candy made from this. **3** a rubbery candy similar to this, in any flavour or colour. [Say LICKER ish]

lid n. **1** a hinged or removable cover, esp. over a container. **2** = EYELID. **3** informal a restraint. □ **blow the lid off** informal expose (a scandal etc.). **put a lid on it**

informal stop talking. □ **lidded** *adj.*
lidless *adj.*

lie¹ ● *v.* (**lies**; *past* **lay**; *past participle* **lain**;
lying) **1** rest flat on a surface. **2** be found.
3 be in a particular state. **4** be situated in a
specific position. ● *n.* the way or direction
or position in which a thing lies. □ **lot lie**
not raise for discussion etc. **lie down**
assume a lying position; have a short rest.
lie heavy cause discomfort or anxiety. **lie
in state** be laid in a public place of
honour before burial. **lie low 1** keep quiet
or unseen. **2** be discreet about one's
intentions. **not take lying down** not
accept without resistance or protest etc.

lie² ● *n.* **1** an intentionally false statement.
2 false belief. ● *v.* (**lies**, **lied**, **lying**) **1** tell a
lie or lies. **2** be deceptive. □ **give** (or **put**)
the lie to serve to show the falsity of. **lie
through one's teeth** lie brazenly.

lied *n.* (*pl.* **lieder**) a type of German song,
usu. for solo voice with piano
accompaniment. [*Say* LEED *or* LEET *for the
singular,* LEEDER *for the plural*]

lie detector *n.* an instrument for
detecting physiological changes associated
with lying.

liege usu. *hist.* ● *adj.* entitled to receive or
bound to give feudal allegiance. ● *n.* (also
liege lord) a feudal superior. [*Say* LEEJ *or*
LEEZH]

lien *n.* *Law* the right to keep someone's
property until a debt is paid. [*Say* LEEN]

lieu *n.* Cdn designating time taken off work
in compensation for overtime worked. □ **in
lieu** instead; in the place of. [*Say* LOO *or*
LYOO]

Lieut. *abbr.* Lieutenant.

lieutenant *n.* **1** a deputy or substitute
acting for a superior. **2** (also **Lieutenant**)
a military or police officer of intermediate
rank. □ **lieutenancy** *n.* [*Say* lef TENNANT
or loo TENNANT]

lieutenant colonel *n.* (also
Lieutenant Colonel) an officer ranking
next below colonel and above major.

lieutenant commander *n.* (also
Lieutenant Commander) a naval
officer ranking below a commander and
above a lieutenant.

lieutenant general *n.* (also
Lieutenant General) an officer ranking
above a major general.

Lieutenant-Governor *n.* (*pl.*
Lieutenant-Governors) the
representative of the Crown in a province.

life *n.* (*pl.* **lives**) **1** the ability to grow,
breathe, reproduce, etc., that distinguishes
animals and plants from objects. **2 a** living
things and their activity. **b** human
presence or activity. **c** the human

condition; existence. **3** the duration of a
thing's existence or functionality. **4** a
person's state of existence as a living
individual. **5** a particular aspect of one's
existence. **6 a** energy, liveliness, animation
b an animating influence. **7** a biography.
8 a sentence of imprisonment for life.
□ **not on your life** *informal* most certainly
not. **take one's life in one's hands**
take a crucial personal risk.

life-and-death *adj.* **1** determining life or
death. **2** vitally important.

lifebelt *n.* a buoyant belt for keeping a
person afloat in water.

lifeblood *n.* the vital factor or influence.

lifeboat *n.* a small rescue or safety boat for
use during emergencies.

lifebuoy *n.* a buoyant support (usu. a ring)
for keeping a person afloat in water, esp. in
an emergency.

life cycle *n.* the complete series of
developmental stages through which an
organism or thing passes.

life expectancy *n.* the average period
that a person may expect to live.

life form *n.* a living thing.

life-giving *adj.* that sustains life or uplifts
and revitalizes.

lifeguard *n.* a person employed to rescue
swimmers from drowning.

life insurance *n.* insurance for a sum to
be paid to named beneficiaries on the
death of the insured person.

life jacket *n.* a buoyant jacket for keeping
a person afloat in water, esp. in an
emergency.

lifeless *adj.* **1** lacking life; no longer living.
2 lacking movement or vitality.
□ **lifelessly** *adv.* **lifelessness** *n.*

lifelike *adj.* closely resembling the person
or thing represented.

lifeline *n.* **1** a rope etc. thrown to rescue
someone in water. **2 a** a sole means of
communication or transport. **b** a vital
source of aid or sustenance.

lifelong *adj.* lasting a lifetime.

life-or-death *adj.* = LIFE-AND-DEATH.

life preserver *n.* a life jacket etc.

lifer *n.* *slang* **1** a person serving a life
sentence. **2** a person seemingly destined to
remain in the same job, position, etc. for
life.

life raft *n.* a raft for use in an emergency.

lifesaver *n.* **1** a buoyant ring for keeping a
person afloat in an emergency. **2** *informal* a
thing that saves one from serious
difficulty. □ **life-saving** *n. & adj.*

life sciences *pl. n.* biology and related
subjects.

life sentence n. **1** a sentence of imprisonment for life. **2** (in Canada) a jail sentence of 25 years. **3** a seemingly inescapable condition.

life-sized adj. (also **life-size**) of the same size as the person or thing represented.

life skills pl. n. the basic skills needed to function normally in society.

lifespan n. the length of time for which an organism or thing lives, exists, or is functional.

life story n. the story of a person's life, esp. told at tedious length.

lifestyle n. **1** the particular way of life of a person or group. **2** designating advertising, products, etc. designed to appeal by association with a particular desirable lifestyle.

life-support ● adj. (of medical equipment) that keeps the body functioning after serious illness or injury. ● n. a life-support system.

lifetime n. **1** the duration of a person's life. **2** the duration of a thing or its usefulness. **3** informal an exceptionally long time. □ **of a lifetime** occurring just once in a person's life.

lifeway n. esp. Anthropology a way of life or lifestyle, esp. of a specific group or community.

lift ● v. **1** raise to a higher position or level. **2** pick up and move to a different position. **3** remove or end a legal restriction, decision, etc. **4** informal steal. ● n. **1** an act or instance of lifting. **2** a free ride in another person's vehicle. **3** a device for carrying people up or down a mountain. **4** a feeling of increased cheerfulness. **5** upward force exerted by the air on an airfoil or other structure. □ **lift down** pick up and bring to a lower position. **lift off** (of a spacecraft or aircraft) rise from the ground. □ **lifter** n.

liftoff n. the takeoff of a spacecraft etc.

ligament n. **1** a short band of tough tissue linking bones together. **2** any membranous fold keeping an organ in position. [Say LIGGA mint]

ligation n. the surgical procedure of tying a ligature tightly, esp. around the Fallopian tubes as a sterilization procedure. [Say li GAY sh'n]

ligature ● n. **1** a cord used to tie up a bleeding artery etc. **2** Music a slur or a tie. **3** Printing two or more letters joined, e.g. æ. ● v. bind or connect with a ligature. [Say LIGGA chur]

light¹ ● n. **1** the radiation that stimulates sight and makes things visible. **2** a source of this. **3** the condition of the space in which this is present. **4** an appearance of brightness. **5** a flame or spark serving to ignite. **6** the aspect in which a thing is regarded or considered. **7** an eminent person. ● v. (**lights**; past participle **lit** or **lighted**; **lighting**) **1** set burning or begin to burn. **2** provide with light or lighting. ● adj. **1** well provided with light; not dark. **2** (of a colour) pale. □ **bring** (or **come**) **to light** reveal or be revealed. **in a good** (or **bad**) **light** giving a favourable (or unfavourable) impression. **in** (**the**) **light of** considering; in view of; drawing information from. **light up 1** become illuminated. **2** informal begin to smoke a cigarette etc. **3** (of the face etc.) brighten with animation. **throw** (or **shed**) **light on** help to explain. □ **lightness** n.

light² ● adj. **1** not heavy or heavy enough. **2** relatively low in weight, amount, density, intensity, etc. **3 a** carrying or suitable for small loads. **b** carrying only light arms, armaments, etc. **4** (of food or drink) small in amount or low in fat, cholesterol, sugar, alcohol, etc. **5** not profound. **6** (of sleep or a sleeper) easily disturbed. **7** easily borne or done. ● adv. **1** in a light manner. **2** with a minimum load. ● v. (**lights**; past and past participle **lit** or **lighted**; **lighting**) (**light upon**) come upon or find by chance. □ **light into** informal attack. **make light of** treat as unimportant. **make light work of** do a thing quickly and easily. □ **lightness** n.

light box n. a translucent surface lit from behind, used to view slides, film, etc.

light bulb n. a glass bulb containing an inert gas, providing light when an electric current is passed through.

light cream n. Cdn a table cream having 7% fat.

light-emitting diode n. = LED.

lighten¹ v. **1** make or become lighter in weight. **2** bring relief to (the heart, mind, etc.). □ **lighten up** informal become less earnest or intense.

lighten² v. shed light on; make less dark.

lighter n. **1** a device for lighting cigarettes, barbecues, etc. **2** a boat, usu. flat-bottomed, for transferring goods to and from ships.

lighter-than-air adj. (of an aircraft) weighing less than the air it displaces, e.g. a blimp.

light-footed adj. nimble.

light-handed adj. having a light, delicate, or deft touch.

light-headed adj. giddy, faint. □ **light-headedness** n.

lighthearted adj. **1** intended to be amusing rather than too serious. **2** cheerful and without problems. □ **lightheartedly** adv. **lightheartedness** n.

lighthouse *n.* a structure containing a beacon light to warn or guide ships.

lighting *n.* **1** equipment for producing light. **2** the arrangement or effect of lights.

lightkeeper *n.* a person in charge of a lighthouse.

lightless *adj.* receiving or producing no light.

lightly *adv.* **1** gently; with very little force or effort. **2** to a small degree. **3** without worry or interest. □ **get off lightly** escape with little punishment. **take lightly** not be serious about.

lightning ● *n.* a flash of bright light produced by an electric discharge from clouds. ● *adj.* very quick.

lightning rod *n.* **1** a metal rod or wire fixed in a high place to divert lightning into the earth. **2** a person or thing that attracts criticism.

light pen *n.* **1** a pen-like device for passing information to a computer. **2** a light-emitting device used for reading bar codes.

lights *pl. n.* the lungs of sheep, pigs, steers, etc., used as a food esp. for pets. □ **punch a person's lights out** beat a person soundly.

light show *n.* a display of changing coloured lights for entertainment.

light station *n.* = LIGHTHOUSE.

light touch *n.* delicate or tactful treatment.

lightweight ● *adj.* **1** of below average weight. **2** of little importance or influence. ● *n.* **1** a lightweight person, animal, or thing. **2 a** a weight in certain sports intermediate between featherweight and welterweight. **b** an athlete of this weight. **3** a person of little influence or significance.

light year *n.* the distance light travels in one mean solar year, approximately 9.46×10^{12} km (5.88×10^{12} miles).

lignin *n.* a substance in some plants that makes them rigid and woody. [*Say* LIG nin]

lignite *n.* a soft brown coal. [*Say* LIG nite]

likable *adj.* = LIKEABLE.

like[1] ● *prep.* **1** resembling or characteristic of. **2** such as. **3** in the manner of. ● *adj.* (**more like, most like**) having similar characteristics; alike. ● *adv. slang* so to speak. ● *conj. informal disputed* **1** as. **2** as if. ● *n.* **1** a similar person or thing. **2** (**the like**) a thing or things of the same kind. □ **feel like** be in the mood for. **like as not** *informal* probably. **like so** *informal* like this; in this manner. **the likes of** *informal* a person such as. **more like it** *informal* nearer what is required.

like[2] ● *v.* (**likes, liked, liking**) **1 a** find agreeable or enjoyable or satisfactory. **b** be fond of (a person). **2** regard. **3** feel inclined. ● *n.* (*in pl.*) the things one likes or prefers.

-like *comb. form* forming adjectives from nouns, meaning "similar to, characteristic of".

likeable *adj.* pleasant; easy to like. □ **likeability** *n.* **likeably** *adv*

likelihood *n.* the state of being likely. □ **in all likelihood** very probably.

likely ● *adj.* (**likelier, likeliest**) **1** probable. **2** to be reasonably expected. **3** promising. ● *adv.* probably. □ **as likely as not** probably.

like-minded *adj.* having the same tastes, opinions, etc.

liken *v.* (foll. by *to*) point out the resemblance of one thing to another.

likeness *n.* (*pl.* **likenesses**) **1** resemblance. **2** a semblance or guise. **3** a portrait or representation.

likewise *adv.* **1** also, moreover, too. **2** similarly.

liking *n.* **1** what one likes; one's taste. **2** regard or fondness.

li'l *adj. informal* little.

lilac *n.* **1** a shrub or small tree with fragrant purple, mauve, pink, or white blossoms. **2** *n. & adj.* a pale pinkish-violet colour. **3** the scent of lilac. [*Say* LIE l'k *or* LIE lock *or* LIE lack]

Lilliputian *adj.* tiny, diminutive. [*Say* lilla PYOO shin]

Lillooet *n.* (*pl.* **Lillooet** *or* **Lillooets**) STL'ATL'IMX. [*Say* LILL oo et]

lilt ● *n.* a rising and falling cadence or inflection. ● *v.* speak or sing etc. with a lilt.

lily *n.* (*pl.* **lilies**) **1** a plant with large trumpet-shaped flowers on a tall, slender stem. **2** the water lily.

lily of the valley *n.* (*pl.* **lilies of the valley**) a plant with broad oval leaves and arching stems of fragrant white bell-shaped flowers.

lily pad *n.* a floating leaf of a water lily.

lily-white *adj.* **1** as white as a lily. **2** *informal* excluding non-whites.

lima bean *n.* a large edible flat whitish bean. [*Say* LIE muh]

limb *n.* **1** an arm, leg, or wing. **2** a large branch of a tree. **3** a projecting part of a thing. □ **out on a limb** in or into a vulnerable or risky position where one is not supported by others. □ **limbed** *adj.* **limbless** *adj.*

limber ● *adj.* **1** agile. **2** flexible. ● *v.* (usu. foll. by *up*) **1** make supple. **2** warm up in preparation for athletic activity. [*Say* LIM burr]

limbo¹ *n.* (*pl.* **limbos**) **1** (in some Christian beliefs) the supposed abode of the souls of infants who were not baptized. **2** an uncertain period of waiting. **3** a state of neglect or oblivion.

limbo² *n.* (*pl.* **limbos**) a West Indian dance in which the dancer bends backwards to pass under a horizontal bar which is progressively lowered.

Limburger *n.* a soft white cheese with a characteristic strong smell.
[*Say* LIM burger]

lime¹ *n.* **1 a** a small green lemon-like citrus fruit. **b** (also **lime tree**) the tree that bears this fruit. **2** *n. & adj.* (also **lime green**) a bright pale green colour.

lime² *n.* **1** (also **quicklime**) a white alkaline substance obtained from limestone and used for making mortar or as a fertilizer or bleach etc. **2** (also **slaked lime**) a white substance made by adding water to quicklime, used esp. in cement. **3** calcium or calcium salts, esp. calcium carbonate in soil etc.

lime³ *n.* (also **lime tree**) a deciduous ornamental tree with heart-shaped leaves and fragrant yellow blossoms.

limelight *n.* **1** an intense white light used formerly in theatres. **2** (**the limelight**) the full glare of publicity.

limerick *n.* a humorous form of five-line poem. [*Say* LIMMA rick]

limestone *n.* a sedimentary rock composed mainly of calcium carbonate.

Limey *slang offensive* ● *n.* (*pl.* **Limeys**) a British person. ● *adj.* British. [*Say* LIME ee]

limit ● *n.* **1** a point, line, etc. beyond which something does not or may not extend or pass. **2** the boundary of an area. **3** a restriction on size or amount. ● *v.* (**limits**, **limited**, **limiting**) **1** set or serve as a limit to. **2** restrict. □ **off limits** out of bounds; forbidden. **within limits** to a moderate extent. □ **limitable** *adj.* **limiting** *adj.*

limitation *n.* **1** the action of limiting something. **2** a condition of limited ability. **3** a limiting rule or circumstance.

limited *adj.* **1** confined within limits. **2** not great in scope or talents. **3 a** few, scanty, restricted. **b** restricted to a few examples. **4** (**Limited**) (after a company name) being a company whose owners are legally responsible only to a limited amount for its debts.

limited edition *n.* an edition of a book etc. limited to some specific number of copies.

limitless *adj.* **1** extending or going on indefinitely. **2** unlimited.
□ **limitlessly** *adv.*

limn *v.* **1** paint or draw; portray. **2** portray or represent in words. [*Say* LIM]

limo *n.* (*pl.* **limos**) *informal* a limousine.

limousine *n.* **1** a large luxurious automobile usu. with a paid driver. **2** a large sedan or minibus for transportation to and from an airport etc.

limp¹ ● *v.* **1** walk lamely. **2** proceed or progress slowly or with difficulty. ● *n.* a lame walk.

limp² *adj.* **1** not stiff or firm. **2** without energy or will. □ **limply** *adv.*

limpet *n.* **1** a marine mollusc with a shallow conical shell and a broad muscular foot. **2** a clinging person. [*Say* LIM pit]

limpid *adj.* **1** clear, transparent. **2** clear and easily comprehended. □ **limpidity** *n.*
[*Say* LIM pid, lim PIDDA tee]

limy *adj.* (**limier**, **limiest**) consisting of or containing lime.

LINC *abbr. Cdn* Language Instruction for Newcomers to Canada. [*Sounds like* LINK]

linchpin *n.* **1** a pin passed through the end of an axle to keep a wheel in position. **2** a vital person or thing. [*Say* LINCH pin]

linden *n.* **1** a basswood tree. **2** an ornamental European tree with heart-shaped leaves and fragrant yellow blossoms. [*Say* LIN din]

lindy *n.* (also **lindy hop**) a dance originating as a form of the jitterbug among blacks in Harlem.

line¹ ● *n.* **1** a long, narrow mark or band. **2** a length of cord, wire, etc. serving a purpose. **3** a row of people or things. **4** a railway track. **5** a notional boundary. **6** a row of soldiers etc. facing an enemy force. **7** a wrinkle in the skin. **8** a range of commercial goods. **9** (**lines**) the words of an actor's part. ● *v.* (**lines**, **lined**, **lining**) **1** be positioned at intervals along. **2** mark or cover with lines. □ **all along the line** at every point. **bring into line** make conform. **end of the line** the point at which one can go no further. **in line 1** arranged or standing in a line. **2** under control. **in line for** likely to receive. **in the line of** in the course of (esp. duty). **in** (or **out of**) **line with** in (or not in) accordance with. **keep in line** control. **lay** (or **put**) **it on the line 1** speak frankly. **2** pay money. **line up 1** arrange or be arranged in a line or lines. **2** have ready; organize. **on the line** at risk. **out of line 1** not in alignment; discordant. **2** failing to conform.

line² *v.* (**lines**, **lined**, **lining**) cover the inside surface of something with a layer of usu. different material. □ **line one's pocket** make money, usu. by corrupt means.

lineage *n.* ancestry. [*Say* LINNY idge]

lineal *adj.* **1** in the direct line of descent or ancestry. **2** linear; of or in lines. [*Say* LINNY ul]

linear *adj.* **1 a** of or in lines. **b** of length. **2** long and narrow and of uniform breadth. **3** involving one dimension only. **4** progressing in a single series of steps or stages; sequential. **5** able to be represented by a straight line on a graph. □ **linearity** *n.* **linearly** *adv.* [*Say* LINNY er, linny AIR uh tee]

linebacker *n. Football* a player or position just behind the defensive line.

line dance ● *n.* a type of social dancing in which participants line up side by side and follow a choreographed pattern of steps. ● *v.* (**line dances, line danced, line dancing**) perform this dance. □ **line dancer** *n.* **line dancing** *n.*

line drive *n. Baseball* a ball hit straight and low above the ground.

lineman *n.* (*pl.* **linemen**) **1** a person who repairs and maintains telephone or electrical etc. lines. **2** *Football* a centre, guard, tackle, or end.

linemate *n. Hockey* a player who plays on the same line as another.

linen ● *n.* **1** cloth woven from flax. **2** articles made or originally made of linen, cotton, etc., e.g. sheets, cloths, undergarments, etc. ● *adj.* made of linen or flax. [*Say* LIN in]

line of credit *n.* (*pl.* **lines of credit**) an amount of credit enabling one to borrow money as often as needed up to a pre-set limit without having to apply each time for a loan.

line of scrimmage *n. Football* the imaginary line separating two teams at the beginning of a scrimmage.

liner[1] *n.* **1** a ship etc. carrying passengers on a regular route. **2** = EYELINER. **3** = LINE DRIVE.

liner[2] *n.* a lining of a garment, container, etc.

linesman *n.* (*pl.* **linesmen**) **1** *Hockey* an on-ice official whose tasks include making offside calls and breaking up fights. **2** (in other games) an official who decides whether a ball falls within the playing area or not. **3** *Football* an official who marks the distances won or lost on each play.

lineup *n.* **1** a line of people waiting e.g. to buy tickets. **2** any group of people or things assembled or organized for a particular purpose.

ling *n.* **1** any of a number of long slender predatory fishes, esp. a large East Atlantic food fish related to the cod. **2** a burbot.

ling cod *n.* a large food fish found in the North Pacific.

linger *v.* **1 a** be slow or reluctant to depart. **b** (foll. by *over, on,* etc.) dally. **2** be protracted; drag on.

lingerie *n.* women's underwear and nightclothes. [*Say* LAWN zhuh ray *or* lawn zhuh RAY]

lingering *adj.* slow to end or disappear. □ **lingeringly** *adv.*

lingo *n.* (*pl.* **lingos** *or* **lingoes**) *informal* the vocabulary of a special subject or group.

lingonberry *n.* (*pl.* **lingonberries**) **1** the cowberry of Scandinavia, used in cooking. **2** an Arctic variety of this of Russia and N America. [*Say* LING gun berry]

lingua franca *n.* (*pl.* **lingua francas**) a common language adopted by speakers whose native languages are different. [*Say* ling gwuh FRANKA]

lingual *adj.* of or formed by the tongue. [*Say* LING gwul]

linguine *pl. n.* (also **linguini**) pasta in the form of narrow ribbons. [*Say* ling GWEENY]

linguist *n.* a person skilled in languages or linguistics. [*Say* LING gwist]

linguistics *n.* the scientific study of language and its structure. □ **linguistic** *adj.* **linguistically** *adv.* [*Say* ling GWIST icks]

liniment *n.* a medicated lotion for rubbing onto the body to relieve pain. [*Say* LINNA mint]

lining *n.* **1** a layer of material used to line a surface etc. **2** an inside layer or surface etc.

link ● *n.* **1** one loop or ring of a chain etc. **2** a connecting part; one in a series. **3** a radio etc. connection. **4** = CUFFLINK. **5** any of the divisions of a chain of sausages. **6** = HYPERLINK. ● *v.* **1** connect or join. **2** connect causally. **3** clasp or intertwine. **4** be joined; attach oneself to. **5** connect by means of a hyperlink.

linkage *n.* the action of linking; a link.

links *pl. n.* a golf course.

link-up *n.* an act or result of linking up.

linoleum *n.* a floor covering consisting of thickened linseed oil and powdered wood etc. applied to a backing. [*Say* lin OLE ee um]

linseed *n.* the seed of flax.

linseed oil *n.* oil extracted from linseed and used in paint and varnish.

lint *n.* **1** tiny threads or fibres; fluff. **2** a soft material used esp. for dressing wounds. **3** an accumulation of dirt, dead skin cells, etc. in the navel.

lintel *n.* a horizontal supporting piece of

timber, stone, etc., across the top of a door or window.

Linux *n.* a freely available Unix-like operating system. [*Say* LIN ux *or* LINE ux]

lion *n.* a large tawny-coloured cat of Africa and northwest India, the male of which has a flowing shaggy mane.

lioness *n.* (*pl.* **lionesses**) a female lion.

lionize *v.* (**lionizes, lionized, lionizing**) treat as a celebrity. □ **lionization** *n.*

lion's share *n.* the largest or best part.

lip *n.* **1 a** either of the two fleshy parts forming the edges of the mouth. **b** a thing resembling these. **c** = LABIUM. **2 a** the edge of a cup, vessel, etc. **b** the edge of an opening or cavity. **3** *informal* impudent talk. □ **bite one's lip** repress an emotion. □ **lipless** *adj.*

lipid *n.* any of a group of organic compounds that are insoluble in water, e.g. fatty acids, oils, waxes, etc. [*Say* LIP id]

lipliner *n.* a cosmetic applied as a line around the lips.

lipoprotein *n.* any of a group of soluble proteins that combine with and transport fat or other lipids in the blood plasma. [*Say* lippo PROTEIN *or* lie po PROTEIN]

liposome *n.* a minute artificial spherical sac esp. used to carry drugs to specific tissues. [*Say* LIPPA soam *or* LIE po soam]

liposuction *n.* the surgical removal of excess fat from under the skin by suction. [*Say* LIPPO suction *or* LIE po suction]

lipped *adj.* having the type of lips mentioned.

lippy *adj.* (**lippier, lippiest**) *informal* **1** insolent, impertinent. **2** having large lips.

lip-read *v.* (**lip-reads, lip-read, lip-reading**) understand speech entirely from observing a speaker's lip movements. □ **lip-reader** *n.* **lip-reading** *n.*

lip service *n.* an insincere expression of support etc.

lip-smacking *adj.* **1** delicious. **2** tantalizing; tempting.

lipstick *n.* a small stick of cosmetic for colouring the lips. □ **lipsticked** *adj.*

lip-synch *v.* (also **lip-sync**) perform (esp. a song) on film by moving one's lips in synchronization with a pre-recorded soundtrack. □ **lip-synching** *n.* [*Say* LIP sink]

liquefy *v.* (**liquefies, liquefied, liquefying**) make or become liquid. □ **liquefaction** *n.* [*Say* LICKWA fie, lickwa FACTION]

liqueur *n.* a strong sweet alcoholic spirit, usu. drunk after a meal. [*Say* li CURE]

liquid ● *adj.* **1** having a consistency like that of water or oil, flowing but of constant volume. **2** like water in appearance; clear, bright, translucent. **3 a** (of sounds) pure and flowing. **b** (of movement) unconstrained. **4 a** (of assets) easily converted into cash. **b** having ready cash or liquid assets. ● *n.* a liquid substance.

liquidation *n.* **1** the process of winding up the affairs of (a company) by ascertaining liabilities and apportioning assets. **2** the action or process of abolishing or eliminating something or someone. □ **liquidate** *v.* (**liquidates, liquidated, liquidating**). **liquidator** *n.*

liquid crystal display *n.* a form of visual display in electronic devices, in which segments of liquid crystals are made visible by temporarily modifying their capacity to reflect light.

liquidity *n.* (*pl.* **liquidities**) **1** the state of being liquid. **2** availability of liquid assets. [*Say* li KWIDDA tee]

liquify *v.* = LIQUEFY.

liquor *n.* **1** an alcoholic drink, esp. produced by distillation. **2** other liquid, esp. that produced in cooking. □ **liquored up** *slang* drunk. [*Say* LICKER]

liquor commission *n. Cdn* **1** (also **liquor control board, liquor board**) a regulatory body controlling the sale of alcoholic beverages. **2** a liquor store operated by this body. Abbreviation: **LC**.

liquorice *n.* = LICORICE. [*Say* LICKER ish]

lira *n.* (*pl.* **lire**) **1** the former chief monetary unit of Italy. **2** the chief monetary unit of Turkey. [*Say* LEE ruh]

LISP *abbr.* a high-level programming language devised for list processing.

lisp ● *n.* **1 a** a speech defect in which *s* is pronounced like *th*. **b** a lisping pronunciation. **2** a sound resembling a lisp. ● *v.* speak or utter with a lisp. □ **lisper** *n.* **lisping** *adj. & n.*

list¹ ● *n.* **1** a number of connected items, names, etc., written as a series. **2** the books published by a particular publisher. ● *v.* **1** make a list of. **2** include in a list, e.g. of items for sale. □ **enter the lists** issue or accept a challenge.

list² ● *v.* (of a ship, building, etc.) lean over to one side. ● *n.* an instance of listing.

listen ● *v.* **1** make an effort to hear something. **2** pay attention to. ● *n.* an act of listening. □ **listen in** listen secretly to a private communication by telephone etc. **2** listen to a broadcast radio program etc. **3** listen to the conversation of others, often covertly and usu. without contributing. **listen up** *informal* pay attention. □ **listener** *n.*

listenable *adj.* easy or pleasant to listen to.

listeria *n.* a type of bacterium that infects humans through contaminated food. [Say liss TEERY uh]

listing[1] *n.* **1** a list or catalogue. **2 a** the drawing up of a list. **b** an entry in a list or catalogue. **3 a** the placing of a property on the list of a real estate agent. **b** a property so listed.

listing[2] *adj.* (of a ship etc.) leaning to one side.

listless *adj.* lacking energy or enthusiasm. □ **listlessly** *adv.* **listlessness** *n.*

list price *n.* the price shown for an article as listed by the maker.

listserv *n.* an email system which automatically sends messages to all subscribers on specific mailing lists. [Say LIST serve]

lit[1] *past and past participle of* LIGHT[1],[2].

lit[2] *n. informal* literature.

litany *n.* (*pl.* **litanies**) **1** a series of prayers or entreaties for use in church services or processions. **2 a** a continuous repetition or long enumeration. **b** a tedious recital. [Say LITTA nee]

litchi *n.* = LYCHEE. [Say LEE chee]

lit crit *n. informal* literary criticism.

lite *adj.* **1** applied to low-fat or low-sugar versions of manufactured food products. **2** *informal* lacking in substance.

liter *n. esp. US* = LITRE.

literacy *n.* **1** the ability to read and write. **2** competence in some field of knowledge, technology, etc.

literal *adj.* **1** taking words in their usual or primary sense without metaphor or allegory. **2** (of a translation etc.) representing the exact words of the original text. **3** without metaphor, exaggeration, or inaccuracy. □ **literalness** *n.*

literalism *n.* insistence on a literal interpretation. □ **literalist** *n.* **literalistic** *adj.*

literally *adv.* **1** in a literal way. **2** used to emphasize the truth of something that may seem surprising. **3** *informal* used to emphasize a figurative word or phrase.

literary *adj.* **1** having to do with literature. **2** well informed about literature. **3** (of a word) used chiefly in literary works. □ **literariness** *n.*

literary criticism *n.* the art or practice of judging and commenting on the qualities and character of literary works. □ **literary critic** *n.*

literary device *n.* any literary technique used to achieve a specific effect, e.g. figures of speech etc.

literate *adj.* **1** able to read and write.

2 a well-read, cultured. **b** educated. **3** competent or well-versed in a specified area. [Say LITTER it]

literati *pl. n.* educated and intelligent people who produce or are well-versed in literature. [Say litter OTTY]

literature *n.* **1** written works, esp. those whose value lies in beauty of language or in emotional effect. **2** literary work or production as a whole. **3** the body of writings produced in a particular country or period. **4** printed matter, leaflets, etc. **5** the published material on a particular subject.

lithe *adj.* **1** moving or bending gracefully. **2** gracefully slim and muscled. □ **lithely** *adv.* [With LI *as in* LIE *and* THE *as in* BATHE]

lithium *n.* a soft silver-white metallic element, the lightest metal. [Say LITH ee um]

litho *n. informal* (*pl.* **lithos**) **1** = LITHOGRAPHY. **2** = LITHOGRAPH. [Say LITH oh]

lithograph *n.* a lithographic print. [Say LITH uh graph]

lithography *n.* a process of obtaining prints from a stone or metal surface so treated that what is to be printed can be inked but the remaining area rejects ink. □ **lithographer** *n.* **lithographic** *adj.* [Say lith OGGRA fee, lith uh GRAPHIC]

lithosphere *n.* the rigid outer portion of the earth. □ **lithospheric** *adj.* [Say LITH us fear, lith us FEAR ick]

Lithuanian *n.* **1** a native or inhabitant of Lithuania. **2** the language of Lithuania. □ **Lithuanian** *adj.* [Say lith oo AY nee in *or* lith you AY nee in]

litigant *n.* a party to a lawsuit. [Say LITTA gint (with G *as in* GIVE)]

litigate *v.* (**litigates**, **litigated**, **litigating**) **1** take a claim or dispute to a law court. **2** contest (a point) in a lawsuit. □ **litigation** *n.* [Say LITTA gate]

litigator *n.* a trial lawyer. [Say LITTA gator]

litigious *adj.* too ready to take disputes to a court of law. □ **litigiously** *adv.* **litigiousness** *n.* [Say luh TIDGE us]

litmus *n.* a dye that is red under acid conditions and blue under alkaline conditions. [Say LIT mus]

litmus test *n.* **1** *informal* a reliable test of value or truth. **2** a test for acids or alkalis using litmus paper.

litre *n.* a metric unit of capacity equal to 1000 ml (about 1.76 imperial pints).

litter ● ** *n.* **1 garbage discarded in a public place. **2** a state of untidiness. **3** all of a group of mammals born at one birth. **4** decomposing leaves etc. forming a distinct layer above the soil, esp. in a forest.

5 esp. *hist.* a vehicle containing a couch shut in by curtains and carried on men's shoulders or by animals. **6** a stretcher for the sick or wounded. **7** straw, rushes, etc., esp. as bedding for animals. ● *v.* **1** leave paper, garbage, etc. lying about, esp. in a public place. **2** (of things) lie about untidily on. **3** (of an animal) give birth to.

litter box *n.* a tray for cat litter.

litterbug *n.* a person who carelessly leaves litter in a public place.

little ● *adj.* (**littler**, **littlest**; **less** or **lesser**; **least**) **1** small in size, amount, degree, etc. **2** a certain though small amount of. **3** relatively unimportant. **4** young or younger. ● *n.* not much; only a small amount. ● *adv.* (**less**, **least**) **1** a to a small extent only. **b** infrequently, rarely. **2** (**a little**) somewhat. □ **little by little** by degrees; gradually. **no little** considerable, a good deal of. **not a little 1** much; a great deal. **2** extremely.

little-bitty *adj. informal* tiny.

Little League *n.* a baseball league for children between ages 8 and 12.

littleneck *n.* (also **littleneck clam**) a small variety of quahog.

littoral ● *adj.* of or on the shore of the sea, a lake, etc. ● *n.* a region lying along a shore. [*Say* LITTER ul]

liturgy *n.* (*pl.* **liturgies**) **1** a form according to which public esp. Christian religious worship is conducted. **2** the Communion office of the Orthodox Church. □ **liturgical** *adj.* **liturgically** *adv.* [*Say* LITTER jee, li TUR ji cull]

livable *adj.* **1** fit to live in. **2** (of a life) worth living. **3** easy to live with. □ **livability** *n.*

live¹ *v.* (**lives**, **lived**, **living**) **1** remain alive. **2** be alive at a specified time. **3** spend one's life in a particular way. **4** make one's home in a place or with a person. **5** supply oneself with the means of subsistence. **6** enjoy life to the full. □ **live and let live** be tolerant towards others of different opinions, lifestyles, etc. **live down** succeed in making others forget (one's embarrassment). **live it up** *informal* pursue pleasure, live extravagantly. **live out 1** experience or execute the rest of (one's life) **2** experience or execute in reality (one's fantasies, ideas, etc.). **live up to 1** put into practice (principles etc.). **2** reach and maintain an expected standard. **live with 1** share a home with. **2** share a home and have a sexual relationship with. **3** tolerate; endure.

live² ● *adj.* **1** living. **2** performed before an audience. **3** broadcast at the time of occurrence. **4** of current importance. **5** connected to a source of electric current.

6 (of coals) burning. ● *adv.* in order to make a live broadcast; as a live performance. □ **go live** (of a system) become operational.

liveable *adj.* = LIVABLE.

lived-in *adj.* showing signs of habitation.

live-in ● *adj.* **1** cohabiting. **2** residing on the premises of one's work. ● *n.* a live-in employee, lover, etc.

livelihood *n.* a way of earning a living. [*Say* LIVELY hood]

livelong *adj.* in its entire length or apparently so. [*Say* LIV long]

lively *adj.* (**livelier**, **liveliest**) **1** full of life and energy. **2** brisk. **3** vivid, stimulating. **4** vivacious, jolly, sociable. **5** bright and vivid. □ **liveliness** *n.*

liven *v.* (usu. foll. by *up*) *informal* **1** make or become more lively. **2** cheer; brighten. [*Rhymes with* DRIVE-IN]

liver¹ *n.* **1** a large organ in the abdomen, functioning in many metabolic processes including the regulation of toxic materials. **2** an animal's liver as food. **3** a dark reddish brown.

liver² *n.* a person who lives in a specified way.

liveried *adj.* (of a servant) wearing the distinctive uniform of a household. [*Say* LIVER eed]

liver spots *pl. n.* brown spots or patches of melanin on the skin.

liverwurst *n.* a cooked sausage having a high proportion of esp. pork liver. [*Say* LIVER wurst]

livery *n.* (*pl.* **liveries**) **1** a distinctive uniform worn by servants in a particular household etc. **2** a distinctive marking, design, etc. **3** a place where horses can be hired. [*Say* LIVER ee]

livery stable *n.* (also **livery barn**) an establishment that keeps or rents horses.

lives *pl. of* LIFE.

livestock *n.* animals kept esp. on a farm for use or profit, e.g. cattle etc.

live trap ● *n.* a box-like trap for catching animals without hurting them. ● *v.* (**live-trap**, **live-traps**, **live-trapped**, **live-trapping**) catch (an animal) in such a trap.

livewell *n.* a container of water in a fishing boat, in which caught fish are kept alive and fresh. [*With* LIVE *rhyming with* DIVE]

live wire *n.* **1** an energetic and forceful person. **2** a wire conveying an electric current.

livid *adj.* **1** *informal* furiously angry. **2** of an intense reddish colour. **3** of a bluish leaden colour, like a bruise. □ **lividly** *adv.* [*Say* LIV id]

living ● *n.* **1** an income which is enough to live on, or the means of earning it. **2** a way or style of life. **3** (**the living**) those who are alive. ● *adj.* **1** that lives or has life. **2** now existent. □ **within living memory** within the memory of people still living.

living colour *n.* vivid or true-to-life colour.

living museum *n.* a historic site at which interpreters dress in period costume, perform period-specific tasks and trades, etc.

living room *n.* a room in a private home for general use during the daytime.

living wage *n.* the lowest wage on which a person can afford a reasonable standard of living.

living will *n.* a written declaration setting out the circumstances in which artificial means of maintaining one's life should be withdrawn.

livre *n.* an old French monetary unit, worth one pound of silver. [*Say* LEEV ruh]

lizard *n.* a reptile that typically has a long body and tail, four legs, movable eyelids, and a rough or scaly hide.

'll *v.* shall, will.

llama *n.* (*pl.* **llamas**) **1** a S American animal of the camel family, kept as a beast of burden and for its soft woolly fleece. **2** the wool from this animal, or cloth made from it. [*Say* LAMMA *or* LOMMA]

LL.B. *abbr.* Bachelor of Laws.

lo¹ *interj.* *archaic* calling attention to an amazing sight. □ **lo and behold** introducing a surprising or unexpected fact.

lo² *adj.* low, used esp. in advertising etc.

load ● *n.* **1** a heavy or bulky thing being or about to be carried. **2** a weight. **3** the total number or amount carried. **4** (**a load/loads of**) *informal* a lot of. **5** the amount of work to be done. **6** a burden of responsibility, worry, etc. ● *v.* **1** put a load on or in. **2** insert something into a device so that it will operate. **3** put ammunition in a firearm. **4** bias toward a particular outcome. □ **get a load of** *slang* take notice of; check out. **load the bases** *Baseball* place baserunners on all three bases. **take a load off** (**one's feet**) *informal* sit or lie down. □ **loadable** *adj.*

loaded *adj.* **1** bearing or carrying a load. **2** *slang* **a** wealthy. **b** drunk. **c** drugged. **3** (of dice etc.) weighted to enable cheating. **4** (of a question or statement) charged with some hidden or improper implication. **5** *informal* (of a car etc.) equipped with optional extras. **6** (of a weapon) charged with ammunition.

loader *n.* **1 a** a machine or device for loading things. **b** = FRONT-END LOADER. **2** a gun, machine, etc. that is loaded in a specified way. □ **-loading** *adj.* (in sense 2).

loading *n.* **1** the application of a load to something. **2** the amount of load applied. **3** *informal* massive consumption of a particular substance etc. to enhance one's performance.

loaf¹ *n.* (*pl.* **loaves**) **1** a portion of bread baked in one esp. oblong piece. **2** a quantity of other food formed into a particular, usu. oblong shape.

loaf² *v.* **1** spend time idly; hang about. **2** move slowly or easily.

loafer *n.* **1** an idle person. **2** a leather shoe shaped like a moccasin with a flat heel.

loam *n.* a fertile soil of clay and sand containing decayed vegetable matter. □ **loamy** *adj.*

loan ● *n.* **1** something lent, esp. a sum of money to be returned. **2** the act of lending. **3** a word, custom, etc., adopted by one people from another. ● *v.* lend (esp. money). □ **on loan** acquired or given as a loan.

loaner *n.* a car, computer, etc. lent to a customer while the customer's is kept for repair.

loan shark *n.* *informal* a person who lends money at exorbitant rates of interest. □ **loansharking** *n.*

loath *adj.* reluctant, unwilling. [With TH *as in* BATH]

loathe *v.* (**loathes, loathed, loathing**) regard with disgust; detest. □ **loather** *n.* **loathing** *n.* [With TH *as in* BATHE]

loathsome *adj.* arousing hatred or disgust. □ **loathsomeness** *n.* [*Say* LOTHE sum *(with* LOTHE *either like* LOATH *or like* LOATHE)]

loaves *pl.* of LOAF¹.

lob ● *v.* (**lobs, lobbed, lobbing**) **1** hit or throw something slowly or in a high arc. **2** fire (a rocket etc.) in a high arc. **3** direct (questions, insults, accusations, etc.) at a person. ● *n.* **1** a ball struck or thrown in a high arc. **2** *Cdn* (also **lob ball**) an intentionally easy question designed to make the respondent look competent.

lobby ● *n.* (*pl.* **lobbies**) **1** a usu. large area inside the main entrance of a building. **2** a body of persons seeking to influence legislators on behalf of a particular interest. **3** (also **division lobby**) each of two areas on either side of the Commons chamber in which MPs may relax or discuss party strategy. ● *v.* (**lobbies, lobbied, lobbying**) **1** solicit the support of or seek to influence. **2** attempt to persuade a politician to support or oppose changes in the law. □ **lobbying** *n.* & *adj.* **lobbyist** *n.*

lobe *n.* **1** a roundish and flattish pendulous part. **2** = EARLOBE. □ **lobed** *adj.*

lobelia *n.* (*pl.* **lobelias**) a low-growing garden plant with esp. blue flowers. [*Say* lo BEELY uh]

lobotomy *n.* (*pl.* **lobotomies**) a rare medical operation that cuts into the frontal lobe of the brain, formerly used to treat mental illness. □ **lobotomize** *v.* [*Say* luh BOTTA mee]

lobster *n.* any large marine crustacean with a long body, stalked eyes, and two pincer-like claws.

lobstering *n.* the catching of lobsters, esp. by commercial fishermen.

lobsterman *n.* (*pl.* **lobstermen**) a person who traps lobster for a living.

lobster pot *n.* a device for trapping lobster, esp. one made of wooden slats.

lobster roll *n.* a long bread roll stuffed with a mixture of lobster meat, celery, onion, mayonnaise, etc.

local ● *adj.* **1** pertaining to a particular locality. **2** only encountered in a particular place. **3** of or belonging to the neighbourhood. **4** of or affecting a part and not the whole, esp. of the body. **5** (of a telephone call) to a nearby place and not subject to long-distance charges. ● *n.* **1** an inhabitant of a particular place. **2** a local train, bus, etc. **3** a local branch of a labour union. **4** a local anaesthetic. □ **locally** *adv.*

local area network *n.* a computer network in which computers in close proximity are able to share resources.

local colour *n.* the typical things, customs, etc. in a place that make it interesting.

locale *n.* a place where something happens. [*Say* lo CAL]

localism *n.* **1 a** attachment to what is local. **b** a limitation of ideas and interests resulting from such attachment. **2** a local idiom, custom, etc.

locality *n.* (*pl.* **localities**) **1** an area or neighbourhood. **2** the position or site of something.

localize *v.* (**localizes, localized, localizing**) **1** restrict or assign to a particular place. **2** (foll. by *in*) (of a disease etc.) be confined to a specified area of the body. □ **localization** *n.*, **localized** *adj.*

locate *v.* (**locates, located, locating**) **1** discover the exact place or position of. **2** establish in a place. **3** (**be located**) be situated.

location *n.* **1** the place where a person or thing is. **2** the act of locating or process of being located. **3** an actual place featured in a film or broadcast, as distinct from a studio simulation. □ **locational** *adj.*

locator *n.* a device used for locating something, e.g. downed aircraft.

loc. cit. *abbr.* in the passage already cited.

loch *n.* (in Scotland) **1** a lake. **2** an arm of the sea, esp. when narrow or partially landlocked. [*Say* LOCK]

loci *pl.* of LOCUS. [*Say* LO sigh]

lock¹ ● *n.* **1** a device for fastening esp. a door, which can only be opened by means of a key, code, etc. **2** a device for preventing a mechanism from operating. **3** a short section of a canal or river with gates at each end which can be opened or closed to change the water level and so raise and lower boats. **4** *Wrestling* a hold that keeps an opponent's limb fixed. **5** *informal* a person or thing that is certain to succeed. ● *v.* **1** fasten with a lock. **2** enclose by locking. **3** store or allocate inaccessibly. **4** make or become immovable. **5** entangle in an embrace or struggle. **6** make (a computer screen) inaccessible unless a password is entered. □ **lock down** confine prisoners to their cells. **have a lock on** *informal* have total control over. **be locked in** be irrevocably committed to. **lock in** convert (a mortgage) from a floating to a fixed rate of interest. **lock on to** locate by radar, a heat-seeking device, etc., and then track. □ **lockable** *adj.*

lock² *n.* **1** a portion of hair that coils or hangs together. **2** (**locks**) the hair of the head.

lockdown *n.* the confining of prisoners to their cells, esp. to gain control during a riot etc.

locker *n.* **1** a small lockable compartment, esp. one of several in a public place. **2** *Nautical* a chest for clothes, stores, ammunition, etc.

locker room ● *n.* a change room for people participating in sports. ● *adj.* (usu. **locker-room**) (of language etc.) coarse, ribald.

locket *n.* a small ornamental case holding a portrait, lock of hair, etc., and usu. hung from the neck.

lockjaw *n.* a variety of tetanus causing the mouth to remain tightly closed.

lockout *n.* the exclusion of employees by their employer from their place of work until certain terms are agreed to.

locksmith *n.* a person who makes, repairs, and replaces locks. □ **locksmithing** *n.*

lockstep ● *n.* marching with each person as close as possible to the one in front. ● *adj.* rigid; inflexible. □ **in lockstep** exactly parallel; in exact synchrony.

lock, stock, and barrel ● *n.* the whole of a thing. **●** *adv.* completely.

lock-up *n.* **1** *informal* = JAIL *n.* 1. **2** *Cdn* an opportunity for the press to examine a government budget in a locked room before it is officially brought down. **3** the locking up of premises for the night.

loco¹ *n.* (*pl.* **locos**) *informal* a locomotive engine.

loco² ● *adj. slang* crazy. **●** *n.* (*pl.* **locos**) (also **locoweed**) a poisonous plant causing brain disease in cattle eating it.

locomotion *n.* motion or the power of motion from one place to another.

locomotive ● *n.* an engine used for pulling trains. **●** *adj.* of or relating to or effecting locomotion.

locus *n.* (*pl.* **loci**) **1** the centre or source of something. **2** *Math* a curve etc. formed by all the points satisfying a particular condition. **3** a position on a chromosome. **4** a position or point. [*Say* LO cuss *for the singular,* LO sigh *for the plural*]

locust *n.* **1** a large grasshopper, swarms of which cause extensive damage to crops. **2** a cicada. **3 a** any of a number of pod-bearing trees of the pea family, esp. the carob tree. **b** the large edible pod of certain plants, esp. a carob bean. **4** a N American tree bearing fragrant white flowers and black pods, grown as an ornamental. [*Say* LO kist]

locution *n.* **1** a word or phrase. **2** style of speech. □ **locutionary** *adj.* [*Say* lo CUE sh'n]

lode *n.* **1** a vein of metal ore. **2** a rich source or plentiful supply.

lodestone *n.* **1** a piece of a naturally magnetized mineral, able to be used as a magnet. **2** a thing that attracts.

lodge ● *n.* **1 a** an esp. resort hotel or inn. **2** the main building in a resort or summer camp, usu. containing a dining area etc. **3** *Cdn* (esp. in proper names) a retirement home. **4** a house occupied in the hunting or fishing season. **5** a teepee or wigwam. **6** a small house for a gatekeeper, gardener, etc. **7** the meeting place of a branch of a society such as the Freemasons. **8** a beaver's or otter's lair. **●** *v.* (**lodges, lodged, lodging**) **1** formally present (a complaint, appeal, etc.). **2** place (power etc.) in a person or group. **3** fix or be fixed in a place. **4** provide with sleeping quarters. **5** reside, esp. as a guest paying for accommodation. **6** serve as a habitation for.

lodgepole *n.* **1** a pole used to support a teepee or wigwam. **2** (also **lodgepole pine**) a pine of mountainous regions of northwestern N America.

lodger *n.* a person receiving accommodation in another's house for payment.

lodging *n.* **1** temporary accommodation. **2** (**lodgings**) a room or rooms rented for long-term lodging. **3** a dwelling.

loess *n.* a very fertile deposit of fine light-coloured wind-blown soil. [*Say* LO ess]

loft ● *n.* **1** a room or space directly under the roof of a house. **2** such a space in a barn etc., used esp. for storing hay and straw. **3** a gallery or upper level in a church or hall. **4** an esp. high-ceilinged apartment built into a former warehouse or commercial building. **●** *v.* **1** send (a ball etc.) high up. **2** clear (an obstacle) in this way.

loftily *adv.* haughtily, condescendingly.

lofty *adj.* (**loftier, loftiest**) **1** of imposing height, towering, soaring. **2** consciously haughty, aloof, or dignified. **3** exalted or noble; sublime.

log¹ ● *n.* **1 a** a cut or fallen part of the trunk or a branch of a tree. **b** something long and cylindrical. **2 a** a record of events occurring during and affecting the voyage of a ship or aircraft. **3** any systematic record of things done, experienced, etc. **●** *v.* (**logs, logged, logging**) **1** clear a region of trees. **2** cut a tree into logs. **3** enter (facts) in a log. **4** achieve (a certain distance, speed, etc.). □ **log in/on** (or **out/off**) go through the procedures of beginning (or concluding) a computer session.

log² *n.* a logarithm.

loganberry *n.* (*pl.* **loganberries**) a hybrid between a blackberry and a raspberry. [*Say* LO gun berry]

logarithm *n.* a figure representing the power to which a fixed number or base must be raised to produce a given number, used to simplify calculations as the addition and subtraction of logarithms is equivalent to multiplication and division. □ **logarithmic** *adj.* [*Say* LOGGA rhythm, logga RHYTHMIC]

logbook *n.* **1** a book containing a detailed record of things done or experienced. **2** a book in which particulars of aircraft flights etc. are recorded.

log boom *n.* a raft of logs fastened together for transportation on water.

log cabin *n.* a house or cabin with walls made of logs.

log drive *n. Cdn* the transporting of logs by floating them down rivers etc. □ **log driver** *n.*

logged-over *adj.* (also **logged-off, logged-out**) (of a tract of forest) that has been logged.

logger *n.* a person who fells trees and prepares timber for milling.

loggerhead *n.* any of various large-headed animals, esp.: **1** a reddish-brown turtle of warm seas. **2** a grey and black N American shrike. □ **at loggerheads** disagreeing or disputing.

loggia *n.* (*pl.* **loggias**) **1** an open-sided gallery or arcade. **2** an open-sided extension of a house. [*Say* LO juh *or* LODGE uh]

logging *n.* the work of cutting and preparing forest timber.

logging road *n.* an unimproved road into a forest area, used for logging purposes.

logic *n.* **1 a** a way of thinking or of explaining something. **b** sensible reasons for doing something. **2** the science of reasoning or proof. **3** a system or set of principles underlying a computer's ability to perform a specified task.

-logic *comb. form* (also **-logical**) forming adjectives corresponding esp. to nouns in *-logy*.

logical *adj.* **1** based on the rules of logic or clear, sound reasoning. **2** (of an action, decision, etc.) natural or sensible given the circumstances. □ **logically** *adv.*

logician *n.* a person who studies the science of reasoning. [*Say* luh JISH'n]

log-in *n.* *Computing* **1** the action of logging in. **2** a code, password, etc. used in logging in.

-logist *comb. form* forming nouns denoting a person skilled or involved in a branch of study etc. with a name in *-logy*.

logistics *pl. n.* **1** the detailed coordination of a complex operation involving many people, facilities, or supplies. **2** the organization of moving, lodging, and supplying military troops and equipment. □ **logistical** *adj.* **logistically** *adv.* [*Say* luh JIST icks]

logjam *n.* **1** a crowded mass of logs in a river. **2** a deadlock.

logo *n.* (*pl.* **logos**) a symbol designed for and used by a company or organization as its special sign.

log-on *n.* = LOG-IN.

log-rolling *n.* **1** *informal* the practice of exchanging favours, esp. (in politics) of exchanging votes to mutual benefit. **2** the action of causing a floating log to rotate by treading; birling.

logy *adj.* (**logier**, **logiest**) *informal* dull and heavy in motion or thought. [*Say* LO ghee]

-logy *comb. form* forming nouns denoting: **1** (usu. as **-ology**) a subject of study or interest. **2** a characteristic of speech or language. **3** discourse.

loin *n.* **1** (in *pl.*) the part of the body on both sides of the spine between the ribs and the hip bones. **2** (**loins**) the region of the sexual organs. **3** a cut of meat that includes the loin vertebrae.

loincloth *n.* a cloth worn around the loins, esp. as a sole garment.

loiter *v.* linger idly. □ **loiterer** *n.*

loll *v.* **1** (often foll. by *about*, *around*) stand, sit, or recline in a lazy attitude. **2** hang loosely. [*Rhymes with* DOLL]

lollapalooza *n.* (*pl.* **lollapaloozas**) *slang* an excellent or attractive person or thing. [*Say* lolla puh LOOZA]

lollipop *n.* a large flat or round candy on a small stick.

Lombardy poplar *n.* a variety of poplar with an especially tall slender form. [*Say* LOM bur dee]

Londoner *n.* a native or inhabitant of London, England, or London, Ontario.

lone *adj.* **1** (of a person) solitary. **2** single, only.

lonely *adj.* (**lonelier**, **loneliest**) **1** sad because without friends or company. **2** (of a place) where only a few people come or visit. **3** causing one to feel sad and alone. □ **loneliness** *n.*

lonely heart *n.* (usu. in *pl.*) a lonely person seeking companionship by advertising in a newspaper etc.

loner *n.* a person who prefers not to associate with others.

lonesome *adj.* **1** solitary, lonely. **2** feeling forlorn. **3** causing such a feeling. □ **by** (or **on**) **one's lonesome** all alone. □ **lonesomeness** *n.*

long¹ ● *adj.* (**longer**; **longest**) **1** of a great or a specified distance or duration. **2** relatively great in extent. **3** (of a ball in sport) travelling a great distance. **4** *Phonetics* having the sound of *a* in *ate*, *e* in *eke*, *i* in *ice*, *o* in *ode*, *u* in *lute*. **5** (of odds) reflecting a low level of probability. **6** (of a drink) large and refreshing, with little or no alcohol. ● *n.* a long time. ● *adv.* (**longer**; **longest**) **1** by or for a long time. **2** throughout a specified time. **3** after an implied point of time. **4** esp. *Sport* at or to a great distance. □ **as** (or **so**) **long as 1** during the whole time that. **2** provided that. **before long** fairly soon. **be long** take a long time. **in the long run** over a long period. **long in the tooth** rather old.

long² *v.* have a strong wish or desire for.

long. *abbr.* longitude.

long-ago *adj.* that is in the distant past.

long-awaited *adj.* that has been awaited for a long time.

longboat n. **1** a sailing ship's largest boat. **2** = LONGSHIP.

longbow n. a bow drawn by hand and shooting a long feathered arrow.

long-chain adj. (of a molecule) containing a chain of many carbon atoms.

long-dead adj. that has been dead for a long time.

long-distance ● adj. **1** (of a telephone call) requiring extra payment because of its distance. **2** relating to such service. **3** covering relatively great distances. ● adv. (also **long distance**) between distant places. ● n. (usu. **long distance**) long-distance telephone service.

long-drawn-out adj. (also **long-drawn**) prolonged, esp. unduly.

longevity n. **1** long life. **2** duration of life. **3** duration or length of service, employment, etc. [Say lon JEVVA tee]

long face n. a dismal expression. □ **long-faced** adj.

longhair n. **1** informal a person with long hair, esp. a hippie. **2** a long-haired cat. □ **long-haired** adj.

longhand n. ordinary handwriting.

long haul n. **1** the transport of goods or passengers over a long distance. **2** a prolonged task. □ **over the long haul** over a long period.

longhorn n. **1** a breed of cattle with long horns. **2** an elongated woodland beetle with very long, slender, backward-flexed antennae.

longhouse n. a dwelling shared by several nuclear families, esp. among the Iroquois and the Aboriginal peoples of the northwest coast of N America.

Longhouse religion n. an Iroquois religion established in the late 18th c., incorporating certain Christian elements and traditional Iroquois beliefs.

longing ● n. a feeling of intense desire. ● adj. having or showing this feeling. □ **longingly** adv.

longish adj. somewhat long.

longitude n. the distance of a place east or west of the Greenwich meridian, measured in degrees. [Say LON ji tude or LONGGA tude]

longitudinal adj. **1** of or in length. **2** running lengthwise. **3** of longitude; measured east to west. □ **longitudinally** adv. [Say lon ji TUDE in ul or longga TUDE in ul]

long johns pl. n. informal close-fitting knit underpants with full-length legs.

long jump n. an athletic contest of jumping as far as possible along the ground in one leap. □ **long-jumper** n.

long-lasting adj. that lasts, or has lasted, for a long time.

long-legged adj. having long legs.

long-life adj. designed or treated to last a long time.

longline n. a deep-sea fishing line with a large number of baited hooks.

longliner n. a fishing boat using longlines.

longlining n. fishing using longlines.

long-lived adj. having a long life.

long-lost adj. that has been lost or not seen for a long time.

long lot n. Cdn hist. a long narrow farm lot extending back from a river.

long-playing adj. (of a record) designed to be played at $33\frac{1}{3}$ revolutions per minute.

long-range adj. **1** (of a missile, aircraft, etc.) having a long range. **2** relating to a period of time far into the future.

long-run adj. occurring or running over a long period of time.

long-running adj. continuing for a long time.

longship n. hist. a long narrow warship used by the Vikings.

longshore adj. relating to or moving along the shore of a body of water.

longshoreman n. (pl. **longshoremen**) a person employed to load and unload ships.

long shot n. **1** a competitor that is unlikely to succeed. **2** an undertaking that has great potential but little chance of success. **3** a wild guess. **4** a bet at long odds. □ **by a long shot** by any means.

long-sleeved adj. with sleeves reaching to the wrist.

longspur n. a N American songbird with brownish plumage and a boldly marked head in the male.

long-standing adj. that has long existed.

long-suffering adj. bearing provocation patiently.

long-term adj. **1** of or for a long period of time. **2** (of an investment, loan, etc.) maturing or coming due after a long period of time.

long-time adj. that has been such for a long time.

long ton n. a unit of weight equal to 2,240 lb. avoirdupois (1016 kg).

long view n. a broad and forward-looking assessment of circumstances etc.

long wave n. a radio wave of frequency less than 300 kHz.

longways adv. (also **longwise**) = LENGTHWISE.

long weekend n. a three-day weekend consisting of Saturday, Sunday, and a statutory holiday on the Friday or Monday.

long-winded adj. **1** (of speech or writing) tediously lengthy. **2** (of a person) verbose. □ **long-windedly** adv. **long-windedness** n.

loo n. (pl. **loos**) esp. Brit. informal a toilet or washroom.

loofah n. the dried fibrous interior of an Asian gourd used as a sponge. [Say LOOFA]

look ● v. **1** direct one's gaze in a specified direction. **2** have an outlook in a specified direction. **3** have the appearance or give the impression of being. ● n. **1** an act of looking. **2** an expression of a feeling or thought by looking. **3** appearance. **4** (**looks**) a person's facial appearance considered aesthetically. **5** a style or fashion. ● interj. (also **look here!**) calling attention, expressing a protest, etc. □ **look after** take care of. **look down on** (or **upon** or **look down one's nose at**) regard with contempt or a feeling of superiority. **look forward to** await (an expected event) eagerly. **look like 1** have the appearance of. **2** indicate the presence of. **3** threaten or promise. **look oneself** appear in good health (esp. after illness etc.). **look out 1** direct one's sight or put one's head out of a window etc. **2** be vigilant or prepared. **3** have or afford a specified outlook. **4** have someone's interests at heart. **look over 1** inspect or survey. **2** examine (a document etc.) esp. cursorily. **look sharp** act promptly. **look up 1** search for (information). **2** improve, esp. in price, prosperity, or well-being. **look a person up and down** scrutinize a person keenly or contemptuously. **look up to** respect or venerate.

look-alike ● n. a person or thing closely resembling another. ● adj. of very similar appearance.

looker n. **1** a person having a specified appearance. **2** informal an attractive person, esp. a woman. **3** a person who looks.

-looking adj. (in comb.) having a specified appearance.

looking glass n. (pl. **looking glasses**) archaic a mirror.

lookit interj. informal **1** demanding attention or protesting. **2** look at.

lookout n. **1** a watch or looking out. **2 a** a post of observation. **b** a person or group stationed to keep watch. **3** a view over a landscape.

look-see n. informal a survey or inspection.

lookup n. the action of systematic electronic information retrieval.

looky v. informal (in imper.; usu. as looky here) demanding attention.

loom¹ n. an apparatus in which threads are woven into fabric.

loom² v. **1** come into sight dimly, esp. threateningly. **2** be ominously close or above. □ **loom large** figure significantly.

loon n. **1** an aquatic diving bird with a sharp bill, esp. the common loon, with a characteristic yodel-like call and a black and white body. **2** informal a crazy person.

loonie n. (pl. **loonies**) Cdn **1** the Canadian one-dollar coin. **2** informal the Canadian dollar.

loony slang ● n. (pl. **loonies**) a mad or silly person. ● adj. (**loonier**, **looniest**) crazy, silly. □ **looniness** n.

loony bin n. slang a mental home or hospital.

loony-tune adj. informal (also **loony-tunes**) crazy, silly; bizarre. □ **loony-tune** n.

loop ● n. **1** a shape produced by a curve that bends round and crosses itself. **2** Figure Skating a type of jump. **3** an endless strip of tape or film allowing continuous repetition. **4** Computing a programmed sequence of instructions that is repeated until a particular condition is satisfied. **5** the circle of influential people or those keeping up to date. ● v. **1** form (thread etc.) into a loop or loops. **2** enclose with a loop. **3** fasten or join with a loop or loops. **4 a** form a loop. **b** move in loop-like patterns. □ **throw** (or **knock**) **one for a loop** surprise, astonish; catch off guard.

looped adj. **1** coiled or wreathed in loops. **2** consisting of a loop. **3** slang drunk.

looper n. an inchworm.

loophole n. a means of evading a rule etc. without infringing the letter of it.

loop-the-loop n. the feat of circling in an aircraft in a vertical loop.

loopy adj. (**loopier**, **loopiest**) **1** slang crazy. **2** having many loops.

loose ● adj. (**looser**, **loosest**) **1** not or no longer controlled or held by bonds or restraint. **2** detached or detachable. **3** not held together or contained. **4** slack, relaxed. **5** not compact or dense. **6** inexact. **7** morally lax. **8** indiscreet. **9** (of the bowels) afflicted with diarrhea. **10** (of a coalition etc.) allowing for substantial independence among members. ● adv. (**looser**, **loosest**) **1** (in comb.) loosely. **2** without constraint. **3** without attachment. ● v. (**looses**, **loosed**, **loosing**) **1** release; free from constraint. **2** untie or undo. **3** relax. **4** discharge (a gun or arrow etc.). □ **on the loose** escaped from captivity. □ **looseness** n.

loose cannon n. a person causing unintentional or misdirected damage.

loose end *n.* an unfinished detail. □ **at loose ends** unsettled, without a place or purpose.

loose-leaf ● *adj.* (of a notebook) with each leaf separate and removable. ● *n.* loose-leaf paper.

loose lips *n.* indiscreet talk. □ **loose-lipped** *adj.*

loosely *adv.* **1** not firmly or tightly. **2** in a way that is not exact.

loosen *v.* **1** make or become less tight or compact or firm. **2** release (the bowels) from constipation. □ **loosen up 1** warm up in preparation for an activity. **2** make or become relaxed.

loosestrife *n.* a tall plant with upright spikes of flowers, growing esp. by water. [*Say* LOOSE strife]

loosey-goosey *adj. informal* laid back; very relaxed.

loot ● *n.* **1** goods taken from an enemy. **2** stolen property or valuables. **3** *slang* money. ● *v.* **1** rob (premises) or steal (goods) left unprotected, esp. after riots etc. **2** plunder.

loot bag *n.* a bag containing candy, trinkets, etc., given to each child at a birthday party etc.

looter *n.* a person who steals unprotected property after a riot, fire, etc. □ **looting** *n.*

lop *v.* (**lops**, **lopped**, **lopping**) **1** cut or remove from a whole. **2** remove something regarded as unnecessary or burdensome.

lope ● *v.* (**lopes**, **loped**, **loping**) move with a long bounding stride. ● *n.* a long bounding stride.

loppet *n.* a cross-country ski race in which all competitors start together. [*Say* LOPPIT]

lopsided *adj.* **1** unevenly balanced. **2** *Sport* with one side greatly outscoring the other. □ **lopsidedly** *adv.* **lopsidedness** *n.*

loquacious *adj.* talkative. □ **loquacity** *n.* [*Say* lo KWAY shus, lo KWASSA tee]

lord ● *n.* **1** a master or ruler. **2** (**Lord**) (often as **the Lord**) **a** a name for God. **b** a name for Christ. **3** a title given to certain British peers or high officials. **4** (**the Lords**) = HOUSE OF LORDS. ● *interj.* (**Lord**) expressing surprise, dismay, etc. □ **lord it over 1** dominate. **2** adopt an attitude of superiority over.

lord and lady *n.* (*pl.* **lords and ladies**) esp. *Cdn* (usu. in *pl.*) the harlequin duck.

lordly *adj.* (**lordlier**, **lordliest**) characteristic of a lord.

Lord's Day *n.* Sunday.

lordship *n.* supreme power or rule. □ **his** (or **your**) **Lordship 1** *Brit.* a respectful form of address to a Lord or a bishop. **2** *Cdn* & *Brit.* a respectful form of address to a judge.

Lord's Prayer *n.* the prayer taught by Christ, beginning "Our Father"

Lord's Supper *n. Christianity* the sacrament in which bread and wine are consecrated and consumed.

Lordy *interj.* expressing surprise, dismay, etc.

lore *n.* a body of traditions and knowledge on a subject.

lorikeet *n.* any of various small brightly coloured parrots. [*Say* LORA keet]

lose *v.* (**loses**, *past* and *past participle* **lost**; **losing**) **1** be deprived of or cease to have. **2** suffer the death of. **3** become unable to find. **4** let pass from one's control or reach. **5** be defeated in. **6** evade. **7** fail to apprehend; not catch (words etc.). **8** forfeit. **9** spend (time, efforts, etc.) to no purpose. **10** suffer loss or detriment; incur a disadvantage. **11** cause (a person) the loss of. **12** (**be lost**) disappear, perish. **13** *informal* get rid of; discard. **14** shed (weight). □ **lose one's balance** fail to remain stable. **lose face** be humiliated. **lose heart** be discouraged. **lose it 1** lose one's composure suddenly and completely. **2** lose one's sanity. **3** cease to excel. **lose out** *informal* **1** not get a fair chance or advantage. **2** be beaten in competition or replaced by. **lose one's temper** become angry. **lose the** (or **one's**) **way** become lost. □ **losing** *n.*

lose-lose *adj. informal* designating a condition which is disadvantageous to everyone involved.

loser *n.* **1** a person or thing that loses or has lost. **2** *informal* **a** a person who regularly fails. **b** a socially awkward person.

loss *n.* (*pl.* **losses**) **1 a** the fact or process of no longer having something. **b** the disadvantage or grief caused by being deprived of something or someone. **2** a person, thing, or amount lost. **3** the death of a person. □ **at a loss 1** uncertain what to think, do, or say. **2** for less money than required to break even.

loss leader *n.* an item sold at a loss to attract customers.

lost ● *v. past* and *past participle of* LOSE. ● *adj.* **1** not knowing where one is. **2** confused or in difficulties. **3** that cannot be found or recovered. **4** suffering damnation. □ **be lost for words** not know what to say. **be lost in** be engrossed in. **be lost on** not be appreciated by. **be lost without** have great difficulty if deprived of.

lost and found *n.* (*pl.* **lost and founds**) a place where misplaced items are collected for retrieval by their owners.

lost cause *n.* an enterprise etc. with no chance of success.

lot ● *n*. 1 *informal* **a** a large number or amount. **b** *informal* much. **2 a** each of a set of objects used in making a chance selection. **b** this method of deciding. **3** a person's destiny. **4 a** a portion of land assigned to a particular owner. **b** a plot of land used for parking vehicles, shooting films, etc. **5** an article or set of articles for sale at an auction etc. **6** a number of associated persons or things. **● *v*. (lots, lotted, lotting)** divide into lots. □ **cast** (or **draw**) **lots** decide by means of lots. **throw in one's lot with** decide to share the fortunes of. **the** (or **the whole**) **lot** the whole number or quantity. **a whole lot** *informal* very much.

Lothario *n. (pl.* **Lotharios**) a man known for many sexual conquests. [*Say* luh THAIR ee oh *or* luh THAR ee oh (*with* TH *as in* THIN)]

lotion *n.* a medicinal or cosmetic creamy liquid applied to the skin.

lottery *n. (pl.* **lotteries**) **1 a** a means of raising money by selling numbered tickets and giving prizes to the holders of numbers drawn at random. **b** any game of chance involving the sale of tickets. **c** any random drawing. **2** an enterprise, process, etc., whose outcome is governed by chance.

lotto *n. (pl.* **lottos**) **1** (also esp. *Que.* **loto**, *pl.* **lotos**) a lottery. **2** a game of chance like bingo.

lotus *n. (pl.* **lotuses**) **1** (in Greek mythology) a plant whose fruit induces a dreamy forgetfulness. **2** a large water lily. [*Say* LO tis]

lotus land *n.* a place of lazy relaxation and enjoyment.

lotus position *n.* a cross-legged position of meditation with both feet resting on the thighs.

Loucheux *n. (pl.* **Loucheux**) = GWICH'IN. [*Say* LOO shoo]

loud ● *adj*. 1 strongly audible. **b** able to produce loud sounds. **c** clamorous, insistent. **2** gaudy, obtrusive. **3** aggressive and noisy. **● *adv*.** in a loud manner. □ **out loud** aloud. □ **loudly** *adv.* **loudness** *n.*

loud hailer *n.* a megaphone.

loudmouth *n. informal* a noisily self-assertive or vociferous person. □ **loudmouthed** *adj.*

loudspeaker *n.* an apparatus that converts electrical impulses into sound.

Lou Gehrig's disease *n.* = AMYOTROPHIC LATERAL SCLEROSIS. [*Say* loo GAIR ig]

lounge ● *v*. (lounges, lounged, lounging) 1 recline comfortably and casually. **2** move about idly. **● *n*. 1** a room in a public place where people may sit and relax. **2** designating easy-listening musical entertainment characteristic of lounges.

lounge lizard *n. informal* **1** an idle person who frequents lounges. **2** a performer of esp. pop songs in lounges.

lounger *n.* **1** a person who lounges. **2** a piece of furniture for relaxing on.

lour *v.* = LOWER³. [*Rhymes with* HOUR]

louse ● *n*. 1 (*pl.* **lice**) **a** a parasitic insect that infests the human hair and skin. **b** any similar insect that is a parasite of animals or plants. **2** (*pl.* **louses**) *slang* a contemptible person. **● *v*. (louses, loused, lousing)** remove lice from. □ **louse up** *slang* mess up.

lousy *adj.* (**lousier, lousiest**) **1** infested with lice. **2** *informal* very bad; contemptible. **3** *informal* well supplied, teeming.

lout *n.* a rough, crude, or ill-mannered man. □ **loutish** *adj.* **loutishness** *n.*

louvre *n.* (also **louver**) each of a set of overlapping slats, esp. in a door, designed to admit air and some light. □ **louvred** *adj.* [*Say* LOOVER]

lovable *adj.* inspiring or deserving love or affection.

lovage *n.* a Mediterranean herb used esp. for flavouring liqueurs. [*Say* LUV idge]

love ● *n*. 1 an intense feeling of deep affection or fondness for a person or thing. **2** sexual passion. **3** sexual relations. **4** a beloved one. **5** (in some sports) no score; nil. **6** a formula for ending an affectionate letter etc. **● *v*. (loves, loved, loving) 1** feel love or deep fondness for. **2** delight in. **3** like very much. □ **fall in love** develop a great (esp. romantic) love (for). **in love** deeply enamoured (of). **make love 1** have sexual intercourse. **2** *archaic* pay amorous attention (to). **no love lost between** mutual dislike between.

loveable *adj.* = LOVABLE.

love affair *n.* **1** an esp. extramarital romantic or sexual relationship between two people. **2** an intense enthusiasm or liking for something.

lovebird *n.* **1** a very small green parrot noted for the affectionate behaviour of mated birds. **2** (in *pl.*) *informal* lovers.

love handles *pl. n. slang* excess fat at the waist.

love-hate relationship *n.* a relationship in which the parties combine feelings of both love and hate.

love-in *n. (pl.* **love-ins**) *informal* **1** a

gathering advocating love and peace. **2** *jocular* a gathering of like-minded people.

love interest *n.* a person in whom another has a romantic or sexual interest.

loveless *adj.* without love. □**lovelessness** *n.*

love life *n.* a person's life with regard to relationships with lovers.

lovelorn *adj.* unhappy because of unrequited love.

lovely ● *adj.* (**lovelier, loveliest**) **1** exquisitely beautiful. **2** pleasing, delightful. ● *n.* (*pl.* **lovelies**) *informal* a pretty woman. □**loveliness** *n.*

lovemaking *n.* amorous sexual activity.

lover *n.* **1** a person in love with another. **2** a person with whom another is having a sexual or romantic relationship. **3** a person who likes something specified.

loveseat *n.* a small sofa for two.

lovesick *adj.* languishing with romantic love.

lovestruck *adj.* completely smitten by love.

love triangle *n.* a situation in which one person is romantically involved with two others.

lovey *informal adj.* (also **lovey-dovey**) fondly affectionate, esp. unduly sentimental.

loving ● *adj.* feeling or showing love. ● *n.* affection. □**lovingly** *adv.*

loving-kindness *n.* tenderness and consideration.

low¹ ● *adj.* **1** not high or tall or far above the ground or horizon. **2** below average in amount, extent, or intensity. **3** (of a sound) deep or quiet. **4** depressed. **5** morally contemptible. ● *n.* **1** a low point, level, or figure. **2** an area of low barometric pressure. ● *adv.* **1** in or into a low position or state. **2** quietly or at low pitch. **3** at or to a moral position considered contemptible □**lowness** *n.*

low² ● *n.* a sound made by cattle; a moo. ● *v.* utter (with) this sound.

Low Arctic *n.* the part of the Canadian Arctic south of the Arctic Circle.

lowball *informal* ● *adj.* **1** designating an unrealistically low price or estimate. **2** inexpensive. ● *v.* deceptively offer someone an unrealistically low price or estimate.

low beam *n.* (usu. in *pl.*) a headlight used for short-range illumination.

low blow *n.* **1** a cruel or unfair attack. **2** a punch below the belt in boxing.

low-born *adj.* born to a family that has a low social status.

lowbrow ● *adj.* not highly intellectual or cultured. ● *n.* a lowbrow person. [*With* LOW *rhyming with* SHOW *and* BROW *rhyming with* COW]

low-cal *adj.* (also **low-calorie**) low in calories.

Low Church *n.* a tradition within Anglicanism stressing the authority of the Bible and the importance of personal conversion.

low-cut *adj.* having a low neckline.

low-density lipoprotein *n.* the form of lipoprotein in which cholesterol is transported in the blood.

lowdown ● *n. informal* the relevant information. ● *adj. informal* dishonourable, contemptible.

low-E *adj.* (also **low-emissivity**) designating a window which has been coated to prevent the escape or entry of heat.

low-end *adj.* relating to relatively cheap models of consumer products, services, etc.

lower¹ ● *adj.* (*comparative of* LOW¹) **1** less high in position or status. **2** situated below another part. **3** situated on less high land, farther south, or downstream. **4** earlier. ● *adv.* in or to a lower position, status, etc.

lower² *v.* **1** let or haul down. **2** make or become lower. **3** degrade. **4** diminish.

lower³ *v.* **1** frown; look sullen. **2** (of the sky etc.) look dark and threatening. [*Rhymes either with* FLOWER *or with* BLOWER]

Lower Canadian *n. Cdn hist.* an inhabitant of the former British colony of Lower Canada (1791–1841), now Labrador and southern Quebec. □**Lower Canadian** *adj.*

lower case *adj.* designating letters that are not capitals.

lower class *n.* the poor or underprivileged class of society. □**lower-class** *adj.*

lowest common denominator *n.* **1** the lowest common multiple of the denominators of several fractions. **2** the least desirable common feature of members of a group.

low frequency *n.* (in radio) 30–300 kilohertz.

low gear *n.* a gear such that the driven end of a transmission revolves more slowly than the driving end.

Low German *n.* the group of German dialects spoken in the northern lowlands.

low-grade *adj.* of low quality or strength.

low-impact *adj.* **1** designating exercises that put little potentially harmful stress on the body. **2** affecting the natural environment as little as possible.

low-key *adj.* (also **low-keyed**) lacking intensity or prominence; restrained.

lowland *n.* (usu. in *pl.*) low-lying country. □ **lowland** *adj.* **lowlander** *n.*

low-life *n.* (*pl.* **low-lifes**) (also **low-lifer**) **1** a degenerate person. **2** such people collectively.

lowlight *n.* **1** a substandard feature or period. **2** (usu. in *pl.*) a dark tint in the hair produced by dyeing.

lowly *adj.* (**lowlier, lowliest**) humble in behaviour or status.

low-lying *adj.* (of land) at low altitude.

low maintenance *adj.* requiring little maintenance, attention, etc.

low-pitched *adj.* **1** (of a sound) low. **2** (of a roof) having only a slight slope.

low-pressure ● *adj.* **1** characterized by or exerting below-average pressure. **2** not demanding or stressful. ● *n.* (**low pressure**) an atmospheric condition with pressure below 101.3 kilopascals.

low profile *n.* an attitude characterized by the avoidance of attention.

low-rise *adj.* **1** (of a building) having few storeys. **2** (of trousers) cut so as to fit low on the hips rather than on the waist. □ **low-rise** *n.*

low season *n.* the period during which the fewest people travel.

low-slung *adj.* **1** suspended; sagging. **2** with a low and wide profile.

low spirits *pl. n.* dejection, depression.

low-tech *n.* (also **low-technology**) relatively unsophisticated tools, machines, etc.

low tide *n.* (also **low water**) the time or level of the tide at its ebb.

low-water mark *n.* **1** the level reached at low water. **2** a minimum recorded level or value etc.

lox[1] *n.* liquid oxygen.

lox[2] *n.* smoked salmon.

loyal *adj.* **1** true or faithful. **2** devoted to the government of one's country. □ **loyally** *adv.* **loyalty** (*pl.* **loyalties**) *n.*

loyalist *n.* **1** a person who remains loyal to the existing sovereign, government, etc. **2** (**Loyalist**) **a** any of the American colonists who supported the British cause during the American Revolution, many of whom afterwards migrated to Canada. **b** *Cdn* a descendant of such a person. □ **loyalism** *n.*

loyal Opposition *n.* = OFFICIAL OPPOSITION.

lozenge *n.* **1** a rhombus or diamond figure. **2** a small candy or tablet for dissolving in the mouth, e.g. for soothing the throat. [*Say* LOZ inj]

LP *n.* a long-playing record.

LPN *n.* (*pl.* **LPNs**) LICENSED PRACTICAL NURSE.

LSAT *abbr.* Law School Admission Test. [*Say* ELL sat]

LSD *n.* lysergic acid diethylamide, a powerful hallucinogenic drug.

Lt *abbr.* **1** (also **Lt.**) LIEUTENANT. **2** (**Lt.**) light.

Ltd. *abbr.* Limited.

Lt.-Gov. *abbr.* Lieutenant-Governor.

luau *n.* (*pl.* **luaus**) a Hawaiian party. [*Say* LOO ow (OW *rhymes with* HOW)]

lubber *n.* **1** a big clumsy fellow. **2** = LANDLUBBER. □ **lubberly** *adj.* & *adv.*

lube *informal* ● *n.* **1** = LUBRICANT. **2** an application of lubricant (esp. to a motor vehicle). ● *v.* (**lubes, lubed, lubing**) = LUBRICATE.

Lubicon *n.* (*pl.* **Lubicon** or **Lubicons**) **1** a Cree Aboriginal group living near Peace River, Alberta. **2** the Algonquian language of the Lubicon. [*Say* LOOBA con]

lubricant ● *n.* a substance used to reduce friction. ● *adj.* lubricating.

lubricate *v.* (**lubricates, lubricated, lubricating**) **1** reduce friction by applying oil etc. **2** (**lubricated** *adj.*) *informal* drunk. □ **lubrication** *n.* **lubricator** *n.*

lubricious *adj.* **1** lewd, prurient. **2** slippery, smooth, oily. □ **lubricity** *n.* [*Say* loo BRISH us, loo BRISSA tee]

lucid *adj.* **1 a** clear; easy to understand. **b** (of a dream) vivid; clear. **2** able to think clearly. □ **lucidity** *n.* **lucidly** *adv.* [*Say* LOO sid, loo SIDDA tee]

Lucifer *n.* Satan. [*Say* LOOSSA fur]

Lucite *n.* *proprietary* a solid transparent plastic. [*Say* LOO site]

luck ● *n.* **1** chance regarded as the bringer of good or bad fortune. **2** circumstances of life brought by this. **3** good fortune. ● *v. informal* **1** (foll. by *into*) acquire by good fortune. **2** (foll. by *out, in*) achieve success by good luck. **3** (foll. by *out*) be disadvantaged by bad luck. □ **as luck would have it** because of luck. **for luck** to bring good fortune. **no such luck** *informal* unfortunately have not. **try one's luck** make a venture. **with luck** if all goes well.

luckily *adv.* fortunately.

luckless *adj.* having no luck; unfortunate.

lucky *adj.* (**luckier, luckiest**) **1** having or resulting from good luck. **2** bringing good luck. **3** fortunate, appropriate. □ **get lucky** *informal* have sex. **thank one's lucky stars** be extremely grateful to fate. □ **luckiness** *n.*

lucrative *adj.* yielding financial gain. [*Say* LOO cruh tiv]

lucre *n. derogatory* financial gain. [*Say* LOO cur]

Luddite *n.* a person opposed to new technology. □ **Luddism** *n.* [*Say* LUD ite]

ludicrous *adj.* absurd or ridiculous. □ **ludicrously** *adv.* [*Say* LOODA cruss]

luff *v.* **1** steer (a ship) nearer the wind. **2** (of a sail) flap from being set too close to the wind.

Luftwaffe *n. hist.* the German air force up to the end of World War II. [*Say* LOOFT voffa]

lug ● *v.* (**lugs, lugged, lugging**) **1** drag (a heavy object) with effort. **2** carry (something heavy) around with one. ● *n.* **1** a projection on an object by which it may be carried, fixed in place, etc. **2** *slang* an awkward or stupid person. **3** an earflap on a hat.

luge ● *n.* **1** a sled with runners, ridden esp. in a lying position with face upwards. **2** the sport in which these are raced. ● *v.* (**luges, luged, luging**) ride on a luge. □ **luger** *n.* [*Say* LOOZH]

Luger *n. proprietary* a type of German automatic pistol. [*Say* LOOG er]

luggage *n.* a traveller's suitcases, bags, etc.

lugubrious *adj.* mournful, dismal. □ **lugubriously** *adv.* **lugubriousness** *n.* [*Say* loo GOO bree us]

lukewarm *adj.* **1** somewhat warm. **2** not enthusiastic. □ **lukewarmness** *n.*

lull ● *v.* **1** soothe or send to sleep gently. **2** deceive into confidence. **3** allay (suspicion etc.) usu. by deception. **4** abate or fall quiet. ● *n.* a temporary quiet period in a storm etc.

lullaby *n.* (*pl.* **lullabies**) a soothing song to send a child to sleep.

lulling *adj.* calming, soothing, esp. in a manner that makes one sleepy.

lulu *n.* (*pl.* **lulus**) *slang* a remarkable person or thing.

lumbar *adj.* relating to the lower back area. [*Say* LUMBER *or* LUM bar]

lumber ● *n.* partly or fully prepared timber. ● *v.* **1** cut and prepare timber. **2** burden with something unwanted or unpleasant. **3** move in a slow clumsy noisy way.

lumbering ● *n.* **1** the lumber or timber trade. **2** the work of cutting and preparing forest timber. ● *adj.* slow and clumsy or awkward.

lumberjack *n. esp. hist.* = LOGGER.

lumberjack jacket *n.* (also **lumberjacket**) a jacket, usu. of warm,

red and black checked material, originally worn by loggers.

lumberjack shirt *n.* a long-sleeved checkered flannel shirt.

lumberman *n.* (*pl.* **lumbermen**) **1** a lumber company owner or manager. **2** = LOGGER.

lumber mill *n.* a factory where logs and lumber are processed.

lumber road *n.* = LOGGING ROAD.

lumberyard *n.* a place where lumber is stored and sold.

luminance *n.* **1** the state or quality of reflecting light. **2** the intensity of light emitted from a surface per unit area in a given direction. [*Say* LOO min ince]

luminary *n.* (*pl.* **luminaries**) a prominent or influential member of a group. [*Say* LOOMA nerry]

luminescence *n.* **1** the emission of light by a substance that has not been heated. **2** the light emitted by a luminescent object. □ **luminescent** *adj.* [*Say* looma NESS ince]

luminous *adj.* **1** radiant, bright, shining. **2** (of a colour) very bright. **3** of visible radiation. □ **luminosity** *n.* **luminously** *adv.* [*Say* LOOM in us]

lummox *n.* (*pl.* **lummoxes**) *informal* a clumsy or stupid person. [*Say* LUM ucks]

lump¹ ● *n.* **1 a** a compact shapeless or misshapen mass. **b** a sugar cube. **2** a quantity or heap. **3** a tumour or swelling. **4** a heavy, dull, or ungainly person. **5** (**lumps**) *slang* hard knocks, attacks, defeats. ● *v.* mass together or group indiscriminately. □ **lump in the throat** a feeling of pressure in the throat, caused by emotion.

lump² *v. informal* □ **like it or lump it** put up with something whether one likes it or not.

lumpectomy *n.* (*pl.* **lumpectomies**) the surgical removal of a usu. cancerous lump from the breast. [*Say* lump ECTA mee]

lumpen *adj. derogatory* ignorantly contented, boorish, stupid. [*Say* LUMP in]

lumpish *adj.* **1** heavy and clumsy. **2** stupid, lethargic. **3** shaped like a lump.

lump sum *n.* **1** a sum covering a number of items. **2** money paid down at once.

lumpy *adj.* (**lumpier, lumpiest**) full of or covered with lumps. □ **lumpiness** *n.*

lunacy *n.* (*pl.* **lunacies**) **1** insanity; the state of being a lunatic. **2** great folly; a foolish act. [*Say* LOONA see]

lunar *adj.* pertaining to the moon.

lunar eclipse *n.* an eclipse in which the moon passes into the earth's shadow.

lunar month *n.* the period between one new moon and the next (about 29¹/₂ days).

lunar year *n.* a period of 12 lunar months.

lunatic ● *n.* **1** an insane person. **2** someone foolish. ● *adj.* mad, foolish.

lunch ● *n.* (*pl.* **lunches**) the meal eaten in the middle of the day. ● *v.* (**lunches, lunched, lunching**) eat one's lunch. □ **do lunch** *informal* have lunch with a person, esp. for business. **out to lunch** *slang* out of touch with reality. □ **luncher** *n.*

lunch box *n.* a box with a handle, for carrying a packed meal.

lunch bucket ● *n.* = LUNCH BOX. ● *adj.* (**lunch-bucket**) = LUNCH-PAIL *adj.*

lunch counter *n.* **1** a counter in a department store etc., where light lunches are served. **2** (also **luncheonette**) a small restaurant or snack bar serving light lunches.

luncheon *n.* an esp. formal lunch. [*Say* LUNCH in]

luncheon meat *n.* a usu. tinned block of ground meat, usu. sliced and eaten cold in sandwiches etc.

lunch pail ● *n.* = LUNCH BOX. ● *adj.* (**lunch-pail**) working-class; blue-collar.

lunchtime *n.* the time around the middle of the day when lunch is usually eaten.

lung *n.* either of the pair of respiratory organs which bring air into contact with the blood. □ **lungful** *n.*

lunge¹ ● *n.* **1** a sudden movement forward. **2** a thrust with a sword etc. ● *v.* (**lunges, lunged, lunging**) make a lunge.

lunge² *n.* = MUSKELLUNGE.

lungfish *n.* (*pl.* **lungfish** or **lungfishes**) a freshwater fish with gills and a modified swim bladder used as lungs.

lunker *n.* *slang* an animal, esp. a fish, which is an exceptionally large example of its species.

lunkhead *n.* (also **lunk**) *slang* a slow-witted person. □ **lunkheaded** *adj.*

lupine¹ *n.* (also **lupin**) a plant with long tapering spikes of flowers. [*Say* LOO pin]

lupine² *adj.* of or like a wolf. [*Say* LOO pine]

lupini bean *n.* the seed of a large-seeded bitter variety of lupine, eaten as food. [*Say* loo PEE nee]

lupus *n.* any of various diseases producing skin ulcers. [*Say* LOO pus]

lurch ● *n.* (*pl.* **lurches**) a sudden unsteady movement or leaning. ● *v.* (**lurches, lurched, lurching**) **1** stagger, move unsteadily. **2** (of a ship etc.) move suddenly to one side. □ **leave in the lurch** desert (a friend etc.) in difficulties.

lure ● *v.* (**lures, lured, luring**) **1** entice usu. with some form of bait. **2** attract back again with the promise of a reward. ● *n.* **1** a thing used to entice. **2** the attractive or compelling qualities of a pursuit etc. **3** an esp. artificial bait used to entice fish.

lurid *adj.* **1** sensational or horrifying. **2** showy, gaudy. **3** vivid or glowing in colour. **4** of an unnatural glare. **5** ghastly, wan. □ **luridly** *adv.* [*Say* LOOR id]

lurk *v.* **1** linger furtively or unobtrusively. **2 a** lie in ambush. **b** hide, esp. for sinister purposes. **3** exist latently or semi-consciously. □ **lurker** *n.*

luscious *adj.* **1** delicious. **2** sensuous. **3** voluptuously attractive. □ **lusciously** *adv.* **lusciousness** *n.*

lush¹ *slang n.* (*pl.* **lushes**) an alcoholic.

lush² *adj.* **1** (of plants, gardens, etc.) growing thickly and strongly in a way that is attractive. **2** luxurious, opulent. **3** providing great pleasure to the senses. □ **lushly** *adv.* **lushness** *n.*

lust ● *n.* **1** strong sexual desire. **2** a passionate desire for. ● *v.* have a strong or excessive (esp. sexual) desire. □ **lustful** *adj.* **lustfully** *adv.*

lustre *n.* (esp. *US* **luster**) **1** the shining quality of a surface. **2** a shiny or reflective surface. **3** splendour, distinction. □ **lustreless** *adj.* **lustrous** *adj.* [*Say* LUSTER]

lusty *adj.* (**lustier, lustiest**) **1** healthy and strong. **2** vigorous or lively. **3** (of a meal etc.) hearty, abundant. **4** lustful; full of sexual desire. □ **lustily** *adv.*

lute *n.* a guitar-like instrument with a long neck and a pear-shaped body.

lutetium *n.* a silvery metallic element. [*Say* loo TEESHY um]

Lutheran *n.* a member of the Protestant denomination based on the beliefs of the German religious reformer Martin Luther (1483–1546). □ **Lutheran** *adj.* **Lutheranism** *n.* [*Say* LOOTH er in]

Lutz *n.* (*pl.* **Lutzes**) *Figure Skating* a type of jump.

lux *n.* (*pl.* **lux**) *Physics* the SI unit of illumination. [*Say* LUCKS]

luxe ● *n.* luxury. ● *adj.* deluxe, sumptuous. [*Sounds like* LUCKS]

luxuriant *adj.* (of vegetation, hair, etc.) lush, profuse in growth. □ **luxuriance** *n.* [*Say* lug ZHURRY int *or* luck SHURRY int]

luxuriantly *adv.* **1** abundantly; in a lush or profuse manner. **2** in a self-indulgently comfortable manner. [*Say* lug ZHURRY int lee *or* luck SHURRY int lee]

luxuriate v. (**luxuriates, luxuriated, luxuriating**) enjoy as a luxury; take self-indulgent delight in. [*Say* lug ZHURRY ate *or* luck SHURRY ate]

luxurious adj. **1** characterized by luxury; sumptuous, rich. **2** extremely comfortable; self-indulgent. □ **luxuriously** adv. **luxuriousness** n. [*Say* lug ZHURRY us *or* luck SHURRY us]

luxury n. (*pl.* **luxuries**) **1** choice or costly surroundings, possessions, food, etc. **2** (often in *pl.*) something desirable for comfort or enjoyment, but not indispensable. **3** (as an *adj.*) providing great comfort; expensive. [*Say* LUCK shur ee *or* LUG zhur ee]

-ly¹ *suffix* forming adjectives esp. from nouns, meaning: **1** having the qualities of. **2** recurring at intervals of.

-ly² *suffix* forming adverbs from adjectives, denoting esp. manner or degree.

lychee n. a sweet fleshy fruit with a thin spiny skin. [*Say* LEE chee]

lycopene n. a red pigment and antioxidant present in tomatoes and some fruits. [*Say* LIE co peen]

Lycra n. *proprietary* an elastic synthetic fibre or fabric used esp. for close-fitting clothing; spandex. [*Say* LIKE ruh]

lye n. any strong alkaline solution, esp. of potassium hydroxide used for cleansing. [*Say* LIE]

lying¹ *pres. part.* of LIE¹.

lying² ● v. *pres. part.* of LIE². ● adj. deceitful, false.

Lyme disease n. a form of arthritis caused by spirochete bacteria transmitted by ticks. [*Say* LIME]

lymph n. a colourless liquid containing white blood cells that cleans the tissues of the body. [*Say* LIMF]

lymphatic adj. of or secreting or conveying lymph. [*Say* lim FAT ick]

lymph node n. (also **lymph gland**) a small mass of tissue in the lymphatic system where lymph is purified and lymphocytes are formed.

lymphocyte n. a form of white blood cell with a single round nucleus, occurring esp. in the lymphatic system. [*Say* LIMF uh site]

lymphoma n. (*pl.* **lymphomas**) any malignant tumour of the lymph nodes, excluding leukemia. [*Say* lim FOME uh]

lynch v. (**lynches, lynched, lynching**) (of a body of people) put (an alleged criminal) to death without a legal trial, esp. by hanging. □ **lyncher** n. **lynching** n. [*Say* LINCH]

lynch mob n. **1** a mob intent on lynching someone. **2** any unruly, angry crowd of people.

lynchpin n. = LINCHPIN. [*Say* LINCH pin]

lynx n. (*pl.* **lynxes** or **lynx**) any of various small to medium-sized northern cats typically having a short tail, tufted ears, and mottled fur. [*Say* LINKS]

lyre n. an ancient stringed instrument like a small U-shaped harp. [*Sounds like* LIAR]

lyric ● adj. **1** (of poetry) expressing the writer's emotions, usu. briefly and in stanzas. **2** (of a poet) writing in this manner. **3** fit to be expressed in song. ● n. **1** a lyric poem or verse. **2** (**lyrics**) lyric verses. **3** (usu. in *pl.*) the words of a song. □ **lyricism** n. [*Say* LEAR ick, LEAR uh sism]

lyrical adj **1** = LYRIC 1, 2. **2** resembling lyric poetry. **3** *informal* highly enthusiastic. □ **lyrically** adv. [*Say* LEAR ick ul]

lyricist n. a person who writes the words to a song. [*Say* LEAR uh sist]

-lysis *comb. form* forming nouns denoting disintegration or decomposition. [*Say* luh sis]

Lysol n. *proprietary* a disinfectant. [*Say* LICE oll]

Mm

M¹ *n.* (also **m**) (*pl.* **Ms** or **M's**) **1** the thirteenth letter of the alphabet. **2** (as a Roman numeral) 1,000.

M² *abbr.* (in sizes) medium.

m¹ *abbr.* (also **m.**) **1 a** masculine. **b** male. **2** married. **3** mile(s). **4** million(s). **5** minute(s). **6** month.

m² *symb.* **1** metre(s). **2** milli-. **3** *Physics* mass.

'm *abbr. informal* am.

M-16 *n.* (*pl.* **M-16s**) an automatic or semi-automatic magazine-fed rifle.

M.A. *n.* (*pl.* **M.A.'s**) Master of Arts.

ma *n.* (*pl.* **mas**) *informal* mother.

ma'am *n.* madam. [*Say* MAM]

Mac *n. informal* **1** a form of address to a male stranger. **2** a McIntosh apple.

macabre *adj.* grim, gruesome, esp. in having to do with death.
[*Say* muh COBBRA *or* muh COB *or* muh CABBRA]

macadam *n.* **1** material for road building with successive layers of compacted broken stone. **2** a material of stone or slag bound with tar, used in paving.
[*Say* muh CAD um]

macadamia *n.* the globular edible nut-like seed of an Australian tree.
[*Say* macka DAY mee uh]

macaque *n.* a medium-sized, forest-dwelling monkey, which has a long tail and prominent cheek pouches.
[*Say* muh CACK]

macaroni *n.* a tubular variety of pasta.

macaroon *n.* a light cookie made with egg whites and ground almonds or coconut.
[*Say* macka ROON]

macaw *n.* a long-tailed brightly coloured parrot native to South and Central America. [*Say* muh KAW]

macchiato *n.* (*pl.* **macchiatos**) coffee served with a very small amount of hot milk or milk froth. [*Say* macky ATTO]

mace¹ *n.* **1** a staff of office. **2** *hist.* a heavy club usu. having a metal head and spikes.

mace² *n.* the dried outer covering of the nutmeg, used as a spice.

mace³ *n. proprietary* an irritant chemical preparation used in aerosol form as a disabling weapon.

macerate *v.* (**macerates, macerated, macerating**) make or become soft by soaking. □ **maceration** *n.*
[*Say* MASSA rate]

Mach *n.* (also **Mach number**) the ratio of the speed of a body to the speed of sound in the surrounding medium. [*Sounds like* MOCK *or* MACK]

machete *n.* a broad heavy knife used as a tool or weapon. [*Say* muh SHETTY]

Machiavellian ● *adj.* **1** elaborately cunning. **2** of or characteristic of Niccolò di Bernardo dei Machiavelli (1469–1527) or his principles. **●** *n.* a person who is scheming and unscrupulous. □ **Machiavellianism** *n.* [*Say* macky a VELLY in]

machination *n.* (usu. in *pl.*) a cunning plot or scheme. [*Say* masha NATION *or* macka NATION]

machine ● *n.* **1** an apparatus using or applying mechanical power, having several parts, each performing a particular task. **2 a** the controlling system of a political party or similar organization. **b** a ruthlessly efficient group of people. **3** a coin-operated dispenser. **●** *v* (**machines, machined, machining**) make or work on with a machine. □ **machining** *n.*

machine code *n.* (also **machine language**) a language that a particular computer can handle or act on directly. □ **machine-coded** *adj.*

machine gun ● *n.* **1** an automatic gun that fires bullets in rapid succession. **2** (**machine-gun**) (as an *adj.*) rapid and repeating like a machine gun. **●** *v.* (**machine-gun, machine-guns, machine-gunned, machine-gunning**) shoot at with a machine gun. □ **machine-gunner** *v.*

machine-readable *adj.* in a form that a computer can process.

machinery *n.* (*pl.* **machineries**) **1** machines collectively. **2** the moving parts of a machine. **3** an organized system.

machine shop *n.* a workshop for making or repairing machines.

machine tool *n.* a mechanically operated tool for working on metal, wood, or plastics.

machinist *n.* a person who operates or makes machinery.

machismo *n.* **1** exaggerated or aggressive

pride in being male. **2** an assertion of manliness. [*Say* muh CHIZ mo *or* muh KIZ mo]

macho *adj.* aggressively proud of one's masculinity. [*Say* MOTCH oh *or* MATCH oh]

mackerel *n.* (*pl.* **mackerel** *or* **mackerels**) a swift-swimming predatory fish esp. of the North Atlantic and Mediterranean. [*Say* MACK rull]

mackinaw *n.* **1 a** a heavy, felted woollen cloth, usu. with a plaid design. **b** a jacket made of this cloth. **2** (**Mackinaw**; in full **Mackinaw trout**) = LAKE TROUT. [*Say* MACK in awe]

mackintosh *n.* (*pl.* **mackintoshes**) esp. *Brit.* a raincoat.

macramé *n.* the art of knotting cord or string in patterns to make decorative articles. [*Say* MACRA may]

macro ● *n.* (*pl.* **macros**) *Computing* a series of abbreviated instructions expanded automatically when required. ● *adj.* **1** large-scale. **2** overall.

macro- *comb. form* **1** long, large. **2** large-scale.

macrobiotic ● *adj.* relating to a dietary system consisting esp. of vegetables and brown rice. ● *n.* (**macrobiotics**; treated as *sing.*) the use or theory of such a dietary system. [*Say* macro bye OTT ick]

macrocosm *n.* **1** the universe; the whole of all nature. **2** a complex structure or whole, esp. one considered to be epitomized by some constituent portion or microcosm. □ **macrocosmic** *adj.* [*Say* MACRO kozzum, macro COSMIC]

macroeconomics *n.* the study of large-scale economic factors, e.g. national productivity. □ **macroeconomic** *adj.* [*Say* macro ECONOMICS, macro ECONOMIST]

macromolecule *n.* a molecule containing a very large number of atoms. [*Say* macro MOLECULE]

macrophage *n.* a large white blood cell responsible for engulfing and digesting bacteria and cell debris. [*Say* MACRO fage]

mad *adj.* (**madder, maddest**) **1** insane. **2** wildly foolish. **3** excessively enthusiastic. **4** *informal* very angry. **5** frantic, desperate. □ **like mad** *informal* with great energy. □ **madly** *adv.*

madam *n.* **1** a respectful form of address to a woman. **2** a woman who keeps a brothel. [*Say* MAD um]

Madame *n.* **1** (*pl.* **Mesdames**) a title or form of address for a French-speaking woman. **2** (**madame**) = MADAM 1.

[*Say* muh DAM *for the singular*, may DAM *for the plural*]

madcap *adj.* reckless, impulsive.

mad cow disease *n. informal* bovine spongiform encephalopathy, a usu. fatal virus disease of cattle involving the central nervous system.

madden *v.* **1** make or become mad. **2** annoy. □ **maddening** *adj.* **maddeningly** *adv.*

made *v.* *past and past participle of* MAKE.

made-to-measure *adj.* made to an individual's specifications etc.

made up *adj.* **1** invented, not true. **2** (of a person) wearing makeup.

madhouse *n.* **1** esp. *hist.* a hospital for the mentally ill. **2** *informal* a scene of extreme confusion.

madman *n.* (*pl.* **madmen**) an insane or furious man.

madness *n.* the quality of being mad.

Madonna *n. Christianity* (**the Madonna**) the Virgin Mary.

madras *n.* a colourful striped or checked cotton fabric. [*Say* muh DRASS]

madrigal *n.* an unaccompanied secular song with several interwoven melodies. [*Say* MADRA gull]

madwoman *n.* (*pl.* **madwomen**) an insane or furious woman.

maelstrom *n.* **1** a great whirlpool. **2** a state of turbulence. [*Say* MAIL strum]

maestro *n.* (*pl.* **maestros**) a distinguished performer or conductor. [*Say* MY stro]

Mafia *n.* **1** an international criminal organization originating in Sicily. **2** (**mafia**) any powerful group exerting a secret and sinister influence. [*Say* MOFFY uh *or* MAFFY uh]

Mafioso *n.* (*pl.* **Mafiosi**) a member of the Mafia. [*Say* maffy OH so, maffy OH see]

magazine *n.* **1** a periodical publication containing articles and pictures. **2** a chamber for holding a supply of cartridges to be fed automatically to the breech of a gun. **3** a similar device feeding a camera, slide projector, etc. **4** a store of arms, ammunition, and explosives.

magenta *n. & adj.* brilliant mauvish-crimson. [*Say* muh JENTA]

maggot *n.* any soft-bodied limbless larva. □ **maggoty** *adj.*

magi *pl. of* MAGUS. [*Say* MAY jie]

magic ● *n.* **1** the supposed art of influencing events using supernatural forces. **2** conjuring tricks. **3** an inexplicable remarkable influence. **4** an enchanting quality. **5** *informal* exceptional skill. ● *adj.*

1 a relating to magic. **b** usable in magic rites. **2** producing surprising results. **3** *informal* wonderful. ● v. (**magics, magicked, magicking**) change or create apparently by magic. □ **magical** *adj.*

magic bullet *n. informal* a universal remedy.

magician *n.* **1** a person with magic powers. **2** a conjuror.

Magic Marker *n. proprietary* a felt-tipped indelible marker pen.

magic mushroom *n.* a mushroom that causes hallucinations.

magic word *n.* a word or phrase the utterance of which effects magic or creates a desired effect.

magisterial *adj.* **1** having or showing power or authority. **2** having to do with a magistrate. □ **magisterially** *adv.* [*Say* madge iss TEERY ul]

magistrate *n.* **1** an official conducting a court for minor cases and preliminary hearings. **2** a civil officer administering the law. [*Say* MADGE iss trate]

Magistrate's Court *n. Cdn* = PROVINCIAL COURT.

magma *n.* very hot fluid or semi-liquid material beneath the earth's crust, from which igneous rock is formed by cooling. □ **magmatic** *adj.* [*Say* MAG muh, mag MAT ick]

Magna Carta *n.* (also **Magna Charta**) a charter of political rights that King John of England was forced to sign by his rebellious barons in 1215.

magna cum laude *adv. & adj.* with or of great distinction. [*Say* magna koom LOUD ay]

magnanimous *adj.* nobly generous; not petty in feelings or conduct. □ **magnanimity** *n.* **magnanimously** *adv.* [*Say* mag NANA muss, magna NIM it ee]

magnate *n.* a wealthy and influential businessperson. [*Say* MAG nate]

magnesium *n.* a silvery metallic element, used for making light alloys. [*Say* mag NEEZY um]

magnet *n.* **1** a piece of iron or other metal that can attract iron. **2** a person or thing that attracts.

magnetic *adj.* **1** having the properties of a magnet or pertaining to magnetism. **2** capable of being attracted by a magnet. **3** very attractive. **4** measured relative to magnetic north. □ **magnetically** *adv.*

magnetic field *n.* a region of variable force around magnets or current-carrying conductors.

magnetic north *n.* the north magnetic pole, indicated by a compass needle.

magnetic pole *n.* **1** each of the points near the geographical North and South poles, where the lines of force of the earth's magnetic fields are vertical. **2** either of two opposite points of a magnet.

magnetic resonance imaging *n.* a form of medical imaging using the nuclear magnetic resonance of protons in the body. Abbreviation: **MRI**.

magnetic tape *n.* a tape coated with magnetic material for use in recording and data storage.

magnetism *n.* **1** the characteristic properties of magnetic phenomena, esp. attraction. **2** an attractive power, esp. charm.

magnetite *n.* magnetic iron oxide, an important ore of iron.

magnetize *v.* (**magnetizes, magnetized, magnetizing**) **1** make magnetic. **2** attract as if by a magnet. □ **magnetization** *n.*

magnetometer *n.* an instrument measuring magnetic forces. [*Say* magna TOM it er]

magnificent *adj.* splendid; impressive. □ **magnificence** *n.* **magnificently** *adv.* [*Say* mag NIFFA s'nt]

magnify *v.* (**magnifies, magnified, magnifying**) **1** make (a thing) appear larger than it is, as with a lens. **2** exaggerate. **3** intensify. □ **magnification** *n.* **magnifier** *n.*

magnifying glass *n.* a convex lens used to increase the apparent size of something.

magnitude *n.* **1** great size or extent. **2** size or importance. **3** the degree of brightness of a star.

magnolia *n.* a tree or shrub with large creamy-pink flowers. [*Say* mag NO lee uh]

magnum *n.* (*pl.* **magnums**) a wine bottle of about twice the standard size.

magnum opus *n.* the most important work of an artist, writer, etc. [*Say* magnum OPE us]

magpie *n.* **1** a black and white bird with a long tail and noisy call. **2** a person who collects things indiscriminately.

magus *n.* (*pl.* **magi**) **1** a priest of ancient Persia. **2** a sorcerer. **3** *Christianity* (**the (three) Magi**) the "wise men" from the East who brought gifts to the infant Christ. [*Say* MAY gus *for the singular*, MAY jie *for the plural*]

Magyar *n.* a member or the language of the predominant cultural group in Hungary. □ **Magyar** *adj.* [*Say* MAG yar]

maharaja *n.* (also **maharajah**) *hist.* a title

of some Indian princes of high rank.
[*Say* maw huh RAW juh]

maharishi *n.* a great Hindu sage or
spiritual leader. [*Say* maw huh REESHY]

mahatma *n.* (in India etc.) a person
regarded with great reverence and respect.
[*Say* muh HATMA]

Mahayana *n.* one of the two major
traditions of Buddhism.
[*Say* maw huh YAWN uh]

Mahdi *n.* (*pl.* **Mahdis**) a messiah expected
by Muslims. □ **Mahdist** *n.* [*Say* MODDY,
MOD ist]

mah-jong *n.* (also **mah-jongg**) a Chinese
game for four, resembling rummy and
played with pieces called tiles.
[*Say* maw JONG]

mahogany ● *n.* (*pl.* **mahoganies**) the
rich, reddish-brown wood of a tropical tree,
used for furniture. ● *adj.* of a rich reddish-
brown colour. [*Say* muh HOGGA nee]

maid *n.* **1** a female domestic servant.
2 *literary* a girl or young woman.

maiden ● *n.* *literary* a young unmarried
woman. ● *adj.* **1** unmarried. **2** first of its
kind. □ **maidenly** *adj.*

maidenhair *n.* a tropical fern that has
fine hairlike stalks.

maidenhead *n.* **1** virginity. **2** the hymen.

maiden name *n.* a married woman's
surname before marriage.

maid of honour *n.* an unmarried woman
attending on a bride, queen, or princess.

mail¹ ● *n.* **1 a** letters, parcels, etc. conveyed
by the postal system. **b** the postal system.
c a delivery or collection of mail. **2** email.
● *v.* **1** send through the postal service.
2 email.

mail² *n.* armour made of interlaced rings or
plates etc. □ **mailed** *adj.*

mailbag *n.* a large sack for carrying mail.

mailbox *n.* **1 a** a public receptacle into
which letters are dropped for delivery by
the postal service. **b** a private receptacle to
which letters are delivered. **2** a file etc. for
receiving and storing electronic or voice
mail.

mailer *n.* **1** an advertising pamphlet sent
by mail. **2** a container in which something
is mailed. **3** a person or thing sending mail.
4 *Computing* a program which provides users
with the facilities necessary for reading,
storing, composing, and sending email.

mailing *n.* **1 a** the action of sending
something by mail. **b** something mailed.
2 a batch of mail sent at one time to many
people.

mailing list *n.* **1** a list of people to whom
advertising matter, information, etc. is to
be mailed regularly. **2** a list of email

addresses, or an email alias for such a list,
that allows the same message to be sent to
each address.

mailman *n.* (*pl.* **mailmen**) a postman.

mail order ● *n.* the buying and selling of
goods by mail. ● *v.* (**mail-order**) buy using
mail-order catalogues.

mailroom *n.* a room in a company etc.
where mail is sorted.

mail slot *n.* a slit through which letters
are delivered.

maim *v.* injure or cripple someone or
something.

main ● *adj.* chief in size, importance, etc.
● *n.* **1** a principal channel for water,
sewage, etc. **2** the ocean. □ **in the main**
for the most part.

mainframe *n.* a large high-speed
computer, esp. one supporting numerous
peripherals.

mainland *n.* a large extent of land,
including the greater part of a country.
□ **mainlander** *n.*

mainline ● *adj.* well established and
adhering to norms. ● *n.* **1** (usu. **main line**)
a principal railway line. **2** *Forestry* the
primary, heavy cable used to haul logs.
3 *slang* a principal vein into which drugs
may be injected. ● *v.* *slang* take drugs
intravenously.

mainly *adv.* for the most part.

mainmast *n.* the principal mast of a ship.

mainsail *n.* the lowest sail on the
mainmast, or a sail set on the after part of
the mainmast. [*Say* MAIN sail *or* MAIN sull]

mainspring *n.* **1** a chief motive. **2** the
principal spring of a clock.

mainstay *n.* a chief support or principal
element.

mainstream ● *n.* the prevailing trend in
opinion, fashion, etc. ● *adj.* **1** relating to an
established field of activity. **2** relating to
the mainstream. ● *v.* place (a child with a
disability) in a class for those without
special needs. □ **mainstreamer** *n.*
mainstreaming *n.*

mainstreeting *n.* *Cdn* political
campaigning in main streets to win
support. □ **mainstreet** *v.*

maintain *v.* **1** cause to continue; preserve.
2 support. **3** uphold in argument. **4** keep in
good repair.

maintenance *n.* **1** the action or state of
maintaining something or being
maintained. **2** the provision of financial
support etc. to one's former spouse after a
separation.

maître d' *n.* (*pl.* **maître d's**) (also **maître
d'hotel** (*pl.* **maîtres d'hotel**)) **1** the
manager etc. of a hotel. **2** a head waiter.

[*Say* may truh DEE *or* may tur DEE, may truh doe TELL]

maize *n.* esp. *Brit.* corn.

Maj *abbr.* (also **Maj.**) (in the Armed Forces) major.

majestic *adj.* stately and dignified. □ **majestically** *adv.*

majesty *n.* (*pl.* **majesties**) **1** impressive dignity or beauty. **2 a** royal power. **b** (**Majesty**) (preceded by *your, her, his, their,* etc.) a title given to a sovereign or a sovereign's wife or widow.

majolica *n.* earthenware with coloured decoration on a white glaze.
[*Say* muh JAW lick uh *or* muh YAW lick uh]

major ● *adj.* **1** important, large. **2** *Music* having or based on a scale with intervals of a semitone between the third and fourth, and seventh and eighth degrees. **3** legally adult. **4** designating levels of amateur hockey for competitors usu. between the ages of 18 and 21. ● *n.* **1** an officer of a rank above captain. Abbreviation: **Maj** *Cdn* or **Maj. 2** a person considered legally an adult. **3** *Music* a major key etc. **4 a** the principal subject studied by a student at a university or college. **b** a student specializing in a specified subject. **5** (in *pl.*) the major leagues. **6** *Hockey* = MAJOR PENALTY. **7** *Cdn Football informal* a touchdown. ● *v.* (foll. by *in*) study or specialize in a subject.

majorette *n.* a member of a female baton-twirling parading group.

major general *n.* an officer of a rank above brigadier general or brigadier.

majoritarian ● *adj.* **1** governed by or believing in majority rule. **2** relating to a majority. ● *n.* a person who supports majority rule. □ **majoritarianism** *n.*
[*Say* muh jorra TERRY in]

majority *n.* (*pl.* **majorities**) **1** (usu. foll. by *of*) the greater number or part. **2** *Politics* **a** the number by which the votes cast for one party, candidate, etc. exceed those of the next in rank. **b** a party etc. receiving the greater number of votes. **3** full legal age.

majority government *n.* a government that has more than half of the total number of parliamentary seats.

major junior *n. Cdn* the highest level of amateur hockey competition.

major league ● *n.* **1** either of the two principal professional baseball leagues in N America. **2** a similar league in other sports. ● *adj.* (usu. **major-league**) **1** relating to a major league. **2** of the highest order. □ **major-leaguer** *n.*

majorly *adv. slang* to a great extent.

major penalty *n. Hockey* a five-minute penalty.

make ● *v.* (**makes, made, making**) **1** form by putting parts together or combining substances. **2** cause to be. **3** force to do something. **4** alter (something) so that it forms (something else). **5** constitute or serve as. **6** estimate as or decide on. **7** gain or earn. **8** arrive at or achieve. **9** prepare to go in a direction or do something. **10** arrange bedclothes tidily on. **11** act. ● *n.* **1** a type, brand, etc. of manufacture. **2** a kind of mental or physical composition. □ **make away with 1** get rid of; kill. **2** squander. **make do** manage with the means available. **make for 1** tend to result in. **2** proceed towards. **make it** *informal* **1** succeed in reaching. **2** be successful. **3** (usu. with *neg.*) survive. **make it up 1** be reconciled. **2** fill in a deficit. **make it up to** remedy an injury, etc. to. **make of 1** construct from. **2** understand about. **make off** depart hastily. **make off with** carry away. **make or break** cause the success or ruin of. **make out 1 a** distinguish by sight or hearing. **b** decipher. **2** understand. **3** assert. **4** *informal* make progress. **5** (usu. foll. by *to*) draw up; write out. **6** *informal* indulge in sexual activity. **make up 1** serve to overcome (a deficiency). **2** complete. **3** compensate. **4** be reconciled. **5** put together. **6** concoct (a story). **7** (of parts) compose (a whole). **8** apply cosmetics to. **on the make** *informal* **1** intent on gain. **2** looking for sex.

make-believe ● *n.* pretense. ● *adj.* pretended.

make-do *adj.* makeshift.

makeover *n.* a complete transformation.

maker *n.* **1** (often in *comb.*) a person or thing that makes. **2** a manufacturer. **3** (**our, the,** etc. **Maker**) God. □ **meet one's maker** *informal* die.

makeshift *adj.* temporary.

makeup *n.* **1** cosmetics for the face etc. **2** the composition or constitution.

make-work *n.* **1** activity devised mainly to keep someone busy. **2** esp. *Cdn* designating an esp. government-sponsored project etc. intended to create jobs.

maki *n.* (in full **maki sushi**) a dish consisting of sushi and raw vegetables wrapped in a sheet of seaweed.
[*Say* MACKY]

making *n.* **1** in senses of MAKE *v.* **2** (in *pl.*) **a** earnings. **b** (usu. foll. by *of*) essential ingredients. □ **be the making of** ensure the success of.

mako *n.* (*pl.* **makos**) a large blue shark of

tropical and temperate oceans.
[Say MACK oh]

malachite n. a bright green mineral containing copper. [Say MALA kite]

maladaptive adj. failing to adjust adequately to the environment.

maladjusted adj. 1 not correctly adjusted. 2 unable to cope with the demands of a social environment. □ **maladjustment** n.

maladroit adj. clumsy. □ **maladroitly** adv. [Say MALA droit]

malady n. (pl. **maladies**) 1 a disease or ailment. 2 something that is wrong. [Say MALA dee]

Malagasy n. 1 the language of Madagascar. 2 (pl. **Malagasies**) a person from Madagascar. □ **Malagasy** adj. [Say mala GASSY]

malaise n. 1 a general feeling of illness or unease. 2 a complex mass of problems. [Say mu LAZE]

malamute n. a dog of a breed developed in Alaska, with a plumed tail curling over the back. [Say MALA mute]

malapropism n. (also **malaprop**) the mistaken use of a word in place of a similar-sounding one.
[Say MALA prop ism]

malaria n. an intermittent fever caused by a parasite transmitted by mosquitoes. □ **malarial** adj. [Say muh LAIRY uh]

malarkey n. informal nonsense.
[Say muh LARKY]

malathion n. an insecticide.
[Say mala THIGH un]

Malay n. 1 a member of a people inhabiting Malaysia and Indonesia. 2 the language of this people. □ **Malay** adj. [Say muh LAY]

Malayan ● n. = MALAY n. 1. ● adj. relating to Malays or Malaya (now part of Malaysia). [Say muh LAY un]

Malaysian n. a person from Malaysia. □ **Malaysian** adj. [Say muh LAY zhun]

malcontent ● n. a discontented person. ● adj. rebellious. [Say MAL kun tent]

male ● adj. 1 of the sex that can beget offspring by fertilization or insemination. 2 of men or male animals, plants, etc. 3 (of plants etc.) containing only fertilizing organs. 4 (of machine parts etc.) designed to enter or fill the corresponding female part. ● n. a male person, animal, or plant. □ **maleness** n.

Malecite n. & adj. = MALISEET.
[Say MALA site]

malefactor n. a criminal; an evildoer.
[Say MALA factor]

malevolent adj. wishing evil to others.

malevolence n. **malevolently** adv.
[Say muh LEVVA l'nt]

malfeasance n. Law evildoing; illegal action. [Say mal FEEZ ince]

malformation n. faulty formation. □ **malformed** adj.

malfunction ● n. a failure to function properly. ● v. fail to function properly.

malice n. the intention to do evil or injury. [Say MAL iss]

malice aforethought n. the intention to commit a crime, esp. murder.

malicious adj. characterized by malice. □ **maliciously** adv. **maliciousness** n. [Say muh LISH us]

malign ● adj. evil. ● v. speak ill of; slander. [Say muh LINE]

malignancy n. (pl. **malignancies**) 1 a tumour. 2 the state of being malevolent. [Say muh LIG nun see]

malignant adj. 1 a very virulent or infectious. b (of a tumour) tending to invade normal tissue and recur after removal. 2 harmful. □ **malignantly** adv. [Say muh LIG nint]

malinger v. feign illness in order to escape duty, work, etc. □ **malingerer** n. [Say muh LINGER]

Maliseet n. (pl. **Maliseet**) a member or the language of an Aboriginal people now occupying northwestern New Brunswick and eastern Quebec. □ **Maliseet** adj. [Say MALA seet]

mall n. 1 a retail complex containing several stores, restaurants, etc. 2 a sheltered promenade.

mallard n. (pl. **mallards**) a wild duck, the male of which has a green head.
[Say MAL urd or MAL ard]

malleable adj. 1 able to be hammered or pressed into shape without breaking or cracking. 2 adaptable. [Say MALLY uh bull]

mallet n. 1 a type of hammer with a large usu. wooden head. 2 a light hammer used for playing the vibraphone etc. 3 a long-handled wooden hammer for striking a croquet or polo ball.

mallow n. a plant with pink or purple flowers.

mall rat n. informal a person who frequents malls to socialize.

malnourished adj. suffering from malnutrition.

malnutrition n. (also **malnourishment**) a dietary condition resulting from a lack of food or essential nutrients.

malodorous adj. foul smelling.
[Say mal ODOROUS]

Malpeque oyster n. Cdn a large edible

oyster raised in Malpeque Bay in PEI.
[*Say* MAUL peck]

malpractice *n.* careless, wrong, or illegal professional behaviour.

malt ● *n.* **1** barley etc. that is steeped, germinated, and dried, esp. for brewing or distilling. **2** = MALT WHISKY. **3** = MALTED MILK. ● *v.* convert (grain) into or become malt. □ **malty** *adj.*

malted ● *adj.* **1** converted into malt. **2** mixed with malt or a malt extract. ● *n.* = MALTED MILK.

malted milk *n.* a powder or drink made from milk and malted cereals.

Maltese *n.* (*pl.* **Maltese**) a person from or the language of Malta. □ **Maltese** *adj.* [*Say* maul TEASE]

Malthusian ● *adj.* relating to English economist T. R. Malthus or his theory that, unrestrained, a population tends to increase at a greater rate than its ability to feed itself. ● *n.* a follower of Malthus. □ **Malthusianism** *n.* [*Say* mal THOOZEY un]

maltreat *v.* ill-treat. □ **maltreatment** *n.*

malt whisky *n.* whisky made from malted barley.

mama *n. informal* mother.

mambo ● *n.* (*pl.* **mambos**) **1** a Latin American dance like the rumba. **2** the music for this. ● *v.* (**mamboes, mamboed, mamboing**) perform the mambo.

mamma *n. informal* = MAMA.

mammal *n.* a warm-blooded animal characterized by mammary glands in the female and a four-chambered heart. □ **mammalian** *adj. & n.* [*For* mammalian *say* muh MAIL yun]

mammary *adj.* of the human female breasts or milk-secreting organs of other mammals. [*Say* MAM ur ee]

mammogram *n.* an image obtained by mammography. [*Say* MAM a gram]

mammography *n.* an X-ray technique of examining the breasts for tumours. [*Say* muh MOGRA fee]

Mammon *n.* wealth regarded as an idol. [*Say* MAM un]

mammoth ● *n.* a large extinct elephant with a hairy coat and curved tusks. ● *adj.* huge.

Man. *abbr.* Manitoba.

man ● *n.* (*pl.* **men**) **1** an adult human male. **2** a husband or lover. **3** a person. **4** human beings in general. **5** a piece used in a board game. ● *v.* (**mans, manned, manning**) provide (a thing or place) with personnel to operate or defend it. ● *interj. informal* expressing surprise, admiration, etc. □ **be**

a man be courageous. **be one's own man** be free to act. **man to man** with candour. **to a man** all without exception.

manacle ● *n.* (usu. in *pl.*) a fetter for the hand; a handcuff. ● *v.* (**manacles, manacled, manacling**) fetter with manacles. [*Say* MAN a cull]

manage *v.* (**manages, managed, managing**) **1** be in charge of; control. **2** succeed in achieving. **3** cope (with) despite difficulties. **4** be free to attend.

manageable *adj.* able to be easily managed, controlled, or accomplished etc. □ **manageability** *n.* **manageably** *adv.*

management *n.* **1** the action of managing. **2** the managers of an organization.

manager *n.* **1** a person who manages staff, an organization, a sports team, etc. **2** a person controlling the business affairs of a professional sports player, actor, etc. □ **managerial** *adj.* [*For* managerial *say* manna JEERY ul]

managing *adj.* (in *comb.*) having executive control or authority.

manatee *n.* a large aquatic plant-eating mammal with paddle-like forelimbs and no hind limbs. [*Say* manna TEE]

Manchu *n.* (*pl.* **Manchus**) a member or the language of a people in China who formed the last imperial dynasty (1644–1912). □ **Manchu** *adj.* [*Say* man CHOO]

mandala *n.* a circular figure symbolizing the universe in Hinduism and Buddhism. [*Say* MANDA luh]

mandarin *n.* **1** (**Mandarin**) the official form of the Chinese language. **2** *hist.* a high-ranking official in the former Chinese empire. **3** a powerful bureaucrat. **4** a small orange with a loose skin. [*Say* MANDA rin]

mandate ● *n.* **1** an order given to a person, organization, etc. to carry out a certain task. **2 a** support for a policy or course of action, seen as given by voters in an election. **b** *Cdn* the period during which a government is in power. **3** a commission to act for another. ● *v.* (**mandates, mandated, mandating**) **1** require, esp. by law. **2** instruct (a delegate) how to act or vote.

mandatory *adj.* required by law or regulation. [*Say* MANDA tory]

mandatory supervision *n. Cdn Law* supervision by a parole officer.

mandible *n.* **1** the lower jaw. **2** the upper or lower part of a bird's beak. **3** either half of the crushing organ in an insect's mouthparts. □ **mandibular** *adj.* [*Say* MANDA bull, man DIB yoo lur]

mandolin *n.* **1** a musical instrument

resembling a lute, having paired metal strings plucked with a pick. **2** (also **mandoline**) a kitchen utensil used for slicing vegetables. □**mandolinist** n. (in sense 1). [Say manda LIN]

mandrake n. a poisonous plant with a forked fleshy root, once thought to resemble the human form and to shriek when plucked.

mandrel n. **1** a shaft inserted into something to secure it to a lathe. **2** a cylindrical rod round which material is forged or shaped. [Say MAN drull]

mandrill n. a large West African baboon with a red and blue face. [Say MAN drill]

mane n. **1** long hair growing in a line on the neck of a horse, lion, etc. **2** a person's long, thick hair. □**maned** adj.

man-eater n. **1** an animal, esp. a shark or tiger, that eats human flesh. **2** informal a woman who has many men as lovers.

maneuver n. = MANOEUVRE.

man Friday n. a male helper or follower.

manful adj. brave; resolute. □**manfully** adv.

manganese n. a grey brittle metallic element used with steel to make alloys. [Say MANGA neez]

mange n. a skin disease in hairy and woolly animals, caused by a parasite. [Rhymes with RANGE]

manger n. a long trough for livestock to eat from.

mangia-cake n. Cdn derogatory or jocular (among Italian-Canadians) a non-Italian white person. [Say MUNJA cake]

mangle[1] n. esp. Brit. hist. a machine for squeezing and pressing wet clothes.

mangle[2] v. (**mangles, mangled, mangling**) **1** destroy or severely damage by tearing or crushing. **2** spoil by misquoting, mispronouncing, etc. □**mangler** n.

mango n. (pl. **mangoes** or **mangos**) the fleshy yellowish-red fruit of a tropical tree.

mangrove n. a tropical tree or shrub that grows in shore mud with many tangled roots above ground. [Say MANG grove]

mangy adj. (**mangier, mangiest**) **1** having mange. **2** in poor condition. [Say MAIN jee]

manhandle v. (**manhandles, manhandled, manhandling**) **1** move (heavy objects) with effort. **2** informal handle roughly.

manhattan n. a cocktail made of vermouth, whisky, etc.

manhole n. a covered opening allowing access to a sewer etc.

manhood n. **1** the state of being a man.

2 a manliness. **b** a man's sexual potency. **3** men collectively.

man-hour n. an hour regarded in terms of the amount of work that could be done by one person within this period.

manhunt n. an organized search for a person, esp. a criminal.

mania n. **1** Psychology mental illness marked by periods of great excitement and violence. **2** an extreme enthusiasm.

-mania comb. form Psychology denoting a special type of mental abnormality or obsession.

maniac ● n. **1** a person exhibiting extreme symptoms of wild behaviour. **2** an obsessive enthusiast. ● adj. of or behaving like a maniac. □**-maniac** comb. form **maniacal** adj. [Say MAY nee ack, muh NYE a cull]

manic adj. **1** of or affected by mania. **2** frenzied, elated, or abnormally energetic. □**manically** adv. [Say MAN ick]

manic depression n. a mental disorder characterized by alternating periods of great happiness and depression. □**manic-depressive** adj. & n.

manicotti n. large tubular pasta. [Say manna COTTY]

manicure ● n. a cosmetic treatment of the hands and fingernails. ● v. (**manicures, manicured, manicuring**) **1** apply a manicure to. **2** trim or cut neatly. □**manicured** adj. **manicurist** n.

manifest ● adj. clear or obvious. ● n. a list of cargo or passengers. ● v. **1** show plainly. **2** reveal itself. □**manifestation** n. **manifestly** adv.

manifesto n. (pl. **manifestos** or **manifestoes**) a public declaration of principles, intentions, etc. [Say manna FESS toe]

manifold ● adj. literary many and various. ● n. a pipe or chamber branching into several openings. [Say MANNA fold]

manikin n. **1** a little person. **2** an anatomical model of the body. [Say MANNA kin]

manila n. **1** the strong fibre of a Philippine tree, used for rope etc. **2** a strong brown paper used for wrapping, envelopes, etc. [Say muh NILLA]

manioc n. a plant with starchy tuberous roots from which tapioca is obtained. Also called CASSAVA. [Say MANNY ock]

manipulate v. (**manipulates, manipulated, manipulating**) **1** handle, treat, or use, esp. skilfully (a tool, question, material, etc.). **2** manage (a person, situation, etc.) to one's own advantage, esp. unfairly or unscrupulously. **3** manually

examine and treat (a part of the body).
4 *Computing* alter, edit, or move (text, data, etc.). □ **manipulable** *adj.* **manipulation** *n.* **manipulator** *n.* [*Say* muh NIP yoo late, muh NIP yoo luh bull, muh nip yoo LAY shun]

manipulative *adj.* **1** characterized by unscrupulous exploitative behaviour. **2** relating to manipulation. [*Say* muh NIP yoo luh tiv]

Manitoba maple *n.* a fast-growing N American maple found east of the Rockies.

Manitoban ● *adj.* relating to Manitoba. **●** *n.* a person from Manitoba.

manitou *n.* (esp. among the Cree and Ojibwa) **1** a spirit. **2** something regarded as having supernatural power. [*Say* MANNA too]

mankind *n.* **1** the human species. **2** male people, as distinct from female.

manlike *adj.* **1** having male qualities. **2** resembling a human being.

manly *adj.* (**manlier, manliest**) **1** having qualities associated with men, such as courage and strength. **2** befitting a man. □ **manliness** *n.*

man-made *adj.* made by humans; synthetic.

manna *n.* **1** *Bible* the substance miraculously supplied as food to the Israelites in the wilderness. **2** (also **manna from heaven**) an unexpected benefit.

manned *adj.* having a human crew.

mannequin *n.* a model of a human body, used for displaying clothes in stores etc. [*Say* MANNA kin]

manner *n.* **1** a way a thing is done or happens. **2** (in *pl.*) polite behaviour. **3** a person's outward bearing, way of speaking, etc. **4** a sort or style. □ **in a manner of speaking** to some extent.

mannered *adj.* **1** behaving in a specified way. **2** artificial and affected.

mannerism *n.* **1** a particular habit or way of speaking or behaving that someone has but is not aware of. **2** too much use of a particular style in painting or writing. **3** (usu. **Mannerism**) a style of 16th-century Italian art characterized by bizarre effects of scale, lighting, and perspective. □ **mannerist** *n.*

mannerly *adj.* well-mannered.

mannikin *n.* = MANIKIN. [*Say* MANNA kin]

manning depot *n.* *Cdn hist.* (during World War II) a training depot for recruits to the Royal Canadian Air Force.

mannish *adj.* **1** usu. *derogatory* (of a woman) masculine in appearance or manner.
2 characteristic of a man. □ **mannishness** *n.*

manoeuvrable *adj.* able to be manoeuvred easily. □ **manoeuvrability** *n.*

manoeuvre (also **maneuver**) **●** *n.* **1** a planned and controlled movement. **2** (in *pl.*) a large-scale exercise of troops, warships, etc. **3** an often deceptive action designed to gain an objective. **●** *v.* (**manoeuvres, manoeuvred, manoeuvring**) **1** perform or cause to perform a manoeuvre. **2** manipulate (a person, thing, etc.) by scheming or skill.

man of the cloth *n.* a clergyman.

man-of-war *n.* *hist.* an armed sailing ship.

manor *n.* **1** (also **manor house**) a large house with lands. **2** *Brit.* **a** part of land consisting of a lord's estate and lands rented to tenants etc. **b** *hist.* a feudal lordship over lands. □ **manorial** *adj.* [For manorial *say* muh NORRY ul]

manpower *n.* **1** the power generated by a person working. **2** people available for work, service, etc. **3** *Cdn hist.* (often **Manpower**) a government department offering job referral services.

manqué *adj.* (placed after noun) that might have been but is not. [*Say* mong KAY]

mansard *n.* a roof which has four sloping sides, each of which becomes steeper halfway down. [*Say* MAN sard]

manse *n.* the house, owned by a congregation, of an esp. Presbyterian or United Church minister.

manservant *n.* (*pl.* **menservants**) a male servant.

mansion *n.* a large house.

man-sized *adj.* (also **man-size**) **1** of the size of a man. **2** big enough for a man.

manslaughter *n.* **1** the killing of a human being. **2** *Law* the unlawful killing of a human being without the intention to do so.

manta *n.* a large ray living in all tropical seas, with wing-like pectoral fins.

mantel *n.* (also **mantelpiece**) **1** a structure of wood, marble, etc. above and around a fireplace. **2** (also **mantelshelf**) a shelf above a fireplace.

mantis *n.* (*pl.* **mantis** or **mantises**) a slender insect related to the cockroach, which feeds on other insects.

mantle ● *n.* **1** a loose sleeveless cloak. **2** a covering. **3** a fragile lace-like tube fixed around a jet of burning gas to give an incandescent light. **4** the region between the crust and the core of the earth. **●** *v.* (**mantles, mantled, mantling**) clothe in or as if in a mantle.

mantra n. **1** a word or sound repeated to aid concentration in meditation. **2** a hymn from the Vedas. **3** a frequently repeated word, phrase, etc.

manual ● adj. **1** having to do with the hand or hands. **2** involving physical rather than mental effort. **3** worked by hand. **4** not involving computers etc. ● n. a book of instructions. □ **manually** adv.

manufacture ● n. **1** the making of articles in a factory etc. **2** a manufactured item or product. ● v. (**manufactures, manufactured, manufacturing**) **1** make (articles), esp. on an industrial scale. **2** invent or fabricate. □ **manufacturer** n.

manure ● n. animal dung used for fertilizing land. ● v. apply manure to (land etc.).

manuscript ● n. **1** a book, document, etc. written by hand. **2** an author's text submitted for publication. **3** handwritten form. ● adj. written by hand.

Manx adj. **1** relating to the Isle of Man, in the Irish Sea. **2** designating a tailless cat.

many ● adj. great in number. ● n. (as pl.) a large number. □ **have one too many** become drunk. **as many** the same number of. **as many again** the same number additionally.

Maoism n. the Communist doctrines of the Chinese statesman Mao Zedong (1893–1976) as formerly practised in China. □ **Maoist** n. & adj. [Say MOW ism (MOW rhymes with COW)]

Maori n. (pl. **Maori** or **Maoris**) a member or the language of the Polynesian aboriginal people of New Zealand. □ **Maori** adj. [Rhymes with FLOWERY]

map ● n. **1 a** a diagram of an area, showing physical features, cities, roads, etc. **b** a diagrammatic representation of a route etc. **2** a diagram or collection of data showing the way in which something is arranged or spread over an area. ● v. (**maps, mapped, mapping**) **1** represent on a map. **2** record in detail the spatial distribution of something. □ **all over the map** lacking central focus. **map out** plan. **put on the map** informal establish as important.

maple n. **1** a tree or shrub with usu. lobed leaves and colourful fall foliage. **2** its wood. **3** the flavour of maple syrup or maple sugar.

maple bush n. Cdn = SUGAR BUSH.

maple butter n. Cdn **1** a spread made by heating and cooling maple syrup. **2** butter blended with maple syrup or maple sugar.

maple leaf n. **1** (pl. **maple leaves**) the leaf of the maple, used as an emblem of Canada. **2** (**Maple Leaf**) the Canadian flag.

maple sugar n. a sugar produced by evaporating the sap of the sugar maple etc.

maple syrup n. a syrup produced from the sap of the sugar maple etc.

map-maker n. a cartographer. □ **map-making** n.

map-reading n. the interpretation of a map.

maquiladora n. a Mexican factory run by a foreign company taking advantage of cheap labour. [Say macky la DORE uh]

Mar. abbr. March.

mar v. (**mars, marred, marring**) ruin; spoil.

maraca n. (pl. **maracas**) a hollow gourd or container filled with beans, pebbles, etc. shaken as a percussion instrument. [Say muh ROCKA or muh RACKA]

maraschino n. (pl. **maraschinos**) a strong sweet liqueur made from a small black cherry. [Say mare a SHEE no]

maraschino cherry n. a cherry preserved in maraschino or maraschino-flavoured syrup.

marathon n. **1** a long-distance running race, usu. of 26 miles 385 yards (42.195 km). **2** a long and difficult task. □ **marathoner** n.

maraud v. search for things to steal or people to attack. □ **marauder** n. [Say muh ROD]

marble ● n. **1** a hard form of limestone capable of taking a polish, used in sculpture and architecture. **2** anything resembling marble in hardness etc. **3 a** a small ball of marble, glass, etc., used as a toy. **b** (in pl.; treated as sing.) a game using these. **4** (in pl.) slang one's mental faculties. **5** (as an adj.) made with two or more colours swirled together. **6** a marble sculpture. ● v. (**marbles, marbled, marbling**) stain or colour to look like marble.

marbled adj. **1** (of meat) streaked with alternating layers of lean and fat. **2** stained or coloured to look like variegated marble.

marbling n. **1** colouring or markings like marble. **2** streaks of fat in lean meat.

March n. the third month.

march[1] ● v. (**marches, marched, marching**) **1** walk in a military manner with a regular measured tread. **2** cause to march. **3** (of events etc.) continue unrelentingly. **4** take part in a protest march. ● n. (pl. **marches**) **1 a** an act of marching. **b** the uniform step of troops etc. **2** a long difficult walk. **3** a procession as a protest or demonstration. **4** (usu. foll. by of) progress. **5** a piece of music composed to accompany a march. □ **march on 1** advance towards. **2** proceed. **on the march 1** marching. **2** in steady progress. □ **marcher** n.

march² n. hist. **1** (usu. in pl.) a boundary (esp. between England and Scotland or Wales). **2** a tract of often disputed land between two countries.

March break n. Cdn a school holiday in March.

March hare n. a hare in the breeding season, characterized by strange behaviour.

marching orders pl. n. **1** a dismissal. **2** instructions given authoritatively. **3** Military the direction for troops to depart for war etc.

marchioness n. (pl. **marchionesses**) **1** the wife or widow of a marquess. **2** a woman holding the rank of marquess in her own right. [Say marsha NESS]

march past n. (pl. **march pasts**) the marching of troops past a saluting point at a review.

Mardi Gras n. the last Tuesday before Lent, celebrated esp. in New Orleans as a day of great revelry. [Say MARDY graw]

mare¹ n. a female horse.

mare² n. (pl. **maria** or **mares**) any of a number of large dark flat areas on the surface of the moon or Mars. [Say MAR ay or MAR ee for the singular, MAR ee uh for the plural]

margarine n. a butter substitute made from vegetable oils.

margarita n. a cocktail made with tequila and lime juice. [Say marga REETA]

margin n. **1** an edge or border. **2** the blank border on each side of the print on a page etc. **3** an amount by which a thing exceeds, falls short, etc.

marginal adj. **1** of or written in a margin. **2** not central. **3** (of a parliamentary seat) having a small majority at risk in an election. **4** barely or only occasionally adequate. **5** outside the mainstream. □ **marginality** adj. **marginally** adv.

marginalia pl. n. marginal notes. [Say margin AILY uh]

marginalize v. (**marginalizes, marginalized, marginalizing**) make or treat as insignificant. □ **marginalization** n.

margin of error n. a small difference allowed for miscalculation etc.

maria pl. of MARE². [Say MAR ee uh]

mariachi n. **1** an itinerant Mexican folk band. **2** a member of such a band. [Say merry ATCH ee]

Marian adj. relating to the Virgin Mary. [Say MERRY un]

marigold n. a plant of the daisy family, with yellow flowers.

marijuana n. **1** dried hemp leaves and flowers, smoked as an intoxicating drug. **2** the plant yielding these.

marimba n. (pl. **marimbas**) an African deep-toned xylophone, consisting of wooden keys on a frame. [Say muh RIMBA]

marina n. (pl. **marinas**) a specially designed harbour with moorings for pleasure boats etc. [Say muh REENA]

marinade ● n. a mixture of ingredients in which food is soaked before cooking, esp. to tenderize or add flavour. ● v. (**marinades, marinaded, marinading**) = MARINATE. [Say MARE a nade]

marinara adj. designating a sauce made from tomatoes, onions, herbs, etc. [Say mare a NAIR uh]

marinate v. (**marinates, marinated, marinating**) soak in a marinade. □ **marination** n. [Say MARE a nate, mare a NATION]

marine ● adj. **1** relating to the sea. **2** relating to shipping or naval matters. ● n. **1** a country's ships. **2 a** a soldier trained to serve on land or sea. **b** (**Marine**) (in the US) a member of the Marine Corps, trained to attack land targets from the sea.

marine park n. **1** a body of water set aside as an ecological preserve. **2** a theme park featuring marine wildlife.

mariner n. a sailor. [Say MARE in ur]

marionette n. a puppet worked from above by strings. [Say marry ANNETTE]

mariposa lily n. a N American lily with three-petalled flowers. [Say mare a POZE uh]

marital adj. of marriage. □ **maritally** adv.

marital status n. a person's situation as regards being single, married, divorced, etc.

maritime adj. **1** relating to the sea or seafaring. **2** living near the sea. **3** (**Maritime**) Cdn relating to the Maritime provinces.

Maritime Command n. Cdn the official name for the Canadian navy.

Maritimer n. Cdn a person from the Maritime provinces.

Maritimes pl. n. (also **Maritime provinces**) New Brunswick, Nova Scotia, and Prince Edward Island.

marjoram n. a plant of the mint family, used as a flavouring. [Say MAR juh rum]

mark¹ ● n. **1** a small area on a surface having a different colour from its surroundings. **2** something that acts as a pointer. **3** a sign that identifies something. **4** an indication of a quality or feeling. **5** a characteristic feature or property of something. **6** a level or stage. **7** a point awarded for an academic assignment, test, etc. **8** a particular model of a machine. ● v. **1** make a mark on. **2** write an identifying word or symbol on. **3** indicate the position of. **4** acknowledge. **5** assess and give a mark to. **6** pay attention to. □ **hit** (or **miss**) **the mark** succeed (or fail). **leave one's mark on** have a long-lasting effect on. **make one's mark** attain distinction. **mark down 1** reduce the price of. **2** make a note of. **3** reduce the examination marks of. **mark off** separate by a boundary etc. **mark time 1** *Military* march on the spot. **2** act routinely. **3** wait to advance. **mark up 1** raise the price of. **2** mark (text etc.) for typesetting or alteration. **off the mark 1** having a start. **2** (also **wide of the mark**) not accurate. **quick** (or **slow**) **off the mark** fast (or slow) to respond. **on the mark 1** accurate. **2** ready to start. **on your mark** (or **marks**) (as an instruction) get ready to start (a race).

mark² n. the former chief monetary unit of Germany.

markdown n. a reduction in price.

marked adj. **1** having a visible mark. **2** clearly noticeable. **3** designating a person watched with hostility. □ **markedly** adv.

marker n. **1** an object used to indicate a position. **2** a felt-tipped pen with a broad tip. **3** any distinguishing mark.

market ● n. **1** the gathering of people for the purchase and sale of provisions, livestock, etc. **2** a space or building used for this. **3** (often foll. by *for*) a demand for a commodity or service. **4** conditions as regards buying or selling. **5** (**the market**) the trade in a specified commodity. **6** = STOCK MARKET. ● v. (**markets, marketed, marketing**) **1** sell. **2** promote an item for sale. □ **be in the market for** wish to buy. **on the market** offered for sale. □ **marketable** adj. **marketability** n. **marketer** n.

marketeer n. a person promoting a specified type of market. □ **marketeering** n.

market garden n. a small farm growing fruit, vegetables, etc. for sale. □ **market gardener** n. **market gardening** n.

marketing n. **1** the promoting and selling of products and services. **2** in senses of MARKET v.

marketing board n. Cdn & Brit. an association of agricultural producers controlling the marketing of a specific commodity.

marketplace n. **1** an open space where a market is held. **2** the world of trade.

market price n. the current price which something fetches in the market.

market research n. the study of consumers' needs and preferences. □ **market researcher** n.

market value n. the value of something as determined by consumer demand.

marking n. (usu. in pl.) **1** an identifying mark or pattern. **2** the action of MARK¹ v.

marksman n. (pl. **marksmen**) a person skilled in shooting. □ **marksmanship** n.

markup n. **1** the amount added to the cost price of goods to cover overhead charges, profit, etc. **2** the act of increasing the price of goods. **3** a system of tagging used to identify the structure of an electronic text.

marl n. soil consisting of clay and lime.

marlin n. a large marine food fish of the swordfish family.

marmalade n. a citrus fruit jam, usu. made with oranges.

marmoset n. a small tropical American monkey with a long bushy tail. [*Say* MARMA zet]

marmot n. a burrowing rodent with a heavy-set body. [*Say* MAR mutt]

maroon¹ adj. & n. brownish crimson.

maroon² v. leave (someone) trapped in an isolated place, especially an island.

marque n. a brand of motor vehicle. [*Sounds like* MARK]

marquee n. **1** a canopy over the entrance to a large building. **2 a** a brightly lit sign at a theatre etc., listing the names of featured performers. **b** (as an adj.) famous. **3** a large tent used for social or commercial functions. [*Say* mar KEY]

marquess n. a British nobleman ranking between a duke and an earl. [*Say* MAR kwiss]

marquetry n. inlaid decorative work in wood, ivory, etc. [*Say* MARKA tree]

marquis n. (pl. **marquises**) a European nobleman ranking between a duke and a count. [*Say* mar KEY]

marquise n. **1** the wife or widow of a marquis. **2** a woman holding the rank of marquis. [*Say* mar KEEZ]

Marquis wheat n. a variety of wheat which ripens quickly. [*Say* MAR kwiss]

marram n. a coarse grass that grows on sand. [*Say* MARE um]

marriage n. **1** the legal or religious union of two people. **2** a ceremony establishing this union. **3** a combination of different elements.

marriageable *adj.* appropriate for marriage.

marriage commissioner *n. Cdn* an official who conducts civil marriages.

marriage of convenience *n.* (*pl.* **marriages of convenience**) a marriage for a financial or political purpose etc.

married ● *adj.* **1** united in marriage. **2** relating to marriage. **3** bound by very strong ties. ● *n.* a married person.

marrow *n.* **1** = BONE MARROW. **2** (also **vegetable marrow**) a large usu. white-fleshed gourd used as food.

marrow bone *n.* a bone containing edible marrow.

marry *v.* (**marries, married, marrying**) **1 a** take as one's spouse in marriage. **b** join (persons) in marriage. **2** combine successfully with something else.

Marsala *n.* a dark sweet fortified dessert wine. [*Say* mar SALA]

marsh *n.* (*pl.* **marshes**) low water-logged land. □ **marshy** *adj.*

marshal ● *n.* **1 a** a high-ranking officer in some armed forces. **b** a high-ranking officer of state. **2** a person arranging ceremonies or procedures. **3** *US* **a** a federal or municipal law officer. **b** the head of a fire department. ● *v.* (**marshals, marshalled, marshalling**) **1** draw up (armed forces) for fighting, exercise, or review. **2** arrange (people) for a procession, race, etc. **3** set (things) in methodical order; prepare.

marshland *n.* land consisting of marshes.

marshmallow *n.* a very soft, fluffy candy made of sugar, egg white, gelatin, etc.

marsh marigold *n.* a golden-flowered plant of the buttercup family.

marsupial *n.* any mammal of an order whose members are born incompletely developed and are usu. carried and suckled in a pouch on the mother's belly. [*Say* mar SOUPY ul]

mart *n.* (usu. in proper names) a store.

marten *n.* a weasel-like carnivore found in forests of Eurasia and N America.

martial *adj.* **1** of or appropriate to warfare or the military. **2** fond of fighting. [*Say* MAR shull]

martial art *n.* a fighting technique such as judo or karate.

martial law *n.* military government, involving the suspension of ordinary law.

Martian ● *adj.* of the planet Mars. ● *n.* a hypothetical inhabitant of Mars. [*Say* MAR sh'n]

martin *n.* a bird of the swallow family.

martini *n.* a cocktail made of dry vermouth and usu. gin. [*Say* mar TEENY]

martyr ● *n.* **1 a** a person who is put to death for refusing to renounce a faith or belief. **b** a person who suffers for a cause. **2** (foll. by *to*) a constant sufferer from. ● *v.* put to death as a martyr. □ **martyred** *adj.* [*Say* MAR tur]

martyrdom *n.* the sufferings or death of a martyr. [*Say* MAR tur dum]

marvel ● *n.* a wonderful person or thing ● *v.* (**marvels, marvelled, marvelling**) feel or express wonder.

marvellous *adj.* (also esp. *US* **marvelous**) **1** astonishing. **2** excellent. □ **marvellously** *adv.* **marvellousness** *n.*

Marxism *n.* the political and economic theories based on the writings of Karl Marx (1818–83). □ **Marxist** *n. & adj.*

Marxist-Leninist ● *n.* an advocate of Marxism as developed by Lenin in the Soviet Union. ● *adj.* relating to this form of Marxism.

Mary Jane *n.* **1** a flat, low-cut shoe for girls. **2** *slang* marijuana.

marzipan *n.* a paste of ground almonds, sugar, etc. [*Say* MARZA pan]

masala *n.* a spice mixture ground into a paste or powder for use in Indian cooking. [*Say* muh SALA]

mascara *n.* (*pl.* **mascaras**) a cosmetic applied to the eyelashes to make them look darker and thicker. □ **mascaraed** *adj.*

mascarpone *n.* a soft mild Italian cream cheese. [*Say* mass car PONY]

mascot *n.* **1** someone or something supposed to bring good luck to a team, school, etc. **2** a costumed figure representing a sports team.

masculine *adj.* **1** relating to men. **2** having qualities associated with men. **3** *Grammar* (of certain words or grammatical forms) treated as male. □ **masculinity** *n.*

maser *n.* a form of laser generating a beam of microwaves. [*Say* MAY zur]

mash ● *n.* **1** a soft mixture. **2** a warm grain mixture fed to horses etc. **3** a mixture of malt grains and hot water used in brewing beer. ● *v.* (**mashes, mashed, mashing**) crush or pound to a mash. □ **masher** *n.*

mask ● *n.* **1** a covering for all or part of the face, esp. for disguise or protection. **2** a respirator used to filter air or supply gas. **3** a likeness of a person's face moulded esp. in clay or wax. **4** a disguise or pretense. **5** a hollow model of a human head worn by ancient Greek and Roman actors. **6** = FACE MASK 2. ● *v.* **1** cover with a mask. **2** disguise or conceal. **3** cover (something) so as to protect it from a process, esp. painting. □ **masked** adj.

masked ball n. a ball at which masks are worn.

masking tape n. adhesive tape used in painting to cover areas on which paint is not wanted.

masochism n. the enjoyment of one's own pain or humiliation. □ **masochist** n. **masochistic** adj. **masochistically** adv. [Say MASSA kism, MASSA kist, massa KISS tick]

mason n. **1** a person who builds with stone or brick. **2 (Mason)** a Freemason.

Masonic adj. relating to Freemasons. [Say muh SONIC]

masonry n. **1 a** the work of a mason. **b** stonework or brickwork. **2 (Masonry)** Freemasonry.

masque n. a dramatic and musical entertainment esp. of the 16th and 17th centuries, originally of pantomime, later with dialogue in poetic verse. [Sounds like MASK]

masquerade ● n. **1** a false show or pretense. **2** a masked ball. ● v. **(masquerades, masqueraded, masquerading)** (often foll. by as) assume a false appearance. □ **masquerader** n. [Say maska RAID]

Mass n. (pl. **Masses**) (also **mass**) **1** the sacrament commemorating the Last Supper, esp. in the Catholic Church. **2** the words or form of service used in the Mass. **3** a musical setting of parts of this.

mass ● n. (pl. **masses**) **1** a body of matter of indefinite shape. **2** a dense aggregation of objects. **3** a large number or amount. **4** an unbroken expanse. **5 (the mass) a** the majority. **b** (in pl.) the ordinary people. **6** Physics the quantity of matter a body contains. **7** (as an adj.) relating to large numbers of people or things; large-scale. ● v. **(masses, massed, massing)** (usu. as **massed** adj.) **1** assemble into a mass. **2** Military (referring to troops) concentrate or be concentrated. □ **in the mass** collectively.

massacre ● n. **1** a general slaughter. **2** informal an utter defeat or destruction. ● v. **(massacres, massacred, massacring) 1** murder (many people) cruelly. **2** informal destroy. **3** informal perform (music etc.) very ineptly. [Say MASSA cur]

massage ● n. the action of rubbing and pressing a person's body with the hands to reduce pain in the muscles and joints. ● v. **(massages, massaged, massaging) 1** apply massage to. **2** apply (a lotion etc.) by rubbing. **3** manipulate (statistics etc.) to

give an acceptable result. **4** flatter. □ **massager** n. [Say muh SOZH]

massasauga n. (pl. **massasaugas**) (also **massasauga rattlesnake**) a small spotted venomous North American rattlesnake. [Say massa SOGGA]

masseur n. a person who provides massage professionally. [Say ma SUR]

masseuse n. a woman who provides massage professionally. [Say ma SOOSE or ma SUHZ]

massif n. a compact group of mountains. [Say ma SEEF]

massive adj. **1** large and heavy or solid. **2** very large or severe. □ **massively** adv. **massiveness** n.

mass market ● n. the market for mass-produced goods. ● adj. **(mass-market)** designed for a large segment of the population. ● v. **(mass-market, mass-markets, mass-marketed, mass-marketing)** market (a product) on a mass scale. □ **mass-marketed** adj. **mass-marketing** n.

mass media n. = MEDIA 2.

mass murder n. the killing of several people at once. □ **mass murderer** n.

mass number n. the total number of protons and neutrons in an atomic nucleus.

mass-produce v. **(mass-produces, mass-produced, mass-producing)** produce (a standardized article) in large quantities, usu. with machinery. □ **mass-produced** adj. **mass production** n.

mast n. **1** a long upright post set up on a ship's keel, esp. to support sails. **2** a post or latticework upright for supporting a radio or television antenna. **3** a flagpole. □ **-masted** comb. form

mastectomy n. (pl. **mastectomies**) the surgical removal of all or part of a breast. [Say mass TECKTA me]

master ● n. **1** a person having control of persons or things. **2** a person who has or gets the upper hand. **3** a person highly accomplished in a particular skill or art, esp. one who teaches others. **4** (also **master's degree**) a graduate degree, usu. awarded after at least one full year of study beyond the undergraduate level. **5** the original copy of a sound recording, film, data file, etc. from which a series of copies can be made. **6 (Master)** a title prefixed to the name of a boy not old enough to be called Mr. **7** (in Ontario) a judicial officer with jurisdiction over decrees given provisionally in legal actions. **8** Mechanics a machine or device directly controlling another. ● adj. **1** main, principal. **2** controlling, supreme. ● v.

1 overcome or defeat. **2** reduce to subjection and obedience. **3** acquire complete knowledge of, facility in using, or skill at. **4** rule as a master. □ **be master of** have control over.

master corporal n. (also **Master Corporal**) *Cdn* (in the Canadian Army and Air Force) a non-commissioned officer of a rank above corporal and below sergeant.

masterful adj. **1** powerful and able to control others. **2** highly skilled.
□ **masterfully** adv. **masterfulness** n.

master key n. a key that opens several locks.

masterly adj. worthy of a master.

mastermind ● n. **1** the person directing an intricate operation. **2** a person with an outstanding intellect. **●** v. plan and direct.

master of ceremonies n. a person in charge of events and introducing speakers or performers at a formal occasion etc.

masterpiece n. **1** an outstanding piece of artistry or workmanship. **2** a person's best work.

master seaman n. (also **Master Seaman**) *Cdn* (in the Canadian Navy) a non-commissioned officer of a rank above leading seaman.

master stroke n. an outstandingly skilful act of policy etc.

masterwork n. a masterpiece.

mastery n. **1** complete knowledge or command of a subject or instrument. **2** control or power.

masthead n. **1 a** the title of a newspaper etc. at the head of the front or editorial page. **b** a list of owners, staff, etc. printed in a newspaper or magazine. **2** the highest part of a ship's mast.

mastic n. **1** a gum from the bark of a Mediterranean tree, used in making varnish. **2** a waterproof, putty-like filler and sealant used in building.
[*Say* MASS tick]

masticate v. (**masticates, masticated, masticating**) chew.
□ **mastication** n. [*Say* MASTA kate]

mastiff n. a large strong dog with drooping ears. [*Say* MASS tiff]

mastodon n. a large extinct mammal resembling the elephant. [*Say* MASTA don]

mastoid ● adj. relating to the mastoid process or bone. **●** n. (also **mastoid process**) a conical prominence on the temporal bone behind the ear, to which muscles are attached.

masturbate v. (**masturbates, masturbated, masturbating**) manually stimulate the genitals for sexual arousal. □ **masturbation** n.

masturbatory adj.
[*Say* MASTER buh tory]

mat¹ ● n. **1** a small piece of carpeting or other heavy material placed on a floor. **2** a usu. thin piece of material placed on a surface to protect it. **3** a piece of padded material for landing on in gymnastics, wrestling, etc. **4** a thick tangled mass of hair, vegetation, etc. **●** v. (**mats, matted, matting**) **1** become matted. **2** cover or furnish with mats.

mat² ● n. material forming a margin around a picture in a frame. **●** v. (**mats, matted, matting**) mount (a print etc.) on a cardboard backing.

matador n. a bullfighter whose task is to kill the bull. [*Say* MATTA door]

match¹ ● n. (pl. **matches**) **1** someone or something equal to another in some quality. **2** an exact equivalent. **3** a person or thing that combines well with another. **4** a contest in which persons or teams compete against each other. **5 a** a marriage or possible marriage partner. **b** a close association of two people. **●** v. (**matches, matched, matching**) **1 a** combine well with, esp. in colour. **b** correspond; harmonize. **2** place in competition with. **3** find a match for. **4** be equal to. **5** provide something equal to **6** provide funds to equal donations from others. □ **match up** (often foll. by *with*) fit to form a coherent whole or relation. **match up to** be as good as. **meet one's match** meet someone who has as much skill, determination, etc. as oneself.

match² ● n. a short thin piece of wood, paper, etc., tipped with a composition that can be ignited by friction. □ **put a match to** set fire to.

matchbook n. a small folder containing paper matches.

matchbox n. (pl. **matchboxes**) a small box for holding matches.

matching adj. **1** that matches. **2** (of financial grants) of an amount based on the amount raised from other sources.

matchless adj. without an equal.
□ **matchlessly** adv.

matchmaker n. a person who tries to arrange marriages or relationships between other people.
□ **matchmaking** n. & adj.

match penalty n. *Hockey* = GAME MISCONDUCT.

match point n. *Tennis etc.* **1** the state of a game when one side needs only one more point to win the match. **2** this point.

matchstick ● n. the stem of a match. **●** adj. **1** very thin. **2** made of or as though of matchsticks.

matchup *n.* **1** the action of setting in opposition. **2** (esp. in sports or politics) **a** two equal persons, teams, or things. **b** a contest between such a pair.

mate¹ ● *n.* **1** (in *comb.*) a fellow member or joint occupant of. **2** a partner in marriage or a lover. **3** either of a pair of mated animals. **4** either of a pair of things. **5 a** an officer on a merchant ship subordinate to the master. **b** an assistant to an officer on board ship. **6** an assistant to a skilled worker. ● *v.* (**mates, mated, mating**) (often foll. by *with*) **1** bring or come together for breeding. **2 a** join in marriage. **b** copulate. □ **mating** *n.*

mate² *n. & v.* (**mates, mated, mating**) *Chess* checkmate.

material ● *n.* **1** the matter from which a thing is or can be made. **2** cloth. **3** (in *pl.*) items needed for doing or creating something. ● *adj.* **1** formed or consisting of matter. **2** relating to physical objects rather than the mind or spirit. **3 a** pertinent, essential. **b** serious.

materialism *n.* **1** a tendency to prefer material possessions and physical comfort to spiritual values. **2** *Philosophy* the doctrine that nothing exists but matter and its movements and modifications. □ **materialist** *n. &* **materialistic** *adj.* **materialistically** *adv.*

materiality *n.* the quality of being material or physical. [*Say* muh teery ALA tee]

materialize *v.* (**materializes, materialized, materializing**) **1** take place or come into existence. **2** appear or be present when expected. □ **materialization** *n.*

materially *adv.* **1** substantially, considerably. **2** in terms of wealth or material possessions.

matériel *n.* available means or resources, esp. in warfare. [*Say* muh teery EL]

maternal *adj.* **1** of or like a mother. **2** having the instincts of motherhood. **3** related or inherited through the mother. □ **maternally** *adv.*

maternity *n.* **1** (as an *adj.*) **a** for women during and just after childbirth. **b** designed for a pregnant woman. **2** a maternity ward or hospital. **3** motherhood.

matey *adj.* (**matier, matiest**) *informal* familiar and friendly.

math *n. informal* mathematics.

mathematician *n.* an expert in or student of mathematics. [*Say* math emma TISH in]

mathematics *n.* **1** the abstract, deductive science of number, quantity, space, and arrangement studied in its own right (**pure mathematics**), or as applied to other disciplines such as physics, engineering, etc. (**applied mathematics**). **2** (as *pl.*) the use of mathematics in calculation etc. □ **mathematical** *adj.* **mathematically** *adv.*

matinee *n.* an afternoon performance at a theatre, concert hall, etc. [*Say* mat in AY]

mat leave *n. informal* maternity leave.

matriarch *n.* **1 a** a woman who is the head of a family or tribe. **b** a woman who dominates an organization. **2** a respected elderly woman. □ **matriarchal** *adj.* [*Say* MAY tree ark, may tree ARK'll]

matriarchy *n.* (*pl.* **matriarchies**) **1** a form of social organization in which the mother is the head of the family and descent is reckoned through the female line. **2** government by a woman or women. [*Say* MAY tree arky]

matriculate *v.* (**matriculates, matriculated, matriculating**) enrol or be enrolled at a college or university. □ **matriculation** *n.* [*Say* muh TRICK yoo late]

matrilineal *adj.* relating to kinship with the female line. □ **matrilineally** *adv.* [*Say* matra LINNY ul]

matrimony *n.* marriage. □ **matrimonial** *adj.* [*Say* MATRA moany, matra MOANY ul]

matrix *n.* (*pl.* **matrices** or **matrixes**) **1** an environment or substance in which a thing is developed. **2** a mould in which a thing is cast or shaped. **3** the rock material in which a gem, fossil, etc. is embedded. **4** *Math* an array of symbols, elements, etc. in rows and columns that is treated as a single element. **5** *Computing* a grid-like array of interconnected circuit elements. [*Say* MAY trix *for the singular,* MAY truh seez *or* MAY trixes *for the plural*]

matron *n.* **1** a middle-aged or elderly married woman. **2** a female prison officer. [*Say* MAY trun]

matronly *adj.* like a matron, esp. as regards being stuffy or portly. [*Say* MAY trun lee]

matron of honour *n.* a married woman attending the bride at a wedding.

Matsqui *n.* (*pl.* **Matsqui**) a member of a Salishan Aboriginal people living in the Lower Fraser valley of BC. [*Say* MAT skwee]

matte (also esp. *Brit.* **matt**) ● *adj.* **1** dull, without lustre. **2** having a flat, not glossy, finish. ● *n.* paint formulated to give a dull flat finish. [*Say* MAT]

matted *adj.* **1** (of hair etc.) tangled and interlaced. **2** covered with a dense growth.

matter ● *n.* **1** a physical substance in general, as distinct from mind and spirit.

b that which has mass and occupies space. **2** a topic under consideration. **3** (**the matter**) the reason for a problem. **4** written or printed material. ● *v.* be important. □ **as a matter of course** as a regular habit. **for that matter 1** as far as that is concerned. **2** and indeed also. **a matter of 1** approximately. **2** a thing that relates to.

matter-of-fact *adj.* **1** not imaginative. **2** not emotional. **3** pertaining to actual fact as distinct from speculation. □ **as a matter of fact** actually. □ **matter-of-factly** *adv.* **matter-of-factness** *n.*

matting *n.* **1** fabric of hemp, grass, etc., for mats. **2** *in senses of* MAT¹, ² *v.*

mattock *n.* an agricultural tool shaped like a pickaxe. [*Say* MAT uck]

mattress *n.* (*pl.* **mattresses**) a large fabric case stuffed with soft, firm, or springy material, used on or as a bed.

maturation *n.* **1** the action or process of maturing. **2** the state of being matured. [*Say* match oo RAY sh'n]

mature ● *adj.* (**maturer**, **maturest**) **1 a** fully developed. **b** sensible, wise. **c** middle-aged or elderly. **2** ripe, ready for consumption. **3** careful and thorough. **4** (of a bond etc.) due for payment. ● *v.* (**matures**, **matured**, **maturing**) **1** bring to or reach a mature state. **2** perfect (a plan etc.). **3** (of a bond etc.) become due for payment. □ **maturely** *adv.* **maturity** *n.*

matzo *n.* (also **matzoh**, **matzah**) (*pl.* **matzos**, **matzohs**, **matzahs** or **matzoth**) a flat, crisp, unleavened bread for the Passover. [*Say* MOTT so *or* MOTT suh *for the singular*, MOTT soze *or* MOTT sawth *for the plural*]

maudlin *adj.* **1** sentimental, esp. insincerely. **2** full of self-pity, especially when drunk. [*Say* MOD lin]

maul *v.* **1** tear and mutilate. **2** handle roughly; damage. **3** subject to damaging criticism. □ **mauling** *n.* [*Sounds like* MALL]

maunder *v.* talk in a rambling manner. [*Say* MAWN dur]

Maundy Thursday *n.* the Thursday before Easter, observed in the Christian Church as a commemoration of the Last Supper. [*Say* MAWN dee]

mausoleum *n.* **1** a large and grand tomb. **2** a building in which are entombed the bodies or remains of several people, often of one family. **3** a very large and sombre building. [*Say* mozza LEE um]

mauve pale purple. □ **mauvish** *adj.* [*Rhymes with* COVE]

maven *n.* *informal* an expert or connoisseur. [*Say* MAY v'n]

maverick *n.* **1** an independent-minded or unorthodox person. **2** a calf or yearling that has not been branded. [*Say* MAV rick]

maw *n.* the jaws or throat.

mawkish *adj.* excessively sentimental. □ **mawkishly** *adv.* **mawkishness** *n.*

max *slang* ● *n.* (a) maximum. ● *adj.* maximal. ● *adv.* at most. ● *v.* (**maxes**, **maxed**, **maxing**) (foll. by *out*) **1** attain a maximum in something. **2** spend to the limit of. □ **to the max 1** completely. **2** to the furthest possible extreme.

maxi *n.* (*pl.* **maxis**) *informal* **1** a long coat or skirt. **2** a maxi-pad.

maxi- *comb. form* very large or long.

maxilla *n.* (*pl.* **maxillae**) **1** the upper jaw or jawbone. **2** the mouthpart of many arthropods used in chewing. □ **maxillary** *adj.* [*Say* mac SILLA *for the singular*, mac SILLY *for the plural*; mac SILLA ree]

maxim *n.* a general truth or rule of conduct.

maximize *v.* (**maximizes**, **maximized**, **maximizing**) increase or enhance to the utmost. □ **maximization** *n.* **maximizer** *n.*

maximum ● *n.* (*pl.* **maximums** or **maxima**) the highest amount or magnitude. ● *adj.* greatest in amount or magnitude. □ **maximal** *adj.* **maximally** *adv.*

maxi-pad *n.* a sanitary pad for heavy menstrual flow.

May *n.* **1** the fifth month. **2** (**may**) the hawthorn or its blossom.

may *aux. v.* (*3rd singular present* **may**; *past* **might**) expressing: **1** (often foll. by *well* for emphasis) possibility or uncertainty. **2** permission. **3** a wish. **4** uncertainty or irony. **5** purpose. □ **be that as it may** (or **that is as may be**) despite that possibility.

Maya *n.* (*pl.* **Maya** or **Mayas**) a member or the language of an Indian people of Central America. □ **Maya** *adj.* **Mayan** *n.* & *adj.* [*Say* MY uh]

maya *n.* *Hindu Philosophy* the supernatural power wielded by gods and demons. [*Say* MY uh]

maybe ● *adv.* perhaps, possibly. ● *n.* (*pl.* **maybes**) an uncertainty.

May Day *n.* 1 May esp. as a festival or a holiday in honour of workers.

mayday *n.* an international radio distress signal used esp. by ships and aircraft.

mayflower *n.* a flower that blooms in May.

mayfly *n.* (*pl.* **mayflies**) a slender aquatic insect which lives briefly.

mayhem *n.* violent or damaging action.

mayn't *contr.* may not.

mayonnaise *n.* (also *informal* **mayo**) a thick creamy dressing made of egg yolks, oil, vinegar, etc.

mayor *n.* the head of a municipal corporation. □ **mayoral** *adj.*

mayoralty *n.* (*pl.* **mayoralties**) **1** the office of mayor. **2** a mayor's period of office. [*Say* MAY ur ul tee]

maypole *n.* a tall pole painted and decked with flowers and ribbons, for dancing around on May Day.

May Two-Four *n. Cdn informal* Victoria Day.

maze *n.* **1 a** a complex network of paths and passages through which one has to find a way. **b** such a pattern, represented on paper. **2** any complex system.

mazel tov *interj.* good luck, congratulations. [*Say* MOZZLE tov *or* MOZZLE toff]

mazurka *n.* **1** a usu. lively Polish dance. **2** a piece of music for this. [*Say* muh ZURKA]

MB *abbr.* **1** (also **Mb**) *Computing* megabyte. **2** Manitoba (in official postal use).

M.B.A. ● *abbr.* Master of Business Administration. ● *n.* (*pl.* **M.B.A.'s**) a person who holds this degree.

MC ● *n.* (*pl.* **MC's**) a master of ceremonies. ● *v.* (**MC's**, **MC'd**, **MC'ing**) act as master of ceremonies for.

McCoy *n. informal* □ **the real McCoy** the real thing.

McIntosh *n.* (*pl.* **McIntoshes**) a medium-sized, deep red apple with green blotches.

MD *abbr.* (*pl.* **MDs**) Doctor of Medicine.

MDA *abbr.* methylenedioxyamphetamine, a synthetic hallucinogenic drug.

MDMA *abbr.* methylenedioxymeth-amphetamine, a drug that causes euphoria and hallucinations.

MDT *abbr.* Mountain Daylight Time.

me¹ ● *pron.* **1** objective case of I². **2** *informal* myself, to or for myself. **3** *informal* used in exclamations. ● *n.* one's personality, the ego.

me² *n.* = MI.

mea culpa ● *n.* (*pl.* **mea culpas**) an acknowledgement of fault or error. ● *interj.* expressing such an acknowledgement. [*Say* may a KOOL puh *or* may a CULL puh (KOOL *rhymes with* WOOL)]

mead *n.* an alcoholic drink of fermented honey and water.

meadow *n.* a piece of grassland.

meadowland *n.* land used for the cultivation of grass for hay.

meadowlark *n.* a N American songbird related to the blackbirds.

meagre *adj.* (also **meager**) small in quantity and poor in quality. □ **meagrely** *adv.* **meagreness** *n.* [*Say* MEE gur]

meal¹ *n.* **1** an occasion when food is eaten. **2** the food eaten on one occasion. □ **make a meal of** consume as a meal.

meal² *n.* **1** any grain or pulse ground to powder. **2** any powdery substance made by grinding.

meal ticket *n.* **1** a ticket entitling one to a meal. **2** *informal* a person or thing that is a source of food or income.

mealtime *n.* a usual time of eating.

mealy *adj.* (**mealier, mealiest**) **1** soft and powdery like meal. **2** containing meal.

mealy bug *n.* a small insect whose body is covered with white powder, and which infests vines etc.

mealy-mouthed *adj.* not willing to speak directly.

mean¹ *v.* (**means, meant, meaning**) **1** intend to express or refer to. **2** (of a word) have as its explanation or its equivalent in another language. **3** intend. **4** have as a consequence. **5** be of specified importance. □ **mean it** not be joking. **mean to say** really admit. **mean well** (often foll. by *by*) have good intentions.

mean² *adj.* **1** uncooperative, unkind, or unfair. **2** not generous. **3** malicious, vicious. **4** characterized by poverty. **5** inferior, poor. **6** *informal* **a** (of a person) skilful, formidable. **b** impressive. □ **no mean** a very good. □ **meanly** *adv.* **meanness** *n.*

mean³ ● *n.* **1** something in the middle of two extremes. **2** *Math* the average value of a set of quantities. ● *adj.* **1** equally far from two extremes. **2** calculated as a mean.

meander ● *v.* **1** wander at random. **2** wind about. ● *n.* (often in *pl.*) a curve in a winding river. □ **meandering** *adj. & n.* [*Say* mee ANDER]

meaning ● *n.* **1** what is meant by a word, action, idea, etc. **2** significance. **3** sense of purpose. ● *adj.* expressive, significant. □ **meaningless** *adj.* **meaninglessly** *adv.* **meaninglessness** *n.*

meaningful *adj.* **1** significant. **2** able to be interpreted. **3** intended to communicate something indirectly. □ **meaningfully** *adv.*

means *pl. n.* **1** (often treated as *sing.*) an action, object, etc. by which a result is brought about. **2** money resources. □ **by all means** certainly. **by any means** in any way. **by means of** by the use or action of. **by no means** certainly not.

mean-spirited *adj.* petty; selfish. □ **mean-spiritedness** *n.*

means test ● *n.* an official inquiry to

establish need before financial assistance from public funds is given. ● *v.* (**means-test**) assess by or subject to a means test.

meant *past and past participle of* MEAN[1].

meantime ● *n.* the intervening period.
● *adv.* = MEANWHILE.

meanwhile ● *adv.* **1** in the intervening period of time. **2** at the same time. ● *n.* the intervening period.

measles *pl. n.* (also treated as *sing.*) an acute infectious viral disease marked by red spots on the skin.

measly *adj.* (**measlier, measliest**) **1** *informal* ridiculously small. **2** *informal* inferior.

measurable *adj.* **1** that can be measured. **2** noticeable. □ **measurably** *adv.*

measure ● *n.* **1** a size or quantity found by measuring. **2** a tape, vessel, etc. used for measuring. **3 a** the degree, extent, or amount of a thing. **b** (foll. by *of*) some degree of. **4** a unit of capacity. **5** a factor by which something is evaluated. **6** suitable action to achieve some end. **7** a legislative enactment. **8** a bar of music. ● *v.* (**measures, measured, measuring**) **1** ascertain the extent or quantity of, by comparing with a standard. **2** be of a specified size. **3** estimate by some standard or rule. **4** mark (a given length). **5** (foll. by *out*) distribute in measured quantities. □ **beyond measure** very greatly. **for good measure** as a finishing touch. **have** (or **get**) **the measure of** have an accurate opinion of. **measure up 1** determine the size etc. of. **2** (often foll. by *to*) have the necessary qualifications (for).

measured *adj.* **1** ascertained by measurement. **2** rhythmical. **3** carefully considered.

measureless *adj.* infinite.

measurement *n.* **1** the action of measuring something. **2** a size, quantity, or extent determined by measuring. **3** (in *pl.*) detailed dimensions. **4** a system of measuring or of measures.

meat *n.* **1** the flesh of animals as food. **2** the essence of. **3** the edible part of fruits, nuts, eggs, shellfish, etc. □ **meatless** *adj.*

meat and potatoes ● *n.* basics. ● *adj.* (**meat-and-potatoes**) fundamental.

meatball *n.* minced meat compressed into a small round ball.

meathead *n.* a stupid person.

meathook *n.* a hook on which to hang meat carcasses etc.

meat loaf *n.* a baked dish of ground meat mixed with onion, bread crumbs, etc.

meat market *n.* **1** a butcher's shop.

2 *slang* a bar etc. where people seek to meet others for sexual encounters.

meat packing *n.* the business of processing, packing, and distributing meat. □ **meat packer** *n.*

meaty *adj.* (**meatier, meatiest**) **1** full of meat. **2** of or like meat. **3** full of substance. □ **meatiness** *n.*

mecca *n.* (*pl.* **meccas**) (also **Mecca**) a place which attracts people of a particular group.

mechanic *n.* a skilled worker who makes or uses or repairs machinery.

mechanical ● *adj.* **1** relating to machines or mechanisms. **2** working by machinery. **3** automatic; lacking originality. **4** of or relating to mechanics as a science. ● *n.* (in *pl.*) the working parts of a machine. □ **mechanically** *adv.*

mechanical engineering *n.* the branch of engineering that deals with the design, construction, and maintenance of machines. □ **mechanical engineer** *n.*

mechanics *pl. n.* **1** (treated as *sing.*) the branch of applied mathematics dealing with motion and tendencies to motion. **2** (treated as *sing.*) the science of machinery. **3** (usu. treated as *pl.*) the construction, workings, and practicalities of a thing.

mechanism *n.* **1** a piece of machinery. **2** a mode of operation; a means.

mechanize *v.* (**mechanizes, mechanized, mechanizing**) **1** make mechanical. **2** introduce machines or machinery in or into. **3** *Military* equip with tanks, armoured cars, etc. □ **mechanization** *n.*

M.Ed. *abbr.* Master of Education.

med *informal* ● *adj.* medical. ● *n.* (usu. in *pl.*) medication.

medal ● *n.* **1** a disc of metal with an inscription etc. to commemorate an event or to reward achievement. **2** (as an *adj.*) designating a competition that will determine medal winners. ● *v.* (**medals, medalled, medalling**) (usu. in *passive*) honour with or receive a medal.
□ **medalled** *adj.*

medallion *n.* **1** a large medal. **2** a small oval cut of meat or fish.
[*Say* muh DAL yun]

medallist *n.* (also esp. *US* **medalist**) **1** a recipient of a (specified) medal. **2** an engraver or designer of medals.

meddle *v.* (**meddles, meddled, meddling**) (often foll. by *with, in*) interfere unduly with others' concerns.
□ **meddler** *n.*

meddlesome *adj.* fond of meddling.

medevac ● *n.* the transportation of sick

or wounded patients by air to hospital. ● *v.* (**medevacs, medevacked, medevacking**) transport by medevac. [*Say* MEDDA vac]

media *pl. n.* **1** *pl. of* MEDIUM. **2** (usu. preceded by *the*; treated as *pl.* or *sing.*) the main means of mass communication regarded collectively.

mediaeval *esp. Brit.* = MEDIEVAL. [*Say* med EVIL]

median ● *adj.* **1** situated in the middle. **2** *Anatomy, Botany, & Zoology* pertaining to the plane which divides something into symmetrical halves. ● *n.* **1** *Math* the middle value of a series of values arranged in order of size. **2** (also **median strip**) a strip of ground or a physical barrier dividing a street or highway. **3** *Math* a straight line drawn from any vertex of a triangle to the middle of the opposite side. [*Say* MEEDY un]

mediate *v.* (**mediates, mediated, mediating**) intervene to produce agreement. □ **mediation** *n.* **mediator** *n.* [*Say* MEEDY ate, meedy AY sh'n, MEEDY ate ur]

medic *n. informal* a doctor or medical student.

Medicaid *n. US* a federal and state system of health insurance for those requiring financial assistance. [*Say* MEDDA kade]

medical ● *adj.* **1** relating to the science and practice of medicine. **2** relating to one's health. ● *n. informal* a medical examination. □ **medically** *adv.*

medical doctor *n.* a physician.

medicalize *v.* (**medicalizes, medicalized, medicalizing**) involve medicine in; view in medical terms. □ **medicalization** *n.*

medical officer *n.* a doctor appointed by a company or public authority to attend to health matters.

medical officer of health *n.* a person in charge of a public health department.

medical practitioner *n.* a physician or surgeon.

medicare *n.* **1** (in Canada) a national health care program administered by the provinces and territories. **2** (**Medicare**) (in the US) a federal system of health insurance for persons over 65 years of age.

medicate *v.* (**medicates, medicated, medicating**) **1** administer medication to. **2** add a medicinal substance to.

medication *n.* **1** a medicine or drug. **2** treatment using drugs.

medicinal ● *adj.* **1** having healing properties. **2** resembling medicine. ● *n.* a

medicinal substance. □ **medicinally** *adv.* [*Say* muh DISSA null]

medicine *n.* **1** the science or practice of the treatment and prevention of disease. **2** a substance taken esp. by mouth to treat or prevent disease. **3** (as an *adj.*) (in Aboriginal societies) used to designate healing power in physical objects, rites, etc. □ **a taste** (or **dose**) **of one's own medicine** treatment such as one is accustomed to giving others. **take one's medicine** submit to something disagreeable.

medicine ball *n.* a large heavy ball used for exercise.

medicine bundle *n.* a collection of objects with sacred and personal power for the owner, used by Plains Aboriginal peoples.

medicine cabinet *n.* (also **medicine chest**) a small cupboard containing medicines etc.

medicine man *n.* a person believed to have magical powers of healing.

medicine wheel *n.* a wheel-shaped arrangement of stones at which acts of ritual and meditation may be performed.

medieval *adj.* **1** relating to the Middle Ages. **2** *informal* old-fashioned. □ **medievalist** *n.* [*Say* med EVIL *or* meddy EVIL]

medina *n.* (*pl.* **medinas**) the old quarter of a northern African town. [*Say* muh DEENA]

mediocre *adj.* **1** of middling quality. **2** second-rate. [*Say* meedy OAKER]

mediocrity *n.* (*pl.* **mediocrities**) **1** the state of being mediocre. **2** a mediocre person or thing. [*Say* meedy OCKRA tee]

meditate *v.* (**meditates, meditated, meditating**) **1 a** exercise the mind in (esp. religious) contemplation. **b** focus on a subject in this manner. **2** plan mentally. □ **meditation** *n.* **meditator** *n.*

meditative *adj.* **1** inclined to meditate. **2** indicative of meditation. □ **meditatively** *adv.* [*Say* MEDDA tay tiv]

Mediterranean ● *n.* **1** (**the Mediterranean**) **a** the Mediterranean Sea. **b** the countries bordering on this. **2** a native of a country bordering on the Mediterranean Sea. ● *adj.* **1** relating to the Mediterranean or nearby inhabitants. **2** (of climate) characterized by hot dry summers and warm wet winters. [*Say* medda tuh RAINY un]

medium ● *n.* (*pl.* **media** or **mediums**) **1** the middle quality, degree, etc. between extremes. **2** the means by which something is communicated. **3** the physical environment of a living organism. **4** an agency or means. **5** the material or form used by an artist etc. **6** (*pl.* **mediums**) a person claiming to be in contact with the spirits of the dead. ● *adj.* **1** between two qualities, degrees, etc. **2** average; moderate.

medium of exchange *n.* (*pl.* **mediums of exchange**) a standard item exchanged in commercial transactions, e.g. money.

medium-sized *adj.* of average size.

medley *n.* (*pl.* **medleys**) **1** a varied mixture. **2** various musical items arranged as a continuous whole.

medulla *n.* **1** the inner region of certain organs or tissues. **2** (also **medulla oblongata**) the continuation of the spinal cord within the skull, forming the lowest part of the brain stem. **3** the soft internal tissue of plants.
[*Say* muh DULLA (oblong GATTA)]

medusa *n.* (*pl.* **medusae**) a free-swimming aquatic invertebrate with stinging tentacles and a jellylike body, e.g. a jellyfish. [*Say* muh DOO suh *for the singular*, muh DOO see *for the plural*]

meek *adj.* **1** humble and submissive. **2** piously gentle. □ **meekly** *adv.* **meekness** *n.*

meet[1] ● *v.* (**meets, met, meeting**) **1** come together with at the same place and time. **2** be introduced to. **3** come into contact with. **4** encounter. **5** satisfy. ● *n.* the assembly of sporting competitors. □ **meet the eye** (or **the ear**) be visible (or audible). **meet a person halfway** make a compromise. **meet up** (often foll. by *with*) *informal* meet or make contact. **more (to it) than meets the eye** hidden qualities or complications.

meet[2] *adj. archaic* suitable, proper.

meeting *n.* **1** in senses of MEET[1]. **2** an assembly of people for discussion etc. **3** an assembly (esp. of Quakers) for worship. **4** the persons assembled.

meeting house *n.* a place of worship for Quakers.

meg *n. slang* megabyte(s).

mega *slang* ● *adj.* of enormous size etc. ● *adv.* extremely.

mega- *comb. form* **1** large. **2** denoting a factor of one million (10^6) in the metric system of measurement. **3** to a great degree.

megabit *n.* 1,048,576 (i.e. 2^{20}) bits as a measure of data capacity, or loosely 1,000,000 bits.

megabuck *n. informal* **1** a million dollars. **2** (in *pl.*) a huge sum of money.

megabyte *n.* 1,048,576 (i.e. 2^{20}) bytes as a measure of data capacity, or loosely 1,000,000 bytes.

megacity *n.* (*pl.* **megacities**) a very large city, often combining separate cities into one metropolitan area.

megadose *n.* a very large dose.
[*Say* MEGA dose]

megahertz *n.* (*pl.* **megahertz**) one million hertz, esp. as a measure of frequency of radio transmissions.

megahit *n.* a highly successful enterprise etc. [*Say* MEGA hit]

megalithic *adj. Archaeology* relating to large stones. [*Say* mega LITH ick]

megalomania *n.* **1** lust for power. **2** a mental disorder producing an exaggerated belief in one's own power.
□ **megalomaniac** *adj. & n.* **megalomaniacal** *adj.*
[*Say* mega loh MANIA, mega loh MANIAC, mega loh muh NYE a cull]

megalopolis *n.* (*pl.* **megalopolises**) a very large city or urban region.
[*Say* mega LOPPA liss]

megaphone *n.* a large funnel-shaped device for amplifying the sound of the voice.

megaproject *n.* a large-scale, costly construction or engineering project.

megastar *n.* a very famous person.
[*Say* MEGA star]

megaton *n.* a unit of explosive power equal to one million tons of TNT.
□ **megatonnage** *n.* [*Say* MEGA tun]

megavolt *n.* one million volts.

megawatt *n.* one million watts.

meiosis *n.* (*pl.* **meioses**) a type of cell division that results in daughter cells with half the chromosome number of the parent cell. □ **meiotic** *adj.* [*Say* my OH sis *for the singular*, my OH seez *for the plural*; my OTT ick]

-meister *comb. form* often *jocular* a person skilled in a specified thing.

melamine *n.* a hard plastic material.
[*Say* MELLA mean]

melancholia *n.* **1** a mental illness marked by depression and ill-founded fears. **2** = MELANCHOLY *n.* 1. □ **melancholic** *adj. & n.* **melancholically** *adv.*
[*Say* melon COALY uh, melon CAWL ick]

melancholy ● *n.* (*pl.* **melancholies**) **1 a** a pensive sadness. **b** a tendency to this. **2** *hist.* one of the four humours once thought to determine a person's qualities. ● *adj.* sad, depressing. [*Say* MELON cawly]

Melanesian *n.* a person from or the language of Melanesia, a region of the western Pacific. □ **Melanesian** *adj.*
[*Say* mella NEE zhun]

mélange *n.* a mixture.
[*Say* may LAWNZH]

melanin *n.* a dark pigment in the hair and skin, responsible for the tanning of skin when exposed to sunlight. [*Say* MELLA nin]

melanoma *n.* (*pl.* **melanomas**) a usu. malignant tumour of melanin-forming cells, usu. in the skin. [*Say* mella NOMA]

melatonin *n.* a substance formed in the pineal gland of various mammals, which inhibits melanin formation. [*Say* mella TOF nin]

Melba toast *n.* very thin crisp toast.

meld ● *v.* merge, blend. ● *n.* a thing formed by merging or blending.

melee *n.* **1** a confused fight. **2** a confused mass of people. [*Say* MAY lay *or* MEL ay *or* mel AY]

mellifluous *adj.* pleasing, musical. [*Say* muh LIFF loo us]

mellow ● *adj.* **1** soft and rich. **2** matured. **3** good-humoured, relaxed. **4** *informal* partly intoxicated. **5** juicy with ripeness. ● *v.* **1** make or become mellow. **2** *informal* relax, become less intense. ▢ **mellowness** *n.*

melodic *adj.* relating to melody. ▢ **melodically** *adv.* [*Say* muh LOD ick]

melodious *adj.* **1** of, producing, or having melody. **2** sweet-sounding. ▢ **melodiously** *adv.* **melodiousness** *n.* [*Say* muh LODEY us]

melodrama *n.* (*pl.* **melodramas**) **1** a sensational or sentimental dramatic piece. **2** exaggerated behaviour. ▢ **melodramatic** *adj.* **melodramatics** *pl. n.* [*Say* MELLOW drama, mellow DRAMATIC]

melody *n.* (*pl.* **melodies**) **1** an arrangement of single notes in a musically expressive succession. **2** the principal part in harmonized music. **3** a song. **4** sweet music.

melon *n.* the sweet fruit of various gourds.

melt ● *v.* **1** make or become liquid by heat. **2** soften; liquefy. **3 a** soften or be softened by pity, love, etc. **b** dissolve into tears. **4** change or merge imperceptibly. **5** (foll. by *away*) leave or disappear. ● *n.* **1** an act or period of melting. **2** a sandwich etc. having melted cheese on top. ▢ **melt away** disappear or make disappear by or as if by liquefaction. **melt down** melt in order to reuse the raw material. ▢ **melter** *n.* **melting** *adj.* **meltingly** *adv.*

meltdown *n.* **1** the melting of a structure, esp. the overheated core of a nuclear reactor. **2** any uncontrolled, disastrous transformation.

melting point *n.* the temperature at which any given solid will melt.

melting pot *n.* a place where different peoples, cultures, ideas, etc. mix together.

melt-in-the-mouth *adj.* (also **melt-in-your-mouth**) (of food) delicious.

meltwater *n.* water formed by the melting of snow and ice.

member *n.* **1** a person or organization belonging to a group. **2** a part of a complex structure. **3 a** any part or organ of the body. **b** the penis.

membership *n.* **1** the state of being a member. **2** the number of members. **3** the body of members collectively.

membrane *n.* **1** any pliable sheet-like structure acting as a boundary, lining, or partition in an organism. **2** a thin pliable sheet or skin. ▢ **membranous** *adj.* [*Say* MEM brain, MEM brun us]

memento *n.* (*pl.* **mementoes** or **mementos**) an object kept as a reminder or souvenir. [*Say* muh MENTOE]

memo *n.* (*pl.* **memos**) a memorandum.

memoir *n.* **1** (in *pl.*) a written account of one's memory of certain events or people. **2** a historical account or biography written from personal knowledge. ▢ **memoirist** *n.* [*Say* MEM warr, MEM warr ist (WARR *rhymes with* FAR)]

memorabilia *pl. n.* souvenirs of memorable events, people, periods, etc. [*Say* memmer a BEEL yuh]

memorable *adj.* **1** worth remembering. **2** easily remembered. ▢ **memorably** *adv.* [*Say* MEMMER a bull]

memorandum *n.* (*pl.* **memoranda**) **1 a** a written note. **b** an informal diplomatic message. **2** a record made for future use. **3** *Law* a document summarizing the terms of a contract etc. [*Say* memma RANDOM *for the singular,* memma RANDA *for the plural*]

memorial ● *n.* an object or institution, or custom established in memory of a person or event. ● *adj.* intending to commemorate a person or thing.

Memorial Cup *n.* a trophy awarded annually to the Canadian major junior amateur hockey champions.

memorialize *v.* (**memorializes, memorialized, memorializing**) produce something that will preserve the memory of a person or thing.

memorial service *n.* a service of commemoration of the dead, usu. without the body or bodies being present.

memorize *v.* (**memorizes, memorized, memorizing**) commit to memory, learn by heart. ▢ **memorization** *n.* **memorizing** *n.*

memory *n.* (*pl.* **memories**) **1 a** the faculty

by which things are recalled to or kept in the mind. **b** an individual's capacity to remember things. **2** one's store of things remembered. **3** a recollection. **4** the capacity of or a device in a computer etc. to store data etc. for retrieval. **5** the remembrance of a person or thing. **6** the reputation of a dead person. **7** the capacity of a substance etc. for manifesting effects of its previous state.

memory bank n. **1** the memory device of a computer etc. **2** informal the store of memories of an individual or group.

memory card n. a memory chip housed in a plastic case which plugs into a computer.

memory chip n. Computing a semiconductor chip made as a memory, e.g. a ROM or a RAM, containing many separately addressable locations.

men pl. of MAN.

menace ● n. **1** a dangerous thing or person. **2** jocular a pest. ● v. threaten. □ **menacing** adj. **menacingly** adv. [Say MEN iss]

ménage n. a family or group living together as a household. [Say may NAZH]

ménage à trois n. (pl. **ménages à trois**) a sexual relationship involving three people, esp. in one household. [Say may nazh a TRWAH]

menagerie n. a collection of wild animals in captivity for exhibition etc. [Say muh NAZH a ree]

mend ● v. **1** restore to a sound condition; repair. **2** regain health. **3** put right. ● n. a darn or repair in material etc. □ **mend (one's) fences** make peace with a person. **mend one's ways** reform. **on the mend** improving.

mendacious adj. untruthful; false. □ **mendaciously** adv. **mendacity** n. [Say men DAY shuss, men DASSA tee]

mendelevium n. an artificially made radioactive metallic element. [Say menda LEEVY um]

mendicant ● adj. **1** begging. **2** (of a religious order, e.g. the Franciscans) originally dependent on charitable contributions. ● n. **1** a beggar. **2** a mendicant friar. [Say MENDA k'nt]

menfolk pl. n. informal **1** men in general. **2** the men of one's family.

menial ● adj. (of work) not requiring much skill and usu. low-paying. ● n. a domestic servant. [Say MEENY ul]

meninges pl. n. the three membranes that line the skull and vertebral canal and enclose the brain and spinal cord. [Say men IN jeez]

meningitis n. an inflammation of the meninges of the brain or spinal cord due to infection by viruses or bacteria. [Say men in JITE us]

meningococcus n. a bacterium involved in some forms of meningitis and cerebrospinal infection. □ **meningococcal** adj. [Say men inga COCKUS, men inga COCKLE]

meniscus n. (pl. **menisci**) **1** the curved upper surface of a liquid in a tube etc. **2** a lens that is convex on one side and concave on the other. **3** a thin fibrous cartilage between the surfaces of some joints, e.g. the knee. [Say muh NISK us for the singular, muh NISK eye for the plural]

Mennonite n. a member of a Protestant denomination originating in Friesland in the 16th century. □ **Mennonite** adj. **Mennonitism** n. [Say MENNA nite]

menopause n. **1** the final cessation of menstruation. **2** the period in a woman's life, usu. around the age of 50, when this occurs. □ **menopausal** adj. [Say MENNA pause, menna PAUSE ul]

menorah n. Judaism a large candelabra used in Jewish worship. [Say men ORE uh]

mensch n. informal an admirable or honourable person.

menservants pl. of MANSERVANT.

menses pl. n. **1** blood etc. discharged from the uterus at menstruation. **2** the time of menstruation. [Say MEN seez]

Menshevik n. a member of a minority faction of the Russian Socialist Party, defeated by the Bolsheviks. [Say MEN shuh vick]

men's room n. (also **men's**) a public washroom for men.

menstrual adj. of or relating to the menses or menstruation. [Say MEN strull or MEN stroo ul]

menstrual cycle n. the process of ovulation and menstruation in sexually mature women and female primates.

menstruate v. (**menstruates**, **menstruated**, **menstruating**) undergo menstruation. [Say MEN strait]

menstruation n. the process of discharging blood and mucosal tissue etc. from the uterus through the vagina that occurs in sexually mature, non-pregnant women, normally at intervals of about four weeks, until menopause. [Say men STRAY sh'n]

menswear n. clothes for men.

-ment suffix **1** forming nouns expressing the means, product, or result of the action of a verb. **2** forming nouns from adjectives.

mental adj. **1** relating to the mind. **2** informal crazy. **3** designating a medical establishment for the treatment of the mentally ill. □ **mentally** adv.

mental block n. a sudden and temporary inability to continue a thought process or mental link, esp. due to subconscious emotional factors.

mental handicap n. the condition in which a person's intellectual capacities are underdeveloped and inhibit normal social functioning. □ **mentally handicapped** adj.

mentality n. (pl. **mentalities**) **1** mental character or disposition. **2** outlook. [Say men TALA tee]

mental note n. a fixing of something in one's mind.

mental retardation n. a developmental disorder in which a person has impaired learning ability and a lower than normal IQ. □ **mentally retarded** adj.

menthol n. a mint-tasting organic alcohol found in oil of peppermint etc. [Say MENTH awl]

mentholated adj. treated with or containing menthol. [Say MENTHA late id]

mention ● v. **1** refer to or remark on incidentally. **2** specify. **3** reveal or disclose. **4** award a minor honour to. ● n. **1** an incidental reference. **2** (in dispatches) a military honour. □ **don't mention it** said in polite dismissal of an apology or thanks. **not to mention** introducing another important fact. □ **mentionable** adj. & n.

mentor ● n. an adviser or guide. ● v. act as a mentor to. □ **mentoring** n. & adj. **mentorship** n. [Say MEN tore]

menu n. **1 a** a list of dishes to be served at a meal, available in a restaurant, etc. **b** the food served. **2** a list of options displayed on a television or computer screen.

menu bar n. a graphical bar in which the primary menus and options for a software program are accessed or displayed.

menu-driven adj. used by making selections from menus.

meow ● n. a characteristic sound made by a domestic cat. ● v. make this sound.

Mephistophelian adj. like a devil, fiendish. [Say muh fista FEELY un]

mercantile adj. relating to trade or commerce. [Say MURK'n tile]

mercantilism n. hist. the economic theory that trade generates wealth and that exports should be promoted, imports restricted, and precious metals accumulated. □ **mercantilist** n. [Say mur CANTA lism]

mercenary ● adj. primarily concerned with money or other material reward. ● n. (pl. **mercenaries**) a professional soldier serving a foreign power for money. [Say MURSE a nerry]

merchandise ● n. goods to be bought and sold. ● v. (**merchandises, merchandised, merchandising**) **1** put on the market. **2** advertise, publicize. □ **merchandiser** n. **merchandising** n. & adj. [Say MURCH'n dice or MURCH'n dize for the noun, MURCH'n dize for the verb]

merchant ● n. **1** a person whose occupation is the purchase and sale of goods for profit. **2** a trader. **3** informal a person showing a liking for a specified practice. ● adj. **1** relating to trade or commerce. **2** (of a ship etc.) involved in the transport of merchandise.

merchant bank n. esp. Brit. an investment bank. □ **merchant banker** n. **merchant banking** n.

merchant marine n. (also **merchant navy**) a fleet of ships used in trade; a nation's commercial shipping. □ **merchant mariner** n.

merchant ship n. a ship conveying merchandise.

merciful adj. having or showing mercy.

mercifully adv. **1** in a merciful manner. **2** fortunately.

merciless adj. **1** unrelenting. **2** showing no mercy. □ **mercilessly** adv. **mercilessness** n.

mercurial adj. **1** lively, quick to react. **2** of or containing mercury. □ **mercurially** adv. [Say mur CURE ee ul]

mercury n. **1** a toxic silvery-white heavy liquid metallic element used in barometers, thermometers, and amalgams. **2 a** the column of mercury in a thermometer or barometer. **b** the temperature or barometric pressure indicated by this, esp. as rising or falling. **3** a weedy plant of the spurge family. □ **mercuric** adj.

mercury vapour lamp n. (also **mercury vapour light**) a lamp in which bluish light is produced by an electric discharge through a vapour of mercury atoms.

mercy n. (pl. **mercies**) **1** compassion or forbearance shown to a powerless person. **2** the disposition to forgive. **3** an act of mercy. **4** (as an adj.) performed out of mercy toward a suffering person. **5** something to be thankful for. □ **at the mercy of** wholly in the power of.

mere adj. (**merest**) **1** having no greater extent, value, power, or importance than the designation implies. **2** insignificant, ordinary. □ **merely** adv.

merengue *n.* a dance of Dominican and Haitian origin, with alternating long and stiff-legged steps. [*Say* muh RENG gay]

meretricious *adj.* showily attractive but valueless. □ **meretriciously** *adv.* **meretriciousness** *n.* [*Say* mare a TRISH us]

merganser *n.* a diving fish-eating duck with a long bill. [*Say* mur GANSE ur]

merge *v.* (**merges, merged, merging**) **1** combine or be combined; integrate. **2** join a lane of traffic. **3** blend into something else. □ **merged** *adj.*

merger *n.* the combining of two commercial companies etc. into one.

meridian *n.* **1** a great circle passing through the celestial poles and zenith of a given place on the earth's surface. **2** half the circle of the earth which extends from pole to pole through a place, corresponding to a line of longitude. **3** any of the pathways in the body along which energy is said to flow. [*Say* mur IDDY un]

meringue *n.* **1** a mixture of stiffly beaten egg white and sugar. **2** this used as a topping for pies or cakes, browned on top but still soft inside. **3** a round of this mixture, baked until crisp, usu. decorated or filled with whipped cream etc. [*Say* muh RANG]

merino *n.* (*pl.* **merinos**) **1** (also **merino sheep**) a variety of sheep with long fine wool. **2** a soft woollen or wool-and-cotton material like cashmere, originally of merino wool. [*Say* muh REENO]

merit ● *n.* **1** the quality of being entitled to reward. **2** excellence. **3** (usu. in *pl.*) a thing entitling one to reward or esteem. **4** esp. *Law* intrinsic rights and wrongs or excellences and defects. ● *v.* (**merits, merited, meriting**) be worthy of. □ **on its merits** with regard only to its intrinsic worth.

meritocracy *n.* (*pl.* **meritocracies**) **1** government or the holding of power by persons selected competitively according to merit. **2** a group of persons selected in this way. **3** a society governed by meritocracy. □ **meritocratic** *adj.* [*Say* merit OCK ruh see, merit a CRAT ick]

meritorious *adj.* deserving reward, praise, or gratitude. [*Say* mare a TORY us]

merlin *n.* a small falcon that hunts small birds.

Merlot *n.* **1** a variety of black grape used in winemaking. **2** a red wine made from Merlot grapes. [*Say* mur LO *or* mare LO]

mermaid *n.* an imaginary sea creature with the head and trunk of a woman and tail of a fish.

merman *n.* (*pl.* **mermen**) an imaginary sea creature, with the head and trunk of a man and the tail of a fish.

merriment *n.* **1** exuberant enjoyment. **2** mirth, fun.

merry *adj.* (**merrier, merriest**) **1** joyous. **2** full of laughter. □ **make merry** be festive. □ **merrily** *adv.*

merry-go-round *n.* **1** a revolving platform with wooden horses etc. for people to ride on. **2** a cycle of bustling activities.

merrymaking *n.* festivity, fun. □ **merrymaker** *n.*

mesa *n.* an isolated flat-topped hill with steep sides, found in arid and semi-arid regions. [*Say* MAY suh]

mescal *n.* **1 a** a succulent plant of Mexico and the southwestern US, used as sources of fermented liquor, food, or fibre. **b** a strong liquor distilled from the sap of this. **2** a peyote cactus. [*Say* MESS cal]

mescaline *n.* (also **mescalin**) a hallucinogenic alkaloid derived from the peyote cactus. [*Say* MESKA leen *or* MESKA lin]

mesclun *n.* a green salad made from a selection of lettuces and flowers. [*Say* MESK lun]

mesh ● *n.* (*pl.* **meshes**) **1** material made of a network of wire or thread. **2** the spacing of the strands of a net. **3** a complex situation. ● *v.* (**meshes, meshed, meshing**) **1 a** fit in, be harmonious, combine. **b** bring together. **2** (of the teeth of a wheel) be engaged. **3** entangle. □ **meshed** *adj.* **meshing** *n. & adj.*

mesmeric *adj.* hypnotic. [*Say* mez MARE ick]

mesmerism *n.* **1** the process of inducing a hypnotic state by the influence of an operator over the will and nervous system of the patient. **2** the state so induced. □ **mesmerist** *n.* [*Say* MEZMER ism]

mesmerize *v.* (**mesmerizes, mesmerized, mesmerizing**) **1** fascinate. **2** hypnotize. [*Say* MEZMER ize]

meso- *comb. form* middle, intermediate. [*Say* MESSO *or* MEZO]

Meso-American *adj.* relating to Meso-America, the region from central Mexico to Nicaragua. □ **Meso-American** *n.* [*Say* mezo AMERICAN]

mesolithic (also **Mesolithic**) ● *adj.* relating to the part of the Stone Age between the paleolithic and neolithic periods, from about 8500 to 2700 BC. ● *n.* the mesolithic period. [*Say* mezo LITH ick]

Mesopotamian *adj.* relating to Mesopotamia, an ancient region of southwest Asia between the Tigris and Euphrates rivers. □ **Mesopotamian** n. [Say messa puh TAMEY un]

mesosphere n. the region of the atmosphere above the stratosphere. □ **mesospheric** adj. [Say MEZO sphere, mezo SFEER ick]

Mesozoic ● adj. relating to the geological era between the Paleozoic and Cenozoic, comprising the Triassic, Jurassic, and Cretaceous periods and lasting from about 248 to 65 million years BP. ● n. this geological era. [Say mezo ZO ick]

mesquite n. **1** a spiny leguminous tree of the southwestern US and Mexico. **2** its wood often used for grilling food. [Say mes KEET]

mess ● n. (pl. **messes**) **1** a dirty, untidy, or bungled state of affairs. **2 a** a person whose life or affairs are confused. **b** an unkempt person. **3** excrement. **4** a place providing meals for soldiers etc. ● v. (**messes, messed, messing**) **1** informal (foll. by with) interfere. **2** take one's meals. **3** informal defecate or soil by defecating. □ **make a mess of** bungle. **mess around** (or **about**) **1** act desultorily. **2** informal make things awkward for. **3** informal **a** engage in sexual activity. **b** engage in adulterous sexual activity. **mess up 1** make a mess (of). **2** ruin or damage.

message n. **1** an oral or written communication. **2** the central import of something. □ **get the message** informal understand what is meant. **send a message** make a significant statement.

message board n. **1** = BULLETIN BOARD 1. **2** an Internet page for the posting of electronic messages. **3** an electronic board displaying instructions.

messaging n. the sending of written messages by computer, phone, etc.

messenger n. **1** a person who carries a message. **2** Biology something that carries genetic information.

mess hall n. a military dining area.

Messiah n. **1 a** the promised deliverer of the Jews, as prophesied in the Hebrew Bible. **b** (usu. as **the Messiah**) (in Christian theology) Jesus Christ regarded as fulfilling this prophecy. **2** (usu. **messiah**) a liberator of an oppressed people etc. [Say muh SIGH uh]

messianic adj. (also **Messianic**) **1** relating to the Messiah. **2** inspired by belief in a messiah. □ **messianism** n. [Say messy ANNICK, muh SIGH a nism]

Messrs. pl. of MR. [Say MESSERS]

mess-up n. a mess, a muddle.

messy adj. (**messier, messiest**) **1** untidy. **2** causing or accompanied by a mess. **3** full of awkward complications. □ **messily** adv. **messiness** n.

mestizo n. (pl. **mestizos**) (in Latin America) a person of mixed European and Aboriginal descent. [Say mess TEEZO]

met past and past participle of MEET[1].

metabolic adj. relating to metabolism. □ **metabolically** adv. [Say meta BAWL ick]

metabolism n. the chemical processes in a living organism resulting in energy production and growth. [Say muh TABBA lism]

metabolite n. a substance formed or used in metabolism. [Say muh TABBA lite]

metabolize v. (**metabolizes, metabolized, metabolizing**) process or be processed by metabolism. [Say muh TABBA lize]

metacarpal n. any of the five bones of the hand, between the wrist and the fingers. [Say meta CAR pull]

metal ● n. **1** any of a class of substances which are in general lustrous, malleable, fusible, ductile solids and good conductors. **2** = HEAVY METAL 1. ● adj. made of metal. ● v. (**metals, metalled, metalling**) provide or fit with metal.

metalanguage n. a language used to describe another language. [Say META language]

metallic adj. **1** of or characteristic of metal or metals. **2** sharp and ringing.

metallurgy n. the science concerned with metals. □ **metallurgical** adj. **metallurgist** n. [Say META lurge ee meta LURGE ick'll]

metalwork n. **1** the art of working in metal. **2** metal objects collectively. □ **metalworker** n. **metalworking** n. & adj.

metamorphic adj. (of rock) that has been transformed by heat and pressure etc. □ **metamorphism** n. [Say meta MORF ick, meta MORF ism]

metamorphose v. (**metamorphoses, metamorphosed, metamorphosing**) **1** change completely. **2** undergo metamorphosis. [Say meta MORF oze]

metamorphosis n. (pl. **metamorphoses**) **1** a complete change. **2** the transformation from an immature form to an adult form. [Say meta MORFA sis or meta more FOE sis for the singular, meta MORFA seez or meta more FOE seez for the plural]

metaphor n. **1** a figure of speech in which

a word or phrase is applied to something to which it is not literally applicable. **2** a thing regarded as symbolic of something else. □ **metaphoric** *adj.* **metaphorical** *adj.* **metaphorically** *adv.* [*Say* META fore, meta FORE ick]

metaphysical *adj.* **1** relating to metaphysics. **2** based on abstract general reasoning. **3** transcending physical matter and laws. □ **metaphysically** *adv.* [*Say* meta PHYSICAL]

metaphysics *pl. n.* (usu. treated as *sing.*) the branch of philosophy dealing with first principals such as being, knowing, essence, etc. [*Say* meta PHYSICS]

metastasis *n.* **1** the transfer of a disease, esp. cancer, from one part of the body to another. **2** a secondary tumour. □ **metastasize** *v.* (**metastasizes**, **metastasized**, **metastasizing**) **metastatic** *adj.* [*Say* muh TASTA sis *for the singular,* muh TASTA size, meta STATIC]

metatarsal *n.* any of the five bones of the foot, between the ankle and the toes. [*Say* meta TAR sull]

mete *v.* (**metes, meted, meting**) apportion or allot.

meteor *n.* a body of matter from outer space made incandescent by friction with the earth's atmosphere.

meteoric *adj.* **1** of meteors or meteorites. **2** rapid like a meteor.

meteorite *n.* a rock or metal fragment that has fallen from space.

meteorology *n.* the study of weather. □ **meteorological** *adj.* **meteorologist** *n.* [*Say* meteor OLLA jee, meteor a LOGICAL]

meter¹ ● *n.* **1** a thing that measures. **2** = PARKING METER. ● *v.* **1** measure by means of a meter. **2** deliver in measured amounts. **3** provide with a meter or meters.

meter² = METRE¹, METRE².

meth *n.* *slang* methamphetamine.

methadone *n.* a potent painkiller, also used as a substitute for morphine or heroin.

methamphetamine *n.* an amphetamine derivative used as a stimulant. [*Say* meth am FETTA mean]

methane *n.* a flammable gas, the main constituent of natural gas. [*Say* METH ane]

methanol *n.* a colourless liquid, used as a solvent. [*Say* METH a nawl]

methinks *v.* (*past* **methought**) *archaic* or *jocular* it seems to me.

method *n.* **1** a mode of procedure. **2** orderliness. □ **method in one's madness** sense in what appears to be strange behaviour.

methodical *adj.* characterized by method or order. □ **methodically** *adv.* [*Say* muh THODDICK'll]

Methodism *n.* a branch of Protestantism originating in the 18th-century and emphasizing a personal relationship with God. □ **Methodist** *n.* & *adj.* [*Say* METHA dism, METHA dist]

methodology *n.* (*pl.* **methodologies**) a body of methods used in a particular activity. □ **methodological** *adj.* [*Say* method OLLA jee]

methought *past of* METHINKS.

methyl *n.* the monovalent hydrocarbon radical −CH_3. [*Say* METH'll]

methyl alcohol *n.* = METHANOL.

methylate *v.* (**methylates, methylated, methylating**) **1** mix with methanol. **2** introduce a methyl group into. [*Say* METH'll ate]

methylated spirits *n.* (also **methylated spirit**) alcohol to which methanol has been added to make it unfit for drinking.

methylene *n.* the highly reactive divalent group of atoms CH_2. [*Say* METH'll een]

meticulous *adj.* very careful and precise. □ **meticulously** *adv.* **meticulousness** *n.* [*Say* muh TICK yoo luss]

métier *n.* a person's work or special ability. [*Say* mate YAY]

Metis *n.* (*pl.* **Metis**) (esp. in Canada) a person of mixed Aboriginal and European descent. [*Say* may TEE]

metonymy *n.* the substitution of an attribute or adjunct for thing meant, e.g. *Crown* for *monarch*. [*Say* muh TAWNA mee]

metre¹ *n.* (also **meter**) a metric unit and the base SI unit of linear measure, equal to about 39.4 inches.

metre² *n.* (also **meter**) **1 a** any form of poetic rhythm. **b** a metrical group or measure. **2** the basic pulse and rhythm of a piece of music.

metre-kilogram-second *adj.* denoting a system of measure using the metre, kilogram, and second as the basic units of length, mass, and time. Abbreviation: **mks.**

metric ● *adj.* **1** relating to the metre or metric system. **2** relating to measurement. ● *n.* = METRIC SYSTEM.

metrical *adj.* **1** relating to a poetic metre. **2** of or involving measurement. □ **metrically** *adv.*

metric system *n.* the decimal measuring system based on the metre, litre, and gram.

metric ton *n.* (also **metric tonne**) 1,000 kilograms (2205 lb.).

metro¹ *n.* (*pl.* **metros**) a subway system in some cities, e.g. Montreal and Paris.

metro² *adj.* metropolitan.

metronome *n. Music* an instrument for marking time with a regular tick. [*Say* METRA nome]

metropolis *n.* a large, busy city. [*Say* muh TROPPA liəs]

metropolitan ● *adj.* **1** relating to a metropolis. **2** encompassing a city and its suburbs. **3** belonging to, forming, or forming part of, a mother country as distinct from its colonies etc. ● *n.* **1** (also **metropolitan bishop**) a bishop having authority over the bishops of a province. **2** an inhabitant of a metropolis. [*Say* metra POLLA tun]

mettle *n.* a person's ability to cope well with difficulties.

mew ● *v.* (of a cat etc.) utter its characteristic cry. ● *n.* this sound.

mewl *v.* cry feebly.

Mexican *n.* **1** a person from Mexico. **2** an indigenous language of Mexico, esp. Nahuatl. □ **Mexican** *adj.*

mezuzah *n.* (*pl.* **mezuzahs**) a parchment inscribed with religious texts, attached to a Jewish house as a sign of faith. [*Say* muh ZOO zuh]

mezzanine *n.* **1** a low storey between two others. **2** the lowest balcony or foremost part of a balcony in a theatre. [*Say* MEZZA neen]

mezzo *n.* (*pl.* **mezzos**) (also **mezzo-soprano**, *pl.* **mezzo-sopranos**) a voice pitched between soprano and contralto. [*Say* METSO]

mezzo-forte *adj. & adv. Music* fairly loud. [*Say* metso FOR tay]

mezzo-piano *adj. & adv.* fairly soft. Abbreviation: **mp**. [*Say* metso PIANO]

MF *abbr.* milk fat.

mg *abbr.* milligram(s).

MHA *n.* (*pl.* **MHAs**) (in Newfoundland and Australia) Member of the House of Assembly.

MHz *abbr.* megahertz.

mi *n.* (also **me**) **1** (in tonic sol-fa) the third note of a major scale. **2** the note E in the fixed-do system.

MIA *abbr.* missing in action.

miasma *n.* (*pl.* **miasmas**) **1** a highly unpleasant smell. **2** an oppressive or unpleasant atmosphere. [*Say* mee AZMA or my AZMA]

mic *n.* microphone. [*Say* MIKE]

mica *n.* (*pl.* **micas**) any of a group of silicate minerals with a layered structure, esp. muscovite. [*Say* MIKE uh]

mice *pl. of* MOUSE.

mickey *n.* (*pl.* **mickeys**) *Cdn* a half bottle of liquor, usu. 375 ml.

Mickey Mouse *adj. informal* **1** of inferior quality. **2** ridiculous, trivial. **3** (of a university course etc.) requiring little work or intellectual ability.

Micmac *n. & adj.* = MI'KMAQ.

micro *adj. informal* **1** microscopic; very small. **2** small-scale.

micro- *comb. form* **1** small. **2** denoting a factor of one millionth (10⁻⁶). **3** dealing with small effects or small quantities. **4** involving the use of a microscope.

microbe *n.* a micro-organism. □ **microbial** *adj.* [*Say* MIKE robe, my CROW bee ul]

microbiology *n.* the scientific study of micro-organisms. □ **microbiological** *adj.* **microbiologist** *n.*

microbrew *n.* a beer produced at a microbrewery. □ **microbrewer** *n.* **microbrewing** *n.*

microbrewery *n.* (*pl.* **microbreweries**) a brewery which produces usu. high-quality beer on a small scale.

microcassette *n.* a small audio cassette for use in a tape recorder etc.

microchip *n.* a tiny wafer of semiconducting material used to make an integrated circuit.

microcircuit *n.* a minute electric circuit. □ **microcircuitry** *n.*

microclimate *n.* the climate of a small local area.

microcomputer *n.* a computer with a microprocessor as its central processing unit.

microcosm *n.* something regarded as embodying in miniature the characteristics of something larger. □ **microcosmic** *adj.* [*Say* MICRO kozzum, micro COSMIC]

microdot *n.* **1** a tiny photograph of a document etc., about the size of a dot. **2** a tiny capsule of LSD. [*Say* MICRO dot]

microeconomics *n.* the branch of economics dealing with small-scale economic factors such as individual commodities etc. □ **microeconomic** *adj.*

microelectronics *n.* the design, manufacture, and use of microchips and microcircuits. □ **microelectronic** *adj.*

microfibre *n.* a lightweight, water-resistant polyester.

microfiche *n.* (*pl.* **microfiche** or **microfiches**) a flat rectangular piece of film bearing very small photographs of printed pages. [*Say* MICRO feesh]

microfilm ● *n.* a length of film bearing

very small photographs of documents etc.
● v. photograph on microfilm.

microform n. very small photographic reproduction on film or paper of a manuscript etc.

microgram n. one-millionth of a gram.

micrograph n. a photograph taken by means of a microscope.

microgravity n. very weak gravity.

micromanage v. (**micromanages, micromanaged, micromanaging**) supervise with excessive attention to small details. □ **micromanagement** n. **micromanager** n.

micrometer n. a gauge for accurately measuring small distances, thicknesses, etc. [Say my KROM it ur]

micrometre n. one-millionth of a metre. [Say MICRO meet ur]

micron n. one-millionth of a metre. Symbol: μ. [Say MY kron]

Micronesian adj. relating to Micronesia, a region of the west Pacific, or its people or their languages. [Say micro NEE zhun]

micronutrient n. a chemical substance required in trace amounts for the growth and development of living organisms.

micro-organism n. a microscopic organisms.

microphone n. an instrument for converting sound waves into electrical energy which may be amplified, transmitted, or recorded.

microprocessor n. an integrated circuit that contains all the functions of a central processing unit of a computer.

microscope n. an instrument magnifying small objects by means of lenses so as to reveal details invisible to the naked eye. □ **under the microscope** examined in great detail.

microscopic adj. **1** so small as to be visible only with a microscope. **2** of the microscope. □ **microscopically** adv.

microscopy n. the use of the microscope. □ **microscopist** n.
[Say my CROSS kuh pee]

microsecond n. one-millionth of a second.

microstructure n. (in a material) the arrangement of crystals etc. visible with a microscope. □ **microstructural** adj. [Say MICRO structure]

microsurgery n. intricate surgery performed using microscopes. [Say MICRO surgery]

microwave ● n. **1** an electromagnetic wave with a wavelength in the range 0.001–0.3m. **2** (also **microwave oven**) an oven that uses microwaves to heat food. ● v.

(**microwaves, microwaved, microwaving**) cook in a microwave oven. □ **microwaveable** adj.

microwinery n. a winery which produces wine on a small scale, and which usu. specializes in high-quality or natural wines.

mid adj. **1** (usu. in comb.) that is the middle of. **2** that is in the middle.

mid-air n. some part of the air above ground level.

midday n. the middle of the day.

midden n. a refuse heap near a dwelling.

middle ● adj. **1** at an equal distance from the extremities of a thing. **2** intermediate in rank, quality, or order. **3** of the period between old and modern. ● n. **1** (often foll. by of) the middle position or part. **2** a person's waist. □ **in the middle of** (often foll. by verbal noun) in the process of; during.

middle age n. the period between youth and old age, about 40 to 60. □ **middle-aged** adj.

Middle Ages pl. n. the period of European history from about 1000 to 1453.

Middle America n. **1** the middle class in the US. **2** Mexico and Central America.

middlebrow informal ● adj. only moderately intellectual. ● n. a middlebrow person.

middle C n. the C near the middle of the piano keyboard, the note between the treble and bass staffs, at about 260 Hz.

middle class ● n. the class of society between the upper and the lower, including professional and business people etc. ● adj. (**middle-class**) of the middle class.

middle distance n. **1** the part of a landscape between the foreground and the background. **2** Athletics a race distance of esp. 400, 800, or 1500 metres.

middle ear n. the cavity of the central part of the ear behind the drum.

Middle East n. an area of southwestern Asia and northern Africa, having a predominantly Muslim population. □ **Middle Eastern** adj.

Middle English n. the English language c.1150–1500.

middle-income adj. relating to the group of people earning average salaries.

middleman n. (pl. **middlemen**) **1** a trader handling a commodity between its producer and the retailer or consumer. **2** a person arranging deals etc. between other people.

middle name n. **1** a person's name placed between the first name and surname. **2** a characteristic quality.

middle-of-the-road adj. **1** moderate;

avoiding extremes. **2** intended to appeal to a wide audience.

middle school *n.* a junior high school.

middleweight *n.* a weight class in certain sports, above welterweight.

middling *adj.* average in size, amount, or rank. [*Say* MID ling]

Mideast *n.* = MIDDLE EAST.

midfield *n.* **1** (in sports) the central part of the playing field. **2** the players positioned in the midfield. □ **midfielder** *n.*

midge *n.* a tiny two-winged insect often seen in swarms near water.

midget *n.* **1** an extremely small person or thing. **2** (as an *adj.*) very small. **3** *Cdn* a level of amateur sport, usu. involving players aged 16 to 17.

MIDI *n.* a data transfer system for electronic musical instruments, computers, etc. [*Say* MIDDY]

midland ● *n.* **1** (**the Midlands**) the inland counties of central England. **2** the middle part of a country. ● *adj.* of or in the midland or Midlands.

mid-life *n.* middle age.

mid-life crisis *n.* an emotional crisis of self-confidence that can occur in early middle age.

midline ● *n.* a line dividing something into symmetrical halves. ● *adj.* (**mid-line**) relating to products or services of average quality.

midnight *n.* 12 o'clock at night.

midnight blue *n. & adj.* very dark blue.

midnight Mass *n.* esp. *Catholicism* a Mass beginning at midnight on Christmas Eve.

midpoint *n.* the middle point.

mid-range ● *adj.* of average cost, capability, etc. ● *n.* the middle part of the range of audible frequencies.

Midrash *n.* (*pl.* **Midrashim**) an ancient commentary on part of the Hebrew scriptures. [*Say* MID rash *for the singular*, mid rash EEM *for the plural*]

midriff *n.* the front of the body between the chest and the waist. [*Say* MID riff]

midsection *n.* the middle part.

midship *n.* the middle part of a ship or boat.

midshipman *n.* (*pl.* **midshipmen**) (in the Royal Navy and *hist.* in the Royal Canadian Navy) a naval officer ranking below sub-lieutenant.

midshore *adj. Cdn* designating the fishery an intermediate distance from shore.

mid-size ● *adj.* (also **mid-sized**) **1** (of a car) of a size between compact and full-size, usu. having a four- or six-cylinder engine

from 2 to 3.5 litres in size. **2** of intermediate size. ● *n.* a mid-size car.

midst □ **in the midst of** among; in the middle of. **in our** (or **your** or **their**) **midst** among us (or you or them).

midstream ● *n.* the middle of a stream etc. ● *adv.* (also **in midstream**) in the middle of an action.

midsummer *n.* the period of or near the summer solstice, about June 21.

mid-term ● *adj.* occurring in the middle of a term. ● *n.* a mid-term exam.

midtown *n.* an area of a city outside the downtown area.

midway ● *adv.* in or toward the middle between two points. ● *n.* a fair with sideshows, rides, etc.

mid-week ● *n.* the middle of the week. ● *adj.* occurring at mid-week. ● *adv.* at mid-week.

Midwest *n.* a region of the northern US west of the Great Lakes. □ **Midwestern** *adj.* **Midwesterner** *n.*

midwife *n.* (*pl.* **midwives**) a person trained to assist women in childbirth. □ **midwifery** *n.* [*Say* MID wife, mid WIF ur ee]

mid-winter *n.* **1** the middle of the winter. **2** the winter solstice, around Dec. 22.

mien *n.* a person's look or bearing. [*Sounds like* MEAN]

miffed *adj. informal* put out of humour.

might¹ *aux. v.* (*3rd. singular* **might**) *past of* MAY, used esp.: **1** expressing possibility or permission. **2** expressing a request. **3** *informal* **a** = MAY 1. **b** (in tentative questions) = MAY 2. **c** = MAY 4. □ **might as well** expressing that it is probably at least as desirable to do a thing as not to do it.

might² *n.* great power or strength. □ **with all one's might** to the utmost of one's power.

might-have-been *n. informal* **1** a past possibility that no longer applies. **2** a person or thing that could have succeeded.

mightn't *contr.* might not.

mighty ● *adj.* (**mightier, mightiest**) **1** powerful or strong, in body, mind, or influence. **2** massive, bulky. **3** *informal* great, considerable. ● *adv. informal* very. □ **mightily** *adv.* **mightiness** *n.*

migraine *n.* a severe headache, often accompanied by nausea and disturbance of vision. [*Say* MY grain]

migrant ● *adj.* that migrates. ● *n.* a migrant person or animal. [*Say* MY grunt]

migrate *v.* (**migrates, migrated, migrating**) **1** move from one place of residence to another. **2** move to a different habitat according to the season. **3** move from the use of one kind of computer, software, database, or programming language to another. □ **migration** n. **migratory** adj. [Say MY grate, my GRAY sh'n, MY gruh tory]

mike informal ● n. a microphone. ● v. (**mikes, miked, miking**) put a microphone near (a person etc.).

Mi'kmaq n. (pl. **Mi'kmaq** or **Mi'kmaqs**) a member or the Algonquian language of an Aboriginal people living in Nova Scotia, New Brunswick, PEI, and the Gaspé Peninsula. □ **Mi'kmaq** adj. [Say MICK mack]

mikveh n. (also **mikvah, mikva**) a bath for use in Jewish ritual purifications. [Say MIK vuh]

mil[1] n. one thousandth of an inch (0.0254 mm).

mil[2] n. (pl. **mil**) (usu. in pl.) informal a million dollars (or pounds).

mild adj. **1** (esp. of a person) gentle and not easily provoked. **2** not severe or harsh. **3** (of the weather) moderately warm. **4** not sharp or strong in taste etc. **5** (of medicine, soap, etc.) operating gently. **6** not keenly felt or seriously intended. □ **mildly** adv.

mildew ● n. a destructive growth of minute fungi on plants, or on damp paper, leather, etc. ● v. taint or be tainted with mildew. □ **mildewed** adj. [Say MIL doo or MIL dyoo]

mile n. **1** (also **statute mile**) a unit of linear measure equal to 1,760 yards (approx. 1.609 kilometres). **2** (in pl.) informal a great distance or amount. □ **miles away** informal lost in thought.

mileage n. **1 a** the distance travelled. **b** the distance a vehicle is capable of travelling per unit of fuel. **2** expenses per distance travelled. **3** informal use, advantage.

milestone n. (also **milepost**) **1** a stone set up beside a road to mark a distance in miles. **2** a significant event in a life, history, etc.

milieu n. (pl. **milieux** or **milieus**) one's social surroundings. [Say mil YOO for the singular, mil YOOS for the plural (with OO as in HOOD)]

militant ● adj. aggressively active and extreme in support of a cause. ● n. a militant activist. □ **militancy** n. **militantly** adv. [Say MILLA t'nt]

militarism n. the desire for strong military capability and its aggressive use in the national interest. □ **militarist** n. & adj. **militaristic** adj. [Say MILLA tuh rism]

militarize v. (**militarizes, militarized, militarizing**) supply with soldiers and other military resources. □ **militarization** n. [Say MILLA tuh rize]

military ● adj. relating to soldiers or armed forces. ● n. (as sing. or pl.; **the military**) members of the armed forces. □ **militarily** adv. [Say MILLA tairy, milla TARE a lee]

militate v. (usu. foll. by against) be a powerful factor in preventing. [Say MILLA tate]

militia n. (pl. **militias**) **1** a supplementary military force raised from the civilian population. **2** a usu. small or rebel military force. [Say muh LISHA]

militiaman n. (pl. **militiamen**) a member of a militia. [Say muh LISHA m'n]

milk ● n. **1** an opaque white fluid secreted by female mammals for the nourishment of their young. **2** the milk of cows etc. as food. **3** the milk-like juice of plants, e.g. in the coconut. ● v. **1** draw milk from. **2 a** exploit. **b** take full advantage from. □ **cry over spilt milk** worry about something that cannot be remedied.

milker n. **1** an animal yielding milk. **2** a person who, or a machine which, milks.

milk fat n. butterfat.

milkmaid n. a girl or woman working in a dairy.

milkman n. (pl. **milkmen**) a person who delivers milk.

milk of magnesia n. a white suspension of magnesium hydroxide in water as an antacid or laxative.

milk powder n. dehydrated milk.

milk run n. **1** the route followed by a milkman. **2** a bus or train route with many stops.

milkshake n. a frothy cold drink of milk blended with flavouring and ice cream.

milk snake n. a harmless, usu. brightly coloured N American snake.

milk tooth n. a temporary tooth in young mammals.

milkweed n. a N American plant with milky juice.

milk-white adj. white like milk.

milky adj. (**milkier, milkiest**) **1** of, like, or mixed with milk. **2** cloudy. □ **milkiness** n.

Milky Way n. (also **Milky Way Galaxy**) the galaxy of which the solar system is part.

mill[1] ● n. **1 a** a building fitted with a mechanical apparatus for grinding grain. **b** such an apparatus. **2** an apparatus for grinding solid substances. **3** a building fitted with machinery for manufacturing processes etc. **4** any group etc. generating something specified. ● v. **1 a** grind etc. in a mill. **b** extract from rock by crushing the rock in a mill. **2** produce ribbed markings on the edge of (a coin). **3** cut or shape (metal) with a rotating tool. **4** move aimlessly. □ **go through the mill** undergo intensive work or a difficult ordeal.

mill² *n.* one thousandth of a dollar, esp. in calculating tax rates.

millenarian ● *adj.* relating to or believing in an imminent golden age, esp. involving the Second Coming of Christ. ● *n.* a person with millenarian views.
□ **millenarianism** *n.*
[*Say* milla NAIRY un]

millennium *n.* (*pl.* **millennia** or **millenniums**) **1** a period of 1,000 years. **2** any millennium reckoned from the supposed date of the birth of Christ.
□ **millennial** *adj.* [*Say* mil ENNY um]

miller *n.* a person who owns or works in a grain mill.

millet *n.* a fast-growing cereal plant with nutritious seeds used for flour or alcohol.

milli- *comb. form* a thousand, esp. denoting a factor of one thousandth. Abbreviation: **m**.

milligram *n.* one thousandth of a gram.

millilitre *n.* one thousandth of a litre.

millimetre *n.* one thousandth of a metre (0.039 in.).

milliner *n.* a person who makes or sells women's hats. □ **millinery** *n.*
[*Say* MILLA nur, MILLA nur ee]

million *card. num.* **1** a thousand thousand. **2** (often in *pl.*) *informal* a very large number.
□ **look** (or **feel** etc.) (**like**) **a million bucks** (or **dollars** etc.) *informal* look (or feel) extremely good.
□ **millionth** *adj., n. & adv.*

millionaire *n.* **1** a person whose assets are worth at least one million dollars, pounds, etc. **2** a person of great wealth.

millipede *n.* an arthropod with a long segmented body having two pairs of legs on each segment.

millisecond *n.* one thousandth of a second.

millpond *n.* a pool of water retained by a dam for the operation of a mill. □ **like a millpond** very calm.

millstone *n.* **1** each of two circular stones used for grinding grain. **2** a heavy burden or responsibility.

mill wheel *n.* a wheel used to drive a water mill.

millwork *n.* **1** work done in a mill. **2** wood products from a mill, e.g. trim.

milquetoast *n.* a timid person.
[*Say* MILK toast]

milt *n.* **1 a** a sperm-filled reproductive gland of a male fish. **b** the semen of a male fish. **2** a spleen or analogous organ.

MIME *n.* a protocol for transmitting different types of data by email, whereby special characters, formatted text, and non-textual data are encoded so that they can be sent and received by a standard email program.

mime ● *n.* **1** the theatrical technique using gesture and expression without words. **2** a performance of mime. **3** (also **mime artist**) a practitioner of mime. ● *v.* (**mimes, mimed, miming**) **1** convey by gesture without words. **2** mouth (song lyrics etc.) along with a soundtrack.

mimesis *n.* **1** *Biology* the close resemblance of an animal or plant to another. **2** the representation of the real world in art, poetry, etc. [*Say* muh MEE sis *or* my MEE sis]

mimetic *adj.* relating to imitation.
[*Say* mim ETT ick]

mimic ● *v.* (**mimics, mimicked, mimicking**) **1** imitate, esp. to entertain. **2** resemble closely. ● *n.* a skilled imitator.
□ **mimicker** *n.*

mimicry *n.* (*pl.* **mimicries**) **1** the act or art of mimicking. **2** a thing that mimics another. [*Say* MIMIC ree]

mimosa *n.* (*pl.* **mimosas**) **1** a shrub with globular flowers and leaves that droop when touched. **2** any of various acacia plants with showy yellow flowers. **3** champagne and orange juice.
[*Say* mim OH zuh *or* mim OH suh]

minaret *n.* a slender turret connected with a mosque. [*Say* minna RET]

mince *v.* (**minces, minced, mincing**) **1** cut up very small or grind. **2** walk with an affected delicacy. □ **not mince words** speak candidly. □ **mincing** *adj.*

mincemeat *n.* a mixture of dried fruit, sugar, candied peel, spices, and often suet.
□ **make mincemeat of** utterly defeat.

mince pie *n.* a pie containing mincemeat.

mind ● *n.* **1** the faculty of consciousness and thought. **2** a person's intellect or memory. **3** a person's attention or will. ● *v.* **1** object to. **2** take care to do. **3** give attention to. **4** take care of temporarily. **5** (in *passive*) be inclined to do. **6** (also **mind you**) qualifying a previous statement. □ **be in** (or **of**) **two minds** be unable to decide. **be of one mind** agree. **give someone a piece of one's mind** rebuke someone. **have** (**half**) **a mind to** be inclined to. **have in mind 1** be thinking of. **2** intend to do. **mind one's Ps & Qs** be polite. **never mind 1** do not be concerned. **2** let alone. **out of one's mind** mad. **to my mind** in my opinion.

mind-altering *adj.* hallucinogenic.

mind-bending *adj. informal* altering one's state of mind.

mind-blowing adj. slang **1** overwhelming. **2** inducing hallucinations. □ **mind-blowingly** adv.

mind-boggling adj. informal overwhelming. □ **mind-bogglingly** adv.

minded adj. **1** (in comb.) **a** inclined to think in some specified way. **b** having a specified kind of mind. **c** interested in or enthusiastic about a specified thing. **2** inclined (to an action).

minder n. a person who attends to a person or thing.

mindful adj. (often foll. by of) taking care. □ **mindfully** adv. **mindfulness** n.

mind game n. **1** (usu. in pl.) informal an attempt to have a psychological effect on another. **2** a test of the intellect.

mindless adj. **1** stupid. **2** not requiring thought. **3** heedless. □ **mindlessly** adv. **mindlessness** n.

mind-numbing adj. very boring. □ **mind-numbingly** adv.

mind reader n. a person capable of discerning the thoughts of another. □ **mind reading** n.

mindscape n. reality as imagined in one's mind.

mindset n. a mental attitude.

mind's eye n. informal the mind as viewer of memories or things imagined. □ **in one's mind's eye** in one's imagination or mental view.

mine[1] poss. pron. the one or ones belonging to or associated with me. □ **of mine** of or belonging to me.

mine[2] ● n. **1** an excavation for extracting natural resources. **2** an abundant source. **3** an explosive device placed in the ground or water. ● v. (**mines, mined, mining**) **1** obtain from a mine. **2** dig. **3** lay explosive mines under or in. **4** = UNDERMINE.

minefield n. **1** an area planted with explosive mines. **2** something presenting unseen hazards.

miner n. **1** a person who works in a mine. **2** any burrowing insect or grub.

mineral ● n. **1** a substance occurring naturally in the earth and not formed from animal or vegetable matter. **2** a substance obtained by mining. **3** any of the elements, e.g. calcium, essential for good nutrition. ● adj. **1** of or containing a mineral or minerals. **2** obtained by mining.

mineralize v. (**mineralizes, mineralized, mineralizing**) **1** change wholly or partly into a mineral. **2** introduce a mineral substance into (water etc.). □ **mineralization** n.

mineralogy n. the scientific study of minerals. □ **mineralogical** adj.

mineralogist n. [Say minner OLLA jee minner a LOGICAL]

mineral oil n. an oily liquid obtained from petroleum and used as a lubricant etc.

mineral rights pl. n. ownership rights to the minerals located on or below a property.

mineral water n. natural water with some dissolved salts present.

mine shaft n. a shaft giving access to a mine.

minestrone n. a soup containing vegetables and pasta, beans, or rice. [Say minna STRONE ee]

minesweeper n. a ship for clearing away mines.

mineworker n. = MINER 1.

Ming n. **1** the Chinese dynasty founded in 1368 and ruling until 1644. **2** Chinese porcelain made during this dynasty.

mingle v. (**mingles, mingled, mingling**) **1** mix, blend. **2** socialize.

mingy adj. (**mingier, mingiest**) informal **1** stingy. **2** small. [Say MIN jee]

mini n. (pl. **minis**) **1** informal a miniskirt. **2** a garment with a miniskirt.

mini- comb. form miniature.

miniature ● adj. **1** much smaller than normal. **2** represented on a small scale. ● n. **1** any object reduced in size. **2** a small-scale portrait. □ **in miniature** on a small scale. □ **miniaturist** n. [Say MINNA chur, MINNA chur ist]

miniature golf n. a game like golf but played on a small obstacle course.

miniaturize v. (**miniaturizes, miniaturized, miniaturizing**) produce in a smaller version. □ **miniaturization** n. [Say MINNA chur ize]

mini-bar n. a small fridge in a hotel room, containing drinks.

minibus n. (pl. **minibuses**) a small bus.

minicam n. a hand-held video camera.

minigolf n. = MINIATURE GOLF.

minima pl. of MINIMUM.

minimal adj. **1** as small as possible. **2 a** Art etc. using simple forms. **b** Music using gradual alteration of short repeated phrases. □ **minimally** adv.

minimalist ● adj. **1** not elaborate. **2** relating to minimal art or music. ● n. a minimalist composer, artist, etc. □ **minimalism** n. **minimalistic** adj.

mini-mart n. = CONVENIENCE STORE.

minimize v. (**minimizes, minimized, minimizing**) **1** reduce to the smallest amount or degree. **2** underestimate or understate the value of. □ **minimization** *n.* **minimizer** *n.*

minimum (*pl.* **minimums** or **minima**) ● *n.* **1** the least possible or attainable amount. **2** the lowest amount attained or recorded. ● *adj.* that is a minimum.

minimum wage *n.* the lowest permitted wage.

mining *n.* the removal of metals, coal, etc. from a mine.

minion *n. derogatory* an unimportant servant. [*Say* MIN yun]

mini-putt *n. Cdn* = MINIATURE GOLF.

miniseries *n.* a film shown on television in several episodes.

miniskirt *n.* a very short skirt.

minister ● *n.* **1** a head of a government department. **2** a member of the clergy. **3** a diplomatic agent. ● *v.* render aid or service.

ministerial *adj.* **1** of a government minister. **2** of a minister of religion or a minister's office. [*Say* min iss TEERY ul]

Minister of the Crown *n.* (*pl.* **Ministers of the Crown**) a member of the Cabinet.

minister without portfolio *n.* (*pl.* **ministers without portfolio**) a government minister with Cabinet status but not in charge of a department.

ministration *n.* (usu. in *pl.*) aid or service. [*Say* min iss TRAY sh'n]

ministry *n.* (*pl.* **ministries**) **1** a government department headed by a minister. **2** (**the ministry**) the work or office of a religious minister. **3** a period of government under one prime minister. **4** the act of ministering to someone. [*Say* MIN iss tree]

minivan *n.* a small passenger van.

mink *n.* **1** a small semi-aquatic ermine-like animal. **2** its thick brown fur. **3** a coat made of this.

minke *n.* a small baleen whale with a pointed snout. [*Say* MIN kuh]

Minnesotan *n.* a person from Minnesota. □ **Minnesotan** *adj.*

minnow *n.* a small freshwater fish.

Minoan *adj.* relating to the Bronze Age civilization centred on Crete (*c.*3000–1100 BC). [*Say* min OWEN]

minor ● *adj.* **1** comparatively small or unimportant. **2 a** based on a scale having intervals of a semitone between the second and third, fifth and sixth, and seventh and eighth degrees. **b** less by a semitone than a major interval. **3** *Cdn* designating organized team sport for children. ● *n.* **1** a person under the age of majority. **2** *Music* a minor key etc. **3** a student's subsidiary subject. **4** *Hockey* = MINOR PENALTY. **5** (in *pl.*) the

minor leagues. ● *v.* (foll. by *in*) study (a subject) as a subsidiary to a main subject.

minority *n.* (*pl.* **minorities**) **1** a smaller number or part. **2** the state of being supported by less than half of the body of opinion, voters, etc. **3** a relatively small group in society identified by a race, religion, language, politics, etc. **4** (as an *adj.*) relating to or done by the minority. **5** the state or period of being under full legal age. [*Say* my NORRA tee or min ORRA tee]

minority government *n.* a government that has fewer seats in parliament than the total number held by all other parties.

minor league ● *n.* **1** a sports league of professional clubs other than the major leagues. **2** *Cdn* an amateur sports league for youth. ● *adj.* (usu. **minor-league**) **1** of a minor league. **2** of inferior quality. □ **minor-leaguer** *n.*

minor penalty *n. Hockey* a two minute penalty given for lesser infractions.

Minotaur *n.* (in Greek mythology) a man with a bull's head, kept in a Cretan labyrinth and fed with human flesh. [*Say* MINE a tore]

minstrel *n.* a medieval singer or musician.

mint¹ ● *n.* **1** an aromatic plant of temperate regions, used as a herb. **2** a mint-flavoured candy. ● *adj.* having the flavour of mint. □ **minted** *adj.* **minty** *adj.*

mint² ● *n.* **1** a place where money is coined under governmental control. **2** a vast sum of money. ● *adj.* in perfect condition. ● *v.* **1** make (coin) by stamping metal. **2** invent. □ **minted** *adj.*

mint green *n. & adj.* a pale pastel green.

mint julep *n.* a sweet iced alcoholic drink of bourbon flavoured with mint.

minuet *n.* **1** a slow stately dance for two in triple time. **2** the music for this. [*Say* min yoo ETT]

minus ● *prep.* **1** with the subtraction of. **2** (of temperature) below zero. **3** lacking. ● *adj.* **1** *Math* negative. **2** *Electronics* having a negative charge. **3** (after a grade etc.) slightly below. ● *n.* (*pl.* **minuses**) **1** *Math* a negative quantity. **2** a disadvantage.

minuscule ● *adj.* **1** extremely small or unimportant. **2** (of a letter) lower case. ● *n.* a lower case letter. [*Say* MINNA skyool]

minute¹ ● *n.* **1** the sixtieth part of an hour or angular degree. **2** a short time. **3** (in *pl.*) a brief summary of proceedings at a meeting. ● *v.* (**minutes**, **minuted**, **minuting**) record in the minutes.

minute² *adj.* (**minutest**) very small or detailed. □ **minutely** *adv.* **minuteness** *n.* [*Say* my NYOOT or my NOOT]

minutiae *pl. n.* precise details.
[*Say* min OOSH uh *or* min OOSHY uh]

minx *n.* (*pl.* **minxes**) a mischievous or pert girl.

Miocene ● *adj.* relating to the fourth epoch of the Tertiary period, lasting from about 24.6 to 5.1 million years ago. ● *n.* this geological epoch. [*Say* MY a seen]

miracle *n.* **1** a remarkable occurrence, esp. one believed to involve supernatural power. **2** any remarkable development or specimen.

miraculous *adj.* **1** supernatural. **2** remarkable. □ **miraculously** *adv.* **miraculousness** *n.*

mirage *n.* **1** an optical illusion, esp. the appearance of water in a desert or on a hot road. **2** an illusory thing. [*Say* mur AWZH]

mire ● *n.* **1** swampy ground; muck. **2** a difficult situation from which it is hard to escape. ● *v.* (**mires, mired, miring**) (esp. as **mired**) **1** sink in a mire. **2** involve in difficulties.

mirror ● *n.* **1** a polished surface reflecting an image. **2** something giving an accurate reflection of something else. ● *v.* reflect as in a mirror. □ **mirrored** *adj.*

mirror image *n.* **1** an identical image, but with the structure reversed, as in a mirror. **2** something identical to another.

mirth *n.* merriment, laughter. □ **mirthful** *adj.* **mirthless** *adj.* **mirthlessly** *adv.*

mis- *prefix* (added to verbs and their derivatives) amiss, badly, wrongly, etc.

misadventure *n.* **1** bad luck. **2** *Law* an accident not caused by crime or negligence.

misalign *v.* give the wrong alignment to. □ **misaligned** *adj.* **misalignment** *n.* [*Say* miss a LINE]

misanthrope *n.* (also **misanthropist**) a person who hates humans or avoids human society. [*Say* MISS un thrope, miss ANTHRA pist]

misanthropy *n.* a dislike of other people. □ **misanthropic** *adj.* [*Say* miss ANTHRA pee, miss un THROP ick]

misapply *v.* (**misapplies, misapplied, misapplying**) apply wrongly. □ **misapplication** *n.*

misapprehend *v.* misunderstand. □ **misapprehension** *n.*

misappropriate *v.* (**misappropriates, misappropriated, misappropriating**) apply to one's own use or to a wrong use. □ **misappropriation** *n.* [*Say* missa PRO pree ate]

misbegotten *adj.* **1** contemptible. **2** badly planned.

misbehave *v.* (**misbehaves, misbehaved, misbehaving**) behave badly. □ **misbehaviour** *n.*

miscalculate *v.* (**miscalculates, miscalculated, miscalculating**) calculate wrongly. □ **miscalculation** *n.*

miscarriage *n.* the expulsion of a fetus from the womb before it can survive independently.

miscarriage of justice *n.* (*pl.* **miscarriages of justice**) any failure of the judicial system to achieve justice.

miscarry *v.* (**miscarries, miscarried, miscarrying**) **1** have a miscarriage. **2** be unsuccessful.

miscast *v.* (**miscasts, miscast, miscasting**) assign an unsuitable role to.

miscegenation *n.* **1** the interbreeding of races. **2** marriage between people of different races. [*Say* miss EDGE in ay sh'n]

miscellaneous *adj.* **1** composed of assorted elements. **2** of various kinds. [*Say* missa LAY nee us]

miscellany *n.* (*pl.* **miscellanies**) a collection of different kinds of things. [*Say* MISSA lay nee]

mischief *n.* **1** troublesome but not malicious conduct. **2** playfulness. **3** harm or injury caused by a person or thing. □ **do a person a mischief** wound or kill a person. **get up to** (or **make**) **mischief** cause trouble. [*Say* MISS chiff]

mischievous *adj.* **1** disposed to mischief. **2** teasing. [*Say* MISS chiv us]

miscommunication *n.* failure to communicate adequately.

misconceived *adj.* badly planned.

misconception *n.* a wrong idea.

misconduct *n.* **1** improper or unprofessional behaviour. **2** *Hockey* a penalty for fighting, arguing with the referee etc.

misconstrue *v.* (**misconstrues, misconstrued, misconstruing**) interpret wrongly.

miscount ● *v.* count wrongly. ● *n.* a wrong count.

miscreant *n.* an immoral or criminal person. [*Say* MISS kree int]

miscue ● *n.* **1** an error. **2** (in pool etc.) the failure to strike the ball properly. ● *v.* (**miscues, miscued, miscueing** or **miscuing**) make a miscue.

misdeed *n.* an evil deed, a wrongdoing; a crime.

misdemeanour *n.* (also **misdemeanor**) **1** a minor wrongdoing. **2** *Law* a minor criminal offence, esp. (in the US) one less serious than a felony. [*Say* miss duh MEAN er]

misdiagnose v. (**misdiagnoses, misdiagnosed, misdiagnosing**) diagnose incorrectly. □ **misdiagnosis** n. (pl. **misdiagnoses**) [Say miss die ug NOCE]

misdirect v. **1** direct wrongly. **2** (of a judge) instruct wrongly. □ **misdirected** adj. **misdirection** n.

miser n. a person who hoards wealth and lives miserably.

miserable adj. **1** wretchedly unhappy. **2** contemptible. **3** causing wretchedness. □ **miserableness** n. **miserably** adv.

miserly adj. like a miser, stingy.

misery n. (pl. **miseries**) **1** great discomfort of mind or body. **2** a thing causing this. □ **put out of its** etc. **misery 1** release from suffering or suspense. **2** kill.

misfire ● v. (**misfires, misfired, misfiring**) **1** fail to fire or function properly. **2** fail to have the intended effect. ● n. an act of misfiring.

misfit n. **1** an unsuitable person. **2** something that does not fit or suit well.

misfortune n. **1** bad luck. **2** an unfortunate condition or event.

misgivings pl. n. mistrust or apprehension.

misguided adj. mistaken in thought or action. □ **misguidedly** adv. **misguidedness** n.

mishandle v. (**mishandles, mishandled, mishandling**) deal with incorrectly or carelessly.

mishap n. an unlucky accident.

mishear v. (**mishears, misheard, mishearing**) hear incorrectly or imperfectly.

mishmash n. a confused mixture.

Mishnah n. an authoritative collection of Jewish oral law, forming the first part of the Talmud. [Say MISH nuh]

misidentify v. (**misidentifies, misidentified, misidentifying**) identify wrongly. □ **misidentification** n.

misinform v. give wrong information to. □ **misinformation** n.

misinformed adj. **1** incorrectly informed. **2** based on incorrect information.

misinterpret v. (**misinterprets, misinterpreted, misinterpreting**) interpret wrongly. □ **misinterpretation** n.

misjudge v. (**misjudges, misjudged, misjudging**) **1** judge wrongly. **2** have a wrong opinion of. □ **misjudgment** n. (also **misjudgement**)

mislabel v. (**mislabels, mislabelled, mislabelling**) give an incorrect label or description to.

mislay v. (**mislays, mislaid, mislaying**) **1** unintentionally put (a thing) where it cannot readily be found. **2** lose.

mislead v. (**misleads, misled, misleading**) give a wrong idea to. □ **misleading** adj. **misleadingly** adv.

mismanage v. (**mismanages, mismanaged, mismanaging**) manage badly. □ **mismanagement** n.

mismatch ● v. (**mismatches, mismatched, mismatching**) match in an unsuitable way. ● n. (pl. **mismatches**) a bad match.

misname v. (**misnames, misnamed, misnaming**) name wrongly or inappropriately.

misnomer n. a term used wrongly. [Say miss NOME er]

miso n. a paste of fermented soybeans and barley or rice malt. [Say MEE so]

misogyny n. disdain or contempt for women. □ **misogynist** n. **misogynistic** adj. [Say miss AWE juh nee, miss AWE juh nist, miss awe juh NISS tick]

misperception n. an incorrect perception.

misplace v. (**misplaces, misplaced, misplacing**) (usu. as **misplaced** adj.) **1** put in the wrong place. **2** bestow inappropriately.

misplaced modifier n. a word, phrase, or clause which apparently refers to a person or thing other than the one intended.

misplay ● v. play wrongly or ineffectively. ● n. an instance of misplaying a ball etc.

misprint ● n. a mistake in printing. ● v. print wrongly.

mispronounce v. (**mispronounces, mispronounced, mispronouncing**) pronounce wrongly. □ **mispronunciation** n.

misquote v. (**misquotes, misquoted, misquoting**) quote wrongly.

misread v. (**misreads, misread, misreading**) read or interpret wrongly. □ **misreading** n.

misrepresent v. represent wrongly. □ **misrepresentation** n.

misrule n. **1** bad government. **2** disorder, esp. intentional.

miss¹ ● v. (**misses, missed, missing**) **1** fail to hit or come into contact with. **2** be too late for. **3** fail to notice, hear, or understand. **4** fail to be present. **5** avoid. **6** omit. **7** notice or feel the loss or absence of. ● n. (pl. **misses**) a failure to hit, attain, connect, etc. □ **miss the boat 1** lose an opportunity. **2** fail to understand the point. **not miss a trick** never fail to seize an opportunity, advantage, etc.

miss² *n. (pl.* **misses) 1 (Miss)** a title for an unmarried woman or girl. **2** the title of a young woman representing a country etc. in a beauty contest. **3** a girl or unmarried woman. **4** used as a term of address to a female schoolteacher, etc.

missal *n. Catholicism* a book containing the texts used in the Mass throughout the year. [*Say* MISS'll]

misshapen *adj.* not having the normal or natural shape. [*Say* mis SHAPEN]

missile *n.* **1** a destructive, self-propelling projectile. **2** an object which is thrown at a target. [*Say* MISS'll *or* MISS ile]

missing *adj.* **1** not in its place; lost. **2** not present, absent. □ **go missing** become lost.

missing link *n.* **1** a thing lacking to complete a series. **2** a hypothetical evolutionary link between humans and apes.

mission *n.* **1 a** a particular task or goal assigned to a person or group. **b** a journey with a purpose. **c** a strongly felt aim or calling. **2** a military or scientific expedition. **3** a body of persons sent abroad to conduct negotiations. **4 a** members of a religious organization working among members of another society, community, etc. **b** a missionary post or organization.

missionary ● *adj.* of religious missions. ● *n. (pl.* **missionaries)** a person doing missionary work.

mission statement *n.* a declaration of general principles.

Mississauga *n. (pl.* **Mississauga** *or* **Mississaugas) 1** a member of an Ojibwa people living in southern Ontario. **2** their Algonquian language. [*Say* missa SOGGA]

Mississippian *adj.* **1** of or pertaining to the state of Mississippi or its inhabitants. **2** designating the period of the Paleozoic era in N America from about 360 to 320 million years BP. □ **Mississippian** *n.* [*Say* miss i SIPPY in]

missive *n.* a letter, esp. a long and serious one.

misspell *v.* (**misspells**; *past* and *past participle* **misspelled** *or* **misspelt**; **misspelling**) spell wrongly. □ **misspelled** *adj.* **misspelling** *n.*

misspent *adj.* spent or passed wastefully.

misstate *v.* (**misstates**, **misstated**, **misstating**) state wrongly or inaccurately. □ **misstatement** *n.*

misstep *n.* an inappropriate or clumsy action.

missus *n. (pl.* **missuses) 1** a form of address to a woman. **2** *slang* or *jocular* a wife.

missy *n. (pl.* **missies)** an affectionate or derogatory form of address to a young girl.

mist ● *n.* **1** a diffuse cloud of water droplets. **2** condensed vapour settling in fine droplets on a surface. ● *v.* cover or become covered with mist.

mistake ● *n.* **1 a** an incorrect idea or opinion. **b** a thing incorrectly done or thought. **2** an error of judgment. ● *v.* (**mistakes**; *past* **mistook**; *past participle* **mistaken**; **mistaking**) **1** misunderstand the meaning or intention of. **2** (foll. by *for*) wrongly take or identify. □ **mistaken** *adj.* **mistakenly** *adv.*

Mistassini Cree *n. (pl.* **Mistassini Cree** *or* **Mistassini Crees)** a member of a Cree people living in north central Quebec. [*Say* mista SEENY]

mister¹ *n.* **1** = MR. **2** a form of address to a man.

mister² *n.* a device for misting plants, hair, etc.

mistily *adv.* **1** in or as through a mist. **2** sentimentally.

mistletoe *n.* a parasitic plant growing on trees and bearing white berries in winter, often used as a Christmas decoration. [*Say* MISS'll toe]

mistranslate *v.* (**mistranslates**, **mistranslated**, **mistranslating**) translate incorrectly. □ **mistranslation** *n.*

mistreat *v.* treat wrongly or badly. □ **mistreatment** *n.*

mistress *n. (pl.* **mistresses) 1** a woman (other than his wife) with whom a married man has a usu. prolonged sexual relationship. **2** a woman in authority over others or with controlling power over something. **3** a female head of a household.

mistrial *n.* **1** a trial rendered invalid through some error in the proceedings. **2** *US* a trial in which the jury cannot agree on a verdict.

mistrust ● *v.* **1** be suspicious of. **2** feel no confidence in. ● *n.* **1** suspicion. **2** lack of confidence. □ **mistrustful** *adj.*

misty *adj.* (**mistier, mistiest) 1** obscured or accompanied by mist. **2** not clear; obscure. □ **mistiness** *n.*

misty-eyed *adj.* **1** emotional. **2** having eyes blurred by tears.

misunderstand *v.* (**misunderstands**, **misunderstood**, **misunderstanding**) understand incorrectly.

misunderstanding *n.* **1** a failure to

understand correctly. **2** a slight disagreement or quarrel.

misunderstood *adj.* **1** misinterpreted. **2** not appreciated.

misuse ● *v.* (**misuses**, **misused**, **misusing**) **1** use wrongly or improperly. **2** maltreat. ● *n.* wrong or improper use or application of power, drugs, etc.

mite ● *adv.* (**a mite**) *informal* somewhat. ● *n.* **1** any of various small arachnids, many of which live in the soil or on plants or animals. **2** a small object or person, esp. a child. **3** an initiation level of sports for children usu. between the ages of 5 and 8. **4** a very small amount.

miter esp. *US* = MITRE.

mitigate *v.* (**mitigates**, **mitigated**, **mitigating**) make less severe, serious, or painful. □ **mitigation** *n.* [*Say* MITTA gate]

mitigating *adj.* (of a fact or circumstance) lessening the seriousness of or blame attached to an action.

mitochondrion *n.* (*pl.* **mitochondria**) an organelle found in large numbers in most cells, responsible for energy production during respiration. □ **mitochondrial** *adj.* [*Say* mite uh CON dree un *for the singular,* mite uh CON dree uh *for the plural*]

mitosis *n.* a type of cell division that results in two cells each having the same number and kind of chromosomes as the parent nucleus. [*Say* my TOE sis]

mitre (also esp. *US* **miter**) ● *n.* **1** a tall pointed headdress worn by bishops. **2** a 90° joint made between two pieces of wood, each cut at a 45° angle. ● *v.* (**mitres**, **mitred**, **mitring**) join by means of a mitre. □ **mitred** *adj.* [*Say* MITE er]

mitt *n.* **1** a covering for the hand with a single section for all four fingers and a separate section for the thumb. **2** *Baseball* a protective catching glove worn by the catcher or first baseman. **3** *slang* a hand or fist.

mitten *n.* **1** = MITT 1. **2** a glove leaving the tips of the fingers and thumb exposed. □ **mittened** *adj.*

mitzvah *n.* (*pl.* **mitzvoth**) *Judaism* **1 a** a precept or commandment. **b** a religious obligation. **2** a good deed or considerate act. [*Say* MITS vuh *for the singular,* MITS vot *for the plural*]

mix ● *v.* (**mixes**, **mixed**, **mixing**) **1** combine or put together. **2** be sociable, esp. at a party. **3** combine two or more sound signals or recordings into one. ● *n.* (*pl.* **mixes**) **1** the result of mixing or combining. **2** the proportion or combination of the components of an integrated whole. **3** a commercially prepared mixture of ingredients for

making a cake etc. **4** a version of a recording in which the component tracks are mixed differently. **5** the soft drink, fruit juice, etc. with which an alcoholic drink is diluted. □ **mix and match** select from a range of alternative combinations. **mix it up** *informal* fight, argue. **mix up 1** mix thoroughly. **2** confuse; mistake the identity of. □ **mixable** *adj.*

mix-and-match ● *adj.* **1** suitable for or selected by mixing and matching. **2** coordinating. ● *n.* (*pl.* **mix-and-matches**) a combination of coordinating items.

mixed *adj.* **1** consisting of diverse qualities or elements. **2** containing persons from various backgrounds etc. **3** for or involving persons of both sexes. **4 a** having both negative and positive aspects. **b** ambiguous, unclear.

mixed blood *n.* a person having parents or ancestors from two or more races. □ **mixed-blood** *adj.*

mixed breed *n.* a crossbreed.

mixed doubles *pl. n. Tennis* a doubles game with a man and a woman on each side.

mixed drink *n.* an alcoholic beverage consisting liquor with fruit juice or a soft drink etc.

mixed feelings *pl. n.* (also **mixed emotions**) a mixture of pleasure and dismay about something.

mixed marriage *n.* a marriage between persons of different races or religions.

mixed media ● *n.* the use of a variety of mediums in a work of art, performance, etc. ● *adj.* (also **mixed-media**) = MULTIMEDIA *adj.*

mixed metaphor *n.* a combination of inconsistent metaphors, e.g. *this tower of strength will forge ahead.*

mixed race *adj.* = MIXED-BLOOD *adj.*

mixed-up *adj. informal* **1** mentally or emotionally confused. **2** socially ill-adjusted.

mixer *n.* **1** a machine for mixing or beating foods etc. **2** = MIX *n.* 5. **3** a device for merging esp. sound signals to produce a combined output. **4** a person who manages socially in a specified manner.

mixture *n.* **1** a substance made by mixing other substances together. **2** the process of mixing or being mixed.

mix-up *n.* a confusion, misunderstanding, or mistake.

mizzen-mast *n.* the mast next aft of the mainmast on a sailing ship.

ml *abbr.* (also **mL**) millilitre(s).

MLA *abbr.* (*pl.* **MLAs**) Member of the Legislative Assembly.

MLB *abbr.* Major League Baseball.

mm *abbr.* millimetre(s).

mmm *interj.* expressing hesitation, reflection, satisfaction, etc.

MNA *abbr.* (*pl.* **MNAs**) *Cdn* (in Quebec) Member of the National Assembly.

mnemonic ● *n.* a pattern of letters or associations which assists in remembering something. ● *adj.* of or designed to aid the memory. [*Say* nuh MONN ick]

MO *abbr.* (*pl.* **MOs**) **1** = MODUS OPERANDI. **2** Medical Officer.

moan ● *n.* **1** a low mournful sound expressing suffering etc. **2** a low plaintive sound made by wind etc. **3** a complaint or grievance. ● *v.* **1** make a moan. **2** *informal* complain or grumble. □ **moaner** *n.*

moat *n.* a deep defensive ditch around a castle, town, etc., usu. filled with water.

mob ● *n.* **1** a disorderly crowd. **2** (**the mob**) usu. *derogatory* the ordinary people. **3** (**the Mob**) *informal* the Mafia or a similar criminal organization. ● *v.* (**mobs, mobbed, mobbing**) **1** crowd round in order to attack or admire. **2** assemble in a mob.

mobile ● *adj.* **1 a** movable; not fixed. **b** (of troops etc.) that may be rapidly moved from place to place. **2** (of a person) able to move into different social levels, fields of employment, etc. ● *n.* a decorative structure with parts that hang so as to turn freely. [*Say* MOE bile; *for the adjective you can also say* MOE bull]

mobile home *n.* a house that can be transported to different locations.

mobile phone *n.* (also **mobile telephone**) = CELLPHONE.

mobility *n.* **1** the ability to move easily from one place, social class, or job to another. **2** the ability to move or travel around easily. **3** *Cdn* (esp. in names of companies) mobile telecommunications systems, e.g. cellphones, pagers, etc. [*Say* mo BILLA tee]

mobilize *v.* (**mobilizes, mobilized, mobilizing**) **1 a** organize or make ready for service, action, battle, etc. **b** be organized or made ready for action. **2** render movable or capable of movement. □ **mobilization** *n.* **mobilizer** *n.*

Möbius strip *n.* (also **Möbius loop**) a surface with only one side, formed by twisting a long, narrow, rectangular strip through 180° and joining the ends. [*Say* MOE bee us]

mobster *n.* *slang* a gangster.

moccasin *n.* **1** a type of soft leather shoe with the sole turned up and sewn to the upper, as originally worn by some Aboriginal peoples. **2** a hard-soled shoe resembling this. **3** a kind of venomous N American snake. □ **moccasined** *adj.*

moccasin telegraph *n.* esp. *Cdn* (esp. *North*) *informal* a means of transmitting rumours by word of mouth; the grapevine.

mocha *n.* **1** a coffee of fine quality. **2** a flavouring made from this, often with chocolate added. **3** a chocolate-flavoured coffee drink. [*Say* MOE kuh]

mochaccino *n.* (*pl.* **mochaccinos**) a cappuccino flavoured with chocolate syrup. [*Say* moe kuh CHEE no]

mock ● *v.* **1** ridicule; scoff at. **2** mimic contemptuously. **3** jeer or defy contemptuously. ● *adj.* **1** sham, imitation (esp. without intention to deceive). **2** pretended, fake. □ **mocker** *n.* **mocking** *adj.* **mockingly** *adv.*

mockery *n.* (*pl.* **mockeries**) **1** derision, ridicule. **2** a counterfeit or absurdly inadequate representation of something. □ **make a mockery of something** make something appear foolish, absurd, or worthless.

mockingbird *n.* a greyish long-tailed songbird which mimics the calls of other birds.

mock orange *n.* a shrub cultivated for its strongly scented white flowers.

mocktail *n.* a non-alcoholic version of a cocktail.

mock-up *n.* an experimental model or replica of a proposed structure.

mod¹ *adj.* modern, esp. in style of dress.

mod² *n.* (in Scotland, Cape Breton, etc.) an often competitive event at which Gaelic music, poetry, and dancing are performed.

mod³ *n.* (usu. **mods**) *informal* modification.

modal *adj.* **1** relating to the way something is done. **2** *Grammar* (of an auxiliary verb, e.g. *would*) used to express the mood of another verb. **3** denoting a style of music using a particular mode. [*Say* moe dull]

modality *n.* (*pl.* **modalities**) **1** a particular mode in which something exists or is experienced or expressed. **2** a prescribed method or technique of procedure, treatment, behaviour, etc. [*Say* muh DALA tee]

mode *n.* **1** a way or manner in which a thing is done. **2** a prevailing fashion, custom, or style. **3 a** any of a number of distinct ways in which a machine operates. **b** a specified way in which a person functions, behaves, etc. **4** *Music* **a** each of the scale systems beginning with a white key and incorporating all the other white keys over an octave. **b** each of the two main modern scale systems, the major and minor.

model ● *n.* **1** a small-scale, three-dimensional representation of thing. **2** a conceptual or mental representation of a thing. **3 a** a car etc. of a particular design or produced in a specified year. **b** each of a series of varying designs of the same type of object. **4** an exemplary person or thing. **5** a person or thing used as an example to copy or imitate. **6** a person employed to pose for an artist, to wear clothes for display, etc. ● *adj.* **1** serving as an example; ideally perfect. **2** designating a small-scale model of the object specified. ● *v.* **(models, modelled, modelling) 1** act or pose as an esp. fashion or photographic model. **2** shape a figure in clay, wax, etc. **3** design in imitation of something else. **4** devise a (usu. mathematical) model or simplified description of. □ **modelling** *n.*

model home *n.* a finished house used to give potential buyers an idea of what other houses in a development will look like.

modeller *n.* a person who makes models of objects.

modem *n.* a device that allows one computer system to transmit data over a telephone line to another.

moderate ● *adj.* **1** avoiding extremes in conduct, opinions, or expression. **2** of medium quantity, size, cost, etc. ● *n.* a person who holds moderate views. ● *v.* **(moderates, moderated, moderating) 1** make or become less violent, intense, rigorous, etc. **2** preside over a deliberative body or at a debate etc. □ **moderately** *adv.* [*Say* MODDER it *for the adjective and noun,* MODDER ate *for the verb*]

moderation *n.* **1** the action of making something less extreme, intense, or violent. **2** the quality of being moderate, esp. in conduct, opinion, etc. □ **in moderation** in a moderate manner or degree.

moderator *n.* **1** a chairperson of a broadcast discussion. **2** a person chosen to preside over a meeting or assembly. **3** (in the United Church) a person elected to serve as the head of the church. **4** an arbitrator or mediator.

modern ● *adj.* **1** of the present and recent times. **2** up-to-date in lifestyle, outlook, opinions, etc. **3** designating art, architecture, etc. marked by a departure from traditional styles and values. ● *n.* **1** (usu. in *pl.*) a person living in or belonging to modern times. **2** a person with modern tastes or opinions. **3** (also

modern dance) a 20th-century style of theatrical dance, not constrained by the rules and techniques of classical ballet. □ **modernness** *n.*

modernism *n.* **1** (**Modernism**) a movement in the arts that aims to break with traditional styles or ideas. **2** modern ideas, methods, or styles. □ **modernist** *n.* **modernistic** *adj.*

modernity *n.* the quality or condition of being modern. [*Say* muh DUR nuh tee *or* muh DAIR nuh tee]

modernize *v.* **(modernizes, modernized, modernizing)** make or become modern. □ **modernization** *n.* **modernizer** *n.*

modest *adj.* **1** having or indicating a humble or moderate estimate of one's own merits. **2** not bold or forward. **3 a** avoiding impropriety or indecency. **b** reserved in sexual matters. **4** not excessive or exaggerated. **5** not showy or ostentatious. □ **modestly** *adv.* **modesty** *n.*

modicum *n.* a small quantity. [*Say* MOD i kum]

modifier *n.* **1** a person or thing that modifies or alters something. **2** a word that qualifies the sense of another word.

modify *v.* **(modifies, modified, modifying) 1** make partial or minor changes in. **2** make less severe or extreme. **3** *Grammar* (of a word) restrict or add to the meaning of another word or phrase. □ **modifiable** *adj.* **modification** *n.*

modish *adj.* fashionable. □ **modishly** *adv.* **modishness** *n.* [*Say* MODE ish]

modulate *v.* **(modulates, modulated, modulating) 1 a** regulate or adjust. **b** moderate. **2** adjust or vary the tone or pitch of (the speaking voice etc.). **3** alter the amplitude or frequency of a wave or signal. **4** *Music* change from one key to another. □ **modulation** *n.* **modulator** *n.* [*Say* MOD you late *or* MODGE oo late]

module *n.* **1** each of a set of sections or units used in the assembly of a building, electronic system, computer program, etc. **2** an independent self-contained unit of a spacecraft. **3** a distinct educational unit which can be combined with others to make up a course. **4** a standard or unit of measurement. □ **modular** *adj.* **modularity** *n.* **modularization** *n.* [*Say* MOD yool *or* MODGE ool]

modus operandi *n.* the particular way in which a person or thing performs a task. [*Say* moe dus oppa RANDY]

modus vivendi *n.* **1** an arrangement allowing conflicting parties to coexist peacefully. **2** a way of living or coping.

[*Say* moe dus viv ENDY *for the singular,* moe dee viv ENDY *for the plural*]

mogul[1] *n.* **1** *informal* an important or influential person. **2** (**Mogul**) *hist.* (often **the Great Mogul**) any of the emperors of Delhi in the 16th–19th centuries. [*Say* MOE gull]

mogul[2] *n.* **1** a mound of hard snow on a ski slope. **2** (in *pl.*) a freestyle skiing event in which skiers negotiate moguls. [*Say* MOE gull]

MOH *abbr.* MEDICAL OFFICER OF HEALTH.

mohair *n.* **1** the hair of the angora goat. **2** a yarn or fabric from this. □ **mohair** *adj.*

Mohawk *n.* **1 a** (*pl.* **Mohawk** or **Mohawks**) a member of an Iroquois people now inhabiting parts of southern Ontario and northern New York. **b** their Iroquoian language. **2** (**mohawk**) a haircut in which the sides of the head are shaved leaving a central brushlike strip. □ **Mohawk** *adj.*

mohel *n. Judaism* a person trained to perform ritual circumcisions. [*Say* maw HELL *or* MOE hell]

moi *interj. jocular* as a tongue-in-cheek rejoinder to being accused of something of which one is clearly guilty. [*Say* MWAH]

moil ● *v.* **1** toil, work hard. **2** move around in agitation or confusion. ● *n.* turmoil, confusion, trouble.

moiré *n.* a fabric having a pattern of glossy wavy bars. □ **moiré** *adj.* [*Say* more AY]

moist *adj.* slightly wet. □ **moistly** *adv.* **moistness** *n.*

moisten *v.* wet superficially or moderately.

moisture *n.* tiny drops of water or other liquid in the air, in a substance, or condensed on a surface.

moisturize *v.* (**moisturizes, moisturized, moisturizing**) make less dry. □ **moisturizer** *n.* **moisturizing** *adj.*

mojo *n.* (*pl.* **mojos**) *esp. US* **1** magic, voodoo. **2** a charm or amulet. **3** *informal* a power, force, or influence of any kind (often with sexual connotations).

mol *abbr.* = MOLE[4].

molar[1] *n.* any of the back grinding teeth of mammals. □ **molar** *adj.*

molar[2] *adj. Physics* of or relating to mass.

molar[3] *adj. Chemistry* **1** of a mass of substance usu. per mole. **2** (of a solution) containing one mole, or a specified number of moles, of solute per litre of solvent.

molasses *n.* **1** a thick, dark syrup drained from raw sugar during refining. **2** a lighter, sweeter version of this used in baking etc. [*Say* muh LASS iss *or* muh LASS izz]

mold etc. = MOULD etc.

mole[1] *n.* **1** a small burrowing insect-eating mammal with very small eyes. **2** a person within an organization who secretly passes confidential information to another organization or country.

mole[2] *n.* a small often slightly raised dark blemish on the skin.

mole[3] *n.* a massive structure serving as a pier, breakwater, causeway, or harbour.

mole[4] *n. Chemistry* the SI unit of amount of substance equal to the quantity containing as many elementary units as there are atoms in 0.012 kg of carbon-12.

molecule *n.* the smallest fundamental unit (usu. a group of atoms) of a chemical compound. □ **molecular** *adj.* [*Say* MOLLA cule, muh LECK yuh ler]

molehill *n.* a small mound thrown up by a mole in burrowing. □ **make a mountain out of a molehill** exaggerate a minor difficulty.

moleskin *n.* **1** a kind of twilled cotton cloth with its surface shaved. **2** a piece of felt put on the feet to reduce abrasion from shoes.

molest *v.* **1** attack or interfere with, esp. sexually. **2** annoy or pester in a hostile way. □ **molestation** *n.* **molester** *n.* [*Say* muh LEST, maul ess TAY sh'n]

moll *n. slang* a gangster's girlfriend.

mollify *v.* (**mollifies, mollified, mollifying**) appease, pacify. [*Say* MOLLA fie]

mollusc *n.* (also esp. *US* **mollusk**) any of various animals having soft bodies and usu. hard shells, including snails, slugs, mussels, and octopuses.

molly *n.* (also **mollie**) a small fish bearing live young, bred in many colours for aquariums.

Molotov cocktail *n.* a simple homemade bomb, esp. a gasoline-filled bottle with a rag stuffed in the neck as a wick. [*Say* MOLLA toff]

Molson muscle *n. Cdn slang* a beer belly.

molt *v. & n. esp. US* = MOULT.

molten *adj.* melted. [*Say* MOLE tin]

molto *adv. Music* very.

molybdenum *n.* a silver-white metallic element used to strengthen steel. [*Say* muh LIBDA num]

mom *n. informal* mother. [*Say* MUM *or* MOM]

mom-and-pop *adj.* designating a family-run store, restaurant, etc.

moment *n.* **1** a very short period of time. **2** an exact point of time. **3** importance.

momentarily *adv.* **1** for a moment; fleetingly. **2** at any moment; very soon.

momentary *adj.* very brief or short-lived.

momentous *adj.* having great importance. □ **momentously** *adv.* **momentousness** *n.* [*Say* moe MEN tuss]

momentum *n.* **1** *Physics* the quantity of motion, measured as a product of mass and velocity. **2** the impetus gained by movement. **3** the impetus gained by the development of a process. [*Say* moe MEN tum]

momma *n.* = MAMA.

mommy *n.* (*pl.* **mommies**) *informal* mother.

Mon. *abbr.* Monday.

monarch *n.* **1** a sovereign, esp. a king or queen. **2** a large orange and black butterfly. [*Say* MON ark]

monarchy *n.* (*pl.* **monarchies**) **1** a form of government with a monarch at the head. **2** a state with this. □ **monarchical** *adj.* **monarchism** *n.* **monarchist** *n.* & *adj.* [*Say* MON arkee, muh NAR kick'll, MON ark ism, MON ark ist]

monastery *n.* (*pl.* **monasteries**) the residence of a religious community, esp. of monks living in seclusion. [*Say* MONNA sterry]

monastic ● *adj.* **1** of or relating to monasteries or the religious communities living in them. **2** austere, solitary, or celibate. ● *n.* a monk or other follower of a monastic rule. □ **monastically** *adv.* **monasticism** *n.* [*Say* muh NASS tick, muh NASSTA sism]

Monday ● *n.* the second day of the week, following Sunday. ● *adv.* **1** on Monday. **2** (**Mondays**) on Mondays; each Monday.

mondo *slang* ● *adj.* big, considerable. ● *adv.* very, extremely.

monetarism *n.* the policy of controlling the amount of money available in a country. □ **monetarist** *n.* & *adj.* [*Say* MONNA tuh rism]

monetary *adj.* of or pertaining to coinage, currency, or money. □ **monetarily** *adv.* [*Say* MONNA terry, monna TERRA lee]

money *n.* **1** a means of payment other than barter, including coins, banknotes, and electronic or printed representations of the values of these. **2** (**monies** or **moneys**) sums of money. □ **for my money** in my opinion. **put one's money where one's mouth is** take action in support of one's statements. (**right**) **on the money** on target.

moneybags *pl. n.* (treated as *sing.*) usu. *derogatory* a wealthy person.

moneybelt *n.* a belt for carrying money etc. beneath the clothes, worn esp. by tourists.

moneyed *adj.* wealthy.

money-grubber *n.* *informal* a person greedily intent on amassing money. □ **money-grubbing** *adj.* & *n.*

money laundering *n.* the practice of transferring funds to conceal their dubious origin. □ **money launderer** *n.*

moneylender *n.* a person who lends money at interest. □ **moneylending** *n.* & *adj.*

money order *n.* an order for payment of a specified sum.

money pit *n.* *informal* a project, program, etc. perceived as wasting large amounts of money.

monger *n.* (usu. in *comb.*) **1** a dealer or trader. **2** usu. *derogatory* a person who promotes something specified. □ **-mongering** *comb. form.* [*Say* MONG grr *or* MUNG grr]

Mongol ● *adj.* **1** of or relating to the Asian people now inhabiting Mongolia or their language. **2** resembling this people. ● *n.* **1** a Mongolian. **2** the Mongolian language. [*Say* MONG gull]

Mongolian *n.* **1** a native or inhabitant of Mongolia, a country in eastern Asia. **2** the language of Mongolia. □ **Mongolian** *adj.* [*Say* mong GOALIE in]

Mongoloid *adj.* of the division of humankind including the indigenous peoples of E and SE Asia and the Arctic region of N America, characteristically having dark eyes, straight hair, and little facial or body hair. □ **Mongoloid** *n.* [*Say* MONG guh loyd]

mongoose *n.* (*pl.* **mongooses**) a short-legged mammal noted for the ability to kill venomous snakes. [*Say* MONG goose]

mongrel ● *n.* an animal, esp. a dog, of no definable breed or type. ● *adj.* of mixed origin, nature, or character. □ **mongrelize** *v.* [*Say* MONG grul]

monied *adj.* = MONEYED. [*Say* MUN eed]

monies *see* MONEY 2. [*Say* MUN ees]

moniker *n.* (also **monicker**) *slang* a name. [*Say* MONNA curr]

monitor ● *n.* **1** a person or device that checks or warns about a situation, operation, etc. **2** a school pupil with disciplinary or other special duties. **3** a video display or audio speaker used to check the quality of a transmission, recording, etc. **4** *Computing* a component displaying data as characters on a screen. **5** a large tropical lizard. ● *v.* watch and check something over a period of time. □ **monitoring** *n.* & *adj.*

monk *n.* a member of a religious community of men living under certain vows esp. of poverty and chastity.

monkey ● *n.* (*pl.* **monkeys**) **1** any of

various mainly long-tailed, agile primates that live in trees in tropical countries. **2** a mischievous person, esp. a child. ● *v.* (**monkeys, monkeyed, monkeying**) **1** tamper or play mischievous tricks. **2** fool around. □ **have a monkey on one's back** *slang* **1** be a drug addict. **2** have a burdensome problem.

monkey bars *pl. n.* a playground structure of joined bars for children to climb on.

monkey business *n. informal* **1** mischief. **2** suspicious or dishonest activities.

monkey suit *n. informal* **1** a tuxedo. **2** any uniform.

monkey wrench *n.* a wrench with an adjustable jaw.

monkfish *n.* (*pl.* **monkfish**) **1** a bottom-dwelling fish that attracts prey by filaments dangling above its mouth. **2** a large bottom-dwelling shark with a flattened body.

monkish *adj.* suggestive of the monastic life, as in austerity or isolation.

monkshood *n.* a cultivated flower with hood-shaped blue or purple flowers. [Say MONK's hood]

mono *n. informal* mononucleosis.

mono- *comb. form* (usu. **mon-** before a vowel) one, alone, single.

monochrome ● *n.* a picture done in one colour or in black and white only. ● *adj.* having or using only one colour or in black and white only. □ **monochromatic** *adj.* **monochromatically** *adv.*

monocle *n.* a single eyeglass, kept in position by the muscles around the eye. [Say MONNA cull]

monoculture *n.* **1** the cultivation of a single crop only. **2** a society which is ethnically or culturally homogeneous. □ **monocultural** *adj.*

monofilament *n.* a single strand of synthetic fibre, e.g. used as fishing line.

monogamy *n.* the practice or state of having only one spouse, mate, or sexual partner at a time. □ **monogamous** *adj.* [Say muh NOGGA mee]

monogram *n.* a person's initials combined in one design, used to identify clothing etc. □ **monogrammed** *adj.*

monograph *n.* a scholarly written study of a single subject.

monolingual *adj.* **1** knowing only one language. **2** written in a single language. [Say mono LING gwul *or* mono LING gyoo ul]

monolith *n.* **1** a single block of stone, esp. a pillar or monument. **2** a large, impersonal social structure regarded as

uniform and immovable. □ **monolithic** *adj.* **monolithically** *adv.* [Say MONNA lith]

monologue *n.* **1** a long speech by one person in a play, conversation etc. **2** a stand-up comedy routine performed esp. by the host of a talk show. □ **monologist** (also **monologuist**) *n.* [Say MONNA log; MONNA log ist *or* mu NOLLA gist]

monomania *n.* an obsession or preoccupation with one thing. □ **monomaniac** *n.* **monomaniacal** *adj.* [Say monna MAY nee uh, monna muh NIE uh cull]

monomer *n.* a molecule that can be linked to other identical molecules to form a polymer. [Say MONNA mer]

mononucleosis *n.* an infectious viral disease characterized by swelling of the lymph glands and prolonged weariness. [Say monno nuke lee OH sis]

monophonic *adj.* (of sound reproduction) using only one transmission channel.

monopolize *v.* (**monopolizes, monopolized, monopolizing**) **1** obtain exclusive control of a commodity etc. **2** dominate a conversation, person's attention, etc. □ **monopolization** *n.* **monopolizer** *n.* [Say muh NOPPA lize]

monopoly *n.* (*pl.* **monopolies**) **1** the exclusive control of the trade in a product or service. **2 a** a product or service that is subject to a monopoly. **b** a company with a monopoly. **3** exclusive possession or control. □ **monopolist** *n.* **monopolistic** *adj.*

monorail *n.* a railway in which the track consists of a single rail.

monosaccharide *n.* a sugar that cannot be hydrolyzed to give a simpler sugar, e.g. glucose. [Say monna SACKA ride]

monosodium glutamate *n.* a chemical compound used in foods as a flavour enhancer. [Say monna sodium GLOOTA mate]

monosyllabic *adj.* **1** having only one syllable. **2** using monosyllabic words. [Say monna sil AB ick]

monosyllable *n.* a word of one syllable. [Say monna SYLLABLE]

monotheism *n.* the belief that there is only one God. □ **monotheist** *n.* **monotheistic** *adj.* [Say monna THEE ism, monna thee ISS tick (*with* TH *as in* THICK)]

monotone ● *n.* **1** a sound or utterance on one note without change of pitch. **2** sameness of style in writing, expression, etc. ● *adj.* without change of pitch or tone.

monotony *n.* **1** lack of interesting variety. **2** sameness of tone or pitch.

□ **monotonous** adj. **monotonously** adv.
[Say muh NOTTA nee]

monounsaturated adj. (esp. of a fat or
oil molecule) containing one double bond.

monovalent adj. Chemistry having a valence
of one. [Say monna VAY lint]

monoxide n. an oxide containing one
oxygen atom.

Monsignor n. Catholicism an honorary title
bestowed on priests, e.g. for distinguished
service. [Say mun SEEN yur]

monsoon n. **1** a wind in south Asia,
blowing from the southwest in summer.
2 a rainy season accompanying this.
□ **monsoonal** adj.

monster n. **1** an imaginary creature, usu.
large and frightening. **2** an inhumanly
cruel or wicked person. **3** a large animal or
thing. **4** (as an adj.) extremely large.

monstrance n. Catholicism a receptacle
with an open or transparent compartment
in which the consecrated Host is exposed
for veneration. [Say MON strince]

monstrosity n. (pl. **monstrosities**) **1** a
huge, hideous, or outrageous thing. **2** the
condition or fact of being monstrous.
[Say mon STROSSA tee]

monstrous adj. **1** of or like a monster in
appearance, frightfulness, etc. **2** huge.
3 a outrageously wrong or absurd.
b atrocious; horrible. □ **monstrously** adv.
monstrousness n.

montage n. **1** Film combination of images
in quick succession. **2** a new composite
whole produced from fragments of
pictures, words, etc. [Say mon TAWZH]

Montagnais n. (pl. **Montagnais**) **1** a
member of an Innu people living in the
barrens between Hudson Bay and the
Labrador coast. **2** their Cree language.
□ **Montagnais** adj. [Say MON tun yay]

Montagnais-Naskapi n. (pl.
Montagnais-Naskapi) = INNU n.

montane adj. **1** of or inhabiting
mountainous country. **2** designating the
belt of upland vegetation below the
timberline.

Monterey Jack n. a mild white cheddar
cheese. [Say monta RAY]

Montessori adj. (of a system of education)
based on the ideas of Maria Montessori
(1870–1952), esp. in seeking to develop
natural interests. [Say monta SORRY]

month n. **1** each of usu. twelve periods into
which a year is divided. **2** a period of four
weeks. **3** = LUNAR MONTH. **4** the period of a
woman's menstrual cycle. □ **month of
Sundays** a very long period.

monthly ● adj. done, produced, or
occurring once a month. ● adv. once a

month; from month to month. ● n. (pl.
monthlies) **1** a monthly periodical. **2** (in
pl.) informal a menstrual period.

Montreal bagel n. Cdn a type of bagel,
originally made in Montreal, which is
thinner, chewier, and sweeter than other
kinds of bagel.

Montrealer n. a native or inhabitant of
Montreal.

Montreal smoked meat n. Cdn =
SMOKED MEAT 2.

monument n. **1** a statue or structure built
to commemorate a person or event. **2** a
structure or site of historical importance.
3 an outstanding, enduring, and
memorable example of something.

monumental adj. **1 a** extremely great;
stupendous. **b** impressive and of lasting
importance. **2** of or serving as a
monument. **3** informal calamitous.
□ **monumentality** n.
monumentally adv.

moo ● v. (**moos, mooed, mooing**) make
the characteristic vocal sound of cattle. ● n.
(pl. **moos**) this sound.

mooch informal ● v. (**mooches,
mooched, mooching**) **1 a** (often foll. by
off) beg, scrounge. **b** steal. **2** loiter or
saunter desultorily. ● n. (pl. **mooches**) a
person who mooches. □ **moocher** n.

mood[1] n. **1** a state of mind or feeling. **2** a
fit of melancholy or bad temper. **3** the
atmosphere or pervading tone of
something. **4** (as an adj.) inducing a
particular mood. □ **in the** (or **no**) **mood**
inclined (or disinclined).

mood[2] n. Grammar a form or set of forms of
a verb serving to indicate whether it is to
express a fact, command, wish, etc.

moody adj. (**moodier, moodiest**) given
to changes of mood; gloomy, sullen.
□ **moodily** adv. **moodiness** n.

moolah n. (also **moola**) slang money.

moon ● n. **1** the natural satellite of the
earth. **2** a satellite of any planet. **3** a
month. ● v. **1** slang expose one's buttocks as
a joke or insult. **2** behave or move listlessly
or dreamily. □ **over the moon** extremely
happy or delighted. □ **moonless** adj.

moonbeam n. a ray of moonlight.

moon face n. a round face. □ **moon-
faced** adj.

Moonie n. slang a member of the
Unification Church, a religious
organization founded in Korea in 1954.

moonlight ● n. **1** the light of the moon.
2 (as an adj.) lighted by the moon. ● v.
(**moonlights, moonlighted,
moonlighting**) informal have a second job,

esp. at night, in addition to one's regular job. □ **moonlighter** *n.*

moonlit *adj.* lighted by the moon.

moonscape *n.* **1** the landscape of the moon. **2** an area resembling this.

moonshine *n.* **1** *slang* illicitly distilled alcoholic liquor. **2** unrealistic talk or ideas. □ **moonshiner** *n.*

moonstone *n.* any of various stones, esp. feldspar, which seem to change colour depending on the viewer's position.

moonstruck *adj.* **1** romantically captivated. **2** mentally deranged.

moonwalk *n.* **1** a walk by an astronaut on the surface of the moon. **2** a dance step in which a person moves backwards while making the motions of walking forwards. □ **moonwalk** *v.*

moony *adj.* (**moonier, mooniest**) listless; stupidly dreamy.

Moor *n.* a member of a Muslim people inhabiting northwest Africa. □ **Moorish** *adj.* [Say MOOR or MORE]

moor[1] *n.* a tract of open, uncultivated, usu. poorly drained upland. □ **moorland** *n.* [Say MOOR or MORE]

moor[2] *v.* tie (a boat etc.) to a fixed object. □ **moorage** *n.*

mooring *n.* **1 a** a fixed object to which a boat etc. is moored. **b** (often in *pl.*) a place where a boat etc. is moored. **2** (in *pl.*) the ropes or cables by which a boat is moored.

moose *n.* (*pl.* **moose**) the largest living deer, the males of which have very large antlers with a broad flat surface.

moosehair *n.* stiff, pale hair from a moose, dyed and used by some Aboriginal peoples to form decorative patterns.

moosehide *n.* the skin of a moose, esp. when tanned.

moose milk *n.* *Cdn* a drink including alcoholic liquor (usu. rum), milk, and often eggs etc.

moot ● *adj.* **1** debatable, undecided. **2** unlikely to happen and therefore not worth considering. **3** *Law* designating a discussion of a hypothetical case. ● *v.* raise a question for discussion.

mop ● *n.* **1** a tool for cleaning floors, consisting of a bunch of thick strings or soft material fastened to a long handle. **2** anything resembling a mop, esp. a thick mass of hair. ● *v.* (**mops, mopped, mopping**) **1** clean with or as with a mop. **2** wipe tears or sweat etc. from one's face or brow. □ **mop up** wipe up with or as with a mop.

mope ● *v.* (**mopes, moped, moping**) **1** behave sulkily. **2** wander about listlessly. ● *n.* **1** a person who mopes. **2** (**the**

mopes) low spirits. □ **moper** *n.* **mopey** (also **mopy**) (**mopier, mopiest**) *adj.*

moped *n.* a small motorcycle equipped with both an engine and pedals. [Say MOE ped]

moppet *n.* *informal* (esp. as a term of endearment) a baby or small child.

MOR *abbr.* MIDDLE-OF-THE-ROAD.

moraine *n.* a ridge or mound of rock debris etc. deposited by a glacier. □ **morainic** *adj.* [Say muh RAIN]

moral ● *adj.* **1** concerned with the principles of right and wrong. **2 a** conforming to accepted standards of conduct. **b** capable of moral action. **3** concerned with morals or ethics. **4** boosting one's morale. ● *n.* **1** a moral lesson of a fable, event, etc. **2** (in *pl.*) moral behaviour, e.g. in sexual conduct. □ **morally** *adv.*

morale *n.* the level of confidence, enthusiasm, etc. of a person or group. [Say more AL]

moralism *n.* the practice of moralizing.

moralist *n.* **1** a person who has strong ideas about moral principles, especially one who judges other people's behaviour. **2** a person who teaches or writes about moral principles. □ **moralistic** *adj.* **moralistically** *adv.*

morality *n.* (*pl.* **moralities**) **1** the degree of conformity of an idea, practice, etc., to moral principles. **2** right moral conduct. **3** a particular system of morals.

morality squad *n.* *Cdn* a police unit dealing with prostitution, pornography, drugs, gambling, etc.

moralize *v.* (**moralizes, moralized, moralizing**) tell other people what is right and wrong. □ **moralizer** *n.*

morass *n.* (*pl.* **morasses**) **1** a disordered situation. **2** a bog or marsh. [Say muh RASS]

moratorium *n.* (*pl.* **moratoriums** or **moratoria**) a temporary prohibition or suspension of an activity. [Say mora TORY um]

moray *n.* a tropical predatory eel-like fish. [Say MORE ay]

morbid *adj.* **1** having an unusual interest in death or other gloomy things. **2** gruesome, grisly. **3** *Medical* indicative of disease. □ **morbidity** *n.* **morbidly** *adv.*

mordant ● *adj.* **1** critical and unkind, but funny. **2** serving to fix colouring matter on another substance. ● *n.* a mordant substance. □ **mordantly** *adv.*

more ● *adj.* existing in a greater or additional quantity, amount, or degree. ● *n.* a greater quantity, number, or amount.

• **adv. 1** in a greater degree. **2** forming the comparative of adjectives and adverbs. **3** again.

morel n. an edible fungus with a honeycombed cap. [Say muh RELL]

moreover adv. what's more.

mores pl. n. the customs and conventions of a community. [Say MORE aze]

morgue n. a place where dead bodies are kept until burial or cremation. [Say MORG]

moribund adj. **1** at the point of death. **2** lacking vitality. [Say MORE i bund]

Mormon n. a member of the Church of Jesus Christ of Latter-day Saints. □ **Mormon** adj. **Mormonism** n. [Say MORE m'n]

morn n. literary morning.

morning n. the early part of the day, esp. from sunrise to noon.

morning glory n. (pl. **morning glories**) a twining plant with trumpet-shaped flowers that fade in the afternoon.

morning sickness n. nausea experienced in the morning during early pregnancy.

morning star n. the planet Venus when seen in the east before sunrise.

Moroccan n. a person from Morocco. □ **Moroccan** adj. [Say muh ROCKIN]

morocco n. (pl. **moroccos**) a fine flexible leather made from goat skins. [Say muh ROCKO]

moron n. informal a very stupid or foolish person. □ **moronic** adj. [Say MORE on, muh RON ick]

morose adj. sullen and ill-tempered. □ **morosely** adv. **moroseness** n. [Say muh ROACE]

morph[1] n. a variant form of an animal or plant.

morph[2] v. **1** alter or transform an image by computer. **2** slang change form. □ **morphing** n.

morpheme n. the smallest unit of meaning that a word can be divided into. [Say MORE feem]

morphine n. a painkilling drug obtained from opium. [Say MORE feen]

morphology n. (pl. **morphologies**) **1** the scientific study of the forms of living organisms or words. **2** the shape, form, or external arrangement of something. □ **morphological** adj. **morphologically** adv. [Say mor FOLLA jee, morfa LOGICAL]

morrow n. (usu. as **the morrow**) literary the following day.

Morse n. (also **Morse code**) a code in which letters are represented by combinations of long and short light or sound signals.

morsel n. a small amount or piece of esp. food.

mortadella n. a large spiced sausage usu. made of pork and pork fat and eaten cold. [Say morta DELLA]

mortal • adj. **1** subject to death. **2** causing death. **3** (of a battle) fought to the death. **4** associated with death. **5** (of an enemy) that cannot be reconciled until death. **6** intense, very serious. • n. a mortal being, esp. a human. □ **mortally** adv.

mortality n. (pl. **mortalities**) **1** the state of being subject to death. **2** loss of life on a large scale. **3** the number of deaths in a given period etc.

mortal sin n. a grave sin regarded as incurring damnation unless repented of.

mortar • n. **1** a mixture of lime with cement, sand, and water, used to bond bricks or stones. **2** a short cannon for firing shells at high angles. **3** a rounded bowl in which ingredients are pounded with a pestle. • v. **1** plaster or join with mortar. **2** attack or bombard with mortar shells. [Say MORTER]

mortarboard n. an academic cap with a stiff flat square top. [Say MORTER board]

mortgage • n. an agreement by which money is lent for buying property, the property itself being the security. • v. (**mortgages, mortgaged, mortgaging**) **1** give a bank etc. the right to take possession of property as a security for money lent. **2** expose to future risk for the sake of immediate advantage. □ **mortgageable** adj. [Say MORE gidge]

mortgagee n. the creditor in a mortgage, e.g. a bank. [Say more gidge EE]

mortgagor n. (also **mortgager**) the debtor in a mortgage. [Say MORE gidge or]

mortician n. an undertaker. [Say more TISH'n]

mortify v. (**mortifies, mortified, mortifying**) **1** cause to feel shamed or humiliated. **2** bring (the body, the passions, etc.) into subjection by self-denial or discipline. □ **mortification** n. **mortifying** adj. **mortifyingly** adv.

mortise n. (also **mortice**) a hole in a piece of wood etc. designed to receive the projection (tenon) of another to form a joint. □ **mortised** adj. [Say MORE tiss]

mortuary • n. (pl. **mortuaries**) a morgue. • adj. of death or burial.

Mosaic adj. of or associated with Moses. [Say moe ZAY ick]

mosaic n. **1** a picture or pattern produced by an arrangement of small pieces of glass

mosasaur n. (also **mosasaurus**, pl. **mosasauruses**) any large extinct marine reptile with a long slender body and flipper-like limbs. [Say MOE suh sore, moe suh SORE us]

mosey v. (**moseys, moseyed, moseying**) informal walk in a leisurely or aimless manner. [Say MOZE ee]

mosh v. (**moshes, moshed, moshing**) slang dance in a violent manner, deliberately hitting other dancers. □ **mosher** n. **moshing** n.

mosh pit n. slang the area in front of the stage at a rock concert, where moshing usually takes place.

Moslem n. & adj. = MUSLIM. [Say MOZZ lum]

mosque n. a Muslim place of worship. [Say MOSK]

mosquito n. (pl. **mosquitoes** or **mosquitos**) **1** any of various slender flying insects, the female of which bites humans and other animals, sometimes transmitting disease. **2** Cdn an initiation level of sports competition for young children.

moss n. (pl. **mosses**) a small, flowerless, green plant that carpets tree trunks, stones, etc. in damp habitats. □ **mossy** adj.

most ● adj. **1** existing in the greatest quantity or degree. **2** nearly all of. ● n. **1** the greatest quantity or number. **2** the majority. ● adv. **1** in the highest degree. **2** forming the superlative of adjectives and adverbs. **3** informal almost. □ **for the most part 1** as regards the greater part. **2** usually.

mostly adv. **1** as regards the greater part. **2** usually.

mote n. a speck of dust.

motel n. a hotel designed for motorists.

motet n. a short sacred choral composition. [Say moe TET]

moth n. a usu. nocturnal insect with two pairs of broad wings that are folded against its thick body when at rest, some species of which have larvae that feed on textiles.

mothball ● n. a ball of naphthalene etc. placed in stored clothes to keep away moths. ● v. **1** place in mothballs. **2** take out of use or active service.

mother ● n. **1** a woman in relation to a child or children to whom she has given birth, adopted, or fostered. **2** any female animal in relation to its offspring. **3** something that gives rise to something else. **4** the head of a female religious community. ● v. **1** be the mother of.

2 protect as a mother. □ **the mother of all …** the largest … of all. □ **motherless** adj.

motherboard n. a printed circuit board containing the principal components of a microcomputer etc.

mother country n. **1** the country which colonized or settled a particular place. **2** one's native country.

motherhood n. **1** the state or condition of being a mother. **2** the qualities characteristic of a mother. **3** (as an adj.) having an undisputed inherent goodness.

mother-in-law n. (pl. **mothers-in-law**) the mother of one's husband or wife.

motherland n. **1** one's native country. **2** the land of one's ancestors.

motherlode n. **1** Mining the main vein of a system. **2** a rich source of something.

motherly adj. like or characteristic of a mother in affection, care, etc. □ **motherliness** n.

mother-of-pearl n. a smooth iridescent substance forming the inner layer of some shells.

mother ship n. **1** a ship in charge of a number of smaller vessels. **2** an aircraft or spacecraft from which another is launched or controlled.

Mother Superior n. the head of a female religious community.

mother-to-be n. (pl. **mothers-to-be**) a woman who is expecting a baby.

mother tongue n. one's native language.

motif n. (pl. **motifs**) **1** a theme which frequently recurs in an artistic, musical, or literary work. **2** a decorative design or pattern. [Say moe TEEF]

motile adj. capable of motion. □ **motility** n. [Say MOE tile, moe TILLA tee]

motion ● n. **1** the action of moving. **2** a particular manner of moving the body. **3** a gesture. **4** a formal proposal put to a committee etc. ● v. direct a person by a sign or gesture. □ **go through the motions** do something perfunctorily. □ **motionless** adj. **motionlessly** adv.

motion picture n. a sequence of photographs taken and projected at very short intervals to create moving images.

motion sickness n. nausea induced by motion, esp. in a vehicle.

motivate v. (**motivates, motivated, motivating**) **1** supply a motive to. **2** cause to act in a particular way. **3** stimulate or energize. □ **motivation** n. **motivational** adj. **motivator** n.

motive ● n. **1** a factor that induces a person to act in a particular way. **2** a motif.

● *adj.* **1** producing motion. **2** motivating, causing. □ **motiveless** *adj.*

mot juste *n.* (*pl.* **mots justes**) the most appropriate expression. [*Say* moe ZHOOST]

motley *adj.* (**motlier**, **motliest**) of varied character.

motocross *n.* cross-country racing on motorcycles. □ **motocrosser** *n.*

motor ● *n.* a machine supplying motive power for a vehicle or for some other device with moving parts. ● *adj.* **1** driven by a motor. **2** of or for motor vehicles. **3** of or for motorists. **4** relating to muscular movement or the nerves activating it. ● *v.* travel by or in a motor vehicle.

motorbike *n. informal* **1** = MOTORCYCLE. **2** = DIRT BIKE.

motorboat *n.* a motor-driven boat.

motorcade *n.* a procession of motor vehicles.

motorcoach *n.* (*pl.* **motorcoaches**) a bus that is comfortably equipped for long journeys.

motorcycle *n.* a two-wheeled motor-driven vehicle. □ **motorcycling** *n.* **motorcyclist** *n.*

motorhome *n.* a large motor vehicle equipped as a self-contained home.

motorist *n.* the driver of a car.

motorization *n.* the introduction or use of motor vehicles.

motorize *v.* (**motorizes**, **motorized**, **motorizing**) **1** provide with a motor. **2** equip (troops etc.) with motor transport.

motormouth *n. slang* a person who talks incessantly.

motor nerve *n.* a nerve carrying impulses from the brain or spinal cord to a muscle.

motorsport *n.* the sport of racing motorized vehicles, esp. cars.

motor vehicle *n.* a road vehicle powered by an engine.

Motown *n.* music with rhythm and blues and soul elements. [*Say* MOE town]

mottled *adj.* marked with spots of colour. □ **mottling** *n.*

motto *n.* (*pl.* **mottoes**) a short phrase used as a guide of behaviour or as an expression of ideals.

mould[1] ● *n.* **1** a hollow container into which liquid material is poured to harden into a required shape. **2** something formed in a mould. ● *v.* **1** form or give shape to. **2** influence the formation of. **3** (esp. of clothing) fit closely to. **4** conform to the shape of. □ **mouldable** *adj.* **moulded** *adj.*

mould[2] *n.* a furry or staining fungal growth, e.g. on old food or damp walls.

mould[3] *n.* **1** loose earth. **2** the upper soil of cultivated land.

moulder[1] *v.* slowly decay or deteriorate, esp. from neglect.

moulder[2] *n.* a person or thing that moulds something.

moulding *n.* a moulded strip used as an ornamental feature around doors etc.

mouldy *adj.* (**mouldier**, **mouldiest**) **1** covered with or smelling of mould. **2** old and decaying. **3** old-fashioned. □ **mouldiness** *n.*

moult ● *v.* shed feathers, hair, etc., in the process of renewing plumage, a coat, etc. ● *n.* a loss of plumage, skin, or hair, esp. as part of an animal's life cycle. [*Say* MOLT]

mound ● *n.* **1** a raised mass of earth or other material. **2** a heap or pile. **3** a small hill. **4** *Baseball* a slight elevation on which the pitcher stands. ● *v.* heap up in a mound.

mount[1] ● *v.* **1** climb up or on to. **2 a** get up on an animal or bicycle to ride it. **b** (**be mounted**) be on horseback. **3** increase in intensity, size, etc. **4** organize and initiate. **5** fix in place or on a support. **6** attach a picture to a backing. ● *n.* **1** something on which an object is mounted for support or display. **2** a horse used for riding. □ **mountable** *adj.*

mount[2] *n.* mountain, hill.

mountain *n.* **1** a very large or high and steep hill. **2** a huge quantity.

mountain ash *n.* a small deciduous tree with compound leaves, white flowers, and scarlet or orange berries.

mountain avens *n.* (*pl.* **mountain avens**) a creeping alpine plant with white or yellow flowers, the floral emblem of the Northwest Territories.

mountain bike *n.* a sturdy bicycle originally designed for mountainous terrain. □ **mountain biker** *n.* **mountain biking** *n.*

mountaineer ● *n.* a mountain climber. ● *v.* climb mountains as a sport. □ **mountaineering** *n.*

mountain goat *n.* **1** a goat-antelope of the Rocky Mountains, with shaggy white hair and backward curving horns. **2** any proverbially agile goat that lives on mountains.

mountain lion *n.* a cougar.

mountainous *adj.* **1** having many mountains. **2** huge.

mountain sheep *n.* a bighorn sheep or a Dall sheep.

mountainside *n.* the side of a mountain.

Mountain Time *n.* the time in a zone

including Alberta, the US Rocky Mountain states, and Mexico.

mountaintop n. the top of a mountain.

mounted ● adj. **1** in senses of MOUNT[1] v. **2** serving on horseback. ● n. Cdn a mounted police force.

Mountie n. informal a member of the RCMP.

Mountie hat n. Cdn the characteristic tan hat of the RCMP, with a broad flat encircling brim.

mourn v. feel or show sorrow following a person's death. □ **mourner** n.

mournful adj. **1** sad, sorrowing. **2** expressing or suggestive of mourning. □ **mournfully** adv. **mournfulness** n.

mourning n. **1** the expression of deep sorrow, esp. for a death. **2** the esp. black clothes worn in mourning.

mourning dove n. a small slender dove with a long pointed tail and a plaintive call.

mouse ● n. (pl. **mice**) **1** a small rodent with a pointed snout, a long tail, and relatively large ears. **2** a timid or feeble person. **3** a small hand-held device moved over a flat surface to produce a corresponding movement of a cursor on a computer screen. ● v. (**mouses, moused, mousing**) **1** hunt for or catch mice. **2** use a mouse to move a cursor on a computer screen. □ **mouselike** adj. & adv. **mouser** n.

mouse pad n. a flat pad across which a computer mouse is moved.

mousetrap n. a trap for catching and usu. killing mice.

moussaka n. an eastern Mediterranean baked dish of ground meat, eggplant, etc. with white sauce. [Say moo SOCK uh]

mousse ● n. **1 a** a dessert of flavoured whipped cream, eggs, etc. **b** a meat or fish purée made with whipped cream etc. **2** a foamy substance for styling the hair. ● v. (**mousses, moussed, moussing**) apply mousse to hair. [Say MOOSE]

moustache n. the hair on the upper lip. □ **moustached** adj.

moustachio n. = MUSTACHIO. [Say muh STASHY oh]

mousy adj. (**mousier, mousiest**) **1** of or like a mouse. **2** shy or timid; ineffectual. **3** nondescript light brown. **4** dark grey with a yellow tinge.

mouth ● n. (pl. **mouths**) **1** an opening in the head through which food is taken in and sounds are emitted. **2** the opening of a sack, cave, volcano, etc. **3 a** the place where a river enters a sea or lake. **b** the entrance to a harbour or bay. **4** informal talkativeness, esp. impudent or boastful. ● v. **1** say words with movement of the mouth but no

sound. **2** utter or speak solemnly with affectations. **3** utter very distinctly. □ **have a big mouth** talk indiscreetly. **mouth off 1** talk insolently or disrespectfully. **2** express one's opinions forcefully. **watch one's mouth** be careful not to say something offensive. □ **mouthed** adj. (also in comb.)

mouthful n. (pl. **mouthfuls**) **1** a quantity, esp. of food, that fills the mouth. **2** a long or complicated word or phrase.

mouthguard n. a piece of esp. sports equipment protecting the mouth, teeth, etc.

mouth organ n. (also **mouth harp**) = HARMONICA.

mouthpart n. any of the usu. paired organs surrounding the mouth of an insect and adapted for feeding.

mouthpiece n. **1** the part of something placed in or near the mouth. **2** a person, organization, etc. that speaks for others.

mouth-to-mouth n. a method of resuscitation in which a person breathes into a subject's lungs through the mouth.

mouthwash n. (pl. **mouthwashes**) a liquid antiseptic etc. for rinsing the mouth or gargling.

mouth-watering adj. **1** (of food etc.) appetizing. **2** tempting, alluring.

mouthy adj. (**mouthier, mouthiest**) informal impudent, cheeky.

movable adj. (also **moveable**) **1** that can be moved. **2** (of a religious feast) variable in date from year to year.

move ● v. (**moves, moved, moving**) **1** go or cause to go in a specified direction or manner. **2** change position. **3** change one's place of residence. **4** change from one state or activity to another. **5** take or cause to take action. **6** make progress. **7** provoke feelings in. **8** propose for discussion at a meeting. ● n. **1** an instance of moving. **2** an action taken towards achieving a purpose. **3** a manoeuvre in a sport. **4** a player's turn during a board game. □ **get a move on** informal **1** hurry up. **2** make a start. **on the move 1** progressing. **2** moving around. **put the move** (or **moves**) **on** make sexual advances towards.

movement n. **1** an act of changing physical location or position. **2** (usu. in pl.) a person's activities and whereabouts. **3** a body of persons with a common goal. **4** a direction of thought. **5** the moving parts of a mechanism. **6** a principal division of a longer musical work. **7** (of the bowels) the action of discharging feces.

mover n. **1** a person or thing that moves. **2** a company that transports furniture etc. for clients changing residence etc. **3** (esp. in

movers and shakers) a person who incites or instigates to action.

movie n. a motion-picture film.

moviegoer n. a person who attends movies. □ **moviegoing** n.

moviemaker n. a filmmaker. □ **moviemaking** n.

moving adj. **1** that moves or causes to move. **2** affecting with emotion. □ **movingly** adv. (in sense 2)

moving picture n. = MOTION PICTURE.

mow v. (**mows**; past **mowed**; past participle **mowed** or **mown**; **mowing**) cut down grass etc. with a machine or scythe. □ **mow down** kill in great numbers esp. by gunfire. [Rhymes with SHOW]

mower n. a machine for mowing grass.

moxie n. slang force of character, energy, ingenuity.

Mozambican n. a native or inhabitant of Mozambique. □ **Mozambican** adj. [Say moe zam BEAK in]

mozzarella n. a very mild white cheese. [Say motsa RELLA]

MP abbr. (pl. **MPs**) **1** Member of Parliament. **2** military police.

MP3 n. a digital audio compression format much used in music files to be downloaded over the Internet.

mph abbr. miles per hour.

MPP abbr. (pl. **MPPs**) Cdn (Ont.) Member of Provincial Parliament.

Mr. n. (pl. **Messrs.**) **1** a title prefixed to the name of a man. **2** a title prefixed to a man's characteristic trait, designation of office, etc.

MRI abbr. MAGNETIC RESONANCE IMAGING.

Mrs. n. (pl. **Mrs.** or **Mesdames**) a title prefixed to the name of a married woman.

MS abbr. **1** (pl. **MSS**) manuscript. **2** MULTIPLE SCLEROSIS.

Ms. n. a title prefixed to the name of a woman regardless of her marital status.

M.Sc. abbr. (pl. **M.Sc.'s**) Master of Science.

MSG abbr. MONOSODIUM GLUTAMATE.

MSRP abbr. manufacturer's suggested retail price.

Mt. abbr. **1** Mount. **2** Mountain.

Mtl. abbr. Montreal.

mu n. **1** the twelfth Greek letter (M, μ). **2** (μ, as a symbol) = MICRO- 2. [Say MYOO]

much ● adj. & pron. **1** a large amount. **2** a poor example of something. ● adv. **1** to a great extent **2** often. ● interj. informal expressing strong disagreement. □ **much as** even though. □ **muchly** adv. jocular

mucho adj. & adv. jocular much. [Say MOOCH oh]

muck ● n. **1** mud. **2** very dark and highly organic soil. **3** informal dirt or filth. **4** manure. ● v. **1** (usu. foll. by up) informal ruin, spoil, mess up. **2** make dirty. □ **muck about** (or **around**) informal **1** putter or fool about. **2** interfere. **muck out** clean (a barn etc.) of manure. □ **mucky** adj.

mucker n. slang **1** a hockey player known more for tenacity than for talent. **2** a person or thing that removes mining waste.

muckraker n. a person who seeks to expose scandals. □ **muckraking** n.

mucky-muck n. (also **muckamuck**, **muckety-muck**) slang a self-important person.

mucosa n. (pl. **mucosae**) a mucous membrane. □ **mucosal** adj. [Say myoo CO suh for the singular, myoo CO see for the plural]

mucous adj. pertaining to mucus. [Say MYOO cuss]

mucous membrane n. a mucus-secreting tissue lining many body cavities.

mucus n. **1** a slimy substance secreted by a mucous membrane or gland. **2** a gummy substance found in plants. [Say MYOO cuss]

mud n. **1** wet soft earthy matter. **2** hard ground from the drying of this. □ **drag through the mud** denigrate publicly. **fling** (or **sling** or **throw**) **mud** speak disparagingly. **one's name is mud** one is in disgrace.

mudbank n. a bank of mud, e.g. on the bed of a river.

mud bath n. a bath in the mud of mineral springs, esp. to relieve rheumatism etc.

mudcat n. **1** Cdn = BULLHEAD 1. **2** a large N American catfish.

muddle ● v. (**muddles, muddled, muddling**) **1** bring into disorder. **2** bewilder, confuse. **3** mismanage. ● n. **1** a state of disorder. **2** mental confusion. □ **muddle through** succeed by perseverance rather than skill.

muddle-headed adj. stupid, confused.

muddy ● adj. (**muddier, muddiest**) **1** like mud. **2** covered in or full of mud. **3** turbid. **4** mentally confused. ● v. (**muddies, muddied, muddying**) make muddy. □ **muddy the waters** confuse matters. □ **muddiness** n.

mud flat n. muddy land left uncovered at low tide.

mudhole n. a water hole dried so as to become mud.

mud pie n. **1** mud made into a pie shape by a child. **2** a rich chocolate ice cream pie.

mud room *n.* a small room in which wet footwear and coats etc. are removed.

mudslide *n.* an avalanche of mud etc.

mudslinging *n. informal* abuse, slander, or malevolent criticism. □ **mudslinger** *n.*

muesli *n.* a breakfast food of crushed cereals, dried fruits, nuts, etc., eaten with milk. [*Say* MYOOZ lee]

muezzin *n.* a Muslim crier who proclaims the hours of prayer usu. from a minaret. [*Say* moo EZZ in]

muff¹ *n.* **1** a fur-covered tube with an opening at each end for the hands to be inserted for warmth. **2** = EARMUFF.

muff² ● *v.* bungle. ● *n.* a failure, esp. to catch a ball.

muffin *n.* a cupcake-like sweet bread.

muffle *v.* (**muffles, muffled, muffling**) **1** wrap for warmth. **2** cover a source of sound to reduce its loudness. **3** stifle an utterance. **4** prevent from speaking.

muffler *n.* **1** a device attached to a motor vehicle's exhaust system to reduce noise. **2** a scarf worn for warmth.

mufti¹ *n.* a Muslim legal expert who gives rulings on religious matters. [*Say* MUFF tee]

mufti² *n.* plain clothes worn by someone who always wears (esp. military) uniform. [*Say* MUFF tee]

mug ● *n.* **1** a cylindrical cup with a handle. **2** *slang* a person's face or mouth. ● *v.* (**mugs, mugged, mugging**) **1** rob a person with violence in a public place. **2** *slang* make faces before a camera etc. □ **a mug's game** *informal* a foolish or unprofitable activity. □ **mugful** *n.* (*pl.* **mugfuls**) **mugger** *n.* (in sense 1 of *v.*).

mugging *n.* a violent robbery of a person in a public place.

muggy *adj.* (**muggier, muggiest**) oppressively humid. □ **mugginess** *n.*

mug shot *n. slang* a photograph of a face.

mug-up *n. Cdn* (esp. *Nfld*) a break for tea etc., esp. while on a journey.

mujahedeen *pl. n.* (also **mujahideen**) guerrilla fighters in Islamic countries. [*Say* mooja huh DEEN]

mukluk *n.* **1** a usu. laced winter boot with a heavy rubber sole and a high fabric upper. **2** a traditional Inuit boot. [*Say* MUCK luck]

muktuk *n.* a traditional Inuit food consisting of the skin and surface blubber of a whale.

mulberry *n.* (*pl.* **mulberries**) **1** a small tree with broad leaves and dark red or white berries. **2** *n.* & *adj.* a dark red or purple colour.

mulch ● *n.* a mixture usu. of vegetable matter spread around a plant to help it grow. ● *v.* (**mulches, mulched, mulching**) treat with mulch.

mule *n.* **1** the offspring of a donkey and a horse. **2** a stupid or obstinate person. **3** *slang* a person acting as a courier for illicit drugs. **4** a light backless shoe.

mule deer *n.* (*pl.* **mule deer**) a long-eared black-tailed deer of western N America.

mulish *adj.* **1** like a mule. **2** stubborn. □ **mulishly** *adv.* **mulishness** *n.*

mull *v.* (often foll. by *over*) ponder or consider.

mullah *n.* a Muslim learned in Islamic theology and sacred law. [*Say* MULLA or MOOLA (with OOL *as in* WOOL)]

mulled *adj.* (of wine) warmed with added sugar, spices, etc.

mullein *n.* a plant with woolly leaves and tall spikes of yellow flowers. [*Say* MULL'n]

mullet¹ *n.* a fish with a thick body and a large blunt-nosed head. [*Say* MULL it]

mullet² *n.* a hairstyle, worn esp. by men, in which the hair is cut short at the front and sides, and left long at the back.

mullion *n.* a vertical bar dividing the lights in a window. □ **mullioned** *adj.* [*Say* MULL yin]

multi- *comb. form* many.

multicellular *adj. Biology* having many cells.

multicoloured *adj.* (also **multicolour**) of many colours.

multiculti *adj.* (also *Cdn* **multicult**) *informal* = MULTICULTURAL.

multicultural *adj.* designating a society consisting of many culturally distinct groups. □ **multiculturalism** *n.* **multiculturalist** *n.* & *adj.* **multiculturally** *adv.*

multi-faceted *adj.* having several facets, aspects, etc.

multifarious *adj.* **1** many and various. **2** having great variety or diversity. □ **multifariously** *adv.* **multifariousness** *n.* [*Say* multi FERRY us]

multilateral *adj.* involving three or more participants. □ **multilateralism** *n.* **multilaterally** *adv.*

multilingual *adj.* **1** in or using several languages. **2** able to speak several languages fluently. □ **multilingualism** *n.*

multimedia *adj.* (of art, education, etc.) using more than one medium of expression.

multinational *n.* a business organization operating in several countries. □ **multinational** *adj.*

multiple ● *adj.* **1** having many parts. **2** many and various. ● *n.* a number that may be divided evenly by another a certain number of times.

multiple-choice *adj.* with the correct answer needing to be chosen from among several listed possibilities.

multiple personality *n.* (also **multiple personality disorder**) a condition in which an individual's personality is apparently split into two or more distinct sub-personalities.

multiple sclerosis *n.* a disease in which sclerosis occurs in the brain and spinal cord, resulting in tremor, paralysis, speech defects, etc.

multiplex ● *adj.* **1** of many elements. **2** relating to a complex of two or more cinemas. ● *n.* (*pl.* **multiplexes**) **1** a multiplex cinema. **2** a multiplex system.

multiplication *n.* the act or process of multiplying.

multiplicity *n.* (*pl.* **multiplicities**) a great number and variety. [*Say* multi PLISSA tee]

multiplier *n.* **1** a thing which or person who multiplies or causes something to increase. **2** a quantity by which a number is multiplied.

multiply¹ *v.* (**multiplies, multiplied, multiplying**) **1** add a number to itself a specified number of times. **2** increase in number. [*Say* MULTA ply]

multiply² *adv.* in several different ways or respects. [*Say* MULL tip lee]

multiracial *adj.* having to do with many human races.

multi-sensory *adj.* affecting more than one of the five senses.

multi-tasking *n.* the execution of a number of tasks at once. □ **multi-task** *v.* **multi-tasking** *adj.*

multitude *n.* **1** a great number. **2** a large gathering of people. **3** (**the multitudes**) the common people.

multitudinous *adj.* very numerous. [*Say* multi TUDE in us]

multivalent *adj.* **1** having many interpretations, meanings, or values. **2** *Chemistry* **a** having a valence of more than two. **b** having a variable valence. □ **multivalence** *n.* [*Say* multi VAY lint]

multivitamin *n.* a nutritional supplement incorporating several vitamins. □ **multivitamin** *adj.*

mum¹ *n. informal* mother.

mum² *adj. informal* silent. □ **mum's the word** say nothing.

mum³ *n. informal* a chrysanthemum.

mumble ● *v.* (**mumbles, mumbled, mumbling**) speak or utter indistinctly. ● *n.* an indistinct utterance. □ **mumbler** *n.* **mumbling** *n.* & *adj.* **mumblingly** *adv.*

mumbo-jumbo *n.* (*pl.* **mumbo-jumbos**) language that is complicated but has no real meaning.

mummer *n.* a masked actor or merrymaker, esp. part of a group going from house to house.

mummify *v.* (**mummifies, mummified, mummifying**) preserve a body in the form of a mummy. □ **mummification** *n.* **mummified** *adj.*

mummy¹ *n.* (*pl.* **mummies**) *informal* mother.

mummy² *n.* (*pl.* **mummies**) (esp. in ancient Egypt) a body that has been ceremonially preserved and wrapping in bandages.

mumps *pl. n.* (treated as *sing.*) a viral disease, esp. of children, characterized by swelling of the glands at the sides of the face.

munch *v.* (**munches, munched, munching**) eat steadily with a marked action of the jaws. □ **muncher** *n.*

munchies *pl. n. informal* **1** snacks. **2** (**the munchies**) hunger for snack food.

munchkin *n. informal* a small or dwarf-like person, animal, etc.

mundane *adj.* **1** dull, routine, everyday. **2** earthly rather than heavenly or spiritual. □ **mundanely** *adv.* **mundanity** *n.* (*pl.* **mundanities**) [*Say* mun DANE *or* MUN dane, mun DANNA tee]

mung *n.* (also **mung bean**) a leguminous plant grown as a source of bean sprouts.

municipal *adj.* having to do with a municipality. □ **municipally** *adv.* [*Say* myoo NISSA pull]

municipality *n.* (*pl.* **municipalities**) a city, town, or district having local government.

munificent *adj.* splendidly generous. □ **munificence** *n.* **munificently** *adv.* [*Say* myoo NIFFA sint]

munitions *pl. n.* military weapons, ammunition, and stores. [*Say* myoo NISH'n]

mural *n.* a painting executed directly on an esp. large section of wall. □ **muralist** *n.*

murder¹ ● *n.* **1** the unlawful premeditated killing of a human being by another. **2** *informal* an unpleasant or damaging situation or thing. ● *v.* **1** kill a human being deliberately. **2** *informal* spoil by bad execution, mispronunciation, performance, etc. □ **get away with murder** *informal* escape punishment.

murder will out murder cannot remain undetected. □ **murderer** n. **murderess** n.

murder² n. a flock (of crows).

murderball n. *Cdn* a game in which players attempt to hit each other with a large inflated ball.

murderous adj. having to do with murder or great harm. □ **murderously** adv. **murderousness** n.

murk n. darkness, gloom; obscurity.

murky adj. (**murkier, murkiest**) **1** dark, gloomy. **2** suspiciously obscure. □ **murkiness** n.

murmur ● n. **1** a softly spoken or nearly indistinct utterance. **2** a quiet complaint. **3** a recurring sound heard in the heart and usu. indicating abnormality. **4** a subdued continuous sound. ● v. **1** speak softly or indistinctly. **2** make a subdued continuous sound. **3** complain in low tones. □ **murmurer** n. **murmuring** adj. & n.

Murphy's Law n. *jocular* the principle that if anything can go wrong, it will.

murre n. an auk or guillemot. [*Rhymes with* HER]

murrelet n. any of several small auks of the north Pacific. [*Say* MUR lit]

muscat n. a sweet fortified white wine. [*Say* MUSS cat]

muscle ● n. **1** fibrous tissue with the ability to contract, producing movement. **2** physical power or strength. ● v. (**muscles, muscled, muscling**) **1** *informal* move by the exercise of physical power. **2** *slang* coerce by violence, intimidation, etc. □ **muscled** adj. **muscly** adj.

muscle-bound adj. having over-developed muscles.

muscle car n. *informal* a powerful car.

muscleman n. (*pl.* **musclemen**) a man with highly developed muscles.

Muscovite n. a native or citizen of Moscow. □ **Muscovite** adj. [*Say* MUSKA vite]

muscular adj. **1** having well-developed muscles. **2** of or affecting the muscles. □ **muscularity** n.

muscular dystrophy n. a hereditary progressive wasting of the muscles.

musculature n. the muscular system of a body. [*Say* MUSS cue luh chur]

musculoskeletal adj. having to do with the musculature and skeleton together. [*Say* muss cue lo SKELETAL]

muse¹ ● n. **1** (**Muse**) *Myth* any of the nine goddesses who encourage the arts and sciences. **2** a person etc. that inspires an artist.

muse² v. (**muses, mused, musing**) **1** ponder, reflect. **2** say or murmur meditatively.

museum n. a building for exhibiting objects of interest or importance.

mush¹ ● n. (*pl.* **mushes**) **1** a soft pulpy mass. **2** feeble sentimentality. ● v. (**mushes, mushed, mushing**) reduce to mush. □ **mushy** adj. **mushiness** n.

mush² ● v. (**mushes, mushed, mushing**) travel through snow with a dogsled. ● n. (*pl.* **mushes**) a journey across snow with a dogsled. □ **musher** n. **mushing** n.

mushroom ● n. the often edible spore-producing body of various fungi, typically with a stalk and domed cap. ● v. appear or increase rapidly. □ **mushrooming** adj. & n.

mushroom cloud n. a cloud of smoke, vapour, etc. suggesting the shape of a mushroom.

music n. **1** the art of combining sounds in a pleasing or expressive way. **2** the sounds so produced, or the notation representing these. □ **face the music** *informal* face the consequences.

musical ● adj. of, like, including, or skilled in music. ● n. a play or film with much singing. □ **musicality** n. **musically** adv.

musical chairs *pl.* n. a game in which players compete for a decreasing number of chairs whenever music stops.

musical ride n. *Cdn* an exhibition of horseback riding choreographed to music.

music box n. a small box that plays a tune when its lid is opened.

music hall n. **1** a public hall or theatre used for musical performances. **2** vaudeville.

musician n. a person who performs esp. instrumental music. □ **musicianship** n.

musicology n. the study of music as an academic subject. □ **musicological** adj. **musicologist** n. [*Say* music OLLA jee]

musing n. **1** an act of being absorbed in thought. **2** an expression of one's thoughts. □ **musingly** adv.

musk n. a strong-smelling substance used in perfumes, originally obtained from a type of deer. □ **musky** adj.

muskeg n. a swamp or bog in northern N America.

muskellunge n. (*pl.* **muskellunge**) a large N American pike. [*Say* MUSKA lunge]

musket n. *hist.* a light gun with a long barrel.

musketeer n. *hist.* a soldier armed with a musket.

muskie n. (pl. **muskie** or **muskies**) = MUSKELLUNGE.

muskmelon n. a yellow or green melon with a raised network of skin markings.

Muskoka chair n. Cdn a slatted wooden lawn chair with a fan-shaped back and broad arms. [Say muh SKO kuh]

muskox n. (pl. **muskox** or **muskoxen**) a large mammal of the tundra, with a thick shaggy coat and small curved horns.

muskrat n. a large semi-aquatic rodent with a musky smell.

Muslim n. a follower of Islam. □ **Muslim** adj. [Say MUZZ lim]

muslin n. a fine, almost transparent cotton fabric. [Say MUZZ lin]

muss informal ● v. (**musses**, **mussed**, **mussing**) mess, make untidy. ● n. disorder, mess.

mussel n. any of various bivalve molluscs, often used for food.

must¹ ● aux. v. (3rd singular present **must**; past **had to** or in indirect speech **must**) **1** be obliged to; should. **2** expressing insistence. **3** expressing a confident opinion. ● n. informal something that should not be missed.

must² n. grape juice before or during fermentation.

must³ n. mustiness, mould.

mustache n. = MOUSTACHE.

mustachio n. (pl. **mustachios**) (often in pl.) an esp. large moustache. □ **mustachioed** adj. [Say muh STASHY oh]

mustang n. a small wild horse of the American plains.

mustard n. **1** a spicy yellow or brown pasty condiment made from the crushed seeds of a plant of the cabbage family. **2** (also **mustard yellow**) the brownish-yellow colour of this condiment. □ **mustardy** adj.

mustard gas n. a vapour used in chemical warfare.

muster ● v. **1** assemble soldiers for inspection. **2** summon up a feeling or attitude. ● n. a group of esp. soldiers brought together, e.g. for inspection. □ **pass muster** come up to the required standard.

must-have n. & adj. (something) regarded as indispensable.

mustn't contr. must not.

must-see n. & adj. (something) that must be seen.

musty adj. (**mustier**, **mustiest**) having a mouldy or stale smell. □ **mustiness** n.

mutable adj. literary **1** liable to change or alteration. **2** fickle. □ **mutability** n. [Say MUTE uh bull]

mutant ● adj. resulting from or showing the effects of mutation. ● n. **1** an individual, gene, etc. which has arisen by or undergone mutation. **2** an individual with freak or grossly abnormal characteristics.

mutate v. (**mutates**, **mutated**, **mutating**) undergo mutation. □ **mutated** adj.

mutation n. **1** the action of changing in form or nature. **2** a genetic change. **3** a distinct form produced by genetic change. □ **mutational** adj.

mute ● adj. **1** not speaking. **2** lacking the faculty of speech. **3** silent. ● n. **1** a person who cannot or will not speak. **2** an apparatus for dampening or softening the sound of a musical instrument **3** = MUTE BUTTON 2. ● v. (**mutes**, **muted**, **muting**) **1** deaden, soften, or eliminate the sound of. **2** tone down, make less intense. □ **mutely** adv. **muteness** n.

mute button n. a button that temporarily turns off the sound on a TV or telephone.

muted adj. **1** subdued, understated. **2** silent, quiet, muffled.

mutilate v. (**mutilates**, **mutilated**, **mutilating**) **1** injure very severely, e.g. by removal of a limb. **2** cause serious damage to. □ **mutilation** n. **mutilator** n. [Say MUTE uh late]

mutiny ● n. (pl. **mutinies**) an open revolt against authority, esp. by soldiers or sailors. ● v. (**mutinies**, **mutinied**, **mutinying**) engage in mutiny. □ **mutinous** adj. **mutinously** adv. [Say MUTE in ee]

mutt n. derogatory or jocular a dog, esp. a mongrel.

mutter ● v. **1** speak in a barely audible manner. **2** grumble about. ● n. **1** low, indistinct muttered words or sounds. **2** an act of muttering. □ **muttering** n. & adj.

mutton n. the flesh of sheep used for food.

mutton busting n. a rodeo event in which a child attempts to remain on the back of a moving sheep for four seconds.

muttonchops n. sideburns that are narrow at the top and wide at the bottom.

mutual adj. **1** experienced by each of two or more parties with reference to the others; reciprocal. **2** shared between two or more persons. □ **mutuality** n. **mutually** adv. [Say MYOO choo ul, myoo choo AL it ee]

mutual fund n. a fund in which the combined contributions from many persons are invested in various securities.

Muzak n. proprietary recorded light background music. [Say MYOO zack]

muzzle ● *n.* **1** the projecting part of an animal's face. **2** a guard fitted over an animal's nose and mouth. **3** the open end of a firearm. ● *v.* (**muzzles, muzzled, muzzling**) **1** put a muzzle on. **2** impose silence upon.

muzzy *adj.* (**muzzier, muzziest**) **1** dazed or fuddled. **2** blurred, indistinct.

MV *abbr.* megavolt(s).

MVP *abbr.* (*pl.* **MVPs**) most valuable player.

MW *abbr.* megawatt(s).

my ● *poss. adj.* of or belonging to me or myself. ● *interj.* expressing surprise, admiration, etc.

myalgia *n.* a pain in a muscle or muscles. □ **myalgic** *adj.* [*Say* my AL juh *or* my AL jee uh]

Mycenaean *adj.* of or relating to a late Bronze Age civilization in Greece. □ **Mycenaean** *n.* [*Say* my suh NEE in]

mycology *n.* the study of fungi. □ **mycologist** *n.* [*Say* my COLLA jee]

myelin *n.* a white substance which forms a sheath around certain nerve fibres. [*Say* MY uh lin]

Mylar *n.* *proprietary* a polyester film. [*Say* MY lar]

mynah *n.* a starling that is able to mimic the human voice. [*Say* MY nuh]

myocardium *n.* (*pl.* **myocardia**) the muscular tissue of the heart. □ **myocardial** *adj.* [*Say* my oh CARDY um *for the singular,* my oh CARDY uh *for the plural*]

myopia *n.* **1** short-sightedness. **2** lack of imagination or foresight. □ **myopic** *adj.* **myopically** *adv.* [*Say* my OPE ee uh, my OP ick]

myriad *n. & adj.* (of) an indefinitely great number. [*Say* MEERY add]

myrrh *n.* a sticky sweet-smelling substance derived from some trees, used in perfume, medicine, etc. [*Rhymes with* HER]

myrtle *n.* **1** an evergreen shrub with glossy aromatic foliage, white flowers, and purple-black oval berries. **2** the lesser periwinkle, a trailing evergreen plant with lilac-blue flowers. [*Rhymes with* TURTLE]

myself *pron.* **1** *emphatic form of* I[2] *or* ME[1]. **2** *reflexive form of* ME[1]. **3** in my normal state.

mysterious *adj.* full of or wrapped in mystery. □ **mysteriously** *adv.* **mysteriousness** *n.*

mystery *n.* (*pl.* **mysteries**) **1** a secret, hidden, or inexplicable matter. **2** secrecy or obscurity. **3** a novel, film, etc. dealing with a puzzling crime.

mystic ● *n.* a person who tries to become united with God and understand deep truths through prayer and meditation. ● *adj.* = MYSTICAL. □ **mysticism** *n.* [*Say* MISS tick, MISSTA sizzum]

mystical *adj.* **1** having to do with mystics or mysticism. **2** inspiring a sense of spiritual mystery and awe. □ **mystically** *adv.* [*Say* MISS tick ul]

mystify *v.* (**mystifies, mystified, mystifying**) bewilder, confuse. □ **mystification** *n.* **mystifying** *adj.* **mystifyingly** *adv.* [*Say* MISSTA fye]

mystique *n.* an attractive mysterious atmosphere surrounding some activity or person. [*Say* miss TEEK]

myth *n.* **1** a traditional story explaining natural or social phenomena. **2** a widely held but false notion. □ **mythic** *adj.* **mythical** *adj.* **mythically** *adv.*

mythology *n.* (*pl.* **mythologies**) **1** a body of myths. **2** the study of myths. □ **mythological** *adj.* **mythologically** *adv.* **mythologize** *v.* **mythologizer** *n.*

mythos *n.* **1** *literary* a myth; a body of myths. **2** a narrative theme or pattern. [*Say* MITH oss *or* MY thoss]

N¹ *n.* (also **n**) (*pl.* **Ns** or **N's**) the fourteenth letter of the alphabet.

N² *abbr.* (also **n**) **1** North or Northern. **2** New.

n¹ *abbr.* (also **n.**) noun.

n² *symb.* **1** *Math* an indefinite number. **2** nano-. □ **to the nth** (or **nth degree**) **1** *Math* to any required power. **2** to any extent.

'n *conj.* (also **'n'**) *informal* and.

NA *abbr.* North America(n).

n/a *abbr.* **1** not applicable. **2** not available.

naan *n.* = NAN².

nab *v.* (**nabs, nabbed, nabbing**) *informal* arrest; capture.

nabob *n.* *informal* a very rich or influential person. [*Say* NAY bob]

nacho *n.* (*pl.* **nachos**) a tortilla chip topped with cheese, salsa, etc. [*Say* NOTCH oh]

nada *n.* *informal* nothing. [*Say* NODDA]

nadir *n.* **1** the point in the sky directly below an observer. **2** the lowest or worst point. [*Say* NAY deer]

NAFTA *abbr.* North American Free Trade Agreement.

nag¹ ● *v.* (**nags, nagged, nagging**) **1** harass with persistent fault-finding or urging. **2** ache dully but persistently. **3** worry or preoccupy. ● *n.* a persistently nagging person. □ **nagging** *n.* **naggingly** *adv.*

nag² *n.* an old or broken-down horse.

Nahuatl *n.* **1** a member of a group of Aboriginal peoples of southern Mexico and Central America, including the Aztecs. **2** their language. □ **Nahuatl** *adj.* [*Say* nuh WOTTLE]

naif *n.* a naive person. [*Say* naw EEF]

nail ● *n.* **1** a small metal spike with a broadened head, driven in with a hammer. **2** a horny covering on the tip of the human finger or toe. ● *v.* **1** fasten with a nail or nails. **2** secure, catch, or get hold of. **3** complete or perform well or perfectly. □ **nailed** *adj.*

nail-biter *n.* **1** something that causes anxiety or tension. **2** someone who bites their fingernails. □ **nail-biting** *adj.*

naive *adj.* **1** showing a lack of experience. **2** natural and unaffected; innocent. □ **naively** *adv.* **naiveness** *n.* [*Say* nigh EEV]

naïveté *n.* (also **naivety**) **1** lack of experience. **2** innocence and lack of affectation. [*Say* nigh ee vuh TAY or nigh EEVA tee]

naked *adj.* **1** unclothed. **2** plain; undisguised. **3** uncovered. **4** defenceless. **5** without leaves, hairs, etc. **6** without prominent features; empty. □ **the naked eye** unassisted vision, e.g. without a telescope, microscope, etc. □ **nakedly** *adv.* **nakedness** *n.*

Nakota *n. & adj.* = ASSINIBOINE. [*Say* na COHTA]

namby-pamby ● *adj.* **1** lacking vigour; weak. **2** blandly pretty or sentimental. ● *n.* (*pl.* **namby-pambies**) a namby-pamby person.

name ● *n.* **1** the word by which someone or something is known, spoken of, etc. **2** a term of abuse. **3** a famous person. **4** an esp. good reputation. ● *v.* (**names, named, naming**) **1** give a name to. **2** mention. **3** nominate, appoint, etc. □ **give a bad name** cause disrepute to. **(have) to one's name** (possess) as one's own. **in the name of 1** calling to witness. **2** by the authority of. **3** for the sake of. **make a name for oneself** (also **make one's name**) become famous. **name of the game** *informal* the purpose of an action etc. □ **nameable** *adj.* **namer** *n.*

name brand *n.* = BRAND NAME.

name-calling *n.* abusive language.

name-dropping *n.* the casual mentioning of famous people one knows in order to impress others. □ **name-drop** *v.* **name-dropper** *n.*

nameless *adj.* **1** having no name. **2** inexpressible. **3** anonymous. **4** individually indistinguishable. □ **namelessly** *adv.* **namelessness** *n.*

namely *adv.* that is to say.

nameplate *n.* a plate or panel identifying the occupant of a room, model of a product, etc.

namesake *n.* a person or thing having the same name as another.

Namibian *n.* a native or inhabitant of Namibia. □ **Namibian** *adj.* [*Say* nuh MIBBY in]

nan[1] n. (also **nana**) informal grandmother.

nan[2] n. a type of flat, oval, leavened bread.

Nanaimo bar n. Cdn a dessert square consisting of a chocolate and cookie-crumb crust covered with a creamy vanilla filling and a chocolate glaze. [Say nuh NIME oh]

nanny n. (pl. **nannies**) **1** a person employed to care for a child in the child's home. **2** = NAN[1]. **3** (**nanny goat**) a female goat.

nano- comb. form **1** denoting a factor of 10^{-9}. **2** very small; minute.

nanosecond n. one billionth of a second.

nanotechnology n. technology on a molecular or atomic scale.

nap[1] ● v. (**naps, napped, napping**) sleep lightly or briefly. ● n. a short daytime sleep.

nap[2] n. the raised pile on textiles, esp. velvet. □ **napped** adj.

napalm ● n. a jellied gasoline used in incendiary bombs. ● v. attack with napalm bombs. [Say NAY palm]

nape n. the back of the neck.

naphtha n. a petroleum distillate used as a fuel and solvent. [Say NAP thuh or NAF thuh]

naphthalene n. a white crystalline aromatic substance used in mothballs. [Say NAF thuh leen or NAP thuh leen]

napkin n. a square piece of linen, paper, etc. used for wiping the lips, fingers, etc. at meals.

Napoleonic adj. having to do with Napoleon I (1769–1821), emperor of France, or his time. [Say nuh poley ON ick]

narc n. slang a police narcotics officer.

narcissism n. excessive interest in oneself. □ **narcissist** n. **narcissistic** adj. [Say NARSA sism]

narcissus n. (pl. **narcissi**) a daffodil, esp. one with pale outer petals surrounding an orange or yellow cup. [Say nar SISS us for the singular, nar SISS eye for the plural]

narcolepsy n. a disease with fits of sleepiness. □ **narcoleptic** adj. & n. [Say NARKA lepsy]

narcosis n. (pl. **narcoses**) drowsiness or unconsciousness induced by a drug. [Say nar CO sis]

narcotic n. **1** an esp. illegal non-medicinal drug affecting mood or behaviour. **2** a drug that induces drowsiness or unconsciousness. □ **narcotic** adj.

nark n. = NARC.

narrate v. (**narrates, narrated, narrating**) **1** give a continuous account of events. **2** provide a spoken commentary or accompaniment for a film etc.

□ **narration** n. [Say NAIR ate or nuh RATE]

narrative n. a spoken or written account of connected events in order of happening. □ **narrative** adj. **narratively** adv. [Say NERRA tiv]

narrator n. a character or voice that recounts events or gives commentary in a book, documentary, etc. [Say NAIR ate er or nuh RATE er]

narrow ● adj. (**narrower, narrowest**) **1 a** of small width in proportion to length. **b** confined or confining. **2** of limited scope. **3** with little margin; close. ● n. (**narrows**) the narrow part of a strait, river, etc. ● v. become or make narrower. □ **narrow down** reduce the number of possibilities. □ **narrowness** n.

narrowly adv. **1** only by a small amount. **2** in a way that is limited. **3** closely; carefully.

narrow-minded adj. rigid or restricted in one's views. □ **narrow-mindedly** adv. **narrow-mindedness** n.

narthex n. (pl. **narthexes**) a lobby inside a church's main entrance. [Say NARTH ex]

narwhal n. a white Arctic whale, the male of which has a long straight tusk. [Say NAR wull]

nary adj. informal or jocular not a; no. [Rhymes with HAIRY]

NASA abbr. National Aeronautics and Space Administration. [Say NASS uh]

nasal ● adj. **1** having to do with the nose. **2** pronounced with the breath passing through the nose. ● n. a nasal letter or sound. □ **nasally** adv.

nascent adj. just beginning to be. [Say NAY sint or NASS int]

NASDAQ n. National Association of Securities Dealers Automated Quotations. [Say NASS dack or NAZZ dack]

Naskapi n. (pl. **Naskapi** or **Naskapis**) **1** a member of an Innu people living along the north shores of the Gulf of St. Lawrence. **2** their language. □ **Naskapi** adj. [Say nuh SKAPPY]

Nass-Gitksan n. an Aboriginal language spoken by the Nisga'a and Gitksan. [Say nass git k'SAN]

nasturtium n. a plant with rounded edible leaves and bright orange, yellow, or red flowers. [Say nuh STIR shum]

nasty ● adj. (**nastier, nastiest**) highly unpleasant. ● n. (pl. **nasties**) informal a nasty person, animal, thing, etc. □ **a nasty piece of work** informal an unpleasant or contemptible person. □ **nastily** adv. **nastiness** n.

natal *adj.* having to do with one's birth. [*Say* NATE ul]

natch *adv. informal* = NATURALLY.

nation *n.* **1 a** a large group of people sharing the same culture, language, history, territory, or political state. **b** the state itself. **2** a group of Aboriginal people with common ancestry who are socially, culturally, and linguistically united. □ **nationhood** *n.*

national ● *adj.* having to do with a nation. ● *n.* **1** a citizen of a specified country. **2** (in *pl.*) a national competition. □ **nationally** *adv.*

national anthem *n.* a nation's esp. official patriotic song.

National Assembly *n.* **1** *Cdn* the provincial legislature of Quebec. **2** an elected house of legislature in various countries.

National Child Benefit *n. Cdn* a joint program of the federal, provincial, and territorial governments and First Nations to increase income support and child-welfare services for low-income working families.

nationalism *n.* **1** patriotic feeling, principles, etc. **2** a policy of national independence. □ **nationalist** *n.* **&** *adj.* **nationalistic** *adj.* **nationalistically** *adv.*

nationality *n.* (*pl.* **nationalities**) **1** the status of belonging to a particular nation **2** an ethnic group forming a part of one or more political nations. **3** nationhood.

nationalize *v.* (**nationalizes**, **nationalized**, **nationalizing**) **1** transfer an industry etc. from private to state ownership. **2** make national. □ **nationalization** *n.*

national park *n.* an area of natural beauty or historical significance protected by the nation.

national service *n.* compulsory service in the armed forces under for a specified period.

National Socialism *n. hist.* the doctrines of nationalism, racial purity, etc., adopted by the Nazis. □ **National Socialist** *n.* **&** *adj.*

nation-state *n.* a sovereign state mainly comprising citizens sharing a common language, culture, descent, etc.

nationwide *adj.* **&** *adv.* extending over the whole nation.

native ● *n.* **1** a person born or living in a specified place. **2** a member of a region's indigenous people, as distinguished from settlers, immigrants, etc. **3** an indigenous animal or plant. ● *adj.* **1** inherent; innate. **2** of one's birth or birthplace. **3** belonging to a specified place. **4** (also **Native**) **a** descended from the original inhabitants of a region. **b** having to do with a region's indigenous people.

Native American *n.* an Aboriginal person of the US.

native-born *adj.* belonging to a particular place by birth.

Native Canadian *n.* an Aboriginal Canadian.

native son *n.* a male native of a particular city, province or state, etc.

native speaker *n.* a person who has spoken a specified language from early childhood.

nativism *n.* the rejection of the cultural influences of foreigners or immigrants. □ **nativist** *adj.* **&** *n.*

nativity *n.* (*pl.* **nativities**) **1** (esp. **the Nativity**) the birth of Christ. **2** a picture of the Nativity. **3** birth. [*Say* nuh TIVVA tee]

NATO *abbr.* North Atlantic Treaty Organization. [*Say* NAY toe]

natter *informal* ● *v.* **1** chatter idly. **2** grumble. ● *n.* **1** aimless chatter. **2** grumbling talk.

natty *adj.* (**nattier**, **nattiest**) *informal* smartly or neatly dressed; fashionable. □ **nattily** *adv.* **nattiness** *n.*

natural ● *adj.* **1** existing in or derived from nature; not artificial. **2** in accordance with nature. **3** born with a particular quality. **4** relaxed and unaffected. **5** related by blood. **6** *Music* not sharpened or flattened. ● *n.* **1** a person with an innate gift or talent. **2** an off-white colour. **3** *Music* a natural note or a sign (♮) denoting one. □ **naturalness** *n.*

natural-born *adj.* having a character or position by birth.

natural childbirth *n.* childbirth with minimal medical or technological intervention.

natural death *n.* death by age or disease, not by accident, violence, etc.

natural gas *n.* an inflammable, mainly methane gas found in the earth's crust.

natural history *n.* the study of animals or plants. □ **natural historian** *n.*

natural increase *n.* population growth resulting from births exceeding deaths.

naturalism *n.* the use of realism and great detail in art and literature.

naturalist ● *n.* **1** an expert or student of natural history. **2** an advocate of naturalism. ● *adj.* = NATURALISTIC.

naturalistic *adj.* **1** imitating nature closely; lifelike. **2** of or according to naturalism.

naturalize v. (**naturalizes**, **naturalized**, **naturalizing**) **1** admit (a foreigner) to the citizenship of a country. **2** introduce an animal or plant into another region. □ **naturalization** n.

natural law n. **1** unchanging, universal moral principles. **2** an observable law relating to natural phenomena.

naturally adv. **1** in a natural manner. **2** as might be expected. **3** by nature; instinctively. **4** without artificial help.

natural resources n. materials occurring in nature and capable of economic exploitation.

natural science n. any of the sciences used in the study of the physical world, e.g. physics, geology, biology.

natural selection n. the Darwinian theory of the survival and propagation of organisms best adapted to their environment.

nature n. **1** (often **Nature**) the physical world, including plants, animals, the landscape, and natural phenomena. **2** (one of) a thing's or person's innate qualities. **3** a sort or class. □ **against nature** unnatural; immoral. **by nature** innately. **from nature** Art using natural objects as models.

natured adj. (in comb.) having a specified disposition.

naturism n. the practice of going unclothed. □ **naturist** n. & adj.

naturopathy n. the treatment or prevention of disease etc. without drugs. □ **naturopath** n. **naturopathic** adj. [Say natch er OP uth ee or nay chur OP uth ee]

Naugahyde n. proprietary a vinyl upholstering material made to resemble leather. [Say NOGGA hide]

naught n. archaic or literary nothing, nought. □ **come to naught** be ruined or unsuccessful.

naughty adj. (**naughtier**, **naughtiest**) **1** disobedient; badly behaved. **2** informal jocular connected with sex in a rude or funny way. □ **naughtily** adv. **naughtiness** n.

nausea n. sickness with an inclination to vomit. [Say NOZZY uh or NOZH uh]

nauseate v. (**nauseates**, **nauseated**, **nauseating**) **1** affect with nausea. **2** disgust; appall. □ **nauseated** adj. **nauseating** adj. **nauseatingly** adv. [Say NOZZY ate]

nauseous adj. **1** affected with nausea. **2** causing nausea. [Say NOSH us]

nautical adj. having to do with sailing and ships. □ **nautically** adv. [Say NOT ick ul]

nautical mile n. a unit of approx. 1 852 metres (2,025 yards).

nautilus n. (pl. **nautiluses** or **nautili**) a mollusc with a spiral shell and numerous short tentacles around the mouth. [Say NOT ill us for the singular, NOT ill eye for the plural]

Navajo n. (also **Navaho**) (pl. **Navajo** or **Navajos**, **Navaho** or **Navahos**) **1** a member of an Athapaskan people of Arizona, Utah, and New Mexico. **2** their language. □ **Navajo** adj. [Say NAVVA hoe]

naval adj. having to do with ships or a navy.

nave n. the central longitudinal part of a church.

navel n. a small rounded depression in the centre of the belly where the umbilical cord used to be attached.

navel-gazing n. self-absorption.

navel orange n. a large orange with a navel-like formation at the top.

navigable adj. that vessels can sail on. [Say NAVVA guh bull]

navigate v. (**navigates**, **navigated**, **navigating**) **1** direct the course of a ship, aircraft, etc. **2** sail on a sea, river, etc. **3** find one's way. **4** assist the driver by map-reading etc. **5** Computing move around a file, file system, website, etc. □ **navigation** n. **navigational** adj. **navigator** n.

navvy n. (pl. **navvies**) Brit. & Cdn informal a labourer working on roads, canals, railways, etc.

navy n. (pl. **navies**) **1** a nation's warships, with officers and other ranks. **2** (also **navy blue**) a dark blue colour. □ **navy** (also **navy blue**) adj.

navy bean n. a small white bean.

nay ● adv. or rather; and more than that. ● interj. Parliament or archaic = NO interj. ● n. **1** the word "nay". **2** a negative vote.

naysayer n. a person who expresses negative or gloomy views. □ **naysaying** n.

Nazarene n. (the Nazarene) Christ. [Say NAZZA reen]

Nazi n. (pl. **Nazis**) **1** hist. a member of the militaristic and racist German National Socialist party, which ruled Germany from 1933–45 under Adolf Hitler. **2** derogatory an extreme racist or authoritarian. □ **Nazi** adj. **Nazism** n. [Say NOTSY or NATSY, NOTSY ism or NATSY ism]

NB abbr. **1** New Brunswick. **2** nota bene.

NBA abbr. National Basketball Association.

NCO abbr. (pl. **NCOs**) non-commissioned officer.

NDP abbr. Cdn NEW DEMOCRATIC PARTY. □ **NDPer** n. (pl. **NDPers**)

NDT abbr. Newfoundland Daylight Time.

NE *abbr.* **1** northeast. **2** northeastern.

Neanderthal *n.* **1** a hominid widely distributed in paleolithic Europe, with a retreating forehead and massive brow ridges. **2** (also **neanderthal**) *jocular or derogatory* **a** a primitive, uncivilized, or uncouth person. **b** a reactionary or extreme conservative. □ **Neanderthal** *adj.* [*Say* nee ANDER tholl]

neap *n.* (also **neap tide**) a tide when there is the least difference between high and low water.

Neapolitan *adj.* of or relating to Naples, Italy. □ **Neapolitan** *n.* [*Say* nee uh POLLA tin]

Neapolitan ice cream *n.* ice cream made in layers of chocolate, vanilla, and strawberry.

near ● *adv.* **1** (often foll. by *to*) close by. **2** closely. **3** *informal* almost. ● *prep.* **1** close to. **2** (in *comb.*) almost. ● *adj.* **1** close. **2** closely related. **3** stingy. ● *v.* approach; draw near to. □ **nearest and dearest** one's closest friends and relatives collectively. □ **nearness** *n.*

nearby ● *adj.* situated in a near position. ● *adv.* (also **near by**) close; not far away.

Nearctic *n.* the wildlife region comprising the Arctic and temperate parts of N America. □ **Nearctic** *adj.* [*Say* nee ARCTIC]

near-death experience *n.* an out-of-body experience taking place on the brink of death.

Near East *n.* the Middle East. □ **Near Eastern** *adj.*

nearly *adv.* **1** almost. **2** closely.

near miss *n.* **1** a bomb etc. that just misses the target. **2** a narrowly avoided collision.

Near North *n. Cdn* the southern edge of the Canadian Subarctic, just north of the heavily settled areas.

nearsighted *adj.* **1** unable to see distant objects clearly. **2** lacking imagination or foresight. □ **nearsightedly** *adv.* **nearsightedness** *n.*

near-term *adj.* pertaining to the near future.

neat *adj.* **1** tidy; clean. **2** elegantly simple in form. **3** cleverly executed. **4** *slang* good, pleasing, excellent. □ **neatly** *adv.* **neatness** *n.*

neaten *v.* make neat.

nebbish *n. informal* an ineffectual or timid person. □ **nebbishy** *adj.*

nebula *n.* (*pl.* **nebulae** or **nebulas**) a cloud of gas and dust in space. □ **nebular** *adj.* [*Say* NEB you luh *for the singular; for* NEBULAE *say* NEB you lee]

nebulous *adj.* **1** hazy, indistinct, vague. **2** *Astronomy* of or like a nebula. □ **nebulously** *adv.* [*Say* NEB you lus]

necessarily *adv.* **1** as a necessary result. **2** by necessity.

necessary ● *adj.* **1** requiring to be done. **2** that must be. ● *n.* (*pl.* **necessaries**) (*usu.* in *pl.*) any of the basic requirements of life.

necessitate *v* (**necessitates**, **necessitated**, **necessitating**) make necessary. [*Say* nuh SESSA tate]

necessity *n.* (*pl.* **necessities**) **1 a** an indispensable thing. **b** indispensability. **2** circumstances enforcing a certain course. **3** imperative need. **4** want; poverty. □ **of necessity** inevitably.

neck ● *n.* **1 a** the part of the body connecting the head to the shoulders. **b** a neckline. **2** any narrow segment of something. **3** the length of a horse's head and neck as a measure of its lead in a race. ● *v. informal* kiss and caress amorously. □ **neck and neck** very close in a competition. □ **-necked** *comb. form* **neckless** *adj.*

neckband *n.* a strip of material around the neck of a garment.

neckerchief *n.* a square of cloth worn around the neck. [*Say* NECKER chiff *or* NECKER chief]

necklace *n.* a chain or string of beads etc., worn as an ornament around the neck.

neckline *n.* the edge or shape of the opening of a garment at the neck.

neck of the woods *n. informal* a community or locality.

necktie *n.* = TIE *n.* 2.

necromancy *n.* **1** divination by the supposed communication with the dead. **2** witchcraft. □ **necromantic** *adj.* **necromancer** *n.* [*Say* NECK ruh mancy]

necrophilia *n.* a morbid and esp. erotic attraction to corpses. □ **necrophiliac** *n.* **necrophilic** *adj.* [*Say* neck ruh FILLY uh]

necropolis *n.* (*pl.* **necropolises**) a cemetery. [*Say* nuh CROPPA liss]

necrosis *n.* the death of tissue due to disease, injury, etc. [*Say* nuh CROW sis]

nectar *n.* **1** a sugary substance produced by plants and made into honey by bees. **2** (in Greek and Roman mythology) the drink of the gods. **3** a drink of usu. undiluted fruit juice.

nectarine *n.* a variety of peach with a thin smooth skin and firm flesh.

née *adj.* (also **nee**) born (to indicate a married woman's maiden name) . [*Say* NAY]

need ● *v.* **1** be in want of; require. **2** be

necessary. ● *n.* **1** a want or requirement. **2** circumstances requiring some necessary thing.

needful ● *adj.* **1** necessary; indispensable. **2** having a need or needs. ● *n.* (**the needful**) what is necessary.

needle ● *n.* **1 a** a very thin small pointed piece of steel with an eye, for guiding thread in sewing. **b** a larger slender stick without an eye, used in knitting. **2** a slender indicator on a dial etc. **3 a** a hypodermic syringe. **b** an injection using a syringe. **4** any of the stiff slender leaves on a conifer. ● *v.* (**needles, needled, needling**) *informal* **1** incite or irritate. **2** tease, harass. □ **needled** *adj.* (also in *comb.*). **needling** *n.*

needle-nose *adj.* (of pliers) having long, thin, pincers.

needlepoint *n.* closely-stitched embroidery worked over canvas.

needless *adj.* unnecessary, uncalled for. □ **needlessly** *adv.*

needlework *n.* sewing or embroidery.

needn't *contr.* need not.

needs *adv.* of necessity.

need-to-know *adj.* designating the practice of telling people only what is necessary for them to carry out a task effectively.

needy *adj.* (**needier, neediest**) **1** poor; destitute. **2** lacking some essential emotional or psychological quality. **3** needing emotional support; insecure. □ **neediness** *n.*

ne'er *adv. literary* = NEVER. [*Say* NAIR]

ne'er-do-well *n.* a good-for-nothing person. □ **ne'er-do-well** *adj.*

nefarious *adj.* wicked; immoral. □ **nefariousness** *n.* [*Say* nuh FERRY us]

neg *n. informal* a photographic negative.

neg. *abbr.* negative.

negate *v.* (**negates, negated, negating**) **1** make ineffective, invalidate. **2** deny the existence of. **3** *Grammar* make negative. [*Say* nuh GATE]

negation *n.* **1** the denial of something. **2** the absence or opposite of something actual or positive. **3** *Grammar* denial of the truth of a clause etc.

negative ● *adj.* **1** expressing or implying denial, prohibition, or refusal. **2** critical, defeatist, not helpful. **3** harmful. **4** marked by absence. **5** of the opposite nature to a thing regarded as positive. **6** *Grammar* expressing negation. **7** *Algebra* less than zero. **8** *Electricity* of the kind of charge carried by electrons. **9** (*Photography*) with lights, shades, and colour values reversed. ● *n.* **1** a negative statement. **2** an image

with lights, shades, and colours reversed. **3** a negative quality or characteristic. **4** a negative result. ● *interj.* no. □ **negatively** *adv.* **negativity** *n.*

negativism *n.* **1** the tendency to be negative in attitude. **2** extreme skepticism, criticism, etc. □ **negativist** *n.*

neglect ● *v.* fail to care for, to do, or to pay attention to. ● *n.* **1** lack of caring; negligence. **2** the state or condition of being neglected. **3** disregard. □ **neglected** *adj.* **neglectful** *adj.*

negligee *n.* a woman's light semi-transparent dressing gown. [*Say* NEG li zhay]

negligence *n.* a lack of proper care and attention. □ **negligent** *adj.* **negligently** *adv.* [*Say* NEG luh jince]

negligible *adj.* not worth considering. [*Say* NEG lidge uh bull]

negotiable *adj.* **1** open to change after discussion. **2** that can be exchanged for money. [*Say* nuh GO shuh bull]

negotiate *v.* (**negotiates, negotiated, negotiating**) **1** try to reach an agreement or settlement through discussion. **2** find a way over, through, etc. □ **negotiated** *adj.* **negotiating** *n.* **negotiation** *n.* **negotiator** *n.* [*Say* nuh GO she ate]

Negro *n.* (*pl.* **Negroes**) a member of the dark-skinned group of peoples that originated in sub-Saharan Africa. □ **Negro** *adj.*

neigh ● *n.* the high whinnying sound of a horse. ● *v.* make such a sound. [*Say* NAY]

neighbour *n.* (also **neighbor**) **1** a person resident next door to or near another. **2** a person regarded as endless to kindness etc.

neighbourhood *n.* (also **neighborhood**) **1** the area surrounding a place, person, or object. **2** a district within a town or city. **3** the vicinity. □ **in the neighbourhood of** roughly; about.

neighbouring *adj.* situated next or near to a place or person.

neighbourly *adj.* (also **neighborly**) characteristic of a good neighbour. □ **neighbourliness** *n.*

neither ● *adj. & pron.* not the one nor the other; not either. ● *adv.* not either. ● *conj.* nor yet; nor. [*Say* NYE ther *or* NEE ther]

nelson *n.* a wrestling hold with one or both arms passed under the opponent's arm(s) from behind and applied to the neck.

nematode *n.* any of various worms with cylindrical bodies, found abundantly in soil and water. [*Say* NEMMA tode]

nemesis *n.* (*pl.* **nemeses**) **1** a long-standing enemy. **2** deserved and not

avoidable punishment or defeat.
[*Say* NEMMA sis *for the singular,*
NEMMA seez]

neo- *comb. form* **1** new, modern. **2** a new or
revived form of. [*Say* NEE oh]

neoclassical *adj.* (also **neoclassic**) of or
relating to a revival or development of a
classical style in the arts.
□ **neoclassicism** *n.* **neoclassicist** *n.*

neocortex *n.* (*pl.* **neocortices**) the part
of the brain involved in sight and hearing.
[*Say* neo CORTEX]

neodymium *n.* a silver-grey naturally-
occurring metallic element.
[*Say* neo DIMMY um]

neolithic *n.* (also **Neolithic**) the later
Stone Age, when ground or polished stone
implements prevailed. □ **neolithic** *adj.*
[*Say* neo LITH ick]

neologism *n.* a new word or expression.
[*Say* nee OLLA jism]

neon ● *n.* **1** an inert gaseous element
giving an orange glow when electricity is
passed through it, used in fluorescent
lighting. **2** neon lighting. ● *adj.* **1** involving
neon. **2** harshly bright, gaudy, or glowing.

neonatal *adj.* having to do with children
immediately after birth. [*Say* neo NATE ul]

neophyte *n.* **1** a novice. **2** a new convert.
[*Say* neo FITE]

neoprene *n.* a strong synthetic rubber.
[*Say* NEO preen]

Nepalese *adj. & n.* (*pl.* **Nepalese**) =
NEPALI. [*Say* neppa LEEZ]

Nepali *n.* (*pl.* **Nepali** or **Nepalis**) **1** a
person from Nepal. **2** the language of
Nepal. □ **Nepali** *adj.* [*Say* nuh POLLY]

nephew *n.* a son of one's brother or sister,
or of one's brother-in-law or sister-in-law.

nepotism *n.* favouritism (esp. in
employment) shown to relatives.
□ **nepotistic** *adj.* [*Say* NEPPA tism]

neptunium *n.* a radioactive metallic
element produced from uranium.
[*Say* nep TUNE ee um]

nerd *n. slang* an unfashionable, socially
awkward person, esp. one excessively
studious or focused on a hobby.
□ **nerdiness** *n.* **nerdish** *adj.* **nerdy** *adj.*
(**nerdier, nerdiest**)

nerve ● *n.* **1** a fibre or bundle of fibres that
transmits signals between the brain or
spinal cord and other parts of the body.
2 a coolness in danger. **b** *informal*
impudence, audacity. **3** (in *pl.*) **a** a state of
heightened nervousness or sensitivity. ● *v.*
(**nerves, nerved, nerving**) brace oneself
to face danger, suffering, etc. □ **get on a
person's nerves** irritate or annoy a
person. **have nerves of steel** be not

easily upset or frightened. **hit** (or **touch**)
a nerve refer to a sensitive subject.
□ **nerved** *adj.*

nerve centre *n.* **1** a group of closely
connected nerve cells associated in
performing some function. **2** the centre of
control of an organization etc.

nerve gas *n.* a poisonous gas that
disrupts the nervous system, esp. for use in
warfare.

nerveless *adj.* inert, lacking vigour or
spirit.

nerve-racking *adj.* (also **nerve-
wracking**) stressful, frightening;
straining the nerves.

nervous *adj.* **1** worried, anxious.
2 excitable; high-strung. **3** pertaining to or
affecting the nerves. □ **nervously** *adv.*
nervousness *n.*

nervous breakdown *n.* a period of
incapacitating mental and emotional
disturbance, stress, etc.

nervous system *n.* the body's network
of specialized cells which transmit nerve
impulses.

nervy *adj.* (**nervier, nerviest**) impudent,
audacious. □ **nervily** *adv.*

-ness *suffix* forming nouns expressing a
state or condition.

nest ● *n.* **1** a structure where a bird lays
eggs and shelters its young. **2** an animal's
breeding ground or lair. **3** a snug or
secluded retreat, shelter, etc. **4** a place
fostering something undesirable. ● *v.* **1** use
or build a nest. **2** take or collect wild birds'
nests or eggs. **3** place or fit a thing inside
another similar one. □ **nested** *adj.*
nester *n.*

nest egg *n.* a sum of money saved for the
future.

nestle *v.* (**nestles, nestled, nestling**)
1 lie in a partly hidden or sheltered
position. **2** settle snugly or affectionately
against something or someone.

nestling *n.* a bird that is too young to leave
its nest. [*Say* NEST ling]

Net *n. informal* (also **net**) (usu. **the Net**) the
Internet.

net¹ ● *n.* **1** an open-meshed material of
twine or cord. **2** a structure of net for
catching fish or insects. **3** *Sport* a goal. **4** a
communications or computer network. ● *v.*
(**nets, netted, netting**) catch or obtain
with or as if with a net. □ **net-like** *adj.*

net² ● *adj.* **1** remaining after all necessary
deductions. **2** (of a weight) excluding that
of the packaging. **3** (of an effect, result,
etc.) overall. **4** after all factors have been
calculated. ● *n.* a net sum, income, result,

etc. ● v. (**nets, netted, netting**) gain or yield as net profit.

nether adj. esp. literary or jocular = LOWER[1] adj. 1. □ **nethermost** adj.

Netherlander n. a person from the Netherlands. □ **Netherlandish** adj.

nether regions pl. n. **1** jocular the buttocks and genitals. **2** hell or the underworld.

netherworld n. the infernal regions; hell.

netiquette n. informal the informal code of conduct governing use of the Internet. [Say NET i kit]

netminder n. a goaltender. □ **netminding** n.

net profit n. the actual profit after working expenses have been paid.

netter n. a boat that fishes using a net.

netting n. **1** netted fabric. **2** the action of fishing with a net or nets.

nettle ● n. a plant with jagged leaves covered with stinging hairs. ● v. (**nettles, nettled, nettling**) irritate, provoke, annoy.

network ● n. **1** an arrangement of intersecting horizontal and vertical lines. **2** a system of interconnected parts, e.g. roads, computers, broadcasting stations. **3** a group of people who interact together. ● v. **1** connect as a network **2** interact with others to exchange information and develop contacts. □ **networker** n. **networking** n.

networked adj. (of a computer etc.) joined to others.

net worth n. the monetary value of something when debts etc. have been deducted.

neural adj. of or like a nerve or the nervous system. [Say NYUR ul or NUR ul]

neuralgia n. an intense intermittent pain along a nerve, esp. in the head or face. □ **neuralgic** adj. [Say nyur AL juh or nur AL juh]

neuro- comb. form a nerve or nerves. [Say NYURO, NURO]

neurobiology n. the biology of the nervous system.

neurochemical adj. of or pertaining to the chemistry of the nervous system. □ **neurochemist** n. **neurochemistry** n.

neurology n. the branch of medicine that deals with nerves and the nervous system. □ **neurological** adj. **neurologically** adv. **neurologist** n. [Say nyur OLLA jee or nur OLLA jee]

neuromuscular adj. having to do with both nerves and muscle tissue.

neuron n. a specialized cell transmitting nerve impulses. [Say NUR on or NYUR on]

neuropsychology n. the study of the relationship between the brain and behaviour.

neuroscience n. any or all of the sciences dealing with the nervous system and brain. □ **neuroscientist** n.

neurosis n. (pl. **neuroses**) a mild mental illness characterized by anxiety, depression, obsessive behaviour, etc. [Say nyur OWE sis or nur OWE sis for the singular, nyur OWE sees or nur OWE sees for the plural]

neurosurgery n. surgery performed on the nervous system. □ **neurosurgeon** n.

neurotic adj. **1** caused by or suffering from neurosis. **2** informal abnormally sensitive or obsessive. □ **neurotically** adv. [Say nur OT ick or nyur OT ick]

neurotoxic adj. poisonous to the nervous system. □ **neurotoxicity** n.

neurotransmitter n. a chemical substance released from a nerve that effects the transfer of an impulse to another nerve or muscle. □ **neurotransmission** n.

neuter ● adj. **1** Grammar neither masculine nor feminine. **2** having no reproductive organs or sexual characteristics. ● v. **1** castrate or spay. **2** deprive of potency, vigour, or force. □ **neutered** adj. **neutering** n. [Say NOOTER or NYOOTER]

Neutral n. a member of an Iroquoian people formerly living on the shores of Lake Erie.

neutral ● adj. **1** not supporting either side in a dispute. **2** lacking strong qualities. **3** (of colours) harmonizing well with most other colours. **4** Chemistry neither acid nor alkaline. **5** having neither a positive nor a negative electrical charge. **6** having neither a positive nor a negative effect. ● n. **1** a neutral country or person. **2** a position of a gear mechanism in which no power is transmitted. **3** a neutral colour. □ **neutrality** n. **neutrally** adv.

neutralize v. (**neutralizes, neutralized, neutralizing**) **1** render ineffective. **2** make chemically or electrically neutral. **3** euphemism kill or render harmless. □ **neutralization** n. **neutralizer** n.

neutral zone n. Hockey the central area of a rink, extending from blue line to blue line.

neutrino n. (pl. **neutrinos**) a stable elementary particle with zero electric charge and probably zero mass. [Say noo TREE no or nyoo TREE no]

neutron n. an elementary particle of about the same mass as a proton but without an electric charge. [*Say* NOO tron *or* NYOO tron]

neutron bomb *n.* a kind of atomic bomb producing large numbers of lethal neutrons but causing relatively little damage to property.

neutron star *n.* a very small star composed mainly of closely packed neutrons.

never *adv.* **1** at no time. **2** not at all. □ **well I never!** expressing great surprise.

nevermore *adv.* at no future time; never again.

never-never land *n.* an imaginary, utopian or illusory place.

nevertheless *adv.* in spite of that.

new *adj.* **1** made, introduced, or discovered recently. **2** not previously owned. **3** seen, experienced, or acquired for the first time. **4** inexperienced at or unaccustomed to. **5** reinvigorated or reformed. □ **newness** *n.*

New Age *n.* a broad movement characterized by alternative approaches to spiritual matters, mysticism, holistic ideas, environmentalism, etc. □ **New Ager** *n.*

newbie *n. slang* a novice on the Internet. [*Say* NEW bee]

newborn ● *adj.* recently born. ● *n.* a newborn child.

New Brunswicker *n.* a person from New Brunswick.

newcomer *n.* a person who has recently arrived.

New Democratic Party *n.* (in Canada) a left-of-centre political party formed from the Co-operative Commonwealth Federation in 1961. Abbreviation: **NDP**. □ **New Democrat** *n.* **New Democratic** *adj.*

newel *n.* **1** the supporting central post of winding stairs. **2** (also **newel post**) a post at the head or foot of a staircase supporting a handrail. [*Say* NEW ul]

newfangled *adj.* objectionably new.

Newfie *n.* (also **Newf**) *informal* **1** a Newfoundlander. **2** Newfoundland. **3** a Newfoundland dog. □ **Newfie** *adj.*

new-found *adj.* newly discovered.

Newfoundland *n.* (also **Newfoundland dog**) a very large breed of dog with a thick coarse coat and webbed feet. [*Say* new f'n LAND *or* NEW f'nd l'nd *or* NEW f'nd land *or* new FOUND l'nd]

Newfoundlander *n.* a native or inhabitant of Newfoundland.

Newfoundland Time *n.* the time in a zone including the island of Newfoundland.

newish *adj.* somewhat new.

new-look *adj.* having a new image.

newly *adv.* **1** recently. **2** afresh, anew.

newlywed *n.* a recently married person.

new moon *n.* **1** the moon when first seen as a crescent. **2** *Astronomy* the time when the moon is in conjunction with the sun.

news *n.* **1** information about recent events. **2** (**the news**) a broadcast report of news.

news agency *n.* an organization that collects and distributes news items.

newsboy *n.* esp. *hist.* a boy who sells or delivers newspapers.

newscast *n.* a radio or television broadcast of news reports. □ **newscaster** *n.*

news conference *n.* a press conference.

news flash *n.* an unscheduled brief broadcast of an important news item.

newsgroup *n.* (on the Internet or other network) a forum for the discussion of a particular subject.

newshound *n. informal* an esp. aggressive news reporter.

newsletter *n.* a printed report issued periodically by a business, organization, etc.

newsmagazine *n.* **1** a glossy magazine reporting and commenting on current events. **2** a television news program consisting of in-depth reports on selected current events.

newsmaker *n.* a person or thing at the centre of newsworthy events. □ **newsmaking** *n.*

newsman *n.* (*pl.* **newsmen**) a reporter, newscaster, or journalist.

newspaper *n.* a daily or weekly publication, usu. on newsprint, containing news, correspondence, etc.

newspapering *n.* the business etc. of producing newspapers.

newspaperman *n.* (*pl.* **newspapermen**) a journalist.

newspaperwoman (*pl.* **newspaperwomen**) *n.* a female journalist.

Newspeak *n.* ambiguous esp. political euphemistic language.

newsprint *n.* a type of low-quality paper on which newspapers are printed.

news reader *n.* = NEWSCASTER.

newsreel *n. hist.* a short motion picture of recent events.

news release *n.* = PRESS RELEASE.

newsroom *n.* a room in a newspaper or broadcasting office where news is processed.

news service *n.* = NEWS AGENCY.

newsstand n. a stall for the sale of newspapers.

newsweekly n. (pl. **newsweeklies**) a weekly newspaper or newsmagazine.

news wire n. a service transmitting the latest news stories, e.g. to newspapers.

newswoman n. (pl. **newswomen**) a female reporter, newscaster, or journalist.

newsworthy adj. of sufficient interest to warrant mention in the news. □ **newsworthiness** n.

newsy adj. (**newsier, newsiest**) full or consisting of esp. gossipy news.

newt n. a small, rough-skinned amphibian with a well-developed tail.

New Testament n. the second part of the Christian Bible, concerned with the life and teachings of Christ and his earliest followers.

newton n. Physics the SI unit of force.

new wave n. **1** a recent trend. **2** a style of pop music of the late 1970s and early 1980s.

New World n. North and South America.

New Year's n. **1** (also **New Year's Eve**) the evening of Dec. 31. **2** (also **New Year's Day**) Jan. 1.

New Yorker n. a native or inhabitant of New York State or New York City.

New York steak n. (also **New York strip**) a steak cut from the outer side of a T-bone.

New Zealander n. a person from New Zealand.

next ● adj. **1** coming immediately after the present one. **2** (of a day of the week, a month, etc.) nearest (but the nearest but one) after the present. ● adv. **1** immediately afterwards. **2** following in the specified order. ● n. the next person or thing. □ **as good** (or **well** or **much** etc.) **as the next person** as good, well, etc. as the average person. **next to 1** adjacent to. **2** almost. **3** following in order after.

next door adv. & adj. in or to the next house, room, etc.

next-generation adj. designating an imminent technology, style, etc.

next of kin n. the closest living relative(s).

next-to-last adj. penultimate.

nexus n. (pl. **nexuses**) a connection or series of connections. [Say NEX us]

NF abbr. Newfoundland.

NFB abbr. National Film Board of Canada.

NFL abbr. (in the US) National Football League.

Nfld. abbr. Newfoundland.

NGO abbr. (pl. **NGOs**) non-governmental organization.

NHL abbr. National Hockey League. □ **NHLer** n. (pl. **NHLers**)

niacin n. a vitamin of the vitamin B complex, found in milk, liver, and yeast. [Say NIGH uh sin]

Niagara n. an outpouring, a deluge.

nib n. the point of a pen or tool.

nibble ● v. (**nibbles, nibbled, nibbling**) **1** take small bites. **2** show cautious interest in. ● n. **1** an instance of nibbling. **2** (also **nibbly,** pl. **nibblies**) a very small amount or item of food. **3** a tentative display of interest. □ **nibbler** n.

niblet n. a small piece of food, e.g. a kernel of corn.

nicad n. a battery, often rechargeable, with a nickel anode and a cadmium cathode. [Say NYE cad]

Nicaraguan n. a person from Nicaragua. □ **Nicaraguan** adj. [Say nicka ROG win]

nice adj. (**nicer, nicest**) **1** pleasant, agreeable, satisfactory. **2** kind, good-natured. **3** fine or subtle. □ **nicely** adv. **niceness** n.

nice-guy adj. characteristic of a nice, agreeable person.

nicety n. (pl. **niceties**) **1** a subtle distinction or detail. **2** a detail of etiquette. [Say NICE uh tee]

niche n. **1** a shallow recess in a wall. **2** a suitable position in life. **3** a particular group of people seen as a potential market for a product. [Say NEESH or NITCH]

nick ● n. a small cut or scratch. ● v. make a nick or nicks in. □ **in the nick of time** only just in time.

nickel n. **1** a silvery-white metallic element. **2** a five-cent coin.

nickel and dime ● v. (**nickels and dimes, nickelled and dimed, nickelling and diming**) strain financially with many small fees. ● adj. (**nickel-and-dime**) petty, insignificant.

nickname ● n. a familiar name given to a person or thing. ● v. (**nicknames, nicknamed, nicknaming**) give a nickname to.

niçoise adj. garnished with tomatoes, capers, anchovies, etc. [Say nee SWOZZ]

nicotine n. a poisonous alkaloid present in tobacco. [Say NICKA teen or nicka TEEN]

niece n. a daughter of one's brother or sister, or of one's brother-in-law or sister-in-law.

nifty adj. (**niftier, niftiest**) informal **1** cleverly designed, executed, etc. **2** stylish. □ **niftily** adv.

Nigerian n. a person from Nigeria. □ **Nigerian** adj. [Say nigh JEERY in]

niggardly adj. stingy. □ **niggardliness** n. [Say NIG erd lee]

niggle ● v. (**niggles**, **niggled**, **niggling**) **1** find fault in a petty way. **2** informal bother. ● n. a trifling complaint. □ **niggling** adj.

nigh often jocular ● adj. near; approaching. ● adv. almost. □ **nigh on** almost

night n. the time from sunset to sunrise.

nightcap n. **1** hist. a cap worn in bed. **2** a drink taken at bedtime. **3** the second game of a doubleheader when played in the evening.

nightclothes n. clothes for wearing in bed.

nightclub n. a club that is open at night for drinking, dancing, entertainment, etc. □ **nightclubber** n. **nightclubbing** n.

night crawler n. an earthworm.

nightfall n. the onset of night.

nightgown n. (also **nightdress**, pl. **nightdresses**) a woman's or girl's loose garment worn in bed.

nighthawk n. **1** a nocturnal insect-eating N American bird. **2** a person who is active at night.

nightie n. informal a nightgown.

nightingale n. a small reddish-brown bird noted for the melodious nighttime song of the male.

nightlife n. activity or entertainment occurring at night, as in nightclubs etc.

night light n. a dim light kept on at night.

nightly adj. & adv. (recurring) every night.

nightmare n. **1** a frightening or unpleasant dream. **2** a very unpleasant experience. **3** an obsessive fear. □ **nightmarish** adj. **nightmarishly** adv.

night owl n. a person active at night.

nightshade n. **1** a plant with red or black usu. poisonous berries. **2** (also **deadly nightshade**) = BELLADONNA.

nightshirt n. a long shirt worn in bed.

nightspot n. a nightclub.

nightstick n. a police officer's truncheon.

night table n. (also **nightstand**) a small low bedside table.

nighttime n. the time between evening and morning.

nightwear n. clothing suitable for wearing in bed.

nihilism n. the belief that nothing has any meaning or value. □ **nihilist** n. **nihilistic** adj. [Say NIGH ill ism]

-nik suffix forming nouns denoting a person associated with a specified thing or quality.

nil n. nothing; no number or amount.

nimble adj. (**nimbler**, **nimblest**) **1** quick and light in movement. **2** clever, versatile. □ **nimbleness** n. **nimbly** adv.

nimbostratus n. a low diffuse dark grey layer of cloud, often with precipitation. [Say nimbo STRAT us]

nimbus n. (pl. **nimbuses** or **nimbi**) **1** a halo. **2** a rain cloud. [Say NIM bus for the singular, NIM bye for the plural]

NIMBY n. (pl. **NIMBYs**) a person whose attitude towards unwanted local developments can be summed up by the statement, 'Not in my backyard' □ **NIMBYism** n.

nimrod n. **1** slang an inept person. **2** often ironic a skilled hunter.

nincompoop n. an idiot.

nine card. num. one more than eight. □ **dressed to the nines** dressed very elaborately or elegantly.

ninefold adj. & adv. **1** nine times as much or as many. **2** consisting of nine parts.

900 number n. a telephone number, with the digits "900" in place of an area code, used to access fee-based services.

nineteen card. num. one more than eighteen. □ **nineteenth** ord. num.

nine-to-five adj. of or involving standard office hours. □ **nine-to-fiver** n.

ninety card. num. (pl. **nineties**) ten more than eighty. □ **ninetieth** ord. num.

ninja n. a person skilled in a martial art characterized by stealthy movement and camouflage.

ninny n. (pl. **ninnies**) a foolish or stupid person.

ninth ord. num. constituting the number nine in a series. □ **ninthly** adv.

niobium n. a rare grey-blue metallic element. [Say nigh OH bee um]

nip ● v. (**nips**, **nipped**, **nipping**) **1** pinch, squeeze, or bite sharply. **2** informal go quickly. **3** informal overtake or defeat by a narrow margin. ● n. **1** a pinch, squeeze, or bite. **2** biting cold. **3** informal a small drink of alcohol. □ **nip in the bud** suppress or destroy at an early stage.

nip and tuck n. (pl. **nips and tucks**) informal a cosmetic surgical operation.

nipple n. **1 a** the tip of the mammary ducts of female mammals, from which milk is secreted for the young. **b** an analogous structure in the male. **2** the rubber tip of a baby's feeding bottle.

nippy adj. (**nippier**, **nippiest**) informal **1** chilly, cold. **2** piquant, sharp tasting.

nirvana n. (in Buddhism) a state of perfect happiness in which there is no suffering or desire, and no sense of self. [Say nur VONNA]

Nisei n. (pl. **Nisei**) a North American whose parents immigrated from Japan. □ **Nisei** adj. [Say nee SAY]

Nisga'a n. (also **Nishga**) (pl. **Nisga'a** or **Nisga'as**, or **Nishga** or **Nishgas**) **1** a member of a Tsimshian Aboriginal people living in the Skeena River valley in northwestern BC. **2** their language.
□ **Nisga'a** adj. [Say NISS guh; for Nishga say NISH guh]

nit n. the egg of a human head louse.

Nitinat n. (pl. **Nitinat** or **Nitinats**) **1** a member of an Aboriginal people, part of the Nuu-chah-nulth, living on southern Vancouver Island. **2** their language.
□ **Nitinat** adj. [Say NITTA nat]

nitpicking n. & adj. informal criticizing small, esp. insignificant faults or errors.
□ **nitpicker** n. **nitpick** v. **nitpicky** adj.

nitrate n. **1** any salt or ester of nitric acid. **2** potassium or sodium nitrate when used as a fertilizer. □ **nitration** n.
[Say ny TRATE]

nitre n. saltpetre, potassium nitrate.
[Say NITE er]

nitric adj. of or containing nitrogen.
[Say NY trick]

nitric acid n. a colourless corrosive poisonous liquid.

nitrite n. any salt or ester of nitrous acid.
[Say NY trite]

nitro n. informal nitroglycerine. [Say NY tro]

nitro- comb. form **1** of or containing nitric acid, nitre, or nitrogen. **2** made with or by use of any of these. **3** of or containing the monovalent $-NO_2$ group.

nitrogen n. a colourless odourless gaseous element that forms four-fifths of the earth's atmosphere. □ **nitrogenous** adj.
[Say ny TRODGE in us]

nitroglycerine n. (also **nitroglycerin**) an explosive yellow liquid.
[Say ny tro GLISSA rin]

nitrous adj. of, like, or impregnated with nitrogen, esp. in the trivalent state.
[Say NY truss]

nitrous acid n. a weak acid existing only in solution and in the gas phase.

nitrous oxide n. a colourless gas used as an anaesthetic and as an aerosol propellant.

nitty-gritty n. slang the realities or practical details of a matter.

nitwit n. informal a stupid person.

nix ● v. (**nixes, nixed, nixing**) slang **1** cancel. **2** reject. ● adv. no.

NL abbr. **1** (in official postal use) Newfoundland and Labrador. **2** Baseball National League.

Nlaka'pamux n. (pl. **Nlaka'pamux**) **1** a member of an Aboriginal people living near the Thompson River in the Fraser River Valley of BC. **2** their language.
□ **Nlaka'pamux** adj. [Say 'n thlaw COP'm]

NMR abbr. nuclear magnetic resonance.

NNE abbr. north-northeast.

NNW abbr. north-northwest.

No n. traditional Japanese drama with dance and song, evolved from Shinto rites.

No. abbr. number.

no ● adj. **1** not any. **2** quite the opposite of. **3** hardly any. ● interj. used to give a negative response. ● adv. not at all. ● n. (pl. **noes**) **1** an utterance of the word no. **2** a denial or refusal. **3** a negative vote.

no-account adj. unimportant, worthless.

nob n. slang the head.

Nobelist n. a winner of a Nobel Prize.
[Say no BELL ist]

nobelium n. an artificially produced radioactive metallic element.
[Say no BEELY um]

Nobel Prize n. (also **Nobel**) any of six international prizes awarded annually for physics, chemistry, physiology or medicine, literature, economics, and the promotion of peace.

nobility n. **1** nobleness. **2** the aristocracy.

noble ● adj. (**nobler, noblest**) **1** belonging to the aristocracy. **2** having lofty ideals; free from pettiness. **3** excellent, admirable. **4** unreactive; inert. ● n. a nobleman or noblewoman.
□ **nobleness** n. **nobly** adv.

noble gas n. any gaseous element that almost never combines with other elements.

nobleman n. (pl. **noblemen**) a man of noble rank or birth.

noblesse oblige n. the moral obligation of the rich or noble to act generously and honourably. [Say no bless oh BLEEZH]

noblewoman n. (pl. **noblewomen**) a woman of noble rank or birth.

nobody ● pron. no person. ● n. (pl. **nobodies**) an unimportant person.

no-brainer n. informal something that requires very little thought.

nock n. a notch at either end of a bow or the butt-end of an arrow.

no-confidence motion n. a non-confidence motion.

nocturnal adj. having to do with the night. □ **nocturnally** adv.
[Say nock TURN ul]

nocturne n. Music a short composition of a dreamy romantic nature. [Say NOCK turn]

nod ● v. (**nods, nodded, nodding**) **1** incline one's head slightly and briefly in assent, greeting, etc. **2** fall forward or bend downwards and sway up and down. ● n. **1** a nodding of the head. **2** an indication of approval. **3** a passing or superficial acknowledgement. □ **get the nod** be approved. **nod off** fall asleep.

nodal *adj.* of or pertaining to a node or nodes. [*Say* NO dull]

noddy *n.* (*pl.* **noddies**) **1** a simpleton. **2** a tropical seabird with mostly dark plumage, resembling a tern.

node *n.* **1** the part of a plant stem from which one or more leaves emerge. **2** a natural swelling or bulge in a bodily organ. **3** the point where lines intersect.

nodule *n.* **1** a small rounded lump of anything. **2** a small swelling or aggregation of cells. [*Say* NOD yul *or* NODGE ul]

Noel *n.* (also **Noël**) Christmas. [*Say* no ELL]

noes *pl. of* NO n.

no-fault *adj.* **1** valid regardless of blame. **2** not assigning blame.

no-frills *adj.* including only what is essential.

noggin *n. informal* the head.

no-good *adj. informal* useless.

Noh *n.* = No.

no-hitter *n. Baseball* a game in which a team's pitchers yield no hits.

no-holds-barred *adj.* with all restrictions relaxed.

no-hoper *n. slang* a person with no chance of succeeding.

nohow *adv.* in no way.

noise *n.* **1** (an) esp. loud or unpleasant sound. **2** disturbances that accompany and interfere with an electrical signal. □ **make noises** speak indirectly about one's intentions. □ **noiseless** *adj.* **noiselessly** *adv.* **noiselessness** *n.*

noisemaker *n.* a device for making a loud noise at a party etc.

noisy *adj.* (**noisier**, **noisiest**) full of or making much noise. □ **noisily** *adv.* **noisiness** *n.*

nomad ● *n.* **1** a member of a people roaming from place to place for food or fresh pasture. **2** a wanderer. ● *adj.* **1** living as a nomad. **2** wandering. □ **nomadic** *adj.* **nomadically** *adv.* **nomadism** *n.* [*Say* NO mad, no MAD ick]

no man's land *n.* the ground between two opposing armies.

nom de guerre *n.* (*pl.* **noms de guerre** *pronunc.* same) a pseudonym. [*Say* nom duh GAIR]

nom de plume *n.* (*pl.* **noms de plume** *pronunc.* same) a pen name. [*Say* nom duh PLOOM]

nomenclature *n.* a system of names used

in a particular science. [*Say* NO m'n clay chur *or* NOM'n clay chur]

nominal *adj.* **1** existing in name only. **2** designating an insignificant sum of money. □ **nominally** *adv.*

nominate *v.* (**nominates**, **nominated**, **nominating**) **1** propose a candidate for election, an honour, etc. **2** name or appoint. □ **nomination** *n.* **nominator** *n.*

nominative *n.* the grammatical case expressing the subject of a verb. □ **nominative** *adj.* [*Say* NOM in a tiv]

nominee *n.* a person or thing that has been nominated for an office, award, etc. [*Say* nomma NEE]

no more ● *n.* nothing further. ● *adj.* not any more ● *adv.* **1** no longer. **2** never again. **3** to no greater extent.

non- *prefix* giving the negative sense of words with which it is combined.

nonagon *n.* a plane figure with nine sides. [*Say* NONNA gon]

non-aligned *adj.* not allied to any of the major world powers. □ **non-alignment** *n.*

no-name ● *adj.* **1** designating a person or thing that is not well known or famous. **2** designating an item not bearing a well-known brand name. ● *n.* a no-name person or thing.

nonce *n.* designating a word coined for one specific occasion. [*Rhymes with* RESPONSE]

nonchalant *adj.* calm and casual, unmoved, not excited, indifferent. □ **nonchalance** *n.* **nonchalantly** *adv.* [*Say* non shuh LONT]

non-combatant *n.* **1** a member of a military force who is not engaged in combat, e.g. a doctor, chaplain, etc. **2** a person not fighting in a war, esp. a civilian.

non-commissioned officer *n. Military* a corporal or sergeant.

noncommittal *adj.* avoiding commitment to a definite opinion or course of action. □ **noncommittally** *adv.* [*Say* non kuh MIT'll]

non-confidence *n. Cdn* a lack of majority support for a government, policy, etc. expressed by a legislature.

nonconformist *n.* **1** a person who does not conform to a prevailing principle. **2** (usu. **Nonconformist**) (in England) a Protestant belonging to a denomination other than the Church of England (Anglican) or Church of Scotland (Presbyterian). □ **nonconformist** *adj.* **nonconformity** *n.*

non-custodial *adj.* **1** (of a parent) not having custody of a child or children, e.g. after a divorce. **2** (of a criminal sentence) served outside of a traditional correctional institution.

nondescript *adj.* lacking distinctive characteristics; dull.
[*Say* non duh SCRIPT]

none ● *pron.* **1** not any. **2** no person. ● *adv.* by no amount; not at all. □ **none other** no other person.

nonentity *n.* (*pl.* **nonentities**) a person or thing of no importance. [*Say* non ENTITY]

nones *pl. n.* in the ancient Roman calendar, the ninth day before the ides by inclusive reckoning. [*Rhymes with* BONES]

nonetheless *adv.* nevertheless.

non-event *n.* an unimportant or anticlimactic occurrence.

non-existence *n.* the condition of not existing.

non-existent *adj.* not existing.

non-fiction *n.* literary work other than fiction, including biography and reference books. □ **non-fictional** *adj.*

non-flammable *adj.* not flammable.

non-import *n. Cdn Football* a player who is a Canadian or who has played with a Canadian team for five years or more.

non-intervention *n.* the principle or practice of not becoming involved in the affairs of other countries. □ **non-interventionist** *adj. & n.*

non-invasive *adj.* not requiring incision into the body.

non-issue *n.* something that is of little or no importance.

no-no *n.* (*pl.* **no-nos**) *informal* something that is not possible or acceptable.

no-nonsense *adj.* serious, sensible; without flippancy.

nonpareil ● *adj.* unrivalled or unique. ● *n.* such a person or thing. [*Say* non pur AY]

nonpayment *n.* failure to pay.

non-performing *adj.* producing no income.

non-person *n.* a person regarded as non-existent or insignificant.

nonplussed *adj.* **1** perplexed. **2** unfazed. [*Say* non PLUSST]

non-professional ● *adj.* not professional (esp. in status). ● *n.* a non-professional person.

non-profit *adj.* not involving or making a profit.

non-proliferation *n.* the prevention of an increase in something, esp. possession of nuclear weapons.

non-scientific *adj.* not involving science or scientific methods. □ **non-scientist** *n.*

nonsense *n.* **1** words that have no meaning, or make no sense. **2** foolish talk,

ideas, etc. **3** unacceptable behaviour. □ **nonsensical** *adj.* **nonsensically** *adv.*

non sequitur *n.* a conclusion, remark, response, etc. not logically following from what has gone before.
[*Say* non SECKWA tur]

non-standard *adj.* **1** not standard. **2** (of language) containing features which are widely used but generally considered incorrect.

non-starter *n. informal* a person or thing that is unlikely to succeed or be effective.

non-status *adj.* (in Canada) designating a person of Indian ancestry who is not registered as an Indian under the Indian Act.

non-steroidal *adj.* of or relating to a drug etc. that is not a steroid but which has similar effects.

non-stop ● *adj.* without any stops, breaks, or pauses. ● *adv.* without stopping or pausing. ● *n.* a non-stop train, flight, etc.

nonsuch *n.* a person or thing that is unrivalled.

non-treaty *adj.* designating status or non-status Indian people who have not signed a treaty with the Canadian government.

non-union *adj.* **1** not belonging to a trade union. **2** not done or produced by members of a trade union. □ **non-unionized** *adj.*

non-use *n.* failure to use.

non-verbal *adj.* not involving words or speech. □ **non-verbally** *adv.*

non-violence *n.* the avoidance of violence, esp. as a principle. □ **non-violent** *adj.*

noodle *n.* **1** a long, thin strip of pasta. **2** *informal* the head **3** (also **pool noodle**) a long solid cylinder of polystyrene foam, used as a flotation toy.

nook *n.* a corner or recess; a secluded or hidden place. [*Rhymes with* LOOK]

nookie *n.* (also **nooky**) *slang* sexual activity. [*Rhymes with* COOKIE]

noon *n.* twelve o'clock in the day, midday.

noonday *n.* midday.

no one *n.* (also **no-one**) no person; nobody.

noontime *n.* midday.

noose *n.* a loop with a knot that tightens as the rope or wire is pulled, esp. in a snare, lasso, or hangman's halter.

Nootka *n. & adj.* (*pl.* **Nootka**) = NUU-CHAH-NULTH. □ **Nootkan** *adj.* [*Say* NOOT kuh]

nope *interj. informal* = NO *interj.*

nor *conj.* **1** and not; and not either. **2** and no more.

nor⁹ (esp. in compounds) north.

NORAD *abbr.* North American Aerospace

Defence Command, an alliance of US and Canadian air defence forces. [*Say* NOR add]

Nordic ● *adj.* **1** of or relating to a tall, fair type of person from Northern Europe. **2** of or relating to Scandinavia or Finland. **3** of or relating to cross-country skiing. ● *n.* a Nordic person.

nordicity *n. Cdn* a measure of the degree of northernness of a high-latitude place. [*Say* nor DISSA tee]

nor'easter *n.* a northeast wind.

Norland *n.* a large red and green cooking and eating apple.

norm *n.* **1** something that is usual, typical, or standard. **2** customary behaviour, appearance, etc. **3** the average level.

normal ● *adj.* **1** regular, usual, typical. **2 a** physically or mentally sound. **b** average. ● *n.* **1** the normal temperature etc. **2** the usual state, level, etc. □ **normalcy** *n.* **normality** *n.* **normally** *adv.*

normalize *v.* (**normalizes, normalized, normalizing**) make or become normal. □ **normalization** *n.*

normal school *n. hist.* a school for training teachers.

Norman ● *n.* **1** a native or inhabitant of Normandy. **2** a descendant of the people of mixed Scandinavian and Frankish origin who conquered England in 1066. **3** the French used by these people. ● *adj.* **1** of or relating to the Normans. **2** of or relating to the style of Romanesque architecture used in Britain under the Normans.

normative *adj.* establishing or relating to a standard or norm. [*Say* NORMA tiv]

Norse ● *n.* **1 a** the Norwegian language. **b** the Scandinavian language group. **2 (the Norse) a** the Norwegians. **b** the Vikings. ● *adj.* of or relating to Norway or ancient Scandinavia. □ **Norseman** *n.* (*pl.* **Norsemen**)

north ● *n.* **1** the point of the horizon 90° counter-clockwise from east. **2** (usu. **the North**) **a** the Arctic. **b** the northern part of a place, esp. a province. ● *adj.* **1** towards, at, or facing north. **2** coming from the north. ● *adv.* **1** towards, at, or near the north. **2** further north than. □ **up north** to or in the north.

North American ● *adj.* of or relating to North America. ● *n.* a person from North America.

North American Free Trade Agreement *n.* an agreement between Canada, the US, and Mexico to remove barriers to trade. Abbreviation: **NAFTA**.

North Atlantic Treaty Organization *n.* an association of European and North American nations, formed in 1949 for the defence of the North Atlantic against the perceived threat of Soviet aggression. Abbreviation: **NATO**.

northbound *adj.* travelling or leading northwards.

northeast ● *n.* **1** the point of the horizon midway between north and **east**. **2 (Northeast)** the part of a place lying to the northeast. ● *adj.* of, towards, or coming from the northeast. ● *adv.* towards, at, or near the northeast. □ **northeastern** *adj.*

northeaster *n.* a northeast wind. □ **northeasterly** *n., adj. & adv.*

northeastward *adj. & adv.* (also **northeastwards**) towards the northeast.

northerly ● *adj. & adv.* **1** in a northern position or direction. **2** (of wind) blowing from the north. ● *n.* a northerly wind.

northern *adj.* **1** of or in the north. **2** lying or directed towards the north. □ **northernmost** *adj.* **northernness** *n.*

northerner *n.* a person from the north.

northern hemisphere the half of the earth north of the equator.

northern lights *pl. n.* an aurora, esp. near the northern magnetic pole.

Northern States *pl. n.* the states in the north of the US, esp. those forming the Union side in the Civil War.

northland *n.* (also **northlands**) the northern lands or parts.

north-northeast *n.* the point or direction midway between north and northeast. □ **north-northeast** *adj. & adv.*

north-northwest *n.* the point or direction midway between north and northwest. □ **north-northwest** *adj. & adv.*

north of 60 *n. Cdn informal* the areas of Canada north of 60 degrees latitude.

North Pole *n. see* POLE² 1.

North Star *n.* the brightest star in the Little Dipper, lying very close to the north celestial pole.

northward *adv. adv.* (also **northwards**) towards the north. □ **northward** *adj.*

northwest ● *n.* **1** the point of the horizon midway between north and west. **2 (Northwest)** the part of a city, country, etc. lying to the northwest. ● *adj.* of, towards, or coming from the northwest. ● *adv.* towards, at, or near the northwest. □ **northwesterly** *n., adj. & adv.* **northwestern** *adj.*

northwester *n.* **1** a northwest wind. **2 (Northwester)** *Cdn hist.* = NOR'WESTER 3.

North West Mounted Police *n. Cdn hist.* a federal police force established in 1873, named the Royal Canadian Mounted Police in 1920. Abbreviation: **NWMP**.

Northwest Rebellion *n. Cdn* an armed uprising of Metis, Indians, and white settlers in Saskatchewan in 1885, led by Louis Riel (1844–85).

northwestward *adj. & adv.* (also **northwestwards**) towards the northwest.

Norwalk virus *n.* a virus which can cause epidemics of gastroenteritis.

Norwegian *n.* **1** a person from Norway. **2** the language of Norway. □ **Norwegian** *adj.* [*Say* nor WEEGE un]

nor'wester *n.* **1** a northwest wind. **2** an oilskin hat. **3** (**Nor'Wester**) *Cdn hist.* an employee of the North West Company, which was engaged in the fur trade until 1821.

nose ● *n.* **1** an organ above the mouth on the face, containing nostrils and used for smelling and breathing. **2 a** the sense of smell. **b** the ability to detect a particular thing. **3** the odour or perfume of something. **4** the front end of a thing, e.g. of a car or aircraft. ● *v.* (**noses, nosed, nosing**) **1 a** perceive the smell of, discover by smell. **b** detect. **2** thrust or rub one's nose against or into. **3** pry or search. **4** move forward slowly. □ **as plain as the nose on your face** easily seen. **by a nose** by a very narrow margin. **count noses** count those present etc. **cut off one's nose to spite one's face** disadvantage oneself in the course of trying to disadvantage another. **keep one's nose clean** *slang* stay out of trouble. **nose out** defeat by a narrow margin. **on the nose** *slang* precisely. **put a person's nose out of joint** *informal* upset or annoy a person. **turn up one's nose** *informal* show disdain. **with one's nose in the air** haughtily.

nosebleed ● *n.* an instance of bleeding from the nose. ● *adj. informal* **1** (of seats etc.) situated in a high level. **2** (of a price etc.) very high.

nose cone *n.* the cone-shaped nose of a rocket etc.

nosedive ● *n.* **1** a steep downward plunge by an aircraft. **2** a sudden plunge or decline. ● *v.* (**nosedives, nosedived, nosediving**) make a nosedive.

no-see-um *n.* a small bloodsucking insect.

nosegay *n.* a posy.

nosh *slang* ● *v.* (**noshes, noshed, noshing**) **1** eat or drink. **2** snack. ● *n.* (*pl.* **noshes**) food or drink. □ **nosher** *n.*

no-show *n.* a person who is expected at an event etc. but does not appear for it.

nostalgia *n.* **1** sentimental yearning for a period of the past. **2** something that evokes these feelings. □ **nostalgic** *adj.* **nostalgically** *adv.* **nostalgist** *n.* [*Say* nuh STAL juh]

nostril *n.* either of two external openings of the nose.

nostrum *n.* **1** a quack remedy. **2** a pet scheme, esp. for reform. [*Say* NOSS trum]

nosy *adj.* (also **nosey**) (**nosier, nosiest**) *informal* inquisitive, prying. □ **nosily** *adv.* **nosiness** *n.*

Nosy Parker *n. informal* a nosy person.

not *adv.* expressing negation. □ **not at all** there is no need for thanks. **not least** notably. **not quite 1** almost. **2** noticeably not.

nota bene *v.* take notice. [*Say* note a BEN ay]

notable ● *adj.* worthy of note; remarkable, eminent. ● *n.* a famous or important person or thing. □ **notably** *adv.*

notarize *v.* (**notarizes, notarized, notarizing**) officially certify. [*Say* NOTE a rize]

notary *n.* (*pl.* **notaries**) **1** (also **notary public**, *pl.* **notaries public**) a person authorized to perform certain legal formalities. **2** (in Quebec) a legal professional who does wills, real estate transactions, etc. but cannot plead in court. [*Say* NOTE a ree]

notation *n.* **1 a** the representation of numbers, pitch and duration etc. of musical notes, dance movements, etc. by symbols. **b** any set of such symbols. **2** a note. □ **notate** *v.* (**notates, notated, notating**)

notch ● *n.* (*pl.* **notches**) **1** an esp. V-shaped indentation on an edge or surface. **2** one of a series of holes for the buckle on a belt, shoe, etc. **3** *informal* a step or degree. **4** a deep gorge. ● *v.* (**notches, notched, notching**) **1** make notches in. **2** record or score. □ **notched** *adj.*

note ● *n.* **1** a brief written record used as an aid to memory etc. **2** an observation of experiences etc. **3** a short or informal letter. **4** a short annotation in a book etc. **5 a** = BANKNOTE. **b** written promise of payment. **6 a** notice, attention. **b** distinction. **7** a single tone of a definite pitch and duration made by a musical instrument or voice, or a symbol representing this. **8** a quality or tone of speaking etc.; a hint. ● *v.* (**notes, noted, noting**) **1** observe, notice. **2** record in writing. **3** (in *passive*) be famous or well known. □ **take note** observe; pay attention (to).

notebook *n.* **1** a small book for making or taking notes. **2** (also **notebook**

computer) a portable computer smaller than a laptop.

noted adj. well known; famous.

notepad n. **1** a pad of paper for writing notes on. **2** a small hand-held personal computer.

notepaper n. paper for writing letters.

noteworthy adj. worthy of attention.

not-for-profit adj. = NON-PROFIT.

nothing ● n. **1** not anything. **2** an unimportant person or thing. ● adv. not at all, in no way. □ **have nothing on 1** be naked. **2** have no engagements. **have nothing on a person 1** have much less of a certain quality etc. than something else. **2** have no incriminating information against someone. **nothing doing** informal **1 a** there is no prospect of success or agreement. **b** I refuse. **2** nothing is happening. **nothing** (or **nothing else**) **for it** no alternative. **nothing** (or **not much**) **to it 1** untrue or unimportant. **2** simple to do. **think nothing of it** do not apologize or feel bound to show gratitude.

nothingness n. **1** non-existence; the non-existent. **2** worthlessness, insignificance.

notice ● n. **1** attention, observation. **2** a displayed sheet etc. bearing an announcement or information. **3 a** an intimation or warning. **b** a formal announcement to end an agreement or leave employment. **4 a** a short review or comment about a new play, book, etc. **b** a small advertisement or announcement in a newspaper or magazine. ● v. (**notices, noticed, noticing**) **1** perceive, observe. **2** remark upon. **3** recognize or acknowledge (a person). □ **put on notice** alert or warn. **take notice** (or **no notice**) show signs (or no signs) of interest.

noticeable adj. easily seen or noticed. □ **noticeably** adv.

notify v. (**notifies, notified, notifying**) inform or give notice to. □ **notification** n.

notion n. **1** an idea or belief. **2** an impulse or desire. **3** small articles related to sewing.

notional adj. **1** existing only in the imagination. **2** existing only in theory or as an idea. □ **notionally** adv.

notoriety n. fame for an unpleasant quality or deed. [Say no tuh RYE a tee]

notorious adj. well known, esp. unfavourably. □ **notoriously** adv. [Say no TORY us]

notwithstanding ● prep. in spite of; without prevention by. ● adv. nevertheless. ● conj. although. [Say not with STANDING]

notwithstanding clause n. Cdn Section 33 of the Canadian Charter of Rights and Freedoms, which allows Parliament and the provincial legislatures to override certain Charter clauses.

nougat n. a candy made from sugar or honey, nuts, and egg white. [Say NOO g't]

nought n. literary nothing.

noun n. Grammar a word (other than a pronoun) that refers to a person, place, or thing.

nourish v. (**nourishes, nourished, nourishing**) **1 a** sustain with food. **b** enrich; promote the development of. **2** foster or cherish. □ **nourishing** adj.

nourishment n. substances necessary for growth, health, and good condition, esp. food.

nouveau adj. modern; up-to-date. [Say NOO voe]

nouveau riche n. (also **nouveaux riches**) people who have recently acquired wealth, esp. those perceived as lacking in good taste. □ **nouveau riche** adj. [Say noo voe REESH]

nouvelle cuisine n. a modern style of (esp. French) cooking that emphasizes the freshness of the ingredients and attractive presentation. [Say noo VELL quiz EEN]

Nov. abbr. November.

nova n. (pl. **novae** or **novas**) a star that suddenly becomes bright and then fades. [Say NO vee or NO vuz for the plural]

Nova Scotian n. a native or inhabitant of Nova Scotia. □ **Nova Scotian** adj.

novel[1] n. a fictitious prose story of considerable length and complexity. □ **novelist** n. **novelistic** adj.

novel[2] adj. of a new kind or nature; strange.

novelize v. (**novelizes, novelized, novelizing**) make into a novel. □ **novelization** n.

novella n. (pl. **novellas**) a short novel or narrative story. [Say nuh VELLA]

novelty n. (pl. **novelties**) **1** newness, originality. **2** a new or unusual thing. **3** a small toy or decoration etc. **4** having novelty; faddish.

November n. the eleventh month.

novena n. Catholicism a devotion consisting of special prayers or services on nine successive days. [Say no VEENA]

novice n. **1** a beginner; an inexperienced person. **2** a person who has entered a religious order but has not taken vows. **3** Cdn a level of children's sports, usu. involving children aged 8 to 9.

novitiate n. **1** the period of being a novice. **2** a religious novice. [Say no VISHY it or no VISHY ate]

novocaine *n.* a local anaesthetic derived from benzoic acid. [*Say* NOVA cane]

now ● *adv.* **1** at the present time. **2** at or from this precise moment. **3** under the present circumstances. ● *conj.* as a result of the fact. □ **now and again** (or **then**) from time to time.

nowadays *adv.* at the present time or age.

nowhere ● *adv.* in, at, or to no place; not anywhere. ● *n.* **1** no place. **2** a remote or nondescript place. ● *adj. slang* remote, insignificant. □ **come out of** (or **from**) **nowhere** be suddenly evident or successful. **in the middle of nowhere** *informal* remote from urban life.

no win *adj.* designating a situation in which success is impossible.

noxious *adj.* **1** harmful, injurious. **2** unpleasant. [*Say* NOCK shuss]

nozzle *n.* a spout on a hose etc. through which a stream of air or liquid issues.

NS *abbr.* Nova Scotia.

NSAID *abbr.* non-steroidal anti-inflammatory drug. [*Say* EN sed]

NSF *abbr.* not sufficient funds, used to denote a cheque that bounces.

NST *abbr.* Newfoundland Standard Time.

NT *abbr.* **1** New Testament. **2** NEWFOUNDLAND TIME. **3** Northwest Territories (in official postal use).

nth *see* N². [*Say* ENTH]

NU *abbr.* (in postal use) Nunavut.

nuance ● *n.* a subtle difference in meaning, feeling, etc. ● *v.* (**nuances, nuanced, nuancing**) give a nuance or nuances to. □ **nuanced** *adj.* [*Say* NOO awnce *or* NYOO awnce]

nub *n.* **1** the point or gist. **2** a small lump. □ **nubby** *adj.*

nubbin *n.* a small lump or stub.

nubile *adj.* (of a girl or young woman) sexually attractive. [*Say* NOO bile *or* NYOO bile]

nuclear *adj.* **1** of, relating to, or constituting a nucleus. **2** using or producing nuclear energy. **3** involving or possessing nuclear weapons. [*Say* NOO klee er *or* NYOO klee er]

nuclear energy *n.* = ATOMIC ENERGY.

nuclear family *n.* a couple and their children, as a basic social unit.

nuclear fission *n.* a nuclear reaction in which a heavy nucleus splits spontaneously or on impact with another particle.

nuclear force *n.* a strong attractive force between nucleons in the atomic nucleus.

nuclear fuel *n.* a substance that will sustain a fission chain reaction so that it can be used as a source of nuclear energy.

nuclear fusion *n.* a nuclear reaction in which atomic nuclei of low atomic number fuse to form a heavier nucleus.

nuclear physics *n.* the physics of atomic nuclei and their interactions. □ **nuclear physicist** *n.*

nuclear power *n.* **1** electric or motive power generated by a nuclear reactor. **2** a country that has nuclear weapons. □ **nuclear-powered** *adj.*

nuclear reactor *n. see* REACTOR 2.

nuclear waste *n.* radioactive waste material.

nuclear weapon *n.* a missile, bomb, etc., using the release of energy by nuclear fission or fusion or both.

nuclear winter *n.* a period of abnormal cold and darkness predicted to follow a nuclear war.

nucleate *v.* (**nucleates, nucleated, nucleating**) **1** form a nucleus. **2** form around a central area. [*Say* NOO klee ate *or* NYOO klee ate]

nucleic acid *n.* either of two complex organic substances (DNA and RNA), present in all living cells. [*Say* noo CLAY ick *or* nyoo CLAY ick]

nucleon *n.* a proton or neutron. [*Say* NOO klee on *or* NYOO klee on]

nucleus *n.* (*pl.* **nuclei**) **1** the central and most important part of an object or group. **2** the positively charged central core of an atom that contains most of its mass. **3** a large dense organelle of cells, containing the genetic material. [*Say* NOO klee us *or* NYOO klee us *for the singular,* NOO klee eye *or* NYOO klee eye *for the plural*]

nude ● *adj.* **1** naked, unclothed, bare. **2** (of hosiery etc.) flesh-coloured. **3** (of beaches etc.) used by nudists. ● *n.* **1** a painting, sculpture, etc. of a nude human figure. **2** (**the nude**) an unclothed state.

nudge ● *v.* (**nudges, nudged, nudging**) **1** prod gently esp. with the elbow. **2** push gently or gradually. **3** coax or encourage. ● *n.* **1** a light touch or push. **2** a gentle reminder. □ **nudge, nudge, wink, wink** used to imply a sexual innuendo.

nudie *n. informal* a film, photograph, etc. featuring nudity.

nudist *n.* a person who advocates or practises going unclothed.

nudity *n.* nakedness.

nugget *n.* **1 a** a lump of gold etc., as found in the earth. **b** a lump of anything. **2** a small but valuable fact etc. **3** a small piece of chicken etc. covered with batter and deep-fried.

nuisance *n.* **1** a person or thing causing

trouble or inconvenience. **2** anything
harmful or offensive to the community.
[*Say* NOOSE ince *or* NYOOSE ince]

nuke *informal* ● *n.* a nuclear weapon. ● *v.*
(**nukes, nuked, nuking**) **1** bomb or
destroy with nuclear weapons. **2** cook
(food) in a microwave.

null *adj.* **1** (esp. **null and void**) invalid.
2 having the value zero.

nullify *v.* (**nullifies, nullified, nullifying**)
1 make legally invalid. **2** cancel out,
neutralize. □ **nullification** *n.*
[*Say* NULL if eye]

nullity *n.* (*pl.* **nullities**) **1** *Law* the fact of
being null and void. **2 a** nothingness. **b** a
mere nothing. [*Say* NULL it ee]

numb ● *adj.* unable to feel, think, or act.
● *v.* **1** make numb. **2** stupefy.
□ **numbing** *adj.* **numbingly** *adv.*
numbness *n.*

number ● *n.* **1** a quantity or value
expressed by a word, symbol, or figure. **2** a
quantity or amount. **3** (**a number of**)
several. **4** a single issue of a magazine. **5** a
song, dance, or other musical item.
6 *informal* an item of clothing of a particular
type. **7** a grammatical classification of
words that consists typically of singular
and plural. ● *v.* **1** amount to. **2** give a
number to. **3** count. **4** include as a member
of a group. □ **by (the) numbers** following
simple instructions (as if) identified by
numbers. **one's days are numbered**
one does not have long to live etc. **do a
number on (a person)** *slang* **1** disparage.
2 deceive. **have a person's number**
informal understand a person's real motives,
character, etc. **one's number is up**
informal one is finished or doomed to die.
□ **numbered** *adj.* **numbering** *n.*
numberless *adj.*

number cruncher *n. slang* **1** *Computing &
Math* a machine capable of complex
calculations etc. **2** an accountant or
statistician. □ **number crunching** *n.*

numbered company *n. Cdn* a
corporation the name of which is simply its
registration number.

number one *informal* ● *n.* **1** oneself. **2** the
best. ● *adj.* leading; most important.

number sign *n.* the sign #.

number theory *n.* the branch of
mathematics that deals with the properties
and relationships of numbers.

number two *n.* **1** something second-rate.
2 a second-in-command.

numbskull *n.* a stupid or foolish person.

numeracy *n.* a good basic knowledge of
math. [*Say* NOOMER a see *or*
NYOOMER a see]

numeral ● *n.* a word, figure, etc. denoting
a number. ● *adj.* of or denoting a number
or numbers.

numerate *adj.* acquainted with the basic
principles of mathematics, esp. arithmetic.
[*Say* NOOMER it *or* NYOOMER it]

numerator *n.* the number above the line
in a fraction. [*Say* NOOMER ate er *or*
NYOOMER ate er]

numerical *adj.* (also **numeric**) **1** having
to do with a number or numbers. **2** (of a
figure etc.) expressing a number.
□ **numerically** *adv.* [*Say* noo MARE ick ul
or nyoo MARE ick ul]

numerology *n.* the study of the supposed
occult or esoteric significance of numbers.
[*Say* noomer OLLA jee *or*
nyoomer OLLA jee]

numero uno *n. informal* **1** oneself. **2** the
best. [*Say* noomer oh OON oh]

numerous *adj.* **1** great in number.
2 consisting of many.

numinous *adj.* having a strong spiritual
quality; awe-inspiring. [*Say* NOO min us *or*
NYOO min us]

numismatics *pl. n.* the study of coins or
medals. □ **numismatic** *adj.* **numismatist**
n. [*Say* noo miz MAT icks *or*
nyoo miz MAT iks, noo MIZ muh tist *or*
nyoo MIZ muh tist]

nun *n.* a member of a Christian community
of women living under vows of poverty,
chastity, and obedience.

nunatak *n.* an isolated peak of rock
projecting above ice or snow.
[*Say* NUN attack]

Nunavummiut *pl. n.* the people
inhabiting the territory of Nunavut.
[*Say* noona VOOMY it]

nunnery *n.* (*pl.* **nunneries**) *hist.* a convent.

nuptial ● *adj.* of or relating to marriage or
weddings. ● *n.* (usu. in *pl.*) a wedding.
[*Say* NUP shull]

nurse ● *n.* **1** a person professionally
trained to care for the sick or infirm, assist
in surgery, etc. **2** (formerly) a person
employed to take charge of young children.
● *v.* (**nurses, nursed, nursing**) **1 a** work
as a nurse. **b** care for (a person) during
sickness or infirmity. **c** give medical
attention to. **2** breastfeed. **3** harbour or
nurture (a grievance etc.). **4 a** foster. **b** tend
or cultivate (a plant). **5** consume (a drink)
slowly.

nurse practitioner *n.* a specially trained
registered nurse who is qualified to
diagnose and treat common diseases,
minor injuries, etc.

nursery *n.* (*pl.* **nurseries**) **1 a** a room or
place equipped for young children. **b** =

DAYCARE 2. **2** a place where plants, trees, etc., are reared for sale or transplantation.

nursery rhyme n. a simple traditional song or poem for children.

nursery school n. a school for children usu. between the ages of three and five.

nursing n. **1 a** the profession of providing health care as a nurse. **b** the duties of a nurse. **2** (as an adj.) concerned with nursing the sick or infirm etc. **3** the action of breastfeeding.

nursing home n. an institution providing long-term health care, esp. for the elderly.

nursing station n. **1** Cdn a clinic or small hospital in a remote community. **2** the central desk on a hospital floor or ward.

nurture ● v. **1** the process of bringing up or training (esp. children). **2** the social environment as an influence on personality. ● v. (**nurtures, nurtured, nurturing**) **1** foster the development of. **2** bring up to maturity. □ **nurturance** n. **nurturant** adj. **nurturer** n.

nut n. **1 a** a fruit consisting of a hard shell around an edible kernel. **b** this kernel. **2 a** small flat piece of metal or other material with a hole through it for screwing on to a bolt. **3** slang **a** an obsessive enthusiast. **b** a crazy person. **4** (in pl.) coarse slang the testicles. **5** slang a person's head. □ **a tough** (or **hard**) **nut to crack** a problem resisting easy solution.

nutbar n. slang an eccentric or crazy person.

nutcase n. slang a crazy or eccentric person.

nutcracker n. a device for cracking the shell of a nut.

nuthatch n. (pl. **nuthatches**) a small bird that climbs tree trunks to feed on nuts, insects, etc. [Say NUT hatch]

nuthouse n. slang a mental home or hospital.

nutmeg n. a spice obtained from the seed of an evergreen East Indian tree.

nutraceutical n. a food containing health-giving additives and having medicinal benefit. [Say nootra SUIT ick'll]

nutrient n. any substance that provides essential nourishment for the maintenance of life.

nutrition n. **1** the process of taking in and absorbing nutrients. **2** the scientific study of this. □ **nutritional** adj. **nutritionally** adv. **nutritionist** n.

nutritious adj. rich in nutrients.

nutritive adj. **1** of or pertaining to nutrition. **2** nutritious. [Say NOOTRA tiv or NYOOTRA tiv]

nuts informal ● adj. crazy, mad. ● interj. an expression of contempt or derision. □ **be nuts about** be enthusiastic about or very fond of.

nuts and bolts ● pl. n. the practical details. ● adj. (usu. **nuts-and-bolts**) pertaining to the practical details.

nutshell n. the hard covering of a nut. □ **in a nutshell** in a few words.

nutso informal ● n. (pl. **nutsos**) a crazy or eccentric person. ● adj. crazy, eccentric.

nutty adj. (**nuttier, nuttiest**) **1** tasting like nuts. **2** informal crazy, eccentric. **3** enthusiastic. **4** full of or having many nuts. □ **nutty as a fruitcake** informal crazy. □ **nuttiness** n.

Nuu-chah-nulth n. (pl. **Nuu-chah-nulth**) **1** a member of a major linguistic group of the Wakashan living on the west coast of Vancouver Island. **2** their language. □ **Nuu-chah-nulth** adj. [Say noo CHAW nul]

Nuxalk n. (pl. **Nuxalk**) **1** a member of a Salishan Aboriginal people of the central BC coast. **2** their language. □ **Nuxalk** adj. [Say noo HAWLK]

nuzzle v. (**nuzzles, nuzzled, nuzzling**) **1** touch or rub gently with the nose. **2** snuggle, cuddle.

NW abbr. **1** northwest. **2** northwestern.

NWT abbr. (also **N.W.T.**) Northwest Territories.

nylon n. **1** a tough, lightweight, elastic synthetic material used for textiles, cord, etc. **2** a nylon fabric. **3** (in pl.) pantyhose or stockings.

nymph n. **1** a mythological spirit regarded as a maiden and associated with aspects of nature. **2** esp. literary a beautiful young woman. **3** an immature form of some insects.

nymphet n. informal a sexually attractive girl or young woman. [Say nim FETT or NIMF it]

nympho n. (pl. **nymphos**) informal a nymphomaniac.

nymphomania n. uncontrollable sexual desire in women. □ **nymphomaniac** n. & adj. [Say nimfa MANIA]

NYSE abbr. New York Stock Exchange.

Oo

O[1] *n.* (also **o**) (*pl.* **Os** or **O's**) **1** the fifteenth letter of the alphabet. **2** (**0**) = OH[2]. **3** a human blood type.

O[2] *interj.* **1** = OH[1]. **2** prefixed to a name when addressing someone.

o' *prep.* of, on.

OAC *abbr.* (also **o.a.c.**) on approved credit.

oaf *n.* (*pl.* **oafs**) an awkward or stupid lout. □ **oafish** *adj.* **oafishness** *n.*

oak *n.* **1** a large tree or shrub that bears acorns. **2** its hard, durable wood.

oak apple *n.* (also **oak gall**) a spherical growth or gall that forms on oak trees, caused by wasp larvae.

oaken *adj.* made of oak.

oaky *adj.* (**oakier, oakiest**) (of wine etc.) having the flavour of oak, acquired from the barrel in which it is aged.

OAP *abbr. Cdn* Old Age Pension.

oar *n.* a pole with a flat blade used for rowing or steering a boat. □ **put one's oar in** interfere, meddle. **rest on one's oars** relax one's efforts. □ **oared** *adj.*

oarlock *n.* a device on a boat's gunwale serving as a fulcrum for an oar.

oarsman *n.* (*pl.* **oarsmen**) a rower.

oarswoman *n.* (*pl.* **oarswomen**) a female rower.

OAS *abbr.* **1** *Cdn* OLD AGE SECURITY. **2** Organization of American States.

oasis *n.* (*pl.* **oases**) **1** a fertile spot in a desert, where water is found. **2** a period of calm in the midst of turbulence. [*Say* oh ACE iss *for the singular,* oh ACE eez *for the plural*]

oat *n.* **1** a cereal plant cultivated in cool climates. **2** the edible grain yielded by this. □ **sow one's oats** (or **wild oats**) indulge in youthful excess or promiscuity.

oath *n.* (*pl.* **oaths**) **1** a solemn promise (often naming God) to do something or that something is true. **2** a swear word. □ **under** (or **on**) **oath** having sworn a solemn oath.

oatmeal *n.* **1 a** rolled oats. **b** meal made from ground oats. **2** porridge made from oats.

obdurate *adj.* stubborn, unyielding. □ **obdurately** *adv.* [*Say* OB dyoor it *or* OB door it]

obeah *n.* a kind of witchcraft practised esp. in the West Indies. [*Say* OH be uh]

obedient *adj.* obeying or ready to obey. □ **obedience** *n.* **obediently** *adv.*

obeisance *n.* **1** deferential respect. **2** a bow, curtsy, or other respectful gesture. [*Say* oh BAY since]

obelisk *n.* a tapering usu. four-sided stone pillar or open metal structure, esp. set up as a monument or landmark etc. [*say* OBBA lisk]

obese *adj.* very fat; corpulent. □ **obesity** *n.* [*say* oh BEESE, oh BEESE it ee]

obey *v.* **1** carry out the command of. **2** do what one is told to do. **3** be prompted by, respond to.

obfuscate *v.* (**obfuscates, obfuscated, obfuscating**) make less clear and more difficult to understand. □ **obfuscation** *n.* [*Say* OB fuss kate]

obi *n.* (*pl.* **obis**) a sash worn with a Japanese kimono. [*Say* OH be]

obituary *n.* (*pl.* **obituaries**) a notice of a death, esp. in a newspaper, usu. in the form of a brief biography. [*Say* oh BIT chew airy]

object ● *n.* **1** a material thing that can be seen or touched. **2** a person or thing to which action or feeling is directed. **3** a purpose. **4** *Grammar* a noun or its equivalent governed by an active transitive verb or by a preposition. ● *v.* **1** express opposition or disapproval; protest. **2** have an objection □ **no object** not forming an important or restricting factor. □ **objector** *n.*

objectify *v.* (**objectifies, objectified, objectifying**) **1** express (something abstract) in a concrete form. **2** treat or regard a person as an object. □ **objectification** *n.*

objection *n.* **1** an expression of opposition or disapproval. **2** the act of objecting.

objectionable *adj.* unpleasant, offensive. □ **objectionably** *adv.*

objective ● *adj.* **1** not influenced by feelings or personal bias. **2** concerned with outward things; dealing with things external to the mind. ● *n.* something sought or aimed at. □ **objectively** *adv.* **objectivity** *n.*

object lesson *n.* a practical example or illustration of some principle.

objet d'art n. (pl. *objets d'art*) a small decorative or artistic object. [*Say* ob zhay DAR]

Oblate n. a member of the Oblates of Mary Immaculate, a missionary order of priests and brothers. □ **Oblate** adj. [*Say* OB late or OBE late]

oblation n. a thing offered to a divine being. [*Say* oh BLAY sh'n]

obligate v. (**obligates, obligated, obligating**) be obliged to do something.

obligation n. **1** a duty; what one is morally or legally required to do. **2** the constraining power of a law etc. **3** a binding agreement. **4 a** a service or kindness done or received. **b** indebtedness for this.

obligatory adj. **1** required by rule, law, or custom. **2** legally or morally binding. [*Say* uh BLIGGA tory]

oblige v. (**obliges, obliged, obliging**) **1** constrain, compel. **2** be binding on. **3 a** make indebted by conferring a favour. **b** gratify. **c** perform a service for □ **much obliged** an expression of thanks.

obliging adj. courteous, accommodating. □ **obligingly** adv.

oblique ● adj. **1 a** slanting. **b** diverging from a straight line or course. **2** roundabout, indirect. **3** *Math* (of a line, plane figure, or surface) inclined at other than a right angle. ● n. an oblique stroke (/). □ **obliquely** adv. **obliqueness** n. [*Say* oh BLEAK]

obliterate v. (**obliterates, obliterated, obliterating**) **1** destroy utterly. **2** cover completely; blot out. □ **obliteration** n. [*Say* oh BLITTER ate]

oblivion n. **1** a state in which one is no longer aware of what is happening. **2** the state of being forgotten. [*Say* oh BLIVVY un]

oblivious adj. unaware or unconscious of. □ **obliviously** adv. **obliviousness** n. [*Say* oh BLIVVY us]

oblong ● adj. **1** rectangular. **2** greater in breadth than in height. ● n. an oblong figure or object.

obnoxious adj. annoying, irritating. □ **obnoxiously** adv. [*Say* ob NOCK shuss]

OBO abbr. or best offer.

oboe n. a woodwind double-reed treble instrument with a plaintive tone. □ **oboist** n.

obscene adj. **1** offensively or repulsively indecent. **2** *informal* highly offensive or repugnant. □ **obscenely** adv.

obscenity n. (pl. **obscenities**) **1** an obscene word, action, etc. **2** the state of being obscene. [*Say* ub SENNA tee]

obscurantism n. the practice of deliberately making something difficult to understand. □ **obscurantist** n. & adj. [*Say* OBSCURE int ism]

obscure ● adj. **1** not clearly expressed or understood. **2** unexplained, doubtful. **3** dark, dim. **4** indistinct; not clear. **5** hidden. ● v. (**obscures, obscured, obscuring**) **1** hide or make unclear. **2** dim the glory of. □ **obscurely** adv.

obscurity n. (pl. **obscurities**) **1** the state of not being well-known. **2** something that is difficult to understand. **3** darkness.

obsequious adj. trying too hard to please someone. □ **obsequiously** adv. **obsequiousness** n. [*Say* ub SEE kwee us]

observance n. **1** behaving in accordance with a law, custom, ritual, etc. **2** an act of a religious or ceremonial character.

observant adj. **1** quick to notice things. **2** adhering strictly to the rules of a religion.

observation n. **1 a** the action of observing something or someone. **b** an observed truth or fact. **2** perception. **3** a remark or statement. □ **under observation** being watched or monitored. □ **observational** adj.

observatory n. (pl. **observatories**) a building equipped for the observation of natural, esp. astronomical, phenomena.

observe v. (**observes, observed, observing**) **1** perceive; take notice of. **2** watch carefully. **3 a** obey (a law etc.). **b** duly perform (a rite). **4** make a comment. □ **observable** adj. **observer** n.

obsess v. (**obsesses, obsessed, obsessing**) **1** preoccupy, haunt. **2** be continually preoccupied with. □ **obsessed** adj.

obsession n. **1** a state of being obsessed. **2** an idea or thought that continually preoccupies a person's mind. □ **obsessional** adj.

obsessive ● adj. **1** thinking continually about someone or something. **2** extremely dedicated, thorough, or careful. ● n. an obsessive person. □ **obsessively** adv.

obsessive-compulsive ● adj. designating a disorder in which a person has an obsessive compulsion to perform meaningless acts. ● n. a person characterized by such obsessive behaviour.

obsidian n. a dark glassy volcanic rock formed from hardened lava. [*Say* ub SIDDY un]

obsolescent adj. becoming obsolete. □ **obsolescence** n. [*Say* obsa LESS'nt, obsa LESS ince]

obsolete *adj.* disused, out of date. [*Say* obsa LEET]

obstacle *n.* a person or thing that obstructs progress.

obstetrician *n.* a physician specializing in obstetrics. [*Say* obsta TRISH un]

obstetrics *n.* the branch of medicine concerned with pregnancy and childbirth. □ **obstetric** *adj.* [*Say* ub STET ricks]

obstinate *adj.* **1** stubbornly refusing to change one's opinion. **2** very difficult to change or overcome. □ **obstinacy** *n.* **obstinately** *adv.* [*Say* OB stin it, OB stinna see]

obstreperous *adj.* noisy and difficult to control. [*Say* ub STREPPER us]

obstruct *v.* **1** block up. **2** prevent the progress of; impede. **3** block.

obstruction *n.* **1** the fact of obstructing or the state of being obstructed. **2** something that blocks or obstructs (a road, passage, etc.).

obstructive *adj.* causing or intended to cause an obstruction.

obtain *v.* **1** acquire, secure; have granted to one. **2** be prevalent or established. □ **obtainable** *adj.*

obtrusive *adj.* unpleasantly or unduly noticeable. □ **obtrusively** *adv.* [*Say* ub TRUCE iv]

obtuse *adj.* **1 a** dull-witted; slow to understand. **b** difficult to understand. **2** of blunt form. **3** (of an angle) more than 90° and less than 180°. □ **obtuseness** *n.* [*Say* ub TOOSE *or* ub TYOOSE]

obverse ● *n.* **1 a** the side of a coin or medal etc. bearing the head or principal design. **b** this design. **2** a counterpart or opposite. ● *adj.* that is an obverse.

obviate *v.* (**obviates, obviated, obviating**) get around or remove (a need etc.). [*Say* OB vee ate]

obvious *adj.* **1** easily seen or understood. **2** not subtle; clear. □ **obviously** *adv.* **obviousness** *n.*

OC *abbr.* Officer of the Order of Canada.

occasion ● *n.* **1 a** a special or noteworthy event. **b** the time or occurrence of this. **2** a reason or justification. **3** an opportunity. **4** an immediate but subordinate cause. ● *v.* bring about esp. incidentally. □ **on occasion** now and then. **rise to the occasion** produce the necessary will, energy, etc., in unusually demanding circumstances.

occasional *adj.* **1** happening, done, etc. infrequently. **2** made or meant for a special occasion. □ **occasionally** *adv.*

Occident *n. literary* **1** (**the Occident**) the West. **2** Europe, the Americas, or both. [*Say* OCK suh d'nt]

occidental ● *adj.* **1** of the Occident, as distinct from oriental. **2** western. ● *n.* (**Occidental**) a native or inhabitant of the Occident. [*Say* ock suh DENTAL]

occiput *n.* the back of the head. □ **occipital** *adj.* [*Say* OXA put, ock SIPPA tull]

occlude *v.* (**occludes, occluded, occluding**) stop up or close (an orifice, passage, etc.). [*Say* uh KLUDE]

occlusion *n.* **1** the position of the teeth when the jaws are closed. **2** the blockage or closing of a hollow organ etc. □ **occlusive** *adj.* [*Say* uh CLUE zh'n, uh CLUE siv]

occult ● *adj.* **1** involving the supernatural. **2** communicated only to the initiated. **3** beyond the range of ordinary knowledge. ● *n.* (**the occult**) supernatural or magical beliefs, practices, or phenomena. □ **occultism** *n.* **occultist** *n.*

occupancy *n.* (*pl.* **occupancies**) **1** the act of occupying something or of being occupied. **2** the number of people meant to occupy a room etc.

occupant *n.* a person who occupies a particular place or job.

occupation *n.* **1** what occupies one. **2** a person's employment; a calling or pursuit. **3** the act of occupying or state of being occupied. **4** the act of taking possession of by military force.

occupational *adj.* **1** having to do with an occupation. **2** (of a disease, etc.) rendered more likely by one's occupation.

occupational therapy *n.* mental or physical activity designed to help people recuperate from physical or mental illness. □ **occupational therapist** *n.*

occupy *v.* (**occupies, occupied, occupying**) **1** reside in. **2** take up or fill (space or time). **3** hold (a position). **4** take military possession of. **5** keep busy or engaged. □ **occupier** *n.*

occur *v.* (**occurs, occurred, occurring**) **1** happen. **2** exist or be encountered in. **3** come into the mind of.

occurrence *n.* **1** an incident or event. **2** the fact or frequency of something happening.

ocean *n.* **1** a large expanse of sea, esp. each of the main areas called the Atlantic, Pacific, Indian, Arctic, and Antarctic Oceans. **2** (usu. as **the ocean**) the sea. **3** a very large expanse or quantity of anything. □ **oceanside** *adj.*

ocean-going *adj.* (of a ship) able to cross oceans.

oceanic *adj.* of, like, or near the ocean. [*Say* oh she ANNICK *or* oh see ANNICK]

oceanography *n.* the study of the physical and biological properties of oceans. □ **oceanographer** *n.* **oceanographic** *adj.* [*Say* ocean OGRA fee, ocean a GRAPHIC]

ocelot *n.* a medium-sized cat native to South and Central America, with black stripes and spots. [*Say* AW suh lot]

ochre *n.* **1** a mineral used as a pigment varying from light yellow to brown or red. **2** a pale brownish yellow. [*Say* OH cur]

o'clock *adv.* of the clock (used to specify the hour).

OCR *abbr.* optical character recognition.

Oct. *abbr.* October.

octa- *comb. form* (also **oct-** before a vowel) eight.

octagon *n.* a plane figure with eight sides and angles. □ **octagonal** *adj.* [*Say* OCTA gon, ock TAGGA null]

octahedron *n.* (*pl.* **octahedrons** or **octahedra**) a solid figure contained by eight plane faces. □ **octahedral** *adj.* [*Say* octa HEED run *for the singular,* octa HEED runs *or* octa HEED ruh *for the plural*]

octane *n.* a colourless inflammable hydrocarbon of the alkane series.

octave *n.* **1** *Music* **a** a series of eight notes occupying the interval between (and including) two notes. **b** this interval. **c** each of the two notes at the extremes of this interval. **2** a stanza of eight lines. [*Say* OCK tiv]

octet *n.* **1 a** a composition for eight voices etc. **b** the performers of such a piece. **2** a group of eight. [*Say* OCK tet]

octo- *comb. form* (also **oct-** before a vowel) eight.

October *n.* the tenth month.

October Crisis *n.* *Cdn* the kidnapping of the British diplomat James Cross and the Quebec politician Pierre Laporte by the Front de Libération du Québec in October of 1970.

octogenarian ● *n.* a person from 80 to 89 years old. ● *adj.* of this age. [*Say* octa juh NAIRY un]

octopus *n.* (*pl.* **octopuses** or **octopi**) a mollusc with eight suckered arms and a soft sac-like body. [*Say* OCTA pusses *or* OCTA pie *for the plural*]

ocular *adj.* having to do with the eyes or sight. [*Say* OCK yoo lur]

OD *slang* ● *n.* (*pl.* **ODs**) an overdose, esp. of a drug. ● *v.* (**OD's**, **OD'd**, **OD'ing**) take an overdose.

O.D. *abbr.* Doctor of Optometry.

Odawa *n.* (*pl.* **Odawa** or **Odawas**) **1** a member of an Aboriginal people formerly living along the Ottawa River, and now living esp. on Manitoulin Island. **2** the Ojibwa dialect of this people. □ **Odawa** *adj.* [*Say* oh DAH wah]

odd *adj.* **1** strange. **2** additional; left over. **3** (of numbers such as 3 and 5) not integrally divisible by two. **4** detached from a set or series. **5** (after a number etc.) somewhat more than. □ **oddly** *adv.* **oddness** *n.*

oddball *informal* ● *n.* an odd or eccentric person. ● *adj.* strange, bizarre.

odd couple *n.* two apparently incompatible people who live, work, etc. together.

oddity *n.* (*pl.* **oddities**) **1** a strange person or thing. **2** a peculiar trait. **3** the state of being odd.

odd jobs *pl. n.* small, esp. domestic, jobs.

odd-man rush *n.* *Hockey* a situation in which the players leading an offensive rush outnumber the skaters defending against it.

oddment *n.* **1** an odd article; something left over. **2** (in *pl.*) miscellaneous articles.

odds *pl. n.* **1** the ratio between the amounts staked as a bet, based on the expected probability either way. **2 a** the probability of something happening. **b** this probability expressed as a ratio. **3** the balance of advantage. **4** an equalizing allowance to a weaker competitor; a handicap. □ **at odds** in conflict or at variance. **by all odds** certainly. **take odds** accept a bet.

odds and ends *pl. n.* miscellaneous articles or remnants.

odds-on *adj.* designating the outcome most favoured by the odds.

ode *n.* **1** a lyric poem, usu. rhymed and in the form of an address. **2** *hist.* a poem meant to be sung. **3** an artistic or literary creation praising or exalting something.

odious *adj.* extremely unpleasant [*Say* OH dee us]

odometer *n.* an instrument for measuring the distance travelled by a vehicle. [*Say* oh DOMMA tur]

odour *n.* (also **odor**) **1** a distinctive, usu. unpleasant smell. **2** a lasting esp. unpleasant quality or trace. □ **odourless** *adj.* (in sense 1). **odorous** *adj.*

odyssey *n.* (*pl.* **odysseys**) a long adventurous journey.

OECD *abbr.* Organization for Economic Co-operation and Development.

Oedipus complex *n.* (according to Freud etc.) the complex of emotions aroused in a young (esp. male) child by a subconscious sexual desire for the parent of the opposite sex. □ **Oedipal** adj. [Say EEDA puss, EED∧ pull]

o'er adv. & prep. literary = OVER.

oeuvre n. (pl. **oeuvres**) **1** the works of an author, painter, composer, etc. **2** a work of art, music, etc. [Say OOV ruh (with OO as in HOOD)]

of prep. **1** expressing the relationship between a part and a whole. **2** belonging to; coming from. **3** expressing the relationship between a scale or measure and a value. **4** made from. **5** used to show position. **6** used to show that something belongs to a category. **7** expressing time in relation to the following hour.

off ● adv. **1** away from the place in question. **2** so as to be removed or separated. **3** starting a journey or race. **4** so as to bring to an end or be discontinued. **5** (of an electrical appliance) not functioning or so as to cease to function. **6** having specified material goods or wealth. ● prep. **1** moving away from. **2** situated or leading in a direction away from. **3** so as to be removed or separated from. **4** informal having a temporary dislike of. ● adj. **1 a** unwell. **b** (of food etc.) no longer fresh. **2** not up to par. **3** decreased in price etc. ● v. slang kill, murder. ● n. a competition. □ **off and on** intermittently.

offal n. **1** the internal organs etc. of a carcass. **2** refuse or waste. [Sounds like AWFUL]

offbeat ● adj. eccentric, unconventional. ● n. Music a beat in a bar that is not accented.

off-centre ● adj. **1** slightly away from the centre. **2** unconventional, eccentric. ● adv. positioned away from the centre.

off chance n. (**the off chance**) the slight possibility.

off-colour adj. slightly indecent or obscene.

offcut n. a remnant of wood, paper, etc., after cutting.

off-day n. **1** a day when one is not at one's best. **2** a day off from work, sports training, etc.

offence n. (also **offense**) **1** an illegal act. **2** a wounding of the feelings. **3** the act of attacking. **4** a thing that constitutes a violation. **5** Sport **a** the role of scoring points, goals, etc. for one's team. **b** the players on a team who perform this role.

offend v. **1** cause offence to or resentment in. **2** displease or anger. **3** commit an illegal act. **4** do wrong. □ **offender** n. **offending** adj.

offensive ● adj. **1** giving or likely to give offence. **2** disgusting, foul-smelling.

3 a aggressive, attacking. **b** (of a weapon) used in attack. **4** Sport pertaining to a team's offence. ● n. **1** (usu. as **the offensive**) an aggressive action or attitude. **2** an attack. □ **offensively** adv. **offensiveness** n.

offer ● v. **1** present for acceptance, refusal, or consideration. **2** express willingness to do something for someone. **3** provide. **4** present to a deity. ● n. **1** an expression of readiness to do or give something. **2** an amount of money that someone is willing to pay for something. **3** a specially reduced price. **4** a proposal of marriage.

offering n. **1** a contribution to a church. **2** a thing offered in worship. **3** anything contributed or offered.

offertory n. (pl. **offertories**) **1** Christianity the offering of the bread and wine at the Eucharist. **2** the collection of money at a religious service. [Say OFFER tory]

offhand ● adj. curt or casual in manner. ● adv. **1** in an offhand manner. **2** without preparation. □ **offhanded** adj. **offhandedly** adv. **offhandedness** n.

office n. **1** a room, set of rooms, or building used as a place for non-manual work. **2** a position of authority or service. **3** tenure of an official position. **4** service done for others. **5** (also **divine office**) Christianity the prayers and psalms said daily by Catholic priests etc.

office block n. a large building designed to contain offices.

office-holder n. an esp. elected official.

officer n. **1** a person holding a position of authority or trust. **2** a policeman or policewoman. **3** a holder of a post in a society or organization. **4** a holder of a public, civil, or ecclesiastical office. **5** (**Officer**) a member of the grade below Companion in the Order of Canada.

official ● adj. **1 a** having to do with an authority or public body. **b** having the authorization of such a body. **2** (often derogatory) characteristic of officials and bureaucracy. **3** formal; ceremonial. ● n. a person holding office or engaged in official duties. □ **officialdom** n. **officially** adv.

official language n. the language or languages under which government services etc. must be provided to citizens.

official opposition n. Cdn & Brit. (in a legislature) the opposition party which has the most seats.

officiate v. (**officiates, officiated, officiating**) **1** act in an official capacity. **2** perform a religious service or ceremony. **3** act as a referee, umpire, etc. [Say oh FISHY ate]

officious adj. asserting authority

aggressively; domineering.
[*Say* oh FISH us]

offing *n.* the more distant part of the sea in view. □**in the offing** not far away; likely to happen soon.

off-key *adj.* out of tune.

off-kilter *adj.* **1** out of alignment, off-centre. **2** offbeat, bizarre.

off-line ● *adj.* Computing not connected to or controlled by a central processing unit. ● *adv.* while not directly controlled by or connected to a central processing unit.

off-load *v.* **1** get rid of (something) by giving it to someone else. **2** unload (cargo etc.).

off-peak *adj. & adv.* at times other than those of greatest demand.

off-putting *adj.* **1** disconcerting. **2** unpleasant. □**off-puttingly** *adv.*

off-ramp *n.* a one-way road leading off a highway.

off-reserve *Cdn* ● *adj.* located on or inhabiting land which is not part of a designated reserve for Aboriginal people. ● *adv.* not on a reserve.

off-road ● *adj.* (of a vehicle etc.) designed for rough terrain. ● *adv.* away from the road. □**off-roader** *n.* **off-roading** *n.*

off-sale *Cdn (BC, Alberta, & North)* ● *n.* the sale of liquor for consumption elsewhere than at the place of sale. ● *adj.* designating a place where liquor is sold in this manner.

off-season *n.* **1** *Sport* the period following the conclusion of the regular season and playoffs. **2** a time when business etc. is slack.

offset ● *n.* **1** a side shoot from a plant. **2** a method of printing in which ink is transferred from a plate or stone to a uniform rubber surface and from there to paper etc. ● *v.* (**offsets**, **offset**, **offsetting**) **1** counterbalance, compensate. **2** place out of line. **3** print by the offset process.

offshoot *n.* **1** a side shoot or branch. **2** a thing which develops from something else.

offshore ● *adj.* **1 a** situated at sea some distance from the shore. **b** of or pertaining to fishing conducted from large vessels at some distance from the shore. **2** (of the wind) blowing seawards. **3** (of goods, funds, etc.) made or registered abroad. ● *adv.* **1** at some distance or in a direction away from the shore. **2** abroad.

offside ● *adj.* *Sport* (of a player) in a position, usu. ahead of the ball or puck, that is not allowed. ● *adv.* in an offside position.

off-site *adj. & adv.* away from a site.

offspring *n.* (*pl.* **offspring**) **1** a person's child or children. **2** an animal's young.

offstage *adj. & adv.* not on the stage and so not visible to the audience.

off-the-rack *adj.* (esp. of clothes) ready-made.

off-the-shelf ● *adj.* (of goods) supplied ready-made. ● *adv.* (**off the shelf**) that can be obtained easily from existing stock.

off-the-wall *adj. slang* crazy, absurd, outlandish.

off-track *adj.* **1** situated or taking place away from a racetrack. **2** (**off track**) away from the subject, goal, etc.

off-white *n. & adj.* a white colour with a grey or yellowish tinge.

oft *adv.* often.

often *adv.* (**oftener**, **oftenest**) **1 a** frequently. **b** at short intervals. **2** in many instances. □**as often as not** in roughly half the instances. [*Say* OFF'n or OFT'n]

oftentimes *adv.* often. [*Say* OFF'n times or OFT'n times]

ogle ● *v.* (**ogles**, **ogled**, **ogling**) **1** stare at in a lecherous way. **2** watch, stare at. ● *n.* an amorous or lecherous look. [*Say* OH gull]

ogre *n.* **1** a man-eating giant. **2** a cruel irascible person. □**ogreish** *adj.* [*Say* OH gur]

oh[1] *interj.* (also **O**) expressing surprise, pain, excitement, etc. □**oh boy** expressing excitement etc. **oh well** expressing resignation.

oh[2] *n.* zero.

ohm *n.* *Electricity* the SI unit of electrical resistance. □**ohmic** *adj.* [*Say* OME]

-oid *suffix* forming adjectives and nouns, denoting resemblance. □**-oidal** *suffix* **-oidally** *suffix*

oil ● *n.* **1** any of various thick liquids insoluble in water, obtained from animal, plant, or mineral sources. **2** petroleum. **3 a** = OIL PAINT. **b** a picture painted in oil paints. ● *v.* **1** apply oil to. **2** treat with oil. □**oil the wheels** help make things go smoothly. □**oiler** *n.*

oil can *n.* a can with a long nozzle for oiling machinery.

oilcloth *n.* a fabric waterproofed with oil.

oil field *n.* an area of land or seabed underlain by strata which contain oil.

oil lamp *n.* a lamp using oil as fuel.

oil paint *n.* a mix of ground colour pigment and oil.

oil painting *n.* **1** the art of painting in oils. **2** a picture painted in oils.

oil patch *n. slang* **1** a petroleum-rich region. **2** the petroleum industry.

oil rig *n.* a structure with equipment for drilling an oil well.

oilseed *n.* any of various seeds from cultivated crops yielding oil.

oilskin *n.* **1** cloth waterproofed with oil. **2** a garment made of this.

oil slick *n.* a smooth patch of floating oil.

oil well *n.* a well from which petroleum is drawn.

oily *adj.* (**oilier, oiliest**) **1** of, like, or containing much oil. **2** covered with oil. **3** excessively polite or flattering; smarmy. □ **oiliness** *n.*

oink ● *v.* grunt like a pig. ● *n.* the grunt of a pig or a sound resembling this.

ointment *n.* a smooth greasy healing or cosmetic preparation for the skin.

OJ *n. informal* orange juice.

Ojibwa *n.* (also **Ojibway**) (*pl.* **Ojibwa** or **Ojibway**) **1** a member of an Algonquian people living esp. around Lake Superior and certain adjacent areas. **2** the Algonquian language of this people. □ **Ojibwa** *adj.* (also **Ojibway**) [*Say* oh JIB way]

Oji-Cree *n.* a mixture of Cree and Ojibwa spoken in northwestern Ontario and Manitoba. [*Say* AW gee cree]

Oka *n. Cdn* a variety of cheese originally made by Trappist monks. [*Say* OH kuh]

Okanagan *n.* (*pl.* **Okanagan**) **1** a member of an Aboriginal people living in southern BC. **2** the Salishan language of this people. [*Say* oh kuh NOGGIN]

okay (also **OK**) *informal* ● *adj.* all right; satisfactory. ● *adv.* well, satisfactorily. ● *n.* (*pl.* **okays** or **OKs**) approval, sanction. ● *interj.* all right, yes. ● *v.* (**okays** or **OK's, okayed** or **OK'd, okaying** or **OK'ing**) approve, sanction. □ **be okay with 1** be acceptable to. **2** be content with.

okey-doke *adj., interj., & adv.* (also **okey-dokey**) *slang* = OKAY.

Okie *n. informal* a person from Oklahoma. [*Sounds like* OAKY]

okra *n.* (*pl.* **okras**) **1** an African plant yielding long ridged seed pods. **2** the seed pods eaten as a vegetable. [*Say* OAK ruh]

Oktoberfest *n.* an annual beer festival celebrated in late September and early October.

old *adj.* (**older, oldest**) **1** having lived for a long time. **2** made or built long ago. **3** possessed or used for a long time. **4** dating from far back. **5** former. **6** of a specified age. **7** *informal* expressing affection or contempt. **8** *Cdn* (of cheddar) aged 10-24 months. □ **of old** formerly; long ago.

old age *n.* the later part of normal life.

old-age home *n.* = OLD PEOPLE'S HOME.

old-age pension *n.* a pension paid by the state to citizens above a certain age. □ **old-age pensioner** *n.*

old age security *n. Cdn* a system of government-funded pensions for those over 65. Abbreviation: **OAS**.

old boys' network *n. informal* (also **old boy network**) an informal network through which men from the same social background, school, etc. help each other.

old country *n.* (**the old country**) the native country of an immigrant etc.

olden *adj. archaic* or *literary* of a former age.

Old English *n.* the language spoken in England by the Anglo-Saxons up to about 1150.

old-fashioned *adj.* **1** in or according to the fashion of an earlier period; antiquated. **2** conservative.

old folks' home *n. informal* an old people's home.

Old French *n.* the French language up to *c.*1400.

old-growth *adj.* (of a tree etc.) mature, never felled.

old guard *n.* the original or conservative members of a group.

old hand *n.* a person with much experience.

old hat *adj. informal* tediously familiar or out of date.

oldie *n. informal* **1** a song or film that is old or familiar. **2** an elderly person.

old lady *n. informal* one's mother, wife, or girlfriend.

old-line *adj.* **1** conservative. **2** well established.

old man *informal* one's father, husband, or boyfriend.

old man's beard *n.* any of various plants with plumed seeds.

Old Master *n.* **1** a great artist of former times, esp. before the 18th c. **2** a painting by such a painter.

old money *n.* **1** wealth accumulated in a family over several generations. **2** people endowed with this.

Old Order *adj.* of or relating to various Mennonite sects which preserve the most conservative codes of behaviour, dress, etc.

old people's home *n.* an institution providing accommodation and nursing care for the elderly.

old school *n.* **1** traditional attitudes. **2** people having such attitudes.

oldsquaw *n.* a duck with very long tail

feathers and mainly white plumage in winter.

oldster *n.* an old person.

Old Testament *n.* the first part of the Christian Bible containing the scriptures of the Hebrews.

old-time *adj.* belonging to or typical of former times. □ **old-timey** *adj.*

old-timer *n.* **1** a person who has lived or worked in a place for a long time. **2** an elderly person. **3** *Sport* **a** a retired professional player, esp. one who participates in sports charity events. **b** a member of a team of middle-aged or elderly amateur players.

Old West *n.* the western US and Canada before the establishment of government.

old wives' tale *n.* a foolish or unscientific tradition or belief.

old woman *n. informal* or *offensive* **1** one's wife, mother, or girlfriend. **2** a fussy or timid person.

Old World *n.* Europe, Asia, and Africa, seen as the part of the world known before the European discovery of the Americas.

old-world *adj.* associated with old times.

oleander *n.* an evergreen shrub of the Mediterranean bearing clusters of white, pink, or red flowers. [*Say* oh lee ANDER]

olfactory *adj.* relating to the sense of smell. [*Say* ole FACTORY *or* awl FACTORY]

oligarch *n.* (*pl.* **oligarchs**) a member of an oligarchy. [*Say* OLLA gark]

oligarchy *n.* (*pl.* **oligarchies**) **1** a small group of people having control of a state or organization. **2** something governed in this way. □ **oligarchic** *adj.* [*Say* OLLA garky, olla GARK ick]

Oligocene *n.* the third epoch of the Tertiary period, about 38 to 24.6 million years ago, when the first primates appeared. □ **Oligocene** *adj.* [*Say* AWL ig a seen]

oligopoly *n.* (*pl.* **oligopolies**) a state of limited competition between a small number of producers. □ **oligopolistic** *adj.* [*Say* olla GOPPA lee, olla goppa LISS tick]

olive ● *n.* **1** a small oval fruit with a hard stone and bitter green or black flesh. **2** (also **olive green**) a greyish-green colour. **3** (also **olive tree**) the evergreen tree that produces this fruit. ● *adj.* **1** (also **olive green**) coloured like an unripe olive. **2** (of the complexion) yellowish brown.

olive branch *n.* **1** the branch of an olive tree as a symbol of peace. **2** a gesture of reconciliation.

olive oil *n.* an oil extracted from olives, used esp. in cooking.

ollie ● *n.* (in skateboarding and snowboarding) a jump performed without the aid of a takeoff ramp. ● *v.* (**ollies**, **ollied**, **ollieing**) perform an ollie.

-ology *comb. form see* -LOGY.

Olympiad *n.* **1** a period of four years between Olympic Games. **2** a celebration of the Olympic Games. [*Say* a LIMPY ad]

Olympian ● *adj.* **1** having to do with Mount Olympus in Greece, traditionally the home of the Greek gods. **2** superior or aloof like a god. **3** of great size. ● *n.* **1** any of the twelve gods regarded as living on Olympus. **2** a competitor in the Olympic Games. [*Say* a LIMPY un]

Olympic ● *adj.* relating to the modern Olympic Games. ● *n.* (**the Olympics**) the Olympic Games.

Olympic Games *n.* **1** a modern international sports competition, with the Summer and Winter Games alternating every second year in different venues. **2** *hist.* an ancient Greek festival held at Olympia every four years.

Olympic-sized *adj.* (also **Olympic-size**) of the dimensions prescribed for Olympic competitions.

om *n. Hinduism & Buddhism* a mystic syllable used as a mantra. [*Say* OME]

Omaha *n.* (*pl.* **Omaha** or **Omahas**) **1** a member of an Aboriginal people of northeastern Nebraska. **2** the Siouan language of this people. □ **Omaha** *adj.* [*Say* OH muh haw]

ombudsman *n.* (*pl.* **ombudsmen**) (also **ombudsperson**) **1** an official appointed to investigate individuals' complaints against public authorities etc. **2** an official within an institution who investigates complaints. [*Say* OMM budz mun]

omega *n.* (*pl.* **omegas**) the last (24th) letter of the Greek alphabet (Ω, ω). [*Say* oh MAY guh]

omega-3 fatty acid *n.* a fatty acid found esp. in fish oil, believed to help reduce blood cholesterol levels.

omelette *n.* a dish of beaten eggs cooked in a frying pan usu. with a filling.

omen *n.* **1** an event or object regarded as portending good or evil. **2** indication of good or evil to come.

omicron *n.* the fifteenth letter of the Greek alphabet (O, o). [*Say* OMM uh kron *or* OME uh kron]

ominous *adj.* suggesting that something bad is going to happen; threatening. □ **ominously** *adv.*

omission *n.* **1** something that has been

left out or excluded. **2** the action of excluding or leaving out. **3** a failure to do something.

omit *v.* (**omits, omitted, omitting**) **1** leave out. **2** fail or neglect.

omni- *comb. form* **1** of all things. **2** in all ways or places.

omnibus ● *n.* (*pl.* **omnibuses**) **1** *hist.* = BUS *n.* 1. **2** a volume containing several novels etc. previously published separately. ● *adj.* serving several purposes at once.

omnidirectional *adj.* of equal sensitivity or power in all directions.

OMNIMAX *n. proprietary* a technique of widescreen cinematography in which 70mm film is projected through a fish-eye lens onto a hemispherical screen.

omnipotent *adj.* having great or absolute power. □ **omnipotence** *n.* [*Say* omm NIPPA t'nt, omm NIPPA tince]

omnipresent *adj.* **1** present everywhere at the same time. **2** widespread. [*Say* OMNI present]

omniscient *adj.* having infinite or very extensive knowledge. □ **omniscience** *n.* [*Say* omm NISHY unt, omm NISHY ince]

omnivorous *adj.* **1** feeding on many kinds of food, esp. on both plants and meat. **2** taking in or using anything available. □ **omnivore** *n.* [*Say* omm NIVVER us, OMNI vore]

ON *abbr.* Ontario (in official postal use).

on ● *prep.* **1** in contact with and supported by (a surface). **2** on to. **3** in the possession of. **4** forming a part of the surface of. **5** about. **6** as a member of (a committee, jury, etc.). **7** having as a target or focus. **8** stored in or broadcast by. **9** in the course of or while travelling in. **10** indicating the day or time of an event. **11** engaged in. **12** regularly taking (a drug or medicine). **13** paid for by. ● *adv.* **1** in contact with and supported by a surface. **2** (of clothing) being worn. **3** with continued movement or action. **4** taking place or being presented. **5** (of an electrical appliance or power supply) functioning. **6** on duty or on stage. □ **be on about** discuss esp. tediously. **be on to** realize the significance or intentions of. **on and off** intermittently. **on and on** at tedious length. **on time** punctual.

on-again, off-again *adj.* occurring at irregular intervals.

on-air *adj.* broadcasting.

once ● *adv.* **1** on one occasion only. **2** at some point in the past. **3** ever or at all. **4** by one degree. ● *conj.* as soon as. ● *n.* one time or occasion. □ **all at once 1** suddenly. **2** all together. **at once 1** immediately. **2** simultaneously. **for once** on this

occasion. **once and for all** (or **once for all**) (done) in a final or conclusive manner. **once** (or **every once**) **in a while** from time to time. **once upon a time 1** at some vague time in the past. **2** formerly.

once-over *n. informal* a rapid preliminary inspection or piece of work.

oncology *n.* the branch of medicine dealing with the diagnosis and treatment of cancerous tumours. □ **oncologist** *n.* [*Say* on COLLA jee, on COLLA jist]

oncoming *adj.* approaching from the front.

one ● *card. num.* **1** the lowest cardinal number; 1. **2** single, or a single person or thing. **3** (before a person's name) a certain. **4** a noteworthy example of. ● *pron.* **1** used to refer to a person or thing previously mentioned or easily identified. **2** a person of a specified kind. **3** used to refer to the speaker, or any person. □ **at one** in agreement. **for one thing** as a single consideration. **one and all** everyone. **one and only 1** unique. **2** unequalled. **one by one** singly, successively.

one-armed bandit *n. informal* a slot machine worked by a long handle at the side.

one-dimensional *adj.* **1** having a single dimension. **2** lacking depth; superficial.

one-eighty *n. informal* **1** a turn of 180 degrees; a U-turn. **2** a complete reversal in attitude or opinion.

one-handed ● *adj.* **1** having only one hand. **2** used or performed with one hand. ● *adv.* using only one hand.

one-horse *adj.* **1** using a single horse. **2** *informal* unimportant; obscure.

Oneida *n.* (*pl.* **Oneida** or **Oneidas**) **1** a member of an Iroquois people formerly living in New York State, and now living near London, Ont. **2** the Iroquoian language of this people. □ **Oneida** *adj.* [*Say* oh NIDE uh]

one-liner *n. informal* a short witty remark or joke.

one-man band *n.* **1** an entertainer who plays a number of musical instruments at the same time. **2** a person who operates without assistance.

oneness *n.* **1** the fact or state of being one. **2** identity or harmony.

one-night stand *n.* **1** *informal* a sexual relationship lasting only one night. **2** a single performance of a play etc. in a place.

one-off *informal* ● *adj.* made or happening only once. ● *n.* a one-off thing.

one-on-one ● *adj.* involving direct communication, confrontation, etc. between two people. ● *adv.* in direct communication, confrontation, etc. ● *n.* a one-on-one meeting etc.

one percent *n.* (also **1 percent**, **1%**) partly skimmed milk containing one percent milk fat.

one-piece ● *n.* (of a bathing suit etc.) made as a single garment. ● *n.* a thing that consists of one piece.

onerous *adj.* burdensome; requiring effort. [*Say* OWN er us *or* ON er us]

oneself *pron.* the reflexive and emphatic form of *one*.

one-shot *adj.* **1** achieved or done with a single attempt etc. **2** used etc. only once.

one-sided *adj.* **1** favouring one side in a dispute. **2** unequal. □ **one-sidedness** *n.*

one-stop *adj.* (of a store etc.) capable of supplying all a customer's needs.

one-time ● *adj.* **1** former. **2** done or occurring etc. only once. ● *v.* (**one-times**, **one-timed**, **one-timing**) shoot (a moving puck, ball, etc.) without stopping it first.

one-track mind *n.* a mind preoccupied with one subject.

one-two *informal* ● *n.* (*pl.* **one-twos**) *Boxing* the delivery of two punches. ● *adj.* (of two competitors etc.) holding first and second place.

one-up *v. informal* (**one-ups**, **one-upped**, **one-upping**) do better than.

one-upmanship *n. informal* the art or practice of maintaining an advantage over someone else.

one-way *adj.* **1** allowing movement or travel in one direction only. **2** characterized by or entailing no reciprocal feeling etc. **3** (of glass etc.) permitting vision from one side only.

one-woman *adj.* involving or operated by only one woman.

ongoing *adj.* **1** continuing without interruption. **2** still in progress.

onion *n.* **1** a swollen edible bulb with a pungent taste and smell. **2** the plant that produces this bulb.

onion ring *n.* a ring of onion coated in batter and deep-fried.

onion skin *n.* **1** the outermost skin of an onion. **2** thin smooth translucent paper.

online ● *adj.* directly controlled by or connected to a computer or the Internet. ● *adv.* while thus controlled or connected. □ **go online 1** establish connection with the Internet. **2** begin using the Internet. **3** in or into operation, production, or existence.

onlooker *n.* a spectator.

only ● *adv.* **1** and no one or nothing more besides. **2** no longer ago than. **3** not until.

4 with the negative result that. ● *adj.* **1** single or solitary. **2** alone deserving consideration. ● *conj. informal* except that. □ **only too** extremely.

onomatopoeia *n.* **1** the formation of a word from a sound associated with what is named (e.g. *sizzle*). **2** the use of such words. □ **onomatopoeic** *adj.* [*Say* onna matta PEE uh]

Onondaga *n.* (*pl.* **Onondaga** or **Onondagas**) **1** a member of an Iroquois people now living near Brantford, Ont. **2** the Iroquoian language of this people. □ **Onondaga** *adj.* [*Say* on on DOGGA]

on-ramp *n.* a sloping one-way road leading onto a highway.

on-reserve *Cdn* ● *adj.* located on land which is part of a designated reserve for Aboriginal people. ● *adv.* on a reserve.

onrush *n.* (*pl.* **onrushes**) an onward rush. □ **onrushing** *adj.*

onscreen ● *adj.* appearing on a television or computer screen. ● *adv.* on or by means of a screen.

onset *n.* the beginning of something.

onshore ● *adj.* **1** on the shore. **2** (of the wind) blowing from the sea towards the land. ● *adv.* on or towards the land.

onside *adj. & adv.* **1** *Sport* (of a player) not offside. **2** (also **on side**) in or into agreement with.

on-site *adj.* taking place or available on a site.

onslaught *n.* a fierce attack. [*Say* ON slot]

onstage *adj. & adv.* on the stage; visible to the audience.

Ont. *abbr.* Ontario.

Ontarian *n.* a native or inhabitant of Ontario. □ **Ontarian** *adj.* [*Say* on TERRY un]

onto *prep.* to a position on or in contact with.

ontology *n.* the branch of metaphysics dealing with the nature of being. □ **ontological** *adj.* [*Say* on TOLLA jee, onta LOGICAL]

onus *n.* a responsibility. [*Say* OH nus]

onward ● *adv.* (also **onwards**) **1** further on. **2** towards the front. **3** with advancing motion. ● *adj.* directed onward.

onyx *n.* (*pl.* **onyxes**) a semi-precious variety of agate with different colours in layers. [*Say* ON ix]

oodles *pl. n. informal* a very great amount.

ooh ● *interj.* expressing surprise, delight, pain, etc. ● *n.* an exclamation of "ooh". ● *v.* (**oohs**, **oohed**, **oohing**) (in phr. **ooh and aah**) express delight etc.

Ookpik *n. Cdn* a doll resembling an owl,

originally handcrafted of sealskin by Inuit artisans.

oolichan *n.* (**oolichan** or **oolichans**) = EULACHON. [*Say* OOLA con]

oompah *n.* (also **oompahpah**) a representation of the repetitive playing of lower brass instruments.

oomph *n. slang* **1** energy, liveliness. **2** attractiveness.

oops *interj. informal* (also **oopsy daisy**) expressing surprise or apology.

ooze ● *v.* (**oozes**, **oozed**, **oozing**) **1** slowly seep out. **2** (of a substance) exude moisture. **3** give a powerful impression of. ● *n.* **1** a sluggish flow of liquid. **2** a deposit of wet mud or slime. □ **oozy** *adj.*

op *n. informal* operation (in surgical and military senses).

opacity *n.* (*pl.* **opacities**) the state of being opaque. [*Say* oh PASSA tee]

opal *n.* a quartz-like form of hydrated silica used as a gemstone, sometimes showing changing colours. [*Say* OH pull]

opalescent *adj.* showing changing colours like an opal. [*Say* oh puh LESS'nt]

opaque *adj.* **1** not clear enough to see through. **2** not easy to understand. [*Say* oh PAKE]

op. cit. *abbr.* in the work already quoted. [*Say* OPP sit]

OPEC *abbr.* Organization of Petroleum Exporting Countries. [*Say* OH peck]

op-ed *n.* a newspaper page containing signed opinion pieces, letters to the editor, etc.

open ● *adj.* **1** not closed, fastened, or restricted. **2** not covered or protected. **3** vulnerable or subject to. **4** spread out, expanded, or unfolded. **5** accessible or available. **6** frank and communicative. **7** not finally settled. **8** making possible. **9** *Music* (of a string) allowed to vibrate along its whole length. **10** *Cdn* (of a mortgage etc.) that may be paid off in full before term without penalty. ● *v.* **1** make or become open. **2** unfold or be unfolded. **3** formally begin or establish. **4** make available. ● *n.* **1** (**the open**) fresh air or open countryside. **2** (**Open**) a championship or competition with no restrictions on who may compete. □ **open fire** start shooting. **open up 1** unlock (premises). **2** make accessible. **3** reveal; bring to notice. **4** talk or speak openly. □ **openable** *adj.* **openness** *n.*

open air ● *n.* (**the open air**) a free, not enclosed space outdoors. ● *adj.* (**open-air**) out of doors.

open-and-shut *adj.* straightforward and conclusive.

open bar *n.* a bar where the drinks are paid for by the host or through an admission fee.

open book ● *n.* a person or thing that is easily understood. ● *adj.* (usu. **open-book**) (of an examination etc.) written with the use of a textbook.

open concept *adj. Cdn* (of a house etc.) having few or no internal walls or partitions.

open custody *n. Cdn* custody in a correctional facility that has relatively little supervision or security, e.g. a group home.

open door *n.* **1** a policy of allowing trade with all nations. **2** free or unrestricted admittance.

open-ended *adj.* having no predetermined limit or boundary. □ **open-endedness** *n.*

opener *n.* **1** a person or thing that opens (something). **2** a device for opening cans, bottles, etc. □ **for openers** *informal* to start with.

open-faced *adj.* (also **open-face**) (of a sandwich etc.) without an upper layer of bread etc.

open-heart *adj.* of surgery in which the heart has been temporarily bypassed and opened.

open house *n.* **1** a reception or party during which guests are invited to drop in to a person's home. **2** a time during which an institution is open to visitors. **3** a time during which a house may be viewed by prospective buyers.

opening ● *n.* **1** a gap. **2** an opportunity. **3** an available job or position. **4** a beginning. **5** the process of becoming open. **6** a ceremony to celebrate a new building, facility, etc. being ready for use. **7** the first performance of a theatrical production etc. **8** *Cdn* a period of fixed length determined by the government during which fishing may be undertaken. ● *adj.* initial, first.

opening line *n.* **1** the first line of a book, movie, etc. **2** a phrase or sentence initiating a conversation.

open letter *n.* a letter addressed to an individual and published in a newspaper etc.

openly *adv.* **1** frankly, honestly. **2** publicly.

open market *n.* an unrestricted market with free competition of buyers and sellers.

open-minded *adj.* accessible to new ideas; not prejudiced. □ **open-mindedness** *n.*

open-mouthed *adj.* with the mouth open, esp. in surprise.

open-necked *adj.* (of a shirt) worn with the top button unfastened.

open-pit mine n. a large pit excavated in the ground from which minerals are mined. □ **open-pit mining** n.

open-plan adj. = OPEN CONCEPT.

open question n. a matter not yet decided.

open season n. **1** the season when restrictions on the killing of game etc. are lifted. **2** a time when there appear to be no restrictions on criticizing particular groups of people etc.

open shop n. a business etc. where employees do not have to be members of a labour union.

open skies n. a system allowing unrestricted access to the airspace over a country.

open system n. a computer system in which the components conform to certain standards, thus allowing greater compatibility.

open university n. (often **Open University**) a university that teaches mainly by broadcasting and correspondence.

openwork n. a pattern with intervening spaces in metal, lace, etc.

opera[1] n. (pl. **operas**) **1** a dramatic work, set to music for singers and instrumentalists. **2** the score for an opera.

opera[2] pl. of OPUS.

operable adj. **1** that can be operated. **2** suitable for treatment by surgical operation. [Say OPERA bull]

opera glasses pl. n. small binoculars for use in a theatre.

opera house n. a theatre for the performance of opera and usu. ballet.

operate v. (**operates**, **operated**, **operating**) **1** manage, work, control. **2** function. **3** produce an effect. **4 a** perform a surgical operation. **b** conduct a military action. **c** be active in business etc. **5** influence or affect (feelings etc.).

operatic adj. **1** of or relating to opera. **2** resembling opera. [Say opper ATTIC]

operating room n. (also **operating theatre**) a room for surgical operations.

operating system n. the basic software that enables the running of a computer program.

operating table n. a table on which surgical operations are performed.

operation n. **1 a** the action of operating. **b** the state of being active or functioning. **2** an active process. **3** a piece of work. **4** an act of surgery performed on a patient. **5** a strategic movement of troops etc. for military action. **6** a financial transaction.

7 a business or enterprise. **8** Math the subjection of a number or quantity etc. to a process affecting its value or form.

operational adj. **1 a** of or used for operations. **b** involved in operations. **2** able or ready to function. □ **operationally** adv.

operative ● adj. **1** in operation. **2** most relevant. **3** of or by surgery. ● n. **1** a worker. **2** a secret agent. [Say OPPER a tiv]

operator n. **1** a person operating a machine etc. **2** a person operating a business. **3** informal a person acting in a specified way. **4** Math a symbol or function denoting an operation.

operetta n. a short opera on a light or humorous theme. [Say opper ETTA]

ophthalmic adj. of or relating to the eye and its diseases. [Say off THAL mick or opp THAL mick]

ophthalmology n. the study and treatment of disorders and diseases of the eye. □ **ophthalmological** adj. **ophthalmologist** n.
[Say off thuh MOLLA jee or opp thuh MOLLA jee, off thuh muh LOGICAL or opp thuh muh LOGICAL]

opiate ● n. **1** a drug containing or derived from opium. **2** a thing which soothes or stupefies. ● adj. containing opium. [Say OH pee it]

opine v. (**opines**, **opined**, **opining**) hold or express as an opinion. [Say oh PINE]

opinion n. **1** a belief or assessment not necessarily based on fact or knowledge. **2** a view held as probable. **3** what one thinks about a particular topic. **4** a formal statement of professional advice. **5** an estimation. □ **be of the opinion that** believe or maintain that. **a matter of opinion** a disputable point.

opinionated adj. conceited and assertive in one's opinions.

opinion poll n. = GALLUP POLL.

opium n. an addictive pain-killing drug prepared from the juice of the opium poppy. [Say OH pee um]

opium den n. a place where opium may be purchased and used.

opium poppy n. a poppy native to Europe and East Asia, with bright flowers.

opossum n. a N American mainly tree-living marsupial that can grasp things with its tail. [Say a POSSUM]

OPP abbr. (in Canada) Ontario Provincial Police.

opponent n. a person who opposes or belongs to an opposing side.

opportune adj. **1** (of a time) well-chosen or

especially favourable or appropriate.
2 occurring at a favourable time.

opportunism n. **1** the adaptation of
policy etc. to circumstances. **2** the seizing
of opportunities when they occur.
□ **opportunist** n. [Say opper TUNE ism]

opportunistic adj. **1** of or relating to
opportunism. **2** (of a species) able to spread
quickly. **3 a** (of a micro-organism) rarely
causing disease except in unusual
circumstances. **b** (of an infection) caused by
such a micro-organism.
□ **opportunistically** adv.
[Say opper too NISS tick or
opper tyoo NISS tick]

opportunity n. (pl. **opportunities**) **1** a
favourable occasion. **2** a chance or opening
offered by circumstances. □ **opportunity
knocks** an opportunity occurs.

opposable adj. **1** able to be opposed. **2** (of
the thumb in primates) capable of facing
and touching the other digits on the same
hand.

oppose v. (**opposes, opposed,
opposing**) **1** resist; set oneself against.
2 be hostile (to). **3** compete with or fight.
4 place in opposition or contrast.
□ **opposed** adj.

opposing adj. **1** in conflict or competition
with. **2** differing from or in conflict with.
3 facing, opposite.

opposite ● adj. **1** facing or back to back.
2 a diametrically different. **b** being the
other of a contrasted pair. **3** (of angles)
between opposite sides of the intersection
of two lines. ● n. an opposite thing or
person. ● adv. in an opposite position.
● prep. in a position opposite to.
□ **oppositely** adv.

opposite number n. a person holding an
equivalent position in another
organization.

opposition n. **1** resistance, antagonism.
2 the state of being hostile. **3** contrast. **4** a
group of opponents or competitors. **5** (**the
Opposition**) the principal parliamentary
party opposed to that in office. **6** the act of
opposing or placing opposite.
□ **oppositional** adj.

oppress v. (**oppresses, oppressed,
oppressing**) **1** treat someone in a cruel
and unfair way. **2** cause to feel distressed or
anxious. □ **oppressed** adj. **oppression** n.
oppressor n.

oppressive adj. **1** harsh or cruel.
2 difficult to endure. **3** (of weather) hot and
humid. □ **oppressively** adv.

opprobrium n. **1** harsh criticism. **2** public
disgrace arising from bad behaviour.
[Say a PRO bree um]

opt v. make a choice. □ **opt out** choose not
to participate. **opt in** choose to participate.

optic ● adj. relating to the eye, vision, or
light. ● n. a lens etc. in an optical
instrument.

optical adj. **1** of sight; visual. **2** of or
concerning optics. **3** (esp. of a lens)
constructed to assist sight. □ **optically** adv.

optical character recognition n. the
identification of printed characters using
photoelectric devices and computer
software.

optical disk n. see DISK n. 1b.

optical fibre n. thin glass fibre through
which light can be transmitted.

optical illusion n. something that
deceives one's eyes by appearing to be
other than it is.

optical scanner n. a device that
performs optical character recognition on
a text.

optician n. a person qualified to make and
supply glasses and contact lenses.
[Say opp TISH'n]

optic nerve n. each of the second pair of
cranial nerves, transmitting impulses from
the eyes to the brain.

optics pl. n. **1** the scientific study of sight
and the behaviour of light. **2** the optical
components of an instrument. **3** the way in
which something is perceived by the
public.

optimal adj. best or most favourable.
□ **optimally** adv. [Say OPP tim'll]

optimism n. an inclination to hopefulness
and confidence.

optimist n. a person inclined to or
professing optimism. □ **optimistic** adj.
optimistically adv.

optimize v. (**optimizes, optimized,
optimizing**) **1 a** make the best use of (an
opportunity etc.). **b** improve to the utmost.
2 make as efficient as possible.
□ **optimization** n. **optimizer** n.

optimum ● n. (pl. **optima** or **optimums**)
the most favourable conditions for growth
or success. ● adj. = OPTIMAL.

option ● n. **1** a thing that is or may be
chosen. **2** freedom of choice. **3** the right to
buy, sell, etc. something in the future. ● v.
buy or sell under option; have an option
on. □ **keep** (or **leave**) **one's options
open** not commit oneself. □ **optional** adj.
optionally adv.

optometry n. the science or profession of
measuring eyesight, detecting eye disease,
and prescribing corrective lenses.
□ **optometrist** n. [Say opp TOMMA tree,
opp TOMMA trist]

opt-out *adj.* designating a provision in a contract etc. allowing one to opt out.

opulent *adj.* **1** made or decorated with expensive materials. **2** abundant. □ **opulence** *n.* **opulently** *adv.* [*Say* OPP yoo l'nt, OPP yoo lince]

opus *n.* (*pl.* **opuses** or **opera**) **1** *Music* a separate composition or set of compositions. **2** any artistic or creative work. [*Say* OH pus *for the singular*, OH pus is *or* OPPER uh *for the plural*]

O.R. *abbr.* operating room.

or *conj.* **1** used to link alternatives. **2** introducing a synonym or explanation of a preceding word or phrase. **3** otherwise. □ **or else 1** otherwise. **2** *informal* expressing a warning or threat. **or so** (after a quantity) or thereabouts.

-or *suffix* forming nouns denoting a person or thing performing the action of a verb.

oracle *n.* **1 a** a place where advice or prophecy was sought from the gods in classical antiquity. **b** a prophet or prophetess at an oracle. **2** a person or thing regarded as an infallible authority. [*Say* ORE a cull]

oracular *adj.* **1** of or concerning an oracle. **2** mysterious or ambiguous. **3** prophetic. [*Say* ore ACK you lur]

oral ● *adj.* **1 a** spoken; not written. **b** designating a culture which has not reached the stage of literacy. **2** relating to or done by the mouth. ● *n. informal* a spoken examination, test, etc. □ **orally** *adv.*

oral sex *n.* sexual activity in which the genitals of one partner are stimulated by the mouth of the other.

oral tradition *n.* the passing on of knowledge, stories, etc. from one generation to another by word of mouth.

orange ● *n.* **1 a** a large round citrus fruit with a bright reddish-yellow rind. **b** any of the trees or shrubs that bear this fruit. **2 a** the reddish yellow colour of an orange. **b** orange pigment. ● *adj.* **1** orange coloured. **2** orange flavoured. □ **orangey** *adj.*

Orangeman *n.* (*pl.* **Orangemen**) a member of the Orange Order.

Orange Order *n.* (also **Orange Lodge**) a society formed in 1795 to support Protestantism in Ireland, established in Canada in the 19th century.

orange pekoe *n.* a black tea made from very small leaves.

orange roughy *n.* an orange-coloured fish much prized for food.

orangutan *n.* a large red long-haired tree-living ape, native to Borneo and Sumatra. [*Say* a RANG oo tan]

oration *n.* **1** a formal speech. **2** a way of speaking. [*Say* ore AY sh'n]

orator *n.* **1** a person making a speech. **2** an eloquent public speaker. [*Say* ORE a tur]

oratorio *n.* (*pl.* **oratorios**) a semi-dramatic work for orchestra and voices esp. on a sacred theme. [*Say* ore a TORY oh]

oratory *n.* (*pl.* **oratories**) **1** the art or practice of formal speaking. **2** exaggerated or eloquent language. **3** a small chapel. □ **oratorical** *adj.* [*Say* ORE a tory, ore a TORE a cull]

orb *n.* **1** a globe surmounted by a cross esp. carried by a sovereign. **2** a sphere; a globe. **3** *literary* a heavenly body.

orbit ● *n.* **1 a** the regularly repeated elliptical course of a celestial object, spacecraft, etc. about a star or a planet. **b** the state of motion in an orbit. **2** the path of an electron around an atomic nucleus. **3** a sphere of action or influence. ● *v.* (**orbits, orbited, orbiting**) **1** go around in orbit. **2** put into orbit. □ **orbital** *adj.*

orbiter *n.* a spacecraft designed to remain in orbit.

orca *n.* (*pl.* **orcas**) the killer whale.

orchard *n.* a piece of enclosed land with fruit trees. □ **orchardist** *n.*

orchestra *n.* **1** a usu. large group of instrumentalists, esp. combining strings, woodwinds, brass, and percussion. **2 a** (also **orchestra pit**) the part of a theatre where the orchestra plays. **b** the seats on the ground floor in a theatre. □ **orchestral** *adj.* [*Say* ORE kiss truh, ore KESS trull]

orchestrate *v.* (**orchestrates, orchestrated, orchestrating**) **1** arrange or compose (music) for orchestral performance. **2** direct (a situation etc.) to produce a desired effect. □ **orchestration** *n.* **orchestrator** *n.* [*Say* ORE kess trate]

orchid *n.* a plant that bears flowers in fantastic shapes and brilliant colours. [*Say* ORE kid]

ordain *v.* **1** bestow the office of minister, priest, or deacon on. **2** (in the Presbyterian church) bestow the office of elder on (a person). **3 a** order or decree something officially. **b** (of God etc.) prescribe, determine.

ordeal *n.* a painful or trying experience.

order ● *n.* **1** the arrangement of people or things according to a particular sequence or method. **2** a state in which everything is in its correct place. **3** a state in which the laws and rules regulating public behaviour are observed. **4** an authoritative command or direction. **5** a request for something to be made, supplied, or served. **6** the prescribed procedure followed in a meeting, law court, or religious service. **7** quality or nature. **8** a social class or system. **9** (**orders** or **holy orders**) the rank of an ordained minister of the Christian Church. **10** a society of monks, nuns, or friars living under the same rule. **11** (esp. **Order**) a company of distinguished people to which appointments are made as an honour or reward. **12** a principal taxonomic category that ranks below class and above family. ● *v.* **1** give an order. **2** request that (something) be made, supplied, or served. **3** arrange methodically. □ **in bad** (or **good**) **order** (not) working. **in order 1** one after another. **2** ready or fit for use. **3** according to the rules. **in order that** so that. **in order to** with a view to. **keep order** enforce orderly behaviour. **made to order 1** made according to individual requirements etc. **2** exactly what is wanted. **of** (or **in** or **on**) **the order of 1** approximately. **2** having the order of magnitude specified by. **on order** ordered but not yet received. **order about 1** dominate. **2** send hither and thither. **Order! Order!** a call for silence or calm. **order out** (or **in**) order food to be delivered to one's home etc. **out of order 1** not working or behaving properly. **2** not in the correct sequence.

order-in-council *n.* (*pl.* **orders-in-council**) *Cdn* an administrative order determined by the cabinet and formally issued by the sovereign or the sovereign's representative.

orderly ● *adj.* **1** methodically arranged; regular. **2** well-behaved. ● *n.* (*pl.* **orderlies**) **1** an attendant in a hospital responsible for various non-medical tasks. **2** a soldier who carries orders for an officer etc. □ **orderliness** *n.*

order of business *n.* a subject or task requiring attention.

Order of Canada *n.* an order of merit honouring Canadians for exemplary achievement.

order of magnitude *n.* a class in a system of classification determined by size, usu. by powers of 10.

order of the day *n.* **1** the prevailing state of affairs. **2** what is called for.

Order Paper *n.* a daily list of topics etc. to be discussed or voted on in a legislature.

ordinal ● *n.* (also **ordinal number**) a number defining a thing's position in a series. ● *adj.* of or relating to an ordinal number.

ordinance *n.* **1** an authoritative order.

2 an enactment by a local authority. [*Say* ORE din ince]

ordinary *adj.* **1** regular, normal. **2** boring; commonplace. □ **out of the ordinary** unusual. □ **ordinarily** *adv.* **ordinariness** *n.*

ordinary seaman *n.* a sailor of the lowest rank. Abbreviation. **OS**.

ordinate *n. Math* **1** a straight line from any point drawn parallel to one coordinate axis and meeting the other. **2** the distance of a point from the horizontal axis.

ordination *n.* the act of ordaining someone as a priest, minister, etc.

ordnance *n.* **1** mounted guns; cannon. **2** military stores and materials. [*Say* ORD nince]

Ordovician *n.* the second period of the Paleozoic era, lasting from about 505 to 438 million years ago, marked by the appearance of the first vertebrates. □ **Ordovician** *adj.* [*Say* orda VISH'n]

ordure *n.* excrement; dung. [*Say* ORE dyoor]

ore *n.* a naturally occurring solid material from which metal or valuable minerals may be extracted.

oregano *n.* the dried leaves of wild marjoram used as a herb in cooking. [*Say* a REGGA no]

organ *n.* **1 a** a usu. large musical instrument having pipes supplied with air from bellows, sounded by keys. **b** a smaller instrument producing similar sounds electronically. **2 a** a part of an organism having a special vital function. **b** esp. *jocular* the penis. **3** a medium of communication, esp. a newspaper or periodical that represents the views of a political party or movement.

organdy *n.* (*pl.* **organdies**) a fine translucent cotton muslin. [*Say* ORGAN dee]

organelle *n.* a specialized structure within a cell. [*Say* orga NELL]

organ grinder *n.* the player of a barrel organ.

organic ● *adj.* **1** of or relating to plants or animals. **2** of, relating to, or affecting a bodily organ or organs. **3** produced or involving production without the use of chemicals etc. **4** (of a compound etc.) containing carbon. **5** (of the parts of a whole) fitting together harmoniously. **6** designating continuous or natural development. ● *n.* an organic substance. □ **organically** *adv.*

organism *n.* **1** an individual plant or animal. **2** a whole with interdependent parts.

organist *n.* the player of an organ.

organization *n.* **1** the action of organizing. **2** the structure or arrangement of items. **3** an efficient and orderly approach to tasks. **4** an organized body or institution. □ **organizational** *adj.* **organizationally** *adv.*

organize *v.* (**organizes, organized, organizing**) **1 a** give an orderly structure to. **b** bring into order; make arrangements for. **2 a** arrange for or initiate. **b** provide. **3** enrol new members in a trade union etc. **4** form elements into an organic whole.

organized crime *n.* widespread criminal activity organized under powerful leadership.

organizer *n.* a person or thing that organizes.

organ stop *n.* **1** a set of pipes of a similar tone in an organ. **2** the handle of the mechanism that brings it into action.

organza *n.* (*pl.* **organzas**) a thin transparent silk or synthetic fabric. [*Say* ore GAN zuh]

orgasm *n.* a sexual climax characterized by feelings of pleasure centred in the genitals. □ **orgasmic** *adj.*

orgy *n.* (*pl.* **orgies**) **1** a wild party, esp. one with excessive drinking and sex. **2** excessive indulgence in an activity. [*Say* ORE jee]

orient ● *n.* (**the Orient**) **1** the Far East. **2** (formerly) the Middle East. ● *v.* **1 a** establish one's position in relation to one's surroundings, the points of a compass, etc. **b** bring into a clearly understood position or relationship. **c** find the bearings of. **2** direct toward a particular interest, action, etc. **3** direct or aim (something) at. □ **oriented** *adj.*

oriental ● *adj.* **1** (often **Oriental**) having to do with East Asia. **2** (often **Oriental**) having to do with Eastern civilizations generally. ● *n.* (esp. **Oriental**) *offensive* a person of East Asian origin.

orientalism *n.* **1** (often **Orientalism**) the representation of the Orient in Western art, literature, etc. **2** this representation perceived as embodying a colonial attitude. □ **orientalist** *n.*

oriental rug *n.* (also **oriental carpet**) a rug or carpet hand-knotted in or as in the Orient.

orientate *v.* (**orientates, orientated, orientating**) = ORIENT *v.*

orientation *n.* **1 a** a person's attitude or adjustment in relation to circumstances etc. **b** = SEXUAL ORIENTATION. **2** an introduction to a subject. **3** the action of orienting or the state of being oriented.

orienteering *n.* a competitive sport in which participants have to find their way across rough country with the aid of map and compass. □ **orienteer** *n. & v.*

orifice *n.* a usu. small opening in the body. [*Say* ORE a fiss]

origami *n.* the Japanese art of folding paper into decorative shapes. [*Say* ore a GAMMY]

origin *n.* **1 a** a beginning. **b** a source or starting point. **2** a person's social background etc.

original ● *adj.* **1** existing from the beginning. **2** inventive. **3 a** that is the origin or source of something. **b** produced by an artist, author, etc., rather than copied. **c** not derivative or imitative. ● *n.* **1** an original model, pattern, picture, etc. from which copies can be made. **2** an unusual person. □ **originally** *adv.*

originality *n.* **1** the quality or fact of being original. **2** newness or freshness.

original sin *n. Christianity* the innate tendency to evil of all humans.

originate *v.* (**originates, originated, originating**) **1** begin, arise, be derived. **2** initiate. **3** begin a scheduled trip at a particular place. □ **origination** *n.* **originator** *n.*

oriole *n.* **1** a bird of the American blackbird family, with orange or yellowish-orange feathers. **2** an Old World bird related to the starling. [*Say* ORE ee ul *or* ORE ee ole]

ormolu *n.* gilded bronze; a gold-coloured alloy of copper, zinc, and tin used in decoration. [*Say* ORMA loo]

ornament ● *n.* **1** a person or thing used or serving to adorn. **2** decoration added to embellish esp. a building. ● *v.* adorn, provide with ornaments. □ **ornamentation** *n.*

ornamental ● *adj.* serving as an ornament; decorative. ● *n.* a plant considered to be ornamental rather than essential.

ornate *adj.* highly decorated. □ **ornately** *adv.* [*Say* ore NATE]

ornery *adj. informal* **1** grumpily stubborn. **2** crotchety. [*Say* ORNER ee]

ornithology *n.* the study of birds. □ **ornithological** *adj.* **ornithologist** *n.* [*Say* ore nith OLLA jee, ore nitha LOGICAL]

orphan ● *n.* **1** a child etc. whose parents are dead. **2** a child bereft of parental care. ● *v.* (of a child etc.) be made an orphan. □ **orphaned** *adj.*

orphanage *n.* an institution which cares for orphans.

ortho- *comb. form* **1** straight, rectangular, upright. **2** proper, correct.

orthodontics *n.* the branch of dentistry that deals with treatment of crooked teeth etc. □ **orthodontic** *adj.* **orthodontist** *n.* [*Say* ortha DON ticks, ortha DON tist]

orthodox *adj.* **1** conforming to what is traditionally accepted as right or true. **2** (of a person) conventional. **3** (usu. **Orthodox**) (of Judaism or Jews) adhering strictly to the rabbinical interpretation of Jewish law. **4** (**Orthodox**) having to do with the Orthodox Church. [*Say* ORTHA docks]

Orthodox Church *n.* the family of Eastern Churches, having the Patriarch of Constantinople as its head.

orthodoxy *n.* (*pl.* **orthodoxies**) **1 a** the quality of being orthodox. **b** orthodox beliefs or practices. **c** the body of orthodox doctrine. **2** a generally accepted theory, doctrine, etc. **3** (also **Orthodoxy**) the Orthodox practice of Judaism. **4** the Orthodox Church or Churches. [*Say* ORTHA docksy]

orthogonal *adj.* rectangular. [*Say* orth OGGA n'll]

orthography *n.* (*pl.* **orthographies**) correct or conventional spelling. □ **orthographic** *adj.* [*Say* orth OGGRA fee, ortha GRAPHIC]

orthopaedics *n.* (also **orthopedics**) the branch of medicine dealing with the correction or treatment of deformities or injuries of bones or muscles. □ **orthopaedic** (also **orthopedic**) *adj.*. **orthopaedist** (also **orthopedist**) *n.* [*Say* ortha PEED icks, ortha PEED ist]

orthotic *n.* (usu. in *pl.*) **1** a moulded insert for a shoe etc. designed to improve posture and gait. **2** an artificial external device, as a brace or splint. [*Say* orth OTT ick]

Orwellian *adj.* of or characteristic of the writings of George Orwell (1903–50), esp. with reference to the totalitarian development of a state. [*Say* ore WELLY un]

oryx *n.* (*pl.* **oryx** or **oryxes**) a large straight-horned antelope native to Africa and Arabia. [*Say* ORE icks]

orzo *n.* a variety of pasta shaped like grains of rice.

OS *abbr. Computing* operating system.

Oscar *n.* any of the statuettes awarded annually as an Academy Award.

oscillate *v.* (**oscillates, oscillated, oscillating**) **1** move to and fro between points. **2** waver between extremes of opinion, action, etc. **3** *Physics* move with periodic regularity. □ **oscillating** *adj.* **oscillation** *n.* **oscillator** *n.* [*Say* OSSA late]

oscilloscope *n.* a device for viewing oscillations by a display on the screen of a cathode ray tube. [*Say* aw SILLA scope]

osier *n.* any of various willows with long flexible shoots used in making baskets etc. [*Say* OZE ee er]

osmium *n.* a hard bluish-white element, used in certain alloys. [*Say* OZ mee um]

osmosis *n.* **1** the passage of a solvent through a semi-permeable partition into a more concentrated solution. **2** gradual, usu. unconscious assimilation of ideas etc. □ **osmotic** *adj.* [*Say* oz MOE sis, oz MOT ick]

osprey *n.* (*pl.* **ospreys**) a large fish-eating bird of prey with a brown back and white markings. [*Say* OSS pray or OSS pree]

Ossie *n.* & *adj.* = AUSSIE.

ossify *v.* (**ossifies, ossified, ossifying**) **1** turn into bone or bony tissue; harden. **2** make or become rigid. □ **ossification** *n.* [*Say* OSSA fie, ossa fuh KAY sh'n]

osso bucco *n.* (also **osso buco**) an Italian dish of veal shanks stewed in wine with vegetables. [*Say* osso BOO koe]

ostensible *adj.* apparently true, but not necessarily so. □ **ostensibly** *adv.* [*Say* oss TEN sib ul]

ostentation *n.* an exaggerated display of wealth which is intended to impress. [*Say* oss ten TAY sh'n]

ostentatious *adj.* showy in a way which is intended to impress. □ **ostentatiously** *adv.* [*Say* oss ten TAY shuss]

osteo- *comb. form* bone.

osteoarthritis *n.* a degenerative disease of joint cartilage causing pain and stiffness. [*Say* OSS tee oh ARTHRITIS]

osteopathy *n.* a system of complementary medicine involving the manipulation of the skeleton and musculature. □ **osteopath** *n.* **osteopathic** *adj.* [*Say* oss tee OPPA thee, OSS tee oh path, oss tee oh PATH ick]

osteoporosis *n.* a condition of fragile, porous bones caused by loss of the protein and mineral content of bone tissue. [*Say* OSS tee oh puh ROE sis]

ostracize *v.* (**ostracizes, ostracized, ostracizing**) exclude from a society etc. by common consent. □ **ostracism** *n.* [*Say* OSTRA size, OSTRA sism]

ostrich *n.* (*pl.* **ostriches**) a large African swift-running flightless bird.

OT *abbr.* **1** overtime. **2 a** occupational therapy. **b** occupational therapist. **3** Old Testament.

OTC *abbr.* = OVER-THE-COUNTER.

other *adj.* & *pron.* **1** used to refer to a person or thing that is different from one already

mentioned or known. **2** additional.
3 alternative of two. **4** those not already
mentioned. □ **other things being
equal** if conditions were alike in all but
the point in question. **someone** (or
something etc.) **or other** some
unspecified person, thing, etc.

other half n. **1** jocular one's wife or
husband. **2** informal (**the other half**) a
group of people having different social etc.
standing. **3** the second of two equal parts.

otherness n. **1** the state or fact of being
different. **2** a thing or existence separate
from the thing mentioned.

otherwise adv. **1** or else. **2** in other
respects. **3** in another way. **4** as an
alternative.

other world n. **1** a supposed life after
death. **2** (also **otherworld**) **a** an alternate
reality. **b** a world or culture in fantasy or
outer space.

otherworldly adj. **1** concerned with
spiritual matters. **2** having to do with an
imaginary world. **3** unworldly; impractical.
□ **otherworldliness** n.

Ottawa n. & adj. (pl. **Ottawa** or **Ottawas**)
= ODAWA.

Ottawan n. a person from Ottawa.

otter n. **1 a** a semi-aquatic fish-eating
mammal with webbed feet. **b** its fur or pelt.
2 = SEA OTTER.

Ottoman ● adj. hist. **1** of or concerning the
Turkish dynasty of Osman or Othman
I (late 13th century), or the empire ruled by
his descendants. **2** Turkish. ● n. an
Ottoman person; a Turk. [Say OTTA m'n]

ottoman n. **1** an upholstered seat, usu.
square and without a back or arms. **2** a
footstool of similar design. [Say OTTA m'n]

ouananiche n. (pl. **ouananiche**) Cdn a
landlocked lake variety of Atlantic salmon.
[Say WANNA nish]

ouch interj. expressing pain or annoyance.

ought aux. v. **1** expressing duty or rightness.
2 expressing shortcoming. **3** expressing
advisability or prudence. **4** expressing
probability

oughtn't contr. ought not.

Ouija n. (also **Ouija board**) proprietary a
board having letters or signs at its rim to
which a pointer moves supposedly in
answer to questions at a seance etc.
[Say WEE jee or WEE juh]

ounce n. **1 a** a unit of weight of one-
sixteenth of a pound avoirdupois (approx.
28 grams). Abbreviation: **oz. b** a unit of
one-twelfth of a pound troy (approx. 31
grams). **2** = FLUID OUNCE. **3** a small
quantity.

our poss. adj. **1** of or belonging to us or

ourselves. **2** (esp. as **Our**) of Us the king or
queen etc.

Our Father n. Christianity **1** the prayer
beginning with the words "Our Father".
2 God.

Our Lady n. Christianity the Virgin Mary.

Our Lord n. Christianity **1** Jesus Christ.
2 God.

ours poss. pron. the one or ones belonging to
or associated with us.

ourselves pron. **1 a** emphatic form of WE or
US. **b** reflexive form of US. **2** in our normal
state of body or mind.

oust v. remove from a job or position of
power. □ **ousted** adj.

ouster n. a removal, esp. from a position of
power.

out ● adv. **1** moving away from a place.
2 away from one's usual base or residence.
3 outdoors. **4** so as to be revealed, heard, or
known. **5** at or to an end. **6** at a specified
distance from the target. **7** to sea, away
from the land. **8** (of the tide) falling or at
its lowest level. **9** no longer in prison.
● prep. out of. ● n. **1** informal a way of escape.
2 Baseball the action of putting a player out.
● adj. **1** not at home or one's place of work.
2 in existence or use. **3** open about one's
homosexuality. **4** not possible or worth
considering. **5** no longer existing or
current. **6** unconscious. **7** mistaken. **8** (of
the ball in tennis, squash, etc.) outside the
playing area. **9** Baseball no longer batting or
on base. ● v. informal reveal the
homosexuality of. □ **on the outs** at
variance or enmity. **out and about**
engaging in normal activity. **out for** intent
on. **out of it** informal **1** dazed. **2** out of
touch. **out to** keenly striving to do. **out
with** an exhortation to expel or dismiss.
out with it say what you are thinking.

out- prefix **1** so as to surpass or exceed.
2 external, separate. **3** away from.

outage n. an interruption in supply, esp. of
electricity.

out-and-out ● adj. complete. ● adv.
completely; totally.

outback n. esp. Austral. the remote and usu.
uninhabited inland districts.

outbid v. (**outbids**, **outbid**, **outbidding**)
bid higher than at an auction etc.

outboard ● adj. & adv. **1** (of a motor)
portable and attachable to the outside of
the stern of a boat. **2** on, near, or towards
the outside of an aircraft, ship, etc. ● n. an
outboard engine or a boat with one.

outbound adj. outward bound.

outbreak n. a usu. sudden eruption of
war, disease, etc.

outbuilding *n.* a detached building that is within the grounds of a main building.

outburst *n.* **1** an explosion of anger etc., expressed in words. **2** a sudden burst of activity etc.

outcast ● *n.* **1** a person rejected by his or her country, society, etc. **2** a vagabond. ● *adj.* rejected; friendless.

outclass *v.* (**outclasses**, **outclassed**, **outclassing**) **1** defeat easily. **2** be superior to.

outcome *n.* a result.

outcrop ● *n.* (also **outcropping**) a part of rock formation that is visible on the surface. ● *v.* (**outcrops**, **outcropped**, **outcropping**) appear as an outcrop.

outcry *n.* (*pl.* **outcries**) a strong expression of public disapproval.

outdated *adj.* out of date.

outdistance *v.* (**outdistances**, **outdistanced**, **outdistancing**) leave (a competitor) behind completely.

outdo *v.* (**outdoes**; *past* **outdid**; *past participle* **outdone**; **outdoing**) do better than.

outdoor *adj.* done, existing, or used out of doors.

outdoors ● *adv.* in or into the open air. ● *adj.*= OUTDOOR. ● *n.* the world outside buildings. □ **outdoorsman** *n.* **outdoorsy** *adj.*

outer *adj.* **1** external. **2** farther from the centre or inside. □ **outermost** *adj.*

outer space *n.* the universe beyond the earth's atmosphere.

outerwear *n.* clothing, such as a coat, that is worn over other clothing.

outfall *n.* the outlet of a river, drain, sewer, etc.

outfield *n.* **1** the part of a baseball field that lies outside of the baseline. **2** the players positioned there. □ **outfielder** *n.*

outfit ● *n.* **1** a set of clothes worn together. **2** a complete set of equipment etc. for a specific purpose. **3** a business or company engaged in a particular activity. **4** a military unit. ● *v.* (**outfits**, **outfitted**, **outfitting**) provide with an outfit.

outfitter *n.* **1** a supplier of equipment for outdoor activities. **2** a guide on wilderness trips etc.

outflank *v.* **1** extend one's flank beyond that of (an enemy). **2** get the better of.

outflow *n.* **1** an outward flow. **2** the amount that flows out.

outfox *v.* (**outfoxes**, **outfoxed**, **outfoxing**) *informal* outwit.

outgoing *adj.* **1** friendly; extrovert. **2** retiring from office. **3** going out or away.

outgrow *v.* (**outgrows**; *past* **outgrew**; *past participle* **outgrown**; **outgrowing**) **1** grow too big for. **2** leave behind as one matures. **3** grow faster or taller than.

outgrowth *n.* **1** something that grows out. **2** a natural development.

outgun *v.* (**outguns**, **outgunned**, **outgunning**) **1** surpass in military power or strength. **2** shoot better than.

outhouse *n.* **1** an outdoor toilet that is separate from the main building. **2** an outbuilding.

outing *n.* **1** a pleasure trip, an excursion. **2** any brief journey from home. **3** a public appearance in something. **4** the practice of revealing the homosexuality someone.

outlander *n.* a foreigner or stranger.

outlandish *adj.* bizarre, strange, not familiar.

outlast *v.* last longer than.

outlaw ● *n.* a fugitive from the law. ● *v.* make illegal; prohibit.

outlay *n.* **1** an amount of money spent. **2** an act of spending money.

outlet *n.* **1** a means of exit or escape. **2** a socket in a wall etc. for connecting an electrical appliance to. **3** a means of expression (of a talent, emotion, etc.). **4** a a place that sells merchandise of a particular type. **b** = FACTORY OUTLET. **5** a stream etc. flowing out of a larger body of water.

outline ● *n.* **1** a rough statement of the main points of something. **2** a sketch containing only contour lines. **3** the lines by which a figure or object is bounded. **4** the main features. ● *v.* (**outlines**, **outlined**, **outlining**) **1** describe the main features of. **2** draw in outline.

outlive *v.* (**outlives**, **outlived**, **outliving**) **1** live or last longer than. **2** live through.

outlook *n.* **1** the prospect for the future. **2** one's mental attitude. **3** a view.

outlying *adj.* situated far from a centre.

outmanoeuvre *v.* (**outmanoeuvres**, **outmanoeuvred**, **outmanoeuvring**) **1** use skill and cunning to secure an advantage over. **2** outdo in manoeuvring.

outmoded *adj.* **1** no longer in fashion. **2** obsolete.

outnumber *v.* exceed in number.

out-of-body experience *n.* a sensation of being outside one's body.

out of date *adj.* old-fashioned, obsolete.

out-of-pocket *adj.* (of costs etc.) paid out in cash.

out-of-sight *adj.* **1** not visible. **2** *informal* excellent.

out-of-the-way *adj.* **1** remote. **2** unusual.

out-of-town *adj.* originating from or occurring in another place. □ **out-of-towner** *n.*

out-of-work *adj.* unemployed.

outpace *v.* (**outpaces, outpaced, outpacing**) **1** go faster than. **2** outdo in a contest.

outpatient *n.* a person receiving treatment at a hospital without being hospitalized.

outperform *v.* perform better than. □ **outperformance** *n.*

outplacement *n.* the act of finding new employment for workers who have been dismissed or made redundant.

outplay *v.* play better than.

outport *n.* **1** *Cdn* **a** (in Newfoundland) any port other than St. John's. **b** (*Maritimes*) a coastal fishing village. **2** a subsidiary port. □ **outporter** *n.*

outpost *n.* **1** a detachment set at a distance from the main army. **2** a distant branch or settlement.

outpost camp *n.* *Cdn* a remote hunting or fishing camp.

outpouring *n.* **1** an expression of very strong feelings. **2** something that pours out.

output ● *n.* **1** the product of a process. **2** the quantity or amount of this. **3** the printout etc. supplied by a computer. **4** the power etc. delivered by an apparatus. **5** *Electronics* a place where energy, information, etc. leaves a system. ● *v.* (**outputs**; *past and past participle* **output** or **outputted; outputting**) **1** put or send out. **2** (of a computer) supply (results etc.).

outrage ● *n.* **1** a shocking violation of others' rights etc. **2** a gross offence or indignity. **3** fierce anger. ● *v.* (**outrages, outraged, outraging**) **1** subject to outrage. **2** injure, insult, etc. flagrantly. □ **outraged** *adj.*

outrageous *adj.* **1** deeply shocking and unacceptable. **2** grossly cruel. **3** highly unusual. □ **outrageously** *adv.* [*Say* out RAGE us]

outran *past of* OUTRUN.

outrank *v.* **1** be superior in rank to. **2** take priority over.

outré *adj.* outside the bounds of what is usual or proper. [*Say* oo TRAY]

outreach ● *v.* (**outreaches, outreached, outreaching**) **1** reach further than. **2** surpass. ● *n.* **1** an organization's involvement with the community, esp. outside its usual centres. **2** the extent or length of reaching out.

outrider *n.* a person in a vehicle or on horseback who escorts another vehicle.

outrigger *n.* **1** a beam, spar, or framework, rigged out and projecting from or over a ship's side. **2** a similar projecting beam etc. in a building.

outright ● *adv.* **1** altogether, entirely. **2** not gradually. **3** openly. ● *adj.* **1** downright, direct. **2** undisputed.

outrun *v.* (**outruns**; *past* **outran**; *past participle* **outrun; outrunning**) **1 a** run faster or farther than. **b** escape from. **2** go beyond; surpass.

outscore *v.* (**outscores, outscored, outscoring**) score more than in a game etc.

outsell *v.* (**outsells**; *past and past participle* **outsold; outselling**) **1** sell more than. **2** be sold in greater quantities than.

outset *n.* the start, beginning.

outshine *v.* (**outshines**; *past and past participle* **outshone; outshining**) **1** shine brighter than. **2** surpass in ability etc.

outside ● *n.* **1** the external side or surface of something. **2** the external appearance of something. **3** the side of a curve where the edge is longer. ● *adj.* **1** situated on or near the outside. **2** not of or belonging to a particular group. ● *prep. & adv.* **1** situated or moving beyond the boundaries of. **2** beyond the limits or scope of. **3** not being a member of. **4** *Cdn* (*North*) in or to the rest of the world, esp. a more heavily populated or urban area. □ **at the outside** at the most. **outside in** = INSIDE OUT. **outside of** *informal* apart from.

outsider *n.* **1 a** a non-member of some circle, profession, etc. **b** an uninitiated person. **2** a competitor etc. thought to have little chance of success.

outsize ● *adj.* unusually large. ● *n.* an exceptionally large person or thing. □ **outsized** *adj.*

outskirts *pl. n.* the outer border or fringe of a town etc.

outsmart *v.* outwit.

outsold *past and past participle of* OUTSELL.

outsource *v.* (**outsources, outsourced, outsourcing**) **1** obtain (goods etc.) by contract from an outside source. **2** contract (work) out. □ **outsourcing** *n.*

outspoken *adj.* frank in stating one's opinions. □ **outspokenness** *n.*

outspread ● *adj.* fully extended or expanded. ● *v.* (**outspreads, outspread, outspreading**) spread out.

outstanding *adj.* **1 a** conspicuous, eminent. **b** remarkable in (a specified field). **2** (esp. of a debt) not yet settled. □ **outstandingly** *adv.*

outstay v. **1** stay beyond the limit of (one's welcome etc.). **2** stay or endure longer than.

outstretch v. (**outstretches, outstretched, outstretching**) **1** reach out or stretch out. **2** go beyond the limit of.

outstrip v. (**outstrips, outstripped, outstripping**) **1** pass in running etc. **2** surpass in competition. **3** be or become faster than.

outta prep. informal out of.

outtake n. a length of film etc. rejected in editing.

out to lunch adj. informal out of touch with reality.

out-turn n. Curling an inward turn of the elbow and an outward turn of the hand made in delivering a stone.

outvote v. (**outvotes, outvoted, outvoting**) defeat by a majority of votes.

outward ● adj. **1** on or towards the outside. **2** going out. **3** external, superficial. ● adv. (also **outwards**) towards the outside. ● n. the exterior. □ **outwardly** adv.

outwash n. (pl. **outwashes**) the material carried from a glacier by meltwater.

outweigh v. exceed in weight, importance, etc.

outwit v. (**outwits, outwitted, outwitting**) be too clever or crafty for.

outwork ● v. work harder or faster than. ● n. an advanced part of a fortification.

outworn adj. obsolete; out-of-date.

ouzo n. (pl. **ouzos**) a Greek aniseed-flavoured spirit. [Say OOZE oh]

ova pl. of OVUM. [Say OVE uh]

oval ● adj. having a rounded and slightly elongated outline. ● n. **1** something with such a shape or outline. **2** an oval speed skating rink etc.

Oval Office n. the office of the US President in the White House.

ovary n. (pl. **ovaries**) **1** each of the female reproductive organs in which ova are produced. **2** the hollow base of the carpel of a flower. □ **ovarian** adj. [Say OVE a ree, oh VERY un]

ovation n. enthusiastic and sustained applause. [Say oh VAY sh'n]

oven n. **1** an enclosed compartment in which food is cooked or heated. **2** a small furnace or kiln.

ovenproof adj. suitable for use in an oven.

over ● prep. **1** extending upwards from or above. **2** above so as to cover or protect. **3** expressing movement or a route across. **4** beyond and falling or hanging from. **5** expressing duration. **6** at a higher level than. **7** higher or more than. **8** expressing authority or control. **9** on the subject of. ● adv. **1** expressing movement or a route across an area. **2** beyond and falling or hanging from a point. **3** in or to the place indicated. **4** expressing action and result. **5** finished. **6** expressing repetition of a process. □ **over again** once again. **over all** taken as a whole. **over and above** in addition to. **over with** (also **over and done with**) finished, completed. **start over** begin again.

over- prefix **1** excessively; to an unwanted degree. **2** upper, outer. **3** "over" in various senses. **4** completely.

overabundant adj. in excessive quantity. □ **overabundance** n.

overachieve v. (**overachieves, overachieved, overachieving**) **1** do more than might be expected. **2** achieve more than. □ **overachievement** n. **overachiever** n.

overact v. act in an exaggerated manner.

overactive adj. excessively active. □ **overactivity** n.

over-age adj. over a certain age limit.

overall ● adj. **1** total, inclusive of all. **2** taking everything into account, general. **3** from end to end. ● adv. **1** taken as a whole. **2** when everything is included. ● n. (in pl.) loose-fitting pants with fabric extending up to cover the front torso, fastened around the neck or over the shoulders. □ **overalled** adj.

overarching adj. **1** all-embracing; comprehensive. **2** forming an arch over.

overarm adj. & adv. (of an arm action) made with the hand brought forward and down from above shoulder level.

overate past of OVEREAT.

overawe v. (**overawes, overawed, overawing**) cause (a person) to feel a great deal of fear, respect, etc.

overbalance v. (**overbalances, overbalanced, overbalancing**) **1** cause to lose balance and fall. **2** fall over. **3** outweigh.

overbearing adj. unpleasantly overpowering.

overbite n. the overlapping of the lower teeth by the upper.

overblown adj. excessively inflated or pretentious.

overboard adv. from on a ship into the water. □ **go overboard 1** be highly enthusiastic. **2** go too far.

overbook v. accept too many bookings or reservations for.

overburden v. burden to excess.

overcapacity n. the resources to produce or handle more than is needed.

overcast adj. **1** (of the sky etc.) cloudy. **2** (in sewing) edged with stitching.

overcharge ● v. (**overcharges, overcharged, overcharging**) **1** charge too high a price. **2** put too much charge into. **3** put excessive detail into. ● n. an excessive charge (of explosive etc.).

overcoat n. **1** a heavy coat. **2** a protective coat of paint etc.

overcome ● v. (**overcomes**; past **overcame**; past participle **overcome**; **overcoming**) **1** prevail over. **2** be victorious. ● adj. affected by or overwhelmed with (emotion etc.).

overcompensate v. (**overcompensates, overcompensated, overcompensating**) **1** compensate excessively for. **2** strive for power etc. in an exaggerated way. □ **overcompensation** n.

overconfident adj. excessively confident. □ **overconfidence** n.

overcook v. cook too much or for too long. □ **overcooked** adj.

overcrowd v. fill beyond what is usual or comfortable. □ **overcrowded** adj. **overcrowding** n.

overdevelop v. (**overdevelops, overdeveloped, overdeveloping**) develop too much. □ **overdevelopment** n.

overdo v. (**overdoes**; past **overdid**; past participle **overdone**; **overdoing**) carry to excess, go too far. □ **overdo it** (or **things**) exhaust oneself.

overdone adj. **1** overcooked. **2** exaggerated.

overdose ● n. an excessive dose (of a drug etc.). ● v. (**overdoses, overdosed, overdosing**) take or give an overdose.

overdraft n. a deficit in a bank account caused by drawing more money than is credited to it.

overdrawn adj. having overdrawn one's bank account.

overdress ● v. (**overdresses, overdressed, overdressing**) **1** dress too warmly. **2** dress with too much formality. ● n. (pl. **overdresses**) a dress worn over another dress etc. □ **overdressed** adj.

overdrive n. **1** an extra high gear in a vehicle, used when driving at high speeds. **2** a state of great activity.

overdub ● v. (**overdubs, overdubbed, overdubbing**) impose (additional sounds) on an existing recording. ● n. an instance of overdubbing.

overdue adj. **1** past the time when due. **2** not having arrived, happened, or been done at the expected time.

overeager adj. excessively eager.

over easy adj. (of a fried egg) flipped when almost cooked and fried lightly on the other side.

overeat v. (**overeats**; past **overate**; past participle **overeaten**; **overeating**) eat too much. □ **overeater** n. **overeating** n.

overemphasis n. excessive emphasis. □ **overemphasize** v. (**overemphasizes, overemphasized, overemphasizing**)

overenthusiasm n. excessive enthusiasm. □ **overenthusiastic** adj.

overestimate ● v. (**overestimates, overestimated, overestimating**) form too high an estimate of. ● n. too high an estimate. □ **overestimation** n.

overexcited adj. too excited.

overexert v. exert too much. □ **overexertion** n.

overexpose v. (**overexposes, overexposed, overexposing**) expose too much. □ **overexposure** n.

overextend v. **1** extend too far. **2** (**overextend oneself**) take on an excessive burden of work etc. □ **overextended** adj.

overfish v. (**overfishes, overfished, overfishing**) deplete by too much fishing. □ **overfishing** n.

overflow ● v. **1** flow over the brim of. **2 a** be too full. **b** (of contents) overflow a container. **3** (of a crowd etc.) extend beyond (a room etc.). **4** flood. **5** be full of or very abundant. ● n. **1** what overflows or is superfluous. **2** the flowing over of a liquid. **3** an outlet for excess water etc. **4** esp. Cdn an overflow of water from beneath the frozen surface of a river, lake, etc.

overfly v. (**overflies**; past **overflew**; past participle **overflown**; **overflying**) fly over or beyond. □ **overflight** n.

overfull adj. filled excessively or to overflowing.

overgrown adj. **1** abnormally large. **2** grown over with vegetation.

overgrowth n. **1** excessive growth. **2** a growth over or on something.

overhand adj. & adv. thrown or played with the hand above the shoulder.

overhang ● v. (**overhangs, overhung, overhanging**) project or hang over. ● n. **1** an overhanging part. **2** the amount by which this projects. □ **overhanging** adj.

overhaul ● v. **1** take to pieces in order to examine. **2** examine the condition of. ● n. a thorough examination, with repairs as necessary.

overhead ● adv. above one's head. ● adj.

1 placed overhead. **2** above the object driven. ● *n.* **1** expenses arising from general operating costs. **2** (also **overhead projector**) a device that projects an enlarged image onto a screen.

overhear *v.* (**overhears**, **overheard**, **overhearing**) hear as an eavesdropper or unintentionally.

overheat *v.* make or become too hot. □ **overheated** *adj.* **overheating** *n.*

overhype *v.* (**overhypes**, **overhyped**, **overhyping**) promote with excessive hype. □ **overhyped** *adj.*

overindulge *v.* (**overindulges**, **overindulged**, **overindulging**) indulge to excess. □ **overindulgence** *n.* **overindulgent** *adj.*

overjoyed *adj.* extremely happy.

overkill *n.* an excess of what is necessary etc.

overland *adj. & adv.* by land.

overlap ● *v.* (**overlaps**, **overlapped**, **overlapping**) **1** extend over so as to partly cover. **2** cover and extend beyond. **3** (of two things) partly coincide. ● *n.* **1** a part or amount which overlaps. **2** a common area of interest etc. □ **overlapping** *n. & adj.*

overlay ● *v.* (**overlays**, **overlaid**, **overlaying**) **1** lay over. **2** cover the surface of. **3** overlie. ● *n.* **1** a thing laid over another. **2** (in printing etc.) a transparent sheet to be superimposed on another sheet.

overlie *v.* (**overlies**; *past* **overlay**; *past participle* **overlain**; **overlying**) lie on top of.

overload ● *v.* (esp. in *passive*) **1** load too heavily. **2** give too much of something. **3** put too great a demand on. ● *n.* an excessive quantity.

overlong *adj. & adv.* too or excessively long.

overlook *v.* **1 a** fail to notice. **b** ignore or disregard. **2** have a view from above.

overlord *n.* a ruler superior to others.

overly *adv.* excessively; too.

overmuch *adv.* too much.

overnight ● *adv.* **1** for the duration of a night. **2** during the night. **3** suddenly. ● *adj.* **1** done, happening, etc. overnight. **2** staying for one night. **3** for use overnight. **4** sudden, instant.

overpackaging *n.* excessive packaging of a product. □ **overpackaged** *adj.*

overpass *n.* (*pl.* **overpasses**) a road or railway line that passes over another by means of a bridge.

overpay *v.* (**overpays**, **overpaid**, **overpaying**) **1** recompense too highly. **2** pay more than. □ **overpayment** *n.*

overplay *v.* **1** play (a part) to excess. **2** give undue importance to.

overpopulated *adj.* having too large a population. □ **overpopulation** *n.*

overpower *v.* **1** defeat with greater strength. **2** be too intense for, overwhelm. □ **overpowering** *adj.* **overpoweringly** *adv.*

overpriced *adj.* too expensive.

overproduce *v.* (**overproduces**, **overproduced**, **overproducing**) produce too much of. □ **overproduction** *n.*

overqualified *adj.* too highly qualified.

overran *past of* OVERRUN.

overrate *v.* (**overrates**, **overrated**, **overrating**) rate or esteem too highly. □ **overrated** *adj.*

overreach *v.* (**overreaches**, **overreached**, **overreaching**) **1** exceed. **2** fail through being too ambitious or trying too hard. □ **overreacher** *n.* **overreaching** *n. & adj.*

overreact *v.* respond more forcibly etc. than is justified. □ **overreaction** *n.*

overrepresent *v.* represented in numbers higher than would be expected.

override ● *v.* (**overrides**; *past* **overrode**; *past participle* **overridden**; **overriding**) **1** use one's authority to reject someone's decision, order, etc.; overrule. **2** be more important than. **3** interrupt the action of (an automatic device). ● *n.* **1** the action of overriding. **2** a device for this.

overriding *adj.* foremost.

overripe *adj.* excessively ripe. □ **overripeness** *n.*

overrule *v.* (**overrules**, **overruled**, **overruling**) reject or disallow by exercising a superior authority.

overrun ● *v.* (**overruns**; *past* **overran**; *past participle* **overrun**; **overrunning**) **1** swarm or spread over. **2** conquer by force. **3** exceed (a fixed limit). ● *n.* **1** an instance of overrunning. **2** the amount of this.

overseas ● *adv.* abroad. ● *adj.* (also **oversea**) foreign; across or beyond the sea.

oversee *v.* (**oversees**; *past* **oversaw**; *past participle* **overseen**; **overseeing**) officially supervise. □ **overseer** *n.*

oversell *v.* (**oversells**, **oversold**, **overselling**) sell more of than one can deliver.

oversexed *adj.* having unusually strong sexual desires.

overshadow *v.* **1** appear more prominent or important than. **2** cast into the shade. **3** cast a feeling of sadness over.

overshoe *n.* a protective shoe worn over another.

overshoot v. (**overshoots, overshot overshooting**) accidentally go further than (an intended place). □ **overshoot the mark** go beyond what is intended.

oversight n. **1** a failure to notice something. **2** an inadvertent mistake.

oversimplify v. (**oversimplifies, oversimplified, oversimplifying**) distort (a problem etc.) by stating it in too simple terms. □ **oversimplification** n. **oversimplified** adj.

oversized adj. (also **oversize**) of more than the usual size.

oversleep v. (**oversleeps, overslept, oversleeping**) sleep too long.

oversold past and past participle of OVERSELL.

overspend v. (**overspends, overspent, overspending**) spend too much. □ **overspending** n.

overstate v. (**overstates, overstated, overstating**) **1** state too strongly. **2** exaggerate. □ **overstatement** n.

overstay v. stay longer than (one's welcome etc.).

overstep v. (**oversteps, overstepped, overstepping**) **1** pass beyond (a limit). **2** violate (certain standards). □ **overstep the mark** (or **bounds**) violate conventions of behaviour.

overstock v. stock excessively. ● n. a supply in excess of demand.

overstretch v. (**overstretches, overstretched, overstretching**) **1** stretch too much. **2** make excessive demands on.

overstuffed adj. (of furniture) made soft and comfortable by extra stuffing.

oversubscribed adj. subscribed for more than the amount available of.

oversupply ● v. (**oversupplies, oversupplied, oversupplying**) supply with too much. ● n. an excessive supply.

overt adj. done openly. □ **overtly** adv. [Say oh VURT or OH vurt]

overtake v. (**overtakes**; past **overtook**; past participle **overtaken; overtaking**) **1** catch up with and pass in the same direction. **2** come suddenly or unexpectedly upon. **3** become level with and exceed.

overtax v. (**overtaxes, overtaxed, overtaxing**) **1** make excessive demands on. **2** tax too heavily.

over-the-counter adj. (of drugs) sold without a prescription.

over-the-top adj. informal outrageous, excessive.

overthrow ● v. (**overthrows**; past **overthrew**; past participle **overthrown; overthrowing**) **1** remove forcibly from power. **2** put an end to. **3** conquer. **4** throw too far or past or over something. ● n. **1** a defeat or downfall. **2** the act of overthrowing.

overtime ● n. **1** time worked in addition to one's regular working hours. **2** payment for this. **3** a further period of play at the end of a game when the score is tied. ● adj. pertaining to or happening in overtime. ● adv. in addition to regular hours.

overtired adj. excessively tired.

overtone n. **1** a subtle or elusive quality or implication. **2** Music any of the tones above the lowest in a harmonic series.

overtook past of OVERTAKE.

overtop ● v. (**overtops, overtopped, overtopping**) **1** be or become higher than. **2** surpass. ● prep. above. ● adv. over the top of.

overture n. **1** an orchestral piece opening an opera, ballet, etc. **2** a one-movement composition in this style. **3** an approach made with the aim of starting a discussion etc. [Say OVER chur]

overturn v. **1** cause to fall down or over. **2** overthrow. **3** invalidate. **4** turn over; capsize.

overuse ● v. (**overuses, overused, overusing**) use too much. ● n. excessive use.

overvalue v. (**overvalues, overvalued, overvaluing**) value too highly.

overview n. a general survey.

overwater ● v. water (a plant etc.) too much. ● adj. situated above the water.

overweening adj. arrogant, conceited.

overweight adj. in excess of a normal, desirable or allowable weight.

overwhelm v. **1** overpower with emotion, an excess of work, etc. **2** crush. **3** bury or drown beneath a huge mass. □ **overwhelming** adj. **overwhelmingly** adv.

overwinter v. **1** spend the winter. **2** (of insects, fungi, etc.) live through the winter.

overwork ● v. **1** work or cause to work too hard. **2** weary or exhaust with too much work. **3** make excessive use of. ● n. excessive work. □ **overworked** adj.

overwrite v. (**overwrites**; past **overwrote**; past participle **overwritten; overwriting**) **1** write on top of. **2** destroy (data) in (a file etc.) by entering new data. **3** write too ornately.

overwrought adj. **1** overexcited, nervous, distraught. **2** too elaborate. [Say over ROT]

overzealous adj. too zealous. [Say over ZELL us]

ovoid ● *adj.* **1** egg-shaped. **2** oval. ● *n.* an ovoid shape. [*Say* OVE oid]

ovulate *v.* (**ovulates**, **ovulated**, **ovulating**) discharge ova or ovules from the ovary. □ **ovulation** *n.* [*Say* OV yoo late]

ovule *n.* the part of the ovary of seed plants that contains the germ cell. [*Say* OVE yool]

ovum *n.* (*pl.* **ova**) **1** a mature reproductive cell of female animals. **2** the egg cell of plants. [*Say* OVE um *for the singular,* OVE uh *for the plural*]

ow *interj.* expressing sudden pain.

owe *v.* (**owes**, **owed**, **owing**) **1** be under obligation to pay or repay (money etc.). **2** render (honour etc.) to a person. **3** be indebted to.

owing *adj.* **1** owed; yet to be paid. **2 a** attributable to. **b** because of.

owl *n.* a nocturnal bird of prey with large eyes and a hooked beak. □ **owlish** *adj.*

own ● *adj.* **1** belonging to oneself or itself. **2** used to emphasize identity rather than possession. ● *pron.* **1** private property **2** kindred. ● *v.* **1** possess. **2 a** admit as valid, true, etc. **b** confess to. □ **come into one's own 1** receive one's due. **2** achieve recognition. **get one's own back** *informal* get revenge. **hold one's own** maintain one's position. **on one's own 1** alone. **2** independently. **own up** confess frankly. □ **-owned** *adj.*

owner *n.* a person who owns something. □ **ownerless** *adj.* **ownership** *n.*

ox *n.* (*pl.* **oxen**) **1** a cow or bull. **2** a castrated bull, typically used as a draft animal. **3** a foolish, clumsy person.

oxbow *n.* **1** a U-shaped collar of an ox yoke. **2** a loop formed by a horseshoe bend in a river.

oxen *pl.* of **ox**.

ox-eye daisy *n.* (*pl.* **ox-eye daisies**) a daisy that has flowers with white petals and a yellow centre.

oxford *n.* (also **oxford shoe**) a low, sturdy shoe laced over the instep.

oxidant *n.* a substance that brings about oxidation. [*Say* OX id unt]

oxidase *n.* an enzyme that reacts with oxygen to form water or hydrogen peroxide. [*Say* OX id ace *or* OX id aze]

oxidation *n.* the process or result of oxidizing or being oxidized.

oxide *n.* a binary compound of oxygen.

oxidize *v.* (**oxidizes**, **oxidized**, **oxidizing**) **1** combine or cause to combine with oxygen. **2** cover or become covered with a coating of oxide; make or become rusty or tarnished. □ **oxidized** *adj.* **oxidizer** *n.* [*Say* OX id ize]

oxtail *n.* the tail of an ox, used in soup.

oxygen *n.* a colourless odourless gaseous element, occurring naturally in air etc., and essential to life.

oxygenate *v.* (**oxygenates**, **oxygenated**, **oxygenating**) supply, treat, or mix with oxygen; oxidize. □ **oxygenation** *n.* [*Say* OXYGEN ate]

oxygen mask *n.* a mask through which oxygen is supplied to relieve breathing difficulties.

oxygen tent *n.* a tent-like enclosure containing oxygen-enriched air, used to aid breathing.

oxymoron *n.* a figure of speech in which apparently contradictory terms appear in conjunction, e.g. *bittersweet*. □ **oxymoronic** *adj.* [*Say* oxy MORE on, oxy muh RON ick]

oxytocin *n.* a hormone that causes increased contraction of the uterus during labour. [*Say* oxy TOE sin]

oy *interj.* calling attention or expressing alarm etc.

oyster *n.* any of various bivalve molluscs with rough irregular shells, several kinds of which are farmed for food or pearls. □ **oystering** *n.*

oyster bed *n.* a part of the sea floor where oysters breed.

oystercatcher *n.* a usu. coastal wading bird with a strong orange-coloured bill.

oyster mushroom *n.* an edible fungus with an oyster-shaped cap.

oyster sauce *n.* a sauce made from soy sauce and oyster extract.

Oz *n.* & *adj.* *slang* Australia or Australian.

oz. *abbr.* ounce(s).

ozone *n.* a strong-smelling poisonous form of oxygen, formed in electrical discharges or by ultraviolet light. [*Say* OH zone]

ozone-friendly *adj.* (of manufactured articles) containing chemicals that are not destructive to the ozone layer.

ozone hole *n.* a region of marked thinning of the ozone layer.

ozone layer *n.* a layer of ozone in the stratosphere that absorbs most of the sun's ultraviolet radiation.

Ozzie *n.* & *adj.* = AUSSIE.

Pp

P *n.* (also **p**) (*pl.* **Ps** or **P's**) the sixteenth letter of the alphabet.

p *abbr.* (also **p.**) (*pl.* **pp**) page.

PA² *n.* (*pl.* **PAs**) a public address system.

pa *n. informal* father.

p.a. *abbr.* per annum.

paan *n.* the leaf of the betel palm wrapped around betel nuts and lime and chewed. [*Sounds like* PAN]

Pablum *n.* **1** *proprietary* a soft cereal for infants. **2** (**pablum**) bland intellectual fare, entertainment, etc.

pace ● *n.* **1 a** a single step in walking or running. **b** the distance covered in this. **2** speed in walking or running. **3** speed or tempo. **4** the rate at which something progresses. **5** any of various gaits, esp. of a horse etc. ● *v.* (**paces, paced, pacing**) **1** walk up and down in a small space. **2** traverse by pacing. **3** set the pace for. **4** measure (a distance) by pacing. **5** (**pace oneself**) do something at a controlled and steady rate. □ **change of pace** a change from what one is used to. **keep pace** advance at an equal rate. **put a person through his** (or **her**) **paces** test a person's qualities or abilities. **set the pace** determine the speed. □ **-paced** *comb. form* **pacing** *n.*

pacemaker *n.* **1** a device for stimulating and regulating heartbeats. **2** a competitor who sets the pace for others.

pacer *n.* **1** a horse bred to take part in harness racing. **2** a person who paces or sets the pace.

pacesetter *n.* **1** a person etc. serving as a model for others. **2** = PACEMAKER 2.

pachyderm *n.* any thick-skinned mammal, esp. an elephant. [*Say* PACKY durm]

pacific *adj.* **1** peaceful. **2** (**Pacific**) relating to the Pacific Ocean.

Pacific dogwood *n.* an ornamental dogwood tree of the west coast of N America; it is the floral emblem of BC.

Pacific Rim *n.* (usu. as **the Pacific Rim**) the countries and regions bordering the Pacific Ocean.

Pacific salmon *n.* a variety of salmon of the North Pacific, esp. the coho, sockeye, and chinook.

Pacific Time *n.* the time in a zone including BC and the Pacific states of the US. **Pacific Standard Time** is eight hours behind GMT; **Pacific Daylight Time** is seven hours behind GMT.

pacifier *n.* **1** something that pacifies. **2** a baby's soother. [*Say* PASSA fie er]

pacifism *n.* the belief that disputes should be settled by peaceful means rather than war. □ **pacifist** *n. & adj.* **pacifistic** *adj.* [*Say* PASSA fism, PASSA fist, pass FISS tick]

pacify *v.* (**pacifies, pacified, pacifying**) **1** appease. **2** bring to a state of peace. □ **pacification** *n.* [*Say* PASSA fie, passa fuh KAY sh'n]

pack¹ ● *n.* **1** a cardboard or paper container and the items inside it. **2** a set of playing cards. **3** a collection of related documents. **4** a group of animals that live and hunt together. **5** usu. *derogatory* a group of similar things or people. **6** the main body of competitors following the leader in a race. **7** an organized group of Cubs, Brownies, etc. **8** a backpack. **9** pack ice. **10** a hot or cold compress, used for treating an injury. ● *v.* **1** fill (a bag) with items needed for travel. **2** place in a container or fold for transport or storage. **3** cram a large number of things into. **4** crowd or fill with people. **5** cover, surround, or fill. **6** *informal* carry (a gun). ● *adj.* (of an animal) used for carrying a load. □ **pack (it) in** (or **up**) *informal* end or stop (it). **pack one's bags** prepare to leave. **send packing** *informal* dismiss summarily. □ **packed** *adj.*

pack² *v.* select (a jury etc.) or fill (a meeting) so as to secure a decision in one's favour.

package ● *n.* **1 a** an object or objects wrapped in paper or packed in a box. **b** a box etc. in which things are packed. **2** (also **package deal**) a set of things offered as a whole. **3** a group of related items viewed as a unit. **4** *Computing* a piece of software suitable for various applications. **5** (also **package tour, package holiday**) a tour, vacation, etc. with all arrangements made at an inclusive price. ● *v.* (**packages, packaged, packaging**) **1** put together in a package. **2** present in such a way as to appeal to the public. □ **packager** n.

packaging n. **1** a wrapping or container for goods. **2** the action or process of packing goods. **3** the creation of an image for promotional purposes; the style and context in which a particular product, person, or idea is marketed.

pack animal n. an animal for carrying packs.

packer n. **1** a person or thing that packs. **2 a** a pack animal. **b** a person who transports goods by means of pack animals.

packet n. **1** a small package. **2** Computing a unit of data transmitted over a network.

packet switching n. a method of data transmission in which a message is broken down into packets that are sent independently, and reassembled at the destination.

Packham pear n. a large, bumpy green pear with smooth white sweet and juicy flesh, grown esp. in the southern hemisphere. [Say PACK um]

pack horse n. a horse for carrying loads.

pack ice n. a large mass of floating ice in the sea.

packing n. **1** the process of packing. **2** material used to protect fragile articles in transit.

packing plant n. a factory where meat or fish is processed and packaged for shipping and sale.

packing snow n. wet snow that holds together when compressed.

pack rat n. a person who hoards things.

packsack n. a knapsack.

packsaddle n. a saddle adapted for supporting packs.

pack train n. a train of pack animals.

pact n. an agreement or treaty between people, groups, or countries.

pad¹ ● n. **1 a** a thick piece of soft or absorbent material. **b** a sanitary pad. **2** a number of sheets of paper fastened together at one edge. **3** a stamp pad. **4** the fleshy underpart of an animal's foot or of a human finger. **5** a guard for the leg, elbow, etc. in sports. **6** a flat surface for helicopter takeoff or rocket-launching. **7** informal an apartment. **8** the floating leaf of a water lily. ● v. (**pads, padded, padding**) **1** provide with a pad or padding. **2** fill out (a piece of writing) with unnecessary material. **3** inflate or falsify figures. □ **padding** n.

pad² ● v. (**pads, padded, padding**) walk with a soft dull steady step. ● n. the sound of soft steady steps.

PA day abbr. Cdn = PROFESSIONAL DEVELOPMENT DAY.

paddle ● n. **1** a short broad-bladed oar used without an oarlock. **2** a paddle-shaped instrument or part of a machine, esp. one used for beating or mixing food. **3 a** a short-handled bat used esp. in table tennis. **b** a numbered bat shaped like this used in an auction. **4** a blade of a paddlewheel. **5** the action of paddling. **6** a plastic-covered electrode used in cardiac stimulation. ● v. (**paddles, paddled, paddling**) **1** move or propel over water by means of paddles. **2** row gently. **3** informal spank. **4** walk, esp. barefoot, in shallow water. □ **paddler** n. **paddling** n.

paddleboat n. a boat propelled by a paddlewheel.

paddlewheel n. a wheel with blades around its circumference, which is rotated to propel a boat. □ **paddlewheeler** n.

paddock n. **1** a small field, esp. for keeping horses in. **2** an enclosure adjoining a racetrack where horses or cars are gathered before a race. [Say PAD ick]

paddy n. (pl. **paddies**) (also **paddy field**) a field where rice is grown.

paddy wagon n. slang a police van for transporting prisoners etc.

padlock ● n. a detachable lock hanging by a pivoted hook on the object fastened. ● v. secure with a padlock.

padre n. **1** a Christian clergyman, esp. a priest. **2** a chaplain in the armed services. [Say POD ray or PAD ray]

pad Thai n. a spicy Thai dish of rice noodles and shrimp, chicken, etc. [Say pad TIE]

paean n. a song of praise or triumph. [Say PEE un]

paella n. (pl. **paellas**) a Spanish dish of rice, saffron, chicken, seafood, etc. [Say pie AY uh or pie ELLA]

pagan ● n. **1** a person holding religious beliefs other than those of any of the main religions of the world. **2** a person considered to be irreligious. ● adj. **1** of or associated with pagans. **2** irreligious. □ **paganism** n. [Say PAY g'n]

page¹ ● n. **1 a** a leaf of a book etc. **b** each side of this. **2** Computing **a** a section of stored data displayed on a screen at one time. **b** a hypertext document which can be accessed on a network, esp. the Internet. ● v. (**pages, paged, paging**) **1** leaf through. **2** Computing display one page at a time.

page² ● n. **1 a** an attendant of a person of rank, a bride, etc., esp. a boy. **b** a person employed in a legislative assembly to deliver members' messages. **2** a boy or man employed to run errands etc. **3** hist. a boy in training for knighthood. ● v. (**pages, paged, paging**) **1** summon by making an announcement. **2** summon by means of a pager. □ **paging** n.

pageant n. **1** a brilliant spectacle or parade. **2** a procession or play depicting historical events. **3** a contest or show. [Say PADGE int]

pageantry n. elaborate display or ceremony. [Say PADGE in tree]

pageboy n. **1** a woman's so short hairstyle. **2** a youth employed as a page.

pager n. a radio device that beeps or vibrates to alert the person wearing it.

page-turner n. **1** a book so engrossing that one is compelled to read it quickly. **2** a person who turns pages for a pianist etc. □ **page-turning** adj.

paginate v. (**paginates, paginated, paginating**) assign numbers to the pages of a book etc. □ **pagination** n. [Say PADGE in ate]

pagoda n. (pl. **pagodas**) a Hindu or Buddhist temple or sacred building, esp. a many-tiered tower. [Say puh GO duh]

paid ● v. past and past participle of PAY. ● adj. recompensed or reimbursed.

pail n. a bucket.

pain ● n. **1 a** physical suffering caused by illness or injury. **b** a feeling of discomfort in a part of the body. **2** mental suffering. **3** careful effort; trouble taken. **4** (also **pain in the neck** etc.) informal a nuisance. ● v. cause pain to. □ **be at** (or **take**) **pains** take great care in doing something. **no pain, no gain** one cannot make progress without experiencing some pain. **on** (or **under**) **pain of** with (death etc.) as the penalty. □ **pained** adj.

painful adj. **1** causing bodily or mental pain. **2** suffering pain. **3** laborious. **4** very bad. □ **painfully** adv.

painkiller n. a medicine or drug for alleviating pain. □ **painkilling** adj.

painless adj. **1** not causing or suffering pain. **2** effortless; easy. □ **painlessly** adv.

painstaking adj. careful, thorough. □ **painstakingly** adv.

paint ● n. **1** colouring matter for imparting colour to a surface. **2** jocular makeup. ● v. **1** cover the surface of with paint. **2** produce (a picture) by painting. **3** describe vividly as if by painting. **4 a** apply makeup to. **b** apply nail polish to. **5** apply (a liquid) to a surface with a brush etc. **6** practise the art of painting. □ **paint a picture** describe in vivid detail. **paint into a corner** force into a situation from which it is not easy to escape. **paint the**

town red informal enjoy oneself flamboyantly. □ **painted** adj.

paintball n. a game in which participants shoot capsules of paint at each other.

paintbox n. (pl. **paintboxes**) a box holding dry paints for painting pictures.

paintbrush n. (pl. **paintbrushes**) **1** a brush for applying paint. **2** a plant of western N America that bears brightly coloured flowering spikes.

paint-by-number adj. **1** denoting a picture in which numbers indicate the colour to be used. **2** unoriginal.

painted lady n. a migratory butterfly with orange-red wings.

painter¹ n. **1** a person who paints pictures. **2** a person who paints walls, buildings, etc. □ **painterly** adj.

painter² n. a rope attached to the bow of a boat for tying it to a quay etc.

painting n. **1** the process or art of using paint. **2** a painted picture.

paint stripper n. something used to remove paint.

paintwork n. a painted surface on a car etc.

pair ● n. **1** a set of two things used together or regarded as a unit. **2** an article consisting of two joined or corresponding parts. **3 a** a dating or married couple. **b** a mated couple of animals. **4** two playing cards of the same denomination. ● v. **1** arrange or be arranged in pairs. **2** match or be matched together. □ **in pairs** in twos. □ **paired** adj. **pairing** n.

pairs skating n. a type of figure skating in which a couple perform a choreographed routine of jumps, lifts, etc. to music. □ **pairs skater** n.

paisley n. **1** a distinctive detailed pattern of curved feather-shaped figures. **2** a fabric having this pattern. [Say PAZE lee]

pajamas pl. n. = PYJAMAS.

Pakistani n. (pl. **Pakistanis**) a person from Pakistan. □ **Pakistani** adj. [Say packa STANNY]

pakora n. a piece of cauliflower, carrot, etc. in seasoned batter and deep-fried. [Say puh CORE uh]

pal ● n. informal **1** a friend. **2** a form of address to a stranger. ● v. (**pals, palled, palling**) associate; form a friendship.

palace n. **1** the official residence of a sovereign, president, archbishop, etc. **2** a splendid mansion.

palace coup n. (also **palace revolution**) the (usu. non-violent) overthrow of a sovereign, government, etc. by senior officials.

paladin n. hist. a knight renowned for

heroism. **2** a dedicated advocate of a cause. [Say PAL a din]

palaeo- esp. *Brit.* = PALEO-. [Say PAILY oh or PALLY oh]

palatable adj. **1** pleasant to taste. **2** acceptable, satisfactory. □ **palatability** n. [Say PALA tuh bull, pala tuh BILLA tee]

palate n. **1** the roof of the mouth. **2** a person's appreciation of taste and flavour. **3** flavour, taste. □ **palatal** adj. [Say PAL it, PALA tull]

palatial adj. like a palace, esp. spacious and splendid. [Say puh LAY shull]

palaver ● n. prolonged and tedious fuss or discussion. ● v. talk unnecessarily at length. [Say puh LAV er]

palazzo n. (pl. **palazzos**) **1** a large palatial building or mansion. **2** loose, wide-legged pants worn by women. [Say puh LAT so or puh LOT so]

pale[1] ● adj. **1** (of a complexion) of a whitish or ashen appearance. **2** (of a colour) not dark or deep. **3** dim. ● v. (**pales, paled, paling**) **1** grow or make pale. **2** be feeble in comparison (with). □ **palely** adv. **paleness** n.

pale[2] n. **1** a pointed piece of wood for fencing etc.; a stake. **2** an enclosed or delimited area. □ **beyond the pale** outside the bounds of acceptable behaviour. □ **paling** n.

Palearctic adj. *Zoology* of the Arctic and temperate parts of the Old World. [Say pailey ARCTIC]

paleface n. a name supposedly used by the North American Indians for the white man.

paleo- comb. form of ancient (esp. prehistoric) times. [Say PAILY oh or PALLY oh]

Paleocene n. *Geology* the earliest epoch of the Tertiary period, lasting from about 65 to 55 million years BP, characterized by a sudden diversification of mammals. □ **Paleocene** adj. [Say PAILEY oh seen]

paleolithic ● adj. of or relating to the early phase of the Stone Age, when primitive stone implements were used. ● n. the paleolithic period. [Say pailey oh LITH ick]

paleontology n. the branch of science that deals with extinct and fossil animals and plants. □ **paleontological** adj. **paleontologist** n. [Say pailey un TOLLA jee, pailey onta LOGICAL, pailey un TOLLA jist]

Paleozoic n. *Geology* the era between the Precambrian and the Mesozoic, lasting from about 590 to 248 million years ago, which ended with the dominance of the reptiles. □ **Paleozoic** adj. [Say pailey a ZO ick]

Palestinian n. a person from Palestine or from the area formerly called Palestine. □ **Palestinian** adj. [Say pala STINNY un]

palette n. **1** a thin board or slab on which an artist lays and mixes colours. **2** the range of colours used by an artist. [Say PAL it]

Pali n. a language used in the canonical books of Buddhism. [Say PALLY]

palindrome n. a word or phrase that reads the same backwards as forwards. □ **palindromic** adj. [Say PAL in drome, pal in DROM ick]

palisade n. a fence of pales or iron railings. [Say pala SAYD]

pall ● n. **1** a cloth spread over a coffin, hearse, or tomb. **2** a dark or gloomy covering. **3** an atmosphere of gloom or fear. ● v. become less appealing through familiarity. [Rhymes with WALL]

Palladian adj. in the neo-classical style of the Italian architect Andrea Palladio (1508–80). [Say puh LADY in]

palladium n. a white metallic element resembling platinum. [Say puh LADY um]

pallbearer n. a person helping to carry or escorting a coffin at a funeral.

pallet n. **1 a** a straw mattress. **b** a makeshift bed. **2** a portable platform for transporting and storing loads. [Say PAL it]

palliative ● n. **1** anything used to alleviate pain without eliminating its source. **2** something that makes a problem less severe but does not solve it. ● adj. serving to alleviate pain, anxiety, etc. [Say PAL ee uh tiv]

palliative care n. medical care provided for the terminally ill, aimed at relieving symptoms.

pallid adj. **1** pale. **2** feeble. [Say PAL id]

pallor n. paleness. [Say PAL er]

pally adj. (**pallier, palliest**) *informal* friendly. [Say PAL ee]

palm[1] n. **1** a tropical evergreen tree with a crown of long feathered or fan-shaped leaves. **2** the leaf of this tree as a symbol of victory or excellence. □ **palmy** adj. (**palmier, palmiest**)

palm[2] ● n. the inner surface of the hand between the wrist and fingers. ● v. **1** conceal in the hand. **2** take or pass on stealthily. □ **in the palm of one's hand** under one's control. **palm off 1** impose or thrust fraudulently (on a person). **2** cause a person to accept unwilling or unknowingly. □ **palmed** adj.

palmate adj. (also **palmated**) **1** shaped

like an open hand. **2** having lobes etc. like spread fingers. [Say PAL mate]

palmetto n. (pl. **palmettos**) a kind of small palm tree. [Say pal METTO or pol METTO]

palmistry n. the art or practice of interpreting a person's character or predicting their future by examining the lines etc. of the hand. □ **palmist** n. [Say PALM iss tree]

palm reader n. a person who practises palmistry.

Palm Sunday n. Christianity the Sunday before Easter.

palmtop n. a computer small enough to be held in one hand.

palomino n. (pl. **palominos**) a golden or tan-coloured horse with a light-coloured mane and tail. [Say pala MEE no]

palooka n. (pl. **palookas**) slang an oaf or lout. [Say puh LOO kuh]

palpable adj. **1** that can be touched or felt. **2** plain to see. **3** so intense as to be almost touched or felt. □ **palpably** adv. [Say PAL puh bull]

palpate v. (**palpates, palpated, palpating**) medically examine by touch. □ **palpation** n. [Say PAL pate]

palpitate v. (**palpitates, palpitated, palpitating**) **1** (of the heart) beat rapidly or irregularly. **2** tremble, quiver. □ **palpitation** n. [Say PAL puh tate]

palsy n. (pl. **palsies**) dated paralysis, esp. with involuntary tremors. □ **palsied** adj. [Say POL zee]

paltry adj. (**paltrier, paltriest**) **1** (of an amount) very small. **2** having no value or useful qualities. [Say POL tree]

pampas pl. n. (singular **pampa**) large treeless plains in S America. [Say PAM pus]

pamper v. treat (someone) with abundant kindness or comfort. □ **pampered** adj. **pampering** n.

pamphlet n. a small booklet or leaflet containing information about a single, esp. controversial, subject.

pamphleteer ● n. a writer or issuer of pamphlets. ● v. write or issue pamphlets. □ **pamphleteering** n.

pan¹ ● n. **1** a cooking vessel of metal, earthenware, etc. **2** any similar shallow container such as the bowl of a pair of scales. **3** a slab of floating ice. **4** a hollow in the ground. ● v. (**pans, panned, panning**) **1** informal criticize severely. **2** wash (gold-bearing gravel) in a shallow pan to search for gold. □ **pan out** (of an action etc.) turn out well.

pan² ● v. (**pans, panned, panning**) swing (a movie camera) to give a panoramic effect or to follow a moving object. ● n. a panning movement.

pan- comb. form all; the whole of; including everyone or everything.

panacea n. (pl. **panaceas**) a cure for all ills. [Say panna SEE uh]

panache n. flamboyant confidence of style or manner. [Say puh NASH]

Pan-Am adj. Pan-American.

Panamanian n. a person from Panama. □ **Panamanian** adj. [Say panna MAY nee in]

Pan-American adj. of, relating to, representing, or involving all of the countries of North and South America.

pancake n. **1** a thin, flat, usu. round cake of batter, grated potatoes, etc., fried on both sides. **2** (also **pancake makeup**) a thick layer of makeup, esp. foundation. □ **flat as a pancake** completely flat.

pancetta n. cured belly of pork, usu. in a long casing. [Say pan CHETTA]

pancreas n. (pl. **pancreases**) a gland supplying the duodenum with digestive fluid and secreting insulin into the blood. □ **pancreatic** adj. [Say PAN cree us, pan cree ATTIC]

panda n. (pl. **pandas**) **1** (also **giant panda**) a bearlike mammal with black and white markings, native to China and Tibet. **2** (also **red panda**) a reddish-brown Himalayan raccoon-like mammal with a bushy tail.

pandemic ● adj. (of a disease) prevalent over a whole country or the world. ● n. a pandemic disease. [Say pan DEM ick]

pandemonium n. uproar or confusion. [Say panda MOE nee um]

pander v. gratify or indulge a person, a desire, etc. □ **panderer** n. **pandering** n.

Pandora's box n. a process that generates many difficult problems. [Say pan DORE uh's]

pane n. a single sheet of glass in a window or door. □ **paned** adj.

panegyric n. a speech or piece of writing expressing high praise. [Say panna JYE rick]

panel ● n. **1 a** a distinct section of a wall, door, garment, etc. **b** a board on which electrical switches, controls, etc. are fixed. **2** a group of people invited to decide on or discuss a matter. **3** a list of available jurors. ● v. (**panels, panelled, panelling**) fit, provide, or cover with panels.

panelling n. (also esp. US **paneling**) panels collectively, esp. wooden panels used for a wall covering.

panellist n. (also esp. US **panelist**) a member of a panel (esp. in broadcasting).

panfish *n.* (*pl.* **panfish**) any small freshwater fish suitable for frying whole in a pan. □ **panfishing** *n.*

pang *n.* a sudden sharp pain or painful emotion.

Pangaea *n.* a single vast continent comprising all of the earth's land masses, which is believed to have existed about 250 million years ago. [*Say* pan JEE uh]

panhandle ● *n.* a narrow strip of territory surrounded on three sides by another country or state etc. **●** *v.* (**panhandles, panhandled, panhandling**) *informal* beg for money in the street. □ **panhandler** *n.*

panic ● *n.* **1** sudden uncontrollable fear or alarm. **2** an agitated busyness as when making preparations for something. **●** *v.* (**panics, panicked, panicking**) affect or be affected with panic. □ **panicky** *adj.*

panic button *n.* a button for summoning help in an emergency. □ **push** (or **press**) **the panic button** react in an unduly alarmed manner.

panic-stricken *adj.* affected with panic.

panjandrum *n.* a person claiming to have great importance or authority. [*Say* pan JAN drum]

pannier *n.* **1** each of a pair of baskets carried by a beast of burden. **2** a bag or box on either side of the rear wheel of a bicycle or motorcycle. [*Say* PAN yer]

panoply *n.* an impressive array. [*Say* PANNA plee]

panorama *n.* **1** an unbroken view of a surrounding region. **2** a complete survey of a subject, sequence of events, etc. **3** a picture or photograph containing a wide view. □ **panoramic** *adj.*

pan pipe *n.* a musical instrument made of a series of short pipes fixed together.

pansy *n.* (*pl.* **pansies**) a garden plant with richly coloured flowers. [*Say* PAN zee]

pant¹ ● *v.* **1** breathe with short quick breaths. **2** yearn or crave. **●** *n.* a panting breath. □ **pantingly** *adv.*

pant² *n.* = PANTS.

pantaloon *n. hist.* men's close-fitting breeches fastened below the calf or at the foot. [*Say* panta LOON]

pantheism *n.* **1** the belief that God is present in all things. **2** worship that admits or tolerates all gods. □ **pantheist** *n.* **pantheistic** *adj.* [*Say* PANTH ee ism]

pantheon *n.* **1** a building in which famous dead people are buried or have memorials. **2** the deities of a people collectively. **3** a temple dedicated to the gods. **4** a group of famous or respected people. [*Say* PANTH ee on]

panther *n.* **1** a cougar. **2** a leopard, esp. with black fur.

panties *pl. n.* legless underwear for women and girls.

pantiliner *n.* a very thin adhesive pad attached to women's underwear to absorb light menstrual flow etc.

pantomime ● *n.* **1 a** the use of gestures and facial expression to convey meaning. **b** a performance of this. **2** an esp. British theatrical entertainment with music, jokes, etc. **●** *v.* (**pantomimes, pantomimed, pantomiming**) represent by pantomime. [*Say* PANTA mime]

pantry *n.* (*pl.* **pantries**) a small room or cupboard in which food, dishes, etc., are kept.

pants *pl. n.* a garment reaching from the waist usu. to the ankles, divided into two parts to cover each leg separately. □ **scare** (or **beat** etc.) **the pants off** *informal* scare, beat, etc., thoroughly. **with one's pants down** *informal* in an embarrassingly unprepared state.

pantsuit *n.* a women's suit of pants and a matching jacket.

panty *n.* = PANTIES.

pantyhose *pl. n.* very sheer nylon tights for women.

panzer *n.* a German armoured unit or tank.

panzerotto *n.* (*pl.* **panzerotti**) *Cdn* a baked pizza-like turnover, filled with tomato sauce, cheese, etc. [*Say* panza ROTTO]

pap *n.* **1** soft or semi-liquid food for infants or invalids. **2** trivial reading matter or entertainment.

papa *n.* (*pl.* **papas**) *archaic* father.

papacy *n.* **1** the office or authority of the Pope. **2** the time during which a Pope is in office. [*Say* PAPE uh see]

papal *adj.* of a pope or the papacy. [*Say* PAPE ul]

paparazzo *n.* (*pl.* **paparazzi**) a freelance photographer who pursues celebrities to get photographs of them. [*Say* pappa RAT so *for the singular,* pappa RAT see *for the plural*]

papaya *n.* (*pl.* **papayas**) an elongated fruit with edible orange flesh and black seeds. [*Say* puh PIE uh]

paper ● *n.* **1** a material manufactured in thin sheets from the pulp of wood etc., used for writing or printing on, or as wrapping material etc. **2** a newspaper. **3** a **a** document printed on paper. **b** (in *pl.*) personal documents. **4** *Commerce* negotiable documents. **5** a scholarly essay or dissertation. **6** a set of questions in an

exam. ● v. **1** apply esp. wallpaper to.
2 a cover with paper. **b** disguise or try to
hide (a fault etc.). □ **on paper 1** in writing.
2 in theory. □ **papery** adj.

paperback ● adj. (of a book) bound in
stiff paper, not boards. ● n. a paperback
book.

paperbark n. any of various trees with
peeling papery bark.

paperboard n. stiff material made by
pasting together sheets of paper.

paper boy n. (also **paper girl**) a boy or
girl who delivers newspapers.

paper clip ● n. a clip of bent wire etc. for
holding several sheets of paper together.
● v. (**paper-clip**) (**paper-clips, paper-
clipped, paper-clipping**) attach with a
paper clip.

paperless adj. using computers rather
than paper to record or exchange
information.

paper route n. a job of regularly
delivering newspapers.

paper-thin adj. & adv. very thin.

paper tiger n. an apparently threatening
but ineffectual person or thing.

paper trail n. documentation linking
someone to an esp. incriminating event.

paperweight n. a small heavy object for
keeping loose papers in place.

paperwork n. **1** routine administrative
work. **2** paper documents collectively.

papier mâché n. strips of paper mixed
with glue, used for making moulded
figures etc. [Say paper ma SHAY or
pap yay ma SHAY]

papilla n. (pl. **papillae**) a small
protuberance on a part of the body or a
plant. [Say puh PILLA for the singular,
puh PILLY for the plural]

papilloma n. (pl. **papillomas**) a wart-like
usu. benign tumour.
[Say pap uh LOW muh]

papoose n. a North American Indian
child. [Say puh POOSE]

pappardelle pl. n. pasta in the form of
broad flat ribbons. [Say pap ar DEL ay]

paprika n. a spice made from dried
ground red sweet peppers. [Say PAP rick uh
or puh PREE kuh]

Pap smear n. (also **Pap test**) a
procedure for detecting cervical cancer.

Papuan n. **1** a native or inhabitant of
Papua. **2** a group of around 750 languages
spoken in and around New Guinea.
□ **Papuan** adj. [Say PAP oo in or
POP oo in]

papyrus n. (pl. **papyri**) **1** a grasslike
aquatic plant with tall, dark green stems.
2 a material prepared in ancient Egypt

from the stem of this plant, used for
writing or painting on. [Say puh PIE rus for
the singular, puh PIE rye for the plural]

par ● n. **1** the average or normal amount
etc. **2** an equal standing. **3** Golf the number
of strokes a first-class player should
normally require for a hole or course. **4** the
face value of a stock or bond. **5** the
recognized value of one country's currency
in terms of another's. ● v. (**pars, parred,
parring**) Golf complete (a hole etc.) with a
score equal to par. □ **par for the course**
informal what is normal in any given
circumstances.

par. abbr. (also **para.**) paragraph.

para- comb. form of or using parachutes.

parable n. **1** a simple story used to
illustrate a moral or spiritual lesson. **2** an
allegory. [Say PERRA bull]

parabola n. (pl. **parabolas**) a
symmetrical curve like the path of a
projectile under the influence of gravity.
□ **parabolic** adj. [Say puh RABBA luh,
perra BOLL ick]

parachute ● n. a cloth canopy that fills
with air and allows a person etc. attached
to it to fall from an airplane at a safe rate.
● v. (**parachutes, parachuted,
parachuting**) **1** drop or land by
parachute. **2** appoint or be appointed as an
outsider to a position, candidacy, etc.
□ **parachutist** n.

parade ● n. **1 a** a public procession. **b** a
series of people or things in succession. **2** a
formal or ceremonial march or assembling
of troops for inspection or display. ● v.
(**parades, paraded, parading**) **1** march
in or assemble for a parade. **2** display
(something) publicly in order to impress.

parade ground n. (also Cdn **parade
square**) an outdoor area where soldiers
etc. gather for inspection etc.

paradigm n. **1** a typical example or
pattern. **2** a model which underlies the
theories and methodology of science etc.
□ **paradigmatic** adj. [Say PERRA dime,
perra dig MAT ick]

paradigm shift n. a fundamental
change.

paradise n. **1** (in some religions) heaven.
2 a an idyllic place or state. **b** an ideal or
perfect place. **3** the Garden of Eden.
□ **paradisal** adj. [Say PERRA dice,
PERRA dice ul]

paradox n. (pl. **paradoxes**) **1** a seemingly
absurd or self-contradictory statement
which may prove to be true. **2** a person or
thing that combines contradictory
qualities. □ **paradoxical** adj.
paradoxically adv.

paraffin n. a flammable waxy or oily

substance distilled from petroleum and shale and used esp. in candles, and for coating and sealing. [Say PERRA fin]

paraffin wax n. paraffin in its solid form.

paragliding n. a sport resembling hang-gliding, using a wide, parachute-like canopy attached to the body by a harness □ **paraglider** n.

paragon n. **1** a person or thing seen as a model of excellence. **2** a model (of virtue etc.). [Say PERRA gon]

paragraph ● n. **1** a distinct passage of a text, beginning on a new line. **2** a distinct section of a legal document. ● v. arrange in paragraphs.

Paraguayan n. a person from Paraguay. □ **Paraguayan** adj. [Say pa ra GWAY in]

parakeet n. a small usu. long-tailed parrot.

paralegal ● n. a person trained in legal matters, but not fully qualified as a lawyer. ● adj. of auxiliary aspects of the law. [Say perra LEGAL]

parallax n. (pl. **parallaxes**) the apparent difference in the position of an object when viewed from different positions. [Say PERRA lax]

parallel ● adj. **1** (of lines or planes) side by side with the same distance continuously between them. **2** precisely similar, analogous, or corresponding. **3** running through the same period of time. ● n. **1** a comparison. **2** a person or thing precisely analogous or equal to another in essential particulars. **3** (also **parallel of latitude**) each of the imaginary parallel circles of latitude on the earth's surface. ● v. (**parallels, paralleled, paralleling**) **1** be parallel to; correspond to. **2** run parallel with. ● adv. in a parallel direction or manner.

parallel bars pl. n. a pair of parallel rails on posts used in gymnastic events.

parallelism n. **1 a** the state, position or character of being parallel. **b** an example of this. **2** correspondence of successive clauses etc. in writing.

parallelogram n. a plane figure having four straight sides with opposite sides parallel. [Say perra LELLA gram]

parallel parking n. the parking of a vehicle parallel to the roadside. □ **parallel park** v.

parallel port n. Computing a connector for a device that sends or receives several bits of data simultaneously by using more than one wire.

parallel structure n. sentence structure in which related parts of a sentence have

the same grammatical function (e.g. all nouns, all adjectives, etc.).

Paralympics pl. n. (also **Paralympic Games**) an international athletic competition for disabled athletes. □ **Paralympian** n. **Paralympic** adj. [Say perra LIM picks, perra LIM pee in]

paralysis n. (pl. **paralyses**) **1** loss of the ability to move a part of the body. **2** inability to act or function. [Say puh RALLA sis]

paralytic adj. of, causing, or suffering from paralysis. [Say perra LIT ick]

paralyze v. (**paralyzes, paralyzed, paralyzing**) (also **paralyse, paralyses, paralysed, paralysing**) **1** affect with paralysis. **2** render incapable of action.

paramecium n. a freshwater protozoan with a slipper-like shape covered with cilia. [Say perra MEE see um]

paramedic n. a paramedical worker, trained in first aid, who works in ambulances.

paramedical adj. supplementing and supporting medical work.

parameter n. **1** a limit or boundary which defines the scope of something. **2** Math a quantity constant in the case considered but varying in different cases. [Say puh RAMMA ter]

paramilitary ● adj. (of forces etc.) organized similarly to military forces. ● n. (pl. **paramilitaries**) **1** a paramilitary organization. **2** a member of such an organization.

paramount adj. **1** superior to others. **2** highest in power or jurisdiction.

paramour n. a lover, esp. an illicit one. [Say PERRA moor]

paranoia n. (pl. **paranoias**) **1** a mental illness characterized by delusions of persecution or exaggerated self-importance. **2** baseless suspicion and mistrust of others. □ **paranoiac** adj. & n. [Say perra NOYA]

paranoid ● adj. **1** resulting or suffering from paranoia. **2** unreasonably anxious or mistrustful. ● n. a person who is paranoid. [Say PERRA noyd]

paranormal adj. outside the scope of known laws of nature or normal objective investigation. [Say perra NORMAL]

parapet n. **1** a low wall at the edge of a roof, bridge, or balcony. **2** a bank of earth or stone erected to provide protection from observation and attack. [Say PERRA pet]

paraphernalia pl. n. miscellaneous belongings, accessories, etc. [Say perra fuh NAILY uh]

paraphrase ● n. rewording. ● v.

(**paraphrases, paraphrased, paraphrasing**) express the meaning of in other words.

paraplegia n. paralysis of the legs and part or all of the torso. □ **paraplegic** adj. & n. [Say perra PLEE juh, perra PLEE jick]

paraprofessional n. a person without professional training to whom a particular aspect of a professional task is assigned.

parapsychology n. the study of mental phenomena outside the area of orthodox psychology. □ **parapsychologist** n.

parasailing n. a sport in which participants wearing open parachutes glide through the air while being towed by a speedboat. □ **parasail** v. & n.

parasite n. **1** an organism living in or on another and benefiting at the expense of the other. **2** a person who lives off others. □ **parasitic** adj. **parasitically** adv. **parasitism** n. [Say PERRA site, perra SIT ick, PERRA site ism]

parasol n. a light umbrella used to give shade from the sun. [Say PARRA sol]

parasympathetic adj. relating to one of the major divisions of the autonomic nervous system, and which is associated more with calmness and rest than with alertness.

parathyroid n. a gland next to the thyroid, secreting a hormone that regulates calcium and phosphate levels in the body.

paratroops pl. n. troops equipped to be dropped by parachute from aircraft. □ **paratrooper** n.

parboil v. partly cook by boiling.

parcel ● n. **1** an item or quantity of goods etc. wrapped up in a single package. **2** a piece of land. **3** (esp. in **part and parcel**) an integral part. ● v. (**parcels, parcelled, parcelling**) **1** wrap as a parcel. **2** divide into portions.

parch v. (**parches, parched, parching**) make or become dry with heat.

parched adj. **1** dried out, esp. by heat. **2** thirsty.

parchment n. **1 a** the skin of a sheep or goat, prepared as a writing etc. surface. **b** a manuscript written on this. **2** (also **parchment paper**) high-grade translucent paper made to resemble parchment. **3** a diploma.

pardner n. jocular a partner.

pardon ● n. **1** the action of forgiving for an error or offence. **2** an official cancellation of the legal consequences of a crime or conviction. ● v. **1** give (an offender) pardon. **2** forgive or excuse. **3** make esp. courteous allowances for.

● interj. (also **pardon me** or **I beg your pardon**) **1** a formula of apology. **2** a request to repeat something said. □ **pardonable** adj.

pare v. (**pares, pared, paring**) **1 a** cut away the skin or outer covering of. **b** trim by cutting away the surface or edge. **2** gradually reduce in size, extent, or number. □ **parer** n.

pared-down adj. simplified.

parent ● n. **1** a father or mother. **2** an animal or plant considered in relation to its offspring. **3** a thing from which another is derived. **4** an initiating organization or enterprise. ● v. **1** be or act as a parent to. **2** beget, produce. □ **parental** adj. **parenthood** n.

parentage n. descent from or through parents.

parent company n. a company of which other companies are subsidiaries.

parenthesis n. (pl. **parentheses**) **1** a word or phrase inserted as an explanation or afterthought, usu. set off in text by brackets, dashes, or commas. **2** either of a pair of round brackets ( ) used for this.

parenthetical adj. of or by way of a parenthesis. □ **parenthetically** adv. [Say pair in THETTA cull]

parenting n. the occupation or concerns of parents.

parent-teacher association n. a local organization of parents and teachers at a school. Abbreviation: **PTA**.

pareve adj. Judaism (of food) being or containing neither meat nor dairy and so kosher for use with either. [Say PAR uh vuh or PAR vuh]

par excellence ● adj. being the supreme example of its kind. [Say par eck sel LONCE]

parfait n. **1** ice cream, sauces, crushed fruit, etc. layered in a tall glass. **2** a frozen dessert of flavoured whipped cream etc. [Say par FAY]

parfleche n. a hide, esp. of buffalo, from which the hair has been removed. [Say PAR flesh]

pariah n. **1** a social outcast. **2** a despised person. [Say puh RYE uh]

parietal adj. of or near the bones forming the central part of the sides and top of the skull. [Say puh RYE it ul]

paring n. a thin portion cut or peeled from a surface. [Say PAIR ing]

paring knife n. a kitchen knife with a short pointed blade.

parish n. (pl. **parishes**) (in the Christian Church) a jurisdiction having a church and clergy.

parishioner *n.* a member or attendee of a particular church. [*Say* puh RISHA ner]

Parisian ● *adj.* relating to Paris. ● *n.* **1** a person from Paris. **2** the kind of French spoken in Paris. [*Say* puh REE zhin]

parity *n.* (*pl.* **parities**) **1** equality or equal status. **2** equivalence of pay for jobs perceived as being comparable. **3** the property of an integer by virtue of which it is odd or even. **4** equivalence of one currency with another. [*Say* PERRA tee]

park ● *n.* **1** a public piece of land with lawns, gardens, etc. in a town or city. **2** a large area of government land kept in its natural state. **3** a large enclosed area of land used to accommodate wild animals in captivity. **4** an area developed for a specified purpose. **5** the gear position in automatic transmission in which the gears are locked. **6** a large enclosed piece of ground attached to a stately home etc. ● *v.* **1** stop and leave (a vehicle) temporarily. **2** *informal* leave or deposit in a convenient place. □ **park oneself** *informal* sit down.

parka *n.* (*pl.* **parkas**) a warm, hooded coat.

parkade *n. Cdn* a parking garage.

park-and-ride *n.* a system whereby commuters, shoppers, etc. leave their cars in designated parking lots and continue into the city by public transportation.

parking *n.* **1** the act of stopping and leaving a vehicle. **2** an area for leaving vehicles. **3** *slang* the act of indulging in sexual activity while in a parked car.

parking brake *n.* = EMERGENCY BRAKE.

parking garage *n.* a structure with space for parking vehicles.

parking lot *n.* a usu. outdoor area for parking vehicles.

parking meter *n.* a coin-operated meter which receives fees for vehicles parked on the street.

parking ticket *n.* a notice of a fine etc. imposed for parking illegally.

Parkinson's disease *n.* (also **Parkinsonism**) a progressive disease of the nervous system which produces tremor, muscular rigidity, and slow, imprecise movements.

parkland *n.* **1** open grassland scattered with clumps of trees etc. **2** a piece of land set aside by the government for public recreation, wildlife conservation, etc.

parks officer *n. Cdn* = PARK WARDEN.

park warden *n.* (also **park ranger**) an official responsible for patrolling and maintaining a national, provincial, etc. park.

parkway *n.* a highway or main road with trees, grass, etc. planted alongside.

parlance *n.* a particular way of speaking. [*Say* PAR lince]

parlay ● *v.* **1** transform (an advantage etc.) into something greater. **2** use (money won on a bet) as a further stake. ● *n.* a bet made by parlaying. [*Say* par LAY *or* PAR lay]

parley ● *n.* (*pl.* **parleys**) an informal conference, under truce, with an enemy, for discussing the terms for armistice etc. ● *v.* (**parleys, parleyed, parleying**) hold a parley. [*Say* PARLY]

parliament *n.* **1** (usu. **Parliament**) the highest legislative body in certain countries, including Canada. **2** a legislative body of a province, state, etc. **3** the members of a parliament. **4** a period during which the members of a parliament are assembled. □ **parliamentary** *adj.*

parliamentarian *n.* **1** a member of a parliament, esp. one well-versed in its procedures. **2** *hist.* (**Parliamentarian**) a member or supporter of the party opposing Charles I in the English Civil War (1642–9).

parliamentary secretary *n.* an MP assisting a senior cabinet minister.

parliament building *n.* **1** a building in which a parliament meets. **2** a complex of buildings housing the parliament and offices of its members and staff.

Parliament Hill *n. Cdn* the hill in Ottawa on which the Parliament Buildings stand.

parlour *n.* (also **parlor**) **1** a sitting room. **2** a business providing specified goods or services. **3** (also **milking parlour**) a room or building equipped for milking cows.

Parmesan *n.* hard dry cheese used esp. in grated form. [*Say* PARMA zon *or* PARMA zan]

parmigiano *n.* Parmesan cheese, esp. grated. [*Say* parma JONNO]

parochial *adj.* **1** of a parish. **2** (of views etc.) local, narrow or restricted in scope. □ **parochialism** *n.* [*Say* puh ROKEY ul]

parochial school *n.* a school established and run by a religious body.

parody ● *n.* (*pl.* **parodies**) **1** an imitation of the style of a particular writer, artist, genre, etc. with deliberate exaggeration for comic effect. **2** a thing done so badly that it seems to be an intentional mockery of what it should be. ● *v.* (**parodies, parodied, parodying**) **1** produce a humorously exaggerated imitation of. **2** mimic humorously. □ **parodic** *adj.* **parodically** *adv.* **parodist** *n.* [*Say* PERRA dee, puh ROD ick]

parole ● *n.* the temporary or permanent release of a prisoner before the end of a sentence, on the promise of good behaviour. ● *v.* (**paroles, paroled,**

paroling) put (a prisoner) on parole. □ **parolee** n. [Say puh ROLE]

paroxysm n. **1** a sudden attack or outburst (of rage, laughter, etc.). **2** a sudden attack or recurrence of disease etc. [Say PAIR uck sism]

parquet n. a flooring of short strips or blocks of wood arranged in a pattern. [Say par KAY or PAR kay]

parr n. a young salmon between the stages of fry and smolt.

parrot ● n. a vividly coloured esp. tropical bird with a short down-curved bill, some kinds of which can mimic the human voice. ● v. (**parrots, parroted, parroting**) repeat mindlessly or mechanically.

parrotfish n. (pl. **parrotfish** or **parrotfishes**) a brightly coloured fish with a mouth like a parrot's hooked bill.

parry ● v. (**parries, parried, parrying**) **1** ward off (a weapon or attack). **2** deal skilfully with (a question etc.). ● n. (pl. **parries**) an act of parrying.

parse v. (**parses, parsed, parsing**) **1** analyze (a word) grammatically. **2** resolve (a sentence) into its component parts and describe them grammatically. □ **parser** n. [Say PARCE]

Parsi n. (pl. **Parsis**) (also **Parsee**, pl. **Parsees**) an adherent of Zoroastrianism, esp. in India. [Say par SEE]

parsimony n. extreme unwillingness to use money or other resources. □ **parsimonious** adj. [Say PARSA moe nee, parsa MOE nee us]

parsley n. a biennial herb with flavourful leaves, used for seasoning and garnishing food.

parsnip n. a large, tapering, pale-yellow root vegetable.

parson n. **1** any (esp. Protestant) member of the clergy. **2** an Anglican parish priest.

parsonage n. a church house provided for a minister. [Say PAR s'n idge]

part ● n. **1** a piece or segment which is combined with others to make up a whole. **2** some but not all of something. **3** a specified fraction of a whole. **4** a measure allowing comparison between the amounts of different ingredients used in a mixture. **5** a role played by an actor or actress. **6** a person's contribution to an action or situation. **7** a melody etc. assigned to a particular voice or instrument. ● v. **1** move apart or divide to leave a central space. **2** leave or cause to leave someone's company. **3** give up possession of. ● adv. partly. □ **for one's part** as far as one is concerned. **look the part** have an appearance suitable for a role etc. **on the part of** proceeding from. **part and parcel** an essential part. **take part** participate (in). **take the part of** support.

partake v. (**partakes**; past **partook**; past participle **partaken; partaking**) **1** participate in. **2** eat or drink. **3** have some (of a quality etc.).

parterre n. a level space in a garden occupied by flower beds arranged formally. [Say par TAIR]

parthenogenesis n. Biology reproduction from an ovum without fertilization. [Say parth uh no GENESIS]

partial adj. **1** forming only part. **2** biased, unfair. **3** having a liking for. □ **partially** adv.

partiality n. bias, favouritism. [Say parshy ALA tee]

participate v. (**participates, participated, participating**) share or take part. □ **participant** n. **participation** n. **participatory** adj.

participle n. a word formed from a verb, e.g. going, gone, and used in compound verb forms, e.g. is going, or as an adjective, e.g. washing machine. □ **participial** adj. [Say PARTA sipple, parta SIPPY ul]

particle n. **1** a very small bit of something. **2** Physics any of numerous subatomic constituents of the physical world that interact with each other, including electrons and photons. **3** the least possible amount. **4** a minor part of speech, esp. a short word that does not change its form.

particle accelerator n. an apparatus for accelerating subatomic particles.

particleboard n. a rigid sheet made from compressed wood chips, sawdust, and resin.

particle physics n. the branch of physics concerned with subatomic particles.

parti-coloured adj. of several colours.

particular ● adj. **1** relating to one thing or person as distinct from others. **2** more than is usual. **3** fastidious. ● n. **1** a detail. **2** (in pl.) points of information. □ **in particular** especially.

particularism n. **1** exclusive devotion to one party, sect, etc. **2** the theological doctrine that only some people are redeemed. □ **particularist** n. & adj. **particularistic** adj.

particularity n. (pl. **particularities**) **1** the quality of being individual. **2** minuteness of detail in a description. **3** a small detail.

particularize v. (**particularizes, particularized, particularizing**) treat individually or in detail.

particularly adv. **1** especially, very. **2** specifically.

particulate ● adj. in the form of separate particles. ● n. matter in this form. [Say par TICK you lit or par TICK you late]

parting ● n. **1** a leave-taking or departure. **2** a division. **3** a point at which things part. ● adj. done or said etc. as one is leaving.

parting shot n. a remark etc. reserved for the moment of departure.

Parti Québécois n. Cdn a political party in Quebec, dedicated to achieving Quebec sovereignty. Abbreviation: **PQ**.

partisan ● n. **1** an esp. zealous supporter of a party, person, or cause. **2** a guerrilla. ● adj. **1** of partisans. **2** biased. □ **partisanship** n. [Say PAR ti zan or PAR ti zun]

partition ● n. **1** division into parts. **2** a structure dividing a space into two parts. ● v. **1** divide into parts. **2** separate with a partition. □ **partitioned** adj.

partly adv. to some extent; not completely.

partner ● n. **1** a person etc. who takes part with another or others in some activity or business. **2** a colleague or associate. **3** a dancer, figure skater, tennis player, etc. paired with another. **4 a** either member of a married couple or an established unmarried couple. **b** a person with whom one has sexual relations. ● v. **1** be or act as the partner of. **2** associate as partners. □ **partnering** n.

partnership n. **1** the state of being a partner or partners. **2** a joint business. **3** a pair or group of partners.

part of speech n. (pl. **parts of speech**) each of the categories to which words are assigned according to their grammatical functions (e.g. noun, verb).

partook past of PARTAKE.

partridge n. (pl. **partridge** or **partridges**) a short-tailed game bird with mainly brown plumage.

part-time ● adj. employed or happening less than full-time. ● adv. on a part-time basis. □ **part-timer** n.

partway adv. **1** part of the way. **2** partly.

party ● n. (pl. **parties**) **1** a social gathering, usu. of invited guests. **2** a group of people taking part in an activity or trip. **3** a political group organized to campaign for election. **4** a person or people forming one side in an agreement or dispute. **5** Law an accessory. **6** informal a person. ● v. (**parties, partied, partying**) **1** go to

parties frequently. **2** revel, carouse. □ **partier** (also **partyer**) n. **partying** n.

party animal n. informal a person who parties.

partygoer n. a person who attends a party or parties.

party line n. **1** the official policies adopted by a political party. **2** an official position or interpretation of events etc. **3** a telephone line shared by two or more subscribers.

party piece n. **1** a musical or other performance intended to be performed on a special occasion. **2** a trick, feat, or other entertaining speciality for which one is renowned.

party politics pl. n. political activity carried out through or for political parties.

party-pooper n. (also **party-poop**) slang a person who spoils other people's enjoyment.

parvenu n. (pl. **parvenus**) **1** a person of obscure origin who has gained wealth or position. **2** an upstart. [Say PARVA noo]

parvovirus n. (pl. **parvoviruses**) a virus that causes contagious disease in dogs. [Say PARVO virus]

pascal n. the SI unit of pressure, equal to one newton per square metre. [Say PASS cull]

paschal adj. **1** of or relating to Easter. **2** of or relating to Passover. [Say PASS cull]

pas de deux n. (pl. **pas de deux**) a theatrical dance for two persons. [Say paw duh DUH for the singular, paw duh DUH or paw duh DUHS for the plural]

pasha n. (pl. **pashas**) **1** hist. the title of a Turkish officer of high rank. **2** informal a powerful or wealthy person. [Say PASH uh]

Pashto n. the language of the Pathans, the official language of Afghanistan. □ **Pashto** adj. [Say PASH toe]

paska n. (pl. **paskas**) Cdn a rich, usu. decorated, egg bread, traditional at Easter among people of Ukrainian origin. [Say PASS kuh]

pasque flower n. a spring-flowering anemone with purple flowers. [Say PASK]

pass[1] ● v. (**passes, passed, passing**) **1** move or go onward, past, through, or across. **2** change from one state or condition to another. **3** transfer (something) to someone. **4** kick, hit, or throw (the puck or ball) to a teammate. **5** (of time) go by. **6** occupy or spend (time). **7** be done or said. **8** come to an end. **9** be successful in (a test or course). **10** declare to be satisfactory. **11** approve (a proposal or law) by voting. **12** utter (remarks) or pronounce (a judgment). **13** forgo one's turn. ● *n.* (*pl.* **passes**) **1** an act of passing. **2** a success in an examination. **3** an official document authorizing the holder to go somewhere or do something. **4** *informal* a sexual advance. **5** a particular state of affairs. □ **in passing 1** by the way. **2** in the course of conversation etc. **pass away** *euphemism* die. **pass by 1** go past. **2** disregard, omit. **pass off** misrepresent (something) as something else. **pass out 1** become unconscious. **2** distribute. **pass over** ignore the claims of (a person) to advancement. **pass up** *informal* refuse or neglect (an opportunity etc.). □ **passer** *n.*

pass² *n.* (*pl.* **passes**) **1** a narrow passage through mountains. **2** a navigable channel. **3** a road or route. □ **head** (or **cut**) **off at the pass** deter or prevent early on.

passable *adj.* **1** barely satisfactory; just adequate. **2** (of a road etc.) that can be passed. □ **passably** *adv.*

passage *n.* **1** the process, action, or means of passing. **2 a** a sea route around a large land mass. **b** a narrow strait between islands etc. **3** the right to pass through. **4 a** the right of conveyance as a passenger. **b** a journey, esp. by sea. **5** a short section from a book, musical work, etc. **6** = PASSAGEWAY. **7** a transition from one state to another.

passageway *n.* a narrow way for passing along; a corridor.

Passamaquoddy *n.* (*pl.* **Passamaquoddy**) **1** a member of a N American Aboriginal people inhabiting parts of southeastern Maine and (formerly) southwestern New Brunswick. **2** the Algonquian language of this people. [*Say* passa muh QUODDY]

passbook *n.* a small book issued by a financial institution to an account holder recording sums deposited and withdrawn.

passé *adj.* **1** no longer fashionable or topical. **2** past one's prime. [*Say* pass AY]

passenger *n.* a traveller in or on a public or private conveyance (other than the driver, pilot, crew, etc.).

passenger pigeon *n.* a wild pigeon of N America, hunted to extinction by 1914.

passerby *n.* (*pl.* **passersby**) a person who goes past, esp. by chance.

passerine ● *n.* any one of a large order of birds that have feet adapted for perching. ● *adj.* of or relating to this order. [*Say* PASS im]

passim *adv.* (of references) to be found at various places throughout the text. [*Say* PASS im]

passing ● *adj.* **1** transient, fleeting. **2** incidental. ● *n.* the death of a person.

passion *n.* **1** strong barely controllable emotion. **2** intense sexual love. **3** strong enthusiasm. **4** a person or thing arousing passion. **5** (**the Passion**) the suffering of Christ during his last days. □ **passionless** *adj.*

passionate *adj.* **1** dominated by or easily moved to strong feeling. **2** showing or caused by passion. □ **passionately** *adv.*

passion flower *n.* a climbing plant of warm regions, which bears distinctive flowers.

passion fruit *n.* the edible purple fruit of some species of passion flower.

passive ● *adj.* **1** suffering action; acted upon. **2** offering no opposition; submissive. **3** not active; inert. **4** *Grammar* designating the voice in which the subject undergoes the action of the verb. ● *n.* the passive voice or form of a verb. □ **passively** *adv.* **passivity** *n.*

passive smoking *n.* the involuntary inhaling of smoke from others' cigarettes etc. □ **passive smoke** *n.*

Passover *n.* the Jewish spring festival commemorating the liberation of the Israelites from slavery in Egypt.

passport *n.* **1** a document issued by a government certifying the holder's identity and citizenship, and entitling the holder to travel abroad. **2** a thing that ensures admission or attainment.

pass-through ● *n.* an opening in a wall between two rooms, through which things etc. are passed. ● *adj.* (of costs) chargeable to the customer.

password *n.* a secret word or phrase used to enter a place or use a computer, network, etc.

past ● *adj.* **1** gone by in time and no longer existing. **2** recently completed or gone by. **3** relating to a former time. **4** *Grammar* expressing a past action or state. ● *n.* **1** (**the past**) a past time or the events in it. **2** a person's past life or career. **3** a past tense or form. ● *prep.* **1** beyond in time or place. **2** beyond the range, duration, or compass of. ● *adv.* so as to pass by. □ **past it** *informal* old and useless.

pasta *n.* (*pl.* **pastas**) **1** a type of dough extruded or stamped into various shapes for cooking. **2** a dish made from this.

paste ● *n.* **1** a moist thick mixture, esp. of powder and liquid. **2** an adhesive. **3** any soft, moist substance or preparation. **4** a hard glass-like composition used in making imitation gems. ● *v.* (**pastes**, **pasted**, **pasting**) **1** fasten or coat with paste. **2** *Computing* insert or reproduce (text) at a new location in a document etc. **3** *slang* beat or thrash. □ **pasting** *n.*

pasteboard *n.* a sheet of stiff material made by pasting together sheets of paper.

pastel ● *n.* **1** a crayon consisting of powdered pigments bound with a gum solution. **2 a** the art or technique of drawing with pastels. **b** a work of art in pastel. **3** a light shade of a colour. ● *adj.* of a light shade or colour.

pastern *n.* the part of a horse's foot between the fetlock and the hoof. [*Say* PASS turn]

pasteurize *v.* (**pasteurizes, pasteurized, pasteurizing**) subject (milk, wine, etc.) to the process of partial sterilization by heating or irradiation. □ **pasteurization** *n.* [*Say* PASS chur ize]

pastiche ● *n.* **1** a medley, esp. in art or music, made up from or imitating various sources. **2** a literary or other work composed in the style of another. ● *v.* (**pastiches, pastiched, pastiching**) copy or imitate the style of. [*Say* pass TEESH]

pastille *n.* a small candy or lozenge. [*Say* pass TEAL]

pastime *n.* a recreational activity or hobby.

pastor *n.* (also **Pastor**) a minister in charge of a church or a congregation.

pastoral ● *adj.* **1** having to do with the keeping or grazing of sheep or cattle. **2** having to do with country life. **3** (of art) portraying country life, usu. in an idealized form. **4** having to do with a pastor or the spiritual care of a congregation. ● *n.* a pastoral poem, play, etc. □ **pastoralism** *n.* **pastoralist** *n.* [*Say* PASS tur ul, PASS tur ul ist]

past perfect *n.* = PLUPERFECT.

pastrami *n.* seasoned smoked beef brisket, usu. cut in thin slices. [*Say* pus TROMMY]

pastry *n.* (*pl.* **pastries**) **1** a dough of flour, fat, and water baked and used in pies etc. **2** food made wholly or partly of this. **3** a sweet bread or cake.

pasture ● *n.* **1** (also **pasture land**) an area of land covered with grass etc. suitable for grazing animals. **2** grass and other plants for animals. ● *v.* (**pastures, pastured, pasturing**) graze in a pasture. □ **out to pasture 1** out to graze. **2** *informal* in retirement or out of service.

pasty[1] *n.* (*pl.* **pasties**) esp. *Brit.* a savoury turnover. [*Say* PAST ee]

pasty[2] *adj.* (**pastier, pastiest**) **1** unhealthily pale. **2** like paste. □ **pastiness** *n.* [*Say* PASTE ee]

PA system *n.* = PUBLIC ADDRESS SYSTEM.

pat[1] ● *v.* (**pats, patted, patting**) tap gently with the hand or a flat surface. ● *n.*

1 a light tap. **2** the sound made by this. **3** a small mass (esp. of butter) formed by patting.

pat[2] *adj.* too quick, easy, or simple. □ **have down pat** know perfectly. **stand pat** stick stubbornly to one's opinion or decision. □ **patly** *adv.*

patch ● *n.* (*pl.* **patches**) **1** a piece of material used to mend or reinforce clothing etc. **2** a pad or shield worn over an eye or eye socket. **3** a dressing etc. put over a wound. **4** a small area, esp. one that contrasts with a surrounding area. **5** a small scrap or remnant. **6** an adhesive patch worn on the skin, which releases a drug into the bloodstream. **7** *informal* a period of time. **8** *Computing* a small piece of code inserted to correct or enhance a program. ● *v.* (**patches, patched, patching**) **1 a** mend with a patch or patches. **b** repair the damage to. **2** settle (differences etc.) after a quarrel. **3** connect by a temporary electrical, radio, etc. connection. □ **patcher** *n.*

patchouli *n.* a strongly scented East Indian plant of the mint family yielding an aromatic oil. [*Say* puh CHOOLY]

patchwork ● *n.* **1** needlework in which small pieces of cloth in different designs are sewn together to form a quilt etc. **2** a thing composed of different pieces or elements. ● *adj.* composed of or resembling patchwork (pieces).

patchy *adj.* (**patchier, patchiest**) **1** uneven in quality. **2** having or existing in patches. □ **patchily** *adv.* **patchiness** *n.*

pate *n. jocular* the head.

pâté *n.* a rich paste of finely ground or puréed meat or fish etc. [*Say* pat AY or PAT ay]

patella *n.* (*pl.* **patellas** or **patellae**) the kneecap. □ **patellar** *adj.* [*Say* puh TELLA *for the singular,* puh TELLAS *or* puh TELLY *for the plural*]

patent ● *n.* **1** a government licence conferring esp. the sole right to make, use, or sell some invention. **2** an invention or process protected by this. ● *adj.* **1** obvious, plain. **2** made and marketed under a patent. ● *v.* obtain a patent for. □ **patentable** *adj.* **patently** *adv.* [*Say* PAT int *or* PATE int, PATE int lee *or* PAT int lee]

patent leather *n.* leather with a glossy varnished surface.

paternal *adj.* **1** fatherly. **2** related through the father. **3** inherited from the male parent.

paternalism *n.* the system of protecting the people one has control over, but also of restricting their freedom or responsibilities. □ **paternalist** adj. & n. **paternalistic** adj.

paternity n. **1** fatherhood. **2** one's paternal origin.

paternity leave n. a leave of absence taken by a father to care for a baby.

path n. (pl. **paths**) **1 a** a track laid down for walking or made by continual treading. **b** a track laid for a special purpose. **2** the line along which a person or thing moves. **3** a course of action or conduct.

Pathan n. a member of a Pashto-speaking people inhabiting northwestern Pakistan and southeastern Afghanistan. [Say puh TAN]

path-breaking adj. innovative; groundbreaking.

pathetic adj. **1** arousing pity. **2** informal miserably inadequate. □ **pathetically** adv.

pathetic fallacy n. a literary device involving metaphor, in which natural phenomena that cannot feel as humans do are described as if they could.

pathfinder n. **1** a person who explores new territory etc. **2** an aircraft or its pilot sent ahead to locate and mark the target area for bombing. **3** (**Pathfinder**) Cdn a member of the branch of the Girl Guides for 12- to 15-year-olds.

pathogen n. a micro-organism that can cause disease. □ **pathogenic** adj. [Say PATH uh jin, path uh JEN ick]

pathogenesis n. the manner of development of a disease. [Say path uh GENESIS]

pathological adj. (also **pathologic**) **1** of pathology. **2** of or caused by a disease. **3** informal **a** extreme and unreasonable. **b** compulsive. □ **pathologically** adv. [Say path uh LOGICAL]

pathology n. (pl. **pathologies**) **1** the science of the causes and effects of bodily diseases. **2** the symptoms or typical behaviour of a disease. **3** any abnormal or unhealthy condition. □ **pathologist** n. [Say puh THOLLA jee]

pathos n. a quality in speech, writing, etc. that excites pity or sadness. [Say PAY thoss]

pathway n. a path or course.

patience n. the capacity to accept delay, provocation, or hardship calmly without anger.

patient ● adj. having or showing patience. ● n. a person receiving medical treatment. □ **patiently** adv.

patina n. (pl. **patinas**) **1** a film, usu. green, formed on the surface of old bronze. **2** a similar film on other surfaces. **3** a gloss produced by age on woodwork etc. [Say puh TEENA or PAT uh nuh]

patio n. (pl. **patios**) a paved area adjoining a house.

patois n. (pl. **patois**) a non-standard local dialect. [Say pat WAH for the singular, pat WAHS for the plural]

patriarch n. **1** the male head of a family or tribe. **2** Bible **a** each of the twelve sons of Jacob, from whom the tribes of Israel were descended. **b** Abraham, Isaac, and Jacob, and their forefathers. **3** the title of a chief or high-ranking bishop. **4 a** a venerable old man. **b** the oldest member of a group. [Say PAY tree ark]

patriarchal adj. of a patriarch or patriarchy. [Say pay tree ARK ul]

patriarchy n. (pl. **patriarchies**) **1** a system of society, government, etc., ruled by a man and with descent through the male line. **2** the attitudes etc. of a society seen as ensuring male dominance. [Say PAY tree arky]

patriate v. (**patriates**, **patriated**, **patriating**) Cdn bring (legislation) under the authority of the autonomous country to which it applies. □ **patriation** n. [Say PAY tree ate]

patrician ● n. an aristocrat. ● adj. **1** noble, aristocratic. **2** refined, well-bred. [Say puh TRISH'n]

Patricias pl. n. Cdn an informal name for the Princess Patricia's Canadian Light Infantry regiment.

patrimony n. (pl. **patrimonies**) **1** a heritage. **2** property inherited from one's father or ancestor. [Say PATRA moe nee]

patriot n. a person who is ardently devoted to his or her country. □ **patriotic** adj. **patriotism** n. [Say PAY tree it, pay tree OT ick]

Patriote n. Cdn hist. a supporter of Louis-Joseph Papineau (1786–1871) in the Rebellion of Lower Canada in 1837. [Say pat ree OT]

patristic adj. of the early Christian theologians or their writings. [Say puh TRISS tick]

patrol ● n. **1** the act of going around an area in order to protect or supervise it. **2** a person or group sent out on patrol. **3** a detachment of troops sent out to reconnoitre. **4** a unit of six to eight Scouts or Guides. ● v. (**patrols**, **patrolled**, **patrolling**) **1** carry out a patrol of. **2** act as a patrol. □ **patroller** n.

patrol car n. a police car used in patrolling.

patrolman n. (pl. **patrolmen**) a police officer on a patrol.

patron n. **1** a person who gives financial or other support to a person, cause, organization, etc. **2** a usu. regular customer of a store etc. [Say PAY trin]

patronage n. **1** the support given by a patron. **2 a** the control of appointments to office, privileges, etc. **b** the appointing of supporters etc. to office etc. **3** a customer's support for a store etc. [Say PAY truh nidge or PATTRA nidge]

patronize v. (**patronizes, patronized, patronizing**) **1** treat a person in a way that suggests they are inferior. **2** act as a patron towards. **3** frequent as a customer. □ **patronizing** adj. **patronizingly** adv. [Say PAY truh nize or PATTRA nize]

patron saint n. a protecting or guiding saint of a person or place.

patronymic n. a name derived from the name of a father or ancestor. [Say pattra NIM ick]

patsy n. (pl. **patsies**) slang a person who is deceived, tricked, etc.

patter ● v. **1** make a rapid succession of taps. **2** run with quick short steps. ● n. **1** a rapid succession of taps etc. **2** rapid speech.

pattern ● n. **1** a repeated decorative design. **2** an esp. regular form, order, or arrangement. **3** a model or design from which copies can be made. **4** an example of excellence. ● v. **1** model on a design etc. **2** decorate with a pattern. □ **patterning** n. **patternless** adj.

patty n. (also **pattie**) (pl. **patties**) **1** a substance formed into a disc-like shape, esp. meat etc. **2** a little pie or pastry.

patty cake n. a child's game in which partners clap their own and each other's hands.

paucity n. smallness of number or quantity. [Say POSSA tee]

paunch n. (pl. **paunches**) the stomach, esp. when protruding. □ **paunchy** adj.

pauper n. a very poor person. □ **pauperization** n. **pauperize** v. (**pauperizes, pauperized, pauperizing**)

pause ● n. **1** a temporary stop or break. **2** (also **pause button**) a control allowing the interruption of a video, CD, etc. ● v. (**pauses, paused, pausing**) **1** make a pause; wait. **2** linger over. □ **give pause to** cause to hesitate.

pave v. (**paves, paved, paving**) cover (a street etc.) with asphalt, concrete, etc. □ **pave the way for** prepare a situation conducive to. □ **paver** n. **paving** n.

pavement n. **1** a paved area or surface. **2** the material used to pave a surface.

pavilion n. **1** a decorative building in a garden. **2** a usu. large tent at a show, fair, etc. **3** a building at a fair or exhibition housing exhibits. **4** a building in a park providing services such as refreshments, washrooms, change rooms, skate rental, etc. [Say puh VILL yin]

Pavlovian adj. of the nature of a reaction or response made unthinkingly or under the influence of others, as described by the Russian physiologist I. P. Pavlov (1849–1936). [Say pav LOE vee in]

paw ● n. **1** a foot of an animal having claws or nails. **2** informal a person's hand. ● v. **1** strike or scrape with a paw, hoof, or foot. **2** informal fondle awkwardly or indecently.

pawn[1] n. **1** Chess a piece of the lowest value. **2** a person used by others for their own purposes.

pawn[2] ● v. deposit an object, esp. with a pawnbroker, as security for money lent. ● n. an object left as security for money etc. lent. □ **pawn off** pass off.

pawnbroker n. a person who lends money at interest on the security of personal property pawned.

pawnshop n. a pawnbroker's shop.

pawpaw n. **1** a N American tree with purple flowers and edible fruit. **2** a papaya.

pay ● v. (**pays, paid, paying**) **1** give money due for work, goods, or a debt. **2** be profitable or advantageous. **3** suffer or account for a fault etc. **4 a** give (attention, respect, a compliment, etc.) to. **b** make (a visit, call, etc.). ● n. wages; payment. ● adj. designating a service etc. which requires payment. □ **pay back 1** return (money). **2** take revenge on. **3** recompense. **pay down** reduce (debt) by repayment. **pay one's dues 1** fulfill one's obligations. **2** undergo hardship to succeed. **pay one's (own) way** cover costs. **pay one's last respects** show respect towards a dead person by attending the funeral etc. **pay off 1** informal yield good results. **2** pay (a debt) in full. **pay out** spend. **pay the piper** pay the cost of an activity or undertaking. **pay one's respects** make a polite visit. **pay through the nose** informal pay much more than a fair price. **put paid to** informal **1** eliminate. **2** terminate; negate. □ **payee** n.

payable ● adj. **1** that must be paid. **2** that may be paid. ● n. (in pl.) debts owed by a business.

pay-as-you-go n. a system or the practice of paying debts etc. as they arise.

payback n. **1** a financial return. **2** the profit from an investment etc. **3** an act of revenge or retaliation.

paycheque n. an esp. regular payment given to an employee.

payday n. **1** a day on which payment, esp. of wages, is collected. **2** *informal* the winning or gaining of a large sum.

pay dirt n. *Mining* ground worth working for ore. □ **hit** (or **strike**) **pay dirt** find a source of profit or reward.

payer n. a person who pays for something.

payload n. **1** the part of a transport vehicle's load from which revenue is derived. **2 a** the explosive warhead carried by an aircraft or rocket. **b** the instruments etc. carried by a spaceship.

paymaster n. an official who pays troops, workers, etc.

payment n. **1** the action or process of paying or of being paid. **2** an amount paid. **3** recompense.

payoff n. *informal* **1** an act of payment. **2** a deserved benefit, outcome, etc. **3** a bribe.

payola n. (*pl.* **payolas**) bribery for unofficial promotion of a product etc. in the media. [*Say* pay OH luh]

payout n. a large payment of money.

pay-per-view n. a television service requiring viewers to pay a fee to watch a specific broadcast.

pay phone n. a telephone operated by the insertion of coins, a credit card, etc.

payroll n. **1** a list of employees receiving regular pay. **2** the personnel costs of a company etc.

pay stub n. (also **pay slip**, **pay statement**) a note given to an employee when paid detailing the amount of pay and deductions for tax etc.

pay-TV n. (also **pay television**) any television service requiring payment from viewers.

PC *abbr.* **1** (*pl.* **PCs**) PERSONAL COMPUTER. **2** *Cdn* Progressive Conservative. **3** politically correct. **4** police constable. **5** privy councillor.

PCB n. (*pl.* **PCBs**) polychlorinated biphenyl, a toxic compound formed as industrial waste.

PCP *abbr.* phencyclidine.

PDA *abbr.* PERSONAL DIGITAL ASSISTANT.

PD day n. *Cdn* professional development day.

PDF *abbr.* portable document format, a file format which allows documents including text, graphics, and images, to be displayed on a computer independent of the application software, hardware or operating system used to create the document.

PDQ *abbr. informal* pretty damn quick.

PDT *abbr.* Pacific Daylight Time.

PE *abbr.* **1** physical education. **2** (in official postal use) Prince Edward Island.

pea n. **1** a round green seed in a pod that is widely eaten as a vegetable. **2** a hardy climbing plant which produces these.

pea brain n. *informal* a stupid or dim-witted person. □ **pea-brained** *adj.*

peace n. **1 a** quiet. **b** mental calm. **2 a** freedom from or the cessation of war. **b** (esp. **Peace**) a peace treaty between countries at war. **3 a** freedom from civil disorder. **b** freedom from quarrels or dissension. □ **at peace 1** in a state of friendliness. **2** serene. **3** *euphemism* dead. **hold one's peace** keep silence. **keep the peace** prevent strife. **make peace** reconcile.

peaceable *adj.* **1** not warlike. **2** free from conflict; peaceful. □ **peaceably** *adv.*

peace bond n. a written undertaking to a court of law to keep the peace.

peace dividend n. public money which becomes available when spending on defence is reduced.

peaceful *adj.* **1** tranquil. **2** not violating peace. **3** pertaining to a state of peace. □ **peacefully** *adv.* **peacefulness** n.

peacekeeping n. the active maintenance of a truce between nations or communities. □ **peacekeeper** n.

peacemaker n. someone who brings about peace. □ **peacemaking** n. & *adj.*

peace officer n. a civil officer appointed to preserve the public peace.

peace pipe n. a N American Aboriginal tobacco pipe, smoked esp. as a sign of peace.

peace sign n. **1** a sign of peace made by holding up the hand with the palm outwards and the first two fingers forming a V. **2** a symbol consisting of a circle divided into thirds by lines.

peacetime n. a period without war.

peach[1] ● n. (*pl.* **peaches**) **1 a** a round juicy fruit with downy yellow and red skin. **b** (also **peach tree**) the tree that bears this fruit. **2** an orange-pink colour. **3** *informal* an impressive or attractive person or thing. ● *adj.* of an orange-pink colour.

peach[2] v. (**peaches**, **peached**, **peaching**) *informal* turn informer; inform.

peaches and cream n. **1** an excellent or desirable situation. **2** a fair complexion. **3** a variety of corn.

peach fuzz n. *informal* the down on the chin of an adolescent boy.

peachy *adj.* (**peachier**, **peachiest**) **1** like a peach in colour or flavour. **2** (also **peachy-keen**) *informal* attractive, outstanding.

peacock *n.* a male peafowl with very long tail feathers (with eye-like markings) that can be fanned out in display.

peafowl *n.* (*pl.* **peafowl**) a large crested pheasant.

pea green *n. & adj.* a bright green colour.

peahen *n.* a female peafowl.

peak ● *n.* **1** a projecting usu. pointed part. **2 a** the highest point in a curve. **b** the time of greatest success. ● *v.* reach the highest value, quality, etc. ● *adj.* maximum.

peaked[1] *adj.* having a peak. [*Say* PEEKT]

peaked[2] *adj.* = PEAKY. [*Say* PEAK id]

peaky *adj.* (**peakier, peakiest**) **1** sickly. **2** white-faced.

peal ● *n.* **1 a** the loud ringing of a bell or bells. **b** a set of bells. **2** a loud repeated sound, esp. of thunder, laughter, etc. ● *v.* **1** sound forth in a peal. **2** ring in peals.

peameal bacon *n. Cdn* back bacon rolled in fine cornmeal.

peanut *n.* **1** the oval edible seed of a plant native to S America. **2** (in *pl.*) *informal* a paltry amount, esp. of money. □ **peanutty** *adj.*

peanut butter *n.* a paste of ground roasted peanuts.

peanut gallery *n. slang* **1** the uppermost balcony in a theatre. **2** a group of hecklers.

pear *n.* **1** a yellowish or brownish-green fleshy fruit, tapering towards the stalk. **2** a tree bearing this fruit.

pearl *n.* **1** a usu. white hard ball formed within the shell of a pearl oyster etc., highly prized as a gem. **2** a precious thing. **3** anything resembling a pearl. **4** an iridescent off-white colour. □ **pearls before swine** something valuable offered to a person unable to appreciate it. □ **pearly** *adj.*

pearl onion *n.* a very small onion.

pearl oyster *n.* a tropical marine bivalve mollusc that is an important source of pearls.

Pearly Gates *pl. n. informal* the gates of Heaven.

pearly whites *pl. n. informal* the teeth.

Peary caribou *n.* a small caribou of the Arctic islands of Canada. [*Say* PEERY]

peasant ● *n.* **1** a farm labourer or small farmer dependent on subsistence farming. **2** *derogatory* an ignorant or unsophisticated person. ● *adj.* **1** of peasants. **2** (of a style of dress etc.) inspired by Western folk traditions. □ **peasantry** *n.* **peasanty** *adj.* [*Say* PEZZ'nt, PEZZ'n tree]

pea soup *n.* **1** a thick soup made from dried split peas. **2** (also **pea-souper**) *informal* a thick yellowish fog.

peat *n.* vegetable matter partly decomposed in wet acid conditions, used for fuel, in gardening, etc. □ **peaty** *adj.*

peat moss *n.* an absorbent moss that grows on boggy ground, dried and used in gardening.

peavey *n.* (also **peavy**) (*pl.* **peaveys, peavies**) a logging implement consisting of a long pole ending in a metal spike and hinged hook. [*Say* PEE vee]

pebble ● *n.* **1** a small smooth stone worn by the action of water. **2** a dimpled texture. ● *v.* (**pebbles, pebbled, pebbling**) give a dimpled texture to. □ **pebbled** *adj.* **pebbly** *adj.*

pecan *n.* an edible nut from a hickory tree of the southern US. [*Say* PEE can *or* pee CAN]

peccadillo *n.* (*pl.* **peccadilloes** or **peccadillos**) a trifling offence. [*Say* pecka DILLO]

peccary *n.* (*pl.* **peccaries**) a dark-furred pig-like mammal inhabiting Central and South America. [*Say* PECKA ree]

peck[1] ● *v.* **1** strike or bite with a beak or pointed instrument. **2** kiss hastily or perfunctorily. **3 a** make (a hole) by pecking. **b** remove by pecking. **4** type at a typewriter etc. ● *n.* **1** an act of pecking. **2** a hasty or perfunctory kiss. □ **peck at** eat listlessly.

peck[2] *n.* a measure of capacity for dry goods, equal to a quarter of a bushel. □ **a peck of** a large number or amount of.

pecking order *n.* a hierarchy based on rank or status.

peckish *adj. informal* moderately hungry.

pecorino *n.* (*pl.* **pecorinos**) an Italian cheese made from ewes' milk. [*Say* pecka REENO]

pectin *n.* a substance that forms in ripe fruit and causes jam or jelly to set.

pectoral ● *adj.* having to do with the chest. ● *n.* **1** a pectoral muscle. **2** a pectoral fin. [*Say* PECK tuh rul]

peculiar *adj.* **1** strange. **2 a** belonging exclusively. **b** belonging to the individual. **3** particular. □ **peculiarly** *adv.*

peculiarity *n.* (*pl.* **peculiarities**) **1** an odd or unusual feature or habit. **2** a distinguishing thing. **3** the state of being peculiar. [*Say* puh cue lee ERRA tee]

pecuniary *adj.* having to do with money. [*Say* puh CUE nee airy]

pedagogue *n.* a teacher. [*Say* PEDDA gog]

pedagogy *n.* (*pl.* **pedagogies**) the science of teaching. □ **pedagogic** *adj.* **pedagogical** *adj.* [*Say* PEDDA godge ee, pedda GODGE ick]

pedal ● *n.* **1** either of a pair of foot-operated levers for powering a bicycle etc.

2 any foot-operated control in a motor vehicle. **3** a bar on a musical instrument, e.g. a piano, organ, or harp, that is operated by the foot. ● v. (**pedals, pedalled, pedalling**) operate a bicycle, organ, etc. by using the pedals. □ **pedal to the metal** informal **1** full speed. **2** with the gas pedal of a vehicle pressed to the floor.

pedant n. a person who is excessively concerned with minor details or with displaying academic learning. □ **pedantic** adj. **pedantically** adv. **pedantry** n. (pl. **pedantries**) [Say PED'nt, puh DAN tick, PED'n tree]

peddle v. (**peddles, peddled, peddling**) **1** sell (goods), esp. by going from place to place. **2** advocate or promote (ideas etc.). **3** sell (drugs) illegally. □ **peddler** n.

pedestal n. **1** a base supporting a column, statue, etc. **2** either of the two supports at either end of the writing surface of a desk. **3** an upright, column-like support for a seat, machine, etc. □ **put** (or **set**) **on a pedestal** idolize.

pedestrian ● n. a person on foot rather than in a vehicle. ● adj. **1** (esp. of writing) dull. **2** having to do with walkers or walking.

pediatrics pl. n. the branch of medicine dealing with children and their diseases. □ **pediatric** adj. **pediatrician** n. [Say peedy AT ricks, peedy uh TRISH'n]

pedicure n. remedial or cosmetic treatment of the feet. □ **pedicured** adj. **pedicurist** n. [Say PED i cure]

pedigree n. **1** a recorded line of descent of a person or animal. **2** the history of a person or thing. **3** a genealogical table. □ **pedigreed** adj.

pediment n. **1** the triangular part crowning the front of a building in the classical style. **2** a similar feature surmounting a door etc. [Say PED i mint]

pedlar n. = PEDDLER. [Say PED ler]

pedophile n. a person who desires children sexually. □ **pedophilia** n. [Say PEDDA file or PEEDA file, pedda FILLY uh or peeda FILLY uh]

pee informal ● v. (**pees, peed, peeing**) **1** urinate. **2** wet by urinating. ● n. **1** an act of urination. **2** urine. □ **peed off** annoyed.

peek ● v. look quickly or furtively. ● n. a quick or furtive look.

peekaboo ● n. the game of hiding one's face and suddenly revealing it. ● interj. the utterance made when doing this.

peel ● v. **1** strip the skin etc. from. **2** (of a surface or object) have the outer layer flake off. **3** remove or separate from a surface or body. **4** (of a vehicle etc.) move quickly. ● n. **1** the outer covering of a fruit, vegetable,

etc. **2** the chemical removal of layers of skin on the face. □ **peeling** n.

peeler n. **1** a utensil for peeling fruit etc. **2** informal a stripper.

peen n. the wedge-shaped or curved end of a hammerhead.

peep[1] ● v. **1** look quickly and secretly. **2** come slowly into view; emerge. ● n. a furtive or peering glance.

peep[2] ● v. make a shrill feeble sound as of a young bird. ● n. **1** such a sound. **2** a slight sound or utterance.

pee-pee n. informal **1** urine. **2** the penis.

peeper[1] n. **1** a person who peeps. **2** informal an eye.

peeper[2] n. = SPRING PEEPER.

peephole n. a small hole to be looked through.

peeping Tom n. a person who secretly observes others.

peep show n. **1** a show of live nudes or an erotic film viewed from a coin-operated booth. **2** a series of small pictures viewed through a small opening of a box etc.

peer[1] v. look keenly or with difficulty.

peer[2] n. **1** a person who is equal in ability, standing, or value. **2** a person of high rank. □ **without peer** unequalled, unrivalled.

peerage n. **1** the nobility. **2** the rank of peer or peeress. **3** a book containing a list of peers etc. [Say PEER idge]

peeress n. (pl. **peeresses**) **1** the wife or widow of a peer. **2** a woman having the rank of a peer by creation or descent.

peer group n. a group of people of the same age, status, etc.

peerless adj. superior to all others of its kind.

peer pressure n. influence from one's peer group.

peer-to-peer adj. designating or relating to a network in which each computer can act as a server for the others, allowing shared access to files and peripherals without the need for a central server.

peeve informal ● n. a cause of annoyance. ● v. (**peeves, peeved, peeving**) annoy.

peevish adj. **1** easily annoyed. **2** characterized by petty vexation or spite. □ **peevishly** adv.

peewee ● n. **1** Cdn a level of amateur sport, usu. involving children aged 12–13. **2** a very small person or thing. ● adj. very small.

peg ● n. **1** a usu. cylindrical pin or bolt of wood, metal, etc., used for hanging things on, securing something in place, or marking a position. **2** Baseball informal a strong, low throw. ● v. (**pegs, pegged,**

pegging) 1 a fix (a thing) with a peg. **b** drive or insert a peg or pegs into. **2** *informal* identify, categorize. **3** *informal* throw (a ball) hard and low. **4** *informal* measure, mark, set. **5** fix (prices etc.) at a certain level. □ **a round** (or **square**) **peg in a square** (or **round**) **hole** a person in a situation unsuited to him or her. **take a person down a peg or two** humble a person. □ **pegged** *adj.*

peg leg *n. informal* an artificial leg, esp. a wooden leg.

PEI *abbr.* Prince Edward Island.

Peigan *n. (pl.* **Peigan** or **Peigans) 1** a member of an Aboriginal people, a part of the Blackfoot confederacy, living in southern Alberta and northwestern Montana. **2** the Algonquian language of this people. □ **Peigan** *adj.* [*Say* pee GAN]

pejorative ● *adj.* expressing contempt and criticism or disapproval. **● *n.*** a derogatory word or form. □ **pejoratively** *adv.* [*Say* puh JORRA tiv]

Peking duck *n.* a Chinese dish consisting of duck coated with honey and hung to dry, and then roasted.

Pekingese *n.* (also **Pekinese**) *(pl.* **Pekingese)** a lapdog of a short-legged breed with long hair and a snub nose. [*Say* pee king EEZ or pee kin EES]

Peking man *n.* the fossilized remains of an extinct human species of the middle Pleistocene period, found in 1926 in China.

pekoe *n.* a high-quality black tea. [*Say* PEE co]

pelagic *adj.* having to with the open sea. [*Say* puh LADGE ick]

pelican *n.* a large water bird with a large bill and a pouch in the throat for storing fish.

pellet *n.* **1** a small, hard, compressed mass of something. **2 a** a bullet or piece of small shot. **b** an imitation bullet for a toy gun.

pell-mell ● *adv.* **1** headlong, recklessly. **2** in disorder. **● *adj.*** confused, tumultuous.

pellucid *adj.* very clear. [*Say* puh LUCID]

pelt[1] *v.* **1 a** hurl small objects at. **b** strike repeatedly. **c** assail with insults etc. **2** (of rain etc.) fall quickly and in torrents.

pelt[2] *n.* the dressed or undressed skin of an animal with hair, wool, etc. still on.

pelvic inflammatory disease *n.* an inflammation of the female reproductive organs. Abbreviation: **PID**.

pelvis *n. (pl.* **pelvises** or **pelves) 1** the wide curved set of bones at the bottom of the torso that the legs and spine are connected to. **2** the part of the abdomen containing the pelvis. □ **pelvic** *adj.*

pemmican *n.* pounded, dried meat (usu.

buffalo) mixed to a paste with melted fat, berries, etc. [*Say* PEM ick in]

pen[1] **● *n.*** **1** an instrument for writing or drawing with ink. **2** the occupation of writing. **3** an instrument resembling a pen. **4** an electronic pen-like device used to enter commands or data into a computer. **● *v.*** **(pens, penned, penning) 1** write. **2** compose.

pen[2] **● *n.*** **1** a small enclosure for farm animals. **2** a place of confinement. **● *v.*** **(pens, penned, penning)** enclose or shut in a pen.

pen[3] *n. slang* a penitentiary.

penal *adj.* having to do with legal punishment or its infliction. [*Say* PEEN'll]

penal code *n.* a system of laws relating to crime and its punishment.

penalize *v.* **(penalizes, penalized, penalizing) 1** subject to a penalty etc. **2** put at a comparative disadvantage. [*Say* PEEN'll ize or PEN'll ize]

penalty *n. (pl.* **penalties) 1** a punishment for a breach of law, contract, etc. **2** a disadvantage, loss, etc. **3** a disadvantage imposed on a competitor for a breach of the rules etc.

penalty box *n.* an area reserved for players temporarily withdrawn from play as a penalty.

penalty kick *n. Soccer* a free kick at the goal, given after a foul in the area around the goal.

penalty killer *n. Hockey* a player who plays while the team's strength is reduced by a penalty. □ **penalty killing** *n.*

penalty shot *n. Hockey* a shot by an offensive player, allowed as a penalty for certain infractions.

penance *n.* **1** an act of self-punishment as reparation for guilt. **2 a** (in the Catholic and Orthodox Churches) a sacrament including confession of one's sins and forgiveness. **b** a punishment imposed esp. by a priest to make up for a sin. **3** an unpleasant task or situation. [*Say* PEN ince]

pen and ink ● *n.* **1** the instruments of writing or drawing. **2** writing. **3** a drawing made using pen and ink. **● *adj.*** **(pen-and-ink)** (esp. of a drawing) done in ink.

pence *n. Brit. pl.* of PENNY.

penchant *n.* a strong or habitual liking. [*Say* PEN ch'nt]

pencil ● *n.* **1** an instrument for writing or drawing, usu. consisting of a thin rod of graphite etc. enclosed in a cylinder. **2** a pencil-like applicator for cosmetics or medication. **● *v.*** **(pencils, pencilled, pencilling) 1** write, sketch, etc. with a pencil. **2** note down or arrange tentatively. □ **pencilled** *adj.*

pencil crayon *n. Cdn* a pencil with a coloured core.

pencil-thin *adj.* very thin or narrow.

pendant *n.* **1** a hanging jewel etc., esp. one attached to a necklace. **2** a light fixture etc. hanging from a ceiling. [*Say* PEN dint]

pending ● *adj.* **1** awaiting decision or settlement. **2** about to happen. ● *prep.* **1** until. **2** during.

pendulous *adj.* **1** tending to droop heavily. **2** hanging down and esp. swinging. [*Say* PEND you luss]

pendulum *n.* a weight suspended so as to swing freely, used to regulate the movement of a clock's works. [*Say* PEND you lum]

penetrate *v.* (**penetrates, penetrated, penetrating**) **1** find access into or through, esp. forcibly. **2** see into, find out, or discern. **3** see through (darkness, fog, etc.). **4** be understood or absorbed by the mind. **5** enter (a market) to establish a new brand, product, etc. **6** (of a male) put the penis into the vagina or anus of (a sexual partner). □ **penetrable** *adj.* **penetration** *n.* **penetrative** *adj.* **penetrator** *n.* [*Say* PENNA trate, PENNA truh bull]

penetrating *adj.* **1** that permeates or forces a way into or through something. **2** suggesting sensitivity or insight. **3 a** (of a voice etc.) easily heard through or above other sounds. **b** (of a smell) sharp, pungent.

penguin *n.* any black-and-white flightless seabird of the southern hemisphere.

penicillin *n.* an antibiotic used to prevent the growth of certain disease-causing bacteria. [*Say* penna SILL in]

penile *adj.* having to do with the penis. [*Say* PEE nile]

peninsula *n.* (*pl.* **peninsulas**) a piece of land almost surrounded by water or projecting far into a sea or lake etc. □ **peninsular** *adj.* [*Say* puh NIN sul uh *or* puh NIN syul uh]

penis *n.* (*pl.* **penises** *or* **penes**) the male genital organ which is used for sexual intercourse and urinating.

penitent ● *adj.* regretting and wishing to atone for sins etc. ● *n.* **1** a person who repents. **2** a person doing penance. □ **penitence** *n.* **penitential** *adj.* [*Say* PEN it int, penna TEN shul]

penitentiary *n.* (*pl.* **penitentiaries**) **1** *Cdn* a federal corrections institution for convicted offenders serving a sentence of two years or more. **2** *US* a prison for serious offenders. [*Say* penna TEN shuh ree]

penknife *n.* (*pl.* **penknives**) a small folding knife.

penmanship *n.* handwriting.

pen name *n.* a literary pseudonym.

pennant *n.* **1 a** a tapering flag, esp. flown on a ship. **b** such a flag identifying a team etc. **2** a flag symbolizing a league championship, esp. in baseball.

penne *n.* pasta in the form of short tubes. [*Say* PEN ay]

penniless *adj.* having no money.

Pennsylvania Dutch *n.* (also **Pennsylvania German**) **1** a dialect of High German spoken by German and Swiss immigrants to Pennsylvania in the 17th and 18th centuries, still spoken by some of their descendants, esp. the Amish. **2** (as *pl.*) these settlers or their descendants. □ **Pennsylvania Dutch** *adj.*

Pennsylvanian *n.* **1** a person from Pennsylvania. **2** (**the Pennsylvanian**) the upper Carboniferous period (320–286 million years ago), characterized by swamp forests and the appearance of reptiles. □ **Pennsylvanian** *adj.*

penny *n.* (*pl.* **pennies**) **1** a one-cent coin. **2** *Brit.* a coin equal to one-hundredth of a pound. **3** *Brit. hist.* a former coin and monetary unit equal to one-twelfth of a shilling. **4** a usu. small sum of money. □ **in for a penny, in for a pound** an exhortation to total commitment to an undertaking. **like a bad penny** continually returning when unwanted. **pennies from heaven** unexpected esp. financial benefits. **a penny for your thoughts** a request to a person to confide in the speaker. **a pretty penny** a considerable sum of money.

penny-pinching ● *adj.* extremely careful with money; thrifty or cheap. ● *n.* thrift, stinginess. □ **penny-pincher** *n.*

pennyroyal *n.* a small-leaved plant of the mint family, cultivated for use in herbal medicine.

penny stock *n.* common stock valued at less than a dollar a share.

pennywhistle *n.* a tin pipe with six holes.

pen pal *n.* a person with whom one builds a friendship by exchanging letters.

pen-pusher *n. informal derogatory* a clerical worker.

pension ● *n.* **1** a regular payment made by a government to senior citizens, the disabled, or to their surviving dependants. **2** a similar payment made by an employer etc. to a retired employee. **3** a regular payment from a fund etc. to which the recipient has contributed. ● *v.* grant a pension to. □ **pension off** dismiss with a pension. □ **pensionable** *adj.*

pensioner *n.* a recipient of (esp. an old-age) pension.

pensive *adj.* having to do with deep or serious thought. □ **pensively** *adv.*

pent *adj.* closely confined; shut in.

penta- *comb. form* five,

pentagon *n.* **1** a plane figure with five sides and angles. **2 (the Pentagon) a** a pentagonal building containing the headquarters of the US armed forces. **b** the leaders of the US armed forces. □ **pentagonal** *adj.* [*Say* PENTA gon, pen TAGGA nul]

pentameter *n.* a verse of five metrical feet. [*Say* pen TAMMA ter]

Pentateuch *n.* the first five books of the Bible, called the Torah by Jews. □ **Pentateuchal** *adj.* [*Say* PENTA tuke]

pentathlon *n.* **1** (in full **modern pentathlon**) an athletic competition in which participants engage in five different events. **2** any athletic event comprising five different events. □ **pentathlete** *n.* [*Say* pen TATH lon, pen TATH leet]

Pentecost *n.* **1** a Christian festival observed on the seventh Sunday after Easter, commemorating the descent of the Holy Spirit on the disciples. **2** *Judaism* = SHAVUOT. [*Say* PENTA cost]

Pentecostal ● *adj.* (also **pentecostal**) **1** relating to Pentecost. **2** of or designating Christian denominations who emphasize charismatic forms of worship, e.g. speaking in tongues, healing, etc. ● *n.* a member of a Pentecostal denomination. □ **Pentecostalism** *n.* [*Say* penta COST ul]

penthouse *n.* an apartment or suite on the top floor of a tall building.

pent-up *adj.* closely confined or held back.

penultimate *adj.* last but one. [*Say* pen ULTIMATE]

penumbra *n.* (*pl.* **penumbrae** or **penumbras**) **1** the partly shaded region around the shadow of an opaque body. **2** a partial shadow. □ **penumbral** *adj.* [*Say* pen UMM bruh *for the singular,* pen UMM bree *or* pen UMM bruhs *for the plural*]

penury *n.* (*pl.* **penuries**) extreme poverty. [*Say* PEN yur ee]

peon *n.* **1** a menial or drudge. **2** a Spanish American farm worker. [*Say* PEE on]

peony *n.* (*pl.* **peonies**) a perennial plant with large showy flowers. [*Say* PEE uh nee]

people ● *n.* **1 a** human beings, esp. as opposed to animals etc. **b** persons in general. **2** persons composing a community, race, nation, etc. **3 (the people)** the ordinary citizens in a country etc. **4** family. ● *v.* (**peoples, peopled, peopling**) **1** fill with people; populate. **2** inhabit. □ **peoplehood** *n.*

people person *n.* a person who enjoys interacting with other people.

people power *n.* **1** political or other pressure applied by the people. **2** physical power exerted by people as opposed to machines etc.

people skills *pl. n.* skills that allow one to deal effectively with other people.

pep *informal* ● *n.* liveliness. ● *v.* (**peps, pepped, pepping**) fill with energy.

pepper ● *n.* **1** the hot-tasting berries of certain plants, ground or used whole to flavour food. **2** the bell-shaped, smooth-skinned, mildly pungent fruit of a tropical American plant of the nightshade family. ● *v.* **1** season with pepper. **2** sprinkle liberally. **3** pelt with missiles.

peppercorn *n.* the dried pepper berry as a condiment.

peppermint *n.* **1** a mint plant, the leaves of which produce a strong-flavoured oil. **2** a candy flavoured with peppermint.

pepperoni *n.* a hard, highly-seasoned sausage made with beef and pork.

pepper spray *n.* an aerosol spray of oils derived from cayenne pepper, used to overcome an assailant.

pepper squash *n. Cdn* a variety of winter squash with dark green to orange skin.

peppery *adj.* **1** of or containing much pepper. **2** hot-tempered. **3** pungent.

peppy *adj.* (**peppier, peppiest**) *informal* vigorous, energetic.

pep rally *n.* a meeting or gathering to inspire enthusiasm.

pep talk *n.* a usu. short talk intended to enthuse, encourage, etc.

peptic ulcer *n.* an ulcer in the stomach or duodenum.

peptide *n.* a compound consisting of two or more linked amino acids.

Péquiste *n. Cdn* a supporter or member of the Parti Québécois. [*Say* pay KEEST]

per *prep.* **1** for each. **2** by means of. **3** (also **as per**) in accordance with.

perambulate *v.* (**perambulates, perambulated, perambulating**) walk through, over, or around a place. □ **perambulation** *n.* [*Say* purr AM byoo late]

per annum *adv.* for each year.

per capita *adv. & adj.* per person.

perceive *v.* (**perceives, perceived, perceiving**) **1** notice or become aware of something; observe. **2** come to realize or understand. **3** regard as. □ **perceivable** adj. **perceiver** n.

percent ● adv. in every hundred. ● n. **1** percentage. **2** one part in every hundred.

percentage n. **1** a rate or proportion percent. **2** a proportion.

percentile n. Statistics one of the 100 equal groups into which a larger group of people can be divided, according to their place on a scale measuring a particular value. [Say purr SEN tile]

perceptible adj. capable of being perceived. □ **perceptibly** adv.

perception n. **1** the ability to see, hear, or become aware of something through the senses. **2** the process of becoming aware in such a way. **3** a way of regarding or understanding something. **4** intuitive understanding and insight.

perceptive adj. **1** capable of perceiving. **2** sensitive; discerning. □ **perceptively** adv. **perceptiveness** n.

perceptual adj. having to do with the ability to perceive. □ **perceptually** adv.

perch¹ ● n. (pl. **perches**) **1** a usu. horizontal bar, branch, etc. used by a bird to rest on. **2** a usu. high or precarious place to rest on. ● v. (**perches, perched, perching**) settle, or cause to settle on or as if on a perch etc.

perch² n. (pl. **perch** or **perches**) **1** a spiny-finned edible freshwater fish of N America. **2** (also **ocean perch**) any similar marine fish.

percolate v. (**percolates, percolated, percolating**) **1 a** filter or ooze gradually (esp. through a porous surface). **b** (of an idea etc.) spread gradually through a group of people. **2 a** prepare (coffee) in a percolator. **b** (of coffee) be made by percolating. □ **percolation** n. [Say PERK uh late]

percolator n. a machine for making coffee by circulating boiling water through ground beans. [Say PERK uh later]

percussion n. **1** musical instruments that are played by being struck or shaken. **2** the forcible striking of one body against another. □ **percussionist** n. **percussive** adj. **percussively** adv.

per diem ● adv. & adj. for each day. ● n. (pl. **per diems**) an allowance or payment for each day. [Say purr DEE em]

peregrine n. (also **peregrine falcon**) a powerful falcon much prized for hawking. [Say PERRA grin]

peremptory adj. expecting to be obeyed immediately and without question or refusal. □ **peremptorily** adv. [Say purr EMP ter ee, purr emp TORA lee]

perennial ● adj. **1** denoting a plant that usu. lives for more than two seasons. **2** constantly occurring; recurring. **3** lasting for a long time. ● n. a perennial plant. □ **perennially** adv. [Say puh RENNY ul]

perestroika n. the economic and political reforms introduced in the former Soviet Union during the 1980s. [Say perra STROY kuh]

perfect ● adj. **1** complete. **2** flawless. **3** very satisfactory. **4** exact; precise. **5** entire; unqualified. **6** Grammar (of a tense) denoting a completed action or event in the past. **7** eminently suitable. ● v. **1** make perfect; improve. **2** carry through. ● n. Grammar the perfect tense. □ **perfectibility** n. **perfectible** adj.

perfection n. **1** the act or process of making perfect. **2** the state of being perfect. **3** a perfect example.

perfectionism n. the uncompromising pursuit of perfection. □ **perfectionist** n. & adj. **perfectionistic** adj.

perfectly adv. **1** completely; absolutely. **2** in a perfect way.

perfect pitch n. the ability to recognize the pitch of a note or produce any given note.

perfidy n. deceitfulness, lack of trustworthiness. □ **perfidious** adj. [Say PURR fi dee, purr FIDDY us]

perforate v. (**perforates, perforated, perforating**) **1** make a hole or holes through; pierce. **2** make a row of small holes in (paper etc.) to facilitate separation. □ **perforated** adj. **perforation** n. [Say PURR fur ate]

perforce adv. necessarily. [Say purr FORCE]

perform v. **1** carry out, execute, or do. **2** fulfill. **3** act in an official way. **4 a** act, dance, or stage for an audience. **b** accomplish (a feat etc.). **5** present entertainment to an audience. **6** function, esp. in a specified way. **7** (of an investment) yield a return. □ **performer** n.

performance n. **1** the act or process of performing. **2** an act of performing a play, song, concert, etc. **3** a person's achievement. **4** informal a fuss. **5** the capabilities of a machine. **6** the return on an investment.

performance art n. a kind of visual art in which the activity of the artist forms a central feature. □ **performance artist** n.

performing arts pl. n. the arts, e.g. drama, music, and dance, that are performed in front of an audience.

perfume ● n. **1** a sweet smell. **2** a scented liquid. ● v. (**perfumes, perfumed,**

perfuming) impart a sweet scent to.
□ **perfumy** adj.

perfumer n. a maker or seller of perfumes.
□ **perfumery** n. (pl. **perfumeries**)

perfunctory adj. done as a matter of duty
or habit, without real interest.
□ **perfunctorily** adv.
[Say purr FUNK tuh ree,
pur FUNK tora lee]

pergola n. (pl. **pergolas**) an arbour or
covered walk, formed of growing plants
trained over trellises. [Say PURR guh luh]

perhaps adv. 1 possibly. 2 introducing a
polite request.

pericardium n. (pl. **pericardia**) the
membrane enclosing the heart.
□ **pericardial** adj. [Say perra CARDY um]

pericarp n. the part of a fruit formed from
the wall of the ripened ovary.

perigee n. the point in the orbit of a
celestial body or satellite where it is nearest
the earth. [Say PERRA jee]

peril n. 1 serious and immediate danger.
2 a thing that causes or may cause damage
or loss. □ **at one's peril** at one's own risk.

perilous adj. dangerous. □ **perilously** adv.

perimenopause n. the years just before
menopause. □ **perimenopausal** adj.
[Say perry MENNA pause]

perimeter n. 1 the circumference or
outline of a closed figure. 2 the outer edges
or boundary of an area.
[Say puh RIMMA ter]

perinatal adj. having to do with the time
immediately before and after birth.
[Say perra NATE ul]

perineum n. the region of the body
between the anus and the scrotum or
vulva. □ **perineal** adj. [Say perra NEE um]

period ● n. 1 a length or portion of time.
2 a distinct portion of history etc. 3 a time
forming part of a geological era. 4 a time
allotted to a particular subject, course, etc.
at school 5 each of the intervals into which
the playing time of a sporting event etc. is
divided. 6 an occurrence of menstruation.
7 a punctuation mark (.) used at the end of
a sentence or an abbreviation. ● adj. having
to do with some past period.

periodic adj. 1 appearing or occurring at
regular intervals. 2 intermittent.
□ **periodicity** n. [Say peery ODD ick,
period ISSA tee]

periodical ● n. a magazine etc. that is
published at regular intervals. ● adj.
1 published at regular intervals. 2 of or
relating to periodicals. □ **periodically** adv.

periodic table n. an arrangement of
chemical elements in order of increasing
atomic number.

periodontics n. the branch of dentistry
concerned with the gums and other
structures surrounding the teeth.
□ **periodontal** adj.
[Say perry uh DON ticks]

period piece n. something considered in
relation to its associations with or
evocativeness of a past period.

peripatetic adj. 1 (of a teacher) working in
more than one school or college etc.
2 going from place to place.
[Say perra puh TET ick]

peripheral ● adj. 1 of minor importance.
2 of the periphery. 3 near the surface of
the body. 4 (of equipment) used with a
computer etc. but not an integral part of it.
● n. a peripheral device or piece of
equipment. □ **peripherally** adv.
[Say puh RIFFA rul]

peripheral vision n. that which is
visible to the eye outside of the main area
of focus.

periphery n. (pl. **peripheries**) 1 the
boundary of an area or surface. 2 an outer
or surrounding region. 3 a marginal or
secondary position or part in a subject or
group. [Say puh RIFFA ree]

periscope n. an apparatus with mirrors
or prisms in a tube so that the user can
view the area above, e.g. from a submerged
submarine.

perish v. (**perishes**, **perished**,
perishing) 1 be destroyed; suffer death or
ruin. 2 disappear. □ **perish the thought**
an exclamation of horror against an
unwelcome idea.

perishable ● adj. liable to perish or rot.
● n. (in pl.) a thing subject to speedy decay.
□ **perishability** n.

peritoneum n. (pl. **peritoneums** or
peritonea) the membrane lining the
cavity of the abdomen.
[Say perra tuh NEE um, perra tuh NEE uh]

peritonitis n. an inflammatory disease of
the peritoneum. [Say perra tuh NITE iss]

periwinkle[1] n. 1 an evergreen trailing
plant with blue or white flowers and glossy
leaves. 2 a purple-blue colour.
[Say PAIR i winkle]

periwinkle[2] n. a small, edible mollusc
with a spiral shell. [Say PAIR i winkle]

perjure reflexive v. (**perjures**, **perjured**,
perjuring) Law **perjure oneself** wilfully
tell a lie when under oath. □ **perjury** n.
[Say PURR jurr]

perk[1] v. raise (esp. one's ears) briskly.
□ **perk up** 1 recover confidence, liveliness,
etc. 2 restore confidence or liveliness in.

perk[2] n. informal a perquisite; a benefit or
privilege.

perk³ *informal* ● *v.* percolate. ● *n. Cdn* a coffee percolator.

perky *adj.* (**perkier, perkiest**) **1** lively; cheerful. **2** bright, attractive. □ **perkily** *adv.* **perkiness** *n.*

perm ● *n.* a method of using chemicals to create curls in hair that last for several months. ● *v.* treat (hair) in such a way.

permafrost *n.* subsoil which remains below freezing point all year.

permanent ● *adj.* **1** lasting, or intended to last, indefinitely or for a long time. **2** persistent, enduring. **3** (of an employee) not contractual. ● *n.* a perm.
□ **permanence** *n.* **permanency** *n.* **permanently** *adv.*

permanent press *n.* (also **perma-press**) a process for producing fabrics which retain their crease, shape, etc.

permanent resident *n.* a landed immigrant.

permeable *adj.* capable of being permeated. □ **permeability** *n.*
[Say PURR me uh bull, purr me uh BILLA tee]

permeate *v.* (**permeates, permeated, permeating**) penetrate throughout; saturate. □ **permeation** *n.*
[Say PURR me ate]

Permian *n.* the final period of the Paleozoic era, lasting from about 286–248 million years ago, characterized by the development of reptiles. □ **Permian** *adj.*
[Say PURMY in]

permissible *adj.* permitted, allowed.
□ **permissibility** *n.* **permissibly** *adv.*

permission *n.* consent; authorization.

permissive *adj.* tolerant; liberal, esp. in sexual matters. □ **permissiveness** *n.*

permit ● *v.* (**permits, permitted, permitting**) **1** give permission or consent to. **2 a** allow. **b** give an opportunity. ● *n.* a document granting permission.

permutation *n.* **1** an ordered arrangement or grouping of a set of numbers, items, etc. **2** any combination of a specified number of things.
□ **permutational** *adj.*
[Say purr myoo TAY sh'n, PURR myoo tate]

pernicious *adj.* having a very harmful effect. [Say purr NISH us]

pernickety *adj. informal* = PERSNICKETY.
[Say purr NICKA tee]

perogy *n.* (*pl.* **perogies**) (also **perogie, perogi**) a dough dumpling stuffed with potato, cheese, etc., boiled and sometimes fried. [Say purr OH ghee]

peroxide ● *n.* **1 a** hydrogen peroxide. **b** a solution of hydrogen peroxide used to bleach the hair. **2** a compound of oxygen with another element. ● *v.* (**peroxides, peroxided, peroxiding**) bleach with peroxide. [Say purr OXIDE]

perp *n. slang* the perpetrator of a crime.

perpendicular ● *adj.* **1** at right angles to the plane of the horizon, a line, a surface or plane. **2** upright, vertical. ● *n.* a perpendicular line or direction.
□ **perpendicularly** *adv.*

perpetrate *v.* (**perpetrates, perpetrated, perpetrating**) commit or perform (a crime etc.). □ **perpetrator** *n.*

perpetual *adj.* **1** eternal; lasting indefinitely. **2** uninterrupted; continuous. **3** frequent. □ **perpetually** *adv.*

perpetuate *v.* (**perpetuates, perpetuated, perpetuating**) make continue indefinitely. □ **perpetuation** *n.*

perpetuity *n.* the state of being perpetual.
□ **in perpetuity** forever.
[Say purr puh CHOO uh tee]

perplex *v.* (**perplexes, perplexed, perplexing**) puzzle, disconcert.
□ **perplexed** *adj.* **perplexing** *adj.*

perplexity *n.* (*pl.* **perplexities**) **1** the state of being perplexed. **2** a thing which perplexes. [Say purr PLEXA tee]

perquisite *n.* **1** a benefit received in addition to one's salary, e.g. the use of a company car. **2** a special right or privilege enjoyed as a result of one's position.
[Say PURR kwuh zit]

per se *adv.* by or in itself. [Say purr SAY]

persecute *v.* (**persecutes, persecuted, persecuting**) **1** subject to hostility or ill-treatment. **2** harass; annoy persistently. □ **persecution** *n.* **persecutor** *n.*

persevere *v.* (**perseveres, persevered, persevering**) continue steadfastly or determinedly; persist.
□ **perseverance** *n.* [Say pursa VEER, pursa VEER ince]

Persian *n.* **1** a person from ancient or modern Persia (now Iran). **2** the language of ancient Persia or modern Iran. **3** (also **Persian cat**) a cat of a breed with a broad round head and long silky hair.
□ **Persian** *adj.*

Persian carpet *n.* (also **Persian rug**) a carpet or rug of a traditional pattern, made by hand from silk or wool.

persimmon *n.* **1** a sweet pulpy edible fruit that resembles a large tomato. **2** the tree bearing this fruit. [Say purr SIMMIN]

persist *v.* **1** continue firmly esp. despite obstacles, objections, etc. **2** survive. **3** be insistent.

persistent *adj.* **1** continuing in spite of obstacles etc. **2** enduring. **3** constantly

repeated. □**persistence** n.
persistently adv.

persnickety adj. informal fussy; fastidious.
[Say purr SNICKA tee]

person n. **1** an individual human being.
2 the body of a human being. **3** Grammar a
category used in the classification of
pronouns, verb forms, etc., according to
whether they indicate the speaker (**first
person**), the addressee (**second
person**), or a third party (**third person**).
□**in person** physically present.
□**personhood** n.

persona n. (pl. **personas** or **personae**)
1 the aspects of a person's character that
are presented to other people. **2** a character
assumed by an author, performer, etc. **3** a
character in a fictional work.
[Say purr SO nuh for the singular; for
personae say purr SO nigh or purr SO nee]

personable adj. pleasant, likeable.

personage n. a person, esp. of rank or
importance.

personal ● adj. **1** one's own; private.
2 done or made in person. **3** directed to,
intended for, or concerning an individual.
4 a referring to an individual's private life.
b close, intimate. **5** of the body. ● n. (also
personal ad) an advertisement or notice
in a newspaper etc. regarding
companionship etc.

personal computer n. a general-
purpose microcomputer designed for use
by one person at a time.

personal digital assistant n. a small
hand-held computer, containing addresses,
appointments, etc.

personal flotation device n. a life
jacket etc. for keeping a person afloat in
water.

personal identification number n. a
number serving as an electronic password.

personality n. (pl. **personalities**) **1 a** all
the qualities that form a person's
character. **b** socially attractive qualities.
c the unique characteristics of a place or
thing. **2** a famous person.

personality cult n. the extreme public
admiration of a famous person.

personality disorder n. a psychiatric
disorder characterized by a tendency to
behave in certain abnormal ways.

personalize v. (**personalizes**,
personalized, **personalizing**) **1** make
personal; adapt to individual persons'
needs etc. **2** mark or inscribe with a
particular person's name etc. **3** cause (a
discussion etc.) to become concerned with
personal matters or feelings.
□**personalization** n.

personally adv. **1** in person. **2** for one's
own part. □**take personally** be offended
by.

personal pronoun n. each of the
pronouns I, you, he, she, it, we, they, me, him,
her, us, them.

personal property n. Law all one's
property except land.

personal space n. the immediate area
around a person where encroachment is
considered uncomfortable.

personal touch n. (pl. **personal
touches**) **1** a characteristic approach to a
situation. **2** a personal element added to
something impersonal.

personal trainer n. a fitness expert who
works one-on-one with a client to plan and
supervise workouts.

personal watercraft n. a jet-propelled
recreational boat for one or two persons,
ridden like a motorcycle.

persona non grata n. (pl. **personae
non gratae**) an unacceptable or
unwelcome person. [Say non GRATTA for
the singular; non GRAT eye or non GRATTY
for the plural]

personify v. (**personifies**, **personified**,
personifying) **1** attribute a human
nature or characteristics to. **2** symbolize (a
quality etc.) by a figure in human form.
3 embody (a quality) in one's own person.
□**personification** n.
[Say purr SONNA fye,
purr sonna fuh CAY sh'n]

personnel n. **1** a body of people who work
for an organization or the armed forces etc.
2 (also **personnel department**) the part
of an organization concerned with hiring
and training employees. [Say person ELL]

personnel carrier n. an armoured
vehicle for transporting troops etc.

perspective ● n. **1** the art of drawing
solid objects on a two-dimensional surface
so as to give the right impression of relative
positions, size, etc. **2** the apparent relation
between visible objects as to position,
distance, etc. **3 a** a point of view. **b** a
mental view of the relative importance of
things. ● adj. of or in perspective.

perspiration n. **1** sweat. **2** sweating.

perspire v. (**perspires**, **perspired**,
perspiring) sweat.

persuade v. (**persuades**, **persuaded**,
persuading) **1** cause (someone) to
believe; convince. **2** induce.
□**persuadable** adj. **persuader** n.

persuasion n. **1** persuading.
2 persuasiveness. **3** a belief or conviction.
4 informal kind or type.

persuasive adj. able to persuade;

convincing. □ **persuasively** adv. **persuasiveness** n. [Say purr SWAY siv]

pert adj. **1** lively or cheeky in a way that is attractive. **2 a** (of clothes) neat and suggesting jauntiness. **b** (of a bodily part) shapely and attractive. **3** (of a person) disrespectful, rude.

pertain v. relate or have reference to.

pertinent adj. relevant to the matter in hand. □ **pertinence** n. **pertinently** adv.

perturb v. make worried or anxious.

perturbation n. **1** anxiety; uneasiness. **2** a slight alteration of a physical system. **3** a minor deviation in the course of a celestial body. [Say purr turb AY sh'n]

pertussis n. whooping cough. [Say purr TUSS iss]

peruse v. (**peruses, perused, perusing**) **1** read or study thoroughly or carefully. **2** read in a casual manner. **3** examine carefully. □ **perusal** n. [Say purr OOZE, purr OOZE ul]

Peruvian n. a person from Peru. □ **Peruvian** adj. [Say purr OOVY in]

perv n. slang a sexual pervert.

pervade v. (**pervades, pervaded, pervading**) **1** spread throughout. **2** become widespread.

pervasive adj. spreading widely through or present everywhere in something. □ **pervasively** adv. **pervasiveness** n.

perverse adj. **1** showing deliberate determination to behave unacceptably. **2** persistent in error. □ **perversely** adv. **perversity** n.

perversion n. **1** the action of perverting. **2** abnormal or unacceptable sexual behaviour.

pervert ● v. **1** alter (something) from its original meaning or state to a distortion of what was first intended. **2** corrupt. ● n. a person showing sexual perversion. □ **perverted** adj.

Pesach n. Judaism Passover. [Say PAY sack]

pesky adj. (**peskier, peskiest**) informal annoying. □ **peskily** adv. **peskiness** n.

peso n. (pl. **pesos**) the basic monetary unit of several Latin American countries and the Philippines. [Say PAY so]

pessimism n. a tendency to take a gloomy view of circumstances. □ **pessimist** n. **pessimistic** adj.

pest n. **1** a troublesome or annoying person or thing. **2** a destructive animal, esp. an insect which attacks crops etc.

pester v. trouble with frequent or persistent requests.

pesticide n. a chemical preparation for destroying insects, weeds, etc.

pestilence n. a fatal epidemic disease. [Say PESTA lince]

pestilential adj. **1** of or relating to pestilence. **2** annoying.

pestle n. a club-shaped instrument for pounding substances in a mortar. [Say PESSLE]

pesto n. (pl. **pestos**) a sauce of crushed basil leaves, pine nuts, garlic, Parmesan cheese, and olive oil, usu. served with pasta.

PET abbr. **1** POSITRON EMISSION TOMOGRAPHY. **2** (also **PETE**) polyethylene terephthalate, a plastic used in recyclable packaging.

pet ● n. **1** an animal kept for pleasure or companionship. **2** a darling, a favourite. ● adj. **1** kept as a pet. **2** of or for pets. **3** favourite or particular. ● v. (**pets, petted, petting**) **1** treat as a pet. **2** stroke (an animal). **3** engage in erotic caressing.

petal n. each of the parts of the corolla of a flower. □ **petalled** adj.

petard n. □ **hoist with one's own petard** adversely affect oneself by schemes against others. [Say puh TARD]

peter v. decrease, diminish, or fade gradually.

Peter Pan n. a person who retains youthful features, or who is immature.

petiole n. the slender stalk joining a leaf to a stem. [Say PETTY ole]

petit bourgeois ● n. (pl. **petits bourgeois**) a member of the lower middle class. ● adj. having to do with the lower middle class. □ **petite bourgeoisie** n. [Say petty BOOR zhwah, petty boor zhwah ZEE]

petite ● adj. **1** (of a woman) of small and dainty build. **2** (of a thing) small in size. **3** designating a size in women's clothing for shorter women. ● n. a petite size in women's clothing. [Say puh TEET]

petition ● n. **1** a formal written request, esp. one signed by many people, appealing to authority in some cause. **2** an application to a court for a writ etc. **3** a formal prayer to God or request to someone in authority. ● v. **1** make a petition to. **2** make a humble appeal to. □ **petitioner** n.

pet name n. an affectionate nickname.

petrel n. a usu. black and white seabird, usu. flying far from land. [Say PET rul]

petri dish n. a shallow covered dish used for the culture of bacteria etc. [Say PEE tree]

petrify v. (**petrifies, petrified, petrifying**) **1** paralyze with fear etc.

2 change (organic matter) into a stony substance.

petrochemical ● *n.* a substance industrially obtained from petroleum or natural gas. ● *adj.* of or relating to petrochemicals.

petrodollar *n.* a unit of currency earned by a country etc. from petroleum exports.

petroglyph *n.* a rock carving. [*Say* PETRO gliff]

petroleum *n.* an oil found in the upper strata of the earth, refined for use as a fuel for heating and in internal combustion engines etc. [*Say* puh TROLL ee um]

petroleum jelly *n.* a soft, translucent mixture of hydrocarbons used as a lubricant, ointment, etc.

petticoat *n.* an undergarment in the form of a skirt or dress. [*Say* PETTY coat]

petting zoo *n.* (also **petting farm**) a collection of wild or farm animals displayed so that visitors, esp. children, may walk among the animals to pet or feed them etc.

petty *adj.* (**pettier, pettiest**) **1** unimportant. **2** small-minded. **3** on a small scale. **4** of lesser importance; minor. □ **pettily** *adv.* **pettiness** *n.*

petty cash *n.* a small amount of money kept for small payments.

petty officer *n.* (also **Petty Officer**) **1** *Cdn* (in the Canadian navy) an officer of either of two ranks: petty officer first class, equivalent to warrant officer in other commands; or petty officer second class, equivalent to sergeant in the other commands. **2** a non-commissioned officer in other navies.

petulant *adj.* childishly sulky, bad-tempered, or unreasonable. □ **petulance** *n.* **petulantly** *adv.* [*Say* PET you lint *or* PETCH oo lint]

petunia *n.* (*pl.* **petunias**) a plant that has esp. white, purple, or red funnel-shaped flowers.

pew *n.* (in a church) a long bench with a back. [*Say* PYOO]

pewter *n.* **1** a grey alloy of tin, antimony and copper. **2** a bluish or silvery grey. [*Say* PYOO ter]

peyote *n.* **1** a small blue-green Mexican cactus with no spines. **2** a hallucinogenic drug containing mescaline prepared from this cactus. [*Say* pay OH tee]

PFD *n.* (*pl.* **PFDs**) PERSONAL FLOTATION DEVICE.

pH *n.* a measure of acidity or alkalinity.

phagocyte *n.* a type of cell capable of engulfing and absorbing foreign matter.

□ **phagocytic** *adj.* [*Say* FAGGA site, fagga SIT ick]

phalanx *n.* (*pl.* **phalanxes** or **phalanges**) **1** a set of people etc. forming a compact mass, or banded for a common purpose. **2** a bone of the finger or toe. [*Say* FAL anx *or* FAIL anx *for the singular,* fuh LAN jeez *for the plural*]

phalarope *n.* a small wading or swimming bird with a straight bill. [*Say* FALA rope]

phallic *adj.* of or resembling a phallus. [*Say* FAL ick]

phallocentric *adj.* **1** centred on a belief in male superiority. **2** centred on the phallus. □ **phallocentrism** *n.* [*Say* fal oh SEN trick]

phallus *n.* (*pl.* **phalluses** or **phalli**) the penis. [*Say* FAL us *for the singular,* FAL us iz *or* FAL eye *for the plurals*]

phantasm *n.* a figment of the imagination. [*Say* FAN tasm]

phantasmagoria *n.* a shifting series of real or imaginary figures as seen in a dream. □ **phantasmagoric** *adj.* **phantasmagorical** *adj.* [*Say* fan tazzma GORY uh]

phantom ● *n.* **1** a ghost; an apparition. **2** a mental illusion. ● *adj.* illusory.

pharaoh *n.* a ruler in ancient Egypt. □ **pharaonic** *adj.* [*Say* FAIR oh, fair ay ON ick]

Pharisee *n.* **1** a member of an ancient Jewish sect, distinguished by strict observance of traditional law. **2** a self-righteous person. [*Say* FAIR uh see]

pharmacare *n.* *Cdn* (in some provinces) a system of subsidization of drug costs.

pharmaceutical ● *adj.* **1** of or engaged in pharmacy. **2** pertaining to medicinal drugs. ● *n.* a medicinal drug. □ **pharmaceutically** *adv.* [*Say* farma SUIT uh cull]

pharmacist *n.* a person qualified to prepare and dispense medicinal drugs.

pharmacology *n.* the scientific study of drugs and their use in medicine. □ **pharmacological** *adj.* **pharmacologist** *n.* [*Say* farma COLLA jee, farma cuh LOGICAL]

pharmacy *n.* (*pl.* **pharmacies**) **1** the preparation and dispensing of (medicinal) drugs. **2** a pharmacist's store or dispensary.

pharynx *n.* (*pl.* **pharynges**) a cavity behind the nose and mouth, connecting them to the esophagus. [*Say* FAIR inx *for the singular,* fuh RIN jeez *for the plural*]

phase ● *n.* **1** a distinct stage in a process of change or development. **2** each of the aspects of the moon or a planet, according to the amount of its illumination. **3** *Physics* a particular stage in the cycle of a periodic phenomenon, esp. an alternating current or a light wave. **4** a difficult or unhappy period. ● *v.* (**phases, phased, phasing**) carry out in phases or stages. □ **phase in** (or **out**) bring gradually into (or out of) use.

phase-out *n.* the gradual removal of something from use.

phaser *n.* (esp. in science fiction) a usu. hand-held weapon incorporating a laser beam.

phat *adj.* (**phatter, phattest**) *slang* excellent.

Ph.D. *abbr.* Doctor of Philosophy.

pheasant *n.* a large, long-tailed game bird.

phencyclidine *n.* a veterinary anaesthetic and a hallucinogenic drug. Abbreviation: **PCP**.
[*Say* fen SIKE luh deen]

phenobarbital *n.* a barbiturate drug used esp. to treat epilepsy.
[*Say* feeno BARBA tawl]

phenol *n.* a poisonous white crystalline solid, used diluted as an antiseptic and disinfectant. □ **phenolic** *adj. & n.*
[*Say* FEE nawl, fuh NAWL ick]

phenom *n. informal* an unusually gifted person. [*Say* FEE nom]

phenomenal *adj.* extraordinary.
□ **phenomenally** *adv.*
[*Say* fuh NOMMA nul]

phenomenology *n.* a philosophical approach that concentrates on the study of what is seen, heard, felt, etc. in contrast to what may be real or true.
□ **phenomenological** *adj.*
[*Say* fuh nomma NOLLA jee, fuh nomma nuh LOGICAL]

phenomenon *n.* (*pl.* **phenomena**) **1** a fact or situation that appears or is perceived. **2** a remarkable person or thing. [*Say* fuh NOMMA non *or* fuh NOMMA nun *for the singular,* fuh NOMMA nuh *for the plural*]

phenotype *n. Biology* the observable characteristics of an individual or group as determined by its genotype and environment. □ **phenotypic** *adj.*
[*Say* FEENO type, feeno TIP ick]

phenylalanine *n.* an amino acid widely distributed in plant proteins.
[*Say* fennel ALA neen *or* fee nul ALA neen]

pheromone *n.* a chemical substance released into the environment by an animal causing a response in others of the same species. □ **pheromonal** *adj.*
[*Say* FERRA mone, ferra MONE ul]

phew *interj.* an expression of relief.

phial *n.* a small glass bottle. [*Sounds like* FILE]

philander *v.* have casual affairs with many women. □ **philanderer** *n.* **philandering** *adj.* [*Say* fill ANDER, fil ANDER er]

philanthropist *n.* a person who donates money to good causes.
[*Say* fill ANTHRA pist]

philanthropy *n.* **1** a love of humankind. **2** the effort to promote the happiness and well-being of one's fellow people, esp. by gifts of money etc. □ **philanthropic** *adj.* [*Say* fill ANTHRA pee, fill un THROP ick]

philately *n.* the collection and study of postage stamps. □ **philatelic** *adj.* **philatelist** *n.* [*Say* fill ATTA lee, filla TELL ick]

-phile *comb. form* forming words with the sense "lover of, that loves" something specified. [*Say* FILE]

philharmonic *adj.* devoted to music (used in the names of orchestras etc.).
[*Say* fill har MON ick *or* filler MON ick]

Philippine *adj.* of or relating to the Philippines or its people. [*Say* FILLA peen]

Philistine ● *n.* **1** a member of a people opposing the Israelites in ancient Palestine. **2** (usu. **philistine**) a person who is hostile or indifferent to culture, the arts, etc. ● *adj.* hostile or indifferent to culture.
□ **philistinism** *n.* [*Say* FILLA steen *or* FILLA stine, FILLA stin ism]

Phillips *n. proprietary* denoting a screw with a cross-shaped slot, or a corresponding screwdriver.

philodendron *n.* (*pl.* **philodendrons**) a tropical American climbing plant, often grown as a houseplant. [*Say* filla DEN drun]

philology *n.* **1** the branch of knowledge that deals with the structure, historical development, and relationships of a language or languages. **2** the branch of knowledge that deals with the linguistic, historical, interpretative, and critical aspects of literature. □ **philological** *adj.* **philologist** *n.* [*Say* fill OLLA jee, filla LOGICAL]

philosopher *n.* a person engaged or learned in philosophy.

philosophical *adj.* (also **philosophic**) **1** having to do with philosophy. **2** skilled in philosophy. **3** calm in difficult circumstances. □ **philosophically** *adv.*

philosophize *v.* (**philosophizes, philosophized, philosophizing**) **1** reason like a philosopher. **2** theorize.
□ **philosophizer** *n.*

philosophy *n.* (*pl.* **philosophies**) **1** the use of reason and argument in seeking truth and knowledge of reality. **2 a** a particular system or set of beliefs reached by this. **b** a personal rule of life. **3** serenity; calmness.

phlegm *n.* **1** the thick sticky substance secreted by the mucous membranes, discharged by coughing. **2** calmness of disposition. □ **phlegmy** *adj.* [*Say* FLEM, FLEMMY]

phlegmatic *adj.* having a calm, not emotional, disposition. [*Say* fleg MAT ick]

phloem *n.* the tissue conducting food material in plants. [*Say* FLOE em]

phlox *n.* (*pl.* **phlox** or **phloxes**) a plant with dense clusters of scented flowers. [*Say* FLOX]

-phobe *comb. form* forming words denoting a person having a fear or dislike of what is specified.

phobia *n.* (*pl.* **phobias**) an abnormal fear or hatred. □ **phobic** *adj.*

-phobia *comb. form* forming words denoting a fear of or aversion to what is specified.

-phobic *comb. form* having a strong or unreasonable fear of the thing described.

phoebe *n.* a small N American tyrant flycatcher with grey-brown or blackish plumage. [*Say* FEEBY]

Phoenician *n.* **1** a member of a people of ancient Phoenicia or of its colonies, esp. Carthage in northern Africa. **2** the Semitic language of the Phoenicians. □ **Phoenician** *adj.* [*Say* fuh NEESH in]

phoenix *n.* (*pl.* **phoenixes**) a mythical bird that burned itself on a funeral pyre and rose from the ashes with renewed youth. [*Say* FEE nix]

phone ● *n.* a telephone. ● *v.* (**phones**, **phoned**, **phoning**) **1** speak to or send (a message) by telephone. **2** make a telephone call. **3** dial. □ **phone in** call a radio show etc. to participate in a broadcast discussion.

phone book *n.* a book listing telephone subscribers with their telephone numbers, and usu. their addresses.

phone booth *n.* a telephone booth.

phone card *n.* a prepaid card for use with a public telephone.

phone-in *n.* a broadcast program during which listeners or viewers phone the studio etc. to participate.

phoneme *n.* any of the units of sound that distinguish one word from another, e.g. *p*, *b*, *d*, *t* as in pad, pat, bad, bat. □ **phonemic** *adj.* [*Say* FOE neem, fuh NEEM ick]

phonetic *adj.* **1** representing vocal sounds. **2 a** designating the difference between any two sounds. **b** (of a system of spelling etc.) that closely matches the sound represented. **3** of or relating to phonetics. □ **phonetically** *adv.* [*Say* fuh NET ick]

phonetics *pl. n.* **1** vocal sounds and their classification. **2** the study of these. [*Say* fuh NET icks]

phoney *adj. & n.* = PHONY.

phonics *pl. n.* a method of teaching reading by associating letters with particular sounds. □ **phonic** *adj.* [*Say* FON icks]

phonograph *n.* a record player. [*Say* FONE uh graph]

phonology *n.* the system or study of speech sounds in a language. □ **phonological** *adj.* [*Say* fuh NOLLA jee, fone uh LOGICAL]

phony *informal* ● *adj.* (**phonier**, **phoniest**) **1** sham; fake. **2** insincere. ● *n.* (*pl.* **phonies**) a phony person or thing. □ **phoniness** *n.*

phooey *interj.* an expression of disgust or contempt. [*Say* FOO ee]

phosphate *n.* any salt or ester of phosphoric acid. [*Say* FOSS fate]

phospholipid *n.* any lipid consisting of a phosphate group and one or more fatty acids. [*Say* foss fuh LIPID]

phosphor *n.* **1** a synthetic fluorescent or phosphorescent substance. **2** phosphorus. [*Say* FOSS fur]

phosphorescence *n.* **1** radiation similar to fluorescence but detectable after excitation ceases. **2** the emission of light without combustion or perceptible heat. □ **phosphorescent** *adj.* [*Say* foss fuh RESS ince]

phosphoric acid *n.* a crystalline solid used in fertilizer, soap manufacture, etc. [*Say* foss FOR ick]

phosphorus *n.* a chemical element found as a poisonous, pale yellow substance that glows in the dark and ignites in the air. □ **phosphorous** *adj.* [*Say* FOSS fur us]

photo *n.* (*pl.* **photos**) a photograph.

photo- *comb. form* denoting: **1** light. **2** photography.

photo-aging *n.* skin damage such as wrinkles etc. caused by the sun's ultraviolet light.

photochemical *adj.* of or relating to the chemical action of light. □ **photochemically** *adv.*

photocopy ● *n.* (*pl.* **photocopies**) a photographic copy of printed or written material. ● *v.* (**photocopies**, **photocopied**, **photocopying**) make photocopies of. □ **photocopied** *adj.* **photocopier** *n.*

photoelectric *adj.* marked by or using emissions of electrons from substances exposed to light.

photoelectric cell *n.* a device which

generates an electric current from a photoelectric effect.

photo essay n. an essay consisting of text and photographs.

photo finish n. a close finish of a race, esp. one where the winner is distinguishable only on a photograph.

photofinishing n. the commercial development and printing of films. □ **photofinisher** n.

photogenic adj. **1** looking attractive in photographs. **2** giving out light. [Say photo JEN ick]

photograph ● n. a picture formed by means of the chemical action of light or other radiation on sensitive film. ● v. **1** take a photograph of. **2** appear when in a photograph. □ **photographer** n. **photographic** adj. **photographically** adv.

photographic memory n. a memory allowing the precise recall of images with the accuracy of a photograph.

photography n. the process or art of taking photographs.

photo ID n. identification containing a photograph of the bearer.

photojournalism n. the art or practice of relating news through the use of photographs. □ **photojournalist** n.

photometer n. an instrument for measuring the strength of light. □ **photometric** adj. **photometry** n. [Say foe TOMMA ter, photo METRIC, foe TOMMA tree]

photon n. an elementary particle representing a quantum of electromagnetic radiation, such as light. □ **photonic** adj. [Say FOE tawn, foe TONNIC]

photo opportunity n. (also informal **photo op**, pl. **photo ops**) an opportunity for media photographers to take pictures of a politician, celebrity, etc.

photo radar n. a computer-operated radar system which takes a photograph of the licence plate of a speeding car.

photorealism n. detailed and not idealized representation in art. □ **photorealist** n. **photorealistic** adj.

photoreceptor n. a structure in a living organism, esp. a sensory cell or sense organ, that reacts to the presence of light.

photosensitive adj. reacting to light. □ **photosensitivity** n.

photosynthesis n. the process in which the energy of sunlight is used by organisms, esp. green plants, to synthesize nutrients from carbon dioxide and water. □ **photosynthesize** v.

(**photosynthesizes**, **photosynthesized**, **photosynthesizing**) **photosynthetic** adj.

photovoltaic adj. relating to the production of electric current at the junction of two substances exposed to light. □ **photovoltaics** n. [Say photo vol TAY ick]

phrasal verb n. an idiomatic phrase consisting of a verb and an adverb or preposition, e.g. *break down*.

phrase ● n. **1** a small group of words forming a conceptual unit, but not a sentence. **2** an idiomatic or short pithy expression. **3** *Music* a group of notes forming a distinct unit within a larger passage. ● v. (**phrases**, **phrased**, **phrasing**) **1** express in words. **2** divide (music) into phrases etc. in performance. □ **phrasal** adj. [Say FRAZE, FRASE ul]

phrase book n. a book listing useful expressions translated into another language.

phraseology n. a particular mode of expression. [Say fray zee OLLA jee]

phrasing n. **1** the words used to express something. **2** the division of a piece of music into phrases.

phreak ● n. (also **phone freak**) a person who makes fraudulent use of a telephone system by electronic means. ● v. use an electronic device to obtain (a telephone call) without payment. □ **phreaking** n. [Say FREAK]

phrenology n. the study of the shape and size of the skull as a supposed indication of character. □ **phrenological** adj. **phrenologist** n. [Say fruh NOLLA jee, frenna LOGICAL]

phyla pl. of PHYLUM. [Say FYE luh]

phylactery n. (plural **phylacteries**) either of two small leather boxes containing Biblical texts in Hebrew, worn by Jewish men during prayer. [Say fill ACTER ee]

phyllo n. Greek flaky pastry in the form of very thin leaves. [Say FEE loe or FIE loe]

phylum n. (pl. **phyla**) a taxonomic rank above class and below kingdom. [Say FYE lum *for the singular*, FYE luh *for the plural*]

phys. ed. n. physical education.

physical ● adj. **1 a** of or concerning the body. **b** having to do with things that can be seen, heard, or touched. **2** of or pertaining to matter or things material. **3 a** of or in accordance with the laws of nature. **b** having to do with physics. **4** inclined to be aggressive or violent. ● n. (also **physical examination**) a medical examination to determine health or physical fitness. □ **get physical 1** become physically aggressive. **2** become sexually involved. **3** exercise. □ **physicality** n. **physically** adv.

physical chemistry n. the application of the techniques and theories of physics to the study of chemical systems etc.

physical education n. instruction in physical exercise and sports.

physical geography n. the branch of geography dealing with natural features and forces of the earth's surface.

physically challenged adj. euphemism having a physical disability.

physical science n. any branch of the sciences that deals with inanimate matter and energy, e.g. physics, chemistry, geology, astronomy, etc.

physical therapy n. esp. US physiotherapy. □ **physical therapist** n.

physician n. a person legally qualified to practise medicine.

physics n. the science dealing with the properties and interactions of matter and energy. □ **physicist** n.

physio n. informal **1** (pl. **physios**) a physiotherapist. **2** physiotherapy.

physiognomy n. (pl. **physiognomies**) **1** a person's face or expression. **2** the external features of a landscape etc. [Say fizzy ONNA me]

physiology n. **1** the branch of biology that studies the normal functions of living organisms and their parts. **2** the way in which a living organism or bodily part functions. □ **physiologic** adj. **physiological** adj. **physiologically** adv. **physiologist** n. [Say fizzy OLLA jee, fizzy uh LOGICAL]

physiotherapy n. the treatment of disease or injury by physical methods such as massage and exercise. □ **physiotherapist** n.

physique n. the form, size, and development of a person's body. [Say fizz EEK]

phytoestrogen n. an estrogen found in plants. [Say fight oh ESSTRA gin]

phytonutrient n. a substance found in certain plants which is believed to be beneficial to human health and help prevent various diseases.

phytoplankton n. plankton consisting of microscopic plants. [Say fight oh PLANK tun]

PI abbr. private investigator.

pi n. **1** the sixteenth letter of the Greek alphabet (Π, π). **2** (as π) the symbol of the ratio of the circumference of a circle to its diameter (approx. 3.14159). [Say PIE]

pianissimo adj. & adv. Music very soft or softly. [Say pee uh NISS i moe]

pianist n. a person who plays the piano. [Say PEE uh nist or pee ANN ist]

pianistic adj. having to do with the art or technique of playing the piano. □ **pianistically** adv. [Say pee uh NISS tick]

piano¹ n. (pl. **pianos**) **1** a large keyboard instrument with metal strings, which are struck by hammers when the keys are pressed. **2** a similar instrument producing sound electronically.

piano² adj. & adv. Music soft or softly.

piano bar n. a cocktail lounge featuring live entertainment.

pianoforte n. formal a piano. [Say piano FOR tay]

piazza n. (pl. **piazzas**) a public square or marketplace esp. in Italy. [Say pee AT suh]

pic n. (pl. **pix** or **pics**) informal **1** a motion picture. **2** a picture or photograph.

pica n. (pl. **picas**) a unit of type size equal to 12 points. [Say PIKE uh]

picaresque adj. relating to fiction involving a central figure involved in a serious of adventures. [Say picka RESK]

picayune adj. petty, insignificant. [Say picka YUNE]

piccolo n. (pl. **piccolos**) a small flute sounding an octave higher than the ordinary flute. [Say PICKA loe]

pick¹ ● v. **1** take hold of and move. **2** remove (a flower or fruit) from where it is growing. **3** choose from a number of alternatives. **4** remove unwanted matter from (one's nose etc.). ● n. **1** an act of selecting something. **2** informal the best person or thing in a group. □ **pick and choose** select carefully or fastidiously. **pick apart 1** find fault. **2** break up. **pick at** nibble. **pick a person's brains** extract ideas etc. from a person by questioning. **pick a fight** (or **quarrel**) start an argument. **pick holes in** find fault with. **pick a lock** open a lock with an instrument other than the proper key. **pick off 1** shoot (people etc.) one by one without haste. **2** eliminate (opposition etc.) singly. **pick on 1** nag at. **2** single out (a person) for victimization etc. **pick out 1** take from a larger number. **2** distinguish from surrounding objects. **3** play (a tune) on the piano etc. **pick over** select the best from. **pick a person's pockets** steal from a person's pockets. **pick up 1** raise (from the ground etc.). **2 a** learn or acquire with little effort. **b** catch (an illness). **3 a** go to collect. **b** stop for and take along with one. **4** make the acquaintance of (a person) casually, esp. as a sexual overture. **5** recover, improve, or increase. **6 a** gather (speed). **b** become stronger. **7** (of the police etc.) arrest. **8** receive (a signal or sound). **pick up on** become aware of. **pick up the pieces** restore to normality or make better, esp. after a setback. **take one's pick** make a choice. □ **picker** n.

pick² n. **1** (also **pickaxe**) a long-handled tool having a usu. curved iron bar pointed at one or both ends, used for breaking up hard ground, masonry, etc. **2** a plectrum. **3** a comb with long, widely spaced teeth. **4** *Figure Skating* a toe pick.

pickerel n. (pl. **pickerel** or **pickerels**) **1** a walleye. **2** a northern pike or other smaller pike. [*Say* PICKER ul]

picket ● n. **1** a person or group of people outside a place as a protest or to persuade esp. workers not to enter during a strike etc. **2** a pointed stake or peg driven into the ground. **3** *Military* a small body of troops sent out to watch for the enemy. ● v. (**pickets, picketed, picketing**) **1 a** form a picket outside. **b** demonstrate as a picket. **2** station (soldiers) as a picket. □ **picketer** n.

picket fence n. **1** a fence consisting of pickets. **2** (also **white picket fence**) this as a symbol of conventional suburban middle-class domesticity.

picket line n. a boundary established by workers on strike, which others are asked not to cross.

pickings pl. n. profits or gains that are easily obtained.

pickle ● n. **1 a** a vegetable, esp. a small cucumber, preserved in brine, vinegar, etc. **b** a condiment of chopped vegetables preserved in brine, mustard, etc. **2** *informal* a difficult predicament. ● v. (**pickles, pickled, pickling**) preserve (food) in brine etc.

pickled adj. **1** (of food) preserved in brine or vinegar. **2** *slang* drunk.

pick-me-up n. **1** an esp. alcoholic drink taken as a tonic or restorative. **2** something that cheers.

pickpocket ● n. a person who steals from the pockets of others. ● v. steal from the pockets of. □ **pickpocketing** n.

pickup n. **1** (also **pickup truck**) a light truck having a usu. open bed with low sides. **2** a device that produces an electrical signal in response to some other kind of signal or change, esp. on a musical instrument or a record or CD player. **3** *slang* a person met casually, esp. for sexual purposes. **4** the act or action of picking up. **5** acceleration. **6** (as an *adj.*) impromptu.

picky adj. (**pickier, pickiest**) *informal* excessively choosy.

picnic ● n. **1** an outing including a packed meal eaten outdoors. **2** any meal eaten outdoors or without tables, chairs, etc. **3** *informal* something easily accomplished. ● v. (**picnics, picnicked, picnicking**) take part in a picnic. □ **picnicker** n.

picnic table n. a rectangular table with benches attached along each long side.

Pict n. a member of an ancient people of northern Britain who eventually amalgamated with the Scots. □ **Pictish** adj.

pictograph n. (also **pictogram**) **1 a** a pictorial symbol or sign. **b** an ancient record consisting of pictorial symbols. **2** a pictorial representation of statistics etc. on a chart, graph, etc. □ **pictographic** adj. [*Say* PICTA graph]

pictorial adj. **1** of or expressed in pictures. **2** containing or illustrated by pictures. □ **pictorially** adv. [*Say* pick TORY ul]

picture ● n. **1** a painting, drawing, or photograph. **2** an image on a television screen. **3** a film. **4** an impression formed from an account or description. ● v. (**pictures, pictured, picturing**) **1** represent in a picture. **2** form a mental image of. □ **get the picture** *informal* become aware of or understand. **in the picture 1** actively involved. **2** fully informed. **out of the picture** no longer involved; irrelevant.

picture-perfect adj. **1** ideal, perfectly ordered. **2** precisely accurate.

picture postcard ● n. a postcard with a picture on one side. ● adj. (**picture-postcard**) conventionally attractive.

picturesque adj. beautiful, esp. in a quaint way. □ **picturesquely** adv. **picturesqueness** n. [*Say* picture ESK]

picture tube n. the cathode ray tube of a TV set.

picture window n. a large window, usu. consisting of one pane of glass.

piddle ● v. (**piddles, piddled, piddling**) **1** *informal* urinate. **2** while or fritter away time etc. ● n. *informal* **1** urination. **2** urine.

piddling adj. (also **piddly**) *informal* trivial; trifling.

pidgin n. a form of a language with vocabulary from two or more languages, used for communication between people not having a common language. [*Say* PIDGE in]

pie n. a dish with a pastry crust or topping or both, with a filling of fruit, meat, etc. □ **easy as pie** *informal* very easy. **pie in the sky** *informal* a promise or hope unlikely to be fulfilled.

piebald ● *adj.* having irregular patches of two colours. ● *n.* a piebald animal. [*Say* PIE bald]

piece ● *n.* **1** a portion separated from the whole. **2** an item used in constructing something or forming part of a set. **3** a musical or written work. **4** a token used to make moves in a board game. **5** a coin of specified value. **6** *informal* a firearm. ● *v.* (**pieces, pieced, piecing**) assemble from individual parts. □ **go to pieces 1** break up, lose cohesion. **2** collapse emotionally or mentally. **in one piece 1** (of a thing) unbroken. **2** (of a person etc.) whole, not harmed. **in pieces** broken, in fragments. (**all**) **of a piece** consistent, in keeping. **a piece of the action** *slang* **1** a share in the profits of something. **2** a share in the excitement. **a piece of one's mind** a sharp rebuke. **say one's piece** give one's opinion or make a statement.

pièce de résistance *n.* (*pl.* **pièces de résistance**) the most important or remarkable item. [*Say* pyess duh ray zis TONCE]

piecemeal ● *adv.* piece by piece; gradually. ● *adj.* consisting of pieces; done bit by bit.

piece of work *n.* (*pl.* **pieces of work**) **1** a difficult thing. **2** a person of a specified kind.

piecework *n.* work paid for by the amount produced.

pie chart *n.* a circle divided into sectors to represent relative quantities.

pied *adj.* having several colours. [*Rhymes with* RIDE]

piedmont *n.* a gentle slope at the foot of mountains. [*Say* PEED mont]

Pied Piper *n.* **1** (in German legend) a piper who rid the town of Hamelin (Hameln) of rats by enticing them away with his music. **2** a person enticing followers esp. to their doom.

pie-eyed *adj.* *slang* drunk.

Piegan *n.* & *adj.* = PEIGAN. [*Say* pee GAN]

pie plate *n.* (also **pie pan**) a shallow usu. round dish in which pies are baked.

pier *n.* **1** a structure leading out into the sea, a lake, etc., used as a landing stage and promenade. **2** a pillar supporting an arch or bridge.

pierce *v.* (**pierces, pierced, piercing**) **1 a** (of a sharp instrument etc.) penetrate the surface of. **b** prick with a sharp instrument. **c** make a hole or opening into or through. **d** affect keenly or sharply. **2** force (a way etc.) through or into. □ **piercer** *n.*

pierced *adj.* **1** having a hole or holes. **2** (of a body part) having a hole in which a ring etc. is worn.

piercing ● *adj.* **1** (of sounds) very high and loud; shrill. **2 a** (of eyes) very bright and clear. **b** (of a look) searching. **3** very perceptive. **4** (of wind etc.) bitter. ● *n.* a hole pierced in a body part in which a ring etc. is worn. □ **piercingly** *adv.*

pierogi *n.* = PEROGY. [*Say* puh ROE ghee]

piety *n.* (*pl.* **pieties**) **1** the quality of being religious. **2** a conventional belief accepted without thinking. [*Say* PIE uh tee]

piffle *n.* *informal* nonsense; empty speech. □ **piffling** *adj.*

pig *n.* **1** a domesticated hoofed mammal with a large head and a broad flat snout. **2** *informal* **a** a selfish and greedy person. **b** an ill-mannered or vulgar person. **3** an oblong mass of iron or lead from a smelting furnace. **4** *slang derogatory* a police officer. □ **buy a pig in a poke** buy something without seeing it. **make a pig of oneself** overeat. **pig out** (**pigs, pigged, pigging**) *informal* eat gluttonously.

pigeon *n.* a stout bird with a small head and a cooing voice.

pigeonhole ● *n.* **1** each of a set of compartments for papers, letters, etc. **2** a small recess for a pigeon to nest in. ● *v.* (**pigeonholes, pigeonholed, pigeonholing**) **1** deposit (a document) in a pigeonhole. **2** assign to a preconceived category.

piggish *adj.* **1** of or relating to pigs. **2** greedy, dirty, or stubborn.

piggy ● *n.* (also **piggie**) (*pl.* **piggies**) *informal* a little pig. ● *adj.* (**piggier, piggiest**) like a pig; piggish.

piggyback ● *n.* (also **piggyback ride**) a ride on the back and shoulders of another person. ● *v.* **1** ride piggyback. **2** give a piggyback ride to. **3** use an established situation as a basis so as to gain an advantage. ● *adv.* **1** on the back and shoulders of another person. **2** on top of a larger object.

piggy bank *n.* a container with a slot in the top, used for saving coins in.

pigheaded *adj.* obstinate.

pig iron *n.* crude iron from a smelting furnace.

piglet *n.* a young pig.

pigment *n.* **1** colouring matter used as paint or dye. **2** the natural colouring matter of animal or plant tissue. □ **pigmentation** *n.*

pigmy *n.* (*pl.* **pigmies**) = PYGMY.

pigskin *n.* **1** the hide of a pig. **2** leather made from this. **3** a football.

pigsty *n.* (*pl.* **pigsties**) **1** (also **pigpen**) a pen or enclosure for pigs. **2** a filthy room etc. [*Say* PIG stye]

pigtail *n.* a braid or ponytail hanging from the back of the head, or two such at the sides. □ **pigtailed** *adj.*

pigweed *n.* a herbaceous plant that grows as a weed.

pika *n. (pl.* **pikas)** a small rabbit-like mammal with small ears and no tail, found in western N America. [*Say* PIKE uh]

pike *n. (pl.* **pike) 1 a** a large freshwater fish with a long narrow snout and sharp teeth. **b** any similar predatory fish. **2** *hist.* a weapon with a pointed steel or iron head on a long wooden shaft. **3** a jackknife position in diving or gymnastics. □ **come down the pike** appear on the scene.

pike pole *n. Cdn* a long pole with a sharp point and hook, used for moving floating logs.

piker *n. informal* a cheap or stingy person.

pilaf *n.* a Middle Eastern or Indian dish of spiced rice or wheat with meat, vegetables, etc. [*Say* PEE laff]

pilaster *n.* a rectangular column. [*Say* pill ASTER]

Pilates *n.* a system of exercises designed to improve strength, flexibility, and posture. [*Say* puh LOT eez]

pilau *n.* = PILAF. [*Say* pi LAU *(LAU rhymes with* HOW*)*]

pilchard *n.* **1** a small European marine fish of the herring family. **2** a sardine of the Pacific coast of N America. [*Say* PILL churd]

pile¹ ● *n.* 1 a heap of things lying one upon another. **2** a large imposing building or group of buildings. **3** *informal* a large quantity. ● *v.* **(piles, piled, piling) 1 a** heap up. **b** load. **2** crowd hurriedly or tightly. □ **pile up 1** accumulate. **2** *informal* cause (a vehicle etc.) to crash.

pile² *n.* a heavy beam driven into the ground to support the foundations of a superstructure. □ **piling** *n.*

pile³ *n.* **1** the soft projecting surface on carpet or fabric. **2** soft hair or down.

pileated woodpecker *n.* a N American woodpecker with a red-topped head. [*Say* PILLY ate ed]

piledriver *n.* a machine for driving piles into the ground.

piles *pl. n.* hemorrhoids.

pileup *n. informal* **1** a multiple crash of road vehicles. **2** an accumulation. **3** a confused mass or heap of people.

pilfer *v.* steal esp. in small quantities. □ **pilferage** *n.*

pilgrim *n.* **1** a person who journeys to a sacred place for religious reasons. **2** (usu.

Pilgrim) one of a group of 102 people who founded a settlement at Plymouth, Massachusetts, in 1620.

pilgrimage *n.* **1** a pilgrim's journey. **2** any journey taken for nostalgic or sentimental reasons. [*Say* PILGRIM idge]

Pilipino *n.* the national language of the Philippines. [*Say* pilla PEE no]

pill¹ *n.* **1 a** a solid round mass of medicine for swallowing whole. **b** (usu. as **(a) the pill)** a contraceptive pill. **2** an unpleasant necessity. **3** *informal* an annoying person.

pill² *v.* (of esp. knitted fabric) form balls of fluff on the surface.

pillage ● *v.* (pillages, pillaged, pillaging) steal or rob with violence, esp. during war. ● *n.* the action of pillaging. □ **pillager** *n.* [*Say* PILL idge]

pillar *n.* **1** a tall upright column used as a support for a building. **2** a strong supporter or important member of something. □ **pillar of strength** a person regarded as giving moral support etc. □ **pillared** *adj.*

pillbox *n. (pl.* **pillboxes) 1** a small shallow cylindrical box for pills. **2** a hat of a similar shape. **3** a small partly underground concrete fort.

pillion *n.* seating for a passenger behind a motorcyclist.

pillory ● *n. (pl.* **pillories) *hist.* a wooden framework with holes for the head and hands, enabling the public to assault or ridicule a person so imprisoned. ● *v.* **(pillories, pilloried, pillorying)** expose to ridicule or public contempt. [*Say* PILLER ee]

pillow ● *n.* 1 a usu. oblong support for the head, esp. in bed. **2** any pillow-shaped block or support. ● *v.* rest (the head etc.) on or as if on a pillow. □ **pillowy** *adj.*

pillowcase *n.* (also **pillow slip)** a washable fabric cover for a pillow.

pillow talk *n.* intimate conversation in bed.

pill-popper *n.* **1** a person who takes pills in abundance. **2** a drug addict. □ **pill-popping** *n. & adj.*

pilot ● *n.* 1 a person who operates the flying controls of an aircraft. **2** a person qualified to take charge of a ship entering or leaving harbour etc. **3 a** an experimental undertaking or test. **b** a test episode of a television series. ● *v.* **(pilots, piloted, piloting) 1** act as a pilot on. **2** produce a pilot for (an idea, scheme, etc.). □ **pilotless** *adj.*

pilot hole *n.* a small hole drilled into something to receive a nail or screw.

pilothouse *n.* = WHEELHOUSE 1.

pilot light *n.* a small flame that burns

continuously, and lights a larger flame when needed.

pilot whale *n.* a small black whale with a low dorsal fin, found in temperate or subtropical waters.

Pilsner *n.* (also **Pilsener**) a pale lager beer with a strong flavour of hops. [*Say* PILLS ner *or* PILCE ner]

pimento *n.* (*pl.* **pimentos**) **1** = SWEET PEPPER. **2** a small tropical tree, native to Jamaica. [*Say* pi MENTO]

pimiento *n.* = PIMENTO. [*Say* pimmy ENTO *or* pim YENTO]

pimp ● *n.* a man who lives off the earnings of prostitutes. ● *v.* **1** act as a pimp. **2** cause to act as a prostitute. □ **pimping** *n.*

pimple *n.* a small, inflamed, usu. raised spot on the skin. □ **pimpled** *adj.* **pimply** *adj.*

PIN *n.* a confidential identification number to validate electronic transactions.

pin ● *n.* **1** a thin piece of metal with a sharp point at one end and a round head at the other, used as a fastener. **2** a metal projection from a plug or an integrated circuit. **3** a small brooch. **4** a steel rod used to join the ends of fractured bones while they heal. **5** a club-shaped usu. wooden peg used as a target in bowling. **6** a metal peg in a hand grenade that prevents it from exploding. ● *v.* (**pins, pinned, pinning**) **1** attach or fasten with a pin or pins. **2** hold someone firmly so they are unable to move. **3** fix (blame etc.) on. □ **neat as a pin** very tidy. **pin down 1** bind (a person etc.) to a promise etc. **2** force (a person) to be specific. **3** restrict the actions or movement of (an enemy etc.). **4** hold down by force. **pin one's hopes** (or **faith** etc.) **on** rely implicitly or completely on.

pina colada *n.* (*pl.* **pina coladas**) a drink made from pineapple juice, rum, and coconut. [*Say* peena kuh LODDA *or* peenya kuh LODDA]

pinafore *n.* an apron-like garment worn over a dress, esp. by small girls.

pinata *n.* (*pl.* **pinatas**) a decorated papier mâché figure filled with small treats, to be broken by a person waving a stick. [*Say* pin YOTTA *or* peen YOTTA]

pinball *n.* a game in which small metal balls are shot across a board and score points by striking targets.

pince-nez *n.* (*pl.* **pince-nez**) a pair of eyeglasses held in place by a clip on the nose. [*Say* PANCE nay]

pincers *pl. n.* **1** (also **pair of pincers**) a gripping tool resembling scissors but with blunt usu. concave jaws. **2** the front claws of lobsters and some other crustaceans.

pinch ● *v.* (**pinches, pinched, pinching**) **1 a** grip tightly, e.g. between finger and thumb etc. **b** (of a shoe etc.) constrict (the flesh) painfully. **2** *slang* **a** steal. **b** arrest (a person). ● *n.* (*pl.* **pinches**) **1** an act of pinching. **2** an amount that can be taken up with fingers and thumb. **3** the stress or pain caused by poverty, hunger, etc. □ **feel the pinch** experience the effects of poverty. **in a pinch** in an emergency. **pinch oneself** check to make sure that one is not dreaming. **pinch pennies** live frugally.

pinched *adj.* (of the features) drawn.

pin cherry *n.* a wild N American cherry tree bearing very small fruit.

pinch-hitter *n.* **1** a baseball player who bats instead of another. **2** a person acting as a substitute for another. □ **pinch-hit** *v.*

pincushion *n.* a small cushion for holding pins.

pine[1] *n.* **1** a coniferous evergreen tree native to northern temperate regions, with clusters of needle-shaped leaves. **2** its wood. □ **piney** (also **piny**) *adj.*

pine[2] *v.* (**pines, pined, pining**) **1** decline or waste away, esp. from grief etc. **2** yearn.

pineal gland *n.* a pea-sized gland in the brain, secreting a hormone-like substance in some mammals. [*Say* PINNY ul *or* PINE ee ul]

pineapple *n.* **1** a large juicy tropical fruit with yellow flesh surrounded by a tough skin. **2** the widely cultivated tropical plant that bears this fruit.

pine cone *n.* the cone-shaped fruit of the pine tree.

pine marten *n.* a weasel-like mammal with predominantly dark brown fur.

pine nut *n.* the edible seed of various pine trees.

ping ● *n.* **1** a single short high ring. **2** the sound of an engine thumping or rattling. ● *v.* **1** make a ping. **2** (of an engine) make a thumping or rattling noise.

pingo *n.* (*pl.* **pingos**) a dome-shaped mound found in permafrost areas.

Ping-Pong *n.* *proprietary* table tennis.

pinhead *n.* **1** the head of a pin. **2** *informal* a stupid or foolish person.

pinhole *n.* a very small hole.

pinion ● *n.* **1** the outer part of a bird's wing. **2** a small cogwheel or spindle engaging with a large cogwheel. ● *v.* **1** cut off the pinion of (a bird) to prevent flight. **2** bind the arms of a person. [*Say* PIN yin]

pink[1] ● *n.* **1** a pale red colour. **2** a type of small carnation with sweet-smelling white, pink, or crimson flowers. **3** *informal* often *derogatory* a person with socialist tendencies.

● *adj.* **1** of a pale red colour. **2** esp. *derogatory* tending to socialism. □ **in the pink** *informal* in very good health. □ **pinkish** *adj.* **pinkly** *adv.*

pink² *v.* cut a scalloped or zigzag edge on.

pink eye *n.* contagious conjunctivitis.

pinking shears *pl. n.* a dressmaker's serrated shears for cutting a zigzag edge.

pinko *n.* (*pl.* **pinkos**) *derogatory* a socialist.

pink salmon *n.* a medium-sized pink-fleshed migratory salmon of the Pacific and Atlantic Oceans.

pink slip ● *n.* a notice of dismissal from employment. ● *v.* (**pink-slip, pink-slips, pink-slipped, pink-slipping**) dismiss from employment.

pinky *n.* (also **pinkie**) (*pl.* **pinkies**) the little finger.

pin money *n.* a very small sum of money.

pinnacle *n.* **1** the culmination or climax. **2** a natural peak. **3** a small ornamental turret on a roof etc. [*Say* PINNA cull]

pinnate *adj.* **1** (of a compound leaf) having leaflets arranged on either side of the stem, usu. in pairs opposite each other. **2** having branches, tentacles, etc., on each side of an axis. [*Say* PIN ate]

pinochle *n.* a card game with a double pack of 48 cards (nine to ace only). [*Say* PEE nuckle]

Pinot *n.* **1** a variety of black or white grape used in winemaking. **2** wine made from these grapes. [*Say* pee NO]

pinpoint ● *n.* **1** the point of a pin. **2** something very small or sharp. ● *adj.* **1** very small. **2** precise, accurate. ● *v.* locate with accuracy.

pinprick *n.* **1** a prick by a pin. **2** a trifling irritation.

pins and needles *pl. n.* a tingling sensation in a limb recovering from numbness. □ **on pins and needles** in a state of suspense.

pinstripe *n.* **1** a very narrow white stripe in dark cloth. **2** a pinstripe suit. □ **pinstriped** *adj.*

pint *n.* **1** a measure of capacity for liquids etc., equal to one-eighth of a gallon. **2** a dry measure, equal to a half quart. **3** esp. *Brit. informal* a pint of beer. [*Say* PINT with the I as in PIKE]

pintail *n.* a duck with a pointed tail.

pinto ● *adj.* having irregular patches of two colours. ● *n.* (*pl.* **pintos**) **1** a horse with irregular patches of two colours. **2** (also **pinto bean**) a variety of kidney bean with mottled seeds.

pint-sized *adj.* (also **pint-size**) *informal* very small.

pin-up *n.* a poster of a popular or sexually attractive person.

pinwheel *n.* **1** a hand-held toy consisting of a stick with a small vaned wheel which rotates. **2** a firework which rotates rapidly when lit.

pinworm *n.* a small parasitic nematode worm.

pioneer ● *n.* **1** an initiator of a new enterprise. **2** a settler in a previously unsettled land. ● *v.* **1** initiate or originate (an enterprise etc.). **2** act as a pioneer. □ **pioneering** *adj.*

pious *adj.* **1** devout; religious. **2** hypocritically virtuous; sanctimonious. □ **piously** *adv.* [*Say* PIE us]

pip¹ *n.* the seed of an apple, orange, grape, etc.

pip² *n.* any of the spots on a playing card, dice, or domino.

pipe ● *n.* **1** a tube used to convey water, gas, exhaust, etc. **2** a narrow tube with a bowl at one end for tobacco, etc., for smoking. **3 a** a wind instrument consisting of a single tube. **b** any of the tubes by which sound is produced in an organ. **c** (in *pl.*) bagpipes. ● *v.* (**pipes, piped, piping**) **1** play a tune etc. on a pipe or pipes. **2** convey by pipes. **3** transmit music etc. by wire or cable. **4** signal the arrival of an officer etc. on board a ship. **5** utter in a shrill voice. **6** arrange (icing, cream, etc.) in decorative lines or twists on a cake etc. □ **pipe down** *informal* be quiet or less insistent. **pipe up** begin to play, sing, speak, etc.

pipe band *n.* a band consisting of bagpipers and drummers.

pipe bomb *n.* a homemade bomb contained in a metal tube.

pipe carrier *n.* a person entrusted with the keeping of a sacred pipe and the leading of pipe ceremonies among Aboriginal peoples.

pipe ceremony *n.* a sacred ritual of some N American Aboriginal peoples, in which tobacco or herbs are smoked in a sacred pipe.

pipe cleaner *n.* a piece of flexible covered wire, used for cleaning a tobacco pipe and for crafts.

pipe dream *n.* an unattainable or fanciful hope.

pipeline *n.* **1** a long usu. underground pipe for conveying oil, gas, etc. **2** a channel supplying goods, information, etc. □ **in the pipeline** being planned, worked on, or produced.

piper *n.* **1** a bagpiper. **2** a person who plays a pipe.

pipette n. a slender tube for transferring or measuring small quantities of liquids. [*Say* pipe ET *or* pip ET]

piping n. **1** the sound of a pipe or pipes being played. **2** lengths of pipe, or a system of pipes. **3** a thin pipe-like fold used as trim or edging on fabric. **4** ornamental lines of icing etc. on a cake or other dish.

piping hot adj. & adv. very or suitably hot.

piping plover n. a small buff-coloured bird with a whistling call.

pipit n. a brown mainly ground-dwelling songbird.

pippin n. **1** an apple grown from seed. **2** a red and yellow dessert apple.

pipsqueak n. *informal* a contemptibly weak or insignificant person or thing.

piquant adj. **1** having a pleasant sharp taste or appetizing flavour. **2** pleasantly exciting and stimulating to the mind. □ **piquancy** n. [*Say* pee CONT *or* pee CANT *or* PEE cant; PEEK'n see]

pique ● v. (**piques, piqued, piquing**) **1** wound the pride of, irritate. **2** arouse interest in. ● n. enmity; resentment. [*Say* PEEK]

piracy n. (pl. **piracies**) **1** the robbing of ships at sea. **2** the infringement of copyright by unauthorized reproduction.

piranha n. (pl. **piranhas**) a predatory S American fish that tears flesh from its prey. [*Say* puh RONNA *or* puh RANNA]

pirate ● n. a person who commits piracy. ● v. (**pirates, pirated, pirating**) use or reproduce another's work or ideas for one's own benefit without permission. □ **piratical** adj. **pirated** adj. [*Say* PIE rut, pie RAT uh cull]

pirogi n. = PEROGY. [*Say* puh ROE ghee]

pirogue n. a long narrow canoe made from a single tree trunk. [*Say* pi ROAG]

pirouette ● n. a rapid turn or spin on one foot, made esp. by a dancer. ● v. (**pirouettes, pirouetted, pirouetting**) perform a pirouette. [*Say* pir oo ET]

Pisces n. (pl. **Pisces**) **1** a large constellation (the Fish or Fishes). **2** the twelfth sign of the zodiac, which the sun enters after Feb. 19. □ **Piscean** n. [*Say* PICE eez]

piss *coarse slang* ● v. (**pisses, pissed, pissing**) urinate. ● n. **1** urine. **2** an act of urinating. □ **piss away** squander; waste. **piss off 1** go away. **2** annoy; anger.

pissed adj. *slang* **1** drunk. **2** annoyed; angry.

pissy adj. (**pissier, pissiest**) *coarse slang* **1** disagreeable; foul. **2** second-rate.

pistachio n. (pl. **pistachios**) the edible pale green seed of an evergreen tree with small brownish-green flowers. [*Say* piss TASHY oh]

piste n. a ski run of compacted snow. [*Say* PEEST]

pistil n. the female organs of a flower, comprising the stigma, style, and ovary. [*Say* PISS tul]

pistol n. a handgun.

pistol-grip n. a handle shaped like the butt of a pistol.

pistol-whip v. (**pistol-whips, pistol-whipped, pistol-whipping**) beat with a pistol.

piston n. a disc or short cylinder fitting closely within a tube in which it moves up and down as part of an engine or pump.

pit ● n. **1** a large hole in the ground. **2** a hollow on any surface. **3** the stone of a fruit. **4** (in full **orchestra pit**) the part of a theatre etc. where the orchestra plays. **5** an area at the side of a track where race cars are serviced. **6** (**the pits**) *slang* a wretched place, situation, person, etc. ● v. (**pits, pitted, pitting**) **1** (usu. foll. by *against*) **a** set people or things in opposition. **b** match one's wits, strengths, etc. against an opponent. **2** make or develop pits or indentations. **3** remove pits from.

pita n. (pl. **pitas**) a flat round hollow unleavened bread which can be split and filled. [*Say* PEETA]

pit bull n. **1** (also **pit bull terrier**) a variety of bull terrier noted for its ferocity. **2** a tenacious or aggressive person.

pitch¹ ● v. (**pitches, pitched, pitching**) **1** set up; erect and fix. **2 a** throw; fling. **b** throw out; get rid of. **3** *Baseball* throw the ball to the batter. **4 a** aim at a particular level, target, or audience. **b** *informal* promote; attempt to win approval for. **5** fall heavily, esp. headlong; lurch. **6** (of a ship etc.) plunge longitudinally. **7** *Music* set at a particular pitch. ● n. (pl. **pitches**) **1** height, degree, intensity, etc. **2** the steepness of a slope. **3** *Baseball* the act or manner of pitching the ball to a batter. **4** *Music* the degree of highness or lowness of a tone. **5** the pitching motion of a ship etc. **6** *informal* behaviour or speech intended to persuade. □ **pitch in** *informal* **1** assist, co-operate. **2** set to work vigorously.

pitch² ● n. (pl. **pitches**) **1** a sticky black substance used for waterproofing. **2** any of various similar substances, such as asphalt or bitumen. **3** the resin or crude turpentine which exudes from pine and fir trees. ● v. (**pitches, pitched, pitching**) cover or coat with pitch.

pitch-black adj. (also **pitch-dark**) very or completely dark.

pitchblende n. a mineral occurring in

pitch-like masses and yielding radium. [Say PITCH blend]

pitcher[1] n. *Baseball* the player who throws the ball to the batter.

pitcher[2] n. a vessel with a lip and a handle, for holding and pouring liquids. □ **pitcherful** n. (pl. **pitcherfuls**)

pitcher plant n. a red-flowered plant with pitcher-shaped leaves that can hold liquids to trap and drown insects, the floral emblem of Newfoundland and Labrador.

pitchfork ● n. a long-handled fork for pitching hay etc. ● v. throw or lift with a pitchfork.

pitchman n. (pl. **pitchmen**) a person delivering a sales pitch.

pitch pine n. any of various pine trees with hard, heavy timber that yields much resin.

pitch pipe n. a small pipe for setting the pitch for singing or tuning.

piteous adj. deserving or causing pity; wretched. □ **piteously** adv. [Say PITY us]

pitfall n. a hidden danger or difficulty.

pith n. 1 spongy white tissue lining the rind of an orange, lemon, etc. 2 spongy tissue in the stems and branches of other plants. 3 the essential part.

pithead n. the top of a mine shaft. [Say PIT head]

pith helmet n. a light helmet made from the dried pith of certain swamp plants, worn by explorers etc. in the tropics.

pithy adj. (**pithier**, **pithiest**) 1 (of an expression, remark, etc.) short but expressed well and full of meaning. 2 of, like, or containing much pith. □ **pithily** adv. **pithiness** n. [Say PITH ee]

pitiable adj. 1 deserving or arousing pity. 2 contemptible. [Say PITY a bull]

pitiful adj. 1 deserving of or arousing pity. 2 contemptible. □ **pitifully** adv. [Say PITTA full]

pitiless adj. 1 showing no pity; cruel. 2 very harsh or severe; unrelenting. □ **pitilessly** adv. [Say PITY less]

piton n. a peg or spike driven into a rock to support a climber. [Say PEE tawn]

pit stop n. 1 *Motor Racing* a stop at a pit for servicing and refuelling. 2 a brief stop during a trip for a snack, rest, etc.

pittance n. a very small or inadequate amount of money.

pitted adj. 1 having pits or indentations in the surface of it. 2 having the pit or stone removed.

pitter-patter ● adv. 1 with a sound like quick light steps. 2 with a rapid beat. ● n. such a sound.

pituitary ● n. (pl. **pituitaries**) a small gland at the base of the brain secreting hormones essential for growth. ● adj. of or relating to this gland. [Say pi TOO a terry or pi TYOO a terry]

pit viper n. any of various venomous snakes that have sensory pits on the head to detect prey.

pity ● n. 1 sorrow and compassion aroused by another's condition. 2 something to be regretted. ● v. (**pities**, **pitied**, **pitying**) feel pity for. □ **take** (or **have**) **pity on** feel or act compassionately towards. □ **pitying** adj. **pityingly** adv.

pivot ● n. 1 a short shaft or pin on which something turns or swings. 2 a crucial or essential person, point, etc. 3 a pivoting movement. ● v. (**pivots**, **pivoted**, **pivoting**) turn on or as if on a pivot. [Say PIV it]

pivotal adj. of crucial importance.

pix pl. n. informal 1 pictures, esp. photographs. 2 movies.

pixel n. any of the tiny areas of light on a television or computer screen. [Say PIX ul]

pixie n. (also **pixy**) (pl. **pixies**) a small fairy, esp. with pointed ears and a pointed hat. □ **pixieish** adj. [Say PIXY, PIXY ish]

pizza n. a flat round base of dough baked with a topping of tomato sauce and cheese and other garnishes, e.g. meat, vegetables, etc.

pizzazz n. (also **pizazz**) informal an attractive combination of liveliness and style or glamour. [Say puh ZAZZ]

pizzeria n. a place where pizzas are made or sold.

pizzicato ● adv. plucking the strings of a violin etc. with the finger. ● adj. (of a note, passage, etc.) performed pizzicato. [Say pits i CATTO or pits i COTTO]

PJs pl. n. informal pyjamas.

pl. abbr. plural.

placard n. a sign for public display, either fixed to a wall or carried in demonstrations etc. [Say PLACK ard or PLACK erd]

placate v. (**placates**, **placated**, **placating**) make less angry; calm. □ **placatingly** adv. [Say pluh KATE or PLACK ate or PLAY kate]

place ● n. 1 a particular position or location. 2 a portion of space occupied by or set aside for someone or something. 3 a position in a sequence. 4 the position of a figure in a decimal number. 5 a square or short street. 6 informal a person's home. ● v. (**places**, **placed**, **placing**) 1 put in a particular position or situation. 2 find an appropriate place or role for. 3 allocate a specified position in a sequence or hierarchy. **4** remember where one has encountered someone or something. **5** arrange for something to be done. **6** finish second in a horse race. □ **go places** *informal* be successful. **put a person in his** (or **her**) **place** deflate or humiliate a person. **take place** occur. □ **placing** *n.* **placeless** *adj.*

placebo *n.* (*pl.* **placebos**) a pill etc. with no medicinal ingredient, used esp. in studies of the effects of real drugs. [*Say* pluh SEE bo]

place kick *n. Football* a kick in which the ball is placed on the ground and held upright. □ **place-kick** *v.* **place-kicker** *n.*

placemat *n.* a small mat used to protect a table on which dishes and eating utensils are set.

placement *n.* **1** the act of finding somebody a suitable job or place to live. **2** a job as part of a course of study or for gaining experience. **3** the act of placing something somewhere.

placenta *n.* (*pl.* **placentas**) an organ in the uterus of a pregnant mammal, nourishing the fetus. □ **placental** *adj.* [*Say* pluh SENTA]

placer *n.* a deposit of sand and gravel in a riverbed or stream bed, containing particles of gold or other minerals. [*Say* PLASS er]

place setting *n.* a set of plates, cutlery, etc. for one person at a meal.

placid *adj.* **1** not easily aroused or disturbed; peaceful. **2** calm; serene. □ **placidly** *adv.* [*Say* PLASS id]

placket *n.* **1** an opening or slit in a garment, for fastenings or access to a pocket. **2** the flap of fabric under this.

plagiarize *v.* (**plagiarizes, plagiarized, plagiarizing**) take and use or claim the thoughts, writings, inventions, etc. of another person as one's own. □ **plagiarism** *n.* **plagiarist** *n.* **plagiarizer** *n.* [*Say* PLAY juh rize]

plague ● *n.* **1 a** (**the plague**) a contagious disease characterized by swollen inflamed lymph nodes (**bubonic plague**) and sometimes infection of the lungs (**pneumonic plague**). **b** any severe contagious disease spreading rapidly. **2** an unusual infestation of a pest etc. ● *v.* (**plagues, plagued, plaguing**) afflict, torment. [*Say* PLAIG]

plaice *n.* (*pl.* **plaice**) a North Atlantic flatfish with a brown back and a white underside. [*Sounds like* PLACE]

plaid *n.* **1** checkered or tartan, esp. woollen, twilled cloth. **2** a checkered or tartan pattern. [*Say* PLAD]

plain ● *adj.* **1** not decorated, garnished, or elaborate; simple. **2** without a pattern. **3** unmarked. **4** easy to perceive or understand; clear. **5** not beautiful or attractive. ● *adv.* simply. ● *n.* **1** a level tract of esp. treeless and flat grassland; prairie. **2** (**the Plains**) the region of western N America originally characterized by such grassland. □ **plainly** *adv.* **plainness** *n.*

plainchant *n.* = PLAINSONG.

plainclothes *adj.* not wearing a uniform.

plains bison *n.* (*pl.* **plains bison**) (also **plains buffalo** *pl.* **plains buffalo** or **plains buffaloes**) a subspecies of the bison, with a yellow-ochre cape of hair over the shoulders.

Plains Cree *n.* (*pl.* **Plains Cree**) **1** a member of a Cree people now living in Manitoba, southern Saskatchewan, and central Alberta. **2** their dialect.

Plains Indian *n.* (*pl.* **Plains Indians**) a member of any of a number of Aboriginal peoples inhabiting the Plains of western N America, including the Assiniboine, Blackfoot, Gros Ventres, Peigan, Blood, and Sarcee.

plainsong *n.* esp. unaccompanied church music sung in unison in medieval modes and in free rhythm.

plain-spoken *adj.* outspoken; blunt.

plaintiff *n.* a person who brings a case against another into court.

plaintive *adj.* expressing sorrow. □ **plaintively** *adv.*

plain-vanilla *adj.* ordinary, plain, not exciting.

plait ● *n.* a length of hair, straw, etc., in three or more interlaced strands; a braid. ● *v.* form hair etc. into a plait. [*Sounds like* PLATE]

plan ● *n.* **1** a detailed scheme for doing or achieving something. **2** an intention. **3** a scheme for making regular payments. **4** a map or diagram. **5** a scale drawing of a horizontal section of a building. ● *v.* (**plans, planned, planning**) **1** decide on and arrange in advance. **2** make preparations. □ **plan on** aim at doing; intend.

planar *adj. Math* having to do with a plane. [*Say* PLANE er]

plane[1] ● *n.* **1** a completely flat surface. **2** an airplane. **3** a level, e.g. of attainment or knowledge. ● *adj.* **1** perfectly level. **2** relating to two-dimensional figures. ● *v.* (**planes, planed, planing**) skim over water.

plane[2] ● *n.* (also **planer**) a tool for smoothing a surface by paring shavings from it. ● v. (**planes, planed, planing**) smooth with a plane.

plane³ n. a tall tree with maple-like leaves and bark that peels in uneven patches.

planeload n. as much as can be carried in an airplane.

planet n. a celestial body in orbit around a star, esp. any of the nine large bodies orbiting the sun.

planetarium n. (pl. **planetariums** or **planetaria**) a domed building in which images of stars, planets, constellations, etc. are projected.

planetary adj. **1** of or like planets. **2** global, worldwide.

plangent adj. plaintive; sad. □**plangently** adv. [Say PLAN jint]

plank n. **1** a long flat piece of timber used esp. in building etc. **2** a single item of a political or other program. □**walk the plank** hist. be made to walk along a plank over the side of a ship to one's death in the sea. □**planked** adj.

plank house n. a large rectangular dwelling covered with planks, used esp. by the Aboriginal peoples of the Pacific coast.

planking n. planks as flooring etc.

plankton n. tiny organisms drifting or floating in the sea or fresh water. □**planktonic** adj. [Say PLANK tun, plank TONIC]

planned adj. in accordance with a plan.

planner n. **1** = URBAN PLANNER. **2** a person who makes plans. **3** a list, table, organizer, etc., helpful in planning.

planning n. **1** in senses of PLAN v. **2** the coordinating of land use and development.

plant ● n. **1** a living thing fixed in the ground, having roots with which it absorbs substances and water and uses it makes nutrients by photosynthesis. **2 a** machinery used in industrial processes. **b** a factory. **c** (also **physical plant**) the premises, fittings, and equipment of a business or institution. **3** informal **a** something incriminating concealed so as to be discovered later. **b** a spy or source of information. ● v. **1** place a seed etc. in the ground so that it may take root and flourish. **2** put or fix in position. **3** station a person as a spy or source of information. **4** cause an idea etc. to be established, esp. in another person's mind. **5** deliver with a deliberate aim. **6** informal conceal something incriminating for later discovery. □**plantlike** adj.

Plantagenet n. hist. a member of the English royal dynasty that held the throne from the accession of Henry II in 1154 until the death of Richard III in 1485.

□**Plantagenet** adj. [Say plan TADGE a nit]

plantain n. **1** a low-growing lawn weed with a rosette of leaves. **2** a kind of banana containing little sugar, used esp. in cooking. [Say plan TANE or PLAN tane]

plantar adj. relating to the sole of the foot. [Sounds like PLANTER]

plantation n. **1** a large farm on which cotton, tobacco, sugar, etc. is cultivated, usu. by resident farm workers. **2** an area planted with trees as part of a reforestation program.

planter n. **1** a large container for growing plants. **2** a person or machine that plants seeds or seedlings.

plaque n. **1** an ornamental tablet, esp. affixed to a building in commemoration. **2** a sticky deposit on teeth where bacteria proliferate. [Say PLACK]

plasma n. **1** the colourless fluid constituent of blood, lymph, or milk. **2** a gas of positive ions and free electrons with an approximately equal positive and negative charge. **3** (attrib.) designating a flat panel display screen which uses an array of cells containing an ionized inert gas such as neon. [Say PLAZMA]

plaster ● n. **1** a soft mixture spread on walls, ceilings, etc., to form a smooth hard surface when dried. **2** = PLASTER OF PARIS. **3** a protective substance spread on a bandage etc. ● v. **1** cover with plaster. **2** cover with a lot of something. **3** stick or apply thickly like plaster. **4** make hair smooth with water, cream, etc. □**plasterer** n.

plastered adj. slang drunk.

plaster of Paris n. fine white plaster made of gypsum and used for making plaster casts etc.

plasterwork n. work done in plaster, esp. the plaster-covered surface of a wall.

plastic ● n. **1** any light strong chemically-produced material that can be moulded when heated. **2** informal credit cards. ● adj. **1** made of plastic. **2** capable of being moulded; supple. **3** artificial, insincere. □**plasticky** adj.

plastic explosive n. a putty-like explosive.

Plasticine n. proprietary a soft mouldable material used, esp. by children, for modelling. [Say plasta SEEN or PLASTA seen]

plasticity n. the ability to be moulded. [Say plass TISSA tee]

plasticize v. (**plasticizes, plasticized, plasticizing**) (often as **plasticized** adj.) coat with plastic. [Say PLASTA size]

plastic surgery n. the process of reconstructing parts of the body by the transfer of tissue. □ **plastic surgeon** n.

plate ● n. **1** a flat dish from which food is eaten or served. **2 a** dishes made of gold or silver. **b** objects of plated metal. **3** a thin, flat piece of metal. **4** a small, flat piece of metal bearing an inscription. **5** a printed photograph or illustration in a book. **6** Geology each of several rigid pieces of the earth's crust. ● v. (**plates, plated, plating**) cover a metal object with a thin coating of a different metal. □ **on a plate** informal available with little trouble to the recipient. **on one's plate** for one to deal with or consider. □ **plateful** n.

plate armour n. armour of metal plates.

plateau ● n. (pl. **plateaus** or **plateaux**) **1** an area of fairly level high ground. **2** a state of little variation after an increase. ● v. (**plateaus, plateaued, plateauing**) reach a level state after an increase. [Say pla TOE for the singular, pla TOES for either plural]

plate glass n. strong thick glass for esp. store windows.

platelet n. a small colourless cell fragment found in large numbers in blood and involved in clotting. [Say PLATE lit]

plate tectonics n. the slow movement of rigid plates on the underlying mantle of the earth's surface.

platform n. **1** a raised surface on which people or things can stand. **2** a structure along the side of a railway track where passengers get on and off trains. **3** a raised structure standing in the sea from which oil or gas wells can be drilled. **4** the declared set of policies of a political party. **5** a very thick sole on a shoe. **6** Computing the hardware standard that determines what kinds of software can be run.

plating n. a coating of gold, silver, etc.

platinum ● n. **1** a precious silvery-white metallic element, used in making jewellery and laboratory apparatus. **2** a greyish-white or silvery colour. ● adj. **1** (of a recording) having attained the highest recognition for sales. **2** platinum-coloured.

platinum blond ● adj. silvery-blond. ● n. a person with silvery-blond hair.

platinum card n. a credit card with a very high or no credit limit.

platitude n. a trite or commonplace remark, esp. one solemnly delivered. [Say PLATTA tude]

Platonic adj. **1** of or associated with the Greek philosopher Plato or his philosophy. **2** (**platonic**) (of love or friendship) not involving sex. **3** pertaining to the ideal form of something. [Say pluh TONIC]

Platonism n. the philosophy of the Greek philosopher Plato. □ **Platonist** n. [Say PLAY tln lsm]

platoon n. **1** a tactical unit usu. divided into three sections of ten to twelve soldiers. **2** a group of persons acting together.

platter n. **1** a large usu. oval dish or plate for presenting or serving food. **2** a serving of food on such a plate. □ **on a platter** informal available with little trouble to the recipient.

platypus n. (pl. **platypuses**) an Australian egg-laying aquatic mammal, with a duck-like bill and webbed feet. [Say PLATTA puss]

plaudit n. (usu. in pl.) an emphatic expression of approval. [Say PLOD it]

plausible adj. seeming reasonable, believable, or probable. □ **plausibility** n. **plausibly** adv. [Say PLOZZA bull]

play ● v. **1** engage in games or other activities for enjoyment. **2** take part in a sport. **3** compete against. **4** take a specified position in a sports team. **5** represent a character in a play etc. **6** perform on a musical instrument. **7** take one's turn in a game. **8** move lightly and quickly. **9** produce sounds from a CD etc. ● n. **1** activities engaged in for enjoyment, e.g. games. **2** the progress of a sports match. **3** a manoeuvre in a sport. **4** a dramatic work for the stage etc. **5** freedom of movement in a mechanism. **6** light and constantly changing movement. **7** the button on a VCR, CD player, etc. which causes it to play. □ **make a play for** informal make an attempt to acquire. **play along 1** co-operate, comply. **2** pretend to agree or co-operate. **play around 1** behave playfully or irresponsibly. **2** have casual or extramarital sexual relations. **play both ends against the middle** keep one's options open by trying to keep favour with opposing sides. **play by ear 1** perform (music) without having seen a score of it. **2** (also **play it by ear**) proceed instinctively or step by step according to results and circumstances. **play down** minimize the importance of. **play fast and loose** act unreliably. **play off 1** oppose one person against another, esp. for one's own advantage. **2** play an extra match to decide a draw or tie. **play on** take advantage of a person's feelings etc. **play out 1** bring or come to an end or resolution. **2** perform to the end. **play up** emphasize, make the most of. **play up to** flatter, esp. to win favour. □ **playability** n. **playable** adj.

play-act v. behave affectedly or insincerely. □ **play-acting** n. **play-actor** n.

playback *n.* the playing of a recording.

playbook *n.* *Sport* a book containing descriptions of a team's strategies and plays.

playboy *n.* an irresponsible, pleasure-seeking, esp. wealthy man.

play-by-play *n.* the broadcast verbal description of a sports match etc. as it unfolds.

playdough *n.* a soft, malleable, coloured dough-like substance used for modelling.

playdown *n.* (usu. in *pl.*) esp. *Cdn & Scot. Sport* a playoff match in a tournament etc.

player *n.* **1** a person taking part in a sport or game. **2** a person playing a musical instrument. **3** an actor. **4** a machine that plays audio or video recordings. **5** a person or company important in a field.

player piano *n.* a piano that can play automatically.

playful *adj.* **1** fond of or inclined to play. **2** done in fun; humorous. □ **playfully** *adv.* **playfulness** *n.*

playground *n.* an outdoor area for children to play on.

playgroup *n.* a group of esp. preschool children who play regularly together under supervision.

playhouse *n.* a theatre.

playing card *n.* each of a set of small cards with an identical pattern on one side and various numbers and symbols on the other, used to play games.

playlist *n.* a list of pieces to be played, esp. on a radio show.

playmaker *n.* a player in a team game who coordinates attacks. □ **playmaking** *n. & adj.*

playmate *n.* a child's companion in play.

playoff *n.* *Sport* **1** (usu. in *pl.*) a tournament played to determine a champion. **2** a match played to decide a draw or tie.

play on words *n.* a pun.

playpen *n.* a portable enclosure for young children to play in.

playroom *n.* a room set aside for playing in.

playschool *n.* a nursery school.

plaything *n.* a toy or other thing to play with.

playtime *n.* time for play or recreation.

playwright *n.* a person who writes plays.

playwriting *n.* the activity of writing plays.

plaza *n.* **1** a shopping centre. **2** an open square in an urban area.

plea *n.* **1** an earnest appeal. **2** a defendant's formal statement in response to a charge.

plea bargain *n.* an arrangement in which a defendant pleads guilty to a lesser charge in the expectation of a lesser sentence. □ **plea bargain** *v.* **plea bargaining** *n.*

plead *v.* (**pleads**; **pleaded** or esp. *US* **pled**; **pleading**) **1** make an earnest appeal. **2** *Law* argue in support of. **3** *Law* declare whether or not one is guilty. **4** offer as an excuse. □ **pleader** *n.*

pleading ● *n.* (usu. in *pl.*) a formal statement of the cause of an action or defence. ● *adj.* expressing an earnest entreaty. □ **pleadingly** *adv.*

pleasant *adj.* **1** pleasing. **2** polite and friendly. □ **pleasantly** *adv.* **pleasantness** *n.*

pleasantry *n.* (*pl.* **pleasantries**) a pleasant or amusing remark, esp. made in casual conversation.

please ● *v.* (**pleases**, **pleased**, **pleasing**) **1** make glad; give pleasure to. **2** be glad or willing to. **3** will, wish. ● *interj.* used as a polite way of making a request. □ **please oneself** do as one likes. □ **pleased** *adj.* **pleasing** *adj.* **pleasingly** *adv.*

pleasurable *adj.* causing pleasure; agreeable. □ **pleasurably** *adv.*

pleasure ● *n.* **1** a feeling of happy satisfaction or enjoyment. **2** a source of pleasure or gratification. **3** sensual gratification. **4** (as an *adj.*) done or used for pleasure. ● *v.* (**pleasures**, **pleasured**, **pleasuring**) give (esp. sexual) pleasure to.

pleat *n.* a flattened fold of cloth doubled on itself in a garment. □ **pleated** *adj.* **pleating** *n.*

plebeian ● *n.* **1** a commoner, esp. in ancient Rome. **2** *derogatory* an esp. uncultured member of the lower classes. ● *adj.* **1** of the common people. **2** uncultured; unrefined. [*Say* pluh BEE in]

plebiscite *n.* a direct vote by the public on a specific issue. [*Say* PLEBBA site]

plectrum *n.* (*pl.* **plectrums** or **plectra**) a guitar pick. [*Say* PLECK trum]

pled esp. *US past of* PLEAD.

pledge ● *n.* **1** a solemn promise or undertaking. **2** a thing given as a guarantee that a debt will be paid or a contract fulfilled. **3** the promise of a financial donation. **4** a thing given as a token of love, favour, etc. **5** a solemn undertaking to abstain from alcohol. ● *v.* (**pledges**, **pledged**, **pledging**) **1** deposit as security. **2** promise solemnly, esp. by the pledge of. **3** bind by a solemn promise. **4** promise to make a financial donation.

Pleistocene *n.* *Geology* the first epoch of the Quaternary period, lasting from about 2,000,000 to 10,000 years ago. □ **Pleistocene** *adj.* [*Say* PLICE tuh seen]

plenary • *adj.* **1** entire, unqualified. **2** to be attended by all members. • *n.* (*pl.* **plenaries**) a plenary session etc.
[*Say* PLENNA ree]

plenitude *n. literary* **1** abundance. **2** fullness, completeness.
[*Say* PLENNA tude]

plenteous *adj. literary* plentiful.
□ **plenteously** *adv.* **plenteousness** *n.*
[*Say* PLENTY us]

plentiful *adj.* **1** abundant. □ **plentifully** *adv.* **plentifulness** *n.*

plenty • *n.* a situation in which there is an ample supply of food, money, etc. • *pron.* a great or sufficient quantity or number.
• *adj. informal* existing in an ample quantity.
• *adv.* **1** *informal* fully, entirely. **2** a lot.

plethora *n.* an abundance.
[*Say* PLETH er uh]

pleurisy *n.* inflammation of the membranes enveloping the lungs.
[*Say* PLURA see]

Plexiglas *n. proprietary* a tough light transparent acrylic thermoplastic.

plexus *n.* (*pl.* **plexus** or **plexuses**) **1** a network of nerves or blood vessels. **2** a structure consisting of a bundle of minute closely interwoven fibres or tubes.

pliable *adj.* **1** bending easily. **2** compliant.
□ **pliability** *n.* [*Say* PLY a bull]

pliant *adj.* **1** flexible. **2** readily influenced.
[*Say* PLY int]

pliers *pl. n.* pincers with gripping jaws used for holding small objects, bending wire, etc.

plight *n.* an esp. unfortunate condition, state, or predicament.

plink • *v.* emit a short, sharp, metallic or ringing sound. • *n.* this sound.

plinth *n.* the lower square slab at the base of a column or pedestal.

Pliocene *n. Geology* the last epoch of the Tertiary period, lasting from about 5.1 to 2 million years ago. □ **Pliocene** *adj.*
[*Say* PLY uh seen]

PLO *abbr.* Palestine Liberation Organization.

plod • *v.* (**plods, plodded, plodding**) **1** walk doggedly or laboriously; trudge. **2** work slowly and steadily, esp. without inspiration. • *n.* a slow heavy walk or pace.
□ **plodder** *n.* **plodding** *adj.*
ploddingly *adv.*

plonk *informal* • *v.* set down hurriedly or clumsily. • *n.* **1** a heavy thud. **2** cheap or inferior wine.

plop • *n.* a sound as of an object dropping into water without a splash. • *v.* (**plops, plopped, plopping**) **1** make a plop. **2** fall or drop with a plop. □ **plop down** sit down abruptly.

plot • *n.* **1** a usu. small piece of ground used for a special purpose, e.g. for a grave. **2** the main sequence of events in a play, novel, etc. **3** a conspiracy or secret plan, esp. for unlawful purposes. • *v.* (**plots, plotted, plotting**) **1** plan or contrive secretly. **2** make a ground plan, map, or diagram of. **3** mark on a chart or diagram. **4** devise the plot of a novel etc.
□ **plotless** *adj.*

plot line *n.* the main features of the plot of a play, novel, film, etc.

plotter *n.* **1** a person who plots something esp. unlawful. **2** an instrument for automatically drawing or plotting a graph etc.

plough *n. & v.* = PLOW. [*Say* PLOW]

ploughman *n.* (*pl.* **ploughmen**) (also **plowman**) a person who uses a plough.
[*Say* PLOWMAN]

ploughshare *n.* (also **plowshare**) the large cutting blade of a plough.
[*Say* PLOW share]

plover *n.* a plump-breasted shorebird with a pigeon-like bill. [*Rhymes with* LOVER]

plow • *n.* **1** (often **plough**) a farm implement with a blade for cutting furrows in the soil and turning it up. **2** a similar implement for deflecting material against which it moves, e.g. a snowplow.
• *v.* **1** (often **plough**) make furrows in and turn up (the earth) with a plow. **2** (often **plough**) (foll. by *under*) bury in the soil by plowing. **3** remove snow from a surface with a plow. **4** (foll. by *through*) advance laboriously. **5** (foll. by *through, into*) travel or be propelled clumsily or violently into or through. □ **plowed** *adj.*

ploy *n. informal* a cunning manoeuvre to gain an advantage.

pluck • *v.* **1** remove by picking or pulling out. **2** pull out a feather, hair, etc. **3** pull at, esp. abruptly or with a jerk. **4** sound a musical instrument string by tugging at it with the finger or pick. • *n.* **1** courage, spirit, boldness. **2** an act of plucking.
□ **pluck up** summon up (one's courage, spirits, etc.). □ **plucker** *n.*

plucky *adj.* (**pluckier, pluckiest**) brave, spirited. □ **pluckily** *adv.*

plug • *n.* **1** a piece of solid material tightly blocking a hole. **2 a** the end of an electrical cord, with metal prongs that fit into a socket to make an electrical connection. **b** *informal* an electric socket. **3** a spark plug. **4** *informal* a piece of publicity for an idea, product, etc. **5** a stick of tobacco for chewing. **6** *Fishing* a lure with one or more hooks. • *v.* (**plugs, plugged, plugging**) **1** stop, fill, or obstruct a hole with a plug etc. **2** *informal* give free publicity to. **3** *slang* shoot or hit. □ **plug away** *informal* persevere doggedly. **plug in 1** connect or be connected electrically by inserting a plug in a socket. **2** *informal* incorporate.

plugged *adj.* stopped up, closed, or filled with a plug.

plugged-in *adj.* **1** connected by means of a plug. **2** *informal* aware of what is happening, in fashion, etc.

plugger *n.* **1** a person who or thing which plugs something. **2** *informal* a person who works diligently.

plug-in ● *adj.* **1** able to be connected by means of a plug. **2** *Computing* (of a module or software) able to be added to a system to give extra features or functions. ● *n.* **1** a plug-in device or unit. **2** *Cdn* an electrical outlet for plugging in a block heater. **3** *Computing* a plug-in module or software.

plum ● *n.* **1** an oval fleshy fruit, usu. purple, reddish, or yellow when ripe, that grows on a tree of the rose family. **2** a deep reddish-purple colour. **3** a highly desirable thing. ● *adj.* **1** (also **plum-coloured**) of a reddish-purple colour. **2** valuable, coveted.

plumage *n.* a bird's feathers. [*Say* PLOO midge]

plumb ● *n.* (also **plumb bob**) a ball of lead etc. attached to the end of a line for finding the depth of water or determining the vertical. ● *adv.* **1** exactly. **2** vertically, straight down. **3** *slang* completely. ● *adj.* **1** vertical, perpendicular. **2** downright, sheer. ● *v.* **1** measure the depth of water with a plumb. **2** test an upright surface to determine the vertical. **3** explore or experience fully or in detail. **4** provide a building or room with plumbing. □ **out of** (or **off**) **plumb** not vertical. [*Say* PLUM]

plumber *n.* a person who fits and repairs the water pipes, water tanks, etc. in a building. [*Say* PLUMMER]

plumbing *n.* **1** the system of water pipes etc. in a building. **2** the work of a plumber. [*Say* PLUMMING]

plumb line *n.* a line with a plumb attached.

plume ● *n.* **1** an esp. large ornamental feather. **2** a spreading trail of vapour etc. ● *v.* (**plumes, plumed, pluming**) **1** provide with a plume or plumes. **2** (of vapour, etc.) form a plume. □ **plumed** *adj.*

plummet ● *v.* (**plummets, plummeted, plummeting**) drop, fall, or plunge rapidly. ● *n.* a plumb or plumb line. [*Say* PLUM it]

plummy *adj.* (**plummier, plummiest**) **1 a** resembling a plum or plums, esp. in taste or colour. **b** rich in plums. **2** *informal* (of a voice) deep, thick-sounding, typical of the

British upper classes. **3** *informal* good, desirable.

plump¹ ● *adj.* having a full rounded shape; filled out. ● *v.* (often foll. by *up, out*) make or become plump. □ **plumpish** *adj.* **plumpness** *n.*

plump² *v.* **1** drop, fall, or set down abruptly. **2** (**plump for**) decide in favour of.

plum pudding *n.* a rich boiled or steamed suet pudding with raisins, currants, spices, etc.

plum tomato *n.* a plum-shaped tomato, used esp. in cooking.

plunder ● *v.* **1** rob esp. systematically or as in war. **2** steal or embezzle. ● *n.* **1** the violent or dishonest acquisition of property. **2** property acquired by plundering. □ **plunderer** *n.*

plunge ● *v.* (**plunges, plunged, plunging**) **1** thrust or drive forcefully or abruptly or impetuously. **2** immerse completely. **3 a** move suddenly and dramatically downward. **b** diminish or drop in value etc. rapidly. ● *n.* **1** a sudden violent movement or fall. **2** an act of jumping or diving. □ **take the plunge** *informal* **1** commit oneself irrevocably to a course of action. **2** get married.

plunger *n.* a rubber cup on a handle for clearing blocked pipes by a plunging and sucking action. [*Say* PLUN jer]

plunk ● *n.* the sound of something dropping, esp. heavily. ● *v.* drop down heavily or abruptly. □ **plunk down** spend (money).

pluperfect ● *adj.* *Grammar* denoting an action completed prior to some past point of time, as: *he had gone by then.* ● *n.* the pluperfect tense. [*Say* ploo PERFECT]

plural ● *adj.* **1** more than one in number. **2** *Grammar* denoting more than one. ● *n.* *Grammar* **1** a plural word or form. **2** the plural number.

pluralism *n.* the existence or toleration in society of a number of different racial, cultural, or religious groups. □ **pluralist** *n.* **pluralistic** *adj.*

plurality *n.* (*pl.* **pluralities**) **1** the state or fact of being plural. **2 a** a large number or quantity. **b** the greater number or part; more than half of the whole. **3** a vote in which the winning candidate receives more ballots than any other but does not receive an absolute majority. [*Say* plur ALA tee]

pluralize *v.* (**pluralizes, pluralized, pluralizing**) **1** make or become plural. **2** express in or form the plural. [*Say* PLURAL ize]

plus ● *prep.* **1** *Math* made more by, increased by. Symbol: +. **2** above zero degrees. ● *adj.*

1 at least. **2** better than. **3** *Math* positive. **4** having a positive electrical charge. **5** designed for people larger than most. ● *n.* (*pl.* **pluses**) an advantage; a positive quality. ● *conj. informal disputed* and furthermore.

plus ça change *interj.* the more things change, the more they stay the same. [*Say* ploo suh SHONZH]

plush ● *n.* a velvet-like type of cloth with a longer pile. ● *adj.* **1** made of or resembling plush. **2** stylish, luxurious. □ **plushness** *n.* **plushy** *adj.* (**plushier, plushiest**)

plus-minus *n. Hockey* (also **plus/minus**) a tally of all even-strength goals scored for (added) and against (subtracted) while a specific player is on the ice.

plutocracy *n.* (*pl.* **plutocracies**) **1** government by the wealthy. **2** a wealthy elite or ruling class. [*Say* ploo TOCKRA see]

plutocrat *n.* often *derogatory* a wealthy and influential person. □ **plutocratic** *adj.* [*Say* PLUTO crat]

plutonium *n.* a radioactive metallic element used in some nuclear reactors and weapons. [*Say* ploo TONY um]

ply¹ *n.* (*pl.* **plies**) **1** a thickness or layer of wood, cloth, or paper. **2** plywood. **3** a strand or twist of rope, yarn, or thread. **4** a reinforcing layer of fabric in a tire.

ply² *v.* (**plies, plied, plying**) **1** work steadily at. **2** travel regularly back and forth. **3 a** supply continuously with food, drink, etc. **b** approach repeatedly with questions, demands, etc. **4** use or wield vigorously (a tool, weapon, etc.).

plywood *n.* a strong warp-resistant board consisting of two or more layers of wood glued together.

PM *abbr.* (*pl.* **PMs**) **1** Prime Minister. **2** post-mortem.

p.m. *abbr.* (also **P.M.**) after noon.

PMO *abbr. Cdn* Prime Minister's Office.

PMS *abbr.* premenstrual syndrome.

pneumatic *adj.* **1** of or relating to air or gases. **2** containing or operated by compressed air. [*Say* new MAT ick]

pneumonia *n.* inflammation of the lungs causing the air sacs to fill with pus and become solid. □ **pneumonic** *adj.* [*Say* new MOANY uh]

PO *abbr.* **1** Post Office. **2** petty officer. **3** purchase order.

poach *v.* (**poaches, poached, poaching**) **1** cook in simmering water. **2 a** catch game or fish illegally. **b** trespass or encroach on another's property, ideas, etc. □ **poacher** *n.*

pock ● *n.* **1** a small pus-filled spot on the skin. **2** a disfiguring scar or pit. ● *v.* mark with pocks or disfiguring spots. □ **pocked** *adj.*

pocket ● *n.* **1** a small bag sewn into or on clothing, for carrying small articles. **2** a pouch-like compartment in a suitcase, car door, etc. **3** one's financial resources. **4** an isolated group or area contrasted with its surroundings. **5** a cavity in a rock or stratum. **6** a pouch at the corner or on the side of a pool table into which balls are driven. ● *v.* (**pockets, pocketed, pocketing**) **1** put into one's pocket. **2** take possession of, esp. dishonestly. **3** *Billiards etc.* drive (a ball) into a pocket. □ **in a person's pocket 1** under a person's control. **2** close to or intimate with a person. **out of pocket** having lost in a transaction. □ **pocketful** *n.*

pocketbook *n.* **1** one's financial resources. **2** (**pocket book**) a small book.

pocket knife *n.* a knife with a folding blade.

pocket money *n.* **1** money for minor expenses. **2** esp. *Brit.* an allowance of money made to a child.

pocket protector *n.* a plastic insert for a shirt pocket, for preventing rips and ink stains caused by pens.

pocket-sized *adj.* (also **pocket-size**) small enough to be carried in a pocket.

pocket watch *n.* a watch intended to be carried in a pocket.

pockmark *n.* a disfiguring scar or hole. □ **pockmarked** *adj.*

pod ● *n.* **1** a long seed vessel esp. of a pea or bean plant. **2** any protruding, detachable, or more or less enclosed part of a tool, craft, vehicle, etc. **3** the cocoon of a silkworm. **4** a small group of whales. ● *v.* (**pods, podded, podding**) **1** bear, form, or have a pod or pods. **2** remove (peas etc.) from pods. □ **podded** *adj.*

podiatry *n.* the medical specialty dealing with the feet. □ **podiatrist** *n.* [*Say* puh DIE a tree]

podium *n.* (*pl.* **podiums** or **podia**) **1** a raised platform at the front of a hall or stage. **2** a platform for an orchestra conductor. **3** a lectern. **4** a desk at an airport departure gate.

poem *n.* a piece of creative writing in short lines, usu. metrical and often using rhyme.

poet *n.* a writer of poems.

poetic *adj.* (also **poetical**) **1 a** of or like poetry or poets. **b** written in verse. **2** elevated in expression. □ **poetically** *adv.*

poetic justice *n.* well-deserved unforeseen retribution or reward.

poetic licence *n.* a writer's

transgression of established rules of language for effect.

poetics *n.* the study of poetry and its techniques.

Poet Laureate *n.* a person honoured by a state as its pre-eminent or most representative poet.

poetry *n.* **1 a** the expression of thought, imagination, or feeling, in language and a form adapted to stir the imagination and the emotions. **b** composition in verse, metrical language, or some equivalent patterned arrangement of language. **2** poems collectively.

pogey *n.* (also **pogy**) *Cdn informal* **1** unemployment insurance benefits. **2** welfare benefits. [*Say* POE ghee]

pogo *n.* (*pl.* **pogos**) **1** (also **pogo stick**) a spring-loaded stick with rests for the feet, for jumping about on. **2** (**Pogo**) *Cdn proprietary* (also **Pogo stick**) a hot dog covered in cornmeal batter and served on a stick.

pogrom *n.* an organized massacre of a particular ethnic group. [*Say* poe GROM]

poignant *adj.* deeply moving, esp. in a way that arouses sadness or regret. □ **poignancy** *n.* **poignantly** *adv.* [*Say* POIN yint]

poinsettia *n.* a small shrub with large esp. scarlet bracts surrounding small yellow flowers, popular as a Christmas houseplant. [*Say* poin SETTA *or* poin SETTY uh]

point ● *n.* **1** the sharp end of a tool, weapon, etc. **2** a particular spot, place, or moment. **3** an item, detail, or idea in a discussion etc. **4** (**the point**) the most significant or relevant factor. **5** purpose. **6** a feature or characteristic. **7** a unit of scoring or of measuring value or achievement. **8** a period or decimal point. **9** a very small dot or mark. **10** (in geometry) something having position but not spatial extent. **11** each of thirty-two directions marked at equal distances around a compass. **12** a narrow piece of land jutting out into the sea, a lake, etc. **13** a unit of measurement for type sizes. **14** any of various positions in a number of sports, esp. (in hockey) either of two areas just inside the blue line where it meets the boards. ● *v.* **1** direct someone's attention in a particular direction by extending one's finger. **2** direct or aim. **3** face in or indicate a particular direction. **4** cite or function as evidence. **5** fill in the joints of brickwork with smoothly finished mortar. □ **beside the point** irrelevant or in an irrelevant way. **case in point** an instance that is relevant or under consideration. **have a**

point be correct in one's contention. **make a point of 1** insist on. **2** make a special project of. **point out** draw attention to. **point up** emphasize. **to the point** relevant or relevantly.

point-blank ● *adj.* **1** fired from very close to the target. **2** straightforward, blunt, direct. ● *adv.* **1** at very close range. **2** directly, bluntly, straightforwardly.

point blanket *n.* a type of Hudson's Bay blanket with short black lines woven in to indicate weight.

point-counterpoint *n.* a situation in which opposing views etc. are heard in alternation.

pointe *n. Ballet* **1** the tip of the toe or toes, or the toe of a pointe shoe. **2** (also **pointe work**) dance performed on the tips of the toes. [*Say* POINT]

pointed *adj.* **1** sharpened or tapering to a point. **2** (of a remark) **a** having particular force. **b** precisely aimed, exactly directed. **3** emphasized. □ **pointedly** *adv.*

pointer *n.* **1** a thing that points or is used to indicate something, e.g. the needle of a gauge, a hand-held rod, or a movable graphic on a computer screen. **2** *informal* a hint, clue, or indication. **3** a dog of a breed that on scenting game stands rigid looking toward it.

pointe shoe *n.* a soft heelless shoe worn by female ballet dancers, with a stiffened toe allowing the dancer to dance on the tip of the toes.

point form *n.* an abbreviated form of writing, not using full sentences or developed paragraphs.

point guard *n. Basketball* a small fast guard who directs the team's offence.

pointillism *n.* a painting technique using tiny dots of various pure colours, which become blended in the viewer's eye. □ **pointillist** *n.* & *adj.* [*Say* PWANT ill ism]

pointless *adj.* **1** lacking force, purpose, or meaning. **2** without a sharp or tapering point. □ **pointlessly** *adv.* **pointlessness** *n.*

point man *n.* **1** the soldier at the head of a patrol. **2** a person who leads a new endeavour. **3** *Hockey* the player taking a position at the point during a power play.

point of order *n.* a query in a debate etc. as to whether correct procedure is being followed.

point of view *n.* **1** a position from which a thing is viewed. **2** a particular way of considering a matter. **3** a narrator's position relative to the story being told.

point spread *n.* the number of points by

which one team is expected to defeat another, for betting purposes.

pointy *adj.* having a noticeably sharp end.

poise ● *n.* **1** a calm and confident manner. **2** the ability to move or stand in a graceful way with good control of one's body. ● *v.* (**poises, poised, poising**) (usu. in *passive*) **1** balance; hold suspended or supported. **2** hover in the air etc.

poised *adj.* **1** composed, self-assured. **2** ready for action.

poison ● *n.* **1** a substance that causes esp. quick death or injury when absorbed by a living organism. **2** a harmful influence or principle etc. ● *v.* **1** administer poison to. **2** infect or treat food, a weapon, etc. with poison. **3** corrupt or pervert; spoil. **4** pollute with toxic substances. □ **poisoner** *n.* **poisoning** *n.*

poison ivy *n.* a climbing plant that secretes an irritant oil.

poison oak *n.* either of two shrubs related to poison ivy and having similar properties.

poisonous *adj.* **1** causing death or illness if absorbed into the body. **2** venomous. **3** unpleasant and vindictive. □ **poisonously** *adv.*

poke ● *v.* (**pokes, poked, poking**) **1** thrust or push with the finger, point of a stick, etc. **2** produce a hole in a thing by poking. **3** push or stick out in a particular direction. **4** move or go slowly or in an aimless manner. **5** search casually. ● *n.* an act of poking. □ **poke fun at** ridicule, tease. **poke holes in** find fault with (an idea etc.).

poke check *n. Hockey* a defensive play in which a player uses the stick to poke the puck out of the puck carrier's control. □ **poke-check** *v.* **poke-checking** *n.*

poker[1] *n.* a stiff metal rod for stirring an open fire.

poker[2] *n.* a card game in which bluff is used as players bet on the value of their hands.

poker face *n.* a facial expression that hides one's true feelings. □ **poker-faced** *adj.*

poker run *n.* (also **poker derby**) a contest in which participants race to a series of points to collect playing cards, the winner being the fastest with the best poker hand.

pokeweed *n.* a plant with red stems, spikes of cream flowers, and purple berries.

pokey *n.* (*pl.* **pokeys**) *slang* prison.

poky *adj.* (**pokier, pokiest**) **1** small and cramped. **2** annoyingly slow.

pol *n. informal* a politician.

polar *adj.* **1 a** of or near a pole of the earth

or a celestial body, or of the celestial sphere. **b** living in the north polar region. **2** having an electrical or magnetic field. **3** directly opposite in character.

polar bear *n.* a very large white Arctic bear.

polar fleece *n.* a thick fleece fabric.

polarity *n.* (*pl.* **polarities**) **1** the tendency of a magnet to point with its extremities to the magnetic poles of the earth. **2** the condition of having two poles with contrary qualities. **3** the state of having two opposite tendencies, opinions, etc. **4** the electrical condition of a body (positive or negative). [*Say* puh LAIR uh tee]

polarize *v.* (**polarizes, polarized, polarizing**) **1** restrict the vibrations of a wave of light to one direction. **2** give magnetic or electric polarity to. **3** divide into two groups of opposing opinion etc. □ **polarization** *n.* **polarizer** *n.*

Polaroid *n. proprietary* **1** a type of camera that produces a finished print rapidly after each exposure. **2** a photograph taken with such a camera.

Pole *n.* a person from Poland.

pole[1] ● *n.* **1** a long slender piece of wood, metal, etc., esp. with the end placed in the ground as a support etc. **2** a long slender flexible rod used in pole vaulting. **3** a fishing rod. ● *v.* (**poles, poled, poling**) use poles, esp. to propel a boat or oneself on skis.

pole[2] *n.* **1 a** (also **north pole, south pole**) each of the two points in the celestial sphere about which the stars appear to revolve. **b** (also **North Pole, South Pole**) each of the extremities of the axis of rotation of the earth. **2** each of the two opposite points on the surface of a magnet. **3** each of two terminals of an electric cell or battery. **4** each of two opposed principles or ideas. □ **be poles apart** differ greatly, esp. in nature or opinion.

poleaxe ● *n.* a battleaxe. ● *v.* (**poleaxes, poleaxed, poleaxing**) **1** hit or kill with or as if with a poleaxe. **2** *informal* surprise or shock greatly.

polecat *n.* a skunk. [*Say* POLE cat]

polemic ● *n.* **1** a controversial discussion. **2** a verbal or written attack. ● *adj.* (also **polemical**) having to do with strongly critical or controversial writing or speech. □ **polemicist** *n.* [*Say* puh LEMMICK, puh LEMMA sist]

polenta *n.* cornmeal boiled in water and often baked or fried. [*Say* puh LENTA]

pole position *n.* the most favourable position at the start of a motor race.

pole vault *n.* the sport of vaulting over a

high bar with the aid of a long flexible pole. □ **pole-vault** v. **pole vaulter** n.

police ● n. (treated as pl.) a force responsible for enforcing the law, maintaining public order, etc. ● v. (**polices, policed, policing**) **1** control by means of police. **2** provide with police. **3** keep order in.

policeman n. (pl. **policemen**) **1** a member of a police force. **2** Hockey = ENFORCER 2.

police state n. a totalitarian state controlled by political police supervising the citizens' activities.

policewoman n. (pl. **policewomen**) a female member of a police force.

policy n. (pl. **policies**) **1** a principle of action adopted or proposed by a government, party, etc. **2** a contract of insurance.

policyholder n. a person or body holding an insurance policy.

polio n. (in full **poliomyelitis**) an infectious viral disease of the central nervous system which can cause permanent paralysis.
[Say POE lee oh (my uh LITE iss)]

polis n. (pl. **poleis**) a city state in ancient Greece. [Say POE liss for the singular, POE leece for the plural]

poli-sci n. informal political science.
[Say polly SIGH]

Polish ● adj. **1** of or relating to Poland. **2** of the Poles or their Slavic language. ● n. this language.

polish ● v. (**polishes, polished, polishing**) **1** make or become smooth or glossy by rubbing. **2** (esp. as **polished** adj.) refine or improve. ● n. (pl. **polishes**) **1** a substance used for polishing. **2** smoothness or glossiness produced by friction. **3** an act of polishing. **4** refinement or elegance of manner, conduct, etc. □ **polish off 1** finish quickly. **2** get rid of. **polish up** revise or improve. □ **polisher** n.

politburo n. (pl. **politburos**) the principal policy-making committee of a Communist party. [Say PAUL it byoor oh]

polite adj. (**politer, politest**) **1** having good manners; courteous. **2** cultured and refined. □ **politely** adv. **politeness** n.

politic ● adj. **1** seeming sensible in the circumstances. **2** political. ● v. (**politics, politicked, politicking**) engage in politics. [Say PAULA tick]

political adj. **1 a** of or concerning the state or its government, or public affairs generally. **b** having to do with politics. **2** based on considerations of power or

public sensibilities rather than principle. □ **politically** adv.

political correctness n. the avoidance of forms of expression that may offend certain groups. □ **politically correct** adj.

politically incorrect adj. failing to exhibit political correctness.

political science n. the study of the state and systems of government. □ **political scientist** n.

politician n. **1** a person engaged in or concerned with politics. **2** a person skilled in politics.

politicize v. (**politicizes, politicized, politicizing**) **1** cause to become political in character. **2** make politically aware. □ **politicization** n. [Say puh LITTA size]

politicking n. political activity, especially to win support. [Say PAULA ticking]

politico n. (pl. **politicos**) informal a politician or political enthusiast.
[Say puh LITTA co]

politics pl. n. **1** (treated as sing. or pl.) **a** the art and science of government. **b** public life and affairs as involving authority and government. **2** (usu. treated as pl.) **a** a particular set of ideas, principles, or commitments in politics. **b** activities concerned with the acquisition or exercise of authority or power.

polity n. (pl. **polities**) **1** a form or process of civil government or constitution. **2** a state as a political entity. [Say PAULA tee]

polka ● n. **1** a lively dance for couples, performed to music with two beats to the bar. **2** the music for this. ● v. dance the polka. [Say POLE kuh or POE kuh]

polka dot n. a round dot as one of many forming a regular pattern on fabric etc. □ **polka-dot** adj. **polka-dotted** adj.
[Say POKE a dot]

poll ● n. **1** an assessment of public opinion by questioning a representative sample. **2 a** the process of voting at an election. **b** a place where votes are cast. **3** a human head. ● v. **1** take the vote or votes of. **2** record the opinion. **3** give one's vote. **4** cut off the top of a tree. **5** (esp. as **polled** adj.) cut the horns off.

pollard ● n. **1** an animal that has lost its horns. **2** a tree with branches cut off to encourage the growth of new young branches. ● v. make (a tree) a pollard.
[Say PAUL erd]

pollen n. the fine powdery substance discharged from the male part of a flower, containing the gamete.

pollinate v. (**pollinates, pollinated, pollinating**) fertilize with pollen. □ **pollination** n. **pollinator** n.

polling n. the registering or casting of votes.

pollock n. (pl. **pollock**) an important North Atlantic food fish of the cod family. [Say PAUL uck]

pollster n. a person who conducts opinion polls. [Say POLE stir]

poll tax n. a tax levied on every adult.

pollutant n. a substance that pollutes air, water, etc. [Say POLLUTE int]

pollute v. (**pollutes, polluted, polluting**) **1** contaminate with poisonous or harmful substances. **2** corrupt. □ **polluted** adj. **polluter** n. **pollution** n.

Pollyanna n. (pl. **Pollyannas**) an excessively cheerful person. □ **Pollyannaish** adj. [Say polly ANNA]

pollywog n. a tadpole.

polo n. **1** a game in which players on horseback try to hit a ball into a goal using long wooden mallets. **2** (also **polo shirt**) a short-sleeved casual shirt with a collar and a short buttoned placket at the neckline.

poltergeist n. a noisy mischievous ghost. [Say POLE tur geist (GEIST rhymes with PRICED)]

poly n. (pl. **polys**) **1** polyester. **2** polyethylene. [Say POLLY]

polybag n. a bag made of polyethylene, used esp. for packaging etc. [Say POLLY bag]

polycarbonate n. any of a class of polymers used mainly in moulding. [Say polly CARBONATE]

polychlorinated biphenyl n. see PCB. [Say polly CHLORINATED by FENNEL]

polychrome ● adj. painted or decorated in many colours. ● n. a work of art in several colours, esp. a statue. □ **polychromed** adj. [Say POLLY chrome]

polycotton n. fabric made from a mixture of cotton and polyester fibre. [Say polly COTTON]

polyester n. **1** a polymer used to make synthetic fibre or resin. **2** a fabric made from this.

polyethylene n. a tough light thermoplastic polymer of ethylene, used for packaging and insulating. [Say polly ETH a leen]

polygamous adj. having more than one spouse at the same time. □ **polygamy** n. [Say puh LIGGA muss, puh LIGGA me]

polyglot ● adj. **1** of many languages. **2** speaking several languages. **3** with the text translated into several languages. ● n. a polyglot person. [Say POLLY glot]

polygon n. a plane figure with usu. four or more sides and angles. □ **polygonal** adj. [Say POLLY gon, puh LIGGA nul]

polygraph n. **1** a lie detector. **2** a test using a polygraph. [Say POLLY graph]

polyhedron n. (pl. **polyhedrons** or **polyhedra**) a solid figure with many (usu. more than six) faces. □ **polyhedral** adj. [Say polly HEE drun]

polymath n. a person of much and varied learning. □ **polymathic** adj. [Say POLLY math]

polymer n. a compound composed of one or more large molecules formed from repeated units of smaller molecules. □ **polymeric** adj. [Say PAULA mer]

polymerase n. any enzyme which catalyzes the formation of a polymer, esp. of DNA or RNA. [Say PAULA mer aze]

polymerize v. (**polymerizes, polymerized, polymerizing**) cause molecules to combine to form a polymer. □ **polymerization** n. [Say PAULA mer ize]

polymorphism n. the existence of various different forms in the successive stages of the development of an organism. □ **polymorphic** adj. **polymorphous** adj. [Say polly MORF ism]

Polynesian ● adj. of or relating to Polynesia. ● n. **1** a person from Polynesia. **2** the group of languages of Polynesia. [Say paula NEE zh'n]

polynomial n. an expression of more than two algebraic terms. □ **polynomial** adj. [Say polly NO me ul]

polynya n. (pl. **polynyas**) a stretch of open water surrounded by ice, esp. in the Arctic seas. [Say puh LEEN yuh]

polyp n. **1** a small and very simple sea creature with a tubular body. **2** a small usu. benign growth protruding from a mucous membrane. [Say PAUL ip]

polyphony n. the combination of a number of musical parts, each forming an individual melody and harmonizing with the others. □ **polyphonic** adj. [Say puh LIFFA nee, polly FON ick]

polypropylene n. any of various propylene polymers including thermoplastic materials used for films, fibres, or moulding materials. [Say polly PRO puh leen]

polysaccharide n. any of a group of carbohydrates, including starch, cellulose, and glycogen, whose molecules consist of long chains of monosaccharides. [Say polly SACKA ride]

polystyrene n. a thermoplastic polymer of styrene, used for insulation and in packaging. [Say polly STYE reen]

polytechnic n. an institution of higher education offering courses in many (esp. vocational) subjects. [Say polly TECK nick]

polytheism n. the belief in or worship of more than one god. □ **polytheist** n.

polytheistic adj. [Say polly THEE ism, polly thee ISS tick (with TH as in THICK)]

polyunsaturated adj. (esp. of a fat or oil molecule) containing several double or triple bonds and thus not encouraging the formation of cholesterol in the blood. [Say polly un SATURATED]

polyurethane n. any polymer containing the urethane group, used in adhesives, paints, plastics, rubbers, foams, etc. [Say polly YURRA thane]

polyvinyl chloride n. a tough transparent solid polymer of vinyl chloride, used for a wide variety of products including pipes, flooring, etc. Abbreviation: **PVC**. [Say polly VINYL]

pomegranate n. an orange-sized fruit with a tough golden-orange outer skin, containing many seeds in a red pulp. [Say POMMA gran it]

pommel n. **1** a knob, esp. at the end of a sword hilt. **2** the upward projecting front part of a saddle. [Say PUM'll]

pomp n. a splendid display; splendour.

pompadour n. **1** a woman's hairstyle with the hair in a high turned-back roll around the face. **2** a man's hairstyle with the hair combed high off the forehead. [Say POMPA door]

pompom n. (also **pompon**) **1** a ball or bobble of tufts of yarn. **2** a bundle of strips of fabric, paper, etc. waved or shaken at a sporting event etc.

pompous adj. **1** self-important, affectedly grand or solemn. **2** unduly grand in style. □ **pomposity** n. **pompously** adv. [Say POM pus, pom POSSA tee]

poncho n. (pl. **ponchos**) **1** a S American cloak made of a blanket-like piece of cloth with a slit in the middle for the head. **2** a garment in this style, esp. a raincoat.

pond n. a fairly small body of still water.

ponder v. think over, consider; muse.

ponderosa n. (pl. **ponderosas**) a tall, slender pine tree of western N America. [Say ponder OH suh]

ponderous adj. **1** heavy; unwieldy. **2** laborious. **3** dull; tedious. □ **ponderously** adv.

pondweed n. an aquatic plant that sometimes has floating leaves.

pontiff n. the Pope. □ **pontifical** adj. [Say PON tiff, pon TIFFA cull]

pontificate ● v. (**pontificates**, **pontificated**, **pontificating**) express one's opinions in a way that is pompous and arrogant. ● n. the term of office of a pope. [Say pon TIFFA kate for the verb, pon TIFFA kit for the noun]

pontoon n. **1** a flat-bottomed boat. **2** a hollow tube or other float for keeping a boat, float plane, temporary bridge, etc., buoyant. [Say pon TOON]

pony n. (pl. **ponies**) a horse of any small breed. □ **pony up** informal hand over (money etc.) esp. in settlement of an account.

ponytail n. a person's hair drawn back, tied, and hanging down like a pony's tail. □ **ponytailed** adj.

Ponzi adj. designating a form of fraud in which belief in the success of a non-existent enterprise is fostered by payment of quick returns to the first investors from money invested by others. [Say PONZY]

poo informal ● n. excrement. ● v. (**poos**, **pooed**, **pooing**) defecate.

pooch n. (pl. **pooches**) informal a dog.

poodle n. a breed of dog with a coat of usu. clipped tight curls.

poof interj. announcing a sudden disappearance or appearance.

pooh interj. expressing impatience or contempt.

pooh-bah n. an influential person, esp. one seen as self-important.

pooh-pooh v. (**pooh-poohs, pooh-poohed, pooh-poohing**) dismiss scornfully.

pooja n. (pl. **poojas**) = PUJA. [Say POO juh]

pool ● n. **1 a** a small body of still liquid. **b** a receptacle or hole filled with water for swimming. **2** any of various games of billiards. **3 a** a common supply of resources etc. **b** esp. Cdn a grain farmers' marketing co-operative. **c** a group of persons sharing resources. **4 a** the players' collective stakes in gambling. **b** a bet in which all of the pool is taken by one winner or divided among a few. ● v. **1** form into a pool. **2** put resources etc. into a common fund.

pool hall n. (also **poolroom**) a place for playing billiards.

poolside n. the area adjoining a swimming pool.

poop ● n. **1** the raised deck at the back of a ship. **2** excrement. **3** slang the latest information. ● v. **1** (esp. as **pooped** adj.) informal exhaust; tire out. **2** defecate.

pooper scooper n. an implement for clearing up dog excrement.

poopy adj. informal soiled with or suggestive of excrement.

poor adj. **1** lacking adequate money. **2** deficient in. **3** inadequate, unsatisfactory. **4** deserving pity or sympathy.

poorhouse n. hist. an institution housing

the poor, often in exchange for manual labour.

poorly ● *adv.* in a poor way. ● *adj.* unwell.

pop¹ ● *n.* **1** a sudden sharp explosive sound. **2** a soft drink or soft drinks collectively. **3** a Popsicle. ● *v.* (**pops, popped, popping**) **1** produce a sudden short explosive sound. **2** go or come quickly or unexpectedly. **3** put or place quickly. **4** *informal* take or inject. **5** (of a person's eyes) open wide and appear to bulge. ● *adj.* sudden, unexpected. □ **a pop** each. **pop off** *informal* **1** die. **2** quietly slip away. **pop the question** *informal* propose marriage. **pop up** appear, esp. unexpectedly.

pop² *informal* ● *adj.* **1** in or relating to a popular or modern style. **2** performing or relating to pop music. ● *n.* **1** (also **pop music**) commercial popular music since the 1950s. **2** (**pops**) pieces of light classical music, show tunes, etc.

pop³ *n.* esp. *US informal* father.

pop art *n.* art based on modern popular culture and the mass media.

popcorn *n.* corn kernels which are heated until they burst open and then eaten as a snack.

pop culture *n.* commercial culture based on popular taste.

pope *n.* (as a title usu. **Pope**) the Bishop of Rome as head of the Roman Catholic Church.

pop-eyed *adj. informal* having bulging or wide-open eyes.

pop fly *n.* = FLY BALL.

popgun *n.* a child's toy gun which shoots a harmless pellet or cork.

poplar *n.* a tall, fast-growing tree with leaves that seem to tremble in the breeze.

popout *n. Baseball* an act of being put out on a short fly ball.

poppa *n. informal* **1** father. **2** grandfather.

popper *n.* **1** a person or thing that pops. **2** a pan or appliance for popping popcorn.

pop-psych *adj.* (also **pop-psychology**) having to do with usu. superficial popular understanding of psychological concepts.

poppy¹ *n.* (*pl.* **poppies**) a plant with showy usu. red flowers, varieties of which are a source of heroin, morphine and codeine, and which is also used as a symbol of remembrance of the war dead.

poppy² *adj.* having a sound characteristic of pop music.

poppycock *n. slang* nonsense.

poppy seed *n.* the small black seed of the poppy, used in fillings and toppings for bread, cakes, etc.

Popsicle *n. proprietary* a piece of frozen flavoured and coloured sweetened water, juice, etc. on a stick.

Popsicle stick *n.* a thin, flat stick with rounded ends on which a Popsicle is frozen, often used in arts and crafts.

populace *n.* the general public. [*Say* POP you lliss]

popular *adj.* **1** liked or admired by many people. **2** having to do with the general public.

popularity *n.* the state of being liked, enjoyed or supported by a large number of people.

popularize *v.* (**popularizes, popularized, popularizing**) **1** make popular. **2** present in a readily understandable form. □ **popularization** *n.* **popularizer** *n.*

popularly *adv.* **1** by a large number of people. **2** by the general public.

popular music *n.* **1** songs, folk tunes, etc., appealing to the tastes of a large number of people. **2** pop music.

popular vote *n.* the total number of votes cast by voters in an election.

populate *v.* (**populates, populated, populating**) form or supply the population of.

population *n.* **1 a** the inhabitants of a place referred to collectively. **b** any specified group within this. **2** the total number of any of these.

populist *n.* a person who seeks political support mainly from the ordinary people. □ **populism** *n.*

populous *adj.* having many inhabitants. [*Say* POP you lus]

pop-up ● *adj.* **1** *Computing* designating a menu, ad, etc. that can appear readily or suddenly on top of other items on the screen. **2** containing three-dimensional figures etc. that rise up when the page is turned. ● *n.* **1** *Baseball* the act of hitting the ball high in the air in or just beyond the infield. **2** *Computing* a pop-up menu, ad, etc.

porcelain *n.* **1** a hard white shiny substance made by baking clay. **2** objects made of this. [*Say* PORSA lin]

porch *n.* (*pl.* **porches**) **1** a covered shelter for the entrance of a building. **2** a veranda.

porcine *adj.* of or like pigs. [*Say* POR sine]

porcini *n.* (*pl.* **porcini**) a mushroom with a glossy brown cap and a fat stem. [*Say* por CHEENY]

porcupine *n.* a large rodent with defensive quills.

pore¹ *n.* a minute opening in the skin or other surface through which gases or fluids may pass.

pore² v. (**pores, pored, poring**) (foll. by *over*) be absorbed in studying.

porgy n. (pl. **porgies**) any of numerous fishes found esp. in N American Atlantic coastal waters. [*Say* PORG ee]

pork n. the flesh of a pig, used as food.

pork barrel n. informal a source of government funds for projects designed to win votes. □ **pork-barrelling** n.

porker n. a pig raised for food.

porky adj. (**porkier, porkiest**) 1 informal fleshy, fat. 2 of or like pork.

porn (also **porno**) informal ● n. pornography. ● adj. pornographic.

pornography n. the explicit description or exhibition of sexual activity in literature, films, etc. □ **pornographer** n. **pornographic** adj. [*Say* pore NOGRA fee, porna GRAPHIC]

porous adj. having many small holes that allow water or air to pass through slowly. □ **porosity** n. [*Say* POR us, por OSSA tee]

porphyry n. (pl. **porphyries**) 1 a hard reddish igneous rock containing crystals of feldspar. 2 an igneous rock with large crystals scattered in a matrix of much smaller crystals. [*Say* PORFA ree]

porpoise n. a small toothed whale with a blunt rounded snout. [*Say* POR pus]

porridge n. a cereal, esp. oats, boiled in water or milk. □ **porridgy** adj.

port¹ n. 1 a harbour. 2 a town with a harbour.

port² n. a strong, sweet, usu. dark red fortified wine of Portugal.

port³ n. the left-hand side (looking forward) of a ship, boat, or aircraft. □ **port** adj.

port⁴ ● n. 1 an opening in the side of a ship for entrance etc. 2 a socket in a computer network where connections can be made with peripherals. ● v. Computing transfer (software) from one operating system etc. to another.

portable ● adj. 1 movable or transportable, esp. easily. 2 capable of being transferred or adapted in altered circumstances. ● n. 1 a portable object, e.g. a radio etc. 2 a small transportable building used as a classroom. □ **portability** n.

portage ● n. 1 the carrying of boats or goods between two stretches of navigable water. 2 a place at which this is necessary. ● v. (**portages, portaged, portaging**) convey a boat or goods at a portage. [*Say* por TOZH]

portal n. 1 an esp. elaborate doorway or gate. 2 a website at which a large directory of links to other sites and usu. a search engine are available, used as a starting point for access to other sites.

porta-potty n. (pl. **porta-potties**) a portable toilet.

portend v. foreshadow as an omen. [*Say* por TEND]

portent n. an omen, a sign of something to come. [*Say* POR tent]

portentous adj. 1 like or serving as a portent. 2 pompously solemn. □ **portentously** adv. [*Say* por TEN tus]

porter n. 1 a person employed to carry luggage at a hotel, move patients at a hospital, etc. 2 a dark brown bitter beer brewed from charred or browned malt. 3 a gatekeeper or doorman.

portfolio n. (pl. **portfolios**) 1 a case for keeping loose sheets of paper, drawings, etc. 2 a range of investments held by a person, company, etc. 3 the office or responsibility of a government minister. 4 samples of an artist's or photographer's work.

porthole n. a usu. round window in the side of a ship or an aircraft. [*Say* PORT hole]

portico n. (pl. **porticoes**) a roof supported by columns at regular intervals usu. forming a porch. [*Say* PORTA co]

portion ● n. 1 a part or share. 2 the amount of food allotted to one person. 3 a specified or limited quantity. ● v. 1 divide into portions. 2 distribute.

Portland cement n. a cement manufactured from chalk and clay.

portly adj. (**portlier, portliest**) rather fat.

portmanteau n. (pl. **portmanteaus**) a travelling bag for clothes, esp. opening into two equal parts. [*Say* port man TOE]

portobello n. (pl. **portobellos**) a large edible variety of the common mushroom. [*Say* porto BELLO]

port of call n. a place where a ship or a person stops on a journey.

portrait n. 1 a drawn, painted, or photographic image of a person or animal, esp. of the face. 2 a description in words of a person. 3 a format in which the height of an illustration etc. is greater than the width. □ **portraitist** n.

portraiture n. the art of painting or taking portraits. [*Say* PORTRA chur]

portray v. 1 make a likeness of. 2 represent, esp. dramatically. □ **portrayal** n.

Portuguese n. (pl. **Portuguese**) 1 a person from Portugal. 2 the Romance language of Portugal and Brazil. □ **Portuguese** adj.

Portuguese man-of-war *n.* (*pl.*
Portuguese men-of-war) a dangerous
marine creature with a floating bladder-
like body and very long stinging tentacles.

pose ● *v.* (**poses, posed, posing**)
1 assume a certain attitude of body, esp.
when being photographed or painted.
2 pretend to be another person. **3** behave
affectedly in order to impress others. **4** put
forward or present. ● *n.* **1** an attitude of
body, esp. assumed when being
photographed etc. **2** an attitude or
pretense.

poser *n.* **1** a person who behaves affectedly
in order to impress others. **2** a puzzling
question or problem.

poseur *n.* a person who behaves affectedly.
[*Say* poe ZER]

posh *adj. informal* luxurious. □ **poshness** *n.*

posit *v.* (**posits, posited, positing**) state
or assume as a fact. [*Say* POZZ it]

position ● *n.* **1** a place where someone or
something is located. **2** the correct place.
3 a way in which something is placed or
arranged. **4** a set of circumstances. **5** high
rank. **6** a job. **7** a point of view or attitude.
● *v.* put or arrange in a particular position.
□ **positional** *adj.*

positive ● *adj.* **1** characterized by the
presence of something. **2** expressing
affirmation, agreement, or permission.
3 constructive, optimistic, or confident.
4 certain. **5** greater than zero. **6** having to
do with the kind of electric charge opposite
to that carried by electrons. **7** (of a
photograph) showing light and shade or
colours true to the original. ● *n.* a positive
quality, attribute, image, etc.
□ **positively** *adv.* **positiveness** *n.*
positivity *n.*

positivism *n.* the philosophical system
that recognizes only things that can be
scientifically or logically proven.
□ **positivist** *n. & adj.* **positivistic** *adj.*
[*Say* POSITIVE ism]

positron *n.* a subatomic particle with a
positive charge equal to the negative
charge of an electron. [*Say* POZZA tron]

positron emission tomography *n.* a
form of tomography used esp. for brain
scans which employs positron-emitting
isotopes introduced into the body as a
source of radiation.

posse *n.* **1** a body of men summoned by a
sheriff to enforce the law. **2** *slang* an esp.
criminal gang. [*Say* POSSY]

possess *v.* (**possesses, possessed,
possessing**) **1** hold as property; own.
2 have an ability or quality. **3 a** have power
over a person. **b** be an obsession of. □ **what**

possessed you? an expression of
incredulity. □ **possessor** *n.*

possession *n.* **1** the act or state of
possessing or being possessed. **2** a thing
possessed. **3** *Law* **a** power or control over a
thing, esp. land, which is similar to lawful
ownership but which may exist separately
from it. **b** *informal* the state of possessing an
illegal drug. **4** temporary control of the ball
or puck by a particular player or team.

possessive *adj.* **1** showing a desire to
possess. **2** showing jealous and
domineering tendencies. **3** *Grammar*
indicating possession.
□ **possessiveness** *n.*

possibility *n.* (*pl.* **possibilities**) **1** the
state or fact of being possible. **2** a thing
that may exist or happen. **3** the capability
of being used, improved, etc.

possible *adj.* **1** capable of existing,
happening, or being achieved. **2** that is
perhaps true or a fact or so.

possibly *adv.* **1** perhaps. **2** in accordance
with possibility.

possum *n.* an opossum. □ **play possum**
informal pretend to be asleep or unaware.

post¹ ● *n.* **1** a long piece of wood or metal
set upright in the ground etc. **2 a** a pole
etc. marking the start or finish of a race.
b a goalpost. ● *v.* **1 a** attach a paper etc. in a
prominent place. **b** announce on a
computer bulletin board etc. **2** achieve (a
score in a game, etc.). **3** announce or
publish (something, esp. a financial result).

post² ● *n.* esp. *Brit.* mail. ● *v.* **1** esp. *Brit.* mail
a letter. **2** (esp. as **posted** *adj.*) supply a
person with information.

post³ ● *n.* **1** a job. **2** a place where a soldier
is stationed or which he or she patrols. **3** a
place where an official is on duty. **4** =
TRADING POST. **5** *Basketball* the area in the
vicinity of the opponent's basket. ● *v.*
1 place or station. **2** appoint to a post or
command.

post⁴ *v.* put up, provide (esp. bail money).

post- *prefix* after in time or order.

postage *n.* the amount charged for
sending a letter etc. by post.

postal *adj.* of or relating to the post office
or mail delivery.

postal code *n.* *Cdn* a series of six
alternating letters and numerals used as
part of a postal address.

postal station *n.* *Cdn* one of a number of
branch post offices in a large community.

postcard *n.* a card with a photograph or
picture on one side, for sending a short
message by mail without an envelope.

post-colonial *adj.* occurring or existing

after the end of colonial rule. □ **post-colonialism** n.

post-consumer adj. designating waste thrown away by consumers and used in recycled products.

postdate v. (**postdates, postdated, postdating**) **1** assign a date later than the actual one to. **2** follow in time.

poster ● n. **1** a printed or written notice or advertisement posted in a public place. **2** a large printed picture for display on a wall. **3** a person who posts a message on a bulletin-board service. ● v. affix posters on or throughout.

poster boy n. **1** a male poster child. **2** a male model who appears in a print advertisement.

poster child n. **1** a child who appears in an advertisement for a charitable organization. **2** a person or thing that represents a quality, cause, etc.

poster girl n. **1** a female poster child. **2** a female model who appears in a print advertisement.

posterior ● adj. situated behind or at the back. ● n. the buttocks.
[Say poss TEERY er]

posterity n. all succeeding generations.
[Say poss TERRA tee]

postglacial adj. formed or occurring after a glacial period or ice age.

postgraduate n. (also **postgrad**) a student continuing a course of study after completing a bachelor's degree.
□ **postgraduate** (also **postgrad**) adj.

posthole n. a hole for the insertion of a fence post.

posthumous adj. occurring after the death of the person involved.
□ **posthumously** adv.
[Say POSS tyuh muss]

postie n. informal a postal worker, esp. a letter carrier.

Post-Impressionism n. the work or style of art that explores colour, line, and form to express the artist's emotional response to objects. □ **Post-Impressionist** n. & adj.

post-industrial adj. having to do with a society which no longer relies on heavy industry. □ **post-industrialism** n.

posting n. **1** an appointment to a position. **2** a message posted to a discussion group etc. on the Internet.

Post-it n. (also **Post-it Note**) proprietary a small sheet of paper with an adhesive strip on the bottom, designed for easy positioning on and removal from smooth surfaces.

postman n. (pl. **postmen**) a person who is employed to deliver letters etc.

postmark ● n. an official mark stamped on a letter, esp. one giving the place and date of dispatch, and serving to cancel the stamp. ● v. mark with this.

postmaster n. a person in charge of a post office.

postmodernism n. a late 20th-century movement in the arts, which represents a rejection of modernism and a distrust of grand theories. □ **postmodern** adj. **postmodernist** adj. & n. **postmodernity** n.

post-mortem n. **1** an examination of a corpse to determine the cause of death. **2** informal a discussion analyzing an event after it has occurred.

postnatal adj. characteristic of or relating to the period after childbirth.
[Say post NATE ul]

post office n. **1** the public body responsible for postal services. **2** a building, counter, etc., where stamps can be bought, letters can be mailed, etc.

post office box n. a box at a post office, where mail is kept until called for.

post-operative adj. (also **post-op**) of the period following a surgical operation.
□ **post-operatively** adv.

postpartum adj. following childbirth.
[Say post PART um]

postpone v. (**postpones, postponed, postponing**) put off to a future time.
□ **postponement** n.

post-production n. work done on a film etc. after recording has taken place, e.g. editing, digital effects, etc.

postscript n. **1** an additional paragraph or remark, usu. at the end of a letter. **2** any additional information, action, etc.

post-season Sport ● adj. of or occurring after the conclusion of the regular season. ● n. the playoffs.

post-secondary adj. of or relating to education occurring after completion of high school.

post-structuralism n. a movement in philosophy and literary criticism that emphasized plurality and instability of meaning, rejecting any theoretical system that claimed to have universal validity.
□ **post-structural** adj. **post-structuralist** n. & adj.

post-traumatic stress disorder n. a condition of mental and emotional stress that sometimes follows injury or severe psychological shock.

postulate ● v. (**postulates, postulated, postulating**) suggest or assume the existence, fact, or truth of something as a basis for reasoning, discussion, or belief. ● *n.* **1** a thing suggested or assumed as true as the basis for reasoning, discussion, or belief. **2** *Math* an assumption used as a basis for mathematical reasoning. [Say POSS tyoo late *for the verb,* POSS tyoo lit *for the noun*]

posture ● *n.* **1** a particular position of the body. **2** the way one holds one's body. **3** an attitude or approach. ● *v.* (**postures, postured, posturing**) behave in a way that is intended to impress or mislead others. ☐ **postural** *adj.* **posturing** *n.*

posy *n.* (*pl.* **posies**) a small bunch of flowers. [Say POE zee]

pot ● *n.* **1** a vessel for holding liquids or solids or for cooking in. **2** the total amount of the bet in a game etc. **3** a fund established by a group of people for a common purpose. **4** *informal* a large sum. **5** *slang* marijuana. ● *v.* (**pots, potted, potting**) **1** place in a flowerpot. **2** *Hockey* score (a goal). **3** seize or secure. ☐ **go to pot** *informal* deteriorate. **the pot calling the kettle black** a case of accusing someone of something of which one is oneself guilty. **pot of gold** an imaginary reward.

potable ● *adj.* drinkable. ● *n.* (usu. in *pl.*) a drinkable substance. ☐ **potability** *n.* [Say POE tuh bull]

potash *n.* an alkaline potassium compound used esp. in the manufacture of fertilizer and soap. [Say POT ash]

potassium *n.* a soft silver-white metallic element, an essential element for living organisms. [Say puh TASSY um]

potato *n.* (*pl.* **potatoes**) a starchy edible plant tuber that is one of the most important food crops.

Potawatomi *n.* **1** a member of an Aboriginal people living originally around Lake Michigan, now found in southwestern Ontario, Kansas, and Oklahoma. **2** the Algonquian language of these people. ☐ **Potawatomi** *adj.* [Say potta WOTTA me]

pot-bellied stove *n.* a small wood-burning stove with a rounded body.

pot-belly *n.* (*pl.* **pot-bellies**) a protruding stomach. ☐ **pot-bellied** *adj.*

potboiler *n.* a mediocre work of literature or art produced merely to earn money.

potent *adj.* **1** powerful; strong. **2** (of a drug, alcoholic drink, poison, etc.) having strong physical or chemical properties. ☐ **potency** *n.* **potently** *adv.* [Say POE tint]

potentate *n.* a person who possesses great power, esp. a monarch or ruler. [Say POE t'n tate]

potential ● *adj.* capable of coming into being or action. ● *n.* **1** the possibility of something developing or happening. **2** qualities that exist and can be developed. **3** the difference in voltage between two points in an electric field or circuit. ☐ **potentiality** *n.* **potentially** *adv.*

potential energy *n.* the energy possessed by a body by virtue of its position or state.

potentilla *n.* a small shrub with yellow or red flowers. [Say poe tun TILLA]

pothead *n.* *slang* a habitual user of marijuana.

pothole *n.* **1** a hole in a road surface. **2** a shallow pond or lake formed by a natural hollow in the ground in which water has collected. **3** a deep hole in the ground or system of caves. ☐ **potholed** *adj.*

potion *n.* a liquid medicine, poison, etc.

potlatch *n.* (*pl.* **potlatches**) (among some Aboriginal peoples of the Pacific coast of N America) a ceremonial feast at which possessions are given away to display wealth or enhance prestige. ☐ **potlatching** *n.*

pot light *n.* *Cdn* a light encased in a cylindrical shell, recessed into a ceiling. ☐ **pot lighting** *n.*

potluck *n.* a party to which each guest brings a dish to be shared.

pot pie *n.* a pie of meat and vegetables.

potpourri *n.* (*pl.* **potpourris**) **1** a mixture of dried petals and spices used to perfume a room etc. **2** a mixture. [Say poe puh REE]

pot roast *n.* a piece of meat cooked slowly in a covered dish with a small amount of liquid.

potshot *n.* **1** a random shot at a person or animal. **2** a shot aimed at an animal within easy reach. **3** a piece of opportunistic criticism.

potted *adj.* **1** planted or grown in a flowerpot. **2** abridged; summarized.

potter[1] *v.* esp. *Brit.* = PUTTER[3].

potter[2] *n.* a maker of ceramic vessels.

potter's wheel *n.* a revolving disc on which wet clay is shaped.

pottery *n.* vessels made of fired clay.

potty[1] *adj.* (**pottier, pottiest**) *slang* esp. *Brit.* foolish or crazy.

potty[2] *n.* (*pl.* **potties**) *informal* a small bowl or a seat fitting over a toilet seat, used by a young child during toilet training.

pouch *n.* (*pl.* **pouches**) **1** a small bag. **2** a pocket of skin in which female marsupials carry their young.

pouf *n.* a soft plump mass of material on a dress, headdress, etc. [Say POOF]

poultice n. a soft medicated mass applied to the body for relieving soreness and inflammation. [Say POLE tiss]

poultry n. chickens, turkeys, ducks, geese, etc., as a source of food.

pounce ● v. (**pounces, pounced, pouncing**) **1** spring or swoop, esp. as in capturing prey. **2** take swift advantage of a mistake. ● n. a sudden swoop or spring.

pound[1] n. **1** a unit of weight equal to 16 oz. avoirdupois (453.6 g). **2** (also **pound sterling**) the chief monetary unit of the UK and several other countries. **3** (also **pound sign**) the sign #, esp. on a telephone keypad or computer keyboard.

pound[2] v. **1 a** beat with repeated heavy blows. **b** grind to a powder or pulp. **2** deliver heavy blows or gunfire. **3** informal cover on foot, esp. in search of work, business, etc. **4** beat heavily or throb. □ **pound into** instill forcefully. **pound out** produce with or as if with heavy blows.

pound[3] n. **1** an enclosure where stray or homeless animals are kept. **2** a place where impounded vehicles are kept.

poundage n. a weight stated in pounds.

pound cake n. a cake made with equal weights of butter, sugar, flour, and eggs.

pounder n. **1** (usu. in comb.) a thing or person weighing a specified number of pounds. **2** a gun carrying a shell of a specified number of pounds.

pounding n. a resounding defeat; an onslaught resulting in heavy losses.

pour v. **1** flow or cause to flow esp. downwards in a stream or shower. **2** dispense by pouring. **3** rain heavily. **4** come or go in profusion or rapid succession. □ **it never rains but it pours** misfortunes rarely come singly. **pour it on** proceed, work, etc. very quickly, with all one's energy. **pour oil on the waters** (or **on troubled waters**) calm a disagreement or disturbance, esp. with conciliatory words. □ **pourable** adj. **pourer** n.

pout ● v. push the lips forward as an expression of displeasure or sulking. ● n. a pouting expression or fit. □ **pouty** adj.

poutine n. Cdn french fries topped with cheese curds and gravy. [Say poo TEEN]

poverty n. the state of being poor.

poverty-stricken adj. extremely poor.

POW abbr. (pl. **POWs**) prisoner of war.

pow interj. expressing the sound of a blow or explosion.

powder ● n. **1** a substance in the form of fine dry particles. **2** a medicine or cosmetic in this form. **3** gunpowder. **4** loose, usu. freshly-fallen snow. ● v. **1** apply powder to. **2** reduce to a fine powder. □ **powdery** adj.

powder blue n. & adj. pale blue.

powder burn n. a burn made by the hot gases emitted by a firearm.

powder keg n. **1** a barrel of gunpowder. **2** a volatile situation.

powder puff n. **1** a soft pad for applying powder to the face. **2** a soft or weak person.

powder room n. **1** a small washroom without a bathtub or shower. **2** euphemism a women's washroom, esp. in a public building.

power ● n. **1** the ability or authority to do or influence something. **2** political control. **3** physical strength or force. **4** a country viewed in terms of its international influence. **5** capacity or performance of an engine etc. **6** mechanical or electrical etc. energy. **7** Physics the rate of doing work. **8** Math the product of a number multiplied by itself a certain number of times. ● v. **1** supply with power. **2** switch on or off. **3** move with speed or force. ● adj. **1** having to do with the generation or distribution of electricity. **2** driven by mechanical or electrical energy. **3** informal involving or expressing authority or influence. **4** intense. □ **in the power of** under the control of. **the powers that be** those in authority. □ **powered** adj.

power-assisted adj. employing a source of power to assist manual operation.

power bar n. an electrical cord containing a number of outlets, an on-off switch, and often a surge suppressor.

power base n. a source of authority or support.

powerboat n. a powerful motorboat.

power broker n. a person who exerts political influence by intrigue. □ **power broking** n. & adj.

powerful adj. **1** having much power or strength. **2** politically or socially influential. **3** having a strong emotional effect. □ **powerfully** adv.

powerhouse n. **1** a power station. **2** a very strong or energetic person or thing.

powerless adj. **1** without power or strength. **2** wholly unable. □ **powerlessly** adv. **powerlessness** n.

powerlifting n. a form of competitive weightlifting emphasizing sheer strength. □ **powerlifter** n.

power line n. a thick wire supplying electrical power, esp. one supported by poles etc.

power of attorney n. the authority to act for another person in legal matters.

power of sale n. the authority by which

a bank etc. may seize and sell a mortgaged property on which the mortgage is in default.

power play n. **1** *Hockey* a temporary numerical advantage while a player on the other team serves a penalty. **2** an often underhanded attempt to gain or maintain power.

power station n. a facility where electricity is generated for distribution.

power surge n. a sudden marked increase in voltage of an electric current.

powertrain n. the mechanism that transmits the drive from the engine of a vehicle to its axle.

power trip n. *slang* something done primarily for the enjoyment of exercising power.

power walking n. brisk walking for exercise. □ **power walker** n.

powwow n. **1** a cultural gathering among some N American Aboriginal peoples, with dancing, music, eating, etc. **2** a conference or meeting. [Say POW wow]

pox n. any virus disease producing a rash of pimples that leave pockmarks on healing.

ppb *abbr.* parts per billion.

ppm *abbr.* parts per million.

PQ *abbr.* **1** Parti Québécois. **2** Province of Quebec.

PR *abbr.* public relations.

practicable *adj.* **1** that can be done or used. **2** possible in practice.
□ **practicability** n. **practicably** *adv.*
[Say PRACK ticka bull]

practical *adj.* **1** of or concerned with practice rather than theory. **2** suited to use or action. **3 a** inclined to action rather than speculation. **b** sensible. **4** feasible.
□ **practicality** n. *(pl.* **practicalities)**
[Say PRACK tick ul, prack tick ALA tee]

practical joke n. a trick played on a person which makes them look foolish.
□ **practical joker** n.

practically *adv.* **1** virtually, almost. **2** in a practical way.

practice ● n. *(also* **practise)** **1** the actual doing of something. **2** the usual way of doing something. **3** a habit or custom. **4** repeated exercise in an activity. **5** the professional work of a doctor, lawyer, etc.
● v. **(practices, practiced, practicing)**
= PRACTISE. □ **out of practice** lacking a former skill from lack of recent practice.

practicum n. a course of practical training through experience working in a particular field. [Say PRACK tick um]

practise v. **(practises, practised, practising)** **1** carry out in action. **2** do repeatedly as an exercise to improve a skill.

3 pursue or be engaged in a profession, religion, etc.

practised *adj.* **1** experienced, expert.
2 gained or perfected through practice.

practising *adj.* currently active or engaged in.

practitioner n. a person practising a profession, esp. medicine.
[Say prack TISHA ner]

pragmatic *adj.* dealing with things in a practical and sensible way rather than by having fixed ideas. □ **pragmatically** *adv.*
pragmatism n. **pragmatist** n.
[Say prag MAT ick, PRAGMA tism]

prairie n. **1** a large area of usu. treeless and flat grassland. **2** (also **the prairies**) the region of western N America originally characterized by such grassland. **3** (**the Prairies**) = PRAIRIE PROVINCES.

prairie chicken n. a medium-sized grouse of the N American prairies.

prairie crocus n. *Cdn* a plant with purple or white crocus-like flowers, the floral emblem of Manitoba.

prairie dog n. a N American rodent that lives in burrows and makes a barking sound.

prairie lily n. a lily bearing upright reddish-orange flowers with spotted petals, the floral emblem of Saskatchewan.

prairie oyster n. **1** a seasoned raw egg with the yolk intact. **2** the testicle of a calf eaten as a delicacy.

Prairie provinces *pl.* n. Alberta, Saskatchewan, and Manitoba.

prairie schooner n. a covered wagon used by 19th-c. pioneers in the prairies.

prairie wool n. *Cdn* the natural grassy plant cover of prairie land.

praise ● v. **(praises, praised, praising)**
1 express warm approval or admiration of.
2 glorify God in words. ● n. the expression of approval or admiration.

praiseworthy *adj.* worthy of praise.

praline n. a confection made by browning nuts in boiling sugar. [Say PRAY leen *or* PRAW leen]

prance v. **(prances, pranced, prancing)** **1** (of a horse) raise the forelegs and spring from the hind legs. **2** walk or behave in an elated or arrogant manner.

prank n. a practical joke or piece of mischief. □ **prankish** *adj.* **prankster** n.

praseodymium n. a soft silvery metallic element of the lanthanide series.
[Say praisy uh DIMMY um]

prate v. **(prates, prated, prating)** talk foolishly or at tedious length.

pratfall n. *informal* **1** a fall on the buttocks. **2** a humiliating failure.

prattle ● v. (**prattles, prattled, prattling**) chatter or say in a childish way. ● n. foolish or trivial talk. □ **prattling** adj.

prawn n. any of various shellfish resembling a large shrimp.

praxis n. accepted practice or custom. [Say PRAX iss]

pray v. **1** say prayers. **2** entreat, beseech.

prayer[1] n. **1 a** a solemn request or thanksgiving to God. **b** a religious service consisting largely of prayers. **2 a** an entreaty. **b** a thing prayed for. □ **not have a prayer** informal have no chance.

prayer[2] n. a person who prays.

prayerful adj. **1** liking to pray. **2** characterized by or expressive of prayer. □ **prayerfully** adv.

praying mantis n. (pl. **praying mantis** or **praying mantises**) a mantis that holds its forelegs in a position suggestive of hands folded in prayer.

pre- prefix before.

preach v. (**preaches, preached, preaching**) **1** deliver a sermon or religious address. **2** give moral advice self-righteously. **3** recommend or advocate.

preacher n. a person who preaches, esp. a minister of religion. □ **preacherly** adj.

preachy adj. (**preachier, preachiest**) informal inclined to preach or moralize. □ **preachiness** n.

preamble n. a preliminary statement or introduction. [Say PREE amble]

preamplifier n. (also **preamp**) an electronic device that amplifies a very weak signal and transmits it to a main amplifier.

Precambrian n. the earliest geological period, from the earth's origin to about 570 million years ago. □ **Precambrian** adj. [Say pree CAME bree un or pree CAM bree un]

precarious adj. **1** not safe or certain; dangerous. **2** not securely held or in position. □ **precariously** adv. **precariousness** n. [Say pruh KERRY us]

precast adj. cast in its final shape before positioning.

precaution n. an action taken in advance to avoid danger or problems. □ **precautionary** adj.

precede v. (**precedes, preceded, preceding**) come or go before in time, order, importance, etc. [Say pree SEED]

precedence n. priority in time, order, or importance, etc. □ **take precedence** (often foll. by over, of) have priority (over). [Say PRESSA dince]

precedent n. **1** a previous legal decision etc. taken as a guide or justification for a subsequent one. **2** a previous similar event. [Say PRESSA dint]

precept n. a general rule intended to regulate behaviour etc. [Say PREE sept]

precinct n. **1** an enclosed or clearly defined area. **2** a specially designated area where traffic is excluded. **3 a** a police subdivision. **b** informal the police station of such a subdivision. **c** (in pl.) a neighbourhood. [Say PREE sinct]

precious adj. **1** of great value or worth. **2** beloved; much prized. **3** affectedly refined in language or manner. □ **precious little** not much. □ **preciousness** n.

precipice n. a tall and very steep face of a rock, cliff, etc. [Say PRESSA piss]

precipitate ● v. (**precipitates, precipitated, precipitating**) **1** hasten the occurrence of. **2** be deposited in solid form from a solution or from suspension in a gas. ● adj. **1** occurring suddenly or abruptly. **2** hasty, thoughtless. ● n. a substance precipitated from a solution etc. □ **precipitately** adv. [Say pree SIPPA tate for the verb, pree SIPPA tit for the adjective and noun]

precipitation n. rain or snow etc. falling to the ground.

precipitous adj. **1** of or like a precipice. **2 a** sudden and great. **b** hasty. □ **precipitously** adv. **precipitousness** n. [Say pruh SIPPA tus]

précis ● n. (pl. **précis**) a summary or abstract, esp. of a text or speech. ● v. (**précises, précised, précising**) make a précis of. [Say PRAY see]

precise adj. **1 a** accurately expressed. **b** definite, exact. **2** scrupulous in being exact. **3** designating an accurate instrument.

precisely adv. **1** in a precise manner. **2** (as a reply) quite so.

precision n. **1** the condition of being precise; accuracy. **2** the degree of refinement in measurement etc. **3** (as an adj.) marked by or adapted for precision.

preclude v. (**precludes, precluded, precluding**) **1** prevent, exclude. **2** make impossible. [Say pree CLUDE]

precocious adj. **1** prematurely developed in some faculty or characteristic. **2** indicating such development. □ **precociously** adv. **precocity** n. [Say pruh CO shus, pruh COSSA tee]

pre-Columbian adj. having to do with the the Americas before the arrival of Columbus in 1492.

preconceived adj. (of an idea) formed

before full knowledge or evidence is available.

preconception *n.* **1** a preconceived idea. **2** a prejudice.

precondition *n.* a prior condition, that must be fulfilled before other things can be done.

pre-contact *adj.* of or relating to an Aboriginal society before contact with Europeans.

precook *v.* cook in advance.

precursor *n.* **1** a forerunner. **2** a substance from which another is formed by decay or chemical reaction etc. [*Say* pree CURSOR]

predate *v.* (**predates, predated, predating**) exist or occur at a date earlier than.

predation *n.* the natural preying of one animal on others. [*Say* pruh DAY sh'n]

predator *n.* an animal naturally preying on others. [*Say* PREDDA ter]

predatory *adj.* preying upon others. [*Say* PREDDA tory]

predecease *v.* (**predeceases, predeceased, predeceasing**) die earlier than. [*Say* pree duh CEASE]

predecessor *n.* **1** a former holder of a position with respect to a later holder. **2** a thing to which another has succeeded. [*Say* PREEDA sesser]

predestination *n. Theology* the belief that everything that happens has been decided or planned in advance, esp. with regard to the salvation of some and not others.

predestine *v.* (**predestines, predestined, predestining**) (often as **predestined** *adj.*) determine or ordain in advance, esp. by divine will or fate. [*Say* pree DES tin]

predetermine *v.* (**predetermines, predetermined, predetermining**) **1** determine beforehand. **2** predestine. □**predetermination** *n.*

predicament *n.* a difficult, unpleasant, or embarrassing situation. [*Say* pree DICKA mint]

predicate ● *v.* (**predicates, predicated, predicating**) found or base on. ● *n. Grammar* what is said about the subject of a sentence etc. [*Say* PREDDA kate *for the verb*, PREDDA kit *for the noun*]

predicative *adj.* (of an adjective or noun) forming or contained in the predicate, as *old* in *the dog is old* (but not in *the old dog*). □**predicatively** *adv.* [*Say* pruh DICKA tiv]

predict *v.* foretell, prophesy. □**predictive** *adj.* **predictor** *n.*

predictable *adj.* **1** that can be predicted or is to be expected. **2** always behaving or

occurring in the way expected. □**predictability** *n.* **predictably** *adv.*

prediction *n.* a thing predicted; a forecast.

predilection *n.* a special liking. [*Say* predda LECTION]

predispose *v.* (**predisposes, predisposed, predisposing**) make someone inclined to a specified attitude, action, or condition. □**predisposition** *n.* [*Say* pree DISPOSE, pree dis POSITION]

prednisone *n.* a synthetic drug used to relieve rheumatic and allergic conditions and to treat leukemia. [*Say* PREDNA zone]

predominant *adj.* **1** being the main or most numerous or widespread element. **2** prevailing, exerting control. □**predominance** *n.*

predominantly *adv.* mainly; for the most part.

predominate *v.* (**predominates, predominated, predominating**) **1** have or exert control. **2** be the strongest, main, or most numerous element.

pre-eclampsia *n.* a condition of pregnancy characterized by high blood pressure. [*Say* pree i CLAMPSY uh]

preemie *n. informal* a baby born prematurely.

pre-eminent *adj.* surpassing all others. □**pre-eminence** *n.* **pre-eminently** *adv.*

pre-empt *v.* **1** take action in order to prevent an anticipated event. **2** act in advance of someone in order to prevent them from doing something. **3** interrupt or replace a broadcast. □**pre-emption** *n.*

pre-emptive *adj.* serving to pre-empt or forestall something. □**pre-emptively** *adv.*

preen *v.* **1** (of a bird) tidy its feathers with its beak. **2** smarten or admire oneself.

pre-existing *adj.* (also **pre-existent**) existing at an earlier time or already.

prefabricated *adj.* (also *informal* **prefab**) **1** manufactured in sections to enable quick and easy assembly on site. **2** produced in an artificially standardized way. □**prefabrication** *n.*

preface ● *n.* **1** an introduction to a book stating its subject, scope, etc. **2** the preliminary part of a speech. ● *v.* (**prefaces, prefaced, prefacing**) introduce or begin. □**prefatory** *adj.* [*Say* PREFF iss, PREFFA tory]

prefect *n.* a chief officer, magistrate, governor, etc. [*Say* PREE fect]

prefecture *n.* a district under the government of a prefect. [*Say* PREE feck chur]

prefer *v.* (**prefers, preferred, preferring**) **1** choose instead; like better. **2** submit for consideration. [*Say* pruh FUR]

preferable *adj.* more desirable or suitable. □ **preferability** *n.* **preferably** *adv.*
[Say PREFF er a bull *or* pruh FURRA bull]

preference *n.* **1** a greater liking for one alternative over others. **2** a thing preferred.

preferential *adj.* of or involving preference. □ **preferentially** *adv.*
[Say preffer EN shul]

preferment *n.* promotion to a position or office. [Say pruh FUR mint]

preferred share *n.* (also **preferred stock**) a share in a company which yields a fixed rate of interest and takes preference over common shares in entitlement to dividends.

prefigure *v.* (**prefigures**, **prefigured**, **prefiguring**) be an early indication or version of.

prefix ● *n.* (*pl.* **prefixes**) **1** a verbal element placed at the beginning of a word to qualify its meaning, e.g. *non-*. **2** a title placed before a name, e.g. *Mr.* ● *v.* (**prefixes**, **prefixed**, **prefixing**) (often foll. by *to*) add as a prefix.

preform *v.* form or shape beforehand.

preggers *adj. informal* = PREGNANT 1.

pregnant *adj.* **1** having a child or young developing in the uterus. **2** full of meaning; significant or suggestive. **3** plentifully provided. □ **pregnancy** *n.*

preheat *v.* heat beforehand.

prehensile *adj.* (of a tail or limb) capable of grasping. [Say pree HEN sile]

prehistoric *adj.* of the period before written records. □ **prehistorically** *adv.* **prehistory** *n.*

pre-industrial *adj.* of the time before industrialization.

prejudge *v.* (**prejudges**, **prejudged**, **prejudging**) form a premature judgment on. □ **prejudgment** *n.*

prejudice ● *n.* **1 a** a preconceived opinion. **b** bias or partiality. **c** dislike or distrust of a person, group, etc. **2** harm or injury that results from some action or judgment. ● *v.* (**prejudices**, **prejudiced**, **prejudicing**) **1** cause to have a prejudice. **2** have a harmful effect on something.
[Say PREDGE uh diss]

prejudiced *adj.* **1** not impartial. **2** bigoted.
[Say PREDGE uh dist]

prejudicial *adj.* **1** causing or characterized by prejudice. **2** harmful to someone or something. □ **prejudicially** *adv.*
[Say predge uh DISH'll]

prelate *n.* a high ecclesiastical dignitary.
[Say PRELLIT]

prelim *n. informal* **1** (often in *pl.*) a preliminary game, contest, round, etc. **2** a

preliminary examination, hearing, or trial.
[Say PREE lim *or* pri LIM]

preliminary ● *adj.* introductory, preparatory. ● *n.* (*pl.* **preliminaries**) (usu. in *pl.*) **1** a preliminary action or arrangement. **2** a preliminary trial or contest. [Say pruh LIMMA nerry]

preliterate *adj.* of a society that has not developed the use of writing.
[Say pre LITERATE]

preload *v.* (esp. as **preloaded** *adj.*) load beforehand.

prelude *n.* **1** an action, event, or situation serving as an introduction. **2** an introductory piece of music.
[Say PRAY lood *or* PRELL yood]

Premarin *n. proprietary* a mixture of estrogen compounds used to treat estrogen deficiency. [Say PREMMA rin]

premarital *adj.* occurring before marriage.
[Say pree MERRA tul]

premature *adj.* **1 a** too early. **b** too hasty. **2** born before the end of the full term of gestation. □ **prematurely** *adv.*

pre-med *n.* **1** a program of studies taken in preparation for medical school. **2** a pre-med student.

premeditated *adj.* thought out or planned beforehand. □ **premeditation** *n.*
[Say pre MEDITATE]

premenstrual *adj.* occurring before a menstrual period.

premenstrual syndrome *n.* any of a range of symptoms (including tension, fluid retention, etc.) experienced by some women in the days immediately before menstruation.

premier ● *n.* **1** *Cdn* the first minister of a province or territory. **2** a prime minister or head of government in any of several countries. ● *adj.* first in importance, order, or time. □ **premiership** *n.*

premiere ● *n.* the first performance or showing of a play, film, etc. ● *v.* (**premieres**, **premiered**, **premiering**) **1** give a premiere of. **2** be presented for the first time.

premise ● *n.* **1** (also **premiss**, *pl.* **premisses**) *Logic* a previous statement or proposition from which another is inferred or follows as a conclusion. **2** the basic circumstances on which a novel, film, etc., is based. **3** (**premises**) a house, building, etc. ● *v.* (**premises**, **premised**, **premising**) (foll. by *on*) base on.
[Say PREM iss]

premium ● *n.* **1** an amount paid for an insurance policy. **2** a sum added to interest, wages, ordinary charges, etc. **3** a reward or prize. ● *adj.* of best quality and therefore more expensive. □ **at a premium 1** highly valued. **2** scarce and in demand. **put a premium on** attach special value to.

premolar *n.* either of two teeth between a canine tooth and first molar.

premonition *n.* a forewarning; a vague foreboding. □ **premonitory** *adj.* [*Say* premma NISH'n, proo MONNA tory]

prenatal *adj.* of the period before childbirth. [*Say* pree NATE ul]

pre-nup *n. informal* a pre-nuptial agreement. [*Say* PREE nup]

pre-nuptial *adj.* (of an agreement etc.) entered into by a couple before marriage, specifying how their assets are to be split in the event of divorce. [*Say* pree NUP choo ul *or* pree NUP shoo ul *or* pree NUP shul]

preoccupation *n.* **1** the state of being preoccupied. **2** a thing that engrosses the mind. [*Say* pre OCCUPATION]

preoccupied *adj.* mentally distracted.

preoccupy *v.* (**preoccupies, preoccupied, preoccupying**) engross the mind of, to the exclusion of other thoughts.

preoperative *adj.* (also **pre-op**) of the period or a condition before an operation.

preordained *adj.* ordained or determined beforehand.

pre-owned *adj.* second-hand, used.

prep *informal* ● *n.* **1** preparation. **2** a preppy. ● *adj.* **1** preparatory. **2** relating to a preparatory school. ● *v.* (**preps, prepped, prepping**) *informal* prepare; make something or oneself ready.

prepackaged *adj.* packaged before retail.

preparation *n.* **1** the action or process of preparing. **2** (often in *pl.*) something done to make ready. **3** a specially prepared substance, esp. a food or medicine.

preparative *adj.* preparatory. [*Say* pruh PERRA tiv]

preparatory *adj.* done in order to prepare for something. [*Say* PREP er a tory *or* pruh PERRA tory]

preparatory school *n.* a usu. private school preparing pupils for college or university.

prepare *v.* (**prepares, prepared, preparing**) make or get ready. □ **be prepared** be ready, disposed, or willing. □ **preparedness** *n.* **preparer** *n.*

prepay *v.* (**prepays, prepaid, prepaying**) pay or pay for in advance. □ **prepayable** *adj.* **prepayment** *n.*

preponderant *adj.* greatest in influence, power, number, or importance. □ **preponderance** *n.* **preponderantly** *adv.* [*Say* pruh PONDER int]

preposition *n.* a word usu. preceding a noun or pronoun and expressing a relation to another word, as in: "the man *on* the platform". □ **prepositional** *adj.* [*Say* preppa ZISH'n]

prepossessing *adj.* attractive, appealing.

preposterous *adj.* utterly absurd; outrageous. □ **preposterously** *adv.* [*Say* pruh POSS ter us]

preppy (also **preppie**) *informal* ● *n.* (*pl.* **preppies**) a person with the neat hair and clothing associated with expensive private schools. ● *adj.* (**preppier, preppiest**) of or like a preppy or preppies.

pre-production *n.* work done on a film, broadcast, etc. before production begins.

preprogram *v.* (**preprograms, preprogrammed, preprogramming**) program beforehand.

prep school *n.* a preparatory school.

prepubescent ● *adj.* (also **prepubertal**) **1** occurring prior to puberty. **2** that has not yet reached puberty. ● *n.* a prepubescent boy or girl. [*Say* pre pyoo BESS int, pre PYOOBERT'll]

pre-qualify *v.* (**pre-qualifies, pre-qualified, pre-qualifying**) qualify in advance, as for a mortgage, sporting event, etc.

prequel *n.* a story, film, etc., whose events precede those of an existing work. [*Say* PREE quil]

Pre-Raphaelite *n.* a member of a group of 19th-century English artists whose works typically depict scenes from classical mythology or medieval romance in a dreamy style. □ **Pre-Raphaelite** *adj.* [*Say* pre RAFFY uh lite]

prerequisite ● *adj.* required as a precondition. ● *n.* a prerequisite thing. [*Say* pre RECKWA zit]

prerogative *n.* a right or privilege exclusive to an individual or class. [*Say* pruh ROGGA tiv]

presage ● *n.* a sign or warning that something will happen. ● *v.* (**presages, presaged, presaging**) be a warning or sign that something will happen. [*Say* PRESS idge *for the noun*, pree SAGE *for the verb*]

presbyter *n.* (in the Presbyterian Church) an elder. [*Say* PRESS buh ter]

Presbyterian ● *n.* a member of a Protestant denomination in which the Church is administered by elected elders of equal rank and ministers. ● *adj.* of Presbyterians. □ **Presbyterianism** *n.* [*Say* press buh TEERY in]

presbytery *n.* (*pl.* **presbyteries**) (in the Presbyterian and United Churches) a regional governing body made up of elders and ministers. [*Say* PRESS buh tree]

preschool ● *adj.* of the time before a child is old enough to go to school. ● *n.* nursery school. □ **preschooler** *n.*

prescient *adj.* having foreknowledge or foresight. □ **prescience** *n.* **presciently** *adv.* [*Say* PRESSY int]

pre-screen *v.* screen beforehand.

prescribe *v.* (**prescribes, prescribed, prescribing**) **1** advise, allow, or recommend the use of. **2** state what should be done or how something should be done.

prescription *n.* **1 a** a doctor's instruction for the composition and use of a medicine. **b** a medicine prescribed. **2** the act or an instance of prescribing.

prescriptive *adj.* **1** prescribing. **2** *Linguistics* attempting to impose rules of correct usage, often at variance with actual usage. □ **prescriptivism** *n.* **prescriptivist** *n.* & *adj.*

pre-season *n.* the period before an esp. sports season begins.

presence *n.* **1** the state or condition of being present. **2** a place where a person is. **3** a person's imposing appearance, bearing, or force of personality. **4** a person, spirit, etc., that is present. **5** the maintenance by a nation of political influence in another region.

presence of mind *n.* calmness and self-control.

present[1] ● *adj.* **1** being or occurring in a particular place. **2** existing or occurring now. **3** *Grammar* expressing an action now going on or habitually performed. ● *n.* **1** the period of time now occurring. **2** *Grammar* a present tense or form of a verb.

present[2] *v.* **1** give formally or ceremonially. **2** offer for acceptance or consideration. **3** formally introduce. **4** put before the public. **5** be the cause of (a problem). **6** *Medicine* exhibit a particular condition or symptom. □ **present arms** hold a rifle etc. vertically in front of the body as a salute. □ **presenter** *n.*

present[3] *n.* a gift; a thing given or presented.

presentable *adj.* **1** of good appearance; fit to be presented to other people. **2** fit for presentation. □ **presentably** *adv.*

presentation *n.* **1** the act or manner of presenting something. **2** a demonstration or display of materials, information, etc. **3** an exhibition or theatrical performance. **4** a formal introduction. **5** the position of the fetus in relation to the cervix at the time of delivery. □ **presentational** *adj.*

present-day *adj.* of this time; modern.

presentiment *n.* a vague expectation; a foreboding. [*Say* pre ZENTA mint *or* pre SENTA mint]

presently *adv.* **1** now. **2** soon.

preservation *n.* the act of preserving or the process or state of being preserved.

preservationist *n.* a supporter or advocate of preservation, esp. of historic sites, natural areas, etc.

preservative ● *n.* a substance for preserving perishable foodstuffs, wood, etc. ● *adj.* tending to preserve. [*Say* pre ZERVA tiv]

preserve ● *v.* (**preserves, preserved, preserving**) **1 a** keep safe or free from harm, decay, etc. **b** keep alive (memory etc.). **2** maintain in its existing state. **3** retain. **4 a** treat or refrigerate to prevent decomposition or fermentation. **b** prepare fruit by boiling it with sugar, for long-term storage. **5** keep a natural area for protection or private use. ● *n.* **1** preserved fruit or vegetables, e.g. jam, pickles. **2** a place where game or fish etc. is preserved. **3** a sphere or area of activity regarded as a person's own. □ **preserver** *n.*

pre-settlement *adj.* designating the time in N America before the arrival of European settlers.

pre-shrunk *adj.* (of a garment) caused to shrink during manufacture so that it does not shrink in use.

preside *v.* (**presides, presided, presiding**) be in a position of authority, esp. at a meeting.

presidency *n.* (*pl.* **presidencies**) **1** the office of president. **2** the period of this.

president *n.* **1** the elected head of a republican state. **2** the head of an association, union, council, company, university, etc. **3** a person in charge of a meeting, assembly, etc. □ **presidential** *adj.*

president-elect *n.* (*pl.* **presidents-elect**) a president who has been elected but has not yet taken office.

press[1] ● *v.* (**presses, pressed, pressing**) **1** exert continuous physical force on something. **2** apply pressure to. **3** move in a specified direction by pushing. **4** continue in one's action. **5** forcefully put forward. **6** make strong efforts to persuade. **7** extract juice or oil by crushing or squeezing fruit, vegetables, etc. **8** (of time) be short. **9** *Weightlifting* raise by gradually pushing upwards from the shoulders. ● *n.* (*pl.* **presses**) **1** a device for applying pressure. **2** a printing press. **3** (**the press**) newspapers or journalists collectively. **4** coverage in newspapers and magazines. **5** a printing or publishing business. **6** a closely packed mass of people or things. **7** *Weightlifting* a raising of a weight from

shoulder height to above the head.
8 *Basketball* any of various forms of close
guarding by the defending team. □ **be
pressed for** have barely enough. **press
(the) flesh** shake hands. □ **presser** *n.*

press² *v.* (**presses**, **pressed**, **pressing**)
hist. force to serve in the army etc.

press agent *n.* a person who deals with
press publicity for an organization.

press box *n.* a reporters' enclosure esp. at
a sports event.

press conference *n.* a session to which
journalists are invited to hear an
announcement, ask questions, etc.

press corps *n.* a group of reporters who
regularly cover the same beat.

press gallery *n.* a gallery for reporters,
esp. in a legislative assembly.

press gang ● *n. hist.* a group of men
employed to force or coerce men to enlist
in the military. ● *v.* (**press-gang**) force or
coerce someone to do something.

pressing ● *adj.* calling for immediate
attention. ● *n.* a series of things made by
pressing. □ **pressingly** *adv.*

press kit *n.* a collection of information on
a certain issue, product, etc., prepared for
distribution to the media.

press office *n.* a department responsible
for dealings with the press. □ **press
officer** *n.*

press release *n.* an official statement
issued to the media by a government
department, business, etc.

press secretary *n.* a person who deals
with publicity and public relations for an
individual or organization.

pressure ● *n.* **1 a** the exertion of
continuous force on or against a body by
another. **b** the force exerted. **2** urgency or
difficulty. **3** constraining influence. ● *v.*
(**pressures**, **pressured**, **pressuring**)
1 apply (esp. psychological or moral)
pressure to. **2** persuade; coerce.

pressure cooker *n.* **1** an airtight pot in
which food can be cooked quickly under
pressure. **2** a very stressful situation.

pressure group *n.* a group that tries to
influence public policy in favour of a
particular interest.

pressure point *n.* **1** a small area on the
skin especially sensitive to pressure. **2** a
target for political pressure or influence.

pressure-treated *adj.* (of wood) treated
with chemical preservatives applied under
high pressure.

pressurize *v.* (**pressurizes**,
pressurized, **pressurizing**) **1** (esp. as
pressurized *adj.*) maintain normal
atmospheric pressure in an aircraft etc. at a
high altitude. **2** raise to a high pressure.
□ **pressurization** *n.*

prestige *n.* **1** respect, reputation, or
influence derived from achievements,
power, wealth, etc. **2** (as an *adj.*) having or
conferring prestige. □ **prestigious** *adj.*
[*Say* press TEEZH or press TEEJ,
press TEE jiss *or* press TIDGE iss]

presto ● *adv. Music* in quick tempo. ● *n.* (*pl.*
prestos) *Music* a movement to be played in
a quick tempo. ● *interj.* (also **presto
chango**) used to announce the successful
completion of a magical trick etc.
[*Say* PRESS toe (change oh)]

presumably *adv.* as may reasonably be
presumed.

presume *v.* (**presumes**, **presumed**,
presuming) **1 a** suppose to be true; take
for granted. **b** assume to be. **2 a** be
impudent enough. **b** dare. **3** take advantage
of a person's good nature etc.

presumption *n.* **1** arrogance;
presumptuous behaviour. **2 a** the act of
presuming a thing to be true. **b** a thing
that is presumed to be true.

presumptuous *adj.* unduly confident,
overbearing. □ **presumptuously** *adv.*
presumptuousness *n.*
[*Say* pre ZUMP choo us]

presuppose *v.* (**presupposes**,
presupposed, **presupposing**)
1 require as a precondition. **2** assume
beforehand. □ **presupposition** *n.*
[*Say* pre SUPPOSE]

prêt-à-porter ● *adj.* (of clothes) sold
ready-to-wear. ● *n.* ready-to-wear clothes.
[*Say* pret uh por TAY]

preteen ● *adj.* of a child just under the age
of thirteen. ● *n.* a preteen child.

pretend ● *v.* **1** imagine, profess, or make it
seem that something is the case when in
fact it is not. **2** lay claim to. ● *adj. informal*
pretended; in pretense.

pretended *adj.* false; not real or genuine.

pretender *n.* **1** a person who claims or
aspires to a title or position. **2** a person
who pretends.

pretense *n.* (also **pretence**) **1 a** a pretext
or excuse. **b** a false show of intentions. **2** a
claim, esp. a false or ambitious one.
3 affectation. [*Say* PREE tense *or*
pre TENSE]

pretension *n.* **1** (usu. in *pl.*) an aspiration
or claim to a greater position.
2 pretentiousness. [*Say* pre TENSION]

pretentious *adj.* attempting to impress
others by making oneself appear more
important, wealthy, talented, etc. than one
really is. □ **pretentiously** *adv.*
pretentiousness *n.* [*Say* pre TEN shus]

preterm *adj.* born or occurring prematurely.

preternatural *adj.* beyond what is normal or natural. □ **preternaturally** *adv.* [Say pree tur NATURAL]

pretext *n.* **1** an ostensible or alleged reason. **2** an excuse offered.

prettify *v.* (**prettifies, prettified, prettifying**) make pretty esp. in an affected or superficial way. □ **prettification** *n.* [Say PRITTA fye]

pretty ● *adj.* (**prettier, prettiest**) having an attractive or pleasant appearance. ● *adv. informal* **1** fairly, moderately. **2** very, considerably. ● *n.* (*pl.* **pretties**) a pretty person. ● *v.* (**pretties, prettied, prettying**) make pretty or attractive. □ **pretty much** (or **nearly** or **well**) *informal* almost; very nearly. **sitting pretty** *informal* in a favourable or advantageous position. □ **prettily** *adv.* **prettiness** *n.*

pretzel ● *n.* a crisp salted biscuit made in the shape of a knot or a stick. ● *v.* (**pretzels, pretzelled, pretzelling**) twist, bend, or contort.

prevail *v.* **1** be victorious. **2** be the more usual or predominant. **3** persuade.

prevailing *adj.* **1** most usual or widespread. **2** (of a wind) that blows in an area most frequently.

prevalent *adj.* generally existing or occurring. □ **prevalence** *n.* **prevalently** *adv.* [Say PREVVA lint]

prevaricate *v.* (**prevaricates, prevaricated, prevaricating**) speak or act in an evasive or misleading way. □ **prevarication** *n.* [Say pre VERRA kate]

prevent *v.* stop from happening or doing something. □ **preventable** *adj.* **preventer** *n.* **prevention** *n.*

preventive *adj.* (also **preventative**) serving to prevent, esp. preventing disease, breakdown, etc. □ **preventively** *adv.*

preview ● *n.* **1 a** the showing of a film, exhibition, etc., before the official opening. **b** a film trailer. **2** a foretaste, a preliminary glimpse. ● *v.* see or show in advance.

previous ● *adj.* **1** coming before in time or order. **2** overly hasty in acting or drawing a conclusion. ● *adv.* (foll. by *to*) before. □ **previously** *adv.*

pre-war *adj.* existing or occurring before a war.

prewash ● *n.* (*pl.* **prewashes**) a preliminary wash. ● *v.* (**prewashes, prewashed, prewashing**) give a preliminary wash to, esp. before selling.

prey ● *n.* an animal that is hunted or killed by another for food. ● *v.* (foll. by *on, upon*) **1** hunt and kill for food. **2** attack, take advantage of, or distress.

prez *n.* (*pl.* **prezzes**) esp. *US slang* a president.

price ● *n.* **1 a** the amount of money etc. for which a thing is bought or sold. **b** value or worth. **2** what is or must be given, done, sacrificed, etc., to obtain or achieve something. ● *v.* (**prices, priced, pricing**) **1** fix or find the price of. **2** estimate the value of. □ **price on a person's head** a reward for a person's capture or death. □ **priced** *adj.*

price-fixing *n.* the maintaining of prices at a certain high level by agreement between competing sellers.

price gouging *n.* the charging of unjustly high prices.

price index *n.* an index showing the variation in the prices of a set of goods etc.

priceless *adj.* **1** beyond price. **2** *informal* very amusing or absurd.

price war *n.* a period of intense commercial competition in which rival enterprises try to undercut each other's prices.

pricey *adj.* (**pricier, priciest**) *informal* expensive. [Say PRICE ee]

prick ● *v.* **1** pierce slightly. **2** trouble mentally. **3** feel a pricking sensation. ● *n.* **1** an act of piercing something with a fine, sharp point. **2** a small mark made by pricking. **3** a pain caused as by pricking. □ **prick (up) one's ears** become suddenly attentive.

prickle ● *n.* **1** a short spine or pointed outgrowth on a plant or animal. **2** a prickling sensation. ● *v.* (**prickles, prickled, prickling**) be affected with a sensation as of pricking.

prickly *adj.* (**pricklier, prickliest**) **1** having prickles. **2 a** ready to take offence; touchy. **b** full of contentious or complicated points; thorny. **3** tingling. □ **prickliness** *n.*

prickly pear *n.* **1** a cactus bearing barbed bristles and large pear-shaped prickly fruits. **2** the edible orange or red fruit of this plant.

pricy *adj.* (**pricier, priciest**) = PRICEY.

pride ● *n.* **1 a** a feeling of satisfaction at achievements or qualities or possessions. **b** an object of this feeling. **c** the foremost or best of a group. **2** a high or overbearing opinion of one's worth or importance. **3** self-respect. **4** a group or company of lions. ● *v.* (**prides, prided, priding**) **pride oneself on** be proud of. □ **prideful** *adj.* **pridefully** *adv.*

pride of place *n.* the most important or prominent position.

priest *n.* **1** an ordained minister of the Catholic, Orthodox, or Anglican Church. **2** a person who performs ceremonies in a non-Christian religion. □**priesthood** *n.* **priestlike** *adj.* **priestly** *adj.*

priestess *n.* (*pl.* **priestesses**) a woman who performs ceremonies in a non-Christian religion.

prig *n.* a self-righteously correct or moralistic person. □**priggish** *adj.* **priggishness** *n.*

prim *adj.* (**primmer, primmest**) **1 a** stiffly formal and precise. **b** ordered, regular, formal. **2** demure. **3** prudish; prissy.

prima ballerina *n.* the chief female dancer in a ballet or ballet company. [*Say* preema balla REENA]

primacy *n.* **1** the state of being first in order, importance, or authority; pre-eminence. **2** the office of a primate. [*Say* PRIME uh see]

prima donna *n.* **1** the chief female singer in an opera or opera company. **2** a temperamentally self-important person. □**prima donna-ish** *adj.* [*Say* preema DONNA]

prima facie ● *adv.* from a first impression. ● *adj.* based on the first impression. [*Say* prime uh FAY she]

primal *adj.* **1** relating to an early stage of evolutionary development and usu. basic or primitive. **2** fundamental, essential. [*Say* PRY mul]

primary ● *adj.* **1 a** of the first importance; chief. **b** fundamental, basic. **2** earliest, original; first in a series. **3** (of education) for young children, esp. below the age of 12. **4** (of an industry) concerned with obtaining natural raw materials. ● *n.* (*pl.* **primaries**) **1** a thing that is primary. **2** (in the US) a preliminary election to appoint delegates to a party conference or to select the candidates for an election. □**primarily** *adv.*

primary colour *n.* any of the colours red, green, and blue, or (for pigments) red, blue and yellow, from which all other colours can be derived.

primate *n.* **1** any animal of the order that includes lemurs, apes, monkeys, and humans. **2** an archbishop or bishop ranked first among all the bishops of a country, region, etc. [*Say* PRY mate; *for sense 2 you can also say* PRY mit]

primavera *adj.* designating a pasta dish made with lightly sautéed spring vegetables. [*Say* preema VERRA]

prime¹ ● *adj.* **1** chief, most important. **2** of the best or highest quality or value.

3 primary, fundamental. **4** (of a number) divisible only by itself and one, e.g. 2, 3, 11. ● *n.* **1** the state of the highest perfection of something. **2** the best part. **3** a prime number. **4** = PRIME RATE.

prime² *v.* (**primes, primed, priming**) **1** prepare for use or action. **2** prepare a gun for firing. **3** pour a liquid into a pump to prepare it for working. **4** prepare a surface for painting by applying a substance that prevents paint from being absorbed.

prime meridian *n.* the meridian passing through Greenwich, from which longitude is reckoned.

prime minister *n.* the head of government in most countries with a parliamentary system. □**prime ministerial** *adj.* **prime ministership** *n.*

primer¹ *n.* **1** a substance used to prime a surface for painting. **2** a person who primes something.

primer² *n.* **1** a textbook for teaching children to read. **2** an introductory book. [*Say* PRIME er *or* PRIMMER]

prime rate *n.* the rate of interest which a bank offers its best customers.

prime rib *n.* a beef roast or steak cut from the seven ribs immediately before the loin.

prime time *n.* the time at which a radio or television audience is expected to be at its highest.

primeval *adj.* **1** of or relating to the first age of the world. **2** primitively instinctual; raw and elementary. [*Say* pry MEE vul]

primitive ● *adj.* **1** relating to the earliest times in history or stages in development. **2** denoting a preliterate, non-industrial society of simple organization. **3** offering an extremely basic level of comfort or convenience. **4** instinctive and unreasoning. ● *n.* a person belonging to a primitive society. □**primitively** *adv.* **primitiveness** *n.*

primly *adv.* **1** in a precise or stiffly formal manner. **2** in a prudish or prissy manner.

primogeniture *n.* the right of the first-born child, esp. the eldest son, to inherit the estate of his or her parents. [*Say* prime oh JENNA chur *or* preemo JENNA chur]

primordial *adj.* **1** existing at or from the beginning. **2** basic and fundamental. [*Say* pry MORDY ul]

primp *v.* groom oneself or one's clothing in a fussy or affected manner.

primrose *n.* **1** (also **primula**) any of a number of low-growing plants with spring flowers in a wide variety of colours. **2** *n. & adj.* (also **primrose yellow**) pale yellow.

prince *n.* **1** a male member of a royal

family other than a reigning king. **2** a son or grandson of a British monarch. **3** a ruler of a small state. **4** a noble usu. ranking next below a duke. **5** the chief or greatest. **6** an admirable man. □ **princelike** adj.

princeling n. **1** a young prince. **2** the ruler of a small principality or domain. [Say PRINCE ling]

princely adj. (**princelier, princeliest**) **1** of or worthy of a prince. **2** sumptuous, generous, splendid.

princess n. (pl. **princesses**) **1** the wife of a prince. **2** a female member of a royal family other than a reigning queen. **3** a daughter or granddaughter of a British monarch. **4** a pre-eminent woman. **5** informal a pampered, egocentric, or demanding girl or woman.

principal ● adj. **1** first in rank or importance; chief. **2** main, leading. **3** constituting the original sum of money invested or lent. ● n. **1** the head of some schools, colleges, and universities. **2** the leading performer in a concert, orchestra section, play, ballet company, etc. **3** a sum of money lent or invested, on which interest is paid.

principality n. (pl. **principalities**) a state ruled by a prince. [Say prince i PALA tee]

principally adv. mainly.

principle n. **1** a fundamental truth as the basis of reasoning or action. **2** a personal code of conduct. **3** a law of nature forming the basis for the construction or working of a machine etc. □ **in principle** as regards fundamentals but not necessarily in detail. **on principle** on the basis of a moral attitude.

principled adj. based on, having, or exhibiting esp. praiseworthy principles of behaviour.

print ● n. **1** the text appearing in a book, newspaper, etc. **2** a mark left on a surface by pressure. **3** a printed picture or design. **4** a photograph printed on paper. **5** a copy of a motion picture on film. **6** a piece of fabric with a coloured pattern or design. ● v. **1** produce books etc. by transferring text or designs to paper. **2** produce a paper copy of information stored on a computer. **3** produce a photographic print from a negative. **4** write clearly without joining the letters. ● adj. **1** made of a printed fabric. **2** of or relating to newspapers or magazines. □ **printable** adj.

printed circuit n. an electric circuit with thin strips of conductor on a flat insulating sheet.

printer n. **1** a person or company that prints books, magazines, etc. **2** a device

that prints, esp. as part of a computer system.

printing n. **1** the production of printed books etc. **2** a single impression of a book. **3** printed letters or writing imitating them.

printing press n. a machine for printing from type or plates etc.

printout n. computer output in printed form.

print run n. the number of copies of a book etc. printed at one time.

prior ● adj. **1** earlier. **2** coming before in time, order, or importance. ● adv. (**prior to**) before. ● n. the superior officer in a religious order.

prioress n. (pl. **prioresses**) a female superior of a house of any of various orders of nuns. [Say PRIOR ess]

prioritize v. (**prioritizes, prioritized, prioritizing**) put tasks etc. in order of importance. [Say pry ORA tize]

priority n. (pl. **priorities**) something that is given prior or special attention.

priory n. (pl. **priories**) a religious house governed by a prior or prioress. [Say PRIOR ee]

prise v. esp. Brit. (**prises, prised, prising**) = PRY 1.

prism n. a transparent object with triangular ends, that breaks up light into the colours of the rainbow.

prison n. **1** a place in which a person is kept in captivity; a jail. **2** any place of real or perceived confinement.

prison camp n. a camp for prisoners of war or political prisoners.

prisoner n. **1** a person kept in prison. **2** a person in custody on a criminal charge and on trial. **3** a person or thing confined by illness, another's grasp, etc. **4** (also **prisoner of war**) a person who is captured in war.

prissy adj. (**prissier, prissiest**) prim, prudish. □ **prissily** adv. **prissiness** n.

pristine adj. **1** in its original condition. **2** fresh and clean, as if new. **3** unspoiled. [Say priss TEEN]

privacy n. **1** the state of being private and not disturbed. **2** freedom from intrusion or public attention. [Say PRY vuh see or PRIVVA see]

private ● adj. **1** for or belonging to one particular person or group only. **2** owned by an individual or commercial company rather than the state. **3** not to be shared or revealed. **4** not choosing to share thoughts and feelings. **5** having no official or public position. **6** not connected with one's work or official position. **7** secluded. ● n. **1** (also

Private) a soldier of the lowest rank. **2** (in *pl.*) *informal* the genitals. ☐ **privately** *adv.*

private company *n.* a company with restricted membership and no issue of shares.

private enterprise *n.* **1** businesses not under government control. **2** free enterprise.

privateer *n.* **1** an armed vessel owned by private individuals and authorized for war service. **2** a commander of such a vessel. [*Say* pry vuh TEER]

private investigator *n.* (also **private eye**) a usu. freelance detective carrying out investigations for a private employer.

private member's bill *n.* a bill introduced by a member of a legislature who is not a cabinet minister.

private parts *pl. n.* the genitals.

privation *n.* lack of the comforts or necessities of life. [*Say* pry VAY sh'n]

privatize *v.* (**privatizes, privatized, privatizing**) assign a business etc. to private as distinct from governmental control or ownership. ☐ **privatization** *n.* [*Say* pry vuh TIZE]

privet *n.* any evergreen shrub of the olive family, bearing small white flowers and black berries. [*Say* PRIV it]

privilege ● *n.* **1** a special right or advantage available only to a particular person or group. **2** the advantages possessed by the rich and powerful. **3** (also **parliamentary privilege**) the freedom of members of a legislative assembly to speak at its meetings without risking legal action. ● *v.* (**privileges, privileged, privileging**) **1** invest with a privilege. **2** consider or treat as more important; favour.

privileged *adj.* **1** having a privilege or privileges. **2** honoured. **3** legally protected from being made public.

privy ● *adj.* sharing in the knowledge of a secret. ● *n.* (*pl.* **privies**) an outhouse. [*Say* PRIVVY]

Privy Council *n.* (in Canada) a chiefly honorary body of advisers appointed by the Governor General, made up of current and former Cabinet ministers and other distinguished people.

Privy Council Office *n.* (in Canada) an administrative body which coordinates the activities of the federal Cabinet, provides advice to the prime minister, and implements government objectives.

prix fixe *n.* **1** a fixed price for a restaurant meal chosen from a usu. limited menu. **2** a meal that is served for such a price. [*Say* pree FIX]

prize ● *n.* **1** something that can be won in a competition, lottery, etc. **2** something striven for. **3** (as an *adj.*) **a** to which a prize is awarded. **b** supremely excellent or outstanding of its kind. ● *v.* (**prizes, prized, prizing**) value highly.

prizefight *n.* a boxing match fought for money. ☐ **prizefighter** *n.* **prizefighting** *n.*

prizewinner *n.* a winner of a prize. ☐ **prizewinning** *adj.*

pro¹ ● *n.* (*pl.* **pros**) a professional. ● *adj.* professional.

pro² ● *adj.* for; in favour. ● *n.* (*pl.* **pros**) a reason or argument for or in favour. ● *prep. & adv.* in favour of.

pro-¹ *prefix* favouring or supporting.

pro-² *prefix* before in time, place, order, etc.

proactive *adj.* creating or controlling a situation by taking the initiative. ☐ **proactively** *adv.*

pro-am ● *adj.* involving professionals and amateurs. ● *n.* a pro-am event.

prob *n. informal* a problem.

probability *n.* (*pl.* **probabilities**) **1** the likelihood of something happening. **2** a probable or most probable event. ☐ **in all probability** most probably.

probable *adj.* that may be expected to happen or prove true; likely. ☐ **probably** *adv.*

probate *n.* **1** the official process of proving that a will is valid. **2** a verified copy of a will.

probation *n.* **1** *Law* the early release of an offender subject to a period of good behaviour under supervision. **2** a period of testing for a new employee etc. ☐ **on probation** undergoing probation, esp. legal supervision. ☐ **probationary** *adj.*

probe ● *n.* **1** a penetrating investigation. **2** any small device, esp. an electrode, for measuring, testing, etc. **3** a blunt-ended surgical instrument for exploring a wound etc. **4** an unmanned exploratory spacecraft. ● *v.* (**probes, probed, probing**) **1** examine or inquire into closely. **2** explore a wound or part of the body with a probe. **3** penetrate with a sharp instrument. ☐ **prober** *n.* **probingly** *adv.*

probity *n.* uprightness, honesty. [*Say* PRO bit ee *or* PROB it ee]

problem *n.* **1** a doubtful or difficult matter requiring a solution. **2** something hard to understand or accomplish or deal with. **3** (as an *adj.*) causing problems; difficult to deal with. **4** a puzzle or question for solution.

problematic *adj.* (also **problematical**) **1** attended by difficulty. **2** doubtful or

questionable. □ **problematically** adv.
[Say prob luh MAT ick]

pro bono adj. done without charge.
[Say pro BONE oh]

proboscis n. (pl. **proboscises** or
probosces) **1** the long flexible trunk or
snout of some mammals, e.g. an elephant.
2 the elongated mouthparts of some
insects. **3** jocular the human nose.
[Say pro BOSS kiss]

procedure n. **1** a way of doing something,
esp. the usual, correct, official, or formal
way. **2** a medical operation. **3** Computing a
subroutine. □ **procedural** adj.
procedurally adv. [Say pro SEE jur]

proceed v. **1** go forward or on further.
2 continue; go on with an activity. **3** be
carried on or continued. **4** adopt a course
of action

proceeding n. **1** an action or piece of
conduct. **2** (in pl.) an action at law; a
lawsuit. **3** (in pl.) a published report of a
conference etc.

proceeds pl. n. money produced by a
transaction or other undertaking.

process¹ ● n. (pl. **processes**) **1** a course
of action or proceeding, esp. a series of
stages in an operation. **2** the progress or
course of something. **3** a natural series of
changes. **4** (as an adj.) that has been
processed. **5** a natural appendage or
outgrowth on an organism. ● v.
(**processes, processed, processing**)
1 put through an industrial or
manufacturing process. **2** deal with a
document etc. officially. **3** operate on data
by means of a program. **4** mix, chop, etc.
using a food processor. **5** develop
photographic film.

process² v. (**processes, processed,
processing**) walk in procession.
[Say pro SESS]

procession n. **1** a number of people or
vehicles etc. moving forward in orderly
succession, esp. at a ceremony or
demonstration. **2** such movement.

processional ● adj. **1** of processions.
2 used, carried, or sung in processions. ● n.
Christianity a hymn etc. sung during a
procession.

processor n. **1** a person, company, or
machine that processes something. **2** a
central processing unit.

pro-choice adj. favouring the right of a
woman to choose to have an abortion.

proclaim v. **1** announce or declare
publicly or officially. **2** declare a person to
be. □ **proclaimer** n.

proclamation n. an official public
statement about something important.
[Say prock luh MAY sh'n]

proclivity n. (pl. **proclivities**) a tendency
or inclination. [Say pro CLIVVA tee]

procrastinate v. (**procrastinates,
procrastinated, procrastinating**)
delay or postpone action.
□ **procrastination** n. **procrastinator** n.
[Say pro CRASS tuh nate]

procreate v. (**procreates, procreated,
procreating**) bring offspring into
existence; reproduce. □ **procreation** n.
procreative adj. [Say PRO create]

proctology n. the branch of medicine
concerned with the anus and rectum.
□ **proctologist** n. [Say prock TOLLA jee]

proctor n. a person who supervises
students in an examination etc.

procure v. (**procures, procured,
procuring**) **1** obtain, esp. by care or effort.
2 bring about. □ **procurable** adj.
procurement n.

prod ● v. (**prods, prodded, prodding**)
1 poke with the finger or a pointed object.
2 stimulate to action. ● n. **1** a poke or
thrust. **2** a stimulus to action. **3** a pointed
or electrified rod for herding cattle etc.
□ **prodder** n.

prodigal ● adj. **1** recklessly wasteful.
2 having returned after an absence. ● n. **1** a
prodigal person. **2** a wasteful person who
repents. **3** a person who returns after an
absence. □ **prodigality** n.
[Say PRODDA gull, prodda GALA tee]

prodigious adj. **1** remarkably or
impressively great in extent, size, or
degree. **2** abnormal. □ **prodigiously** adv.
[Say pruh DIDGE us]

prodigy n. (pl. **prodigies**) a person
endowed with exceptional qualities or
abilities, esp. a precocious child.
[Say PRODDA jee]

produce ● v. (**produces, produced,
producing**) **1** bring into existence; cause.
2 manufacture. **3** yield fruit, a harvest, etc.
4 give birth to. **5** bring forward for
consideration or use. **6 a** bring a play etc.
before the public. **b** supervise the making
of a film, broadcast, etc. ● n. **1** agricultural
and natural products collectively. **2** fruits
and vegetables. □ **producer** n.

product n. **1** a thing that is grown or
produced, usu. for sale. **2** a thing or
substance produced during a natural,
chemical, or manufacturing process. **3** a
result. **4** Math a quantity obtained by
multiplying quantities together.

production n. **1** the action of making or
manufacturing. **2** a total yield. **3 a** the
process of making a film, play, record, etc.
b a film, play, record, etc., produced.
4 informal a needlessly complicated situation

or event. **5** the sets, costumes, etc. of a theatrical entertainment.

production line *n.* an assembly line.

productive *adj.* **1** of or engaged in the production of goods. **2** producing much. □ **productively** *adv.* **productivity** *n.*

Prof. *abbr.* Professor.

prof *n. a professor.*

profane ● *adj.* **1** secular; not sacred. **2 a** showing a lack of respect for God or holy things; irreverent. **b** obscene. ● *v.* (**profanes, profaned, profaning**) **1** treat a sacred thing with irreverence. **2** violate what is entitled to respect. □ **profanely** *adv.* **profaner** *n.*
[*Say* pro FANE]

profanity *n.* (*pl.* **profanities**) **1** profane language. **2** a swear word.
[*Say* pro FANNA tee]

profess *v.* (**professes, professed, professing**) **1** claim openly to have or be. **2** affirm one's faith in or allegiance to.

professed *adj.* **1** self-acknowledged. **2** claimed or asserted openly but often falsely. □ **professedly** *adv.*
[*Say* pruh FEST, pruh FESSID lee]

profession *n.* **1** a job or vocation, esp. one that involves formal qualification. **2** a body of people engaged in a profession. **3** a declaration or avowal.

professional ● *adj.* **1** having to do with a profession. **2** showing the skill of a professional. **3** engaged in a specified activity as one's main paid occupation. ● *n.* **1** a person qualified or employed in one of the professions. **2** a professional player or performer. **3** a highly experienced person. □ **professionally** *adv.*

professional development day *n.* esp. *Cdn* a day on which classes are cancelled so that teachers may attend seminars etc.

professionalism *n.* **1** the skill or qualities required or expected of members of a profession. **2** great skill and ability.

professor *n.* a university teacher. □ **professorial** *adj.* **professorship** *n.*
[*Say* proffa SORRY ul]

proffer *v.* offer.

proficient *adj.* adept, expert. □ **proficiency** *n.* **proficiently** *adv.*
[*Say* pruh FISH'nt]

profile ● *n.* **1** an outline as seen from one side. **2** a short biographical or character sketch. **3** the extent to which a person, organization, etc., attracts public notice or comment. **4** a vertical cross-section of a structure etc. ● *v.* (**profiles, profiled, profiling**) describe in a short article. □ **in profile** as seen from one side. **keep a**

low profile remain inconspicuous. □ **profiler** *n.*

profiling *n.* the recording and analysis of a person's psychological and behavioural characteristics.

profit ● *n.* **1** financial gain. **2** an advantage or benefit. ● *v.* (**profits, profited, profiting**) **1** be beneficial to. **2** obtain an esp. financial benefit. □ **profitless** *adj.*

profitable *adj.* **1** yielding profit. **2** beneficial; useful. □ **profitability** *n.* **profitably** *adv.*

profiteer ● *v.* seek to make excessive profits, esp. illegally. ● *n.* a person who profiteers.

profit margin *n.* the difference between the cost of buying or producing something and the price for which it is sold.

profit-sharing *n.* the sharing of profits esp. between employer and employees.

profligate *adj.* **1** shamelessly immoral. **2** recklessly extravagant and wasteful. □ **profligacy** *n.* **profligately** *adv.*
[*Say* PROFF lig it]

pro forma ● *adj.* **1** done as a matter of form. **2** sent in advance of goods supplied. ● *adv.* as a matter of form.
[*Say* pro FORMA]

profound *adj.* **1 a** showing great knowledge or insight. **b** demanding deep study or thought. **2** deep, intense, unqualified. **3** at or extending to a great depth. □ **profoundly** *adv.* **profundity** *n.*

profuse *adj.* **1** lavish; extravagant. **2** exuberantly plentiful; abundant. □ **profusely** *adv.* **profusion** *n.*
[*Say* pro FYOOSS, pro FUSION]

progenitor *n.* **1** an ancestor. **2** an originator. **3** something that serves as a model. [*Say* pro JENNA tur]

progeny *n.* offspring.
[*Say* PRODGE a nee]

progesterone *n.* a hormone which stimulates the uterus to prepare for pregnancy. [*Say* pro JESTER own]

progestin *n.* (also **progestogen**) a hormone that maintains pregnancy and prevents further ovulation.
[*Say* pro JESS tin, pro JESTA jin]

prognosis *n.* (*pl.* **prognoses**) a forecast, esp. of the course of a medical condition. □ **prognostic** *adj.* [*Say* prog NO sis *for the singular,* prog NO seez *for the plural;* prog NOSS tick]

prognostication *n.* **1** the action of predicting. **2** a prediction. □ **prognosticator** *n.*

program (also **programme**) ● *n.* **1 a** a printed list of events at a performance etc. **b** the performance itself. **2** a radio or television broadcast. **3 a** a course of actions towards a long-term aim. **b** a plan of events or system of activities. **4** a course of study. **5** a series of coded instructions to control the operation of a computer etc. ● v. (**programs** or **programmes**, **programmed**, **programming**) **1** make a program; plan. **2** provide (a computer etc.) with coded instructions. **3** train. **4** choose for performance. □ **programmability** n. **programmable** adj. **programmer** n. **programming** n.

programmatic adj. having to do with a program or method.
□ **programmatically** adv.

progress ● n. (pl. **progresses**) **1** movement towards a destination. **2** development, improvement. ● v. (**progresses**, **progressed**, **progressing**) **1** move onward; continue. **2** develop, improve. **3** cause to advance or improve. □ **in progress** going on. [Say PRAW gress or PRO gress for the noun, pruh GRESS for the verb]

progression n. **1** the gradual movement from one stage to another. **2** a series of things. **3 a** = ARITHMETIC PROGRESSION. **b** = GEOMETRIC PROGRESSION.
[Say pruh GRESH'n]

progressive ● adj. **1** moving forward. **2** proceeding step by step. **3 a** favouring new ideas or social reform. **b** liberal or modern. **c** avant-garde. **4** increasing in severity. **5** (of taxation) at rates increasing with the sum taxed. ● n. an advocate of progressive politics. □ **progressively** adv. [Say pruh GRESS iv]

Progressive Conservative n. a member or supporter of the Progressive Conservative Party. □ **Progressive Conservative** adj.

Progressive Conservative Party n. (in Canada) a political party advocating right-of-centre policies.

prohibit v. (**prohibits**, **prohibits**, **prohibited**, **prohibiting**) (often foll. by from + verbal noun) **1** formally forbid. **2** prevent.

prohibition n. **1** the act of forbidding. **2** Law a law or rule that stops something being done or used. **3** (usu. **Prohibition**) the prevention by law of the manufacture and sale of alcoholic drink, esp. as in the US 1920–33. □ **prohibitionism** n. **prohibitionist** n. [Say pro hib ISH'n]

prohibitive adj. **1** too expensive. **2** intended to prevent something. □ **prohibitively** adv. [Say pro HIBBA tiv]

project ● n. **1** a plan. **2 a** an undertaking with a particular aim. **b** any planned activity. **3** a piece of research work. **4** =

HOUSING PROJECT. ● v. **1** plan. **2** jut out. **3** throw; cast; impel. **4** extrapolate; forecast. **5** cause (light etc.) to fall on a surface. **6** cause (sound) to be heard at a distance. **7** express forcefully or effectively. **8** Psychology attribute (an emotion etc.) to something external. □ **projection** n. [Say PRAW ject or PRO ject for the noun, pruh JECT for the verb; pruh JECK shun]

projectile ● n. a missile fired or thrown at a target. ● adj. projected with great force. [Say pruh JECK tile]

projectionist n. a person whose job is to show films by operating a projector.

projector n. an apparatus for projecting images from slides or film onto a screen.

prolapse ● n. **1** the forward or downward displacement of a part or organ. **2** the prolapsed part or organ. ● v. (**prolapses**, **prolapsed**, **prolapsing**) undergo prolapse. [Say PRO laps]

prole derogatory informal ● adj. proletarian. ● n. a proletarian.

proletarian ● adj. relating to the proletariat. ● n. a member of the proletariat. [Say prole a TERRY un]

proletariat n. **1** the class of wage earners, esp. (in Marxist theory) labourers engaged in industrial production. **2** poor landless freemen in ancient Rome.
[Say prole a TERRY it]

pro-life adj. opposed to abortion and euthanasia. □ **pro-lifer** n.

proliferate v. (**proliferates**, **proliferated**, **proliferating**) **1** increase rapidly in numbers. **2** produce or reproduce rapidly. □ **proliferation** n. [Say pruh LIFFER ate]

prolific adj. **1** extremely productive. **2** producing much fruit, foliage, offspring, or creative work. **3** plentiful. □ **prolifically** adv. [Say pruh LIF ick]

prolix adj. too wordy; tedious. □ **prolixity** n. [Say PRO licks, pro LICKS a tee]

prologue n. **1** an introduction to a literary or musical work. **2** (usu. foll. by to) any event leading to another.

prolong v. extend in time.

prom n. informal a formal dance event at a high school etc.

promenade ● n. **1** a walk, ride, or drive, taken for leisure. **2** esp. Brit. a paved public walk along a seafront. ● v. (**promenades**, **promenaded**, **promenading**) go or take for a walk to show off. [Say promma NAD or promma NOD]

prominence n. **1** the state of being important or famous. **2** a jutting out feature of the landscape.
[Say PROMMA nince]

prominent *adj.* **1** distinguished; important. **2** conspicuous. **3** jutting out. □ **prominently** *adv.* [*Say* PROMMA n'nt]

promiscuous *adj.* **1** having or involving frequent short sexual relationships with different partners. **2** implying an approach that is not selective. □ **promiscuity** *n.* **promiscuously** *adv.* [*Say* pruh MISS cue us, promise CUE a tee]

promise ● *n.* **1** an assurance, esp. regarding future action. **2** a sign of future achievements. ● *v.* (**promises, promised, promising**) **1** make a promise. **2** afford expectations of. **3** *informal* assure.

promised land *n.* **1** (**Promised Land**) *Bible* Canaan, the land promised by God to Abraham and his descendants. **2** any happy place or coveted situation.

promising *adj.* likely to turn out well. □ **promisingly** *adv.*

promissory note *n.* a signed promise to pay a stated sum. [*Say* PROMISE or ee]

promo *informal* ● *n.* (*pl.* **promos**) an advertising campaign, trailer, etc. ● *adj.* relating to publicity.

promontory *n.* (*pl.* **promontories**) a point of high land jutting out into the sea. [*Say* PROM'n tory]

promote *v.* (**promotes, promoted, promoting**) **1** (often foll. by *to*) raise to a higher office, rank, etc. **2** encourage; support actively. **3** publicize. □ **promoter** *n.* **promotion** *n.* **promotional** *adj.*

prompt ● *adj.* **1** acting without delay. **2** done at once. ● *v.* **1** incite. **2 a** supply a forgotten word, sentence, etc. **b** assist (a hesitating speaker) with a suggestion. **3** give rise to. ● *n.* **1 a** an act of prompting. **b** a thing said to help the memory of an actor etc. **2** a visual indication that a computer is waiting for input. □ **prompter** *n.* **prompting** *n.* **promptly** *adv.* **promptness** *n.*

promulgate *v.* (**promulgates, promulgated, promulgating**) **1** make known to the public. **2** proclaim. □ **promulgation** *n.* [*Say* PROM'll gate]

prone *adj.* **1 a** lying face downwards. **b** lying flat. **2** disposed or liable; vulnerable to. □ **proneness** *n.*

prong *n.* each of two or more projecting pointed parts at the end of a fork etc.

pronged *adj.* **1** having a prong or prongs. **2** (in *comb.*) having a specified number of points of attack etc.

pronghorn *n.* (also **pronghorn antelope**) a small deer-like mammal with black horns, inhabiting Western Canada and the northwestern US.

pronoun *n.* a word used instead of and to indicate a noun already mentioned or known.

pronounce *v.* (**pronounces, pronounced, pronouncing**) **1** utter in a certain way. **2** deliver or proclaim (a judgment etc.). □ **pronouncement** *n.*

pronounced *adj.* **1** very noticeable. **2** strongly felt. **3** uttered. □ **pronouncedly** *adv.* [*Say* pruh NOUNST, pruh NOUN sid lee]

pronto *adv. informal* promptly.

pronunciation *n.* **1** the way in which something is pronounced. **2** a person's way of pronouncing words etc. [*Say* pruh nunsy AY sh'n]

proof ● *n.* **1** evidence etc. establishing a fact. **2** an act of proving. **3** the standard of strength of distilled alcoholic liquors. **4** a printout used for making corrections before final printing. **5** the stages in the resolution of a mathematical or philosophical problem. **6** a photographic print made for selection etc. ● *adj.* **1** able to resist. **2** (of a distilled alcoholic liquor) of standard strength. ● *v.* **1** make (something) proof or waterproof. **2** proofread.

proof positive *n.* absolutely certain proof.

proofread *v.* (**proofreads, proofread, proofreading**) read and mark any errors. □ **proofreader** *n.* **proofreading** *n.*

prop ● *n.* **1** a rigid support. **2** a source of support. **3** a movable object used on a theatre stage etc. **4** *informal* a propeller. ● *v.* (**props, propped, propping**) **1** (often foll. by *up*) support with a prop. **2** lean (something) against a support.

propaganda *n.* usu. *derogatory* information, esp. misleading, promoting a particular point of view. [*Say* proppa GANDA]

propagandist *n.* a person who spreads propaganda. □ **propagandist** *adj.* **propagandistic** *adj.* [*Say* proppa GAN dist, proppa gan DISS tick]

propagandize *v.* (**propagandizes, propagandized, propagandizing**) promote a cause using propaganda. [*Say* proppa GAN dize]

propagate *v.* (**propagates, propagated, propagating**) **1** breed by natural processes from the parent stock. **2** spread. □ **propagation** *n.* **propagator** *n.* [*Say* PROPPA gate]

propane *n.* a gaseous hydrocarbon used as bottled fuel.

propel *v.* (**propels, propelled, propelling**) **1** drive or push forward. **2** urge on.

propellant *n.* **1** a thing that propels. **2** a compressed gas that forces out the contents of an aerosol. **3** an explosive that fires bullets etc. from a firearm. **4** a substance providing thrust in a rocket engine.

propeller *n.* a revolving shaft with blades for propelling a ship or aircraft.

propensity *n.* (*pl.* **propensities**) a tendency. [*Say* pruh PENSA tee]

proper *adj.* **1** right. **2** decent; respectable. **3** belonging or relating distinctively. **4** strictly so called.

properly *adv.* **1** fittingly. **2** accurately. **3** respectably.

proper name *n.* (also **proper noun**) a name used for an individual person, place, etc., and spelled with a capital letter.

property *n.* (*pl.* **properties**) **1 a** something owned. **b** possessions collectively. **2** an attribute.

prophecy *n.* (*pl.* **prophecies**) **1 a** a divinely inspired utterance. **b** a prediction of future events. **2** the faculty of prophesying. [*Say* PROFFA see]

prophesy *v.* (**prophesies, prophesied, prophesying**) foretell future events. [*Say* PROFFA sigh]

prophet *n.* **1 a** a teacher or interpreter of the supposed will of God. **b** (in several religions) a person sent by God to teach or give a message. **2** a person who foretells events or speaks innovatively. □ **prophetess** *n.* (*pl.* **prophetesses**) [*Sounds like* PROFIT]

prophetic *adj.* **1** accurately predicting the future. **2** of or concerning a prophet. □ **prophetically** *adv.* [*Say* pruh FET ick]

prophylactic ● *adj.* **1** tending to prevent disease. **2** protective; precautionary. ● *n.* **1** a preventive medicine or course of action. **2** a condom. [*Say* pro fill ACK tick]

propitious *adj.* favourable. [*Say* pruh PISH us]

proponent *n.* a person advocating a theory or proposal. [*Say* pruh PONE int]

proportion ● *n.* **1 a** a part, share, or number considered in relation to a whole. **b** a comparative ratio. **2** (usu. in *pl.*) a correct or ideal relationship in size, degree, etc. **3** (in *pl.*) dimensions. ● *v.* adjust or regulate in proportion to something. □ **in proportion 1** by the same factor. **2** without exaggerating. **out of (all) proportion 1** badly proportioned; disproportionate. **2** exaggerated. □ **proportional** *adj.* **proportionally** *adv.*

proportional representation *n.* an electoral system in which parties gain seats in proportion to the number of votes cast for them. Abbreviation: **PR**.

proportionate *adj.* = PROPORTIONAL. □ **proportionately** *adv.* [*Say* PROPORTION it]

proportioned *adj.* having proportions of a specified type.

proposal *n.* **1** an esp. formal plan or suggestion. **2** an offer of marriage.

propose *v.* (**proposes, proposed, proposing**) **1** put forward for consideration. **2** intend. **3** make an offer of marriage. □ **proposed** *adj.* **proposer** *n.*

proposition ● *n.* **1** a plan proposed. **2** a statement or assertion. **3** a task, opponent, etc. to be dealt with. **4** *informal* a proposal to have sexual relations. ● *v. informal* make a proposal (esp. of sexual relations) to.

propound *v.* offer for consideration.

proprietary *adj.* **1** owned or manufactured by a particular company. **2** relating to ownership or property. [*Say* pruh PRY a terry]

proprietor *n.* the owner of a business or property. □ **proprietorial** *adj.* **proprietorship** *n.* [*Say* pruh PRY a tur, pruh pry a TORY ul]

propriety *n.* (*pl.* **proprieties**) **1** correct moral and social behaviour. **2** (in *pl.*) the rules of correct conduct. [*Say* pruh PRY a tee]

propulsion *n.* **1** the action of driving forward. **2** the force that does this. □ **propulsive** *adj.*

propylene *n.* a gaseous hydrocarbon used in the manufacture of chemicals. [*Say* PRO puh leen]

pro-rate *v.* (**pro-rates, pro-rated, pro-rating**) calculate or distribute proportionally. □ **pro-rated** *adj.*

prorogue *v.* (**prorogues, prorogued, proroguing**) discontinue the meetings of (a parliament etc.) without dissolving it. □ **prorogation** *n.* [*Say* pro ROAG, pro ruh GAY sh'n]

prosaic *adj.* **1** like prose. **2** dull. □ **prosaically** *adv.* [*Say* pruh ZAY ick]

proscenium *n.* **1** (also **proscenium arch**) an arch that frames the front of a stage. **2** the part of the stage in front of the curtain. [*Say* pro SEENY um]

prosciutto *n.* Italian cured ham. [*Say* pruh SHOO toe]

proscribe *v.* (**proscribes, proscribed, proscribing**) **1** denounce or forbid, esp. by law. **2** banish. [*Say* pro SCRIBE]

proscription *n.* the action of proscribing. [*Say* pro SCRIP sh'n]

prose *n.* ordinary written or spoken language.

prosecute v. (**prosecutes, prosecuted, prosecuting**) **1** institute legal proceedings against or with reference to. **2** carry on.

prosecution n. **1 a** the prosecuting of a person with respect to a criminal charge. **b** the prosecuting party in a court case. **2** the action of carrying out a course of action.

prosecutor n. a person who prosecutes. □ **prosecutorial** adj.
[Say PROSSA cute er, prossa cue TORY ul]

proselytize v. (**proselytizes, proselytized, proselytizing**) **1** attempt to persuade others to adopt one's own belief, esp. in religion. **2** champion a cause. □ **proselytizer** n. [Say PROSSA luh tize]

prose poem n. a piece of imaginative poetic writing in prose.

prosody n. **1** the systematic study of verses. **2** patterns of stress and intonation in ordinary speech. [Say PROZZA dee or PROSSA dee]

prospect ● n. **1 a** the chance that something will happen. **b** (often in pl.) chances of success. **c** a vision or idea of the future. **2 a** something viewed in terms of its profitability. **b** someone likely to succeed. **c** a potential customer. **3** an extensive view of landscape. ● v. **1** explore a region for minerals. **2** search around for something. □ **prospecting** n. **prospector** n.

prospective adj. **1** expected. **2** relating to the future. □ **prospectively** adv.

prospectus n. (pl. **prospectuses**) **1** a document advertising a commercial enterprise to investors. **2** a listing of the courses etc. of an educational institution.

prosper v. **1** succeed. **2** make successful.

prosperity n. the state of being prosperous. [Say pruh SPARE a tee]

prosperous adj. **1** successful. **2** thriving.

prostaglandin n. a hormone-like substance that causes muscle contraction. [Say prossta GLAND in]

prostate n. a gland surrounding the neck of the bladder in male mammals and releasing a fluid forming part of the semen. [Say PROSS tate]

prosthesis n. (pl. **prostheses**) an artificial body part. □ **prosthetic** adj. [Say pross THEESIS for the singular, pross THEESEEZ for the plural, pross THETTICK]

prosthetics pl. n. **1** (usu. treated as sing.) artificial body parts. **2** the branch of surgery dealing with these. [Say pross THETTICKS]

prostitute ● n. a person who engages in sexual activity for payment. ● v. (**prostitutes, prostituted, prostituting**) **1** put oneself or one's talents to an unworthy use for money. **2** make a prostitute of. □ **prostitution** n.

prostrate ● adj. **1** lying face downwards. **2** overcome by grief etc. ● v. (**prostrates, prostrated, prostrating**) **1** (**prostrate oneself**) throw (oneself) down in submission etc. **2** reduce to exhaustion or weakness. □ **prostration** n.
[Say PROSS trate for the adjective, praw STRATE for the verb, pross TRAY sh'n]

prosy adj. (**prosier, prosiest**) **1** like prose. **2** tedious. [Say PROSE ee]

protagonist n. **1** the principal character. **2** a leading figure. [Say pro TAGGA nist]

protease n. any enzyme able to hydrolyze proteins and peptides by splitting them. [Say PRO tee ace]

protect v. **1** keep safe from harm. **2 a** attempt to preserve. **b** restrict access to or development of. **3** Computing restrict access (to a file etc.). **4** shield from competition. □ **protected** adj. **protector** n.

protection n. **1 a** the act of protecting, or the state of being protected. **b** a thing that protects. **2 a** the payment of money to criminals so that they will not attack a property or person. **b** the money paid for this. **3** insurance coverage.

protectionism n. the practice of shielding a country's own industry by taxing foreign goods. □ **protectionist** n. & adj.

protective adj. **1** intended to protect. **2** tending to protect. **3** of or relating to the protection of domestic industries from foreign competition. □ **protectively** adv. **protectiveness** n.

protective custody n. the detention of a person for his or her own protection.

protectorate n. **1** a territory that is controlled and protected by a larger state. **2** (**Protectorate**) hist. the period in England 1653–59 under the rule of Oliver Cromwell or his son. [Say PROTECTOR it]

protege n. a person whose welfare and career are looked after by an influential person. [Say PRO tuh zhay or PRAW tuh zhay]

protein n. **1** any of a group of organic compounds composed of one or more chains of amino acids and forming an essential part of all living organisms. **2** such substances collectively. [Say PRO teen]

pro tem adj. & adv. for the time being.

Proterozoic n. the eon constituting the later part of Precambrian time, from about 2.5 billion to 550 million years ago. □ **Proterozoic** adj. [Say pro tur oh ZO ick]

protest ● n. **1** a statement of dissent or complaint. **2** a usu. public demonstration of objection to government etc. policy. ● v. **1 a** make a protest against. **b** object to; stubbornly disagree. **2** affirm solemnly. □ **under protest** unwillingly. □ **protester** n.

Protestant (also **protestant**) ● n. a member of any of the western Christian Churches that are separate from the Catholic Church in accordance with the principles of the Reformation. ● adj. relating to any of the Protestant Churches or their members. □ **Protestantism** n. [Say PROTTA st'nt]

protestation n. **1** an emphatic declaration that something is or is not the case. **2** a protest. [Say protta STAY sh'n or pro tess TAY sh'n]

protist n. an organism with both plant and animal characteristics. [Say PRO tist]

proto- comb. form **1** first. **2** designating the earliest form of a language.

protocol n. **1** official formality and etiquette. **2** the original draft of a diplomatic document. **3** Computing a set of rules governing data communication between devices.

proton n. a stable elementary particle with a positive electric charge, occurring in all atomic nuclei. [Say PRO tawn]

protoplasm n. the material comprising the living part of a cell. □ **protoplasmic** adj. [Say PRO tuh plasm, pro tuh PLASMIC]

prototype ● n. **1** an original form from which other forms are developed or copied. **2** a trial model. ● v. (**prototypes**, **prototyped**, **prototyping**) make a prototype of. □ **prototypical** adj. [Say PRO tuh type, pro tuh TYPICAL]

protozoan n. (pl. **protozoa** or **protozoans**) (also **protozoon**, pl. **protozoa**) a single-celled microscopic organism such as an amoeba. □ **protozoan** adj. [Say pro tuh ZO un]

protract v. lengthen. □ **protracted** adj.

protractor n. a semicircular instrument for measuring angles. [Say pruh TRACTOR or PRO tractor]

protrude v. (**protrudes**, **protruded**, **protruding**) extend beyond or above a surface. □ **protrusion** n.

protuberance n. **1** something that protrudes. **2** the fact or state of protruding. □ **protuberant** adj. [Say pruh TOOBER ince, pruh TOOBER int]

proud adj. **1** feeling greatly honoured or pleased. **2 a** valuing oneself too highly. **b** suitably satisfied with one's achievements. **3** justly arousing pride. **4** (of a thing) imposing. □ **do proud** informal **1** be a source of pride to. **2** treat with lavish generosity. □ **proudly** adv.

Prov. abbr. **1** (also **prov.**) Provincial, provincial. **2** (also **prov.**) Province, province.

prove v. (**proves**; past **proved**; past participle **proven** or **proved**; **proving**) **1 a** demonstrate the truth of by evidence or argument. **b** assert or reveal. **c** show to be (right, wrong, etc.). **2 a** be found. **b** turn out to be. **3** test the accuracy of. **4** establish the genuineness of. □ **prove oneself** show one's abilities. □ **provable** adj.

proven adj. **1** shown to be such through trial and experience. **2** (also in comb.) demonstrated to be effective.

provenance n. **1** the place of origin or history. **2** origin. [Say PROVVA nince]

Provençal ● adj. **1** relating to the language, people, etc. of Provence in southeast France. **2** (also **provençale**) containing olive oil, garlic, and often tomato, with tarragon, rosemary, etc. ● n. a person from or the language of Provence. [Say praw von SAL]

proverb n. a short pithy saying generally held to embody a truth.

proverbial adj. **1** as well-known as a proverb; notorious. **2** of or referred to in a proverb. □ **proverbially** adv.

provide v. (**provides**, **provided**, **providing**) **1 a** supply. **b** offer or present. **2** ensure or specify. □ **provide for 1** financially etc. support. **2** plan so as to deal with. **3** make it possible for something to be done later. □ **provider** n.

provided conj. (also **providing**) (often foll. by that) on the condition (that).

providence n. esp. Christianity (also **Providence**) God or some natural force that some people believe controls human lives. [Say PROVVA dince]

providential adj. **1** of or by divine intervention. **2** lucky. □ **providentially** adv. [Say provva DEN shull]

province n. **1** a principal administrative division of a country or empire, esp. (in Canada) one of the ten principal political units which, along with the Territories, constitute Canada. **2** (in pl.) the whole of a country outside the capital city. **3** a person's particular area of knowledge or responsibility.

provincehood n. Cdn the quality or status of being a province.

Province House n. the name of the legislative building in Nova Scotia and PEI.

province-wide adj. esp. Cdn extending throughout or pertaining to a whole province.

provincial ● adj. **1** of or relating to a province or provinces. **2** derogatory narrow or limited; unsophisticated. **● n. 1** Cdn (in pl.) a provincial competition. **2** an inhabitant of esp. a European region outside the capital city. **3** an unsophisticated person.
□ **provincially** adv.

provincial building n. Cdn a building housing provincial government offices.

provincial court n. Cdn a court established by provincial legislation where hearings on minor offences are conducted by judge alone.

provincialism n. **1** a lack of sophistication in attitude or manners. **2** allegiance to one's province rather than one's country. □ **provincialist** n. & adj.

provincialization n. Cdn the transfer (of responsibilities, etc.) to the provincial level. □ **provincialize** v. (**provincializes, provincialized, provincializing**)

provincial park n. Cdn an area of land owned and preserved by a provincial government for recreation, wildlife protection, etc.

provincial parliament n. Cdn a provincial legislative assembly.

provincial police n. Cdn (esp. Ont. & Que.) a police force under provincial authority.

provincial right n. Cdn (usu. in pl.) the right of a province to have authority over specified areas under provincial jurisdiction.

proving ground n. any area or situation in which a person or thing is tested.

provision ● n. **1 a** the providing of something for use. **b** something provided. **c** preparation for the future. **2** (in pl.) food, drink, etc. **3** a condition or requirement in a legal document. **● v.** supply with provisions.

provisional adj. temporary.
□ **provisionally** adv.

proviso n. (pl. **provisos**) a condition that must be accepted before an agreement can be made. [Say pruh VIZE oh]

provocateur n. a person who provokes controversy or disturbance.
[Say pruh VOKKA tur]

provocation n. **1** action or speech that provokes. **2** the act of provoking.
[Say provva KAY sh'n]

provocative adj. **1** intentionally causing anger, controversy, etc. **2** tending to arouse

sexual desire. **3** intellectually stimulating.
□ **provocatively** adv. **provocativeness** n. [Say pruh VOKKA tiv]

provoke v. (**provokes, provoked, provoking**) **1** annoy, disturb, or harass. **2** cause a particular reaction in a person etc. **3** give rise to. □ **provoking** adj. **provokingly** adv.

provolone n. a type of mellow cow's-milk cheese originally made in southern Italy.
[Say pro vo LO nay, pro uh LO nee]

provost n. a high-ranking administrative officer in a university. [Say PROV ust]

prow n. the foremost part or bow of a ship.
□ **prowed** comb. form [Rhymes with HOW]

prowess n. great skill. [Say prow ESS or PROW iss (PROW rhymes with HOW)]

prowl ● v. **1** move (or move through) quietly and carefully. **2** walk or wander anxiously. **● n.** an act of prowling. □ **on the prowl** moving about secretively.

prowler n. a person who moves stealthily about or loiters near a place with a view to committing a crime.

proximate adj. nearest or next before or after. [Say PROCK sim it]

proximity n. nearness in space, time, etc.
[Say prock SIMMA tee]

proxy n. (pl. **proxies**) **1** the authority to represent or act for someone else. **2** a person authorized to represent someone else.

Prozac n. proprietary the antidepressant drug fluoxetine hydrochloride.
[Say PRO zack]

prude n. a person easily shocked by sexual matters or nudity. □ **prudery** n. **prudish** adj. **prudishness** n.

prudent adj. **1** careful to provide for the future. **2** discreet or cautious. **3** having good judgment. □ **prudence** n. **prudently** adv.

prudential adj. involving or showing care or forethought. [Say proo DEN shull]

prune[1] n. a dried plum.

prune[2] v. (**prunes, pruned, pruning**) **1** trim a tree etc. by cutting away dead or overgrown branches etc. **2** reduce by cutting or removing unnecessary parts.
□ **pruner** n.

prurient adj. **1** having or showing an excessive interest in sexual matters. **2** encouraging such an excessive interest.
□ **prurience** n. [Say PROOR ee int]

Prussian ● adj. relating to Prussia, a former German state. **● n.** a native of Prussia. [Say PRUSH'n]

pry v. (**pries, pried, prying**) **1** move, open, raise, etc., by leverage. **2** remove,

obtain, or separate with difficulty.
3 inquire impertinently.

prying *adj.* unduly inquisitive.

PS *abbr.* postscript.

psalm *n.* a sacred song contained in the Biblical Book of Psalms. [*Say* SOM]

pseudo ● *adj.* sham. ● *n.* (*pl.* **pseudos**) a pretentious or insincere person. [*Say* SOO doe]

pseudo- *comb. form* (also **pseud-** before a vowel) **1** not genuine. **2** resembling or imitating. [*Say* SOO doe]

pseudonym *n.* a fictitious name assumed by an author. [*Say* SOO duh nim]

pshaw *interj.* an expression of contempt or impatience.

psi *n.* the twenty-third letter of the Greek alphabet (Ψ, ψ). [*Say* SIGH *or* puh SIGH]

psoriasis *n.* a skin disease marked by red scaly patches. ◻ **psoriatic** *adj.* [*Say* suh RYE a sis, sorry ATTIC]

PST *abbr.* **1** *Cdn* provincial sales tax. **2** Pacific Standard Time.

psych *informal* ● *v.* (**psychs, psyched, psyching**) **1** (usu. foll. by *up*) prepare mentally for an ordeal. **2** (usu. foll. by *out*) analyze someone's motivation for one's own advantage. **3** influence a person psychologically; intimidate. ● *n.* psychology. ● *adj.* psychiatric. [*Say* SIKE]

psyche *n.* **1** the soul; the spirit. **2** the mind. [*Say* SIKE ee]

psychedelia *pl. n.* psychedelic posters, paintings, etc. [*Say* sike a DELLY uh]

psychedelic ● *adj.* **1 a** (of an experience) hallucinatory. **b** (of a drug) producing hallucinations. **2** *informal* having vivid colours or designs etc. ● *n.* a hallucinogenic drug. ◻ **psychedelically** *adv.* [*Say* sike a DEL ick]

psychiatric *adj.* relating to mental illness or its treatment. [*Say* sike ee AT rick]

psychiatrist *n.* a medical doctor specializing in psychiatry. [*Say* sigh KIE a trist]

psychiatry *n.* the study and treatment of mental disease. [*Say* sigh KIE a tree]

psychic ● *adj.* **1 a** (of a person) considered to have occult powers, such as telepathy. **b** inexplicable by natural laws. **2** relating to the soul or mind. ● *n.* a person considered to have psychic powers. ◻ **psychically** *adv.* [*Say* SIKE ick]

psycho *informal* ● *n.* (*pl.* **psychos**) a psychopath. ● *adj.* psychopathic. [*Say* SIKE oh]

psycho- *comb. form* relating to the mind or psychology. [*Say* SIKE oh]

psychoactive *adj.* (of a drug) affecting the mind. [*Say* sike oh ACTIVE]

psychoanalysis *n.* a therapeutic method of treating mental disorders by investigating the interaction of conscious and unconscious mind. ◻ **psychoanalyst** *n.* **psychoanalytic** *adj.* **psychoanalytical** *adj.* **psychoanalytically** *adv.* **psychoanalyze** *v.* [*Say* sike oh ANALYSIS, sike oh ANALYTIC, sike oh ANALYZE]

psychobabble *n.* *informal derogatory* writing or talk filled with psychiatric jargon. [*Say* SIKE oh babble]

psychodynamics *pl. n.* (treated as *sing.*) the study of the interrelation between the various parts of an individual's psyche. [*Say* sike oh DYNAMICS]

psychological *adj.* **1** relating to the mind. **2** relating to psychology. **3** *informal* having a basis in the mind; imaginary. ◻ **psychologically** *adv.* **psychologist** *n.* [*Say* sike uh LOGICAL]

psychology *n.* (*pl.* **psychologies**) **1** the scientific study of the human mind and its functions. **2** the mental characteristics or attitude of a person or group. [*Say* sigh COLLA jee]

psychopath *n.* **1** a person suffering from chronic mental disorder esp. with violent behaviour. **2** a mentally or emotionally unstable person. ◻ **psychopathic** *adj.* [*Say* SIKE oh path, sike oh PATH ick]

psychopathology *n.* (*pl.* **psychopathologies**) **1** the scientific study of mental disorders. **2** features of people's mental health considered collectively. **3** mental or behavioural disorder. [*Say* sike oh puh THOLLA jee]

psychopathy *n.* psychopathic behaviour. [*Say* sigh COP uth ee]

psychosis *n.* (*pl.* **psychoses**) a severe mental derangement resulting in loss of contact with reality. [*Say* sigh CO sis *for the singular,* sigh CO seez *for the plural*]

psychosomatic *adj.* caused or aggravated by mental conflict, stress, etc. [*Say* sike oh suh MAT ick]

psychotherapy *n.* (*pl.* **psychotherapies**) the treatment of mental disorder by psychological means. ◻ **psychotherapeutic** *adj.* **psychotherapist** *n.* [*Say* sike oh THERAPY, sike oh therra PYOOT ick]

psychotic ● *adj.* of, denoting, or suffering from a severe mental derangement. ● *n.* a person with a psychosis. ◻ **psychotically** *adv.* [*Say* sigh COT ick]

psychotropic *n.* (of a drug) acting on the mind. [*Say* sike oh TROP ick]

PTA *abbr.* PARENT-TEACHER ASSOCIATION.

ptarmigan *n.* (*pl.* **ptarmigan** or **ptarmigans**) a game bird of Arctic regions resembling a grouse, with white plumage in winter. [*Say* TAR mig un]

pterodactyl *n.* a large extinct flying reptile with a long slender head and neck. [*Say* tare a DACK til]

Ptolemaic *adj.* relating to the Greek astronomer Ptolemy (2nd century) or his theories, esp. that the earth is the stationary centre of the universe. [*Say* tolla MAY ick]

pub *n.* an establishment licensed to sell alcoholic drinks.

pubbing *n.* the action of going drinking in pubs.

pub-crawl ● *n.* a drinking tour of several pubs or bars. ● *v.* make such a tour.

puberty *n.* the period during which adolescents reach sexual maturity and become capable of reproduction. [*Say* PYOO bur tee]

pubes *n.* (*pl.* **pubes**) **1** the lower part of the abdomen at the front of the pelvis, covered with hair from puberty. **2** *informal* the pubic hair. [*Say* PYOO beez]

pubescence *n.* the time when puberty begins. □ **pubescent** *adj.* [*Say* pyoo BESS ince, pyoo BESS'nt]

pubic *adj.* relating to the pubes or pubis. [*Say* PYOO bick]

pubis *n.* (*pl.* **pubes**) either of a pair of bones forming the two sides of the pelvis. [*Say* PYOO biss *for the singular,* PYOO beez *for the plural*]

public ● *adj.* **1** of or concerning the people as a whole. **2** open to or shared by all the people. **3** existing openly. **4 a** provided by or concerning a government. **b** in government. **5** well-known. **6** *Cdn* relating to the public school system. ● *n.* **1** the community in general. **2** a group of people with a particular interest. □ **go public 1** become a public company. **2** reveal information. **in public** openly. □ **publicly** *adv.*

public address system *n.* an amplification system used at public meetings etc.

publication *n.* **1 a** the preparation and issuing of literature, music, etc. to the public. **b** a thing published. **2** the action of making something generally known.

public company *n.* a company whose shares are traded freely on a stock exchange.

public corporation *n.* a government-owned corporation.

public domain *n.* the legal status of a work not protected by copyright.

public enemy *n.* a notorious wanted criminal.

public housing *n.* government-subsidized housing for low-income families.

publicist *n.* a person who promotes a product, performer, etc.

publicity *n.* **1 a** the publicizing of someone or something. **b** material or information used for this. **2** public exposure; media attention.

publicize *v.* (**publicizes, publicized, publicizing**) make publicly known.

public mischief *n.* *Cdn* the criminal offence of making a false accusation, reporting an offence that did not occur, etc.

public ownership *n.* ownership by the state.

public purse *n.* *informal* the national treasury.

public relations *pl. n.* **1** the work of presenting a good image of an organization, person, etc., to the public. **2** the relationship between an organization and the public.

public school *n.* **1** a primary or secondary school that is supported by public funds. **2** *Cdn* (*Ont.*) **a** a school that is part of the public school system (*compare* SEPARATE SCHOOL 1). **b** an elementary school that is part of the public school system.

public school board *n.* *Cdn* an elected board of trustees responsible for the public schools of a particular area.

public school system *n.* *Cdn* a system of publicly-funded non-denominational schools.

public sector *n.* that part of the economy under direct control by the state.

public servant *n.* a government employee.

public service *n.* **1** public servants collectively. **2** a service provided to the public without charge by a corporation etc.

public service announcement *n.* a message aired by a radio or television station as a service to the public or a non-profit organization.

public transit *n.* (also **public transportation, public transport**) a system of buses, trains, etc., running on fixed routes.

Public Trustee *n.* *Cdn* a provincial government official who administers the estates of people who die without a will, missing persons, etc.

public works *n.* building work paid for by the government.

publish v. (**publishes, published, publishing**) **1** prepare and issue for public sale. **2** make generally known. **3** *Law* communicate (a libel etc.) to a third party. □ **publishable** adj. **publishing** n.

publisher n. **1** a person or esp. a company that produces and distributes copies of a book, newspaper, etc. for sale. **2** a newspaper proprietor.

puce n. & adj. a dark reddish purple. [*Say* PYOOS]

puck n. **1** a hard rubber disc used in hockey. **2** *Cdn* something shaped like a hockey puck.

puck carrier n. *Hockey* the player in possession of the puck.

pucker ● v. (often foll. by *up*) **1** gather into wrinkles or folds. **2** contract (the lips) as when preparing to kiss. ● n. a wrinkle or fold.

puckster n. *Cdn slang* a hockey player.

pudding n. **1** a cooked dessert, heavier and more moist than cake. **2** a dessert made of flavoured milk thickened with cornstarch.

puddle ● n. a small pool of rainwater etc. ● v. (**puddles, puddled, puddling**) form a small pool. □ **puddly** adj.

pudendum n. (pl. **pudenda**) (usu. in pl.) the genitals, esp. of a woman. [*Say* pyoo DEN dum]

pudgy adj. (**pudgier, pudgiest**) *informal* plump.

pueblo n. (pl. **pueblos**) **1** an Indian settlement or village in Latin America. **2** (**Pueblo**) a member of a North American Indian people living esp. in New Mexico and Arizona. □ **Pueblo** adj. [*Say* PWEB lo]

puerile adj. trivial, childish. □ **puerility** n. [*Say* PURE ile, pure ILLA tee]

Puerto Rican n. a person from Puerto Rico. □ **Puerto Rican** adj. [*Say* porto REEK'n or pware toe REEK'n]

puff ● n. **1 a** a short blast of air, smoke, etc. **b** an inhalation or exhalation from a cigarette etc. **2** a light, fluffy food. **3** a gathered mass of material in a dress etc. ● v. **1** emit a puff. **2** send out or move with puffs (of vapour, smoke, etc.). **3** make or be out of breath. **4** swell. **5** smoke (a pipe, cigarette, etc.). **6** advertise or promote with false praise. □ **puffer** n.

puffball n. **1** a ball-shaped fungus which bursts to release spores. **2** anything round and fluffy, such as a powder puff.

puffed-up adj. **1** swollen. **2** having an exaggerated sense of importance. **3** inflated or bombastic in language or style. **4** involving or consisting of exaggerated or undue praise.

pufferfish n. (pl. **pufferfish** or **pufferfishes**) a spiny tropical fish that inflates itself when threatened.

puffery n. exaggerated praise.

puffin n. a black and white northern seabird with a large head and bright triangular bill.

puffy adj. (**puffier, puffiest**) **1** swollen. **2** soft, rounded, and light. □ **puffiness** n.

pug n. (also **pug dog**) a small dog with a broad flat nose and deeply wrinkled face.

pugilist n. a professional boxer. □ **pugilistic** adj. [*Say* PYOO jil ist, pyoo jil ISS tick]

pugnacious adj. inclined to fight. □ **pugnaciously** adv. **pugnacity** n. [*Say* pug NAY shuss, pug NASSA tee]

puja n. a Hindu rite of worship. [*Say* POO juh]

puke *slang* ● v. (**pukes, puked, puking**) vomit. ● n. vomit. □ **pukey** adj.

pull ● v. **1** exert force on (something) so as to move it toward the origin of the force. **2** remove by pulling. **3** *informal* bring out for use. **4** move steadily. **5** attract as a customer. **6** strain (a muscle etc.). **7** inhale deeply while drawing on (a cigarette). **8** *informal* cancel or withdraw. ● n. **1** an act of pulling. **2** a deep draft or inhalation. **3** a force, influence, or compulsion. □ **pull back** retreat. **pull a face** assume a distinctive expression. **pull for** support. **pull in 1** arrive. **2** earn or acquire. **3** *informal* arrest. **pull one's hair out** be exasperated. **pull a person's leg** deceive a person playfully. **pull off 1** remove by pulling. **2** succeed in achieving or accomplishing. **3** remove from participation in. **pull oneself together** recover control of oneself. **pull out 1** take out by pulling. **2** depart. **3** withdraw. **4** (of a vehicle) move out from the side of the road, or from its normal position to overtake. **pull out all the stops** exert extreme effort. **pull over 1** move to the side of the road. **2** (of the police etc.) stop (a vehicle) for a traffic violation etc. **pull the plug** *informal* put an end to an enterprise; cut off supplies. **pull punches** (usu. in *neg.*) avoid using one's full force. **pull strings** exert influence. **pull through** get through a difficult or dangerous situation. **pull up 1** stop or cause to stop moving. **2** cause to appear on a computer screen. **pull one's (own) weight** do one's fair share of work. □ **puller** n.

pull-down adj. **1** that may be pulled down. **2** *Computing* designating a menu only displayed when required.

pulley n. (pl. **pulleys**) a grooved wheel for a cord etc. to pass over, used for changing the direction of a force.

Pullman n. **1** a comfortable railway car. **2** a sleeping car. **3** a large suitcase. [Say PULL m'n]

pullout ● adj. that may be pulled out. ● n. **1** a loose section of a magazine. **2** a withdrawal.

pullover n. a knitted garment put on over the head and covering the top half of the body.

pull-up n. **1** an exercise involving raising oneself with one's arms by pulling up against a horizontal bar etc. **2** a sudden stop.

pulmonary adj. relating to the lungs. [Say PUL mun airy (PUL rhymes with HULL)]

pulmonary artery n. the artery conveying blood from the heart to the lungs.

pulp ● n. **1** the soft fleshy part of fruit etc. **2** any soft thick wet mass. **3** a soft shapeless mass made of ground wood etc., used in papermaking. **4** popular writing regarded as of poor quality. **5** vascular tissue filling the interior of a tooth. **6** = PULPWOOD. ● v. **1** reduce to pulp. **2** remove pulp from. □ **pulpy** adj.

pulpit n. a raised lectern in a church etc. from which the preacher delivers a sermon. [Say PUL pit]

pulpwood n. timber suitable for making pulp.

pulsar n. a type of star emitting regular pulses of radio waves. [Say PULSE arr]

pulsate v. (**pulsates, pulsated, pulsating**) **1** expand and contract rhythmically. **2** vibrate. □ **pulsation** n.

pulse[1] ● n. **1** a rhythmical throbbing of the arteries as blood is propelled through them. **2** a single vibration or throb of sound, light, etc. **3** a general feeling or opinion. **4** a musical beat. **5** any regular rhythm. ● v. (**pulses, pulsed, pulsing**) **1** pulsate. **2** transmit or operate rhythmically.

pulse[2] n. the edible seeds of various leguminous plants, e.g. lentils.

pulverize v. (**pulverizes, pulverized, pulverizing**) **1** reduce to fine particles. **2** informal demolish.

puma n. a cougar. [Say PYOO muh]

pumice n. (also **pumice stone**) a light porous volcanic rock, used as an abrasive or to remove hard skin. [Say PUM iss]

pummel v. (**pummels, pummelled, pummelling**) **1** thump repeatedly. **2** defeat or criticize thoroughly.

pump[1] ● n. a device for raising or moving liquids or gases, inflating tires, etc. ● v. **1** raise or remove with a pump. **2 a** fill with air. **b** increase the volume, strength, etc. of.

3 cause to move, pour forth, etc., in great quantities. **4** elicit information from. **5** move vigorously up and down. **6** apply and release (brakes) quickly and repeatedly. **7** cause a major input of (money etc.). □ **pump iron** informal lift weights.

pump[2] n. a lightweight, low-cut women's shoe, with no laces or straps.

pumped adj. (also **pumped up**) **1** in senses of PUMP[1] v. **2** informal eager, excited.

pumper n. **1** in senses of PUMP[1] v. **2** a fire truck used to pump water or chemicals to douse a fire.

pumpernickel n. a dark, sour rye bread.

pumpkin n. a large rounded orange gourd, with a thick rind and edible flesh.

pumpkinseed n. a colourful N American sunfish with an orange belly.

pump-priming n. the introduction of fluid etc. into a pump to prepare it for working.

pun ● n. a joke using the different meanings of a word or the fact that one word sounds like another. ● v. (**puns, punned, punning**) (foll. by on) make a pun with.

punch[1] ● v. (**punches, punched, punching**) **1** strike, esp. with a closed fist. **2** prod or poke. **3** pierce a hole in. **4** strike with the fingertip. ● n. (pl. **punches**) **1** a blow with a fist. **2** the ability to deliver this. **3** informal vigour. **4** a device for punching holes. **5** a tool or machine for impressing a design or stamping a die on a material. □ **punch in 1** record the time of one's arrival at work. **2** enter (data) using a keyboard. **punch out 1** remove or detach by punching. **2** record the time of one's departure from work. **3** informal assault with punches.

punch[2] n. (pl. **punches**) a drink of mixed beverages.

punch[3] n. □ **as pleased as punch** showing great pleasure.

punch-drunk adj. stupefied from being punched many times.

punchline n. the climactic final phrase of a joke etc.

punch-up n. informal (also **punchout**) a fist fight.

punchy adj. (**punchier, punchiest**) **1** vigorous; forceful. **2** PUNCH-DRUNK. **3** in a state of nervous tension or extreme fatigue. **4 a** (of a sentence etc.) terse, short. **b** composed of punchy segments: a punchy news program.

punctilious adj. very attentive to detail or correct behaviour. □ **punctiliously** adv. [Say punk TILLY us]

punctual adj. precisely or habitually on time. □ **punctuality** n. **punctually** adv.

punctuate v. (**punctuates**, **punctuated**, **punctuating**) **1** insert punctuation marks in. **2** interrupt at intervals.

punctuation n. the system of marks used in writing to separate sentences and phrases etc. and to clarify meaning.

puncture ● n. a small hole caused by a sharp object. ● v. (**punctures**, **punctured**, **puncturing**) **1** make a small hole in. **2** suddenly make someone feel less confident, proud, etc. **3** penetrate.

pundit n. **1** a very learned Hindu. **2** an expert who expresses opinions esp. on current affairs. □ **punditry** n.

pungent adj. **1** having a sharp or strong taste or smell. **2** strongly critical. □ **pungency** n. **pungently** adv. [Say PUN jint]

punish v. (**punishes**, **punished**, **punishing**) **1** cause to suffer for an offence. **2** inflict a penalty for. **3** informal inflict severe blows on. **4** subject to severe treatment. □ **punishable** adj. **punisher** n. **punishing** adj. **punishingly** adv. **punishment** n.

punitive adj. inflicting punishment. [Say PYOON it iv]

Punjabi n. (pl. **Punjabis**) **1** a native or the language of the state of Punjab in India or the province of Punjab in Pakistan. **2** the language spoken in these areas. □ **Punjabi** adj. [Say poon JABBY]

punk ● n. **1** a young man regarded as contemptible. **2** a young ruffian. **3 a** (also **punk rock**) a loud fast-moving form of angry rock music. **b** the style associated with this, characterized by coloured spiked hair and leather clothing. **c** a member of this subculture. **4** an inexperienced person. **5** crumbly wood that has been attacked by fungus. ● adj. **1** rotten. **2** denoting punk rock or subculture. □ **punker** n. **punkish** adj. **punky** adj.

punt¹ ● n. a long narrow flat-bottomed riverboat propelled by a long pole. ● v. **1** propel (a punt) with a pole. **2** travel or convey in a punt.

punt² ● v. kick (a ball) after it has dropped from the hands and before it reaches the ground. ● n. such a kick.

puny adj. (**punier**, **puniest**) **1** undersized. **2** weak. [Say PYOO nee]

pup ● n. **1** a young dog. **2** a young wolf, rat, seal, etc. ● v. (**pups**, **pupped**, **pupping**) bring forth (pups).

pupa n. (pl. **pupae**) an inactive immature form of an insect. □ **pupal** adj.

[Say PYOO puh for the singular, PYOO pee for the plural]

pupil¹ n. a person who is taught by another.

pupil² n. the dark circular opening in the centre of the iris of the eye.

puppet n. **1** a small figure representing a human being or animal and moved by various means as entertainment. **2** a person, state, etc. controlled by another.

puppeteer n. (also **puppet master**) a person who works puppets. □ **puppeteering** n.

puppetry n. the making and using of puppets.

puppy n. (pl. **puppies**) a young dog. □ **puppyish** adj.

pup tent n. a small triangular tent.

purchase ● v. (**purchases**, **purchased**, **purchasing**) **1** buy. **2** obtain at some cost. ● n. **1** the action of buying. **2** something bought. **3** a firm hold or grip. □ **purchaser** n.

purdah n. a practice in certain Muslim and Hindu societies of screening women from strangers or men. □ **in purdah** (of a woman) screened from contact with strangers. [Say PUR duh]

pure adj. (**purer**, **purest**) **1** unmixed. **2** chaste; good. **3** guiltless. **4** sincere. **5** mere, sheer. **6** perfectly in tune. **7** theoretical rather than practical. **8** free of impurities.

purebred ● adj. bred from parents of the same breed or variety. ● n. such an animal.

purée ● n. a pulp of vegetables or fruit etc. reduced to a smooth thick liquid. ● v. (**purées**, **puréed**, **puréeing**) make a purée of. [Say pure AY or PURE ay]

pure laine Cdn ● adj. **1** designating a francophone Quebecer descended from the French settlers in New France and having exclusively French ancestry. **2** of or consisting of pure laine Quebecers. ● n. such a person. [Say pure LEN]

purely adv. **1** in a pure manner. **2** merely. **3** entirely.

pure science n. a science depending on deductions from demonstrated truths.

purgation n. **1** the action of purifying or cleansing a person or thing. **2** purging of the bowels. [Say pur GAY sh'n]

purgative ● n. **1** a laxative. **2** a thing that rids a person of unwanted feelings or memories. ● adj. strongly laxative. [Say PURGA tiv]

purgatory n. **1** the condition or supposed place of spiritual cleansing, esp. (Catholicism) of those having to atone for venial sins etc. **2** a temporary situation of suffering before

a more favourable situation.
□ **purgatorial** adj. [Say PURGA tory]

purge ● v. (**purges, purged, purging**)
1 rid someone (of unwanted feelings etc.).
2 remove (something unwanted). **3** empty
the stomach or bowels by vomiting or
taking a laxative. ● n. an abrupt or violent
removal of people. □ **purger** n.

purify v. (**purifies, purified, purifying**)
1 cleanse. **2** make ceremonially clean. **3** rid
something of an unwanted element.
□ **purification** n. **purifier** n.

Purim n. a Jewish festival commemorating
the defeat of a plot to massacre the Jews in
Persia. [Say POOR im]

purine n. an organic nitrogenous base
forming uric acid on oxidation.
[Say POOR een]

purist n. a stickler for scrupulous
correctness or authenticity, e.g. in
language or art. □ **purism** n.

puritan ● n. **1** (**Puritan**) hist. a member of
a group of English Protestants who sought
to simplify forms of worship. **2** an
extremely strict person, esp. in terms of
religion or morality. ● adj. **1** (**Puritan**) hist.
relating to the Puritans. **2** scrupulous and
austere in religion or morals.
□ **puritanism** n. [Say PURE a tin]

puritanical adj. often derogatory extremely
strict about religious or moral behaviour.
□ **puritanically** adv.
[Say pure a TAN ick ul]

purity n. (pl. **purities**) **1** a clean and pure
state. **2** freedom from external influences.
[Say PURE it ee]

purl ● n. **1** a knitting stitch made by
putting the needle through the front of the
previous stitch and passing the yarn
around the back of the needle. **2** a babbling
motion or sound. ● v. **1** knit with a purl
stitch. **2** flow with a swirling motion or
babbling sound.

purlieu n. (pl. **purlieus**) (in pl.) the
surrounding area. [Say PURL yoo]

purloin v. steal. [Say pur LOIN]

purple ● n. **1** a colour intermediate
between red and blue. **2** (**the purple**) a
position of authority or privilege. ● adj. **1** of
a purple colour. **2** excessively elaborate. ● v.
(**purples, purpled, purpling**) make or
become purple. □ **purplish** adj.

purple loosestrife n. a wetland plant
with a long spike of purple flowers.

purport v. **1** claim to do something, esp.
falsely. **2** have as its meaning.
□ **purportedly** adv.

purpose ● n. **1 a** something to be
attained; a thing intended. **b** the reason for
something. **2** determination. ● v.
(**purposes, purposed, purposing**)

intend. □ **on purpose** intentionally. **to
no purpose** with no result or effect. **to
the purpose 1** relevant. **2** useful.
□ **purposeful** adj. **purposefully** adv.
purposeless adj. **purposely** adv.

purpose-built adj. (also **purpose-made**,
purpose-designed, etc.) made for a
specific purpose.

purr ● v. **1** (of a cat) make a low vibratory
sound usu. expressing contentment.
2 make a similar sound. **3** express pleasure
or with pleasure. ● n. a purring sound.

purse ● n. **1** a small woman's bag for
holding small personal articles. **2** hist. a
small leather pouch for coins. **3** money,
funds. **4** a sum collected as a present or
given as a prize. ● v. (**purses, pursed,
pursing**) **1** pucker or contract. **2** become
contracted and wrinkled.

purser n. **1** an officer on a ship who keeps
the accounts. **2** the head steward in a ship
or airplane.

purse seine n. a fishing net or seine
which may be drawn into the shape of a
sack. □ **purse seiner** n. **purse
seining** n.

purse strings pl. n. control of or access to
funds.

purslane n. a small, fleshy-leaved plant
used in salads. [Say PURSE lane]

pursuant adv. (foll. by to) conforming to or
in accordance with. [Say PURSUE int]

pursue v. (**pursues, pursued,
pursuing**) **1** follow in order to catch or
attack. **2** continue or proceed along.
3 engage in (study or other activity). **4** seek
after. **5** persistently seek the attention of.
6 persistently assail. □ **pursuer** n.

pursuit n. **1** the act of looking for
something. **2** an occupation or activity.
3 the act of following or chasing someone.

purvey v. provide or supply. □ **purveyor** n.
[Say pur VAY]

purview n. the range of responsibilities or
concerns of a person or thing.
[Say PUR view]

pus n. a thick yellowish or greenish liquid
produced from infected tissue.

push ● v. (**pushes, pushed, pushing**)
1 exert force on (someone or something) so
as to move them away from the source of
the force. **2** move (one's body or a part of it)
forcefully into a specified position. **3** move
forward by using force. **4** urge (someone) to
greater effort. **5** demand persistently.
6 informal promote. **7** informal sell illegally.
8 (**be pushing**) informal be nearly (an age).
● n. (pl. **pushes**) **1** an act of pushing. **2** a
vigorous effort. **3** forcefulness and
enterprise. □ **be pushed for** informal have
very little of. **push around** informal bully.

push one's luck 1 take undue risks.
2 act presumptuously. **when push comes to shove** when action must be taken. □ **pusher** n.

push button ● n. a button pushed to operate an electrical device. ● adj. (**push-button**) **1** operated by pressing a push button. **2** easily obtainable; instant.

pushcart n. a small handcart.

pushover n. informal **1** something easily done or won. **2** a person easily overcome, persuaded, etc.

push-pin n. a tack with a usu. plastic head, used on bulletin boards etc.

push-pull adj. **1** Electronics consisting of two valves etc. operated alternately. **2** operated by pushing and pulling.

push-start ● n. the starting of a motor vehicle by pushing it to turn the engine. ● v. start (a vehicle) in this way.

push-up ● n. an exercise in which a person lies facing the floor and raises the upper body by pushing down with the hands. ● adj. designating a brassiere or similar garment designed to provide uplift for the breasts.

pushy adj. (**pushier, pushiest**) informal unpleasantly self-assertive. □ **pushiness** n.

puss n. (pl. **pusses**) informal a cat.

pussy n. (pl. **pussies**) informal a cat.

pussycat n. informal **1** a cat. **2** a meek or amiable person.

pussyfoot v. (**pussyfoots, pussyfooted, pussyfooting**) **1** act cautiously or noncommittally. **2** move warily.

pussy willow n. a willow with soft, furry, white or yellow catkins.

pustule n. a pimple containing pus. [Say PUS chool or PUST yool]

put ● v. (**puts, put, putting**) **1** move to or place in a particular position. **2** bring into a particular state or condition. **3** assign a value or limit to. **4** express. **5** proceed in a particular direction. **6** throw in an athletic competition. ● n. a throw of the shot or weight. □ **put about 1** spread. **2** Nautical turn around. **put across 1** make acceptable or effective. **2** express in an understandable way. **put aside** save for later use or collection. **2** disregard. **put away 1** put back in the place where it is normally kept. **2** lay aside for future use. **3 a** confine. **b** commit to a home or mental institution. **4** informal consume in large quantities. **put down 1** suppress. **2** informal snub. **3** record or enter in writing. **4** account or reckon. **5** attribute. **6** put to death. **7** pay as a deposit. **8** put to bed. **9** land. **put forth 1** send out (buds etc.).

2 formal put into circulation. **put forward 1** suggest or propose. **2** put into a prominent position. **put in 1** enter or submit. **2** be a candidate for. **3** spend (time). **4** interpose (a remark etc.). **5** call at a port etc. **6** plant. **put off 1** postpone. **2** evade with an excuse. **3** hinder or distract. **4** disconcert; cause to lose interest. **put on 1** clothe oneself with. **2** apply. **3** cause to function. **4** stage (a play etc.). **5** pretend; fake; assume. **6** increase one's weight by. **7** put in touch with. **8** informal trick. **put out 1 a** annoy. **b** inconvenience. **2** extinguish. **3** Baseball cause to be out. **4** dislocate. **5** exert. **6** publish or broadcast. **put one over** (foll. by on) informal trick. **put through 1** carry out or complete. **2** connect (a person) by telephone. **3** subject to an ordeal. **4** arrange, offer, or pay for. **put up 1** build or erect. **2** take or provide accommodation. **3** engage in as a form of resistance. **4** present. **5** raise. **6** display. **put upon** make unfair demands on. **put up or shut up** informal defend oneself or remain silent. **put a person up to** instigate a person in. **put up with** endure.

putative adj. generally considered to be. □ **putatively** adv. [Say PYOOT a tiv]

put-down n. informal a snub or criticism.

put-in n. a place from which to launch a canoe or other small craft.

put-on n. informal a hoax.

putrefaction n. the process of rotting. [Say pyoo truh FACTION]

putrefy v. (**putrefies, putrefied, putrefying**) decay and smell very bad. [Say PYOO truh fie]

putrid adj. **1** decomposed, rotten. **2** foul, noxious. **3** morally corrupt. [Say PYOO trid]

putsch n. (pl. **putsches**) a violent uprising. □ **putschist** n. & adj. [Rhymes with BUTCH]

putt ● v. (**putts, putted, putting**) strike (a golf ball) gently. ● n. a putting stroke.

puttanesca adj. denoting a pasta sauce of tomatoes, garlic, olives, anchovies, etc. [Say poo tan ESKA]

putter[1] n. **1** a golf club used in putting. **2** a golfer who putts.

putter[2] n. & v. = PUTT-PUTT.

putter[3] v. **1** (often foll. by around, about) work in a desultory but pleasant manner. **2** go slowly.

putt-putt ● n. the sound of a small gasoline engine. ● v. (**putt-putts, putt-putted, putt-putting**) make this sound.

putty ● n. (pl. **putties**) a paste that hardens when dry, used for fixing glass into window frames, filling holes in woodwork, etc. ● *v.* (**putties, puttied, puttying**) cover, join, or fill up with putty. □ **putty in a person's hands** someone very compliant.

put-up *adj.* fraudulently presented.

putz ● *n.* (*pl.* **putzes**) *slang* a fool. ● *v.* (**putzes, putzed, putzing**) (usu. foll. by *around*) waste time. [*Rhymes with* NUTS]

puzzle ● *n.* **1** a difficult problem. **2** a problem or toy designed to test knowledge or ingenuity. ● *v.* (**puzzles, puzzled, puzzling**) **1** confound. **2** be perplexed (about). **3** (usu. as **puzzling** *adj.*) require much thought to comprehend. **4** understand by hard thought. □ **puzzled** *adj.* **puzzlement** *n.*

puzzler *n.* **1** a difficult problem. **2** a person who likes solving puzzles.

PVC *abbr.* POLYVINYL CHLORIDE.

PWYC *abbr.* esp. *Cdn* pay what you can, designating theatrical etc. events where audience members pay what they can afford.

pygmy *n.* (*pl.* **pygmies**) **1** a member of a small-statured people in equatorial Africa and parts of Southeast Asia. **2** a very small person, animal, or thing. □ **pygmy** *adj.* [*Say* PIG mee]

pyjamas *pl. n.* **1** a suit of loose pants and a top for sleeping in. **2** (**pyjama**) designating parts of a suit of pyjamas.

pylon *n.* **1** a plastic cone used to mark areas of roads etc. **2** esp. *Brit.* a tall structure for supporting power cables. **3** a structure on the wing of an aircraft supporting an engine or weapon.

pyramid *n.* **1** a monumental stone structure with a square base and sloping sides meeting centrally at an apex, esp. an ancient Egyptian royal tomb. **2** a polyhedron or solid figure of this type with

a base of three or more sides. □ **pyramidal** *adj.*

pyramid selling *n.* (also **pyramid scheme**) a system of selling goods in which agency rights are sold to an increasing number of distributors at successively lower levels.

pyre *n.* a heap of combustible material, esp. on which a corpse is burned. [*Rhymes with* FIRE]

Pyrex *n.* *proprietary* a hard heat-resistant glass. [*Say* PIE rex]

pyrite *n.* (also **pyrites, iron pyrites**) a yellow lustrous form of iron disulphide. [*Say* PIE rite]

pyromania *n.* an obsessive desire to set things on fire. □ **pyromaniac** *n.* [*Say* pie roe MAY nee uh]

pyrotechnic *adj.* relating to fireworks. □ **pyrotechnical** *adj.* [*Say* pie roe TECK nick]

pyrotechnics *pl. n.* **1** (treated as *sing.*) the art of making fireworks. **2** a display of fireworks. **3** any brilliant display. [*Say* pie roe TECK nicks]

pyrrhic *adj.* won at too great a cost to be of use to the victor. [*Say* PIR ick]

pysanka *n.* (*pl.* **pysanky**) *Cdn* a hand-painted Ukrainian Easter egg. [*Say* PIS un kuh *for the singular,* PIS un key *for the plural*]

Pythagorean ● *adj.* relating to the Greek philosopher Pythagoras or his philosophy, esp. about reincarnation. ● *n.* a follower of Pythagoras. [*Say* pie thagga REE un]

Pythagorean theorem *n.* the theorem that the square of the hypotenuse of a right-angled triangle is equal to the sum of the squares of the other two sides.

python *n.* a large snake that crushes its prey.

Qq

Q¹ *n.* (also **q**) (*pl.* **Qs** or **Q's**) the seventeenth letter of the alphabet.

Q² *abbr.* (also **Q.**) **1** Queen, Queen's. **2** question.

Q & A *abbr.* question and answer.

QC *abbr.* **1** (also **Qc**) Quebec. **2** Queen's Counsel.

qi *n.* (in Chinese philosophy) the life force flowing through the body. [*Say* CHEE]

qigong *n.* a system of techniques to focus and strengthen qi. [*Say* chee GOONG]

QPF *abbr. Cdn* Quebec Police Force; the Sûreté du Québec.

QST *n. Cdn* Quebec Sales Tax.

qt. *abbr.* quart(s).

quack¹ ● *n.* the harsh sound made by ducks. ● *v.* utter this sound.

quack² *n.* an unqualified practitioner of medicine. □ **quackery** *n.*

quack grass *n.* a coarse grass with long creeping roots.

quad *n.* **1** *informal* a quadrangle. **2** *informal* a quadruplet. **3** *informal* a quadriplegic. **4** *Figure Skating* a quadruple jump. **5** a quadriceps muscle.

quadrangle *n.* **1** a four-sided plane figure. **2** a four-sided court, usu. enclosed. □ **quadrangular** *adj.*

quadrant *n.* **1** a quarter of a circle's circumference. **2** a plane figure enclosed by two radii of a circle at right angles and the arc cut off by them. **3** a quarter of a sphere.

quadraphonic *adj.* using four transmission channels. [*Say* kwodra FON ick]

quadratic *adj. Math* involving the second and no higher power of an unknown quantity or variable. [*Say* kwod RAT ick]

quadriceps *n.* (*pl.* **quadriceps**) a large four-headed muscle at the front of the thigh. [*Say* KWODRA seps]

quadrilateral ● *adj.* having four sides. ● *n.* a four-sided figure. [*Say* kwodra LATERAL]

quadrille *n.* a square dance usu. performed by four couples. [*Say* kwod RILL]

quadrillion *n.* (*pl.* **quadrillion** or **quadrillions**) **1** a thousand raised to the fifth power. **2** *informal* a very large amount. [*Say* kwod RILL yun]

quadriplegia *n.* paralysis of all four limbs. □ **quadriplegic** *adj. & n.* [*Say* kwodra PLEE juh]

quadruped ● *n.* a four-footed mammal. ● *adj.* four-footed. [*Say* KWOD ruh ped]

quadruple ● *adj.* **1** fourfold. **2** having four parts. **3** having four beats in a bar. ● *n.* a fourfold number or amount. ● *v.* (**quadruples, quadrupled, quadrupling**) multiply by four; increase fourfold. [*Say* kwod RUPE ul]

quadruplet *n.* each of four children born at one birth. [*Say* kwod RUPE lit]

quadruplex *n.* (*pl.* **quadruplexes**) *Cdn* a building divided into four self-contained residences. [*Say* KWODRA plex]

quaff *v.* drink deeply. □ **quaffable** *adj.* **quaffer** *n.* [*Say* KWOFF]

quagmire *n.* **1** a soft wet area that gives way underfoot. **2** an awkward situation. [*Say* KWAG mire *or* KWOG mire]

quahog *n.* (also **quahaug**) an edible N American clam. [*Say* KWAH hog]

quail¹ *n.* (*pl.* **quail** or **quails**) a short-tailed game bird.

quail² *v.* be apprehensive with fear.

quaint *adj.* attractively unusual or old-fashioned. □ **quaintly** *adv.* **quaintness** *n.*

quake ● *v.* (**quakes, quaked, quaking**) shake, tremble. ● *n.* an earthquake.

Quaker ● *n.* a member of the Society of Friends, a Christian movement devoted to peaceful principles and rejecting formal doctrine etc. ● *adj.* relating to Quakers. □ **Quakerism** *n.*

qualification *n.* **1** the act of qualifying. **2** a quality that makes someone suitable for a job or activity. **3** a statement that makes another less absolute. **4** a condition necessary to acquire a right etc.

qualifier *n.* **1** a person or team that has qualified. **2** a game etc. that must be won in order to enter a competition. **3** *Grammar* a word that describes or qualifies another word.

qualify *v.* (**qualifies, qualified, qualifying**) **1** make suitable for a position or purpose. **2** make legally entitled. **3** satisfy the requirements. **4** modify. **5** attribute a quality to.

qualifying *adj.* determining those that qualify.

qualitative *adj.* concerned with quality or qualities. □ **qualitatively** *adv.*

quality *n.* (*pl.* **qualities**) **1** the standard of something when compared to other things like it. **2 a** general excellence. **b** (as an *adj.*) of high quality. **3** a distinctive characteristic. **4** the distinctive timbre of a voice or sound.

quality control *n.* a system of maintaining standards in manufactured products by testing and inspection.

qualm *n.* an uneasy doubt. [*Say* KWOM]

quandary *n.* (*pl.* **quandaries**) **1** a perplexing problem. **2** a practical dilemma. [*Say* KWON dree]

quantify *v.* (**quantifies, quantified, quantifying**) express or measure the quantity of. □ **quantifiable** *adj.* **quantification** *n.*

quantitative *adj.* concerned with or measurable by quantity. □ **quantitatively** *adv.*

quantity *n.* (*pl.* **quantities**) **1** a certain number or amount. **2** a specified measurable number or amount. **3** an abundance. **4** *Math* a value etc. that may be expressed in numbers.

quantum (*pl.* **quanta**) ● *n.* a distinct quantity of energy corresponding to that involved in the absorption or emission of energy by an atom. ● *adj.* dramatic. [*Say* KWON tum]

quantum leap *n.* (also **quantum jump**) a sudden large increase or advance.

quantum mechanics *pl. n.* the branch of mechanics dealing with the description of the behaviour of subatomic particles.

quantum theory *n.* a theory of matter and energy based on the concept of quanta.

quarantine ● *n.* **1** isolation imposed on persons or animals that may carry disease. **2** the period of this. ● *v.* (**quarantines, quarantined, quarantining**) impose such isolation on. [*Say* KWORE in teen]

quark *n.* any of a class of subatomic particles with a fractional electric charge, of which protons, neutrons, etc. are thought to be composed. [*Rhymes with* PORK *or* PARK]

quarrel ● *n.* **1** an angry disagreement. **2** an occasion of complaint. ● *v.* (**quarrels, quarrelled, quarrelling**) **1** have a dispute. **2** find fault. □ **quarreller** *n.*

quarrelsome *adj.* given to quarrelling.

quarry[1] ● *n.* (*pl.* **quarries**) an open-air excavation where stone etc. is extracted. ● *v.* (**quarries, quarried, quarrying**) extract (stone) from a quarry.

quarry[2] *n.* (*pl.* **quarries**) the object of a hunt or chase.

quart *n.* **1** a measure of capacity for liquids etc., equal to a quarter of a gallon, or 1.135 litres (0.946 litres in the US). **2** a unit of dry measure, about 1.1 litres.

quarter ● *n.* **1** each of four equal parts into which something may be divided. **2** a period of three months. **3** a quarter-hour. **4** a Canadian or US coin worth 25 cents. **5** each of four equal periods in a game of football, basketball, etc. **6** a part of a town with a specified character or use. **7** (in *pl.*) lodgings. **8** a source. ● *v.* **1** divide into quarters. **2** (in *passive*) be stationed or lodged. ● *adj.* forming a quarter.

quarterback ● *n.* the player who directs the offence of a football team. ● *v.* **1** play a game as a quarterback. **2** lead (a team) as quarterback. **3** lead.

quarterdeck *n.* part of a ship's upper deck near the stern.

quarter horse *n.* a small stocky breed of horse noted for agility and speed.

quarterly ● *adj.* produced or occurring once every quarter of a year. ● *adv.* once every quarter of a year. ● *n.* (*pl.* **quarterlies**) a quarterly publication.

quartermaster *n.* **1** a regimental officer in charge of lodging, rations, etc. **2** a naval petty officer in charge of steering, signals, etc.

quarter note *n.* a note having the time value of a quarter of a whole note, drawn as a large dot with a stem.

quarter section *n.* a quarter of a square mile.

quartet *n.* **1 a** a composition for four voices or instruments. **b** the performers of such a piece. **2** any group of four.

quarto *n.* (*pl.* **quartos**) **1** a size of book page resulting from folding a sheet into four leaves. **2** a book of this size.

quartz *n.* (*pl.* **quartzes**) a mineral consisting of silica, crystallizing in colourless or white hexagonal prisms.

quartzite *n.* a hard granular rock consisting mainly of quartz.

quasar *n.* a celestial object of great size and remoteness, giving off enormous amounts of energy. [*Say* KWAY zar]

quash *v.* (**quashes, quashed, quashing**) suppress. [*Say* KWOSH]

quasi *adj.* resembling; being nearly. [*Say* KWOZZY]

quasi- *comb. form* **1** seemingly. **2** almost.

quaternary ● *adj.* **1 a** having four parts. **b** fourth in a series. **2** (**Quaternary**) *Geology* relating to the most current period in the Cenozoic era, beginning about 2

million years ago. ● n. (pl. **quaternaries**)
1 a set of four things. **2** (**Quaternary**)
Geology the Quaternary period.
[*Say* KWOTTER nairy *or*
kwuh TURNER ee]

quatrain n. a stanza of four lines. usu.
with alternating rhymes. [*Say* KWOT rain]

quaver ● v. **1** shake, tremble. **2** say or sing
tremulously. ● n. a tremble in speech.
[*Say* KWAY vur]

quavery adj. tremulous.
[*Say* KWAY vur ee]

quay n. a platform lying alongside or
projecting into water for loading and
unloading ships etc. [*Sounds like* KEY]

quayside ● n. the land forming or near a
quay. ● adj. at or by a quay. [*Say* KEY side]

Que. abbr. Quebec.

queasy adj. (**queasier, queasiest**)
1 feeling nauseous. **2** slightly nervous.
3 feeling disgust. □ **queasily** adv.
queasiness n.

Quebecer (also **Quebecker**) a person
from Quebec. [*Say* kwuh BECKER *or*
kuh BECKER *or* kay BECKER]

Quebec heater n. Cdn a cylindrical stove.
[*Say* kwuh BECK *or* kuh BECK]

Québécois n. Cdn (pl. **Québécois**) a
francophone person from Quebec.
□ **Québécoise** adj. [*Say* kay beck WAH]

Quechua n. (pl. **Quechua** or **Quechuas**)
1 a member of a S American Indian people
of Peru and neighbouring countries. **2** the
language of this people. □ **Quechua** adj.
[*Say* KETCH wuh]

queen ● n. **1** (as a title usu. **Queen**) a
female sovereign. **2** (also **queen consort**)
a king's wife. **3** a pre-eminent woman or
thing. **4** the fertile female among ants,
bees, etc. **5** the most powerful piece in
chess. **6** a playing card bearing a picture of
a queen. ● v. make (a woman) queen. ● adj.
denoting a queen-size bed, mattress,
sheets, etc. □ **queenly** adj.

Queen Anne's lace n. a plant of the
parsley family, with lacy clusters of white
flowers.

queen bee n. **1** (of bees) the fertile female
in a hive. **2** a woman who holds a superior
position.

Queen's Bench n. (also **Court of
Queen's Bench**) (in Alberta,
Saskatchewan, Manitoba, and New
Brunswick) the superior-court trial
division, which has the jurisdiction to hear
the most serious indictable offences and
civil cases.

Queen's Birthday n. Cdn (in BC and
Newfoundland and Labrador) a holiday

falling on the Monday immediately
preceding 25 May.

Queen's Counsel n. an appointment
bestowed on a barrister by the Attorney
General in recognition of excellence.

Queen's English n. the English language
as correctly written or spoken in Britain.

queen-size adj. (also **queen-sized**)
1 designating the second-largest standard
size of mattress etc., usu. 153 by 208 cm (60
by 80 in.). **2** of an extra-large size.

Queen's Park n. the Ontario legislature
or government.

Queen's Printer n. Cdn an official printer
of government documents etc.

queer ● adj. **1** odd. **2** slang homosexual. **3** of
questionable character. ● n. slang a
homosexual. □ **queerly** adv. **queerness** n.

quell v. **1 a** put an end to. **b** cause to
submit. **2** suppress (feelings).

quench v. (**quenches, quenched,
quenching**) **1** satisfy (thirst) by drinking.
2 extinguish. □ **quencher** n.

querulous adj. of a whining or peevish
nature. □ **querulously** adj.
querulousness n. [*Say* KWARE uh lus]

query ● n. (pl. **queries**) a question. ● v.
(**queries, queried, querying**) **1** express
as a question. **2** express doubt about. **3** ask
a question of. [*Say* KWEER ee]

quesadilla n. a dish of vegetables and
grated cheese etc., stuffed between two
tortillas. [*Say* case a DEE yuh]

quest ● n. **1** a search or expedition. **2** the
thing or goal sought. ● v. go on a quest.
□ **quester** n.

question ● n. **1** a sentence worded or
expressed so as to seek information.
2 a doubt. **b** the raising of such doubt. **3** a
matter to be settled. **4** (foll. by *of*) a matter
depending on conditions. ● v. **1** ask
questions of. **2** express or feel doubt about.
3 challenge. □ **in question** that is being
discussed. **call into question** cast doubt
on. **no question of** no possibility of. **out
of the question** impossible.
□ **questioner** n. **questioning** n.

questionable adj. **1** open to doubt.
2 possibly dishonest or unwise.
□ **questionably** adv.

question mark n. **1** a punctuation mark
(?) indicating a question. **2** a cause for
uncertainty.

questionnaire n. a formulated series of
questions.

question period n. Cdn a period of time
in which members of a legislature may
question government ministers.

queue ● n. **1** a line of people or vehicles
waiting their turn for something.

2 *Computing* a list of data items, commands, etc., stored so as to be retrievable in a definite order. ● *v.* (**queues**, **queued**, **queuing** or **queueing**) form or join a queue. [*Sounds like* CUE]

quibble ● *n.* a trivial point of criticism. ● *v.* (**quibbles**, **quibbled**, **quibbling**) argue about small differences. □ **quibbler** *n.* **quibbling** *adj.*

quiche *n.* a pastry shell with a savoury filling thickened with eggs. [*Say* KEESH]

quiche lorraine *n.* a quiche with bacon in the filling. [*Say* keesh luh RAIN]

quick ● *adj.* **1** moving fast. **2** lasting a short time. **3** prompt. **4** intelligent. **5** keenly perceptive. **6** (of temper) easily roused. ● *adv.* at a rapid rate. ● *n.* **1** the tender flesh below the growing part of a fingernail or toenail. **2** the central or most sensitive part. □ **cut to the quick** deeply offend or upset someone. □ **quickly** *adv.* **quickness** *n.*

quicken *v.* **1** make or become quicker. **2** (of a fetus) begin to show signs of life.

quickie *informal* ● *n.* **1** a thing done quickly. **2** a brief act of sexual intercourse. ● *adj.* made or executed quickly.

quicklime *n.* = LIME[2] n. 1.

quicksand *n.* **1** loose wet sand that sucks in anything resting on it. **2** a treacherous situation.

quicksilver ● *n.* mercury. ● *adj.* in constant flux.

quickstep *n.* a fast foxtrot.

quick study *n.* a fast learner.

quick-witted *adj.* able to think and respond quickly. □ **quick-wittedness** *n.*

quid pro quo *n.* a thing given in return for something.

quiescent *adj.* in a state or period of inactivity or dormancy. □ **quiescence** *n.* [*Say* kwee ESS int]

quiet ● *adj.* (**quieter**, **quietest**) **1** making little or no noise. **2** free from activity or disturbance. **3** discreet. **4** tranquil and reserved. ● *n.* an absence of noise or disturbance. ● *v.* make or become quiet. □ **be quiet** cease talking etc. **keep quiet 1** refrain from making a noise. **2** suppress information etc. □ **quietly** *adv.* **quietness** *n.*

quieten *v.* esp. *Brit.* (often foll. by *down*) = QUIET *v.*

Quiet Revolution *n.* *Cdn* in Quebec, the period 1960–66, characterized by province-wide reforms and mounting separatist sentiment.

quietude *n.* a state of quiet.

quill *n.* **1** (usu. in *pl.*) the spines of a porcupine. **2** a large wing or tail feather, or its hollow stem. **3** a pen made of a quill.

quillwork *n.* art using porcupine quills, done esp. by the Mi'kmaq.

quilt ● *n.* a bed cover made of padding enclosed between layers of fabric. ● *v.* make a quilt. □ **quilted** *adj.* **quilter** *n.* **quilting** *n.*

quince *n.* a hard acid pear-shaped fruit of a small tree, used in jams and jellies.

quinine *n.* an alkaloid found in the bark of the cinchona, used in treating malaria. [*Say* KWIN ine *or* KWINE ine *or* KWIN een]

quinoa *n.* the starchy seeds of several goosefoots, used as food. [*Say* KEEN wuh]

quinsy *n.* an inflammation of the throat. [*Say* KWIN zee]

quint *n.* *informal* a quintuplet.

quintessence *n.* **1** the purest or most typical example. **2** the most essential part. □ **quintessential** *adj.* **quintessentially** *adv.* [*Say* kwint ESSENCE, kwint ESSENTIAL]

quintet *n.* **1 a** a group of five musicians playing or singing together. **b** a composition for a quintet. **2** any group of five.

quintuple ● *adj.* **1** consisting of five parts. **2** five times as much or as many. ● *v.* (**quintuples**, **quintupled**, **quintupling**) multiply by five.

quintuplet *n.* each of five children born at one birth.

quinzhee *n.* (*pl.* **quinzhees**) a shelter created by hollowing out a pile of snow. [*Say* KWINZY]

quip ● *n.* a clever saying. ● *v.* (**quips**, **quipped**, **quipping**) **1** make quips. **2** say (something) as a quip.

quire *n.* **1** four sheets of paper folded to form eight leaves. **2** 25 (also 24) sheets of paper.

quirk *n.* **1** a peculiarity of behaviour or character. **2** a trick of fate. □ **quirkily** *adv.* **quirkiness** *n.* **quirky** *adj.* (**quirkier**, **quirkiest**)

quisling *n.* a traitor co-operating with an occupying enemy. [*Say* QUIZ ling]

quit ● *v.* (**quits**, **quit**, **quitting**) **1** leave or abandon. **2** cease. **3** give up (one's employment). ● *adj.* (foll. by *of*) rid.

quite *adv.* **1** completely; in the fullest sense. **2** somewhat; to some extent. **3** said to indicate agreement. □ **quite a** a remarkable (person or thing). **quite a few** *informal* a fairly large number of.

quits *adj.* on even terms by retaliation or repayment. □ **call it quits 1** acknowledge that things are now even. **2** cease an activity.

quitter *n.* a person who gives up easily.

quiver ● *v.* tremble slightly. ● *n.* **1** a quivering motion or sound. **2** a case for holding arrows.

quixotic *adj.* idealistic and impractical. □ **quixotically** *adv.* [*Say* quick SOT ick]

quiz ● *n.* (*pl.* **quizzes**) **1** a short test or examination. **2** a test of knowledge as a form of entertainment. ● *v.* (**quizzes, quizzed, quizzing**) test or examine by questioning.

quizzical *adj.* indicating mild puzzlement. □ **quizzically** *adv.*

Quonset *n. proprietary* (also **Quonset hut**) a prefabricated metal building with a semi-cylindrical corrugated roof. [*Say* KWON set]

quorum *n.* the minimum number of members that must be present to validate the proceedings of an assembly etc. [*Say* KWORE um]

quota *n.* **1** the share that one is obliged to contribute or entitled to receive. **2 a** a limited quantity of goods etc. that may be produced, exported, or imported. **b** *Cdn* authorization granted by a marketing board to produce a specified quantity of an agricultural product. **3** a fixed number of a group allowed to do something.

quotable *adj.* suitable for quoting.

quotation *n.* **1** a passage or remark repeated by someone other than the original author or speaker. **2** the action of quoting. **3** a short tune taken from one piece of music to another. **4** *Stock Market* an amount stated as the current price of stocks or commodities. **5** an estimate of the cost of something.

quotation mark *n.* each of a set of punctuation marks, single (' ') or double (" "), used to mark a quoted passage, a title, etc.

quote ● *v.* (**quotes, quoted, quoting**) **1** repeat or copy out a passage or remark. **2** give someone (an estimated price). **3** list (a company) on a stock exchange. ● *n. informal* **1** a quotation. **2** (usu. in *pl.*) quotation marks.

quotidian *adj.* commonplace, everyday. [*Say* quo TIDDY un]

quotient *n.* **1** a result obtained by dividing one quantity by another. **2** the presence of a specified characteristic. [*Say* QUO sh'nt]

Quran *n.* (also **Qur'an**) the Islamic sacred book, believed to be the word of God as told to Muhammad and written down in Arabic. □ **Quranic** *adj.* [*Say* kuh RAN, kuh RAN ick]

q.v. *abbr. quod vide*, "which see" (in cross-references).

QWERTY *adj.* (also **qwerty**) denoting the standard English-language computer keyboard. [*Say* KWUR tee]

Rr

R¹ *n.* (also **r**) (*pl.* **Rs** or **R's**) the eighteenth letter of the alphabet. □**the three Rs** reading, writing, and arithmetic, as the fundamentals of learning.

R² *abbr.* (also **R.**) **1** (of films) restricted. **2** *Regina*. **3** *Rex*. **4** River.

rabbet ● *n.* a step-shaped channel cut in wood to receive the edge or tongue of another piece. ● *v.* (**rabbets**, **rabbeted**, **rabbeting**) **1** join or fix with a rabbet. **2** make a rabbet in.

rabbi *n.* (*pl.* **rabbis**) a Jewish religious leader or teacher of Jewish law.

rabbinate *n.* **1** the office of a rabbi. **2** rabbis collectively. [*Say* RAB in it]

rabbinical *adj.* (also **rabbinic**) relating to rabbis. [*Say* ruh BIN ick ul]

rabbit *n.* a burrowing gregarious plant-eating mammal with long ears and a short tail. □**rabbity** *adj.*

rabble *n.* **1** a large disorderly group of people. **2** (**the rabble**) the lower classes.

rabble-rouser *n.* a person who stirs up popular opinion for political reasons. □**rabble-rousing** *adj.* & *n.*

rabid *adj.* **1** extremely fanatical. **2** affected with rabies. □**rabidly** *adv.*

rabies *n.* a contagious and fatal viral disease of animals, transmissible through saliva to humans and causing madness and convulsions.

raccoon *n.* a greyish-brown mammal of N America, with a ringed bushy tail and black mask-like markings across the eyes.

race¹ ● *n.* **1** a contest of speed between athletes, horses, vehicles, etc. **2** any contest or competition. **3** a determined effort. ● *v.* (**races**, **raced**, **racing**) **1** take part in a race. **2** have a race with. **3** compete in speed with. **4** cause to race. **5** move at full speed. **6** operate at excessive speed. □**racer** *n.*

race² *n.* **1** each of the major divisions of humankind, based on distinct physical characteristics. **2** a tribe, nation, etc., regarded as of a distinct ethnic stock. **3** the concept of division into races. **4** a subdivision of a species. **5** a group of persons etc. with some common feature.

race car *n.* a car built for racing on a prepared track.

racehorse *n.* a horse bred for racing.

raceme *n.* a flower cluster with the separate flowers attached by short equal stalks to a central stem. [*Say* ray SEEM]

racetrack *n.* (also **racecourse**) a ground or track used for racing.

raceway *n.* **1** a racetrack. **2** a track or channel along which something runs.

racial *adj.* **1** of or concerning race. **2** relating to difference in race. **3** racist. □**racially** *adv.*

racial profiling *n.* **1** selection for scrutiny by law enforcement based on racial or ethnic rather than behavioural or evidentiary criteria. **2** discrimination or stereotyping on racial or ethnic grounds.

racism *n.* (also **racialism**) **1** a belief in the superiority of a particular race. **2** prejudice or antagonism towards other races based on this. □**racist** (also **racialist**) *n.* & *adj.*

rack ● *n.* **1** a framework for holding or storing things. **2** a toothed bar engaging with a pinion etc. **3** *hist.* an instrument of torture that stretches the victim's joints. **4** a triangular frame for arranging balls before a game of pool etc. **5** a set of antlers. **6** destruction. **7** a roast of lamb cut from the loin. ● *v.* **1** inflict suffering on. **2** *hist.* torture on the rack. **3** place in or on a rack. □**off the rack** ready-made. **rack one's brains** make a great mental effort. **rack up** accumulate.

racket ● *n.* **1** a loud unpleasant noise. **2** *informal* a fraudulent scheme for obtaining money etc. **3** a form of organized crime. **4** *informal* a line of business. ● *v.* (**rackets**, **racketed**, **racketing**) move noisily. □**rackety** *adj.*

racketeer *n.* a person who makes money through dishonest activities. □**racketeering** *n.*

raconteur *n.* a teller of anecdotes. [*Say* rack on TUR]

racquet *n.* **1** a bat with a stringed oval frame, used in tennis, squash, etc. **2** (in *pl.*) a ball game for two or four persons played with racquets in a plain four-walled court.

racquetball *n.* a game played with a small hard ball and a short-handled racquet in a four-walled handball court.

racy *adj.* (**racier**, **raciest**) exciting, esp. in a sexual way. □**racily** *adv.*

rad n. **1** (pl. **rad**) radian. **2** a unit of absorbed dose of ionizing radiation. **3** informal radiator.

radar n. **1** an apparatus for detecting the position and speed of things, using pulses of high-frequency electromagnetic waves. **2** an ability to notice a phenomenon.

raddled adj. untidy, unkempt.

radial ● adj. **1** relating to rays. **2 a** arranged like rays or radii. **b** acting or moving along lines diverging from a centre. **3** relating to the radius bone. **4** (of a tire) having the tread strengthened and the core fabric layers arranged radially. ● n. a radial tire. □ **radially** adv. [Say RAY dee ul]

radian n. Math a unit of angle, equivalent to 57.296° [Say RAY dee un]

radiant adj. **1** emitting rays of light. **2** beaming with joy or hope. **3** dazzling. **4** issuing in rays. **5** operating or extending radially. **6** in the form of radiation. □ **radiance** n. **radiantly** adv. [Say RAY dee unt]

radiate ● v. (**radiates**, **radiated**, **radiating**) **1** emit or be emitted in rays. **2** emit (light, heat, or sound) from a centre. **3** transmit or demonstrate (an emotion, feeling, etc.). **4** diverge or cause to diverge or spread from a centre. ● adj. having divergent rays or parts radially arranged. [Say RAY dee ate]

radiation n. the emission of energy as electromagnetic waves or as moving subatomic particles.

radiation sickness n. nausea, nerve damage, etc. caused by exposure of the body to ionizing radiation.

radiator n. **1** a person or thing that radiates. **2** a device for heating a room etc., esp. consisting of a metal case through which hot water circulates. **3** a device in a motor vehicle or aircraft with a large surface for cooling circulating water from the engine. [Say RAIDY ate er]

radical ● adj. **1** of the root or roots. **2** far-reaching. **3 a** advocating thorough reform. **b** extreme. **4** Math of the root of a number or quantity. ● n. **1** a person holding radical views. **2** a group of atoms behaving as a unit in certain compounds. **3** Math a quantity expressed as the root of another. □ **radicalism** n. **radicalization** n. **radicalize** v. (**radicalizes**, **radicalized**, **radicalizing**) **radically** adv.

radical sign n. a symbol, $\sqrt{\ }$, $\sqrt[3]{\ }$, etc., indicating the square, cube, etc., root of the number following.

radicchio n. (pl. **radicchios**) a variety of chicory with dark red leaves. [Say ruh DEEKY oh]

radii pl. of RADIUS. [Say RAY dee eye]

radio ● n. (pl. **radios**) **1 a** the transmission and reception of sound messages etc. by electromagnetic waves of radio frequency. **b** an apparatus for receiving, broadcasting, or transmitting radio signals. **2** sound broadcasting in general. ● v. (**radioes**, **radioed**, **radioing**) **1** send by radio. **2** send a message to by radio.

radio- comb. form **1** denoting radio or broadcasting. **2** connected with radioactivity, rays, or radiation.

radioactivity n. **1** the spontaneous disintegration of atomic nuclei, with the emission of radiation or particles. **2** the radiation emitted. □ **radioactive** adj. **radioactively** adv.

radiocarbon n. a radioactive isotope of carbon.

radiocarbon dating n. = CARBON DATING.

radio collar n. a collar equipped with a radio transmitter. □ **radio-collar** v.

radio-controlled adj. controlled from a distance by radio.

radio frequency n. the frequency band of telecommunication, ranging from 10^4–10^{11} or 10^{12} Hz.

radiograph ● n. a picture obtained by X-rays, gamma rays, etc. ● v. obtain a picture of by X-ray, gamma ray, etc. □ **radiographer** n. **radiographic** adj. **radiography** n. [Say RADIO graph, raidy OGRA fur, raidy OGRA fee]

radioisotope n. a radioactive isotope. [Say radio ICE uh tope]

radiology n. the scientific study of X-rays and other high-energy radiation. □ **radiological** adj. **radiologist** n. [Say raidy OLLA jee, raidy a LOGICAL, raidy OLLA jist]

radiometer n. an instrument for measuring the intensity or force of radioactivity. □ **radiometric** adj. [Say raidy OMMA tur, radio METRIC]

radio telescope n. an instrument for detecting radio waves from space.

radiotherapy n. the treatment of cancer etc. by X-rays or other radiation. □ **radiotherapist** n.

radish n. (pl. **radishes**) a small red root with a pungent taste, eaten raw.

radium n. a radioactive metallic element used in luminous materials and radiotherapy. [Say RAY dee um]

radius n. (pl. **radii** or **radiuses**) **1** a straight line from the centre to the circumference of a circle or sphere. **2** a usu. specified distance from a centre in all directions. **3** the thicker and shorter of the two bones in the human forearm. [Say RAY dee us; for radii say RAY dee eye]

radon n. a gaseous radioactive element used in radiotherapy. [Say RAY don]

RAF abbr. (in the UK) Royal Air Force.

raffia n. fibre from the leaves of a tropical palm tree, used for making hats, baskets, etc. [Say RAFFY uh]

raffish adj. attractively disreputable. □ **raffishness** n.

raffle ● n. a fundraising lottery with goods as prizes. ● v. (**raffles, raffled, raffling**) offer as a prize in a raffle.

raft¹ ● n. **1** a flat platform of logs etc. tied together, used as a boat or floating platform. **2** a lifeboat or inflatable boat. **3** a mass of squared timber or logs fastened together for transportation on water. ● v. **1** transport as or on a raft. **2** use a raft. **3** form into a raft. **4** engage in the sport of whitewater rafting. □ **rafting** n.

raft² n. informal a large amount.

rafter¹ n. each of the usu. sloping beams forming the framework of a roof. □ **raftered** adj.

rafter² n. a person who rafts.

rag¹ n. **1** a frayed or worn piece of cloth. **2 a** (in pl.) old, worn clothes. **b** informal a garment of any kind. **3** derogatory an inferior newspaper etc.

rag² v. (**rags, ragged, ragging**) slang scold; criticize. □ **rag the puck 1** Hockey stickhandle skilfully to waste time. **2** Cdn slang waste time intentionally.

rag³ n. a ragtime tune.

ragamuffin n. **1** a child in ragged dirty clothes. **2** = RAGGAMUFFIN.

rage ● n. **1** violent anger. **2** the violent action of a natural force. **3 a** vehement passion. **b** a widespread temporary enthusiasm. ● v. (**rages, raged, raging**) **1** be full of anger. **2** speak furiously. **3** continue unchecked. □ **all the rage** very popular.

ragga n. a style of popular music combining elements of reggae and hip hop.

raggamuffin n. **1** a follower of ragga. **2** = RAGGA.

ragged adj. **1** torn; frayed. **2** rough. **3** in ragged clothes. **4** with a broken or jagged outline or surface. **5** faulty. **6** rough and uneven. **7** exhausted. □ **raggedly** adv. **raggedness** n. **raggedy** adj. [Say RAG id]

raggle-taggle adj. assorted.

raging adj. extreme.

raglan adj. having or denoting sleeves attached to a garment by a diagonal seam running from the neck to the underarm.

ragout n. a stew. [Say rag OO]

rags-to-riches adj. relating to a person who starts out poor and ends up rich.

ragtag ● adj. (also **ragtail**) **1** disorganized, scraggly. **2** ragged or shabby; unkempt. ● n. derogatory the rabble.

ragtime ● n. an early form of jazz music played esp. on the piano. ● adj. resembling ragtime.

ragtop n. **1** a convertible car with a top made of cloth. **2** the top of such a car.

ragweed n. a N American plant of the daisy family, a major cause of hay fever.

raid ● n. **1** a rapid surprise attack. **2** a surprise visit by police etc. to arrest suspected persons or seize illicit goods. **3** Stock Market an attempt to lower prices by the concerted selling of shares. ● v. make a raid on. □ **raider** n.

rail ● n. **1** a bar in a fence or attached to a wall, for hanging things on, holding onto, etc. **2** a steel bar or continuous line of bars forming a railway track. **3** a railway. **4** a drab bird found in marshes. ● v. **1** furnish with a rail or rails. **2** enclose with rails. **3** complain vehemently. □ **off the rails** deranged.

railcar n. a railway carriage.

railhead n. the furthest point reached by a railway.

railing n. **1** a handrail. **2** (often in pl.) a fence or barrier made of rails.

railroad ● n. = RAILWAY. ● v. **1** rush or coerce. **2** send to prison by means of false evidence. □ **railroader** n.

railway n. esp. Cdn & Brit. **1** a track made of steel rails upon which trains run. **2** a system of such tracks or the company operating it.

railwayman n. (pl. **railwaymen**) esp. Brit. & Cdn a railway employee.

railway yard n. (also **rail yard**) the area where rolling stock is kept and made up into trains.

raiment n. literary & archaic clothing. [Say RAY m'nt]

rain ● n. **1** the condensed moisture of the atmosphere falling visibly in separate drops. **2** (in pl.) (**the rains**) the rainy season in tropical countries. ● v. **1** (of rain) fall. **2** fall like rain. **3** lavishly bestow. **4** send down rain. □ **rain on someone's parade** informal spoil a person's good time. **rain out** cause to be terminated because of rain.

rainbow ● n. **1** an arch of colours formed in the sky etc. by refraction and dispersion of sunlight by water droplets. **2** a wide variety of related things. ● *adj.* many-coloured. □ **chase a rainbow** pursue an illusory goal.

rainbow trout *n.* (*pl.* **rainbow trout**) a large trout widespread throughout N America.

rain check *n.* **1** a ticket given for later use when a sports event etc. is postponed by rain. **2** a promise that an offer will be maintained though deferred. □ **take a rain check on** reserve the right to take up (an offer) later.

raincoat *n.* a water-resistant coat.

raindrop *n.* a single drop of rain.

rainfall *n.* **1** a fall of rain. **2** the quantity of rain falling within a given area in a given time.

rainforest *n.* a luxuriant forest in an area of consistent heavy rainfall.

rainmaker *n.* **1** a person who seeks to cause rain to fall, either by magic or by a technique such as seeding. **2** *slang* a highly successful person. □ **rainmaking** *n.*

rainout *n.* the cancellation of an event because of rain.

rainproof *adj.* resistant to rainwater.

rainstorm *n.* a storm with heavy rain.

rainwater *n.* water obtained from collected rain.

rainwear *n.* clothes for wearing in the rain.

rainy *adj.* (**rainier, rainiest**) **1** in or on which rain is falling or usually falls. **2** laden with or bringing rain.

raise ● *v.* (**raises, raised, raising**) **1** lift or move to a higher position or level. **2** set upright. **3** increase the amount, level, or strength of. **4** promote to a higher rank. **5** cause to be heard, felt, or considered. **6** build. **7** collect or levy. **8** bring up. **9** breed or grow. **10** wake from sleep or bring back from death. **11** abandon or force to abandon. **12** *Curling* strike (a rock) with another rock to move it deeper. ● *n.* **1** an increase in salary. **2** *Curling* the act or an instance of raising a rock. □ **raise one's hand to** make as if to strike. **raise hell** *informal* make a disturbance. **raise one's voice** speak louder. □ **raiser** *n.* (also in *comb.*)

raisin *n.* **1** a partially dried grape. **2** the dark purplish-brown colour of raisins. □ **raisiny** *adj.*

raison d'être *n.* (*pl.* **raisons d'être**) a purpose that justifies a thing's existence. [*Say* raise on DETRA *(with* ON *as in French)*]

raita *n.* an Indian side dish of chopped cucumber and spices in yogurt. [*Say* ruh EET uh]

Raj *n.* (**the Raj**) *hist.* the period of British rule in the Indian subcontinent before 1947. [*Say* RAWZH]

raja *n.* (also **rajah**) *hist.* an Indian king or prince. [*Say* RAWZH uh]

rake¹ ● *n.* **1** an implement consisting of a pole with a hooked crossbar or fine tines at the end, for gathering leaves, smoothing soil, etc. **2** a similar implement used by a croupier to gather money. ● *v.* (**rakes, raked, raking**) **1** collect etc. with or as with a rake. **2** tidy with a rake. **3** use a rake. **4** search. **5** sweep with gunfire, a look, etc. **6** scratch or scrape. □ **rake in** *informal* amass (profits). **rake up** (or **over**) revive the memory of. □ **raker** *n.*

rake² *n.* a stylish but immoral man. □ **rakish** *adj.*

rake³ ● *v.* (**rakes, raked, raking**) set at a sloping angle. ● *n.* **1** a raking position. **2** the amount by which a thing, e.g. a stage or auditorium, rakes. □ **raked** *adj.*

rallentando *adv. & adj.* with a gradual decrease of speed. [*Say* ral in TAN doe]

rally ● *v.* (**rallies, rallied, rallying**) **1** (with reference to troops) gather again so as to continue fighting. **2** gather for support or united action. **3** recover or cause to recover. **4** increase after a fall. ● *n.* (*pl.* **rallies**) **1** a mass meeting held as a protest or in support of a cause. **2** a quick or marked recovery. **3** *Baseball* the scoring of two or more runs in one inning. **4** *Tennis etc.* an extended exchange of strokes between players. **5** a competition for motor vehicles, often over rough terrain.

rallying cry *n.* a slogan.

RAM *abbr. Computing* random access memory.

ram ● *n.* a male sheep that has not been castrated. ● *v.* (**rams, rammed, ramming**) **1** force or squeeze into place by pressure. **2** beat down or drive in by heavy blows. **3** strike violently. **4** push (a bill etc.) through a legislature. □ **ram home** stress forcefully.

-rama *comb. form informal* or *jocular* forming nouns denoting abundance, extravaganza.

Ramadan *n.* the ninth month of the Muslim year, during which strict fasting is observed from sunrise to sunset. [*Say* RAMMA dan]

ramble ● *v.* (**rambles, rambled, rambling**) **1** walk for pleasure. **2** talk or write in a confused way and at length. **3** spread in various directions. ● *n.* a walk taken for pleasure. □ **rambler** *n.*

rambling *adj.* **1** wandering. **2** disconnected, incoherent. **3** irregularly arranged. **4** straggling, climbing.

rambunctious *adj. informal* **1** active. **2** boisterous. □ **rambunctiously** *adv.* **rambunctiousness** *n.*

ramen *pl. n.* quick-cooking noodles, often served in broth. [*Say* ROM in]

ramification *n.* a consequence of an action or event. [*Say* ramma fuh KAY sh'n]

ramify *v.* (**ramifies, ramified, ramifying**) form branches or subdivisions. [*Say* RAMMA fie]

ramp ● *n.* **1** a slope for joining two levels of ground. **2** a short sloping road leading on or off a highway. **3** movable stairs for entering or leaving an aircraft. ● *v.* **1** (usu. as **ramped** *adj.*) furnish with a ramp. **2** (often foll. by *up*) increase.

rampage ● *v.* (**rampages, rampaged, rampaging**) rush wildly about. ● *n.* a period of uncontrolled or violent behaviour.

rampant *adj.* flourishing or spreading uncontrollably. □ **rampantly** *adv.* [*Say* RAMP int]

rampart *n.* **1** a wall with a broad top and usu. a walkway, built around a castle, fort, etc. **2** a defence or protection.

ramrod ● *n.* a rod for ramming down the charge of a muzzle-loading firearm. ● *adj.* very straight. ● *adv.* like a ramrod. ● *v.* (**ramrods, ramrodded, ramrodding**) force or drive as with a ramrod.

ramshackle *adj.* **1** tumbledown, rickety. **2** poorly designed or organized.

ran *past of* RUN.

ranch ● *n.* (*pl.* **ranches**) **1** a cattle-breeding farm esp. in the western US and Canada. **2** a house on a cattle ranch. **3** a type of creamy salad dressing. ● *v.* (**ranches, ranched, ranching**) **1** work on or run a ranch. **2** breed or rear (animals) on or as on a ranch. **3** use (land) as a ranch. □ **rancher** *n.* **ranching** *n.*

ranchland *n.* land used for or suitable for ranching.

rancid *adj.* smelling or tasting rank and stale as a result of oxidation. [*Say* RAN sid]

rancorous *adj.* bitter, full of spite. □ **rancorously** *adv.*

rancour *n.* (also esp. *US* **rancor**) bitterness, animosity. [*Say* RANKER]

R & B *abbr.* rhythm and blues.

R & D *abbr.* research and development.

random *adj.* **1** made, done, etc., without method or conscious choice. **2** *Statistics* with equal chances for each item. □ **at random** without aim or purpose or principle. □ **randomly** *adv.* **randomness** *n.*

random access *n.* a process allowing information in a computer to be stored or recovered without reading through items stored previously.

randomize *v.* (**randomizes, randomized, randomizing**) put things in random order.

R & R *abbr.* **1** rest and relaxation. **2** rescue and resuscitation.

randy *adj.* (**randier, randiest**) *informal* **1** lustful. **2** bawdy, risqué.

rang *past of* RING[2].

range ● *n.* **1** the area of variation between limits on a particular scale. **2** a set of different things of the same general type. **3** the extent of a person's or thing's abilities etc. **4** the distance within which something is able to operate. **5 a** a row, series, etc., esp. of mountains or buildings. **b** *Cdn* a row of prison cells. **6** a large area of open land for grazing or hunting. **7** an area used as a military testing ground or for target practice. **8** the area over which a plant or animal is distributed. **9** an electric or gas stove. ● *v.* (**ranges, ranged, ranging**) **1** vary or extend between limits. **2 a** place or arrange in order. **b** align with a certain group etc. **3** rove, wander. **4** traverse in all directions.

rangefinder *n.* an instrument for estimating the distance of an object.

rangeland *n.* an extensive area of open country used for grazing or hunting animals.

ranger *n.* **1 a** = FOREST RANGER. **b** (also **park ranger**) = PARK WARDEN. **2 a** mounted soldier. **3** *Cdn* (*North*) an Indian or Inuit who serves as a military scout or observer on a voluntary basis. **4** (**Ranger**) *Cdn & Brit.* a member of the senior branch of the Girl Guides, aged 15 or older.

rangy[1] *adj.* (**rangier, rangiest**) **1** slender and tall or long. **2** tending to wander about. [*Say* RANGE ee]

rangy[2] *adj.* (**rangier, rangiest**) *Cdn informal* (of a person, esp. a child) restless, uncontrollable, and bad-tempered. [*Say* RANG ee]

rank[1] ● *n.* **1 a** a position in a hierarchy. **b** a grade of dignity or achievement. **2** a row or line. **3** a single line of soldiers drawn up abreast. **4** order, array. ● *v.* **1** have rank or place. **2** classify. **3** arrange in a rank or ranks. □ **break rank** (or **ranks**) **1** fail to remain in line. **2** fail to maintain solidarity. **close ranks** maintain solidarity. **the ranks 1** the common soldiers. **2** a group of people of a specified type.

rank[2] *adj.* **1** growing too thickly and coarsely. **2** foul-smelling. **3** unmistakable.

rank and file *n.* (usu. treated as *pl.*) **1** the ordinary soldiers who are not officers. **2** any ordinary members as opposed to the leaders.

ranking ● *n.* ordering by rank. ● *adj.* having a high rank.

rankle *v.* (**rankles, rankled, rankling**) **1** cause persistent annoyance. **2** cause bitter feelings in (a person).

ransack *v.* **1** pillage or plunder. **2** thoroughly search.

ransom ● *n.* a payment demanded for the release of a prisoner. ● *v.* buy the freedom or restoration of.

rant ● *v.* speak vehemently at length. ● *n.* a piece of ranting. □ **rant and rave** express anger noisily and forcefully. □ **ranter** *n.*

rap ● *n.* **1** a sharp knock. **2** *slang* criticism, punishment. **3** (also **rap music**) a style of popular music characterized by spoken rhythmic lyrics against a background with a pronounced beat. ● *v.* (**raps, rapped, rapping**) **1** strike briskly. **2** knock; make a sharp tapping sound. **3** *informal* **a** criticize adversely. **b** accuse. **4** perform or utter in the style of rap music. □ **beat the rap** escape punishment. **rap on the knuckles** a reprimand. □ **rapper** *n.*

rapacious *adj.* greedy, extortionate. □ **rapacity** *n.* [*Say* ruh PAY shuss, ruh PASS it ee]

rape¹ ● *n.* **1** the action or an act of forcing a person to have sexual intercourse unwillingly. **2** plunder or violation. ● *v.* (**rapes, raped, raping**) **1** commit rape on. **2** destroy.

rape² *n.* a plant of the cabbage family, the seeds of which yield an oil.

rapeseed *n.* **1** the seed of the rape plant. **2** the rape plant.

rapeseed oil *n.* (also **rape oil**) an oil made from rapeseed and used as a lubricant and in foodstuffs.

rapid ● *adj.* **1** quick. **2** acting or completed in a short time. **3** descending steeply. ● *n.* (usu. in *pl.*) a swift, turbulent section of river. □ **rapidly** *adv.*

rapid eye movement *n.* a type of jerky movement of the eyes during periods of dreaming.

rapid-fire *adj.* fired, uttered, etc., in quick succession.

rapidity *n.* swiftness. [*Say* ruh PIDDA tee]

rapier ● *n.* a light slender sword used for thrusting. ● *adj.* very quick and intelligent. [*Say* RAY pee er]

rapini *pl. n.* the edible leaves of an immature white turnip. [*Say* ruh PEENY]

rapist *n.* a person who commits rape.

rappel ● *v.* (**rappels, rappelled, rappelling**) descend a steep rock face by using a doubled rope fixed at a higher point. ● *n.* a descent made by rappelling. [*Say* ruh PEL]

rapport *n.* a relationship, esp. a harmonious one. [*Say* ruh PORE]

rapprochement *n.* a renewal of harmonious relations, esp. between nations. [*Say* ra prosh MON (*with* ON *as in* French)]

rapt *adj.* fully absorbed, enraptured.

raptor *n.* any bird of prey.

rapture *n.* **1** ecstatic delight. **2** (in *pl.*) expressions of this. □ **rapturous** *adj.* **rapturously** *adv.*

rare *adj.* (**rarer, rarest**) **1** seldom done or found. **2** (of meat) slightly cooked. □ **rarely** *adv.*

rarefied *adj.* (also **rarified**) **1** thinner or less dense than usual. **2** distant from the lives of ordinary people. [*Say* RARE a fide]

raring *adj. informal* eager.

rarity *n.* (*pl.* **rarities**) **1** the state of being rare. **2** an uncommon thing.

rascal *n.* often *jocular* a mischievous person, esp. a child. □ **rascally** *adj.*

rash¹ *adj.* reckless. □ **rashly** *adv.* **rashness** *n.*

rash² *n.* (*pl.* **rashes**) **1** an eruption of the skin in spots or patches. **2** (usu. foll. by *of*) a sudden unwelcome phenomenon.

rasp ● *n.* **1** a harsh, grating noise. **2** a coarse file. ● *v.* **1** scrape something with a rasp. **2** make a harsh grating sound. □ **raspy** *adj.*

raspberry *n.* (*pl.* **raspberries**) **1** a bramble or its soft edible red berry. **2** *informal* a sputtering sound made with the lips and tongue expressing derision.

Rastafarian (also **Rasta**) ● *n.* a member of a Jamaican sect regarding black people as divinely chosen and the former Emperor Haile Selassie of Ethiopia as God. ● *adj.* of this sect. □ **Rastafarianism** *n.* [*Say* rasta FAIRY un]

raster *n.* a pattern of horizontal lines of pixels composing an image.

rat ● *n.* **1** a rodent resembling a large mouse. **2** a deserter; a turncoat. **3** *informal* an unpleasant person. **4** *informal* a person frequently found in a specified place. ● *v.* (**rats, ratted, ratting**) *informal* **1** inform (against someone); betray. **2** *informal* desert a cause etc.

ratatouille *n.* a dish of stewed onions, zucchini, tomatoes, eggplant, and peppers. [*Say* ratta TOO ee]

ratchet ● *n.* **1** a device consisting of a bar or wheel with angled teeth in which a cog etc. fits, allowing movement in one direction only. **2** a wheel with a rim so toothed. ● *v.* (**ratchets, ratcheted, ratcheting**) cause to rise or fall as a step in a process.

rate ● *n.* **1** a measure, quantity, or frequency measured against another. **2** a fixed price or charge. **3** rapidity of movement or change. **4** rank. ● *v.* (**rates**, **rated**, **rating**) **1** estimate the worth of **2** regard as. **3 a** rank or classify. **b** rank highly. **4** be worthy of. □ **at any rate** whatever happens. **at this rate** if this example is typical. □ **rater** *n.*

ratepayer *n.* a person paying local property taxes.

rather *adv.* **1** by preference. **2** as a more likely alternative. **3 a** more precisely. **b** on the contrary. **4** slightly. □ **had rather** would rather.

ratify *v.* (**ratifies**, **ratified**, **ratifying**) confirm or accept (an agreement made in one's name) by formal consent, signature, etc. □ **ratification** *n.* [*Say* RATTA fie, ratta fuh KAY sh'n]

rating *n.* **1** a classification or ranking based on quality, standard, or performance. **2** the estimated standing of a person etc. as regards credit. **3** the estimated audience size of a television or radio show. **4** *Cdn & Brit.* a non-commissioned sailor.

ratio *n.* (*pl.* **ratios**) **1** the relationship between two amounts, determined by the number of times one contains the other. **2** a proportional relationship between things not precisely measurable. [*Say* RAY shee oh]

ration ● *n.* **1** a fixed official allowance of something in a time of shortage. **2** (usu. in *pl.*) a fixed daily allowance of food, esp. in the armed forces. ● *v.* **1** limit (persons or provisions) to a fixed ration. **2** (usu. foll. by *out*) share out (food etc.) in fixed quantities. [*Say* RASH'n]

rational *adj.* **1** of or based on reasoning or reason. **2** able to think reasonably. □ **rationality** *n.* **rationally** *adv.* [*Say* RASH'n ul, rash'n ALA tee]

rationale *n.* a set of reasons for a course of action or a belief. [*Say* rasha NAL]

rationalism *n.* **1** *Philosophy* the theory that reason is the foundation of certainty. **2** a belief in reason rather than religion or emotion as a guiding principle. □ **rationalist** *n.* [*Say* RASH'n ul ism]

rationalize *v.* (**rationalizes**, **rationalized**, **rationalizing**) **1** create a rational but specious explanation of. **2** make logical and consistent. **3** make (a business) more efficient by reducing labour, time, or materials. □ **rationalization** *n.* [*Say* RASH'n ul ize, rash'n ul ize AY sh'n]

rat race *n.* a fiercely competitive struggle.

rats *interj.* expressing annoyance.

rattan *n.* any East Indian climbing palm with long thin jointed pliable stems used for wicker furniture etc. [*Say* ruh TAN]

rat-tat-tat *n.* a rapping staccato sound.

rattle ● *v.* (**rattles**, **rattled**, **rattling**) **1** make or cause to make a rapid succession of short sharp hard sounds. **2** move with a rattling noise. **3** recite or talk rapidly. **4** *informal* alarm. ● *n.* **1** a rattling sound. **2** an instrument or toy made to rattle. **3** the set of rings in a rattlesnake's tail. □ **rattling** *adj.* **rattly** *adj.*

rattlesnake *n.* (also *informal* **rattler**) a poisonous N American snake with a rattling structure of rings in its tail.

rattletrap *informal* ● *n.* a rickety old vehicle etc. ● *adj.* rickety.

ratty *adj.* (**rattier**, **rattiest**) **1** like a rat. **2** *informal* shabby.

raucous *adj.* harsh-sounding. □ **raucously** *adv.* **raucousness** *n.* [*Say* ROCK us]

raunchy *adj.* (**raunchier**, **raunchiest**) *informal* **1** coarse; sexually provocative. **2** (of sound) distorted.

ravage ● *v.* (**ravages**, **ravaged**, **ravaging**) cause severe damage to. ● *n.* destructive effect.

rave ● *v.* (**raves**, **raved**, **raving**) **1** talk wildly. **2** speak with rapturous admiration. **3** roar. **4** *slang* attend a rave. ● *n.* **1** *informal* a very enthusiastic review. **2** an all-night party held usu. in a warehouse or open field, with dancing to electronic music. □ **raver** *n.*

raven ● *n.* a large glossy blue-black crow. ● *adj.* glossy black. [*Say* RAVE un]

ravening *adj.* extremely hungry for prey. [*Say* RAV un ing]

ravenous *adj.* **1** very hungry. **2** voracious. □ **ravenously** *adv.* [*Say* RAV un us]

ravine *n.* a narrow, steep-sided valley.

raving ● *n.* (usu. in *pl.*) wild or delirious talk. ● *adj.* frenzied. ● *adv. informal* as an intensifier.

ravioli *n.* small squares of pasta stuffed with minced meat, cheese, spinach, etc. [*Say* ravvy OH lee]

ravish *v.* (**ravishes**, **ravished**, **ravishing**) **1** force a woman to have sex. **2** fill with delight. □ **ravisher** *n.*

ravishing *adj.* **1** entrancing. **2** extraordinarily beautiful. □ **ravishingly** *adv.*

raw *adj.* **1** (of food) uncooked. **2** in the natural state. **3** not analyzed or processed etc. **4** inexperienced. **5 a** stripped of skin. **b** abnormally sensitive. **6** chilly and damp. **7** crude, unrefined. □ **in the raw 1** in its natural state. **2** naked. **raw deal** unfair treatment □ **rawness** *n.*

rawhide n. hide that has not been tanned.

raw material n. material from which products are manufactured.

ray[1] ● n. **1** a line of light or radiation coming from a point. **2** (in *pl.*) radiation of a specified type. **3** a trace of a good quality. ● v. (**rays, rayed, raying**) **1** issue in rays. **2** radiate.

ray[2] n. a broad flat fish with a long tail.

rayon n. a synthetic fibre made from viscose.

raze v. (**razes, razed, razing**) completely destroy.

razor ● n. an instrument with a sharp blade for shaving unwanted hair from the skin. ● v. cut with a razor.

razorback n. a hog with a sharp ridged back.

razorbill n. an auk with a sharp-edged bill.

razor wire n. a type of coiled wire with extremely sharp edges or points.

razz v. *slang* (**razzes, razzed, razzing**) ridicule.

razzle-dazzle n. (also **razzle**) *informal* **1** a flamboyant often insincere display. **2** glamorous excitement.

razzmatazz n. *informal* = RAZZLE-DAZZLE.

RBI n. (*pl.* **RBIs** or **RBI**) *Baseball* run batted in. [*Say* arr bee EYE *or* RIBBY]

RC *abbr.* Roman Catholic.

RCAF *abbr. hist.* Royal Canadian Air Force.

RCMP ● *abbr.* Royal Canadian Mounted Police. ● n. (*pl.* **RCMPs**) *Cdn informal* an RCMP officer.

RCN *abbr. hist.* Royal Canadian Navy.

RDA *abbr.* (*pl.* **RDAs**) recommended daily allowance.

RDI *abbr.* (*pl.* **RDIs**) recommended daily intake.

re[1] *prep.* **1** in the matter of. **2** *informal* concerning. [*Say* REE]

re[2] n. **1** (in tonic sol-fa) the second note of a major scale. **2** the note D in the fixed-do system. [*Say* RAY]

re- *prefix* **1** once more; anew. **2** with return to a previous state.

reach ● v. (**reaches, reached, reaching**) **1** stretch out an arm in order to touch or grasp something. **2** be able to touch (something) with an outstretched arm or leg. **3** arrive at or attain. **4** make contact with. **5** succeed in influencing. ● n. (*pl.* **reaches**) **1** an act of reaching. **2** the distance someone can reach. **3** the extent of something or someone's effect or influence. **4** (also **reaches**) a continuous extent of land or water. □ **reachable** *adj.* **reacher** n.

reacquaint v. (usu. foll. by *with*) make acquainted again.

react v. **1** respond to something in a particular way. **2** suffer adverse physical effects after ingesting, breathing, or touching a substance. **3** interact and undergo a chemical or physical change.

reaction n. **1** something done or experienced in response to a situation or event. **2** a mode of thinking deliberately different from a previous one. **3** a response by the body, usu. a bad one, to a drug, chemical substance, etc. **4** a tendency to oppose change. **5** a process in which substances interact and are changed. **6** *Physics* a force equal but opposite to another force. **7** the ability to respond quickly.

reactionary usu. *derogatory* ● *adj.* tending to oppose progress or reform. ● n. (*pl.* **reactionaries**) a reactionary person.

reactivate v. (**reactivates, reactivated, reactivating**) restore to a state of activity. □ **reactivation** n.

reactive *adj.* **1** showing reaction. **2** reacting rather than taking the initiative. **3** having a tendency to react chemically. □ **reactivity** n.

reactor n. **1** a person or thing that reacts. **2** (also **nuclear reactor**) an apparatus or structure in which a controlled nuclear chain reaction releases energy.

read[1] ● v. (**reads, read, reading**) **1** look at and understand the meaning of (written or printed matter) by interpreting its characters or symbols. **2** speak (written or printed words) aloud. **3** contain or consist of specified words. **4** interpret the significance of. **5** inspect and record the figure indicated on (a measuring instrument). **6** hear and understand. **7** copy or transfer (data). ● n. **1** an act of reading. **2** a book etc. as regards its readability. □ **read between the lines** look for or find hidden meaning. **read into** assume meanings which are not intended by the speaker or writer. **read my lips** *informal* listen carefully. **read up on** study.

read[2] *adj.* (often in *comb.*) educated in a subject by reading. □ **take as read** accept without discussing.

readable *adj.* **1** able to be read. **2** pleasant to read. **3** (of data) able to be processed. □ **readability** n.

reader n. **1** a person who reads. **2** a device that interprets encoded data. **3** a book containing written extracts used for teaching purposes. **4** a device for producing an image that can be read from microfilm etc.

readership n. **1** the readers of a

newspaper etc. **2** the number or extent of these.

readily adv. **1** without showing reluctance. **2** promptly; without difficulty. [Say RED a lee]

reading n. **1** the action or skill of reading. **2** an instance of something being read to an audience. **3** an interpretation of a text. **4** a figure recorded on a measuring instrument. **5** a stage of debate in parliament through which a bill must pass to become law.

reading week n. Cdn a week in a university term during which there are no classes.

readjust v. **1** adjust again. **2** adapt to a changed situation. □ **readjustment** n. [Say re ADJUST]

readmit v. (**readmits, readmitted, readmitting**) admit again. □ **readmission** n. [Say re ADMIT]

read-only memory n. Computing a memory read at high speed but not capable of being changed by program instructions. Abbreviation: **ROM**.

readout n. **1** the display of data by an automatic device. **2** a record of output produced by a computer or scientific instrument.

read/write adj. Computing capable of reading existing data and accepting alterations or further input.

ready ● adj. (**readier, readiest**) **1** prepared for an activity or situation. **2** made available for immediate use. **3** within reach. **4** willing to do. **5** immediate. ● adv. (**done, prepared, etc.**) beforehand. ● v. (**readies, readied, readying**) make ready; prepare. □ **at the ready** ready for action. **get ready** prepare. □ **readiness** n.

ready-made adj. **1** made in a standard size. **2** prepared in advance. **3** very appropriate and already available.

ready-mix adj. (also **ready-mixed**) having some or all of the constituents already mixed together.

ready-to-wear ● n. clothing made in standard sizes. ● adj. pertaining to this style of clothing.

reaffirm v. affirm again. □ **reaffirmation** n.

reagent n. Chemistry a substance that produces a chemical reaction, used in tests and experiments. [Say re AGENT]

real adj. **1** actually existing. **2** genuine, sincere. **3** not artificial. **4** serious. **5** Law of or relating to immovable property such as land or houses. **6** appraised by purchasing power. □ **realness** n.

real estate n. **1** immovable property, such as land or houses. **2** the business of trading in this.

realign v. **1** adjust or alter the direction of. **2** restructure or regroup. □ **realignment** n. [Say re a LINE]

realism n. **1** the acceptance of a situation as it is and acting accordingly. **2** fidelity to nature in representation. **3** (also **Realism**) an artistic movement of the 19th century featuring non-idealized scenes of modern life. □ **realist** n. & adj.

realistic adj. **1** having or showing a sensible and practical idea of what can be achieved. **2** true to real life or nature. □ **realistically** adv.

reality n. (pl. **realities**) **1** the state of things as they actually exist. **2** a thing that is real. **3** the state of being real. □ **in reality** in fact.

realize v. (**realizes, realized, realizing**) **1** become fully aware of. **2** understand clearly. **3** make happen in reality. **4** a convert into money. **b** acquire. **c** be sold for. □ **realizable** adj. **realization** n.

reallocate v. (**reallocates, reallocated, reallocating**) allocate again or differently. □ **reallocation** n. [Say re ALOE kate]

really adv. **1** in actual fact. **2** very. **3** (as a strong affirmative) seriously, I assure you. **4** an expression of disbelief.

realm n. **1** formal a kingdom. **2** a field of activity or of some abstract conception. [Say RELM]

realpolitik n. politics based on realities and material needs. [Say ray al paula TEEK]

real time ● n. the actual time during which a process or event occurs. ● adj. (usu. **real-time**) Computing **1** in which input data is processed almost immediately. **2** responding virtually immediately to changes.

realtor n. a real estate agent.

realty n. real estate.

ream ● n. **1** twenty quires or 500 (formerly 480) sheets of paper. **2** (in pl.) a large quantity of paper etc. ● v. widen with a borer. □ **ream a person out** informal reprimand a person harshly. □ **reamer** n.

reanalyze v. (**reanalyzes, reanalyzed, reanalyzing**) analyze again. □ **reanalysis** n.

reanimate v. (**reanimates, reanimated, reanimating**) **1** revive. **2** restore to liveliness etc. □ **reanimation** n.

reap v. **1** cut as a harvest. **2** harvest the crop of (a field). **3** receive. □ **reaper** n.

reappear v. appear again or as previously. □ **reappearance** n.

reapply v. (**reapplies, reapplied, reapplying**) apply again.

reappraisal n. a new appraisal.

rear[1] ● n. **1** the back part of anything. **2** the space behind anything. **3** (also **rear end**) informal the buttocks. ● adj. at the back. □ **bring up the rear** come last.

rear[2] v. **1 a** bring up and educate. **b** breed and care for. **2** (usu. foll. by up) rise. **3** set upright, build. **4** extend to a great height. □ **rear** (or **raise**) **its** (**ugly**) **head** make an (unwelcome) appearance. □ **rearing** n.

rear admiral n. (also **Rear Admiral**) a naval officer ranking below a vice admiral.

rear-end v. crash into the back of.

rear-ender n. informal a collision in which one vehicle rear-ends another.

rearguard n. **1** a body of troops detached to protect the rear. **2** a defensive or conservative element. **3** Hockey slang a defenceman.

rearm v. arm again. □ **rearmament** n.

rearmost adj. furthest back.

rearrange v. (**rearranges, rearranged, rearranging**) arrange differently. □ **rearrangement** n. **rearranging** n.

rear-view mirror n. (also **rear-view**) a mirror fixed inside the windshield of a car, truck, etc.

rearward ● adv. towards the rear. ● adj. located at or towards the rear.

rear-wheel drive n. a drive system in a car etc. in which engine power operates through the rear wheels alone.

reason ● n. **1** a motive, cause, or justification. **2** the power to think sensibly. ● v. **1** try to reach conclusions by connected thought. **2** use an argument by way of persuasion. □ **by reason of** owing to. **in** (or **within**) **reason** within the bounds of sense. **it stands to reason** it is evident or logical. □ **reasoned** adj. **reasoning** n.

reasonable adj. **1** having sound judgment. **2** in accordance with reason. **3 a** inexpensive. **b** fairly good. □ **reasonableness** n. **reasonably** adv.

reassemble v. (**reassembles, reassembled, reassembling**) put back together. □ **reassembly** n.

reassert v. assert again. □ **reassertion** n.

reassess v. (**reassesses, reassessed, reassessing**) assess again. □ **reassessment** n. [Say re ASSESS]

reassign v. assign again. □ **reassignment** n.

reassure v. (**reassures, reassured, reassuring**) restore confidence to.

□ **reassurance** n. **reassuring** adj. **reassuringly** adv.

reattach v. (**reattaches, reattached, reattaching**) attach again.

reawaken v. awaken again. □ **reawakening** n.

Reb n. a traditional Jewish courtesy title used preceding a man's name.

rebar n. a steel reinforcing rod in concrete. [Say REE bar]

rebate n. **1** a partial refund of money paid. **2** a discount. ● v. (**rebates, rebated, rebating**) pay back as a rebate.

rebbe n. **1** a Jewish religious leader or rabbi. **2** (**Rebbe**) a title of respect used for a Hasidic religious leader. [Say REBBA]

rebel ● n. a person who fights against established authority. ● adj. **1** rebellious. **2** of or concerning rebels. **3** in rebellion. ● v. (**rebels, rebelled, rebelling**) resist openly or violently; be a rebel.

rebellion n. **1** an act of rebelling against a government or authority. **2** opposition to authority or control.

rebellious adj. rebelling or inclined to rebel. □ **rebelliously** adv. **rebelliousness** n.

rebirth n. **1** the process of being born again. **2** a revival.

reboot Computing ● v. boot up again. ● n. an act of rebooting.

reborn adj. **1** having experienced a profound transformation or a complete spiritual change. **2** existing or active again.

rebound ● v. **1** spring back after action or impact. **2** make a recovery. **3** Basketball recover (a ball) that has bounced off the backboard etc. **4** (foll. by upon) have an adverse effect upon (the doer). ● n. **1** a positive reaction after something negative. **2** Sport a puck, ball, etc. which has bounced back from the goal, basket, etc. or been let loose by the goaltender. ● adj. occurring again. □ **on the rebound 1** while still recovering from an emotional shock. **2** while bouncing back. □ **rebounder** n. **rebounding** n.

rebrand ● v. **1** apply a new brand identity (as a different name, logo, livery, etc.) to (an existing product, service, or company). **2** radically change the presentation of. ● n. the act or an instance of rebranding.

rebuff ● n. an abrupt rejection. ● v. reject abruptly.

rebuild v. (**rebuilds, rebuilt, rebuilding**) **1** build again. **2** re-establish or revive.

rebuke ● v. (**rebukes, rebuked, rebuking**) scold or reprimand harshly. ● n. a stern reprimand.

rebus n. (pl. **rebuses**) a type of puzzle in which a word is represented by pictures etc. suggesting its parts. [Say REE bus]

rebut v. (**rebuts, rebutted, rebutting**) refute or disprove. □ **rebuttal** n. [Say re BUT, re BUT ul]

rec adj. **1** recreation. **2** recreational.

recalcitrant adj. **1** obstinately disobedient. **2** difficult to manage. [Say re KALSA trint]

recalculate v. (**recalculates, recalculated, recalculating**) calculate again. □ **recalculation** n.

recall ● v. **1** recollect, remember. **2** request the return of (a person, product, etc.). **3** serve as a reminder of. **4** revoke or annul. ● n. **1** the action of recalling. **2** a request for the return of a faulty product. **3** the ability to remember. **4** removal of an elected official from office.

recant v. say publicly that one no longer holds an opinion or belief. □ **recantation** n. **recanter** n.

recap informal ● v. (**recaps, recapped, recapping**) recapitulate. ● n. a recapitulation.

recapitulate v. (**recapitulates, recapitulated, recapitulating**) summarize what has been said etc. [Say re kuh PITCHA late]

recapitulation n. **1** the act of recapitulating. **2** Music part of a movement in which themes from the exposition are restated. [Say re kuh pitcha LAY sh'n]

recapture v. (**recaptures, recaptured, recapturing**) **1** capture again. **2** experience again.

recast v. (**recasts, recast, recasting**) put into a new form.

recede v. (**recedes, receded, receding**) **1** withdraw or move backwards, or appear to do so. **2** fade, become remote. **3** slope backwards. **4** decline. **5** withdraw or retreat from. **6** (of a person's hair) cease to grow at the front, sides, etc. [Sounds like RESEED]

receipt n. **1** the action of receiving something or the fact of its being received. **2** a printed or written acknowledgement of the acceptance of goods or payment of money. **3** (usu. in pl.) an amount of money etc. received. □ **in receipt of** having received. [Say re SEAT]

receivable ● adj. **1** capable of being received. **2** for which money has not yet been received. ● n. (in pl.) debts owed to a business.

receive v. (**receives, received, receiving**) **1** be given, or presented with, or paid. **2** accept or take delivery of. **3** pick up (broadcast signals). **4** Tennis be the player to whom the server serves the ball. **5** serve as a receptacle for. **6** suffer or be subject to. **7** meet with (a reaction). **8** entertain as a guest. **9** admit as a member. **10** Football be the player or team to whom the offensive team kicks the ball.

received adj. generally accepted as true.

receiver n. **1** a person or thing that receives. **2** the part of a machine that receives sound, signals, etc. **3** an apparatus, such as a radio, that receives signals transmitted as electromagnetic waves. **4** Football (also **wide receiver**) a player on the offensive team who catches passes from the quarterback.

receiver general n. (pl. **receivers general**) the official to whom all money owed to the government is sent.

receivership n. the state of a business having its property controlled by someone appointed by the government because it has gone bankrupt.

recent adj. **1** not long past. **2** not long established. □ **recently** adv.

receptacle n. **1** a container in which something is stored or deposited. **2** an electrical outlet. [Say re SEPTA cull]

reception n. **1** the action or process of receiving or being received. **2** the manner in which a person or thing is received or welcomed. **3** a formal social event to which guests are invited to mark some occasion, e.g. a wedding. **4** a place where guests or clients etc. report on arrival at a hotel, office, etc. **5 a** the receiving of broadcast signals. **b** the quality of this. **6** Football a catch of a ball thrown by the quarterback.

receptionist n. a person employed in an organization to welcome visitors, answer the telephone, etc.

receptive adj. **1** quick or able to receive ideas. **2** willing to hear or accept; open. **3** concerned with receiving stimuli etc. □ **receptivity** n. [Say re SEP tiv, re sep TIVVA tee]

receptor n. an organ or cell in the body that responds to a stimulus such as light and transmits a signal to a sensory nerve.

recess ● n. (pl. **recesses**) **1** a short break between classes. **2** a temporary cessation from work. **3** a space set back in a wall. **4** (often in pl.) a hidden or secret place. ● v. (**recesses, recessed, recessing**) **1** make a recess in. **2** set back. **3** adjourn. □ **recessed** adj. [Say RE sess]

recession n. **1** a temporary decline in economic activity. **2** a withdrawal from a place or point. **3** a receding part of an object. [Say re SESH'n]

recessionary *adj.* relating to a recession. [*Say* re SESH'n airy]

recessive *adj.* **1** (of an inherited characteristic) appearing in offspring only when not masked by a dominant characteristic. **2** tending to recede. **3** relating to an economic recession. [*Say* re SESS iv]

recharge ● *v.* (**recharges, recharged, recharging**) **1** refill. **2** restore an electric charge to. **3** be recharged. **4** recover energy by resting. ● *n.* a renewed charge. □ **rechargeable** *adj. & n.*

recharger *n.* a device for recharging batteries or equipment powered by batteries.

rechristen *v.* give a new name to. [*Say* re CHRIS in]

recidivist *n.* a person who relapses into crime. □ **recidivism** *n.* [*Say* re SID iv ist]

recipe *n.* **1** a statement of the ingredients and procedure required for preparing a dish. **2** a means of achieving something. [*Say* RESSA pee]

recipient *n.* a person who receives something. [*Say* re SIPPY unt]

reciprocal ● *adj.* **1** in return. **2** mutual. ● *n. Math* an expression or function so related to another that their product is one. □ **reciprocally** *adv.* [*Say* re SIPRA cull]

reciprocate *v.* (**reciprocates, reciprocated, reciprocating**) **1** return. **2** offer in return. **3** move backwards and forwards. [*Say* re SIPRA kate]

reciprocity *n.* (*pl.* **reciprocities**) the practice of exchanging things with others for mutual benefit. [*Say* ressa PROSSA tee]

recirculate *v.* (**recirculates, recirculated, recirculating**) circulate again. □ **recirculation** *n.*

recital *n.* **1** the performance of music, dance, etc. by a soloist or small group. **2** a long spoken description of a series of events. [*Say* re SITE ul]

recitative *n.* declamatory speech-like singing used esp. in opera. [*Say* ressa tuh TEEV]

recite *v.* (**recites, recited, reciting**) **1** repeat aloud from memory, esp. to an audience. **2** mention in order. **3** give a detailed account of. □ **recitation** *n.* [*Say* re SITE, ressa TAY shun]

reckless *adj.* disregarding the consequences. □ **recklessly** *adv.* **recklessness** *n.*

reckon *v.* **1** compute by calculation. **2 a** conclude after calculation. **b** *informal* think, suppose. **3** count on; base plans on.

4 consider. **5** include in computation. **6** make calculations. □ **to be reckoned with** (or **to reckon with**) important; not to be ignored.

reckoning *n.* **1** the act of calculating something. **2** an opinion. **3** the avenging of past mistakes or misdeeds.

reclaim *v.* **1** seek the return of. **2** make wasteland fit for cultivating. **3** recover raw material from waste products. □ **reclaimed** *adj.* **reclamation** *n.* [ree CLAME, reckla MAY sh'n]

reclassify *v.* (**reclassifies, reclassified, reclassifying**) classify again. □ **reclassification** *n.*

recline *v.* (**reclines, reclined, reclining**) lean or lie back in a relaxed position. □ **reclining** *adj.*

recliner *n.* a comfortable chair for reclining in.

recluse *n.* a person preferring seclusion. □ **reclusive** *adj.* [*Say* RECK loose *or* ruh KLOOSE, ruh KLOO siv]

recognition *n.* **1** the act of recognizing a person or thing. **2** the acknowledgement of a service, achievement, etc. **3** formal approval. [*Say* reck ug NISH'n]

recognizance *n.* **1** a legal commitment to appear when summoned etc. **2** a sum pledged as surety for this. [*Say* ruh COG niz ince]

recognize *v.* (**recognizes, recognized, recognizing**) **1** identify as already known. **2** discover the nature of. **3** realize or admit. **4** acknowledge the existence, validity, etc. of. **5** show appreciation of; acknowledge. **6** allow to speak in a debate etc. □ **recognizable** *adj.* **recognizably** *adv.*

recoil ● *v.* **1** suddenly move back in fear, horror, or disgust. **2** react to something with strong dislike or fear. **3** (of a gun) move suddenly backwards when it is fired. ● *n.* a sudden movement backwards.

recollect *v.* remember. [*Say* recka LECT]

recollection *n.* **1** the act of remembering something. **2** a memory.

recommend *v.* **1** suggest as suitable for some purpose, use, or position. **2** advise as a course of action etc. **3** make acceptable or desirable. □ **recommendable** *adj.* **recommendation** *n.*

recompense ● *v.* (**recompenses, recompensed, recompensing**) compensate a person for a loss, an expense, or for work completed. ● *n.* compensation or reward. [*Say* reck um PENCE]

reconcile *v.* (**reconciles, reconciled, reconciling**) **1** restore friendly relations between. **2** make someone accept something unwelcome. **3** cause to coexist in harmony. **4** settle (a quarrel). [*Say* RECK'n sile]

reconciliation *n.* **1** an end to a disagreement and the return to friendly relations. **2** the action of reconciling opposing ideas, facts, etc. **3** (in the Catholic and Orthodox Churches) a sacrament including confession of one's sins and forgiveness. **4** the action or practice of making one account consistent with another, esp. by allowing for transactions begun but not yet completed. [*Say* reck'n silly AY sh'n]

recondition *v.* **1** overhaul, renovate. **2** make usable again.

reconfigure *v.* (**reconfigures, reconfigured, reconfiguring**) configure again or differently. □ **reconfiguration** *n.*

reconnaissance *n.* a survey of a region, esp. a military examination to locate or ascertain strategic features. [*Say* re CONNA since]

reconnoitre ● *n.* an esp. military observation of an area. ● *v.* (**reconnoitres, reconnoitred, reconnoitring**) make a reconnoitre of. [*Say* recka NOY ter]

reconsider *v.* consider again. □ **reconsideration** *n.*

reconstitute *v.* (**reconstitutes, reconstituted, reconstituting**) **1** build up again from parts. **2** restore (dried food etc.) to its original state by adding water. □ **reconstitution** *n.*

reconstruct *v.* **1** build or form again. **2** create or act out (a past event) from the evidence. □ **reconstructive** *adj.*

reconstruction *n.* **1** the act of reconstructing. **2** (**Reconstruction**) *US hist.* the period (1865-77) following the Civil War.

reconvene *v.* (**reconvenes, reconvened, reconvening**) convene again, esp. after a pause.

record ● *n.* **1** a piece of evidence or information constituting an account of something. **2** the previous conduct or performance of a person or thing. **3** (also **criminal record**) a list of a person's previous criminal convictions. **4** the best performance or most remarkable event of its kind officially recognized. **5** a thin plastic disk carrying recorded sound in grooves. ● *v.* **1** make a record of. **2** convert (sound, a broadcast, etc.) into permanent form for later reproduction. □ **for the record** as an official statement etc. **go on record** state one's opinion officially. **a matter of record** a thing established as

a fact. **off the record** as an unofficial statement etc. **set the record straight** correct a misapprehension. □ **recordable** *adj.*

record-breaking *adj.* that breaks a record (*see* RECORD *n.* 4). □ **record-breaker** *n.*

recorder *n.* **1** an apparatus for recording. **2 a** a keeper of records. **b** a person who makes an official record. **3** a reedless wind instrument, played by blowing directly into one end while covering holes with the fingers.

recording *n.* **1** the process by which audio or video signals are recorded. **2** something recorded. **3** the disc, record, or tape so produced.

recount[1] *v.* give an account of something. [*Say* re COUNT]

recount[2] ● *v.* count again. ● *n.* a recounting, esp. of votes. [*Say* REE count]

recoup *v.* recover or regain something lost or spent. [*Say* re COOP]

recourse *n.* **1** the action of turning to a possible source of help, advice, protection, etc. **2** a person or thing turned to. □ **have recourse to** turn to (a person or thing) for help. [*Say* RE course]

re-cover *v.* **1** cover again. **2** provide with a new cover.

recover *v.* **1** regain possession or control of. **2** return to a normal state of health or consciousness. **3** regain (an amount of money spent or owed). **4** retrieve or make up for. **5** (**recover oneself**) regain composure. □ **recoverable** *adj.* **recovering** *adj.*

recovery *n.* (*pl.* **recoveries**) **1** the action or an act of recovering. **2** the room in a hospital where patients are kept immediately after an operation. **3** the process of overcoming an addiction to drugs etc. or recovering from mental illness.

recreate *v.* (**recreates, recreated, recreating**) create over again. [*Say* re CREATE]

recreation[1] *n.* something created again. [*Say* re CREATION]

recreation[2] *n.* **1** the process of entertaining oneself. **2** an activity or pastime pursued for pleasure. □ **recreational** *adj.* **recreationally** *adv.* [*Say* reck ree AY sh'n, reck ree AY sh'n ul]

recreational vehicle *n.* a van or camper used for recreational purposes.

recrimination *n.* an accusation in response to one from someone else. [*Say* re crimmin AY sh'n]

rec room *n.* a room in a house used for recreation.

recruit ● *n.* a newly recruited member, esp. of the armed forces. ● *v.* **1** enlist as a recruit. **2** attempt to hire or enrol (a person). □ **recruiter** *n.* **recruitment** *n.* [*Say* re CROOT]

recta *pl. of* RECTUM.

rectangle *n.* a plane figure with four straight sides and four right angles, esp. one with adjacent sides unequal. □ **rectangular** *adj.*

rectify *v.* (**rectifies, rectified, rectifying**) **1** adjust or make right; correct. **2** convert (alternating current) to direct current. □ **rectifiable** *adj.* **rectification** *n.* [*Say* RECK ti fie, reck ti FIE a bull, reck ti fi KAY sh'n]

rectilinear *adj.* bounded, moving in, or characterized by straight lines. [*Say* reck tuh LINNY er]

rectitude *n.* morally correct behaviour. [*Say* RECK ti tood *or* RECK ti tyood]

recto *n.* (*pl.* **rectos**) **1** the right-hand page of an open book. **2** the front of a printed leaf of paper.

rector *n.* **1** (in the Anglican Church) a clergyman in charge of a parish. **2** *Catholicism* a priest in charge of a church or religious institution. **3** the head of some schools, universities, and colleges. [*Say* RECKTER]

rectory *n.* (*pl.* **rectories**) a rector's house. [*Say* RECKTER ee]

rectum *n.* (*pl.* **rectums** or **recta**) the final section of the large intestine, ending at the anus. □ **rectal** *adj.*

recumbent *adj.* lying down. [*Say* re CUM bint]

recuperate *v.* (**recuperates, recuperated, recuperating**) recover from illness or exhaustion etc. □ **recuperation** *n.* **recuperative** *adj.* [*Say* re COOPER ate]

recur *v.* (**recurs, recurred, recurring**) **1** occur again; be repeated. **2** come back to one's mind. □ **recurrence** *n.* **recurrent** *adj.* **recurrently** *adv.* [*Say* re CURR, re CURRENT, re CURR ince]

recycle *v.* (**recycles, recycled, recycling**) **1** convert (waste) material into a form in which it can be reused. **2** use again. **3** convert into something new. □ **recyclable** *adj. & n.* **recycler** *n.* **recycling** *n.*

red ● *adj.* **1** of the colour of blood, fire, or rubies. **2** (of a face) red due to embarrassment etc. **3** (of hair or fur) reddish-brown. **4** (of wine) made from dark grapes. **5** *informal derogatory* communist or

socialist. **6** *Cdn* of the Liberal Party. ● *n.* **1** a red colour, pigment, or material. **2** *informal derogatory* communist or socialist. □ **in the red** in debt. □ **reddish** *adj.* **redness** *n.*

red alert *n.* **1** an urgent warning of imminent danger. **2** an instruction to prepare for an emergency.

Red Army *n.* **1** *hist.* the army of the Soviet Union (1917–1946). **2** the army of China or other (esp. Communist) countries.

red blood cell *n.* (also **red cell**) one of the principal cells in the blood of vertebrates, containing hemoglobin and transporting oxygen and carbon dioxide to and from tissues.

red-blooded *adj.* full of life, spirited.

redbud *n.* an early-flowering N American tree of the pea family.

redcap *n.* a railway porter.

red carpet *n.* a strip of red carpet laid down on formal occasions to greet important visitors.

red cedar *n.* a N American coniferous tree with reddish-brown bark and reddish wood.

red cent *n.* **1** the (originally copper) coin of the lowest value. **2** a trivial sum.

Red Chamber *n.* *Cdn* the Senate chamber of the Parliament Buildings.

redcoat *n.* *hist.* **1** *Cdn* a member of the North West Mounted Police. **2** a British soldier.

redcurrant *n.* a widely cultivated shrub bearing small, sweet, red berries.

red deer *n.* a large deer with a reddish-brown coat.

redden *v.* **1** make or become red. **2** blush.

redecorate *v.* (**redecorates, redecorated, redecorating**) decorate again or differently. □ **redecoration** *n.* [*Say* re DECORATE]

redeem *v.* **1 a** compensate for the faults or bad aspects of. **b** (**redeem oneself**) compensate for past failings. **2** save or deliver from sin or evil. **3** exchange a coupon etc. for goods or money. **4** gain or regain possession of in exchange for payment. **5** repay a debt. □ **redeemable** *adj.*

redeemer *n.* **1** a person who redeems. **2** (**Redeemer**) Jesus Christ.

redemption *n.* **1** the action of saving or being saved from sin, error, or evil. **2** an act or the process of erasing or compensating for the flaws of a person, a thing, or oneself. **3** a thing that saves someone from error or evil. **4** the action of regaining or gaining possession of something in exchange for payment, or clearing a debt. □ **beyond/past redemption** (of a person or thing) too bad to be saved or improved. □ **redemptive** *adj.*

Red Ensign *n.* a red flag having the Union Jack in the upper corner, e.g. one used as Canada's national flag until 1965 or one used as the ensign of the British merchant navy.

redeploy *v.* move (troops etc.) from one area of activity to another.
□ **redeployment** *n.* [*Say* re duh PLOY]

redevelop *v.* (**redevelops, redeveloped, redeveloping**) develop anew (esp. an urban area).
□ **redevelopment** *n.*

red-eye *n.* **1** a red reflection on a person's eye, seen on colour photographs taken with a flash. **2** (also **red-eye flight**) *informal* an overnight airline flight. **3** *Cdn* a drink made with tomato juice and beer.

red-faced *adj.* embarrassed, ashamed.

red flag *n.* **1** a warning of danger. **2** a red flag waved as a signal to stop.

red fox *n.* the common fox of Eurasia and N America.

red giant *n.* a very large star of high luminosity.

red-handed *adj.* in or just after the act of doing wrong.

redhead *n.* a person with red hair. □ **red-headed** *adj.*

red herring *n.* **1** dried smoked herring. **2** a misleading clue or distraction.

red-hot *adj.* **1 a** sufficiently hot to glow red. **b** very hot. **2** highly exciting. **3** (of news) sensational.

redial ● *v.* (**redials, redialed** or **redialled, redialing** or **redialling**) dial again. ● *n.* the facility on a telephone which enables a user to automatically dial the number just dialed by pressing a single button.

redid *past of* REDO. [*Say* re DID]

red ink *n.* financial deficit or debt.

redirect *v.* **1** use in a different, more desirable way. **2** send in a different direction. **3** change the address of (a letter).
□ **redirection** *n.*

redistribute *v.* (**redistributes, redistributed, redistributing**) distribute again or differently.
□ **redistribution** *n.* **redistributionist** *n.* & *adj.* **redistributive** *adj.*

red-letter day *n.* a day that is pleasantly noteworthy or memorable.

red-light district *n.* a district containing many brothels, strip clubs, etc.

red line ● *n.* **1** *Hockey* the centre line on the ice surface. **2** a red mark on a gauge etc. indicating the maximum safe value of speed or other quantity. ● *v.* (**redline**)

(**redlines, redlined, redlining**) refuse credit, loans, etc., to businesses or residents of a neighbourhood considered high-risk or less lucrative.

red maple *n.* a maple of eastern N America, with red twigs, buds, and flowers.

red mullet *n.* a red marine fish of the Mediterranean and northeastern Atlantic.

redneck *derogatory* ● *n.* a person holding reactionary political views. ● *adj.* reactionary.

redo *v.* (**redoes**; *past* **redid**; *past participle* **redone**; **redoing**) do again or differently.

redolent *adj.* **1** strongly reminiscent or suggestive. **2** having a strong fragrance or odour. □ **redolence** *n.* [*Say* REDDA lint, REDDA lince]

redouble *v.* (**redoubles, redoubled, redoubling**) make or grow greater or more numerous; intensify.

redoubt *n.* *Military* a type of fortification without flanking defences. [*Say* re DOUT]

redoubtable *adj.* **1** formidable. **2** (of a person) commanding respect.
[*Say* re DOUT a bull]

red pepper *n.* the ripe fruit of the sweet pepper.

redpoll *n.* a finch with a red crest.

redress ● *v.* (**redresses, redressed, redressing**) remedy or rectify (a wrong or grievance etc.). ● *n.* remedy or compensation for a wrong. [*Say* re DRESS *or* REE dress]

Red River cart *n.* *Cdn hist.* a sturdy two-wheeled wooden cart pulled by oxen or horses.

Red River Rebellion *n.* *Cdn hist.* an uprising in 1869–70 by the Metis in the Red River valley in Manitoba under Louis Riel.

red snapper *n.* an edible marine fish of the west Atlantic.

red squirrel *n.* a small N American squirrel with reddish fur.

redstart *n.* **1** any of various N and S American warblers with red markings. **2** a red-tailed European songbird.

red tape *n.* excessive bureaucracy or adherence to formalities.

red tide *n.* a discoloration of marine waters caused by an outbreak of toxic red organisms.

Red Tory *n.* *Cdn* a Conservative who holds more liberal views on certain esp. social issues. □ **Red Toryism** *n.*

reduce *v.* (**reduces, reduced, reducing**) **1** make or become smaller or less. **2** change (something) to (a simpler or more basic form). **3** bring to (an undesirable state). **4** boil (a sauce or other

liquid) so that it becomes thicker.
5 *Chemistry* cause to combine chemically
with hydrogen. **6** *Chemistry* cause to undergo
a reaction in which electrons are gained
from another substance or molecule.
□ **reducer** *n.* **reducible** *adj.*

reduced circumstances *pl. n.* a poorer
financial condition or situation.

reduction *n.* **1** the action or fact of
reducing. **2** an amount by which prices etc.
are reduced. **3** a smaller copy of a picture
etc. **4** an arrangement of an orchestral
score for piano etc. **5** a thick sauce made by
boiling.

reductionism *n.* often *derogatory* the
practice of describing a complex
phenomenon in terms of phenomena
which are held to represent a simpler or
more fundamental level. □ **reductionist**
n. **reductionistic** *adj.*

reductive *adj.* often *derogatory* that tries to
explain something complicated in an oversimplified way.

redundant *adj.* **1** no longer needed or
useful. **2** (of words) that can be omitted.
3 (of a person) no longer needed at work
and therefore unemployed. **4** *Engineering &
Computing* (of a component) not needed but
included in case of failure in another
component. □ **redundancy** *n.*
redundantly *adv.* [*Say* re DUN dint,
re DUN din see]

reduplicate *v.* (**reduplicates**,
reduplicated, **reduplicating**) repeat (a
letter or syllable) exactly or with a slight
change. □ **reduplication** *n.*
[*Say* re DUPLICATE]

red-winged blackbird *n.* a very
common North and Central American
blackbird, the male of which has a red
patch on the wings.

redwood *n.* an exceptionally large conifer
of California and Oregon, yielding red
wood.

reed *n.* **1** a water or marsh plant with tall
firm stems. **2** a pipe of reed or straw.
3 a the vibrating part of the mouthpiece of
some wind instruments, e.g. the oboe and
clarinet. **b** a reed instrument.

re-educate *v.* (**re-educates**, **re-
educated**, **re-educating**) educate
again, esp. to change a person's views or
beliefs. □ **re-education** *n.*

reedy *adj.* (**reedier**, **reediest**) **1** full of
reeds. **2** like a reed. **3** (of a voice) high, thin,
and harsh.

reef ● *n.* (*pl.* **reefs**) **1** a ridge of jagged rock,
coral, or sand just above or below the
surface of the sea. **2** a vein of ore, esp. one
containing gold. **3** each of several strips
across a sail that can be drawn in to reduce

the area exposed to the wind. ● *v.* take in a
reef of (a sail).

reefer *n.* **1** *slang* a marijuana cigarette. **2** a
close-fitting double-breasted jacket.

reef knot *n.* a double knot made to hold
securely and cast off easily.

reek ● *v.* smell strongly and unpleasantly.
● *n.* an unpleasant smell. □ **reeky** *adj.*

reel ● *n.* **1** a cylindrical device on which
film, tape, etc., is wound. **2** a device for
winding and unwinding a line as required.
3 a revolving part in various machines. **4** a
lively folk or Scottish dance. ● *v.* **1** wind on
a reel. **2** draw (fish etc.) in by the use of a
reel. **3** stagger. **4** be shaken mentally or
physically. □ **reel off** say or recite very
rapidly.

re-elect *v.* elect again. □ **re-election** *n.*

reel-to-reel *adj.* designating a tape
recorder in which the tape passes between
two reels mounted separately.

re-emerge *v.* (**re-emerges**, **re-
emerged**, **re-emerging**) emerge again;
come back out. □ **re-emergence** *n.*

re-enact *v.* act out (a past event). □ **re-
enactment** *n.*

re-engineer *v.* **1** design and construct
again. **2** change the structure of a business
or other organization. □ **re-
engineering** *n.*

re-enter *v.* **1** enter again. **2** participate in
again.

re-entry *n.* (*pl.* **re-entries**) the act of
entering again, esp. re-entering the earth's
atmosphere.

reeve *n.* *Cdn* (in some provinces) the elected
leader of the council of a town or other
municipality. □ **reeveship** *n.*

re-examine *v.* (**re-examines**, **re-
examined**, **re-examining**) examine
again or further (esp. a witness). □ **re-
examination** *n.*

ref *Sport informal* ● *n.* a referee. ● *v.* (**refs**,
reffed, **reffing**) supervise as a referee.

refer *v.* (**refers**, **referred**, **referring**)
1 allude (to) or describe. **2** represent;
pertain (to). **3** send or direct (someone) to a
person for help, advice, etc. **4** direct
(questions to be answered etc.) to someone.
5 consult (notes etc.) for information or
advice. **6** trace or attribute something to.

referee ● *n.* **1** an official who supervises a
game or sporting match to ensure that
players obey the rules. **2** a person whose
opinion or judgment is sought. **3** a person
appointed to assess an academic work for
publication. ● *v.* (**referees**, **refereed**,
refereeing) act as referee.
□ **refereed** *adj.*

reference ● *n.* **1 a** an allusion. **b** a

correspondence. **2 a** a book or passage of a book, esp. one used as a source of information for a research paper etc. **b** a useful source of information. **3 a** a testimonial supporting an applicant for employment etc. **b** a person giving this. ● *v.* (**references, referenced, referencing**) **1** cite. **2** provide (a book etc.) with references. □ **with** (or **in**) **reference to** regarding; as regards. □ **referential** *adj.* [*Say* reffer EN shul]

reference book *n.* a book meant to be consulted for information on individual matters.

reference library *n.* a library in which the books are for consultation, not loan.

referendum *n.* (*pl.* **referendums** or **referenda**) **1** the process of referring a political question to the electorate for a direct vote. **2** a vote taken by referendum.

referent *n.* the idea or thing that a word etc. symbolizes. [*Say* REFFER int]

referral *n.* the referring of an individual to an expert or specialist for advice. [*Say* re FUR ul]

refill ● *v.* fill again. ● *n.* **1** a replacement for something that has been used up. **2** a second serving, esp. of a beverage etc. □ **refillable** *adj.*

refinance *v.* (**refinances, refinanced, refinancing**) **1** finance again. **2** repay (a loan) by obtaining fresh loans. □ **refinancing** *n.* [*Say* re FINANCE]

refine *v.* (**refines, refined, refining**) **1** free from impurities or defects. **2** make or become more polished or cultured. **3** improve or perfect. □ **refined** *adj.* **refining** *n.*

refinement *n.* **1** the process of refining. **2** an improvement. **3** polish or elegance in behaviour or taste.

refiner *n.* a person or company whose business is to refine crude oil, sugar, etc.

refinery *n.* (*pl.* **refineries**) a place where oil etc. is refined.

refinish *v.* (**refinishes, refinished, refinishing**) **1** apply a new finish to (a surface). **2** remove old layers of paint or varnish from and apply new stain etc. to.

refit ● *v.* (**refits, refitted, refitting**) restore or be restored to a serviceable condition. ● *n.* a restoration or repair. □ **refitting** *n.*

reflect *v.* **1** throw back (heat, light, sound, etc.) from a surface. **2** (esp. of a mirror, water, etc.) reproduce or show an image of. **3** result from. **4** bring credit or discredit to. **5 a** meditate on. **b** consider.

reflection *n.* **1** the process of light, heat, or sound being reflected. **2 a** reflected

light, heat, or colour. **b** a reflected image. **3** careful consideration. **4** an indication. **5** an account or representation of something.

reflective *adj.* **1** (of a surface etc.) reflecting light, images, etc. **2** given to meditation. **3** indicative. □ **reflectively** *adv.*

reflector *n.* **1** a piece of glass or metal etc. for reflecting light in a required direction. **2** a telescope etc. using a mirror to produce images. **3** any surface which reflects light, heat, etc.

reflex ● *n.* (*pl.* **reflexes**) **1** an involuntary or automatic response to something. **2** (in *pl.*) the ability to react quickly, esp. dexterously. ● *adj.* **1** done as a reflex. **2** (of a reaction) immediate, unthinking.

reflexive *adj.* **1** triggered by, or as if by, reflex. **2** *Grammar* (of a word or form) referring back to the subject of a sentence. **3** *Grammar* (of a verb) having a reflexive pronoun as its object (as in *to wash oneself*). □ **reflexively** *adv.* **reflexivity** *n.* [*Say* re FLEX iv, reflex IVVA tee]

reflexology *n.* a system of massage used to relieve tension and treat illness. □ **reflexologist** *n.* [*Say* reflex OLLA jee, reflex OLLA jist]

refocus *v.* (**refocuses, refocused, refocusing**) **1** adjust the focus of. **2** focus attention on something new or different.

reforest *v.* plant again with trees. □ **reforestation** *n.*

reform ● *v.* **1** make or become better; improve. **2** abolish or cure (an abuse or vice). ● *n.* the action or an act of reforming. □ **reformed** *adj.* **reformer** *n.*

re-form *v.* form again.

reformation *n.* **1** the act of reforming or process of being reformed. **2** (**the Reformation**) *hist.* the 16th-century movement to reform the Catholic Church, which resulted in the establishment of the Protestant Churches. [*Say* reffer MAY sh'n]

reformatory *n.* (*pl.* **reformatories**) an institution for reforming young offenders. [*Say* re FORMA tory]

reformist ● *n.* an advocate of social, political, or religious reform. ● *adj.* of or pertaining to reformists. □ **reformism** *n.*

Reform Judaism *n.* a branch of Judaism which has reformed aspects of Orthodox Jewish worship and ritual.

reform school *n.* = REFORMATORY.

refract *v.* (of water, air, glass, etc.) deflect (a ray of light etc.) at a certain angle when it enters obliquely. □ **refracted** *adj.* **refraction** *n.* **refractive** *adj.*

refractor *n.* a refracting medium or lens. [*Say* re FRACTOR]

refractory *adj.* **1** stubborn, rebellious, unmanageable. **2** (of a wound, disease, etc.) not yielding to treatment. **3** (of a substance) hard to fuse or work. [*Say* re FRACTOR ee]

refrain[1] *v.* avoid doing; abstain.

refrain[2] *n.* **1** a recurring phrase, esp. at the ends of stanzas. **2** an often repeated idea or expression.

refresh *v.* (**refreshes, refreshed, refreshing**) **1 a** impart strength or energy to; invigorate. **b** revive with food, rest, etc. **2** stimulate (the memory), esp. by consulting the source of one's information. **3** replenish. □ **refreshed** *adj.*

refresher *n.* **1** something that refreshes, esp. a drink. **2** an update or review of previous education.

refreshing *adj.* **1** serving to refresh. **2** pleasantly new. **3** (of food or drink) cooling. □ **refreshingly** *adv.*

refreshment *n.* **1** the act of refreshing or the process of being refreshed. **2** food or drink.

refrigerate *v.* (**refrigerates, refrigerated, refrigerating**) make or become cool or cold, esp. so as to preserve. □ **refrigerant** *n.* **refrigerated** *adj.* **refrigeration** *n.*

refrigerator *n.* a cabinet or room in which food etc. is kept cold.

refuel *v.* (**refuels, refuelled, refuelling**) **1** replenish a fuel supply. **2** supply with more fuel.

refuge *n.* **1** a shelter from pursuit, danger, or trouble. **2** a person or place etc. offering this. □ **take refuge in** resort to as a means of escape or shelter. [*Say* REF yoodge]

refugee *n.* (*pl.* **refugees**) a person taking refuge, esp. in a foreign country, from war, persecution, etc.

refund ● *v.* **1** pay back (money). **2** reimburse (a person). ● *n.* **1** an act of refunding. **2** a sum refunded. □ **refundable** *adj.*

refurbish *v.* (**refurbishes, refurbished, refurbishing**) **1** brighten up, redecorate. **2** restore, repair. □ **refurbished** *adj.* **refurbishment** *n.* [*Say* re FUR bish]

refuse[1] *v.* (**refuses, refused, refusing**) **1** decline to take or accept (something offered). **2** adamantly decline. **3** withhold permission or consent. **4** decline to give (something requested); deny. □ **refusal** *n.*

refuse[2] *n.* formal garbage. [*Say* REF yooss]

refusenik *n.* **1** *hist.* a Jew in the former Soviet Union who was refused permission to emigrate to Israel. **2** a person who refuses to comply with rules or regulations. [*Say* re FUZE nick]

refute *v.* (**refutes, refuted, refuting**) **1** prove by argument that a statement or theory or the person proposing it is wrong; disprove, rebut. **2** deny or contradict a statement or accusation without argument or proof. □ **refutation** *n.* [*Say* re FYOOT, ref you TAY sh'n]

regain *v.* **1** obtain possession or use of after loss. **2** get back to.

regal *adj.* having to do with a monarch. □ **regally** *adv.* [*Say* REE gull, REE guh lee]

regale *v.* (**regales, regaled, regaling**) **1** entertain or divert with (talk etc.). **2** entertain lavishly with feasting. [*Say* re GAIL]

regalia *pl. n.* **1** any distinctive or elaborate clothes or accoutrements. **2** the decoration of royalty used esp. at coronations. [*Say* re GAIL yuh]

regard ● *v.* **1** look upon or view; consider. **2** esteem, value. **3** (of a thing) relate to. **4** gaze on steadily. ● *n.* **1** concern (for); proper consideration (of). **2** esteem. **3** a respect. **4** (in *pl.*) an expression of politeness in a letter. **5** a steady look. □ **with** (or **in**) **regard to** as concerns.

regarding *prep.* about, concerning.

regardless ● *adj.* without regard for. ● *adv.* anyway, nevertheless.

regatta *n.* (*pl.* **regattas**) a series of races of boats, yachts, etc. [*Say* re GATTA]

regency *n.* (*pl.* **regencies**) **1** the office or jurisdiction of regent. **2** a commission acting as regent. **3** the period of office of a regent or regency commission. [*Say* REE jin see]

regenerate ● *v.* (**regenerates, regenerated, regenerating**) **1** reconstitute in a new and improved form; revive. **2** bring or come into renewed existence. **3** grow again or cause (new tissue) to grow again. ● *adj.* **1** spiritually born again. **2** reformed. □ **regeneration** *n.* **regenerative** *adj.* [*Say* re JENNER ate *for the verb*, re JENNER it *for the adjective*; re jenner AY shun, re JENNER uh tiv]

regent ● *n.* a person appointed to administer a state because the monarch is a minor, absent, or incapacitated. ● *adj.* (after a noun) acting as regent. [*Say* REE jint]

reggae *n.* a West Indian style of popular music indigenous to the black culture of Jamaica. [*Say* REG ay]

regime *n.* **1 a** a method of government, esp. one that is considered to be oppressive. **b** a period in which such a government is in power. **2** a system of managing or organizing something. **3** a (medical) regimen. [*Say* ray ZHEEM]

regimen *n.* **1** *Medical* a prescribed course of exercise, diet, etc. **2** a strict routine or schedule. [*Say* REDGE a men]

regiment *n.* **1** a permanent unit of an army. **2** a large array or number. □ **regimental** *adj.* **regimentation** *n.* [*Say* REDGE a mint]

regimented *adj.* **1** characterized by strict discipline or order. **2** organized according to an order or system. [*Say* REDGE uh ment ed]

Regina *n.* the reigning queen (following a name or in the titles of lawsuits). [*Say* re JYE nuh *or* re JEE nuh]

Regina Manifesto *n. Cdn hist.* the declaration of principles and objectives adopted by the Co-operative Commonwealth Federation in 1933. [*Say* re JYE nuh]

Reginan *n.* a native or inhabitant of Regina. □ **Reginan** *adj.* [*Say* re JYE nun]

region *n.* **1** an area of land or division of the earth's surface having definable features. **2 a** the area of land outside a principal city. **b** (in *pl.*) esp. *Cdn* the areas away from the political centre. **3** a part of the body. **4** a relatively large administrative division of a country or province. □ **in the region of** approximately. □ **regional** *adj.* **regionally** *adv.*

regionalism *n.* **1** the theory or practice of regional rather than central systems of administration. **2** allegiance to or concern for one's region rather than one's country. **3** a linguistic feature, custom, etc. peculiar to a particular region. □ **regionalist** *n. & adj.*

regionalize *v.* (**regionalizes, regionalized, regionalizing**) **1** bring under the control of a region for administrative purposes. **2** divide into regions. □ **regionalization** *n.*

register ● *n.* **1** an official list or record. **2** a device that records information automatically. **3** a device used to store information within a computer system. **4** an adjustable plate for regulating the passage of air, heat, smoke, etc. **5 a** the range of tones of a voice or instrument. **b** a part of this range. **6** *Linguistics* each of several forms of a language (colloquial, formal, etc.) usually used in particular circumstances. ● *v.* **1** set down or record in a register. **2 a** check into a hotel. **b** enrol in a course etc. **3 a** (of an instrument) record automatically; indicate. **b** (of temperature, winds, etc.) be or reach a certain figure when measured. **4 a** express (an emotion) facially or by gesture. **b** (of an emotion)

show. **5** make an impression. **6** entrust (a letter etc.) to a post office for transmission by registered mail. □ **registrant** *n.*

registered *adj.* **1** recorded; officially set down. **2** officially licensed; certified. **3** signed up; enrolled.

Registered Education Savings Plan *n. Cdn* = RESP.

registered mail *n.* a postal procedure with special precautions for safety and for compensation in case of loss.

registered nurse *n.* a nurse who is licensed to practise and is a registered member of a nurses' association.

Registered Retirement Income Fund *n. Cdn* = RRIF.

Registered Retirement Savings Plan *n. Cdn* = RRSP.

registrar *n.* **1** an official responsible for keeping official records. **2** an official at an educational institution responsible for maintaining records. **3** *Cdn & Brit. Law* a judicial and administrative officer responsible for issuing and filing court documents. [*Say* REDGE iss trar]

registration *n.* **1** the action of registering. **2** the form or certificate that verifies that something has been registered.

registry *n.* (*pl.* **registries**) **1** a place or office where registers or records are kept. **2** registration. **3** a list of gifts requested e.g. by a couple to be married, kept at a store for consultation by gift buyers.

registry office *n. Cdn* **1** a government office where private property may be registered and where records of ownership are kept. **2** a government office where records of births, deaths, and marriages are kept.

regress *v.* (**regresses, regressed, regressing**) return to a previous or less advanced state. □ **regression** *n.* [*Say* re GRESS, re GRESH'n]

regressive *adj.* **1** returning to a former or less developed state. **2** (of a tax) taking a proportionally greater amount from those on lower incomes. [*Say* re GRESS iv]

regret ● *v.* (**regrets, regretted, regretting**) **1** feel or express sorrow or distress over. **2** express polite apologies for. ● *n.* **1** a feeling of sorrow, repentance, disappointment, etc. **2** an (esp. formal) expression of disappointment at an inability to comply etc. □ **give** (or **send**) **one's regrets** formally decline an invitation.

regretful *adj.* feeling or showing regret. □ **regretfully** *adv.*

regrettable *adj.* (of events or conduct)

unfortunate, unwelcome.
□ **regrettably** adv.

regroup v. **1** group or arrange again or differently. **2** become organized before attempting something again.

regular ● adj. **1** arranged or recurring in a constant or definite pattern. **2** doing the same thing often or at uniform intervals. **3** done or happening frequently. **4** conforming to or governed by an accepted standard. **5** usual. **6** Grammar (of a word) following the normal pattern of inflection. **7** of or belonging to the permanent professional armed forces of a country. **8** of an ordinary kind. **9** Geometry (of a figure) having all sides and all angles equal. ● n. **1** informal a regular customer, visitor, etc. **2** a regular soldier. □ **regularity** n. **regularization** n. **regularize** v. (**regularizes, regularized, regularizing**). **regularly** adv.

regulate v. (**regulates, regulated, regulating**) **1** govern or control by law. **2** keep regular; maintain the health of. **3** adapt to requirements. **4** alter the speed of (a machine or clock). □ **regulator** n.

regulation n. **1** the action or process of regulating or being regulated. **2** a rule or directive made and maintained by an authority. **3** (as an adj.) in accordance with regulations.

regulation time n. Sport the time normally allotted for the completion of a game.

regulatory adj. having to do with a regulation or regulations.
[Say REGG you luh tory]

regurgitate v. (**regurgitates, regurgitated, regurgitating**) **1** bring (swallowed food) up again to the mouth. **2** repeat information without comprehending it. □ **regurgitation** n.
[Say re GURGE uh tate]

rehab n. informal rehabilitation.
[Say REE hab]

rehabilitate v. (**rehabilitates, rehabilitated, rehabilitating**) **1** restore (a person) to effectiveness or normal life by training etc., esp. after imprisonment, injury, or illness. **2** recondition. **3** restore the reputation of. □ **rehabilitation** n. **rehabilitative** adj. [Say re huh BILLA tate, re huh billa TAY sh'n, re huh BILLA tay tiv]

rehash ● v. (**rehashes, rehashed, rehashing**) put (old material) into a new form without significant change or improvement. ● n. (pl. **rehashes**) the reuse of old ideas or material.

rehearsal n. a trial performance or practice of a play, ceremony, etc.

rehearse v. (**rehearses, rehearsed, rehearsing**) **1** practise (a play, recital, etc.) for later public performance. **2** hold a rehearsal. **3** train by rehearsal. **4** recite or say over. **5** state a list of points.

rehydrate v. (**rehydrates, rehydrated, rehydrating**) absorb or cause to absorb water again after dehydration.
□ **rehydration** n.

reign ● v. **1** hold royal office; be a monarch. **2** (often **reign supreme**) prevail; hold sway. **3** (of a winner etc.) be currently holding the title etc. ● n. **1** sovereignty, rule. **2** the period of rule of a sovereign. **3** a period during which something holds sway. □ **reigning** adj.
[Sounds like RAIN]

reign of terror n. (pl. **reigns of terror**) **1** a period of remorseless repression or bloodshed. **2** (**Reign of Terror**; also **the Terror**) the period of the French Revolution when the ruling Jacobin faction ruthlessly executed anyone considered a threat to their regime.

reiki n. a supposed healing technique in which a therapist channels energy into a patient by means of touch. [Say RAY key]

reimburse v. (**reimburses, reimbursed, reimbursing**) repay; pay back. □ **reimbursement** n.
[Say re im BURSE]

rein ● n. (in sing. or pl.) **1** a long narrow strap attached to a horse's bit, used to guide a horse etc. **2** a means of control. ● v. **1** check or manage with reins. **2** pull up or back with reins. **3** govern, restrain, control. □ **free** (or **full**) **rein** complete freedom of action. **keep a tight rein on** allow little freedom to. [Sounds like RAIN]

reincarnation n. **1** the rebirth of a soul in a new body. **2** a new embodiment of a person, idea, etc. □ **reincarnate** v.
[Say re in car NAY sh'n, re in CAR nate or re in car NATE]

reindeer n. (pl. **reindeer**) a subarctic deer, of which both sexes have large antlers.

reinforce v. (**reinforces, reinforced, reinforcing**) strengthen or support, esp. with additional personnel or material.

reinforcement n. **1** the act of reinforcing. **2** a thing that reinforces. **3** (in pl.) extra personnel etc. sent to strengthen an army or similar force.

reinstate v. (**reinstates, reinstated, reinstating**) restore to a former position or state. □ **reinstatement** n.
[Say re in STATE]

reintroduce v. (**reintroduces, reintroduced, reintroducing**) **1** introduce again. **2** introduce (a species) to

a place it formerly inhabited.
□ **reintroduction** n.

reinvent v. **1** invent again. **2** change something so much that it appears to be something completely new. □ **reinvent the wheel** waste effort by doing something that has already been done. □ **reinvention** n.

reinvigorate v. (**reinvigorates, reinvigorated, reinvigorating**) impart fresh vigour to.

reissue ● v. (**reissues, reissued, reissuing**) issue again or in a different form. ● n. a new issue.

reiterate v. (**reiterates, reiterated, reiterating**) say again or repeatedly. □ **reiteration** n. [Say re ITTER ate]

reject ● v. **1** refuse to accept (something faulty or unsatisfactory). **2** refuse to believe in. **3** fail to give due care or affection. **4** (of the body) not accept (a transplanted organ). ● n. a thing or person rejected. □ **rejection** n.

rejig v. (**rejigs, rejigged, rejigging**) Cdn & Brit. reconfigure, rearrange.

rejoice v. (**rejoices, rejoiced, rejoicing**) **1** feel or show great joy. **2** be glad. □ **rejoicing** n.

rejoin[1] v. **1** reunite. **2** join again.

rejoin[2] v. say in answer.

rejoinder n. a reply, esp. a witty one.

rejuvenate v. (**rejuvenates, rejuvenated, rejuvenating**) **1** make young or as if young again. **2** inject new vigour or liveliness into. □ **rejuvenation** n.

relapse ● v. (**relapses, relapsed, relapsing**) **1** experience a return of an illness after a recovery. **2** fall back to a worse state, practice, etc. ● n. **1** a deterioration in someone's health after a temporary improvement. **2** a lapse back into a previous less desirable state. [Say REE laps]

relate v. (**relates, related, relating**) **1** narrate or recount. **2** connect by blood or marriage. **3** establish a connection between. **4** have reference to. **5** understand or have empathy for.

related adj. **1** connected by blood or marriage. **2** associated or connected. □ **relatedness** n.

relation n. **1** the way in which one person or thing is related to another. **2** a relative. **3** (in pl.) **a** dealings, rapport. **b** sexual intercourse. **4** = RELATIONSHIP. **5 a** narration. **b** a narrative. □ **in relation to** as regards. □ **relational** adj.

relationship n. **1** the fact or state of being related. **2 a** a connection or association.

b an emotional (esp. sexual) association between two people. **3** kinship.

relative ● adj. **1** considered or having significance in relation to something else. **2** proportionate to (something else). **3 a** comparative. **b** in relation to. **4** related to each other. **5** relating, relevant. ● n. **1** a person connected by blood or marriage. **2** a species related to another by common origin. □ **relatively** adv.

relative clause n. a clause attached to an antecedent by a relative pronoun.

relative pronoun n. a pronoun referring to an antecedent and attaching a subordinate clause to it, e.g. who in the man who screamed.

relativism n. the doctrine or belief that truth, morality, etc., are relative and not absolute. □ **relativist** n. **relativistic** adj.

relativity n. **1** the fact or state of being relative. **2** Physics (also **special theory of relativity**) a description of matter, energy, space, and time according to Einstein's theories.

relaunch ● v. (**relaunches, relaunched, relaunching**) launch again in a new or different way. ● n. a relaunching of something.

relax v. (**relaxes, relaxed, relaxing**) **1 a** make or become less stiff or rigid or tense. **b** become at ease etc. **2** make or become less formal or strict. **3** reduce (one's attention etc.). **4** cease work or effort. □ **relaxed** adj. **relaxer** n. **relaxing** adj.

relaxant n. a drug etc. that reduces tension and produces relaxation.

relaxation n. **1** the act of relaxing or state of being relaxed. **2** recreation or rest.

relay ● n. **1** a set of people etc. appointed to relieve others or to operate in shifts. **2** (also **relay race**) a race between teams of which each member in turn covers part of the distance. **3** a device activating changes in an electric circuit etc. in response to other changes affecting itself. **4** a device etc. which receives, amplifies, and transmits a signal. ● v. receive (a message etc.) and transmit it to others. **2 a** arrange in relays. **b** provide with relays.

release ● v. (**releases, released, releasing**) **1** set free from confinement. **2** free from an obligation or duty. **3** allow to move freely. **4** allow (information) to be generally available. **5** make (a film or recording) available to the public. ● n. **1** the action of releasing or being released. **2** a film or other product released to the public. **3** a handle or catch that releases part of a mechanism.

relegate v. (**relegates, relegated, relegating**) consign or dismiss to an

inferior position, category, etc.
□ **relegation** n. [Say RELLA gate]

relent v. **1** finally agree to something after refusing. **2** relax one's severity. [Say re LENT]

relentless adj. **1** unrelenting; insistent. **2** oppressively constant. □ **relentlessly** adv. **relentlessness** n. [Say re LENT liss]

relevant adj. **1** closely connected or appropriate to the matter at hand. **2** having ideas that are useful to people in their lives and work. □ **relevance** n. **relevantly** adv. [Say RELLA vint, RELLA vince]

reliable adj. that may be relied on. □ **reliability** n. **reliably** adv.

reliance n. dependence; the act or state of relying on something. □ **reliant** adj.

relic n. **1** an object interesting because of its association with the past. **2** a part of a deceased holy person's body or belongings etc. kept as an object of reverence. **3** a surviving custom, belief, etc. from a past age. **4** a memento or souvenir. [Say RELLICK]

relict n. a thing surviving from a previous period. [Say RELL ict]

relief n. **1** a feeling of reassurance and relaxation following release from anxiety or distress. **2** a cause of relief. **3** a break in a tense or boring situation. **4** assistance given to those in need or difficulty. **5** a person or group replacing others who have been on duty. **6** a method of moulding, carving, etc. in which the design stands out from the surface. **7** Geog. difference in height from the surrounding terrain.

relieve v. (**relieves, relieved, relieving**) **1** bring or provide aid or assistance to. **2** alleviate or reduce (pain etc.). **3** mitigate the tedium of. **4** bring military support for (a besieged place). **5** release (a person) from a duty by taking their place. **6** take (a burden) away from. **7** bring into relief. □ **relieve oneself** urinate or defecate. □ **relieved** adj. **reliever** n.

religion n. **1** the belief in a superhuman controlling power, esp. in a God or gods. **2** a particular system of faith and worship.

religiosity n. the condition of being esp. excessively religious. [Say re lidge ee OSSA tee]

religious ● adj. **1** devoted to religion; devout. **2** of or concerned with religion. **3** scrupulous, conscientious. ● n. (pl. **religious**) a person bound by religious vows. □ **religiously** adv.

relinquish v. (**relinquishes, relinquishing, relinquishing**) give up, let go of. □ **relinquishment** n. [Say re LINK wish]

relish ● n. (pl. **relishes**) **1** great liking or enjoyment. **2 a** an appetizing flavour. **b** an attractive quality. **3** a condiment eaten with plain food to add flavour. ● v. (**relishes, relished, relishing**) **1** enjoy greatly. **2** look forward to. [Say RELL ish]

relive v. (**relives, relived, reliving**) live (an experience etc.) over again, esp. in the imagination.

relocate v. (**relocates, relocated, relocating**) **1** locate in a new place. **2** move to a new place. □ **relocation** n.

reluctant adj. unwilling or disinclined. □ **reluctance** n. **reluctantly** adv.

rely v. (**relies, relied, relying**) **1** depend on with confidence. **2** be dependent on.

REM abbr. RAPID EYE MOVEMENT.

remain v. **1** be left over. **2** be left behind. **3** continue to be. □ **remain to be seen** be not yet known. □ **remaining** adj.

remainder ● n. **1** a part or number remaining or left over. **2** a number left after division or subtraction. **3** a book left unsold when it is no longer in great demand. ● v. dispose of at a reduced price.

remains pl. n. **1** what remains. **2** relics of antiquity. **3** a person's body after death.

remake ● v. (**remakes, remade, remaking**) make again or differently. ● n. a thing that has been remade.

remand ● v. return (a prisoner) to custody, esp. while awaiting trial. ● n. **1** a re-committal to custody. **2** the state of having been remanded. [Say re MAND]

remark ● v. **1 a** say by way of comment. **b** take notice of. **2** make a comment. ● n. **1** a comment. **2** the act of noticing or commenting.

remarkable adj. **1** worth notice. **2** striking. □ **remarkably** adv.

remarry v. (**remarries, remarried, remarrying**) marry again. □ **remarriage** n.

remaster v. (often as **remastered** adj.) rework or adjust the master of (a recording). □ **remastering** n.

rematch n. (pl. **rematches**) a second match between the same opponents.

remedial adj. **1** serving or meant as a remedy. **2** for learners requiring special attention. [Say re MEEDY ul]

remedy ● n. (pl. **remedies**) **1** a medicine or treatment (for a disease etc.). **2** a means of counteracting anything undesirable. ● v. (**remedies, remedied, remedying**) rectify; make good. [Say REMMA dee]

remember v. **1** keep in the memory; not forget. **2 a** call to mind. **b** have in mind. **3** think of or acknowledge (a person) in some connection. **4** convey greetings from (one person) to (another).

remembrance n. **1** the act of remembering. **2** a memory. **3** a keepsake or souvenir. **4** a gift made in remembrance of another.

Remembrance Day n. (in Canada) 11 Nov., the anniversary of the armistice at the end of World War I.

remind v. **1** cause (a person) to remember or think of. **2** cause (a person) to remember to do something.

reminder n. **1** a thing that reminds, esp. a letter or bill. **2** a memento or souvenir.

reminisce v. (**reminisces, reminisced, reminiscing**) indulge in remembering events from one's past. [*Say* remma NISS]

reminiscence n. **1** the recalling of one's past, esp. with enjoyment. **2 a** a past fact or experience that is remembered. **b** the process of narrating this. **3** (**reminiscences**) a collection in literary form of incidents that a person remembers. □ **reminiscent** adj. [*Say* remma NISS ince, remma NISS'nt]

remiss adj. careless of duty; negligent. [*Say* re MISS]

remission n. **1** a period during which a serious illness improves for a time. **2** Cdn & Brit. the reduction of a prison sentence on account of good behaviour etc. **3** the remitting of a debt or penalty etc. **4** forgiveness (of sins etc.). [*Say* re MISSION]

remit v. (**remits, remitted, remitting**) **1** cancel (a debt or punishment etc.). **2** send (money etc.) in payment. **3** refer (a matter for decision etc.) to some authority. [*Say* re MITT]

remittance n. **1** money sent in payment. **2** the act of sending money. [*Say* re MITT ince]

remix ● v. (**remixes, remixed, remixing**) mix (esp. a recording) again. ● n. (pl. **remixes**) a sound recording that has been remixed. □ **remixer** n.

remnant n. **1** a small remaining quantity. **2** a piece of cloth etc. left when the greater part has been used or sold. **3** a surviving trace.

remodel v. (**remodels, remodelled, remodelling**) **1** model again or differently. **2** change the structure of; reconstruct. □ **remodelling** n.

remonstrate v. (**remonstrates, remonstrated, remonstrating**) make a protest; argue forcibly. □ **remonstrance** n. [*Say* REM in strate]

remorse n. deep regret for a wrong

committed. □ **remorseful** adj. [*Say* re MORSE]

remorseless adj. **1** cruel without remorse. **2** relentless. □ **remorselessly** adv.

remote (**remoter, remotest**) ● adj. **1** far away in place or time. **2** out of the way; situated away from the main centres. **3** distantly related. **4** slight, faint. **5** aloof; not friendly. **6** widely different. **7** situated or occurring at or from a distance. ● n. a remote control. □ **remotely** adv. **remoteness** n.

remote control n. **1** control of a machine or apparatus from a distance by means of signals transmitted from a radio or electronic device. **2** such a device. □ **remote-controlled** adj.

removal n. **1** the action of removing. **2** dismissal. **3** the abolition of something.

remove ● v. (**removes, removed, removing**) **1** take off or away from the position occupied. **2 a** move or take to another place. **b** get rid of; eliminate. **3** take away. **4** dismiss from office. **5** informal kill, assassinate. ● n. **1** a degree of remoteness. **2** a stage in a gradation. □ **removable** adj. **remover** n.

removed adj. (esp. of cousins) separated by a specified number of steps of descent.

remunerate v. (**remunerates, remunerated, remunerating**) pay for services rendered. □ **remuneration** n. **remunerative** adj. [*Say* re MYOONA rate, re MYOONA ruh tiv]

Renaissance n. **1** the period in Western European history in the 14th–16th centuries marked by advances in art and literature under the influence of classical models. **2** the style of art, architecture, etc. developed during this era. **3** (**renaissance**) a revival. [*Say* RENNA sonce or re NAY sonce]

Renaissance man n. a person with many talents or pursuits.

renal adj. of or concerning the kidneys. [*Say* REE null]

rend v. (**rends, rent, rending**) **1** split or divide in pieces. **2** cause emotional pain to. □ **rend the air** sound piercingly.

render v. **1** cause to be or become; make. **2** give or pay (money, service, etc.). **3 a** give (assistance). **b** show (obedience etc.). **4 a** submit; send in. **b** hand down (a verdict). **5** represent or portray artistically etc. **6** translate. **7** melt down (fat etc.) esp. to clarify. □ **rendering** n.

rendezvous ● n. (pl. **rendezvous**) **1** a meeting place. **2** a meeting by arrangement. **3** a place appointed for assembling troops etc. ● v.

(**rendezvouses, rendezvoused, rendezvousing**) meet at a rendezvous. [*Say* RON day voo *for the singular,* RON day vooz *for the plural*]

rendition *n.* **1** a performance of a dramatic role, piece of music, etc. **2** a translation. **3** a visual representation.

renegade ● *n.* **1** a person who leaves one political, religious, etc. group to join another. **2** a person who opposes a group or society that they used to belong to. ● *adj.* traitorous, rebellious. [*Say* RENNA gade]

renege *v.* (**reneges, reneged, reneging**) go back on one's word; change one's mind. [*Say* re NEG *or* re NAIG]

renegotiate *v.* (**renegotiates, renegotiated, renegotiating**) negotiate again or on different terms. □ **renegotiation** *n.* [*Say* re nuh GO she ate]

renew *v.* **1** revive; make new again. **2** reinforce; replace. **3** resume after an interruption. **4** get, begin, etc. anew. **5 a** extend the period of validity of (a licence, subscription, etc.). **b** extend the period of loan of (a library book). □ **renewal** *n.*

renewable *adj.* **1** able to be renewed. **2** (of energy etc.) not depleted by utilization.

rennet *n.* **1** curdled milk found in the stomach of a calf, used in curdling milk for cheese etc. **2** a preparation made from the stomach membrane of a calf, used for the same purpose. [*Say* REN it]

reno *n.* (*pl.* **renos**) *Cdn informal* **1** a renovated house. **2** renovation. [*Say* RENNO]

renounce *v.* (**renounces, renounced, renouncing**) **1** consent formally to abandon; surrender. **2** refuse to recognize any longer. **3 a** decline further association with. **b** discontinue; forsake.

renovate *v.* (**renovates, renovated, renovating**) **1** remodel or install new fixtures etc. in. **2** restore to good condition. □ **renovation** *n.* **renovator** *n.*

renown *n.* fame; high distinction. □ **renowned** *adj.* [*Say* re NOWN (NOWN *rhymes with* CROWN)]

rent¹ ● *n.* **1** a regular payment made by a tenant for the use of land or premises. **2** payment for the use of equipment etc. ● *v.* **1** pay someone for the use of. **2** let someone use (something) in return for rent. □ **rentable** *adj.* **renter** *n.*

rent² *n.* a large tear.

rent³ *past and past participle of* REND.

rental ● *n.* **1** the amount paid or received as rent. **2** the act of renting. **3** something rented. ● *adj.* **1** of or relating to rent. **2** available for rent.

renunciation *n.* the formal rejection of something. [*Say* re nun see AY sh'n]

reoccur *v.* (**reoccurs, reoccurred, reoccurring**) occur again or habitually. □ **reoccurrence** *n.*

reoffend *v.* offend again; commit a further (esp. criminal) offence.

reorder ● *v.* **1** put in order again. **2** repeat an order for (a product). ● *n.* a repeated order for a product etc.

reorganize *v.* (**reorganizes, reorganized, reorganizing**) **1** organize differently. **2** restructure the management of (a corporation). □ **reorganization** *n.* **reorganizer** *n.*

reorient *v.* **1** give a new direction to. **2** help (a person) find his or her bearings. **3** change the outlook of. **4** (**reorient oneself**) adjust oneself to something. □ **reorientate** *v.* **reorientation** *n.*

rep¹ *n. informal* **1** a representative. **2** repertory. **3** reputation. **4** repetition (of an exercise).

rep² *n. Cdn* = REP LEAGUE.

repackage *v.* (**repackages, repackaged, repackaging**) **1** package again or differently. **2** present in a new form. □ **repackaging** *n.*

repaid *past and past participle of* REPAY.

repair ● *v.* **1 a** restore to good condition after damage or wear. **b** renovate or mend by replacing or fixing parts. **c** set right. **2** go, make one's way. ● *n.* **1** the action of repairing something. **2** the result of this. **3** the condition of an object. □ **repairable** *adj.* **repairer** *n.*

repairman *n.* (*pl.* **repairmen**) a person who repairs things.

reparation *n.* **1** the making of amends for a wrong. **2** compensation for war damage paid by the defeated country. [*Say* reppa RAY sh'n]

repartee *n.* quick, witty comments or replies. [*Say* rep ar TAY *or* rep ar TEE]

repast *n. formal* a meal. [*Say* re PAST]

repatriate *v.* (**repatriates, repatriated, repatriating**) **1 a** restore (a person) to his or her native land. **b** return to one's own native land. **2** bring (legislation) under the authority of the autonomous country to which it applies. □ **repatriation** *n.* [*Say* re PAY tree ate]

repay *v.* (**repays, repaid, repaying**) **1** pay back (money). **2** return (a visit etc.). **3** make repayment to (a person). **4** give in recompense. □ **repayable** *adj.* **repayment** *n.*

rep by pop *n. Cdn hist.* = REPRESENTATION BY POPULATION.

repeal ● *v.* revoke or annul (a law etc.). ● *n.* the action of repealing a law.

repeat ● *v.* **1** say or do again. **2** (**repeat oneself**) say the same thing again. **3** (**repeat itself**) occur again in the same way or form. **4** (of food) be tasted again after being swallowed, as a result of indigestion. ● *n.* **1** an instance of repeating or being repeated. **2** a repeated broadcast. **3** *Music* a passage intended to be repeated. □ **repeatability** *n.* **repeatable** *adj.* **repeated** *adj.* **repeatedly** *adv.*

repeater *n.* **1** a person or thing that repeats. **2** a firearm which fires several shots without loading again. **3** a device for the automatic further transmission of an electrically transmitted message.

repel *v.* (**repels, repelled, repelling**) **1** drive back; ward off. **2** refuse admission or acceptance to. **3** be repulsive to. **4** resist mixing with or admitting. □ **repeller** *n.* [*Say* re PELL]

repellent ● *adj.* **1** able to repel a particular thing. **2** disgusting, repulsive. ● *n.* (also **repellant**) **1** a substance that repels. **2** a substance used to waterproof fabric etc. □ **repellency** *n.* [*Say* re PELL'nt, re PELL'n see]

repent *v.* **1** regret (one's wrongdoing etc.); resolve not to continue. **2** feel deep regret or remorse. □ **repentance** *n.* **repentant** *adj.*

repercussion *n.* **1** an indirect effect following an event or action. **2** the recoil after impact. **3** an echo or reverberation. [*Say* ree pur KUSH'n or ree pur KUSH'n (KUSH *rhymes with* MUSH)]

repertoire *n.* **1** a stock of pieces etc. that a company or performer knows or regularly performs. **2** all of the works existing in a particular artistic genre. [*Say* REPPER twar *or* REPPA twar (TWAR *rhymes with* FAR)]

repertory *n.* (*pl.* **repertories**) **1** = REPERTOIRE. **2** the performance of various theatrical productions for short periods in rotation by one company. **3** a company performing repertory. **4** a collection. [*Say* REPPER tory *or* REPPA tory]

repertory theatre *n.* **1** a theatre at which plays are performed for short runs. **2** a movie theatre at which esp. second-run films are shown.

repetition *n.* **1 a** the fact or an instance of repeating something. **b** the recurrence of an action or event. **2** a thing repeated. **3** a training exercise which is repeated. [*Say* reppa TISH'n]

repetitious *adj.* (esp. of speech or writing) having much repetition. [*Say* reppa TISH us]

repetitive *adj.* **1** saying or doing the same thing many times. **2** repeated many times. □ **repetitively** *adv.* **repetitiveness** *n.* [*Say* re PETTA tive]

repetitive strain injury *n.* injury arising from the prolonged use of particular muscles.

rephrase *v.* (**rephrases, rephrased, rephrasing**) express in an alternative way. [*Say* re PHRASE]

replace *v.* (**replaces, replaced, replacing**) **1** put back in place. **2** take the place of; succeed. **3** provide a substitute for. **4** fill up the place of. □ **replaceable** *adj.*

replacement *n.* **1** the act of replacing one thing with another. **2** a person or thing that replaces another.

replay ● *v.* **1** play back (a recording etc.). **2** play (a game etc.) again. **3** go over in one's mind. ● *n.* **1** the playing again of a section of a recording. **2** an occurrence which closely follows the pattern of a previous event.

rep league *n. Cdn* a league in children's sports for players with stronger abilities, usu. more competitive than house leagues, and requiring players to pass tryouts.

replenish *v.* (**replenishes, replenished, replenishing**) **1** fill up again. **2** renew. □ **replenishment** *n.* [*Say* re PLEN ish]

replete *adj.* **1** filled or well-supplied with. **2** very full of food. [*Say* re PLEET]

replica *n.* (*pl.* **replicas**) **1** a facsimile, an exact copy. **2** a duplicate of a work made by the original artist. [*Say* REP li kuh]

replicate *v.* (**replicates, replicated, replicating**) **1** repeat (an experiment etc.). **2** make a replica of. □ **replication** *n.* **replicator** *n.* [*Say* REP lick ate]

reply ● *v.* (**replies, replied, replying**) **1** make an answer, respond. **2** say in answer. ● *n.* (*pl.* **replies**) **1** the act of replying. **2** a response.

report ● *v.* **1** give a spoken or written account of something. **2** convey information about an event or situation. **3** make a formal complaint about. **4** present oneself as having arrived or as ready to do something. **5** be responsible to (a supervisor). ● *n.* **1** an account given of a matter after investigation. **2** a piece of information about an event or situation. **3** the sound of an explosion or gunfire. □ **reportable** *adj.* **reportedly** *adv.*

reportage *n.* the reporting of news for the media. [*Say* rep or TAWZH]

report card *n.* **1** a written statement of a student's marks etc. at school. **2** an evaluation of performance.

reporter *n.* **1** a person employed to report news etc. for newspapers or broadcasts. **2** a person who reports.

repose ● *n.* **1** the cessation of activity or toil. **2** sleep. **3** a peaceful state. ● *v.* (**reposes, reposed, reposing**) **1** lie down in rest. **2** lay (one's head etc.) to rest. **3** lie; be lying or laid. **4** be supported or based on. **5** place (trust etc.) in. **6** be kept in a place. [*Say* re POZE]

reposition *v.* **1** move or place in a different position. **2** adjust one's position. **3** change the image of (a company etc.).

repository *n.* (*pl.* **repositories**) **1** a place where things are stored. **2** a receptacle. **3** a book, person, etc. regarded as a store of information etc. [*Say* re POZZA tory or re POZZA tree]

repossess *v.* (**repossesses, repossessed, repossessing**) regain possession of (esp. property or goods on which required payments have not been made). □ **repossession** *n.*

reprehensible *adj.* deserving condemnation. [*Say* rep re HENSA bull]

represent *v.* **1** be entitled or appointed to act and speak for. **2** be an elected member of a legislature for. **3** constitute. **4** be a specimen or example of. **5** portray or depict. **6** symbolize.

representation *n.* **1** the action of representing or the state of being represented. **2** the description or portrayal of someone or something. **3** a thing (esp. a painting etc.) that represents another. **4** (esp. in *pl.*) statements made to a higher authority, esp. to communicate an opinion or make a protest □ **representational** *adj.*

representation by population *n. Cdn hist.* the concept, esp. in the Province of Canada after 1851, that legislative representation should be based proportionally on population.

representative ● *adj.* **1** typical of a class or category. **2** containing typical specimens of all types. **3 a** consisting of elected deputies etc. **b** based on the representation of a nation etc. by such deputies. **4** serving as a portrayal or symbol of. ● *n.* **1** a sample or typical embodiment of. **2 a** the agent of a person or society. **b** a salesperson. **3** a delegate. **4** a deputy in a representative assembly. □ **representativeness** *n.*

repress *v.* (**represses, repressed, repressing**) **1** subdue by force. **2** restrain or suppress (thoughts, feelings, etc.). □ **repression** *n.* **repressive** *adj.* **repressiveness** *n.*

repressed *adj.* **1** (of a person) having emotions or desires that are not expressed. **2** (of emotions) not expressed openly.

reprieve ● *v.* (**reprieves, reprieved, reprieving**) **1** cancel or postpone the punishment of. **2** abandon or postpone plans to close. ● *n.* **1** a cancellation of a punishment. **2** a temporary escape from difficulty or danger. [*Say* re PREEV]

reprimand ● *n.* an official or sharp rebuke. ● *v.* express severe disapproval of. [*Say* REP ruh mand]

reprint ● *v.* print again. ● *n.* **1** the act of printing more copies of. **2** a book etc. reprinted.

reprisal *n.* an act of retaliation. [*Say* re PRIZE ul]

reprise ● *n.* **1** a repeated passage in music. **2** a repeated item in a musical program. ● *v.* (**reprises, reprised, reprising**) repeat (a performance, song, etc.). [*Say* re PRIZE or re PREEZ]

reproach ● *v.* (**reproaches, reproached, reproaching**) **1** express one's disapproval of. **2** scold; rebuke. ● *n.* **1** a rebuke. **2** blame, criticism. □ **above** (or **beyond**) **reproach** perfect. □ **reproachful** *adj.* **reproachfully** *adv.*

reprobate ● *n.* a person of highly immoral character. ● *adj.* immoral. [*Say* REP ruh bate]

reproduce *v.* (**reproduces, reproduced, reproducing**) **1** produce a copy of. **2** cause to be seen or heard etc. again. **3** produce further members of the same species by natural means. **4** (**reproduce oneself**) produce offspring. □ **reproducible** *adj.*

reproduction *n.* **1** the action or process of reproducing something. **2** a copy of a work of art. **3** (of furniture etc.) made in imitation of a certain style. □ **reproductive** *adj.*

reproof *n.* (*pl.* **reproofs**) an expression of blame or disapproval. [*Say* re PROOF]

reprove *v.* (**reproves, reproved, reproving**) express disapproval of; reprimand. □ **reproving** *adj.* [*Say* re PROOVE]

reptile *n.* any cold-blooded animal of a class that includes snakes, lizards, crocodiles, turtles, etc. □ **reptilian** *adj. & n.* [*For* reptilian *say* rep TILLY in]

republic *n.* **1 a** a state in which supreme power is held by the people or their elected representatives, not by a monarch etc. **b** the system of government of such a state. **2** a society with equality between its members.

republican ● *adj.* **1** having to do with or like a republic. **2** advocating or supporting republican government. ● *n.* **1** a person in favour of republican government. **2** (**Republican**) (in the US) a member or supporter of the Republican Party. **3** (also **Republican**) an advocate of a united Ireland. □ **republicanism** n.

Republican Party n. one of the two main US political parties.

repudiate v. (**repudiates, repudiated, repudiating**) **1** deny the truth or validity of. **2** refuse to accept or be associated with. **3** refuse to fulfill or honour an obligation. □ **repudiation** n. [Say re PYOODY ate]

repugnance n. intense disgust. [Say re PUG nunce]

repugnant adj. **1** extremely distasteful; unacceptable. **2** incompatible. [Say re PUG nunt]

repulse v. (**repulses, repulsed, repulsing**) **1** drive back (an attack) by force of arms. **2 a** rebuff. **b** refuse. **3** repel. □ **repulsive** adj. **repulsively** adv.

repulsion n. **1** aversion; disgust. **2** esp. Physics the force by which bodies tend to repel each other.

reputable adj. having a good reputation. [Say REP you tuh bull]

reputation n. **1** what is generally said or believed about someone or something. **2** the state of being well thought of. **3** fame, credit, or notoriety.

repute n. reputation. [Say re PYOOT]

reputed adj. **1** generally considered or reckoned. **2** passing as being. □ **reputedly** adv. [Say re PYOOT id]

request ● n. **1** an act of asking politely or formally for something. **2** a thing asked for. ● v. **1** ask for something. **2** ask a person to do something.

requiem n. **1** (**Requiem**) esp. Catholicism a Mass for the repose of the souls of the dead. **2** a musical setting for this. [Say RECK we em]

require v. (**requires, required, requiring**) **1** need. **2** lay down as an imperative. **3** command; instruct; order. **4** demand (of or from a person) as a right. □ **requirement** n.

requisite ● adj. required by circumstances or regulations. ● n. a thing needed (for some purpose). [Say RECK wuh zit]

requisition ● n. **1** an official order for the use of property or materials. **2** a formal written demand for something. ● v. demand the use or supply of. [Say reck wuh ZISH'n]

re-release ● v. (**re-releases, re-released, re-releasing**) release (a record, film, etc.) again. ● n. a re-released record, film, etc.

reroute v. (**reroutes, rerouted, rerouting**) send or carry by a different route. [Say re ROOT or re ROUT]

rerun ● v. (**reruns**; past **reran**; past participle **rerun**; **rerunning**) **1** show a program, film, etc. again. **2** run again. ● n. something that is rerun, esp. a race or a television program.

resale n. the sale of a thing previously bought.

reschedule v. (**reschedules, rescheduled, rescheduling**) alter the schedule of.

rescind v. revoke, cancel. □ **rescission** n. [Say re SIND, re SIZH'n]

rescue ● v. (**rescues, rescued, rescuing**) **1** save or set free from a dangerous or distressing situation. **2** informal keep from being lost or abandoned. ● n. an act of saving or being saved. □ **rescuer** n.

research ● n. the study of materials, sources, etc., in order to establish facts and reach new conclusions. ● v. (**researches, researched, researching**) do research. □ **researcher** n.

reseed v. sow (land) with seed again.

resell v. (**resells, resold, reselling**) sell (an object etc.) after buying it. □ **reseller** n.

resemblance n. a likeness or similarity.

resemble v. (**resembles, resembled, resembling**) be like; have a similarity to.

resent v. show or feel indignation at; be aggrieved by. □ **resentful** adj. **resentfully** adv. **resentment** n.

reservation n. **1** the act of reserving. **2** an express or tacit qualification or exception to an agreement etc. **3** an area of land reserved for occupation by American Indians in the US, Australian Aboriginals, etc.

reserve ● v. (**reserves, reserved, reserving**) **1** keep for future use. **2** order to be specially retained for a particular person. **3** retain or secure. **4** postpone delivery of (judgment etc.). ● n. **1** a thing reserved for future use. **2** a limitation, qualification, or exception attached to something. **3** coolness or distance of manner. **4** a place reserved for special use. **5** (in Canada) an area of land set aside for the use of a specific group of Aboriginal people. **6** assets kept readily available as cash, or as gold or foreign exchange. **7 a** troops withheld from action to reinforce or protect others. **b** additional forces available in an emergency. **8** an extra player chosen to be a possible substitute in a team. ● adj. **1** having to do with a reserve. **2** kept in reserve.

reserved adj. **1** reticent; slow to reveal emotion or opinions. **2** set apart, destined for some use or fate.

reservist n. a member of a country's reserve forces.

reservoir n. **1** a large lake or pool used for collecting and storing water for public and industrial use etc. **2 a** any receptacle esp. for or of fluid. **b** a place where fluid etc. collects. **3** a part of a machine etc. holding fluid. **4** a reserve or supply. [*Say* REZZER vwar *(*VWAR *rhymes with* FAR*)*]

reset ● v. (**resets, reset, resetting**) **1** set again or differently. **2** cause (a device etc.) to return to a condition of readiness. ● n. the action or an act of resetting something.

resettle v. (**resettles, resettled, resettling**) settle in a different place. □ **resettlement** n.

reshuffle ● v. (**reshuffles, reshuffled, reshuffling**) **1** shuffle (cards) again. **2** interchange the posts of (government ministers etc.). **3** interchange. ● n. an act of reshuffling.

reside v. (**resides, resided, residing**) **1** have one's home, dwell permanently. **2** be present or situated in. **3** (of power, a right, etc.) belong to a person or group.

residence n. **1** the fact of residing somewhere. **2** the place where a person resides. **3** a building providing accommodation for students. □ **in residence** dwelling or working at a specified place.

residency n. (pl. **residencies**) **1** = RESIDENCE 1. **2** a period of specialized medical training. **3** Brit. & Cdn a regular engagement at a club, theatre, etc. for a musician etc.

resident ● n. **1** a permanent inhabitant. **2** a medical graduate engaged in specialized practice in a hospital. ● adj. **1** residing; in residence. **2 a** working regularly in a particular place. **b** frequenting a particular place. **3** located; inherent. □ **residential** adj.

residential school n. esp. Cdn hist. a boarding school usu. operated or subsidized by religious orders to accommodate Aboriginal students.

residual ● adj. **1** remaining; still left. **2** esp. Chemistry left as a residue. **3** Math resulting from subtraction. ● n. **1** a quantity left over or resulting from subtraction. **2** (in pl.) a royalty paid to an actor, musician, etc. for a repeat broadcast. □ **residually** adv. [*Say* re ZIDGE oo ul]

residue n. **1** what is left over. **2** esp. Chemistry a substance left after combustion, evaporation, etc. [*Say* REZZA due]

resign v. **1** voluntarily leave a job. **2** (**resign oneself**) accept something as

inevitable. □ **resigned** adj. **resignedly** adv. [For resignedly *say* re ZINE id lee]

resignation n. **1** an act of resigning. **2** the document etc. stating an intention to resign. **3** the uncomplaining endurance of a sorrow or difficulty.

resilient adj. **1** (of a substance etc.) resuming its original shape after bending, stretching, etc. **2** readily recovering from shock, depression, etc. □ **resilience** n. [*Say* re ZILL yint, re ZILL yince]

resin ● n. **1** a sticky substance that is secreted by some trees (esp. fir and pine). **2** (also **synthetic resin**) a solid or liquid organic compound made by polymerization etc. and used in adhesives, plastics, and varnishes. ● v. (**resins, resined, resining**) rub or treat with resin. □ **resinous** adj. [*Say* REZZIN]

resist v. **1** withstand the action or effect of; repel. **2** prevent from reaching, penetrating, etc. **3** abstain from. **4** strive against. **5** refuse to comply. □ **resister** n.

resistance n. **1** the action or power of resisting. **2 a** the ability to withstand adverse conditions. **b** lack of sensitivity to a drug, insecticide, etc. **3** the impeding effect exerted by one material thing on another. **4** Physics **a** the property of hindering the conduction of electricity, heat, etc. **b** the measure of this in a body. Symbol: **R**. **5** (also **resistance movement**) a secret organization resisting authority. **6** armed or violent opposition. □ **the path of least resistance** the easiest course of action. □ **resistant** adj.

resistor n. a device that resists the passage of an electrical current.

resold past and past participle of RESELL.

resolute adj. determined. □ **resolutely** adv. **resoluteness** n. [*Say* REZZA loot]

resolution n. **1** a formal expression of opinion or intention by a legislative body. **2** a firm decision. **3** the quality of being resolute. **4** the resolving of a problem, dispute, etc. **5** esp. Chemistry the process of separating something into constituent parts. **6** Physics etc. the smallest interval measurable by a scientific (esp. optical) instrument. **7 a** the degree of detail visible in a photographic or television image. **b** the amount of graphical information that can be shown on a computer screen.

resolve ● v. (**resolves, resolved, resolving**) **1** settle or find a solution to. **2 a** decide firmly on a course of action. **b** (of an assembly) pass a resolution by vote. **3** separate into constituent parts. **4** (of something seen at a distance) turn into a different form when seen more clearly. ● n. **1** a firm mental decision or intention.

2 resoluteness. □ **resolvable** *adj.* **resolved** *adj.*

resonant *adj.* **1** (of sound) deep, clear, and ringing; echoing. **2** (of a body, room, etc.) tending to reinforce or prolong sounds. **3** suggesting images, feelings, memories, etc. **4** (of a place) resounding. □ **resonance** *n.* [*Say* REZZA nint, REZZA nince]

resonate *v.* (**resonates, resonated, resonating**) **1** make a deep, full, reverberating sound. **2** evoke or suggest images, memories, and emotions. **3** make an impression on someone. □ **resonator** *n.* [*Say* REZZA nate, REZZA nate er]

resort ● *n.* **1** a place frequented esp. for holidays or for a specified purpose. **2 a** a person or thing to which one has recourse. **b** recourse to. ● *v.* turn to as an expedient. □ **in the** (or **as a**) **last resort** when all else has failed.

resound *v.* **1** (of a place) ring or echo. **2** (of a voice etc.) produce echoes. **3** (of fame etc.) be much talked of. □ **resounding** *adj.* **resoundingly** *adv.* [*Say* re ZOUND, re ZOUND ing]

resource ● *n.* **1** (usu. in *pl.*) a stock or supply of materials and assets that can be drawn on when needed. **2** something occurring in nature and capable of economic exploitation. **3** (in *pl.*) a country's collective means of supporting itself, as represented by its minerals, land, and other assets. **4** a book etc. which supplies information on a particular topic. **5** one's personal attributes regarded as able to help one in adverse circumstances. ● *v.* (**resources, resourced, resourcing**) provide with resources needed for effective operation. □ **resourcing** *n.*

resourceful *adj.* good at finding ways to do things and solve problems. □ **resourcefully** *adv.* **resourcefulness** *n.*

resource teacher *n. Cdn* a teacher who provides educational resources to other teachers. **2** a teacher who works with special-needs or gifted children.

RESP *abbr. Cdn* Registered Educational Savings Plan, a tax-sheltered plan for saving money for a child's post-secondary education.

respect ● *n.* **1** a feeling of admiration for someone because of their qualities or achievements. **2** due regard for the feelings or rights of others. **3** (in *pl.*) polite greetings. **4** a particular aspect or point. ● *v.* **1** feel or have respect for. **2** avoid harming or interfering with. **3** agree to recognize and abide by. □ **with** (or **with all due**) **respect** a mollifying formula preceding

an expression of disagreement. **with respect to** (or **in respect of**) as concerns.

respectable *adj.* **1** regarded by society as being proper, correct, and good. **2** of some merit or importance. **3** adequate or acceptable. □ **respectability** *n.* **respectably** *adv.*

respectful *adj.* feeling or showing respect. □ **respectfully** *adv.*

respecting *prep.* with reference to.

respective *adj.* concerning or appropriate to each of several individually.

respectively *adv.* separately and in the order mentioned.

respiration *n.* **1** the action of breathing. **2** the process in animals and plants in which energy is produced, in animals involving the intake of oxygen.

respirator *n.* **1** an apparatus for maintaining artificial breathing. **2** an apparatus worn over the face to prevent gas, dust, etc., from being inhaled.

respiratory *adj.* having to do with respiration. [*Say* RESPER a tory]

respire *v.* (**respires, respired, respiring**) **1** breathe. **2** (of living organisms) carry out respiration.

respite *n.* a short period of rest or relief from something difficult or unpleasant. [*Say* RESS pite *or* RESS pit]

resplendent *adj.* making an attractive or impressive display. □ **resplendently** *adv.* [*Say* re SPLEN dint]

respond *v.* **1** answer, give a reply. **2** do something in reply. **3** react esp. favourably. □ **responder** *n.*

respondent *n.* **1** a person who responds to a survey or questionnaire. **2** a defendant in a lawsuit.

response *n.* **1** an answer given in word or act. **2** a reaction.

responsibility *n.* (*pl.* **responsibilities**) **1 a** the state or fact of being responsible. **b** the ability to act independently. **2** something for which one is responsible.

responsible *adj.* **1** liable to be called to account. **2** morally accountable for one's actions. **3** respectable; evidently trustworthy. **4** being the primary cause. **5** involving responsibility. □ **responsibly** *adv.*

responsible government *n. Cdn* a form of government in which the cabinet or executive branch is held collectively responsible and accountable to an elected legislature.

responsive *adj.* **1** responding readily. **2** responding with enthusiasm. □ **responsiveness** *n.*

rest[1] • v. **1** cease work or movement in order to relax or recover strength. **2** allow to be inactive in order to regain or save energy. **3** place or be placed so as to stay in a specified position. **4** depend or be based on. **5** place (trust, hope, or confidence) in or on. **6** (of power, responsibility, etc.) belong to. **7** (of a matter) be left without further action. • n. **1** the action or a period of resting. **2** a motionless state. **3** *Music* an interval of silence of a specified duration. **4** an object that is used to hold or support something. □ **at rest 1** not moving. **2** lying dead. **give it a rest** *informal* leave (a contentious issue) for the moment. **put** (or **lay**) **to rest 1** put a decisive end to. **2** bury in a grave. **rest one's case** conclude one's argument etc. **rest up** rest oneself thoroughly. □ **rested** adj. **restful** adj.

rest[2] • n. (**the rest**) the remaining part or parts; the others. • v. remain in a specified state. □ **rest easy** remain or become calm.

restate v. (**restates, restated, restating**) express again or differently. □ **restatement** n.

restaurant n. a commercial establishment where meals are prepared, served, and eaten.

restaurateur n. (also **restauranteur**) a person who owns or manages a restaurant. [Say ress ter a TUR, ress ter on TUR]

rest home n. a home for old or infirm people.

Restigouche salmon n. a variety of Atlantic salmon associated with the Restigouche River. [Say RESTA goosh]

restitution n. **1** the restoration of something lost or stolen to its proper owner. **2** payment for an injury or loss. [Say resta TOO sh'n or resta TYOO sh'n]

restive adj. **1** restless, impatient. **2** (of a horse) refusing to advance. **3** unmanageable.

restless adj. **1** uneasy, agitated. **2** fidgeting; constantly moving. □ **restlessly** adv. **restlessness** n.

restoration n. **1** the return of something to a former state, condition, or owner. **2** a model or drawing representing the supposed original form of a ruined building etc. **3** (**the Restoration**) *hist.* **a** the re-establishment of Charles II as king of England in 1660. **b** the period following this. [Say ress ter AY sh'n]

restorative • adj. tending to or able to restore health or strength. • n. a restorative medicine, food, etc. [Say re STORA tive]

restore v. (**restores, restored, restoring**) **1** return to a previous condition, place, or owner. **2** bring back to good health etc. **3** reinstate. **4** put back; replace. □ **restored** adj. **restorer** n.

restrain v. **1 a** prevent (someone or oneself) from doing something. **b** keep (someone or oneself) under control. **2** impose a limit upon. **3** forcibly control or confine.

restrained adj. **1** kept under control or within bounds. **2** characterized by restraint or reserve.

restraining order n. a temporary court order issued to prevent an individual from committing a particular action.

restraint n. **1** self-control. **2** reserve of manner. **3** a device that restrains. **4** confinement. [Say re STRAINT]

restrict v. **1 a** limit to a specific person or group of people. **b** put a limit on. **2** control, curtail, or reduce. **3** prevent.

restricted • adj. **1** confined, controlled, or limited in some way. **2** available or accessible only to certain authorized individuals. • n. (**Restricted**) *Cdn* a film classification designating movies that have been deemed unsuitable for people under the age of 18.

restriction n. **1** the action of restricting, or the state of being restricted. **2** a limiting condition or regulation.

restrictive adj. **1** tending to limit, prevent, or restrict. **2** *Grammar* (of a clause or phrase) specifying which particular thing or things are being discussed.

restroom n. esp. *US* a public washroom.

restructure v. (**restructures, restructured, restructuring**) **1** give a new structure to; rebuild. **2** fundamentally reorganize. □ **restructuring** n.

result • n. **1** a consequence or outcome. **2** a satisfactory outcome. **3** a quantity, formula, etc., obtained by calculation. **4** (in pl.) **a** a list of scores or winners etc. **b** the findings of a research study etc. • v. **1** arise as the consequence of. **2** have a specified end or outcome. □ **as a result** consequently, therefore.

resultant adj. occurring as a result.

resume v. (**resumes, resumed, resuming**) **1** begin again after an interruption. **2** occupy again.

resumé n. **1** a brief account of one's education, previous employment, etc., usu. submitted with a job application. **2** a summary. [Say REZZA may or REZZ you may]

resumption n. the act of beginning something again after it has stopped.

resurface v. (**resurfaces, resurfaced,**

resurfacing) 1 rise again; turn up again. **2** lay a new surface on.

resurgence *n.* **1** a renewed prominence or popularity. **2** a recovery. □ **resurgent** *adj.* [Say re SURGE ince]

resurrect *v.* **1** revive. **2** raise from the dead. [Say rezza RECT]

resurrection *n.* **1** the action of resurrecting. **2** (usu. **Resurrection**) (in Christian belief) Christ's rising from the dead. **3** a revival of something. [Say rezza REC sh'n]

resuscitate *v.* (**resuscitates, resuscitated, resuscitating**) **1** revive from unconsciousness. **2** revive or restore. □ **resuscitation** *n.* **resuscitator** *n.* [Say re SUSSA tate]

retail ● *n.* the sale of goods to the public. ● *adj.* **1** of or pertaining to the retailing of goods. **2** sold by retail. ● *adv.* by retail; at a retail price ● *v.* **1** sell (goods) in retail trade. **2** (of goods) be sold in this way. □ **retailer** *n.* **retailing** *n.*

retain *v.* **1** maintain possession of; keep. **2** allow to remain or prevail. **3** keep in place. **4** secure (professional services etc.) with a preliminary payment.

retainer *n.* **1** *Law* a fee for retaining a lawyer etc. **2 a** *hist.* a dependant or follower of a person of rank. **b** a long-standing servant. **3** a thing that holds something in place. **4** *Dentistry* **a** a device that fits over the teeth to keep them aligned once they have been straightened. **b** a structure cemented to a tooth to keep a bridge in place.

retake *v.* (**retakes**; *past* **retook**; *past participle* **retaken**; **retaking**) **1** take again. **2** regain possession of. **3** film (a scene) or make (a recording) again.

retaliate *v.* (**retaliates, retaliated, retaliating**) attack in return. □ **retaliation** *n.* **retaliatory** *adj.* [Say re TALLY ate, re TALLY a tory]

retard ● *v.* delay the progress or development of. ● *n. slang offensive* **1** a mentally retarded person. **2** a stupid person. □ **retardation** *n.*

retardant ● *adj.* tending to slow or resist. ● *n.* something that slows a process.

retarded *adj.* less developed, esp. mentally, than is normal.

retch *v.* make an attempt to vomit. □ **retching** *n.*

retention *n.* **1** the continued possession, use, or control of something. **2** the action of retaining.

retentive *adj.* **1** tending to retain. **2** not forgetful.

rethink ● *v.* (**rethinks, rethought, rethinking**) think about (something) again. ● *n.* a reassessment.

reticence *n.* the avoidance of saying all one knows or feels; reserve in speech etc. □ **reticent** *adj.* [Say RETTA since]

retina *n.* (*pl.* **retinas**) a light-sensitive layer at the back of the eyeball that triggers nerve impulses which are sent to the brain where the visual image is formed. □ **retinal** *adj.* [Say RET uh uh]

retinol *n.* a vitamin essential for growth and vision in dim light; vitamin A. [Say RETTA nawl]

retinue *n.* a group of attendants accompanying an important person. [Say RETTA new]

retire *v.* (**retires, retired, retiring**) **1 a** leave office or employment, esp. because of age. **b** cease to employ or use. **2** withdraw or retreat. **3** go to bed. **4** *Baseball* cause (a side) to end a turn at bat. **5** withdraw from circulation or currency. □ **retired** *adj.* **retirement** *n.*

retiree *n.* a person who has retired from work. [Say re tire EE]

retiring *adj.* shy.

retool *v.* **1** equip (a factory etc.) with new tools. **2** equip or prepare oneself again. **3** adapt something to make it more useful.

retort ● *n.* a sharp or witty reply. ● *v.* reply angrily or wittily. [Say TORT]

retouch *v.* (**retouches, retouched, retouching**) **1** touch up. **2** alter or restore a photograph etc. by making minor changes after development. □ **retouching** *n.*

retrace *v.* (**retraces, retraced, retracing**) **1** go back over (one's steps etc.). **2** go back over in one's memory. **3** trace back to a source.

retract *v.* **1** withdraw or revoke. **2** draw or be drawn back or in. □ **retractable** *adj.* **retraction** *n.*

retractor *n.* **1** a muscle used for retracting. **2** a device for retracting.

retread ● *v.* (**retreads, retreaded, retreading**) **1** put a fresh tread on. **2** alter something so that it is superficially different. ● *n.* a retreaded tire. [Say re TRED]

retreat ● *v.* **1** (esp. of military forces) retire or draw back; turn away from difficulty or opposition. **2** back down. **3** become smaller in size or extent. **4** withdraw into privacy or security. ● *n.* **1 a** the act of moving back or withdrawing. **b** *Military* a signal for this. **2** a quiet or secluded place in which one can rest and relax. **3 a** a period of seclusion for prayer and meditation. **b** a period during which co-workers or people with common interests meet to exchange ideas.

retrench v. (**retrenches**, **retrenched**, **retrenching**) cut down expenses. □ **retrenchment** n.

retrial n. a second or further trial.

retribution n. **1** punishment that is considered to be fully deserved. **2** retaliation. □ **retributive** adj. [Say ret ri BYOO sh'n, re TRIB you tiv]

retrieve v. (**retrieves**, **retrieved**, **retrieving**) **1** recover and bring back. **2** fetch. **3** Computing find or extract (information stored in a computer). □ **retrievable** adj. **retrieval** n.

retriever n. **1** a breed of dog used for retrieving game. **2** a person or thing that retrieves something.

retro ● n. (pl. **retros**) style or fashion imitating the past. ● adj. imitative of a style from the past.

retro- comb. form **1** denoting action back or backwards. **2** denoting location behind.

retroactive adj. (of legislation etc.) taking effect from a past date. □ **retroactively** adv.

retrofit ● v. (**retrofits**, **retrofitted**, **retrofitting**) **1** modify (machinery etc.) to incorporate changes and developments introduced after manufacture. **2** provide (an older building etc.) with new fixtures, equipment, etc. ● n. **1** a modification made to retrofit a product. **2** a retrofitted product.

retrograde ● adj. **1** directed backwards. **2** reverting to a less developed or inferior state. ● n. Astronomy the apparent backward motion of a planet in the zodiac.

retrospect n. a survey of past time or events. □ **in retrospect** when looked back on.

retrospective ● adj. (of an exhibition etc.) showing an artist's development over his or her lifetime. ● n. a retrospective film series, exhibition, etc. □ **retrospectively** adv.

retrovirus n. (pl. **retroviruses**) any of a group of RNA viruses which insert a DNA copy of their genome into the host cell, e.g. HIV. □ **retroviral** adj.

return ● v. **1** come or go back to a place. **2** go back to (a particular state or activity). **3** give or send back or put back. **4** feel, say, or do (the same feeling, action, etc.) in response. **5** (of a judge or jury) give a verdict. **6** yield (a profit). **7** elect to office. ● n. **1** an act or the action of returning. **2** a thing returned. **3** a formal report or statement. **4** a profit from an investment. **5** (in pl.) decision; results. **6** (in tennis etc.) the act of hitting a ball back in the direction of the server. ● adj. characterized by return or returning: *return airfare.* ● adv. Cdn & Brit. (of travel) to a particular destination and back. □ **in return** as an exchange. **many happy returns** a greeting on a birthday. □ **returnable** adj. **returner** n.

returned adj. **1** that has come or been brought back. **2** Cdn (of a member of the armed forces) discharged after active service.

returnee n. **1** a person who returns to or from a place. **2** a person who returns home after war or service abroad. [Say return EE]

returning officer n. Cdn an official organizing and overseeing the conduct of an election etc. in a constituency.

Reuben n. (also **Reuben sandwich**) a hot sandwich on rye bread, containing corned beef, sauerkraut, and usu. Swiss cheese. [Say ROO bin]

reunify v. (**reunifies**, **reunified**, **reunifying**) restore (esp. separated territories) to a political unity. □ **reunification** n.

reunion n. **1** the act of people coming together again after a period of separation. **2** a social gathering esp. of relatives or friends after a long separation.

reunite v. (**reunites**, **reunited**, **reuniting**) bring or come back together.

reupholster v. repair or replace the stuffing or covering of (furniture). [Say re up HOLSTER]

reuse ● v. (**reuses**, **reused**, **reusing**) use again or more than once. ● n. a second or further use. □ **reusable** adj. **reused** adj.

Rev. abbr. Reverend.

rev informal ● n. (in pl.) the number of revolutions of an engine per minute. ● v. (**revs**, **revved**, **revving**) **1** (of an internal combustion engine) revolve with increasing speed. **2** increase the speed of revolution of an internal combustion engine. **3** stimulate, activate, or accelerate.

revalue v. (**revalues**, **revalued**, **revaluing**) Economics **1** assess the value of something again. **2** give a different or esp. higher value to. □ **revaluation** n.

revamp ● v. **1** repair, restore. **2** renovate, overhaul. ● n. **1** a revamped version. **2** an act of revamping something.

reveal v. **1** display, show, or expose. **2** disclose, divulge. **3** appear or become apparent. □ **revealer** n.

revealing adj. **1** providing insight esp. into something obscure or private. **2** (of a garment) allowing more of the body to be seen than is usual. □ **revealingly** adv.

reveille n. a signal given on a drum or bugle to waken soldiers. [Say REVVA lee]

réveillon n. (among francophones) a festive meal on Christmas morning or on New Year's Eve. [Say REV ay on (with on as in French)]

revel ● v. (revels, revelled, revelling) take great delight in. ● n. (usu. in pl.) a lively and noisy festivity. □ **reveller** n. **revelling** n. [Say REV'll]

revelation n. 1 the revealing of something that was previously unknown. 2 a surprising and previously unknown fact. 3 a completely new or surprising experience. [Say revva LAY sh'n]

revelatory adj. serving to reveal. [Say REVVA luh tory]

revelry n. (pl. revelries) boisterous gaiety or mirth.

revenge ● n. 1 retaliation for an offence or injury. 2 an act of retaliation. 3 a vindictive feeling. ● v. (revenges, revenged, revenging) 1 take revenge for (an offence). 2 retaliate on behalf of.

revenge of the cradle n. Cdn (**the revenge of the cradle**) the extremely high birth rate of French Canadians from the 19th to the mid-20th centuries.

revenue n. 1 a income, esp. of a large amount, from any source. b (in pl.) items constituting this. 2 a government's annual income from which public expenses are met. 3 the department of the civil service collecting this.

reverb n. Music informal 1 reverberation. 2 a device to produce this. [Say re VERB or REE verb]

reverberate v. (reverberates, reverberated, reverberating) 1 a (of sound etc.) be returned or echoed repeatedly. b return (a sound etc.) in this way. 2 (of an event) have continuing effects. □ **reverberation** n. [Say re VERB a rate]

revere v. (reveres, revered, revering) hold in deep respect. [Say re VEER]

reverence ● n. a feeling of great respect or admiration. ● v. (reverences, reverenced, reverencing) regard or treat with reverence. [Say REVVER ince]

Reverend ● adj. (as the title of a member of the clergy). ● n. informal (also **reverend**) a clergyman. [Say REVVER und]

reverent adj. feeling or showing reverence. □ **reverential** adj. **reverentially** adv. **reverently** adv. [Say REVVER unt, revver EN shull, REVVER unt lee]

reverie n. a daydream. [Say REVVER ee]

reversal n. 1 a change to an opposite direction, position, or course of action. 2 a harmful change of fortune.

reverse ● v. (reverses, reversed, reversing) 1 turn the other way around or inside out. 2 change to the opposite character or effect. 3 move backwards. 4 make (an engine etc.) work in a contrary direction. 5 revoke or annul (a verdict etc.). ● adj. 1 placed or turned in an opposite direction or position. 2 opposite or contrary in character or order. ● n. 1 the opposite or contrary. 2 an occurrence of misfortune. 3 reverse gear or motion. 4 the reverse side of something. 5 the side of a coin or medal etc. bearing the secondary design. □ **reverser** n. **reversible** adj.

reverse psychology n. the practice of suggesting that a person do the opposite of what one really wants him or her to do.

reversing falls n. Cdn a set of rapids on a tidal river, the flow of which reverses regularly due to the pressure of the incoming tide.

reversion n. 1 a return to a previous state, habit, etc. 2 Biology the action of returning to a former or ancestral type. [Say re VERSION]

revert v. return to a former state, condition, or habit.

review ● n. 1 a general survey or assessment of a subject or thing. 2 a retrospective survey or report on past events. 3 an examination, so as to make changes if necessary. 4 an action of reviewing something already learned. 5 a display and formal inspection of troops etc. 6 an account or criticism of a book, performance, restaurant, etc. ● v. 1 survey or look back on. 2 reconsider or revise. 3 present or study material again. 4 hold a review of (troops etc.). 5 publish or broadcast a review of (a book etc.). 6 Law submit (a sentence etc.) to review. □ **reviewable** adj.

reviewer n. a person who reviews books, performances, etc. for publication.

revile v. (reviles, reviled, reviling) criticize abusively.

revise v. (revises, revised, revising) 1 examine or amend (text). 2 consider and alter (an opinion etc.).

revision n. 1 the action of revising something. 2 a change or set of changes made to something.

revisionism n. often derogatory 1 a revised interpretation of classical Marxist theory. 2 the theory or practice of revising one's attitude to a previously accepted situation or point of view. □ **revisionist** n. & adj.

revisit v. (revisits, revisited, revisiting) 1 visit again. 2 take up (a subject etc.) again.

revitalize v. (**revitalizes, revitalized, revitalizing**) make something stronger, healthier, or more active.
□ **revitalization** n.

revival n. **1** an improvement in the condition or strength of something. **2** the process of bringing something back into existence, use, etc. **3** a reawakening of religious fervour. **4** a new production of an old play etc.

revivalism n. the promotion of a revival, esp. of religious fervour.
□ **revivalist** n. & adj.

revive v. (**revives, revived, reviving**) **1** come or bring back to consciousness or life or strength. **2** come or bring back to existence, use, notice, etc. **3** produce (a play etc.) that has not been performed for some time.

revivify v. (**revivifies, revivified, revivifying**) restore to activity, vigour, or life. □ **revivification** n. [Say re VIVVA fie, re vivva fuh KAY sh'n]

revoke v. (**revokes, revoked, revoking**) withdraw or cancel (a licence etc.).
□ **revocable** adj. **revocation** n. [Say re VOKE, re VOKE a bull or REV ick a bull, revva KAY sh'n]

revolt ● v. **1** rise in rebellion against authority. **2** affect with strong disgust. ● n. **1** an act of rebelling. **2** a state of insurrection. **3** a sense of loathing.

revolting adj. disgusting, horrible.

revolution n. **1 a** the forcible overthrow of a government or social order. **b** (in Marxism) the replacement of one ruling class by another. **2** any fundamental change or reversal of conditions. **3** a circular movement made by something fixed to a central point. **4 a** motion in orbit; rotation. **b** the single completion of an orbit.

revolutionary ● adj. **1** involving a complete or dramatic change. **2** of or causing political revolution. **3** (**Revolutionary**) of or relating to a particular revolution. ● n. (pl. **revolutionaries**) an instigator or supporter of revolution.

revolutionize v. (**revolutionizes, revolutionized, revolutionizing**) introduce fundamental change to.

Révolution tranquille n. Cdn = QUIET REVOLUTION.
[Say ray voll oo SYON tron KEEL (with SYON as in French)]

revolve v. (**revolves, revolved, revolving**) **1** turn or cause to turn around, esp. on an axis. **2** move in a circular orbit. **3** have as its chief concern.

revolver n. a pistol with revolving

chambers enabling several shots to be fired without loading again.

revue n. a theatrical entertainment of a series of short sketches and songs.
[Say re VIEW]

revulsion n. a sense of loathing.
[Say re VULL sh'n]

reward ● n. **1** a thing given in recognition of service, effort, or achievement. **2** a fair return for good or bad behaviour. ● v. **1** give a reward to. **2** make return for (an action).

rewarding adj. providing satisfaction.

rewind ● v. (**rewinds, rewound, rewinding**) wind (a film or tape etc.) back to the beginning. ● n. a mechanism for doing this. □ **rewinder** n.

rewire v. (**rewires, rewired, rewiring**) provide with new wiring.

reword v. change the wording of.

rework v. revise; fashion again.
□ **reworking** n.

rewrite ● v. (**rewrites**; past **rewrote**; past participle **rewritten**; **rewriting**) **1** write again or differently. **2** present (history) in a new or different light. ● n. the action of rewriting something.

rez n. (pl. **rezzes**) informal an Indian reserve or reservation.

Rh abbr. rhesus factor.

rhapsodize v. (**rhapsodizes, rhapsodized, rhapsodizing**) talk or write about with great enthusiasm.
[Say RAPSA dize]

rhapsody n. (pl. **rhapsodies**) **1** a highly enthusiastic or ecstatic expression of feeling. **2** an emotional piece of music in one extended movement. □ **rhapsodic** adj. [Say RAPSA dee, RAP sod ick]

rhea n. (pl. **rheas**) a S American flightless bird, similar to but smaller than an ostrich.
[Say REE uh]

rheostat n. Electricity an instrument used to control a current by varying the resistance.
□ **rheostatic** adj. [Say REE uh stat, ree uh STATIC]

rhesus factor n. = RH FACTOR.

rhesus monkey n. a small monkey common in northern India. [Say REE sus]

rhetoric n. **1** the art of effective or persuasive speaking or writing. **2** language designed to persuade or impress.
[Say RETTER ick]

rhetorical adj. **1** expressed to persuade or impress. **2** having to do with rhetoric.
□ **rhetorically** adv. [Say ruh TORA cull]

rhetorical question n. a question asked not for information but to produce an effect.

rheumatism n. any disease marked by

inflammation and pain in the joints, muscles, or fibrous tissue. □ **rheumatic** *adj. & n.* [*Say* ROOMA tism, roo MAT ick]

rheumatoid arthritis *n.* a chronic progressive disease causing inflammation and stiffening of the joints.
[*Say* ROOMA toid]

Rh factor *n.* (also **rhesus factor**) an antigen occurring on the red blood cells of most humans and some other primates.

rhinestone *n.* an imitation diamond.
[*Say* RINE stone]

rhino *n.* (*pl.* **rhino** or **rhinos**) *informal* a rhinoceros.

rhinoceros *n.* (*pl.* **rhinoceros** or **rhinoceroses**) a large thick-skinned plant-eating mammal of Africa and South Asia, with one or two horns on the nose.

rhinoplasty *n.* (*pl.* **rhinoplasties**) plastic surgery of the nose. [*Say* RYE no plasty]

rhizome *n.* an underground rootlike stem bearing both roots and shoots.
□ **rhizomatous** *adj.* [*Say* RYE zome, rye ZOE muh tus]

rhodium *n.* a hard white metallic element, occurring naturally in platinum ores.
[*Say* ROADY um]

rhododendron *n.* an evergreen shrub or small tree, with usu. large clusters of trumpet-shaped flowers.
[*Say* ROAD uh DEN drun]

rhomboid ● *adj.* having or resembling the shape of a rhombus. ● *n.* a quadrilateral of which only the opposite sides and angles are equal. [*Say* ROM boyd]

rhombus *n.* (*pl.* **rhombuses** or **rhombi**) *Math* a parallelogram with oblique angles and equal sides. □ **rhombic** *adj.*
[*Say* ROM bus *for the singular; for* RHOMBI *say* ROM bye; ROM bick]

rhubarb *n.* a large-leaved plant producing long fleshy dark red stalks that can be cooked and eaten. [*Say* ROO barb]

rhumba *n. & v.* = RUMBA. [*Say* RUMBA]

rhyme ● *n.* **1** words or syllables that have or end with the same sound as each other. **2** verse or a poem having rhymes. **3** a word that has the same sound as another. ● *v.* (**rhymes, rhymed, rhyming**) **1 a** (of words or lines) produce a rhyme. **b** act as a rhyme (with another). **2** make or write rhymes. □ **rhyme off** *Cdn* recite rapidly and spontaneously (a list of items). **rhyme or reason** sense or logic. □ **rhymer** *n.*

rhythm *n.* **1** a measured flow of words and phrases in verse or prose determined by length of and stress on syllables. **2** the aspect of musical composition concerned with periodical accent and the duration of notes. **3** movement with a regular

succession of strong and weak elements. **4** a regularly recurring sequence of events. **5** a sense of rhythm.

rhythm and blues *n.* popular music with a blues theme and strong rhythm.

rhythmic *adj.* (also **rhythmical**) relating to or characterized by rhythm.
□ **rhythmically** *adv.*

rhythmic gymnastics *n.* a form of gymnastics emphasizing dance-like rhythmic routines, typically accentuated by the use of ribbons or hoops. □ **rhythmic gymnast** *n.*

rhythm method *n.* birth control by avoiding sexual intercourse when ovulation is likely to occur.

rhythm section *n.* the part of a band etc. mainly supplying rhythm, usu. consisting of drums, bass, etc.

rib ● *n.* **1** each of the curved bones articulated in pairs to the spine and protecting the thoracic cavity and its organs. **2 a** a roast of meat from this part of an animal. **b** (usu. in *pl.*) spareribs. **3** a piece often of stronger material serving to support or strengthen a structure. **4** a curved strut forming part of the framework of a ship's hull. **5** *Knitting* a combination of plain and purl stitches producing a ribbed fabric. ● *v.* (**ribs, ribbed, ribbing**) **1** provide with ribs. **2** *informal* tease. **3** mark with ridges. □ **ribbing** *n.*

ribald *adj.* referring to sexual matters in a rude but humorous way. □ **ribaldry** *n.*
[*Say* RYE b'ld *or* RIBBLED, RYE b'll dree *or* RIBBLE dree]

ribbed *adj.* **1** having ribs or rib-like markings. **2** *Knitting* having ribbing.

ribbit *n.* the sound made by a frog.

ribbon *n.* **1** a narrow strip of fabric, used esp. for trimming or decoration. **2** a ribbon of a special colour etc. worn to indicate something. **3** a long narrow strip of anything. **4** (in *pl.*) ragged strips.
□ **ribboned** *adj.*

rib cage *n.* the wall of bones formed by the ribs.

rib-eye *n.* (also **rib-eye steak**) a roundish steak cut from the rib.

riboflavin *n.* a B vitamin found in liver, milk, and eggs. [*Say* rye bo FLAY vin]

ribonucleic acid *n.* a nucleic acid present in living cells. Abbreviation: **RNA**.
[*Say* rye bo new CLAY ick]

ribosome *n.* each of the minute particles consisting of RNA and associated proteins found in the cytoplasm of living cells.
□ **ribosomal** *adj.* [*Say* RYE buh soam, rye buh SOAM ull]

rice *n.* the grain of a widely cultivated swamp grass, a major world cereal.

rice cake *n.* a round, crisp biscuit made of puffed rice.

rice paper *n.* edible paper made from the pith of an oriental tree and used for painting and in cookery.

rich *adj.* **1** having much wealth. **2** splendid, costly, elaborate. **3** valuable. **4** ample. **5** abundantly supplied with. **6** (of food) containing much fat, sugar, etc. **7** (of colour, sound, or smell) deep and strong. **8** (of soil) very fertile. **9** (of a country etc.) abounding in natural resources.

riches *pl. n.* wealth; money and valuable possessions.

richly *adv.* **1** in a rich way. **2** fully.

Richter scale *n.* a scale for representing the strength of an earthquake. [*Say* RICK ter]

rick *n.* a stack of hay, straw, etc.

rickets *n.* a disease of children caused by vitamin D deficiency, characterized by softening of the bones and bow legs.

rickettsia *n.* (*pl.* **rickettsiae** or **rickettsias**) a parasitic micro-organism causing typhus and other diseases. □ **rickettsial** *adj.* [*Say* ri KETSY uh]

rickety *adj.* insecure or shaky in construction.

rickshaw *n.* a light two-wheeled vehicle drawn by one or more persons.

ricochet ● *n.* the action of a projectile, esp. a shell or bullet, in rebounding off a surface. ● *v.* (**ricochets**, **ricocheted**, **ricocheting**) ricochet from a surface. [*Say* RICK a shay]

ricotta *n.* a soft white Italian cheese. [*Say* ri COTTA]

rid *v.* (**rids**, **rid**, **ridding**) make (a person or place) free of something unwanted. □ **be** (**or get**) **rid of** be freed or relieved of; dispose of.

riddance *n.* □ **good riddance** expressing welcome relief from an unwanted person or thing.

ridden ● *v. past participle of* RIDE. ● *adj.* (in *comb.*) infested or afflicted.

riddle[1] *n.* **1** a cleverly worded question or statement testing ingenuity. **2** a puzzling thing or person.

riddle[2] *v.* (**riddles**, **riddled**, **riddling**) **1** make many holes in. **2** fill.

ride ● *v.* (**rides**; *past* **rode**; *past participle* **ridden**; **riding**) **1** sit on and control the movement of (a horse, bicycle, or motorcycle). **2** travel in or on a vehicle or horse. **3** be carried or supported by. **4** sail or float. **5** be full of or dominated by. ● *n.* **1** an act of riding. **2** a roller coaster, merry-go-round, etc. ridden at a fair. **3** a demonstration of (esp. horse) riding. **4** a person giving a lift in a vehicle. □ **come** (**or go** etc.) **along for the ride** participate disinterestedly or just for fun. **let a thing ride** leave it alone. **ride high** be elated or successful. **ride on** be dependent on. **ride out** come safely through. **ride shotgun 1** travel as a guard in the seat next to the driver. **2** ride in the passenger seat of a vehicle. **ride up** (of a garment) work or move upwards. **take for a ride** *informal* hoax or deceive.

rider *n.* **1** a person who rides (a horse, bicycle, etc.). **2 a** an additional clause added to a document. **b** a condition, proviso, etc. □ **riderless** *adj.*

ridership *n.* the number of passengers using a particular form of mass transportation.

ridge *n.* **1** the line of the junction of two surfaces sloping upwards towards each other. **2** a long narrow hilltop or mountain range. **3** any narrow elevation across a surface. **4** *Meteorology* an elongated region of high pressure. **5** *Agriculture* a raised strip of arable land.

ridged *adj.* with a surface marked by ridges.

ridgepole *n.* **1** the horizontal pole of a tent. **2** a beam along the ridge of a roof.

ridicule ● *n.* derision or mockery. ● *v.* (**ridicules**, **ridiculed**, **ridiculing**) make fun of.

ridiculous *adj.* **1** unreasonable, absurd. **2** deserving or inviting ridicule. □ **ridiculously** *adv.* **ridiculousness** *n.*

riding[1] *n.* the practice or skill of riding horses.

riding[2] *n.* (in Canada) a constituency or electoral district.

riding association *n.* Cdn a unit of a political party at the riding level, responsible for nominating a candidate for election.

Riel Rebellion *n.* Cdn **1** = RED RIVER REBELLION. **2** = NORTHWEST REBELLION. **3** these collectively. [*Say* ree ELL]

Riesling *n.* a kind of dry white wine from colder climates. [*Say* REEZ ling]

rife *adj.* **1** (esp. of something undesirable) widespread. **2** full of.

riff ● *n.* **1** a short repeated phrase in rock, jazz, etc. **2** *informal* any commentary, improvisation, etc. on a theme. ● *v.* **1** play riffs. **2** *informal* comment.

riffle *v.* (**riffles**, **riffled**, **riffling**) **1 a** turn (pages) in quick succession. **b** shuffle (playing cards). **2** (esp. of wind) disturb the smoothness of.

riff-raff n. (often as **the riff-raff**) the rabble.

rifle ● n. **1** a gun with a long rifled barrel. **2** (in pl.) infantry armed with rifles. ● v. (**rifles, rifled, rifling**) **1** make spiral grooves in (a gun) to make a bullet spin **2** shoot, throw, etc. forcefully in a straight line. **3** search through something hurriedly to steal or find something.

rift n. **1** a crack or split in an object. **2** a cleft or fissure. **3** a breach in friendly relations.

rift valley n. a steep-sided valley formed by the downward displacement of the earth's crust between two nearly parallel faults.

rig ● v. (**rigs, rigged, rigging**) **1 a** provide (a ship) with sails, rigging, etc. **b** prepare (a ship) for sailing. **2** fit with clothes or equipment. **3** set up hastily. **4** connect with ropes, wires, etc. **5** manage or conduct fraudulently. ● n. **1** the arrangement of a boat's sails, rigging, etc. **2** equipment for a special purpose; gear. **3** an oil rig. **4** a large vehicle, esp. a transport truck. □ **rigged** adj.

rigamarole n. = RIGMAROLE. [Say RIGGA muh role]

rigatoni n. pasta in the form of short hollow tubes. [Say rigga TONY]

rigger n. **1** a person who rigs or who arranges rigging. **2** a ship rigged in a specified way.

rigging n. **1** a ship's spars, ropes, etc., supporting the sails. **2** an arrangement of ropes, wires, etc. in any structure. **3** the lines and other equipment used in moving logs.

right ● adj. **1** on or towards the side of a person or thing which is to the east when the person or thing is facing north. **2** morally good or justified. **3** factually correct. **4** most appropriate. **5** in a satisfactory, sound, or normal condition. **6** relating to a right-wing person or group. ● n. **1** that which is morally right. **2** (in pl.) the authority to perform, publish, or film a particular work or event. **3** the right-hand side or direction. **4** a right turn. **5** a person's right fist, or a blow given with it. **6** (often **Right**) a group favouring conservative views. ● v. **1** restore to a normal or upright position. **2** restore to a normal or correct condition. **3** make amends for (a wrong). ● adv. **1** on or to the right side. **2** to the furthest extent; completely. **3** exactly; directly. **4** correctly or satisfactorily. **5** immediately. ● interj. informal **1** expressing agreement or assent. **2** ironic expressing scorn. □ **as right as rain** perfectly sound. **by right** (or **rights**) justly, in fairness. **do right by** act dutifully towards. **in one's own right** on account of one's own status, effort, etc. **in the right** having justice or truth on one's side. **in one's right mind** sane. **put** (or **set**) **to rights** make correct. **right and left** (or **right, left, and centre**) on all sides. **right away** (also **right off**) immediately. □ **rightness** n. **rightward** adv. & adj.

right angle n. a 90° angle. □ **at right angles** (**to**) placed to form a right angle (with). □ **right-angled** adj.

right brain n. the right half of the cerebrum, controlling the left side of the body, in humans often associated with spatial perception and intuition.

righteous adj. **1** morally right; virtuous. **2** self-righteous. □ **righteously** adv. **righteousness** n. [Say RYE chuss]

rightful adj. **1** having a clear right to something. **2** equitable, fair. □ **rightfully** adv.

right-hand adj. **1** on or towards the right side. **2** done with the right hand.

right-handed ● adj. **1** using the right hand by preference. **2** made to be used by right-handed people. **3** (of a blow) struck with the right hand. **4** turning to the right. ● adv. with the right hand or to the right side. □ **right-handedly** adv.

right-hander n. **1** a right-handed person. **2** a right-handed blow etc.

right-hand man n. an indispensable assistant.

Right Honourable adj. (in Canada) a title given to the Governor General, the prime minister, and the chief justice. Abbreviation: **Rt. Hon.**

rightist ● adj. supporting the principles of the right. ● n. a person or thing supporting such principles.

rightly adv. justly, properly.

right-of-way n. (pl. **rights-of-way**) **1** a right to pass over another's ground. **2** a path subject to such a right. **3** the right of one vehicle to proceed before another.

right-thinking adj. having sound views and principles.

right whale n. a baleen whale with a large head and a deeply curved jaw.

right wing ● n. **1** the conservative or reactionary section of a political party or system. **2** Hockey **a** the forward position to the right of centre. **b** the player at this position. **3** the right side of an army. ● adj. (usu. **right-wing**) conservative or reactionary. □ **right winger** n.

righty informal ● n. (pl. **righties**) **1** a right-handed person. **2** Politics a right winger.

● *adv.* esp. *Baseball* with the right hand or to the right side.

rigid *adj.* **1** that cannot be bent. **2** inflexible, strict. □ **rigidity** *n.* **rigidly** *adv.*

rigmarole *n.* **1** a lengthy and complicated procedure. **2** a long, rambling story. [*Say* RIG muh role]

rigor mortis *n.* stiffening of the body after death. [*Say* rigger MORE tiss]

rigorous *adj.* **1** characterized by rigour; strict. **2** strictly exact or accurate. **3** harsh, severe. □ **rigorously** *adv.* [*Say* RIGGER us]

rigour *n.* (also **rigor**) **1 a** severity, strictness, harshness. **b** (in *pl.*) harsh measures or conditions. **2** logical exactitude. **3** strict enforcement of rules etc. [*Say* RIGGER]

rile *v.* (**riles**, **riled**, **riling**) **1** *informal* anger, irritate. **2** make (water) turbulent.

rill *n.* **1** a small stream. **2** a shallow channel

rim ● *n.* **1** a raised edge or border, esp. of something circular. **2** the part of a pair of eyeglasses surrounding the lenses. **3** the outer edge of a wheel. **4** a boundary line. ● *v.* (**rims**, **rimmed**, **rimming**) form a rim around something. □ **rimless** *adj.* **rimmed** *adj.*

rime *n.* **1** frost. **2** *literary* hoarfrost.

rind *n.* the tough outer layer of fruit, cheese, bacon, etc. [*Rhymes with* FIND]

ring¹ ● *n.* **1** a small circular band of precious metal worn on a finger. **2** a circular band, object, or mark. **3** an enclosed space in which a sport, performance, or show takes place. **4** a group of people or things arranged in a circle. **5** a group of people working together illegally. **6** a number of atoms bonded together to form a closed loop in a molecule. ● *v.* **1** surround. **2** draw a circle around. □ **run** (or **make**) **rings around** *informal* outclass or outwit. □ **ringed** *adj.*

ring² ● *v.* (**rings**; *past* **rang**; *past participle* **rung**; **ringing**) **1** make or cause to make a clear resonant sound. **2** reverberate with (a sound). **3 a** (of a telephone) emit a ring etc. indicating an incoming call. **b** esp. *Brit.* call by telephone. **4** call for attention by sounding a bell. **5** sound (the hour etc.) on a bell or bells. **6** usher in (or out) by or as if by ringing a bell. **7** (of the ears) be filled with a buzzing or humming sound. ● *n.* **1** an act or instance of ringing. **2** a loud clear sound or tone. **3** *informal* a telephone call. **4** a quality conveyed by something heard. □ **ring off the hook** (of a telephone) ring incessantly. **ring true** (or **false**) convey an impression of truth (or falsehood). **ring up 1** record (an amount spent) on a cash register. **2** accomplish. □ **ringing** *adj.*

ringed seal *n.* an Arctic seal with irregular ring-shaped markings.

ringer *n.* **1** *informal* **a** a fraudulent substitute. **b** a person resembling another. **2** a person or device that rings.

ringette *n.* *Cdn* a game resembling hockey, played with a straight stick and a rubber ring.

ring finger *n.* the finger next to the little finger.

ringleader *n.* a leading instigator in an esp. illicit activity.

ringlet *n.* a curly lock of hair.

ringmaster *n.* **1** the person directing a circus performance. **2** *informal* a leader.

ring-necked *adj.* (of an animal, bird, etc.) having a band of colour around the neck.

ringside *n.* the area immediately beside a boxing ring, circus ring, etc.

ring-tailed *adj.* having a tail ringed in alternate colours.

ringworm *n.* a fungous infection of the skin causing circular inflamed patches.

rink *n.* **1** an area of natural or artificial ice for skating, playing hockey, etc. **2** an area for roller skating. **3** a team in curling.

rink rat *n. see* RAT *n.* 4.

rinkside ● *n.* the area adjacent to the ice at a rink. ● *adv.* along the edge of the rink.

rinky-dink *adj.* *informal* second-rate, small-time.

rinse ● *v.* (**rinses**, **rinsed**, **rinsing**) wash with clean water, esp. to remove soap. ● *n.* **1** an act of rinsing something. **2** a dye for temporarily tinting hair. **3** a solution for cleansing the mouth.

riot ● *n.* **1** an esp. violent disturbance of the peace by a crowd. **2** a lavish display. **3** *informal* a very amusing thing or person. ● *v.* (**riots**, **rioted**, **rioting**) make or engage in a riot. □ **run riot** throw off all restraint. □ **rioter** *n.*

Riot Act *n.* a proclamation in the Criminal Code of Canada ordering rioters to disperse. □ **read the riot act** give someone a severe warning.

riotous *adj.* **1** marked by or involving rioting. **2** uproarious. □ **riotously** *adv.* [*Say* RYE uh tus]

RIP *abbr.* may they rest in peace.

rip¹ ● *v.* (**rips**, **ripped**, **ripping**) **1** tear. **2 a** make (a hole etc.) by ripping. **b** make a long tear in. **3** split. **4** rush along. **5** *informal* criticize. ● *n.* **1** a long tear or cut. **2** an act of ripping. **3** *informal* a fraud or swindle □ **let rip** *informal* **1** act without restraint. **2** speak violently. **rip off** *informal* **1** defraud (a person etc.). **2** steal. □ **ripper** *n.*

rip² *n.* a stretch of rough water caused by the meeting of currents.

riparian *adj.* of or on a riverbank.
[*Say* ri PERRY in]

rip cord *n.* a cord for opening a parachute.

ripe *adj.* **1** (of grain, fruit, etc.) ready to be reaped or picked or eaten. **2** mature; fully developed. **3** (of a person's age) advanced. **4** fit or ready. □ **ripely** *adv.* **ripeness** *n.*

ripen *v.* make or become ripe.

rip-off *n. informal* **1** something that is grossly overpriced. **2** an inferior imitation.

riposte ● *n.* a quick sharp reply. ● *v.* (**ripostes, riposted, riposting**) deliver a riposte. [*Say* ri POST *(POST rhymes with* LOST*)*]

ripple ● *n.* **1** a ruffling of the water's surface. **2** a gentle lively sound that rises and falls. **3** something with an undulating pattern. ● *v.* (**ripples, rippled, rippling**) **1** form or cause to form ripples. **2** show or sound like ripples. □ **ripply** *adj.*

ripple effect *n.* the spreading consequences of an event or action.

rip-roaring *adj.* **1** wildly boisterous. **2** excellent, first-rate.

ripstop ● *adj.* (of fabric etc.) woven so that a tear will not spread. ● *n.* ripstop fabric.

riptide *n.* **1** a strong surface current from the shore. **2** a stretch of rough water caused by the meeting of currents.

rise ● *v.* (**rises;** *past* **rose;** *past participle* **risen; rising**) **1** come or go up. **2** get up from. **3** increase in number, size, or quality. **4** (of land) slope upwards. **5** (of the sun etc.) appear above the horizon. **6** reach a higher social or professional position. **7** respond adequately to (a challenge). **8** rebel. **9** (of a river) have its source. ● *n.* **1** an act or instance of rising. **2** an upward slope or hill. □ **get a rise out of** *informal* provoke an emotional reaction from. **on the rise** on the increase. **rise above 1** be superior to (petty feelings etc.). **2** show dignity or strength in the face of (difficulty etc.). **rise and shine** *informal* wake up. □ **rising** *adj.*

riser *n.* **1** a person who rises, esp. from bed. **2** a vertical section between the treads of a staircase. **3 a** a low platform on a stage etc. **b** one of a series of these arranged in step-like fashion.

risible *adj.* deserving to be laughed at.
[*Say* RIZZA bull]

risk ● *n.* **1** a chance of danger or other bad outcome. **2** a person or thing causing a risk. ● *v.* **1** expose to risk. **2** accept the chance of. **3** venture on. □ **at risk** exposed to danger. **at one's (own) risk** accepting responsibility. **at the risk of** with the possibility of. **risk one's neck** put one's own life in danger. **run a (or the) risk** expose oneself to danger or loss etc.

risky *adj.* (**riskier, riskiest**) involving risk. □ **riskiness** *n.*

risotto *n.* (*pl.* **risottos**) an Italian dish of rice cooked in broth with meat, onions, etc. [*Say* ri ZOTTO]

risqué *adj.* slightly indecent. [*Say* riss KAY]

Ritalin *n. proprietary* a drug used esp. to treat attention deficit disorder. [*Say* RITTA lin]

rite *n.* a religious or solemn observance or act.

rite of passage *n.* a ritual or event marking a stage of a person's life, e.g. marriage.

ritual ● *n.* **1** a prescribed order of performing rites. **2** a procedure regularly followed. ● *adj.* of or done as a ritual. □ **ritualize** *v.* (**ritualizes, ritualized, ritualizing**). **ritually** *adv.*

ritualism *n.* the regular or excessive practice of ritual. □ **ritualistic** *adj.* **ritualistically** *adv.*

ritzy *adj.* (**ritzier, ritziest**) *informal* **1** luxurious. **2** fashionable in a showy or gaudy way.

rival ● *n.* **1** a person, team, etc. competing with another for the same objective. **2** a person or thing that equals another in quality etc. **3** (as an *adj.*) being a rival. ● *v.* (**rivals, rivalled, rivalling**) **1** be the rival of or comparable to. **2** seem to be as good as.

rivalrous *adj.* competitive.
[*Say* RIVAL russ]

rivalry *n.* (*pl.* **rivalries**) competition for the same objective or for superiority in the same field.

river *n.* **1** a natural stream of water flowing in a channel to the ocean or a lake etc. **2** a copious flow. □ **sell down the river** *informal* betray or let down. **up the river** *informal* to or in prison.

riverbank *n.* the edge of a river.

riverbed *n.* the channel in which a river flows.

riverboat *n.* a boat for use on rivers.

river drive *n. Cdn* a log drive down a river.

riverine *adj.* of or on a river.
[*Say* RIVER ine]

river lot *n. Cdn hist.* a long narrow farm lot extending back from a river.

riverside *n.* the ground along a riverbank.

rivet ● *n.* a nail or bolt for holding together metal plates etc. ● *v.* (**rivets, riveted, riveting**) **1 a** join or fasten with rivets. **b** fix; make immovable. **2 a** direct intently (one's eyes etc.). **b** engross. □ **riveter** *n.*

rivulet *n.* a small stream. [*Say* RIV yuh lit]

RN *abbr.* **1** Registered Nurse. **2** (in the UK) Royal Navy.

RNA *abbr.* ribonucleic acid.

roach¹ *n.* (*pl.* **roach** or **roaches**) **1** a small European freshwater fish of the carp family. **2** a freshwater fish of N America.

roach² *n.* (*pl.* **roaches**) **1** *informal* a cockroach. **2** *slang* the butt of a marijuana cigarette.

road ● *n.* **1** a path or way with a specially prepared surface; a street. **2 a** one's way or route. **b** a way of accomplishing something. **3** a partly sheltered piece of water in which ships can ride at anchor. ● *adj. Sport* having to do with games played at an opponent's venue. □ **in the** (or **my** etc.) **road** *informal* obstructing a person or thing. **one for the road** *informal* a final drink before departure. **on the road** **1** travelling. **2** (of a car etc.) in working condition. **take to the road** set out. □ **roadless** *adj.*

road allowance *n. Cdn* a strip of land retained by government authorities for the construction of a road. **2** an area at either side of a road which remains a public right-of-way.

roadblock *n.* **1** a barrier or barricade on a road. **2** any obstruction.

road hockey *n. Cdn* street hockey.

roadhouse *n.* a restaurant or bar located on a major road.

roadie *n. informal* a person employed by a touring pop group etc. to set up and maintain equipment. [Say ROAD ee]

roadkill *n.* an animal killed by a vehicle on a road.

road rage *n.* violent anger caused by the stress of driving.

roadrunner *n.* a bird of Mexican and US deserts, which flies poorly but runs fast.

road show *n.* **1** a performance given by a group of touring entertainers. **2** a radio or television program done on location. **3** a touring political or advertising campaign.

roadside *n.* the strip of land beside a road.

roadster *n.* **1** an open two-seater car. **2** a motorcycle for use on roads.

road test ● *n.* **1** a test of the performance of a vehicle on the road. **2** a test of any new product. ● *v.* (**road-test**) **1** test (a vehicle) on the road. **2** test (any new product).

road trip *n.* **1** a series of games played away from home. **2** any journey made by car, bus, etc.

roadway *n.* **1** a road. **2** the portion of a road used by vehicles.

roadwork *n.* **1** the construction or repair of roads. **2** athletic training involving running on roads.

roadworthy *adj.* fit to be used on the road. □ **roadworthiness** *n.*

roam ● *v.* **1** ramble; wander over. **2** (of a cellphone user) move from one geographic area to another without losing phone service. ● *n.* an act of roaming.

roan ● *adj.* (of a horse) having a coat of which the prevailing colour is interspersed with hairs of another colour. ● *n.* a roan animal.

roar ● *n.* **1** a loud deep hoarse sound, as made by a lion, a loud engine, thunder, etc. **2** a loud laugh. ● *v.* **1** utter or make a roar. **2** laugh loudly. **b** travel in a vehicle at high speed.

roaring *adj. in senses of* ROAR *v.* □ **roaring drunk** *informal* very drunk and noisy. **roaring success** *informal* a great success. **roaring trade** *informal* very brisk trade.

roast ● *v.* **1 a** cook (food, esp. meat) in an oven or over a fire. **b** heat (coffee beans) before grinding. **2** criticize severely. **3** undergo roasting. ● *adj.* (of food) roasted. ● *n.* **1** roast meat. **2** a party where roasted food is eaten. **3** a mock-serious ceremonial tribute. □ **roast alive** subject to intense heat. □ **roaster** *n.*

roasting ● *adj.* **1** very hot. **2** used for or fit for roasting. ● *n.* **1** *in senses of* ROAST *v.* **2** a severe criticism or denunciation.

rob *v.* (**robs, robbed, robbing**) **1** take unlawfully from. **2** deprive of what is due or normal. **3** commit robbery. **4** *informal* overcharge. □ **rob Peter to pay Paul** discharge one debt by incurring another. □ **robber** *n.*

robbery *n.* (*pl.* **robberies**) **1** the action of robbing. **2** unashamed swindling or overcharging.

robe ● *n.* **1** a long loose outer garment. **2** a dressing gown or bathrobe. **3** a long outer garment worn as an indication of the wearer's rank, office, etc. **4** a blanket or wrap of fur. ● *v.* (**robes, robed, robing**) clothe in a robe; dress.

Robertson *n. Cdn proprietary* **1** a type of screw with a square notch on the head. **2** a type of screwdriver designed to fit this.

robin *n.* **1** a red-breasted thrush. **2** (also **robin redbreast**) a small brown European bird with a red throat and breast.

Robin Hood *n.* a person who acts unfavourably toward the rich for the benefit of the poor.

robin's egg blue *n. & adj.* a pale greenish-blue colour.

robot *n.* **1** a machine functioning like a human. **2** a machine capable of carrying out a complex series of actions automatically. **3** a person who works mechanically but insensitively. □ **robotic** *adj.* **robotically** *adv.* [Say ROE bot, roe BOT ick]

robotics *pl. n.* the study of robots; the

science of their design and operation. □**roboticist** n. [*Say* roe BOT icks, roe BOTTA sist]

robust adj. (**robuster, robustest**) **1 a** strong and sturdy. **b** healthy, vigorous. **2** (of exercise etc.) vigorous. **3** (of intellect) straightforward. **4** (of a statement etc.) bold, firm. **5** (of wine etc.) rich and full-bodied. **6** (of a computer system) resistant to malfunctioning. □**robustly** adv. **robustness** n.

robusta n. coffee beans from an African species of coffee plant.

rock[1] n. **1** the hard mineral material of the earth's crust. **2** a mass of rock projecting out of the ground or water. **3** a boulder. **4** (**the Rock**) **a** Cdn the island of Newfoundland. **b** Gibraltar. **5** a large polished circular stone, used in the game of curling. **6** Geology any natural material with a distinctive composition of minerals. **7** informal a diamond or other precious stone. □**between a rock and a hard place** in a dilemma. **on the rocks** informal **1** (esp. of a marriage) in danger of breaking up. **2** (of a drink) served undiluted with ice cubes. □**rocklike** adj.

rock[2] ● v. **1** move to and fro. **2** distress, perturb. **3** dance to or play rock music. **4** (of popular music) possess a strong beat. **5** slang be impressive. ● n. **1** a rocking movement. **2** a period of rocking. **3** rock 'n' roll. □**rock the boat** informal disturb the equilibrium of a situation.

rockabilly n. a type of popular music combining rock 'n' roll and hillbilly music. [*Say* ROCKA billy]

rock bass n. a N American freshwater fish frequenting rocky shallows.

rock-bottom ● adj. the very lowest. ● n. (**rock bottom**) the very lowest level.

rocker n. **1** a person or thing that rocks. **2** a curved bar on which something can rock. **3** a rocking chair. **4** a person who performs or enjoys rock music. □**off one's rocker** slang crazy.

rockery n. (pl. **rockeries**) a rock garden.

rocket ● n. **1** a cylindrical projectile that can be propelled by combustion of its contents. **2** (also **rocket engine** or **rocket motor**) an engine using a similar principle. **3** a rocket-propelled missile, spacecraft, etc. **4** anything that moves very quickly. ● v. (**rockets, rocketed, rocketing**) **1** bombard with rockets. **2 a** move quickly. **b** increase rapidly.

rocket science n. a difficult or complicated matter.

rocket scientist n. jocular a person who is highly intelligent, esp. in scientific matters.

rocket ship n. a spaceship powered by rockets.

rock face n. a vertical surface of natural rock.

rockfish n. a fish frequenting rocks or rocky bottoms.

rock garden n. a garden composed of large stones with plants growing between them.

rockhound n. informal a collector of rocks. □**rockhounding** n.

rocking chair n. a chair mounted on rockers or springs for rocking in.

rocking horse n. a model of a horse mounted on rockers or springs for a child to rock on.

rock 'n' roll ● n. a type of popular music originating in the 1950s, characterized by a heavy beat and simple melodies. ● v. informal get down to business. □**rock 'n' roller** n.

rock salt n. common salt as a solid mineral.

rock-solid adj. (also **rock-steady**) very solid or firm.

rocky[1] adj. (**rockier, rockiest**) **1** of or like rock. **2** full of or abounding in rock or rocks. □**rockiness** n.

rocky[2] adj. (**rockier, rockiest**) informal **1** fraught with difficulties etc. **2** unsteady.

rocky road n. **1** a mixture of chocolate chips, marshmallow, and nuts used in ice cream etc. **2** a course of action fraught with difficulties etc.

rococo ● n. a style of art and architecture prevalent in 18th-century Europe, and characterized esp. by lightness and elegance. ● adj. **1** (of furniture or architecture) elaborately ornate. **2** (of art) light, delicate, and highly ornamented. [*Say* ruh CO co]

rod n. **1** a slender straight bar esp. of wood or metal. **2** this as a symbol of office. **3 a** a stick used in caning. **b** punishment. **4** a fishing rod. **5** any of numerous rod-shaped structures in the eye, detecting dim light. □**rod-like** adj.

rode past of RIDE.

rodent n. a gnawing animal of an order that includes rats, mice, squirrels, and other mammals with strong incisors and no canine teeth. □**rodent-like** adj.

rodeo n. (pl. **rodeos**) **1** a display exhibiting the skills of riding broncos, roping cattle, etc. **2** a similar (usu. competitive) exhibition of other skills, e.g. motorcycle riding. **3** a roundup of cattle. [*Say* ROADY oh]

roe n. **1** (also **hard roe**) the mass of eggs in a female fish's ovary, used as food. **2** (also soft roe) the ripe testes of a male fish, used as food.

roentgen n. a unit of ionizing radiation. [Say RONT gun or RUNT gun]

roger interj. **1** your message has been received and understood (used in radio communication etc.). **2** slang OK.

rogue n. **1** a dishonest or unprincipled person. **2** jocular a mischievous person. **3 a** a wild animal living apart from the herd. **b** a stray or undisciplined person or thing. [Say ROAG]

rogues' gallery n. **1** a collection of photographs of known criminals etc. **2** any collection of people notable for a certain quality, esp. a disreputable one.

roguish adj. **1** playfully mischievous. **2** characteristic of a rogue. □ **roguishly** adv. [Say ROE gish]

roil v. **1** make (a liquid) muddy by disturbing the sediment. **2** (esp. of liquid) move in a turbulent manner. [Sounds like ROYAL]

roistering ● adj. enjoying oneself or celebrating in a noisy or boisterous way. ● n. noisy or boisterous celebration.

role n. **1** a performer's part in a play, film, etc. **2** a person's or thing's function. **3** the part played by a person in society, life, etc.

role model n. a person looked to by others as an example.

role-playing n. a learning activity in which a person acts as they would expect another to behave in a particular situation. □ **role-play** v. **role player** n.

roll ● v. **1** move by turning over and over. **2** move forward on wheels or with a smooth, undulating motion. **3** (of an aircraft or vehicle) sway from side to side. **4** (of a machine or device) begin operating. **5** turn (something flexible) over and over on itself to form a cylindrical shape. **6** flatten (something) by passing a roller over it or by passing it between rollers. **7** (of a loud, deep sound) reverberate. **8** pronounce (an r) with a trill. **9** throw (dice). **10** set out. ● n. **1** a cylinder formed by rolling flexible material. **2** a rolling movement. **3** a gymnastic exercise in which the body is rolled into a tucked position and turned in a forward or backward circle. **4** a long, deep, reverberating sound. **5** (in drumming) a sustained, rapid alternation of single or double strokes of each stick. **6** a very small loaf of bread. **7** an official list or register of names. □ **be rolling in** informal have plenty of (esp. money). **on a roll** slang experiencing a bout of success or progress. **roll back 1** reduce. **2** turn or force back. **roll in the aisles** informal laugh uproariously. **roll**

out 1 a unveil (a new aircraft). **b** launch (a new product etc.). **2** slang get out of bed. **roll up 1** informal arrive. **2** make into or form a roll. **roll with the punches** informal adapt oneself to difficult circumstances.

rollback n. a reduction or decrease in prices, wages, etc.

roll bar n. an overhead metal bar protecting the occupants if the vehicle overturns.

roll call n. the reading aloud of a list of names to establish who is present.

rolled oats pl. n. oats that have been husked and crushed.

roller n. **1 a** a revolving cylinder used to move, flatten, or spread something. **b** a cylinder for diminishing friction when moving a heavy object. **2** a small cylinder on which hair is rolled for setting. **3** a long swelling wave.

Rollerblade ● n. proprietary an in-line skate. ● v. (**rollerblade, rollerblades, rollerbladed, rollerblading**) skate using in-line skates. □ **rollerblader** n.

roller coaster ● n. **1** a ride at an amusement park etc. having small open railway cars which travel on an elevated, winding track up and down steep hills. **2** something marked by sudden ups and downs. ● adj. (**roller-coaster**) that goes up and down, or changes, suddenly and repeatedly.

roller hockey n. hockey played on in-line skates.

roller skate ● n. each of a pair of boots with wheels attached for riding on paved surfaces etc. ● v. (**roller skates, roller skated, roller skating**) move on roller skates. □ **roller skater** n.

rollicking adj. lively, fast-paced, and amusing.

rolling adj. **1** that turns over and over, esp. so as to move forward on a surface or down a slope. **2** that moves or runs upon wheels. **3** (esp. of strikes, power cuts, etc.) taking place in different places in succession; staggered, rotating. **4** (of a landscape) gently undulating.

rolling pin n. a cylinder for rolling out pastry, dough, etc.

rolling stock n. the locomotives, cars, or other vehicles used on a railway.

rolling stone n. a person who is unwilling to settle in one place.

rollout n. **1** the official wheeling out of a new aircraft or spacecraft. **2** the official launch of a new product.

rollover n. **1** Economics the further investment of stocks, bonds, mutual funds, etc. **2** *informal* the overturning of a vehicle etc.

Rolodex *n.* (*pl.* **Rolodexes**) *proprietary* a desktop card index, used for storing telephone numbers etc. [*Say* ROLA dex]

roly-poly *adj.* pudgy, plump.

ROM *n. Computing* read-only memory [*Say* ROM]

romaine *n.* a variety of lettuce with crisp narrow leaves. [*Say* roe MAIN]

Roman ● *adj.* **1** of ancient Rome or its territory or people. **2** of medieval or modern Rome. **3** of papal Rome. **4** (**roman**) (of type) of a plain upright kind used in ordinary print. **5** (of the alphabet etc.) based on the ancient Roman system with letters A–Z. ● *n.* **1** a person who lives or lived in Rome. **2** a soldier of the Roman Empire. **3** (**roman**) roman type.

Roman Catholic ● *adj.* relating to the part of the Christian Church acknowledging the Pope as its head. ● *n.* a member of this Church. □ **Roman Catholicism** *n.*

romance ● *n.* **1 a** a love affair. **b** idealized love. **c** a prevailing sense of wonder or mystery surrounding a love affair **2** a feeling of excitement and adventure. **3** a literary genre with romantic love or highly imaginative episodes forming the central theme. **4** a medieval tale of some hero of chivalry. ● *adj.* (**Romance**) of any of the languages descended from Latin (e.g. French, Italian, Spanish, etc.). ● *v.* (**romances, romanced, romancing**) **1** attempt to win the love of someone. **2** romanticize.

Romanesque *n.* a style of architecture prevalent in Europe *c.* 900–1200, with massive vaulting and round arches. [*Say* roman ESK]

Romanian *n.* **1** a person from Romania. **2** the Romance language of Romania. □ **Romanian** *adj.* [*Say* roe MAINY in]

Roman numeral *n.* any of the Roman letters representing numbers: I = 1, V = 5, X = 10, etc.

Romano *n.* a strong-tasting hard cheese. [*Say* roe MAN oh]

romano bean *n.* a variety of green or yellow snap bean, with a strong flavour and a meaty texture.

Romansh ● *n.* a Romance language spoken in the Swiss canton of Grisons. ● *adj.* having to do with this language. [*Say* roe MANSH]

romantic ● *adj.* **1** inclined towards or suggestive of romance in love. **2** having to do with an idealized or fantastic view of reality. **3** (of a person) imaginative, idealistic. **4 a** (of style in art, music, etc.)

concerned more with feeling and emotion than with form and aesthetic qualities. **b** (also **Romantic**) of or relating to the Romanticism of the 18th and 19th centuries. **5** not practical, fantastic. ● *n.* **1** a romantic person. **2** a writer or artist of the Romantic school. □ **romantically** *adv.*

romanticism *n.* **1** (also **Romanticism**) adherence to a romantic style in art, music, etc. **2** a tendency towards romance. **3** (**Romanticism**) a movement in the arts and literature, originating in the late 18th century, favouring creative inspiration, subjectivity, and the primacy of the individual.

romanticize *v.* (**romanticizes, romanticized, romanticizing**) deal with or describe something in an idealized or unrealistic fashion. □ **romanticization** *n.*

Romany *n.* (*pl.* **Romanies**) **1** a gypsy. **2** the Indo-European language of the gypsies. □ **Romany** *adj.* [*Say* ROMMA nee]

Romeo *n.* (*pl.* **Romeos**) a passionate male lover.

romp ● *v.* **1** play about roughly and energetically. **2** *informal* proceed easily. **3** win a race etc. with ease. ● *n.* **1** a period of romping. **2** a song, play, etc. that is lively and lighthearted. **3** *Sport* an easy victory. **4** a playful sexual encounter.

romper *n.* (also **romper suit, rompers** *pl. n.*) a young child's one-piece garment covering the legs and trunk.

rondo *n.* (*pl.* **rondos**) a musical form with a recurring theme. [*Say* RON doe]

roof ● *n.* (*pl.* **roofs**) **1 a** the upper outside covering of a building. **b** any external covering forming a top. **2** the overhead inner surface of a covered space. ● *v.* cover with or as with a roof. □ **go through the roof** *informal* (of prices etc.) reach extreme heights. **hit** (or **go through**) **the roof** *informal* become very angry. **raise the roof** make a lot of noise inside a building. **under one roof** in the same building. □ **roofed** *adj.* **roofless** *adj.*

roofer *n.* a person who constructs or repairs roofs.

roofing *n.* **1** the material for making roofs. **2** the process of building roofs.

roofline *n.* the outline of a roof or roofs.

roof rack *n.* a frame for carrying luggage etc. on the roof of a car.

rooftop *n.* the outer surface of a roof.

rook ● *n.* **1** a chess piece that can move in a straight line forwards, backwards, or sideways. **2** a black Eurasian bird of the crow family. ● *v.* charge (a customer) in an extortionate way; swindle.

rookery n. (pl. **rookeries**) **1** a colony of seabirds or seals. **2 a** a colony of rooks. **b** a clump of trees having rooks' nests.

rookie n. *informal* **1** a new member in a particular athletic league. **2** a new recruit. **3** a novice.

room ● n. **1** space viewed in terms of its capacity to do or hold things. **2** opportunity, scope. **3** a part of a building enclosed by walls, floor, and ceiling. **4** (in pl.) a set of rooms rented out to lodgers. ● v. rent a room or rooms; lodge. □ **make room** clear a space for. □ **-roomed** comb. form **roomful** n.

room and board n. **1** accommodation and meals. **2** the cost of this.

roomie n. *informal* a roommate.

rooming house n. a house etc. divided into furnished rooms for rent.

roommate n. a person who lives in the same apartment etc. as another.

room service n. (in a hotel etc.) a service providing drinks or a meal to guests in their rooms.

room temperature n. a temperature that would be considered normal in a house usu. approx. 20° C.

roomy adj. (**roomier, roomiest**) having plenty of room; spacious. □ **roominess** n.

roost ● n. a place where birds or bats regularly settle, esp. to sleep. ● v. (of a bird) settle for rest or sleep. □ **come home to roost** (of a scheme etc.) have negative consequences for the person who originated it.

rooster n. a male chicken.

root ● n. **1** a part of a plant normally below ground, which acts as a support and collects water and nourishment. **2** the embedded part of a bodily structure such as a hair. **3** a vegetable which grows as the root of a plant. **4** the basic cause or origin. **5** (in pl.) family, ethnic, or cultural origins. **6** *Linguistics* the part of a word that has the main meaning. **7** *Music* the lowest note of a chord in its original form. **8** *Math* a number that when multiplied by itself one or more times gives a specified number. ● v. **1** develop roots. **2** fix firmly with or as if with roots. **3** dig up by the roots. **4** (of an animal) turn up (the ground) with the snout, beak, etc. **5 a** rummage around. **b** find by rummaging. **6** *informal* encourage with cheering etc. □ **put down roots** become settled or established. **take root** become fixed or established. **root out** find and get rid of. □ **rooter** n. **rootless** adj. **rootlessness** n. **rootlike** adj.

root beer n. a carbonated drink made from an extract of roots.

root canal n. **1** the pulp-filled cavity in the root of a tooth. **2** a procedure to replace the infected pulp of a tooth.

root cellar n. an underground room in a house for storing esp. vegetables.

rooted adj. **1** firmly established. **2** having a root or roots. □ **rootedness** n.

rootstock n. **1** a stock onto which another variety has been grafted. **2** a rhizome.

rootsy adj. (**rootsier, rootsiest**) *informal* (esp. of music) non-commercial, esp. showing traditional origins.

rope ● n. **1** a length of strong thick cord made by twisting together strands of hemp, nylon, etc. **2** a quantity of similar things strung together. **3** (**the ropes**) **a** the rules and procedures of a business, operation, etc. **b** the ropes enclosing a boxing or wrestling ring etc. ● v. (**ropes, roped, roping**) **1** fasten, secure, or catch with rope. **2** enclose (a space) with rope. **3** persuade or entice someone to take part in something. □ **on the ropes** near defeat. □ **ropelike** adj. **roping** n. **ropy** adj.

roper n. a person who uses a lasso to catch and secure cattle etc.

roquefort n. a soft blue cheese made from ewes' milk. [*Say* ROKE furt]

rorqual n. a baleen whale characterized by a pleated throat and small dorsal fin. [*Say* ROAR kwull]

Rorschach adj. designating a type of personality test in which participants are asked to interpret a standard set of ink blots. [*Say* ROAR shack *or* ROAR shock]

rosacea n. a condition in which certain blood vessels enlarge, giving the cheeks and nose a flushed appearance. [*Say* rose AISHA]

rosary n. (pl. **rosaries**) **1** *Catholicism* a form of devotion in which sets of Hail Marys are repeated. **2** a string of beads for keeping count of prayers said. [*Say* ROZA ree]

rose[1] ● n. **1** a prickly bush or shrub that bears fragrant flowers. **2** the flower of this. **3** a light crimson colour; pink. **4** a rose-shaped design or ornament. ● adj. pink or pale red. □ **come up roses** develop in a very favourable way.

rose[2] past of RISE.

rosé n. **1** any pale red or pink wine. **2** designating a pasta sauce made by combining tomato sauce and cream sauce. [*Say* roe ZAY]

roseate adj. **1** having a partly pink plumage. **2** rose-coloured. [*Say* ROZY it]

rosebud n. **1** a bud of a rose. **2** representing something resembling a rosebud in nature or appearance.

rose-coloured adj. rose-pink. □ **see through rose-coloured glasses**

regard (circumstances etc.) with unfounded optimism.

rosehip *n.* the fruit of a rose.

rosemary *n.* **1** a fragrant shrub of the mint family. **2** the leaves of this used as a herb.

rosette *n.* **1** an ornament resembling or representing a rose. **2** a rose-shaped arrangement of ribbon worn esp. as a badge, or as a symbol of a prize won. **3** markings resembling a rose. [*Say* rose ETT]

rosewater *n.* water distilled from roses, or scented with the essence of roses.

rosewood *n.* a fragrant wood derived esp. from tropical leguminous trees, used in making furniture.

Rosh Hashanah *n.* the festival celebrating the Jewish New Year. [*Say* rosh huh SHONNA]

rosin ● *n.* a kind of resin, used on the bows of stringed instruments, dancers' shoes, etc. to prevent slipping. ● *v.* (**rosins, rosined, rosining**) treat with rosin. [*Say* ROZZIN]

roster *n.* **1** *Sport* a list of players belonging or available to a team. **2** any list of people belonging to a specified group. **3** a list or plan showing turns of duty or leave for individuals or groups in an organization.

rostrum *n.* (*pl.* **rostra** or **rostrums**) a platform or pulpit for public speaking. [*Say* ROSS trum]

rosy *adj.* (**rosier, rosiest**) **1 a** pink or red. **b** pink as an indication of health. **2** promising.

rot ● *v.* (**rots, rotted, rotting**) **1** decay. **2** (of society etc.) deteriorate. ● *n.* **1 a** the process or state of rotting. **b** rotten or decayed matter. **2** a disease in plants causing the decay of tissue. **3** a decline in standards. **4** *slang* nonsense.

rotary *adj.* **1** acting by rotation. **2** operating through the rotation of some part. [*Say* ROE tuh ree]

rotate *v.* (**rotates, rotated, rotating**) **1** move around an axis or centre. **2 a** change the position etc. of a person or thing in a regularly recurring order. **b** act or occur in turns. □ **rotatable** *adj.* **rotator** *n.* [*Say* ROW tate, ROTATE a bull]

rotation *n.* **1** the action of rotating. **2** a regular organized order of things, events, or people. **3** a system of growing different crops in regular order. **4** a tour of duty. □ **rotational** *adj.*

rotator cuff *n.* the muscles that support the arm at the shoulder joint.

rote *adj.* by routine or mechanical repetition etc. □ **by rote 1** in a mechanical

manner. **2** acquired through memorization without understanding.

rotgut *n. slang* cheap usu. inferior alcoholic liquor.

roti *n.* (*pl.* **rotis**) a dish of Indian origin consisting of unleavened bread folded over usu. a spicy filling. [*Say* ROE tee]

rotini *n.* a variety of pasta in small spirals. [*Say* roe TEENY]

rotisserie *n.* **1** a rotating spit for roasting meat. **2** a fantasy baseball league. [*Say* roe TISSER ee]

rotor *n.* **1** a rotary part of a machine. **2** a hub with a set of radiating airfoils on a helicopter etc. that provides lift when rotated.

Rototiller *n.* a machine with rotating blades used for breaking up soil. □ **rototill** *v.* [*Say* ROE toe tiller]

rotten *adj.* (**rottener, rottenest**) **1 a** in a state of decomposition or decay. **b** falling to pieces. **2** miserable, wretched. **3** despicable, vile. **4** (also **rotting**) *Cdn* designating ice or snow which has become granular and weak. **5** corrupt. □ **spoil someone rotten** spoil a person excessively.

Rottweiler *n.* a large, stocky, powerful dog having short hair with black and tan markings. [*Say* ROT wile er]

rotund *adj.* (of a person) fat. [*Say* roe TUND]

rotunda *n.* **1** a circular hall or room. **2** a building with a circular ground plan, esp. with a dome. [*Say* roe TUNDA]

rouge ● *n.* **1** a red powder or cream used for colouring the cheeks. **2** (**rouge**) *Cdn* esp. *hist.* a Quebec supporter of a Liberal party. **3** *Cdn Football* a single point scored when the receiving team fails to run a kick out of the end zone. ● *v.* (**rouges, rouged, rouging**) colour with rouge. [*Say* ROOZH]

rough ● *adj.* **1** not smooth or level. **2** not gentle. **3 a** (of the sea, weather, etc.) violent, stormy. **b** (of a flight etc.) bumpy. **4** lacking refinement. **5** plain and basic. **6** harsh in sound or taste. **7** not worked out in every detail; approximate. **8** *informal* difficult and unpleasant. ● *adv.* **1** in a rough manner. **2** (live or sleep etc.) outdoors. ● *n.* **1** a rough, preliminary state. **2** *Golf* the area of longer grass around the fairway and the green. ● *v.* shape or plan roughly. □ **rough and ready** simple or crude but effective. **rough around the edges 1** (of a person) irritable. **2** (of a thing) having a few imperfections. **rough it** live in rough accommodation without basic comforts. **rough up** *slang* treat with violence or abuse. □ **roughness** *n.*

roughage *n.* **1** dietary fibre. **2** coarse fodder. [Say RUFF idge]

rough-and-tumble ● *adj.* disregarding rules. ● *n.* a free-for-all.

roughcast *n.* plaster of lime and gravel, used on outside walls.

rough cut ● *n.* the first version of a film. ● *adj.* (usu. **rough-cut**) (of a log etc.) having been cut with a coarse blade to an approximate size.

roughen *v.* make or become rough.

rough-hewn *adj.* **1** uncouth, unrefined. **2** cut or shaped out roughly.

roughhouse ● *n.* boisterous play or wrestling. ● *v.* (**roughhouses, roughhoused, roughhousing**) engage in rambunctious behaviour. □ **roughhousing** *n.* [Say RUFF house]

roughing *n. Hockey* an unnecessary use of force for which a player is given a penalty.

roughly *adv.* **1** approximately. **2** in a coarse or uneven manner. **3** in a harsh manner.

roughneck *informal* ● *n.* **1** a rough or rowdy person. **2** a worker on an oil rig. ● *v.* work as a roughneck.

roughrider *n.* a person who breaks in unbroken horses.

roughshod *adj.* (of a horse) having shoes with nail heads projecting to prevent slipping. □ **ride roughshod over** push around. [Say RUFF shod]

roughy *n.* (*pl.* **roughies**) a kind of rough-skinned marine fish. [Say RUFFY]

roulette *n.* a gambling game in which a ball is dropped onto a revolving wheel with numbered compartments, players betting on the number at which the ball will come to rest. [Say roo LET]

round ● *adj.* **1** shaped like a circle, cylinder, or sphere. **2** having a curved surface. **3** (of shoulders) bent forward. **4** (of a voice or musical tone) rich and mellow. **5** (of a number) expressed in convenient units rather than exactly, e.g. to the nearest whole number. ● *n.* **1** a circular piece or section. **2** a route by which a number of people or places are visited in turn. **3** a regular sequence of activities. **4** each of a sequence of sessions in a process. **5** a single division of a boxing or wrestling match. **6** a song for three or more unaccompanied voices or parts, each singing the same theme but starting one after another. **7** the amount of ammunition needed to fire one shot. **8** a set of drinks bought for all the members of a group. **9** a single outburst of applause. ● *adv. & prep. esp. Brit.* = AROUND. ● *v.* **1** make or become round. **2** pass around (a corner etc.). **3** express (a number) in a less exact but more convenient form. □ **in the round 1** with all features shown.

2 *Theatre* with the audience around at least three sides of the stage. **3** (of sculpture) with all sides shown. **make one's rounds** take a customary route for inspection etc. **round about 1** all round. **2** with a change to an opposite position. **3** approximately. **round off 1** bring to a complete or well-ordered state. **2** smooth the corners of. **3** = ROUND *v.* **3**. **round on** make a sudden verbal attack on. **round out** provide more detail about. **round up 1** collect or bring together. **2** express a number in a less exact but more convenient form by increasing it. □ **roundish** *adj.* **roundness** *n.*

roundabout *adj.* indirect.

rounded *adj.* **1** that has been rounded. **2** round or curved. **3** possessing a pleasing depth or wide range of characteristics etc.

roundel *n.* **1** a small circular object. **2** a circular identifying mark painted on military aircraft. **3** a poem of eleven lines in three stanzas. [Say ROUND ul]

rounder *n.* **1** *slang* a person who makes the rounds of prisons or bars. **2** a boxing match of a specified number of rounds.

Roundhead *n.* a member or supporter of the party opposing Charles I in the English Civil War.

roundhouse *n.* a circular repair shed for railway locomotives.

roundly *adv.* **1** bluntly, severely. **2** vigorously. **3** in a circular way.

round robin *n.* a tournament in which each competitor plays in turn against every other.

round-shouldered *adj.* with shoulders bent forward.

round table *n.* an assembly for discussion.

round-the-clock *adj.* lasting all day and usu. all night.

round trip *n.* a trip to a place and back again.

roundup *n.* **1** a systematic rounding up of people or things. **2** the people and horses engaged in the rounding up of cattle etc. **3** a summary.

roundwood *n.* timber used in the round without being squared by sawing or hewing.

roundworm *n.* a nematode worm, infesting the gut of a mammal or bird.

rouse *v.* (**rouses, roused, rousing**) **1** bring out of sleep; wake. **2** stir up, arouse. **3** provoke to anger. □ **rouse oneself** become active.

rousing *adj.* exciting, stirring.

roust *v.* rouse, stir up.

rout[1] ● *n.* **1** a disorderly retreat of defeated troops. **2** a decisive defeat. ● *v.* **1** cause to

retreat in disorder. **2** defeat decisively.
□ **put to rout** put to flight.

rout² *v.* **1** = ROOT *v.* 4, 5. **2** cut a groove in (a surface).

route ● *n.* **1 a** a way taken in getting from a starting point to a destination, **b** a series of steps taken to achieve something. **2** a round of stops regularly travelled. ● *v.* (**routes, routed, routing**) send along a particular route. [*Rhymes with* SHOOT *or* SHOUT]

router¹ *n.* a tool for cutting grooves etc. [*Rhymes with* SHOUTER]

router² *n.* a device which forwards data packets to the appropriate parts of a computer network. [*Rhymes with* SHOUTER]

routine ● *n.* **1** a regular course or procedure. **2** a set sequence in a dance, comedy act, etc. **3** *informal* a hackneyed, predictable response. ● *adj.* **1** performed as part of a routine. **2** of a customary kind. □ **routinely** *adv.*

rove *v.* (**roves, roved, roving**) **1** wander without a settled destination. **2** (of eyes) look in all directions. □ **rover** *n.* **roving** *adj.*

row¹ *n.* **1** a number of persons or things in a line. **2** a line of seats across a theatre etc. **3** a street with a continuous line of houses along one or each side. **4** a line of plants in a field or garden. □ **a hard** (or **long etc.**) **row to hoe** a difficult task. **in a row 1** forming a row. **2** in succession.

row² ● *v.* propel a boat with oars. ● *n.* a period of rowing. □ **rower** *n.*

row³ *informal* ● *n.* a fierce quarrel. ● *v.* make or engage in a row. [*Rhymes with* NOW]

rowan *n.* **1** (also **rowan tree**) = MOUNTAIN ASH. **2** (also **rowanberry** *pl.* **rowanberries**) the scarlet berry of this tree. [*Say* ROW un *(*ROW *rhymes with* CROW *or* COW)]

rowboat *n.* a small boat propelled by oars.

rowdy ● *adj.* (**rowdier, rowdiest**) noisy and disorderly. ● *n.* (*pl.* **rowdies**) a rowdy person. □ **rowdily** *adv.* **rowdiness** *n.* **rowdyism** *n.*

row house *n.* a number of houses joined in a row.

rowing machine *n.* an exercise machine for simulating the action of rowing.

royal ● *adj.* **1** of or suited to a king or queen. **2** in the service of a king or queen. **3** majestic, stately. **4** on a great scale, first-rate. ● *n. informal* a member of the royal family. □ **royally** *adv.*

Royal Air Force *n.* the British air force.

royal assent *n.* the formal consent of the sovereign or his or her representative to a bill passed by Parliament.

royal blue *n.* & *adj.* a deep vivid blue.

Royal Canadian Mounted Police *n.* Canada's national police force.

Royal Commission *n.* a commission of inquiry appointed by the Crown at the request of the government.

royalist *n.* **1** a supporter of monarchy. **2** *hist.* a supporter of the King against Parliament in the English Civil War (1642–9).

royal jelly *n.* a substance secreted by honeybee workers and fed by them to future queen bees.

royalty *n.* (*pl.* **royalties**) **1** the office or power of a king or queen. **2 a** royal persons. **b** a member of a royal family. **3** a sum paid for the use of a patent or to an author etc. for each copy of a book etc. sold or for each public performance of a work.

rpm *abbr.* revolutions per minute.

RR *abbr.* **1** railroad. **2** rural route.

RRIF *abbr.* (*pl.* **RRIFs**) *Cdn* Registered Retirement Income Fund, a tax-sheltered savings plan which provides retirement income. [*Say* RIFF]

RRSP *abbr.* (*pl.* **RRSPs**) *Cdn* Registered Retirement Savings Plan, a tax-sheltered plan for saving for retirement.

RSI *abbr.* (*pl.* **RSIs**) REPETITIVE STRAIN INJURY.

RSVP ● *n.* (*pl.* **RSVPs**) a reply to an invitation. ● *v.* (**RSVP's, RSVP'd; RSVP'ing**) reply to an invitation.

Rte. *abbr.* route.

RTF *abbr.* rich text format, a file format which permits easy transfer of graphics and formatted text between different applications and operating systems.

Rt. Hon. *abbr.* Right Honourable.

Rt. Rev. *abbr.* Right Reverend.

rub ● *v.* (**rubs, rubbed, rubbing**) **1** apply pressure with a repeated back and forth motion. **2** reproduce the design of (a carving) by rubbing paper laid on it with coloured chalk etc. ● *n.* **1** an act of rubbing. **2** an impediment or difficulty. **3** a substance applied by rubbing. **4** a massage. □ **not have two coins to rub together** have no money. **rub elbows** (or **shoulders**) **with** associate or come into contact with. **rub it in** (or **rub a person's nose in it**) emphasize or repeat an embarrassing fact etc. **rub off 1** be transferred by contact. **2** remove by rubbing. **rub out 1** erase. **2** *slang* kill, eliminate. **rub salt into** (or **in**) **the wound** (or **wounds**) behave so as to aggravate a hurt already inflicted. **rub the wrong way** irritate.

rubber *n.* **1** a tough elastic substance made from the latex of plants or synthetically.

2 a piece of this for erasing pencil marks. **3** *informal* a condom. **4** (in *pl.*) galoshes. **5** (**the rubber**) *Hockey slang* the puck. **6** a deciding game when scores are even. □ **burn** (or **lay**) **rubber 1** travel very quickly in a car. **2** leave tire tracks on a surface, usu. by accelerating or braking rapidly. □ **rubbery** *adj.*

rubber band *n.* a loop of rubber for holding things together.

rubber cement *n.* an adhesive containing rubber in a solvent.

rubberize *v.* (**rubberizes**, **rubberized**, **rubberizing**) treat or coat with rubber.

rubberneck *informal* ● *n.* a person who stares inquisitively or stupidly. ● *v.* act in this way. □ **rubbernecker** *n.*

rubber plant *n.* **1** an evergreen plant with dark green shiny leaves. **2** (also **rubber tree**) a tropical tree yielding latex used to make rubber.

rubber stamp ● *n.* **1** a device for inking and imprinting on a surface. **2** an automatic approval. ● *v.* (**rubber-stamp**) approve automatically without proper consideration.

rubbing *n.* an impression of a carved design made by rubbing chalk etc. on a piece of paper laid over it.

rubbing alcohol *n.* alcohol used in massaging, as an antiseptic, etc.

rubbish *n.* **1** esp. *Brit.* waste material. **2** worthless material. **3** nonsense. □ **rubbishy** *adj.*

rubble *n.* rough fragments of stone or brick etc.

rubby *n.* (*pl.* **rubbies**) (also **rubbydub**) *Cdn slang* a person who drinks rubbing alcohol etc.; a derelict alcoholic.

rubdown *n.* a massage.

rube *n. informal* a country bumpkin.

rubella *n.* German measles. [*Say* roo BELLA]

ruble *n.* the chief monetary unit of Russia and some other former republics of the USSR. [*Say* ROO bull]

rubric *n.* a category or designation. [*Say* ROO brick]

ruby *n.* (*pl.* **rubies**) **1** a rare precious stone of a deep red colour. **2** *n. & adj.* a glowing purplish-red colour.

ruby red *n.* a sweet variety of grapefruit with dark red flesh.

ruche *n.* a frill or gathering of lace etc. □ **ruched** *adj.* **ruching** *n.* [*Say* ROOSH]

ruck *n.* (**the ruck**) **1** an undistinguished crowd of persons or things. **2** (in racing) the main body of competitors not likely to overtake the leaders.

rucked up *adj.* creased or folded; wrinkled.

rucksack *n.* a backpack.

ruckus *n.* (*pl.* **ruckuses**) *informal* a noisy disturbance.

rudbeckia *n.* (*pl.* **rudbeckias**) a N American plant of the daisy family, bearing flowers with a dark cone-like centre. [*Say* rud BECKY uh]

rudder *n.* a flat piece hinged vertically to the back of a boat or airplane, used for steering. □ **rudderless** *adj.*

ruddy *adj.* (**ruddier**, **ruddiest**) **1** (of a complexion) freshly or healthily red. **2** reddish. □ **ruddiness** *n.*

rude *adj.* (**ruder**, **rudest**) **1** impolite or offensive. **2** roughly made or done. **3** unsophisticated. **4** *informal* indecent, lewd. □ **rudely** *adv.* **rudeness** *n.*

rude awakening *n.* a severe disillusionment or arousal from complacency.

rudiment *n.* **1** (in *pl.*) the basic elements of a subject. **2** an imperfect beginning of something not developed. **3** *Biology* a part or organ not yet developed. [*Say* ROODA m'nt]

rudimentary *adj.* **1** involving basic principles; fundamental. **2** incompletely developed. [*Say* rooda MENTA ree]

rue¹ *v.* (**rues**, **rued**, **rueing** or **ruing**) repent of; bitterly regret.

rue² *n.* a perennial evergreen shrub with bitter leaves formerly used in medicine.

rueful *adj.* expressing sorrow or regret. □ **ruefully** *adv.*

ruff *n.* **1** a starched frill worn around the neck. **2** a ring of feathers or hair around a bird's or animal's neck. **3** a fringe of fur around the hood of a jacket.

ruffed grouse *n.* a N American woodland grouse with a black or reddish ruff on the neck.

ruffian *n.* a violent lawless person.

ruffle ● *v.* (**ruffles**, **ruffled**, **ruffling**) **1** disturb the smoothness or tranquility of. **2** upset the calmness of. **3** gather (fabric) into a ruffle. **4 a** (of a bird) erect (its feathers) in anger etc. **b** disorder or disarrange (hair). ● *n.* an ornamental frill used to decorate the edge of a garment etc. □ **ruffle feathers** (or **a person's feathers**) *informal* upset or annoy.

rufous *adj.* reddish brown. [*Say* ROO fuss]

rug *n.* **1** a piece of thick material or animal skin, placed as a covering on the floor. **2** *slang* a toupée. □ **pull the rug** (**out**) **from under** deprive of support.

rugby *n.* (also **rugby football**) a team game played with an oval ball that may be kicked, carried, and passed by hand.

rugby shirt n. a men's usu. cotton casual shirt with a collar.

rugelach n. a type of small cookie consisting of pastry rolled up to form a crescent shape over a filling of cinnamon sugar, nuts, etc. [Say ROOGA loch]

rugged adj. **1** having a rough uneven surface. **2** (of features) strongly marked. **3** unpolished. **b** austere. **4** (esp. of a machine) robust. □ **ruggedly** adv. **ruggedness** n.

rug rat n. slang a small child.

ruin ● n. **1 a** a destroyed or wrecked state. **2** a person's or thing's downfall. **3** the complete loss of one's property or position. **4** the remains of a building etc. that has suffered ruin. **5** a cause of ruin. ● v. **1 a** bring to ruin. **b** utterly wreck. **2** reduce to ruins.

ruination n. the act of ruining or the state of being ruined.

ruinous adj. **1** bringing ruin. **2** in ruins. □ **ruinously** adv.

rule ● n. **1** a principle to which something etc. conforms or is required to conform. **2** a prevailing custom or standard. **3** government or dominion. **4** the period during which a government or monarch holds power. **5** = RULER 2. **6** a code of discipline of a religious order. ● v. (**rules, ruled, ruling**) **1** exercise decisive influence over. **2** have sovereign control of. **3** pronounce authoritatively. **4** make lines across (paper). **5** be prevalent. **6** slang be pre-eminent □ **as a rule** usually. **rule out 1** exclude. **2** make impossible. **rule the roost** be in control.

rule of thumb n. a general guide based on practice rather than theory.

ruler n. **1** a person exercising government or dominion. **2** a straight-edged strip of rigid material marked at regular intervals, used to draw lines or measure distance.

ruling ● n. an authoritative decision or announcement. ● adj. prevailing.

rum n. a liquor distilled from sugar cane or molasses.

rumba ● n. **1** an Afro-Cuban dance. **2** a ballroom dance imitative of this. ● v. (**rumbas, rumbaed** or **rumba'd, rumbaing**) dance the rumba.

rumble ● v. (**rumbles, rumbled, rumbling**) **1** make a continuous deep sound, like thunder. **2** move with a rumbling noise. **3** slang engage in a street fight. ● n. **1** a rumbling sound. **2** slang a street fight between gangs.

rumblings pl. n. early indications of something.

rumen n. the first stomach of a ruminant. [Say ROO mun]

ruminant ● n. an animal that chews the cud, e.g. a cow. ● adj. of ruminants. [Say ROOMA n'nt]

ruminate v. (**ruminates, ruminated, ruminating**) **1** meditate, ponder. **2** (of ruminants) chew the cud. □ **rumination** n. **ruminative** adj. [Say ROO min ate, roo min AY sh'n, ROO min a tiv]

rummage ● v. (**rummages, rummaged, rummaging**) search, esp. in a disorganized way. ● n. a disorganized search.

rummage sale n. a sale of miscellaneous usu. second-hand articles.

rummy n. a card game in which players try to form sets and sequences of cards.

rumour (also **rumor**) ● n. **1** general talk or hearsay. **2** a current but not verified assertion. ● v. report by way of rumour.

rump n. **1** the hind part of a mammal. **2** a small remnant of a parliament.

rumple v. (**rumples, rumpled, rumpling**) make or become creased. □ **rumpled** adj.

rumpus n. (pl. **rumpuses**) informal a disturbance, brawl, etc.

rumpus room n. a room for games and play.

rum-runner n. a person or ship engaged in smuggling alcohol. □ **rum-running** n.

run ● v. (**runs**; past tense **ran**; past participle **run**; **running**) **1** move at a speed faster than a walk. **2** move about in a hurried way. **3** pass. **4** move forcefully. **5** (of a bus, train, etc.) make a regular journey on a particular route. **6** be in charge of. **7** continue or proceed. **8** function or cause to function. **9** pass into or reach a specified state or level. **10** (of a liquid) flow. **11** emit or exude a liquid. **12** (of dye or colour) dissolve and spread when wet. **13** stand as a candidate. **14** publish or be published in a newspaper or magazine. **15** (of a computer) execute (a series of commands). **16** transport in a car. **17** smuggle (goods). **18** (of stockings) develop a run. **19** navigate (rapids, a waterfall, etc.) in a boat. **20** smuggle (goods). ● n. **1** an act or instance of running. **2** a running pace. **3** a journey or route. **4** a short excursion made in a car. **5** a course or track regularly used. **6** a length, spell, or stretch of something. **7** an enclosed area in which animals may run. **8** a rapid series of musical notes. **9** (**the run of**) free and unrestricted use of. **10** Baseball a point scored by the batter returning to home plate after touching the bases. **11** a vertical strip of unravelled fabric in hosiery. **12** (**the runs**) informal diarrhea. □ **on the run 1** escaping. **2** hurrying about. **run across** happen to meet. **run along** *informal* depart. **run around 1** bustle. **2** deceive or evade repeatedly. **3** *informal* engage in sexual relations (esp. illicitly). **run away 1** flee, abscond. **2** elope. **3** (of a child) leave the parental home. **run away with 1** carry off. **2** win (a prize) easily. **3** leave home to have a relationship with. **4** deprive of self-control. **run down 1** knock down. **2** reduce the strength or numbers of. **3** (of an unwound clock etc.) stop. **4** become feeble from undernourishment or overwork. **5** disparage. **run dry** cease to flow. **run for it** seek safety by fleeing. **a run** (or **a good run**) **for one's money** vigorous competition. **run high** (of feelings) be strong. **run into 1** collide with. **2** encounter. **3** reach as many as. **run into the ground** *informal* bring to exhaustion. **run its course** follow its natural progress. **run low** (or **short**) become depleted. **run off 1** produce (copies etc.) on a machine. **2** decide (a race or other contest) after a series of heats. **3** write or recite fluently. **run off at the mouth** *informal* talk incessantly. **run on one's feet** very busy. **run on 1** continue in operation. **2** speak volubly. **run out 1** come to an end; become used up. **2** exhaust one's stock of. **run out on** *informal* desert (a person). **run over 1** overflow. **2** study quickly. **3** (of a vehicle) knock down or crush. **run ragged** exhaust (a person). **run through 1** examine or rehearse briefly. **2** peruse. **3** consume (money) by reckless spending. **4** pervade. **5** pierce with a sword etc. **run up 1** accumulate (a debt etc.) quickly. **2** build or make hurriedly. **3** raise (a flag). **run up against** meet with (a difficulty). **run wild 1** grow unchecked. **2** act or behave without any control. **run with 1** proceed with. **2** associate with.

runabout *n.* **1** a light car. **2** a small pleasure boat.

runaround *n.* deceit or evasion.

runaway ● *adj.* **1** (of a person) having run away. **2** (of an animal or vehicle) out of control. **3** happening very rapidly. **4** happening very easily. ● *n.* **1** a person who has run away. **2** an animal or vehicle that is running out of control. **3** an easy victory.

rundown ● *n.* **1** a reduction in numbers. **2** a detailed analysis. ● *adj.* **1** decayed after prosperity. **2** enfeebled. **3** dilapidated.

rune *n.* any of the letters of the earliest Germanic alphabet used by Scandinavians and Anglo-Saxons from about the 3rd century. □ **runic** *adj.* [Say ROON, ROON ick]

rung[1] *n.* **1** each of the horizontal supports of a ladder. **2** a strengthening crosspiece. **3** a level or rank.

rung[2] *past participle of* RING[2].

run-in *n.* (*pl.* **run-ins**) a quarrel.

runner *n.* **1** a person, horse, etc., that runs. **2** *Baseball* a baserunner. **3** *Cdn* a running shoe. **4 a** a creeping plant stem that can take root. **b** a twining plant. **5** each of the long pieces on a sleigh etc. on which it slides. **6** a rod or groove or blade on which a thing slides. **7** a long narrow rug. **8** a messenger or agent for a bookmaker, drug dealer, etc.

runner-up *n.* (*pl.* **runners-up**) the competitor or team taking second place.

running ● *n.* **1** the action of runners in a race etc. **2** management or operation. **3** an act or an instance of racing. ● *adj.* **1** continuing. **2** consecutive. **3** done with a run. **4** (of water) flowing naturally or supplied to a building through pipes and taps. **5** (of a sore) exuding liquid or pus. □ **in** (or **out of**) **the running** (of a competitor) having a good (or poor) chance of winning. **up and running** in operation.

running back *n.* *Football* a back whose main task is to run carrying the ball.

running mate *n.* *US* a candidate for a supporting position in an election.

running shoe *n.* a shoe having an upper made of cloth and a rubber or synthetic sole.

runny *adj.* (**runnier, runniest**) **1** tending to run or flow. **2** excessively fluid.

runoff *n.* **1** an amount of rainfall or melted snow running off a mountain, roof, etc. **2** the spring thaw. **3** an additional race etc. held to break a tie.

run-of-the-mill *adj.* undistinguished, ordinary.

runt *n.* **1** the smallest animal in a litter. **2** an undersized person. □ **runty** *adj.*

run-through *n.* (*pl.* **run-throughs**) **1** a rehearsal with as few stops as possible. **2** a brief survey.

run-up *n.* (*pl.* **run-ups**) the period preceding an important event.

runway *n.* **1** a specially prepared surface along which aircraft take off and land. **2** a long raised platform in a theatre etc.

rupee *n.* the basic monetary unit of India, Pakistan, and several other countries. [Say roo PEE]

rupture ● *n.* **1** a sudden and complete breaking or bursting. **2** an ending of good relations between people. **3** an abdominal hernia. ● *v.* (**ruptures, ruptured,**

rupturing) **1** break or burst suddenly.
2 suffer the bursting of a bodily part.
3 undergo a rupture.

rural *adj.* **1** having to do with the country rather than town. **2** of or concerning agriculture. □ **rurally** *adv*

rural route *n.* a mail delivery route in an area outside of a town or city.

ruse *n.* a stratagem or trick. [*Say* ROOZ]

rush¹ ● *v.* (**rushes, rushed, rushing**) **1** move or act with urgent haste. **2** transport with urgent haste. **3** deal with hurriedly. **4** (of air or a liquid) flow strongly. **5** dash towards in an attempt to attack or capture. **6** *Hockey* bring the puck up the ice. ● *n.* (*pl.* **rushes**) **1** an act or instance of rushing. **2** a period of great activity. **3** (as an *adj.*) done with great haste or speed. **4** *informal* a thrill of excitement. **5** a sudden strong demand for a product. **6** (as an *adj.*) designating a seat at a performance purchased at a reduced price on the day of the performance. □ **rusher** *n.*

rush² *n.* (*pl.* **rushes**) **1** a marsh or waterside plant, used for making chair seats and baskets etc. **2** a stem of this plant.

rush hour *n.* a time of day when traffic is at its heaviest.

russet ● *adj.* reddish brown. ● *n.* **1** a reddish-brown colour. **2** a kind of rough-skinned russet-coloured apple. **3** a variety of potato with a reddish skin.

Russian *n.* **1** a person from Russia or the Russian Federation. **2** *hist.* a person from the former Soviet Union. **3** the official language of Russia. □ **Russian** *adj.*

Russian roulette *n.* an act of daring in which one squeezes the trigger of a revolver held to one's head with one chamber loaded, having first spun the chamber.

Russian thistle *n.* a prickly tumbleweed.

rust ● *n.* **1** a reddish-brown coating formed on iron or steel by oxidation. **2** a plant disease with rust-coloured spots caused by fungi. **3** a reddish-brown colour. ● *v.* be affected with rust.

rust belt *n.* *informal* an area of once profitable heavy industry.

rustbucket *n.* *informal* an old and rusty car etc.

rustic ● *adj.* **1** having associations with the country or country life. **2** unsophisticated, simple. **3** made in a plain or simple fashion. ● *n.* an unsophisticated country person.

rustle ● *v.* (**rustles, rustled, rustling**) **1** make or cause to make a gentle crackling sound. **2** move with a rustling sound. **3** steal (cattle or horses). ● *n.* a rustling sound or movement. □ **rustle up** *informal* produce quickly when needed. □ **rustler** *n.*

rustproof ● *adj.* (of a metal) not susceptible to corrosion by rust. ● *v.* make rustproof.

rusty *adj.* (**rustier, rustiest**) **1** rusted or affected by rust. **2** (of knowledge etc.) faded or impaired by neglect. **3** rust-coloured.

rut¹ ● *n.* **1** a deep track made by the passage of wheels. **2** any groove, furrow, etc. **3** an established (esp. tedious) mode of practice. ● *v.* (**ruts, rutted, rutting**) mark with ruts. □ **in a rut** following a fixed (esp. tedious) pattern of behaviour that is difficult to change.

rut² ● *n.* **1** the periodic sexual activity of a male deer, goat, etc. **2** the period during which this happens. ● *v.* (**ruts, rutted, rutting**) be affected with rut.

rutabaga *n.* (*pl.* **rutabagas**) a large, round, yellow-fleshed root that is eaten as a vegetable; an orange turnip. [*Say* ROOTA bay guh *or* ROOTA bag uh]

ruthenium *n.* a rare hard white metallic element. [*Say* roo THEENY um]

ruthless *adj.* having no pity or compassion. □ **ruthlessly** *adv.* **ruthlessness** *n.*

RV *abbr.* (*pl.* **RVs**) recreational vehicle.

R-value *n.* a measure of the insulating capability of a wall, building material, etc.

Rwandan *n.* a person from Rwanda. □ **Rwandan** *adj.* [*Say* roo ON dun]

Rx *abbr.* prescription.

rye *n.* **1** a cereal plant with spikes bearing wheat-like grains. **2** (also **rye whisky**) a whisky made from rye and sometimes other grains. **3** rye bread.

ryegrass *n.* (*pl.* **ryegrasses**) a kind of grass used for fodder and lawns.

Ss

S¹ *n.* (also **s**) (*pl.* **Ss** or **S's**) **1** the nineteenth letter of the alphabet. **2** an S-shaped object or curve.

S² *abbr.* (also **S.**) **1** soprano. **2** South, Southern.

s *abbr.* (also **s.**) second(s).

Saanich *n.* (*pl.* **Saanich**) **1** a member of a division of Straits people living on Vancouver Island. **2** the dialect spoken by the Saanich. [*Say* SAN itch]

sabayon *n.* ZABAGLIONE. [*Say* SAB eye yon]

Sabbath *n.* **1** a day of rest and worship kept by Jews and some Christians on Saturday. **2** a day of worship celebrated by most Christians on Sunday.

sabbatical ● *adj.* (of leave) granted at intervals to a professor or teacher for study or travel. ● *n.* a period of sabbatical leave. [*Say* suh BAT ick ul]

saber *n.* esp. *US* = SABRE.

sable¹ *n.* a small furry brown mammal of northern Europe and parts of northern Asia.

sable² ● *n.* esp. *literary* black. ● *adj.* black.

sabotage ● *n.* deliberate damage to property. ● *v.* (**sabotages**, **sabotaged**, **sabotaging**) **1** commit sabotage on. **2** make useless. [*Say* SABBA tawzh]

saboteur *n.* a person who sabotages. [*Say* sabba TUR]

sabre *n.* (also esp. *US* **saber**) **1** a cavalry sword with a curved blade. **2** a light fencing sword with a tapering blade.

sabre-rattling *n.* a display or threat of force.

sabre-toothed *adj.* designating an extinct mammal with long sabre-shaped upper canines.

sac *n.* a bag-like cavity, enclosed by a membrane, in an animal or plant.

saccharide *n.* *Chemistry* = SUGAR 2. [*Say* SACK a ride]

saccharin *n.* a very sweet substance, used as a substitute for sugar. [*Say* SACK a rin]

saccharine *adj.* **1** sweet; sugary. **2** sentimental etc. [*Say* SACK a rin]

sachem *n.* the supreme chief of some N American Aboriginal peoples. [*Say* SAY chum]

sachet *n.* a small bag or packet of something, esp. potpourri. [*Say* sash AY]

sack¹ ● *n.* **1** a large strong bag for storing or conveying goods. **2** (**the sack**) *informal* dismissal from employment. **3** (**the sack**) *slang* bed. ● *v.* *informal* dismiss from employment. □ **hit the sack** *informal* go to bed. **sack out** *informal* go to sleep.

sack² ● *v.* plunder and destroy (a town etc.). ● *n.* the sacking of a captured place.

sackcloth *n.* **1** a coarse fabric, as of flax or hemp. **2** clothes of this.

sacking *n.* material for making sacks.

sacrament *n.* **1** a religious ceremony regarded as an outward and visible sign of spiritual grace, e.g. baptism or the Eucharist. **2** (also **the Blessed Sacrament**) the consecrated elements of the Eucharist. □ **sacramental** *adj.* [*Say* SACKRA m'nt, sackra MENTAL]

sacred *adj.* **1 a** connected with a god or goddess and so made holy by association. **b** religious rather than secular. **2** regarded with great respect or reverence. **3** (of writings etc.) embodying the doctrines of a religion. **4** sacrosanct. □ **sacredness** *n.*

sacred cow *n.* *informal* an idea or institution unreasonably held to be above criticism.

sacrifice ● *n.* **1 a** the act of giving up something valued for the sake of something more important. **b** the loss entailed in this. **2** the slaughter of an animal or person or giving up of a possession as an offering to a deity. **3** (in games) a loss incurred deliberately to avoid a greater loss. ● *v.* (**sacrifices**, **sacrificed**, **sacrificing**) **1** give up or offer as a sacrifice. **2** devote or give over to. □ **sacrificial** *adj.* [*Say* SACKRA fice, sackra FISH ul]

sacrilege *n.* a violation or misuse of what is regarded as sacred. □ **sacrilegious** *adj.* [*Say* SACKRA lidge, sackra LIDGE us]

sacristy *n.* (*pl.* **sacristies**) a room in a church where the vestments, sacred vessels, etc., are kept. [*Say* SACK riss tee]

sacrosanct *adj.* most sacred; exempt from criticism etc. [*Say* SACK roe sankt]

sacrum *n.* the triangular bone situated between the hip bones. □ **sacral** *adj.* [*Say* SAKE rum]

SAD *abbr.* seasonal affective disorder.

sad *adj.* (**sadder, saddest**) **1** unhappy. **2** causing sorrow. **3** regrettable. **4** shameful; contemptible. □ **sadness** *n.*

sadden *v.* make or become sad.

saddle ● *n.* **1** a seat of leather etc. fastened on a horse etc. for riding. **2** a seat on a bicycle etc. **3** a cut of meat consisting of the two loins. **4** a ridge rising to a summit at each end. ● *v.* (**saddles, saddled, saddling**) **1** put a saddle on (a horse etc.). **2** burden (a person) with a task, debt, etc. □ **in the saddle 1** mounted. **2** in office or control.

saddleback *n.* **1** a hill or ridge with a concave upper outline. **2** an animal or bird with saddle-like markings on its back.

saddlebag *n.* **1** each of a pair of bags attached to the saddle (on a horse, bicycle, etc.). **2** *informal* excess fat around the hips and thighs.

saddle horse *n.* a horse for riding.

saddler *n.* a maker of or dealer in saddles etc. for horses. □ **saddlery** *n.*

saddle shoe *n.* a two-tone oxford shoe, originally popular in the 1950s.

Sadducee *n.* a member of a Jewish sect of the time of Christ that denied the resurrection of the dead. [*Say* SAD yoo see]

sadhu *n.* (*pl.* **sadhus**) (in India) a wise and holy man. [*Say* SAW doo]

sadism *n.* the enjoyment of inflicting pain or suffering on others. □ **sadist** *n.* **sadistic** *adj.* **sadistically** *adv.* [*Say* SAY dism, SAY dist, suh DIS tick]

sadly *adv.* **1** showing or feeling sadness. **2** unfortunately. **3** greatly.

sado-masochism *n.* sexual gratification achieved through inflicting and receiving pain. □ **sado-masochist** *n.* **sado-masochistic** *adj.* [*Say* say doe MASSA kism, say doe massa KISS tick]

sad sack *n. informal* a very inept person.

safari *n.* (*pl.* **safaris**) an expedition to observe or hunt animals, esp. in Africa.

safe ● *adj.* (**safer, safest**) **1** protected from danger or risk. **2** affording security. **3** reliable, certain. **4** prevented from escaping or doing harm. **5** (also **safe and sound**) not injured. **6** cautious and unenterprising. ● *n.* **1** a strong lockable cabinet etc. for valuables. **2** (esp. *Cdn*) *slang* a condom. ● *adv. informal* in a safe manner. □ **safely** *adv.*

safe deposit *n.* safety deposit.

safeguard ● *n.* a proviso etc. that tends to prevent something undesirable. ● *v.* guard or protect with a safeguard.

safe house *n.* **1** a place of refuge or rendezvous for people in hiding. **2** a place providing free temporary emergency accommodation for those fleeing abuse.

safekeeping *n.* preservation in a safe place.

safe sex *n.* (also **safer sex**) sexual activity in which people protect themselves against sexually transmitted diseases.

safety *n.* (*pl.* **safeties**) **1** the condition of being safe. **2** a device for preventing injury from machinery. **3** *Football* **a** a defensive back who plays in a deep position. **b** a play in which the offensive team moves the ball into its own end zone.

safety belt *n.* a seat belt.

safety deposit *n.* (also **safe deposit**) a place in which valuables are stored.

safety glass *n.* glass that will not splinter when broken.

safety net *n.* **1** a net placed to catch an acrobat etc. in case of a fall. **2** any means of protection against difficulty or loss.

safety pin ● *n.* a pin with a point that is held in a guard when closed. ● *v.* (**safety-pin**) fasten with a safety pin.

safety valve *n.* a valve opening automatically to relieve excessive pressure.

safflower *n.* a thistle-like plant whose seeds yield an edible oil.

saffron *n.* **1** an orange-yellow spice made from the dried stigmas of the crocus. **2** the orange-yellow colour of this.

sag ● *v.* (**sags, sagged, sagging**) **1 a** sink under weight or pressure. **b** hang down loosely. **2** have a downward bulge in the middle. **3** decline, weaken. **4** fall in price. ● *n.* **1** the amount that something sags. **2** a sinking condition. □ **saggy** *adj.*

saga *n.* **1** a long story of heroic achievement. **2** a long involved story. [*Say* SAG uh *or* SAW guh]

sagacious *adj.* wise. □ **sagacity** *n.* [*Say* suh GAY shuss, suh GASSA tee]

sage[1] *n.* **1** an aromatic plant with leaves that are used as a herb in cooking. **2** *n. & adj.* (also **sage green**) a dull greyish-green colour.

sage[2] ● *n.* a profoundly wise person. ● *adj.* (**sager, sagest**) wise. □ **sagely** *adv.*

sagebrush *n.* **1** a shrubby aromatic plant of N America. **2** scrub that is dominated by such shrubs.

Sagittarius *n.* **1** a constellation (the Centaur). **2** the ninth sign of the zodiac, which the sun enters around Nov. 22. □ **Sagittarian** *n.* [*Say* sadge a TERRY us]

sago *n.* (*pl.* **sagos**) **1** a kind of starch, made from the sago palm and used in puddings etc. **2** (also **sago palm**) a palm growing in freshwater swamps of Southeast Asia. [*Say* SAY go]

Saharan *adj.* of or relating to the Sahara Desert. [*Say* suh HAIR un *or* suh HAR un]

sahib *n.* (*pl.* **sahibs**) **1** (in India) a polite form of address for a man. **2** a gentleman. [*Say* SAW hib]

Sahtu Dene *n.* (*pl.* **Sahtu Dene**) **1** a member of a Dene people living near Great Bear Lake, NWT. **2** the Athapaskan language of this people. □ **Sahtu Dene** *adj.* [*Say* saw too DEN ay]

said ● *v. past and past participle of* SAY. ● *adj.* (**the said**) the previously mentioned.

sail ● *n.* **1** a piece of material extended on rigging to catch the wind and propel a boat or ship. **2** a ship's sails collectively. **3** a trip in a sailing ship. **4** a wind-catching apparatus attached to the arm of a windmill. ● *v.* **1** travel on water by the use of sails or engine power. **2 a** navigate (a ship etc.). **b** travel on (a sea). **3** glide or move smoothly. **4** *informal* move or succeed easily. □ **sail close to the wind 1** sail as nearly against the wind as possible. **2** risk overstepping the mark.

sailboard *n.* a board with a mast and sail, used in windsurfing.

sailboat *n.* a boat driven by sails.

sailcloth *n.* **1** canvas for sails. **2** a dress material like canvas.

sailer *n.* a sailing vessel.

sailfish *n.* (*pl.* **sailfish** *or* **sailfishes**) a kind of fish with a large dorsal fin that resembles a sail.

sailing ship *n.* a vessel driven by sails.

sailor *n.* **1** a member of a ship's crew. **2** a person who sails for recreation. **3** a person considered as liable or not to be seasick.

sailplane *n.* a glider designed for sustained flight.

saint *n.* **1** a holy or canonized person regarded as having a place in heaven. **2** (**Saint** *or* **St.**) the title of a saint or archangel. **3** a very virtuous person. □ **sainthood** *n.*

St. Bernard *n.* a breed of very large dog originally kept to rescue travellers on the Great St. Bernard Pass in the Alps.

sainted *adj.* good or kind; like a saint.

Saint-Jean-Baptiste Day *n.* *Cdn* (in Quebec) the former official name for the Fête nationale, June 24. [*Say* san zhon ba TEEST]

St. John's wort *n.* **1** a yellow-flowered plant often cultivated for ornament. **2** an extract from this flower used esp. as an antidepressant.

saintly *adj.* (**saintlier, saintliest**) very holy or virtuous. □ **saintliness** *n.*

St. Patrick's Day *n.* March 17, the feast day of St. Patrick, on which Irish heritage is celebrated.

saint's day *n.* (*pl.* **saints' days**) a Church festival in memory of a saint.

sake[1] *n.* **1** out of consideration for. **2** in order to please, get, or keep. □ **for Christ's** (*or* **God's** *or* **goodness'** etc.) **sake** an expression of urgency, impatience, etc. **for old times' sake** in memory of former times.

sake[2] *n.* a Japanese alcoholic drink made from fermented rice. [*Say* SACKY *or* SOCKY]

salaam ● *n.* **1** (in Muslim countries and India) the greeting "Peace". **2** a low bow with the right palm on the forehead. ● *v.* make a salaam. [*Say* suh LOM]

salacious *adj.* **1** lustful; lecherous. **2** (of writings etc.) tending to cause sexual desire. □ **salaciously** *adv.* [*Say* suh LAY shuss]

salad *n.* **1** a cold dish of various mixtures of raw or cooked vegetables, and usu. seasoned with a dressing. **2** a mixture of fish, meat, etc. with mayonnaise, often as a sandwich filling.

salad days *pl. n.* a period of youthful inexperience.

salal *n.* a shrub of western N America, with edible purple-black berries. [*Say* suh LAL]

salamander *n.* **1** a newt-like amphibian, usu. with bright markings. **2** a mythical lizard-like creature thought to live in fire. [*Say* SAL a mander]

salami *n.* (*pl.* **salamis**) a highly seasoned dried sausage.

salaried *adj.* receiving a salary.

salary *n.* (*pl.* **salaries**) a fixed regular payment made by an employer to an employee, usu. expressed as an annual sum.

Salchow *n.* *Figure Skating* a type of jump. [*Say* SOW cow (SOW *rhymes with* COW)]

sale *n.* **1** the exchange of something for money etc. **2** the amount sold. **3** an offering of goods at reduced prices for a period. **4 a** an event at which goods are sold. **b** a public auction. □ **on sale** for sale at a reduced price.

saleable *adj.* fit to be sold.

salesman *n.* (*pl.* **salesmen**) a man employed to sell goods or services. □ **salesmanship** *n.*

salesperson *n.* (*pl.* **salespeople** *or* **salespersons**) a salesman or saleswoman.

sales pitch *n.* an argument used to persuade someone.

sales representative *n.* (also *informal*

sales rep) a person who represents a business to prospective customers.

sales tax n. a tax on sales, added to the cost of a purchase.

saleswoman n. (pl. **saleswomen**) a woman employed to sell goods or services.

salicylic acid n. a bitter chemical used as a fungicide and in the production of dyes. [Say sal a SILL ick]

salient ● adj. **1** most important or notable. **2** (of an angle etc.) pointing outwards. ● n. **1** a salient angle in fortification. **2** an outward bulge in a line of military attack or defence. □ **salience** n. [Say SAY lee int, SAY lee ince]

saline ● adj. containing salt or salts. ● n. (also **saline solution**) a solution of salt in water. □ **salinity** n. [Say SAY leen, suh LINNA tee]

Salish n. (pl. **Salish**) = SNE NAY MUXW. [Say SAL ish]

Salishan n. an Aboriginal language group of the west coast of N America, including Comox, Halkomelem, Lillooet, Nuxalk, Okanagan, Sechelt, Shuswap, Squamish, Straits, and Nlaka'pamux. □ **Salishan** adj. [Say SAL ish un]

saliva n. liquid secreted into the mouth by glands to facilitate chewing and swallowing. □ **salivary** adj. [Say suh LIE va, SAL iv airy]

salivate v. (**salivates**, **salivated**, **salivating**) secrete saliva esp. in anticipation. [Say SAL iv ate]

sallow adj. (**sallower**, **sallowest**) (of the skin) of a sickly yellow or pale brown.

sally ● n. (pl. **sallies**) **1 a** a lively remark esp. by way of attack in argument. **b** a sudden charge from a fortification upon its besiegers. **2** an excursion. ● v. (**sallies**, **sallied**, **sallying**) **1** go for a walk etc. **2** make a military sally.

Sally Ann n. Cdn & Brit. informal (usu. as **the Sally Ann**) the Salvation Army.

salmon n. (pl. **salmon** or **salmons**) **1** a large, edible food and sport fish with pink flesh. **2** (also **salmon pink**) the colour of salmon flesh, usu. pink with a tinge of orange.

salmonella n. (pl. **salmonellae** or **salmonellas**) a bacterium which can cause food poisoning and typhoid. [Say salma NELLA for the singular, salma NELLY or salma NELLAS for the plural]

salon n. **1** a boutique specializing in fashionable products, or services such as hairdressing. **2** the reception room of a large house. **3** an exhibition of painting,

sculpture, books, etc. **4** a gathering of intellectuals etc.

saloon n. **1** hist. a bar of the Old West. **2** any bar or tavern.

salsa n. (pl. **salsas**) **1** a Latin American spicy sauce made with tomatoes and chilies etc. **2 a** a kind of dance music of Latin American origin, incorporating jazz and rock elements. **b** a dance performed to this. [Say SAWL suh]

salsa verde n. **1** a green Italian sauce, usu. served with fish. **2** a spicy Mexican sauce. [Say sal suh VAIR day]

SALT abbr. Strategic Arms Limitation Talks (or Treaty).

salt ● n. **1 a** sodium chloride, found esp. in water or as a reddish brown mineral. **b** this substance used esp. for seasoning and preserving food. **2** a chemical compound formed from the reaction of an acid with a base. **3** an experienced sailor. ● adj. **1** containing or tasting of salt. **2** treated, cured, or preserved with salt. ● v. **1** cure or preserve with salt or brine. **2** season with salt. **3** sprinkle with salt, esp. to melt snow or ice. □ **salt away** informal. save or stash (money etc.) for the future. **the salt of the earth** a person of great worthiness, honesty, etc. **take (with a grain (or pinch) of salt** be justifiably skeptical of. **worth one's salt** deserving what one earns. □ **salting** n.

salt and pepper adj. having dark and light (esp. grey) colours interspersed.

saltbox ● adj. designating a house etc. with two storeys at the front and one at the back. ● n. (pl. **saltboxes**) a saltbox house.

saltcellar n. a small container for holding salt.

Salteaux (pl. **Salteaux**) = SAULTEAUX. [Say SO toe]

salted adj. seasoned, treated, or preserved with salt.

salter n. esp. Cdn a truck which dispenses salt on roads.

salt fish n. preserved cod that has been split, salted, and dried.

saltine n. a salted cracker. [Say sawl TEEN]

salt lick n. **1** a place where animals go to lick naturally occurring salt deposits. **2** a block of salt given to domestic horses etc. to lick.

salt marsh n. (also **saltwater marsh**) a marsh that has been flooded by the tide.

saltpetre n. potassium nitrate, used esp. in manufacturing gunpowder. [Say salt PETER]

salt pork n. cured pork fat, highly salted.

salt water ● n. **1** water with a high

concentration of salt, esp. sea water. **2** the ocean, sea, etc. ● *adj.* (usu. **saltwater**) **1** having to do with salt water. **2** living in or by salt water.

salty *adj.* (**saltier, saltiest**) **1** tasting of or containing salt. **2 a** (of humour etc.) racy, risqué. **b** (of language) coarse. □ **saltiness** *n.*

salubrious *adj.* **1** favourable to good health. **2** agreeable. [*Say* suh LOOB ree us]

salutary *adj.* producing good effects. [*Say* SAL yoo terry]

salutation *n.* **1** a sign or expression of greeting. **2** the initial words of a letter. **3** a gesture of respect. [*Say* sal yoo TAY sh'n]

salute ● *n.* **1** a gesture of respect or solidarity. **2** a specified movement of the hand, weapons, or flags as a formal military gesture of respect. **3** the discharge of a gun or guns as a formal sign of respect or celebration. **4** a tribute or testimonial (to). ● *v.* (**salutes, saluted, saluting**) **1 a** make a salute to. **b** perform a salute. **2** receive or greet with.

Salvadoran (also **Salvadorean**) ● *adj.* of or relating to El Salvador. ● *n.* a person from El Salvador. [*Say* salva DORE un, salva DORE ee un]

salvage ● *v.* (**salvages, salvaged, salvaging**) **1** save or recover (materials) from a shipwreck, fire, etc. **2** save from being lost or destroyed. ● *n.* **1** the action of salvaging. **2** something that has been salvaged. □ **salvageable** *adj.* **salvager** *n.*

salvation *n.* **1** the act of saving or being saved. **2** preservation from harm etc. **3** the saving of the soul through deliverance from sin. **4** a person or thing that saves.

Salvation Army *n.* an international evangelical organization which assists the poor and homeless.

salve ● *n.* **1** a healing ointment. **2** a thing that soothes (hurt feelings etc.). ● *v.* (**salves, salved, salving**) soothe or calm (pride, conscience, etc.). [*Say* SALV]

salver *n.* a tray. [*Say* SAL vur]

salvia *n.* (*pl.* **salvias**) a plant of the mint family with red or blue flowers. [*Say* SAL vee uh]

salvo *n.* (*pl.* **salvoes** or **salvos**) **1** the simultaneous discharge of artillery in battle or as a salute. **2** a sudden aggressive series of acts. [*Say* SAL vo]

SAM *abbr.* (*pl.* **SAMs**) surface-to-air missile.

Samaritan *n.* (also **good Samaritan**) a charitable or helpful person. **2** a native of Samaria. □ **Samaritan** *adj.* [*Say* suh MARE a tun]

samba ● *n.* (*pl.* **sambas**) **1** a Brazilian dance of African origin. **2** a related

ballroom dance. ● *v.* (**sambas, sambaed** or **samba'd, sambaing**) dance the samba. [*Say* SAM buh]

sambuca *n.* (*pl.* **sambucas**) an Italian aniseed-flavoured liqueur. [*Say* zam BOOK uh]

same ● *adj.* **1** (often **as the same**) not different. **2** unvarying. **3** (of a person or thing) previously mentioned. ● *pron.* (**the same**) the same person or thing. ● *adv.* in the same way. □ **all** (or **just**) **the same** nevertheless. **at the same time** **1** simultaneously. **2** notwithstanding. **be all the same to** be a matter of indifference. **same difference** *informal* no difference. **same here** *informal* the same applies to me. □ **sameness** *n.*

same-day *adj.* designating a service provided on the day of purchase etc.

same-sex *adj.* designating a relationship in which both partners are of the same sex.

Sami *n.* the Lapps collectively. □ **Sami** *adj.* [*Say* SOMMY]

Samoan *n.* a person from Samoa. □ **Samoan** *adj.* [*Say* suh MOE un]

samosa *n.* (*pl.* **samosas**) an Indian triangular fried pastry stuffed with spiced vegetables or meat. [*Say* suh MOE suh]

samovar *n.* a metal, usu. ornate, Russian urn for making tea. [*Say* SAMMA varr]

Samoyed *n.* a breed of white dog having a thick coat and a tail curling over the back. [*Say* SAMMA yed]

sampan *n.* a small boat or skiff propelled by a scull or oars set in the stern, used in the Far East. [*Say* SAM pan]

sample ● *n.* **1** a small part or quantity intended to show what the whole is like. **2** a small amount of a product given to prospective customers. **3** a specimen taken for scientific testing. **4** a piece of music that has been digitalized. ● *v.* (**samples, sampled, sampling**) **1** try or examine (something) taking or experiencing a sample. **2 a** convert (an analog signal) to a digital one. **b** record (sound) digitally for subsequent electronic processing. □ **sampling** *n.*

sampler *n.* **1** a piece of embroidery sewn in various stitches as a demonstration of skill. **2** a device for sampling music. **3** a collection of representative items etc.

samurai *n.* (*pl.* **samurai**) **1** (in feudal Japan) a member of a military caste. **2** a Japanese army officer. [*Say* SAM uh rye]

San *n.* (*pl.* **San**) **1** a member of the aboriginal Bushmen of southern Africa. **2** the group of languages spoken by the San. □ **San** *adj.* [*Sounds like* SAWN]

sanatorium *n.* (*pl.* **sanatoriums** or

sanatoria) an establishment for the treatment of convalescents and those suffering chronic disorders etc. [*Say* sanna TORY um]

sanctify *v.* (**sanctifies, sanctified, sanctifying**) **1** consecrate; make holy. **2** purify. **3** legitimize. □ **sanctification** *n.* [*Say* SANK tif eye, sank tiffa KAY sh'n]

sanctimonious *adj.* pretending piety, sanctity, or holiness. □ **sanctimoniously** *adv.* **sanctimoniousness** *n.* **sanctimony** *n.* [*Say* sankta MOANY us, SANKTA moany]

sanction ● *n.* **1** official approval for a particular action. **2** the action of making something legally binding. **3** measures taken by a country to coerce another to do something. **4** a penalty enacted to enforce obedience to a law or rule. ● *v.* authorize or agree to.

sanctity *n.* **1** holiness. **2** the quality of being too important to subject to dishonour or to violate. [*Say* SANKTA tee]

sanctuary *n.* (*pl.* **sanctuaries**) **1** a holy place. **2 a** esp. *Jewish Hist.* the inmost recess or holiest part of a temple etc. **b** the part of a church containing the altar. **3** a place where birds, animals, etc., are bred and protected. **4** a place of refuge.

sanctum *n.* (*pl.* **sanctums, sancta**) **1** a holy place. **2** *informal* a person's private place.

Sanctus *n.* (*pl.* **Sanctuses**) a prayer beginning "Holy, holy, holy", said or sung during some Christian liturgies.

sand ● *n.* **1** a loose granular substance resulting from the weathering of rocks, found on beaches, deserts, etc. **2** (in *pl.*) an area predominantly of sand. ● *v.* **1** smooth with sandpaper. **2** sprinkle with sand. □ **sands of time** the moments or passage of time.

sandal *n.* a light open shoe with light straps.

sandalwood *n.* the scented wood of a widely cultivated Indian tree used esp. in carving and incense.

sandbag ● *n.* a bag filled with sand, used for protection against floods or gunfire, or as ballast. ● *v.* (**sandbags, sandbagged, sandbagging**) place sandbags around something to fortify or protect it. □ **sandbagger** *n.*

sandbank *n.* a deposit of sand formed in shallow water.

sandbar *n.* a large bank of sand forming in a river or sea.

sandblast *v.* roughen, treat, or clean with a jet of sand driven by compressed air or steam.

sandbox *n.* (*pl.* **sandboxes**) a shallow box of sand for children to play in.

sandcastle *n.* a shape like a castle made in sand.

sandcherry *n.* (*plural* **sandcherries**) any of several shrubby wild cherries of North America, purple-leaved varieties of which are often cultivated in gardens.

sand dollar *n.* a flattened sea urchin that lives partly buried in sand.

sand dune *n.* a shifting mound or ridge of sand.

sander *n.* **1** a power tool using sandpaper to smooth surfaces etc. **2** a vehicle that sprinkles sand on icy streets.

sanderling *n.* a small wading bird of the sandpiper family.

sandhill crane *n.* a grey N American crane.

sandlot *n.* a small plot of vacant land used by children for games etc.

S&M *abbr.* sadism and masochism or sado-masochism.

sandman *n.* a make-believe figure that is supposed to make children sleep by sprinkling sand or sleep in their eyes.

sandpaper ● *n.* strong paper coated with sand or another abrasive, used for smoothing surfaces. ● *v.* smooth with sandpaper. □ **sandpapery** *adj.*

sandpiper *n.* a wading bird with a long bill and long legs.

sandstone *n.* a sedimentary rock of consolidated grains of sand, esp. of quartz.

sandstorm *n.* a storm of wind with clouds of sand.

sand trap *n.* a shallow pit of fine sand serving as a hazard on a golf course.

sandwich ● *n.* (*pl.* **sandwiches**) **1** two slices of bread with a filling between them. **2** anything resembling a sandwich. ● *v.* (**sandwiches, sandwiched, sandwiching**) **1** place or insert (a thing) between two dissimilar ones. **2** squeeze in between others. [*Say* SAND witch *or* SAN witch *or* SAM witch]

sandwich board *n.* **1** a pair of signs, usu. bearing advertisements, joined at the top by straps to be worn on a person's shoulders. **2** a similar pair of signs joined at the top to be free-standing.

sandwich generation *n.* the generation of adults trying to raise children while also caring for aged parents.

sandy *adj.* (**sandier, sandiest**) **1** composed of or containing sand. **2** having the texture of sand. **3** (of hair) light reddish-blond.

sane *adj.* (**saner, sanest**) **1** of sound

mind; not mad. **2** (of views etc.) sensible. □ **sanely** adv.

sang past of SING.

sang-froid n. coolness of mind or action. [Say sang FRWAH]

sangria n. a drink of esp. red wine with sugar, fruit juice, and usu. soda. [Say san GREE uh]

sanguine adj. optimistic; confident. [Say SANG gwin]

sanitarium n. = SANATORIUM. [Say sanna TERRY um]

sanitary adj. **1** of or pertaining to sanitation. **2** hygienic.

sanitary pad n. (also **sanitary napkin**) an absorbent pad worn during menstruation.

sanitation n. **1** systems designed to protect or promote health. **2** the disposal of sewage and garbage.

sanitize v. (**sanitizes, sanitized, sanitizing**) **1** make (something) hygienic. **2** make (information etc.) more acceptable by removing disturbing material. □ **sanitizer** n.

sanity n. **1 a** the state of being sane. **b** mental health. **2** reasonableness.

sank past of SINK.

sans prep. jocular without. [Say SONZ]

Sansei n. (pl. **Sansei**) a North American whose grandparents immigrated from Japan. [Say SAN say]

Sanskrit ● n. the ancient language of the Indian subcontinent, the principal language of religious writings and scholarship. ● adj. of or in this language. □ **Sanskritic** adj. [Say SAN scrit, san SCRIT ick]

sans serif ● n. a form of type without serifs. ● adj. without serifs. [Say san SAIR if]

Santa Claus (pl. **Santa Clauses**) (also **Santa**, pl. **Santas**) a folk figure, usu. represented as a fat, white-bearded old man in a red suit, said to bring presents on Christmas Eve.

Santee n. (pl. **Santee** or **Santees**) **1** a member of a Dakota group originally from Minnesota, now also living in Manitoba and Saskatchewan. **2** the Siouan language of this people. [Say san TEE]

sap ● n. **1** the fluid that circulates in a plant and is essential to its growth. **2** slang a foolish person. **3** a tunnel or trench to conceal assailants' approach to a fortified place. ● v. (**saps, sapped, sapping**) gradually weaken a person's strength etc.

sapient adj. literary wise, intelligent. [Say SAY pee int]

sapling n. a young tree.

sapper n. **1** a person who digs tunnels and trenches. **2** a military engineer who lays or detects and disarms mines.

sapphire ● n. **1** a transparent blue precious stone. **2** (also **sapphire blue**) an intense blue colour. ● adj. (also **sapphire-blue**) of sapphire blue. [Say SAFF ire]

sappy adj. (**sappier, sappiest**) informal too sentimental.

sapsucker n. a small woodpecker that pecks holes in trees for sap and insects.

sapwood n. the soft outer layers of recently formed wood.

SAR abbr. SEARCH AND RESCUE.

Saracen n. hist. an Arab or Muslim at the time of the Crusades. [Say SARAH sun]

saran n. (also **saran wrap**) clear thin plastic film, used to wrap foods. [Say suh RAN]

sarcasm n. the use of bitter or wounding, esp. ironic, remarks. □ **sarcastic** adj. **sarcastically** adv. [Say SAR kaz um, sar KASS tick]

Sarcee n. (pl. **Sarcee** or **Sarcees**) **1** a member of a small Athapaskan group living near Calgary. **2** the language of this people. □ **Sarcee** adj. [Say SAR see]

sarcoma n. a malignant tumour of connective or other tissue. [Say sar CO muh]

sarcophagus n. (pl. **sarcophagi**) a stone coffin. [Say sar COFFA gus for the singular, sar COFFA guy for the plural]

sardine n. a herring or herring-like fish, esp. preserved in oil or brine and canned. □ **like sardines** crowded close together.

Sardinian n. **1** a person from Sardinia. **2** the Romance language of Sardinia. □ **Sardinian** adj. [Say sar DINNY un]

sardonic adj. mocking or sarcastic. □ **sardonically** adv. [Say sar DON ick]

sarge n. slang sergeant.

sari n. (pl. **saris**) (also **saree** pl. **sarees**) a length of cotton or silk draped around the body, traditionally worn by Indian women. [Say SAR ee]

sarong n. a Malay and Javanese garment, worn by both sexes, consisting of a long strip of cloth worn tucked around the waist or under the armpits. [Say suh RONG]

SARS abbr. SEVERE ACUTE RESPIRATORY SYNDROME. [Say SARZ]

sarsaparilla n. (pl. **sarsaparillas**) **1** the dried roots of various tropical American shrubs, used as a flavouring. **2** a soft drink flavoured with sarsaparilla. [Say saspa RILLA]

sartorial adj. having to do with clothes or clothing. □ **sartorially** adv. [Say sar TORY ul]

sash *n.* (*pl.* **sashes**) **1** a long strip of cloth worn around the waist or over one shoulder. **2** a frame holding the glass in a sash window.

sashay *v. informal* **1** saunter. **2** walk or move so as to attract attention. [*Say* sash AY]

sashimi *n.* a Japanese dish of garnished raw fish. [*Say* sa SHEE mee]

sash window *n.* a window consisting of two frames of glass, one or both of which can slide up and down.

Sask. *abbr.* Saskatchewan.

Saskatchewan Day *n. Cdn* (*Sask.*) a statutory holiday occurring on the first Monday in August.

Saskatchewanian ● *adj.* of or relating to Saskatchewan. ● *n.* a person from Saskatchewan.
[*Say* suh scatch a WONNY un]

Saskatchewan Party *n.* a political party of Saskatchewan formed in 1997 by the Conservatives and some Liberals.

saskatoon *n. Cdn* (*Prairies*) **1** a shrub of western N America, which produces purple edible berries. **2** (also **saskatoon berry**) this berry.

sasquatch *n.* (*pl.* **sasquatch** or **sasquatches**) a mythical large hairy creature said to live in northwestern N America. [*Say* SASK watch]

sass *informal* ● *n.* impudence, cheek. ● *v.* (**sasses, sassed, sassing**) be impudent to.

sassafras *n.* (*pl.* **sassafrases**) a small N American tree whose aromatic leaves and bark yield an oil used in medicines and perfumes. [*Say* SASSA frass]

sassy *adj.* (**sassier, sassiest**) *informal* **1** showing a lack of respect; cheeky. **2** confident. □ **sassiness** *n.*

SAT *abbr. proprietary* SCHOLASTIC APTITUDE TEST.

sat *past and past participle of* SIT.

Satan the Devil. [*Say* SAY tun]

satanic *adj.* **1** having to do with Satan. **2** extremely evil. [*Say* suh TAN ick]

Satanism *n.* the worship of Satan. □ **Satanist** *n.* [*Say* SAY tun ism]

satay *n.* (also **saté**) an Indonesian and Malaysian dish of small pieces of meat grilled on a skewer, usu. served with a spicy peanut sauce. [*Say* sa TAY *or* SAT ay]

SATB *abbr. Music* soprano, alto, tenor, and bass.

satchel *n.* a usu. leather bag, used to carry books etc. on the back or from the shoulder.

sate *v.* (**sates, sated, sating**) satisfy a desire or appetite etc. fully.

satellite ● *n.* **1** a celestial body orbiting the earth or another planet. **2** an artificial body placed in orbit around the earth or another planet. **3** something that is subordinate to or reliant on another place or thing. ● *adj.* **1** transmitted by satellite. **2** (of a region etc.) subordinate to another.

satellite dish *n.* a saucer-shaped aerial for receiving broadcasting signals transmitted by satellite.

sati *n.* (*pl.* **satis**) = SUTTEE. [*Say* suh TEE *or* SUT ee]

satiate *v.* (**satiates, satiated, satiating**) satisfy a person or their desire or appetite etc. fully. □ **satiation** *n.* [*Say* SAY shee ate]

satin ● *n.* **1** a smooth, glossy fabric. **2** a paint with a low lustre. ● *adj.* **1** smooth as satin. **2** made of satin. □ **satiny** *adj.*

satinwood *n.* **1** a glossy yellow timber used in carpentry. **2** a hardwood tree producing this timber.

satire *n.* **1** the use of humour, irony, exaggeration, or ridicule to expose and criticize people's bad points. **2** a play, novel, etc. using satire. □ **satiric** *adj.* (also **satirical**) **satirically** *adv.* **satirist** *n.*

satirize *v.* (**satirizes, satirized, satirizing**) [*Say* SAT ire, suh TEER ick, SAT er ist, SAT er ize]

satisfaction *n.* **1** the state of being satisfied. **2** a thing that settles an obligation or pays a debt. **3** what is felt to be owed or due to one.

satisfactory *adj.* satisfying expectations or needs. □ **satisfactorily** *adv.* [*Say* satis FACTORY, satis FACTOR a lee]

satisfy *v.* (**satisfies, satisfied, satisfying**) **1** meet the expectations, needs, or desires of. **2** fulfill (a desire or need). **3** provide with adequate information about. **4** comply with. □ **satisfy oneself** be certain in one's own mind. □ **satisfied** *adj.* **satisfying** *adj.* **satisfyingly** *adv.*

satrap *n.* **1** a provincial governor in the ancient Persian Empire. **2** a minor or subordinate ruler. [*Say* SAT rap]

saturate *v.* (**saturates, saturated, saturating**) **1** soak thoroughly with liquid. **2** fill a person or thing until no more can be held or absorbed. **3** cause a substance to absorb, hold, or combine with the greatest possible amount of another substance. **4** supply (a market) beyond the point at which there is demand for a product.

saturated *adj.* **1** completely wet. **2** filled with the greatest possible amount of something. **3 a** (of an organic molecule) containing the greatest number of hydrogen atoms. **b** (of fat) containing a high proportion of fatty acid molecules. **4** (of colour) very strong or bright. [Say SATCH a rate id]

saturation point *n.* the stage beyond which no more can be absorbed or accepted.

Saturday ● *n.* the day of the week following Friday. ● *adv.* **1** on Saturday. **2** (**Saturdays**) each Saturday.

satyr *n.* **1** one of a class of Greek woodland gods with a horse's ears and tail, or (in Roman representations) with a goat's ears, tail, legs, and budding horns. **2** a man with strong sexual desires. [Say SAT er or SATE er]

sauce ● *n.* **1** a thick liquid preparation eaten with food. **2** stewed fruit, e.g. apples. **3** *informal* impudence, impertinence. **4** *informal* alcohol. ● *v.* (**sauces, sauced, saucing**) *informal* be impudent to.

sauced *adj.* **1** served with a sauce. **2** *slang* drunk.

saucepan *n.* a usu. round metal cooking pot, often with a lid and long handle.

saucer *n.* **1** a shallow circular dish, esp. for standing a teacup on. **2** something saucer-shaped.

saucy *adj.* (**saucier, sauciest**) **1 a** sexually suggestive, esp. in a lighthearted way. **b** cheeky, rude. **2** bold and full of spirit. □ **saucily** *adv.*

Saudi (also **Saudi Arabian**) ● *adj.* of Saudi Arabia or its ruling dynasty. ● *n.* (*pl.* **Saudis**) **1** a person from Saudi Arabia. **2** a member of the ruling dynasty of Saudi Arabia. [Say SOWDY or SODDY (SOWDY *rhymes with* HOWDY)]

sauerkraut *n.* pickled cabbage. [Say SOUR krout]

sauger *n.* a large-mouthed N American fish. [Say SOGGER]

Saulteaux *n.* (*pl.* **Saulteaux**) **1** a member of an Aboriginal people formerly living on the shore of Lake Superior, now esp. in Manitoba. **2** the Ojibwa dialect of this people. □ **Saulteaux** *adj.* [Say SO toe]

sauna *n.* **1** a special room filled with steam to clean and refresh the body. **2** a session in a sauna.

saunter ● *v.* walk or go slowly. ● *n.* a leisurely ramble.

sauropod *n.* any of a group of plant-eating dinosaurs with a long neck and tail. [Say SORE oh pod]

sausage *n.* **1** a tube of seasoned ground meat in a skin. **2** a sausage-shaped object.

sausage roll *n.* minced pork enclosed in pastry and baked.

sauté ● *v.* (**sautés, sautéed, sautéing**) fry (food) quickly in a little hot fat. ● *n.* food cooked in this way. [Say SAW tay or saw TAY or so TAY]

Sauvignon *n.* (also **Sauvignon Blanc**) a type of dry white wine. [Say SO veen yon, so veen yon BLONK *(with* ON *as in French)*]

savage ● *adj.* **1** fierce; cruel. **2** wild. **3** *archaic offensive* uncivilized; primitive. ● *n.* **1** *archaic offensive* a member of a primitive tribe. **2** a cruel person. ● *v.* (**savages, savaged, savaging**) **1** attack and bite or maul etc. **2** criticize fiercely. □ **savagely** *adv.* **savagery** *n.*

savannah *n.* (also **savanna**) a grassy plain in tropical regions with few or no trees.

savant *n.* a learned person or expert in some field. [Say sa VONT]

save¹ ● *v.* (**saves, saved, saving**) **1** rescue, protect, etc. from danger etc. **2** keep for future use. **3 a** prevent exposure to (annoyance etc.). **b** obviate the need or likelihood of. **4** preserve from damnation. **5** *Computing* store (data) on a hard drive etc. **6 a** prevent an opponent from scoring (a goal etc.). **b** stop (a ball etc.) from entering the goal. ● *n. Hockey etc.* an act of preventing a goal. □ **save one's breath** not waste time speaking to no effect. **save the day** (or **situation**) find a solution to difficulty or disaster. **save face** avoid humiliation. **save one's neck** (or **skin**) escape from danger. □ **saver** *n.*

save² *prep. & conj. literary* except.

saving ● *adj.* making economical use of. ● *n.* **1** anything that is saved, esp. money. **2** an economy. ● *prep.* except.

saving grace *n.* a redeeming quality.

savings account *n.* an interest-paying bank account.

savings bond *n.* a certificate issued by a government etc. promising to repay borrowed money at a fixed rate of interest.

saviour *n.* (also **savior**) **1** a person who saves or delivers from danger etc. **2** (**Saviour**) *Christianity* Christ.

savoir faire *n.* the ability to act suitably in any situation. [Say sav warr FAIR (WARR *rhymes with* CAR)]

savory *n.* (*pl.* **savories**) a plant related to mint used as a herb in cooking.

savour (also **savor**) ● *v.* **1** appreciate and enjoy the taste of (food). **2** enjoy or appreciate (an experience etc.). ● *n.* a characteristic taste etc.

savoury (also **savory**) ● *adj.* **1** having an appetizing taste or smell. **2** (of food) salty or piquant. **3** pleasant; acceptable. ● *n.* (*pl.* **savouries**) a savoury dish.

savvy *slang* ● *n.* shrewdness and practical

knowledge. ● *adj.* (**savvier**, **savviest**) having or showing savvy.

saw[1] ● *n.* a tool for cutting with a toothed blade. ● *v.* (**saws**; *past* **sawed**; *past participle* **sawn** *or* **sawed**; **sawing**) **1** cut with a saw. **2** move to and fro as if cutting with a saw. □ **saw logs** *slang* snore. **saw off** *Cdn* compromise by trading concessions.

saw[2] *past of* SEE[1].

saw[3] *n.* a short phrase or proverb.

sawdust *n.* powdery wood particles produced in sawing.

sawed-off *adj.* (of a gun) having part of the barrel sawn off to make it easier to handle and give a wider field of fire.

sawhorse *n.* a rack supporting wood for sawing.

sawlog *n.* a felled tree suitable for cutting into timber.

sawmill *n.* a factory in which wood is sawn mechanically □ **sawmilling** *adj.*

sawn *past participle of* SAW[1].

saw-off *n. Cdn* **1** an arrangement between political rivals in which each agrees not to contest a seat etc. held by the other. **2** any compromise involving mutual concessions. **3** a tie, deadlock, etc.

sawtooth *adj.* (also **sawtoothed**) shaped like the teeth of a saw.

saw-whet owl *n.* a small brown North American owl of coniferous and deciduous woods.

sawyer *n.* a person who saws timber. [*Say* SOY er *or* SAW yur]

sax *n.* (*pl.* **saxes**) *informal* a saxophone.

saxifrage *n.* a plant that grows on rocky ground and bears small flowers. [*Say* SAXA frayge *or* SAXA fradge]

Saxon ● *n.* **1** *hist.* **a** a member of a Germanic people that conquered and occupied parts of England in the 5th–6th centuries. **b** the language of the Saxons. **2** Anglo-Saxon. **3** a native of modern Saxony in Germany. ● *adj.* **1** *hist.* of the Saxons. **2** of modern Saxony or Saxons.

saxophone *n.* a metal woodwind reed instrument, used esp. in jazz and popular music. □ **saxophonist** *n.*

say ● *v.* (**says**, **said**, **saying**) **1** utter words so as to communicate something. **2** (of a text or symbol) convey information or instructions. **3** (of a clock or watch) indicate (a time). **4** be asserted or reported. **5** present (a consideration) in favour of. **6** assume as a hypothesis. ● *interj.* esp. *US* an exclamation of surprise etc. ● *n.* an opportunity to state one's opinion or to influence events. □ **say much** (or **something**) **for** indicate the high quality of. **says you!** *informal* I disagree. **say**

when *informal* indicate when enough drink or food has been given. **say the word 1** indicate agreement or give permission. **2** give the order etc. **that is to say 1** in other words. **2** or at least. **when all is said and done** after all. **you don't say** *informal* an expression of amazement.

saying *n.* a well-known expression which offers advice or wisdom. □ **go without saying** be too obvious to need mention. **there is no saying** it is impossible to know.

sayonara *interj.* goodbye. [*Say* sigh a NARR uh]

say-so *n.* **1** the power to decide or allow something. **2** an arbitrary or unauthorized assertion.

scab ● *n.* **1** a crust formed over a cut, sore, etc. in healing. **2** *informal derogatory* a person who refuses to strike or join a trade union. ● *v.* (**scabs**, **scabbed**, **scabbing**) **1** act as a scab. **2** (of a wound etc.) form a scab. □ **scabby** *adj.*

scabbard *n. hist.* a sheath for a sword, bayonet, etc. [*Say* SCAB urd]

scabies *n.* a contagious skin disease causing severe itching. [*Say* SKAY beez]

scabrous *adj.* **1** having a rough surface. **2** not attractive. **3** indecent; scandalous. [*Say* SKAB russ]

scad *n.* a fish with very large spiky scales.

scads *pl. n. informal* large quantities.

scaffold *n.* **1** scaffolding. **2** *hist.* a raised wooden platform used for the execution of criminals. [*Say* SKAFF old]

scaffolding *n.* **1** a temporary structure formed of poles, planks, etc., used while building or repairing a house etc. **2** any supporting framework. [*Say* SKAFF old ing]

scalable *adj.* **1** capable of being climbed. **2** *Computing* able to be changed in size, capability, etc.

scalar *Math & Physics* ● *adj.* having only magnitude, not direction. ● *n.* a scalar quantity. [*Say* SKAY lur]

scalawag *n.* a rascal. [*Say* SKAL a wag]

scald ● *v.* **1** burn with hot liquid or steam. **2** heat (esp. milk) to near boiling point. **3** clean (a pan etc.) by rinsing with boiling water. **4** dip briefly in boiling water. ● *n.* a burn etc. caused by scalding. [*Rhymes with* BALD]

scalding *adj.* extremely hot. [*Rhymes with* BALDING]

scale[1] ● *n.* **1** each of the small overlapping plates protecting the skin of fish and reptiles. **2** a thick white deposit formed in a kettle etc. by the action of heat on water. **3** dental plaque. ● *v.* (**scales**, **scaled**,

scaling) 1 remove scale or scales from. **2** remove plaque from (teeth) by scraping. □ **scales fall from a person's eyes** a person is no longer deceived. □ **scaleless** *adj.*

scale² *n.* **1** (also in *pl.*) a weighing machine or device. **2** (**the Scales**) the zodiacal sign or constellation Libra. □ **tip the scales 1** weigh. **2** affect the result of something in one way.

scale³ ● *n.* **1** a series of degrees; a graded classification system. **2 a** a ratio of size in a map, drawing, or plan. **b** relative dimensions. **3** a set of marks on a line used in measuring etc. **4** an arrangement of notes in a system of music in ascending or descending order. **5** the minimum pay rate for a particular job, as determined by a union contract. ● *v.* (**scales, scaled, scaling**) **1** climb. **2** represent in proportional dimensions. **3** *Forestry* **a** estimate the amount of (standing timber). **b** measure (a log) to estimate how much cut timber it will yield. □ **scale back** reduce the scale, scope, or size of. **scale down** make smaller in proportion. **scale up** make larger in proportion. **to scale** with a uniform reduction or enlargement.

scalene *adj.* (of a triangle) having three unequal sides. [*Say* SKAY leen *or* skay LEEN]

scaler *n.* a person who scales timber or logs.

scallion *n.* a shallot or green onion. [*Say* SKAL yun]

scallop ● *n.* **1** an edible bivalve mollusc with a ribbed fan-shaped shell. **2** (also **scallop shell**) a single valve from the fan-shaped shell of a scallop. **3** (in *pl.*) an ornamental edging cut in imitation of the edge of a scallop shell. ● *v.* (**scallops, scalloped, scalloping**) **1** ornament (an edge or material) with scallops. **2** bake (food, esp. potatoes) in a cream sauce. [*Say* SKAL up *or* SKAWL up]

scallywag *n.* = SCALAWAG.

scalp ● *n.* **1** the skin covering the top of the head. **2** *hist.* the scalp of an enemy cut or torn away as a trophy. ● *v.* **1** *hist.* take the scalp of (an enemy). **2** *informal* resell (tickets) at inflated prices. □ **scalper** *n.* (in sense 2 of *v.*).

scalpel *n.* a surgeon's small sharp knife.

scaly *adj.* **1** covered in scales or flakes. **2** of or like a deposit of scale.

scam *slang* ● *n.* a trick or swindle. ● *v.* (**scams, scammed, scamming**) **1** swindle. **2** obtain in an unethical manner. □ **scammer** *n.*

scamp *n.* *informal* a rascal; a rogue.

scamper *v.* **1** run and skip playfully. **2** move quickly.

scampi *pl. n.* **1** large prawns. **2** a dish of these, usu. fried.

scan ● *v.* (**scans, scanned, scanning**) **1** look at intently or quickly. **2** move a detector or beam across something. **3** convert (an image, text, etc.) into digital form for processing, transmission, etc. **4** read (a line of verse etc.) with emphasis on its rhythm. **5** (of verse etc.) follow metrical rules. ● *n.* **1** the act of scanning. **2** an image obtained by scanning.

scandal *n.* **1** a person or circumstance etc. causing general public outrage. **2** the outrage or gossip so caused.

scandalize *v.* (**scandalizes, scandalized, scandalizing**) offend the moral feelings etc. of.

scandalous *adj.* **1** causing general outrage by a perceived offence against morality or law. **2** (of a state of affairs) disgracefully bad. □ **scandalously** *adv.*

Scandinavian *n.* **1** a person from Scandinavia. **2** the family of languages of Scandinavia. □ **Scandinavian** *adj.* [*Say* skanda NAVY un]

scanner *n.* **1** a device for scanning something. **2** a device for converting text, an image, etc. into digital data.

scant *adj.* **1** barely sufficient; deficient. **2** barely amounting to.

scanty *adj.* (**scantier, scantiest**) **1** of small extent or amount. **2** barely sufficient. □ **scantily** *adv.*

scapegoat ● *n.* a person who is blamed for the wrongdoings or mistakes of others. ● *v.* make a scapegoat of. □ **scapegoating** *n.*

scapula *n.* (*pl.* **scapulae** *or* **scapulas**) the shoulder blade. [*Say* SKAP yoo luh *for the singular*, SKAP yoo lee *for the plural*]

scapular ● *adj.* relating to the shoulder or shoulder blade. ● *n.* a monastic cloak consisting of a piece of cloth covering the shoulders and extending in front and behind almost to the feet. [*Say* SKAP yoo lur]

scar ● *n.* **1** a usu. permanent mark on the skin left after the healing of a wound etc. **2** the lasting effect of grief etc. **3** a mark left by damage etc. **4** a mark left on the stem etc. of a plant by the fall of a leaf etc. ● *v.* (**scars, scarred, scarring**) **1** mark with a scar or scars. **2** form a scar.

scarab *n.* **1** the dung beetle, treated as sacred in ancient Egypt. **2** a gem or other ornament made to resemble this beetle. [*Say* SCARE ub]

scarce *adj.* (**scarcer, scarcest**) **1** (esp.

of food etc.) insufficient for the demand; scanty. **2** rare. □**make oneself scarce** *informal* keep out of the way.

scarcely *adv.* **1** only just. **2** surely not.

scarcity *n.* (*pl.* **scarcities**) a lack or inadequacy. [*Say* SCARE si tee]

scare ● *v.* (**scares**, **scared**, **scaring**) **1** frighten or become frightened. **2** drive away by frightening. ● *n.* **1** a sudden attack of fright. **2** a general period of alarm. □**scare up** (or **out**) **1** frighten (game etc.) out of cover. **2** *informal* manage to find. □**scared** *adj.* **scarily** *adv.*

scarecrow *n.* **1** an object set up in a field to scare birds away. **2** *informal* a badly dressed or very thin person.

scaremonger *n.* a person who spreads frightening rumours. □**scaremongering** *n.* [*Say* SCARE mong gur *or* SCARE mung gur]

scarf¹ *n.* (*pl.* **scarves** or **scarfs**) a length or square of material worn around the neck or head.

scarf² *v. informal* eat or drink greedily.

scarify *v.* (**scarifies**, **scarified**, **scarifying**) **1** make cuts in the surface of. **2** loosen (esp. soil) with a machine. □**scarification** *n.* **scarifier** *n.* [*Say* SCARE a fie, scare a fuh KAY sh'n]

scarlet *n. & adj.* brilliant red tinged with orange.

scarlet fever *n.* an infectious bacterial fever with a scarlet rash.

scarlet woman *n. jocular* a promiscuous woman.

scarves *pl. of* SCARF¹.

scary *adj.* (**scarier**, **scariest**) **1** frightening. **2** surprising or alarming.

scat ● *n.* **1** animal droppings. **2** (also **scat singing**) improvised jazz singing using sounds instead of words. ● *v.* (**scats**, **scatted**, **scatting**) **1** sing scat. **2** depart quickly. ● *interj.* go!

scathing *adj.* witheringly scornful. □**scathingly** *adv.* [*Rhymes with* SUNBATHING]

scatological *adj.* marked by a preoccupation with excretion and human waste. [*Say* scatta LOGICAL]

scatter *v.* **1** throw here and there. **2** disperse or cause to disperse. **3** *Physics* deflect or diffuse. □**scattering** *n.*

scatterbrain *n.* a person given to silly or disorganized thought. □**scatterbrained** *adj.*

scattered *adj.* **1** not clustered together. **2** scatterbrained.

scattergun ● *n.* a shotgun. ● *adj.* (also **scattershot**) random, haphazard.

scatty *adj.* (**scattier**, **scattiest**) *informal* scatterbrained.

scaup *n.* a kind of duck with a dark head and breast and a white-sided body. [*Say* SCOP]

scavenge ● *v.* (**scavenges**, **scavenged**, **scavenging**) **1** search for and collect (useful items) from waste material. **2** (of an animal or bird) feed on (carrion). ● *n.* the action or process of scavenging. □**scavenger** *n.*

scavenger hunt *n.* a game in which people try to collect certain miscellaneous objects.

scenario *n.* (*pl.* **scenarios**) **1** an outline of the plot of a play etc. **2** a postulated sequence of future events. **3** *informal* a situation. [*Say* sen AIRY oh *or* sen ARR ee oh]

scene *n.* **1** a place in which events occur. **2** an incident. **3** a public incident displaying emotion, temper, etc. **4 a** a continuous portion of a theatrical production in a fixed setting. **b** a similar section of a film, book, etc. **5** a landscape or view. **6** *informal* **a** an area of action or interest. **b** a milieu. □**behind the scenes** not known to the public. **behind-the-scenes** secret. **change of scene** (or **scenery**) a move to different surroundings. **come on the scene** arrive. **quit the scene** depart.

scenery *n.* **1** the general appearance of the natural features of a landscape. **2** the painted representations of landscape etc. used as the background in a play etc.

scenic *adj.* **1** (of natural scenery) picturesque. **2** *Theatre* of or on the stage.

scent ● *n.* **1** a distinctive, esp. pleasant, smell. **2 a** a scent trail left by an animal. **b** clues etc. that can be followed like a scent trail. **3** esp. *Brit.* perfume. ● *v.* **1 a** discern by scent. **b** sense the presence of. **2** make fragrant. □**put** (or **throw**) **off the scent** deceive by false clues etc. □**scented** *adj.* **scentless** *adj.*

sceptic etc. = SKEPTIC.

sceptre *n.* a staff borne esp. at a coronation as a symbol of sovereignty. □**sceptred** *adj.* [*Say* SEP tur]

schedule ● *n.* **1** a list or plan of intended events, times, etc.; a timetable. **2** any list or tabular statement. **3** any of a number of forms attached to a tax return. ● *v.* (**schedules**, **scheduled**, **scheduling**) **1** arrange (an event etc.) for a certain time. **2** make a schedule of. □**according to** (or **on**) **schedule** as planned. □**scheduler** *n.* **scheduling** *n.* [*Say* SKED zhoo ul *or* SHED zhool *or* SHED jool]

schema *n.* (*pl.* **schemata** or **schemas**)

an outline or model of a plan or theory. [*Say* SKEEM uh *for the singular,* SKEEM a tuh *or* SKEEM uhs *for the plural*]

schematic ● *adj.* **1** of or concerning a scheme or schema. **2** representing objects by symbols etc. ● *n.* a schematic diagram. □ **schematically** *adv.* [*Say* skeem AT ick *or* skim AT ick]

scheme ● *n.* **1 a** a systematic plan for work, action, etc. **b** a systematic arrangement. **2** a plot. **3** a timetable, outline, etc. ● *v.* (**schemes, schemed, scheming**) make usu. secret plans. □ **scheme of things** the way things are. □ **schemer** *n.*

scheming *adj.* cunning or deceitful.

scherzo *n.* (*pl.* **scherzos**) a light or playful movement in a symphony, sonata, etc. [*Say* SKAIRT so]

schism *n.* **1** the division of a group into opposing sections. **2** the separation of a Church into two Churches owing to differences of belief. [*Say* SKIZ um]

schist *n.* a metamorphic rock composed of layers of different minerals. [*Say* SHIST]

schizo *informal offensive* ● *adj.* schizophrenic. ● *n.* (*pl.* **schizos**) a schizophrenic. [*Say* SKITS oh]

schizoid ● *adj.* **1** tending to or resembling schizophrenia or a schizophrenic. **2** having inconsistent or contradictory elements. ● *n.* a schizoid person. [*Say* SKITS oid]

schizophrenia *n.* **1** a mental disease marked by a breakdown in the relation between thoughts, feelings, and actions. **2** *informal* an approach characterized by contradictory elements. □ **schizophrenic** *adj. & n.* [*Say* skitsa FREENY uh, skitsa FREN ick]

schlemiel *n. informal* an awkward or unlucky person. [*Say* shluh MEAL]

schlep *informal* ● *v.* (**schleps, schlepped, schlepping**) **1** carry (a burden). **2** go or work with great effort. ● *n.* **1** a tedious journey. **2** an inept or stupid person. □ **schlepper** *n.* [*Say* SHLEP]

schlock *n. informal* **1** cheap or shoddy goods. **2** junk. □ **schlocky** *adj.* (**schlockier, schlockiest**) [*Say* SHLOCK]

schlockey *n. Cdn* a children's game like hockey played on a framed plywood sheet. [*Say* SHLOCK ee]

schlub *n. slang* a clumsy or untidy person. [*Say* SHLUB]

schlump *n. slang* a slow or slovenly person. [*Say* SHLUMP]

schmaltz *n. informal* sentimentality. □ **schmaltzy** *adj.* (**schmaltzier, schmaltziest**) [*Rhymes with* WALTZ]

schmo *n. slang* (*pl.* **schmoes**) an ordinary person. [*Say* SHMO]

schmooze *v. informal* (**schmoozes, schmoozed, schmoozing**) **1** talk, chat. **2** talk to (an esp. important person). □ **schmoozer** *n.* [*Say* SHMOOZ]

schmuck *slang* ● *n.* a contemptible person. ● *v. Cdn* hit, flatten.

schnapps *n.* a strong alcoholic spirit made from grain, with added flavouring such as peppermint etc. [*Say* SHNAPS *or* SHNOPPS]

schnauzer *n.* a German breed of dog with a close wiry coat and heavy whiskers. [*Say* SHNOW zur *or* SHNOUT zur (SHNOW *rhymes with* NOW)]

schnitzel *n.* a thin cutlet, breaded and fried. [*Say* SHNIT zul]

schnozz *n.* (*pl.* **schnozzes**) (also **schnozzle, schnozzola**) *slang* the nose.

scholar *n.* **1** a learned person; an academic. **2** the holder of a scholarship. □ **scholarly** *adj.*

scholarship *n.* **1** academic achievement or study. **2** a financial award to maintain a student in full-time education.

scholastic *adj.* of or concerning schools, education, etc. [*Say* skuh LASS tick] □ **scholastically** *adv.*

scholastic aptitude test *n. proprietary* a standardized test of a student's verbal and mathematical skills, used for admission to American colleges. Abbreviation: **SAT**.

school[1] ● *n.* **1** an institution for educating children or adults. **2** a day's work at school. **3** any institution at which instruction is given in a particular discipline. **4** a department of a university. **5** a group of artists, philosophers, etc. sharing similar ideas. ● *v.* send to school; educate. □ **school of hard knocks** experience gained from adversity. □ **schooler** *n.*

school[2] *n.* a large group of fish, whales, etc.

school board *n.* **1** an elected board responsible for policy concerning the schools in a given area. **2** an administrative unit responsible for the schools in a given area.

schoolboy *n.* a boy attending school.

schoolchild *n.* (*pl.* **schoolchildren**) a child attending school.

schoolgirl *n.* a girl attending school.

schoolhouse *n.* a small, usu. one-room school.

schooling *n.* **1** education, esp. at school. **2** training or discipline.

schoolmarm *n.* a prim and fussy female schoolteacher. □ **schoolmarmish** *adj.*

schoolmaster *n.* a male teacher in an esp. private school.

schoolmate *n.* a companion at school.

schoolroom *n.* a classroom.

schoolteacher *n.* a person who teaches in a school.

schoolyard *n.* a playing area beside a school.

school year *n.* academic year.

schooner *n.* **1** a ship with two or more masts. **2** a tall beer glass. [*Say* SKOONER]

schuss ● *n.* (*pl.* **schusses**) a straight downhill run on skis. ● *v.* (**schusses, schussed, schussing**) make a schuss. [*Rhymes with* PUSS]

sciatica *n.* pain in the sciatic nerve. [*Say* sigh ATTIC uh]

sciatic nerve *n.* the largest nerve in the human body, running from the pelvis to the thigh. [*Say* sigh ATTIC]

science *n.* **1** the systematic study of the structure and behaviour of the physical and natural world through observation and experiment. **2** systematic and formulated knowledge. **3** skilful technique.

science fiction *n.* fiction based on imagined future scientific or technological advances, frequently showing space or time travel.

scientific *adj.* **1 a** relating to or based on science. **b** systematic, accurate. **2** constituted of scientists. □ **scientifically** *adv.*

scientist *n.* a person with expert knowledge of a (usu. physical or natural) science.

Scientology *n.* *proprietary* a religious system whose adherents seek self-knowledge and spiritual fulfillment through courses of study and training. □ **Scientologist** *n.* [*Say* sigh un TOLLA jee, sigh un TOLLA jist]

sci-fi *n.* *informal* science fiction.

scimitar *n.* an oriental curved sword. [*Say* SIM it er]

scintillate *v.* (**scintillates, scintillated, scintillating**) **1** talk cleverly or wittily. **2** sparkle; twinkle. □ **scintillation** *n.* [*Say* SINT a late]

scintillating *adj.* **1** sparkling. **2** brilliantly and excitingly clever.

scion *n.* **1** a shoot of a plant etc., esp. one cut for grafting. **2** a descendant of a (esp. notable) family. [*Say* SIGH un]

scissor *v.* move or cause to move like scissors.

scissors *pl. n.* (also **pair of scissors** *singular*) an instrument for cutting, having two pivoted blades with finger and thumb holes in the handles.

sclerosis *n.* (*pl.* **scleroses**) an abnormal hardening of body tissue. □ **sclerotic** *adj.* [*Say* skluh ROE sis, skluh ROT ick]

scoff *v.* *informal* **1** speak derisively; be scornful. **2** eat greedily. □ **scoffer** *n.*

scofflaw *n.* *informal* a person who flouts the law.

scold ● *v.* rebuke or reprimand (esp. a child). ● *n.* a person who scolds. □ **scolding** *n.*

sconce *n.* **1** a lighting fixture attached to a wall. **2** a bracket to support a candle, attached to a wall. [*Rhymes with* FONTS]

scone *n.* a tea biscuit often containing raisins or currants. [*Rhymes with* CON *or* CONE]

scoop ● *n.* **1** an object resembling a spoon for transferring substances. **2** a movement of scooping. **3 a** a piece of news published by a newspaper etc. in advance of its rivals. **b** *informal* news. ● *v.* **1** hollow out. **2 a** lift with a scoop. **b** pick up rapidly. **3** forestall (a rival newspaper etc.) with a scoop. □ **scooper** *n.*

scoop neck *n.* a rounded low-cut neckline on a garment. □ **scoop-necked** *adj.*

scoot *v.* *informal* move quickly.

scooter *n.* **1** (also **motor scooter**) a light motorcycle. **2** a motorized cart used by a disabled or elderly person. **3** a means of transport consisting of a footboard mounted on two wheels and a steering column with handles, propelled by pushing one foot along the ground.

scope ● *n.* **1** the extent to which it is possible to range. **2** the sweep or reach of observation, thought, etc. **3** space or freedom to act. ● *v.* *slang* investigate or assess.

scorch ● *v.* (**scorches, scorched, scorching**) **1** burn the surface of with flame or heat. **2** become discoloured etc. with heat. ● *n.* (*pl.* **scorches**) a mark made by scorching. □ **scorched** *adj.*

scorcher *n.* *informal* **1** a very hot day. **2** *Sport* an extremely fast shot or hit.

score ● *n.* **1** the number of points, goals, runs, etc. achieved by an individual or side in a game. **2** (*pl.* **score**) a group or set of twenty. **3** (**scores of**) a large amount or number of. **4** a written representation of a musical composition showing all the vocal or instrumental parts. **5** a notch or line cut into a surface. **6** (**the score**) *informal* the state of affairs. ● *v.* (**scores, scored, scoring**) **1** gain (a point, goal, run, etc.) in a game. **2** be worth (a number of points). **3** record the score during a game. **4** cut a mark on (a surface). **5** orchestrate or arrange (a piece of music). **6** *informal* succeed in obtaining something. □ **know the score** *informal* be aware of the essential facts. **on that score** so far as that is concerned. **settle a score** avenge an injury. **score points** outdo another person. □ **scoreless** *adj.* **scorer** *n.* **scoring** *n.*

scoreboard *n.* a large board for publicly displaying the score in a game etc.

scorecard *n.* (also **scoresheet**) a printed card on which scores are recorded.

scorn ● *n.* disdain, contempt. ● *v.* **1** hold in contempt or disdain. **2** refuse to do as unworthy. □ **scornful** *adj.* **scornfully** *adv.*

Scorpio *n.* (*pl.* **Scorpios**) **1** (usu. **Scorpius**) a constellation (the Scorpion). **2** the eighth sign of the zodiac, which the sun enters around Oct. 23. [*Say* SCORE pee oh]

scorpion *n.* **1** an arachnid with pincers and a poisonous sting on its tail. **2** (**the Scorpion**) the zodiacal sign or constellation Scorpio. [*Say* SCORE pee un]

Scot *n.* a person from Scotland.

Scotch *n.* Scotch whisky.

scotch *v.* (**scotches, scotched, scotching**) put an end to.

Scotch tape ● *n.* *proprietary* transparent adhesive tape. ● *v.* (**Scotch-tape, Scotch-tapes, Scotch-taped, Scotch-taping**) fasten with Scotch tape.

Scotch whisky *n.* whisky distilled in Scotland, esp. from malted barley.

scoter *n.* (*pl.* **scoter** or **scoters**) a northern duck that breeds in the Arctic and Subarctic. [*Say* SCOTE er]

scot-free *adv.* without being punished or harmed.

Scotland Yard *n.* (in the UK) **1** the headquarters of the London Metropolitan Police. **2** its Criminal Investigation Department.

Scots ● *adj.* = SCOTTISH. ● *n.* the form of English spoken in (esp. Lowlands) Scotland.

Scotsman *n.* (*pl.* **Scotsmen**) a person from Scotland.

Scotswoman *n.* (*pl.* **Scotswomen**) a woman from Scotland.

Scottish ● *adj.* of Scotland or its people. ● *n.* (**the Scottish**) the people of Scotland.

Scottish terrier *n.* (also *informal* **Scottie, Scottie dog**) a small terrier with a rough coat.

scoundrel *n.* a dishonest person.

scour *v.* **1** cleanse or brighten by rubbing with something rough or a detergent. **2** clear out (a pipe, channel, etc.) by flushing water through it. **3** search thoroughly. **4** wear away.

scourge ● *n.* **1** a whip used for punishment. **2** a person or thing that causes trouble or suffering. ● *v.* (**scourges, scourged, scourging**) **1** whip. **2** punish; afflict. [*Say* SKURGE]

scout ● *n.* **1** a person sent out to get information about the enemy. **2** a talent scout. **3** a person or vehicle sent out for reconnoitring. **4** (**Scout**) a member of a Scouting organization. ● *v.* **1** act as a scout. **2** make a search. □ **scouter** *n.* **scouting** *n.*

Scouting *n.* an international movement aiming to develop character in young people, esp. through outdoor activity.

scoutmaster *n.* a person in charge of a group of Scouts.

scow *n.* a flat-bottomed boat. [*Rhymes with* COW]

scowl ● *n.* a severe frown producing a sullen look. ● *v.* make a scowl.

scrabble ● *v.* (**scrabbles, scrabbled, scrabbling**) **1** scratch or grope to find or hold on to something. **2** scramble on hands and feet. ● *n.* an act of scrabbling.

scraggly *adj.* sparse and irregular; ragged.

scraggy *adj.* (**scraggier, scraggiest**) **1** thin and bony. **2** = SCRAGGLY.

scram *v.* (**scrams, scrammed, scramming**) *informal* go away.

scramble ● *v.* (**scrambles, scrambled, scrambling**) **1** move or make one's way quickly and awkwardly, using one's hands as well as one's feet. **2** make or become confused. **3** make (a broadcast transmission or telephone conversation) unintelligible without a decoding device. **4** cook (beaten eggs) in a pan. **5** (of a fighter aircraft) take off immediately in an emergency. **6** *informal* act in a hurried manner. ● *n.* **1** an act of scrambling. **2** a difficult climb or walk. **3** a disorganized struggle or competition.

scrambler *n.* a device used to scramble television signals, telephone conversations, etc.

scrap ● *n.* **1** a fragment or remnant. **2** rubbish or waste. **3** a cutting from something written or printed. **4** discarded metal or paper for reuse. **5** the smallest piece or amount. **6** (in *pl.*) **a** odds and ends. **b** bits of leftover food. **7** *informal* a fight. ● *v.* (**scraps, scrapped, scrapping**) **1** discard. **2** get rid of; cancel. **3** engage in a fight.

scrapbook *n.* a book of blank pages for sticking clippings, drawings, photographs, etc. in.

scrape ● *v.* (**scrapes, scraped, scraping**) **1** move a hard or sharp edge across (a surface), as to smooth or clean. **2** rub (a surface) harshly against or with another. **3** make (a hollow) by scraping. **4** draw or move with a sound of scraping. **5** just manage to achieve or pass. **6** amass with difficulty. ● *n.* **1** the act or sound of scraping. **2** a scraped place (on the skin etc.). **3** *informal* an awkward predicament. □ **scrape (the bottom of) the barrel** *informal* be obliged to use one's last resources. □ **scraper** *n.* **scraping** *n.*

scrap heap *n.* a collection of discarded things.

scrapie *n.* a disease of sheep involving the central nervous system. [*Say* SCRAPE ee]

scrapper *n. informal* **1** a person who fights. **2** a competitive person.

scrappy *adj.* (**scrappier, scrappiest**) **1** pugnacious or tenacious. **2** consisting of scraps. **3** incomplete. □ **scrappiness** *n.*

scratch ● *v.* (**scratches, scratched, scratching**) **1** score or mark a surface, skin, etc. with a sharp or pointed object. **2** rub with the hand to relieve itching. **3** make or form by scratching. **4** write hurriedly. **5** obtain or achieve with difficulty. **6** strike (out) something written. **7** withdraw from competition. ● *n.* **1** a mark or wound made by scratching. **2** a sound of scratching. **3** an act of scratching oneself. **4** *informal* a superficial wound. ● *adj.* **1** collected by chance. **2** collected or made from whatever is available. □ **from scratch 1** from the beginning. **2** (of food) prepared from the basic ingredients. **scratch one's head** be perplexed. **scratch my back and I will scratch yours** do me a favour and I will return it. **scratch the surface** understand or deal with only superficially. **up to scratch** up to the required standard. □ **scratcher** *n.*

scratch pad *n.* **1** a pad of paper for scribbling. **2** *Computing* a small memory for the temporary storage of data.

scratchy *adj.* (**scratchier, scratchiest**) **1** tending to make scratches or a scratching noise. **2** (of a garment) tending to itch.

scrawl ● *v.* write in a hurried untidy way. ● *n.* **1** a piece of hurried or illegible writing. **2** a scrawled note.

scrawny *adj.* (**scrawnier, scrawniest**) very skinny, not attractive. □ **scrawniness** *n.*

scream ● *n.* **1** a loud piercing cry expressing fear, pain, etc. **2** *informal* an irresistibly funny thing, person, etc. ● *v.* **1** emit a scream. **2** speak or sing in a screaming tone. **3** *informal* move very quickly. □ **screamer** *n.*

screamingly *adv.* **1** extremely. **2** blatantly.

scree *n.* (in *sing.* or *pl.*) **1** small loose stones. **2** a mountain slope covered with these.

screech ● *n.* (*pl.* **screeches**) **1** a harsh high-pitched scream etc. **2** (in Canada) a potent dark rum of Newfoundland. ● *v.* (**screeches, screeched, screeching**) utter with or make a screech □ **screecher** *n.* **screechy** *adj.* (**screechier, screechiest**).

screech owl *n.* an owl that screeches instead of hooting.

screed *n.* a long usu. tiresome piece of writing or speech.

screen ● *n.* **1** an upright partition for separating, concealing, or sheltering. **2** a thing used as a shelter, for concealment, etc. **3 a** a blank surface on which films etc. are projected. **b** (**the screen**) the film industry. **4** the surface of a television or computer monitor on which images appear. **5** a frame with fine wire netting to keep out flies etc. ● *v.* **1** afford shelter to; hide. **2** shut off or hide behind a screen. **3** *Hockey* obstruct the view of (a goalie). **4 a** show (a film etc.) on a screen. **b** broadcast (a television program). **5 a** test for the presence or absence of a disease. **b** check for the presence or absence of a quality. □ **screener** *n.*

screening *n.* **1** the showing of a film. **2** the testing of a group for a disease etc.

screenplay *n.* the script of a film, with acting instructions, scene directions, etc.

screen printing *n.* a process like stencilling with ink forced through a prepared sheet of fine material. □ **screen-print** *v.*

screen saver *n. Computing* a program which, after a set time, replaces an unchanging screen display with a moving image to prevent damage to the phosphor.

screen test *n.* a filmed audition of a prospective actor.

screenwriter *n.* a person who writes a screenplay. □ **screenwriting** *n.*

screw ● *n.* **1** a metal pin or cylinder with a spiral thread running around the outside, used esp. for fastening. **2** (also **screw propeller**) a ship's or aircraft's propeller. **3** *slang* a prison guard. ● *v.* **1** fasten or tighten with a screw or screws. **2** *slang* cheat or take advantage of. **3** *slang* extort from. □ **have a screw loose** *informal* be slightly crazy. **put the screws on** *informal* exert pressure on someone. **screw around** *slang* **1** be promiscuous. **2** fool around. **3** toy with someone psychologically. **screw up 1** *slang* **a** bungle or mismanage. **b** spoil or ruin. **2** summon up (one's courage etc.).

3 contort (one's face etc.). **4** crush into a tight mass (paper etc.).

screwball ● n. **1** Baseball a curving pitch. **2** slang a crazy or eccentric person. ● adj. slang crazy, eccentric.

screw cap n. a screw-top.

screwdriver n. **1** a tool with a shaped tip to fit into the head of a screw to turn it. **2** a cocktail of vodka and orange juice.

screwed adj. **1** slang ruined. **2** twisted.

screw-top n. a cap or lid that can be screwed on to a bottle, jar, etc.

screw-up n. slang a bungle or mess.

screwy adj. (**screwier**, **screwiest**) slang **1** crazy or eccentric. **2** absurd.

scribble ● v. (**scribbles**, **scribbled**, **scribbling**) **1** write or draw carelessly or hurriedly. **2** be an author or writer. ● n. **1** a scrawl. **2** a hasty note etc.

scribbler n. **1** informal a person or thing that scribbles. **2** Cdn a small, soft-covered notebook for school.

scribblings pl. n. scribbled writing.

scribe n. **1** a person who writes or copies out documents. **2** Jewish Hist. an ancient Jewish record-keeper. **3** informal a writer, esp. a journalist. □ **scribal** adj.

scrim n. **1** a theatrical drop made of a fabric that becomes transparent when lit from behind. **2** the fabric of which such drops are made.

scrimmage ● n. **1** a rough or confused struggle. **2** Football **a** a sequence of play beginning with a backward pass from the centre. **b** (also **scrimmage line**) the line of scrimmage. ● v. (**scrimmages**, **scrimmaged**, **scrimmaging**) engage in a scrimmage.

scrimp v. spend money carefully in order to save. □ **scrimp and save** practise thrift to save money.

scrimshaw ● v. adorn (whalebone, ivory, etc.) with carved or coloured designs. ● n. work of this kind.

scrip[1] n. **1** a provisional certificate of money subscribed to a bank or company etc. entitling the holder to dividends. **2** temporary paper currency.

scrip[2] n. (also **land scrip**) **1** a certificate entitling the holder to acquire possession of public land. **2** Cdn hist. a certificate issued to Metis entitling the bearer to 240 acres or money for the purchase of land.

script ● n. **1** handwriting as distinct from print. **2** type imitating handwriting. **3 a** the text of a play, film, or broadcast. **b** a planned series of statements etc. ● v. write a script for.

scripture n. writings sacred to a religion or group, esp. (as **Scripture** or **the Scriptures**) the Bible. □ **scriptural** adj.

scriptwriter n. a person who writes a script. □ **scriptwriting** n.

scritch n. a quiet scratching sound. □ **scritching** n. & adj.

scroll ● n. **1** a roll of parchment or paper. **2** a book in the ancient roll form. **3** an ornamental design or carving imitating a roll of parchment. ● v. move (displayed text etc.) on a computer screen in order to view different parts of it.

scroll bar n. a long thin section at the edge of a computer display by which material can be scrolled using a mouse.

scrollwork n. decoration of spiral lines.

Scrooge n. a miserly person.

scrotum n. a pouch of skin containing the testicles. [Say SKROTE um]

scrounge informal ● v. (**scrounges**, **scrounged**, **scrounging**) **1** search or forage for. **2** search about to find something at no cost. ● n. an act of scrounging. □ **scrounger** n.

scrub[1] ● v. (**scrubs**, **scrubbed**, **scrubbing**) **1** rub a surface hard so as to clean. **2** thoroughly clean (the hands, face, etc.) by scrubbing. **3** informal scrap or cancel. ● n. **1** an act of scrubbing. **2** something used in scrubbing. **3** (in pl.) special hygienic clothing worn by surgeons and nurses during operations. □ **scrubbable** adj. **scrubber** n.

scrub[2] n. **1 a** vegetation consisting mainly of brush or stunted trees. **b** land covered with this. **2** an animal of inferior breed. **3** Sport **a** informal a player not of the first class. **b** Cdn a pickup game. □ **scrubby** adj.

scrubland n. land consisting of scrub vegetation.

scruff n. the back of the neck.

scruffy adj. (**scruffier**, **scruffiest**) informal shabby, slovenly; ragged. □ **scruffiness** n.

scrum ● n. **1** Rugby an arrangement of the forwards of each team in opposing groups, each with arms interlocked and heads down, with the ball thrown in. **2** Brit. & Cdn informal a disorderly crowd. **3** Cdn a situation where a crowd of reporters surround and interrogate a politician. ● v. (**scrums**, **scrummed**, **scrumming**) **1** Rugby form a scrum. **2** Cdn engage in a scrum.

scrumptious adj. informal **1** delicious. **2** pleasing.

scrunch v. (**scrunches**, **scrunched**, **scrunching**) **1 a** make or become crumpled. **b** crouch. **2** make or cause to make a crunching sound.

scrunchy n. (also **scrunchie**) (pl. **scrunchies**) an elastic band covered in loose fabric, used to fasten the hair.

scruple ● n. **1** a regard to the morality or propriety of an action. **2** a feeling of doubt caused by this. ● v. (**scruples, scrupled, scrupling**) be reluctant because of scruples. [Say SCREW pull]

scrupulous adj. **1** conscientious or thorough. **2** careful to avoid doing wrong. □ **scrupulosity** n. **scrupulously** adv. [Say SCREW pyoo lus, screw pyoo LOSSA tee]

scrutineer n. esp. Cdn & Brit. a person who scrutinizes esp. the conduct and result of a ballot. [Say screw tin EAR]

scrutinize v. (**scrutinizes, scrutinized, scrutinizing**) look closely at. [Say SCREW tin ize]

scrutiny n. (pl. **scrutinies**) **1** a critical investigation or examination. **2** an official examination of ballot papers. [Say SCREW tuh nee]

SCSI n. (pl. **SCSIs**) a standard interface connecting peripheral devices to computers. [Sounds like SCUZZY]

scuba n. (pl. **scubas**) a portable breathing apparatus for divers.

scud ● v. (**scuds, scudded, scudding**) **1** be driven swiftly by the wind. **2** skim along. ● n. (usu. **Scud**) a type of long-range surface-to-surface missile.

scuff ● v. **1** graze or brush against. **2** scrape (a shoe etc.) against something. **3** walk with dragging feet. ● n. a mark of scuffing. □ **scuffed** adj.

scuffle ● n. **1** a confused struggle or fight; a tussle. **2** the shuffling of feet. ● v. (**scuffles, scuffled, scuffling**) **1** engage in a scuffle. **2** move with a shuffling gait. □ **scuffler** n.

scull ● n. **1** either of a pair of small oars used by a single rower. **2** an oar placed over the stern of a boat to propel it, usu. by a twisting motion. **3** a small boat propelled with a scull or sculls. ● v. **1** propel (a boat) with sculls. **2** stay afloat or propel oneself through water by making a waving motion in the water with the hands. □ **sculler** n.

scullery n. (pl. **sculleries**) a small kitchen or room at the back of a house for washing dishes etc.

sculpin n. a fish with a large spiny head native to non-tropical regions.

sculpt v. create or represent something by carving, casting, or other shaping techniques. □ **sculpting** n. **sculptor** n. **sculptress** n.

sculpture ● n. **1** the art of making forms in stone, wood, clay, etc. **2** a work or works of sculpture. ● v. (**sculptures, sculptured, sculpturing**) **1** represent in sculpture. **2** give a markedly contoured form to. □ **sculptural** adj.

scum n. **1** a layer of dirt, froth, etc. on the top of liquid. **2** the most worthless part of something. **3** informal a worthless person etc. □ **scummy** adj.

scumbag n. (also **scumball, scumbucket**) slang a contemptible person.

scupper ● n. a hole in a ship's side to carry off water from the deck. ● v. slang **1** sink (a ship). **2** defeat or ruin (a plan etc.).

scurf n. **1** flakes on the skin's surface, esp. those of the head. **2** any scaly matter on a surface.

scurrilous adj. **1** spreading scandalous claims about someone in order to damage their reputation. **2** given to rude and insulting humour. □ **scurrility** n. [Say SKUR a lus, skur ILLA tee]

scurry ● v. (**scurries, scurried, scurrying**) run or move hurriedly. ● n. (pl. **scurries**) a scurrying movement.

scurvy n. a disease caused by lack of vitamin C, with bleeding gums and the opening of previously healed wounds.

scuttle ● v. (**scuttles, scuttled, scuttling**) **1** abandon or thwart (a plan etc.). **2** let water into (a ship) to sink it. **3** run hurriedly with short quick steps. ● n. **1** a hole with a lid in a ship's deck or side. **2** a small bucket for carrying coal.

scuttlebutt n. informal rumour, gossip.

scuzzy adj. (**scuzzier, scuzziest**) slang squalid, sleazy, or disgusting. □ **scuzz** n. **scuzziness** n.

scythe ● n. an agricultural tool with a long curving blade at the end of a long pole, used to cut grass, grain, etc. ● v. (**scythes, scythed, scything**) cut with, or as if with, a scythe. [Say SYTHE (with TH as in SOOTHE)]

SE abbr. **1** southeast. **2** southeastern.

sea n. **1** the expanse of salt water that surrounds the earth's land masses. **2** a particular area of this. **3** a vast expanse or quantity. □ **at sea 1** in a ship on the sea. **2** (also **all at sea**) perplexed, confused. **on the sea 1** in a ship at sea. **2** situated on the coast. **put** (or **put out**) **to sea** leave land or port.

sea bass n. (pl. **sea bass** or **sea basses**) a marine fish resembling or related to the bass.

seabed n. the sea floor.

seabird n. a bird that lives on or near the sea.

seaboard n. the land along the sea.

sea change *n.* a notable or unexpected transformation.

sea cucumber *n.* a wormlike marine invertebrate.

sea dog *n.* an old or experienced sailor.

Sea-Doo *n.* (*pl.* **Sea-Doos**) *proprietary* a personal watercraft.

seafaring ● *adj.* **1** travelling by sea. **2** having to do with the occupation of a sailor. ● *n.* **1** travel by sea. **2** the occupation of a sailor. □ **seafarer** *n.*
[*Say* SEA fare ing]

sea floor *n.* the bottom of the sea.

seafood *n.* an edible animal obtained from the sea, including fish, crustaceans, etc.

seafront *n.* the part of a coastal town directly facing the sea.

seagoing *adj.* **1** fit for crossing the sea. **2 a** relating to sea travel. **b** having to do with the occupation of a sailor.

seagrass *n.* (*pl.* **seagrasses**) a grasslike plant growing in or by the sea.

seagull *n.* a gull.

sea horse *n.* a small upright marine fish with a head and neck suggestive of a horse.

sea ice *n.* a large expanse of ice formed from frozen salt water.

seal¹ ● *n.* **1** a device or substance used to join two things together or make something impervious. **2** a piece of wax or lead with an individual design stamped into it, attached to a document as a guarantee of authenticity. **3** a confirmation or guarantee. ● *v.* **1** fasten or close securely. **2** isolate (an area) by preventing entrance to and exit from it. **3** apply a coating to (a surface) to make it impervious. **4** conclude, establish definitively. **5** authenticate with a seal. □ **one's lips are sealed** one promises to keep a secret.

seal² ● *n.* **1** a fish-eating amphibious sea mammal with flippers. **2** sealskin. ● *v.* hunt for seals. □ **sealing** *n.*

sealant *n.* a material or substance used to make something airtight or watertight.

sea legs *n.* the ability to keep one's balance and avoid being sick while at sea.

sealer¹ *n.* **1** (also **sealer jar**) *Cdn* (esp. *Prairies* & *BC*) a preserving jar with a glass or metal lid secured by a metal band screwed onto the mouth of the jar. **2** an undercoat of paint etc. used to give porous building materials a surface more receptive to finishing coats. **3** a sealant.

sealer² *n.* **1** a person who hunts seals. **2** a ship used for this.

sea level *n.* the average level of the sea's surface, used in calculating altitude.

sealift *n.* a large-scale transportation of supplies, troops, etc. by sea.

sea lion *n.* a large-eared seal having a broader muzzle and sparser fur than fur seals.

seal of approval *n.* **1** a seal or stamp indicating that something has been approved by an authority. **2** an expression of endorsement etc.

sealskin *n.* **1** the skin or prepared fur of a seal. **2** a garment made from this.

seam *n.* **1** a line along which two pieces of cloth etc. are stitched together. **2** a line or ridge where two parallel edges meet. **3** a stratum of coal etc. □ **come apart at the seams** collapse emotionally.

seaman *n.* (*pl.* **seamen**) **1** a sailor. **2** an enlisted member of the navy below the rank of petty officer. □ **seamanship** *n.*

seamless *adj.* **1** without a seam. **2** uninterrupted, smooth. □ **seamlessly** *adv.* **seamlessness** *n.*

seamstress *n.* (*pl.* **seamstresses**) a woman who makes and mends clothing.
[*Say* SEAM struss *or* SEM struss]

seamy *adj.* (**seamier**, **seamiest**) disreputable.

seance *n.* a meeting at which people attempt to make contact with the dead.
[*Say* SAY awnce]

sea otter *n.* a Pacific otter with thick dark fur.

seaplane *n.* an aircraft designed to take off from and land on water.

seaport *n.* **1** a harbour or port for sea-going ships. **2** a town or city having this.

sear *v.* **1** burn or scorch the surface of. **2** cause great pain or anguish (to). **3** brown (meat) quickly at a high temperature. **4** leave an esp. disturbing impression on.
[*Rhymes with* HEAR]

search ● *v.* (**searches**, **searched**, **searching**) **1** look through or examine thoroughly to find something. **2** *Computing* locate a specified piece of information in a file or document. **3** examine or question thoroughly. **4** look probingly for. ● *n.* (*pl.* **searches**) an act of searching. □ **search me!** *informal* I don't know.
□ **searchable** *adj.* **searcher** *n.*

search and rescue *n.* an operation designed to find and rescue people who are lost or in danger etc.

search engine *n.* a program for the retrieval of data, files, etc. from a database or network.

searching *adj.* thorough, penetrating.

searchlight *n.* a powerful outdoor electric light with a movable beam.

search party *n.* (*pl.* **search parties**) a

group of people organized to look for a lost person or thing.

search warrant *n.* a judge's order authorizing a person to enter and search a building etc.

searing *adj.* **1** scorching. **2** agonizing. **3** (of words) powerful and critical. □ **searingly** *adv.* [Rhymes with HEARING]

sea salt *n.* salt produced by evaporating sea water.

seascape *n.* a picturesque view or picture of the sea.

seashell *n.* the shell of a marine mollusc.

seashore *n.* land close to or bordering on the sea.

seasick *adj.* suffering from nausea from the motion of a ship at sea. □ **seasickness** *n.*

seaside *n.* a beach area.

season ● *n.* **1** each of the four divisions of the year (spring, summer, fall, and winter). **2** a time of year characterized by climatic features. **3** a time when something is plentiful or regularly indulged in. **4** a schedule of shows, sporting events, etc. **5** (also **Season**) the time of year surrounding a particular holiday. ● *v.* **1** flavour (food) with salt, herbs, etc. **2 a** make or become suitable. **b** make or become mature or experienced. **3** make more interesting. □ **in season 1** (of food) plentiful and ready to eat. **2** (of an animal) in heat.

seasonable *adj.* usual for or appropriate to a particular season.

seasonal *adj.* **1** having to do with the seasons of the year or a particular season. **2** varying with the season. **3** employed only during a particular season. □ **seasonality** *n.* **seasonally** *adv.*

seasonal affective disorder *n.* a depressive state associated with late fall and winter.

seasoning *n.* an ingredient added to food to enhance its flavour.

season ticket *n.* (usu. in *pl.*) (also esp. *Cdn* **season's ticket**) tickets for esp. a schedule of sporting or cultural events during a specified period.

sea star *n.* a starfish.

seat ● *n.* **1 a** a thing made or used for sitting on. **b** the part of a chair etc. on which one sits. **2** a place for a person to sit in a theatre, vehicle, etc. **3 a** the right to sit as a member of a deliberative body. **b** *Cdn & Brit.* a Member of Parliament's constituency. **4** the buttocks. **5** the part of the pants etc. covering the buttocks. **6** the base. **7** a site or location. ● *v.* **1** arrange for (someone) to sit somewhere. **2** provide seats for. **3** sit

down. □ **be seated** sit down. **by the seat of one's pants** *informal* by instinct rather than logic. **take a seat** sit down. □ **seating** *n.*

seat belt *n.* a strap designed to secure a person in a seat of a vehicle, aircraft, etc.

seated *adj.* **1** sitting. **2** positioned.

seatmate *n.* a person sitting in a nearby seat.

seat sale *n.* *Cdn & Brit.* a sale of esp. airline tickets.

sea urchin *n.* a small marine creature with a spiny shell.

seawall *n.* a wall or embankment erected as a breakwater to prevent encroachment by the sea.

seaward ● *adv.* (also **seawards**) towards the sea. ● *adj.* **1** going out to sea. **2** facing towards the sea. ● *n.* the direction in which the sea lies.

seaway *n.* an inland waterway for sea-going ships.

seaweed *n.* an algae growing in the sea or on the rocks on a shore. □ **seaweedy** *adj.*

seaworthy *adj.* (esp. of a ship) in a suitable condition to sail on the sea. □ **seaworthiness** *n.*

sec *n.* *informal* a second.

sec. *abbr.* second(s).

secede *v.* (**secedes, seceded, seceding**) withdraw formally from an alliance, a federal union, or a political or religious organization. [Say suh SEED]

secession *n.* **1** the action of seceding. **2** (**Secession**) *hist.* the withdrawal of eleven southern States from the US Union in 1860. □ **secessionist** *n. & adj.* [Say suh SESSION]

Sechelt *n.* (*pl.* **Sechelt**) **1** a member of an Aboriginal people living on the coast of BC. **2** their Sne Nay Muxw language. □ **Sechelt** *adj.* [Say SEE shelt]

secluded *adj.* **1** hidden from view. **2** isolated or withdrawn from human contact. □ **seclude** *v.* (**secludes, secluded, secluding**)

seclusion *n.* a secluded state.

second¹ ● *ord. num.* **1** coming next after the first. **2** coming next in rank, quality, or importance. **3** (in *pl.*) *informal* a second helping of food at a meal. **4** a slightly flawed item. **5** an assistant or attendant, esp. in a boxing match or duel. **6** the second player on a curling rink. ● *v.* **1** support, assist. **2** formally support or endorse. □ **second to none** superior.

second² *n.* **1** a sixtieth part of a minute of time or angular measurement. **2** *informal* a brief moment.

second³ *v.* transfer a worker etc.

temporarily to another position.
□ **secondment** n. [Say suh KOND, suh KOND m'nt]

secondarily adv. in the second place.

secondary ● adj. **1** coming after or less important than something primary. **2** not original. **3** relating to education for students in their mid to late teens. **4** arising after or in consequence of an earlier infection etc. ● n. (pl. **secondaries**) **1** a secondary person or thing. **2** a secondary school.

secondary sexual characteristics pl. n. the physical characteristics developed at puberty which distinguish between the sexes but are not essential to reproduction.

second-best ● adj. next in quality to the best. ● n. **1** a second-best person or thing. **2** a less desirable alternative.

second class ● n. **1** a set of persons or things grouped together as second-best. **2** the second-best accommodation in a train, ship, etc. ● adj. (usu. **second-class**) **1** belonging to or travelling by the second class. **2** inferior in quality, status, etc. ● adv. (usu. **second-class**) by second class.

second coming n. **1** (usu. **Second Coming**) the prophesied return of Christ to earth. **2** the return of a person or thing.

second cousin n. a child of one's parent's first cousin.

second-degree adj. **1** designating the second-most serious category of crime. **2** denoting burns that cause blistering but not scarring.

second fiddle n. see FIDDLE.

second generation ● n. **1** the offspring of the first generation born in a country. **2** (of technology) an advanced or refined stage of development. ● adj. (usu. **second-generation**) **1** designating the offspring of a first generation. **2** designating something in an improved stage of development.

second-growth ● n. a growth of trees etc. replacing one that has been destroyed by fire, logging, etc. ● adj. designating a second growth.

second-guess v. (**second-guesses**, **second-guessed**, **second-guessing**) **1** predict by guesswork. **2** question with hindsight.

second hand n. the hand on an analog clock or watch that indicates the passing of seconds.

second-hand ● adj. **1** (of goods) previously owned or used. **2 a** not heard or obtained directly. **b** not undergone personally. ● adv. **1** through an intermediary. **2** not new.

second-hand smoke n. the smoke from a smoker's cigarette etc. inhaled unwillingly by others.

second language n. a language used in addition to one's native language.

secondly adv. **1** furthermore. **2** as a second item.

second nature n. an acquired ability or habit etc. that has become instinctive.

second-rate adj. of mediocre quality. □ **second rater** n.

second sight n. the ability to perceive future or distant events.

second string ● n. Sport a roster of backup players available to replace players from the starting lineup. ● adj. (**second-string**) **1** designating a player etc. who is a backup or substitute. **2** (of a person or thing) second-class. □ **second stringer** n.

second thoughts pl. n. **1** a new opinion or resolution reached after further consideration. **2** doubt about a decision etc. already made.

second wind n. a renewed energy or vigour needed to continue an effort.

secret ● adj. **1** kept or meant to be kept hidden from others. **2** (of a person) **a** having a role unknown to others. **b** able to preserve secrecy. ● n. **1** something secret. **2** a thing known only to a few. **3** a mystery. **4** the best or only way to achieve something. □ **secrecy** n. **secretly** adv.

secret agent n. a person operating covertly; a spy.

secretariat n. an esp. governmental administrative department. [Say sekra TERRY it]

secretary n. (pl. **secretaries**) **1** a person employed to manage or assist with files, make appointments, etc. **2** an official appointed by an organization to conduct its correspondence, keep its records, etc. **3** Cdn & Brit. = PARLIAMENTARY SECRETARY. **4** a senior member of the staff of an embassy. □ **secretarial** adj.

Secretary-General n. (pl. **Secretaries-General**) the principal administrator of an organization.

Secretary of State n. (pl. **Secretaries of State**) **1** Cdn (usu. **secretary of state**) a government minister responsible for a specific area within a department. **2** US the chief government official responsible for foreign affairs.

secrete v. (**secretes**, **secreted**, **secreting**) **1** (of a cell, organ, etc.) produce and discharge (a substance). **2** conceal. □ **secretion** n. **secretory** adj. [Say suh KREET, suh KREE shun, suh KREET a ree]

secretive *adj.* inclined to make or keep secrets. □ **secretively** *adv.* **secretiveness** *n.* [*Say* SEE kruh tiv]

secret police *n.* a police force operating in secret for political purposes.

secret service *n.* **1** a government department concerned with espionage. **2** (**Secret Service**) (in the US) a branch of the Treasury Department dealing with counterfeiting and protecting the President etc.

secret society *n.* an organization whose members are sworn to secrecy about its proceedings.

sect *n.* **1** a body of people holding religious doctrines usu. different from those of a larger group from which they have separated. **2** usu. *derogatory* a religious faction regarded as heretical. **3** the system or body of adherents of a philosopher or philosophy etc.

sectarian *adj.* **1** of or concerning a sect. **2** pertaining to or created by differences of religion or denomination. **3** bigoted or narrow-minded. □ **sectarianism** *n.* [*Say* sec TERRY un]

section ● *n.* **1** a part cut off or separated from something. **2** a group of musicians playing similar instruments forming part of a band or orchestra. **3** a subdivision of a newspaper, book, etc. **4** a department of a store, library, etc. in which similar items may be found together. **5** one of the naturally divided segments of a citrus fruit. **6 a** (*West*) one square mile of esp. agricultural land, 640 acres (approx. 260 hectares). **b** a particular district or community of a town. **7** a representation of the internal structure of something as it would appear if cut across a vertical or horizontal plane. ● *v.* arrange in or divide into sections.

sectional ● *adj.* **1** of or relating to a section. **2** relating to a section or sections of a country, society, etc. **3** assembled or made from several sections. ● *n.* a piece of furniture composed of sections.

sector *n.* **1** a distinct part or branch of an economy. **2** a part of a circle between two lines drawn from its centre to its circumference. **3** a subdivision of an area for military operations. □ **sectoral** *adj.*

secular *adj.* **1** not religious or spiritual. **2** (of literature, music, etc.) not concerned with or promoting religious belief. **3** (of clergy) not bound by a religious rule. □ **secularism** *n.* **secularist** *n.*

secular humanism *n.* a political and social philosophy emphasizing the freedom of the individual. □ **secular humanist** *n.* & *adj.*

secularize *v.* remove something from the control of religion. □ **secularization** *n.*

secure ● *adj.* **1** assured, confident. **2** reliable. **3** fixed or fastened so as not to give way or yield under strain. **4** not likely to be lost or stolen etc. **5** (of a place) **a** affording protection or safety. **b** difficult to escape from. ● *v.* (**secures**, **secured**, **securing**) **1** make secure or safe. **2** fasten or close securely. **3** obtain or achieve. **4** ensure (an outcome etc.). □ **securely** *adv.*

security *n.* (*pl.* **securities**) **1** the state of being or feeling secure. **2** something that provides protection or safety. **3** measures taken to ensure safety and prevent crime etc. **4** the guarantee or assurance of something. **5 a** a certificate proving that one owns stocks or bonds. **b** a document acknowledging a debt. **6** something valuable given as a guarantee of the fulfillment of an obligation, such as an appearance in court or the payment of a debt, and given up in the event of a default that one will repay a loan.

security blanket *n.* **1** a familiar blanket clung to by a child for comfort. **2** *informal* something comforting or reassuring.

Security Council *n.* a permanent body of the UN seeking to maintain peace and security.

security guard *n.* a person employed to ensure the security of a person, building, etc.

Secwepemc *n.* & *adj.* (*pl.* **Secwepemc**) = SHUSWAP. [*Say* SEC weppum uck]

sedan *n.* **1** a car for four or more people. **2** (also **sedan chair**) *hist.* an enclosed chair carried on poles by two porters.

sedate ● *adj.* calm and not hurried. ● *v.* (**sedates**, **sedated**, **sedate**) administer a sedative to. □ **sedately** *adv.* **sedation** *n.* [*Say* suh DATE, suh DAY sh'n]

sedative ● *n.* a drug etc., that tends to calm or soothe. ● *adj.* calming, soothing. [*Say* SEDDA tiv]

sedentary *adj.* **1** (of work etc.) characterized by much sitting. **2** (of a person) spending much time seated. [*Say* SED'n terry]

Seder *n.* a Jewish ritual service and ceremonial dinner for the first night or first two nights of the Passover. [*Say* SAY dur]

sedge *n.* a grasslike plant growing esp. in wet areas.

sediment *n.* **1** matter that settles to the bottom of a liquid. **2** matter that is carried by water or wind and deposited on land. □ **sedimentation** *n.* [*Say* SEDDA m'nt, sedda mun TAY sh'n]

sedimentary *adj.* **1** of or like sediment.

2 (esp. of rocks) formed from sediment. [Say sedda MENTA ree]

sedition n. conduct or speech inciting rebellion against the authority of a ruler or state. □ **seditious** adj. [Say suh DISH'n, suh DISH us]

seduce v. (**seduces, seduced, seducing**) **1** tempt into sexual activity. **2 a** persuade to do something unwise. **b** deceive. □ **seducer** n. **seductress** n.

seduction n. **1** the action of seducing someone. **2** a tempting thing. □ **seductive** adj. **seductively** adv. **seductiveness** n.

sedulous adj. showing dedication and diligence. □ **sedulously** adv. [Say SED yoo lus]

sedum n. a plant with fleshy leaves and star-shaped flowers. [Say SEED um]

see[1] v. (**sees**; past **saw**; past participle **seen**; **seeing**) **1** perceive with the eyes. **2** experience or witness. **3** deduce after reflection or from information. **4** regard in a specified way. **5** envisage. **6** meet (someone one knows) socially or by chance. **7** meet regularly as a boyfriend or girlfriend. **8** consult (a specialist or professional). **9** give an interview or consultation to. **10** escort to a specified place. **11** attend to. **12** ensure that. □ **as far as I can see** to the best of my understanding. **see here!** look here! **see life** gain experience of the world. **see the light 1** realize one's mistakes etc. **2** suddenly see the way to proceed. **3** undergo religious conversion. **see the light of day** come into existence. **see off** be present at the departure of (a person). **see out 1** accompany out of. **2** finish something completely. **see red** become suddenly enraged. **see things** have hallucinations. **see through 1** not be deceived by. **2** penetrate visually. **see a thing through** persist with it until it is completed. **see one's way clear to** feel able or entitled to. **see you** (or **see you later**) informal an expression on parting. **you see 1** you understand. **2** you will understand.

see[2] n. the district or jurisdiction of a bishop or archbishop.

seed ● n. **1** a flowering plant's unit of reproduction. **2** a prime cause or beginning. **3** archaic semen or sperm. **4** Sport a seeded player. ● v. **1** sow seeds. **2** produce seed. **3** remove seeds from. **4** place a crystal or crystalline substance in to cause condensation (esp. in a cloud). **5** Sport assign to (a strong competitor) a position which ensures that strong competitors do not meet each other in early rounds. **6** go

to seed. □ **go** (or **run**) **to seed 1** cease flowering as seed develops. **2** become degenerate etc. □ **seeder** n. **seedless** adj.

seedbed n. **1** a bed of fine soil in which to sow seeds. **2** a place of development.

seed head n. a flower head in seed.

seedling n. a young plant raised from seed.

seed money n. money allocated to initiate a project.

seedy adj. (**seedier, seediest**) **1** having a filthy or disreputable appearance. **2** (of a place) shabby, rundown. □ **seediness** n.

seeing ● conj. considering that. ● n. the sense of sight.

seek v. (**seeks, sought, seeking**) **1** make a search or inquiry (for). **2 a** try to find or get. **b** ask for. **3** endeavour. **4** make for or resort to. □ **seek out 1** search for and find. **2** single out for companionship etc. □ **seeker** n.

seem v. **1** give the impression of being. **2** appear or be perceived.

seeming adj. apparent but not genuine. □ **seemingly** adv.

seemly adj. (**seemlier, seemliest**) conforming to propriety or good taste. □ **seemliness** n.

seen past participle of SEE[1].

seep v. **1** ooze, filter, or percolate slowly. **2** permeate.

seepage n. **1** the act of seeping. **2** the quantity that seeps out.

seer n. a person of supposed supernatural insight.

seersucker n. material of linen, cotton, etc., with a puckered surface.

see-saw ● n. **1** a long plank balanced on a central support for children to sit on and move up and down by pushing the ground with their feet. **2** an up-and-down motion. ● v. **1** play on a see-saw. **2** move up and down as on a see-saw. **3** vacillate.

seethe v. (**seethes, seethed, seething**) **1** boil, bubble over. **2** be very agitated, esp. with anger.

see-through adj. (esp. of clothing) translucent.

segment ● n. **1** each of the parts into which a thing is divided. **2** Math a part of a figure cut off by a line or plane intersecting it. **3** an item within a broadcast program. ● v. divide into segments. □ **segmental** adj. **segmentation** n. [Say SEG m'nt, seg MENTAL, seg men TAY sh'n]

segregate v. (**segregates, segregated, segregating**) **1** set apart from the rest or from each other.

2 separate along racial, sexual, or religious lines. [*Say* SEGRA gate]

segregation *n.* **1** enforced separation of racial groups in a place. **2** the act of separating. **3** an area of a prison where inmates are isolated from others. □ **segregationist** *n. & adj.* [*Say* segra GAY sh'n]

segue ● *v.* (**segues, segued, segueing** or **seguing**) **1** *Music* go on without pause into the next section. **2** move smoothly from one thing to another. ● *n.* an instance of this. [*Say* SEG way]

seigneur *n.* **1** *Cdn hist.* a holder of land under the seigneurial system. **2** a feudal lord. □ **seigneurial** *adj.* **seigneury** *n.* (*pl.* **seigneuries**). [*Say* seen YUR, seen YURI ul, SENIOR ee]

seigneurial system *n. Cdn hist.* a system of land tenure established in New France, based on feudalism.

seine ● *n.* (also **seine net**) a fishing net with floats at the top and weights at the bottom edge. ● *v.* (**seines, seined, seining**) fish or catch with a seine. □ **seiner** *n.* **seining** *n.* [*Sounds like* SANE]

seismic *adj.* **1** of or relating to earthquakes. **2** of enormous proportions or effect. □ **seismically** *adv.* [*Say* SIZE mick]

seismograph *n.* an instrument that records the force etc. of earthquakes. [*Say* SIZE muh graph]

seismology *n.* the scientific study of earthquakes and related phenomena. □ **seismological** *adj.* **seismologist** *n.* [*Say* size MOLLA jee, size muh LOGICAL, size MOLLA jist]

seize *v.* (**seizes, seized, seizing**) **1** take hold of forcibly or suddenly. **2** take possession of forcibly. **3** take possession of by warrant or legal right. **4** affect suddenly. **5** take advantage of (an opportunity). **6** comprehend quickly. **7 a** (of a machine or part) become stuck or jammed. **b** (of a body part) become stiff.

seizure *n.* **1** the action of seizing. **2** a sudden attack of epilepsy etc.

Sekani *n.* (*pl.* **Sekani** or **Sekanis**) **1** a member of an Aboriginal group living on the western slope of the Rocky Mountains. **2** the Athapaskan language of this people. □ **Sekani** *adj.* [*Say* suh CANNY]

seldom *adv.* not often.

select ● *v.* **1** choose, esp. as the best or most suitable. **2** choose something from a number. ● *adj.* **1** chosen for excellence or suitability. **2** (of a society etc.) exclusive. □ **selectable** *adj.*

select committee *n.* a small parliamentary committee appointed for a special purpose.

selection *n.* **1** the action or fact of selecting. **2** a number of selected people or things. **3** a range of things from which a choice may be made.

selective *adj.* **1** having to do with selection. **2** able to select. **3** (of one's memory, hearing, etc.) selecting what is convenient. □ **selectively** *adv.* **selectivity** *n.*

selective serotonin reuptake inhibitor *n.* any of a group of antidepressant drugs that increase the levels of serotonin in the brain.

selector *n.* a person or thing that selects, esp. a device for selecting a setting on a machine.

selenium *n.* a non-metallic element with semiconducting properties. [*Say* suh LEENY um]

self ● *n.* (*pl.* **selves**) **1** a person's or thing's own individuality or essence. **2** one's own interests or pleasure. **3** used in phrases equivalent to *myself, yourself,* etc. ● *pron. informal* myself, yourself, himself, herself, etc.

self- *comb. form* expressing reflexive action having to do with or by oneself or itself.

self-absorption *n.* preoccupation with one's own emotions, interests, or situation. □ **self-absorbed** *adj.*

self-actualization *n.* the realization of one's talents and potentialities. □ **self-actualize** *v.* (**self-actualizes, self-actualized, self-actualizing**)

self-addressed *adj.* (of an envelope etc.) having one's own address on it.

self-aggrandizement *n.* the act of making oneself more important in appearance or reality. □ **self-aggrandizing** *adj.*

self-appointed *adj.* designated so by oneself.

self-assertion *n.* confidence in expressing one's views. □ **self-assertive** *adj.*

self-assessment *n.* assessment or evaluation of oneself or one's actions etc.

self-assurance *n.* confidence in one's own abilities etc. □ **self-assured** *adj.*

self-aware *adj.* conscious of one's character, feelings, etc. □ **self-awareness** *n.*

self-centred *adj.* preoccupied with oneself or one's affairs.

self-confessed *adj.* openly admitting oneself to be.

self-confidence *n.* = SELF-ASSURANCE. □ **self-confident** *adj.* **self-confidently** *adv.*

self-congratulation n. = SELF-SATISFACTION. □ **self-congratulatory** adj.

self-conscious adj. nervous or awkward because very aware of oneself or one's actions. □ **self-consciously** adv. **self-consciousness** n.

self-contained adj. **1** independent. **2** complete in itself.

self-control n. the power of controlling one's reactions, emotions, etc. □ **self-controlled** adj.

self-deception n. deceiving oneself esp. concerning one's true feelings etc.

self-defeating adj. (of an attempt etc.) doomed to failure because of internal inconsistencies etc.

self-defence n. **1** a defence of oneself esp. through the use of physical force. **2** the skill of being able to protect oneself without using weapons.

self-denial n. the denial of one's own interests or needs. □ **self-denying** adj.

self-deprecating n. modest about or critical of oneself. □ **self-deprecatingly** adv. **self-deprecation** n. **self-deprecatory** adj.

self-destruct ● v. explode or disintegrate automatically, esp. when pre-set to do so. ● adj. enabling a thing to self-destruct.

self-destruction n. the process of destroying oneself or itself. □ **self-destructive** adj.

self-determination n. **1** the freedom of a people to decide their own allegiance or form of government. **2** the freedom to live or act as one chooses. □ **self-determining** adj.

self-discipline n. the ability to apply oneself, control one's feelings, etc. □ **self-disciplined** adj.

self-doubt n. lack of confidence in oneself. □ **self-doubting** adj.

self-educated adj. taught by oneself without formal instruction.

self-effacing adj. retiring; modest. □ **self-effacingly** adv.

self-employed adj. working for oneself, as a freelancer or owner of a business etc. □ **self-employment** n.

self-esteem n. confidence in one's own character and abilities.

self-evident adj. obvious. □ **self-evidently** adv.

self-examination n. **1** the study of one's own conduct, reasons, etc. **2** the examining of one's body or a part of one's body for signs of illness etc.

self-explanatory adj. not needing explanation.

self-expression n. the expression of one's feelings, thoughts, etc.

self-fulfilling adj. (of a prophecy etc.) bound to come true as a result of actions brought about by its being made.

self-fulfillment n. the fulfillment of one's own hopes and ambitions.

self-government n. government of a country or region by its own people. □ **self-governing** adj.

selfhood n. separate and conscious existence.

self-image n. one's own idea or picture of oneself.

self-immolation n. an act of suicide by setting oneself on fire, as a protest.

self-importance n. a high opinion of oneself. □ **self-important** adj. **self-importantly** adv.

self-imposed adj. (of a task or condition etc.) imposed on and by oneself, not externally.

self-improvement n. the improvement of one's own position or disposition by one's own efforts.

self-induced adj. induced by oneself or itself.

self-indulgence n. **1** the quality of being self-indulgent. **2** a self-indulgent act.

self-indulgent adj. indulging or tending to indulge in pleasure, idleness, etc. □ **self-indulgently** adv.

self-inflicted adj. (of a wound, damage, etc.) inflicted on oneself, esp. deliberately.

self-interest n. (concern for) one's personal interest or advantage. □ **self-interested** adj.

selfish adj. chiefly concerned with or due to one's own personal profit or pleasure. □ **selfishly** adv. **selfishness** n.

self-knowledge n. the understanding of oneself, one's motives, etc.

selfless adj. disregarding oneself or one's own interests. □ **selflessly** adv. **selflessness** n.

self-made adj. successful or rich by one's own effort.

self-medication n. the use of medication to treat oneself without seeking any medical supervision. □ **self-medicate** v.

self-mocking adj. mocking oneself or itself. □ **self-mockery** n.

self-motivated adj. acting on one's own initiative without external pressure. □ **self-motivation** n.

self-perpetuating adj. perpetuating itself or oneself without external intervention. □ **self-perpetuation** n.

self-pity n. extreme sorrow for one's own

troubles etc. □ **self-pitying** adj. **self-pityingly** adv.

self-portrait n. a portrait or description of an artist, writer, etc., by himself or herself.

self-possessed adj. calm and confident, esp. at times of stress or difficulty. □ **self-possession** n.

self-preservation n. the preservation of one's own life, safety, best interests, etc.

self-proclaimed adj. proclaimed by oneself to be such.

self-propelled adj. moving or able to move without external propulsion.

self-realization n. the development of one's faculties, abilities, etc.

self-referential adj. making reference to itself.

self-regard n. **1** a proper regard for oneself; self-respect. **2** vanity, conceit. □ **self-regarding** adj.

self-regulating adj. regulating oneself or itself without intervention. □ **self-regulation** n. **self-regulatory** adj.

self-reliance n. reliance on one's own resources etc. □ **self-reliant** adj.

self-respect n. respect for oneself.

self-respecting adj. **1** having self-respect. **2** meriting a particular role or name.

self-restraint n. self-control.

self-righteous adj. excessively confident of one's own righteousness or virtue. □ **self-righteously** adv. **self-righteousness** n.

self-rule n. self-government.

self-sacrifice n. the negation of one's own interests, wishes, etc., in favour of those of others. □ **self-sacrificing** adj.

selfsame adj. the very same.

self-satisfaction n. excessive or smug satisfaction with oneself. □ **self-satisfied** adj.

self-seeking adj. seeking one's own welfare before that of others.

self-serve (also **self-service**) ● adj. where customers serve themselves. ● n. informal a self-serve gas station etc.

self-serving adj. self-seeking.

self-starter n. an ambitious person who needs no external motivation.

self-styled adj. called so by oneself.

self-sufficient adj. able to do or produce what one needs without outside help. □ **self-sufficiency** n. **self-sufficiently** adv.

self-supporting adj. **1** capable of maintaining oneself financially. **2** standing without external aid.

self-sustaining adj. sustaining oneself.

self-taught adj. educated or trained by oneself.

self-willed adj. obstinately pursuing one's own wishes. □ **self-will** n.

self-worth n. self-esteem.

sell ● v. (**sells**, **sold**, **selling**) **1** hand over in exchange for money. **2** be a dealer in. **3** achieve sales. **4** (**sell for**) have a specified price. **5** betray for some reward. **6** persuade someone of the merits of. ● n. a manner of selling. □ **sell off** sell the remainder of at reduced prices. **sell out 1 a** sell all one's stock of a commodity. **b** be completely or all sold. **2** (often foll. by to) abandon one's principles, honourable aims, etc. for personal gain. **sell short** disparage, underestimate. □ **sellable** adj.

seller n. **1** a person who sells. **2** a commodity that sells well or badly.

selling point n. a feature of something that makes it attractive, esp. to buyers or customers.

sell-off n. **1** the privatization of a state company by a sale of shares. **2** a sale or disposal of bonds, shares, etc., usu. causing a fall in price. **3** a sale, esp. to dispose of property.

sellout n. **1** the selling of all tickets for a show. **2** a betrayal.

seltzer n. **1** natural effervescent mineral water. **2** an artificial substitute for this. [Say SELT sir]

selvage n. (also **selvedge**) an edging that prevents cloth from unravelling. [Say SELL vidge]

selves pl. of SELF.

semantic adj. **1** relating to meaning in language. **2** of or relating to semantics. □ **semantically** adv. [Say suh MAN tick]

semantics pl. n. (usu. treated as sing.) **1** the branch of linguistics concerned with meaning. **2** the interpretation or meaning of a sentence, word, etc. [Say suh MAN ticks]

semaphore n. a system of sending messages by holding the arms or two flags in certain positions according to an alphabetic code. [Say SEMMA for]

semblance n. the outward or superficial appearance of something. [Say SEM blince]

semen n. the reproductive fluid of male animals, containing spermatozoa in suspension.

semester n. an academic session occupying half of the academic year.

semestered adj. esp. Cdn (of a school) structured so that the whole year's course material in any given subject is concentrated into one or the other of two semesters. □ **semestering** n.

semi n. (pl. **semis**) informal **1** Cdn & Brit. a semi-detached house. **2** a semifinal. **3** a semi-trailer.

semi- prefix **1** half. **2** partly. **3** almost. **4** occurring or appearing twice in a specified period.

semi-annual adj. occurring, published, etc., twice a year. □ **semi-annually** adv.

semi-aquatic adj. **1** living partly on land and partly in water. **2** growing in very wet ground.

semi-automatic ● adj. (of a firearm) having a mechanism for automatic loading but not for continuous firing. ● n. a semi-automatic firearm.

semicircle n. half of a circle or of its circumference. □ **semicircular** adj.

semicolon n. a punctuation mark (;) of intermediate value between a comma and a period.

semiconductor n. a solid that conducts electricity in certain conditions, but not as well as most metals do. □ **semiconducting** adj.

semi-conscious adj. partly conscious. □ **semi-consciousness** n.

semi-desert n. a semi-arid area intermediate between grassland and desert.

semi-detached ● adj. (of a house) joined to another by a shared wall on one side only. ● n. a semi-detached house.

semifinal n. a match or round immediately preceding the final. □ **semifinalist** n.

semigloss n. a paint that has or produces a moderately satiny finish.

semi-liquid ● adj. of a consistency between solid and liquid. ● n. a semi-liquid substance.

semi-monthly ● adj. occurring, published, etc., twice a month. ● adv. twice a month.

seminal adj. **1** strongly influencing later developments. **2** of semen. [Say SEMMA nul]

seminar n. a small group, esp. at a university, meeting to discuss or study something.

seminary n. (pl. **seminaries**) a training college for priests, rabbis, etc. □ **seminarian** n. [Say SEMMA nerry]

semiotics n. the study of signs and symbols in language. □ **semiotic** adj. [Say semmy OTT icks]

semi-permanent adj. rather less than permanent. □ **semi-permanently** adv.

semi-permeable adj. permeable to small molecules but not large ones.

semi-precious adj. (of a gem) less valuable than a precious stone.

semi-private adj. **1** partially or somewhat private. **2** designating a hospital room shared by two patients.

semi-professional ● adj. receiving payment for an activity but not relying on it for a living. ● n. a semi-professional musician, athlete, etc. □ **semi-professionally** adv.

semi-retired adj. partially but not completely retired. □ **semi-retirement** n.

semi-skilled adj. having or needing some training but less than for a skilled worker.

semi-sweet adj. slightly sweetened.

semi-synthetic adj. Chemistry prepared synthetically but deriving from a naturally occurring material.

Semite n. a member of any of the peoples speaking a Semitic language, esp. the Jews and Arabs. [Say SEM ite or SEEM ite]

Semitic ● adj. **1** of or relating to the Semites, esp. the Jews. **2** of or relating to the languages of the family including Hebrew and Arabic. ● n. the Semitic language family. [Say suh MIT ick]

semitone n. a musical interval of half a tone. [Say SEMMY tone]

semi-trailer n. a trailer having wheels at the back but supported at the front by a towing vehicle.

semi-transparent adj. partly transparent.

semi-vowel n. a sound intermediate between a vowel and a consonant (e.g. w, y).

semi-weekly ● adj. occurring, published, etc., twice a week. ● adv. twice a week.

semolina n. the hard grains left after the milling of flour, used esp. in making pasta. [Say semma LEENA]

senate n. **1** (**Senate**) **a** (in Canada) the appointed upper chamber of Parliament. **b** (in the US) the elected upper house of Congress or of a state legislature. **c** a similar legislative body in other countries. **2** the governing body of a university or college. [Say SENNIT]

senator n. a member of a senate. □ **senatorial** adj. **senatorship** n. [Say SENNA tur, senna TORY ul]

send v. (**sends**, **sent**, **sending**) **1** order or cause to go or be conveyed. **2** propel. **3** cause to be in a specified state. □ **send for 1** summon. **2** order by mail. **send in 1** cause to go in. **2** submit (an entry etc.) for a competition etc. **send up** informal satirize or ridicule, esp. by mimicking. □ **sender** n.

send-off n. a demonstration of goodwill etc. at a person's departure, the start of a project, etc.

send-up *n. informal* a satire or parody.

Seneca *n.* (*pl.* **Seneca** or **Senecas**) **1** a member of one of the founding peoples of the Iroquois Five Nations confederacy. **2** their language. □ **Seneca** *adj.* [*Say* SENNA kuh]

Senegalese *n.* (*pl.* **Senegalese**) a person from Senegal. □ **Senegalese** *adj.* [*Say* senna guh LEEZ]

senile *adj.* having the esp. mental weaknesses of old age. □ **senility** *n.* [*Say* SEE nile, suh NILLA tee]

senior ● *adj.* **1** more or most advanced in age, standing, rank, position, etc. **2** senior to another of the same name. **3** (of a school) having students over age 11. **4** esp. *US* of the final year at a university or high school. ● *n.* **1** a person over 65. **2** one's elder, or one's superior in length of service, membership, etc. **3** esp. *US* a student in the final year at a university or high school. □ **seniority** *n.* [*Say* SEE nyur, see NYORA tee]

senior citizen *n.* an elderly person, esp. a person over 65.

senior high school *n.* a secondary school comprising usu. the three highest grades.

senna *n.* a laxative prepared from the dried pods of the cassia tree.

sensation *n.* **1** the consciousness of perceiving some state or condition of one's body. **2** an awareness or impression. **3 a** a stirring intense interest, esp. among a large group of people. **b** a person, event, etc., causing such interest.

sensational *adj.* **1 a** causing a sensation. **b** deliberately trying to provoke interest by being shocking, salacious, etc. **2** very good. □ **sensationally** *adv.*

sensationalism *n.* the use of or interest in sensational material in journalism, political agitation, etc. □ **sensationalist** *n.* & *adj.* **sensationalistic** *adj.* **sensationalize** *v.*

sense ● *n.* **1** any of the special bodily faculties by which sensation is roused. **2** the ability to perceive or to be conscious of the presence or properties of things. **3** an understanding or instinct regarding a specified matter. **4** practical wisdom or judgment, common sense. **5** a meaning. ● *v.* (**senses, sensed, sensing**) **1** perceive by a sense or senses. **2** be vaguely aware of. **3** detect. □ **come to one's senses 1** regain consciousness. **2** become sensible after acting foolishly. **make sense** be intelligible or practicable. **out of one's senses** in or into a state of madness.

senseless *adj.* **1** unconscious. **2** wildly foolish. **3** without meaning or purpose. □ **senselessly** *adv.* **senselessness** *n.*

sense organ *n.* a bodily organ conveying external stimuli to the sensory system.

sensibility *n.* (*pl.* **sensibilities**) **1** openness to emotional impressions. **2 a** (in *pl.*) emotional feelings. **b** a person's moral, emotional, or aesthetic ideas or standards.

sensible *adj.* **1** having or showing wisdom or common sense. **2** perceptible by the senses. **3** practical and functional. □ **sensibleness** *n.* **sensibly** *adv.*

sensitive *adj.* **1** very open to or acutely affected by external stimuli. **2 a** easily affected emotionally, aesthetically, etc. **b** attuned to others' emotions. **3** responsive to or recording slight changes. **4** (of a topic etc.) needing careful handling to avoid causing offence etc. □ **sensitively** *adv.* **sensitivity** *n.* (*pl.* **sensitivities**)

sensitize *v.* (**sensitizes, sensitized, sensitizing**) make sensitive.

sensor *n.* a device which detects or measures a physical property.

sensory *adj.* of sensation or the senses. [*Say* SENSA ree]

sensual *adj.* **1 a** of or depending on the senses only and not on the intellect. **b** given to the pursuit of sensual pleasures. **c** suggesting an interest in physical esp. sexual pleasure. **2** of sense or sensation, sensory. □ **sensuality** *n.* **sensually** *adv.* **sensualism** *n.* **sensualist** *n.* [*Say* SEN shoo ul]

sensuous *adj.* **1** of or derived from or affecting the senses, esp. aesthetically rather than sensually. **2** attractive or gratifying physically, esp. sexually. □ **sensuously** *adv.* **sensuousness** *n.* [*Say* SEN shoo us]

sent *past and past participle of* SEND.

sentence ● *n.* **1** a set of words complete in itself as the expression of a thought. **2** the punishment allotted to a person convicted in a criminal trial. ● *v.* (**sentences, sentenced, sentencing**) declare the sentence of a convicted criminal etc. □ **sentencing** *n.*

sentient *adj.* having the power of perception by the senses. □ **sentience** *n.* [*Say* SEN shint]

sentiment *n.* **1** an opinion or point of view. **2** an opinion or feeling. **3** emotional or tender feelings collectively, esp. when considered excessive or inappropriate.

sentimental *adj.* **1** of or characterized by sentiment. **2** showing or affected by emotion rather than reason. **3** appealing to esp. excessive sentiment. □ **sentimentalism** *n.* **sentimentalist** *n.*

sentimentality n. **sentimentalize** v. (**sentimentalizes**, **sentimentalized**, **sentimentalizing**) **sentimentally** adv.

sentinel n. a sentry or lookout. [Say SEN tin ul]

sentry n. (pl. **sentries**) a soldier stationed to keep guard.

sepal n. each of the divisions or leaves of the calyx. [Say SEEPLE or SEPPLE]

separable adj. able to be separated. □ **separability** n. **separably** adv.

separate ● adj. **1** forming a unit that is apart or by itself. **2** Cdn of or relating to a separate school. ● n. (in pl.) separate articles of clothing suitable for wearing together in various combinations. ● v. (**separates**, **separated**, **separating**) **1** make separate. **2** prevent union or contact of. **3** go different ways, disperse. **4** cease to live together as a married couple. **5** secede. **6** divide or sort into constituent parts or sizes. □ **separately** adv. **separateness** n. **separation** n.

separate school n. Cdn a publicly funded school for a religious minority, esp. Catholics.

separatist n. a person who favours separation, esp. for political or ecclesiastical independence. □ **separatism** n. **separatist** adj. [Say SEPRA tist]

separator n. a machine or device for separating, e.g. cream from milk or egg yolk from egg white.

Sephardi n. (pl. **Sephardim**) a Jew of Iberian descent. □ **Sephardic** adj. [Say suh FARDY for the singular, suh FAR dim for the plural]

sepia ● n. (pl. **sepias**) **1** a dark reddish-brown colour associated with early photography. **2** a brown pigment used in monochrome drawing and in watercolours. ● adj. of a dark reddish-brown colour. [Say SEEPY uh]

Sept. abbr. September.

septa pl. of SEPTUM.

September n. the ninth month.

septet n. a group of seven performers etc. [Say sep TET]

septic adj. **1** contaminated with bacteria from a festering wound etc. **2** of or relating to a system in which the organic matter in sewage is decomposed through bacterial activity.

septuagenarian n. a person from 70 to 79 years old. □ **septuagenarian** adj. [Say sept wuh juh NERRY in]

Septuagint n. a Greek version of the Hebrew Scriptures including the Apocrypha. [Say SEPT wuh jint]

septum n. (pl. **septa**) a partition, such as that between the nostrils.

sepulchral adj. **1** of a tomb. **2** funereal, gloomy. [Say se PUL krul (PUL rhymes with HULL)]

sepulchre n. a tomb, esp. a burial vault or cave. [Say SEPPLE cur]

sequel n. a novel, film, etc., that continues the story of an earlier one.

sequence ● n. **1** order of succession. **2** a set of related things that follow each other in a particular order. ● v. (**sequences**, **sequenced**, **sequencing**) arrange in a definite order.

sequencer n. a electronic device for storing sequences of musical notes etc. and transmitting them to an electronic musical instrument.

sequential adj. **1** following in a sequence or as a logical conclusion. **2** esp. Computing occurring or performed in a particular order. □ **sequentially** adv. [Say si KWEN shul]

sequester v. seclude, isolate, set apart. [Say si KWESS ter]

sequin n. a circular spangle attached to clothing as an ornament. □ **sequined** adj. [Say SEEK win]

sequoia n. (pl. **sequoias**) a huge Californian redwood tree. [Say suh KWOY uh]

sera pl. of SERUM. [Say SEE ruh]

seraph n. (pl. **seraphim** or **seraphs**) **1** Bible a supernatural being with three pairs of wings. **2** Christianity a member of the highest order of the nine ranks of heavenly beings. [Say SAIR uff for the singular, SERRA fim for the plural]

Serb n. a person from Serbia. □ **Serb** adj.

Serbian n. **1** the dialect of the Serbs. **2** = SERB. □ **Serbian** adj.

Serbo-Croat n. (also **Serbo-Croatian**) the Slavic language of the Serbs and Croats. [Say sir bo CROW at, sir bo crow AY sh'n]

sere adj. literary withered. [Say SEER]

serenade ● n. **1** a piece of music sung or played by a lover at night under the window of his beloved. **2** a piece of music for a string or wind ensemble. ● v. (**serenades**, **serenaded**, **serenading**) sing or play a serenade to. [Say serra NADE]

serendipity n. (pl. **serendipities**) the fact of something interesting or pleasant happening by chance. □ **serendipitous** adj. **serendipitously** adv. [Say sair un DIPPA tee]

serene adj. (**serener**, **serenest**) placid, tranquil. □ **serenely** adv. **serenity** n. [Say suh REEN, suh RENNA tee]

serf n. (pl. **serfs**) **1** (under the feudal system) a labourer who was not free to move from the land on which he worked. **2** an oppressed person, a drudge. □ **serfdom** n.

serge n. a durable twilled woollen or worsted fabric. [Say SURGE]

sergeant n. **1** (in the Canadian Army and Air Force and other armies) a non-commissioned officer ranking above corporal. **2** (in some Canadian police forces) an officer ranking above the lowest ranks. [Say SAR jint]

sergeant-at-arms n. (pl. **sergeants-at-arms**) a ceremonial official of a court or city or parliament.

sergeant major n. **1** a middle-ranking police officer. **2** (in various military organizations) a high-ranking non-commissioned officer.

serial ● n. a story, play, or film which is published, broadcast, or shown in regular instalments. ● adj. **1** consisting of or taking place in a series. **2** given to or characterized by the repetition of certain behaviour. □ **serially** adv.

serialize v. (**serializes, serialized, serializing**) publish or produce in instalments. □ **serialization** n.

serial killer n. a person who murders repeatedly. □ **serial killing** n.

serial number n. a number showing position in a series, esp. one identifying a manufactured object.

series n. (pl. **series**) **1** a number of similar or related things coming one after another. **2** a set of programs with the same actors or on related subjects but each complete in itself. **3** Math a set of quantities constituting a progression or having values determined by a common relation.

serif n. a slight projection finishing off a stroke of a letter, as in T contrasted with T. [Say SAIR if]

serious adj. **1** thoughtful, earnest, responsible. **2** important, demanding consideration. **3** not slight or negligible. **4** sincere, in earnest **5** involving profound love, the intention to marry, etc. **6** informal remarkable; impressive. □ **seriousness** n.

seriously adv. **1** in a serious manner (esp. introducing a sentence, implying that irony etc. is now to cease). **2** to a serious extent. **3** informal very, really.

sermon n. **1** a discourse based on a passage of Scripture and delivered during a religious service. **2** an esp. long talk that tries to present moral advice.

seropositive adj. giving a positive result in a test of blood serum, e.g. for presence of a virus. □ **seropositivity** n. [Say seero POSITIVE]

serotonin n. a compound present in blood platelets and serum, which constricts the blood vessels and acts as a neurotransmitter. [Say serra TOE nin]

serpent n. usu. literary a snake, esp. of a large kind.

serpentine adj. **1** of or like a serpent. **2** coiling, meandering, writhing. [Say SIRP'n tine or SIRP'n teen]

serrated adj. with a saw-like edge. □ **serration** n. [Say suh RATE id]

serum n. (pl. **sera** or **serums**) **1** the liquid in which blood cells are suspended and which separates out when blood coagulates. **2** the serum of an animal used in inoculation or as a diagnostic agent. [Say SEER um for the plural, SEER uh for the plural]

servant n. **1** a person employed in a house on domestic duties or as a personal attendant. **2** a devoted follower, a person willing to serve another.

serve ● v. (**serves, served, serving**) **1** perform duties or services for. **2** be employed as a member of the armed forces. **3** spend a period in office, in an apprenticeship, or in prison. **4** present food or drink to. **5** attend to a customer. **6** be useful for. **7** be enough for. **8** Law formally deliver. **9** hit a ball etc. to begin or resume play. ● n. an act of hitting a ball or shuttlecock to start play. □ **serve one's needs** be adequate. **serve a person right** be a person's deserved punishment or misfortune.

server n. **1** a person who serves another, esp. a waiter. **2** (in tennis etc.) the player who serves the ball. **3** Computing a program or device which manages shared access to a centralized resource or service in a network. **4** a utensil for serving food.

service ● n. (often as an adj.) **1** the action of serving. **2** a period of employment. **3** an act of assistance. **4** a religious ceremony according to a prescribed form. **5** a system supplying a public need such as transport, or utilities such as water. **6** (in pl.) the armed forces. **7** a set of matching crockery used for serving a particular meal. **8** (in tennis etc.) a serve. **9** a periodic routine inspection and maintenance of a vehicle etc. **10** the sector of the economy that supplies the needs of the consumer but produces no tangible goods. **11** the act of serving customers. ● v. (**services, serviced, servicing**) **1** provide service or services for, esp. maintain. **2** maintain or repair a car etc. **3** pay interest on a debt. **4** supply with a service. **5** (of a male animal) copulate with a female animal. □ **in service 1** employed as a servant. **2** available for use. **out of service** not available for use. **see service 1** have experience of service, esp. in the armed forces. **2** (of a thing) be much used.

serviceable *adj.* **1** useful or usable. **2** able to render service. **3** durable. **4** suited for ordinary use rather than ornament. □ **serviceability** *n.* [*Say* SERVICE a bull]

serviceberry *n.* (*pl.* **serviceberries**) an edible fruit growing on a shrub of the rose family; a saskatoon.

service centre *n.* a commercial operation where cars, appliances, etc. can be taken for maintenance and repair.

service club *n.* an association of business or professional people promoting community welfare and goodwill.

serviced *adj.* Cdn & Brit. hooked up to utilities such as gas, water, and hydro.

serviceman *n.* (*pl.* **servicemen**) a man serving in the armed forces.

service provider *n.* a company which provides access to the Internet.

service road *n.* a road parallel to a highway, giving access to houses, stores, etc.

service station *n.* a gas station.

servicewoman *n.* (*pl.* **servicewomen**) a woman serving in the armed forces.

serviette *n.* Cdn an esp. paper napkin. [*Say* servy ET]

servile *adj.* **1** having or showing an excessive willingness to serve or please others. **2** of a slave or slaves. □ **servilely** *adv.* **servility** *n.* [*Say* SIR vile, sir VILLA tee]

serving *n.* **1** the action of SERVE *v.* **2** a quantity of food served to one person. **3** (as an *adj.*) used for serving food.

servitude *n.* **1** slavery. **2** the state of being subject to someone more powerful.

servo *n.* (*pl.* **servos**) **1** (also **servo-mechanism**) a powered mechanism producing motion or forces at a higher level of energy than the input level, e.g. in the brakes and steering of large motor vehicles. **2** (also **servo-motor**) the motive element in a servo-mechanism. [*Say* SIR vo]

sesame *n.* a plant that produces small edible oil-rich seeds. [*Say* SESSA me]

sesquicentennial *n.* a one-hundred-and-fiftieth anniversary. □ **sesquicentennial** *adj.* [*Say* sess kwi sen TENNY ul]

session *n.* **1** a period devoted to a particular activity. **2** a meeting of a council, court, or law-making body to conduct its business. **3** a period during which such meetings are regularly held. **4** an academic year or term. **5** the governing body of a Presbyterian or United Church congregation, composed of the minister and the elders. □ **in session** assembled for business. □ **sessional** *adj.*

set¹ *v.* (**sets**, **set**, **setting**) **1** put in a certain position or location. **2** put into a specified state. **3** cause someone to do something. **4** decide on or fix a time, price, etc. **5** establish as an example or record. **6** adjust a device as required. **7** prepare a table for a meal. **8** harden. **9** arrange damp hair into the required style. **10** put a broken bone into the correct position for healing. **11** (of the sun, moon, etc.) drop towards and below the earth's horizon. **12** Printing arrange text. □ **set back 1** place further back in place or time. **2** impede or reverse the progress of. **3** informal cost a person a specified amount. **set forth 1** begin a journey. **2** make known; expound. **set little** (or **much**) **by** consider to be of little (or much) value. **set off 1** begin a journey. **2** detonate a bomb etc. **3** initiate, stimulate. **4** serve as an adornment or foil to; enhance. **set on** (or **upon**) attack violently. **set out 1** begin a journey. **2** aim or intend. **3** demonstrate, arrange, or exhibit. **4** mark out. **set sail** begin a sea voyage. **set to** begin doing something vigorously. **set up 1** place in position or view. **2** organize or start an enterprise. **3** cause or make arrangements for a situation. **set oneself up as** make pretensions to being.

set² *n.* **1** a number of things or people grouped together as similar or forming a unit. **2** a group of people with common interests. **3** a radio or television receiver. **4** (in tennis etc.) a group of games counting as a unit towards a match. **5** a collection of scenery, stage furniture, etc., used in a play or film. **6** Math a collection of distinct entities satisfying specified conditions and regarded as a unit. **7** a sequence of musical pieces performed before or after an intermission.

set³ *adj.* **1** in senses of SET¹. **2** prescribed or determined in advance. **3** fixed, unchanging, unmoving. **4** prepared for action. **5** (foll. by *on*, *upon*) determined to acquire or achieve etc.

setback *n.* **1** a reversal or arrest of progress. **2** a relapse. **3** the distance by which a building is set back from the property line.

set piece *n.* a sequence of rehearsed movements etc., as in sports or military operations.

settee *n.* a usu. upholstered seat with a

back and usu. arms, for more than one person. [*Say* set EE]

setter *n.* a large, long-haired dog trained to stand rigid when scenting game.

setting *n.* **1** the position or manner in which a thing is set. **2** the immediate surroundings; the environment of a thing. **3** the place and time in which a story, drama, etc. is set. **4** a frame in which a jewel is set. **5** the music to which words of a poem, song, etc., are set. **6** a set of cutlery, dishes, etc. for one person. **7** the way in which a machine is set to operate.

settle[1] *v.* (**settles**, **settled**, **settling**) **1** reach an agreement about an argument etc. **2** (often foll. by *down*) adopt a more steady or secure life, e.g. in a permanent home. **3** sit, come to rest, or arrange comfortably or securely. **4** become or make calmer or quieter. **5** pay a debt. **6** (foll. by *for*) accept something less than ideal. **7** sink slowly in a liquid to form sediment. **8 a** people with inhabitants. **b** take up residence in a new place. **9** sink down gradually. **10** become firm or compact. □ **settle in** become accustomed to a new home, new surroundings, etc. **settle up** pay a debt etc.

settle[2] *n.* a bench with a high back and arms and often with a box fitted below the seat.

settled *adj.* **1** that has settled or been settled. **2** indicating a settled mind, character, or disposition. **3** (of weather) calm and fair.

settlement *n.* **1** an official agreement intended to resolve a dispute. **2** a place where people establish a community. **3** the process of paying money owed.

settler *n.* a person who goes to settle in a new country or place.

set-to *n.* (*pl.* **set-tos**) *informal* a fight or argument.

set-up *n.* **1** an arrangement or organization. **2** an act of setting up. **3** *informal* a conspiracy whereby a person is caused to incriminate himself or herself. **4** *Sport* a pass or play intended to provide an opportunity for another player to score.

seven *card. num.* one more than six.

sevenfold *adj. & adv.* **1** seven times as much or as many. **2** consisting of seven parts.

seventeen *card. num.* one more than sixteen. □ **seventeenth** *ord. num.*

seventh *ord. num.* **1** constituting number seven in a sequence. **2** one of seven equal parts of a thing. **3** an interval spanning seven consecutive notes in the diatonic scale (e.g. C to B).

Seventh-day Adventist *n.* a member of a Christian group believing in the imminent return of Christ to earth and observing the Sabbath on Saturday. □ **Seventh-day Adventist** *adj.*

seventy *card. num.* ten less than eighty. □ **seventieth** *ord. num.*

sever *v.* **1** divide, break, or make separate, esp. by cutting. **2** end a relationship or connection. [*Say* SEV er]

several *adj.* **1** more than two but not many. **2** separate or respective; distinct. □ **severally** *adv.*

severance *n.* **1** the action of ending a connection or relation. **2** (also **severance pay**) an amount paid to an employee who is dismissed. **3** the act or an instance of severing. [*Say* SEV er ince]

severe *adj.* **1** rigorous, strict, and harsh in attitude or treatment. **2** serious, critical. **3** forceful. **4** extreme (in an unpleasant quality). □ **severely** *adv.* **severity** *n.* [*Say* suh VEER, suh VERRA tee]

severe acute respiratory syndrome *n.* a highly contagious viral ailment causing severe pneumonia-like and flu-like symptoms. Abbr.: **SARS**.

sew *v.* (**sews**; *past* **sewed**; *past participle* **sewn** or **sewed**; **sewing**) **1** fasten, join, attach, etc., by making stitches with a needle and thread or a sewing machine. **2** make by sewing. □ **sew up 1** join or enclose by sewing. **2** *informal* bring to a desired conclusion or condition.

sewage *n.* waste matter, esp. excrement, conveyed in sewers.

sewer[1] *n.* a conduit, usu. underground, for carrying off drainage water and sewage.

sewer[2] *n.* a person that sews.

sewing *n.* **1** a piece of material or work to be sewn. **2** the action of sewing.

sewing machine *n.* a machine for sewing or stitching.

sex ● *n.* (*pl.* **sexes**) **1** either of the main divisions (male and female) into which living things are placed on the basis of their reproductive functions. **2** the fact of belonging to one of these. **3** males or females collectively. **4** sexual intercourse. **5** sexual instincts, desires, etc., or their manifestation. ● *adj.* **1** of or relating to sex. **2** arising from a difference or consciousness of sex.

sex act *n.* sexual intercourse.

sexagenarian *n.* a person from 60 to 69 years old. □ **sexagenarian** *adj.* [*Say* sexa juh NERRY in]

sex appeal *n.* sexual attractiveness.

sex change *n.* an apparent change of sex by surgical means and hormone treatment.

sex chromosome *n.* a chromosome concerned in determining the sex of an organism (in mammals the x chromosome and the y chromosome).

sexed *adj.* **1** having a sexual appetite. **2** having sexual characteristics.

sex hormone *n.* a hormone affecting sexual development or behaviour.

sexism *n.* prejudice or discrimination, esp. against women, on the grounds of sex. □ **sexist** *adj. & n.*

sexless *adj.* **1** *Biology* neither male nor female. **2** lacking in sexual desire or attractiveness.

sex life *n.* a person's sexual activities viewed collectively.

sex object *n.* a person regarded mainly in terms of sexual attractiveness.

sex offender *n.* a person who commits a sexual crime.

sexology *n.* the study of sexual life or relationships. □ **sexologist** *n.*

sexpot *n.* *informal* a sexy person (esp. a woman).

sex symbol *n.* a person widely noted for sex appeal.

sextant *n.* an instrument with a graduated arc of 60° for measuring the angular distance of objects by means of mirrors.

sextet *n.* a group of six performers etc.

sexton *n.* a person who looks after a church and churchyard.

sex trade *n.* prostitution.

sextuple ● *adj.* **1** sixfold. **2** having six parts. **3** being six times as many or much. ● *n.* a sixfold number or amount. ● *v.* multiply by six. [*Say* sex TUPPLE]

sextuplet *n.* each of six children born at one birth. [*Say* sex TUP lit]

sexual *adj.* **1** of or relating to sex or the desire for sex. **2** of or relating to the sexes or the relations between them. **3** (of reproduction) involving the fusion of male and female cells. □ **sexually** *adv.*

sexual abuse *n.* the forcing of a person, esp. a child, to engage in sexual activity or relations.

sexual assault *n.* threatened or actual sexual contact without consent.

sexual harassment *n.* harassment in a workplace etc. involving the making of unwanted sexual advances, obscene remarks, etc.

sexual intercourse *n.* genital contact between individuals, esp. involving the insertion of a man's penis into a woman's vagina.

sexuality *n.* **1** capacity for sexual feelings. **2** sexual feelings, desires, etc. collectively. **3** = SEXUAL ORIENTATION.

sexualize *v.* (**sexualizes, sexualized, sexualizing**) **1** make sexual. **2** attribute sex or a sexual role to.

sexually transmitted disease *n.* a disease transmitted by sexual contact, e.g. AIDS, gonorrhea.

sexual orientation *n.* (also **sexual preference**) the fact of being attracted to people of the opposite sex, of one's own sex, or both sexes.

sex work *n.* prostitution. □ **sex worker** *n.*

sexy *adj.* (**sexier, sexiest**) **1** sexually attractive or stimulating. **2** sexually aroused. **3** concerned with or engrossed in sex. **4** *informal* exciting, appealing, trendy. □ **sexily** *adv.* **sexiness** *n.*

SF *abbr.* science fiction.

SGML *abbr. Computing* Standard Generalized Mark-up Language, a form of generic coding used for producing printed material in electronic form.

Shabbat *n.* (also **Shabbos, Shabbes**) the Jewish Sabbath. [*Say* shaw BOT]

shabby *adj.* (**shabbier, shabbiest**) **1** in bad repair or condition. **2** dressed in old or worn clothes. **3** of poor quality. **4** contemptible, dishonourable. □ **shabbily** *adv.* **shabbiness** *n.*

shack *n.* a roughly built hut or cabin. □ **shack up** *slang* live together in a sexual relationship without being married. □ **shacky** *adj.*

shackle ● *n.* **1** a fetter enclosing the ankle or wrist. **2** (usu. in *pl.*) a restraint or impediment. ● *v.* (**shackles, shackled, shackling**) **1** impede, restrain. **2** fasten with a shackle.

shacktown *n. Cdn* a community composed of shacks or other temporary housing.

shad *n.* (*pl.* **shad** or **shads**) a deep-bodied edible fish of the herring family.

shade ● *n.* **1** comparative darkness and coolness caused by shelter from direct light and heat. **2** a place or area sheltered from the sun. **3** a darker part of a picture etc. **4** a colour, esp. as distinguished from one nearly like it. **5** a slight amount. **6 a** a lampshade. **b** a blind. **7** (in *pl.*) *informal* sunglasses. **8** *literary* a ghost. ● *v.* (**shades, shaded, shading**) **1** screen from light. **2** cover the light of. **3** darken. □ **shades of** suggesting reminiscence or unfavourable comparison.

shading *n.* the representation of light and shade in a drawing etc.

shadow ● *n.* **1** a dark figure projected by a body intercepting rays of light. **2** an inseparable companion. **3** a person secretly following another. **4** the slightest trace. **5** a weak or less good remnant or thing. **6** (as an *adj.*) denoting members of the opposition holding responsibilities parallel to those of the government. **7** eyeshadow. ● *v.* **1** cast a shadow over. **2** follow and watch the movements of. □ **shadowless** *adj.*

shadowbox *v.* (**shadowboxes, shadowboxed, shadowboxing**) box against an imaginary opponent as a form of training. □ **shadowboxing** *n.*

shadowy *adj.* **1** like or having a shadow. **2** full of shadows. **3** vague, indistinct.

shady *adj.* (**shadier, shadiest**) **1** giving shade. **2** situated in shade. **3** disreputable; of doubtful honesty.

shaft ● *n.* **1** the stem or handle of a tool, implement, etc. **2** a long vertical space for an elevator in a building, for ventilation, etc. **3** a long and narrow part connecting or driving parts of greater thickness. **4** an arrow or spear. **5** a remark intended to hurt or provoke. **6 a** a ray of light. **b** a bolt of lightning. **7** *informal* (**the shaft**) harsh or unfair treatment. ● *v. informal* treat unfairly.

shag *n.* **1** a rough growth or mass of hair etc. **2** a carpet with a long rough pile.

shaggy *adj.* (**shaggier, shaggiest**) **1** hairy, rough-haired. **2** unkempt. **3** (of the hair) coarse and abundant. **4** (of cloth) having a long and coarse nap.

shaggy-dog story *n.* a long rambling esp. pointless story.

shah *n.* a title of the former monarch of Iran.

shake ● *v.* (**shakes;** *past* **shook;** *past participle* **shaken; shaking**) **1** move forcefully or quickly up and down or to and fro. **2** tremble or vibrate markedly. **3** agitate, shock, or upset. **4** weaken or impair; make less firm. **5** make tremulous or rapidly alternating sounds. **6** brandish. **7** shake hands. **8** *informal* = SHAKE OFF. ● *n.* **1** an act of shaking. **2** (**the shakes**) a fit of or tendency to trembling or shivering. **3** a milkshake. **4** = CEDAR SHAKE. □ **no great shakes** *informal* not very good or significant. **shake hands** clasp right hands at meeting or parting, in reconciliation or congratulation, or over a concluded bargain. **shake one's head** move one's head from side to side in refusal, denial, disapproval, incredulity, or concern. **shake off 1** get rid of. **2** manage to evade. **shake up 1** mix by shaking. **2** rouse from lethargy, apathy, conventionality, etc.

shakedown *n.* **1** a period or process of adjustment or change. **2** *slang* a swindle. **3** a search.

shaker *n.* **1** a person or thing that shakes. **2** a container from which something is shaken. **3** a container for shaking together the ingredients of cocktails etc. **4** (**Shaker**) **a** a member of an American religious sect living simply, in celibate mixed communities. **b** (as an *adj.*) (of furniture etc.) produced by or of a type produced by Shakers, characterized by simplicity and lack of ornamentation. **5** (as an *adj.*) (also **shaker knit**) designating a style of knitting having parallel rows of ribbing.

Shakespearean (also **Shakespearian**) ● *adj.* of or relating to the English poet and dramatist William Shakespeare (1564–1616). ● *n.* a student of Shakespeare's works etc.

shakeup *n.* an upheaval or drastic reorganization.

shaky *adj.* (**shakier, shakiest**) **1** unsteady; apt to shake; trembling. **2** unsound, infirm. **3** unreliable, wavering. □ **shakily** *adv.* **shakiness** *n.*

shale *n.* soft finely layered rock that splits easily, consisting of consolidated clay.

shall *aux. v.* **1** indicating future predictions. **2** indicating will or determination. **3** indicating or offering suggestions. **4** indicating orders or instructions.

shallot *n.* a variety of onion that forms clumps of small bulbs. [*Say* shuh LOT *or* SHALL it]

shallow ● *adj.* **1** of little depth. **2** superficial, trivial. ● *n.* (often in *pl.*) shallow waters. □ **shallowly** *adv.* **shallowness** *n.*

shalom *n. & interj.* a Jewish salutation at meeting or parting. [*Say* shuh LOM]

sham ● *n.* **1** a person or thing pretending or pretended to be something else. **2** a decorative cover for a pillow. ● *adj.* pretended, counterfeit. ● *v.* (**shams, shammed, shamming**) pretend.

shaman *n.* (esp. among some peoples of northern Asia and N America) a person regarded as having access to spirits. □ **shamanic** *adj.* **shamanism** *n.* **shamanistic** *adj.* [*Say* SHAY min, shuh MAN ick]

shamble *v.* (**shambles, shambled, shambling**) walk or run with a shuffling or awkward gait.

shambles *n.* a scene of complete disorder.

shame ● *n.* **1** a feeling of humiliation resulting from guilt or foolishness. **2** a capacity for experiencing this. **3** a state of disgrace, discredit, or intense regret. **4 a** a person or thing that brings disgrace etc. **b** a thing or action that is regrettable. ● *v.* (**shames, shamed, shaming**) **1** bring shame on. **2** force by shame. □ **put to**

shame humiliate by revealing superior qualities etc. □ **shameful** *adj.* **shamefully** *adv.*

shamefaced *adj.* feeling or showing shame or embarrassment. □ **shamefacedly** *adv.* [Say SHAME faced, shame FACE id lee]

shameless *adj.* **1** showing no sense of shame. **2** impudent, brazen. □ **shamelessly** *adv.* **shamelessness** *n.*

shampoo ● *n. (pl.* **shampoos**) **1** liquid used to wash the hair. **2** a similar substance for washing a car or carpet etc. **3** an act of cleaning with shampoo. ● *v.* (**shampoos**, **shampooed**, **shampooing**) wash with shampoo. □ **shampooer** *n.*

shamrock *n.* a clover-like plant with a three-lobed leaf on each stem, used as an Irish emblem.

shanghai *v.* (**shanghais**, **shanghaied**, **shanghaiing**) trick or force into doing something.

Shanghai noodles *pl. n.* a Chinese dish consisting of thick spaghetti-like noodles stir-fried with meat and vegetables.

Shangri-La *n. (pl.* **Shangri-Las**) an imaginary paradise on earth.

shank ● *n.* **1 a** the lower part of the leg. **2** a cut of meat from an animal's leg. **3** a shaft or stem. ● *v. Golf* mis-hit the ball with the heel of the club. □ **shanked** *adj.*

shan't *contr.* shall not.

shanty¹ *n. (pl.* **shanties**) **1** a crudely built shack. **2** a hut or cabin. **3** esp. *Cdn hist.* a logging camp.

shanty² *n. (pl.* **shanties**) a song with alternating solo and chorus, of a kind originally sung by sailors.

shantytown *n.* a poor or depressed area of a city or town, consisting of shanties.

shape ● *n.* **1** the external form of a person or thing as produced by its outline. **2** a definite or proper arrangement. **3 a** a specified condition. **b** (when unqualified) good condition. **c** the nature or characteristics of something. **4** a piece of material, paper, etc., made or cut in a particular form. ● *v.* (**shapes**, **shaped**, **shaping**) **1** give a certain shape or form to. **2** give signs of future development. **3** assume or develop into a shape. □ **shape up 1** take a (specified) form. **2** make good progress; improve. **take shape** assume a distinct form. □ **shaped** *adj.* **shaper** *n.*

shapeless *adj.* lacking definite or attractive shape. □ **shapelessness** *n.*

shapely *adj.* (**shapelier**, **shapeliest**) **1** well formed or proportioned. **2** of elegant or pleasing shape or appearance.

shape-shifter *n.* an imaginary creature capable of changing its form. □ **shape-shifting** *n.*

shard *n.* a broken piece of pottery or glass etc.

share¹ ● *n.* **1** an individual's portion of a common amount. **2** any of the equal parts into which a company's capital is divided, entitling its owner to a proportion of the profits. ● *v.* (**shares**, **shared**, **sharing**) **1** get or have or give a share of. **2** use or benefit from jointly with others. **3** have in common. **4** let others use one's things. **5** (foll. by *in*) participate. **6** (often foll. by *out*) divide and distribute. **7** tell, recount; share personal information. □ **share and share alike** make an equal division. □ **shareable** *adj.* **sharer** *n.*

share² *n.* a ploughshare.

sharecropper *n.* a tenant farmer who gives a part of each crop as rent. □ **sharecropping** *n.*

shareholder *n.* an owner of shares in a company. □ **shareholding** *n.*

shareware *n.* software that is available free of charge for evaluation, after which a fee is requested for continued use.

shark *n.* **1** a large usu. voracious marine fish with a long body and prominent dorsal fin. **2** *informal* a person who unscrupulously exploits or swindles others.

sharkskin *n.* **1** the rough scaly skin of a shark. **2** a smooth slightly lustrous fabric.

sharp ● *adj.* **1** having an edge or point able to cut or pierce. **2** tapering to a point or edge. **3** abrupt, steep, angular. **4** well defined, clean-cut. **5 a** severe or intense. **b** pungent, acid. **c** keen. **6** shrill and piercing. **7** harsh. **8** quick to perceive or comprehend. **9** vigorous or brisk. **10** *Music* **a** above the desired or true pitch. **b** (as **C sharp** etc.) a semitone higher than C etc. **11** *informal* stylish. ● *n.* **1** *Music* **a** a note raised a semitone above natural pitch. **b** the sign (♯) indicating this. **2** *informal* a swindler or cheat. ● *adv.* **1** punctually. **2** suddenly, abruptly, promptly. **3** *Music* above the true pitch. □ **sharply** *adv.* **sharpness** *n.*

sharp-edged *adj.* biting, caustic.

sharpen *v.* make or become sharp. □ **sharpener** *n.*

sharpie *n.* a swindler.

sharpshooter *n.* a skilled shooter or marksman. □ **sharpshooting** *n.* & *adj.*

sharp-tailed grouse *n.* a medium-sized grouse of grasslands in western N America, with a short pointed tail.

shasta *n.* (*pl.* **shastas**) a tall European plant that bears a single daisy-like flower.

shatter v. **1** break suddenly in pieces. **2** severely damage or utterly destroy. □ **shattering** adj. **shatteringly** adv.

shatterproof adj. designed to resist shattering.

shave ● v. (**shaves**; past **shaved**; past participle **shaved** or (as adj.) **shaven**; **shaving**) **1** remove bristles or hair with a razor. **2** reduce by a small amount. **3** cut thin slices from the surface of wood etc. **4** pass close to without touching. **5** cut (hair, grass, etc.) very short. ● n. **1** an act of shaving. **2** a close approach without contact.

shaver n. an electric razor.

shaving n. a thin, curled strip cut off the surface of wood, chocolate, etc.

shaving kit n. a small bag or case for holding shaving supplies and other toiletries.

Shavuot n. (also **Shavuoth**) the Jewish harvest festival, on the fiftieth day after the second day of Passover. [Say shaw voo OTT or shaw voo OTH]

shawl n. a piece of fabric, usu. folded into a triangle, worn over the shoulders or wrapped around a baby. □ **shawled** adj.

she ● pron. **1** the female previously named or in question. **2** a thing regarded as female, e.g. a vehicle or ship. ● n. a female.

sheaf n. (pl. **sheaves**) **1** a pile or bundle of paper. **2** a bundle of stalks and ears of grain tied after reaping.

shear ● v. (**shears**; past **sheared**; past participle **shorn** or **sheared**; **shearing**) **1** clip the wool off a sheep etc. **2** remove by cutting. **3** cut with scissors or shears etc. **4** (foll. by of) strip bare. **5** (often foll. by off) break from a structural strain. ● n. **1** a strain produced by pressure in the structure of a substance, so that each layer slides over the next. **2** (in pl.) large scissors for use in gardens etc. □ **shearer** n.

shearling n. **1** a sheep that has been shorn once. **2** a fleece or wool from a shearling. [Say SHEER ling]

shearwater n. any of a number of seabirds which habitually skim low over the open sea with wings outstretched.

sheath n. **1** a close-fitting cover, esp. for the blade of a knife or sword. **2** a condom. **3** Botany, Anatomy, & Zoology an enclosing case or tissue. **4** a woman's close-fitting dress.

sheathe v. (**sheathes**, **sheathed**, **sheathing**) **1** put into a sheath. **2** encase.

sheathing n. **1** a protective casing or covering. **2** a layer of plywood etc. covering a frame.

shebang n. slang □ **the whole shebang** the whole situation, thing, etc. [Say shuh BANG]

shed[1] n. a simple one-storeyed structure for storage, as shelter for animals, or as a workshop etc. **2** a large structure often with at least one side open, for storing machinery, vehicles, etc.

shed[2] v. (**sheds**, **shed**, **shedding**) **1** allow leaves, hair, skin, etc. to fall off naturally. **2** cause to fall or flow. **3** disperse, diffuse, radiate. **4** remove or get rid of.

she'd contr. **1** she had. **2** she would.

sheen n. **1** a gloss or lustre on a surface. **2** radiance, brightness.

sheep n. (pl. **sheep**) **1** a ruminant mammal with a thick woolly coat, kept in flocks for wool or meat. **2** a bashful, defenceless, or esp. easily led person. □ **separate the sheep from the goats** divide into desirable and undesirable groups. □ **sheeplike** adj.

sheepdog n. a dog of a breed trained to guard and herd sheep.

sheepish adj. **1** embarrassed through shame or foolishness. **2** bashful, shy. □ **sheepishly** adv. **sheepishness** n.

sheepskin n. a garment or rug of sheep's skin with the wool on.

sheer ● adj. **1** complete, absolute. **2** perpendicular; very steep. **3** (of a textile) very thin. ● n. **1 a** a sheer fabric. **b** (in pl.) sheer curtains or nylon hosiery. **2** a deviation from a course. ● v. **1** esp. Nautical swerve or change course. **2** go away, esp. from a person or topic one dislikes or fears. □ **sheerly** adv.

sheesh interj. expressing mild frustration, exasperation, surprise, embarrassment, etc.

sheet[1] ● n. **1** a large rectangular piece of fabric used on a bed to lie on or under. **2** a broad thin flat piece of material, e.g. paper or metal. **3** the long rectangular ice surface on which curling is played. **4** a wide continuous surface or expanse of water, ice, flame, falling rain, etc. **5** a large very shallow pan for baking. ● v. **1** provide or cover with sheets. **2** form into sheets. **3** (of rain etc.) fall in sheets.

sheet[2] n. a rope or chain attached to the lower corner of a sail for securing or controlling it. □ **three sheets to the wind** slang drunk.

sheeting n. **1** material for making bed linen. **2** material covering another in sheets.

sheet lightning n. a lightning flash whose bolt is unseen, observed as a sudden flash of brightness illuminating a wide area.

sheet music *n.* esp. unbound printed musical scores.

sheik *n.* (also **sheikh**) **1** a chief or head of an Arab tribe, family, or village. **2** a Muslim leader. □ **sheikdom** *n.* [*Say* SHEEK *or* SHAKE]

shekel *n.* **1** the chief monetary unit of modern Israel. **2** *hist.* a silver coin and unit of weight used in ancient Israel etc. [*Say* SHECK'll]

shelf *n.* (*pl.* **shelves**) **1** a thin flat piece of wood etc. projecting from a wall, or as part of a unit, used to store or display things. **2 a** a ledge of rock. **b** = CONTINENTAL SHELF. □ **off the shelf** available immediately from a retailer's stock.

shelf life *n.* the amount of time for which a stored item of food etc. remains usable.

shell ● *n.* **1** the hard outer covering of molluscs, eggs, nuts, turtles, etc. **2 a** an explosive projectile for use in a big gun. **b** a cartridge. **3** a mere outer form without substance. **4** any outer case. **5** a very light all-weather jacket, often with a removable lining. **6** a program which provides an interface between the user and the operating system. ● *v.* **1** remove the shell or pod from. **2** bombard with shells. □ **come out of one's shell** cease to be shy. **shell out** *informal* hand over (a required sum). □ **shell-like** *adj.*

she'll *contr.* she will; she shall.

shellac ● *n.* varnish made from melted lac resin. ● *v.* (**shellacs**, **shellacked**, **shellacking**) **1** varnish with shellac. **2** *slang* defeat or thrash soundly. [*Say* shuh LACK]

shellacking *n. slang* a severe defeat or beating. [*Say* shuh LACKING]

shelled *adj.* **1** having a shell or shells, esp. of a specific kind. **2** having had its shell removed.

shellfish *n.* (*pl.* **shellfish** or **shellfishes**) **1** an aquatic shelled mollusc, e.g. an oyster, scallop, etc. **2** a crustacean, e.g. a crab etc.

shell game *n.* **1** a sleight-of-hand trick in which bystanders are encouraged to place bets as to which of several shuffled walnut shells conceals a small object. **2** *informal* a confidence game.

shell shock *n.* psychological disturbance resulting from exposure to battle. □ **shell-shocked** *adj.*

shelter ● *n.* **1** a structure built to give protection. **2 a** a place of refuge provided for the homeless, abused women, etc. **b** an animal sanctuary. **3** a shielded condition. **4** (also **tax shelter**) a financial arrangement intended to avoid or minimize taxes. ● *v.* **1** provide with protection from the weather, danger,

difficulty, unpleasantness, etc. **2** take cover. **3** protect (invested income) from taxation. □ **sheltered** *adj.*

shelterbelt *n.* a line of trees etc. serving to break the force of the wind.

shelve *v.* (**shelves**, **shelved**, **shelving**) **1** put on a shelf. **2 a** abandon or defer (a plan etc.). **b** remove from active work etc. **3** (of ground etc.) slope in a specified direction.

shelves *pl.* of SHELF.

shelving *n.* **1** *in senses of* SHELVE. **2** shelves collectively.

shemozzle *n. slang* **1** a brawl or commotion. **2** a muddle. [*Say* shuh MOZZLE]

shenanigans *pl. n. informal* **1** high-spirited behaviour. **2** secret or dishonest activity. [*Say* shuh NANNA gun]

shepherd ● *n.* **1** a person who tends sheep at pasture. **2** = GERMAN SHEPHERD. ● *v.* **1** tend (sheep etc.) as a shepherd. **2** marshal or direct the movement of. [*Say* SHEP erd]

shepherdess *n.* a woman who tends sheep at pasture. [*Say* SHEP erd ess]

shepherd's pie *n.* a dish of ground meat under a layer of mashed potatoes.

sherbet *n.* **1** a usu. fruit-flavoured frozen dessert similar to ice cream. **2** a flavoured sweet powder eaten as a candy or used to make an effervescing drink. [*Say* SHUR bit *or* SHUR bert]

sheriff *n.* **1** *Cdn* an appointed court official. **2** *US* a usu. elected officer responsible for keeping the peace in a county.

Sherpa *n.* (*pl.* **Sherpa** or **Sherpas**) a member of a Himalayan people living on the border of Nepal and Tibet renowned for their skill in mountaineering. [*Say* SHUR puh]

sherry *n.* (*pl.* **sherries**) a fortified wine originally from southern Spain.

she's *contr.* she is; she has.

Shetland ● *adj.* of or pertaining to the Shetland Islands. ● *n.* a fine loosely twisted wool from Shetland sheep. [*Say* SHET lind]

Shetland sheepdog *n.* a small collie-like breed of dog.

Shia (also **Shiah**, **Shi'a**) ● *n.* (*pl.* **Shia** or **Shias**) **1** one of the two main branches of Islam, which rejects the first three Sunni caliphs and regards Ali as Muhammad's first successor. **2** an adherent of this branch of Islam. ● *adj.* of or relating to Shia. [*Say* SHEE uh]

shiatsu *n.* a kind of therapy in which pressure is applied to certain points of the body. [*Say* she AT soo]

shibboleth *n.* **1** an outdated or old-fashioned idea, principle, or phrase. **2** a custom, word, pronunciation, etc. that distinguishes a particular group of people. [*Say* SHIBBA leth]

shied *past and past participle* of SHY.

shield ● *n.* **1 a** a broad piece of armour carried on the arm to deflect blows. **b** a thing serving to protect. **2** a piece of fabric etc. worn as a liner to protect a garment against staining. **3 (the Shield)** (in Canada) the Canadian Shield. **4** a stylized representation of a shield, characteristically of a flat-topped heart shape. ● *v.* protect, shelter, or screen with or as with a shield.

shift ● *v.* **1** change or move from one position or state to another. **2** change gear in a vehicle. **3** contrive or manage as best one can. ● *n.* **1** a slight change in position, direction, or tendency. **2 a** one of two or more recurring periods in which different groups of workers, hockey players, etc. do the same jobs in relay. **b** one of such groups. **3 a** a woman's straight unwaisted dress. **b** a woman's slip. **4** a key on a keyboard used to switch between lower and upper case, conduct special operations, etc. □ **make shift** manage or contrive. **shift for oneself** rely on one's own efforts.

shifter *n.* **1** a person or thing that shifts. **2** a gearshift.

shiftless *adj.* lacking resourcefulness; lazy; inefficient. □ **shiftlessness** *n.*

shift work *n.* work conducted in often variable periods independent of a standard workday, usu. at night. □ **shift worker** *n.*

shifty *adj.* (**shiftier**, **shiftiest**) *informal* not straightforward; evasive; deceitful. □ **shiftily** *adv.* **shiftiness** *n.*

Shiism *n.* (also **Shi'ism**) the doctrines or principles of the Shia branch of Islam. [*Say* SHEE ism]

shiitake *n.* an edible mushroom that grows on fallen timber. [*Say* shi TOCKY *or* shi TACKY]

Shiite (also **Shi'ite**) ● *n.* an adherent of the Shia branch of Islam. ● *adj.* of or relating to Shia. [*Say* SHEE ite]

shiksa *n.* often *offensive* a non-Jewish girl or woman. [*Say* SHICK suh]

shill ● *n.* **1** an accomplice, esp. one posing as an enthusiastic or successful customer to encourage or entice potential buyers, gamblers, etc. **2** an adherent of a party or point of view etc. posing as a disinterested advocate. ● *v.* **1** (often foll. by *for*) promote a cause, esp. with pretended objectivity. **2** act as an accomplice or shill in a scam.

shillelagh *n.* a thick stick or club of wood used in Ireland esp. as a weapon. [*Say* shi LAY lee *or* shi LAY luh]

shilling *n.* *hist.* a former British coin and monetary unit equal to one-twentieth of a pound or twelve pence.

shilly-shally *v.* (**shilly-shallies**, **shilly-shallied**, **shilly-shallying**) act with indecision or hesitation. □ **shilly-shallying** *n.*

shim ● *n.* a thin strip, wedge, or washer inserted in machinery etc. to make parts fit or align. ● *v.* (**shims**, **shimmed**, **shimming**) wedge, raise, or fill up with a shim.

shimmer ● *v.* **1** shine with a tremulous or faint diffused light. **2** quiver or tremble. ● *n.* a faint tremulous light or image. □ **shimmering** *adj.* **shimmery** *adj.*

shimmy ● *n.* (*pl.* **shimmies**) an abnormal vibration of esp. the front wheels of a vehicle. ● *v.* (**shimmies**, **shimmied**, **shimmying**) **1** shake or sway the body. **2** (esp. of a car etc.) shake or vibrate abnormally.

shin *n.* the front of the leg below the knee.

shindig *n.* (also **shindy** *pl.* **shindies**) *informal* **1** a lively or festive gathering. **2** a noisy disturbance.

shine ● *v.* (**shines**, **shone**, **shining**) **1 a** emit, give off, or reflect light. **b** (of the sun) not be obscured by clouds etc. **2** be unusually vibrant or animated, esp. with excitement, joy, etc. **3** direct light in a particular direction. **4** (*past* and *past participle* **shined**) make bright; polish. **5** excel. ● *n.* **1** brightness or radiance emanating from a source of light. **2** a lustre reflecting off a surface, esp. the result of polishing. **3** an act of rubbing something to give it a shiny surface. □ **take a shine to** *informal* take a fancy to; like. □ **shining** *adj.*

shiner *n.* **1** *informal* a black eye. **2** any of various silvery fishes, esp. a minnow.

shingle ● *n.* **1** a thin rectangular tile used to cover esp. roofs. **2** a small sign or nameplate hanging outside a store or office. **3** small rounded pebbles, esp. on a seashore. ● *v.* (**shingles**, **shingled**, **shingling**) install shingles on (a roof etc.). □ **shingled** *adj.*

shingles *pl. n.* (usu. treated as *sing.*) a disease characterized by a band of painful minute blisters on the skin.

shinny ● *v.* (**shinnies**, **shinnied**, **shinnying**) *informal* climb up or down a tree etc. by clasping it with the arms and legs. ● *n.* Cdn **1** *informal* pickup hockey played usu. without nets, referees, or equipment except for skates, sticks, and a ball or puck etc. **2** *informal* hockey.

shin splints *pl. n.* (usu. treated as *sing.*) acute pain in the lower leg caused esp. by prolonged running.

Shinto *n.* a Japanese religion involving the

worship of ancestors and nature spirits.
□ **Shintoism** n. **Shintoist** n.

shiny adj. (**shinier**, **shiniest**) having a polished or gleaming surface.
□ **shininess** n.

ship • n. **1** a large sea-going vessel. **2** a spacecraft. • v. (**ships**, **shipped**, **shipping**) **1** transport, deliver, or convey by or on a ship. **2** transport by truck, rail, or other means. □ **run a tight ship** manage a company etc. with strict authority. **when a person's ship comes in** (or **home**) when a person's fortune is made.

-ship suffix forming nouns denoting: **1** a quality or condition. **2** status, title, or office. **3** a skill in a certain capacity. **4** the collective individuals of a group.

shipboard adj. occurring or used on board a ship.

shipbuilder n. a person or company that designs and builds ships.
□ **shipbuilding** n.

shiplap n. wooden siding consisting of boards with overlapping L-shaped notches along their edges to allow for flush placement against the wall.

shipmate n. a fellow member of a ship's crew.

shipment n. an amount of goods transported, delivered, or received.

shipper n. a person or company that transports or receives goods by land, sea, or air.

shipping n. **1** the transport of goods by sea, land, or air. **2** ships collectively.

ship's biscuit n. hist. a hard coarse cracker kept and eaten on board ship.

shipshape adj. in good order.

shipwreck • n. **1** the destruction of a ship by a storm, sinking, etc. **2** the remains of a ship so destroyed. • v. **1** cause to suffer shipwreck. **2** destroy a person's hopes, dreams, fortunes, etc.

shipyard n. a large area adjoining a body of water in which ships are built or repaired.

shiraz n. (pl. **shirazes**) a variety of red wine produced in Australia and South Africa. [Say shuh RAZZ]

shirk v. avoid, evade, or attempt to get out of work, responsibility, etc. □ **shirker** n.

shirt n. **1** a garment for the upper body with sleeves, a collar, and buttons down the front. **2** any garment for the upper body. □ **get one's shirt in a knot** become agitated or upset. **lose one's shirt** lose all one's money, esp. in a bet, investment, etc. □ **shirtless** adj.

shirted adj. wearing a shirt.

shirt sleeve n. **1** the sleeve of a shirt. **2** (as an adj.; usu. **shirt-sleeve**) designating an environment that is warm, informal, or laborious enough for not wearing a jacket. □ **in shirt sleeves** wearing a shirt with no jacket etc. over it.

shirttail n. (also in pl.) the lower curved part of a shirt below the waist.

shish kebab n. pieces of marinated meat and vegetables cooked and served on a skewer. [Say SHISH kuh bob]

shiv n. slang a knife, switchblade, or razor.

shiva n. (pl. **shivas**) (also **shivah**, pl. **shivahs**) Judaism a period of seven days' mourning beginning immediately after a funeral. □ **sit shiva** mourn. [Say SHIVVA]

shiver • v. **1** tremble with cold, fear, etc. **2** break into splinters. • n. **1** a momentary quivering or trembling of the body. **2** (in pl.) an attack of shivering. **3** each of the small pieces into which esp. glass is shattered when broken. □ **shivery** adj.

shoal¹ • n. **1** a school of fish, porpoises, etc. **2** a large number. • v. (of fish) gather in schools.

shoal² n. **1** an area of shallow water. **2** a submerged sandbank visible at low tide. [Rhymes with GOAL]

shock¹ • n. **1** a sudden and usu. disturbing effect on the mind, feelings, or emotions. **2** a serious medical condition associated with a fall in blood pressure, caused by loss of blood, severe injury, etc. **3** a sudden and violent collision, impact, tremor, etc. **4** = ELECTRIC SHOCK 1. **5** a shock absorber. • v. **1 a** arouse surprise or bewilderment etc. **b** arouse outrage, disgust, anger, etc. **2** affect with an electric shock.

shock² n. an unkempt or shaggy mass of hair.

shock absorber n. a device for absorbing jolts and vibrations on a road vehicle. □ **shock-absorbing** adj.

shocked adj. scandalized, horrified, disgusted.

shocker n. informal a revelation etc. that causes surprise or outrage.

shocking adj. causing indignation, scandal, or disgust. □ **shockingly** adv.

shock treatment n. (also **shock therapy**) **1** a method of treating depressive patients by giving electric shocks to the brain. **2** sudden and harsh or drastic measures taken to improve a situation.

shock troops pl. n. troops trained for assault.

shock wave n. **1** a moving wave of very high pressure caused by explosion or by a body moving faster than sound. **2** the repercussions of an event.

shod ● v. *past and past participle of* SHOE. ● *adj.* having or wearing shoes or other footwear.

shoddy *adj.* (**shoddier**, **shoddiest**) of poor or inferior quality. □ **shoddily** *adv.* **shoddiness** *n.*

shoe ● *n.* **1** one of a matching pair of coverings for the foot with a sturdy sole, usu. reaching below the ankle. **2** a horseshoe. **3** anything resembling a shoe in shape or use. **4** = BRAKE SHOE. ● v. (**shoes**; *past and past participle* **shod** or **shoed**; **shoeing**) **1** fit (esp. a horse etc.) with shoes. **2** cover or protect with a shoe or shoes. □ **be in a person's shoes** be in his or her situation, predicament, role, etc. **if the shoe fits** if a criticism or description seems applicable, one should be guided by it. □ **shoeless** *adj.*

shoebox *n.* (*pl.* **shoeboxes**) the oblong box in which a new pair of shoes is packaged.

shoehorn ● *n.* a curved piece of metal, plastic, etc., used to ease the heel into a shoe. ● v. force into a tight, inadequate, or unsuitable space or position.

shoelace *n.* a short length of string used for tying shoes and boots etc.

shoemaker *n.* a person who makes and repairs shoes and boots. □ **shoemaking** *n.*

shoeshine *n.* an act of cleaning and polishing shoes.

shoestring *n.* **1** a shoelace. **2** *informal* a small esp. inadequate amount of money.

shofar *n.* (*pl.* **shofars** or **shofroth**) a trumpet made of a ram's horn. [*Say* SHOW fur *for the singular*, SHOW frot *for the plural*]

shogun *n.* any of a succession of hereditary commanders-in-chief in feudal Japan. [*Say* SHOW gun]

shone *past and past participle of* SHINE. [*Say* SHON]

shoo ● *interj.* an exclamation used to frighten or drive away. ● v. (**shoos**, **shooed**, **shooing**) drive or urge in a desired direction.

shoo-in *n. informal* something sure to succeed or win.

shook ● v. *past of* SHAKE. ● *adj. informal* (foll. by *up*) agitated, upset.

shoot ● v. (**shoots**, **shot**, **shooting**) **1** kill or wound with a bullet or arrow. **2** cause a gun to fire. **3** move suddenly and rapidly. **4** direct a glance, question, or remark at someone. **5** film or photograph something. **6** (of a boat) sweep swiftly down (rapids etc.). **7** direct a puck or ball toward

the net, basket, etc. **8** send out buds or shoots. **9** make a specified score in a round of golf. **10** (usu. foll. by *for*) plan, aim. ● *n.* **1** a competition in shooting. **2** a film or photography session. **3** a new growth of a plant. ● *interj. informal* **1** an invitation for a comment, question, etc. **2** an exclamation of disappointment, anger, etc. □ **shoot down 1** kill by shooting. **2** cause an aircraft to crash by shooting. **3** reject an argument, proposal, etc. **shoot from the hip** *informal* speak or act spontaneously or hastily. **shoot it out** engage in a decisive confrontation. **shoot oneself in the foot** inadvertently make a situation worse. **shoot one's mouth off** talk too much or indiscreetly. **shoot the breeze** (or **bull**) chat idly.

shoot-'em-up *n. slang* a fast-moving movie which features extensive shooting and gunplay.

shooter *n.* **1** a person who discharges a firearm. **2** (*in comb.*) a gun or other device for shooting. **3** *Sport* a player who takes a shot. **4** a small drink of alcohol, esp. liquor.

shooting ● *n.* **1 a** a wounding or killing by gunfire. **b** the discharge of a firearm. **2** the hobby or sport of hunting game or firing at targets. **3** (in sports) the ability to shoot accurately. ● *adj.* (of a pain etc.) sharp and spreading quickly.

shooting gallery *n.* a long room or fairground booth used for recreational shooting at usu. moving targets.

shooting star *n.* a small meteor burning up upon entering the earth's atmosphere.

shootout *n.* **1** a decisive gunfight. **2** (also **penalty shootout**) (in soccer, hockey, etc.) a method of deciding games ending in a tie in which each team takes a specified number of penalty shots. **3** a close high-scoring game.

shop ● *n.* **1** a place where goods are sold. **2** a place where repairs or manufacturing takes place. **3 a** a room or course in a school for teaching woodworking or mechanical skills etc. **b** the study of these skills. **4** one's occupation as a subject of conversation. ● v. (**shops**, **shopped**, **shopping**) **1** buy goods. **2** sell or propose an idea to several prospective buyers. □ **shop around** visit several stores, service providers, etc. in search of the best price or service.

shopaholic *n. jocular* an avid or compulsive shopper.

shop floor *n.* **1** the working environment in a factory, esp. as distinct from a management environment. **2** the workers in a factory etc.

shopkeeper *n.* a person who owns or

manages a shop or store.
□ **shopkeeping** n.

shoplift v. steal from a store by posing as a customer. □ **shoplifter** n. **shoplifting** n.

shopper n. **1** a person who makes purchases in a shop. **2** an advertising supplement; a flyer.

shopping n. **1** the purchase of merchandise etc. **2** goods purchased.

shopping centre n. (also **shopping mall**, **shopping plaza**) = MALL 1.

shop steward n. a person elected by workers in a factory etc. to represent them in dealings with management.

shoptalk n. conversation about one's job etc.

shopworn adj. **1** faded or dirty from being on display in a store. **2** no longer fresh or new; hackneyed or stale.

shore[1] n. **1** the land at the edge of a large body of water. **2** land, as opposed to sea.

shore[2] ● v. (**shores**, **shored**, **shoring**) (often foll. by up) **1** reinforce; strengthen or fortify. **2** support a wall etc. with a beam or beams set at an angle. ● n. a beam set obliquely against a wall etc. as a support.

shorebird n. a bird which frequents the shore.

shoreline n. the line along which a stretch of water meets the shore.

shore lunch n. Cdn a fish meal cooked on a lakeshore or riverbank etc. as part of a fishing or other boating excursion.

shorn ● v. past participle of SHEAR. ● adj. **1** having had all or most of the hair of the head, wool, etc. removed. **2** deprived.

short ● adj. **1** of a small length, duration, or extent. **2** small in height. **3** in insufficient supply. **4** terse; uncivil. **5** (of a ball in sport) travelling only a short distance, or not far enough. **6** (of odds) reflecting a high level of probability. **7** Phonetics having the sound of a in pat, e in pet, i in pit, o in pot, u in but. **8** (of pastry) containing a high proportion of fat to flour and therefore crumbly. ● adv. (in sport) not far or not far enough. ● n. **1** a short-circuit. **2** a short film. **3** Baseball the position of shortstop. ● v. short-circuit. □ **be caught** (or **taken**) **short** be at a disadvantage, esp. by being without something important. **fall** (or **come**) **short of** fail to reach or amount to. **in short supply** scarce. **in the short term** (or **run**) over a short period of time. **pull up** (or **bring up**) **short** stop abruptly or before the expected destination. **short end of the stick** the less favourable part of a deal. **short of 1** having a partial or total lack. **2** without going so far as. **3** distant from.

short of breath out of breath.
□ **shortish** adj. **shortness** n.

shortage n. (often foll. by of) a deficiency or lack.

shortbread n. a crisp rich crumbly cookie made with butter, flour, and sugar.

shortcake n. a cake with a filling of fruit and whipped cream.

shortchange v. (**shortchanges**, **shortchanged**, **shortchanging**) **1** give insufficient change to a customer, accidentally or intentionally. **2** treat unfairly.

short-circuit ● n. a faulty circuit in an electrical connection, in which the current flows along a shorter route than it should follow. ● v. fail or cease working as a result of a short-circuit.

shortcoming n. a fault or defect.

shortcut n. **1** a route that shortens the distance travelled. **2** a quick or easy way of accomplishing something.

shorten v. become or make shorter or short.

shortening n. **1** a soft fat that produces a crisp flaky effect in baked products. **2** an act of making something short or shorter.

shortfall n. a failure to reach esp. a financial goal or expectations.

short fuse n. informal a quick temper.

shortgrass n. (pl. **shortgrasses**) any of a number of short grasses especially resistant to drought.

shorthair n. a short-haired domestic cat or dog.

shorthand n. **1** a method of writing or typing in abbreviations and symbols. **2** (often foll. by for) any abbreviated or symbolic mode of expression.

short-handed ● adj. **1** not having the usual number of workers etc. **2** Hockey playing or occurring with fewer players on the ice than one's opponent. ● adv. with fewer players, workers, etc. than usual.

short-haul n. the transport of goods or passengers over a short distance.

Shorthorn n. a breed of cattle with short horns.

short list ● n. a list of selected candidates for a position from which a final choice is made. ● v. (usu. **shortlist**) add (a person) to a list of candidates for a position.

short-lived adj. lasting only for a short time.

shortly adv. **1** soon. **2** a short time. **3** in a few words.

short notice n. □ **on** (or **at**) **short notice** with little advance warning.

short-order adj. of restaurant food that

can be prepared and served quickly. □ **in short order** immediately.

short-range *adj.* **1** operating or capable of operating within a small or limited area. **2** relating to a fairly immediate future time.

short rib *n.* **1** any of the lower ribs which are not attached to the breastbone. **2** a piece of meat containing any of these.

shorts *pl. n.* **1** a pair of pants extending nor farther than the knees. **2** men's underpants.

short shrift *n.* brusque or dismissive treatment.

short-sighted *adj.* **1** unable to focus on distant objects. **2** lacking imagination, foresight, or proper consideration. □ **short-sightedly** *adv.* **short-sightedness** *n.*

short-sleeved *adj.* with sleeves not reaching below the elbow.

short-staffed *adj.* having insufficient staff.

shortstop *n. Baseball* the player that covers the part of the infield between second and third.

short story *n.* a prose narrative shorter than a novel.

short temper *n.* a tendency to lose one's temper quickly or easily. □ **short-tempered** *adj.*

short-term *adj.* having to do with a relatively short period of time.

short-track speed skating *n.* a form of speed skating competition performed on a standard-size hockey rink.

shortwave *n.* a radio wave with a wavelength of less than about 100 metres, a frequency of 3 to 30 MHz.

shorty *n.* (*pl.* **shorties**) *informal* or *derogatory* a person shorter than average.

shot^1 *n.* **1** the firing of a gun etc. **2** *Sport* an attempt to score by hitting, stroking, or kicking the ball etc. **3** *informal* an attempt. **4** (*pl.* **shot**) a ball of metal fired from a gun. **5** a heavy ball thrown by a shot putter. **6** a photograph. **7** a film sequence photographed continuously. **8** *informal* a small drink of alcohol. **9** *informal* an injection of a drug or vaccine. □ **have** (or **take**) **a shot at** make an attempt at; try. **give something a shot** try something. **shot in the arm** stimulus or encouragement. **shot in the dark** a mere guess.

shot^2 ● *v.* past and past participle of SHOOT. ● *adj. informal* **1** ruined; worn out. **2** exhausted. □ **shot through** permeated or suffused.

shotgun ● *n.* a gun for firing small shot, used esp. for hunting. ● *adj.* **1** of or like a shotgun. **2** wide-ranging, but random.

shotgun marriage *n.* (also **shotgun wedding**) *informal* **1** an enforced or hurried wedding, esp. because of the bride's pregnancy. **2** any enforced alliance, partnership, etc.

shot put *n.* an athletic contest in which a very heavy ball is thrown as far as possible. □ **shot putter** *n.*

shot rock *n. Curling* the rock lying nearest to the centre of the rings.

should *aux. v.* past of SHALL, used esp.: **1 a** to express a duty, obligation, or likelihood. **b** (in the 1st person) to express a tentative suggestion. **2** forming a conditional or indefinite clause. **3** expressing purpose = MAY, MIGHT^1.

shoulder ● *n.* **1** the joint where an arm, wing, or foreleg is attached to the body. **2** the upper foreleg and shoulder blade of a pig, lamb, etc. when butchered. **3** a strip of ground bordering a road. **4** a part of anything resembling a shoulder in form or function. ● *v.* **1** push with the shoulder; jostle. **2** take a burden etc. on one's shoulders. □ **shouldered** *adj.*

shoulder blade *n.* either of the large flat bones of the upper back.

shouldn't *contr.* should not.

shout ● *v.* cry out or speak loudly. ● *n.* a loud cry expressing joy etc. or calling attention. □ **shout down** reduce to silence by shouting. □ **shouter** *n.*

shove ● *v.* (**shoves, shoved, shoving**) **1** push vigorously. **2** *informal* put somewhere. ● *n.* an act of shoving or of prompting a person into action. □ **shove it** *slang* expressing contemptuous rejection or dismissal. **shove off 1** start from the shore in a boat. **2** leave.

shovel ● *n.* **1** a spade-like tool for shifting quantities of snow, earth, etc. **2** a machine having a similar form or function. **3** *Cdn* the wide flat part of a moose's antler. ● *v.* (**shovels, shovelled, shovelling**) **1** shift or clear snow etc. with or as if with a shovel. **2** *informal* move something in large quantities or roughly. □ **shovelful** *n.* (*pl.* **shovelfuls**) **shoveller** *n.*

show ● *v.* (**shows**; past **showed**; past participle **shown**; **showing**) **1** be or make visible. **2** exhibit or produce for viewing. **3** depict in art. **4** manifest. **5** prove. **6** treat with a specified quality. **7** demonstrate. **8** conduct or lead. **9** finish third or in the first three in a race. ● *n.* **1** a spectacle or display. **2** an esp. musical stage performance. **3** a radio or television program. **4** an event or competition involving the public display of animals, plants, or products. **5** *informal* an undertaking, project, or organization. **6** an outward display of a quality. **7** the third position, esp. in a horse race. □ **show around** act as a guide. **show cause** *Law* allege with justification. **show one's colours** make one's opinion clear. **show one's hand** (or **cards**) disclose one's plans. **show off 1** display to advantage. **2** ostentatiously display one's knowledge, talent, etc. **show oneself** be seen in public. **show up 1** make or be conspicuous or clearly visible. **2** expose a fraud, imposter, inferiority, etc. **3** appear; arrive. **4** embarrass or humiliate. □ **showing** *n.*

show and tell *n.* an elementary-school activity in which a student brings an object from home and describes it to his or her classmates.

showbiz *n. informal* = SHOW BUSINESS.

showboat ● *n.* **1** a river steamer on which theatrical performances are given. **2** *informal* a show-off. ● *v.* act pretentiously; show off.

show business *n.* the entertainment industry.

showcase ● *n.* **1** a glass case used for exhibiting goods etc. **2** a medium for presenting to general attention. ● *v.* (**showcases, showcased, showcasing**) exhibit or display.

showdown *n.* a final test or confrontation.

shower ● *n.* **1** a brief fall of esp. rain, snow, hail, etc. **2 a** a cubicle, bath, etc. in which one stands under a spray of water. **b** the act of washing oneself in a shower. **3** a brisk flurry of bullets, stones, sparks, etc. **4** a party for giving presents to a prospective bride, pregnant woman, etc. ● *v.* **1** discharge in a shower. **2** use a shower. **3** lavishly bestow. **4** descend or come in a shower.

showery *adj.* (of weather) characterized by frequent showers of rain.

showgirl *n.* an actress who sings and dances in musicals, variety shows, etc.

show home *n.* (also **show house**) = MODEL HOME.

show jumping *n.* the sport of riding horses over a course of fences and other obstacles. □ **show jumper** *n.*

showman *n.* (*pl.* **showmen**) **1** a person who presents an esp. theatrical show. **2** an entertainer who performs with panache and style. **3** a person skilled in self-promotion. □ **showmanship** *n.*

shown *past participle of* SHOW.

show-off *informal n.* a person who shows off. □ **show-offy** *adj.*

show of hands *n.* (*pl.* **shows of hands**) raised hands as a means of voting, showing interest, etc.

showpiece *n.* **1** an item presented for exhibition or display. **2** an outstanding specimen.

showplace *n.* a place to display something to its best advantage.

showroom *n.* a room in a factory etc. used to display goods for sale.

showstopper *n. informal* a strikingly impressive performance. □ **show-stopping** *adj.*

showtime *n.* the time at which a show is scheduled to begin.

show tune *n.* a popular tune from a musical.

showy *adj.* (**showier, showiest**) very bright or colourful and attracting much attention. □ **showily** *adv.* **showiness** *n.*

shrank *past of* SHRINK.

shrapnel *n.* fragments of a bomb etc. thrown out by an explosion. [*Say* SHRAP nul]

shred ● *n.* a scrap, fragment, or strip of cloth, paper, etc. ● *v.* (**shreds, shredded, shredding**) tear or cut into shreds.

shredder *n.* a machine used to shred objects, e.g. paper documents.

shrew *n.* **1** a mouselike mammal with a long pointed snout and tiny eyes. **2** a bad-tempered woman.

shrewd *adj.* having good judgment; astute. □ **shrewdly** *adv.* **shrewdness** *n.*

shriek ● *v.* utter a shrill screeching sound esp. in pain, terror or delight. ● *n.* a high-pitched piercing cry or sound. [*Say* SHREEK]

shrike *n.* a bird which impales small birds and insects on thorns.

shrill ● *adj.* piercing and high-pitched in sound. ● *v.* make a shrill noise. □ **shrillness** *n.* **shrilly** *adv.*

shrimp *n.* **1** (*pl.* **shrimp** or **shrimps**) a small edible shellfish. **2** *informal* a very small slight person.

shrine *n.* **1 a** a chapel, church, altar, etc., sacred to a saint, holy person, relic, etc. **b** a niche containing a holy statue etc. **2** a place associated with a particular person, event, etc. **3** a Shinto place of worship.

Shriner *n.* a member of the Order of Nobles of the Mystic Shrine, a charitable society founded in the US in 1872. [*Say* SHRINE er]

shrink ● *v.* (**shrinks**; *past* **shrank** or **shrunk**; *past participle* **shrunk**; **shrinking**) **1** make or become reduced in size or number. **2** (usu. foll. by *from, back*) recoil. **3** be averse from doing. ● *n. informal* a

psychiatrist. □ **shrinkable** *adj.*
shrinkage *n.*

shrinking violet *n. informal* a very shy person.

shrink wrap ● *n.* thin transparent plastic film shrunk tightly on to an article as packaging, protection, etc. ● *v.* (**shrink-wrap, shrink-wraps, shrink-wrapped, shrink-wrapping**) enclose in shrink wrap. □ **shrink-wrapped** *adj.*

shrivel *v.* (**shrivels, shrivelled, shrivelling**) contract or wither into a wrinkled, contorted, or dried-up state.

shroud ● *n.* **1** a sheet for wrapping a corpse for burial. **2** (in *pl.*) a set of ropes supporting the mast or topmast of a sailing ship. ● *v.* cover, conceal.

Shrove Tuesday *n.* the day before Ash Wednesday.

shrub *n.* a woody plant smaller than a tree and having a very short stem with low branches. □ **shrubby** *adj.*

shrubbery *n.* (*pl.* **shrubberies**) **1** an area planted with shrubs. **2** shrubs collectively.

shrug ● *v.* (**shrugs, shrugged, shrugging**) slightly and momentarily raise the shoulders to express indifference, helplessness, contempt, etc. ● *n.* an act of shrugging one's shoulders. □ **shrug off** dismiss as unimportant.

shrunk *past participle of* SHRINK.

shrunken *adj.* (esp. of a face, person, etc.) having grown smaller esp. because of age, illness, etc.

shtetl *n. hist.* a small Jewish town in eastern Europe. [*Say* SHTET'll *or* SHTAIT'll]

shtick *n. slang* an attention-getting or theatrical routine, gimmick, or talent.

shuck ● *n.* **1** a husk or pod, esp. of an ear of corn. **2** the shell of an oyster or clam. ● *v.* remove the shucks of. □ **shucker** *n.*

shucks *interj. informal* an expression of regret or self-deprecation in response to praise.

shudder ● *v.* **1** shiver esp. convulsively from fear, cold, repugnance, etc. **2** feel strong repugnance etc. **3** vibrate or quiver. ● *n.* an act of shuddering. □ **shudderingly** *adv.* **shuddery** *adj.*

shuffle ● *v.* (**shuffles, shuffled, shuffling**) **1** walk without lifting one's feet completely from the ground. **2 a** rearrange a pack of cards by sliding them over each other quickly. **b** rearrange. **3** assume or remove esp. clumsily or evasively. **4** restlessly shift one's position. ● *n.* **1** a shuffling movement. **2** an act of shuffling cards. **3** a general change of relative positions. **4** a dance performed with a quick brushing movement of the feet . □ **lost in the shuffle** overlooked in a crowd, confusion, etc. □ **shuffler** *n.*

shuffleboard *n.* a game in which competitors use a long-handled implement to push discs into numbered scoring sections.

shul *n.* **1** a synagogue. **2** a service at a synagogue. [*Say* SHOOL]

shun *v.* (**shuns, shunned, shunning**) avoid.

shunt ● *v.* **1** move a train from one set of tracks to another. **2** push aside or out of the way. **3** pass blood, fluid, etc. through a shunt. ● *n.* an alternative path for the flowing of an electrical current or blood etc.

shush ● *interj.* = HUSH *interj.* ● *v.* (**shushes, shushed, shushing**) **1** make or be silent. **2** move with the sound of a rush of air.

Shuswap *n.* (*pl.* **Shuswap** or **Shuswaps**) **1** a member of an Aboriginal people living in the Thompson River area of BC. **2** their Salishan language. □ **Shuswap** [*Say* SHOO swop]

shut *v.* (**shuts, shut, shutting**) **1** close. **2** (usu. foll. by *in, out*) keep in or out of a room etc. by shutting a door etc. □ **shut the door on** refuse to consider; make impossible. **shut down** stop from operating. **shut off** **1** stop the flow of by shutting a valve. **2** switch off. **shut out** **1** exclude from a place, situation, etc. **2** prevent the opposing team from scoring. **shut up** *informal* stop talking. **shut your face** (or **mouth** or **trap**)! *slang* stop talking.

shutdown *n.* **1** the closure of a factory etc. **2** the turning off of a machine, computer, etc.

shut-eye *n. informal* sleep.

shut-in *n.* a person who is confined indoors because of ill health.

shut-off *n.* a cessation of flow, supply, or activity.

shutout *n.* any game in which one side does not score.

shutter ● *n.* **1** an esp. hinged panel fixed beside a window for security or privacy or to keep the light in or out. **2** a device on a camera that opens to allow light to enter. ● *v.* **1** close the shutters of. **2** close a business etc. permanently. **3** provide with shutters.

shutterbug *n.* an enthusiastic photographer.

shutter speed *n.* the time for which a shutter on a camera is open.

shuttle ● *n.* **1** a bobbin with two pointed ends used for carrying the weft thread across between the warp threads in weaving. **2** a plane, bus, etc., going to and fro over a short route continuously. **3** = SPACE SHUTTLE. ● *v.* (**shuttles, shuttled, shuttling**) travel or transport back and forth between places.

shuttlecock *n.* a small piece of cork, rubber, etc. fitted with a ring of feathers, or a similar plastic object, used in badminton.

shy ● *adj.* (**shyer, shyest**) **1** timid. **2** reluctant. **3** (in *comb.*) showing fear of or distaste for. **4** (often foll. by *of*) *informal* short of a stated amount, measurement, etc. ● *v.* (**shies, shied, shying**) **1** (of a horse) suddenly turn aside in fright. **2** (usu. foll. by *away from*) avoid doing something due to nervousness or lack of confidence. □ **shyness** *n.*

shyster *n. informal* a person, esp. a lawyer, who uses unscrupulous methods. [*Say* SHICE ter]

SI *abbr.* Système International, the international system of units of measurement.

si *n. Music* = TI. [*Say* SEE]

Siamese *n.* (*pl.* **Siamese**) **1 a** a native of Siam (now Thailand). **b** the language of Siam. **2** (also **Siamese cat**) a breed of cream-coloured, short-haired cat, with brown ears, face, paws, and tail. □ **Siamese** *adj.* [*Say* sigh a MEEZ]

Siamese twins *pl. n.* = CONJOINED TWINS.

sib *n.* **1** esp. *Genetics* a sibling. **2** a blood relative.

Siberian *n.* a native of Siberia. □ **Siberian** *adj.* [*Say* sigh BEERY in]

Siberian husky *n.* a hardy breed of husky, originally from Siberia, with a stocky body and blue eyes.

Siberian tiger *n.* a very large tiger of SE Siberia and NE China.

sibilant ● *adj.* articulated with a hissing sound. ● *n.* a sibilant letter or sound, e.g. *s*. [*Say* SIBBLE int]

sibling *n.* a brother or sister.

sibyl *n.* any of the women in ancient times supposed to utter the oracles and prophecies of a god. [*Say* SIBBLE]

sic[1] *adv.* (usu. in brackets) used, spelled, etc., as written (placed after a quoted word that appears odd or erroneous). [*Say* SICK]

sic[2] *v.* (**sics, sicced, siccing**) **1** (esp. to a dog) attack a person or animal. **2** (usu. foll. by *on*) set (an animal) on another animal or person. [*Say* SICK]

Sicilian *n.* a person from Sicily. □ **Sicilian** *adj.* [*Say* si SILL yin]

sick[1] *adj.* **1** ill. **2** vomiting or tending to vomit. **3** mentally disturbed. **4** *informal* (of humour etc.) jeering at misfortune, illness,

death, etc. **5** (usu. foll. by *of*) disgusted by too much exposure to. □ **sick to one's stomach** vomiting or nauseous.

sick[2] *v.* = SIC[2].

sick bay *n.* part of a ship used as a hospital.

sickbed *n.* an invalid's bed.

sick day *n.* a usu. paid day off for a worker because of illness.

sicken *v.* **1** affect with or feel loathing, nausea, or disgust. **2** afflict with an illness. □ **sickening** *adj.*

sickle *n.* **1** a short-handled tool with a semicircular blade, used esp. for cutting grass, grain, etc. **2** (also **sickle bar**) the cutting mechanism of a combine, mower, etc., consisting of a heavy bar with many blades.

sick leave *n.* leave of absence granted because of illness.

sickle-cell anemia *n.* a severe hereditary form of anemia, with red blood cells distorted into a crescent shape.

sickly *adj.* (**sicklier, sickliest**) **1 a** of weak health; apt to be ill. **b** languid, faint, or pale, suggesting sickness. **2** causing ill health. **3** sentimental or mawkish. **4** inducing nausea.

sickness *n.* **1** the state of being ill. **2** a disease. **3** vomiting or a tendency to vomit.

sicko *n.* (*pl.* **sickos**) *slang* a mentally ill or perverted person.

side ● *n.* **1** a position to the left or right of an object, place, or central point. **2** either of the two halves of something. **3** an upright surface of a structure that is not the top, bottom, front, or back. **4** each of the flat surfaces of a solid object. **5** each of the lines forming the boundary of a plane rectilinear figure. **6** each of the two surfaces of something flat and thin. **7** (as an *adj.*) subsidiary or less important. **8** one person, team, etc. opposing another in a dispute or game. **9** a particular aspect. **10** a person's kinship or line of descent as traced through either their father or mother. ● *v.* (**sides, sided, siding**) share an opinion or stance, esp. in a particular dispute. □ **on the … side** fairly, somewhat. **on the side 1** in addition to one's regular work etc. **2** secretly or illicitly. **3** as a side dish. **take sides** favour or support one party in a dispute. □ **sided** *adj.*

sidearm *Baseball* ● *adj.* having to do with a pitch delivered with the arm swung to the side, parallel to the ground. ● *adv.* with the arm swung to the side.

side bacon *n. Cdn* bacon from the belly of a pig, having alternate strips of fat and lean.

sidebar *n.* a short, usu. boxed, article in a newspaper etc. placed alongside a main article and containing additional information.

sideboard *n.* a piece of dining-room furniture used to store dishes, cutlery, table linen, etc.

sideburns *pl. n.* hair grown by a man down the sides of his face in front of the ears.

sidecar *n.* a small usu. open car attached to the side of a motorcycle, for one or more passengers.

side dish *n.* an extra dish accompanying the main course.

side effect *n.* **1** *Medical* a usu. adverse reaction caused by a drug in addition to the intended effect. **2** an unintended secondary result.

sidekick *n. informal* a close, often subordinate companion.

sidelight *n.* **1** a light coming from the side. **2** a piece of incidental information on a subject. **3** a window by the side of a door or other window. □ **sidelighting** *n.*

sideline ● *n.* **1** an activity pursued as a secondary job, hobby, etc. **2** *Sport* a line along the side of the playing surface marking the area that is in bounds. ● *v.* (**sidelines**, **sidelined**, **sidelining**) **1** remove a player from a game, esp. through injury or a suspension. **2** remove from action or consideration etc. □ **on** (or **from**) **the sidelines** in (or from) a position removed from the main action.

sidelock *n.* a long curly lock of hair falling from the side of the head down along the cheek, worn esp. by Orthodox Jews.

sidelong *adj. & adv.* sideways.

sideman *n.* (*pl.* **sidemen**) a supporting musician in a band.

side order *n.* a separate serving of food supplementing a restaurant meal.

sidereal *adj.* of or concerning the constellations or stars. [*Say* sigh DEERY ul]

side ribs *pl. n.* Cdn a cut of pork from the belly including the ribs and adhering meat.

sidesaddle *adv.* riding with both legs on the same side of the horse.

sideshow *n.* a minor show or attraction in an exhibition or circus.

sideslip ● *n.* a sideways movement of a ski, wheeled vehicle, airplane, etc. ● *v.* (**sideslips**, **sideslipped**, **sideslipping**) move sideways.

sidesplit *n.* Cdn a house with floors raised half a level on one side.

sidestep *v.* (**sidesteps**, **sidestepped**, **sidestepping**) evade or dodge; refuse to address or confront.

side street *n.* a minor street.

side stroke *n.* a swimming stroke in which the swimmer lies on his or her side, drawing the arms through the water in opposite directions from the chest while kicking.

side-swipe ● *n.* **1** a passing jibe or verbal attack. **2** a glancing blow along the side of esp. a vehicle. ● *v.* (**side-swipes**, **side-swiped**, **side-swiping**) **1** strike a glancing blow on the side of a vehicle in passing. **2** attack indirectly.

sidetrack *v.* **1** distract from an objective, issue, topic, etc. **2** divert a plan etc. from its intended purpose.

sidewalk *n.* a paved pedestrian walkway along a street.

sideways ● *adv.* **1** to or from a side. **2** with one side facing forward. ● *adj.* to or from a side.

sidewinder *n.* a desert rattlesnake which moves with a side-to-side slithering motion.

siding *n.* **1** material used to cover the outside of a building. **2** a short length of railway track connected to an adjacent line for storing trains and enabling trains on the same line to pass each other.

sidle *v.* (**sidles**, **sidled**, **sidling**) walk in a sly, sneaky, or timid manner. [*Say* SIDE 'll]

SIDS *n.* = SUDDEN INFANT DEATH SYNDROME. [*Say* SIDZ]

siege *n.* **1** an operation in which an army etc. attempts to force the surrender of a fortified place by surrounding it and cutting off supplies. **2** a prolonged and determined attack. [*Say* SEEDGE *or* SEEZH]

siemens *n.* the SI unit of conductance, equal to one reciprocal ohm. Abbreviation: **S**. [*Say* SEE mins]

sienna *n.* a kind of iron-rich earth used as a pigment in painting, naturally yellowish brown but reddish brown when roasted (**burnt sienna**). [*Say* see ENNA]

sierra *n.* (*pl.* **sierras**) a long jagged mountain chain. [*Say* see ERRA]

siesta *n.* (*pl.* **siestas**) an afternoon nap or rest, esp. in a warm country. [*Say* see ESTA]

sieur *n. hist.* a title for a seigneur in New France. [*Say* SYER]

sieve *n.* a meshed or perforated surface enclosed in a frame, used to separate coarse particles from finer ones or from a liquid. [*Say* SIV]

sift *v.* **1** pass through a sieve or sifter. **2** (usu. foll. by *out, from*) remove selectively.

3 subject to a close or thorough examination, esp. as part of a selection process.

sifter *n.* a container with a meshed or perforated top or bottom for sprinkling dry ingredients onto a surface.

sigh ● *v.* emit a long deep audible breath as an expression of sadness, weariness, longing, relief, etc. ● *n.* a long and audible exhalation expressing sadness, weariness, etc.

sight ● *n.* **1** the ability to see. **2 a** a thing seen. **b** *informal* a person or thing having a ridiculous, repulsive, or dishevelled appearance. **3** (usu. in *pl.*) the noteworthy features of a city etc. **4** a range of space within which a person etc. can see. **5** a view of something. **6** (also in *pl.*) a device on a gun or surveying instrument used to make one's aim or observation more precise. ● *v.* **1** observe, notice, or glimpse. **2** watch or locate an object, target, etc., esp. by viewing it through a sight. □ **lower one's sights** become less ambitious. **out of sight, out of mind** it is easy to forget what is absent. **set one's sights on** strive for. **sight for sore eyes** a welcome person or thing.

sighted *adj.* **1** capable of seeing; not blind. **2** (in *comb.*) having a specified kind of sight. □ **sightedness** *n.* (in sense 2)

sight gag *n.* a humorous effect produced by a visual action etc. as opposed to something verbal.

sighting *n.* **1** an occasion when something esp. unusual or fleeting is seen. **2** the act of adjusting the aim or sights of a gun etc.

sightline *n.* a line of vision extending from a person's eye to what is seen, esp. in a theatre or stadium.

sight-read *v.* (**sight-reads**, **sight-read**, **sight-reading**) play or sing music from a score one has not seen before. □ **sight-reading** *n.*

sightseeing *n.* the action of visiting places of interest. □ **sightseer** *n.*

sight unseen *adv.* without a chance to look at or inspect a purchase etc. beforehand.

sign ● *n.* **1** a thing indicating the presence, occurrence, or advent of something else. **2** a notice or signal conveying information or an instruction. **3** a symbol or word used to represent something in algebra, music, or other subjects. **4** *Astrology* each of the twelve equal sections into which the zodiac is divided. ● *v.* **1** write one's name for the purposes of identification or authorization. **2** hire or be hired by signing a contract. **3** use gestures to convey information or instructions. □ **sign in** sign

a register upon arrival. **sign off** say or write one's name to mark the end of a letter, broadcast, etc. **sign off on** approve; give one's approval to. **sign on 1** agree to a contract, employment, etc. **2** begin work, broadcasting, etc., esp. by writing or announcing one's name. **sign over** (or **away**) surrender (one's right, property, etc.) by signing a document etc. **sign out 1** sign a register upon leaving. **2** borrow (a book from a library). **sign up 1** hire. **2** enlist in the armed forces. **3** enrol.

signage *n.* signs collectively, esp. those used commercially.

signal ● *n.* **1** a sound, device, or gesture used to convey warning, direction, or information. **2** a modulated electric current or electromagnetic wave, conveying information. **3** an immediate occasion or cause of action. ● *v.* (**signals**, **signalled**, **signalling**) **1** make a signal. **2** be a sign or indication of. ● *adj.* noteworthy, striking. □ **signally** *adv.*

signalman *n.* (*pl.* **signalmen**) a person employed to transmit and receive signals, e.g. with a railway.

signatory *n.* (*pl.* **signatories**) a person, party, or country that has signed a deal, contract, treaty, etc. [*Say* nuh tory]

signature *n.* **1** a person's name, initials, or distinctive mark used in signing a letter, document, etc. **2** (also as an *adj.*) a distinctive or identifying feature or characteristic. **3** *Music* **a** = KEY SIGNATURE. **b** = TIME SIGNATURE.

signboard *n.* **1** a board displaying the name or logo of a business. **2** a board mounted on a signpost indicating directions.

signee *n.* a person who has signed a contract, register, etc. [*Say* sigh NEE]

signet *n.* **1** a small seal, usu. set in a ring, used to authenticate a document. **2** the impression of a seal. [*Say* SIG nit]

significance *n.* **1** consequence, importance. **2** a concealed or real meaning. **3** the state of being significant.

significant *adj.* **1** of great importance or consequence. **2** having information that may be gathered. **3** noteworthy. □ **significantly** *adv.*

significant other *n.* a spouse, partner, or lover.

signification *n.* **1** the act of signifying. **2** the implication, sense, or meaning.

signifier *n.* a thing that signifies or conveys meaning.

signify *v.* (**signifies**, **signified**, **signifying**) **1** be a sign or symbol of; represent, denote. **2** mean. **3** be of importance; matter.

signing *n.* **1** the action of writing one's signature on a document or contract. **2** sign language. **3** a session of signing autographs.

sign language *n.* a system of communication by visual gestures, used esp. by the hearing impaired.

sign-off *n.* the ending of a letter or broadcast etc.

sign of the cross *n.* a Christian sign made in blessing or prayer, by tracing a cross with the hand.

sign of the times *n.* an incident, event, person, etc. that typifies or foreshadows a social trend.

signpost ● *n.* a post with a sign giving directions or information. ● *v.* provide with or as with a signpost or signposts.

Sikh *n.* a member of a Punjabi religion combining Hindu and Islamic elements and based on belief in one god. □ **Sikh** *adj.* **Sikhism** *n.* [*Say* SEEK, SEEK ism]

Siksika *n.* (*pl.* **Siksika** or **Siksikas**) **1** a member of a Blackfoot people living in central Alberta. **2** their language. □ **Siksika** *adj.* [*Say* sick SICKA]

silage *n.* grass or other fodder, not dried but compacted and stored in a silo, used as animal feed. [*Say* SIGH lidge]

silence ● *n.* **1** absence of sound, noise, or speech. **2** the avoidance of discussing a particular topic or thing. ● *v.* (**silences, silenced, silencing**) **1** make quiet or silent. **2** defy critics by successfully defending one's position. **3** prevent a person from freely expressing an opinion.

silencer *n.* a device used to reduce the sound of a gun.

silent *adj.* **1** characterized by an absence of sound or noise. **2** not talking. **3** taciturn; speaking little. **4** omitting mention of a particular subject. **5** not having a recorded soundtrack or audible dialogue. **6** producing no detectable signs or symptoms. **7** written but not pronounced, like *b* in doubt. □ **silently** *adv.*

silent auction *n.* an auction in which bids are submitted in writing.

silhouette *n.* **1** a representation of a thing showing the outline only, usu. done in solid black against a contrasting background. **2** the dark shadow or outline of a person or thing. [*Say* silla WET]

silhouetted *adj.* shown in silhouette.

silica *n.* a hard mineral substance occurring naturally as flint, opal, or quartz, etc., used in the manufacture of glass and ceramics. □ **siliceous** *adj.* [*Say* SILLA kuh, suh LISH us]

silicate *n.* any compound of one or more

metals with silicon and oxygen, including mica, feldspar, etc. [*Say* SILLA kit]

silicon *n.* a non-metallic element used in electronic components for its semiconducting properties. [*Say* SILLA con]

silicon chip *n.* a silicon microchip.

silicone *n.* any of the many polymeric organic compounds of silicon and oxygen used as electrical insulators, waterproofing agents, etc. [*Say* SILLA cone]

silk *n.* **1** a fine lustrous strong fibre produced by silkworms in making cocoons. **2** a similar fibre spun by some spiders. **3** thread or cloth made from silk fibre or resembling this. **4** (in *pl.*) a jockey's cap and jacket bearing the colours of the horse's owner. **5** the long silky hairs forming in a tuft on an ear of corn.

silken *adj.* made of or resembling silk.

silkscreen *n.* **1** the process of screen-printing. **2** a print made by this process.

silkworm *n.* the caterpillar which spins a silk cocoon that is processed to yield silk fibre.

silky *adj.* (**silkier, silkiest**) **1** like silk in smoothness, softness, fineness, or lustre. **2** suave, smooth.

sill *n.* **1** a strong horizontal beam forming the base or foundation of esp. a house. **2** the bottom part of a window or door frame.

silly *adj.* (**sillier, silliest**) **1** displaying a lack of judgment or common sense. **2** ridiculous. **3** stupefied. □ **silliness** *n.*

silo *n.* (*pl.* **silos**) **1** a tall cylinder or pit in which green corn or hay etc. is pressed and kept for fodder, undergoing fermentation. **2** a pit or tower for the storage of grain etc. **3** an underground chamber in which a missile is kept ready for firing. [*Say* SIGH lo]

silt ● *n.* fine sand, clay, or other soil carried by moving water and deposited as sediment on the bottom or on the shore of a body of water. ● *v.* (often foll. by *up*) fill or clog with silt. □ **siltation** *n.* **silty** *adj.*

Silurian *n.* the third period of the Paleozoic era, lasting from about 438 to 408 million years BP. □ **Silurian** *adj.* [*Say* suh LOORY in]

silver ● *n.* **1** a greyish-white precious metal. **2** the colour of silver. **3** coins collectively; change. **4** utensils and vessels made of or plated with silver. **5** any household cutlery. **6** (also **silver medal**) a medal of silver awarded as second prize. ● *adj.* **1** made wholly or chiefly of silver. **2** coloured like silver. **3** designating the twenty-fifth appearance of an annual

event. ● v. coat or plate with silver.
□ **silvery** adj.

silver bullet n. informal a cure-all or universal remedy.

silverfish n. (pl. **silverfish** or **silverfishes**) **1** a small silvery wingless insect. **2** a silver-coloured fish.

silver fox n. a red fox at a time when its fur is black with white tips.

silver-grey n. & adj. a pale or lustrous grey.

silver lining n. a consolation in misfortune.

silver plate n. **1** vessels or utensils made of or plated with silver. **2** the material of which these are made. □ **silver-plated** adj.

silver screen n. the movie industry; motion pictures collectively.

silversmith n. a manufacturer of silver articles.

silverware n. tableware made or coated with silver, stainless steel, etc.

silviculture n. the branch of forestry concerned with the growing and cultivation of trees. □ **silvicultural** adj. **silviculturist** n. [Say SILVA culture]

sim n. simulation.

simcha n. (pl. **simchas**) a Jewish party or celebration. [Say SIM chuh or SIM kuh]

simian ● adj. of or like apes and monkeys. ● n. an ape or monkey. [Say SIMMY in]

similar adj. **1** of the same nature or kind; alike. **2** (foll. by to) resembling. **3** (of two geometrical figures etc.) containing the same angles. □ **similarly** adv.

similarity n. (pl. **similarities**) **1** the state or fact of being similar. **2** a point of resemblance.

simile n. a figure of speech involving an explicit comparison using the words "like" or "as", e.g. as brave as a lion. [Say SIMMA lee]

similitude n. similarity or resemblance. [Say suh MILLA tood or suh MILLA tyood]

simmer ● v. **1** cook at or just below the boiling point. **2** be in a state of suppressed anger or excitement. ● n. a simmering condition. □ **simmer down** become calm or less agitated.

simper ● v. smile in a silly or affected way. ● n. such a smile.

simple adj. **1** easily understood or done. **2** not complicated or elaborate. **3 a** consisting of or involving only one element, part, or operation. **b** (of a tense) formed without an auxiliary verb. **4** unqualified. **5** foolish or ignorant. **6** plain in appearance or manner. **7** not of high social standing.

simpleton n. a foolish, gullible, or halfwitted person.

simplex adj. simple; not compounded.

simplicity n. the fact or condition of being simple. □ **be simplicity itself** be extremely easy.

simplify v. (**simplifies**, **simplified**, **simplifying**) make simple. □ **simplification** n.

simplistic adj. **1** excessively or affectedly simple. **2** oversimplified so as to conceal difficulties. □ **simplistically** adv.

simply adv. **1** in a simple manner. **2** absolutely; without doubt. **3** merely.

simulate v. (**simulates**, **simulated**, **simulating**) **1** pretend to have or feel. **2** imitate or counterfeit. **3 a** imitate the conditions of a situation, e.g. for training or amusement. **b** produce a computer model of a process. □ **simulated** adj. **simulation** n. **simulator** n.

simulcast ● n. **1** a simultaneous broadcast on radio and television or in two or more languages etc. **2** a live transmission of a sports event for usu. off-track betting purposes. ● v. (**simulcasts**, **simulcast**, **simulcasting**) broadcast as a simulcast. □ **simulcasting** n. [Say SIGH mul kast or SIMMLE cast]

simultaneous adj. occurring or operating at the same time. □ **simultaneity** n. **simultaneously** adv. [Say sigh mul TAY nee us or simmle TAY nee us; sigh mul tuh NAY uh tee or simmle tuh NAY uh tee]

SIN abbr. Cdn SOCIAL INSURANCE NUMBER. [Say SIN]

sin¹ ● n. **1** the breaking of divine or moral law, esp. by a conscious act. **2** an action regarded as a serious offence or fault. ● v. (**sins**, **sinned**, **sinning**) **1** commit a sin. **2** (foll. by against) offend. □ **cover** (or **hide** etc.) **a multitude of sins** conceal the real, usu. unpleasant, facts or situation. **do** (or **be**) **something for one's sins** jocular do (or be) something as a supposed punishment for something. **live in sin** jocular live together in a sexual relationship without being married.

sin² abbr. sine. [Say SINE]

sin bin n. informal Hockey the penalty box.

since ● prep. in the period between a past time and the present. ● conj. **1** during or in the time after. **2** because. ● adv. **1** from that time until now or the time being considered. **2** ago, before now.

sincere adj. (**more sincere**, **sincerest**) **1** free from pretense or deceit. **2** genuine, honest, frank. □ **sincerely** adv. **sincerity** n. [Say sin SEER, sin SERRA tee]

sine n. the trigonometric function that is equal to the ratio of the side opposite a given angle (in a right-angled triangle) to the hypotenuse.

sinecure n. a position that requires little or no work but usu. yields profit or honour. [Say SINNA cure]

sine qua non n. an indispensable condition or qualification. [Say sin ay kwah NON]

sinew n. **1** a tendon. **2** (in pl.) muscles; bodily strength. **3** (in pl.) something providing strength to an organization etc. □**sinewy** adj. [Say SIN you]

sinful adj. **1** committing sin, esp. habitually. **2** (of an act) involving or characterized by sin. **3** informal self-indulgently delicious. □**sinfully** adv. **sinfulness** n.

sing v. (**sings**; past **sang**; past participle **sung**; **singing**) **1** utter musical sounds with the voice. **2** (of the wind, a kettle, etc.) make melodious, humming, buzzing, or whistling sounds. **3** slang turn informer; confess. □**singable** adj. **singer** n. **singing** n. & adj.

singalong n. an informal occasion when a group of people sing together.

Singaporean ● adj. of or relating to Singapore. ● n. a person from Singapore. [Say sing a PORRY in]

singe ● v. (**singes**, **singed**, **singeing**) burn superficially or lightly. ● n. a superficial burn.

single ● adj. **1** one only. **2** united or undivided. **3** designed or suitable for one person. **4** regarded separately. **5** not married; not involved in a romantic or sexual relationship. **6** even one. ● n. **1** a single thing, or item in a series. **2** a record, compact disc, etc., containing only one or two songs. **3** Baseball a one-base hit. **4** (usu. in plural) a game with one player on each side. **5** an unmarried person. ● v. (**singles**, **singled**, **singling**) **1** select from a group as worthy of special attention, praise, etc. **2** Baseball hit a single. □**singleness** n. **singly** adv.

single-breasted adj. (of a coat etc.) having only one set of buttons and buttonholes.

single file ● n. a line of people or things arranged one behind another. ● adv. one behind another.

single-handed ● adv. without help from another. ● adj. done etc. single-handed. □**single-handedly** adv.

single-minded adj. having or intent on only one purpose. □**single-mindedly** adv. **single-mindedness** n.

single parent n. a person bringing up a child or children without a partner. □**single parenthood** n.

single point n. Cdn Football = ROUGE n. 3.

single space v. lay out or print text on consecutive lines. □**single-spaced** adj.

singleton n. a single or only person or thing.

singsong ● adj. characterized by or uttered with a rising and falling rhythm, cadence, or intonation. ● n. **1** a singsong manner. **2** a singalong. □**singsongy** adj.

singular ● adj. **1** exceptionally good or great. **2** eccentric or strange. **3** (of a word or form) referring to a single person or thing. ● n. Grammar a singular word or form. □**singularly** adv.

singularity n. (pl. **singularities**) **1** the state or condition of being singular. **2** an odd trait or peculiarity. [Say sing gyoo LERRA tee]

Sinhalese n. (pl. **Sinhalese**) **1** a member of a people forming the majority of the population of Sri Lanka. **2** their language. □**Sinhalese** adj. [Say sin huh LEEZ or sinna LEEZ]

sinister adj. **1** suggestive of evil. **2** wicked or criminal. □**sinisterly** adv.

sink ● v. (**sinks**; past **sank** or sometimes **sunk**; past participle **sunk**; **sinking**) **1** go or send down below the surface of a liquid. **2** lower oneself or drop down. **3** insert beneath a surface. **4** cause something sharp to penetrate a surface. **5** gradually decrease or decline in amount or intensity. **6** fall into a particular condition. **7** (foll. by in, into) put money or energy into. **8** cause a ball to enter a pocket, a hole, a basket, etc. ● n. **1** a fixed basin with a water supply and outflow pipe. **2** a body or process by which energy or a component is removed from a system. □**sink in 1** penetrate; be absorbed. **2** become gradually comprehensible. **sink one's teeth into** take up (a challenge, cause, etc.) fervently or energetically. **sink or swim** fail totally or survive by one's own efforts. □**sinkable** adj.

sinker n. **1** a person or thing which sinks. **2** a weight used to sink a fishing line etc. **3** (also **sinkerball**) Baseball a pitch in which the ball drops markedly.

sinkhole n. **1 a** a large depression in the ground, e.g. resulting from the collapse of a subterranean cave. **b** a cavity into which a stream etc. disappears. **2** informal a place of vice or corruption. **3** informal an enterprise etc. which swallows all invested money to no effect.

sinless adj. free from sin. □**sinlessness** n.

sinner n. a person who sins, esp. habitually.

Sino- comb. form Chinese; Chinese and. [Say SINE oh]

sinuous *adj.* **1** with many curves. **2** moving in a smooth, flowing way. □ **sinuously** *adv.* [Say SIN you us]

sinus *n.* (*pl.* **sinuses**) a cavity of bone or tissue, esp. in the skull connecting with the nostrils. [Say SIGH nus]

Sion = ZION. [Say SIGH un]

Siouan *n.* an Aboriginal language family including Dakota, Assiniboine, Sioux, and Omaha. □ **Siouan** *adj.* [Say SOO in]

Sioux *n.* (*pl.* **Sioux**) **1** a member of a group of Aboriginal peoples chiefly inhabiting the upper Mississippi and Missouri river basins. **2** their language. □ **Sioux** *adj.* [Say SOO]

sip ● *v.* (**sips**, **sipped**, **sipping**) drink in one or more small amounts. ● *n.* **1** a small mouthful of liquid. **2** the act of taking this.

siphon ● *n.* a tube used for conveying liquid up from the surface level of one container and then down to a lower one. ● *v.* (often foll. by *off*) **1** conduct or flow through a siphon. **2** divert or set aside funds etc. [Say SIFE in]

sir *n.* **1** a polite, respectful, or formal form of address to a man. **2** (**Sir**) a titular prefix to the first name of a knight or baronet.

sire ● *n.* **1** the male parent of a domestic quadruped. **2** *archaic* a respectful form of address to a king. ● *v.* (**sires**, **sired**, **siring**) (of a domestic quadruped) be the father of.

siree *interj.* (also **sirree**) *informal* as an emphatic, esp. after *yes* or *no*. [Say sir EE]

siren *n.* **1** a device for making a loud prolonged signal or warning sound. **2** (in Greek mythology) a woman or winged creature whose singing lured sailors onto rocks. **3** a sweet singer. **4** a dangerously fascinating woman. ● *adj.* irresistibly tempting.

sirloin *n.* the choicer part of a loin of beef.

sis *n.* *informal* a sister.

sisal *n.* **1** a Mexican plant with large fleshy leaves, cultivated for fibre production. **2** the fibre made from this, used esp. for making rope. [Say SICE 'll]

siskin *n.* any of various small streaked yellowish-green finches.

sissy *informal* ● *n.* (*pl.* **sissies**) an effeminate or cowardly person. ● *adj.* effeminate; cowardly. □ **sissified** *adj.*

sister *n.* **1** a woman or girl in relation to other children of her parents. **2 a** a close female friend or associate. **b** a female fellow member of a trade union, the human race, etc. **3** a member of a female religious order. **4** (as an *adj.*) of the same type or design or origin etc. □ **sisterly** *adj. & adv.*

sisterhood *n.* **1** the relationship between sisters. **2** a group of women linked by a shared interest or belief. **3** community of feeling and mutual support between women.

sister-in-law *n.* (*pl.* **sisters-in-law**) **1** the sister of one's spouse. **2** the wife of one's brother or brother-in-law.

sit *v.* (**sits**, **sat**, **sitting**) **1** rest with one's weight supported by one's buttocks and one's back upright. **2** be or remain in a particular position or state. **3** (of a parliament, committee, court, etc.) be engaged in its business. **4** serve as a member of a council, jury, etc. **5** have enough seats for. **6** pose for an artist or photographer. **7** *Sport* be prevented from participating because of poor play, a suspension, etc. □ **be sitting pretty** be comfortably or advantageously placed. **sit around** sit doing nothing, esp. while waiting. **sit back** relax one's efforts. **sit in** **1** (foll. by *for*) take the place of. **2** (foll. by *on*) be present as an observer at. **sit on 1** be a member of. **2** *informal* delay action about. **sit out** take no part in (a dance, sports match, etc.). **sit tight** *informal* hold back from taking action. **sit up 1** rise from a lying to a sitting position. **2** sit firmly upright. **3** stay awake later than usual, esp. while waiting for someone. **sit well** (often foll. by *with*; usu. in *neg.*) be acceptable or not disturbing to.

sitar *n.* a long-necked Indian guitar-like instrument with movable frets. [Say si TAR *or* SIT ar]

sitcom *n.* *informal* a situation comedy.

sit-down ● *adj.* **1** designating a meal eaten sitting at a table. **2** designating a protest in which demonstrators occupy their workplace or sit down on the ground in a public place. ● *n.* a sit-down protest etc.

site ● *n.* **1** the ground chosen or used for a town or building. **2** a place where some activity is conducted. **3** a single source for files, services, etc. on the Internet. ● *v.* (**sites**, **sited**, **siting**) **1** locate or place. **2** provide with a site.

sit-in *n.* a protest, strike, demonstration, etc. in which people occupy a workplace, public building, etc.

Sitka *n.* (*pl.* **Sitkas**) a fast-growing spruce widely cultivated for its timber. [Say SIT kuh]

sitter *n.* **1** a person who sits, esp. for a portrait. **2 a** a babysitter. **b** (esp. in *comb.*) a person who takes care of a house, pet, etc. while the owners are away.

sitting ● *n.* **1** a continuous period of being seated. **2** a session in which a meal is served. **3** a period during which a law court, legislature, etc. is engaged in business. ● *adj.* **1** having sat down. **2** (of a legislator) currently holding office.

sitting duck *n.* (also **sitting target**) *informal* something very easy to attack.

sitting room *n.* a room in a house for relaxed sitting in.

situate *v.* (**situates, situated, situating**) **1** put in a certain position or circumstances. **2** put in a context.

situation *n.* **1** a place and its surroundings. **2** a set of circumstances. **3** an employee's position or job. □ **situational** *adj.*

situation comedy *n.* a TV comedy in which the characters are involved in amusing situations.

sit-up *n.* an exercise in which a person lying on the back lifts the torso to a sitting position.

SIU *abbr.* SPECIAL INVESTIGATIONS UNIT.

six *card. num.* (*pl.* **sixes**) one more than five. □ **at sixes and sevens** in confusion or disagreement. **six of one and half a dozen of the other** a situation of little real difference between alternatives. □ **sixfold** *adj. & adv.*

Six Nations *n.* the Iroquois confederacy after the Tuscarora joined in 1722.

six-pack *n.* a pack of six identical items, esp. cans or bottles of beer.

six-shooter *n.* (also **six-gun**) a revolver with six chambers.

sixteen *card. num.* one more than fifteen. □ **sixteenth** *ord. num.*

sixteenth note *n. Music* a note having the time value of half an eighth note and represented by a large dot with a two-hooked stem.

sixth *ord. num.* **1** constituting number six in a sequence. **2** each of six equal parts of a thing. **3** an interval spanning six consecutive notes in a diatonic scale. □ **sixthly** *adv.*

sixth sense *n.* a supposed faculty giving intuitive or extrasensory knowledge.

sixty *card. num.* (*pl.* **sixties**) **1** ten less than seventy. **2** (**Sixty**) *Cdn* the parallel of latitude 60° north, dividing the western provinces from the territories. □ **sixtieth** *ord. num.*

sizable *adj.* (also **sizeable**) fairly large. □ **sizably** *adv.*

size¹ ● *n.* **1** the relative bigness or extent of a thing. **2** each of the classes into which articles, esp. garments, are divided according to size. ● *v.* (**sizes, sized, sizing**) sort according to size. □ **of a size** having the same size. **the size of it** *informal* a true account of the matter. **size**

up 1 estimate the size of. **2** *informal* form a judgment of. □ **sized** *adj.*

size² ● *n.* a gelatinous solution used in glazing paper, stiffening textiles, etc. ● *v.* (**sizes, sized, sizing**) glaze or stiffen with size.

sizzle ● *v.* (**sizzles, sizzled, sizzling**) **1 a** make a sputtering or hissing sound when or as if frying. **b** fry or burn. **2** *informal* be in a state of great excitement. ● *n.* **1** a sizzling sound. **2** *informal* intense excitement. □ **sizzler** *n.* **sizzling** *adj. & adv.*

SK *abbr.* Saskatchewan (in official postal use).

ska *n.* a style of popular music of Jamaican origin, with a fast tempo and strongly accentuated offbeat.

skank¹ ● *n.* a dance performed to reggae music, characterized by rhythmically bending forward, raising the knees, and extending the hands palms downwards. ● *v.* play reggae music or dance in this style.

skank² *n. slang* a person, esp. a woman, regarded as not attractive, sleazy, sexually promiscuous, or immoral.

skanky *adj. slang* disgusting and not attractive, esp. because dirty.

skate¹ ● *n.* **1** a boot with a steel blade for gliding on ice. **2** a roller skate or in-line skate. **3** a period of skating. ● *v.* (**skates, skated, skating**) **1** move on or as if on skates. **2** (foll. by *around, over*) refer fleetingly to, disregard. **3** skateboard. □ **hang up one's skates** *Cdn* retire from professional life. □ **skating** *n.*

skate² *n.* (*pl.* **skate** or **skates**) a large marine fish of the ray family, with a roughly diamond-shaped body and a long thin tail.

skate-a-thon *n.* esp. *Cdn* a prolonged period of skating as a fundraiser.

skateboard ● *n.* a short narrow board mounted on wheels, for riding on while standing. ● *v.* ride on a skateboard. □ **skateboarder** *n.* **skateboarding** *n.*

skate park *n.* an area designated and equipped for skateboarding.

skater *n.* **1** a person who skates. **2** *Hockey* a player other than the goalie. **3** a skateboarder.

skating rink *n.* **1** an area of ice for skating. **2** a building containing a rink for skating.

skedaddle *v. informal* (**skedaddles, skedaddled, skedaddling**) run away, depart quickly, flee. [*Say* skuh DADDLE]

skeet *n.* (also **skeet shooting**) a shooting sport in which a clay target is thrown from a trap to simulate the flight of a bird.

skeeter n. slang a mosquito.

skein n. a loosely coiled bundle of yarn or thread. [Say SKANE]

skeletal adj. **1** of, forming, or resembling a skeleton. **2** very thin, emaciated. **3** consisting of only a bare minimum.

skeleton n. **1** a hard internal or external framework of bones, cartilage, shell, etc., supporting or containing the body of an animal. **2** the supporting framework or structure of a thing. **3** a very thin or emaciated person or animal. **4** an outline sketch. **5** (as an adj.) having only the minimum number of persons, parts, etc.

skeleton in the closet n. a discreditable fact kept secret.

skeptic n. a person who doubts the validity of accepted beliefs in a particular subject. □ **skeptical** adj. **skeptically** adv. **skepticism** n.

sketch ● n. (pl. **sketches**) **1** a rough, merely outlined, or unfinished drawing or painting. **2** a brief account without many details. **3** an item in a comedy program. ● v. (**sketches, sketched, sketching**) **1** make or give a sketch of. **2** draw sketches. **3** (often foll. by in, out) indicate briefly or in outline.

sketchbook n. (also **sketch pad**) a book or pad of drawing paper for doing sketches on.

sketchy adj. (**sketchier, sketchiest**) not complete or thoroughly detailed. □ **sketchily** adv. **sketchiness** n.

skew v. **1** make biased or distorted. **2** make crooked or set at an angle. [Say SKYOO]

skewer ● n. **1** a long pin for holding meat, vegetables, etc. compactly together while cooking. **2** any similar pin for securing something in place. ● v. **1** fasten together or pierce with a skewer. **2** criticize sharply. [Say SKYOO er]

ski ● n. (pl. **skis**) **1** each of a pair of long narrow pieces of wood or plastic etc. fastened under the feet for travelling over snow. **2** a similar device under a vehicle or aircraft. **3** = WATER SKI. ● v. (**skis, skied, skiing**) travel on skis. □ **skiable** adj.

ski bum n. slang an avid skier.

skid ● v. (**skids, skidded, skidding**) **1** (of a vehicle etc.) slide on slippery ground, esp. sideways or obliquely. **2** slip, slide. **3** informal decline or deteriorate. **4** slide or haul logs. ● n. **1** an act of skidding or sliding. **2** a pallet or portable platform for transporting and storing goods. **3** a runner beneath an aircraft for use when landing on snow or grass. **4** Sport informal a losing streak. □ **on the skids** in a steadily worsening state. □ **skidding** n.

skidder n. a powerful four-wheel tractor used to haul logs from a cutting area.

Ski-Doo ● n. proprietary a snowmobile. ● v. (**skidoo, skidoos, skidooed, skidooing**) **1** ride on a snowmobile. **2** slang go away; depart. □ **skidooer** n. **skidooing** n.

skid row n. a part of a town or city frequented by vagrants etc.

skier n. a person who skis.

skiff n. **1** any of various types of small light boat. **2** a light dusting of snow.

skiing n. the activity of moving on skis.

ski jump n. **1** a steep ramp levelling off at the end to allow a skier to leap through the air. **2** a jump executed from this. □ **ski jumper** n. **ski jumping** n.

skilful adj. (also **skillful**) having or showing skill. □ **skilfully** adv. **skilfulness** n.

ski lift n. a device for carrying skiers up a slope.

skill n. **1** (often foll. by in) expertness or practised ability in an action. **2** (usu. in pl.) a specific aptitude.

skilled adj. **1** having or showing skill. **2** highly trained or experienced. **3** (of work) requiring skill or special training.

skillet n. a frying pan.

skim ● v. (**skims, skimmed, skimming**) **1** take a floating layer from the surface of a liquid. **2 a** keep touching lightly or nearly touching a surface in passing over. **b** (or foll. by over) deal with a subject superficially. **3** (often foll. by over, along) glide along in the air. **4** throw a flat stone low over water so that it bounces on the surface several times. **5** read superficially. ● n. **1** an act of reading something quickly. **2** skim milk.

ski mask n. a usu. knitted covering for the head and face, with holes for the eyes and mouth.

skimmer n. **1** a device for skimming liquids. **2** a marine bird that feeds by skimming over water with its knifelike lower mandible immersed. **3** a hydroplane, hydrofoil, hovercraft, etc. **4** a device that records credit card or debit card numbers for fraudulent use.

skim milk n. milk from which the cream has been skimmed.

skimming n. the fraudulent copying of credit or debit card details with a card swipe or other device.

skimp v. use too little time, money, or material in an attempt to economize.

skimpy adj. (**skimpier, skimpiest**)

1 meagre; not ample or sufficient. **2** (of clothing) very short or revealing.

skin ● *n.* **1** the flexible continuous covering of a human or other animal body. **2** the skin of a flayed animal with or without the hair. **3** an outer layer or covering. **4** a container for liquid, made of an animal's whole skin. **5** *slang* a skinhead. **6** *see* SKINS GAME. ● *v.* (**skins, skinned, skinning**) **1 a** remove the skin from. **b** graze a part of the body. **2** *slang* fleece or swindle. ● *adj.* depicting pornographic material. □ **by the skin of one's teeth** by a very narrow margin. **get under a person's skin** annoy a person intensely. **have a thick** (or **thin**) **skin** be insensitive (or sensitive) to criticism etc. **no skin off one's nose** a matter of indifference to one. □ **skinless** *adj.* **skinner** *n.*

skin deep *adj.* superficial, not deep or lasting.

skin diver *n.* a person who swims underwater without a diving suit. □ **skin diving** *n.*

skinflint *n.* a miserly person.

skinhead *n.* a person with shaven or close-cropped hair worn as a symbol of anarchy or racism.

skink *n.* a smooth-bodied lizard with short or absent limbs, usu. burrowing in sandy ground.

skinned *adj.* having a skin of a specified type.

skinny *adj.* (**skinnier, skinniest**) **1** thin or emaciated. **2** (of an object) narrow, slim. □ **skinniness** *n.*

skinny-dip *informal* ● *v.* (**skinny-dips, skinny-dipped, skinny-dipping**) swim nude. ● *n.* (**skinny dip**) a swim in the nude. □ **skinny-dipper** *n.* **skinny-dipping** *n.*

skins game *n. Sport* a form of golf, curling, bowling, etc., in which the winner of each hole, end, or frame is awarded a financial prize, or "skin".

skin-tight *adj.* very close-fitting.

skip[1] ● *v.* (**skips, skipped, skipping**) **1** move along lightly, stepping from one foot to the other with a hop or bounce. **2** jump repeatedly over a rope which is held at both ends and turned over the head and under the feet. **3** jump lightly over. **4** omit or move quickly over. **5** fail to attend; miss. **6** (of a record or compact disc) play erratically because of a defect. ● *n.* a skipping movement or action. □ **skip it** *slang* abandon a topic etc.

skip[2] ● *n.* the captain of a curling or bowling team. ● *v.* (**skips, skipped, skipping**) be the skip of.

skipjack *n.* a small striped Pacific tuna used as food.

skipper ● *n.* **1** the captain of an esp. small ship. **2** the captain of an aircraft. **3** the captain of a side in a game or sport. ● *v.* act as captain of.

skip rock *n. Curling* one of a rink's last two rocks of an end, usu. delivered by the skip.

skirl ● *n.* the shrill sound characteristic of bagpipes. ● *v.* make a skirl.

skirmish ● *n.* **1** an unplanned fight between small groups of troops. **2** a short argument etc. ● *v.* engage in a skirmish. □ **skirmisher** *n.*

skirt ● *n.* **1** a woman's outer garment hanging from the waist. **2** the part of a dress, coat, etc. that hangs below the waist. ● *v.* **1** go along or around or past the edge of. **2** be situated along. **3** avoid dealing with. □ **skirted** *adj.*

skit *n.* a light, usu. short, piece of satire or comedy.

skitter *v.* move lightly or hastily.

skittery *adj.* skittish, restless.

skittish *adj.* **1** lively, playful. **2** (of a horse etc.) nervous, inclined to shy, fidgety. **3** fickle, changeable. □ **skittishly** *adv.* **skittishness** *n.*

skittle *n.* **1** a pin used in the game of skittles. **2** (**skittles**) a game played with usu. nine wooden pins set up at the end of an alley to be bowled down usu. with a wooden ball or disc.

skivvy *n.* (*pl.* **skivvies**) **1** a menial or poorly-paid worker. **2** (in *pl.*) esp. men's underwear.

SKU *abbr.* stock-keeping unit, designating a number used in retail stock control. [Say SKEW]

skua *n.* a large seabird known for robbing other seabirds of food by forcing them to disgorge the fish they have caught. [Say SKYOO uh]

skulduggery *n.* trickery; unscrupulous behaviour.

skulk *v.* **1** move stealthily or lurk, esp. in a cowardly or sinister way. **2** sneak away in time of danger. □ **skulker** *n.*

skull *n.* a bone framework enclosing the brain of a person or animal. □ **skulled** *adj.*

skullcap *n.* a small close-fitting brimless cap.

skunk ● *n.* **1** a mammal with distinctive black and white striped fur, capable of emitting a powerful stench as a defence. **2** *informal* a thoroughly contemptible person. ● *v. slang* defeat soundly.

skunk cabbage *n.* a plant of the arum family, the flower of which has a distinctive unpleasant smell.

skunky *adj.* (**skunkier, skunkiest**) *informal* (of beer) foul-tasting, esp. as a result of exposure to light.

sky *n.* (*pl.* **skies**) the atmosphere and outer space seen from the earth.

skybox *n.* (*pl.* **skyboxes**) a private room near the top of a stadium or arena, from where the event may be viewed.

skydiving *n.* the sport of jumping from an aircraft and falling for as long as possible before opening one's parachute. □ **skydive** *v.* **skydiver** *n.*

sky-high *adv. & adj.* very high.

skyhook *n.* an imaginary or fanciful device for suspension in or attachment to the sky.

skylark ● *n.* a lark noted for singing while hovering in flight. ● *v.* play tricks or practical jokes; frolic.

skylight *n.* a window in a roof for letting in daylight. □ **skylit** *adj.*

skyline *n.* **1** the outline of hills, buildings, etc., defined against the sky. **2** an overhead cable for transporting logs.

skyrocket ● *v.* (**skyrockets, skyrocketed, skyrocketing**) rise or increase very steeply or rapidly. ● *n.* a firework exploding high in the air.

skyscraper *n.* a very tall building.

skyward ● *adv.* (also **skywards**) towards the sky. ● *adj.* moving skyward.

skyway *n.* **1** a route used by aircraft. **2** (also **skywalk**) a covered overhead walkway between buildings. **3** a long highly elevated section of highway, esp. spanning water.

skywriting *n.* legible smoke trails made by an airplane esp. for advertising.

slab *n.* **1** a flat broad fairly thick piece of solid material, e.g. concrete or stone. **2** a large flat piece of cake, chocolate, etc.

slack ● *adj.* **1** not taut. **2** inactive or sluggish. **3** negligent or remiss. **4** (of tide etc.) neither ebbing nor flowing. ● *n.* the slack part of a rope etc. ● *v.* **1 a** slacken. **b** loosen (rope etc.). **2** *informal* be lazy; shirk. ● *adv.* slackly. □ **slack off** reduce activity, effort, speed, etc. **take** (or **pick**) **up the slack** make up a deficiency. □ **slackly** *adv.* **slackness** *n.*

slacken *v.* make or become slack.

slacker *n.* a shirker; a lazy person.

slacks *pl. n.* trousers.

slag ● *n.* stony waste matter separated from metals during the smelting or refining of ore. ● *v.* (**slags, slagged, slagging**) *informal* criticize in an abusive and insulting way.

slain *past participle of* SLAY.

slake *v.* (**slakes, slaked, slaking**) **1** quench or satisfy thirst, desire, etc. **2** disintegrate (quicklime) by chemical combination with water.

slalom ● *n.* **1** a downhill ski race on a zigzag course marked by flags. **2** a similar obstacle race for canoeists, water skiers, skateboarders, etc. ● *v.* (**slaloms, slalomed, slaloming**) perform or compete in a slalom. □ **slalomer** *n.* [*Say* SLAW lum]

slam ● *v.* (**slams, slammed, slamming**) **1** shut or put down forcefully. **2** move violently. **3** *slang* criticize severely. **4** *slang* hit. ● *n.* **1** a sound of or as of a slammed door. **2** a criticism or insult. **3** the winning of every trick in a card game.

slam-bang ● *adv.* with the sound of a slam. ● *adj. informal* **1** impressive, exciting, or energetic. **2** noisy, violent.

slam-dancing *n.* a form of dancing to rock music in which participants deliberately collide violently with one another. □ **slam-dance** *n. & v.* **slam-dancer** *n.*

slam dunk ● *n.* **1** *Basketball* a forceful and often dramatic dunk shot. **2** *informal* a sure thing; an easy victory. ● *v.* (**slam-dunk**) **1** *Basketball* dunk the ball in a forceful, often dramatic manner. **2** *informal* easily defeat a person or thing. **3** *informal* achieve something in a forceful, often dramatic way.

slammer *n. slang* (usu. as **the slammer**) prison.

slander ● *n.* **1** a malicious, false, and injurious statement spoken about a person. **2** the uttering of such statements. ● *v.* utter slander about. □ **slanderer** *n.* **slanderous** *adj.* **slanderously** *adv.*

slang *n.* words, phrases, and uses that are regarded as very informal. □ **slangy** *adj.*

slanging match *n.* a prolonged exchange of insults.

slant ● *v.* **1** slope or lean. **2** (often as **slanted** *adj.*) present information from a particular angle, esp. unfairly. ● *n.* **1** a slope; an oblique position. **2** a point of view, esp. a biased one. □ **slantwise** *adv.* **slanty** *adj.*

slap ● *v.* (**slaps, slapped, slapping**) **1** strike with the palm of the hand or a flat object. **2** put down forcefully. **3** put hastily or carelessly. **4** strike with a sharp slap. **5** *informal* punish with a fine, sentence, etc. ● *n.* **1** a blow with the palm of the hand or a flat object. **2** a slapping sound. ● *adv.* suddenly, fully, directly.

slapdash *adj.* hasty and careless.

slap-happy *adj. informal* **1** cheerfully casual or flippant. **2** dazed or disoriented.

slapshot *n. Hockey* a hard shot taken by raising the stick to waist height before striking the puck.

slapstick *n.* boisterous physical comedy, characterized by pratfalls etc.

slash ● *v.* (**slashes, slashed, slashing**) **1** make a sweeping cut with a knife, sword, whip, etc. **2** reduce prices etc. drastically. **3** *Hockey* swing at an opponent with the stick. **4** clear land of vegetation. ● *n.* (*pl.* **slashes**) **1 a** a slashing cut. **b** a wound or slit made by this. **2** an oblique stroke (/). **3** a severe or drastic reduction. **4** *Hockey* an act of slashing. □ **slashing** *n.*

slash-and-burn *adj.* **1** designating cultivation in which vegetation is cut down, allowed to dry, and then burned off before seeds are planted. **2** aggressive or ruthless.

slasher *n.* **1** a person or thing that slashes. **2** (also **slasher film, slasher movie**) a film depicting violent assault with a knife etc.

slat *n.* any thin narrow piece of wood, plastic, or metal, such as one of those found on a fence or Venetian blind. □ **slatted** *adj.*

slate ● *n.* **1** a dark fine-grained rock that splits readily into flat smooth plates. **2** a piece of such a plate used as a tile in roofing or paving. **3** a framed piece of such a plate, formerly used for writing on. **4** a bluish-grey or bluish-purple colour. **5** a list of nominees for election or appointment. **6** *informal* an agenda, schedule, or list ● *v.* (**slates, slated, slating**) **1** (usu. foll. by *for, to*) plan, schedule. **2** propose or nominate for a position, political office etc. **3** cover a roof etc. with slates. □ **wipe the slate clean** forgive or cancel the record of past offences.

slather *v. informal* cover a surface with a large portion of a substance. [*Rhymes with* GATHER]

slattern *n.* an untidy and slovenly woman. □ **slatternly** *adj.*

slaty *adj.* resembling slate in colour, texture, or appearance.

slaughter ● *n.* **1** the killing of an animal or animals for food. **2** a brutal or ruthless killing. **3** a massacre. ● *v.* **1** kill an animal for food. **2** kill ruthlessly or brutally. **3** kill large numbers of people. □ **slaughterer** *n.* [*Say* SLOTTER]

slaughterhouse *n.* a place where animals are butchered for food. [*Say* SLOTTER house]

Slav ● *n.* a member of a group of peoples in central and eastern Europe speaking Slavic languages. ● *adj.* of or relating to the Slavs or the Slavic languages.

slave ● *n.* **1** a person who is the legal property of another and is bound to absolute obedience. **2** a person working very hard, esp. without appropriate reward. **3** a person completely under the domination of a specified influence. **4** a device which is controlled by or which follows the movements of another. ● *v.* (**slaves, slaved, slaving**) toil or work very hard.

slave-driver *n.* a demanding and unyielding supervisor, employer, teacher, etc.

slaveholder *n.* a person who owns slaves. □ **slaveholding** *n. & adj.*

slaver[1] *n. hist.* **1** a ship used in the slave trade. **2** a person dealing in or owning slaves. [*Say* SLAVE er]

slaver[2] ● *n.* saliva running from the mouth. ● *v.* **1** drool. **2** show excessive eagerness or obsequiousness. □ **slavering** *adj.* [*Say* SLAVVER]

slavery *n.* **1** the practice or institution of keeping slaves. **2** the condition or fact of being a slave.

Slavey *n.* (*pl.* **Slavey** or **Slaveys**) **1** a member of a number of Dene Aboriginal groups living between Lake Athabasca and Great Slave Lake. **2** any of their Athapaskan languages. □ **Slavey** *adj.* [*Say* SLAY vee]

Slavic ● *adj.* **1** of the branch of Indo-European languages including Russian, Polish, Ukrainian, Czech, etc. **2** of the Slavs. ● *n.* a Slavic language or these collectively.

slavish *adj.* **1** befitting a slave. **2** showing no attempt at originality. □ **slavishly** *adv.*

Slavonic *adj. & n.* = SLAVIC. [*Say* sluh VON ick]

slaw *n.* coleslaw.

slay *v.* (**slays**; *past* **slew**; *past participle* **slain**; **slaying**) **1** kill. **2** *slang* overwhelm with amusement.

slayer *n.* **1** *literary* a person who kills mythological creatures, monsters, dragons, etc. **2** *jocular* a nemesis or conqueror.

slaying *n.* **1** a murder. **2** the killing of a mythical monster.

sleaze ● *n.* *informal* **1** sleazy material, conditions, or behaviour. **2** a person who behaves in a sleazy way.

sleazebag *n.* (also **sleazeball**) *slang* a sordid, despicable, or shady person.

sleazy *adj.* (**sleazier, sleaziest**) **1** disreputable or corrupt. **2** sexually immoral or promiscuous. **3** filthy, grimy; seedy; dilapidated. □ **sleaziness** *n.*

sled ● *n.* **1** a low vehicle mounted on runners for transport over snow or ice. **2** a similar but smaller device used esp. by children to coast down hills. **3** a snowmobile. ● v. (**sleds, sledded, sledding**) ride, race, or carry on a sled.

sledder n. a person who races or rides a sled or snowmobile.

sledding n. **1** the activity or action of racing or riding a sled or snowmobile. **2** progress in any sphere of action.

sledge¹ ● n. a sled. ● v. travel or convey by sledge.

sledge² n. (also **sledgehammer**) a large heavy hammer with a long handle used to break stone etc.

sleek adj. **1 a** having a smooth and shiny appearance. **b** having a well-groomed and healthy appearance. **2** smooth and polished in manners and behaviour. **3** streamlined, smooth, aerodynamic. □ **sleekly** adv. **sleekness** n.

sleep ● n. **1** the recurring condition of unconscious rest and inactivity assumed by people and many animals. **2** *euphemism* death. **3** a gummy secretion found in the corners of the eyes after sleep. ● v. (**sleeps, slept, sleeping**) **1** be or fall asleep. **2** (foll. by *with, together*) have a sexual encounter or relationship. **3** (foll. by *on*) postpone a decision until the next day. **4** provide sleeping accommodation for. **5** be inactive or dormant. □ **go to sleep** **1** achieve a state of sleep. **2** (of a limb) become numb as a result of prolonged pressure. **put to sleep 1** kill an animal in a humane manner. **2** anaesthetize. **sleep around** be sexually promiscuous. **sleep in** remain asleep later than usual. **sleep over** spend the night at another's house. **sleep tight!** sleep well.

sleeper n. **1** a person that sleeps, esp. in a specified way. **2** a thing that is introduced with little attention, but which turns out to be successful. **3** (also **sleeping car**) a railway car provided with beds for passengers. **4** one-piece pyjamas for infants or children. **5** a strong usu. horizontal beam used to support a wall or floorboards. **6** a spy or saboteur etc. who remains inactive while establishing a secure position.

sleeping bag n. a warm lined or padded body-length bag designed for sleeping esp. outdoors.

sleeping pill n. a sedative.

sleeping sickness n. **1** a tropical African disease transmitted by tsetse flies, leading eventually to lethargy and death. **2** an infectious viral encephalitis, with headache and drowsiness leading to coma.

sleepless adj. **1** without sleep. **2** unable to sleep. **3** continually active or moving. □ **sleeplessly** adv. **sleeplessness** n.

sleepover n. an occasion on which a child spends the night at a friend's house.

sleepwalk v. walk or perform other actions in one's sleep. □ **sleepwalker** n.

sleepy adj. (**sleepier, sleepiest**) **1** drowsy. **2** lazy. **3** lacking activity or bustle. **4** conducive to sleep. □ **sleepily** adv. **sleepiness** n.

sleepyhead n. a sleepy or inattentive person.

sleet n. precipitation in the form of melting snow or freezing rain. □ **sleety** adj.

sleeve n. **1** the part of a garment that covers the arm. **2** the envelope used to protect a record. **3** any tubular piece of plastic or metal etc. used to cover or protect a rod or shaft etc. □ **roll up one's sleeves** prepare to fight or work. **up one's sleeve** concealed but ready for use. □ **sleeved** adj. **sleeveless** adj.

sleigh ● n. a sled, esp. a large one drawn by horses and used to convey passengers. ● v. travel on a sleigh. [Say SLAY]

sleigh bell n. any of a number of small bells attached to a sleigh or to a horse drawing it.

sleight of hand n. **1** skilful movements of the hand, esp. in performing a trick or magic. **2** a cunning manoeuvre, scheme, or deception. [Say SLITE]

slender adj. (**more slender, slenderest**) **1** thin. **2** relatively small; meagre. □ **slenderness** n.

slept past and past participle of SLEEP.

sleuth *informal* ● n. a detective or investigator. ● v. investigate, research. [Say SLOOTH]

slew¹ v. **1** (often foll. by *around*) turn or swing around, esp. without moving from a position. **2** skid or slide uncontrollably. **3** send toppling or spinning.

slew² past of SLAY.

slew³ n. *informal* (usu. foll. by *of*) a large number or quantity.

slice ● n. **1** a thin broad piece of an item of food. **2** a share. **3** a cut or incision. ● v. (**slices, sliced, slicing**) **1** cut into slices. **2** cut a piece off. **3** make a cut or incision. **4** strike a ball at an angle so that it curves as it travels. □ **slice of life** a movie, play, incident, etc. that offers a realistic representation of everyday life. □ **slicer** n.

sliced adj. cut cleanly into slices.

slick ● adj. **1 a** clever, crafty. **b** deftly or skilfully executed. **2 a** superficially smooth or suave. **b** plausible but insincere. **3 a** smooth and glossy. ● n. **1 a** patch or stretch of oil or ice etc., esp. floating on a body of water. **2** a smooth

racing tire having little or no tread. ● *v.*
informal **1** (often foll. by *up*) smarten or tidy
up; make sleek. **2** (usu. foll. by *back, down*)
flatten one's hair. □ **slickly** *adv.*
slickness *n.*

slicker *n.* **1** a raincoat of oilskin, rubber,
plastic, etc., usu. in a bright colour.
2 *informal* = CITY SLICKER.

slide ● *v.* (**slides, slid, sliding**) **1** move
along a smooth surface while maintaining
continuous contact with it. **2** move
smoothly or quickly. **3** change gradually to
a worse condition or lower level. ● *n.* **1** a
structure with a smooth sloping surface for
children to slide down. **2** a move along a
smooth surface while maintaining
continuous contact with it. **3** a small
rectangular piece of glass on which an
object is placed for examination under a
microscope. **4** a mounted transparency for
projecting on a screen. **5** a landslide or
avalanche. **6** *Cdn* a track or slope prepared
with snow or ice for tobogganing. □ **let
things slide** allow deterioration.

slider *n.* **1** a part or device that slides.
2 *Baseball* a fast pitch that curves away from
the direction in which it was thrown.

sliding scale *n.* a scale of fees, taxes, etc.,
that varies in accordance with variation of
some standard.

slight ● *adj.* **1** small in quantity, degree, or
importance. **2** slender. ● *v.* treat or speak of
with disrespect or a lack of courtesy. ● *n.* a
marked display of disregard or disrespect.
□ **slightingly** *adv.* **slightly** *adv.*

slim ● *adj.* (**slimmer, slimmest**) **1** of
small girth or thickness. **2** of thin or
slender build. **3** poor, meagre. **4** small. ● *v.*
(**slims, slimmed, slimming**) (often foll.
by *down*) make or become slim or slimmer.
□ **slimness** *n.*

slime ● *n.* **1** thick slippery mud or any
similar substance, esp. when considered
noxious or unpleasant. **2** a viscous mucous
secretion exuded by fish, snails, slugs, etc.
3 *slang* = SLIMEBALL. ● *v.* (**slimes, slimed,
sliming**) cover with or as if with slime.

slimeball *n.* *slang* a filthy, corrupt, morally
degenerate, or despicable person; a sleaze.

slimline *adj.* of sleek and slender design.

slimy *adj.* (**slimier, slimiest**) **1** of the
consistency of slime. **2** covered with or full
of slime. **3** disgustingly foul or dishonest.
□ **sliminess** *n.*

sling ● *n.* **1** a loop or net in which an
object may be raised, lowered, or
suspended. **2** a bandage looped around the
neck to support an injured arm. **3** a loop of
leather or other material in which a stone
is whirled and then released. **4** a pouch
supported by a strap around the neck for

carrying a young child. **5** a drink of gin
diluted with water or soda and lemon
juice. ● *v.* (**slings, slung, slinging**)
1 hurl or cast from a sling. **2** speak or utter
(insults, criticism, etc.). **3** hang or allow to
hang, esp. loosely or sloppily. **4** hoist or
transfer with a sling. □ **sling hash** work
as a chef or server in a restaurant.

slingback *n.* a woman's shoe held in place
by a strap above the heel.

slinger *n.* **1** *informal* a person who serves
food or drinks. **2** a person who uses or
carries etc. a specified thing.

slingshot *n.* a Y-shaped frame supporting
an elastic which can be used to launch a
small projectile.

slink *v.* (**slinks, slunk, slinking**) (often
foll. by *off, away*) **1** sneak away as if
ashamed, embarrassed, timid, or guilty.
2 walk or move in a provocative or alluring
manner.

slinky *adj.* (**slinkier, slinkiest**) **1** moving
in an alluring or seductive manner. **2** (of
clothes) close-fitting and provocative.
□ **slinkiness** *n.*

slip ● *v.* (**slips, slipped, slipping**) **1** lose
one's balance or footing and slide
unintentionally. **2** accidentally slide out of
position or from someone's grasp. **3** fail to
grip a surface. **4** pass gradually to a worse
condition. **5** (usu. foll. by *up*) make a
careless error. **6** move or place quickly or
stealthily. **7** get loose from. **8** fail to be
remembered by. ● *n.* **1** a short
unintentional slide. **2** an accidental or
slight error. **3** an article of lingerie
extending from the shoulder or the waist
to the hemline of a dress or skirt. **4** a space
at a dock etc. where a boat may be kept. **5** a
pillowcase. **6** a small piece of paper. □ **give
a person the slip** escape from or evade
a person. **let slip** accidentally utter or
reveal or disclose. **slip of the tongue** a
small mistake in which something is said
unintentionally.

slipcase *n.* a close-fitting case for a book
that allows the spine to remain visible.

slipcover *n.* a removable cover for a chair,
couch, etc.

slip-on ● *adj.* that can be easily slipped on
and off. ● *n.* a shoe without laces or straps
etc.

slippage *n.* **1** the process of something
slipping or subsiding. **2** a falling off or
decline. [*Say* SLIP idge]

slipped disc *n.* = HERNIATED DISC.

slipper *n.* **1** a light loose comfortable
indoor shoe. **2** a light, slip-on, heelless shoe
for dancing etc. □ **slippered** *adj.*

slippery *adj.* (**slipperier, slipperiest**)
1 difficult to hold firmly or to stand or

move on because of smoothness. **2** (of a subject) difficult to handle or comprehend. **3** unreliable, unscrupulous, shifty. □ **slipperiness** n.

slippery slope n. an irreversible course leading to disaster.

slippy adj. (**slippier, slippiest**) informal slippery.

slipshod adj. **1** careless, esp. in working or in handling ideas or words. **2** shabby, untidy.

slipstream n. **1** a current of air or water driven back by a revolving propeller or a moving vehicle. **2** an assisting force regarded as drawing something behind something else.

slip-up n. informal a blunder.

slipway n. a slip for building ships or landing boats.

slit ● n. **1** a long straight narrow incision. **2** a long narrow opening comparable to a cut. ● v. (**slits, slit, slitting**) **1** make a slit in. **2** cut into strips.

slither ● v. **1** move smoothly over a surface with a twisting motion. **2** move or go stealthily. ● n. a slithering movement. □ **slithery** adj.

sliver ● n. **1** a usu. long thin piece or sharp fragment that has been split or broken off something. **2** (foll. by of) a small amount. ● v. (esp. as **slivered** adj.) cut or break up into slivers.

slob n. **1** informal an untidy, lazy, or fat person. **2** Cdn sludgy masses of densely packed sea ice. □ **slobbish** adj. **slobby** adj.

slobber ● v. **1** let saliva or food run from the mouth. **2** (foll. by over) be overly affectionate toward or sentimental about a person or thing. ● n. saliva running from the mouth. □ **slobbery** adj.

slog ● v. (**slogs, slogged, slogging**) **1** (often foll. by away, on) work hard or steadily at something. **2** walk or move steadily with great effort or toil. ● n. **1** hard, steady work or effort. **2** a long, tiring walk or march.

slogan n. a short, memorable phrase used in advertising or associated with a political group.

sloganeer n. one who devises or uses slogans. □ **sloganeering** n. [Say slogan EER]

slo-mo n. informal = SLOW MOTION.

sloop n. a small, one-masted vessel with mainsail and jib.

slop ● v. (**slops, slopped, slopping**) **1** (often foll. by over) spill or splash over the edge of a container, vessel, etc. **2** walk or wander through a wet or muddy place. ● n. **1** food that is poorly cooked or not

appetizing. **2** semi-liquid food for pigs, esp. the remains of food intended for people. **3** (in pl.) liquid household waste matter. □ **slop about** move about in a slovenly manner.

slope ● n. **1** a piece of rising or falling ground etc. **2** a place for skiing on the side of a hill or mountain. ● v. (**slopes, sloped, sloping**) lie obliquely, esp. downwards. □ **sloped** adj.

slo-pitch n. a form of baseball in which the batter has three chances to hit a lobbed softball.

sloppy adj. (**sloppier, sloppiest**) **1** careless, slipshod. **2** splashed with liquid. **3** untidy. **4** wet with rain or slush. **5** (of clothes) loose; baggy. **6** having a muddy consistency. □ **sloppily** adv. **sloppiness** n.

sloppy joe n. a sandwich consisting of a thick filling of loose ground beef and sauce served on a bun.

slosh v. (**sloshes, sloshed, sloshing**) **1** move with a splashing sound. **2** make liquid move noisily.

sloshed adj. slang drunk.

slot ● n. **1** a slit, groove or channel into which something fits or is inserted. **2** a position to be filled in a schedule or order. **3** Hockey the area directly in front of the net, considered an excellent shooting position. **4** (as an adj.) designating a screwdriver with a straight flat blade. **5** informal = SLOT MACHINE. **6** Computing (in full **expansion slot**) a place in a computer where an extra circuit board can be inserted. ● v. (**slots, slotted, slotting**) **1** place or be placed into a slot. **2** provide with a slot or slots.

sloth n. **1** laziness; reluctance to make an effort. **2** a slow-moving nocturnal mammal with claws and long limbs for hanging from trees. [Rhymes with CLOTH]

slot machine n. a gambling machine, usu. activated by a lever, that produces random combinations of symbols which must match for the player to win.

slotted adj. **1** having a slot or slots. **2** (of a screw) having a narrow slot on the head.

slouch ● v. (**slouches, slouched, slouching**) **1** stand or sit with the back, shoulders, and neck bent or drooping forwards. **2** walk or move with a shuffling gait and slouching posture. ● n. a slouching posture or movement. □ **no slouch** informal a competent person or performer. □ **slouchy** adj. (**slouchier, slouchiest**)

slough[1] n. **1** an area of soft ground; a swamp or quagmire. **2** Cdn (West) & US Northwest a small marshy pool or lake produced by rain or melting snow flooding a depression in the soil. **3** *Cdn* (*BC*) a shallow inlet or estuary lined with grass. [*Say* SLOO; *for senses 1 and 3 you can also rhyme* SLOUGH *with* HOW]

slough² ● *n.* **1** a part that an animal sheds, esp. a snake's skin. **2** a layer of dead tissue that will fall away from the skin. ● *v.* **1** (often foll. by *off*) shed, remove, or cast off skin, tissue, etc. **2** (foll. by *off*) get rid of or abandon something. [*Say* SLUFF]

Slovak *n.* **1** (also **Slovakian**) a person from Slovakia. **2** the language of Slovakia. □ **Slovak** (also **Slovakian**) *adj.* [*Say* SLOE vack, sloe VACKY un]

sloven *n.* a person who is habitually untidy or careless. [*Say* SLOV in *or* SLUV in]

Slovenian *n.* (also **Slovene**) **1** a person from Slovenia. **2** the language of Slovenia. □ **Slovenian** *adj.* [*Say* sluh VEENY in; SLOE veen]

slovenly *adj.* careless, untidy, negligent. □ **slovenliness** *n.* [*Say* SLOV in lee *or* SLUV in lee]

slow ● *adj.* **1** moving or capable of moving only at a low speed. **2** lasting or taking a long time. **3** (of a clock or watch) showing a time earlier than the correct time. **4** not quick to understand, think, or learn. **5** showing little activity. **6** *Photography* (of a film) needing long exposure. **7** (of a fire or oven) burning or giving off heat gently. ● *adv.* slowly. ● *v.* **1** reduce speed. **2** reduce one's pace of life. **3** become or cause to be slow. □ **slowly** *adv.* **slowness** *n.*

slow burn *n.* slowly mounting intensity. □ **slow-burning** *adj.*

slowdown *n.* **1** the action of slowing down. **2** a form of industrial action in which employees deliberately work slowly.

slow motion *n.* **1** the technique of playing a film or video so that actions appear to be slower than in real life. **2** the simulation of this in real action.

slow-pitch *n.* = SLO-PITCH.

slowpoke *n.* a slow or lazy person etc.

slow-release *adj.* designating a drug, fertilizer, etc. that releases a substance slowly.

sludge *n.* **1** thick greasy mud, ooze, etc. **2** muddy or slimy sediment. **3** the sediment in a sewage or septic tank. **4** an accumulation of dirty oil, esp. formed as industrial waste. □ **sludgy** *adj.* (**sludgier**, **sludgiest**)

slug¹ ● *n.* **1 a** a small shell-less mollusc. **b** *informal* a slow or lazy person. **2** a bullet. **3** a drink; a swig. **4** a piece of metal used as a counterfeit coin. ● *v.* (**slugs**, **slugged**, **slugging**) **1** move slowly or sluggishly. **2** drink quickly.

slug² *informal* ● *v.* (**slugs**, **slugged**, **slugging**) strike with a hard blow. ● *n.* a hard blow. □ **slug it out 1** fight it out. **2** stick it out.

slugfest *n.* *informal* a violent or intense fight or quarrel.

sluggard *n.* a lazy sluggish person.

slugger *n.* **1** a person who delivers heavy blows. **2** a baseball player who hits powerful home runs.

sluggish *adj.* slow-moving. □ **sluggishly** *adv.* **sluggishness** *n.*

sluice ● *n.* **1** (also **sluice gate**) a sliding device for controlling the flow of water. **2** (also **sluiceway**) a channel or waterway controlled by means of a sluice. **3** (also **sluice box**) an artificial water channel for washing ore. ● *v.* (**sluices**, **sluiced**, **sluicing**) **1** wash or rinse with water. **2** (of water) pour or flow abundantly. [*Rhymes with* JUICE]

slum ● *n.* **1** an overcrowded and squalid district etc., usu. in a city and inhabited by very poor people. **2** a house or building unfit to be lived in. ● *v.* (**slums**, **slummed**, **slumming**) put up with less comfortable conditions, associate with persons of a lower social class, etc. than one is used to. □ **slummy** *adj.*

slumber ● *v.* sleep. ● *n.* a sleep.

slumlord *n.* a landlord who rents slum property to tenants.

slump ● *n.* **1** a sudden fall in prices or a long period of low economic activity. **2** a reduction in performance. ● *v.* **1** undergo a slump. **2** sit, lean, or fall heavily or limply. □ **slumped** *adj.*

slung *past and past participle of* SLING.

slunk *past and past participle of* SLINK.

slur ● *v.* (**slurs**, **slurred**, **slurring**) **1** pronounce or write indistinctly. **2** *Music* perform (a group of two or more notes) legato. **3** pass over lightly. ● *n.* **1** an unfair remark intended to damage someone's reputation. **2** an act of speaking or tendency to speak indistinctly. **3** *Music* a curved line to show that notes are to be slurred.

slurp ● *v.* drink or eat noisily. ● *n.* **1** the sound of this. **2** a slurping gulp. □ **slurpy** *adj.*

slurry *n.* (*pl.* **slurries**) **1** a semi-liquid mixture, esp. of manure, mud, etc., and water. **2** thin liquid cement.

slush *n.* **1** partially melted snow or ice. **2** (also **slushy** (*pl.* **slushies**)) a confection consisting of flavoured slushy ice. □ **slushy** *adj.* (**slushier**, **slushiest**)

slush fund *n.* a sum of money kept for illegal purposes.

slut *n. derogatory* a promiscuous woman. □ **sluttish** *adj.* **slutty** *adj.*

sly *adj.* (**slyer, slyest**) **1** cunning; crafty. **2** (of an action etc.) done etc. in secret. **3** roguish. □ **on the sly** covertly. □ **slyly** *adv.* **slyness** *n.*

smack ● *n.* **1** a sharp slap or blow. **2** a hard hit in baseball etc. **3** a loud kiss. **4** a loud sharp sound. **5** a noisy parting of the lips in anticipation. **6** *slang* a hard drug, esp. heroin. ● *v.* **1** strike sharply. **2** part (one's lips) noisily. **3 a** taste of. **b** suggest the presence of. ● *adv. informal* **1** with a smack. **2** suddenly; violently. **3** exactly.

smacker *n.* (also **smackeroo**) *slang* **1** a loud kiss. **2** one dollar.

small ● *adj.* **1** of less than normal size. **2** not great in amount, number, strength, or power. **3** young. **4** unimportant. **5** (of a business) operating on a modest scale. ● *adv.* into small pieces. □ **be small potatoes** be insignificant. **feel** (or **look**) **small** be humiliated. □ **smallish** *adj.* **smallness** *n.*

small-bore *adj.* **1** (of a firearm) with a narrow bore. **2** *informal* petty, small-time.

small change *n.* **1** coins. **2** an insignificant amount of money. **3** a trivial thing.

small claims court *n.* a general name given to a court with jurisdiction over civil claims involving relatively small amounts of money.

small fry *pl. n.* **1** young children or fish. **2** insignificant things or people.

small hours *pl. n.* the early hours of the morning after midnight.

small intestine *n.* the narrow part of the intestine that food first passes into from the stomach.

small-minded *adj.* petty; of narrow outlook. □ **small-mindedness** *n.*

smallmouth *n.* (*plural* **smallmouth** or **smallmouths**) a North American freshwater bass with a small mouth.

small of the back *n.* the part of the back below the waist.

smallpox *n.* an acute viral disease, with fever and pustules that leave permanent scars.

small print *n.* = FINE PRINT.

small-scale *adj.* of limited size or extent.

small screen *n. informal* television.

small talk *n.* light social conversation.

small-time *adj. informal* unimportant or petty.

small-town *adj.* having to do with a small town; unsophisticated.

smarmy *adj.* (**smarmier, smarmiest**) *informal* polite in a way that is not sincere. □ **smarm** *v.*

smart ● *adj.* **1 a** intelligent. **b** impudent. **c** shrewd. **2** well-groomed; neat. **3** bright and fresh in appearance. **4** stylish; fashionable. **5** quick. **6** painfully severe. **7 a** (of a device) capable of independent action. **b** (of a missile etc.) guided to a target by an optical system. **8** (of a drug, drink, etc.) that supposedly improves memory or mental acuteness. ● *v.* **1** feel or give pain or distress. **2** (of an insult etc.) rankle. ● *n.* **1** a bodily or mental sharp pain. **2** (in *pl.*) intelligence. □ **smartly** *adv.* **smartness** *n.*

smart aleck *n.* (also **smart alec, smartass**) *informal* a person displaying impudent or smug cleverness. □ **smart-alecky** *adj.*

smart card *n.* a plastic card on which information is stored in electronic form.

smart cookie *n. informal* a smart or shrewd person.

smart drug *n.* a drug which supposedly improves memory etc.

smarten *v.* make or become smarter.

smart-mouth *v. informal* give a cheeky retort to someone.

smarty *n.* (*pl.* **smarties**) (also **smarty-pants**, *pl.* **smarty-pants**) *informal* a know-it-all.

smash ● *v.* (**smashes, smashed, smashing**) **1 a** break. **b** bring to complete destruction, defeat, or disaster. **2** hit or collide with forcefully. ● *n.* (*pl.* **smashes**) **1** an act or sound of smashing. **2** (also **smash hit**) a very successful movie, song, etc. **3** a powerful hit. **4** bankruptcy.

smash-and-grab *n.* (*pl.* **smash-and-grabs**) (usu. as an *adj.*) a robbery in which the thief smashes a window and seizes goods.

smashed *adj.* **1** broken into pieces. **2** *slang* drunk.

smasher *n.* **1** a person or thing that smashes. **2** *informal* a very attractive or pleasing person or thing.

smashing *adj. informal* excellent.

smattering *n.* **1** a slight knowledge of a language or subject. **2** a small amount.

smear ● *v.* **1** daub or mark with a greasy or sticky substance. **2** blot; smudge. **3** defame the character of; slander. ● *n.* **1** material smeared on a microscopic slide etc. for examination. **2** a greasy or sticky mark. **3** a false accusation. □ **smeary** *adj.*

smell ● *n.* **1** the faculty of perceiving odours or scents. **2** the quality that is perceived by this. **3** an odour. **4** a suggestion of something. • v. (**smells**, **smelled**, **smelling**) **1** perceive the smell of. **2** emit odour. **3** seem by smell to be. **4 a** be redolent of. **b** be suggestive of. **5** stink. **6** detect, discern. **7** sniff or search about. □ **smell blood** (of an aggressor) be encouraged by another's vulnerability. **smell a rat** suspect trickery etc. **smell the roses** appreciate what is often ignored.

smelling salts pl. n. a chemical with a very strong smell used to revive someone who has fainted.

smelly adj. (**smellier**, **smelliest**) having a strong or unpleasant smell.

smelt¹ v. extract metal from ore by melting. □ **smelter** n. **smelting** n.

smelt² n. (pl. **smelt** or **smelts**) a small silvery fish.

smidgen n. (also **smidge**) informal a tiny bit.

smile • v. (**smiles**, **smiled**, **smiling**) **1** relax the features into a pleased or kind expression, usu. with the corners of the mouth turned up. **2** encourage. • n. an act of smiling. □ **be all smiles** (of a person) look very cheerful. □ **smiley** adj. **smiling** adj. **smilingly** adv.

smirk • n. a conceited, smug, or silly smile. • v. put on a smirk. □ **smirky** adj.

smite v. (**smites**; past **smote**; past participle **smitten**; **smiting**) strike or hit forcefully.

smith n. **1** a worker in metal. **2** a blacksmith.

smithereens pl. n. small fragments. [SMITHER rhymes with WITHER]

smithy n. (pl. **smithies**) a blacksmith's workshop.

smitten • v. past participle of SMITE. • adj. **1** affected with or by something. **2** in love.

smock • n. **1** a loose garment worn to protect one's clothes. **2** a loose shirt-like garment, with the upper part closely gathered in smocking. • v. adorn with smocking.

smocking n. an ornamental effect on cloth made by gathering the material tightly into pleats.

smog n. fog intensified by atmospheric pollutants. □ **smoggy** adj. (**smoggier**, **smoggiest**)

smoke • n. **1** a visible vapour in air, emitted from a burning substance. **2** an act of smoking tobacco. **3** informal a cigarette or cigar. **4** Baseball informal a very effective fastball. • v. (**smokes**, **smoked**, **smoking**) **1** emit smoke. **2** inhale and exhale the smoke of a cigarette, cigar, etc. **3** cure or darken by the action of smoke. **4** drive out of a place by using smoke.

5 informal **a** shoot with a firearm. **b** defeat overwhelmingly. **6** esp. Sport make (a powerful shot, stroke, etc.). □ **go up in smoke 1** be destroyed by fire. **2** (of a plan etc.) come to nothing. **where there's smoke there's fire** rumours are not entirely baseless. **smoke up** Cdn informal smoke esp. marijuana. □ **smokable** adj. **smokeless** adj. **smoking** n. & adj.

smoke and mirrors pl. n. something intended to deceive or confuse.

smoked meat n. **1** meat that has been cured by smoking. **2** Cdn (esp. Que. & Ont.) cured beef similar to pastrami but more heavily smoked.

smokehouse n. a place for curing meat etc. by smoking.

smoker n. **1** a person or thing that smokes. **2** a small box used for smoking fish etc.

smokescreen n. **1** a cloud of smoke diffused to conceal (esp. military) operations. **2** a ruse for disguising one's activities.

smoke shop n. **1** a store selling tobacco products. **2** a convenience store.

smoke signal n. a column of smoke used as a signal.

smokestack n. a chimney for discharging smoke from a locomotive, factory, ship, etc.

smoking gun n. a piece of evidence that proves something beyond doubt.

smoky adj. (also **smokey**) (**smokier**, **smokiest**) **1** emitting or filled with smoke. **2** stained with smoke. **3** having the taste of smoked food. **4** (of a voice) husky. □ **smokiness** n.

smolder v. & n. = SMOULDER.

smolt n. (pl. **smolts** or **smolt**) a young salmon migrating to the sea for the first time.

smooch informal • v. (**smooches**, **smooched**, **smooching**) **1** kiss. **2** cuddle. • n. (pl. **smooches**) a kiss. □ **smoocher** n. **smoochy** adj.

smooth • adj. **1** having an even and regular surface. **2** (of a liquid) without lumps. **3** (of movement) without jerks. **4** without difficulties. **5** charming in a suave way. **6** (of a flavour) without harshness or bitterness. • v. (**smooths**, **smoothed**, **smoothing**) **1** make or become smooth. **2** get rid of (difficulties etc.). • adv. smoothly. □ **smoothly** adv. **smoothness** n.

smoothie n. (pl. **smoothies**) informal **1** a person who is suave or polite. **2** (also **smoothy**) a thick smooth drink of fresh fruit puréed with milk, yogourt, or ice cream.

smooth muscle n. a muscle in hollow organs, usu. performing involuntary functions.

smooth sailing n. easy progress.

smooth talk informal ● n. charming or flattering language. ● v. (**smooth-talk**) address or persuade with this. □ **smooth talker** n. **smooth-talking** adj.

s'more n. a graham cracker topped with melted chocolate and a marshmallow.

smorgasbord n. **1** (also **smorg** Cdn) a buffet offering a wide variety of dishes. **2** a wide range of something. [Say SMORE gus bord]

smote past of SMITE.

smother v. **1** suffocate. **2** overwhelm with (kisses, kindness, etc.). **3** cover entirely with. **4** extinguish (a fire) by covering it. **5 a** suppress or conceal. **b** repress. **6** Hockey immobilize (the puck) on the ice by falling on top of it, covering it with a glove, etc.

smoulder v. **1** burn slowly with smoke but no flame. **2** (of emotions etc.) exist in a suppressed or concealed state. **3** (of a person) show suppressed anger, passion, etc. □ **smouldering** adj.

smudge ● n. **1** a blurred or smeared mark. **2** (also **smudge fire**) an outdoor fire with dense smoke made to keep off insects etc. **3** a burning bundle of sweetgrass etc., used in ritually purifying a house, room, person, etc. ● v. (**smudges, smudged, smudging**) **1** make a smudge on. **2** become smeared or blurred. **3** smear or blur the lines of. **4** burn sweetgrass etc. with the intention of ritually purifying. □ **smudging** n. **smudgy** adj.

smug adj. (**smugger, smuggest**) self-satisfied; complacent. □ **smugly** adv. **smugness** n.

smuggle v. (**smuggles, smuggled, smuggling**) **1** move (goods) illegally into or out of a country. **2** convey secretly. □ **smuggler** n. **smuggling** n.

smut n. **1** indecent stories, pictures, or comments. **2** a fungous disease of cereals characterized by a black powdery deposit. **3** a small flake of soot etc. □ **smutty** adj. (**smuttier, smuttiest**) (esp. in sense 1)

snack ● n. **1** a light, casual, or hurried meal. **2** food eaten between meals. ● v. eat a snack. □ **snacker** n.

snack bar n. a usu. small kiosk, counter, etc. where snacks are sold.

snaffle ● n. (also **snaffle bit**) (on a bridle) a simple bit with a single rein. ● v. (**snaffles, snaffled, snaffling**) **1** put a snaffle on. **2** informal secretly take for oneself.

snafu n. slang (pl. **snafus**) **1** a confused or muddled state. **2** a mistake or blunder. [Say sna FOO]

snag ● n. **1** an unexpected problem. **2 a** a jagged or projecting point. **b** a tree trunk or branch under water, forming an obstruction to navigation. **3** a tear or pull in material etc. ● v. (**snags, snagged, snagging**) **1** catch or tear on a snag. **2** catch or obtain, esp. by quick action.

snaggle-toothed adj. having irregular or projecting teeth. □ **snaggletooth** n.

snail n. a slow-moving mollusc with a spiral shell.

snail mail n. slang the ordinary postal system as opposed to email.

snake ● n. **1** a reptile with a long slender limbless body, many kinds of which have a poisonous bite. **2** (also **snake in the grass**) a treacherous person or secret enemy. **3** (in full **plumber's snake**) a long flexible wire for clearing obstacles in pipes etc. ● v. (**snakes, snaked, snaking**) move or twist like a snake. □ **snakelike** adj.

snakebite n. a wound resulting from being bitten by an esp. poisonous snake.

snake fence n. (also **snake-rail fence**) Cdn a fence of stacked roughly-split logs laid in a zigzag pattern.

snake oil n. informal **1** quack medicine. **2** a fraudulent product.

snakeskin ● n. the skin of a snake. ● adj. made of or resembling this.

snaky adj. (also **snakey**) **1** of or like a snake. **2** winding; sinuous. **3** showing coldness or guile. □ **go** (or **drive someone**) **snaky** Cdn lose (or cause to lose) self-control.

snap ● v. (**snaps, snapped, snapping**) **1** break suddenly or with a snap. **2** emit a sudden sharp sound or crack. **3** open or close with a snapping sound. **4** speak to or say irritably. **5** (esp. of a dog etc.) make a sudden bite. **6** move quickly. **7** take a snapshot of. **8** Football put (the ball) into play. **9** bring an end to. **10** lose one's composure suddenly. ● n. **1** an act or sound of snapping. **2** slang an easy task. **3** a crisp biscuit. **4** a snapshot. **5** (also **cold snap**) a sudden brief spell of cold weather. **6** a card game in which players call "snap" when two similar cards are exposed. **7** Football an act of snapping the ball. ● adj. done on the spur of the moment. □ **in a snap** with no hesitation or difficulty. **snap one's fingers** producing an audible snap with the fingers. **snap out of** informal get rid of (a mood etc.) by a sudden effort. **snap up**

1 accept quickly or eagerly. **2** pick up hastily.

snapdragon *n.* a garden plant with bag-shaped flowers.

snapper *n.* **1** a person or thing that snaps. **2** a marine fish that is valued as food. **3** a snapping turtle.

snapping turtle *n.* a large aggressive Central and North American freshwater turtle with a large head and long tail.

snappish *adj.* **1** curt; ill-tempered. **2** (of a dog etc.) inclined to snap. □ **snappishness** *n.*

snappy *adj.* (**snappier, snappiest**) *informal* **1** brisk, full of zest. **2** fashionable, up-to-date. **3** snappish. □ **make it snappy** be quick about it. □ **snappily** *adv.*

snapshot *n.* **1** a casual photograph taken quickly. **2** a description or profile of a thing etc. **3** (**snap shot**) a quick shot on goal, esp. (*Hockey*) a shot taken by lifting the stick a short distance off the ice before striking the puck quickly with a hard flicking motion.

snare ● *n.* **1** a trap for catching birds or animals, esp. with a noose of wire or cord. **2** a thing that acts as a temptation. **3** twisted strings stretched across the lower head of a drum to produce a rattling sound. **4** (also **snare drum**) a drum fitted with snares. ● *v.* (**snares, snared, snaring**) **1** catch in a snare. **2** lure or trap with a snare. **3** grab.

snarky *adj.* (**snarkier, snarkiest**) *informal* irritable.

snarl ● *v.* **1** make an angry growl with bared teeth. **2** make bad-tempered complaints or criticisms. **3** utter by snarling. **4** twist; entangle. **5** become entangled, congested, etc. ● *n.* **1** the act or sound of snarling. **2** a tangle. □ **snarly** *adj.*

snatch ● *v.* (**snatches, snatched, snatching**) **1** take or seize something quickly or roughly. **2 a** steal. **b** kidnap (esp. a child). **3** quickly take when the chance presents itself. **4** take away or from esp. suddenly. ● *n.* (*pl.* **snatches**) **1** an act of snatching. **2** a fragment of a song or talk etc. **3** *slang* a kidnapping. **4** a short period of doing something. □ **snatcher** *n.* (esp. in sense 2b of *v.*)

snazzy *adj.* (**snazzier, snazziest**) *slang* smart or fashionable. □ **snazzily** *adv.* **snazziness** *n.*

sneak ● *v.* (**sneaks;** *past* and *past participle* **snuck** or **sneaked; sneaking**) **1** go quietly and secretly. **2** *informal* take or do something secretly. ● *n.* a cowardly deceitful person. ● *adj.* acting or done secretly. □ **sneak up** approach quietly and stealthily. □ **sneaking** *adj.*

sneaker *n.* a running shoe. □ **sneakered** *adj.*

sneak preview *n.* a special showing of a new film, exhibition, etc. before it is shown to the public.

sneaky *adj.* (**sneakier, sneakiest**) behaving in a secret and sometimes dishonest or unpleasant way. □ **sneakily** *adv.* **sneakiness** *n.*

sneer ● *n.* a contemptuous smile or remark. ● *v.* **1** smile contemptuously. **2** say sneeringly or contemptuously. □ **sneering** *adj.* **sneeringly** *adv.*

sneeze ● *n.* a sudden involuntary expulsion of air from the nose and mouth caused by irritation of the nostrils. ● *v.* (**sneezes, sneezed, sneezing**) make a sneeze. □ **not to be sneezed at** not insignificant. □ **sneezy** *adj.*

Sne Nay Muxw *n.* (*pl.* **Sne Nay Muxw**) **1** a member of an Aboriginal people inhabiting southwestern BC. **2** the Salishan language of this people. □ **Sne Nay Muxw** *adj.* [*Say* snuh NYE mo]

snicker ● *n.* **1** a half-suppressed laugh. **2** a whinny, a neigh. ● *v.* **1** make such a laugh. **2** whinny.

snide *adj.* sneering; slyly derogatory. □ **snidely** *adv.*

sniff ● *v.* **1** draw up air audibly through the nose. **2** clear one's nose by sniffing. **3** express disdain, contempt, etc. **4** smell by sniffing. **5** *informal* take (a drug etc.) by breathing it in through the nose. **6** discover, suspect. **7** say (something) in a complaining or disdainful way. ● *n.* **1** an act or sound of sniffing. **2** a hint or intimation. □ **sniff around** search around secretly. **sniff at** show contempt for. **sniff out** detect. □ **sniffily** *adv.*

sniffer *n.* **1** a person who sniffs esp. a drug. **2** *informal* the nose. **3** *informal* any device for detecting gas etc. **4** a dog trained to detect drugs or track missing people.

sniffle ● *v.* (**sniffles, sniffled, sniffling**) sniff slightly or repeatedly. ● *n.* **1** the act of sniffling. **2** a slight head cold. □ **sniffly** *adj.*

sniffy *adj. informal* disdainful. □ **sniffily** *adv.*

snifter *n.* **1** a short-stemmed glass with a large bowl. **2** *slang* a small drink of alcohol.

snigger ● *n.* = SNICKER *n.* 1. ● *v.* = SNICKER *v.* 1.

snip ● *v.* (**snips, snipped, snipping**) cut with scissors or shears in small quick strokes. ● *n.* **1** an act of snipping. **2** a small piece snipped off.

snipe ● *n.* **1** (*pl.* **snipe** or **snipes**) a brown wading bird with a long straight bill. **2** (*pl.* **snipes**) a sly or petty criticism. ● *v.* (**snipes, sniped, sniping**) **1** fire shots from hiding. **2** make a sly critical attack. □ **sniper** n. **sniping** n.

snippet n. a small fragment or bit.

snippy adj. (**snippier, snippiest**) informal impertinently brusque. □ **snippily** adv.

snit n. a state of agitation, pique, etc.

snitch ● v. (**snitches, snitched, snitching**) slang **1** steal. **2** inform on a person. ● n. (pl. **snitches**) an informer.

snivel v. (**snivels, snivelled, snivelling**) **1** cry and sniff. **2** complain in a miserable, crying voice. **3** have a runny nose. □ **snivelling** adj.

snob n. **1** a person with an exaggerated respect for social position or wealth. **2** a person who is condescending to others whose tastes or attainments are considered inferior. □ **snobbery** n. (pl. **snobberies**) **snobbish** adj. **snobbishly** adv. **snobbishness** n. **snobbism** n. **snobby** adj. (**snobbier, snobbiest**)

sno-cone = SNOW CONE.

snooker ● n. **1** a game played with cues on a pool table in which the players use a cue ball to pocket the other balls in a set order. **2** a position in this game in which a direct shot at a permitted ball is impossible. ● v. **1** subject to a snooker. **2** slang **a** defeat; thwart. **b** trick; dupe. [SNOOK rhymes with LOOK or LUKE]

snoop informal ● v. investigate secretly. ● n. **1** an act of snooping. **2** a person who snoops. □ **snooper** n. **snoopy** adj.

snoot n. slang the nose.

snooty adj. (**snootier, snootiest**) informal snobbish; conceited; contemptuous. □ **snootily** adv. **snootiness** n.

snooze informal ● n. **1** a short sleep. **2** informal something boring. **3** a function on an alarm clock etc. which turns off the alarm for a short, fixed period. ● v. (**snoozes, snoozed, snoozing**) take a snooze. □ **snoozer** n.

snore ● n. a snorting sound in breathing during sleep. ● v. (**snores, snored, snoring**) make this sound. □ **snorer** n.

snorkel ● n. a breathing tube for an underwater swimmer. ● v. (**snorkels, snorkelled, snorkelling**) use a snorkel. □ **snorkeller** n.

snort ● n. **1** an explosive sound made by the sudden forcing of breath through the nose, esp. expressing disbelief. **2** a similar sound made by an engine etc. **3** informal a small drink of liquor. **4** slang an inhaled dose of a drug. ● v. **1** make a snort. **2** slang inhale (esp. cocaine). □ **snorter** n.

snot n. slang **1** nasal mucus. **2** a contemptible person.

snot-nosed adj. slang **1** (of a person) snotty. **2** conceited.

snotty adj. (**snottier, snottiest**) slang **1** producing or covered with snot. **2** showing a superior attitude.

snout n. **1** the projecting nose and mouth of an animal. **2** the pointed front of a thing. □ **snouted** adj.

snow ● n. **1** atmospheric vapour frozen into ice crystals and falling in light white flakes. **2** a layer of this on the ground. **3** a thing resembling snow, esp. the white spots on a television screen. **4** slang cocaine. ● v. **1** (of snow) fall. **2** confine or block with snow. **3** fall as or like snow. **4** slang deceive or charm. □ **be snowed under** be overwhelmed.

snow angel n. the outline of an angel made by lying in the snow and moving the arms and legs.

snowball ● n. a ball of packed snow. ● v. grow or increase rapidly. □ **not a snowball's chance in hell** informal no chance at all.

snowbank n. a heap or mound of snow.

snowbelt n. a region subject to heavy snowfalls.

snowbird n. informal a person from Canada or the northern US who moves to a southern state in the winter.

snow-blind adj. temporarily blinded by the glare of light reflected on snow. □ **snow blindness** n.

snow blower n. a machine that clears snow by blowing it to one side.

snowboard n. a wide board like a ski used for sliding downhill on snow. □ **snowboarder** n. **snowboarding** n.

snowbound adj. prevented by snow from going out or travelling.

snowcap n. the tip of a mountain covered with snow. □ **snow-capped** adj.

snowcat n. a vehicle with caterpillar tracks for travelling through snow, used esp. for grooming ski trails etc.

snow cone n. a paper cone filled with crushed ice flavoured with fruit syrup.

snow crab n. an edible spider crab found off the eastern coast of Canada.

snowdrift n. a bank of snow heaped up by the wind.

snowdrop n. a plant with white drooping flowers in the early spring.

snowfall n. **1** a fall of snow. **2** the amount of snow that falls at a given time.

snow fence n. a usu. portable fence serving as a barrier to drifting snow. □ **snow fencing** n.

snowfield n. a permanent wide expanse of snow.

snowflake *n.* each of the many small crystals in which snow falls.

snow goose *n.* a white Arctic goose with black-tipped wings.

snow job *n.* an attempt to deceive or persuade, esp. through flattery.

snow leopard *n.* a large rare Asian cat with leopard-like markings on a cream coat.

snow line *n.* the level above which snow never melts entirely.

snow-making *n.* the production of artificial snow.

snowman *n.* (*pl.* **snowmen**) a figure resembling a person, made of packed snow.

snowmelt *n.* **1** the melting of fallen snow. **2** the water that results from this.

snowmobile *n.* a motor vehicle equipped with runners and Caterpillar tracks for travelling over snow. □ **snowmobiler** *n.* **snowmobiling** *n.*

snowpack *n.* the accumulation of winter snow.

snow pants *pl. n.* a pair of pants worn over other pants in wintery conditions, usu. of padded nylon.

snow pea *n.* a variety of pea eaten whole including the pod.

snowplow (also **snowplough**) ● *n.* **1** a device or vehicle for clearing roads etc. of snow. **2** *Skiing* a technique for slowing down in which the points of the skis are turned inwards. ● *v.* **1** clear (a road etc.) using a snowplow. **2** *Skiing* execute a snowplow.

snowshoe ● *n.* a flat device like a racquet attached to a boot for walking on snow. ● *v.* (**snowshoes, snowshoed, snowshoeing**) travel on snowshoes. □ **snowshoer** *n.*

snowshoe hare *n.* (also **snowshoe rabbit**) a N American hare with large hind feet and a white coat in winter.

snowstorm *n.* a heavy fall of snow.

snowsuit *n.* a winter outer garment combining both coat and pants.

snow tire *n.* a tire equipped with deep treads etc. to give increased traction on snow or ice.

snow-white *adj.* pure white.

snowy *adj.* (**snowier, snowiest**) **1 a** of or like snow. **b** pure white. **2** (of the weather etc.) with much snow. **3** covered with snow.

snowy owl *n.* a large white owl, native to the Arctic.

snub ● *v.* (**snubs, snubbed, snubbing**) rebuff or humiliate scornfully. ● *n.* an act of snubbing. ● *adj.* short and blunt in shape.

snub nose *n.* a short turned-up nose. □ **snub-nosed** *adj.*

snuck *past and past participle of* SNEAK.

snuff ● *n.* **1** the charred part of a candle wick. **2** powdered tobacco that is sniffed up the nostrils. ● *v.* **1** smother the flame of (a candle). **2** *slang* kill (a person). □ **snuff out 1** extinguish by snuffing. **2** kill. **up to snuff** *informal* up to standard.

snuffer *n.* a small hollow cone with a handle used to snuff a candle.

snuffle ● *v.* (**snuffles, snuffled, snuffling**) **1** make sniffing sounds. **2** speak or say nasally. **3** breathe noisily as through a partially blocked nose. **4** sniff. ● *n.* **1** a snuffling sound. **2** (in *pl.*) a partial blockage of the nose.

snug ● *adj.* (**snugger, snuggest**) **1** warm and cozy. **2** secure and sheltered. **3** compact and well-organized. **4** close-fitting. ● *v.* (**snugs, snugged, snugging**) make snug. □ **snugly** *adv.*

snuggle *v.* (**snuggles, snuggled, snuggling**) **1** lie or get close to for warmth, comfort, or affection. **2** place in a warm comfortable position.

snuggly *adj.* (**snugglier, snuggliest**) comfortably warm, cozy. [Say SNUGGLE ee]

Snugli *n. proprietary* a pouch for carrying a baby.

snye *n. Cdn* a narrow or meandering side channel.

so[1] ● *adv.* **1** to such a great extent. **2** extremely; very much. **3** to the same extent. **4** referring back to something previously mentioned. **5** similarly. **6** thus. ● *conj.* **1** therefore. **2** with the result or aim that. **3** and then. **4** in the same way. ● *pron.* something that is near to the number in question. □ **and so on** (also **and so forth**) **1** and similar things. **2** and in similar ways. **so be it** an expression of acceptance. **so long!** *informal* goodbye. **so to speak** (or **say**) indicating that one is not talking literally. **so what?** *informal* why should that be considered significant?

so[2] *n. Music* **1** (in tonic sol-fa) the fifth note of a major scale. **2** the note G in the fixed-do system.

soak ● *v.* **1** make or become thoroughly wet. **2** (of rain etc.) drench. **3** (**soak oneself in**) immerse oneself in (a subject etc.). **4** (of liquid) spread completely throughout. **5** remove by soaking in water etc. **6** *informal* extract money from by an extortionate charge etc. ● *n.* the act of soaking or the state of being soaked. □ **soak up 1** absorb (liquid). **2** acquire (knowledge etc.). **3** expose oneself to (the sun etc.). □ **soaker** *n.*

soaked adj. **1** thoroughly wet. **2** very drunk.

soaking ● adj. (also **soaking wet**) very wet; wet through. ● n. an act of wetting something.

so-and-so n. (pl. **so-and-sos**) **1** a person or thing not needing to be specified. **2** informal a person disliked.

soap ● n. **1** a cleansing agent that is a compound of fatty acid with soda or potash which yields a lather used in washing. **2** informal a soap opera. ● v. **1** apply soap to. **2** scrub with soap.

soapbox n. (pl. **soapboxes**) **1** a makeshift stand for a public speaker. **2** something that provides an outlet for a person's opinions etc.

soap opera n. **1** a television drama dealing with events in the daily lives of a group of characters. **2** informal a series of sensational, unexpected, or melodramatic events.

soapstone n. a soft rock with a smooth greasy feel.

soapy adj. (**soapier**, **soapiest**) **1** of or like soap. **2** containing or smeared with soap.

soar v. **1** fly or rise high. **2** reach a high level. **3** maintain height in the air by gliding. □ **soaring** adj.

sob ● v. (**sobs**, **sobbed**, **sobbing**) **1 a** draw breath in convulsive gasps usu. with weeping. **b** weep in this way. **2** utter with sobs. ● n. an act or sound of sobbing.

sober ● adj. (**soberer**, **soberest**) **1** not drunk. **2** not given to excessive drinking of alcohol. **3** moderate, sedate. **4** not fanciful. **5** (of a colour etc.) quiet and inconspicuous. ● v. make or become sober. □ **soberly** adv.

sobriety n. **1** the state of being sober. **2** moderation. [Say suh BRYE a tee]

sobriquet n. **1** a nickname. **2** an assumed name. [Say SO brick ay]

sob story n. informal a story intended to arouse sympathy or sadness.

so-called adj. commonly designated or known as.

soccer n. a form of football played by two teams of 11, in which a round ball may be kicked but not handled except by the goaltender.

sociable adj. **1** ready and willing to talk and act with others. **2** friendly. **3** not stiff or formal. □ **sociability** n. **sociably** adv. [Say SO shuh bull, so shuh BILLA tee]

social ● adj. **1** of or relating to society or its organization. **2** concerned with the mutual relations of human beings. **3** living in organized communities. **4** indicating activities in which people meet each other for pleasure. **5** (of birds, insects, etc.) living in organized communities. ● n. a social gathering. □ **socially** adv.

social assistance n. Cdn social security.

social climber n. derogatory a person anxious to gain a higher social status. □ **social climbing** n. **social-climbing** adj.

social conscience n. a sense of responsibility for the problems and injustices of society.

social contract n. (also **social compact**) an unspoken understanding among the members of a society that co-operation produces social benefits, e.g. sacrificing some individual freedoms for state protection.

social credit ● n. **1** an economic theory that the purchasing power of consumers should be increased. **2** (**Social Credit**) Cdn the Social Credit party. ● adj. (**Social Credit**) Cdn of the Social Credit Party.

Social Credit Party n. Cdn a political party formed in the 1930s espousing conservative financial and social policies. □ **Social Crediter** n.

social Darwinism n. a late 19th-century theory that individuals, groups, and peoples are subject to the same laws of natural selection as plants and animals. □ **social Darwinist** n.

social democracy n. a socialist system achieved by democratic means. □ **social democrat** n.

social engineering n. the attempt to change society according to particular political beliefs.

social housing n. Cdn & Brit. public housing.

social insurance number n. Cdn a nine-digit number by which the federal government identifies individuals for the purposes of taxation, pensions, etc. Abbreviation: **SIN**.

socialism n. **1** a political and economic theory which advocates that the community as a whole, and not private capitalists, should own and control the resources and industries of a country. **2** policy or practice based on this theory. □ **socialist** n. & adj. **socialistic** adj.

socialite n. a person who is well-known in fashionable society. [Say SOCIAL ite]

socialize v. (**socializes**, **socialized**, **socializing**) **1** act in a sociable manner. **2** make (someone) behave in a way that is acceptable to society. □ **socialization** n.

social justice n. the notion that society should be organized in a way that allows equal opportunity for all.

social life *n.* leisure activities in which one associates with one's friends etc.

social realism *n.* the realistic depiction of social conditions in art and literature. □ **social realist** *n.*

social science *n.* **1** the scientific study of human society and social relationships **2** a branch of this (e.g. politics). □ **social scientist** *n.*

social security *n.* state assistance to those lacking in economic security and welfare.

social service *n.* a service provided by the state etc. for the community, esp. education, health care, etc.

social studies *pl. n.* a school course including geography, history, anthropology, etc.

social work *n.* work done to help people with special needs. □ **social worker** *n.*

societal *adj.* having to do with society. [*Say* suh SIGH a tull]

society *n.* (*pl.* **societies**) **1** the sum of human conditions and activity regarded as a whole functioning interdependently. **2** a social community. **3 a** a social mode of life. **b** the customs of an ordered community. **4** the socially advantaged members of a community. **5** participation in hospitality. **6** companionship, company. **7** an association or group.

Society of Friends *n.* a movement of Christians (called **Quakers**) devoted to peaceful principles.

Society of Jesus *n.* a Catholic order of priests (also called **Jesuits**) founded in 1534 to do missionary work.

socio- *comb. form* **1** of society (and). **2** of or relating to sociology (and). [*Say* SO see oh *or* SO shee oh]

socio-economic *adj.* having to do with the interaction of social and economic factors. □ **socio-economically** *adv.*

sociolinguistics *n.* the study of language in relation to social factors. □ **sociolinguistic** *adj.*

sociology *n.* **1** the study of the development and structure of human society. **2** the study of social problems. □ **sociological** *adj.* **sociologist** *n.* [*Say* so see OLLA jee *or* so shee OLLA jee, so see a LOGICAL *or* so shee a LOGICAL]

sociopath *n.* a person with a personality disorder manifesting itself in extreme anti-social attitudes and behaviour. □ **sociopathic** *adj.* [*Say* SO see oh path, so see oh PATH ick]

sock¹ *n.* ● **1** a short knitted covering for the foot. **2** a windsock. ● *v.* (usu. foll. by

away) put money aside as savings. □ **knock** (or **blow**) **one's socks off** astound, amaze. **pull up one's socks** *informal* make an effort to improve. **put a sock in it** *informal* be quiet.

sock² *informal* ● *v.* hit forcefully. ● *n.* a hard blow. □ **sock it to** attack or address vigorously.

socked in *adj.* (of an airport etc.) not operating because of snow, fog, etc.

socket *n.* **1** a hollow for something to fit into or revolve in. **2** a device receiving a plug, light bulb, etc.

sockeye *n.* (*pl.* **sockeye**) a blue-backed salmon of the N American Pacific coast.

sock hop *n.* a social dance at which participants dance in their stocking feet.

Socratic ● *adj.* of or relating to the Greek philosopher Socrates (469–399 BC) or his philosophy. ● *n.* a follower of Socrates. [*Say* so CRAT ick]

Socred *Cdn* ● *adj.* = SOCIAL CREDIT *adj.* ● *n.* a supporter of the Social Credit Party. [*Say* SO cred]

sod ● *n.* the surface of the ground with grass, or a piece of this. ● *v.* (**sods**, **sodded**, **sodding**) cover with sod.

soda *n.* **1** any compound of sodium in common use. **2** (also **soda water**) carbonated water. **3** (also **soda pop**) esp. *US* = POP¹ *n.* 2. **4** a sweet fizzy drink.

soda cracker *n.* a thin crisp cracker made with baking soda.

soda fountain *n.* a shop or counter serving soft drinks, ice cream, etc.

sodbuster *n.* *informal* a crop farmer, esp. one of the early homesteaders on the Prairies.

sodden *adj.* **1** soaked through. **2** intoxicated.

sod house *n.* (also **sod hut**) a house made of sod, built esp. by settlers on the Prairies.

sodium *n.* a soft silver-white reactive metallic element, occurring naturally in salt etc. [*Say* SO dee um]

sodium chloride *n.* the chemical name for common salt.

sodium nitrate *n.* a white powdery compound used mainly in fertilizers.

sodomite *n.* a person who engages in sodomy. [*Say* SOD um ite]

sodomy *n.* anal intercourse. □ **sodomize** *v.* (**sodomizes**, **sodomized**, **sodomizing**) [*Say* SODDA mee]

sod-turning *n.* *Cdn* = GROUNDBREAKING *n.*

sofa *n.* a long upholstered seat with a back and arms, for two or more people.

sofa bed *n.* a sofa that can be folded out into a bed.

soffit *n.* the underside of an arch, overhanging eaves, etc.

soft ● *adj.* **1** lacking hardness or firmness. **2** not rough in texture. **3** quiet and gentle. **4** (of light or colour) not harsh. **5** sympathetic, lenient. **6** *informal* (of a job or way of life) requiring little effort. **7** *informal* foolish. **8** (of a drink) not alcoholic. **9** (of a drug) not likely to cause addiction. **10** (of water) free from mineral salts. **11** (also **soft-core**) (of pornography) not explicit. ● *adv.* softly. ● *n.* a soft or yielding thing. □ **have a soft spot for** be fond of. □ **softness** *n.* **softly** *adv.*

softball *n.* **1** a form of baseball played on a smaller diamond with a larger, softer ball. **2** the ball used in this.

soft-boiled *adj.* **1** (of an egg) lightly boiled leaving the yolk soft. **2** *informal* (of a person) easygoing.

softcover *adj. & n.* paperback.

soft drink *n.* a carbonated, non-alcoholic drink.

soften *v.* **1** make or become soft or softer. **2** make or become less severe. **3** modify, tone down. **4** reduce the resistance of (a person). □ **softener** *n.* [Say SOFF'n]

soft-focus ● *adj.* **1** having to do with a deliberate slight blurring in a photograph. **2** deliberately unclear. ● *n.* (**soft focus**) **1** a deliberate slight blurring in a photograph. **2** deliberate lack of clarity.

soft-hearted *adj.* tender, compassionate.

softie *n.* (also **softy**) (*pl.* **softies**) *informal* a kind, soft-hearted, or weak person.

soft palate *n.* the rear part of the palate.

soft pedal ● *n.* a pedal on a piano that softens the tone. ● *v.* (**soft-pedal, soft-pedals, soft-pedalled, soft-pedalling**) refrain from emphasizing.

soft rock *n.* a type of rock music characterized by a melodic sound and usu. romantic lyrics.

soft sell ● *n.* subtly persuasive salesmanship. ● *v.* (**soft-sell, soft-sells, soft-sold, soft-selling**) sell by this method.

soft-shell crab *n.* a crab that has recently moulted and has a new shell that is soft and edible.

soft-shoe ● *n.* a kind of tap dance performed in soft-soled shoes. ● *v.* (**soft-shoes, soft-shoed, soft-shoeing**) **1** perform this dance. **2** move quietly.

soft soap ● *n.* **1** a semi-liquid soap. **2** *informal* persuasive flattery. ● *v.* (**soft-soap**) *informal* persuade with flattery.

soft-spoken *adj.* speaking with a quiet voice.

soft touch *n.* *slang* a person easily manipulated.

software *n.* programs and other operating information used by a computer.

softwood *n.* **1** the wood of pine, spruce, or other conifers. **2** a tree producing such wood.

soggy *adj.* (**soggier, soggiest**) **1** sodden, saturated. **2** (of weather) rainy.

soh *n.* = SO².

soil ● *n.* **1** the upper layer of earth in which plants grow. **2** the ground. **3** ground belonging to a nation; territory. **4** a dirty mark. **5** filth. ● *v.* **1** make dirty. **2** dirty (diapers etc.) by defecation. **3** tarnish, defile. □ **soilless** *adj.*

soiree *n.* a party in the evening. [Say swah RAY]

sojourn ● *n.* a temporary stay. ● *v.* stay temporarily. □ **sojourner** *n.* [Say SO jurn]

sol *n.* = SO². [Say SAUL]

solace ● *n.* comfort in distress. ● *v.* (**solaces, solaced, solacing**) give solace to. [Say SAUL us]

solar *adj.* having to do with the sun.

solar cell *n.* a photoelectric device converting solar radiation into electricity.

solar eclipse *n.* an eclipse in which the sun is obscured by the moon.

solarium *n.* a glass-enclosed room, balcony, etc. [Say suh LARRY um]

solar panel *n.* (also **solar collector**) a panel that harnesses the sun's energy, either to generate electricity or to heat water.

solar plexus *n.* (*pl.* **solar plexus** or **solar plexuses**) **1** the network of nerves at the pit of the stomach. **2** the region of the torso in front of this.

solar power *n.* power obtained by harnessing the energy of the sun's rays. □ **solar-powered** *adj.*

solar system *n.* the collection of nine planets and their moons, comets, and asteroids in orbit around the sun.

solar year *n.* the time taken for the earth to travel once around the sun, measured from equinox to equinox.

sold *past and past participle* of SELL. □ **sold on** *informal* enthusiastic about.

solder ● *n.* a low-melting alloy used for joining metals. ● *v.* join with solder. □ **solderless** *adj.* [Say SODDER, SODDER less]

soldering iron *n.* a tool used for applying solder. [Say SODDER ing]

soldier ● *n.* **1** a person serving in an army.

2 a private or non-commissioned officer in an army. **3** a person who fights for a cause. **4** (also **soldier ant**) a wingless ant or termite with a large head and jaws for fighting. ● *v.* serve as a soldier. □ **soldier on** *informal* persevere doggedly. □ **soldierly** *adj.*

soldier of fortune *n.* a person ready to take service under any state or person.

sold-out *adj.* having all tickets sold.

sole¹ ● *n.* **1 a** the underside of the foot. **b** the part of footwear corresponding to this. **2** (*pl.* **sole** or **soles**) an edible marine flatfish. ● *v.* provide (a shoe etc.) with a sole. □ **-soled** *adj.*

sole² *adj.* one and only. □ **solely** *adv.*

solecism *n.* **1** a mistake of grammar or idiom. **2** a piece of bad manners or incorrect behaviour. [*Say* SOLLA sism]

solemn *adj.* **1** serious and dignified. **2** formal. **3** cheerless. **4** weighty. **5** grave, sober. □ **solemnly** *adv.*

solemnity *n.* (*pl.* **solemnities**) **1** the state of being solemn. **2** a rite or celebration. [*Say* suh LEM nuh tee]

solemnize *v.* (**solemnizes, solemnized, solemnizing**) **1** duly perform (a ceremony). **2** celebrate or commemorate by special observances. [*Say* SOLEMN nize]

solenoid *n.* a coil of wire acting as a magnet when carrying current. [*Say* SOLE annoyed]

solicit *v.* (**solicits, solicited, soliciting**) **1** ask for or try to obtain something from someone. **2** accost a person and offer one's services as a prostitute. □ **solicitation** *n.* [*Say* suh LISS it, suh lissa TAY sh'n]

solicitor *n.* **1** *Cdn* a lawyer. **2** a person who solicits. **3** the chief law officer of a city, town, or government department. [*Say* suh LISSA tur]

Solicitor General *n.* (*pl.* **Solicitors General**) (in Canada) a cabinet member who is responsible for correctional services, law enforcement, etc.

solicitous *adj.* showing interest or concern. □ **solicitously** *adv.* [*Say* suh LISSA tuss]

solicitude *n.* care or concern. [*Say* suh LISSA tood *or* suh LISSA tyood]

solid ● *adj.* **1** firm and stable in shape. **2** strongly built or made. **3** not hollow or having spaces or gaps. **4** consisting of the same substance throughout. **5** (of time) continuous. **6** able to be relied on. **7** *Geometry* three-dimensional. ● *n.* **1** a solid substance or object. **2** (in *pl.*) food that is

not liquid. **3** a three-dimensional body or figure. ● *adv.* solidly. □ **solidly** *adv.*

solidarity *n.* (*pl.* **solidarities**) **1** support for the beliefs or plight of an individual or group. **2** agreement among individuals with a common interest. [*Say* solla DARE a tee]

solidify *v.* (**solidifies, solidified, solidifying**) **1** make or become solid. **2** secure or strengthen (a position etc.). □ **solidification** *n.* [*Say* suh LIDDA fie, suh lidda fuh KAY sh'n]

solidity *n.* the quality or state of being solid. [*Say* suh LIDDA tee]

soliloquy *n.* (*pl.* **soliloquies**) the act of talking when alone or regardless of any hearers, esp. in drama. □ **soliloquize** *v.* (**soliloquizes, soliloquized, soliloquizing**) [*Say* suh LIL a kwee, suh LIL a kwize]

solipsism *n.* the view that the self is all that can be known to exist. □ **solipsistic** *adj.* [*Say* SOLLIP sism, sollip SIS tick]

solitaire *n.* **1** a diamond or other gem set by itself. **2** a ring having a single gem. **3** a game for one player in which cards have to be arranged in certain groups or sequences. **4** a game for one player played by removing pegs etc. one at a time from a board by jumping others over them. [*Say* SOLLA tare]

solitary ● *adj.* **1** done or existing alone. **2** performed alone. **3** (of a place) secluded. **4** single or sole. **5** *Botany* growing singly. ● *n.* (*pl.* **solitaries**) **1** a recluse or hermit. **2** *informal* (also **solitary confinement**) isolation of a prisoner in a separate cell as a punishment. □ **solitariness** *n.*

solitude *n.* the state of being alone.

solo ● *n.* (*pl.* **solos**) **1** (*pl.* **solos** or **soli**) a piece of music, song, or dance for one performer. **2** an unaccompanied flight by a pilot. ● *v.* (**soloes, soloed, soloing**) perform a solo. ● *adv.* unaccompanied, alone.

soloist *n.* a performer of a solo.

solstice *n.* either of the two times in the year, approx. June 21 and Dec. 22, when the sun reaches its highest or lowest point in the sky at noon, marked by the longest and shortest days. [*Say* SOLE stiss *or* SAUL stiss]

soluble *adj.* that can be dissolved. □ **solubility** *n.* [*Say* SAUL yoo bull, saul yoo BILLA tee]

solute *n.* a dissolved substance. [*Say* SAUL yoot]

solution *n.* **1 a** a means of solving a problem. **b** an explanation or answer. **2** a mixture formed when a substance is dissolved in a liquid. **3** the act of dissolving or the state of being dissolved.

solve v. (**solves, solved, solving**) find an answer to or a way of dealing with (a problem). □ **solvable** adj. **solver** n.

solvency n. the state of not being in debt. [Say SAUL vun see]

solvent ● adj. **1** having more money than one owes. **2** able to dissolve a substance. ● n. **1** the liquid in which a solute is dissolved to form a solution. **2** a liquid used to dissolve other substances.

solvent abuse n. the use of solvents as intoxicants by inhalation.

Somali n. **1** (pl. **Somali** or **Somalis**) a **a** member of a Muslim people of Somalia. **b** a person from Somalia. **2** the language of this people. □ **Somali** adj. **Somalian** adj. & n. [Say suh MAWL ee or suh MAL ee]

somatic adj. having to do with the body rather than the mind. [Say suh MAT ick]

sombre adj. (also esp. US **somber**) **1** gloomy, shadowy. **2** dark in colour. **3** oppressively solemn. □ **sombrely** adv.

sombrero n. (pl. **sombreros**) a broad-brimmed hat worn esp. in Mexico. [Say som BRARE oh]

some ● adj. **1** an unspecified amount or number of. **2** that is unknown or unspecified. **3** a considerable amount or number of. **4** informal notably such. ● pron. some people or things, some number or amount. □ **and then some** informal and plenty more than that.

-some suffix forming nouns from numerals, meaning "a group of (so many)".

somebody (also **someone**) ● pron. some person. ● n. (pl. **somebodies**) a person of importance.

someday adv. at some time in the future.

somehow adv. **1** in some way. **2** for some reason or other.

someplace adv. & pron. somewhere.

somersault ● n. an acrobatic movement in which a person turns head over heels in the air or on the ground. ● v. perform a somersault. [Say SUMMER salt]

something ● n. & pron. **1 a** some unspecified or unknown thing. **b** (also **something or other**) as a substitute for an unknown description. **2** a known or understood but not expressed quantity, quality, or extent. **3** informal an important person or thing. **4** (in comb.) used to denote a person's approximate age. ● adv. **1** somewhat. **2** informal to a high degree. □ **something like 1** an amount in the region of. **2** somewhat like.

sometime ● adv. at some unspecified time. ● adj. **1** former. **2** occasional.

sometimes adv. occasionally.

somewhat ● adv. to some extent. ● n. & pron. something.

somewhere ● adv. in or to some place. ● pron. some unspecified place. □ **get somewhere** informal achieve success. **somewhere around** approximately.

somnambulism n. sleepwalking. □ **somnambulist** n. [Say som NAM byoo lism, som NAM byoo list]

somnolent adj. **1** sleepy. **2** inducing drowsiness. □ **somnolence** n. [Say SOMNA lint]

son n. **1** a boy or man in relation to his parents. **2** a male descendant. **3** (also **my son**) a form of address to a boy. **4** (**the Son**) (in Christian belief) Jesus Christ.

sonar n. **1** a system for the underwater detection of objects by reflected sound pulses. **2** an apparatus for this. [Say SO nar]

sonata n. a composition for one instrument or two, usu. in several movements. [Say suh NOTTA or suh NATTA]

song n. **1** a musical composition comprising a set of words set to music. **2** singing. **3** a sound suggestive of singing. **4** the usu. repeated musical call of some birds. □ **for a song** informal very cheaply. □ **song-like** adj.

song and dance n. informal a fuss.

songbird n. a bird with a musical call.

songbook n. a collection of songs with music.

songwriter n. a writer of songs or the music for them. □ **songwriting** n.

sonic adj. relating to or using sound waves. □ **sonically** adv. [Say SAWN ick]

sonic boom n. a loud explosive noise caused by the shock wave from an aircraft breaking the sound barrier.

son-in-law n. (pl. **sons-in-law**) the husband of one's daughter.

sonnet n. a lyric poem of 14 lines, usu. written in iambic pentameter, using a formal rhyme scheme.

sonny n. informal a familiar form of address to a young boy.

son of a gun informal ● n. **1** a jocular form of address or reference. **2** a rascal. ● interj. an exclamation of amazement.

son of God n. (**Son of God**) Jesus Christ.

sonorous adj. having a loud, full, or deep sound. □ **sonority** n. **sonorously** adv. [Say SAWN er us or SONE er us, suh NOR a tee]

soon adv. **1** within a short period of time. **2** early. **3** readily or willingly. □ **as** (or **so**)

soon as at the moment that. **how soon?** how early. **no sooner ... than** at the very moment that. **sooner or later** eventually.

soot *n.* a black substance rising in fine flakes in the smoke of wood, coal, oil, etc. [*Rhymes with* FOOT]

soothe *v.* (**soothes, soothed, soothing**) **1** calm. **2** reduce the intensity of. **3** provide relief or tranquility. □ **soothing** *adj.* **soothingly** *adv.*

soother *n. Cdn & Brit.* a ring or nipple made of rubber or plastic given to a baby to suck.

soothsayer *n.* a person who predicts future events. □ **soothsaying** *n.*

sooty *adj.* (**sootier, sootiest**) covered with or full of soot. [*With* OO *as in* FOOT]

sop ● *n.* a thing given or done to pacify or appease a person. ● *v.* (**sops, sopped, sopping**) absorb (liquid) in a sponge, piece of bread, etc.

sophist *n.* a person who uses clever but false arguments. [*Say* SOFF ist]

sophisticate *n.* a sophisticated person. [*Say* suh FISTA kit]

sophisticated *adj.* **1 a** worldly, cultured, and refined. **b** knowledgeable, experienced. **2** appealing to sophisticated people or sophisticated tastes. **3 a** complex. **b** highly developed. □ **sophistication** *n.* [*Say* suh FISTA kate id, suh fista KAY sh'n]

sophistry *n.* (*pl.* **sophistries**) **1** the use of clever but false arguments. **2** such an argument. [*Say* SOFF us tree]

sophomore *n.* (esp. in the US) a second-year student in high school, college, or university. [*Say* SOFFA more]

sophomoric *adj.* **1** having to do with a sophomore. **2** intellectually pretentious while immature, juvenile, or shallow. [*Say* soffa MORE ick]

soporific ● *adj.* tending to induce or produce sleep. ● *n.* a soporific drug or influence. [*Say* soppa RIFF ick]

sopping *adj.* (also **sopping wet**) soaked with liquid.

soppy *adj.* (**soppier, soppiest**) *informal* mawkishly sentimental.

soprano *n.* **1 a** the highest singing voice. **b** a singer with this voice. **2** an instrument of a high or the highest pitch in its family. [*Say* suh PRAN oh]

sorbet *n.* a soft water ice made with fruit juice or fruit purée. [*Say* sore BAY]

sorcery *n.* (*pl.* **sorceries**) magic esp. that uses evil spirits. □ **sorcerer** *n.* **sorceress** *n.* (*pl.* **sorceresses**) [*Say* SORE sir ee, SORE sir ur, SORE sir ess]

sordid *adj.* **1** immoral or dishonest. **2** dirty, filthy.

sore ● *adj.* **1** painful or aching. **2** (of a person) suffering bodily pain. **3** *informal* angry, irritated. ● *n.* **1** a raw or tender place on the body. **2** a source of annoyance. □ **soreness** *n.*

sore loser *n.* a person who cannot accept losing graciously.

sorely *adv.* extremely, desperately.

sore point *n.* (also **sore spot**) a contentious issue.

sorghum *n.* a tropical cereal grass that is a major source of grain and animal feed. [*Say* SORE gum]

sorority *n.* (*pl.* **sororities**) a society for female students in a university or college. [*Say* suh ROAR a tee]

sorrel ● *adj.* of a light reddish-brown colour. ● *n.* **1** this colour. **2** an animal of this colour. **3** a meadow plant with triangular leaves and an acidic flavour. [*Say* SORE ul]

sorrow ● *n.* **1** mental distress caused by loss or disappointment; grief. **2** a cause of sorrow. ● *v.* feel or express sorrow. □ **sorrowful** *adj.* **sorrowfully** *adv.*

sorry ● *adj.* (**sorrier, sorriest**) **1** feeling sadness or regret. **2** full of shame, guilt, and remorse. **3** pathetic. ● *interj.* **1** used to express apology or regret. **2** what did you say?

sort ● *n.* **1** a group of things or people with common attributes. **2** an unusual example of a specified thing. **3** *informal* a person of a specified character. ● *v.* arrange systematically in groups. □ **of sorts** (or **of a sort**) *informal* of an unusual kind. **out of sorts 1** slightly irritable. **2** slightly unwell. **sort of** *informal* to some extent. **sort out 1** separate into groups according to kind. **2** separate from a group. **3** resolve (a problem). □ **sorter** *n.*

sortie ● *n.* **1** a sudden attack made by troops from a besieged garrison. **2** an operational flight by a single military aircraft. **3** *informal* an excursion. ● *v.* (**sorties, sortied, sortieing**) make a sortie. [*Say* SORE tee]

SOS *n.* (*pl.* **SOS's**) **1** an international code signal of extreme distress. **2** an urgent appeal for help.

so-so *adj.* neither very good nor very bad.

sot *n.* a habitual drunk.

sotto voce *adv. & adj.* in a low or quiet voice. [*Say* sotto VOE chay]

soufflé *n.* a light spongy dish usu. made by adding egg yolks and a filling to stiffly beaten egg whites then baked until puffy. [*Say* soo FLAY]

sough ● *v.* make a moaning or whistling

sound as of the wind. ● *n.* a gentle rushing sound. [*Rhymes with* COW]

sought *past and past participle of* SEEK.

sought-after *adj.* in high demand.

soul *n.* **1** the spiritual element of a human being or animal, regarded as the seat of the emotions or intellect. **2 a** the spiritual part of a human being, esp. regarded as immortal. **b** the disembodied spirit of a dead person. **3** a person regarded as the personification of a certain quality. **4** an individual. **5** a person regarded with familiarity etc. **6** emotional or intellectual energy or intensity. **7** (also as an *adj.*) the emotional or spiritual quality of black American life and culture. **8** soul music. □ **upon my soul!** an exclamation of surprise.

soul-destroying *adj.* excruciatingly monotonous.

soul food *n.* food traditionally eaten by American blacks.

soulful *adj.* full of soul or feeling. □ **soulfully** *adv.* **soulfulness** *n.*

soulless *adj.* **1** having no soul. **2** dull, not interesting. **3** (of a thing) made or done without imagination.

soulmate *n.* a person with whom one shares a passion or bond.

soul music *n.* a type of black American pop music which combines rhythm and blues with elements of gospel.

soul-searching ● *n.* a penetrating examination of one's beliefs, motives, or emotions. ● *adj.* characterized by such scrutiny.

sound¹ ● *n.* **1** a sensation caused in the ear by vibrations passing through the surrounding air. **2** vibrations causing this sensation. **3** anything that can be heard. **4** an idea or impression conveyed by words. **5** a distinctive style of esp. pop music. **6** (also **sound crew**) the department of engineers responsible for producing sound for a movie or concert etc. ● *v.* **1** convey a specific impression when heard. **2** make or cause to make a sound. **3** give an audible signal for. □ **sound and fury** noisy or boisterous talk or activity. **sound off** express one's opinions vehemently. □ **soundless** *adj.*

sound² ● *adj.* **1** free from disease or injury. **2** in good condition. **3** sensible, fair. **4** financially secure. **5 a** (of sleep) not disturbed. **b** (of a person sleeping) tending to sleep deeply. **6** severe, hard, thorough. ● *adv.* in a sound manner. □ **soundly** *adv.* **soundness** *n.*

sound³ *v.* **1** test or measure the depth of (the sea or a river etc.). **2 a** inquire (esp.

cautiously) into the opinions of others. **b** investigate. □ **sounder** *n.*

sound⁴ *n.* **1** a narrow stretch of water, esp. one between the mainland and an island or connecting two large bodies of water. **2** an inlet.

sound barrier *n.* **1** the point at which an aircraft reaches the speed of sound. **2** a wall erected or insulated to prevent the passage of sound. □ **break the sound barrier** travel faster than the speed of sound.

sound bite *n.* a short extract from a recorded interview, speech, etc.

sound card *n.* a device inserted in a computer to allow the use of audio components for multimedia applications.

sound effect *n.* a sound other than speech or music made artificially for use in a movie or play etc.

sounding *n.* **1** a measurement of the depth of water, now usu. by means of echo. **2** cautious investigation. **3** measurements taken by sounding.

sounding board *n.* **1** a means of making one's opinions, beliefs, etc. more widely known. **2** a person whose feedback will serve as an accurate assessment of how well a plan etc. will be received.

soundman *n.* (*pl.* **soundmen**) an engineer responsible for producing sound for a concert, movie, etc.

soundproof ● *adj.* impervious to sound. ● *v.* make soundproof. □ **soundproofing** *n.*

soundscape *n.* **1** a musical composition consisting of a texture of sounds. **2** the sounds heard in a locale or environment.

sound system *n.* a set of equipment used for the reproduction and amplification of sound.

soundtrack *n.* **1** the sound element of a film. **2** such a recording made available for sale.

sound wave *n.* a vibration in the air or water etc. that is heard as sound.

soup ● *n.* **1** a usu. savoury liquid dish made by boiling meat, fish, or vegetables etc. in stock or water. **2** *informal* anything having a consistency resembling that of soup. ● *v. informal* **1** modify (an engine, car, etc.) so as to increase its power or efficiency. **2** enhance. □ **from soup to nuts** *informal* from beginning to end. **in the soup** *informal* in trouble. □ **soupy** *adj.*

soupçon *n.* a very small amount. [*Say* SOUP sawn]

soup du jour *n.* (*pl.* **soups du jour**) the soup of the day in a restaurant.

souped-up adj. modified so as to increase efficiency, power, appeal, etc.

soup kitchen n. a place where warm meals are served to the needy.

sour ● adj. **1** having a tart or acid taste like that of lemon or vinegar. **2 a** having gone bad because of fermentation. **b** smelling or tasting rancid. **3** angry, resentful. **4** unpleasant. **5** out of tune. ● n. an alcoholic drink with lemon or lime juice. ● v. **1** make or become sour. **2** make or become unpleasant. □ **go** (or **turn**) **sour 1** (of food etc.) become bad. **2** turn out badly. □ **sourly** adv. **sourness** n.

source ● n. **1 a** a place, person, or thing from which something originates. **b** a cause of or reason for. **2 a** a document from which original information may be obtained. **b** an esp. anonymous person who supplies information. **3** the beginning or origin of a river or stream. ● v. (**sources, sourced, sourcing**) **1** contract a particular manufacturer or company to supply (a product etc.). **2** have, cite, or identify (a book etc.).

source code n. the complex series of instructions supplied to a computer by a programmer.

sour cream n. cream soured by lactic acid bacteria.

sourdough n. **1** a mixture of flour and water left to ferment so that natural yeasts develop, used to make bread dough which has a slightly sour taste. **2** bread made from sourdough.

sour grapes pl. n. used to suggest that someone is pretending not to want what they in fact do want.

sourpuss n. (pl. **sourpusses**) informal an irritable or sullen person.

soused adj. informal drunk.

south ● n. **1** the point of the horizon 90° clockwise from east. **2** (usu. **the South**) **a** the southern part of the world, a country, or a town. **b** the Southern States of the US, bounded on the north by Maryland, the Ohio River, and Missouri. ● adj. **1** toward, at, near, or facing the south. **2** coming from the south. ● adv. toward, at, or near the south.

South African n. a person from South Africa. □ **South African** adj.

South American n. a person from South America. □ **South American** adj.

South Asian n. a person from the Indian subcontinent, including India, Pakistan, Bangladesh, and Sri Lanka. □ **South Asian** adj.

southbound adj. & adv. travelling or leading southward.

southeast ● n. **1** the point of the horizon midway between south and east. **2** (**Southeast**) the part of a country or city lying to the southeast. ● adj. of, toward, or coming from the southeast. ● adv. toward, at, or near the southeast. □ **southeastern** adj.

Southeast Asian n. a person from Southeast Asia. □ **Southeast Asian** adj.

southeasterly ● adj. & adv. southeast. ● n. (pl. **southeasterlies**) (also **southeaster**) a southeast wind.

southeastward adj. & adv. (also **southeastwards**) toward the southeast.

southerly ● adj. & adv. **1** in a southern position or direction. **2** (of a wind) blowing from the south. ● n. (pl. **southerlies**) a southerly wind. [Rhymes with MOTHERLY]

southern adj. **1 a** of or in the south. **b** (also **Southern**) having to do with the States of the US South. **2** lying or directed toward the south. **3** (of a wind) blowing from the south. □ **southernmost** adj.

southerner n. a person from the south of a region.

southern hemisphere n. the half of the earth below the equator.

south of 60 n. (also **south of sixty**) Cdn the areas of Canada south of 60 degrees latitude.

southpaw n. informal a left-handed person, esp. a left-handed pitcher.

South Pole n. see POLE² 1.

south-southeast ● n. the direction midway between south and southeast. ● adj. & adv. from, toward, in, or facing this direction.

south-southwest ● n. the direction midway between south and southwest. ● adj. & adv. from, toward, in, or facing this direction.

southward ● adj. & adv. (also **southwards**) toward the south. ● n. a southward direction.

southwest ● n. **1** the point of the horizon midway between south and west. **2** (**Southwest**) the part of a country etc. lying to the southwest. ● adj. of, toward, or coming from the southwest. ● adv. toward, at, or near the southwest. □ **southwestern** adj.

southwesterly ● adj. & adv. southwest. ● n. (also **southwester**) a southwest wind or storm.

southwestward adj. & adv. (also **southwestwards**) toward the southwest.

souvenir n. a memento or keepsake. [Say soova NEAR]

souvlaki n. a Greek dish of pieces of

marinated meat grilled on a skewer.
[*Say* soov LACKY]

sou'wester *n.* **1** a waterproof hat with a broad flap covering the neck and flaps tied under the chin. **2** a southwesterly wind. [*Say* sow WESTER *(SOW rhymes with* COW)]

sovereign ● *n.* the recognized supreme ruler of a people or country; a monarch. ● *adj.* **1** supreme, greatest, absolute. **2** characterized by or concerned with independence or autonomy. **3** having superior or supreme rank or power. [*Say* SOV rin]

sovereignist (also **sovereigntist**) *Cdn* ● *n.* a supporter of Quebec's right to self-government. ● *adj.* having to do with the movement for Quebec independence. [*Say* SOV rin ist, SOV rin tist]

sovereignty *n.* (*pl.* **sovereignties**) **1** the authority of a state to govern itself. **2** supreme authority. [*Say* SOV rin tee]

sovereignty-association *n. Cdn* a proposed arrangement whereby Quebec would achieve political independence while maintaining a formal esp. economic association with the rest of Canada.

Soviet *hist.* ● *n.* **1** a citizen of the former USSR. **2** (**soviet**) an elected council in the former USSR. **3** (**soviet**) a revolutionary council of workers, peasants, etc. before 1917. ● *adj.* of or concerning the former USSR or its people. [*Say* SO vee it]

sow[1] *v.* (**sows**; *past* **sowed**; *past participle* **sown** or **sowed**; **sowing**) **1 a** scatter or deposit (seed) on or in the earth. **b** plant (a field etc.) with seed. **2** initiate; spread. □ **sow the seed** (or **seeds**) **of** instigate, introduce. [*Say* SO]

sow[2] *n.* a female adult pig. [*Rhymes with* COW]

soy *n.* (also **soya**) **1** soy sauce. **2** soybean.

soya burger *n.* (also **soyburger**) a vegetarian hamburger made with tofu.

soybean *n.* (also esp. *Brit.* **soya bean**) **1** a plant cultivated for the edible oil and flour it yields. **2** the seed of this plant.

soybean milk *n.* (also **soy milk**) a substitute for milk made by suspending soybean flour in water.

soy sauce *n.* (also **soya sauce**) a dark brown salty sauce made from pickled soybeans.

spa *n.* **1** a curative or medicinal mineral spring. **2** a commercial establishment offering health and beauty treatment.

space ● *n.* **1 a** ground or an area that is not occupied. **b** an interval between one, two, or three-dimensional points or objects. **2** area sufficient or available for some purpose or thing. **3** the immense expanse of the physical universe beyond the earth's atmosphere. **4** an interval of time. **5** an interval or blank space between words or lines. ● *v.* (**spaces**, **spaced**, **spacing**) **1** set or arrange at determinate intervals. **2** separate by means of a space or spaces. □ **space out 1** spread out with more or wider spaces between. **2** experience an esp. drug-induced stupor or daze. □ **spacing** *n.*

space age ● *n.* (also **Space Age**) the present period, in which exploration of space is possible. ● *adj.* (**space-age**) designed with advanced technology.

space bar *n.* a key on a typewriter or computer keyboard used to insert a space between characters or words etc.

space cadet *n. informal* a person who seems out of touch with reality.

spacecraft *n.* a manned or unmanned vehicle designed to travel in outer space.

spaced *adj. slang* (also **spaced out**) in a dazed or confused state.

space heater *n.* a small portable appliance used to heat a contained space.

spaceman *n.* (*pl.* **spacemen**) *dated* **1** an astronaut. **2** a visitor from outer space.

spacer *n.* a device used to make or keep a space in something.

space-saving *adj.* designed to occupy little space or save space.

spaceship *n.* a manned spacecraft.

space shuttle *n.* a spacecraft that is designed to carry equipment and astronauts into orbit and back.

space station *n.* a manned artificial satellite used as a long-term base for operations in space.

spacesuit *n.* a sealed and pressurized suit that allows an astronaut to survive in space.

space-time *n.* (also **space-time continuum**) time and three-dimensional space regarded as fused in a four-dimensional continuum.

spacey *adj.* (also **spacy**) (**spacier**, **spaciest**) *slang* absent-minded or out of touch with reality. □ **spaciness** *n.*

spacious *adj.* **1** having ample space. **2** (of land etc.) covering a wide area. □ **spaciousness** *n.* [*Say* SPAY shuss]

spade ● *n.* **1** a tool resembling a shovel used for digging or cutting the ground. **2** any tool resembling this in shape or function. **3** a black inverted heart-shaped figure with a small stalk used to denote a playing card of a particular suit. **4** (in *pl.*) the suit denoted by this figure. ● *v.* (**spades**, **spaded**, **spading**) dig up or remove with a spade. □ **call a spade a**

spade speak plainly or bluntly. **in spades** *informal* in large amounts or to a high degree. □ **spadeful** *n.* (*pl.* **spadefuls**)

spadix *n.* a spike of flowers usu. enclosed in a spathe. [*Say* SPAY dix]

spaghetti *n.* **1** pasta made in solid thin strings. **2** a dish of this with sauce.

spaghettini *n.* very thin spaghetti. [*Say* spag get TEENY]

spaghetti strap *n.* a thin string like shoulder strap on a dress etc.

spam ● *n.* **1** (**Spam**) *proprietary* a tinned meat product made mainly from ham. **2** *Computing* **a** an esp. advertising message sent to a large number of newsgroups, mailing lists, etc. **b** such messages collectively. ● *v.* (**spams**, **spammed**, **spamming**) *Computing* send spam. □ **spammer** *n.* **spamming** *n.*

span ● *n.* **1** the full extent from end to end in space or time. **2** the length of time for which something lasts. **3** each arch or part of a bridge between piers or supports. **4** a wingspan. **5** the maximum distance between the tips of the thumb and little finger. **6** a short distance or time. ● *v.* (**spans**, **spanned**, **spanning**) extend across or over.

spanakopita *n.* a Greek phyllo pastry stuffed with spinach, feta, etc. [*Say* spanna co PEET uh]

spandex *n.* an elastic polyurethane fabric.

spangle *n.* **1** a small thin piece of glittering material esp. used to ornament a dress etc.; a sequin. **2** a small sparkling object. □ **spangled** *adj.* **spangly** *adj.*

Spaniard *n.* a person from Spain. [*Say* SPAN yurd]

spaniel *n.* a dog with a long silky coat and drooping ears. [*Say* SPAN yull]

Spanish *n.* **1** the principal language of Spain and Spanish America. **2** (**the Spanish**) the people of Spain. □ **Spanish** *adj.*

Spanish Inquisition *n.* *hist.* an ecclesiastical court established in 1478 for the detection of heretics.

Spanish moss *n.* a tropical American plant that grows as silvery-green festoons on trees.

Spanish onion *n.* a large, mild variety of onion.

spank ● *v.* slap esp. on the buttocks with the open hand etc. ● *n.* a slap of this type.

spanking ● *adv. informal* very, exceedingly. ● *n.* an act of slapping on the buttocks.

spar ● *v.* (**spars**, **sparred**, **sparring**) **1** make the motions of boxing without landing heavy blows. **2** engage in argument. ● *n.* **1 a** a sparring motion. **b** a

boxing match. **2** an argument. **3** a stout pole esp. used for the mast, yard, etc. of a ship.

spare ● *adj.* **1** not required for ordinary use; extra. **2** thin. **3** scanty; frugal. **4** not wanted or used by others. ● *n.* **1** a spare part. **2** *Bowling* the knocking down of all the pins with two balls. **3** *Cdn* a period with no scheduled classes in one's school day schedule. **4** *Curling* a substitute player. ● *v.* (**spares**, **spared**, **sparing**) **1** afford to give or do without. **2 a** abstain from killing or harming. **b** protect from something unpleasant. **3** be frugal or grudging of. □ **to spare** left over.

spareribs *pl. n.* trimmed ribs of esp. pork.

spare tire *n.* **1** an extra tire carried in a vehicle. **2** *informal* a roll of fat around the waist.

sparing *adj.* moderate, restrained. □ **sparingly** *adv.*

spark ● *n.* **1** a fiery particle thrown off from a fire etc. **2** a particle of a quality etc. **3** *Electricity* **a** a light produced by an electrical discharge. **b** such a discharge that ignites the explosive mixture in an internal combustion engine. **4 a** anything which excites. **b** energy or enthusiasm. **5** (**Spark**) *Cdn* a member of the branch of Girl Guides for 5- or 6-year-olds. ● *v.* **1** emit sparks. **2** ignite. □ **sparks flew** (or **will fly** etc.) there was (or will be etc.) a heated confrontation etc. □ **sparky** *adj.*

sparkle ● *v.* (**sparkles**, **sparkled**, **sparkling**) **1 a** emit or seem to emit sparks. **b** be witty. **2** (of wine etc.) be bubbly. ● *n.* **1** a flash of light. **2** a glittering particle. **3** vivacity. □ **sparkling** *adj.* **sparkly** *adj.*

sparkler *n.* a hand-held firework that produces sparks when lit.

spark plug *n.* **1** a device used to ignite the explosive mixture in an internal combustion engine. **2** *informal* a person or thing which initiates an activity.

sparrow *n.* a small bird with brown and grey plumage.

sparrow hawk *n.* a small falcon that is capable of hovering.

sparse *adj.* (**sparser**, **sparsest**) **1** thinly dispersed or scattered. **2** scanty. □ **sparsely** *adv.* **sparseness** *n.* **sparsity** *n.*

Spartan ● *adj.* **1** of or relating to the city of Sparta in ancient Greece. **2** (**spartan**) **a** possessing courage, endurance, etc. **b** lacking comfort; austere. ● *n.* **1** a citizen of Sparta. **2** *Cdn* a red eating or cooking apple with tiny white dots.

spasm *n.* **1** a sudden involuntary muscular contraction. **2** *informal* a sudden brief spell.

spasmodic adj. **1** caused by or subject to a spasm or spasms. **2** occurring or done by fits and starts. □ **spasmodically** adv. [Say spaz MOD ick]

spastic adj. **1** Medical affected by or pertaining to spasms or sudden involuntary movements. **2** offensive uncoordinated. [Say SPASS tick]

spat[1] past and past participle of SPIT[1].

spat[2] n. (usu. in pl.) hist. a short cloth covering to protect the ankle and instep from mud etc.

spat[3] informal ● n. a petty quarrel. ● v. (**spats, spatted, spatting**) quarrel pettily.

spate n. **1** a sudden flood in a river. **2** a large or excessive amount.

spathe n. a large bract enclosing the flower cluster of certain plants. [Rhymes with BATHE]

spatial adj. **1** of or concerning space. **2** occupying space. □ **spatially** adv. [Say SPAY shull]

spatter ● v. **1** splash with spots of liquid etc. **2** scatter (liquid, mud, etc.), esp. in drops. ● n. a splash.

spatula n. **1** an implement with a rubber blade, used to scrape the sides of a bowl etc. **2** a knifelike implement used to spread icing etc. **3** an implement used to lift or flip pancakes, eggs, etc.

spatulate adj. having a broad rounded end. [Say SPATCH oo lut]

spawn ● v. **1** (of a fish, frog, etc.) produce or fertilize (eggs). **2** produce or generate. ● n. **1** the eggs of fish, frogs, etc. **2** derogatory human offspring. **3** a result of something. □ **spawner** n.

spay v. sterilize (a female animal) by removing the ovaries. □ **spayed** adj.

speak v. (**speaks;** past **spoke;** past participle **spoken; speaking**) **1** say something. **2 a** mention in writing etc. **b** articulate the feelings of (another person etc.). **3** use or be able to use (a specified language). **4** literary communicate feeling etc. □ **nothing to speak of** nothing worth mentioning. **speak for itself** need no supporting evidence. **speak in tongues** Christianity speak in a language one does not know, identified as a gift of the Holy Spirit. **speak one's mind** speak bluntly or frankly. **speak out** give one's opinion. **speak volumes** be very significant.

-speak comb. form forming nouns denoting a particular mode of speaking.

speakeasy n. (pl. **speakeasies**) esp. hist. slang a bar etc. selling liquor illicitly.

speaker n. **1** a person who speaks. **2** a person who speaks a specified language.

3 (**Speaker**) the presiding officer in a legislative assembly. **4** a loudspeaker.

speakerphone n. a telephone with a loudspeaker and microphone, which does not need to be held in the hand.

speaking ● n. the action of uttering words etc. ● adj. **1** that speaks. **2** able to speak in a specified language. **3** with a reference to something specified. □ **on speaking terms 1** slightly acquainted. **2** on friendly terms.

spear ● n. **1** a weapon with a pointed tip and a long shaft. **2** a pointed stem of asparagus etc. ● v. **1** pierce or strike with or as if with a spear. **2** Hockey jab or poke with the blade of the stick. □ **spearing** n.

spearhead ● n. **1** (also **spear point**) the point of a spear. **2** an individual or group leading a campaign, attack, etc. ● v. act as the spearhead of.

spearmint n. a common garden mint, used in cooking and as a flavouring.

spec n. a specification or specifications. □ **on spec** informal without the assurance of success or reward.

special ● adj. **1 a** particularly good; exceptional. **b** peculiar; specific. **2** for a particular purpose. **3** in which a person specializes. **4** denoting education for children with particular needs. ● n. **1** a special person or thing. **2** the offering of something at a temporarily reduced price. **3** a program scheduled and aired in place of regular programming. □ **on special** available at a temporarily reduced price. □ **specially** adv. **specialness** n.

special constable n. Cdn & Brit. a police officer sworn in to assist in times of emergency etc.

special edition n. **1** an extra edition of a newspaper etc. **2** a specially modified version of a product.

special education n. (also informal **special ed**) **1** the education of children with special needs. **2** a program providing such education.

special effects pl. n. scenic or optical illusions for films, television, etc., created by computers, props, camera work, etc.

special investigations unit n. an independent police unit responsible for investigating the conduct of police officers.

specialist n. **1** a person who is trained in a particular branch of a profession. **2** a person who is knowledgeable about a particular subject.

speciality (pl. **specialities**) = SPECIALTY. [Say speshy ALA tee]

specialize v. (**specializes, specialized, specializing**) **1** concentrate on and become an expert in a particular subject or skill. **2** make a habit of engaging in a particular activity. **3** *Biology* adapt or set apart an organ or part to serve a special function. □ **specialization** *n.* **specialized** *adj.*

special needs *pl. n.* **1** the special esp. educational requirements of people with disabilities. **2** (as an *adj.*) (**special-needs**) designating such people or their education.

Special Olympics *pl. n.* an international multi-event sporting competition for people with mental disabilities.

specialty *n.* (*pl.* **specialties**) **1** a special pursuit, product, etc., to which a company or a person gives special attention. **2** a special feature or skill. [*Say* SPESH ul tee]

specie *n.* coin money. [*Say* SPEE see]

species *n.* (*pl.* **species**) **1** a group of living organisms consisting of similar individuals capable of interbreeding. **2** a kind or sort. [*Say* SPEE seez *or* SPEE sheez]

specific ● *adj.* **1** clearly defined. **2** peculiar, particular. **3** of or concerning a species. ● *n.* (esp. in *pl.*) a precise detail. □ **specifically** *adv.*

specification *n.* **1** an act of specifying. **2 a** (esp. in *pl.*) a detailed description of the design and materials to make something. **b** a specified standard of workmanship to be achieved. [*Say* spess iffa KAY sh'n]

specific gravity *n. Chemistry* the ratio of the density of a substance to the density of a standard.

specificity *n.* the quality of being specific. [*Say* spess if ISSA tee]

specify *v.* (**specifies**, **specified**, **specifying**) **1** name or mention expressly. **2** name as a condition.

specimen *n.* **1** an individual or part taken as an example of a class or whole. **2** a sample for medical testing. **3** *informal* usu. *derogatory* a person of a specified sort.

specious *adj.* **1** seeming reasonable but actually wrong. **2** misleadingly attractive in appearance. □ **speciously** *adv.* [*Say* SPEE shuss]

speck *n.* **1** a small spot or dot. **2** a particle. □ **specked** *adj.*

speckle *n.* a small spot, mark, or stain. □ **speckled** *adj.*

speckled trout *n.* a brook trout.

specs *pl. n. informal* a pair of eyeglasses.

spec sheet *n.* a list of an item's specifications.

spectacle *n.* **1** a public show, ceremony, etc. **2** anything attracting public attention. □ **make a spectacle of oneself** make oneself an object of ridicule.

spectacles *pl. n.* a pair of eyeglasses.

spectacular ● *adj.* **1** beautiful or impressive in a dramatic way. **2** striking. ● *n.* a spectacular thing or event. □ **spectacularly** *adv.*

spectate *v.* (**spectates**, **spectated**, **spectating**) be a spectator.

spectator *n.* a person who looks on at a show, game, incident, etc.

spectra *pl. of* SPECTRUM.

spectral *adj.* **1 a** of or relating to spectres. **b** ghostlike. **2** of or concerning spectra or the spectrum.

spectral line *n.* each of a series of lines in a spectrum.

spectre *n.* **1** a ghost. **2** a possible unpleasant or dangerous occurrence.

spectrometer *n.* an instrument used for measuring observed spectra. □ **spectrometry** *n.* [*Say* speck TROMMA tur, speck TROMMA tree]

spectroscope *n.* an instrument for producing and recording spectra for examination. □ **spectroscopic** *adj.* **spectroscopy** *n.* [*Say* SPECTRO scope, spectro SCOP ick, speck TROSS kuh pee]

spectrum *n.* (*pl.* **spectra** *or* **spectrums**) **1** a band of colours produced by separating light into elements with different wavelengths. **2** the entire range of wavelengths of electromagnetic radiation. **3** an image or distribution of components of electromagnetic radiation, sound, etc., arranged according to frequency, charge, energy, etc. **4** the entire range or a wide range of anything.

speculate *v.* (**speculates**, **speculated**, **speculating**) **1** form a theory without firm evidence. **2** invest in stocks, property, or other ventures in the hope of gain but with the possibility of loss. □ **speculation** *n.* **speculator** *n.*

speculative *adj.* **1** of, based on or inclined to speculation. **2** (of an investment) involving the risk of loss. □ **speculatively** *adv.* [*Say* SPECK yoo luh tiv]

speculum *n.* an instrument to hold open or dilate a part of the body for examination. [*Say* SPECK yoo lum]

sped *past and past participle of* SPEED.

speech *n.* (*pl.* **speeches**) **1** the faculty or act of speaking. **2** a usu. formal address delivered to an audience. **3** a manner of speaking. **4** a remark.

Speech from the Throne *n. Cdn* a statement summarizing the government's proposed measures, read at the opening of a session of Parliament or a legislature.

speechify *v.* (**speechifies, speechified, speechifying**) *jocular* or *derogatory* make esp. boring speeches.

speech-language pathology *n.* (also **speech pathology**) the treatment of disorders of speech and communication. □ **speech-language pathologist** *n.*

speechless *adj.* unable to speak, esp. because of emotion etc.

speech therapy *n.* speech-language pathology. □ **speech therapist** *n.*

speed ● *n.* **1** rapidity of movement. **2** a rate of progress or motion. **3** each of the possible gear ratios in a bicycle etc. **4** *Photography* **a** the sensitivity of film to light. **b** the light gathering power of a lens. **5** *slang* an amphetamine drug. ● *v.* (**speeds**; *past* and *past participle* **sped** or **speeded**; **speeding**) **1** go fast. **2** (of a motorist etc.) travel at an illegal speed. **3** send fast or on its way. □ **speed up** move or work at greater speed. **up to speed 1** operating at full speed. **2** operating at an anticipated level. **3** fully informed. □ **speeder** *n.*

speedboat *n.* a motorboat designed for high speed.

speed bump *n.* **1** a ridge across a roadway requiring drivers to slow down. **2** any sort of minor impediment to a course of action.

speed-dial *n.* a function on some telephones which stores frequently-called numbers in a memory for faster dialing. □ **speed-dialing** *n.*

speeding *n.* the traffic offence of driving at an illegal speed.

speed limit *n.* the maximum speed at which a road vehicle may legally be driven in a particular area etc.

speedometer *n.* an instrument displaying the speed of motor vehicle etc. [*Say* spuh DOMMA tur]

speed-read *v.* (**speed-reads, speed-read, speed-reading**) read rapidly. □ **speed-reader** *n.*

speed skating *n.* racing performed on skates around a usu. oval track. □ **speed skater** *n.*

speedster *n.* **1** a fast motor vehicle. **2** a person or animal that moves quickly.

speed trap *n.* a part of a highway etc. where police check the speed of passing vehicles.

speed-up *n.* an increase in the speed or rate of working.

speedway *n.* **1** a road or track used for motor racing. **2** a highway for fast motor traffic.

speedy *adj.* (**speedier, speediest**) **1** moving quickly. **2** prompt. □ **speedily** *adv.*

spell¹ *v.* (**spells**; *past* and *past participle* **spelled** or **spelt**; **spelling**) **1** write or name the letters that form (a word etc.) in correct sequence. **2** (of letters) form (a word etc.). **3** result in. □ **spell out 1** make out (words etc.) letter by letter. **2** explain in detail. □ **speller** *n.*

spell² *n.* **1 a** words which when spoken are thought to have magical power. **b** a state caused by a person speaking such words. **2** a fascinating influence that a person or thing has. □ **under a spell** mastered by or as if by a spell.

spell³ ● *n.* **1** a short period of time. **2** a period of a specified type of weather. **3** a bout of something. ● *v.* (**spells, spelled, spelling**) relieve or take the place of.

spellbind *v.* (**spellbinds, spellbound, spellbinding**) hold the complete attention of. □ **spellbinding** *adj.*

spellbound *adj.* entranced, fascinated.

spell-check ● *n.* a check of the spelling in a file using a spell-checker. ● *v.* check the spelling in a file using a spell-checker.

spell-checker *n.* (also **spelling checker**) a computer program which checks the spelling of words in files of text.

spelling *n.* **1** the process of writing or naming the letters of a word etc. **2** the way a word is spelled.

spelling bee *n.* a competition in which competitors spell words orally and are eliminated for misspellings.

spelt¹ *past* and *past participle* of SPELL¹.

spelt² *n.* an older species of wheat, favoured as a health food.

spelunker *n.* a person who explores caves. □ **spelunking** *n.* [*Say* spil LUNK er]

spend *v.* (**spends, spent, spending**) **1** pay out money. **2 a** use or consume (time or energy). **b** use up. **3** pass (time etc.). □ **spender** *n.*

spendthrift ● *n.* a person who spends money too freely. ● *adj.* extravagant.

spent ● *v.* *past* and *past participle* of SPEND. ● *adj.* used up.

sperm *n.* (*pl.* **sperm** or **sperms**) **1** a spermatozoon. **2** semen.

spermaceti *n.* a white waxy substance produced by the sperm whale to help it float. [*Say* sperma SETTY]

spermatozoon *n.* (*pl.* **spermatozoa**) a cell that is produced by the sex organs of a male and that can fertilize an ovum. [*Say* sperm atto ZO un]

sperm bank *n.* a place where semen is stored for use in artificial insemination.

spermicide *n.* a substance able to kill spermatozoa. □ **spermicidal** *adj.* [*Say* SPERMA side, sperma SIDE ul]

sperm whale *n.* a large toothed whale with a massive head, formerly hunted for the spermaceti and oil in its head.

spew ● *v.* **1** vomit. **2** expel or be expelled rapidly and forcibly. ● *n.* vomited food etc.

SPF *abbr.* sun protection factor.

sphagnum *n.* (also **sphagnum moss**) a spongy moss growing in bogs, used esp. as a soil conditioner. [*Say* SFAG num *or* SPAG num]

sphere *n.* **1** a round solid figure with every point on its surface equidistant from its centre. **2** a ball or globe. **3** any celestial body. **4 a** a field of action or influence. **b** a stratum of society or social class. □ **sphere of influence** the area of a state's or a person's interests etc.

spherical *adj.* **1** shaped like a sphere. **2** of or relating to spheres. [*Say* SFEER ick ul *or* SFAIR ick ul]

spheroid *n.* a body approximating to a sphere in shape. □ **spheroidal** *adj.* [*Say* SFEER oid, sfeer OID ul]

sphincter *n.* a ring of muscle surrounding and serving to close an opening, esp. the anus. [*Say* SFINK tur]

sphinx *n.* (*pl.* **sphinxes**) **1** (**Sphinx**) (in Greek mythology) a winged monster having a woman's head and a lion's body. **2** an ancient Egyptian stone figure having a lion's body and a human or animal head. **3** a mysterious person. [*Say* SFINKS]

spic and span *adj.* (also **spick-and-span**) **1** smart and new. **2** neat and clean.

spice ● *n.* **1** a strongly flavoured vegetable substance used to season food. **2** an interesting or piquant quality. ● *v.* (**spices, spiced, spicing**) **1** flavour with spice. **2** add an interesting quality to.

spicule *n.* any small sharp-pointed body. [*Say* SPICK yule]

spicy *adj.* (**spicier, spiciest**) **1** flavoured with spice. **2** sensational. □ **spiciness** *n.*

spider *n.* an eight-legged arthropod, capable of spinning webs to capture insects as food. □ **spidery** *adj.*

spider mite *n.* (also **red spider mite**) a plant-feeding mite that resembles a tiny spider.

spider monkey *n.* a monkey of Central and South America with long slender limbs and a long tail.

spider plant *n.* a plant having long narrow leaves with a central yellow stripe.

spiderweb *n.* **1** a web spun by a spider. **2** something resembling this.

spiel¹ *n.* slang a long or prepared speech or story, esp. a sales pitch. [*Say* SHPEEL *or* SPEEL]

spiel² *n.* informal a bonspiel. [*Say* SPEEL]

spiff *v.* informal make attractive or smart.

spiffy *adj.* (**spiffier, spiffiest**) informal **1** excellent. **2** well-dressed; elegant. □ **spiffily** *adv.*

spigot *n.* **1** a small peg or plug. **2 a** US a tap. **b** a device for controlling the flow of liquid in a tap. [*Say* SPIG ut]

spike¹ ● *n.* **1 a** a sharp point. **b** a pointed piece of metal. **2** a tap nail. **3 a** any of several metal points set into the sole of a running shoe to prevent slipping. **b** (in *pl.*) a pair of running shoes with spikes. **4 a** a sharp increase. **b** *Electronics* a pulse of high voltage of very short duration. **5** (in volleyball) an act of spiking the ball. ● *v.* (**spikes, spiked, spiking**) **1 a** fasten or provide with spikes. **b** fix on or pierce with spikes. **c** form into spikes. **2** informal lace (a drink) with alcohol, a drug, etc. **3** (in volleyball) hit (the ball) forcefully downward into the opposite court. **4** drive a long nail into (a tree). **5 a** experience (a high fever). **b** (of a fever) rapidly rise.

spike² *n.* a flower cluster formed of many flower heads attached closely on a long stem. □ **spikelet** *n.*

spiky *adj.* (**spikier, spikiest**) **1** like a spike. **2** having a spike or spikes.

spile *n.* **1** a small spout for tapping sap from a sugar maple. **2** a wooden peg or spigot.

spill ● *v.* (**spills;** *past* and *past participle* **spilled** or **spilt; spilling**) **1 a** flow or cause to flow out of a container, esp. unintentionally. **b** cast (light) or (of light) be cast into a darker area. **2** move out quickly from a place etc. **3** *slang* disclose (information etc.). ● *n.* **1** an act of spilling a liquid; spilled liquid. **2** a tumble or fall. □ **spill the beans** informal reveal information etc. **spill blood** kill or wound people. **spill one's guts** reveal one's thoughts or feelings. □ **spillage** *n.*

spillover *n.* **1** something that has spread or overflowed into another area. **2** a consequence or by-product.

spillway *n.* a passage for surplus water from a dam etc.

spin ● *v.* (**spins, spun, spinning**) **1** turn or cause to turn around quickly. **2** make thread from wool, cotton, etc. **3** (of a spider, silkworm, etc.) make (a web, cocoon, etc.) by extruding a fine viscous thread. **4** tell or write (a story etc.). **5** impart spin to (a ball). **6** be dizzy. **7** (of a wheel) revolve rapidly without providing traction. **8** informal play (records). ● *n.* **1** a spinning motion. **2** a tailspin. **3** a revolving motion through the air. **4** informal a brief excursion, esp. for pleasure. **5** a favourable slant given to a news story etc. **6** Figure Skating a movement involving rotating rapidly in one spot. □ **spin off 1** produce as a spinoff. **2** create (a company) from a parent company in this way. **spin out 1** prolong. **2** make (something) last as long as possible. **3** (esp. of a driver or car) lose or go out of control. **spin one's wheels** waste one's time or efforts.

spina bifida *n.* a congenital defect of the spine, in which part of the spinal cord is exposed through a gap in the backbone. [*Say* spine a BIFFA duh]

spinach *n.* a green vegetable with succulent leaves.

spinal ● *adj.* of or relating to the spine. ● *n. informal* an epidural anaesthetic.

spinal column *n.* the spine.

spinal cord *n.* a structure of the central nervous system enclosed in the spine, connecting all parts of the body with the brain.

spinal tap *n.* the insertion of a needle into the spine.

spin control *n. slang* an attempt to give a particular slant to esp. political news coverage.

spindle *n.* **1** a pin for twisting and winding thread. **2** a pin or axis that revolves or on which something revolves. **3** a turned piece of wood used as a banister, chair leg, etc.

spindly *adj.* (**spindlier, spindliest**) long or tall and thin.

spin doctor *n. informal* a spokesperson employed to give a favourable interpretation of events to the media.

spindrift *n.* spray blown along the surface of the sea.

spine *n.* **1** the backbone. **2** *Zoology & Botany* any hard, pointed structure. **3** a sharp ridge or projection. **4** firmness of character. **5** the part of a book's cover that encloses the inner edges of the pages. □ **spined** *adj.*

spineless *adj.* **1** lacking energy or decisiveness. **2** having no spine.

spine-tingling *adj.* thrilling or pleasurably frightening.

spinnaker *n.* a large triangular sail carried opposite the mainsail of a racing yacht running before the wind. [*Say* SPINNA cur]

spinner *n.* **1** a person or thing that spins. **2** (also **spinnerbait**) a fishing bait or lure fixed so as to revolve when pulled through the water.

spinneret *n.* an organ through which the silk, gossamer, or thread of spiders, silkworms, etc. is produced. [*Say* SPINNER ett]

spinning *n.* **1** *in senses of* SPIN *v.* **2** a form of physical exercise in which participants ride stationary bicycles in a group session accompanied by music.

spinning wheel *n.* a device formerly used for spinning yarn or thread with a spindle driven by a wheel attached to a crank or treadle.

spinny *adj.* (**spinnier, spinniest**) *Cdn* crazy, ditzy.

spinoff *n.* **1** an incidental result. **2** something derived from another product of a similar type.

spinster *n. Law* an unmarried woman. □ **spinsterhood** *n.*

spiny *adj.* (**spinier, spiniest**) **1** full of spines. **2** difficult to understand or handle. **3** sharp-pointed.

spiny lobster *n.* a large edible crustacean with a spiny shell.

spiral ● *adj.* **1** winding about a centre in an enlarging or decreasing continuous circular motion. **2** winding continuously along a cylinder. **3** spiral-bound. ● *n.* **1** a spiral curve, shape or pattern. **2** a spiral spring. **3** a progressive increase or deterioration. ● *v.* (**spirals, spiralled, spiralling**) **1** move in a spiral course. **2** make spiral. **3** increase rapidly. □ **spiralling** *adj.* **spirally** *adv.*

spiral binding *n.* a type of binding in which the pages are held together by a spiral of wire. □ **spiral-bound** *adj.*

spire *n.* **1** a tapering pointed structure built esp. on a church tower. **2** any conical, pointed, or tapering thing.

spirea *n.* a shrub with clusters of small white or pink flowers. [*Say* spy REE uh]

spirit ● *n.* **1 a** the vital animating essence of a person or animal. **b** the soul. **2 a** a rational or intelligent being without a material body. **b** a supernatural being. **c** (**the Spirit**) the Holy Spirit. **3** a mood; a tendency. **4 a** (usu. in *pl.*) strong distilled liquor. **b** a distilled volatile liquid. **c** purified alcohol. **5 a** a person's mental or moral nature or qualities. **b** energy, vivacity. **c** courage. **6** the general intent or true meaning of a statement etc. **7** feelings of loyalty to a team, group, etc. ● *v.* (**spirits, spirited, spiriting**) take away rapidly and secretly. ● *adj.* of or relating to supernatural spirits. □ **in spirit** in one's thoughts. **keep a person's spirits up** cheer a person up. **the spirit moves a person** he or she feels inclined (to do something).

spirited *adj.* **1** full of spirit. **2** having a spirit of a specified kind. □ **spiritedly** *adv.* **spiritedness** *n.*

spiritless *adj.* lacking courage or vigour.

spirit level *n.* a device containing a bent glass tube nearly filled with alcohol, used to test a horizontal surface by the position of an air bubble.

spiritual ● *adj.* **1** of or relating to the human spirit or soul. **2** concerned with sacred or religious things. ● *n.* an emotional Christian song derived from the musical traditions of Blacks in the southern US. □ **spirituality** *n.* **spiritually** *adv.*

spiritualism *n.* the belief that the spirits of the dead can communicate with the living. □ **spiritualist** *n. & adj.* [Say SPIRIT chew ull ism]

spirochete *n.* any of various flexible spiral bacteria, esp. one that causes syphilis. [Say SPY ro keet]

spit[1] ● *v.* (**spits**; past and past participle **spat** or **spit**; **spitting**) **1** eject saliva from the mouth. **2 a** eject (blood, food, etc.) from the mouth. **b** utter vehemently. **3** (of a fire, pan, etc.) send out sparks, hot fat, etc. **4** (of rain) fall lightly. **5** (esp. of a cat) make a spitting noise in anger. ● *n.* **1** saliva. **2** an act of spitting. □ **spit it out** *informal* say what is on one's mind. **spit up** (esp. of a baby) vomit. □ **spitter** *n.*

spit[2] ● *n.* **1** a slender rod on which meat is roasted on a fire etc. **2** a small point of land projecting into the water. ● *v.* (**spits**, **spitted**, **spitting**) thrust a spit through meat.

spitball *n.* **1** a ball of chewed paper etc. usu. blown through a straw at a person. **2** Baseball an illegal swerving pitch made with a ball moistened with saliva.

spite ● *n.* ill will, malice. ● *v.* (**spites**, **spited**, **spiting**) thwart, mortify, annoy. □ **in spite of** notwithstanding. **in spite of oneself** etc. though one would rather have done otherwise.

spiteful *adj.* motivated by spite. □ **spitefully** *adv.*

spitting distance *n.* a very short distance.

spitting image *n.* informal the exact likeness of.

spittle *n.* saliva, esp. as ejected from the mouth.

spittoon *n.* a pot used for spitting into. [Say spit TOON]

splash ● *v.* (**splashes**, **splashed**, **splashing**) **1** fall or cause to fall in scattered drops. **2** cover with scattered drops. **3** strike or move around in water, causing it to fly around. **4** (of a spacecraft) land on water. **5** display (a story or photograph) in a prominent place in a newspaper or magazine. ● *n.* (pl. **splashes**) **1** an instance of splashing. **2** a small quantity of liquid that has splashed on to a surface. **3** a small quantity of liquid

added to a drink. **4** a bright patch of colour. **5** informal a prominent news feature or story. □ **make a splash** attract much attention.

splashy *adj.* (**splashier**, **splashiest**) **1** attracting attention. **2** involving splashing.

splat *n.* informal a sound as of something wet hitting a surface.

splatter ● *v.* **1** make wet or dirty by splashing. **2** splash. ● *n.* **1** a noisy splashing sound. **2** a quantity splattered.

splay ● *v.* (**splays**, **splayed**, **splaying**) **1** spread apart. **2** (of an opening or its sides) diverge in shape or position. ● *adj.* turned outward or widened.

spleen *n.* **1** an organ involved in the production and removal of red blood cells in most vertebrates. **2** ill temper, spite.

splendid *adj.* **1** magnificent, gorgeous. **2** impressive. **3** excellent. □ **splendidly** *adv.*

splendour *n.* (also **splendor**) **1** magnificence; grandeur. **2** dazzling brightness. [Say SPLEN dur]

splice ● *v.* (**splices**, **spliced**, **splicing**) **1** join the ends of (ropes) by interweaving strands. **2** join (pieces of film etc.) by sticking together the ends. **3** join (girders, beams, etc.) by overlapping and fastening the ends. **4** informal join in marriage. ● *n.* a place where film, rope, etc. has been joined. □ **splicer** *n.*

spliff *n.* slang a marijuana cigarette.

splint ● *n.* **1** a strip of rigid material used for holding a broken bone etc. when set. **2** a thin strip of wood etc. used to light a fire etc. ● *v.* secure with a splint or splints.

splinter ● *n.* **1** a small thin sharp piece broken off from wood, glass, etc. **2** (also **splinter group**, **splinter party**) a group or party that has broken away from a larger one. ● *v.* break into splinters. □ **splintery** *adj.*

split ● *v.* (**splits**, **split**, **splitting**) **1** break forcibly into parts. **2** divide into parts or groups. **3** end a marriage or other relationship. **4** slang leave. ● *n.* **1** a tear, crack, or fissure. **2** a separation. **3** (in pl.) the feat of leaping in the air or sitting down with the legs straight, spread apart, and at right angles to the body. ● *adj.* **1** that has split or been split. **2** divided in opinion etc. □ **split the difference** take the average of two proposed amounts. **split hairs** make insignificant distinctions. **split the vote** *Cdn & Brit.* (of a candidate or party) attract votes from another so that both are defeated by a third. □ **splitter** *n.*

split end *n.* (usu. in pl.) a hair which has split at the end from dryness etc.

split infinitive *n.* a phrase consisting of

an infinitive with an adverb etc. inserted between *to* and the verb.

split-level ● *adj.* (of a room or a building) having the floor level of one part different from the floor level of an adjacent part. ● *n.* a split-level building.

split pea *n.* a pea dried and split in half.

split-rail *adj.* designating a type of fence etc. made from split logs.

split-screen *n.* a screen on a computer etc. on which two or more images are displayed.

split second ● *n.* a very brief moment. ● *adj.* (**split-second**) **1** very rapid. **2** (of timing) very precise.

splitting *adj.* (of a headache) very painful.

splotch ● *n.* (*pl.* **splotches**) a daub, blot, or smear. ● *v.* (**splotches, splotched, splotching**) make a large spot or patch on. □ **splotchy** *adj.* (**splotchier, splotchiest**)

splurge *informal* ● *n.* an act of spending money extravagantly. ● *v.* (**splurges, splurged, splurging**) **1** spend large sums of money. **2** spend extravagantly.

splutter ● *v.* **1 a** speak in a hurried, vehement, or choking manner. **b** make a series of spitting or choking sounds. **2 a** speak rapidly or incoherently. **b** emit (sparks etc.) with a spitting sound. ● *n.* a spluttering sound.

spoil ● *v.* (**spoils;** *past* and *past participle* **spoiled** or esp. *Brit.* **spoilt; spoiling**) **1** damage, ruin. **2 a** harm the character of (esp. a child) by excessive indulgence. **b** pamper. **3** (of food) go bad. **4** render (a ballot) invalid. ● *n.* (usu. in *pl.*) plunder taken from an enemy in war. □ **be spoiling for** aggressively seek (a fight etc.).

spoilage *n.* the decay of food etc.

spoiler *n.* **1** a person or thing that spoils something. **2 a** a flap on an aircraft wing which can be raised to create drag and so reduce speed. **b** a similar device on a vehicle intended to improve road-holding at high speed.

spoilsport *n.* a person who spoils others' enjoyment.

spoke[1] *n.* **1** each of the wire rods or bars running from the hub to the rim of a wheel. **2** a rung of a ladder. □ **spoked** *adj.*

spoke[2] *past of* SPEAK.

spoken ● *v. past participle of* SPEAK. ● *adj.* **1** (in *comb.*) speaking in a specified way. **2** (of language etc.) oral as opposed to written. □ **spoken for** claimed, requisitioned.

spokesman *n.* (*pl.* **spokesmen**) a person who speaks on behalf of others.

spokesperson *n.* (*pl.* **spokespersons** or **spokespeople**) a spokesman or spokeswoman.

spokeswoman *n.* (*pl.* **spokeswomen**) a woman who speaks on behalf of others.

sponge ● *n.* **1** a primitive sea animal with a soft porous body. **2 a** a piece of a soft, light, porous, and absorbent substance, used in bathing, cleaning, etc. **b** a piece of sponge or similar material inserted in the vagina as a contraceptive. **3** a spongelike food etc. **4** a sponger. ● *v.* (**sponges; sponged; sponging** or **spongeing**) **1** wipe or cleanse with a sponge. **2** wipe off or efface. **3** live at the expense of (another person) with no intention of reimbursement etc. □ **spongelike** *adj.*

sponge cake *n.* a very light cake with a spongelike consistency and little or no fat.

sponge hockey *n. Cdn* a form of hockey played on ice with rubber-soled boots and a sponge puck.

sponge puck *n. Cdn* a hockey puck made of hard sponge.

sponger *n.* a person who contrives to live at another's expense.

spongy *adj.* (**spongier, spongiest**) like a sponge. □ **sponginess** *n.*

sponsor ● *n.* **1** a person who supports an activity done for charity by pledging money in advance. **2** a person or organization that financially supports an activity or broadcast program etc. in return for advertising. **3** a person who introduces a proposal for legislation. ● *v.* be a sponsor for. □ **sponsorship** *n.*

spontaneous *adj.* **1** done or occurring because of a sudden impulse. **2** voluntary. **3** instinctive, automatic. **4** (of movement, literary style, etc.) gracefully natural and unconstrained. □ **spontaneity** *n.* **spontaneously** *adv.* [Say spon TAINY us, sponta NAY a tee]

spontaneous combustion *n.* the ignition of a substance from heat engendered within itself.

spoof *informal* ● *n.* a humorous imitation of something in which its characteristic features are exaggerated for comic effect. ● *v.* **1** parody. **2 a** hoax, swindle. **b** *Computing* deceive (a server) by assuming another user's identity.

spook ● *n.* **1** *informal* a ghost. **2** *slang* a spy. ● *v. slang* frighten.

spooky *adj.* (**spookier, spookiest**) **1** *informal* ghostly, eerie. **2** *slang* nervous. □ **spookily** *adv.* **spookiness** *n.*

spool ● *n.* **1** a reel for winding thread, wire, tape, film, etc., on. **2** the revolving cylinder of an angler's reel. ● *v.* wind on or as on a spool. □ **spooler** *n.* **spooling** *n.*

spoon ● *n.* **1** a utensil consisting of an oval or round bowl and a handle. **2** a spoon-shaped thing, esp. (also **spoon bait**) a piece of metal used as a lure in fishing. ● *v.* **1** lift and move with a spoon. **2** *informal* behave in an amorous way. **3** lie close together. □ **born with a silver spoon in one's mouth** born in wealthy circumstances. □ **spoonful** *n.* (*pl.* **spoonfuls**)

spoonbill *n.* a wading bird with a long spoon-shaped bill.

spoon-feed *v.* (**spoon-feeds**, **spoon-fed**, **spoon-feeding**) provide help etc. to (a person etc.) without requiring any effort on the recipient's part.

spoor *n.* the track or scent of a person or animal.

sporadic *adj.* occurring only here and there or occasionally. □ **sporadically** *adv.* [*Say* spuh RAD ick]

spore *n.* a tiny reproductive cell of many plants and micro-organisms.

sport ● *n.* **1** a game or competitive activity, esp. one involving physical exertion. **2** recreation, amusement. **3** *informal* **a** a fair, cheerful person. **b** a person behaving in a specified way. ● *v.* wear, exhibit, or produce, esp. ostentatiously. □ **make sport of** make fun of.

sportcoat *n.* a sports jacket.

sport fish *n.* a kind of fish caught for sport. □ **sport fisherman** *n.* **sport fishing** *n.*

sporting *adj.* **1** connected with or interested in sports. **2** fair and generous.

sporting chance *n.* a reasonable chance of success.

sports car *n.* a low, fast car.

sportscast *n.* a broadcast of a sports event. □ **sportscaster** *n.*

sports coat *n.* a sports jacket.

sports day *n.* *Cdn* & *Brit.* a day on which schoolchildren participate in games, races, etc.

sports jacket *n.* (also **sport jacket**) a man's jacket for informal wear.

sportsman *n.* (*pl.* **sportsmen**) **1** a person who takes part in sports. **2** a person who behaves fairly and generously. **3** a person who hunts or fishes recreationally. □ **sportsmanlike** *adj.* **sportsmanship** *n.*

sportsplex *n.* (*pl.* **sportsplexes**) a building offering different sports facilities under one roof.

sportswear *n.* **1** clothes worn for playing sports. **2** clothing of an informal type.

sportswoman *n.* (*pl.* **sportswomen**) a woman who takes part in sports.

sportswriter *n.* a journalist who writes on sports.

sport-utility *n.* (*pl.* **sport-utilities**) (also **sport-utility vehicle**, **sport ute** *informal*) a hybrid between a Jeep and a minivan.

sporty *adj.* (**sportier**, **sportiest**) *informal* **1** fond of sports. **2** (esp. of clothes) suitable for informal wear. **3** (of a car) resembling a sports car.

spot ● *n.* **1** a small round mark on a surface. **2** a particular place, point, or position. **3** a moral blemish. **4** a particular part or aspect. **5** an awkward or difficult situation. ● *v.* (**spots**, **spotted**, **spotting**) **1** notice or recognize (someone or something) that is difficult to detect or that one is searching for. **2** mark with spots. **3** *informal* loan. □ **hit the spot** *informal* be exactly what is required. **on the spot 1** at the scene of an action or event. **2** immediately. **put on the spot** *informal* force to answer an awkward question etc. □ **spotted** *adj.*

spot check ● *n.* a test made on a randomly selected subject. ● *v.* (**spot-check**) subject to a spot check.

spotless *adj.* absolutely clean or pure. □ **spotlessly** *adv.*

spotlight ● *n.* **1** a beam of light directed on a small area. **2** a lamp projecting this. **3** full attention or publicity. ● *v.* (**spotlights**; *past* and *past participle* **spotlighted** or **spotlit**; **spotlighting**) **1** direct a spotlight on. **2** draw attention to.

spotted fever *n.* (also **Rocky Mountain spotted fever**) a rickettsial disease characterized by fever and spots on the skin.

spotted owl *n.* a large, dark brown hornless owl of N America.

spotter *n.* **1** (often in *comb.*) a person who spots people or things. **2** an aviator or aircraft employed in locating enemy positions etc. **3** (in gymnastics etc.) a person stationed to provide safety assistance to the performer.

spotting *n.* a slight discharge of blood from the vagina.

spotty *adj.* (**spottier**, **spottiest**) **1** marked with spots. **2** patchy.

spouse *n.* a husband or wife. □ **spousal** *adj.*

Spouse's Allowance *n.* *Cdn* a federal benefit paid to low-income 60–64-year-old spouses of Old Age Security pensioners.

spout ● *n.* **1** a projecting tube or lip through which a liquid etc. is poured. **2** a jet or column of liquid, grain, etc. **3** a whale's blowhole. ● *v.* **1** spray out in a steady flow or stream. **2** express one's views in a lengthy and tedious manner.

sprain ● v. wrench (an ankle, wrist, etc.) so as to cause pain and swelling. ● n. such a wrench.

sprang past of SPRING.

sprawl ● v. **1** sit or lie or fall with limbs flung out. **2** spread out irregularly to cover a large area. ● n. **1** a sprawling movement. **2** a straggling group. **3** the straggling expansion of an urban or industrial area. □ **sprawling** adj.

spray ● n. **1 a** liquid flying in small drops. **b** a quantity of small objects flying through the air. **2 a** a sprig of flowers or leaves. **b** a bunch of flowers decoratively arranged. ● v. **1** throw in the form of spray. **2** sprinkle (an object) with small drops or particles. **3** (of a male animal) mark its environment with the smell of its urine. □ **sprayer** n.

spray-on adj. (of a product) applied in the form of a spray.

spray paint ● n. paint in an aerosol can for spraying upon a surface. ● v. (**spray-paint**) paint using spray paint.

spread ● v. (**spreads, spread, spreading**) **1** open out so as to increase in surface area, width, or length. **2** stretch out (limbs, hands, fingers, or wings) so that they are far apart. **3** extend over a wide area or a specified period of time. **4** reach or cause to reach more and more people. **5** apply (a substance) in an even layer. ● n. **1** the action of spreading. **2** the degree or extent of spreading. **3** diffusion or expansion. **4** a garnish that is spread on bread etc. **5** an article etc. displayed esp. on two facing pages. **6** informal a large meal. **7** a bedspread. □ **spread oneself too thin** attempt to undertake too many projects at once. □ **spreadable** adj. **spreader** n.

spread-eagle ● n. **1** a representation of an eagle with legs and wings extended. **2** Figure Skating a straight glide made with the feet a short distance apart and the arms held out to either side. ● v. (**spread-eagles, spread-eagled, spread-eagling**) **1** place (a person) in a position with arms and legs spread out. **2** Figure Skating perform a spread-eagle. □ **spread-eagled** adj.

spreadsheet n. a computer program allowing manipulation of esp. tabulated numerical data.

spree n. **1** a period of extravagant indulgence. **2** a period of a (usu. specified) activity.

sprig n. **1** a small branch or shoot. **2** a representation of this.

sprightly adj. (**sprightlier,**

sprightliest) brisk, lively, spirited. □ **sprightliness** n.

spring ● v. (**springs;** past **sprang** or **sprung;** past participle **sprung; springing**) **1** move suddenly or rapidly upwards or forwards. **2** move or do suddenly. **3** operate by or as if by means of a spring mechanism. **4** originate or appear from. **5** suddenly develop or appear. **6** present unexpectedly to (someone). **7** informal bring about the escape of (a prisoner). ● n. **1** the season after winter and before summer. **2** a spiral metal coil that can be pressed or pulled but that returns to its former shape when released. **3** a sudden jump upwards. **4** a place where water wells up from an underground source. **5** elastic quality. **6** liveliness. □ **spring a leak** develop a leak.

springboard n. **1** a starting point or impetus for an activity, discussion, etc. **2** a springy board used by gymnasts in vaulting etc.

spring breakup n. Cdn = BREAKUP 3.

spring chicken n. □ **no spring chicken** not a young person.

springer spaniel n. a sturdy dog of medium height used esp. in hunting to rouse game.

spring fever n. a restless feeling sometimes associated with spring.

springform pan n. a round metal cake pan with sides that may be released from the bottom.

spring-loaded adj. (of a device etc.) containing a spring that presses one part against another.

spring peeper n. a small brown North American tree frog with a high piping call.

spring roll n. a deep-fried Oriental snack, consisting of a very thin wrapper rolled around a mixture of chopped vegetables etc.

spring salmon n. Cdn a chinook salmon.

spring tide n. a tide occurring just after the new and full moon, in which there is the greatest difference between high and low water.

springtime n. **1** the season of spring. **2** the earliest and usu. most pleasant stage of something.

spring wheat n. wheat that is planted in the spring.

springy adj. (**springier, springiest**) **1** elastic, resilient. **2** (of movement etc.) buoyant and vigorous. □ **springiness** n.

sprinkle ● v. (**sprinkles, sprinkled, sprinkling**) **1** scatter liquid, powder, etc. in small drops or particles. **2** distribute in small amounts. **3** (of rain) fall in a fine mist. ● *n.* **1** the action or an act of sprinkling. **2** a dusting or light shower. **3** (usu. in *pl.*) a tiny coloured candy used to decorate cookies, cupcakes, etc. □ **sprinkling** *n.*

sprinkler *n.* **1** a device etc. used to sprinkle esp. water. **2** an overhead plumbing fixture for extinguishing fires.

sprint ● *v.* run a short distance at full speed. ● *n.* **1** a fast race in which the participants run, cycle, ride, etc. at full speed. **2** a short burst of speed. □ **sprinter** *n.*

sprite *n.* an elf or fairy.

spritz ● *v.* (**spritzes, spritzed, spritzing**) **1** sprinkle or spray with a liquid. **2** apply (a liquid) by spraying. ● *n.* (*pl.* **spritzes**) a small spray.

spritzer *n.* a mixture of wine and soda water.

sprocket *n.* each of several teeth on a wheel engaging with links of a chain on a bicycle or with holes in film etc.

sprout ● *v.* **1** put forth, produce, or develop (shoots etc.). **2** begin to grow. **3** spring up or emerge. **4** give rise to. ● *n.* **1** a shoot of a plant. **2** (usu. in *pl.*) Brussels sprouts.

spruce[1] ● *adj.* neat in dress and appearance. ● *v.* (**spruces, spruced, sprucing**) make or become neat or smart.

spruce[2] *n.* **1** a coniferous evergreen tree, which has a distinctive pyramid shape and hanging cones. **2** its wood.

spruce beer *n.* an alcoholic or non-alcoholic drink made by sweetening the water of boiled spruce twigs and needles.

spruce budworm *n.* the brown larva of a N American moth, which is a serious pest of spruce and other conifers.

sprung ● *v.* past and past participle of SPRING. ● *adj.* **1** fitted with springs. **2** (of a floor) suspended above a subfloor in order to be resilient or springy.

spry *adj.* (**spryer, spryest**) nimble, lively.

spud *n. slang* a potato.

spume *n.* foam or froth on a liquid. [*Say* SPYOOM]

spumoni *n.* a kind of rich layered ice cream with candied fruit and nuts. [*Say* spuh MOANY]

spun ● *v.* past and past participle of SPIN. ● *adj.* converted into threads.

spunk *n. informal* energy, courage.

spunky *adj.* (**spunkier, spunkiest**) *informal* full of energy, courage. □ **spunkily** *adv.* **spunkiness** *n.*

spur ● *n.* **1** a small spike or a spiked wheel worn on a rider's heel for urging a horse forward. **2** a stimulus or encouragement.

3 (also **spur line**) a short stretch of track branching off a railway line. **4** a ridge that projects from a mountain or hill. **5** an abnormal growth on the heel or elbow. ● *v.* (**spurs, spurred, spurring**) **1** prick (a horse) with spurs. **2 a** encourage. **b** stimulate. □ **earn** (or **win**) **one's spurs** attain distinction. **on the spur of the moment** on a sudden whim or impulse. □ **spurred** *adj.*

spurge *n.* a plant or shrub that produces a milky juice, used as a source of latex.

spurious *adj.* **1** not genuine; false or fake. **2** based on false reasoning. [*Say* SPUR ee us *or* SPYOOR ee us]

spurn *v.* reject or refuse with contempt.

spur-of-the-moment *adj.* impromptu, sudden.

spurt ● *v.* **1 a** gush out in a stream. **b** squirt. **2** move or act with greater speed or exertion for a short time. ● *n.* **1** a short gushing stream of liquid etc. **2** a marked or sudden increase of speed or exertion. **3** a marked increase or improvement.

sputter ● *v.* **1 a** emit a spitting or slight explosive sound or series of such sounds. **b** proceed with difficulty, struggle. **2** say or speak in a hurried or incoherent manner. ● *n.* a series of soft explosive sounds.

sputum *n.* **1** saliva, spittle. **2** a mixture of saliva and mucus coughed up from the respiratory tract. [*Say* SPEW tum]

spy ● *n.* (*pl.* **spies**) **1** a person employed to collect and report secret information on esp. the activities of an enemy or rival. **2** a person who keeps watch on others. **3** (**Spy**) (also **Northern Spy**) a large red cooking apple streaked with green. ● *v.* (**spies, spied, spying**) **1** catch sight of. **2** work as a spy. □ **spy on** maintain a secret observation of.

spyglass *n.* (*pl.* **spyglasses**) a small telescope.

spymaster *n. informal* the head of a spy organization.

spyware *n.* software that secretly tracks a user's Internet browsing for the purpose of targeting advertising.

SQ *abbr. Cdn* Sûreté du Québec.

sq. *abbr.* square.

squab *n.* a newly hatched or very young bird, esp. a pigeon. [*Say* SKWOB]

squabble ● *n.* a petty or noisy quarrel. ● *v.* (**squabbles, squabbled, squabbling**) engage in a squabble.

squad *n.* **1** a small group of people sharing a task etc. **2** a small number of soldiers assembled for drill or working together. **3** *Sport informal* a team. **4** a unit or division within a police force.

squad car n. a police car.

squadron n. **1** a principal division of an armoured or cavalry regiment. **2** the basic administrative unit of an air force. **3** a formal unit in a navy. **4** informal a large group.

squalid adj. **1** very dirty and unpleasant. **2** sordid. [Say SKWOL id]

squall ● n. **1** a sudden and short-lived violent storm or gust of wind. **2** a shrill cry or scream, as of a baby. ● v. scream. □ **squally** adj.

squalor n. a filthy or squalid state. [Say SKWOL er]

Squamish n. (pl. **Squamish**) **1** a member of an Aboriginal people living in southwestern BC. **2** the Salishan language of the Squamish. □ **Squamish** adj. [Say SKWOM ish]

squamous adj. covered with, composed of, or characterized by scales. [Say SKWAY muss]

squander v. **1** spend (time, money, etc.) recklessly or lavishly. **2** let (an opportunity) pass. [Say SKWON dur]

square ● n. **1** a plane figure with four right angles and four equal straight sides. **2** an open usu. four-sided area enclosed by buildings. **3** an L-shaped or T-shaped instrument used to draw or verify right angles. **4** the product of a number multiplied by itself. **5** slang a conventional or old-fashioned person. **6** a dessert cut into square pieces. ● adj. (**squarer**, **squarest**) **1** having the shape of a square. **2** having or forming a right angle. **3 a** solid, stocky. **b** (of the jaw etc.) having a square outline. **4** designating a unit of measure equal to the area of a square whose side is one of the unit specified. **5 a** even, straight, level. **b** perpendicular. **6** (also **all square**) **a** with all accounts settled. **b** (of scores) tied. **7** fair and honest. **8** slang old-fashioned. ● adv. **1** informal exactly, directly. **2** upright, straight. **3** fairly, honestly. ● v. (**squares**, **squared**, **squaring**) **1** make square or rectangular. **2** multiply (a number) by itself. **3** correspond, be consistent. **4** settle (an account, debt, etc.). **5** place (one's shoulders) squarely facing forwards. **6** (usu. in passive) mark out in squares. **7** tie (a game or series). □ **back to square one** informal back to the starting point. **squared away** taken care of, dealt with. **square off 1** assume the stance or crouch of a boxer. **2** meet in competition or opposition. □ **squarely** adv. **squareness** n. **squarish** adj.

square brackets pl. n. brackets of the form [ ].

square dance ● n. a type of dance which starts with four couples facing one another in a square. ● v. participate in a square dance. □ **square dancer** n. **square dancing** n.

square meal n. a hearty and satisfying meal.

square-rigged adj. (of a ship) with the principal sails at right angles to the length of the ship.

square root n. the number which produces a specified quantity when multiplied by itself.

squash ● v. (**squashes**, **squashed**, **squashing**) **1** crush or squeeze into a pulp, flat mass, or distorted shape. **2** pack tightly. **3** reject or suppress. **4** flatten or be crushed. ● n. **1** a game for two or four players with racquets and a small fairly soft ball played in a closed court. **2** (pl. **squash** or **squashes**) an edible gourd, the flesh of which may be cooked and eaten as a vegetable. □ **squashy** adj.

squat ● v. (**squats**, **squatted**, **squatting**) **1** crouch on the balls of one's feet with the legs bent. **2** unlawfully occupy an uninhabited building or an area of land. ● adj. (**squatter**, **squattest**) short and fat. ● n. **1** slang nothing. **2** a property occupied by squatters. **3** a squatting posture. □ **squatter** n.

squawk ● n. **1** a loud harsh cry esp. of a bird. **2** a loud complaint or protest. ● v. **1** utter a squawk. **2** complain or protest loudly.

squeak ● n. **1** a sharp shrill sound or cry. **2** (also **narrow squeak**) a narrow escape. ● v. **1** make or emit a squeak. **2** utter or sing in a shrill voice. **3** informal manage or pass by only a narrow margin.

squeaker n. **1** a game etc. won by a narrow margin. **2** a person or thing that squeaks.

squeaky adj. (**squeakier**, **squeakiest**) tending to squeak.

squeaky clean adj. **1** above reproach. **2** completely clean.

squeal ● n. a long shrill sound or cry. ● v. **1** make a squeal. **2** utter with a squeal. **3** slang turn informer against. □ **squealer** n.

squeamish adj. **1** easily turned sick or disgusted. **2** not wanting to do something that might be considered dishonest. □ **squeamishness** n.

squeegee ● n. an implement with a wide rubber blade used to clean windows. ● v. (**squeegees**, **squeegeed**, **squeegeeing**) clean with a squeegee.

squeeze ● v. (**squeezes**, **squeezed**, **squeezing**) **1** firmly press from opposite

or all sides. **2** extract (liquid or a soft substance) from something by squeezing. **3** manage to get into or through (a restricted space). **4** manage to find time for. **5** obtain from someone with difficulty. **6** hug firmly. ● *n.* **1** an act of squeezing or being squeezed. **2** a small amount of liquid extracted by squeezing. **3** a strong financial demand. **4** *informal* a girlfriend or boyfriend. **5** a bind. **6** *Baseball* (also **squeeze play**) a play in which the batter attempts to bring a player home from third on a sacrifice bunt. □ **put the squeeze on** *informal* coerce or pressure (a person).
□ **squeezable** *adj.* **squeezer** *n.*

squeezebox *n.* (*pl.* **squeezeboxes**) *informal* an accordion or concertina.

squelch ● *v.* (**squelches, squelched, squelching**) **1 a** walk or tread heavily in mud etc., so as to make a sucking sound. **b** make a sucking sound. **2** crush, silence, suppress. ● *n.* a squelching sound.
□ **squelchy** *adj.*

squib *n.* **1** a small firework burning with a hissing sound. **2 a** a brief news item used as a filler in a newspaper. **b** a short satirical composition.

squid *n.* an elongated marine mollusc related to the octopus, with eight arms in a ring around two longer tentacles.

squidgy *adj.* (**squidgier, squidgiest**) *informal* soft or moist.

squiggle ● *n.* a short curly or wavy line. ● *v.* (**squiggles, squiggled, squiggling**) write in squiggles; scrawl.
□ **squiggly** *adj.*

squinch *v.* (**squinches, squinched, squinching**) **1** screw up one's eyes etc. **2** (of the eyes etc.) squint.

squint ● *v.* **1** look obliquely or with the eyes partly closed. **2** hold (one's eyes) half-shut. **3** suffer from a disorder which causes each eye to look in a different direction. ● *n.* **1** a permanent deviation or defective alignment of one or both eyes. **2** a look through half-closed eyes. **3** *informal* a glance or look. □ **squinty** *adj.* (**squintier, squintiest**)

squire ● *n.* **1** (in Britain) a country gentleman, esp. the chief landowner in a country district. **2** *hist.* a young nobleman serving as a knight's attendant. ● *v.* (**squires, squired, squiring**) (of a man) attend upon (a woman).

squirm *v.* **1** wriggle, writhe. **2** show embarrassment. □ **squirmy** *adj.*

squirrel ● *n.* an esp. tree-dwelling rodent with a long bushy tail. ● *v.* (**squirrels, squirrelled, squirrelling**) **1** hoard (objects, food, etc.). **2** bustle, scurry.

squirrelly *adj. informal* **1** restless, fidgety. **2** eccentric, crazy.

squirt ● *v.* **1** eject or propel (a liquid or semi-liquid substance) in a jet-like stream, esp. from a small opening. **2** (of liquid or a semi-liquid substance) be discharged in this way. **3** splash with liquid ejected by squirting. **4** (often foll. by *free* or *loose*) be lost or dropped; slip or fall, esp. from one's hand. ● *n.* **1 a** a jet or stream of liquid. **b** a small quantity produced by squirting. **2** *informal* **a** a young person, esp. a meddlesome child. **b** an insignificant but presumptuous person. **3 a** an initiation level of sports for young children. **b** a player at this level.

squish *v.* (**squishes, squished, squishing**) **1** make a gushing or squelching sound. **2** crush, squash, or squeeze. **3** pack or be packed tightly.
□ **squishy** *adj.*

Sr. *abbr.* Senior.

Sri Lankan *n.* a person from Sri Lanka (formerly Ceylon). □ **Sri Lankan** *adj.* [*Say* shree LANK un *or* sree LANK un]

SSE *abbr.* south-southeast.

SSRI *abbr.* SELECTIVE SEROTONIN REUPTAKE INHIBITOR.

SSW *abbr.* south-southwest.

St. *abbr.* **1** Street. **2** Saint.

stab ● *v.* (**stabs, stabbed, stabbing**) **1** thrust a knife etc. into. **2** cause a feeling like being stabbed. **3** thrust a pointed object at. **4** pierce a hole in something. ● *n.* **1 a** an instance of stabbing. **b** a blow or thrust with a knife etc. **2 a** a sharply painful sensation. **3** *informal* an attempt. **4 a** vigorous thrust. □ **stab in the back 1** *n.* a treacherous or slanderous attack. **2** *v.* slander or betray. **stab in the dark** a blind attempt. □ **stabber** *n.* **stabbing** *n.*

stability *n.* the quality or state of being stable. [*Say* stuh BILLA tee]

stabilization payment *n. Cdn* a payment made esp. by the federal government to stabilize a faltering economy.

stabilize *v.* (**stabilizes, stabilized, stabilizing**) make or become stable.
□ **stabilization** *n.*

stabilizer *n.* **1** the horizontal tailplane of an aircraft. **2** a gyroscopic device to prevent rolling of a ship. **3** a substance which prevents the breakdown of emulsions, esp. as a food additive.

stable ● *adj.* (**stabler, stablest**) **1** firmly fixed or established. **2 a** firm, resolute. **b** mentally and emotionally sound. **3** *Chemistry* (of a compound) not readily decomposing. **4** *Physics* not subject to radioactive decay. **5** not deteriorating in health after an injury or operation. ● *n.* **1** a building for keeping horses. **2** an establishment where racehorses are kept and trained. **3** the racehorses of a particular stable. ● *v.* (**stables, stabled, stabling**) keep in a stable. □ **stabling** *n.* **stably** *adv.*

stablemate *n.* a horse of the same stable.

staccato ● *adv. & adj.* **1** *Music* with each note sharply detached or separated from the others. **2** with short and sharp sounds. ● *n.* (*pl.* **staccatos**) **1** a staccato passage in music etc. **2** staccato delivery. [*Say* stuh KATTO *or* stuh KOTTO]

stack ● *n.* **1** a neat pile or heap. **2** a circular or rectangular pile of hay etc. **3** *informal* a large quantity. **4** a smokestack. **5** a number of aircraft flying at different altitudes while waiting for permission to land. **6** (in *pl.*) a part of a library where most of the books are stored on shelving. ● *v.* **1** pile in a stack or stacks. **2** arrange (cards) secretly for cheating. **3** cause (aircraft) to fly at different levels while waiting to land. **4** skew the representation on (a committee etc.) so that it will act in one's interests. □ **stack the deck** (or **cards**) cause (circumstances etc.) to favour one person etc. over another. **stack up** *informal* measure up. □ **stackable** *adj.* **stacker** *n.*

stacked *adj.* **1 a** put into a stack or stacks. **b** piled with goods etc. **2** (of odds, circumstances, etc.) biased. **3** *informal* (of a woman) having large breasts.

stadium *n.* (*pl.* **stadiums**) a sports ground with tiers of seats for spectators.

stadium seating *n.* an arrangement of seats, esp. in a movie theatre, in which each row of seats is on a tier one step higher than the one in front of it.

staff ● *n.* **1** (*pl.* also **staves**) **a** a stick used as a support or weapon. **b** a rod held as a sign of office or authority. **2 a** a group of people employed in a business etc. **b** a group of military officers assisting a commanding officer. **3** *Music* a set of usu. five parallel lines on which a note is placed to indicate its pitch. ● *v.* **1** provide with staff. **2** work as a member of staff in. □ **on staff** serving as a member of a staff. □ **staffed** *adj.* **staffing** *n.*

staffer *n.* a member of an esp. newspaper staff.

staff room *n.* esp. *Cdn & Brit.* a common room for staff, esp. in a school.

stag ● *n.* **1** an adult male deer. **2** = STAG PARTY. ● *adj. informal* of, for, or composed of men only. ● *adv. informal* without a date.

stage ● *n.* **1** a point or period in a process. **2 a** a raised floor or platform on which plays etc. are performed. **b** (**the stage**) the acting or theatrical profession. **3** a regular stopping place on a route. **4** a section of a rocket with a separate engine, jettisoned when its propellant is exhausted. **5** a stagecoach. ● *v.* (**stages, staged, staging**) **1** present on stage. **2** arrange the occurrence of. **3** present or arrange a contrived or mock version of. □ **on** (**the**) **stage** performing as an actor, dancer, etc. **set the stage** prepare the way or conditions for.

stagecoach *n.* (*pl.* **stagecoaches**) *hist.* a large closed horse-drawn coach running regularly between two places.

stagecraft *n.* skill in mounting theatrical performances etc.

stage direction *n.* an instruction in the text of a play as to the position, tone, etc., of an actor, or sound effects etc.

stage-dive *v.* (of a performer etc.) leap from a stage so as to land on top of the crowd at a rock concert.

stage door *n.* an entrance from the street to a theatre behind the stage.

stage fright *n.* nervousness on facing an audience.

stagehand *n.* a person handling scenery etc. during a play etc.

stage left *n.* the part of a stage to the left of a person facing the audience.

stage-manage *v.* (**stage-manages, stage-managed, stage-managing**) **1** be the stage manager of. **2** arrange and control for effect. □ **stage management** *n.*

stage manager *n.* the person responsible for giving cues to all those involved in a performance.

stage right *n.* the part of a stage to the right of a person facing the audience.

stagette *n.* *Cdn* an all-female celebration in honour of a woman about to marry.

stage whisper ● *n.* **1** a loud whisper addressed by one actor to another, meant to be heard by the audience. **2** any loud whisper meant to be heard by people. ● *v.* (**stage-whisper**) utter in a loud whisper.

stagey *adj.* (**stagier, stagiest**) = STAGY.

stagflation *n.* inflation combined with economic stagnation.

stagger ● *v.* **1** walk unsteadily, totter. **2** shock, confuse. **3** arrange (events etc.) so that they do not coincide. **4** arrange (objects etc.) so that they are not in line. ● *n.* **1** a tottering movement. **2** (in *pl.*) **a** any of various diseases of farm animals marked by staggering. **b** giddiness.

staggering *adj.* **1** astonishing, bewildering. **2** that staggers. □ **staggeringly** *adv.*

staging n. **1** an instance or method of presenting a play etc. **2** (as an *adj.*) referring to a stopping place en route to a destination.

stagnant *adj.* **1** (of liquid or air) motionless, having no current. **2** showing no activity, sluggish.

stagnate v. (**stagnates, stagnated, stagnating**) be or become stagnant. □ **stagnation** n.

stag party n. an all-male celebration in honour of a man about to marry.

stagy *adj.* (**stagier, stagiest**) theatrical; exaggerated. [*Say* STAGE ee]

staid *adj.* usu. *derogatory* settled and dignified; not adventurous.

stain ● v. **1** discolour or be discoloured by the action of liquid sinking in. **2** spoil, damage (a reputation etc.). **3** colour (wood, glass, etc.) with a dye or chemical. ● n. **1** a discoloration; a spot or mark not easily removed. **2** damage to a reputation etc. **3** a substance used in staining.

stained glass n. dyed or coloured glass, used esp. in windows.

stainless *adj.* without or resistant to stains.

stainless steel n. an iron alloy containing chromium and resistant to rust.

stair n. **1** each of a set of fixed steps. **2** (esp. in *pl.*) a set of such steps.

staircase n. a flight of stairs and the supporting structure.

stairclimber n. an exercise machine for simulating the action of climbing stairs.

Stairmaster n. *proprietary* = STAIRCLIMBER.

stairway n. a flight of stairs, a staircase.

stairwell n. the shaft in which a staircase is built.

stake¹ ● n. **1** a stout stick or post sharpened at one end and driven into the ground. **2** *hist.* the post to which a person was tied to be burned alive. ● v. (**stakes, staked, staking**) **1** fasten, secure, or support with a stake or stakes. **2** mark off (an area) with stakes. **3** state or establish (a claim). □ **pull** (or **pull up**) **stakes** depart. **stake out** *informal* **1** place under surveillance. **2** declare a special interest in or right to.

stake² ● n. **1** a sum of money etc. wagered. **2 a** an interest or concern, esp. financial. **b** (in *pl.*) what is being risked. **3** (in *pl.*) money offered as a prize. ● v. (**stakes, staked, staking**) **1** wager. **2** risk. □ **at stake 1** risked. **2** in question.

stakeholder n. a person with an interest in something.

stakeout n. *informal* a continuous secret watch by the police.

stalactite n. a tapering deposit hanging down from the roof of a cave etc., formed by dripping water. [*Say* stuh LACK tite *or* STAL ack tite]

stalagmite n. a mound or tapering column rising from the floor of a cave etc., deposited by dripping water. [*Say* stuh LAG mite *or* STAL ag mite]

stale ● *adj.* (**staler, stalest**) **1 a** not fresh, not quite new. **b** musty, insipid. **2** lacking novelty or interest. **3** no longer performing well. ● v. (**stales, staled, staling**) make or become stale.

stalemate ● n. **1** *Chess* a position counting as a draw, in which a player is not in check but cannot move except into check. **2** a deadlock. ● v. (**stalemates, stalemated, stalemating**) bring to a stalemate.

Stalinism n. the policies followed by the Soviet dictator Joseph Stalin (1879–1953), esp. centralization, totalitarianism, and the pursuit of Communism. □ **Stalinist** n. [*Say* STAL in ism *or* STOL in ism]

stalk¹ n. **1** the main stem of a plant. **2** the attachment or support of a leaf, flower, fruit, etc. **3** a similar support for an organ etc. in an animal.

stalk² v. **1** pursue or approach stealthily. **2** walk in a stately or haughty manner. **3** harass with unwanted and obsessive attention. □ **stalker** n. **stalking** n.

stall ● n. **1** a trader's stand or booth in a market etc. **2 a** a stable. **b** a compartment for one animal in this. **c** a compartment for one horse at the start of a race. **3** a compartment or cubicle with a single shower or toilet. **4** a fixed seat in the choir or chancel of a church. **5** a parking space. **6** the stalling of an engine. ● v. **1 a** (of a motor vehicle or its engine) stop running. **b** (of an aircraft) be moving at a speed too low to allow effective operation of the controls. **c** cause to stall. **2** stop moving or progressing. **3 a** play for time when being questioned etc. **b** delay.

stallion n. an adult male horse that has not been castrated.

stalwart ● *adj.* **1** strongly built. **2** courageous, resolute. ● n. a stalwart person. [*Say* STAWL wurt]

stamen n. the male fertilizing organ of a flowering plant. [*Say* STAY mun]

stamina n. the ability to endure prolonged physical or mental strain. [*Say* STAM uh]

stammer ● v. **1** speak with halting articulation. **2** utter (words) in this way. ● n. a tendency to stammer.

stamp ● v. **1** bring down (one's foot) heavily on the ground etc. **2** impress a pattern, mark, etc. on. **3** affix a postage or other stamp to. **4 a** assign a specific character to. **b** (usu. in *passive*) mark with a particular feeling. ● *n.* **1** an instrument for stamping a pattern or mark. **2** a mark or pattern made by this. **3** a postage stamp. **4** a heavy downward blow with the foot. **5 a** a characteristic mark or impress. **b** character. **6** an audio or digital mark made on a recorded message, data file, etc. □ **stamp out 1** produce by cutting out with a die etc. **2** put an end to.

stampede ● *n.* **1** a sudden flight of a number of horses, cattle, etc. **2** a sudden rapid movement or reaction of a mass of people due to interest or panic. **3** *Cdn & US West* an exhibition or fair involving rodeo events etc. ● *v.* (**stampedes, stampeded, stampeding**) **1** take part in or cause a stampede. **2** cause to act hurriedly. □ **stampeder** *n.*

stamp pad *n.* an ink-soaked pad, used for inking a rubber stamp etc.

stance *n.* **1** the way a person stands. **2** a moral or intellectual attitude to something.

stanch *v.* = STAUNCH. [*Rhymes with* RANCH]

stanchion *n.* an upright bar, post, or frame forming a support or barrier. [*Say* STAN chun]

stand ● *v.* (**stands, stood, standing**) **1** be in or rise to an upright position, supported by one's feet. **2** place or be situated in a particular position. **3** move to a specified place. **4** remain stationary or unchanged. **5** be in a specified state or condition. **6** adopt a particular attitude towards an issue. **7** be likely to do something. **8** act in a specified capacity. **9** tolerate. **10** be a candidate for (an office). ● *n.* **1** an attitude towards a particular issue. **2** a determined effort to hold one's ground or resist something. **3** a stopping of motion or progress. **4** a large raised tiered structure for spectators. **5** a raised platform for a band, orchestra, or speaker. **6** a rack, base, or item of furniture for holding or displaying something. **7** a small temporary stall or booth from which goods are sold or displayed. **8** a witness box. **9** a group of trees etc. □ **as it stands 1** in its present condition. **2** (also **as things stand**) in the present circumstances. **stand alone** be unequalled. **stand by 1** look on without interfering. **2** uphold, side with (a person). **3** abide by (terms or promises). **4** be ready to act. **stand corrected** accept correction. **stand down 1** withdraw from a team, election, etc. **2** leave the witness box. **3** *Military* go off duty. **stand firm** (or **fast**) be steadfast. **stand for 1** represent. **2** *informal* endure, tolerate. **stand one's ground** not yield.

stand in act in place of another. **stand on** insist on. **stand on one's own two feet** (or **own feet**) be self-reliant. **stand out 1** be prominent or conspicuous. **2** hold out. **stand up 1 a** rise to one's feet. **b** place in a standing position. **2** (of an argument etc.) be valid. **3** *informal* fail to keep an appointment with. **stand up for** support, defend (a person or cause). **stand up to 1** meet or face (an opponent) courageously. **2** be resistant to the harmful effects of. **take a** (or **one's**) **stand** commit to a position in a debate etc.

stand-alone *adj.* **1** (of a computer) operating independently of a network etc. **2** designed or intended not to rely on an external structure or system.

standard ● *n.* **1** a level of quality or attainment. **2** a required or agreed level of quality or attainment. **3** something used as a measure in comparative evaluations. **4** (in *pl.*) principles of good behaviour. **5** a military or ceremonial flag. **6** a tune or song of established popularity. ● *adj.* **1** used or accepted as normal or average. **2** (of a size, measure, etc.) regularly used or produced. **3** (of a work, writer, etc.) viewed as authoritative and so widely read. ● *adv.* in its standard state, form, etc. □ **set the standard** reach a level of excellence which others must try to match.

standard-bearer *n.* **1** a soldier who carries a standard. **2** a prominent leader in a cause.

standardbred *n.* a horse of a breed able to attain a specific speed, developed esp. for harness racing.

standard issue *n.* **1** that which is issued as a matter of course. **2** (as an *adj.*) ordinary.

standardize *v.* (**standardizes, standardized, standardizing**) cause to conform to a standard. □ **standardization** *n.*

standard of living *n.* (*pl.* **standards of living**) the degree of material comfort available to a person or community.

standard time *n.* a uniform time officially adopted for a country or region.

standby ● *n.* (*pl.* **standbys**) **1** a person or thing ready if needed in an emergency etc. **2** a thing which has proven to be reliable. ● *adj.* **1** ready for immediate use. **2** designating a system of air travel whereby unreserved seats are allocated just before departure. **3** *Cdn & Brit.* designating theatre tickets sold on the basis of availability on the day of performance. ● *adv.* without having booked seats in advance. □ **on standby** prepared for immediate use or activity and awaiting instructions etc.

stand-in *n.* a substitute, esp. for an actor.

standing ● *n.* **1** esteem or repute; status. **2** duration. **3** length of service etc. **4** (in *pl.*) a ranking of teams etc. in a league etc. **5** one's position in a ranking. ● *adj.* **1** upright. **2** established, permanent. **3** (of a jump, start, etc.) performed from rest or from a standing position. **4** (of water) stagnant. □ **in good standing 1** fully paid-up as a member etc. **2** in favour.

standing committee *n.* a committee that is permanent during the existence of the appointing body.

standing joke *n.* something that regularly causes amusement or provokes ridicule.

standing order *n.* **1** (in *pl.*) the rules governing the conduct of business in a parliament etc. **2** an esp. military order that remains valid without having to be repeated. **3** an order with a supplier to supply a product whenever it is available.

standing ovation *n.* prolonged applause during which the audience rises to its feet.

standoff *n.* **1** a deadlock. **2** a confrontation in which each side is entrenched and threatening.

standoffish *adj.* cold or distant in manner. □ **standoffishness** *n.*

standout *n. informal* a remarkable or outstanding person or thing.

standpoint *n.* **1** the position from which a thing is viewed. **2** a mental attitude.

standstill *n.* a stoppage.

stand-up ● *adj.* **1** (of comedy) performed by standing before an audience and telling jokes. **2** that stands or is used upright. **3** (of a fight) violent or fair and square. **4** (of a person) honest, trustworthy. ● *n.* **1** a stand-up comedian. **2** stand-up comedy.

stank *past of* STINK.

Stanley Cup *n.* a trophy awarded annually to the hockey team that wins the NHL championships.

stanza *n.* a group of lines forming the basic metrical unit in a poem or verse. [*Say* STAN zuh]

staph *n. informal* staphylococcus. [*Sounds like* STAFF]

staphylococcus *n.* (*pl.* **staphylococci**) a bacterium which causes pus formation. □ **staphylococcal** *adj.* [*Say* staff illa COCK us *for the singular,* staff illa COCK eye *for the plural,* staff illa COCKLE]

staple ● *n.* **1 a** the main or an important article of commerce. **b** the chief element or a main component. **2** a small thin piece of U-shaped wire that is used for fastening etc. ● *v.* (**staples, stapled, stapling**) fasten or attach with a staple or staples. ● *adj.* **1** main or principal. **2** important.

stapler *n.* a small device for stapling paper etc.

star ● *n.* **1** a fixed luminous point in the night sky. **2** a stylized representation of a star, often used to indicate a category of excellence. **3** a famous or talented entertainer or sports player. **4** an outstanding person or thing. ● *v.* (**stars, starred, starring**) **1 a** (of a film etc.) feature as a principal performer. **b** (of a performer) be featured in a film etc. **2** mark or adorn with a star or stars. □ **my stars!** *informal* an expression of surprise. □ **starless** *adj.* **starlike** *adj.*

starboard ● *n.* the right-hand side (looking forward) of a ship or aircraft. ● *adj.* on or turned towards the starboard side.

starburst *n.* **1** a pattern of radiating lines or rays around a central object etc. **2** an explosion producing this effect.

starch ● *n.* (*pl.* **starches**) **1** a carbohydrate obtained chiefly from cereals and potatoes, forming an important constituent of the human diet. **2** a preparation of this for stiffening fabric. ● *v.* (**starches, starched, starching**) stiffen with starch.

starchy *adj.* (**starchier, starchiest**) **1** (of food) containing a lot of starch. **2** (of clothing) stiff with starch. **3** very stiff, formal.

stardom *n.* the state of being famous as a star.

stardust *n.* a romantic mystical look or sensation.

stare ● *v.* (**stares, stared, staring**) **1** look fixedly. **2** (of eyes) be wide open and fixed. **3** be unpleasantly prominent or striking. ● *n.* a staring gaze. □ **stare down** stare at someone until they are forced to look away. **stare one in the face** be evident or imminent.

starfish *n.* (*pl.* **starfish** or **starfishes**) a marine creature with five or more radiating arms.

starfruit *n.* a juicy yellow Southeast Asian fruit with a star-shaped cross-section.

stargazer *n. informal* **1** an astronomer or astrologer. **2** a daydreamer. □ **stargazing** *n.*

stark ● *adj.* **1** desolate, bare. **2** sharply evident. **3** downright, sheer. **4** brutally simple. **5** completely naked. ● *adv.* completely, wholly. □ **starkly** *adv.* **starkness** *n.*

starlet *n.* a promising young female performer.

starlight *n.* **1** the light of the stars. **2** (as an *adj.*) starlit.

starling *n.* a small bird with dark shiny plumage.

starlit *adj.* **1** lighted by stars. **2** with stars visible.

Star of Courage *n.* Canada's second-highest award for bravery. Abbreviation: **SC**.

Star of David *n.* a figure consisting of two interlaced triangles, used as a Jewish and Israeli symbol.

starry *adj.* (**starrier**, **starriest**) **1** covered with stars. **2** resembling a star.

starry-eyed *adj. informal* **1** enthusiastic but impractical. **2** euphoric.

starship *n.* (in science fiction) a large spacecraft for interstellar space travel.

star sign *n.* a sign of the zodiac.

star-spangled *adj.* **1** covered or glittering with stars. **2** featuring many famous performers.

star-struck *adj.* fascinated or greatly impressed by celebrities.

star-studded *n.* featuring many famous performers.

start ● *v.* **1** begin to do, be, happen, or engage in. **2** begin to operate or work. **3** cause to happen or operate. **4** begin to move or travel. **5** jump or jerk from surprise. **6** *literary* move or appear suddenly. **7** (of eyes) bulge. ● *n.* **1** an act of beginning or the point at which something begins. **2** a head start. **3** a jerk of surprise etc. □ **by fits and starts** intermittently or spasmodically. **for a start** *informal* as a beginning. **start off 1** begin. **2** begin to move. **start out 1** begin a journey. **2** *informal* proceed (to do something). **start up 1** arise; occur. **to start with 1** in the first place. **2** at the beginning.

starter ● *n.* **1** a person or thing that starts. **2** an esp. automatic device for starting an engine. **3** a player who plays at the beginning of a game. **4** a horse or competitor starting in a race. **5** the first course of a meal. ● *adj.* having to do with a start or beginning. □ **for starters** *informal* to start with.

starting block *n.* a block for bracing the feet of a runner at the start of a race.

starting lineup *n.* a list of players chosen to start a game.

startle *v.* (**startles**, **startled**, **startling**) give a shock or surprise to. □ **startled** *adj.* **startling** *adj.* **startlingly** *adv.*

start-up *n.* **1** the action or process of setting something in motion. **2** a newly established business.

star turn *n.* the principal item in an entertainment or performance.

starve *v.* (**starves**, **starved**, **starving**) **1** (cause to) suffer or die of hunger. **2** suffer from extreme poverty. **3** feel very hungry. **4** suffer from want. **5** deprive of. □ **starvation** *n.* & *adj.* **-starved** *comb. form*

stash *informal* ● *v.* (**stashes**, **stashed**, **stashing**) **1** put in a safe or hidden place. **2** hoard, stow. ● *n.* (*pl.* **stashes**) **1** a hiding place. **2** a cache, e.g. of an illegal drug.

stasis *n.* **1** a state of inactivity or equilibrium. **2** a stoppage of circulation of body fluids. [*Say* STAY sis *or* STASS iss]

stat ● *n. informal* **1** a statistic. **2** *Cdn* a statutory holiday. ● *adv. esp. Medical* immediately.

state ● *n.* **1** the existing condition or position of a person or thing. **2** *informal* **a** an agitated mental condition. **b** an untidy condition. **3 a** an organized political community under one government. **b** a political unit forming part of a federation. **c** (**the States**) the US. **4** (as an *adj.*) **a** having to do with the state. **b** reserved for or involving ceremony. ● *v.* (**states**, **stated**, **stating**) express in speech or writing. □ **of state** concerning politics or government. □ **statehood** *n.* **statewide** *adj.*

statecraft *n.* the art of diplomacy and government.

stated *adj.* **1** fixed, established. **2** explicitly set forth.

State Department *n.* (in the US) the department of foreign affairs.

stateless *adj.* **1** (of a person) having no nationality or citizenship. **2** without a state.

state line *n.* the boundary between two US states.

stately *adj.* (**statelier**, **stateliest**) dignified; imposing. □ **stateliness** *n.*

statement *n.* **1** a clear expression of something in speech or writing. **2** an official account of facts, views, or plans. **3** a formal account of events given to the police or in a court of law. **4** a record of transactions in a bank account etc.

statement of claim *n. Cdn* a legal document served in a civil suit which sets out the relief applied for by the plaintiff.

state of affairs *n.* circumstances.

state of the art ● *n.* the current stage of development of a subject. ● *adj.* (usu. **state-of-the-art**) using the latest techniques or equipment.

stateroom *n.* a private compartment in a passenger ship, train, etc.

stateside *esp. US informal* ● *adj.* of, in, or

relating to the US. ● *adv.* in or towards the continental US.

statesman *n.* (*pl.* **statesmen**) **1** a person skilled in affairs of state. **2** a distinguished politician. □ **statesmanship** *n.*

stateswoman *n.* (*pl.* **stateswomen**) **1** a woman skilled in affairs of state. **2** a distinguished female politician.

state trooper *n. US* a member of a state police force.

static ● *adj.* **1** stationary; not acting or changing. **2** of or relating to static electricity. **3** *Physics* concerned with bodies at rest or forces in equilibrium. ● *n.* **1** static electricity. **2** interference with the reception of telecommunications and broadcasts. **3** *slang* aggravation; criticism. □ **statically** *adv.*

static electricity *n.* a stationary electric charge, usu. produced by friction.

staticky *adj.* **1** producing static cling. **2** (of a radio broadcast etc.) crackling.

station ● *n.* **1 a** a regular stopping place on a railway or subway line. **b** (also **bus station**) a place where intercity buses depart and arrive. **2** a place or building etc. where a person or thing stands or is placed. **3** a place where a particular service or activity is based. **4 a** a broadcasting studio or company. **b** a specific frequency assigned to a broadcaster. **5** a plant for generating electricity. **6** position in life. ● *v.* **1** assign a station to. **2** put in position.

stationary *adj.* **1** not moving. **2** not portable. **3** not changing.

stationer *n.* a person who sells stationery.

stationery *n.* writing paper or materials.

station of the cross *n.* each of a series of usu. 14 images representing the events in the last days of Christ's life, before which devotions are performed in some churches.

station wagon *n.* a car with the passenger area extended and combined with space for luggage.

statism *n.* centralized state administration of social and economic affairs. □ **statist** *n.* & *adj.* [*Say* STATE ism]

statistic *n.* a statistical fact or item.

statistical *adj.* of or relating to statistics. □ **statistically** *adv.*

statistician *n.* a person who studies statistics. [*Say* stat iss TISH'n]

statistics *pl. n.* the science of collecting and analyzing numerical data, esp. in or for large quantities.

statuary ● *adj.* of or for statues. ● *n.* statues collectively.

statue *n.* a sculptured, cast, or carved figure of a person or animal.

statuesque *adj.* **1** like a statue. **2** (esp. of a woman) tall and graceful. [*Say* statue ESK]

statuette *n.* a small statue. [*Say* statue ETT]

stature *n.* **1** the natural height of the body. **2** importance or reputation.

status *n.* (*pl.* **statuses**) **1** a person's social or professional position in relation to others. **2** high rank or social position. **3** *Law* a person's legal standing. **4** *Cdn* (as an *adj.*) (of an Aboriginal person) registered as an Indian under the Indian Act. **5** the position of affairs at a particular time. [*Say* STAT us *or* STATE us]

status quo *n.* the existing state of affairs. [*Say* stat us KWO *or* state us KWO]

status symbol *n.* a possession that is thought to show a person's high social rank, wealth, etc.

statute *n.* **1** a written law. **2** any of the rules of an organization or institution.

statute law *n.* **1** the body of principles and rules of law laid down in statutes. **2** a statute.

statute of limitations *n.* (*pl.* **statutes of limitations**) a law that fixes the time within which legal action must be taken.

statutory *adj.* **1** required or permitted by statute. **2** (of an offence) punishable under a statute.

statutory holiday *n. Cdn* a public holiday established by statute.

statutory release *n. Cdn Law* parole as required by statute.

staunch ● *adj.* **1** trustworthy, loyal. **2** (of a ship etc.) strong, watertight, etc. ● *v.* (**staunches, staunched, staunching**) restrain the flow of (esp. blood).

staunchly *adv.* in a strongly loyal manner.

stave ● *n.* **1** each of the curved pieces of wood forming the sides of a cask, pail, etc. **2** *Music* a set of usu. five parallel lines on which a note is placed to indicate its pitch. ● *v.* (**staves**; *past* and *past participle* **stove** or **staved**; **staving**) **1** break a hole in. **2** crush or knock out of shape. □ **stave off** (*past* and *past participle* **staved**) avert or defer (esp. misfortune).

stay ● *v.* (**stays, stayed, staying**) **1** remain. **2** have temporary residence as a visitor etc. **3** stop or check (progress etc.). **4** postpone (judgment etc.). **5** assuage (hunger etc.). **6** show endurance. **7 a** keep up with. **b** continue with. ● *n.* **1** a period of staying somewhere. **2** a suspension or postponement of a sentence, judgment, etc. **3** a rope or wire that supports a ship's mast etc. **4** (in *pl.*) *hist.* a laced corset esp. with whalebone stiffening. □ **has come** (or **is here**) **to stay** *informal* must be regarded as permanent. **stay the course** pursue a course of action to the end. **stay in** remain indoors. **stay on** remain in a place or position. **stay put** remain somewhere without moving. **stay up** not go to bed.

staying power *n.* endurance, stamina.

STD *abbr.* a sexually transmitted disease.

stead *n.* □ **in a person's** (or **thing's**) **stead** as a substitute. **stand a person in good stead** be advantageous to him or her. [*Say* STED]

steadfast *adj.* **1** constant, firm. **2** (of a gaze etc.) fixed in intensity. □ **steadfastly** *adv.* **steadfastness** *n.* [*Say* STED fast]

steady ● *adj.* (**steadier, steadiest**) **1** firmly in place. **2** done in a uniform and regular manner. **3** not changeable or changing. **4** serious, sensible. **5** not faltering. **6** steadily. ● *v.* (**steadies, steadied, steadying**) make or become steady. ● *interj.* as a warning to take care. ● *n.* (*pl.* **steadies**) *informal* a regular boyfriend or girlfriend. □ **go steady** *informal* have as a regular boyfriend or girlfriend. □ **steadily** *adv.* **steadiness** *n.*

steady state *n.* an unvarying condition, esp. in a physical process.

steak *n.* a slice of meat or fish.

steakette *n. Cdn* a thin patty of ground beef.

steak tartare *n.* a dish of raw chopped steak mixed with raw egg, onion, and seasonings. [*Say* steak tar TAR]

steal ● *v.* (**steals**; *past* **stole**; *past participle* **stolen; stealing**) **1** take illegally without right or permission. **2** obtain surreptitiously. **3** win or gain possession of. **4** move, esp. silently or stealthily. **5** *Baseball* advance to (a base) while the ball is being pitched. ● *n. informal* an unexpectedly easy task or good bargain. □ **steal the show** outshine other performers. **steal a person's thunder** take the limelight or attention from another person. □ **stealer** *n.* (also in *comb.*)

stealth *n.* **1** secrecy. **2** (as an *adj.*) designed with technology which makes detection by radar or sonar difficult. [*Rhymes with* HEALTH]

stealthy *adj.* (**stealthier, stealthiest**) quiet or secret. □ **stealthily** *adv.* [*Rhymes with* HEALTHY]

steam ● *n.* **1 a** the gas into which water is changed by boiling. **b** a mist of liquid particles of water produced by condensation of this gas. **2 a** energy or power provided by steam power. **b** *informal* power or energy generally. ● *v.* **1 a** cook (food) in steam. **b** treat with steam. **2** give off steam or other vapour. **3 a** move under

the power of a steam engine. **b** *informal* proceed with speed or vigour. **4** cover or become covered with condensed water vapour. **5** *informal* be or cause to be angry. □ **blow** (or **let**) **off steam** release one's pent-up energy. **full steam ahead** with as much speed and vigour as possible. **get up steam** work oneself into an energetic or angry state. **lose steam** slow down. **pick up steam** speed up. **run out of steam** lose one's energy. **under one's own steam** without help. □ **steamed** *adj.*

steam bath *n.* **1** a room etc. filled with steam for cleaning oneself by sweating. **2** a bath taken in such a room.

steamboat *n.* a boat propelled by a steam engine.

steamed up *adj.* **1** (of a surface) covered with condensed vapour. **2** angry.

steam engine *n.* **1** an engine using the expansion or condensation of steam to generate power. **2** a steam locomotive.

steamer *n.* **1** a thing that steams. **2** a ship etc. propelled by steam. **3** a container in which food is cooked by steam.

steam iron *n.* an electric iron that emits steam from its flat surface.

steamroller ● *n.* a heavy slow-moving vehicle with a roller, used for levelling roads. ● *v.* (also **steamroll**) **1** crush forcibly or indiscriminately. **2** force (a measure etc.) through a legislature by overriding opposition.

steam room *n.* a room filled with steam for taking steam baths.

steamship *n.* a ship propelled by a steam engine.

steamy *adj.* (**steamier, steamiest**) **1** like or full of steam. **2** *informal* erotic, passionate. **3** hot and humid.

steed *n. archaic* or *literary* a fast powerful horse.

steel ● *n.* **1** a durable alloy of iron with carbon, used as a structural and fabricating material. **2** toughness. **3** a steel rod for sharpening knives. **4** *Cdn* a railway track. ● *adj.* **1** made of steel. **2** like steel. ● *v.* make resolute.

steel band *n.* a band playing esp. calypso music on steel drums.

steel drum *n.* (also **steel pan**) a percussion instrument made out of an oil drum with one end beaten down and divided into grooved sections to give different notes.

steelhead *n.* a large silvery N American rainbow trout.

steelie *n. informal* **1** a steel ball bearing used as a marble. **2** a steelhead.

steel wool n. an abrasive substance consisting of a mass of fine steel threads.

steelworks pl. n. (usu. treated as sing.) (also **steel mill**) a plant where steel is manufactured. □ **steelworker** n.

steely adj. (**steelier, steeliest**) **1** of or like steel. **2** severe.

steep ● adj. **1** sloping sharply. **2** (of a rise or fall) rapid. **3** informal exorbitant; unreasonable. ● v. **1** soak in liquid. **2** surround or fill with a quality or influence. □ **steepen** v. **steeply** adv. **steepness** n.

steeple n. a tall tower above the roof of a church. □ **steepled** adj.

steeplechase n. **1** a horse race across the countryside or on a racecourse with ditches, hedges, etc., to jump. **2** a cross-country foot race. □ **steeplechaser** n. **steeplechasing** n.

steer ● v. **1** direct or control the movement of. **2** guide by advice or instruction etc. **3** guide the movement or trend of. ● n. **1** a piece of advice. **2** a castrated male of domestic cattle. □ **steer clear of** take care to avoid. □ **steerable** adj. **steering** n.

steerage n. esp. hist. the part of a ship allotted to passengers travelling at the cheapest rate.

steering column n. the shaft connecting the steering wheel, handlebars, etc. of a vehicle to the rest of the steering gear.

steering committee n. (also **steering group**) a committee that decides the order of certain business activities and guides their general course.

steering wheel n. a wheel by which a vehicle etc. is steered.

steersman n. a person who steers a vessel.

steer wrestling n. a rodeo event in which a contestant on a horse chases a steer, dismounts, and wrestles the steer to the ground. □ **steer wrestler** n.

stegosaurus n. (also **stegosaur**) a plant-eating dinosaur with a double row of large bony plates along the back. [Say stegga SORE us]

stein n. a large mug. [Say STINE]

stellar adj. **1** relating to a star or stars. **2 a** having star performers. **b** informal outstanding.

Steller's jay n. a blue jay found in central and western N America.

stem ● n. **1** the main body or stalk of a plant or shrub. **2** the stalk supporting a fruit, flower, or leaf. **3 a** the slender part of a wineglass between the body and the base. **b** the tube of a tobacco pipe. **c** a vertical stroke in a letter or musical note. **4** the root or main part of a word. ● v. (**stems, stemmed, stemming**) **1** (foll. by from) originate from. **2** remove the stem or stems from. **3** stop. **4** dam up. □ **stem the tide** work against a difficult trend. □ **stemmed** adj.

stem cell n. an undifferentiated cell from which specialized cells develop.

stemware n. crystal or glass vessels with rounded bowls on stems.

stench n. a foul smell.

stencil ● n. **1** a thin sheet of plastic etc., in which a pattern or lettering is cut, used to produce a corresponding pattern on the surface beneath it by applying ink, paint, etc. to the cut-out areas. **2** the pattern etc. produced by a stencil. ● v. (**stencils, stencilled, stencilling**) produce or decorate with a stencil.

stenography n. the art of writing in and then transcribing shorthand. □ **stenographer** n. [Say sten OGGRA fee]

stent n. a splint placed inside a duct, canal, or blood vessel to aid healing or relieve an obstruction.

stentorian adj. (of a voice etc.) loud and powerful. [Say sten TORY in]

step ● n. **1** the complete movement of one leg in walking or running. **2** a unit of movement in dancing. **3** a measure taken in a course of action. **4** a flat-topped structure for passing from one level to another. **5** a short distance. **6** the sound or mark made by a foot in walking etc. ● v. (**steps, stepped, stepping**) **1** lift and set down one's foot in walking. **2** come or go in a specified direction by stepping. **3** make progress in a specified way. **4** perform (a dance). □ **in step 1** stepping in time with music or other marchers. **2** conforming. **in a person's steps** following a person's example. **step by step** gradually; by stages or degrees. **step down** (also **step aside**) resign. **step forward** offer one's help etc. **step in 1** enter. **2** intervene to help or hinder. **step on it** (or **on the gas**) informal **1** accelerate a motor vehicle. **2** hurry up. **step up 1** increase, intensify. **2** come forward for some purpose. **watch one's step** be careful. □ **stepped** adj.

stepbrother n. a son of one's stepmother or stepfather by an earlier marriage.

step-by-step adj. proceeding through or involving a series of distinct stages.

stepchild n. (pl. **stepchildren**) **1** a child of one's husband or wife by a previous marriage. **2** informal a neglected or scorned member of a group.

step dance ● n. a dance displaying

special steps by an individual performer, popular in Celtic cultures. ● v. (**step-dance**, **step-dances**, **step-danced**, **step-dancing**) perform a step dance. □ **step dancer** n. **step-dancing** n.

stepdaughter n. a female stepchild.

stepfather n. a male step-parent.

step-in ● n. a garment or shoe put on by stepping into it. ● adj. put on by being stepped into without unfastening.

stepladder n. a short folding ladder.

stepmother n. a female step-parent.

step-parent n. a mother's or father's later spouse.

steppe n. a level grassy plain, esp. in southeast Europe and Siberia. [Say STEP]

stepped-up adj. increased, intensified.

stepper n. **1** an exercise machine used to simulate the activity of climbing stairs. **2** informal a dancer who steps.

stepping stone n. **1** a raised stone on which to step while crossing a stream, muddy ground, etc. **2** something used as a means of advancement.

stepsister n. a daughter of one's stepmother or stepfather by an earlier marriage.

stepson n. a male stepchild.

stepwise adj. & adv. in a series of distinct stages.

stereo ● n. (pl. **stereos**) **1** a stereophonic CD player, tape deck, etc. **2** stereophonic sound. ● adj. **1** stereophonic. **2** stereoscopic.

stereophonic adj. (of sound reproduction) using two or more channels so that the sound seems to come from more than one source. [Say stereo FON ick]

stereoscope n. a device by which two photographs of the same object taken at slightly different angles are viewed together, giving an impression of depth. □ **stereoscopic** adj. **stereoscopically** adv.

stereotype ● n. **1** a widely held but oversimplified image of a particular type of person or thing. **2** a person or thing appearing to conform to such an image. ● v. (**stereotypes**, **stereotyped**, **stereotyping**) (esp. as **stereotyped** adj.) view or represent as a stereotype. □ **stereotypic** adj. **stereotypical** adj. **stereotypically** adv.

sterile adj. **1** not able to produce offspring. **2** free from bacteria etc. **3** unproductive. **4** lacking originality. **5** (of plants) not producing fruit or seeds. □ **sterility** n. [Say STARE ile or STARE ill, stuh RILLA tee]

sterilize v. (**sterilizes**, **sterilized**, **sterilizing**) **1** make something free from

bacteria etc. **2** deprive a person or animal of the ability to produce offspring. □ **sterilization** n. **sterilizer** n. [Say STARE uh lize]

sterling ● adj. **1** of or in British money. **2** denoting silver of 92^1/$_4$% purity. **3** made of sterling silver. **4** excellent, valuable. ● n. **1** British money. **2** sterling silver. [Say STIR ling]

stern^1 adj. serious, strict. □ **sternly** adv. **sternness** n.

stern^2 n. the rear part of a boat.

sternum n. (pl. **sternums** or **sterna**) the breastbone.

sternwheeler n. a steamer propelled by a paddlewheel positioned at the stern.

steroid n. any of a group of organic compounds that includes many hormones and vitamins, used to treat various diseases and to increase muscle size. □ **steroidal** adj. [Say STARE oid, stare OID'll]

stethoscope n. an instrument used to listen to the action of the heart, lungs, etc. [Say STETH uh scope]

stetson n. a hat with a wide brim and a high crown, associated with cowboys.

stevedore ● n. a person employed in loading and unloading ships. ● v. (**stevedores**, **stevedored**, **stevedoring**) load or unload the cargo of. □ **stevedoring** n. & adj. [Say STEVE uh dor]

stew ● v. **1** simmer in a pot. **2** informal be oppressed by heat or humidity. **3** informal **a** suffer prolonged embarrassment, anxiety, etc. **b** fret or be anxious. ● n. **1** a dish of stewed meat, fish, vegetables, etc. **2** informal an agitated state. **3** a mixture.

steward ● n. **1** a passengers' attendant. **2** an official appointed to supervise arrangements at a large public event. **3** a person responsible for supplies of food etc. for a college or club etc. **4** a person employed to manage another's property, take care of something, etc. ● v. act as a steward of. □ **stewardship** n.

stewardess n. a female flight attendant.

stewpot n. **1** a pot for cooking stew. **2** a mixture.

stick^1 n. **1** a slender branch broken or cut from a tree. **2** a thin wooden rod. **3** something resembling a stick. **4** (**the sticks**) informal remote rural areas.

stick^2 v. (**sticks**; past and past participle **stuck**; **sticking**) **1** insert or thrust. **2** stab. **3** fix or be fixed on or by a pointed thing. **4** adhere. **5** endure. **6** lose the power of motion or action. **7** informal **a** put somewhere quickly or haphazardly. **b** remain or be confined in a place.

8 *informal* **a** be convincing or regarded as valid. **b** place the blame for (a thing) on. **9** persevere with. □ **stick around** *informal* linger. **stick by** stay loyal or close to. **stick 'em up!** *informal* hands up! **stick it to (a person)** *informal* **1** treat unfairly. **2** get even with. **stick one's neck out** become vulnerable by acting boldly. **stick out** protrude. **stick together** *informal* remain united. **stick up for** support or defend.

stickball *n.* a form of baseball using a rubber ball and a broomstick etc., usu. played by children.

sticker ● *n.* **1** an adhesive label or notice. **2** a person or thing that sticks. ● *v.* attach a sticker to.

stick figure *n.* a figure drawn in thin simple lines.

stickhandle *v.* (**stickhandles, stickhandled, stickhandling**) **1** *Hockey* skilfully control the puck with the stick. **2** *Cdn* manoeuvre skilfully around. □ **stickhandler** *n.* **stickhandling** *n.*

sticking point *n.* the limit of progress, agreement, etc.

stick-in-the-mud *n.* (*pl.* **stick-in-the-muds**) *informal* a person who resists change.

stickleback *n.* a small fish with sharp spines along the back.

stickler *n.* **1** a person who insists on something. **2** a difficult problem.

stick-on *adj.* adhesive.

stick shift *n.* **1** a manual transmission for a car etc. **2** a lever used to change gear.

stickup *n.* *informal* a robbery using a gun.

stickwork *n.* *Hockey* interference with the stick.

sticky ● *adj.* (**stickier, stickiest**) **1** tending or intended to stick. **2** glutinous, viscous. **3 a** humid. **b** damp with sweat. **4** *informal* awkward. ● *n.* (*pl.* **stickies**) *informal* = Post-it. □ **have sticky fingers** be in the habit of stealing. □ **stickiness** *n.*

sticky tape *n.* clear adhesive tape.

stiff ● *adj.* **1** rigid. **2** hard to move or turn etc. **3** demanding effort. **4** severe. **5** not relaxed. **6** aching due to previous exertion. **7** exorbitant. ● *n.* *slang* **1** a corpse. **2 a** a useless person. **b** an ordinary person. ● *v. slang* **1** cheat. **2** murder. □ **stiffish** *adj.* **stiffly** *adv.* **stiffness** *n.*

stiffen *v.* make or become stiff. □ **stiffener** *n.* **stiffening** *n.*

stiff upper lip *n.* control of one's emotions when facing difficulties.

stifle *v.* (**stifles, stifled, stifling**) **1** prevent or constrain. **2** suppress. **3** suffocate. [*Say* STIFE 'll]

stifling *adj.* **1** unbearably hot. **2** oppressive. □ **stiflingly** *adv.* [*Say* STIFE ling]

stigma *n.* (*pl.* **stigmata** or **stigmas**) **1 a** a mark of disgrace. **b** an unfavourable reputation. **2** the part of a pistil that receives pollen. **3** (usu. as **stigmata**) (in Christian belief) marks corresponding to those left on Christ's body by the Crucifixion. □ **stigmatic** *adj.*

stigmatize *v.* (**stigmatizes, stigmatized, stigmatizing**) describe or regard someone or something as worthy of disgrace or great disapproval. □ **stigmatization** *n.* [*Say* STIGMA tize]

stile *n.* an arrangement of steps allowing people to climb over a fence or wall.

stiletto *n.* (*pl.* **stilettos**) **1** a short dagger with a thick blade. **2** (also **stiletto heel**) a thin, high heel on a women's shoe. [*Say* still ETTO]

still ● *adj.* **1** not or hardly moving. **2** calm and tranquil. ● *n.* **1** deep silence and calm. **2** an ordinary static photograph. ● *adv.* **1** without moving. **2** even now or at a particular time. **3** nevertheless. **4** increasingly. **5** an apparatus for distilling alcoholic drinks. ● *v.* make or become still. □ **stillness** *n.*

stillbirth *n.* the birth of a dead child.

stillborn *adj.* **1** born dead. **2** not able to succeed.

still life *n.* (*pl.* **still lifes**) a painting, drawing, or photograph of inanimate objects.

stilt *n.* **1** either of a pair of poles with supports for the feet enabling the user to walk at a distance above the ground. **2** each of a set of piles or posts supporting a building etc. **3** a long-billed wading bird with long slender legs.

stilted *adj.* **1** stiff and unnatural. **2** standing on stilts.

stimulant ● *n.* **1** a substance that stimulates. **2** a stimulating influence. ● *adj.* that stimulates.

stimulate *v.* (**stimulates, stimulated, stimulating**) **1** make something develop or become more active. **2** make someone interested in something. □ **stimulating** *adj.* **stimulation** *n.* **stimulator** *n.*

stimulus *n.* (*pl.* **stimuli**) a thing that rouses activity or causes a reaction. [*Say* STIM you lus]

sting ● *n.* **1** a sharp painful wound inflicted by any of a number of insects, animals, and plants. **2** a sharp pain. **3** the painful quality or effect of something. **4** an undercover operation in which police officers take part in an illegal transaction in order to catch a presumed criminal.

5 slang a swindle. **6** = STINGER 1a. ● v.
(**stings**; past and past participle **stung**;
stinging) **1** prick or pierce with a stinger.
2 cause a sharp pain. **3** feel such pain.
4 informal cause financial hardship to; cheat.
□ **stinging** adj. **stingless** adj.

stinger n. **1 a** a sharp organ capable of
inflicting a wound. **b** (in plants) a tiny hair
which emits an irritating fluid when
touched. **c** something capable of stinging.
2 a sharp painful blow or comment.
[Say STING er]

stinging nettle n. a nettle with stinging
hairs and strongly serrated oval leaves.

stingray n. a broad flatfish with a
diamond-shaped body with a long
poisonous serrated spine.

stingy adj. (**stingier, stingiest**)
1 unwilling to give, spend, or use
resources. **2** meagre. □ **stinginess** n.
[Say STIN jee]

stink ● v. (**stinks**; past **stank** or **stunk**;
past participle **stunk**; **stinking**) **1** emit a
strong offensive smell. **2** informal be
offensively bad or unpleasant. **3** (foll. by up)
fill with an offensive odour. ● n. **1** an
offensive smell. **2** informal a fuss or scandal.
□ **stinker** n. **stinky** adj.

stinking ● adj. **1** that stinks. **2** slang
despicable. ● adv. slang to an objectionable
degree. □ **stinkingly** adv.

stint ● v. **1** use or distribute grudgingly.
2 be sparing or cheap; economize. ● n. **1** a
short period of time. **2** a limitation of
supply or effort.

stipe n. the stalk of a mushroom or
toadstool.

stipend n. **1** a fixed regular sum paid for
the services of a teacher, public official, or
clergyman. **2** any fixed regular payment.
[Say STIPE end]

stipple v. (**stipples, stippled,
stippling**) **1** mark with small spots or
flecks. **2** produce a roughened or gritty
texture on.

stipulate v. (**stipulates, stipulated,
stipulating**) demand or specify as part of
an agreement. □ **stipulated** adj.
stipulation n. [Say STIP yuh late]

stir ● v. (**stirs, stirred, stirring**) **1** mix
using a spoon etc. **2** move or cause to move
slightly. **3** arouse or provoke. ● n.
1 commotion or excitement. **2** an act of
stirring. **3** the slightest movement.
□ **stirrer** n.

stir-crazy adj. **1** restless from prolonged
confinement. **2** deranged after
imprisonment.

stir-fry ● v. (**stir-fries, stir-fried, stir-
frying**) fry rapidly at high heat while
stirring. ● n. (pl. **stir-fries**) a dish of stir-
fried food.

stirring ● adj. inspiring, exciting. ● n. an
initial stage or feeling. □ **stirringly** adv.

stirrup n. **1** either of a pair of loops
attached to either side of a horse's saddle
to support the rider's foot. **2** a thing shaped
like a stirrup. **3** a loop at the bottom of a
pant leg meant to keep the pants from
rising above the ankle. **4** (also **stirrup
bone**) a small stirrup-shaped bone in the
ear. [Say STIR up]

stir stick n. a small plastic stick used for
stirring coffee etc.

stitch ● n. (pl. **stitches**) **1 a** a single pass
of a threaded needle in and out of a fabric.
b the resulting loop of thread. **2** (usu. in pl.)
each of the loops of material used in
sewing up a wound. **3** a painful cramp in
the side of the body often resulting from
vigorous exercise. **4 a** a single complete
movement of the needle used in knitting
etc. **b** a particular method of knitting etc.
● v. (**stitches, stitched, stitching**) join
or decorate using stitches. □ **in stitches**
informal laughing uncontrollably. **stitch in
time** a timely remedy. □ **stitcher** n.
stitching n.

Stl'atl'imx n. (pl. **Stl'atl'imx**) a member
or the Salishan language of an Aboriginal
people living in southwestern BC,
northeast of Vancouver. □ **Stl'atl'imx** adj.
[Say STAT lee um]

stock ● n. **1** a supply of merchandise,
resources, etc. available for sale or use.
2 the raw materials for a particular
product. **3** livestock. **4 a** capital raised by a
business by selling shares. **b** shares in a
company. **5** one's reputation or popularity.
6 liquid made by stewing bones, vegetables,
etc. **7 a** one's ancestry. **b** a family. **8** a roll of
film that has not been exposed or
processed. **9 a** the trunk or stem of a tree
or shrub. **b** a plant from which cuttings are
taken. **10** a plant with fragrant white,
pink, or lilac flowers. **11** (in pl.) hist. a
wooden structure used for securing and
punishing criminals in public. **12** a handle
or base. ● adj. **1** kept regularly in stock.
2 common or conventional. ● v. **1** have or
keep available for sale or use. **2 a** furnish
with goods, equipment, or livestock. **b** fill
with fish. □ **in stock** on the premises and
available for immediate sale. **out of
stock** not available for immediate sale.
stock up obtain stocks or supplies. **take
stock 1** make an inventory of one's stock.
2 assess or review.

stockade ● n. **1** a barrier of upright
stakes, erected for defensive purposes. **2** a
military prison. ● v. (**stockades**,

stockaded, stockading) fortify with a stockade.

stockbroker n. a member of a stock exchange who deals in stocks and shares. □ **stockbrokerage** n. **stockbroking** n.

stock car n. **1** an ordinary car modified for a form of racing in which collisions often occur. **2** a boxcar used to transport livestock.

stock exchange n. **1** (also **Stock Exchange**) a building where stocks and shares are traded publicly. **2** the dealers working there. **3** the composite index of share prices etc. at an exchange.

stockholder n. an owner of stocks or shares. □ **stockholding** n.

stock index n. (also called **composite index**) a stock market index based on the performance of a selection of stocks.

stocking n. **1 a** either of a pair of separate, close-fitting coverings for the feet and legs, worn by women. **b** (in pl.) pantyhose. **2** a stocking hung at Christmas to be filled with small gifts. □ **stockinged** adj.

stocking cap n. a knitted toque with a long tapered end which hangs down.

stock-in-trade n. **1 a** the equipment required for a particular business. **b** merchandise. **2** something characteristic of a person or group.

stockman n. (pl. **stockmen**) **1** a person who looks after livestock on a farm. **2** an owner of livestock.

stock market n. a stock exchange.

stock option n. the right to buy, sell, etc. specified stocks etc. at a specified price within a set time.

stockpile ● n. a reserve of stock for use esp. during an emergency. ● v. (**stockpiles, stockpiled, stockpiling**) accumulate a stockpile of.

stockpot n. a large pot with handles.

stock-still adv. completely motionless.

stock-taking n. **1** the process of making an inventory of stock. **2** an assessment of one's situation etc.

stocky adj. (**stockier, stockiest**) short and strongly built. □ **stockiness** n.

stockyard n. an enclosure with pens and sheds for livestock about to be sold, shipped, slaughtered, etc.

stodgy adj. (**stodgier, stodgiest**) **1** heavy, filling, and high in carbohydrates. **2** excessively conventional and dull. □ **stodginess** n.

stogie n. informal a cigar. [Say STOE ghee]

stoic ● n. **1** (**Stoic**) a member of the ancient Greek school of philosophy which encouraged virtue and the control of one's passions. **2** (**stoic**) a person who represses emotion and displays indifference to pleasure and pain. ● adj. **1** (**stoic**; also **stoical**) behaving like a stoic. **2** (**Stoic**) relating to the Stoics. □ **stoically** adv. **Stoicism** n. (also **stoicism**). [Say STOE ick, STOE uh sism]

stoke v. (**stokes, stoked, stoking**) **1** tend (a fire) to increase the heat. **2** encourage, fuel. □ **stoker** n.

stoked adj. informal exhilarated.

stole¹ n. **1** a woman's long scarf or shawl. **2** an ecclesiastical vestment worn over the shoulders.

stole² past of STEAL.

stolen ● v. past participle of STEAL. ● adj. **1** obtained by theft. **2** accomplished or enjoyed in secret.

stolid adj. not expressing emotion or interest. □ **stolidly** adv. **stolidness** n. [Rhymes with SOLID]

Sto:lo n. (pl. **Sto:lo**) a member or the Halkomelem language of an Aboriginal people living along the lower Fraser River, BC. □ **Sto:lo** adj. [Say STAW loe or STOE loe]

stomach ● n. **1** the internal organ in which the first part of digestion occurs. **2** the belly or abdomen. **3 a** an appetite. **b** the ability to digest food without becoming sick. **4 a** courage. **b** tolerance. ● v. (**stomachs, stomached, stomaching**) **1** tolerate, endure. **2** find sufficiently palatable to swallow or keep down.

stomach-churning adj. causing nausea.

stomach flu n. informal a bout of gastrointestinal trouble characterized by diarrhea and/or vomiting.

stomach upset n. indigestion or nausea.

stomp ● v. **1** walk with loud, heavy steps. **2** trample on. **3** dance or play a stomp. ● n. **1** any lively dance involving a heavy stamping step. **2** (also **stomper**) a rhythmic piece of music suitable for such a dance. □ **stomper** n.

stomping ground n. (usu. in pl.) a favourite haunt or place of action.

stone ● n. **1 a** solid non-metallic mineral matter, of which rock is made. **b** a piece of this. **2 a** a piece of stone artificially shaped for use in building etc. **b** a tombstone. **3** a gem. **4** (often in pl.) a small piece of hard material forming in the bladder or kidney and causing pain. **5** a hard seed in certain fruits. **6** (also **curling stone**) a curling rock. ● adv. completely, totally. ● v. (**stones, stoned, stoning**) **1** pelt with stones. **2** remove the stones from. □ **a stone's throw** a short distance.

Stone Age n. **1** a prehistoric period

characterized by the use of weapons and tools made of stone. **2** (as an *adj.*) (also **stone-age**) primitive, outmoded.

stoneboat *n.* a flat-bottomed sled used for removing stones from fields.

stonecut *n.* **1** an esp. Inuit printing technique using an image engraved on stone. **2** a print made using this technique.

stonecutter *n.* a person or machine that cuts or shapes stone.

stoned *adj. slang* under the influence of drugs.

stone-ground *adj.* ground using millstones.

stonemason *n.* a person who cuts, prepares, and builds with stone.

Stone sheep *n.* (also **Stone's sheep**) a sheep of the south central Yukon and northern BC.

stonewall *v.* **1** hold up by making lengthy speeches and evasive answers. **2** hinder or prevent. **3** *Sport* thwart (an opponent) with strong defence. □ **stonewalling** *n.*

stoneware *n.* a dense kind of pottery made from clay containing much silica.

stonewash ● *n.* a faded appearance given to denim by washing it with abrasives (also as an *adj.*). ● *v.* (**stonewashes, stonewashed, stonewashing**) wash with abrasives. □ **stonewashed** *adj.*

stonework *n.* **1** masonry. **2** the parts of a building made of stone. **3** the art of working with stone.

Stoney *n.* (*pl.* **Stoneys** or **Stoney**) **1** a member of a Siouan Aboriginal people now living in southern Alberta. **2** their language. □ **Stoney** *adj.*

stony *adj.* (also **stoney**) (**stonier, stoniest**) **1** full of or covered with stones. **2** lacking sensitivity or feeling. **3** (also **stony-faced**) cold, expressionless. **4** harsh and grim. □ **stonily** *adv.*

stood *past and past participle of* STAND.

stooge *n.* **1** an unquestioningly loyal or fawning assistant. **2** a subordinate who performs unpleasant labour. **3** an entertainer who feeds lines to another comedian and serves as a butt of the other's jokes.

stook ● *n. Cdn & Brit.* a small stack of bales of hay or straw etc. collected in a field. ● *v. Cdn & Brit.* arrange in stooks. □ **stooking** *n.* [*Rhymes either with* BOOK *or with* SPOOK]

stool *n.* **1** a seat without a back or arms. **2** a short low bench. **3** (often in *pl.*) feces. □ **fall between two stools** fail to be or take either of two desirable alternatives.

stool pigeon *n.* **1** a criminal who informs against other criminals. **2** a decoy.

stoop ● *v.* **1** lower one's body by bending forwards. **2** lower oneself or one's standards. ● *n.* **1** a stooping posture. **2** a small raised platform. □ **stoop and scoop** *Cdn* pick up the excrement of one's pet. □ **stooped** *adj.*

stop ● *v.* (**stops, stopped, stopping**) **1** come or bring to an end. **2** prevent. **3** cease moving or operating. **4** call at a designated place to pick up or set down passengers. **5** *informal* stay somewhere for a short time. **6** withhold or deduct. **7** block. ● *n.* **1** a cessation of movement or operation. **2** a place designated for a bus or subway etc. to stop. **3** an order stopping payment. **4 a** a set of organ pipes producing tones of the same character. **b** the handle or knob operating these. □ **stop by** (or **in**) visit. **stop dead** (or **short**) cease abruptly. **stop over** rest or make a break in one's journey.

stop-and-go *adj.* alternately stopping and starting.

stopgap *n.* a temporary solution.

stoplight *n.* a set of traffic lights.

stopover *n.* (also **stopoff**) **1** a brief stop in a journey. **2** a place where one stops during a journey.

stoppage *n.* **1** an interruption. **2** the condition of being blocked. [*Say* STOP idge]

stop-payment *n.* an order stopping payment.

stopper ● *n.* **1** a plug. **2** *Baseball* a relief pitcher. ● *v.* close or plug with a stopper.

stopwatch *n.* (*pl.* **stopwatches**) a watch with a mechanism for recording elapsed time.

storage *n.* **1 a** the action of storing a thing. **b** space available for storing. **2** the cost of storing something. **3** *Computing* **a** the electronic retention of retrievable data by a device. **b** = MEMORY 4. [*Say* STOR idge]

store ● *n.* **1** a retail establishment. **2** a quantity of something available for future use. **3** (in *pl.*) articles accumulated for a particular purpose. ● *v.* (**stores, stored, storing**) **1 a** accumulate a supply of. **b** place in a storage facility. **2** retain (data) in some physical form that enables subsequent retrieval. **3** hold, contain. **4** provide with something useful. □ **in store 1** kept in readiness. **2** coming in the future. **set** (or **put**) **store by** consider to be of importance or value. □ **storable** *adj.*

store-bought *adj.* not homemade.

storefront *n.* **1** the side of a store facing onto the street. **2** a commercial property with a window facing onto the street.

storehouse *n.* a place where things are stored.

storekeeper n. **1** a store manager. **2** a store owner. **3** a person who looks after stored goods.

storeroom n. a room in which supplies are kept.

storey n. (pl. **storeys**) **1** a single level of a house or building. **2** a rough estimate of height based on the approximate height of a storey (about 3 metres). □ **storeyed** adj.

storied adj. celebrated; legendary.

stork n. a large wading bird with long legs and a long heavy bill.

storm ● n. **1** a violent weather disturbance with high winds, heavy rain or snow, thunder and lightning, etc. **2 a** a violent outburst. **b** a violent shower of projectiles or blows. **3** informal a storm window. **4** a direct assault by troops on a stronghold. ● v. **1 a** move violently or angrily. **b** say or shout in an angry or violent manner. **2** rush, attack. **3** be violent or tempestuous. □ **take by storm 1** capture by direct assault. **2** achieve sudden or overwhelming success with. **up a storm** with great enthusiasm and energy.

storm cloud n. **1** a dark heavy cloud. **2** a threatening state of affairs.

storm drain n. = STORM SEWER.

storm petrel n. a small seabird of the open ocean.

storm sewer n. a drain built to carry away excess rainwater etc.

storm trooper n. **1** hist. a member of the Nazi political militia. **2** a militant activist or vigilante.

storm window n. a detachable outer window put up in winter as insulation and to protect an inner window from the effects of storms.

stormy adj. (**stormier**, **stormiest**) **1** disturbed by a storm. **2** subject to or affected by storms. **3 a** turbulent, tempestuous. **b** angry.

story n. (pl. **stories**) **1** an account of imaginary or real people or events etc. told for entertainment. **2** a representation of facts. **3** informal a lie. **4** an item of news. □ **another story** a matter requiring separate treatment. **the same old story** the familiar course of events. **the story goes** it is said.

storyboard n. a sequence of pictures etc. outlining the plan of a movie etc.

storybook ● n. a book of stories for children. ● adj. denoting a perfect thing typical of a stories in storybooks.

storyline n. the plot of a novel, movie, etc.

storyteller n. **1** a person who tells stories. **2** informal a liar. □ **storytelling** n. & adj.

stout ● adj. **1** rather fat. **2** thick or strong.

3 brave, vigorous. ● n. a strong dark beer. □ **stoutly** adv.

stove[1] n. an apparatus burning fuel or using electricity for heating or cooking.

stove[2] past and past participle of STAVE v.

stovepipe n. a pipe conducting smoke and gases from a stove to a chimney.

stovetop n. the top surface of a stove, esp. the cooking elements.

stow v. **1** pack tidily and compactly. **2** place in its proper place.

stowage n. **1** the act of stowing. **2** a place for this. [Say STOE idge]

stowaway n. a person who hides on board a ship or aircraft etc. to get free passage. [Say STOE away]

straddle v. (**straddles**, **straddled**, **straddling**) **1 a** sit or stand with the legs one on either side of. **b** be situated across. **2** participate in (two different cultures etc.).

strafe ● v. (**strafes**, **strafed**, **strafing**) attack repeatedly with bullets or bombs from low-flying aircraft. ● n. an act of strafing.

straggle ● v. (**straggles**, **straggled**, **straggling**) **1** trail slowly behind others. **2** grow or spread in an irregular, untidy way. ● n. a group of straggling people or things. □ **straggler** n. **straggly** adj.

straight ● adj. **1** extending uniformly in the same direction. **2** successive. **3** arranged in proper order. **4** honest, candid. **5** logical, not emotional. **6** unchanged, undiluted. **7** informal **a** heterosexual. **b** conventional. **8** not curly or wavy. **9** not flared. **10** coming direct from its source. ● n. a straight part of something. ● adv. **1** in a straight line; directly. **2** continuously. **3** correctly. **4** honestly and logically. **5** upright. □ **go straight** live an honest life after being a criminal. **set** (or **put**) **a person straight** correct somebody's wrong idea or impression. **the straight and narrow** morally correct behaviour. **straight away** immediately. **straight off** informal without hesitation. **straight up** informal **1** unmixed, undiluted. **2** truthfully, honestly. □ **straightness** n.

straight-ahead adj. simple or unadorned.

straight-arm v. push away with the arm outstretched.

straight arrow n. informal a person who lives an honest, sober life. □ **straight-arrow** adj.

straightaway n. a straight section.

straightedge n. a bar with one edge accurately straight.

straighten v. **1** make or become straight. **2** make tidy. □ **straighten out 1** clear up (confusion). **2** settle or resolve. **3** improve in character or conduct. □**straightener** *n.*

straight face *n.* an intentionally expressionless face. □**straight-faced** *adj.*

straight flush *n.* a hand of cards that is a numerical sequence in a single suit.

straightforward *adj.* **1** honest or frank. **2** not complicated. □**straightforwardly** *adv.* **straightforwardness** *n.*

straight man *n.* a comedian's stooge.

straight-on *adv. & adj.* from directly in front.

straight razor *n.* a razor with a long blade and a folding handle.

straight shooter *n. slang* a person who states bluntly what they think. □**straight-shooting** *adj.*

straight-up *adj. informal* **1** trustworthy. **2** undiluted.

strain¹ ● *v.* **1** make or force to make an unusually great effort. **2** tug, pull. **3** stretch tightly. **4** make severe or excessive demands on. **5** injure by overexertion. **6 a** clear (liquid) of solid matter by passing it through a sieve etc. **b** filter (solids) out from a liquid. ● *n.* **1** a force tending to strain something. **2** an injury caused by straining a muscle etc. **3** a severe demand on strength or resources. **4** a short musical phrase. **5** a tone or tendency in speech or writing. **6** *Physics* **a** the condition of a body subjected to stress. **b** a quantity measuring this. □**strain oneself 1** injure oneself by effort. **2** make undue efforts. □**strainer** *n.*

strain² *n.* **1** a breed of animals, plants, etc. **2** a tendency in a person's character. **3** a distinct variety of a micro-organism.

strained *adj.* **1** constrained, forced. **2** mutually distrustful or tense. **3** far-fetched, laboured. **4** that has been passed through a strainer.

strait *n.* **1** a narrow passage of water connecting two large bodies of water. **2** (usu. in *pl.*) difficulty or distress.

straitened *adj.* of or marked by a shortage of money.

straitjacket ● *n.* **1** a strong garment with long sleeves which are tied together to prevent the person wearing it from acting violently. **2** a severe restriction. ● *v.* (**straitjackets, straitjacketed, straitjacketing**) **1** restrain with a straitjacket. **2** severely restrict.

straitlaced *adj.* having strict moral attitudes.

Straits *n.* an Aboriginal language of BC, part of the Salishan language group.

strand¹ ● *v.* **1** (esp. as **stranded** *adj.*) leave (a person) helpless in a place. **2** run

aground. ● *n. literary* the margin of a sea, lake, or river.

strand² *n.* **1** a single length of thread, wire, etc. **2** an element that forms part of a complex whole. **3** a lock of hair.

strange *adj.* (**stranger, strangest**) **1** unusual, surprising. **2** not familiar. **3** having unpleasant feelings. **4** not at ease or comfortable. **5** (foll. by *to*) unaccustomed. □**make strange** *Cdn* (of a child) fuss or be shy in company. □**strangely** *adv.* **strangeness** *n.*

stranger *n.* **1** a person who does not know, or is not known in, a particular place, company, or experience. **2** (often foll. by *to*) a person one does not know.

strangle *v.* (**strangles, strangled, strangling**) **1** kill by squeezing or gripping the throat. **2** restrict the proper growth or operation of. **3** suppress. □**strangler** *n.*

stranglehold *n.* **1** a wrestling hold that throttles an opponent. **2** a deadly grip. **3** exclusive control.

strangulate *v.* (**strangulates, strangulated, strangulating**) **1** constrict or compress so as to prevent circulation or the passage of a fluid. **2** strangle. □**strangulation** *n.*

strap ● *n.* **1** a strip of flexible material fastening, securing, or carrying something. **2** a loop for grasping to steady oneself while standing in a moving vehicle. **3** (**the strap**) punishment by beating with a leather strap. **4** a strip of metal used to secure or connect. ● *v.* (**straps, strapped, strapping**) **1** secure or bind with a strap. **2** beat with a strap.

strapless *adj.* without esp. shoulder straps.

strapped *adj.* subject to a shortage.

strapping ● *adj.* large and sturdy. ● *n.* **1** material for making straps. **2** a punishment by beating with a strap.

strata *n.* **1** *plural of* STRATUM. **2** a dish made of alternating layers of foods, esp. of bread with cheese etc., soaked in eggs and milk and baked. [*Say* STRATTA]

stratagem *n.* a cunning plan or scheme. [*Say* STRATTA jem]

strategic *adj.* **1** of or serving the ends of strategy. **2** essential in fighting a war. **3** relating to gaining a longer-term military objective. □**strategically** *adv.*

strategize *v.* (**strategizes, strategized, strategizing**) make strategy. □**strategist** *n.* [*Say* STRATTA jize]

strategy *n.* (*pl.* **strategies**) **1** a plan designed to achieve a particular long-term aim. **2** the art of planning and directing military activity in a battle or war. [Say STRATTA jee]

stratify v. (**stratifies**, **stratified**, **stratifying**) **1** (esp. as **stratified** adj.) form or arrange into strata. **2** arrange or classify. □ **stratification** n. [Say STRATTA fie, stratta fuh CAY sh'n]

stratosphere n. **1** a layer of atmospheric air above the troposphere extending to about 50 km above the earth's surface. **2** a very high or the highest level. □ **stratospheric** adj. [Say STRATTA sphere, stratta SFEER ick or stratta SFAIR ick]

stratum n. (pl. **strata**) **1** esp. Geology a layer or series of layers of rock etc. **2** a layer within any structure. **3** a social class etc. [Say STRAT um]

straw n. **1** dry cut stalks of grain. **2** a single dried stalk. **3** a hollow plastic or paper tube for sucking drink from a glass etc. □ **draw the short straw** be chosen by lot for a disagreeable task. **grasp** (or **clutch**) **at straws** resort to an inadequate expedient in desperation. **the last** (or **final**) **straw** a slight addition to a burden that makes it finally unbearable.

strawberry n. (pl. **strawberries**) an edible soft red fruit of a low-growing plant.

strawberry blond ● n. **1** pinkish-blond hair. **2** a woman with such hair. ● adj. of a pinkish-blond colour.

strawberry social n. (also **strawberry tea**) a public event sponsored by a church etc. as a fundraiser, where desserts featuring strawberries are served.

straw-colour n. pale yellow. □ **straw-coloured** adj.

straw man n. (pl. **straw men**) something set up as the object of an argument in order to be defeated.

straw poll n. an unofficial test of opinion.

stray ● v. **1** wander from the right course or place. **2** be sexually unfaithful. **3** wander aimlessly. ● n. **1** a domestic animal that has strayed from its home etc. **2** a homeless person. ● adj. **1** lost, isolated. **2** having no home. **3** that is not in the right place.

streak ● n. **1** a long irregular line of colour etc. **2** an element in a person's character. **3** a run or series. **4** a flash of lightning. ● v. **1** mark with streaks. **2** move very rapidly. **3** form streaks. **4** tint with streaks. □ **streaking** n. **streaky** adj.

stream ● n. **1** a small river. **2** a continuous flow of fluid, things, people, etc. **3** Cdn & Brit. a group of similarly able schoolchildren taught together. ● v. **1** move or flow as a stream. **2** run with liquid. **3** float or wave in the wind. **4** emit a

stream of. **5** extend in rays or beams. **6** Cdn & Brit. arrange in streams. □ **on stream** into operation or effect or participation.

streamer n. **1** a long narrow strip of material used as a decoration or flag. **2** a fishing fly with feathers attached. **3** (in pl.) the aurora. **4** Cdn an elongated band of clouds generating much localized snow.

streamline v. (**streamlines**, **streamlined**, **streamlining**) **1** give the form which presents the least resistance to motion. **2** make more efficient or better organized. □ **streamlined** adj.

street ● n. a public road in a city, town, or village. ● adj. **1** of or adjoining the street. **2** suitable for everyday wear. **3** occurring or appearing on a street. **4** homeless. □ **on the street** (or **streets**) **1** homeless. **2** out of prison.

streetcar n. a passenger vehicle running on rails laid in an urban street.

street hockey n. Cdn a version of hockey played on a street usu. with a ball.

street legal adj. **1** (of a vehicle) legally roadworthy. **2** informal above-board.

street racing n. the illegal racing of automobiles on public roads, esp. late at night. □ **street racer** n.

street smarts pl. n. informal **1** shrewd awareness of how to survive in an urban environment. **2** common sense. □ **street-smart** adj.

street value n. the price for which something can be illegally sold.

streetwalker n. a prostitute seeking customers in the street. □ **streetwalking** n. & adj.

streetwear n. casual clothing inspired by urban fashions and worn esp. by youth.

streetwise adj. having the skills for dealing with modern urban life.

strength n. **1** the state of being strong. **2** a positive quality or attribute. **3** the extent to which something is strong. **4** a full complement. □ **from strength to strength** with ever-increasing success. **on the strength of** on the basis of.

strengthen v. make or become stronger.

strenuous adj. **1** requiring or using great effort. **2** energetic. □ **strenuously** adv. **strenuousness** n. [Say STREN you us]

strep informal ● n. **1** = STREPTOCOCCUS. **2** = STREP THROAT. ● adj. STREPTOCOCCAL.

strep throat n. an acute sore throat with fever caused by streptococcal infection.

streptococcus n. (pl. **streptococci**) a bacterium some species of which cause infectious diseases, the souring of milk, and tooth decay. □ **streptococcal** adj.

[*Say* strep tuh COCK us *for the singular,* strep tuh COCK eye *for the plural*]

streptomycin *n.* an antibiotic effective against many disease-producing bacteria. [*Say* strep tuh MICE in]

stress ● *n.* (*pl.* **stresses**) **1** pressure or tension exerted on a material object. **2 a** demand on physical or mental energy. **b** a state of mental or emotional strain. **3 a** emphasis. **b** emphasis laid on a syllable or word. ● *v.* (**stresses, stressed, stressing**) **1** emphasize. **2** subject to stress. □ **stressed** *adj.*

stressed out *adj. informal* debilitated or exhausted by stress.

stress fracture *n.* a fracture of a bone caused by the repeated application of a high load.

stressful *adj.* causing stress. □ **stressfully** *adv.* **stressfulness** *n.*

stressor *n.* something that causes stress. [*Say* STRESSER]

stretch ● *v.* (**stretches, stretched, stretching**) **1** be made or be able to be made longer or wider without breaking. **2** pull tightly from one point to another. **3** extend one's body or a part of it to its full length. **4** last longer than expected. **5** extend over an area or period of time. **6** be sufficient for a particular purpose. **7** make demands on. ● *n.* (*pl.* **stretches**) **1** an act of stretching one's limbs or body. **2** the condition of being stretched. **3** the capacity to stretch. **4** a continuous expanse or period. **5** (as an *adj.*) a motor vehicle modified with extended seating etc. **6** *informal* an exaggeration or distortion. **7** a straight part at the end of a racetrack. □ **stretch one's legs** exercise oneself by walking. **stretch a point** agree to something not normally allowed. □ **stretchable** *adj.* **stretchy** *adj.*

stretcher *n.* a framework of two poles with canvas etc. between, for carrying a sick, injured, or dead person.

stretch marks *pl. n.* marks on the skin resulting from weight gain or pregnancy.

streusel *n.* a crumbly sweet mixture used in cake fillings and toppings etc. [*Say* STROOSSLE *or* STROOZLE]

strew *v.* (**strews**; *past* **strewed**; *past participle* **strewn** *or* **strewed**; **strewing**) **1** scatter or be scattered. **2** spread with scattered things.

striation *n.* a linear mark, ridge, or groove on a surface. □ **striated** *adj.* [*Say* stry AY sh'n, STRY ated]

stricken *adj.* overcome with illness or misfortune etc.

strict *adj.* **1** demanding that rules of behaviour etc. are obeyed. **2** following rules

or beliefs exactly. **3** precisely limited. **4** without deviation. **5** requiring complete compliance. **6** absolute. □ **strictly** *adv.* **strictness** *n.*

stricture *n.* **1** (usu. in *pl.*) a sternly critical remark. **2** (usu. in *pl.*) rules that restrict action. **3** an abnormal narrowing of a duct in the body.

stride ● *v.* (**strides**; *past* **strode**; *past participle* **stridden**; **striding**) **1** walk with long firm steps. **2** cross with one step. ● *n.* **1** a single long step. **2** the length of such a step. **3** (usu. in *pl.*) progress. □ **break stride 1** change one's gait. **2** slow down. **hit** (or **get into**) **one's stride** reach a steady rate of progress etc. **take in one's stride** manage without difficulty.

strident *adj.* **1** loud and harsh. **2** urgent and aggressive. □ **stridency** *n.* **stridently** *adv.* [*Say* STRY dint]

strife *n.* conflict, enmity.

strike ● *v.* (**strikes, struck, striking**) **1** deliver a blow to. **2** come into forcible contact with. **3** hit or kick (a ball) so as to score a run, point, or goal. **4** ignite (a match) by rubbing it briskly against an abrasive surface. **5** suddenly attack. **6** (foll. by *into*) cause (fear etc.) in. **7** cause to become suddenly. **8** suddenly come into the mind of. **9** discover. **10** (esp. in *passive*) find interesting. **11** refuse to work, as a form of organized protest. **12** cancel by crossing out with a pen. **13** proceed vigorously. **14** reach (agreement). **15** indicate the time by sounding a chime. **16** *Cdn* create (a committee). ● *n.* **1** an organized refusal by employees to work. **2** a sudden attack. **3** *Baseball* a batter's unsuccessful attempt to hit a pitched ball. **4** (in bowling) an act of knocking down all the pins with one's first ball. **5** an act of striking a ball. **6** a discovery. **7** a thing to one's discredit. □ **on strike** taking part in an industrial strike. **strike it rich** *informal* find a source of abundance or success. **strike it lucky** have a lucky success. **strike out 1** hit out. **2** act vigorously. **3** delete. **4** begin. **5** *Baseball* **a** dismiss by means of three strikes. **b** be dismissed in this way. **6** be unsuccessful. **strike up** start casually. **strike while the iron is hot** act promptly at a good opportunity. □ **striker** *n.*

strikebound *adj.* immobilized or closed by a strike.

strikebreaker *n.* one working in place of others who are on strike. □ **strikebreaking** *n.* & *adj.*

strikeout *n. Baseball* an out called when a batter has had three strikes.

strike zone *n. Baseball* an imaginary

rectangle above home plate extending from the armpits to the knees of a batter.

striking ● *adj.* **1** impressive; attracting attention. **2** conspicuous. **3** on strike. ● *n.* the act of striking. □ **within striking distance** near enough to hit or achieve. □ **strikingly** *adv.*

string ● *n.* **1** twine or narrow cord. **2** a length of catgut or wire etc. on a musical instrument, producing a note by vibration. **3** (in *pl.*) stringed instruments in an orchestra etc. **4** (in *pl.*) an awkward associated complication. **5** a set, series, or sequence. **6** a group of racehorses trained at one stable. **7** a piece of nylon etc. interwoven with others to form the head of a tennis etc. racquet. **8** *Computing* a linear sequence of characters, records, or data. ● *v.* (**strings, strung, stringing**) **1** supply with a string or strings. **2** arrange in or as a string. **3** provide or adorn with something suspended or slung. **4** thread on or tie with strings. **5** place a string ready for use on. □ **on a string** under one's control. **string along** *informal* mislead (a person) about one's own intentions. **string out** prolong (esp. unduly). **string up 1** hang up on strings etc. **2** *informal* kill by hanging.

string band *n.* an esp. jazz or bluegrass music ensemble of string instruments.

string bean *n.* **1** any of various beans eaten in their pods. **2** *informal* a tall thin person.

stringed *adj.* having strings.

stringent *adj.* strict, precise. □ **stringency** *n.* **stringently** *adv.* [*Say* STRIN jint]

stringer *n.* **1** a horizontal member connecting uprights in a framework. **2** a longitudinal structural member in a framework. **3** *informal* a freelance newspaper correspondent. **4** (usu. in *comb.*) an athlete etc. ranked according to ability. [*Rhymes with* SINGER]

string quartet *n.* **1** a chamber music ensemble consisting of two violins, viola, and cello. **2** a piece of music for such an ensemble.

stringy *adj.* (**stringier, stringiest**) **1** fibrous, tough. **2** of or like string. **3** tall and thin. [*Say* STRING ee]

strip ● *v.* (**strips, stripped, stripping**) **1 a** remove the clothes or covering from. **b** pull off or remove. **2** undress oneself. **3** deprive of property, titles, etc. **4** leave bare of accessories or fittings. **5** sell off (a company's assets) for profit. **6** remove paint, wax, etc. from a surface. **7** tear the thread from (a screw). ● *n.* **1** a long narrow piece. **2** a narrow flat bar of iron or steel. **3** (also **strip cartoon**) a comic strip. **4** an area of commercial development along a town road. **5** an airstrip. **6** a performance of a striptease. □ **tear a strip off a person** *informal* angrily rebuke someone.

strip club *n.* (also **strip joint**) a club featuring striptease performances.

stripe ● *n.* **1** a long narrow band or strip differing in colour or texture from its surroundings. **2** a chevron etc. denoting military rank. **3** a category of character, opinion, etc. ● *v.* (**stripes, striped, striping**) mark with stripes. □ **striped** *adj.* **stripey** *adj.* **stripy** *adj.*

strip mall *n.* a series of stores running parallel to a street.

stripped-down *adj.* reduced to essentials.

stripper *n.* **1** a person who performs striptease. **2** a device or solvent for removing paint etc.

striptease *n.* a form of erotic entertainment in which a performer removes his or her clothes.

strive *v.* (**strives;** *past* **strove** or **strived;** *past participle* **striven; striving**) **1** try hard. **2** struggle or contend.

strobe ● *n.* (also **strobe light**) a bright light that flashes on and off. ● *v.* (**strobes, strobed, strobing**) **1** light as if with a strobe. **2** flash intermittently.

strode *past of* STRIDE.

stroganoff *n.* (also **beef stroganoff**) a dish of strips of beef cooked in a sauce containing mushrooms and sour cream. [*Say* STROE guh noff]

stroke ● *n.* **1** an act of hitting. **2** *Golf* an act of hitting the ball with a club, as a unit of scoring. **3** a sound made by a striking clock. **4** an act of stroking with the hand. **5** a mark made by drawing a pen, pencil, or paintbrush once across paper or canvas. **6** a line forming part of a written or printed character. **7** a short diagonal line separating characters or figures. **8** one of a series of repeated movements. **9** a style of swimming. **10** a feat or event. **11** the action of moving the oar in rowing. **12** a sudden disabling attack or loss of consciousness caused by an interruption in blood flow to the brain. ● *v.* (**strokes, stroked, stroking**) **1** move one's hand with gentle pressure over. **2** *informal* manipulate by means of flattery etc. **3** hit (a ball) with a smooth, controlled movement. □ **at a stroke** by a single action. □ **stroker** *n.* (also in *comb.*).

stroll ● *v.* walk in a leisurely way. ● *n.* a short leisurely walk.

stroller *n.* **1** a folding chair on wheels in which a small child can be pushed along. **2** a person who strolls.

strolling *adj.* itinerant.

strong ● adj. (**stronger**, **strongest**)
1 physically powerful. **2** done with or able to withstand great force. **3** secure or firmly established. **4** great in power or ability. **5** very intense. **6** forceful and extreme. **7** pungent and full-flavoured. **8** containing much alcohol. **9** used after a number to indicate the size of a group. **10** Cdn slightly more than the stated measurement. ● adv. strongly. □ **come on strong** behave aggressively. **going strong** informal continuing action vigorously. □ **strongly** adv.

strong-arm ● adj. using threats or force. ● v. threaten, intimidate.

strongbox n. (pl. **strongboxes**) a metal box for safeguarding valuables.

stronghold n. **1** a fortified place. **2** a secure refuge. **3** a centre of support for a cause etc.

strongman n. (pl. **strongmen**) **1** a forceful leader. **2** a performer of feats of strength.

strongroom n. a room designed to protect valuables against fire and theft.

strong-willed adj. **1** determined. **2** stubborn.

strontium n. a soft silver-white metallic element. [Say STRON shee um]

stroud n. Cdn a coarse woollen cloth used esp. in the North to make blankets, leggings, etc.

strove past of STRIVE.

struck ● v. past and past participle of STRIKE. ● adj. pertaining to or affected by an industrial strike.

structural adj. relating to or forming part of a structure. □ **structurally** adv.

structuralism n. a theory that texts, languages, and social systems should be regarded as a structure whose various parts have meaning only when considered in relation to each other. □ **structuralist** n. & adj.

structure ● n. **1** a whole constructed unit. **2** the state of being well organized. **3** a set of interconnecting parts of any complex thing. ● v. (**structures**, **structured**, **structuring**) give structure to. □ **structured** adj. (also in comb.)

strudel n. a dessert of thin pastry rolled up around a usu. fruit filling and baked. [Say STROODLE]

struggle ● v. (**struggles**, **struggled**, **struggling**) **1** make forceful efforts to get free of restraint. **2** make violent or determined efforts under difficulties. **3** fight strenuously. **4** (esp. as **struggling** adj.) have difficulty. ● n. **1** the act or a period of struggling. **2** a hard contest. **3** a determined effort under difficulties.

strum v. (**strums**, **strummed**, **strumming**) **1** play a guitar, banjo, etc. by sweeping the thumb or a pick up or down the strings. **2** play (a tune etc.) in this way. □ **strummer** n.

strung past and past participle of STRING.

strung out adj. informal **1** addicted to, using, or high on drugs. **2** in a state of extreme nervous tension.

strut ● n. **1** a bar used to support or strengthen a structure. **2** a strutting gait. ● v. (**struts**, **strutted**, **strutting**) walk in a proud upright way. □ **strut one's stuff** informal display one's ability. □ **strutter** n.

strychnine n. a bitter and highly poisonous substance obtained from a plant. [Say STRICK nine or STRICK neen]

stub ● n. **1** the remnant of a pencil or cigarette etc. after use. **2** the small part of a cheque, receipt, ticket etc. that remains after the main part has been detached. **3** a shortened or unusually short thing. ● v. (**stubs**, **stubbed**, **stubbing**) **1** strike (one's toe) against something. **2** extinguish (a lighted cigarette) by pressing the lighted end against something.

stubble n. **1** the cut stalks of cereal plants left after the harvest. **2** a short bristly growth. □ **stubbled** adj. **stubbly** adj.

stubble-jumper n. Cdn slang a prairie farmer.

stubborn adj. **1** unreasonably obstinate. **2** unyielding. **3** that will not respond to treatment. □ **stubbornly** adj. **stubbornness** n.

stubby ● adj. (**stubbier**, **stubbiest**) short and thick. ● n. (pl. **stubbies**) Cdn hist. informal a small squat bottle of beer.

stucco ● n. (pl. **stuccoes**) plaster or cement used for coating or decorating wall surfaces. ● v. (**stuccoes**, **stuccoed**, **stuccoing**) coat with stucco.

stuck ● v. past and past participle of STICK². ● adj. **1** unable to progress. **2** confined in a place. **3** butchered by having its throat cut. □ **be stuck for** be in need of. **be stuck on** informal be infatuated with. **be stuck with** informal be unable to get rid of.

stuck-up adj. informal snobbish.

stud¹ ● n. **1** a large-headed nail or knob projecting from a surface. **2** a small piece of jewellery for wearing in pierced ears or nostrils. **3** a small object like a button with two heads. **4** a two-by-four to which drywall etc. is nailed. **5** a metal piece set into a tire to improve traction. ● v. (**studs**, **studded**, **studding**) **1** set with or as with studs. **2** be scattered over or about. □ **studded** adj.

stud² *n.* **1 a** a number of horses kept for breeding. **b** a place where these are kept. **2** (also **stud horse**) a stallion. **3** *informal* a very sexually active man. **4** (also **stud poker**) a form of poker with betting after the dealing of successive rounds of cards face up. □ **studly** *adj.*

studding *n.* the wood framing of a wall in a house etc.

student *n.* **1 a** a person who is studying. **b** a school pupil. **2** (as an *adj.*) studying in order to become. **3** a person who has a particular interest in something.

student-at-law *n.* (*pl.* **students-at-law**) *Cdn* an articling student.

studied *adj.* deliberate. □ **studiedly** *adv.*

studio *n.* (*pl.* **studios**) **1** a place where film and sound recordings are produced. **2** a company which produces films. **3** the workroom of a painter or photographer etc. **4** a large room where dancers rehearse. **5** (also **studio apartment**) an apartment with only one main room.

studious *adj.* **1** devoted to study or reading. **2** deliberate, painstaking. □ **studiously** *adv.* **studiousness** *n.*

study ● *n.* (*pl.* **studies**) **1** the devotion of time and attention to acquiring knowledge. **2** (in *pl.*) the pursuit of academic knowledge. **3** a detailed investigation. **4** a room used for reading, writing, etc. ● *v.* (**studies, studied, studying**) **1** investigate or examine. **2** apply oneself to study. **3** try to learn. **4** read attentively.

stuff ● *n.* **1** material. **2** a substance or things of an indeterminate kind not needing to be specified. **3** a particular knowledge or activity. **4** a person's capabilities or inward character. **5** valueless matter, nonsense. ● *v.* **1 a** pack tightly. **b** fill (envelopes) with printed matter. **2** force or cram (a thing). **3** fill out the skin of (an animal or bird etc.) with material to restore the original shape. **4** fill with a savoury or sweet mixture. **5** fill with food. **6** push clumsily. **7** block up. **8** *slang* dispose of as unwanted. **9** place bogus votes in. □ **get stuffed** *slang* an exclamation of dismissal or contempt. □ **stuffer** *n.*

stuffed shirt *n. informal* a pompous or prim person.

stuffing *n.* **1** padding used to stuff cushions etc. **2** a savoury mixture put inside a chicken, turkey, etc. before it is cooked. □ **knock** (or **take**) **the stuffing out of** *informal* make feeble or weak; defeat.

stuffy *adj.* (**stuffier, stuffiest**) **1** lacking fresh air or ventilation. **2** dull, formal, and boring. **3** blocked up. □ **stuffiness** *n.*

stultifying *adj.* extremely boring. □ **stultifyingly** *adv.* [*Say* STUL tuh fie ing]

stumble ● *v.* (**stumbles, stumbled, stumbling**) **1** have a partial fall from misplacing one's foot. **2** walk unsteadily. **3** act in a blundering or hesitating manner. **4** (foll. by *on, upon, across*) discover by chance. ● *n.* an act of stumbling.

stumblebum *n. informal* a clumsy person.

stumbling block *n.* an obstacle.

stump ● *n.* **1** the portion remaining fixed in the ground when a tree falls or is cut. **2** the part remaining when a limb etc. is amputated or severed. **3** anything that has been worn down or reduced to a small part of its original length. **4** (in *pl.*) *jocular* the legs. ● *v.* **1** be too hard for. **2** traverse (a district) making speeches for an election campaign. **3** remove the stumps from. □ **on the stump** *informal* engaged in political campaigning. □ **stumped** *adj.*

stumpage *n.* **1** standing timber considered with reference to its value. **2** (also **stumpage fee**) a tax charged for the cutting of timber on government-owned land. [*Say* STUMP idge]

stumpy *adj.* (**stumpier, stumpiest**) short and thick.

stun *v.* (**stuns, stunned, stunning**) **1** knock senseless. **2** bewilder or shock. **3** deafen temporarily.

stung *past and past participle of* STING.

stun gun *n.* a gun which stuns a person or animal by means of an electric shock etc.

stunk *past and past participle of* STINK.

stunned *adj.* Cdn informal stupid.

stunner *n. informal* **1** a thing that stuns, dazes, or amazes. **2** a very attractive woman.

stunning *adj. informal* **1** extremely impressive or attractive. **2** shocking. □ **stunningly** *adv.*

stunt¹ *v.* retard the growth of.

stunt² ● *n.* **1** something unusual done to attract attention. **2** a notably impressive act. ● *v.* perform stunts.

stuntman *n.* (*pl.* **stuntmen**) a man employed to take an actor's place in performing dangerous stunts.

stupefy *v.* (**stupefies, stupefied, stupefying**) **1** make someone unable to think or feel properly. **2** stun with astonishment. □ **stupefaction** *n.* **stupefying** *adj.* **stupefyingly** *adv.* [*Say* STUPE uh fie, stupe uh FACTION]

stupendous *adj.* amazing or prodigious, esp. in terms of size or degree. □ **stupendously** *adv.* [*Say* stew PEN dus]

stupid *adj.* (**stupider, stupidest**) **1** not intelligent. **2** showing lack of good judgment. **3** boring or not interesting. **4** obtuse. **5** *informal* a general term of disparagement. □ **stupidity** *n.* (*pl.* **stupidities**). **stupidly** *adv.*

stupor *n.* **1** a condition of near-unconsciousness caused by disease, narcotics, alcohol, etc. **2** a dazed, stunned, or torpid state. [*Say* STEW per]

sturdy *adj.* (**sturdier, sturdiest**) **1** strongly built. **2** vigorous. □ **sturdily** *adv.* **sturdiness** *n.*

sturgeon *n.* a large primitive shark-like fish, caught for its caviar and flesh. [*Say* STIR gin]

stutter ● *v.* **1** stammer by involuntarily repeating the first consonants of words. **2** move or start with difficulty. ● *n.* a tendency to stutter when speaking. □ **stutterer** *n.*

sty *n.* **1** (*pl.* **sties**) **a** an enclosure for pigs. **b** a filthy dwelling. **2** (*pl.* **sties** or **styes**) an inflamed swelling on the edge of an eyelid.

style ● *n.* **1** a kind or sort. **2** a distinctive manner. **3 a** a superior quality. **b** fashionableness or attractiveness. **4** a particular make, shape, or pattern. **5** *Botany* the narrow extension of the ovary supporting the stigma. ● *v.* (**styles, styled, styling**) **1** make in a particular style. **2** give a particular title, name, or description to.

stylish *adj.* **1** fashionable. **2** having a superior quality. □ **stylishly** *adv.* **stylishness** *n.*

stylist *n.* **1 a** a person who creates new styles, esp. of clothes or cars. **b** a hairdresser. **2** a writer noted for good literary style. **3** a person whose job is to arrange and coordinate food, clothes, etc. in a stylish and attractive way in photographs or films.

stylistic *adj.* concerning esp. literary or artistic style. □ **stylistically** *adv.*

stylized *adj.* not natural or realistic. □ **stylization** *n.*

stylus *n.* (*pl.* **styli** or **styluses**) **1** any sharp instrument or point for engraving, tracing, etc. **2** a pen-shaped electrical device for designing graphical images on a computer screen. [*Say* STY lus *for the singular; for* STYLI *say* STY lie]

stymie ● *v.* (**stymies, stymied, stymying** or **stymieing**) **1** obstruct or thwart. **2** puzzle. **3** *Golf* block with a stymie. ● *n.* (*pl.* **stymies**) *Golf* a situation on a green in which the path of a putt to the hole is obstructed by an opponent's ball. [*Say* STY mee]

styrene *n.* a liquid hydrocarbon used in making plastics etc. [*Say* STY reen]

Styrofoam *n.* *proprietary* a variety of expanded polystyrene often used in F etc.

suasion *n.* *formal* persuasion as opposed to force. [*Say* SWAY zh'n]

suave *adj.* confident, elegant and polite. □ **suavely** *adv.* **suavity** *n.* [*Say* SWOV, SWOVVA tee]

sub *informal* ● *n.* **1** a submarine. **2** a sandwich made with a long roll. **3** a substitute. **4** a subscription. ● *v.* (**subs, subbed, subbing**) act or work as a substitute.

subalpine *adj.* **1** pertaining to the mountain slopes just below the timberline. **2** of or pertaining to the area at the foot of the Alps.

subarctic *n.* (usu. **Subarctic**) the region immediately south of the Arctic Circle. □ **subarctic** *adj.*

subatomic *adj.* **1** existing or occurring within an atom. **2** smaller than an atom.

subcategory *n.* (*pl.* **subcategories**) a secondary category.

subclass *n.* (*pl.* **subclasses**) **1** a secondary class. **2** a taxonomic category below a class.

subcommittee *n.* a committee appointed by a larger committee.

subcompact ● *adj.* designating a car usu. having a wheelbase of less than 85 inches, and a 1 litre engine. ● *n.* a subcompact car.

subconscious ● *n.* the part of the mind which influences actions etc. without one's full awareness. ● *adj.* **1** of or existing in the subconscious. **2** operating without one's full awareness. □ **subconsciously** *adv.*

subcontinent *n.* **1** a large section of a continent considered as a particular area. **2** a large land mass smaller than a continent. □ **subcontinental** *adj.*

subcontract ● *v.* **1** hire a person, company, etc. to do (work) as part of a larger contract. **2** make or carry out a subcontract. ● *n.* an agreement that one party will perform some or all of a previous contract.

subcontractor *n.* the party to whom a principal contractor has sublet a contract.

subculture *n.* **1** a cultural group as distinguished from a larger culture. **2** a culture of micro-organisms started from another culture.

subcutaneous *adj.* just under the skin. □ **subcutaneously** *adv.* [*Say* sub cue TAY nee us]

subdirectory *n.* (*pl.* **subdirectories**) *Computing* a directory contained in another directory.

subdiscipline *n.* a subordinate branch of a discipline.

subdivide v. (**subdivides, subdivided, subdividing**) **1** divide into smaller parts. **2** divide into plots for sale or development.

subdivision n. **1** an area of land divided into plots for sale or development. **2** a housing development built on such an area. **3** each of the parts into which a thing is or may be divided. **4** the action of subdividing.

subduc v. (**subdues, subdued, subduing**) **1** overpower. **2** bring under control.

subdued adj. **1** lacking intensity or force. **2** not showing much excitement.

subfamily n. (pl. **subfamilies**) a subdivision of a family in a classification.

subfloor n. a rough floor serving as a foundation for a finished floor. □ **subflooring** n.

subfreezing adj. below the freezing point.

sub-genre n. a subordinate style of esp. literature or art.

subgroup n. **1** a subordinate group. **2** Math a series of operations forming part of a larger group.

subheading n. (also **subhead**) **1** a subordinate heading, caption, etc. **2** a subordinate division in a classification.

subhuman ● adj. **1** closely related to, but of a lower order of being than, a human. **2** uncivilized, bestial. ● n. a subhuman person or creature.

subject ● n. **1** the focus of attention in a discussion etc. **2** something studied in an academic institution. **3** Grammar a word or phrase in a sentence indicating who or what performs the action of a verb or upon whom or which a verb is predicated. **4** a person owing allegiance to and under the protection of a monarch or government. ● adj. (usu. foll. by to) **1** susceptible to some condition. **2** liable. **3** conditional upon. **4** bound by law or regulation. **5** under the domination of an individual or group etc. ● adv. (foll. by to) conditionally upon. ● v. **1** cause to experience or endure a specified thing. **2** make vulnerable to. **3** extend one's influence over. □ **subjection** n.

subjective adj. **1** proceeding from an individual's personal thoughts and opinions. **2** constructed as appropriate to the subject of a sentence or verb. □ **subjectively** n. adv. **subjectivity** n.

subjugate v. (**subjugates, subjugated, subjugating**) bring under one's control. □ **subjugation** n. [Say SUB juh gate]

subjunctive Grammar ● n. **1** (also **subjunctive mood**) a mood of verbs used to express a condition, wish, fear, possibility, command, suggestion or uncertainty. **2** a verb in this mood. ● adj. expressed in the subjunctive. [Say sub JUNK tiv]

subkingdom n. a taxonomic category below a kingdom.

sublet ● v. (**sublets, sublet, subletting**) **1** acquire a lease on (an apartment etc.) from the person leasing it from its owner. **2** rent out (an apartment etc.) that one is leasing from its owner. ● n. an apartment etc. that is being sublet.

sub-lieutenant n. Cdn & Brit. a naval officer ranking next below lieutenant. Abbreviation: **SLt.**

sublimate v. (**sublimates, sublimated, sublimating**) **1** divert the energy of (a primitive impulse) into a more valued or acceptable activity. **2** change between solid and gaseous states without liquefaction. □ **sublimation** n. [Say SUB luh mate]

sublime ● adj. (**sublimer, sublimest**) **1** of the most exalted or high moral or spiritual level. **2** of such excellence or beauty as to inspire great admiration. **3** usu. ironic of the most extreme kind. ● n. a quality in art or nature inspiring awe, emotion, etc. □ **sublimely** adv. **sublimity** n. [Say sub LIME, sub LIMMA tee]

subliminal adj. affecting someone's mind without their being aware of it. □ **subliminally** adv. [Say sub LIMMA nul]

submachine gun n. a hand-held lightweight machine gun.

submarine ● n. **1** a vessel capable of operating under water. **2** = SUB n. 2. ● adj. existing under the surface of the sea.

submariner n. a member of the navy who serves on submarines. [Say sub MERRA ner]

submerge v. (**submerges, submerged, submerging**) **1** immerse in a liquid. **2** overwhelm with work, problems, etc. **3** conceal or suppress. **4** dive below the surface of water. □ **submerged** adj. **submergence** n.

submerse v. (**submerses, submersed, submersing**) submerge. □ **submersion** n.

submersible ● n. a submarine exploring under water for short periods. ● adj. intended to operate under water.

submicroscopic adj. too small to be seen by an ordinary microscope.

submissive adj. meekly obedient or passive. □ **submissively** adv. **submissiveness** n.

submit v. (**submits, submitted, submitting**) **1 a** cease resistance; give way. **b** surrender (oneself) to. **2** present for consideration. **3** subject to an operation,

treatment, etc. **4** suggest politely.
□ **submission** *n.*

suborder *n.* a taxonomic category below an order.

subordinate ● *adj.* (often. foll. by *to*) **1** of inferior rank. **2** secondary, minor. **3** dependent upon a principal thing of the same kind. ● *n.* a subordinate person or thing. ● *v.* (**subordinates**, **subordinated**, **subordinating**) (usu. foll. by *to*) **1** treat as less important. **2** make dependent on something else. □ **subordination** *n.* [*Say* sub ORDA nit *for the adjective and noun,* sub ORDA nate *for the verb;* sub orda NAY sh'n.]

subordinate clause *n.* a clause that does not constitute a sentence itself but which depends on the principal clause.

suborn *v.* pay or persuade someone to do something illegal. [*Say* suh BORN]

subphylum *n.* (*pl.* **subphyla**) a taxonomic category below a phylum. [*Say* sub FIE lum *for the singular,* sub FIE luh *for the plural*]

subplot *n.* a secondary plot in a novel, play, etc.

subpoena ● *n.* (*pl.* **subpoenas**) a writ ordering a person to attend court. ● *v.* (**subpoenas**, **subpoenaed**, **subpoenaing**) **1** summon to appear in court as a witness. **2** summon with a subpoena. [*Say* suh PEENA]

subroutine *n. Computing* (also **subprogram**) a routine performing a frequent operation within a program.

sub-Saharan *adj.* relating to the African regions south of the Sahara desert.

subscribe *v.* (**subscribes**, **subscribed**, **subscribing**) **1** arrange to receive something regularly in exchange for payment. **2** agree with an idea or resolution. **3 a** pay or guarantee for an issue of shares. **b** contribute (money) to a cause. □ **subscriber** *n.*

subscript ● *n.* a character, number, or symbol written or printed below the line. ● *adj.* written or printed below the line.

subscription *n.* **1** an action of subscribing. **2** a payment to subscribe to something.

subsea *adj. & adv.* beneath the surface of the sea.

subsection *n.* a division of a section.

subsequent *adj.* following a specified event etc. in time. □ **subsequently** *adv.*

subservient *adj.* **1** too willing to obey other people. **2** less important than something else. □ **subservience** *n.* [*Say* sub SIR vee int]

subset *n.* **1** a secondary part of a set. **2** *Math* a set consisting of elements all of which are contained in another set.

subside *v.* (**subsides**, **subsided**, **subsiding**) **1** become calm or tranquil. **2** be reduced to a lower level. **3** cave in. **4** sink into the ground or water. **5** be reduced. **6** settle into a comfortable position.

subsidence *n.* the gradual caving in or sinking of an area of land. [*Say* sub SIGH dince *or* SUB suh dince]

subsidiary ● *adj.* **1** less important than but related to. **2** (of a company) controlled by a parent company. ● *n.* (*pl.* **subsidiaries**) a company whose controlling interest is owned by a parent company. [*Say* sub SIDDY airy *or* sub SIDGE er ee]

subsidize *v.* (**subsidizes**, **subsidized**, **subsidizing**) **1** pay part of the cost of producing something to reduce prices for the consumer. **2** support financially. □ **subsidization** *n.* **subsidized** *adj.* [*Say* SUB suh dize]

subsidy *n.* (*pl.* **subsidies**) **1** money granted by the government to help an industry or business keep prices low, avoid cutting jobs, etc. **2** money granted to an organization held to be in the public interest. **3** any contribution of money. [*Say* SUB suh dee]

subsist *v.* **1** manage to stay alive. **2** *formal* exist; remain in effect. [*Say* sub SIST]

subsistence *n.* **1** the means of supporting life. **2** the production of sufficient goods to sustain oneself, without a surplus for trade. **3** a minimal standard of living or income. [*Say* sub SIST ince]

subsoil *n.* the layer of soil under the topsoil.

subsonic *adj.* relating to speeds less than that of sound. □ **subsonically** *adv.*

subspecies *n.* (*pl.* **subspecies**) a distinct subdivision of a species.

substance *n.* **1** the essential esp. solid matter of which a physical thing consists. **2** a particular kind of material having a definite chemical composition and usu. uniform properties. **3** an intoxicating or narcotic chemical or drug. **4 a** the content of a thing as opposed to its superficial appearance. **b** strength of character. **5 a** the essential point. **b** concrete evidence. **6** wealth and possessions.

substandard *adj.* inadequate, inferior.

substantial *adj.* **1** ample or considerable. **2** of solid build. **3** having substance or truth. □ **substantially** *adv.* [*Say* sub STAN shul]

substantiate *v.* (**substantiates**, **substantiated**, **substantiating**) prove

the truth of. □ **substantiation** n.
[*Say* sub STAN shee ate]

substantive adj. **1** having a firm basis in reality and so important or meaningful. **2** *Law* relating to rights and duties as opposed to forms of procedure. □ **substantively** adv. [*Say* SUB stun tiv or sub STAN tiv]

substation n. **1** an establishment subordinate to a principal station. **2** a station that reduces high voltages of electrical current so as to be suitable for supply to consumers.

substitute ● n. a person or thing that is or may be used in place of another. ● v. (**substitutes**, **substituted**, **substituting**) **1** use or insert in place of another. **2** act as a substitute. □ **substitution** n.

substrate n. **1** a layer of earth or rock beneath the surface. **2** the substance on which an organism grows or an enzyme acts. **3** an underlying surface. [*Say* SUB strate]

substratum n. (pl. **substrata**) **1** a foundation or basis. **2** substrate. [*Say* SUB strat um]

substructure n. an underlying structure.

subsume v. (**subsumes**, **subsumed**, **subsuming**) include something in a particular group or category. □ **subsumption** n.

subsurface ● n. that which lies immediately below the surface of something. ● adj. existing beneath the surface of earth, water, etc.

subsystem n. a self-contained system within a larger system.

subterfuge n. deceit resorted to in an attempt to avoid blame, justify an argument, etc. [*Say* SUB ter fuge]

subterranean adj. existing or happening under the earth's surface. [*Say* sub tuh RAINY in]

subtext n. an underlying theme.

subtitle n. **1** a secondary title. **2** a translation or transcription of movie dialogue etc. printed at the bottom of the screen. □ **subtitled** adj. **subtitling** n.

subtle adj. (**subtler**, **subtlest**) **1 a** difficult to detect. **b** done imperceptibly or secretly. **2** faint. **3 a** capable of making fine distinctions. **b** organized cleverly. □ **subtlety** n. (pl. **subtleties**) **subtly** adv. [*Say* SUTTLE]

subtotal n. the total of one part of a group of figures to be added.

subtract v. deduct; remove (usu. to calculate the difference). □ **subtraction** n.

subtropics pl. n. the regions adjacent to the tropics. □ **subtropical** adj.

subtype n. a subordinate type.

suburb n. a residential district on the edge of a city or town. □ **suburban** adj. **suburbanite** n. **suburbanization** n. **suburbanize** v. (**suburbanizes**, **suburbanized**, **suburbanizing**)

suburbia n. **1** suburbs collectively. **2** *derogatory* the social and cultural aspects of suburban life.

subversive ● adj. seeking to subvert. ● n. a subversive person. □ **subversiveness** n. [*Say* sub VER siv]

subvert v. undermine the authority of. □ **subversion** n. [*Say* sub VERT]

subway n. **1** an underground railway. **2** a station on a subway line.

subwoofer n. a loudspeaker component reproducing very low frequencies.

sub-zero adj. lower than zero.

succeed v. **1** achieve success. **2** take or inherit the place of.

success n. **1** the accomplishment of an aim. **2** the attainment of wealth, fame, or position. **3** a thing or person that turns out well.

successful adj. having or resulting in success. □ **successfully** adv.

succession n. **1** a number of people or things following one after the other. **2** the action or right of inheriting a title, property, etc. **3** the rotation of crops. □ **in quick succession** following one another at short intervals. □ **successional** adj.

successive adj. following one after another. □ **successively** adv.

successor n. a person or thing succeeding another.

succinct adj. briefly expressed. □ **succinctly** adv. **succinctness** n. [*Say* suh SINCT or suck SINCT]

succour ● n. assistance. ● v. assist. [*Say* SUCKER]

succulent ● adj. **1** tender, juicy, and tasty. **2** having thick, fleshy leaves or stems adapted to storing water. ● n. a succulent plant. □ **succulence** n. **succulently** adv. [*Say* SUCK yuh lint]

succumb v. **1** be overcome. **2** die as the result of a disease, wound, etc. [*Say* suh KUM]

such ● adj. **1** of the kind or degree in question. **2** so great. **3** of a more than normal kind or degree. **4** of the kind already indicated or implied. ● pron. **1** the thing or action in question. **2 a** *Commerce* the aforesaid thing or things. **b** similar things. □ **as such** as being what has been indicated or named. **such as 1** of a kind that; like. **2** for example. **3** those who. **such as it is** despite its shortcomings.

such-and-such ● *adj.* of a particular kind but not needing to be specified. ● *n.* a person or thing of this kind.

suchlike *informal* ● *adj.* of such a kind. ● *n.* things, people, etc. of such a kind.

suck ● *v.* **1** draw into the mouth. **2** perform a sucking action on. **3** *slang* be very bad. **4** make a sucking action or sound. **5** make a gurgling or drawing sound. **6** engulf, smother, or drown in a sucking movement. **7** draw in some direction. ● *n.* **1** *Cdn informal* a crybaby or sore loser. **2** *Cdn informal* a person who behaves obsequiously to those in authority. □ **suck dry 1** exhaust the contents of by sucking. **2** exhaust as if by sucking. **suck in 1** absorb. **2** = sense 6 of *v.* **3** draw in. **4** take in; cheat or deceive. **5** involve in an activity etc. **suck up 1** behave obsequiously. **2** absorb.

sucker ● *n.* **1** a person or thing that sucks. **2 a** *informal* a gullible person. **b** a person especially susceptible to. **3** *informal* a thing not specified by name. **4** *informal* a hard candy on a small stick. **5** a device or organ that adheres to a surface by suction. **6** a N American freshwater fish with thick lips used to suck up food. **7** a shoot springing from the root of a plant. ● *v. informal* fool, trick.

sucker punch *n.* an unexpected punch. □ **sucker-punch** *v.* (**sucker-punches, sucker-punched, sucker-punching**)

suckle *v.* (**suckles, suckled, suckling**) feed from the breast or udder.

suckling *n.* a child or animal which has not yet been weaned.

sucky *adj. informal* **1** wimpy or childish. **2** trying too hard to impress. **3** unpleasant.

sucrose *n.* common sugar. [*Say* SUKE roace]

suction ● *n.* **1** the process of removing air or liquid from a space or container. **2** the production of a partial vacuum by the removal of air. ● *v.* draw using suction; suck.

suction cup *n.* a usu. rubber concave disc that adheres to a smooth surface by suction.

Sudanese *adj.* of Sudan, a republic in northeastern Africa, or the Sudan region south of the Sahara. □ **Sudanese** *n.* [*Say* soo duh NEEZ]

sudden *adj.* happening unexpectedly or without warning. □ **all of a sudden** unexpectedly; suddenly. □ **suddenly** *adv.* **suddenness** *n.*

sudden death *n.* a session of play to break a tie, in which the first to take the lead wins.

sudden infant death syndrome *n.* the unexplained death of a baby while sleeping.

suds *pl. n.* **1** froth of soap and water. **2** *informal* beer. □ **sudsy** *adj.*

sue *v.* (**sues, sued, suing**) **1** institute legal proceedings against. **2** make application to a law court for redress. **3** make entreaty for.

suede *n.* soft leather with a velvety surface on one side. [*Sounds like* SWAYED]

suet *n.* fat on the kidneys or loins of oxen, sheep, etc., used in puddings etc. [*Say* SOO it]

suffer *v.* **1** undergo. **2** put up with. □ **not suffer fools gladly** refuse to be patient with people one considers foolish, stupid, etc. □ **sufferer** *n.* **suffering** *n.*

sufferance *n.* □ **on sufferance** with someone's (usu. reluctant) consent.

suffice *v.* (**suffices, sufficed, sufficing**) be enough or adequate. [*Say* suh FICE]

sufficient *adj.* adequate. □ **sufficiency** *n.* **sufficiently** *adv.* [*Say* suh FISH'nt]

suffix ● *n.* (*pl.* **suffixes**) a verbal element added at the end of a word. ● *v.* (**suffixes, suffixed, suffixing**) append as a suffix.

suffocate *v.* (**suffocates, suffocated, suffocating**) **1** choke or kill by stopping breathing. **2** produce a breathless sensation in. **3** be or feel suffocated. **4** *informal* restrict. □ **suffocating** *adj.* **suffocatingly** *adv.* **suffocation** *n.*

suffrage *n.* the right of voting in political elections. [*Say* SUFF ridge]

suffragette *n. hist.* a woman acting in favour of women's suffrage. [*Say* suffra JET]

suffuse *v.* (**suffuses, suffused, suffusing**) fill or spread through or over something. □ **suffusion** *n.* [*Say* suh FUZE, suh FUSION]

Sufi *n.* (*pl.* **Sufis**) a member of an Islamic spiritual order based on mysticism, simplicity, and self-discipline. □ **Sufic** *adj.* **Sufism** *n.* [*Say* SOOF ee, SOOF ism]

sugar ● *n.* **1** a sweet crystalline substance obtained from various plants. **2** any of a group of soluble usu. sweet-tasting crystalline carbohydrates found esp. in plants. **3** *informal* darling, dear. ● *interj.* expressing exasperation etc. ● *v.* **1** sweeten or coat with sugar. **2** (also **sugar off**) make maple syrup or maple sugar by collecting and boiling maple sap. □ **sugarless** *adj.*

sugar beet *n.* a kind of beet from which sugar is extracted.

sugar bush *n.* a grove of sugar maples.

sugar cane *n.* a perennial tropical grass with stout stems from which sugar is extracted.

sugar-coat *v.* (often as **sugar-coated** *adj.*) **1** cover in sugar. **2** make superficially attractive. □ **sugar-coating** *n.*

sugar daddy *n. slang* an elderly man who lavishes gifts on a young person esp. in return for sex.

sugaring *n.* **1** (also **sugaring off**) the making of maple sugar or syrup by boiling the sap of a sugar maple. **2** a method of removing hair using a sticky sugar mixture.

sugar maple *n.* a N American maple that produces a sap from which maple sugar and maple syrup are made.

sugar pie *n. Cdn* (esp. *Que.*) a pie with a filling of brown or maple sugar mixed with cream.

sugar plum *n. archaic* a small round hard candy.

sugar shack *n. Cdn* **1** a building in which maple sap is boiled. **2** esp. *Que.* a usu. small establishment in a sugar bush serving maple-flavoured dishes etc.

sugary *adj.* **1** containing esp. a high proportion of sugar. **2** excessively sweet or sentimental. □ **sugariness** *n.*

suggest *v.* **1** propose. **2 a** cause to present itself. **b** hint at. □ **suggest itself** come into the mind. [*Say* suh JEST *or* sug JEST]

suggestion *n.* **1** the action of putting forward a plan for consideration. **2 a** a theory, plan, etc., suggested. **b** an implication or hint. **3** the process of calling up an idea in someone's mind by associating it with other things. [*Say* suh JESTION *or* sug JESTION]

suggestive *adj.* **1** causing someone to think of something. **2** making people think about sex. □ **suggestively** *adv.* **suggestiveness** *n.* [*Say* suh JESTIVE *or* sug JESTIVE]

suicidal *adj.* **1** deeply depressed and likely to commit suicide. **2** likely to lead to suicide. **3** likely to have a disastrously damaging effect on oneself. □ **suicidally** *adv.* [*Say* soo uh SIDE 'll]

suicide *n.* **1 a** the intentional killing of oneself. **b** a person who commits suicide. **2** a self-destructive action. **3** (as an *adj.*) *Military* designating a highly dangerous or deliberately suicidal operation. [*Say* SOO uh side]

suit ● *n.* **1 a** a set of outer clothes of matching material. **b** clothes worn for a particular activity etc. **2** any of the four sets into which a pack of cards is divided. **3** a lawsuit. **4** *slang* a business executive. **5** (usu. foll. by *of*) a set of armour, sails, etc. **6** the process of trying to win a woman's affection. ● *v.* **1** go well with. **2** meet the requirements of. **3** make appropriate. □ **suit oneself 1** do as one chooses. **2** find something that satisfies one. **suit up** dress for a particular activity.

suitable *adj.* (usu. foll. by *to*, *for*) well fitted for the purpose. □ **suitability** *n.* **suitably** *adv.*

suitcase *n.* a usu. oblong case for carrying clothes etc.

suite *n.* **1 a** a set of rooms in a hotel etc. for use by one person or group. **b** a set of furniture of the same design. **2** an apartment. **3** a set of instrumental compositions etc. to be played in succession. **4** a set of pieces from an opera etc. arranged as one instrumental work. **5** *Computing* a set of programs with a uniform design and the ability to share data. [*Say* SWEET]

suited *adj.* appropriate.

suitor *n.* **1** a man seeking to marry a specified woman. **2** a plaintiff. **3** a prospective buyer. [*Say* SOOTER]

sukiyaki *n.* a Japanese dish of sliced meat simmered with vegetables and sauce. [*Say* soo kee OCKY]

Sukkot *n.* the Jewish autumn harvest and thanksgiving festival. [*Say* SOO cot]

sulfate = SULPHATE.

sulfur etc. = SULPHUR etc.

sulk ● *v.* indulge in a period of sullen, resentful silence. ● *n.* a period of sulking.

sulky *adj.* (**sulkier**, **sulkiest**) sullen, morose, or silent. □ **sulkily** *adv.*

sullen *adj.* **1** morose, resentful, sulky. **2** dark and gloomy. □ **sullenly** *adv.* **sullenness** *n.*

sully *v.* (**sullies**, **sullied**, **sullying**) **1** disgrace or tarnish. **2** dirty.

sulphate *n.* a salt or ester of sulphuric acid.

sulphide *n.* a binary compound of sulphur.

sulphite *n.* a substance containing sulphur, found typically in foods and wines.

sulphur *n.* **1** a pale yellow non-metallic element, used in making gunpowder, matches, and sulphuric acid, and in the treatment of skin diseases. **2** the material of which hellfire and lightning were believed to consist.

sulphur dioxide ● *n.* a colourless pungent gas formed by burning sulphur.

sulphuric *adj.* containing sulphur.
[*Say* sul FYOOR ick]

sulphuric acid *n.* a dense oily colourless highly acid and corrosive fluid much used in the chemical industry.

sulphurous *adj.* **1 a** relating to or suggestive of sulphur. **b** suggestive of burning sulphur, hellfire, etc. **2** *Chemistry* containing tetravalent sulphur.
[*Say* SUL fruss]

Sulpician *n.* a member of a Roman Catholic society of priests concerned esp. with the training of priests.
[*Say* sool PISH'n]

sultan *n.* **1 a** a Muslim sovereign. **b** (the Sultan) *hist.* the sultan of Turkey. **2** an absolute ruler. [*Say* SUL tin]

sultana *n.* (*pl.* **sultanas**) a seedless raisin.
[*Say* sul TANA]

sultanate *n.* **1** the rank of or land owned by a sultan. **2** the period when someone is a sultan. [*Say* SUL tuh nate]

sultry *adj.* (**sultrier, sultriest**) **1** hot and humid. **2** passionate; sensual.
[*Say* SUL tree]

sum *n.* **1** the total amount resulting from the addition of two or more items, facts, feelings, etc. **2** an amount of money. **3** an arithmetical problem. □ **in sum** in brief.
sum up (**sums up, summed up, summing up**) **1** review or summarize the evidence in a case etc. **2** form or express an idea of the character of. **3** express as a total.

sumac *n.* (also **sumach**) a shrub or tree with cone-shaped clusters of reddish fruits, the leaves of which are used in tanning and dyeing. [*Say* SOO mack]

Sumatran *adj.* of Sumatra, a large island of Indonesia, or its people or language. □ **Sumatran** *n.* [*Say* soo MAW trin]

Sumerian *adj.* relating to the early and non-Semitic element in ancient Babylonian civilization. □ **Sumerian** *n.*
[*Say* soo MERRY in]

summa cum laude *adv. & adj.* of the highest standard.
[*Say* sooma koom LOUD ay]

summarily *adv.* briefly or suddenly.
[*Say* suh MERRA lee]

summarize *v.* (**summarizes, summarized, summarizing**) make or be a summary of.

summary ● *n.* (*pl.* **summaries**) a brief account. ● *adj.* **1** dispensing with needless details or formalities. **2** without the customary legal formalities.

summary conviction *n.* a conviction made by a judge or magistrates without a jury.

summary conviction offence *n.* (also

summary offence) *Cdn* a relatively minor criminal offence tried by a magistrate.

summation *n.* a summary of what has been done or said. [*Say* suh MAY sh'n]

summer ● *n.* the warmest season of the year. ● *v.* pass the summer.
□ **summery** *adj.*

summerfallow esp. *Cdn* ● *n.* agricultural land left uncultivated in the summer. ● *v.* lay fallow during the summer.

summer house *n.* a light building in a garden, park, etc.

summer school *n.* a course of classes held in the summer.

summer student *n.* *Cdn* an esp. university student working at a job for the summer.

summertime *n.* the period of summer.

summit *n.* **1** the highest point or degree. **2** a discussion esp. between heads of government.

summiteer *n.* a participant in a summit meeting.

summitry *n.* the practice of convening or holding summit meetings, or using them as a diplomatic device.

summon *v.* **1** call upon to appear. **2** call upon or together. **3** gather (courage etc.).

summons ● *n.* (*pl.* **summonses**) **1** a call to attend or do something. **2** an order to appear before a judge or magistrate. ● *v.* (**summonses, summonsed, summonsing**) esp. *Law* serve with a summons.

sumo *n.* a Japanese form of wrestling in which bulky wrestlers try to force one another out of a ring (also as an *adj.*).
[*Say* SOO moe]

sump *n.* a pit etc. in which superfluous liquid collects.

sump pump *n.* a pump for removing waste water.

sumptuous *adj.* lavish. □ **sumptuously** *adv.* **sumptuousness** *n.*

sum total *n.* the total amount.

Sun. *abbr.* Sunday.

sun ● *n.* **1 a** the star around which the earth orbits and from which it receives light and warmth. **b** any similar star. **2** the light or warmth received from the sun. ● *v.* (**suns, sunned, sunning**) bask in the sun. □ **beneath** (or **under**) **the sun** anywhere in the world.

sun-baked *adj.* dried by or exposed to the heat of the sun.

sunbathe *v.* (**sunbathes, sunbathed, sunbathing**) bask in the sun.
□ **sunbather** *n.*

sunbeam *n.* a ray of sunlight.

sunbelt *n.* an area receiving plenty of sunshine.

sunblock *n.* a lotion etc. for protecting the skin from the sun.

sunburn ● *n.* inflammation of the skin caused by overexposure to the sun. ● *v.* suffer from sunburn. □ **sunburned** *adj.* (also **sunburnt**)

sunburst *n.* **1** something resembling the sun and its rays. **2** a sudden burst of sunshine. **3** *Cdn* a trimming of fur around the hood of a parka.

sundae *n.* a dish of ice cream topped with sauce, fruit, nuts, etc.

sun dance *n.* an annual ceremony held at midsummer by some Plains Aboriginal peoples.

Sunday ● *n.* the first day of the week, observed by Christians as a day of worship. ● *adv.* on Sunday.

Sunday best *n.* a person's best clothes.

Sunday school *n.* a class held on Sunday to teach children about Christianity.

sundeck *n.* a terrace or balcony positioned to catch the sun.

sunder *v. literary* separate.

sundew *n.* a small insect-consuming bog plant, with leaves bearing sticky hairs that trap insects.

sundial *n.* an instrument showing time by the shadow of a pointer cast by the sun on to a graduated disc.

sun dog *n.* a bright rainbow-coloured spot, usu. one of two, on either side of the sun, caused by reflection of light by atmospheric ice crystals.

sundown *n.* sunset.

sun-drenched *adj.* **1** illuminated by sunshine. **2** having very sunny weather.

sundress *n.* (*pl.* **sundresses**) a light, loose sleeveless dress.

sun-dried *adj.* dried by the sun, not by artificial heat.

sundry ● *adj.* various; several. ● *n.* (*pl.* **sundries**) (in *pl.*) items not mentioned individually. □ **all and sundry** everyone. [*Say* SUN dree]

sunfish *n.* (*pl.* **sunfish** or **sunfishes**) **1** a large, almost spherical ocean fish with a tall dorsal fin and a very short tail. **2** a small, deep-bodied, N American freshwater fish.

sunflower *n.* a very tall N American plant of the daisy family, grown for its seeds and oil.

sung *past participle of* SING.

sunglasses *pl. n.* glasses tinted to protect the eyes from sunlight.

sunk *past and past participle of* SINK.

sunken *adj.* **1** that has been sunk. **2** beneath the surface. **3** hollow. **4** placed on a lower level.

sun-kissed *adj.* warmed or affected by the sun.

sun lamp *n.* a lamp giving ultraviolet rays for an artificial suntan etc.

sunlight *n.* light from the sun. □ **sunlit** *adj.*

Sunna *n.* a traditional portion of Muslim law based on Muhammad's words or acts, accepted (with the Koran) as authoritative by Muslims. [*Say* SOON uh]

Sunni ● *n.* **1** one of the two main branches of Islam. **2** (*pl.* **Sunni** or **Sunnis**) an adherent of this branch of Islam. ● *adj.* of or relating to Sunni. [*Say* SOONY]

sunny *adj.* (**sunnier, sunniest**) **1 a** bright with sunlight. **b** exposed to or warmed by the sun. **2** cheery, bright, and optimistic. □ **sunnily** *adv.* **sunniness** *n.*

sun protection factor *n.* a number indicating the effectiveness of sunscreens etc.

sunrise *n.* **1** the sun's rising at dawn. **2** the coloured sky associated with this. **3** the time at which sunrise occurs.

sunroof *n.* a sliding part of the roof of a car that can be opened to let in air and sunlight.

sunroom *n.* a room with large windows, designed to receive sunlight.

sunscreen *n.* a cream or lotion rubbed on to the skin to protect it from the sun.

sunset *n.* **1** the time in the evening when the sun sets. **2** the coloured sky associated with this. **3** (as an *adj.*) designating a provision under which something is to be terminated after a fixed period unless formally renewed.

sunshade *n.* something that provides shade.

sunshine *n.* **1 a** the light or warmth of the sun. **b** an area lit by the sun. **2** fine weather. **3** cheerfulness. **4** *informal* a form of address. □ **sunshiny** *adj.*

sunspot *n.* one of the dark patches observed on the sun's surface.

sunstroke *n.* acute prostration or collapse from the excessive heat of the sun.

suntan *n.* a brown colour of the skin caused by exposure to the sun. □ **suntanned** *adj.* **suntanning** *n.*

sun-up *n.* sunrise.

sup ● *v.* (**sups, supped, supping**) take by sips or spoonfuls. ● *n.* a sip of liquid.

super ● *adj.* **1** *informal* exceptional. **2** of or to the highest degree, power, etc. ● *n. informal* **1** a superintendent. **2** an actor who appears on stage but does not speak. ● *adv. informal* extremely.

super- comb. form forming nouns, adjectives, and verbs, meaning: **1** above, beyond, or over in place or time or conceptually. **2** to a great degree. **3** extra good or large of its kind. **4** of a higher kind.

superannuated *adj.* **1** retired with a pension. **2** dismissed as too old for use etc. [*Say* super ANYOO ate id]

superannuation *n.* **1** a pension paid to a retired person. **2** a regular payment made towards this by an employed person. [*Say* super anyoo AY sh'n]

superb *adj.* **1** excellent; fine. **2** of the most impressive kind. □ **superbly** *adv.* [*Say* soo PERB]

supercar *n.* a high-performance sports car.

supercharge *v.* (**supercharges, supercharged, supercharging**) **1** charge with energy, emotion, etc. **2** use a supercharger on. □ **supercharged** *adj.*

supercharger *n.* a device supplying air or fuel to an internal combustion engine at above normal pressure to increase efficiency.

supercilious *adj.* assuming an air of contemptuous superiority. □ **superciliously** *adv.* **superciliousness** *n.* [*Say* super SILLY us]

supercluster *n. Astronomy* a cluster of galaxies which themselves occur as clusters.

supercomputer *n.* a powerful computer which can deal with complex problems. □ **supercomputing** *n.*

superconductivity *n.* the property of zero electrical resistance in some substances at very low temperatures. □ **superconducting** *adj.* **superconductor** *n.*

supercontinent *n.* each of several large land masses thought to have divided to form the present continents.

supercool ● *v.* **1** cool below its freezing point without solidification or crystallization. **2** be cooled in this way. ● *adj. slang* very cool, relaxed, etc.

super-duper *adj. informal* exceptional.

superego *n.* (*pl.* **superegos**) *Psychology* the part of the mind that acts as a conscience and reflects social rules. [*Say* SUPER ego]

superfamily *n.* (*pl.* **superfamilies**) a taxonomic category between family and order.

superficial *adj.* **1** of or on the surface. **2** rapid. **3** apparent but not real. **4** lacking substance or profundity. □ **superficiality**

n. **superficially** *adv.* [*Say* super FISH'll, super fishy ALA tee]

superfine *adj.* **1** in very small granules. **2** *Commerce* of extra quality.

superfluous *adj.* more than necessary. [*Say* soo PUR flu us]

supergiant *n.* a very large and bright star.

super giant slalom *n. Skiing* (also *informal* **super G**) a downhill event with a longer course and wider turns than a giant slalom.

superglue ● *n.* a very strong glue. ● *v.* (**superglues, superglued, supergluing**) stick with superglue.

supergroup *n.* **1** a group made up of several related groups. **2 a** an exceptional rock group. **b** a group of star musicians from different bands.

superheat *v.* heat above its boiling point, esp. without vaporization. □ **superheater** *n.*

superhero *n.* (*pl.* **superheroes**) a character with extraordinary abilities or attributes.

superhighway *n.* a highway with several lanes in each direction.

superhuman *adj.* **1** beyond normal human capability. **2** higher than human. □ **superhumanly** *adv.*

superimpose *v.* (**superimposes, superimposed, superimposing**) lay on something else. □ **superimposition** *n.* [*Say* super im POZE, super im POSITION]

superintend *v.* manage, supervise. □ **superintendence** *n.*

superintendent *n.* **1 a** a person who superintends. **b** a director or administrator. **2** a police officer ranking above either staff inspector or inspector. **3** a caretaker. **4** the chief administrator of a school division.

superior ● *adj.* **1** in a higher position or rank. **2 a** above average; better. **b** having a high opinion of oneself. ● *n.* **1** a person superior to another in rank, character, etc. **2** the head of a monastery etc. □ **superiority** *n.*

superior court *n.* the supreme court of a province.

superlative ● *adj.* **1** of the highest quality or degree. **2** expressing the highest degree of a quality. ● *n.* **1** *Grammar* the superlative form of a word. **2** (usu. in *pl.*) an expression of abundant praise. □ **superlatively** *adv.* [*Say* soo PUR luh tiv]

superman *n.* (*pl.* **supermen**) **1** an ideal man of the future, achieving domination through integrity and creativity. **2** *informal* a man of exceptional strength or ability.

supermarket *n.* a large store selling foods, household goods, etc.

superminister n. *Cdn* a cabinet minister responsible for a very important portfolio or portfolios.

supermodel n. a highly-paid, very famous model.

supermom n. *informal* a mother who fulfills all the duties of motherhood, esp. while also employed outside of the home.

supernatural ● adj. attributed to or thought to reveal some force above the laws of nature. ● n. supernatural, occult, or magical forces, effects, etc. □**supernaturalism** n. **supernaturally** adv.

supernova n. (pl. **supernovas** or **supernovae**) a star that suddenly becomes much brighter because of an explosion ejecting most of its mass. [*Say* SUPER no vuh; *for* SUPERNOVAE *say* SUPER no vee]

supernumerary ● adj. **1** in excess of the normal number. **2** engaged for extra work. **3** appearing on stage but not speaking. ● n. (pl. **supernumeraries**) a supernumerary person or thing. [*Say* super NUMER airy]

superpose v. (**superposes**, **superposed**, **superposing**) esp. *Math* place on or above something else. □**superposition** n.

superpower n. a state with supreme power and influence.

supersaturated adj. concentrated beyond saturation point. □**supersaturation** n.

superscript ● n. a character, number, or symbol written or printed above the line. ● adj. written or printed above the line.

supersede v. (**supersedes**, **superseded**, **superseding**) take the place of. [*Say* super SEED]

supersize ● adj. larger than average or standard sizes. ● n. a thing which is extremely large. ● v. select or provide a larger portion than normal of (food).

supersonic adj. designating or having a speed greater than that of sound. □**supersonically** adv.

superstar n. an extremely famous performer etc. □**superstardom** n.

superstition n. **1** an irrational belief or fear regarding supernatural influences. **2** a practice, opinion, or religion based on these. □**superstitious** adj. **superstitiously** adv.

superstore n. a very large supermarket or other store.

superstructure n. **1** the part of a building above its foundations. **2** a structure built on top of something else.

supervise v. (**supervises**, **supervised**, **supervising**) watch and direct the performance of or the work of. □**supervision** n. **supervisor** n. **supervisory** adj.

superwoman n. (pl. **superwomen**) *informal* a woman of exceptional strength or ability.

supine adj. **1** lying face upwards. **2** having the front part upwards. [*Say* SOO pine]

supper n. the evening meal. □**sing for one's supper** do something in return for a benefit.

suppertime n. the time at which supper is customarily served.

supplant v. dispossess and take the place of. [*Say* suh PLANT]

supple adj. (**suppler**, **supplest**) **1** flexible, easily bent. **2** graceful. □**suppleness** n.

supplement ● n. **1** a part added to remedy deficiencies or add information. **2** a separate section added to a newspaper or periodical. **3** an additional charge payable for an extra service or facility. ● v. provide a supplement for. □**supplemental** adj. **supplementary** adj. **supplementation** n.

supplicant n. a person making a humble plea.

supplicate v. (**supplicates**, **supplicated**, **supplicating**) ask humbly. □**supplication** n. [*Say* SUP luh kate]

supplier n. a person or company that supplies goods.

supply¹ ● v. (**supplies**, **supplied**, **supplying**) **1** provide. **2** meet or make up for. **3** fill as a substitute. ● n. (pl. **supplies**) **1** the action of providing what is needed. **2** a store or amount of something. **3** (in pl.) **a** food etc. necessary for maintenance or an activity. **b** the provisions and equipment for an army etc. **c** a grant of money by Parliament for the costs of government. **4** (often as an adj.) a teacher, clergy member, etc. acting as a substitute. □**in short supply** available in limited quantity. [*Say* suh PLY]

supply² adv. in a supple manner. [*Say* SUPPLE ee]

supply and demand n. the amount of a product available and needed, as factors regulating its price.

support ● v. **1** bear all or part of the weight of. **2** provide with a home and the necessities of life. **3** confirm or back up. **4** give assistance, encouragement, or approval to. **5** endure. **6** contribute to. **7** allow the use or operation of. ● n. **1** the action of supporting. **2** a person or thing that supports. **3** encouragement, assistance, financial aid etc. **4** money paid to a former spouse and/or their children. ● *adj.* reinforced with elastic fibres. □ **supportable** *adj.* **supporter** *n.*

supporting *adj.* **1** having an important but not leading part. **2** helping to confirm. **3** carrying weight.

supportive *adj.* providing support or encouragement. □ **supportiveness** *n.*

suppose *v.* (**supposes, supposed, supposing**) **1** assume, esp. without knowledge. **2** take as a possibility. **3** as a formula of proposal. **4** require as a condition. **5** if. □ **I suppose so** an expression of hesitant agreement.

supposed *adj.* **1** used to show doubt about a generally accepted claim etc. **2** generally believed. **3 a** expected or required. **b** allowed. **4** intended. □ **supposedly** *adv.*

supposition *n.* an uncertain belief. [*Say* suppa ZISH'n]

suppository *n.* (*pl.* **suppositories**) a medical preparation to be inserted into the rectum or vagina to melt. [*Say* suh POZZA tory *or* suh POZZA tree]

suppress *v.* (**suppresses, suppressed, suppressing**) **1** end the activity or existence of. **2** prevent from being known or expressed. **3** *Psychology* keep out of one's consciousness. □ **suppression** *n.* **suppressive** *adj.* **suppressor** *n.* [*Say* suh PRESS]

suppressant *n.* a suppressing or restraining substance. [*Say* suh PRESS int]

suppurating *adj.* forming pus. [*Say* SUP yuh rating]

supranational *adj.* involving more than one country. [*Say* soop ruh NATIONAL]

supremacist *n.* a believer in the supremacy of a particular race, sex, etc. [*Say* soo PREMMA sist]

supremacy *n.* (*pl.* **supremacies**) the condition of being superior to all others. [*Say* soo PREMMA see]

supreme *adj.* **1** highest in importance, power, or quality. **2** greatest in amount or degree. **3** ultimate; resulting in death. □ **reign** (or **rule**) **supreme 1** be dominant. **2** be widespread. □ **supremely** *adv.* [*Say* soo PREEM]

Supreme Being *n.* an all-powerful God.

Supreme Court *n.* the highest judicial court of appeal in a country, province, etc.

surcharge *n.* a fee charged in addition to the normal cost of something.

sure ● *adj.* **1** certain. reliable or secure. ● *adv. informal* certainly. ● *interj.* yes. □ **make sure of** establish the truth of. **sure enough** *informal* **1** in fact. **2** almost certainly. **sure of oneself** self-confident.

to be sure it is undeniable. □ **sureness** *n.*

surefire *adj. informal* reliable.

sure-footed *adj.* **1** treading safely without slipping. **2** not likely to make a mistake. □ **sure-footedness** *n.*

surely *adv.* **1** indeed. **2** used to express a strong belief in the statement qualified. **3** without fail.

Sûreté *n.* (also **Sûreté du Québec**) *Cdn* the provincial police force of Quebec. [*Say* soora TAY]

surety *n.* (*pl.* **sureties**) **1** a person who assumes responsibility for the obligation of another. **2** money given as a guarantee. **3** certainty. [*Say* SHOORA tee]

surf ● *n.* the swell of the sea breaking on the shore etc. ● *v.* **1** ride the crest of a wave towards, esp. on a surfboard. **2 a** flip between television channels using a remote control. **b** search (the Internet) to sample various sites. □ **surfer** *n.* **surfing** *n.*

surface ● *n.* **1** the upper or outside part of something. **2** the superficial level or appearance of a person or thing. **3** a relatively flat horizontal space. **4** *Geometry* a continuous two-dimensional extent. ● *v.* (**surfaces, surfaced, surfacing**) **1** cover with a particular type of surface. **2 a** rise to the surface of esp. water. **b** become apparent. □ **surfaced** *adj.*

surface tension *n.* the property causing the surface of a liquid to behave as if covered with a weak elastic skin.

surfactant *n.* a substance which reduces surface tension of a liquid. [*Say* sir FACK tint]

surf and turf *n.* a restaurant meal combining seafood and steak.

surfboard *n.* a long narrow fibreglass board on which a surfer is carried with a breaking wave.

surfeit *n.* an excessive amount. □ **surfeited** *adj.* [*Say* SIR fit]

surge ● *n.* **1** a sudden or violent rush etc. **2** a high rolling swell of water. **3** a rapid increase in price, voltage, etc. **4** a heavy forward or upward motion of a large mass, volume, etc. ● *v.* (**surges, surged, surging**) **1** rise and move forward in great waves. **2** move forward or increase suddenly and dramatically.

surgeon *n.* a medical practitioner qualified to practise surgery. [*Say* SIR jin]

Surgeon General *n.* (*pl.* **Surgeons General**) **1** (in the US) the senior medical officer of the Bureau of Public Health. **2** the senior officer in medical service of the armed forces.

surgery *n.* (*pl.* **surgeries**) **1** the medical

treatment of injuries or disorders by cutting open the body and repairing or replacing parts. **2** the area where surgery is performed.

surge suppressor n. (also **surge protector**) a device that protects against damage from a power surge. □**surge suppression** n.

surgical adj. **1** relating to surgeons or surgery. **2** used or worn by surgeons or during surgery. **3** designating a swift and precise military attack. □**surgically** adv.

surly adj. (**surlier, surliest**) **1** rude, unfriendly. **2** hostile. □**surliness** n. [Say SIR lee]

surmise ● v. (**surmises, surmised, surmising**) suppose without having sufficient evidence. ● n. a guess.

surmount v. **1** overcome. **2** rest on top of or be situated on or above.

surname n. a hereditary name common to all members of a family.

surpass v. (**surpasses, surpassed, surpassing**) **1** be greater or better than. **2** go beyond, exceed. □**surpassing** adj. **surpassingly** adv.

surplice n. Christianity a loose white vestment with wide sleeves, worn by some clergy and choristers. [Say SIR pliss]

surplus ● n. (pl. **surpluses**) **1** an amount left over when requirements have been met. **2** an excess of revenue over expenditure. ● adj. exceeding what is needed or used.

surprise ● n. **1** an unexpected or astonishing thing. **2** astonishment. **3** a gift. **4** (as an adj.) unexpected. **5** a dish prepared with ingredients not made known. ● v. (**surprises, surprised, surprising**) **1** cause to feel astonishment. **2 a** startle with a sudden approach. **b** attack by surprise. ● interj. used as an exclamation as a surprise is revealed. □**surprise, surprise** ironic just as one might expect. **take** (or **catch**) **by surprise** startle or astonish with a surprise. □**surprised** adj. **surprising** adj. **surprisingly** adv.

surreal adj. very strange, more like a dream than reality. □**surreally** adv. [Say sir REAL]

Surrealism n. a 20th-century movement in art and literature aiming to express the subconscious and move beyond conventions of reality. □**Surrealist** n. & adj. [Say sir REALISM]

surrealistic adj. **1** (**Surrealistic**) based on, influenced by, or pertaining to Surrealism or the Surrealists. **2** characteristic or suggestive of Surrealism. □**surrealistically** adv. [Say sir REALISTIC]

surrender ● v. **1 a** cease resistance. **b** give up possession or control of. **2** (also **surrender oneself**) abandon oneself entirely to some influence etc. **3** Sport give up or allow (a goal etc.). ● n. the action of surrendering.

surreptitious adj. obtained, done, etc. in secret. □**surreptitiously** adv. [Say sir up TISH iss]

surrogacy n. the practice of surrogate motherhood. [Say SIR uh guh see]

surrogate n. a person or thing taking the place of another. [Say SIR uh git]

surrogate mother n. **1** a woman who bears a child for another woman. **2** a person or animal acting the role of mother.

surround ● v. **1** stand or be situated around. **2** place people or things on all sides of. **3** form the entourage of. **4** exist as a predominant aspect of. ● n. a structure placed around something.

surrounding ● adj. located or situated around. ● n. (in pl.) all the objects, conditions, etc. that are around.

surround sound n. a system of sound reproduction in which several speakers create a sense of space and depth.

surtax ● n. (pl. **surtaxes**) **1** a higher rate of tax levied on high personal incomes. **2** any additional tax on something already taxed. ● v. (**surtaxes, surtaxed, surtaxing**) impose a surtax on. [Say SIR tax]

surveillance n. **1** close observation or supervision. **2** a security device used to monitor premises etc. [Say sir VAIL ince]

survey ● n. **1** a general discussion, treatment, etc. **2** a collection and analysis of data relating to the opinions, habits, etc. of a population. **3 a** the process of surveying land or property. **b** a map or plan based on such a survey. **4** a close inspection. ● v. **1** make a general and comprehensive assessment of. **2** record or ascertain the opinions of. **3** determine the boundaries, extent, and ownership of (land etc.). □**surveying** n. **surveyor** n.

survivable adj. able to be survived. □**survivability** n.

survival n. **1** the state of continuing to live or exist. **2** the practice of coping with harsh conditions as a leisure activity etc. □**survival of the fittest** the continued existence of the organisms best adapted to their environment, as a concept in the Darwinian theory of evolution.

survivalism n. **1** a policy of trying to ensure survival. **2** the practising of outdoor survival skills as a sport. □**survivalist** n. & adj.

survival kit n. first aid supplies,

emergency rations, etc., for use when stranded or lost.

survive v. (**survives, survived, surviving**) **1** continue to live or exist. **2** live or exist longer than. **3** remain alive after going through. □ **survivor** n.

susceptible adj. **1** likely to be affected; vulnerable. **2** impressionable, sensitive. □ **susceptibility** n. [Say suh SEPTA bull, suh septa BILLA tee]

sushi n. a Japanese snack of cold boiled rice with seaweed, vegetables, and often raw fish. [Say SOOSHY]

suspect ● v. **1** imagine to be possible; believe tentatively. **2** doubt the innocence or genuineness of. ● n. a person suspected of an offence etc. ● adj. subject to suspicion. □ **suspected** adj.

suspend v. **1** attach to something above so that it hangs freely. **2** cause to float or be elevated without attachment. **3** postpone or delay. **4** halt temporarily. **5** temporarily remove or expel as a punishment etc. □ **suspend disbelief** refrain from being skeptical.

suspended animation n. a temporary cessation of the vital functions.

suspended sentence n. a judicial sentence that is not enforced if the offender commits no further offence within a specified period.

suspenders pl. n. a pair of straps worn to hold the pants up.

suspense n. **1** a state of anxious uncertainty about what will happen. **2** a quality in fiction etc. that arouses excited expectation. □ **suspenseful** adj.

suspension n. **1** the action of suspending or the state of being suspended. **2** (also **suspension system**) the system of springs and shocks that supports a vehicle on its axles. **3** a mixture in which small particles are distributed throughout a fluid.

suspension bridge n. a bridge with a deck suspended from cables supported by towers.

suspicion n. **1** a feeling that someone is guilty of a crime etc. **2** a faint belief. **3** a cautious distrust. □ **above suspicion** too obviously good etc. to be suspected. **under suspicion** thought to be guilty of wrongdoing.

suspicious adj. **1** feeling or prone to suspicion. **2** indicating suspicion. **3** inviting suspicion. □ **suspiciously** adv. **suspiciousness** n.

suss v. (**susses, sussed, sussing**) informal (usu. foll. by out) **1** investigate, check out. **2** figure out.

sustain v. **1** support, keep alive. **2** endure. **3** undergo or suffer. **4** keep going continuously. **5** uphold or decide in favour of. **6** give strength to. **7** substantiate. **8** hold the weight of. □ **sustained** adj.

sustainable adj. **1** avoiding depletion of natural resources. **2** that may be maintained. □ **sustainability** n. **sustainably** adv.

sustenance n. **1** nourishment needed to stay alive. **2** the process of sustaining esp. life. [Say SUSTA nince]

Sutra n. (pl. **Sutras**) **1** a wise phrase, or collection of these, in Hindu literature. **2** a narrative part of Buddhist literature. **3** Jainist scripture. [Say SOOTRA]

suttee n. (pl. **suttees**) esp. hist. the Hindu practice of a widow committing suicide on her husband's funeral pyre. [Say suh TEE or SUT ee]

suture ● n. **1 a** a stitch or row of stitches joining of the edges of a wound etc. **b** the material used for this. **2** the junction of two bones forming an immovable articulation. ● v. (**sutures, sutured, suturing**) stitch up with a suture. □ **sutured** adj. [Say SOO chur]

SUV abbr. (pl. **SUVs**) a sport-utility vehicle.

svelte adj. slender. [Say SVELT]

Svengali n. (pl. **Svengalis**) a person who exercises a controlling influence on another. [Say sven GALLEY]

SW abbr. **1** southwest. **2** southwestern. **3** shortwave.

swab ● n. **1** an absorbent pad. **2** a mop etc. ● v. (**swabs, swabbed, swabbing**) clean, absorb, or apply with a swab. [Say SWOB]

swaddle v. (**swaddles, swaddled, swaddling**) **1** wrap in garments or cloth. **2** surround with. [Say SWODDLE]

swaddling clothes pl. n. hist. strips of bandage wrapped around a newborn child to quieten it. [Say SWODDLING]

swag n. **1** slang the stolen goods carried off by a thief. **2** a curtain or drapery fastened to hang loosely and sag in the middle. **3** an ornamental arrangement of flowers, leaves, or fruit.

swagger ● v. **1** walk or behave with confidence or toughness. **2** talk boastfully. ● n. **1** an attitude of cockiness or toughness. **2** a swaggering gait. □ **swaggering** adj. **swaggeringly** adv.

Swahili n. (pl. **Swahili**) a member of a people of eastern Africa, or their widely spoken language. □ **Swahili** adj. [Say swuh HEELY]

swain n. literary a young lover.

swale n. a low or hollow place.

swallow¹ ● *v.* **1** cause or allow to pass down the throat. **2** perform the muscular movement of the esophagus required to do this. **3** accept. **4** repress. **5** engulf or consume. ● *n.* **1** the act of swallowing. **2** an amount swallowed in one action. □ **swallower** *n.*

swallow² *n.* a migratory swift-flying bird with a forked tail.

swallowtail *n.* **1** anything resembling a swallow's deeply forked tail. **2** a butterfly with wings in this shape. □ **swallow-tailed** *adj.*

swam *past of* SWIM.

swami *n.* (*pl.* **swamis**) a Hindu male religious teacher. [*Say* SWOMMY]

swamp ● *n.* a tract of low-lying ground in which water collects. ● *v.* **1 a** overwhelm. **b** fill or become filled with water. **2** clear (a road) in a forest by felling trees etc. □ **swampy** *adj.*

swamped *adj.* overwhelmed with work.

swamper *n. Cdn* a person who clears logging roads.

swampland *n.* land consisting of swamps.

Swampy Cree *n.* a member or dialect of a Cree people living in northern Manitoba and near western James Bay and Hudson Bay.

swan *n.* a large web-footed white (or sometimes black) swimming bird with a long neck.

swan dive *n.* **1** a forward dive with the arms extended sideways until the diver is close to the surface of the water, at which point the arms are brought together over the head. **2** *jocular* a dramatic or spectacular fall, plunge, or dive.

swank *informal* ● *n.* **1** style, elegance. **2** flashiness. ● *adj.* stylish. □ **swanky** *adj.* (**swankier, swankiest**)

swan song *n.* a final work or performance before retirement or death.

swap ● *v.* (**swaps, swapped, swapping**) exchange. ● *n.* an act of swapping. □ **swapper** *n.*

swarm ● *n.* **1** a cluster of bees leaving the hive with the queen to establish a new colony. **2** a large number of insects or birds moving in a cluster. **3** any large or dense group. ● *v.* **1** gather or move in a swarm. **2** be crowded or infested. **3** (of a group) fill (an area). **4** climb rapidly using hands and feet.

swarming *n.* an attack on an individual by a group of attackers who taunt, shove, etc. until the victim is too intimidated or confused to resist theft or assault.

swarthy *adj.* (**swarthier, swarthiest**) of a dark complexion. □ **swarthiness** *n.* [*Say* SWOR thee]

swashbuckler *n.* an ostentatiously daring adventurer. □ **swashbuckling** *adj. & n.*

swastika *n.* (*pl.* **swastikas**) **1** an ancient symbol of a cross with each of its four arms of equal length bent at right angles, usu. in a clockwise direction. **2** this used as the emblem of Nazi Germany and anti-Semitic etc. hate groups. [*Say* swaw STEEKA *or* SWOSS tick uh]

SWAT *n.* (also **SWAT team**) (in the US) a special police detachment trained to deal with terrorism, hostage-takings, etc. [*Say* SWOT]

swat ● *v.* (**swats, swatted, swatting**) **1** crush with a sharp blow. **2** slap, smack. **3** direct a blow at a target. ● *n.* a sharp slap or hit. □ **swatter** *n.*

swatch *n.* (*pl.* **swatches**) a sample of cloth, paint colour, etc. [*Say* SWOTCH]

swath ● *n.* (*pl.* **swaths**) **1** a row or line of grass, wheat, etc. as it falls when cut down. **2** a broad strip or area. ● *v.* cut (grain etc.) with a swather. [*Say* SWOTH]

swathe *v.* (**swathes, swathed, swathing**) **1** wrap in bandages etc. **2** cover in or under. [*Rhymes either with* CLOTH *or with* BATHE]

swather *n.* a machine used to cut grain and deposit it in a row to dry and be collected. [*Rhymes with* FATHER, *though it may have the* TH *of* THIN]

sway ● *v.* **1** move or swing slowly back and forth. **2** waver. **3** influence or control. **4** bend or lean to one side. ● *n.* **1** power or influence. **2** a to-and-fro movement.

Swazi *n.* (*pl.* **Swazi** *or* **Swazis**) a person from or the language of Swaziland and parts of Eastern Transvaal in South Africa. □ **Swazi** *adj.* [*Say* SWOZZY]

swear *v.* (**swears;** *past* **swore;** *past participle* **sworn; swearing**) **1** promise solemnly or on oath. **2** *informal* state emphatically. **3** cause to take an oath. **4** use profane language. **5** *informal* have great confidence in. □ **swear in** induct into office etc. by administering an oath. **swear off** *informal* vow to abstain from. □ **swearing** *n.*

swearing-in *n.* a ceremony at which a person swears to accept the conditions of an office.

swear word *n.* a profanity.

sweat ● *n.* **1** moisture exuded through the pores of the skin. **2** a state of sweating. **3** *informal* a state of anxiety. **4** *informal* drudgery, effort. **5** condensed moisture on a surface. **6** (in *pl.*) *informal* **a** = a sweatsuit.

b sweatpants. **c** a sweatshirt. ● *v.* (**sweats**; *past* and *past participle* **sweated** or **sweat**; **sweating**) **1** exude sweat. **2** be terrified, suffering, etc. **3** exhibit surface moisture. **4** drudge, toil. **5** *informal* worry about. □ **by the sweat of one's brow** by one's own hard work. **no sweat** *informal* **1** there is no need to worry. **2** without any difficulty. **sweat it out** *informal* endure a difficult experience to the end.

sweatband *n.* a band of absorbent material worn to soak up sweat.

sweater *n.* **1** a usu. knitted garment covering the upper half of the body. **2** a sports jersey. □ **sweatered** *adj.*

sweat lodge *n.* a structure heated by pouring water over hot stones, used by some Aboriginal groups to induce sweating, as for religious or medical purposes.

sweatpants *pl. n.* loose fleece pants worn as casual attire or for sports.

sweatshirt *n.* a loosely fitting long-sleeved fleece top.

sweatshop *n.* a factory where workers work long hours in unpleasant conditions for low pay.

sweatsuit *n.* a suit of a sweatshirt and sweatpants.

sweaty *adj.* (**sweatier**, **sweatiest**) **1** damp with or smelling of sweat. **2** causing sweat. □ **sweatily** *adv.*

Swede *n.* a person from Sweden.

swede saw *n.* *Cdn* a type of hand saw with a bow-like tubular frame and many cutting teeth.

Swedish *adj.* relating to Sweden or its people or language. □ **Swedish** *n.*

sweep ● *v.* (**sweeps**, **swept**, **sweeping**) **1** clean or push with or as with a broom. **2** dismiss. **3** drive along with force. **4** remove or clear forcefully. **5** move or cross swiftly. **6** impart a sweeping motion to. **7** pass over in order to search for something. **8** include in the line of fire. **9** win every event, award, etc. in (a contest). ● *n.* **1 a** a long, swift movement. **b** an act of sweeping. **2** a long curved stretch of road etc. **3** range or scope. **4** victory in every event etc. contested. **5** a comprehensive search or survey. **6** a chimney sweep. □ **make a clean sweep of 1** completely abolish. **2** win all the prizes etc. in. **sweep away 1** abolish swiftly. **2** (usu. in *passive*) powerfully affect emotionally. **sweep a person off his** (or **her**) **feet** affect a person with powerful emotion.

sweeper *n.* **1** a person or device that sweeps. **2** *Cdn* **a** a tree overhanging a stream etc. **b** a drifting log in a stream etc. **3** *Curling* a player who sweeps in front of a moving rock with a broom or brush.

sweeping ● *adj.* **1** wide in range. **2** ignoring particular cases or exceptions. **3** complete. **4** passing over a wide area. ● *n.* (in *pl.*) dirt etc. collected by sweeping. □ **sweepingly** *adv.*

sweepstakes *n.* (also **sweepstake**) **1** a form of gambling in which all the money bet on a result is paid to the winners. **2** a race with betting of this kind.

sweet ● *adj.* **1** having the pleasant taste of sugar or honey. **2** smelling or sounding pleasant. **3 a** not salty, sour, or bitter. **b** fresh and pure. **4** highly gratifying. **5** pleasant. **6** *informal* pretty, charming. **7** (foll. by *on*) *informal* fond of. ● *n.* **1** (in *pl.*) sweet foods. **2** a sweet part of something. **3** sweetheart. □ **sweetish** *adj.*

sweet-and-sour *adj.* cooked in a sauce containing sugar and vinegar or lemon juice etc.

sweetbread *n.* the pancreas or thymus of an animal, used for food.

sweet chestnut *n.* a large European tree that produces edible chestnuts within bristly cases.

sweeten *v.* **1** make or become sweet or sweeter in smell, taste, or sound. **2** make fresh or wholesome; purify. **3** make agreeable or less painful. **4** increase the attractiveness or value of (a deal, proposal, etc.). **5** *Cards informal* increase the stakes in (a pot).

sweetener *n.* **1** a substance used to sweeten food or drink, esp. any of various low-calorie sugar substitutes. **2** a thing that makes something more pleasant, agreeable, or tolerable. **3** *informal* a bribe or inducement.

sweetgrass *n.* **1** any of several fragrant grasses used in basket making. **2** any of various grasses or other plants relished by cattle for their sweet succulent foliage.

sweetheart *n.* **1** a person with whom one is in love. **2** a term of endearment. **3** a lovable, amiable, or obliging person.

sweetheart deal *n.* (also **sweetheart contract**) *informal* an industrial agreement reached privately by employers and union leaders in their own interests.

sweetie *n. informal* **1** (also **sweetie pie**) a term of endearment (esp. as a form of address). **2** = SWEETHEART 3.

sweetly *adv.* **1** in a pleasant way. **2** in a way that smells sweet. **3** without difficulties or problems.

sweetmeat *n.* **1** a confectionery item, e.g. a preserved or candied fruit, a sugared nut, etc. **2** a small fancy cake.

sweetness *n.* the quality of being sweet. □ **sweetness and light** a pleasant or enjoyable experience, situation, or person.

sweet pea *n.* a climbing plant of the pea family with colourful fragrant flowers.

sweet pepper *n.* a relatively mild-tasting pepper.

sweet potato *n.* an edible tuberous root of a Central American trailing plant, with a slightly sweet white or orange flesh.

sweet talk *informal* ● *n.* flattery. ● *v.* (**sweet-talk**) flatter in order to persuade. □ **sweet-talking** *adj.*

sweet tooth *n.* a liking for sweet-tasting things.

swell ● *v.* (**swells**; *past* **swelled**; *past participle* **swollen** or **swelled**; **swelling**) **1** grow or become more intense. **2** rise up from the surrounding surface. **3** bulge. **4** be filled with an emotion. ● *n.* **1** an act or the state of swelling. **2** the heaving of the sea with waves that do not break. **3** a crescendo. **4** *informal* a fashionable or outstanding person. ● *adj.* **1** *informal* fine, excellent. **2** *informal* fashionable.

swelled head *n.* *informal* excessive pride.

swelling *n.* an abnormal enlargement of a body part, due to injury or illness.

sweltering *adj.* uncomfortably hot. □ **swelteringly** *adv.*

swept *past and past participle of* SWEEP.

swerve ● *v.* (**swerves**, **swerved**, **swerving**) change direction abruptly. ● *n.* **1** a swerving movement. **2** divergence from a course.

swift ● *adj.* **1** soon coming or passing. **2** speedy. **3** *informal* smart. ● *n.* **1** a swift-flying insect-eating bird with long wings that resembles a swallow. **2** *Cdn* an area of rapidly flowing current in a river. □ **swiftly** *adv.* **swiftness** *n.*

swig *informal* ● *v.* (**swigs**, **swigged**, **swigging**) drink in large drafts. ● *n.* a large swallow, esp. of liquor.

swill ● *v.* drink greedily. ● *n.* **1** scraps of waste food. **2** inferior liquor. **3** worthless matter.

swim ● *v.* (**swims**; *past* **swam**; *past participle* **swum**; **swimming**) **1** propel oneself through water using the body. **2** float on or be immersed in a liquid. **3** have a dizzy effect or sensation. ● *n.* an act or period of swimming. □ **swimmer** *n.* **swimming** *n.*

swim bladder *n.* a gas-filled sac in fish used to maintain buoyancy.

swimmingly *adv.* easily.

swimsuit *n.* an esp. one-piece bathing suit worn by women.

swim trunks *pl. n.* (also **swimming trunks**) loose-fitting shorts worn by men for swimming.

swimwear *n.* clothing worn for swimming.

swindle ● *v.* (**swindles**, **swindled**, **swindling**) cheat a person of money etc. ● *n.* **1** an act of swindling. **2** a fraudulent scheme. □ **swindler** *n.*

swine *n.* **1** (*pl.* **swine**) a pig. **2** (*pl.* **swine** or **swines**) *informal* a contemptible person. □ **swinish** *adj.*

swing ● *v.* (**swings**, **swung**, **swinging**) **1** move with a to-and-fro or curving motion. **2** revolve. **3** move around to the opposite direction. **4** change from one opinion or mood to another. **5** attempt to hit. **6** *informal* **a** be trendy and modern. **b** be promiscuous. **7** *informal* be lively. **8** have a decisive influence on. **9** *informal* deal with or achieve. **10** *informal* be executed by hanging. ● *n.* **1** an act of swinging. **2** a swift tour involving a number of stops. **3** a swinging gait or rhythm. **4** a seat slung by ropes or chains etc. for swinging on or in. **5 a** jazz music with an easy flowing but vigorous rhythm. **b** dance performed to this. **c** the rhythmic drive of this music. **6** a discernible change in opinion (often as an *adj.*). **7** an attempted punch. □ **get (back) into the swing of things** get used to (or return to) being easy and relaxed about an activity. □ **swinger** *n.* (esp. in sense 6 of *verb*) **swinging** *adj.*

swinging bridge *n.* a footbridge suspended from cables, which swings from side to side when walked on.

swingman *n.* (*pl.* **swingmen**) a versatile player.

swingy *adj.* (**swingier**, **swingiest**) **1** (of music) characterized by swing. **2** designed to swing with body movement. **3** *Curling* (of ice) on which the lateral movement of a rock is greater than normal.

swipe ● *v.* (**swipes**, **swiped**, **swiping**) **1** hit hard and recklessly with a sweeping motion. **2** *informal* steal. **3** pass (a card with magnetic data) through an electronic device that reads and processes the data. ● *n.* **1** a swinging blow. **2** a sharp criticism. □ **swiper** *n.*

swipe card *n.* a plastic card bearing magnetically encoded information which is read when the edge of the card is slid through an electronic device.

swirl ● *v.* **1** move or flow or carry along with or as with a whirling motion. **2** give a twisted form to. ● *n.* **1** a twist or curl. **2** commotion. □ **swirly** *adj.*

swish ● *v.* (**swishes**, **swished**, **swishing**) **1** move with a rustling or hissing sound. **2** cause to make such a sound. **3** swing audibly through the air, grass, etc. **4** *Basketball* sink (a shot) without the ball touching the backboard or rim. ● *n.* **1** a swishing action or sound. **2** *Basketball informal* a shot that goes through the basket without touching the backboard or rim.

swishy *adj.* **1** making a swishing sound. **2** *slang* effeminate.

Swiss *adj.* relating to Switzerland or its people. □ **Swiss** *n.*

Swiss Army knife *n.* a pocket knife incorporating multiple blades and other tools.

Swiss chard *n.* a kind of beet with edible white stalks.

Swiss cheese ● *n.* a mild hard yellow cheese with many large holes in it. ● *adj.* (**Swiss-cheese**) characterized by large holes or spaces.

switch ● *n.* (*pl.* **switches**) **1** a device for making and breaking an electrical connection. **2 a** a transfer or deviation. **b** an exchange. **3** a flexible shoot cut from a tree. **4** a light tapering rod. **5** a device for transferring a train from one railway track to another. ● *v.* (**switches, switched, switching**) **1** turn on or off. **2** change or transfer position, subject, etc. **3** reverse the positions of. □ **switch off** *informal* cease to pay attention. □ **switchable** *adj.* **switcher** *n.*

switchback *n.* a railway or road with 180° bends.

switchblade *n.* a pocket knife with the blade released by a spring.

switchboard *n.* a central panel in an office etc. for the manual control of telephone connections.

switch-hit *v.* (**switch-hits, switch-hit, switch-hitting**) *Baseball* bat or be able to bat either right- or left-handed. □ **switch hitter** *n.* **switch-hitting** *adj.*

switchover *n.* a change.

swivel ● *n.* (often as an *adj.*) a fastening or coupling device between two parts enabling one to revolve without turning the other. ● *v.* (**swivels, swivelled, swivelling**) turn on or as on a swivel. [*Say* SWIV'll]

swivel chair *n.* a chair with a seat able to be turned horizontally.

swizzle stick *n.* a stick used for stirring drinks.

swollen ● *v. past participle of* SWELL. ● *adj.* enlarged by or as if by swelling.

swoon ● *v.* **1** be emotionally overwhelmed by. **2** *literary* faint. ● *n.* an instance of swooning. □ **swoony** *adj.*

swoop ● *v.* **1** descend rapidly like a bird of prey. **2** make a sudden attack. ● *n.* an act of swooping.

swoosh ● *n.* (*pl.* **swooshes**) **1** the noise of a sudden rush of liquid, air, etc. **2** a curved, wavy, or elliptical design as part of a corporate logo. ● *v.* (**swooshes, swooshed, swooshing**) move or cause to move with this noise.

sword *n.* **1** a weapon with a usu. metal blade and hilt with a hand guard. **2** (**the sword**) military power and violence.

swordfish *n.* (*pl.* **swordfish** or **swordfishes**) a large edible marine fish with a streamlined body and a flattened sword-like snout.

swordplay *n.* fencing.

swordsman *n.* (*pl.* **swordsmen**) a person who fights with a sword. □ **swordsmanship** *n.*

swore *past of* SWEAR.

sworn ● *v. past participle of* SWEAR. ● *adj.* bound by oath.

swum *past participle of* SWIM.

swung *past and past participle of* SWING.

sybarite *n.* a self-indulgent person fond of luxury. □ **sybaritic** *adj.* **sybaritism** *n.* [*Say* SIBBA rite, sibba RIT ick]

sycamore *n.* **1** an eastern N American plane tree, which has greyish-brown peeling bark. **2** (also **sycamore maple**) a large maple of Eurasia, with winged seeds. **3** *Bible* a Middle Eastern fig tree. [*Say* SICKA more]

sycophant *n.* a person who insincerely praises important people to win their favour. □ **sycophantic** *adj.* **sycophantically** *adv.* [*Say* SICKA fant *or* SIKE uh fant]

syllabi *pl.* of SYLLABUS. [*Say* SILLA bye]

syllabic ● *adj.* **1** of, relating to, or based on syllables. **2** (of a symbol) representing a whole syllable. ● *n.* **1** a list of characters representing the syllables used in a language and sometimes serving the purpose of an alphabet. **2** a syllabic symbol. [*Say* suh LABBICK]

syllabication *n.* (also **syllabification**) division into or articulation by syllables. [*Say* suh labba CAY sh'n, suh labba fuh CAY sh'n]

syllable *n.* **1** a unit of pronunciation uttered without interruption. **2** a character or characters representing a syllable. **3** (usu. with *neg.*) the least amount of speech or writing. □ **in words of one syllable** expressed bluntly. [*Say* SILLA bull]

syllabus *n.* (*pl.* **syllabuses** or **syllabi**) the program or outline of a course of study etc. [*Say* SILLA bus; SILLA bye]

syllogism *n.* a form of reasoning in which a conclusion is drawn from two premises. □ **syllogistic** *adj.* [*Say* SILLA jism]

sylph *n.* **1** an elemental spirit of the air. **2** a slender graceful woman or girl. □ **sylphlike** *adj.* [*Say* SILF]

sylvan *adj.* esp. *literary* **1** having or associated with woods; wooded. **2** pleasantly rural. [*Say* SILV'n]

symbiosis *n.* (*pl.* **symbioses**) **1** an interaction between two different organisms living in close physical association, usu. to the advantage of both. **2** a mutually advantageous relationship. □ **symbiotic** *adj.* **symbiotically** *adv.* [*Say* sim by OH sis, sim by OH seez; sim by OT ick]

symbol *n.* **1** a thing regarded as typifying or representing something. **2** a mark or character taken as the conventional sign of some object, idea, etc. □ **symbolic** *adj.* **symbolically** *adv.*

symbolism *n.* **1** the use of symbols to represent ideas. **2** symbolic meaning attached to objects. □ **symbolist** *n.*

symbolize *v.* (**symbolizes**, **symbolized**, **symbolizing**) **1** be a symbol of. **2** represent by means of symbols.

symbology *n.* (*pl.* **symbologies**) **1** the use or study of symbols. **2** symbols collectively. [*Say* sim BOLLA jee]

symmetry *n.* (*pl.* **symmetries**) **1** the quality of being made up of identical parts facing each other or around an axis. **2** pleasing proportion of the parts of a thing. **3** close or exact correspondence between different things. □ **symmetrical** *adj.* **symmetrically** *adv.* [*Say* SIMMA tree, suh METRIC'll]

sympathetic *adj.* **1** feeling or showing sympathy. **2** due to sympathy. **3** likeable. **4** inclined to favour. **5** (of pain etc.) caused by a pain in someone else or in another part of the body. **6** sounding by a vibration communicated from another vibrating object. **7** referring to the part of the nervous system supplying the internal organs, blood vessels, and glands. □ **sympathetically** *adv.*

sympathize *v.* (**sympathizes**, **sympathized**, **sympathizing**) **1** feel or express sympathy. **2** agree with a sentiment etc. □ **sympathizer** *n.*

sympathy *n.* (*pl.* **sympathies**) **1** the act of sharing in an emotion etc. of another person or thing. **2** a favourable attitude. **3** agreement in opinion or desire. **4** (as an *adj.*) in support of another cause.

symphonic *adj.* of or having the form or character of a symphony.

symphonically *adv.* [*Say* sim FONNICK]

symphony *n.* (*pl.* **symphonies**) **1** an elaborate composition usu. for full orchestra, and in several movements. **2** (also **symphony orchestra**) a large orchestra suitable for playing symphonies etc. [*Say* SIMFA nee]

symposium *n.* (*pl.* **symposia**) **1** a conference or meeting to discuss a particular subject. **2** a collection of essays or papers for this purpose. [*Say* sim POZEY um *for the singular,* sim POZEY uh *for the plural*]

symptom *n.* **1** a change in the physical or mental condition of a person, regarded as evidence of a disorder. **2** a sign of the existence of something. □ **symptomatic** *adj.* **symptomless** *adj.* [*Say* SIMP tum, simp tuh MAT ick]

synagogue *n.* the building where a Jewish assembly meets for religious observance and instruction. [*Say* SINNA gog]

synapse *n.* **1** a gap between two nerve cells, across which impulses are conducted. **2** (in *pl.*) the synapses in the brain, considered as an indicator of mental activity. □ **synaptic** *adj.* [*Say* SIN aps *or* suh NAPS, suh NAP tick]

sync (also **synch**) *informal* ● *n.* synchronization. ● *v.* (**synch**, **synchs**, **synched**, **synching**) synchronize. □ **in** (or **out of**) **sync** working well (or badly) together. [*Say* SINK]

synchro *n.* (*pl.* **synchros**) **1** a synchronizing device. **2** synchronized swimming. **3** synchronized skating. [*Say* SINK roe]

synchronicity *n.* the simultaneous occurrence of events which appear related but have no obvious connection. [*Say* sink ruh NISSA tee]

synchronize *v.* (**synchronizes**, **synchronized**, **synchronizing**) **1** occur or cause to occur at the same time. **2** coordinate, combine. □ **synchronization** *n.* [*Say* SINK ruh nize]

synchronized skating *n.* figure skating performed in unison by a team of 12 or more skaters. □ **synchronized skater** *n.*

synchronized swimming *n.* a sport in which teams of swimmers perform coordinated movements in time to music. □ **synchronized swimmer** *n.*

synchronous *adj.* existing or occurring at the same time. □ **synchronously** *adv.* [*Say* SINK ruh nus]

synchrony *n.* simultaneous action or occurrence. [*Say* SINK ruh nee]

syncline n. a fold of layered rock in the earth's crust, forming a trough-shaped depression in which the strata slope upwards from the middle. [Say SINK line]

syncopated adj. (of musical rhythm) having the strong accent shifted so that it falls on a normally weak beat. □ **syncopation** n. [Say SINKA pate]

syncretism n. the amalgamation of different cultures, religions, or schools of thought. □ **syncretic** adj. **syncretistic** adj. [Say SINK ruh tism, sin CRET ick]

syndicate ● n. **1** a combination of individuals or organizations to promote some common interest. **2** an association supplying material to a number of publications. **3** an organized crime group. ● v. (**syndicates, syndicated, syndicating**) **1** form into a syndicate. **2** publish or broadcast in a number of media at the same time. □ **syndication** n. **syndicator** n. [Say SIN duh kit for the noun, SIN duh kate for the verb]

syndrome n. **1** a group of symptoms which consistently occur together. **2** a characteristic combination of opinions, behaviour, etc. [Say SIN drome or SIN drum]

synecdoche n. a figure of speech in which a part is made to represent the whole or vice versa. [Say suh NECK duh key]

synergy n. (pl. **synergies**) the interaction of two things to produce an effect that exceeds the sum of their individual effects. □ **synergistic** adj. **synergistically** adv. [Say SINNER jee, sinner JISS tick]

synod n. **1** a church council attended by delegated clergy and sometimes laity. **2** a group of churches whose representatives meet regularly. **3** a Presbyterian church court above the presbyteries and subject to General Assembly. [Say SIN id]

synonym n. a word or phrase that means exactly or nearly the same as another in the same language. [Say SINNA nim]

synonymous adj. **1** having the same meaning. **2** suggestive of or associated with another. □ **synonymously** adv. [Say sin ONNA mus]

synopsis n. (pl. **synopses**) **1** a summary or outline. **2** a brief general survey. □ **synopsize** v. (**synopsizes, synopsized, synopsizing**) [Say sin OP sis for the singular, sin OP seez for the plural]

synoptic adj. **1** of, forming, or giving a synopsis. **2** taking a comprehensive mental view. **3** (**Synoptic**) designating any of the Gospels of Matthew, Mark, and Luke, which describe events from a similar point of view. [Say sin OPTIC]

synovial adj. relating to a viscous fluid lubricating joints and tendon sheaths. [Say sigh NO vee ul]

syntactic adj. of or according to syntax. □ **syntactical** adj. **syntactically** adv. [Say sin TACTIC]

syntax n. the arrangement of words and phrases to create sentences.

synth n. informal a synthesizer. [Say SINTH]

synthesis n. (pl. **syntheses**) **1** the process or result of building up separate elements into a connected whole. **2** a combination. **3** Chemistry the formation of a compound by combination of its elements. [Say SINTH uh sis for the singular, SINTH uh seez for the plural]

synthesize v. (**synthesizes, synthesized, synthesizing**) **1** make a synthesis of. **2** combine into a coherent whole. **3** (esp. as **synthesized** adj.) imitate electronically using a synthesizer. **4** make (something) by synthesis, esp. chemically. [Say SINTH uh size]

synthesizer n. an electronic musical instrument, usu. with a keyboard, producing sounds by generating and combining signals of different frequencies. [Say SINTH uh sizer]

synthetic ● adj. **1 a** made by chemical synthesis. **b** artificial. **2** insincere. **3** relating to synthesis. ● n. a synthetic substance. □ **synthetically** adv.

syphilis n. a sexually transmitted disease progressing from infection of the genitals via the skin and mucous membrane to the bones, muscles, and brain. □ **syphilitic** adj. & n. [Say SIFFA liss, siffa LIT ick]

Syrah n. a variety of black grape used in winemaking, or the wine produced from this. [Say SEERA]

Syrian n. a person from Syria. □ **Syrian** adj. [Say SEERY in]

syringe ● n. **1** a tube with a nozzle and piston or bulb for sucking in and ejecting liquid in a fine stream. **2** (also **hypodermic syringe**) a similar device with a hollow needle for insertion under the skin. ● v. (**syringes, syringed, syringing**) sluice or spray with a syringe. [Say suh RINDGE]

syrup n. any of various sweet liquids used in food, preserving, or medicine. □ **syrupy** adj.

system n. **1** a set of connected things, parts, institutions, etc. working together. **2** a person's body. **3** a method or classification. **4 a** a particular form of government, religion, etc. **b** (**the system**) the prevailing political or social order.

system administrator *n.* a person who administers a computer system or network.

systematic *adj.* done or acting according to a plan or system; methodical. □ **systematically** *adv.*

systematize *v.* (**systematizes**, **systematized**, **systematizing**) arrange according to an organized system. [*Say* SYSTEM a tize]

systemic *adj.* **1** of or concerning the whole body. **2** entering a plant via the roots or shoots and passing through the tissues.

3 of or pertaining to a system in its entirety. □ **systemically** *adv.* [*Say* siss TEM ick]

systems analysis *n.* the analysis of a complex process in order to improve its efficiency. □ **systems analyst** *n.*

Szechuan *n.* (also **Szechwan**) (as an *adj.*) designating food cooked in the distinctively spicy style originating in Sichuan, a province of west central China. [*Say* SETCH wahn *or* SESH wahn]

T *n.* (also **t**) (*pl.* **Ts** or **T's**) **1** the twentieth letter of the alphabet. **2** a T-shaped thing. **3** a T-shirt. □ **to a T** exactly.

t. *abbr.* **1** ton(s). **2** tonne(s).

T4 *n.* (*pl.* **T4's**) (also **T4 slip**) *Cdn* an official statement of an employee's earnings and deductions for the year, issued by an employer.

TA *informal* ● *n.* (*pl.* **TA's**) a teaching assistant, a graduate student hired to assist a professor, esp. by marking assignments and teaching seminars. ● *v.* (**TA's, TA'd, TA'ing**) work as a teaching assistant.

tab ● *n.* **1** a small flap or strip of material attached to something. **2** *informal* a bill or price. **3** a function on a keyboard etc. pre-setting a movement of the cursor. **4** a tabloid. **5** *slang* a tablet. ● *v.* (**tabs, tabbed, tabbing**) **1** provide with a tab or tabs. **2** label. □ **keep tabs on** *informal* **1** keep account of. **2** have under observation.

tabbouleh *n.* a Middle Eastern salad made with bulgur, parsley, onion, mint, lemon juice, oil, and spices. [*Say* tuh BOO lee]

tabby *n.* (*pl.* **tabbies**) (also **tabby cat**) a striped cat.

tabernacle *n.* **1** a tent used by the Israelites to house the Ark of the Covenant during the Exodus. **2** *Christianity* a niche or receptacle for the consecrated Eucharistic elements. **3** a place of worship.

tabla *n.* (*pl.* **tablas**) a pair of small drums played with the hands. [*Say* TAB luh *or* TOB luh]

table ● *n.* **1** a piece of furniture with a flat top and one or more legs. **2** a group seated at table for dinner etc. **3** a set of facts and figures systematically displayed in columns. **4** a flat surface for working on. **5** a table around which negotiations are conducted. ● *v.* (**tables, tabled, tabling**) **1** *Cdn & Brit.* formally propose for discussion at a meeting. **2** esp. *US* postpone consideration of. □ **on the table** offered for discussion. **turn the tables** reverse a situation to one's advantage. **under the table** *informal* done surreptitiously to avoid taxes etc.

tableau *n.* (*pl.* **tableaux**) a picturesque scene reminiscent of a painting.

[*Say* TAB loe *for the singular,* TAB loze *for the plural*]

tablecloth *n.* a cloth spread over a table.

table d'hôte *n.* (*pl.* **tables d'hôte**) a meal consisting of a set menu at a fixed price. [*Say* tab luh DOTE]

tableland *n.* an area of level high land.

table linen *n.* tablecloths and napkins.

table manners *pl. n.* correct behaviour while eating.

table saw *n.* a fixed circular saw mounted so that the blade projects through a slot in a metal table.

tablespoon *n.* **1** a large spoon used for serving food. **2** a measuring spoon equal to $^1/_2$ fluid ounce (approx. 15 ml). □ **tablespoonful** *n.* (*pl.* **tablespoonfuls**)

tablet *n.* **1** a small round or cylindrical pill. **2** a flat slab of stone or wood.

table tennis *n.* an indoor game played with small bats, a ball, and a table divided by a net.

tabletop *n.* the surface of a table.

tabletop hockey *n.* a game using a table resembling a miniature hockey rink with players controlled by connected rods.

tableware *n.* dishes, plates, etc., for use at meals.

table wine *n.* ordinary wine for a meal.

tabloid *n.* **1** a newspaper, usu. popular in style, having pages half the size of a broadsheet. **2** (as an *adj.*) designating sensational or lurid journalism etc.

taboo ● *n.* (*pl.* **taboos**) **1** a social or religious custom placing a ban or restriction on someone or something. **2** a prohibited thing. ● *adj.* prohibited, esp. by social custom. ● *v.* (**taboos, tabooed, tabooing**) prohibit.

tabular *adj.* arranged in tables or lists. [*Say* TAB you ler]

tabula rasa *n.* the human mind viewed as having no innate ideas. [*Say* tab you luh RAZZA]

tabulate *v.* (**tabulates, tabulated, tabulating**) arrange in the form of a table. □ **tabulation** *n.*

tachometer *n.* an instrument for measuring the working speed of an engine. [*Say* tuh COMMA ter]

tachycardia *n.* an abnormally rapid heart rate. [*Say* tacky CARDY uh]

tacit *adj.* understood or implied without being stated. □ **tacitly** *adv.* [*Say* TASS it]

taciturn *adj.* reserved in speech. □ **taciturnity** *n.* [*Say* TASSA turn, tassa TURN it ee]

tack¹ ● *n.* **1 a** a small broad-headed sharp nail. **b** a thumbtack. **2** a long stitch used in fastening fabrics temporarily. **3** (of a ship) an act or the direction of tacking. **4** a course of action. **5** a sticky condition of varnish etc. ● *v.* **1** fasten with or as if with tacks. **2** stitch lightly together. **3** annex, append (a thing). **4 a** change a ship's course by turning its head to the wind. **b** make a series of tacks in order to progress to windward. **5** change one's conduct or policy etc.

tack² ● *n.* the saddle, bridle, etc., of a horse. ● *v.* put tack on.

tackle ● *n.* **1** equipment for a task or sport. **2** a mechanism of ropes and pulleys etc. for lifting weights, managing sails, etc. **3** a windlass with its ropes and hooks. **4** an act of tackling in football etc. **5** *Football* the player next to the end of either the offensive or defensive line. ● *v.* (**tackles, tackled, tackling**) **1** try to deal with. **2 a** throw one's body at to stop or take down. **b** (in soccer etc.) obstruct or intercept (a player with the ball). **3** secure or lift by means of tackle. □ **tackler** *n.*

tackle box *n.* a box with many compartments for storing fishing tackle.

tacky *adj.* (**tackier, tackiest**) **1** still slightly sticky after application. **2** *informal* showing poor taste or quality. □ **tackiness** *n.*

taco *n.* (*pl.* **tacos**) a fried corn tortilla filled with ground meat or beans, etc. [*Say* TACKO *or* TOCKO]

taco shell *n.* a usu. crisp folded tortilla for tacos.

tact *n.* skill in dealing with others or with difficult issues. □ **tactful** *adj.* **tactfully** *adv.* **tactfulness** *n.* **tactless** *adj.*

tactic *n.* a method used to achieve something.

tactical *adj.* **1** done or planned to gain a specific end. **2** done or for use in immediate support of military or naval operations. **3** (of voting) aimed at preventing the strongest candidate from winning. □ **tactically** *adv.*

tactician *n.* someone skilled at planning how to achieve something. [*Say* tack TISH'n]

tactics *pl. n.* **1** (also treated as *sing.*) the art of disposing armed forces. **2** the immediate

or short-range means adopted in carrying out a scheme.

tactile *adj.* **1** of the sense of touch. **2** perceived by touch. **3** given to touching others, esp. as an unselfconscious expression of sympathy or affection. [*Say* TACK tile]

tad *n. informal* a small amount.

ta-dah *interj.* (also **ta-da**) expressing a dramatic revelation.

tadpole *n.* the larva of a frog, toad, etc., at the stage when it lives in water and has gills, a tail, and no legs.

tae kwon do *n.* a modern Korean martial art similar to karate. [*Say* tie kwon DOE]

taffeta *n.* (*pl.* **taffetas**) a fine lustrous silk or silk-like fabric. [*Say* TAFFA tuh]

taffy *n.* (*pl.* **taffies**) **1** a chewy confection similar to toffee. **2** *Cdn* a confection made by pouring hot maple syrup onto packed snow.

tag¹ ● *n.* **1 a** a label attached to a person or thing to indicate price, ownership, identity, etc. **b** an electronic device that can be attached to a person or thing for monitoring purposes. **2** *informal* a nickname or popular designation. **3** a motto or slogan. **4** a gang's or individual's identifying graffiti. ● *v.* (**tags, tagged, tagging**) **1** provide with a tag or label. **2** (often foll. by *on, on to*) add, esp. as an afterthought. **3** *informal* follow closely or trail behind. □ **tag along** (often foll. by *with*) go along with or accompany. □ **tagged** *adj.*

tag² ● *n.* a children's game in which one player chases the others, and whoever is caught then becomes "it". ● *v.* (**tags, tagged, tagging**) **1** touch a player in a game of tag. **2** *Baseball* touch a runner with the ball. **3** *informal* strike with a powerful punch or blow.

Tagalog *n.* (*pl.* **Tagalog** or **Tagalogs**) **1** a member of the principal people of the Philippines. **2** their language. □ **Tagalog** *adj.* [*Say* ta GAL og]

tagalong ● *n.* an esp. unwanted follower or companion. ● *adj.* **1** that is towed behind something else. **2** designating an unwelcome follower or companion.

tagger *n.* **1** a person who paints graffiti tags. **2** a computer program that inserts tags in text.

Tagish *n.* (*pl.* **Tagish**) **1** a member of an Aboriginal people living esp. in the southern Yukon. **2** their Athapaskan language. □ **Tagish** *adj.* [*Say* TAG ish]

tagliatelle *n.* a type of pasta made in narrow ribbons. [*Say* tal yuh TELLY]

tag line *n.* a catchphrase or slogan, esp. in advertising or as the punchline of a joke.

tag team *n.* **1** a pair of wrestlers who take turns fighting against the members of another pair. **2** two people working as a team.

tahini *n.* a paste or sauce made from ground sesame seeds. [*Say* tuh HEENY]

Tahitian *n.* **1** a native or inhabitant of Tahiti. **2** the Polynesian language of Tahiti. □ **Tahitian** *adj.* [*Say* tuh HEE sh'n *or* tuh HEETY un]

Tahltan *n.* (*pl.* **Tahltan** or **Tahltans**) **1** a member of an Aboriginal people living in the area of the Stikine River, BC. **2** their Athapaskan language. □ **Tahltan** *adj.* [*Say* TAWL tan]

tai chi *n.* (also **tai chi chuan**) a Chinese martial art and system of exercises consisting of sequences of very slow controlled movements. [*Say* tie CHEE, tie chee CHWON]

taiga *n.* (*pl.* **taigas**) any of the swampy subarctic coniferous forests below the Arctic tundra; the boreal forest. [*Say* TIE guh]

tail ● *n.* **1** the part at the rear of an animal that sticks out from the rest of the body. **2** the rear end or part of anything. **3** a luminous trail of dust extending from the head of a comet. **4** the hanging part of the back of a coat. **5** (in *pl.*) a tailcoat. **6** a twisted or braided tress of hair. **7** (often in *pl.*) the image on the reverse of a coin. **8** *informal* a detective, spy, etc. who secretly watches or follows a person. **9** *slang* the buttocks. ● *v.* **1** *informal* follow closely and secretly. **2** (of an object in flight) drift or curve away from a target. □ **on a person's tail** closely following a person. **tail off** (or **away**) diminish gradually. **with one's tail between one's legs** in a state of dejection or humiliation. □ **tailed** *adj.* **tailless** *adj.*

tailbone *n.* the small triangular bone at the base of the spinal column in humans.

tailcoat *n.* a man's coat with long tails at the back, worn as part of formal dress.

tail end *n.* **1** the conclusion or final part. **2** the back end of a thing.

tail fin *n.* **1** the rear fin of a fish. **2** a projection on the rear of a car or aircraft.

tailgate ● *n.* the hinged door at the back of a pickup truck, station wagon, etc. ● *v.* (**tailgates**, **tailgated**, **tailgating**) *informal* follow another vehicle too closely. □ **tailgater** *n.*

tailings *pl. n.* crushed stone and other waste produced in drilling, mining, or smelting ore.

tail light *n.* (also **tail lamp**) a usu. red light at the rear of esp. a motor vehicle.

tailor ● *n.* a person who makes and alters men's clothing. ● *v.* **1** design and make clothing esp. to meet the size requirements of a particular customer. **2** design or adapt something to suit a specific need. □ **tailoring** *n.*

tailored *adj.* **1** made by a tailor. **2** (of clothing) well cut and closely fitted. **3** having a neat design or appearance. **4** made to suit a specific purpose.

tailor-made ● *adj.* **1** made by a tailor for a particular customer. **2** altered or designed to meet a specific requirement. **3** ideally suited. ● *n.* a tailor-made article of clothing.

tailpiece *n.* an appendage attached to a thing to extend or conclude it.

tailpipe *n.* the rear section of the exhaust pipe of a motor vehicle.

tailplane *n.* a horizontal airfoil at the tail of an aircraft.

tailrace *n.* a watercourse leading away from a water wheel, dam, turbine, etc.

tailspin ● *n.* **1 a** a sharp or rapid decline. **b** *Sport* a slump. **2** a nose-first spiralling descent of an aircraft. ● *v.* (**tailspins**, **tailspun**, **tailspinning**) perform or fall into a tailspin.

tailwind *n.* a wind blowing in the direction of travel of an aircraft or vehicle.

taint ● *n.* a trace or suggestion of some undesirable or corrupting quality. ● *v.* **1** contaminate or pollute. **2** ruin, spoil.

Taiwanese *n.* (*pl.* **Taiwanese**) a person from Taiwan. □ **Taiwanese** *adj.* [*Say* tie wah NEEZ]

Tajik *n.* (*pl.* **Tajiks** or **Tajik**) **1** a person from Tajikistan. **2** the Iranian language of the Tajiks. □ **Tajik** *adj.* [*Say* taw JEEK]

take ● *v.* (**takes**; *past* **took**; *past participle* **taken**; **taking**) **1** lay hold of with one's hands. **2** occupy a place. **3** capture. **4** carry or bring with one. **5** remove from a place. **6** subtract. **7** consume. **8** bring into a specified state. **9** use as a route or a means of transport. **10** receive. **11** assume (a position, state, or form). **12** require or use up. **13** hold or accommodate. **14** act on (an opportunity). **15** regard, view, or deal with in a specified way. **16** submit to, tolerate, or endure. **17** undertake, or perform (an action or task). **18** be taught in (a subject). ● *n.* **1** a sequence of sound or vision photographed or recorded continuously. **2** a particular version of or approach to something. **3** an amount acquired. □ **on the take** receiving bribes. **take after** resemble (a parent or relative etc.). **take apart** dismantle. **take away 1** (foll. by

from) diminish; detract from. **2** subtract.
take the cake be the most remarkable,
outrageous, amusing, annoying, etc. **take
heart** be encouraged. **take ill** (or **sick**)
informal become ill or sick. **take in 1** *informal*
go out to see (a movie etc.). **2** offer
hospitality or shelter to (a person or
animal). **3** make (an article of clothing)
smaller. **4** cheat. **5** include or comprise.
take in hand start doing or dealing with.
take it 1 (often foll. by *that* + clause)
assume. **2** *informal* put up with or endure.
take it out on relieve one's frustration
by treating harshly. **take a lot** (or **it**) **out
of** exhaust the strength of. **take off
1 a** remove clothing. **b** lose weight.
2 remove. **3** deduct (part of an amount).
4 *informal* depart, esp. hastily. **5** *informal*
mimic humorously. **6** become airborne.
7 become successful or popular. **take on
1** undertake (work etc.). **2** hire. **3** challenge
or confront. **4** acquire (a new meaning etc.).
take out 1 buy food at a restaurant for
eating elsewhere. **2** receive (a loan) from a
bank. **3** borrow from a library. **4** *slang*
a *Sport* remove (an opponent) from the play.
b assassinate, murder. **take over** take
control. **take one's time** not hurry.
take to form a liking for. **take up
1** become interested in. **2** occupy (time or
space). **3** begin (residence etc.). **4** resume.
5 join in. **6** accept. **7** shorten. **8** pursue
further. **take up with** begin to associate
with. □ **taker** *n.*

take-charge *adj.* characterized by
leadership or authority.

takedown *n.* **1** the bringing of an
opponent down off his or her feet. **2** a
police arrest.

take-no-prisoners *adj.* very aggressive;
merciless.

takeoff *n.* **1** the action of becoming
airborne. **2 a** a caricature or parody. **b** an
imitation.

takeout *n.* **1** a meal bought at a restaurant
to be eaten off the premises. **2** *Curling* a shot
which removes an opponent's rock from
play.

takeover *n.* **1** the buying out of one
company by another. **2** a hostile
assumption of power. **3** an act of taking
over.

takeover bid *n.* an offer made to the
shareholders of a company to buy their
shares at a specified price in order to gain
control of that company.

taking ● *adj.* attractive or captivating. ● *n.*
1 the action or process of TAKE *v.* **2** (in *pl.*)
the amount of money earned by a business.

talc *n.* **1** a soft mineral form of magnesium
silicate with a greasy feel. **2** talcum powder.

talcum *n.* (also **talcum powder**) a
preparation of powdered talc for general
cosmetic use.

tale *n.* **1** a story or narrative. **2 a** a report of
an alleged fact. **b** a lie. **3** a true account of
extraordinary events.

talent *n.* **1** a special skill. **2** a person
possessing exceptional skill. **3** an ancient
unit of weight and currency. □ **talented**
adj. **talentless** *adj.*

talisman *n.* (*pl.* **talismans**) **1** an object
supposedly endowed with the power to
fend off evil or bring good luck. **2** a thing
supposed capable of working wonders.
□ **talismanic** *adj.* [*Say* TAL iz mun,
tal iz MANIC]

talk ● *v.* **1** speak in order to give
information or express ideas or feelings.
2 have the power of speech. **3** (foll. by *into*,
out of) persuade to do (or not to do)
something. **4** *informal* have in mind,
envisage. **5** gossip. ● *n.* **1** conversation or
talking. **2** a particular mode of speech. **3** an
informal address or lecture. **4** rumour or
gossip. **5** (often in *pl.*) formal negotiations
between conflicting parties etc. **6** empty
promises or boasting. □ **talk at** talk
incessantly without consideration for the
opinions of the listener. **talk back** reply
defiantly or with impudence. **talk big** talk
boastfully. **talk down to** speak
condescendingly to. **talk a good game**
talk convincingly yet fail to act effectively.
talk of the town a prominent topic of
local interest and popular discussion. **talk
over** discuss at length. **talk the talk** say
things and make promises that will please
others. **talk through one's hat
1** exaggerate, bluff. **2** talk wildly or
nonsensically. **talk tough** speak in a
brash, boastful, or menacing manner. **talk
up** discuss a subject in order to arouse
interest in it. □ **talker** *n.* **talking** *adj. & n.*

talkative *adj.* given to talking; chatty.
□ **talkativeness** *n.*

talkie *n.* *informal* a movie with a soundtrack,
as distinct from a silent film.

talking book *n.* a recorded reading of a
book.

talking head *n.* *informal* a TV reporter or
newscaster shown from the shoulders up.

talking point *n.* a topic that provokes
discussion or argument.

talking stick *n.* (among some
N American Aboriginal peoples) a carved
staff entitling the holder to speak to a
gathering.

talking-to *n.* (*pl.* **talking-tos**) *informal* a
reproof or reprimand.

talk radio *n.* a radio format featuring
interviews and listener phone-ins.

talk show n. a TV or radio show in which people, esp. celebrities, are invited to talk informally.

talky adj. (**talkier, talkiest**) **1** wordy or long-winded. **2** talkative.

tall ● adj. **1** of greater than average height. **2** of a specified height. **3** high relative to width or surrounding objects. **4** informal (of a statement or story) exaggerated, extravagant, unlikely. ● adv. straight and erect.

tallis n. (pl. **tallitim**) a shawl worn by Jewish men, esp. at prayer. [Say TAL iss for the singular, ta LEET im for the plural]

tall order n. an exorbitant or unreasonable demand.

tallow n. the harder kinds of animal fat used in making candles, soap, etc.

tall ship n. a high-masted ship.

tally ● n. (pl. **tallies**) **1 a** a total score or amount. **b** the record of an amount, debt, score, etc. **2** Sport a goal or run scored. **3** a mark or marks used to represent a number of things. ● v. (**tallies, tallied, tallying**) **1 a** record a number etc. **b** calculate the total of. **2** achieve a total of. **3** agree or correspond. **4** Sport score a point.

Talmud n. the body of Jewish civil and ceremonial law and legend comprising the Mishnah and a rabbinical commentary on it. □ **Talmudic** adj. **Talmudist** n. [MUD rhymes with HOOD]

talon n. a claw of a bird of prey. □ **taloned** adj.

talus n. (pl. **taluses**) a scree slope at the base of a mountain etc. consisting of material which has fallen from the face of the cliff above. [Say TAY lus]

tam n. a round cap of Scottish origin fitting closely around the brows but large and full above.

tamale n. a Mexican food of seasoned ground meat wrapped in cornmeal dough and steamed or baked in corn husks. [Say tuh MOLLY or tuh MALLY]

tamarack n. a slender larch found in wet places. [Say TAMMA rack]

tamari n. a rich fermented Japanese soy sauce. [Say tuh MAR ee]

tamarind n. a tropical tree bearing a pod encasing a sticky brown acidic pulp used in cooking. [Say TAMMA rind]

tamarisk n. a shrub that produces long slender branches with small pink or white flowers. [Say TAMMA risk]

tambourine n. a percussion instrument like a shallow drum with small jingling discs around the circumference, played by shaking, striking, etc. [Say tam buh REEN]

tame ● adj. (**tamer, tamest**) **1** domesticated. **2** (of an animal) accustomed to people; without the shyness, fear, or fierceness of a wild animal. **3** not exciting, adventurous, or controversial. **4** co-operative or servile. ● v. (**tames, tamed, taming**) **1** bring a wild animal into the service of humans. **2** reduce the intensity of an emotion etc.; calm, temper. **3** control, subdue a person etc. **4** cultivate land. □ **tamely** adv. **tamer** n.

Tamil n. **1** a member of a Dravidian people inhabiting the southern Indian subcontinent and parts of Sri Lanka. **2** their language. □ **Tamil** adj. [Say TAM ul]

tamoxifen n. a synthetic drug used to treat breast cancer and infertility in women. [Say tuh MOX if en]

tamp v. (often foll. by down) pound down or pack earth, gravel, etc.

tamper v. (foll. by with) meddle with something to cause damage or make unauthorized alterations. □ **tampering** n.

tamper-proof adj. (also **tamper-resistant**) not readily susceptible to tampering.

tampon n. a plug of soft material inserted into the vagina to absorb menstrual blood.

tan¹ ● n. **1** a brown skin colour resulting from exposure to the sun. **2** a yellowish-brown colour. ● adj. **1** of a yellowish-brown colour. **2** brown in colour due to exposure to the sun. ● v. (**tans, tanned, tanning**) **1** make or become brown by exposure to the sun. **2** convert rawhide into leather by soaking in tannic acid or by the use of mineral salts etc. □ **tanning** n.

tan² abbr. tangent.

tanager n. a small songbird of the bunting family, the male of which usu. has brightly coloured plumage. [Say TANNA jur]

tandem ● n. **1** a team of two people or machines working together. **2** a bicycle equipped with seats and pedals for two riders. ● adj. **1** co-operative, joint, dual. **2** involving two similar things. ● adv. together.

tandoor n. **1** a clay oven of a kind used originally in northern India and Pakistan. **2** (as an adj.) designating food cooked in such an oven. [Say TAN dure]

tandoori n. (pl. **tandooris**) (often as an adj.) a style of Indian cooking based on the use of a tandoor. [Say tan DURE ee]

tang n. **1** a sharp or penetrating flavour or smell. **2** a pointed projection on the blade of a knife etc., by which the blade is held in the handle.

tangent ● n. Math **1** a straight line that touches a curve but if extended does not intersect it. **2** a completely different line of thought or action. **3** the ratio of the sides opposite and adjacent to an angle in a right-angled triangle. ● *adj. Math* (of a line) that is a tangent. [*Say* TAN junt]

tangential *adj.* **1** *Math* of, pertaining to, or of the nature of a tangent. **2** straying or digressing from the main topic. **3** of relatively minor importance.
□ **tangentially** *adv.* [*Say* tan JEN shull]

tangerine *n.* a tangy mandarin orange. [*Say* tan juh REEN]

tangible ● *adj.* **1** that can be touched or felt. **2** clear and definite; real. ● *n.* (usu. in *pl.*) a tangible thing, esp. an asset.
□ **tangibly** *adv.* [*Say* TAN juh bull]

tangle ● *v.* (**tangles, tangled, tangling**) **1 a** twist or intertwine a strand or strands into a confused mass. **b** become so twisted or intertwined. **2** become embroiled in a difficult situation or controversy. **3** complicate. ● *n.* **1** a confused mass of twisted or intertwined strands that not easily separated. **2** a single long strand knotted in a confusing manner. **3** a confused or complicated state or situation.
□ **tangled** *adj.*

tango ● *n.* (*pl.* **tangos**) a ballroom dance of Argentinian origin, performed with long dramatic gliding movements and abrupt pauses and changes in direction. ● *v.* (**tangoes, tangoed, tangoing**) dance the tango.

tangy *adj.* (**tangier, tangiest**) having a strong, sharp flavour or scent.

tank ● *n.* **1** a large receptacle usu. for liquid or gas. **2** a heavy armoured fighting vehicle moving on a tracked carriage. **3** a container for a vehicle's fuel. **4** (also **tank top**) a sleeveless upper garment with a scoop neck. **5** a pond or reservoir. **6** *informal* a prison or cell. ● *v.* **1** (usu. foll. by *up*) fill a tank with fuel. **2** *informal* (foll. by *up*) drink heavily. **3** *Sport slang* lose a game or match deliberately. **4** *slang* decline or decrease. **5** fail utterly.

tankard *n.* a tall mug with a handle and sometimes a hinged lid. [*Say* TANK urd]

tanker *n.* a vehicle for carrying liquids or gases in bulk.

tank farm *n.* an area of oil or gas storage tanks.

tanned *adj.* having a brown skin colour as a result of being in the sun.

tanner *n.* **1** a person who tans hides. **2** a person who sunbathes.

tannery *n.* (*pl.* **tanneries**) a place where hides are tanned.

tannic *adj.* (of wine) having an astringent flavour due to the presence of tannin.

tannin *n.* (also **tannic acid**) a yellowish or

brownish bitter-tasting substance present in tea, some galls, barks, and other plant tissues.

tansy *n.* (*pl.* **tansies**) a plant with yellow button-like flowers and aromatic leaves.

tantalize *v.* (**tantalizes, tantalized, tantalizing**) **1** torment or tease with something that is not obtainable. **2** tempt; excite the senses or desires of.
□ **tantalizing** *adj.* **tantalizingly** *adv.*
[*Say* TANTA lize]

tantalum *n.* a naturally occurring hard white metallic element. [*Say* TANTA lum]

tantamount *adj.* (foll. by *to*) equivalent to.

Tantra *n.* (*pl.* **Tantras**) any of a class of Hindu or Buddhist mystical writings.
□ **Tantric** *adj.* **Tantrism** *n.*

tantrum *n.* an outburst of bad temper.

Tanzanian *n.* a native or inhabitant of Tanzania. □ **Tanzanian** *adj.*
[*Say* tanza NEE un]

Tao *n.* **1** (in Taoism) ultimate reality. **2** (in Confucianism) the norm to be followed. [*Say* TOW *or* DOW *(rhyming with* COW*)*]

Taoism *n.* a Chinese philosophy advocating humility and religious piety.
□ **Taoist** *n.* [*Say* TOW ism *or* DOW ism *(the first bit rhymes with* COW*)*]

tap[1] ● *n.* **1** a device by which a flow of liquid or gas from a pipe or vessel can be controlled. **2** an act of tapping a telephone etc. **3** the surgical withdrawal of fluid from a cavity etc. ● *v.* (**taps, tapped, tapping**) **1** let out (a liquid) by means of, or as if by means of, a tap. **2** draw sap from a tree by cutting into it. **3** obtain information or resources. **4** secretly connect a listening device to a telephone. □ **on tap** (of beer etc.) ready to be drawn from a keg. **tap into** obtain something from.

tap[2] ● *v.* (**taps, tapped, tapping**) **1** strike gently but audibly. **2** = TAP DANCE. **3** write using a typewriter or computer keyboard. ● *n.* **1 a** a light blow; a rap. **b** the sound of this. **2** = TAP DANCE. **3** (in *pl.*, usu. treated as *sing.*) *US* a bugle call played at lights out or a military funeral. □ **tapper** *n.*

tapas *pl. n.* small savoury Spanish appetizers. [*Say* TAP us]

tap dance ● *n.* a display dance performed wearing metal-soled shoes, with rhythmical tapping of the toes and heels. ● *v.* (**tap dances, tap danced, tap dancing**) perform a tap dance. □ **tap dancer** *n.* **tap dancing** *n.*

tape ● *n.* **1** a narrow strip of material for tying up, fastening, etc. **2** a strip of material stretched across the finishing line of a race. **3** (also **adhesive tape**) a strip of paper or plastic etc. coated with adhesive for fastening, sticking, etc. **4 a** = MAGNETIC

TAPE. **b** an audio or video cassette. **5** (also **tape measure**) a strip of tape marked for measuring lengths. ● *v.* (**tapes, taped, taping**) **1** tie up or join etc. with tape. **2** (foll. by *off*) seal or mark off an area with tape. **3** record on magnetic tape.

tapenade *n.* an hors d'oeuvre made mainly from puréed black olives, capers, and anchovies. [*Say* TAPPA nad]

taper ● *n.* **1** a wick coated with wax etc. for conveying a flame. **2** a slender candle. **3** gradual diminution in width or thickness. ● *v.* (often foll. by *off*) **1** diminish or reduce in thickness towards one end. **2** make or become gradually less. □ **tapering** *adj.*

tape recorder *n.* a machine for recording sounds on magnetic tape. □ **tape recording** *n.*

tapestry *n.* (*pl.* **tapestries**) a piece of thick fabric with designs woven or embroidered on it. [*Say* TAP us tree]

tapeworm *n.* a flatworm with a segmented ribbon-like body, living as a parasite in the intestines.

tap-in *n.* (*pl.* **tap-ins**) a close-range shot requiring little force.

taping *n.* **1** the act or an instance of recording something on magnetic tape. **2** the act of applying tape.

tapioca *n.* white grains obtained from cassava and used for puddings etc. [*Say* tappy OAK uh]

tapir *n.* a nocturnal hoofed mammal with a short flexible protruding snout. [*Sounds like* TAPER]

taproom *n.* a room in which alcoholic drinks are available.

taproot *n.* a tapering root growing vertically.

tar ● *n.* **1 a** a dark thick inflammable liquid distilled from wood or coal etc., used as a preservative of wood, in making roads, etc. **b** a similar substance formed in the burning of tobacco etc. **2** *informal* a sailor. ● *v.* (**tars, tarred, tarring**) **1** cover with tar. **2** damage the appearance, image, or reputation of. □ **tar and feather** smear with tar and then cover with feathers as a punishment. **tarred with the same brush** having the same faults.

tarantula *n.* (*pl.* **tarantulas**) a very large hairy tropical spider. [*Say* tuh RAN choo luh]

tardy *adj.* (**tardier, tardiest**) **1** late; not punctual. **2** slow to act or come or happen. □ **tardiness** *n.*

target ● *n.* **1** a thing fired or aimed at. **2** a person, group, etc. which is the object of attention, a campaign, etc. **3** an objective or result aimed at. **4** an object of criticism or abuse. ● *v.* (**targets, targeted, targeting**) **1** identify or single out as an object of attention or attack. **2** aim or direct. □ **on target** on the correct course to meet an objective.

tariff *n.* **1** a duty on a particular class of imports or exports. **2** a table of fixed charges. [*Say* TARE iff]

tarmac *n.* **1** *proprietary* asphalt. **2** a surface made of this, e.g. a runway. [*Say* TAR mack]

tarnish ● *v.* (**tarnishes, tarnished, tarnishing**) **1** lessen or destroy the lustre of metal etc. **2** sully. **3** lose lustre. ● *n.* **1** a loss of lustre. **2** a film of colour formed on an exposed surface of a mineral or metal.

taro *n.* (*pl.* **taros**) a tropical plant of the arum family that has edible tuberous roots. [*Say* TARE oh]

tarot *n.* a set of special playing cards used for fortune-telling. [*Say* TARE oh]

tarp *n.* *informal* a tarpaulin.

tarpaper *n.* paper coated with tar, often used as a building material.

tarpaulin *n.* a covering of heavy-duty waterproof cloth. [*Say* tar POLLEN]

tarpon *n.* a large silvery tropical fish. [*Say* TAR pon]

tarragon *n.* a bushy plant with narrow aromatic leaves that are used as a herb. [*Say* TARE a gone]

tarry¹ *adj.* of or like or smeared with tar.

tarry² *v.* (**tarries, tarried, tarrying**) *literary* delay leaving a place.

tarsal ● *adj.* of or relating to the bones in the ankle. ● *n.* a tarsal bone. [*Say* TAR sull]

tar sand *n.* a deposit of sand containing bitumen.

tarsus *n.* the group of bones forming the ankle and upper foot.

tart ● *n.* **1** a small, usu. open pie containing a fruit or sweet filling. **2** *slang* a prostitute or promiscuous woman. ● *v.* (foll. by *up*) *informal* smarten up, esp. flashily or gaudily. ● *adj.* **1** sharp or acid in taste. **2** (of a remark etc.) cutting, bitter. □ **tartlet** *n.* **tartly** *adv.* **tartness** *n.*

tartan *n.* **1** a pattern of coloured stripes crossing at right angles. **2** woollen cloth woven in this pattern.

Tartar (also **Tatar**) ● *n.* **1** a member of a group of Turkic peoples inhabiting parts of European and Asiatic Russia. **2** *hist.* a member of a combined group of central Asian peoples who conquered much of Asia and eastern Europe in the early 13th century. **3** (**tartar**) a person in a position of authority who has a very bad temper.

● *adj.* of or relating to the Tartars.
[*Say* TAR tur]

tartar *n.* **1** a hard deposit that forms on the teeth. **2** a hard crust that forms during the fermentation of wine. [*Say* TAR tur]

tartar sauce *n.* a sauce of mayonnaise and chopped pickles, capers, etc.

tartufo *n.* (*pl.* **tartufos**) a ball of ice cream with one flavour in the centre surrounded by another flavour. [*Say* tar TOO foe]

tarty *adj.* (**tartier, tartiest**) *informal* of or suggestive of a prostitute or promiscuous woman.

task ● *n.* **1** a piece of work to be done. **2** an unpleasant piece of work. ● *v.* **1** make great demands on. **2** assign a task to. □ **put to the task** cause to do something. **take to task** rebuke, scold.

task force *n.* (also **task group**) **1** *Military* an armed force organized for a special operation. **2** a unit specially organized for a task.

taskmaster *n.* a person who imposes a demanding workload.

Tasmanian *n.* a person from Tasmania. □ **Tasmanian** *adj.* [*Say* taz MAINY un]

Tasmanian devil *n.* a bearlike nocturnal flesh-eating marsupial with powerful jaws.

tassel *n.* **1** a decorative tuft of loosely hanging threads etc. **2** a tassel-like head of some plants. □ **tasselled** *adj.* [*Rhymes with* HASSLE]

taste ● *n.* **1 a** the sensation of flavour perceived in the mouth on contact with a substance. **b** the sense perceiving this. **2** a small sample of food or drink. **3** a slight experience. **4** a liking. **5** aesthetic discernment in art, literature, fashion, etc. **6** a sense of what is tactful or polite etc. ● *v.* (**tastes, tasted, tasting**) **1** sample or test the flavour of. **2** perceive the flavour of. **3** eat or drink a small portion of. **4** have experience of. **5** have a specified flavour. □ **to taste** in the amount needed for a pleasing result.

taste bud *n.* any of the nerve endings on the tongue by which things are tasted.

tasteful *adj.* having, or done in, good taste. □ **tastefully** *adv.* **tastefulness** *n.*

tasteless *adj.* **1** lacking flavour. **2** having, or done in, bad taste. □ **tastelessly** *adv.* **tastelessness** *n.*

tastemaker *n.* a person or institution that helps determine what is fashionable.

taster *n.* a person employed to test food or drink by tasting it.

taste test *n.* a usu. blind comparison of the flavours of similar products. □ **taste-test** *v.*

tasting *n.* a gathering at which food or drink (esp. wine) is tasted and evaluated.

tasty *adj.* (**tastier, tastiest**) pleasing in flavour.

tatami *n.* (*pl.* **tatamis** or **tatami**) a rush-covered straw mat forming a traditional Japanese floor covering. [*Say* tuh TOMMY]

Tatar *see* TARTAR. [*Say* TAR tur]

tater *n. informal* = POTATO. [*Say* TAY tur]

tatter *n.* (usu. in *pl.*) an irregularly torn piece of cloth or paper etc. □ **in tatters** *informal* torn to shreds. □ **tattered** *adj.*

tattle *v.* (**tattles, tattled, tattling**) (often foll. by *on*) inform against a person. □ **tattler** *n.*

tattletale *n.* someone who tattles on another.

tattoo¹ *n.* (*pl.* **tattoos**) a military display consisting of music, marching, and exercises.

tattoo² ● *v.* (**tattoos, tattooed, tattooing**) mark the skin by puncturing it and inserting pigment. ● *n.* (*pl.* **tattoos**) a design made by tattooing. □ **tattooist** *n.*

tatty *adj.* (**tattier, tattiest**) *informal* **1** worn and shabby. **2** of poor quality.

taught *past and past participle of* TEACH.

taunt ● *n.* a thing said in order to anger or wound a person. ● *v.* assail with taunts. □ **taunter** *n.* **tauntingly** *adv.*

taupe *n. & adj.* a grey tinged esp. with brown. [*Say* TOPE]

Taurus *n.* **1** a constellation (the Bull). **2** the second sign of the zodiac, which the sun enters around Apr. 20. □ **Taurean** *adj. & n.*

taut *adj.* **1** (of a rope, muscles, etc.) tight. **2** (of nerves) tense. □ **tautly** *adv.* **tautness** *n.*

tautology *n.* (*pl.* **tautologies**) the saying of the same thing twice in different words. □ **tautological** *adj.* [*Say* taw TOLLA jee, totta LOGICAL]

tavern *n.* a drinking establishment; a pub.

taverna *n.* a Greek café or restaurant. [*Say* tuh VARE nuh]

tawdry *adj.* (**tawdrier, tawdriest**) **1** showy but cheap and of poor quality. **2** involving low moral standards. □ **tawdriness** *n.*

tawny *n.* (**tawnier, tawniest**) an orange- or yellow-brown colour. □ **tawny** *adj.*

tawny owl *n.* **1** a reddish-brown European owl. **2** (**Tawny Owl**) *Cdn* an assistant adult leader of a Brownie pack.

tax ● *n.* (*pl.* **taxes**) **1** a compulsory contribution to government revenue. **2** a strain or heavy demand; a burdensome obligation. ● *v.* (**taxes, taxed, taxing**) **1** impose a tax on. **2** deduct tax from.

3 make heavy demands on. **4** accuse of wrongdoing □ **taxable** *adj.* **taxation** *n.*

taxa *pl. of* TAXON.

tax break *n. informal* a tax concession allowed by government.

tax credit *n.* a sum that may be deducted from the amount of tax owing. □ **tax-creditable** *adj. Cdn*

tax-deductible *adj.* (of expenses) that may be deducted from income before the amount of tax to be paid is calculated.

taxi ● *n.* (*pl.* **taxis**) **1** (also **taxicab**) a car and driver that may be hired. **2** a boat, airplane, etc. similarly used. ● *v.* (**taxis**, **taxied**, **taxiing**) **1** (of an aircraft) move along the ground before takeoff or after landing. **2** go in a taxi.

taxidermy *n.* the art of stuffing and mounting the skins of animals in lifelike poses. □ **taxidermist** *n.* [*Say* TAXA durmy]

taxing *adj.* tiring or demanding.

taxman *n.* (*pl.* **taxmen**) *informal* an inspector or collector of taxes.

taxon *n.* (*pl.* **taxa**) a taxonomic group of any rank, e.g. a species or family. [*Say* TAX un]

taxonomy *n.* (*pl.* **taxonomies**) the science of the classification of organisms into orders, families, genera, species, etc. □ **taxonomic** *adj.* **taxonomist** *n.* [*Say* tax ONNA mee]

taxpayer *n.* a person who pays taxes. □ **taxpaying** *adj.*

tax return *n.* a declaration of income for taxation purposes.

tax shelter *n.* an investment etc. intended to minimize payment of tax. □ **tax-sheltered** *adj.*

TB *abbr.* **1** tubercle bacillus. **2** tuberculosis.

TBA *abbr.* to be announced.

T-ball *n.* a form of baseball for young children, in which the ball is placed on a stand in front of the batter.

T-bar *n.* (also **T-bar lift**) a type of ski lift in the form of a series of inverted T-shaped metal bars for towing skiers.

T-bill *n.* a treasury bill.

T-bone *n.* a T-shaped bone, esp. in steak.

tbsp *abbr.* = TABLESPOON 2.

T cell *n.* a type of white blood cell produced by the thymus gland and active in the body's immune response.

tchotchke *n. informal* a knick-knack. [*Say* CHOTCH kee]

TCP/IP *abbr. proprietary* Transmission Control Protocol/Internet Protocol, the obligatory standard to be used by any system connecting to the Internet.

TD *abbr.* (*pl.* **TDs**) touchdown.

TDD *abbr.* (*pl.* **TDDs**) Telephone Device for the Deaf.

te (*pl.* **tes**) = TI. [*Say* TEE]

tea *n.* (*pl.* **teas**) **1 a** a drink made by infusing the dried leaves of a tea plant in boiling water. **b** the dried leaves used to make this. **c** the Asian shrub that produces these leaves. **2** a similar drink made by infusing other leaves or substances. **3** an afternoon reception at which tea is served.

tea bag *n.* a small perforated bag containing tea leaves for infusion.

tea biscuit *n. Cdn* a small baked food, leavened with baking powder or soda, often containing raisins.

teach *v.* (**teaches**, **taught**, **teaching**) **1** impart knowledge to or instruct. **2** give instruction in. **3** cause to learn by example. **4** advocate as a principle. □ **teachable** *adj.*

teacher *n.* a person who teaches, esp. in a school. □ **teacherly** *adj.*

teaching *n.* **1** the profession of a teacher. **2** what is taught; a doctrine.

tea cozy *n.* a cover placed over a teapot to keep it hot.

teacup *n.* a cup from which tea is drunk, usu. with a matching saucer.

teak *n.* the hard lightweight durable timber of an Asian tree, used to make furniture.

teakettle *n.* = KETTLE 1.

teal *n.* (*pl.* **teal** or **teals**) **1** a small freshwater duck. **2** *n. & adj.* (also **teal blue**) a dark greenish-blue colour.

tea leaf *n.* **1** a dried leaf of tea. **2** (esp. in *pl.*) these after infusion or as dregs, the patterns formed by which are interpreted by fortune tellers.

tea light *n.* a small candle in a shallow round metal case.

team ● *n.* **1** a set of players forming one side in a contest. **2** two or more persons working together. **3** a set of draft animals. ● *v.* **1** (usu. foll. by *up*) join in a team or in common action. **2** harness (horses etc.) in a team.

teammate *n.* a fellow member of a team.

team player *n.* a person who works well as a member of a team.

teamster *n.* **1** a truck driver. **2** a driver of a team of animals.

teamwork *n.* the combined action of a team, group, etc.

teapot *n.* a pot with a handle, spout, and lid, in which tea is brewed and from which it is poured.

tear¹ ● *v.* (**tears**; *past* **tore**; *past participle* **torn**; **tearing**) **1** pull to pieces with some force. **2** pull with some force. **3** violently disrupt or divide. **4** *informal* go hurriedly or impetuously. **5** undergo tearing. ● *n.* **1** a hole or other damage caused by tearing. **2** a **a** spree. **b** *Sport* a winning streak. □ **be torn between** have difficulty in choosing between. **tear down** demolish. **tear one's hair out** behave with extreme desperation or anger. **tear into** attack verbally; reprimand.

tear² ● *n.* a drop of clear salty liquid in or from the eyes, resulting from emotion, physical irritation, pain, etc. ● *v.* (**tears, teared, tearing**) (of the eyes) fill with tears.

teardrop *n.* **1** a single tear. **2** a thing in the shape of a teardrop, esp. a jewel.

tearful *adj.* **1** crying or inclined to cry. **2** causing or accompanied with tears. □ **tearfully** *adv.* **tearfulness** *n.*

tear gas ● *n.* a gas that causes severe irritation to the eyes, used in warfare or riot control. ● *v.* (**tear-gas, tear-gases, tear-gassed, tear-gassing**) attack with tear gas.

tear-jerker *n. informal* a sentimental story, film, etc., calculated to evoke tears. □ **tear-jerking** *n.* & *adj.*

tea room *n.* a small restaurant or café where tea and other refreshments are served.

teary *adj.* tearful; sad.

tease ● *v.* (**teases, teased, teasing**) **1 a** make fun of or attempt to provoke in a playful or unkind way. **b** say something ironically as a provocation. **2** tantalize sexually. **3** comb the hair from the ends towards the scalp to make it look thicker. **4** pick wool etc. into separate fibres. ● *n.* **1** *informal* a person fond of teasing. **2** an act of making fun of or tempting someone. □ **tease out 1** separate by disentangling. **2** extract or obtain by painstaking effort. □ **teasingly** *adv.*

teaser *n.* **1** *informal* a hard question or task. **2** a teasing person. **3** a short introductory advertisement designed to stimulate curiosity.

tea service *n.* (also **tea set**) a matching teapot, milk jug, and sugar bowl for serving tea.

teaspoon *n.* **1** a small spoon for stirring coffee, tea, etc. **2** a unit of measure for cooking, equal to about 5 ml. Abbreviation: **tsp.** □ **teaspoonful** *n.* (*pl.* **teaspoonfuls**)

teat *n.* a mammary nipple. [*Say* TEET or TIT]

tea towel *n.* a thin linen or cotton towel for drying washed dishes etc.

tech (*pl.* **techs**) *informal* ● *n.* **1** technology. **2** a technician. **3** a technical college or school. ● *adj.* technical, technological.

techie *n.* (*pl.* **techies**) *informal* an expert in or enthusiast for technology, esp. computers. [*Say* TECKY]

technical *adj.* **1** of or involving or concerned with the applied sciences. **2** of or relating to a particular subject or craft etc. **3** requiring special knowledge to be understood. **4** due to mechanical failure. **5** such in strict interpretation. **6** of or relating to the technique of an art form. **7** of or relating to technological equipment.

technicality *n.* (*pl.* **technicalities**) **1** the state of being technical. **2** a technical expression. **3** a technical point or detail.

technical knockout *n. Boxing* a victory due to the opponent's inability to continue.

technically *adv.* **1** with reference to the technique displayed. **2** according to the exact meaning of words etc.; strictly.

technician *n.* **1** a person operating technical equipment in a laboratory etc. **2** an expert in the practical application of a science.

Technicolor *n.* **1** *proprietary* a process of colour cinematography. **2** (usu. **technicolor** or **technicolour**) *informal* vivid colour. [*Say* TECKNA colour]

technique *n.* **1** a particular esp. skilful method of doing something. **2** skill in a particular field.

techno ● *n.* a style of popular dance music making extensive use of electronic instruments and synthesized sound. ● *adj.* having to do with technology.

techno- *comb. form* relating to or using technology.

technobabble *n. informal* incomprehensible technical jargon.

technocracy *n.* a social or political system in which scientific or technical experts hold a great deal of power. [*Say* teck NOCKRA see]

technocrat *n.* a politically powerful expert in science, technology, engineering, etc. □ **technocratic** *adj.*

technology *n.* (*pl.* **technologies**) **1** the study or use of the applied sciences. **2** the application of scientific knowledge for practical purposes. **3** a tool etc. used for this. □ **technological** *adj.* **technologically** *adv.* **technologist** *n.* [*Say* teck NOLLA jee]

technophile *n.* an enthusiast about new technology. [*Say* TECHNO file]

technophobe *n.* a person who fears or avoids new technology. □ **technophobia** *n.* **technophobic** *adj.* [*Say* techno FOBE, techno FOE bee uh, techno FOE bick]

techy *adj. informal* technical. [*Say* TECKY]

tectonic plate *n.* each of a number of solid plates forming the earth's surface.

tectonics *pl. n.* (usu. treated as *sing.*) processes involving large-scale structural features of the earth's surface. □ **tectonic** *adj.* [*Say* teck TONICS]

teddy *n.* (*pl.* **teddies**) **1** (also **teddy bear**) a soft toy bear. **2** a woman's undergarment combining camisole and panties.

tedious *adj.* tiresomely long or boring. □ **tediously** *adv.* **tediousness** *n.* [*Say* TEEDY us]

tedium *n.* the state of being tedious. [*Say* TEEDY um]

tee[1] *n.* (*pl.* **tees**) = T.

tee[2] ● *n.* **1 a** a cleared space from which a golf ball is struck at the beginning of play at a hole. **b** a small support from which a ball is struck at a tee. **2** a mark aimed at in curling etc. ● *v.* (**tees, teed, teeing**) (often foll. by *up*) place a ball on a tee ready to strike it. □ **tee off 1** play a ball from a tee. **2** *informal* make angry; annoy.

tee-hee ● *n.* a titter or giggle. ● *v.* (**tee-hees, tee-heed, tee-heeing**) titter or laugh.

teem *v.* **1** be abundant. **2** (foll. by *with*) be full of or swarming with. **3** (of rain) fall heavily. □ **teeming** *adj.*

teen ● *adj.* teenage. ● *n.* a teenager.

teenage *adj.* relating to or characteristic of teenagers. □ **teenaged** *adj.*

teenager *n.* a person from 13 to 19 years old.

teens *pl. n.* the numbers from 13 to 19, as in years, degrees of temperature, etc.

teeny *adj.* (**teenier, teeniest**) (also **teensy, teensier, teensiest**) *informal* tiny.

teenybopper *n. informal* a young teenage girl who keenly follows the latest fashions.

teeny-weeny *adj.* (also **teensy-weensy**) *informal* very tiny.

teepee *n.* (*pl.* **teepees**) a conical tent formerly used by Plains Indians.

tee-shirt *n.* = T-SHIRT.

teeter *v.* **1** totter; be unsteady. **2** hesitate; be indecisive.

teeter-totter *n.* a see-saw.

teeth *pl.* of TOOTH.

teethe *v.* (**teethes, teethed, teething**) grow baby teeth. □ **teething** *n.* [*Rhymes with* BREATHE]

teetotaller *n.* a person who doesn't drink alcohol. □ **teetotal** *adj.* **teetotalling** *n. & adj.* [*Say* tee TOTAL er]

TEFL *abbr.* teaching of English as a foreign language. [*Say* TEFF ul]

Teflon *n.* **1** *proprietary*

polytetrafluoroethylene, used as a non-stick coating for kitchen utensils. **2** (as an *adj.*) having a reputation that is not damaged in spite of scandal or misjudgment. [*Say* TEFF lawn]

telebanking *n.* (also **telephone banking**) the conducting of banking transactions by telephone.

telecast ● *n.* a television broadcast. ● *v.* (**telecasts, telecast, telecasting**) transmit by television. □ **telecaster** *n.*

telecom *n.* telecommunications.

telecommunication *n.* **1** communication by telephone, radio, television, etc. **2** (usu. in *pl.*) the branch of technology concerned with this.

telecommute *v.* (**telecommutes, telecommuted, telecommuting**) work from home, communicating by Internet, telephone, fax, etc. □ **telecommuter** *n.* **telecommuting** *n.*

teleconference *n.* a conference with participants linked by telecommunication devices. □ **teleconferencing** *n.*

telegenic *adj.* having an appearance that looks pleasing on television. [*Say* tella JEN ick]

telegram *n.* a message sent by telegraph and then delivered in written form.

telegraph ● *n.* a system of transmitting messages to a distant place esp. by making and breaking an electrical connection. ● *v.* **1** send a message by telegraph. **2** give an advance indication of. □ **telegraphy** *n.* [*Say* tuh LEGRA fee]

telegraphic *adj.* **1** of or by telegraphs or telegrams. **2** very concise; omitting inessential words. □ **telegraphically** *adv.*

telehealth *n.* (also **telemedicine**) the delivery of health services, expertise, and information at a distance through the use of information technology and telecommunications.

telekinesis *n.* movement of objects at a distance supposedly by mental power. □ **telekinetic** *adj.* [*Say* tele kin EE sis, tele kin ETT ick]

telemark *n. Skiing* a swing turn with one ski advanced and the knee bent, used to change direction or stop short.

telemarketing *n.* marketing by means of usu. unsolicited telephone calls. □ **telemarketer** *n.*

teleology *n.* the belief that all things in nature have a purpose and happen because of that. □ **teleological** *adj.* [*Say* telly OLLA jee *or* teely OLLA jee]

telepath *n.* a person able to communicate telepathically.

telepathy *n.* the supposed

communication or perception of thoughts by extrasensory means. □ **telepathic** *adj.* **telepathically** *adv.* [*Say* tuh LEPPA thee]

telephone ● *n.* an apparatus for transmitting speech over a distance. ● *v.* (**telephones, telephoned, telephoning**) = PHONE *v.* □ **telephonic** *adj.* **telephony** *n.* [*Say* tele FON Ick, tel EFFA nee]

telephoto ● *n.* (*pl.* **telephotos**) a lens giving a magnified image of distant objects. ● *adj.* of or using such a lens.

teleport *v.* move objects at a distance by mental power or other non-physical means. □ **teleportation** *n.*

teleprinter *n.* a device for transmitting telegraph messages as they are keyed, and for printing messages received.

teleprompter *n.* a device displaying a script to a speaker on TV.

telesales *pl. n.* selling by telephone.

telescope ● *n.* **1** an optical instrument using lenses or mirrors or both to make distant objects appear nearer and larger. **2** = RADIO TELESCOPE. ● *v.* (**telescopes, telescoped, telescoping**) **1** press or drive together so that one section slides into another like the segments of a folding telescope. **2** be capable of closing in this way. **3** compress so as to occupy less space or time.

telescopic *adj.* **1 a** of, relating to, or made with a telescope. **b** visible only through a telescope. **2** able to focus on and magnify distant objects. **3** consisting of sections that telescope. □ **telescopically** *adv.* [*Say* tele SCOP ick]

teletheatre *n.* a betting facility where horse races are shown on television.

telethon *n.* a very long television program to raise money for a charity.

teletype ● *n.* a kind of teleprinter. ● *v.* (**teletypes, teletyped, teletyping**) **1** operate a teleprinter. **2** send by means of a teleprinter.

televangelist *n.* an evangelical preacher who preaches on television. [*Say* tele VAN jell ist]

televise *v.* (**televises, televised, televising**) transmit by television.

television *n.* **1** a system of broadcasting visual images. **2** a device with a screen for receiving these broadcasts. **3** the programs broadcast on television. □ **televisual** *adj.* **televisually** *adv.*

telework *v.* = TELECOMMUTE. □ **teleworker** *n.* **teleworking** *n.*

telex ● *n.* (*pl.* **telexes**) **1** a telegraph system using teleprinters on the public telecommunications network. **2** a message

sent this way. ● *v.* (**telexes, telexed, telexing**) send or communicate with by telex.

tell[1] *v.* (**tells, told, telling**) **1** express in words. **2** reveal or signify to. **3** (foll. by *on*) *informal* inform against. **4** instruct. **5** decide, determine, distinguish. **6 a** (often foll. by *on*) produce a noticeable effect. **b** reveal the truth. **c** have an influence. **7** count votes. □ **as far as one can tell** judging from the available information. **tell apart** distinguish between. **tell off** *informal* reprimand, scold. **tell tales** report a discreditable fact about another. **tell (the) time** determine the time from a clock or watch. **there is no telling** it is impossible to know.

tell[2] *n.* a mound formed by the accumulated remains of ancient settlements.

teller *n.* **1** a person who receives and pays out money in a bank. **2** a person who tells esp. stories.

telling *adj.* **1** having a marked effect. **2** significant. □ **tellingly** *adv.*

telltale *adj.* that reveals or betrays.

tellurium *n.* a rare silver-white element used in semiconductors. [*Say* tel LURE ee um]

telnet ● *n.* a protocol that allows a user on one computer to log in to another computer that is part of the same network. ● *v.* (**telnets, telnetted, telnetting**) log in or connect to a remote computer using a telnet program. [*Say* TELL net]

temerity *n.* excessive confidence or boldness. [*Say* tuh MARE a tee]

temp *informal* ● *n.* **1** a temporary employee. **2** a temperature. ● *v.* work as a temp.

tempeh *n.* a fermented soybean product. [*Say* TEM puh]

temper ● *n.* **1** a state of mind. **2** irritation or anger. **3** a tendency to have fits of anger. **4** composure or calmness. **5** a metal's hardness and elasticity. ● *v.* **1** bring metal etc. to a proper hardness or consistency. **2** moderate.

tempera *n.* (*pl.* **temperas**) **1** a method of painting with powdered pigment mixed with egg yolk and water. **2** this type of paint. [*Say* TEMPER uh]

temperament *n.* **1** a person's natural disposition. **2** a creative or spirited personality. [*Say* TEMPRA m'nt *or* TEMPER m'nt]

temperamental *adj.* **1** of or having temperament. **2 a** liable to erratic or moody behaviour. **b** working unpredictably; unreliable. □ **temperamentally** *adv.* [*Say* tempra MENTAL *or* temper MENTAL]

temperance n. abstinence from alcoholic drink. [Say TEMPER ince]

temperate adj. **1** showing moderation or self-restraint. **2** characterized by mild temperatures. [Say TEMPER it]

temperature n. **1** the degree or intensity of heat. **2** informal an internal body temperature above the normal.

-tempered comb. form having a specified temper or disposition.

tempest n. **1** a violent windy storm. **2** activity or an incident involving strong and often conflicting emotions, agitation, violence, etc. □ **tempest in a teapot** great agitation over a trivial matter.

tempestuous adj. **1** stormy. **2** turbulent, violent, passionate. □ **tempestuously** adv. **tempestuousness** n. [Say tem PESS chew us]

template n. **1 a** a thin board or plate used as a guide in cutting or drilling metal, stone, wood, etc. **b** a flat card for cutting cloth for patchwork etc. **2** Computing a stored pattern for a document from which new documents may be made. [Say TEM plate or TEM plit]

temple n. **1** a building devoted to the worship of a god or gods. **2** a place in which God is regarded as residing. **3** any large imposing building devoted to a particular interest. **4** the flat part of either side of the head between the forehead and the ear.

tempo n. **1** (pl. **tempos** or **tempi**) the speed at which music is played. **2** (pl. **tempos**) the pace of an activity.

temporal adj. **1** of worldly as opposed to spiritual affairs. **2** of or relating to time. **3** of the temples of the head. □ **temporality** n. **temporally** adv. [Say TEMPER ul]

temporary adj. lasting or meant to last only for a limited time. □ **temporarily** adv.

temporize v. (**temporizes, temporized, temporizing**) gain time by avoiding to commit oneself. [Say TEMPER ize]

tempt v. **1** entice or incite to do a wrong or forbidden thing. **2** allure, attract. **3** risk provoking. □ **tempter** n. **tempting** adj. **temptingly** adv. **temptress** n.

temptation n. **1** a desire to do something wrong or self-indulgent. **2** a tempting thing.

tempura n. (in Japanese cuisine) fish, shellfish, or vegetables, fried in batter. [Say tem POO ruh]

ten card. num. one more than nine.

tenable adj. that can be maintained or defended against attack or objection. [Say TEN a bull]

tenacious adj. **1** holding firmly and resolutely to something. **2** continuing to exist for longer than one might expect. □ **tenaciously** adv. [Say ten AY shuss]

tenacity n. the quality of not giving up easily, of holding on stubbornly. [Say ten ASS it ee]

tenant ● n. a person, business, etc. who rents a residence, premises, etc. from the owner. ● v. occupy as a tenant. □ **tenancy** n.

Ten Commandments pl. n. Bible the divine rules of conduct given by God to Moses.

tend v. **1 a** (usu. foll. by to, toward) be apt or inclined. **b** be moving; be directed. **2 a** take care of, look after. **b** give attention.

tendency n. (pl. **tendencies**) **1** (often foll. by to, toward) an inclination; a way in which a person etc. is likely to behave. **2** a direction in which something moves or changes.

tendentious adj. derogatory calculated to promote a particular viewpoint; biased. □ **tendentiously** adv. **tendentiousness** n. [Say ten DEN shuss]

tender ● adj. (**tenderer, tenderest**) **1** easily cut or chewed, not tough. **2 a** easily wounded. **b** easily damaged. **c** somewhat painful. **3** loving, affectionate, fond. **4** (of age) early, immature. ● v. **1 a** offer, present. **b** offer as payment. **2** make an offer for the supply of a thing or the execution of work. **3** invite bids for a contract. ● n. **1** an offer to execute work or supply goods at a fixed price. **2** the auctioning of a contract to bidders. **3** money or other commodities that may be legally tendered in payment. **4** a person who looks after people or things. □ **put out to tender** seek tenders with respect to work etc. □ **tenderer** n. **tenderly** adv. **tenderness** n.

tenderfoot n. (pl. **tenderfoots** or **tenderfeet**) a newcomer or novice, esp. in the bush or in the Scouts or Guides.

tender-hearted adj. easily moved by pity etc. □ **tender-heartedness** n.

tenderize v. (**tenderizes, tenderized, tenderizing**) make meat tender by pounding, marinating, etc. □ **tenderizer** n.

tenderloin n. **1** a tender cut of meat from the inside of a loin of beef or pork. **2** slang a disreputable district of a city.

tendinitis n. (also **tendonitis**) inflammation of a tendon. [Say tendon ITE iss]

tendon n. a cord of strong fibrous tissue attaching a muscle to a bone etc.

tendril *n.* each of the slender often spiral shoots by which some climbing plants cling for support.

tenement *n.* a building with apartments rented cheaply.

tenet *n.* a central belief or principle.

tenfold *adj. & adv.* **1** ten times as much or as many. **2** consisting of ten parts.

10-gallon hat *n.* = COWBOY HAT.

tennis *n.* either of two games in which two or four players strike a ball with racquets over a net stretched across a court.

tennis elbow *n.* a painful inflammation of the tendons in the elbow.

tenon *n.* a projection on a piece of wood made for insertion into a corresponding cavity (mortise) in another piece to form a joint. □**tenoned** *adj.*

tenor *n.* **1 a** a singing voice between baritone and alto or counter-tenor. **b** a singer with this voice. **2** an instrument with a similar range. **3** the general meaning of a document, talk, etc. **4** a settled or prevailing course or direction.

tenpin *n.* **1** (often in *pl.*) (also **10-pin bowling**) a variety of bowling in which players have two chances to knock down a set of ten pins using a large hard rubber ball. **2** a pin used in this game.

tense ● *adj.* **1** stretched tight, strained. **2** in a state of, causing, or characterized by nervous strain or tension. ● *v.* (**tenses, tensed, tensing**) make or become tense. ● *n. Grammar* a form taken by a verb to indicate when the action takes place and whether it is completed. □**tense up** become tense. □**tensely** *adv.*

tensile *adj.* **1** of or relating to tension. **2** that can be drawn out or stretched. [*Say* TENSE ile]

tensile strength *n.* resistance to breaking under tension.

tension *n.* **1 a** the state of being stretched tight. **b** the state of having the muscles stretched tight. **2** mental strain or excitement. **3** a strained state or relationship. **4** *Mechanics* the strained condition resulting from forces acting in opposite directions.

tensor *n.* a muscle that tightens or stretches a part of the body.

Tensor bandage *n. Cdn proprietary* a wide elasticized bandage used to provide support to injured joints.

ten-spot *n. informal* **1** a ten-dollar bill. **2** a playing card with ten pips.

tent ● *n.* a portable shelter or dwelling of canvas, cloth, etc., supported by poles and stretched by cords pegged to the ground. ● *v.* **1** cover with or as with a tent. **2** camp in a tent. **3** form into a tent-like shape, esp. with sides etc. meeting at a top point or ridge. □**tented** *adj.*

tentacle *n.* **1** a long slender flexible appendage of an (esp. invertebrate) animal. **2** (usu. in *pl.*) a pervasive sinister influence. □**tentacled** *adj.* **tentacular** *adj.* [*Say* TENT a cull, ten TACK yoo lur]

tentative *adj.* **1** experimental, provisional. **2** hesitant, not definite. □**tentatively** *adv.* **tentativeness** *n.*

tent caterpillar *n.* a moth larva that lives in groups inside tent-like silken webs in a tree.

tenterhook *n.* □**on tenterhooks** mentally agitated due to uncertainty.

tenth *ord. num.* the position in a sequence corresponding to the number 10 in the sequence 1-10. □**tenthly** *adv.*

tent ring *n. Cdn* a ring of stones for holding down a tent, teepee, etc., esp. as indicating a past campsite.

tenuous *adj.* **1** very weak or slight. **2** very slender or fine; insubstantial. □**tenuously** *adv.* [*Say* TEN yoo us]

tenure *n.* **1** a condition under which property is held. **2** the holding or possession of an office or property. **3** guaranteed permanent employment. [*Say* TEN yur]

tenured *adj.* (of a position) carrying a guarantee of permanent employment. [*Say* TEN yurd]

tepee *n.* (*pl.* **tepees**) = TEEPEE.

tepid *adj.* **1** slightly warm. **2** not enthusiastic. □**tepidly** *adv.* [*Say* TEP id]

tequila *n.* a Mexican alcoholic liquor made by distilling the fermented sap of a succulent plant. [*Say* tuh KEELA]

tera- *comb. form* **1** denoting a factor of 10^{12}. **2** *Computing* denoting a factor of 2^{40} (i.e. 1 099 511 627 776).

terbium *n.* a silvery metallic element. [*Say* TURBY um]

teriyaki *n.* **1** (in Japanese cuisine) fish or meat marinated in soy sauce etc. and grilled. **2** this sauce. [*Say* terry YACKY *or* terry YOCKY]

term ● *n.* **1** a word used to express a definite concept. **2** (in *pl.*) relations. **3** (in *pl.*) conditions or stipulations. **4 a** a limited period of some state or activity. **b** a period of some weeks, alternating with holiday, during which instruction is given in a school etc. **c** a period of imprisonment. **5** *Math* **a** each of the two quantities in a ratio. **b** each quantity in a series. **c** a part of an expression joined to the rest by + or −. **6** the completion of an normal length of pregnancy. ● *v.* give a name to. □**bring to**

terms cause to accept conditions. **come to terms** agree on conditions. **come to terms with** reconcile oneself to. **in terms of** as regards, with reference to. **make terms** conclude an agreement. **be on good** (or **friendly** etc.) **terms with** have a good relationship with.

term deposit *n. Cdn* an amount of money deposited with a bank etc. for a fixed term at a fixed interest rate.

terminal ● adj. 1 leading to death. **2** relating to a limit or end. **● n. 1** a terminus for trains or long-distance buses. **2** a departure and arrival building for passengers at an airport. **3** a keyboard and screen connected to a central computer. **4** an installation where grain, oil, etc. is stored at the end of a rail line or pipeline, or at a port. □ **terminally** *adv.*

terminate *v.* (**terminates, terminated, terminating**) **1** end. **2** fire an employee. □ **termination** *n.* **terminator** *n.*

terminology *n.* (*pl.* **terminologies**) the terms used in a particular subject.

terminus *n.* (*pl.* **termini** or **terminuses**) **1 a** the end of a railway, bus route, etc. **b** a station at this point. **2** the end point of any of various things. [*Say* TERM in us *for the singular,* TERM in eye *or* TERM in us iz *for the plural*]

termite *n.* a small insect that lives in large colonies and feeds on wood.

term of endearment *n.* a name used to convey love or fondness.

term paper *n.* an essay representative of the work done during a term.

terms of reference *n.* the limits set on the scope of a committee, report, etc.

tern *n.* a gull-like seabird with long pointed wings and a forked tail.

terrace ● n. 1 a each of a series of flat areas formed on a slope and used for cultivation. **b** a similar levelled top of a natural slope. **2** a level paved area next to a house. **3** the flat roof of a house used as a cool resting area. **4** a row of houses on a raised level or along a slope. **● v.** (**terraces, terraced, terracing**) (esp. as **terraced** *adj.*) form into or provide with a terrace or terraces. □ **terracing** *n.*

terracotta ● n. 1 usu. brownish-red earthenware that has not been glazed. **2** the brownish-red colour of terracotta. **● adj.** of a brownish-red colour.

terrain *n.* a tract of land, esp. with regard to its physical features.

terrapin *n.* an edible freshwater turtle. [*Say* TERRA pin]

terrarium *n.* (*pl.* **terrariums** or **terraria**) **1** a container artificially prepared for keeping very small land animals such as newts and snakes. **2** a sealed transparent globe etc. containing growing plants. [*Say* tuh RARE ee um]

terrazzo *n.* (*pl.* **terrazzos**) a smooth flooring material of stone chips set in concrete. [*Say* tuh RAT so *or* tuh RAZ oh]

terrestrial *adj.* **1** living on the land or on the ground, rather than in water, in trees, or in the air. **2** (of a planet) similar in size or composition to the earth. **3** of the earth.

terrible *adj.* **1 a** dreadful, awful. **b** very bad. **2** very incompetent. **3** ill. **4** full of remorse. **5** *formal* causing or fit to cause terror.

terribly *adv.* **1** *informal* very, extremely. **2** in a terrible manner.

terrier *n.* any of various breeds of dog known for their eagerness and tenacity.

terrific *adj. informal* **1** excellent. **2** of great size or intensity. **3** excessive. □ **terrifically** *adv.*

terrify *v.* (**terrifies, terrified, terrifying**) fill with terror. □ **terrifying** *adj.* **terrifyingly** *adv.*

terrine *n.* **1** a kind of pâté, usu. coarse textured. **2** a usu. oval earthenware vessel. [*Say* tuh REEN]

territorial *adj.* **1** of land. **2** having to do with a particular district or locality. **3** especially defensive of an area. **4** (usu. **Territorial**) of or relating to any of the Territories of Canada or other countries.

territoriality *n.* a pattern of behaviour in which an animal or group of animals defends an area against others of the same species.

territorial waters *pl. n.* the the part of the sea under the jurisdiction of a country.

territory *n.* (*pl.* **territories**) **1** the extent of the land under the jurisdiction of a ruler, country, city, etc. **2** (**Territory**) an organized division of a country not having the full status of a province, state, etc. **3** an area of knowledge, activity, or experience. **4** *Zoology* an area defended by an animal. **5** an area of land, esp. with a specified characteristic.

terror *n.* **1** extreme fear or dread. **2 a** a person or thing that causes terror. **b** *informal* an exasperating or troublesome person. **3** terrorism. **4** (**the Terror**) REIGN OF TERROR 2.

terrorism *n.* the employment of violence and intimidation to achieve political aims. □ **terrorist** *n.*

terrorize *v.* (**terrorizes, terrorized, terrorizing**) **1** fill with terror. **2** use terrorism against. **3** bully, harass.

terry cloth *n.* (also **terry**) an absorbent

cotton pile fabric with the loops uncut, used for towels etc.

terse *adj.* (**terser**, **tersest**) using few words; curt, abrupt. □ **tersely** *adv.* **terseness** *n.*

tertiary ● *adj.* **1** third in order or rank etc. **2** (**Tertiary**) of or relating to the first period in the Cenozoic era, lasting from about 65 to 2 million years ago. ● *n.* the Tertiary period. [*Say* TUR shur ee]

TESL *abbr.* teaching of English as a second language. [*Say* TESS ul]

tesla *n.* (*pl.* **teslas**) the SI unit of density of magnetic flux density. [*Say* TESS luh]

test ● *n.* **1** a examination or trial of the qualities, genuineness, condition, or suitability of a person or thing. **2** a procedure for assessing a person's aptitude, competence, skill, or intelligence. **3** a situation requiring a particular ability or strength. **4** a standard for comparison or trial. **5** *Chemistry* a procedure for identifying a substance or revealing whether it is present. **6** (as an *adj.*) designating fishing line having a specified strength. ● *v.* **1** subject to a close or critical examination. **2** subject to a chemical test. **3** apply or carry out a test on a person or thing. **4** try the patience or endurance of. □ **testable** *adj.*

testament *n.* **1** *Bible* (**Testament**) either of the main divisions of the Christian Bible. **2** evidence, proof; a tribute. **3** a will.

test bed *n.* a testing site.

test case *n.* **1** *Law* a case that sets a precedent for other cases involving the same legal principle. **2** a set of circumstances used to test something.

test drive ● *v.* **1** drive a vehicle in order to assess its quality before buying it. **2** *informal* sample a product prior to purchase. ● *n.* a drive taken to assess the performance of a vehicle one is thinking of buying.

tester *n.* **1** a person or device that tests something. **2** a small amount of a perfume or cosmetic for a customer to sample before purchase.

testes *pl. of* TESTIS. [*Say* TESS teez]

testicle *n.* either of the two sperm-producing oval organs in male mammals, enclosed in the scrotum. □ **testicular** *adj.* [*Say* TESTA cull, tess TICK yoo lur]

testify *v.* (**testifies**, **testified**, **testifying**) **1** give evidence in a court of law. **2** affirm or declare, esp. based on first-hand knowledge. **3** bear witness; attest. **4** serve as proof or evidence of.

testimonial *n.* **1** a statement attesting to the quality of a product, character of a person, etc. **2** a public tribute. [*Say* testa MOANY ul]

testimony *n.* (*pl.* **testimonies**) **1** evidence presented by a witness in a court of law. **2** a declaration or statement of fact. **3** (usu. foll. by *to*) a demonstration. [*Say* TESTA moany]

testing ground *n.* a place or situation where something may be tried out before being used, implemented, or adopted on a larger scale.

testis *n.* (*pl.* **testes**) a testicle. [*Say* TESS tiss *for the singular*, TESS teez *for the plural*]

testosterone *n.* **1** a hormone that stimulates the development of male secondary sexual characteristics. **2** *informal* stereotypical male behaviour etc. [*Say* tess TOSSTA rone]

test tube *n.* **1** a cylindrical glass vessel with a rounded bottom, used to hold small amounts of liquid for experimentation. **2** (as an *adj.*, usu. **test-tube**) designating procedures carried out in laboratories.

test-tube baby *n.* *informal* a baby that grows from an egg that is fertilized outside the mother's body and then inserted back in the uterus.

testy *adj.* (**testier**, **testiest**) irritable, touchy. □ **testily** *adv.* **testiness** *n.*

tetanus *n.* a disease causing the muscles to stiffen and go into spasms. [*Say* TET nuss *or* TET a nuss]

tetchy *adj.* (**tetchier**, **tetchiest**) easily angered or annoyed. □ **tetchily** *adv.* **tetchiness** *n.*

tête-à-tête (*pl.* **tête-à-têtes**) ● *n.* a conversation between two people. ● *adv.* **1** together in private. **2** face to face. [*Say* tet a TET]

tether ● *n.* a rope etc. used to tie an animal to the spot. ● *v.* **1** tie with a tether. **2** bind by circumstances or conditions.

Tetlit Gwich'in *n.* a member of a Gwich'in people from Fort McPherson, NWT. □ **Tetlit Gwich'in** *adj.* [TEET lit GWITCH in]

tetracycline *n.* any of various of antibiotics used in the treatment of acne etc. [*Say* tetra SIKE lean *or* tetra SIKE lin]

tetrahedron *n.* (*pl.* **tetrahedrons** *or* **tetrahedra**) a solid figure with four plane faces. □ **tetrahedral** *adj.* [*Say* tetra HEE drun *for the singular,* tetra HEE druh *or* tetra HEE druns *for the plural*]

tetrahydrocannabinol *n.* = THC. [*Say* tetra hydro kuh NAB in awl]

tetravalent *adj.* *Chemistry* having a valence of four. [*Say* tetra VAY lunt]

Teuton *n.* a member of a Teutonic nation, esp. a German. [*Say* TOO tun *or* TYOO tun]

Teutonic *adj.* **1** German. **2** stereotypically German. [*Say* too TONIC *or* tyoo TONIC]

Texan *n.* a native or inhabitant of Texas. □ **Texan** *adj.*

Tex-Mex ● *n.* a Texan style of cooking with Mexican influences. ● *adj.* blending Texan and Mexican elements.

text *n.* **1** the wording of something written. **2** the main written or printed part of a book as distinct from notes, illustrations, etc. **3** the original words of a document. **4** data in textual form. **5 a** a textbook. **b** (in *pl.*) books prescribed for study. **6** a short passage from the Scriptures.

textbook ● *n.* a book giving instruction in a particular subject. ● *adj.* conforming to a standard or model.

textile *n.* fabric; cloth.

text messaging *n.* the sending of a message in text over the Internet to appear on the display screen of a wireless phone or pager. □ **text message** *n.*

textual *adj.* relating to a text or texts. □ **textually** *adv.*

textural *adj.* relating to texture. □ **texturally** *adv.*

texture ● *n.* **1 a** the roughness, smoothness, softness, etc. of a surface. **b** the feel of food in the mouth. **2** the composition of the constituent parts of something, such as soil or rock. ● *v.* (**textures, textured, texturing**) provide with a texture. □ **textured** *adj.*

Thai *n.* (*pl.* **Thai** *or* **Thais**) **1** a person from Thailand. **2** the language of Thailand. □ **Thai** *adj.* [*Sounds like* TIE]

thalamus *n.* (*pl.* **thalami**) either of two masses of grey matter in the brain, involved in sensory information and pain perception. [*Say* THALLA muss, THALLA my]

thalassemia *n.* (*pl.* **thalassemias**) any of a group of hereditary diseases caused by faulty hemoglobin synthesis. [*Say* thalla SEEMY uh]

thalidomide *n.* **1** a drug formerly used as a sedative but found in 1961 to cause fetal malformation. **2** (as an *adj.*) born with an abnormality due to the effects of thalidomide. [*Say* thuh LIDDA mide]

thallium *n.* a rare soft white metallic element. [*Say* THALLY um]

than *conj. & prep.* **1** introducing the second element in a comparison. **2** introducing the second element in a statement of difference. **3** in a statement expressing hypothesis or consequence. **4** when.

thank ● *v.* **1** express gratitude to. **2** hold responsible. ● *n.* (in *pl.*) **1** gratitude. **2** an expression of gratitude. ● *interj.* (in *pl.*) used

as an expression of gratitude. □ **no thanks to** despite. **thank goodness** (or **God** or **heavens** etc.) an expression of relief or pleasure. **thanks to** as a result of.

thankful *adj.* **1** grateful, appreciative, relieved. **2** expressive of thanks. □ **thankfulness** *n.*

thankfully *adv.* **1** *disputed* fortunately. **2** in a thankful manner.

thankless *adj.* **1** not expressing or feeling gratitude. **2** (of a task etc.) not likely to win or receive thanks. □ **thanklessly** *adv.*

Thanksgiving *n.* **1** *Cdn* an annual holiday, originally for giving thanks for the harvest, celebrated in Canada on the second Monday in October, and in the US on the fourth Thursday in November. **2** (**thanksgiving**) the expression of thanks or gratitude, esp. to God.

thank you ● *interj.* **1** a polite formula expressing gratitude for something. **2** used to emphasize a preceding refusal. ● *n.* *informal* an act of expressing gratitude.

that ● *pron. & demonstrative adj.* (*pl.* **those**) **1** used to identify a specific person or thing. **2** referring to the more distant of two things. **3** referring to a previously-mentioned thing. **4** (as a *pronoun*) (*pl.* **that**) used instead of *which* or *whom* to introduce a defining clause. ● *adv.* **1** to such a degree. **2** *informal* very. ● *conj.* **1** introducing a subordinate clause. **2** *literary* expressing a wish or regret. □ **all that** very. **and all that** *informal* and all or various associated things. **like that 1** of that kind. **2** in that manner. **3** *informal* without effort. **that is** (or **that is to say**) a formula introducing or following an explanation. **that's that** a formula indicating completion. **that will do** no more is needed or desirable.

thataway *adv.* *informal* in that direction.

thatch ● *n.* (*pl.* **thatches**) **1** a roof covering of straw, reeds, etc. **2** a matted layer of plant debris etc. on a lawn. ● *v.* (**thatches, thatched, thatching**) **1** cover with thatch. **2** remove thatch from a lawn.

thatched *adj.* made of, covered, or roofed with thatch.

thaw ● *v.* **1** (often foll. by *out*) **a** pass from a frozen to an unfrozen state. **b** warm up after being very cold. **2** (of the weather) become warm enough to melt snow and ice etc. **3** (often foll. by *out*) defrost. **4** make or become amicable after a period of animosity. ● *n.* **1** a period of warmer weather marked by the melting of snow and ice. **2** a reduction in the hostility or formality of relations.

THC *abbr.* tetrahydrocannabinol, a

crystalline compound that is the main active ingredient of cannabis.

the ● *definite article* **1** denoting one or more people or things already mentioned, under discussion, implied, or familiar. **2** serving to describe as unique. **3 a** which is, who are, etc. **b** denoting a class described. **4** best known or best entitled to the name. **5** used to indicate that a singular noun represents a species, class, etc. ● *adv.* in or by that (or such a) degree; on that account.

theatre *n.* (also **theater**) **1 a** a building or facility where plays etc. are performed in front of an audience. **b** a building or facility where movies are screened. **2** forms of entertainment performed in theatres. **3** the writing, production, and performance of plays. **4** a scene or field of action. **5** (also **operating theatre**) a room for surgical operations.

theatregoer *n.* a person who often attends theatres. □ **theatregoing** *n. & adj.*

theatrical ● *adj.* **1** of or for the theatre; of acting or actors. **2 a** (of a manner, speech, or gesture) calculated for effect; showy. **b** (of a person) artificial, affected. ● *n.* **1** (usu. in *pl.*) a dramatic performance. **2** (in *pl.*) theatrics. □ **theatricality** *n.* **theatrically** *adv.*

theatrics *pl. n.* showy dramatic gestures, exaggerated behaviour and display of emotion.

thee *pron. archaic objective case of* THOU[1].

theft *n.* the action of stealing.

their *poss. adj.* **1** of or belonging to them. **2** *disputed* his or her.

theirs *poss. pron.* **1** the one or ones belonging to or associated with them. **2** *disputed* the one or ones belonging to an indefinite singular antecedent. □ **of theirs** of or belonging to them.

theism *n.* belief in the existence of gods or a god, esp. one who created and intervenes in the universe. □ **theist** *n.* **theistic** *adj.* [*Say* THEE ism, THEE ist, thee ISS tick (*with* TH *as in* THIEF)]

them *pron.* **1** objective case of THEY. **2** *disputed* him or her.

thematic *adj.* of or relating to subjects or topics. □ **thematically** *adv.* [*Say* theme ATTIC]

theme ● *n.* **1 a** a subject on which a person speaks, writes, or thinks. **b** a dominant subject in work of art. **2** a frequently recurring melody. **3** (also **theme song**) a distinctive tune used to introduce a particular program, person, etc. ● *v.* (**themes, themed, theming**) design (an event etc.) around a theme.

theme park *n.* an amusement park organized around a theme.

themselves *pron.* **1 a** *emphatic form of* THEY or THEM. **b** *reflexive form of* THEM. **2** *disputed* himself or herself. □ **be themselves** act in their normal manner.

then ● *adv.* **1** at that time. **2 a** next. **b** and also. **c** after all. **3** in that case. ● *adj.* that or who was such at the time in question. ● *n.* that time. □ **then again** on the other hand.

thence *adv.* (also **from thence**) *archaic* or *literary* **1** from that place. **2** for that reason. **3** thenceforth.

thenceforth *adv.* (also **from thenceforth**) *archaic* or *literary* from that time onward.

theocracy *n.* (*pl.* **theocracies**) **1** a form of government by God or by a priestly order etc. which rules in the name of God. **2** a state so governed. □ **theocratic** *adj.* [*Say* thee OCKRA see, thee uh CRAT ick (*with* TH *as in* THIEF)]

theologian *n.* a person who studies theology. [*Say* thee uh LOW jun (*with* TH *as in* THIEF)]

theology *n.* (*pl.* **theologies**) **1** the study of God and religious belief. **2** religious beliefs and theory. □ **theological** *adj.* [*Say* thee OLLA jee, thee uh LOGICAL (*with* TH *as in* THIEF)]

theorem *n.* esp. *Math* **1** a general proposition not self-evident but proved by a chain of reasoning. **2** a rule in algebra etc., esp. one expressed by symbols or formulas. [*Say* THEER um]

theoretical *adj.* (also **theoretic**) **1** concerned with knowledge but not with its practical application. **2** based on theory rather than experience or practice. **3** existing only in theory. □ **theoretically** *adv.* [*Say* thee uh RET ick ul (*with* TH *as in* THIEF)]

theoretician *n.* a person concerned with the theoretical aspects of a subject. [*Say* theer a TISH'n]

theorist *n.* a theoretician. [*Say* THEER ist]

theorize *v.* (**theorizes, theorized, theorizing**) **1** form or construct theories. **2** consider in theory. [*Say* THEER ize]

theory *n.* (*pl.* **theories**) **1** a supposition or system of ideas explaining something. **2** a speculative (esp. fanciful) view. **3** (the sphere of) abstract knowledge. **4** the principles on which a subject of study is based.

theosophy *n.* a philosophy professing to achieve a knowledge of God by spiritual ecstasy, direct intuition, or special individual relations. [*Say* thee OSSA fee (*with* TH *as in* THIEF)]

therapeutic *adj.* **1** of, for, or contributing to the cure of disease. **2** contributing to

general well-being. □ **therapeutically** adv.
therapeutics pl. n.
[Say therra PYOOT ick]

therapy n. (pl. **therapies**) **1** the treatment of physical or mental disorders. **2** a particular type of such treatment. □ **therapist** n. [Say THERRA pee, THERRA pist]

there ● adv. **1** in, at, or to that place or position. **2** at that point. **3** in that respect. **4** used for emphasis in calling attention. **5** used to indicate the fact or existence of something. ● interj. **1** expressing triumph, satisfaction, etc. ● n. **2** used to soothe. □ **be there for someone** be ready to give support etc. **have been there before** slang know all about it. **there it is** that is the situation.

thereabouts adv. (also **thereabout**) **1** near that place. **2** near that number, quantity, etc.

thereafter adv. formal after that.

thereby adv. by that means, as a result of that.

therefore adv. for that reason.

therein adv. formal **1** in or into that place etc. **2** in that respect.

thereof adv. formal of that or it.

thereon adv. formal on that or it.

there's contr. there is.

thereto adv. formal that or it.

thereupon adv. immediately or shortly after that.

thermal ● adj. **1** of, for, or producing heat. **2** promoting the retention of heat. ● n. **1** a rising current of heated air. **2** thermal underwear. □ **thermally** adv.

thermodynamics pl. n. (usu. treated as sing.) the science of the relations between heat and other forms of energy. □ **thermodynamic** adj.

thermometer n. an instrument for measuring temperature.

thermonuclear adj. **1** relating to or using nuclear reactions that occur only at very high temperatures. **2** relating to weapons using these reactions.

thermoplastic ● adj. (of a substance) that becomes soft and plastic on heating. ● n. a thermoplastic substance.

Thermos n. (pl. **Thermoses**) proprietary an insulated flask for keeping a liquid hot or cold.

thermostat n. a device that automatically regulates temperature, or that activates a device at a set temperature. □ **thermostatic** adj. **thermostatically** adv.

thesaurus n. (pl. **thesauruses** or **thesauri**) a book that lists words in

groups of synonyms and related concepts. [Say thuh SORE us for the singular, thuh SORE us iz or thuh SORE eye for the plural]

these pl. of THIS.

thesis n. (pl. **theses**) **1** a proposition to be maintained or proved. **2** a dissertation, esp. by a candidate for a degree. [Say THEE sis for the singular, THEE seez for the plural (with TH as in THIEF)]

thespian ● adj. of or relating to tragedy or drama. ● n. an actor or actress. [Say THESPY un]

they pron. **1** the people, animals, or things previously named or in question. **2** people in general. **3** those in authority. **4** disputed as a third person singular indefinite pronoun meaning "he or she".

they'd contr. **1** they had. **2** they would.

they'll contr. **1** they will. **2** they shall.

they're contr. they are.

they've contr. they have.

thiamine n. a vitamin of the vitamin B complex, occurring in unrefined cereals, beans, and liver. [Say THIGH a min]

thick ● adj. **1** of great or specified extent between opposite surfaces. **2 a** crowded together; dense. **b** numerous. **3** densely covered or filled. **4** firm in consistency. **5** impenetrable by sight. **6** informal stupid. **7** (of an accent) very marked. **8** informal intimate or very friendly. ● n. a thick or dense part of anything. □ **in the thick of 1** at the busiest or most intense part of. **2** heavily occupied with. **lay it** (or **something**) **on thick** exaggerate. **through thick and thin** under all conditions. □ **thickly** adv. **thickness** n.

thicken v. **1** make or become thick or thicker. **2** become more complicated. □ **thickener** n.

thickening n. **1** the process of becoming thick or thicker. **2** a substance used to thicken liquid. **3** a thickened part.

thicket n. a tangle of shrubs or trees.

thickset adj. **1** heavily or solidly built. **2** set or growing close together.

thick skin n. **1** a thick or hard skin. **2** informal insensitivity to criticism. □ **thick-skinned** adj.

thief n. (pl. **thieves**) a person who steals.

thieve v. (**thieves**, **thieved**, **thieving**) **1** be a thief. **2** steal. □ **thievery** n.

thigh n. the part of the leg between the hip and the knee.

thigh bone n. the femur.

thimble n. **1** a metal or plastic cap, usu. with a closed end, worn to protect the finger in sewing. **2** (also **thimbleful** (pl. **thimblefuls**)) a small quantity.

thin ● *adj.* (**thinner, thinnest**) **1** having the opposite surfaces close together. **2** made of thin material. **3** lean. **4 a** not dense or copious. **b** not full or closely packed. **5** of slight consistency. ● *adv.* thinly. ● *v.* (**thins, thinned, thinning**) **1** make or become thin or thinner. **2** reduce. **3** remove some plants etc. to improve the growth of the rest. □ **thin on top** balding. □ **thinness** *n.*

thin air *n.* a state of invisibility or non-existence.

thin blue line *n.* the police or military seen as the only defence against invasion etc.

thine *poss. pron. archaic* **1** the one or ones belonging to thee. **2** (before a vowel) = THY.

thing *n.* **1** an inanimate material object. **2** an unspecified object. **3** (**things**) personal belongings or clothing. **4** an action, activity, or thought. **5** (**things**) unspecified matters **6** (**the thing**) *informal* what is needed, acceptable, or fashionable. □ **do one's own thing** *informal* pursue one's own interests. **do things to** *informal* affect remarkably. **have a thing about** (or **for, with**) *informal* be obsessed about. **make a thing of** *informal* **1** regard as essential. **2** cause a fuss about. **one** (or **just one**) **of those things** *informal* something not avoidable.

thingy *n.* (*pl.* **thingies**) (also **thingamajig, thingamabob, thingummy** (*pl.* **thingummies**)) *informal* a person or thing whose name one has forgotten or does not know.

think ● *v.* (**thinks, thought, thinking**) **1** have a particular opinion, belief, or idea about someone or something. **2** direct one's mind toward someone or something. **3** take into account or consideration. **4** consider the possibility or advantages of. **5** have a particular opinion of. **6** call something to mind. ● *n. informal* an act of thinking. □ **have another think coming** be greatly mistaken. **think again** revise one's plans or opinions. **think aloud** utter one's thoughts as soon as they occur. **think better of** change one's mind about (an intention) after reconsideration. **think over** reflect upon in order to reach a decision. **think through** reflect fully upon. **think twice** avoid hasty action etc. **think up** *informal* devise. □ **thinkable** *adj.* **thinker** *n.*

thinking ● *adj.* **1** using thought or rational judgment. **2** thoughtful, intellectual. ● *n.* opinion or judgment. □ **put on one's thinking cap** *informal* meditate on a problem.

think tank *n.* a body of experts providing advice and ideas on specific national or commercial problems.

thinly *adv.* **1** in a way that produces a thin piece or layer of something. **2** with very few things or people close together. **3** in a way that is not sincere. **4** in a way that does not hide the truth very well.

thinner *n.* a liquid used to dilute paint etc.

thin red line *n.* the military seen as the only defence against lawlessness, invasion, etc.

thin-skinned *adj.* **1** having a thin skin. **2** sensitive to criticism.

third *ord. num.* **1** constituting number three in a sequence; 3rd. **2** each of three equal parts into which something is divided. **3** an interval spanning three consecutive notes in a diatonic scale, e.g. C to E. □ **thirdly** *adv.*

third degree ● *n.* long and severe questioning to obtain information or a confession. ● *adj.* (**third-degree**) denoting burns of the most severe kind.

third eye *n.* **1** *Hinduism & Buddhism* the "eye of insight" in the forehead of an image of a deity. **2** the faculty of intuitive insight.

third party ● *n.* **1** a party or person besides the two primarily concerned. **2** a person involved incidentally. ● *adj. Cdn & Brit.* (of insurance) covering damage or injury suffered by a person other than the insured.

third-rate *adj.* inferior.

Third Reich *n.* the Nazi regime, 1933–45.

third-string *adj.* (esp. of an athlete) inferior. □ **third-stringer** *n.*

Third Wave *n.* the current phase of economic, social, and cultural change, in which knowledge is the primary productive force.

third way *n.* any option regarded as an alternative to two extremes.

third wheel *n. informal* a third person joining a couple in a social situation more suitable for just the couple.

Third World *n.* (usu. as **the Third World**) the developing countries of Asia, Africa, and Latin America.

thirst ● *n.* **1** a physical craving to drink something. **2** a strong desire or craving. ● *v.* (usu. foll. by *for*) **1** feel thirst. **2** have a strong desire.

thirsty *adj.* (**thirstier, thirstiest**) **1** having a need or desire to drink. **2** dry; needing moisture. **3** (often foll. by *for*) eager. **4** *informal* causing thirst. □ **thirstily** *adv.*

thirteen *card. num.* one more than twelve. □ **thirteenth** *ord. num.*

thirty *card. num.* (*pl.* **thirties**) ten more than twenty. □ **thirtieth** *ord. num.*

thirtyish *adj. informal* about thirty, esp. in age.

thirty-second note *n. Music* a note having the time value of half a sixteenth note and represented by a large dot with a three-hooked stem.

thirtysomething *informal* ● *n.* **1** an undetermined age between thirty and forty. **2** a person of this age. ● *adj.* between thirty and forty years of age.

this ● *demonstrative pron. & demonstrative adj.* (*pl.* **these**) **1** used to identify a specific person or thing close at hand or being indicated or experienced. **2** referring to the nearer of two things. **3** referring to a thing or situation just mentioned. **4** used with periods of time related to the present. ● *adv.* to the degree or extent indicated. □ **this and that** *informal* various unspecified things.

thistle *n.* **1** a prickly plant with chiefly purple flowers in globular heads. **2** one of these plants as the national emblem of Scotland. **3** any of several other prickly plants. [With TH *as in* THIN]

thistledown *n.* the light feathery down of a thistle seed.

thither *adv. archaic* or *formal* to or towards that place.

Thompson *n.* = NLAKA'PAMUX. [Say TOM sun]

thong *n.* **1** a narrow strip of hide or leather used esp. as a lace, cord, etc. **2** = FLIP-FLOP 2. **3** a skimpy undergarment that covers the genitals but not the buttocks. □ **thonged** *adj.*

thorax *n.* **1 a** the part of the body of a mammal between the neck and the abdomen. **b** the corresponding part of a bird, reptile, amphibian, or fish. **2** the middle section of the body of an arthropod. □ **thoracic** *adj.* [Say THOR axe, thor ASS ick]

thorium *n.* a radioactive metallic element used in electronic equipment and as a source of nuclear energy. [Say THORRY um]

thorn *n.* **1** a stiff sharp projection on a plant. **2** a thorn-bearing bush, shrub, or tree. **3** a cause of grief, irritation, or trouble. □ **thornless** *adj.*

thorny *adj.* (**thornier, thorniest**) **1** having many thorns. **2** difficult to handle or resolve.

thorough *adj.* **1** applied to or affecting every detail. **2** done with great care and completeness. **3** taking pains to do something completely. **4** absolute, utter. □ **thoroughly** *adv.* **thoroughness** *n.*

thoroughbred ● *n.* **1** a purebred animal, esp. a horse. **2** (**Thoroughbred**) a racehorse of a breed originating from English mares and Arab stallions. ● *adj.* **1** of pure breed. **2** of outstanding quality.

thoroughfare *n.* a road or path.

thoroughgoing *adj.* extremely thorough.

those *pl. of* THAT.

thou[1] *pron. archaic* the second person singular nominative pronoun; you. [With TH *as in* THAT]

thou[2] *n.* (*pl.* **thou** or **thous**) *informal* a thousand, esp. a thousand dollars. [With TH *as in* THOUSAND]

though ● *conj.* **1** despite the fact that. **2** even if. **3** nevertheless. **4** in spite of being. ● *adv.* **1** however; all the same. **2** indeed, truly □ **as though** = AS IF (*see* AS[1]).

thought ● *n.* **1** the process or power of thinking. **2** the way of thinking associated with a particular time, people, etc. **3** sober reflection or contemplation. **4** an idea. **5 a** regard, consideration. **b** (in *pl.*) sympathy. ● *v. past and past participle of* THINK. □ **give thought to** consider. **on second thought** contrary to what one originally decided.

thoughtful *adj.* **1** (often foll. by *of*) considerate, kind. **2** showing signs of careful thought or consideration. **3 a** absorbed in meditation. **b** given to contemplation. □ **thoughtfully** *adv.* **thoughtfulness** *n.*

thoughtless *adj.* **1** lacking in consideration for others. **2** showing a lack of concern for consequences. **3** resulting from a lack of thought. □ **thoughtlessly** *adv.* **thoughtlessness** *n.*

thought out *adj.* produced by mental effort.

thousand *card. num.* **1** the product of a hundred and ten; 1,000. **2** (**thousands**) *informal* an unspecified large number. □ **thousandfold** *adj. & adv.* **thousandth** *ord. num.*

Thousand Island *n.* designating a salad dressing made of mayonnaise, chili sauce, etc.

thrall *n. literary* a condition of or like slavery. □ **thralldom** *n.* [Rhymes with MALL]

thrash ● *v.* (**thrashes, thrashed, thrashing**) **1** beat severely with a stick or whip. **2 a** *informal* defeat convincingly. **b** criticize or scold severely. **3** move or fling the body, limbs, etc., about violently, esp. in panic. **4** = THRESH 1. ● *n.* a style of fast loud heavy metal rock music. □ **thrash out** discuss at length in order to reach a solution or consensus. □ **thrashing** *n.*

thrasher *n.* **1** = THRESHER 2. **2 a** N American songbird with greyish or brownish plumage and a slightly down-curved bill.

thread ● *n.* **1** a long, thin strand of fibres used in sewing or weaving. **2** a long thin line or piece of something. **3** a spiral ridge on the outside of a screw, bolt, etc., or on the inside of a nut etc. **4** a theme running throughout a situation or piece of writing. **5** a group of linked messages posted on the Internet that share a common subject. **6** (**threads**) *informal* clothes. ● *v.* **1** pass a thread through. **2** move or weave in and out of obstacles. **3** *Sport* complete (a pass) to a teammate through a crowd of players. □ **threaded** *adj.* **threadlike** *adj.*

threadbare *adj.* **1** (of fabric, carpeting, etc.) so worn that the nap is lost and the thread visible. **2 a** having lost effect through overuse. **b** weak or insubstantial. **3** wearing threadbare clothing.

threat *n.* **1** an expression of an intention to inflict pain, injury, damage, etc. **2** an indication of the imminent occurrence of something unwelcome. **3** a person or thing likely to cause of harm etc.

threaten *v.* **1** (often foll. by *with*) make a threat or threats against. **2** appear likely to cause something undesirable. **3** jeopardize or endanger. **4** be an indication of the imminent occurrence of something undesirable. **5** intimidate or frighten.

threatened *adj.* **1** in danger of becoming rare or extinct. **2** vulnerable, intimidated. **3** having been vowed, predicted, or foreshadowed. **4** in jeopardy or danger.

threatening *adj.* **1** designed or tending to menace or intimidate. **2** foreboding. □ **threateningly** *adv.*

three *card. num.* (*pl.* **threes**) one more than two.

3-D ● *adj.* **1** three-dimensional. **2** used to produce a three-dimensional image or appearance. ● *n.* a format that presents three-dimensional images.

three-dimensional *adj.* having or appearing to have length, width, and depth. □ **three-dimensionality** *n.*

threefold ● *adj.* **1** three times as much or as many. **2** consisting of three parts. ● *adv.* to or by three times the number.

three-on-three *n.* a scaled-down game of basketball involving two teams of three players shooting at only one basket.

three-peat *Sport informal* ● *n.* a third consecutive win of a particular championship. ● *v.* win a particular championship for a third consecutive time.

three-piece *adj.* **1** consisting of three matching parts. **2** (of a suit) consisting of matching pants, jacket, and vest.

three-pitch *n. Cdn* a variety of softball in

which the batter has only three chances to hit a ball delivered underhand by a teammate.

three-point turn *n.* a method of turning a vehicle around by moving in three arcs, forwards, backwards, and forwards again.

three-pronged *adj.* having three aspects, stages, aims, etc.

three-ring circus *n.* **1** a circus with three rings for simultaneous performances. **2** a public spectacle, esp. one with little substance.

three-sixty *n.* (*pl.* **three-sixties**) *informal* a spin or turn of 360°

threesome *n.* a group of three people.

three-star *adj.* (of a hotel, restaurant, etc.) given three stars in a grading; of fairly high quality.

three-way *adj.* involving or having three participants, settings, parts, etc.

three-wheeler *n.* a vehicle with three wheels.

thresh *v.* (**threshes, threshed, threshing**) **1** shake or beat wheat etc. to separate the grain from the husk and straw. **2** = THRASH *v.* 1, 3. [*Rhymes with* MESH *or* MASH]

thresher *n.* **1 a** a person that threshes grain. **b** a threshing machine. **2** (also **thresher shark**) a shark with a long upper lobe to its tail. [*THRESH rhymes with* MESH *or* MASH]

threshold *n.* **1 a** the bottom of a doorway, crossed upon entering a house or room. **b** the entrance to a building etc. **c** the boundary of a region. **2** the point just before a new situation, period of life, etc. begins. **3** a level that must be exceeded for a certain reaction, phenomenon, result, or condition to take place.

threw *past of* THROW.

thrice *adv. archaic* three times.

thrift *n.* the habit of saving money and spending it carefully. □ **thriftiness** *n.* **thrifty** *adj.*

thrift shop *n.* (also **thrift store**) a store that sells second-hand merchandise, with proceeds often going to charity.

thrill ● *n.* **1** a powerful and often sudden feeling of excitement, exhilaration, or emotion. **2** an exciting or exhilarating event or experience. **3** intense excitement. ● *v.* **1** cause to feel intense excitement. **2** thoroughly please or delight. **3** feel or become excited. **4** quiver or throb with or as if with emotion. □ **thrilled** *adj.* **thrilling** *adj.* **thrillingly** *adv.*

thriller *n.* an exciting or sensational movie or novel etc., esp. a suspenseful one involving mystery, crime, or espionage.

thrips *n.* (*pl.* **thrips**) a minute dark insect which sucks plant sap and can be a pest.

thrive *v.* (**thrives**; *past* **thrived** or **throve**; *past participle* **thrived**; **thriving**) **1** grow vigorously, flourish. **2** be or become successful or prosperous. □ **thrive on** **1** depend upon for growth or sustenance. **2** be driven or encouraged by. □ **thriving** *adj.*

throat *n.* **1** the front part of the neck beneath. **2** the windpipe or gullet. **3** anything resembling or compared to a throat. □ **be at each other's** (or **one another's**) **throats** quarrel violently. **ram** (or **thrust** etc.) **down a person's throat** force a person to accept. □ **-throated** *adj.* (in *comb.*)

throaty *adj.* **1** (of a voice) rough, husky. **2** produced or modified in the throat; deep, guttural.

throb ● *v.* (**throbs, throbbed, throbbing**) **1** beat or palpitate, esp. with more than usual force or rapidity. **2** pulsate or vibrate, esp. with a deep audible rhythm. **3** ache with a recurrent or pulsating pain. ● *n.* **1** a palpitation or (esp. violent) pulsation. **2** a rhythmic esp. audible beat or vibration.

throes *pl. n.* intense or violent pains or struggles, esp. accompanying death, birth, or great change.

thrombosis *n.* a clotting of the blood in a part of the circulatory system. [*Say* throm BO sis]

throne *n.* **1** an ornate chair occupied by a monarch, esp. on ceremonial occasions. **2** the position, office, power, or dignity of a sovereign. **3** *informal* a toilet.

Throne Speech *n. Cdn* = SPEECH FROM THE THRONE.

throng ● *n.* a crowd or multitude of people. ● *v.* **1** gather or assemble in or around. **2** travel in large numbers.

throttle ● *n.* a device controlling the flow of fuel or steam etc. in an engine. ● *v.* (**throttles, throttled, throttling**) **1** choke or strangle. **2** control the flow of gas or steam to an engine. □ **throttle back** (or **down**) close the throttle of (an engine or vehicle) in order to slow down.

through ● *prep.* **1 a** from one end to the other of. **b** beyond; past. **2** between or among. **3** from beginning to end of. **4 a** by means of. **b** due to. **5** up to and including. ● *adv.* **1 a** from side to side, end to end, or beginning to end of. **b** all the way; to the end of a journey. **2** past or across a barrier or space. **3** successfully past a particular stage or test. **4** so as to be connected by telephone. ● *adj.* **1** (of a flight etc.) that travels the whole distance or journey

without interruption or change. **2** (of traffic) going through a place to a destination. **3** (of a road, route, etc.) open at both ends, allowing a continuous journey. □ **be through** *informal* **1** have finished. **2** cease to have dealings. **3** have no further prospects. **through and through** thoroughly; in every respect.

throughout ● *prep.* **1** through all of; in or to every part of; everywhere in. **2** during the whole time, extent, or length of. ● *adv.* **1** in every part or respect. **2** during the whole time.

throughput *n.* **1** the amount of material put through a process, esp. in manufacturing or computing. **2** processing or handling capacity.

throve *past of* THRIVE.

throw ● *v.* (**throws**; *past* **threw**; *past participle* **thrown**; **throwing**) **1** propel with force through the air by a rapid movement of the arm and hand. **2** move or put into place quickly, hurriedly, or roughly. **3** project, direct, or cast in a particular direction. **4** send suddenly into a particular condition. **5** disconcert or confuse. **6** have a fit or tantrum. **7** *informal* give or hold a party. ● *n.* **1** an act of throwing. **2** a small rug or light cover for furniture. **3** (preceded by *a*) *informal* a single turn, round, or item. □ **throw away 1** dispose of or discard. **2** waste or fail to make use of. **throw back 1** (usu. in *passive*; foll. by *on*) force to rely on something. **2** pull aside (curtains, bedclothes, etc.), esp. with a sharp movement. **throw a person a curve** confuse someone by doing or saying something unexpected. **throw down the gauntlet** (or **glove**) issue a challenge. **throw in 1** include at no extra cost. **2** add or make a remark casually. **throw in the towel** (or **sponge**) admit defeat. **throw off 1** confuse or distract from the matter in hand. **2** discard; contrive to get rid of. **3** write or utter in an offhand manner. **throw oneself at** make eager or overt advances upon. **throw oneself into** engage vigorously in. **throw oneself on** (or **upon**) **1** rely completely on. **2** attack. **throw open 1** open wide and usu. suddenly. **2** make vulnerable or accessible. **3** invite general discussion on (a question). **throw out 1** discard or dispose of. **2 a** force to leave the premises. **b** evict from a house or apartment. **c** *Sport* eject from a game as a disciplinary measure. **3** wrench or dislocate. **4** put forward tentatively. **5 a** reject in Parliament. **b** dismiss in a court of law. **6** *Baseball* put out by throwing the ball to the base before he or she reaches it. **throw over** desert or abandon. **throw together 1** prepare or assemble hastily. **2** introduce. **throw up 1** vomit. **2** abandon. **3** resign from. **4** erect hastily. **5** bring to notice. **6** lift (a sash window) quickly. **throw one's weight around** (or **about**) *informal* act with unpleasant self-assertiveness. □ **thrower** *n.*

throwaway ● *adj.* **1** disposable. **2** (of a line, word, etc.) deliberately insufficiently emphasized for effect. **3** disposed to throwing things away. ● *n.* something that is meant to be discarded after esp. one use.

throwback *n.* (often foll. by *to*) **1** a person who embodies the principles etc. of an earlier era. **2** something that recalls a similar thing of a previous era.

throw rug *n.* a light rug used as a casual covering for furniture.

thrum[1] ● *v.* (**thrums, thrummed, thrumming**) **1** play (a stringed instrument) monotonously. **2** drum idly. **3** produce or emit a low hum or thrumming sound. ● *n.* **1** a low monotonous hum or drone, such as that of a car. **2** music consisting of the unskilled or monotonous playing of a guitar etc.

thrum[2] ● *n.* loose strands or wisps of wool that has not been spun, raw fleece etc. twisted and knitted into a toque or mitten etc. ● *v.* (**thrums, thrummed, thrumming**) knit thrums into a mitten or toque etc. at regular intervals. □ **thrummed** *adj.* **thrumming** *n.*

thrush *n.* (*pl.* **thrushes**) **1** a songbird with a brown back, a spotted breast, and a loud song. **2** a fungal disease characterized by white patches on the inside of the mouth and throat and on the tongue. **3** this disease affecting any other part of the body, esp. the vagina.

thrust ● *v.* (**thrusts, thrust, thrusting**) **1** push or shove with a sudden force. **2 a** (foll. by *on*) impose forcibly on a person. **b** force into some condition or course of action. **3 a** make (one's way) forcibly. **b** make a sudden lunge forward. **c** stab. ● *n.* **1** a sudden or forcible push or lunge. **2** the propulsive force exerted by a propeller, jet, etc. **3** the principal theme or underlying principle. **4** a caustic or critical remark. **5** a lunge or attack. **6** the sideways pressure exerted by an arch or other structure against an abutment or support.

thruster *n.* **1** a small rocket engine on a spacecraft. **2 a** (also **bow thruster**) a propeller located on the bow of a ship. **b** each of several jets or propellers on an offshore rig etc.

thud ● *n.* a dull low sound like that of a blow on something soft. ● *v.* (**thuds, thudded, thudding**) produce or fall with a thud.

thug *n.* **1** a vicious ruffian. **2** *derogatory* a punk or bully. □ **thuggery** *n.* **thuggish** *adj.*

thumb ● *n.* **1 a** the short thick first digit of the human hand. **b** a corresponding digit of the foot or hand of other animals. **2** the part of a glove meant for a thumb. ● *v.* **1** turn the pages of a book with or as if with a thumb. **2** make dirty or worn with repeated handling. **3** solicit (a ride etc.) by signalling with a closed fist and raised thumb to passing vehicles. □ **be all thumbs** be clumsy. **thumb one's nose 1** make a gesture of contempt with one's thumb against the bottom of the nose, the hand open, and fingers spread out. **2** scorn. **thumbs-down** an indication of rejection or failure. **thumbs-up** an indication of success or approval. **under a person's thumb** completely under a person's influence. □ **thumbed** *adj.* (also in *comb.*)

thumb index *n.* (*pl.* **thumb indexes**) a set of labelled notches cut into the side of a dictionary etc. for easy reference. □ **thumb-indexed** *adj.*

thumbnail ● *n.* **1** the nail of a thumb. **2** a very small or concise summary or representation. **3** *Computing* a small picture of a larger image or page layout, often used as a link on a web page. ● *adj.* very small or concise.

thumbprint *n.* **1** an impression of a thumb used esp. for identification. **2** a distinguishing trait etc.

thumbscrew *n.* **1** an instrument of torture for crushing the thumbs. **2** a screw with a flattened head for turning with the thumb and forefinger.

thumbtack ● *n.* a pin with a flat head that may be pushed into a bulletin board for fastening a notice etc. ● *v.* fasten to a wall etc. using a thumbtack.

thump ● *v.* **1** beat or strike heavily. **2** throb or pulsate strongly. **3** step or tread heavily. **4** pound with the hand. **5** *informal* achieve a resounding victory over. **6** play with a heavy touch. ● *n.* **1** a dull heavy blow. **2** the sound of this. □ **thumper** *n.*

thumping ● *adj.* **1** *informal* exceptionally large. **2** that thumps. ● *n.* **1** a series of repeated thumps or the sound of this. **2** *informal* a thorough beating. □ **thumpingly** *adv.*

thunder ● *n.* **1** a loud rumbling noise accompanying a flash of lightning, caused by the sudden heating and expansion of gases. **2** a resounding loud deep noise. ● *v.* **1** (of thunder) sound. **2** make or proceed with a noise suggestive of thunder. **3** utter in a loud voice or forceful manner. **4** criticize vehemently. □ **steal a**

person's thunder spoil the effect of another's action by doing it first.

thunderbird *n.* a mythical bird, in many N American Aboriginal legends, which created thunder and lightning.

thunderbolt *n.* **1** a flash of lightning with a simultaneous crash of thunder. **2** a bolt of lightning believed to be used as an agent of divine punishment. **3** a sudden occurrence.

thunderclap *n.* **1** a crash of thunder. **2** a very loud, sudden noise. **3** something that happens unexpectedly.

thundercloud *n.* **1** a towering cumulonimbus cloud, which produces thunder and lightning. **2** something threatening or dreadful.

thunderhead *n.* a tall cumulonimbus cloud with an anvil-shaped top extending horizontally.

thundering *adj. informal* **1** very great or excessive. **2** as loud as thunder. □ **thunderingly** *adv.*

thunderous *adj.* **1** powerful, very hard or heavy. **2** very loud like thunder. □ **thunderously** *adv.*

thundershower *n.* a rain shower accompanied by thunder and lightning.

thunderstorm *n.* a storm with thunder and lightning.

thunderstruck *adj.* amazed, astonished.

Thurs. *abbr.* (also **Thur.**) Thursday.

Thursday ● *n.* the fifth day of the week, following Wednesday. ● *adv.* **1** on Thursday. **2** (**Thursdays**) on Thursdays.

thus *adv. formal* **1 a** in this way. **b** as follows. **2** therefore; as a result. **3** so; to the degree indicated.

thwack ● *n.* **1** a sharp resonant sound as produced by a blow. **2** a heavy blow producing such a sound. ● *v.* strike (a person or thing), esp. with something flat.

thwart ● *v.* successfully oppose. ● *n.* a structural member extending across a boat.

thy *poss. pron.* (also **thine** before a vowel) *archaic* of or belonging to thee.

thyme *n.* a low-growing aromatic plant, grown for use as a herb. [*Sounds like* TIME]

thymine *n.* a compound found in all living tissue as a component base of DNA. [*Say* THIGH mean]

thymus *n.* (also **thymus gland**) a gland in the neck which produces white blood cells. [*Say* THIGH muss]

thyroid *n.* **1** (also **thyroid gland**) a gland in the neck which secretes hormones regulating growth and development. **2** (also **thyroid cartilage**) the largest of the cartilages of the larynx. [*Say* THIGH roid]

thyself *pron. archaic emphatic & reflexive form of* THOU[1], THEE; = YOURSELF.

ti *n.* (*pl.* **tis**) **1** (in tonic sol-fa) the seventh note of a major scale. **2** the note B in the fixed-do system. [*Say* TEE]

tiara *n.* (*pl.* **tiaras**) a woman's jewelled ornamental coronet or headband worn on the front of the hair. [*Say* tee AIR uh *or* tee ARR uh]

Tibetan *n.* **1** a person from Tibet. **2** the language of Tibet. □ **Tibetan** *adj.* [*Say* tib BET un]

tibia *n.* (*pl.* **tibiae** *or* **tibias**) **1** the inner of the two bones of the lower leg extending from the knee to the ankle. **2** the corresponding part in other animals. □ **tibial** *adj.* [*Say* TIBBY uh *for the singular,* TIBBY ee *for the plural,* TIBBY ul]

tic *n.* **1** a habitual twitching of one or more muscles, esp. of the face. **2** a habit or quirk.

tick ● *n.* **1** the regular click made by a watch or clock. **2** a mark ($\sqrt{}$) made to check off items on a list, indicate that something is correct, etc. **3** a tiny spider-like animal that attaches itself to the skin and sucks blood. **4** a case filled with feathers etc. to form a mattress or pillow. ● *v.* **1 a** (of a clock etc.) make a tick. **b** (of time) pass. **2** (of a mechanism) operate. **3** mark with a tick. □ **tick off** *informal* annoy, irritate. **what makes a person tick** *informal* a person's motivation. □ **tick-borne** *adj.*

ticked *adj.* (also **ticked off**) *informal* angry.

ticker *n.* **1** *informal* **a** the heart. **b** a watch. **2** an electronic device that prints out stock prices or news stories.

tickertape *n.* **1** a long narrow strip of paper on which a ticker prints esp. stock prices. **2** this or similar material thrown from windows to greet a celebrity in a motorcade.

ticket ● *n.* **1** a piece of paper or card giving the holder a right to admission to a place or event or to travel by public transport. **2** an official notification of a traffic violation. **3 a** a list of candidates for election. **b** the declared principles or policies of a political party. **4** a tag or label attached to an item and giving its price, size, etc. **5** (**the ticket**) *informal* the ideal thing. **6** a certificate of qualification as a ship's officer, pilot, etc. ● *v.* (**tickets, ticketed, ticketing**) **1** issue a ticket to. **2** attach a ticket to. □ **write one's own ticket** dictate one's own terms.

ticking *n.* a strong durable fabric used esp. to cover pillows.

tickle ● *v.* (**tickles, tickled, tickling**) **1 a** lightly touch, stroke, or poke in a way that causes itching and laughter. **b** (of a part of the body) be affected by this sensation. **2** amuse or excite. ● *n.* **1** an act of tickling. **2** a tickling sensation. □ **tickled pink** (or **to death**) *informal* extremely pleased. □ **tickler** *n.*

ticklish *adj.* **1** sensitive to tickling. **2** (of a matter) tricky, delicate. **3** (of a person) touchy.

tick-tock *n.* the ticking sound of a clock.

tic-tac-toe (also **tick-tack-toe**) ● *n.* a children's game in which players attempt to complete a row of three Xs or three Os on a grid of nine squares. ● *adj. Hockey* designating skilful play.

tidal *adj.* of or affected by the tides. □ **tidally** *adv.*

tidal wave *n.* **1** an exceptionally large ocean wave, esp. one caused by an earthquake; a tsunami. **2** a widespread manifestation of feeling, opinion, etc.

tidbit *n.* **1** a small piece of food. **2** an interesting item of news.

tiddlywink *n.* **1** a small plastic counter flicked into a cup by a larger one. **2** (in *pl.*) this game.

tide *n.* **1 a** the alternate rising and falling of the sea, due to the attraction of the moon and sun. **b** the water as affected by this. **2** the course or trend of opinion etc. **3** (in *comb.*) a particular season. □ **tide over** (**tides over**, **tided over**, **tiding over**) help (a person) through esp. a difficult period.

tidewater *n.* water carried or affected by tides.

tidings *pl. n. literary* news.

tidy ● *adj.* (**tidier**, **tidiest**) **1** neat, orderly. **2** (of a person) **a** having a neat appearance. **b** inclined to keep things neat. **3** convenient. **4** *informal* considerable. ● *v.* (**tidies**, **tidied**, **tidying**) make (a room, oneself, etc.) neat. ● *n.* (*pl.* **tidies**) an act or period of tidying. □ **tidily** *adv.* **tidiness** *n.*

tie ● *v.* (**ties**, **tied**, **tying**) **1** bind or fasten with rope or string etc. **2 a** form into a knot or bow. **b** secure by tying a lace, belt, etc. **3 a** be closely linked to. **b** restrict with an obligation etc. **4 a** finish a game etc. with the same score as (an opponent). **b** make (a game or score) even. ● *n.* **1** a thing that ties. **2** a strip of material worn around the neck, tied with a knot in front. **3** a link or connection, esp. a bond. **4** a game or competition etc. in which two or more opponents have the same score. **5** a beam laid horizontally to support the rails of a train track. □ **fit to be tied** *informal* very angry. **tie in** make relevant to or consistent with. **tie one on** get drunk. **tie up 1** bind or fasten securely with cord etc. **2** fully occupy or engage (a person).

3 prevent from acting freely. **4** complete (an undertaking etc.). **5** moor (a boat). **6** secure or tether. **7** invest or reserve (capital etc.) so that it is not immediately available for use.

tiebreaker *n.* (also **tiebreak**) esp. *Sport* **1** a means of determining the winner when two competitors are tied. **2** a goal or point etc. that breaks a tie. □ **tiebreaking** *adj.*

tied *adj.* **1** fastened with string etc. **2** (of a game or contest) with both competitors achieving the same score. **3** *Music* (of two or more notes) performed as one unbroken note.

tie-down *n.* a cord or strap used to secure or fasten something.

tie-dye ● *n.* **1** a method of producing patterns on fabric by tying parts of it so that they receive less dye than other parts. **2** a garment etc. dyed in this way. ● *v.* (**tie-dyes**, **tie-dyed**, **tie-dying**) dye (fabric) using this method. □ **tie-dyed** *adj.*

tie-in *n.* **1** a connection or association. **2** a joint promotion of related items.

tier *n.* **1** each of a series of rows or levels placed one above another. **2** a rank, grade, or stratum. □ **tiered** *adj.* [Rhymes with PIER]

tie-up *n.* **1** a stoppage. **2** a traffic jam.

tiff *n.* a petty quarrel.

tiffany *n.* (*pl.* **tiffanies**) (also **tiffany lamp**) any of various lamps with stained glass shades.

tiger *n.* a large powerful carnivorous feline, tawny yellow in colour with blackish stripes, native to Asia. □ **tigerish** *adj.*

tiger cat *n.* any moderate-sized feline resembling the tiger.

tiger lily *n.* a tall lily with flowers of dull orange spotted with black.

tiger shark *n.* an aggressive striped shark of warm seas.

tiger shrimp *n.* a large shrimp marked with dark bands.

tight ● *adj.* **1** not loose. **2** (of money etc.) scarce. **3** dense, compact. **4 a** (of control etc.) strictly imposed. **b** (of a deadline etc.) allowing no leeway. **5** difficult to deal with or manage. **6** impervious to a specified thing. **7** (of a corner) having a short radius. **8** *informal* intimate. **9** *informal* drunk. ● *adv.* tightly □ **run a tight ship** strictly manage an organization etc. **sit tight 1** remain in one's seat. **2** do nothing. □ **tighten** *v.* **tightly** *adv.* **tightness** *n.*

tight-fisted *adj.* stingy. □ **tight-fistedness** *n.*

tight-lipped *adj.* **1** refusing to discuss esp. a particular matter. **2** with the lips pursed.

tightly knit *adj.* (also **tight-knit**) close-knit.

tightrope n. **1** a rope or wire stretched tightly high above the ground, on which acrobats perform. **2** a delicate or risky situation.

tights pl. n. a close-fitting garment made usu. of knitted nylon, designed to cover the hips, legs, and feet.

tightwad n. slang a cheap person.

tigress n. (pl. **tigresses**) a female tiger.

tikka n. an Indian dish of marinated meat, grilled on skewers. [Say TICK uh or TEAK uh]

tilde n. a mark (~), placed over esp. certain Spanish and Portuguese letters. [Say TIL duh]

tile • n. **1** a thin slab of baked clay used for paving a floor, covering a roof, walls, etc. **2** a piece of glazed ceramic, cork, etc., used for similar purposes. **3** tiles collectively. **4** a hollow pipe used for drainage. **5** a thin flat piece used in a game. • v. (**tiles, tiled, tiling**) **1** cover with tiles. **2** lay drainage tile in. □ **on the tiles** informal enjoying a night out in a wild or reckless manner, esp. drinking. □ **tiling** n.

till¹ prep. & conj. = UNTIL.

till² n. a drawer for money in a store etc.

till³ v. **1** prepare and use (land) for growing crops. **2** plow. □ **tillage** n.

tiller n. **1** a horizontal bar fitted to the head of a boat's rudder to turn it in steering. **2** a machine or implement used for breaking up soil.

tilt • v. **1** move into a sloping position. **2** incline towards a particular opinion. **3** bias or influence in favour of a particular person or thing. **4** hist. rush or charge at in a joust. • n. **1** a slanting position; a lean. **2** a bias. **3 a** an encounter between opponents. **b** hist. a joust. □ **full** (or **at full**) **tilt 1** at full speed. **2** with the utmost force. **tilt at windmills** attack an imaginary enemy.

tilth n. **1** the condition of cultivated soil. **2** cultivation of land.

timber • n. **1** wood prepared for use in building, carpentry, etc. **2 a** a beam forming or capable of forming part of a structure. **b** (usu. in pl.) the pieces of wood forming the ribs, bends, or frames of a ship's hull. **3** large standing trees. • interj. a warning cry that a tree is about to fall. □ **timbered** adj.

timber frame n. **1** a usu. factory-prepared section of timber framework used in the construction of houses etc. **2** a house or barn etc. built using this.

timberland n. land covered with forest yielding timber.

timberline n. **1** the level on a mountain above which no trees grow. **2** the latitudinal limit north of which no trees grow.

timber wolf n. = WOLF 1.

timbre n. the distinctive character or quality of a sound. [Say TAM bur or TAM bruh]

Timbuktu (also **Timbuctoo**) any remote or outlandish place. [Say tim buck TOO]

time • n. **1** the indefinite continued progress of existence and events in the past, present, and future, regarded as a whole. **2** a point of time as measured in hours and minutes past midnight or noon. **3** the favourable or appropriate moment to do something. **4** (**a time**) an indefinite period. **5** (also **times**) a portion of time characterized by particular events or circumstances. **6** (**one's time**) a period regarded as characteristic of a particular stage in one's life. **7** the length of time taken to complete an activity. **8** time as allotted, available, or used. **9** an instance of something happening or being done. **10** informal a prison sentence. **11** an apprenticeship. **12** the normal rate of pay for time spent working. **13** the rhythmic pattern or tempo of a piece of music. • v. (**times, timed, timing**) **1** arrange a time for. **2** perform at a particular time. **3** measure the time taken by. □ **ahead of one's time** having ideas too advanced to be accepted by one's contemporaries. **ahead of time** earlier, beforehand. **all the time 1** constantly. **2** at all times. **at times** occasionally. **before one's time 1** prematurely. **2** before one was born. **for the time being** for the present. **half the time** informal **1** very often. **2** in a relatively short period. **have the time 1** be able to spend the time needed. **2** know what time it is. **in no** (or **less than no**) **time 1** very soon. **2** very quickly. **in one's own good** (or **sweet**) **time** at a pace decided by oneself. **in one's own time 1** punctual. **2** eventually. **keep time** move or sing etc. in time. **know the time of day** be well informed. **no time** informal a very short interval. **time after time 1** repeatedly. **2** in many instances. **time and** (or **time and time**) **again** on many occasions. **the time of one's life** a thrilling or extremely enjoyable occasion. **time of the month** informal or euphemism a woman's menstrual period.

time and a half n. one and a half times normal pay, paid to an employee for overtime work.

time bomb n. **1** a bomb designed to explode at a pre-set time. **2 a** a situation on the verge of becoming a crisis. **b** an unpredictable or moody person.

time capsule *n.* a sealed box etc. containing objects chosen as representative of life at a particular time.

time-consuming *adj.* that requires a large amount of time.

time frame *n.* a specific period of time.

time-honoured *adj.* (also **time-honored**) (of a custom, tradition, etc.) that is revered as a result of having been observed etc. for many years.

time immemorial *n.* a longer time than anyone can remember.

timekeeper *n.* **1** an official responsible for recording time. **2** a device that records time. □ **timekeeping** *n.*

time lag *n.* an interval of time between related events.

time-lapse *adj.* pertaining to a method of taking a sequence of photographs at long intervals to photograph a slow process.

timeless *adj.* not affected by the passage of time. □ **timelessly** *adv.* **timelessness** *n.*

timeline *n.* **1** a line graduated in years on which esp. historical events are marked. **2** a schedule for a project etc. showing the dates by which certain stages must be completed.

timely *adj.* (**timelier**, **timeliest**) occurring or made at a suitable or appropriate time. □ **timeliness** *n.*

time machine *n.* an imaginary machine capable of transporting a person through time.

time off *n.* a period of time spent away from work.

time out *n.* **1** *Sport* a short stoppage in play so that a team can discuss strategy etc. **2** a short break from an activity.

timepiece *n.* an instrument, such as a clock, for measuring the passage of time.

timer *n.* **1** a device that measures elapsed time. **2** a device that can be set to turn an appliance etc. on or off at a pre-set time. **3** a person who keeps track of time.

times ● *n.* used following a number to express multiplication. ● *adv.* multiplied by.

time scale *n.* the time allowed for or taken by a sequence of events.

time-sensitive *adj.* that must be completed, sent, etc. at or by a certain time.

time-sharing *n.* an arrangement in which a vacation home is jointly owned or rented by several people, each of whom is entitled to use it for a period of time each year. □ **time-share** *n.*

time signature *n. Music* an indication of tempo following a clef.

time slot *n.* an allotted place in a broadcasting schedule.

times table *n.* a chart showing the products of a number when multiplied by each of the numbers from one to twelve.

timetable ● *n.* **1** a list or plan of the times or dates when successive things are to occur. **2** a student's schedule indicating the days and times of classes. ● *v.* (**timetables**, **timetabled**, **timetabling**) schedule.

time-tested *adj.* that has been proven to be effective etc. over time.

time trial *n.* a race in which participants are individually timed.

time warp *n.* **1** (in science fiction) an imaginary distortion of space in relation to time that causes a person to travel backwards or forwards in time. **2** a state in which the styles etc. of a past period are retained.

time-worn *adj.* **1** antiquated. **2** adversely affected by time. **3** trite.

time zone *n.* each of the longitudinal divisions of the globe throughout which a standard time is used.

timid *adj.* **1** meek, shy. **2** characterized by fear or shyness. □ **timidity** *n.* **timidly** *adv.*

timing *n.* **1** the ability to act or speak at the right time in order to achieve the greatest effect. **2** the time chosen for an event etc. **3** the act of recording time.

Timorese *n.* (*pl.* **Timorese**) a member of the indigenous people of Timor. □ **Timorese** *adj.* [*Say* tee more EEZ]

timorous *adj.* nervous and easily frightened. □ **timorously** *adv.* **timorousness** *n.* [*Say* TIMMER us]

timothy *n.* a Eurasian grass, naturalized in N America, widely grown for grazing.

timpani *pl. n.* kettledrums. □ **timpanist** *n.* [*Say* TIMPA nee]

tin ● *n.* **1** a silvery-white metallic element resisting corrosion. **2 a** a container made of tin. **b** esp. *Brit.* a hermetically sealed container in which food is preserved and sold; a can. **3** = TIN PLATE. ● *v.* (**tins**, **tinned**, **tinning**) **1** seal (food) in an airtight tin. **2** cover or coat with tin. □ **tinned** *adj.*

tincture *n.* **1** a tinge or trace. **2** a substance dissolved in alcohol for use as a medicine. [*Say* TINK chur]

tinder *n.* a dry substance that readily catches fire, used to start a fire. [*Say* TIN dur]

tinderbox *n.* (*pl.* **tinderboxes**) **1** *hist.* a box containing tinder, flint, and steel. **2** a situation that may erupt into violence etc. [*Say* TIN dur box]

tine *n.* a point or prong, such as on a fork. □ **tined** *adj.*

tinfoil *n.* aluminum foil.

ting *n.* a thin clear high-pitched ringing sound.

tinge *n.* **1** a trace of some colour. **2** a touch or trace of something. □ **tinged** *adj.*

tingle ● *v.* **1 a** a slight prickling or stinging sensation. **2** a slight tickling sensation or goosebumps as a result of excitement. ● *v.* (**tingles, tingled, tingling**) experience or cause this sensation. □ **tingly** *adj.* (**tinglier, tingliest**)

tinker ● *v.* **1 a** work in an amateurish or desultory way. **b** meddle, tamper. **2** make minor adjustments to. ● *n.* **1** a travelling mender of kettles and pans etc. **2** a period of tinkering. □ **tinkerer** *n.* **tinkering** *n.*

tinkle ● *v.* (**tinkles, tinkled, tinkling**) **1** make light clear ringing sounds. **2** *informal* urinate. ● *n.* **1** a tinkling sound. **2** *informal* or *euphemism* an act of urinating. □ **tinkly** *adj.*

tinnitus *n.* a ringing in the ears. [*Say* tin ITE us]

tinny *adj.* (**tinnier, tinniest**) **1 a** having a sound like that of tin being struck. **b** (of music) thin and metallic. **2** (of an object) flimsy, insubstantial.

tin plate *n.* sheet iron or steel coated with tin.

tin-plated *adj.* coated with tin.

tinpot *adj.* second-rate, inferior.

tinsel *n.* **1** glittering metallic strands used for decoration. **2** cheap or superficial brilliance. □ **tinselly** *adj.*

tinsmith *n.* a person who makes or repairs items of tin.

tint ● *n.* **1** a shade, colour, or hue. **2** a faint colour. **3** a semi-permanent hair dye. ● *v.* **1** apply a tint to; colour. **2** give (glass) a darker tone or colour.

tiny *adj.* (**tinier, tiniest**) very small; minuscule.

tip¹ ● *n.* **1** an extremity or end. **2** a small piece attached to or over the end of something. ● *v.* (**tips, tipped, tipping**) **1** provide with a tip. **2** colour or mark the tip of. □ **on the tip of one's tongue** about to be remembered. **the tip of the iceberg** a small part of something much larger.

tip² ● *v.* (**tips, tipped, tipping**) **1** (cause to) assume a slanting position. **2** overturn. **3 a** tilt (a container) in order to empty its contents. **b** pour out or spill. **4** strike or touch lightly. **5 a** *Hockey* deflect (a shot) toward the net. **b** *Baseball* (of a batter) barely hit (a pitch or the ball) foul. ● *n.* **1** a gentle push or slight tilt. **2** *Hockey* an act of deflecting the puck. □ **tip the scales**

1 (also **tip the balance**) be the deciding factor. **2** weigh. **tip one's hand** unintentionally reveal one's intentions. **tip one's hat** (or **cap**) acknowledge or thank. **tip off** *Basketball* (of two teams) begin a game with a jump ball.

tip³ ● *n.* **1** a small sum of money given in thanks for a service given. **2** a useful suggestion. **3** a piece of private or special information. ● *v.* (**tips, tipped, tipping**) give a small sum of money to. □ **tip off** *informal* give advance warning or confidential information. □ **tipper** *n.*

tipi *n.* (*pl.* **tipis**) = TEEPEE. [*Say* TEE pee]

tipoff *n.* **1** a warning or piece of secret information etc. **2** something that serves as a warning. **3** *Basketball* a jump ball at the start of a game.

tipple ● *v.* (**tipples, tippled, tippling**) **1** drink liquor habitually. **2** drink (liquor) in small amounts. ● *n.* *informal* an alcoholic drink. □ **tippler** *n.*

tippy *adj.* (**tippier, tippiest**) *informal* unstable.

tippytoe *n., v., & adv.* *informal* = TIPTOE.

tipster *n.* a person who provides tips about betting at horse races.

tipsy *adj.* (**tipsier, tipsiest**) **1** slightly drunk. **2** tippy.

tiptoe ● *n.* the tips of the toes. ● *v.* (**tiptoes, tiptoed, tiptoeing**) **1** walk gently with the heels raised. **2** cautiously avoid. ● *adv.* (also **on tiptoe**) (stand etc.) on the toes and balls of the feet.

tip-top *adj.* excellent.

tirade *n.* a long vehement rant or outburst. [*Say* TIE raid]

tiramisu *n.* an Italian dessert consisting of layers of sponge cake or biscuit, filled with mascarpone cheese. [*Say* teera mee SOO *or* teera MEE soo]

tire¹ *v.* (**tires, tired, tiring**) **1** make or become weak or exhausted through exertion. **2 a** exhaust the patience or interest of. **b** become bored or impatient with. □ **tiring** *adj.*

tire² *n.* a rubber covering placed around each of the wheels of a vehicle.

tired *adj.* **1** weak, exhausted, or fatigued. **2** (of an idea etc.) overused. □ **tiredly** *adv.* **tiredness** *n.*

tireless *adj.* showing or having inexhaustible energy. □ **tirelessly** *adv.*

tiresome *adj.* **1** wearisome, tedious. **2** annoying. □ **tiresomely** *adv.*

'tis *archaic* it is.

tissue *n.* **1** the material of which an animal or plant body is composed, consisting of specialized cells. **2 a** (also **facial tissue**) a piece of absorbent paper used as a disposable handkerchief. **b** (also **toilet tissue**) toilet paper. **3** (also **tissue paper**) thin translucent paper, often coloured. **4** an intricate mass or network of things.

tit *n.* **1** a small songbird. **2** *informal* a nipple; a teat. **3** *coarse slang* a woman's breast.

Titan *n.* **1** (usu. **titan**) a person or organization of very great power or strength. **2** *Greek Myth* a member of a family of early gigantic gods. [*Say* TITE un]

titanic *adj.* of exceptional strength, size, or power. [*Say* tie TAN ick]

titanium *n.* a grey metallic element used to make strong corrosion-resistant alloys. [*Say* tie TAINY um]

titanium dioxide *n.* (also **titanium oxide**) a naturally occurring inert compound of titanium and oxygen.

tit-for-tat *n.* a situation in which a blow, insult, etc. is given in retaliation for another.

tithe ● *n.* 1 *hist.* one-tenth of what people produced or earned in a year, formerly taken as a tax to support the Church. **2 a** a tenth of an individual's income, pledged or donated to a church. **b** any tax or donation, usu. of one-tenth of a person's income. **● *v.* (tithes, tithed, tithing)** pay one-tenth of (one's earnings etc.), esp. towards the support of a church. □ **tithing** *n.* [*Rhymes with* WRITHE]

titillate *v.* (**titillates, titillated, titillating**) excite a person, esp. with pictures etc. of a sexual nature. □ **titillating** *adj.* **titillation** *n.* [*Say* TITTLE ate]

title ● *n.* 1 the name given to a book, work of art, etc. **2** a publication. **3** a caption or credit in a movie etc. **4 a** a word used to indicate a person's status, rank, or position, e.g. *Dr., Mrs.,* etc. **b** a description indicating a person's role or function, e.g. *Queen, Assistant Coach.* **5** *Sport* a championship. **6** *Law* **a** the right to the possession of land or property. **b** a just or recognized claim. **● *v.* (titles, titled, titling**) give a title to.

titled *adj.* having a title of nobility or rank.

titmouse *n.* (*pl.* **titmice**) a small songbird that searches in trees for insects.

**titter ● *v.* laugh or giggle. ● *n.* a nervous giggle.

tittle *n.* the smallest part of something.

tittle-tattle *n.* petty gossip.

titular *adj.* **1** holding a formal position or title without any real authority. **2** from whom or which a title is taken. **3** relating to a title. [*Say* TIT yoo lur]

tizzy *n.* (*pl.* **tizzies**) (also **tizz**; *pl.* **tizzes**) *informal* a flustered, agitated, or hysterical state.

TKO ● *n.* (*pl.* **TKOs) *Boxing* a technical knockout. **● *v.* (TKO's, TKO'd, TKO'ing**) **1** *Boxing* defeat by technical knockout. **2** *informal* thwart (a person).

TLC *abbr. informal* tender loving care.

Tlingit *n.* (*pl.* **Tlingit** or **Tlingits**) **1** a member of an Aboriginal people living on the islands and coast of southeastern Alaska and northern BC. **2** the language of this people. □ **Tlingit** *adj.* [*Say* TLING git]

TM *abbr.* **1** trademark. **2** Transcendental Meditation.

TNT *abbr.* trinitrotoluene, a high explosive.

to ● *prep.* 1 introducing a noun: **a** expressing what is reached, approached, or touched. **b** expressing what is aimed at. **c** as far as; until. **d** to the extent of. **e** expressing what is followed. **f** expressing what is considered or affected. **g** expressing what is caused or produced. **2** introducing the infinitive. **3** as a substitute for *to* + infinitive. **● *adv.* 1** in the normal or required position. **2** in a nearly closed position.

toad *n.* any frog-like tailless amphibian that breeds in water but lives chiefly on land.

toadstool *n.* a non-technical name for various fungi, usu. poisonous, with a round flat cap on a slender stalk.

toady ● *n.* (*pl.* **toadies) an obsequious person. **● *v.* (toadies, toadied, toadying**) treat someone in an obsequious way in order to win favour or approval. □ **toadying** *adj.*

to and fro ● *adv.* 1 backwards and forwards. **2** repeatedly between the same points. **● *n.* (usu. **to-and-fro**) **1** movement to and fro. **2** vacillation or debate on an issue. □ **toing and froing** constant bustling movement.

toast ● *n.* 1 sliced bread browned on both sides by exposure to heat. **2 a** a very brief speech or tribute offered in honour of a person etc. before drinking. **b** a call by the speaker to other guests to raise their glasses before drinking. **3 a** a person etc. in whose honour a company is asked to drink. **b** a person or thing that is extremely popular or celebrated. **4** *informal* a person or thing in severe difficulty. **● *v.* 1** cook or brown by exposure to a source of heat. **2** (of bread etc.) become brown in this way. **3** drink a toast to.

toaster *n.* a device used to toast bread etc.

toasty *adj.* (**toastier, toastiest**) comfortably warm.

tobacco *n.* (*pl.* **tobaccos**) **1** the dried leaves of a plant of the nightshade family, smoked or chewed for pleasure and used for ceremonial purposes by some Aboriginal groups. **2** the plant producing these leaves.

tobacconist *n.* a shopkeeper who deals in tobacco. [*Say* tuh BACKA nist]

toboggan ● *n.* a long narrow sled without runners, bent or curled upwards at the front. ● *v.* ride on a toboggan. □ **tobogganing** *n.*

toboggan slide *n. Cdn* **1** = SLIDE *n.* 6. **2** *informal* a rapid decline.

toccata *n.* (*pl.* **toccatas**) a brisk musical composition for a keyboard instrument, designed to show the performer's touch and technique. [*Say* tuh CATTA]

tock ● *n.* a short, hollow sound. ● *v.* make this sound.

tocopherol *n.* an alcohol occurring in plant oils, wheat germ, egg yolk, and leafy vegetables, vitamin E. [*Say* toe COFFER awl]

today ● *adv.* **1** on or during this present day. **2** nowadays. ● *n.* **1** this present day. **2** modern times. □ **a week today** one week from today.

toddle *v.* (**toddles, toddled, toddling**) **1** walk with short unsteady steps. **2** *informal* **a** take a casual or leisurely walk. **b** depart.

toddler *n.* a child who has just recently learned to walk. □ **toddlerhood** *n.*

toddy *n.* (*pl.* **toddies**) a drink made with esp. rum or whisky and hot water and sugar.

to-do *n.* (*pl.* **to-dos**) a commotion or fuss.

to-do list *n.* a list of chores, projects, etc. that one must do.

toe ● *n.* **1** any of the five digits at the end of the foot. **2** the corresponding part of an animal. **3** the part of footwear that covers the toes. **4** *Figure Skating* **a** a toe pick. **b** a toe loop. **5** the lower end, tip, or point of something. ● *v.* (**toes, toed, toeing**) touch with one's toe. □ **make a person's toes curl** excite or thrill a person. **on one's toes** alert, ready. **toe the line** conform to a general policy or principle. □ **toed** *adj.*

toecap *n.* the reinforced covering of the toe of a boot or shoe.

toehold *n.* **1** a small foothold. **2** a favourable position from which a minor advantage may be gained or influence or support increased minimally.

toe loop *n.* Figure Skating a type of jump.

toenail *n.* the nail at the tip of each toe.

toe pick *n.* a jagged toothed edge on the front tip of a skate blade.

toffee *n.* a hard and often brittle candy that softens in the mouth, made by boiling sugar and butter.

tofu *n.* a pale curd made from soybean milk and used as a source of protein. [*Say* TOE foo]

toga *n.* (*pl.* **togas**) Roman History a loose flowing outer garment made of a single piece of cloth. [*Say* TOE guh]

together ● *adv.* **1** in company. **2** at the same time. **3** collectively. **4** so as to form a connected or coherent whole. **5** *informal* **a** into an organized state. **b** into a rational state of mind. ● *adj.* *informal* composed, well-organized.

togetherness *n.* **1** a feeling of comfort proceeding from a close and harmonious association with others. **2** the condition of being together.

togged *adj.* *informal* dressed up.

toggle ● *n.* **1** a short decorative crosspiece attached to a garment, pushed through a loop to act as a fastener. **2** *Computing* a key or command that that has opposite effects on successive occasions. ● *v.* (**toggles, toggled, toggling**) **1** *Computing* switch from one function or state of operation to another by using a toggle. **2** provide or fasten with a toggle.

toggle switch *n.* an electric switch operated by means of a projecting lever that is moved usu. up and down.

togs *pl. n.* *informal* clothes, esp. a single outfit.

toil ● *v.* **1** work laboriously or incessantly. **2** make slow painful progress. ● *n.* prolonged labour. □ **toiler** *n.*

toilet *n.* **1 a** a bathroom fixture for defecation and urination, usu. with a flushing mechanism. **b** a room containing such a fixture. **2** (also **toilette**) the process of washing, dressing, etc. □ **go into** (or **down**) **the toilet** *informal* go into sharp decline. [*For* TOILETTE *say* twah LET]

toiletry *n.* (*pl.* **toiletries**) an article used in washing and dressing, such as soap, shampoo, etc.

toilet training *n.* the process of teaching a young child to use the toilet. □ **toilet train** *v.*

toke *slang* ● *n.* **1** a drag on a cigarette containing esp. marijuana. **2** a marijuana cigarette. ● *v.* (**tokes, toked, toking**) smoke or take a drag on a marijuana cigarette.

token ● *n.* **1 a** a thing used to represent something abstract or immaterial. **b** a thing given as an expression of affection. **2** a coin-like object, used on public transit, in a casino, etc. **3** a person chosen as a nominal representative of an under-represented group. ● *adj.* **1** chosen as a nominal representative of a minority group. **2** done or made as a matter of form.

3 conducted briefly to demonstrate strength of feeling. □ **by the same token 1** in the same way. **2** moreover.

tokenism *n.* the principle of granting minimum concessions as a token gesture to appease public pressure, comply with legal requirements, etc. □ **tokenistic** *adj.*

told *past and past participle of* TELL¹.

tolerable *adj.* **1** able to be endured. **2** fairly good. □ **tolerably** *adv.* [Say TOLLER a bull]

tolerance *n.* **1** the ability to accept things one dislikes or disagrees with. **2** the ability of an organism to endure something, e.g. a transplant, without adverse reaction. **3** a decrease in the body's response to a drug after prolonged use. [Say TOLLER ince]

tolerant *adj.* **1** showing tolerance. **2** patient, forgiving. **3** able to withstand certain conditions etc. [Say TOLLER unt]

tolerate *v.* (**tolerates, tolerated, tolerating**) **1** allow the existence, practice, or occurrence of. **2** endure or allow with patience. **3** sustain or endure (pain etc.). **4** be capable of continued subjection to (a drug etc.) without harm. □ **toleration** *n.* [Say TOLLER ate]

toll¹ *n.* **1** a charge for permission to travel along a road or highway etc. **2** the loss or damage caused by a disaster etc. **3** a charge for a long-distance telephone call.

toll² ● *v.* **1** ring with slow, even strokes. **2** announce (the time, a death etc.) in this way. ● *n.* the action or sound of a bell as it tolls.

toll booth *n.* a booth on a road etc. where tolls are collected.

tollgate ● *n.* a gate preventing passage until a toll is paid. ● *v.* (**tollgates, tollgated, tollgating**) *Cdn* block or hinder pending payment of a bribe or tribute. □ **tollgating** *n.*

toluene *n.* (also **toluol**) a liquid hydrocarbon used esp. as a solvent and in explosives. [Say TOL yoo een, TOL yoo awl]

tom *n.* **1** a tomcat. **2** a male of various other animals.

tomahawk *n.* a hatchet-like tool or weapon, formerly used by some North American Indians.

tomatillo *n.* (*pl.* **tomatillos**) esp. *US* **1** a purplish edible fruit. **2** a Mexican plant that bears this. [Say tomma TILLO]

tomato *n.* (*pl.* **tomatoes**) **1** a glossy, usu. bright red and pulpy edible fruit. **2** the plant that bears this fruit. □ **tomatoey** *adj.* [Say tuh MAY toe *or* tuh MAT oh, tuh MAY toe ee *or* tuh MAT oh ee]

tomato clam cocktail *n.* a drink

consisting of tomato juice mixed with clam juice.

tomb *n.* **1** a large esp. underground vault for the burial of the dead. **2** a monument erected over a person's grave. **3** (**the tomb**) *literary* death. [Say TOOM]

tomboy *n.* a girl whose behaviour, appearance, etc. are considered boyish. □ **tomboyish** *adj.*

tombstone *n.* a usu. engraved stone slab placed over a person's grave as a memorial. [Say TOOM stone]

tomcat ● *n.* a male cat. ● *v.* (**tomcats, tomcatted, tomcatting**) *slang* (of a man) pursue women promiscuously.

Tom, Dick, and Harry *n.* usu. *derogatory* ordinary people in general.

tome *n.* a large heavy book. [Rhymes with HOME]

tomfoolery *n.* silly behaviour.

tommycod *n.* (*pl.* **tommycod**) (also **tomcod**) a small edible greenish-brown N American fish.

tomography *n.* a technique which provides images of a cross-section of the human body or other solid object using X-rays or ultrasound. [Say tuh MOGRA fee]

tomorrow ● *n.* **1** the day after today. **2** the near future. ● *adv.* **1** on the day after today. **2** at some future time.

tom-tom *n.* a simple hand-beaten drum associated with N American Aboriginal, African, or Eastern cultures.

ton ● *n.* **1** a unit of weight equal to 2,000 lb. avoirdupois (907.19 kg). **2** (also **long ton**) *Brit.* a unit of weight equal to 2,240 lb. avoirdupois (1016 kg). **3** a metric ton. **4** (usu. in *pl.*) *informal* a large number or amount. ● *adv.* (usu. in *pl.*) *informal* much, a lot. □ **weigh a ton** *informal* be very heavy.

tonal *adj.* **1** of or relating to tone or tonality. **2** (of music) written in a definite key or keys. [Say TONE ul]

tonality *n.* (*pl.* **tonalities**) **1 a** the relationship between the tones of a musical scale. **b** a single tonic key as the basis of a composition. **2** the colour scheme of a picture. [Say toe NALA tee]

tone ● *n.* **1** a musical or vocal sound, esp. with reference to its pitch, quality, and strength. **2** the sound of a voice expressing a feeling or mood. **3** a manner of expression in writing. **4** *Music* an interval of a major second, e.g. do–re. **5 a** the general effect of colour or of light and shade in a picture. **b** the tint or shade of a colour. **6** the general spirit of something. **7** (of the body) the state of being firm and strong. ● *v.* (**tones, toned, toning**) **1** give the desired tone to. **2** modify the tone of.

3 strengthen, firm. □ **tone down 1** make or become softer in tone. **2** make less strong or extreme.

tone-deaf *adj.* unable to perceive differences of musical pitch accurately. □ **tone-deafness** *n.*

tone poem *n.* an orchestral composition on a descriptive theme.

toner *n.* **1** a powder used in photocopiers, laser printers, etc. **2** an astringent applied to the face to control oiliness.

Tongan ● *adj.* of or relating to the island group of Tonga or its people or language. ● *n.* **1** a person from Tonga. **2** the Polynesian language spoken in Tonga. [*Say* TONG gun]

tongs *pl. n.* (also **pair of tongs** *singular*) an instrument with two hinged arms for grasping etc.

tongue *n.* **1** the fleshy organ in the mouth used in tasting, licking, swallowing, and (in humans) for speech. **2** the tongue of an ox etc. as food. **3** the faculty of speech. **4** a language. **5 a** a long low promontory. **b** a strip of leather etc. under the laces in a shoe. **6** a thing like a tongue in shape etc. □ **find** (or **lose**) **one's tongue** be able (or unable) to express oneself after a shock etc. **the gift of tongues** the power of speaking in unknown languages, regarded as one of the gifts of the Holy Spirit. **(with) tongue in cheek** insincerely or ironically. □ **tongued** *adj.*

tongue-and-groove *n.* panelling etc. with a projecting strip down one side and a groove down the other.

tongue-in-cheek ● *adj.* ironic; humorous. ● *adv.* insincerely or ironically.

tongue-lashing *n.* a severe scolding.

tongue-tied *adj.* too shy or embarrassed to speak.

tongue twister *n.* a sequence of words difficult to pronounce quickly.

tonguing *n.* the technique of playing a wind instrument using the tongue.

tonic *n.* **1** an invigorating medicine. **2** anything serving to invigorate. **3** (also **tonic water**) a carbonated drink containing quinine. **4** *Music* the first degree of a scale.

tonic sol-fa *n.* a system of notation used to teach singing, with do as the keynote of all major keys and la as the keynote of all minor keys.

tonight ● *n.* the evening or night of the present day. ● *adv.* on the present or coming evening or night.

tonnage *n.* **1** weight in tons. **2** a ship's freight-carrying capacity. **3** a charge per ton on freight. [*Say* TUN idge]

tonne *n.* a metric ton. [*Say* TUN]

tonsil *n.* either of two small masses of tissue on each side of the root of the tongue.

tonsillectomy *n.* (*pl.* **tonsillectomies**) the surgical removal of the tonsils. [*Say* tonsil ECKTA me]

tonsillitis *n.* tonsil inflammation. [*Say* tonsil ITE us]

tonsure *n.* **1** the shaving of the crown of the head, esp. of a monk. **2** a bare patch made in this way. □ **tonsured** *adj.* [*Say* TAWN sure]

tony *adj.* (**tonier, toniest**) *informal* stylish, high-class.

too *adv.* **1** more than is desirable, permissible, or possible. **2** in addition. **3** *informal* very. **4** moreover.

toodle-oo *interj.* *informal* goodbye.

took *past of* TAKE.

tool ● *n.* **1** any device or implement used to carry out a particular function. **2** a thing used in an occupation. **3** a person used by another. ● *v.* **1** work or shape with a tool. **2** impress a design on (leather). **3** *slang* drive or ride, esp. in a casual manner. **4** equip with tools. □ **tooling** *n.*

toolbar *n.* a row of computer icons used to execute certain commands.

tool kit *n.* **1** a set of tools. **2** a set of software tools. **3** a repertoire of techniques used to solve problems etc.

toonie *n.* *Cdn informal* the Canadian two-dollar coin.

toot ● *n.* a short sharp sound as made by a horn. ● *v.* make or cause to make a toot. □ **toot one's own horn** praise oneself.

tooth *n.* (*pl.* **teeth**) **1** each of a set of hard enamel-coated structures in the jaws, used for biting and chewing. **2** a toothlike part or projection. **3** (in *pl.*) force or effectiveness. □ **armed to the teeth** completely armed or equipped. **fight tooth and nail** fight very fiercely. **get one's teeth into** devote oneself seriously to. □ **toothed** *adj.* **toothlike** *adj.*

toothache *n.* a pain in a tooth.

toothbrush *n.* (*pl.* **toothbrushes**) a small brush with a long handle, for cleaning the teeth.

toothed whale *n.* any of a number of whales that have teeth, including sperm whales, killer whales, dolphins, etc.

tooth fairy *n.* (in folk legend) a fairy who leaves a coin for a child in exchange for a baby tooth placed under the child's pillow at night.

toothless *adj.* **1** having no teeth. **2** lacking genuine force or effectiveness.

toothpaste *n.* a paste for cleaning the teeth.

toothpick *n.* a small pointed stick for removing bits of food stuck between the teeth.

toothsome *adj.* **1** (of food) appetizing. **2** sexy.

toothy *adj.* (**toothier, toothiest**) having or showing large or prominent teeth.

tootle *v.* (**tootles, tootled, tootling**) **1** *informal* move casually or aimlessly. **2** toot gently. **3** play (a wind instrument).

tootsie *n.* (*pl.* **tootsies**) **1** (usu. in *pl.*) *informal* a foot; a toe. **2** *slang* **a** a woman. **b** a prostitute. [*Rhymes with* FOOTSIE]

top¹ ● *n.* **1** the highest point or part. **2** the highest rank or place. **3** the upper surface of a thing. **4** the upper part of a thing, esp.: **a** a garment covering the upper part of the body. **b** the upper part of a shoe or boot. **c** a lid or stopper. **5** the utmost degree. **6** the beginning. **7** (esp. in *pl.*) the leaves etc. of a plant. ● *adj.* highest in position, rank, or degree. ● *v.* (**tops, topped, topping**) **1** provide with a top etc. **2** remove the top of. **3 a** be higher or better than. **b** be at the top of. **4** reach the top of (a hill etc.). □ (**at**) **tops** at the most. **from top to toe** from head to foot. **on top 1** in a superior position; above. **2** on the upper part of the head. **on top of 1** fully in command of. **2** in close proximity to. **3** in addition to. **on top of the world** *informal* exuberant. **over the top** to excess, beyond reasonable limits. **top up 1** add to; bring up to a certain level. **2** fill up.

top² *n.* a toy spinning on a point when set in motion.

topaz *n.* (*pl.* **topazes**) a transparent or translucent usu. yellow precious stone. [*Say* TOE paz]

top brass *n.* *informal* persons in authority or of high rank.

topcoat *n.* **1** an overcoat. **2** an outer coat of paint etc.

top dog *n.* *informal* a victor or master.

top dollar *n.* a high price.

top drawer ● *n.* *informal* high social position or origin. ● *adj.* (**top-drawer**) *informal* of the highest quality or esp. social level.

top dressing *n.* **1** the application of manure or fertilizer to the top of the earth around a plant or plants. **2** manure so applied. □ **top-dress** *v.*

top-end *adj.* having to do with the most expensive section of the market.

top-flight *adj.* in the highest rank or level.

top gun *n.* *informal* **1** an ace fighter pilot. **2** an important person etc.

top hat *n.* a man's formal tall hat. □ **top-hatted** *adj.*

top-heavy *adj.* **1** too heavy at the top and so likely to be unstable. **2** (of an organization etc.) having too large a number of senior executives.

topiary ● *n.* (*pl.* **topiaries**) **1** the art of clipping shrubs or trees into attractive shapes. **2** a piece or example of topiary work. ● *adj.* concerned with topiaries. [*Say* TOPE ee airy]

topic *n.* **1** a theme for a book etc. **2** the subject of a conversation.

topical *adj.* **1** of or pertaining to current affairs. **2** relating to a particular subject. **3** (of an ailment etc.) affecting or applied externally to a part of the body. □ **topicality** *n.* **topically** *adv.*

topknot *n.* **1** a bun or tuft of hair worn on the crown of the head. **2** a tuft or crest growing on the head.

topless *adj.* **1** without or seeming to be without a top. **2 a** (of a person) bare-breasted. **b** (of a place) where women go topless.

topmast *n.* the mast next above the lower mast on a sailing ship.

topmost *adj.* uppermost.

top-notch *adj.* *informal* first-rate.

top-of-the-line *adj.* the most expensive of a group of products.

topography *n.* (*pl.* **topographies**) **1** a detailed description, representation on a map, etc., of the natural and artificial features of an area. **2** such features. □ **topographic** *adj.* **topographical** *adj.* **topographically** *adv.* [*Say* tuh POGRA fee, toppa GRAPHIC]

topology *n.* (*pl.* **topologies**) *Math* the study of geometrical properties and spatial relations unaffected by the continuous change of shape or size of figures. [*Say* tuh POLLA jee]

topper *n.* **1** a thing that tops. **2** *informal* a top hat.

topping *n.* a garnish, sauce, etc. put on top of food.

topple *v.* (**topples, toppled, toppling**) **1** totter and fall, or cause to do so. **2** overthrow or be overthrown.

topsail *n.* **1** the rectangular sail next above the lowest on a sailing ship. **2** a fore-and-aft sail above the gaff. [*Say* TOP sail *or* TOP sull]

top secret *adj.* of the highest secrecy.

top shelf *Hockey informal* ● *n.* the highest part of the net. ● *adv.* at or into this part of the net.

topside ● *n.* the side of a ship above the

waterline. ● *adv.* on or to the upper deck of a ship.

topsoil *n.* the surface layer of soil.

topspin *n.* a fast forward spin imparted to a ball in tennis etc.

topsy-turvy ● *adv. & adj.* **1** upside down. **2** in utter confusion. ● *n.* utter confusion.

toque *n.* **1** *Cdn* **a** a close-fitting knitted hat, often with a tassel or pompom. **b** a long knitted stocking cap. **2** a tall white hat, worn by chefs. [*Sense 1 rhymes with* FLUKE; *sense 2 rhymes with* POKE]

Torah *n.* the law of God as revealed to Moses and recorded in the first five books of the Hebrew scriptures. [*Say* TORE uh]

torch ● *n.* (*pl.* **torches**) **1 a** a piece of wood, cloth, etc., soaked in a flammable substance and lighted. **b** any similar lamp. **2** a blowtorch. ● *v.* (**torches**, **torched**, **torching**) *slang* set fire to. □ **carry a torch for** suffer from unrequited love for. **pick up the torch** carry on with the work of someone unable to continue.

torch song *n.* a melancholy or sentimental romantic song. □ **torch singer** *n.*

tore *past of* TEAR¹.

torment ● *n.* **1** severe physical or mental suffering. **2** a cause of this. ● *v.* **1** subject to torment. **2** tease excessively. □ **tormentor** *n.*

torn ● *v. past participle of* TEAR¹. ● *adj.* **1** that has been torn. **2** anxious because having to make a painful choice between two options.

tornado *n.* (*pl.* **tornadoes**) a violent storm with very strong winds, often accompanied by a funnel-shaped cloud.

Torontonian *n.* a person from Toronto. [*Say* tuh ron TONY un]

torpedo ● *n.* (*pl.* **torpedoes**) **1** a self-propelled underwater missile, fired at a ship and exploding on impact. **2** (also **aerial torpedo**) a similar device dropped from an aircraft. ● *v.* (**torpedoes**, **torpedoed**, **torpedoing**) **1** destroy or attack with a torpedo. **2** make ineffective or inoperative.

torpid *adj.* **1** mentally or physically inactive. **2** numb.

torpor *n.* a state of inactivity; lethargy. [*Say* TORE pur]

torque ● *n.* a twisting or rotating force. ● *v.* (**torques**, **torqued**, **torquing**) **1** apply torque or a twisting force to. **2** *informal* heighten; increase. [*Say* TORK]

torrent *n.* **1** a rushing stream of water, lava, etc. **2** a great downpour of rain. **3** a copious flow. □ **torrential** *adj.* [*Say* TORE unt, tuh REN shull]

torrid *adj.* **1** very hot and dry. **2** emotionally charged; passionate. **3** hard to contain or stop. [*Say* TORE id]

torsion *n.* **1** the action of twisting or the state of being twisted. **2** the extent to which a curve departs from being planar. □ **torsional** *adj.* **torsionally** *adv.* [*Say* TORE shun]

torso *n.* (*pl.* **torsos**) **1** the trunk of the human body. **2** a statue of a human consisting of the trunk alone.

tort *n.* *Law* a breach of duty (other than under contract) leading to legal liability.

torte *n.* an elaborate rich cake, esp. one with ground nuts.

tortellini *n.* small crescent-shaped pasta pouches stuffed with meat, cheese, etc. [*Say* torta LEENY]

tortilla *n.* (*pl.* **tortillas**) (esp. in Mexican cooking) a thin round bread made with either cornmeal or wheat flour and usu. served with a filling. [*Say* tore TEE uh]

tortilla chip *n.* (usu. in *pl.*) a fried segment of a corn tortilla, eaten like a potato chip.

tortoise *n.* any slow-moving land or freshwater reptile with a domed shell into which it can draw its head. [*Say* TORE tuss]

tortoiseshell ● *n.* **1** the yellowish-brown mottled outer shell of some turtles, used for decorative combs, jewellery, etc. **2** (also **tortoiseshell cat**) a domestic cat with a mottled black, orange, and cream coat. ● *adj.* **1** having the appearance of tortoiseshell. **2** made of tortoiseshell. [*Say* TORE tuss shell]

tortuous *adj.* **1** full of twists and turns. **2** unnecessarily complex. □ **tortuously** *adv.* [*Say* TORE chew us]

torture ● *n.* **1** the infliction of severe bodily pain esp. as a punishment or a means of interrogation. **2** severe suffering. ● *v.* (**tortures**, **tortured**, **torturing**) subject to torture. □ **torturer** *n.* **torturous** *adj.* [*Say* TORCHER, TORCHER us]

Tory *informal* ● *n.* (*pl.* **Tories**) a member or supporter of a Conservative party. ● *adj.* of or relating to a Conservative party. □ **Toryism** *n.*

toss ● *v.* (**tosses**, **tossed**, **tossing**) **1** throw lightly or carelessly or easily. **2** roll about, throw, or be thrown, restlessly or from side to side. **3** throw (a coin) into the air to decide a choice etc. by the side on which it lands. **4** stir or turn (food) to coat it with dressing etc. **5** debate. **6** discard. ● *n.* (*pl.* **tosses**) **1** the act of tossing. **2** a game etc. in which something is tossed. □ **toss in** add to a mixture casually. **toss**

off 1 dispatch rapidly. **2** utter in an offhand manner.

toss-up n. **1** a situation in which either of two outcomes is equally possible. **2** the tossing of a coin.

tot¹ n. **1** a small child. **2** a small drink of liquor.

tot² v. (**tots, totted, totting**) **1** (usu. foll. by *up*) add. **2** (foll. by *up*) mount up.

total ● adj. **1** complete, comprising the whole or all. **2** absolute. **3** (of an eclipse) in which the whole sun, moon, etc. is obscured. ● n. a total number or amount. ● v. (**totals, totalled, totalling**). **1 a** amount in number to. **b** find the total of. **2** slang wreck completely. ● adv. in total.

totalitarian ● adj. (of government) consisting of one political party that has complete power. ● n. an advocate of such a system. □ **totalitarianism** n. [Say toe tala TERRY in]

totality n. **1** the complete amount. **2** the quality of being total. [Say toe TALA tee]

totally ● adv. completely. ● interj. yes.

tote informal ● v. (**totes, toted, toting**) **1** carry. **2** find the total of. ● n. **1** (also **tote bag**) a large usu. canvas bag with handles. **2** Cdn any large container for storage. **3** slang (also **tote board**) a device showing the bets staked on a race.

totem n. **1** the ancestral emblem of a clan or family, usu. an animal or plant. **2** an emblem or symbol. □ **totemic** adj. **totemism** n. [Say TOE tum, toe TEM ick, TOE tum ism]

totem pole n. **1** a pole on which family crests or totems are carved or hung. **2** a grouping in order of status.

tote road n. a rough temporary road, esp. to a work camp.

-toting comb. form carrying the object specified.

totter ● v. **1** stand or walk unsteadily. **2** shake or rock as if about to collapse. ● n. an unsteady or shaky movement or gait. □ **tottering** adj. **tottery** adj.

toucan n. a brightly coloured tropical American fruit-eating bird, with a huge beak. [Say TOO can]

touch ● v. (**touches, touched, touching**) **1** come into or be in physical contact with. **2** bring esp. the hand into contact with something. **3** rouse tender feelings in. **4** (usu. with neg.) **a** interfere with. **b** have any dealings with. **c** use or consume. **5** attain or equal. **6** affect slightly. ● n. (pl. **touches**) **1** the act or manner of touching. **2** the faculty of perception through physical contact. **3** a small amount. **4 a** a manner of playing an instrument keyboard. **b** the manner in which the keys respond to touch. **5 a** a distinguishing detail. **b** a special proficiency. **6** (esp. in pl.) **a** a light stroke with a pen etc. **b** a slight alteration. □ **in touch 1** in communication. **2** up to date. **3** aware. **lose touch** cease to be informed or be in contact with. **lose one's touch** not show one's customary skill. **out of touch** not up to date, aware, in communication, etc. **touch down** make contact with the ground in landing. **touch off 1** explode by touching with a match etc. **2** initiate suddenly. **touch on 1** treat or refer to briefly. **2** verge on. **touch up** give finishing details to. □ **touchable** adj.

touch and go adj. uncertain regarding the outcome.

touchdown n. **1 a** Football the act of being in possession of the ball in the opposing side's end zone. **b** Rugby an act of touching the ground behind the opposing side's goal with the ball held in the hands. **2** the moment at which the wheels etc. touch the ground during landing.

touché interj. **1** the acknowledgement of a hit by a fencing opponent. **2** the acknowledgement of a justified accusation etc. made by another. [Say too SHAY]

touched adj. **1** in senses of TOUCH v. **2** informal slightly mad.

touch football n. a form of football in which the ball carrier need only be touched to be stopped.

touching adj. rousing tender feelings. □ **touchingly** adv.

touchpad n. a pad that needs only to be touched to activate an electrical device.

touch screen n. a computer screen that allows the user to interact by touching it with a finger or stylus.

touchstone n. **1** a piece of stone used for testing alloys of gold etc. by observing the colour of the mark which they make on it. **2** anything which serves to test genuineness.

Touch-Tone adj. proprietary designating a telephone system in which a different tone is generated by each of the numbered buttons.

touch type v. (**touch types, touch typed, touch typing**) type without looking at the keys. □ **touch typing** n. **touch typist** n.

touch-up n. a quick restoration or improvement.

touchy adj. (**touchier, touchiest**) **1** apt to take offence. **2** delicate. □ **touchily** adv. **touchiness** n.

touchy-feely adj. openly expressing emotions, affection, etc.

tough ● *adj.* **1** hard to break, cut, tear, or chew. **2** able to endure hardship. **3** unyielding; difficult. **4** stern or severe. **5** *informal* aggressive, violent. ● *n.* a violent criminal. ● *interj. ironic* that is unfortunate (used unsympathetically). □ **be a tough sell** be difficult to convince others about. **tough (it) out** *informal* endure or withstand. □ **toughly** *adv.* **toughness** *n.*

toughen *v.* make or become tough.

toughie *n.* (also **toughy**) (*pl.* **toughies**) *informal* a tough person or problem.

tough-minded *adj.* **1** realistic, not sentimental. **2** determined. □ **tough-mindedness** *n.*

toupée *n.* a wig or artificial hairpiece to cover a bald spot. [*Say* too PAY]

tour ● *n.* **1 a** a journey from place to place as a holiday. **b** an excursion. **2** a period of duty on military or diplomatic service. **3** a series of performances, games, etc., at different places on a route. ● *v.* make a tour (of).

tour de force *n.* (*pl.* **tours de force** *pronunc.* same) a feat of skill or strength.

Tourette's syndrome *n.* (also **Tourette Syndrome**) a neurological disorder characterized by involuntary tics and utterances of obscene language. [*Say* too RET]

tourism *n.* the commercial organization and operation of holidays and visits to places of interest.

tourist *n.* a person making a visit as a holiday.

tourist trap *n.* a place where tourists are exploited.

touristy *adj.* usu. *derogatory* appealing to many tourists.

tourmaline *n.* a boron aluminum silicate mineral of various colours, used in electrical devices and as a gemstone. [*Say* TOOR muh leen]

tournament *n.* **1** a series of contests between a number of competitors. **2** *hist.* a pageant in which jousting with blunted weapons took place.

tournedos *n.* (*pl.* **tournedos**) a small round thick cut of beef tenderloin. [*Say* TOOR nuh doe]

tourney *n.* (*pl.* **tourneys**) a tournament. [*Rhymes with* JOURNEY]

tourniquet *n.* a cord or tight bandage tied around limb etc. to stop the flow of blood through an artery. [*Say* TURN a kay]

tourtière *n.* a French-Canadian meat pie traditionally served at Christmas. [*Say* tor TYAIR]

tousle ● *v.* (**tousles**, **tousled**, **tousling**) make untidy; rumple. ● *n.* a tousled mass of hair etc. [*Say* TOUSE 'll]

tout ● *v.* **1** recommend the merits of (someone or something). **2** attempt to sell (something). ● *n.* a person soliciting business aggressively. □ **touted** *adj.*

tow ● *v.* **1** pull along by a rope, chain, etc. **2** remove to a pound, garage, etc. ● *n.* an act of or mechanism for towing. □ **in tow 1** (also **under tow**) being towed. **2** accompanying. □ **towable** *adj.*

toward *prep.* (also **towards**) **1** in the direction of. **2** as regards. **3** as a contribution to. **4** near.

towboat *n.* a boat used to tow other boats etc.

towel ● *n.* **1** a rough-surfaced absorbent cloth used for drying. **2** absorbent paper. ● *v.* (**towels**, **towelled**, **towelling**) wipe or dry with a towel.

towelette *n.* a small moistened tissue.

towelling *n.* **1** *in senses of* TOWEL *v.* **2** absorbent cloth, usu. cotton, used for towels.

tower ● *n.* **1** a tall narrow building or structure. **2** a lofty pile or mass. **3** an upright casing for computer components. ● *v.* be high or above; be superior. □ **towered** *adj.* **towering** *adj.*

towheaded *adj.* having very light-coloured or unkempt hair.

towhee *n.* a N American woodland bunting. [*Say* TOW hee *(*TOW *rhymes with* PLOW*)*]

town *n.* **1 a** an urban area with defined boundaries. **b** the people of a town. **c** the government etc. of a town. **2** the central business area. □ **go to town** *informal* act with enthusiasm. **on the town** *informal* enjoying the entertainments of a town.

town hall *n.* **1** a building for the administration of local government. **2** (also **town hall meeting**) a meeting or television broadcast allowing people to express their opinions on political issues to political leaders.

townhouse *n.* **1** (also **townhome**) any of a row of usu. similar joined houses. **2** an urban residence.

townie *n.* (also **townee**) *derogatory* a person living in a town.

townsfolk *n.* the inhabitants of a town.

township *n.* **1** a division of a county with some corporate powers. **2** a district six miles square, containing thirty-six sections. **3** *hist.* an urban area in South Africa set aside for black occupation.

townsite *n.* esp. *Cdn* **1** the site of a town.

2 an unincorporated town in a national park etc.

townsman *n.* (*pl.* **townsmen**) an inhabitant of a town.

townspeople *pl. n.* the people of a town.

towpath *n.* a path beside a river or canal.

tow truck *n.* a truck used to tow away motor vehicles.

toxemia *n.* **1** blood poisoning. **2** a condition in pregnancy characterized by increased blood pressure. □ **toxemic** *adj.* [Say tox EEMY uh]

toxic 1 of or relating to poison. **2** poisonous. **3** caused by poison. □ **toxically** *adv.* **toxicity** *n.* [TOX ick, tox ISSA tee,]

toxicology *n.* the scientific study of poisons. □ **toxicological** *adj.* **toxicologist** *n.* [Say toxa COLLA jee, toxa kuh LOGICAL, toxa COLLA jist]

toxic shock syndrome *n.* acute blood poisoning in women, usu. caused by bacterial infection from a retained tampon, IUD, etc. Abbreviation: **TSS**.

toxin *n.* a poison produced by a living organism.

toxoplasmosis *n.* a disease transmitted esp. through poorly prepared food or in cat feces and dangerous in unborn children. [Say toxo plaz MOE sis]

toy ● *n.* 1 a a plaything. **b** a model or miniature replica. **2** a thing regarded as providing amusement. ● *v.* (usu. foll. by *with*) **1 a** consider without seriousness. **b** deal thoughtlessly. **2** move idly or nibble at without enthusiasm.

toy boy *n. informal* a much younger male lover.

trace¹ ● *v.* (traces, traced, tracing) 1 a find by investigation. **b** follow the track or position of. **2** copy by drawing over its lines using translucent paper. **3** mark out, sketch, etc. laboriously. ● *n.* **1 a** a sign of something having existed or passed by. **b** a very small quantity. **2** a footprint, track etc. **3** a line or pattern on paper or a screen, esp. showing something recorded by machine. □ **traceable** *adj.*

trace² *n.* each of the two side straps, chains, or ropes by which a horse, sled dog, etc. draws a vehicle.

trace element *n.* a chemical element present or required in minute amounts.

tracer *n.* **1** a person or thing that traces. **2** a bullet etc. visible in flight because of flames etc. emitted.

tracery *n.* (*pl.* **traceries**) **1** ornamental stone openwork. **2** a delicate decorative pattern.

trachea *n.* the passage through which air

reaches the bronchial tubes from the larynx. □ **tracheal** *adj.* [Say TRAKE ee uh *or* TRACK ee uh]

tracheotomy *n.* (*pl.* **tracheotomies**) a surgical operation to make an opening in the trachea. [Say trake ee OTTA mee]

tracing *n.* **1** a copy of a drawing etc. made by tracing. **2** = TRACE¹ *n.* 3.

track ● *n.* 1 a mark left by a person, animal, or thing in passing. **2** a rough path. **3** a continuous railway line. **4 a** a racecourse etc. **b** *Sport* the athletic events which take place on a track. **5 a** a section of a compact disc etc. containing one song etc. **b** a sequence of data recorded on a strip of magnetic tape etc. **6** a line of travel or motion. **7** a continuous band around the wheels of a tank, tractor, etc. **8** a course of action or reasoning. **9** (usu. in *pl.*) *slang* a line on the skin made by repeated injections. ● *v.* **1** follow the track of. **2** follow the course or development of. **3** move in relation to the subject being filmed. **4** make a track with (dirt etc.) from the feet. □ **keep** (or **lose**) **track of** follow (or fail to follow) the course or development of. **on the right** (or **wrong**) **track** following the right (or wrong) line of inquiry. **on** (or **off**) **track** following (or deviating from) the desired direction. **track down** reach or capture by tracking. □ **tracked** *adj.* **trackless** *adj.*

trackball *n. Computing* a small ball that is rotated to move a cursor.

tracker *n.* **1** a person or thing that tracks. **2** a police dog tracking by scent.

tracking *n.* **1** in senses of TRACK *v.* **2** the formation of a conducting path over the surface of an insulating material. **3** in a VCR, the alignment of the tape with the tape head.

track light *n.* (usu. in *pl.*) one of a line of lights fitted on a metal or plastic strip. □ **track lighting** *n.*

trackpad *n. Computing* a small pad with which the actions of a cursor etc. can be controlled by the movement of a finger along its surface.

track pants *pl. n.* loose pants, usu. with elasticized cuffs.

track record *n.* the past achievements.

track suit *n.* a loose warm two-piece suit worn by an athlete etc. for exercising.

tract *n.* **1** a large extent of land. **2** an area of an organ or system. **3** a short treatise.

tractable *adj.* easy to deal with. □ **tractability** *n.*

traction *n.* **1** the grip of a tire, footwear, etc. on the ground. **2** the act of pulling a thing over a surface. **3** a sustained pulling on a limb, muscle, etc., to maintain the positions of fractured bones etc.

tractor *n.* a powerful motor vehicle, usu. with large treaded rear wheels, used for hauling farm machinery etc.

tractor-trailer *n.* an articulated truck consisting of a powerful cab pulling a large detachable trailer.

trad *adj. informal* traditional.

trade ● *n.* **1 a** buying and selling. **b** business conducted for profit, or of a specified nature. **2** a skilled handicraft. **3** (usu. as **the trade**) the people engaged in a specific trade. **4** a transaction or exchange. ● *v.* (**trades, traded, trading**) **1** buy and sell. **2** exchange, or exchange things with (a person). **3** be bought and sold. □ **trade off** exchange as part of a compromise **trade on** take advantage of. **trade up** sell something in order to buy a better or more expensive replacement. □ **tradable** *adj.*

trade barrier *n.* something that restricts trade.

tradecraft *n.* **1** skill in a trade or calling. **2** skill in espionage.

trade deficit *n.* (also **trade gap**) the extent by which a country's imports exceed its exports.

trade-in *n.* a thing exchanged in part payment for another.

trademark ● *n.* **1** a logo, word, etc., legally established as representing a company, product, etc. **2** a distinctive characteristic. ● *adj.* distinctive. ● *v.* (usu. as **trademarked** *adj.*) provide or register with a trademark.

trade name *n.* **1** a name used in a trade. **2** a name given to a product or business.

trade-off *n.* a compromise.

trader *n.* **1** a person engaged in trading. **2** a person who trades stocks.

trade show *n.* an exhibition and gathering for a particular trade.

tradesman *n.* (*pl.* **tradesmen**) a person engaged in a trade.

tradespeople *pl. n.* people engaged in trade.

trade union *n.* = LABOUR UNION. □ **trade unionism** *n.* **trade unionist** *n.*

trade war *n.* a situation in which governments act aggressively to promote their own countries' trading interests.

trade wind *n.* a wind blowing continually towards the equator and deflected westward.

trading *n.* the act of engaging in trade.

trading card *n.* a small card depicting a famous figure etc., for collecting or swapping.

trading post *n.* a place for conducting trade, esp. one established in a remote area to trade with Aboriginal peoples.

tradition *n.* **1 a** a custom or belief handed down to posterity. **b** this process of handing down. **2** an established practice. □ **traditional** *adj.* **traditionally** *adv.*

traditionalism *n.* respect or support for tradition. □ **traditionalist** *n.*

traffic ● *n.* **1 a** vehicles moving on a public road. **b** the movement of ships, aircraft, etc. **c** people moving on foot. **2** trade, esp. illegal. **3 a** the transportation of goods and people by road, rail, air, sea, etc. **b** the persons or goods so transported. **4** dealings or communication. **5** signals etc. transmitted through a communications system. ● *v.* (**traffics, trafficked, trafficking**) **1** trade illegally in something. **2** offer for consumption or use. □ **trafficker** *n.*

traffic calming *n.* the deliberate slowing of traffic using speed bumps etc.

traffic circle *n.* a road junction at which traffic moves in one direction around a central island.

traffic island *n.* a paved or grassed area in a road to divert traffic, provide a refuge for pedestrians, etc.

traffic jam *n.* traffic at a standstill.

trafficked *adj.* used by an esp. specified amount of traffic.

traffic light *n.* (usu. in *pl.*) each of a set of automatic lights, usu. red, amber, and green, for controlling road traffic.

tragedy *n.* (*pl.* **tragedies**) **1** an event causing great suffering or sorrow. **2** a tragic element. **3** a dramatic representation dealing with tragic events.

tragic *adj.* **1** greatly distressing. **2** of, or in the style of, tragedy. □ **tragically** *adv.*

tragicomedy *n.* (*pl.* **tragicomedies**) **1** a play having a mixture of comedy and tragedy. **2** an event etc. having tragic and comic elements. □ **tragicomic** *adj.*

trail ● *n.* **1** a track left by a thing, person, etc., moving over a surface. **2** a path, track, or route. **3** a part dragging behind a thing or person. ● *v.* **1** draw or be drawn behind. **2** walk wearily. **3** follow the trail of. **4 a** be losing. **b** have fewer points than. **5** peter out. **6 a** grow or hang over a wall etc. **b** hang loosely.

trailblazer *n.* **1** a person who marks a new track through wild country. **2** an innovator. □ **trailblazing** *n.* & *adj.*

trail-breaker *n.* a person who clears a path through rough terrain, deep snow, etc. □ **trail-breaking** *n.*

trailer ● *n.* **1** a vehicle or container towed

by a vehicle. **2** a platform for transporting a boat etc. **3** a camper, mobile home, etc. **4** a preview advertising a film etc. **5** a person or thing that trails. **6** a trailing plant. ● *v.* transport or travel by trailer.

trailer park *n.* (also **trailer court**) a place where mobile homes etc. may be parked for holiday or more permanent accommodation.

trailhead *n.* the starting point of a trail.

trail mix *n.* a mixture of nuts, dried fruit, chocolate chips, etc.

trail ride *n.* a ride on horseback along a trail. □ **trail riding** *n.*

train ● *v.* **1 a** teach a specified skill by practice. **b** undergo this process. **2** bring or come into a state of physical efficiency. **3** cause to grow in a required shape. **4** aim or point. ● *n.* **1** a series of railway cars drawn by a locomotive. **2** something dragged along behind or forming the back part of a dress, robe, etc. **3** a series or succession. **4** a body of followers. **5** a series of connected parts in machinery. □ **in train** properly arranged or directed. **in a person's train** following behind a person. □ **trainable** *adj.* **trainer** *n.* **training** *n.*

trainee *n.* a person undergoing training.

training ground *n.* any setting where one develops specific skills.

training wheel *n.* a small wheel used to stabilize a bicycle.

trainload *n.* a number of people, or quantity of goods etc., transported by train.

traipse *informal* ● *v.* (**traipses, traipsed, traipsing**) walk or move wearily or casually. ● *n.* a tedious journey on foot. [*Rhymes with* GRAPES]

trait *n.* **1** a distinguishing characteristic. **2** a genetically determined characteristic.

traitor *n.* a person who betrays esp. their country. □ **traitorous** *adj.* **traitorously** *adv.* [*Say* TRAY ter]

trajectory *n.* (*pl.* **trajectories**) **1** the path of an object sent into the air. **2** a course of action. [*Say* truh JECKTER ee]

tram *n.* **1** esp. *Brit.* a streetcar. **2** each of a series of small enclosed passenger cabins suspended from a cable and drawn up and down a mountainside by an engine at one end.

tramp ● *v.* **1 a** walk heavily and firmly. **b** go or cross on foot. **2** tread on. ● *n.* **1** a person who travels by foot as a vagrant. **2** *slang derogatory* a promiscuous woman. **3** the sound of a marching feet, hooves, etc. **4** a long journey on foot. **5** a merchant ship running on no regular line or route. □ **trampy** *adj.*

trample ● *v.* (**tramples, trampled, trampling**) **1** tread or crush under foot. **2** disregard with contempt. ● *n.* the sound or act of trampling.

trampoline ● *n.* a strong fabric sheet connected by springs to a horizontal frame, used as a springboard, etc. ● *v.* use a trampoline.

tramway *n.* **1** a crude road with tracks for wheels. **2** rails for a streetcar.

trance *n.* **1** a sleep-like state in which a person does not respond to stimuli. **2** a state of extreme exaltation or mental absorption. **3** a stunned state. □ **trancelike** *adj.*

tranche *n.* a portion. [*Say* TRANSH]

tranquil *adj.* calm, serene. □ **tranquilly** *adv.*

tranquility *n.* calmness. [*Say* tran KWILLA tee]

tranquilize *v.* (**tranquilizes, tranquilized, tranquilizing**) make tranquil with a drug. □ **tranquilizer** *n.* **tranquilizing** *adj.*

trans- *prefix* across.

transact *v.* carry through (business).

transaction *n.* **1 a** a piece of commercial business done. **b** an exchange. **c** the management of business etc. **2** (in *pl.*) published reports of a society's discussions etc. □ **transactional** *adj.*

transatlantic *adj.* **1** crossing or spanning the Atlantic. **2** beyond the Atlantic.

transborder *adj.* pertaining to both sides of a border.

transceiver *n.* a transmitter and receiver of signals. [*Say* tran SEEVER]

transcend *v.* be or go beyond the range of. [*Say* tran SEND]

transcendent *adj.* **1** beyond or above the range of normal or physical human experience. **2** surpassing the ordinary. **3** existing apart from the physical universe. □ **transcendence** *n.* **transcendental** *adj.* **transcendently** *adv.* [*Say* tran SEN dint, tran sin DENTAL]

Transcendental Meditation *n.* *proprietary* a technique for calming oneself etc. using meditation and the repetition of words and sounds.

transcontinental ● *adj.* extending across a continent. ● *n.* a transcontinental railway or train.

transcribe *v.* (**transcribes, transcribed, transcribing**) **1** put into written or printed form. **2** make a copy of (something) in a different alphabet or language. **3** arrange for a different instrument etc. **4** represent in a written

form using phonetic characters.
□ **transcriber** n.

transcript n. **1** a written or recorded copy. **2** any copy. **3** an official record of a student's grades etc.

transcription n. **1 a** the action or process of transcribing something. **b** a written or printed representation of something. **2** an arrangement of a piece of music for different instrumentation etc.

transcultural adj. pertaining to more than one culture.

transduce v. (**transduces**, **transduced**, **transducing**) convert (energy) into a different medium or form of energy. □ **transduction** n.

transducer n. a device for converting esp. a non-electrical signal into an electrical one.

transect v. cut across or transversely. □ **transection** n.

transept n. **1** either arm of the part of a cross-shaped church at right angles to the nave. **2** this part as a whole.
[*Say* TRAN sept]

trans fat n. (also **trans fatty acid**) any unsaturated fatty acid with the same atoms on opposite sides of its double bonds.

transfer ● v. (**transfers**, **transferred**, **transferring**) **1** (often foll. by *to*) **a** move from one place to another. **b** hand over. **2** change from one route, airport, station, etc., to another on a journey. **3** reroute to another line, department, etc. **4** convey or apply from one surface to another. ● n. **1** an act of transferring. **2** a ticket allowing a journey to be continued on another route etc. **3** a design etc. conveyed or to be conveyed from one surface to another. **4** a person who is or is to be transferred. **5** the conveyance of property, a right, etc. **6** (also **transfer payment**) a direct payment from a government not made in exchange for goods or services, (in Canada) esp. to another level of government.

transferable adj. that can be transferred. □ **transferability** n. [*Say* trans FUR a bull, transfer a BILLA tee]

transference n. **1** the action of transferring something. **2** *Psychology* the redirection of childhood emotions to a new object, esp. to a psychoanalyst.
[*Say* TRANSFER ince]

transfer station n. a facility where garbage is collected for compression etc. before being trucked to a landfill.

transfigure v. (**transfigures**, **transfigured**, **transfiguring**) change in form or appearance, esp. so as to elevate or

idealize. □ **transfiguration** n.
[*Say* trans FIGURE]

transfix v. (**transfixes**, **transfixed**, **transfixing**) **1** pierce with a sharp implement or weapon. **2** root to the spot with astonishment, fear, etc.

transform v. **1 a** make a thorough change in the form or appearance. **b** undergo such a change. **2** change the voltage etc. of. □ **transformable** adj.

transformation n. a thorough change in form or appearance.
□ **transformational** adj.

transformative adj. causing change or able to cause change.

transformer n. an apparatus for altering the voltage of an alternating current.

transfuse v. (**transfuses**, **transfused**, **transfusing**) **1** transfer blood from one person or animal to another. **2** inject liquid into a blood vessel to replace lost fluid. □ **transfusion** n.

transgendered adj. having an identity which does not conform unambiguously to conventional notions of male or female gender.

transgenic adj. having genetic material introduced from another species.
[*Say* trans JEN ick]

transgress v. (**transgresses**, **transgressed**, **transgressing**) go beyond the limit of (what is acceptable, a law, etc.). □ **transgressor** n.

transgression n. the breaking of a moral law or rule of behaviour.

transient ● adj. of short duration; impermanent. ● n. **1** a temporary visitor, worker, etc. **2** a vagrant. □ **transience** n., **transiently** adv. [*Say* TRANZY int]

transistor n. **1** a small electronic device made of semiconductor material such as silicon, used for controlling an electric current. **2** (also **transistor radio**) a portable radio with transistors.
[*Say* tran ZIST er]

transit ● n. **1** the act or process of going, conveying, or being conveyed. **2** a route. **3** the local conveyance of passengers on public routes. **4** the apparent passage of a celestial body across the meridian of a place or across the face of a sun or planet. ● v. (**transits**, **transited**, **transiting**) pass across or through an area. □ **in transit** while going or being conveyed.

transition n. **1** a change from one place, condition, etc., to another. **2** a passage from one subject or section to another. □ **transitional** adj.

transition house n. (also **transition**

home) *Cdn* a home operated by a social service agency, esp. for abused women.

transitive *adj.* (of a verb) that takes a direct object. □**transitively** *adv.* **transitivity** *n.* [*Say* TRANZA tiv, tranza TIVVA tee]

transitory *adj.* not permanent. □**transitoriness** *n.* [*Say* TRANZA tory, TRANZA tory niss]

translate *v.* (**translates, translated, translating**) **1** express in another language or form. **2** be translatable. **3** interpret the significance of. **4** *Christianity* **a** remove (a bishop) to another see. **b** remove (a saint's relics etc.) to another place. **5** *Bible* convey to heaven without death. □**translatable** *adj.* **translation** *n.* **translator** *n.*

transliterate *v.* (**transliterates, transliterated, transliterating**) represent in the closest corresponding letters of a different alphabet or language. □**transliteration** *n.* [*Say* trans LITTER ate]

translocate *v.* (**translocates, translocated, translocating**) move from one place to another. □**translocation** *n.*

translucent *adj.* allowing light, but not detailed shapes, to pass through. □**translucence** *n.* **translucently** *adv.* [*Say* trans LOO sint]

transmigration *n.* **1** the passage of the soul into a different body after death. **2** migration. [*Say* trans MIGRATE]

transmission *n.* **1** the action or process of transmitting something. **2** a broadcast radio or television program. **3** the mechanism by which power is transmitted from an engine to the axle in a motor vehicle. [*Say* trans MISSION]

transmit *v.* (**transmits, transmitted, transmitting**) **1 a** pass or hand on. **b** communicate. **2 a** allow to pass through. **b** be a medium for. **3** broadcast. □**transmissible** *adj.* **transmittable** *adj.* **transmittal** *n.*

transmitter *n.* **1** a person or thing that transmits. **2** a set of equipment used to generate and transmit electromagnetic waves carrying messages, signals, etc. **3** = NEUROTRANSMITTER.

transmogrify *v.* (**transmogrifies, transmogrified, transmogrifying**) *jocular* transform, esp. in a magical or surprising manner. □**transmogrification** *n.* [*Say* trans MOGRA fie, trans mogra fi CAY sh'n]

transmute *v.* (**transmutes, transmuted, transmuting**) change the form, nature, or substance of. □**transmutation** *n.*

transnational ● *adj.* extending beyond national boundaries. ● *n.* a transnational company. □**transnationally** *adv.*

transoceanic *adj.* **1** situated beyond the ocean. **2** concerned with crossing the ocean. [*Say* trans oh see ANN ick]

transom *n.* **1** a horizontal bar across a window or the top of a door. **2** a strengthening crossbar. **3** a window divided by or placed above a transom. [*Say* TRAN sum]

trans-Pacific *adj.* on the other side of or crossing the Pacific Ocean.

transparency *n.* (*pl.* **transparencies**) **1** the condition of being transparent. **2** a positive transparent photograph viewed using a slide projector. **3** a clear plastic page viewed using an overhead projector. **4** the quality of transactions and activities in business, government, etc., being open to examination by the public.

transparent *adj.* **1** allowing light to pass through so that bodies can be distinctly seen. **2** easily seen through or discerned. **3** having motives that are easily understood. **4** (of transactions and activities in business, government, etc.) open to examination by the public. □**transparently** *adv.*

transpire *v.* (**transpires, transpired, transpiring**) **1 a** (preceded by *it* as subject) prove to be the case. **b** come to be known. **2** happen. **3** release water vapour. □**transpiration** *n.*

transplant ● *v.* **1** plant in or move to another place. **2** transfer to another part of the body or another body. ● *n.* **1** the transplanting of an organ or tissue. **2** a transplanted thing. □**transplantable** *adj.* **transplantation** *n.* **transplanter** *n.*

transponder *n.* a device for receiving a radio signal and automatically transmitting a different signal.

transport ● *v.* **1** take or carry from one place to another. **2** *hist.* take to a penal colony. ● *n.* **1** the action of transporting or the state of being transported. **2** a system of moving people, goods, etc. **3 a** a ship, aircraft, etc. used to carry soldiers, supplies, etc. **b** = TRANSPORT TRUCK. **4** (esp. in *pl.*) a very strong emotion. □**transportable** *adj.* **transportation** *n.* **transported** *adj.*

transporter *n.* **1** a person or device that transports. **2** a vehicle used to transport other vehicles, machinery, etc.

transport truck *n.* a large, long truck.

transpose *v.* (**transposes, transposing**) **1** cause to change places. **2** change the order or position of (words or a word) in a sentence. **3** *Music* write or perform in a different key from the original. □ **transposable** *adj*. **transposition** *n*.

transsexual ● *adj*. having the physical characteristics of one sex and the supposed psychological characteristics of the other. ● *n*. **1** a transsexual person. **2** a person whose sex has been changed by surgery.

transship *v.* (**transships, transshipped, transshipping**) transfer from one ship or form of transport to another. □ **transshipment** *n*.

transubstantiation *n*. (in Catholic and Orthodox belief) the conversion in the Eucharist, after consecration, of the bread and wine into the body and blood of Christ. [*Say* tran sub stanshy AY sh'n]

transverse *adj*. situated or acting in a crosswise direction. □ **transversely** *adv.* [*Say* TRANS vers]

transvestite *n*. a person, esp. a man, who dresses in the clothes of the opposite sex. □ **transvestism** *n*. [*Say* trans VEST ite, trans VEST ism]

trap ● *n*. **1 a** an enclosure or device, often baited, for catching animals. **b** a device with bait for killing vermin. **2 a** a trick betraying a person into speech or an act. **b** a situation difficult to escape from. **3** an arrangement to catch an unsuspecting person. **4** a device for hurling a clay pigeon etc. into the air. **5** a curve in a drainpipe etc. that fills with liquid and prevents the upward passage of gases. **6** *slang* the mouth **7** *Golf* a bunker. **8** *Hockey* a defensive strategy in which a team positions all its skaters in the neutral zone. **9** *Football* an offensive play permitting a defensive player to cross the line of scrimmage only to be blocked off so as create a gap for the ball carrier. **10** a two-wheeled carriage. **11** a trap door. **12** (esp. in *pl.*) *informal* a percussion instrument in a band. ● *v.* (**traps, trapped, trapping**) **1** catch using a trap. **2** stop and retain in a trap. **3** provide with traps. **4** prevent from escaping. **5** *Baseball* catch (a ball) just after it has hit the ground. □ **trap out** deplete the supply of fur-bearing animals through trapping.

trap door *n*. a door or hatch in a floor, ceiling, or roof.

trapeze *n*. a crossbar suspended by ropes used as a swing for acrobatics etc. [*Say* tra PEEZ]

trapezium *n*. (*pl.* **trapezia** or **trapeziums**) a quadrilateral with no two sides parallel. [*Say* truh PEEZY um; truh PEEZY uh]

trapezius *n*. (*pl.* **trapezii**) either of the large triangular muscles extending over the back of the neck and shoulders. [*Say* truh PEEZY us *for the singular*, truh PEEZY eye *for the plural*]

trapezoid *n*. a quadrilateral with only one pair of sides parallel. □ **trapezoidal** *adj*. [*Say* TRAPPA zoid]

trapline *n*. **1** a series of traps set outdoors for catching animals. **2** the trail along which a trapper walks to check his or her traplines.

trapper *n*. **1** a person who traps wild animals for furs. **2** *Hockey* a goalie's catching glove.

trappings *pl. n*. **1** outward signs. **2** the ornamental harness of a horse.

Trappist ● *n*. a member of a branch of the Cistercian order of monks noted for their vow of silence. ● *adj*. relating to this order.

trap shooting *n*. the sport of shooting at clay pigeons launched from a trap. □ **trap shooter** *n*.

trash ● *n*. **1** garbage. **2** poor-quality or worthless stuff. **3** nonsense. **4** a worthless person or persons. ● *v.* (**trashes, trashed, trashing**) *informal* **1** wreck, destroy. **2** expose the worthless nature of.

trashed *adj*. **1** *informal* very drunk. **2** destroyed.

trash talk *informal* ● *n*. **1** *Sport* insulting talk intended to demoralize an opponent. **2** any contemptuous or boastful statement. ● *v.* (**trash-talk**) **1** deliver trash talk. **2** badmouth an opponent. □ **trash-talker** *n*. **trash-talking** *n*. & *adj*.

trashy *adj*. (**trashier, trashiest**) **1** of poor quality. **2** disreputable. □ **trashily** *adv.* **trashiness** *n*.

trattoria *n*. an Italian restaurant. [*Say* tratta REE uh]

trauma *n*. (*pl.* **traumas**) **1 a** *Psychology* emotional shock following a stressful event. **b** a disturbing experience. **2** any physical injury, or the shock following it, characterized by a drop in body temperature, mental confusion, etc. [*Say* TROMMA]

traumatic *adj*. **1** of or causing trauma. **2** emotionally disturbing. [*Say* truh MAT ick]

traumatize *v.* (**traumatizes, traumatized, traumatizing**) shock very much. [*Say* TROMMA tize]

travail *n*. *literary* painful or laborious effort. [*Say* truh VAIL *or* TRAV ail]

travel ● *v.* (**travels, travelled, travelling**) **1** move or go from one place to another. **2 a** journey along or through. **b** cover in travelling. **3** withstand a long journey. **4** *Basketball* move two or more steps while carrying the ball, in violation of the rules. ● *n.* **1 a** the act of travelling, esp. in foreign countries. **b** (often in *pl.*) a period of this. **2** (as an *adj.*) suitable for use when travelling. □ **travelling** *n.*

travel agency *n.* a company which makes arrangements for travellers. □ **travel agent** *n.*

travelled *adj.* experienced in travelling.

traveller *n.* **1** a person who travels. **2** (also **New Age traveller**) a person with New Age values who leads an unconventional wandering lifestyle.

traveller's cheque *n.* a cheque for a fixed amount that may be cashed on signature, usu. internationally.

travelogue *n.* a film, book, or illustrated lecture about travel. [*Say* TRAVEL og]

traverse ● *v.* (**traverses**, **traversed**, **traversing**) travel or lie across. ● *n.* **1** a sideways movement. **2** an act of crossing something. [*Say* truh VERSE]

travertine *n.* a chalky rock deposited from springs. [*Say* TRAVER teen]

travesty ● *n.* (*pl.* **travesties**) a grotesque misrepresentation or imitation. ● *v.* (**travesties**, **travestied**, **travestying**) make or be a travesty of. [*Say* TRAVA stee]

travois *n.* (*pl.* **travois**) *hist.* a V-shaped frame of teepee poles pulled by dogs or horses, used by Plains Aboriginal peoples to carry loads. [*Say* TRAV wah *for the singular,* TRAV wahs *for the plural*]

trawl ● *v.* **1** fish by dragging a large net or a long line supporting baited hooks. **2** search thoroughly. ● *n.* **1** an act of trawling. **2** (also **trawl net**) a large wide-mouthed fishing net. **3** (also **trawl line**) a long buoyed sea-fishing line supporting baited hooks.

trawler *n.* **1** a boat used for trawling. **2** a person who trawls.

tray *n.* a flat shallow vessel usu. with a raised rim for carrying things.

treacherous *adj.* **1** guilty of or involving betrayal. **2** dangerous, hazardous. □ **treacherously** *adv.* [*Say* TRETCHER us]

treachery *n.* (*pl.* **treacheries**) betrayal of trust. [*Say* TRETCHER ee]

treacle *n.* esp. *Brit.* **1** a syrup produced in refining sugar. **2** molasses. □ **treacly** *adj.* [*Say* TREEKLE]

tread ● *v.* (**treads**; *past* **trod**; *past participle* **trodden** or **trod**; **treading**) **1 a** set down one's foot. **b** (of the foot) be set down. **2 a** walk on. **b** press or crush with the feet. **3** perform by walking. **4** make by treading. **5** subdue mercilessly. **6** make a track with

(dirt etc.) from the feet. ● *n.* **1** a manner or sound of walking. **2** the top surface of a step or stair. **3** the thick moulded part of a vehicle tire for gripping the road. **4** the part of a wheel that touches the rail. **5** the part of the sole of a shoe that rests on the ground. □ **tread water 1** maintain an upright position in the water by moving the feet with a walking movement. **2** fail to advance. □ **treaded** *adj.* **treader** *n.* [*Say* TRED]

treadle ● *n.* a lever worked by the foot to operate a machine. ● *v.* (**treadles**, **treadled**, **treadling**) work a treadle. [*Say* TREDDLE]

treadmill *n.* **1** a device for producing motion by the weight of persons or animals stepping on steps on the inner surface of a revolving upright wheel. **2** an exercise machine with a moving belt on which a person walks or jogs. **3** monotonous routine work. [*Say* TRED mill]

treason *n.* **1** (also **high treason**) the crime of betraying one's country. **2** any betrayal of trust. □ **treasonous** *adj.*

treasonable *adj.* involving or guilty of treason.

treasure ● *n.* **1** stored riches, esp. in the form of gems, precious metals, etc. **2** a very valued or valuable object or person. ● *v.* (**treasures**, **treasured**, **treasuring**) value highly.

treasure hunt *n.* **1** a search for treasure. **2** a game in which players seek a hidden object from a series of clues.

treasurer *n.* **1** a person who administers the funds of a society, corporation, etc. **2** an officer authorized to receive and disburse public revenues.

treasure trove *n.* **1** *Law* treasure of unknown ownership found hidden in the ground etc. and declared the property of the Crown. **2** a collection of valuable things.

treasury *n.* (*pl.* **treasuries**) **1** a place or building where treasure is stored. **2** the funds or revenue of a state, institution, or society. **3** (**Treasury**) the department managing the public revenue of a country.

treasury bill *n.* a bill of exchange issued by the government to raise money for temporary needs.

Treasury Board *n. Cdn* a committee of the Privy Council that reviews planned government expenditures and programs etc.

treasury bond *n.* a government bond issued by the Treasury.

treat ● *v.* **1** behave towards or deal with in a certain way. **2** apply a process to. **3** apply medical care to. **4** present (a subject).

5 (often foll. by *to*) provide with food, entertainment, an indulgence, etc. at one's own expense. ● *n.* **1** an event that gives great pleasure. **2** a meal, entertainment, etc., provided by someone for another's enjoyment. **3** a candy or other sweet food item. □ **treatable** *adj.* **treater** *n.* **treating** *n.*

treatise *n.* a written work dealing systematically with a subject.
[*Say* TREE tiss]

treatment *n.* **1** a way of behaving towards someone or dealing with something. **2** the application of medical care. **3** a manner of treating a subject. **4** subjection to the action of a chemical, physical, or biological agent.

treaty *n.* (*pl.* **treaties**) a formal agreement, esp. between states.

treaty band *n. Cdn* an Aboriginal band that has signed a treaty with the federal government.

treaty Indian *n. Cdn* a status Indian who is a member of a treaty band.

treaty rights *pl. n. Cdn* the rights granted to a group of Aboriginal people under the terms of a treaty.

treble ● *adj.* **1** high-pitched. **2** soprano. **3** *esp. Brit.* **a** threefold. **b** triple. **c** three times as much or many. ● *n.* **1 a** soprano. **b** a high-pitched voice. **2** the high-frequency output of a radio, record player, etc. [*Say* TREBBLE]

treble clef *n. Music* a sign that indicates that the second lowest line of the staff represents the G above middle C.

tree ● *n.* **1** a perennial plant with a trunk and branches, often growing to a considerable height. **2** a branching diagram in which relationships etc. are shown by points joined by lines. **3** a family tree. ● *v.* (**trees, treed, treeing**) force to take refuge in a tree. □ **grow on trees** be plentiful. **out of one's tree** *informal* crazy. □ **treeless** *adj.* **treelike** *adj.*

treed *adj.* containing trees.

tree farm *n.* an area of land where trees are grown commercially.

tree fern *n.* a large fern with an upright trunk-like stem.

tree frog *n.* a tree-dwelling tailless amphibian with adhesive discs on its digits.

tree house *n.* a structure built in a tree for children to play in.

tree hugger *n. informal* an environmentalist.

treeline *n.* **1** the latitudinal limit beyond which no trees grow. **2** the level on a mountain above which no trees grow.

treetop *n.* the topmost part of a tree.

trefoil ● *n.* **1** a yellow flower with three-lobed leaves, resembling clover. **2** a thing arranged in or with three lobes. ● *adj.* of or concerning a three-lobed plant etc. [*Say* TREFF oil *or* TREE foil]

trek ● *v.* (**treks, trekked, trekking**) travel arduously. ● *n.* a journey made by trekking. □ **trekker** *n.*

trellis ● *n.* (*pl.* **trellises**) a lattice of light bars used to support for fruit trees, creepers, etc. ● *v.* (**trellises, trellised, trellising**) provide or support with a trellis.

tremble ● *v.* (**trembles, trembled, trembling**) **1** shake involuntarily. **2** be in a state of extreme apprehension. ● *n.* a trembling state or movement.
□ **tremblingly** *adv.* **trembly** *adj.*

trembling aspen *n.* (also **trembling poplar**) a poplar found across Canada, with leaves that tremble in a breeze.

tremendous *adj.* remarkable, excellent.
□ **tremendously** *adv.*

tremolo *n.* (*pl.* **tremolos**) a shaky effect produced on musical instruments or in singing. [*Say* TREMMA loe]

tremor ● *n.* **1** a quivering. **2** a thrill. **3** a slight earthquake. ● *v.* undergo tremors. [*Say* TREMMER]

tremulous *adj.* **1** trembling or quivering. **2** drawn by a shaky hand. □ **tremulously** *adv.* **tremulousness** *n.*
[*Say* TREM yuh lus]

trench ● *n.* (*pl.* **trenches**) **1** a long narrow deep depression or ditch. **2** this dug by troops for shelter from enemy fire. ● *v.* (**trenches, trenched, trenching**) dig a trench or trenches in. □ **in the trenches** actively involved in the hard work of a project.

trenchant *adj.* expressed strongly and clearly. □ **trenchancy** *n.* **trenchantly** *adv.* [*Say* TREN chunt]

trench coat *n.* a loose belted double-breasted raincoat.

trencher *n.* a machine used in digging trenches.

trench warfare *n.* hostilities carried on from more or less permanent trenches.

trend ● *n.* a general direction and tendency. ● *v.* bend or develop in a specified direction.

trendoid *informal* often *derogatory* ● *adj.* trendy. ● *n.* a person who sets or follows fashions.

trendsetter *n.* a person who leads the way in fashion etc. □ **trendsetting** *adj.*

trendy *informal* ● *adj.* (**trendier, trendiest**) often *derogatory* following fashionable trends. ● *n.* (*pl.* **trendies**) a

fashionable person. □**trendily** adv.
trendiness n.

trepidation n. a feeling of fear about what
may happen. [Say treppa DAY sh'n]

très adv. very. [Say TRAY]

trespass ● v. (**trespasses**,
trespassed, **trespassing**) **1** make an
unlawful intrusion. **2** make claims that
cannot be justified. **3** (foll. by against) archaic
offend. ● n. (pl. **trespasses**) **1** Law
unlawful entry to a person's land or
property. **2** archaic an offence.
□**trespasser** n.

tress n. (pl. **tresses**) **1** a long lock of
human hair. **2** (in pl.) a woman's or girl's
head of hair. □**tressed** adj.

trestle n. **1** a supporting structure for a
table etc. **2** (also **trestle table**) a table
consisting of a board laid on trestles.
3 (also **trestlework**) an open braced
framework to support a bridge etc. **4** (also
trestle bridge) a bridge supported on
trestles. [Rhymes with WRESTLE]

T. Rex n. (pl. **T. Rexes**) Tyrannosaurus rex
(see TYRANNOSAUR.)

tri- comb. form **1** forming nouns and
adjectives meaning three or three times.
2 Chemistry containing three atoms or
groups of a specified kind.

triactor n. Cdn a bet on the first three
finishers in a horse race, specifying the
order of finish. [Say TRY actor]

triad n. **1** a group of three people or things.
2 a chord of three notes, consisting of a
given note with the third and fifth above it.
3 (usu. **Triad**) any of several Chinese secret
criminal societies. □**triadic** adj.
[Say TRY ad, try AD ick]

triage n. the process of determining the
order in which a large number of patients
will receive medical treatment.
[Say TREE azh or TREE ozh]

trial n. **1** a formal examination of evidence
by a judge and often a jury, in order to
decide guilt in a case of criminal or civil
proceedings. **2** a test of the performance,
qualities, suitability, etc. **3** a frustrating
thing. □**on trial 1** being tried in a court of
law. **2** being tested.

trial and error n. a process of
experimenting with various unsuccessful
approaches until a suitable one is found.

trial balloon n. an announcement etc.
made in order to see how a new policy will
be received.

trial run n. **1** a preliminary test of the
performance of a new procedure etc. **2** a
drive taken to assess the performance of a
car or truck etc. one is thinking of buying.

triangle n. **1** a plane closed figure with

three sides and angles. **2** a percussion
instrument consisting of a steel rod bent
into a triangle, sounded with a rod. **3** a
situation or relationship involving three
people.

triangular adj. **1** shaped like a triangle.
2 involving three people etc.

triangulation n. (**triangulates**,
triangulated, **triangulating**) a method
of finding out distance and position by
measuring first the distance between two
points and then the angle from these to a
third point.

Triassic n. the earliest period of the
Mesozoic era, which lasted from about 248
to 213 million years ago. □**Triassic** adj.
[Say try ASSICK]

triathlon n. an athletic contest in which
competitors engage in three different
events, usu. swimming, cycling, and long-
distance running. □**triathlete** n.
[Say try ATH lon]

tribal adj. relating to a tribe or tribes.
□**tribally** adv.

tribal council n. an organization of
Aboriginal communities grouped together
for common aims.

tribalism n. **1** the condition of existing as
a separate tribe or tribes. **2** loyalty to one's
tribe or social group.

tribe n. **1** a group of families claiming
common descent, sharing a common
culture, etc. **2** a community of people
united by a shared profession or hobby etc.
3 a group of related animals or plants.

tribesman n. (pl. **tribesmen**) a member
of a tribe.

tribespeople pl. n. the members of a
tribe.

tribulation n. great trouble.
[Say trib yuh LAY sh'n]

tribunal n. **1** a board established to settle
certain types of dispute. **2** a court of
justice. [Say try BYOO nul or trib YOO nul]

tribune n. **1** a popular leader who attempts
to protect the interests of the people.
2 Roman History **a** an official appointed to
protect the interests of the plebeians.
b (also **military tribune**) a legionary
officer. [Say TRIB yoon or truh BYOON]

tributary n. (pl. **tributaries**) **1** a stream
etc. flowing into a larger river or lake. **2** hist.
a person or nation required to pay a tax or
tribute to another. □**tributary** adj.
[Say TRIB yuh terry]

tribute n. **1** an act, statement, or gift
intended to show gratitude, respect, etc.
2 (foll. by to) a thing resulting from a
praiseworthy quality or act. **3** hist. a

payment made periodically by one nation or ruler to another.

trice n. □ **in a trice** in a moment.

triceps n. (pl. **triceps**) the large extensor muscle at the back of the upper arm. [Say TRY seps]

triceratops n. (pl. **triceratopses**) a plant-eating dinosaur with a bony horn on the snout, two longer ones above the eyes, and a bony frill around the neck. [Say try SERRA tops]

trick ● n. **1** a scheme undertaken to deceive. **2** an optical illusion or figment of the imagination. **3** a special technique. **4 a** a feat of skill. **b** an unusual action learned by an animal. **5** a practical joke. **6** a characteristic habit. **7** (as an adj.) done to deceive. **8** slang a prostitute's client, or a session with a client. **9** the cards played in a single round of a card game. **10** (as an adj.) designating a limb or joint that is unsound. ● v. **1** deceive by a trick; cheat. **2** lure or induce by trickery. □ **do the trick** informal achieve the required result. **how's tricks?** informal how are you? **turn a trick** slang (of a prostitute) have a session with a client.

trickery n. the use of tricks.

trickle ● v. (**trickles, trickled, trickling**) **1** flow in a thin stream or drops. **2** come, go, or pass gradually. **3** (foll. by down) (esp. of wealth or information) be dispersed or distributed among recipients at various levels in diminishing amounts. ● n. **1** a thin or dripping stream of liquid. **2** a slow passage or flow.

trick-or-treat ● n. a Halloween custom in which children, dressed in costumes, knock on the doors of neighbours soliciting a treat of esp. candy, threatening to commit a prank if denied. ● interj. (usu. **trick or treat!**) shouted by children while trick-or-treating. □ **trick-or-treater** n. **trick-or-treating** n.

trickster n. **1** a person who enjoys playing pranks on others. **2** a person who deceives others.

tricky adj. (**trickier, trickiest**) **1** difficult, challenging. **2** awkward. **3** deceitful. □ **trickiness** n.

tricolour ● n. a flag of three colours, esp. the French national flag of blue, white, and red. ● adj. (also **tricoloured**) having three colours. [Say TRY colour; for the noun you can also say TRICKA ler]

tricycle n. a vehicle similar to a bicycle but with three wheels, two at the back and one at the front.

trident n. a three-pronged spear.

tried ● v. past and past participle of TRY. ● adj. tested by experience.

tried-and-true adj. proven reliable by experience.

trifle ● n. **1** a dessert of sponge cake soaked in liquor and covered with custard, jam, whipped cream, and fruit. **2** a small amount. **3** a thing of little importance. ● v. (**trifles, trifled, trifling**) (foll. by with) treat with a lack of respect. □ **trifler** n.

trifling adj. **1** petty, trivial. **2** frivolous. □ **triflingly** adv.

trifocal ● n. (in pl.) a pair of eyeglasses having lenses with three parts, each with a different focal length. ● adj. having three focuses. [Say TRY focal]

trig n. informal trigonometry.

trigger ● n. **1** a movable lever for releasing a spring or catch and so setting off a gun or mechanism. **2** an event that causes something to happen. ● v. **1** set in motion; initiate. **2** fire by the use of a trigger. □ **quick on the trigger** quick to react. □ **triggered** adj.

trigger-happy adj. **1** apt to shoot with little provocation. **2** liable to act or react rashly.

triglyceride n. any ester formed from glycerol and three acid radicals, including the main constituents of fats and oils. [Say try GLISSER ide]

trigonometry n. the branch of mathematics dealing with the relations between the sides and angles of triangles and with the functions of angles. □ **trigonometric** adj. [Say trigga NOMMA tree, trigga nuh METRIC]

trike n. informal a tricycle.

trilateral adj. **1** of, on, or with three sides. **2** involving or shared by three parties. [Say try LATTER ul]

trilight n. Cdn a light bulb that can shine at any of three degrees of brightness.

trilingual adj. **1** able to speak three languages. **2** spoken or written in three languages. [Say try LING gwul or try LING gyoo ul]

trill ● n. **1** a quavering sound produced by a rapid alternation of two notes a tone or semitone apart. **2** any high-pitched sound resembling this. ● v. **1** produce a trill. **2** sing or play with a trill.

trillion n. **1** a million million. **2** (in pl.) informal a very large number. □ **trillionth** adj. & n.

trillium n. a plant of the lily family, bearing a whorl of three leaves and a solitary flower; it is the floral emblem of Ontario.

trilobite n. an extinct marine arthropod

with a rear part divided into three segments. [Say TRY luh bite]

trilogy n. (pl. **trilogies**) a group of three related novels, plays, films, etc. [Say TRILLA jee]

trim ● v. (**trims**, **trimmed**, **trimming**) **1** make neat or regular by cutting away unwanted parts. **2** remove or cut away. **3 a** reduce the size, amount, or number of. **b** eliminate. **4 a** decorate with ornaments etc. **b** (often foll. by *up*) make neat in appearance. **5** adjust the balance of by distributing cargo evenly. **6** arrange (sails) to suit the wind. ● n. **1** a haircut to shorten a person's hair without changing the hairstyle. **2** decoration along the edge of something. **3** ornamental finishing pieces on a car or truck. **4** a person's clothing. **5** the balance or inclination of an aircraft. ● adj. **1** neat, tidy. **2** in proper order. **3** slender, slim. □ **in trim** having a neat or healthy appearance. □ **trimmer** n.

trimester n. **1** a period of three months. **2** one third of the length of a human pregnancy. **3** each of three terms of an academic year at some universities and high schools. [Say TRY mester or try MESTER]

trimming n. **1** ornamentation or decoration. **2** (in pl.) informal the garnishes and side dishes traditionally served with a particular meal. **3** (in pl.) pieces cut off in trimming.

Trinidadian n. a person from Trinidad. □ **Trinidadian** adj. [Say trinna DADDY in or trinna DAY dee in]

Trinitarian ● n. Christianity a person who believes in the doctrine of the Trinity. ● adj. of or believing in the doctrine of the Trinity. [Say trinna TERRY in]

Trinity n. (pl. **Trinities**) **1** Theology (in orthodox Christian belief) the three modes of being (Father, Son, and Holy Spirit) that together make up God. **2** (often foll. by *of*) a group of three people or things.

trinket n. a small ornament or piece of jewellery etc. of little value.

trio n. (pl. **trios**) **1** a set or group of three. **2** Music a group of, or composition for, three performers.

trip ● v. (**trips**, **tripped**, **tripping**) **1 a** cause to stumble or fall by entangling the feet. **b** stumble or fall. **2** make or cause to make a mistake. **3 a** run or dance with quick light steps. **b** flow lightly and gracefully. **4** esp. Cdn make a journey through rough country, esp. in a canoe. **5** release or depress (a switch etc.) to activate a mechanism. **6** (often foll. by *out*) informal undergo a hallucinatory experience induced by drugs. ● n. **1** a journey or

excursion. **2 a** an act of causing a person to stumble or blunder. **b** a stumble or blunder. **3** an illusory or self-indulgent activity or attitude. **4** informal a hallucinatory experience caused by a drug. **5** an exhilarating experience. **6** a contrivance for a tripping mechanism etc. □ **trip the light fantastic** jocular dance.

tripartite adj. **1** consisting of three parts. **2** shared by or involving three parties. [Say try PAR tite]

tripe n. **1** the stomach of a ruminant, prepared as food. **2** informal something considered worthless or foolish.

triple ● adj. **1** consisting of three parts or things. **2** involving three parties. **3** three times as much or many. ● adv. to three times the amount or extent. ● n. **1** a threefold number or amount. **2** a set of three. **3** Figure Skating, Dance, etc. a jump, spin, etc. involving three revolutions. ● v. (**triples**, **tripled**, **tripling**) multiply or increase by three. □ **triply** adv.

Triple A n. a minor league just below major league baseball.

triple crown n. the title awarded to the winner of three important events.

triple-decker n. something with three decks, layers, or levels.

triple jump n. a sport in which athletes attempt to achieve the greatest distance on a jump that involves a hop, a long step, and a leap. □ **triple jumper** n.

triple play n. Baseball a play in which three players, usu. the batter and two baserunners, are put out.

triplet n. **1** (usu. in pl.) each of three children or animals born at one birth. **2 a** a group of three equal notes played in the time of two. **b** a group of three rhyming lines of verse.

triplex ● n. (pl. **triplexes**) a residential building divided into three apartments. ● adj. triple or threefold. [Say TRY plex or TRIP lex]

triplicate ● adj. **1** existing in three examples or copies. **2** having three corresponding parts. ● n. each of a set of three copies or corresponding parts. ● v. (**triplicates**, **triplicated**, **triplicating**) **1** make in three copies. **2** multiply by three. [Say TRIPLA kit for the adjective and noun, TRIPLA kate for the verb]

triploid ● n. an organism or cell having three times the haploid set of chromosomes. ● adj. of or being a triploid. [Say TRIP loyd]

tripod n. **1** a stand with three legs for supporting a camera etc. **2** a three-legged stool, table, etc. [Say TRY pod]

tripper n. **1** esp. Cdn (North) a person who

journeys through rough country, esp. by canoe. **2** a person who goes on a short trip for pleasure.

tripping n. **1** esp. *Cdn (North)* the activity of travelling through rough country, esp. by canoe. **2** *Hockey* an illegal act of causing an opponent to fall by obstructing him or her with one's stick, leg, or foot, etc.

trippingly adv. with great ease and rapidity.

trippy adj. (**trippier**, **trippiest**) *informal* producing an effect resembling that of a psychedelic drug.

triptych n. **1** a picture or relief carving on three panels. **2** a set of three artistic works meant to be viewed or performed together. [Say TRIP tick]

tripwire n. a wire placed in order to trip up trespassers etc., or to activate an alarm when disturbed.

trisodium phosphate n. a water-soluble compound, occurring as crystals, used esp. as a detergent. [Say try SODIUM]

trite adj. (**triter**, **tritest**) **1** stale through constant use or repetition. **2** characterized by stale or commonplace ideas. □ **triteness** n.

triticale n. a high-protein hybrid between wheat and rye. [Say tritta KAY lee]

tritium n. a radioactive isotope of hydrogen used in fusion reactors. [Say TRITTY um]

triumph ● n. **1** a great success, achievement, or victory. **2** the state of being successful. **3** the thrill of victory. ● v. (often foll. by *over*) **1** be successful or victorious. **2** rejoice at victory or success.

triumphal adj. done, used, or made to celebrate a triumph.

triumphalism n. ostentatious pride in one's success or achievements. □ **triumphalist** adj. & n. [Say try UMF ul ism]

triumphant adj. **1** victorious or successful. **2** exultant. □ **triumphantly** adv.

triumvirate n. **1** a group of three people in a joint position of power. **2** *informal* any set of three. [Say try UM ver it]

trivalent adj. **1** having a valence of three. **2** providing immunity against three strains of an infective agent. [Say try VAIL int]

trivet n. **1** a small stand with three legs, placed under a hot kettle etc. to protect the surface of a table. **2** a similar stand used to keep something raised while being heated. [Say TRIVVIT]

trivia n. **1** unimportant but interesting tidbits of information. **2** unimportant details.

trivial adj. of little importance or

consequence. □ **triviality** n. (*pl.* **trivialities**) **trivially** adv.

trivialize v. (**trivializes**, **trivialized**, **trivializing**) diminish the importance of; belittle. □ **trivialization** n.

trod past and past participle of TREAD.

trodden past participle of TREAD.

troglodyte ● n. **1** a prehistoric cave dweller. **2** *derogatory* a wilfully ignorant or old-fashioned person. **3** a hermit. ● adj. **1** dwelling in caves. **2** ignorant, old-fashioned, or uncouth. □ **troglodytic** adj. [Say TROGLA dite, trogla DIT ick]

troika n. **1** a Russian carriage drawn by three horses. **2** a group of three people working together. [Say TROY kuh]

Trojan ● adj. of the ancient city of Troy on the coast of Turkey or its inhabitants. ● n. **1** a person from Troy. **2** a person of great energy or endurance. [Say TRO jin]

Trojan Horse n. something seemingly harmless that eludes a person's defences to bring about his or her downfall.

troll[1] n. *Scandinavian Myth* a grotesque dwarf (or, formerly, giant) usu. dwelling in caves or under bridges. [*Rhymes with* ROLL]

troll[2] v. **1** fish by drawing bait along in the water behind a moving boat. **2** (foll. by *for*) **a** attempt to catch a particular type of fish using this method. **b** pursue, seek. □ **troller** n. [*Rhymes with* ROLL]

trolley n. (*pl.* **trolleys**) **1** a small cart on wheels. **2** a grooved metal pulley conveying electric current through a pole to the motor of a streetcar etc. **3** (also **trolley bus**) a bus powered by electricity from an overhead cable. [*Rhymes with* DOLLY]

trombone n. a large brass wind instrument with a sliding tube used to vary its pitch. □ **trombonist** n.

tromp v. *informal* **1** march with a heavy step. **2** trample.

trompe l'oeil n. an optical illusion. [Say tromp LOY]

troop ● n. **1** an assembled company of people or animals. **2 a** a detachment of police officers or soldiers etc. **b** (in *pl.*) soldiers or armed forces. ● v. march or proceed in large numbers.

trooper n. **1** (also **Trooper**) a private in an armoured or cavalry unit. **2** *US* = STATE TROOPER. **3** *informal* a hard-working, reliable person.

trope n. a figurative or metaphorical use of a word or expression. [*Rhymes with* ROPE]

trophy n. (*pl.* **trophies**) **1** an ornamental commemorative object awarded as a prize. **2** an animal or animal part captured in hunting and displayed. **3** *derogatory* a person or thing regarded as having been obtained to enhance a person's status by association.

tropic *n.* **1** (**Tropic**) either of two parallels of latitude 23°26′ north (**Tropic of Cancer**) or south (**Tropic of Capricorn**) of the equator. **2** (in *pl.*) the torrid zone between these.

tropical *adj.* **1** relating to the tropics. **2** very hot and humid. **3** suitable for use in the tropics.

troposphere *n.* the lowest region of the atmosphere, extending to a height of between 8 and 18 km. □ **tropospheric** *adj.* [*Say* TROPPA sfeer *or* TROPE a sfeer, troppa SFAIR ick *or* trope a SFAIR ick]

trot ● *v.* (**trots, trotted, trotting**) **1** run with short strides at a moderate pace. **2** (of a horse) proceed at a pace faster than a walk in which the legs move in diagonal pairs. **3** *informal* walk, go. **4** cause to proceed at a trot. ● *n.* **1** a trotting pace or gait. **2** a run at this pace. **3** (**the trots**) *slang* an attack of diarrhea. □ **hot to trot** *informal* **1** eager, enthusiastic. **2** sexually active or excited. **on the trot** *informal* continually busy. **trot out 1** show off the paces of (a horse). **2** produce for inspection, esp. predictably.

troth *n. archaic* □ **plight** (or **pledge**) **one's troth** pledge one's word in marriage etc. [*Rhymes with* BOTH]

trotter *n.* **1** a horse bred for harness racing. **2** (usu. in *pl.*) a pig's foot.

troubadour *n.* **1** a French medieval lyric poet, composing and singing in Provençal. **2** a singer or poet. [*Say* TROOBA dor]

trouble ● *n.* **1 a** difficulty, problems, complications. **b** disturbance of the mind or feelings. **2** a cause of trouble. **3** an annoying or problematic aspect. **4** a faulty condition. **5 a** fighting. **b** (in *pl.*) political or social unrest. **6** disagreement, strife. ● *v.* (**troubles, troubled, troubling**) **1** cause distress to. **2** subject or be subjected to inconvenience, bother, etc. **3** afflict. **4** be disturbed or worried. □ **in trouble 1** involved in a matter likely to bring punishment. **2** *euphemism* pregnant while unmarried.

troubled *adj.* **1** feeling or showing worry or distress. **2** fraught with problems. **3** physically unsettled or disturbed.

troublemaker *n.* a person who habitually causes trouble. □ **troublemaking** *n. & adj.*

troubleshooter *n.* **1** a person who corrects faults in machinery, computer equipment, etc. **2** a mediator who specializes in resolving disputes. □ **troubleshoot** *v.* **troubleshooting** *n.*

troublesome *adj.* **1** that causes problems.

2 distressing, worrisome. **3** fraught with problems.

trough *n.* **1 a** a long open receptacle for water, animal feed, etc. **b** *jocular* a source of wealth. **2** a narrow channel or conduit for conveying a liquid. **3** *Meteorology* an elongated region of low barometric pressure. **4** a hollow between two wave crests. **5** the lowest point of something. **6** a broad elongated depression or valley. [*Say* TROFF]

trounce *v.* (**trounces, trounced, trouncing**) defeat decisively. □ **trouncing** *n.*

troupe *n.* a company of actors or dancers etc. [*Say* TROOP]

trouper *n.* a member of a troupe. [*Say* TROOPER]

trousers *pl. n.* **1** an outer garment reaching from the waist usu. to the ankles, divided into two parts to cover the legs. **2** (**trouser**) (as an *adj.*) designating a part of such a garment.

trousseau *n.* (*pl.* **trousseaux** or **trousseaus**) the clothes collected by a bride for her marriage. [*Say* TROO so *or* troo SO; TROO soze *or* troo SOZE]

trout *n.* (*pl.* **trout** or **trouts**) a chiefly freshwater fish of the salmon family, used as food.

trove *n.* = TREASURE TROVE.

trowel ● *n.* **1** a small hand-held tool with a flat metal blade, used to apply mortar etc. **2** a hand-held gardening tool resembling a small shovel. ● *v.* (**trowels, trowelled, trowelling**) dig, move, or apply with a trowel. [*Rhymes with* TOWEL]

troy *n.* (also **troy weight**) a system of weights used for precious metals and gems, based on a pound of 12 ounces or 5,760 grains.

truant *n.* **1** a student who stays away from school without leave. **2** a person absent from work. □ **truancy** *n.* [*Say* TROO int]

truce *n.* **1** a temporary suspension of hostilities. **2** an agreement achieving this.

truck ● *n.* **1** a large sturdy road vehicle. **2 a** a wheeled cart or platform used to transport goods. **b** (also **hand truck**) a sturdy metal frame with two wheels used to move large appliances etc. **3** a pivoted undercarriage with wheels, mounted to the underside of a railway car. ● *v.* **1** convey by truck. **2** drive a truck. **3** *informal* go or proceed at a casual pace. □ **have no truck with** avoid dealing or associating with.

trucker *n.* **1** a person who drives a transport truck or tractor-trailer etc. for a living. **2** a company dealing in long-

distance transportation of goods.
□ **trucking** n.

truckload n. **1** the quantity of goods that can be transported in a truck. **2** (usu. foll. by of) informal a large quantity.

truck stop n. a roadside restaurant, often having a gas station on the premises.

truculent adj. bad-tempered and defiant. □ **truculence** n. **truculently** adv. [Say TRUCK yuh lint]

trudge ● v. (**trudges**, **trudged**, **trudging**) **1** walk laboriously but steadily. **2** travel in this way. ● n. a steady laborious walk.

true ● adj. (**truer**, **truest**) **1** in accordance or consistent with reality. **2** genuine; rightly or strictly so called. **3** loyal or faithful. **4** closely conforming (to an expectation). **5** correctly positioned; level, square. **6** accurate. **7** certainly, admittedly. **8** measured relative to true north. **9** reliable. ● adv. **1** in a sincere manner. **2** accurately. **3** conforming with the ancestral type. ● v. (**trues**, **trued**, **truing** or **trueing**) (often foll. by up) bring into the correct form, alignment, etc. □ **come true** actually happen. **out of true** not in the correct position. □ **trueness** n.

true-blue adj. **1** steadfastly loyal. **2** real; genuine.

true north n. **1** north according to the earth's axis, not magnetic north. **2** (**the True North**) Cdn jocular Canada.

truffle n. **1** a strong-smelling underground fungus regarded as a gourmet food item. **2** a round soft chocolate, often flavoured with alcohol. □ **truffled** adj.

truism n. a self-evident or hackneyed truth. [Say TROO ism]

truly adv. **1 a** sincerely. **b** very. **2** indeed. **3** faithfully. **4** accurately. **5** rightly. **6** used in formulaic closings of letters.

trump ● n. **1** (in pl.) Cards the suit determined to rank above the other three during a deal or game. **2** (also **trump card**) a playing card of this suit. **3** (also **trump card**) an important resource held secretly for use at an opportune moment. **4** informal an admirable, helpful person. ● v. **1** defeat with a trump. **2** informal **a** foil or thwart with an unexpected move. **b** surpass. □ **trump up** fabricate (an accusation etc.).

trumped-up adj. fabricated, invented.

trumpet ● n. **1** a brass wind instrument having a straight or curved tube with a flared bell. **2** anything resembling a trumpet in shape, such as a flower head. **3** anything resembling the sound of a trumpet. ● v. (**trumpets**, **trumpeted**, **trumpeting**) **1** announce or proclaim loudly. **2 a** blow a trumpet. **b** make a sound like that of a trumpet.

trumpeter n. **1** a person who plays a trumpet. **2** a bird having a loud trumpet-like cry.

trumpeter swan n. a large N American wild swan with a black bill and a loud, trumpet-like call.

truncate v. (**truncates**, **truncated**, **truncating**) shorten or diminish. □ **truncated** adj. **truncation** n. [Say TRUN kate or trun KATE]

truncheon n. a short club carried by a police officer. [Say TRUN chin]

trundle v. (**trundles**, **trundled**, **trundling**) **1** move or roll heavily on wheels. **2** go or move, esp. heavily. **3** push along.

trunk n. **1** the main stem of a tree as distinct from its branches and roots. **2** a person's or animal's body apart from the limbs and head. **3** the long snout of an elephant. **4** a large box with a hinged lid for transporting clothes etc. **5** a compartment at the rear of most cars, used to transport luggage etc. **6** (in pl.) a man's shorts or briefs worn for swimming, boxing, etc. **7** the main part of any structure. **8** the main body of a blood vessel.

trunk line n. **1** a main railway line or route. **2** a main pipeline for oil or gas. **3** a telephone line running between exchanges.

trunk road n. Cdn an access road for logging.

truss ● n. (pl. **trusses**) **1** a metal or wooden structural framework. **2** a padded belt fitted with straps to apply pressure on a hernia. ● v. (**trusses**, **trussed**, **trussing**) **1** bind the wings and legs of (a fowl etc.) to the body for cooking. **2** tie up by binding the arms close to the body. **3** support with a truss or trusses.

trust ● n. **1** confidence in the loyalty, reliability, strength, etc., of a person or thing. **2** the state of being responsible for someone or something. **3** reliance on the truth of something without examination. **4** Law an arrangement whereby a person holds or uses property for the benefit of one or more others. **5** an organization managed by trustees. **6** a group of companies organized to defeat competition etc. ● v. **1** have or place confidence in. **2** (foll. by with) allow to have or be responsible for. **3** believe. **4** have confidence or hope that a thing is occurring or will occur. **5** allow credit to (a customer) for goods. □ **in trust** Law held by one person for the enjoyment and benefit of another. **on trust 1** on credit. **2** on the basis of trust. **take on trust** accept without evidence. □**trustable** *adj.* **trusted** *adj.*

trust company *n.* a company formed to act as a trustee or to deal with trusts, esp. one that offers banking services.

trustee *n.* **1** *Law* a person given control or powers of administration of property held in trust with a legal obligation to administer it solely for the purposes specified. **2** a person appointed to manage the affairs of an institution etc. **3** *Cdn* an elected member of a school board. **4** a state made responsible for the government of an area. □**trusteeship** *n.*

trustful *adj.* inclined to trust. □**trustfully** *adv.*

trust fund *n.* a fund of money etc. held in trust.

trusting *adj.* inclined to trust others. □**trustingly** *adv.*

trustworthy *adj.* reliable, dependable. □**trustworthiness** *n.*

trusty *adj.* (**trustier, trustiest**) *archaic* or *jocular* trustworthy.

truth *n.* (*pl.* **truths**) **1** the quality or a state of being true. **2 a** what is true. **b** a true statement. **3** an established principle. **4** accuracy of delineation or representation. □**in truth** *literary* truly.

truthful *adj.* **1** habitually speaking the truth. **2** accurate; true. □**truthfully** *adv.* **truthfulness** *n.*

truth serum *n.* (also **truth drug**) any of various drugs supposedly able to induce a person to tell the truth.

try ● *v.* (**tries, tried, trying**) **1** make an attempt to do something. **2** test by use or experiment. **3** make severe demands on. **4** examine the effectiveness of. **5** ascertain the state of fastening of. **6 a** investigate and decide judicially. **b** subject to trial. **7** make an experiment in order to find out. **8** (foll. by *for*) **a** apply for. **b** seek to attain. **9** extract (oil) from fat by heating. ● *n.* (*pl.* **tries**) **1** an attempt. **2** *Rugby* the act of touching the ball down within the opposing goal line to score. □**try one's hand** see how skilful one is, esp. at the first attempt. **try on** put on (clothes etc.) to see if they fit. **try out 1** put to the test. **2** undergo a test.

trying *adj.* hard to endure.

tryout *n.* (often in *pl.*) **1** a test of qualities or performance. **2** a gathering of prospective members of a team, troupe, etc. for such testing.

trypsin *n.* a digestive enzyme which hydrolyzes proteins, secreted by the pancreas. [*Say* TRIP sin]

tryst ● *n.* a secret meeting between lovers. ● *v.* keep a tryst. [*Say* TRIST]

tsar *n.* = CZAR. [*Say* ZAR]

tsetse *n.* an African fly that feeds on blood and transmits sleeping sickness. [*Say* TSEET see *or* SEET see]

T-shirt *n.* a short-sleeved casual top. □**T-shirted** *adj.*

Tsilhqot'in *n.* (*pl.* **Tsilhqot'in**) a member or the language of an Athapaskan people inhabiting the basin of the Chilcotin River valley in BC. □**Tsilhqot'in** *adj.* [*Say* tsill COAT in]

Tsimshian *n.* (*pl.* **Tsimshian** or **Tsimshians**) **1** a member of a group of Aboriginal peoples living in coastal and interior northern BC. **2** their group of languages. □**Tsimshian** *adj.* [*Say* TSIMSHY in *or* TSIM shin]

tsk *interj., n.,* & *v.* (also **tsk tsk**; *v.* **tsk-tsk**) = TUT (see TUT-TUT). [*Say* TISK]

TSP *abbr.* trisodium phosphate.

tsp. *abbr.* teaspoonful.

T-square *n.* a T-shaped instrument for drawing right angles etc.

tsunami *n.* (*pl.* **tsunamis**) a long high sea wave caused by underwater earthquakes etc. [*Say* tsoo NOMMY]

Tsuu T'ina *n.* & *adj.* (*pl.* **Tsuu T'ina**) = SARCEE. [*Say* tsoo TINNA]

TSX *abbr.* Toronto Stock Exchange.

tub ● *n.* **1** a flat-bottomed usu. round container. **2** a bathtub. **3** *informal* a clumsy slow boat. ● *v.* (**tubs, tubbed, tubbing**) place in a tub.

tuba *n.* (*pl.* **tubas**) a large, very low-pitched valved brass wind instrument.

tubal *adj.* relating to a tube. [*Say* TUBE ul]

tubal ligation *n.* a surgical procedure for making a female incapable of bearing offspring by cutting the Fallopian tubes.

tubby *adj.* (**tubbier, tubbiest**) fat. □**tubbiness** *n.*

tube *n.* **1** a long hollow rigid or flexible cylinder. **2** a soft metal or plastic cylinder sealed at one end and having a screw cap at the other. **3** a hollow cylindrical organ or structure in the body or plant. **4** (as an *adj.*) designating a close-fitting skirt or sleeveless cylindrical dress or top. **5** (**the tube**) *informal* television. □**down the tube** (or **tubes**) lost, wasted.

tuber *n.* the short rounded part of a stem or rhizome, usu. found underground. [*Say* TUBE er]

tubercle *n.* **1** a small rounded bump on a bone. **2** a small rounded swelling on the body or in an organ. [*Say* TUBE er cul]

tubercle bacillus *n.* a bacterium causing tuberculosis.

tubercular ● *adj.* (also **tuberculous**) of or having tubercles or tuberculosis. ● *n.* a person with tuberculosis. [*Say* too BERK yuh ler]

tuberculosis *n.* an infectious disease characterized by the growth of small rounded swellings or tubercles in the tissues, esp. in the lungs, causing fever, weight loss, etc. [*Say* too berk yuh LOE sis]

tuberose *n.* a Mexican plant with heavily scented white waxy flowers. [*Say* TUBA roze *or* TUBE roze]

tuberous *adj.* **1** having or consisting of a tuber or tubers. **2** characterized by rounded swellings. [*Say* TUBE er us]

tube skate *n. Cdn* an ice skate with the blade running along a hollow metal tube.

tubing *n.* **1 a** a length of tube. **b** a quantity of tubes. **2** the activity of floating or sliding in a large inflated inner tube.

tub-thumper *n. informal* a ranting preacher etc. □ **tub-thumping** *adj. & n.*

tubular *adj.* **1** tube-shaped. **2** having or consisting of tubes. **3** made of tubular pieces. [*Say* TUBE yuh ler]

tuck ● *v.* **1** push, fold, or turn under or between two surfaces. **2** draw together in a small space. **3** stow or hide away in a specified place or way. **4** make a stitched fold in. ● *n.* **1** a flattened usu. stitched fold in material. **2** (also **tuck position**) a position with the knees against the chest. **3** *informal* a cosmetic surgical operation. □ **tuck in** *informal* eat food heartily.

tuckered out *adj.* exhausted.

tucking *n.* a series of usu. stitched tucks in material.

tuck shop *n. Cdn* a small store within a hospital, hotel, etc., selling snacks etc.

'tude *n.* = ATTITUDE 3.

Tudor *hist.* ● *adj.* **1** of or relating to the royal family of England that ruled from 1485 to 1603. **2** of or relating to the architecture of this period, known for half-timbering and elaborately decorated houses. ● *n.* **1** a member of the Tudor royal family. **2** a house with Tudor architecture. [*Say* TOO der *or* TYOO der]

Tues. *abbr.* (also **Tue.**) Tuesday.

Tuesday ● *n.* the third day of the week, following Monday. ● *adv.* **1** on Tuesday. **2** (**Tuesdays**) on Tuesdays.

tufa *n.* **1** a porous rock composed of calcium carbonate and formed around mineral springs. **2** (also **tuff**) rock formed from volcanic ash. [*Say* TOO fuh *or* TYOO fuh]

tuffet *n.* **1** a low seat. **2** a clump of something. [*Say* TUFFIT]

tuft ● *n.* a bunch of threads, hair, etc., held together at the base. ● *v.* **1** provide with a tuft or tufts. **2** make depressions at regular intervals in (upholstery etc.) by passing a thread through. **3** grow in tufts. □ **tufted** *adj.*

tufting *n.* **1** *in senses of* TUFT *v.* **2** a handicraft using tufts of dyed moosehair or caribou hair stitched in patterns on a background of fabric or leather.

tug ● *v.* (**tugs**, **tugged**, **tugging**) **1** pull hard or violently. **2** tow by means of a tugboat. ● *n.* **1** a hard or jerky pull. **2** a sudden strong feeling. **3** (also **tugboat**) a small powerful boat for towing larger boats. **4** an aircraft towing a glider. □ **tugger** *n.*

tug-of-war *n.* **1** a contest in which two teams pull at opposite ends of a rope until one drags the other over a central line. **2** an intense struggle between opponents.

tuition *n.* **1** a fee paid for education. **2** teaching or instruction. [*Say* too ISH'n]

tulip *n.* a bulbous plant with showy cup-shaped flowers.

tulip tree *n.* a tree of eastern N America, with tulip-like flowers.

tulle *n.* a soft fine net used in veils, tutus, etc. [*Say* TOOL]

tum *n. informal* the stomach.

tumble ● *v.* (**tumbles**, **tumbled**, **tumbling**) **1** fall or cause to fall suddenly or headlong. **2 a** fall in amount. **b** collapse. **3** roll or toss erratically. **4** rush headlong. **5** (foll. by *to*) *informal* understand the meaning of. **6** overturn. **7** perform gymnastic or acrobatic feats. **8** rumple or disarrange. ● *n.* **1** a sudden or headlong fall. **2** a somersault or other acrobatic feat. **3** an untidy state.

tumbledown *adj.* falling or fallen into ruin.

tumble dry *v.* (**tumble dries**, **tumble dried**, **tumble drying**) dry in a clothes dryer with a heated rotating drum.

tumbler *n.* **1** a drinking glass with no handle or foot. **2** an acrobat or gymnast. **3** a pivoted piece in a lock that holds the bolt until lifted by a key. **4** a revolving drum containing an abrasive substance, in which castings, gemstones, etc., are cleaned by friction. □ **tumblerful** *n.* (*pl.* **tumblerfuls**)

tumbleweed *n.* a plant of arid regions, forming a globular bush that breaks off in late summer and is tumbled about by the wind.

tumescent *adj.* **1** swollen or swelling. **2** (of a man) sexually aroused. □ **tumescence** *n.* [*Say* too MESS'nt *or* tyoo MESS'nt]

tummy *n.* (*pl.* **tummies**) *informal* the stomach.

tummy tuck *n. informal* cosmetic surgery to remove excess abdominal fat.

tumour *n.* (also **tumor**) an abnormal swelling or enlargement in the body, esp. caused by excessive continued growth and proliferation of cells in a tissue. □ **tumorous** *adj.* [*Say* TOOM er, TUMOUR us]

tumpline *n.* a sling for carrying a load on the back, with a strap which passes around the forehead.

tumult *n.* **1 a** a loud, confused noise. **b** a large crowd. **2** confusion or disorder. [*Say* TOO mult *or* TUM ult]

tumultuous *adj.* **1** very loud or noisy. **2** characterized by confusion, disorder, etc. **3** agitated. □ **tumultuously** *adv.* [*Say* tuh MUL choo us *or* too MUL choo us *or* tyoo MUL choo us]

tun *n.* **1** a large beer or wine cask. **2** a brewer's fermenting vat. **3** a measure of capacity, equal to 210 imperial gallons or 252 US gallons (about 955 litres).

tuna *n.* (*pl.* **tuna** *or* **tunas**) **1** a large marine fish with a rounded body and a pointed snout, found in warm seas. **2** (also **tuna fish**) the flesh of the tuna.

tundra *n.* a vast level treeless Arctic region usu. with a marshy surface and underlying permafrost.

Tundra Buggy *n. Cdn proprietary* a large-wheeled tourist bus used in polar bear country.

tune ● *n.* **1** a melody with or without harmony. **2** a song. **3** the proper musical pitch. ● *v.* (**tunes**, **tuned**, **tuning**) **1** put in tune. **2** adjust to a particular frequency etc. **3** adjust to run efficiently. **4** adjust or adapt to a required purpose. □ **in** (or **out of**) **tune 1** having (or not having) the correct pitch. **2** in (or not in) agreement or harmony. **stay tuned 1** continue to watch or listen. **2** *informal* more information is coming. **to the tune of** *informal* to the considerable sum of. **tune in** (often foll. by *to*) *informal* become acquainted with or aware of. **tune out 1** stop watching a broadcast etc. **2** become oblivious. **tune up 1** bring one's instrument to the proper or uniform pitch. **2** bring to the most efficient condition. □ **tuning** *n.*

tuneful *adj.* melodious, musical. □ **tunefully** *adv.* **tunefulness** *n.*

tuneless *adj.* **1** not melodious. **2** out of tune. □ **tunelessly** *adv.*

tuner *n.* **1** a person who tunes musical instruments. **2** a device for tuning a radio receiver. **3** an electronic device for tuning a musical instrument.

tunesmith *n. informal* a songwriter.

tune-up *n.* an act of adjusting a motor vehicle etc. to ensure optimum performance.

tung *n.* a Chinese tree yielding an oil used in paints and varnishes.

tungsten *n.* a steel grey dense metallic element with a very high melting point, used in lamps etc. [*Say* TUNG stin]

tunic *n.* **1** a close-fitting short coat of police or military etc. uniform. **2** a loose sleeveless garment reaching to the thigh or knees.

tuning fork *n.* a two-pronged steel fork that gives a particular note when struck, used for tuning instruments.

Tunisian *adj.* relating to Tunisia. □ **Tunisian** *n.* [*Say* tuh NEEZH in *or* tuh NEEZY in]

tunnel ● *n.* **1** a passage that is built underground or dug by a burrowing animal. **2** a long enclosed passageway. **3** a prolonged period of difficulty. **4** a canal or hollow groove in the body. ● *v.* (**tunnels**, **tunnelled**, **tunnelling**) **1** make a tunnel through. **2** move by tunnelling. □ **tunneller** *n.*

tunnel vision *n.* **1** defective vision that fails to include objects away from the centre of the field of view. **2** *informal* the tendency to focus on a single aim or limited aspect.

tupelo *n.* (*pl.* **tupelos**) an Asian and N American deciduous tree with colourful foliage, which grows in swampy conditions. [*Say* TOOPA loe *or* TYOOPA loe]

tupik *n.* a traditional skin tent used in summer by Inuit. [*Say* TOO pick]

Tupperware *n. proprietary* a range of plastic containers for storing food.

tuque *n.* = TOQUE 1.

turban *n.* **1** a long length of material wound around a cap or the head, worn by Muslim and Sikh men. **2** a woman's headdress or hat resembling this. □ **turbaned** *adj.*

turbid *adj.* muddy, thick. □ **turbidity** *n.*

turbine *n.* a rotary motor or engine driven by a flow of water, steam, gas, wind, etc., esp. to produce electrical power.

turbo *n.* (*pl.* **turbos**) a turbocharger, or a vehicle equipped with this.

turbocharged *adj.* **1** equipped with a turbocharger for increased power. **2** *informal* featuring a higher than usual level of energy, power, etc.

turbocharger *n.* a system driven by a turbine that uses exhaust gases to increase an engine's power.

turboprop *n.* a jet engine in which a turbine is used to drive a propeller.

turbot *n.* (*pl.* **turbot**) **1** halibut. **2** a large diamond-shaped European flatfish used for food. [*Say* TUR bit]

turbulence *n.* **1** an irregularly fluctuating flow of air or fluid. **2** stormy conditions. **3** a disturbance or tumult. [*Say* TUR byoo lince]

turbulent *adj.* **1** characterized by conflict or confusion. **2** moving unsteadily or violently. [*Say* TUR byoo lint]

turd *n. coarse slang* **1** a lump of excrement. **2** a term of contempt for a person.

tureen *n.* a deep covered dish. [*Say* toor EEN]

turf ● *n.* (*pl.* **turfs** or **turves**) **1 a** a layer of grass etc. with earth and matted roots. **b** a piece of this cut from the ground. **2** a slab of peat for fuel. **3** (**the turf**) horse racing or racetracks. **4 a** one's personal territory. **b** one's sphere of influence. ● *v.* **1** (often as **turfed** *adj.*) cover with turf. **2** *informal* expel or eject.

turgid *adj.* **1** swollen, inflated. **2** tediously pompous. [*Say* TUR jid]

Turk *n.* a person from Turkey.

turkey *n.* (*pl.* **turkeys**) **1 a** large domesticated game bird, originally of N America, eaten esp. on festive occasions. **2** *slang* **a** a theatrical failure. **b** a stupid person. □ **talk turkey** *informal* talk frankly and straightforwardly.

turkey vulture *n.* (also **turkey buzzard**) a N American vulture with dark feathers, a white beak and legs, and a bare red head.

Turkic *adj.* relating to a group of languages including Turkish, or the peoples speaking them. [*Say* TURK ick]

Turkish ● *adj.* relating to Turkey, the Turks, or their language. ● *n.* this language.

Turkish bath *n.* a hot-air or steam bath followed by washing, massage, etc.

turmeric *n.* a tropical Asian plant with aromatic roots yielding a spice used in curries. [*Say* TUR mur ick]

turmoil *n.* a state of great disturbance.

turn ● *v.* **1** move around a central axis. **2** move so as to face or go in a different direction. **3** (of a road) bend, curve. **4** go around (a corner). **5** focus or conclude focusing on a particular subject etc. **6** (foll. by *to*) **a** apply oneself to. **b** have recourse to. **7** (foll. by *into*) transform. **8** cause to become or become. **9** (foll. by *against*) make or become hostile to. **10** (foll. by *on*) attack. **11** change colour. **12** make or become sour. **13** be or cause to be nauseated.

14 reach the age of. **15 a** flip (a page) in order to read or write on the other side. **b** (foll. by *to*) go to. **16** become an informer. **17** become giddy. **18** twist or sprain. **19** (foll. by *on*) depend on. **20** execute or perform. **21** make or earn. **22** divert. **23** shape on a lathe. ● *n.* **1** an act of turning around on an axis. **2 a** a change of direction. **b** a point at which a turning or change occurs. **3** a bend in a road or river. **4** a change in the course of events. **5** the transition from one period to the next. **6** an opportunity or obligation etc. that comes successively to each of several people. **7** a work shift. **8** a short walk or ride. **9** an act or deed. **10** *informal* a momentary shock. **11** a particular manner of linguistic expression. **12** a tendency or disposition. □ **at every turn** at every change of circumstance. **in turn** in succession. **not know which way** (or **where**) **to turn** be unsure how to act. **out of turn 1** at a time when it is not one's turn. **2** inappropriately. **take turns** act or work alternately or in succession. **turn around 1** completely change direction. **2** process (passengers, goods, etc.) and send out again. **turn away 1** face another direction. **2** reject, rebuff. **turn the corner 1** make a turn at an intersection. **2** begin to improve. **turn a person's crank** *slang* amuse or excite a person. **turn down 1** reject. **2** reduce the volume or strength of. **3** fold down. **turn in 1** submit. **2** achieve or register. **3** *informal* go to bed. **4** fold inwards. **5** incline inwards. **6** hand over to the authorities. **turn loose** set free. **turn off 1** stop the flow or operation of; switch off. **2 a** enter a side road. **b** lead off from another road. **3** *informal* cause to lose interest. **turn on 1 a** start the flow or operation of; switch on. **b** activate, begin to use. **2** *informal* excite, arouse. **3** *informal* introduce to. **turn out 1** prove to be the case. **2** extinguish. **3** *informal* assemble; attend a meeting etc. **4** expel. **5** produce. **6** dress or equip. **7** empty. **turn over 1** turn from one side onto another. **2** upset. **3 a** cause (an engine) to run. **b** (of an engine) start running. **4** consider thoroughly. **5** transfer the care of (a person or thing) to (a person). **6** *Sport* lose possession of. **7** do business to the amount of. **turn tail** flee. **turn the tide** reverse the trend of events. **turn up 1** increase the volume or strength of. **2** place upwards. **3** discover. **4** be found. **5** happen or appear. □ **turner** *n.*

turnabout *n.* **1** a change of direction. **2** an abrupt change of opinion or policy etc.

turnaround *n.* **1** an abrupt or unexpected

reversal. **2** the process of completing or the time needed to complete a task.

turncoat n. a traitor.

turndown ● n. **1** a rejection or refusal. **2** an act of turning down the sheets of a bed. **3** a downturn. ● adj. that is or may be turned down.

turning n. **1** the act of using a lathe. **2** work produced on a lathe.

turning point n. a moment at which a decisive change occurs.

turnip n, **1** = RUTABAGA. **2** a vegetable with a large white globular root and sprouting edible leaves.

turnkey adj. **1** providing for a supply of equipment in a state ready for operation. **2** assembled and ready for immediate use.

turnoff n. **1** a road that leads from a more important one. **2** informal something that causes disgust.

turn-on n. informal a thing or person that thrills or causes sexual arousal.

turnout n. **1** the number of people attending an event. **2** the quantity of goods produced in a given time. **3** a place where animals may be turned out to graze. **4** Dance the outward rotation of the leg in the hip socket.

turnover n. **1** the amount of money made in a business in a given time. **2** the rate at which a particular asset or product is sold and replaced. **3** the rate at which people join and leave a company etc. **4** a small pie made by folding pastry over onto itself to enclose a filling. **5** Sport a loss of possession of the ball or puck to the opposing team.

turnpike n. **1** US a toll highway. **2** a tollgate.

turnstile n. a mechanical gate consisting of revolving arms fixed to a vertical post allowing people through singly.

turntable n. **1** a circular revolving platform spinning a phonograph record. **2** a circular revolving platform for turning a railway locomotive or other vehicle.

turpentine n. **1** a volatile essential oil obtained from gum turpentine or pine wood, used esp. as a solvent, paint thinner, and in medical liniments. **2** (also **crude turpentine** or **gum turpentine**) a sticky substance which exudes from coniferous trees, esp. pines.

turpitude n. formal wickedness. [Say TERPA tude]

turquoise n. **1** a semi-precious stone, usu. opaque and greenish-blue. **2** n. & adj. the greenish-blue colour of this. [Say TUR koyz or TUR kwoyz]

turret n. **1** a small tower projecting from a wall, esp. in a castle. **2** a low usu. revolving armoured enclosure for a gun and gunners in a ship, tank, etc. □ **turreted** adj.

turtle n. a marine or freshwater reptile encased in a shell of bony plates. □ **turn turtle** turn over, capsize.

turtledove n. a wild dove noted for its soft cooing and its affection for its mate and young.

turtleneck n. a high round turned-over collar, or a garment having this.

turtle shell ● n. the yellowish-brown outer shell of some turtles, used for jewellery etc. ● adj. (**turtleshell**) made of or having the appearance of turtle shell.

Tuscan n. an inhabitant or the classical language of Tuscany in central Italy. □ **Tuscan** adj. [Say TUS kin]

Tuscarora n. (pl. **Tuscarora** or **Tuscaroras**) a member or the language of an Iroquois people living in southern Ontario and western New York. □ **Tuscarora** adj. [Say TUSKA rora]

tush n. slang the buttocks. [Rhymes with PUSH]

tusk n. a long pointed tooth protruding from a closed mouth, as in the elephant. □ **tusked** adj. (also in comb.)

tussle ● n. a minor struggle or conflict. ● v. (**tussles, tussled, tussling**) engage in a tussle.

tussock n. a clump of grass etc. □ **tussocky** adj. [Say TUSS uck]

tut interj., n., & v. (**tuts, tutted, tutting**) = TUT-TUT.

Tutchone n. (pl. **Tutchone** or **Tutchones**) a member or the language of an Aboriginal people living near the Yukon River. □ **Tutchone** adj. [Say too CHONEY]

tutelage n. **1** instruction. **2** protection. [Say TOOTA lidge or TYOOTA lidge]

tutelary adj. **1** serving as a guardian, protector, or patron. **2** relating to a guardian. [Say TOOTA lerry or TYOOTA lerry]

tutor ● n. **1** a private teacher. **2** esp. Brit. a university teacher supervising the studies of assigned undergraduates. ● v. **1** act as a tutor to. **2** work as a tutor.

tutorial ● adj. of or relating to a tutor or tuition. ● n. **1** a period of instruction given by a tutor or teaching assistant. **2** any training session or seminar. **3** a program offering onscreen instruction relating to software. [Say too TORY ul]

Tutsi n. (pl. **Tutsi** or **Tutsis**) a member of a Bantu-speaking people in Rwanda. [Sounds like TOOTSIE]

tutti-frutti n. (pl. **tutti-fruttis**) a type of ice cream containing chopped preserved fruits and nuts. [Say tooty FROOTY]

tut-tut ● *interj.* expressing rebuke. ● *n.* an exclamation of "tut-tut" or the sound of consecutive clicks of the tongue against the alveolar ridge. ● *v.* (**tut-tuts, tut-tutted, tut-tutting**) **1** exclaim "tut-tut". **2** express disapproval.

tutu *n.* (*pl.* **tutus**) a ballerina's costume with a flowing bell-shaped skirt or a short, stiff skirt of layered net standing out from the hips.

tux *n.* (*pl.* **tuxes**) *informal* a tuxedo.

tuxedo *n.* (*pl.* **tuxedos**) **1** a formal suit worn by men, including of a usu. black jacket and matching pants. **2** the formal jacket worn as part of this suit.

TV *n.* (*pl.* **TVs**) television.

TV dinner *n.* a prepared frozen single-serving meal packaged in a compartmentalized tray in which it is heated.

TV table *n.* (also **TV tray**) a small portable folding table with a detachable tray forming the tabletop.

twaddle *n.* silly or dull talk or writing.

twang ● *n.* **1** a ringing sound made by a plucked string. **2** a nasal quality of pronunciation or intonation. ● *v.* **1** make or cause to make a twang. **2** utter with a nasal twang. □ **twangy** *adj.* (**twangier, twangiest**)

'twas *archaic* it was.

tweak ● *v.* **1** pinch and twist sharply. **2** make fine adjustments to. ● *n.* **1** a sharp twist or pull. **2** a slight improvement.

twee *adj.* usu. *derogatory* affectedly quaint or sentimental.

tweed *n.* **1** a rough-surfaced woollen cloth with mixed colours. **2** (in *pl.*) clothes made of tweed.

tweedy *adj.* (**tweedier, tweediest**) **1** of or relating to tweed cloth. **2** often dressed in tweeds; dowdy.

tween *n.* (also **tween-ager, tweenie**) a person between 8 and 14 years of age.

tweet ● *n.* the chirp of a small bird. ● *v.* make a chirping noise.

tweeter *n.* a loudspeaker designed to reproduce high frequencies.

tweeze *v.* (**tweezes, tweezed, tweezing**) pinch or pluck with or as if with tweezers.

tweezers *pl. n.* a small pair of pincers used for picking and plucking.

twelfth *ord. num.* constituting number 12 in a series.

twelve *card. num.* one more than eleven.

12-step *adj.* relating to a progression through twelve stages towards recovery from addiction. □ **12-stepper** *n.*

twenty *card. num.* (*pl.* **twenties**) ten less than thirty. □ **twenty-first, -second,** etc. the ordinal numbers between twentieth and thirtieth. **twenty-one, -two,** etc. the cardinal numbers between twenty and thirty. □ **twentieth** *ord. num.* **twentyfold** *adj. & adv.*

24-7 *adv.* twenty-four hours a day, seven days a week.

twenty-one *n.* blackjack.

twenty-six *n.* (*pl.* **twenty-sixes**) *Cdn* a 26-ounce (or 750-ml) bottle of liquor.

twentysomething *n.* **1** an undetermined age between twenty and thirty. **2** a person of this age or generation.

20/20 *adj.* (also **twenty-twenty**) denoting vision of normal sharpness.

twenty-two *n.* a .22-calibre gun or cartridge.

twerp *n.* *slang* a foolish or insignificant person.

twice *adv.* **1** on two successive occasions; two times. **2** in double degree or quantity.

twiddle *v.* (**twiddles, twiddled, twiddling**) **1 a** cause to rotate lightly with the fingers. **b** play idly; fiddle. **2** move in a twirling way. □ **twiddle one's thumbs 1** move one's thumbs around each other as a sign of boredom. **2** have nothing to do. □ **twiddly** *adj.*

twig[1] *n.* a small branch or shoot of a tree or shrub.

twig[2] *v.* (**twigs, twigged, twigging**) *informal* **1** understand. **2** recognize, perceive.

twilight *n.* **1 a** the soft light from the sky when the sun is below the horizon. **b** any faint light. **2** the early evening when this occurs. **3** an intermediate condition, esp. one of decline. [Say TWY lite]

twilight zone *n.* any area lying undefined or intermediate between two distinct regions.

twilit *adj.* dimly illuminated. [Say TWY lit]

twill *n.* **1** a woven fabric with a surface of diagonal parallel ridges. **2** the method of weaving this fabric. □ **twilled** *adj.*

twin ● *n.* **1** each of two children or animals born at the same time to the same mother. **2** either of two closely similar things; a counterpart. **3** either of two parts working in unison. **4** (as an *adj.*) denoting a twin-size mattress, bed, etc. **5** a twin-engined aircraft. ● *v.* (**twins, twinned, twinning**) **1 a** unite closely or intimately. **b** (often foll. by *with*) be or become coupled. **2** (usu. in *passive*) establish official links between for the purposes of friendship and cultural exchange. □ **twinning** *n.*

twin city *n.* **1** (**Twin Cities**) two neighbouring cities situated close together.

2 each of a pair of usu. international cities with official ties for the purposes of friendship and cultural exchange.

twine ● n. a strong cord or string made of the twisted strands of hemp, cotton, sisal, etc. **●** v. **(twines, twined, twining) 1** join together by twisting. **2** become joined or tangled. **3** wind or wrap. **4** form by twisting or weaving flowers, leaves, etc. **5** (of a plant) grow in a twisting manner.

twin-engined adj. (also **twin-engine**) having two engines.

twinge ● n. a sudden sharp pain or pang. **●** v. **(twinges, twinged, twinging)** cause or experience a twinge.

twinkle ● v. **(twinkles, twinkled, twinkling) 1** shine with rapid alternation between brightness and faintness. **2** have a bright amused expression. **3** move lightly and rapidly. **●** n. **1** a sparkle or gleam of the eyes. **2** a brief flash or gleam of light. □ **twinkler** n. **twinkly** adj.

twinkling ● n. the action of twinkling. **●** adj. that twinkles. □ **in a twinkling** (or **the twinkling of an eye**) in an instant.

twinship n. the condition of being twin or a twin.

twin-size adj. (also **twin-sized**) designating the smallest standard size of mattress, usu. 98 by 191 cm (38.5 by 75 in.), or of the bed frame, sheets, etc. designed for such a mattress.

twirl ● v. **1** spin, turn, or rotate rapidly. **2** roll or twist between the thumb and forefinger. **●** n. **1** a twirling motion. **2** a twirling shape. □ **twirler** n. **twirly** adj.

twist ● v. **1 a** distort the shape of by turning two ends in opposite directions. **b** coil or cause to coil around an axis into a spiral shape. **2** wind together to form a rope. **3** wind or coil around something. **4** turn around in order to face another direction. **5 a** accidentally turn (one's ankle etc.) sharply, injuring the ligaments or tendons. **b** contort in pain, anger, or contempt. **6** misrepresent. **7** apply a rotating movement to; rotate. **8** follow a very winding path. **9** dance the twist. **●** n. **1** an act or an instance of twisting. **2** a thing formed by or as by twisting; a twisted shape. **3** a bend or curve in a road or path. **4 a** a complication or unexpected development. **b** a slight change made to an existing model. **5** usu. derogatory an eccentric attitude. **6 a** a curled piece of lemon peel to flavour a drink. **b** an item of food having a spiral or twisted shape. **7 (the twist)** a dance in which the upper and lower body are swivelled back and forth in opposite directions, popular in the early 1960s. **8** a sprain or strain of a limb.

9 Physics a twisting strain or force. □ **twist a person's arm** informal apply coercion to a person. **twist of fate** an ironic reversal of fortune. **twist the knife** cause additional damage or pain. **twist in the wind** be left in a state of painful suspense or uncertainty.

twisted adj. **1** morally warped. **2** having many complications and unexpected changes of plot. **3** misshapen, mangled. **4** sprained. **5** entwined. **6** contorted.

twister n. **1** a tornado. **2** a person or thing that twists.

twist-tie ● n. a small strip of plastic-covered wire used to fasten. **●** v. **(twist-ties, twist-tied, twist-tying)** fasten with a twist-tie.

twisty adj. **(twistier, twistiest)** having many bends.

twit ● n. slang a silly or foolish person. **●** v. **(twits, twitted, twitting)** reproach or tease.

twitch ● v. **(twitches, twitched, twitching) 1** move or contract spasmodically. **2** give a short sharp pull at. **●** n. **1 a** a sudden involuntary contraction or movement of a muscle etc. **b** a pang. **2 a** sudden sharp pull or jerk.

twitchy adj. **(twitchier, twitchiest) 1** having a tendency to twitch. **2** nervous, fidgety.

twitter ● v. **1** (of a bird) chirp with light tremulous sounds. **2** talk rapidly in a high tremulous voice. **●** n. **1** a light tremulous chirping. **2** informal a state of excitement. □ **twitterer** n. **twittery** adj.

two card. num. one more than one. □ **in two** in or into two pieces. **or two** denoting several. **put two and two together** make an inference from what is evident. **two by two** in pairs.

two-bagger n. informal (also **two-base hit**) Baseball a successful hit which allows a player to get to second base safely.

two-bit adj. informal cheap, small-time.

two bits n. informal twenty-five cents.

two-by-four n. a length of timber that has a rectangular cross-section of $1\frac{1}{2}$ inches by $3\frac{1}{2}$ inches (3.8 cm by 8.9 cm) when trimmed, or 2 inches by 4 inches (5.1 cm by 10.2 cm) when not trimmed.

two cents pl. n. (also **two cents' worth**) informal an unsolicited opinion.

two-dimensional adj. **1** having or appearing to have length and width but no depth. **2** lacking depth; superficial.

two-faced adj. insincere.

two-fisted adj. tough, aggressive.

twofold adj. & adv. **1** twice as much or as many. **2** consisting of two parts.

two-four *n.* *Cdn informal* a case of twenty-four bottles of beer.

two-handed *adj.* using or requiring two hands.

two percent *n.* (also **2 percent**, **2%**) partly skimmed milk containing two percent milk fat.

two-ply ● *adj.* consisting of two strands or thicknesses. ● *n.* two-ply wool or wood etc.

two-pronged *adj.* having two aspects.

two-sided *adj.* **1** having two sides. **2** having two aspects.

two solitudes *pl. n.* *Cdn* the anglophone and francophone populations of Canada, portrayed as two cultures coexisting independently.

twosome *n.* **1** two people together. **2** a game, dance, etc., for two people.

two-step ● *n.* a ballroom dance for couples involving a sliding step in march or polka time. ● *v.* (**two-steps**, **two-stepped**, **two-stepping**) dance the two-step. ● *adj.* involving two successive actions or stages.

two-stroke *adj.* **1** having its power cycle completed in one up-and-down movement of the piston. **2** having a two-stroke engine.

two-time *informal* ● *v.* (**two-times**, **two-timed**, **two-timing**) **1** be unfaithful to. **2** swindle, double-cross. ● *adj.* having achieved a specified distinction twice. □ **two-timer** *n.*

two-tone *adj.* having two colours or two shades of the same colour.

two-way *adj.* **1** involving two participants. **2** capable of transmitting and receiving signals. **3** moving in opposite directions.

two-way mirror *n.* a panel of glass that is transparent from one side but reflects light and images from the other.

Twp. *abbr.* Township.

tycoon *n.* a business magnate.

tyee *n.* *Cdn* (*BC*) a chinook salmon, esp. one weighing more than 13.6 kg (30 lb.). [*Say* TIE ee]

tying *pres. part. of* TIE.

tyke *n.* **1** *informal* a small child. **2** *Cdn* an initiation level of sports competition for young children.

Tylenol *n. proprietary* acetaminophen.

tympanic membrane *n.* the eardrum. [*Say* tim PANIC]

tympanum *n.* (*pl.* **tympana** or **tympanums**) **1** the middle ear. **2** the eardrum. [*Say* TIMPA num; TIMPA nuh]

Tyndall stone *n.* (also **Tyndall limestone**) *Cdn* a variety of limestone near Winnipeg, noted for the presence of fossils. [*Say* TINDLE]

type ● *n.* **1 a** a class of people or things distinguished by common essential characteristics. **b** a kind or sort. **2** an illustration, symbol, or characteristic specimen. **3** (in *comb.*) made of, resembling, or functioning as. **4 a** a person of a specified or implied character. **b** the kind of person to whom one is attracted. **5 a** the general distinguishing form etc. **b** something serving as a model. **6 a** a character for printing, originally a metal casting. **b** such pieces collectively. **c** printed characters collectively. ● *v.* (**types**, **typed**, **typing**) **1 a** write with a typewriter. **b** use a computer keyboard. **2 a** classify. **b** *Biology & Medical* determine the type to which (blood, tissue, etc.) belongs.

Type A *n.* (*pl.* **Type A's**) **1** a personality type characterized by ambition, impatience, and aggressive competitiveness, thought to be particularly susceptible to stress. **2** a person of this type.

Type B *n.* (*pl.* **Type B's**) **1** a personality type characterized as easygoing and thought to have low susceptibility to stress. **2** a person of this type.

typecast *v.* (**typecasts**, **typecast**, **typecasting**) **1** assign repeatedly to the same type of role. **2** consider as fitting a stereotype. □ **typecasting** *n.*

typed *adj.* **1** classified as or having a certain character or type. **2** typewritten.

typeface *n.* **1** the particular style, appearance, size, etc. of a type or set of types. **2** *Computing* the design of a particular font.

typescript *n.* a typewritten document.

typeset *v.* (**typesets**, **typeset**, **typesetting**) prepare a book for printing by arranging the characters etc. on the page. □ **typesetter** *n.* **typesetting** *n.* [*Say* TYPE set]

typewriter *n.* a machine with keys for producing print-like characters. □ **typewriting** *n.*

typewritten *adj.* produced with a typewriter.

typhoid *n.* (also **typhoid fever**) a severe infectious fever involving a rash, muscle pain, intestinal inflammation, etc. [*Say* TIE foid]

typhoon *n.* a violent storm occurring in or around the Indian subcontinent. [*Say* tie FOON]

typhus *n.* an acute infectious fever often transmitted by lice or fleas, characterized by a purple rash. [*Say* TIFE us]

typical *adj.* **1** serving as a characteristic example. **2** characteristic of a type. **3** conforming to expectations. □ **typically** *adv.*

typify v. (**typifies, typified, typifying**)
1 be a typical example of something. **2** be a
typical feature of something.
[*Say* TIPPA fie]

typist n. a person who types or uses a
typewriter.

typo n. (pl. **typos**) *informal* an error in typed
or printed material.

typography n. the art or work of
designing how text will appear when it is
printed. □ **typographic** adj.
typographical adj. **typographically**
adv. [*Say* type OGGRA fee,
type a GRAPHIC]

typology n. (pl. **typologies**) **1** the branch
of knowledge that deals with classes with
common characteristics. **2** the branch of
religion that deals with esp. Biblical
symbolic representation. □ **typological**
adj. **typologist** n. [*Say* type OLLA jee,
type a LOGICAL]

tyrannical adj. using power over people in
a cruel way. □ **tyrannically** adv.
[*Say* ti RANNA cull]

tyrannize v. (**tyrannizes, tyrannized,
tyrannizing**) rule or behave oppressively
towards. [*Say* TEERA nize]

tyrannosaur n. (also **tyrannosaurus**, pl.
tyrannosauruses) a huge bipedal
carnivorous dinosaur, *Tyrannosaurus rex*,
with powerful hind legs and jaws and
small claw-like front legs.
[*Say* tuh RANNA sore, tuh ranna SORE us]

tyranny n. (pl. **tyrannies**) **1** the arbitrary,
cruel, and excessive exercise of power.
2 *Greek History* **a** absolute rule by someone
who seizes power without legal right. **b** a
state ruled by a such a leader.
□ **tyrannous** adj. **tyrannously** adv.
[*Say* TEERA nee]

tyrant n. **1** an oppressive or cruel ruler.
2 any person exercising power oppressively
or cruelly. **3** *Greek History* an absolute ruler
who seizes power without legal right.
[*Say* TIE runt]

tyrant flycatcher n. a small bird that
catches insects by a short flight from a
perch.

tyro n. (pl. **tyros**) a beginner. [*Say* TIE roe]

tzatziki n. a Greek side dish of yogourt
with cucumber, garlic, etc.
[*Say* tsat SEEKY]

Uu

U¹ *n.* (also **u**) (*pl.* **Us** or **U's**) **1** the twenty-first letter of the alphabet. **2** (usu. in *comb.*) a U-shaped object or curve.

U² *abbr.* (also **U.**) university.

ubiquitous *adj.* seeming to be everywhere at the same time; very common. □ **ubiquitously** *adv.* **ubiquity** *n.* [*Say* you BICK wi tus, you BICK wi tee]

U-boat *n. hist.* a German submarine.

udder *n.* the hanging mammary gland of cattle, sheep, etc.

UFO *n.* (*pl.* **UFOs**) an unidentified flying object.

Ugandan *adj.* relating to Uganda. □ **Ugandan** *n.* [*Say* you GAN din]

ugh *interj.* expressing disgust.

ugly *adj.* (**uglier, ugliest**) **1** not pleasing; repulsive. **2** threatening, dangerous. **3** morally repulsive. **4** characterized by violence. □ **ugliness** *n.*

ugly duckling *n.* a person who turns out to be beautiful or talented etc. against all expectations.

uh *interj.* expressing the sound made by a speaker who hesitates or is uncertain what to say.

UHF *abbr.* ultra-high frequency.

uh-huh *interj. informal* expressing assent or a noncommittal response to a question or remark.

uh-oh *interj.* expressing concern.

UHT *abbr.* ultra-high-temperature sterilization.

uh-uh *interj.* no.

Uke *n.* (also **Ukie**) *Cdn dated informal* a Ukrainian.

Ukrainian *n.* a person from, or the language of, Ukraine. □ **Ukrainian** *adj.* [*Say* you CRAY nee in]

Ukrainian Catholic *adj.* of or pertaining to a Ukrainian Eastern Church of the Catholic communion. □ **Ukrainian Catholic** *n.*

Ukrainian Christmas *n.* Christmas as celebrated by Ukrainian Christians on 7 January.

Ukrainian Orthodox *adj.* (also **Ukrainian Greek Orthodox**) of or pertaining to various Eastern Orthodox Churches of Ukrainian ethnicity.

ukulele *n.* a small four-stringed Hawaiian guitar. [*Say* yooka LAY lee]

ulcer *n.* an open sore on an external or internal surface of the body. □ **ulcerous** *adj.*

ulcerate *v.* (**ulcerates, ulcerated, ulcerating**) (often as **ulcerated** *adj.*) develop into or affect with an ulcer. □ **ulceration** *n.* **ulcerative** *adj.* [*Say* ULCER ate, ULCER a tiv]

ulna *n.* (*pl.* **ulnae**) the thinner and longer bone in the forearm, on the side opposite to the thumb. □ **ulnar** *adj.* [*Say* ULL nuh *for the singular,* ULL nee *for the plural*]

ulterior *adj.* existing in the background, or beyond what is evident. [*Say* ul TEERY ur]

ultimate ● *adj.* **1** last, final. **2** beyond which no other exists. **3** fundamental. **4** maximum. **5** *informal* not surpassed. ● *n.* **1** (**the ultimate**) the best achievable or imaginable. **2** a final or fundamental fact or principle. **3** a non-contact field sport using a Frisbee. □ **ultimately** *adj.*

ultimatum *n.* (*pl.* **ultimatums**) a final demand by one party, the rejection of which could cause a breakdown in relations, war, etc. [*Say* ulta MAY tum]

ultra ● *adj.* **1** favouring extreme views or measures. **2** extreme. ● *adv.* very, extremely.

ultra- *comb. form* extreme(ly), excessive(ly).

ultra-high *adj.* **1** extremely high. **2** (of a frequency) in the range 300 to 3000 megahertz.

ultralight ● *n.* a very small aircraft with an open frame. ● *adj.* extremely light.

ultramarine *n.* **1** a brilliant blue pigment. **2** *n. & adj.* the colour of this. [*Say* ultra MARINE]

ultramontane ● *adj.* **1** advocating supreme papal authority. **2** *Cdn hist.* (in Quebec) advocating the subordination of the state to the Catholic Church. ● *n.* a person advocating ultramontane views. □ **ultramontanism** *n.* **ultramontanist** *n.* [*Say* ultra MON tane, ultra MON tuh nism]

ultrasonic *adj.* of or involving sound waves with a frequency above the upper limit of human hearing. □ **ultrasonically** *adv.*

ultrasonics *pl. n.* (usu. treated as *sing.*) the science of ultrasonic waves.

ultrasound *n.* **1** sound having an ultrasonic frequency. **2** ultrasonic waves. **3** a diagnostic procedure using echoes of ultrasonic pulses to delineate objects etc.

ultraviolet *adj.* of or using electromagnetic radiation having a wavelength shorter than that of the violet end of the visible spectrum but longer than that of X-rays.

ulu *n.* a crescent-shaped Inuit knife traditionally used by women. [*Say* OO loo]

ululate *v.* (**ululates, ululated, ululating**) howl, wail. ☐ **ululation** *n.* [*Say* ULL yuh late *or* YOOL yuh late]

um *interj.* expressing hesitation or a pause in speech.

umbel *n.* a flower cluster in which stalks spring from a common centre and form a flat or curved surface. ☐ **umbelliferous** *adj.* [*Rhymes with* HUMBLE]

umber *n.* a natural pigment darker and browner than ochre.

umbilical *adj.* affecting or having to do with the navel or umbilical cord. [*Say* um BILLA cull]

umbilical cord *n.* **1** a flexible cord-like structure containing blood vessels and attaching a fetus to the placenta. **2** a supply cable linking a missile to its launcher, or an astronaut in space to a spacecraft. **3** a close link or connection.

umbra *n.* (*pl.* **umbras** or **umbrae**) **1** the fully shaded inner region of a shadow cast by an opaque object. **2** the dark central part of a sunspot. [*Say* UM bruh *for the singular; for* UMBRAE *say* UM bree]

umbrage *n.* offence. [*Say* UM bridge]

umbrella *n.* **1** a light portable device for protection against rain etc., consisting of a cloth canopy mounted on a folding frame on a central stick. **2** protection or patronage. **3** (often as an *adj.*) a unifying agency.

umiak *n.* a large, open, flat-bottomed boat traditionally used by Inuit women. [*Say* OOMY ack]

umlaut *n.* a mark (¨) used over a vowel in some languages to indicate pronunciation. [*Say* OOM lout]

ump *informal* ● *n.* an umpire. ● *v.* umpire.

umpire ● *n.* **1** a person chosen to enforce the rules and settle disputes in various sports. **2** a person chosen to arbitrate. ● *v.* (**umpires, umpired, umpiring**) act as umpire.

umpteen *slang* ● *adj.* indefinitely many. ● *pron.* indefinitely many. ☐ **umpteenth** *adj.*

un- *prefix* **1** added to adjectives and participles and their derivative nouns and adverbs, meaning: **a** not. **b** the reverse of. **2** added to nouns, meaning "a lack of". **3** added to verbs, forming verbs denoting: **a** the reversal or cancellation of an action or state. **b** deprivation or separation. **c** release from.

'un *pron. informal* one.

unabashed *adj.* not ashamed or embarrassed. ☐ **unabashedly** *adv.* [*Say* un uh BASHED, un uh BASH id lee]

unabated *adj.* without any reduction in intensity or strength.

unable *adj.* not able; lacking ability.

unabridged *adj.* (of a text etc.) not shortened.

unacceptable *adj.* not acceptable. ☐ **unacceptability** *n.* **unacceptably** *adv.*

unaccompanied *adj.* **1** not accompanied, alone. **2** *Music* without accompaniment.

unaccountable *adj.* **1** not required or expected to justify actions or decisions. **2** unable to be explained. ☐ **unaccountably** *adv.*

unaccounted for *adj.* **1** (esp. of a person) missing. **2** unexplained.

unaccustomed *adj.* **1** not accustomed. **2** not customary; unusual.

unacknowledged *adj.* not acknowledged. [*Say* un ack KNOWLEDGED]

unadorned *adj.* not adorned.

unadulterated *adj.* **1** absolute, total. **2** not mixed with any different or extra elements.

unaffected *adj.* **1** not affected. **2** free from affectation.

unaffiliated *adj.* not affiliated. [*Say* un a FILLY ated]

unalloyed *adj.* not mixed with anything else. [*Say* un a LOID]

unambiguous *adj.* not ambiguous; clear in meaning. ☐ **unambiguously** *adv.* [*Say* un am BIG you us]

un-American *adj.* **1** not in accordance with American characteristics etc. **2** (in the US) treasonable.

unanimous *adj.* **1** all in agreement. **2** (of an opinion, vote, etc.) held or given by general consent. ☐ **unanimity** *n.* **unanimously** *adv.* [*Say* you NANNA muss, yoona NIMMA tee]

unannounced *adj.* not announced; without warning.

unanswerable *adj.* **1** unable to be answered. **2** unable to be refuted.

unanswered *adj.* **1** not answered. **2** (of a

goal scored by one team) not matched by a goal scored by the other team.

unapologetic *adj.* not apologetic or sorry. □ **unapologetically** *adv.* [*Say* un a polla JET ick]

unapproachable *adj.* **1** not friendly or inviting. **2 a** remote. **b** that cannot be equalled.

unarguable *adj.* not arguable. □ **unarguably** *adv.*

unarmed *adj.* not armed; without weapons.

unashamed *adj.* **1** feeling no guilt, shameless. **2** bold. □ **unashamedly** *adv.* [*Say* un a SHAMED, un a SHAME id lee]

unassailable *adj.* unable to be attacked or questioned.

unassertive *adj.* not assertive or forthcoming.

unassisted *adj.* **1** not assisted. **2** *Hockey* (of a goal) scored by a player who takes possession of the puck from the opposing team.

unassuming *adj.* not pretentious or arrogant. □ **unassumingly** *adv.*

unattached *adj.* **1** not attached. **2** not engaged or married or in a committed relationship with someone.

unattended *adj.* **1** not supervised; alone. **2** with the owner not present. **3** (usu. foll. by *to*) not made the object of one's attention, concern, etc.; not dealt with.

unauthorized *adj.* **1** not authorized. **2** (of a biography) written without the consent of the subject.

unaware ● *adj.* not aware. ● *adv.* (also **unawares**) **1** unexpectedly. **2** inadvertently.

unbalance ● *v.* (**unbalances, unbalances/ unbalancing**) upset the physical or mental balance of. ● *n.* instability, esp. mental.

unbalanced *adj.* **1** not balanced. **2** (of a mind) unstable or deranged.

unbearable *adj.* not bearable. □ **unbearably** *adv.*

unbeatable *adj.* **1** not beatable. **2** superlative, excellent.

unbeaten *adj.* **1** not beaten. **2** not surpassed.

unbecoming *adj.* **1** not flattering. **2** unsuitable, inappropriate.

unbeknownst *adj.* (also **unbeknown**) without the knowledge of. [*Say* un bee NOANST]

unbelief *n.* lack of belief. □ **unbeliever** *n.* **unbelieving** *adj.*

unbelievable *adj.* not believable; incredible. □ **unbelievably** *adv.*

unbend *v.* (**unbends, unbent, unbending**) **1** straighten. **2** relax from strain or severity.

unbending *adj.* **1** not bending; inflexible. **2** strict in behaviour or attitudes.

unbiased *adj.* not biased.

unbidden *adj.* **1** not commanded or invited. **2** spontaneous.

unblinking *adj.* **1** not blinking. **2** steadfast. **3** stolid. □ **unblinkingly** *adv.*

unborn *adj.* not yet born.

unbound *adj.* **1** not bound or tied up. **2** unconstrained.

unbounded *adj.* not bounded; infinite.

unbowed *adj.* undaunted. [*Say* un BOWED (BOWED *rhymes with* PLOWED)]

unbridgeable *adj.* unable to be bridged.

unbridled *adj.* unconstrained.

unbroken *adj.* **1** not broken. **2** not tamed. **3** not subdued or weakened. **4** not interrupted.

unbudgeable *adj.* *informal* that cannot be moved. [*Say* un BUDGE a bull]

unburden *v.* **1** relieve of a burden. **2** confess (a secret) to someone. □ **unburdened** *adj.*

uncalled *adj.* not summoned or invited. □ **uncalled for** impertinent or unnecessary.

un-Canadian *adj.* not in accordance with Canadian characteristics etc.

uncanny *adj.* (**uncannier, uncanniest**) **1** seemingly supernatural. **2** of an unsettling accuracy etc. □ **uncannily** *adv.*, **uncanniness** *n.* [*Say* un CANNY, un CANNA lee]

uncaring *adj.* **1** neglectful. **2** lacking compassion.

unceasing *adj.* continuous. □ **unceasingly** *adv.*

uncensored *adj.* not censored.

unceremonious *adj.* **1** lacking ceremony. **2** abrupt; impolite. □ **unceremoniously** *adv.* [*Say* un serra MOANY us]

uncertain *adj.* **1** not certainly knowing or known. **2** unreliable. **3** changeable. **4** not confident. □ **in no uncertain terms** clearly and forcefully. □ **uncertainly** *adv.*

uncertainty *n.* (pl. **uncertainties**) **1** the fact of being uncertain. **2** something that is uncertain.

unchallenged *adj.* not challenged.

unchangeable *adj.* not able to be changed.

unchanged *adj.* not changed.

unchanging *adj.* remaining the same.

uncharacteristic *adj.* not characteristic. □ **uncharacteristically** *adv.*

uncharitable *adj.* unkind and unsympathetic. □ **uncharitably** *adv.*

uncharted *adj.* not mapped or surveyed.

uncharted waters *pl. n.* (also **uncharted territory**) a situation that one has not experienced before.

unchecked *adj.* **1** not checked. **2** unrestrained.

unchristian *adj.* **1** uncaring or selfish. **2** not Christian.

uncivil *adj.* impolite.

uncivilized *adj.* **1** not civilized. **2** rough; uncultured.

unclasp *v.* **1** loosen a clasp. **2** release the grip of (a hand etc.).

unclassified *adj.* **1** not classified. **2** not secret.

uncle *n.* **1** the brother of one's father or mother. **2** an aunt's husband. □ **cry** (or **say**) **uncle** *informal* surrender.

unclean *adj.* **1** not clean. **2** morally wrong. **3** (of food) regarded as impure and forbidden by a particular religion.

unclear *adj.* **1** not clear or easy to understand. **2** doubtful, uncertain.

Uncle Sam *n.* *informal* a personification of the government or citizens of the US.

unclog *v.* (**unclogs, unclogged, unclogging**) clear a blockage from (a pipe etc.).

unclothed *adj.* naked.

unclouded *adj.* **1** not clouded; bright. **2** untroubled.

uncomfortable *adj.* **1** not comfortable. **2** uneasy. □ **uncomfortably** *adv.*

uncommon *adj.* **1** not common; unusual. **2** remarkably great. □ **uncommonly** *adv.*

uncommunicative *adj.* not wanting to communicate.
[*Say* un kuh MYOONA kay tiv]

uncomplaining *adj.* not complaining; resigned. □ **uncomplainingly** *adv.*

uncomplimentary *adj.* rude; insulting.

uncomprehending *adj.* not comprehending.
□ **uncomprehendingly** *adv.*

uncompromising *adj.* unwilling to compromise. □ **uncompromisingly** *adv.*

unconcern *n.* indifference; apathy.
□ **unconcerned** *adj.* **unconcernedly** *adv.* [*Say* un CONCERN, un CONCERN id lee]

unconditional *adj.* not subject to conditions. □ **unconditionally** *adv.*

uncongenial *adj.* **1** not friendly, pleasant, or agreeable. **2** not suitable.
[*Say* un k'n JEENY ul]

unconnected *adj.* **1** not physically joined.

2 not connected or associated. **3** (of speech etc.) disconnected.

unconscionable *adj.* **1** shamefully wrong. **2** unreasonably excessive.
□ **unconscionably** *adv.*
[*Say* un CONSH'n a bull]

unconscious ● *adj.* not conscious. ● *n.* that part of the mind which is inaccessible to the conscious mind but which affects behaviour, emotions, etc.
□ **unconsciously** *adv.*
unconsciousness *n.*

unconstitutional *adj.* not in accordance with a constitution or with rules.

unconstrained *adj.* not constrained or compelled.

uncontaminated *adj.* not contaminated.

uncontested *adj.* not contested.

uncontrollable *adj.* not controllable.
□ **uncontrollably** *adv.*

unconventional *adj.* not bound by convention; unusual.
□ **unconventionality** *n.*
unconventionally *adv.*

uncool *adj.* *slang* not stylish or hip.

uncooperative *adj.* not co-operative.

uncoordinated *adj.* **1** not coordinated. **2** clumsy.

uncork *v.* draw the cork from (a bottle etc.).

uncountable *adj.* inestimable, immense.

uncounted *adj.* **1** not counted. **2** very many.

uncouple *v.* (**uncouples, uncoupled, uncoupling**) **1** unfasten, disconnect. **2** release (railway cars) from couplings.

uncouth *adj.* lacking in ease and polish; uncultured. [*Say* un COOTH]

uncover *v.* **1** remove a cover or covering from. **2** disclose. □ **uncovered** *adj.*

uncredited *adj.* not acknowledged as the author, actor, etc.

uncritical *adj.* **1** not critical. **2** not willing to criticize. □ **uncritically** *adv.*

unction *n.* **1 a** a solemn or fervent manner of expression arising from deep emotion. **b** excessive flattery. **2** the action of anointing someone with oil or ointment.
[*Say* UNK shin]

unctuous *adj.* **1** unpleasantly or excessively flattering. **2** having a greasy feel. □ **unctuously** *adv.* **unctuousness** *n.*
[*Say* UNK choo us]

uncultivated *adj.* not cultivated.

uncultured *adj.* not cultured, unrefined.

uncut *adj.* **1** not cut. **2** (of a book, film, etc.) uncensored. **3** (of a stone) not shaped by cutting. **4** (of alcohol or a drug) pure.

undaunted *adj.* not daunted.
[*Say* un DON tid]

undead ● *adj.* (esp. of a vampire etc.) technically dead but still animate. ● *n.* (preceded by *the*) those who are undead.

undecided ● *adj.* **1** not settled or certain. **2** hesitating; irresolute. ● *n.* a person who is undecided.

undecipherable *adj.* that cannot be read or understood. [*Say* un dee CIPHER a bull]

undecorated *adj.* **1** not adorned. **2** not honoured with an award.

undefiled *adj.* not defiled; pure.

undefined *adj.* **1** not defined. **2** vague. □ **undefinable** *adj.*

undemocratic *adj.* not democratic.

undeniable *adj.* **1** unable to be denied or disputed. **2** excellent. □ **undeniably** *adv.*

under ● *prep.* **1** lower than; below; beneath. **2 a** inferior to; less than. **b** at a lower cost than. **3 a** controlled or bound by. **b** undergoing. **c** classified in. **4** sheltered by. ● *adv.* **1** in or to a lower position or condition. **2** *informal* in or into a state of unconsciousness. ● *adj.* lower. □ **under the sun** anywhere in the world.

under- *prefix in senses of* UNDER: **1** below, beneath. **2** lower in status. **3** insufficiently, incompletely.

underachieve *v.* (**underachieves, underachieved, underachieving**) do less well than might be expected. □ **underachievement** *n.* **underachiever** *n.*

underage *adj.* not old enough, esp. not yet of adult status.

underarm ● *adj. & adv.* **1** (of a throw, pitch, etc.) performed with the hand lower than the level of the shoulders. **2** in, of, or for the armpit. ● *n.* the armpit.

underbelly *n.* (*pl.* **underbellies**) **1** the underside of an animal etc. **2** an area etc. vulnerable to attack. **3** a hidden, unpleasant, or criminal part of society.

underbrush *n.* undergrowth in a forest.

undercarriage *n.* **1** the supporting frame of a vehicle. **2** a structure of wheels or floats beneath an aircraft which supports the aircraft on the ground, water, etc.

underclass *n.* (*pl.* **underclasses**) a subordinate social class.

underclothes *pl. n.* underwear. □ **underclothing** *n.*

undercoat *n.* **1** a preliminary layer of paint under the finishing coat. **2** an animal's under layer of hair or down. □ **undercoating** *n.*

undercover ● *adj.* involved in or involving spying, esp. as part of a police investigation. ● *adv.* as an undercover agent.

undercurrent *n.* **1** a current below the surface. **2** an underlying often contrary feeling or influence.

undercut *v.* (**undercuts, undercut, undercutting**) **1** sell or work at a lower price or lower wages than. **2** cut away the part below or under. **3** render unstable, undermine.

underdeveloped *adj.* **1** not fully developed. **2** (of a country etc.) below its potential economic level. □ **underdevelopment** *n.*

underdog *n.* a person, team, etc. thought to be in a weaker position, and therefore not likely to win.

underdressed *adj.* dressed too plainly or too lightly.

underemployed *adj.* **1** employed at a task that uses less than one's full abilities. **2** not having enough work. **3** used less than it could be. □ **underemployment** *n.*

underestimate ● *v.* (**underestimates, underestimated, underestimating**) **1** fail to recognize the strength, skill, etc. of a person. **2** form too low an opinion of. ● *n.* an estimate that is too low. □ **underestimation** *n.*

underfed *adj.* insufficiently fed.

underfoot *adv.* **1** beneath one's feet. **2** in the way.

underfunded *adj.* not having sufficient funding. □ **underfund** *v.* **underfunding** *n.*

undergarment *n.* an article of underclothing.

undergird *v.* provide support for.

undergo *v.* (**undergoes;** *past* **underwent;** *past participle* **undergone; undergoing**) experience.

undergrad *n. & adj.* *informal* an undergraduate.

undergraduate *n.* (also **undergrad** *informal*) a university student who has not yet completed a bachelor's degree.

underground ● *adv.* **1** beneath the surface of the ground. **2** into hiding or some secret activity. ● *adj.* **1** situated beneath the surface of the ground. **2 a** secret, hidden. **b** designating a secret group, movement, or activity. **3** unconventional, experimental. ● *n.* **1** a secret group or activity. **2** a subculture seeking to provide radical alternatives to the established mode.

Underground Railroad *n.* (also *Cdn* **Underground Railway**) *hist.* a secret network of safe houses and transportation established to help fugitive slaves escape from the southern U.S.

undergrowth *n.* a dense growth of shrubs etc.

underhand ● *adj.* **1** *Sport* (of a throw etc.) performed with the hand lower than the level of the shoulders. **2** = UNDERHANDED. ● *adv.* with an underhand motion. ● *v.* throw underhand.

underhanded ● *adj.* **1** deceptive, crafty. **2** secret, clandestine. ● *adv.* underhand.

underlay ● *v.* (**underlays, underlaid, underlaying**) lay something under (a thing) to support it. ● *n.* a thing laid under another.

underlie *v.* (**underlies**; *past* **underlay**; *past participle* **underlain**; **underlying**) **1** lie or be situated under. **2** be the cause or basis of.

underline ● *v.* (**underlines, underlined, underlining**) **1** draw a line under (a word etc.) for emphasis. **2** emphasize. ● *n.* a line drawn under a word etc. □ **underlining** *n.*

underling *n.* usu. *derogatory* a subordinate.

underlying ● *v. pres. part. of* UNDERLIE. ● *adj.* **1** lying under or beneath the surface. **2** fundamental, basic.

undermine *v.* (**undermines, undermined, undermining**) **1** weaken, injure, destroy. **2** wear away the base or foundation of. **3** dig a tunnel or excavate beneath.

underneath ● *prep.* **1** directly below. **2** below or behind a covering of. ● *adv.* **1** at or to a lower place. **2** directly beneath. ● *n.* the lower surface or part. ● *adj.* lower.

undernourished *adj.* insufficiently nourished. □ **undernourishment** *n.*

underpants *pl. n.* an article of underclothing worn to cover the hips, crotch, and sometimes thighs.

underpart *n.* the lower part of anything.

underpass *n.* (*pl.* **underpasses**) a section of road etc. providing a passage beneath another road etc.

underpay *v.* (**underpays, underpaid, underpaying**) pay (an employee etc.) too little. □ **underpaid** *adj.*

underperform *v.* perform less well or be less profitable than expected. □ **underperformance** *n.*

underpin *v.* (**underpins, underpinned, underpinning**) **1** form the basis for. **2** support or strengthen (a building etc.) from below. □ **underpinning** *n.*

underplay *v.* **1** play down the importance of. **2** *Theatre* perform with deliberate restraint.

underprivileged *adj.* **1** less privileged than others. **2** not enjoying the normal standard of living or rights in a society.

underrate *v.* (**underrates, underrated, underrating**) have too low an opinion of. □ **underrated** *adj.* [*Say* under RATE]

underscore ● *v.* (**underscores, underscored, underscoring**) underline. ● *n.* **1** an underline. **2** the character _, used to represent a word break or blank space.

undersea *adj.* below the sea or the surface of the sea.

undersecretary *n.* (*pl.* **undersecretaries**) a subordinate official, esp. a junior minister or senior civil servant.

undersell *v.* (**undersells, undersold, underselling**) sell at a lower price than.

undershirt *n.* a light shirt with no collar worn as an article of underclothing.

undershorts *pl. n.* men's underpants.

underside *n.* (also in *pl.*) the lower side or bottom.

undersigned *adj.* whose signature is appended below.

undersized *adj.* (also **undersize**) of less than the usual size.

undersold *past and past participle of* UNDERSELL.

understaffed *adj.* having too few staff. □ **understaffing** *n.*

understand *v.* (**understands, understood, understanding**) **1** perceive the meaning of (words, a person, etc.). **2** perceive the significance or cause of. **3 a** know how to deal with, be sympathetic to. **b** accept without anger or resentment. **4** be conversant or familiar with. **5** accept as true without positive knowledge. **6** supply (a word) mentally. □ **understand each other 1** know each other's views. **2** be in agreement.

understandable *adj.* **1** that one might expect; natural or reasonable. **2** comprehensible. □ **understandability** *n.* **understandably** *adv.*

understanding ● *n.* **1** the ability to reason and comprehend; intellect. **2 a** an individual's perception of a situation etc. **b** a person's knowledge of a subject. **3** an agreement. **4** harmony in opinion or feeling. **5** empathy. ● *adj.* **1** sympathetic to others' feelings. **2** having understanding. □ **understandingly** *adv.*

understate *v.* (**understates, understated, understating**) **1** express in greatly or unduly restrained terms. **2** represent (a thing) as being less than it actually is. □ **understatement** *n.*

understated *adj.* **1** restrained in style or colour; not showy. **2** stated in unduly restrained terms. □ **understatedly** *adv.*

understudy esp. *Theatre* ● *n.* (*pl.* **understudies**) a person who studies another's role etc. in order to perform in

the absence of the other. ● *v.*
(**understudies, understudied,
understudying**) study (a role etc.) as an
understudy.

undertake *v.* (**undertakes**; *past*
undertook; *past participle* **undertaken**;
undertaking) **1** take on; commit oneself
to perform. **2** accept an obligation.

undertaker *n.* a funeral director.

undertaking *n.* **1** work etc. undertaken.
2 a pledge or promise. **3** the management
of funerals as a profession.

undertone *n.* **1** a subdued tone of sound
or colour. **2** an underlying quality. **3** an
undercurrent of feeling.

undertook *past of* UNDERTAKE.

undertow *n.* an undercurrent.
[*Say* UNDER toe]

underuse ● *v.* (**underuses,
underused, underusing**) use below the
optimum level. ● *n.* insufficient use.

underutilized *adj.* underused.
[*Say* under UTILIZED]

undervalue *v.* (**undervalues,
undervalued, undervaluing**) **1** value
insufficiently. **2** underestimate.

underwater ● *adj.* **1** living or situated
below the surface of the water. **2** designed
to be used or done under the surface of the
water. ● *adv.* under water.

under way *adj.* **1** in progress. **2** *Nautical* (of
a ship) in motion.

underwear *n.* **1** underclothing.
2 underpants.

underweight *adj.* weighing less than is
normal or desirable.

underwent *past of* UNDERGO.

underwhelm *v. jocular* fail to impress.
□ **underwhelming** *adj.*

underwire *n.* **1** a thin semicircular
support of wire stitched into the underside
of each cup of a bra. **2** a bra with such a
support.

underworld *n.* **1** the world of criminals or
of organized crime. **2** the mythical abode
of the dead under the earth.

underwrite *v.* (**underwrites**; *past*
underwrote; *past participle*
underwritten; underwriting) **1 a** sign,
issue, and accept liability under (an
insurance policy). **b** insure. **2** guarantee (an
undertaking or venture etc.) by assuming
responsibility for any debts incurred. **3** pay
for. □ **underwriter** *n.*

undeserved *adj.* not deserved.
□ **undeservedly** *adv.* [*Say* un DESERVED,
un DESERVE id lee]

undesirable ● *adj.* not desirable. ● *n.* an
objectionable or unpleasant person etc.
□ **undesirability** *n.* **undesirably** *adv.*

undetected *adj.* not detected.

undetermined *adj.* undecided.

undeterred *adj.* not deterred.
[*Say* un dee TURD]

undid *past of* UNDO.

undies *pl. n. informal* underclothes.

undifferentiated *adj.* not differentiated.

undigested *adj.* **1** not digested. **2** (esp. of
information) not properly understood or
considered.

undiluted *adj.* **1** not diluted. **2** complete,
utter

undisciplined *adj.* lacking discipline.

undisclosed *adj.* not revealed or made
known.

undiscriminating *adj.* **1** lacking taste or
good judgment. **2** not selective.

undisguised *adj.* not disguised or
concealed. [*Say* un DISGUISED]

undisputed *adj.* **1** not disputed or called
into question. **2** universally acknowledged.

undistinguished *adj.* **1** lacking any
distinguishing feature. **2** not remarkable.

undivided *adj.* not divided or shared;
whole.

undo ● *v.* (**undoes**; *past* **undid**; *past
participle* **undone; undoing**) **1 a** unfasten
or untie. **b** become unfastened. **2** annul,
cancel. **3** ruin the prospects or morals of.
● *n. Computing* a feature of some programs
that allows the user to reverse the effect of
the last action.

undocumented *adj.* **1** not having the
appropriate legal documents. **2** not proved
by or recorded in documents.

undoing *n.* **1** ruin, downfall. **2** the cause of
this.

undone *adj.* **1** not done; incomplete. **2** not
fastened or tied.

undoubtedly *adv.* beyond doubt; certainly.

undreamed of *adj.* (also **undreamt of**)
not previously considered or imagined.

undress ● *v.* (**undresses, undressed,
undressing**) **1** take off one's clothes.
2 take the clothes off (a person). ● *n.*
1 *Military* a uniform worn on ordinary rather
than ceremonial occasions. **2** the state of
being naked or only partially clothed.

undressed *adj.* **1** not or no longer dressed.
2 (of leather etc.) not treated. **3** (of food) not
having a dressing.

undue *adj.* **1** excessive, disproportionate.
2 inappropriate.

undulate *v.* (**undulates, undulated,
undulating**) **1** have a wavy or rippling
outline. **2** have a wavelike motion.
□ **undulation** *n.* [*Say* UN dyoo late *or*
UN joo late]

unduly *adv.* excessively. [*Say* un DUE lee]

undying *adj.* eternal, never-ending.

unearned *adj.* not earned.

unearth *v.* **1** discover by investigation or searching; bring to light. **2** dig up.

unearthly *adj.* **1 a** not of this world. **b** eerie, mysterious. **2** not typical of this world. **3** *informal* absurdly early.

unease *n.* anxiety, discomfort.

uneasy *adj.* (**uneasier, uneasiest**) **1** (of a person) apprehensive. **2** disturbing. **3** tenuous, shaky. □ **uneasily** *adv.* **uneasiness** *n.*

uneatable *adj.* that is not in a condition to be eaten.

uneconomic *adj.* incapable of being profitably operated etc.

uneducated *adj.* not educated.

unemployable *adj.* not qualified or suitable for paid employment.

unemployed ● *adj.* **1** not having paid employment. **2** not in use. ● *n.* (preceded by *the*) unemployed people.

unemployment *n.* **1** the state of being unemployed. **2** the number or percentage of unemployed people. **3** *Cdn informal* unemployment insurance.

unemployment benefit *n.* a regular payment made by the state or, in the US, a trade union, to an unemployed person.

unemployment insurance *n. Cdn* the former name for employment insurance. Abbreviation: **UI**.

unencumbered *adj.* **1** not having any burden or impediment. **2** free of debt.

unending *adj.* having or seeming to have no end.

unenforceable *adj.* (of a contract, law, etc.) impossible to enforce.

unenlightened *adj.* not enlightened.

unenterprising *adj.* not enterprising.

unenviable *adj.* unpleasant, undesirable. [*Say* un ENVY a bull]

unequal *adj.* **1** not equal in amount, size, value, etc. **2** inadequate in ability or resources etc. **3 a** not evenly balanced. **b** inconsistent. □ **unequally** *adv.*

unequalled *adj.* **1** superior to all others. **2** not matched or surpassed.

unequivocal *adj.* plain, unmistakable. □ **unequivocally** *adv.* [*Say* un ee KWIVVA cull]

unerring *adj.* always right or accurate. □ **unerringly** *adv.*

unethical *adj.* not ethical. □ **unethically** *adv.*

uneven *adj.* **1** not level or smooth. **2** not consistent, regular, or uniform. **3** unequal. □ **unevenly** *adv.* **unevenness** *n.*

unexceptionable *adj.* to whom or to which no exception can be taken.

unexceptional *adj.* not out of the ordinary.

unexpected *adj.* not expected; surprising. □ **unexpectedly** *adv.* **unexpectedness** *n.*

unexplained *adj.* not explained. □ **unexplainable** *adj.*

unexplored *adj.* not explored.

unfailing *adj.* **1** unlimited. **2** unceasing, constant. **3** reliable. □ **unfailingly** *adv.*

unfair *adj.* **1** not just or reasonable. **2** not according to the rules. **3** dishonest. □ **unfairly** *adv.* **unfairness** *n.*

unfaithful *adj.* **1** not faithful, esp. to a sexual partner. **2** disloyal. □ **unfaithfulness** *n.*

unfaltering *adj.* steady, resolute.

unfasten *v.* **1** loosen. **2** open the fastening of. **3** detach. □ **unfastened** *adj.*

unfathomable *adj.* incapable of being fathomed. □ **unfathomably** *adv.* [*Say* un FATHOM a bull]

unfavourable *adj.* (also **unfavorable**) not favourable; adverse. □ **unfavourably** *adv.*

unfazed *adj. informal* untroubled.

unfeasible *adj.* not feasible.

unfeeling *adj.* **1** unsympathetic, harsh. **2** lacking sensitivity.

unfettered *adj.* unrestrained, unrestricted.

unfiltered *adj.* **1** not filtered. **2** (of a cigarette) having no filter.

unfinished *adj.* **1** not finished. **2** (of wood etc.) not stained etc.

unfinished business *n.* **1** something that must be completed. **2** *Psychology informal* unresolved issues.

unfit *adj.* **1 a** not fit, proper, or suitable. **b** not qualified. **2** in poor physical shape.

unflagging *adj.* tireless, persistent. □ **unflaggingly** *adv.*

unflappable *adj. informal* calm in a crisis. □ **unflappability** *n.*

unflinching *adj.* not showing reluctance, hesitation, or fear. □ **unflinchingly** *adv.*

unfold *v.* **1** open or spread out. **2** develop, become clear. **3** become opened out. **4** reveal or make clear.

unforced *adj.* **1** easy, natural. **2** not compelled or constrained.

unforeseen *adj.* not foreseen. □ **unforeseeable** *adj.*

unforgettable *adj.* memorable, wonderful. □ **unforgettably** *adv.*

unforgivable *adj.* inexcusable, disgraceful. □ **unforgivably** *adv.*

unforgiving *adj.* not forgiving.

unformed *adj.* **1** not formed. **2** shapeless. **3** not developed.

unforthcoming *adj.* **1** not willing to divulge information. **2** not ready or made available when needed or wanted.

unfortunate ● *adj.* **1 a** unlucky. **b** unhappy. **2** regrettable. **3** inappropriate. ● *n.* an unfortunate person. □ **unfortunately** *adv.*

unfounded *adj.* having no basis in fact.

unfreeze *v.* (**unfreezes**; *past* **unfroze**; *past participle* **unfrozen**; **unfreezing**) **1** thaw. **2** remove restrictions from (assets etc.).

unfriendly *adj.* (**unfriendlier**, **unfriendliest**) **1** not friendly. **2** *informal* not helpful to. □ **unfriendliness** *n.*

unfrozen ● *v. past participle of* UNFREEZE. ● *adj.* not frozen.

unfulfilled *adj.* not fulfilled. □ **unfulfilling** *adj.*

unfunny *adj.* (**unfunnier**, **unfunniest**) not amusing.

unfurl *v.* **1** spread or open out (a sail, flag, etc.). **2** become spread out.

unfurnished *adj.* **1** without furniture. **2** not provided or supplied.

ungainly *adj.* awkward, clumsy. □ **ungainliness** *n.*

unglamorous *adj.* **1** lacking glamour. **2** mundane.

unglued *adj.* having no glue, unstuck. □ **come** (or **become**) **unglued 1 a** lose one's composure. **b** become crazy. **2** fall into chaos.

ungodly *adj.* **1** impious, wicked. **2** *informal* outrageous. □ **ungodliness** *n.*

ungracious *adj.* not cordial, courteous, or polite. □ **ungraciously** *adv.*

ungrammatical *adj.* contrary to the rules of grammar. □ **ungrammatically** *adv.*

ungrateful *adj.* **1** not feeling or showing gratitude. **2** not acceptable.

unguarded *adj.* **1 a** candid, open. **b** resulting from such candidness. **2** careless, thoughtless. **3** not guarded.

unguent *n.* a soft substance used esp. as an ointment. [*Say* UNG gwint]

ungulate ● *adj.* hoofed. ● *n.* a hoofed mammal. [*Say* UNG gyoo lit *or* UNG gyoo late]

unhappy *adj.* (**unhappier**, **unhappiest**) **1 a** not happy. **b** displeased, regrettable. □ **unhappily** *adv.* **unhappiness** *n.*

unhealthy *adj.* (**unhealthier**, **unhealthiest**) **1** not in good health. **2** not conducive to good health. **3** unwholesome.

4 inappropriate, perverse. □ **unhealthily** *adv.* **unhealthiness** *n.*

unheard of *adj.* **1** unknown, unfamiliar. **2** unprecedented. **3** outrageous.

unheeded *adj.* not heeded; disregarded.

unheralded *adj.* unannounced.

unhesitating *adj.* **1** without doubt or hesitation. **2** without interruption. □ **unhesitatingly** *adv.*

unhinge *v.* (**unhinges**, **unhinged**, **unhinging**) **1** take (a door etc.) off its hinges. **2 a** unsettle (a person); make crazy. **b** throw into chaos. □ **unhinged** *adj.*

unhip *adj. informal* not hip.

unholy *adj.* (**unholier**, **unholiest**) **1** evil, wicked. **2** *informal* dreadful. **3** not holy.

unhook *v.* **1** remove from a hook. **2** unfasten by releasing a hook.

unhuman *adj.* **1** not human. **2** superhuman. **3** inhuman.

uni- *comb. form* one; having or consisting of one.

unicameral *adj.* with a single legislative chamber. [*Say* yoona CAMMER ul]

unicellular *adj.* consisting of a single cell. [*Say* yoona CELL yuh ler]

unicorn *n.* a legendary animal usu. represented as a horse with a single horn projecting from its forehead.

unicycle *n.* a single-wheeled cycle. □ **unicyclist** *n.*

unidealized *adj.* not represented as perfect or ideal. [*Say* un IDEAL ized]

unidentified *adj.* not identified.

unidirectional *adj.* only moving etc. in one direction. [*Say* yoona DIRECTION ul]

unification *n.* the process of being united or made into a whole. [*Say* yoona fuh KAY sh'n]

uniform ● *adj.* **1** not changing in form or character; unvarying. **2** conforming to the same standard, rules, or pattern. ● *n.* **1** uniform distinctive clothing worn by members of the same body, e.g. by soldiers etc. **2** clothing worn by nurses and other medical professionals. □ **uniformed** *adj.* **uniformly** *adv.*

uniformity *n.* the state of being uniform. [*Say* yoona FORMA tee]

unify *v.* (**unifies**, **unified**, **unifying**) make united or uniform. □ **unified** *adj.* **unifying** *adj.* [*Say* YOONA fie]

unilateral *adj.* performed by or affecting only one person or party. □ **unilaterally** *adv.* [*Say* yoona LATTER ul]

unilingual *esp. Cdn adj.* **1** able to speak only one language. **2** spoken or written in only one language. ● *n.* a unilingual

person. [*Say* yoona LING gwul *or*
yoona LING gyoo ul]

unimaginable *adj.* impossible to imagine.
  □ **unimaginably** *adv.*

unimpeachable *adj.* beyond reproach.

unimpeded *adj.* not impeded.
  [*Say* un im PEED id]

unimportant *adj.* not important.
  □ **unimportance** *n.*

unimproved *adj.* **1** not improved. **2** (of
land) not developed.

unincorporated *adj.* not formed into a
corporation. [*Say* un in CORE pur ate id]

uninformed *adj.* **1** not informed.
  2 ignorant.

uninhabitable *adj.* that cannot be
inhabited.

uninhabited *adj.* not inhabited.

uninhibited *adj.* not inhibited.
  □ **uninhibitedly** *adv.*

uninitiated *adj.* not admitted or
instructed. [*Say* un in ISHY ate id]

uninspired *adj.* dull.

unintelligible *adj.* not intelligible.
  [*Say* un in TELLA juh bull]

uninterested *adj.* **1** not interested.
  2 unconcerned.

uninviting *adj.* not inviting; not attractive.

union *n.* **1** the action or fact of joining
together or being joined together. **2 a** a
whole resulting from the combination of
parts or members. **b** a political unit formed
in this way. **3 a** a labour union. **b** a group
of people united for a common cause. **4** a
marriage. **5** a state of harmony or
agreement. **6** (**the Union**) *US hist.* the body
of northern states in the American Civil
War.

unionist *n.* **1 a** a member of a labour
union. **b** an advocate of labour unions.
  2 (usu. **Unionist**) an advocate of esp.
political union. □ **unionism** *n.*

unionize *v.* (**unionizes**, **unionized**,
unionizing) bring or come under the
organization of a labour union.
  □ **unionization** *n.* **unionized** *adj.*

Union Jack *n.* the national flag of the
United Kingdom.

Union Nationale *n.* *Cdn* (in Quebec) a
provincial party identified with French-
Canadian nationalism which held power
1944–60 under Maurice Duplessis.
  [*Say* oon yon nass yuh NAL *(with* on *as in
French)*]

unique *adj.* **1** of which there is only one;
unequalled. **2** *disputed* unusual, remarkable.
  3 limited to a particular area, situation,
etc. □ **uniquely** *adv.* **uniqueness** *n.*
  [*Say* yoo NEEK]

unisex *adj.* designed to be suitable for both
sexes. [*Say* YOONA sex]

unison ● *n.* **1** identity in pitch of two or
more sounds or notes. **2** agreement,
concord. ● *adj.* coinciding in pitch. □ **in
unison** together; as one.
  [*Say* YOONA sun]

unit *n.* **1 a** an individual thing, person, or
group regarded as single and complete.
  b each of the (smallest) separate
individuals or groups into which a whole
may be analyzed. **2** a quantity chosen as a
standard for measurement. **3** an apartment
etc. **4** a device with a specified function.
  5 a piece of furniture for fitting with
others like it or made of complementary
parts. **6 a** a group with a special function
in an organization. **b** a subdivision of a
larger military grouping. **7** a portion of a
school course on a particular theme.

unitard *n.* a tight-fitting one-piece
garment which covers the body from the
shoulders to the toes or ankles.
  [*Say* YOONA tard]

Unitarian *n.* a member of a religious
group who believe that God is not a Trinity
but one person. □ **Unitarian** *adj.*
  Unitarianism *n.* [*Say* yoona TERRY un]

unitary *adj.* **1** marked by unity or
uniformity. **2** of or relating to a system of
government in which the powers of the
separate constituent parts are vested in one
central body. [*Say* YOONA terry]

unite *v.* (**unites**, **united**, **uniting**) **1** make
or become one. **2** join together for a
common purpose. **3** join in marriage.

united *adj.* **1** joined together. **2** joined
politically. **3** in agreement. **4** (**United**) *Cdn*
having to do with the United Church.

United Church *n.* (also **United Church
of Canada**) a Protestant denomination
formed in 1925 by the merger of
Methodists and Presbyterians.

United Empire Loyalist *n.* *Cdn* **1** a
colonist of the American revolutionary
period who supported the British cause
and migrated to Canada. **2** *Cdn* a
descendant of such a person.

United Nations *n.* an international
organization of countries set up in 1945 to
promote international peace, security, and
co-operation. Abbreviation: **UN**.

unity *n.* (*pl.* **unities**) **1** oneness; being
formed of parts that constitute a whole.
  2 harmony or concord. **3** a thing forming a
complex whole. **4** *Math* the number "one".

universal *adj.* of or done etc. by all persons
or things in the world or in the class
concerned. □ **universality** *n.*
  universally *adv.* [*Say* yoona VERSE'll,
yoona vur SALLA tee]

universalist n. **1** a person advocating loyalty to others without regard to national allegiance. **2** *Theology* a person who believes that all mankind will eventually be saved. □ **universalism** n. **universalistic** adj. [*Say* UNIVERSAL ist, universal ISS tick]

universalize v. (**universalizes, universalized, universalizing**) **1** apply universally. **2** make available for all. [*Say* UNIVERSAL ize]

Universal Product Code n. a bar code printed on the packaging of many consumer goods. Abbreviation: **UPC**.

universe n. **1** all existing things. **2** all of humanity.

university n. (*pl.* **universities**) **1** an educational institution designed for advanced learning, conferring degrees in various faculties. **2** the members of this collectively.

Unix n. *Computing proprietary* a multi-user operating system. [*Say* YOO nix]

unjust adj. unfair. □ **unjustly** adv.

unkempt adj. **1** untidy. **2** dishevelled.

unknowable ● adj. that cannot be known. ● n. an unknowable thing.

unknowing adj. not knowing. □ **unknowingly** adv.

unknown ● adj. not known. ● n. **1** an unknown thing or person. **2** an unknown quantity.

unlawful adj. not lawful; illegal. □ **unlawfully** adv.

unleaded ● adj. (of gasoline etc.) without added lead. ● n. unleaded gasoline. [*Say* un LED id]

unlearn v. (**unlearns**; *past* and *past participle* **unlearned** or **unlearnt**; **unlearning**) **1** discard from one's memory. **2** rid oneself of (a habit etc.).

unleash v. (**unleashes, unleashed, unleashing**) **1** release (something powerful or destructive). **2** set free to engage in pursuit or attack.

unleavened adj. made without yeast or other raising agent. [*Say* un LEV ind]

unless conj. if not; except when.

unlettered adj. **1** illiterate. **2** not well educated.

unlicensed adj. (also **unlicenced**) without a licence to sell alcoholic drink.

unlike ● prep. **1** different from; not like. **2** in contrast to. **3** uncharacteristic of. ● adj. not alike.

unlikely adj. (**unlikelier, unlikeliest**) **1** improbable. **2** not expected to do something. **3** unpromising.

unlimited adj. without limit; unrestricted.

unlined adj. **1** without lines or wrinkles. **2** (of a garment etc.) without lining.

unlisted adj. **1** not listed in a telephone directory. **2** (of a security) not eligible for trading on an exchange.

unlistenable adj. (esp. of music) impossible or unbearable to listen to.

unload v. **1** remove a load from. **2** remove the charge from (a firearm etc.). **3** *informal* get rid of. □ **unloader** n.

unlock v. **1 a** release the lock of. **b** release or disclose by unlocking. **2** become unlocked.

unloved adj. not loved.

unlucky adj. (**unluckier, unluckiest**) **1** not fortunate or successful. **2** wretched. **3** bringing bad luck.

unmade adj. not made.

unmanageable adj. not (easily) managed or controlled. □ **unmanageably** adv.

unmanned adj. **1** not manned. **2** deprived of supposedly manly qualities (e.g. self-control, courage).

unmannerly adj. without good manners.

unmapped adj. **1** not represented on a map. **2** unexplored.

unmarked adj. **1** not marked. **2** not noticed.

unmask v. **1** remove the mask from. **2** expose the true character of.

unmatched adj. not matched or equalled.

unmediated adj. directly perceived. [*Say* un MEEDY ate id]

unmentionable ● adj. that cannot (properly) be mentioned. ● n. (in *pl.*) *jocular* undergarments.

unmerciful adj. merciless. □ **unmercifully** adv.

unmindful adj. (often foll. by *of*) not mindful; unaware.

unmissable adj. that cannot or should not be missed.

unmistakable adj. that cannot be mistaken. □ **unmistakably** adv.

unmitigated adj. **1** pure, complete. **2** absolute. [*Say* un MITTA gate id]

unmotivated adj. without motivation; without a motive.

unmoved adj. **1** not moved. **2** not changed in one's purpose. **3** not affected by emotion. □ **unmoving** adj.

unmusical adj. **1** not pleasing to the ear. **2** unskilled in or indifferent to music.

unnatural adj. **1** contrary to nature; not normal. **2** extremely cruel or wicked. **3** artificial. □ **unnaturally** adv.

unnecessary adj. **1** not necessary. **2** more than is necessary. □ **unnecessarily** adv.

[*Say* un NESSA sare ee, un nessa SARE uh lee]

unnerve v. (**unnerves, unnerved, unnerving**) deprive of strength or resolution. ☐ **unnerving** adj. **unnervingly** adv.

unobtrusive adj. not making oneself noticed. ☐ **unobtrusively** adv. [*Say* un ub TRUCE iv]

unofficial adj. not officially authorized or confirmed ☐ **unofficially** adv.

unoriginal adj. lacking originality.

unorthodox adj. not orthodox. ☐ **unorthodoxy** n. [*Say* un ORTHA docks, un ORTHA docksy]

unpack v. **1** open and remove the contents of (luggage etc.). **2** take out from a package etc.

unpaid adj. (of a debt or a person) not paid.

unpalatable adj. **1** not pleasant to taste. **2** (of an idea etc.) disagreeable. [*Say* un PALA tuh bull]

unparalleled adj. having no parallel or equal.

unpardonable adj. that cannot be pardoned. ☐ **unpardonably** adv.

unplanned adj. not planned.

unpleasant adj. not pleasant; disagreeable. ☐ **unpleasantly** adv. **unpleasantness** n.

unplug v. (**unplugs, unplugged, unplugging**) **1** disconnect an electrical device by removing its plug from the socket. **2** unclog.

unplugged adj. **1** that has been unplugged. **2** (of rock music etc.) played on instruments without electric amplification.

unpolished adj. **1** not polished. **2** without refinement; crude.

unpopular adj. not popular; not liked. ☐ **unpopularity** n.

unprecedented adj. **1** having no precedent. **2** new. ☐ **unprecedentedly** adv. [*Say* un PRESSA dent id]

unpredictable adj. that cannot be predicted. ☐ **unpredictability** n. **unpredictably** adv.

unpremeditated adj. not deliberately planned; unintentional. [*Say* un pre MEDITATE id]

unprepossessing adj. not attractive. [*Say* un pre POSSESSING]

unpretentious adj. simple, modest. [*Say* un pre TEN shuss]

unprincipled adj. lacking or not based on good moral principles. [*Say* un PRIN sip pulled]

unprintable adj. that cannot be printed, esp. because too indecent etc.

unproductive adj. not productive.

unprofessional adj. **1** contrary to professional standards of behaviour etc. **2** amateur. ☐ **unprofessionally** adv.

unpromising adj. not likely to turn out well.

unprotected adj. **1** not protected. **2** (of sexual intercourse) performed without a condom etc.

unproven adj. (also **unproved**) not proven.

unprovoked adj. (of an act) without provocation.

unpublished adj. not published.

unqualified adj. **1 a** not having the necessary qualifications. **b** not competent. **2** complete.

unquestionable adj. that cannot be disputed or doubted. ☐ **unquestionably** adv.

unquestioned adj. **1** not disputed or doubted. **2** not interrogated.

unquestioning adj. asking no questions. ☐ **unquestioningly** adv.

unquiet adj. **1** restless, agitated. **2** anxious.

unquote adv. (in speech etc.) indicating the end of a quotation.

unravel v. (**unravels, unravelled, unravelling**) **1** cause to be no longer tangled. **2** solve (a mystery etc.). **3** undo (a knitted fabric). **4** become undone. **5** come apart.

unread adj. **1** not read. **2** (of a person) not well-read. [*Say* un RED]

unreadable adj. **1** too dull or difficult to be worth reading. **2** illegible.

unreal adj. **1** not real. **2** imaginary. **3** slang incredible. ☐ **unreality** n.

unrealistic adj. not realistic. ☐ **unrealistically** adv.

unrealized adj. not achieved.

unreason n. lack of reasonable thought. ☐ **unreasoning** adj.

unreasonable adj. **1** going beyond the limits of what is reasonable or equitable. **2** not based on reason. ☐ **unreasonableness** n. **unreasonably** adv.

unrecognized adj. not recognized.

unreconstructed adj. not converted to the current political orthodoxy.

unrefined adj. not refined.

unregenerate ● adj. not reforming; obstinately wrong or bad. ● n. an unregenerate person. [*Say* un re JENNER it]

unreleased *adj.* (of a recording, film, etc.) not released.

unrelenting *adj.* **1** not relenting or yielding. **2** unmerciful. **3** not abating. □ **unrelentingly** *adv.*

unreliable *adj.* not reliable. □ **unreliability** *n.* **unreliably** *adv.*

unrelieved *adj.* **1** lacking variation; boring. **2** not aided.

unremitting *adj.* never relaxing or slackening, incessant. □ **unremittingly** *adv.*

unrepeatable *adj.* **1** that cannot be done again. **2** too indecent to be said again.

unrepentant *adj.* not repentant. □ **unrepentantly** *adv.*

unrepresentative *adj.* not representative.

unrequited *adj.* **1** (of love etc.) not reciprocated. **2** (of a yearning etc.) not satisfied. [*Say* un re QUITE id]

unreserved *adj.* **1** not reserved. **2** without reservations; absolute. □ **unreservedly** *adv.* [*Say* un re ZURVD, un re ZURV id lee]

unresolved *adj.* (of a problem, dispute, etc.) not resolved.

unrest *n.* a state of disturbance accompanied by angry protest etc.

unrestrained *adj.* not restrained.

unrestricted *adj.* not limited or restricted.

unrivalled *adj.* having no equal; peerless. [*Say* un RYE vuld]

unroll *v.* **1** open out from a rolled-up state. **2** spread out, display.

unruffled *adj.* **1** calm. **2** not physically ruffled.

unruly *adj.* (**unrulier, unruliest**) disorderly. □ **unruliness** *n.* [*Say* un RUE lee, un RUE lee ness]

unsaid *adj.* not said or uttered.

unsaleable *adj.* (also **unsalable**) not saleable.

unsatisfactory *adj.* poor, unacceptable.

unsaturated *adj.* (of a fat or oil) having double or triple bonds in its molecule and therefore more easily processed by the body. [*Say* un SATCH a rate id]

unsavoury *adj.* (also **unsavory**) **1** morally offensive; unpleasant. **2** (of a taste or smell) unpleasant.

unscathed *adj.* without suffering any injury. [*SCATHE rhymes with* BATHE]

unschooled *adj.* **1** uneducated, untaught. **2** not trained; undisciplined.

unscientific *adj.* not in accordance with scientific principles. □ **unscientifically** *adv.*

unscramble *v.* (**unscrambles, unscrambled, unscrambling**) restore from a scrambled state.

unscrew *v.* **1** unfasten or be unfastened by twisting like a screw. **2** loosen (a screw etc.).

unscrupulous *adj.* having no scruples, unprincipled. □ **unscrupulously** *adv.* [*Say* un SCREW pyoo lus]

unseasonable *adj.* (of weather) not appropriate to the season. □ **unseasonably** *adv.*

unseasonal *adj.* unusual or inappropriate for the time or season.

unseasoned *adj.* **1** not flavoured with salt, herbs, etc. **2** (of timber) not matured. **3** inexperienced.

unseat *v.* **1** remove from power or office. **2** dislodge from a saddle or seat.

unseeing *adj.* **1** not observant. **2** blind. □ **unseeingly** *adv.*

unseemly *adj.* (**unseemlier, unseemliest**) **1** indecent. **2** unbecoming.

unseen *adj.* **1** not seen. **2** invisible.

unselfconscious *adj.* not shy or embarrassed. □ **unselfconsciously** *adv.*

unserviceable *adj.* unfit for use.

unsettle *v.* (**unsettles, unsettled, unsettling**) make anxious; disturb. □ **unsettling** *adj.*

unsettled *adj.* **1** uneasy. **2** lacking stability. **3** unresolved. **4** (of a region) not populated.

unsexy *adj.* (**unsexier, unsexiest**) **1** not sexually attractive. **2** not fashionable or exciting.

unshakable *adj.* (also **unshakeable**) that cannot be shaken.

unsheathe *v.* (**unsheathes, unsheathed, unsheathing**) remove (a knife etc.) from a sheath.

unsightly *adj.* unpleasant to look at, ugly.

unsigned *adj.* **1** not signed. **2** without a contract.

unskilled *adj.* lacking or not needing special skill or training.

unsociable *adj.* disliking the company of others. [*Say* un SO shuh bull]

unsocial *adj.* **1** not social. **2** outside the normal working day. **3** anti-social.

unsolicited *adj.* not asked for. [*Say* un suh LISS it id]

unsophisticated *adj.* **1** not having much experience of the world and social situations. **2** not complicated; basic. [*Say* un suh FISTA kate id]

unsought *adj.* **1** not sought for. **2** without being requested. [*Say* un SOT]

unsound *adj.* **1** unhealthy, diseased. **2** rotten, not safe. **3 a** not based on sound evidence or reasoning. **b** unorthodox. □ **of unsound mind** insane.

unsparing *adj.* **1** giving freely. **2** uncaring.

unspeakable *adj.* **1** that cannot be expressed in words. **2** indescribably bad. □ **unspeakably** *adv.*

unspecified *adj.* not specified.

unspoiled *adj.* (also esp. *Brit.* **unspoilt**) not spoiled, esp. not marred by development.

unspoken *adj.* **1** understood without being expressed verbally. **2** not uttered.

unsportsmanlike *adj.* (of behaviour etc.) unseemly; unfair.

unstable *adj.* **1** not stable. **2** changeable. **3** showing a tendency to sudden mental or emotional changes. **4** (of an air mass) likely to produce precipitation.

unsteady *adj.* (**unsteadier**, **unsteadiest**) **1** not steady or firm. **2** not uniform or regular. □ **unsteadily** *adv.* **unsteadiness** *n.*

unstick *v.* (**unsticks**, **unstuck**, **unsticking**) separate (a thing stuck to another). □ **come unstuck** *informal* come to grief.

unstinting *adj.* lavish. □ **unstintingly** *adv.*

unstoppable *adj.* that cannot be stopped or prevented. □ **unstoppably** *adv.*

unstressed *adj.* **1** (of a word etc.) not pronounced with stress. **2** not subjected to stress.

unstructured *adj.* **1** not structured. **2** informal.

unsuccessful *adj.* not successful. □ **unsuccessfully** *adv.*

unsuitable *adj.* not suitable.

unsuited *adj.* not suited (to); not fit (for).

unsung *adj.* unrecognized, unknown.

unsure *adj.* not sure.

unsuspecting *adj.* not suspecting.

unswerving *adj.* **1** steady, constant. **2** not turning aside. □ **unswervingly** *adv.*

unsympathetic *adj.* not sympathetic. □ **unsympathetically** *adv.*

untangle *v.* (**untangles**, **untangled**, **untangling**) **1** free from a tangled state. **2** free from entanglement.

untapped *adj.* not (yet) tapped.

untaught *adj.* **1** not instructed by teaching. **2** natural.

untenable *adj.* (of an argument, position, etc.) not tenable. [*Say* un TEN a bull]

untended *adj.* neglected.

untested *adj.* not tested or proved.

unthinkable *adj.* **1** that cannot be imagined. **2** *informal* highly unlikely or undesirable.

unthinking *adj.* **1** not thinking.

2 characterized by thoughtlessness. □ **unthinkingly** *adv.*

untidy *adj.* (**untidier**, **untidiest**) **1** not arranged tidily. **2** not inclined to be tidy. □ **untidily** *adv.* **untidiness** *n.*

untie *v.* (**unties**, **untied**, **untying**) **1** undo (a knot etc.). **2** unfasten the cords etc. of.

until ● *prep.* **1** up to or as late as. **2** up to the time of. ● *conj.* **1** up to the time when. **2** so long that.

untimely *adj.* **1** happening or done at an unsuitable time. **2** (esp. of death) happening too soon. □ **untimeliness** *n.*

unto *prep.* *archaic* to.

untold *adj.* **1** not told. **2** not (able to be) counted or measured.

untouchable ● *adj.* **1** that may not be harmed, criticized, etc. **2** that cannot be matched or rivalled. ● *n.* a member of the lowest caste of Hindu society. □ **untouchability** *n.*

untouched *adj.* **1** not touched. **2** not harmed, modified, used, or tasted. **3** not affected by emotion.

untoward *adj.* **1** unseemly, improper. **2** unexpected or awkward.

untracked *adj.* **1** not marked with tracks. **2** unexplored. **3** not traced or followed.

untrammelled *adj.* not impeded or constrained.

untried *adj.* **1** not tried or tested. **2** inexperienced.

untrue *adj.* **1** not true. **2** not faithful or loyal.

untruth *n.* a false statement.

unturned *adj.* not turned. □ **leave no stone unturned** explore every possibility.

untutored *adj.* **1** uneducated. **2** simple, unsophisticated.

unused *adj.* **1 a** not in use. **b** not used. **2** not accustomed.

unusual *adj.* **1** not usual. **2** remarkable, strange. □ **unusually** *adv.*

unutterable *adj.* beyond description. □ **unutterably** *adv.*

unvarnished *adj.* **1** not varnished. **2** plain and straightforward.

unveil *v.* **1** remove a veil or covering from. **2** show or announce publicly for the first time. □ **unveiling** *n.*

unvoiced *adj.* **1** not expressed. **2** (of a vocal sound) uttered without vibration of the vocal cords.

unwanted *adj.* not or no longer desired.

unwarranted *adj.* **1** unauthorized. **2** not justified.

unwary *adj.* **1** not cautious. **2** not aware of

danger etc. □ **unwariness** n. [Say un WARE ee]

unwashed adj. **1** not washed. **2** not usually washed.

unwavering adj. not wavering. □ **unwaveringly** adv.

unwelcome adj. not welcome or acceptable.

unwell adj. ill.

unwholesome adj. **1** unhealthy. **2** unhealthy-looking.

unwieldy adj. (**unwieldier**, **unwieldiest**) cumbersome or hard to manage, owing to size, shape, etc. [Say un WHEEL dee]

unwilling adj. not willing; reluctant. □ **unwillingly** adv. **unwillingness** n.

unwind v. (**unwinds, unwound, unwinding**) **1** draw out (a thing that has been wound). **2** informal relax.

unwise adj. not wise; foolish. □ **unwisely** adv.

unwitting adj. **1 a** not aware of being the thing described. **b** unaware. **2** unintentional, inadvertent. □ **unwittingly** adv.

unwonted adj. not customary or usual. [Sounds like UNWANTED]

unworkable adj. impracticable.

unworldly adj. **1** spiritually-minded. **2** spiritual.

unworthy adj. (**unworthier**, **unworthiest**) **1** not worthy or befitting the character of a person etc. **2** having insufficient merit or worth. □ **unworthiness** n.

unwound[1] adj. not wound or wound up.

unwound[2] past and past participle of UNWIND.

unwrap v. (**unwraps, unwrapped, unwrapping**) **1** remove the wrapping from. **2** open or unfold. **3** reveal, disclose.

unwritten adj. **1** not written. **2** (of a law etc.) resting originally on custom or judicial decision. **3** (of a convention etc.) implicit.

unyielding adj. **1** not yielding. **2** firm, obstinate.

unzip v. (**unzips, unzipped, unzipping**) **1** unfasten the zipper of. **2** Computing decompress (a compressed file).

up ● adv. 1 at, in, or towards a higher place or position **2** to or in a place regarded as higher. **3** informal ahead etc. as indicated. **4 a** to or in an erect position. **b** to or in a prepared position. **5** in a stronger or winning position. **6** to the place where someone is. **7** at or to a higher price or value. **8** in a state of completion. **9** into a compact or secure state. **10** out of bed.

11 (of the sun etc.) having risen. **12** happening. **13** informed. **14** upstairs. **● prep. 1** upward along, through, or into. **2** from the bottom to the top of. **3** along. **● adj. 1** directed upward. **2** ready, enthusiastic. **● v. (ups, upped, upping) 1** informal begin abruptly to say or do. **2** increase or raise. □ **on the up and up** informal on the level. **something is up** informal something unusual is happening. **up against 1** in or into contact with. **2** informal confronted with. **up and around** (or **about, doing**) having risen from bed. **up and down 1** back and forth (along). **2** in every direction. **3** informal in varying health or spirits. **up on** informed about. **up with** interj. expressing support for. **what's up?** informal **1** what is going on? **2** what is the matter?

up-and-coming adj. informal likely to succeed. □ **up-and-comer** n.

up and running adj. & adv. functioning.

upbeat ● n. a beat not accented in music. **● adj.** informal cheerful.

upbraid v. chide or reproach.

upbringing n. the way in which a child is brought up; education.

UPC n. (pl. **UPCs**) UNIVERSAL PRODUCT CODE.

upchuck v. & n. slang vomit.

upcoming adj. forthcoming.

upcountry adv. & adj. inland.

update ● v. (updates, updated, updating) 1 make more modern or up-to-date. **2** provide with the latest information. **● n. 1** an act of updating. **2** an updated version. □ **updated** adj.

updraft n. an upward draft.

upend v. **1** set or become upside down. **2** knock over.

upfront informal **● adv.** (usu. **up front**) **1** at the front; in front. **2** (of payments) in advance. **● adj. 1** honest, frank. **2** (of payments) made in advance.

upgrade ● v. (upgrades, upgraded, upgrading) 1 raise in rank etc. **2** improve (equipment etc.). **3** replace with improved versions. **4** move to a higher category in a hierarchy. **● n. 1** an act of upgrading something. **2** an upgraded piece of equipment etc.□ **upgradeable** adj. **upgrader** n.

upheaval n. **1** a violent or sudden change or disruption. **2** an upward displacement of the earth's crust.

uphill ● adv. towards the top of a hill, slope, etc. **● adj. 1** sloping up. **2** difficult. **● n.** an upward slope.

uphold v. (**upholds, upheld, upholding**) **1** confirm or maintain. **2** give support to. **3** maintain (a custom etc.). □ **upholder** n.

upholster v. provide (furniture) with upholstery. □**upholsterer** n. [Say up HOLE stir]

upholstery n. **1** textile covering, padding, etc., for furniture. **2** an upholsterer's work. [Say up HOLE stir ee]

U-pick ● adj. designating an orchard or farm where customers pick produce directly. ● n. such a farm or orchard.

upkeep n. **1** maintenance in good condition **2** the cost of this.

upland n. high or hilly country.

uplift ● v. **1** raise. **2** elevate morally or spiritually. ● n. **1** an act of uplifting. **2** the raising of part of the earth's surface. **3** informal a morally or spiritually elevating influence. **4** support for the bust etc. from a garment. □**uplifting** adj.

uplink ● n. a communications link to a satellite. ● v. send by an uplink.

upload ● v. **1** transfer (data) to a larger storage device. **2** Cdn shift (costs) from a lower level of government to higher one. ● n. a transfer of this type.

upmarket adj. & adv. upscale.

upon prep. = ON.

upper ● adj. **1** situated above another part. **2** higher in position or status. **3** (Upper) situated on higher ground. ● n. **1** the part of a boot or shoe above the sole. **2** slang a stimulant drug.

Upper Canadian n. Cdn **1** hist. a native or inhabitant of the former British colony of Upper Canada (1791–1841), now the southern part of Ontario. **2** esp. Maritimes a native or inhabitant of Ontario. □**Upper Canadian** adj.

upper case ● adj. designating capital letters. ● n. a capital letter.

upper class ● n. the highest class of society. ● adj. (**upper-class**) of the upper class.

upper crust n. informal the upper class.

uppercut n. an upward blow delivered with the arm bent.

upper hand n. dominance; an advantage.

upper house n. (also **upper chamber**) the usu. smaller body in a bicameral legislature, esp. (in Canada) the Senate.

upper middle class ● n. the class between the middle and upper classes. ● adj. (**upper-middle-class**) of the upper middle class.

uppermost ● adj. **1** highest in place or rank. **2** predominant. ● adv. at or to the uppermost position.

uppity adj. informal arrogant, snobbish, rude. □**uppitiness** (also **uppityness**) n.

upraise v. (**upraises**, **upraised**, **upraising**) raise to a higher level.

upright ● adj. **1** erect, vertical. **2** (of a piano) with vertical strings. **3** righteous; strictly honourable or honest. ● n. **1** a post or rod fixed upright. **2** an upright piano. □**uprightness** n.

uprising n. **1** a rebellion or revolt. **2** the action of rising.

upriver adj. & adv. at or towards a point nearer the source of a river.

uproar n. a loud and noisy disturbance.

uproarious adj. **1** very noisy. **2** provoking loud laughter. □**uproariously** adv. [Say up ROAR ee us]

uproot v. **1** pull (a plant etc.) up from the ground. **2** displace (a person) from an accustomed location.

upsadaisy interj. upsy-daisy.

upscale adj. & adv. toward or relating to the more affluent sector of the market.

upset ● v. (**upsets**, **upset**, **upsetting**) **1** overturn or be overturned. **2** disturb or disrupt. ● n. **1** a state of upsetting or being upset. **2** a surprising victory over a favoured opponent. ● adj. **1** disturbed. **2** distressed. □**upsetting** adj.

upshot n. the eventual outcome or conclusion.

upside n. informal the positive aspect of something.

upside down ● adv. **1** with the upper part where the lower part should be. **2** in or into total disorder. ● adj. inverted.

upstage ● adj. & adv. nearer the back of a theatre stage. ● v. (**upstages**, **upstaged**, **upstaging**) divert attention from (a person) to oneself.

upstairs ● adv. **1** to or on an upper floor. **2** to or in a more influential position. ● adj. situated upstairs. ● n. an upper floor.

upstanding adj. honest or straightforward.

upstart ● n. a person who has risen suddenly to prominence. ● adj. **1** that is an upstart. **2** of or like an upstart.

upstate adj. & adv. of or to the part of a US state remote from its large cities.

upstream ● adv. against the flow of a stream etc. ● adj. moving upstream.

upsurge n. **1** an upward surge. **2** a rapid increase.

upswing n. an upward trend.

upsy-daisy interj. expressing encouragement to a child who is being lifted.

uptake n. **1** informal understanding; comprehension. **2** absorption of something by a living system.

uptempo adj. & adv. at a fast or increased tempo.

uptick *n.* a small increase.

uptight *adj. informal* **1** nervously tense or angry. **2** rigidly conventional.

up-to-date *adj.* meeting or familiar with the latest developments or fashion.

up-to-the-minute *adj.* latest.

uptown ● *adj.* **1** of or in the upper or northward part of a city outside of downtown. **2** of or characteristic of an affluent area or people. ● *n.* **1** *Cdn* the central business district, esp. of a small town. **2** the upper or northward part of a city outside of downtown. ● *adv.* in or into the area designated as uptown.

upturn *n.* an upward trend; an improvement.

upturned *adj.* turned upwards or upside down.

upward ● *adv.* (also **upwards**) towards what is higher or superior. ● *adj.* moving or leading upward. □ **upwards of** more than.

upwardly mobile *adj.* able or aspiring to advance socially. □ **upward mobility** *n.*

upwelling *n.* **1** a welling upward. **2** the water that has risen in this way.

upwind *adj. & adv.* against the direction of the wind.

uranium *n.* a heavy radioactive metallic element which is used as a source of nuclear energy. [*Say* yoor AINY um]

urban *adj.* having to do with a town or city. **2** designating music, or radio stations playing it, performed by black artists.

urbane *adj.* elegant and refined; courteous, sophisticated. [*Say* er BANE]

urbanism *n.* **1** urbanization. **2** the character etc. of a city. **3** a study of city development etc.

urbanite *n.* a resident of a city.

urbanity *n.* (*pl.* **urbanities**) **1** an urbane quality or manner. **2** urban life.

urbanize *v.* (**urbanizes, urbanized, urbanizing**) make a mainly rural area more like a city. □ **urbanization** *n.*

urban legend *n.* a story, not verifiable and usu. untrue, widely recounted as if true.

urban planner *n.* a person who plans the development of urban communities as a profession. □ **urban planning** *n.*

urban renewal *n.* the process of rejuvenating derelict districts of a city.

urchin *n.* a poor, dirty, and ill-clothed child.

Urdu *n.* a language of Pakistan and India closely related to Hindi. [*Say* ER doo]

urea *n.* a waste product of mammals excreted in the urine. [*Say* yoo REE uh]

urethane ● *n.* a synthetic resin used esp. in paints, adhesives, and foams. ● *v.* (**urethanes, urethaned, urethaning**) cover a surface with a paint or varnish containing urethane. [*Say* YOORA thane]

urethra *n.* the tube or canal through which urine is carried out of the body from the bladder, and which in the male also conveys semen. □ **urethral** *adj.* [*Say* yoo REETH ruh, yoo REETH rull]

urge ● *v.* (**urges, urged, urging**) **1** drive or hasten with force or encouragement. **2** encourage or entreat earnestly. ● *n.* a strong impulse, desire, etc. □ **urging** *n.*

urgent *adj.* **1** demanding or requiring immediate action or attention. **2** insistent. □ **urgency** *n.* (*pl.* **urgencies**) **urgently** *adv.*

uric acid *n.* an almost insoluble crystalline acid which is excreted in the urine of mammals, birds, reptiles, and insects. [*Say* YOOR ick]

urinal *n.* **1** a plumbing fixture for men to urinate into. **2** any receptacle for urination.

urinalysis *n.* (*pl.* **urinalyses**) the analysis of urine. [*Say* urine ALA sis *for the singular,* urine ALA seez *for the plural*]

urinary *adj.* **1** of or relating to urine. **2** affecting or occurring in the urinary system.

urinate *v.* (**urinates, urinated, urinating**) discharge urine. □ **urination** *n.*

urine *n.* the pale yellow fluid containing waste products filtered from the blood by the kidneys, stored in the bladder, and discharged at intervals through the urethra.

URL *n. Computing* the address used to specify the location of a website on the Internet.

urn *n.* **1** a large decorative vase with a rounded body and a pedestal. **2** any usu. ornamental vessel used to store the ashes of the cremated dead. **3** a large metal container with a tap, in which coffee etc is made and kept hot.

urology *n.* the branch of medicine that deals with the kidneys and urinary tract. □ **urologist** *n.* [*Say* yoor OLLA jee, yoor OLLA jist]

Ursuline ● *n.* a nun of an Augustinian order founded in 1535 for nursing the sick and teaching girls. ● *adj.* of this order. [*Say* URSE yoo lin *or* URSE yoo line]

Uruguayan *n.* a person from Uruguay. □ **Uruguayan** *adj.* [*Say* yoora GWAY un]

us *pron.* objective case of WE.

usable *adj.* (also **useable**) that can be used. □ **usability** *n.*

usage *n.* **1** the action of using something or of being used. **2 a** habitual or customary practice. **b** established or customary use of words in a language.

use ● *v.* (**uses, used, using**) **1** employ (something) for a purpose. **2 a** (in *past*) did repeatedly or existed in the past. **b** (usu. in *passive*) accustomed. **3** exploit for one's own ends. **4** treat in a specified manner. **5** take (drugs etc.) regularly. ● *n.* **1** the act of using or the state of being used. **2** the manner of using something. **3** the right or power of using. **4** value, usefulness. **5** need or occasion for employing something. **6** habitual or common practice. □ **have no use for 1** do not need. **2** be impatient with. **it's** (or **there's**) **no use** it would be pointless to. **make use of 1** employ. **2** benefit from. **use up 1** use all of. **2** find a use for. **3** exhaust.

used *adj.* having been previously owned; second-hand.

useful *adj.* **1** that can be used for a practical purpose. **2** of use to someone. **3** *informal* reasonably successful. □ **make oneself useful** be helpful. □ **usefully** *adv.* **usefulness** *n.*

useless *adj.* **1** failing to fulfill the intended purpose. **2** serving no purpose. **3** *informal* incompetent, ineffectual. □ **uselessly** *adv.* **uselessness** *n.*

Usenet *n.* a service designed to help users access information on a network. [Say YOOZ net]

user *n.* **1** a person who uses or operates something. **2** *informal* a drug addict. **3** a person who exploits others.

user-friendly *adj.* **1** designed to make the user's task as easy as possible. **2** easy to use or understand. □ **user-friendliness** *n.*

user group *n.* *Computing* a newsgroup exchanging technical information etc.

username *n.* (also **user ID**) *Computing* an identification used in conjunction with a password by a person with access to a computer network.

usher ● *n.* **1** a person who shows people to their seats in a theatre, stadium, church, etc. **2** an attendant at a wedding, responsible for showing guests to their seats. ● *v.* **1** show or guide somewhere. **2** be the forerunner of (an era etc.).

usherette *n.* a woman who shows people to their seats.

Usher of the Black Rod *n.* *Cdn* = BLACK ROD.

usual ● *adj.* such as commonly occurs; customary, regular. ● *n.* *informal* **1** (the

usual) what is commonly said or done etc. **2** (preceded by *the* etc.) the drink or meal a person habitually orders. □ **usually** *adv.*

usurious *adj.* **1** relating to usury. **2** exorbitant, excessive. [Say yoo ZUR ee us or yoo ZHUR ee us]

usurp *v.* **1** seize or assume (another's position or authority) by force. **2** take possession of (land etc.) unlawfully. □ **usurpation** *n.* **usurper** *n.* [Say yoo SURP or yoo ZURP]

usury *n.* the practice of lending money at esp. an exorbitant rate of interest. □ **usurer** *n.* [Say YOO zur ee or YOO zhur ee]

utensil *n.* a tool or implement for domestic use.

uterus *n.* (*pl.* **uteruses** or **uteri**) the womb. □ **uterine** *adj.* [Say YOO tur us for the singular, YOO tur eye for the plural, YOO tur in]

utilitarian *adj.* **1** designed to be useful or practical rather than attractive. **2** of or pertaining to utilitarianism. [Say yoo tilla TERRY un]

utilitarianism *n.* the doctrine that the guiding principle of conduct should be to achieve the greatest happiness for the greatest number of people. [Say yoo tilla TERRY un ism]

utility ● *n.* (*pl.* **utilities**) **1** the condition of being useful or beneficial. **2** in *pl.*) electricity, natural gas, water, etc. as provided to the public. ● *adj.* designating things made for utility.

utilize *v.* (**utilizes, utilized, utilizing**) make practical and effective use of. □ **utilization** *n.*

utmost ● *adj.* **1** greatest; most extreme. **2** furthest; outermost. ● *n.* (**the utmost**) **1** the greatest in degree, amount, or extent. **2** the extreme limit. □ **do one's utmost** do all that one can.

utopia *n.* (*pl.* **utopias**) **1** an imaginary or hypothetical perfect place. **2** an impossibly ideal scheme. [Say yoo TOPE ee uh]

utopian ● *adj.* **1** having to do with a utopia. **2** idealistic. ● *n.* an idealistic reformer. □ **utopianism** *n.* [Say yoo TOPE ee un]

utter[1] *adj.* complete, total. □ **utterly** *adv.*

utter[2] *v.* **1** emit audibly. **2** speak or say.

utterance *n.* **1** the action of saying something aloud. **2** a spoken word, statement, or vocal sound.

uttermost *adj.* & *n.* utmost.

U-turn ● *n.* **1** an act of driving a vehicle in a U-shaped course so as to face the opposite way. **2** a reversal of policy. ● *v.* perform a U-turn.

UV *abbr.* ultraviolet.

UV Index *n.* an index used to represent the intensity of the sun's ultraviolet rays.

uvula *n.* (*pl.* **uvulae**) a fleshy extension of the soft palate hanging above the throat.

[*Say* YOO view luh *or* UV yoo luh *for the singular,* YOO view lee *for the plural*]

Uzbek *n.* **1** a member of a Turkic people living mainly in Uzbekistan. **2** the language of this people. [*Say* OOZ beck *(with* OO *as in* FOOT*)*]

Uzi *n.* a type of submachine gun. [*Sounds like* OOZY]

Vv

V¹ *n.* (also **v**) (*pl.* **Vs** or **V's**) **1** the twenty-second letter of the alphabet. **2** (as a Roman numeral) five.

V² *symb.* volt(s).

v. *abbr.* **1** verse. **2** verso. **3** versus.

V6 *n.* (*pl.* **V6's**) an engine with six cylinders forming a V shape.

V8 *n.* (*pl.* **V8's**) an engine with eight cylinders forming a V shape.

vac *n. informal* a vacuum cleaner.

vacancy *n.* (*pl.* **vacancies**) **1** the state of being vacant or empty. **2** an available room in a hotel, apartment building, etc. **3** a job opening. [*Say* VAY kun see]

vacant *adj.* **1** empty. **2** (of land etc.) uninhabited. **3** not occupied. **4** (of a position) available. **5** exhibiting a lack of attention or thought. □ **vacantly** *adv.* [*Say* VAY k'nt]

vacate *v.* (**vacates, vacated, vacating**) **1** leave (a place). **2** give up tenure of (a post etc.). [*Say* VAY kate *or* vuh KATE]

vacation ● *n.* a period of time spent away from work or school etc; a holiday. ● *v.* take or spend a vacation. □ **vacationer** *n.*

vacation pay *n. Cdn* the wages which an employee is entitled, under federal law, to receive either as paid vacation, or in lieu of paid vacation.

vaccinate *v.* (**vaccinates, vaccinated, vaccinating**) immunize. □ **vaccination** *n.* [*Say* VAC sin ate]

vaccine *n.* a substance used to stimulate the production of antibodies and procure immunity from a disease. [*Say* vac SEEN *or* VAC seen]

vacillate *v.* (**vacillates, vacillated, vacillating**) waver between different opinions, actions, etc. □ **vacillating** *adj.* **vacillation** *n.* [*Say* VASS ill ate]

vacuity *n.* (*pl.* **vacuities**) a lack of intelligence or thought. [*Say* vuh CUE it ee]

vacuole *n.* a small cavity or vesicle in organic tissue. [*Say* VAC yoo ul]

vacuous *adj.* **1** not intelligent, expressionless. **2** meaningless. □ **vacuousness** *n.* [*Say* VAC yoo us]

vacuum ● *n.* **1** a space entirely devoid of matter. **2** a space from which the air has been completely or partly removed. **3 a** a place marked by an absence of the usual or expected contents. **b** a state of isolation. **4** (also **vacuum cleaner**) an electrical appliance for removing dust by suction. ● *v.* clean with a vacuum cleaner.

vacuum packed *adj.* **1** (esp. of food) sealed in an airtight package from which air has been removed. **2** sealed and made airtight.

vacuum tube *n.* a sealed glass tube containing a near-vacuum for the free passage of electric current.

vagabond ● *n.* a tramp or hobo, esp. an idle or dishonest one. ● *adj.* roving or wandering.

vagaries *pl. n.* unexpected and inexplicable changes. [*Say* VAY guh reez]

vagina *n.* the canal leading from the vulva to the cervix in women and most female mammals. □ **vaginal** *adj.* [*Say* vuh JIE nuh, VAJ in ul]

vagrant ● *n.* **1** a person with no settled home or regular work. **2** a person who roams or wanders. ● *adj.* **1** like or relating to a vagrant or vagrancy. **2** wandering. □ **vagrancy** *n.* [*Say* VAY grunt, VAY grun see]

vague *adj.* **1** (of a statement etc.) couched in general or imprecise terms. **2** not definite or clear. **3** lacking physical definiteness of form. **4** inexact in thought or understanding. □ **vaguely** *adv.* **vagueness** *n.*

vain *adj.* **1** having an excessively high opinion of oneself. **2** useless, ineffectual. **3** empty, trivial. □ **in vain** without success; ineffectually. **take a person's name in vain** mention a person's name casually or irreverently. □ **vainly** *adv.*

vainglory *n. literary* extreme vanity. □ **vainglorious** *adj.* [*Say* VAIN glory, vain GLORIOUS]

valance *n.* a short ornamental curtain hung around a bedstead or above a window etc. [*Say* VAL ince *or* VALE ince]

vale *n. literary* a valley.

valedictorian *n.* a person who gives a valedictory. [*Say* valla dick TORY un]

valedictory *n.* (*pl.* **valedictories**) **1** a speech or address given by a student as a part of graduation exercises. **2** any statement or address made upon leaving. [*Say* valla DICK tuh ree]

valence *n.* the number of hydrogen atoms that an atom or group combines with or displaces in the formation of compounds. [*Say* VALE ince]

Valencia orange *n.* a variety of orange with a sweet juicy flesh, few seeds, and thin, smooth peel.

valentine *n.* **1** a note, card, or gift given as a token of love on Valentine's Day. **2** a person to whom one sends such a card.

Valentine's Day *n.* (also **St. Valentine's Day**) Feb. 14, celebrated with the exchange of valentines etc.

valerian *n.* **1** a Eurasian plant that typically bears clusters of small pink or white flowers. **2** a bitter-tasting drug derived from this plant, used as a sedative etc. [*Say* vuh LEERY un]

valet *n.* **1** a male servant who attends to a gentleman's clothes etc. **2** a hotel employee with similar duties for guests. **3** an attendant who parks cars for patrons of a restaurant etc. **4** a rack on which clothing may be hung. [*Say* val AY *or* VAL ay]

Valhalla *n.* **1** *Scandinavian Myth* the hall in which the souls of those who have died in battle feast with Odin. **2** *informal* a place representing a state of bliss. [*Say* val HAL uh]

valiant *adj.* brave, courageous. □ **valiantly** *adv.* [*Say* VALLEY unt]

valid *adj.* **1** (of an argument etc.) sound. **2** legally binding and acceptable. **3** having legitimacy or authority. □ **validly** *adv.*

validate *v.* (**validates, validated, validating**) **1** check or prove the validity of. **2** lend force or validity to. □ **validation** *n.*

validity *n.* **1** the state of being valid. **2** legitimacy, credibility. [*Say* vuh LID it ee]

valise *n.* a small piece of luggage similar to a suitcase. [*Say* vuh LEEZ]

Valium *n.* *proprietary* the drug diazepam used as a tranquilizer and relaxant. [*Say* VALLEY um]

Valkyrie *n.* *Scandinavian Myth* one of the maidens who conducted fallen warriors to Valhalla. [*Say* VAL keery]

valley *n.* (*pl.* **valleys**) **1 a** a low usu. elongated area more or less enclosed by hills. **b** the tract of land drained by a single large river system. **2** any depression or hollow resembling this.

valorize *v.* (**valorizes, valorized, valorizing**) give value or validity to something. □ **valorization** *n.*

valorous *adj.* brave, courageous.

valour *n.* personal courage.

valuable ● *adj.* **1** of material or monetary values. **2** of great use or benefit. ● *n.* (usu. in *pl.*) a valuable thing.

valuation *n.* an estimation of a thing's value.

value ● *n.* **1** the worth, usefulness, or importance of a thing. **2** the amount of money etc. that something is worth. **3** the ability of a thing to serve a specified purpose. **4** (in *pl.*) principles or moral standards. **5** *Music* the length or duration of a note. ● *v.* (**values, valued, valuing**) **1** estimate the value of. **2** consider of worth or importance. □ **valueless** *adj.*

value-added *adj.* **1** (of food, goods, etc.) having extra features or ingredients added to the basic line or model to justify an increase in price. **2** (of a company) offering specialized or extended services.

value-added tax *n.* a tax on the amount by which the value of an article has been increased at each stage of production.

value judgment *n.* an estimate of merit based on personal opinion rather than facts.

valve *n.* **1** a device for controlling the passage of fluid through a pipe. **2** *Anatomy & Zoology* a fold in a hollow organ or blood vessel etc. which allows blood to flow in one direction only. **3** a device for extending the range of pitch of a brass instrument by varying the length of the tube. □ **valved** *adj.*

vamoose *v.* (**vamooses, vamoosed, vamoosing**) *slang* leave, disappear, take off. [*Say* va MOOSE]

vamp¹ ● *n.* **1** the upper front part of a boot or shoe. **2** *Music* a short simple introductory passage or accompaniment. ● *v.* *Music* play as a vamp.

vamp² *informal* ● *n.* a woman who uses sexual attraction to exploit men. ● *v.* behave as a vamp. □ **vampish** *adj.* **vampy** *adj.*

vampire *n.* a ghost or reanimated corpse supposed to leave its grave at night to suck the blood of the living. □ **vampiric** *adj.* [*Say* vam PEER ick]

vampire bat *n.* a small bat that feeds on the blood of mammals or birds using its two sharp incisor teeth. [*Say* vam PEER ick]

van¹ *n.* a covered vehicle for moving goods or people.

van² *n.* a vanguard.

vanadium *n.* a hard grey metallic element, used to strengthen some steels. [*Say* vuh NAY dee um]

Vancouverite *n.* a person from Vancouver.

vandal ● *n.* **1** a person who wilfully destroys or damages property. **2 (Vandal)** a member of a Germanic people that ravaged southern Europe in the 4th–5th centuries. ● *adj.* of or relating to the Vandals. □**vandalism** *n.* **vandalize** *v.* **(vandalizes, vandalized, vandalizing)**

vane *n.* **1** a weather vane. **2** a blade of a screw propeller or a windmill etc. **3** the sight of surveying instruments etc. □**vaned** *adj.*

vanguard *n.* **1** the foremost part of an advancing army or fleet. **2** the leaders of a movement or of opinion etc. [*Say* VAN gard]

Vanier Cup *n.* Cdn a trophy awarded annually to the winner of the Canadian inter-university football championship. [*Say* VAN yay]

vanilla ● *n.* **1 a** a tropical climbing orchid with fragrant flowers. **b** (also **vanilla bean**) the fruit of these. **2** a substance obtained from the vanilla bean, used as a flavouring. ● *adj.* ordinary.

vanish *v.* **(vanishes, vanished, vanishing) 1 a** disappear suddenly. **b** fade away. **2** cease to exist.

vanity *n.* (*pl.* **vanities**) **1 a** excessive pride in one's achievements or appearance. **b** excessive concern with one's physical appearance. **2** the quality of being unimportant or futile. **3** a unit in a bathroom consisting of a sink and countertop with cupboards beneath. **4** a dressing table.

vanquish *v.* **(vanquishes, vanquished, vanquishing)** *literary* conquer or overcome. [*Say* VANG kwish]

vantage *n.* (also **vantage point**) a place affording a good view or prospect. [*Say* VAN tidge]

vapid *adj.* insipid; lacking interest. □**vapidity** *n.* [*Say* VAP id, vuh PIDDA tee]

vaporize *v.* **(vaporizes, vaporized, vaporizing)** convert or be converted into vapour. □**vaporization** *n.* **vaporizer** *n.*

vapour *n.* (also **vapor**) **1** moisture or another substance diffused or suspended in air. **2** *Physics* a gaseous form of a normally liquid or solid substance. □**vaporous** *adj.*

variable ● *adj.* **1 a** that can be varied or adapted. **b** (of a gear) designed to give varying speeds. **2** apt to vary. **3** *Math* (of a quantity) indeterminate. **4** (of wind) tending to change direction. ● *n.* a variable thing or quantity. □**variability** *n.* **variably** *adv.*

variance *n.* **1** difference of opinion. **2** a discrepancy. **3** an official dispensation.

variant ● *adj.* **1** differing in form or details from the main one. **2** having different forms. ● *n.* a variant form etc.

variation *n.* **1** a change or slight difference in condition, amount, or level. **2** a different or distinct form or version. **3** *Music* a repetition of a theme in a changed form. □**variations on a theme** a variety of things that differ slightly but have a strong common element.

varicose *adj.* (of a vein) affected by a condition causing them to become dilated and swollen. [*Say* VARE a cose (COSE rhymes with DOSE)]

varied *adj.* showing variety.

variegated *adj.* **1** (of plants) having leaves containing two or more colours. **2** marked by variety or diversity. [*Say* VARY a gate id]

varietal ● *adj.* **1** esp. Botany & Zoology of or being a variety. **2** (of wine) made from a single variety of grape. ● *n.* a varietal wine. [*Say* va RIOT'll]

variety *n.* (*pl.* **varieties**) **1** diversity. **2** a quantity or collection of different things. **3** a thing which has some differences from others of the same general class. **4** a different form of a thing, quality, etc. **5** *Biology* **a** a subspecies. **b** a cultivar. **6** a mixed sequence of dances, songs, etc.

variety store *n.* a convenience store.

various *adj.* **1** different, diverse. **2** more than one. □**variously** *adv.*

varmint *n.* informal jocular **1** a destructive wild animal. **2** a troublesome person.

varnish ● *n.* a resinous solution used to give a clear hard shiny coating to wood, metal, etc. ● *v.* **(varnishes, varnished, varnishing)** apply varnish to.

varsity *adj.* **1** designating sports played at the university or college level. **2** designating the most advanced level of athletic competition in a high school etc.

Varsol *n.* Cdn proprietary a liquid distilled from petroleum and used esp. as a paint thinner.

vary *v.* **(varies, varied, varying) 1** differ or make different. **2** become or be different. **3** be in proportion to. □**varying** *adj.*

varying hare *n.* the Arctic hare.

vascular *adj.* of or containing vessels for conveying blood or sap etc. [*Say* VASS cue lur]

vas deferens *n.* the duct carrying sperm from the testicle to the urethra. [*Say* vass DEFFA renz]

vase *n.* a vessel used as an ornament or container, esp. for flowers. [*Say* VOZ or VAZE]

vasectomy *n.* (*pl.* **vasectomies**) the surgical removal of part of each vas deferens esp. as a means of sterilization. [*Say* vuh SEKTA me]

Vaseline *n.* *proprietary* a type of petroleum jelly used as an ointment, lubricant, etc.

vassal *n.* **1** *hist.* a man in the Middle Ages who promised to fight for a king or landowner, in return for being given land to live on. **2** a dependent person or country. □ **vassalage** *n.* [*Rhymes with* HASSLE]

vast *adj.* immense, huge; very great. □ **vastly** *adv.* **vastness** *n.*

vat *n.* a large tank or other vessel, esp. for holding liquids.

Vatican *n.* (**the Vatican**) **1** the official residence of the Pope in Rome. **2** papal government.

vaudeville *n.* **1** a form of variety entertainment popular esp. from about 1880 to the early 1930s. **2** a stage play on a trivial theme with interspersed songs. □ **vaudevillian** *adj. & n.* [*Say* VOD vill, vod VILLY un]

vault ● *n.* **1 a** an arched roof. **b** a continuous arch. **c** a set or series of arches. **2** a vault-like covering. **3** an underground chamber. **4** a place of storage, esp. for valuables. **5** an act of vaulting. ● *v.* leap or spring over, esp. using one's hands or a pole to push oneself.

vaulting *n.* **1** arched work in a vaulted roof. **2** a gymnastic exercise in which participants vault over obstacles.

vaunt *v.* *literary* boast about or praise.

vaunted *adj.* highly praised.

V-chip *n.* a device that can be programmed to block any TV program that contains violence, sex, or bad language.

VCR *n.* (*pl.* **VCRs**) an electrical device used for recording and playing back videocassettes.

VD *abbr.* venereal disease.

VDT *abbr.* video display terminal.

veal *n.* calf's flesh.

vector *n.* **1** *Math & Physics* a quantity having direction as well as magnitude, esp. as determining the position of one point in space relative to another. **2** a carrier of disease.

Veda *n.* (in *sing.* or *pl.*) the most ancient Hindu scriptures. □ **Vedic** *adj.* [*Say* VAY duh *or* VEE duh, VAY dick *or* VEE dick]

VE day *n.* May 8, the day marking the Allied victory in Europe in 1945.

veep *n.* *informal* a vice-president.

veer ● *v.* **1** change direction or course, esp. suddenly. **2** (of the wind) change direction

clockwise. ● *n.* a change of course or direction.

veg[1] *n.* *informal* a vegetable or vegetables.

veg[2] *v.* (**vegges, vegged, vegging**) relax in a mindless manner.

vegan ● *n.* a person who does not eat or use animal products. ● *adj.* using or containing no animal products. □ **veganism** *n.* [*Say* VEE gun *or* VAY gun *or* VEDGE un]

vegetable ● *n.* **1** a plant or fungus used for food. **2** *informal* a person who is incapable of normal intellectual activity. ● *adj.* **1** having to do with plants or plant life. **2** of or relating to vegetables as food.

vegetable oil *n.* an oil derived from plants.

vegetal *adj.* of or having the nature of plants. [*Say* VEDGE a tul]

vegetarian ● *n.* a person who does not eat meat. ● *adj.* containing no meat. □ **vegetarianism** *n.*

vegetate *v.* (**vegetates, vegetated, vegetating**) **1** live a predictable or monotonous life. **2** relax in a mindless manner.

vegetation *n.* plant life.

vegetative *adj.* **1** having to do with growth and development as distinct from reproduction. **2** of or relating to vegetation. **3** (of a person) unthinking or inactive. □ **vegetatively** *adv.*

veggie *informal* ● *n.* **1** a vegetable. **2** a vegetarian. ● *adj.* made of vegetables; vegetarian.

vehement *adj.* showing or caused by strong feeling. □ **vehemence** *n.* **vehemently** *adv.* [*Say* VEE a m'nt, VEE a munce]

vehicle *n.* **1** any conveyance for transporting people, goods, etc., esp. on land. **2** a medium for thought, feeling, etc. **3** a liquid etc. as a medium for suspending pigments etc. □ **vehicular** *adj.* [*Say* VEE a cull, vuh HICK yoo lur]

veil ● *n.* **1** a piece of fabric worn, esp. by women, to protect or hide the face. **2** a piece of fabric as part of a nun's headdress, resting on the head and shoulders. **3** a curtain. **4** something that conceals or disguises. ● *v.* cover with or as if with a veil. □ **take the veil** become a nun. □ **veiled** *adj.*

vein ● *n.* **1 a** any of the anatomical tubes by which blood is conveyed to the heart. **b** (in general use) any blood vessel. **2** a rib in the framework of a leaf. **3** a streak of a different colour in wood, marble, etc. **4** a fissure in rock filled with ore or other deposited material. **5** a source of a particular characteristic. **6** a distinctive feature. ● v. fill or cover with or as with veins. □ **veined** adj. **veining** n. **veiny** adj. (**veinier, veiniest**)

Velcro proprietary ● n. a fastener for clothes etc. consisting of two strips of nylon fabric which adhere when pressed together. ● v. (**Velcroes, Velcroed, Velcroing**) fasten with Velcro. □ **Velcroed** adj.

veld n. (also **veldt**) South Africa grassland. [Say VELT]

vellum n. **1** fine parchment originally from the skin of a calf. **2** smooth writing paper imitating vellum.

velocity n. (pl. **velocities**) **1** the measure of the rate of movement in a given direction. **2** speed in a given direction. **3** (in general use) speed. [Say vuh LOSSA tee]

velour n. a fabric with a velvet-like finish. [Say vuh LOOR]

velvet ● n. **1** a closely woven fabric of silk, cotton, etc., with a thick short pile on one side. **2** anything smooth and soft like velvet. ● adj. of or like velvet. □ **velvety** adj.

velveteen n. a cotton fabric with a pile like velvet.

velvet revolution n. a non-violent political revolution, esp. (**Velvet Revolution**) the sequence of events in Czechoslovakia which led to the ending of Communist rule in late 1989.

venal adj. **1** (of a person) willing to act immorally for money. **2** associated with corruption or bribery. □ **venality** n. [Say VEEN ul, vee NALLA tee]

vend v. **1** offer (merchandise) for sale. **2** Law sell.

vendetta n. (pl. **vendettas**) **1** a blood feud in which the family of a murdered person seeks vengeance on the murderer. **2** a prolonged bitter quarrel. [Say ven DETTA]

vending machine n. a coin-operated machine for the sale of small items.

vendor n. **1** Law the seller in a sale. **2** a person who sells, esp. at an outdoor stand etc.

veneer ● n. **1** a thin covering of fine wood etc. applied to a coarser wood. **2** a deceptive outward appearance of a good quality etc. ● v. apply a veneer to.

venerable adj. **1** entitled to veneration on account of character, age, etc. **2** Catholicism as the title of a deceased person who has attained a certain degree of sanctity. **3** as the title of an archdeacon in the Anglican Church. [Say VENNER a bull]

venerate v. (**venerates, venerated, venerating**) **1** regard with deep respect.

2 revere. □ **veneration** n. [Say VENNER ate]

venereal disease n. = SEXUALLY TRANSMITTED DISEASE.

Venetian ● n. **1** a person from Venice. **2** the Italian dialect of Venice. **3** (**venetian**) (also **venetian blind**) a window blind consisting of a number of adjustable horizontal slats. ● adj. of Venice. [Say ven EESH un]

Venezuelan n. a person from Venezuela. □ **Venezuelan** adj. [Say ven iz WAIL un]

vengeance n. **1** punishment inflicted or retribution exacted for a wrong or injury. **2** the desire for revenge. □ **with a vengeance** with great intensity. [Say VEN jince]

vengeful adj. vindictive; seeking vengeance. □ **vengefulness** n.

venial adj. (of a sin or fault) not very serious; not mortal. [Say VEENY ul]

venison n. a deer's flesh as food. [Say VEN iss un or VEN iz un]

Venn diagram n. a diagram representing mathematical sets as intersecting circles, with the intersections representing common elements of the sets.

venom n. **1** a poisonous fluid secreted by snakes, scorpions, etc., usu. transmitted by a bite or sting. **2** malice, spite.

venomous adj. **1** containing or injecting venom. **2** malicious, spiteful. □ **venomously** adv.

venous adj. **1** of or full of veins. **2** (of blood) deoxygenated and of a dusky red colour. [Sounds like VENUS]

vent ● n. **1** (also **vent hole**) a hole or opening allowing motion of air etc. out of or into a confined space. **2** an outlet. **3** a slit in a garment. **4** a flue of a chimney. ● v. **1** a make a vent in. **b** provide with a vent. **2** give free expression to. □ **vent one's spleen on** scold or ill-treat without cause.

ventilate v. (**ventilates, ventilated, ventilating**) **1** a cause air to circulate freely in (a room etc.). **b** provide with a vent or vents. **2** submit (a grievance etc.) to public discussion. **3** Medical **a** oxygenate. **b** force air into (the lungs). □ **ventilation** n.

ventilator n. **1** an appliance or aperture for ventilating a room etc. **2** an apparatus for maintaining artificial breathing.

ventral adj. **1** Anatomy & Zoology of or on the abdomen. **2** Botany of the front or lower surface. □ **ventrally** adv.

ventricle n. either of the two muscular lower chambers of the heart, which pump the blood to the arteries. □ **ventricular** adj. [Say VEN trickle, ven TRICK yoo lur]

ventriloquism *n.* the skill of speaking so that the sounds seem to come from the speaker's dummy or another source. □ **ventriloquist** *n.* [Say ven TRILLA quiz um, ven TRILLA quist]

venture ● *n.* **1** an undertaking of a risk. **2** a business enterprise involving risk. ● *v.* (**ventures**, **ventured**, **venturing**) **1** dare; not be afraid. **2** dare to put forward (an opinion etc.). **3** stake (a bet etc.).

venture capital *n.* money invested in a project in which there is a substantial element of risk. □ **venture capitalist** *n.*

venturer *n.* **1** *hist.* a person who takes part in a trading venture. **2** (**Venturer**) *Cdn* a member of a level (ages 14–17) in Scouting.

venturesome *adj.* **1** disposed to take risks. **2** risky.

venue *n.* the place where a meeting or event etc. is held.

Venus flytrap *n.* a plant with hinged leaves that spring shut on and digest insects that land on them.

veracity *n.* **1** honesty. **2** accuracy. [Say vuh RASSA tee]

veranda *n.* (also **verandah**) a usu. roofed porch or gallery along the outside of a house.

verb *n.* a word used to indicate an action, state, or occurrence, e.g. *hear, become, happen.*

verbal *adj.* **1** of or concerned with words. **2** oral, not written. **3** relating to a verb. **4** articulate. □ **verbally** *adv.*

verbalize *v.* (**verbalizes**, **verbalized**, **verbalizing**) express in words. □ **verbalization** *n.*

verbal noun *n. Grammar* a noun formed as an inflection of a verb, e.g. *smoking* in *smoking is forbidden.*

verbatim *adv. & adj.* in exactly the same words. [Say vur BATE um]

verbena *n.* a plant that bears clusters of fragrant showy flowers. [Say vur BEENA]

verbiage *n.* needless accumulation of words. [Say VURBY idge]

verbose *adj.* using more words than are needed. □ **verbosity** *n.* [Say vur BOSE, vur BOSSA tee (BOSE rhymes with DOSE)]

verboten *adj.* forbidden. [Say vur BO tun]

verdant *adj.* **1** bright green. **2** (of countryside) green with grass or other vegetation. [Say VUR dunt]

verdict *n.* **1** a decision in a civil or criminal cause or an inquest. **2** a decision or opinion given after testing or trying something.

verdigris *n.* **1** a green crystallized

substance formed on copper. **2** green rust on copper or brass. [Say VUR degrees]

verge ● *n.* **1** an edge or border. **2** a limit beyond which something happens. ● *v.* (**verges**, **verged**, **verging**) border on.

verify *v.* (**verifies**, **verified**, **verifying**) make sure or show that something is true, accurate, or justified. □ **verifiable** *adj.* **verification** *n.*

verisimilitude *n.* the appearance of being true or real. [Say vare uh suh MILLA tood or vare uh suh MILLA tyood]

veritable *adj.* rightly so called. □ **veritably** *adv.* [Say VARE it a bull]

vérité *n.* realism or naturalism in the arts. [Say very TAY]

verity *n.* (*pl.* **verities**) **1** a true principle or belief. **2** truth. [Say VARE it ee]

vermicelli *n.* pasta made in long slender threads. [Say vurma CHELLY]

vermiculite *n.* a yellow or brown mineral, used for insulation or as a medium for growing plants. [Say vur MICK yoo lite]

vermilion *n.* **1** a bright red mineral. **2** a brilliant red pigment or colour. [Say vur MILLION]

vermin *n.* **1** mammals and birds injurious to crops, etc. **2** parasitic worms or insects. **3** vile or contemptible persons.

vermouth *n.* a fortified wine flavoured with herbs. [Say vur MOOTH]

vernacular ● *n.* **1** the language or dialect of a particular country. **2** the language used by people belonging to a specified group. **3** informal speech. ● *adj.* (of language) of one's native country. [Say vur NACK yoo lur]

vernal *adj.* having to do with spring.

versatile *adj.* **1** turning easily from one subject or occupation to another. **2** (of a device etc.) having many uses. □ **versatility** *n.* [Say VERSE a tile, verse a TILLA tee]

verse *n.* **1** writing arranged with a metrical rhythm, often having a rhyme. **2 a** a metrical line. **b** a stanza of a poem or song. **c** a poem. **3** each of the short numbered divisions of a chapter in the Bible etc.

versed *adj.* experienced or skilled in; knowledgeable about.

versify *v.* (**versifies**, **versified**, **versifying**) **1** turn into or express in verse. **2** compose verses.

version *n.* **1** an account of a matter from a particular person's point of view. **2** a book etc. in a particular edition or translation. **3** a form or variant of a thing.

verso *n.* (*pl.* **versos**) the left-hand page of an open book. [Say VERSE oh]

versus *prep.* **1** against. *Abbreviation:* **v.**, **vs.** **2** as opposed to.

vertebra *n.* (*pl.* **vertebrae**) **1** each segment of the backbone. **2** (in *pl.*) the backbone. □ **vertebral** *adj.*
[*Say* VURTA bruh *for the singular,* VURTA bray *for the plural,* VURTA brul]

vertebrate ● *n.* any animal having a spinal column, including mammals, birds, reptiles, amphibians, and fishes. ● *adj.* of or relating to the vertebrates.
[*Say* VURTA brate *or* VURTA brut]

vertex *n.* (*pl.* **vertices**) **1** the highest point. **2** *Math* **a** each angular point of a polygon etc. **b** a meeting point of two lines that form an angle. [*Say* VUR tex *for the singular,* VUR tuh seez *for the plural*]

vertical ● *adj.* **1** at right angles to a horizontal plane, perpendicular. **2** in a direction from top to bottom. **3** of or at the vertex or highest point. ● *n.* **1** a vertical line or plane. **2** (in *pl.*) (also **vertical blinds**) window blinds consisting of a number of adjustable vertical slats. **3** (also **vertical drop**) the difference in elevation between the top and bottom of a mountain etc. □ **verticality** *n.* **vertically** *adv.*

vertically integrated *adj.* denoting a company that controls all aspects of production, including those normally operated by separate firms, from harvesting raw materials to manufacturing finished goods. □ **vertical integration** *n.*

vertiginous *adj.* of or causing vertigo. □ **vertiginously** *adv.*
[*Say* vur TIDGE in us]

vertigo *n.* dizziness. [*Say* VUR tig oh]

verve *n.* enthusiasm, vigour, spirit.

very ● *adv.* **1** in a high degree. **2** in the fullest sense. ● *adj.* real, true, actual.

Very Reverend *n.* **1** (in Canada) the title of a moderator of the United Church. **2** the title of a dean etc.

vesicle *n.* **1** a small fluid-filled sac or vacuole in an animal or plant. **2** *Medical* a blister. □ **vesicular** *adj.* [*Say* VESS ick ul, vuh SICK yoo lur]

vespers *pl. n.* a service of evening prayer.

vessel *n.* **1** a hollow receptacle esp. for liquid. **2** a ship or boat. **3** a duct or canal etc. holding or conveying fluid within an animal body or plant structure.

vest ● *n.* **1** a sleeveless usu. V-necked garment covering the shoulders and reaching the waist or hip, worn over a shirt. **2** any sleeveless garment. ● *v.* **1** bestow or confer (powers etc.) on. **2** confer (property or power) on. □ **close to the vest** cautious(ly), guarded(ly).

vestal virgin *n.* (in ancient Rome) a virgin

consecrated to the goddess of the household, and vowed to chastity.

vested interest *n.* a personal interest in a state of affairs.

vestibule *n.* **1** a hall or lobby just inside the outer door of a building. **2** *Anatomy* the central cavity of the labyrinth of the inner ear. □ **vestibular** *adj.* [*Say* VESTA byool, vess TIB yoo lur]

vestige *n.* **1** a trace or piece of evidence. **2** a slight amount. **3** a part or organ that is reduced or that has no function but was well developed in its ancestors. □ **vestigial** *adj.* [*Say* VESS tidge, ves TIDGE ee ul]

vestment *n.* **1** an official robe worn by clergy, choristers, etc. during a service. **2** an official or state robe.

vestry *n.* (*pl.* **vestries**) **1** a room in a church for keeping vestments in. **2** esp. *Anglicanism* a meeting of the members of a parish. [*Say* VESS tree]

vet¹ ● *n.* a veterinarian. ● *v.* (**vets**, **vetted**, **vetting**) **1** make a careful and critical examination of. **2** examine or treat (an animal).

vet² *n. informal* an esp. military veteran.

vetch *n.* (*pl.* **vetches**) a plant of the pea family, grown for silage or fodder.

veteran *n.* **1** a person who has long experience in a particular field. **2** an ex-serviceman or servicewoman.

veterinarian *n.* a person qualified to treat diseased or injured animals.

veterinary *adj.* of or for diseases and injuries of animals, or their treatment.

veto ● *n.* (*pl.* **vetoes**) **1 a** a constitutional right to reject a legislative enactment. **b** the right of a permanent member of the UN Security Council to reject a resolution. **2** a prohibition. ● *v.* (**vetoes**, **vetoed**, **vetoing**) **1** exercise a veto against. **2** forbid.

vex *v.* (**vexes**, **vexed**, **vexing**) **1** irritate, annoy. **2** puzzle, confound. **3** distress mentally. □ **vexation** *n.* **vexing** *adj.*

vexatious *adj.* causing or tending to cause annoyance or worry. [*Say* vex AY shuss]

vexed *adj.* **1** irritated, angered. **2** (of a problem, issue, etc.) difficult; problematic.

VHF *abbr.* very high frequency (designating radio waves of frequency *c.* 30– *c.*300 MHz).

VHS *abbr. proprietary* Video Home System (a standard format for videocassettes).

via *prep.* **1** by way of. **2** by means of. [*Say* VEE uh *or* VIE uh]

viable *adj.* **1** (of a plan etc.) feasible; practicable. **2 a** (of a seed or spore) able to germinate. **b** (of a plant, animal, etc.) capable of living or developing normally.

3 *Medical* (of a fetus) able to live after birth. □ **viability** *n.* [Say VIE a bull, vie ABILITY]

viaduct *n.* **1** a long bridge-like structure carrying a road or railway across a valley etc. **2** such a road or railway. [Say VIE a duct]

Viagra *n.* *proprietary* a drug taken in the treatment of male impotence. [Say vie AGRA]

vial *n.* a small vessel esp. for holding liquid medicines.

vibe *n.* *informal* **1** a feeling or atmosphere communicated. **2** (in *pl.*) a vibraphone.

vibrant *adj.* **1** full of life and energy. **2** (of colours etc.) bright. **3** vibrating. **4** (of sound) resonant. □ **vibrancy** *n.* **vibrantly** *adv.*

vibraphone *n.* an electrical percussion instrument of tuned metal bars giving a vibrato effect. □ **vibraphonist** *n.* [Say VIE bruh phone, VIE bruh phone ist]

vibrate *v.* (**vibrates**, **vibrated**, **vibrating**) **1** move or cause to move rapidly to and fro. **2** *Physics* move unceasingly to and fro. **3** (of a sound) throb. **4** quiver, thrill.

vibration *n.* **1** an instance or the state of vibrating. **2** (**vibrations**) a person's emotional state, the atmosphere of a place, as felt by others. □ **vibrational** *adj.*

vibrato *n.* (*pl.* **vibratos**) a rapid slight variation in pitch in singing or playing some instruments. [Say vib ROT oh]

vibrator *n.* a device that vibrates or causes vibration. □ **vibratory** *adj.* [Say VIE brate er, VIBE ruh tory]

viburnum *n.* a shrub or small tree with clusters of white flowers. [Say vie BURN um]

vicar *n.* **1 a** (in the Church of England) a clergyman appointed to act as priest of a parish. **b** (in other Anglican churches) a clergyman who substitutes for or assists the rector of a parish. **2** *Catholicism* a representative of a bishop. [Say VICKER]

vicarious *adj.* **1** experienced or enjoyed by imagining one's own participation in the experiences of another. **2** performed or undergone on behalf of another. □ **vicariously** *adv.* [Say vick AIRY us *or* vie CARE ee us]

vice¹ *n.* **1 a** illegal or grossly immoral conduct. **b** criminal activity esp. involving prostitution or drugs etc. **2** a personal flaw or bad habit.

vice² esp. *Brit.* = VISE.

vice- *comb. form* next in rank to and acting as a deputy for.

vice admiral *n.* (also **Vice Admiral**) a naval officer ranking below admiral and above rear admiral.

vice-chancellor *n.* **1** the deputy of a chancellor. **2** *Cdn & Brit.* the representative of the chancellor of a university, discharging most of the administrative duties.

vice-president *n.* an official or executive serving as a deputy to a president. □ **vice-presidency** *n.* **vice-presidential** *adj.*

viceregal *adj.* of or relating to a Governor General or viceroy. [Say vice REE gull]

viceroy *n.* a person who governs a colony or province etc. on behalf of a sovereign. [Say VICE roy]

vice squad *n.* a special unit of a police force investigating prostitution, drug trafficking, etc.

vice versa *adv.* the other way around. [Say vice VERSE uh]

vichyssoise *n.* a thick soup of puréed leeks and potatoes with cream, usu. served chilled. [Say VEESHY swoz]

vicinity *n.* (*pl.* **vicinities**) the area near or surrounding a place. □ **in the vicinity of 1** near. **2** approximately.

vicious *adj.* **1** malevolent, wicked. **2** savage, brutal. **3** fierce, intense. □ **viciously** *adv.* **viciousness** *n.*

vicious circle *n.* (also **vicious cycle**) a situation in which one problem leads to another, which then makes the first one worse.

vicissitudes *pl. n.* changes in circumstance or fortune. [Say viss ISSA toodz *or* viss ISSA tyoodz]

victim *n.* **1** a person who suffers or dies as a result of an event or circumstance. **2** a person fooled; a dupe. □ **fall victim to** succumb to or suffer as a result of. □ **victimhood** *n.*

victimize *v.* (**victimizes**, **victimized**, **victimizing**) **1** make a victim of. **2** single out for punishment or unfair treatment. □ **victimization** *n.* **victimizer** *n.*

victimology *n.* the study of the victims of crime or discrimination.

victor *n.* a person or country etc. that defeats an adversary or opponent.

Victoria Cross *n.* a medal awarded to members of the Commonwealth armed forces for conspicuous acts of bravery.

Victoria Day *n.* *Cdn* a holiday falling on the Monday immediately preceding May 25.

Victorian ● *adj.* **1** relating to the reign of Queen Victoria (1837–1901). **2** of the attitudes attributed to this time, esp. prudery. **3** typical of the architectural style of this time. ● n. **1** a person of this time. **2** a resident of a place called Victoria.

Victorian Order of Nurses n. *Cdn* a non-profit health organization that provides home care for the elderly and chronically ill.

victorious adj. having won a victory. □**victoriously** adv.

victory n. (pl **victories**) **1** an act of defeating an enemy or opponent. **2** a success in some endeavour.

victual ● n. (usu. in pl.) food, provisions. ● v. (**victuals**, **victualled**, **victualling**) supply or feed with victuals. [*Say* VICK chew ul *or* VITTLE]

Vidal n. a hybrid variety of white wine grape widely grown in Ontario, used esp. in icewines. [*Say* vee DAL]

video ● n. (pl. **videos**) **1** the process of recording and reproducing visual images on magnetic tape or disk. **2 a** a recording made on videotape or disk. **b** a music video. **3** a videocassette or DVD. ● v. (**videoes**, **videoed**, **videoing**) record on videotape.

video camera n. (also **videocam**) a camera used to record images on videotape.

videocassette n. a length of videotape enclosed in a sealed plastic casing.

videocassette recorder n. a VCR.

video conference n. an arrangement in which television sets linked by telephone lines are used to enable people in different places to communicate with and see each other. □**video conferencing** n.

video display terminal n. (also **video display unit**) a device for displaying on a screen data stored in a computer.

video game n. a computer game that can be played on a television screen, computer monitor, etc.

videographer n. a person who videotapes events. □**videography** n. [*Say* viddy OGRA fur]

video lottery terminal n. a government-regulated gambling machine that offers a selection of esp. card games on a video screen.

videophone n. a telephone incorporating a screen allowing communication in both sound and vision.

video recorder n. a VCR.

videotape ● n. **1** magnetic tape for recording television pictures and sound. **2 a** a length of this. **b** a videocassette. **3** a recording made on videotape. ● v. (**videotapes**, **videotaped**, **videotaping**) make a recording of on videotape.

vie v. (**vies**, **vied**, **vying**) compete, contend.

Viennese ● adj. having to do with Vienna, Austria. ● n. (pl. **Viennese**) a person from Vienna. [*Say* vee en EEZ]

Vietnamese n. (pl. **Vietnamese**) **1** a person from Vietnam. **2** the language of Vietnam. □**Vietnamese** adj. [*Say* vee etna MEEZ]

view ● n. **1** range of vision. **2 a** what is seen from a particular point. **b** a picture etc. representing this. **3 a** an opinion or belief. **b** a mental attitude. **c** a manner of considering a thing. **4** a visual examination or survey. ● v. **1** inspect or examine. **2** catch sight of. **3** regard or approach in a particular manner. **4** watch on television. □**have in view** have as one's object. **in view of 1** considering. **2** so as to be seen by. **on view** being displayed or exhibited. **with a view to 1** with the hope of. **2** with the aim of attaining or achieving. □**viewable** adj.

viewer n. **1** a person who views something; a spectator. **2** a person watching television. **3** a device for looking at photographic slides or transparencies etc.

viewership n. the audience for a television program or channel etc.

viewfinder n. a device on a camera showing the field of view of the lens.

viewing n. **1** an opportunity or occasion to view. **2** the activity or a period of watching television. **3** an opportunity for mourners to see the body of a deceased person prior to a funeral.

viewpoint n. **1** a point of view. **2** a position from which a view may be seen.

vigil n. **1** a stationary and peaceful demonstration in support of a particular cause. **2** a period of keeping awake, esp. to keep watch or pray. **3** *Christianity* the eve of a festival or holy day as an occasion for religious observance. [*Say* VIDGE ul]

vigilant adj. keeping careful watch for signs of danger or difficulty. □**vigilance** n. **vigilantly** adv. [*Say* VIDGE a lunt, VIDGE a lunce]

vigilante n. a person, often a member of a group, who attempts to prevent crime or punish criminals without the legal authority to do so. □**vigilantism** n. [*Say* vidge a LANTY]

vignette n. **1 a** a brief descriptive account, anecdote, etc. **b** a short evocative usu. self-contained episode. **2** an illustration or design on a blank space in a book. **3** an evocative image. [*Say* vin YET]

vigorous adj. **1 a** physically strong, healthy and robust. **b** (of a plant) growing actively; flourishing. **2** involving physical force or energy. **3** (of language etc.) powerful, rousing. ☐ **vigorously** *adv.*

vigour *n.* (also **vigor**) **1** physical strength. **2** good physical condition. **3** strength, intensity, or vitality.

Viking *n.* any of the Scandinavian seafaring pirates and traders who raided and settled in parts of northwestern Europe in the 8th–11th centuries. ☐ **Viking** *adj.*

vile *adj.* **1 a** disgusting. **b** abominably bad. **2** wicked. ☐ **vileness** *n.*

vilify *v.* (**vilifies, vilified, vilifying**) speak or write about in an abusively critical way. ☐ **vilification** *n.* [*Say* VILLA fie, villa fuh KAY sh'n]

villa *n.* (*pl.* **villas**) a luxurious country residence, esp. in continental Europe.

village *n.* **1** a group of houses and associated buildings, esp. in a rural area. **2** a self-contained district within a city or town. ☐ **villager** *n.*

villain *n.* **1** a wicked person. **2** the character in a play, novel, etc., whose evil actions or motives are important in the plot. ☐ **villainous** *adj.* **villainy** *n.*

villein *n. hist.* a feudal tenant entirely subject to a lord. [*Sounds like* VILLAIN]

vim *n. informal* vigour, energy.

vinaigrette *n.* a dressing made with oil, vinegar, and seasoning. [*Say* vinna GRETT]

vindaloo *n.* (*pl.* **vindaloos**) a spicy Indian curry made with meat, fish, or poultry. [*Say* vin duh LOO]

vindicate *v.* (**vindicates, vindicated, vindicating**) **1** clear of blame or suspicion. **2** show or prove to be right or justified. ☐ **vindication** *n.* [*Say* VINDA kate]

vindictive *adj.* having a strong or unreasonable desire for revenge. ☐ **vindictiveness** *n.* [*Say* vin DICK tiv]

vine *n.* **1** a climbing or trailing plant, esp. one that bears grapes. **2** the slender stem of such a plant.

vinegar *n.* **1** a sour liquid of dilute acetic acid, used as a condiment or preservative. **2** energy, vitality. ☐ **vinegared** *adj.* **vinegary** *adj.*

vineyard *n.* a plantation of grapevines. [*Say* VIN yurd]

vinifera ● *adj.* having to do with a type of grape used in winemaking, native to Europe and also cultivated in N America. ● *n.* (*pl.* **vinifera** *or* **viniferas**) the vinifera wine or grape. [*Say* vie NIFFER uh]

vinification *n.* the conversion of grape juice etc. into wine. ☐ **vinify** *v.* (**vinifies, vinified, vinifying**) [*Say* vin iffa KAY sh'n, VIN if eye]

vino *n. informal* wine. [*Say* VEE no]

vintage ● *n.* **1** the year in which a particular wine was produced. **2** a wine of high quality from a single year and district. **3** the gathering of grapes for winemaking. **4** the time when a thing was made or produced. ● *adj.* **1** being of high quality and earlier time. **2** representing the best period of a person's work. **3** (of wine) produced in an exceptional year.

vintner *n.* a person who makes or sells wine.

vinyl *n.* **1** a strong plastic made by polymerizing esp. polyvinyl chloride. **2 a** a phonograph record. **b** phonograph records collectively.

viol *n.* a musical instrument of the Renaissance and Baroque periods, resembling a violin, but with five, six, or seven strings. [*Sounds like* VIAL]

viola[1] *n.* (*pl.* **violas**) an instrument of the violin family, larger than the violin and of lower pitch. [*Say* vee OH luh]

viola[2] *n.* (*pl.* **violas**) any plant of a genus that includes the pansy and violet. [*Say* vie OH luh *or* vee OH luh]

violate *v.* (**violates, violated, violating**) **1** fail to observe or comply with. **2 a** treat irreverently. **b** disregard. **3** disturb (a person's privacy etc.). **4** assault sexually; rape. ☐ **violation** *n.* **violator** *n.*

violence *n.* **1** the esp. illegal exercise of physical force to cause injury or damage. **2** strength or intensity of emotion.

violent *adj.* **1** using or involving violence. **2** (of a person) tending to use aggressive physical force. **3** operating with great and usu. destructive physical force. **4** passionate, intense. ☐ **violently** *adv.*

violet ● *n.* **1** a plant usu. having purple, blue, yellow, or white five-petalled flowers. **2** a bluish-purple colour. ● *adj.* of a bluish-purple colour.

violin *n.* a musical instrument with four strings, rested on the shoulder and played with a bow. ☐ **violinist** *n.*

violist *n.* a person who plays a viola. [*Say* vee OLE ist]

violoncello *n.* (*pl.* **violoncellos**) *formal* a cello. [*Say* vee uh lun CHELL oh *or* vie uh lun CHELL oh]

VIP *n.* (*pl.* **VIPs**) a very important person.

viper *n.* **1** a venomous snake with large hinged fangs and dark patterns on its skin. **2** a spiteful or treacherous person.

viral *adj.* of or caused by a virus. [*Say* VIE rull]

vireo *n.* (*pl.* **vireos**) a small plain songbird inhabiting woodlands in the western hemisphere. [*Say* VEERY oh]

virgin ● *n.* **1** a person who has never had

sexual intercourse. **2** **(the Virgin)** the Virgin Mary. **3** *informal* a naive or inexperienced person. ● *adj.* **1 a** being a virgin. **b** of or befitting a virgin. **2** not yet used or exploited. **3** undefiled, spotless. **4** (of olive oil) obtained from the first pressing of olives. **5** (of wool) that has never been spun or woven. □ **virginal** *adj.*

Virginia creeper *n.* a N American vine with red autumn foliage.

virginity *n.* **1** the state of being a virgin. **2** a naive or inexperienced state.

Virgo *n.* (*pl.* **Virgos**) **1** a constellation (the Virgin). **2** the sixth sign of the zodiac, which the sun enters around Aug. 23. □ **Virgoan** *n. & adj.*

virile *adj.* (of a man) having strength, energy, and a strong sex drive. □ **virility** *n.* [*Say* VEER ile, vuh RILLA tee]

virology *n.* the branch of science that deals with the study of viruses. □ **virologist** *n.* [*Say* vie RAWLA jee, vie RAWLA jist]

virtual *adj.* **1** almost or nearly the thing described, but not completely. **2 a** not physically existing but made by software to appear to do so. **b** designating or experienced in an environment created by virtual reality. □ **virtuality** *n.* **virtually** *adv.*

virtual reality *n.* **1** a notional image or environment generated by computer software with which a user can interact while wearing or using specialized equipment. **2** the technology used to generate this environment.

virtue *n.* **1** conformity of life and conduct with moral principles. **2** a particular form of moral excellence. **3** chastity or sexual purity. **4** a particular beneficial quality or feature. □ **by** (or **in**) **virtue of** on the basis of. **make a virtue of necessity** derive some credit from an unwelcome obligation.

virtuoso *n.* (*pl.* **virtuosi** or **virtuosos**) **1** a person who has mastered the technique of a fine art, esp. music. **2** a person with outstanding skill in any sphere. □ **virtuosic** *adj.* **virtuosity** *n.* [*Say* virtue OH so *for the singular,* virtue OH see *or* virtue OH soze *for the plural;* virtue OSS ick, virtue OSSA tee]

virtuous *adj.* **1** having high moral standards. **2** chaste.

virulent *adj.* **1** violently bitter. **2 a** (of a disease) malignant or severe. **b** (of micro-organisms) capable of producing disease. □ **virulence** *n.* **virulently** *adv.* [*Say* VEER oo l'nt *or* VEER yoo l'nt]

virus *n.* (*pl.* **viruses**) **1 a** a submicroscopic organism that can multiply only inside living host cells and is usu. pathogenic. **b** an infection with such an organism. **2** a computer virus. **3** a harmful or malignant influence.

visa *n.* (*pl.* **visas**) **1** a note on a passport etc. showing that the holder is allowed to enter or leave a country. **2** the term for which such a note remains valid.

visage *n. literary* a face. [*Say* VIZ idge]

vis-à-vis *prep.* **1** in relation to. **2** as compared with. [*Say* veez a VEE]

viscera *pl. n.* the internal organs in the body, esp. those in the abdomen. [*Say* VISSER uh]

visceral *adj.* **1** of the viscera. **2** relating to inward feelings rather than conscious reasoning. □ **viscerally** *adv.* [*Say* VISSER ul]

viscid *adj.* sticky. [*Say* VISS id]

viscose *n.* **1** a form of cellulose in a highly viscous state suitable for drawing into yarn. **2** rayon made from this. [*Say* VISS kose (KOSE *rhymes with* DOSE *or* DOZE)]

viscosity *n.* (*pl.* **viscosities**) **1** the state of being viscous. **2** (of a fluid) internal friction. [*Say* viss KOSSA tee]

viscount *n.* a nobleman ranking between an earl and a baron. □ **viscountess** *n.* [*Say* VIE count]

viscous *adj.* **1** glutinous, sticky. **2** semi-liquid. [*Say* VISS cuss]

vise ● *n.* an instrument, esp. on a workbench, with two movable jaws between which an object may be clamped. ● *v.* (**vises**, **vised**, **vising**) secure in a vise. □ **viselike** *adj.*

visibility *n.* (*pl.* **visibilities**) **1** the state of being visible. **2** the distance one can see depending on light and weather conditions. **3** the degree to which something attracts attention.

visible *adj.* **1** that can be seen by the eye. **2** that can be perceived. **3** attracting attention. □ **visibly** *adv.*

visible minority *n.* esp. *Cdn* an ethnic group whose members are racially distinct from those of the predominant race in a society.

visible spectrum *n.* the range of wavelengths of electromagnetic radiation to which the human eye is normally sensitive.

Visigoth *n.* **1** a member of the Goths who settled in France and Spain in the 5th century. **2** *informal* an uncivilized person. [*Say* VIZ a goth]

vision *n.* **1** the act or faculty of seeing. **2 a** something seen in a dream or trance, or in the imagination. **b** an apparition. **3** imaginative insight. **4** ability to plan in a far-sighted way. **5** a person etc. of unusual beauty.

visionary ● *adj.* **1** thinking about the future with imagination or wisdom. **2** having to do with visions in a dream or trance, or as a supernatural apparition. ● *n.* (*pl.* **visionaries**) a visionary person.

vision quest *n.* (among some N American Aboriginal peoples) a sacred ceremony in which an individual goes to a secluded place to fast and communicate with the spiritual world.

visit ● *v.* (**visits**, **visited**, **visiting**) **1** go or come to see (a person, place, etc.). **2** reside temporarily with or at. **3** access and view a site on the World Wide Web. **4** come upon, attack. **5** *Bible* punish (a person). **6** chat. ● *n.* **1 a** an act of visiting. **b** a temporary stay with a person or at a place. **2** an occasion of going to a doctor, dentist, etc. **3** a chat. □ **visiting** *n.* & *adj.* **visitor** *n.*

visitation *n.* **1** a visit, esp. a formal one. **2** a divorced person's visit with his or her child in the custody of a former spouse. **3** (**Visitation**) the visit of the Virgin Mary to Elizabeth related in Luke 1:39-56. **4** trouble regarded as a divine punishment.

visor *n.* **1 a** a movable part of a helmet covering the face. **b** the projecting front part of a cap. **c** a half-moon shaped shade on a headband, worn to protect the eyes from strong light. **2** a movable flap at the top of a windshield inside a car to protect the eyes from glare. □ **visored** *adj.*

vista *n.* (*pl.* **vistas**) **1** a long narrow view. **2** a scenic wide view. **3** a far-reaching mental view.

visual ● *adj.* relating to seeing or sight. ● *n.* (usu. in *pl.*) **1** a visual image or display. **2** the visual element of a film or television broadcast. □ **visually** *adv.*

visual art *n.* (often in *pl.*) any art meant to be appreciated mainly through sight. □ **visual artist** *n.*

visualize *v.* (**visualizes**, **visualized**, **visualizing**) make visible esp. to one's mind; form an image of. □ **visualization** *n.*

vital ● *adj.* **1 a** extremely important. **b** paramount. **2** essential for life. **3** full of life or activity. ● *n.* (in *pl.*) the body's vital organs. □ **vitally** *adv.*

vitality *n.* **1** liveliness, animation. **2** the ability to sustain life.

vital signs *pl. n.* clinical measurements that indicate the state of a person's essential body functions, esp. pulse rate, temperature, respiration rate, and blood pressure.

vital statistics *pl. n.* **1** the number of

births, marriages, deaths, etc. **2** *jocular* the measurements of a woman's bust, waist, and hips.

vitamin *n.* **1** any of a group of organic compounds essential in small amounts for many living organisms. **2** a pill providing any of these as a dietary supplement.

vitamin A *n.* retinol.

vitamin B₁ *n.* thiamine.

vitamin B₂ *n.* riboflavin.

vitamin B₃ *n.* niacin.

vitamin B₁₂ *n.* a vitamin of the B complex, found in foods of animal origin.

vitamin B complex *n.* a group of vitamins which are often found together in the same foods.

vitamin C *n.* ascorbic acid.

vitamin D *n.* any of a group of vitamins found in liver and fish oils and sunlight, essential for the absorption of calcium.

vitamin E *n.* tocopherol.

vitamin K *n.* any of a group of vitamins found esp. in green leaves, essential for blood clotting.

vitiate *v.* (**vitiates**, **vitiated**, **vitiating**) **1** spoil or impair the quality or efficiency of. **2** destroy or impair the legal validity of. [*Say* VISHY ate]

viticulture *n.* the cultivation of grapevines; the study of this. □ **viticultural** *adj.* [*Say* VITTA culture, vitta CULTURAL]

vitreous *adj.* of, or of the nature of, glass. [*Say* VITRY us]

vitrify *v.* (**vitrifies**, **vitrified**, **vitrifying**) convert or be converted into glass or a glass-like substance esp. by heat. [*Say* VITRA fie]

vitriol *n.* **1** sulphuric acid. **2** cruel and bitter criticism. □ **vitriolic** *adj.* [*Say* VITRY ul, vitry AWL ick]

vittle *informal* = VICTUAL.

vituperation *n.* bitter and abusive language. [*Say* vit tooper AY sh'n]

vituperative *v.* bitter and abusive. [*Say* vit TOOPER a tiv]

vivacious *adj.* attractively lively. □ **vivacity** *n.* [*Say* viv AY shuss *or* vive AY shuss, viv ASSA tee *or* vive ASSA tee]

vivid *adj.* **1 a** (of light or colour) strong, intense. **b** brilliant. **2 a** (of an impression etc.) clear, striking. **b** (of a mental faculty) active. □ **vividly** *adv.* **vividness** *n.*

vivify *v.* (**vivifies**, **vivified**, **vivifying**) enliven or animate. [*Say* VIVA fie]

vivisection *n.* the practice of doing experiments on live animals for research.

☐**vivisect** v. [Say VIV a section, VIV a sect]

vixen n. **1** a female fox. **2** a spiteful or quarrelsome woman.

viz. adv. namely; in other words.

vizier n. hist. a high official in some Muslim countries. [Say VIZZY ur or viz EAR]

VJ n. (pl. **VJs**) a person who introduces music videos on television etc.

VLT n. (pl. **VLTs**) video lottery terminal.

V-neck n. **1** a neckline with straight sides meeting at an angle to form a V. **2** a garment with this. ☐**V-necked** adj.

vocab n. informal vocabulary. [Say VO cab]

vocabulary n. (pl. **vocabularies**) **1** the (principal) words used in a particular language or in a particular activity. **2** a list of these with definitions or translations. **3** the range of words known to an individual.

vocal ● adj. **1** relating to the human voice. **2** expressing one's feelings freely. **3** (of music) written for or produced by the voice. ● n. the sung part of a musical composition. ☐**vocally** adv.

vocal cords pl. n. (also **vocal folds**) folds of the lining of the larynx which vibrate in the airstream to produce voiced sounds.

vocalic adj. of or consisting of a vowel or vowels. [Say vo KAL ick]

vocalist n. a singer.

vocalize v. (**vocalizes, vocalized, vocalizing**) **1** produce (a sound or word) with the voice. **2** articulate, express. **3** Music sing with several notes to one vowel. ☐**vocalization** n.

vocation n. **1 a** a strong feeling of suitability for a particular career or occupation. **b** a divine call to the religious life. **2 a** a person's employment. **b** a trade or profession.

vocational adj. **1** of or relating to an occupation or employment. **2** (of education or training) directed at a manual or technical occupation.

vociferous adj. **1** noisy, clamorous. **2** vehement. ☐**vociferously** adv. [Say vo SIFFER us]

vodka n. (pl. **vodkas**) a colourless alcoholic liquor made from rye etc.

vogue n. **1** (**the vogue**) the prevailing fashion. **2** popular use. ☐**in vogue** in fashion. ☐**voguish** adj. [Say VOAG, VOAG ish]

voice ● n. **1 a** a sound formed in the larynx etc. and uttered by the mouth as speech or song. **b** the ability to produce this. **2 a** utterance. **b** an opinion. **c** the right to express an opinion. **3** Grammar a form of a verb showing the relation of the subject to the action. **4** Music a vocal part in a composition. **5** Phonetics sound uttered with resonance of the vocal cords. ● v. (**voices, voiced, voicing**) **1** give utterance to; express. **2** (esp. as **voiced** adj.) Phonetics utter with vibration of the vocal cords. ☐**with one voice** unanimously. ☐-**voiced** comb. form **voicing** n.

voice box n. the larynx.

voiceless adj. **1** mute, speechless. **2** Phonetics uttered without vibration of the vocal cords.

voice mail n. a system for electronically storing verbal messages left by telephone callers.

voice-over n. narration in a film etc. not accompanied by a picture of the speaker.

void ● adj. **1 a** empty, vacant. **b** lacking; free from. **2** not valid or legally binding. **3** useless. ● n. an empty space. ● v. **1** render invalid. **2** empty the contents of esp. the bowels or bladder.

voila interj. expressing satisfaction. [Say vwah LAH]

voile n. a thin semi-transparent material. [Say VOIL or VWOL]

volatile ● adj. **1** evaporating rapidly. **2** liable to change rapidly and unpredictably. **3** (of a person) liable to display rapid changes of emotion. ● n. a volatile substance. ☐**volatility** n. [Say VOLLA tile, volla TILLA tee]

volcanic adj. of, like, or produced by a volcano. ☐**volcanically** adv.

volcanism n. volcanic activity.

volcano n. (pl. **volcanoes**) a mountain or hill having an opening through which lava, cinders, steam, gases, etc., are or have been expelled from the earth's crust.

volcanology n. the scientific study of volcanoes. ☐**volcanologist** n. [Say vol can OLLA jee, vol can OLLA jist]

vole n. a small mouselike burrowing rodent.

volition n. the faculty or power of using one's will. ☐**of** (or **by**) **one's own volition** voluntarily. [Say vuh LISH un]

volley ● n. (pl. **volleys**) **1 a** the simultaneous discharge of a number of weapons. **b** the bullets etc. discharged in a volley. **2** a rapid emission of many things at once. **3 a** the return of a ball etc. before it touches the ground. **b** a series of these. **4** Volleyball a pass etc. made with the fingertips. ● v. (**volleys, volleyed, volleying**) **1** Sport return or send (a ball) by a volley. **2** discharge (bullets, abuse, etc.) in a volley.

volleyball n. **1** a game for two teams in which a large inflated ball is hit back and forth over a net with the fingers, fist, or forearm. **2** the ball used in this game.

volt *n.* the SI unit of electromotive force, the difference of potential that would carry one ampere of current against one ohm resistance. Abbreviation: **V**.

voltage *n.* electromotive force or potential difference expressed in volts.

volte-face *n.* a complete reversal of position or policy. [Say volta FASS]

voluble *adj.* **1** talking a lot, and with enthusiasm. **2** expressed in many words. □ **volubility** *n.* **volubly** *adv.* [Say VOL yoo bull, vol yoo BILLA tee]

volume *n.* **1 a** a book, esp. one of a series. **b** several issues of a magazine etc. esp. designed to be bound together as a book. **2 a** solid content, bulk. **b** the space occupied by a substance. **c** an amount or quantity. **3** degree of loudness. □ **volumed** *adj.*

volumetric *adj.* relating to measurement by volume. □ **volumetrically** *adv.* [Say vol yoo METRIC]

voluminous *adj.* **1** large in volume. **2** (of clothing etc.) loose and ample. **3** (of writing) very lengthy. □ **voluminously** *adv.* [Say vuh LOO min us]

voluntarism *n.* the principle of relying on voluntary action rather than compulsion, esp. as regards social welfare. □ **voluntarist** *n.* [Say VOL un tuh rism]

voluntary ● *adj.* **1** done or acting of one's own free will. **2** unpaid. **3** brought about etc. by voluntary action. **4** (of a muscle or limb) controlled by the will. **5** intentional. ● *n.* (*pl.* **voluntaries**) an organ solo played before, during, or after a church service. □ **voluntarily** *adv.* [Say VOL un terry, vol un TARE a lee]

volunteer ● *n.* **1** a person who voluntarily offers to do something. **2** a person who enrols voluntarily for military service. **3** a person who works for an organization without pay. **4** (as an *adj.*) designating an organization etc. composed of volunteers. ● *v.* **1** undertake or offer voluntarily. **2** be a volunteer. **3** assign or commit (a person) to a particular esp. "voluntary" undertaking. □ **volunteering** *n.* **volunteerism** *n.*

voluptuous *adj.* **1** (of a woman) curvaceous and sexually desirable. **2** giving sensual pleasure. □ **voluptuously** *adv.* **voluptuousness** *n.* [Say vuh LUP chew us *or* vuh LUP tyoo us]

vomit ● *v.* (**vomits, vomited, vomiting**) **1** eject (matter) from the stomach through the mouth. **2** eject violently, belch forth. ● *n.* matter vomited from the stomach.

VON *Cdn* ● *abbr.* Victorian Order of Nurses.

● *n.* (*pl.* **VONs**) a nurse belonging to this organization.

voodoo *n.* a religion practised in the West Indies and the southern US, characterized by sorcery and spirit possession, and combining elements of traditional African religious rites with Catholic ritual.

voodoo doll *n.* a small figure, the tormenting or hexing of which supposedly affects a specific real person.

voracious *adj.* **1** greedy in eating. **2** insatiable. □ **voraciously** *adv.* **voracity** *n.* [Say vuh RAY shuss, vuh RASSA tee]

vortex *n.* (*pl.* **vortices** *or* **vortexes**) **1** a mass of whirling water or air. **2** any whirling motion or mass. [Say VORE tex *for the singular*, VORE tuh seez *for the plural*]

votary *n.* (*pl.* **votaries**) **1** a devoted follower of a religion or cult, esp. one who has taken vows. **2** a devoted follower, adherent, or advocate. [Say VOTE a ree]

vote ● *n.* **1 a** a formal expression of choice esp. between two or more candidates or courses of action. **b** a ballot etc. used for recording one's choice. **2** the collective votes that are given by or for a particular group. **3** (usu. as **the vote**) the right to vote. ● *v.* (**votes, voted, voting**) **1 a** express by casting a vote. **b** register or express one's opinion regarding. **2** support habitually or in a particular election. □ **put to a** (or **the**) **vote** submit to a decision by voting. **vote down** defeat (a proposal etc.). **vote in** elect by votes. **vote out** dismiss from office etc. by voting. □ **voter** *n.*

vote of confidence *n.* (*pl.* **votes of confidence**) **1** a vote showing that the majority support the policy of the governing body etc. **2** an indication of support or approval.

vote of non-confidence *n.* (*pl.* **votes of non-confidence**) *Cdn* a vote indicating that the majority does not support a policy of the governing party.

votive *adj.* offered or undertaken in fulfillment of a vow or in gratitude. [Say VO tiv]

votive candle *n.* a candle that may be lit as a symbol of prayer or for decoration.

vouch *v.* (foll. by *for*) **1** assert or confirm the truth or accuracy of. **2** confirm the identity or good character of.

voucher *n.* a document which can be exchanged for goods or services, or which entitles the holder to a discount.

vouchsafe *v. formal* **1** give as a gift or privilege. **2** permit or agree.

vow ● *n.* **1** a solemn promise. **2** a solemn undertaking or resolve. ● *v.* **1** promise or undertake solemnly. **2** make a solemn resolve or threat.

vowel *n.* **1** a speech sound made with vibration of the vocal cords but without audible friction. **2** a letter representing such a sound, such as *a, e, i, o, u.*

vox pop *n. informal* **1** popular opinion as represented by informal comments from the public. **2** statements of this kind.

voyage ● *n.* a journey, esp. a long one. ● *v.* (**voyages, voyaged, voyaging**) make a voyage. □ **voyager** *n.*

voyageur *n.* **1** esp. *Cdn hist.* a usu. French-speaking or Metis canoeist employed to transport goods to and from trading posts in the interior. **2** an outdoorsman or adventurer. [*Say* voy a ZHUR *or* vwah ya ZHUR]

voyeur *n.* **1** a person who derives pleasure from watching others as they undress or engage in sexual activities. **2** an observer who derives enjoyment from observing a situation without participating in it. □ **voyeurism** *n.* **voyeuristic** *adj.* [*Say* voy YUR, VOY er ism, voy er ISS tick]

VP *abbr.* Vice-President.

VQA *abbr. Cdn* (as an *adj.*) designating a Canadian wine certified by the Vintners Quality Alliance as meeting certain standards.

vroom ● *v.* **1** (esp. of a car or engine) make a roaring or revving noise. **2** (of a car etc.) travel at high speed. ● *n.* the sound of an engine. ● *interj.* an imitation of such a sound.

vs. *abbr.* versus.

V-shaped *adj.* having a shape resembling the letter V.

vulcanize *v.* (**vulcanizes, vulcanized, vulcanizing**) harden (rubber or rubber-like material) by treating it with sulphur at a high temperature.

vulgar *adj.* **1** likely to offend; obscene. **2** displaying ignorance or a lack of refinement. **3** having to do with the common people. □ **vulgarity** *n.* (*pl.* **vulgarities**). **vulgarly** *adv.*

vulgarize *v.* (**vulgarizes, vulgarized, vulgarizing**) **1** make less refined. **2** make widely known or available.

Vulgate *n.* **1** the Latin version of the Bible prepared in the late 4th century. **2** the official Catholic Latin text of the Bible. [*Say* VULL gate *or* VULL gut]

vulnerable *adj.* **1** able to be hurt. **2** liable to damage or harm. **3** exposed to a destructive agent or influence etc. □ **vulnerability** *n.* (*pl.* **vulnerabilities**). **vulnerably** *adv.*

vulture *n.* **1** a large bird of prey with a mainly bald head and neck, which feeds chiefly on carrion. **2** a ruthless or greedy person.

vulva *n.* (*pl.* **vulvas**) the external female genitals. □ **vulval** *adj.*

Vuntut Gwich'in *n.* a member of a Gwich'in people living in Yukon, esp. in and around the community of Old Crow. [*Say* VOON toot GWITCH in *(with* OO *as in* BOOK.]

vying *pres. part. of* VIE.

Ww

W¹ *n.* (also **w**) (*pl.* **Ws** or **W's**) the twenty-third letter of the alphabet.

W² *abbr.* (also **W.**) **1** watt(s). **2** West(ern).

wacked *adj.* = WHACKED.

wacko *slang* ● *adj.* crazy, insane. ● *n.* (*pl.* **wackos** or **wackoes**) a crazy person.

wacky *adj.* (**wackier, wackiest**) *informal* crazy, madcap. □ **wackiness** *n.*

wad ● *n.* **1 a** a small mass of soft material. **b** a compact bundle of material. **2 a** a bundle of banknotes or papers etc. **b** a large quantity of esp. money. **3** a plug of paper, cloth, or felt retaining the powder and shot in a gun. ● *v.* (**wads, wadded, wadding**) **1** press or crumple (soft material). **2** plug with a wad. □ **wadding** *n.* [Say WOD, WODDING]

waddle ● *v.* (**waddles, waddled, waddling**) walk with short steps and a clumsy swaying motion. ● *n.* a waddling gait.

wade *v.* (**wades, waded, wading**) **1** walk through water, mud, or snow. **2** go or read laboriously or doggedly through. □ **wade in** (or **into**) *informal* involve oneself energetically.

wader *n.* **1** (in *pl.*) high waterproof boots, worn esp. for fishing. **2** any large, long-legged wading bird, as a heron, stork, or crane.

wading bird *n.* any usu. long-legged bird that finds its food in shallow waters or along the shore.

wafer *n.* **1** a very thin light crisp cookie. **2** a thin disc of unleavened bread used in the Eucharist.

waferboard *n.* esp. *Cdn* a rigid sheet or panel of randomly arranged chips of wood bonded with resin.

wafer-thin *adj.* & *adv.* very thin or thinly.

waffle¹ ● *v.* (**waffles, waffled, waffling**) **1** waver in opinion or resolve. **2** indulge in rambling aimless speech or writing. ● *n.* **1** verbose but aimless talk or writing. **2** (**Waffle**) *Cdn hist.* a caucus of NDP members organized in 1969 to promote a socialist and nationalist agenda. □ **waffler** *n.*

waffle² *n.* **1** a crisp pancake with a grid-like texture on each side. **2** (as an *adj.*)

designating esp. fabrics with a texture resembling this.

waffle iron *n.* an appliance used to bake and form indentations on waffles.

waft ● *v.* **1** float or glide gently through the air. **2** carry or send gently through the air. ● *n.* a scent carried by a breeze. [*Rhymes with* LOFT *or* RAFT]

wag¹ ● *v.* (**wags, wagged, wagging**) shake, wave, or sway to and fro, esp. rapidly. ● *n.* a single wagging motion. □ **tongues** (or **chins** or **jaws**) **wag** there is talk or gossip.

wag² *n.* a joker or wit.

wage ● *n.* **1** a payment, usu. fixed and regular, for work performed. **2** *literary* reward, recompense. ● *v.* (**wages, waged, waging**) conduct, carry on (a war etc.).

wager ● *v.* **1** stake (esp. money) on the outcome of an uncertain event. **2 a** make a bet. **b** *informal* be certain. ● *n.* **1** a betting transaction. **2** a thing laid down as a bet. □ **wagering** *n.*

waggish *adj.* amusing, witty.

waggle *informal* ● *v.* (**waggles, waggled, waggling**) move with short movements from side to side or up and down. ● *n.* a waggling motion.

Wagnerian ● *adj.* **1** having to do with the German composer Richard Wagner (1813–83) or his music. **2** grandiose, highly dramatic. ● *n.* an admirer of Wagner or his music. [Say vog NAIRY un]

wagon *n.* **1** a large sturdy four-wheeled vehicle, usu. drawn by horse or tractor and sometimes covered, for transporting goods or passengers. **2** a child's small four-wheeled cart, drawn by hand. □ (**off** or) **on the wagon** *informal* (not) abstaining from alcoholic drinks.

wagon train *n.* esp. *hist.* a succession of esp. covered wagons used by migrating pioneers.

Wahhabi *n.* (*pl.* **Wahhabis**) a member of a strictly orthodox Sunni Muslim sect. [Say wuh HOBBY]

wahoo *interj.* = YAHOO². [Say wuh HOO]

wah-wah *n.* **1** an effect achieved on an electric guitar by using a pedal to control the output from the amplifier. **2** a device for producing this effect.

waif *n.* a neglected, abandoned, or starved child. □**waifish** *adj.* **waiflike** *adj.*

wail ● *n.* **1** a long loud high-pitched cry of pain, grief, or despair. **2** a sound resembling this. ● *v.* **1** utter a wail. **2** produce a sound like wailing. **3** complain or lament persistently. □**wailer** *n.*

wainscot *n.* wood panelling esp. covering the lower part of a wall of a room. □**wainscotted** *adj.* (also **wainscoted**) [*Say* WAYNE scott]

wainscotting *n.* (also **wainscoting**) **1** wainscot. **2** the material used for this. [*Say* WAYNE scott ing]

waist *n.* **1** the part of the human body below the ribs and above the hips. **2** the part of a garment encircling or covering the waist. **3** the narrow middle part of a violin, hourglass, etc. □**waisted** *comb. form*

waistband *n.* a band of material fitting around the waist on a skirt, pair of pants, etc.

waistcoat *n.* a man's formal vest, usu. buttoned and worn under a jacket.

waistline *n.* **1** a person's waist, usu. with reference to its circumference. **2** = WAIST 2.

wait ● *v.* **1** stay where one is or delay action until a particular time or event. **2** stop or slow down so that a person catches up. **3** await. **4** be ready or available. **5 a** (of a matter etc.) be neglected or unresolved for some time. **b** be delayed. ● *n.* a period of waiting. □**wait and see** await the progress of events before acting. **waiting to happen** likely to happen imminently. **wait on 1 a** attend to the needs of. **b** take orders from and serve meals to. **c** serve. **2** wait for. **wait out** *informal* wait for the end of. **wait tables** (or **on tables**) work in a restaurant as a waiter or waitress. **you wait!** used to imply a threat or promise.

waiter *n.* **1** a person who serves customers at their tables in a restaurant. **2** a tray or salver.

waiting list *n.* a list of people waiting for something not immediately available.

waiting room *n.* a room where one may wait for an appointment etc.

wait-list ● *n.* a waiting list. ● *v.* place on a waiting list.

waitperson *n.* (*pl.* **waitpersons** or **waitpeople**) a waiter or waitress.

waitress ● *n.* (*pl.* **waitresses**) a woman who serves customers at their tables in a restaurant. ● *v.* (**waitresses**, **waitressed**, **waitressing**) work as a waitress. □**waitressing** *n.*

wait staff *n.* the waiters and waitresses of a restaurant collectively.

waive *v.* (**waives**, **waived**, **waiving**) **1** decline to take advantage of (a right etc.). **2** refrain from insisting upon or imposing (a rule, penalty, etc.).

waiver *n.* **1** the act or an instance of waiving a right, claim, etc. **2** a formal document recording this.

Wakashan *n.* an Aboriginal language family of the west coast of N America, including Haisla, Heiltsuk, Kwakwala, and Nuu-chah-nulth. [*Say* WOKKA shan]

wake¹ ● *v.* (**wakes**; *past* **woke** or **waked**; *past participle* **woken** or **waked**; **waking**) **1** come out of or rouse from the state of sleep or unconsciousness. **2** become or cause to become alert or aware. **3** disturb with noise. **4** stir or evoke. **5** rise or raise from the dead. ● *n.* **1** a watch or vigil held beside the body of a dead person before burial. **2** a party to celebrate and remember the life of a person who has died. □**waking** *adj.*

wake² *n.* **1** the track left on the water's surface by a moving vessel. **2** turbulent air left behind a moving aircraft. □**in the wake of 1** behind, following. **2** in the aftermath of.

wakeboarding *n.* a water sport in which participants ride on a short, wide board, towed by a motorboat. □**wakeboard** *n.*

wakeful *adj.* **1** unable to sleep. **2** (of a night etc.) passed with little sleep. □**wakefulness** *n.*

waken *v.* make or become awake.

wake-up call *n.* **1** a telephone call made to wake a person up. **2** an incident etc. symptomatic of and drawing attention to a larger problem requiring immediate action.

Waldorf salad *n.* a salad of diced apples, walnuts, etc., with mayonnaise. [*Say* WOL dorf]

Waldorf school *n.* a private school based on the ideas of the Austrian philosopher Rudolf Steiner (1861–1925). [*Say* WOL dorf]

walk ● *v.* **1** move along at a slow or moderate pace using one's legs. **2** travel or go on foot. **3 a** escort or accompany on foot. **b** lead (a dog etc.) at a walking pace. **4** (of a ghost) roam. **5** *Baseball* **a** (of a batter) reach first base by taking four balls. **b** (of a pitcher) send (a batter) to first base by throwing four balls. ● *n.* **1** a short journey on foot. **2** a person's particular manner of walking. **3** a place intended or suitable for walking. **4** a sidewalk or paved path. **5** a distance to be walked. **6** *Baseball* a free pass to first base awarded to a batter who has taken four balls from a pitcher. □**walk**

around (or **about**) stroll. **walk all over** *informal* **1** defeat easily. **2** take advantage of. **walk away with** *informal* = WALK OFF WITH. **walk in** enter or arrive. **walk in the park** a feat achieved with ease. **walk into** *informal* encounter through unwariness. **walk a person off his** (or **her**) **feet** (or **legs**) exhaust a person with walking. **walk off the job** go on strike. **walk off with** *informal* **1** steal. **2** win easily. **walk out 1** depart suddenly in anger or protest. **2** go on strike. **walk out on** abandon. **walk the streets 1** be a prostitute. **2** traverse the streets esp. in search of work etc. **walk through 1** rehearse (a scene etc.). **2** guide carefully through a procedure. **walk the walk** carry through on promises made. □ **walking** n. & adj.

walkable adj. (of a distance) capable of being walked.

walker n. **1** a person who walks. **2** a wheeled framework that supports a baby so that he or she can learn to walk. **3** a frame with or without wheels used by disabled or old people to help them walk.

walkie-talkie n. a small two-way radio.

walk-in ● adj. **1** (of a storage area) large enough to walk into. **2** designating an establishment or medical facility etc. that serves customers and patients without appointments. ● n. (pl. **walk-ins**) **1** a facility that serves customers without appointments. **2** a client of such a facility.

walking wounded pl. n. **1** war casualties capable of walking despite their injuries. **2** *informal* a group of people suffering from illnesses or emotional difficulties.

Walkman n. (pl. **Walkmans**) *proprietary* a type of personal stereo with headphones.

walk of life n. (plural **walks of life**) a person's profession or social rank.

walk-on n. a small role usu. with no speaking in a film, play, etc.

walkout n. **1** a sudden angry departure, esp. in protest. **2** a strike called by workers. **3** a doorway or passageway providing access to the outside.

walkover n. an easy victory.

walk-through n. a rough rehearsal of a play or film.

walk-up n. **1** a building with no elevator. **2** an apartment etc. located in such a building.

walkway n. any passage or path designed for or used by pedestrians.

wall ● n. **1** a continuous and usu. vertical structure, enclosing, protecting, or dividing a space or supporting a roof. **2** a vertical rock face. **3** *Anatomy* the outermost layer or enclosing membrane etc. of an organ etc. **4** an obstacle or barrier. **5** an immaterial thing dividing or isolating like a wall. ● v. **1** fortify or enclose with or as if with a wall or walls. **2** block, seal, or close with a wall. **3** confine within a sealed space. □ **between you and me and the wall** *informal* in strict confidence. **go to the wall** do everything in one's power to help another. **hit the wall** reach a point at which one can proceed no further. **off the wall** *informal* unorthodox, unconventional. **up the wall** *informal* crazy or furious. **walls have ears** one should be cautious about what one says lest it be overheard. □ **walled** adj.

wallaby n. (pl. **wallabies**) a kind of marsupial that is similar to, but smaller than, a kangaroo. [Say WOLLA bee]

wallboard n. drywall.

wallcovering n. any of various materials used to cover and decorate interior walls.

wallet n. a flat pocket-sized folding case for keeping money, identification, etc. on one's person.

walleye n. **1** a large N American freshwater fish that has large prominent eyes. **2** an eye with a streaked or white iris. **3** an eye squinting outwards. □ **walleyed** adj.

wallflower n. **1** a plant with fragrant clustered flowers in spring. **2** *informal* a shy or socially awkward person. **3** a person sitting out at a dance for lack of partners.

wall hanging n. a usu. large decorative tapestry etc. hung for display.

Walloon n. **1** a member of a French-speaking people inhabiting southern and eastern Belgium and neighbouring parts of France. **2** their French dialect. □ **Walloon** adj. [Say wuh LOON]

wallop *informal* ● v. (**wallops**, **walloped**, **walloping**) **1 a** pound or strike with great force. **b** spank; beat. **2** esp. *Sport* defeat decisively. ● n. a heavy or resounding blow. □ **walloping** n. & adj.

wallow ● v. **1** lie or roll around in mud, water, etc. **2** indulge in unrestrained self-pity etc. ● n. **1** an act of wallowing. **2** a place used by buffalo, rhinoceros, etc., for wallowing.

wallpaper ● n. **1** decorative paper pasted on interior walls as decoration. **2** *Computing* an optional background pattern or picture displayed onscreen. ● v. decorate with wallpaper.

Wall Street n. the American money market or financial interests. □ **Wall Streeter** n.

wall-to-wall adj. **1** (of carpeting) covering the entire floor area. **2** filling a space entirely.

walnut *n.* **1** a tall tree, valued for its edible nuts and its ornamental timber. **2** the nut of this tree, consisting of a wrinkled edible kernel in a ridged shell. **3** the wood of the walnut tree.

walrus *n.* (*pl.* **walrus** or **walruses**) a large amphibious long-tusked Arctic mammal.

waltz ● *n.* (*pl.* **waltzes**) **1** a dance in triple time performed by couples who rotate and progress around the floor. **2** the music for this. ● *v.* (**waltzes, waltzed, waltzing**) **1** dance a waltz. **2** *informal* move lightly, casually, etc.

wampum *n. hist.* small beads cut from a quahog shell and woven into strings or belts by Aboriginal peoples of eastern N America to be used as a unit of exchange. [*Say* WOM pum]

WAN *n.* wide-area network. [*Rhymes with* PAN]

wan *adj.* (**wanner, wannest**) **1** (of a person) pale, sickly. **2** (of light) faint. □ **wanly** *adv.* [*Rhymes with* PAWN]

wand *n.* **1 a** a supposedly magic stick used in casting spells. **b** a stick used by a conjuror for effect. **2** a slender rod carried or used as a marker in the ground. **3** a small applicator for mascara etc. **4** a hand-held electronic device for reading a bar code, detecting metal, etc.

wander ● *v.* **1** go about from place to place aimlessly. **2 a** wind about; meander. **b** (of esp. a person) get lost; stray from a path etc. **3** be inattentive or incoherent. ● *n.* an act of wandering. □ **wanderer** *n.* **wandering** *n.*

wanderlust *n.* a desire to travel.

wane *v.* (**wanes, waned, waning**) **1** (of the moon) decrease in apparent size after the full moon. **2** decrease in power, brilliance, etc. □ **on the wane** waning.

wangle *v. informal* (**wangles, wangled, wangling**) obtain (a favour etc.) by scheming etc.

wannabe *n. slang* often *derogatory* a person who tries to emulate a particular celebrity etc.

want ● *v.* **1 a** desire; wish for possession of. **b** desire sexually. **c** *informal* ought; should; need. **2** lack; be deficient. ● *n.* **1 a** a lack or deficiency. **b** poverty. **2** a desire for a thing etc.

want ad *n.* a classified advertisement.

wanted *adj.* (of a suspected criminal etc.) sought by the police.

wanting *adj.* **1** lacking (in quality or quantity). **2** absent, not provided. □ **be found wanting** fail to meet requirements.

wanton *adj.* **1** random; motiveless. **2** sexually promiscuous. □ **wantonly** *adv.* **wantonness** *n.*

wapiti *n.* (*pl.* **wapitis**) an elk. [*Say* WOP it ee]

war ● *n.* **1 a** armed hostilities between esp. nations. **b** a specific conflict or the period during which such conflict exists. **2** warfare as a profession or art. **3 a** a sustained campaign against crime, poverty, etc. **b** sustained rivalry or competition. ● *v.* (**wars, warred, warring**) make war. □ **at war** engaged in a war. **go to war 1** declare a war. **2** (of a soldier etc.) see active service.

warbird *n. informal* a fighter aircraft.

warble *v.* (**warbles, warbled, warbling**) sing in a quavering or bird-like manner.

warbler *n.* a small bird with a warbling song.

war bonnet *n.* a headdress, esp. one with feathers attached to a headband, worn as traditional garb by some North American Indian peoples.

war chest *n.* a store of funds for a war or other activity.

war crime *n.* a crime violating the international laws of war. □ **war criminal** *n.*

war cry *n.* **1** something shouted to rally one's troops. **2** a party slogan etc.

ward *n.* **1** a separate room or division of a hospital etc. **2** an esp. municipal administrative or electoral division. **3** a minor under the care of a guardian appointed by the parents or a court. □ **ward off 1** parry (a blow). **2** avert, turn away (danger etc.).

warden *n.* **1** a supervising official. **2** *Cdn* the head of a county council. **3 a** a prison governor. **b** the governor of an institution at a university or college. **4** *Anglicanism* an elected lay representative of a parish.

warder *n.* a prison guard.

wardrobe *n.* **1** a large cupboard for storing clothes. **2** a person's entire stock of clothes. **3** the costume department or costumes of a performing arts company etc.

wardroom *n.* a room in a warship for the use of commissioned officers.

ware *n.* **1** things of the same kind. **2** (usu. in *pl.*) **a** articles for sale. **b** a person's skills etc. **3** ceramics etc. of a specified type. **4** (in *comb.*) a kind of software.

warehouse ● *n.* **1** a building in which esp. retail goods are stored. **2** a wholesale or large retail store. ● *v.* (**warehouses, warehoused, warehousing**) **1** deposit or store in a warehouse. **2** *informal* shut up in a prison or hospital etc.

warfare *n.* **1** the activity of fighting a war. **2** an aggressive or violent conflict.

warfarin *n.* an anticoagulant used esp. as a rat poison. [*Say* WORF er in]

war game *n.* **1** a military exercise testing or improving tactics etc. **2** a battle etc. conducted with counters representing military units. □ **war-gaming** *n.*

warhead *n.* the explosive head of a missile, torpedo, or similar weapon.

warhorse *n.* **1** *hist.* a knight's or trooper's powerful horse. **2** *informal* a veteran of any activity; a dependable or stalwart person or thing. **3** a frequently used or very familiar thing, esp. a work of art which is frequently performed.

warlike *adj.* **1** hostile. **2** of or like warfare.

warlock *n.* a man who practises witchcraft.

warlord *n.* the leader of a military group within a country or an area.

warm ● *adj.* **1** of or at a fairly or comfortably high temperature. **2** (of clothes etc.) providing warmth. **3 a** sympathetic; friendly; loving. **b** enthusiastic. **4** *informal* close to finding what is sought. **5** (of a colour etc.) reddish, pink, or yellowish, etc. **6** *Hunting* (of a scent) fresh and strong. ● *v.* **a** make or become warm. **b** make or become cheerful, excited, etc. ● *n.* **1** the act of warming. **2** warmth. □ **warm up 1** (of an athlete, performer, etc.) prepare oneself by preliminary light exercise or practice. **2** become or cause to become warmer. **3** become enthusiastic etc. (about). **4** heat (food) esp. again. □ **warmer** *n.* **warming** *n.* **warmly** *adv.*

warm-blooded *adj.* **1** having warm blood. **2** passionate. □ **warm-bloodedness** *n.*

warmed-over *adj.* stale; second-hand.

warm front *n.* the leading edge of a mass of warm air.

warm fuzzy *informal* ● *n.* (*pl.* **warm fuzzies**) a gut feeling of emotional warmth or satisfaction. ● *adj.* (also **warm and fuzzy**) having to do with such a reaction.

warm-hearted *adj.* kind, friendly.

warmonger *n.* a person who seeks to bring about war. □ **warmongering** *n.* & *adj.* [*Say* WAR mong gur *or* WAR mung gur]

warmth *n.* **1 a** the state of being warm. **b** moderate heat. **2** a friendly or loving attitude etc.

warm-up *n.* **1** a session of exercise or practice before a contest, performance, etc. **2** (as an *adj.*) **a** designating clothing worn during an athletic warm-up. **b** designating an act that performs prior to the main attraction.

warn *v.* **1** inform of danger, a possible problem, etc. **2** admonish. **3** give (a person) cautionary notice regarding conduct etc. □ **warn off** warn to keep away (from).

warning ● *n.* **1** anything that serves to warn. **2** an indication of any impending event. ● *adj.* serving to warn or indicate.

war of attrition *n.* a prolonged war, usu. involving massive losses on both sides, with each side calculating that the other's resources will be exhausted first.

warp ● *v.* **1** make or become bent or twisted as a result of heat, damp, etc. **2** make or become perverted or strange. ● *n.* **1** a state of being warped. **2** the threads stretched lengthwise in a loom to be crossed by the weft. **3** (in science fiction) an imaginary distortion in space in relation to time. □ **warped** *adj.*

warpath *n.* **1** *hist.* the route taken on a warlike expedition by North American Indians. **2** *informal* any hostile course.

warplane *n.* a military aircraft.

warp speed *n.* (in science fiction) travelling speed faster than that of light.

warrant ● *n.* **1** a written authorization allowing police to search premises, arrest a suspect, etc. **2** an acceptable reason for doing something. **3** a written authorization, money voucher, etc. ● *v.* **1** justify. **2** guarantee or attest to.

warrant officer *n.* **1** (also **Warrant Officer**) (in the Canadian Army and Air Force) a non-commissioned officer of a rank above sergeant. Abbreviation: **WO**. **2** an officer of a similar rank in other armies.

warranty *n.* (*pl.* **warranties**) a manufacturer's written promise as to the extent to which defective goods will be repaired, replaced, etc.

warren *n.* **1** a network of interconnecting rabbit burrows. **2** a maze-like building etc.

warring *adj.* **1** fighting. **2** conflicting.

warrior *n.* a brave or experienced soldier or fighter.

warship *n.* an armoured ship used in war.

wart *n.* **1** a small benign growth on the skin, caused by a virus. **2** any protuberance on the skin of an animal, surface of a plant, etc. □ **warts and all** *informal* with no attempt to conceal blemishes or inadequacies. □ **warty** *adj.* (**wartier, wartiest**)

warthog *n.* an African wild pig with a large head and warty lumps on its face, and large curved tusks.

wartime *n.* the period during which a war is waged.

war-torn *adj.* devastated by war.

war-weary *adj.* exhausted and dispirited by war.

wary *adj.* (**warier, wariest**) **1** on one's guard. **2** cautious, suspicious. □ **warily** *adv.* **wariness** *n.* [*Say* WARE ee]

was *1st & 3rd singular past of* BE.

wasabi *n.* a plant whose root (resembling horseradish) is used in Japanese cooking. [*Say* wuh SOBBY]

wash ● *v.* (**washes, washed, washing**) **1** cleanse with liquid, esp. water and usu. soap. **2** remove (dirt) in this way. **3** (of fabric) bear washing without damage. **4** (of a stain etc.) be removed by washing. **5** (of moving liquid) carry or be carried along. **6** sweep, move, or splash. ● *n.* (*pl.* **washes**) **1** the act of washing; the process of being washed. **2** a quantity of clothes for washing. **3** the water or air disturbed by the passage of a ship etc. or aircraft. **4** a liquid to spread over a surface to cleanse, heal, or colour. **5** a situation or result which is of no net benefit to either of two opposing sides. □ **come out in the wash** *informal* be clarified or resolved in the course of time. **wash down 1** wash completely. **2** accompany or follow (food) with a drink. **wash one's hands of** renounce responsibility for. **wash up 1** wash (dishes etc.) after use. **2** wash one's face and hands. **won't wash** *informal* (of an argument etc.) will not be accepted. □ **washable** *adj.*

wash-and-wear *adj.* **1** (of a fabric) easily washed and not needing ironing. **2** (of a haircut) requiring little or no styling.

wash basin *n.* a basin for washing the hands, face, etc.

washboard *n.* **1 a** a board of ribbed wood or a sheet of corrugated zinc on which clothes are scrubbed in washing. **b** this used as a percussion instrument. **2** a road whose surface has become corrugated by weather and use.

washcloth *n.* a face cloth.

washed out *adj.* **1** faded by washing. **2** pale.

washed up *adj. slang* having failed.

washer *n.* **1 a** a person or thing that washes. **b** a washing machine. **2** a flat ring to tighten or prevent leakage at a joint. **3** a similar ring placed under a nut or the head of a screw, etc. □ **washerless** *adj.*

washerwoman *n.* (*pl.* **washerwomen**) a woman whose occupation is washing clothes etc.

washing *n.* **1** a quantity of clothes for washing or just washed. **2** the act of washing clothes.

washing machine *n.* a machine for washing clothes etc.

washout *n.* **1** a narrow river channel. **2** a breach in a road etc., caused by flooding. **3** *informal* a complete failure.

washroom *n.* **1** esp. *Cdn* a room with toilet facilities. **2** a room with facilities for washing oneself. □ **go to the washroom** esp. *Cdn euphemism* defecate or urinate.

washstand *n.* a piece of furniture to hold a basin, soap, etc. for washing oneself with.

washtub *n.* a tub for washing clothes etc.

wasn't *contr.* was not.

WASP *n.* usu. *derogatory* **1** a white Protestant of Anglo-Saxon descent. **2** a middle-class N American white Protestant. □ **WASP** *adj.* **WASPy** *adj.*

wasp *n.* a stinging insect with black and yellow stripes and a very thin waist.

waspish *adj.* bad-tempered; irritable. □ **waspishly** *adv.*

wastage *n.* **1** an amount wasted. **2** loss or destruction of something. [*Say* WASTE idge]

waste ● *v.* (**wastes, wasted, wasting**) **1** use to no purpose or extravagantly. **2** fail to use or make use of. **3 a** give (advice etc.), utter (words etc.), without effect. **b** fail to be appreciated. **4** wear gradually away; wither. **5** *slang* **a** beat up. **b** kill. ● *adj.* **1** superfluous. **2** (of an area) not inhabited or cultivated. ● *n.* **1** the act or an instance of wasting. **2 a** waste material or food. **b** excrement. **3** a waste region. □ **go to waste** be wasted. **lay waste** ravage, devastate. **waste not, want not** extravagance leads to poverty. □ **waster** *n.*

wastebasket *n.* a receptacle for waste paper.

wasted *adj.* **1** *in sense of* WASTE *v.* **2** *slang* **a** very tired. **b** intoxicated.

wasteful *adj.* **1** extravagant. **2** causing or showing waste. □ **wastefully** *adj.* **wastefulness** *n.*

wasteland *n.* **1** a barren or devastated area of land. **2** a place or time considered spiritually barren.

wastepaper basket *n.* a wastebasket.

waste product *n.* (esp. in *pl.*) a useless by-product of manufacture etc.

wastrel *n.* a wasteful or good-for-nothing person. [*Say* WASTE rull]

watch ● *v.* (**watches, watched, watching**) **1** look at. **2 a** keep under observation. **b** pay attention to. **3** be vigilant; take heed. **4** look after. ● *n.* (*pl.* **watches**) **1** a small timepiece worn on one's person. **2** a state of alert observation or attention. **3** *Nautical* a usu. four-hour spell of duty. **4** *hist.* a watchman or group of watchmen. **5** a former division of the night. □ **on the watch** waiting for an expected occurrence. **watch one's back** be alert to danger. **watch it** (or **oneself**) *informal* be careful. **watch out 1** be on one's guard. **2** as a warning of immediate danger. **watch one's step** proceed cautiously. □ **watchable** *adj.* **watcher** *n.*

watchdog *n.* **1** a dog kept to guard property etc. **2** a person or body monitoring others' behaviour etc.

watchful *adj.* alert; on the watch. □ **watchfully** *adv.* **watchfulness** *n.*

watchmaker *n.* a person who makes and repairs watches. □ **watchmaking** *n.*

watchman *n.* (*pl.* **watchmen**) a man employed to look after an empty building.

watchtower *n.* a tower from which observation can be kept.

watchword *n.* a slogan.

water ● *n.* **1** a colourless tasteless liquid compound of oxygen and hydrogen, found in seas, lakes, and rivers, in rain, and in secretions of organisms. **2** an expanse of water. **3** (in *pl.*) part of a sea or river. **4** (often as **the waters**) mineral water at a spa etc. **5 a** urine. **b** (usu. in *pl.*) the amniotic fluid discharged from the womb before childbirth. ● *v.* **1** sprinkle or soak with water. **2** give water to. **3** (of the mouth or eyes) secrete saliva or tears. **4** dilute. □ **in deep water** (or **waters**) in serious trouble. **like water** lavishly. **make one's mouth water** stimulate one's appetite or anticipation. **make water 1** urinate. **2** (of a ship) take in water. **on the water** on a ship etc. **water down 1** dilute with water. **2** make less vivid or forceful. **water under the bridge** past events accepted as past.

water-based *adj.* having water as the main ingredient.

waterbed *n.* a bed with a rubber or plastic mattress filled with water.

water bomber *n. Cdn* an aircraft used to drop water on forest fires. □ **water bombing** *n.*

water buffalo *n.* a large black domesticated buffalo with heavy swept-back horns.

water chestnut *n.* **1** an aquatic plant producing an edible rounded seed. **2 a** the tuber of a tropical sedge that is widely used in Asian cuisine. **b** the sedge that yields this tuber.

watercolour *n.* (also **watercolor**) **1** artists' paint made of pigment to be diluted with water. **2** a picture painted with this. **3** the art of painting with watercolours. □ **watercolourist** *n.*

water cooler *n.* a tank of cooled drinking water in a workplace esp. as a setting for gossip.

watercourse *n.* a brook, stream, or artificial water channel.

watercraft *n.* (*pl.* **watercraft**) any boat.

watercress *n.* a cress that grows in flowing water, with strong-flavoured leaves used in salads etc.

waterfall *n.* a stream of water flowing over a precipice or down a steep hillside.

waterfowl *n.* birds frequenting water.

waterfront *n.* esp. urban land adjoining a body of water.

water hazard *n.* a pond or stream on a golf course that acts as an obstruction.

water hole *n.* a shallow depression in which water collects.

water ice *n.* a confection of flavoured and frozen water and sugar etc.

watering can *n.* a portable container with a long spout, used for watering plants.

watering hole *n.* **1** a pool of water from which animals drink. **2** *slang* a bar.

water lily *n.* an aquatic plant with broad floating leaves and large cup-shaped flowers.

waterline *n.* **1 a** the line along which water touches the side of something. **b** such a line marked on a ship. **2** a pipe etc. used to convey water.

waterlogged *adj.* **1** saturated with or full of water. **2** (of a boat etc.) hardly able to float.

Waterloo *n.* (*pl.* **Waterloos**) a decisive defeat. [*Say* water LOO]

water main *n.* a water supply system's main pipe.

watermark ● *n.* a faint design made in some paper, seen when held against the light. ● *v.* mark with this.

watermelon *n.* a large smooth green melon with sweet edible red pulp.

water park *n.* a public recreation area with water slides, swimming pools, etc.

water pipe *n.* **1** a pipe that conveys water. **2** an oriental tobacco pipe with a long tube passing through water.

water pistol *n.* a toy pistol shooting a jet of water.

water polo *n.* a game played in a swimming pool, in which teams attempt to throw a ball into the other team's goal.

water power *n.* mechanical force derived from the motion of water.

waterproof ● *adj.* impervious to water. ● *v.* make waterproof.

water repellent *adj.* not easily penetrated by water.

water-resistant *adj.* (of a fabric, wristwatch, etc.) able to resist the penetration of water.

watershed *n.* **1** a line of separation between waters flowing to different rivers, basins, or seas, **2** a turning point in affairs. **3** the area drained by a single lake or river.

waterside *n.* the margin of a sea, lake, or river.

water ski ● *n.* each of a pair of skis, or a single board, which enable a person pulled by a motorboat to skim over the surface of the water. ● *v.* (**water-ski, water-skis, water-skied, water-skiing**) travel on a water ski or skis. □ **water skier** *n.* **water skiing** *n.*

waterslide *n.* a slide down which water cascades, esp. into a swimming pool.

waterspout *n.* a rotating column of water and spray formed by a whirlwind between sea and cloud.

water table *n.* a level below which the ground is saturated with water.

water taxi *n.* a small boat for hire for transporting passengers.

watertight *adj.* **1** fastened or fitted or made so as to prevent the passage of water. **2** (of an argument etc.) unassailable.

water torture *n.* a form of torture in which the victim is exposed to the incessant dripping of water on the head, or the sound of dripping.

water tower *n.* a tower with an elevated tank for distributing water.

waterway *n.* **1** a navigable channel. **2** a route for transport by water.

water wheel *n.* a wheel driven by water to work machinery, or to raise water.

waterworks *n.* **1** an establishment for managing a city's water supply. **2** *informal* the shedding of tears.

watery *adj.* **1** containing too much water. **2** too thin in consistency. **3** of, or of the consistency of water. **4** (of colour) pale.

watt *n.* the SI unit of power, equivalent to one joule per second, corresponding to the rate of energy in an electric circuit where the potential difference is one volt and the current one ampere. Symbol: **W**.

wattage *n.* an amount of electrical power expressed in watts.

wattle[1] *n.* interlaced rods and split rods as a material for making fences, walls, etc. [*Rhymes with* BOTTLE]

wattle[2] *n.* a fleshy lobe on the head or throat of a turkey or other birds. □ **wattled** *adj.* [*Rhymes with* BOTTLE]

wave ● *v.* (**waves, waved, waving**) **1** move a hand etc. to and fro in greeting or as a signal. **2 a** show a motion as of a flag etc. in the wind. **b** impart a waving motion to. **3** brandish (a sword etc.). **4** tell or direct by waving. **5** express (a greeting etc.) by waving. **6** make or be wavy. ● *n.* **1** a moving ridge of water, curling into an arched form and breaking on the shore. **2 a** a thing compared to this. **b** (usu. as **the wave**) a wavelike effect produced by a crowd at a sporting event etc. **3** a gesture of waving. **4 a** the process of waving the hair. **b** a slight curl in the hair. **5 a** a temporary occurrence or increase of a condition, emotion, or influence. **b** a specified period of widespread weather. **6** *Physics* a periodic disturbance of the particles of a substance without net movement of the particles, as in the passage of heat, sound, etc. □ **make waves** *informal* **1** cause trouble. **2** create a significant impression. **wave aside** dismiss as irrelevant. □ **wavelike** *adj.*

waveband *n.* a range of (esp. radio) wavelengths between certain limits.

wavelength *n.* **1** the distance between successive crests of a wave, esp. points in a sound wave or electromagnetic wave. **2** this as a distinctive feature of radio waves. **3** *informal* a particular mode of thinking and communicating.

wavelet *n.* a small wave.

waver *v.* **1** be or become unsteady; falter. **2** be undecided or indecisive. **3** flicker. □ **wavery** *adj.*

wavy *adj.* (**wavier, waviest**) having waves or curves. □ **waviness** *n.*

wax[1] ● *n.* (*pl.* **waxes**) **1** beeswax. **2** a white translucent material obtained from this and used for candles etc. **3** any similar substance, typically a lipid or hydrocarbon. **4** a session of waxing to remove hair. ● *v.* (**waxes, waxed, waxing**) **1** cover, polish, or treat with wax. **2** remove unwanted hair by applying wax and peeling off the wax and hairs together. **3** *informal* defeat resoundingly. □ **the whole ball of wax** the full complement of related things.

wax[2] *v.* (**waxes, waxed, waxing**) **1** (of the moon) have an ever larger part of its visible surface illuminated. **2** become philosophical, eloquent, etc. while speaking or writing.

wax bean *n.* a yellow-podded bean.

waxed paper *n.* (also **wax paper**) paper coated with wax used for wrapping food etc.

waxen *adj.* having a smooth pale surface as of wax.

waxwing *n.* a crested songbird with small

tips like red sealing wax to some wing feathers.

waxwork *n.* **1** a lifelike dummy modelled in wax. **2** (in *pl.*) an exhibition of waxworks.

waxy *adj.* (**waxier, waxiest**) resembling wax in consistency or in its surface.

way ● *n.* **1** a road etc., for passing along. **2** a route for reaching a place. **3** a place of passage into a building etc. **4** a method or plan for doing something. **5 a** a person's desired course of action. **b** a personal peculiarity. **6** a specific manner of life or procedure. **7** the normal course of events. **8** (also *informal* **ways**) a travelling distance. **9** an unimpeded opportunity of advance. **10** a region or ground over which advance is desired. **11** advance in some direction. **12** movement of a ship etc. **13** a specified direction. **14** (in *pl.*) parts into which a thing is divided. **15** *informal* the scope or range of something. **16** a specified condition or state. ● *adv. informal* to a considerable extent. □ **across the way** facing or opposite. **be on one's way** set off; depart. **by the way** incidentally. **by way of 1** through; by means of. **2** with the intention of. **come one's way** become available to one. **get** (or **have**) **one's way** (or **have it one's own way** etc.) get what one wants. **give way 1 a** make concessions. **b** yield. **2** concede precedence (to). **3** collapse. **4** be superseded by. **go all the way 1** go the whole distance. **2** do something wholeheartedly. **3** *informal* engage in sexual intercourse. **go out of one's way** make a special effort. **go one's own way** act independently. **in no way** not at all. **in the** (or **one's**) **way** forming an obstacle or hindrance. **lead the way 1** act as guide or leader. **2** show how to do something. **look the other way** ignore what one should notice. **make way 1** allow room for others to proceed. **2** achieve progress. **one way or another** by some means. **on the** (or **one's**) **way 1** in the course of a journey etc. **2** having progressed. **3** *informal* (of a child) conceived but not yet born. **on the way out** *informal* going out of fashion. **the other way around** (or **about**) in an inverted or reversed position or direction. **out of the way 1** no longer an obstacle. **2** disposed of. **3** (of a person) imprisoned or killed. **4** (with *neg.*) common or not remarkable. **5** (of a place) remote. **way back** *informal* long ago.

waybill *n.* **1** a document on which a shipper, courier, etc. records details of the item to be transported. **2** a list of passengers or parcels on a vehicle.

wayfarer *n.* a traveller, esp. on foot. □ **wayfaring** *n.* [*Say* WAY fare er]

waylay *v.* (**waylays, waylaid, waylaying**) **1** lie in wait for. **2** stop to rob or talk to.

way of life *n.* (*pl.* **ways of life**) the principles or habits governing all one's actions etc.

way-out *adj. informal* **1** unusual, eccentric. **2** excellent.

waypoint *n.* **1** a stopping place. **2** the coordinates of each stage of a flight etc.

wayside *n.* the side of a road. □ **fall by the wayside 1** fail to continue in an endeavour etc. **2** be discarded.

way station *n.* **1** a minor station on a railway. **2** a point marking progress.

wayward *adj.* difficult to control or predict. □ **waywardness** *n.*

we *pron.* **1** used by and with reference to more than one person speaking or writing. **2** used for or by a royal person or writer in a formal context. **3** people in general.

weak *adj.* **1** deficient in strength, power, or number; fragile. **2** sickly, feeble. **3 a** easily led. **b** indicating a lack of resolution. **4** not convincing. **5** (of a liquid or solution) watery. **6** (of a syllable etc.) unstressed. □ **weakly** *adv.*

weaken *v.* make or become weak.

weakfish *n.* (*pl.* **weakfish** or **weakfishes**) a North American marine fish, popular as a food and sport fish.

weak-kneed *adj. informal* lacking resolution.

weakling *n.* a feeble person or animal.

weak link *n.* a weak element which renders the whole vulnerable.

weakness *n.* (*pl.* **weaknesses**) **1** the state or condition of being weak. **2** a weak point; a defect. **3** the inability to resist a temptation. **4** a self-indulgent liking.

weal¹ *n.* = WELT. [*Sounds like* WHEEL]

weal² *n. literary* welfare; good fortune. [*Sounds like* WHEEL]

wealth *n.* **1** riches. **2** the state of being rich. **3** an abundance or profusion.

wealthy *adj.* (**wealthier, wealthiest**) rich.

wean *v.* **1** accustom (a young mammal) to food other than its mother's milk. **2** disengage (from a habit etc.) esp. gradually. **3** expose to from an early age.

weapon *n.* **1** a thing designed or used for inflicting bodily harm. **2** a means used to gain an advantage. □ **weaponless** *adj.* **weaponry** *n.*

weapons-grade *adj.* designating fissile material suitable for making nuclear weapons.

wear ● *v.* (**wears;** *past* **wore;** *past participle* **worn; wearing**) **1** have on one's person as clothing or an ornament etc. **2** be dressed habitually in. **3** exhibit or present (a facial expression or appearance). **4 a** injure the surface of, or partly obliterate, by rubbing or use. **b** undergo such injury or change. **5** rub or be rubbed off. **6** exhaust. **7** overcome by persistence. **8 a** last long. **b** endure continued use. **9** (of time) pass, esp. tediously. ● *n.* **1** the act of wearing or the state of being worn. **2** things worn. **3** (also **wear and tear**) damage sustained from continuous use. **4** the capacity for resisting wear and tear. □ **wear off** lose effectiveness or intensity. **wear out 1** use or be used until no longer usable. **2** tire or be tired out. **wear thin 1** (of patience etc.) begin to fail. **2** tax one's patience. **wear** (or **wear one's years**) **well** *informal* remain young-looking. □ **wearable** *adj. & n.* **wearer** *n.*

wearing *adj.* **1** tiring; stressful; frustrating. **2** tedious. [*Say* WARE ing]

wearisome *adj.* tedious. [*Say* WEER ee sum]

weary ● *adj.* (**wearier**, **weariest**) **1** tired. **2** no longer interested in. **3** tiring or tedious. ● *v.* (**wearies**, **wearied**, **wearying**) make or grow weary. □ **wearily** *adv.* **weariness** *n.* [*Say* WEER ee, WEER a lee, WEERY ness]

weasel ● *n.* **1** a small carnivorous mammal, noted for its ferocity. **2** *informal* a deceitful or treacherous person. ● *v.* (**weasels**, **weaseled**, **weaseling**) default on an obligation. □ **weasel one's way into** obtain by cunning etc. □ **weaselly** *adj.*

weather ● *n.* **1** the state of the atmosphere at a place and time as regards temperature, wind, rain, etc. **2** bad weather. ● *v.* **1** expose to or affect by atmospheric changes. **2** come safely through. □ **keep a** (or **one's**) **weather eye on** (or **open**) be watchful. **under the weather** *informal* **1** slightly unwell. **2** in low spirits. □ **weathering** *n.*

weather-beaten *adj.* worn, damaged, or discoloured by exposure to the weather.

weatherboard ● *n.* **1** (also **weatherboarding**) **a** a siding material consisting of a series of horizontal boards with edges overlapping. **b** one of these boards. **2** a sloping board attached to the bottom of an outside door. ● *v.* fit or supply with weatherboards.

weatherman *n.* (*pl.* **weathermen**) **1** a man who broadcasts a forecast of the weather. **2** a meteorologist.

weatherproof ● *adj.* resistant to the effects of bad weather. ● *v.* make weatherproof.

weather station *n.* an observation post for recording meteorological data.

weatherstrip ● *n.* a piece of material used to make a door or window proof against rain or wind. ● *v.* (**weatherstrips**, **weatherstripped**, **weatherstripping**) apply a weatherstrip to. □ **weatherstripping** *n.*

weather vane *n.* a revolving pointer to show wind direction.

weather-worn *adj.* weather-beaten.

weave¹ ● *v.* (**weaves**; *past* **wove**; *past participle* **woven** or **wove**; **weaving**) **1** form fabric by interlacing long threads in two directions. **2** make (a basket or wreath etc.) by interlacing rods or flowers etc. **3 a** contrive, devise, esp. skilfully. **b** intermingle as if by weaving. ● *n.* a style of weaving. □ **weaving** *n.*

weave² *v.* (**weaves**; *past* **weaved** or **wove**; *past participle* **weaved** or **woven**; **weaving**) move from side to side to get around obstructions.

weaver *n.* **1** a person who weaves. **2** (also **weaver bird**) a tropical finch-like bird that builds elaborately woven nests.

web *n.* **1** a network of fine threads constructed by a spider to catch its prey. **2 a** a complete network or connected series. **b** (also **Web**) the World Wide Web. **3** a membrane between the toes of a swimming animal or bird.

webbed *adj.* **1** (of a bird's foot etc.) having the digits connected by a web. **2** (of fingers or toes) united by a fold of skin.

webbing *n.* a web or woven fabric, used for supporting upholstery, for belts, etc.

webcam *n.* a video camera connected to a computer connected to the Internet, so that its images can be seen by Internet users.

webcast *n.* a live video broadcast of an event transmitted over the Internet. □ **webcasting** *n.*

weber *n.* the SI unit of magnetic flux, causing the electromotive force of one volt in a circuit of one turn when generated or removed in one second. Abbreviation: **Wb**. [*Say* VAY bur]

web-footed *adj.* having the toes connected by webs.

weblog *n.* a frequently updated website typically consisting of someone's online journal with links to other sites. □ **weblogger** *n.*

webmaster *n.* a person who develops or is in charge of websites.

web page *n.* a hypertext document that is accessible via the World Wide Web.

web server *n.* **1** a program providing access to World Wide Web documents. **2** the computer or system on which such a program runs, and on which documents are stored.

website *n.* a hypertext document that can be accessed via the World Wide Web.

Wed. *abbr.* Wednesday.

wed *v.* (**weds**; *past and past participle* **wedded** or **wed**; **wedding**) **1** usu. *formal or literary* **a** marry. **b** join in marriage. **2** unite.

we'd *contr.* **1** we had. **2** we should; we would.

wedded *adj.* **1** of or in marriage. **2** obstinately attached (to a pursuit etc.).

wedding *n.* **1** a marriage ceremony. **2** an act of uniting.

wedding party *n.* the principal figures at a wedding, including the bride and groom, and their attendants.

wedding ring *n.* (also **wedding band**) a ring given during a wedding ceremony and worn afterwards to show that the wearer is married.

wedge ● *n.* **1** a piece of wood or metal etc. tapering to a sharp edge, that is driven between two objects or parts of an object to secure or separate them. **2** anything resembling or acting as a wedge. **3** a golf club with a wedge-shaped head. **4** a women's shoe with a solid wedge-shaped sole. ● *v.* (**wedges, wedged, wedging**) **1** tighten, secure, or fasten by means of a wedge. **2** force open or apart with a wedge. **3** pack or thrust tightly in or into. □ **thin edge** (or **end**) **of the wedge** *informal* an action unimportant in itself, but likely to lead to more serious developments.

wedge-shaped *adj.* **1** shaped like a solid wedge. **2** V-shaped.

wedgie *n.* *informal* a practical joke in which the victim's underpants are pulled up tightly between the buttocks.

wedlock *n.* the married state. □ **born in** (or **out of**) **wedlock** born of married (or unmarried) parents.

Wednesday ● *n.* the fourth day of the week, following Tuesday. ● *adv.* **1** on Wednesday. **2** (**Wednesdays**) on Wednesdays.

wee[1] *adj.* (**weer; weest**) *informal* very small.

wee[2] *v.* (**wees, weed, weeing**) esp. *Brit. slang* urinate.

weed ● *n.* **1** a wild plant growing where it is not wanted. **2** *slang* **a** marijuana. **b** tobacco. ● *v.* **1** clear (an area) of weeds.

2 sort out (inferior or unwanted parts or members etc.) for removal. □ **weeder** *n.* **weedless** *adj.*

weedbed *n.* an area of a lake etc. with many weeds.

weedy *adj.* (**weedier, weediest**) **1** having many weeds. **2** (esp. of a person) thin or feeble-looking.

week *n.* **1** a period of seven days generally reckoned from Sunday or Monday. **2** one week of the year devoted to a specific event, holiday, etc. **3** the period of five days from Monday through Friday. **4** the period during which one works in a week.

weekday *n.* any of the days from Monday to Friday.

weekend ● *n.* the period from Friday evening to Sunday evening. ● *adj.* **1** held on or over a weekend. **2** carrying out a specific activity only on weekends. **3** for use on weekends. ● *v.* spend a weekend.

weekender *n.* a person who spends weekends away from home.

weekend warrior *n.* *informal* or *jocular* a person who participates in an activity only on weekends.

weekly ● *adj.* **1** done, produced, or occurring once a week. **2** calculated by the week. ● *adv.* once a week. ● *n.* (*pl.* **weeklies**) a weekly newspaper etc.

weeknight *n.* each of the nights of a week not falling on a weekend.

weenie *n.* **1** a frankfurter. **2** *derogatory* a feeble person. **3** *slang* the penis.

weeny *adj.* (**weenier, weeniest**) (also **weensy, weensier, weensiest**) *informal* tiny.

weep ● *v.* (**weeps, wept, weeping**) **1** express grief or misery etc. by tears. **2** shed tears for. **3** exude (liquid etc.). ● *n.* a fit or period of weeping. □ **weeper** *n.* **weeping** *adj.*

weepie *n.* (*pl.* **weepies**) *informal* a sentimental or emotional movie, novel, etc.

weeping willow *n.* an ornamental willow with drooping branches and slender leaves.

weepy *adj.* (**weepier, weepiest**) *informal* **1** inclined to cry. **2** sentimental.

weevil *n.* **1** a small destructive beetle, the larvae of which typically develop inside seeds, stems, etc. **2** any insect damaging stored grain. [*Rhymes with* EVIL]

wee-wee *n.* *informal* urine.

weft *n.* **1** the threads woven across a warp to make fabric. **2** strips of cane, straw, etc. used in weaving baskets or mats etc.

weigh *v.* **1** determine the heaviness of (a body or substance). **2 a** measure and remove a quantity from a larger supply.

b distribute in exact amounts by weight. **3 a** consider the relative value of. **b** compare (one consideration) with another. **4** have or be equal to a specified degree of heaviness. **5** have a usu. specified degree of importance. **6** be a source of worry or concern (to). □ **weigh anchor** take the anchor up. **weigh down** be oppressive or burdensome to. **weigh in 1** (of a boxer, jockey, etc.) have one's weight checked officially. **2** bring one's weight or influence to bear. **weigh up** *informal* consider carefully. **weigh one's words** carefully choose a tactful way of expressing something.

weigh-in *n.* an official weighing, such as a boxer prior to a bout.

weight ● ** *n.* **1 *Physics* the force experienced by a body as a result of the earth's gravitational pull. **2** the heaviness of a body. **3** a unit or system of units used for measuring or expressing how much a body weighs. **4** a body of a known weight for use in weighing. **5** a heavy body used to hold something down etc. **6 a** a heavy mass or load. **b** an emotional burden. **7 a** influence, sway. **b** preponderance. **8** (in *pl.*) heavy blocks or discs of metal, barbells, etc., used in weightlifting ● *v.* **1 a** supply with an additional weight. **b** hold down with a weight or weights. **2** devise or manipulate (a rule etc.) so that it favours someone or something. **3** impede or burden. □ **worth one's** (or **its**) **weight in gold** extremely valuable or helpful. □ **weighted** *adj.*

weightless *adj.* **1** lacking or apparently lacking weight. **2** not apparently acted on by gravity. □ **weightlessly** *adv.* **weightlessness** *n.*

weightlifting *n.* the sport or exercise of lifting heavy weights. □ **weightlifter** *n.*

weighty *adj.* (**weightier, weightiest**) **1** heavy. **2** of great importance. **3** convincing, persuasive. **4** influential. □ **weightiness** *n.*

weir *n.* **1** a dam built across a river to raise the level of water upstream or regulate its flow. **2** an enclosure of stakes set in a stream etc., used for trapping fish. [*Say* WEER]

weird *adj.* **1** strange, unusual. **2** suggestive of the supernatural. □ **weird out** *slang* **1** make or become upset. **2** induce a sense of disbelief in. □ **weirdly** *adv.* **weirdness** *n.*

weirdo *n.* (*pl.* **weirdos**) (also **weirdy**) (*pl.* **weirdies**) *informal* a strange or abnormal person.

welch *v.* = WELSH.

welcome ● ** *n.* **1 a kind reception given to someone upon arriving. **2** a greeting or reception of a specified kind. ● *interj.* used to greet a visitor or guest. ● *v.* (**welcomes, welcomed, welcoming**) **1** greet or receive with pleasure or with something specified. **2** be pleased at or receptive to. ● *adj.* **1** that one receives with pleasure. **2** freely allowed or cordially invited. □ **you're** (or **you are**) **welcome** a polite response to an expression of thanks. □ **welcomer** *n.*

welcome mat *n.* **1** a doormat typically bearing some message of greeting. **2** anything used to invite, entice, or solicit.

welcoming *adj.* **1** (of a person) friendly. **2** (of a place) attractive and looking comfortable.

weld ● ** *v.* **1 a hammer or press (pieces of heated metal) into one piece. **b** join (pieces of metal or plastic etc.) by melting. **c** form or repair by welding. **2** bring together into an effectual or homogeneous whole. ● *n.* a welded joint. □ **welder** *n.*

welfare *n.* **1** well-being, happiness. **2 a** the organized provision for the basic well-being of needy members of a community. **b** financial support given for this purpose. □ **on welfare** receiving financial assistance from the government for basic living needs.

welfare state *n.* **1** a system whereby the government of a country etc. undertakes to protect the health and well-being of its citizens. **2** a country practising this system.

well¹ ● *adv.* (**better, best**) **1** in an acceptable or satisfactory manner. **2** with some distinction. **3** in a kind way. **4** thoroughly, carefully. **5** favourably. **6** with equanimity or good nature. **7** probably. **8** to a considerable extent. **9** intimately. **10** fortunately. **11** comfortably. ● *adj.* (**better, best**) **1** in good health. **2 a** in a satisfactory state or position. **b** proper, advisable. ● *interj.* **1** expressing surprise, resignation, etc. **2** used to resume speaking, esp. after a pause. □ **as well 1** also. **2** (also **just as well**) with equal reason or result. **as well as** in addition to. **leave** (or **let**) **well enough alone** refrain from interfering with. **well and good** expressing acceptance of a statement or decision etc. **well and truly** completely.

well² ● *n.* **1** a shaft sunk into the ground to obtain water, oil, etc. **2** a natural source or spring of water. **3** a space in a building enclosing a staircase or housing an elevator or providing light and air. **4** a receptacle, reservoir, or depression designed to hold liquid. **5** a source, esp. a copious one. ● *v.* **1** gather, gush, or spring. **2** be filled with tears.

we'll contr. we shall; we will.

well-adjusted adj. mentally and emotionally stable.

well-advised adj. prudent, wise.

well-appointed adj. furnished with all of the necessary equipment or desirable features.

well aware adj. certainly aware.

well-balanced adj. **1** regulated to ensure a proper balance. **2** sane, sensible.

well-behaved adj. showing good manners or conduct.

well-being n. a happy, healthy, and prosperous state.

well-bred adj. demonstrating qualities indicative of a good upbringing.

well-built adj. **1** of solid and reliable construction. **2** (of a person) well-proportioned.

well-connected adj. having powerful or influential connections.

well-defined adj. clearly marked, outlined, or indicated.

well-deserved adj. rightfully merited or earned.

well done ● adj. **1** (of meat) thoroughly cooked. **2** carried out skilfully or effectively. ● interj. expressing approval.

well-endowed adj. well provided with talent or resources.

well-established adj. **1** (of a custom, rule, etc.) long-standing. **2** proven.

well-fed adj. **1** having had plenty to eat. **2** euphemism plump.

well-founded adj. having a foundation in reason; based on strong evidence.

well-groomed adj. **1** looking clean and neat. **2** (of ski trails etc.) properly maintained.

well-grounded adj. **1** well-founded. **2** having a good training in or knowledge of a subject.

wellhead n. **1** a structure built over an oil or gas well. **2** a wellspring.

well-heeled adj. informal wealthy.

well-informed adj. having much knowledge in a subject.

wellington n. (also **wellington boot**) (usu. in pl.) esp. Brit. a waterproof rubber or plastic boot usu. reaching the knee.

well-intentioned adj. having or showing good intentions.

well-kept adj. carefully preserved; not revealed.

well-known adj. **1** widely known, famous. **2** thoroughly known.

well-maintained adj. **1** kept in good repair. **2** kept up to date.

well-mannered adj. courteous, polite.

well-matched adj. **1** compatible, suited. **2** (of opponents) evenly matched.

well-meaning adj. **1** having or demonstrating good intentions. **2** (also **well-meant**) (of advice etc.) based on good intentions but usu. ineffective.

wellness n. the state of being well or in good health.

well-nigh adv. almost.

well off adj. **1** wealthy. **2** in a fortunate situation or position.

well-oiled adj. informal **1 a** sufficiently or generously lubricated. **b** running smoothly. **2** drunk.

well-ordered adj. neatly, carefully, or properly ordered.

well-paid adj. **1** amply rewarded for a job. **2** (also **well-paying**) (of a job) that pays well.

well-preserved adj. **1** remaining in good condition. **2** (of an old person) showing little sign of aging.

well-read adj. knowledgeable from much reading.

well-rounded adj. **1** (of a person) having a fully developed personality and a wide range of knowledge and interests. **2** well-balanced.

well-spoken adj. (of a person) speaking articulately or with an accent considered to be refined.

wellspring n. **1** the place where a spring breaks out of the ground. **2** an esp. abundant source.

well-suited adj. suitable.

well-thought-of adj. esteemed, respected.

well-thought-out adj. carefully planned in advance.

well-thumbed adj. (of a book) bearing marks of frequent handling.

well-to-do adj. comfortably wealthy, prosperous.

well-travelled adj. **1** having travelled extensively. **2** (of a path etc.) much frequented.

well versed adj. knowledgeable about.

well-wisher n. a person conveying his or her congratulations etc. to another.

well-worn adj. **1** worn out from extensive use or handling. **2** (of a phrase etc.) trite, hackneyed.

Welsh ● adj. of or relating to Wales or its people or language. ● n. **1** the Celtic language of Wales. **2** (**the Welsh**) the people of Wales.

welsh v. (**welshes**, **welshed**, **welshing**) fail or refuse to honour a debt or obligation.

Welshman n. (pl. **Welshmen**) a man from Wales.

welt n. a ridge raised on the flesh by the impact of a rod, whip, etc.

welter n. a confused mixture of things or people.

welterweight n. **1** a weight class in certain sports between lightweight and middleweight. **2** a boxer etc. of this weight.

wench n. (pl. **wenches**) **1** jocular a girl or young woman. **2** archaic a prostitute.

wend v. □ **wend one's way** make one's way.

wendigo n. = WINDIGO.

Wen-Do n. Cdn proprietary a program of self-defence for women, emphasizing awareness and avoidance of potentially dangerous situations. [Say wen DOE]

went past of GO.

wept past of WEEP.

were 2nd singular past, plural past, and past subjunctive of BE.

we're contr. we are.

weren't contr. were not.

werewolf n. (pl. **werewolves**) a mythical being who at times changes from a person to a wolf. [Say WARE wolf or WEER wolf]

Wesleyan adj. Methodist. [Say WEZZLY un or WESSLY un]

west ● n. **1** the point of the horizon where the sun sets at the equinoxes. **2** the compass point corresponding to this. **3** (usu. **the West**) **a** Europe and the countries of the western hemisphere seen in contrast to other civilizations. **b** hist. the non-Communist countries of Europe and N America. **4** (usu. **the West**) the western part of a country or city etc. ● adj. **1** towards, at, or facing west. **2** coming from the west. ● adv. **1** towards, at, or near the west. **2** further west than. □ **westernmost** adj.

westbound adj. travelling or leading westwards.

westerly ● adj. & adv. **1** in a western position or direction. **2** (of a wind) blowing from the west. ● n. (pl. **westerlies**) a wind blowing from the west.

western ● adj. **1** of or in the west. **2** lying or facing the west. **3** coming from the west. **4** (**Western**) **a** of or relating to the Occident or (formerly) the non-Communist countries of Europe and N America. **b** of or related to the western part of a country or town. **5** designating an omelette containing onions, ham, and peppers, or a sandwich containing such an omelette. ● n. **1** a film or novel featuring cowboys in heroic roles, gunfights, etc. **2** a western omelette or sandwich. ● adv. (ride etc.) in the manner of a cowboy. □ **westernmost** adj.

Western Church n. the part of the Christian Church including the Catholic and Protestant Churches.

westerner n. (also **Westerner**) a person from the west of a region.

western hemisphere n. the half of the earth containing N and S America and the surrounding waters.

westernize v. (**westernizes**, **westernized**, **westernizing**) influence with or convert to Western ideas and customs etc. □ **westernization** n.

Western provinces pl. n. Manitoba, Alberta, Saskatchewan, and British Columbia.

West Indian n. a person from any island of the West Indies. □ **West Indian** adj.

West Nile virus n. a mosquito-borne virus and the disease it causes, usu. a mild fever but sometimes a fatal encephalitis.

west-northwest n. the direction midway between west and northwest.

west-southwest n. the direction midway between west and southwest.

westward ● adj. & adv. (also **westwards**) towards the west. ● n. a westward direction.

wet ● adj. (**wetter**, **wettest**) **1** covered or soaked with liquid. **2** rainy. **3** (of paint, ink, etc.) not yet dried. **4** used with or involving water or liquid. **5** informal favouring or permitting the sale of alcohol. ● v. (**wets**; **wet** or **wetted**; **wetting**) **1** dampen, make wet. **2 a** urinate in or on. **b** urinate involuntarily. ● n. **1** moisture. **2** precipitation. □ **all wet** informal completely wrong. **wet behind the ears** immature, inexperienced. **wet one's whistle** informal drink. □ **wetly** adv. **wetness** n. **wettable** adj. **wetting** n.

wet dream n. an erotic dream with involuntary ejaculation of semen.

wetland n. (often in pl.) marshy or swampy land.

wet nurse n. a woman employed to breastfeed another's baby.

wetsuit n. a close-fitting rubber garment worn by scuba divers etc. to protect them from the cold.

Wet'suwet'en n. (pl. **Wet'suwet'en**) **1** a member of an Aboriginal people living in north-central BC. **2** the Tsimshian language of this people. □ **Wet'suwet'en** adj. [Say wut SOO wuh tun]

we've contr. we have.

whack informal ● v. **1** strike or beat forcefully with a sharp blow. **2** slang kill. ● n. **1** a sharp blow. **2** slang a large number or amount. □ **have** (or **take**) **a whack at** *slang* attempt. **out of whack** *slang* **1** out of order. **2** (of figures etc.) maladjusted, skewed.

whacked *adj. informal* **1 a** mad, crazy. **b** high or intoxicated on drugs or alcohol. **2** exhausted.

whacko *adj. and n.* = WACKO.

whacky *adj.* = WACKY.

whale[1] *n.* (*pl.* **whales** or **whale**) a large marine mammal which breathes through a nasal opening on top of its head. □ **a whale of a** *informal* an exceptionally good or large etc.

whale[2] *v. informal* beat, thrash.

whalebone *n.* an elastic horny substance which grows in a series of thin parallel plates in the upper jaw of baleen whales, serving to strain plankton from the sea water.

whale-watch ● *n.* (*pl.* **whale-watches**) an excursion made by boat to observe whales in their natural habitat. ● *v.* (**whale-watches, whale-watched, whale-watching**) go on such an excursion.

whaling *n.* the hunting and killing of whales.

wham *informal* ● *n.* the sound of forcible impact. ● *interj.* expressing such a sound. ● *v.* (**whams, whammed, whamming**) **1** make such a sound or impact. **2** strike with force.

whammy *n.* (*pl.* **whammies**) esp. *US informal* **1** an evil or unlucky influence. **2** (esp. in phr. **double whammy**) a powerful or unpleasant effect.

whap ● *n.* **1** a hard slap. **2** the sound of this. ● *v.* (**whaps, whapped, whapping**) strike or slap forcefully. [*Say* WOP *or* WAP]

wharf *n.* (*pl.* **wharves** or **wharfs**) a level quayside structure to which a ship may be moored to load and unload. [*Say* WORF]

what ● *interrog. adj.* used in asking the identity of a choice made. ● *adj.* (usu. in exclamation) how great or remarkable ● *rel. adj.* the or any . . . that. ● *pron.* **1** used in asking for information specifying something. **2** (asking for a remark to be repeated) = what did you say? **3** asking for repetition, clarification, or confirmation of something. **4 a** how much. **b** how great. ● *rel. pron.* that or those which. ● *adv.* to what extent ● *interj.* **1** expressing surprise or astonishment. **2** expressing disbelief. □ **what for** *informal* **1** why? for what reason? **2** a severe reprimand. **what have you** *informal* anything else similar. **what is more** and as an additional point. **what of it?** why should that be considered

significant? **what's his** (or **her**) **name** (also **what's his** (or **her**) **face**) *informal* a person whose name one cannot recall etc. **what's what** *informal* what things are useful or important. **what's with** *informal* what is the matter with? **what with** *informal* on account of.

whatchamacallit *n. informal* (also **whatchacallit, what-d'you-call-it**) a thing the proper name of which one cannot recall or does not know.

whatever ● *pron.* **1** anything or everything that. **2** no matter what. **3** representing an unknown formal alternative. **4** what in any way ● *adj.* **1** any . . . that. **2** any; no matter what. **3** denoting an unspecified person or thing. **4** whatsoever.

whatnot *n.* **1** other similar items. **2** an unspecified or trivial thing. **3** a stand with shelves used for keeping small objects.

whatsit *n.* **1** a whatchamacallit. **2** a person whose name one cannot recall or does not know.

whatsoever *adj.* (with *neg.*) at all.

wheat *n.* **1** a cereal plant bearing dense four-sided seed spikes. **2** its grain, used in making flour etc.

Wheat Board *n. Cdn* a Crown corporation responsible for the sale of all wheat and barley produced in western Canada.

wheat germ *n.* the embryo of the wheat grain.

wheat pool *n. Cdn* a grain farmers' co-operative in Western Canada for the sale of wheat etc.

wheedle *v.* (**wheedles, wheedled, wheedling**) **1** attempt to coax or persuade (a person) by flattery or endearments. **2** obtain or acquire by wheedling. □ **wheedling** *adj.*

wheel ● *n.* **1** a circular object attached or able to be attached to an axle around which it revolves, used to facilitate the motion of a vehicle or for mechanical purposes. **2** anything resembling a wheel. **3** a machine etc. of which a wheel is an essential part. **4** (in *pl.*) *slang* a car. **5** a steering wheel. **6** (in *pl.*) the driving or animating force. ● *v.* **1** turn or rotate on an axis or pivot. **2** change direction, esp. suddenly. **3** push or pull (a wheeled thing). **4** move in circles or curves. □ **at the wheel 1** (also **behind the wheel**) driving a car or truck etc. **2** directing a ship. **3** in control of affairs. **wheel and deal** engage in political or commercial scheming. □ **wheeled** *adj.*

wheelbarrow *n.* a shallow open container for moving small loads, with a wheel at one end and two handles at the other.

wheelbase *n.* the distance between the front and rear axles of a vehicle.

wheelchair *n.* a chair on wheels for an invalid or a disabled person.

wheeler *n.* (in *comb.*) a vehicle having a specified number of wheels.

wheeler-dealer *n.* a person who engages in political or commercial scheming. □ **wheeler-dealing** *n.*

wheelhouse *n.* the structure on a ship containing the steering wheel.

wheelie *n. slang* the stunt of riding a bicycle or motorcycle with the front wheel off the ground.

wheel of Fortune *n.* **1** a notional wheel which the goddess Fortune is said to turn in order to determine the fates of humans. **2** a gambling game in which an upright wheel is spun, and points are won depending on where the wheel stops spinning.

wheeze ● *v.* (**wheezes, wheezed, wheezing**) **1** breathe with an audible chesty whistling sound. **2** make a similar whistling or rasping sound. ● *n.* **1** a sound of wheezing. **2** *informal* a hackneyed running joke or comic phrase. □ **wheezy** *adj.*

whelk *n.* a shellfish with a spiral shell.

whelp ● *n.* a young dog, seal, or mink. ● *v.* (of a female animal) give birth to (a whelp or whelps).

when ● *interrog. adv.* **1** at what time? **2** how soon? **3** how long ago? **4** in what circumstances? ● *adv. informal* in the past. ● *rel. adv.* (preceded by *time* etc.) at or on which. ● *conj.* **1 a** at the time that. **b** at any time that. **2** although. **3** at which time. **4** whereas. ● *pron.* what time? ● *n.* time.

whence *formal* ● *adv.* from what place? ● *conj.* **1** to the place from which. **2** from which. **3** and thence.

whenever *conj. & adv.* **1** at whatever time. **2** every time that. □ **or whenever** *informal* or at any similar time.

where ● *interrog. adv.* **1** in or at what place or position? **2** to what place? **3 a** in what book or passage? **b** from whom? from what source? **4** in what direction or respect? **5** in what situation? **6** at what point? ● *conj.* **1** in, at, or to the place in which. **2** in the situation in which. **3** *informal* that. ● *pron.* what place? ● *n.* a place.

whereabouts ● *adv.* where or approximately where? ● *n.* the place where a person or thing is.

whereas *conj.* **1** in contrast or comparison with the fact that. **2** taking into consideration the fact that.

whereby *conj.* **1** by which. **2** according to which.

wherefore ● *adv. archaic* **1** for what reason? **2** as a result of which. ● *n.* a reason.

wherein *formal* ● *conj.* in which thing, matter, place, etc. ● *adv.* in what place or respect?

whereof *formal* ● *conj.* of which or whom. ● *adv.* of what? □ **know whereof one speaks** know what one is talking about.

whereupon *conj.* upon the occurrence of which.

wherever ● *adv.* in or to whatever place. ● *conj.* in every place that. □ **or wherever** *informal* or in any similar place.

wherewithal *n.* the means by which to do something. [*Say* WHERE with all]

whet *v.* (**whets, whetted, whetting**) **1** sharpen (a tool or weapon). **2** stimulate (the appetite etc.).

whether *conj.* **1** expressing a doubt or choice between alternatives. **2** expressing an enquiry or investigation. **3** introducing a statement that is applicable whichever of the possibilities given is true.

whetstone *n.* a shaped fine-grained stone used to sharpen tools.

whew *interj.* expressing relief, surprise, or exhaustion.

whey *n.* the watery liquid that remains when milk forms curds. [*Sounds like* WAY]

which ● *interrog. adj.* used in asking the identity of a choice from a set of alternatives. ● *rel. adj.* being the thing or things just referred to. ● *interrog. pron.* **1** which person or persons **2** which thing or things. ● *rel. pron.* (*possessive* **of which, whose**) introducing a clause that gives additional information about the antecedent.

whichever *adj. & pron.* **1** either or any of a definite set of people or things that. **2** no matter which.

whiff ● *n.* **1** a puff or breath of air, smoke, etc. **2** a smell or odour. **3** a trace or suggestion. ● *v.* **1** sniff. **2** blow or puff lightly.

whiffle ● *v.* (**whiffles, whiffled, whiffling**) **1** (of the wind) blow gently. **2** make the sound of this. ● *n.* a slight movement of air.

Whig *n. hist.* **1** a member of the English, later British, reforming party that after 1688 sought the supremacy of Parliament, succeeded in the 19th century by the Liberal Party. **2 a** a member of a 19th-century US political party established in 1834, succeeded by the Republican Party.

b a colonist who supported the American Revolution.

while ● *n.* a period of time. ● *conj.* **1** during the time that. **2** in spite of the fact that. **3** whereas. ● *v.* (**whiles, whiled, whiling**) pass (time) in a leisurely or pleasant manner. □ **all the while** during the whole time (that). **worth while** (or **one's while**) worth the time or effort spent.

whilst *adv. & conj.* esp. *Brit.* while. [*With* l *as in* WHILE]

whim *n.* **1** a spontaneous idea or decision. **2** capriciousness.

whimbrel *n.* a small curlew with a striped head and a trilling call. [*Say* WIM brull]

whimper ● *v.* make feeble or plaintive sounds expressive of fear, pain, or distress. ● *n.* **1** a whimpering sound. **2** a dull or anticlimactic note or tone.

whimsical *adj.* **1** spontaneous. **2 a** imaginative or playful. **b** unconventional, fanciful, or quaint. □ **whimsicality** *n.* **whimsically** *adv.* [*Say* WIMZA cull, wimza KALLA tee]

whimsy *n.* (*pl.* **whimsies**) **1** a fanciful or playful quality or condition. **2** a whim.

whine ● *n.* **1** a prolonged cry or wail suggesting pain or complaint. **2** a shrill prolonged sound resembling this. **3 a** a complaining tone of voice. **b** a feeble complaint. ● *v.* (**whines, whined, whining**) **1** emit or utter a whine. **2** complain in a querulous tone. **3** say in a whining tone. □ **whiner** *n.* **whiny** *adj.* (**whinier, whiniest**)

whinny ● *n.* (*pl.* **whinnies**) **1** a gentle high-pitched neigh. **2** a sound resembling this. ● *v.* (**whinnies, whinnied, whinnying**) give a whinny. [*Say* WIN ee]

whip ● *n.* **1** a flexible switch or a rod with a leather lash attached, used for urging animals on or flogging. **2** a member of a political party appointed to monitor and control its conduct and tactics. **3** a light fluffy dessert made with whipped cream or beaten eggs. ● *v.* (**whips, whipped, whipping**) **1** beat or urge with a whip. **2** bring (a person) into a usu. specified condition or state. **3** beat (cream or eggs etc.) into a froth. **4** move suddenly. **5** *informal* throw or propel with great force. **6** *slang* defeat convincingly. □ **whip off** remove (an article of clothing) hurriedly. **2** produce in a short amount of time. **whip on** urge into action. **whip out** draw out. **whip up** **1** make or prepare quickly or with ease. **2** excite or stir up (feeling etc.). □ **whipper** *n.*

whiplash *n.* damage to the neck or spine caused by a severe jerk of the head.

whipped *adj.* **1** that has been whipped. **2** *informal* tired, exhausted.

whipped cream *n.* heavy cream beaten until stiff.

whippersnapper *n.* **1** a presumptuous or intrusive young person. **2** a child.

whippet *n.* a small slender breed of dog used for racing. [*Say* WIP it]

whipping *n.* **1** a beating with a whip. **2** *Sport* a sound defeat.

whipping boy *n.* a scapegoat.

whipping cream *n.* heavy cream, usu. with 35% milk fat, suitable for whipping.

whippoorwill *n.* a N American bird with a loud repeated cry. [*Say* WIPPER will]

whippy *adj.* (**whippier, whippiest**) flexible, springy.

whipsaw *n.* a saw with a narrow blade and a handle at both ends.

whir *n. & v.* = WHIRR.

whirl ● *v.* **1** turn around rapidly. **2** convey or travel swiftly. **3** (of the brain, senses, etc.) seem to spin. ● *n.* **1** a swift whirling movement. **2** *informal* an attempt. **3** a state of intense activity. **4** a state of confusion. □ **whirling** *adj.*

whirligig *n.* **1** anything having a rapid circling movement. **2** a toy that whirls around. **3** anything characterized by constant frantic activity.

whirling dervish *n.* a member of a Muslim religious fraternity which includes the practice of dancing as a spiritual exercise.

whirlpool *n.* **1** a powerful circular eddy in a body of water that draws or sucks objects to its centre. **2** a large bathtub with underwater jets of hot usu. aerated water.

whirlwind *n.* **1** a small rotating storm of wind in which a funnel-shaped column of air whirls rapidly over land or water. **2** (as an *adj.*) very rapid or hasty. **3** a confused tumultuous process. **4** an active, impetuous person.

whirr ● *n.* a continuous droning, humming, or buzzing sound. ● *v.* (**whirrs, whirred, whirring**) **1** make this sound. **2** move swiftly with such a sound.

whisk ● *v.* **1** brush lightly with a sweeping movement. **2** move or take with a sudden sweeping motion. **3** whip with a whisk. **4** go quickly. ● *n.* **1** a whisking action or motion. **2** a utensil consisting of wire hoops attached to a handle. **3** (also **whisk broom**) a small broom used to sweep dust or debris from a surface.

whisker *n.* **1 a** any of the hairs growing on a person's face. **b** (in *pl.*) these hairs collectively. **2** each of the long projecting hairs growing on the face of many mammals. **3** *informal* a small distance or amount. □ **whiskered** *adj.* **whiskery** *adj.*

whisky *n.* (*pl.* **whiskies**) (also **whiskey**, *pl.* **whiskeys**) an alcoholic liquor distilled esp. from rye, malted barley, or corn.

whisky jack *n. Cdn* a grey jay.

whisper ● v. 1 say or speak in a soft breathy voice. **2** speak or converse in private. **3** (of leaves etc.) make a soft rustling sound. **● n. 1** whispering speech. **2** something whispered. **3 a** a rumour or piece of gossip. **b** a hint. **4** a soft rustling sound. □ **whisperer** *n.* **whispering** *n.*

whist *n.* a card game for four players grouped into pairs, in which points are scored according to the number of tricks won. [*Rhymes with* LIST]

whistle ● n. 1 a clear shrill sound made by forcing breath through pursed lips etc. **2** a similar sound made by a bird, the wind, etc. **3** a small device that produces such a sound when blown. **● v. (whistles, whistled, whistling) 1** sound or emit a whistle. **2** give a signal by whistling. **3** produce (a tune etc.) by whistling. **4** summon, announce, or signal by whistling. **5** (of the wind etc.) move or fly past with a whistle. □ **as clean** (or **clear** or **dry**) **as a whistle** very clean. **blow the whistle on** *informal* call attention to (a questionable or illicit activity), or inform on (those responsible).

whistle-blower *n.* a person who calls attention to a questionable or illicit activity. □ **whistle-blowing** *adj. & n.*

whistle stop *n.* **1 a** the train station of a small town at which trains stop only when a passenger is waiting to board. **b** a small or unimportant town. **2** a politician's brief stop in a town to give an electioneering speech. **3** (as an *adj.*) designating a journey with brief stops at small towns along the way.

whit *n.* the least possible amount.

white ● adj. 1 having a colour like that of fresh snow or milk. **2** (esp. of the skin) approaching such a colour. **3 a** designating any of various peoples having light-coloured skin. **b** predominantly inhabited by white people. **4** (of wine) made from white grapes or dark grapes with the skins removed. **5** (of coffee) having milk or cream added. **● n. 1** a white colour. **2** the white or light-coloured part of anything. **3** the translucent viscous fluid surrounding the yolk of an egg; albumen. **4** the visible part of the eyeball around the iris. **5** white clothing or material. **6** a member of a light-skinned race. □ **white out 1** make or become white. **2** obliterate or conceal with whiteness, as with snow. **3** cover with

correction fluid. □ **whitely** *adv.* **whiteness** *n.* **whitish** *adj.*

white blood cell *n.* (also **white cell**) any of the colourless cells found in the blood, lymph, and connective tissue, which produce antibodies.

whiteboard *n.* a wipeable board with a white surface.

white bread ● n. bread of a light colour, made from usu. bleached wheat flour without bran. **● adj. (white-bread) 1** having to do with the white middle class. **2** conventional; bland.

whitecap *n.* a wave or breaker with a foamy white crest.

white-collar *adj.* **1** having to do with non-manual administrative or professional work. **2** (of a crime) non-violent, esp. involving fraud etc.

white elephant *n.* an item etc. that is no longer useful or wanted.

whitefish *n.* (*pl.* **whitefish** or **whitefishes**) **1** a mainly freshwater fish of the trout family. **2** (**white fish**) any fish with pale flesh.

white flag *n.* the flag traditionally used to signal surrender. □ **raise** (or **wave** or **run up**) **the white flag** admit defeat.

whitefly *n.* (*pl.* **whiteflies**) a small insect with wings covered with powdery white wax, which damages plants.

white goods *pl. n.* **1** household linen. **2** large domestic appliances.

whitehead *n.* a white or white-topped pimple.

white heat *n.* the very high temperature at which metal radiates a white light.

white-hot *adj.* **1** (of metal) at white heat. **2** (of an emotion) passionate, ardent.

White House *n.* **1** the official residence of the US President in Washington, DC. **2** the executive branch of the US government.

white knight *n.* a person who comes to the aid of someone.

white-knuckle *adj.* causing fear or terror.

white lie *n.* a harmless or trivial untruth.

white light *n.* colourless light, e.g. sunlight.

white meat *n.* any meat that is pale when cooked, such as veal or poultry.

whiten *v.* make or become white. □ **whitener** *n.*

white noise *n.* noise having nearly equal intensities at all frequencies.

whiteout *n.* **1** a dense blizzard that reduces visibility. **2** a usu. white liquid that is painted over a typed or written error.

white pages *pl. n.* a telephone directory

containing the phone numbers and addresses of residential and business subscribers listed alphabetically.

whitepainting n. *Cdn* the reclamation of a house, building, etc. in a derelict part of a city's urban core.

white paper n. **1** (also **White Paper**) an official report summarizing the results of an investigation into an issue, and outlining government policy regarding it. **2** an authoritative report on an item of particular interest.

white sale n. a sale of household linen.

white sauce n. a sauce made with flour, melted butter, and milk or cream.

white supremacy n. a belief that whites are innately superior to non-whites. □ **white supremacist** n.

white-tailed deer n. (also **whitetail**, **whitetail deer**) a species of deer that has a white underside to the tail.

white tie n. **1** a man's white bow tie worn as part of full evening dress. **2** full evening dress.

white trash n. *derogatory* lower-class white people.

whitewall n. (also **whitewall tire**) an automotive tire with a white side wall.

whitewash ● n. (pl. **whitewashes**) **1** a solution used for painting houses and walls white. **2** something that conceals faults or mistakes. **3** a victory in which the opponent fails to score or is defeated by a lopsided margin. ● v. (**whitewashes**, **whitewashed**, **whitewashing**) **1** cover with whitewash. **2** attempt to conceal faults or mistakes. **3** *Sport* defeat convincingly.

whitewater n. a stretch of turbulent foamy water in a river.

white whale n. = BELUGA 1.

whither adv. & conj. *archaic* **1** to what place? **2** to what result?

whiting n. **1** a fish of the cod family with pearly-white flesh. **2** ground chalk used to make whitewash, putty, etc. [*Say* WHITE ing]

whittle v. (**whittles**, **whittled**, **whittling**) **1** carve (wood etc.) by cutting thin shavings from it. **2** reduce or diminish by repeated subtractions.

whiz *informal* ● n. (pl. **whizzes**) **1** the humming or buzzing sound made by a body moving quickly through the air. **2** *informal* a person who is remarkable or skilful at something. **3** *slang* an act of urinating. ● v. (**whizzes**, **whizzed**, **whizzing**) **1** make or move with a humming or buzzing sound. **2** cause to make such a sound. **3** *slang* urinate.

whiz-bang adj. *informal* **1** fast-paced. **2** technologically innovative.

whiz kid n. *informal* an exceptionally bright or successful young person.

who pron. (obj. **whom** or *informal* **who**; possessive **whose**) **1 a** what or which person or persons? **b** what sort of person or persons? **2** (a person) that.

whoa interj. commanding a horse etc. to stop. [*Sounds like* WOE]

who'd contr. **1** who had. **2** who would.

whodunit n. *informal* a crime story or murder mystery. [*Say* who DUN it]

whoever pron. (obj. **whomever** or *informal* **whoever**; possessive **whosever**) **1** the or any person or persons who. **2** *informal* any or some similar person.

whole ● adj. **1** entire. **2** unbroken, intact. **3** containing all the proper constituents. ● n. **1** a thing complete in itself. **2** all there is of a thing. ● adv. entirely. □ **as a whole** in its entirety. **on the whole** taking everything into account; in general. **a whole new** (or **different**) **ball game** *informal* a separate issue very different from the one currently under discussion. **the whole nine yards** *slang* everything. □ **wholeness** n.

whole cloth □ **out of whole cloth** with no basis in fact or reality.

whole food n. food that has not been processed or refined.

whole-grain adj. (of cereal products) containing the whole grain.

wholehearted adj. completely sincere or committed. □ **wholeheartedly** adv.

whole milk n. milk which has not been skimmed.

whole note n. *Music* a note having the time value of four quarter notes.

whole number n. a number without fractions.

wholesale ● n. the selling of goods in large quantities to be retailed by others. ● adj. **1** having to do with wholesale. **2** extensive. ● adv. **1** at a wholesale price. **2** on a large scale. ● v. sell (goods) wholesale. □ **wholesaler** n.

wholesome adj. promoting good health and physical or mental well-being. □ **wholesomely** adv. **wholesomeness** n.

whole wheat n. wheat with none of the bran or germ removed.

wholly adv. entirely, completely.

whom objective case of WHO.

whomever objective case of WHOEVER.

whomp *informal* ● n. a dull heavy sound. ● v. **1** bang or strike heavily. **2** make such a sound.

whoop ● *n.* **1** a loud excited cry. **2** a long rasping intake of air. ● *v.* utter a whoop. □ **no big whoop** *slang* no big deal. **whoop it up** *Informal* engage in revelry. [Say WOOP or HOOP (with OO *as in* HOOT or HOOD)]

whoopee *informal* ● *interj.* expressing exuberant joy. ● *n.* exuberant enjoyment. □ **make whoopee** *informal* **1** rejoice noisily. **2** make love. [Say woo PEE *for the interjection,* WOOP ee *for the noun (with* OO *as in* HOOT or HOOD)]

whoopee cushion *n.* a rubber cushion that when sat on makes a sound like the breaking of wind. [Say WOOP ee (with OO *as in* HOOT or HOOD)]

whooper *n.* a whooping crane or swan. [Say WOOP er or HOOP er (with OO *as in* LOOP)]

whooping cough *n.* an infectious bacterial disease with short violent coughs followed by a whoop. [Say WOOP ing or HOOP ing (with OO *as in* LOOP)]

whooping crane *n.* a large endangered mainly white N American crane. [Say WOOP ing or HOOP ing (with OO *as in* LOOP)]

whoops *interj. informal* expressing dismay or apology. [Say WOOPS (with OO *as in* HOOD)]

whoop-up *n. Cdn informal* a noisy party.

whoosh ● *v.* (**whooshes, whooshed, whooshing**) (cause to) move with a rushing sound. ● *n.* (*pl.* **whooshes**) a whooshing movement. [*Rhymes with* SPLOOSH or PUSH]

whopper *n. slang* **1** something big. **2** a blatant lie.

whopping *adj. slang* very big.

whore ● *n.* **1** a prostitute. **2** *derogatory* a promiscuous woman. ● *v.* (**whores, whored, whoring**) **1** use the services of prostitutes. **2** act as a whore. [*Rhymes with* LORE or LURE]

whorehouse *n.* a brothel. [*WHORE rhymes with* LORE or LURE]

whorl *n.* **1** a ring of leaves etc. around a stem. **2** one turn of a spiral shell. **3** a coil. **4** a complete circle in a fingerprint. □ **whorled** *adj.* [Say WORL or WURL]

who's *contr.* **1** who is. **2** who has.

whose ● *pron.* of or belonging to which person ● *adj.* of whom or which.

whosever *possessive of* WHOEVER.

who's who *n.* **1** the significant people in a given field. **2** a list with facts about notable persons.

whump ● *n.* a dull thudding sound. ● *v.* make or move or strike with such a sound.

whup *v.* (**whups, whupped, whupping**) esp. *US informal* **1** whip or beat a person. **2** defeat soundly.

why ● *adv.* **1 a** for what reason or purpose? **b** on what grounds? **2** for which. expressing: **1** surprise. **2** impatience. **3** objection ● *n.* (*pl.* **whys**) a reason or explanation.

Wicca *n.* the religious cult of modern witchcraft, a benevolent nature-oriented goddess-worshipping religion. □ **Wiccan** *adj. & n.* [Say WICK uh]

wick ● *n.* a thread feeding a flame with fuel in a candle, lamp, etc. ● *v.* absorb moisture through narrow openings in a fabric etc.

wicked *adj.* (**wickeder, wickedest**) **1** sinful. **2** spiteful, ill-tempered. **3** playfully malicious. **4** *slang* excellent. □ **wickedly** *adv.* **wickedness** *n.*

wicker *n.* braided twigs or osiers etc. used for chairs, baskets, etc.

wicket *n.* **1** a station for an employee in a ticket office, bank, etc. **2** a small door or gate. **3** *Cricket* a set of three stumps with the bails in position defended by a batsman. **4** a croquet hoop.

wide *adj.* (**wider, widest**) **1** measuring much across or from side to side. **2** (following a measurement) in width. **3** extensive. **4** not tight; loose. **5** not specialized. **6** open to the full extent. **7 a** not within a reasonable distance of. **b** at a considerable distance from. □ **widely** *adv.*

wide-angle *adj.* (of a lens) having a short focal length and hence a field covering a wide angle.

wide-area network *n. Computing* a communications network, typically between different sites. Abbreviation: WAN.

wide-body *n.* (*pl.* **wide-bodies**) a large jet with a cabin divided by two aisles. □ **wide-bodied** *adj.*

wide-eyed *adj.* **1** having one's eyes wide open in surprise etc. **2** naive, innocent.

widen *v.* make or become wider.

wide open *adj.* **1** fully open. **2** (of a contest) having an unpredictable outcome. **3** exposed or vulnerable.

wide-ranging *adj.* covering an extensive range.

widescreen *adj.* designed with or for a screen presenting a wide field of vision.

widespread *adj.* widely distributed.

widget *n. informal* any gadget.

widow *n.* **1** a woman whose husband has died and who has not remarried. **2** *informal* a woman whose husband is often away on a

specified activity. □ **widowed** *adj.*
widowhood *n.*

widower *n.* a man whose wife has died and who has not remarried.

width *n.* **1** measurement or distance from side to side. **2** a large extent. **3** a strip of material of a particular width.
□ **widthways** *adv.* **widthwise** *adv.*

wield *v.* **1** hold and use (a weapon or tool). **2** exert or command (power etc.).
□ **wielder** *n.* [Rhymes with FIELD]

wiener *n.* **1** a frankfurter. **2** *slang* the penis.

Wiener schnitzel *n.* a breaded and fried pork or veal cutlet. [Say VEEN er shnit zul]

wienie *n.* = WEENIE.

wife *n.* (*pl.* **wives**) a married woman esp. in relation to her husband. □ **wifely** *adj.*

wig *n.* **1** an artificial head of hair. **2** a hairpiece. □ **wig out** (**wigs, wigged, wigging**) *slang* lose control of one's emotions. □ **wigged** *adj.*

wiggle *informal* ● *v.* (**wiggles, wiggled, wiggling**) move irregularly from side to side etc. ● *n.* an act of wiggling. □ **wiggler** *n.* **wiggly** *adj.* (**wigglier, wiggliest**)

wiggle room *n.* a limited capacity to manoeuvre or negotiate; an allowance made for the possibility of error or change.

wigwam *n.* (among some N American Aboriginal peoples) a dome-shaped house covered with birch bark. [Say WIG wom]

wild ● *adj.* **1** (of an animal or plant) in its original natural state. **2** not civilized. **3** (of land etc.) not cultivated or settled by people. **4** unrestrained. **5** tempestuous. **6 a** intensely eager. **b** (of looks, appearance, etc.) indicating distraction. **7** *informal* angry. **8** haphazard. **9** *informal* amazing. ● *adv.* in a wild manner. ● *n.* (usu. in *pl.*) a wilderness. □ **in the wild** in an uncultivated etc. state. **run wild** grow unchecked or undisciplined. □ **wildly** *adv.* **wildness** *n.*

wild card *n.* **1** a playing card having any rank chosen by the player holding it. **2** *Computing* a character that will match any character or sequence of characters in a search. **3** an unpredictable person or thing.

wildcat ● *n.* **1** a smallish cat of a non-domesticated kind, esp. the bobcat. **2** a hot-tempered person. **3** an exploratory oil well. **4** a sudden and unofficial strike. ● *adj.* **1** having to do with prospecting for oil. **2** (of a strike) called at short notice.
□ **wildcatter** *n.*

wildebeest *n.* a large antelope native to southern Africa. [Say WILL duh beast or VILL duh beast]

wilderness *n.* an uncultivated and uninhabited region.

wildfire *n.* a destructive or uncontrollable fire. □ **spread like wildfire** spread quickly.

wildflower *n.* a flowering plant growing in a natural state.

wildfowl *n.* (*pl.* **wildfowl**) a game bird.

wild goose chase *n.* a foolish or hopeless quest.

wildlife *n.* wild animals.

wild rice *n.* a tall grass related to rice, yielding edible grains.

Wild West *n.* the lawless frontier districts of the western US in the 19th century.

wildwood *n.* woodland that is not cultivated.

wiles *pl. n.* clever tricks used to manipulate someone.

wilful *adj.* **1** intentional, deliberate. **2** headstrong. □ **wilfully** *adv.* **wilfulness** *n.*

will[1] *v.* **1** expressing the future tense. **2** expressing a wish or intention. **3** expressing desire or consent. **4** expressing ability or capacity. **5** expressing inevitable tendency. **6** expressing probability.

will[2] ● *n.* **1** the faculty by which a person decides on and takes action. **2** (also **willpower**) self-control. **3** a desire or intention. **4** the power of effecting one's intentions. **5** directions (usu. written) in legal form for the disposition of one's property after death. ● *v.* **1** intend. **2** cause by the exercise of willpower. **3** bequeath by the terms of a will. □ **at will** whenever one pleases. **where there's a will there's a way** determination will overcome any obstacle. **a will of one's own** obstinacy. **with a will** energetically or resolutely.
□ **willed** *adj.*

willet *n.* (*pl.* **willet**) a large grey and white N American shorebird with a loud call.

willful = WILFUL.

willies *pl. n. informal* nervous discomfort.

willing *adj.* **1** ready to consent or undertake. **2** given, done, etc. by a willing person. □ **willingly** *adv.* **willingness** *n.*

will-o'-the-wisp *n.* **1** a bluish light seen hovering at night on marshy ground, thought to result from the combustion of natural gases. **2** something that is difficult to find or catch.

willow *n.* a tree or shrub with small flowers borne on catkins.

willow herb *n.* a plant with narrow leaves and pink or purple flowers.

willowy *adj.* **1** tall, slender, and graceful. **2** having willows.

willpower *n.* = WILL[2] *n.* 2.

willy *n.* (*pl.* **willies**) *slang* the penis.

willy-nilly ● *adv.* **1** whether one likes it or not. **2** haphazardly. **●** *adj.* occurring willy-nilly.

wilt ● *v.* **1** (of a plant etc.) wither, droop. **2** (of a person) lose one's energy. **3** cause to wilt. **●** *n.* the action of wilting.

wily *adj.* (**wilier, wiliest**) crafty, cunning.

wimp *n. Informal* a feeble or cowardly person. □ **wimp out** chicken out. □ **wimpish** *adj.* **wimpishness** *n.* **wimpy** *adj.* (**wimpier, wimpiest**)

wimple *n.* a linen or silk headdress covering the neck and the sides of the face.

win ● *v.* (**wins;** *past* and *past participle* **won; winning**) **1** gain as a result of a fight, contest, bet, etc. **2** be victorious in (a fight, game, etc.). **3** make one's way or become or reach by effort. **●** *n.* a victory in a game or bet etc. □ **win the day** be victorious. **win out** overcome obstacles. **win over** persuade. □ **winnable** *adj.*

wince ● *v.* (**winces, winced, wincing**) grimace or flinch involuntarily in pain or distress. **●** *n.* a wincing movement.

winch ● *n.* (*pl.* **winches**) a hauling or lifting device consisting of a rope or chain winding around a horizontal axle, turned by a crank or motor. **●** *v.* (**winches, winched, winching**) lift with a winch.

wind¹ ● *n.* **1** air in more or less rapid natural motion. **2** breath as needed in physical exertion or speech. **3** mere empty words. **4** intestinal gas. **5 a** a breath of air for sounding a wind instrument. **b** (a player of) a wind instrument. **●** *v.* **1** cause someone to have difficulty breathing because of exertion or a punch to the stomach. **2** renew the wind of by rest. □ **sail close to the wind 1** sail nearly against the wind. **2** *informal* verge on indecency, dishonesty, or disaster. **get wind of 1** detect by smell. **2** begin to suspect. **how** (or **which way**) **the wind blows** (or **lies**) **1** what is the state of opinion. **2** what developments are likely. **in the wind** happening or about to happen. **like the wind** swiftly. **take the wind out of a person's sails** frustrate a person by anticipating an action or remark etc. **wind** (or **winds**) **of change** a force or influence for reform. □ **windless** *adj.*

wind² ● *v.* (**winds, wound, winding**) **1** go in a circular or spiral course. **2** make (one's way) by such a course. **3** wrap closely. **4** coil. **5** wind up (a clock etc.). **6** hoist with a windlass etc. **●** *n.* **1** a bend or turn in a course. **2** a single turn when winding. □ **wind down 1** lower by winding. **2** unwind. **3** (of a person) relax. **4** draw to a close. **wind up 1** coil the whole of. **2** esp. *Brit.* tighten the coiling or coiled spring of

(esp. a clock etc.). **3 a** *informal* increase the tension of. **b** provoke (a person) to the point of anger. **4** bring to a conclusion. **wound up** *adj.* (of a person) excited or tense. □ **winding** *n.* **&** *adj.*

windbag *n. informal* a person who talks a lot but says little of any value.

windblown *adj.* carried or made untidy by the wind.

windbreak *n.* an obstacle, such as a row of trees etc., which provides shelter from the wind.

windbreaker *n.* a wind-resistant outer jacket with close-fitting neck, cuffs, and hip band.

windburn *n.* inflammation of the skin caused by exposure to wind. □ **windburned** *adj.* (also **windburnt**)

wind chill *n.* the cooling effect of wind blowing on a surface.

wind chimes *pl. n.* small pieces of glass, metal, etc. suspended so as to tinkle in the wind.

windfall *n.* **1** an unexpected gift of money, piece of good luck, etc. **2** an apple etc. blown to the ground by the wind. **3** a branch or tree blown down by the wind.

wind farm *n.* a group of energy-producing windmills or wind turbines.

Windigo *n.* (in the folklore of Northern Algonquian peoples) a cannibalistic giant. [*Say* WIN di go]

wind instrument *n.* a musical instrument in which sound is produced by the player blowing into the instrument.

windjammer *n.* a merchant sailing ship.

windlass *n.* (*pl.* **windlasses**) a winch, esp. on a ship or in a harbour. [*Sounds like* WINDLESS]

windmill ● *n.* a mill, pump, or generator driven by sails or blades that rotate in the wind. **●** *v.* fling (one's limbs) around in a manner suggestive of a windmill. □ **tilt at windmills** attack an imaginary enemy or grievance.

window *n.* **1** an opening in a wall, door, etc., usu. with glass, to admit light or air etc. and allow people to see out. **2** a space for display behind the front window of a store. **3** an aperture through which customers are served in a bank, ticket office, etc. **4** an opportunity to observe or learn. **5** a transparent part in an envelope to show an address. **6** *Computing* a defined area on a display screen for viewing information. **7** any interval or opportunity for action. □ **windowed** *adj.* **windowless** *adj.*

window box *n.* a narrow box placed on an

outside windowsill, used for growing flowers.

window dressing *n.* **1** the art of arranging a display in a store window etc. **2** a presentation of facts etc. to give a deceptively favourable impression.

window ledge *n.* a windowsill.

windowpane *n.* a pane of glass in a window.

window-shop *v.* (**window-shops, window-shopped, window-shopping**) look at goods displayed in store windows, usu. without buying. □ **window-shopper** *n.*

windowsill *n.* a sill below a window.

windpipe *n.* the trachea.

windproof *adj.* impervious to wind.

windrow *n.* **1** a line of raked hay etc. laid out for drying by the wind. **2** a row of leaves, dust, etc. heaped up by the wind. **3** *Cdn* a ridge of snow, gravel, etc. heaped along the side of a road by a snowplow etc. [*Say* WIN droe]

windshield *n.* a glass window across the front of a motor vehicle or aircraft.

windsock *n.* a nylon cylinder or cone on a mast to show the direction of the wind etc.

windstorm *n.* a storm with very strong wind but little precipitation.

windsurf *v.* ride on the water on a sailboard. □ **windsurfer** *n.* **windsurfing** *n.*

windswept *adj.* exposed to or swept back by wind.

wind tunnel *n.* a tunnel-like device for producing an airstream in the study of wind flow or wind effects on objects.

windup ● *n.* **1** a conclusion. **2** the drawing back of the arm or stick as part of a throwing or shooting motion. ● *adj.* operated by being wound up.

windward ● *adj. & adv.* on the side from which the wind is blowing. ● *n.* the windward side.

windy¹ *adj.* (**windier, windiest**) **1** stormy with wind. **2** exposed to the wind. **3** *informal* wordy.

windy² *adj.* (**windier, windiest**) that winds, winding.

wine *n.* **1** fermented grape juice as an alcoholic drink. **2** a fermented drink made from other fruits. □ **wine and dine** entertain or be entertained with food and drink.

wine cellar *n.* **1** a cellar for storing wine. **2** the contents of this.

wine cooler *n.* a drink of wine, soda water, and fruit flavours.

wineglass *n.* (*pl.* **wineglasses**) a glass for wine, usu. with a stem and foot.

wine grower *n.* a cultivator of grapes for wine. □ **wine-growing** *n. & adj.*

winemaker *n.* a producer of wine. □ **winemaking** *n.*

winery *n.* (*pl.* **wineries**) an establishment where wine is made.

winey *adj.* (**winier, winiest**) resembling wine.

wing ● *n.* **1** each of the limbs or organs by which a bird, bat, or insect is able to fly. **2** anything similar to a wing in form or function. **3** either of a pair of rigid horizontal structures extending on either side of an aircraft that support it in the air. **4** part of a building. **5** a section of a political party or group holding particular views. **6** esp. *Hockey & Soccer* **a** the area along the side of a playing surface. **b** a player at this position. **7** (in *pl.*) the sides of a theatre stage out of view of the audience. ● *v.* **1 a** fly. **b** make (one's way) through the air. **2** throw. □ **on the wing** flying or in flight. **on a wing and a prayer** with only the slightest chance of success. **spread** (or **stretch**) **one's wings** test one's abilities. **take under one's wing** treat as a protege. **wing it** *informal* improvise. □ **winged** *adj.* **wingless** *adj.* **wing-like** *adj.*

wingbeat *n.* one complete cycle of movements made by the wing of a bird etc. in flying.

wingding *n. informal* a wild party.

winger *n.* **1** *Sport* a forward who plays on the wing. **2** a person affiliated with a political wing.

wing nut *n.* **1** a threaded nut with projections for the fingers to turn it on a screw. **2** *slang* a stupid person.

wingspan *n.* (also **wingspread**) the maximum extent from tip to tip of the wings of a bird or aircraft.

wing tip *n.* **1** the tip of a wing. **2** a shoe with a usu. perforated toecap with a backward extending point and curved sides.

wingy *adj.* (**wingier, wingiest**) *Cdn informal* crazy. [*Say* WING ee]

wink ● *v.* **1** close and open one eye to convey a message or as a signal of friendliness. **2** (of a light etc.) twinkle. **3** disappear or go out suddenly. ● *n.* **1** an act of closing and opening the eye. **2** a brief moment. **3** *informal* a very brief sleep.

winkle ● *n.* a small edible mollusc with a spiral shell. ● *v.* (**winkles, winkled, winkling**) extract.

winless adj. characterized by an absence of victories.

Winnebago n. (pl. **Winnebagos**) proprietary a large motorhome.
[Say winna BAY go]

winner n. **1** a person etc. who wins. **2** a goal etc. that decides the outcome of a game etc. **3** informal a successful or highly promising thing.

winning ● adj. **1** victorious, successful. **2** that determines the outcome of a game etc. **3** attractive, persuasive. ● n. **1** the action of being victorious. **2** (in pl.) money won esp. in gambling. □ **winningly** adv.

winningest adj. Sport informal that has won the most often. [Say WINNING est]

Winnipegger n. a person from Winnipeg.

winnow v. **1** blow air through (grain) to remove the chaff. **2** separate (chaff) from grain. **3** subject to a process which separates esp. the good from the bad.

wino n. (pl. **winos**) slang a habitual excessive drinker of cheap wine.
[Say WINE oh]

winsome adj. attractive or appealing. □ **winsomely** adv. **winsomeness** n.
[Say WIN sum]

winter ● n. **1** the fourth and coldest season of the year, between autumn and spring. **2** cold or wintry weather typical of this season. ● adj. characteristic of, done, or suitable for use in winter. ● v. spend the winter.

winter club n. Cdn an organization that offers recreational activities such as skating and curling throughout the winter.

wintergreen n. a N American evergreen plant that yields a pungent oil, which is used medicinally and as a flavouring.

winterize v. (**winterizes**, **winterized**, **winterizing**) adapt or prepare for use in cold weather. □ **winterization** n. **winterized** adj.

winterkill n. the death of plants or animals by exposure to frost, snow, and extreme cold.

winter road n. Cdn a secondary road made of compact snow or ice, often plowed over a frozen lake or ground impassable in the summer.

wintertime n. the season of winter.

winter wheat n. wheat that is planted in the fall and harvested the following summer.

wintry adj. (also **wintery**) (**wintrier**, **wintriest**) **1** characteristic of or affected by winter. **2** (of a smile, greeting, etc.) lacking warmth or enthusiasm.

win-win adj. designating a situation which is beneficial to both parties involved.

wipe ● v. (**wipes**, **wiped**, **wiping**) **1** clean or dry by rubbing with a cloth etc. **2** spread or apply by rubbing with a soft cloth or the hand etc. **3 a** clear or remove (moisture, dirt, etc.) from something. **b** remove or eliminate completely. **4** remove or erase from one's mind. **5** erase (data etc.) from a storage medium. ● n. **1** an act of wiping. **2** a disposable cloth for wiping something clean. □ **wipe down** clean by wiping. **wipe the floor with** informal inflict a humiliating defeat on. **wipe out 1 a** greatly reduce the strength or significance of. **b** efface, obliterate. **2** slang murder. **3** informal fall or crash. □ **wipeable** adj.

wiped out adj. **1** destroyed. **2** financially ruined. **3** informal tired.

wipeout n. **1** a fall, crash, or accident. **2** informal a dismal failure.

wiper n. (in full **windshield wiper**) a rubber blade on an arm which keeps a windshield clear of rain etc.

wire ● n. **1** metal drawn out into the form of a fine thread or thin flexible rod. **2** a single line of esp. copper wire, or several of these, used as a conductor of electrical current. **3 a** dated a telegram. **b** (also **wire service**) a service transmitting the latest news stories. **4** an electronic listening device. **5** a line or cable made of several strands of wire twisted together for strength. ● v. (**wires**, **wired**, **wiring**) **1** fit, fasten, or secure with a wire. **2** furnish with electrical circuits etc. **3** fit (a person) with a concealed listening device. **4** informal arrange to have (money) sent. □ **get one's wires crossed** become confused or misunderstood. **under the wire** just in time.

wired adj. **1** slang hyper or antsy. **2 a** fitted with electrical connections or cables. **b** informal having access to the Internet.

wireless ● adj. having to do with devices etc. not requiring wires, esp. those employing radio transmission. ● n. (also **wireless telegraphy**) radio transmission.

wiretap ● n. **1** an act of tapping a telephone line, esp. as a means of surveillance. **2** a device used to do this. ● v. (**wiretaps**, **wiretapped**, **wiretapping**) tap a telephone line. □ **wiretapper** n. **wiretapping** n.

wiring n. a system of electrical wires in a device or building.

wiry adj. (**wirier**, **wiriest**) **1** resembling wire. **2** (of a person) thin and sinewy.

wisdom n. **1** the state of being wise. **2** experience and knowledge together with

the power of applying them. **3** prudence.
4 wise sayings etc. regarded collectively.

wisdom tooth *n.* each of four hindmost teeth in humans, which usu. appear around the age of 20.

wise[1] *adj.* (**wiser**, **wisest**) **1** having experience and knowledge and the ability to apply them. **2** prudent, sensible. **3** learned. **4** *informal* **a** alert. **b** impudent. □**wise to** *informal* aware of. **wise up** become informed or enlightened. **without anyone's being the wiser** undetected. □**wisely** *adv.*

wise[2] *n. archaic* way, manner. □**in no wise** not at all.

-wise[1] *suffix informal* forming adverbs meaning "in terms of".

-wise[2] *suffix* forming adjectives meaning "mindful and careful of".

wiseacre *n.* **1** a know-it-all. **2** a wise guy.

wiseass *n.* (*pl.* **wiseasses**) *slang* a wise guy.

wisecrack *informal* ● *n.* a witty or sarcastic remark. ● *v.* make a wisecrack. □**wisecracker** *n.* **wisecracking** *n. & adj.*

wise guy *n. informal* a cocky person who makes sarcastic comments, esp. to display cleverness.

wish ● *v.* (**wishes**, **wished**, **wishing**) **1** desire (esp. something that cannot or will not occur). **2** intend or hope. **3** demand or request. **4** have or express a desire or yearning for. **5** express one's hopes for (the success of another). **6** (usu. with *neg.*) foist on a person. ● *n.* (*pl.* **wishes**) **1 a** a desire or hope. **b** an expression of this. **2** a thing desired. □**best** (or **good**) **wishes** hopes felt for another's happiness etc.

wishbone *n.* **1** a forked bone between the neck and breastbone of a bird. **2** an object of similar shape.

wishful *adj.* having or expressing a wish. □**wishfully** *adv.*

wish list *n.* a list of wishes or aspirations.

wishy-washy *adj.* **1** indecisive. **2** feeble.

wisp *n.* **1** several strands of hair etc. **2** a thin faint trace of smoke etc. **3** a slender, delicate person. **4** a hint. □**wispy** *adj.* (**wispier**, **wispiest**)

wisteria *n.* a climbing plant with hanging bunches of flowers. [*Say* wis TEERY uh]

wistful *adj.* having or showing vague or regretful longing. □**wistfully** *adv.* **wistfulness** *n.*

wit[1] *n.* **1** the apt, clever, and funny expression of thought, calculated to delight an audience. **2** a person possessing such an ability. **3** (often in *pl.*) mental or intellectual power. □**at one's wits'** (or **wit's**) **end** in a state of utter perplexity or despair. **have** (or **keep**) **one's wits about one** be mentally alert. **live by one's wits** live by ingenious or crafty expedients. **scare** (or **frighten**) **the wits out of** frighten severely. □**-witted** *comb. form*

wit[2] *v.* □**to wit** namely.

witch *n.* (*pl.* **witches**) **1** a person, usu. a woman, who practises magic. **2** a follower or practitioner of modern witchcraft; a Wiccan. **3** a hag. □**witchlike** *adj.* **witchy** *adj.*

witchcraft *n.* **1** the practices of a witch, esp. the use of magic. **2** the practices and beliefs of the Wiccans.

witch doctor *n.* one who claims to cure disease and counteract witchcraft by magic.

witch hazel *n.* **1** a N American shrub with fragrant yellow flowers. **2** an astringent lotion made from the bark and leaves of this plant.

witch hunt *n.* **1** *hist.* a search for and persecution of people suspected of witchcraft. **2** a malicious campaign directed against a group of people with unpopular or unorthodox views. □**witch-hunting** *n.*

witching hour *n.* midnight, when witches are supposedly active.

with *prep.* expressing: **1** an instrument or means used. **2** association or company. **3** separation or release. **4** origin. **5** possession. **6** circumstances. **7** manner adopted or displayed. **8** agreement. **9** antagonism, competition. **10** responsibility or care for. **11** material. **12** addition or supply. □**be with a person 1** agree with and support a person. **2** *informal* follow a person's meaning **one with** part of the same whole as. **with it** *informal* **1 a** up to date. **b** (**with-it**) fashionable. **2** alert.

withdraw *v.* (**withdraws**; *past* **withdrew**; *past participle* **withdrawn**; **withdrawing**) **1** pull or draw back. **2** discontinue, cancel. **3** remove from a position, competition, etc. **4** take (money) out of an account. **5 a** retire. **b** become reserved. **6** retract (a remark).

withdrawal *n.* **1 a** the action of withdrawing something. **b** the removal of money from a place of deposit. **2** the process of ceasing to take an addictive drug. **3** a state of apathy or retreat from objective reality. [*Say* with DRAWL]

withdrawn *adj.* abnormally shy and unsociable.

wither *v.* **1** (of a plant) become dry and shrivelled. **2** lose or deprive of vigour or freshness. **3** cease to flourish.

withering adj. **1** scornful, scathing. **2** fading, decaying. □ **witheringly** adv.

withers pl. n. the highest part of the back of a horse etc., lying between the shoulder blades.

withhold v. (**withholds**, **withheld**, **withholding**) **1** restrain or hold back from action. **2** keep back; refuse to give.

within prep. **1** inside. **2 a** not beyond or exceeding. **b** not transgressing. **3** not further off than. **4** before the end of (a period of time).

without prep. **1** not having, feeling, or showing. **2** with freedom from. **3** in the absence of. **4** with neglect or avoidance of.

withstand v. (**withstands**, **withstood**, **withstanding**) **1** resist, oppose. **2** tolerate, endure. **3** offer resistance.

witless adj. **1** foolish; stupid. **2** crazy. □ **witlessly** adv. **witlessness** n.

witness ● n. (pl. **witnesses**) **1** a person who sees an event or occurrence take place. **2 a** a person giving testimony in a court of law. **b** testimony. **3 a** a person selected or appointed to be present at a transaction etc. **b** a person who signs a document attesting to its proper execution. ● v. (**witnesses**, **witnessed**, **witnessing**) **1** be a witness of. **2** sign (a document) as a witness of its authenticity. **3** be the scene or setting of. **4** give or serve as evidence. □ **bear witness to 1** attest the truth of. **2** state one's belief in. **call to witness** appeal to for confirmation etc.

witness box n. Cdn & Brit. (also **witness stand**) an enclosure in a court of law from which witnesses give evidence.

witticism n. a witty remark. [Say WITTA sism]

witting adj. **1** aware of the full facts of a situation. **2** deliberate, intentional. □ **wittingly** adv.

witty adj. (**wittier**, **wittiest**) **1** given to saying or writing clever and amusing things. **2** characterized by wit or humour. □ **wittily** adv. **wittiness** n.

wives pl. of WIFE.

wizard n. **1** a man who practises magic. **2** a person noted for remarkable ability. **3** Computing a software tool that operates automatically to guide a user through a particular process. □ **wizardly** adj.

wizardry n. **1** the art or practice of a wizard. **2** remarkable skill in a particular field or activity.

wizened adj. shrivelled or wrinkled. [Say WIZZ'nd]

w/o abbr. without.

wobble ● v. (**wobbles**, **wobbled**, **wobbling**) **1** move erratically from side to side. **2** stagger. **3** (of a sound) quaver. ● n. **1** an unsteady movement from side to side. **2** a tremble or quaver in the voice.

wobbly adj. (**wobblier**, **wobbliest**) **1** wobbling or tending to wobble. **2** (of a line, handwriting, etc.) shaky, wavy. **3** wavering. □ **wobbliness** n.

woe n. **1** bitter grief. **2** (in pl.) troubles. □ **woe betide** (or **to**) there will be unfortunate consequences for. **woe is me** an exclamation of distress.

woebegone adj. sad or miserable in appearance. [Say WOE be gon]

woeful adj. **1** afflicted with sorrow. **2** causing sorrow or affliction. **3** very bad. □ **woefully** adv.

wok n. a large bowl-shaped frying pan used in esp. Chinese cooking.

woke past of WAKE[1].

woken past participle of WAKE[1].

wolf ● n. (pl. **wolves**) **1** a wild flesh-eating mammal related to the dog. **2** slang **a** a ferocious person. **b** a womanizer. ● v. (**wolfs**, **wolfed**, **wolfing**) devour (food) ravenously. □ **cry wolf** raise repeated false alarms (so that a genuine one is disregarded). **keep the wolf from the door** have enough money to be able to buy food. **wolf in sheep's clothing** a person whose hostile intentions are concealed by a pretense of friendliness. □ **wolfish** adj. **wolfishly** adv. **wolflike** adj. & adv.

wolfhound n. a dog of a large breed used for hunting wolves.

wolf whistle ● n. a whistle imitating the howl of a wolf, used to express admiration of a woman's appearance. ● v. (**wolf-whistle**, **wolf-whistles**, **wolf-whistled**, **wolf-whistling**) make such a whistling sound.

wolf willow n. Cdn a N American tree with pinkish bark and silvery leaves.

wolverine n. a carnivorous animal of the weasel family with dark brown fur and a long bushy tail, native to northern tundra and forests. [Say wool ver EEN]

wolves pl. of WOLF.

woman n. (pl. **women**) **1** an adult female person. **2** (as an adj.) female. **3** informal a wife or lover. □ **womanless** adj. **womanlike** adj.

womanhood n. **1 a** the state or condition of being a woman. **b** female maturity. **2** the qualities traditionally attributed to women. **3** women collectively.

womanize v. (**womanizes**, **womanized**, **womanizing**) (of a man) engage in casual sexual encounters with women. □ **womanizer** n.

womankind *n.* women collectively.

womanly *adj.* (of a woman) having qualities traditionally associated with women. □ **womanliness** *n.*

womb *n.* the organ in the body of a woman or female mammal in which offspring are carried and nourished before birth; the uterus. □ **womblike** *adj.* [*Say* WOOM]

wombat *n.* a burrowing plant-eating Australian marsupial that resembles a small bear. [*Say* WOM bat]

women *pl. of* WOMAN.

womenfolk *pl. n.* **1** women collectively. **2** the women of a particular family etc.

women's liberation *n.* feminism, esp. in the 1970s.

women's movement *n.* a movement campaigning for women's liberation and for the extension of women's rights.

women's shelter *n.* an establishment offering refuge to women who are victims of esp. domestic abuse.

women's studies *pl. n.* a course of academic studies focusing on women and their role in society.

womenswear *n.* clothes for women.

won *past and past participle of* WIN.

wonder ● *n.* **1** the emotion excited by the perception of something unexpected or inexplicable, esp. surprise or astonishment **2** an amazing person or thing. **3** (as an *adj.*) having marvellous or amazing properties or qualities. ● *v.* **1** desire or be curious to know. **2** speculate with curiosity or doubt. **3** used to express a polite request **4** be filled with wonder. □ **I shouldn't wonder** *informal* it would not surprise me. **no** (or **small**) **wonder** it is natural or hardly surprising. **work** (or **do**) **wonders 1** perform miracles. **2** achieve remarkable success.

wonderful *adj.* **1** very remarkable or admirable. **2** marvellous, terrific. □ **wonderfully** *adv.* **wonderfulness** *n.*

wondering *adj.* filled with wonder; marvelling. □ **wonderingly** *adv.*

wonderland *n.* **1** an imaginary world of marvels. **2** a place of remarkable beauty.

wonderment *n.* a state of surprise or awe.

wonderstruck *adj.* reduced to silence by wonder.

wondrous *adj.* *literary* wonderful. □ **wondrously** *adv.* [*Say* WUN drus]

wonk *n.* *slang* usu. *derogatory* **1** a studious or hard-working person. **2** (also **policy wonk**) esp. *US* a person who takes an unnecessary interest in minor details of policy. □ **wonkery** *n.*

wonky *adj.* (**wonkier**, **wonkiest**) *informal*

1 crooked, loose. **2** faulty, askew. □ **wonkiness** *n.*

wont ● *adj.* accustomed. ● *n.* one's normal behaviour. [*Sounds like* WANT]

won't *contr.* will not.

wonted *adj.* usual. [*Sounds like* WANTED]

won ton *n.* (in Chinese cooking) a small round dumpling containing a savoury filling, usu. boiled and served in a broth. [*Say* WON ton *(both parts of this word rhyme with* DAWN*)*]

woo *v.* (**woos**, **wooed**, **wooing**) **1** seek the love of (esp. a woman). **2** seek the support of. **3** try to win (fame etc.).

wood *n.* **1 a** a hard fibrous material that forms the main substance of the trunk or branches of a tree etc. **b** this cut for timber or for fuel. **2** a small forest. **3** (**the wood**) wooden storage, esp. a cask, for wine etc. **4** a wooden-headed golf club.

wood bison *n.* (*pl.* **wood bison**) (also **wood buffalo**, *pl.* **wood buffalo** or **wood buffaloes**) a subspecies of N American bison found in wooded parts of western Canada.

woodblock *n.* a block from which woodcuts are made.

woodcarving *n.* **1** the act or art of carving wood. **2** a design carved in wood. □ **woodcarver** *n.*

woodchuck *n.* a reddish-brown and grey N American marmot.

woodcock *n.* (*pl.* **woodcock**) a woodland game bird of the sandpiper family, with a long bill.

woodcut *n.* **1** a relief cut on a block of wood. **2** a print made from this.

woodcutter *n.* **1** a person who cuts down trees. **2** a woodcut maker. □ **woodcutting** *adj. & n.*

wood duck *n.* a N American wild duck, the male of which has a green and blue head.

wooded *adj.* having woods or many trees.

wooden *adj.* **1** made of wood. **2** like wood. **3 a** stiff or stilted. **b** expressionless. □ **woodenly** *adv.*

woodland *n.* wooded country, woods. □ **woodlander** *n.*

woodland caribou *n.* (*pl.* **woodland caribou**) a large caribou found in wooded areas of Canada.

Woodland Cree *n.* (*pl.* **Woodland Cree** or **Woodland Crees**) **1** a member of a Cree people who live in forested areas. **2** the dialect of Cree spoken by this people.

woodlot *n.* a treed plot of land.

woodpecker *n.* a bird with a strong bill, which taps tree trunks in search of insects.

woodpile *n.* a pile of wood, esp. for fuel.

wood pulp *n.* wood fibre reduced chemically or mechanically to pulp as raw material for paper.

woodruff *n.* a white-flowered plant grown for the fragrance of its whorled leaves.

woods *pl. n.* trees densely occupying a tract of land. □**out of the woods** out of danger.

woodshed *n.* a shed where firewood is stored.

woodsman *n.* (*pl.* **woodsmen**) **1** a person who lives in or frequents the woods. **2** a person skilled in woodworking.

woodsmoke *n.* the smoke from a wood fire.

woodsy *adj.* (**woodsier, woodsiest**) like or characteristic of woods.

woodwind *n.* a wind instrument originally made of wood, e.g. flute or clarinet.

woodwork *n.* **1** the making of things in wood. **2** things made of wood. □**crawl** (or **come**) **out of the woodwork** *informal* (of something unwelcome) emerge from obscurity into prominence.
□**woodworker** *n.* **woodworking** *n.*

woodworm *n.* **1** the wood-boring larva of a small brown beetle. **2** damaged wood affected by this.

woody *adj.* (**woodier, woodiest**) **1** abounding in woods. **2** like or of wood. □**woodiness** *n.*

woof¹ ● *n.* the gruff bark of a dog. ● *v.* give a woof. [*With* OO *as in* WOOL]

woof² *n.* = WEFT 1. [*With* OO *as in either* WOOL *or* PROOF]

woofer *n.* a loudspeaker designed to reproduce low frequencies. [*With* OO *as in* WOOL]

wool *n.* **1** fine soft wavy hair from the fleece of sheep, goats, etc. **2** yarn produced from this hair. **3** a wool-like substance.
□**pull the wool over a person's eyes** deceive a person.

woolgather *v.* be absent-minded or inattentive. □**woolgathering** *n.*

woollen (also **woolen**) ● *adj.* made wholly or partly of wool. ● *n.* (in *pl.*) woollen garments.

woolly ● *adj.* (**woollier, woolliest**) **1** bearing or naturally covered with wool; downy. **2** resembling wool. **3** made of wool. **4** (of a sound) indistinct. **5** (of thought) vague or confused. ● *n.* (*pl.* **woollies**) *informal* a woollen garment, esp. a sweater.
□**woolliness** *n.*

woosh *v., n., & interj.* (**wooshes, wooshed, wooshing**) = WHOOSH.

woozy *adj.* (**woozier, wooziest**) *informal* dizzy, unsteady, or dazed. □**woozily** *adv.* **wooziness** *n.*

Worcestershire sauce *n.* a pungent sauce containing soy and vinegar.
[*Say* WUSS tuh sher *or* WURST er sher]

word ● *n.* **1** a sound or combination of sounds forming a meaningful element of speech. **2** speech. **3** one's promise. **4** a thing said, a remark or conversation. **5** (in *pl.*) the text of a song or an actor's part. **6** (in *pl.*) angry talk. **7 a** news. **b** a rumour. **8** a command, password, or motto. **9** (**the Word**) **a** any divine message. **b** the Gospel. ● *v.* put into words. □**be as good as one's word** fulfill what one has promised. **break one's word** fail to do what one has promised. **have a word** speak briefly (to). **in so many words** explicitly or bluntly. **in a** (or **one**) **word** briefly. **keep one's word** do what one has promised. **my** (or **upon my**) **word** an exclamation of surprise. **of few words** taciturn. **of one's word** reliable in keeping promises. **on** (or **upon**) **my word** used to introduce a solemn declaration. **take a person at his** or **her word** interpret a person's words literally. **take a person's word for it** believe a person's statement etc. **waste words** talk in vain. **word for word** in exactly the same or corresponding words. **words fail me** an expression of disbelief etc. **a word to the wise** a piece of advice etc. □**wordless** *adj.*

wording *n.* **1** a form of words used. **2** the way in which something is worded.

word of mouth *n.* spoken communication between people.

wordplay *n.* witty use of words.

word processor *n.* a computer system for storing, editing, and usu. displaying and printing text entered from a keyboard. □**word-processed** *adj.* **word processing** *n.*

wordsmith *n.* a skilled user of words.

wordy *adj.* (**wordier, wordiest**) using many or too many words. □**wordiness** *n.*

wore *past of* WEAR.

work ● *n.* **1** the application of mental or physical effort to a purpose. **2 a** a task to be undertaken. **b** the materials for this. **3** a thing done or made by work. **4** a person's employment or occupation etc. **5 a** a literary or musical composition. **b** (in *pl.*) all such by an author or composer etc. **6** actions or experiences of a specified kind. **7** things or parts made of a specified material. **8** (in *pl.*) the operative part of a clock or machine. **9** *Physics* the exertion of force overcoming resistance. **10** a defensive structure. ● *v.* **1** do work. **2** be employed in certain work. **3** make efforts. **4** be a craftsman (in a material). **5** operate or function. **6** (of a part of a machine) run, revolve. **7** carry on, manage, or control. **8 a** cause to toil. **b** cultivate (land). **9** bring to a desired shape or consistency. **10** gradually become (loose etc.) by constant movement. **11** have influence. □ **get worked up** become angry, excited, or tense. **have one's work cut out** be faced with a hard task. **in the works** being planned. **set to work** begin or cause to begin operations. **work away** (or **on**) continue to work. **work in** find a place for. **work it** *informal* bring it about. **work out 1** solve by calculation. **2** be calculated. **3** give or have as a definite result. **4** provide for the details of. **5** accomplish with difficulty. **6** exhaust with work. **7** engage in physical exercise. **work over 1** examine thoroughly. **2** *informal* treat with violence. **work to rule** follow official working rules exactly so as to reduce output and efficiency. **work up 1** bring gradually to an efficient state. **2** advance gradually to a climax. **3** excite by degrees.

workable *adj.* **1** that can be worked or will work. **2** practicable, feasible. □ **workability** *n.*

workaday *adj.* **1** ordinary, everyday. **2** fit for or seen on workdays.

workaholic *n. informal* a person who willingly works too hard. □ **workaholism** *n.*

workbench *n.* (*pl.* **workbenches**) a bench for doing mechanical or practical work.

workbook *n.* **1** a student's book giving information on a subject and exercises. **2** a student's notebook.

workboot *n.* a sturdy leather boot.

work camp *n.* a prison camp enforcing a regime of hard labour.

workday *n.* **1** a day on which work is usually done. **2** the part of the day devoted to work.

worker *n.* **1** one who works. **2 a** one who works in a specified way. **b** one who works hard. **3** a neuter or not yet developed female of various social insects.

workers' compensation *n.* money paid to a person to compensate for injury suffered on the job.

work ethic *n.* the principle that hard work is intrinsically virtuous.

workfare *n.* a welfare system which requires some work from those receiving benefits.

workforce *n.* the workers engaged or available in an industry etc.

workgroup *n.* a group of people who have simultaneous access to shared software and data.

workhorse *n.* **1** a horse used for heavy work. **2** a person, machine, etc. that does much work.

workhouse *n. Brit. hist.* an institution where poor people used to have to live and work if they couldn't afford living anywhere else.

working ● *adj.* **1 a** having a job. **b** doing manual work. **2** functioning or able to function. **3** that is good enough as a basis for work, argument, etc. and may be improved later. **●** *n.* **1** the activity of work. **2** the act or manner of functioning. **3** (usu. in *pl.*) **a** a mine or quarry. **b** the part of this in which work is being done.

working capital *n.* capital needed and used in running a business.

working class ● *n.* the class of people employed for wages, esp. in manual or industrial work. **●** *adj.* (**working-class**) of or relating to this class.

working order *n.* the condition in which a machine works.

work-in-progress *n.* (*pl.* **works-in-progress**) work undertaken but not yet completed.

workload *n.* the amount of work to be done by an individual etc.

workman *n.* (*pl.* **workmen**) **1** a man employed to do manual labour. **2** a person who works in a specified way.

workmanlike *adj.* showing practised skill.

workmanship *n.* the degree of skill in doing a task or of quality in the product made.

workmate *n.* a person with whom one works.

work of art *n.* (*pl.* **works of art**) a fine picture, poem, or building etc.

workout *n.* a session of physical exercise or training.

workplace *n.* a place at which a person works.

workroom *n.* a room equipped for a certain kind of work.

worksheet *n.* **1** a paper for recording work done or in progress. **2** a paper listing questions or activities for students.

workshop ● *n.* **1** a room or building in which goods are made. **2 a** a meeting for concerted discussion and practical work on a particular subject. **b** the members of such a group. **●** *v.* (**workshops, workshopped, workshopping**) present a workshop performance of (a dramatic work).

workspace *n.* **1** space in which to work.

2 an area rented or sold for commercial purposes. **3** *Computing* a memory storage facility for temporary use.

workstation *n.* **1** a computer terminal. **2** a location on an assembly line at which a manufacturing operation is carried out.

work-to-rule *n.* the act of following official working rules exactly so as to reduce output and efficiency.

workup *n.* a diagnostic examination of a patient.

workweek *n.* the number of days or hours per week devoted to work.

world *n.* **1 a** the earth, or a planetary body like it. **b** its countries and peoples. **2 a** the universe or all that exists. **b** everything that exists outside oneself. **3 a** the time, state, or scene of human existence. **b** mortal life. **4** secular interests and affairs. **5** active life. **6** average or fashionable people or their customs or opinions. **7** a vast amount. □ **be worlds apart** be completely different. **bring into the world** give birth to or attend at the birth of. **come into the world** be born. **for all the world** precisely. **man** (or **woman**) **of the world** a person experienced in human affairs. **out of this world** *informal* extremely good etc. **see the world** travel widely. **think the world of** have a very high regard for. **the** (or **all the**) **world over** throughout the world. **world without end** forever.

world beat *n.* world music.

world-class *adj.* of a very high quality or standard.

world-famous *adj.* known throughout the world.

World Heritage Site *n.* a natural or man-made site of outstanding international importance.

worldly *adj.* (**worldlier**, **worldliest**) **1** of or concerned with material values rather than a spiritual existence. **2** experienced and sophisticated. □ **worldliness** *n.*

world music *n.* traditional local or ethnic music, esp. from the developing world.

world power *n.* a nation having power and influence in world affairs.

World Series *n.* the N American Major League Baseball championship.

world's fair *n.* an international exhibition of the industrial, scientific, etc. achievements of the participating nations.

world war *n.* a war between many important nations.

world-weary *adj.* feeling or indicating weariness or cynicism as a result of long experience of life. □ **world-weariness** *n.*

worldwide ● *adj.* occurring in or known

throughout the world. ● *adv.* throughout the world.

World Wide Web *n.* an international computer network using hypertext links to access and retrieve information.

worm ● *n.* **1** an earthworm or other creeping or burrowing invertebrate animal with a long slender body and no limbs. **2** the long slender larva of an insect. **3** (in *pl.*) intestinal or other internal parasites. **4** a maggot supposed to eat dead bodies in the grave. **5** an insignificant or contemptible person. ● *v.* **1** move with a crawling motion. **2** insinuate oneself into a person's favour etc. **3** obtain (a secret etc.) by cunning persistence. □ **wormer** *n.* **wormlike** *adj.* **wormy** *adj.* (**wormier**, **wormiest**)

wormwood *n.* **1** a woody shrub with a bitter taste used in vermouth, absinthe, and medicine. **2** a state or source of bitterness, grief, or sadness.

worn ● *v. past participle of* WEAR. ● *adj.* **1** damaged by use or wear. **2** looking tired. **3** (also **well-worn**) (of a joke etc.) stale.

worn out *adj.* **1** exhausted. **2** worn, esp. so as to be no longer usable.

worried *adj.* **1** uneasy, troubled in the mind. **2** suggesting worry. □ **worriedly** *adv.*

worrisome *adj.* causing or apt to cause worry.

worry ● *v.* (**worries**, **worried**, **worrying**) **1** give way to anxiety or unease. **2** be a trouble or anxiety to. **3 a** (of a dog etc.) shake or pull repeatedly with the teeth. **b** attack repeatedly. ● *n.* (*pl.* **worries**) **1** a thing that causes anxiety. **2** anxiety. □ **not to worry** *informal* there is no need to worry. □ **worrier** *n.* **worrying** *adj.* **worryingly** *adv.*

worrywart *n. informal* a person who tends to worry unduly.

worse ● *adj.* **1** bad to a greater degree. **2** in or into worse health or a worse condition. ● *adv.* more badly or more ill. ● *n.* **1** a worse thing or things. **2** (**the worse**) a worse condition. □ **none the worse** not adversely affected (by). **the worse for wear 1** damaged by use. **2** injured. **3** drunk. **worse off** in a worse position.

worsen *v.* make or become worse.

worship ● *n.* **1 a** reverence paid to a deity. **b** the rites or ceremonies of worship. **2** great adoration or devotion. ● *v.* (**worships**, **worshipped**, **worshipping**) **1** adore as divine. **2** idolize or regard with adoration. **3** attend public worship. □ **Your** (or **His** or **Her**) **Worship** esp. *Cdn* & *Brit.* a title of respect used to or of a mayor etc. □ **worshipper** *n.*

worshipful *adj.* **1** (usu. **Worshipful**) a

title given to officers of certain organizations. **2** adoring.

worst ● *adj.* most bad. ● *adv.* most badly. ● *n.* the worst part, possibility, etc. ● *v.* get the better of. □ **at worst** (or **the worst**) in the worst possible case. **if (the) worst comes to (the) worst** if the worst happens. **in the worst way** to an extreme degree.

worsted *n.* **1** a fine smooth yarn spun from combed long staple wool. **2** fabric made from this. [*Say* WORSE tid]

worth ● *adj.* **1** of a value equivalent to. **2** deserving. **3** possessing or having property amounting to. ● *n.* **1** what a person or thing is worth. **2** the equivalent of money in a commodity. □ **for all one is worth** *informal* with one's utmost efforts. **for what it is worth** without a guarantee of its truth or value.

worthless *adj.* without value or merit. □ **worthlessness** *n.*

worthwhile *adj.* that is worth the time or effort spent.

worthy ● *adj.* (**worthier, worthiest**) **1** having some moral worth. **2** esp. *jocular* (of a person) entitled to recognition. **3 a** deserving. **b** adequate or suitable to the dignity etc. of. ● *n.* (*pl.* **worthies**) **1** a worthy person. **2** a person of some distinction. □ **worthily** *adv.* **worthiness** *n.*

would *aux. v.* used esp. **: 1 a** in a reported speech. **b** to express the conditional mood. **2** to express habitual action. **3** to express a question or polite request **4** to express probability. **5** *literary* to express a wish.

would-be *adj.* often *derogatory* desiring or aspiring to be.

wouldn't *contr.* would not.

wound[1] ● *n.* **1** an injury done to living tissue by a cut or blow etc. **2** an injury to a person's reputation or feelings. ● *v.* inflict a wound on. □ **wounded** *n.* [*Say* WOOND]

wound[2] *past and past participle of* WIND[2]. [*Rhymes with* SOUND]

wove *past of* WEAVE[1].

woven *past participle of* WEAVE[1].

wow ● *interj.* expressing astonishment or admiration. ● *v. slang* impress or excite greatly.

wrack[1] *n.* **1** seaweed on the shore. **2** a wreck or wreckage.

wrack[2] *var of.* RACK *v.*

wraith *n.* **1** a ghost or apparition. **2** the spectral appearance of someone supposed to portend that person's death. □ **wraithlike** *adj.* [*Say* RAITH]

wrangle ● *n.* a heated or prolonged dispute. ● *v.* (**wrangles, wrangled,**

wrangling) **1** engage in a wrangle. **2** get (a thing) by argument or persuasion. **3** herd (horses, cattle, etc.). □ **wrangling** *n.*

wrangler *n.* **1** a cowboy. **2** a person who wrangles.

wrap ● *v.* (**wraps, wrapped, wrapping**) **1** envelop in folded or soft encircling material. **2 a** arrange or draw (a pliant covering) around. **b** encircle or wind around. **3** *slang* crash (a vehicle) into a stationary object. **4** finish filming (a movie etc.). **5** *Computing* cause (a word) to be carried over to a new line automatically. ● *n.* **1** a shawl or scarf. **2** material used for wrapping. **3** the completion of the filming of a movie etc. **4** a sandwich of fillings wrapped in a tortilla. □ **take the wraps off** disclose. **under wraps** in secrecy. **wrapped up in** engrossed or absorbed in. **wrap up 1** finish off. **2** put on warm clothes.

wraparound ● *adj.* (of a garment) designed to wrap around the body. ● *n.* anything that wraps around.

wrapper *n.* a thing in which something is wrapped.

wrapping *n.* (often in *pl.*) material used to wrap.

wrapping paper *n.* decorative paper for wrapping gifts etc.

wrap-up ● *n.* a summary; a conclusion. ● *adj.* that concludes a program, book, etc.

wrath *n. literary* extreme anger. □ **wrathful** *adj.* **wrathfully** *adv.* [*Say* RATH]

wreak *v.* (**wreaks, wreaked, wreaking**) **1** give expression to (vengeance etc.). **2** cause (damage etc.). [*Say* REEK]

wreath *n.* (*pl.* **wreaths**) **1** flowers or leaves fastened in a ring esp. as an ornament or for laying on a grave. **2** something shaped like a wreath. [*Say* REETH]

wreathe *v.* (**wreathes, wreathed, wreathing**) encircle. [*Say* REETHE (*with the* TH *of* BATHE*)*]

wreck ● *n.* **1 a** the destruction esp. of a ship. **b** a ship that has suffered a wreck. **2** a greatly damaged or disabled building, vehicle, etc. **3** a person whose esp. mental health has been damaged. **4** a crash or collision. ● *v.* **1** cause the wreck of (a ship etc.); damage or destroy. **2** completely ruin. **3** suffer a wreck. □ **wrecker** *n.*

wreckage *n.* **1** wrecked material. **2** the remnants of a wreck.

wrecked *adj.* **1** involved in a shipwreck. **2** *informal* intoxicated. **3** destroyed.

wrecking *n.* the demolition of old cars, buildings, etc. to obtain usable scrap.

wrecking ball *n.* a heavy metal ball

swung from a crane to demolish a building.

wren *n.* a small usu. brown songbird with an erect tail.

wrench ● *n.* (*pl.* **wrenches**) **1** a violent twist or oblique pull. **2** a tool for gripping and turning a nut on a bolt etc. **3** a painful uprooting or parting. ● *v.* (**wrenches, wrenched, wrenching**) **1** twist or pull violently. **2** pull off with a wrench. **3** injure (a limb etc.) by undue twisting.

wrest *v.* **1** pull away from a person's grasp. **2** obtain by effort.

wrestle ● *n.* **1** a contest in which two opponents grapple and try to throw each other to the ground. **2** a hard struggle. ● *v.* (**wrestles, wrestled, wrestling**) **1** take part in a wrestle. **2** fight (a person) in a wrestle. **3** struggle, contend. □**wrestler** *n.* **wrestling** *n.*

wretch *n.* (*pl.* **wretches**) **1** an unfortunate person. **2** often *jocular* an evil or wicked person.

wretched *adj.* **1** unhappy. **2** of very poor quality. **3** ill. **4** despicable. **5** used to express annoyance. □**wretchedly** *adv.* **wretchedness** *n.* [*Say* RETCH id]

wriggle ● *v.* (**wriggles, wriggled, wriggling**) **1** twist or turn with short writhing movements. **2** move or go in this way. ● *n.* an act of wriggling. □**wriggle out** *informal* avoid on a contrived pretext. □**wriggler** *n.* **wriggly** *adj.*

wring *v.* (**wrings, wrung, wringing**) **1** squeeze and twist to force liquid from. **2** break something by twisting it forcibly. **3** squeeze tightly. **4** obtain with difficulty or effort. □**wring one's hands** clasp them as a gesture of distress.

wringer *n.* a device for wringing water from wet clothes etc. □**put through the wringer** *informal* subject to a very stressful experience.

wrinkle ● *n.* **1** a slight crease in the skin or fabric etc. **2** *informal* a minor difficulty. **3** a clever innovation. ● *v.* (**wrinkles, wrinkled, wrinkling**) **1** make wrinkles in. **2** form wrinkles. □**wrinkled** *adj.*

wrinkly *adj.* (**wrinklier, wrinkliest**) having many wrinkles.

wrist *n.* the joint connecting the hand with the forearm. □**slap on the wrist** a mild rebuke.

wristband *n.* **1** a band worn around the wrist; a cuff. **2** a bracelet used for identification.

wrist shot *n.* a shot taken by sweeping the puck along the ice with a fluid motion before releasing it.

wristwatch *n.* a watch worn on the wrist.

writ[1] *n.* **1** a form of written command in the name of a sovereign, court, etc., to act in some way. **2** a government document ordering an election.

writ[2] □**writ large** in magnified or emphasized form.

write *v.* (**writes**; *past* **wrote**; *past participle* **written**; **writing**) **1** mark a surface by means of a pen, pencil, etc., with symbols, letters, or words. **2** form (such symbols etc.). **3** fill out or complete with writing. **4** record (data) in a computer memory. **5** compose (a text etc.) for publication; set down in writing. **6 a** write and send a letter. **b** communicate by writing. **7** *Cdn & South Africa* take (an exam). **8** write in a cursive hand. □**nothing to write home about** *informal* of little interest. **write in** send a suggestion, query, etc., in writing. **write off 1** write and send a letter. **2** note the deduction of money in an account, financial statement or tax return, esp. to record the cancelling of a sum as a business expense, bad debt, depreciated stock, etc. **3** damage (a vehicle etc.) so badly that it cannot be repaired. **4** dismiss as insignificant. **write out 1** write in full. **2** exhaust (oneself) by writing. **write up** write a full account of.

write-off *n.* **1** a thing written off, esp. a vehicle too badly damaged to be repaired. **2** a person or thing that is given up as being hopeless etc. **3 a** an act of cancelling a debt because there is no chance that it will be paid. **b** an act of writing off an expense, etc.

write protect *n.* a means to protect the data in a storage device from being erased. □**write-protected** *adj.*

writer *n.* **1** one who writes or has written something. **2** one who writes professionally.

writerly *adj.* **1** characteristic of a professional author. **2** consciously literary.

writer's block *n.* an inability to express thoughts in writing due to lack of inspiration.

writer's cramp *n.* a muscular spasm in the hands due to excessive writing.

write-up *n. informal* a written account, a review.

writhe *v.* (**writhes, writhed, writhing**) **1** twist about in or as if in acute pain. **2** suffer severe mental discomfort. [*Say* RITHE (*with the* I *of* RIDE *and the* TH *of* BATHE)]

writing *n.* **1** a group or sequence of letters or symbols. **2** handwriting. **3** a piece of literary work. **4** the work or profession of a writer. □**in writing** in written form. **the**

writing is on the wall *see* HANDWRITING.

written ● *v. past participle of* WRITE. ● *adj.* that is done in writing.

wrong ● *adj.* **1** mistaken; not true. **2** unsuitable. **3** contrary to law or morality. **4** in or into a bad or abnormal condition. ● *adv.* in a wrong manner or direction; with an incorrect result. ● *n.* **1** a wrong action. **2** unjust action or treatment. ● *v.* **1** treat unjustly. **2** mistakenly attribute bad motives to. □ **do wrong to** malign or mistreat. **get off on the wrong foot** begin badly. **get** (or **get hold of**) **the wrong end of the stick** misunderstand completely. **go down the wrong way** (of food) enter the windpipe instead of the gullet. **in the wrong** responsible for a mistake or offence. **on the wrong side of 1** out of favour with. **2** somewhat more than (a stated age). □ **wrongly** *adv.* **wrongness** *n.*

wrongdoer *n.* a person who behaves immorally or illegally. □ **wrongdoing** *n.*

wrongful *adj.* **1** characterized by unfairness or injustice. **2** contrary to law. □ **wrongfully** *adv.*

wrong-headed *adj.* perverse and obstinate.

wrote *past of* WRITE. □ **that's all she wrote** *informal* that's it.

wrought *adj.* **1** (of metals) beaten out or shaped by hammering. **2** made, crafted. [*Say* ROT]

wrought iron *n.* a tough form of iron suitable for forging or rolling, not for casting.

wrung *past and past participle of* WRING. □ **wrung out** exhausted.

wry *adj.* (**wryer, wryest** or **wrier, wriest**) **1** (of humour) dry and mocking. **2** (of a face) contorted in disappointment, mockery, etc. □ **wryly** *adv.* [*Say* RYE]

wunderkind *n. informal* a person who achieves great success while young. [*Say* VOONDER kint]

wuss *n.* (*pl.* **wusses**) (also **wussy** *pl.* **wussies**) *slang* a feeble or cowardly person. □ **wussy** *adj.* [*Say* WOOSS (with OO *as in* WOOL)]

WW I *abbr.* World War I.

WW II *abbr.* World War II.

WWW *abbr.* World Wide Web.

WYSIWYG *adj.* (also **wysiwyg**) *Computing* denoting the representation of text onscreen in a form looking exactly like the printout. [*Say* WIZZY wig]

Xx

X *n.* (also **x**) (*pl.* **Xs** or **X's**) **1** the twenty-fourth letter of the alphabet. **2** (as a Roman numeral) ten. **3** (usu. **x**) *Algebra* the first unknown quantity. **4** *Math* the first coordinate. **5** an unknown or unspecified number or person etc.

X-acto knife *n. proprietary* a small utility knife with a fine very sharp blade, used for crafts, hobbies, etc.

X chromosome *n.* a sex chromosome of which the number in female cells is twice that in male cells.

xenon *n.* a heavy colourless odourless inert gaseous element used in fluorescent lamps. [*Say* ZEN on]

xenophobe *n.* a person who dislikes foreigners. □ **xenophobia** *n.* **xenophobic** *adj.* [*Say* ZENNA fobe, zenna FOE bee uh]

xeriscaping *n.* a landscaping method requiring little or no irrigation. □ **xeriscape** *n.* [*Say* ZERRA scape ing]

Xerox ● *n.* (*pl.* **Xeroxes**) *proprietary* **1** a photocopier. **2** a photocopy. ● *v.* (**xerox**, **xeroxes**, **xeroxed**, **xeroxing**) photocopy. [*Say* ZEE rocks]

Xhosa *n.* **1** (*pl.* **Xhosa** or **Xhosas**) a member of a Bantu-speaking people forming the second largest ethnic group in South Africa. **2** the language of this people. □ **Xhosa** *adj.* [*Say* CO suh *or* COSSA]

Xmas *n. informal* Christmas. [*Say* CHRISTMAS *or* ECKS mus]

XML *abbr.* Extensible Mark-up Language.

X-rated *adj.* indecent, pornographic.

X-ray (also **x-ray**) ● *n.* **1** (in *pl.*) electromagnetic radiation of short wavelength, able to pass through opaque bodies. **2** an image made by passing X-rays through something. ● *v.* photograph or examine with X-rays.

X's and O's *n.* tic-tac-toe.

Xwe Nal Mewx *n. & adj.* = Sne Nay Muxw.

xylem *n. Botany* the woody tissue in the stem of a plant. [*Say* ZYE lem]

xylene *n.* a volatile liquid hydrocarbon obtained from wood etc. [*Say* ZYE leen]

xylophone *n.* a musical instrument of wooden or metal bars struck with a small hammer. [*Say* ZYE luh phone]

Yy

Y *n.* (also **y**) (*pl.* **Y s** or **Y's**) **1** the twenty-fifth letter of the alphabet. **2** (usu. **y**) *Algebra* the second unknown quantity. **3** *Math* the second coordinate. **4** a Y-shaped thing.

yacht ● *n.* **1** a light sailing vessel, esp. equipped for racing. **2** a power-driven vessel equipped for cruising. ● *v.* race or cruise in a yacht. □ **yachting** *n.* [*Say* YOT]

yachtsman *n.* (*pl.* **yachtsmen**) a person who sails yachts. [*Say* YOTS m'n]

yack *n. & v.* (also **yackety-yack**) *informal* = YAK *n.* 2, *v.*

yahoo[1] *n.* (*pl.* **yahoos**) a coarse or uncivilized person. ● *adj.* characteristic of a yahoo.

yahoo[2] *interj.* an exclamation of excitement.

Yahweh *n.* (also **Yahveh**) a form of the Hebrew name of God used in the Bible. [*Say* YAW way *or* YAW vay]

yak ● *n.* **1** a large domesticated ox with shaggy hair and large horns, used in Tibet as a pack animal and for its milk, meat, and hide. **2** *informal* trivial or unduly persistent talk. ● *v.* (**yaks, yakked, yakking**) *informal* chatter.

yakuza *n.* (*pl.* **yakuza**) a member of a Japanese organized crime gang. [*Say* yuh COOZA]

yam *n.* **1** a tropical climbing plant bearing edible starchy tubers. **2** esp. *US* a sweet potato.

yammer *v. informal* **1** grumble. **2 a** make a loud noise. **b** talk incessantly.

yang *n.* (in Chinese philosophy) the active male principle of the universe (*compare* YIN).

Yank *n. informal* often *derogatory* a resident of the US.

yank *informal* ● *v.* **1** pull with a jerk. **2** remove or withdraw abruptly. ● *n.* a sudden hard pull.

Yankee *n. informal* **1** often *derogatory* a Yank. **2** *US* an inhabitant of New England or one of the northern States. **3** *hist.* a Federal soldier in the American Civil War. □ **Yankee** *adj.*

yap ● *v.* (**yaps, yapped, yapping**) **1** bark shrilly. **2** *informal* talk noisily; complain. ● *n.* **1** a shrill bark. **2** *slang* the mouth □ **yapper** *n.* **yappy** *adj.* (**yappier, yappiest**)

yard[1] *n.* **1** a unit of linear measure equal to 3 feet (0.9144 metre). **2** a square or cubic yard, esp. of sand, topsoil, etc. **3** a spar slung across a mast for a sail to hang from.

yard[2] *n.* **1** a piece of enclosed ground, esp. attached to a building. **2** the area at the front or back of a house. **3** an enclosed area used for a particular business or purpose. **4** a railway yard.

yardage *n.* **1** a number of yards of material etc. **2** a distance measured in yards. [*Say* YARD idge]

yard sale *n.* a sale of used household items.

yardstick *n.* **1** a measuring rod a yard long. **2** a standard used for comparison.

yardwork *n.* gardening and other maintenance work.

yarmulke *n.* (also **yarmulka**) a skullcap worn by Jewish men and boys. [*Say* YAR mull kuh]

yarn ● *n.* **1** any spun thread, esp. for knitting etc. **2** *informal* a long or rambling story. ● *v. informal* tell yarns.

yarrow *n.* a perennial plant with feathery leaves and heads of small white or pale pink flowers.

yaw ● *v.* **1** (of a ship) deviate temporarily from its course. **2** (of an aircraft etc.) rotate about a vertical axis. ● *n.* the yawing of a ship etc. [*Rhymes with* SAW]

yawn ● *v.* **1** open the mouth wide and inhale esp. when sleepy or bored. **2** (of a chasm etc.) gape. ● *n.* **1** an act of yawning. **2** *informal* a boring idea, activity, etc.

yawp ● *n.* a harsh or hoarse cry. ● *v.* make a yawp.

yaws *pl. n.* a contagious tropical skin disease with large red swellings.

yay ● *interj. slang* (also **yea, yeah**) expressing triumph, approval, or encouragement. ● *adv. informal* (with adjectives of size, height, etc.) so, this.

Y chromosome *n.* a sex chromosome occurring only in male cells.

yd. *abbr.* yard (measure).

ye[1] *pron. archaic pl.* of THOU[1].

ye[2] *adj. pseudo-archaic* = THE.

yea ● *interj.* yes. ● *adv.* indeed, even. ● *n.* (*pl.* **yeas**) **1** the word "yea". **2** an affirmative answer. □ **the yeas have it** the affirmative votes are in the majority. [*Say* YAY]

yeah *adv. informal* yes. □ **oh yeah?** expressing incredulity.

year *n.* **1** (also **solar year**) the time occupied by the earth in one revolution around the sun. **2** (also **calendar year**) the period of 365 or 366 days from Jan. 1 to Dec. 31. **3** a period of the same length as this starting at any point. **4** (in *pl.*) age. **5** (usu. in *pl.*) *informal* a very long time. **6** a group of students entering university etc. in the same year. □ **year in, year out** continually over a period of years.

yearbook *n.* an annual publication dealing with or commemorating the events or aspects of the (usu. preceding) year.

year-end *n.* the end of esp. the financial year.

yearling *n.* an animal between one and two years old.

yearly ● *adj.* **1** done or occurring once a year. **2** lasting a year. ● *adv.* once a year.

yearn *v.* have a strong emotional longing. □ **yearning** *n. & adj.*

year-round *n.* ● *adj.* existing etc. throughout the year. ● *adv.* throughout the year.

yeast *n.* **1** a fungous substance obtained esp. from fermenting malt liquors and used to raise bread etc. **2** a single-celled fungus in which reproduction takes place by budding or fission. □ **yeasty** *adj.*

yeast infection *n.* a fungal disease of esp. the vagina, characterized by pain and severe itching.

yech *interj.* expressing disgust.

yee-haw *interj.* expressing enthusiasm.

yeesh *interj. informal* expressing exasperation etc.

yell ● *n.* a loud sharp cry. ● *v.* make or utter with a yell. □ **yelling** *n.*

yellow ● *adj.* **1** of the colour of lemons, egg yolks, or gold. **2** *informal* cowardly. ● *n.* **1** a yellow colour or pigment. **2** a yellow light as part of a set of traffic lights. ● *v.* make or become yellow. □ **yellowish** *adj.* **yellowy** *adj.*

yellow-belly *n.* (*pl.* **yellow-bellies**) *informal* a coward. □ **yellow-bellied** *adj.*

yellow fever *n.* an often fatal tropical virus disease characterized by fever and jaundice.

yellowfin *n.* (also **yellowfin tuna**) a widely distributed, commercially important tuna with yellow fins.

yellowhammer *n.* a flicker with yellow plumage.

yellow jacket *n.* a wasp with black and yellow markings.

Yellowknifer *n.* a native of Yellowknife, NWT.

yellowlegs *n.* (*pl.* **yellowlegs**) a migratory sandpiper with yellow legs.

Yellow Pages *n. proprietary* a telephone book or section of one printed on yellow paper, listing businesses according to the goods or services they offer.

yelp ● *n.* a sharp shrill cry. ● *v.* utter a yelp.

Yemeni (*pl.* **Yemenis**) ● *n.* a person from Yemen. ● *adj.* of Yemen or its people. [*Say* YEMMA nee]

yen[1] *n.* (*pl.* **yen**) the chief monetary unit of Japan.

yen[2] *n.* (*pl.* **yens**) *informal* a longing or yearning.

yenta *n.* (also **yente**) *slang* a gossip.

yeoman *n.* (*pl.* **yeomen**) **1** *Brit.* esp. *hist.* a man holding and cultivating a small landed estate. **2** (**Yeoman**) (also **Chief Yeoman of Signals**) a signalman in the Canadian Navy or the Royal Navy. [*Say* YO min]

Yeoman of the Guard *n.* **1** a member of the British sovereign's bodyguard, now having only ceremonial duties. **2** (in general use) a warder in the Tower of London.

yeoman service *n.* (also **yeoman work**) efficient or useful help in need.

yep *adv. & n. informal* yes.

yes ● *adv.* used to give an affirmative response. ● *n.* (*pl.* **yeses**) **1** an utterance of the word *yes*. **2** an affirmation. **3** a vote in favour of a proposition.

yeshiva *n.* (also **yeshivah**) **1** an Orthodox Jewish college or seminary. **2** an Orthodox Jewish elementary school. [*Say* yuh SHEEVA]

yes-man *n.* (*pl.* **yes-men**) *informal* a weak person who always agrees with people in authority.

yesterday ● *adv.* **1** on the day before today. **2** in the recent past. ● *n.* **1** the day before today. **2** the recent past.

yesteryear *n. literary* the past.

yet ● *adv.* **1** up until now or then. **2** so soon as. **3** again. **4** in the remaining time available. **5** nevertheless. **6** what's more. ● *conj.* but at the same time. □ **nor yet** and also not.

yeti *n.* (*pl.* **yetis**) an abominable snowman.

yew *n.* **1** a dark-leaved evergreen coniferous tree or shrub. **2** its wood.

Yiddish *n.* a language used by Jews in or from central and eastern Europe, originally a German dialect with words from Hebrew and several modern languages. □ **Yiddish** *adj.*

yield ● v. **1** produce. **2** give up. **3 a** surrender. **b** change one's course of action in deference to. **4** give right-of-way to other traffic. ● n. an amount yielded or produced.

yielding adj. **1** compliant, submissive. **2** able to bend.

yikes interj. slang an expression of surprise or alarm.

yin n. (in Chinese philosophy) the passive female principle of the universe (compare YANG).

yingyang n. □ **up the yingyang** slang in large quantities or to a large degree.

yin-yang n. the harmonious interaction of the female and male forces of the universe.

yip v. & n. (**yips, yipped, yipping**) yelp.

yippee interj. expressing delight or excitement.

yo interj. slang used to get someone's attention.

yodel ● v. (**yodels, yodelled, yodelling**) sing with frequent changes between falsetto and the normal voice. ● n. a yodelling cry. □ **yodeller** n. [Say YODE 'll]

yoga n. **1** a Hindu system of philosophical meditation and asceticism. **2** a system of esp. posture and breathing exercises used to attain control of the body and mind. □ **yogic** adj.

yogi n. (pl. **yogis**) a person proficient in yoga.

yogourt n. (also **yoghurt, yogurt**) a semi-solid slightly tart food prepared from milk fermented by added bacteria.

yoke ● n. **1** a wooden crosspiece fastened over the necks of two oxen etc. and attached to the plow or wagon to be drawn. **2** (pl. **yoke** or **yokes**) a pair (of oxen etc.). **3** an object like a yoke in form or function. **4** a part of a garment, usu. placed across the shoulders or around the hips, from which the rest hangs. **5** something that exercises control in an oppressive or burdensome manner. **6** a bond or union. ● v. (**yokes, yoked, yoking**) **1** put a yoke on. **2** couple or unite. **3** link to.

yokel n. a country bumpkin. [Say YOKE 'll]

yolk n. the yellow inner part of an egg. □ **yolked** adj. **yolky** adj.

Yom Kippur n. the most solemn Jewish religious holiday, eight days after the Jewish New Year, marked by fasting and repentance. [Say yom ki POOR]

yon adj. & adv. yonder.

yonder ● adv. over there. ● adj. situated yonder. ● n. a remote place.

yoo-hoo interj. used to attract attention.

yore n. □ **of yore** formerly.

York boat n. Cdn hist. a large inland cargo boat used esp. during the fur trade.

Yorkshire pudding n. a puffy baked pudding, usu. eaten with roast beef. [Say YORK sher]

Yoruba n. **1** (pl. **Yorubas** or **Yoruba**) a member of a people inhabiting esp. Nigeria. **2** the language of this people. □ **Yoruba** adj. [Say YORRA buh]

you pron. **1** used with reference to the person or persons addressed, or one such person and one or more associated persons. **2** (in general statements) one, anyone. □ **you and yours** you together with your family etc.

you'd contr. **1** you had. **2** you would.

you-know-what n. (also **you-know-who**) a thing or person unspecified but understood.

you'll contr. you will; you shall.

young ● adj. (**younger, youngest**) **1** not yet old. **2 a** immature or inexperienced. **b** youthful. **3** characteristic of youth. ● n. offspring, esp. of animals. □ **youngish** adj.

young blood n. a younger member or members of a group.

young offender n. a young criminal.

youngster n. a child or young person.

Young Turk n. **1** a member of a group of reformers in the Ottoman Empire. **2** a young person eager for radical change.

young 'un n. informal a youngster.

your poss. adj. **1** of or belonging to you. **2** informal usu. derogatory much talked of. **3** belonging to or associated with any person.

you're contr. you are.

yours poss. pron. **1** the one or ones belonging to or associated with you. **2** your letter. □ **of yours** of or belonging to you.

yourself pron. (pl. **yourselves**) **1 a** emphatic form of YOU. **b** reflexive form of YOU. **2** in your normal state of body or mind. □ **be yourself** act in your normal manner.

yours truly n. informal myself, me; I. □ **yours truly** used as a formula to end a letter.

youse pron. (also **yous**) non-standard you.

youth n. (pl. **youths**) **1** the state of being young; the period between childhood and adult age. **2** the vigour, inexperience, or other characteristic of this period. **3** a young person or young people.

youthful adj. **1** young or seeming young. **2** having the characteristics of youth. □ **youthfully** adv. **youthfulness** n.

youth hostel n. a place where (esp. young) travellers can stay cheaply.

you've *contr.* you have.

yowl • *n.* a loud wailing cry of pain or distress. • *v.* utter a yowl.

yo-yo • *n.* (*pl.* **yo-yos**) **1** a toy consisting of a pair of discs with a deep groove between them in which string is attached and wound, and which can be spun up and down as the string unwinds and rewinds. **2** a thing that repeatedly falls and rises again. • *adj.* characterized by repeated upward and downward movement etc. • *v.* (**yo-yoes, yo-yoed, yo-yoing**) alternate between two positions or situations.

YT *abbr.* Yukon territory.

YTD *abbr.* year to date.

ytterbium *n.* a silvery metallic element. [*Say* it TERBY um]

yttrium *n.* a greyish metallic element, used in making superconductors. [*Say* ITTRY um]

yuan *n.* (*pl.* **yuan**) the chief monetary unit of China. [*Say* yoo ON]

yucca *n.* (*pl.* **yuccas**) a N American plant with white flowers and sword-like leaves. [*Say* YUCKA]

yuck[1] *interj. slang* an expression of strong distaste or disgust. □ **yucky** *adj.* (**yuckier, yuckiest**)

yuck[2] *v. & n.* = YUK.

Yugoslav *n.* (also **Yugoslavian**) a person from Yugoslavia. □ **Yugoslav** *adj.* [*Say* YOOGA slov *or* YOOGA slav]

yuk *informal* • *v.* (**yuks, yukked, yukking**) **1** laugh heartily. **2** fool around. • *n.* **1** a hearty laugh. **2** something that causes hearty laughter.

Yukoner *n.* a person from the Yukon Territory.

Yukon Gold *n.* a large, yellow-fleshed variety of potato.

yule *n.* (also **yuletide**) *archaic* or *literary* Christmas.

yule log *n.* **1** a large log burned in the hearth on Christmas Eve. **2** a log-shaped rolled cake eaten at Christmas.

yum *interj.* (also **yum-yum**) expressing pleasure from eating.

yummy *adj.* (**yummier, yummiest**) *informal* tasty, delicious.

Yupik *n.* **1** a member of a group of Aboriginal peoples living in coastal areas of Alaska and northeastern Siberia. **2** any of the languages spoken by the Yupik. □ **Yupik** *adj.* [*Say* YOU pick]

yuppie *n.* (*pl.* **yuppies**) *informal*, usu. *derogatory* a young, affluent, middle-class professional person. □ **yuppiedom** *n.*

yuppify *v.* (**yuppifies, yuppified, yuppifying**) *informal* make characteristic of yuppies. □ **yuppification** *n.* [*Say* YUPPA fie, yup i fi CAY sh'n]

yurt *n.* a circular tent of felt, skins, etc., on a collapsible framework.

Zz

Z n. (also **z**) (pl. **Zs** or **Z's**) **1** the twenty-sixth letter of the alphabet. **2** (usu. **z**) *Algebra* the third unknown quantity. **3** *Math* the third coordinate. [*Say* ZED *or* ZEE]

zabaglione n. (pl. **zabagliones**) a dessert consisting of whipped egg yolks, sugar, and (esp. Marsala) wine. [*Say* za BA lee oh nay]

zaftig adj. informal (of a woman) plump. [*Say* ZAFF tig]

zag ● n. a sharp change of direction. ● v. (**zags, zagged, zagging**) perform a zag.

Zambian n. a person from Zambia. □ **Zambian** adj. [*Say* ZAMBY in]

Zamboni n. (pl. **Zambonis**) proprietary a tractor-like machine for smoothing an ice surface. [*Say* zam BONEY]

zany ● adj. (**zanier, zaniest**) crazily ridiculous. ● n. (pl. **zanies**) a foolish or eccentric person. □ **zanily** adv. **zaniness** n. [*Say* ZAY nee, ZANE uh lee, ZANY niss]

zap slang ● v. (**zaps, zapped, zapping**) **1 a** kill or destroy. **b** hit forcibly. **2 a** move quickly and vigorously. **b** use a remote control to change television channels, operate a video recorder, etc. **3** overwhelm emotionally. **4** informal cook (food) in a microwave. ● n. **1** energy, vigour. **2** a strong emotional effect. □ **zapper** n.

zeal n. **1** earnestness or fervour in advancing a cause. **2** great energy and enthusiasm.

zealot n. an uncompromising or extreme partisan. □ **zealotry** n. [*Say* ZELLIT, ZELLA tree]

zealous adj. full of zeal; enthusiastic. □ **zealously** adv. [*Say* ZELLIS]

zebra n. (pl. **zebras** or **zebra**) **1** an African quadruped with black and white stripes and an erect mane. **2** (as an adj.) with alternate dark and pale stripes.

zebra mussel n. a tiny freshwater mussel that proliferates rapidly and adheres to any surface.

zed n. Cdn & Brit. the letter Z.

zeda n. (pl. **zedas**) (among Jewish people) grandfather. [*Say* ZAY duh]

zee n. the letter Z. □ **catch** (or **bag**) **some zees** slang get some sleep.

zeitgeist n. the defining spirit or mood of a particular period in history. [*Say* ZITE geist (GEIST *rhymes with* PRICED)]

Zen n. a form of Buddhism emphasizing the value of meditation and intuition. □ **Zenlike** adj.

zenith n. **1** the part of the celestial sphere directly above an observer. **2** the highest or culminating point. [*Say* ZEE nith *or* ZEN ith]

zephyr n. literary a mild gentle breeze. [*Say* ZEFFER]

Zeppelin n. hist. a large dirigible airship of the early 20th century. [*Say* ZEP lin]

zero ● n. (pl. **zeros**) **1 a** the figure 0. **b** no quantity or number; nil. **2** (also **zero hour**) **a** the hour at which a planned operation is timed to begin. **b** a crucial moment. **3** the lowest point. ● adj. no, not any. ● v. (**zeroes, zeroed, zeroing**) **1** adjust (an instrument etc.) to zero. **2** set the sights of (a gun) for firing. □ **zero in on 1** take aim at. **2** focus attention on.

zero-sum adj. (of a game etc.) in which whatever is gained by one side is lost by the other.

zero tolerance n. a policy of punishing all infractions against a law etc., no matter how minor.

zest n. **1** an exciting or stimulating flavour or quality. **2** great enthusiasm or energy. **3** the outer, coloured, covering of the peel of a citrus fruit. □ **zestful** adj. **zestfully** adv.

zester n. a kitchen utensil for obtaining zest from citrus fruit.

zesty adj. (**zestier, zestiest**) **1** (of food) piquant. **2** energetic, stimulating.

zig ● n. an abrupt angled movement. ● v. (**zigs, zigged, zigging**) perform a zig.

ziggurat n. a rectangular stepped tower in ancient Mesopotamia, surmounted by a temple. [*Say* ZIGGA rat]

zigzag ● n. a line or course having abrupt alternate right and left turns. ● adj. having the form of a zigzag. ● adv. with a zigzag course. ● v. (**zigzags, zigzagged, zigzagging**) move in a zigzag course.

zilch n. slang nothing.

zillion n. informal an indefinite large number. □ **zillionth** adj.

Zimbabwean n. a person from

Zimbabwe. □**Zimbabwean** *adj.*
[*Say* zim BOB wee in *or* zim BOB way in]

zinc *n.* a white metallic element used as a component of brass and in electric batteries.

zinc oxide *n.* a powder used as a white pigment and in medicinal ointments.

zine *n. informal* a magazine. [*Say* ZEEN]

Zinfandel *n.* a wine, esp. a sweet rosé, made esp. in California. [*Say* ZIN fan dell]

zing *informal* ● *n.* **1** vigour, energy. **2** a short, high-pitched buzzing or ringing sound. **3** zest. ● *v.* **1** move swiftly. **2** criticize or rebuke severely. □**zingy** *adj.* (**zingier, zingiest**)

zinger *n. slang* **1** a witty or pointed remark. **2** an unexpected turn of events.

zinnia *n.* (*pl.* **zinnias**) a plant of the daisy family with bright showy flowers.
[*Say* ZIN yuh]

Zion *n.* **1** Jerusalem; allegorically, the heavenly city or kingdom of heaven. **2** the Jewish religion or people. **3** the region of Palestine as the Jewish homeland and as the symbol of Judaism. [*Say* ZYE in]

Zionism *n.* a movement for the development of a Jewish nation in what is now Israel. □**Zionist** *n.* [*Say* ZYE in ism]

zip ● *n.* **1** a light fast sound. **2** energy, vigour. **3** zest. **4** *informal* nothing, zero. **5** esp. *Brit.* a zipper. **6** a zip code. ● *v.* (**zips, zipped, zipping**) **1** fasten with a zipper. **2** move at high speed. **3** *Computing* compress (a file or files).

zip code *n. US* a system of postal codes consisting of five- or nine-digit numbers.

zip-lock *adj.* (also **zip-top**) designating a plastic bag with a special strip along the two open edges so that it can be sealed shut by pressing them together and readily opened again.

zipper *n.* a fastening device of two flexible strips with interlocking projections closed or opened by pulling a slide along them. □**zippered** *adj.*

zippo *n. informal* nothing.

zippy *adj.* (**zippier, zippiest**) *informal* **1** bright, fresh, lively. **2** speedy. □**zippily** *adv.* **zippiness** *n.*

zip-up *adj.* able to be fastened with a zip fastener.

zircon *n.* a zirconium silicate of which some translucent varieties are cut into gems. [*Say* ZER con]

zirconia *n.* zirconium dioxide, a white solid used as a synthetic substitute for diamonds in jewellery.
[*Say* zer CONEY uh]

zirconium *n.* a grey metallic element occurring in zircon. [*Say* zer CONEY um]

zit *n. slang* a pimple.

zither *n.* a musical instrument consisting of a flat box with numerous strings stretched across it, placed horizontally. [*Rhymes with* HITHER]

zodiac *n.* **1** a belt of the heavens including all apparent positions of the sun, moon, and planets, and divided into twelve parts named after constellations and used in astrology. **2** (**Zodiac**) *proprietary* a kind of inflatable rubber dinghy usu. with an outboard motor. □**zodiacal** *adj.*
[*Say* ZOE dee ack, zuh DIE a cull]

zombie *n.* **1** *informal* a dull or exceedingly tired person. **2** a corpse said to be revived by witchcraft. **3** *Cdn slang* (during World War II) a conscript. □**zombielike** *adj.* **zombified** *adj.* **zombify** *v.* (**zombifies, zombified, zombifying**)

zone ● *n.* **1** an area having particular features or a particular use. **2** an area between two exact or approximate concentric circles. **3** (also **time zone**) a range of longitudes where a common standard time is used. **4** *Geology etc.* a range between specified limits of depth, height, etc. ● *v.* (**zones, zoned, zoning**) **1** encircle as or with a zone. **2** arrange or distribute by zones. **3** divide (a city, land, etc.) into areas subject to particular planning restrictions. □**zone out** *slang* lose concentration. □**zonal** *adj.* **zoning** *n.* (in sense 3 of *verb*)

zonk *v. slang* **1** hit or strike. **2** (foll. by *out*) **a** knock out. **b** fall asleep.

zoo *n.* **1** a place where wild animals are kept for exhibition to the public. **2** any busy, noisy place.

zookeeper *n.* a person employed in a zoo to care for the animals.

zoology *n.* the scientific study of animals. □**zoological** *adj.* **zoologist** *n.*
[*Say* zoo OLLA jee *or* zo OLLA jee, zoo a LOGICAL *or* zo a LOGICAL]

zoom ● *v.* **1** move quickly. **2** cause (an airplane) to mount at high speed and a steep angle. **3** alter the field of view of a camera by varying the focal length of a zoom lens. **4** alter the representation of an image etc. on a computer screen so as to make it appear larger or smaller. ● *n.* **1** a zooming camera shot. **2** (also **zoom lens**) a lens with a variable focal length.

zooplankton *n.* the animal component of plankton. [*Say* zoo a PLANK tun *or* zo a PLANK tun]

zoot suit *n. informal* a man's suit of an exaggerated style popular in the 1940s.

Zoroastrian ● *adj.* of or relating to the Persian prophet Zoroaster (or Zarathustra; *c.*628–*c.*551 BC) or the religious system

taught by him. ● *n.* a follower of Zoroaster.
□ **Zoroastrianism** *n.*
[*Say* zoro ASTRY un]

zouk *n.* an exuberant style of popular
music combining Caribbean and Western
elements. [*Rhymes with* FLUKE]

zowie *interj.* expressing astonishment or
delight.

zucchini *n.* (*pl.* **zucchini** or **zucchinis**) a
green-skinned summer squash.
[*Say* zoo KEENY]

Zulu *n.* (*pl.* **Zulus** or **Zulu**) **1** a member of a
Bantu-speaking people forming the largest
ethnic group in South Africa. **2** the
language of this people. □ **Zulu** *adj.*
[*Say* ZOO loo]

Zuni *n.* (*pl.* **Zuni** or **Zunis**) **1** a member of a
Pueblo people of New Mexico. **2** the
language of this people. □ **Zuni** *adj.*
[*Say* ZOO nee *or* ZOON yee]

Zyban *n.* *proprietary* an antidepressant drug,
used as an aid in quitting smoking.
[*Say* ZYE ban]

zygote *n.* a cell formed by the union of two
gametes. [*Say* ZYE goat]

zzz *interj.* imitating the sound of snoring.

PRAISE FOR THE
CANADIAN OXFORD DICTIONARY

"...a unique reference book for all Canadians; an essential tool for anyone writing for Canadian readers; and a book I know I will consult endlessly."

Robert MacNeil, *Time Magazine*

"It is a treat to find the way we speak validated in a thick, stylish, authoritative volume which can take its place on the bookshelf with other great dictionaries... On the evidence of a week's serious browsing, the Canadian Oxford earns an A."

Winnipeg Free Press

"We can all write and speak a bit more confidently with the arrival of the *Canadian Oxford Dictionary*."

The Globe and Mail

"The *Canadian Oxford Dictionary*... has set new standards in Canadian lexicography while unexpectedly shooting to the top of bestseller lists."

Toronto Star

"Canadian libraries will want to update their reference collections with the latest edition, which is also a worthy addition to any Canadian home reference collection."

Booklist

Official Dictionary of
The Canadian Press and *The Globe and Mail*

Over 200,000 copies sold

OXFORD UNIVERSITY PRESS PUBLISHES A RANGE OF REFERENCE WORKS FOR CANADIANS.